THE

Reference Passage Bible New Testament

With Old Testament References

Comprising all of the Books of the New Testament Complete, arranged in Topics, with the Reference Passages given in full text upon the same page to facilitate their use, without comment.

The Gospels

ARE ARRANGED IN PARALLEL COLUMNS, IN CHRONOLOGICAL ORDER, GIVING TIME AND PLACE.

The Acts, Epistles and Revelation

ARE ARRANGED IN CONSECUTIVE ORDER

WITH

Instructions, Maps and Indices.

COMPILED BY

I. N. JOHNS

LOGOS INTERNATIONAL
PLAINFIELD, NEW JERSEY

The Reference Passage Bible
Library of Congress catalog card number: 78-56146
International Standard Book Number: 0-88270-275-0
Printed in the United States of America
Published by Logos International, Plainfield, New Jersey 07060

The Reference Passage Bible
New Testament.

This Book comprises the New Testament portion of The Reference Passage Bible and appears in two forms: In two volumes known as "THE PARALLEL GOSPELS AND REFERENCE PASSAGES," and "THE ACTS, EPISTLES, REVELATION AND REFERENCE PASSAGES"; and a combined volume entitled as seen above.

GENERAL PURPOSE. Scripture is its own best interpreter, but the constant use of a concordance or a Marginal Reference is laborious and time consuming. And that there may be a conservation of mental energy as well, the full text of each reference passage is given upon the same page with the Scriptural text that is being studied. There are many advantages in having Scripture along one line of thought grouped together, under the eye and hand, for reflection; so as to make deductions by comparison or association, generalizing or specializing, so that one may draw logical conclusions, and have the assurance that they are Scriptural beyond doubt.

AUTHORITIES. The Authorized text and marginal notes are used throughout. In the matter of harmony and chronology, Robinson, Andrews, Butler, Kephart and others were consulted. The Reference Texts and reference passages are those found in the Bibles in common use, with some exception, and thousands more drawn from Canne, Browne, Blayney, Scott, Cobbin and others. The principle governing the collations is that of direct relevancy to the thought of the text indicated, without reflection or purpose as to doctrine. The work is without note or comment, and the association of Scriptures that chances by grouping them, is not intended to confirm or deny any doctrine. Each student is left to draw his own conclusions. We desire to acknowledge the very valuable assistance of Mr. J. F. Kempfer in the compilation of the Gospels.

METHODS OF STUDY. Several well defined methods of study may be pursued with facility. *First* the ordinary method of reading chapters and verses in their consecutive order. In reading the Gospels thus, recourse may be had to the Chapter and verse index, since Chronological order breaks up the consecutive order in a slight manner. The *Second* method is analytical in its character; and has as its object the acquiring of more complete knowledge of the books of the Bible, by a close investigation of their contents. For this purpose there is a division into Sections (§) called topics, which may be seen to advantage in the Topic Index. The *Third* method is topical in its character. For this purpose superior reference letters will be found throughout the consecutive Scripture text (largest type); these designate important texts, subjects or thoughts, and refer to groups of passages along the same line of thought, but in such different connections that one's knowledge of the subject is thereby expanded. The *fourth* method is Synthetic in its character, and its application will be found a little farther on. Other methods might be mentioned, but these are sufficient for rudimentary study; and perhaps, too, it is better that each individual should be directed in large measure by his own spirit in particulars.

GENERAL DIRECTIONS. There are 604 topics marked as sections (§). The Gospels covering 225 of this number, and the Acts, Epistles and Revelation, the remaining 379. The consecutive Scripture text, or *Text of the Topic*, as it is often referred to, is found in 10 pt. (largest) type. The Reference Passages are given in 8 pt. (next to largest) type; and other references and marginal notes are given in 6 pt. (smallest) type. The two open pages always serve for one; as will be seen by the sectional title lines, which are made to extend across both.

The superior reference letters ([a], [b], [c], etc.,) in *The Text of the Topic*, point out important texts, subjects, persons, places, words, phrases, etc., for study and refer to the groups of passages from various portions of the Scriptures in 8 pt. type, under corresponding capital letters (A, B, C, etc.). A passage is never repeated on the same open pages; if it is needed a second time, it is referred to in its first place. Thus: "Acts 2. 4. *See under D.*" (See it under H, 3d col. pages 638, 639). It may be referred to thus: "Acts 2. 24. *See text of topic*," which means you shall look into the large type of the section you are studying, for it. (See S, 4th col. page 628, 629). Reference is also made to some other part of the book, where the same subject has been fully developed, to avoid increasing the size of the book beyond convenient handling, thus: "Acts 1. 8. *See k, K, § 227, page 628.*" (See T, 4th col., pages 638, 639); the small *k* in this reference refers to the superior reference letter in *the Text of the topic*, pointing out the subject. The large *K* refers to the group of passages in 8 pt. type, and teaches that the subject should always be read first and the passages afterwards; otherwise the latter might not associate with proper sense. A passage usually contains other thoughts besides the one for which it was chosen.

THE ANALYTICAL METHOD. This method implies studying by books. Its purpose is to ascertain what a book contains. It may be concerning its authorship, to whom addressed, when and where written, the purpose, geographical and historical setting; conditions surrounding the writer—those addressed, its teachings, doctrines, etc. But should the young reader not wish to enter into so close an inspection, then let him read each book carefully, time and again, until he can make for himself a few very general divisions, as the following upon *The Acts:*

I. The ascension and closing events of our Lord's life on earth.

II. The disciples awaiting, and receiving the Holy Spirit—Marking the inception of the Christian Church.

III. Peter and John the principal workers. Disciples increase greatly. Troubles arise without, difficulties within, all of which is entrusted to the Holy Spirit. Joy, peace and love rule the congregation—The character of the early Church is here set forth.

IV. The Church expands. Deacons, or stewards, are chosen. Stephen and Philip are the principals. Evangelistic work begins. Persecutions grow sore. The first martyrdom comes like a thunder clap and scatters the lovely community into all the world to become witnesses of the gospel.

V. Saul now appears upon the scene. Peter introduces the Gentile branch of the Church that the former is to champion. Barnabas appears in his strength, and as a foster brother to Saul.

VI. Missionary work begins. The supremacy of Paul's ministry asserts itself. The mighty apostle to the Gentiles stands out conspicuously with satellites of his own, almost a dictator; nevertheless, beautifully submissive to the mother Church at Jerusalem, the oracle of the Son of Righteousness.

VII. Persecution always, everywhere present, closes this intensely interesting history of the early Church. Paul is a prisoner at Rome, where he established the gospel.

It will be noticed that the chapters and verses designating the beginning and the closing of these divisions are not given; let each reader do that for himself. The topic index for each book will give some help along this line; but in most instances, the divisions are too numerous to be easily retained in the mind for ready use.

THE TOPICAL METHOD. This method consists in studying any text, subject, or topic, in the light the Scripture itself may throw upon it. To illustrate: turn to pages 626, 627, § 226. Acts 1. 3. (*Text of the topic*) under f. "Speaking of the things pertaining to he kingdom of God." Now turn to the group of passages under F in the 4th column. Read these carefully. Notice what Daniel says about the kingdom: "God shall set it up." "Never be destroyed." "A powerful kingdom." "Stands forever." Matthew says: "It is at hand." "Those Jews lose it, another nation gets it." Luke says: "It cometh not with observation." "Is within you." Romans says: "It is not meat and drink but righteousness and peace and joy in the Holy Ghost." Meditate over the several statements and a clearer understanding of the Kingdom of God may be found.

The character of these deductions will change; on some texts they are simple, upon others more complex. Sometimes the collated passages are merely similar incidents, others the peculiar use of a word. The biography of a person. Sometimes they stand to show the relation of one event to another. Often they are prophecies, or Mosaic law relevant to the subject.

This method is well adapted for those who teach, lead meetings, or exhort. And it is here the study of the scattered truth takes the form of synthesis.

THE SYNTHETIC METHOD. This method is the very opposite of the Analytic. To illustrate simply: Take an apple, divide it, remove the core, carefully lay it to one side; now pare the rind from it equally careful; you have the pulp remaining; three distinct parts; each different from the other; you have Analyzed. Now return each part to its proper place as well as you can, so that you can recognize the apple again. This latter is a simple act of Synthesis. But the Synthetic study of the scattered truth of the Scripture is not so simple; in the illustration you had the pattern of the apple before you first; whereas, in the matter of truth we are not possessed of the pattern until it is taught us, or we see it in the Lord, deducted from the Word of God. And this truth must be laid together for our several needs. Read Isa. 28: 9-13. And we trust it may be done after the manner God has laid down. Read I. John 2:27. Synthetical study will then, as you see, be applied after you have acquired some scattered truth of a subject or topic; arranging them into logical thought, or series of thoughts, so as to enable you to give forth the truth in an intelligent manner.

TEACHING S. S. LESSONS. Most S. S. Lesson Helps tend to omit the use of the Bible itself. This work holds that purpose especially in view. Let every child who can read readily be provided with a Bible. If they possess one of their own, use it. For example of application turn to Acts 12:11, page 706, (1st col)., under *k* and *l*, The Text or Subject is, The Lord delivering out of trouble. Now look to the passages under K and L (2nd, 3rd cols.): let the first child find Ps. 34:7 in his own Bible; by simple questions draw out how those who fear God are protected. Let another find Ps. 33:18, 19; still another, Job 5:19, questioning to a point of instruction each time. When the subject has been exhausted, review it by summing up the scattered facts and expounding them more fully and completely unto the perfect truth. By this method the young learn to handle the Bible with aptness; they are taught to think upon what is read; God's will and promises are known by his Word; and their own Bibles will become endeared to them, and possess a value not likely to be acquired in any other way.

Adult classes may be supplied with the Book; these are more apt to choose a method of their own, so that we shall only add, that reasoning and comparison of different views may profitably engage their attention after they have satisfied themselves with the facts that constitute the setting of the lesson.

DIRECTIONS FOR THE STUDY OF THE GOSPELS. Turn to pages 54 and 55. You observe four columns; one for each of the gospels respectively. It is the 16th §; that is the sixteenth event in our Lord's life, viz., "The Temptation." It probably occurred in January or February of A. D. 27, in the desert of Judea. You will now notice that this event is recorded by Matthew in the 4th chapter: 1-11; by Mark 1:12, 13 and by Luke 3:23; 4:1-13. This you will know by the large type text in their respective columns. In John's column you see no large text type; thereby it may be known that John gave no record of this event. The gospel names at the head of the columns apply only to large type text. Looking over the gospel text as given here by the three first named gospels, beginning with Matthew, superior reference letters, *a*, *b*, *c*, etc., will be seen located here and there, indicating the more important thoughts of the topic; these refer to the groups of passages in smaller type designated correspondingly by capital letters thus: A, B C, etc., e. g. the *b* in the 1st verse of Matthew 4, at the head of the left hand column refers to the thought of being "led by the Spirit." Under B in the lower half of the same column will be found Scripture quoting other instances of the same character. Under the "A" will be found reference made to the *text of topic;* this indicates that the first verses given in Matthew's and Mark's columns and the second one in Luke's column are along the same line of thought. Turning to pages 56 and 57 it will be found that there the subject is concluded. On this page Mark has no parallel account, his record being very brief.

HOW TO STUDY. *For the family circle*, and for those who desire to begin a regular reading of the Scriptures, we recommend that first of all, section after section of the gospel text (large type) be read in whatever column or columns it may be found. This course will render every portion of the gospels, and present a continuous Chronological narrative of our Lord's Life without any change from the Bible except the order of arrangement. *To be interested in a matter one must be busied therein.* Therefore parents should encourage children to collect pictures illustrating events in our Lord's life, and tell the story they represent in a simple manner. Sunday-school lesson pictures, journals, papers and the family Bible are fruitful sources. Family worship should largely be instruction for children.

HOW TO STUDY. *With the Map.* Another exercise in which the older children will participate with zeal is the study of places as associated with our Lord's journeys up and down the Holy Land. Procure a map of "Palestine in the time of Christ;" lesson journals contain them. Begin with section 4; "Annunciation to Mary" at Nazareth. Read the text and trace every movement of Mary and Jesus in the order given. Observe the outline given on page VI. Devote a map to each of the periods given. Or if desired, all of his life up to the first passover, § 4—§ 20 on the first map; and each passover year on each succeeding map as follows: § 21—§ 36; § 37—§ 85; § 86—§ 202. The value of this exercise cannot be over-estimated. The work of the hand in tracing over the map makes a lasting impression, and aids the mind to properly associate the teachings of the gospels.

MAPS AND INDICES. Several maps are provided that easy reference may be made to places mentioned. An Index of the Books of the New Testament giving their arrangement Sections (§) and pages will be found on page VII. A Chapter and verse index for Matthew, Mark, Luke and John on page 1418, and a topic Index on page 1402. If at any time it should be desired to locate a subject, the text of which is not known, a concordance should be used to ascertain the texts, then by referring to the indices here given, the subject can readily be found. To have added a concordance, or even a word index, would have so increased the size of the book that it would not serve as a handbook convenient to carry.

CONCLUSION. In conclusion we will add that the Lord is the Christian's portion. In this work it was sought to draw each one closer to him. His words are Spirit and Life (John 6:63); they abide for ever, and they are our meat and drink (I. Peter 2:2). Therefore as did Paul to the Ephesian elders—"I commend you to God, and to the word of his grace, which is able to build you up and to give you an inheritance among all them which are sanctified."

I. N. J.

GENERAL OUTLINE OF THE LIFE OF CHRIST.

INTRODUCTIONS. [§§ 1, 2.]

Period of Obscurity.

CHILDHOOD AND YOUTH TO MANHOOD; THIRTY YEARS, B. C. 5–A. D. 27. [§§ 4–17.]
EARLY GALILEAN MINISTRY; THREE MONTHS, FEBRUARY–APRIL, A. D. 27. [§§ 18–20.]
EARLY JUDEAN MINISTRY; NINE MONTHS, APRIL–DECEMBER, A. D. 27. [§§ 21–24.]

Period of Public Favor.

LATER GALILEAN MINISTRY; ONE YEAR AND NINE MONTHS, DECEMBER, A. D. 27–OCTOBER, A. D. 29. [§§ 25–108.]

Period of Opposition.

N. B.—Opposition to Jesus began during the later Galilean ministry, being strongly marked about the time of the third Passover. [See § 84.]

LATER JUDEAN MINISTRY; THREE MONTHS, OCTOBER, A. D. 29–JANUARY, A. D. 30. [§§ 109–122.]
PERÆAN MINISTRY; THREE MONTHS, JANUARY–MARCH, A. D. 30, [§§ 123–151.]
THE LAST WEEK; FIRST WEEK OF APRIL. A. D. 30. [§§ 152–211.]

THE FORTY DAYS. [§§ 212–224.]
CONCLUSION. [§ 225.]

A TABLE OF THE ORDER AND ARRANGEMENT OF THE BOOKS OF THE NEW TESTAMENT.

The consecutive Text of these books is found in the bold type. In Matthew, Mark, Luke and John, where the consecutive order is broken because of their chronological arrangement, refer to the chapter and verse index on page 1418.

A

Prov. 8. 22 The LORD possessed me in the beginning of his way, before his works of old.

23 I was set up from everlasting, from the beginning, or ever the earth was.

24 When *there were* no depths, I was brought forth; when *there were* no fountains abounding with water.

25 Before the mountains were settled, before the hills was I brought forth:

26 While as yet he had not made the earth, nor the fields, nor the highest part of the dust of the world.

27 When he prepared the heavens, I *was* there: when he set a compass upon the face of the depth:

28 When he established the clouds above: when he strengthened the fountains of the deep:

29 When he gave to the sea his decree, that the waters should not pass his commandment: when he appointed the foundations of the earth:

30 Then I was by him, *as* one brought up *with him:* and I was daily *his* delight, rejoicing always before him;

31 Rejoicing in the habitable part of his earth; and my delights *were* with the sons of men.

Col. 1. 17 And he is before all things, and by him all things consist:

I Jno. 1. 1 That which was from the beginning, which we have heard, which we have seen with our eyes, which we have looked upon, and our hands have handled, of the Word of life;

Rev. 1. 2 Who bare record of the word of God, and of the testimony of Jesus Christ, and of all things that he saw.

Rev. 19. 13 And he *was* clothed with a vesture dipped in blood: and his name is called The Word of God.

B

Prov. 8. 30. *See under A.*

Zech. 13. 7 Awake, O sword, against my Shepherd, and against the man *that is* my fellow, saith the LORD of hosts: smite the Shepherd, and the sheep shall be scattered: and I will turn mine hand upon the little ones.

John 17. 5 And now, O Father, glorify thou me with thine own self with the glory which I had with thee before the world was.

I Jno. 1. 2 (For the life was manifested, and we have seen *it*, and bear witness, and shew unto you that eternal life, which

§1. GOD THE

was with the Father, and was manifested unto us;)

C

Isa. 9. 6 For unto us a child is born, unto us a son is given: and the government shall be upon his shoulder: and his name shall be called Wonderful, Counsellor, The mighty God, The everlasting Father, The Prince of Peace.

Phil. 2. 6 Who, being in the form of God, thought it not robbery to be equal with God:

Titus 2. 13 Looking for that blessed hope, and the glorious appearing of the great God and our Saviour Jesus Christ;

I Jno. 5. 7 For there are three that bear record in heaven, the Father, the Word, and the Holy Ghost: and these three are one.

D

Gen. 1. 1 In the beginning God created the heaven and the earth.

E

Ps. 33. 6 By the word of the LORD were the heavens made; and all the host of them by the breath of his mouth.

John 1. 10. *See text of topic.*

Eph. 3. 9 And to make all *men* see what *is* the fellowship of the mystery, which from the beginning of the world hath been hid in God, who created all things by Jesus Christ:

Col. 1. 16 For by him were all things created, that are in heaven, and that are in earth, visible and invisible, whether *they be* thrones, or dominions, or principalities, or powers: all things were created by him, and for him:

Heb. 1. 2 Hath in these last days spoken unto us by *his* Son, whom he hath appointed heir of all things, by whom also he made the worlds;

Rev. 4. 11 Thou art worthy, O LORD, to receive glory and honour and power: for thou hast created all things, and for thy pleasure they are and were created.

F

John 5. 26 For as the Father hath life in himself; so hath he given to the Son to have life in himself;

I Jno. 5. 11 And this is the record, that God hath given to us eternal life, and this life is in his Son.

G

John 8. 12 Then spake Jesus again unto them, saying, I am the light of the world: he that followeth me shall not walk in darkness, but shall have the light of life.

WORD.

G—CONCLUDED.

John 9. 5 As long as I am in the world, I am the light of the world.

John 12. 35 Then Jesus said unto them, Yet a little while is the light with you. Walk while ye have the light, lest darkness come upon you: for he that walketh in darkness knoweth not whither he goeth.

John 12. 46 I am come a light into the world, that whosoever believeth on me should not abide in darkness.

H

John 3. 19 And this is the condemnation, that light is come into the world, and men loved darkness rather than light, because their deeds were evil.

I

Mal. 3. 1 Behold, I will send my messenger, and he shall prepare the way before me: and the Lord, whom ye seek, shall suddenly come to his temple, even the messenger of the covenant, whom ye delight in: behold, he shall come, saith the LORD of hosts.

Matt. 3. 1 In those days came John the Baptist, preaching in the wilderness of Judea,

Luke 3. 2 Annas and Caiaphas being the high priests, the word of God came unto John the son of Zacharias in the wilderness.

John 1. 33 And I knew him not: but he that sent me to baptize with water, the same said unto me, Upon whom thou shalt see the Spirit descending, and remaining on him, the same is he which baptizeth with the Holy Ghost.

K

Acts 19. 4 Then said Paul, John verily baptized with the baptism of repentance, saying unto the people, that they should believe on him which should come after him, that is, on Christ Jesus.

L

Acts 13. 25 And as John fulfilled his course, he said, Whom think ye that I am? I am not *he*. But, behold, there cometh one after me, whose shoes of *his* feet I am not worthy to loose.

M

Isa. 49. 6 And he said, it is a light thing that thou shouldest be my servant to raise up the tribes of Jacob, and to restore the preserved of Israel: I will also give thee for a light to the Gentiles, that thou mayest be my salvation unto the end of the earth.

1: 1–14.

1 In the beginning [a]was the Word, and the Word was [b]with God, [c]and the Word was God.

2 [d]The same was in the beginning with God.

3 [e]All things were made by him; and without him was not anything made that was made.

4 [f]In him was life; and [g]the life was the light of men.

5 And [h]the light shineth in darkness; and the darkness comprehended it not.

6 ¶ [i]There was a man sent from God, whose name *was* John.

7 [k]The same came for a witness, to bear witness of the Light, that all *men* through him might believe.

8 He [l]was not that Light, but *was sent* to bear witness of that Light.

9 [m]*That* was the true Light, which lighteth every man that cometh into the world.

10 He was in the world, and [n]the world was made by him, and the world knew him not.

M—CONCLUDED.

John 1. 4. *See text of topic.*

I Jno. 2. 8 Again, a new commandment I write unto you, which thing is true in him and in you: because the darkness is past, and the true light now shineth.

N

Ps. 33. 6. *See under E.*

John 1. 3. *See text of topic.*

I Cor. 8. 6 But to us *there is but* one God, the Father, of whom *are* all things, and we in him; and one Lord Jesus Christ, by whom *are* all things, and we by him.

Eph. 3. 9. *See under E.*

Col. 1. 17. *See under A.*

Heb. 1. 2. *See under E.*

Heb. 11. 3 Through faith we understand that the worlds were framed by the word of God, so that things which are seen were not made of things which do appear.

Rev. 4. 11. *See under E.*

§ 1. GOD THE

O

Luke19. 14 But his citizens hated him, and sent a message after him, saying, We will not have this *man* to reign over us.

Acts 3. 26 Unto you first God, having raised up his Son Jesus, sent him to bless you, in turning away every one of you from his iniquities.

Acts 13. 46 Then Paul and Barnabas waxed bold, and said, It was necessary that the word of God should first have been spoken to you; but seeing ye put it from you, and judge yourselves unworthy of everlasting life, lo, we turn to the Gentiles.

P

Isa. 56. 5 Even unto them will I give in mine house and within my walls a place and a name better than of sons and of daughters: I will give them an everlasting name, that shall not be cut off.

Rom. 8. 15 For ye have not received the spirit of bondage again to fear; but ye have received the Spirit of adoption, whereby we cry, Abba, Father.

Gal. 3. 26 For ye are all the children of God by faith in Christ Jesus.

II Pet.1. 4 Whereby are given unto us exceeding great and precious promises; that by these ye might be partakers of the divine nature, having escaped the corruption that is in the world through lust.

I Jno. 3. 1 Behold, what manner of love the Father hath bestowed upon us, that we should be called the sons of God: therefore the world knoweth us not, because it knew him not.

1.

Or, *the right;* or, *privilege.*

Q

Deut. 30. 6 And the Lord thy God will circumcise thine heart, and the heart of thy seed, to love the Lord thy God with all thine heart, and with all thy soul, that thou mayest live.

John 3. 5 Jesus answered, Verily, verily, I say unto thee, Except a man be born of water and *of* the Spirit, he cannot enter into the kingdom of God.

Jas. 1. 18 Of his own will begat he us with the word of truth, that we should be a kind of first-fruits of his creatures.

I Pet. 1. 23 Being born again, not of corruptible seed, but of incorruptible, by the word of God, which liveth and abideth for ever.

R

Matt. 1. 16 And Jacob begat Joseph the husband of Mary, of whom was born Jesus, who is called Christ.

Matt. 1. 20 But while he thought on these things, behold, the angel of the Lord appeared unto him in a dream, saying, Joseph, thou son of David, fear not to take unto thee Mary thy wife: for that which is conceived in her is of the Holy Ghost.

Luke 1. 31 And, behold, thou shalt conceive in thy womb, and bring forth a son, and shalt call his name JESUS.

Luke 1. 35 And the angel answered and said unto her, The Holy Ghost shall come upon thee, and the power of the Highest shall overshadow thee: therefore also that holy thing which shall be born of thee shall be called the Son of God.

Luke 2. 7 And she brought forth her firstborn son, and wrapped him in swaddling clothes, and laid him in a manger; because there was no room for them in the inn.

§ 2. SAINT LUKE'S PREFACE

A

Heb. 2. 3 How shall we escape, if we neglect so great salvation; which at the first began to be spoken by the Lord, and was confirmed unto us by them that heard *him;*

I Pet. 5. 1 The elders which are among you I exhort, who am also an elder, and a witness of the sufferings of Christ, and also a partaker of the glory that shall be revealed:

II Pet. 1. 16 For we have not followed cunningly devised fables, when we made known unto you the power and coming of our Lord Jesus Christ, but were eye-witnesses of his majesty.

I Jno. 1. 1 That which was from the beginning, which we have heard, which we have seen with our eyes, which we have looked upon, and our hands have handled, of the Word of life;

B

Mark 1. 1 The beginning of the gospel of Jesus Christ, the Son of God:

John 15. 27 And ye also shall bear witness, because ye have been with me from the beginning.

WORD (CONCLUDED).

R—CONCLUDED.

1Tim. 3. 16 And without controversy great is the mystery of godliness: God was manifest in the flesh, justified in the Spirit, seen of angels, preached unto the Gentiles, believed on in the world, received up into glory.

I Jno. 1. 1. *See under A.*

S

Rom. 1. 3 Concerning his Son Jesus Christ our Lord, which was made of the seed of David according to the flesh:

Gal. 4. 4 But when the fulness of the time was come, God sent forth his Son, made of a woman, made under the law,

T

Heb. 2. 11 For both he that sanctifieth and they who are sanctfied *are* all of one: for which cause he is not ashamed to call them brethren,

Heb. 2. 14 Forasmuch then as the children are partakers of flesh and blood, he also himself likewise took part of the same; that through death he might destroy him that had the power of death, that is, the devil;

Heb. 2. 16 For verily he took not on *him the nature of* angels; but he took on *him* the seed of Abraham.

17 Wherefore in all things it behooved him to be made like unto *his* brethren, that he might be a merciful and faithful high priest in things *pertaining* to God, to make reconciliation for the sins of the people.

U

Isa. 40. 5 And the glory of the LORD shall be revealed, and all flesh shall see *it* together: for the mouth of the LORD hath spoken *it*.

CHAP. 1.

11 [o] He came unto his own, and his
own received him not.
12 But [p] as many as received him,
to them gave he [1] power to become the
sons of God, *even* to them that believe
on his name:
13 [q] Which were born, not of blood,
nor of the will of the flesh, nor of the
will of man, but of God.
14 [r] And the Word [s] was made [t] flesh,
and dwelt among us, (and [u] we beheld
his glory, the glory as of the only begotten of the Father,) [x] full of grace
and truth (p. 59).

U—CONCLUDED.

Matt.17. 2 And was transfigured before them; and his face did shine as the sun, and his raiment was white as the light.

John 2. 11 This beginning of miracles did Jesus in Cana of Galilee, and manifested forth his glory; and his disciples believed on him.

John 11. 40 Jesus saith unto her, Said I not unto thee, that, if thou wouldest believe, thou shouldest see the glory of God?

II Pet. 1. 17 For he received from God the Father honour and glory, when there came such a voice to him from the excellent glory, This is my beloved Son, in whom I am well pleased.

X

Col. 1. 19 For it pleased *the Father* that in him should all fulness dwell;

TO THEOPHILUS.

1: 1–4.

1 Forasmuch as many have taken
in hand to set forth in order a declaration of those things which are most
surely believed among us,
2 [a] Even as they delivered them unto
us, which [b] from the beginning were
eyewitnesses, and ministers of the word;
3 [c] It seemed good to me also, having

C

Acts 15. 19 Wherefore my sentence is, that we trouble not them, which from among the Gentiles are turned to God:

Acts 15. 25 It seemed good unto us, being assembled with one accord, to send chosen men unto you with our beloved Barnabas and Paul,

Acts 15. 28 For it seemed good to the Holy Ghost, and to us, to lay upon you no greater burden than these necessary things;

I Cor. 7. 40 But she is happier if she so abide, after my judgment: and I think also that I have the Spirit of God.

§ 2. SAINT LUKE'S PREFACE

D

Acts 11. 4 But Peter rehearsed *the matter* from the beginning, and expounded *it* by order unto them, saying,

E

Acts 1. 1 The former treatise have I made, O Theophilus, of all that Jesus began both to do and teach,
2 Until the day in which he was taken up, after that he through the Holy Ghost had given commandments unto the apostles whom he had chosen:
3 To whom also he showed himself alive after his passion by many infallible proofs, being seen of them forty days, and speaking of the things pertaining to the kingdom of God:

Acts 23. 26 Claudius Lysias unto the most excellent governor Felix *sendeth* greeting.

Acts 24. 3 We accept *it* always, and in all

§ 3. AN ANGEL APPEARS TO ZACHARIAS.

A

Matt. 2. 1 Now when Jesus was born in Bethlehem of Judæa in the days of Herod the king, behold, there came wise men from the east to Jerusalem :

B

I Chr. 24. 10 The seventh to Hakkoz, the eighth to Abijah,

I Chr. 24. 19 These *were* the orderings of them in their service to come into the house of the LORD, according to their manner, under Aaron their father, as the LORD God of Israel had commanded him.

Neh. 12. 4 Iddo, Ginnetho, Abijah,

Neh. 12. 17 Of Abijah, Zichri; of Miniamin, of Moadiah Piltai;

C

Gen. 7. 1 And the LORD said unto Noah, Come thou and all thy house into the ark; for thee have I seen righteous before me in this generation.

Gen. 17. 1 And when Abram was ninety years old and nine, the LORD appeared to Abram, and said unto him, I *am* the Almighty God; walk before me, and be thou perfect.

I Ki. 9. 4 And if thou wilt walk before me, as David thy father walked, in integrity of heart, and in uprightness, to do according to all that I have commanded thee, *and* wilt keep my statutes and my judgments;

II Ki. 20. 3 I beseech thee, O LORD, remember now how I have walked before thee in truth and with a perfect heart, and have done *that which is* good in thy sight. And Hezekiah wept sore.

Job 1. 1 There was a man in the land of Uz, whose name *was* Job; and that man was perfect and upright, and one that feared God, and eschewed evil.

C—CONCLUDED.

Acts 23. 1 And Paul, earnestly beholding the council, said, Men *and* brethren, I have lived in all good conscience before God until this day.

Acts 24. 16 And herein do I exercise myself, to have always a conscience void of offence toward God, and *toward* men.

Phil. 3. 6 Concerning zeal, persecuting the church; touching the righteousness which is in the law, blameless.

D

I Chr. 24. 19. *See under B.*

II Chr. 8. 14 And he appointed, according to the order of David his father, the courses of the priests to their service, and the Levites to their charges, to praise and minister before the priests, as the duty of every day required: the porters also by their courses at every gate: for so had David the man of God commanded.

II Chr. 31. 2 And Hezekiah appointed the courses of the priests and the Levites after their courses, every man according to his service, the priests and Levites for burnt offerings and for peace offerings, to minister, and to give thanks, and to praise in the gates of the tents of the LORD.

E

Ex. 30. 7 And Aaron shall burn thereon sweet incense every morning: when he dresseth the lamps, he shall burn incense upon it.
8 And when Aaron lighteth the lamps at even, he shall burn incense upon it, a perpetual incense before the LORD throughout your generations.

I Sa. 2. 28 And did I choose him out of all the tribes of Israel *to be* my priest, to offer upon mine altar, to burn incense, to wear an ephod before me? and did

TO THEOPHILUS (CONCLUDED).

CHAP. 1.

had perfect understanding of all things
from the very first, to write unto thee
[d]in order, [e]most excellent Theophilus,
4 [f]That thou mightest know the certainty of those things, wherein thou
hast been instructed.

places, most noble Felix, with all thankfulness.

Acts 26. 25 But he said, I am not mad, most noble Festus; but speak forth the words of truth and soberness.

F

John 20. 31 But these are written, that ye might believe that Jesus is the Christ, the Son of God; and that believing ye might have life through his name.

TIME, OCTOBER, B. C. 6; PLACE, JERUSALEM.

1: 5-25.

5 There [a]was in the days of Herod,
the king of Judæa, a certain priest
named Zacharias, [b]of the course of
Abia: and his wife *was* of the daughters of Aaron, and her name *was* Elisabeth.
6 And they were both [c]righteous
before God, walking in all the commandments and ordinances of the Lord
blameless.
7 And they had no child, because
that Elisabeth was barren; and they
both were *now* well stricken in years.
8 And it came to pass, that, while he
executed the priest's office before God,
[d]in the order of his course,
9 According to the custom of the
priest's office, his lot was [e]to burn incense when he went into the temple of
the Lord.
10 [f]And the whole multitude of the
people were praying without at the
time of incense.
11 And there appeared unto him an
angel of the Lord standing on the
right side of [g]the altar of incense.

E—CONTINUED.

I give unto the house of thy father all the offerings made by fire of the children of Israel?

E—CONCLUDED.

I Chr. 23. 13 The sons of Amram; Aaron, and Moses: and Aaron was separated, that he should sanctify the most holy things, he and his sons for ever, to burn incense before the LORD, to minister unto him, and to bless in his name for ever.

II Chr. 29. 11 My sons, be not now negligent: for the LORD hath chosen you to stand before him, to serve him, and that ye should minister unto him, and burn incense.

F

Lev. 16. 17 And there shall be no man in the tabernacle of the congregation when he goeth in to make an atonement in the holy *place*, until he come out, and have made an atonement for himself, and for his household, and for all the congregation of Israel.

Heb. 4. 14 Seeing then that we have a great high priest, that is passed into the heavens, Jesus the Son of God, let us hold fast *our* profession.

Heb. 9. 24 For Christ is not entered into the holy places made with hands, *which are* the figures of the true; but into heaven itself, now to appear in the presence of God for us:

Rev. 8. 3 And another angel came and stood at the altar, having a golden censer; and there was given unto him much incense, that he should offer *it* with the prayers of all saints upon the golden altar which was before the throne.

4 And the smoke of the incense, *which came* with the prayers of the saints, ascended up before God out of the angel's hand.

G

Ex. 30. 1 And thou shalt make an altar to burn incense upon: *of* shittim wood shalt thou make it.

§ 3. AN ANGEL APPEARS TO ZACHARIAS

H

Judg. 6. 22 And when Gideon perceived that he *was* an angel of the LORD, Gideon said, Alas, O Lord GOD! for because I have seen an angel of the LORD face to face.

Judg.13. 22 And Manoah said unto his wife, We shall surely die, because we have seen God.

Dan. 10. 8 Therefore I was left alone, and saw this great vision, and there remained no strength in me: for my comeliness was turned in me into corruption, and I retained no strength.

Luke 1. 29 And when she saw *him*, she was troubled at his saying, and cast in her mind what manner of salutation this should be.

Luke 2. 9 And, lo, the angel of the Lord came upon them, and the glory of the Lord shone round about them; and they were sore afraid.

Acts 10. 4 And when he looked on him, he was afraid, and said, What is it, Lord? And he said unto him, Thy prayers and thine alms are come up for a memorial before God.

Rev. 1. 17 And when I saw him, I fell at his feet as dead. And he laid his right hand upon me, saying unto me, Fear not; I am the first and the last:

I

Gen. 25. 21 And Isaac entreated the LORD for his wife, because she *was* barren: and the LORD was entreated of him, and Rebekah his wife conceived.

I Sa. 1. 19 And they rose up in the morning early, and worshipped before the LORD, and returned, and came to their house to Ramah: and Elkanah knew Hannah his wife; and the LORD remembered her.

K

Luke 1. 60 And his mother answered and said, Not *so;* but he shall be called John.

Luke 1. 63 And he asked for a writing table, and wrote, saying, His name is John. And they marvelled all.

L

Luke 1. 58 And her neighbours and her cousins heard how the Lord had showed great mercy upon her; and they rejoiced with her.

M

Matt.11. 11 Verily I say unto you, Among them that are born of women there

M—CONCLUDED.

hath not risen a greater than John the Baptist: notwithstanding, he that is least in the kingdom of heaven is greater than he.

N

Num. 6. 3 He shall separate *himself* from wine and strong drink, and shall drink no vinegar of wine, or vinegar of strong drink, neither shall he drink any liquor of grapes, nor eat moist grapes, or dried.

Judg.13. 4 Now therefore beware, I pray thee, and drink not wine nor strong drink, and eat not any unclean *thing.*

Luke 7. 33 For John the Baptist came neither eating bread nor drinking wine; and ye say, He hath a devil.

O

Jer. 1. 5 Before I formed thee in the belly I knew thee; and before thou camest forth out of the womb I sanctified thee, *and* I ordained thee a prophet unto the nations.

Gal. 1. 15 But when it pleased God, who separated me from my mother's womb, and called *me* by his grace,

P

Mal. 4. 5 Behold, I will send you Elijah the prophet before the coming of the great and dreadful day of the LORD:

6 And he shall turn the heart of the fathers to the children, and the heart of the children to their fathers, lest I come and smite the earth with a curse.

Q

Mal. 4. 5, 6. *See under P.*

Matt.11. 13 For all the prophets and the law prophesied until John.

14 And if ye will receive *it*, this is Elias, which was for to come.

Mark 9. 12 And he answered and told them, Elias verily cometh first, and restoreth all things; and how it is written of the Son of man, that he must suffer many things, and be set at nought.

1

Or, *by*.

R

Isa. 40. 3 The voice of him that crieth in the wilderness, Prepare ye the way of the LORD, make straight in the desert a highway for our God.

Amos 4. 12 Therefore thus will I do unto thee, O Israel: *and* because I will do this unto thee, prepare to meet thy God, O Israel.

(CONTINUED). TIME, OCTOBER, B. C. 6; PLACE, JERUSALEM.

CHAP. 1.

12 And when Zacharias saw *him*, [h]he was troubled, and fear fell upon him.

13 But the angel said unto him, Fear not, Zacharias: for [i]thy prayer is heard; and thy wife Elisabeth shall bear thee a son, and [k]thou shalt call his name John.

14 And thou shalt have joy and gladness; and [l]many shall rejoice at his birth.

15 For he shall be [m]great in the sight of the Lord, and [n]shall drink neither wine nor strong drink; and he shall be filled with the Holy Ghost, [o]even from his mother's womb.

16 [p]And many of the children of Israel shall he turn to the Lord their God.

17 [q]And he shall go before him in the spirit and power of Elias, to turn the hearts of the fathers to the children, and the disobedient [1]to the wisdom of the just; to make ready a people [r]prepared for the Lord.

18 And Zacharias said unto the angel, [s]Whereby shall I know this? for I am an old man, and my wife well stricken in years.

19 And the angel answering said unto him, I am [t]Gabriel, that stand in the presence of God; and am sent to speak unto thee, and to show thee these glad tidings.

20 And, behold, [u]thou shalt be dumb, and not able to speak, until the day that these things shall be performed, because thou believest not my words, which shall be fulfilled in their season.

R—CONCLUDED.

Rom. 9. 5 Whose *are* the fathers, and of whom as concerning the flesh Christ *came*, who is over all, God blessed for ever. Amen.

II Tim.2. 21 If a man therefore purge himself from these, he shall be a vessel unto honour, sanctified, and meet for the master's use, *and* prepared unto every good work.

S

Gen. 17. 17 Then Abraham fell upon his face, and laughed, and said in his heart, Shall *a child* be born unto him that is a hundred years old? and shall Sarah, that is ninety years old, bear?

T

Dan. 8. 16 And I heard a man's voice between *the banks of* Ulai, which called, and said, Gabriel, make this *man* to understand the vision.

Dan. 9. 21 Yea, while I *was* speaking in prayer, even the man Gabriel, whom I had seen in the vision at the beginning, being caused to fly swiftly, touched me about the time of the evening oblation.

22 And he informed *me*, and talked with me, and said, O Daniel, I am now come forth to give thee skill and understanding.

23 At the beginning of thy supplications the commandment came forth, and I am come to show *thee;* for thou *art* greatly beloved: therefore understand the matter, and consider the vision.

Matt.18. 10 Take heed that ye despise not one of these little ones; for I say unto you, That in heaven their angels do always behold the face of my Father which is in heaven.

Heb. 1. 14 Are they not all ministering spirits, sent forth to minister for them who shall be heirs of salvation?

U

Eze. 3. 26 And I will make thy tongue cleave to the roof of thy mouth, that thou shalt be dumb, and shalt not be to them a reprover: for they *are* a rebellious house.

Eze. 24. 27 In that day shall thy mouth be opened to him which is escaped, and thou shalt speak, and be no more dumb: and thou shalt be a sign unto them; and they shall know that I *am* the LORD.

§ 3. AN ANGEL APPEARS TO ZACHARIAS

X

Num. 6. 22 And the LORD spake unto Moses, saying,

23 Speak unto Aaron and unto his sons, saying, On this wise ye shall bless the children of Israel, saying unto them,

24 The LORD bless thee, and keep thee:

25 The LORD make his face shine upon thee, and be gracious unto thee:

26 The LORD lift up his countenance upon thee, and give thee peace.

27 And they shall put my name upon the children of Israel, and I will bless them.

Y

II Ki. 11. 5 And he commanded them, saying, This *is* the thing that ye shall do; A third part of you that enter in on the sabbath shall even be keepers of the watch of the king's house;

6 And a third part *shall be* at the gate of Sur; and a third part at the gate behind the guard: so shall ye keep the watch of the house, that it be not broken down.

Y—CONCLUDED.

II Ki. 11. 7 And two parts of all you that go forth on the sabbath, even they shall keep the watch of the house of the LORD about the king.

1 Chr. 9. 25 And their brethren, *which were* in their villages, *were* to come after seven days from time to time with them.

Z

Gen. 30. 23 And she conceived, and bare a son; and said, God hath taken away my reproach:

Isa. 4. 1 And in that day seven women shall take hold of one man, saying, We will eat our own bread, and wear our own apparel; only let us be called by thy name, to take away our reproach.

Isa. 54. 1 Sing, O barren, thou *that* didst not bear; break forth into singing, and cry aloud, thou *that* didst not travail with child: for more *are* the children of the desolate than the children of the married wife, saith the LORD.

2 Enlarge the place of thy tent, and let them stretch forth the curtains of thine habitations: spare not, lengthen thy cords, and strengthen thy stakes;

§ 4. AN ANGEL APPEARS TO MARY.

A

Matt. 1. 18 Now the birth of Jesus Christ was on this wise: When as his mother Mary was espoused to Joseph, before they came together, she was found with child of the Holy Ghost.

Luke 2. 4 And Joseph also went up from Galilee, out of the city of Nazareth, into Judæa, unto the city of David, which is called Bethlehem, (because he was of the house and lineage of David,)

5 To be taxed with Mary his espoused wife, being great with child.

B

Dan. 9. 21 Yea, while I *was* speaking in prayer, even the man Gabriel, whom I had seen in the vision at the beginning, being caused to fly swiftly, touched me about the time of the evening oblation.

22 And he informed *me*, and talked with me, and said, O Daniel, I am now come forth to give thee skill and understanding.

B—CONCLUDED.

Dan. 9. 23 At the beginning of thy supplications the commandment came forth, and I am come to show *thee;* for thou *art* greatly beloved: therefore understand the matter, and consider the vision.

Dan. 10. 19 And said, O man greatly beloved, fear not: peace *be* unto thee; be strong, yea, be strong. And when he had spoken unto me, I was strengthened, and said, Let my lord speak; for thou hast strengthened me.

1

Or, *graciously accepted;* or, *much graced.*

Luke 1. 30. *See text of topic.*

C

Judg. 6. 12 And the angel of the LORD appeared unto him, and said unto him, The LORD *is* with thee, thou mighty man of valour.

Isa. 43. 5 Fear not; for I *am* with thee: I will bring thy seed from the east, and gather thee from the west:

(CONCLUDED). TIME, OCTOBER, B. C. 6; PLACE, JERUSALEM.

CHAP. 1.

21 And the people [x]waited for Zacharias, and marvelled that he tarried so long in the temple.

22 And when he came out, he could not speak unto them: and they perceived that he had seen a vision in the temple; for he beckoned unto them, and remained speechless.

23 And it came to pass, that, as soon as [y]the days of his ministration were accomplished, he departed to his own house.

24 And after those days his wife Elisabeth conceived, and hid herself five months, saying,

25 Thus hath the Lord dealt with me in the days wherein he looked on *me*, to [z]take away my reproach among men.

Z—CONCLUDED.

Isa. 54. 3 For thou shalt break forth on the right hand and on the left; and thy seed shall inherit the Gentiles, and make the desolate cities to be inhabited.

4 Fear not; for thou shalt not be ashamed: neither be thou confounded; for thou shalt not be put to shame: for thou shalt forget the shame of thy youth, and shalt not remember the reproach of thy widowhood any more.

5 For thy Maker *is* thine husband; The LORD of hosts *is* his name; and thy Redeemer the Holy One of Israel; The God of the whole earth shall he be called.

6 For the LORD hath called thee as a woman forsaken and grieved in spirit, and a wife of youth, when thou wast refused, saith thy God.

7 For a small moment have I forsaken thee; but with great mercies will I gather thee.

Gal. 3. 16 Now to Abraham and his seed were the promises made. He saith not, And to seeds, as of many; but as of one, And to thy seed, which is Christ.

TIME, APRIL, B. C. 5; PLACE, NAZARETH.

1: 26–38.

26 And in the sixth month the angel Gabriel was sent from God unto a city of Galilee, named Nazareth,

27 To a virgin [a]espoused to a man whose name was Joseph, of the house of David; and the virgin's name *was* Mary.

28 And the angel came in unto her, and said, [b]Hail, *thou that art* [1]highly favoured, [c]the Lord *is* with thee: blessed *art* thou among women.

29 And when she saw *him*, [d]she was troubled at his saying, and cast in her mind what manner of salutation this should be.

30 And the angel said unto her, Fear

C—CONCLUDED.

Jer. 1. 18 For, behold, I have made thee this day a defenced city, and an iron pillar, and brazen walls against the whole land, against the kings of Judah, against the princes thereof, against the priests thereof, and against the people of the land.

19 And they shall fight against thee; but they shall not prevail against thee; for I *am* with thee, saith the LORD, to deliver thee.

Acts 18. 10 For I am with thee, and no man shall set on thee to hurt thee: for I have much people in this city.

D

Luke 1. 12 And when Zacharias saw *him*, he was troubled, and fear fell upon him.

Acts 10. 4 And when he looked on him, he was afraid, and said, What is it, Lord? And he said unto him, Thy prayers and thine alms are come up for a memorial before God.

§ 4. AN ANGEL APPEARS TO MARY (Concluded).

E

Isa. 7. 14 Therefore the Lord himself shall give you a sign; Behold, a virgin shall conceive, and bear a son, and shall call his name Immanuel.

Matt. 1. 21. *See text of* § 8.

Gal. 4. 4 But when the fulness of the time was come, God sent forth his Son, made of a woman, made under the law,

F

Luke 2. 21. *See text of* § 10.

G

I Tim. 6. 15 Which in his times he shall show, *who is* the blessed and only Potentate, the King of kings, and Lord of lords;

Phil. 2. 9 Wherefore God also hath highly exalted him, and given him a name which is above every name:

10 That at the name of Jesus every knee should bow, of *things* in heaven, and *things* in earth, and *things* under the earth;

11 And *that* every tongue should confess that Jesus Christ *is* Lord, to the glory of God the Father.

H

Mark. 5. 7 And cried with a loud voice, and said, What have I to do with thee, Jesus, *thou* Son of the most high God? I adjure thee by God, that thou torment me not.

I

II Sa. 7. 11 And as since the time that I commanded judges *to be* over my people Israel, and have caused thee to rest from all thine enemies. Also the Lord telleth thee that he will make thee a house.

12 And when thy days be fulfilled, and thou shalt sleep with thy fathers, I will set up thy seed after thee, which shall proceed out of thy bowels, and I will establish his kingdom.

Ps. 132. 11 The Lord hath sworn *in* truth unto David; he will not turn from it; Of the fruit of thy body will I set upon thy throne.

Isa. 9. 6 For unto us a child is born, unto us a son is given: and the government shall be upon his shoulder: and his name shall be called Wonderful, Counsellor, The mighty God, The everlasting Father, The Prince of Peace.

I—Concluded.

Isa. 9. 7 Of the increase of *his* government and peace *there shall be* no end, upon the throne of David, and upon his kingdom, to order it, and to establish it with judgment and with justice from henceforth even for ever. The zeal of the Lord of hosts will perform this.

Isa. 16. 5 And in mercy shall the throne be established: and he shall sit upon it in truth in the tabernacle of David, judging, and seeking judgment, and hasting righteousness.

Jer. 23. 5 Behold, the days come, saith the Lord, that I will raise unto David a righteous Branch, and a King shall reign and prosper, and shall execute judgment and justice in the earth.

Rev. 3. 7 And to the angel of the church in Philadelphia write; These things saith he that is holy, he that is true, he that hath the key of David, he that openeth, and no man shutteth; and shutteth, and no man openeth;

K

Dan. 2. 44 And in the days of these kings shall the God of heaven set up a kingdom, which shall never be destroyed: and the kingdom shall not be left to other people, *but* it shall break in pieces and consume all these kingdoms, and it shall stand for ever.

Dan. 7. 14 And there was given him dominion, and glory, and a kingdom, that all people, nations, and languages, should serve him: his dominion *is* an everlasting dominion, which shall not pass away, and his kingdom *that* which shall not be destroyed.

Dan. 7. 27 And the kingdom and dominion, and the greatness of the kingdom under the whole heaven, shall be given to the people of the saints of the Most High, whose kingdom *is* an everlasting kingdom, and all dominions shall serve and obey him.

Obad. 21 And saviours shall come up on mount Zion to judge the mount of Esau; and the kingdom shall be the Lord's.

Mic. 4. 7 And I will make her that halted a remnant, and her that was cast far off a strong nation: and the Lord shall reign over them in mount Zion from henceforth even for ever.

John 12. 34 The people answered him, We have heard out of the law that Christ abideth for ever: and how sayest

TIME, APRIL, B. C. 5; PLACE, NAZARETH.

CHAP. 1.

not, Mary: for thou hast found favour with God.

31 [e]And, behold, thou shalt conceive in thy womb, and bring forth a son, and [f]shalt call his name JESUS.

32 He shall [g]be great, and [h]shall be called the Son of the Highest; and [i]the Lord God shall give unto him the throne of his father David:

33 [k]And he shall reign over the house of Jacob for ever; and of his kingdom there shall be no end.

34 Then said Mary unto the angel, How shall this be, seeing I know not a man?

35 And the angel answered and said unto her, [l]The Holy Ghost shall come upon thee, and the power of the Highest shall overshadow thee: therefore also that holy thing which shall be born of thee shall be called [m]the Son of God.

36 And, behold, thy cousin Elisabeth, she hath also conceived a son in her old age; and this is the sixth month with her, who was called barren.

37 For [n]with God nothing shall be impossible.

38 And Mary said, Behold the handmaid of the Lord; be it unto me according to thy word. And the angel departed from her.

K—CONCLUDED.

thou, The Son of man must be lifted up? who is this Son of man?

Heb. 1. 8 But unto the Son *he saith*, Thy throne, O God, *is* for ever and ever: a sceptre of righteousness *is* the sceptre of thy kingdom.

L

Matt. 1. 20. *See text of 28.*

M

Matt. 14. 33 Then they that were in the ship came and worshipped him, saying, Of a truth thou art the Son of God.

Matt. 26. 63 But Jesus held his peace. And the high priest answered and said unto him, I adjure thee by the living God, that thou tell us whether thou be the Christ, the Son of God.

64 Jesus saith unto him, Thou hast said: nevertheless I say unto you, Hereafter shall ye see the Son of man sitting on the right hand of power, and coming in the clouds of heaven.

Mark 1. 1 The beginning of the gospel of Jesus Christ, the Son of God;

John 1. 34 And I saw, and bare record that this is the Son of God.

John 20. 31 But these are written, that ye might believe that Jesus is the Christ, the Son of God; and that believing ye might have life through his name.

Acts 8. 37 And Philip said, If thou believest with all thine heart, thou mayest. And he answered and said, I believe that Jesus Christ is the Son of God.

Rom. 1. 4 And declared *to be* the Son of God with power, according to the Spirit of holiness, by the resurrection from the dead:

N

Gen. 18. 14 Is any thing too hard for the LORD? At the time appointed I will return unto thee, according to the time of life, and Sarah shall have a son.

Jer. 32. 17 Ah Lord GOD! behold, thou hast made the heaven and the earth by thy great power and stretched-out arm, *and* there is nothing too hard for thee:

Zech. 8. 6 Thus saith the LORD of hosts: If it be marvellous in the eyes of the remnant of this people in these days, should it also be marvellous in mine eyes? saith the LORD of hosts.

Matt. 19. 26 But Jesus beheld *them*, and said unto them, With men this is impossible; but with God all things are possible.

Mark 10. 27 And Jesus looking upon them saith, With men *it is* impossible, but not with God: for with God all things are possible.

Luke 18. 27 And he said, The things which are impossible with men are possible with God.

Rom. 4. 21 And being fully persuaded, that what he had promised, he was able also to perform.

§ 5. MARY VISITS ELISABETH REMAINING THREE MONTHS.

A

Josh.21. 9 And they gave out of the tribe of the children of Judah, and out of the tribe of the children of Simeon, these cities which are *here* mentioned by name,

10 Which the children of Aaron, *being* of the families of the Kohathites, *who were* of the children of Levi, had: for theirs was the first lot.

11 And they gave them the city of Arba the father of Anak, which *city is* Hebron, in the hill *country* of Judah, with the suburbs thereof round about it.

B

Acts 6. 3 Wherefore, brethren, look ye out among you seven men of honest report, full of the Holy Ghost and wisdom, whom we may appoint over this business.

C

Judg. 5. 24 Blessed above women shall Jael the wife of Heber the Kenite be: blessed shall she be above women in the tent.

Luke 1. 28 And the angel came in unto her, and said, Hail, *thou that art* highly favoured, the Lord *is* with thee: blessed *art* thou among women.

D

Ruth 2. 10 Then she fell on her face, and bowed herself to the ground, and said unto him, Why have I found grace in thine eyes, that thou shouldest take knowledge of me, seeing I *am* a stranger?

1 Sa. 25. 40 And when the servants of David were come to Abigail to Carmel, they spake unto her, saying, David sent us unto thee, to take thee to him to wife.

41 And she arose, and bowed herself on *her* face to the earth, and said, Behold, *let* thine handmaid *be* a servant to wash the feet of the servants of my lord.

Phil. 2. 3 *Let* nothing *be done* through strife or vainglory; but in lowliness of mind let each esteem other better than themselves.

1

Or, *which believed that there.*

E

1 Sa. 2. 1 And Hannah prayed, and said, My heart rejoiceth in the LORD, mine horn

E—CONCLUDED.

is exalted in the LORD; my mouth is enlarged over mine enemies; because I rejoice in thy salvation.

Ps. 34. 2 My soul shall make her boast in the LORD: the humble shall hear *thereof*, and be glad.

3 O magnify the LORD with me, and let us exalt his name together.

Ps. 35. 9 And my soul shall be joyful in the LORD: it shall rejoice in his salvation.

Isa. 24. 15 Wherefore glorify ye the LORD in the fires, *even* the name of the LORD God of Israel in the isles of the sea.

16 From the uttermost part of the earth have we heard songs, *even* glory to the righteous. But I said, My leanness, my leanness, woe unto me! the treacherous dealers have dealt treacherously; yea, the treacherous dealers have dealt very treacherously.

Isa. 45. 25 In the LORD shall all the seed of Israel be justified, and shall glory.

Isa. 61. 10 I will greatly rejoice in the LORD, my soul shall be joyful in my God; for he hath clothed me with the garments of salvation, he hath covered me with the robe of righteousness, as a bridegroom decketh *himself* with ornaments, and as a bride adorneth *herself* with her jewels.

Hab. 3. 17 Although the fig tree shall not blossom, neither *shall* fruit *be* in the vines; the labour of the olive shall fail, and the fields shall yield no meat; the flock shall be cut off from the fold, and *there shall be* no herd in the stalls:

18 Yet I will rejoice in the LORD, I will joy in the God of my salvation.

F

I Sa. 1. 11 And she vowed a vow, and said, O LORD of hosts, if thou wilt indeed look on the affliction of thine handmaid, and remember me, and not forget thine handmaid, but wilt give unto thine handmaid a man child, then I will give him unto the LORD all the days of his life, and there shall no razor come upon his head.

Ps. 138. 6 Though the LORD *be* high, yet hath he respect unto the lowly: but the proud he knoweth afar off.

G

Mal. 3. 12 And all nations shall call you blessed: for ye shall be a delightsome land, saith the LORD of hosts.

TIME, APRIL–JUNE, B. C. 5; PLACE, PROBABLY HEBRON.

1 : 39–56.

39 And Mary arose in those days, and went into the hill country with haste, [a]into a city of Juda;

40 And entered into the house of Zacharias, and saluted Elisabeth.

41 And it came to pass, that, when Elisabeth heard the salutation of Mary, the babe leaped in her womb; and Elisabeth was filled [b]with the Holy Ghost:

42 And she spake out with a loud voice, and said, [c]Blessed *art* thou among women, and blessed *is* the fruit of thy womb.

43 And [d]whence *is* this to me, that the mother of my Lord should come to me?

44 For, lo, as soon as the voice of thy salutation sounded in mine ears, the babe leaped in my womb for joy.

45 And blessed *is* she [1]that believed: for there shall be a performance of those things which were told her from the Lord.

46 And Mary said, [e]My soul doth magnify the Lord,

47 And my spirit hath rejoiced in God my Saviour.

48 For [f]he hath regarded the low estate of his handmaiden: for, behold, from henceforth [g]all generations shall call me blessed.

49 For he that is mighty [h]hath done to me great things; and [i]holy *is* his name.

50 And [k]his mercy *is* on them that fear him from generation to generation.

G—CONCLUDED.

Luke 11. 27 And it came to pass, as he spake these things, a certain woman of the company lifted up her voice, and said unto him, Blessed *is* the womb that bare thee, and the paps which thou hast sucked.

H

Ps. 71. 19 Thy righteousness also, O God, *is* very high, who hast done great things: O God, who *is* like unto thee!

Ps. 126. 2 Then was our mouth filled with laughter, and our tongue with singing: then said they among the heathen, The LORD hath done great things for them.

3 The LORD hath done great things for us; *whereof* we are glad.

I

Ps. 111. 9 He sent redemption unto his people: he hath commanded his covenant for ever: holy and reverend *is* his name.

K

Gen. 17. 7 And I will establish my covenant between me and thee and thy seed after thee in their generations, for an everlasting covenant, to be a God unto thee and to thy seed after thee.

Ex. 20. 6 And showing mercy unto thousands of them that love me, and keep my commandments.

Ps. 103. 17 But the mercy of the LORD *is* from everlasting to everlasting upon them that fear him, and his righteousness unto children's children

18 To such as keep his covenant, and to those that remember his commandments to do them.

L

Ps. 98. 1 O sing unto the LORD a new song; for he hath done marvellous things: his right hand, and his holy arm, hath gotten him the victory.

Ps. 118. 15 The voice of rejoicing and salvation *is* in the tabernacles of the righteous: the right hand of the LORD doeth valiantly.

Isa. 40. 10 Behold, the Lord GOD will come with strong *hand*, and his arm shall rule for him: behold, his reward *is* with him, and his work before him.

Isa. 51. 9 Awake, awake, put on strength, O arm of the LORD; awake, as in the ancient days, in the generations of old.

See next page (18) for L Concluded.

§ 5. MARY VISITS ELISABETH REMAINING THREE MONTHS

L—CONCLUDED. See preceding page (17).
Art thou not it that hath cut Rahab, *and* wounded the dragon?

Isa. 52. 10 The LORD hath made bare his holy arm in the eyes of all the nations; and all the ends of the earth shall see the salvation of our God.

M

Ps. 33. 10 The LORD bringeth the counsel of the heathen to nought: he maketh the devices of the people of none effect.

I Pet. 5. 5 Likewise, ye younger, submit yourselves unto the elder. Yea, all *of you* be subject one to another, and be clothed with humility: for God resisteth the proud, and giveth grace to the humble.

N

I Sa. 2. 6 The LORD killeth, and maketh alive: he bringeth down to the grave, and bringeth up.

7 The LORD maketh poor, and maketh rich: he bringeth low, and lifteth up.

I Sa. 2. 8 He raiseth up the poor out of the dust, *and* lifteth up the beggar from the dunghill, to set *them* among princes, and to make them inherit the throne of glory: for the pillars of the earth *are* the LORD'S, and he hath set the world upon them.

Job 5. 11 To set up on high those that be low; that those which mourn may be exalted to safety.

Ps. 113. 6 Who humbleth *himself* to behold *the things that are* in heaven, and in the earth!

O

I Sa. 2. 5 *They that were* full have hired out themselves for bread; and *they that were* hungry ceased: so that the barren hath borne seven; and she that hath many children is waxed feeble.

Ps. 34. 10 The young lions do lack, and suffer hunger: but they that seek the LORD shall not want any good *thing*.

P

Ps. 98. 3 He hath remembered his mercy and his truth toward the house of

§ 6. BIRTH OF JOHN THE BAPTIST.

A

Ruth 4. 14 And the women said unto Naomi, Blessed *be* the LORD, which hath not left thee this day without a kinsman, that his name may be famous in Israel.

15 And he shall be unto thee a restorer of *thy* life, and a nourisher of thine old age: for thy daughter in law, which loveth thee, which is better to thee than seven sons, hath borne him.

16 And Naomi took the child, and laid it in her bosom, and became nurse unto it.

17 And the women her neighbours gave it a name, saying, There is a son born to Naomi; and they called his name Obed: he *is* the father of Jesse, the father of David.

B

Gen. 21. 6 And Sarah said, God hath made me to laugh, *so that* all that hear will laugh with me.

Rom. 12. 15 Rejoice with them that do rejoice, and weep with them that weep.

I Co. 12. 26 And whether one member suffer all the members suffer with it; or one member be honoured, all the members rejoice with it.

Luke 1. 14 And thou shalt have joy and gladness; and many shall rejoice at his birth.

C

Gen. 17. 12 And he that is eight days old shall be circumcised among you, every man child in your generations, he that is born in the house, or bought with money of any stranger, which *is* not of thy seed.

Lev. 12. 3 And in the eighth day the flesh of his foreskin shall be circumcised.

Acts 7. 8 And he gave him the covenant of circumcision: and so *Abraham* begat Isaac, and circumcised him the eighth day; and Isaac *begat* Jacob; and Jacob *begat* the twelve patriarchs.

D

Luke 1. 13 But the angel said unto him, Fear not, Zacharias: for thy prayer is heard; and thy wife Elisabeth shall bear thee a son, and thou shalt call his name John.

E

Prov. 3. 1 My son, forget not my law; but let thine heart keep my commandments:

2 For length of days, and long life, and peace, shall they add to thee.

(CONCLUDED). TIME, APRIL–JUNE, B. C. 5; PLACE, PROBABLY HEBRON.

CHAP. 1.

51 [l]He hath showed strength with his arm; [m]he hath scattered the proud in the imagination of their hearts.

52 [n]He hath put down the mighty from *their* seats, and exalted them of low degree.

53 [o]He hath filled the hungry with good things; and the rich he hath sent empty away.

54 He hath holpen his servant Israel, [p]in remembrance of *his* mercy,

55 [q]As he spake to our fathers, to Abraham, and to his seed for ever.

56 And Mary abode with her about three months, and returned to her own house.

P—CONCLUDED.

Israel: all the ends of the earth have seen the salvation of our God.

Jer. 31. 3 The LORD hath appeared of old unto me, *saying*, Yea, I have loved thee with an everlasting love: therefore with loving-kindness have I drawn thee.

Jer. 31. 20 *Is* Ephraim my dear son? *is he* a pleasant child? for since I spake against him, I do earnestly remember him still: therefore my bowels are troubled for him; I will surely have mercy upon him, saith the LORD.

Q

Gen. 17. 19 And God said, Sarah thy wife shall bear thee a son indeed; and thou shalt call his name Isaac: and I will establish my covenant with him for an everlasting covenant, *and* with his seed after him.

Ps. 132. 11 The LORD hath sworn *in* truth unto David; he will not turn from it; Of the fruit of thy body will I set upon thy throne.

TIME, JUNE, B. C. 5; PLACE, PROBABLY HEBRON.

1: 57–80.

57 Now Elisabeth's full time came that she should be delivered; and she brought forth a son.

58 And her [a]neighbours and her cousins heard how the Lord had showed great mercy upon her; and [b]they rejoiced with her.

59 And it came to pass, that [c]on the eighth day they came to circumcise the child; and they called him Zacharias, after the name of his father.

60 And his mother answered and said, [d]Not *so;* but he shall be called John.

61 And they said unto her, There is none of thy kindred that is called by this name.

62 And they made signs to his father, how he would have him called.

E—CONCLUDED.

Prov. 3. 3 Let not mercy and truth forsake thee: bind them about thy neck; write them upon the table of thine heart:

4 So shalt thou find favour and good understanding in the sight of God and man.

Jer. 17. 1 The sin of Judah *is* written with a pen of iron, *and* with the point of a diamond: *it is* graven upon the table of their heart, and upon the horns of your altars;

Hab. 2. 2 And the LORD answered me, and said, Write the vision, and make *it* plain upon tables, that he may run that readeth it.

F

Luke 1. 13. *See under D.*

G

Luke 1. 20. *See text of § 3.*

1

Or, *things.*

H

Luke 1. 39. *See text of § 5.*

I

Luke 2. 19. *See text of § 9.*
Luke 2. 51. *See text of § 13.*

§ 6. BIRTH OF JOHN THE BAPTIST (CONTINUED).

For E, F, G, 1, H and I see preceding page (19).

K

Gen. 39. 2 And the LORD was with Joseph, and he was a prosperous man; and he was in the house of his master the Egyptian.

Ps. 80. 17 Let thy hand be upon the man of thy right hand, upon the son of man *whom* thou madest strong for thyself.

Ps. 89. 21 With whom my hand shall be established: mine arm also shall strengthen him.

Acts 11. 21 And the hand of the Lord was with them: and a great number believed, and turned unto the Lord.

L

IIChr.20 14 Then upon Jahaziel the son of Zechariah, the son of Benaiah, the son of Jeiel, the son of Mattaniah, a Levite of the sons of Asaph, came the Spirit of the LORD in the midst of the congregation;

Joel 2. 28 And it shall come to pass afterward, *that* I will pour out my Spirit upon all flesh; and your sons and your daughters shall prophesy, your old men shall dream dreams, your young men shall see visions:

M

I Ki. 1. 48 And also thus said the king, Blessed *be* the LORD God of Israel, which hath given *one* to sit on my throne this day, mine eyes even seeing *it*.

Ps. 41. 13 Blessed *be* the LORD God of Israel from everlasting, and to everlasting. Amen, and Amen.

Ps. 72. 18 Blessed *be* the LORD God, the God of Israel, who only doeth wondrous things.

Ps. 106. 48 Blessed *be* the LORD God of Israel from everlasting to everlasting: and let all the people say, Amen. Praise ye the LORD.

N

Ex. 3. 16 Go, and gather the elders of Israel together, and say unto them, The LORD God of your fathers, the God of Abraham, of Isaac, and of Jacob, appeared unto me, saying, I have surely visited you, and *seen* that which is done to you in Egypt:

Ex. 4. 31 And the people believed: and when they heard that the LORD had visited the children of Israel, and that he had looked upon their affliction, then they bowed their heads and worshipped.

Ps. 111. 9 He sent redemption unto his people: he hath commanded his covenant for ever: holy and reverend *is* his name.

N—CONCLUDED.

Luke 7. 16 And there came a fear on all: and they glorified God, saying, That a great prophet is risen up among us; and, That God hath visited his people.

O

Ps. 132. 17 There will I make the horn of David to bud: I have ordained a lamp for mine anointed.

P

Jer. 23. 5 Behold, the days come, saith the LORD, that I will raise unto David a righteous Branch, and a King shall reign and prosper, and shall execute judgment and justice in the earth.

6 In his days Judah shall be saved, and Israel shall dwell safely: and this *is* his name whereby he shall be called, THE LORD OUR RIGHTEOUSNESS.

Jer. 30. 10 Therefore fear thou not, O my servant Jacob, saith the LORD; neither be dismayed, O Israel: for, lo, I will save thee from afar, and thy seed from the land of their captivity; and Jacob shall return, and shall be in rest, and be quiet, and none shall make *him* afraid.

Dan. 9. 24 Seventy weeks are determined upon thy people and upon thy holy city, to finish the transgression, and to make an end of sins, and to make reconciliation for iniquity, and to bring in everlasting righteousness, and to seal up the vision and prophecy, and to anoint the Most Holy.

Acts 3. 21 Whom the heaven must receive until the times of restitution of all things, which God hath spoken by the mouth of all his holy prophets since the world began.

Rom. 1. 1 Paul, a servant of Jesus Christ, called *to be* an apostle, separated unto the gospel of God,

2 (Which he had promised afore by his prophets in the holy Scriptures,)

Q

Lev. 26. 42 Then will I remember my covenant with Jacob, and also my covenant with Isaac, and also my covenant with Abraham will I remember; and I will remember the land.

Ps. 98. 3 He hath remembered his mercy and his truth toward the house of Israel: all the ends of the earth have seen the salvation of our God.

TIME, JUNE, B. C. 5; PLACE, PROBABLY HEBRON.

CHAP. 1.

63 And he asked for a [e]writing table, and wrote, saying, [f]His name is John. And they marvelled all.

64 [g]And his mouth was opened immediately, and his tongue *loosed,* and he spake, and praised God.

65 And fear came on all that dwelt round about them: and all these [1]sayings were noised abroad throughout all the [h]hill country of Judæa.

66 And all they that heard *them* [i]laid *them* up in their hearts, saying, What manner of child shall this be! And [k]the hand of the Lord was with him.

67 And his father Zacharias [l]was filled with the Holy Ghost, and prophesied, saying,

68 [m]Blessed *be* the Lord God of Israel; for [n]he hath visited and redeemed his people,

69 [o]And hath raised up a horn of salvation for us in the house of his servant David;

70 [p]As he spake by the mouth of his holy prophets, which have been since the world began:

71 That we should be saved from our enemies, and from the hand of all that hate us;

72 [q]To perform the mercy *promised* to our fathers, and to remember his holy covenant;

73 [r]The oath which he sware to our father Abraham,

74 That he would grant unto us, that we, being delivered out of the hand of our enemies, might [s]serve him without fear,

Q—CONCLUDED.

Ps. 105. 8 He hath remembered his covenant for ever, the word *which* he commanded to a thousand generations.

9 Which *covenant* he made with Abraham, and his oath unto Isaac;

Eze. 16. 60 Nevertheless, I will remember my covenant with thee in the days of thy youth, and I will establish unto thee an everlasting covenant.

Luke 1. 54. *See text of* § 5.

R

Gen. 12. 3 And I will bless them that bless thee, and curse him that curseth thee: and in thee shall all families of the earth be blessed.

S

Rom. 6. 18 Being then made free from sin, ye became the servants of righteousness.

Rom. 6. 22 But now being made free from sin, and become servants to God, ye have your fruit unto holiness, and the end everlasting life.

Heb. 9. 14 How much more shall the blood of Christ, who through the eternal Spirit offered himself without spot to God, purge your conscience from dead works to serve the living God?

T

Jer. 32. 39 And I will give them one heart, and one way, that they may fear me for ever, for the good of them, and of their children after them:

U

Isa. 40. 3 The voice of him that crieth in the wilderness, Prepare ye the way of the LORD, make straight in the desert a highway for our God.

Mal. 3. 1 Behold, I will send my messenger, and he shall prepare the way before me: and the Lord, whom ye seek, shall suddenly come to his temple, even the messenger of the covenant, whom ye delight in: behold, he shall come, saith the LORD of hosts.

Mal. 4. 5 Behold, I will send you Elijah the prophet before the coming of the great and dreadful day of the LORD:

6 And he shall turn the heart of the fathers to the children, and the heart of the children to their fathers, lest I come and smite the earth with a curse.

Matt. 11. 10 For this is *he,* of whom it is written, Behold, I send my messenger before thy face, which shall prepare thy way before thee.

Luke 1. 17. *See text of* § 3.

§ 6. BIRTH OF JOHN THE BAPTIST (Concluded).

For T and U see preceding page (21).

X

Mark 1. 4 John did baptize in the wilderness, and preach the baptism of repentance for the remission of sins.

Luke 3. 3 And he came into all the country about Jordan, preaching the baptism of repentance for the remission of sins;

2

Or, *for*.

3

Or, *bowels of the mercy*.

4

Or, *sunrising*, or *branch*.

Num.24. 17 I shall see him, but not now: I shall behold him, but not nigh: there shall come a Star out of Jacob, and a Sceptre shall rise out of Israel, and shall smite the corners of Moab, and destroy all the children of Sheth.

Isa. 11. 1 And there shall come forth a rod out of the stem of Jesse, and a Branch shall grow out of his roots:

Zech. 3. 8 Hear now, O Joshua the high priest, thou, and thy fellows that sit before thee: for they *are* men wondered at: for, behold, I will bring forth my servant the BRANCH.

Zech. 6. 12 And speak unto him, saying, Thus speaketh the Lord of hosts, saying, Behold the man whose name *is* The BRANCH; and he shall grow up out of his place, and he shall build the temple of the Lord:

Mal. 4. 2 But unto you that fear my name shall the Sun of righteousness arise with healing in his wings; and ye shall go forth, and grow up as calves of the stall.

Y

Isa. 9. 2 The people that walked in darkness have seen a great light: they that dwell in the land of the shadow of death, upon them hath the light shined.

Isa. 42. 6 I the Lord have called thee in righteousness, and will hold thine hand, and will keep thee, and give thee for a covenant of the people, for a light of the Gentiles;

7 To open the blind eyes, to bring out the prisoners from the prison, *and* them that sit in darkness out of the prison house.

Isa. 49. 9 That thou mayest say to the pris-

§ 7. THE TWO

[In this section the text of the Revised Version is substituted for that of the

Matt. 1: 1–17.

(1) The book of the generation of Jesus Christ, [a]the son of David, the [b]son of Abraham.

A

Ps. 132. 11 The Lord hath sworn *in* truth unto David; he will not turn from it; Of the fruit of thy body will I set upon thy throne.

Isa. 11. 1 And there shall come forth a rod out of the stem of Jesse, and a Branch shall grow out of his roots:

Jer. 23. 5 Behold, the days come, saith the Lord, that I will raise unto David a righteous Branch, and a King shall reign and prosper, and shall execute judgment and justice in the earth.

Matt.22. 42 Saying, What think ye of Christ? whose son is he? They say unto him, *The son* of David.

John 7. 42 Hath not the Scripture said, That Christ cometh of the seed of David, and out of the town of Bethlehem, where David was?

Acts 2. 30 Therefore being a prophet, and knowing that God had sworn with an oath to him, that of the fruit of his loins, according to the flesh, he would raise up Christ to sit on his throne;

A—Concluded.

Acts 13. 23 Of this man's seed hath God, according to *his* promise, raised unto Israel a Saviour, Jesus:

Rom. 1. 3 Concerning his Son Jesus Christ our Lord, which was made of the seed of David according to the flesh:

B

Gen. 12. 3 And I will bless them that bless thee, and curse him that curseth thee: and in thee shall all families of the earth be blessed.

Gen. 22. 18 And in thy seed shall all the nations of the earth be blessed; because thou hast obeyed my voice.

Gal. 3. 16 Now to Abraham and his seed were the promises made. He saith not, And to seeds, as of many; but as of one, And to thy seed, which is Christ.

C

Gen. 1. 26 And God said, Let us make man in our image, after our likeness: and let them have dominion over the fish of the sea, and over the fowl of the air,

TIME, JUNE, B. C. 5; PLACE, PROBABLY HEBRON.

CHAP. 1.

75 [t]In holiness and righteousness before him, all the days of our life.

76 And thou, child, shalt be called the prophet of the Highest: for [u]thou shalt go before the face of the Lord to prepare his ways;

77 To give knowledge of salvation unto his people [x2]by the remission of their sins,

78 Through the [g]tender mercy of our God; whereby the [h]dayspring from on high hath visited us,

79 [y]To give light to them that sit in darkness and *in* the shadow of death, to guide our feet into the way of peace.

80 And [z]the child grew, and waxed strong in spirit, and [a]was in the deserts till the day of his showing unto Israel.

Y—CONCLUDED.

oners, Go forth; to them that *are* in darkness, Show yourselves. They shall feed in the ways, and their pastures *shall be* in all high places.

Matt. 4. 16 The people which sat in darkness saw great light; and to them which sat in the region and shadow of death light is sprung up.

Acts 26. 18 To open their eyes, *and* to turn *them* from darkness to light, and *from* the power of Satan unto God, that they may receive forgiveness of sins, and inheritance among them which are sanctified by faith that is in me.

Z

Luke 2. 40 And the child grew, and waxed strong in spirit, filled with wisdom; nd the grace of God was upon him.

A

Matt. 3. 1 In those days came John the Baptist, preaching in the wilderness of Judæa.

Matt. 11. 7 And as they departed, Jesus began to say unto the multitudes concerning John, What went ye out into the wilderness to see? A reed shaken with the wind?

GENEALOGIES.

Authorized Version for the sake of the Old Testament form of the names.]

LUKE 3: 23–38, inverted.

(38) The [c]*son* of God, the *son* of [d]Adam, the *son* of Seth, the *son* of Enos,

C—CONCLUDED.

and over the cattle, and over all the earth, and over every creeping thing that creepeth upon the earth.

27 So God created man in his *own* image, in the image of God created he him; male and female created he them.

Gen. 5. 1, 2. *See under D.*

Isa. 64. 8 But now, O LORD, thou *art* our Father; we *are* the clay, and thou our potter; and we all *are* the work of thy hand.

D

Gen. 5. 1 This *is* the book of the generations of Adam. In the day that God created man, in the likeness of God made he him,

2 Male and female created he them; and blessed them, and called their name Adam, in the day when they were created.

Gen. 5. 3 And Adam lived a hundred and thirty years, and begat *a son* in his own likeness, after his image; and called his name Seth:

Gen. 5. 6 And Seth lived a hundred and five years, and begat Enos:

Gen. 5. 9 And Enos lived ninety years, and begat Cainan:

Gen. 5. 12 And Cainan lived seventy years, and begat Mahalaleel:

Gen. 5. 15 And Mahalaleel lived sixty and five years, and begat Jared:

Gen. 5. 18 And Jared lived a hundred sixty and two years, and he begat Enoch:

Gen. 5. 21 And Enoch lived sixty and five years, and begat Methuselah:

Gen. 5. 25 And Methuselah lived a hundred eighty and seven years, and begat Lamech:

Gen. 5. 28 And Lamech lived a hundred eighty and two years, and begat a son:

29 And he called his name Noah, saying, This *same* shall comfort us concerning our work and toil of our hands, because of the ground which the LORD hath cursed.

Gen. 5. 32 And Noah was five hundred years

See next page (24) for D concluded.

§ 7. THE TWO GENEALOGIES

Chap. 1.

(2) [e]Abraham begat Isaac; and [f]Isaac begat Jacob; and [g]Jacob begat Judah and his brethren; (3) and [h]Judah begat Perez and Zerah of Tamar; and [i]Perez begat Hezron; and Hezron begat Ram; (4) and Ram begat Amminadab; and Amminadab begat [k]Nahshon; and Nahshon begat Salmon; (5) and Salmon begat Boaz of [l]Rahab; and Boaz begat Obed of Ruth; and Obed begat Jesse; (6) and [m]Jesse begat David the king. And [n]David begat Solomon of her *that had been the wife* of Uriah;

D—Concluded. See preceding page (23).

old: and Noah begat Shem, Ham, and Japheth.

Gen. 11. 10 These *are* the generations of Shem: Shem *was* a hundred years old, and begat Arphaxad two years after the flood:

Gen. 11. 12 And Arphaxad lived five and thirty years, and begat Salah:

Gen. 11. 14 And Salah lived thirty years, and begat Eber:

Gen. 11. 16 And Eber lived four and thirty years, and begat Peleg:

Gen. 11. 18 And Peleg lived thirty years, and begat Reu:

Gen. 11. 20 And Reu lived two and thirty years, and begat Serug:

Gen. 11. 22 And Serug lived thirty years, and begat Nahor:

Gen. 11. 24 And Nahor lived nine and twenty years, and begat Terah:

Gen. 11. 26 And Terah lived seventy years, and begat Abram, Nahor, and Haran.

E

Gen. 21. 2 For Sarah conceived, and bare Abraham a son in his old age, at the set time of which God had spoken to him.

3 And Abraham called the name of his son that was born unto him, whom Sarah bare to him, Isaac.

Gen. 25. 26 And after that came his brother out, and his hand took hold on Esau's heel; and his name was called Jacob: and Isaac *was* threescore years old when she bare them.

E—Concluded.

Gen. 29. 35 And she conceived again, and bare a son: and she said, Now will I praise the Lord: therefore she called his name Judah; and left bearing.

Gen. 38. 29 And it came to pass, as he drew back his hand, that, behold, his brother came out: and she said, How hast thou broken forth? *this* breach *be* upon thee: therefore his name was called Pharez.

Ruth 4. 18 Now these *are* the generations of Pharez: Pharez begat Hezron,

19 And Hezron begat Ram, and Ram begat Amminadab,

20 And Amminadab begat Nahshon, and Nahshon begat Salmon,

21 And Salmon begat Boaz, and Boaz begat Obed,

22 And Obed begat Jesse, and Jesse begat David.

I Chr. 3. 5 And these were born unto him in Jerusalem; Shimea, and Shobab, and Nathan, and Solomon, four, of Bath-shua the daughter of Ammiel:

I Chr. 3. 10 And Solomon's son *was* Rehoboam, Abia his son, Asa his son, Jehoshaphat his son,

11 Joram his son, Ahaziah his son, Joash his son,

12 Amaziah his son, Azariah his son, Jotham his son,

13 Ahaz his son, Hezekiah his son, Manasseh his son,

14 Amon his son, Josiah his son.

15 And the sons of Josiah *were*, the first-born Johanan, the second Jehoiakim, the third Zedekiah, the fourth Shallum.

16 And the sons of Jehoiakim: Jeconiah his son, Zedekiah his son.

17 And the sons of Jeconiah; Assir, Salathiel his son,

18 Malchiram also, and Pedaiah, and Shenazar, Jecamiah, Hoshama, and Nedabiah.

19 And the sons of Pedaiah *were*, Zerubbabel, and Shimei: and the sons of Zerubbabel, Meshullam, and Hananiah, and Shelomith their sister:

Neh. 12. 1 Now these *are* the priests and the Levites that went up with Zerubbabel the son of Shealtiel, and Jeshua: Seraiah, Jeremiah, Ezra,

Matt. 1. 13-16. *See text of topic.*

F

Gen. 25. 26. *See under E.*

G

Gen. 29. 35. *See under E.*

(Continued).

Chap. 3.

(37) the *son* of Cainan, the *son* of Mahalaleel, the *son* of Jared, the *son* of Enoch, the *son* of Methuselah, (36) the *son* of Lamech, the *son* of Noah, the *son* of [o]Shem, the *son* of [p]Arphaxad, the *son* of Cainan, (35) the *son* of Shelah, the *son* of Eber, the *son* of Peleg, the *son* of Reu, the *son* of Serug, (34) the *son* of Nahor, the *son* of [q]Terah, the *son* of Abraham, the *son* of Isaac, the *son* of Jacob, (33) the *son* of Judah, the *son* of Perez, the *son* of Hezron, the *son* of Arni, the *son* of Amminadab, (32) the *son* of Nahshon, the *son* of Salmon, the *son* of Boaz, the *son* of Obed, the *son* of [r]Jesse, (31) the *son* of [s]David, the *son* of [t]Nathan, the *son* of Mattatha, the *son* of Menna, the *son* of Melea, (30) the *son* of Eliakim, the *son* of

H

Gen. 38. 27 And it came to pass in the time of her travail, that, behold, twins *were* in her womb.

28 And it came to pass, when she travailed, that *the one* put out *his* hand: and the midwife took and bound upon his hand a scarlet thread, saying, This came out first.

Gen. 38. 29. *See under E.*

I

Ruth 4.18-22. *See under E.*

I Chr. 2. 5 The sons of Pharez; Hezron, and Hamul.

I Chr. 2. 9 The sons also of Hezron, that were born unto him; Jerahmeel, and Ram, and Chelubai.

10 And Ram begat Amminadab; and Amminadab begat Nahshon, prince of the children of Judah;

11 And Nahshon begat Salma, and Salma begat Boaz,

12 And Boaz begat Obed, and Obed begat Jesse.

K

Num. 1. 7 Of Judah; Nahshon the son of Amminadab.

L

Josh. 6. 22 But Joshua had said unto the two men that had spied out the country, Go into the harlot's house, and bring out thence the woman, and all that she hath, as ye sware unto her.

Heb. 11. 31 By faith the harlot Rahab perished not with them that believed not, when she had received the spies with peace.

M

I Sa. 16. 1 And the Lord said unto Samuel, How long wilt thou mourn for Saul, seeing I have rejected him from reigning over Israel? fill thine horn with oil, and go, I will send thee to Jesse the Beth-lehemite: for I have provided me a king among his sons.

I Sa. 17. 12 Now David *was* the son of that Ephrathite of Beth-lehem-judah, whose name *was* Jesse; and he had eight sons: and the man went among men *for* an old man in the days of Saul.

N

II Sa. 12. 24 And David comforted Bath-sheba his wife, and went in unto her, and lay with her: and she bare a son, and he called his name Solomon: and the Lord loved him.

O

Gen. 11. 10. *See under D.*

P

Gen. 5. 6. *See under D, page 23.*
Gen. 11. 10. *See under D.*

Q

Gen. 11. 24, 26. *See under D.*

R

Ruth 4.18, etc. *See under E.*
I Chr. 2.10, etc. *See under I.*

S

II Sa. 5. 14 And these *be* the names of those that were born unto him in Jerusalem; Shammuah, and Shobab, and Nathan, and Solomon,

I Chr. 3. 5. *See under E.*

T

Zech. 12. 12 And the land shall mourn, every family apart; the family of the house of David apart, and their wives apart; the family of the house of Nathan apart, and their wives apart;

§ 7. THE TWO GENEALOGIES

CHAP. 1.

(7) and [u]Solomon begat Rehoboam; and Rehoboam begat Abijah; and Abijah begat Asa; (8) and Asa begat Jehoshaphat; and Jehoshaphat begat Joram; and Joram begat Uzziah; (9) and Uzziah begat Jotham; and Jotham begat Ahaz; and Ahaz begat Hezekiah; (10) and [x]Hezekiah begat Manasseh; and Manasseh begat Amon; and Amon begat Josiah; (11) and [1y]Josiah begat Jechoniah and his brethren, at the time of the [z]carrying away to Babylon.

(12) And after the carrying away to Babylon, [a]Jechoniah begat Shealtiel; and Shealtiel begat [b]Zerubbabel; (13) and Zerubbabel begat Abiud; and Abiud begat Eliakim; and Eliakim begat Azor; (14) and Azor begat Sadoc; and Sadoc begat Achim; and Achim begat Eliud; (15) and Eliud begat Eleazar; and Eleazar begat Matthan; and Matthan begat Jacob; (16) and Jacob begat Joseph the husband of Mary, of whom was born [c]Jesus, who is called Christ.

(17) So all the generations from Abraham unto David are fourteen generations; and from David unto the carrying away to Babylon fourteen generations; and from the carrying away to Babylon unto the Christ fourteen generations.

U

I Chr. 3. 10–16. *See under E, page 24.*

X

II Ki. 20. 21 And Hezekiah slept with his fathers: and Manasseh his son reigned in his stead.

I Chr. 3. 13. *See under E, page 24.*

1

Some read, *Josias begat Jakim and Jakim begat Jechonias.*

Y

I Chr. 3. 15, 16. *See under E, page 24.*

Z

II Ki. 24. 15 And he carried away Jehoiachin to Babylon, and the king's mother, and the king's wives, and his officers, and the mighty of the land, *those* carried he into captivity from Jerusalem to Babylon.

16 And all the men of might, *even* seven thousand, and craftsmen and smiths a thousand, all *that were* strong *and* apt for war, even them the king of Babylon brought captive to Babylon.

II Ki. 25. 11 Now the rest of the people that were left in the city, and the fugitives that fell away to the king of Babylon, with the remnant of the multitude, did Nebuzar-adan the captain of the guard carry away.

II Chr. 36. 10 And when the year was expired, king Nebuchadnezzar sent, and brought him to Babylon, with the goodly vessels of the house of the LORD, and made Zedekiah his brother king over Judah and Jerusalem.

II Chr. 36. 20 And them that had escaped from the sword carried he away to Babylon; where they were servants to him and his sons until the reign of the kingdom of Persia:

Jer. 27. 20 Which Nebuchadnezzar king of Babylon took not, when he carried away captive Jeconiah the son of Jehoiakim king of Judah from Jerusalem to Babylon, and all the nobles of Judah and Jerusalem;

Jer. 39. 9 Then Nebuzar-adan the captain of the guard carried away captive into Babylon the remnant of the people that remained in the city, and those that fell away, that fell to him, with the rest of the people that remained.

Jer. 52. 11 Then he put out the eyes of Zedekiah; and the king of Babylon bound him in chains, and carried him to Babylon, and put him in prison till the day of his death.

Jer. 52. 15 Then Nebuzar-adan the captain of the guard carried away captive *certain* of the poor of the people, and the residue of the people that remained in the city, and those that fell away, that fell to the king of Babylon, and the rest of the multitude.

Jer. 52. 28 This *is* the people whom Nebu-

(CONCLUDED).

CHAP 3.

Jonam, the *son* of Joseph, the *son* of
Judas, the *son* of Symeon, (29) the
son of Levi, the *son* of Matthat, the
son of Jorim, the *son* of Eliezer, the
son of Jesus, (28) the *son* of Er, the
son of Elmadam, the *son* of Cosam, the
son of Addi, the *son* of Melchi, (27)
the *son* of Neri, the *son* of Shealtiel,
the *son* of [2]Zerubbabel, the *son* of
Rhesa, the *son* of Joanan, (26) the *son*
of Joda, the *son* of Josech, the *son* of
Semein, the *son* of Mattathias, the *son*
of Maath, (25) the *son* of Naggai,
the *son* of Esli, the *son* of Nahum, the
son of Amos, the *son* of Mattathias,
(24) the *son* of Joseph, the *son* of
Jannai, the *son* of Melchi, the *son* of
Levi, the *son* of Matthat, (23) the [3]*son*
of Heli,—And Jesus himself . . . .
being the [d]son (as was supposed) of
Joseph. (p. 55.)

Z—CONCLUDED.

chadrezzar carried away captive: in the seventh year three thousand Jews and three and twenty:

Jer. 52. 29 In the eighteenth year of Nebuchadrezzar he carried away captive from Jerusalem eight hundred thirty and two persons:

30 In the three and twentieth year of Nebuchadrezzar, Nebuzar-adan the captain of the guard carried away captive of the Jews seven hundred forty and five persons: all the persons *were* four thousand and six hundred.

Dan. 1. 1 In the third year of the reign of Jehoiakim king of Judah came Nebuchadnezzar king of Babylon unto Jerusalem, and besieged it.

2 And the Lord gave Jehoiakim king of Judah into his hand, with part of the vessels of the house of God: which he carried into the land of Shinar to the house of his god; and he brought the vessels into the treasure house of his god.

A

I Chr. 3. 17, 19. *See under E, page 24.*

B

Ezr. 3. 2 Then stood up Jeshua the son of Jozadak, and his brethren the priests, and Zerubbabel the son of Shealtiel, and his brethren, and builded the altar of the God of Israel, to offer burnt offerings thereon, as *it is* written in the law of Moses the man of God.

Ezr. 5. 2 Then rose up Zerubbabel the son of Shealtiel, and Jeshua the son of Jozadak, and began to build the house of God which *is* at Jerusalem: and with them *were* the prophets of God helping them.

Neh. 12. 1 Now these *are* the priests and the Levites that went up with Zerubbabel the son of Shealtiel, and Jeshua: Seraiah, Jeremiah, Ezra,

Hag. 1. 1 In the second year of Darius the king, in the sixth month, in the first day of the month, came the word of the LORD by Haggai the prophet unto Zerubbabel the son of Shealtiel, governor of Judah, and to Joshua the son of Josedech, the high priest, saying,

C

Gen. 3. 15 And I will put enmity between thee and the woman, and between thy seed and her seed, it shall bruise thy head, and thou shalt bruise his heel.

Isa. 53. 2 For he shall grow up before him as a tender plant, and as a root out of a dry ground: he hath no form nor comeliness; and when we shall see him, *there is* no beauty that we should desire him.

I Tim. 3. 16 And without controversy great is the mystery of godliness: God was manifest in the flesh, justified in the Spirit, seen of angels, preached unto the Gentiles, believed on in the world, received up into glory.

2

It is uncertain whether Zerubbabel and Shealtiel are the same as those mentioned in Matt. i. 12 (*see text of topic*) and I Chr. 3. 17, 19 (*see under E, page 24*).

3

Son-in-law.

D

Matt. 13. 55 Is not this the carpenter's son? is not his mother called Mary? and his brethren, James, and Joses, and Simon, and Judas?

John 6. 42 And they said, Is not this Jesus, the son of Joseph, whose father and mother we know? how is it then that he saith, I came down from heaven?

§ 8. THE BIRTH OF JESUS.
(*Including Joseph's Vision*.

1: 18–25.

18 Now the [a] birth of Jesus Christ was on this wise: When as his mother Mary was espoused to Joseph, before they came together, she was found with child [b] of the Holy Ghost.

19 Then Joseph her husband, being a just *man*, and not willing [c] to make her a public example, was minded to put her away privily.

20 But while he thought on these things, behold, the angel of the Lord appeared unto him in a dream, saying, Joseph, thou son of David, fear not to take unto thee Mary thy wife; [d] for that which is [1] conceived in her is of the Holy Ghost.

21 [e] And she shall bring forth a son, and thou shalt call his name [2] JESUS: for [f] he shall save his people from their sins.

22 Now all this was done, that [g] it might be fulfilled which was spoken of the Lord by the prophet, saying,

23 [h] Behold, a virgin shall be with child, and shall bring forth a son, and [3] they shall call his name Emmanuel, which being interpreted is, [i] God with us.

24 Then Joseph being raised from sleep did as the angel of the Lord had bidden him, and took unto him his wife:

25 And knew her not till she had brought forth [k] her firstborn son: and he called his name JESUS. (p. 36.)

A

Luke 1. 26 And in the sixth month the angel Gabriel was sent from God unto a city of Galilee, named Nazareth,
27 To a virgin espoused to a man whose name was Joseph, of the house of David; and the virgin's name *was* Mary.

B

Luke 1. 35 And the angel answered and said unto her, The Holy Ghost shall come upon thee, and the power of the Highest shall overshadow thee; therefore also that holy thing which shall be born of thee shall be called the Son of God.

C

Deut. 24. 1 When a man hath taken a wife, and married her, and it come to pass that she find no favour in his eyes, because he hath found some uncleanness in her: then let him write her a bill of divorcement, and give *it* in her hand, and send her out of his house.

D

Luke 1. 35. *See under B.*

1

Gr. *begotten.*

E

Luke 1. 31 And, behold, thou shalt conceive in thy womb, and bring forth a son, and shalt call his name JESUS.

2

That is, *Saviour.*

F

Gen. 49. 10 The sceptre shall not depart from Judah, nor a lawgiver from between his feet, until Shiloh come; and unto him *shall* the gathering of the people *be.*

Acts 4. 12 Neither is there salvation in any other: for there is none other name under heaven given among men, whereby we must be saved.

Acts 5. 31 Him hath God exalted with his right hand *to be* a Prince and a Saviour, for to give repentance to Israel, and forgiveness of sins.

Acts 13. 23 Of this man's seed hath God, according to *his* promise, raised unto Israel a Saviour, Jesus:

Acts 13. 38 Be it known unto you therefore, men *and* brethren, that through this man is preached unto you the forgiveness of sins:

Heb. 7. 25 Wherefore he is able also to save them to the uttermost that come unto God by him, seeing he ever liveth to make intercession for them.

Rev. 1. 5 And from Jesus Christ, *who is* the faithful witness, *and* the first begotten of the dead, and the prince of the kings of the earth. Unto him that loved us, and washed us from our sins in his own blood,

TIME, DECEMBER, B. C. 5; PLACE, BETHLEHEM.
Time, April, B. C. 5; Place, Nazareth.)

2: 1–7.

1 And it came to pass in those days,
that there went out a decree from
Cæsar Augustus, that all the world
should be [4] taxed.

2 ([l] *And* this taxing was first made
when Cyrenius was governor of Syria.)

3 And all went to be taxed, every
one into his own city.

4 And Joseph also went up from
Galilee, out of the city of Nazareth,
into Judæa, unto [m] the city of David,
which is called Bethlehem, ([n] because
he was of the house and lineage of
David,)

5 To be taxed with Mary [o] his espoused wife, being great with child.

6 And so it was, that, while they
were there, the days were accomplished
that she should be delivered.

7 And [p] she brought forth her first-
born son, and wrapped him in swaddling clothes, and laid him in a
manger; because there was no room
for them in the inn.

G

Heb. 6. 18 That by two immutable things, in which *it was* impossible for God to lie, we might have a strong consolation, who have fled for refuge to lay hold upon the hope set before us:

H

Isa. 7. 14 Therefore the Lord himself shall give you a sign; Behold, a virgin shall conceive, and bear a son, and shall call his name Immanuel.

3

Or, *his name shall be called.*

I

Isa. 9. 6 For unto us a child is born, unto us a son is given: and the government shall be upon his shoulder: and his name shall be called Wonderful, Counsellor, The mighty God, The everlasting Father, The Prince of Peace.

I—CONCLUDED.

I Tim. 3. 16 And without controversy great is the mystery of godliness: God was manifest in the flesh, justified in the Spirit, seen of angels, preached unto the Gentiles, believed on in the world, received up into glory.

K

Ex. 13. 2 Sanctify unto me all the firstborn, whatsoever openeth the womb among the children of Israel, *both* of man and of beast: it *is* mine.

Luke 2. 7. *See text of topic.*

Luke 2. 21 And when eight days were accomplished for the circumcising of the child, his name was called JESUS, which was so named of the angel before he was conceived in the womb.

4.

Or, *enrolled.*

L

Acts 5. 37 After this man rose up Judas of Galilee in the days of the taxing, and drew away much people after him: he also perished; and all, *even* as many as obeyed him, were dispersed.

M

I Sam. 16. 1 And the LORD said unto Samuel, How long wilt thou mourn for Saul, seeing I have rejected him from reigning over Israel? Fill thine horn with oil, and go, I will send thee to Jesse the Beth-lehemite: for I have provided me a king among his sons.

I Sam. 16. 4 And Samuel did that which the LORD spake, and came to Beth-lehem. And the elders of the town trembled at his coming, and said, Comest thou peaceably?

Mic. 5. 2 But thou, Beth-lehem Ephratah, *though* thou be little among the thousands of Judah, *yet* out of thee shall he come forth unto me *that is* to be ruler in Israel; whose goings forth *have been* from of old, from everlasting.

John 7. 42 Hath not the Scripture said, That Christ cometh of the seed of David, and out of the town of Bethlehem, where David was?

N

Matt. 1. 16 And Jacob begat Joseph the husband of Mary, of whom was born Jesus, who is called Christ.

Luke 1. 27. *See under A.*

O

Matt. 1. 18. *See text of topic.*
Luke 1. 27. *See under A.*

P

Matt. 1. 25. *See text of topic.*

§ 9. AN ANGEL APPEARS TO THE SHEPHERDS.

1

Or, *the night watches.*

A

Luke 1. 12 And when Zacharias saw *him*, he was troubled, and fear fell upon him.

B

Gen. 12. 3 And I will bless them that bless thee, and curse him that curseth thee: and in thee shall all families of the earth be blessed.

Matt. 28. 19 Go ye therefore, and teach all nations, baptizing them in the name of the Father, and of the Son, and of the Holy Ghost:

Mark 1. 15 And saying, The time is fulfilled, and the kingdom of God is at hand: repent ye, and believe the gospel.

Luke 2. 31 Which thou hast prepared before the face of all people;
32 A light to lighten the Gentiles, and the glory of thy people Israel.

Luke 24. 47 And that repentance and remission of sins should be preached in his name among all nations, beginning at Jerusalem.

Col. 1. 23 If ye continue in the faith grounded and settled, and *be* not moved away from the hope of the gospel, which ye have heard, *and* which was preached to every creature which is under heaven; whereof I Paul am made a minister;

C

Isa. 9. 6 For unto us a child is born, unto us a son is given: and the government shall be upon his shoulder: and his name shall be called Wonderful, Counsellor, The mighty God, The everlasting Father, The Prince of Peace.

D

Matt. 1. 21. *See text of* § *8.*

E

Matt. 1. 16 And Jacob begat Joseph the husband of Mary, of whom was born Jesus, who is called Christ.

Matt. 16. 16 And Simon Peter answered and said, Thou art the Christ, the Son of the living God.

Luke 1. 43 And whence *is* this to me, that the mother of my Lord should come to me?

Acts 2. 36 Therefore let all the house of Israel know assuredly, that God hath made that same Jesus, whom ye have crucified, both Lord and Christ.

E—Concluded.

Acts 10. 36 The word which *God* sent unto the children of Israel, preaching peace by Jesus Christ: (he is Lord of all:)

Phil. 2. 11 And *that* every tongue should confess that Jesus Christ *is* Lord, to the glory of God the Father.

F

Gen. 28. 12 And he dreamed, and behold a ladder set up on the earth, and the top of it reached to heaven: and behold the angels of God ascending and descending on it.

Gen. 32. 1 And Jacob went on his way, and the angels of God met him.
2 And when Jacob saw them, he said, This *is* God's host: and he called the name of that place Mahanaim.

Ps. 103. 20 Bless the LORD, ye his angels, that excel in strength, that do his commandments, hearkening unto the voice of his word.
21 Bless ye the LORD, all *ye* his hosts; *ye* ministers of his, that do his pleasure.

Ps. 148. 2 Praise ye him, all his angels: praise ye him, all his hosts.

Dan. 7. 10 A fiery stream issued and came forth from before him: thousand thousands ministered unto him, and ten thousand times ten thousand stood before him: the judgment was set and the books were opened.

Heb. 1. 14 Are they not all ministering spirits, sent forth to minister for them who shall be heirs of salvation?

Rev. 5. 11 And I beheld, and I heard the voice of many angels round about the throne, and the beasts, and the elders: and the number of them was ten thousand times ten thousand, and thousands of thousands;

G

Luke 19. 38 Saying, Blessed *be* the King that cometh in the name of the Lord: peace in heaven, and glory in the highest.

Eph. 1. 6 To the praise of the glory of his grace, wherein he hath made us accepted in the beloved:

Eph. 3. 10 To the intent that now unto the principalities and powers in heavenly *places* might be known by the church the manifold wisdom of God.

Eph. 3. 21 Unto him *be* glory in the church by Christ Jesus throughout all ages, world without end. Amen.

TIME, DECEMBER, B. C. 5; PLACE, NEAR BETHLEHEM.

2: 8–20.

8 And there were in the same country shepherds abiding in the field, keeping [1]watch over their flock by night.

9 And, lo, the angel of the Lord came upon them, and the glory of the Lord shone round about them; [a]and they were sore afraid.

10 And the angel said unto them, Fear not: for, behold, I bring you good tidings of great joy, [b]which shall be to all people.

11 [c]For unto you is born this day in the city of David [d]a Saviour, [e]which is Christ the Lord.

12 And this *shall be* a sign unto you; Ye shall find the babe wrapped in swaddling clothes, lying in a manger.

13 [f]And suddenly there was with the angel a multitude of the heavenly host praising God, and saying,

14 [g]Glory to God in the highest, and on earth [h]peace, [i]good will toward men.

15 And it came to pass, as the angels were gone away from them into heaven, the [2]shepherds said one to another, Let us now go even unto Bethlehem, and see this thing which is come to pass, which the Lord hath made known unto us.

G—CONCLUDED.

Rev. 5. 13 And every creature which is in heaven, and on the earth, and under the earth, and such as are in the sea, and all that are in them, heard I saying, Blessing, and honour, and glory, and power, *be* unto him that sitteth upon the throne, and unto the Lamb for ever and ever.

H

Isa. 57. 19 I create the fruit of the lips: Peace, peace to *him that is* far off, and

H—CONCLUDED.

to *him that is* near, saith the LORD; and I will heal him.

Luke 1. 79 To give light to them that sit in darkness and *in* the shadow of death, to guide our feet into the way of peace.

Rom. 5. 1 Therefore being justified by faith, we have peace with God through our Lord Jesus Christ:

Eph. 2. 17 And came and preached peace to you which were afar off, and to them that were nigh.

Col. 1. 20 And, having made peace through the blood of his cross, by him to reconcile all things unto himself; by him, *I say*, whether *they be* things in earth, or things in heaven.

I

John 3. 16 For God so loved the world, that he gave his only begotten Son, that whosoever believeth in him should not perish, but have everlasting life.

Eph. 2. 4 But God, who is rich in mercy, for his great love wherewith he loved us,

Eph. 2. 7 That in the ages to come he might show the exceeding riches of his grace, in *his* kindness toward us, through Christ Jesus.

II Thes. 2. 16 Now our Lord Jesus Christ himself, and God, even our Father, which hath loved us, and hath given *us* everlasting consolation and good hope through grace.

Tit. 3. 4 But after that the kindness and love of God our Saviour toward man appeared,

5 Not by works of righteousness which we have done, but according to his mercy he saved us, by the washing of regeneration, and renewing of the Holy Ghost;

6 Which he shed on us abundantly through Jesus Christ our Saviour;

7 That being justified by his grace, we should be made heirs according to the hope of eternal life.

I Jno. 4. 9 In this was manifested the love of God toward us, because that God sent his only begotten Son into the world, that we might live through him.

10 Herein is love, not that we loved God, but that he loved us, and sent his Son *to be* the propitiation for our sins.

2 Or, *the men the shepherds*

§ 9. AN ANGEL APPEARS TO THE SHEPHERDS

K

Eccl 9. 10 Whatsoever thy hand findeth to do, do *it* with thy might; for *there is* no work, nor device, nor knowledge, nor wisdom, in the grave, whither thou goest.

L

Mal. 3. 16 Then they that feared the LORD spake often one to another: and the LORD hearkened, and heard *it*, and a book of remembrance was written before him for them that feared the LORD, and that thought upon his name.

17 And they shall be mine, saith the LORD of hosts, in that day when I make up my jewels; and I will spare them, as a man spareth his own son that serveth him.

18 Then shall ye return, and discern between the righteous and the wicked, between him that serveth God and him that serveth him not.

M

Gen. 37. 11 And his brethren envied him; but his father observed the saying.

1 Sa. 21. 12 And David laid up these words in his heart, and was sore afraid of Achish the king of Gath.

Prov. 4. 4 He taught me also, and said unto

M—CONCLUDED.

me, Let thine heart retain my words: keep my commandments, and live.

Hos. 14. 9 Who *is* wise, and he shall understand these *things?* prudent, and he shall know them? for the ways of the LORD *are* right, and the just shall walk in them: but the transgressors shall fall therein.

Luke 2. 51 And he went down with them, and came to Nazareth, and was subject unto them: but his mother kept all these sayings in her heart.

Luke 1. 66 And all they that heard *them* laid *them* up in their hearts, saying, What manner of child shall this be! And the hand of the Lord was with him.

N

1 Chr. 29. 10 Wherefore David blessed the LORD before all the congregation: and David said, Blessed *be* thou, LORD God of Israel our father, for ever and ever.

11 Thine, O LORD, *is* the greatness, and the power, and the glory, and the victory, and the majesty: for all *that is* in the heaven and in the earth *is thine;* thine *is* the kingdom, O LORD, and thou art exalted as head above all.

§ 10. THE CIRCUMCISION AND PRESENTATION IN THE TEMPLE.

A

Gen. 17. 12 And he that is eight days old shall be circumcised among you, every man child in your generations, he that is born in the house, or bought with money of any stranger, which *is* not of thy seed.

Lev. 12. 3 And in the eighth day the flesh of his foreskin shall be circumcised.

Luke 1. 59. *See text of § 6.*

B

Matt. 1. 21. *See text of § 8.*

Matt. 1 25. *See text of § 8.*

Luke 1. 31. *See text of § 4.*

C

Lev. 12. 2 Speak unto the children of Israel, saying, If a woman have conceived seed, and borne a man child, then she shall be unclean seven days; according to the days of the separation for her infirmity shall she be unclean.

3 And in the eighth day the flesh of his foreskin shall be circumcised.

4 And she shall then continue in the blood of her purifying three and thirty days; she shall touch no hallowed

C—CONCLUDED.

thing, nor come into the sanctuary, until the days of her purifying be fulfilled.

Lev. 12. 6 And when the days of her purifying are fulfilled, for a son, or for a daughter, she shall bring a lamb of the first year for a burnt offering, and a young pigeon, or a turtle-dove, for a sin offering, unto the door of the tabernacle of the congregation, unto the priest:

D

Ex. 13. 2 Sanctify unto me all the first-born, whatsoever openeth the womb among the children of Israel, *both* of man and of beast: it *is* mine.

Ex. 22. 29 Thou shalt not delay *to offer* the first of thy ripe fruits, and of thy liquors: the first-born of thy sons shalt thou give unto me.

Ex. 34. 19 All that openeth the matrix *is* mine; and every firstling among the cattle, *whether* ox or sheep, *that is male.*

Num. 3. 13 Because all the first-born *are* mine; *for* on the day that I smote all the

(CONCLUDED). TIME, DECEMBER, B. C. 5; PLACE, NEAR BETHLEHEM.

CHAP. 2.

16 And they came [k]with haste, and found Mary and Joseph, and the babe lying in a manger.

17 [l]And when they had seen *it*, they made known abroad the saying which was told them concerning this child.

18 And all they that heard *it* wondered at those things which were told them by the shepherds.

19 [m]But Mary kept all these things, and pondered *them* in her heart.

20 [n]And the shepherds returned, glorifying and praising God for all the things that they had heard and seen, as it was told unto them.

N—CONTINUED.

I Chr. 29. 12 Both riches and honour *come* of thee, and thou reignest over all; and in thine hand *is* power and might;

N—CONCLUDED.

and in thine hand *it is* to make great, and to give strength unto all.

13 Now therefore, our God, we thank thee, and praise thy glorious name.

Ps. 106. 48 Blessed *be* the LORD God of Israel from everlasting to everlasting: and let all the people say, Amen. Praise ye the LORD.

Ps. 107. 8 Oh that *men* would praise the LORD *for* his goodness, and *for* his wonderful works to the children of men!

9 For he satisfieth the longing soul, and filleth the hungry soul with goodness.

Ps. 107. 15 Oh that *men* would praise the LORD *for* his goodness, and *for* his wonderful works to the children of men!

16 For he hath broken the gates of brass, and cut the bars of iron in sunder.

Ps. 107. 21 Oh that *men* would praise the LORD *for* his goodness, and *for* his wonderful works to the children of men!

22 And let them sacrifice the sacrifices of thanksgiving, and declare his works with rejoicing.

TIME, JANUARY, FEBRUARY, B. C. 4; PLACE, BETHLEHEM, JERUSALEM.

2: 21–38.

21 [a]And when eight days were accomplished for the circumcising of the child, his name was called [b]JESUS, which was so named of the angel before he was conceived in the womb.

22 And when the [c]days of her purification according to the law of Moses were accomplished, they brought him to Jerusalem, to present *him* to the Lord;

23 (As it is written in the law of the Lord, [d]Every male that openeth the womb shall be called holy to the Lord;)

24 And to offer a sacrifice according to [e]that which is said in the law of the Lord. A pair of turtle-doves, or two young pigeons.

D—CONCLUDED.

first-born in the land of Egypt I hallowed unto me all the first-born in Israel, both man and beast: mine they shall be: I *am* the LORD.

Num. 8. 17 For all the first-born of the children of Israel *are* mine, *both* man and beast: on the day that I smote every first-born in the land of Egypt I sanctified them for myself.

Num. 18. 15 Every thing that openeth the matrix in all flesh, which they bring unto the LORD, *whether it be* of men or beasts, shall be thine: nevertheless the first-born of man shalt thou surely redeem, and the firstling of unclean beasts shalt thou redeem.

E

Lev. 12. 2. *See under C.*
Lev. 12. 6. *See under C.*
Lev. 12. 8 And if she be not able to bring a lamb, then she shall bring two turtles, or two young pigeons; the one for the burnt offering, and the other for a sin offering: and the priest shall make an atonement for her, and she shall be clean.

§ 10. THE CIRCUMCISION AND PRESENTATION IN THE TEMPLE

F

Isa. 40. 1 Comfort ye, comfort ye my people, saith your God.

Mark15. 43 Joseph of Arimathea, an honourable counsellor, which also waited for the kingdom of God, came, and went in boldly unto Pilate, and craved the body of Jesus.

Luke 2. 38. *See text of topic.*

G

Ps. 89. 48 What man *is he that* liveth, and shall not see death? shall he deliver his soul from the hand of the grave? Selah.

Heb. 11. 5 By faith Enoch was translated that he should not see death; and was not found, because God had translated him: for before his translation he had this testimony, that he pleased God.

H

Matt. 4. 1 Then was Jesus led up of the Spirit into the wilderness to be tempted of the devil.

Acts 8. 29 Then the Spirit said unto Philip, Go near, and join thyself to this chariot.

Acts 10. 19 While Peter thought on the vision, the Spirit said unto him, Behold, three men seek thee.

Rev. 1. 10 I was in the Spirit on the Lord's day, and heard behind me a great voice, as of a trumpet.

I

Gen. 15. 15 And thou shalt go to thy fathers in peace; thou shalt be buried in a good old age.

Gen. 46. 30 And Israel said unto Joseph, Now let me die, since I have seen thy face, because thou *art* yet alive.

Ps. 37. 37 Mark the perfect *man*, and behold the upright: for the end of *that* man *is* peace.

Isa. 57. 1 The righteous perisheth, and no man layeth *it* to heart: and merciful men *are* taken away, none considering that the righteous is taken away from the evil *to come*.

Phil. 1. 23 For I am in a strait betwixt two, having a desire to depart, and to be with Christ; which is far better:

Rev. 14. 13 And I heard a voice from heaven saying unto me, Write, Blessed *are* the dead which die in the Lord from henceforth: Yea, saith the Spirit, that they may rest from their labours; and their works do follow them.

K

Ps. 48. 3 God is known in her palaces for a refuge.

Isa. 52. 10 The LORD hath made bare his holy arm in the eyes of all the nations; and all the ends of the earth shall see the salvation of our God.

Luke 3. 6 And all flesh shall see the salvation of God.

Acts 4. 12 Neither is there salvation in any other: for there is none other name under heaven given among men, whereby we must be saved.

L

Isa. 9. 2 The people that walked in darkness have seen a great light: they that dwell in the land of the shadow of death, upon them hath the light shined.

Isa. 42. 6 I the LORD have called thee in righteousness, and will hold thine hand, and will keep thee, and give thee for a covenant of the people, for a light of the Gentiles;

Isa. 49. 6 And he said, It is a light thing that thou shouldest be my servant to raise up the tribes of Jacob, and to restore the preserved of Israel: I will also give thee for a light to the Gentiles, that thou mayest be my salvation unto the end of the earth.

Isa. 60. 1 Arise, shine; for thy light is come, and the glory of the LORD is risen upon thee.

2 For, behold, the darkness shall cover the earth, and gross darkness the people: but the LORD shall arise upon thee, and his glory shall be seen upon thee.

3 And the Gentiles shall come to thy light, and kings to the brightness of thy rising.

Isa. 60. 19 The sun shall be no more thy light by day; neither for brightness shall the moon give light unto thee: but the LORD shall be unto thee an everlasting light, and thy God thy glory.

Matt. 4. 16 The people which sat in darkness saw great light; and to them which sat in the region and shadow of death light is sprung up.

Acts 13. 47 For so hath the Lord commanded us, *saying*, I have set thee to be a light of the Gentiles, that thou shouldest be for salvation unto the ends of the earth.

(CONTINUED). TIME, JANUARY, FEBRUARY, B. C. 4; PLACE, BETHLEHEM, JERUSALEM.

CHAP 2.

25 And, behold, there was a man in Jerusalem, whose name *was* Simeon; and the same man *was* just and devout, [f]waiting for the consolation of Israel: and the Holy Ghost was upon him.

26 And it was revealed unto him by the Holy Ghost, that he should not [g]see death, before he had seen the Lord's Christ.

27 And he came [h]by the Spirit into the temple: and when the parents brought in the child Jesus, to do for him after the custom of the law,

28 Then took he him up in his arms, and blessed God, and said,

29 Lord, [i]now lettest thou thy servant depart in peace, according to thy word:

30 For mine eyes [k]have seen thy salvation,

31 Which thou hast prepared before the face of all people;

32 [l]A light to lighten the Gentiles, and the glory of thy people Israel.

33 And Joseph and his mother marvelled at those things which were spoken of him.

34 And Simeon blessed them, and said unto Mary his mother, Behold, this *child* is set for the [m]fall and rising again of many in Israel; and for [n]a sign which shall be spoken against;

35 (Yea, [o]a sword shall pierce through thy own soul also;) that the thoughts of many hearts may be revealed.

L—CONCLUDED.

Acts 28. 28 Be it known therefore unto you, that the salvation of God is sent unto the Gentiles, and *that* they will hear it.

M

Isa. 8. 14 And he shall be for a sanctuary; but for a stone of stumbling and for a rock of offence to both the houses of Israel, for a gin and for a snare to the inhabitants of Jerusalem.

Hos. 14. 9 Who *is* wise, and he shall understand these *things?* prudent, and he shall know them? for the ways of the LORD *are* right, and the just shall walk in them: but the transgressors shall fall therein.

Matt. 21. 44 And whosoever shall fall on this stone shall be broken: but on whomsoever it shall fall, it will grind him to powder.

Rom. 9. 32 Wherefore? Because *they sought it* not by faith, but as it were by the works of the law. For they stumbled at that stumblingstone;

33 As it is written, Behold, I lay in Sion a stumblingstone and rock of offence: and whosoever believeth on him shall not be ashamed.

I Cor. 1. 23 But we preach Christ crucified, unto the Jews a stumblingblock, and unto the Greeks foolishness;

24 But unto them which are called, both Jews and Greeks, Christ the power of God, and the wisdom of God.

II Cor. 2. 16 To the one *we are* the savour of death unto death; and to the other the savour of life unto life. And who *is* sufficient for these things?

I Pet. 2. 7 Unto you therefore which believe *he is* precious: but unto them which be disobedient, the stone which the builders disallowed, the same is made the head of the corner,

8 And a stone of stumbling, and a rock of offence, *even to them* which stumble at the word, being disobedient: whereunto also they were appointed.

N

Acts 28. 22 But we desire to hear of thee what thou thinkest: for as concerning this sect, we know that every where it is spoken against.

O

Ps. 42. 10 *As* with a sword in my bones, mine enemies reproach me; while they say daily unto me, Where *is* thy God?

John 19. 25 Now there stood by the cross of Jesus his mother, and his mother's sister, Mary the *wife* of Cleophas, and Mary Magdalene.

§ 10. THE CIRCUMCISION AND PRESENTATION IN THE TEMPLE

P

Ex. 15. 20 And Miriam the prophetess, the sister of Aaron, took a timbrel in her hand; and all the women went out after her with timbrels and with dances.

Judg. 4. 4 And Deborah, a prophetess, the wife of Lapidoth, she judged Israel at that time.

II Ki. 22. 14 So Hilkiah the priest, and Ahikam, and Achbor, and Shaphan, and Asahiah, went unto Huldah the prophetess, the wife of Shallum the son of Tikvah, the son of Harhas, keeper of the wardrobe; (now she dwelt in Jerusalem in the college;) and they communed with her.

Acts 2. 18 And on my servants and on my handmaidens I will pour out in those days of my Spirit; and they shall prophesy:

Acts 21. 8 And the next *day* we that were of

P—Concluded.

Paul's company departed, and came unto Cæsarea; and we entered into the house of Philip the evangelist, which was *one* of the seven; and abode with him.

9 And the same man had four daughters, virgins, which did prophesy.

Q

Job 5. 26 Thou shalt come to *thy* grave in a full age, like as a shock of corn cometh in in his season.

R

Ex. 38. 8 And he made the laver *of* brass, and the foot of it *of* brass, of the looking-glasses of *the women* assembling, which assembled *at* the door of the tabernacle of the congregation.

Ps. 27. 4 One *thing* have I desired of the Lord, that will I seek after; that I may dwell in the house of the Lord all the days of my life, to behold the

§ 11. THE WISE MEN FROM THE EAST

2: 1–12.

1 Now when [a]Jesus was born in Bethlehem of Judæa in the days of Herod the king, behold, there came wise men [b]from the east to Jerusalem,

2 Saying, [c]Where is he that is born King of the Jews? for we have seen [d]his star in the east, and are come to worship him.

3 When Herod the king had heard *these things*, he was troubled, and all Jerusalem with him.

4 And when he had gathered all [e]the chief priests and [f]scribes of the people together, [g]he demanded of them where Christ should be born.

5 And they said unto him, In Bethlehem of Judæa: for thus it is written by the prophet,

6 [h]And thou Bethlehem, *in* the land of Juda, art not the least among the princes of Juda: for out of thee shall

A

Luke 2. 4 And Joseph also went up from Galilee, out of the city of Nazareth, into Judæa, unto the city of David, which is called Bethlehem, (because he was of the house and lineage of David,)

5 To be taxed with Mary his espoused wife, being great with child.

6 And so it was, that, while they were there, the days were accomplished that she should be delivered.

7 And she brought forth her firstborn son, and wrapped him in swaddling clothes, and laid him in a manger; because there was no room for them in the inn.

B

Gen. 10. 30 And their dwelling was from Mesha, as thou goest unto Sephar, a mount of the east.

Gen. 25. 6 But unto the sons of the concubines, which Abraham had, Abraham gave gifts, and sent them away from Isaac his son, while he yet lived, eastward, unto the east country.

I Ki. 4. 30 And Solomon's wisdom excelled the wisdom of all the children of the east country, and all the wisdom of Egypt.

Isa. 11. 10 And in that day there shall be a root of Jesse, which shall stand for an ensign of the people; to it shall the

(CONCLUDED). TIME, JANUARY, FEBRUARY, B. C. 4; PLACE, BETHLEHEM, JERUSALEM.

CHAP. 2.

36 And there was one Anna, a [p]prophetess, the daughter of Phanuel, of the tribe of Aser: [q]she was of a great age, and had lived with a husband seven years from her virginity;

37 And she *was* a widow of about fourscore and four years, [r]which departed not from the temple, but served *God* with fastings and prayers [s]night and day.

38 And she coming in that instant gave thanks likewise unto the Lord, and spake of him to all them that [t]looked for redemption in [1]Jerusalem.

R—CONCLUDED.

beauty of the LORD, and to inquire in his temple.

S

Acts 26. 7 Unto which *promise* our twelve tribes, instantly serving *God* day and night, hope to come. For which hope's sake, king Agrippa, I am accused of the Jews.

I Tim.5. 5 Now she that is a widow indeed, and desolate, trusteth in God, and continueth in supplications and prayers night and day.

T

Mark 15. 43. *See under F, page 34.*
Luke 2. 25. *See text of topic.*

Luke24. 21 But we trusted that it had been he which should have redeemed Israel: and beside all this, to-day is the third day since these things were done.

1

Or, *Israel.*

TIME, FEBRUARY, B. C. 4; PLACE, JERUSALEM, BETHLEH

Gentiles seek: and his rest shall be glorious.

C

Luke 2. 11 For unto you is born this day in the city of David a Saviour, which is Christ the Lord.

D

Num.24. 17 I shall see him, but not now: I shall behold him, but not nigh: there shall come a Star out of Jacob, and a Sceptre shall rise out of Israel, and shall smite the corners of Moab, and destroy all the children of Sheth.

Isa. 60. 3 And the Gentiles shall come to thy light, and kings to the brightness of thy rising.

E

II Chr. 36. 14 Moreover all the chief of the priests, and the people, transgressed very much after all the abominations of the heathen; and polluted the house of the LORD which he had hallowed in Jerusalem.

Ps. 2. 1. Why do the heathen rage, and the people imagine a vain thing?

F

II Chr.34.13 Also *they were* over the bearers of burdens, and *were* overseers of all that wrought the work in any manner of service: and of the Levites *there were* scribes, and officers, and porters.

G

Mal. 2. 7 For the priest's lips should keep knowledge, and they should seek the law at his mouth: for he *is* the messenger of the LORD of hosts.

H

Mic. 5. 2 But thou, Beth-lehem Ephratah, *though* thou be little among the thousands of Judah, *yet* out of thee shall he come forth unto me *that is* to be ruler in Israel; whose goings forth *have been* from of old, from everlasting.

John 7. 42 Hath not the Scripture said, That Christ cometh of the seed of David, and out of the town of Bethlehem, where David was?

I

Rev. 2. 27 And he shall rule them with a rod of iron; as the vessels of a potter shall they be broken to shivers: even as I received of my Father.

1

Or, *feed.*

Ps. 78. 70 He chose David also his servant, and took him from the sheepfolds:

71 From following the ewes great with young he brought him to feed Jacob his people, and Israel his inheritance.

72 So he fed them according to the integrity of his heart; and guided

See next page (38) for 1 concluded.

§ 11. THE WISE MEN FROM THE EAST (CONCLUDED).

CHAP. 2.

come a Governor, [i]that shall [1]rule my people Israel.

7 [k]Then Herod, when he had privily called the wise men, inquired of them diligently what time the star appeared.

8 And he sent them to Bethlehem, and said, Go and search diligently for the young child; and when ye have found *him*, bring me word again, that I may come and worship him also.

9 When they had heard the king, they departed; and, lo, the star, which they saw in the east, went before them, till it came and stood over where the young child was.

10 When they saw the star, they rejoiced with exceeding great joy.

11 And when they were come into the house, they saw the young child with Mary his mother, and fell down, and worshipped him: and when they had opened their treasures, [l]they [2]presented unto him gifts; gold, and frankincense, and myrrh.

12 And being warned of God [m]in a dream that they should not return to Herod, they departed into their own country another way.

1—CONCLUDED.

See preceding page (37); also for I.

Isa. 40. them by the skilfulness of his hands.
11 He shall feed his flock like a shepherd: he shall gather the lambs with his arm, and carry *them* in his bosom, *and* shall gently lead those that are with young.

K

Ex. 1. 10 Come on, let us deal wisely with them; lest they multiply, and it come to pass, that, when there falleth out any war, they join also unto our enemies, and fight against us, and *so* get them up out of the land.

I Sa. 18. 20 And Michal Saul's daughter loved David: and they told Saul, and the thing pleased him.
21 And Saul said, I will give him her, that she may be a snare to him, and that the hand of the Philistines may be against him. Wherefore Saul said to David, Thou shalt this day be my son in law in *the one of* the twain.

Ps. 10. 9 He lieth in wait secretly as a lion in his den: he lieth in wait to catch the poor: he doth catch the poor, when he draweth him into his net.
10 He croucheth, *and* humbleth himself, that the poor may fall by his strong ones.
11 He hath said in his heart, God hath forgotten: he hideth his face; he will never see *it*.

Ps. 55. 21 *The words* of his mouth were smoother than butter, but war *was* in his heart: his words were softer than oil, yet *were* they drawn swords.

Ps. 64. 2 Hide me from the secret counsel of the wicked; from the insurrection of the workers of iniquity:
3 Who whet their tongue like a sword, *and* bend *their bows to shoot* their arrows, *even* bitter words:

§ 12. FLIGHT INTO EGYPT. HEROD'S CRUELTY. THE RETURN.

2: 13–23.

13 And when they were departed, behold, [a]the angel of the Lord appeareth to Joseph in a dream, saying, [b]Arise, and take the young child and his mother, and flee into Egypt, and be thou there until I bring thee word: for

A

Acts 5. 19 But the angel of the Lord by night opened the prison doors, and brought them forth, and said,

Acts 10. 7 And when the angel which spake unto Cornelius was departed, he called two of his household servants, and a devout soldier of them that waited on him continually;

Acts 10. 22 And they said, Cornelius the centurion, a just man, and one that feareth

TIME, FEBRUARY, B. C. 4; PLACE, JERUSALEM, BETHLEHEM.

K—CONTINUED.

Ps. 64. 4 That they may shoot in secret at the perfect: suddenly do they shoot at him, and fear not.

5 They encourage themselves *in* an evil matter: they commune of laying snares privily; they say, Who shall see them?

6 They search out iniquities; they accomplish a diligent search: both the inward *thought* of every one *of them*, and the heart, *is* deep.

7 But God shall shoot at them *with* an arrow; suddenly shall they be wounded.

Ps. 83. 3 They have taken crafty counsel against thy people, and consulted against thy hidden ones.

4 They have said, Come, and let us cut them off from *being* a nation; that the name of Israel may be no more in remembrance.

Isa. 7. 5 Because Syria, Ephraim, and the son of Remaliah, have taken evil counsel against thee, saying,

6 Let us go up against Judah, and vex it, and let us make a breach therein for us, and set a king in the midst of it, *even* the son of Tabeal:

7 Thus saith the Lord GOD, It shall not stand, neither shall it come to pass.

Rev. 12. 1 And there appeared a great wonder in heaven; a woman clothed with the sun, and the moon under her feet, and upon her head a crown of twelve stars:

2 And she being with child cried, travailing in birth, and pained to be delivered.

3 And there appeared another wonder in heaven; and behold a great red dragon, having seven heads and ten horns, and seven crowns upon his heads.

K—CONCLUDED.

Rev. 12. 4 And his tail drew the third part of the stars of heaven, and did cast them to the earth: and the dragon stood before the woman which was ready to be delivered, for to devour her child as soon as it was born.

5 And she brought forth a man child, who was to rule all nations with a rod of iron: and her child was caught up unto God, and *to* his throne.

L

Ps. 2. 12 Kiss the Son, lest he be angry, and ye perish *from* the way, when his wrath is kindled but a little. Blessed *are* all they that put their trust in him.

Ps. 72. 10 The kings of Tarshish and of the isles shall bring presents: the kings of Sheba and Seba shall offer gifts.

Isa. 60. 6 The multitude of camels shall cover thee, the dromedaries of Midian and Ephah; all they from Sheba shall come: they shall bring gold and incense; and they shall show forth the praises of the LORD.

2

Or, *offered.*

M

Job. 33. 15 In a dream, in a vision of the night, when deep sleep falleth upon men, in slumberings upon the bed;

16 Then he openeth the ears of men, and sealeth their instruction,

17 That he may withdraw man *from his* purpose, and hide pride from man.

Matt. 1. 20 But while he thought on these things, behold, the angel of the Lord appeared unto him in a dream, saying, Joseph, thou son of David, fear not to take unto thee Mary thy wife: for that which is conceived in her is of the Holy Ghost.

TIME, FEBRUARY–MAY, B. C. 4; PLACE, BETHLEHEM, NAZARETH.

[2: 39, 40.]

A—CONTINUED.

God, and of good report among all the nation of the Jews, was warned from God by a holy angel to send for thee into his house, and to hear words of thee.

Acts 12. 11 And when Peter was come to himself, he said, Now I know of a surety, that the Lord hath sent his angel, and hath delivered me out of the hand of Herod, and *from* all the expectation of the people of the Jews.

Heb. 1. 13 But to which of the angels said he at any time, Sit on my right hand, until I make thine enemies thy footstool?

14 Are they not all ministering spirits, sent forth to minister for them who shall be heirs of salvation?

See next page (40) for B.

§ 12. FLIGHT INTO EGYPT. HEROD'S CRUELTY. THE RETURN.

CHAP. 2.

Herod will seek the young child to destroy him.

14 When he arose, he took the young child and his mother by night, and departed into Egypt:

15 And was there until the death of Herod: that it might be fulfilled which was spoken of the Lord by the prophet, saying, [c]Out of Egypt have I called my son.

16 Then Herod, when he saw that he was mocked of the wise men, [d]was exceeding wroth, and sent forth, and slew all the children that were in Bethlehem, and in all the coasts thereof, from two years old and under, according to the time which he had diligently inquired of the wise men.

17 Then was fulfilled that which was spoken by [e]Jeremy the prophet, saying,

18 In Rama was there a voice heard, lamentation, and weeping, and great mourning, Rachel weeping *for* her children, and would not be comforted, because they are not.

19 But when [f]Herod was dead, behold, an angel of the Lord appeareth in a dream to Joseph in Egypt,

20 Saying, Arise, and take the young child and his mother, and go into the land of Israel: for they are dead which sought the young child's life.

21 And he arose, and took the young child and his mother, and came into the land of Israel.

22 But when he heard that Archelaus did reign in Judæa in the room of his father Herod, [g]he was afraid to

B

Rev. 12. 6 And the woman fled into the wilderness, where she hath a place prepared of God, that they should feed her there a thousand two hundred *and* threescore days.

7 And there was war in heaven: Michael and his angels fought against the dragon; and the dragon fought and his angels,

Rev. 12. 14 And to the woman were given two wings of a great eagle, that she might fly into the wilderness, into her place, where she is nourished for a time, and times, and half a time, from the face of the serpent.

C

Num. 24. 8 God brought him forth out of Egypt; he hath as it were the strength of a unicorn: he shall eat up the nations his enemies, and shall break their bones, and pierce *them* through with his arrows.

Hos. 11. 1 When Israel *was* a child, then I loved him, and called my son out of Egypt.

D

Gen. 49. 7 Cursed *be* their anger, for *it was* fierce; and their wrath, for it was cruel: I will divide them in Jacob, and scatter them in Israel.

II Ki. 8. 12 And Hazael said, Why weepeth my lord? And he answered, Because I know the evil that thou wilt do unto the children of Israel: their strong holds wilt thou set on fire, and their young men wilt thou slay with the sword, and wilt dash their children, and rip up their women with child.

13 And Hazael said, But what, *is* thy servant a dog, that he should do this great thing? And Elisha answered, The LORD hath showed me that thou *shalt be* king over Syria.

Prov. 27. 3 A stone *is* heavy, and the sand weighty; but a fool's wrath *is* heavier than them both.

4 Wrath *is* cruel, and anger *is* outrageous; but who *is* able to stand before envy?

Prov. 28. 15 *As* a roaring lion, and a ranging bear; *so is* a wicked ruler over the poor people.

Prov. 28. 17 A man that doeth violence to the blood of *any* person shall flee to the pit; let no man stay him.

(CONTINUED). TIME, FEBRUARY–MAY, B. C. 4; PLACE, BETHLEHEM, NAZARETH.

D—CONCLUDED.

Isa. 26. 20 Come, my people, enter thou into thy chambers, and shut thy doors about thee: hide thyself as it were for a little moment, until the indignation be overpast.

21 For, behold, the LORD cometh out of his place to punish the inhabitants of the earth for their iniquity: the earth also shall disclose her blood, and shall no more cover her slain.

Isa. 61. 7 For your shame *ye shall have* double; and *for* confusion they shall rejoice in their portion: therefore in their land they shall possess the double: everlasting joy shall be unto them.

Dan. 3. 13 Then Nebuchadnezzar in *his* rage and fury commanded to bring Shadrach, Meshach, and Abed-nego. Then they brought these men before the king.

14 Nebuchadnezzar spake and said unto them, *Is it* true, O Shadrach, Meshach, and Abed-nego? do not ye serve my gods, nor worship the golden image which I have set up?

Dan. 3. 19 Then was Nebuchadnezzar full of fury, and the form of his visage was changed against Shadrach, Meshach, and Abed-nego: *therefore* he spake, and commanded that they should heat the furnace one seven times more than it was wont to be heated.

20 And he commanded the most mighty men that *were* in his army to bind Shadrach, Meshach, and Abed-nego, *and* to cast *them* into the burning fiery furnace.

E

Jer. 31. 15 Thus saith the LORD; A voice was heard in Ramah, lamentation, *and* bitter weeping; Rachel weeping for her children refused to be comforted for her children, because they *were* not.

F

Ps. 76. 10 Surely the wrath of man shall praise thee: the remainder of wrath shalt thou restrain.

Isa. 51. 12 I, *even* I, *am* he that comforteth you: who *art* thou, that thou shouldest be afraid of a man *that* shall die, and of the son of man *which* shall be made *as* grass:

Dan. 8. 25 And through his policy also he shall cause craft to prosper in his hand; and he shall magnify *himself* in his heart, and by peace shall destroy many: he shall also stand up against the Prince of princes; but he shall be broken without hand.

F—CONCLUDED.

Dan. 11. 44 But tidings out of the east and out of the north shall trouble him: therefore he shall go forth with great fury to destroy, and utterly to make away many

45 And he shall plant the tabernacles of his palace between the seas in the glorious holy mountain; yet he shall come to his end, and none shall help him.

G

I Sa. 16. 2 And Samuel said, How can I go? if Saul hear *it*, he will kill me. And the LORD said, Take a heifer with thee, and say, I am come to sacrifice to the LORD.

Acts 9. 13 Then Ananias answered, Lord, I have heard by many of this man, how much evil he hath done to thy saints at Jerusalem:

14 And here he hath authority from the chief priests to bind all that call on thy name.

H

Ps. 48. 14 For this God *is* our God for ever and ever: he will be our guide *even* unto death.

Ps. 73. 24 Thou shalt guide me with thy counsel, and afterward receive me *to* glory.

Ps. 107. 6 Then they cried unto the LORD in their trouble, *and* he delivered them out of their distresses.

7 And he led them forth by the right way, that they might go to a city of habitation.

I

Matt. 3. 13 Then cometh Jesus from Galilee to Jordan unto John, to be baptized of him.

Luke 2. 39. *See text of topic.*

K

John 1. 45 Philip findeth Nathaniel, and saith unto him, We have found him, of whom Moses in the law, and the prophets, did write, Jesus of Nazareth, the son of Joseph.

L

Judg. 13. 5 For, lo, thou shalt conceive, and bear a son; and no razor shall come on his head: for the child shall be a Nazarite unto God from the womb: and he shall begin to deliver Israel out of the hand of the Philistines.

See next page (42) for L concluded.

§ 12. FLIGHT INTO EGYPT. HEROD'S CRUELTY. THE RETURN.

CHAP. 2.

go thither: notwithstanding, [h]being warned of God in a dream, he turned aside [i]into the parts of Galilee:

23 And he came and dwelt in a city called [k]Nazareth: that it might be fulfilled [l]which was spoken by the prophets, He shall be called a Nazarene.

For H, I, K and L see preceding page (41).

L—CONCLUDED.

I Sa. 1. 11 And she vowed a vow, and said, O LORD of hosts, if thou wilt indeed look on the affliction of thine handmaid, and remember me, and not forget thine handmaid, but wilt give unto thine handmaid a man child, then I will give him unto the LORD all the days of his life, and there shall no razor come upon his head.

§ 13. JESUS IN THE TEMPLE WITH THE DOCTORS.

A

Ex. 23. 15 Thou shalt keep the feast of unleavened bread: (thou shalt eat unleavened bread seven days, as I commanded thee, in the time appointed of the month Abib; for in it thou camest out from Egypt: and none shall appear before me empty:)

Ex. 23. 17 Three times in the year all thy males shall appear before the Lord GOD.

Ex. 34. 23 Thrice in the year shall all your men children appear before the Lord GOD, the God of Israel.

Deut. 16. 1 Observe the month of Abib, and keep the passover unto the LORD thy God: for in the month of Abib the LORD thy God brought thee forth out of Egypt by night.

Deut. 16. 16 Three times in a year shall all thy males appear before the LORD thy God in the place which he shall choose; in the feast of unleavened bread, and in the feast of weeks, and in the feast of tabernacles: and they shall not appear before the LORD empty:

B

IIChr. 30. 21 And the children of Israel that were present at Jerusalem kept the feast of unleavened bread seven days with great gladness: and the Levites and the priests praised the LORD day by day, *singing* with loud instruments unto the LORD

22 And Hezekiah spake comfortably unto all the Levites that taught the good knowledge of the LORD: and they did eat throughout the feast seven days, offering peace offerings, and making confession to the LORD God of their fathers.

B—CONCLUDED.

IIChr. 30. 23 And the whole assembly took counsel to keep other seven days: and they kept *other* seven days with gladness.

II Chr. 35. 17 And the children of Israel that were present kept the passover at that time, and the feast of unleavened bread seven days.

18 And there was no passover like to that kept in Israel from the days of Samuel the prophet; neither did all the kings of Israel keep such a passover as Josiah kept, and the priests, and the Levites, and all Judah and Israel that were present, and the inhabitants of Jerusalem.

C

Ps. 42. 4 When I remember these *things*, I pour out my soul in me: for I had gone with the multitude, I went with them to the house of God, with the voice of joy and praise, with a multitude that kept holyday.

Ps. 122. 1 I was glad when they said unto me, Let us go into the house of the LORD.

2 Our feet shall stand within thy gates, O Jerusalem.

3 Jerusalem is builded as a city that is compact together:

4 Whither the tribes go up, the tribes of the LORD, unto the testimony of Israel, to give thanks unto the name of the LORD.

Isa. 2. 3 And many people shall go and say, Come ye, and let us go up to the mountain of the LORD, to the house of the God of Jacob; and he will teach us of his ways, and we will walk in his paths: for out of Zion shall go forth the law, and the word of the LORD from Jerusalem.

(CONCLUDED). TIME, FEBRUARY–MAY, B. C. 4; PLACE, BETHLEHEM, NAZARETH.

CHAP. 2.

39 And when they had performed all things according to the law of the Lord, they returned into Galilee, to their own city Nazareth.

40 [m]And the child grew, and waxed strong in spirit, filled with wisdom; and the grace of God was upon him.

M

Luke 1. 80 And the child grew, and waxed strong in spirit, and was in the deserts till the day of his showing unto Israel.

Luke 2. 52 And Jesus increased in wisdom and stature, and in favour with God and man.

IITim. 2. 1 Thou therefore, my son, be strong in the grace that is in Christ Jesus.

TIME, APRIL, A. D. 8; PLACE, JERUSALEM.

2: 41–52.

41 Now his parents went to Jerusalem [a]every year at the feast of the passover.

42 And when he was twelve years old, they went up to Jerusalem after the custom of the feast.

43 [b]And when they had fulfilled the days, as they returned, the child Jesus tarried behind in Jerusalem; and Joseph and his mother knew not *of it.*

44 But they, supposing him to have been [c]in the company, went a day's journey; and they sought him among *their* kinsfolk and acquaintance.

45 And when they found him not, they turned back again to Jerusalem, seeking him.

46 And it came to pass, that after three days they found him in the temple, sitting in the midst of the doctors, [d]both hearing them, and asking them questions.

47 And [e]all that heard him were astonished at his understanding and answers.

48 And when they saw him, they were amazed: and his mother said unto him, Son, why hast thou thus

D

Isa. 11. 1 And there shall come forth a rod out of the stem of Jesse, and a Branch shall grow out of his roots:

2 And the Spirit of the LORD shall rest upon him, the spirit of wisdom and understanding, the spirit of counsel and might, the spirit of knowledge and of the fear of the LORD;

3 And shall make him of quick understanding in the fear of the LORD: and he shall not judge after the sight of his eyes, neither reprove after the hearing of his ears:

4 But with righteousness shall he judge the poor, and reprove with equity for the meek of the earth: and he shall smite the earth with the rod of his mouth, and with the breath of his lips shall he slay the wicked.

Isa. 49. 1 Listen, O isles, unto me; and hearken, ye people, from far; The LORD hath called me from the womb; from the bowels of my mother hath he made mention of my name.

2 And he hath made my mouth like a sharp sword; in the shadow of his hand hath he hid me, and made me a polished shaft; in his quiver hath he hid me;

Isa. 50. 4 The Lord GOD hath given me the tongue of the learned, that I should know how to speak a word in season to *him that is* weary: he wakeneth morning by morning, he wakeneth mine ear to hear as the learned.

E

Matt. 7. 28 And it came to pass, when Jesus had ended these sayings, the people were astonished at his doctrine:

Mark 1. 22 And they were astonished at his doctrine: for he taught them as one

See next page (44) for E concluded.

§ 13. JESUS IN THE TEMPLE WITH THE DOCTORS

E—CONCLUDED. See preceding page (43).

that had authority, and not as the scribes.

Luke 4. 22 And all bare him witness, and wondered at the gracious words which proceeded out of his mouth. And they said, Is not this Joseph's son?

Luke 4. 32 And they were astonished at his doctrine: for his word was with power.

John 7. 15 And the Jews marvelled, saying, How knoweth this man letters, having never learned?

46 The officers answered, Never man spake like this man.

F

John 2. 16 And said unto them that sold doves, Take these things hence; make not my Father's house a house of merchandise.

John 4. 34 Jesus saith unto them, My meat is to do the will of him that sent me, and to finish his work.

G

Luke 9. 45 But they understood not this saying, and it was hid from them, that they perceived it not: and they feared to ask him of that saying.

Luke 18. 34 And they understood none of these things: and this saying was hid from them, neither knew they the things which were spoken.

H

Dan. 7. 28 Hitherto *is* the end of the matter. As for me Daniel, my cogitations much troubled me, and my countenance changed in me: but I kept the matter in my heart.

Luke 2. 19 But Mary kept all these things, and pondered *them* in her heart.

I

I Sa. 2. 26 And the child Samuel grew on, and was in favour both with the LORD, and also with men.

§ 14. MINISTRY OF JOHN THE BAPTIST.

3 : 1–12.

1 In those days came [a]John the Baptist, preaching [b]in the wilderness of Judæa,

2 And saying, Repent ye: for [c]the kingdom of heaven is at hand.

3 For this is he that was spoken of by the prophet Esaias, saying, [d]The voice of one crying in the wilderness, [e]Prepare ye the way of the Lord, make his paths straight.

A

Mal. 3. 1 Behold, I will send my messenger, and he shall prepare the way before me: and the Lord, whom ye seek, shall suddenly come to his temple, even the messenger of the covenant, whom ye delight in: behold, he shall come, saith the LORD of hosts.

Mark 1. 4. *See text of topic.*

Mark 1. 15 And saying, The time is fulfilled, and the kingdom of God is at hand: repent ye, and believe the gospel.

Luke 3. 2, 3. *See text of topic.*

John 1. 28. *See text of § 17.*

1 : 1–8.

1 The beginning of the gospel of Jesus Christ, [f]the Son of God;

2 As it is written in the prophets, [g]Behold, I send my messenger before thy face, which shall prepare thy way before thee.

3 [h]The voice of one crying in the wilderness, Prepare ye the way of the Lord, make his paths straight.

4 [i]John did baptize in the wilderness, and preach the baptism of repentance [1]for the remission of sins.

B

Josh. 14. 10 And now, behold, the LORD hath kept me alive, as he said, these forty and five years, even since the LORD spake this word unto Moses, while *the children of* Israel wandered in the wilderness: and now, lo, I *am* this day fourscore and five years old.

C

Dan. 2. 44 And in the days of these kings shall the God of heaven set up a kingdom, which shall never be destroyed:

(CONCLUDED). TIME, APRIL, A. D. 8; PLACE, JERUSALEM.

CHAP. 2.

dealt with us? behold, thy father and I have sought thee sorrowing.

49 And he said unto them, How is it that ye sought me? wist ye not that I must be about [f]my Father's business?

50 And [g]they understood not the saying which he spake unto them.

51 And he went down with them, and came to Nazareth, and was subject unto them: but his mother [h]kept all these sayings in her heart.

52 And Jesus [i]increased in wisdom and [1]stature, and in [k]favour with God and man.

I—CONCLUDED.

Luke 2. 40 And the child grew, and waxed strong in spirit, filled with wisdom; and the grace of God was upon him.

1

Or, *age.*

K

Prov. 3. 3 Let not mercy and truth forsake thee: bind them about thy neck; write them upon the table of thine heart:

4 So shalt thou find favour and good understanding in the sight of God and man.

Acts 7. 9 And the patriarchs, moved with envy, sold Joseph into Egypt: but God was with him,

10 And delivered him out of all his afflictions, and gave him favour and wisdom in the sight of Pharaoh king of Egypt; and he made him governor over Egypt and all his house.

TIME, SUMMER, A. D. 26; PLACE, THE DESERT, THE JORDAN.

3: 1–18.

1 Now in the fifteenth year of the reign of Tiberius Cæsar, Pontius Pilate being governor of Judæa, and Herod being tetrarch of Galilee, and his brother Philip tetrarch of Iturea and of the region of Trachonitis, and Lysanias the tetrarch of Abilene,

2 [k]Annas and Caiaphas being the high priests, the word of God came unto John the son of Zacharias in the wilderness.

3 [l]And he came into all the country about Jordan, preaching the baptism of repentance [m]for the remission of sins;

4 As it is written in the book of the words of Esaias the prophet, saying, [n]The voice of one crying in the wilderness, Prepare ye the way of the Lord, make his paths straight.

5 Every valley shall be filled, and

C—CONCLUDED.

and the kingdom shall not be left to other people, *but* it shall break in pieces and consume all these kingdoms, and it shall stand for ever.

Matt. 4. 17 From that time Jesus began to preach, and to say, Repent: for the kingdom of heaven is at hand.

Matt.10. 7 And as ye go, preach, saying, The kingdom of heaven is at hand.

D

Isa. 40. 3 The voice of him that crieth in the wilderness, Prepare ye the way of the LORD, make straight in the desert a highway for our God.

Mark 1. 3. *See text of topic.*
Luke 3. 4. *See text of topic.*
John 1. 23. *See text of ¶ 17.*

E

Luke 1. 76 And thou, child, shalt be called the prophet of the Highest: for thou shalt go before the face of the Lord to prepare his ways;

F

Ps. 2. 7 I will declare the decree: the LORD hath said unto me, Thou *art* my Son; this day have I begotten thee.

Matt.14. 33 Then they that were in the ship came and worshipped him, saying, Of a truth thou art the Son of God.

For F concluded, G, H, I, 1, K, L, M and N see next page (46).

§ 14. MINISTRY OF JOHN THE BAPTIST (Continued).

Chap. 3.

4 And [o]the same John [p]had his raiment of camel's hair, and a leathern girdle about his loins; and his meat was [q]locusts and wild [r]honey.

5 [s]Then went out to him Jerusalem, and all Judæa, and all the region round about Jordan,

6 [t]And were baptized of him in Jordan, confessing their sins.

Chap. 1.

5 [u]And there went out unto him all the land of Judæa, and they of Jerusalem, and were all baptized of him in the river of Jordan, confessing their sins.

6 And John was [x]clothed with camel's hair, and with a girdle of a skin about his loins; and he did eat [y]locusts and wild honey; p. 50.

F—Concluded. See preceding page (45).

Luke 1. 35 And the angel answered and said unto her, The Holy Ghost shall come upon thee, and the power of the Highest shall overshadow thee: therefore also that holy thing which shall be born of thee shall be called the Son of God.

John 1. 34 And I saw, and bare record that this is the Son of God.

G

Mal. 3. 1. *See under A, page 44.*

Matt. 11. 10 For this is *he*, of whom it is written, Behold, I send my messenger before thy face, which shall prepare thy way before thee.

Luke 7. 27 This is *he*, of whom it is written, Behold, I send my messenger before thy face, which shall prepare thy way before thee.

H

Isa. 40. 3. *See under D, page 45.*
Matt. 3. 3. *See text of topic.*
Luke 3. 4. *See text of topic.*
John 1. 15, 23. *See text of § 17.*

I

Matt. 3. 1. *See text of topic.*
Luke 3. 3. *See text of topic.*

John 3. 23 And John also was baptizing in Enon near to Salim, because there was much water there: and they came, and were baptized.

1

Or, *unto*.

K

John 11. 49 And one of them, *named* Caiaphas, being the high priest that same year, said unto them, Ye know nothing at all.

John 11. 51 And this spake he not of himself: but being high priest that year, he prophesied that Jesus should die for that nation;

K—Concluded.

John 18. 13 And led him away to Annas first; for he was father-in-law to Caiaphas, which was the high priest that same year.

Acts 4. 6 And Annas the high priest, and Caiaphas, and John, and Alexander, and as many as were of the kindred of the high priest, were gathered together at Jerusalem.

L

Mal. 4. 5 Behold, I will send you Elijah the prophet before the coming of the great and dreadful day of the Lord:
6 And he shall turn the heart of the fathers to the children, and the heart of the children to their fathers, lest I come and smite the earth with a curse.

Matt. 3. 1. *See text of topic.*
Mark 1. 4. *See text of topic.*
Acts 19. 4. *See under T.*

M

Luke 1. 77 To give knowledge of salvation unto his people by the remission of their sins,

N

Isa. 40. 3. *See under D, page 45.*
Matt. 3. 3. *See text of topic.*
Mark 1. 3. *See text of topic.*
John 1. 23. *See text of § 17.*

O

Mark 1. 6. *See text of topic.*

P

II Ki. 1. 8 And they answered him, *He was* a hairy man, and girt with a girdle of leather about his loins. And he said, It *is* Elijah the Tishbite.

Zech. 13. 4 And it shall come to pass in that day, *that* the prophets shall be ashamed every one of his vision, when he hath prophesied; neither shall they wear a rough garment to deceive:

TIME, SUMMER, A. D. 26; PLACE, THE DESERT, THE JORDAN.

CHAP. 3.

every mountain and hill shall be brought low; and the crooked shall be made straight, and the rough ways *shall be* made smooth;

6 And [z]all flesh shall see the salvation of God.

Q

Lev. 11. 22 *Even* these of them ye may eat; the locust after his kind, and the bald locust after his kind, and the beetle after his kind, and the grasshopper after his kind.

R

I Sa. 14. 25 And all *they of* the land came to a wood; and there was honey upon the ground.

26 And when the people were come into the wood, behold, the honey dropped; but no man put his hand to his mouth: for the people feared the oath.

S

Mark 1. 5. *See text of topic.*
Luke 3. 7. *See text of topic.*

T

Eze. 36. 25 Then will I sprinkle clean water upon you, and ye shall be clean: from all your filthiness, and from all your idols, will I cleanse you.

Acts 2. 38 Then Peter said unto them, Repent, and be baptized every one of you in the name of Jesus Christ for the remission of sins, and ye shall receive the gift of the Holy Ghost.

39 For the promise is unto you, and to your children, and to all that are afar off, *even* as many as the Lord our God shall call.

40 And with many other words did he testify and exhort, saying, Save yourselves from this untoward generation.

41 Then they that gladly received his word were baptized: and the same day there were added *unto them* about three thousnnd souls.

Acts 11. 16 Then remembered I the word of the Lord, how that he said, John indeed baptized with water; but ye shall be baptized with the Holy Ghost.

Acts 19. 4 Then said Paul, John verily baptized with the baptism of repentance, saying unto the people, that they

T—CONCLUDED.

should believe on him which should come after him, that is, on Christ Jesus.

Acts 19. 18 And many that believed came, and confessed, and showed their deeds.

1Cor. 10. 2 And were all baptized unto Moses in the cloud and in the sea;

Col. 2. 12 Buried with him in baptism, wherein also ye are risen with *him* through the faith of the operation of God, who hath raised him from the dead.

Heb 6. 2 Of the doctrine of baptisms, and of laying on of hands, and of resurrection of the dead, and of eternal judgment.

U

Matt. 3. 5. *See text of topic.*

X

Matt. 3. 4. *See text of topic.*

Y

Lev. 11. 22. *See under Q.*

Z

Ps. 98. 2 The LORD hath made known his salvation: his righteousness hath he openly showed in the sight of the heathen.

3 He hath remembered his mercy and his truth toward the house of Israel: all the ends of the earth have seen the salvation of our God.

Isa. 40. 5 And the glory of the LORD shall be revealed, and all flesh shall see *it* together: for the mouth of the LORD hath spoken *it*.

Isa. 49. 6 And he said, It is a light thing that thou shouldest be my servant to raise up the tribes of Jacob, and to restore the preserved of Israel: I will also give thee for a light to the Gentiles, that thou mayest be my salvation unto the end of the earth.

Isa. 52. 10 The LORD hath made bare his holy arm in the eyes of all the nations; and all the ends of the earth shall see the salvation of our God.

Mark16. 15 And he said unto them, Go ye into all the world, and preach the gospel to every creature.

Luke 2. 10 And the angel said unto them, Fear not: for, behold, I bring you good tidings of great joy, which shall be to all people.

Rom. 10. 12 For there is no difference between the Jew and the Greek: for the same Lord over all is rich unto all that call upon him.

§ 14. MINISTRY OF JOHN THE BAPTIST (Continued).

Chap. 3.

7 But when he saw many of the Pharisees and Sadducees come to his baptism, he said unto them, [a]O generation of vipers, who hath warned you to flee from [b]the wrath to come?

8 Bring forth therefore fruits [2]meet for repentance:

9 And think not to say within yourselves, [c]We have Abraham to *our* father: for I say unto you, that God is able of these stones to raise up children unto Abraham.

10 And now also the axe is laid unto the root of the trees: [d]therefore every tree which bringeth not forth good fruit is hewn down, and cast into the fire.

A

Matt.12. 34 O generation of vipers, how can ye, being evil, speak good things? for out of the abundance of the heart the mouth speaketh.

Matt.23. 33 *Ye* serpents, *ye* generation of vipers, how can ye escape the damnation of hell?

Luke 3. 7, 8, 9. *See text of topic.*

B

Rom. 5. 9 Much more then, being now justified by his blood, we shall be saved from wrath through him.

IThes.1. 10 And to wait for his Son from heaven, whom he raised from the dead, *even* Jesus, which delivered us from the wrath to come.

2

Or, *answerable to amendment of life.*

II Cor.7. 1 Having therefore these promises, dearly beloved, let us cleanse ourselves from all filthiness of the flesh and spirit, perfecting holiness in the fear of God.

II Cor.7. 11 For behold this selfsame thing, that ye sorrowed after a godly sort, what carefulness it wrought in you, yea, *what* clearing of yourselves, yea, *what* indignation, yea, *what* fear, yea, *what* vehement desire, yea, *what* zeal, yea, *what* revenge! In all *things* ye have approved yourselves to be clear in this matter.

[Chap. 1.]

C

John 8. 33 They answered him, We be Abraham's seed, and were never in bondage to any man: how sayest thou, Ye shall be made free?

John 8. 39 They answered and said unto him, Abraham is our father. Jesus saith unto them, If ye were Abraham's children, ye would do the works of Abraham.

Acts 13. 26 Men *and* brethren, children of the stock of Abraham, and whosoever among you feareth God, to you is the word of this salvation sent.

Rom. 4. 1 What shall we say then that Abraham our father, as pertaining to the flesh, hath found?

Rom. 4. 11 And he received the sign of circumcision, a seal of the righteousness of the faith which *he had yet* being uncircumcised: that he might be the father of all them that believe, though they be not circumcised; that righteousness might be imputed unto them also:

Rom. 4. 16 Therefore *it is* of faith, that *it might be* by grace; to the end the promise might be sure to all the seed; not to that only which is of the law, but to that also which is of the faith of Abraham; who is the father of us all,

D

Ps. 1. 3 And he shall be like a tree planted by the rivers of water, that bringeth forth his fruit in his season; his leaf also shall not wither; and whatsoever he doeth shall prosper.

Jer. 17. 7 Blessed *is* the man that trusteth in the Lord, and whose hope the Lord is.

8 For he shall be as a tree planted by the waters, and *that* spreadeth out her roots by the river, and shall not see when heat cometh, but her leaf shall be green; and shall not be careful in the year of drought, neither shall cease from yielding fruit.

Eze.15. 2 Son of man, What is the vine tree more than any tree, *or than* a branch which is among the trees of the forest?

3 Shall wood be taken thereof to do any work? or will *men* take a pin of it to hang any vessel thereon?

4 Behold, it is cast into the fire for fuel; the fire devoureth both the ends of it, and the midst of it is burned. Is it meet for *any* work?

TIME, SUMMER, A.D. 26; PLACE, THE DESERT, THE JORDAN.

CHAP. 3.

7 Then said he to the multitude that came forth to be baptized of him, [e]O generation of vipers, who hath warned you to flee from the wrath to come?

8 [f]Bring forth therefore fruits [3]worthy of repentance, and begin not to say within yourselves, We have Abraham to *our* father: for I say unto you, That God is able of these stones to raise up children unto Abraham.

9 And now also the axe is laid unto the root of the trees: [g]every tree therefore which bringeth not forth good fruit is hewn down, and cast into the fire.

D—CONTINUED.

Eze. 15. 5 Behold, when it was whole, it was meet for no work: how much less shall it be meet yet for *any* work, when the fire hath devoured it, and it is burned?

6 Therefore thus saith the Lord GOD; As the vine tree among the trees of the forest, which I have given to the fire for fuel, so will I give the inhabitants of Jerusalem.

7 And I will set my face against them; they shall go out from *one* fire, and *another* fire shall devour them; and ye shall know that I *am* the LORD, when I set my face against them.

Matt. 7. 19 Every tree that bringeth not forth good fruit is hewn down, and cast into the fire.

Luke 13. 7 Then said he unto the dresser of his vineyard, Behold, these three years I come seeking fruit on this fig tree, and find none: cut it down; why cumbereth it the ground?

John 15. 6 If a man abide not in me, he is cast forth as a branch, and is withered; and men gather them, and cast *them* into the fire, and they are burned.

Heb. 6. 8 But that which beareth thorns and briers *is* rejected, and *is* nigh unto cursing; whose end *is* to be burned.

I Pet. 4. 17 For the time *is come* that judgment must begin at the house of God: and if *it* first *begin* at us, what shall the end *be* of them that obey not the gospel of God?

D—CONCLUDED.

I Pet. 4. 18 And if the righteous scarcely be saved, where shall the ungodly and the sinner appear?

E

Matt. 3. 7. *See text of topic.*

F

Acts 26. 20 But showed first unto them of Damascus, and at Jerusalem, and throughout all the coasts of Judæa, and *then* to the Gentiles, that they should repent and turn to God, and do works meet for repentance.

3

Or, *meet for.*

G

Matt. 7. 19. *See under D.*

H

Mark 1. 8. *See text of topic.*
Luke 3. 16. *See text of topic.*
John 1. 15, 26. *See text of* § *17.*
John 1. 33. *See text of* § *15.*

Acts 1. 5 For John truly baptized with water; but ye shall be baptized with the Holy Ghost not many days hence.

Acts 11. 16 Then remembered I the word of the Lord, how that he said, John indeed baptized with water; but ye shall be baptized with the Holy Ghost.

Acts 19. 4 Then said Paul, John verily baptized with the baptism of repentance, saying unto the people, that they should believe on him which should come after him, that is, on Christ Jesus.

I

Isa. 4. 4 When the Lord shall have washed away the filth of the daughters of Zion, and shall have purged the blood of Jerusalem from the midst thereof by the spirit of judgment, and by the spirit of burning.

Isa. 44. 3 For I will pour water upon him that is thirsty, and floods upon the dry ground: I will pour my Spirit upon thy seed, and my blessing upon thine offspring:

Mal. 3. 2 But who may abide the day of his coming? and who shall stand when he appeareth? for he *is* like a refiner's fire, and like fullers' soap:

Acts 2. 3 And there appeared unto them cloven tongues like as of fire, and it sat upon each of them.

See next page (50) for I concluded.

§ 14. MINISTRY OF JOHN THE BAPTIST (CONCLUDED).

CHAP. 3.

11 [h]I indeed baptize you with water unto repentance: but he that cometh after me is mightier than I, whose shoes I am not worthy to bear: [i]he shall baptize you with the Holy Ghost, and *with* fire:

12 [k]Whose fan *is* in his hand, and he will thoroughly purge his floor, and gather his wheat into the garner; but he will [l]burn up the chaff with unquenchable fire.

For H and I see preceding page (49).

I—CONCLUDED.

Acts 2. 4 And they were all filled with the Holy Ghost, and began to speak with other tongues, as the Spirit gave them utterance.

I Cor.12. 13 For by one Spirit are we all baptized into one body, whether *we be* Jews or Gentiles, whether *we be* bond or free; and have been all made to drink into one Spirit.

Tit. 3. 5 Not by works of righteousness which we have done, but according to his mercy he saved us, by the washing of regeneration, and renewing of the Holy Ghost;

K

Mal. 3. 3 And he shall sit *as* a refiner and purifier of silver: and he shall purify the sons of Levi, and purge them as gold and silver, that they may offer unto the LORD an offering in righteousness.

L

Mal. 4. 1 For, behold, the day cometh, that shall burn as an oven; and all the proud, yea, and all that do wickedly, shall be stubble: and the day that cometh shall burn them up, saith the LORD of hosts, that it shall leave them neither root nor branch.

Matt.13. 30 Let both grow together until the harvest: and in the time of harvest I will say to the reapers, Gather ye together first the tares, and bind them in bundles to burn them: but gather the wheat into my barn.

CHAP. 1.

7 And preached, saying, [m]There cometh one mightier than I after me, the latchet of whose shoes I am not worthy to stoop down and unloose.

8 [n]I indeed have baptized you with water: but he shall baptize you [o]with the Holy Ghost.

M

Matt. 3. 11. *See text of topic.*
John 1. 27. *See text of § 17.*

Acts 13. 25 And as John fulfilled his course, he said, Whom think ye that I am? I am not *he*. But, behold, there cometh one after me, whose shoes of *his* feet I am not worthy to loose.

N

Acts 1. 5; 11. 16; and 19. 4. *See under H, page 49.*

O

Isa. 44. 3. *See under I, page 49.*

Joel 2. 28 And it shall come to pass afterward, *that* I will pour out my Spirit upon all flesh; and your sons and your daughters shall prophesy; your old men shall dream dreams, your young men shall see visions:

Acts 2. 4. *See under I.*

Acts 10. 45 And they of the circumcision which believed were astonished, as many as came with Peter, because that on the Gentiles also was poured out the gift of the Holy Ghost.

Acts 11. 15 And as I began to speak, the Holy Ghost fell on them, as on us at the beginning.

Acts 11. 16. *See under H, page 49.*
I Cor. 12. 13. *See under I.*

P

Acts 2. 37 Now when they heard *this* they were pricked in their heart, and said unto Peter and to the rest of the apostles, Men *and* brethren, what shall we do?

Q

Luke 11. 41 But rather give alms of such things as ye have: and, behold, all things are clean unto you.

II Cor.8. 14 But by an equality, *that* now at this time your abundance *may be a supply* for their want, that their abundance also may be *a supply* for your want; that there may be equality:

Jas. 2. 15 If a brother or sister be naked, and destitute of daily food,

TIME, SUMMER, A. D. 26; PLACE, THE DESERT, THE JORDAN.

CHAP. 3.

10 And the people asked him, saying, [p]What shall we do then?

11 He answereth and saith unto them, [q]He that hath two coats, let him impart to him that hath none; and he that hath meat, let him do likewise.

12 [r]Then came also publicans to be baptized, and said unto him, Master, what shall we do?

13 And he said unto them, [s]Exact no more than that which is appointed you.

14 And the soldiers likewise demanded of him, saying, And what shall we do? And he said unto them, [4]Do violence to no man, [t]neither accuse *any* falsely; and be content with your [5]wages.

15 And as the people were in [6]expectation, and all men [7]mused in their hearts of John, whether he were the Christ, or not;

16 John answered, saying unto *them* all, [u]I indeed baptize you with water; but one mightier than I cometh, the latchet of whose shoes I am not worthy to unloose: he shall baptize you with [x]the Holy Ghost and with fire:

17 Whose fan *is* in his hand, and he will thoroughly purge his floor, and [y]will gather the wheat into his garner; but the chaff he will burn with fire unquenchable.

18 And many other things in his exhortation preached he unto the people.

Q—CONTINUED.

Jas. 2. 16 And one of you say unto them, Depart in peace, be *ye* warmed and filled; notwithstanding ye give them not those things which are needful to the body: what *doth it* profit?

Q—CONCLUDED.

I Jno. 3. 17 But whoso hath this world's good, and seeth his brother have need, and shutteth up his bowels *of compassion* from him, how dwelleth the love of God in him?

I Jno. 4. 20 If a man say, I love God, and hateth his brother, he is a liar: for he that loveth not his brother whom he hath seen, how can he love God whom he hath not seen?

R

Matt.21. 32 For John came unto you in the way of righteousness, and ye believed him not; but the publicans and the harlots believed him: and ye, when ye had seen *it*, repented not afterward, that ye might believe him.

Luke 7. 29 And all the people that heard *him*, and the publicans, justified God, being baptized with the baptism of John.

S

Mic. 6. 8 He hath showed thee, O man, what *is* good; and what doth the LORD require of thee, but to do justly, and to love mercy, and to walk humbly with thy God?

Luke 19. 8 And Zaccheus stood, and said unto the Lord; Behold, Lord, the half of my goods I give to the poor; and if I have taken any thing from any man by false accusation, I restore *him* fourfold.

4

Or, *Put no man in fear.*

T

Ex. 23. 1 Thou shalt not raise a false report; put not thine hand with the wicked to be an unrighteous witness.

Lev. 19. 11 Ye shall not steal, neither deal falsely, neither lie one to another.

5

Or, *allowance.*

6

Or, *in suspense.*

7

Or, *reasoned*, or, *debated.*

U

Matt. 3. 11. *See text of topic.*

X

I Cor. 12. 13. *See under I.*

Y

Mic. 4. 12 But they know not the thoughts of the LORD, neither understand they his counsel: for he shall gather them as the sheaves into the floor.

Matt. 13. 30. *See under L.*

3: 13–17.

13 [a]Then cometh Jesus [b]from Galilee to Jordan unto John, to be baptized of him.

14 But John forbade him, saying, I have need to be baptized of thee, and comest thou to me?

15 And Jesus answering said unto him, Suffer *it to be so* now: for thus it becometh us to [c]fulfill all righteousness. Then he suffered him.

16 [d]And Jesus, when he was baptized, went up straightway out of the water: and, lo, the heavens were opened unto him, and he saw [e]the Spirit of God descending like a dove, and lighting upon him:

17 [f]And lo a voice from heaven, saying, [g]This is my beloved Son, in whom I am well pleased.

A

Mark 1. 9. *See text of topic.*
Luke 3. 21. *See text of topic.*

B

Matt. 2. 22 But when he heard that Archelaus did reign in Judea in the room of his father Herod, he was afraid to go thither: notwithstanding, being warned of God in a dream, he turned aside into the parts of Galilee:

C

Ex. 29. 4 And Aaron and his sons thou shalt bring unto the door of the tabernacle of the congregation, and shalt wash them with water.

Deut. 6. 25 And it shall be our righteousness, if we observe to do all these commandments before the LORD our God, as he hath commanded us.

Dan. 9. 24 Seventy weeks are determined upon thy people, and upon thy holy city, to finish the transgression, and to make an end of sins, and to make reconciliation for iniquity, and to bring in everlasting righteousness, and to seal up the vision and prophecy, and to anoint the Most Holy.

D

Mark 1. 10. *See text of topic.*

§ 15. BAPTISM OF JESUS CHRIST.

1 : 9–11.

9 [h]And it came to pass in those days, that Jesus came from Nazareth of Galilee, and was baptized of John in Jordan.

10 [i]And straightway coming up out of the water, he saw the heavens [1]opened, and the Spirit like a dove descending upon him:

11 And there came a voice from heaven, *saying*, [k]Thou art my beloved Son, in whom I am well pleased.

E

Isa. 11. 2 And the Spirit of the LORD shall rest upon him, the spirit of wisdom and understanding, the spirit of counsel and might, the spirit of knowledge and of the fear of the Lord:

Isa. 42. 1 Behold my servant, whom I uphold; mine elect, *in whom* my soul delighteth; I have put my spirit upon him: he shall bring forth judgment to the Gentiles.

Luke 3. 22. *See text of topic.*
John 1. 32, 33. *See text of topic.*

F

John 12. 28 Father, glorify thy name. Then came there a voice from heaven, *saying*, I have both glorified *it*, and will glorify *it* again.

Acts 13. 33 God hath fulfilled the same unto us their children, in that he hath raised up Jesus again; as it is also written in the second psalm, Thou art my Son, this day have I begotten thee.

Rom. 1. 4 And declared *to be* the Son of God with power, according to the Spirit of holiness, by the resurrection from the dead:

G

Ps. 2. 7 I will declare the decree: the LORD hath said unto me, thou *art* my Son; this day have I begotten thee.

Isa. 42. 1. *See under E.*

Matt. 12. 18 Behold my servant, whom I have chosen; my beloved, in whom my soul is well pleased: I will put my Spirit upon him, and he shall shew judgment to the Gentiles.

Matt. 17. 5 While he yet spake, behold, a bright cloud overshadowed them: and behold a voice out of the cloud,

TIME, JANUARY, A. D. 27; PLACE, THE JORDAN.

3: 21, 22.

21 Now when all the people were baptized, [l]it came to pass, that Jesus also being baptized, and praying, the [m]heaven was opened,

22 And the Holy Ghost descended in a bodily shape l. e a dove upon him, and a voice came [n]from heaven, which said, Thou art my beloved Son; in thee I am well pleased.

G—CONCLUDED.

which said, This is my beloved Son, in whom I am well pleased; hear ye him.

Mark 1. 11. *See text of topic.*
Mark 9. 7. *See under K.*
Luke 9. 35 And there came a voice out of the cloud, saying, This is my beloved Son: hear him.
John 3. 35 The Father loveth the Son, and hath given all things into his hand.
John 10. 17 Therefore doth my Father love me, because I lay down my life, that I might take it again.
Eph. 1. 6 To the praise of the glory of his grace, wherein he hath made us accepted in the beloved:
Col. 1. 13 Who hath delivered us from the power of darkness, and hath translated *us* into the kingdom of his dear Son.
II Pet. 1. 17 For he received from God the Father honour and glory, when there came such a voice to him from the excellent glory, This is my beloved Son, in whom I am well pleased.

H

Matt. 3. 13. *See text of topic.*
Luke 3. 21. *See text of topic.*

I

Matt. 3. 16. *See text of topic.*
John 1. 32. *See text of topic.*

1

Or, *cloven*, or, *rent*.

K

Ps. 2. 7. *See under G.*
Matt. 3. 17. *See text of topic.*
Mark 9. 7 And there was a cloud that overshadowed them: and a voice came out of the cloud, saying, This is my beloved Son: hear him.
II Pet. 1. 17. *See under G.*

L

Matt. 3. 13. *See text of topic.*
John 1. 32. *See text of topic.*

1: 32–34.

32 [o]And John bare record, saying, I saw the Spirit descending from heaven like a dove, and it abode upon him.

33 And I knew him not: but he that sent me to baptize with water, the same said unto me, Upon whom thou shalt see the Spirit descending, and remaining on him, [p]the same is he which baptizeth with the Holy Ghost.

34 And I saw, and bare record that this is the Son of God. (p. 63.)

M

Acts. 7. 56 And said, Behold, I see the heavens opened, and the Son of man standing on the right hand of God.
Acts 10. 11 And saw heaven opened, and a certain vessel descending unto him, as it had been a great sheet knit at the four corners and let down to the earth:

N

II Pet. 1. 17. *See under G.*

O

Matt. 3. 16. *See text of topic.*
Mark 1. 10. *See text of topic.*
Luke 3. 22. *See text of topic.*
John 5. 32 There is another that beareth witness of me; and I know that the witness which he witnesseth of me is true.

P

Matt. 3. 11 I indeed baptize you with water unto repentance: but he that cometh after me is mightier than I, whose shoes I am not worthy to bear: he shall baptize you with the Holy Ghost, and *with* fire:
Acts 1. 5 For John truly baptized with water; but ye shall be baptized with the Holy Ghost not many days hence.
Acts 2. 4 And they were all filled with the Holy Ghost, and began to speak with other tongues, as the Spirit gave them utterance.
Acts 10. 44 While Peter yet spake these words, the Holy Ghost fell on all them which heard the word.
Acts 19. 6 And when Paul had laid *his* hands upon them, the Holy Ghost came on them; and they spake with tongues, and prophesied.

§ 16. THE TEMPTATION.

4: 1–11.

1 Then was [a]Jesus led up of [b]the Spirit into the wilderness to be [c]tempted of the devil.

2 And when he had [d]fasted forty days and forty nights, he was afterward a hungered.

3 And when the tempter came to him, he said, If thou be the Son of God, command that these stones be made bread.

4 But he answered and said, [e]It is written, Man shall not live by bread alone, but by every word that proceedeth out of the mouth of God.

A

Mark 1. 12. *See text of topic.*
Luke 4. 1. *See text of topic.*

B

I Ki. 18. 12 And it shall come to pass, *as soon as* I am gone from thee, that the Spirit of the LORD shall carry thee whither I know not; and *so* when I come and tell Ahab, and he cannot find thee, he shall slay me: but I thy servant fear the LORD from my youth.

Eze. 3. 14 So the spirit lifted me up, and took me away, and I went in bitterness, in the heat of my spirit; but the hand of the LORD was strong upon me.

Eze. 8. 3 And he put forth the form of a hand, and took me by a lock of mine head; and the spirit lifted me up between the earth and the heaven, and brought me in the visions of God to Jerusalem, to the door of the inner gate that looketh toward the north; where *was* the seat of the image of jealousy, which provoketh to jealousy.

Eze. 11. 1 Moreover the spirit lifted me up, and brought me unto the east gate of the LORD's house, which looketh eastward: and behold at the door of the gate five and twenty men; among whom I saw Jaazaniah the son of Azur, and Pelatiah the son of Benaiah, princes of the people.

Eze. 11. 24 Afterwards the spirit took me up, and brought me in a vision by the Spirit of God into Chaldea, to them

1: 12, 13.

12 [f]And immediately the Spirit driveth him into the wilderness.

13 And he was there in the wilderness forty days tempted of Satan; and was with the wild beasts; [g]and the angels ministered unto him. (p. 78.)

B—CONCLUDED.

of the captivity. So the vision that I had seen went up from me.

Eze. 40. 2 In the visions of God brought he me into the land of Israel, and set me upon a very high mountain, by which *was* as the frame of a city on the south.

Eze. 43. 5 So the spirit took me up, and brought me into the inner court; and, behold, the glory of the LORD filled the house.

Acts 8. 39 And when they were come up out of the water, the Spirit of the Lord caught away Philip, that the eunuch saw him no more: and he went on his way rejoicing.

C

Heb. 4. 15 For we have not a high priest which cannot be touched with the feeling of our infirmities; but was in all points tempted like as *we are, yet* without sin.

D

Ex. 34. 28 And he was there with the LORD forty days and forty nights; he did neither eat bread, nor drink water. And he wrote upon the tables the words of the covenant, the ten commandments.

E

Deut. 8. 3 And he humbled thee, and suffered thee to hunger, and fed thee with manna, which thou knewest not, neither did thy fathers know; that he might make thee know that man doth not live by bread only, but by every *word* that proceedeth out of the mouth of the LORD doth man live.

Eph. 6. 17 And take the helmet of salvation, and the sword of the Spirit, which is the word of God:

F

Matt. 4. 1. *See text of topic.*
Luke 4. 1. *See text of topic.*

G

Matt. 4. 11. *See text of topic.*

TIME, JANUARY–FEBRUARY, A. D. 27; PLACE, DESERT OF JUDÆA.

3: 23; 4: 1–13.

23 And Jesus himself began to be
[h]about thirty years of age, being (as
was supposed) the son of Joseph, which
was *the son* of Heli, (p. 23.)

CHAP. 4.

1 And [i]Jesus being full of the Holy
Ghost returned from Jordan, and [k]was
led by the Spirit into the wilderness,
2 Being forty days [l]tempted of the
devil. And [m]in those days he did eat
nothing: and when they were ended,
he afterward hungered.
3 And the devil said unto him, If
thou be the Son of God, command this
stone that it be made bread.
4 And Jesus answered him, saying,
[n]It is written, That man shall not live
by bread alone, but by every word of
God.

G—CONCLUDED.

I Tim. 3. 16 And without controversy great is the mystery of godliness: God was manifest in the flesh, justified in the Spirit, seen of angels, preached unto the Gentiles, believed on in the world, received up into glory.

H

Num. 4. 1 And the LORD spake unto Moses and unto Aaron, saying,
2 Take the sum of the sons of Kohath from among the sons of Levi, after their families, by the house of their fathers,
3 From thirty years old and upward even until fifty years old, all that enter into the host, to do the work in the tabernacle of the congregation.

Num. 4. 22 Take also the sum of the sons of Gershon, throughout the houses of their fathers, by their families;
23 From thirty years old and upward until fifty years old shalt thou number them; all that enter in to perform the service, to do the work in the tabernacle of the congregation.

I

Isa. 11. 2 And the Spirit of the Lord shall rest upon him, the spirit of wisdom

I—CONCLUDED.

and understanding, the spirit of counsel and might, the spirit of knowledge and of the fear of the LORD;

Isa. 61. 1 The Spirit of the Lord GOD *is* upon me; because the LORD hath anointed me to preach good tidings unto the meek; he hath sent me to bind up the brokenhearted, to proclaim liberty to the captives, and the opening of the prison to *them that are* bound;
2 To proclaim the acceptable year of the LORD, and the day of vengeance of our God; to comfort all that mourn;
3 To appoint unto them that mourn in Zion, to give unto them beauty for ashes, the oil of joy for mourning, the garment of praise for the spirit of heaviness; that they might be called Trees of righteousness, The planting of the LORD, that he might be glorified.

Matt. 4. 1. *See text of topic.*
Mark 1. 12. *See text of topic.*

John 3. 34 For he whom God hath sent speaketh the words of God: for God giveth not the Spirit by measure *unto him.*

K

Luke 2. 27 And he came by the Spirit into the temple: and when the parents brought in the child Jesus, to do for him after the custom of the law,

Luke 4. 14 And Jesus returned in the power of the Spirit into Galilee: and there went out a fame of him through all the region round about.

L

Gen. 3. 15 And I will put enmity between thee and the woman, and between thy seed and her seed; it shall bruise thy head, and thou shalt bruise his heel.

Heb. 2. 18 For in that he himself hath suffered being tempted, he is able to succour them that are tempted.

M

Ex. 34. 28. *See under D.*

I Ki. 19. 8 And he arose, and did eat and drink, and went in the strength of that meat forty days and forty nights unto Horeb the mount of God.

N

Deut. 8. 3. *See under E.*
Eph. 6. 17. *See under E.*

O

Neh. 11. 1 And the rulers of the people dwelt at Jerusalem: the rest of the people

For O concluded see next page (56).

Chap. 4.

5 Then the devil taketh him up [o]into the holy city, and setteth him on a pinnacle of the temple,

6 And saith unto him, If thou be the Son of God, cast thyself down: for it is written, [p]He shall give his angels charge concerning thee: and in *their* hands they shall bear thee up, lest at any time thou dash thy foot against a stone.

7 Jesus said unto him, [q]It is written again, Thou shalt not tempt the Lord thy God.

8 Again, the devil taketh him up into an exceeding high mountain, and [r]showeth him all the kingdoms of the world, and the glory of them;

9 And saith unto him, All these things will I give thee, if thou wilt fall down and worship me.

10 Then saith Jesus unto him, Get thee hence, Satan: for it is written, [s]Thou shalt worship the Lord thy God, and him only shalt thou serve.

11 Then the devil [t]leaveth him, and, behold, angels came and ministered unto him. (p. 78.)

O—Continued. See preceding page (55).

also cast lots, to bring one of ten to dwell in Jerusalem the holy city, and nine parts *to dwell* in *other* cities.

Neh. 11. 18 All the Levites in the holy city *were* two hundred fourscore and four.

Isa. 48. 2 For they call themselves of the holy city, and stay themselves upon the God of Israel: The Lord of hosts *is* his name.

Isa. 52. 1 Awake, awake, put on thy strength, O Zion; put on thy beautiful garments, O Jerusalem, the holy city: for henceforth there shall no more come into thee the uncircumcised and the unclean.

Matt. 27. 53 And came out of the graves after

§ 16. THE TEMPTATION (Concluded).

[Chap. 1.]

O—Concluded.

his resurrection, and went into the holy city, and appeared unto many.

Rev. 11. 2 But the court which is without the temple leave out, and measure it not; for it is given unto the Gentiles: and the holy city shall they tread under foot forty *and* two months.

P

Ps. 91. 11 For he shall give his angels charge over thee, to keep thee in all thy ways.

12 They shall bear thee up in *their* hands, lest thou dash thy foot against a stone.

Q

Deut. 6. 16 Ye shall not tempt the Lord your God, as ye tempted *him* in Massah.

R

Esth. 1. 3 In the third year of his reign, he made a feast unto all his princes and his servants; the power of Persia and Media, the nobles and princes of the provinces, *being* before him:

4 When he showed the riches of his glorious kingdom and the honour of his excellent majesty many days, *even* a hundred and fourscore days.

Esth. 5. 11 And Haman told them of the glory of his riches, and the multitude of his children, and all *the things* wherein the king had promoted him, and how he had advanced him above the princes and servants of the king.

Ps. 49. 16 Be not thou afraid when one is made rich, when the glory of his house is increased;

17 For when he dieth he shall carry nothing away: his glory shall not descend after him.

18 Though while he lived he blessed his soul, (and *men* will praise thee, when thou doest well to thyself,)

19 He shall go to the generation of his fathers; they shall never see light.

20 Man *that is* in honour, and understandeth not, is like the beasts *that* perish.

Dan. 4. 30 The king spake, and said, Is not this great Babylon, that I have built for the house of the kingdom by the might of my power, and for the honour of my majesty?

S

Deut. 6. 13 Thou shalt fear the Lord thy God, and serve him, and shalt swear by his name.

TIME, JANUARY–FEBRUARY, A. D. 27; PLACE, DESERT OF JUDÆA.

CHAP. 4.

5 And the devil, taking him up into a high mountain, showed unto him all the kingdoms of the world in a moment of time.

6 And the devil said unto him, All this power will I give thee, and the glory of them: for [u]that is delivered unto me; and to whomsoever I will, I give it.

7 If thou therefore wilt [1]worship me, all shall be thine.

8 And Jesus answered and said unto him, Get thee behind me, Satan: for [x]it is written, Thou shalt worship the Lord thy God, and him only shalt thou serve.

9 [y]And he brought him to Jerusalem, and set him on a pinnacle of the temple, and said unto him, If thou be the Son of God, cast [z]thyself down from hence:

10 For [a]it is written, He shall give his angels charge over thee, to keep thee:

11 And in *their* hands they shall bear thee up, lest at any time thou dash thy foot against a stone.

12 And Jesus answering said unto him, [b]It is said, Thou shalt not tempt the Lord thy God.

13 And when the devil had ended all the temptation, he [c]departed from him [d]for a season. (p. 79.)

S—CONTINUED.

Deut.10. 20 Thou shalt fear the LORD thy God; him shalt thou serve, and to him shalt thou cleave, and swear by his name.

Josh. 24. 14 Now therefore fear the LORD, and serve him in sincerity and in truth; and put away the gods which your fathers served on the other side of the flood, and in Egypt; and serve ye the LORD.

S—CONCLUDED.

I Sa. 7. 3 And Samuel spake unto all the house of Israel, saying, If ye do return unto the LORD with all your hearts, *then* put away the strange gods and Ashtaroth from among you, and prepare your hearts unto the LORD, and serve him only: and he will deliver you out of the hand of the Philistines.

T

Jas. 4. 7 Submit yourselves therefore to God. Resist the devil, and he will flee from you.

U

John 12. 31 Now is the judgment of this world: now shall the prince of this world be cast out.

John 14. 30 Hereafter I will not talk much with you: for the prince of this world cometh, and hath nothing in me.

Rev. 13. 2 And the beast which I saw was like unto a leopard, and his feet were as *the feet* of a bear, and his mouth as the mouth of a lion: and the dragon gave him his power, and his seat, and great authority.

Rev. 13. 7 And it was given unto him to make war with the saints, and to overcome them: and power was given him over all kindreds, and tongues, and nations.

1

Or, *fall down before me.*

X

Deut. 6. 13. *See under S.*
Deut. 10. 20. *See under S.*

Y

Matt. 4. 5. *See text of topic.*

Z

I Pet. 5. 8 Be sober, be vigilant; because your adversary the devil, as a roaring lion, walketh about, seeking whom he may devour:

A

Ps. 91. 11, 12. *See under P.*

B

Deut. 6. 16. *See under Q.*

C

Jas. 4. 7. *See under T.*

D

John 14. 30. *See under U.*

Heb. 4. 15 For we have not a high priest which cannot be touched with the feeling of our infirmities; but was in all points tempted like as *we are, yet* without sin.

§ 17. TESTIMONY OF JOHN THE BAPTIST TO JESUS.

A

John 1. 32 And John bare record, saying, I saw the Spirit descending from heaven like a dove, and it abode upon him.

John 3. 32 And what he hath seen and heard, that he testifieth; and no man receiveth his testimony.

John 5. 33 Ye sent unto John, and he bare witness unto the truth.

B

Matt. 3. 11. *See text of § 14.*
Mark 1. 7. *See text of § 14.*
Luke 3. 16. *See text of § 14.*
John 1.27,30. *See text of topic.*

John 3. 31 He that cometh from above is above all: he that is of the earth is earthly, and speaketh of the earth: he that cometh from heaven is above all.

C

John 8. 58 Jesus said unto them, Verily, verily, I say unto you, Before Abraham was, I am.

Col. 1. 17 And he is before all things, and by him all things consist:

D

John 3. 34 For he whom God hath sent speaketh the words of God: for God giveth not the Spirit by measure *unto him.*

Eph. 1. 6 To the praise of the glory of his grace, wherein he hath made us accepted in the beloved:

7 In whom we have redemption through his blood, the forgiveness of sins, according to the riches of his grace;

8 Wherein he hath abounded toward us in all wisdom and prudence;

Col. 1. 19 For it pleased *the Father* that in him should all fulness dwell:

Col. 2. 9 For in him dwelleth all the fulness of the Godhead bodily.

10 And ye are complete in him, which is the head of all principality and power:

E

Ex. 20. 1 And God spake all these words, saying,

Deut. 4. 44 And this *is* the law which Moses set before the children of Israel:

Deut. 5. 1 And Moses called all Israel, and said unto them, Hear, O Israel, the statutes and judgments which I speak in your ears this day, that ye may learn them, and keep and do them.

Deut.33. 4 Moses commanded us a law, *even* the inheritance of the congregation of Jacob.

F

Rom. 3. 24 Being justified freely by his grace through the redemption that is in Christ Jesus:

Rom. 5. 21 That as sin hath reigned unto death, even so might grace reign through righteousness unto eternal life by Jesus Christ our Lord.

Rom. 6. 14 For sin shall not have dominion over you: for ye are not under the law, but under grace.

G

John 8. 32 And ye shall know the truth, and the truth shall make you free.

John 14. 6 Jesus saith unto him, I am the way, the truth, and the life: no man cometh unto the Father, but by me.

H

Ex. 33. 20 And he said, Thou canst not see my face: for there shall no man see me, and live.

Deut. 4. 12 And the LORD spake unto you out of the midst of the fire: ye heard the voice of the words, but saw no similitude; only *ye heard* a voice.

Matt.11. 27 All things are delivered unto me of my Father: and no man knoweth the Son, but the Father; neither knoweth any man the Father, save the Son, and *he* to whomsoever the Son will reveal *him.*

Luke 10. 22 All things are delivered to me of my Father: and no man knoweth who the Son is, but the Father; and who the Father is, but the Son, and *he* to whom the Son will reveal *him.*

John 6. 46 Not that any man hath seen the Father, save he which is of God, he hath seen the Father.

I Tim.1. 17 Now unto the King eternal, immortal, invisible, the only wise God, *be* honour and glory for ever and ever. Amen.

I Tim.6. 16 Who only hath immortality, dwelling in the light which no man can approach unto; whom no man hath seen, nor can see: to whom *be* honour and power everlasting. Amen.

I Jno. 4. 12 No man hath seen God at any time. If we love one another, God dwelleth in us, and his love is perfected in us.

I Jno. 4. 20 If a man say, I love God, and hateth his brother, he is a liar: for he that loveth not his brother whom he hath seen, how can he love God whom he hath not seen?

TIME, FEBRUARY, A. D. 27 ; PLACE, BETHANY BEYOND JORDAN [BETHABARA].

I

John 1. 14. *See text of § 1.*

John 3. 16 For God so loved the world, that he gave his only begotten Son, that whosoever believeth in him should not perish, but have everlasting life.

John 3. 18 He that believeth on him is not condemned: but he that believeth not is condemned already, because he hath not believed in the name of the only begotten Son of God.

I Jno. 4. 9 In this was manifested the love of God toward us, because that God sent his only begotten Son into the world, that we might live through him.

K

Prov. 8. 30 Then I was by him, *as* one brought up *with him:* and I was daily *his* delight, rejoicing always before him;

L

John 5. 33. *See under A.*

M

Luke 3. 15. *See text of § 14.*

John 3. 28 Ye yourselves bear me witness, that I said, I am not the Christ, but that I am sent before him.

Acts 13. 25 And as John fulfilled his course, he said, Whom think ye that I am? I am not *he.* But, behold, there cometh one after me, whose shoes of *his* feet I am not worthy to loose.

N

Mal. 4. 5 Behold, I will send you Elijah the prophet before the coming of the great and dreadful day of the LORD:

Matt. 17. 10 And his disciples asked him, saying, Why then say the scribes that Elias must first come?

O

Luke 1. 17. *See text of § 3.*

P

Deut. 18. 15 The LORD thy God will raise up unto thee a Prophet from the midst of thee, of thy brethren, like unto me; unto him ye shall hearken;

Deut. 18. 18 I will raise them up a Prophet from among their brethren, like unto thee, and will put my words in his mouth; and he shall speak unto them all that I shall command him.

1

Or, *a prophet?*

Q

Matt. 3. 3. *See text of § 14.*
Mark 1. 3. *See text of § 14.*
Luke 3. 4. *See text of § 14.*
John 3. 28. *See under M.*

R

Isa. 40. 3. *See under D, page 45.*

1 : 15–31.

15 [a]John bare witness of him, and
cried, saying, This was he of whom I
spake, [b]He that cometh after me is
preferred before me; [c]for he was before me.

16 And of his [d]fulness have all we
received, and grace for grace.

17 For [e] the law was given by Moses, [f] *but* grace and [g]truth came by Jesus Christ.

18 [h]No man hath seen God at any
time; [i]the only begotten Son, which is
in [k]the bosom of the Father, he hath
declared *him.*

19 And this is [l]the record of John,
when the Jews sent priests and Levites
from Jerusalem to ask him, Who art
thou?

20 And [m]he confessed, and denied
not; but confessed, I am not the Christ.

21 And they asked him, What then?
Art thou [n]Elias? And he saith, [o]I am
not. Art thou [p] [1]that Prophet? And
he answered, No.

22 Then said they unto him, Who
art thou? that we may give an answer
to them that sent us. What sayest
thou of thyself?

23 [q]He said, I *am* the voice of one
crying in the wilderness, Make straight
the way of the Lord, as [r]said the prophet Esaias.

S

Matt. 3. 11. *See text of § 14.*

T

Mal. 3. 1 Behold, I will send my messenger, and he shall prepare the way before me: and the Lord, whom ye seek shall suddenly come to his temple, even the messenger of the covenant, whom ye delight in: behold, he shall come, saith the LORD of hosts.

§ 17. TESTIMONY OF JOHN THE BAPTIST TO JESUS (Concluded).

For S and T see preceding page (59).

U

John 1. 15, 30. *See text of topic.*

Acts 19. 4 Then said Paul, John verily baptized with the baptism of repentance, saying unto the people, that they should believe on him which should come after him, that is, on Christ Jesus.

X

Judg. 7. 24 And Gideon sent messengers throughout all mount Ephraim, saying, Come down against the Midianites, and take before them the waters unto Beth-barah and Jordan. Then all the men of Ephraim gathered themselves together, and took the waters unto Beth-barah and Jordan.

John 10. 40 And went away again beyond Jordan into the place where John at first baptized; and there he abode.

Y

Gen. 22. 7 And Isaac spake unto Abraham his father, and said, My father: and he said, Here *am* I, my son. And he said, Behold the fire and the wood: but where *is* the lamb for a burnt offering?

8 And Abraham said, My son, God will provide himself a lamb for a burnt offering: so they went both of them together.

Ex. 12. 3 Speak ye unto all the congregation of Israel, saying, In the tenth *day* of this month they shall take to them every man a lamb, according to the house of *their* fathers, a lamb for a house:

Isa. 53. 7 He was oppressed, and he was afflicted, yet he opened not his mouth: he is brought as a lamb to the slaughter, and as a sheep before her shearers is dumb, so he openeth not his mouth.

John 1. 36 And looking upon Jesus as he walked, he saith, Behold the Lamb of God!

Acts 8. 32 The place of the Scripture which he read was this, He was led as a sheep to the slaughter; and like a lamb dumb before his shearer, so opened he not his mouth:

1 Pet. 1. 19 But with the precious blood of Christ, as of a lamb without blemish and without spot:

Rev. 5. 6 And I beheld, and, lo, in the midst of the throne and of the four beasts, and in the midst of the elders, stood a Lamb as it had been slain, having seven horns and seven eyes, which are

Y—Concluded.

the seven Spirits of God sent forth into all the earth.

7 And he came and took the book out of the right hand of him that sat upon the throne.

8 And when he had taken the book, the four beasts and four *and* twenty elders fell down before the Lamb, having every one of them harps, and golden vials full of odours, which are the prayers of saints.

9 And they sung a new song, saying, Thou art worthy to take the book, and to open the seals thereof: for thou wast slain, and hast redeemed us to God by thy blood out of every kindred, and tongue, and people, and nation;

10 And hast made us unto our God kings and priests: and we shall reign on the earth.

11 And I beheld, and I heard the voice of many angels round about the throne, and the beasts, and the elders: and the number of them was ten thousand times ten thousand, and thousands of thousands;

12 Saying with a loud voice, Worthy is the Lamb that was slain to receive power, and riches, and wisdom, and strength, and honour, and glory, and blessing.

13 And every creature which is in heaven, and on the earth, and under the earth, and such as are in the sea, and all that are in them, heard I saying, Blessing, and honour, and glory, and power, *be* unto him that sitteth upon the throne, and unto the Lamb for ever and ever.

14 And the four beasts said, Amen. And the four *and* twenty elders fell down and worshipped him that liveth for ever and ever.

Z

Isa. 53. 11 He shall see of the travail of his soul, *and* shall be satisfied: by his knowledge shall my righteous servant justify many; for he shall bear their iniquities.

Hos. 14. 1 O Israel, return unto the Lord thy God; for thou hast fallen by thine iniquity.

2 Take with you words, and turn to the Lord: say unto him, Take away all iniquity, and receive *us* graciously: so will we render the calves of our lips.

TIME, FEBRUARY, A. D. 27; PLACE, BETHANY BEYOND JORDAN [BETHABARA].

Z—CONCLUDED.

I Cor.15. 3 For I delivered unto you first of all that which I also received, how that Christ died for our sins according to the Scriptures;

Gal. 1. 4 Who gave himself for our sins, that he might deliver us from this present evil world, according to the will of God and our Father:

Heb. 1. 3 Who being the brightness of *his* glory, and the express image of his person, and upholding all things by the word of his power, when he had by himself purged our sins, sat down on the right hand of the Majesty on high;

Heb. 2. 17 Wherefore in all things it behooved him to be made like unto *his* brethren, that he might be a merciful and faithful high priest in things *pertaining* to God, to make reconciliation for the sins of the people.

Heb. 9. 28 So Christ was once offered to bear the sins of many; and unto them that look for him shall he appear the second time without sin unto salvation.

I Pet. 2. 24 Who his own self bare our sins in his own body on the tree, that we, being dead to sins, should live unto righteousness: by whose stripes ye were healed.

I Pet. 3. 18 For Christ also hath once suffered for sins, the just for the unjust, that he might bring us to God, being put to death in the flesh, but quickened by the Spirit:

I Jno. 2. 2 And he is the propitiation for our sins: and not for ours only, but also for *the sins of* the whole world.

I Jno. 3. 5 And ye know that he was manifested to take away our sins; and in him is no sin.

I Jno. 4. 10 Herein is love, not that we loved God, but that he loved us, and sent his Son *to be* the propitiation for our sins.

Rev. 1. 5 And from Jesus Christ, *who is* the faithful witness, *and* the first-begotten of the dead, and the prince of the kings of the earth. Unto him that loved us, and washed us from our sins in his own blood.

2

Or, *beareth.*

A

John 1. 15, 27. *See text of topic.*

B

Isa. 40. 3. *See under D, page 45.*

Isa. 40. 4 Every valley shall be exalted, and every mountain and hill shall be made

CHAP. 1.

24 And they which were sent were
of the Pharisees.

25 And they asked him, and said
unto him, Why baptizest thou then, if
thou be not that Christ, nor Elias,
neither that Prophet?

26 John answered them, saying, [s]I
baptize with water: [t]but there standeth
one among you, whom ye know not;

27 [u]He it is, who coming after me
is preferred before me, whose shoe's
latchet I am not worthy to unloose.

28 These things were done [x]in Bethabara beyond Jordan, where John was
baptizing.

29 The next day John seeth Jesus
coming unto him, and saith, Behold
[y]the Lamb of God, [z]which [2]taketh
away the sin of the world!

30 [a]This is he of whom I said, After
me cometh a man which is preferred
before me; for he was before me.

31 And I knew him not: [b]but that
he should be made manifest to Israel,
[c]therefore am I come baptizing with
water.

(p. 53.)

B—CONCLUDED.

low: and the crooked shall be made straight, and the rough places plain:

5 And the glory of the LORD shall be revealed, and all flesh shall see *it* together: for the mouth of the LORD hath spoken *it.*

C

Mal. 3. 1. *See under T, page 59.*
Matt. 3. 6. *See text of* § *14.*
Luke 1. 17. *See text of* § *3.*

Luke 1. 76 And thou, child, shalt be called the prophet of the Highest: for thou shalt go before the face of the Lord to prepare his ways;

77 To give knowledge of salvation unto his people by the remission of their sins,

Luke 3. 3, 4. *See text of* § *14.*

§ 18. ANDREW AND ANOTHER DISCIPLE AND SIMON PETER.

A

John 18. 15 And Simon Peter followed Jesus, and *so did* another disciple: that disciple was known unto the high priest, and went in with Jesus into the palace of the high priest.

B

Isa. 45. 22 Look unto me, and be ye saved, all the ends of the earth: for I *am* God, and *there is* none else.

Isa. 65. 1 I am sought of *them that* asked not *for me;* I am found of *them that* sought me not: I said, Behold me, behold me, unto a nation *that* was not called by my name.

2 I have spread out my hands all the day unto a rebellious people, which walketh in a way *that was* not good, after their own thoughts;

John 1. 29. *See text of § 17.*

Heb. 12. 2 Looking unto Jesus the author and finisher of *our* faith; who for the joy that was set before him endured the cross, despising the shame, and is set down at the right hand of the throne of God.

C

Prov. 15. 23 A man hath joy by the answer of his mouth: and a word *spoken* in due season, how good *is it!*

Zech. 8. 21 And the inhabitants of one *city* shall go to another, saying, Let us go speedily to pray before the LORD, and to seek the LORD of hosts: I will go also.

Rom. 10. 17 So then faith *cometh* by hearing, and hearing by the word of God.

Rev. 22. 17 And the Spirit and the bride say, Come. And let him that heareth say, Come. And let him that is athirst come. And whomsoever will, let him take the water of life freely.

D

Ruth 1. 16 And Ruth said, Entreat me not to leave thee, *or* to return from following after thee: for whither thou goest, I will go; and where thou lodgest, I will lodge: thy people *shall be* my people, and thy God my God:

I Ki. 10. 8 Happy *are* thy men, happy *are* these thy servants, which stand continually before thee, *and* that hear thy wisdom.

Ps. 27. 4 One *thing* have I desired of the LORD, that will I seek after; that I may dwell in the house of the LORD all the days of my life, to behold the beauty of the LORD, and to inquire in his temple.

Prov. 8. 34 Blessed *is* the man that heareth me, watching daily at my gates, waiting at the posts of my doors.

Prov. 13. 20 He that walketh with wise *men* shall be wise: but a companion of fools shall be destroyed.

1

Or, *abidest.*

E

Prov. 8. 17 I love them that love me; and those that seek me early shall find me.

Acts 28. 30 And Paul dwelt two whole years in his own hired house, and received all that came in unto him,

31 Preaching the kingdom of God, and teaching those things which concern the Lord Jesus Christ, with all confidence, no man forbidding him.

Rev. 3. 20 Behold, I stand at the door, and knock: if any man hear my voice, and open the door, I will come in to him, and will sup with him, and he with me.

2

That was two hours before night.

§ 19. PHILIP AND NATHANAEL.

A

John 12. 21 The same came therefore to Philip, which was of Bethsaida of Galilee, and desired him, saying, Sir, we would see Jesus.

B

John 21. 2 There were together Simon Peter, and Thomas called Didymus, and Nathanael of Cana in Galilee, and the *sons* of Zebedee, and two other of his disciples.

C

Gen. 3. 15 And I will put enmity between thee and the woman, and between thy seed and her seed; it shall bruise thy head, and thou shalt bruise his heel.

Gen. 22. 18 And in thy seed shall all the nations of the earth be blessed; because thou hast obeyed my voice.

Gen. 49. 10 The sceptre shall not depart from Judah, nor a lawgiver from between his feet, until Shiloh come; and unto him *shall* the gathering of the people *be.*

Deut. 18. 18 I will raise them up a Prophet

TIME, FEBRUARY, A. D. 27; PLACE, THE JORDAN.

F

Matt. 4. 18. *See text of § 30.*

Acts 1. 13 And when they were come in they went up into an upper room, where abode both Peter, and James, and John, and Andrew, Philip, and Thomas, Bartholomew, and Matthew, James *the son* of Alpheus, and Simon Zelotes, and Judas *the brother* of James.

3

Or, *the Anointed.*

Ps. 2. 2 The kings of the earth set themselves, and the rulers take counsel together, against the LORD, and against his Anointed, *saying,*

Ps. 45. 7 Thou lovest righteousness, and hatest wickedness: therefore God, thy God, hath anointed thee with the oil of gladness above thy fellows.

Ps. 89. 20 I have found David my servant; with my holy oil have I anointed him:

Acts 10. 38 How God anointed Jesus of Nazareth with the Holy Ghost and with power: who went about doing good, and healing all that were oppressed of the devil; for God was with him.

Heb. 1. 8 But unto the Son *he saith,* Thy throne, O God, *is* for ever and ever: a sceptre of righteousness *is* the sceptre of thy kingdom.

9 Thou hast loved righteousness, and hated iniquity; therefore God, *even* thy God, hath anointed thee with the oil of gladness above thy fellows.

G

Matt.16. 18 And I say also unto thee, That thou art Peter, and upon this rock I will build my church; and the gates of hell shall not prevail against it.

4

Or, *Peter.*

1: 35–42.

35 Again the next day after, John
stood, [a]and two of his disciples;

36 And looking upon Jesus as he
walked, he saith, [b]Behold the Lamb of
God!

37 And the two disciples heard him
speak, [c]and they followed Jesus.

38 Then Jesus turned, and saw them
following, and saith unto them, What
seek ye? They said unto him, Rabbi,
(which is to say, being interpreted,
Master,) [d]where [1]dwellest thou?

39 He saith unto them, Come and
see. They came and saw where he
dwelt, and [e]abode with him that day:
for it was [2]about the tenth hour.

40 One of the two which heard John
speak, and followed him, was [f]Andrew,
Simon Peter's brother.

41 He first findeth his own brother
Simon, and saith unto him, We have
found the Messias, which is, being interpreted, [3]the Christ.

42 And he brought him to Jesus.
And when Jesus beheld him, he said,
Thou art Simon the son of Jona: [g]thou
shalt be called Cephas, which is by interpretation, [4]A stone.

TIME, FEBRUARY, A. D. 27; PLACE, THE JORDAN.

C—CONCLUDED.

from among their brethren, like unto thee, and will put my words in his mouth; and he shall speak unto them all that I shall command him.

19 And it shall come to pass, *that* whosoever will not hearken unto my words which he shall speak in my name, I will require *it* of him.

Luke 24. 27 And beginning at Moses and all the prophets, he expounded unto them in all the Scriptures the things concerning himself.

1: 43–51.

43 The day following Jesus would go
forth into Galilee, and findeth Philip,
and saith unto him, Follow me.

44 Now [a]Philip was of Bethsaida,
the city of Andrew and Peter.

45 Philip findeth [b]Nathanael, and
saith unto him, We have found him,
of whom [c]Moses in the law, and the

§ 19. PHILIP AND NATHANAEL (CONCLUDED).

D

Isa. 4. 2 In that day shall the branch of the LORD be beautiful and glorious, and the fruit of the earth *shall be* excellent and comely for them that are escaped of Israel.

Isa. 7. 14 Therefore the Lord himself shall give you a sign; Behold, a virgin shall conceive, and bear a son, and shall call his name Immanuel.

Isa. 9. 6 For unto us a child is born, unto us a son is given: and the government shall be upon his shoulder: and his name shall be called Wonderful, Counsellor, The mighty God, The everlasting Father, The Prince of Peace.

Isa. 53. 2 For he shall grow up before him as a tender plant, and as a root out of a dry ground: he hath no form nor comeliness; and when we shall see him, *there is* no beauty that we should desire him.

Mic. 5. 2 But thou, Beth-lehem Ephratah, *though* thou be little among the thousands of Judah, *yet* out of thee shall he come forth unto me *that is* to be ruler in Israel; whose goings forth *have been* from of old, from everlasting.

Zech. 6. 12 And speak unto him, saying, Thus speaketh the LORD of hosts, saying, Behold the man whose name *is* The BRANCH; and he shall grow up out of his place, and he shall build the temple of the LORD:

Zech. 9. 9 Rejoice greatly, O daughter of Zion; shout, O daughter of Jerusalem: behold, thy King cometh unto thee: he *is* just, and having salvation; lowly, and riding upon an ass, and upon a colt the foal of an ass.

E

Matt. 2. 23. *See text of § 12.*
Luke 2. 4. *See text of § 8.*

F

John 7. 41 Others said, This is the Christ. But some said, Shall Christ come out of Galilee?

John 7. 42 Hath not the Scripture said, That Christ cometh of the seed of David, and out of the town of Bethlehem, where David was?

John 7. 52 They answered and said unto him, Art thou also of Galilee? Search, and look: for out of Galilee ariseth no prophet.

G

Ps. 32. 2 Blessed *is* the man unto whom the LORD imputeth not iniquity, and in whose spirit *there is* no guile.

Ps. 33. 1 Rejoice in the LORD, O ye righteous: *for* praise is comely for the upright.

John 8. 39 They answered and said unto him, Abraham is our father. Jesus saith unto them, If ye were Abraham's children, ye would do the works of Abraham.

Rom. 2. 28 For he is not a Jew, which is one outwardly; neither *is that* circumcision, which is outward in the flesh.

29 But he *is* a Jew, which is one inwardly; and circumcision *is that* of the heart, in the spirit, *and* not in the letter; whose praise *is* not of men, but of God.

Rom. 9. 6 Not as though the word of God hath taken none effect. For they *are* not all Israel, which are of Israel:

H

Matt. 14. 33 Then they that were in the ship came and worshipped him, saying, Of a truth thou art the Son of God.

§ 20. THE MARRIAGE AT CANA OF GALILEE.

A

Gen. 1. 27 So God created man in his *own* image, in the image of God created he him; male and female created he them.

28 And God blessed them, and God said unto them, Be fruitful, and multiply, and replenish the earth, and subdue it: and have dominion over the fish of the sea, and over the fowl of the air, and over every living thing that moveth upon the earth.

Ps. 128 1 Blessed *is* every one that feareth

A—CONTINUED.

the LORD; that walketh in his ways.

2 For thou shalt eat the labour of thine hands: happy *shalt* thou *be*, and *it shall be* well with thee.

3 Thy wife *shall be* as a fruitful vine by the sides of thine house: thy children like olive plants round about thy table.

4 Behold, that thus shall the man be blessed that feareth the LORD.

Prov. 18. 22 *Whoso* findeth a wife findeth a good *thing*, and obtaineth favour of the LORD.

TIME, FEBRUARY, A. D. 27; PLACE, THE JORDAN.

I

Matt.21. 5 Tell ye the daughter of Sion, Behold, thy King cometh unto thee, meek, and sitting upon an ass, and a colt the foal of an ass.

Matt.27. 11 And Jesus stood before the governor: and the governor asked him, saying, Art thou the King of the Jews? And Jesus said unto him, Thou sayest.

Matt.27. 42 He saved others; himself he cannot save. If he be the King of Israel, let him now come down from the cross, and we will believe him.

John 18. 37 Pilate therefore said unto him, Art thou a king then? Jesus answered, Thou sayest that I am a king. To this end was I born, and for this cause came I into the world, that I should bear witness unto the truth. Every one that is of the truth heareth my voice.

John 19. 3 And said, Hail, King of the Jews! and they smote him with their hands.

K

Gen. 28. 12 And he dreamed, and behold a ladder set up on the earth, and the top of it reached to heaven: and behold the angels of God ascending and descending on it.

Matt. 4. 11. *See text of* § *16.*
Luke 2. 9, 13. *See text of* § *9.*

Luke 22. 43 And there appeared an angel unto him from heaven, strengthening him.

Luke 24. 4 And it came to pass, as they were much perplexed thereabout, behold, two men stood by them in shining garments:

Acts 1. 10 And while they looked steadfastly toward heaven as he went up, behold, two men stood by them in white apparel;

CHAP. 1.

[d]prophets, did write, [e]Jesus of Nazareth, the son of Joseph.

46 And Nathanael said unto him, [f]Can there any good thing come out of Nazareth? Philip saith unto him, Come and see.

47 Jesus saw Nathanael coming to him, and saith of him, Behold an [g]Israelite indeed, in whom is no guile!

48 Nathanael saith unto him, Whence knowest thou me? Jesus answered and said unto him, Before that Philip called thee, when thou wast under the fig tree, I saw thee.

49 Nathanael answered and saith unto him, Rabbi, [h]thou art the Son of God; [i]thou art the King of Israel.

50 Jesus answered and said unto him, Because I said unto thee, I saw thee under the fig tree, believest thou? thou shalt see greater things than these.

51 And he saith unto him, Verily, verily, I say unto you, [k]Hereafter ye shall see heaven open, and the angels of God ascending and descending upon the Son of man.

TIME, FEBRUARY, A. D. 27.

A—CONTINUED,

Prov.19. 14 House and riches *are* the inheritance of fathers: and a prudent wife *is* from the LORD.

Prov.31. 10 Who can find a virtuous woman? for her price *is* far above rubies.

11 The heart of her husband doth safely trust in her, so that he shall have no need of spoil.

12 She will do him good and not evil all the days of her life.

Eph 5. 33 Nevertheless, let every one of you in particular so love his wife even as

2: 1–12.

1 And the third day there was a [a]marriage in [b]Cana of Galilee; and the mother of Jesus was there:

A—CONCLUDED.

himself; and the wife *see* that she reverence *her* husband.

B

Josh. 19. 28 And Hebron, and Rehob, and Hammon, and Kanah, *even* unto great Zidon:

§ 20. THE MARRIAGE AT CANA OF GALILEE

C

John 19. 26 When Jesus therefore saw his mother, and the disciples standing by, whom he loved, he saith unto his mother, Woman, behold thy son!

D

II Sa. 16. 10 And the king said, What have I to do with you, ye sons of Zeruiah? so let him curse, because the LORD hath said unto him, Curse David. Who shall then say, Wherefore hast thou done so?

II Sa. 19. 22 And David said, What have I to do with you, ye sons of Zeruiah, that ye should this day be adversaries unto me? shall there any man be put to death this day in Israel? for do not I know that I *am* this day king over Israel?

E

Eccl. 3. 1 To every *thing there is* a season, and a time to every purpose under the heaven:

John 7. 6 Then Jesus said unto them, My time is not yet come: but your time is always ready.

John 12. 23 And Jesus answered them, saying, The hour is come, that the Son of man should be glorified.

F

Gen. 6. 22 Thus did Noah; according to all that God commanded him, so did he.

Judg. 13. 14 She may not eat of any *thing* that cometh of the vine, neither let her drink wine or strong drink, nor eat any unclean *thing:* all that I commanded her let her observe.

Luke 5. 5 And Simon answering said unto him, Master, we have toiled all the night, and have taken nothing: nevertheless at thy word I will let down the net.

6 And when they had this done, they inclosed a great multitude of fishes: and their net brake.

Acts 9. 6 And he trembling and astonished said, Lord, what wilt thou have me to do? And the Lord *said* unto him, Arise, and go into the city, and it shall be told thee what thou must do.

Heb. 5. 9 And being made perfect, he became the author of eternal salvation unto all them that obey him;

Heb. 11. 8 By faith Abraham, when he was called to go out into a place which he should after receive for an inheritance, obeyed; and he went out, not knowing whither he went.

G

Mark 7. 3 For the Pharisees, and all the Jews, except they wash *their* hands oft, eat not, holding the tradition of the elders.

Eph. 5. 25 Husbands, love your wives, even as Christ also loved the church, and gave himself for it;

26 That he might sanctify and cleanse it with the washing of water by the word,

27 That he might present it to himself a glorious church, not having spot, or wrinkle, or any such thing; but that it should be holy and without blemish.

Heb. 6. 1 Therefore leaving the principles of the doctrine of Christ, let us go on unto perfection; not laying again the foundation of repentance from dead works, and of faith toward God,

2 Of the doctrine of baptisms, and of laying on of hands, and of resurrection of the dead, and of eternal judgment.

Heb. 9. 8 The Holy Ghost this signifying, that the way into the holiest of all was not yet made manifest, while as the first tabernacle was yet standing:

9 Which *was* a figure for the time then present, in which were offered both gifts and sacrifices, that could not make him that did the service perfect, as pertaining to the conscience;

10 *Which stood* only in meats and drinks, and divers washings, and carnal ordinances, imposed *on them* until the time of reformation.

Heb. 9. 19 For when Moses had spoken every precept to all the people according to the law, he took the blood of calves and of goats, with water, and scarlet wool, and hyssop, and sprinkled both the book and all the people,

Heb. 10. 22 Let us draw near with a true heart in full assurance of faith, having our hearts sprinkled from an evil conscience, and our bodies washed with pure water.

H

John 4. 46 So Jesus came again into Cana of Galilee, where he made the water wine. And there was a certain nobleman, whose son was sick at Capernaum.

I

Ex. 4. 9 And it shall come to pass, if they will not believe also these two signs, neither hearken unto thy voice, that

(CONCLUDED). TIME, FEBRUARY, A. D. 27.

I—CONCLUDED.

thou shalt take of the water of the river, and pour *it* upon the dry *land:* and the water which thou takest out of the river shall become blood upon the dry *land.*

K

Deut 5. 24 And ye said, Behold, the LORD our God hath showed us his glory and his greatness, and we have heard his voice out of the midst of the fire: we have seen this day that God doth talk with man, and he liveth.

Ps. 72. 19 And blessed *be* his glorious name for ever: and let the whole earth be filled *with* his glory. Amen, and Amen.

Ps. 96. 3 Declare his glory among the heathen, his wonders among all people.

John 1. 14 And the Word was made flesh, and dwelt among us, (and we beheld his glory, the glory as of the only begotten of the Father,) full of grace and truth.

II Cor.3. 18 But we all, with open face beholding as in a glass the glory of the Lord, are changed into the same image from glory to glory, *even* as by the Spirit of the Lord.

II Cor.4. 6 For God, who commanded the light to shine out of darkness, hath shined in our hearts, to *give* the light of the knowledge of the glory of God in the face of Jesus Christ.

L

John 11. 15 And I am glad for your sakes that I was not there, to the intent ye may believe; nevertheless let us go unto him.

John 20. 30 And many other signs truly did Jesus in the presence of his disciples, which are not written in this book:

31 But these are written, that ye might believe that Jesus is the Christ, the Son of God; and that believing ye might have life through his name.

I Jno. 5. 13 These things have I written unto you that believe on the name of the Son of God; that ye may know that ye have eternal life, and that ye may believe on the name of the Son of God.

M

Matt.12. 46 While he yet talked to the people, behold, *his* mother and his brethren stood without, desiring to speak with him.

CHAP. 2.

2 And both Jesus was called, and his disciples, to the marriage.

3 And when they wanted wine, the mother of Jesus saith unto him, They have no wine.

4 Jesus saith unto her, [c]Woman, [d]what have I to do with thee? [e]mine hour is not yet come.

5 His mother saith unto the servants, [f]Whatsoever he saith unto you, do *it.*

6 And there were set there six waterpots of stone, [g]after the manner of the purifying of the Jews, containing two or three firkins apiece.

7 Jesus saith unto them, Fill the waterpots with water. And they filled them up to the brim.

8 And he saith unto them, Draw out now and bear unto the governor of the feast. And they bare *it.*

9 When the ruler of the feast had tasted [h]the water that was made wine, and knew not whence it was, (but the servants which drew the water knew,) the governor of the feast called the bridegroom.

10 And saith unto him, Every man at the beginning doth set forth good wine; and when men have well drunk, then that which is worse: *but* thou hast kept the good wine until now.

11 This [i]beginning of miracles did Jesus in Cana of Galilee, [k]and manifested forth his glory; [l]and his disciples believed on him.

12 After this he went down to Capernaum, he, and his mother, and [m]his brethren, and his disciples; and they continued there not many days.

§ 21. THE FIRST PASSOVER AND CLEANSING OF THE TEMPLE.

A

Ex. 12. 14 And this day shall be unto you for a memorial; and ye shall keep it a feast to the LORD throughout your generations: ye shall keep it a feast by an ordinance for ever.

Deut.16. 1 Observe the month of Abib, and keep the passover unto the LORD thy God: for in the month of Abib the LORD thy God brought thee forth out of Egypt by night.

Deut.16. 16 Three times in a year shall all thy males appear before the LORD thy God in the place which he shall choose; in the feast of unleavened bread, and in the feast of weeks, and in the feast of tabernacles: and they shall not appear before the LORD empty:

John 5. 1 After this there was a feast of the Jews; and Jesus went up to Jerusalem.

John 6. 4 And the passover, a feast of the Jews, was nigh.

John 11. 55 And the Jews' passover was nigh at hand: and many went out of the country up to Jerusalem before the passover, to purify themselves.

John 2. 23. *See text of topic.*

B

Matt.21. 12 And Jesus went into the temple of God, and cast out all them that sold and bought in the temple, and overthrew the tables of the money-changers, and the seats of them that sold doves.

Mark11. 15 And they come to Jerusalem: and Jesus went into the temple, and began to cast out them that sold and bought in the temple, and overthrew the tables of the money-changers, and the seats of them that sold doves;

Luke19. 45 And he went into the temple, and began to cast out them that sold therein, and them that bought;

C

Ps. 93. 5 Thy testimonies are very sure: holiness becometh thine house, O LORD, for ever.

Jer. 7. 11 Is this house, which is called by my name, become a den of robbers in your eyes? Behold, even I have seen *it*, saith the LORD.

Hos. 12. 7 *He is* a merchant, the balances of deceit *are* in his hand: he loveth to oppress.

8 And Ephraim said, Yet I am become rich, I have found me out substance: *in* all my labours they shall find none iniquity in me that *were* sin.

C—CONCLUDED.

Luke 2. 49 And he said unto them, How is it that ye sought me? wist ye not that I must be about my Father's business?

Acts 19. 24 For a certain *man* named Demetrius, a silversmith, which made silver shrines for Diana, brought no small gain unto the craftsmen;

25 Whom he called together with the workmen of like occupation, and said, Sirs, ye know that by this craft we have our wealth.

26 Moreover ye see and hear, that not alone at Ephesus, but almost throughout all Asia, this Paul hath persuaded and turned away much people, saying that they be no gods, which are made with hands:

27 So that not only this our craft is in danger to be set at nought; but also that the temple of the great goddess Diana should be despised, and her magnificence should be destroyed, whom all Asia and the world worshippeth.

I Tim.6. 9 But they that will be rich fall into temptation and a snare, and *into* many foolish and hurtful lusts, which drown men in destruction and perdition.

10 For the love of money is the root of all evil: which while some coveted after, they have erred from the faith, and pierced themselves through with many sorrows.

D

Ps. 69. 9 For the zeal of thine house hath eaten me up; and the reproaches of them that reproached thee are fallen upon me.

Ps. 119. 139 My zeal hath consumed me, because mine enemies have forgotten thy words.

E

Matt.12. 38 Then certain of the scribes and of the Pharisees answered, saying, Master, we would see a sign from thee.

John 6. 30 They said therefore unto him, What sign showest thou then, that we may see, and believe thee? what dost thou work?

F

Matt.26. 61 And said, This *fellow* said, I am able to destroy the temple of God, and to build it in three days.

Matt.27. 40 And saying, Thou that destroyest the temple, and buildest *it* in three days, save thyself. If thou be the Son of God, come down from the cross.

Mark14. 58 We heard him say, I will destroy this temple that is made with hands,

TIME, APRIL, A. D. 27; PLACE, JERUSALEM.

F—CONCLUDED.

and within three days I will build another made without hands.

Mark15. 29 And they that passed by railed on him, wagging their heads, and saying, Ah, thou that destroyest the temple, and buildest *it* in three days,

G

I Cor. 3. 16 Know ye not that ye are the temple of God, and *that* the Spirit of God dwelleth in you?

I Cor. 6. 19 What! know ye not that your body is the temple of the Holy Ghost *which is* in you, which ye have of God, and ye are not your own?

IICor.6. 16 And what agreement hath the temple of God with idols? for ye are the temple of the living God; as God hath said, I will dwell in them, and walk in *them;* and I will be their God, and they shall be my people.

Col. 2. 9 For in him dwelleth all the fulness of the Godhead bodily.

Heb. 8. 2 A minister of the sanctuary, and of the true tabernacle, which the Lord pitched, and not man.

H

Luke 24. 8 And they remembered his words,

Luke 24. 25 Then he said unto them, O fools, and slow of heart to believe all that the prophets have spoken:

Luke 24. 45 Then opened he their understanding, that they might understand the Scriptures,

John 14. 26 But the Comforter, *which is* the Holy Ghost, whom the Father will send in my name, he shall teach you all things, and bring all things to your remembrance, whatsoever I have said unto you.

I

I Sa. 16. 7 But the LORD said unto Samuel, Look not on his countenance, or on the height of his stature; because I have refused him: for *the LORD seeth* not as man seeth; for man looketh on the outward appearance, but the LORD looketh on the heart.

I Chr.28. 9 And thou, Solomon my son, know thou the God of thy father, and serve him with a perfect heart and with a willing mind: for the LORD searcheth all hearts, and understandeth all the imaginations of the thoughts: if thou seek him, he will be found of thee; but if thou forsake him, he will cast thee off for ever.

Matt. 9. 4 And Jesus knowing their thoughts

2: 13–25.

13 [a]And the Jews' passover was at hand, and Jesus went up to Jerusalem,

14 [b]And found in the temple those that sold oxen and sheep and doves, and the changers of money sitting:

15 And when he had made a scourge of small cords, he drove them all out of the temple, and the sheep, and the oxen; and poured out the changers' money, and overthrew the tables;

16 And said unto them that sold doves, Take these things hence; [c]make not my Father's house a house of merchandise.

17 And his disciples remembered that it was written, [d] The zeal of thine house hath eaten me up.

18 Then answered the Jews and said unto him, [e] What sign showest thou unto us, seeing that thou doest these things?

19 Jesus answered and said unto them, [f]Destroy this temple, and in three days I will raise it up.

20 Then said the Jews, Forty and six years was this temple in building, and wilt thou rear it up in three days?

21 But he spake [g]of the temple of his body.

22 When therefore he was risen from the dead, [h]his disciples remembered that he had said this unto them; and they believed the Scripture, and the word which Jesus had said.

23 ¶ Now when he was in Jerusalem at the passover, in the feast *day*, many believed in his name, when they saw the miracles which he did.

§ 21. THE FIRST PASSOVER AND CLEANSING OF THE TEMPLE

I—CONTINUED. See preceding page (69).
said, Wherefore think ye evil in your hearts?

Mark 2. 8 And immediately, when Jesus perceived in his spirit that they so reasoned within themselves, he said unto them, Why reason ye these things in your hearts?

John 6. 64 But there are some of you that believe not. For Jesus knew from the beginning who they were that believed not, and who should betray him.

I—CONTINUED.

John 16. 30 Now are we sure that thou knowest all things, and needest not that any man should ask thee: by this we believe that thou camest forth from God.

Acts 1. 24 And they prayed, and said, Thou,

§ 22. OUR LORD'S DISCOURSE WITH NICODEMUS.

A

John 7. 50 Nicodemus saith unto them, (he that came to Jesus by night, being one of them,)

John 19. 39 And there came also Nicodemus, (which at the first came to Jesus by night,) and brought a mixture of myrrh and aloes, about a hundred pound *weight*.

B

John 9. 16 Therefore said some of the Pharisees, This man is not of God, because he keepeth not the sabbath day. Others said, How can a man that is a sinner do such miracles? And there was a division among them.

John 9. 33 If this man were not of God, he could do nothing.

Acts 2. 22 Ye men of Israel, hear these words; Jesus of Nazareth, a man approved of God among you by miracles and wonders and signs, which God did by him in the midst of you, as ye yourselves also know:

C

Acts 10. 38 How God anointed Jesus of Nazareth with the Holy Ghost and with power: who went about doing good, and healing all that were oppressed of the devil; for God was with him.

D

John 1. 13 Which were born, not of blood, nor of the will of the flesh, nor of the will of man, but of God.

II Cor. 5. 17 Therefore if any man *be* in Christ, *he is* a new creature: old things are passed away; behold, all things are become new.

Gal. 6. 15 For in Christ Jesus neither circumcision availeth any thing, nor uncircumcision, but a new creature.

Eph. 2. 5 Even when we were dead in sins, hath quickened us together with Christ, (by grace ye are saved;)

D—CONCLUDED.

Eph. 2. 10 For we are his workmanship, created in Christ Jesus unto good works, which God hath before ordained that we should walk in them.

Tit. 3. 5 Not by works of righteousness which we have done, but according to his mercy he saved us, by the washing of regeneration, and renewing of the Holy Ghost;

Jas. 1. 18 Of his own will begat he us with the word of truth, that we should be a kind of first-fruits of his creatures.

I Pet. 1. 23 Being born again, not of corruptible seed, but of incorruptible, by the word of God, which liveth and abideth for ever.

I Jno. 3. 9 Whosoever is born of God doth not commit sin; for his seed remaineth in him: and he cannot sin, because he is born of God.

1

Or, *from above*.

E

Mark 16. 16 He that believeth and is baptized shall be saved; but he that believeth not shall be damned.

Acts 2. 38 Then Peter said unto them, Repent, and be baptized every one of you in the name of Jesus Christ for the remission of sins, and ye shall receive the gift of the Holy Ghost.

I Pet. 3. 21 The like figure whereunto *even* baptism doth also now save us, (not the putting away of the filth of the flesh, but the answer of a good conscience toward God,) by the resurrection of Jesus Christ:

F

Eze. 11. 19 And I will give them one heart, and I will put a new spirit within you; and I will take the stony heart out of their flesh, and will give them a heart of flesh:

20 That they may walk in my stat-

(CONCLUDED). TIME, APRIL, A. D. 27; PLACE, JERUSALEM.

I—CONCLUDED.

Lord, which knowest the hearts of all *men*, show whether of these two thou hast chosen,

Rev. 2. 23 And I will kill her children with death; and all the churches shall know that I am he which searcheth the reins and hearts: and I will give unto every one of you according to your works.

CHAP. 2.

24 But Jesus did not commit himself
unto them, because he knew all *men*,
25 And needed not that any should
testify of man; [i]for he knew what was
in man.

TIME, APRIL, A. D. 27; PLACE, JERUSALEM.

F—CONTINUED.

utes, and keep mine ordinances, and do them: and they shall be my people, and I will be their God.

Eze. 36. 26 A new heart also will I give you, and a new spirit will I put within you: and I will take away the stony heart out of your flesh, and I will give you a heart of flesh.

27 And I will put my Spirit within you, and cause you to walk in my statutes, and ye shall keep my judgments, and do *them*.

Rom. 8. 5 For they that are after the flesh do mind the things of the flesh; but they that are after the Spirit, the things of the Spirit.

Rom. 8. 9 But ye are not in the flesh, but in the Spirit, if so be that the Spirit of God dwell in you. Now if any man have not the Spirit of Christ, he is none of his.

I Cor. 6. 17 But he that is joined unto the Lord is one spirit.

Gal. 5. 17 For the flesh lusteth against the Spirit, and the Spirit against the flesh: and these are contrary the one to the other; so that ye cannot do the things that ye would.

18 But if ye be led of the Spirit, ye are not under the law.

19 Now the works of the flesh are manifest, which are *these*, Adultery, fornication, uncleanness, lasciviousness,

20 Idolatry, witchcraft, hatred, variance, emulations, wrath, strife, seditions, heresies,

21 Envyings, murders, drunkenness, revellings, and such like: of the which I tell you before, as I have also told *you* in time past, that they which do such things shall not inherit the kingdom of God.

3: 1–21.

1 There was a man of the Pharisees,
named Nicodemus, a ruler of the Jews:
2 [a] The same came to Jesus by night,
and said unto him, Rabbi, we know
that thou art a teacher come from God:
for [b]no man can do these miracles that
thou doest, except [c]God be with him.
3 Jesus answered and said unto him,
[d]Verily, verily, I say unto thee, Except a man be born [1]again, he cannot
see the kingdom of God.
4 Nicodemus saith unto him, How
can a man be born when he is old?
can he enter the second time into his
mother's womb, and be born?
5 Jesus answered, Verily, verily, I
say unto thee, [e] Except a man be born
of water and *of* the Spirit, he cannot
enter into the kingdom of God.
6 That which is born of the flesh is
flesh; and [f]that which is born of the
Spirit is spirit.
7 Marvel not that I said unto thee,
Ye must be born [2]again.

F—CONCLUDED.

Gal. 5. 22 But the fruit of the Spirit is love, joy, peace, longsuffering, gentleness, goodness, faith,

23 Meekness, temperance: against such there is no law.

2 Or, *from above*.

§ 22. OUR LORD'S DISCOURSE WITH NICODEMUS (Continued).

G

Eccl. 11. 5 As thou knowest not what *is* the way of the spirit, *nor* how the bones *do grow* in the womb of her that is with child: even so thou knowest not the works of God who maketh all.

I Cor. 2. 11 For what man knoweth the things of a man, save the spirit of man which is in him? even so the things of God knoweth no man, but the Spirit of God.

H

John 6. 52 The Jews therefore strove among themselves, saying, How can this man give us *his* flesh to eat?

John 6. 60 Many therefore of his disciples, when they had heard *this*, said, This is a hard saying; who can hear it?

I

Matt. 11. 27 All things are delivered unto me of my Father: and no man knoweth the Son, but the Father; neither knoweth any man the Father, save the Son, and *he* to whomsoever the Son will reveal *him*.

John 1. 18 No man hath seen God at any time; the only begotten Son, which is in the bosom of the Father, he hath declared *him*.

John 7. 16 Jesus answered them, and said, My doctrine is not mine, but his that sent me.

John 8. 28 Then said Jesus unto them, When ye have lifted up the Son of man, then shall ye know that I am *he*, and *that* I do nothing of myself; but as my Father hath taught me, I speak these things.

John 12. 49 For I have not spoken of myself; but the Father which sent me, he gave me a commandment, what I should say, and what I should speak.

John 14. 24 He that loveth me not keepeth not my sayings: and the word which ye hear is not mine, but the Father's which sent me.

K

John 3. 32 And what he hath seen and heard, that he testifieth; and no man receiveth his testimony.

L

Prov. 30. 4 Who hath ascended up into heaven, or descended? who hath gathered the wind in his fists? who hath bound the waters in a garment? who hath established all the ends of the earth? what *is* his name, and what *is* his son's name, if thou canst tell?

L—Concluded.

John 6. 33 For the bread of God is he which cometh down from heaven, and giveth life unto the world.

John 6. 38 For I came down from heaven, not to do mine own will, but the will of him that sent me.

John 6. 51 I am the living bread which came down from heaven: if any man eat of this bread, he shall live for ever: and the bread that I will give is my flesh, which I will give for the life of the world.

John 6. 62 *What* and if ye shall see the Son of man ascend up where he was before?

John 16. 28 I came forth from the Father, and am come into the world: again, I leave the world, and go to the Father.

Acts 2. 34 For David is not ascended into the heavens: but he saith himself, The Lord said unto my Lord, Sit thou on my right hand.

I Cor. 15. 47 The first man *is* of the earth, earthy: the second man *is* the Lord from heaven.

Eph. 4. 9 (Now that he ascended, what is it but that he also descended first into the lower parts of the earth?

10 He that descended is the same also that ascended up far above all heavens, that he might fill all things.)

M

Num. 21. 9 And Moses made a serpent of brass, and put it upon a pole; and it came to pass, that if a serpent had bitten any man, when he beheld the serpent of brass, he lived.

N

John 8. 28. *See under I.*

John 12. 32 And I, if I be lifted up from the earth, will draw all *men* unto me.

33 This he said, signifying what death he should die.

34 The people answered him, We have heard out of the law that Christ abideth for ever: and how sayest thou, The Son of man must be lifted up? who is this Son of man?

O

John 3. 36 He that believeth on the Son hath everlasting life: and he that believeth not the Son shall not see life: but the wrath of God abideth on him.

John 6. 47 Verily, verily, I say unto you, He that believeth on me hath everlasting life.

P

Rom. 5. 8 But God commendeth his love to-

TIME, APRIL, A. D. 27; PLACE, JERUSALEM.

P—CONCLUDED.

ward us, in that, while we were yet sinners, Christ died for us.

I Jno. 4. 9 In this was manifested the love of God toward us, because that God sent his only begotten Son into the world, that we might live through him.

Q

Luke 9. 56 For the Son of man is not come to destroy men's lives, but to save *them*. And they went to another village.

John 5. 45 Do not think that I will accuse you to the Father: there is *one* that accuseth you, *even* Moses, in whom ye trust.

John 8. 15 Ye judge after the flesh; I judge no man.

John 12. 47 And if any man hear my words, and believe not, I judge him not: for I came not to judge the world, but to save the world.

I Jno. 4. 14 And we have seen and do testify that the Father sent the Son *to be* the Saviour of the world.

R

John 5. 24 Verily, verily, I say unto you, He that heareth my word, and believeth on him that sent me, hath everlasting life, and shall not come into condemnation; but is passed from death unto life.

John 6. 40 And this is the will of him that sent me, that every one which seeth the Son, and believeth on him, may have everlasting life: and I will raise him up at the last day.

John 6. 47. *See under O.*

John 20. 31 But these are written, that ye might believe that Jesus is the Christ, the Son of God; and that believing ye might have life through his name.

S

Rom. 5. 1 Therefore being justified by faith, we have peace with God through our Lord Jesus Christ:

Rom. 8. 1 *There is* therefore now no condemnation to them which are in Christ Jesus, who walk not after the flesh, but after the Spirit.

Rom. 8. 34 Who *is* he that condemneth? *It is* Christ that died, yea rather, that is risen again, who is even at the right hand of God, who also maketh intercession for us.

1 Jno. 5. 11 And this is the record, that God hath given to us eternal life, and this life is in his Son.

12 He that hath the Son hath life; *and* he that hath not the Son of God hath not life.

CHAP. 3.

8 [g]The wind bloweth where it listeth, and thou hearest the sound thereof, but canst not tell whence it cometh, and whither it goeth: so is every one that is born of the Spirit.

9 Nicodemus answered and said unto him, [h]How can these things be?

10 Jesus answered and said unto him, Art thou a master of Israel, and knowest not these things?

11 [i]Verily, verily, I say unto thee, We speak that we do know, and testify that we have seen; and [k]ye receive not our witness.

12 If I have told you earthly things, and ye believe not, how shall ye believe, if I tell you *of* heavenly things?

13 And [l]no man hath ascended up to heaven, but he that came down from heaven, *even* the Son of man which is in heaven.

14 [m]And as Moses lifted up the serpent in the wilderness, even so [n]must the Son of man be lifted up:

15 That whosoever believeth in him should not perish, [o]but have eternal life.

16 [p]For God so loved the world, that he gave his only begotten Son, that whosoever believeth in him should not perish, but have everlasting life.

17 [q]For God sent not his Son into the world to condemn the world; but that the world through him might be saved.

18 [r]He that believeth on him [s]is not condemned: but he that believeth not is condemned already, because he hath not believed in the name of the only begotten Son of God.

§ 22. OUR LORD'S DISCOURSE WITH NICODEMUS (CONCLUDED).

T

Isa. 5. 20 Woe unto them that call evil good, and good evil; that put darkness for light, and light for darkness; that put bitter for sweet, and sweet for bitter!

John 1. 4 In him was life; and the life was the light of men.

John 1. 9 *That* was the true Light, which lighteth every man that cometh into the world.

10 He was in the world, and the world was made by him, and the world knew him not.

11 He came unto his own, and his own received him not.

John 8. 12 Then spake Jesus again unto them, saying, I am the light of the world: he that followeth me shall not walk in darkness, but shall have the light of life.

U

Job 24. 13 They are of those that rebel against the light; they know not the ways thereof, nor abide in the paths thereof.

Job 24. 17 For the morning *is* to them even as the shadow of death: if *one* know *them, they are in* the terrors of the shadow of death.

Eph. 5. 13 But all things that are reproved are made manifest by the light: for whatsoever doth make manifest is light.

3

Or, *discovered.*

X

Ps. 1. 1 Blessed *is* the man that walketh not in the counsel of the ungodly, nor standeth in the way of sinners, nor sitteth in the seat of the scornful.

§ 23. CHRIST AND JOHN BAPTIZING.

A

John 4. 2. *See text of § 24.*

B

Gen. 14. 18 And Melchizedek king of Salem brought forth bread and wine: and he *was* the priest of the most high God.

Gen. 33. 18 And Jacob came to Shalem, a city of Shechem, which *is* in the land of Canaan, when he came from Padanaram; and pitched his tent before the city.

I Sa. 9. 4 And he passed through mount Ephraim, and passed through the land of Shalisha, but they found *them* not: then they passed through the land of Shalim, and *there they were* not: and he passed through the land of the Benjamites, but they found *them* not.

C

Matt. 3. 5 Then went out to him Jerusalem, and all Judæa, and all the region round about Jordan,

6 And were baptized of him in Jordan, confessing their sins.

D

Matt.14. 3 For Herod had laid hold on John, and bound him, and put *him* in prison for Herodias' sake, his brother Philip's wife.

Luke 3. 19 But Herod the tetrarch, being reproved by him for Herodias his brother Philip's wife, and for all the evils which Herod had done,

D—CONCLUDED.

Luke 3. 20 Added yet this above all, that he shut up John in prison.

E

John 1. 7 The same came for a witness, to bear witness of the Light, that all *men* through him might believe.

John 1. 15 John bare witness of him, and cried, saying, This was he of whom I spake, He that cometh after me is preferred before me; for he was before me.

John 1. 27 He it is, who coming after me is preferred before me, whose shoe's latchet I am not worthy to unloose.

John 1. 34 And I saw, and bare record that this is the Son of God.

F

I Cor.4. 7 For who maketh thee to differ *from another?* and what hast thou that thou didst not receive? now if thou didst receive *it*, why dost thou glory, as if thou hadst not received *it?*

Heb. 5. 4 And no man taketh this honour unto himself, but he that is called of God, as *was* Aaron.

Jas. 1. 17 Every good gift and every perfect gift is from above, and cometh down from the Father of lights, with whom is no variableness, neither shadow of turning.

1

Or, *take unto himself.*

Time, April, A. D. 27; Place, Jerusalem.

X—Concluded.

Ps. 1. 2 But his delight *is* in the law of the Lord; and in his law doth he meditate day and night.

3 And he shall be like a tree planted by the rivers of water, that bringeth forth his fruit in his season; his leaf also shall not wither; and whatsoever he doeth shall prosper.

Isa. 8. 20 To the law and to the testimony: if they speak not according to this word, *it is* because *there is* no light in them.

Y

I Cor.15. 10 But by the grace of God I am what I am: and his grace which *was bestowed* upon me was not in vain; but I labored more abundantly than they all: yet not I, but the grace of God which was with me.

Chap. 3.

19 And this is the condemnation, [t]that light is come into the world, and men loved darkness rather than light, because their deeds were evil.

20 For [u]every one that doeth evil hateth the light, neither cometh to the light, lest his deeds should be [s]reproved.

21 But [x]he that doeth truth cometh to the light, [y]that his deeds may be made manifest, that they are wrought in God.

Time, Summer, A. D. 27; Place, Judæa, Ænon in Samaria.

G

John 1. 20 And he confessed, and denied not; but confessed, I am not the Christ.

John 1. 27. *See under E.*

H

Mal. 3. 1 Behold, I will send my messenger, and he shall prepare the way before me: and the Lord, whom ye seek, shall suddenly come to his temple, even the messenger of the covenant, whom ye delight in: behold, he shall come, saith the Lord of hosts.

Mark 1. 2 As it is written in the prophets, Behold, I send my messenger before thy face, which shall prepare thy way before thee.

Luke 1. 17 And he shall go before him in the spirit and power of Elias, to turn the hearts of the fathers to the children, and the disobedient to the wisdom of the just; to make ready a people prepared for the Lord.

I

Matt.22. 2 The kingdom of heaven is like unto a certain king, which made a marriage for his son,

IICor.11. 2 For I am jealous over you with godly jealousy: for I have espoused you to one husband, that I may present *you as* a chaste virgin to Christ.

Eph. 5. 25 Husbands, love your wives, even as Christ also loved the church, and gave himself for it;

For I concluded see next page (76).

3 : 22–36.

22 After these things came Jesus and his disciples into the land of Judæa; and there he tarried with them, [a]and baptized.

23 And John also was baptizing in Ænon near to [b]Salim, because there was much water there: [c]and they came, and were baptized.

24 For [d]John was not yet cast into prison.

25 Then there arose a question between *some* of John's disciples and the Jews about purifying.

26 And they came unto John, and said unto him, Rabbi, he that was with thee beyond Jordan, [e]to whom thou barest witness, behold, the same baptizeth, and all *men* come to him.

27 John answered and said, [f]A man can [1]receive nothing, except it be given him from heaven.

§ 23. CHRIST AND JOHN BAPTIZING (CONCLUDED).

For G, H, and I see preceding page (75).

I—CONCLUDED.

Eph. 5. 27 That he might present it to himself a glorious church, not having spot, or wrinkle, or any such thing; but that it should be holy and without blemish.

Rev. 21. 9 And there came unto me one of the seven angels which had the seven vials full of the seven last plagues, and talked with me, saying, Come hither, I will show thee the bride, the Lamb's wife.

K

Song 5. 1 I am come into my garden, my sister, *my* spouse: I have gathered my myrrh with my spice; I have eaten my honeycomb with my honey; I have drunk my wine with my milk: eat, O friends; drink, yea, drink abundantly, O beloved.

L

Isa. 9. 7 Of the increase of *his* government and peace *there shall be* no end, upon the throne of David, and upon his kingdom, to order it, and to establish it with judgment and with justice from henceforth even for ever. The zeal of the LORD of hosts will perform this.

M

Phil. 3. 8 Yea doubtless, and I count all things *but* loss for the excellency of the knowledge of Christ Jesus my Lord: for whom I have suffered the loss of all things, and do count them *but* dung, that I may win Christ,

N

John 3. 13 And no man hath ascended up to heaven, but he that came down from heaven, *even* the Son of man which is in heaven.

John 8. 23 And he said unto them, Ye are from beneath; I am from above: ye are of this world; I am not of this world.

O

Matt.28. 18 And Jesus came and spake unto them, saying, All power is given unto me in heaven and in earth.

John 1. 15, 27. *See under E, page 74.*

Rom. 9. 5 Whose *are* the fathers, and of whom as concerning the flesh Christ *came,* who is over all, God blessed for ever. Amen.

P

I Cor.15. 47 The first man *is* of the earth, earthy: the second man *is* the Lord from heaven.

Q

John 6. 33 For the bread of God is he which cometh down from heaven, and giveth life unto the world.

I Cor. 15. 47. *See under P.*

Eph. 1. 20 Which he wrought in Christ, when he raised him from the dead, and set *him* at his own right hand in the heavenly *places,*

Phil. 2. 9 Wherefore God also hath highly exalted him, and given him a name which is above every name:

R

John 3. 11 Verily, verily, I say unto thee, We speak that we do know, and testify that we have seen; and ye receive not our witness.

John 8. 26 I have many things to say and to judge of you: but he that sent me is true; and I speak to the world those things which I have heard of him.

John 15. 15 Henceforth I call you not servants; for the servant knoweth not what his lord doeth: but I have called you friends; for all things that I have heard of my Father I have made known unto you.

S

Rom. 3. 4 God forbid: yea, let God be true, but every man a liar; as it is written, That thou mightest be justified in thy sayings, and mightest overcome when thou art judged.

II Cor.1. 22 Who hath also sealed us, and given the earnest of the Spirit in our hearts.

I Jno. 5. 10 He that believeth on the Son of God hath the witness in himself: he that believeth not God hath made him a liar; because he believeth not the record that God gave of his Son.

T

John 7. 16 Jesus answered them, and said, My doctrine is not mine, but his that sent me.

U

John 1. 16 And of his fulness have all we received, and grace for grace.

Col. 1. 19 For it pleased *the Father* that in him should all fulness dwell;

X

Dan. 7. 14 And there was given him dominion, and glory, and a kingdom, that all people, nations, and languages, should serve him: his dominion *is* an everlasting dominion, which shall not pass away, and his kingdom *that* which shall not be destroyed.

Time, Summer, A. D. 27; Place, Judæa, Ænon in Samaria.

X—Concluded.

Matt.11. 27 All things are delivered unto me of my Father: and no man knoweth the Son, but the Father; neither knoweth any man the Father, save the Son, and *he* to whomsoever the Son will reveal *him*.

Matt. 28. 18. *See under O.*

Luke10. 22 All things are delivered to me of my Father: and no man knoweth who the Son is, but the Father; and who the Father is, but the Son, and *he* to whom the Son will reveal *him*.

John 5. 20 For the Father loveth the Son, and showeth him all things that himself doeth: and he will show him greater works than these, that ye may marvel.

John 5. 22 For the Father judgeth no man, but hath committed all judgment unto the Son:

John13. 3 Jesus knowing that the Father had given all things into his hands, and that he was come from God, and went to God:

John17. 2 As thou hast given him power over all flesh, that he should give eternal life to as many as thou hast given him.

Heb. 2. 8 Thou hast put all things in subjection under his feet. For in that he put all in subjection under him, he left nothing *that is* not put under him. But now we see not yet all things put under him.

Y

Hab. 2. 4 Behold, his soul *which* is lifted up is not upright in him: but the just shall live by his faith.

John 1. 12 But as many as received him to them gave he power to become the sons of God, *even* to them that believe on his name:

John 3. 15, 16. *See text of* § 22.

John 6. 47 Verily, verily, I say unto you, He that believeth on me hath everlasting life.

Rom. 1. 17 For therein is the righteousness of God revealed from faith to faith: as it is written, The just shall live by faith.

I Jno. 5. 10. *See under S.*

Z

Gal. 3. 10 For as many as are of the works of the law are under the curse: for it is written, Cursed *is* every one that continueth not in all things which are written in the book of the law to do them.

Chap. 3.

28 Ye yourselves bear me witness, that I said, [g] I am not the Christ, [h]but that I am sent before him.

29 [i] He that hath the bride is the bridegroom: [k]but the friend of the bridegroom, which standeth and heareth him, rejoiceth greatly because of the bridegroom's voice: this my joy therefore is fulfilled.

30 He [l]must increase, but [m] I *must* decrease.

31 [n] He that cometh from above [o]is above all: [p]he that is of the earth is earthly, and speaketh of the earth: [q] he that cometh from heaven is above all.

32 And [r] what he hath seen and heard, that he testifieth; and no man receiveth his testimony.

33 He that hath received his testimony [s]hath set to his seal that God is true.

34 [t] For he whom God hath sent speaketh the words of God: for God giveth not the Spirit [u]by measure *unto him*.

35 [x] The Father loveth the Son, and hath given all things into his hand.

36 [y] He that believeth on the Son hath everlasting life: and he that believeth not the Son shall not see life; but the [z]wrath of God abideth on him.

Z—Concluded.

Heb. 10. 29 Of how much sorer punishment, suppose ye, shall he be thought worthy, who hath trodden under foot the Son of God, and hath counted the blood of the covenant, wherewith he was sanctified, an unholy thing, and hath done despite unto the Spirit of grace?

§ 24. IMPRISONMENT OF JOHN. JESUS SETS OUT FOR GALILEE.

MATTHEW 4: 12; 14: 3–5.

12 [a] Now when Jesus had heard that John was [1]cast into prison, he departed into Galilee; (p. 92.)

CHAP. 14.

3 [b] For Herod had laid hold on John, and bound him, and put *him* in prison for Herodias' sake, his brother Philip's wife.

4 For John said unto him, [c] It is not lawful for thee to have her.

5 And when he would have put him to death, he feared the multitude, [d]because they counted him as a prophet.

MARK 1: 14; 6: 17–20.

14 [e] Now after that John was put in prison, Jesus came into Galilee, [f] preaching the gospel of the kingdom of God.

CHAP. 6. (p. 86.)

17 For Herod himself had sent forth and laid hold upon John, and bound him in prison for Herodias' sake, his brother Philip's wife; for he had married her.

18 For John had said unto Herod, [g] It is not lawful for thee to have thy brother's wife.

19 Therefore Herodias had [2]a quarrel against him, and would have killed him; but she could not:

20 For Herod [h]feared John, knowing that he was a just man and a holy, and [3]observed him; and when he heard him, he did many things, and heard him gladly. (p. 242.)

A (p. 242.)

Mark 1. 14. *See text of topic.*
Luke 3. 20. *See text of topic.*
Luke 4. 14. *See text of topic.*

Luke 4. 30 But he, passing through the midst of them, went his way,

31 And came down to Capernaum, a city of Galilee, and taught them on the sabbath days.

John 4. 42 And said unto the woman, Now we believe, not because of thy saying: for we have heard *him* ourselves, and know that this is indeed the Christ, the Saviour of the world.

43 Now after two days he departed thence, and went into Galilee.

1
Or, *delivered up*.

B

Prov. 10. 17 He *is in* the way of life that keepeth instruction: but he that refuseth reproof erreth.

Prov. 15. 10 Correction *is* grievous unto him that forsaketh the way: *and* he that hateth reproof shall die.

Mark 6. 17. *See text of topic.*
Luke 3. 19, 20. *See text of topic.*

C

Lev. 18. 16 Thou shalt not uncover the nakedness of thy brother's wife: it *is* thy brother's nakedness.

Lev. 20. 21 And if a man shall take his brother's wife, it *is* an unclean thing: he hath uncovered his brother's nakedness; they shall be childless.

Dan. 5. 22 And thou his son, O Belshazzar, hast not humbled thine heart, though thou knewest all this;

C—CONCLUDED.

Dan. 5. 23 But hast lifted up thyself against the Lord of heaven; and they have brought the vessels of his house before thee, and thou and thy lords, thy wives and thy concubines, have drunk wine in them; and thou hast praised the gods of silver, and gold, of brass, iron, wood, and stone, which see not, nor hear, nor know: and the God in whose hand thy breath *is*, and whose *are* all thy ways, hast thou not glorified:

24 Then was the part of the hand sent from him; and this writing was written.

Eph. 5. 11 And have no fellowship with the unfruitful works of darkness, but rather reprove *them*.

II Tim. 4. 2 Preach the word; be instant in season, out of season; reprove, rebuke, exhort with all long-suffering and doctrine.

D

Matt. 21. 26 But if we shall say, Of men; we fear the people; for all hold John as a prophet.

TIME, DECEMBER, A. D. 27; PLACE, CASTLE OF MACHÆRUS IN PERÆA, JUDÆA.

3: 19, 20; 4: 14.

19 [i]But Herod the tetrarch, being reproved by him for Herodias his brother Philip's wife, and for all the evils which Herod had done,
20 Added yet this above all, that he shut up John in prison. (p. 53.)

CHAP. 4.

14 [k]And Jesus returned [l]in the power of the Spirit into [m]Galilee: and there went out a fame of him through all the region round about. (p. 87.)

4: 1–3.

1 When therefore the Lord knew how the Pharisees had heard that Jesus made and [n]baptized more disciples than John,
2 (Though Jesus himself baptized not, but his disciples,)
3 He left Judæa, and departed again into Galilee.

D—CONCLUDED.

Luke 20. 6 But and if we say, Of men; all the people will stone us: for they be persuaded that John was a prophet.

E

Matt. 4. 12. *See text of topic.*

F

Matt. 4. 22 And they immediately left the ship and their father, and followed him.
23 And Jesus went about all Galilee, teaching in their synagogues, and preaching the gospel of the kingdom, and healing all manner of sickness and all manner of disease among the people.

G

Lev. 18. 16 and Lev. 20. 21. *See under C.*
Deut. 25. 7 And if the man like not to take his brother's wife, then let his brother's wife go up to the gate unto the elders, and say, My husband's brother refuseth to raise up unto his brother a name in Israel, he will not perform the duty of my husband's brother.
8 Then the elders of his city shall call him, and speak unto him: and *if* he stand *to it*, and say, I like not to take her;
9 Then shall his brother's wife come unto him in the presence of the elders, and loose his shoe from off his foot, and spit in his face, and shall answer and say, So shall it be done unto that man that will not build up his brother's house.
10 And his name shall be called in Israel, The house of him that hath his shoe loosed.
Dan. 5. 22, Eph. 5. 11, and II Tim. 4. 2. *See under C.*
Heb. 13. 4 Marriage *is* honourable in all, and

G—CONCLUDED.

the bed undefiled: but whoremongers and adulterers God will judge.

2

Or, *an inward grudge.*

H

Matt. 14. 5. *See text of topic.*
Matt. 21. 26. *See under D.*

3

Or, *kept him*, or, *saved him.*

I

Prov. 28. 15 *As* a roaring lion, and a ranging bear; *so is* a wicked ruler over the poor people.
16 The prince that wanteth understanding *is* also a great oppressor: *but* he that hateth covetousness shall prolong *his* days.
Matt. 14. 3 and Mark 6. 17. *See text of topic.*

K

Matt. 4. 12. *See text of topic.*
John 4. 43. *See under A.*

L

Luke 4. 1 And Jesus being full of the Holy Ghost returned from Jordan, and was led by the Spirit into the wilderness,

M

Acts 10. 37 That word, *I say*, ye know, which was published throughout all Judæa, and began from Galilee, after the baptism which John preached;
38 How God anointed Jesus of Nazareth with the Holy Ghost and with power: who went about doing good, and healing all that were oppressed of the devil; for God was with him.

N

John 3. 22 After these things came Jesus and his disciples into the land of Judæa; and there he tarried with them, and baptized.
John 3. 26 And they came unto John, and said unto him, Rabbi, he that was with thee beyond Jordan, to whom thou barest witness, behold, the same baptizeth, and all *men* come to him.

§ 25. DISCOURSE WITH THE SAMARITAN WOMAN.

A

Gen. 33. 19 And he bought a parcel of a field, where he had spread his tent, at the hand of the children of Hamor, Shechem's father, for a hundred pieces of money.

Gen. 48. 22 Moreover I have given to thee one portion above thy brethren, which I took out of the hand of the Amorite with my sword and with my bow.

Josh. 24. 32 And the bones of Joseph, which the children of Israel brought up out of Egypt, buried they in Shechem, in a parcel of ground which Jacob bought of the sons of Hamor the father of Shechem for a hundred pieces of silver; and it became the inheritance of the children of Joseph.

B

II Ki. 17. 24 And the king of Assyria brought *men* from Babylon, and from Cuthah, and from Ava, and from Hamath, and from Sepharvaim, and placed *them* in the cities of Samaria instead of the children of Israel: and they possessed Samaria, and dwelt in the cities thereof.

Ezr. 4. 3 But Zerubbabel, and Jeshua, and the rest of the chief of the fathers of Israel, said unto them, Ye have nothing to do with us to build a house unto our God; but we ourselves together will build unto the LORD God of Israel, as king Cyrus the king of Persia hath commanded us.

Luke 9. 52 And sent messengers before his face: and they went, and entered into a village of the Samaritans, to make ready for him.

53 And they did not receive him, because his face was as though he would go to Jerusalem.

Acts 10. 28 And he said unto them, Ye know how that it is an unlawful thing for a man that is a Jew to keep company, or come unto one of another nation; but God hath showed me that I should not call any man common or unclean.

C

Isa. 9. 6 For unto us a child is born, unto us a son is given: and the government shall be upon his shoulder: and his name shall be called Wonderful, Counsellor, The mighty God, The everlasting Father, The Prince of Peace.

Isa. 42. 6 I the LORD have called thee in righteousness, and will hold thine hand, and will keep thee, and give thee for a covenant of the people, for a light of the Gentiles;

C—CONCLUDED.

Rom. 8. 32 He that spared not his own Son, but delivered him up for us all, how shall he not with him also freely give us all things?

D

Ex. 17. 6 Behold, I will stand before thee there upon the rock in Horeb; and thou shalt smite the rock, and there shall come water out of it, that the people may drink. And Moses did so in the sight of the elders of Israel.

Ps. 36. 8 They shall be abundantly satisfied with the fatness of thy house; and thou shalt make them drink of the river of thy pleasures.

9 For with thee *is* the fountain of life: in thy light shall we see light.

Ps. 46. 4 *There is* a river, the streams whereof shall make glad the city of God, the holy *place* of the tabernacles of the Most High.

Isa. 12. 3 Therefore with joy shall ye draw water out of the wells of salvation.

Isa. 35. 6 Then shall the lame *man* leap as a hart, and the tongue of the dumb sing: for in the wilderness shall waters break out, and streams in the desert.

Isa. 41. 17 *When* the poor and needy seek water, and *there is* none, *and* their tongue faileth for thirst, I the LORD will hear them, *I* the God of Israel will not forsake them.

18 I will open rivers in high places, and fountains in the midst of the valleys: I will make the wilderness a pool of water, and the dry land springs of water.

Isa. 44. 3 For I will pour water upon him that is thirsty, and floods upon the dry ground: I will pour my Spirit upon thy seed, and my blessing upon thine offspring:

Jer. 2. 13 For my people have committed two evils; they have forsaken me the fountain of living waters, *and* hewed them out cisterns, broken cisterns, that can hold no water.

Zech. 13. 1 In that day there shall be a fountain opened to the house of David and to the inhabitants of Jerusalem for sin and for uncleanness.

Zech. 14. 8 And it shall be in that day, *that* living waters shall go out from Jerusalem; half of them toward the former sea, and half of them toward the hinder sea: in summer and in winter shall it be.

TIME, DECEMBER, A. D. 27; PLACE, SHECHEM OR NEAPOLIS.

D—CONCLUDED.

I Cor.10. 4 And did all drink the same spiritual drink; for they drank of that spiritual Rock that followed them: and that Rock was Christ.

Rev. 7. 17 For the Lamb which is in the midst of the throne shall feed them, and shall lead them unto living fountains of waters: and God shall wipe away all tears from their eyes.

Rev. 21. 6 And he said unto me, It is done. I am Alpha and Omega, the beginning and the end. I will give unto him that is athirst of the fountain of the water of life freely.

Rev. 22. 1 And he showed me a pure river of water of life, clear as crystal, proceeding out of the throne of God and of the Lamb.

2 In the midst of the street of it, and on either side of the river, *was there* the tree of life, which bare twelve *manner of* fruits, *and* yielded her fruit every month: and the leaves of the tree *were* for the healing of the nations.

3 And there shall be no more curse: but the throne of God and of the Lamb shall be in it; and his servants shall serve him:

4 And they shall see his face; and his name *shall be* in their foreheads.

5 And there shall be no night there; and they need no candle, neither light of the sun; for the Lord God giveth them light: and they shall reign for ever and ever.

Rev. 22. 17 And the Spirit and the bride say, Come. And let him that heareth say, Come. And let him that is athirst come. And whosoever will, let him take the water of life freely.

E

Isa. 49. 10 They shall not hunger nor thirst; neither shall the heat nor sun smite them: for he that hath mercy on them shall lead them, even by the springs of water shall he guide them.

11 And I will make all my mountains a way, and my highways shall be exalted.

John 6. 35 And Jesus said unto them, I am the bread of life: he that cometh to me shall never hunger; and he that believeth on me shall never thirst.

John 6. 58 This is that bread which came down from heaven: not as your fathers did eat manna, and are dead: he that eateth of this bread shall live for ever.

4: 4–42.

4 And he must needs go through Samaria.

5 Then cometh he to a city of Samaria, which is called Sychar, near to the parcel of ground [a]that Jacob gave to his son Joseph.

6 Now Jacob's well was there. Jesus therefore, being wearied with *his* journey, sat thus on the well: *and* it was about the sixth hour.

7 There cometh a woman of Samaria to draw water: Jesus saith unto her, Give me to drink.

8 (For his disciples were gone away unto the city to buy meat.)

9 Then saith the woman of Samaria unto him, How is it that thou, being a Jew, askest drink of me, which am a woman of Samaria? for [b]the Jews have no dealings with the Samaritans.

10 Jesus answered and said unto her, If thou knewest the [c]gift of God, and who it is that saith to thee, Give me to drink; thou wouldest have asked of him, and he would have given thee [d] living water.

11 The woman saith unto him, Sir, thou hast nothing to draw with, and the well is deep: from whence then hast thou that living water?

12 Art thou greater than our father Jacob, which gave us the well, and drank thereof himself, and his children, and his cattle?

13 Jesus answered and said unto her, Whosoever drinketh of this water shall thirst again:

14 But [e]whosoever drinketh of the

§ 25. DISCOURSE WITH THE SAMARITAN WOMAN (CONTINUED).

F

John 7. 38 He that believeth on me, as the Scripture hath said, out of his belly shall flow rivers of living water.

G

John 6. 34 Then said they unto him, Lord, evermore give us this bread.

John 17. 2 As thou hast given him power over all flesh, that he should give eternal life to as many as thou hast given him.

3 And this is life eternal, that they might know thee the only true God, and Jesus Christ, whom thou hast sent.

Rom. 6. 23 For the wages of sin *is* death; but the gift of God *is* eternal life through Jesus Christ our Lord.

I Jno. 5. 20 And we know that the Son of God is come, and hath given us an understanding, that we may know him that is true; and we are in him that is true, *even* in his Son Jesus Christ. This is the true God, and eternal life.

H

Luke 7. 16 And there came a fear on all: and they glorified God, saying, That a great prophet is risen up among us; and, That God hath visited his people.

Luke 24. 19 And he said unto them, What things? And they said unto him, Concerning Jesus of Nazareth, which was a prophet mighty in deed and word before God and all the people:

John 6. 14 Then those men, when they had seen the miracle that Jesus did, said, This is of a truth that Prophet that should come into the world.

John 7. 40 Many of the people therefore, when they heard this saying, said, Of a truth this is the Prophet.

I

Gen. 12. 6 And Abram passed through the land unto the place of Sichem, unto the plain of Moreh. And the Canaanite *was* then in the land.

Judg. 9. 7 And when they told *it* to Jotham, he went and stood in the top of mount Gerizim, and lifted up his voice, and cried, and said unto them, Hearken unto me, ye men of Shechem, that God may hearken unto you.

K

Deut. 12. 5 But unto the place which the LORD your God shall choose out of all your tribes to put his name there, *even* unto his habitation shall ye seek, and thither thou shalt come:

K—CONCLUDED.

Deut. 12. 11 Then there shall be a place which the LORD your God shall choose to cause his name to dwell there; thither shall ye bring all that I command you; your burnt offerings, and your sacrifices, your tithes, and the heave offering of your hand, and all your choice vows which ye vow unto the LORD:

I Ki. 9. 3 And the LORD said unto him, I have heard thy prayer and thy supplication, that thou hast made before me: I have hallowed this house, which thou hast built, to put my name there for ever; and mine eyes and mine heart shall be there perpetually.

II Chr. 7. 12 And the LORD appeared to Solomon by night, and said unto him, I have heard thy prayer, and have chosen this place to myself for a house of sacrifice.

L

Mal. 1. 11 For, from the rising of the sun even unto the going down of the same, my name *shall be* great among the Gentiles; and in every place incense *shall be* offered unto my name, and a pure offering: for my name *shall be* great among the heathen, saith the LORD of hosts.

I Tim. 2. 8 I will therefore that men pray every where, lifting up holy hands, without wrath and doubting.

M

II Ki. 17. 29 Howbeit every nation made gods of their own, and put *them* in the houses of the high places which the Samaritans had made, every nation in their cities wherein they dwelt.

N

Isa. 2. 3 And many people shall go and say, Come ye, and let us go up to the mountain of the LORD, to the house of the God of Jacob; and he will teach us of his ways, and we will walk in his paths: for out of Zion shall go forth the law, and the word of the LORD from Jerusalem.

Luke 24. 47 And that repentance and remission of sins should be preached in his name among all nations, beginning at Jerusalem.

Rom. 9. 4 Who are Israelites; to whom *pertaineth* the adoption, and the glory, and the covenants, and the giving of the law, and the service *of God*, and the promises;

TIME, DECEMBER, A. D. 27; PLACE, SHECHEM OR NEAPOLIS.

N—CONCLUDED.

Rom. 9. 5 Whose *are* the fathers, and of whom as concerning the flesh Christ *came*, who is over all, God blessed for ever. Amen.

O

Phil. 3. 3 For we are the circumcision, which worship God in the spirit, and rejoice in Christ Jesus, and have no confidence in the flesh.

P

Josh. 24. 14 Now therefore fear the LORD, and serve him in sincerity and in truth; and put away the gods which your fathers served on the other side of the flood, and in Egypt; and serve ye the LORD.

I Sa. 12. 24 Only fear the LORD, and serve him in truth with all your heart: for consider how great *things* he hath done for you.

Ps. 17. 1 Hear the right, O LORD, attend unto my cry; give ear unto my prayer, *that goeth* not out of feigned lips.

Ps. 32. 2 Blessed *is* the man unto whom the LORD imputeth not iniquity, and in whose spirit *there is* no guile.

Ps. 51. 6 Behold, thou desirest truth in the inward parts: and in the hidden *part* thou shalt make me to know wisdom.

Isa. 10. 20 And it shall come to pass in that day, *that* the remnant of Israel, and such as are escaped of the house of Jacob, shall no more again stay upon him that smote them; but shall stay upon the LORD, the Holy One of Israel, in truth.

John 1. 17 For the law was given by Moses, *but* grace and truth came by Jesus Christ.

Q

II Cor. 3. 17 Now the Lord is that Spirit: and where the Spirit of the Lord *is*, there *is* liberty.

R

Deut. 18. 15 The LORD thy God will raise up unto thee a Prophet from the midst of thee, of thy brethren, like unto me; unto him ye shall hearken;

Dan. 9. 24 Seventy weeks are determined upon thy people and upon thy holy city, to finish the transgression, and to make an end of sins, and to make reconciliation for iniquity, and to bring in everlasting righteousness and to seal up the vision and prophecy, and to anoint the Most Holy.

CHAP. 4.

water that I shall give him shall never thirst; but the water that I shall give him [f]shall be in him a well of water springing up into everlasting life.

15 [g]The woman saith unto him, Sir, give me this water, that I thirst not, neither come hither to draw.

16 Jesus saith unto her, Go, call thy husband, and come hither.

17 The woman answered and said, I have no husband. Jesus said unto her, Thou hast well said, I have no husband:

18 For thou hast had five husbands; and he whom thou now hast is not thy husband: in that saidst thou truly.

19 The woman saith unto him, Sir, [h]I perceive that thou art a prophet.

20 Our fathers worshipped in [i]this mountain; and ye say, that in [k]Jerusalem is the place where men ought to worship.

21 Jesus saith unto her, Woman, believe me, the hour cometh, [l]when ye shall neither in this mountain, nor yet at Jerusalem, worship the Father.

22 Ye worship [m]ye know not what: we know what we worship; for [n]salvation is of the Jews.

23 But the hour cometh, and now is, when the true worshippers shall worship the Father in [o]spirit [p]and in truth: for the Father seeketh such to worship him.

24 [q]God *is* a Spirit: and they that worship him must worship *him* in spirit and in truth.

25 The woman saith unto him, I know that [r]Messias cometh, which is called

§ 25. DISCOURSE WITH THE SAMARITAN WOMAN (Continued).

S

John 4. 29, 30. *See text of topic.*

T

Matt.26. 63 But Jesus held his peace. And the high priest answered and said unto him, I adjure thee by the living God, that thou tell us whether thou be the Christ, the Son of God.

64 Jesus saith unto him, Thou hast said: nevertheless I say unto you, Hereafter shall ye see the Son of man sitting on the right hand of power, and coming in the clouds of heaven.

Mark14. 61 But he held his peace, and answered nothing. Again the high priest asked him, and said unto him, Art thou the Christ, the Son of the Blessed?

62 And Jesus said, I am: and ye shall see the Son of man sitting on the right hand of power, and coming in the clouds of heaven.

John 9. 37 And Jesus said unto him, Thou hast both seen him, and it is he that talketh with thee.

U

John 4. 25. *See text of topic.*

X

Jer. 15. 16 Thy words were found, and I did eat them; and thy word was unto me the joy and rejoicing of mine heart: for I am called by thy name, O LORD God of hosts.

Y

Job 23. 12 Neither have I gone back from the commandment of his lips; I have esteemed the words of his mouth more than my necessary *food*.

Ps. 40. 8 I delight to do thy will, O my God: yea, thy law *is* within my heart.

John 6. 38 For I came down from heaven, not to do mine own will, but the will of him that sent me.

John 17. 4 I have glorified thee on the earth: I have finished the work which thou gavest me to do.

John 19. 30 When Jesus therefore had received the vinegar, he said, It is finished: and he bowed his head, and gave up the ghost.

Acts 20. 35 I have showed you all things, how that so labouring ye ought to support the weak, and to remember the words of the Lord Jesus, how he said, It is more blessed to give than to receive.

Z

Matt. 9. 37 Then saith he unto his disciples,

Z—Concluded.

The harvest truly *is* plenteous, but the labourers *are* few;

Luke 10. 2 Therefore said he unto them, The harvest truly *is* great, but the labourers *are* few: pray ye therefore the Lord of the harvest, that he would send forth labourers into his harvest.

A

Prov. 11. 30 The fruit of the righteous *is* a tree of life; and he that winneth souls *is* wise.

31 Behold, the righteous shall be recompensed in the earth: much more the wicked and the sinner.

Dan. 12. 3 And they that be wise shall shine as the brightness of the firmament; and they that turn many to righteousness, as the stars for ever and ever.

Rom. 1. 13 Now I would not have you ignorant, brethren, that oftentimes I purposed to come unto you, (but was let hitherto,) that I might have some fruit among you also, even as among other Gentiles.

Rom. 6. 22 But now being made free from sin, and become servants to God, ye have your fruit unto holiness, and the end everlasting life.

23 For the wages of sin *is* death; but the gift of God *is* eternal life through Jesus Christ our Lord.

I Cor. 9. 19 For though I be free from all *men*, yet have I made myself servant unto all, that I might gain the more.

20 And unto the Jews I became as a Jew, that I might gain the Jews; to them that are under the law, as under the law, that I might gain them that are under the law;

21 To them that are without law, as without law, (being not without law to God, but under the law to Christ,) that I might gain them that are without law.

22 To the weak became I as weak, that I might gain the weak: I am made all things to all *men*, that I might by all means save some.

23 And this I do for the gospel's sake, that I might be partaker thereof with *you*.

Phil. 2. 15 That ye may be blameless and harmless, the sons of God, without rebuke, in the midst of a crooked and perverse nation, among whom ye shine as lights in the world;

16 Holding forth the word of life; that I may rejoice in the day of

TIME, DECEMBER, A. D. 27; PLACE, SHECHEM OR NEAPOLIS.

A—CONCLUDED.

Christ, that I have not run in vain, neither laboured in vain.

I Thes.2. 19 For what *is* our hope, or joy, or crown of rejoicing? *Are* not even ye in the presence of our Lord Jesus Christ at his coming?

20 For ye are our glory and joy.

I Tim. 4. 16 Take heed unto thyself, and unto the doctrine; continue in them: for in doing this thou shalt both save thyself, and them that hear thee.

II Tim.4. 7 I have fought a good fight, I have finished *my* course, I have kept the faith:

8 Henceforth there is laid up for me a crown of righteousness, which the Lord, the righteous judge, shall give me at that day: and not to me only, but unto all them also that love his appearing.

Jas. 5. 19 Brethren, if any of you do err from the truth, and one convert him;

20 Let him know, that he which converteth the sinner from the error of his way shall save a soul from death, and shall hide a multitude of sins.

B

I Cor. 3. 5 Who then is Paul, and who *is* Apollos, but ministers by whom ye believe, even as the Lord gave to every man?

6 I have planted, Apollos watered; but God gave the increase.

7 So then neither is he that planteth any thing, neither he that watereth; but God that giveth the increase.

8 Now he that planteth and he that watereth are one: and every man shall receive his own reward according to his own labour.

9 For we are labourers together with God: ye are God's husbandry, *ye are* God's building.

C

Judg. 6. 3 And *so* it was, when Israel had sown, that the Midianites came up, and the Amalekites, and the children of the east, even they came up against them:

Mic. 6. 15 Thou shalt sow, but thou shalt not reap; thou shalt tread the olives, but thou shalt not anoint thee with oil; and sweet wine, but shalt not drink wine.

Luke 19. 21 For I feared thee, because thou art an austere man: thou takest up that thou layest not down, and reapest that thou didst not sow.

CHAP. 4.

Christ: when he is come, [s]he will tell us all things.

26 Jesus saith unto her, [t]I that speak unto thee am *he*.

27 And upon this came his disciples, and marvelled that he talked with the woman: yet no man said, What seekest thou? or, Why talkest thou with her?

28 The woman then left her waterpot, and went her way into the city, and saith to the men,

29 Come, see a man [u]which told me all things that ever I did: is not this the Christ?

30 Then they went out of the city, and came unto him.

31 In the mean while his disciples prayed him, saying, Master, eat.

32 But he said unto them, [x]I have meat to eat that ye know not of.

33 Therefore said the disciples one to another, Hath any man brought him *aught* to eat?

34 Jesus saith unto them, [y]My meat is to do the will of him that sent me, and to finish his work.

35 Say not ye, There are yet four months, and *then* cometh harvest? behold, I say unto you, Lift up your eyes, and look on the fields; [z]for they are white already to harvest.

36 [a]And he that reapeth receiveth wages, and gathereth fruit unto life eternal: [b]that both he that soweth and he that reapeth may rejoice together.

37 And herein is that saying true, [c]One soweth, and another reapeth.

§ 25. DISCOURSE WITH THE SAMARITAN WOMAN (Concluded).

D

Acts 10. 43 To him give all the prophets witness, that through his name whosoever believeth in him shall receive remission of sins.

I Pet. 1. 12 Unto whom it was revealed, that not unto themselves, but unto us they did minister the things, which are now reported unto you by them that have preached the gospel unto you with the Holy Ghost sent down from heaven; which things the angels desire to look into.

E

Gen. 49. 10 The scepter shall not depart from Judah, nor a lawgiver from between his feet, until Shiloh come; and unto him *shall* the gathering of the people *be*.

F

John 4. 29. *See text of topic.*

G

Gen. 32. 26 And he said, Let me go, for the day breaketh. And he said, I will not let thee go, except thou bless me.

H

Isa. 42. 1 Behold my servant, whom I uphold; mine elect, *in whom* my soul de-

H—Concluded.

lighteth; I have put my Spirit upon him: he shall bring forth judgment to the Gentiles.

I

John 17. 8 For I have given unto them the words which thou gavest me; and they have received *them*, and have known surely that I came out from thee, and they have believed that thou didst send me.

I Jno. 4. 14 And we have seen and do testify that the Father sent the Son *to be* the Saviour of the world.

Acts 17. 11 These were more noble than those in Thessalonica; in that they received the word with all readiness of mind, and searched the Scriptures daily, whether those things were so.

12 Therefore many of them believed; also of honourable women which were Greeks, and of men, not a few.

K

Isa. 45. 22 Look unto me, and be ye saved, all the ends of the earth: for I *am* God, and *there is* none else.

23 I have sworn by myself, the word is gone out of my mouth *in* righteousness, and shall not return, That unto

§ 26. JESUS ARRIVES IN GALILEE AND TEACHES PUBLICLY.

4: 17.

17 [a]From that time Jesus began to preach, and to say, [b]Repent: for the kingdom of heaven is at hand. (p. 94.)

A

Mark 1.14,15. *See text of topic.*

B

Matt. 3. 2 And saying, Repent ye: for the kingdom of heaven is at hand.

Matt. 10. 7 And as ye go, preach, saying, The kingdom of heaven is at hand.

C

Matt. 4. 12. *See text of § 24.*

D

Ps. 110. 3 Thy people *shall be* willing in the day of thy power, in the beauties of holiness from the womb of the morning: thou hast the dew of thy youth.

Dan. 9. 25 Know therefore and understand, *that* from the going forth of the commandment to restore and to build Jerusalem, unto the Messiah the Prince, *shall be* seven weeks, and threescore and two weeks: the street shall be

1: 14, 15.

14 [c]Now after that John was put in prison, Jesus came into Galilee, preaching the gospel of the kingdom of God,

15 And saying, [d]The time is fulfilled, and [e]the kingdom of God is at hand: repent ye, and believe the gospel. p. 94.

D—Concluded.

built again, and the wall, even in troublous times.

Gal. 4. 4 But when the fulness of the time was come, God sent forth his Son, made of a woman, made under the law,

Eph. 1. 10 That in the dispensation of the fulness of times he might gather together in one all things in Christ, both which are in heaven, and which are on earth; *even* in him:

E

Matt. 3. 2. *See under B.*

Matt. 4. 17. *See text of topic.*

TIME, DECEMBER, A. D. 27; PLACE, SHECHEM OR NEAPOLIS.

K—CONCLUDED.

me every knee shall bow, every tongue shall swear.

Acts 4. 12 Neither is there salvation in any other: for there is none other name under heaven given among men, whereby we must be saved.

Rom.10. 11 For the Scripture saith, Whosoever believeth on him shall not be ashamed.

12 For there is no difference between the Jew and the Greek: for the same Lord over all is rich unto all that call upon him.

13 For whosoever shall call upon the name of the Lord shall be saved.

II Cor.5. 18 And all things *are* of God, who hath reconciled us to himself by Jesus Christ, and hath given to us the ministry of reconciliation;

19 To wit, that God was in Christ, reconciling the world unto himself, not imputing their trespasses unto them; and hath committed unto us the word of reconciliation.

L

I Jno. 2. 2 And he is the propitiation for our sins: and not for ours only, but also for *the sins of* the whole world.

CHAP. 4.

38 I sent you to reap that whereon ye bestowed no labour: [d]other men laboured, and ye are entered into their labours.

39 [e]And many of the Samaritans of that city believed on him [f]for the saying of the woman which testified, He told me all that ever I did.

40 So [g]when the Samaritans were come unto him, they besought him that he would tarry with them: and he abode there two days.

41 [h]And many more believed because of his own word;

42 And said unto the woman, Now we believe, not because of thy saying: for [i]we have heard *him* ourselves, [k]and know that this is indeed the Christ, the [l]Saviour of the world.

TIME, JANUARY–APRIL, A. D. 28.

4: 14, 15.

14 [f]And Jesus returned in the power of the Spirit into Galilee: and there went out a fame of him through all the region round about.

15 And he taught in their synagogues, being [g]glorified of all. (p. 91.)

F

Matt. 4. 12. *See text of* § 24.
John 4. 43. *See text of topic.*

G

Isa. 52. 13 Behold, my servant shall deal prudently, he shall be exalted and extolled, and be very high.

H

Matt.13. 57 And they were offended in him. But Jesus said unto them, A prophet is not without honour, save in his own country, and in his own house.

I

John 2. 23. *See text of* § 21.
John 3. 2. *See text of* § 22.

4: 43–45.

43 Now after two days he departed thence, and went into Galilee.

44 For [h]Jesus himself testified, that a prophet hath no honour in his own country.

45 Then when he was come into Galilee, the Galileans received him, [i]having seen all the things that he did at Jerusalem at the feast: [k]for they also went unto the feast.

K

Deut.16. 16 Three times in a year shall all thy males appear before the LORD thy God in the place which he shall choose; in the feast of unleavened bread, and in the feast of weeks, and in the feast of tabernacles: and they shall not appear before the LORD empty:

§ 27. HEALING OF THE NOBLEMAN'S SON LYING ILL AT CAPERNAUM.

A

Josh. 19. 28 And Hebron, and Rehob, and Hammon, and Kanah, *even* unto great Zidon;

John 2. 1 And the third day there was a marriage in Cana of Galilee; and the mother of Jesus was there:

2 And both Jesus was called, and his disciples, to the marriage.

John 2. 11 This beginning of miracles did Jesus in Cana of Galilee, and manifested forth his glory; and his disciples believed on him.

1

Or, *courtier*, or, *ruler*.

B

Ps. 50. 15 And call upon me in the day of trouble: I will deliver thee, and thou shalt glorify me.

Ps. 78. 34 When he slew them, then they sought him: and they returned and inquired early after God.

Hos. 5. 15 I will go *and* return to my place, till they acknowledge their offense, and seek my face: in their affliction they will seek me early.

Matt. 9. 18 While he spake these things unto them, behold, there came a certain ruler, and worshipped him, saying, My daughter is even now dead: but come and lay thy hand upon her, and she shall live.

Luke 7. 2 And a certain centurion's servant, who was dear unto him, was sick, and ready to die.

C

Ps. 40. 17 But I *am* poor and needy; *yet* the Lord thinketh upon me: thou *art* my help and my deliverer; make no tarrying, O my God.

Ps. 88. 10 Wilt thou show wonders to the dead? shall the dead arise *and* praise thee? Selah.

11 Shall thy loving-kindness be declared in the grave? *or* thy faithfulness in destruction?

12 Shall thy wonders be known in the dark? and thy righteousness in the land of forgetfulness?

Mark 5. 23 And besought him greatly, saying, My little daughter lieth at the point of death: *I pray thee,* come and lay thy hands on her, that she may be healed; and she shall live.

Mark 5. 36 As soon as Jesus heard the word that was spoken he saith unto the ruler of the synagogue, Be not afraid, only believe.

C—CONCLUDED.

Mark 5. 37 And he suffered no man to follow him, save Peter, and James, and John the brother of James.

D

Num. 14. 11 And the LORD said unto Moses, How long will this people provoke me? and how long will it be ere they believe me, for all the signs which I have showed among them?

Matt. 16. 1 The Pharisees also with the Sadducees came, and tempting desired him that he would show them a sign from heaven.

Luke 10. 18 And he said unto them, I beheld Satan as lightning fall from heaven.

John 2. 18 Then answered the Jews and said unto him, What sign showest thou unto us, seeing that thou doest these things?

John 20. 29 Jesus saith unto him, Thomas, because thou hast seen me, thou hast believed: blessed *are* they that have not seen, and *yet* have believed.

Acts 2. 22 Ye men of Israel, hear these words; Jesus of Nazareth, a man approved of God among you by miracles and wonders and signs, which God did by him in the midst of you, as ye yourselves also know:

I Cor. 1. 22 For the Jews require a sign, and the Greeks seek after wisdom:

E

I Ki. 17. 13 And Elijah said unto her, Fear not; go *and* do as thou hast said: but make me thereof a little cake first, and bring *it* unto me, and after make for thee and for thy son.

14 For thus saith the LORD God of Israel, The barrel of meal shall not waste, neither shall the cruse of oil fail, until the day *that* the LORD sendeth rain upon the earth.

15 And she went and did according to the saying of Elijah: and she, and he, and her house, did eat *many* days.

16 *And* the barrel of meal wasted not, neither did the cruse of oil fail, according to the word of the LORD, which he spake by Elijah.

Matt. 8. 13 And Jesus said unto the centurion, Go thy way; and as thou hast believed, *so* be it done unto thee. And his servant was healed in the selfsame hour.

Mark 7. 29 And he said unto her, For this saying go thy way; the devil is gone out of thy daughter.

Time, January–April, A. D. 28; Place, Cana of Galilee.

E—Concluded.

Luke 17. 14 And when he saw *them*, he said unto them, Go show yourselves unto the priests. And it came to pass, that, as they went, they were cleansed.

Rom. 4. 20 He staggered not at the promise of God through unbelief; but was strong in faith, giving glory to God;

21 And being fully persuaded, that what he had promised, he was able also to perform.

Heb. 11. 18 Of whom it was said, That in Isaac shall thy seed be called:

19 Accounting that God *was* able to raise *him* up, even from the dead; from whence also he received him in a figure.

F

I Ki. 17. 23 And Elijah took the child, and brought him down out of the chamber into the house, and delivered him unto his mother: and Elijah said, See, thy son liveth.

G

Ps. 33 9 For he spake, and it was *done*; he commanded, and it stood fast.

Ps. 107. 20 He sent his word, and healed them, and delivered *them* from their destructions.

Matt. 8. 8 The centurion answered and said, Lord, I am not worthy that thou shouldest come under my roof: but speak the word only, and my servant shall be healed.

9 For I am a man under authority, having soldiers under me: and I say to this *man*, Go, and he goeth; and to another, Come, and he cometh; and to my servant, Do this, and he doeth *it*.

H

Luke 19. 9 And Jesus said unto him, This day is salvation come to this house, forasmuch as he also is a son of Abraham.

Acts 2. 39 For the promise is unto you, and to your children, and to all that are afar off, *even* as many as the Lord our God shall call.

Acts 16. 15 And when she was baptized, and her household, she besought *us*, saying, If ye have judged me to be faithful to the Lord, come into my house, and abide *there*. And she constrained us.

Acts 16. 34 And when he had brought them into his house, he set meat before them, and rejoiced, believing in God with all his house.

Acts 18. 8 And Crispus, the chief ruler of the

4 : 46–54.

46 So Jesus came again into Cana of Galilee, [a]where he made the water wine. And there was a certain [1]nobleman, [b]whose son was sick at Capernaum.

47 When he heard that Jesus was come out of Judæa into Galilee, he went unto him, and besought him [c]that he would come down, and heal his son: for he was at the point of death.

48 Then said Jesus unto him, [d]Except ye see signs and wonders, ye will not believe.

49 The nobleman saith unto him, Sir, come down ere my child die.

50 Jesus saith unto him, [e]Go thy way; thy son liveth. And the man believed the word that Jesus had spoken unto him, and he went his way.

51 And as he was now going down, his servants met him, and told *him*, saying, [f]Thy son liveth.

52 Then inquired he of them the hour when he began to amend. And they said unto him, Yesterday at the seventh hour the fever left him.

53 So the father knew that *it was* [g]at the same hour, in the which Jesus said unto him, Thy son liveth: and [h]himself believed, and his whole house.

54 This *is* again the second miracle *that* Jesus did, when he was come out of Judæa into Galilee. (p. 107.)

H—Concluded.

synagogue, believed on the Lord with all his house; and many of the Corinthians hearing believed, and were baptized.

A

Matt. 2. 23 And he came and dwelt in a city called Nazareth: that it might be fulfilled which was spoken by the prophets, He shall be called a Nazarene.

Matt.13. 54 And when he was come into his own country, he taught them in their synagogue, insomuch that they were astonished, and said, Whence hath this *man* this wisdom, and *these* mighty works?

Mark 6. 1 And he went out from thence, and came into his own country; and his disciples follow him.

B

Acts 13. 14 But when they departed from Perga, they came to Antioch in Pisidia, and went into the synagogue on the sabbath day, and sat down.

Acts 17. 2 And Paul, as his manner was, went in unto them, and three sabbath days reasoned with them out of the Scriptures,

C

Ps. 45. 7 Thou lovest righteousness, and hatest wickedness: therefore God, thy God, hath anointed thee with the oil of gladness above thy fellows.

Isa. 11. 2 And the Spirit of the LORD shall rest upon him, the spirit of wisdom and understanding, the spirit of counsel and might, the spirit of knowledge and of the fear of the LORD;

3 And shall make him of quick understanding in the fear of the LORD: and he shall not judge after the sight of his eyes, neither reprove after the hearing of his ears:

4 But with righteousness shall he judge the poor, and reprove with equity for the meek of the earth: and he shall smite the earth with the rod of his mouth, and with the breath of his lips shall he slay the wicked.

5 And righteousness shall be the girdle of his loins, and faithfulness the girdle of his reins.

Isa. 42. 1 Behold my servant, whom I uphold; mine elect, *in whom* my soul delighteth; I have put my Spirit upon him: he shall bring forth judgment to the Gentiles.

2 He shall not cry, nor lift up, nor cause his voice to be heard in the street.

3 A bruised reed shall he not break, and the smoking flax shall he not quench: he shall bring forth judgment unto truth.

§ 28. JESUS REJECTED AT NAZARETH.

C—CONCLUDED.

Isa. 42. 4 He shall not fail nor be discouraged, till he have set judgment in the earth: and the isles shall wait for his law.

Isa. 50. 4 The Lord GOD hath given me the tongue of the learned, that I should know how to speak a word in season to *him that is* weary: he wakeneth morning by morning, he wakeneth mine ear to hear as the learned.

Isa. 59. 21 As for me, this *is* my covenant with them, saith the LORD; My Spirit that *is* upon thee, and my words which I have put in thy mouth, shall not depart out of thy mouth, nor out of the mouth of thy seed, nor out of the mouth of thy seed's seed, saith the LORD, from henceforth and for ever.

Isa. 61. 1 The Spirit of the Lord GOD *is* upon me; because the LORD hath anointed me to preach good tidings unto the meek; he hath sent me to bind up the brokenhearted, to proclaim liberty to the captives, and the opening of the prison to *them that are* bound;

2 To proclaim the acceptable year of the LORD, and the day of vengeance of our God; to comfort all that mourn;

3 To appoint unto them that mourn in Zion, to give unto them beauty for ashes, the oil of joy for mourning, the garment of praise for the spirit of heaviness; that they might be called Trees of righteousness, The planting of the LORD, that he might be glorified.

Dan. 9. 24 Seventy weeks are determined upon thy people, and upon thy holy city, to finish the transgression, and to make an end of sins, and to make reconciliation for iniquity, and to bring in everlasting righteousness, and to seal up the vision and prophecy, and to anoint the Most Holy.

D

Lev. 25. 8 And thou shalt number seven sabbaths of years unto thee, seven times seven years; and the space of the seven sabbaths of years shall be unto thee forty and nine years.

9 Then shalt thou cause the trumpet of the jubilee to sound on the tenth *day* of the seventh month, in the day of atonement shall ye make the trumpet sound throughout all your land.

II Cor.6. 2 (For he saith, I have heard thee in a time accepted, and in the day of sal-

TIME, JANUARY–APRIL, A. D. 28.

4: 16–30.

16 And he came to [a]Nazareth, where he had been brought up: and, as his custom was, [b]he went into the synagogue on the sabbath day, and stood up for to read.

17 And there was delivered unto him the book of the prophet Esaias. And when he had opened the book, he found the place where it was written,

18 [c]The Spirit of the Lord *is* upon me, because he hath anointed me to preach the gospel to the poor; he hath sent me to heal the brokenhearted, to preach deliverance to the captives, and recovering of sight to the blind, to set at liberty them that are bruised,

19 To preach the [d]acceptable year of the Lord.

20 And he closed the book, and he gave *it* again to the minister, and sat down. And the eyes of all them that were in the synagogue were fastened on him.

21 And he began to say unto them, This day is this Scripture fulfilled in your ears.

22 And all bare him witness, and [e]wondered at the [f]gracious words which proceeded out of his mouth. And they said, [g]Is not this Joseph's son?

23 And he said unto them, Ye will surely say unto me this proverb, Physician, heal thyself: whatsoever we have heard done in [h]Capernaum, do also here in [i]thy country.

24 And he said, Verily I say unto you, [k]No prophet is accepted in his own country.

D—CONCLUDED.

vation have I succoured thee: behold, now *is* the accepted time; behold, now *is* the day of salvation.)

E

Ps. 45. 2 Thou art fairer than the children of men: grace is poured into thy lips: therefore God hath blessed thee for ever.

Matt. 13. 54. *See under A.*

Mark 6. 2 And when the sabbath day was come, he began to teach in the synagogue: and many hearing *him* were astonished, saying, From whence hath this *man* these things? and what wisdom *is* this which is given unto him, that even such mighty works are wrought by his hands?

Luke 2. 47 And all that heard him were astonished at his understanding and answers.

F

Prov. 16. 21 The wise in heart shall be called prudent: and the sweetness of the lips increaseth learning.

Prov. 25. 11 A word fitly spoken *is like* apples of gold in pictures of silver.

G

John 6. 42 And they said, Is not this Jesus, the son of Joseph, whose father and mother we know? how is it then that he saith, I came down from heaven?

H

Matt. 4. 13 And leaving Nazareth, he came and dwelt in Capernaum, which is upon the sea coast, in the borders of Zabulon and Nephthalim:

Matt. 11. 23 And thou, Capernaum, which art exalted unto heaven, shalt be brought down to hell: for if the mighty works, which have been done in thee, had been done in Sodom, it would have remained until this day.

I

Matt. 13. 54. *See under A.*
Mark 6. 1. *See under A.*

K

Matt. 13. 57 And they were offended in him. But Jesus said unto them, A prophet is not without honour, save in his own country, and in his own house.

Mark 6. 4 But Jesus said unto them, A prophet is not without honour, but in his own country, and among his own kin, and in his own house.

John 4. 44 For Jesus himself testified, that a prophet hath no honour in his own country.

§ 28. JESUS REJECTED AT NAZARETH (Concluded).

L

I Ki. 17. 9 Arise, get thee to Zarephath, which *belongeth* to Zidon, and dwell there: behold, I have commanded a widow woman there to sustain thee.

I Ki. 18. 1 And it came to pass *after* many days, that the word of the Lord came to Elijah in the third year, saying, Go, show thyself unto Ahab; and I will send rain upon the earth.

Jas. 5. 17 Elias was a man subject to like passions as we are, and he prayed earnestly that it might not rain: and it rained not on the earth by the space of three years and six months.

M

I Ki. 19. 19 So he departed thence, and found Elisha the son of Shaphat, who *was* ploughing *with* twelve yoke *of oxen* before him, and he with the twelfth: and Elijah passed by him, and cast his mantle upon him.

20 And he left the oxen, and ran after Elijah, and said, Let me, I pray thee, kiss my father and my mother, and *then* I will follow thee. And he said unto him, Go back again: for what have I done to thee?

21 And he returned back from him, and took a yoke of oxen, and slew them, and boiled their flesh with the instruments of the oxen, and gave unto the people, and they did eat. Then he arose, and went after Elijah, and ministered unto him.

N

II Ki. 5. 14 Then went he down, and dipped himself seven times in Jordan, according to the saying of the man of God: and his flesh came again like unto the flesh of a little child, and he was clean.

Job 21. 22 Shall *any* teach God knowledge? seeing he judgeth those that are high.

Job 33. 13 Why dost thou strive against him? for he giveth not account of any of his matters.

Job 36. 22 Behold, God exalteth by his power: who teacheth like him?

23 Who hath enjoined him his way? or who can say, Thou hast wrought iniquity?

24 Remember that thou magnify his work, which men behold.

Dan. 4. 35 And all the inhabitants of the earth *are* reputed as nothing: and he doeth according to his will in the army of heaven, and *among* the inhabitants of the earth: and none can stay his hand, or say unto him, What doest thou?

36 At the same time my reason returned unto me; and for the glory of my kingdom, mine honour and brightness returned unto me; and my counsellors and my lords sought unto me; and I was established in my kingdom, and excellent majesty was added unto me.

§ 29. JESUS LEAVES NAZARETH AND DWELLS

4: 13–16.

13 And leaving Nazareth, he came and dwelt in Capernaum, which is upon the sea coast, in the borders of Zabulon and Nephthalim:

14 That it might be fulfilled which was spoken by Esaias the prophet, saying,

15 [a]The land of Zabulon, and the land of Nephthalim, *by* the way of the sea, beyond Jordan, Galilee of the Gentiles;

16 [b]The people which sat in darkness saw great light; and to them which sat in the region and shadow of death light is sprung up. (p. 86.)

A

Isa. 9. 1 Nevertheless the dimness *shall* not *be* such as *was* in her vexation, when at the first he lightly afflicted the land of Zebulun, and the land of Naphtali, and afterward did more grievously afflict *her by* the way of the sea, beyond Jordan, in Galilee of the nations.

2 The people that walked in darkness have seen a great light: they that dwell in the land of the shadow of death, upon them hath the light shined.

3 Thou hast multiplied the nation, *and* not increased the joy: they joy before thee according to the joy in harvest, *and* as *men* rejoice when they divide the spoil.

4 For thou hast broken the yoke of his burden, and the staff of his shoul-

Time, January–April, A. D. 28.

Chap. 4.

25 But I tell you of a truth, [l]many widows were in Israel in the days of Elias, when the heaven was shut up three years and six months, when great famine was throughout all the land;

26 But unto none of them was Elias sent, save unto Sarepta, *a city* of Sidon, unto a woman *that was* a widow.

27 And many lepers were in Israel in the time of [m]Eliseus the prophet; and none of them was [n]cleansed, saving Naaman the Syrian.

28 And all they in the synagogue, when they heard these things, [o]were filled with wrath,

29 And rose up, and thrust him out of the city, and led him unto the [1]brow of the hill whereon their city was built, that they might cast him down headlong.

30 But he, [p]passing through the midst of them, went his way,

N—Concluded.

Dan. 4. 37 Now I Nebuchadnezzar praise and extol and honour the King of heaven, all whose works *are* truth, and his ways judgment: and those that walk in pride he is able to abase.

O

IIChr.16. 10 Then Asa was wroth with the seer, and put him in a prison house; for *he was* in a rage with him because of this *thing*. And Asa oppressed *some* of the people the same time.

IIChr.24. 20 And the Spirit of God came upon Zechariah the son of Jehoiada the priest, which stood above the people, and said unto them, Thus saith God, Why transgress ye the commandments of the Lord, that ye cannot prosper? because ye have forsaken the Lord, he hath also forsaken you.

21 And they conspired against him, and stoned him with stones at the commandment of the king in the court of the house of the Lord.

1

Or, *edge*.

P

John 8. 59 Then took they up stones to cast at him: but Jesus hid himself, and went out of the temple, going through the midst of them, and so passed by.

John 10. 39 Therefore they sought again to take him; but he escaped out of their hand,

AT CAPERNAUM. Time, January–April, A. D. 28.

4: 31.

31 And [c]came down to Capernaum, a city of Galilee, and taught them on the sabbath days. (p. 97.)

A—Concluded.

der, the rod of his oppressor, as in the day of Midian.

5 For every battle of the warrior *is* with confused noise, and garments rolled in blood; but *this* shall be with burning *and* fuel of fire.

B

Ps. 107. 10 Such as sit in darkness and in the shadow of death, *being* bound in affliction and iron;

11 Because they rebelled against the words of God, and contemned the counsel of the Most High:

12 Therefore he brought down their heart with labour; they fell down, and *there was* none to help.

B—Concluded.

13 Then they cried unto the Lord in their trouble, *and* he saved them out of their distresses.

Isa. 42. 6 I the Lord have called thee in righteousness, and will hold thine hand, and will keep thee, and give thee for a covenant of the people, for a light of the Gentiles;

7 To open the blind eyes, to bring out the prisoners from the prison, *and* them that sit in darkness out of the prison house.

Luke 2. 32 A light to lighten the Gentiles, and the glory of thy people Israel.

C

Matt. 4. 13. *See text of topic.*

Mark 1. 21 And they went into Capernaum: and straightway on the sabbath day he entered into the synagogue, and taught.

§ 30. PETER, ANDREW, JAMES AND JOHN CALLED. DRAUGHT OF

4: 18–22.

18 [a]And Jesus, walking by the sea of Galilee, saw two brethren, Simon called [b]Peter, and Andrew his brother, casting a net into the sea: for they were fishers.

19 And he saith unto them, Follow me, and [c]I will make you fishers of men.

20 [d]And they straightway left *their* nets, and followed him.

21 [e]And going on from thence, he saw other two brethren, James *the son* of Zebedee, and John his brother, in a ship with Zebedee their father, mending their nets; and he called them.

A

Mark 1. 16, 17, 18. *See text of topic*
Luke 5. 2. *See text of topic.*

B

John 1. 35 Again the next day after, John stood, and two of his disciples;

36 And looking upon Jesus as he walked, he saith, Behold the Lamb of God!

37 And the two disciples heard him speak, and they followed Jesus.

38 Then Jesus turned, and saw them following, and saith unto them, What seek ye? They said unto him, Rabbi, (which is to say, being interpreted, Master,) where dwellest thou?

39 He saith unto them, Come and see. They came and saw where he dwelt, and abode with him that day: for it was about the tenth hour.

40 One of the two which heard John *speak*, and followed him, was Andrew, Simon Peter's brother.

41 He first findeth his own brother Simon, and saith unto him, We have found the Messias, which is, being interpreted, the Christ.

42 And he brought him to Jesus. And when Jesus beheld him, he said, Thou art Simon the son of Jona: thou shalt be called Cephas, which is by interpretation, A stone.

43 The day following Jesus would go forth into Galilee, and findeth Philip, and saith unto him, Follow me.

1: 16–20.

16 [f]Now as he walked by the sea of Galilee, he saw Simon and Andrew his brother casting a net into the sea: for they were fishers.

17 And Jesus said unto them, Come ye after me, and I will make you to become fishers of men.

18 And straightway [g]they forsook their nets, and followed him.

19 [h]And when he had gone a little further thence, he saw James the *son* of Zebedee, and John his brother, who also were in the ship mending their nets.

B—Concluded.

John 1. 44 Now Philip was of Bethsaida, the city of Andrew and Peter.

C

Eze. 47. 9 And it shall come to pass, *that* every thing that liveth, which moveth, whithersoever the rivers shall come, shall live: and there shall be a very great multitude of fish, because these waters shall come thither: for they shall be healed; and every thing shall live whither the river cometh.

10 And it shall come to pass, *that* the fishers shall stand upon it from En-gedi even unto En-eglaim; they shall be a *place* to spread forth nets; their fish shall be according to their kinds, as the fish of the great sea, exceeding many.

Luke 5. 10, 11. *See text of topic.*

D

Mark 10. 28 Then Peter began to say unto him, Lo, we have left all, and have followed thee.

Luke 18. 28 Then Peter said, Lo, we have left all, and followed thee.

E

Mark 1. 19, 20. *See text of topic.*
Luke 5. 10. *See text of topic.*

F

Matt. 4. 18. *See text of topic.*
Luke 5. 4. *See text of topic.*
John 1. 35–44. *See under B.*

G

Matt. 19. 27 Then answered Peter and said unto him, Behold, we have forsaken

FISHES. Time, January–April, A. D. 28; Place, Near Capernaum.

5: 1–11.

1 And [i]it came to pass, that, as the people pressed upon him to hear the word of God, he stood by the lake of Gennesaret,

2 And saw two ships standing by the lake: but the fishermen were gone out of them, and were washing *their* nets.

3 And he entered into one of the ships, which was Simon's, and prayed him that he would thrust out a little from the land. And he sat down, and taught the people out of the ship.

4 Now when he had left speaking, he said unto Simon, [k]Launch out into the deep, and let down your nets for a draught.

5 And Simon answering said unto him, Master, [l]we have toiled all the night, and have taken nothing: [m]nevertheless at thy word I will let down the net.

6 And when they had this done, they inclosed a great multitude of fishes: and their net brake.

7 And they beckoned unto *their* partners, which were in the other ship, that they should come and help them. And they came, and filled both the ships, so that they began to sink.

8 When Simon Peter saw *it*, he fell down at Jesus' knees, saying, [n]Depart from me; for I am a sinful man, O Lord.

9 For he was astonished, and all that were with him, at the draught of the fishes which they had taken:

10 And so *was* also James, and John, the sons of Zebedee, which were partners with Simon. And Jesus said unto Simon, Fear not; from henceforth thou shalt catch men.

all, and followed thee; what shall we have therefore?

Luke 5. 11. *See text of topic.*

H

Matt. 4. 21. *See text of topic.*

I

Matt. 4. 18 and Mark 1. 16. *See text of topic.*

K

John 21. 6 And he said unto them, Cast the net on the right side of the ship, and ye shall find. They cast therefore, and now they were not able to draw it for the multitude of fishes.

L

Ps. 127. 1 Except the LORD build the house, they labour in vain that build it: except the LORD keep the city, the watchman waketh *but* in vain.

2 *It is* vain for you to rise up early, to sit up late, to eat the bread of sorrows: *for* so he giveth his beloved sleep.

Eze. 37. 11 Then he said unto me, Son of man, these bones are the whole house of Israel: Behold, they say, Our bones are dried, and our hope is lost: we are cut off for our parts.

12 Therefore prophesy and say unto them, Thus saith the Lord GOD; Behold, O my people, I will open your graves, and cause you to come up out of your graves, and bring you into the land of Israel.

John 21. 3 Simon Peter saith unto them, I go a fishing. They say unto him, We also go with thee. They went forth, and entered into a ship immediately; and that night they caught nothing.

M

II Ki. 5. 10 And Elisha sent a messenger unto him, saying, Go and wash in Jordan seven times, and thy flesh shall come again to thee, and thou shalt be clean.

11 But Naaman was wroth, and went away, and said, Behold, I thought, He will surely come out to me, and stand, and call on the name of the LORD his God, and strike his hand over the place, and recover the leper.

12 *Are* not Abana and Pharpar, rivers of Damascus, better than all the waters of Israel? may I not wash in them, and be clean? So he turned and went away in a rage.

13 And his servants came near, and spake unto him, and said, My father, *if* the prophet had bid thee *do some* great thing, wouldest thou not have done *it?* how much rather then, when he saith to thee, Wash, and be clean?

For M concluded and N see following pages (96, 97).

§ 30. PETER, ANDREW, JAMES AND JOHN CALLED. DRAUGHT OF

CHAP. 4.

22 And they immediately left the ship and their father, and followed him. (p. 98.)

M—CONTINUED.

II Ki. 5. 14 Then went he down, and dipped himself seven times in Jordan, according to the saying of the man of God: and his flesh came again like unto the

CHAP. 1.

20 And straightway he called them: and they left their father Zebedee in the ship with the hired servants, and went after him.

M—CONCLUDED.

flesh of a little child, and he was clean.

§ 31. HEALING OF A DEMONIAC IN THE SYNAGOGUE.

A

Matt. 4. 13 And leaving Nazareth, he came and dwelt in Capernaum, which is upon the sea coast, in the borders of Zabulon and Nephthalim:

Luke 4. 31. *See text of topic.*

B

Matt. 7. 28 And it came to pass, when Jesus had ended these sayings, the people were astonished at his doctrine:

29 For he taught them as *one* having authority, and not as the scribes.

C

Luke 4. 33. *See text of topic.*

D

Matt. 8. 29 And, behold, they cried out, saying, What have we to do with thee, Jesus, thou Son of God? art thou come hither to torment us before the time?

E

Ps. 16. 10 For thou wilt not leave my soul in hell; neither wilt thou suffer thine Holy One to see corruption.

Acts 2. 31 He, seeing this before, spake of the resurrection of Christ, that his soul was not left in hell, neither his flesh did see corruption.

Jas. 2. 19 Thou believest that there is one God; thou doest well: the devils also believe, and tremble.

F

Mark 1. 34 And he healed many that were sick of divers diseases, and cast out many devils; and suffered not the devils to speak, because they knew him.

G

Mark 9. 20 And they brought him unto him: and when he saw him, straightway the spirit tare him; and he fell on the ground, and wallowed foaming.

1 : 21–28.

21 [a]And they went into Capernaum; and straightway on the sabbath day he entered into the synagogue, and taught.

22 [b]And they were astonished at his doctrine: for he taught them as one that had authority, and not as the scribes.

23 [c]And there was in their synagogue a man with an unclean spirit; and he cried out,

24 Saying, Let *us* alone; [d]what have we to do with thee, thou Jesus of Nazareth? art thou come to destroy us? I know thee who thou art, the [e]Holy One of God.

25 And Jesus [f]rebuked him, saying, Hold thy peace, and come out of him.

26 And when the unclean spirit [g]had torn him, and cried with a loud voice, he came out of him.

27 And they were all amazed, insomuch that they questioned among themselves, saying, What thing is this? what new doctrine *is* this? for with authority commandeth he even the unclean spirits, and they do obey him.

28 And immediately his fame spread abroad throughout all the region round about Galilee.

FISHES (CONCLUDED). TIME, JANUARY–APRIL, A. D. 28; PLACE, NEAR CAPERNAUM.

CHAP. 5.

11 And when they had brought their
ships to land, they forsook all, and
followed him. (p. 101.)

N

II Sa. 6. 9 And David was afraid of the LORD that day, and said, How shall the ark of the LORD come to me?

N—CONCLUDED.

I Ki. 17. 18 And she said unto Elijah, What have I to do with thee, O thou man of God? art thou come unto me to call my sin to remembrance, and to slay my son?

Job 42. 5 I have heard of thee by the hearing of the ear; but now mine eye seeth thee:

6 Wherefore I abhor *myself*, and repent in dust and ashes.

TIME, JANUARY–APRIL, A. D. 28; PLACE, CAPERNAUM.

4: 31–37.

31 And [h]came down to Capernaum,
a city of Galilee, and taught them on
the sabbath days.

32 And they were astonished at his
doctrine: [i]for his word was with
power.

33 [k]And in the synagogue there was
a man, which had a spirit of an unclean devil, and cried out with a loud
voice,

34 Saying, Let *us* alone; what have
we to do with thee, *thou* Jesus of
Nazareth? art thou come to destroy
us? [l]I know thee who thou art; [m]the
Holy One of God.

35 And Jesus rebuked him, saying,
Hold thy peace, and come out of him.
And when the devil had thrown him
in the midst, he came out of him, and
hurt him not.

36 And they were all amazed and
spake among themselves, saying, What
a word *is* this! for with authority and
power he commandeth the unclean
spirits, and they come out.

37 And [n]the fame of him went out
into every place of the country round
about.

H

Matt. 4. 13. *See under A.*
Mark 1. 21. *See text of topic.*

I

Matt. 7. 28, 29. *See under B.*

Tit. 2. 15 These things speak, and exhort, and rebuke with all authority. Let no man despise thee.

K

Mark 1. 23. *See text of topic.*

L

Luke 4. 41 And devils also came out of many, crying out, and saying, Thou art Christ the Son of God. And he rebuking *them* suffered them not to speak: for they knew that he was Christ.

M

Ps. 16. 10. *See under E.*

Isa. 49. 7 Thus saith the LORD, the Redeemer of Israel, *and* his Holy One, to him whom man despiseth, to him whom the nation abhorreth, to a servant of rulers, Kings shall see and arise, princes also shall worship, because of the LORD that is faithful, *and* the Holy One of Israel, and he shall choose thee.

Dan. 9. 24 Seventy weeks are determined upon thy people, and upon thy holy city, to finish the transgression, and to make an end of sins, and to make reconciliation for iniquity, and to bring in everlasting righteousness, and to seal up the vision and prophecy, and to anoint the Most Holy.

Luke 1. 35 And the angel answered and said unto her, The Holy Ghost shall come upon thee, and the power of the Highest shall overshadow thee: therefore also that holy thing which shall be born of thee shall be called the Son of God.

N

Mic. 5. 4 And he shall stand and feed in the strength of the LORD, in the majesty of the name of the LORD his God; and they shall abide: for now shall he be great unto the ends of the earth.

§ 32. THE HEALING OF PETER'S WIFE'S MOTHER AND MANY

8: 14–17.

14 [a]And when Jesus was come into Peter's house, he saw [b]his wife's mother laid, and sick of a fever.

15 And he touched her hand, and the fever left her: and she arose, and ministered unto them.

16 [c]When the even was come, they brought unto him many that were possessed with devils: and he cast out the spirits with *his* word, and healed all that were sick:

17 That it might be fulfilled which was spoken by Esaias the prophet, saying, [d]Himself took our infirmities, and bare *our* sicknesses. (p. 212.)

A

Mark 1. 29, 30, 31. *See text of topic.*
Luke 4. 38, 39. *See text of topic.*

B

I Cor. 9. 5 Have we not power to lead about a sister, a wife, as well as other apostles, and *as* the brethren of the Lord, and Cephas?

C

Mark 1. 32, etc. and Luke 4. 40, 41. *See text of topic.*

D

Isa. 53. 4 Surely he hath borne our griefs, and carried our sorrows: yet we did

1: 29–34.

29 [e]And forthwith, when they were come out of the synagogue, they entered into the house of Simon and Andrew, with James and John.

30 But Simon's wife's mother lay sick of a fever; and anon they tell him of her.

31 And he came and took her by the hand, and lifted her up; and [f]immediately the fever left her, and she ministered unto them.

32 [g]And at even, when the sun did set, they brought unto him all that were diseased, and them that were possessed with devils.

33 And all the city was gathered together at the door.

34 And he healed many that were sick of divers diseases, and cast out many devils; and [h]suffered not the devils to speak, because they knew him.

D—CONTINUED.

esteem him stricken, smitten of God, and afflicted.

§ 33. JESUS AND HIS DISCIPLES GO FROM CAPERNAUM

4: 23–25.

23 And Jesus went about all Galilee, [a]teaching in their synagogues, and preaching [b]the gospel of the kingdom, [c]and healing all manner of sickness and all manner of disease among the people.

24 And his [d]fame went throughout all Syria: and they brought unto him all sick people that were taken with divers diseases and torments, and those which were possessed with devils, and those which were lunatic, and those

1: 35–39.

35 And in the morning, rising up a great while before day, he went out, and departed into a solitary place, and there prayed.

36 And Simon and they that were with him followed after him.

37 And when they had found him, they said unto him, All *men* seek for thee.

A

Matt. 9. 35 And Jesus went about all the cities and villages, teaching in their synagogues, and preaching the gospel

OTHERS. Time, January-April, A. D. 28; Place, Capernaum.

4: 38–41.

38 And he arose out of the synagogue, and entered into Simon's house. And Simon's wife's mother was taken with a great fever; and they besought him for her.

39 And he stood over her, and rebuked the fever; and it left her: and immediately she arose and ministered unto them.

40 Now when the sun was setting, all they that had any sick with divers diseases brought them unto him; and he laid his hands on every one of them, and healed them.

41 [i]And devils also came out of many, crying out, and saying, Thou art Christ the Son of God. And [k]he rebuking *them* suffered them not [1]to speak: for they knew that he was Christ.

D—Concluded.

I Pet. 2. 24 Who his own self bare our sins in his own body on the tree, that we, being dead to sins, should live unto righteousness: by whose stripes ye were healed.

E

Matt. 8. 14. *See text of topic.*
Luke 4. 38. *See text of topic.*

F

Ps. 103. 3 Who forgiveth all thine iniquities; who healeth all thy diseases·

G

Matt. 8. 16. *See text of topic.*
Luke 4. 40. *See text of topic.*

H

Mark 3. 12 And he straitly charged them that they should not make him known.

Acts 16. 17 The same followed Paul and us, and cried, saying, These men are the servants of the most high God, which show unto us the way of salvation.

18 And this did she many days. But Paul, being grieved, turned and said to the spirit, I command thee in the name of Jesus Christ to come out of her. And he came out the same hour.

I

Mark 1. 34. *See text of topic.*

Mark 3. 11 And unclean spirits, when they saw him, fell down before him, and cried, saying, Thou art the Son of God.

K

Mark 1. 25 And Jesus rebuked him, saying, Hold thy peace, and come out of him.

Mark 1. 34. *See text of topic.*

Luke 4. 35 And Jesus rebuked him, saying, Hold thy peace, and come out of him. And when the devil had thrown him in the midst, he came out of him, and hurt him not.

1

Or, *to say that they knew him to be Christ.*

THROUGHOUT GALILEE. Time, January-April, A. D. 28.

4: 42–44.

42 And when it was day, he departed and went into a desert place: and the people sought him, and came unto him, and stayed him, that he should not depart from them.

A—Concluded.

of the kingdom, and healing every sickness and every disease among the people.

Mark 1. 21 And they went into Capernaum; and straightway on the sabbath day he entered into the synagogue, and taught.

Luke 4. 15 And he taught in their synagogues, being glorified of all.

B

Matt. 24. 14 And this gospel of the kingdom shall be preached in all the world for a witness unto all nations; and then shall the end come.

Mark 1. 14 Now after that John was put in prison, Jesus came into Galilee, preaching the gospel of the kingdom of God,

C

Mark. 1. 34. *See text of* § 32.

D

Isa. 52. 13 Behold, my servant shall deal prudently, he shall be exalted and extolled, and be very high.

E

Mark 3. 7 But Jesus withdrew himself with his disciples to the sea: and a great multitude from Galilee followed him, and from Judæa.

§ 33. JESUS AND HIS DISCIPLES GO FROM CAPERNAUM

CHAP. 4.

that had the palsy; and he healed them.

25 [e]And there followed him great multitudes of people from Galilee, and *from* Decapolis, and *from* Jerusalem, and *from* Judæa, and *from* beyond Jordan. (p. 124.)

CHAP. 1.

38 And he said unto them, Let us go into the next towns, that I may preach there also: for [f]therefore came I forth.

39 And he preached in their synagogues throughout all Galilee, and cast out devils.

§ 34. HEALING OF A LEPER.

8: 2–4.

2 [a]And, behold, there came a leper and worshipped him, saying, Lord, if thou wilt, thou canst make me clean.

3 And Jesus put forth *his* hand, and touched him, saying, I will; be thou clean. And immediately his leprosy was cleansed.

4 And Jesus saith unto him, [b]See thou tell no man; but go thy way, show thyself to the priest, and offer the gift that [c]Moses commanded, for a testimony unto them. (p. 150.)

A

Mark 1. 40, etc. *See text of topic.*
Luke 5. 12, etc. *See text of topic.*

B

Matt. 9. 30 And their eyes were opened; and Jesus straitly charged them, saying, See *that* no man know *it*.

Mark 5. 43 And he charged them straitly that no man should know it; and commanded that something should be given her to eat.

C

Lev. 14. 3 And the priest shall go forth out of the camp; and the priest shall look, and, behold, *if* the plague of leprosy be healed in the leper;

4 Then shall the priest command to take for him that is to be cleansed two birds alive *and* clean, and cedar wood, and scarlet, and hyssop:

Lev. 14. 10 And on the eighth day he shall take two he lambs without blemish, and one ewe lamb of the first year without blemish, and three tenth deals

1: 40–45.

40 [d]And there came a leper to him, beseeching him, and kneeling down to him, and saying unto him, If thou wilt, [e]thou canst make me clean.

41 And Jesus, [f]moved with compassion, put forth *his* hand, and touched him, and saith unto him, I will; be thou clean.

42 And as soon as he had spoken, immediately the leprosy departed from him, and he was cleansed.

43 And he straitly charged him, and forthwith sent him away;

44 And saith unto him, See thou say nothing to any man: but go thy way, show thyself to the priest, and offer for thy cleansing those things which Moses commanded, for a testimony unto them.

45 But he went out, and began to publish *it* much, and to blaze abroad the matter, insomuch that Jesus could no more openly enter into the city, but was without in desert places: [g]and they came to him from every quarter.

C—CONTINUED.

of fine flour *for* a meat offering, mingled with oil, and one log of oil.

Lev. 14. 21 And if he *be* poor, and cannot get so much; then he shall take one lamb

THROUGHOUT GALILEE (CONCLUDED). TIME, JANUARY–APRIL, A. D. 28.

CHAP. 4.

43 And he said unto them, I must preach the kingdom of God to other cities also: for therefore am I sent.

44 And he preached in the synagogues of Galilee. (p. 95.)

F

Isa. 61. 1. The Spirit of the Lord GOD *is* upon me; because the LORD hath anointed me to preach good tidings unto the meek; he hath sent me to bind up the brokenhearted, to proclaim liberty to the captives, and the opening of the prison to *them that are* bound:

John 16. 28 I came forth from the Father, and am come into the world: again, I leave the world, and go to the Father.

John 17. 4 I have glorified thee on the earth: I have finished the work which thou gavest me to do.

TIME, JANUARY–APRIL, A. D. 28; PLACE, GALILEE.

5: 12–16.

12 And it came to pass, when he was in a certain city, behold a man full of leprosy; who seeing Jesus fell on *his* face, and besought him, saying, Lord, if thou wilt, thou canst [h]make me clean.

13 And he put forth *his* hand, and touched him, saying, I will: be thou clean. And immediately the leprosy departed from him.

14 And he charged him to tell no man: but go, and show thyself to the priest, and offer for thy cleansing, according as Moses commanded, for a testimony unto them.

15 But so much the more went there a fame abroad of him: [i]and great multitudes came together to hear, and to be healed by him of their infirmities.

16 And he withdrew himself into the wilderness, and prayed.

C—CONCLUDED.

for a trespass offering to be waved, to make an atonement for him, and one tenth deal of fine flour mingled with oil for a meat offering, and a log of oil;

22 And two turtle-doves, or two young pigeons, such as he is able to get; and the one shall be a sin offering, and the other a burnt offering.

D

Matt. 8. 2. *See text of topic.*
Luke 5. 12. *See text of topic.*

E

Gen. 18. 14 Is any thing too hard for the LORD? At the time appointed I will return unto thee, according to the time of life, and Sarah shall have a son.

Jer. 32. 17 Ah Lord GOD! behold, thou hast made the heaven and the earth by thy great power and stretched-out arm, *and* there is nothing too hard for thee:

F

Heb. 2. 17 Wherefore in all things it behooved him to be made like unto *his* brethren, that he might be a merciful and faithful high priest in things *pertaining* to God, to make reconciliation for the sins of the people.

Heb. 4. 15 For we have not a high priest which cannot be touched with the feeling of our infirmities; but was in all points tempted like as *we are, yet* without sin.

G

Mark 2. 13 And he went forth again by the sea-side; and all the multitude resorted unto him, and he taught them.

H

Jer. 32. 27 Behold, I *am* the LORD, the God of all flesh: is there any thing too hard for me?

Heb. 7. 25 Wherefore he is able also to save them to the uttermost that come unto God by him, seeing he ever liveth to make intercession for them.

I

Matt. 4. 25 And there followed him great multitudes of people from Galilee, and *from* Decapolis, and *from* Jerusalem, and *from* Judæa, and *from* beyond Jordan.

§ 35. THE HEALING OF A PARALYTIC.

9: 2–8.

2 [a]And, behold, they brought to him a man sick of the palsy, lying on a bed: [b]and Jesus seeing their faith said unto the sick of the palsy; Son, be of good cheer; [c]thy sins be forgiven thee.

3 And, behold, certain of the scribes said within themselves, This *man* blasphemeth.

4 And Jesus knowing their thoughts

A

Mark 2. 3. *See text of topic.*
Luke 5. 18. *See text of topic.*

B

Matt. 8. 10 When Jesus heard *it*, he marvelled, and said to them that followed, Verily I say unto you, I have not found so great faith, no, not in Israel.

C

Rom. 5. 11 And not only *so*, but we also joy in God through our Lord Jesus Christ, by whom we have now received the atonement.

Eph. 1. 7 In whom we have redemption through his blood, the forgiveness of sins, according to the riches of his grace;

D

Matt. 8. 34 And, behold, the whole city came out to meet Jesus: and when they saw him, they besought *him* that he would depart out of their coasts.

Matt. 9. 1 And he entered into a ship, and passed over, and came into his own city.

Luke 5. 18. *See text of topic.*

E

Isa. 61. 1 The Spirit of the Lord GOD *is* upon me; because the LORD hath anointed me to preach good tidings unto the meek; he hath sent me to bind up the brokenhearted, to proclaim liberty to the captives, and the opening of the prison to *them that are* bound:

Eph. 2. 17 And came and preached peace to you which were afar off, and to them that were nigh.

Heb. 2. 3 How shall we escape, if we neglect so great salvation; which at the first began to be spoken by the Lord, and was confirmed unto us by them that heard *him;*

2: 1–12.

1 And again [d]he entered into Capernaum after *some* days; and it was noised that he was in the house.

2 And straightway many were gathered together, insomuch that there was no room to receive *them*, no, not so much as about the door: and he [e]preached the word unto them.

3 And they come unto him, bringing one sick of the palsy, which was borne of four.

4 And when they could not come nigh unto him for the press, they uncovered the roof where he was: and when they had broken *it* up, they let down the bed wherein the sick of the palsy lay.

5 When Jesus [f]saw their faith, he said unto the sick of the palsy, [g]Son, thy sins be forgiven thee.

6 But there were certain of the scribes sitting there, and reasoning in their hearts,

7 Why doth this *man* thus speak blasphemies? [h]who can forgive sins but God only?

8 And immediately, [i]when Jesus perceived in his spirit that they so reasoned within themselves, he said unto them, Why reason ye these things in your hearts?

F

Gen. 22. 12 And he said, Lay not thine hand upon the lad, neither do thou any thing unto him: for now I know that thou fearest God, seeing thou hast not withheld thy son, thine only *son*, from me.

Heb. 4. 13 Neither is there any creature that is not manifest in his sight: but all things *are* naked and opened unto the eyes of him with whom we have to do.

TIME, JANUARY–APRIL, A. D. 28; PLACE, CAPERNAUM.

5: 17–26.

17 And it came to pass on a certain day, as he was teaching, that there were Pharisees and doctors of the law sitting by, which were come out of every town of Galilee, and Judæa, and Jerusalem: and the power of the Lord was *present* to heal them.

18 [k]And, behold, men brought in a bed a man which was taken with a palsy: and they sought *means* to bring him in, and to lay *him* before him.

19 And when they could not find by what *way* they might bring him in because of the multitude, they went upon the housetop, and let him down through the tiling with *his* couch into the midst before Jesus.

20 And when [l]he saw their faith, he said unto him, Man, [m]thy sins are forgiven thee.

21 [n]And the scribes and the Pharisees began to reason, saying, Who is this which speaketh blasphemies? [o]Who can forgive sins, but God alone?

22 But when Jesus perceived their thoughts, he answering said unto them, What reason ye in your hearts?

G

Ps. 103. 3 Who forgiveth all thine iniquities; who healeth all thy diseases;

Isa. 53. 11 He shall see of the travail of his soul, *and* shall be satisfied: by his knowledge shall my righteous servant justify many; for he shall bear their iniquities.

H

Job 14. 4 Who can bring a clean *thing* out of an unclean? not one.

Ps. 130. 4 But *there is* forgiveness with thee, that thou mayest be feared.

Isa. 43. 25 I, *even* I, *am* he that blotteth out thy transgressions for mine own sake, and will not remember thy sins.

I

I Sa. 16. 7 But the LORD said unto Samuel, Look not on his countenance, or on the height of his stature; because I have refused him: for *the LORD seeth* not as man seeth; for man looketh on the outward appearance, but the LORD looketh on the heart.

I Chr. 29. 17 I know also, my God, that thou triest the heart, and hast pleasure in uprightness. As for me, in the uprightness of mine heart I have willingly offered all these things; and now have I seen with joy thy people, which are present here, to offer willingly unto thee.

Ps. 7. 9 Oh let the wickedness of the wicked come to an end; but establish the just: for the righteous God trieth the hearts and reins.

Ps. 139. 1 O LORD, thou hast searched me, and known *me*.

Jer. 17. 10 I the LORD search the heart, *I* try the reins, even to give every man according to his ways, *and* according to the fruit of his doings.

Matt. 9. 4. *See text of topic.*
Heb. 4. 13. *See under F.*

Rev. 2. 23 And I will kill her children with death; and all the churches shall know that I am he which searcheth the reins and hearts: and I will give unto every one of you according to your works.

K

Matt. 9. 2. *See text of topic.*
Mark 2. 3. *See text of topic.*

L

Rev. 2. 23. *See under I.*

M

Acts 5. 31. *See under Q, page 105.*

N

Matt. 9. 3. *See text of topic.*
Mark 2. 6, 7. *See text of topic.*

O

Ex. 34. 7 Keeping mercy for thousands, forgiving iniquity and transgression and sin, and that will by no means clear *the guilty;* visiting the iniquity of the fathers upon the children, and upon the children's children, unto the third and to the fourth *generation.*

Ps. 32. 5 I acknowledged my sin unto thee, and mine iniquity have I not hid. I said, I will confess my transgressions unto the LORD; and thou forgavest the iniquity of my sin. Selah.

Ps. 103. 3. *See under G.*

For O concluded see next page (104).

§ 35. THE HEALING OF A PARALYTIC (CONCLUDED).

CHAP. 9.

said, [p]Wherefore think ye evil in your hearts?

5 For whether is easier, to say, *Thy* sins be forgiven thee; or to say, Arise, and walk?

6 But that ye may know that [q]the Son of man hath power on earth to forgive sins, (then saith he to the sick of the palsy,) Arise, take up thy bed, and go unto thine house.

7 And he arose, and departed to his house.

8 But when the multitudes saw *it*, they marvelled, and glorified God, which had given such power unto men.

O—CONCLUDED. See preceding page (103).

Isa. 43. 25 I, *even* I, *am* he that blotteth out thy transgressions for mine own sake, and will not remember thy sins.

Dan. 9. 9 To the Lord our God *belong* mercies and forgivenesses, though we have rebelled against him;

P

Ps. 139. 2 Thou knowest my downsitting and mine uprising; thou understandest my thought afar off.

Matt. 12. 25 And Jesus knew their thoughts, and said unto them, Every kingdom divided against itself is brought to desolation; and every city or house divided against itself shall not stand:

CHAP. 2.

9 [r]Whether is it easier to say to the sick of the palsy, *Thy* sins be forgiven thee; or to say, Arise, and take up thy bed, and walk?

10 But that ye may know that [s]the Son of man hath power on earth to forgive sins, (he saith to the sick of the palsy,)

11 I say unto thee, Arise, and take up thy bed, and go thy way into thine house.

12 And [t]immediately he arose, took up the bed, and went forth before them all; insomuch that they were all amazed, and glorified God, saying, We never saw it on this fashion.

P—CONTINUED.

Mark 12. 15 Shall we give, or shall we not give? But he, knowing their hypocrisy, said unto them, Why tempt ye me? bring me a penny, that I may see *it*.

Luke 5. 22 But when Jesus perceived their thoughts, he answering said unto them, What reason ye in your hearts?

Luke 6. 8 But he knew their thoughts, and said to the man which had the withered hand, Rise up, and stand forth in the midst. And he arose and stood forth.

Luke 9. 47 And Jesus, perceiving the thought of their heart, took a child, and set him by him,

§ 36. MATTHEW, THE PUBLICAN.

9 : 9.

9 [a]And as Jesus passed forth from thence, he saw a man, named Matthew, sitting at the receipt of custom: and he saith unto him, Follow me. And he arose, and followed him. (p. 220.)

A

Mark 2. 14. *See text of topic.*
Luke 5. 27. *See text of topic.*

2: 13, 14.

13 [b]And he went forth again by the sea side; and all the multitude resorted unto him, and he taught them.

14 [c]And as he passed by, he saw Levi the *son* of Alpheus sitting [1]at the receipt of custom, and said unto him, Follow me. And he arose and followed him. (p. 220.)

TIME, JANUARY–APRIL, A. D. 28; PLACE, CAPERNAUM.

CHAP. 5.

23 Whether is easier, to say, Thy sins be forgiven thee; or to say, Rise up and walk?

24 But that ye may know that the [u]Son of man hath power upon earth to forgive sins, (he said unto the sick of the palsy,) I say unto thee, Arise, and take up thy couch, and go into thine house.

25 And immediately he rose up before them, and took up that whereon he lay, and departed to his own house, [x]glorifying God.

26 And they were all amazed, and they glorified God, and were filled with fear, saying, We have seen strange things to-day.

P—CONCLUDED.

Luke 11. 17 But he, knowing their thoughts, said unto them, Every kingdom divided against itself is brought to desolation; and a house *divided* against a house falleth.

Q

Acts 5. 31 Him hath God exalted with his right hand *to be* a Prince and a Saviour, for to give repentance to Israel, and forgiveness of sins.

R

Matt. 9. 5. *See text of topic.*

S

Isa. 53. 11 He shall see of the travail of his soul, *and* shall be satisfied: by his knowledge shall my righteous servant justify many; for he shall bear their iniquities.

Dan. 7. 13 I saw in the night visions, and, behold, *one* like the Son of man came with the clouds of heaven, and came to the Ancient of days, and they brought him near before him.

T

Ps. 33. 9 For he spake, and it was *done;* he commanded, and it stood fast.

U

Acts 5. 31. *See under Q.*

Col. 3. 13 Forbearing one another, and forgiving one another, if any man have a quarrel against any: even as Christ forgave you, so also *do* ye.

X

Ps. 50. 23 Whoso offereth praise glorifieth me: and to him that ordereth *his* conversation *aright* will I show the salvation of God.

Ps. 103. 1 Bless the LORD, O my soul: and all that is within me, *bless* his holy name.

Ps. 107. 20 He sent his word, and healed them, and delivered *them* from their destructions.

21 Oh that *men* would praise the LORD *for* his goodness, and *for* his wonderful works to the children of men!

22 And let them sacrifice the sacrifices of thanksgiving, and declare his works with rejoicing.

John. 9. 24 Then again called they the man that was blind, and said unto him, Give God the praise: we know that this man is a sinner.

TIME, JANUARY–APRIL, A. D. 28; PLACE, CAPERNAUM.

5: 27, 28.

27 And after these things he went forth, and saw a publican, named Levi, sitting at the receipt of custom: and he said unto him, Follow me.

28 And he left all, rose up, and followed him. (p. 221.)

B

Matt. 9. 9. *See text of topic.*

C

Acts 1. 13 And when they were come in, they went up into an upper room, where abode both Peter, and James, and John, and Andrew, Philip, and Thomas, Bartholomew, and Matthew, James *the son* of Alpheus, and Simon Zelotes, and Judas *the brother* of James.

1

Or, *at the place where the custom was received.*

§ 37. THE SECOND PASSOVER. HEALING OF THE IMPOTENT MAN AT

A

Ex. 23. 14 Three times thou shalt keep a feast unto me in the year.

15 Thou shalt keep the feast of unleavened bread: (thou shalt eat unleavened bread seven days, as I commanded thee, in the time appointed of the month Abib; for in it thou camest out from Egypt: and none shall appear before me empty:)

16 And the feast of harvest, the first-fruits of thy labours, which thou hast sown in the field: and the feast of ingathering, *which is* in the end of the year, when thou hast gathered in thy labours out of the field.

17 Three times in the year all thy males shall appear before the Lord God.

Ex. 34. 18 The feast of unleavened bread shalt thou keep. Seven days thou shalt eat unleavened bread, as I commanded thee, in the time of the month Abib: for in the month Abib thou camest out from Egypt.

Ex. 34. 22 And thou shalt observe the feast of weeks, of the first-fruits of wheat harvest, and the feast of ingathering at the year's end.

23 Thrice in the year shall all your men children appear before the Lord God, the God of Israel.

Lev. 23. 2 Speak unto the children of Israel, and say unto them, *Concerning* the feasts of the LORD, which ye shall proclaim *to be* holy convocations, *even* these *are* my feasts.

Deut.16. 1 Observe the month of Abib, and keep the passover unto the LORD thy God: for in the month of Abib the LORD thy God brought thee forth out of Egypt by night.

John 2. 13 And the Jews' passover was at hand, and Jesus went up to Jerusalem.

B

Neh. 3. 1 Then Elishib the high priest rose up with his brethren the priests, and they builded the sheep gate; they sanctified it, and set up the doors of it; even unto the tower of Meah they sanctified it, unto the tower of Hananeel.

Neh. 12. 39 And from above the gate of Ephraim, and above the old gate, and above the fish gate, and the tower of Hananeel, and the tower of Meah, even unto the sheep gate: and they stood still in the prison gate.

1

Or, *gate*.

C

Isa. 22. 9 Ye have seen also the breaches of the city of David, that they are many: and ye gathered together the waters of the lower pool.

10 And ye have numbered the houses of Jerusalem, and the houses have ye broken down to fortify the wall.

11 Ye made also a ditch between the two walls for the water of the old pool: but ye have not looked unto the maker thereof, neither had respect unto him that fashioned it long ago.

2

That is, *House of mercy*.

D

Ps. 119. 60 I made haste, and delayed not to keep thy commandments.

Prov. 6. 4 Give not sleep to thine eyes, nor slumber to thine eyelids.

Eccl. 9. 10 Whatsoever thy hand findeth to do, do *it* with thy might; for *there is* no work, nor device, nor knowledge, nor wisdom, in the grave, whither thou goest.

E

Heb. 4. 13 Neither is there any creature that is not manifest in his sight: but all things *are* naked and opened unto the eyes of him with whom we have to do.

F

Ps. 72. 13 He shall spare the poor and needy, and shall save the souls of the needy.

Ps. 113. 5 Who *is* like unto the LORD our God, who dwelleth on high,

6 Who humbleth *himself* to behold *the things that are* in heaven, and in the earth!

G

Matt. 9. 6 But that ye may know that the Son of man hath power on earth to forgive sins, (then saith he to the sick of the palsy,) Arise, take up thy bed, and go unto thine house.

Mark 2. 11 I say unto thee, Arise, and take up thy bed, and go thy way into thine house.

Luke 5. 24 But that ye may know that the Son of man hath power upon earth to forgive sins, (he said unto the sick of the palsy,) I say unto thee, Arise, and take up thy couch, and go into thine house.

H

John 9. 14 And it was the sabbath day when Jesus made the clay, and opened his eyes.

THE POOL OF BETHESDA. TIME, APRIL, A. D. 28; PLACE, JERUSALEM.

I

Ex. 20. 10 But the seventh day *is* the sabbath of the LORD thy God: *in it* thou shalt not do any work, thou, nor thy son, nor thy daughter, thy manservant, nor thy maidservant, nor thy cattle, nor thy stranger that *is* within thy gates:

Neh. 13. 19 And it came to pass, that when the gates of Jerusalem began to be dark before the sabbath, I commanded that the gates should be shut, and charged that they should not be opened till after the sabbath: and *some* of my servants set I at the gates, *that* there should no burden be brought in on the sabbath day.

Jer. 17. 21 Thus saith the LORD; Take heed to yourselves, and bear no burden on the sabbath day, nor bring *it* in by the gates of Jerusalem;

22 Neither carry forth a burden out of your houses on the sabbath day, neither do ye any work, but hallow ye the sabbath day, as I commanded your fathers.

Matt.12. 2 But when the Pharisees saw *it*, they said unto him, Behold, thy disciples do that which is not lawful to do upon the sabbath day.

Mark 2. 24 And the Pharisees said unto him, Behold, why do they on the sabbath day that which is not lawful?

Mark 3. 1 And he entered again into the synagogue; and there was a man there which had a withered hand.

2 And they watched him, whether he would heal him on the sabbath day; that they might accuse him.

3 And he saith unto the man which had the withered hand, Stand forth.

4 And he saith unto them, Is it lawful to do good on the sabbath days, or to do evil? to save life, or to kill? But they held their peace.

Luke 6. 2 And certain of the Pharisees said unto them, Why do ye that which is not lawful to do on the sabbath days?

Luke 13. 14 And the ruler of the synagogue answered with indignation, because that Jesus had healed on the sabbath day, and said unto the people, There are six days in which men ought to work: in them therefore come and be healed, and not on the sabbath day.

John 7. 23 If a man on the sabbath day receive circumcision, that the law of Moses should not be broken; are ye angry at me, because I have made a man every whit whole on the sabbath day?

5: 1–16.

1 After [a]this there was a feast of the Jews; and Jesus went up to Jerusalem.

2 Now there is at Jerusalem [b]by the sheep [1]*market*, a [c]pool, which is called in the Hebrew tongue [2]Bethesda, having five porches.

3 In these lay a great multitude of impotent folk, of blind, halt, withered, waiting for the moving of the water.

4 For an angel went down at a certain season into the pool, and troubled the water: whosoever then [d]first after the troubling of the water stepped in was made whole of whatsoever disease he had.

5 And a certain man was there, which had an infirmity thirty and eight years.

6 When Jesus saw him lie, and [e]knew that he had been now a long time *in that case*, he saith unto him, [f]Wilt thou be made whole?

7 The impotent man answered him, Sir, I have no man, when the water is troubled, to put me into the pool: but while I am coming, another steppeth down before me.

8 Jesus saith unto him, [g]Rise, take up thy bed, and walk.

9 And immediately the man was made whole, and took up his bed, and walked: and [h]on the same day was the sabbath.

10 The Jews therefore said unto him that was cured, It is the sabbath day: [i]it is not lawful for thee to carry *thy* bed.

11 He answered them, He that made me whole, the same said unto me, Take up thy bed, and walk.

§ 37. THE SECOND PASSOVER. HEALING OF THE IMPOTENT MAN AT

3

Or, *from the multitude that was.*

K

Ps. 103. 2 Bless the LORD, O my soul, and forget not all his benefits:

L

Ezr. 9. 13 And after all that is come upon us for our evil deeds, and for our great trespass, seeing that thou our God hast punished us less than our iniquities *deserve*, and hast given us *such* deliverance as this;

14 Should we again break thy commandments, and join in affinity with the people of these abominations? wouldest not thou be angry with us till thou hadst consumed *us*, so that *there should be* no remnant nor escaping?

Neh. 9. 28 But after they had rest, they did evil again before thee: therefore leftest thou them in the hand of their enemies, so that they had the dominion over them: yet when they returned, and cried unto thee, thou heardest *them* from heaven; and many times didst thou deliver them according to thy mercies;

Matt.12. 45 Then goeth he, And taketh with himself seven other spirits more wicked than himself, and they enter in and

L—CONCLUDED.

dwell there: and the last *state* of that man is worse than the first. Even so shall it be also unto this wicked generation.

John 8. 11 She said, No man, Lord. And Jesus said unto her, Neither do I condemn thee: go, and sin no more.

I Pet. 4. 3 For the time past of *our* life may suffice us to have wrought the will of the Gentiles, when we walked in lasciviousness, lusts, excess of wine, revellings, banquetings, and abominable idolatries:

4 Wherein they think it strange that ye run not with *them* to the same excess of riot, speaking evil of *you:*

5 Who shall give account to him that is ready to judge the quick and the dead.

M

Lev. 26. 23 And if ye will not be reformed by me by these things, but will walk contrary unto me;

24 Then will I also walk contrary unto you, and will punish you yet seven times for your sins.

25 And I will bring a sword upon you, that shall avenge the quarrel of *my* covenant: and when ye are gathered together within your cities, I

§ 38. DISCOURSE SUBSEQUENT TO THE MIRACLE AT

A

Gen. 2. 1 Thus the heavens and the earth were finished, and all the host of them.

2 And on the seventh day God ended his work which he had made; and he rested on the seventh day from all his work which he had made.

Ps. 65. 6 Which by his strength setteth fast the mountains; *being* girded with power:

Isa. 40. 26 Lift up your eyes on high, and behold who hath created these *things*, that bringeth out their host by number: he calleth them all by names by the greatness of his might, for that *he is* strong in power; not one faileth.

John 9. 4 I must work the works of him that sent me, while it is day: the night cometh, when no man can work.

John 14. 10 Believest thou not that I am in the Father, and the Father in me? the words that I speak unto you I speak not of myself: but the Father that dwelleth in me, he doeth the works.

B

John 7. 19 Did not Moses give you the law, and *yet* none of you keepeth the law? Why go ye about to kill me?

C

Zech.13. 7 Awake, O sword, against my Shepherd, and against the man *that is* my fellow, saith the LORD of hosts: smite the Shepherd, and the sheep shall be scattered: and I will turn mine hand upon the little ones.

John 10. 30 I and *my* Father are one.

John 10. 33 The Jews answered him, saying, For a good work we stone thee not; but for blasphemy; and because that thou, being a man, makest thyself God.

Phil. 2. 6 Who, being in the form of God, thought it not robbery to be equal with God:

D

John 5. 30. *See text of topic.*

John 8. 28 Then said Jesus unto them, When ye have lifted up the Son of man, then shall ye know that I am *he*, and *that* I do nothing of myself; but as

THE POOL OF BETHESDA (Concluded). Time, April, A. D. 28; Place, Jerusalem.

M—Concluded.

will send the pestilence among you; and ye shall be delivered into the hand of the enemy.

26 *And* when I have broken the staff of your bread, ten women shall bake your bread in one oven, and they shall deliver *you* your bread again by weight: and ye shall eat, and not be satisfied.

27 And if ye will not for all this hearken unto me, but walk contrary unto me;

28 Then I will walk contrary unto you also in fury; and I, even I, will chastise you seven times for your sins.

29 And ye shall eat the flesh of your sons, and the flesh of your daughters shall ye eat.

30 And I will destroy your high places, and cut down your images, and cast your carcasses upon the carcasses of your idols, and my soul shall abhor you.

31 And I will make your cities waste, and bring your sanctuaries unto desolation, and I will not smell the savour of your sweet odours.

32 And I will bring the land into desolation: and your enemies which dwell therein shall be astonished at it.

Chap. 5.

12 Then asked they him, What man is that which said unto thee, Take up thy bed, and walk?

13 And he that was healed wist not who it was: for Jesus had conveyed himself away, [g]a multitude being in *that* place.

14 Afterward Jesus findeth him [k]in the temple, and said unto him, Behold, thou art made whole: [l]sin no more, [m]lest a worse thing come unto thee.

15 The man departed, and told the Jews that it was Jesus, which had made him whole.

16 And therefore did the Jews persecute Jesus, and sought to slay him, because he had done these things on the sabbath day.

BETHESDA. Time, April, A. D. 28; Place, Jerusalem.

D—Concluded.

my Father hath taught me, I speak these things.

John 9. 4. *See under A.*

John 12. 49 For I have not spoken of myself; but the Father which sent me, he gave me a commandment, what I should say, and what I should speak.

John 14. 10. *See under A.*

E

Matt. 3. 17 And lo a voice from heaven, saying, This is my beloved Son, in whom I am well pleased.

Matt. 17. 5 While he yet spake, behold, a bright cloud overshadowed them: and behold a voice out of the cloud, which said, This is my beloved Son, in whom I am well pleased; hear ye him.

John 3. 35 The Father loveth the Son, and hath given all things into his hand.

II Pet. 1. 17 For he received from God the Father honour and glory, when there came such a voice to him from the excellent glory, This is my beloved Son, in whom I am well pleased.

5: 17–47.

17 But Jesus answered them, [a]My Father worketh hitherto, and I work.

18 Therefore the Jews [b]sought the more to kill him, because he not only had broken the sabbath, but said also that God was his Father, [c]making himself equal with God.

19 Then answered Jesus and said unto them, Verily, verily, I say unto you, [d]The Son can do nothing of himself, but what he seeth the Father do: for what things soever he doeth, these also doeth the Son likewise.

20 For [e]the Father loveth the Son, and showeth him all things that himself doeth: and he will show him

§ 38. DISCOURSE SUBSEQUENT TO THE MIRACLE AT BETHESDA

F

Luke 7. 14 And he came and touched the bier: and they that bare *him* stood still. And he said, Young man, I say unto thee, Arise.

Luke 8. 54 And he put them all out, and took her by the hand, and called, saying, Maid, arise.

John 11. 25 Jesus said unto her, I am the resurrection, and the life: he that believeth in me, though he were dead, yet shall he live:

John 11. 43 And when he thus had spoken, he cried with a loud voice, Lazarus, come forth.

G

Matt. 11. 27 All things are delivered unto me of my Father: and no man knoweth the Son, but the Father; neither knoweth any man the Father, save the Son, and *he* to whomsoever the Son will reveal *him*.

Matt. 28. 18 And Jesus came and spake unto them, saying, All power is given unto me in heaven and in earth.

John 3. 35. *See under E, page 109.*
John 5. 27. *See text of topic.*

John 17. 2 As thou hast given him power over all flesh, that he should give eternal life to as many as thou hast given him.

Acts 17. 31 Because he hath appointed a day, in the which he will judge the world in righteousness by *that* man whom he hath ordained: *whereof* he hath given assurance unto all *men*, in that he hath raised him from the dead.

I Pet. 4. 5 Who shall give account to him that is ready to judge the quick and the dead.

H

Matt. 28. 19 Go ye therefore, and teach all nations, baptizing them in the name of the Father, and of the Son, and of the Holy Ghost:

I Jno. 2. 23 Whosoever denieth the Son, the same hath not the Father: [*but*] *he that acknowledgeth the Son hath the Father also.*

Rev. 5. 8 And when he had taken the book, the four beasts and four *and* twenty elders fell down before the Lamb, having every one of them harps, and golden vials full of odours, which are the prayers of saints.

I

John 3. 16 For God so loved the world, that he gave his only begotten Son, that whosoever believeth in him should not perish, but have everlasting life.

I—Concluded.

John 3. 18. *See text of § 22.*

John 6. 40 And this is the will of him that sent me, that every one which seeth the Son, and believeth on him, may have everlasting life: and I will raise him up at the last day.

John 6. 47 Verily, verily, I say unto you, He that believeth on me hath everlasting life.

John 8. 51 Verily, verily, I say unto you, If a man keep my saying, he shall never see death.

John 20. 31 But these are written, that ye might believe that Jesus is the Christ, the Son of God; and that believing ye might have life through his name.

K

I Jno. 3. 14 We know that we have passed from death unto life, because we love the brethren. He that loveth not *his* brother abideth in death.

L

John 5. 28. *See text of topic.*

Gal. 2. 20 I am crucified with Christ: nevertheless I live: yet not I, but Christ liveth in me: and the life which I now live in the flesh I live by the faith of the Son of God, who loved me, and gave himself for me.

Eph. 2. 1 And you *hath he quickened*, who were dead in trespasses and sins;

Eph. 2. 5 Even when we were dead in sins, hath quickened us together with Christ, (by grace ye are saved;)

Eph. 5. 14. Wherefore he saith, Awake thou that sleepest, and arise from the dead, and Christ shall give thee light.

Col. 2. 13 And you, being dead in your sins and the uncircumcision of your flesh, hath he quickened together with him, having forgiven you all trespasses;

Rev. 3. 1 And unto the angel of the church in Sardis write; These things saith he that hath the seven Spirits of God, and the seven stars; I know thy works, that thou hast a name that thou livest, and art dead.

M

Jer. 10. 10 But the Lord *is* the true God, he *is* the living God, and an everlasting King: at his wrath the earth shall tremble, and the nations shall not be able to abide his indignation.

John 5. 22. *See text of topic.*

Acts 10. 42 And he commanded us to preach unto the people, and to testify that it is he which was ordained of God *to be* the Judge of quick and dead.

(CONTINUED). TIME, APRIL, A. D. 28; PLACE, JERUSALEM.

M—CONCLUDED.

Acts 17. 31. *See under G.*

1 Pet. 3. 22 Who is gone into heaven, and is on the right hand of God; angels and authorities and powers being made subject unto him.

N

Dan. 7. 13 I saw in the night visions, and, behold, *one* like the Son of man came with the clouds of heaven, and came to the Ancient of days, and they brought him near before him.

14 And there was given him dominion, and glory, and a kingdom, that all people, nations, and languages, should serve him: his dominion *is* an everlasting dominion, which shall not pass away, and his kingdom *that* which shall not be destroyed.

O

Isa. 26. 19 Thy dead *men* shall live, *together with* my dead body shall they arise. Awake and sing, ye that dwell in dust: for thy dew *is as* the dew of herbs, and the earth shall cast out the dead.

I Cor.15. 52 In a moment, in the twinkling of an eye, at the last trump: for the trumpet shall sound, and the dead shall be raised incorruptible, and we shall be changed.

I Thes.4. 16 For the Lord himself shall descend from heaven with a shout, with the voice of the archangel, and with the trump of God: and the dead in Christ shall rise first:

P

Dan. 12. 2 And many of them that sleep in the dust of the earth shall awake, some to everlasting life, and some to shame *and* everlasting contempt.

Matt.25. 32 And before him shall be gathered all nations: and he shall separate them one from another, as a shepherd divideth *his* sheep from the goats:

33 And he shall set the sheep on his right hand, but the goats on the left.

Matt.25. 46 And these shall go away into everlasting punishment: but the righteous into life eternal.

Q

John 5. 19. *See text of topic.*

R

Matt.26. 39 And he went a little further, and fell on his face, and prayed, saying, O my Father, if it be possible, let this cup pass from me: nevertheless, not as I will, but as thou *wilt.*

For R concluded see next page (112).

CHAP. 5.

greater works than these, that ye may
marvel.
21 For as the Father raiseth up the
dead, and quickeneth *them;* [f]even so
the Son quickeneth whom he will.
22 For the Father judgeth no man,
but [g]hath committed all judgment
unto the Son:
23 That all *men* should [h]honour the
Son, even as they honour the Father.
He that honoureth not the Son honoureth not the Father which hath sent
him.
24 Verily, verily, I say unto you,
[i]He that heareth my word, and believeth on him that sent me, hath
everlasting life, and shall not come
into condemnation; [k]but is passed from
death unto life.
25 Verily, verily, I say unto you,
The hour is coming, and now is, when
[l]the dead shall hear the voice of the
Son of God: and they that hear shall
live.
26 For as the Father hath life in
himself; so hath he given to the Son
to have life in himself,
27 And [m]hath given him authority
to execute judgment also, [n]because he
is the Son of man.
28 Marvel not at this: for the hour
is coming, in the which all that are in
the graves shall hear his voice,
29 [o]And shall come forth; [p]they that
have done good, unto the resurrection
of life; and they that have done evil,
unto the resurrection of damnation.
30 [q]I can of mine own self do
nothing: as I hear, I judge: and my

§ 38. DISCOURSE SUBSEQUENT TO THE MIRACLE AT BETHESDA

R—CONCLUDED. See preceding page (111).

John 4. 34 Jesus saith unto them, My meat is to do the will of him that sent me, and to finish his work.

John 6. 38 For I came down from heaven, not to do mine own will, but the will of him that sent me.

S

John 8. 14 Jesus answered and said unto them, Though I bear record of myself, *yet* my record is true: for I know whence I came, and whither I go; but ye cannot tell whence I come, and whither I go.

Rev. 3. 14 And unto the angel of the church of the Laodiceans write; These things saith the Amen, the faithful and true witness, the beginning of the creation of God;

T

Matt. 3. 17 And lo a voice from heaven, saying, This is my beloved Son, in whom I am well pleased.

Matt. 17. 5 While he yet spake, behold, a bright cloud overshadowed them: and behold a voice out of the cloud, which said, This is my beloved Son, in whom I am well pleased; hear ye him.

John 8. 18 I am one that bear witness of myself, and the Father that sent me beareth witness of me.

I Jno. 5. 6 This is he that came by water and blood, *even* Jesus Christ: not by water only, but by water and blood. And it is the Spirit that beareth witness, because the Spirit is truth.

7 For there are three that bear record in heaven, the Father, the Word, and the Holy Ghost: and these three are one.

I Jno. 5. 9 If we receive the witness of men, the witness of God is greater: for this is the witness of God which he hath testified of his Son.

U

John 1. 15 John bare witness of him, and cried, saying, This was he of whom I spake, He that cometh after me is preferred before me; for he was before me.

John 1. 19 And this is the record of John, when the Jews sent priests and Levites from Jerusalem to ask him, Who art thou?

John 1. 27 He it is, who coming after me is preferred before me, whose shoe's latchet I am not worthy to unloose.

John 1. 32 And John bare record, saying, I saw the Spirit descending from heaven like a dove, and it abode upon him.

X

II Pet. 1. 19 We have also a more sure word of prophecy; whereunto ye do well that ye take heed, as unto a light that shineth in a dark place, until the day dawn, and the daystar arise in your hearts:

Y

Eze. 33. 31 And they come unto thee as the people cometh, and they sit before thee *as* my people, and they hear thy words, but they will not do them: for with their mouth they show much love, *but* their heart goeth after their covetousness.

32 And, lo, thou *art* unto them as a very lovely song of one that hath a pleasant voice, and can play well on an instrument: for they hear thy words, but they do them not.

Matt. 13. 20 But he that received the seed into stony places, the same is he that heareth the word, and anon with joy receiveth it:

Matt. 21. 26 But if we shall say, Of men; we fear the people; for all hold John as a prophet.

Mark 6. 20 For Herod feared John, knowing that he was a just man and a holy, and observed him; and when he heard him, he did many things, and heard him gladly.

Z

I Jno. 5. 9. *See under T.*

A

John 3. 2 The same came to Jesus by night, and said unto him, Rabbi, we know that thou art a teacher come from God: for no man can do these miracles that thou doest, except God be with him.

John 10. 25 Jesus answered them, I told you, and ye believed not: the works that I do in my Father's name, they bear witness of me.

John 15. 24 If I had not done among them the works which none other man did, they had not had sin: but now have they both seen and hated both me and my Father.

B

Matt. 3. 17. *See under T.*
Matt. 17. 5. *See under T.*

John 6. 27 Labor not for the meat which perisheth, but for that meat which endureth unto everlasting life, which the Son of man shall give unto you: for him hath God the Father sealed.

John 8. 18. *See under T.*
I Jno. 5. 6. *See under T.*

(CONTINUED). TIME, APRIL, A. D. 28; PLACE, JERUSALEM.

C

Ex. 33. 17 And the LORD said unto Moses, I will do this thing also that thou hast spoken: for thou hast found grace in my sight, and I know thee by name.

18 And he said, I beseech thee, show me thy glory.

19 And he said, I will make all my goodness pass before thee, and I will proclaim the name of the LORD before thee; and will be gracious to whom I will be gracious, and will show mercy on whom I will show mercy.

20 And he said, Thou canst not see my face: for there shall no man see me, and live.

21 And the LORD said, Behold, *there is* a place by me, and thou shalt stand upon a rock:

22 And it shall come to pass, while my glory passeth by, that I will put thee in a cleft of the rock, and will cover thee with my hand while I pass by:

23 And I will take away mine hand, and thou shalt see my back parts; but my face shall not be seen.

Deut. 4. 12 And the LORD spake unto you out of the midst of the fire: ye heard the voice of the words, but saw no similitude; only *ye heard* a voice.

John 1. 18 No man hath seen God at any time; the only begotten Son, which is in the bosom of the Father, he hath declared *him*.

John 14. 9 Jesus saith unto him, Have I been so long time with you, and yet hast thou not known me, Philip? he that hath seen me hath seen the Father; and how sayest thou *then*, Show us the Father?

I Tim. 1. 17 Now unto the King eternal, immortal, invisible, the only wise God, *be* honour and glory for ever and ever. Amen.

I Tim. 6. 15 Which in his times he shall show, *who is* the blessed and only Potentate, the King of kings, and Lord of lords;

16 Who only hath immortality, dwelling in the light which no man can approach unto; whom no man hath seen, nor can see: to whom *be* honour and power everlasting. Amen.

I Jno. 1. 1 That which was from the begining, which we have heard, which we have seen with our eyes, which we have looked upon, and our hands have handled, of the Word of life;

2 (For the life was manifested, and

CHAP. 5.

judgment is just; because [r]I seek not
mine own will, but the will of the
Father which hath sent me.
31 [s]If I bear witness of myself, my
witness is not true.
32 [t]There is another that beareth
witness of me; and I know that the
witness which he witnesseth of me is
true.
33 Ye sent unto John, [u]and he bare
witness unto the truth.
34 But I receive not testimony from
man: but these things I say, that ye
might be saved.
35 He was a burning and [x]a shining
light: and [y]ye were willing for a season to rejoice in his light.
36 But [z]I have greater witness than
that of John: for [a]the works which
the Father hath given me to finish, the
same works that I do, bear witness of
me, that the Father hath sent me.
37 And the Father himself, which
hath sent me, [b]hath borne witness of
me. Ye have neither heard his voice
at any time, [c]nor seen his shape.
38 And ye have not his word abiding in you: for whom he hath sent,
him ye believe not

C—CONCLUDED.

we have seen *it*, and bear witness, and show unto you that eternal life, which was with the Father, and was manifested unto us;)

I Jno. 4. 12 No man hath seen God at any time. If we love one another, God dwelleth in us, and his love is perfected in us.

I Jno. 4. 20 If a man say, I love God, and hateth his brother, he is a liar: for he that loveth not his brother whom he hath seen, how can he love God whom he hath not seen?

§ 38. DISCOURSE SUBSEQUENT TO THE MIRACLE AT BETHESDA

D

Deut. 11. 18 Therefore shall ye lay up these my words in your heart and in your soul, and bind them for a sign upon your hand, that they may be as frontlets between your eyes.

19 And ye shall teach them your children, speaking of them when thou sittest in thine house, and when thou walkest by the way, when thou liest down, and when thou risest up.

20 And thou shalt write them upon the door posts of thine house, and upon thy gates:

21 That your days may be multiplied, and the days of your children, in the land which the LORD sware unto your fathers to give them, as the days of heaven upon the earth.

Josh. 1. 8 This book of the law shall not depart out of thy mouth; but thou shalt meditate therein day and night, that thou mayest observe to do according to all that is written therein: for then thou shalt make thy way prosperous, and then thou shalt have good success.

Ps. 1. 2 But his delight *is* in the law of the LORD; and in his law doth he meditate day and night.

Ps. 119. 11 Thy word have I hid in mine heart, that I might not sin against thee.

Prov. 6. 23 For the commandment *is* a lamp; and the law *is* light; and reproofs of instruction *are* the way of life;

Prov. 8. 33 Hear instruction, and be wise, and refuse it not.

Isa. 8. 20 To the law and to the testimony: if they speak not according to this word, *it is* because *there is* no light in them.

Isa. 34. 16 Seek ye out of the book of the LORD, and read: no one of these shall fail, none shall want her mate: for my mouth it hath commanded, and his spirit it hath gathered them.

D—CONCLUDED.

Luke 16. 29 Abraham saith unto him, They have Moses and the prophets; let them hear them.

John 5. 46. *See text of topic.*

Acts 17. 11 These were more noble than those in Thessalonica, in that they received the word with all readiness of mind, and searched the Scriptures daily, whether those things were so.

E

Deut. 18. 15 The LORD thy God will raise up unto thee a Prophet from the midst of thee, of thy brethren, like unto me; unto him ye shall hearken;

Deut. 18. 18 I will raise them up a Prophet from among their brethren, like unto thee, and will put my words in his mouth; and he shall speak unto them all that I shall command him.

Luke 24. 27 And beginning at Moses and all the prophets, he expounded unto them in all the Scriptures the things concerning himself.

Luke 24. 44 And he said unto them, These *are* the words which I spake unto you, while I was yet with you, that all things must be fulfilled, which were written in the law of Moses, and *in* the prophets, and *in* the psalms, concerning me.

John 1. 45 Philip findeth Nathanael, and saith unto him, We have found him, of whom Moses in the law, and the prophets, did write, Jesus of Nazareth, the son of Joseph.

F

John 1. 11 He came into his own, and his own received him not.

John 3. 19 And this is the condemnation, that light is come into the world, and men loved darkness rather than light, because their deeds were evil.

§ 39. PLUCKING EARS OF CORN ON THE SABBATH.

12: 1–8.

1 At that time [a]Jesus went on the sabbath day through the corn; and his disciples were a hungered, and began to pluck the ears of corn, and to eat.

A

Deut. 23. 25. *See under C.*
Mark. 2. 23. *See text of topic.*
Luke 6. 1. *See text of topic.*

2: 23–28.

23 [b]And it came to pass, that he went through the corn fields on the sabbath day; and his disciples began, as they went, to pluck the ears of corn.

B

Deut. 23. 25. *See under C.*
Matt. 12. 1. *See text of topic.*
Luke 6. 1. *See text of topic.*

(CONCLUDED). TIME, APRIL, A. D. 28; PLACE, JERUSALEM.

G

John 5. 34. *See text of topic.*

I Thes.2. 6 Nor of men sought we glory, neither of you, nor *yet* of others, when we might have been burdensome, as the apostles of Christ.

H

John 12. 43 For they loved the praise of men more than the praise of God.

I

Rom. 2. 29 But he *is* a Jew, which is one inwardly; and circumcision *is that* of the heart, in the spirit, *and* not in the letter; whose praise *is* not of men, but of God.

K

Rom. 2. 12 For as many as have sinned without law shall also perish without law; and as many as have sinned in the law shall be judged by the law;

L

Gen. 3. 15 And I will put enmity between thee and the woman, and between thy seed and her seed; it shall bruise thy head, and thou shalt bruise his heel.

Gen. 12. 3 And I will bless them that bless thee, and curse him that curseth thee: and in thee shall all families of the earth be blessed.

Gen. 18. 18 Seeing that Abraham shall surely become a great and mighty nation, and all the nations of the earth shall be blessed in him?

Gen. 22. 18 And in thy seed shall all the nations of the earth be blessed; because thou hast obeyed my voice.

Gen. 49. 10 The sceptre shall not depart from Judah, nor a lawgiver from between his feet, until Shiloh come; and unto him *shall* the gathering of the people *be*.

Deut. 18. 15, 18 and John 1. 45. *See under E.*

Acts 26. 22 Having therefore obtained help of God, I continue unto this day, wit-

CHAP. 5.

39 [d]Search the Scriptures; for in them ye think ye have eternal life: and [e]they are they which testify of me.

40 [f]And ye will not come to me, that ye might have life.

41 [g]I receive not honour from men.

42 But I know you, that ye have not the love of God in you.

43 I am come in my Father's name, and ye receive me not: if another shall come in his own name, him ye will receive.

44 [h]How can ye believe, which receive honour one of another, and seek not [i]the honour that *cometh* from God only?

45 Do not think that I will accuse you to the Father: [k]there is *one* that accuseth you, *even* Moses, in whom ye trust.

46 For had ye believed Moses, ye would have believed me; [l]for he wrote of me.

47 But if ye believe not his writings, how shall ye believe my words? p. 245.

L—CONCLUDED.

nessing both to small and great, saying none other things than those which the prophets and Moses did say should come:

TIME, APRIL–MAY, A. D. 28; PLACE, ON THE WAY TO GALILEE.

6: 1–5.

1 And it [c]came to pass on the second sabbath after the first, that he went through the corn fields; and his disciples plucked the ears of corn, and did eat, rubbing *them* in *their* hands.

C

Deut.23. 24 When thou comest into thy neighbour's vineyard, then thou mayest eat

C—CONCLUDED.

grapes thy fill at thine own pleasure; but thou shalt not put *any* in thy vessel.

25 When thou comest into the standing corn of thy neighbour, then thou mayest pluck the ears with thine hand; but thou shalt not move a sickle unto thy neighbour's standing corn.

Mark 2. 23. *See text of topic.*

Luke 6. 1. *See text of topic.*

§ 39. PLUCKING EARS OF CORN ON THE SABBATH (CONCLUDED).

CHAP. 12.

2 But when the Pharisees saw *it*, they said unto him, Behold, thy disciples do that which is not lawful to do upon the sabbath day.

3 But he said unto them, Have ye not read [d]what David did, when he was a hungered, and they that were with him;

4 How he entered into the house of God, and did eat [e] the showbread, which was not lawful for him to eat, neither for them which were with him, [f]but only for the priests?

5 Or have ye not read in the [g]law, how that on the sabbath days the priests in the temple profane the sabbath, and are blameless?

6 But I say unto you, That in this place is [h]*one* greater than the temple.

7 But if ye had known what *this* meaneth, [i]I will have mercy, and not sacrifice, ye would not have condemned the guiltless.

8 For the [k]Son of man is Lord even of the sabbath day.

CHAP. 2.

24 And the Pharisees said unto him, Behold, why do they on the sabbath day that which is not lawful?

25 And he said unto them, Have ye never read [l]what David did, when he had need, and was a hungered, he, and they that were with him?

26 How he went into the house of God in the days of Abiathar the high priest, and did eat the showbread, [m]which is not lawful to eat but for the priests, and gave also to them which were with him?

27 And he said unto them, The sabbath was made for man, and not man for the sabbath:

28 Therefore [n]the Son of man is Lord also of the sabbath.

D

1 Sa 21. 3 Now therefore what is under thine hand? give *me* five *loaves of* bread in mine hand, or what there is present.

4 And the priest answered David, and said, *There is* no common bread under mine hand, but there is hallowed bread; if the young men have kept themselves at least from women.

5 And David answered the priest, and said unto him, Of a truth women *have been* kept from us about these three days, since I came out, and the vessels of the young men are holy, and *the bread is* in a manner common, yea, though it were sanctified this day in the vessel.

6 So the priest gave him hallowed *bread:* for there was no bread there but the showbread, that was taken

D—CONCLUDED.

from before the LORD, to put hot bread in the day when it was taken away.

E

Ex. 25. 30 And thou shalt set upon the table showbread before me always.

Lev. 24. 5 And thou shalt take fine flour, and bake twelve cakes thereof: two tenth deals shall be in one cake.

6 And thou shalt set them in two rows, six on a row, upon the pure table before the LORD.

7 And thou shalt put pure frankincense upon *each* row, that it may be on the bread for a memorial, *even* an offering made by fire unto the LORD.

F

Ex. 29. 32 And Aaron and his sons shall eat the flesh of the ram, and the bread that *is* in the basket, *by* the door of the tabernacle of the congregation.

33 And they shall eat those things wherewith the atonement was made, to consecrate *and* to sanctify them: but a stranger shall not eat *thereof*, because they *are* holy.

Lev. 8. 31 And Moses said unto Aaron and to his sons, Boil the flesh *at* the door of the tabernacle of the congregation; and there eat it with the bread that *is*

TIME, APRIL–MAY, A. D. 28; PLACE, ON THE WAY TO GALILEE.

CHAP. 6.

2 And certain of the Pharisees said
unto them, Why do ye that [o]which is
not lawful to do on the sabbath days?
3 And Jesus answering them said,
Have ye not read so much as this,
[p]what David did, when himself was a
hungered, and they which were with him;
4 How he went into the house of
of God, and did take and eat the
showbread, and gave also to them that
were with him; [q]which it is not lawful
to eat but for the priests alone?
5 And he said unto them, That the
Son of man is Lord also of the sabbath.

F—CONCLUDED.

in the basket of consecrations, as I commanded, saying, Aaron and his sons shall eat it.

Lev. 24. 9 And it shall be Aaron's and his sons'; and they shall eat it in the holy place: for it *is* most holy unto him of the offerings of the LORD made by fire by a perpetual statute.

G

Num. 28. 9 And on the sabbath day two lambs of the first year without spot, and two tenth deals of flour *for* a meat offering, mingled with oil, and the drink offering thereof:

10 *This is* the burnt offering of every sabbath, beside the continual burnt offering, and his drink offering.

John 7. 22 Moses therefore gave unto you circumcision; (not because it is of Moses, but of the fathers;) and ye on the sabbath day circumcise a man.

H

II Chr. 6. 18 But will God in very deed dwell with men on the earth? Behold, heaven and the heaven of heavens cannot contain thee; how much less this house which I have built!

Mal. 3. 1 Behold, I will send my messenger, and he shall prepare the way before me: and the Lord, whom ye seek, shall suddenly come to his temple, even the messenger of the covenant, whom ye delight in. behold, he shall come, saith the LORD of hosts.

I

Hos. 6. 6 For I desired mercy, and not sacrifice; and the knowledge of God more than burnt offerings.

Mic. 6. 6 Wherewith shall I come before the LORD, *and* bow myself before the high God? shall I come before him with burnt offerings, with calves of a year old?

7 Will the LORD be pleased with thousands of rams, *or* with ten thousands of rivers of oil? shall I give my first-born *for* my transgression, the fruit of my body *for* the sin of my soul?

8 He hath showed thee, O man, what *is* good; and what doth the LORD require of thee, but to do justly, and to love mercy, and to walk humbly with thy God?

Matt. 9. 13 But go ye and learn what *that* meaneth, I will have mercy, and not sacrifice: for I am not come to call the righteous, but sinners to repentance.

K

Dan. 7. 13 I saw in the night visions, and, behold, *one* like the Son of man came with the clouds of heaven, and came to the Ancient of days, and they brought him near before him.

L

Isa. 21. 6. *See under D.*

M

Ex. 25. 30. *See under E.*
Ex. 29. 32, 33. *See under F.*
Lev. 24. 9. *See under F.*

N

Matt. 12. 8. *See text of topic.*

O

Ex. 20. 10 But the seventh day *is* the sabbath of the LORD thy God: *in it* thou shalt not do any work, thou, nor thy son, nor thy daughter, thy manservant, nor thy maidservant, nor thy cattle, nor thy stranger that *is* within thy gates:

Mark 7. 2 And when they saw some of his disciples eat bread with defiled, that is to say, with unwashen hands, they found fault.

P

I Sa. 21. 6. *See under D.*

Q

Ex. 29. 23 And one loaf of bread, and one cake of oiled bread, and one wafer out of the basket of the unleavened bread that *is* before the LORD:

24 And thou shalt put all in the hands of Aaron, and in the hands of his sons; and shalt wave them *for* a wave offering before the LORD.

Ex. 29. 33 and Lev. 24. 9. *See under F.*

§ 40. THE WITHERED HAND HEALED ON THE SABBATH.

12 : 9–14.

9 [a]And when he was departed thence, he went into their synagogue:

10 And, behold, there was a man which had *his* hand withered. And they asked him, saying, [b]Is it lawful to heal on the sabbath days? that they might accuse him.

11 And he said unto them, What man shall there be among you, that shall have one sheep, and [c]if it fall into a pit on the sabbath day, will he not lay hold on it, and lift *it* out?

12 How much then is a man better than a sheep? Wherefore it is lawful to do well on the sabbath days.

13 Then saith he to the man, Stretch forth thine hand. And he stretched *it* forth; and it was restored whole, like as the other.

14 Then [d]the Pharisees went out, and [1]held a council against him, how they might destroy him.

A

Mark 3. 1 and Luke 6. 6. *See text of topic.*

B

Luke 13. 14 And the ruler of the synagogue answered with indignation, because that Jesus had healed on the sabbath day, and said unto the people, There are six days in which men ought to work: in them therefore come and be healed, and not on the sabbath day.

Luke 14. 3 And Jesus answering spake unto the lawyers and Pharisees, saying, Is it lawful to heal on the sabbath day?

John 9. 16 Therefore said some of the Pharisees, This man is not of God, because he keepeth not the sabbath day. Others said, How can a man that is a sinner do such miracles? And there was a division among them.

C

Ex. 23. 4 If thou meet thine enemy's ox or his ass going astray, thou shalt surely bring it back to him again.

5 If thou see the ass of him that hateth thee lying under his burden,

3 : 1–6.

1 And [e]he entered again into the synagogue; and there was a man there which had a withered hand.

2 And they watched him, whether he would heal him on the sabbath day; that they might accuse him.

3 And he saith unto the man which had the withered hand, [2]Stand forth.

4 And he saith unto them, Is it lawful to do good on the sabbath days, or to do evil? to save life or to kill? But they held their peace.

5 And when he had looked round about on them with [f]anger, being grieved for the [3]hardness of their hearts, he saith unto the man, Stretch forth thine hand. And he stretched *it* out: and his hand was restored whole as the other.

6 [g]And the Pharisees went forth, and straightway took counsel with [h]the Herodians against him, how they might destroy him.

C—CONCLUDED.

and wouldest forbear to help him, thou shalt surely help with him.

Deut. 22. 4 Thou shalt not see thy brother's ass or his ox fall down by the way, and hide thyself from them: thou shalt surely help him to lift *them* up again.

D

Matt. 27. 1 When the morning was come, all the chief priests and elders of the people took counsel against Jesus to put him to death:

Mark 3. 6. *See text of topic.*

Luke 6. 11. *See text of topic.*

John 5. 18 Therefore the Jews sought the more to kill him, because he not only had broken the sabbath, but said also that God was his Father, making himself equal with God.

John 10. 39 Therefore they sought again to take him; but he escaped out of their hand,

TIME, APRIL–MAY, A. D. 28; PLACE, GALILEE.

6 : 6–11.

6 [i]And it came to pass also on another sabbath, that he entered into the synagogue and taught: and there was a man whose right hand was withered.

7 And the scribes and Pharisees watched him, whether he would heal on the sabbath day; that they might find an accusation against him.

8 But he [k]knew their thoughts, and said to the man which had the withered hand, Rise up, and stand forth in the midst. And he arose and stood forth.

9 Then said Jesus unto them, I will ask you one thing; [l]Is it lawful on the sabbath days to do good, or to do evil? to save life, or to destroy *it?*

10 And looking round about upon them all, he said unto the man, Stretch forth thy hand. And he did so: and his hand was restored whole as the other.

11 And they were filled with madness; and communed one with another what they might do to Jesus.

(p. 123.)

D—CONCLUDED.

John 11. 53 Then from that day forth they took counsel together for to put him to death.

1

Or, *took counsel.*

E

Matt. 12. 9 and Luke 6. 6. *See text of topic.*

2

Or, *Arise, stand forth in the midst.*

Dan. 6. 10 Now when Daniel knew that the writing was signed, he went into his house; and, his windows being open in his chamber toward Jerusalem, he kneeled upon his knees three times a day, and prayed, and gave thanks before his God, as he did aforetime.

Phil. 1. 14 And many of the brethren in the Lord, waxing confident by my bonds,

2—CONCLUDED.

are much more bold to speak the word without fear.

F

Ps. 69. 9 For the zeal of thine house hath eaten me up; and the reproaches of them that reproached thee are fallen upon me.

3

Or, *blindness.*

G

Matt. 12. 14. *See text of topic.*

H

Matt. 22. 16 And they sent out unto him their disciples with the Herodians, saying, Master, we know that thou art true, and teachest the way of God in truth, neither carest thou for any *man:* for thou regardest not the person of men.

I

Matt. 12. 9 and Mark 3. 1. *See text of topic.*
Luke 13. 14, Luke 14. 3 and John 9. 16. *See under B.*

K

I Sa. 16. 7 But the LORD said unto Samuel, Look not on his countenance, or on the height of his stature; because I have refused him: for *the LORD seeth* not as man seeth; for man looketh on the outward appearance, but the LORD looketh on the heart.

John 2. 24 But Jesus did not commit himself unto them, because he knew all *men,*

25 And needed not that any should testify of man; for he knew what was in man.

John 21. 17 He saith unto him the third time, Simon, *son* of Jonas, lovest thou me? Peter was grieved because he said unto him the third time, Lovest thou me? And he said unto him, Lord, thou knowest all things; thou knowest that I love thee. Jesus saith unto him, Feed my sheep.

Acts 1. 24 And they prayed, and said, Thou, Lord, which knowest the hearts of all *men,* show whether of these two thou hast chosen.

Rev. 2. 23 And I will kill her children with death; and all the churches shall know that I am he which searcheth the reins and hearts: and I will give unto every one of you according to your works.

L

John 7. 23 If a man on the sabbath day receive circumcision, that the law of Moses should not be broken; are ye angry at me, because I have made a man every whit whole on the sabbath day?

§ 41. JESUS ARRIVES AT THE SEA OF TIBERIUS FOLLOWED BY

12: 15–21.

15 But when Jesus [a]knew *it*, [b]he withdrew himself from thence: [c]and great multitudes followed him, and he healed them all;

16 And [d]charged them that they should not make him known:

17 That it might be [e]fulfilled which was spoken by Esaias the prophet, saying,

18 [f]Behold [g]my servant, whom I have chosen; my beloved, [h]in whom my soul is well pleased: I will put [i]my Spirit upon him, and he shall show judgment to the Gentiles.

19 He shall not strive, nor cry; neither shall any man hear his voice in the streets.

20 A [k]bruised reed shall he not break, and smoking flax shall he not quench, till he send forth judgment unto victory.

21 And in his name shall the Gentiles trust. (p. 166.)

3: 7–12.

7 But Jesus withdrew himself with his disciples to the sea; and a great multitude from Galilee followed him, [l]and from Judæa,

8 And from Jerusalem, and from Idumæa, and *from* beyond Jordan, and they about Tyre and Sidon, a great multitude, when they had heard what great things he did, came unto him.

9 And he spake to his disciples, that a small ship should wait on him because of the multitude, lest they should throng him.

10 For he had healed many; insomuch that they [1]pressed upon him for to touch him, as many as had plagues.

11 [m]And unclean spirits, when they saw him, fell down before him, and cried, saying, [n]Thou art the Son of God.

12 And [o]he straitly charged them that they should not make him known.

A

Ps. 139. 2 Thou knowest my downsitting and mine uprising: thou understandest my thought afar off.

Heb. 4. 13 Neither is there any creature that is not manifest in his sight: but all things *are* naked and opened unto the eyes of him with whom we have to do.

B

Matt. 10. 23 But when they persecute you in this city, flee ye into another: for verily I say unto you, Ye shall not have gone over the cities of Israel, till the Son of man be come.

Mark 3. 7. *See text of topic.*

C

Matt. 19. 2 And great multitudes followed him; and he healed them there.

D

Matt. 9. 30 And their eyes were opened; and Jesus straitly charged them, saying, See *that* no man know *it*.

E

Num. 23. 19 God *is* not a man, that he should lie; neither the son of man, that he should repent: hath he said, and shall he not do *it?* or hath he spoken, and shall he not make it good?

F

Isa. 42. 1. Behold my servant, whom I uphold; mine elect, *in whom* my soul delighteth; I have put my Spirit upon him; he shall bring forth judgment to the Gentiles.

2 He shall not cry, nor lift up, nor cause his voice to be heard in the street.

3 A bruised reed shall he not break, and the smoking flax shall he not quench: he shall bring forth judgment unto truth.

4 He shall not fail nor be discouraged, till he have set judgment in the earth: and the isles shall wait for his law.

MULTITUDES. TIME, SUMMER, A. D. 28; PLACE, ALSO CALLED LAKE OF GALILEE.

G

Isa. 49. 5 And now, saith the LORD that formed me from the womb *to be* his servant, to bring Jacob again to him, Though Israel be not gathered, yet shall I be glorious in the eyes of the LORD, and my God shall be my strength.

6 And he said, It is a light thing that thou shouldest be my servant to raise up the tribes of Jacob, and to restore the preserved of Israel: I will also give thee for a light to the Gentiles, that thou mayest be my salvation unto the end of the earth.

Isa. 52. 13 Behold, my servant shall deal prudently, he shall be exalted and extolled, and be very high.

Isa. 53. 10 Yet it pleased the LORD to bruise him; he hath put *him* to grief: when thou shalt make his soul an offering for sin, he shall see *his* seed, he shall prolong *his* days, and the pleasure of the LORD shall prosper in his hand.

11 He shall see of the travail of his soul, *and* shall be satisfied: by his knowledge shall my righteous servant justify many; for he shall bear their iniquities.

12 Therefore will I divide him *a portion* with the great, and he shall divide the spoil with the strong; because he hath poured out his soul unto death: and he was numbered with the transgressors; and he bare the sin of many, and made intercession for the transgressors.

Zech. 3. 8 Hear now, O Joshua the high priest, thou, and thy fellows that sit before thee: for they *are* men wondered at: for, behold, I will bring forth my servant the BRANCH.

Phil. 2. 6 Who, being in the form of God, thought it not robbery to be equal with God:

7 But made himself of no reputation, and took upon him the form of a servant, and was made in the likeness of men:

H

Matt. 3. 17 And lo a voice from heaven, saying, This is my beloved Son, in whom I am well pleased.

Matt. 17. 5 While he yet spake, behold, a bright cloud overshadowed them: and behold a voice out of the cloud, which said, This is my beloved Son, in whom I am well pleased; hear ye him.

I Pet. 2. 4 To whom coming, *as unto* a living stone, disallowed indeed of men, but chosen of God, *and* precious,

I

Isa. 61. 1 The Spirit of the Lord GOD *is* upon me; because the LORD hath anointed me to preach good tidings unto the meek; he hath sent me to bind up the brokenhearted, to proclaim liberty to the captives, and the opening of the prison to *them that are* bound;

K

Isa. 40. 11 He shall feed his flock like a shepherd: he shall gather the lambs with his arm, and carry *them* in his bosom, *and* shall gently lead those that are with young.

Isa. 42. 3. *See under F.*

L

Luke 6. 17 And he came down with them, and stood in the plain, and the company of his disciples, and a great multitude of people out of all Judæa and Jerusalem, and from the sea coast of Tyre and Sidon, which came to hear him, and to be healed of their diseases;

1

Or, *rushed.*

M

Mark 1. 23 And there was in their synagogue a man with an unclean spirit; and he cried out,

24 Saying, Let *us* alone; what have we to do with thee, thou Jesus of Nazareth? art thou come to destroy us? I know thee who thou art, the Holy One of God.

Luke 4. 41 And devils also came out of many, crying out, and saying, Thou art Christ the Son of God. And he rebuking *them* suffered them not to speak: for they knew that he was Christ.

N

Matt. 14. 33 Then they that were in the ship came and worshipped him, saying, Of a truth thou art the Son of God.

Mark 1. 1 The beginning of the gospel of Jesus Christ, the Son of God;

O

Matt. 12. 16. *See text of topic.*

Mark 1. 25 And Jesus rebuked him, saying, Hold thy peace, and come out of him.

Mark 1. 34 And he healed many that were sick of divers diseases, and cast out many devils; and suffered not the devils to speak, because they knew him.

§ 42. THE TWELVE APOSTLES CHOSEN.

10 : 2–4.

2 Now the names of the twelve apostles are these; The first, Simon, [a]who is called Peter, and Andrew his brother; James *the son* of Zebedee, and John his brother;

3 Philip, and Bartholomew; Thomas, and Matthew the publican; James *the son* of Alpheus, and Lebbeus, whose surname was [1]Thaddeus;

4 [b]Simon the Canaanite, and Judas [c]Iscariot, who also betrayed him. p. 232.

A

John 1. 42 And he brought him to Jesus. And when Jesus beheld him, he said, Thou art Simon the son of Jona: thou shalt be called Cephas, which is by interpretation, A stone.

1

Or, *Judas.*

Jude 1. *See under G.*

B

Luke 6. 15. *See text of topic.*

Acts 1. 13 And when they were come in, they went up into an upper room, where abode both Peter, and James, and John, and Andrew, Philip, and Thomas, Bartholomew, and Matthew, James *the son* of Alpheus, and Simon Zelotes, and Judas *the brother* of James.

C

John 13. 26 Jesus answered, He it is, to whom I shall give a sop, when I have dipped *it.* And when he had dipped the sop, he gave *it* to Judas Iscariot, *the son* of Simon.

D

Matt. 10. 1 And when he had called unto *him* his twelve disciples, he gave them power *against* unclean spirits, to cast them out, and to heal all manner of sickness and all manner of disease.

Luke 6. 12, 13. *See text of topic.*

Luke 9. 1 Then he called his twelve disciples together, and gave them power and authority over all devils, and to cure diseases.

E

John 1. 42. *See under A.*

3 : 13–19.

13 [d]And he goeth up into a mountain, and calleth *unto him* whom he would: and they came unto him.

14 And he ordained twelve, that they should be with him, and that he might send them forth to preach,

15 And to have power to heal sicknesses, and to cast out devils:

16 And Simon [e]he surnamed Peter;

17 And James the *son* of Zebedee, and John the brother of James; and he surnamed them Boanerges, which is, [f]The sons of thunder:

18 And Andrew, and Philip, and Bartholomew, and Matthew, and Thomas, and James the *son* of Alpheus, and [g]Thaddeus, and Simon the Canaanite,

19 And Judas Iscariot, which also betrayed him: and they went [2]into a house. (p. 166.)

F

Isa. 58. 1 Cry aloud, spare not, lift up thy voice like a trumpet, and show my people their transgression, and the house of Jacob their sins.

G

Jude 1 Jude, the servant of Jesus Christ, and brother of James, to them that are sanctified by God the Father, and preserved in Jesus Christ, *and* called:

2

Or, *home.*

H

Ps. 55. 15 Let death seize upon them, *and* let them go down quick into hell: for wickedness *is* in their dwellings, *and* among them.

16 As for me, I will call upon God; and the LORD shall save me.

17 Evening, and morning, and at noon, will I pray, and cry aloud: and he shall hear my voice.

Ps. 109. 3 They compassed me about also with words of hatred; and fought against me without a cause.

4 For my love they are my adversaries: but I *give myself unto* prayer.

TIME, SUMMER, A. D. 28; PLACE, NEAR CAPERNAUM [HORNS OF HATTIN].

6: 12–19.

12 And it came to pass in those days, [h]that he went out into a mountain to pray, and [i]continued all night in prayer to God.

13 And when it was day, he called *unto him* his disciples: [k]and of them he chose twelve, whom also he named apostles;

14 Simon, ([l]whom he also named Peter,) and Andrew his brother, James and John, Philip and Bartholomew,

15 Matthew and Thomas, James the *son* of Alpheus, and Simon called Zelotes,

16 And Judas [m]*the brother* of James, and Judas Iscariot, which also was the traitor.

17 ¶ And he came down with them, and stood in the plain, and the company of his disciples, [n]and a great multitude of people out of all Judæa and Jerusalem, and from the sea coast of Tyre and Sidon, which came to hear him, and to be healed of their diseases;

18 And they that were vexed with unclean spirits: and they were healed.

19 And the whole multitude [o]sought to touch him: for [p]there went virtue out of him, and healed *them* all.

H—CONTINUED.

Dan 6. 10 Now when Daniel knew that the writing was signed, he went into his house; and, his windows being open in his chamber toward Jerusalem, he kneeled upon his knees three times a day, and prayed, and gave thanks before his God, as he did aforetime.

11 Then these men assembled, and found Daniel praying and making supplication before his God.

Heb. 5. 7 Who in the days of his flesh, when he had offered up prayers and supplications with strong crying and tears unto him that was able to save him from death, and was heard in that he feared;

I

Gen. 32. 24 And Jacob was left alone; and there wrestled a man with him until the breaking of the day.

25 And when he saw that he prevailed not against him, he touched the hollow of his thigh; and the hollow of Jacob's thigh was out of joint, as he wrestled with him.

26 And he said, Let me go, for the day breaketh. And he said, I will not let thee go, except thou bless me.

Ps. 22. 2 O my God, I cry in the daytime, but thou hearest not; and in the night season, and am not silent.

Matt. 14. 23 And when he had sent the multitudes away, he went up into a mountain apart to pray: and when the evening was come, he was there alone.

24 But the ship was now in the midst of the sea, tossed with waves: for the wind was contrary.

25 And in the fourth watch of the night Jesus went unto them, walking on the sea.

Col. 4. 2 Continue in prayer, and watch in the same with thanksgiving;

K

Matt. 10. 1. *See under D.*

L

John 1. 42. *See under A.*

M

Jude 1. *See under G.*

N

Matt. 4. 25 And there followed him great multitudes of people from Galilee, and *from* Decapolis, and *from* Jerusalem, and *from* Judæa, and *from* beyond Jordan.

Mark 3. 7 But Jesus withdrew himself with his disciples to the sea: and a great multitude from Galilee followed him, and from Judæa,

O

Matt. 14. 36 And besought him that they might only touch the hem of his garment: and as many as touched were made perfectly whole.

P

Mark 5. 30 And Jesus, immediately knowing in himself that virtue had gone out of him, turned him about in the press, and said, Who touched my clothes?

Luke 8. 46 And Jesus said, Somebody hath touched me: for I perceived that virtue is gone out of me.

§ 43. THE SERMON ON THE MOUNT: THE BEATITUDES.

5 : 1 — 10.

1 And seeing the multitudes, [a]he went up into a mountain: and when he was set, his disciples came unto him:

2 And he opened his mouth, and taught them, saying,

3 [b]Blessed *are* the poor in spirit: for theirs is the kingdom of heaven.

4 [c]Blessed *are* they that mourn: for they shall be comforted.

5 [d]Blessed *are* the meek: for [e]they shall inherit the earth.

6 Blessed *are* they which do hunger and thirst after righteousness: [f]for they shall be filled.

7 Blessed *are* the merciful: [g]for they shall obtain mercy.

8 [h]Blessed *are* the pure in heart: for [i]they shall see God.

9 Blessed *are* the [k]peacemakers: for they shall be called the children of God.

10 [l]Blessed *are* they which are persecuted for righteousness' sake: for theirs is the kingdom of heaven.

A

Mark 3. 13 And he goeth up into a mountain, and calleth *unto him* whom he would: and they came unto him.

B

Luke 6. 20. *See text of topic.*

Ps. 51. 17 The sacrifices of God *are* a broken spirit: a broken and a contrite heart, O God, thou wilt not despise.

Prov. 16. 19 Better *it is to be* of an humble spirit with the lowly, than to divide the spoil with the proud.

Prov. 29. 23 A man's pride shall bring him low: but honour shall uphold the humble in spirit.

Isa. 57. 15 For thus saith the high and lofty One that inhabiteth eternity, whose name *is* Holy; I dwell in the high and holy *place*, with him also *that is* of a contrite and humble spirit, to revive the spirit of the humble, and to revive the heart of the contrite ones.

B—Concluded.

Isa. 66. 2 For all those *things* hath mine hand made, and all those *things* have been, saith the LORD: but to this *man* will I look, *even* to *him that is* poor and of a contrite spirit, and trembleth at my word.

C

Isa. 61. 2 To proclaim the acceptable year of the LORD, and the day of vengeance, of our God; to comfort all that mourn;

3 To appoint unto them that mourn in Zion, to give unto them beauty for ashes, the oil of joy for mourning, the garment of praise for the spirit of heaviness; that they might be called Trees of righteousness, The planting of the LORD, that he might be glorified.

Luke 6. 21. *See text of topic.*

John 16. 20 Verily, verily, I say unto you, That ye shall weep and lament, but the world shall rejoice; and ye shall be sorrowful, but your sorrow shall be turned into joy.

II Cor. 1. 7 And our hope of you *is* steadfast, knowing, that as ye are partakers of the sufferings, so *shall ye be* also of the consolation.

Rev. 21. 4 And God shall wipe away all tears from their eyes; and there shall be no more death, neither sorrow, nor crying, neither shall there be any more pain: for the former things are passed away.

D

Ps. 37. 11 But the meek shall inherit the earth; and shall delight themselves in the abundance of peace.

I Pet. 3. 4 But *let it be* the hidden man of the heart, in that which is not corruptible, *even the ornament* of a meek and quiet spirit, which is in the sight of God of great price.

E

Rom. 4. 13 For the promise, that he should be the heir of the world, *was* not to Abraham, or to his seed, through the law, but through the righteousness of faith.

F

Isa. 55. 1 Ho, every one that thirsteth, come ye to the waters, and he that hath no money; come ye, buy, and eat; yea, come, buy wine and milk without money and without price.

TIME, SUMMER, A. D. 28; PLACE, NEAR CAPERNAUM [HORNS OF HATTIN].

6 : 20–49.

20 And he lifted up his eyes on his
disciples, and said, [m]Blessed *be ye* poor:
for yours is the kingdom of God.
21 [n]Blessed *are ye* that hunger now:
for ye shall be filled. [o]Blessed *are ye*
that weep now: for ye shall laugh.

F—CONCLUDED.

Isa. 65. 13 Therefore thus saith the Lord GOD, Behold, my servants shall eat, but ye shall be hungry: behold, my servants shall drink, but ye shall be thirsty: behold, my servants shall rejoice, but ye shall be ashamed:

G

Ps. 41. 1 Blessed *is* he that considereth the poor: the LORD will deliver him in time of trouble.

Matt. 6. 14. *See text of topic.*

Mark 11. 25 And when ye stand praying, forgive, if ye have aught against any; that your Father also which is in heaven may forgive you your trespasses.

II Tim. 1. 16 The Lord give mercy unto the house of Onesiphorus; for he oft refreshed me, and was not ashamed of my chain:

Heb. 6. 10 For God *is* not unrighteous to forget your work and labour of love, which ye have showed toward his name, in that ye have ministered to the saints, and do minister.

11 And we desire that every one of you do show the same diligence to the full assurance of hope unto the end:

Jas. 2. 13 For he shall have judgment without mercy, that hath showed no mercy; and mercy rejoiceth against judgment.

H

Ps. 15. 2 He that walketh uprightly, and worketh righteousness, and speaketh the truth in his heart.

Ps. 24. 4 He that hath clean hands, and a pure heart; who hath not lifted up his soul unto vanity, nor sworn deceitfully.

Heb. 12. 14 Follow peace with all *men*, and holiness, without which no man shall see the Lord:

I

I Cor. 13. 12 For now we see through a glass, darkly; but then face to face: now I know in part; but then shall I know even as also I am known.

I—CONCLUDED.

I Jno. 3. 2 Beloved, now are we the sons of God, and it doth not yet appear what we shall be: but we know that, when he shall appear, we shall be like him; for we shall see him as he is.

3 And every man that hath this hope in him purifieth himself, even as he is pure.

K

Ps. 34. 14 Depart from evil, and do good; seek peace, and pursue it.

Heb. 12. 14. *See under H.*

L

II Cor. 4. 17 For our light affliction, which is but for a moment, worketh for us a far more exceeding *and* eternal weight of glory;

II Tim. 2. 12 If we suffer, we shall also reign with *him:* if we deny *him,* he also will deny us:

I Pet. 3. 14 But and if ye suffer for righteousness' sake, happy *are ye:* and be not afraid of their terror, neither be troubled:

M

Matt. 5. 3. *See text of topic.*

Matt. 11. 5 The blind receive their sight, and the lame walk, the lepers are cleansed, and the deaf hear, the dead are raised up, and the poor have the gospel preached to them.

Jas. 2. 5 Hearken, my beloved brethren, Hath not God chosen the poor of this world rich in faith, and heirs of the kingdom which he hath promised to them that love him?

N

Isa. 55. 1 and Isa. 65. 13. *See under F.*
Matt. 5. 6. *See text of topic.*

O

Eccl. 7. 2 *It is* better to go to the house of mourning, than to go to the house of feasting: for that *is* the end of all men; and the living will lay *it* to his heart.

3 Sorrow *is* better than laughter: for by the sadness of the countenance the heart is made better.

Isa. 61. 3. *See under C.*
Matt. 5. 4. *See text of topic.*

Rev. 7. 14 And I said unto him, Sir, thou knowest. And he said to me, These are they which came out of great tribulation, and have washed their robes, and made them white in the blood of the Lamb.

Rev. 7. 17 For the Lamb which is in the midst of the throne shall feed them, and shall lead them unto living fountains of waters: and God shall wipe away all tears from their eyes.

§ 43. THE SERMON ON THE MOUNT: WOES PRONOUNCED, (CONTINUED).

CHAP. 5.

11 [p]Blessed are ye, when *men* shall
revile you, and persecute *you*, and shall
say all manner of [q]evil against you
[1]falsely, for my sake.

12 [r]Rejoice, and be exceeding glad:
for great *is* your reward in heaven:
for [s]so persecuted they the prophets
which were before you.

13 Ye are the salt of the earth: [t]but
if the salt have lost his savour, wherewith shall it be salted? it is thenceforth good for nothing, but to be cast
out, and to be trodden under foot of
men.

14 [u]Ye are the light of the world.
A city that is set on a hill cannot be
hid.

15 Neither do men [x]light a candle,
and put it under [2]a bushel, but on a
candlestick; and it giveth light unto
all that are in the house.

P

Luke 6. 22. *See text of topic.*

Q

I Pet. 4. 14 If ye be reproached for the name of Christ, happy *are ye;* for the Spirit of glory and of God resteth upon you: on their part he is evil spoken of, but on your part he is glorified.

1

Gr., *lying.*

R

Luke 6. 23. *See text of topic.*

Acts 5. 41 And they departed from the presence of the council, rejoicing that they were counted worthy to suffer shame for his name.

Rom. 5. 3 And not only *so*, but we glory in tribulations also; knowing that tribulation worketh patience:

Jas. 1. 2 My brethren, count it all joy when ye fall into divers temptations;

I Pet. 4. 13 But rejoice, inasmuch as ye are partakers of Christ's sufferings; that, when his glory shall be revealed, ye may be glad also with exceeding joy.

S

II Chr. 36. 16 But they mocked the messengers of God, and despised his words, and misused his prophets, until the wrath of the LORD arose against his people, till *there was* no remedy.

Neh. 9. 26 Nevertheless they were disobedient, and rebelled against thee, and cast thy law behind their backs, and slew thy prophets which testified against them to turn them to thee, and they wrought great provocations.

Matt. 23. 34 Wherefore, behold, I send unto you prophets, and wise men, and scribes: and *some* of them ye shall kill and crucify; and *some* of them shall ye scourge in your synagogues, and persecute *them* from city to city:

Matt. 23. 37 O Jerusalem, Jerusalem, *thou* that killest the prophets, and stonest them which are sent unto thee, how often would I have gathered thy children together, even as a hen gathereth her chickens under *her* wings, and ye would not!

Acts 7. 52 Which of the prophets have not your fathers persecuted? and they have slain them which showed before of the coming of the Just One; of whom ye have been now the betrayers and murderers:

I Thes. 2. 15 Who both killed the Lord Jesus, and their own prophets, and have persecuted us; and they please not God, and are contrary to all men:

T

Mark 9. 50 Salt *is* good: but if the salt have lost his saltness, wherewith will ye season it? Have salt in yourselves, and have peace one with another.

Luke 14. 34 Salt *is* good: but if the salt have lost his savour, wherewith shall it be seasoned?

35 It is neither fit for the land, nor yet for the dunghill; *but* men cast it out. He that hath ears to hear, let him hear.

U

Prov. 4. 18 But the path of the just *is* as the shining light, that shineth more and more unto the perfect day.

Phil. 2. 15 That ye may be blameless and harmless, the sons of God, without rebuke, in the midst of a crooked and perverse nation, among whom ye shine as lights in the world;

X

Mark 4. 21 And he said unto them, Is a candle brought to be put under a bushel, or under a bed? and not to be set on a candlestick?

TIME, SUMMER, A. D. 28; PLACE, NEAR CAPERNAUM [HORNS OF HATTIN].

CHAP. 6.

22 [y]Blessed are ye, when men shall
hate you, and when they [z]shall separate
you *from their company*, and shall reproach *you*, and cast out your name
as evil, for the Son of man's sake.

23 [a]Rejoice ye in that day, and leap
for joy: for, behold, your reward *is*
great in heaven: for [b]in the like manner did their fathers unto the prophets.

24 [c]But woe unto you [d]that are rich!
for [e]ye have received your consolation.

25 [f]Woe unto you that are full! for
ye shall hunger. [g]Woe unto you that
laugh now! for ye shall mourn and
weep.

26 [h]Woe unto you, when all men
shall speak well of you! for so did
their fathers to the false prophets.

(p. 135.)

X—CONCLUDED.

Luke 8. 16 No man, when he hath lighted a candle, covereth it with a vessel, or putteth *it* under a bed; but setteth *it* on a candlestick, that they which enter in may see the light.

Luke 11. 33 No man, when he hath lighted a candle, putteth *it* in a secret place, neither under a bushel, but on a candlestick, that they which come in may see the light.

2

The word in the original signifies *a measure containing about a pint less than a peck.*

Y

Matt. 5. 11. *See text of topic.*

I Pet. 2. 19 For this *is* thankworthy, if a man for conscience toward God endure grief, suffering wrongfully.

I Pet. 3. 14 But and if ye suffer for righteousness' sake, happy *are ye:* and be not afraid of their terror, neither be troubled;

I Pet. 4. 14. *See under Q.*

Z

John 16. 2 They shall put you out of the synagogues: yea, the time cometh, that whosoever killeth you will think that he doeth God service.

A

Matt. 5. 12. *See text of topic.*
Acts 5. 41. *See under R.*

Col. 1. 24 Who now rejoice in my sufferings for you, and fill up that which is behind of the afflictions of Christ in my flesh for his body's sake, which is the church:

Jas. 1. 2. *See under R.*

B

Acts 7. 51 Ye stiffnecked and uncircumcised in heart and ears, ye do always resist the Holy Ghost: as your fathers *did*, so *do* ye.

C

Amos 6. 1 Woe to them *that are* at ease in Zion, and trust in the mountain of Samaria, *which are* named chief of the nations, to whom the house of Israel came!

Luke 12. 20 But God said unto him, *Thou* fool, this night thy soul shall be required of thee: then whose shall those things be, which thou hast provided?

21 So *is* he that layeth up treasure for himself, and is not rich toward God.

Jas. 5. 1 Go to now, *ye* rich men, weep and howl for your miseries that shall come upon *you*.

D

Luke 12. 21. *See under C.*

E

Matt. 6. 2, 5, 16. *See text of topic.*

Luke 16. 25 But Abraham said, Son, remember that thou in thy lifetime receivedst thy good things, and likewise Lazarus evil things: but now he is comforted, and thou art tormented.

F

Isa. 65. 13. *See under F, page 125.*

G

Prov. 14. 13 Even in laughter the heart **is** sorrowful; and the end of that mirth *is* heaviness.

H

Mic. 2. 11 If a man walking in the spirit and falsehood do lie, *saying,* I will prophesy unto thee of wine and of strong drink; he shall even be the prophet of this people.

John 15. 19 If ye were of the world, the world would love his own; but because ye are not of the world, but I have chosen you out of the world, therefore the world hateth you.

I Jno. 4. 5 They are of the world: therefore speak they of the world, and the world heareth them.

§ 43. THE SERMON ON THE MOUNT: THE LAW IN ITS SPIRIT,

CHAP. 5.

16 Let [i]your light so shine before men, [k]that they may see your good works, and [l]glorify your Father which is in heaven.

17 [m]Think not that I am come to destroy the law, or the prophets: I am not come to destroy, but to fulfil.

18 For verily I say unto you, [n]Till heaven and earth pass, one jot or one tittle shall in no wise pass from the law, till all be fulfilled.

19 [o]Whosoever therefore shall break one of these least commandments, and shall teach men so, he shall be called the least in the kingdom of heaven: but whosoever shall do and teach *them*, the same shall be called great in the kingdom of heaven.

20 For I say unto you, That except your righteousness shall exceed [p]*the righteousness* of the scribes and Pharisees, ye shall in no case enter into the kingdom of heaven.

21 Ye have heard that it was said [3]by them of old time, [q]Thou shalt not kill; and whosoever shall kill shall be in danger of the judgment:

22 But I say unto you, That [r]whosoever is angry with his brother without a cause shall be in danger of the judgment: and whosoever shall say to his brother, [4s]Raca, shall be in danger of the council: but whosoever shall say, Thou [5]fool, shall be in danger of hell fire.

23 Therefore [t]if thou bring thy gift to the altar, and there rememberest that thy brother hath aught against thee;

I

Prov. 4. 18 But the path of the just *is* as the shining light, that shineth more and more unto the perfect day.

19 The way of the wicked *is* as darkness: they know not at what they stumble.

Isa. 58. 8 Then shall thy light break forth as the morning, and thine health shall spring forth speedily: and thy righteousness shall go before thee; the glory of the LORD shall be thy rearward.

9 Then shalt thou call, and the LORD shall answer; thou shalt cry, and he shall say, Here I *am*. If thou take away from the midst of thee the yoke, the putting forth of the finger, and speaking vanity;

10 And *if* thou draw out thy soul to the hungry, and satisfy the afflicted soul; then shall thy light rise in obscurity, and thy darkness *be* as the noonday:

Isa. 60. 1 Arise, shine; for thy light is come, and the glory of the LORD is risen upon thee.

2 For, behold, the darkness shall cover the earth, and gross darkness the people: but the LORD shall arise upon thee, and his glory shall be seen upon thee.

3 And the Gentiles shall come to thy light, and kings to the brightness of thy rising.

Rom.13. 11 And that, knowing the time, that now *it is* high time to awake out of sleep: for now *is* our salvation nearer than when we believed.

12 The night is far spent, the day is at hand: let us therefore cast off the works of darkness, and let us put on the armour of light.

13 Let us walk honestly, as in the day; not in rioting and drunkenness, not in chambering and wantonness, not in strife and envying:

14 But put ye on the Lord Jesus Christ, and make not provision for the flesh, to *fulfil* the lusts *thereof*.

Eph. 5. 8 For ye were sometime darkness, but now *are ye* light in the Lord: walk as children of light;

I Thes.2. 12 That ye would walk worthy of God, who hath called you unto his kingdom and glory.

I Thes.5. 6 Therefore let us not sleep, as *do* others; but let us watch and be sober.

7 For they that sleep sleep in the night; and they that be drunken are drunken in the night.

(CONTINUED). TIME, SUMMER, A. D. 28; PLACE, NEAR CAPERNAUM [HORNS OF HATTIN].

[CHAP. 6.]

I—CONCLUDED.

I Thes. 5. 8 But let us, who are of the day, be sober, putting on the breastplate of faith and love; and for a helmet, the hope of salvation.

I Jno. 1. 5 This then is the message which we have heard of him, and declare unto you, that God is light, and in him is no darkness at all.

6 If we say that we have fellowship with him, and walk in darkness, we lie, and do not the truth:

7 But if we walk in the light, as he is in the light, we have fellowship one with another, and the blood of Jesus Christ his Son cleanseth us from all sin.

K

I Pet. 2. 12 Having your conversation honest among the Gentiles: that, whereas they speak against you as evil doers, they may by *your* good works, which they shall behold, glorify God in the day of visitation.

L

John 15. 8 Herein is my Father glorified, that ye bear much fruit; so shall ye be my disciples.

I Cor. 14. 25 And thus are the secrets of his heart made manifest; and so falling down on *his* face he will worship God, and report that God is in you of a truth.

M

Dan. 9. 24 Seventy weeks are determined upon thy people, and upon thy holy city, to finish the transgression, and to make an end of sins, and to make reconciliation for iniquity, and to bring in everlasting righteousness, and to seal up the vision and prophecy, and to anoint the Most Holy.

Rom. 3. 31 Do we then make void the law through faith? God forbid: yea, we establish the law.

Rom. 10. 4 For Christ *is* the end of the law for righteousness to every one that believeth.

Gal. 3. 24 Wherefore the law was our schoolmaster *to bring us* unto Christ, that we might be justified by faith.

N

Luke 16. 17 And it is easier for heaven and earth to pass, than one tittle of the law to fail.

O

Jas. 2. 10 For whosoever shall keep the whole law, and yet offend in one *point*, he is guilty of all.

P

Luke 11. 39 And the Lord said unto him, Now do ye Pharisees make clean the outside of the cup and the platter; but your inward part is full of ravening and wickedness.

40 *Ye* fools, did not he, that made that which is without, make that which is within also?

Luke 11. 44 Woe unto you, scribes and Pharisees, hypocrites! for ye are as graves which appear not, and the men that walk over *them* are not aware *of them.*

Rom. 9. 31 But Israel, which followed after the law of righteousness, hath not attained to the law of righteousness.

Rom. 10. 3 For they, being ignorant of God's righteousness, and going about to establish their own righteousness, have not submitted themselves unto the righteousness of God.

Phil. 3. 9 And be found in him, not having mine own righteousness, which is of the law, but that which is through the faith of Christ, the righteousness which is of God by faith:

3

Or, *to them.*

Q

Ex. 20. 13 Thou shalt not kill.

Deut. 5. 17 Thou shalt not kill.

R

I Jno. 3. 15 Whosoever hateth his brother is a murderer: and ye know that no murderer hath eternal life abiding in him.

4

That is, *vain fellow.*

S

II Sa. 6. 20 Then David returned to bless his household. And Michal the daughter of Saul came out to meet David, and said, How glorious was the king of Israel to day, who uncovered himself to day in the eyes of the handmaids of his servants, as one of the vain fellows shamelessly uncovereth himself!

Jas. 2. 20 But wilt thou know, O vain man, that faith without works is dead?

5

Or, *graceless wretch.*

T

Matt. 8. 4 And Jesus saith unto him, See thou tell no man; but go thy way, show thyself to the priest, and offer the gift that Moses commanded, for a testimony unto them.

Matt. 23. 19 *Ye* fools and blind: for whether *is* greater, the gift, or the altar that sanctifieth the gift?

§ 43. THE SERMON ON THE MOUNT: THE LAW IN ITS SPIRIT, CONCLUDED.

CHAP. 5.

24 [u]Leave there thy gift before the altar, and go thy way; first be reconciled to thy brother, and then come and offer thy gift.

25 [x]Agree with thine adversary quickly, [y]while thou art in the way with him; lest at any time the adversary deliver thee to the judge, and the judge deliver thee to the officer, and thou be cast into prison.

26 Verily I say unto thee, [z]Thou shalt by no means come out thence, till thou hast paid the uttermost farthing.

27 Ye have heard that it was said by them of old time, [a]Thou shalt not commit adultery:

28 But I say unto you, That whosoever [b]looketh on a woman to lust after her hath committed adultery with her already in his heart.

29 [c]And if thy right eye [6]offend thee, [d]pluck it out, and cast *it* from thee: for it is profitable for thee that one of thy members should perish, and not *that* thy whole body should be cast into hell.

30 And if thy right hand offend thee, cut it off, and cast *it* from thee: for it is profitable for thee that one of thy members should perish, and not *that* thy whole body should be cast into hell.

31 It hath been said, [e]Whosoever shall put away his wife, let him give her a writing of divorcement:

U

Job 42. 8 Therefore take unto you now seven bullocks and seven rams, and go to my servant Job, and offer up for yourselves a burnt offering; and my servant Job shall pray for you: for him will I accept: lest I deal with you *after your* folly, in that ye have not spoken of me *the thing which is* right, like my servant Job.

Matt.18. 19 Again I say unto you, That if two of you shall agree on earth as touching anything that they shall ask, it shall be done for them of my Father which is in heaven.

I Tim.2. 8 I will therefore that men pray every where, lifting up holy hands, without wrath and doubting.

I Pet. 3. 7 Likewise, ye husbands, dwell with *them* according to knowledge, giving honour unto the wife, as unto the weaker vessel, and as being heirs together of the grace of life; that your prayers be not hindered.

X

Job 22. 21 Acquaint now thyself with him, and be at peace: thereby good shall come unto thee.

Prov.25. 8 Go not forth hastily to strive, lest *thou know not* what to do in the end thereof, when thy neighbor hath put thee to shame.

Luke 12. 58 When thou goest with thine adversary to the magistrate, *as thou art* in the way, give diligence that thou mayest be delivered from him; lest he hale thee to the judge, and the judge deliver thee to the officer, and the officer cast thee into prison.

59 I tell thee, thou shalt not depart thence, till thou hast paid the very last mite.

Y

Ps. 32. 6 For this shall every one that is godly pray unto thee in a time when thou mayest be found: surely in the floods of great waters they shall not come nigh unto him.

Isa. 55. 6 Seek ye the LORD while he may be found, call ye upon him while he is near:

Z

II Thes.1. 9 Who shall be punished with everlasting destruction from the presence of the Lord, and from the glory of his power;

A

Ex. 20. 14 Thou shalt not commit adultery.

Deut. 5. 18 Neither shalt thou commit adultery.

B

Gen. 34. 2 And when Shechem the son of Hamor the Hivite, prince of the country, saw her, he took her, and lay with her, and defiled her.

(CONTINUED). TIME, SUMMER, A. D. 28; PLACE, NEAR CAPERNAUM [HORNS OF HATTIN].

[CHAP. 6.]

B—CONCLUDED.

Job 31. 1 I made a covenant with mine eyes, why then should I think upon a maid?

Prov. 6. 25 Lust not after her beauty in thine heart; neither let her take thee with her eyelids.

II Sa. 11 2 And it came to pass in an eveningtide, that David arose from off his bed, and walked upon the roof of the king's house: and from the roof he saw a woman washing herself; and the woman *was* very beautiful to look upon.

Eph. 5. 5 For this ye know, that no whoremonger, nor unclean person, nor covetous man, who is an idolater, hath any inheritance in the kingdom of Christ and of God.

C

Matt.18. 8 Wherefore if thy hand or thy foot offend thee, cut them off, and cast *them* from thee: it is better for thee to enter into life halt or maimed, rather than having two hands or two feet to be cast into everlasting fire.

9 And if thine eye offend thee, pluck it out, and cast *it* from thee: it is better for thee to enter into life with one eye, rather than having two eyes to be cast into hell fire.

Mark 9. 43 And if thy hand offend thee, cut it off: it is better for thee to enter into life maimed, than having two hands to go into hell, into the fire that never shall be quenched:

44 Where their worm dieth not, and the fire is not quenched.

45 And if thy foot offend thee, cut it off: it is better for thee to enter halt into life, than having two feet to be cast into hell, into the fire that never shall be quenched:

46 Where their worm dieth not, and the fire is not quenched.

47 And if thine eye offend thee, pluck it out: it is better for thee to enter into the kingdom of God with one eye, than having two eyes to be cast into hell fire:

6

Or, *do cause thee to offend.*

D

Matt.19. 12 For there are some eunuchs, which were so born from *their* mother's womb: and there are some eunuchs, which were made eunuchs of men: and there be eunuchs, which have made themselves eunuchs for the kingdom of heaven's sake. He that is able to receive *it*, let him receive *it*.

D—CONCLUDED.

Rom. 6. 6 Knowing this, that our old man is crucified with *him*, that the body of sin might be destroyed, that henceforth we should not serve sin.

Rom. 8. 13 For if ye live after the flesh, ye shall die: but if ye through the Spirit do mortify the deeds of the body, ye shall live.

I Cor. 9. 27 But I keep under my body, and bring *it* into subjection: lest that by any means, when I have preached to others, I myself should be a castaway

Col. 3. 5 Mortify therefore your members which are upon the earth; fornication, uncleanness, inordinate affection, evil concupiscence, and covetousness, which is idolatry:

I Pet. 4. 1 Forasmuch then as Christ hath suffered for us in the flesh, arm yourselves likewise with the same mind: for he that hath suffered in the flesh hath ceased from sin;

2 That he no longer should live the rest of *his* time in the flesh to the lusts of men, but to the will of God.

3 For the time past of *our* life may suffice us to have wrought the will of the Gentiles, when we walked in lasciviousness, lusts, excess of wine, revellings, banquetings, and abominable idolatries:

E

Deut.24. 1 When a man hath taken a wife, and married her, and it come to pass that she find no favour in his eyes, because he hath found some uncleanness in her; then let him write her a bill of divorcement, and give *it* in her hand, and send her out of his house.

Jer. 3. 1 They say, If a man put away his wife, and she go from him, and become another man's, shall he return unto her again? shall not that land be greatly polluted? but thou hast played the harlot with many lovers; yet return again to me, saith the LORD.

Matt.19. 3 The Pharisees also came unto him, tempting him, and saying unto him, Is it lawful for a man to put away his wife for every cause?

Mark10. 2 And the Pharisees came to him, and asked him, Is it lawful for a man to put away *his* wife? tempting him.

3 And he answered and said unto them, What did Moses command you?

4 And they said, Moses suffered to write a bill of divorcement, and to put *her* away.

§ 43. THE SERMON ON THE MOUNT: THE LAW FURTHER EXPLAINED, F—CONCLUDED.

CHAP. 5.

32 But I say unto you, That [f] whosoever shall put away his wife, saving for the cause of fornication, causeth her to commit adultery: and whosoever shall marry her that is divorced committeth adultery.

33 Again, ye have heard that [g] it hath been said by them of old time, [h] Thou shalt not forswear thyself, but [i] shalt perform unto the Lord thine oaths:

34 But I say unto you, [k] Swear not at all; neither by heaven; for it is [l] God's throne:

35 Nor by the earth; for it is his footstool: neither by Jerusalem; for it is [m] the city of the great King.

36 Neither shalt thou swear by thy head, because thou canst not make one hair white or black.

37 [n] But let your communication be, Yea, yea; Nay, nay: for whatsoever is more than these cometh of evil.

38 Ye have heard that it hath been said, [o] An eye for an eye, and a tooth for a tooth:

39 But I say unto you, [p] That ye resist not evil: [q] but whosoever shall smite thee on thy right cheek, turn to him the other also.

40 And if any man will sue thee at the law, and take away thy coat, let him have *thy* cloak also.

41 And whosoever [r] shall compel thee to go a mile, go with him twain.

F

Matt.19. 9 And I say unto you, Whosoever shall put away his wife, except *it be* for fornication, and shall marry another, committeth adultery: and whoso marrieth her which is put away doth commit adultery.

Luke 16. 18 Whosoever putteth away his wife, and marrieth another, committeth adultery: and whosoever marrieth her that is put away from *her* husband committeth adultery.

Rom. 7. 3 So then if, while *her* husband liveth, she be married to another man, she shall be called an adulteress: but if her husband be dead, she is free from that law; so that she is no adulteress, though she be married to another man.

I Cor. 7. 10 And unto the married I command, *yet* not I, but the Lord, Let not the wife depart from *her* husband:

11 But and if she depart, let her remain unmarried, or be reconciled to *her* husband: and let not the husband put away *his* wife.

G

Matt.23. 16 Woe unto you, *ye* blind guides, which say, Whosoever shall swear by the temple, it is nothing; but whosoever shall swear by the gold of the temple, he is a debtor!

H

Ex. 20. 7 Thou shalt not take the name of the LORD thy God in vain: for the LORD will not hold him guiltless that taketh his name in vain.

Lev. 19. 12 And ye shall not swear by my name falsely, neither shalt thou profane the name of thy God: I *am* the LORD.

Num.30. 2 If a man vow a vow unto the LORD, or swear an oath to bind his soul with a bond; he shall not break his word, he shall do according to all that proceedeth out of his mouth.

Deut. 5. 11 Thou shalt not take the name of the LORD thy God in vain: for the LORD will not hold *him* guiltless that taketh his name in vain.

I

Deut.23. 23 That which is gone out of thy lips thou shalt keep and perform; *even* a freewill offering, according as thou hast vowed unto the LORD thy God, which thou hast promised with thy mouth.

K

Matt. 23. 16. *See under G.*

Matt.23. 18 And, Whosoever shall swear by the altar, it is nothing; but whosoever sweareth by the gift that is upon it, he is guilty.

Matt.23. 22 And he that shall swear by heaven, sweareth by the throne of God, and by him that sitteth thereon.

(CONTINUED). TIME, SUMMER, A. D. 28; PLACE, NEAR CAPERNAUM [HORNS OF HATTIN].

CHAP. 6.

29 [s]And unto him that smiteth thee on the *one* cheek offer also the other; [t]and him that taketh away thy cloak forbid not *to take thy* coat also.

K—CONCLUDED.

Jas. 5. 12 But above all things, my brethren, swear not, neither by heaven, neither by the earth, neither by any other oath: but let your yea be yea; and *your* nay, nay; lest ye fall into condemnation.

L

Isa. 66. 1 Thus saith the LORD, The heaven *is* my throne, and the earth *is* my footstool: where *is* the house that ye build unto me? and where *is* the place of my rest?

M

Ps. 48. 2 Beautiful for situation, the joy of the whole earth, *is* mount Zion, *on* the sides of the north, the city of the great King.

Ps. 87. 3 Glorious things are spoken of thee, O city of God. Selah.

N

II Cor.1. 18 But *as* God *is* true, our word toward you was not yea and nay.

19 For the Son of God, Jesus Christ, who was preached among you by us, *even* by me and Silvanus and Timotheus, was not yea and nay, but in him was yea.

20 For all the promises of God in him *are* yea, and in him Amen, unto the glory of God by us.

Col. 4. 6 Let your speech *be* always with grace, seasoned with salt, that ye may know how ye ought to answer every man.

Jas. 5. 12. *See under K.*

O

Ex. 21. 24 Eye for eye, tooth for tooth, hand for hand, foot for foot,

Lev. 24. 20 Breach for breach, eye for eye, tooth for tooth: as he hath caused a blemish in a man, so shall it be done to him *again.*

Deut.19. 21 And thine eye shall not pity; *but* life *shall go* for life, eye for eye, tooth for tooth, hand for hand, foot for foot.

P

Prov.20. 22 Say not thou, I will recompense evil; *but* wait on the LORD, and he shall save thee.

Prov.24. 29 Say not, I will do so to him as he hath done to me: I will render to the man according to his work.

Luke 6. 29. *See text of topic.*

Rom.12. 17 Recompense to no man evil for evil. Provide things honest in the sight of all men.

Rom.12. 19 Dearly beloved, avenge not yourselves, but *rather* give place unto wrath: for it is written, Vengeance *is* mine; I will repay, saith the Lord.

I Cor. 6. 7 Now therefore there is utterly a fault among you, because ye go to law one with another. Why do ye not rather take wrong? Why do ye not rather *suffer yourselves to* be defrauded?

I Thes.5. 15 See that none render evil for evil unto any *man;* but ever follow that which is good, both among yourselves, and to all *men.*

I Pet. 3. 9 Not rendering evil for evil, or railing for railing: but contrariwise blessing; knowing that ye are thereunto called, that ye should inherit a blessing.

Q

Isa. 50. 6 I gave my back to the smiters, and my cheeks to them that plucked off the hair: I hid not my face from shame and spitting.

Lam. 3. 30 He giveth *his* cheek to him that smiteth him: he is filled full with reproach.

R

I Ki. 22. 24 But Zedekiah the son of Chenaanah went near, and smote Micaiah on the cheek, and said, Which way went the Spirit of the LORD from me to speak unto thee?

Job 16. 10 They have gaped upon me with their mouth; they have smitten me upon the cheek reproachfully; they have gathered themselves together against me.

Matt.27. 32 And as they came out, they found a man of Cyrene, Simon by name: him they compelled to bear his cross.

Mark15. 21 And they compel one Simon a Cyrenian, who passed by, coming out of the country, the father of Alexander and Rufus, to bear his cross.

S

Matt. 5. 39. *See text of topic.*

T

I Cor. 6. 7. *See under P.*

Heb. 10. 34 For ye had compassion of me in my bonds, and took joyfully the spoiling of your goods, knowing in yourselves that ye have in heaven a better and an enduring substance.

§ 43. THE SERMON ON THE MOUNT: THE LAW FURTHER EXPLAINED,

CHAP. 5.

42 [u]Give to him that asketh thee, and from him that would borrow of thee turn not thou away.

43 Ye have heard that it hath been said, [x]Thou shalt love thy neighbour, [y]and hate thine enemy.

44 But I say unto you, [z]Love your enemies, bless them that curse you, do good to them that hate you, and pray [a]for them which despitefully use you, and persecute you:

45 That ye may be the children of your Father which is in heaven: for [b]he maketh his sun to rise on the evil and on the good, and sendeth rain on the just and on the unjust.

46 [c]For if ye love them which love you, what reward have ye? do not even the publicans the same?

47 And if ye salute your brethren only, what do ye more *than others?* do not even the publicans so?

U

Deut.15. 7 If there be among you a poor man of one of thy brethren within any of thy gates in thy land which the LORD thy God giveth thee, thou shalt not harden thine heart, nor shut thine hand from thy poor brother:

8 But thou shalt open thine hand wide unto him, and shalt surely lend him sufficient for his need, *in that* which he wanteth.

9 Beware that there be not a thought in thy wicked heart, saying, The seventh year, the year of release, is at hand; and thine eye be evil against thy poor brother, and thou givest him nought; and he cry unto the LORD against thee, and it be sin unto thee.

10 Thou shalt surely give him, and thine heart shall not be grieved when thou givest unto him: because that for this thing the LORD thy God shall bless thee in all thy works, and in all that thou puttest thine hand unto.

X

Lev. 19. 18 Thou shalt not avenge, nor bear any grudge against the children of thy people, but thou shalt love thy neighbour as thyself: I *am* the LORD.

Y

Deut.23. 6 Thou shalt not seek their peace nor their prosperity all thy days for ever.

Ps. 41. 10 But thou, O LORD, be merciful unto me, and raise me up, that I may requite them.

Z

Prov.25. 21 If thine enemy be hungry, give him bread to eat; and if he be thirsty, give him water to drink:

Luke 6. 27, 35. *See text of topic.*

Rom.12. 14 Bless them which persecute you: bless, and curse not.

Rom.12. 20 Therefore if thine enemy hunger, feed him; if he thirst, give him drink: for in so doing thou shalt heap coals of fire on his head.

A

Luke 23. 34 Then said Jesus, Father, forgive them; for they know not what they do. And they parted his raiment, and cast lots.

Acts 7. 60 And he kneeled down, and cried with a loud voice, Lord, lay not this sin to their charge. And when he had said this, he fell asleep.

I Cor. 4. 12 And labour, working with our own hands: being reviled, we bless; being persecuted, we suffer it:

13 Being defamed, we entreat: we are made as the filth of the world, *and are* the offscouring of all things unto this day.

I Pet. 2. 23 Who, when he was reviled, reviled not again; when he suffered, he threatened not; but committed *himself* to him that judgeth righteously:

I Pet. 3. 9. *See under P, page 133.*

B

Job 25. 3 Is there any number of his armies? and upon whom doth not his light arise?

C

Luke 6. 32. *See text of topic.*

D

Deut. 15. 7, 8, 10. *See under U.*

Prov. 3. 27 Withhold not good from them to whom it is due, when it is in the power of thine hand to do *it.*

Prov.21. 26 He coveteth greedily all the day long: but the righteous giveth and spareth not.

Matt. 5. 42. *See text of topic.*

(CONTINUED). TIME, SUMMER, A. D. 28; PLACE, NEAR CAPERNAUM [HORNS OF HATTIN].

CHAP. 6.

30 [d]Give to every man that asketh of thee; and of him that taketh away thy goods ask *them* not again. (p. 145.)

* * * * *

27 [e]But I say unto you which hear, Love your enemies, do good to them which hate you,

28 Bless them that curse you, and [f]pray for them which despitefully use you. (p. 133.)

* * * * *

32 [g]For if ye love them which love you, what thank have ye? for sinners also love those that love them.

33 And if ye do good to them which do good to you, what thank have ye? for sinners also do even the same.

34 [h]And if ye lend *to them* of whom ye hope to receive, what thank have ye? for sinners also lend to sinners, to receive as much again.

35 But [i]love ye your enemies, and do good, and [k]lend, hoping for nothing again; and your reward shall be great, and [l]ye shall be the children of the Highest: [m]for he is kind unto the unthankful and *to* the evil.

E

Ex. 23. 4 If thou meet thine enemy's ox or his ass going astray, thou shalt surely bring it back to him again.

Prov. 24. 17 Rejoice not when thine enemy falleth, and let not thine heart be glad when he stumbleth:

Prov. 25. 21. *See under Z.*
Matt. 5. 44 and Luke 6. 35. *See text of topic.*
Rom. 12. 20. *See under Z.*

F

Luke 23. 34 and Acts 7. 60. *See under A.*

G

Matt. 5. 46. *See text of topic.*

H

Matt. 5. 42. *See text of topic.*

I

Luke 6. 27. *See text of topic.*

K

Lev. 25. 25 If thy brother be waxen poor, and hath sold away *some* of his possession, and if any of his kin come to redeem it, then shall he redeem that which his brother sold.

Lev. 25. 35 And if thy brother be waxen poor, and fallen in decay with thee; then thou shalt relieve him: *yea, though he be* a stranger, or a sojourner; that he may live with thee.

Ps. 37. 25 I have been young, and *now* am old; yet have I not seen the righteous forsaken, nor his seed begging bread.

26 *He is* ever merciful, and lendeth; and his seed *is* blessed.

L

Matt. 5. 45. *See text of topic.*

John 13. 35 By this shall all *men* know that ye are my disciples, if ye have love one to another.

John 15. 8 Herein is my Father glorified, that ye bear much fruit; so shall ye be my disciples.

I Jno. 3. 1 Behold, what manner of love the Father hath bestowed upon us, that we should be called the sons of God: therefore the world knoweth us not, because it knew him not.

I Jno. 3. 10 In this the children of God are manifest, and the children of the devil: whosoever doeth not righteousness is not of God, neither he that loveth not his brother.

11 For this is the message that ye heard from the beginning, that we should love one another.

12 Not as Cain, *who* was of that wicked one, and slew his brother. And wherefore slew he him? Because his own works were evil, and his brother's righteous.

13 Marvel not, my brethren, if the world hate you.

14 We know that we have passed from death unto life, because we love the brethren. He that loveth not *his* brother abideth in death.

M

Ps. 145. 8 The LORD *is* gracious, and full of compassion; slow to anger, and of great mercy.

9 The LORD *is* good to all: and his tender mercies *are* over all his works.

Acts 14. 17 Nevertheless he left not himself without witness, in that he did good, and gave us rain from heaven, and fruitful seasons, filling our hearts with food and gladness.

§ 43. THE SERMON ON THE MOUNT: ALMSGIVING, PRAYER,

CHAP. 5.

48 [n]Be ye therefore perfect, even [o]as your Father which is in heaven is perfect.

CHAP. 6.

1 Take heed that ye do not your [7]alms before men, to be seen of them: otherwise ye have no reward [8]of your Father which is in heaven.

2 Therefore [p]when thou doest *thine* alms, [q]do not sound a trumpet before thee, as the hypocrites do in the synagogues and in the streets, that they may have glory of men. Verily I say unto you, They have their reward.

3 But when thou doest alms, let not thy left hand know what thy right hand doeth:

4 That thine alms may be in secret: and thy Father which seeth in secret himself [q]shall reward thee openly.

5 And when thou prayest, thou shalt not be as the hypocrites *are:* for they love to pray standing in the synagogues and in the corners of the streets, that they may be seen of men. Verily I say unto you, They have their reward.

6 But thou, when thou prayest, [r]enter into thy closet, and when thou hast shut thy door, pray to thy Father which is in secret; and thy Father which [s]seeth in secret shall reward thee openly.

7 But when ye pray, [t]use not vain repetitions, as the heathen *do:* for they think that they shall be heard for their much speaking.

8 Be not ye therefore like unto them: for your [u]Father knoweth what things ye have need of, before ye ask him.

N

Gen. 17. 1 And when Abram was ninety years old and nine, the LORD appeared to Abram, and said unto him, I *am* the Almighty God; walk before me, and be thou perfect.

Lev. 11. 44 For I *am* the LORD your God: ye shall therefore sanctify yourselves, and ye shall be holy; for I *am* holy: neither shall ye defile yourselves with any manner of creeping thing that creepeth upon the earth.

Lev. 19. 2 Speak unto all the congregation of the children of Israel, and say unto them, Ye shall be holy: for I the LORD your God *am* holy.

Luke 6. 36. *See text of topic.*

Col. 1. 28 Whom we preach, warning every man, and teaching every man in all wisdom; that we may present every man perfect in Christ Jesus;

Col. 4. 12 Epaphras, who is *one* of you, a servant of Christ, saluteth you, always labouring fervently for you in prayers, that ye may stand perfect and complete in all the will of God.

Jas. 1. 4 But let patience have *her* perfect work, that ye may be perfect and entire, wanting nothing.

I Pet. 1. 15 But as he which hath called you is holy, so be ye holy in all manner of conversation;

16 Because it is written, Be ye holy; for I am holy.

O

Eph. 5. 1 Be ye therefore followers of God, as dear children;

2 And walk in love, as Christ also hath loved us, and hath given himself for us an offering and a sacrifice to God for a sweet-smelling savour.

7

Or, *righteousness.*

Deut. 24. 12 And if the man *be* poor, thou shalt not sleep with his pledge:

13 In any case thou shalt deliver him the pledge again when the sun goeth down, that he may sleep in his own raiment, and bless thee: and it shall be righteousness unto thee before the LORD thy God.

Ps. 112. 9 He hath dispersed, he hath given to the poor; his righteousness endureth forever; his horn shall be exalted with honour.

Dan. 4. 27 Wherefore, O king, let my counsel be acceptable unto thee, and break off thy sins by righteousness, and thine iniquities by showing mercy to the poor; if it may be a lengthening of thy tranquillity.

(CONTINUED). TIME, SUMMER, A. D. 28; PLACE, NEAR CAPERNAUM [HORNS OF HATTIN].

CHAP. 6.

36 [x]Be ye therefore merciful, as your Father also is merciful. (p. 143.)

O—CONCLUDED.

II Cor. 9. 9 (As it is written, He hath dispersed abroad; he hath given to the poor: his righteousness remaineth forever.

10 Now he that ministereth seed to the sower both minister bread for *your* food, and multiply your seed sown, and increase the fruits of your righteousness:)

8

Or, *with.*

P

Rom. 12. 8 Or he that exhorteth, on exhortation: he that giveth, *let him do it* with simplicity; he that ruleth, with diligence; he that showeth mercy, with cheerfulness.

9

Or, *cause not a trumpet to be sounded.*

Q

Luke 14. 14 And thou shalt be blessed; for they cannot recompense thee: for thou shalt be recompensed at the resurrection of the just.

R

II Ki. 4. 33 He went in therefore, and shut the door upon them twain, and prayed unto the LORD.

Isa. 26. 20 Come, my people, enter thou into thy chambers, and shut thy doors about thee: hide thyself as it were for a little moment, until the indignation be overpast.

S

Jer. 17. 10 I the LORD search the heart, *I* try the reins, even to give every man according to his ways, *and* according to the fruit of his doings.

T

I Ki. 18. 26 And they took the bullock which was given them, and they dressed *it*, and called on the name of Baal from morning even until noon, saying, O Baal, hear us. But *there was* no voice, nor any that answered. And they leaped upon the altar which was made.

27 And it came to pass at noon, that Elijah mocked them, and said, Cry aloud: for he *is* a god; either he is talking, or he is pursuing, or he is in a journey, *or* peradventure he sleepeth, and must be awaked.

T—CONCLUDED.

I Ki. 18. 28 And they cried aloud, and cut themselves after their manner with knives and lancets, till the blood gushed out upon them.

29 And it came to pass, when midday was past, and they prophesied until the *time* of the offering of the *evening* sacrifice, that *there was* neither voice, nor any to answer, nor any that regarded.

Eccl. 5. 2 Be not rash with thy mouth, and let not thine heart be hasty to utter *any* thing before God: for God *is* in heaven, and thou upon earth: therefore let thy words be few.

3 For a dream cometh through the multitude of business; and a fool's voice *is known* by multitude of words.

Eccl. 5. 7 For in the multitude of dreams and many words *there are* also *divers* vanities: but fear thou God.

Acts 19. 34 But when they knew that he was a Jew, all with one voice about the space of two hours cried out, Great *is* Diana of the Ephesians.

U

Ps. 38. 9 Lord, all my desire *is* before thee; and my groaning is not hid from thee.

Ps. 69. 17 And hide not thy face from thy servant; for I am in trouble: hear me speedily.

18 Draw nigh unto my soul, *and* redeem it: deliver me because of mine enemies.

19 Thou hast known my reproach, and my shame, and my dishonour: mine adversaries *are* all before thee.

Ps. 139. 2 Thou knowest my downsitting and mine uprising; thou understandest my thought afar off.

Luke 12. 30 For all these things do the nations of the world seek after: and your Father knoweth that ye have need of these things.

John 16. 23 And in that day ye shall ask me nothing. Verily, verily, I say unto you, Whatsoever ye shall ask the Father in my name, he will give *it* you.

24 Hitherto have ye asked nothing in my name: ask, and ye shall receive, that your joy may be full.

Phil. 4. 6 Be careful for nothing; but in every thing by prayer and supplication with thanksgiving let your requests be made known unto God.

X

Matt. 5. 48. *See text of topic.*
Eph. 5. 1, 2. *See under O.*

§ 43. THE SERMON ON THE MOUNT: FASTING, (CONTINUED).

CHAP. 6.

9 After this manner therefore pray
ye: [y]Our Father which art in heaven,
[z]Hallowed be thy name.

10 Thy kingdom come. [a]Thy will
be done in earth, [b]as *it is* in heaven.

11 Give us this day our [c]daily bread.

12 And [d]forgive us our debts, as we
forgive our debtors.

13 [e]And lead us not into temptation,
but [f]deliver us from evil: [g]For thine
is the kingdom, and the power, and
the glory, for ever. Amen.

14 [h]For if ye forgive men their trespasses, your heavenly Father will also
forgive you:

15 But [i]if ye forgive not men their
trespasses, neither will your Father
forgive your trespasses.

16 Moreover [k]when ye fast, be not,
as the hypocrites, of a sad countenance: for they disfigure their faces,
that they may appear unto men to
fast. Verily I say unto you, They
have their reward.

17 But thou, when thou fastest,
[l]anoint thine head, and wash thy
face;

18 That thou appear not unto men
to fast, but unto thy Father which is
in secret: and thy Father which seeth
in secret shall reward thee openly.

19 [m]Lay not up for yourselves treasures upon earth, where moth and rust
doth corrupt, and where thieves break
through and steal:

Y

Luke 11. 2 And he said unto them, When ye pray, say, Our Father which art in heaven, Hallowed be thy name. Thy kingdom come. Thy will be done, as in heaven, so in earth.

Y—CONCLUDED.

Luke 11. 3 Give us day by day our daily bread.

4 And forgive us our sins; for we also forgive everyone that is indebted to us. And lead us not into temptation; but deliver us from evil.

Z

Isa. 6. 3 And one cried unto another, and said, Holy, holy, holy, *is* the LORD of hosts: the whole earth *is* full of his glory.

A

Matt. 26. 39 And he went a little further, and fell on his face, and prayed, saying, O my Father, if it be possible, let this cup pass from me: nevertheless, not as I will, but as thou *wilt*.

Matt. 26. 42 He went away again the second time, and prayed, saying, O my Father, if this cup may not pass away from me, except I drink it, thy will be done.

Acts 21. 14 And when he would not be persuaded, we ceased, saying, The will of the Lord be done.

B

Ps. 103. 20 Bless the LORD, ye his angels, that excel in strength, that do his commandments, hearkening unto the voice of his word.

21 Bless ye the LORD, all *ye* his hosts; *ye* ministers of his, that do his pleasure.

C

Job 23. 12 Neither have I gone back from the commandment of his lips; I have esteemed the words of his mouth more than my necessary *food*.

Prov. 30. 8 Remove far from me vanity and lies; give me neither poverty nor riches; feed me with food convenient for me:

D

Matt. 18. 21 Then came Peter to him, and said, Lord, how oft shall my brother sin against me, and I forgive him? till seven times?

22 Jesus saith unto him, I say not unto thee, Until seven times: but, Until seventy times seven.

E

Matt. 26. 41 Watch and pray, that ye enter not into temptation: the spirit indeed *is* willing, but the flesh *is* weak.

Luke 22. 40 And when he was at the place, he said unto them, Pray that ye enter not into temptation.

TIME, SUMMER, A. D. 28; PLACE, NEAR CAPERNAUM [HORNS OF HATTIN].

[CHAP. 6.]

E—CONCLUDED.

Luke 22. 46 And said unto them, Why sleep ye? rise and pray, lest ye enter into temptation.

I Cor.10. 13 There hath no temptation taken you but such as is common to man: but God *is* faithful, who will not suffer you to be tempted above that ye are able; but will with the temptation also make a way to escape, that ye may be able to bear *it*.

II Pet.2. 9 The Lord knoweth how to deliver the godly out of temptation, and to reserve the unjust unto the day of judgment to be punished:

Rev. 3. 10 Because thou hast kept the word of my patience, I also will keep thee from the hour of temptation, which shall come upon all the world, to try them that dwell upon the earth.

F

John 17. 15 I pray not that thou shouldest take them out of the world, but that thou shouldest keep them from the evil.

G

I Chr.29. 11 Thine, O LORD, *is* the greatness, and the power, and the glory, and the victory, and the majesty: for all *that is* in the heaven and in the earth *is thine;* thine *is* the kingdom, O LORD, and thou art exalted as head above all.

H

Mark 11. 25 And when ye stand praying, forgive, if ye have aught against any; that your Father also which is in heaven may forgive you your trespasses.

26 But if ye do not forgive, neither will your Father which is in heaven forgive your trespasses.

Eph. 4. 32 And be ye kind one to another, tender-hearted, forgiving one another, even as God for Christ's sake hath forgiven you.

Col. 3. 13 Forbearing one another, and forgiving one another, if any man have a quarrel against any: even as Christ forgave you, so also *do* ye.

I

Matt.18. 35 So likewise shall my heavenly Father do also unto you, if ye from your hearts forgive not every one his brother their trespasses.

Jas. 2. 13 For he shall have judgment without mercy, that hath showed no mercy; and mercy rejoiceth against judgment.

K

Isa. 58. 5 Is it such a fast that I have chosen? a day for a man to afflict his soul? *is it* to bow down his head as a bulrush, and to spread sackcloth and ashes *under him?* wilt thou call this a fast, and an acceptable day to the LORD?

L

Ruth 3. 3 Wash thyself therefore, and anoint thee, and put thy raiment upon thee, and get thee down to the floor: *but* make not thyself known unto the man, until he shall have done eating and drinking.

Dan. 10. 3 I ate no pleasant bread, neither came flesh nor wine in my mouth, neither did I anoint myself at all, till three whole weeks were fulfilled.

M

Job 31. 24 If I have made gold my hope, or have said to the fine gold, *Thou art* my confidence;

25 If I rejoiced because my wealth *was* great, and because mine hand had gotten much;

26 If I beheld the sun when it shined, or the moon walking *in* brightness;

27 And my heart hath been secretly enticed, or my mouth hath kissed my hand:

28 This also *were* an inquity *to be punished by* the judge: for I should have denied the God *that is* above.

Prov.23. 4 Labor not to be rich: cease from thine own wisdom.

I Tim. 6. 17 Charge them that are rich in this world, that they be not high-minded, nor trust in uncertain riches, but in the living God, who giveth us richly all things to enjoy.

Heb. 13. 5 *Let your* conversation *be* without covetousness; *and be* content with such things as ye have: for he hath said, I will never leave thee, nor forsake thee.

Jas. 5. 1 Go to now, *ye* rich men, weep and howl for your miseries that shall come upon *you*.

2 Your riches are corrupted, and your garments are moth-eaten.

3 Your gold and silver is cankered; and the rust of them shall be a witness against you, and shall eat your flesh as it were fire. Ye have heaped treasure together for the last days.

4 Behold, the hire of the labourers who have reaped down your fields, which is of you kept back by fraud, crieth: and the cries of them which have reaped are entered into the ears of the Lord of Sabaoth.

For M concluded see next page (140).

§ 43. THE SERMON ON THE MOUNT: TREASURE, SERVICE, (Continued).

Chap. 6.

20 [n]But lay up for yourselves treasures in heaven, where neither moth nor rust doth corrupt, and where thieves do not break through nor steal:

21 For where your treasure is, there will your heart be also.

22 [o]The light of the body is the eye: if therefore thine eye be single, thy whole body shall be full of light.

23 But if thine eye be evil, thy whole body shall be full of darkness. If therefore the light that is in thee be darkness, how great *is* that darkness!

24 [p]No man can serve two masters: for either he will hate the one, and love the other; or else he will hold to the one, and despise the other. [q]Ye cannot serve God and mammon.

25 Therefore I say unto you, [r]Take no thought for your life, what ye shall eat, or what ye shall drink; nor yet for your body, what ye shall put on. Is not the life more than meat, and the body than raiment?

26 [s]Behold the fowls of the air: for they sow not, neither do they reap, nor gather into barns; yet your heavenly Father feedeth them. Are ye not much better than they?

27 Which of you by taking thought can add one cubit unto his stature?

28 And why take ye thought for raiment? Consider the lilies of the field, how they grow; they toil not, neither do they spin:

29 And yet I say unto you, That even Solomon in all his glory was not arrayed like one of these.

M—Concluded.

Jas. 5. 5 Ye have lived in pleasure on the earth, and been wanton; ye have nourished your hearts, as in a day of slaughter.

N

Job 31. 24 If I have made gold my hope, or have said to the fine gold, *Thou art* my confidence;

Ps. 39. 6 Surely every man walketh in a vain show: surely they are disquieted in vain: he heapeth up *riches,* and knoweth not who shall gather them.

Ps. 62. 10 Trust not in oppression, and become not vain in robbery: if riches increase, set not your heart *upon them.*

Prov. 11. 4 Riches profit not in the day of wrath: but righteousness delivereth from death.

Prov. 23. 5 Wilt thou set thine eyes upon that which is not? for *riches* certainly make themselves wings; they fly away as an eagle toward heaven.

Eccl. 2. 26 For *God* giveth to a man that *is* good in his sight, wisdom, and knowledge, and joy: but to the sinner he giveth travail, to gather and to heap up, that he may give to *him that is* good before God. This also *is* vanity and vexation of spirit.

Eccl. 5. 10 He that loveth silver shall not be satisfied with silver; nor he that loveth abundance with increase: this *is* also vanity.

11 When goods increase, they are increased that eat them: and what good *is there* to the owners thereof, saving the beholding *of them* with their eyes?

12 The sleep of a labouring man *is* sweet, whether he eat little or much: but the abundance of the rich will not suffer him to sleep.

13 There is a sore evil *which* I have seen under the sun, *namely,* riches kept for the owners thereof to their hurt.

14 But those riches perish by evil travail: and he begetteth a son, and *there is* nothing in his hand.

Zeph. 1. 18 Neither their silver nor their gold shall be able to deliver them in the day of the Lord's wrath; but the whole land shall be devoured by the fire of his jealousy: for he shall make even a speedy riddance of all them that dwell in the land.

Matt. 19. 21 Jesus said unto him, If thou wilt be perfect, go *and* sell that thou hast, and give to the poor, and thou shalt

Time, Summer, A. D. 28; Place, Near Capernaum [Horns of Hattin].

[Chap. 6.]

N—Concluded.

have treasure in heaven: and come
and follow me.
Luke12. 33 Sell that ye have, and give alms;
provide yourselves bags which wax
not old, a treasure in the heavens that
faileth not, where no thief approacheth, neither moth corrupteth.
34 For where your treasure is, there
will your heart be also.
Luke 18. 22 Now when Jesus heard these
things, he said unto him, Yet lackest
thou one thing: sell all that thou
hast, and distribute unto the poor,
and thou shalt have treasure in heav-
en: and come, follow me.
I Tim.6. 7 For we brought nothing into *this*
world, *and it is* certain we can carry
nothing out.
8 And having food and raiment, let
us be therewith content.
9 But they that will be rich fall into
temptation and a snare, and *into* many
foolish and hurtful lusts, which drown
men in destruction and perdition.
10 For the love of money is the root
of all evil: which while some coveted
after, they have erred from the faith,
and pierced themselves through with
many sorrows.
I Tim.6. 19 Laying up in store for themselves
a good foundation against the time to
come, that they may lay hold on eternal life.
I Pet. 1. 4 To an inheritance incorruptible,
and undefiled, and that fadeth not
away, reserved in heaven for you,

O

Luke 11. 34 The light of the body is the eye:
therefore when thine eye is single, thy
whole body also is full of light; but
when *thine eye* is evil, thy body also *is*
full of darkness.
35 Take heed therefore, that the
light which is in thee be not darkness.
36 If thy whole body therefore *be*
full of light, having no part dark, the
whole shall be full of light, as when
the bright shining of a candle doth
give thee light.

P

Luke 16. 13 No servant can serve two masters:
for either he will hate the one, and
love the other; or else he will hold to
the one, and despise the other. Ye
cannot serve God and mammon.

Q

Gal. 1. 10 For do I now persuade men, or

Q—Concluded.

God? or do I seek to please men? for
if I yet pleased men, I should not be
the servant of Christ.
I Tim. 6. 17 Charge them that are rich in this
world, that they be not high-minded,
nor trust in uncertain riches, but in
the living God, who giveth us richly
all things to enjoy;
18 That they do good, that they be
rich in good works, ready to distribute,
willing to communicate:
Jas. 4. 4 Ye adulterers and adulteresses,
know ye not that the friendship of the
world is enmity with God? whosoever
therefore will be a friend of the world
is the enemy of God.
I Jno. 2. 15 Love not the world, neither the
things *that are* in the world. If any
man love the world, the love of the
Father is not in him.

R

Ps. 55. 22 Cast thy burden upon the Lord,
and he shall sustain thee: he shall
never suffer the righteous to be moved.
Luke12. 22 And he said unto his disciples,
Therefore I say unto you, Take no
thought for your life, what ye shall
eat; neither for the body, what ye
shall put on.
23 The life is more than meat, and
the body *is more* than raiment.
Phil. 4. 6 Be careful for nothing; but in
every thing by prayer and supplication with thanksgiving let your requests be made known unto God.
I Pet. 5. 7 Casting all your care upon him;
for he careth for you.

S

Job 38. 41 Who provideth for the raven his
food? when his young ones cry unto
God, they wander for lack of meat.
Ps. 104. 10 He sendeth the springs into the
valleys, *which* run among the hills.
11 They give drink to every beast of
the field: the wild asses quench their
thirst.
Ps. 147. 9 He giveth to the beast his food,
and to the young ravens which cry.
Luke12. 24 Consider the ravens: for they
neither sow nor reap; which neither
have storehouse nor barn; and God
feedeth them: how much more are ye
better than the fowls?
25 And which of you with taking
thought can add to his stature one
cubit?
26 If ye then be not able to do that
thing which is least, why take ye
thought for the rest?

§ 43. THE SERMON ON THE MOUNT: TRUST, JUDGE NOT, (CONTINUED).

CHAP. 6.

30 Wherefore, if God so clothe the grass of the field, which to day is, and to morrow is cast into the oven, *shall he* not much more *clothe* you, O ye of little faith?

31 Therefore take no thought, saying, What shall we eat? or, What shall we drink? or, Wherewithal shall we be clothed?

32 (For after all these things do the Gentiles seek:) for your [t]heavenly Father knoweth that ye have need of all these things.

33 But [u]seek ye first the kingdom of God, and his righteousness; and all these things shall be added unto you.

34 Take therefore no [10]thought for the morrow: for the morrow shall take thought for the things of itself. Sufficient unto the day *is* the evil thereof.

CHAP. 7.

1 Judge [x]not, that ye be not judged.

2 For with what judgment ye judge, ye shall be judged; [y]and with what measure ye mete, it shall be measured to you again.

3 [z]And why beholdest thou the mote that is in thy brother's eye, but considerest not the beam that is in thine own eye?

4 Or how wilt thou say to thy brother, Let me pull out the mote out of thine eye; and, behold, a beam *is* in thine own eye?

5 Thou hypocrite, first cast out the beam out of thine own eye; and then shalt thou see clearly to cast out the mote out of thy brother's eye.

T

Phil. 4. 19 But my God shall supply all your need according to his riches in glory by Christ Jesus.

U

I Ki. 3. 13 And I have also given thee that which thou hast not asked, both riches, and honor: so that there shall not be any among the kings like unto thee all thy days.

Ps. 34. 9 O fear the LORD, ye his saints: for *there is* no want to them that fear him.

Ps. 37. 25 I have been young, and *now* am old; yet have I not seen the righteous forsaken, nor his seed begging bread.

Mark10. 30 But he shall receive a hundredfold now in this time, houses, and brethren, and sisters, and mothers, and children, and lands, with persecutions; and in the world to come eternal life.

Luke12. 31 But rather seek ye the kingdom of God; and all these things shall be added unto you.

Rom. 8. 32 He that spared not his own Son, but delivered him up for us all, how shall he not with him also freely give us all things?

IITim.4. 8 Henceforth there is laid up for me a crown of righteousness, which the Lord, the righteous judge, shall give me at that day: and not to me only, but unto all them also that love his appearing.

10

Anxious thought.

X

Luke 6. 37. *See text of topic.*

Rom. 2. 1 Therefore thou art inexcusable, O man, whosoever thou art that judgest: for wherein thou judgest another, thou condemnest thyself; for thou that judgest doest the same things.

Rom.14. 10 But why dost thou judge thy brother? or why dost thou set at nought thy brother? for we shall all stand before the judgment seat of Christ.

Rom.14. 13 Let us not therefore judge one another any more: but judge this rather, that no man put a stumblingblock or an occasion to fall in *his* brother's way.

I Cor. 4. 3 But with me it is a very small thing that I should be judged of you, or of man's judgment: yea, I judge not mine own self.

I Cor. 4. 5 Therefore judge nothing before the time, until the Lord come, who both will bring to light the hidden

TIME, SUMMER, A. D. 28; PLACE, NEAR CAPERNAUM [HORNS OF HATTIN].

CHAP. 6.

37 [a]Judge not, and ye shall not be
judged: condemn not, and ye shall
not be condemned: forgive, and ye
shall be forgiven:
38 [b]Give, and it shall be given unto
you; good measure, pressed down, and
shaken together, and running over,
shall men give into your [c]bosom. For
[d]with the same measure that ye mete
withal it shall be measured to you
again.
39 And he spake a parable unto
them; [e]Can the blind lead the blind?
shall they not both fall into the ditch?
40 [f]The disciple is not above his
master: but every one [11]that is perfect shall be as his master.
41 [g]And why beholdest thou the
mote that is in thy brother's eye, but
perceivest not the beam that is in thine
own eye?
42 Either how canst thou say to thy
brother, Brother, let me pull out the
mote that is in thine eye, when thou
thyself beholdest not the beam that is
in thine own eye? Thou hypocrite,
[h]cast out first the beam out of thine
own eye, and then shalt thou see
clearly to pull out the mote that is in
thy brother's eye. (p. 147.)

X—CONTINUED.

things of darkness, and will make manifest the counsels of the hearts: and then shall every man have praise of God.

Jas. 4. 11 Speak not evil one of another, brethren. He that speaketh evil of *his* brother, and judgeth his brother, speaketh evil of the law, and judgeth the law: but if thou judge the law, thou art not a doer of the law, but a judge.

X—CONCLUDED.

Jas. 4. 12 There is one lawgiver, who is able to save and to destroy: who art thou that judgest another?

Y

Mark 4. 24 And he said unto them, Take heed what ye hear. With what measure ye mete, it shall be measured to you; and unto you that hear shall more be given.

Luke 6. 38. *See text of topic.*

Z

Luke 6. 41, 42. *See text of topic.*

A

Matt. 7. 1. *See text of topic.*
Jas. 4. 11. *See under X.*

B

Prov. 19. 17 He that hath pity upon the poor lendeth unto the LORD; and that which he hath given will he pay him again.

C

Ps. 79. 12 And render unto our neighbours sevenfold into their bosom their reproach, wherewith they have reproached thee, O Lord.

D

Matt. 7. 2. *See text of topic.*
Mark 4. 24. *See under Y.*

Jas 2. 13 For he shall have judgment without mercy, that hath showed no mercy; and mercy rejoiceth against judgment.

E

Matt. 15. 14 Let them alone: they be blind leaders of the blind. And if the blind lead the blind, both shall fall into the ditch.

F

Matt. 10. 24 The disciple is not above *his* master, nor the servant above his lord.

John 13. 16 Verily, verily, I say unto you, The servant is not greater than his lord; neither he that is sent greater than he that sent him.

John 15. 20 Remember the word that I said unto you, The servant is not greater than his lord. If they have persecuted me, they will also persecute you; if they have kept my saying, they will keep yours also.

11

Or, *shall be perfect as his master.*

G

Matt. 7. 3. *See text of topic.*

H

Prov. 18. 17 *He that is* first in his own cause *seemeth* just; but his neighbour cometh and searcheth him.

§ 43. THE SERMON ON THE MOUNT: ASK, ENTER IN, THE GOLDEN RULE, I—CONCLUDED.

CHAP. 7.

6 [i]Give not that which is holy unto the
dogs, neither cast ye your pearls before
swine, lest they trample them under
their feet, and turn again and rend you.
7 [k]Ask, and it shall be given you;
seek, and ye shall find; knock, and it
shall be opened unto you:
8 For [l]every one that asketh receiveth; and he that seeketh findeth; and
to him that knocketh it shall be opened.
9 [m]Or what man is there of you,
whom if his son ask bread, will he
give him a stone?
10 Or if he ask a fish, will he give
him a serpent?
11 If ye then, [n]being evil, know
how to give good gifts unto your children, how much [o]more shall your
Father which is in heaven give good
things to them that ask him?
12 Therefore all things [p]whatsoever
ye would that men should do to you,
do ye even so to them: for [q]this is the
law and the prophets.
13 [r]Enter ye in at the strait gate:
for [s]wide *is* the gate, and broad *is* the
way, that leadeth to destruction, and
many there be which go in thereat:
14 [12]Because strait *is* the gate, and
narrow *is* the way, which leadeth unto
life, and few there be that find it.

I

Prov. 9. 7 He that reproveth a scorner getteth to himself shame: and he that rebuketh a wicked *man getteth* himself a blot.

8 Reprove not a scorner, lest he hate thee: rebuke a wise man, and he will love thee.

Prov. 23. 9 Speak not in the ears of a fool: for he will despise the wisdom of thy words.

Acts 13. 45 But when the Jews saw the multitudes, they were filled with envy, and spake against those things which were spoken by Paul, contradicting and blaspheming.

46 Then Paul and Barnabas waxed bold, and said, It was necessary that the word of God should first have been spoken to you: but seeing ye put it from you, and judge yourselves unworthy of everlasting life, lo, we turn to the Gentiles.

K

Matt. 21. 22 And all things, whatsoever ye shall ask in prayer, believing, ye shall receive.

Mark 11. 24 Therefore I say unto you, What things soever ye desire, when ye pray, believe that ye receive *them*, and ye shall have *them*.

Luke 11. 9 And I say unto you, Ask, and it shall be given you; seek, and ye shall find; knock, and it shall be opened unto you.

10 For every one that asketh receiveth; and he that seeketh findeth; and to him that knocketh it shall be opened.

Luke 18. 1 And he spake a parable unto them *to this end*, that men ought always to pray, and not to faint;

John 14. 13 And whatsoever ye shall ask in my name, that will I do, that the Father may be glorified in the Son.

John 15. 7 If ye abide in me, and my words abide in you, ye shall ask what ye will, and it shall be done unto you.

John 16. 23 And in that day ye shall ask me nothing. Verily, verily, I say unto you, Whatsoever ye shall ask the Father in my name, he will give *it* you.

24 Hitherto have ye asked nothing in my name: ask, and ye shall receive, that your joy may be full.

Jas. 1. 5 If any of you lack wisdom, let him ask of God, that giveth to all *men* liberally, and upbraideth not; and it shall be given him.

6 But let him ask in faith, nothing wavering: for he that wavereth is like a wave of the sea driven with the wind and tossed.

I Jno. 3. 22 And whatsoever we ask, we receive of him, because we keep his commandments, and do those things that are pleasing in his sight.

I Jno. 5. 14 And this is the confidence that we have in him, that, if we ask anything according to his will, he heareth us:

(CONTINUED). TIME, SUMMER, A. D. 28; PLACE, NEAR CAPERNAUM [HORNS OF HATTIN].

CHAP. 6.

31 [t]And as ye would that men should do to you, do ye also to them likewise. (p. 135.)

K—CONCLUDED.

I Jno. 5. 15 And if we know that he hear us, whatsoever we ask, we know that we have the petitions that we desired of him.

L

Prov. 8. 17 I love them that love me; and those that seek me early shall find me.

Jer. 29. 12 Then shall ye call upon me, and ye shall go and pray unto me, and I will hearken unto you.

13 And ye shall seek me, and find *me*, when ye shall search for me with all your heart.

M

Luke 11. 11 If a son shall ask bread of any of you that is a father, will he give him a stone? or if *he ask* a fish, will he for a fish give him a serpent?

12 Or if he shall ask an egg, will he offer him a scorpion?

13 If ye then, being evil, know how to give good gifts unto your children; how much more shall *your* heavenly Father give the Holy Spirit to them that ask him?

N

Gen. 6. 5 And GOD saw that the wickedness of man *was* great in the earth, and *that* every imagination of the thoughts of his heart *was* only evil continually.

Gen. 8. 21 And the LORD smelled a sweet savour; and the LORD said in his heart, I will not again curse the ground any more for man's sake; for the imagination of man's heart *is* evil from his youth: neither will I again smite any more every thing living, as I have done.

O

Ps. 86. 5 For thou, Lord, *art* good, and ready to forgive; and plenteous in mercy unto all them that call upon thee.

Isa. 49. 15 Can a woman forget her sucking child, that she should not have compassion on the son of her womb? yea, they may forget, yet will I not forget thee.

Rom. 8. 32 He that spared not his own Son, but delivered him up for us all, how shall he not with him also freely give us all things?

P

Luke 6. 31. *See text of topic.*

Q

Lev. 19. 18 Thou shalt not avenge, nor bear any grudge against the children of thy people, but thou shalt love thy neighbour as thyself: I *am* the LORD.

Matt. 22. 40 On these two commandments hang all the law and the prophets.

Rom. 13. 8 Owe no man any thing, but to love one another: for he that loveth another hath fulfilled the law.

9 For this, Thou shalt not commit adultery, Thou shalt not kill, Thou shalt not steal, Thou shalt not bear false witness, Thou shalt not covet; and if *there be* any other commandment, it is briefly comprehended in this saying, namely, Thou shalt love thy neighbour as thyself.

10 Love worketh no ill to his neighbour: therefore love *is* the fulfilling of the law.

Gal. 5. 14 For all the law is fulfilled in one word, *even* in this; Thou shalt love thy neighbour as thyeslf.

I Tim. 1. 5 Now the end of the commandment is charity out of a pure heart, and *of* a good conscience, and *of* faith unfeigned:

R

Prov. 4. 26 Ponder the path of thy feet, and let all thy ways be established.

27 Turn not to the right hand nor to the left: remove thy foot from evil.

Prov. 9. 6 Forsake the foolish, and live; and go in the way of understanding.

Luke 13. 24 Strive to enter in at the strait gate: for many, I say unto you, will seek to enter in, and shall not be able.

S

Ps. 14. 2 The LORD looked down from heaven upon the children of men, to see if there were any that did understand, *and* seek God.

3 They are all gone aside, they are *all* together become filthy: *there is* none that doeth good, no, not one.

I Jno. 5. 19 *And* we know that we are of God, and the whole world lieth in wickedness.

12

Or, *how*.

T

Matt. 7. 12. *See text of topic.*

Phil. 4. 8 Finally, brethren, whatsoever things are true, whatsoever things *are* honest, whatsoever things *are* just, whatsoever things *are* pure, whatsoever things *are* lovely, whatsoever things *are* of good report; if *there be* any virtue, and if *there be* any praise, think on these things.

§ 43. THE SERMON ON THE MOUNT: FALSE PROPHETS, (CONTINUED).

CHAP. 7.

15 [u]Beware of false prophets, [x]which come to you in sheep's clothing, but inwardly they are [y]ravening wolves.

16 [z]Ye shall know them by their fruits. [a]Do men gather grapes of thorns, or figs of thistles?

17 Even so [b]every good tree bringeth forth good fruit; but a corrupt tree bringeth forth evil fruit.

18 A good tree cannot bring forth evil fruit, neither *can* a corrupt tree bring forth good fruit.

19 [c]Every tree that bringeth not forth good fruit is hewn down, and cast into the fire.

20 Wherefore by their fruits ye shall know them.

U

Deut.13. 3 Thou shalt not hearken unto the words of that prophet, or that dreamer of dreams: for the LORD your God proveth you, to know whether ye love the LORD your God with all your heart and with all your soul.

Jer. 23. 16 Thus saith the LORD of hosts, Hearken not unto the words of the prophets that prophesy unto you; they make you vain: they speak a vision of their own heart, *and* not out of the mouth of the LORD.

Matt.24. 4 And Jesus answered and said unto them, Take heed that no man deceive you.

5 For many shall come in my name, saying, I am Christ; and shall deceive many.

Matt.24. 11 And many false prophets shall rise, and shall deceive many.

Matt.24. 24 For there shall arise false Christs, and false prophets, and shall show great signs and wonders; insomuch that, if *it were* possible, they shall deceive the very elect.

Mark13. 22 For false Christs and false prophets shall rise, and shall show signs and wonders, to seduce, if *it were* possible, even the elect.

Rom.16. 17 Now I beseech you, brethren, mark them which cause divisions and offences contrary to the doctrine which ye have learned; and avoid them.

U—CONCLUDED.

Rom.16. 18 For they that are such serve not our Lord Jesus Christ, but their own belly; and by good words and fair speeches deceive the hearts of the simple.

Eph. 5. 6 Let no man deceive you with vain words: for because of these things cometh the wrath of God upon the children of disobedience.

Col. 2. 8 Beware lest any man spoil you through philosophy and vain deceit, after the tradition of men, after the rudiments of the world, and not after Christ.

IIPet. 2. 1 But there were false prophets also among the people, even as there shall be false teachers among you, who privily shall bring in damnable heresies, even denying the Lord that bought them, and bring upon themselves swift destruction.

2 And many shall follow their pernicious ways; by reason of whom the way of truth shall be evil spoken of.

3 And through covetousness shall they with feigned words make merchandise of you: whose judgment now of a long time lingereth not, and their damnation slumbereth not.

I Jno. 4. 1 Beloved, believe not every spirit, but try the spirits whether they are of God: because many false prophets are gone out into the world.

X

Mic. 3. 5 Thus saith the LORD concerning the prophets that make my people err, that bite with their teeth, and cry, Peace; and he that putteth not into their mouths, they even prepare war against him:

II Tim. 3. 5. *See under D.*

Y

Acts 20. 29 For I know this, that after my departing shall grievous wolves enter in among you, not sparing the flock.

30 Also of your own selves shall men arise, speaking perverse things, to draw away disciples after them.

Z

Matt. 7. 20. *See text of topic.*

Matt.12. 33 Either make the tree good, and his fruit good; or else make the tree corrupt, and his fruit corrupt: for the tree is known by *his* fruit.

A

Luke 6. 43, 44. *See text of topic.*

Time, Summer, A. D. 28: Place, Near Capernaum [Horns of Hattin].

Chap. 6.

43 [d]For a good tree bringeth not forth corrupt fruit; neither doth a corrupt tree bring forth good fruit.

44 For [e]every tree is known by his own fruit. For of thorns men do not gather figs, nor of a bramble bush gather they [13]grapes.

45 [f]A good man out of the good treasure of his heart bringeth forth that which is good; and an evil man out of the evil treasure of his heart bringeth forth that which is evil: for [g]of the abundance of the heart his mouth speaketh.

B

Jer. 11. 19 But I *was* like a lamb *or* an ox *that* is brought to the slaughter; and I knew not that they had devised devices against me, *saying*, Let us destroy the tree with the fruit thereof, and let us cut him off from the land of the living, that his name may be no more remembered.

Matt. 12. 33. *See under Z.*

C

Matt. 3. 10 And now also the axe is laid unto the root of the trees: therefore every tree which bringeth not forth good fruit is hewn down, and cast into the fire.

Luke 3. 9. *See text of* § 14.

John 15. 2 Every branch in me that beareth not fruit he taketh away: and every *branch* that beareth fruit, he purgeth it, that it may bring forth more fruit.

John 15. 6 If a man abide not in me, he is cast forth as a branch, and is withered; and men gather them, and cast *them* into the fire, and they are burned.

D

Matt. 7. 16, 17. *See text of topic.*

II Tim. 3. 1 This know also, that in the last days perilous times shall come.

2 For men shall be lovers of their own selves, covetous, boasters, proud, blasphemers, disobedient to parents, unthankful, unholy,

3 Without natural affection, trucebreakers, false accusers, incontinent, fierce, despisers of those that are good,

D—Concluded.

II Tim. 3. 4 Traitors, heady, high-minded, lovers of pleasures more than lovers of God:

5 Having a form of godliness, but denying the power thereof: from such turn away.

6 For of this sort are they which creep into houses, and lead captive silly women laden with sins, led away with divers lusts,

7 Ever learning, and never able to come to the knowledge of the truth.

8 Now as Jannes and Jambres withstood Moses, so do these also resist the truth: men of corrupt minds, reprobate concerning the faith.

9 But they shall proceed no further: for their folly shall be manifest unto all *men*, as theirs also was.

E

Matt. 12. 33. *See under Z.*

13

Gr., *a grape.*

F

Ps. 37. 30 The mouth of the righteous speaketh wisdom, and his tongue talketh of judgment.

31 The law of his God *is* in his heart; none of his steps shall slide.

Ps. 40. 7 Then said I, Lo, I come: in the volume of the book *it is* written of me,

8 I delight to do thy will, O my God: yea, thy law *is* within my heart.

9 I have preached righteousness in the great congregation: lo, I have not refrained my lips, O Lord, thou knowest.

Matt. 12. 35 A good man out of the good treasure of the heart bringeth forth good things: and an evil man out of the evil treasure bringeth forth evil things.

Rom. 8. 5 For they that are after the flesh do mind the things of the flesh; but they that are after the Spirit, the things of the Spirit.

6 For to be carnally minded *is* death; but to be spiritually minded *is* life and peace.

7 Because the carnal mind *is* enmity against God: for it is not subject to the law of God, neither indeed can be.

8 So then they that are in the flesh cannot please God.

G

Matt. 12. 34 O generation of vipers, how can ye, being evil, speak good things? for out of the abundance of the heart the mouth speaketh.

§43. THE SERMON ON THE MOUNT: THE WISE AND FOOLISH BUILDERS,

Chap. 7.

21 Not every one that saith unto me, [h]Lord, Lord, shall enter into the kingdom of heaven; but he that doeth the will of my Father which is in heaven.

22 Many will say to me in that day, Lord, Lord, have we [i]not prophesied in thy name? and in thy name have cast out devils? and in thy name done many wonderful works?

23 And [k]then will I profess unto them, I never knew you: [l]depart from me, ye that work iniquity.

24 Therefore [m] whosoever heareth these sayings of mine, and doeth them, I will liken him unto a wise man, which built his house upon a rock:

25 And the [n]rain descended, and the floods came, and the winds blew, and beat upon that house; and [o]it fell not: for it was founded upon a rock.

26 And every one that heareth these sayings of mine, and doeth them not, shall be likened unto a foolish man, which built his house upon the sand:

27 And the rain descended, and the floods came, and the winds blew, and beat upon that house; and it fell: and [p]great was the fall of it.

28 And it came to pass, when Jesus had ended these sayings, the people were astonished at his doctrine:

29 [q]For he taught them as *one* having authority, and not as the scribes.

Chap. 8.

1 When he was come down from the mountain, great multitudes followed him. (p. 100.)

H

Hos. 8. 2 Israel shall cry unto me, My God, we know thee.

Matt.25. 11 Afterward came also the other virgins, saying, Lord, Lord, open to us.

12 But he answered and said, Verily I say unto you, I know you not.

Luke 6. 46. *See text of topic.*

Luke 13. 25 When once the master of the house is risen up, and hath shut to the door, and ye begin to stand without, and to knock at the door, saying, Lord, Lord, open unto us; and he shall answer and say unto you, I know you not whence ye are:

Acts 19. 13 Then certain of the vagabond Jews, exorcists, took upon them to call over them which had evil spirits the name of the Lord Jesus, saying, We adjure you by Jesus whom Paul preacheth.

Rom. 2. 13 (For not the hearers of the law *are* just before God, but the doers of the law shall be justified.

Jas. 1. 22 But be ye doers of the word, and not hearers only, deceiving your own selves.

I

Num.24. 4 He hath said, *which* heard the words of God, which saw the vision of the Almighty, falling *into a trance*, but having his eyes open:

John 11. 51 And this spake he not of himself: but being high priest that year, he prophesied that Jesus should die for that nation;

I Cor.13. 2 And though I have *the gift of* prophecy, and understand all mysteries, and all knowledge; and though I have all faith, so that I could remove mountains, and have not charity, I am nothing.

K

Matt. 25. 12 and Luke 13. 25. *See under H.*

Luke 13. 27 But he shall say, I tell you, I know you not whence ye are; depart from me, all *ye* workers of iniquity.

II Tim.2. 19 Nevertheless the foundation of God standeth sure, having this seal, The Lord knoweth them that are his. And, Let every one that nameth the name of Christ depart from iniquity.

L

Ps. 5. 5 The foolish shall not stand in thy sight: thou hatest all workers of iniquity.

Ps. 6. 8 Depart from me, all ye workers of iniquity; for the Lord hath heard the voice of my weeping.

(CONCLUDED). TIME, SUMMER, A. D. 28; PLACE, NEAR CAPERNAUM [HORNS OF HATTIN].

CHAP. 6.

46 [r]And why call ye me, Lord, Lord,
and do not the things which I say?

47 [s]Whosoever cometh to me, and
heareth my sayings, and doeth them, I
will show you to whom he is like:

48 He is like a man which built a
house, and digged deep, and laid the
foundation on a rock: and when the
[t]flood arose, the stream beat vehemently upon that house, and could
not shake it; for it was founded upon
[u]a rock.

49 But he that heareth, and doeth
not, is like a man that without a foundation built a house upon the earth;
against which the stream did beat vehemently, and immediately it fell;
and [x]the ruin of that house was
great.

L—CONCLUDED.

Matt. 25. 41 Then shall he say also unto them on the left hand, Depart from me, ye cursed, into everlasting fire, prepared for the devil and his angels:

M

Luke 6. 47. *See text of topic.*

N

Acts 14. 22 Confirming the souls of the disciples, *and* exhorting them to continue in the faith, and that we must through much tribulation enter into the kingdom of God.

II Tim. 3. 12 Yea, and all that will live godly in Christ Jesus shall suffer persecution.

O

Rom. 8. 35 Who shall separate us from the love of Christ? *shall* tribulation, or distress, or persecution, or famine, or nakedness, or peril, or sword?

II Tim. 2. 19. *See under K.*

I Pet. 1. 5 Who are kept by the power of God through faith unto salvation ready to be revealed in the last time.

P

Heb. 10. 31 *It is* a fearful thing to fall into the hands of the living God.

P—CONCLUDED.

II Pet. 2. 20 For if after they have escaped the pollutions of the world through the knowledge of the Lord and Saviour Jesus Christ, they are again entangled therein, and overcome, the latter end is worse with them than the beginning.

Q

Isa. 50. 4 The Lord GOD hath given me the tongue of the learned, that I should know how to speak a word in season to *him that is* weary: he wakeneth morning by morning, he wakeneth mine ear to hear as the learned.

Mark 1. 22. *See text of § 31.*

John 7. 46 The officers answered, Never man spake like this man.

R

Mal. 1. 6 A son honoureth *his* father, and a servant his master: if then I *be* a father, where *is* mine honour? and if I *be* a master, where *is* my fear? saith the LORD of hosts unto you, O priests, that despise my name. And ye say, Wherein have we despised thy name?

Matt. 7. 21. *See text of topic.*

Matt. 25. 11, Luke 13. 25, Rom. 2. 13 and Jas. 1. 22. *See under H.*

S

Matt. 7. 24. *See text of topic.*

T

II Sa. 22. 5 When the waves of death compassed me, the floods of ungodly men made me afraid;

Ps. 32. 6 For this shall every one that is godly pray unto thee in a time when thou mayest be found: surely in the floods of great waters they shall not come nigh unto him.

Nah. 1. 8 But with an overrunning flood he will make an utter end of the place thereof, and darkness shall pursue his enemies.

Acts 14. 22 and II Tim. 3. 12. *See under N.*

U

Ps. 125. 1 They that trust in the LORD *shall be* as Mount Zion, *which* cannot be removed, *but* abideth for ever.

II Tim. 2. 19. *See under K.*

1 Pet. 1. 5. *See under O.*

Jude 1 Jude, the servant of Jesus Christ, and brother of James, to them that are sanctified by God the Father, and preserved in Jesus Christ, *and* called:

X

Job 8. 13 So *are* the paths of all that forget God; and the hypocrite's hope shall perish:

Heb. 10. 31 and II Pet. 2. 20. *See under P.*

§ 44. HEALING OF THE CENTURION'S SERVANT.

8: 5-13.

5 [a]And when Jesus was entered into Capernaum, there came unto him a centurion, beseeching him,

6 And saying, Lord, my servant lieth at home sick of the palsy, grievously tormented.

7 And Jesus saith unto him, I will come and heal him.

8 The centurion answered and said, Lord, [b]I am not worthy that thou shouldest come under my roof: but [c]speak the word only, and my servant shall be healed.

9 For I am a man under authority, having soldiers under me: and I say to this *man*, Go, and he goeth; and to another, Come, and he cometh; and to my servant, Do this, and he doeth *it*.

10 When Jesus heard *it*, he marvelled, and said to them that followed, Verily I say unto you, I have not found so great faith, no, not in Israel.

11 And I say unto you, That [d]many shall come from the east and west, and shall sit down with Abraham, and Isaac, and Jacob, in the kingdom of heaven:

A

Luke 7. 1, etc. *See text of topic.*

B

Luke 15. 19 And am no more worthy to be called thy son: make me as one of thy hired servants.

Luke 15. 21 And the son said unto him, Father, I have sinned against heaven, and in thy sight, and am no more worthy to be called thy son.

C

Ps. 33. 9 For he spake, and it was *done;* he commanded, and it stood fast.

Ps. 107. 20 He sent his word, and healed them, and delivered *them* from their destructions.

D

Gen. 12. 3 And I will bless them that bless thee, and curse him that curseth thee: and in thee shall all families of the earth be blessed.

Gen. 22. 18 And in thy seed shall all the nations of the earth be blessed; because thou hast obeyed my voice.

Gen. 28. 14 And thy seed shall be as the dust of the earth; and thou shalt spread abroad to the west, and to the east, and to the north, and to the south: and in thee and in thy seed shall all the families of the earth be blessed.

Isa. 2. 2 And it shall come to pass in the last days, *that* the mountain of the LORD's house shall be established in the top of the mountains, and shall be exalted above the hills; and all nations shall flow unto it.

3 And many people shall go and say, Come ye, and let us go up to the mountain of the LORD, to the house of the God of Jacob; and he will teach us of his ways, and we will walk in his paths: for out of Zion shall go forth the law, and the word of the LORD from Jerusalem.

Isa. 11. 10 And in that day there shall be a root of Jesse, which shall stand for an ensign of the people; to it shall the Gentiles seek: and his rest shall be glorious.

Jer. 16. 19 O LORD, my strength, and my fortress, and my refuge in the day of affliction, the Gentiles shall come unto thee from the ends of the earth, and shall say, Surely our fathers have inherited lies, vanity, and *things* wherein *there is* no profit.

Mal. 1. 11 For, from the rising of the sun even unto the going down of the same, my name *shall be* great among the Gentiles; and in every place incense *shall be* offered unto my name, and a pure offering: for my name *shall be* great among the heathen, saith the LORD of hosts.

Luke 13. 29 And they shall come from the east, and *from* the west, and from the north, and *from* the south, and shall sit down in the kingdom of God.

Acts 10. 45 And they of the circumcision which believed were astonished, as many as came with Peter, because that on the Gentiles also was poured out the gift of the Holy Ghost.

Acts 11. 18 When they heard these things, they held their peace, and glorified God, saying, Then hath God also to

TIME, SUMMER, A. D. 28; PLACE, CAPERNAUM.

7 : 1–10.

1 Now when he had ended all his sayings in the audience of the people, he entered into Capernaum.

2 And a certain centurion's servant, who was dear unto him, was sick, and ready to die.

3 And when he heard of Jesus, he sent unto him the elders of the Jews, beseeching him that he would come and heal his servant.

4 And when they came to Jesus, they besought him instantly, saying, That he was worthy for whom he should do this:

5 For he loveth our nation, and he hath built us a synagogue.

6 Then Jesus went with them. And when he was now not far from the house, the centurion sent friends to him, saying unto him, Lord, trouble not thyself; for I am not worthy that thou shouldest enter under my roof:

7 Wherefore neither thought I myself worthy to come unto thee: but say in a word, and my servant shall be healed.

8 For I also am a man set under authority, having under me soldiers, and I say unto [1]one, Go, and he goeth; and to another, Come, and he cometh; and to my servant, Do this, and he doeth *it*.

9 When Jesus heard these things, he marvelled at him, and turned him about, and said unto the people that followed him, I say unto you, I have not found so great faith, no, not in [f]**Israel.**

D—CONCLUDED.

the Gentiles granted repentance unto life.

Acts 14. 27 And when they were come, and had gathered the church together, they rehearsed all that God had done with them, and how he had opened the door of faith unto the Gentiles.

Rom.15. 9 And that the Gentiles might glorify God for *his* mercy; as it is written, For this cause I will confess to thee among the Gentiles, and sing unto thy name.

10 And again he saith, Rejoice, ye Gentiles, with his people.

11 And again, Praise the Lord, all ye Gentiles; and laud him, all ye people.

12 And again, Esaias, saith, There shall be a root of Jesse, and he that shall rise to reign over the Gentiles; in him shall the Gentiles trust.

Eph. 2. 11 Wherefore remember, that ye *being* in time past Gentiles in the flesh, who are called Uncircumcision by that which is called the Circumcision in the flesh made by hands;

12 That at that time ye were without Christ, being aliens from the commonwealth of Israel, and strangers from the covenants of promise, having no hope, and without God in the world:

13 But now, in Christ Jesus, ye who sometime were far off are made nigh by the blood of Christ.

14 For he is our peace, who hath made both one, and hath broken down the middle wall of partition *between us;*

Eph. 3. 6 That the Gentiles should be fellow heirs, and of the same body, and partakers of his promise in Christ by the gospel:

E

Matt. 8. 5. *See text of topic.*

1

Gr., *this man.*

F

Rom. 3. 1 What advantage then hath the Jew? or what profit *is there* of circumcision?

2 Much every way: chiefly, because that unto them were committed the oracles of God.

Rom. 9. 4 Who are Israelites; to whom *pertaineth* the adoption, and the glory, and the covenants, and the giving of the law, and the service *of God,* and the promises;

§ 44. HEALING OF THE CENTURION'S SERVANT

CHAP. 8.

12 But [g]the children of the kingdom [h]shall be cast out into outer darkness: there shall be weeping and gnashing of teeth.

13 And Jesus said unto the centurion, Go thy way; and as thou hast believed, *so* be it done unto thee. And his servant was healed in the selfsame hour. (p. 98.)

G

Matt.21. 43 Therefore say I unto you, The kingdom of God shall be taken from you, and given to a nation bringing forth the fruits thereof.

H

Matt.13. 42 And shall cast them into a furnace of fire: there shall be wailing and gnashing of teeth.

Matt.13. 50 And shall cast them into the furnace of fire: there shall be wailing and gnashing of teeth.

Matt.22. 13 Then said the king to the servants, Bind him hand and foot, and take him away, and cast *him* into

§ 45. RAISING OF THE WIDOW'S SON.

A

Job 29. 13 The blessing of him that was ready to perish came upon me: and I caused the widow's heart to sing for joy.

Acts 9. 39 Then Peter arose and went with them. When he was come, they brought him into the upper chamber: and all the widows stood by him weeping, and showing the coats and garments which Dorcas made, while she was with them.

40 But Peter put them all forth, and kneeled down, and prayed; and turning *him* to the body said, Tabitha, arise. And she opened her eyes: and when she saw Peter, she sat up.

41 And he gave her *his* hand, and lifted her up; and when he had called the saints and widows, he presented her alive.

B

Lam. 3. 32 But though he cause grief, yet will he have compassion according to the multitude of his mercies.

John 11. 33 When Jesus therefore saw her weeping, and the Jews also weeping which came with her, he groaned in the spirit, and was troubled,

34 And said, Where have ye laid him? They say unto him, Lord, come and see.

35 Jesus wept.

Heb. 4. 15 For we have not a high priest which cannot be touched with the feeling of our infirmities; but was in all points tempted like as *we are, yet* without sin.

1

Or, *coffin.*

C

I Ki. 17. 17 And it came to pass after these things, *that* the son of the woman, the mistress of the house, fell sick; and his sickness was so sore, that there was no breath left in him.

18 And she said unto Elijah, What have I to do with thee, O thou man of God? art thou come unto me to call my sin to remembrance, and to slay my son?

19 And he said unto her, Give me thy son. And he took him out of her bosom, and carried him up into a loft, where he abode, and laid him upon his own bed.

20 And he cried unto the LORD, and said, O LORD my God, hast thou also brought evil upon the widow with whom I sojourn, by slaying her son?

21 And he stretched himself upon the child three times, and cried unto the LORD, and said, O LORD my God, I pray thee, let this child's soul come into him again.

22 And the LORD heard the voice of Elijah; and the soul of the child came into him again, and he revived.

Job 14. 12 So man lieth down, and riseth not: till the heavens *be* no more, they shall not awake, nor be raised out of their sleep.

Job 14. 14 If a man die, shall he live *again?* all the days of my appointed time will I wait, till my change come.

Isa. 26. 19 Thy dead *men* shall live, *together with* my dead body shall they arise. Awake and sing, ye that dwell in dust: for thy dew *is as* the dew of herbs, and the earth shall cast out the dead.

(CONCLUDED). TIME, SUMMER, A. D. 28; PLACE, CAPERNAUM.

CHAP. 7.

10 And they that were sent, returning to the house, found the servant whole that had been sick.

H—CONTINUED.

outer darkness; there shall be weeping and gnashing of teeth.

Matt.24. 51 And shall cut him asunder, and appoint *him* his portion with the hypocrites: there shall be weeping and gnashing of teeth.

Matt.25. 30 And cast ye the unprofitable servant into outer darkness: there shall

H—CONCLUDED.

be weeping and gnashing of teeth.

Luke 13. 28 There shall be weeping and gnashing of teeth, when ye shall see Abraham, and Isaac, and Jacob, and all the prophets, in the kingdom of God, and you *yourselves* thrust out.

IIPet. 2. 17 These are wells without water, clouds that are carried with a tempest; to whom the mist of darkness is reserved for ever.

Jude 13 Raging waves of the sea, foaming out their own shame; wandering stars, to whom is reserved the blackness of darkness for ever.

TIME, SUMMER, A. D. 28; PLACE, NAIN.

7: 11–17.

11 And it came to pass the day after, that he went into a city called Nain; and many of his disciples went with him, and much people.

12 Now when he came nigh to the gate of the city, behold, there was a dead man carried out, the only son of his mother, and she was a [a]widow: and much people of the city was with her.

13 And when the Lord saw her, he [b]had compassion on her, and said unto her, Weep not.

14 And he came and touched the [1]bier: and they that bare *him* stood still. And he said, [c]Young man, I say unto thee, Arise.

15 And he that was dead sat up, and began to speak. And he delivered him to his mother.

16 [d]And there came a fear on all: and they glorified God, saying, [e]That a great prophet is risen up among us; and [f]That God hath visited his people.

17 And this rumour of him went forth throughout all Judæa, and throughout all the region round about.

C—CONCLUDED.

Luke 8. 54 And he put them all out, and took her by the hand, and called, saying, Maid, arise.

John 11. 43 And when he thus had spoken, he cried with a loud voice, Lazarus, come forth.

Acts 9. 40. *See under A.*

Rom. 4. 17 (As it is written, I have made thee a father of many nations,) before him whom he believed, *even* God, who quickeneth the dead, and calleth those things which be not as though they were:

D

Luke 1. 65 And fear came on all that dwelt round about them: and all these sayings were noised abroad throughout all the hill country of Judæa.

E

Luke 24. 19 And he said unto them, What things? And they said unto him, Concerning Jesus of Nazareth, which was a prophet mighty in deed and word before God and all the people:

John 4. 19 The woman saith unto him, Sir, I perceive that thou art a prophet.

John 6. 14 Then those men, when they had seen the miracle that Jesus did, said, This is of a truth that Prophet that should come into the world.

John 9. 17 They say unto the blind man again, What sayest thou of him, that he hath opened thine eyes? He said, He is a prophet.

F

Luke 1. 68 Blessed *be* the Lord God of Israel; for he hath visited and redeemed his people,

§46. MESSENGERS FROM JOHN THE BAPTIST AND SUBSEQUENT DISCOURSE.

11 : 2–19.

2 [a]Now when John had heard [b]in the prison the works of Christ, he sent two of his disciples,

3 And said unto him, Art thou [c]he that should come, or do we look for another?

4 Jesus answered and said unto them, Go and show John again those things which ye do hear and see:

5 [d]The blind receive their sight, and the lame walk, the lepers are cleansed, and the deaf hear, the dead are raised up, and [e]the poor have the gospel preached to them.

A

Luke 7. 18, 19, etc. *See text of topic.*

B

Matt.14. 3 For Herod had laid hold on John, and bound him, and put *him* in prison for Herodias' sake, his brother Philip's wife.

C

Gen. 49. 10 The scepter shall not depart from Judah, nor a law giver from between his feet, until Shiloh come; and unto him *shall* the gathering of the people *be.*

Num.24. 17 I shall see him, but not now: I shall behold him, but not nigh: there shall come a Star out of Jacob, and a Sceptre shall rise out of Israel, and shall smite the corners of Moab, and destroy all the children of Sheth.

Dan. 9. 24 Seventy weeks are determined upon thy people and upon thy holy city, to finish the transgression, and to make an end of sins, and to make reconciliation for iniquity, and to bring in everlasting righteousness, and to seal up the vision and prophecy, and to anoint the Most Holy.

John 6. 14 Then those men, when they had seen the miracle that Jesus did, said, This is of a truth that Prophet that should come into the world.

D

Isa. 29. 18 And in that day shall the deaf hear the words of the book, and the eyes of the blind shall see out of obscurity, and out of darkness.

D—Concluded.

Isa. 35. 4 Say to them *that are* of a fearful heart, Be strong, fear not: behold, your God will come *with* vengeance, *even* God *with* a recompense; he will come and save you.

5 Then the eyes of the blind shall be opened, and the ears of the deaf shall be unstopped.

6 Then shall the lame *man* leap as a hart, and the tongue of the dumb sing: for in the wilderness shall waters break out, and streams in the desert.

Isa. 42. 6 I the Lord have called thee in righteousness, and will hold thine hand, and will keep thee, and give thee for a covenant of the people, for a light of the Gentiles;

7 To open the blind eyes, to bring out the prisoners from the prison, *and* them that sit in darkness out of the prison house.

John 2. 23 Now when he was in Jerusalem at the passover, in the feast *day*, many believed in his name, when they saw the miracles which he did.

John 3. 2 The same came to Jesus by night, and said unto him, Rabbi, we know that thou art a teacher come from God: for no man can do these miracles that thou doest, except God be with him.

John 5. 36 But I have greater witness than *that* of John: for the works which the Father hath given me to finish, the same works that I do, bear witness of me, that the Father hath sent me.

John 10. 25 Jesus answered them, I told you, and ye believed not: the works that I do in my Father's name, they bear witness of me.

John 10. 38 But if I do, though ye believe not me, believe the works; that ye may know, and believe, that the Father *is* in me, and I in him.

John 14. 11 Believe me that I *am* in the Father, and the Father in me: or else believe me for the very works' sake.

E

Ps. 22. 26 The meek shall eat and be satisfied: they shall praise the Lord that seek him: your heart shall live for ever.

Isa. 61. 1 The Spirit of the Lord God *is* upon me; because the Lord hath anointed me to preach good tidings unto the meek; he hath sent me to bind up the brokenhearted, to pro-

Time, Summer, A. D. 28; Place, Castle of Machærus in Peræa, Galilee.

7 : 18–35.

18 [f] And the disciples of John showed him of all these things.

19 And John calling *unto him* two of his disciples sent *them* to Jesus, saying, Art thou [g]he that should come? or look we for another?

20 When the men were come unto him, they said, John Baptist hath sent us unto thee, saying, Art thou he that should come? or look we for another?

21 And in that same hour he cured many of *their* infirmities and plagues, and of evil spirits; and unto many *that were* blind he gave sight.

22 [h]Then Jesus answering said unto them, Go your way, and tell John what things ye have seen and heard; [i]how that the blind see, the lame walk, the lepers are cleansed, the deaf hear, the dead are raised, to the poor the gospel is preached.

E—Concluded.

claim liberty to the captives, and the opening of the prison to *them that are* bound;

Isa. 66. 2 For all those *things* hath mine hand made, and all those *things* have been, saith the Lord: but to this *man* will I look, *even* to *him that is* poor and of a contrite spirit, and trembleth at my word.

Zech. 11. 7 And I will feed the flock of slaughter, even you, O poor of the flock. And I took unto me two staves; the one I called Beauty, and the other I called Bands; and I feed the flock.

Luke 4. 18 The Spirit of the Lord *is* upon me, because he hath anointed me to preach the gospel to the poor; he hath sent me to heal the brokenhearted, to preach deliverance to the captives, and recovering of sight to the blind, to set at liberty them that are bruised,

Jas. 2. 5 Hearken, my beloved brethren, Hath not God chosen the poor of this world rich in faith, and heirs of the kingdom which he hath promised to them that love him?

F

Matt. 11. 2. *See text of topic.*

G

Eze. 21. 27 I will overturn, overturn, overturn it: and it shall be no *more*, until he come whose right it is; and I will give it *him*.

Eze. 34. 23 And I will set up one Shepherd over them, and he shall feed them, *even* my servant David; he shall feed them, and he shall be their shepherd.

Eze. 34. 29 And I will raise up for them a plant of renown, and they shall be no more consumed with hunger in the land, neither bear the shame of the heathen any more.

Dan. 9. 24. *See under C.*

Dan. 9. 25 Know therefore and understand, *that* from the going forth of the commandment to restore and to build Jerusalem, unto the Messiah the Prince, *shall be* seven weeks, and threescore and two weeks: the street shall be built again, and the wall, even in troublous times.

26 And after threescore and two weeks shall Messiah be cut off, but not for himself: and the people of the prince that shall come shall destroy the city and the sanctuary; and the end thereof *shall be* with a flood, and unto the end of the war desolations are determined.

Hag. 2. 7 And I will shake all nations, and the Desire of all nations shall come: and I will fill this house with glory, saith the Lord of hosts.

Zech. 9. 9 Rejoice greatly, O daughter of Zion; shout, O daughter of Jerusalem: behold, thy King cometh unto thee: he *is* just, and having salvation; lowly, and riding upon an ass, and upon a colt the foal of an ass.

Mal. 3. 1. *See under O, page 157.*

Mal. 3. 2 But who may abide the day of his coming? and who shall stand when he appeareth? for he *is* like a refiner's fire, and like fullers' soap:

3 And he shall sit *as* a refiner and purifier of silver: and he shall purify the sons of Levi, and purge them as gold and silver, that they may offer unto the Lord an offering in righteousness.

H

Matt. 11. 4, 5. *See text of topic.*

I

Isa. 29. 18, Isa. 35. 5 and Isa. 42. 6. *See under D.*

§46. MESSENGERS FROM JOHN THE BAPTIST AND SUBSEQUENT DISCOURSE

CHAP. 11.

6 And blessed is *he*, whosoever shall not [k]be offended in me.

7 [l]And as they departed, Jesus began to say unto the multitudes concerning John, What went ye out into the wilderness to see? [m]A reed shaken with the wind?

8 But what went ye out for to see? A man clothed in soft raiment? behold, they that wear soft *clothing* are in kings' houses.

9 But what went ye out for to see? A prophet? yea, I say unto you, [n]and more than a prophet.

10 For this is *he*, of whom it is written, [o]Behold, I send my messenger before thy face, which shall prepare thy way before thee.

11 Verily I say unto you, Among them that are born of women there hath not risen a greater than John the Baptist: notwithstanding, he that is least in the kingdom of heaven is greater than he.

12 [p]And from the days of John the Baptist until now the kingdom of heaven [1]suffereth violence, and the violent take it by force.

K

Isa. 8. 14 And he shall be for a sanctuary; but for a stone of stumbling and for a rock of offence to both the houses of Israel, for a gin and for a snare to the inhabitants of Jerusalem.

15 And many among them shall stumble, and fall, and be broken, and be snared, and be taken.

Matt.13. 57 And they were offended in him. But Jesus said unto them, A prophet is not without honor, save in his own country, and in his own house.

Matt.24. 10 And then shall many be offended, and shall betray one another, and shall hate one another.

K—CONCLUDED.

Matt.26. 31 Then saith Jesus unto them, All ye shall be offended because of me this night: for it is written, I will smite the Shepherd, and the sheep of the flock shall be scattered abroad.

Rom. 9. 32 Wherefore? Because *they sought it* not by faith, but as it were by the works of the law. For they stumbled at that stumblingstone;

33 As it is written, Behold, I lay in Sion a stumblingstone and rock of offence: and whosoever believeth on him shall not be ashamed.

I Cor. 1. 23 But we preach Christ crucified, unto the Jews a stumblingblock, and unto the Greeks foolishness;

I Cor. 2. 14 But the natural man receiveth not the things of the Spirit of God: for they are foolishness unto him: neither can he know *them*, because they are spiritually discerned.

Gal. 5. 11 And I, brethren, if I yet preach circumcision, why do I yet suffer persecution? then is the offence of the cross ceased.

12 I would they were even cut off which trouble you.

I Pet. 2. 8 And a stone of stumbling, and a rock of offence, *even to them* which stumble at the word, being disobedient: whereunto also they were appointed.

L

Luke 7. 24. *See text of topic.*

M

Eph. 4. 14 That we *henceforth* be no more children, tossed to and fro, and carried about with every wind of doctrine, by the sleight of men, *and* cunning craftiness, whereby they lie in wait to deceive:

Jas. 1. 6 But let him ask in faith, nothing wavering: for he that wavereth is like a wave of the sea driven with the wind and tossed.

N

Matt.14. 5 And when he would have put him to death, he feared the multitude, because they counted him as a prophet.

Matt.21. 26 But if we shall say, Of men; we fear the people; for all hold John as a prophet.

Luke 1. 76 And thou, child, shalt be called the prophet of the Highest: for thou shalt go before the face of the Lord to prepare his ways;

Luke 7. 26. *See text of topic.*

(CONTINUED). TIME, SUMMER, A.D. 28; PLACE, CASTLE OF MACHÆRUS IN PERÆA, GALILEE.

CHAP. 7.

23 And blessed is *he*, whosoever shall not be offended in me.

24 [q]And when the messengers of John were departed, he began to speak unto the people concerning John, What went ye out into the wilderness for to see? A reed shaken with the wind?

25 But what went ye out for to see? A man clothed in soft raiment? Behold, they which are gorgeously apparelled, and live delicately, are in kings' courts.

26 But what went ye out for to see? A prophet? Yea, I say unto you, and much more than a prophet.

27 This is *he*, of whom it is written, [r]Behold, I send my messenger before thy face, which shall prepare thy way before thee.

28 For I say unto you, Among those that are born of women there is not a greater prophet than John the Baptist: but he that is least in the kingdom of God is greater than he.

29 And all the people that heard *him*, and the publicans, justified God, [s]being baptized with the baptism of John.

O

Mal. 3. 1 Behold, I will send my messenger, and he shall prepare the way before me: and the Lord, whom ye seek, shall suddenly come to his temple, even the messenger of the covenant, whom ye delight in: behold, he shall come, saith the LORD of hosts.

Mark 1. 2 As it is written in the prophets, Behold, I send my messenger before thy face, which shall prepare thy way before thee.

Luke 1. 76. *See under N.*

Luke 7. 27. *See text of topic.*

P

Luke 16. 16 The law and the prophets *were* until John: since that time the kingdom of God is preached, and every man presseth into it.

1

Or, *is gotten by force, and they that thrust men.*

Q

Matt. 11. 7. *See text of topic.*

R

Isa. 40. 3 The voice of him that crieth in the wilderness, Prepare ye the way of the LORD, make straight in the desert a highway for our God.

4 Every valley shall be exalted, and every mountain and hill shall be made low: and the crooked shall be made straight, and the rough places plain:

5 And the glory of the LORD shall be revealed, and all flesh shall see *it* together: for the mouth of the LORD hath spoken *it*.

6 The voice said, Cry. And he said, What shall I cry? All flesh *is* grass, and all the goodliness thereof *is* as the flower of the field:

7 The grass withereth, the flower fadeth; because the spirit of the LORD bloweth upon it: surely the people *is* grass.

8 The grass withereth, the flower fadeth: but the word of our God shall stand for ever.

Mal. 3. 1. *See under O.*

Mal. 4. 5. *See under U, page 158.*

S

Matt. 3. 5 Then went out to him Jerusalem, and all Judæa, and all the region round about Jordan,

6 And were baptized of him in Jordan, confessing their sins.

Luke 3. 12 Then came also publicans to be baptized, and said unto him, Master, what shall we do?

Luke 1. 15 For he shall be great in the sight of the Lord, and shall drink neither wine nor strong drink; and he shall be filled with the Holy Ghost, even from his mother's womb.

16 And many of the children of Israel shall he turn to the Lord their God.

17 And he shall go before him in the spirit and power of Elias, to turn the hearts of the fathers to the children, and the disobedient to the wisdom of the just; to make ready a people prepared for the Lord.

§ 46. MESSENGERS FROM JOHN THE BAPTIST AND SUBSEQUENT DISCOURSE

CHAP. 11.

13 [t]For all the prophets and the law prophesied until John.

14 And if ye will receive *it,* this is [u]Elias, which was for to come.

15 [x]He that hath ears to hear, let him hear.

16 But [y]whereunto shall I liken this generation? It is like unto children sitting in the markets, and calling unto their fellows,

17 And saying, [z]We have piped unto you, and ye have not danced; we have mourned unto you, and ye have not lamented.

18 For [a]John came neither eating nor drinking, and they say, He hath a devil.

19 The Son of man [b]came eating and drinking, and they say, Behold a man gluttonous, and a winebibber, [c]a friend of publicans and sinners. [d]But wisdom is justified of her children.

T

Mal. 4. 6 And he shall turn the heart of the fathers to the children, and the heart of the children to their fathers, lest I come and smite the earth with a curse.

Rom. 3. 21 But now the righteousness of God without the law is manifested, being witnessed by the law and the prophets;

U

Mal. 4. 5 Behold, I will send you Elijah the prophet before the coming of the great and dreadful day of the LORD:

Matt.17. 12 But I say unto you, That Elias is come already, and they knew him not, but have done unto him whatsoever they listed. Likewise shall also the Son of man suffer of them.

Luke 1. 17 And he shall go before him in the spirit and power of Elias, to turn the hearts of the fathers to the children, and the disobedient to the wisdom of the just; to make ready a people prepared for the Lord.

X

Matt.13. 9 Who hath ears to hear, let him hear.

Luke 8. 8 And other fell on good ground, and sprang up, and bare fruit a hundredfold. And when he had said these things, he cried, He that hath ears to hear, let him hear.

Rev. 2. 7 He that hath an ear, let him hear what the Spirit saith unto the churches; To him that overcometh will I give to eat of the tree of life, which is in the midst of the paradise of God.

Rev. 2. 11 He that hath an ear, let him hear what the Spirit saith unto the churches; He that overcometh shall not be hurt of the second death.

Rev. 2. 17 He that hath an ear, let him hear what the Spirit saith unto the churches; To him that overcometh will I give to eat of the hidden manna, and will give him a white stone, and in the stone a new name written, which no man knoweth saving he that receiveth *it.*

Rev. 2. 29 He that hath an ear, let him hear what the Spirit saith unto the churches.

Rev. 3. 6 He that hath an ear, let him hear what the Spirit saith unto the churches.

Rev. 3. 13 He that hath an ear, let him hear what the Spirit saith unto the churches.

Rev. 3. 22 He that hath an ear, let him hear what the Spirit saith unto the churches.

Y

Luke 7. 31. *See text of topic.*

Z

Isa. 28. 9 Whom shall he teach knowledge? and whom shall he make to understand doctrine? *them that are* weaned from the milk, *and* drawn from the breasts.

10 For precept *must be* upon precept, precept upon precept; line upon line, line upon line; here a little, *and* there a little:

11 For with stammering lips and another tongue will he speak to this people.

12 To whom he said, This *is* the rest *wherewith* ye may cause the weary to rest; and this *is* the refreshing: yet they would not hear.

13 But the word of the LORD was unto them precept upon precept, precept upon precept; line upon line,

(CONCLUDED). TIME, SUMMER, A.D. 28; PLACE, CASTLE OF MACHÆRUS IN PERÆA, GALILEE.

CHAP. 7.

30 But the Pharisees and lawyers [2]rejected [e]the counsel of God [3]against themselves, being not baptized of him.

31 And the Lord said, Whereunto then shall I liken the men of this generation? and to what are they like?

32 They are like unto children sitting in the marketplace, and calling one to another, and saying, We have piped unto you, and ye have not danced; we have mourned to you, and ye have not wept.

33 For [f]John the Baptist came neither eating bread nor drinking wine; and ye say, He hath a devil.

34 The Son of man is come eating and drinking; and ye say, Behold a gluttonous man, and a winebibber, a friend of publicans and sinners!

35 [g]But wisdom is justified of all her children. (p. 163.)

Z—CONCLUDED.

line upon line; here a little, *and* there a little; that they might go, and fall backward, and be broken, and snared, and taken.

A

Jer. 15. 17 I sat not in the assembly of the mockers, nor rejoiced; I sat alone because of thy hand: for thou hast filled me with indignation.

Jer. 16. 8 Thou shalt not also go into the house of feasting, to sit with them to eat and to drink.

9 For thus saith the LORD of hosts, the God of Israel; Behold, I will cause to cease out of this place in your eyes, and in your days, the voice of mirth, and the voice of gladness, the voice of the bridegroom, and the voice of the bride.

I Cor. 9. 27 But I keep under my body, and bring *it* into subjection: lest that by any means, when I have preached to others, I myself should be a castaway.

B

Luke 5. 29 And Levi made him a great feast in his own house: and there was a great company of publicans and of others that sat down with them.

John 12. 2 There they made him a supper; and Martha served: but Lazarus was one of them that sat at the table with him.

Rom. 15. 2 Let every one of us please *his* neighbour for *his* good to edification.

C

Matt. 9. 10 And it came to pass, as Jesus sat at meat in the house, behold, many publicans and sinners came and sat down with him and his disciples.

D

Luke 7. 35. *See text of topic.*

Phil. 2. 15 That ye may be blameless and harmless, the sons of God, without rebuke, in the midst of a crooked and perverse nation, among whom ye shine as lights in the world;

2

Or, *frustrated.*

E

Acts 20. 27 For I have not shunned to declare unto you all the counsel of God.

3

Or, *within themselves.*

F

Matt. 3. 4 And the same John had his raiment of camel's hair, and a leathern girdle about his loins; and his meat was locusts and wild honey.

Mark 1. 6 And John was clothed with camel's hair, and with a girdle of a skin about his loins; and he did eat locusts and wild honey;

Luke 1. 15 For he shall be great in the sight of the Lord, and shall drink neither wine nor strong drink; and he shall be filled with the Holy Ghost, even from his mother's womb.

G

Prov. 8. 32 Now therefore hearken unto me, O ye children: for blessed *are they that* keep my ways.

33 Hear instruction, and be wise, and refuse it not.

34 Blessed *is* the man that heareth me, watching daily at my gates, waiting at the posts of my doors.

35 For whoso findeth me findeth life, and shall obtain favor of the LORD.

36 But he that sinneth against me wrongeth his own soul: all they that hate me love death.

Matt. 11. 19. *See text of topic.*

§ 47. FAVOURED CITIES OF GALILEE UPBRAIDED.

11 : 20–24.

20 Then began he to [a]upbraid the cities wherein most of his mighty works were done, because they repented not:

21 [b]Woe unto thee, Chorazin! woe unto thee, Bethsaida! for if the mighty works, which were done in you, had been done in Tyre and Sidon, they would have repented long ago [c]in sackcloth and ashes.

22 But I say unto you, [d]It shall be more tolerable for Tyre and Sidon at the day of judgment, than for you.

23 And thou, Capernaum, [e]which art exalted unto heaven, shalt be brought down to hell: for if the mighty works, which have been done in thee, had been done in Sodom, it would have remained until this day.

24 But I say unto you, [f]That it shall be more tolerable for the land of Sodom in the day of judgment, than for thee.

A

Ps. 81. 10 I *am* the LORD thy God, which brought thee out of the land of Egypt: open thy mouth wide, and I will fill it.

11 But my people would not hearken to my voice; and Israel would none of me.

12 So I gave them up unto their own hearts' lust: *and* they walked in their own counsels.

13 O that my people had hearkened unto me, *and* Israel had walked in my ways!

Isa. 1. 2 Hear, O heavens, and give ear, O earth: for the LORD hath spoken; I have nourished and brought up children, and they have rebelled against me,

3 The ox knoweth his owner, and the ass his master's crib: *but* Israel doth not know, my people doth not consider.

4 Ah sinful nation, a people laden with iniquity, a seed of evil doers, children that are corrupters: they have forsaken the LORD, they have provoked the Holy One of Israel unto anger, they are gone away backward.

5 Why should ye be stricken any more? ye will revolt more and more: the whole head is sick, and the whole heart faint.

Mic. 6. 1 Hear ye now what the LORD saith; Arise, contend thou before the mountains, and let the hills hear thy voice.

§ 48. CALL TO THE MEEK AND SUFFERING.

11 : 25–30.

25 [a]At that time Jesus answered and said, I thank thee, O Father, Lord of heaven and earth, because [b]thou hast hid these things from the wise and prudent, [c]and hast revealed them unto babes.

26 Even so, Father; for so it seemed good in thy sight.

A

Luke 10. 21 In that hour Jesus rejoiced in spirit, and said, I thank thee, O Father, Lord of heaven and earth, that thou hast hid these things from the wise and prudent, and hast revealed them unto babes: even so, Father; for so it seemed good in thy sight.

B

Job 5. 12 He disappointeth the devices of the crafty, so that their hands cannot perform *their* enterprise.

13 He taketh the wise in their own craftiness: and the counsel of the froward is carried headlong.

Ps. 8. 2 Out of the mouth of babes and sucklings hast thou ordained strength because of thine enemies, that thou mightest still the enemy and the avenger.

Isa. 5. 21 Woe unto *them that are* wise in their own eyes, and prudent in their own sight!

Isa. 29. 14 Therefore, behold, I will proceed to do a marvellous work among this people, *even* a marvellous work and a wonder: for the wisdom of their wise *men* shall perish, and the understanding of their prudent *men* shall be hid.

Jer. 8. 9 The wise *men* are ashamed, they

Time, Summer, A. D. 28; Place, Capernaum.

A—Concluded.

Mic. 6. 2 Hear ye, O mountains, the Lord's controversy, and ye strong foundations of the earth: for the Lord hath a controversy with his people, and he will plead with Israel.

3 O my people, what have I done unto thee? and wherein have I wearied thee? testify against me.

4 For I brought thee up out of the land of Egypt, and redeemed thee out of the house of servants; and I sent before thee Moses, Aaron, and Miriam.

Mark 9. 19 He answereth him, and saith, O faithless generation, how long shall I be with you? how long shall I suffer you? bring him unto me.

B

Luke 10. 13 Woe unto thee, Chorazin! woe unto thee, Bethsaida! for if the mighty works had been done in Tyre and Sidon, which have been done in you, they had a great while ago repented, sitting in sackcloth and ashes.

14 But it shall be more tolerable for Tyre and Sidon at the judgment, than for you.

15 And thou, Capernaum, which art exalted to heaven, shalt be thrust down to hell.

Jude 11 Woe unto them! for they have gone in the way of Cain, and ran greedily after the error of Balaam for reward, and perished in the gainsaying of Core.

C

Jon. 3. 7 And he caused *it* to be proclaimed and published through Nineveh by the decree of the king and his nobles, saying, Let neither man nor beast, herd nor flock, taste any thing: let them not feed, nor drink water:

8 But let man and beast be covered with sackcloth, and cry mightily unto God: yea, let them turn every one from his evil way, and from the violence that *is* in their hands.

D

Matt. 11. 24. *See text of topic.*

Matt. 10. 15 Verily I say unto you, It shall be more tolerable for the land of Sodom and Gomorrah in the day of judgment, than for that city.

E

Isa. 14. 13 For thou hast said in thine heart, I will ascend into heaven, I will exalt my throne above the stars of God: I will sit also upon the mount of the congregation, in the sides of the north:

Lam. 2. 1 How hath the Lord covered the daughter of Zion with a cloud in his anger, *and* cast down from heaven unto the earth the beauty of Israel, and remembered not his footstool in the day of his anger!

F

Matt. 10. 15. *See under D.*

Time, Summer, A. D. 28; Place, Capernaum.

B—Concluded.

are dismayed and taken: lo, they have rejected the word of the Lord; and what wisdom *is* in them?

I Cor. 1. 19 For it is written, I will destroy the wisdom of the wise, and will bring to nothing the understanding of the prudent.

I Cor. 1. 27 But God hath chosen the foolish things of the world to confound the wise; and God hath chosen the weak things of the world to confound the things which are mighty;

I Cor. 2. 8 Which none of the princes of this world knew: for had they known *it*, they would not have crucified the Lord of glory.

II Cor. 3. 14 But their minds were blinded: for until this day remaineth the same vail untaken away in the reading of the old testament; which *vail* is done away in Christ.

C

Matt. 16. 17 And Jesus answered and said unto him, Blessed art thou, Simon Bar-jona: for flesh and blood hath not revealed *it* unto thee, but my Father which is in heaven.

D

Matt. 28. 18 And Jesus came and spake unto them, saying, All power is given unto me in heaven and in earth.

Luke 10. 22 All things are delivered to me of my Father: and no man knoweth who the Son is, but the Father; and who the Father is, but the Son, and *he* to whom the Son will reveal *him*.

John 3. 35 The Father loveth the Son, and hath given all things into his hand.

John 13. 3 Jesus knowing that the Father had given all things into his hands, and that he was come from God, and went to God;

For D concluded see next page (162).

§ 48. CALL TO THE MEEK AND SUFFERING

CHAP. 11.

27 [d]All things are delivered unto me of my Father: and no man knoweth the Son, but the Father; [e]neither knoweth any man the Father, save the Son, and *he* to whomsoever the Son will reveal *him*.

28 Come unto me, all *ye* that labour and are heavy laden, and I will give you rest.

29 Take my yoke upon you, [f]and learn of me; for I am meek and [g]lowly in heart; [h]and ye shall find rest unto your souls.

30 [i]For my yoke *is* easy, and my burden is light. (p. 114.)

D—CONCLUDED. See preceding page (161).

John 17. 2 As thou hast given him power over all flesh, that he should give eternal life to as many as thou hast given him.

I Cor.15. 27 For he hath put all things under his feet. But when he saith, All things are put under *him, it is* manifest that he is excepted, which did put all things under him.

Eph. 1. 20 Which he wrought in Christ, when he raised him from the dead, and set *him* at his own right hand in the heavenly *places*,

21 Far above all principality, and power, and might, and dominion, and every name that is named, not only in this world, but also in that which is to come:

22 And hath put all *things* under his feet, and gave him *to be* the head over all *things* to the church,

23 Which is his body, the fulness of him that filleth all in all.

§ 49. ANOINTING OF THE FEET OF JESUS AT THE PHARISEE'S

A

Matt.26. 6 Now when Jesus was in Bethany, in the house of Simon the leper,

7 There came unto him a woman having an alabaster box of very precious ointment, and poured it on his head, as he sat at meat.

8 But when his disciples saw *it*, they had indignation, saying, To what purpose *is* this waste?

9 For this ointment might have been sold for much, and given to the poor.

10 When Jesus understood *it*, he said unto them, Why trouble ye the woman? for she hath wrought a good work upon me.

11 For ye have the poor always with you; but me ye have not always.

12 For in that she hath poured this ointment on my body, she did *it* for my burial.

13 Verily I say unto you, Wheresoever this gospel shall be preached in the whole world, *there* shall also this, that this woman hath done, be told for a memorial of her.

Mark 14. 3 And being in Bethany, in the house of Simon the leper, as he sat at meat, there came a woman having an alabaster box of ointment of spikenard very precious; and she brake the box, and poured *it* on his head.

A—CONTINUED.

Mark 14. 4 And there were some that had indignation within themselves, and said, Why was this waste of the ointment made?

5 For it might have been sold for more than three hundred pence, and have been given to the poor. And they murmured against her.

6 And Jesus said, Let her alone; why trouble ye her? she hath wrought a good work on me.

7 For ye have the poor with you always, and whensoever ye will ye may do them good: but me ye have not always.

8 She hath done what she could: she is come aforehand to anoint my body to the burying.

9 Verily I say unto you, Wheresoever this gospel shall be preached throughout the whole world, *this* also that she hath done shall be spoken of for a memorial of her.

John 12. 1 Then Jesus six days before the passover came to Bethany, where Lazarus was which had been dead, whom he raised from the dead.

2 There they made him a supper; and Martha served: but Lazarus was one of them that sat at the table with him.

(CONCLUDED). TIME, SUMMER, A. D. 28; PLACE, CAPERNAUM.

E

John 1. 18 No man hath seen God at any time; the only begotten Son, which is in the bosom of the Father, he hath declared *him.*

John 6. 46 Not that any man hath seen the Father, save he which is of God, he hath seen the Father.

John 10. 15 As the Father knoweth me, even so I know the Father: and I lay down my life for the sheep.

F

John 13. 15 For I have given you an example, that ye should do as I have done to you.

Phil. 2. 5 Let this mind be in you, which was also in Christ Jesus:

I Pet. 2. 21 For even hereunto were ye called: because Christ also suffered for us, leaving us an example, that ye should follow his steps:

I Jno. 2. 6 He that saith he abideth in him ought himself also so to walk, even as he walked.

G

Zech. 9. 9 Rejoice greatly, O daughter of

G—CONCLUDED.

Zion; shout, O daughter of Jerusalem: behold, thy King cometh unto thee: he *is* just, and having salvation; lowly, and riding upon an ass, and upon a colt the foal of an ass.

Phil. 2. 7 But made himself of no reputation, and took upon him the form of a servant, and was made in the likeness of men:

8 And being found in fashion as a man, he humbled himself, and became obedient unto death, even the death of the cross.

H

Jer. 6. 16 Thus saith the LORD, Stand ye in the ways, and see, and ask for the old paths, where *is* the good way, and walk therein, and ye shall find rest for your souls. But they said, We will not walk *therein.*

I

I Jno. 5. 3 For this is the love of God, that we keep his commandments: and his commandments are not grievous.

TABLE. TIME, SUMMER, A. D. 28; PLACE, CAPERNAUM.

7 : 36–50.

36 [a]And one of the Pharisees desired him that he would eat with him. And he went into the Pharisee's house, and sat down to meat.

37 And, behold, a woman in the city, which was a sinner, when she knew that *Jesus* sat at meat in the Pharisee's house, brought an alabaster box of ointment,

38 And stood at his feet behind *him* weeping, and began to wash his feet with tears, and did wipe *them* with the hairs of her head, and kissed his feet, and anointed *them* with the ointment.

39 Now when the Pharisee which had bidden him saw *it,* he spake within himself, saying, [b]This man, if he were a prophet, would have known who and what manner of woman *this is* that toucheth him; for she is a sinner.

A—CONCLUDED.

John 12. 3 Then took Mary a pound of ointment of spikenard, very costly, and anointed the feet of Jesus, and wiped his feet with her hair: and the house was filled with the odour of the ointment.

4 Then saith one of his disciples, Judas Iscariot, Simon's *son,* which should betray him,

5 Why was not this ointment sold for three hundred pence, and given to the poor?

6 This he said, not that he cared for the poor; but because he was a thief, and had the bag, and bare what was put therein.

7 Then said Jesus, Let her alone: against the day of my burying hath she kept this.

8 For the poor always ye have with you: but me ye have not always.

B

Luke 15. 2 And the Pharisees and scribes murmured, saying, This man receiveth sinners, and eateth with them.

John 9 23 Therefore said his parents, He is of age; ask him.

24 Then again called they the man that was blind, and said unto him, Give God the praise: we know that this man is a sinner.

§ 49. ANOINTING OF THE FEET OF JESUS AT THE PHARISEE'S

C

Matt.18. 28 But the same servant went out, and found one of his fellow servants, which owed him a hundred pence: and he laid hands on him, and took *him* by the throat, saying, Pay me that thou owest.

D

Isa. 43. 25 I, *even* I, *am* he that blotteth out thy transgressions for mine own sake, and will not remember thy sins.

Isa. 44. 22 I have blotted out, as a thick cloud, thy transgressions, and, as a cloud, thy sins: return unto me; for I have redeemed thee.

E

Gen. 18. 4 Let a little water, I pray you, be fetched, and wash your feet, and rest yourselves under the tree:

I Tim.5. 10 Well reported of for good works; if she have brought up children, if she have lodged strangers, if she have washed the saints' feet, if she have relieved the afflicted, if she have diligently followed every good work.

F

ICor.16. 20 All the brethren greet you. Greet ye one another with a holy kiss.

G

Ps. 23. 5 Thou preparest a table before me in the presence of mine enemies: thou anointest my head with oil; my cup runneth over.

Eccl. 9. 8 Let thy garments be always white; and let thy head lack no ointment.

H

Ex. 34. 6 And the LORD passed by before him, and proclaimed, The LORD, The LORD God, merciful and gracious, long-suffering, and abundant in goodness and truth,

7 Keeping mercy for thousands, forgiving iniquity and transgression and sin, and that will by no means clear *the guilty;* visiting the iniquity of the fathers upon the children, and upon the children's children, unto the third and to the fourth *generation.*

Isa. 1. 16 Wash ye, make you clean; put away the evil of your doings from before mine eyes; cease to do evil;

17 Learn to do well; seek judgment, relieve the oppressed, judge the fatherless, plead for the widow.

18 Come now, and let us reason together, saith the LORD: though your sins be as scarlet, they shall be as white as snow; though they be red like crimson, they shall be as wool.

H—CONTINUED.

Isa. 1. 19 If ye be willing and obedient, ye shall eat the good of the land:

20 But if ye refuse and rebel, ye shall be devoured with the sword: for the mouth of the LORD hath spoken *it.*

Isa. 55. 6 Seek ye the LORD while he may be found, call ye upon him while he is near:

7 Let the wicked forsake his way, and the unrighteous man his thoughts: and let him return unto the LORD, and he will have mercy upon him; and to our God, for he will abundantly pardon.

Eze. 16. 62 And I will establish my covenant with thee; and thou shalt know that I *am* the LORD:

63 That thou mayest remember, and be confounded, and never open thy mouth any more because of thy shame, when I am pacified toward thee for all that thou hast done, saith the Lord GOD.

Eze. 36. 29 I will also save you from all your uncleannesses: and I will call for the corn, and will increase it, and lay no famine upon you.

30 And I will multiply the fruit of the tree, and the increase of the field, that ye shall receive no more reproach of famine among the heathen.

31 Then shall ye remember your own evil ways, and your doings that *were* not good, and shall loathe yourselves in your own sight for your iniquities and for your abominations.

32 Not for your sakes do I *this,* saith the Lord GOD, be it known unto you: be ashamed and confounded for your own ways, O house of Israel.

Mic. 7. 18 Who *is* a God like unto thee, that pardoneth iniquity, and passeth by the transgression of the remnant of his heritage? he retaineth not his anger for ever, because he delighteth *in* mercy.

19 He will turn again, he will have compassion upon us; he will subdue our iniquities; and thou wilt cast all their sins into the depths of the sea.

Acts 5. 31 Him hath God exalted with his right hand *to be* a Prince and a Saviour, for to give repentance to Israel, and forgiveness of sins.

I Cor. 6. 9 Know ye not that the unrighteous shall not inherit the kingdom of God? Be not deceived: neither fornicators, nor idolaters, nor adulterers, nor effeminate, nor abusers of themselves with mankind,

TABLE (Concluded). Time, Summer, A. D. 28; Place, Capernaum.

Chap. 7.

40 And Jesus answering said unto him, Simon, I have somewhat to say unto thee. And he saith, Master, say on.

41 There was a certain creditor which had two debtors: the one owed five hundred [c]pence, and the other fifty.

42 And when they had nothing to pay, he frankly [d]forgave them both. Tell me therefore, which of them will love him most?

43 Simon answered and said, I suppose that *he*, to whom he forgave most. And he said unto him, Thou hast rightly judged.

44 And he turned to the woman, and said unto Simon, Seest thou this woman? I entered into thine house, thou gavest me no [e]water for my feet: but she hath washed my feet with tears, and wiped *them* with the hairs of her head.

45 Thou gavest me no [f]kiss: but this woman, since the time I came in, hath not ceased to kiss my feet.

46 [g]My head with oil thou didst not anoint: but this woman hath anointed my feet with ointment.

47 [h]Wherefore I say unto thee, Her sins, which are many, are forgiven; for [i]she loved much: but to whom little is forgiven, *the same* loveth little.

48 And he said unto her, [k]Thy sins are forgiven.

49 [l]And they that sat at meat with him began to say within themselves, Who is this that forgiveth sins also?

50 And he said to the woman, [m]Thy faith hath saved thee; go in peace.

H—Concluded.

I Cor. 6. 10 Nor thieves, nor covetous, nor drunkards, nor revilers, nor extortioners, shall inherit the kingdom of God.

11 And such were some of you: but ye are washed, but ye are sanctified, but ye are justified in the name of the Lord Jesus, and by the Spirit of our God.

I Tim. 1. 14 And the grace of our Lord was exceeding abundant with faith and love which is in Christ Jesus.

I Jno. 1. 7 But if we walk in the light, as he is in the light, we have fellowship one with another, and the blood of Jesus Christ his Son cleanseth us from all sin.

I

Gal. 5. 6 For in Jesus Christ neither circumcision availeth anything, nor uncircumcision; but faith which worketh by love.

K

Matt. 9. 2 And, behold, they brought to him a man sick of the palsy, lying on a bed: and Jesus seeing their faith said unto the sick of the palsy; Son, be of good cheer; thy sins be forgiven thee.

Mark 2. 5 When Jesus saw their faith, he said unto the sick of the palsy, Son, thy sins be forgiven thee.

L

Isa. 53. 3 He is despised and rejected of men: a man of sorrows, and acquainted with grief: and we hid as it were *our* faces from him; he was despised, and we esteemed him not.

Matt. 9. 3 And, behold, certain of the scribes said within themselves, This *man* blasphemeth.

Mark 2. 7 Why doth this *man* thus speak blasphemies? who can forgive sins but God only?

M

Matt. 9. 22 But Jesus turned him about, and when he saw her, he said, Daughter, be of good comfort; thy faith hath made thee whole. And the woman was made whole from that hour.

Mark 5. 34 And he said unto her, Daughter, thy faith hath made thee whole; go in peace, and be whole of thy plague.

Mark 10. 52 And Jesus said unto him, Go thy way; thy faith hath made thee whole. And immediately he received his sight, and followed Jesus in the way.

Luke 8. 48 And he said unto her, Daughter, be of good comfort: thy faith hath made thee whole; go in peace.

§ 50. JESUS WITH THE TWELVE MAKES A SECOND

A

Isa. 52. 7 How beautiful upon the mountains are the feet of him that bringeth good tidings, that publisheth peace; that bringeth good tidings of good, that publisheth salvation; that saith unto Zion, Thy God reigneth!

Isa. 61. 1 The Spirit of the Lord GOD *is* upon me; because the LORD hath anointed me to preach good tidings unto the meek; he hath sent me to bind up the brokenhearted, to proclaim liberty to the captives, and the opening of the prison to *them that are* bound;

2 To proclaim the acceptable year of the LORD, and the day of vengeance of our God; to comfort all that mourn;

3 To appoint unto them that mourn in Zion, to give unto them beauty for ashes, the oil of joy for mourning, the

A—CONTINUED.

garment of praise for the spirit of heaviness; that they might be called Trees of righteousness, The planting of the LORD, that he might be glorified.

Nah. 1. 15 Behold upon the mountains the feet of him that bringeth good tidings, that publisheth peace! O Judah, keep thy solemn feasts, perform thy vows: for the wicked shall no more pass through thee; he is utterly cut off.

Luke 4. 18 The Spirit of the Lord *is* upon me, because he hath anointed me to preach the gospel to the poor; he hath sent me to heal the brokenhearted, to preach deliverance to the captives, and recovering of sight to the blind, to set at liberty them that are bruised,

19 To preach the acceptable year of the Lord.

§ 51. THE HEALING OF A DEMONIAC. BLASPHEMOUS SCRIBES AND

12 : 22–37.

22 [a]Then was brought unto him one possessed with a devil, blind, and dumb: and he healed him, insomuch that the blind and dumb both spake and saw.

23 And all the people were amazed, and said, Is not this the [b]Son of David?

A

Matt. 9. 32 As they went out, behold, they brought to him a dumb man possessed with a devil.

33 And when the devil was cast out, the dumb spake: and the multitudes marvelled, saying, It was never so seen in Israel.

34 But the Pharisees said, He casteth out devils through the prince of the devils.

Mark 3. 11 And unclean spirits, when they saw him, fell down before him, and cried, saying, Thou art the Son of God.

Luke 11. 15. *See text of topic.*

B

Rom. 9. 5 Whose *are* the fathers, and of whom as concerning the flesh Christ *came*, who is over all, God blessed forever. Amen.

1

Or, *home.*

3 : 19–30.

19 And Judas Iscariot, which also betrayed him: and they went [1]into a house.

20 And the multitude cometh together again, [c]so that they could not so much as eat bread.

21 And when his [2]friends heard *of it*, they went out to lay hold on him: [d]for they said, He is beside himself.

C

Mark 6. 31 And he said unto them, Come ye yourselves apart into a desert place, and rest a while: for there were many coming and going, and they had no leisure so much as to eat.

2

Or, *kinsmen.*

D

II Ki. 9. 11 Then Jehu came forth to the servants of his lord: and *one* said unto him, *Is* all well? wherefore came this mad *fellow* to thee? And he said unto them, Ye know the man, and his communication.

Jer. 29. 26 The LORD hath made thee priest in the stead of Jehoiada the priest, that ye should be officers in the house of the LORD, for every man *that is* mad, and maketh himself a prophet, that thou shouldest put him in prison, and in the stocks.

CIRCUIT IN GALILEE. TIME, AUTUMN, A. D. 28.

8 : 1–3.

1 And it came to pass afterward, that he went throughout every city and village, preaching and showing the [a]glad tidings of the kingdom of God: and the twelve *were* with him,

2 And [b]certain women, which had been healed of evil spirits and infirmities, Mary called Magdalene, [c]out of whom went seven devils,

3 And Joanna the wife of Chuza Herod's steward, and Susanna, and many others, which ministered unto him of their substance. (p. 197.)

A—CONCLUDED.

Rom.10. 15 And how shall they preach, except they be sent? as it is written, How beautiful are the feet of them that preach the gospel of peace, and bring glad tidings of good things!

B

Matt.27. 55 And many women were there beholding afar off, which followed Jesus from Galilee, ministering unto him:
56 Among which was Mary Magdalene, and Mary the mother of James and Joses, and the mother of Zebedee's children.

C

Mark 16. 9 Now when *Jesus* was risen early the first *day* of the week, he appeared first to Mary Magdalene, out of whom he had cast seven devils.

PHARISEES REPROVED. TIME, AUTUMN, A. D. 28; PLACE, GALILEE.

11 : 14, 15, 17–23.

14 [e]And he was casting out a devil, and it was dumb. And it came to pass, when the devil was gone out, the dumb spake; and the people wondered.

D—CONTINUED.

Hos. 9. 7 The days of visitation are come, the days of recompense are come; Israel shall know *it:* the prophet *is* a fool, the spiritual man *is* mad, for the multitude of thine iniquity, and the great hatred.
8 The watchman of Ephraim *was* with my God: *but* the prophet *is* a snare of a fowler in all his ways, *and* hatred in the house of his God.

John 7. 5 For neither did his brethren believe in him.

John 10. 20 And many of them said, He hath a devil, and is mad; why hear ye him?

Acts 26. 24 And as he thus spake for himself, Festus said with a loud voice, Paul, thou art beside thyself; much learning doth make thee mad.
25 But he said, I am not mad, most noble Festus; but speak forth the words of truth and soberness.

I Cor. 2. 13 Which things also we speak, not in the words which man's wisdom teacheth, but which the Holy Ghost teacheth; comparing spiritual things with spiritual.

D—CONCLUDED.

I Cor. 2. 14 But the natural man receiveth not the things of the Spirit of God: for they are foolishness unto him: neither can he know *them,* because they are spiritually discerned.

II Cor. 5. 13 For whether we be beside ourselves, *it is* to God: or wether we be sober, *it is* for your cause.
14 For the love of Christ constraineth us; because we thus judge, that if one died for all, then were all dead:
15 And *that* he died for all, that they which live should not henceforth live unto themselves, but unto him which died for them, and rose again.

E

Matt. 9. 32. *See under A.*
Matt. 12. 22. *See text of topic.*

F

Matt. 9. 34. *See under A.*
Mark 3. 22 and Luke 11. 15. *See text of topic.*

3

Gr., *Beelzebul.*

G

Matt. 9. 4 And Jesus knowing their thoughts said, Wherefore think ye evil in your hearts?

John 2. 25 And needed not that any should testify of man; for he knew what was in man.

Rev. 2. 23 And I will kill her children with death; and all the churches shall know that I am he which searcheth the reins and hearts: and I will give unto every one of you according to your works.

§ 51. THE HEALING OF A DEMONIAC. BLASPHEMOUS SCRIBES AND

CHAP. 12.

24 [f]But when the Pharisees heard
it, they said, This *fellow* doth not cast
out devils, but by [g]Beelzebub the
prince of the devils.

25 And Jesus [g]knew their thoughts,
and said unto them, Every kingdom
divided against itself is brought to
desolation; and every city or house
divided against itself shall not stand:

26 And if Satan cast out Satan, he
is divided against himself; how shall
then his kingdom stand?

27 And if I by Beelzebub cast out
devils, by whom do your children cast
them out? therefore they shall be your
judges.

28 But if I cast out devils by the
Spirit of God, then [h]the kingdom of
God is come unto you.

29 [i]Or else, how can one enter into a
strong man's house, and spoil his
goods, except he first bind the strong
man? and then he will spoil his house.

For F, 3 and G see preceding page (167).

H

Dan. 2. 44 And in the days of these kings shall the God of heaven set up a kingdom, which shall never be destroyed: and the kingdom shall not be left to other people, *but* it shall break in pieces and consume all these kingdoms, and it shall stand for ever.

Dan. 7. 14 And there was given him dominion, and glory, and a kingdom, that all people, nations, and languages, should serve him: his dominion *is* an everlasting dominion, which shall not pass away, and his kingdom *that* which shall not be destroyed.

Luke 1. 33 And he shall reign over the house of Jacob for ever; and of his kingdom there shall be no end.

Luke 11. 20. *See text of topic.*

CHAP. 3.

22 And the scribes which came down
from Jerusalem said, [k]He hath Beelzebub, and by the prince of the devils
casteth he out devils.

23 [l]And he called them *unto him*,
and said unto them in parables, How
can Satan cast out Satan?

24 And if a kingdom be divided
against itself, that kingdom cannot
stand.

25 And if a house be divided against
itself, that house cannot stand.

26 And if Satan rise up against himself, and be divided, he cannot stand,
but hath an end.

27 [m]No man can enter into a strong
man's house, and spoil his goods, except he will first bind the strong man;
and then he will spoil his house.

H—CONCLUDED.

Luke 17. 20 And when he was demanded of the Pharisees, when the kingdom of God should come, he answered them and said, The kingdom of God cometh not with observation:

21 Neither shall they say, Lo here! or, lo there! for, behold, the kingdom of God is within you.

Heb. 12. 28 Wherefore we receiving a kingdom which cannot be moved, let us have grace, whereby we may serve God acceptably with reverence and godly fear:

29 For our God *is* a consuming fire.

I

Isa. 49. 24 Shall the prey be taken from the mighty, or the lawful captive delivered?

Luke 11. 21, 22, 23. *See text of topic.*

K

Matt. 9. 34. *See under A, page 166.*

Matt. 10. 25 It is enough for the disciple that he be as his master, and the servant as his lord. If they have called the master of the house Beelzebub, how much more *shall they call* them of his household?

PHARISEES REPROVED (CONTINUED).

CHAP. 11.

15 But some of them said, [n]He casteth out devils through [4]Beelzebub the
chief of the devils. (p. 173.)

* * * * *

17 But [o]he, knowing their thoughts,
said unto them, Every kingdom divided against itself is brought to desolation; and a house *divided* against a
house falleth.

18 If Satan also be divided against
himself, how shall his kingdom stand?
because ye say that I cast out devils
through Beelzebub.

19 And if I by Beelzebub cast out
devils, by whom do [p]your sons cast
them out? therefore shall they be your
judges.

20 But if I [q]with the finger of God
cast out devils, no doubt the kingdom
of God is come upon you.

21 [r]When a strong man armed keepeth his palace, his goods are in peace:

22 But [s]when a stronger than he
shall come upon him, and overcome
him, he taketh from him all his
armour wherein he trusted, and divideth his spoils.

K—CONTINUED.

Matt. 12. 24 and Luke 11. 15. *See text of topic.*

John 7. 20 The people answered and said, Thou hast a devil: who goeth about to kill thee?

John 8. 48 Then answered the Jews, and said unto him, Say we not well that thou art a Samaritan, and hast a devil?

49 Jesus answered, I have not a devil; but I honour my Father, and ye do dishonour me.

50 And I seek not mine own glory: there is one that seeketh and judgeth.

51 Verily, verily, I say unto you, If a man keep my saying, he shall never see death.

52 Then said the Jews unto him, Now we know that thou hast a devil.

TIME, AUTUMN, A. D. 28; PLACE, GALILEE.

K—CONCLUDED.

Abraham is dead, and the prophets; and thou sayest, If a man keep my saying, he shall never taste of death.

John 10. 20. *See under D, page 167.*

L

Matt. 12. 25. *See text of topic.*

M

Isa. 49. 24. *See under I.*
Matt. 12. 29. *See text of topic.*

N

Matt. 9. 34. *See under A, page 166.*
Matt. 12. 24. *See text of topic.*

4

Gr., *Beelzebul.*

O

Matt. 12. 25 and Mark 3. 24. *See text of topic.*
John 2. 25 and Rev. 2. 23. *See under G, page 167.*

P

Mark 9. 38 And John answered him, saying, Master, we saw one casting out devils in thy name, and he followeth not us; and we forbade him, because he followeth not us.

Luke 9. 49 And John answered and said, Master, we saw one casting out devils in thy name; and we forbade him, because he followeth not with us.

Q

Ex. 8. 19 Then the magicians said unto Pharaoh, This *is* the finger of God: and Pharaoh's heart was hardened, and he hearkened not unto them; as the LORD had said.

R

Matt. 12. 29 and Mark 3. 27. *See text of topic.*

Eph. 6. 12 For we wrestle not against flesh and blood, but against principalities, against powers, against the rulers of the darkness of this world, against spiritual wickedness in high *places.*

I Pet. 5. 8 Be sober, be vigilant; because your adversary the devil, as a roaring lion, walketh about, seeking whom he may devour:

S

Isa. 53. 12 Therefore will I divide him *a portion* with the great, and he shall divide the spoil with the strong; because he hath poured out his soul unto death: and he was numbered with the transgressors; and he bare the sin of many, and made intercession for the transgressors.

Col. 2. 15 *And* having spoiled principalities and powers, he made a show of them openly, triumphing over them in it.

§ 51. THE HEALING OF A DEMONIAC. BLASPHEMOUS SCRIBES AND

CHAP. 12.

30 He that is not with me is against me; and he that gathereth not with me scattereth abroad.

31 Wherefore I say unto you, [t]All manner of sin and blasphemy shall be forgiven unto men: [u]but the blasphemy *against* the *Holy* Ghost shall not be forgiven unto men.

32 And whosoever [x]speaketh a word against the Son of man, [y]it shall be forgiven him: but whosoever speaketh against the Holy Ghost, it shall not be forgiven him, neither in this world, neither in the *world* to come.

33 Either make the tree good, and [z]his fruit good; or else make the tree corrupt, and his fruit corrupt: for the tree is known by *his* fruit.

34 O [a]generation of vipers, how can ye, being evil, speak good things? [b]for out of the abundance of the heart the mouth speaketh.

35 [c]A good man out of the good treasure of the heart bringeth forth good things: and an evil man out of the evil treasure bringeth forth evil things.

36 But I say unto you, That every idle word that men shall speak, they shall give account thereof in the day of judgment.

37 For by thy words thou shalt be justified, and by thy words thou shalt be condemned.

T

Mark 3. 28. *See text of topic.*

Luke 12. 10 And whosoever shall speak a word against the Son of man, it shall be forgiven him: but unto him that blasphemeth against the Holy Ghost it shall not be forgiven.

CHAP. 3.

28 [d]Verily I say unto you, All sins shall be forgiven unto the sons of men, and blasphemies wherewith soever they shall blaspheme:

29 But he that shall blaspheme against the Holy Ghost hath [e]never forgiveness, but is in danger of eternal damnation:

30 Because they said, He hath an unclean spirit. (p. 176.)

T—CONCLUDED.

Heb. 6. 4 For *it is* impossible for those who were once enlightened, and have tasted of the heavenly gift, and were made partakers of the Holy Ghost,

5 And have tasted the good word of God, and the powers of the world to come,

6 If they shall fall away, to renew them again unto repentance; seeing they crucify to themselves the Son of God afresh, and put *him* to an open shame.

Heb. 10. 26 For if we sin wilfully after that we have received the knowledge of the truth, there remaineth no more sacrifice for sins.

Heb. 10. 29 Of how much sorer punishment, suppose ye, shall he be thought worthy, who hath trodden under foot the Son of God, and hath counted the blood of the covenant, wherewith he was sanctified, an unholy thing, and hath done despite unto the Spirit of grace?

I Jno. 5. 16 If any man see his brother sin a sin *which is* not unto death, he shall ask, and he shall give him life for them that sin not unto death. There is a sin unto death: I do not say that he shall pray for it.

U

Acts 7. 51 Ye stiffnecked and uncircumcised in heart and ears, ye do always resist the Holy Ghost: as your fathers *did*, so *do* ye.

Heb. 6. 4. *See under T.*

X

Matt. 11. 19 The Son of man came eating and drinking, and they say, Behold a man gluttonous, and a winebibber, a friend of publicans and sinners. But wisdom is justified of her children.

PHARISEES REPROVED (CONCLUDED). TIME, AUTUMN, A. D. 28; PLACE, GALILEE.

CHAP. 11.

23 *f* He that is not with me is against me; and he that gathereth not with me scattereth. (p. 175.)

X—CONCLUDED.

Matt.13. 55 Is not this the carpenter's son? is not his mother called Mary? and his brethren, James, and Joses, and Simon, and Judas?
56 And his sisters, are they not all with us? Whence then hath this *man* all these things?

John 7. 12 And there was much murmuring among the people concerning him: for some said, He is a good man: others said, Nay; but he deceiveth the people.

John 7. 52 They answered and said unto him, Art thou also of Galilee? Search, and look: for out of Galilee ariseth no prophet.

Y

I Tim.1. 13 Who was before a blasphemer, and a persecutor, and injurious: but I obtained mercy, because I did *it* ignorantly in unbelief.

Z

Eze. 18. 31 Cast away from you all your transgressions, whereby ye have transgressed; and make you a new heart and a new spirit: for why will ye die, O house of Israel?

Amos 5. 15 Hate the evil, and love the good, and establish judgment in the gate: it may be that the LORD God of hosts will be gracious unto the remnant of Joseph.

Matt. 7. 17 Even so every good tree bringeth forth good fruit; but a corrupt tree bringeth forth evil fruit.

Luke 6. 43 For a good tree bringeth not forth corrupt fruit; neither doth a corrupt tree bring forth good fruit.
44 For every tree is known by his own fruit. For of thorns men do not gather figs, nor of a bramble bush gather they grapes.

A

Matt. 3. 7 But when he saw many of the Pharisees and Sadducees come to his baptism, he said unto them, O generation of vipers, who hath warned you to flee from the wrath to come?

Matt.23. 33 *Ye* serpents, *ye* generation of vipers, how can ye escape the damnation of hell?

B

Luke 6. 45 A good man out of the good treasure of his heart bringeth forth that which is good; and an evil man out of the evil treasure of his heart bringeth forth that which is evil: for of the abundance of the heart his mouth speaketh.

C

Ps. 37. 30 The mouth of the righteous speaketh wisdom, and his tongue talketh of judgment.
31 The law of his God *is* in his heart; none of his steps shall slide.

Prov.10. 20 The tongue of the just *is as* choice silver: the heart of the wicked *is* little worth.
21 The lips of the righteous feed many: but fools die for want of wisdom.

Prov.12. 6 The words of the wicked *are* to lie in wait for blood: but the mouth of the upright shall deliver them.

Prov.12. 17 *He that* speaketh truth showeth forth righteousness: but a false witness deceit.
18 There is that speaketh like the piercings of a sword: but the tongue of the wise *is* health.
19 The lip of truth shall be established for ever: but a lying tongue *is* but for a moment.

Prov.15. 4 A wholesome tongue *is* a tree of life: but perverseness therein *is* a breach in the spirit.

Prov.15. 23 A man hath joy by the answer of his mouth: and a word *spoken* in due season, how good *is it!*

D

Matt. 12. 31. *See text of topic.*
Luke 12. 10 and I Jno. 5. 16. *See under T.*

E

Matt.25. 46 And these shall go away into everlasting punishment: but the righteous into life eternal.

Mark 12. 40 Which devour widows' houses, and for a pretence make long prayers: these shall receive greater damnation.

Acts 7. 51. *See under U.*

IIThes.1. 9 Who shall be punished with everlasting destruction from the presence of the Lord, and from the glory of his power;
10 When he shall come to be glorified in his saints, and to be admired in all them that believe (because our testimony among you was believed) in that day.

Heb. 6. 4. *See under T.*

F

Matt. 12. 30. *See text of topic.*

§ 52. THE SIGN OF JONAH: ANSWER TO THE SCRIBES AND PHARISEES

12: 38–42.

38 [a]Then certain of the scribes and of the Pharisees answered, saying, Master, we would see a sign from thee.

39 But he answered and said unto them, An evil and [b]adulterous generation seeketh after a sign; and there shall no sign be given to it, but the sign of the prophet Jonas:

40 [c]For as Jonas was three days and three nights in the whale's belly; so shall the Son of man be three days and three nights in the heart of the earth.

41 [d]The men of Nineveh shall rise in judgment with this generation, and [e]shall condemn it: [f]because they repented at the preaching of Jonas; and, behold, [g]a greater than Jonas *is* here.

42 [h]The queen of the south shall rise up in the judgment with this generation, and shall condemn it: for she came from the uttermost parts of the earth to hear the wisdom of Solomon; and, behold, [i]a greater than Solomon *is* here.

A

Matt.16. 1 The Pharisees also with the Sadducees came, and tempting desired him that he would show them a sign from heaven.

Mark 8. 11 And the Pharisees came forth, and began to question with him, seeking of him a sign from heaven, tempting him.

Luke 11. 16. *See text of topic.*
Luke 11. 29. *See text of topic.*

John 2. 18 Then answered the Jews and said unto him, What sign showest thou unto us, seeing that thou doest these things?

I Cor. 1. 22 For the Jews require a sign, and the Greeks seek after wisdom:

B

Isa. 57. 3 But draw near hither, ye sons of the sorceress, the seed of the adulterer and the whore.

B—Concluded.

Matt.16. 4 A wicked and adulterous generation seeketh after a sign; and there shall no sign be given unto it, but the sign of the prophet Jonas. And he left them, and departed.

Mark 8. 38 Whosoever therefore shall be ashamed of me and of my words, in this adulterous and sinful generation, of him also shall the Son of man be ashamed, when he cometh in the glory of his Father with the holy angels.

John 4. 48 Then said Jesus unto him, Except ye see signs and wonders, ye will not believe.

Jas. 4. 4 Ye adulterers and adulteresses, know ye not that the friendship of the world is enmity with God? whosoever therefore will be a friend of the world is the enemy of God.

C

Jon. 1. 17 Now the Lord had prepared a great fish to swallow up Jonah. And Jonah was in the belly of the fish three days and three nights.

D

Luke 11. 32. *See text of topic.*

E

Jer. 3. 11 And the Lord said unto me, The backsliding Israel hath justified herself more than treacherous Judah.

Eze. 16. 51 Neither hath Samaria committed half of thy sins; but thou hast multiplied thine abominations more than they, and hast justified thy sisters in all thine abominations which thou hast done.

52 Thou also, which hast judged thy sisters, bear thine own shame for thy sins that thou hast committed more abominable than they: they are more righteous than thou: yea, be thou confounded also, and bear thy shame, in that thou hast justified thy sisters.

Rom. 2. 27 And shall not uncircumcision which is by nature, if it fulfill the law, judge thee, who by the letter and circumcision dost transgress the law?

F

Jon. 3. 5 So the people of Nineveh believed God, and proclaimed a fast, and put on sackcloth, from the greatest of them even to the least of them.

6 For word came unto the king of Nineveh, and he arose from his throne, and he laid his robe from him, and covered *him* with sackcloth, and sat in ashes.

WHO SEEK A SIGN. TIME, AUTUMN, A. D. 28; PLACE, GALILEE.

11 : 16, 29–32.

16 And others, tempting *him*, [k]sought
of him a sign from heaven. (p. 169.)

* * * * *

29 [l]And when the people were gathered thick together, he began to say, This is an evil generation: they seek a sign; and there shall no sign be given it, but the sign of Jonas the prophet.

30 For as [m]Jonas was a sign unto the Ninevites, so shall also the Son of man be to this generation.

31 [n]The queen of the south shall rise up in the judgment with the men of this generation, and condemn them: for she came from the utmost parts of the earth to hear the wisdom of Solomon; and, behold, [o]a greater than Solomon *is* here.

32 The men of Nineveh shall rise up in the judgment with this generation, and shall condemn it: for [p]they repented at the preaching of Jonas; and, behold, a greater than Jonas *is* here.

G

Isa. 9. 6 For unto us a child is born, unto us a son is given: and the government shall be upon his shoulder: and his name shall be called Wonderful, Counsellor, The mighty God, The everlasting Father, The Prince of Peace.

John 3. 31 He that cometh from above is above all: he that is of the earth is earthly, and speaketh of the earth: he that cometh from heaven is above all.

Rom. 9. 5 Whose *are* the fathers, and of whom as concerning the flesh Christ *came*, who is over all, God blessed for ever. Amen.

Heb. 3. 6 But Christ as a son over his own house; whose house are we, if we hold fast the confidence and the rejoicing of the hope firm unto the end.

H

I Ki. 10. 1 And when the queen of Sheba heard of the fame of Solomon concerning the name of the LORD, she came to prove him with hard questions.

H—CONCLUDED.

II Chr. 9. 1 And when the queen of Sheba heard of the fame of Solomon, she came to prove Solomon with hard questions at Jerusalem, with a very great company, and camels that bare spices, and gold in abundance, and precious stones: and when she was come to Solomon, she communed with him of all that was in her heart.

Luke 11. 31. *See text of topic.*

I

Col. 2. 2 That their hearts might be comforted, being knit together in love, and unto all riches of the full assurance of understanding, to the acknowledgment of the mystery of God, and of the Father, and of Christ;

3 In whom are hid all the treasures of wisdom and knowledge.

Heb. 1. 1 God, who at sundry times and in divers manners spake in time past unto the fathers by the prophets,

2 Hath in these last days spoken unto us by *his* Son, whom he hath appointed heir of all things, by whom also he made the worlds;

3 Who being the brightness of *his* glory, and the express image of his person, and upholding all things by the word of his power, when he had by himself purged our sins, sat down on the right hand of the Majesty on high;

4 Being made so much better than the angels, as he hath by inheritance obtained a more excellent name than they.

K

Matt. 12. 38. *See text of topic.*
Matt. 16. 1. *See under A.*

L

Matt. 12. 38, 39. *See text of topic.*

M

Jon. 1. 17. *See under C.*

Jon. 2. 10 And the LORD spake unto the fish, and it vomited out Jonah upon the dry *land*.

N

I Ki. 10. 1. *See under H.*

O

Isa. 9. 6 and Rom. 9. 5. *See under G.*

Tit. 2. 13 Looking for that blessed hope, and the glorious appearing of the great God and our Saviour Jesus Christ;

P

Jon. 3. 5. *See under F.*

§ 53. THE UNCLEAN SPIRIT'S RETURN: A REFLECTION

12: 43–45.

43 [a]When the unclean spirit is gone out of a man, [b]he walketh through dry places, seeking rest, and findeth none.

44 Then he saith, I will return into my house from whence I came out; and when he is come, he findeth *it* empty, swept, and garnished.

45 Then [c]goeth he, and taketh with himself seven other spirits more wicked than himself, and they enter in and dwell there: [d]and the last *state* of that man is worse than the first. Even so shall it be also unto this wicked generation.

A

Luke 11. 24. *See text of topic.*

B

Job 1. 7 And the LORD said unto Satan, Whence comest thou? Then Satan answered the LORD, and said, From going to and fro in the earth, and from walking up and down in it.

I Pet. 5. 8 Be sober, be vigilant; because your adversary the devil, as a roaring lion, walketh about, seeking whom he may devour:

C

Isa. 66. 3 He that killeth an ox *is as if* he slew a man; he that sacrificeth a lamb, *as if* he cut off a dog's neck; he that offereth an oblation, *as if he*

C—CONCLUDED.

offered swine's blood; he that burneth incense, *as if* he blessed an idol. Yea, they have chosen their own ways, and their soul delighteth in their abominations.

4 I also will choose their delusions, and will bring their fears upon them; because when I called, none did answer; when I spake, they did not hear: but they did evil before mine eyes, and chose *that* in which I delighted not.

D

Heb. 6. 4 For *it is* impossible for those who were once enlightened, and have tasted of the heavenly gift, and were made partakers of the Holy Ghost,

5 And have tasted the good word of God, and the powers of the world to come,

6 If they shall fall away, to renew them again unto repentance; seeing they crucify to themselves the Son of God afresh, and put *him* to an open shame.

Heb. 10. 26 For if we sin wilfully after that we have received the knowledge of the truth, there remaineth no more sacrifice for sins,

27 But a certain fearful looking for of judgment and fiery indignation, which shall devour the adversaries.

II Pet. 2. 20 For if after they have escaped the pollutions of the world through the knowledge of the Lord and Saviour Jesus Christ, they are again entangled therein, and overcome, the latter end is worse with them than the beginning.

§ 54. THE LIGHT OF THE BODY: A REFLECTION OF

A

Matt. 5. 15 Neither do men light a candle, and put it under a bushel, but on a candlestick; and it giveth light unto all that are in the house.

Mark 4. 21 And he said unto them, Is a candle brought to be put under a bushel, or under a bed? and not to be set on a candlestick?

Luke 8. 16 No man, when he hath lighted a candle, covereth it with a vessel, or putteth *it* under a bed; but setteth *it* on a candlestick, that they which enter in may see the light.

1

The word in the original signifies *a measure containing about a pint less than a peck.*

B

Phil. 2. 15 That ye may be blameless and harmless, the sons of God, without rebuke, in the midst of a crooked and perverse nation, among whom ye shine as lights in the world;

16 Holding forth the word of life; that I may rejoice in the day of Christ, that I have not run in vain, neither laboured in vain.

OF OUR LORD. Time, Autumn, A. D. 28; Place, Galilee.

11: 24–28.

24 [e]When the unclean spirit is gone out of a man, he walketh through dry places, seeking rest; and finding none, he saith, I will return unto my house whence I came out.

25 And when he cometh, he findeth *it* swept and garnished.

26 Then goeth he, and taketh *to him* seven other spirits more wicked than himself; and they enter in, and dwell there: and [f]the last *state* of that man is worse than the first.

27 And it came to pass, as he spake these things, a certain woman of the company lifted up her voice, and said unto him, [g]Blessed *is* the womb that bare thee, and the paps which thou hast sucked.

28 But he said, Yea, [h]rather, blessed *are* they that hear the word of God, and keep it. (p. 173.)

D—Continued.

II Pet.2. 21 For it had been better for them not to have known the way of righteousness, than, after they have known *it*, to turn from the holy commandment delivered unto them.

D—Concluded.

II Pet.2. 22 But it is happened unto them according to the true proverb, The dog *is* turned to his own vomit again; and the sow that was washed to her wallowing in the mire.

E

Matt. 12. 43. *See text of topic.*

F

John 5. 14 Afterward Jesus findeth him in the temple, and said unto him, Behold, thou art made whole: sin no more, lest a worse thing come unto thee.

Heb. 6. 4, Heb. 10. 26 and II Pet. 2. 20. *See under D.*

G

Luke 1. 28 And the angel came in unto her, and said, Hail, *thou that art* highly favoured, the Lord *is* with thee: blessed *art* thou among women.

Luke 1. 48 For he hath regarded the low estate of his handmaiden: for, behold, from henceforth all generations shall call me blessed.

H

Matt. 7. 21 Not every one that saith unto me, Lord, Lord, shall enter into the kingdom of heaven; but he that doeth the will of my Father which is in heaven.

Luke 8. 21 And he answered and said unto them, My mother and my brethren are these which hear the word of God, and do it.

Jas. 1. 25 But whoso looketh into the perfect law of liberty, and continueth *therein*, he being not a forgetful hearer, but a doer of the work, this man shall be blessed in his deed.

OUR LORD. Time, Autumn, A. D. 28; Place, Galilee.

11: 33–36.

33 [a]No man, when he hath lighted a candle, putteth *it* in a secret place, neither under a [1]bushel, but on a candlestick, that they which come in [b]may see the light.

34 [c]The light of the body is the eye: therefore when thine eye is [d]single, thy whole body also is full of light; [e]but when *thine eye* is evil, thy body also *is* full of darkness.

C

Matt. 6. 22 The light of the body is the eye: if therefore thine eye be single, thy whole body shall be full of light.

23 But if thine eye be evil, thy whole body shall be full of darkness. If therefore the light that is in thee be darkness, how great *is* that darkness!

D

Acts 2. 46 And they, continuing daily with one accord in the temple, and breaking bread from house to house, did eat their meat with gladness and singleness of heart,

For D concluded and E see succeeding pages (176, 177).

§ 54. THE LIGHT OF THE BODY: A REFLECTION OF OUR LORD

D—CONTINUED. See preceding page (175).

II Cor.1. 12 For our rejoicing is this, the testimony of our conscience, that in simplicity and godly sincerity, not with fleshly wisdom, but by the grace of God, we have had our conversation in the world, and more abundantly to you-ward.

IICor.11. 3 But I fear, lest by any means, as the serpent beguiled Eve through his subtilty, so your minds should be corrupted from the simplicity that is in Christ.

D—CONCLUDED.

Eph. 6. 5 Servants, be obedient to them that are *your* masters according to the flesh, with fear and trembling, in singleness of your heart, as unto Christ;

Col. 3. 22 Servants, obey in all things *your* masters according to the flesh; not with eyeservice, as men-pleasers; but in singleness of heart, fearing God:

E

Prov.28. 22 He that hasteth to be rich *hath* an evil eye, and considereth not that poverty shall come upon him.

§ 55. THE TRUE DISCIPLES OF CHRIST HIS NEAREST

12: 46–50.

46 While he yet talked to the people,
behold, [a]*his* mother and [b]his brethren
stood without, desiring to speak with
him.
47 Then one said unto him, Behold,
thy mother and thy brethren stand
without, desiring to speak with thee.
48 But he answered and said unto
him that told him, Who is my mother?
and who are my brethren?
49 And he stretched forth his hand
toward his disciples, and said, Behold
my mother and my brethren!
50 For [c]whosoever shall do the will
of my Father which is in heaven, the
same is my brother, and sister, and
mother. (p. 196.)

A

Mark 3. 31 and Luke 8. 19, etc. *See text of topic.*

B

Matt.13. 55 Is not this the carpenter's son? Is not his mother called Mary? and his brethren, James, and Joses, and Simon, and Judas?

Mark 6. 3 Is not this the carpenter, the son of Mary, the brother of James, and Joses, and of Juda, and Simon? and are not his sisters here with us? And they were offended at him.

John 2. 12 After this he went down to Capernaum, he, and his mother, and his brethren, and his disciples; and they continued there not many days.

3: 31–35.

31 [d]There came then his brethren
and his mother, and, standing without, sent unto him, calling him.
32 And the multitude sat about him,
and they said unto him, Behold, [e]thy
mother and thy brethren without seek
for thee.
33 And he answered them, saying,
Who is my mother, or my brethren?
34 And he looked round about on
them which sat about him, and said,
[f]Behold my mother and my brethren!
35 For whosoever shall do the will
of God, the same is my brother, and
my sister, and mother. (p. 196.)

B—CONCLUDED.

John 7. 3 His brethren therefore said unto him, Depart hence, and go into Judæa, that thy disciples also may see the works that thou doest.

John 7. 5 For neither did his brethren believe in him.

Acts 1. 14 These all continued with one accord in prayer and supplication, with the women, and Mary the mother of Jesus, and with his brethren.

I Cor. 9. 5 Have we not power to lead about a sister, a wife, as well as other apostles, and *as* the brethren of the Lord, and Cephas?

Gal. 1. 19 But other of the apostles saw I none, save James the Lord's brother.

(CONCLUDED). TIME, AUTUMN, A. D. 28; PLACE, GALILEE.

CHAP. 11.

35 Take heed therefore, that the light which is in thee be not darkness.

36 If thy whole body therefore *be* full of light, having no part dark, the whole shall be full of light, as when the bright shining of a candle doth give thee light. (p. 179.)

E—CONCLUDED.

Isa. 6. 9 And he said, Go, and tell this people, Hear ye indeed, but understand not; and see ye indeed, but perceive not.

10 Make the heart of this people fat, and make their ears heavy, and shut their eyes; lest they see with their eyes, and hear with their ears, and understand with their heart, and convert, and be healed.

RELATIVES. TIME, AUTUMN, A. D. 28; PLACE, GALILEE.

8: 19–21.

19 [g]Then came to him *his* mother and his brethren, and could not come at him for the press.

20 And it was told him *by certain* which said, Thy mother and thy brethren stand without, desiring to see thee.

21 And he answered and said unto them, My mother and my brethren are these which hear the word of God, and do it. (p. 213.)

C

John 15. 14 Ye are my friends, if ye do whatsoever I command you.

Gal. 5. 6 For in Jesus Christ neither circumcision availeth any thing, nor uncircumcision; but faith which worketh by love.

Gal. 6. 15 For in Christ Jesus neither circumcision availeth any thing, nor uncircumcision, but a new creature.

Col. 3. 11 Where there is neither Greek nor Jew, circumcision nor uncircumcision, Barbarian, Scythian, bond *nor* free; but Christ *is* all, and in all.

Heb. 2. 11 For both he that sanctifieth and they who are sanctified *are* all of one: for which cause he is not ashamed to call them brethren,

D

Matt. 12. 46 and Luke 8. 19. *See text of topic.*

E

Matt. 13. 55, Mark 6. 3 and John 7. 3. *See under B.*

F

Deut. 33. 8 And of Levi he said, *Let* thy Thummim and thy Urim *be* with thy holy one, whom thou didst prove at Massah, *and with* whom thou didst strive at the waters of Meribah;

F—CONCLUDED.

Deut. 33. 9 Who said unto his father and to his mother, I have not seen him; neither did he acknowledge his brethren, nor knew his own children: for they have observed thy word, and kept thy covenant.

Ps. 22. 22 I will declare thy name unto my brethren: in the midst of the congregation will I praise thee.

Song 4. 9 Thou hast ravished my heart, my sister, *my* spouse; thou hast ravished my heart with one of thine eyes, with one chain of thy neck.

10 How fair is thy love, my sister, *my* spouse! how much better is thy love than wine! and the smell of thine ointments than all spices!

Matt. 25. 39 Or when saw we thee sick, or in prison, and came unto thee?

40 And the King shall answer and say unto them, Verily I say unto you, Inasmuch as ye have done *it* unto one of the least of these my brethren, ye have done *it* unto me.

Matt. 28. 10 Then said Jesus unto them, Be not afraid: go tell my brethren that they go into Galilee, and there shall they see me.

Luke 11. 27 And it came to pass, as he spake these things, a certain woman of the company lifted up her voice, and said unto him, Blessed *is* the womb that bare thee, and the paps which thou hast sucked.

28 But he said, Yea, rather, blessed *are* they that hear the word of God, and keep it.

Rom. 8. 29 For whom he did foreknow, he also did predestinate *to be* conformed to the image of his Son, that he might be the first-born among many brethren.

Heb. 2. 11. *See under C.*

G

Matt. 12. 46 and Mark 3. 31. *See text of topic.*

§ 56. AT A PHARISEE'S TABLE JESUS DENOUNCES WOES AGAINST

A

Mark 7. 3 For the Pharisees, and all the Jews, except they wash *their* hands oft, eat not, holding the tradition of the elders.

B

Matt.23. 25 Woe unto you, scribes and Pharisees, hypocrites! for ye make clean the outside of the cup and of the platter, but within they are full of extortion and excess.

26 *Thou* blind Pharisee, cleanse first that *which is* within the cup and platter, that the outside of them may be clean also.

C

IITim.3. 5 Having a form of godliness, but denying the power thereof: from such turn away.

Tit. 1. 15 Unto the pure all things are pure: but unto them that are defiled and unbelieving *is* nothing pure; but even their mind and conscience is defiled.

D

Isa. 58. 7 *Is it* not to deal thy bread to the hungry, and that thou bring the poor that are cast out to thy house? when thou seest the naked, that thou cover him; and that thou hide not thyself from thine own flesh?

Dan. 4. 27 Wherefore, O king, let my counsel be acceptable unto thee, and break off thy sins by righteousness, and thine iniquities by showing mercy to the poor; if it may be a lengthening of thy tranquillity.

Luke 12. 33 Sell that ye have, and give alms; provide yourselves bags which wax not old, a treasure in the heavens that faileth not, where no thief approacheth, neither moth corrupteth.

1

Or, *as you are able.*

E

I Sa. 15. 22 And Samuel said, Hath the LORD *as great* delight in burnt offerings and sacrifices, as in obeying the voice of the LORD? Behold, to obey *is* better than sacrifice, *and* to hearken than the fat of rams.

Isa. 1. 10 Hear the word of the LORD, ye rulers of Sodom; give ear unto the law of our God, ye people of Gomorrah.

11 To what purpose *is* the multitude of your sacrifices unto me? saith the LORD: I am full of the burnt offerings of rams, and the fat of fed beasts; and I delight not in the blood of bullocks, or of lambs, or of he goats.

E—CONCLUDED.

Isa. 1. 12 When ye come to appear before me, who hath required this at your hand, to tread my courts?

13 Bring no more vain oblations; incense is an abomination unto me; the new moons and sabbaths, the calling of assemblies, I cannot away with; *it is* iniquity, even the solemn meeting.

14 Your new moons and your appointed feasts my soul hateth: they are a trouble unto me; I am weary to bear *them.*

15 And when ye spread forth your hands, I will hide mine eyes from you; yea, when ye make many prayers, I will not hear: your hands are full of blood.

16 Wash ye, make you clean; put away the evil of your doings from before mine eyes; cease to do evil;

17 Learn to do well; seek judgment, relieve the oppressed, judge the fatherless, plead for the widow.

Hos. 6. 6 For I desired mercy, and not sacrifice; and the knowledge of God more than burnt offerings.

Matt.23. 23 Woe unto you, scribes and Pharisees, hypocrites! for ye pay tithe of mint and anise and cummin, and have omitted the weightier *matters* of the law, judgment, mercy, and faith: these ought ye to have done, and not to leave the other undone.

24 *Ye* blind guides, which strain at a gnat, and swallow a camel.

F

Mal. 3. 10 Bring ye all the tithes into the storehouse, that there may be meat in mine house, and prove me now herewith, saith the LORD of hosts, if I will not open you the windows of heaven, and pour you out a blessing, that *there shall* not *be room* enough *to receive it.*

G

Matt.23. 5 But all their works they do for to be seen of men: they make broad their phylacteries, and enlarge the borders of their garments,

6 And love the uppermost rooms at feasts, and the chief seats in the synagogues,

7 And greetings in the markets, and to be called of men, Rabbi, Rabbi.

8 But be not ye called Rabbi: for one is your Master, *even* Christ; and all ye are brethren.

9 And call no *man* your father upon the earth: for one is your Father, which is in heaven.

THE PHARISEES AND OTHERS. TIME, AUTUMN, A. D. 28; PLACE, GALILEE.

11: 37–54.

37 And as he spake, a certain Pharisee besought him to dine with him: and he went in, and sat down to meat.

38 And [a]when the Pharisee saw *it*, he marvelled that he had not first washed before dinner.

39 [b]And the Lord said unto him, Now do ye Pharisees make clean the outside of the cup and the platter; but [c]your inward part is full of ravening and wickedness.

40 *Ye* fools, did not he, that made that which is without, make that which is within also?

41 [d]But rather give alms [1]of such things as ye have; and, behold, all things are clean unto you.

42 [e]But woe unto you, Pharisees! for ye tithe mint and rue and all manner of herbs, and pass over judgment and the love of God: [f]these ought ye to have done, and not to leave the other undone.

43 [g]Woe unto you, Pharisees! for ye love the uppermost seats in the synagogues, and greetings in the markets.

44 [h]Woe unto you, scribes and Pharisees, hypocrites! [i]for ye are as graves which appear not, and the men that walk over *them* are not aware *of them*.

45 Then answered one of the lawyers, and said unto him, Master, thus saying thou reproachest us also.

46 And he said, Woe unto you also, ye lawyers! [k]for ye lade men with burdens grievous to be borne, and ye yourselves touch not the burdens with one of your fingers.

G—CONCLUDED.

Matt.23. 10 Neither be ye called masters: for one is your Master, *even* Christ.

11 But he that is greatest among you shall be your servant.

12 And whosoever shall exalt himself shall be abased; and he that shall humble himself shall be exalted.

Mark 12. 38 And he said unto them in his doctrine, Beware of the scribes, which love to go in long clothing, and *love* salutations in the marketplaces,

39 And the chief seats in the synagogues, and the uppermost rooms at feasts:

40 Which devour widows' houses, and for a pretence make long prayers: these shall receive greater damnation.

H

Matt.23. 27 Woe unto you, scribes and Pharisees, hypocrites! for ye are like unto whited sepulchres, which indeed appear beautiful outward, but are within full of dead *men's* bones, and of all uncleanness.

28 Even so ye also outwardly appear righteous unto men, but within ye are full of hypocrisy and iniquity.

I

Num.19. 16 And whosoever toucheth one that is slain with a sword in the open fields, or a dead body, or a bone of a man, or a grave, shall be unclean seven days.

Ps. 5. 9 For *there is* no faithfulness in their mouth; their inward part *is* very wickedness; their throat *is* an open sepulchre; they flatter with their tongue.

Acts 23. 3 Then said Paul unto him, God shall smite thee, *thou* whited wall: for sittest thou to judge me after the law, and commandest me to be smitten contrary to the law?

K

Matt.23. 1 Then spake Jesus to the multitude, and to his disciples,

2 Saying, The scribes and the Pharisees sit in Moses' seat:

3 All therefore whatsoever they bid you observe, *that* observe and do; but do not ye after their works: for they say, and do not.

4 For they bind heavy burdens and grievous to be borne, and lay *them* on men's shoulders; but they *themselves* will not move them with one of their fingers.

§ 56. AT A PHARISEE'S TABLE JESUS DENOUNCES WOES AGAINST THE

L

Matt.23. 29 Woe unto you, scribes and Pharisees, hypocrites! because ye build the tombs of the prophets, and garnish the sepulchres of the righteous,

30 And say, If we had been in the days of our fathers, we would not have been partakers with them in the blood of the prophets.

31 Wherefore ye be witnesses unto yourselves, that ye are the children of them which killed the prophets.

32 Fill ye up then the measure of your fathers.

33 *Ye* serpents, *ye* generation of vipers, how can ye escape the damnation of hell?

M

Acts 7. 51 Ye stiffnecked and uncircumcised in heart and ears, ye do always resist the Holy Ghost: as your fathers *did*, so *do* ye.

52 Which of the prophets have not your fathers persecuted? and they have slain them which showed before of the coming of the Just One; of whom ye have been now the betrayers and murderers:

53 Who have received the law by the disposition of angels, and have not kept *it*.

I Thes.2. 14 For ye, brethren, became followers of the churches of God which in Judæa are in Christ Jesus: for ye also have suffered like things of your own countrymen, even as they *have* of the Jews:

15 Who both killed the Lord Jesus, and their own prophets, and have persecuted us; and they please not God, and are contrary to all men:

16 Forbidding us to speak to the Gentiles that they might be saved, to fill up their sins always: for the wrath is come upon them to the uttermost.

N

Prov. 1. 20 Wisdom crieth without; she uttereth her voice in the streets:

21 She crieth in the chief place of concourse, in the openings of the gates: in the city she uttereth her words, *saying*,

22 How long, ye simple ones, will ye love simplicity? and the scorners delight in their scorning, and fools hate knowledge?

23 Turn you at my reproof: behold, I will pour out my spirit unto you, I will make known my words unto you.

N—Concluded.

I Cor. 1. 22 For the Jews require a sign, and the Greeks seek after wisdom:

23 But we preach Christ crucified, unto the Jews a stumblingblock, and unto the Greeks foolishness;

24 But unto them which are called, both Jews and Greeks, Christ the power of God, and the wisdom of God.

25 Because the foolishness of God is wiser than men; and the weakness of God is stronger than men.

O

Matt.23. 34 Wherefore, behold, I send unto you prophets, and wise men, and scribes: and *some* of them ye shall kill and crucify; and *some* of them shall ye scourge in your synagogues, and persecute *them* from city to city:

35 That upon you may come all the righteous blood shed upon the earth, from the blood of righteous Abel unto the blood of Zacharias son of Barachias, whom ye slew between the temple and the altar.

36 Verily I say unto you, All these things shall come upon this generation.

P

Gen. 4. 8 And Cain talked with Abel his brother: and it came to pass, when they were in the field, that Cain rose up against Abel his brother, and slew him.

Q

IIChr.24. 20 And the Spirit of God came upon Zechariah the son of Jehoiada the priest, which stood above the people, and said unto them, Thus saith God, Why transgress ye the commandments of the LORD, that ye cannot prosper? because ye have forsaken the LORD, he hath also forsaken you.

21 And they conspired against him, and stoned him with stones at the commandment of the king in the court of the house of the LORD.

R

Matt.23. 13 But woe unto you, scribes and Pharisees, hypocrites! for ye shut up the kingdom of heaven against men: for ye neither go in *yourselves*, neither suffer ye them that are entering to go in.

14 Woe unto you, scribes and Pharisees, hypocrites! for ye devour widows' houses, and for a pretense make long prayer: therefore ye shall receive the greater damnation.

PHARISEES AND OTHERS (CONCLUDED). TIME, AUTUMN, A. D. 28; PLACE, GALILEE.

CHAP. 11.

47 [l]Woe unto you! for ye build the
sepulchres of the prophets, and your
fathers killed them.

48 Truly ye bear witness that ye
allow the deeds of your fathers: for
[m]they indeed killed them, and ye build
their sepulchres.

49 Therefore also said [n]the wisdom
of God, [o]I will send them prophets
and apostles, and *some* of them they
shall slay and persecute:

50 That the blood of all the prophets, which was shed from the foundation of the world, may be required
of this generation;

51 [p]From the blood of Abel unto
[q]the blood of Zacharias, which perished between the altar and the temple: verily I say unto you, It shall be
required of this generation.

52 [r]Woe unto you, lawyers! for ye
have taken away the key of knowledge: ye entered not in yourselves,
and them that were entering in ye
[2]hindered.

53 And as he said these things unto
them, the scribes and the Pharisees
began to urge *him* vehemently, and
to provoke him to speak of many
things:

54 Laying wait for him, and [s]seeking
to catch something out of his mouth,
that they might accuse him.

R—CONTINUED.

Matt.23. 15 Woe unto you, scribes and Pharisees, hypocrites! for ye compass sea
and land to make one proselyte; and
when he is made, ye make him twofold more the child of hell than yourselves.

R—CONCLUDED.

Matt.23. 16 Woe unto you, *ye* blind guides,
which say, Whosoever shall swear by
the temple, it is nothing; but whosoever shall swear by the gold of the
temple, he is a debtor!

17 *Ye* fools and blind: for whether
is greater, the gold, or the temple that
sanctifieth the gold?

18 And, Whosoever shall swear by
the altar, it is nothing; but whosoever sweareth by the gift that is upon
it, he is guilty.

19 *Ye* fools and blind: for whether
is greater, the gift, or the altar that
sanctifieth the gift?

20 Whoso therefore shall swear by
the altar, sweareth by it, and by all
things thereon.

21 And whoso shall swear by the
temple, sweareth by it, and by him
that dwelleth therein.

22 And he that shall swear by heav-
en, sweareth by the throne of God,
and by him that sitteth thereon.

2

Or, *forbad*

S

Ps. 37. 32 The wicked watcheth the righteous, and seeketh to slay him.

33 The LORD will not leave him in
his hand, nor condemn him when he
is judged.

Ps. 56. 5 Every day they wrest my words:
all their thoughts *are* against me for
evil.

6 They gather themselves together,
they hide themselves, they mark my
steps, when they wait for my soul.

7 Shall they escape by iniquity? in
thine anger cast down the people, O God.

Matt.22. 15 Then went the Pharisees, and
took counsel how they might entangle
him in *his* talk.

16 And they sent out unto him their
disciples with the Herodians, saying,
Master, we know that thou art true,
and teachest the way of God in truth,
neither carest thou for any *man:*
for thou regardest not the person of
men.

17 Tell us therefore, What thinkest
thou? Is it lawful to give tribute unto
Cæsar, or not?

18 But Jesus perceived their wickedness, and said, Why tempt ye me,
ye hypocrites?

Mark 12. 13 And they send unto him certain
of the Pharisees and of the Herodians,
to catch him in *his* words.

§ 57. JESUS DISCOURSES TO HIS DISCIPLES AND THE MULTITUDE.

A

Matt.16. 6 Then Jesus said unto them, Take heed and beware of the leaven of the Pharisees and of the Sadducees.

Mark 8. 15 And he charged them, saying, Take heed, beware of the leaven of the Pharisees, and *of* the leaven of Herod.

B

Matt.16. 12 Then understood they how that he bade *them* not beware of the leaven of bread, but of the doctrine of the Pharisees and of the Sadducees.

I Cor. 5. 7 Purge out therefore the old leaven, that ye may be a new lump, as ye are unleavened. For even Christ our passover is sacrificed for us:

8 Therefore let us keep the feast, not with old leaven, neither with the leaven of malice and wickedness; but with the unleavened *bread* of sincerity and truth.

C

Eccl. 12. 14 For God shall bring every work into judgment, with every secret thing, whether *it be* good, or whether *it be* evil.

Matt.10. 26 Fear them not therefore: for there is nothing covered, that shall not be revealed; and hid, that shall not be known.

27 What I tell you in darkness, *that* speak ye in light: and what ye hear in the ear, *that* preach ye upon the housetops.

28 And fear not them which kill the body, but are not able to kill the soul: but rather fear him which is able to destroy both soul and body in hell.

29 Are not two sparrows sold for a farthing? and one of them shall not fall on the ground without your Father.

30 But the very hairs of your head are all numbered.

31 Fear ye not therefore, ye are of more value than many sparrows.

32 Whosoever therefore shall confess me before men, him will I confess also before my Father which is in heaven.

33 But whosoever shall deny me before men, him will I also deny before my Father which is in heaven.

Mark 4. 22 For there is nothing hid, which shall not be manifested; neither was any thing kept secret, but that it should come abroad.

C—Concluded.

Luke 8. 17 For nothing is secret, that shall not be made manifest; neither *any thing* hid, that shall not be known and come abroad.

I Cor. 4. 5 Therefore judge nothing before the time, until the Lord come, who both will bring to light the hidden things of darkness, and will make manifest the counsels of the hearts: and then shall every man have praise of God.

Rev. 20. 12 And I saw the dead, small and great, stand before God; and the books were opened: and another book was opened, which is *the book* of life: and the dead were judged out of those things which were written in the books, according to their works.

13 And the sea gave up the dead which were in it; and death and hell delivered up the dead which were in them: and they were judged every man according to their works.

D

Isa. 51. 7 Hearken unto me, ye that know righteousness, the people in whose heart *is* my law; fear ye not the reproach of men, neither be ye afraid of their revilings.

8 For the moth shall eat them up like a garment, and the worm shall eat them like wool: but my righteousness shall be for ever, and my salvation from generation to generation.

Isa. 51. 12 I, *even* I, *am* he that comforteth you: who *art* thou, that thou shouldest be afraid of a man *that* shall die, and of the son of man *which* shall be made *as* grass;

13 And forgettest the Lord thy Maker, and hath stretched forth the heavens, and laid the foundations of the earth; and hast feared continually every day because of the fury of the oppressor, as if he were ready to destroy? and where *is* the fury of the oppressor?

Jer. 1. 8 Be not afraid of their faces: for I *am* with thee to deliver thee, saith the Lord.

Matt. 10. 28. *See under C.*

E

John 15. 14 Ye are my friends, if ye do whatsoever I command you.

15 Henceforth I call you not servants; for the servant knoweth not what his lord doeth: but I have called you friends; for all things that I have heard of my Father I have made known unto you.

TIME, AUTUMN, A. D. 28; PLACE, GALILEE.

12: 1–59.

1 In the mean time, when there were
gathered together an innumerable
multitude of people, insomuch that
they trode one upon another, he [a]be-
gan to say unto his disciples first of
all, [b]Beware ye of the leaven of the
Pharisees, which is hypocrisy.
2 [c]For there is nothing covered, that
shall not be revealed; neither hid,
that shall not be known.
3 Therefore, whatsoever ye have
spoken in darkness shall be heard in
the light; and that which ye have
spoken in the ear in closets shall be
proclaimed upon the housetops.
4 [d]And I say unto you [e]my friends,
Be not afraid of them that kill the
body, and after that have no more
that they can do.
5 But I will forewarn you whom ye
shall fear: Fear him, which after he
hath killed hath [f]power to cast into
hell; yea, I say unto you, Fear him.
6 Are not five sparrows sold for two
[1]farthings, and [g]not one of them is forgotten before God?
7 But even the very hairs of your
head are all numbered. Fear not
therefore: ye are of more value than
many sparrows.
8 [h]Also I say unto you, Whosoever
shall confess me before men, him shall
the Son of man also confess before the
angels of God:
9 But he that denieth me before men
shall be denied before the angels of
God.
10 And [i]whosoever shall speak a
word against the Son of man, it shall

F

Rev. 1. 18 *I am* he that liveth, and was dead; and, behold, I am alive for evermore, Amen; and have the keys of hell and of death.

1

It is in value *a half penny farthing* in the original, as being the tenth part of the Roman penny (denarius); in American money *one and seven-tenth cents*, or, two farthings, *three and four-tenth cents.*

G

Ps. 50. 10 For every beast of the forest *is* mine, *and* the cattle upon a thousand hills.

11 I know all the fowls of the mountains: and the wild beasts of the field *are* mine.

Ps. 113. 6 Who humbleth *himself* to behold *the things that are* in heaven, and in the earth!

Acts 15. 18 Known unto God are all his works from the beginning of the world.

H

Matt. 10. 32. *See under C.*

Mark 8. 38 Whosoever therefore shall be ashamed of me and of my words, in this adulterous and sinful generation, of him also shall the Son of man be ashamed, when he cometh in the glory of his Father with the holy angels.

II Tim. 2. 12 If we suffer, we shall also reign with *him:* if we deny *him,* he also will deny us:

I Jno. 2. 23 Whosoever denieth the Son, the same hath not the Father: [*but*] *he that acknowledgeth the Son hath the Father also.*

I

Matt. 12. 31 Wherefore I say unto you, All manner of sin and blasphemy shall be forgiven unto men: but the blasphemy *against* the *Holy* Ghost shall not be forgiven unto men.

32 And whosoever speaketh a word against the Son of man, it shall be forgiven him: but whosoever speaketh against the Holy Ghost, it shall not be forgiven him, neither in this world, neither in the *world* to come.

Mark 3. 28 Verily I say unto you, All sins shall be forgiven unto the sons of men, and blasphemies wherewith soever they shall blaspheme:

I Jno. 5. 16 If any man see his brother sin a sin *which is* not unto death, he shall ask, and he shall give him life for them that sin not unto death. There is a sin unto death: I do not say that he shall pray for it.

§ 57. JESUS DISCOURSES TO HIS DISCIPLES AND THE MULTITUDE

K

Matt.10. 19 But when they deliver you up, take no thought how or what ye shall speak: for it shall be given you in that same hour what ye shall speak.

20 For it is not ye that speak, but the Spirit of your Father which speaketh in you.

Mark 13. 11 But when they shall lead *you*, and deliver you up, take no thought beforehand what ye shall speak, neither do ye premeditate: but whatsoever shall be given you in that hour, that speak ye: for it is not ye that speak, but the Holy Ghost.

Luke 21. 14 Settle *it* therefore in your hearts, not to meditate before what ye shall answer:

L

Ex. 4. 11 And the LORD said unto him, Who hath made man's mouth? or who maketh the dumb, or deaf, or the seeing, or the blind? have not I the LORD?

12 Now therefore go, and I will be with thy mouth, and teach thee what thou shalt say.

I Pet. 5. 7 Casting all your care upon him; for he careth for you.

M

John 18. 36 Jesus answered, My kingdom is not of this world: if my kingdom were of this world, then would my servants fight, that I should not be delivered to the Jews: but now is my kingdom not from hence.

N

Josh. 7. 21 When I saw among the spoils a goodly Babylonish garment, and two hundred shekels of silver, and a wedge of gold of fifty shekels weight, then I coveted them, and took them; and, behold, they *are* hid in the earth in the midst of my tent, and the silver under it.

Job 31. 24 If I have made gold my hope, or have said to the fine gold, *Thou art* my confidence;

25 If I rejoiced because my wealth *was* great, and because mine hand had gotten much;

Ps. 10. 3 For the wicked boasteth of his heart's desire, and blesseth the covetous *whom* the LORD abhorreth.

Ps. 62. 10 Trust not in oppression, and become not vain in robbery: if riches increase, set not your heart *upon them.*

Ps. 119. 36 Incline my heart unto thy testimonies, and not to covetousness.

N—CONCLUDED.

Ps. 119. 37 Turn away mine eyes from beholding vanity; *and* quicken thou me in thy way.

Prov.23. 4 Labour not to be rich: cease from thine own wisdom.

5 Wilt thou set thine eyes upon that which is not? for *riches* certainly make themselves wings; they fly away as an eagle toward heaven.

Prov.28. 16 The prince that wanteth understanding *is* also a great oppressor: *but* he that hateth covetousness shall prolong *his* days.

I Tim.6. 6 But godliness with contentment is great gain.

7 For we brought nothing into *this* world, *and it is* certain we can carry nothing out.

8 And having food and raiment, let us be therewith content.

9 But they that will be rich fall into temptation and a snare, and *into* many foolish and hurtful lusts, which drown men in destruction and perdition.

10 For the love of money is the root of all evil: which while some coveted after, they have erred from the faith, and pierced themselves through with many sorrows.

11 But thou, O man of God, flee these things; and follow after righteousness, godliness, faith, love, patience, meekness.

Heb. 13. 5 *Let your* conversation *be* without covetousness; *and be* content with such things as ye have: for he hath said, I will never leave thee, nor forsake thee.

6 So that we may boldly say, The Lord *is* my helper, and I will not fear what man shall do unto me.

O

Prov.27. 1 Boast not thyself of to morrow; for thou knowest not what a day may bring forth.

Eccl. 11. 9 Rejoice, O young man, in thy youth; and let thy heart cheer thee in the days of thy youth, and walk in the ways of thine heart, and in the sight of thine eyes: but know thou, that for all these *things* God will bring thee into judgment.

Isa. 5. 11 Woe unto them that rise up early in the morning, *that* they may follow strong drink; that continue until night, *till* wine inflame them!

Isa. 22. 13 And behold joy and gladness, slaying oxen, and killing sheep, eating flesh, and drinking wine: let us eat and drink; for to morrow we shall die.

(CONTINUED). TIME, AUTUMN, A. D. 28; PLACE, GALILEE.

CHAP. 12.

be forgiven him: but unto him that blasphemeth against the Holy Ghost it shall not be forgiven.

11 [k]And when they bring you unto the synagogues, and *unto* magistrates, and powers, take ye no thought how or what thing ye shall answer, or what ye shall say:

12 For [l]the Holy Ghost shall teach you in the same hour what ye ought to say.

13 And one of the company said unto him, Master, speak to my brother, that he divide the inheritance with me.

14 And he said unto him, [m]Man, who made me a judge or a divider over you?

15 And he said unto them, [n]Take heed, and beware of covetousness: for a man's life consisteth not in the abundance of the things which he possesseth.

16 And he spake a parable unto them, saying, The ground of a certain rich man brought forth plentifully:

17 And he thought within himself, saying, What shall I do, because I have no room where to bestow my fruits?

18 And he said, This will I do: I will pull down my barns, and build greater; and there will I bestow all my fruits and my goods.

19 And I will say to my [o]soul, Soul, thou hast much goods laid up for many years; take thine ease, eat, drink, *and* be merry.

O—CONCLUDED.

Amos 6. 3 Ye that put far away the evil day, and cause the seat of violence to come near;

4 That lie upon beds of ivory, and stretch themselves upon their couches, and eat the lambs out of the flock, and the calves out of the midst of the stall;

I Cor.15. 32 If after the manner of men I have fought with beasts at Ephesus, what advantageth it me, if the dead rise not? let us eat and drink; for to morrow we die.

Jas. 5. 5 Ye have lived in pleasure on the earth, and been wanton; ye have nourished your hearts, as in a day of slaughter.

2

Or, *do they require thy soul.*

P

Job 20. 22 In the fulness of his sufficiency he shall be in straits: every hand of the wicked shall come upon him.

Job 21. 13 They spend their days in wealth, and in a moment go down to the grave.

Job 27. 8 For what *is* the hope of the hypocrite, though he hath gained, when God taketh away his soul?

Ps. 52. 7 Lo, *this is* the man *that* made not God his strength; but trusted in the abundance of his riches, *and* strengthened himself in his wickedness.

Dan. 4. 29 At the end of twelve months he walked in the palace of the kingdom of Babylon.

30 The king spake, and said, Is not this great Babylon, that I have built for the house of the kingdom by the might of my power, and for the honour of my majesty?

31 While the word *was* in the king's mouth, there fell a voice from heaven, *saying*, O king Nebuchadnezzar, to thee it is spoken; The kingdom is departed from thee.

32 And they shall drive thee from men, and thy dwelling *shall be* with the beasts of the field: they shall make thee to eat grass as oxen, and seven times shall pass over thee, until thou know that the Most High ruleth in the kingdom of men, and giveth it to whomsoever he will.

33 The same hour was the thing fulfilled upon Nebuchadnezzar: and he was driven from men, and did eat grass as oxen, and his body was wet with the dew of heaven, till his hairs

For P concluded see next page (186).

§ 57. JESUS DISCOURSES TO HIS DISCIPLES AND THE MULTITUDE

For 2 and P see preceding page (185).

P—CONCLUDED.

were grown like eagles' *feathers*, and his nails like birds' *claws*.

Jas. 4. 14 Whereas ye know not what *shall be* on the morrow. For what *is* your life? It is even a vapour, that appeareth for a little time, and then vanisheth away.

Q

Ps. 39. 6 Surely every man walketh in a vain show: surely they are disquieted in vain: he heapeth up *riches*, and knoweth not who shall gather them.

Jer. 17. 11 *As* the partridge sitteth *on eggs*, and hatcheth *them* not; *so* he that getteth riches, and not by right, shall leave them in the midst of his days, and at his end shall be a fool.

R

Matt. 6. 19 Lay not up for yourselves treasures upon earth, where moth and rust doth corrupt, and where thieves break through and steal:

20 But lay up for yourselves treasures in heaven, where neither moth nor rust doth corrupt, and where thieves do not break through nor steal:

21 For where your treasure is, there will your heart be also.

Luke 12. 33. *See text of topic.*

IICor. 6. 10 As sorrowful, yet alway rejoicing; as poor, yet making many rich; as having nothing, and *yet* possessing all things.

ITim. 6. 18 That they do good, that they be rich in good works, ready to distribute, willing to communicate;

19 Laying up in store for themselves a good foundation against the time to come, that they may lay hold on eternal life.

Jas. 2. 5 Hearken, my beloved brethren, Hath not God chosen the poor of this world rich in faith, and heirs of the kingdom which he hath promised to them that love him?

S

Matt. 6. 25 Therefore I say unto you, Take no thought for your life, what ye shall eat, or what ye shall drink; nor yet for your body, what ye shall put on. Is not the life more than meat, and the body than raiment?

26 Behold the fowls of the air: for they sow not, neither do they reap, nor gather into barns; yet your heavenly Father feedeth them. Are ye not much better than they?

S—CONCLUDED.

Matt. 6. 27 Which of you by taking thought can add one cubit unto his stature?

28 And why take ye thought for raiment? Consider the lilies of the field, how they grow; they toil not, neither do they spin:

29 And yet I say unto you, That even Solomon in all his glory was not arrayed like one of these.

30 Wherefore, if God so clothe the grass of the field, which to day is, and to morrow is cast into the oven, *shall he* not much more *clothe* you, O ye of little faith?

31 Therefore take no thought, saying, What shall we eat? or, What shall we drink? or, Wherewithal shall we be clothed?

32 (For after all these things do the Gentiles seek:) for your heavenly Father knoweth that ye have need of all these things.

33 But seek ye first the kingdom of God, and his righteousness; and all these things shall be added unto you.

Phil. 4. 6 Be careful for nothing; but in every thing by prayer and supplication with thanksgiving let your requests be made known unto God.

T

Job 38. 41 Who provideth for the raven his food? when his young ones cry unto God, they wander for lack of meat.

Ps. 147. 9 He giveth to the beast his food, *and* to the young ravens which cry.

U

Ps. 39. 6 Surely every man walketh in a vain show: surely they are disquieted in vain: he heapeth up *riches*, and knoweth not who shall gather them.

Eccl. 7. 13 Consider the work of God: for who can make *that* straight which he hath made crooked?

I Pet. 5. 7 Casting all your care upon him; for he careth for you.

X

I Ki. 10. 4 And when the queen of Sheba had seen all Solomon's wisdom, and the house that he had built,

5 And the meat of his table, and the sitting of his servants, and the attendance of his ministers, and their apparel, and his cupbearers, and his ascent by which he went up into the house of the LORD; there was no more spirit in her.

6 And she said to the king, It was a true report that I heard in mine own land of thy acts and of thy wisdom.

(CONTINUED). TIME, AUTUMN, A. D. 28; PLACE, GALILEE.

CHAP. 12.

20 But God said unto him, *Thou* fool, this night [2p]thy soul shall be required of thee: [q]then whose shall those things be, which thou hast provided?

21 So *is* he that layeth up treasure for himself, [r]and is not rich toward God.

22 And he said unto his disciples, Therefore I say unto you, [s]Take no thought for your life, what ye shall eat; neither for the body, what ye shall put on.

23 The life is more than meat, and the body *is more* than raiment.

24 Consider the ravens: for they neither sow nor reap; which neither have storehouse nor barn; and [t]God feedeth them: how much more are ye better than the fowls?

25 And which of you with taking thought can add to his stature one cubit?

26 If ye then be not able to do that thing which is least, [u]why take ye thought for the rest?

27 Consider the lilies how they grow: they toil not, they spin not; and yet I say unto you, that [x]Solomon in all his glory was not arrayed like one of these.

28 If then God so clothe the grass, [y]which is to day in the field, and to morrow is cast into the oven; how much more *will he clothe* you, O ye of little faith?

29 And seek not ye what ye shall eat, or what ye shall drink, [3]neither be ye of doubtful mind.

30 For all these things do the nations of the world seek after: and your Father knoweth [z]that ye have need of these things.

X—CONCLUDED.

I Ki. 10. 7 Howbeit I believed not the words, until I came, and mine eyes had seen *it;* and, behold, the half was not told me: thy wisdom and prosperity exceedeth the fame which I heard.

II Chr. 9. 3 And when the queen of Sheba had seen the wisdom of Solomon, and the house that he had built,

4 And the meat of his table, and the sitting of his servants, and the attendance of his ministers, and their apparel; his cupbearers also, and their apparel; and his ascent by which he went up into the house of the LORD; there was no more spirit in her.

5 And she said to the king, *It was* a true report which I heard in mine own land of thine acts, and of thy wisdom:

6 Howbeit I believed not their words, until I came, and mine eyes had seen *it:* and, behold, the one half of the greatness of thy wisdom was not told me: *for* thou exceedest the fame that I heard.

Y

Isa. 40. 6 The voice said, Cry. And he said, What shall I cry? All flesh *is* grass, and all the goodliness thereof *is* as the flower of the field:

7 The grass withereth, the flower fadeth; because the spirit of the LORD bloweth upon it: surely the people *is* grass.

8 The grass withereth, the flower fadeth: but the word of our God shall stand for ever.

I Pet. 1. 24 For all flesh *is* as grass, and all the glory of man as the flower of grass. The grass withereth, and the flower thereof falleth away:

25 But the word of the Lord endureth for ever. And this is the word which by the gospel is preached unto you.

3

Or, *live not in careful suspense.*

Z

II Chr. 16. 9 For the eyes of the LORD run to and fro throughout the whole earth, to show himself strong in the behalf of *them* whose heart *is* perfect toward him. Herein thou hast done foolishly: therefore from henceforth thou shalt have wars.

Phil. 4. 19 But my God shall supply all your need according to his riches in glory by Christ Jesus.

§ 57. JESUS DISCOURSES TO HIS DISCIPLES AND THE MULTITUDE

A

Matt. 6. 33. *See under S, page 186.*

B

Rom. 8. 30 Moreover, whom he did predestinate, them he also called: and whom he called, them he also justified: and whom he justified, them he also glorified.

31 What shall we then say to these things? If God *be* for us, who *can be* against us?

I Tim. 4. 8 For bodily exercise profiteth little: but godliness is profitable unto all things, having promise of the life that now is, and of that which is to come.

C

Matt.11. 25 At that time Jesus answered and said, I thank thee, O Father, Lord of heaven and earth, because thou hast hid these things from the wise and prudent, and hast revealed them unto babes.

26 Even so, Father; for so it seemed good in thy sight.

D

Matt.19. 21 Jesus said unto him, If thou wilt be perfect, go *and* sell that thou hast, and give to the poor, and thou shalt have treasure in heaven: and come *and* follow me.

Acts 2. 45 And sold their possessions and goods, and parted them to all *men*, as every man had need.

Acts 4. 34 Neither was there any among them that lacked: for as many as were possessors of lands or houses sold them, and brought the prices of the things that were sold,

E

Matt. 6. 20. *See under R, page 186.*

Luke 16. 9 And I say unto you, Make to yourselves friends of the mammon of unrighteousness; that, when ye fail, they may receive you into everlasting habitations.

I Tim. 6. 19 Laying up in store for themselves a good foundation against the time to come, that they may lay hold on eternal life.

F

Eph. 6. 14 Stand therefore, having your loins girt about with truth, and having on the breastplate of righteousness:

I Pet. 1. 13 Wherefore gird up the loins of your mind, be sober, and hope to the end for the grace that is to be brought unto you at the revelation of Jesus Christ:

G

Matt.25. 1 Then shall the kingdom of heaven be likened unto ten virgins, which took their lamps, and went forth to meet the bridegroom.

2 And five of them were wise, and five *were* foolish.

3 They that *were* foolish took their lamps, and took no oil with them:

4 But the wise took oil in their vessels with their lamps.

5 While the bridegroom tarried, they all slumbered and slept.

6 And at midnight there was a cry made, Behold, the bridegroom cometh; go ye out to meet him.

7 Then all those virgins arose, and trimmed their lamps.

8 And the foolish said unto the wise, Give us of your oil; for our lamps are gone out.

9 But the wise answered, saying, *Not so;* lest there be not enough for us and you: but go ye rather to them that sell, and buy for yourselves.

10 And while they went to buy, the bridegroom came; and they that were ready went in with him to the marriage: and the door was shut.

11 Afterward came also the other virgins, saying, Lord, Lord, open to us.

12 But he answered and said, Verily I say unto you, I know you not.

13 Watch therefore; for ye know neither the day nor the hour wherein the Son of man cometh.

H

Matt.24. 46 Blessed *is* that servant, whom his lord when he cometh shall find so doing.

I

Matt.24. 43 But know this, that if the goodman of the house had known in what watch the thief would come, he would have watched, and would not have suffered his house to be broken up.

I Thes.5. 2 For yourselves know perfectly that the day of the Lord so cometh as a thief in the night.

II Pet.3. 10 But the day of the Lord will come as a thief in the night; in the which the heavens shall pass away with a great noise, and the elements shall melt with fervent heat, the earth also and the works that are therein shall be burned up.

Rev. 3. 3 Remember therefore how thou hast received and heard, and hold fast, and repent. If therefore thou

(CONTINUED). TIME, AUTUMN, A. D. 28; PLACE, GALILEE.

CHAP. 12.

31 [a]But rather seek ye the kingdom of God; and [b]all these things shall be added unto you.

32 Fear not, little flock; for [c]it is your Father's good pleasure to give you the kingdom.

33 [d]Sell that ye have, and give alms; [e]provide yourselves bags which wax not old, a treasure in the heavens that faileth not, where no thief approacheth, neither moth corrupteth.

34 For where your treasure is, there will your heart be also.

35 [f]Let your loins be girded about, and [g]*your* lights burning;

36 And ye yourselves like unto men that wait for their lord, when he will return from the wedding; that, when he cometh and knocketh, they may open unto him immediately.

37 [h]Blessed *are* those servants, whom the lord when he cometh shall find watching: verily I say unto you, that he shall gird himself, and make them to sit down to meat, and will come forth and serve them.

38 And if he shall come in the second watch, or come in the third watch, and find *them* so, blessed are those servants.

39 [i]And this know, that if the goodman of the house had known what hour the thief would come, he would have watched, and not have suffered his house to be broken through.

40 [k]Be ye therefore ready also: for the Son of man cometh at an hour when ye think not.

I—CONCLUDED.

shalt not watch, I will come on thee as a thief, and thou shalt not know what hour I will come upon thee.

Rev. 16. 15 Behold, I come as a thief. Blessed *is* he that watcheth, and keepeth his garments, lest he walk naked, and they see his shame.

K

Matt. 24. 44 Therefore be ye also ready: for in such an hour as ye think not the Son of man cometh.

Matt. 25. 13. *See under G.*

Mark 13. 33 Take ye heed, watch and pray: for ye know not when the time is.

Luke 21. 34 And take heed to yourselves, lest at any time your hearts be overcharged with surfeiting, and drunkenness, and cares of this life, and *so* that day come upon you unawares.

Luke 21. 36 Watch ye therefore, and pray always, that ye may be accounted worthy to escape all these things that shall come to pass, and to stand before the Son of man.

Rom. 13. 11 And that, knowing the time, that now *it is* high time to awake out of sleep: for now *is* our salvation nearer than when we believed.

12 The night is far spent, the day is at hand: let us therefore cast off the works of darkness, and let us put on the armour of light.

13 Let us walk honestly, as in the day; not in rioting and drunkenness, not in chambering and wantonness, not in strife and envying:

14 But put ye on the Lord Jesus Christ, and make not provision for the flesh, to *fulfil* the lusts *thereof*.

I Thes. 5. 6 Therefore let us not sleep, as *do* others; but let us watch and be sober.

II Pet. 3. 12 Looking for and hasting unto the coming of the day of God, wherein the heavens being on fire shall be dissolved, and the elements shall melt with fervent heat?

13 Nevertheless we, according to his promise, look for new heavens and a new earth, wherein dwelleth righteousness.

14 Wherefore, beloved, seeing that ye look for such things, be diligent that ye may be found of him in peace, without spot, and blameless.

Rev. 19. 7 Let us be glad and rejoice, and give honour to him: for the marriage of the Lamb is come, and his wife hath made herself ready.

§ 57. JESUS DISCOURSES TO HIS DISCIPLES AND THE MULTITUDE

L

Matt.24. 45 Who then is a faithful and wise servant, whom his lord hath made ruler over his household, to give them meat in due season?

Matt.25. 21 His lord said unto him, Well done, *thou* good and faithful servant: thou hast been faithful over a few things, I will make thee ruler over many things: enter thou into the joy of thy lord.

I Cor. 4. 2 Moreover it is required in stewards, that a man be found faithful.

M

Matt.24. 47 Verily I say unto you, That he shall make him ruler over all his goods.

I Pet. 5. 4 And when the chief Shepherd shall appear, ye shall receive a crown of glory that fadeth not away.

N

Eze. 12. 22 Son of man, what *is* that proverb *that* ye have in the land of Israel, saying, The days are prolonged, and every vision faileth?

Eze. 12. 27 Son of man, behold, *they of* the house of Israel say, The vision that he seeth *is* for many days *to come*, and he prophesieth of the times *that are* far off.

28 Therefore say unto them, Thus saith the Lord GOD; There shall none of my words be prolonged any more, but the word which I have spoken shall be done, saith the Lord GOD.

Matt.24. 48 But and if that evil servant shall say in his heart, My lord delayeth his coming:

49 And shall begin to smite *his* fellow servants, and to eat and drink with the drunken;

50 The lord of that servant shall come in a day when he looketh not for *him*, and in an hour that he is not aware of,

51 And shall cut him asunder, and appoint *him* his portion with the hypocrites: there shall be weeping and gnashing of teeth.

II Pet 2. 3 And through covetousness shall they with feigned words make merchandise of you: whose judgment now of a long time lingereth not, and their damnation slumbereth not.

4 For if God spared not the angels that sinned, but cast *them* down to hell, and delivered *them* into chains of darkness, to be reserved unto judgment;

O

Jer. 20. 1 Now Pashur the son of Immer the priest, who *was* also chief governor in the house of the LORD, heard that Jeremiah prophesied these things.

2 Then Pashur smote Jeremiah the prophet, and put him in the stocks that *were* in the high gate of Benjamin, which *was* by the house of the LORD.

Eze. 34. 3 Ye eat the fat, and ye clothe you with the wool, ye kill them that are fed: *but* ye feed not the flock.

4 The diseased have ye not strengthened, neither have ye healed that which was sick, neither have ye bound up *that which was* broken, neither have ye brought again that which was driven away, neither have ye sought that which was lost; but with force and with cruelty have ye ruled them.

IICor.11. 20 For ye suffer, if a man bring you into bondage, if a man devour *you*, if a man take *of you*, if a man exalt himself, if a man smite you on the face.

III Jno. 9 I wrote unto the church: but Diotrephes, who loveth to have the preeminence among them, receiveth us not.

10 Wherefore, if I come, I will remember his deeds which he doeth, prating against us with malicious words: and not content therewith, neither doth he himself receive the brethren, and forbiddeth them that would, and casteth *them* out of the church.

P

Isa. 56. 11 Yea, *they are* greedy dogs *which* can never have enough, and they *are* shepherds *that* cannot understand: they all look to their own way, every one for his gain, from his quarter.

12 Come ye, *say they*, I will fetch wine, and we will fill ourselves with strong drink; and to morrow shall be as this day, *and* much more abundant.

Eze. 34. 8 *As* I live, saith the Lord GOD, surely because my flock became a prey, and my flock became meat to every beast of the field, because *there was* no shepherd, neither did my shepherds search for my flock, but the shepherds fed themselves, and fed not my flock;

Rom.16. 18 For they that are such serve not our Lord Jesus Christ, but their own belly; and by good words and fair speeches deceive the hearts of the simple.

(CONTINUED). TIME, AUTUMN, A. D. 28; PLACE, GALILEE.

CHAP. 12.

41 Then Peter said unto him, Lord, speakest thou this parable unto us, or even to all?

42 And the Lord said, [l]Who then is that faithful and wise steward, whom *his* lord shall make ruler over his household, to give *them their* portion of meat in due season?

43 Blessed *is* that servant, whom his lord when he cometh shall find so doing.

44 [m]Of a truth I say unto you, that he will make him ruler over all that he hath.

45 [n]But and if that servant say in his heart, My lord delayeth his coming; and shall begin to [o]beat the menservants and maidens, and to [p]eat and drink, and to be drunken;

46 The lord of that servant will come in a day when he looketh not for *him*, and at an hour when he is not aware, and will [4]cut him in sunder, and will appoint him his portion with the unbelievers.

47 And [q]that servant, which knew his lord's will, and prepared not *himself*, neither did according to his will, shall be beaten with many *stripes*.

48 [r]But he that knew not, and did commit things worthy of stripes, shall be beaten with few *stripes*. For unto whomsoever much is given, of him shall be much required; and to whom men have committed much, of him they will ask the more.

49 [s]I am come to send fire on the earth; and what will I, if it be already kindled?

P—CONCLUDED.

II Pet.2. 13 And shall receive the reward of unrighteousness, *as* they that count it pleasure to riot in the daytime. Spots *they are* and blemishes, sporting themselves with their own deceivings while they feast with you;

4

Or, *cut him off.*

Matt. 24. 51. *See under N.*

Q

Num.15. 30 But the soul that doeth *aught* presumptuously, *whether he be* born in the land, or a stranger, the same reproacheth the LORD; and that soul shall be cut off from among his people.

Deut.25. 2 And it shall be, if the wicked man *be* worthy to be beaten, that the judge shall cause him to lie down, and to be beaten before his face, according to his fault, by a certain number.

John 9. 41 Jesus said unto them, If ye were blind, ye should have no sin: but now ye say, We see; therefore your sin remaineth.

John 15. 22 If I had not come and spoken unto them, they had not had sin; but now they have no cloak for their sin.

Acts 17. 30 And the times of this ignorance God winked at; but now commandeth all men every where to repent:

Jas. 4. 17 Therefore to him that knoweth to do good, and doeth *it* not, to him it is sin.

R

Lev. 5. 17 And if a soul sin, and commit any of these things which are forbidden to be done by the commandments of the LORD; though he wist *it* not, yet is he guilty, and shall bear his iniquity.

Rom. 2. 12 For as many as have sinned without law shall also perish without law; and as many as have sinned in the law shall be judged by the law;

13 (For not the hearers of the law *are* just before God, but the doers of the law shall be justified.

I Tim. 1. 13 Who was before a blasphemer, and a persecutor, and injurious: but I obtained mercy, because I did *it* ignorantly in unbelief.

S

Isa. 11. 4 But with righteousness shall he judge the poor, and reprove with equity for the meek of the earth: and he shall smite the earth with the rod of his mouth, and with the breath of his lips shall he slay the wicked.

Luke 12. 51. *See text of topic.*

§ 57. JESUS DISCOURSES TO HIS DISCIPLES AND THE MULTITUDE

T

Matt.20. 22 But Jesus answered and said, Ye know not what ye ask. Are ye able to drink of the cup that I shall drink of, and to be baptized with the baptism that I am baptized with? They say unto him, We are able.

Mark 10. 38 But Jesus said unto them, Ye know not what ye ask: can ye drink of the cup that I drink of? and be baptized with the baptism that I am baptized with?

5

Or, *pained.*

U

Matt.10. 34 Think not that I am come to send peace on earth: I came not to send peace, but a sword.

Luke 12. 49. *See text of topic.*

X

Mic. 7. 6 For the son dishonoureth the father, the daughter riseth up against her mother, the daughter in law against her mother in law; a man's enemies *are* the men of his own house.

John 7. 43 So there was a division among the people because of him.

John 9. 16 Therefore said some of the Pharisees, This man is not of God, because he keepeth not the sabbath day. Others said, How can a man that is a sinner do such miracles? And there was a division among them.

John 10. 19 There was a division therefore again among the Jews for these sayings.

Y

Matt.10. 35 For I am come to set a man at variance against his father, and the daughter against her mother, and the daughter in law against her mother in law.

Z

Matt.16. 2 He answered and said unto them, When it is evening, ye say, *It will be* fair weather: for the sky is red.

A

I Cor. 1. 21 For after that in the wisdom of God the world by wisdom knew not God, it pleased God by the foolishness of preaching to save them that believe.

22 For the Jews require a sign, and the Greeks seek after wisdom:

23 But we preach Christ crucified, unto the Jews a stumblingblock, and unto the Greeks foolishness;

24 But unto them which are called, both Jews and Greeks, Christ the power of God, and the wisdom of God.

A—Concluded.

I Cor. 1. 25 Because the foolishness of God is wiser than men; and the weakness of God is stronger than men.

26 For ye see your calling, brethren, how that not many wise men after the flesh, not many mighty, not many noble *are called:*

27 But God hath chosen the foolish things of the world to confound the wise; and God hath chosen the weak things of the world to confound the things which are mighty;

B

Luke 19. 41 And when he was come near, he beheld the city, and wept over it,

42 Saying, If thou hadst known, even thou, at least in this thy day, the things *which belong* unto thy peace! but now they are hid from thine eyes.

43 For the days shall come upon thee, that thine enemies shall cast a trench about thee, and compass thee round, and keep thee in on every side,

44 And shall lay thee even with the ground, and thy children within thee; and they shall not leave in thee one stone upon another; because thou knewest not the time of thy visitation.

Gal. 4. 4 But when the fulness of the time was come, God sent forth his Son, made of a woman, made under the law,

C

Prov.25. 8 Go not forth hastily to strive, lest *thou know not* what to do in the end thereof, when thy neighbour hath put thee to shame.

9 Debate thy cause with thy neighbour *himself;* and discover not a secret to another:

Matt. 5. 25 Agree with thine adversary quickly, while thou art in the way with him, lest at any time the adversary deliver thee to the judge, and the judge deliver thee to the officer, and thou be cast into prison.

26 Verily I say unto thee, Thou shalt by no means come out thence, till thou hast paid the uttermost farthing.

D

Ps. 32. 6 For this shall every one that is godly pray unto thee in a time when thou mayest be found: surely in the floods of great waters they shall not come nigh unto him.

Isa. 55. 6 Seek ye the Lord while he may be found, call ye upon him while he is near:

(Concluded). Time, Autumn, A. D. 28; Place, Galilee.

Chap. 12.

50 But [t]I have a baptism to be baptized with; and how am I [5]straitened till it be accomplished!

51 [u]Suppose ye that I am come to give peace on earth? I tell you, Nay; [x]but rather division:

52 [y]For from henceforth there shall be five in one house divided, three against two, and two against three.

53 The father shall be divided against the son, and the son against the father; the mother against the daughter, and the daughter against the mother; the mother in law against her daughter in law, and the daughter in law against her mother in law.

54 [z]And he said also to the people, When ye see a cloud rise out of the west, straightway ye say, There cometh a shower; and so it is.

55 And when *ye see* the south wind blow, ye say, There will be heat; and it cometh to pass.

56 *Ye* [a]hypocrites, ye can discern the face of the sky and of the earth; but how is it that ye do not discern [b]this time?

57 Yea, and why even of yourselves judge ye not what is right?

58 [c]When thou goest with thine adversary to the magistrate, [d]*as thou art* in the way, give diligence that thou mayest be delivered from him; lest he hale thee to the judge, and the judge deliver thee to the officer, and the officer cast thee into prison.

59 I tell thee, thou shalt not depart thence [e]till thou hast paid the very last mite.

D—Concluded.

Heb. 3. 7 Wherefore as the Holy Ghost saith, To day if ye will hear his voice,

8 Harden not your hearts, as in the provocation, in the day of temptation in the wilderness:

9 When your fathers tempted me, proved me, and saw my works forty years.

10 Wherefore I was grieved with that generation, and said, They do alway err in *their* heart; and they have not known my ways.

11 So I sware in my wrath, They shall not enter into my rest.

12 Take heed, brethren, lest there be in any of you an evil heart of unbelief, in departing from the living God.

13 But exhort one another daily, while it is called To day; lest any of you be hardened through the deceitfulness of sin.

14 For we are made partakers of Christ, if we hold the beginning of our confidence steadfast unto the end;

15 While it is said, To day if ye will hear his voice, harden not your hearts, as in the provocation.

E

Matt.18. 34 And his lord was wroth, and delivered him to the tormentors, till he should pay all that was due unto him.

Matt.25. 41 Then shall he say also unto them on the left hand, Depart from me, ye cursed, into everlasting fire, prepared for the devil and his angels:

Matt.25. 46 And these shall go away into everlasting punishment: but the righteous into life eternal.

IIThes.1. 7 And to you who are troubled rest with us, when the Lord Jesus shall be revealed from heaven with his mighty angels,

8 In flaming fire taking vengeance on them that know not God, and that obey not the gospel of our Lord Jesus Christ:

9 Who shall be punished with everlasting destruction from the presence of the Lord, and from the glory of his power;

10 When he shall come to be glorified in his saints, and to be admired in all them that believe (because our testimony among you was believed) in that day.

§ 58. THE GALILEANS THAT PERISHED. PARABLE OF THE

A

Acts 5. 37 After this man rose up Judas of Galilee in the days of the taxing, and drew away much people after him: he also perished; and all, *even* as many as obeyed him, were dispersed.

B

Acts 28. 4 And when the barbarians saw the *venomous* beast hang on his hand, they said among themselves, No doubt this man is a murderer, whom, though he hath escaped the sea, yet vengeance suffereth not to live.

C

Eze. 18. 30 Therefore I will judge you, O house of Israel, every one according to his ways, saith the Lord GOD. Repent, and turn *yourselves* from all your transgressions; so iniquity shall not be your ruin.

31 Cast away from you all your transgressions, whereby ye have transgressed; and make you a new heart and a new spirit: for why will ye die, O house of Israel?

32 For I have no pleasure in the death of him that dieth, saith the Lord GOD: wherefore turn *yourselves*, and live ye.

Eze. 33. 11 Say unto them, *As* I live, saith the Lord GOD, I have no pleasure in the death of the wicked; but that the wicked turn from his way and live: turn ye, turn ye from your evil ways; for why will ye die, O house of Israel?

1

Or, *debtors*.

Matt.18. 23 Therefore is the kingdom of heaven likened unto a certain king, which would take account of his servants.

24 And when he had begun to reckon, one was brought unto him, which owed him ten thousand talents.

Luke 11. 4 And forgive us our sins; for we also forgive every one that is indebted to us. And lead us not into temptation; but deliver us from evil.

D

Isa. 5. 1 Now will I sing to my well beloved a song of my beloved touching his vineyard. My well beloved hath a vineyard in a very fruitful hill:

2 And he fenced it, and gathered out the stones thereof, and planted it with the choicest vine, and built a tower in the midst of it, and also made a winepress therein: and he looked

D—CONCLUDED.

that it should bring forth grapes, and it brought forth wild grapes.

3 And now, O inhabitants of Jerusalem, and men of Judah, judge, I pray you, betwixt me and my vineyard.

4 What could have been done more to my vineyard, that I have not done in it? wherefore, when I looked that it should bring forth grapes, brought it forth wild grapes?

5 And now go to; I will tell you what I will do to my vineyard: I will take away the hedge thereof, and it shall be eaten up; *and* break down the wall thereof, and it shall be trodden down:

6 And I will lay it waste: it shall not be pruned, nor digged; but there shall come up briars and thorns: I will also command the clouds that they rain no rain upon it.

7 For the vineyard of the LORD of hosts *is* the house of Israel, and the men of Judah his pleasant plant: and he looked for judgment, but behold oppression; for righteousness, but behold a cry.

Matt.21. 19 And when he saw a fig tree in the way, he came to it, and found nothing thereon, but leaves only, and said unto it, Let no fruit grow on thee henceforward for ever. And presently the fig tree withered away.

E

Rom. 2. 4 Or despisest thou the riches of his goodness and forbearance and longsuffering; not knowing that the goodness of God leadeth thee to repentance?

5 But, after thy hardness and impenitent heart, treasurest up unto thyself wrath against the day of wrath and revelation of the righteous judgment of God;

II Pet. 3. 9 The Lord is not slack concerning his promise, as some men count slackness; but is long-suffering to us-ward, not willing that any should perish, but that all should come to repentance.

10 But the day of the Lord will come as a thief in the night; in the which the heavens shall pass away with a great noise, and the elements shall melt with fervent heat, the earth also and the works that are therein shall be burned up.

BARREN FIG TREE. Time, Autumn, A. D. 28; Place, Galilee.

13 : 1–9.

1 There were present at that season some that told him of [a]the Galileans, whose blood Pilate had mingled with their sacrifices.

2 And Jesus answering said unto them, Suppose [b]ye that these Galileans were sinners above all the Galileans, because they suffered such things?

3 I tell you, Nay: but, except [c]ye repent, ye shall all likewise perish.

4 Or those eighteen, upon whom the tower in Siloam fell, and slew them, think ye that they were [1]sinners above all men that dwelt in Jerusalem?

5 I tell you, Nay: but, except ye repent, ye shall all likewise perish.

6 He spake also this parable; [d]A certain *man* had a fig tree planted in his vineyard; and he came and sought fruit thereon, and found none.

7 Then said he unto the dresser of his vineyard, Behold, these [e]three years I come seeking fruit on this fig tree, and find none: cut it down; why cumbereth it the ground?

8 And he answering said unto him, Lord, let [f]it alone this year also, till I shall dig about it, and dung *it:*

9 And if it bear fruit, *well:* and if not, *then* after that thou shalt cut it down. (p. 367.)

F

Ex. 32. 11 And Moses besought the Lord his God, and said, Lord, why doth thy wrath wax hot against thy people, which thou hast brought forth out of the land of Egypt with great power, and with a mighty hand?

12 Wherefore should the Egyptians speak, and say, For mischief did he bring them out, to slay them in the mountains, and to consume them from the face of the earth? Turn from thy

F—Concluded.

fierce wrath, and repent of this evil against thy people.

13 Remember Abraham, Isaac, and Israel, thy servants, to whom thou swarest by thine own self, and saidst unto them, I will multiply your seed as the stars of heaven, and all this land that I have spoken of will I give unto your seed, and they shall inherit *it* for ever.

14 And the Lord repented of the evil which he thought to do unto his people.

Ex. 32. 30 And it came to pass on the morrow, that Moses said unto the people, Ye have sinned a great sin: and now I will go up unto the Lord; peradventure I shall make an atonement for your sin.

31 And Moses returned unto the Lord, and said, Oh, this people have sinned a great sin, and have made them gods of gold.

32 Yet now, if thou wilt forgive their sin—; and if not, blot me, I pray thee, out of thy book which thou hast written.

33 And the Lord said unto Moses, Whosoever hath sinned against me, him will I blot out of my book.

34 Therefore now go, lead the people unto *the place* of which I have spoken unto thee: behold, mine Angel shall go before thee: nevertheless, in the day when I visit, I will visit their sin upon them.

35 And the Lord plagued the people, because they made the calf which Aaron made.

Ex. 34. 8 And Moses made haste, and bowed his head toward the earth, and worshipped.

9 And he said, If now I have found grace in thy sight, O Lord, let my Lord, I pray thee, go among us; for it *is* a stiffnecked people: and pardon our iniquity and our sin, and take us for thine inheritance.

Joel 2. 17 Let the priests, the ministers of the Lord, weep between the porch and the altar, and let them say, Spare thy people, O Lord, and give not thine heritage to reproach, that the heathen should rule over them: wherefore should they say among the people, Where *is* their God?

Heb. 7. 25 Wherefore he is able also to save them to the uttermost that come unto God by him, seeing he ever liveth to make intercession for them.

§ 59. THE PARABLE OF THE SOWER.

13: 1–23.

1 The same day went Jesus out of the house, [a]and sat by the sea side.

2 [b]And great multitudes were gathered together unto him, so that [c]he went into a ship, and sat; and the whole multitude stood on the shore.

3 And he spake many things unto them in parables, saying, [d]Behold, a sower went forth to sow;

4 And when he sowed, some *seeds* fell by the way side, and the fowls came and devoured them up:

5 Some fell upon [e]stony places, where they had not much earth: and forthwith they sprung up, because they had no deepness of earth:

6 And when the sun was up, they were scorched; and because they had no [f]root, they withered away.

7 And some fell among [g]thorns; and the thorns sprung up, and choked them:

8 But other fell into good ground and brought forth fruit, some [h]a hundredfold, some sixtyfold, some thirtyfold.

9 [i]Who hath ears to hear, let him hear.

10 And the disciples came, and said unto him, Why speakest thou unto them in parables?

A

Mark 4. 1. *See text of topic.*

B

Luke 8. 4. *See text of topic.*

C

Luke 5. 3 And he entered into one of the ships, which was Simon's, and prayed him that he would thrust out a little from the land. And he sat down and taught the people out of the ship.

D

Luke 8. 5. *See text of topic.*

4: 1–20.

1 And [k]he began again to teach by the sea side: and there was gathered unto him a great multitude, so that he entered into a ship, and sat in the sea; and the whole multitude was by the sea on the land.

2 And he taught them many things by parables, [l]and said unto them in his doctrine,

3 Hearken; Behold, there went out a sower to sow:

4 And it came to pass, as he sowed, some fell by the way side, and the fowls of the air came and devoured it up.

5 And some fell on stony ground, where it had not much earth; and immediately it sprang up, because it had no depth of earth:

6 But when the sun was up, it was scorched; and because it had no root, it withered away.

7 And some fell among thorns, and the thorns grew up, and choked it, and it yielded no fruit.

8 And other fell on good ground, [m]and did yield fruit that sprang up and increased, and brought forth, some thirty, and some sixty, and some a hundred.

9 And he said unto them, He that hath ears to hear, let him hear.

10 [n]And when he was alone, they that were about him with the twelve asked of him the parable.

E

Eze. 11. 19 And I will give them one heart, and I will put a new spirit within you; and I will take the stony heart out of their flesh, and will give them a heart of flesh:

TIME, AUTUMN, A. D. 28; PLACE, LAKE OF GALILEE: NEAR CAPERNAUM.

8: 4–15.

4 [o]And when much people were gathered together, and were come to him out of every city, he spake by a parable:

5 A sower went out to sow his seed: and as he sowed, some fell by the way side; and it was trodden down, and the fowls of the air devoured it.

6 And some fell upon a rock; and as soon as it was sprung up, it withered away, because it lacked moisture.

7 And some fell among thorns; and the thorns sprang up with it, and choked it.

8 And other fell on good ground, and sprang up, and bare fruit a hundredfold. And when he had said these things, he cried, He that hath ears to hear, let him hear.

9 [p]And his disciples asked him, saying, What might this parable be?

F

Eph. 3. 17 That Christ may dwell in your hearts by faith; that ye, being rooted and grounded in love,

Col. 1. 23 If ye continue in the faith grounded and settled, and *be* not moved away from the hope of the gospel, which ye have heard, *and* which was preached to every creature which is under heaven; whereof I Paul am made a minister:

Col. 2. 6 As ye have therefore received Christ Jesus the Lord, *so* walk ye in him:

7 Rooted and built up in him, and stablished in the faith, as ye have been taught, abounding therein with thanksgiving.

G

Gen. 3. 18 Thorns also and thistles shall it bring forth to thee: and thou shalt eat the herb of the field:

H

Gen. 26. 12 Then Isaac sowed in that land, and received in the same year a hundredfold: and the LORD blessed him.

H—CONCLUDED.

Gal. 5. 22 But the fruit of the Spirit is love, joy, peace, long-suffering, gentleness, goodness, faith,

23 Meekness, temperance: against such there is no law.

Phil. 1. 11 Being filled with the fruits of righteousness, which are by Jesus Christ, unto the glory and praise of God.

I

Matt. 11. 15 He that hath ears to hear, let him hear.

Mark 4. 9. *See text of topic.*

K

Matt. 13. 1 and Luke 8. 4. *See text of topic.*

L

Matt. 7. 28 And it came to pass, when Jesus had ended these sayings, the people were astonished at his doctrine:

Mark 12. 38 And he said unto them in his doctrine, Beware of the scribes, which love to go in long clothing, and *love* salutations in the marketplaces,

John 7. 16 Jesus answered them, and said, My doctrine is not mine, but his that sent me.

17 If any man will do his will, he shall know of the doctrine, whether it be of God, or *whether* I speak of myself.

M

John 15. 5 I am the vine, ye *are* the branches. He that abideth in me, and I in him, the same bringeth forth much fruit; for without me ye can do nothing.

Col. 1. 6 Which is come unto you, as *it is* in all the world; and bringeth forth fruit, as *it doth* also in you, since the day ye heard *of it*, and knew the grace of God in truth:

N

Prov. 2. 11 Discretion shall preserve thee, understanding shall keep thee:

12 To deliver thee from the way of the evil *man*, from the man that speaketh froward things:

13 Who leave the paths of uprightness, to walk in the ways of darkness;

Prov. 4. 7 Wisdom *is* the principal thing; *therefore* get wisdom: and with all thy getting get understanding.

Prov. 13. 20 He that walketh with wise *men* shall be wise: but a companion of fools shall be destroyed.

Matt. 13. 10 and Luke 8. 9, etc. *See text of topic.*

O

Matt. 13. 2 and Mark 4. 1. *See text of topic.*

P

Matt. 13. 10 and Mark 4. 10. *See text of topic.*

§ 59. THE PARABLE OF THE SOWER (CONTINUED).

CHAP. 13.

11 He answered and said unto them, Because [q]it is given unto you to know the mysteries of the kingdom of heaven, but to them it is not given.

12 [r]For whosoever hath, to him shall be given, and he shall have more abundance: but whosoever hath not, from him shall be taken away even that he hath.

13 Therefore speak I to them in parables: because they seeing see not; and hearing they hear not, neither do they understand.

14 And in them is fulfilled the prophecy of Esaias, which saith, [s]By hearing ye shall hear, and shall not understand; and seeing ye shall see, and shall not perceive:

15 For this people's heart is waxed gross, and *their* ears [t]are dull of hearing, and their eyes they have closed; lest at any time they should see with *their* eyes, and hear with *their* ears, and should understand with *their* heart, and should be converted, and I should heal them.

16 But [u]blessed *are* your eyes, for they see: and your ears, for they hear.

17 For verily I say unto you, [x]That many prophets and righteous *men* have desired to see *those things* which ye see, and have not seen *them;* and to hear *those things* which ye hear, and have not heard *them.*

Q

Matt.11. 25 At that time Jesus answered and said, I thank thee, O Father, Lord of heaven and earth, because thou hast hid these things from the wise and prudent, and hast revealed them unto babes.

CHAP. 4.

11 And he said unto them, Unto you it is given to know the mystery of the kingdom of God: but unto [y]them that are without, all *these* things are done in parables:

12 [z]That seeing they may see, and not perceive; and hearing they may hear, and not understand; lest at any time they should be converted, and *their* sins should be forgiven them.

13 And he said unto them, Know ye not this parable? and how then will ye know all parables?

Q—CONCLUDED.

Matt.16. 17 And Jesus answered and said unto him, Blessed art thou, Simon Barjona: for flesh and blood hath not revealed *it* unto thee, but my Father which is in heaven.

Mark 4. 11. *See text of topic.*

I Cor. 2. 10 But God hath revealed *them* unto us by his Spirit: for the Spirit searcheth all things, yea, the deep things of God.

Col. 1. 26 *Even* the mystery which hath been hid from ages and from generations, but now is made manifest to his saints:

I Jno. 2. 27 But the anointing which ye have received of him abideth in you, and ye need not that any man teach you: but as the same anointing teacheth you of all things, and is truth, and is no lie, and even as it hath taught you, ye shall abide in him.

R

Matt.25. 29 For unto every one that hath shall be given, and he shall have abundance: but from him that hath not shall be taken away even that which he hath.

Mark 4. 25 For he that hath, to him shall be given; and he that hath not, from him shall be taken even that which he hath.

Luke 8. 18 Take heed therefore how ye hear: for whosoever hath, to him shall be given; and whosoever hath not, from him shall be taken even that which he seemeth to have.

TIME, AUTUMN, A. D. 28; PLACE, LAKE OF GALILEE: NEAR CAPERNAUM.

CHAP. 8.

10 And he said, Unto you it is given to know the mysteries of the kingdom of God: but to others in parables; [a]that seeing they might not see, and hearing they might not understand.

R—CONCLUDED.

Luke 19. 26 For I say unto you, That unto every one which hath shall be given; and from him that hath not, even that he hath shall be taken away from him.

S

Isa. 6. 9 And he said, Go, and tell this people, Hear ye indeed, but understand not; and see ye indeed, but perceive not.

Eze. 12. 2 Son of man, thou dwellest in the midst of a rebellious house, which have eyes to see, and see not; they have ears to hear, and hear not: for they *are* a rebellious house.

Mark 4. 12 and Luke 8. 10. *See text of topic.*

John 12. 40 He hath blinded their eyes, and hardened their heart; that they should not see with *their* eyes, nor understand with *their* heart, and be converted, and I should heal them.

Acts 28. 26 Saying, Go unto this people, and say, Hearing ye shall hear, and shall not understand; and seeing ye shall see, and not perceive:

27 For the heart of this people is waxed gross, and their ears are dull of hearing, and their eyes have they closed; lest they should see with *their* eyes, and hear with *their* ears, and understand with *their* heart, and should be converted, and I should heal them.

Rom. 11. 8 (According as it is written, God hath given them the spirit of slumber, eyes that they should not see, and ears that they should not hear;) unto this day.

II Cor. 3. 14 But their minds were blinded: for until this day remaineth the same vail untaken away in the reading of the old testament; which *vail* is done away in Christ.

15 But even unto this day, when Moses is read, the vail is upon their heart.

T

Heb. 5. 11 Of whom we have many things to say, and hard to be uttered, seeing ye are dull of hearing.

U

Matt. 16. 17. *See under Q.*

Luke 10. 23 And he turned him unto *his* disciples, and said privately, Blessed *are* the eyes which see the things that ye see:

24 For I tell you that many prophets and kings have desired to see those things which ye see, and have not seen *them;* and to hear those things which ye hear, and have not heard *them.*

John 20. 29 Jesus saith unto him, Thomas, because thou hast seen me, thou hast believed: blessed *are* they that have not seen, and *yet* have believed.

X

Heb. 11. 13 These all died in faith, not having received the promises, but having seen them afar off, and were persuaded of *them,* and embraced *them,* and confessed that they were strangers and pilgrims on the earth.

I Pet. 1. 10 Of which salvation the prophets have inquired and searched diligently, who prophesied of the grace *that should come* unto you:

11 Searching what, or what manner of time the Spirit of Christ which was in them did signify, when it testified beforehand the sufferings of Christ, and the glory that should follow.

Y

I Cor. 2. 10 But God hath revealed *them* unto us by his Spirit: for the Spirit searcheth all things, yea, the deep things of God.

I Cor. 5. 12 For what have I to do to judge them also that are without? do not ye judge them that are within?

13 But them that are without God judgeth. Therefore put away from among yourselves that wicked person.

Col. 4. 5 Walk in wisdom toward them that are without, redeeming the time.

I Thes. 4. 12 That ye may walk honestly toward them that are without, and *that* ye may have lack of nothing.

I Tim. 3. 7 Moreover he must have a good report of them which are without; lest he fall into reproach and the snare of the devil.

Z

Isa. 6. 9. *See under S.*
Matt. 13. 14 and Luke 8. 10. *See text of topic.*
John 12. 40, Acts 28. 26 and Rom. 11. 8. *See under S.*

A

Isa. 6. 9. *See under S.*
Mark 4. 12. *See text of topic.*

§ 59. THE PARABLE OF THE SOWER (CONCLUDED).

CHAP 13.

18 [b]Hear ye therefore the parable of the sower.

19 When any one heareth the word [c]of the kingdom, and understandeth *it* not, then cometh [d]the wicked one, and catcheth away that which was sown in his heart. This is he which received seed by the way side.

20 But he that received the seed into stony places, the same is he that heareth the word, and anon [e]with joy receiveth it;

21 Yet hath he not root in himself, but dureth for a while: for when tribulation or persecution ariseth because of the word, by and by [f]he is offended.

22 He also that received seed [g]among the thorns is he that heareth the word; and the [h]care of this world, and the deceitfulness of riches, choke the word, and he becometh unfruitful.

23 But he that received seed into the good ground is he that heareth the word, and understandeth *it;* which also beareth fruit, and bringeth forth, some a hundredfold, some sixty, some thirty.

CHAP. 4.

14 [i]The sower soweth the word.

15 And these are they by the way side, where the word is sown; but when they have heard, Satan cometh immediately, and taketh away the word that was sown in their hearts.

16 And these are they likewise which are sown on stony ground; who, when they have heard the word, immediately receive it with gladness;

17 And have no root in themselves, and so endure but for a time: afterward, when affliction or persecution ariseth for the word's sake, immediately they are offended.

18 And these are they which are sown among thorns; such as hear the word,

19 And the cares of this world, [k]and the deceitfulness of riches, and the lusts of other things entering in, choke the word, and it becometh unfruitful.

20 And these are they which are sown on good ground; such as hear the word, and receive *it*, and bring forth fruit, some thirtyfold, some sixty, and some a hundred.

B

Mark 4. 14 and Luke 8. 11. *See text of topic.*

C

Matt. 4. 23 And Jesus went about all Galilee, teaching in their synagogues, and preaching the gospel of the kingdom, and healing all manner of sickness and all manner of disease among the people.

D

IICor. 2. 11 Lest Satan should get an advantage of us: for we are not ignorant of his devices.

E

Isa. 58. 2 Yet they seek me daily, and delight to know my ways, as a nation that did righteousness, and forsook not the ordinance of their God: they ask of me the ordinances of justice; they take delight in approaching to God.

Eze. 33. 31 And they come unto thee as the people cometh, and they sit before thee *as* my people, and they hear thy words, but they will not do them: for with their mouth they show much love, *but* their heart goeth after their covetousness.

32 And, lo, thou *art* unto them as a very lovely song of one that hath a pleasant voice, and can play well on

TIME, AUTUMN, A. D. 28; PLACE, LAKE OF GALILEE: NEAR CAPERNAUM.

CHAP. 8.

11 [l]Now the parable is this: The [m]seed is the word of God.

12 Those by the [n]way side are they that hear; then cometh the devil, and taketh away the word out of their hearts, lest they should believe and be saved.

13 They on the rock *are they*, which, when they hear, receive the word with joy; and these have no root, which for a while believe, and in time of temptation fall away.

14 And that which fell among thorns are they, which, when they have heard, go forth, and are choked with cares [o]and riches and pleasures of *this* life, and bring no fruit to perfection.

15 But that on the good ground are they, which in an honest and good heart, having heard the word, keep *it*, and [p]bring forth fruit with patience.

E—CONCLUDED.

an instrument: for they hear thy words, but they do them not.

John 5. 35 He was a burning and a shining light: and ye were willing for a season to rejoice in his light.

F

Matt. 11. 6 And blessed is *he*, whosoever shall not be offended in me.

II Tim. 1. 15 This thou knowest, that all they which are in Asia be turned away from me, of whom are Phygellus and Hermogenes.

G

Jer. 4. 3 For thus saith the LORD to the men of Judah and Jerusalem, Break up your fallow ground, and sow not among thorns.

H

Matt. 19. 23 Then said Jesus unto his disciples, Verily I say unto you, That a rich man shall hardly enter into the kingdom of heaven.

Mark 10. 23 And Jesus looked round about, and saith unto his disciples, How hardly shall they that have riches enter into the kingdom of God!

H—CONCLUDED.

Luke 18. 24 And when Jesus saw that he was very sorrowful, he said, How hardly shall they that have riches enter into the kingdom of God!

I Tim. 6. 9 But they that will be rich fall into temptation and a snare, and *into* many foolish and hurtful lusts, which drown men in destruction and perdition.

II Tim. 4. 10 For Demas hath forsaken me, having loved this present world, and is departed unto Thessalonica; Crescens to Galatia, Titus unto Dalmatia.

I

Matt. 13. 19. *See text of topic.*

K

I Tim. 6. 9. *See under H.*

I Tim. 6. 17 Charge them that are rich in this world, that they be not high-minded, nor trust in uncertain riches, but in the living God, who giveth us richly all things to enjoy;

L

Matt. 13. 18 and Mark 4. 14. *See text of topic.*

M

I Pet. 1. 23 Being born again, not of corruptible seed, but of incorruptible, by the word of God, which liveth and abideth for ever.

N

Jas. 1. 23 For if any be a hearer of the word, and not a doer, he is like unto a man beholding his natural face in a glass:

24 For he beholdeth himself, and goeth his way, and straightway forgetteth what manner of man he was.

O

Matt. 19. 23 and I Tim. 6. 9. *See under H.*

I Tim. 6. 10 For the love of money is the root of all evil: which while some coveted after, they have erred from the faith, and pierced themselves through with many sorrows.

II Tim. 4. 10. *See under H.*

P

II Pet. 1. 5 And besides this, giving all diligence, add to your faith virtue; and to virtue, knowledge;

6 And to knowledge, temperance; and to temperance, patience; and to patience, godliness;

7 And to godliness, brotherly kindness; and to brotherly kindness, charity.

Jas. 1. 3 Knowing *this*, that the trying of your faith worketh patience.

4 But let patience have *her* perfect work, that ye may be perfect and entire, wanting nothing.

§ 60. PARABLE OF THE CANDLE HID UNDER A BUSHEL.

A

Matt. 5. 15 Neither do men light a candle, and put it under a bushel, but on a candlestick; and it giveth light unto all that are in the house.

Luke 8. 16. *See text of topic.*

Luke 11. 33 No man, when he hath lighted a candle, putteth *it* in a secret place, neither under a bushel, but on a candlestick, that they which come in may see the light.

1

The word in the original signifies, *a measure containing about a pint less than a peck.*

B

Matt. 10. 26 Fear them not therefore: for there is nothing covered, that shall not be revealed; and hid, that shall not be known.

Luke 12. 2 For there is nothing covered, that shall not be revealed; neither hid, that shall not be known.

I Jno. 1. 2 (For the life was manifested, and we have seen *it*, and bear witness, and show unto you that eternal life, which was with the Father, and was manifested unto us;)

C

Matt. 11. 15 He that hath ears to hear, let him hear.

Mark 4. 9 And he said unto them, He that hath ears to hear, let him hear.

D

I Jno. 4. 1 Beloved, believe not every spirit, but try the spirits whether they are of God: because many false prophets are gone out into the world.

4: 21–25.

21 [a]And he said unto them, Is a candle brought to be put under a [1]bushel, or under a bed? and not to be set on a candlestick?

22 [b]For there is nothing hid, which shall not be manifested; neither was any thing kept secret, but that it should come abroad.

23 [c]If any man have ears to hear, let him hear.

24 And he said unto them, [d]Take heed what ye hear. [e]With what measure ye mete, it shall be measured to you; and unto you that hear shall more be given.

25 [f]For he that hath, to him shall be given; and he that hath not, from him shall be taken even that which he hath.

E

Matt. 7. 2 For with what judgment ye judge, ye shall be judged: and with what measure ye mete, it shall be measured to you again.

Luke 6. 38 Give, and it shall be given unto you; good measure, pressed down, and shaken together, and running over, shall men give into your bosom.

§ 61. OUR LORD SPEAKS THE PARABLE OF THE WHEAT

13: 24–30.

24 Another parable put he forth unto them, saying, The kingdom of heaven is likened unto a man which sowed good seed in his field:

25 But while men slept, his [a]enemy came and sowed tares among the wheat, and went his way.

26 [b]But when the blade was sprung up, and brought forth fruit, then appeared the tares also.

A

Prov. 6. 16 These six *things* doth the LORD hate; yea, seven *are* an abomination unto him:

17 A proud look, a lying tongue, and hands that shed innocent blood,

18 A heart that deviseth wicked imaginations, feet that be swift in running to mischief,

19 A false witness *that* speaketh lies, and he that soweth discord among brethren.

II Cor. 11. 13 For such *are* false apostles, deceitful workers, transforming themselves into the apostles of Christ.

14 And no marvel; for Satan himself is transformed into an angel of light.

TIME, AUTUMN, A. D. 28; PLACE, LAKE OF GALILEE: NEAR CAPERNAUM.

8: 16–18.

16 [g]No man, when he hath lighted a
candle, covereth it with a vessel, or
putteth *it* under a bed; but setteth *it*
on a candlestick, that they which enter
in may see the light.

17 [h]For nothing is secret, that shall
not be made manifest; neither *any
thing* hid, that shall not be known and
come abroad.

18 Take heed therefore how ye hear:
[i]for whosoever hath, to him shall be
given; and whosoever hath not, from
him shall be taken even that which he
[2]seemeth to have. (p. 177.)

E—CONCLUDED.

For with the same measure that ye mete withal it shall be measured to you again.

II Cor.9. 6 But this *I say*, He which soweth sparingly shall reap also sparingly; and he which soweth bountifully shall reap also bountifully.

7 Every man according as he purposeth in his heart, *so let him give;* not grudgingly, or of necessity: for God loveth a cheerful giver.

F

Matt.13. 12 For whosoever hath, to him shall be given, and he shall have more abundance: but whosoever hath not,

F—CONCLUDED.

from him shall be taken away even that he hath.

Matt.25. 29 For unto every one that hath shall be given, and he shall have abundance: but from him that hath not shall be taken away even that which he hath.

Luke 8. 18. *See text of topic.*

Luke 19. 26 For I say unto you, That unto every one which hath shall be given; and from him that hath not, even that he hath shall be taken away from him.

G

Matt. 5. 15. *See under A.*
Mark 4. 21. *See text of topic.*
Luke 11. 33. *See under A.*

Phil. 2. 14 Do all things without murmurings and disputings:

15 That ye may be blameless and harmless, the sons of God, without rebuke, in the midst of a crooked and perverse nation, among whom ye shine as lights in the world;

16 Holding forth the word of life; that I may rejoice in the day of Christ, that I have not run in vain, neither laboured in vain.

H

Matt. 10. 26 and Luke 12. 2. *See under B.*

I

Matt. 13. 12, Matt. 25. 29 and Luke 19. 26. *See under F.*

John15. 2 Every branch in me that beareth not fruit he taketh away: and every *branch* that beareth fruit, he purgeth it, that it may bring forth more fruit.

2 Or, *thinketh that he hath.*

AND TARES. TIME, AUTUMN, A.D. 28; PLACE, NEAR CAPERNAUM.

A—CONCLUDED.

IICor.11. 15 Therefore *it is* no great thing if his ministers also be transformed as the ministers of righteousness; whose end shall be according to their works.

I Pet. 5. 8 Be sober, be vigilant; because your adversary the devil, as a roaring lion, walketh about, seeking whom he may devour:

Rev. 12. 8 And prevailed not; neither was their place found any more in heaven.

9 And the great dragon was cast out, that old serpent, called the Devil, and Satan, which deceiveth the whole world: he was cast out into the earth, and his angels were cast out with him.

B

Mark 4. 26 And he said, So is the kingdom of God, as if a man should cast seed into the ground;

27 And should sleep, and rise night and day, and the seed should spring and grow up, he knoweth not how.

28 For the earth bringeth forth fruit of herself, first the blade, then the ear, after that the full corn in the ear.

29 But when the fruit is brought forth, immediately he putteth in the sickle, because the harvest is come.

Col. 1. 10 That ye might walk worthy of the Lord unto all pleasing, being fruitful in every good work, and increasing in the knowledge of God;

§ 61. OUR LORD SPEAKS THE PARABLE OF THE WHEAT AND

CHAP. 13.

27 [c]So the servants of the householder came and said unto him, Sir, didst not thou sow good seed in thy field? from [d]whence then hath it tares?

28 He said unto them, An enemy hath done this. The servants said unto him, Wilt thou then that we go and gather them up?

29 But he said, Nay; lest while ye gather up the tares, ye root up also the wheat with them.

30 Let both grow together until the harvest: and in the time of harvest I will say to the reapers, Gather ye together first the tares, and bind them in bundles to [e]burn them: [f]but gather the wheat into my barn.

C

I Cor. 3. 5 Who then is Paul, and who *is* Apollos, but ministers by whom ye believed, even as the Lord gave to every man?

C—CONCLUDED.

I Cor. 3. 6 I have planted, Apollos watered; but God gave the increase.

7 So then neither is he that planteth anything, neither he that watereth; but God that giveth the increase.

8 Now he that planteth and he that watereth are one: and every man shall receive his own reward according to his own labour.

9 For we are labourers together with God: ye are God's husbandry, *ye are* God's building.

D

Rom.16. 17 Now I beseech you, brethren, mark them which cause divisions and offences contrary to the doctrine which ye have learned; and avoid them.

Gal. 3. 1 O foolish Galatians, who hath bewitched you, that ye should not obey the truth, before whose eyes Jesus Christ hath been evidently set forth, crucified among you?

E

Isa. 27. 10 Yet the defenced city *shall be* desolate, *and* the habitation forsaken, and left like a wilderness: there shall the calf feed, and there shall he lie down, and consume the branches thereof.

11 When the boughs thereof are withered, they shall be broken off:

§ 62. PARABLE OF THE GROWTH OF SEED.

A

Matt.13. 24 Another parable put he forth unto them, saying, The kingdom of heaven is likened unto a man which sowed good seed in his field:

B

Prov.11. 18 The wicked worketh a deceitful work: but to him that soweth righteousness *shall be* a sure reward.

Eccl. 11. 6 In the morning sow thy seed, and in the evening withhold not thine hand: for thou knowest not whether shall prosper, either this or that, or whether they both *shall be* alike good.

C

Ps. 1. 3 And he shall be like a tree planted by the rivers of water, that bringeth forth his fruit in his season; his leaf also shall not wither; and whatsoever he doeth shall prosper.

Ps. 92. 13 Those that be planted in the house of the LORD shall flourish in the courts of our God.

4: 26–29.

26 And he said, [a]So is the kingdom of God, [b]as if a man should cast seed into the ground;

27 And should sleep, and rise night and day, and the seed should spring and grow up, he knoweth not how.

28 For the earth bringeth forth fruit of herself; [c]first the blade, then the ear, after that the full corn in the ear.

29 But when the fruit is [1]brought forth, immediately [d]he putteth in the sickle, because the harvest is come.

C—CONCLUDED.

Ps. 92. 14 They shall still bring forth fruit in old age; they shall be fat and flourishing;

TARES (CONCLUDED). TIME, AUTUMN, A. D. 28; PLACE, NEAR CAPERNAUM.

E—CONTINUED.

the women come, *and* set them on
fire; for it *is* a people of no understanding: therefore he that made
them will not have mercy on them,
and he that formed them will show
them no favour.

Eze. 15. 4 Behold, it is cast into the fire for
fuel; the fire devoureth both the ends
of it, and the midst of it is burned.
Is it meet for *any* work?

5 Behold, when it was whole, it was
meet for no work: how much less
shall it be meet yet for *any* work,
when the fire hath devoured it, and it
is burned?

6 Therefore thus saith the Lord
GOD; As the vine tree among the
trees of the forest, which I have given
to the fire for fuel, so will I give the
inhabitants of Jerusalem.

7 And I will set my face against
them; they shall go out from *one* fire,
and *another* fire shall devour them;
and ye shall know that I *am* the LORD,
when I set my face against them.

Mal. 4. 1 For, behold, the day cometh, that
shall burn as an oven; and all the
proud, yea, and all that do wickedly,
shall be stubble: and the day that
cometh shall burn them up, saith the
LORD of hosts, that it shall leave

E—CONCLUDED.

them neither root nor branch.

Matt. 25. 40 And the King shall answer and
say unto them, Verily I say unto you,
Inasmuch as ye have done *it* unto one
of the least of these my brethren, ye
have done *it* unto me.

41 Then shall he say also unto them
on the left hand, Depart from me, ye
cursed, into everlasting fire, prepared
for the devil and his angels:

John 15. 6 If a man abide not in me, he is cast
forth as a branch, and is withered;
and men gather them, and cast *them*
into the fire, and they are burned.

F

Matt. 3. 11 I indeed baptize you with water
unto repentance: but he that cometh
after me is mightier than I, whose
shoes I am not worthy to bear: he
shall baptize you with the Holy Ghost,
and *with* fire:

12 Whose fan *is* in his hand, and he
will thoroughly purge his floor, and
gather his wheat into the garner; but
he will burn up the chaff with unquenchable fire.

Luke 3. 17 Whose fan *is* in his hand, and he
will thoroughly purge his floor, and
will gather the wheat into his garner;
but the chaff he will burn with fire
unquenchable.

TIME, AUTUMN, A. D. 28; PLACE, NEAR CAPERNAUM.

1

Or, *ripe*.

Eph. 4. 13 Till we all come in the unity of
the faith, and of the knowledge of the
Son of God, unto a perfect man, unto
the measure of the stature of the fulness of Christ:

D

Isa. 57. 1 The righteous perisheth, and no
man layeth *it* to heart: and merciful
men *are* taken away, none considering
that the righteous is taken away from
the evil *to come*.

2 He shall enter into peace: they
shall rest in their beds, *each one* walking *in* his uprightness.

Joel 3. 13 Put ye in the sickle, for the harvest is ripe: come, get you down; for
the press is full, the fats overflow; for
their wickedness *is* great.

14 Multitudes, multitudes in the valley of decision: for the day of the
LORD *is* near in the valley of decision.

15 The sun and the moon shall be
darkened, and the stars shall with-

D—CONCLUDED.

draw their shining.

Rev. 14. 15 And another angel came out of
the temple, crying with a loud voice
to him that sat on the cloud, Thrust
in thy sickle, and reap: for the time
is come for thee to reap; for the harvest of the earth is ripe.

16 And he that sat on the cloud
thrust in his sickle on the earth; and
the earth was reaped.

17 And another angel came out of
the temple which is in heaven, he
also having a sharp sickle.

18 And another angel came out from
the altar, which had power over fire;
and cried with a loud cry to him that
had the sharp sickle, saying, Thrust
in thy sharp sickle, and gather the
clusters of the vine of the earth; for
her grapes are fully ripe.

19 And the angel thrust in his sickle
into the earth, and gathered the vine
of the earth, and cast *it* into the great
winepress of the wrath of God.

§ 63. PARABLE OF THE GRAIN OF MUSTARD SEED.

13 : 31, 32.

31 Another parable put he forth unto them, saying, [a]The kingdom of heaven is like to a grain of mustard seed, which a man took, and sowed in his field:

32 Which indeed is the least of all seeds: but when it is grown, it is the greatest among herbs, and becometh a tree, so that the birds of the air come and lodge in the branches thereof.

A

Isa. 2. 2 And it shall come to pass in the last days, *that* the mountain of the LORD's house shall be established in the top of the mountains, and shall be exalted above the hills; and all nations shall flow unto it.

3 And many people shall go and say,

4: 30–32.

30 And he said, [b]Whereunto shall we liken the kingdom of God? or with what comparison shall we compare it?

31 *It is* like a grain of mustard seed, which, when it is sown in the earth, is less than all the seeds that be in the earth:

32 But when it is sown, it [c]groweth up, and becometh greater than all herbs, and shooteth out great branches; so that the fowls of the air may lodge under the shadow of it.

A—CONTINUED.

Come ye, and let us go up to the mountain of the LORD, to the house of the God of Jacob; and he will

§ 64. PARABLE OF THE LEAVEN HID IN THE MEAL.

13: 33.

33 [a]Another parable spake he unto them; The kingdom of heaven is like unto leaven, which a woman took, and hid in three [1]measures of meal, [b]till the whole was leavened.

A

Luke 13. 20 And again he said, Whereunto shall I liken the kingdom of God?

21 It is like leaven, which a woman took and hid in three measures of meal, till the whole was leavened.

1

The word in the Greek is, *a measure containing about a peck and one-half, wanting a little more than a pint.*

§ 65. ON THE TEACHING BY PARABLES.

13: 34, 35.

34 [a]All these things spake Jesus unto the multitude in parables; and without a parable spake he not unto them:

35 That it might be fulfilled which was spoken by the prophet, saying, [b]I will open my mouth in parables; [c]I will utter things which have been kept secret from the foundation of the world.

A

Mark 4. 33, 34. *See text of topic.*

B

Ps. 78. 2 I will open my mouth in a parable: I will utter dark sayings of old:

4: 33, 34.

33 [d]And with many such parables spake he the word unto them, as they were able to hear *it.*

34 But without a parable spake he not unto them: and when they were alone, he expounded all things to his disciples. (p. 212.)

C

Rom. 16. 25 Now to him that is of power to stablish you according to my gospel, and the preaching of Jesus Christ, according to the revelation of the mystery, which was kept secret since the world began,

TIME, AUTUMN, A. D. 28; PLACE, NEAR CAPERNAUM.

A—CONCLUDED.

teach us of his ways, and we will walk in his paths: for out of Zion shall go forth the law, and the word of the LORD from Jerusalem.

Mic. 4. 1 But in the last days it shall come to pass, *that* the mountain of the house of the LORD shall be established in the top of the mountains, and it shall be exalted above the hills; and people shall flow unto it.

Mark 4. 30, etc. *See text of topic.*

Luke 13. 18 Then said he, Unto what is the kingdom of God like? and whereunto shall I resemble it?

19 It is like a grain of mustard seed, which a man took, and cast into his garden; and it grew, and waxed a great tree; and the fowls of the air lodged in the branches of it.

II Pet. 3. 18 But grow in grace, and *in* the knowledge of our Lord and Saviour Jesus Christ. To him *be* glory both now and for ever. Amen.

B

Matt. 13. 31. *See text of topic.*
Luke 13. 18. *See under A.*

Acts 2. 41 Then they that gladly received his word were baptized: and the same day there were added *unto them* about three thousand souls.

Acts 4. 4 Howbeit many of them which heard the word believed; and the number of the men was about five thousand.

Acts 5. 14 And believers were the more added to the Lord, multitudes both of men and women;)

Acts 19. 20 So mightily grew the word of God and prevailed.

C

Mal. 1. 11 For, from the rising of the sun even unto the going down of the same, my name *shall be* great among the Gentiles; and in every place incense *shall be* offered unto my name, and a pure offering: for my name *shall be* great among the heathen, saith the LORD of hosts.

TIME, AUTUMN, A. D. 28; PLACE, NEAR CAPERNAUM.

B

Job 17. 9 The righteous also shall hold on his way, and he that hath clean hands shall be stronger and stronger.

Prov. 4. 18 But the path of the just *is* as the shining light, that shineth more and more unto the perfect day.

Hos. 6. 3 Then shall we know, *if* we follow on to know the LORD: his going forth is prepared as the morning; and he

B—CONCLUDED.

shall come unto us as the rain, as the latter *and* former rain unto the earth.

Phil. 1. 6 Being confident of this very thing, that he which hath begun a good work in you will perform *it* until the day of Jesus Christ:

Phil. 1. 9 And this I pray, that your love may abound yet more and more in knowledge and *in* all judgment;

TIME, AUTUMN, A. D. 28; PLACE, NEAR CAPERNAUM.

C—CONCLUDED.

Rom. 16. 26 But now is made manifest, and by the Scriptures of the prophets, according to the commandment of the everlasting God, made known to all nations for the obedience of faith:

I Cor. 2. 7 But we speak the wisdom of God in a mystery, *even* the hidden *wisdom*, which God ordained before the world unto our glory:

Eph. 3. 9 And to make all *men* see what *is* the fellowship of the mystery, which from the beginning of the world hath been hid in God, who created all things by Jesus Christ:

Col. 1. 26 *Even* the mystery which hath been hid from ages and from generations, but now is made manifest to his saints:

D

Matt. 13. 34. *See text of topic.*

John 16. 12 I have yet many things to say unto you, but ye cannot bear them now.

I Cor. 3. 1 And I, brethren, could not speak unto you as unto spiritual, but as unto carnal, *even* as unto babes in Christ.

2 I have fed you with milk, and not with meat: for hitherto ye were not able *to bear it*, neither yet now are ye able.

Heb. 5. 13 For every one that useth milk, *is* unskilful in the word of righteousness: for he is a babe.

14 But strong meat belongeth to them that are of full age, *even* those who by reason of use have their senses exercised to discern both good and evil.

§ 66. THE WHEAT AND THE TARES EXPLAINED.

13: 36–43.

36 Then Jesus sent the multitude away, and went into the house: and his disciples came unto him, saying, Declare unto us the parable of the tares of the field.

37 He answered and said unto them, He that [a]soweth the good seed is the Son of man;

38 [b]The field is the world; the good seed are the children of the kingdom; but the tares are the [c]children of the wicked one;

39 The enemy that sowed them is the devil; [d]the harvest is the end of the world; and the reapers are the angels.

40 As therefore the tares are gathered and burned in the fire; so shall it be in the end of this world.

41 The Son of man shall send forth his angels, [e]and they shall gather out of his kingdom all [1]things that offend, and them which do iniquity;

42 [f]And shall cast them into a furnace of fire: [g]there shall be wailing and gnashing of teeth.

43 [h]Then shall the righteous shine forth as the sun in the kingdom of their Father. [i]Who hath ears to hear, let him hear.

A

Isa. 61. 1 The Spirit of the Lord GOD *is* upon me; because the LORD hath anointed me to preach good tidings unto the meek; he hath sent me to bind up the brokenhearted, to proclaim liberty to the captives, and the opening of the prison to *them that are* bound:

B

Matt.24. 14 And this gospel of the kingdom shall be preached in all the world for a witness unto all nations; and then shall the end come.

B—CONCLUDED.

Matt.28. 19 Go ye therefore, and teach all nations, baptizing them in the name of the Father, and of the Son, and of the Holy Ghost:

Mark 16. 15 And he said unto them, Go ye into all the world, and preach the gospel to every creature.

Mark 16. 20 And they went forth, and preached every where, the Lord working with *them*, and confirming the word with signs following. Amen.

Luke 24. 47 And that repentance and remission of sins should be preached in his name among all nations, beginning at Jerusalem.

Rom.10. 18 But I say, Have they not heard? Yes verily, their sound went into all the earth, and their words unto the ends of the world.

Col. 1. 6 Which is come unto you, as *it is* in all the world; and bringeth forth fruit, as *it doth* also in you, since the day ye heard *of it*, and knew the grace of God in truth:

C

Gen. 3. 13 And the LORD God said unto the woman, What *is* this *that* thou hast done? And the woman said, The serpent beguiled me, and I did eat.

14 And the LORD God said unto the serpent, Because thou hast done this, thou *art* cursed above all cattle, and above every beast of the field; upon thy belly shalt thou go, and dust shalt thou eat all the days of thy life:

15 And I will put enmity between thee and the woman, and between thy seed and her seed; it shall bruise thy head, and thou shalt bruise his heel.

John 8. 44 Ye are of *your* father the devil, and the lusts of your father ye will do: he was a murderer from the beginning, and abode not in the truth, because there is no truth in him. When he speaketh a lie, he speaketh of his own: for he is a liar, and the father of it.

Acts 13. 10 And said, O full of all subtilty and all mischief, *thou* child of the devil, *thou* enemy of all righteousness, wilt thou not cease to pervert the right ways of the Lord?

I Jno. 3. 8 He that committeth sin is of the devil; for the devil sinneth from the beginning. For this purpose the Son of God was manifested, that he might destroy the works of the devil.

TIME, AUTUMN, A. D. 28; PLACE, NEAR CAPERNAUM.

D

Joel 3. 13 Put ye in the sickle, for the harvest is ripe: come, get you down; for the press is full, the fats overflow; for their wickedness *is* great.

Rev. 14. 15 And another angel came out of the temple, crying with a loud voice to him that sat on the cloud, Thrust in thy sickle, and reap: for the time is come for thee to reap; for the harvest of the earth is ripe.

E

Matt.18. 7 Woe unto the world because of offences! for it must needs be that offences come; but woe to that man by whom the offence cometh!

Rom.16. 17 Now I beseech you, brethren, mark them which cause divisions and offences contrary to the doctrine which ye have learned; and avoid them.

II Pet. 2. 1 But there were false prophets also among the people, even as there shall be false teachers among you, who privily shall bring in damnable heresies, even denying the Lord that bought them, and bring upon themselves swift destruction.

2 And many shall follow their pernicious ways; by reason of whom the way of truth shall be evil spoken of.

1

Or, *scandals.*

F

Matt. 3. 12 Whose fan *is* in his hand, and he will thoroughly purge his floor, and gather his wheat into the garner; but he will burn up the chaff with unquenchable fire.

Rev. 19. 20 And the beast was taken, and with him the false prophet that wrought miracles before him, with which he deceived them that had received the mark of the beast, and them that worshipped his image. These both were cast alive into a lake of fire burning with brimstone.

Rev. 20. 10 And the devil that deceived them was cast into the lake of fire and brimstone, where the beast and the false prophet *are*, and shall be tormented day and night for ever and ever.

G

Matt. 8. 12 But the children of the kingdom shall be cast out into outer darkness: there shall be weeping and gnashing of teeth.

Matt.13. 50 And shall cast them into the furnace of fire: there shall be wailing and gnashing of teeth.

H

Dan. 12. 3 And they that be wise shall shine as the brightness of the firmament; and they that turn many to righteousness, as the stars for ever and ever.

Matt.25. 34 Then shall the King say unto them on his right hand, Come, ye blessed of my Father, inherit the kingdom prepared for you from the foundation of the world:

35 For I was a hungered, and ye gave me meat: I was thirsty, and ye gave me drink: I was a stranger, and you took me in:

36 Naked, and ye clothed me: I was sick, and ye visited me: I was in prison, and ye came unto me.

I Cor.15. 42 So also *is* the resurrection of the dead. It is sown in corruption, it is raised in incorruption:

43 It is sown in dishonour, it is raised in glory: it is sown in weakness, it is raised in power:

I Cor.15. 58 Therefore, my beloved brethren, be ye steadfast, unmovable, always abounding in the work of the Lord, forasmuch as ye know that your labour is not in vain in the Lord.

Rev. 7. 9 After this I beheld, and, lo, a great multitude, which no man could number, of all nations, and kindreds, and people, and tongues, stood before the throne, and before the Lamb, clothed with white robes, and palms in their hands;

Rev. 21. 3 And I heard a great voice out of heaven saying, Behold, the tabernacle of God *is* with men, and he will dwell with them, and they shall be his people, and God himself shall be with them, *and be* their God.

4 And God shall wipe away all tears from their eyes; and there shall be no more death, neither sorrow, nor crying, neither shall there be any more pain: for the former things are passed away.

5 And he that sat upon the throne said, Behold, I make all things new. And he said unto me, Write: for these words are true and faithful.

Rev. 21. 22 And I saw no temple therein: for the Lord God Almighty and the Lamb are the temple of it.

23 And the city had no need of the sun, neither of the moon, to shine in it: for the glory of God did lighten it, and the Lamb *is* the light thereof.

I

Matt.13. 9 Who hath ears to hear, let him hear.

§ 67. PARABLE OF THE HID TREASURE, THE PEARL AND

13: 44–53.

44 Again, the kingdom of heaven is like unto treasure hid in a field; the which when a man hath found, he hideth, and for joy thereof goeth and [a]selleth all that he hath, and [b]buyeth that field.

45 Again, the kingdom of heaven is like unto a merchantman, seeking goodly pearls:

46 Who, when he had found [c]one pearl of great price, went and sold all that he had, and bought it.

47 Again, the kingdom of heaven is like unto a net, that was cast into the sea, and [d]gathered of every kind:

48 Which, when it was full, they drew to shore, and sat down, and gathered the good into vessels, but cast the bad away.

49 So shall it be at the end of the world: the angels shall come forth, and [e]sever the wicked from among the just,

50 [f]And shall cast them into the furnace of fire: there shall be wailing and gnashing of teeth.

51 Jesus saith unto them, Have ye understood all these things? They say unto him, Yea, Lord.

52 Then said he unto them, Therefore every [g]scribe [h]*which is* instructed unto the kingdom of heaven, is like unto a man *that is* a householder, which bringeth forth out of his treasure [i]*things* new and old.

53 And it came to pass, *that* when Jesus had finished these parables, he departed thence. (p. 228.)

A

Phil. 3. 7 But what things were gain to me, those I counted loss for Christ.

8 Yea doubtless, and I count all things *but* loss for the excellency of the knowledge of Christ Jesus my Lord: for whom I have suffered the loss of all things, and do count them *but* dung, that I may win Christ,

B

Isa. 55. 1 Ho, every one that thirsteth, come ye to the waters, and he that hath no money; come ye, buy, and eat; yea, come, buy wine and milk without money and without price.

Rev. 3. 18 I counsel thee to buy of me gold tried in the fire, that thou mayest be rich; and white raiment, that thou mayest be clothed, and *that* the shame of thy nakedness do not appear; and anoint thine eyes with eyesalve, that thou mayest see.

C

Prov. 2. 1 My son, if thou wilt receive my words, and hide my commandments with thee;

2 So that thou incline thine ear unto wisdom, *and* apply thine heart to understanding;

3 Yea, if thou criest after knowledge, *and* liftest up thy voice for understanding;

4 If thou seekest her as silver, and searchest for her as *for* hid treasures;

Prov. 3. 13 Happy *is* the man *that* findeth wisdom, and the man *that* getteth understanding:

14 For the merchandise of it *is* better than the merchandise of silver, and the gain thereof than fine gold.

15 She *is* more precious than rubies: and all the things thou canst desire are not to be compared unto her.

Prov. 8. 10 Receive my instruction, and not silver; and knowledge rather than choice gold.

11 For wisdom *is* better than rubies; and all the things that may be desired are not to be compared to it.

12 I wisdom dwell with prudence, and find out knowledge of witty inventions.

13 The fear of the LORD *is* to hate evil: pride, and arrogancy, and the evil way, and the froward mouth, do I hate.

14 Counsel *is* mine, and sound wisdom: I *am* understanding; I have strength.

THE NET. Time, Autumn, A. D. 28; Place, Near Capernaum.

C—Concluded.

Prov. 8. 15 By me kings reign, and princes decree justice.

16 By me princes rule, and nobles, *even* all the judges of the earth.

17 I love them that love me; and those that seek me early shall find me.

18 Riches and honour *are* with me; *yea*, durable riches and righteousness.

19 My fruit *is* better than gold, yea, than fine gold; and my revenue than choice silver.

D

Matt.22. 10 So those servants went out into the highways, and gathered together all as many as they found, both bad and good: and the wedding was furnished with guests.

E

Matt.25. 32 And before him shall be gathered all nations: and he shall separate them one from another, as a shepherd divideth *his* sheep from the goats:

Rev. 20. 12 And I saw the dead, small and great, stand before God; and the books were opened: and another book was opened, which is *the book* of life: and the dead were judged out of those things which were written in the books, according to their works.

13 And the sea gave up the dead which were in it; and death and hell delivered up the dead which were in them: and they were judged every man according to their works.

14 And death and hell were cast into the lake of fire. This is the second death.

15 And whosoever was not found written in the book of life was cast into the lake of fire.

F

Matt.13. 42 And shall cast them into a furnace of fire: there shall be wailing and gnashing of teeth.

G

Ezr. 7. 6 This Ezra went up from Babylon; and he *was* a ready scribe in the law of Moses, which the Lord God of Israel had given: and the king granted him all his request, according to the hand of the Lord his God upon him.

Ezr. 7. 10 For Ezra had prepared his heart to seek the law of the Lord, and to do *it*, and to teach in Israel statutes and judgments.

Ezr. 7. 21 And I, *even* I Artaxerxes the king, do make a decree to all the treasurers which *are* beyond the river, that whatsoever Ezra the priest, the

G—Concluded.

scribe of the law of the God of heaven, shall require of you, it be done speedily.

H

Prov.15. 7 The lips of the wise disperse knowledge: but the heart of the foolish *doeth* not so.

Prov.16. 20 He that handleth a matter wisely shall find good: and whoso trusteth in the Lord, happy *is* he.

21 The wise in heart shall be called prudent: and the sweetness of the lips increaseth learning.

22 Understanding *is* a wellspring of life unto him that hath it: but the instruction of fools *is* folly.

23 The heart of the wise teacheth his mouth, and addeth learning to his lips.

24 Pleasant words *are as* a honeycomb, sweet to the soul, and health to the bones.

Prov.18. 4 The words of a man's mouth *are as* deep waters, *and* the wellspring of wisdom *as* a flowing brook.

Eccl. 12. 9 And moreover, because the Preacher was wise, he still taught the people knowledge; yea, he gave good heed, and sought out, *and* set in order many proverbs.

10 The Preacher sought to find out acceptable words: and *that which was* written *was* upright, *even* words of truth.

11 The words of the wise *are* as goads, and as nails fastened *by* the masters of assemblies, *which* are given from one shepherd.

Eph. 3. 8 Unto me, who am less than the least of all saints, is this grace given, that I should preach among the Gentiles the unsearchable riches of Christ;

Col. 3. 16 Let the word of Christ dwell in you richly in all wisdom; teaching and admonishing one another in psalms and hymns and spiritual songs, singing with grace in your hearts to the Lord.

I

Song 7. 13 The mandrakes give a smell, and at our gates *are* all manner of pleasant *fruits*, new and old, *which* I have laid up for thee, O my beloved.

I Jno. 2. 7 Brethren, I write no new commandment, unto you, but an old commandment which ye had from the beginning. The old commandment is the word which ye have heard from the beginning.

§ 68. JESUS DIRECTS TO CROSS THE LAKE. UNREADY DISCIPLES.

8 : 18–23.

18 Now when Jesus saw great multitudes about him, he gave commandment to depart unto the other side.

19 [a]And a certain scribe came, and said unto him, Master, I will follow thee withersoever thou goest.

20 And Jesus saith unto him, The foxes have holes, and the birds of the air *have* nests; but the [b]Son of man hath not where to lay *his* head.

21 [c]And another of his disciples said unto him, Lord, [d]suffer me first to go and bury my father.

22 But Jesus said unto him, Follow me; and let the [e]dead bury their dead.

23 And when he was entered into a ship, his disciples followed him.

A

Luke 9. 57, 58. *See text of topic.*

B

Ps. 22. 6 But I *am* a worm, and no man; a reproach of men, and despised of the people.

C

Luke 9. 59, 60. *See text of topic.*

D

I Ki. 19. 20 And he left the oxen, and ran after Elijah, and said, Let me, I pray thee, kiss my father and my mother, and *then* I will follow thee. And he said unto him, Go back again: for what have I done to thee?

4 : 35, 36.

35 [f]And the same day, when the even was come, he saith unto them, Let us pass over unto the other side.

36 And when they had sent away the multitude, they took him even as he was in the ship. And there were also with him other little ships.

E

Eph. 2. 1 And you *hath he quickened,* who were dead in trespasses and sins;

Eph. 2. 5 Even when we were dead in sins, hath quickened us together with Christ, (by grace ye are saved;)

F

Isa. 42. 4 He shall not fail nor be discouraged, till he have set judgment in the earth: and the isles shall wait for his law.

Matt. 8. 18, 23 and Luke 8. 22. *See text of topic.*

G

Matt. 8. 19. *See text of topic.*

H

Ps. 84. 3 Yea, the sparrow hath found a house, and the swallow a nest for herself, where she may lay her young, *even* thine altars, O LORD of hosts, my King, and my God.

II Cor. 8. 9 For ye know the grace of our Lord Jesus Christ, that, though he was rich, yet for your sakes he became poor, that ye through his poverty might be rich.

Jas. 2. 5 Hearken, my beloved brethren, Hath not God chosen the poor of this world rich in faith, and heirs of the kingdom which he hath promised to them that love him?

I

Matt. 8. 21. *See text of topic.*

§ 69. JESUS STILLS THE TEMPEST.

8 : 24–27.

24 [a]And, behold, there arose a great tempest in the sea, insomuch that the ship was covered with the waves: but he was asleep.

25 And his disciples came to *him,* and awoke him, saying, Lord, save us: we perish.

4 : 37–41.

37 And there arose a great storm of wind, and the waves beat into the ship, so that it was now full.

38 And he was in the hinder part of the ship, asleep on a pillow: and they awake him, and say unto him, Master, carest thou not that we perish?

TIME, AUTUMN, A. D. 28; PLACE, LAKE OF GALILEE.

9: 57–62; 8: 22.

57 [g]And it came to pass, that, as they went in the way, a certain *man* said unto him, Lord, I will follow thee whithersoever thou goest.

58 [h]And Jesus said unto him, Foxes have holes, and birds of the air *have* nests; but the Son of man hath not where to lay *his* head.

59 [i]And he said unto another, Follow me. But he said, Lord, suffer me first to go and bury my father.

60 Jesus said unto him, Let the dead bury their dead: but go thou and preach the kingdom of God.

61 And another also said, Lord, [k]I will follow thee; but let me first go bid them farewell, which are at home at my house.

62 And Jesus said unto him, [l]No man, having put his hand to the plough, and looking back, is fit for the kingdom of God. (p. 305.)

CHAP. 8.

22 [m]Now it came to pass on a certain day, that he went into a ship with his disciples: and he said unto them, Let us go over unto the other side of the lake. And they launched forth.

K

I Ki. 19. 20. *See under D.*

L

Ps. 78. 8 And might not be as their fathers, a stubborn and rebellious generation; a generation *that* set not their heart aright, and whose spirit was not steadfast with God.

9 The children of Ephraim, *being* armed, *and* carrying bows, turned back in the day of battle.

Luke 17. 32 Remember Lot's wife.

II Pet. 2. 20 For if after they have escaped the pollutions of the world through the knowledge of the Lord and Saviour Jesus Christ, they are again entangled therein, and overcome, the latter end is worse with them than the beginning.

Heb. 6. 4 For *it is* impossible for those who were once enlightened, and have tasted of the heavenly gift, and were made partakers of the Holy Ghost,

5 And have tasted the good word of God, and the powers of the world to come,

6 If they shall fall away, to renew them again unto repentance; seeing they crucify to themselves the Son of God afresh, and put *him* to an open shame.

7 For the earth which drinketh in the rain that cometh oft upon it, and bringeth forth herbs meet for them by whom it is dressed, receiveth blessing from God:

8 But that which beareth thorns and briers *is* rejected, and *is* nigh unto cursing; whose end *is* to be burned.

9 But, beloved, we are persuaded better things of you, and things that accompany salvation, though we thus speak.

M

Matt. 8. 23 and Mark 4. 35. *See text of topic.*

TIME, AUTUMN, A. D. 28; PLACE, LAKE OF GALILEE: ALSO CALLED SEA OF TIBERIUS.

8: 23–25.

23 But as they sailed, he fell asleep: and there came down a storm of wind on the lake; and they were filled *with water*, and were in jeopardy.

24 And they came to him, and awoke him, saying, Master, Master, we perish.

A

Mark 4. 37, etc. *See text of topic.*

A—CONCLUDED.

Luke 8. 23, etc. *See text of topic.*

Jon. 1. 4 But the LORD sent out a great wind into the sea, and there was a mighty tempest in the sea, so that the ship was like to be broken.

5 Then the mariners were afraid, and cried every man unto his god, and cast forth the wares that *were* in the ship into the sea, to lighten *it* of them. But Jonah was gone down into the sides of the ship; and he lay, and was fast asleep.

§ 69. JESUS STILLS THE TEMPEST (Concluded).

Chap. 8.

26 And he saith unto them, [b]Why are ye fearful, O ye of little faith? Then [c]he arose, and rebuked the winds and the sea; and there was a great calm.

27 But the men marvelled, saying, What manner of man is this, that even the winds and the sea obey him!

B

Phil. 4. 6 Be careful for nothing: but in every thing by prayer and supplication with thanksgiving let your requests be made known unto God.

C

Ps. 65. 7 Which stilleth the noise of the seas, the noise of their waves, and the tumult of the people.
Ps. 89. 9 Thou rulest the raging of the sea: when the waves thereof arise, thou stillest them.
Ps. 107. 29 He maketh the storm a calm, so that the waves thereof are still.
Nah. 1. 4 He rebuketh the sea and maketh

Chap. 4.

39 And he arose, and [d]rebuked the wind, and said unto the sea, Peace, be still. And the wind ceased, and there was a great calm.

40 And he said unto them, Why are ye so fearful? how is it that ye have no faith?

41 And they [e]feared exceedingly, and said one to another, What manner of man is this, that even the wind and the sea obey him?

C—Concluded.

it dry, and drieth up all the rivers: Bashan languisheth, and Carmel, and the flower of Lebanon languisheth.

D

Job 28. 11 He bindeth the floods from overflowing; and *the thing that is* hid bringeth he forth to light.
Job 38. 11 And said, Hitherto shalt thou come, but no further: and here shall thy proud waves be stayed?

§ 70. THE TWO DEMONIACS OF GADARA

8: 28–34; 9: 1.

28 [a]And when he was come to the other side into the country of the [b]Gergesenes, there met him two possessed with devils, coming out of the tombs, exceeding fierce, [c]so that no man might pass by that way.

A

Mark 5. 1, etc. and Luke 8. 26, etc. *See text of topic.*
Acts 10. 38 How God anointed Jesus of Nazareth with the Holy Ghost and with power: who went about doing good, and healing all that were oppressed of the devil; for God was with him.

B

Gen. 10. 16 And the Jebusite, and the Amorite, and the Girgasite,
Gen. 15. 21 And the Amorites, and the Canaanites, and the Girgashites, and the Jebusites.
Deut. 7. 1 When the Lord thy God shall bring thee into the land whither thou

5: 1–21.

1 And [d]they came over unto the other side of the sea, into the country of the Gadarenes.

2 And when he was come out of the ship, immediately there met him out of the tombs a man with an unclean spirit,

3 [e]Who had *his* dwelling among the tombs; and no man could bind him, no, not with chains:

4 Because that he had been often bound with fetters and chains, and the chains had been plucked asunder by him, and the fetters broken in pieces: neither could any *man* tame him.

B—Continued.

goest to possess it, and hath cast out many nations before thee, the Hittites,

TIME, AUTUMN, A. D. 28; PLACE, LAKE OF GALILLE: ALSO CALLED SEA OF TIBERIUS.

CHAP. 8.

Then he [f] arose, and rebuked the wind and the raging of the water: and they ceased, and there was a calm.

25 And he said unto them, Where is your faith? And they being [g] afraid wondered, saying one to another, What manner of man is this! for he commandeth even the winds and water, and they obey him.

D—CONTINUED.

Ps. 29. 10 The LORD sitteth upon the flood; yea, the LORD sitteth King for ever.

Ps. 65. 5 *By* terrible things in righteousness wilt thou answer us, O God of our salvation; *who art* the confidence of all the ends of the earth, and of them that are afar off *upon* the sea:

Ps. 65. 7 and Ps. 89. 9. *See under C.*

Ps. 107. 23 They that go down to the sea in ships, that do business in great waters;
24 These see the works of the LORD, and his wonders in the deep.

Ps. 107. 29. *See under C.*

D—CONCLUDED.

Ps. 135. 5 For I know that the LORD *is* great, and *that* our Lord *is* above all gods.
6 Whatsoever the LORD pleased, *that* did he in heaven, and in earth, in the seas, and all deep places.

Nah. 1. 4. *See under C.*

E

Ps. 33. 8 Let all the earth fear the LORD: let all the inhabitants of the world stand in awe of him.
9 For he spake, and it was *done;* he commanded, and it stood fast.

F

Job 28. 11, Job 38. 11 and Ps. 29. 10. *See under D.*

Ps. 46. 1 God *is* our refuge and strength, a very present help in trouble.

Ps. 65. 7 and Ps. 89. 9. *See under C.*

Ps. 93. 4 The LORD on high *is* mightier than the noise of many waters, *yea, than* the mighty waves of the sea.

Ps. 107. 29 and Nah. 1. 4. *See under C.*

G

Ps. 33. 8, 9. *See under E.*
Mark 4. 41. *See text of topic.*

Mark 6. 51 And he went up unto them into the ship; and the wind ceased; and they were sore amazed in themselves beyond measure, and wondered.

TIME, AUTUMN, A. D. 28; PLACE, SOUTHEAST COAST OF THE LAKE OF GALILEE.

8: 26–40.

26 [f] And they arrived at the country of the Gadarenes, which is over against Galilee.

27 And when he went forth to land, there met him out of the city a certain man, which had devils long time, and ware no clothes, neither abode in *any* house, but in the tombs.

B—CONCLUDED.

and the Girgashites, and the Amorites, and the Canaanites, and the Perizzites, and the Hivites, and the Jebusites, seven nations greater and mightier than thou;

C

Judg. 5. 6 In the days of Shamgar the son of Anath, in the days of Jael, the highways were unoccupied, and the travellers walked through byways.

D

Matt. 8. 28 and Luke 8. 26. *See text of topic.*

E

Num. 19. 16 And whosoever toucheth one that is slain with a sword in the open fields, or a dead body, or a bone of a man, or a grave, shall be unclean seven days.

Isa. 65. 4 Which remain among the graves, and lodge in the monuments; which eat swine's flesh, and broth of abominable *things is in* their vessels;

Dan. 4. 32 And they shall drive thee from men, and thy dwelling *shall be* with the beasts of the field: they shall make thee to eat grass as oxen, and seven times shall pass over thee, until thou know that the Most High ruleth in the kingdom of men, and giveth it to whomsoever he will.
33 The same hour was the thing fulfilled upon Nebuchadnezzar: and he was driven from men, and did eat grass as oxen, and his body was wet with the dew of heaven, till his hairs were grown like eagles' *feathers*, and his nails like birds' *claws*.

F

Matt. 8. 28 and Mark 5. 1. *See text of topic.*

§ 70. THE TWO DEMONIACS OF GADARA (CONTINUED).

CHAP. 8.

29 And, behold, they cried out, saying, [g]What have we to do with thee, Jesus, thou Son of God? art thou come hither to torment us before the time?

30 And there was a good way off from them a herd of many [h]swine feeding.

31 So the devils [i]besought him, saying, If thou cast us out, suffer us to go away into the herd of swine.

32 And he said unto them, Go. And when they were come out, they went into the herd of swine: and, behold, the whole herd of swine ran violently down a steep place into the sea, and perished in the waters.

33 And they that kept them fled, and went their ways into the city, and told every thing, and what was befallen to the possessed of the devils.

G

II Pet.2. 4 For if God spared not the angels that sinned, but cast *them* down to hell, and delivered *them* into chains of darkness, to be reserved unto judgment;

H

Deut.14. 8 And the swine, because it divideth the hoof, yet cheweth not the cud, it *is* unclean unto you: ye shall not eat of their flesh, nor touch their dead carcass.

I

Phil. 2. 10 That at the name of Jesus every knee should bow, of *things* in heaven, and *things* in earth, and *things* under the earth;

K

Acts 16. 17 The same followed Paul and us, and cried, saying, These men are the servants of the most high God, which show unto us the way of salvation.

Phil. 2. 10. *See under I.*

Phil. 2. 11 And *that* every tongue should confess that Jesus Christ *is* Lord, to the glory of God the Father.

CHAP. 5.

5 And always, night and day, he was in the mountains, and in the tombs, crying, and cutting himself with stones.

6 But when he saw Jesus afar off, he ran and [k]worshipped him,

7 And cried with a loud voice, and said, What have I to do with thee, Jesus, *thou* Son of the most high God? I adjure thee by God, that thou torment me not.

8 (For he said unto him, Come out of the man, *thou* unclean spirit.)

9 And he asked him, What *is* thy name? And he answered, saying, My name *is* Legion: for we are many.

10 And he besought him much that he would not send them away out of the country.

11 Now there was there nigh unto the mountains a great herd of [l]swine feeding.

12 And all the devils besought him, saying, Send us into the swine, that we may enter into them.

13 And forthwith Jesus [m]gave them leave. And the unclean spirits went out, and entered into the swine; and the herd ran violently down a steep place into the sea, (they were about two thousand,) and were choked in the sea.

14 And they that fed the swine fled, and told *it* in the city, and in the country. And they went out to see what it was that was done.

L

Lev. 11. 7 And the swine, though he divide the hoof, and be clovenfooted, yet he cheweth not the cud; he *is* unclean to you.

TIME, AUTUMN, A. D. 28; PLACE, SOUTHEAST COAST OF THE LAKE OF GALILEE.

CHAP. 8.

28 When he saw Jesus, he [n]cried out, and fell down before him, and with a loud voice said, What have I to do with thee, Jesus, *thou* Son of God most high? I beseech thee, torment me not.

29 (For he had commanded the unclean spirit to come out of the man. For oftentimes it had caught him: and he was kept bound with chains and in fetters; and he brake the bands, and was driven of the devil into the wilderness.)

30 And Jesus asked him, saying, What is thy name? And he said, Legion: because many devils were entered into him.

31 And they besought him that he would not command them to go out [o]into the deep.

32 And there was there a herd [p]of many swine feeding on the mountain: and they besought him that he would suffer them to enter into them. And [q]he suffered them.

33 Then went the devils out of the man, and entered into the swine: and the herd ran violently down a steep place into the lake, and were choked.

34 When they that fed *them* saw what was done, they fled, and went and told *it* in the city and in the country.

35 Then they went out to see what was done;

L—CONTINUED.

Deut. 14. 8. *See under H.*

Isa. 65. 3 A people that provoketh me to anger continually to my face; that sacrificeth in gardens, and burneth incense upon altars of brick;

L—CONCLUDED.

Isa. 65. 4 Which remain among the graves, and lodge in the monuments; which eat swine's flesh, and broth of abominable *things is in* their vessels;

M

I Ki. 22. 21 And there came forth a spirit, and stood before the LORD, and said, I will persuade him.

22 And the LORD said unto him, Wherewith? And he said, I will go forth, and I will be a lying spirit in the mouth of all his prophets. And he said, Thou shalt persuade *him*, and prevail also: go forth, and do so.

Job 1. 12 And the LORD said unto Satan, Behold, all that he hath *is* in thy power; only upon himself put not forth thine hand. So Satan went forth from the presence of the LORD.

Job 2. 6 And the LORD said unto Satan, Behold, he *is* in thine hand; but save his life.

Job 12. 16 With him *is* strength and wisdom: the deceived and the deceiver *are* his.

N

Acts 16. 16 And it came to pass, as we went to prayer, a certain damsel possessed with a spirit of divination met us, which brought her masters much gain by soothsaying:

Acts 16. 17. *See under K.*

Acts 16. 18 And this did she many days. But Paul, being grieved, turned and said to the spirit, I command thee in the name of Jesus Christ to come out of her. And he came out the same hour.

Phil. 2. 10. *See under I.*
Phil. 2. 11. *See under K.*

O

Rev. 9. 2 And he opened the bottomless pit; and there arose a smoke out of the pit, as the smoke of a great furnace; and the sun and the air were darkened by reason of the smoke of the pit.

Rev. 20. 3 And cast him into the bottomless pit, and shut him up, and set a seal upon him, that he should deceive the nations no more, till the thousand years should be fulfilled: and after that he must be loosed a little season.

P

Lev. 11. 7. *See under L.*
Deut. 14. 8. *See under H.*

Q

Job 1. 12 and Job 12. 16. *See under M.*

Rev. 20. 7 And when the thousand years are expired, Satan shall be loosed out of his prison.

§ 70. THE TWO DEMONIACS OF GADARA (Concluded).

Chap. 8.

34 And, behold, the whole city came out to meet Jesus: and when they saw him, [r]they besought *him* that he would depart out of their coasts.

Chap. 9.

1 And he entered into a ship, and passed over, [s]and came into his own city.

(p. 102.)

R

Deut. 5. 25 Now therefore why should we die? for this great fire will consume us: if we hear the voice of the Lord our God any more, then we shall die.

I Ki. 17. 18 And she said unto Elijah, What have I to do with thee, O thou man of God? art thou come unto me to call my sin to remembrance, and to slay my son?

Mark 5. 10. *See text of topic.*

Acts 16. 39 And they came and besought them, and brought *them* out, and desired *them* to depart out of the city.

S

Matt. 4. 13 And leaving Nazareth, he came and dwelt in Capernaum, which is upon the sea coast, in the borders of Zabulon and Nephthalim:

T

Rom. 16. 20 And the God of peace shall bruise Satan under your feet shortly. The grace of our Lord Jesus Christ *be* with you. Amen.

I Jno. 3. 8 He that committeth sin is of the devil; for the devil sinneth from the beginning. For this purpose the Son of God was manifested, that he might destroy the works of the devil.

U

Deut. 5. 25 and I Ki. 17. 18. *See under R.*

Job 21. 13 They spend their days in wealth, and in a moment go down to the grave.

14 Therefore they say unto God, Depart from us; for we desire not the knowledge of thy ways.

Matt. 8. 34. *See text of topic.*
Acts 16. 39. *See under R.*

X

Ps. 116. 12 What shall I render unto the Lord *for* all his benefits toward me?

Luke 8. 38. *See text of topic.*

Phil. 1. 23 For I am in a strait betwixt two, having a desire to depart, and to be with Christ; which is far better:

Chap 5.

15 And they come to Jesus, and see him that was possessed with the devil, and had the legion, sitting, and clothed, and [t]in his right mind; and they were afraid.

16 And they that saw *it* told them how it befell to him that was possessed with the devil, and *also* concerning the swine.

17 And [u]they began to pray him to depart out of their coasts.

18 And when he was come into the ship, [x]he that had been possessed with the devil prayed him that he might be with him.

19 Howbeit Jesus suffered him not, but saith unto him, [y]Go home to thy friends, and tell them how great things the Lord hath done for thee, and hath had compassion on thee.

20 And he departed, and [z]began to publish in Decapolis how great things Jesus had done for him: and all *men* did marvel.

21 [a]And when Jesus was passed over again by ship unto the other side, much people gathered unto him; and he was nigh unto the sea.

(p. 222.)

Y

Ps. 66. 16 Come *and* hear, all ye that fear God, and I will declare what he hath done for my soul.

Isa. 38. 15 What shall I say? he hath both spoken unto me, and himself hath done *it:* I shall go softly all my years in the bitterness of my soul.

16 O Lord, by these *things men* live, and in all these *things is* the life of my spirit: so wilt thou recover me, and make me to live.

17 Behold, for peace I had great bitterness; but thou hast in love to my soul *delivered it* from the pit of corruption: for thou hast cast all my sins behind thy back.

TIME, AUTUMN, A. D. 28; PLACE, SOUTHEAST COAST OF THE LAKE OF GALILEE.

CHAP. 8.

and came to Jesus, and found the man, out of whom the devils were departed, sitting at the feet of Jesus, clothed, and [b]in his right mind: and they were afraid.

36 They also which saw *it* told them by what means he that was possessed of the devils was healed.

37 [c]Then the whole multitude of the country of the Gadarenes round about [d]besought him to depart from them; for they were taken with great fear: and he went up into the ship, and returned back again.

38 Now [e]the man, out of whom the devils were departed, besought him that he might be with him: but Jesus sent him away, saying,

39 Return to thine own house, and show how great things God hath done unto thee. And he went his way, and published throughout the whole city how great things Jesus had done unto him.

40 And it came to pass, that, when Jesus was returned, the people *gladly* received him: for they were all waiting for him.

(p. 223.)

Y—CONCLUDED.

Isa. 38. 18 For the grave cannot praise thee, death cannot celebrate thee: they that go down into the pit cannot hope for thy truth.

Dan. 4. 1 Nebuchadnezzar the king, unto all people, nations, and languages, that dwell in all the earth; Peace be multiplied unto you.

2 I thought it good to show the signs and wonders that the high God hath wrought toward me.

3 How great *are* his signs! and how mighty *are* his wonders! his kingdom *is* an everlasting kingdom, and his dominion *is* from generation to generation.

Z

Isa. 63. 7 I will mention the loving-kindness of the LORD, *and* the praises of the LORD, according to all that the LORD hath bestowed on us, and the great goodness toward the house of Israel, which he hath bestowed on them according to his mercies, and according to the multitude of his loving-kindnesses.

A

Matt. 9. 1 and Luke 8. 40. *See text of topic.*

B

Rom. 16. 20 and I Jno. 3. 8. *See under T.*

C

Matt. 8. 34. *See text of topic.*

D

I Sa. 16. 4 And Samuel did that which the LORD spake, and came to Beth-lehem. And the elders of the town trembled at his coming, and said, Comest thou peaceably?

Job 21. 14. *See under U.*

Mark 1. 23 And there was in their synagogue a man with an unclean spirit; and he cried out,

24 Saying, Let *us* alone; what have we to do with thee, thou Jesus of Nazareth? art thou come to destroy us? I know thee who thou art, the Holy One of God.

Luke 4. 33 And in the synagogue there was a man, which had a spirit of an unclean devil, and cried out with a loud voice,

34 Saying, Let *us* alone; what have we to do with thee, *thou* Jesus of Nazareth? art thou come to destroy us? I know thee who thou art; the Holy One of God.

I Cor. 2. 14 But the natural man receiveth not the things of the Spirit of God: for they are foolishness unto him: neither can he know *them*, because they are spiritually discerned.

E

Ps. 103. 1 Bless the LORD, O my soul: and all that is within me, *bless* his holy name.

2 Bless the LORD, O my soul, and forget not all his benefits:

Ps. 116. 12. *See under X.*

Dan. 4. 37 Now I Nebuchadnezzar praise and extol and honour the King of heaven, all whose works *are* truth, and his ways judgment: and those that walk in pride he is able to abase.

Mark 5. 18. *See text of topic.*

Luke 18. 43 And immediately he received his sight, and followed him, glorifying God: and all the people, when they saw *it*, gave praise unto God.

§ 71. LEVI'S FEAST.

9 : 10–13.

10 [a]And it came to pass, as Jesus sat at meat in the house, behold, many publicans and sinners came and sat down with him and his disciples.

11 And when the Pharisees saw *it*, they said unto his disciples, [b]Why eateth your master with publicans and [c]sinners?

12 But when Jesus heard *that*, he said unto them, They that be whole need not a physician, but they that are sick.

13 But go ye and learn what *that* meaneth, [d]I will have mercy, and not sacrifice: for I am not come to call the righteous, [e]but sinners to repentance.

A

Mark 2. 15, etc. and Luke 5. 29, etc. *See text of topic.*

B

Matt.11. 19 The Son of man came eating and drinking, and they say, Behold a man gluttonous, and a winebibber, a friend of publicans and sinners. But wisdom is justified of her children.

Luke 5. 30. *See text of topic.*

2: 15–17.

15 [f]And it came to pass, that, as Jesus sat at meat in his house, many publicans and sinners sat also together with Jesus and his disciples; for there were many, and they followed him.

16 And when [g]the scribes and Pharisees saw him eat with publicans and sinners, they said unto his disciples, How is it that he eateth and drinketh with publicans and sinners?

17 When Jesus heard *it*, he saith unto them, [h]They that are whole have no need of the physician, but they that are sick: I came not to call the righteous, but sinners to repentance.

B—CONCLUDED.

Luke 15. 2 And the Pharisees and scribes murmured, saying, This man receiveth sinners, and eateth with them.

C

Gal. 2. 15 We *who are* Jews by nature, and not sinners of the Gentiles,

D

Prov.21. 3 To do justice and judgment *is* more acceptable to the LORD than sacrifice.

§ 72. THE DISCIPLES OF JESUS FAST NOT. GARMENTS AND

9 : 14–17.

14 Then came to him the disciples of John, saying, [a]Why do we and the Pharisees fast oft, but thy disciples fast not?

15 And Jesus said unto them, Can [b]the children of the bridechamber mourn, as long as the bridegroom is with them?

A

Mark 2. 18, etc. and Luke 5. 33, etc. *See text of topic.*

Luke 18. 12 I fast twice in the week, I give tithes of all that I possess.

B

John 3. 29 He that hath the bride is the bridegroom: but the friend of the bridegroom, which standeth and hear-

2 : 18–22.

18 [c]And the disciples of John and of the Pharisees used to fast: and they come and say unto him, Why do the disciples of John and of the Pharisees fast, but thy disciples fast not?

19 And Jesus said unto them, Can the children of [d]the bridechamber fast, while the bridegroom is with them? as long as they have [e]the bridegroom with them, they cannot fast.

B—CONCLUDED.

eth him, rejoiceth greatly because of the bridegroom's voice: this my joy therefore is fulfilled.

TIME, AUTUMN, A. D. 28; PLACE, CAPERNAUM.

5: 29–32.

29 [i]And Levi made him a great feast in his own house: and [k]there was a great company of publicans and of others that sat down with them.

30 But their scribes and Pharisees murmured against his disciples, saying, Why do ye eat and drink with publicans and sinners?

31 And Jesus answering said unto them, They that are whole need not a physician; but they that are sick.

32 [l]I came not to call the righteous, but sinners to repentance.

D—CONTINUED.

Hos. 6. 6 For I desired mercy, and not sacrifice; and the knowledge of God more than burnt offerings.

Mic. 6. 6 Wherewith shall I come before the LORD, *and* bow myself before the high God? shall I come before him with burnt offerings, with calves of a year old?

7 Will the LORD be pleased with thousands of rams, *or* with ten thousands of rivers of oil? shall I give my first-born *for* my transgression, the fruit of my body *for* the sin of my soul?

D—CONCLUDED.

Mic. 6. 8 He hath showed thee, O man, what *is* good; and what doth the LORD require of thee, but to do justly, and to love mercy, and to walk humbly with thy God?

Matt.12. 7 But if ye had known what *this* meaneth, I will have mercy, and not sacrifice, ye would not have condemned the guiltless.

E

I Tim. 1. 15 This *is* a faithful saying, and worthy of all acceptation, that Christ Jesus came into the world to save sinners; of whom I am chief.

F

Matt. 9. 10. *See text of topic.*

G

Isa. 65. 5 Which say, Stand by thyself, come not near to me; for I am holier than thou. These *are* a smoke in my nose, a fire that burneth all the day.

H

Matt. 9. 12, 13. *See text of topic.*

Matt.18. 11 For the Son of man is come to save that which was lost.

Luke 5. 31, 32. *See text of topic.*

Luke 19. 10 For the Son of man is come to seek and to save that which was lost.

I Tim. 1. 15. *See under E.*

I

Matt. 9. 10 and Mark 2. 15. *See text of topic.*

K

Luke 15. 1 Then drew near unto him all the publicans and sinners for to hear him.

L

Matt. 9. 13. *See text of topic.*
I Tim. 1. 15. *See under E.*

BOTTLES. TIME, AUTUMN, A. D. 28; PLACE, CAPERNAUM.

5: 33–39.

33 And they said unto him, [f]Why do the disciples of John fast often, and make prayers, and likewise *the disciples* of the Pharisees; but thine eat and drink?

34 And he said unto them, Can ye make the children of the bridechamber fast, while [g]the bridegroom is with them?

C

Matt. 9. 14 and Luke 5. 33. *See text of topic.*

D

Song 1. 4 Draw me, we will run after thee: the King hath brought me into his chambers: we will be glad and rejoice in thee, we will remember thy love more than wine: the upright love thee.

E

Rev. 19. 7 Let us be glad and rejoice, and give honour to him: for the marriage of the Lamb is come, and his wife hath made herself ready.

F

Matt. 9. 14 and Mark 2. 18. *See text of topic.*

G

Matt.22. 2 The kingdom of heaven is like unto a certain king, which made a marriage for his son,

II Cor.11. 2 For I am jealous over you with godly jealousy: for I have espoused you to one husband, that I may present *you as* a chaste virgin to Christ.

Rev. 19. 7. *See under E.*

Rev. 21. 2 And I John saw the holy city, new Jerusalem, coming down from God out of heaven, prepared as a bride adorned for her husband.

§ 72. THE DISCIPLES OF JESUS FAST NOT. GARMENTS AND

CHAP. 9.

but the days will come, when the bridegroom shall be taken from them, and [h]then shall they fast.

16 No man putteth a piece of [1]new cloth unto an old garment; for that which is put in to fill it up taketh from the garment, and the rent is made worse.

17 Neither do men put new wine into old bottles: else the bottles break, and the wine runneth out, and the bottles perish: but they put new wine into new bottles, and both are preserved.

H

Acts 13. 2 As they ministered to the Lord, and fasted the Holy Ghost said, Separate me, Barnabas and Saul for the work whereunto I have called them.
3 And when they had fasted and prayed, and laid *their* hands on them, they sent *them* away.

Acts 14. 23 And when they had ordained them elders in every church, and had prayed with fasting, they commended them to the Lord, on whom they believed.

CHAP. 2.

20 But the days will come, when the bridegroom shall be taken away from them, and then shall they fast in those days.

21 No man also seweth a piece of new cloth on an old garment; else the new piece that filled it up taketh away from the old, and the rent is made worse.

22 And no man putteth new wine into old bottles; else the new wine doth burst the bottles, and the wine is spilled, and the bottles will be marred: but new wine must be put into new bottles. (p. 114.)

H—CONCLUDED.

I Cor. 7. 5 Defraud ye not one the other, except *it be* with consent for a time, that ye may give yourselves to fasting and prayer; and come together again, that Satan tempt you not for your incontinency.

II Cor.11. 27 In weariness and painfulness, in watchings often, in hunger and thirst, in fastings often, in cold and nakedness.

1

Or, *raw*, or, *unwrought cloth.*

§ 73. THE RAISING OF JAIRUS' DAUGHTER. THE WOMAN HEALED

9: 18–26.

18 [a]While he spake these things unto them, behold, there came a certain ruler, and worshipped him, saying, My daughter is even now dead: but come and lay thy hand upon her, and she shall live.

19 And Jesus arose, and followed him, and *so did* his disciples.

A

Mark 5. 22, etc. and Luke 8. 41, etc. *See text of topic.*

B

Matt. 9. 18 and Luke 8. 41. *See text of topic.*

Acts 13. 15 And after the reading of the law and the prophets, the rulers of the

5: 22–43.

22 [b]And, behold, there cometh one of the rulers of the synagogue, Jairus by name; and when he saw him, [c]he fell at his feet,

23 And [d]besought him greatly, saying, My little daughter lieth at the point of death: *I pray thee,* come and lay thy hands on her, that she may be healed; and she shall live.

24 And *Jesus* went with him; and much people followed him, and thronged him.

BOTTLES (CONCLUDED). TIME, AUTUMN, A. D. 28; PLACE, CAPERNAUM.

CHAP. 5.

35 But the days will come, when
the bridegroom shall [i]be taken away
from them, and [k]then shall they fast
in those days.

36 [l]And he spake also a parable unto them; No man putteth a piece of a
new garment upon an old; if otherwise, then both the new maketh a rent,
and the piece that was *taken* out of
the new agreeth not with the old.

37 And no man putteth new wine
into old bottles; else the new wine will
burst the bottles, and be spilled, and
the bottles shall perish.

38 But new wine must be put into
new bottles; and both are preserved.

39 No man also having drunk old
wine straightway desireth new; for he
saith, The old is better. (p. 115.)

I

Dan. 9. 26 And after threescore and two weeks shall Messiah be cut off, but not for himself: and the people of the prince that shall come shall destroy

I—CONCLUDED.

the city and the sanctuary; and the end thereof *shall be* with a flood, and unto the end of the war desolations are determined.

Zech. 13. 7 Awake, O sword, against my Shepherd, and against the man *that is* my fellow, saith the LORD of hosts: smite the Shepherd, and the sheep shall be scattered: and I will turn mine hand upon the little ones.

John 7. 33 Then said Jesus unto them, Yet a little while am I with you, and *then* I go unto him that sent me.

K

Isa. 22. 12 And in that day did the Lord GOD of hosts call to weeping, and to mourning, and to baldness, and to girding with sackcloth:

Matt. 6. 16 Moreover when ye fast, be not, as the hypocrites, of a sad countenance: for they disfigure their faces, that they may appear unto men to fast. Verily I say unto you, They have their reward.

17 But thou, when thou fastest, anoint thine head, and wash thy face:

Acts 13. 2, 3. *See under H.*

II Cor. 6. 4 But in all *things* approving ourselves as the ministers of God, in much patience, in affliction, in necessities, in distresses,

5 In stripes, in imprisonments, in tumults, in labours, in watchings, in fastings;

L

Matt. 9. 16, 17 and Mark 2. 21, 22. *See text of topic.*

ON THE WAY. TIME, AUTUMN, A. D. 28; PLACE, CAPERNAUM.

8; 41–56.

41 [e]And, behold, there came a man
named Jairus, and he was a ruler of
the synagogue; and he fell down at
Jesus' feet, and besought him that he
would come into his house:

42 For he had one only daughter,
about twelve years of age, and she lay
a dying. But as he went the people
thronged him.

B—CONCLUDED.

synagogue sent unto them, saying, *Ye* men *and* brethren, if ye have any word of exhortation for the people, say on.

C

Acts 10. 25 And as Peter was coming in, Cornelius met him, and fell down at his feet, and worshipped *him*.

26 But Peter took him up, saying, Stand up; I myself also am a man.

Rev. 22. 8 And I John saw these things, and heard *them*. And when I had heard and seen, I fell down to worship before the feet of the angel which showed me these things.

D

Ps. 50. 15 And call upon me in the day of trouble: I will deliver thee, and thou shalt glorify me.

Ps. 107. 19 Then they cry unto the LORD in their trouble, *and* he saveth them out of their distresses.

E

Matt. 9. 18 and Mark 5. 22. *See text of topic.*

§ 73. THE RAISING OF JAIRUS' DAUGHTER. THE WOMAN HEALED

CHAP. 9.

20 [f]And, behold, a woman, which was diseased with an issue of blood twelve years, came behind *him*, and touched the hem of his garment:

21 For she said within herself, If I may but touch his garment, I shall be whole.

22 But Jesus turned him about, and when he saw her, he said, Daughter, be of good comfort; [g]thy faith hath made thee whole. And the woman was made whole from that hour.

F

Mark 5. 25 and Luke 8. 43. *See text of topic.*

G

Luke 7. 50 And he said to the woman, Thy faith hath saved thee; go in peace.

Luke 8. 48. *See text of topic.*

Luke 17. 19 And he said unto him, Arise, go thy way: thy faith hath made thee whole.

Luke 18. 42 And Jesus said unto him, Receive thy sight: thy faith hath saved thee.

H

Lev. 15. 25 And if a woman have an issue of her blood many days out of the time of her separation, or if it run beyond the time of her separation; all the days of the issue of her uncleanness shall be as the days of her separation: she *shall be* unclean.

Matt. 9. 20. *See text of topic.*

I

Ps. 108. 12 Give us help from trouble: for vain *is* the help of man.

K

Acts 5. 15 Insomuch that they brought forth the sick into the streets, and laid *them* on beds and couches, that at the least the shadow of Peter passing by might overshadow some of them.

Acts 19. 11 And God wrought special miracles by the hands of Paul:

12 So that from his body were brought unto the sick handkerchiefs or aprons, and the diseases departed from them, and the evil spirits went out of them.

L

Ex. 15. 26 And said, If thou wilt diligently hearken to the voice of the LORD thy God, and wilt do that which is right

CHAP. 5.

25 And a certain woman, [h]which had an issue of blood twelve years,

26 And had suffered many things of many physicians, and had spent all that she had, and [i]was nothing bettered, but rather grew worse,

27 When she had heard of Jesus, came in the press behind, and [k]touched his garment.

28 For she said, If I may touch but his clothes, I shall be whole.

29 And [l]straightway the fountain of her blood was dried up; and she felt in *her* body that she was healed of that plague.

30 And Jesus, immediately knowing in himself that [m]virtue had gone out of him, turned him about in the press, and said, Who touched my clothes?

31 And his disciples said unto him, Thou seest the multitude thronging thee, and sayest thou, Who touched me?

32 And he looked round about to see her that had done this thing.

33 But the woman fearing and trembling, knowing what was done in her, came and fell down before him, [n]and told him all the truth.

34 And he said unto her, Daughter, [o]thy faith hath made thee whole; [p]go in peace, and be whole of thy plague.

35 [q]While he yet spake, there came from the ruler of the synagogue's *house certain* which said, Thy daughter is dead; why troublest thou the Master any further?

L—CONCLUDED.

in his sight, and wilt give ear to his commandments, and keep all his statutes, I will put none of these diseases upon thee, which I have brought upon the Egyptians: for I *am* the LORD that healeth thee.

ON THE WAY (CONTINUED). TIME, AUTUMN, A. D. 28; PLACE, CAPERNAUM.

CHAP. 8.

43 [r]And a woman having an issue of blood twelve years, which had spent all her living upon physicians, neither could be healed of any,

44 Came behind *him*, and [s]touched the border of his garment: and immediately her issue of blood stanched.

45 And Jesus said, Who touched me? When all denied, Peter and they that were with him said, Master, the multitude throng thee and press *thee*, and sayest thou, Who touched me?

46 And Jesus said, Somebody hath touched me: for I perceive that [t]virtue is gone out of me.

47 And when the woman saw that she was not hid, she came trembling, and falling down before him, she declared unto him before all the people for what cause she had touched him, and how she was healed immediately.

48 And he said unto her, Daughter, be of good comfort: thy faith hath made thee whole; go in peace.

49 [u]While he yet spake, there cometh one from the ruler of the synagogue's *house*, saying to him, Thy daughter is dead; trouble not the Master.

M

Luke 6. 19 And the whole multitude sought to touch him: for there went virtue out of him, and healed *them* all.

Luke 8. 46. *See text of topic.*

N

Ps. 30. 2 O LORD my God, I cried unto thee, and thou hast healed me.

Ps. 103. 2 Bless the LORD, O my soul, and forget not all his benefits:

3 Who forgiveth all thine iniquities; who healeth all thy diseases;

4 Who redeemeth thy life from destruction; who crowneth thee with loving-kindness and tender mercies;

5 Who satisfieth thy mouth with

N—CONCLUDED.

good *things; so that* thy youth is renewed like the eagle's.

Ps. 116. 12 What shall I render unto the LORD *for* all his benefits toward me?

13 I will take the cup of salvation, and call upon the name of the LORD.

14 I will pay my vows unto the LORD now in the presence of all his people.

O

Matt. 9. 22. *See text of topic.*

Mark 10. 52 And Jesus said unto him, Go thy way; thy faith hath made thee whole. And immediately he received his sight, and followed Jesus in the way.

Acts 14. 8 And there sat a certain man at Lystra, impotent in his feet, being a cripple from his mother's womb, who never had walked:

9 The same heard Paul speak: who steadfastly beholding him, and perceiving that he had faith to be healed,

10 Said with a loud voice, Stand upright on thy feet. And he leaped and walked.

P

I Sa. 1. 17 Then Eli answered and said, Go in peace: and the God of Israel grant *thee* thy petition that thou hast asked of him.

Eccl. 9. 7 Go thy way, eat thy bread with joy, and drink thy wine with a merry heart; for God now accepteth thy works.

Q

Luke 8. 49. *See text of topic.*

R

Lev. 15. 25. *See under H.*
Matt. 9. 20 and Mark 5. 25. *See text of topic.*

S

Acts 5. 15 and Acts 19. 12. *See under K.*

T

Mark 5. 30. *See text of topic.*
Luke 6. 19. *See under M.*

U

Mark 5. 35. *See text of topic.*

X

Mark 5. 38 and Luke 8. 51. *See text of topic.*

Y

II Chr. 35. 25 And Jeremiah lamented for Josiah: and all the singing men and the singing women spake of Josiah in their lamentations to this day, and made them an ordinance in Israel: and, behold, they *are* written in the lamentations.

Z

Acts 20. 10 And Paul went down, and fell on him, and embracing *him* said, Trouble not yourselves; for his life is in him.

§ 73. THE RAISING OF JAIRUS' DAUGHTER. THE WOMAN HEALED

CHAP. 9.

23 [x]And when Jesus came into the ruler's house, and saw [y]the minstrels and the people making a noise,

24 He said unto them, [z]Give place: for the maid is not dead, but sleepeth. And they laughed him to scorn.

25 But when the people were put forth, he went in, and took her by the hand, and the maid arose.

26 And [1]the fame hereof went abroad into all that land.

For X, Y and Z see preceding page (225).

1

Or, *this fame.*

A

John 11. 25 Jesus said unto her, I am the resurrection, and the life: he that believeth in me, though he were dead, yet shall he live:

John 11. 40 Jesus saith unto her, Said I not unto thee, that, if thou wouldest believe, thou shouldest see the glory of God?

Rom. 4. 20 He staggered not at the promise of God through unbelief: but was strong in faith, giving glory to God;

21 And being fully persuaded, that what he had promised, he was able also to perform.

22 And therefore it was imputed to him for righteousness.

23 Now it was not written for his sake alone, that it was imputed to him;

24 But for us also, to whom it shall be imputed, if we believe on him that raised up Jesus our Lord from the dead;

25 Who was delivered for our offences, and was raised again for our justification.

B

Mark 9. 2 And after six days Jesus taketh *with him* Peter, and James, and John, and leadeth them up into a high mountain apart by themselves: and he was transfigured before them.

Mark 14. 33 And he taketh with him Peter and James and John, and began to be sore amazed, and to be very heavy;

C

Dan. 12. 2 And many of them that sleep in the dust of the earth shall awake, some to everlasting life, and some to shame *and* everlasting contempt.

CHAP. 5.

36 As soon as Jesus heard the word that was spoken, he saith unto the ruler of the synagogue, [a]Be not afraid, only believe.

37 And he suffered no man to follow him, [b]save Peter, and James, and John the brother of James.

38 And he cometh to the house of the ruler of the synagogue, and seeth the tumult, and them that wept and wailed greatly.

39 And when he was come in, he saith unto them, Why make ye this ado, and weep? the damsel is not dead, but [c]sleepeth.

40 And they laughed him to scorn. [d]But when he had put them all out, he taketh the father and the mother of the damsel, and them that were with him, and entereth in where the damsel was lying.

41 And he took the damsel by the hand, and said unto her, Talitha cumi; which is, being interpreted, Damsel, (I say unto thee,) arise.

42 And straightway the [e]damsel arose, and walked; for she was *of the age* of twelve years. And they were astonished with a great astonishment.

43 And [f]he charged them straitly that no man should know it; and [g]commanded that something should be given her to eat.

C—CONTINUED.

John 11. 11 These things said he: and after that he saith unto them, Our friend Lazarus sleepeth; but I go, that I may awake him out of sleep.

Acts 20. 10 And Paul went down, and fell on him, and embracing *him* said, Trouble not yourselves; for his life is in him.

I Cor. 11. 30 For this cause many *are* weak and sickly among you, and many sleep.

ON THE WAY (Concluded). Time, Autumn, A. D. 28; Place, Capernaum.

Chap. 8.

50 But when Jesus heard *it*, he answered him, saying, Fear not: [h]believe only, and she shall be made whole.

51 And when he came into the house, he suffered no man to go in, save Peter, and James, and John, and the father and the mother of the maiden.

52 And all wept, and bewailed her: but he said, Weep not; she is not dead, [i]but sleepeth.

53 And they laughed him to scorn, knowing that she was dead.

54 And he put them all out, and took her by the hand, and called, saying, Maid, [k]arise.

55 And her spirit came again, and she arose straightway: and he commanded to give her meat.

56 And her parents were astonished: but he charged them that they should tell no man what was done. (p. 233.)

C—Concluded.

I Thes. 4. 13 But I would not have you to be ignorant, brethren, concerning them which are asleep, that ye sorrow not, even as others which have no hope.

14 For if we believe that Jesus died and rose again, even so them also which sleep in Jesus will God bring with him.

I Thes. 5. 9 For God hath not appointed us to wrath, but to obtain salvation by our Lord Jesus Christ,

10 Who died for us, that, whether we wake or sleep, we should live together with him.

D

Acts 9. 40 But Peter put them all forth, and kneeled down, and prayed; and turning *him* to the body said, Tabitha, arise. And she opened her eyes: and when she saw Peter, she sat up.

E

Gen. 1. 3 And God said, Let there be light: and there was light.

Ps. 33. 9 For he spake, and it was *done;* he commanded, and it stood fast.

E—Concluded.

Phil. 3. 21 Who shall change our vile body, that it may be fashioned like unto his glorious body, according to the working whereby he is able even to subdue all things unto himself.

F

Matt. 8. 4 And Jesus saith unto him, See thou tell no man; but go thy way, show thyself to the priest, and offer the gift that Moses commanded, for a testimony unto them.

Matt. 9. 30 And their eyes were opened; and Jesus straitly charged them, saying, See *that* no man know *it*.

Matt. 17. 9 And as they came down from the mountain, Jesus charged them, saying, Tell the vision to no man, until the Son of man be risen again from the dead.

Luke 5. 14 And he charged him to tell no man: but go, and show thyself to the priest, and offer for thy cleansing, according as Moses commanded, for a testimony unto them.

G

Luke 24. 42 And they gave him a piece of a broiled fish, and of a honeycomb.

43 And he took *it*, and did eat before them.

Acts 10. 41 Not to all the people, but unto witnesses chosen before of God, *even* to us, who did eat and drink with him after he rose from the dead.

H

II Chr. 20. 20 And they rose early in the morning, and went forth into the wilderness of Tekoa: and as they went forth, Jehoshaphat stood and said, Hear me, O Judah, and ye inhabitants of Jerusalem; Believe in the Lord your God, so shall ye be established; believe his prophets, so shall ye prosper.

Mark 9. 23 Jesus said unto him, If thou canst believe, all things *are* possible to him that believeth.

I

John 11. 11. *See under C.*

John 11. 13 Howbeit Jesus spake of his death: but they thought that he had spoken of taking of rest in sleep.

K

Luke 7. 14 And he came and touched the bier: and they that bare *him* stood still. And he said, Young man, I say unto thee, Arise.

John 11. 43 And when he thus had spoken, he cried with a loud voice, Lazarus, come forth.

§ 74. TWO BLIND MEN HEALED AND A DUMB SPIRIT

Matthew 9 : 27–34.

27 And when Jesus departed thence, two blind men followed him, crying, and saying, [a]*Thou* Son of David, have mercy on us.

28 And when he was come into the house, the blind men came to him: and Jesus saith unto them, Believe ye that I am able to do this? They said unto him, Yea, Lord.

29 Then touched he their eyes, saying, According to your faith be it unto you.

30 And [b]their eyes were opened; and Jesus straitly charged them, saying, [c]See *that* no man know *it*.

31 [d]But they, when they were departed, spread abroad his fame in all that country.

32 [e]As they went out, behold, they brought to him a dumb man possessed with a devil.

33 And when the devil was cast out, the [f]dumb spake: and the multitudes marvelled, saying, [g]It was never so seen in Israel.

34 But the Pharisees said, [h]He casteth out devils through the prince of the devils. (p. 230.)

A

Matt.15. 22 And, behold, a woman of Canaan came out of the same coasts, and cried unto him, saying, Have mercy on me, O Lord, *thou* Son of David; my daughter is grievously vexed with a devil.

Matt.20. 30 And, behold, two blind men sitting by the way side, when they heard that Jesus passed by, cried out, saying, Have mercy on us, O Lord, *thou* Son of David.

31 And the multitude rebuked them, because they should hold their peace: but they cried the more, saying, Have mercy on us, O Lord, *thou* Son of David.

Mark10. 47 And when he heard that it was Jesus of Nazareth, he began to cry out, and say, Jesus, *thou* Son of David, have mercy on me.

48 And many charged him that he should hold his peace: but he cried the more a great deal, *Thou* Son of David, have mercy on me.

Luke18. 38 And he cried, saying, Jesus, *thou* Son of David, have mercy on me.

39 And they which went before rebuked him, that he should hold his peace: but he cried so much the more, *Thou* Son of David, have mercy on me.

B

Ps. 146. 8 The LORD openeth *the eyes of* the blind: the LORD raiseth them that are bowed down: the LORD loveth the righteous:

C

Matt. 8. 4 And Jesus saith unto him, See thou tell no man; but go thy way, show thyself to the priest, and offer the gift that Moses commanded, for a testimony unto them.

§ 75. JESUS AGAIN AT NAZARETH AND AGAIN REJECTED.

Matthew 13 : 54–58.

54 [a]And when he was come into his own country, he taught them in their synagogue, insomuch that they were astonished, and said,

A

Deut.18. 15 The LORD thy God will raise up unto thee a Prophet from the midst of thee, of thy brethren, like unto me; unto him ye shall hearken;

Mark 6 : 1–6.

1 And [b]he went out from thence, and came into his own country; and his disciples follow him.

2 And when the sabbath day was come, he began to teach in the synagogue: and many hearing *him* were astonished, saying,

CAST OUT. TIME, AUTUMN, A. D. 28; PLACE, CAPERNAUM.

C—CONCLUDED.

Matt.12. 14 Then the Pharisees went out, and held a council against him, how they might destroy him.

15 But when Jesus knew *it*, he withdrew himself from thence: and great multitudes followed him, and he healed them all;

16 And charged them that they should not make him known.

Matt.17. 9 And as they came down from the mountain, Jesus charged them, saying, Tell the vision to no man, until the Son of man be risen again from the dead.

Luke 5. 14 And he charged him to tell no man: but go, and show thyself to the priest, and offer for thy cleansing, according as Moses commanded, for a testimony unto them.

D

Mark 7. 36 And he charged them that they should tell no man: but the more he charged them, so much the more a great deal they published *it*;

E

Matt.12. 22 Then was brought unto him one possessed with a devil, blind, and dumb: and he healed him, insomuch that the blind and dumb both spake and saw.

Luke 11 14 And he was casting out a devil, and it was dumb. And it came to pass, when the devil was gone out, the dumb spake; and the people wondered.

F

Ex. 4. 11 And the LORD said unto him, Who hath made man's mouth? or who maketh the dumb, or deaf, or the seeing, or the blind? have not I the LORD?

12 Now therefore go, and I will be with thy mouth, and teach thee what thou shalt say.

F—CONCLUDED.

Isa. 35. 6 Then shall the lame *man* leap as a hart, and the tongue of the dumb sing: for in the wilderness shall waters break out, and streams in the desert.

G

II Ki. 5. 8 And it was *so*, when Elisha the man of God had heard that the king of Israel had rent his clothes, that he sent to the king, saying, Wherefore hast thou rent thy clothes? let him come now to me, and he shall know that there is a prophet in Israel.

Ps. 76. 1 In Judah *is* God known: his name *is* great in Israel.

Jer. 32. 20 Which hast set signs and wonders in the land of Egypt, *even* unto this day, and in Israel, and among *other* men; and hast made thee a name, as at this day;

Luke 7. 9 When Jesus heard these things, he marvelled at him, and turned him about, and said unto the people that followed him, I say unto you, I have not found so great faith, no, not in Israel.

H

Matt.12. 24 But when the Pharisees heard *it*, they said, This *fellow* doth not cast out devils, but by Beelzebub the prince of the devils.

Mark 3. 22 And the scribes which came down from Jerusalem said, He hath Beelzebub, and by the prince of the devils casteth he out devils.

Luke 11. 15 But some of them said, He casteth out devils through Beelzebub the chief of the devils.

John 3. 20 For every one that doeth evil hateth the light, neither cometh to the light, lest his deeds should be reproved.

TIME, AUTUMN, A. D. 28; PLACE, NAZARETH.

A—CONTINUED.

Ps. 40. 10 I have not hid thy righteousness within my heart; I have declared thy faithfulness and thy salvation: I have not concealed thy loving-kindness and thy truth from the great congregation.

John 1. 11 He came unto his own, and his own received him not.

Matt. 2. 23 And he came and dwelt in a city called Nazareth: that it might be fulfilled which was spoken by the prophets, He shall be called a Nazarene.

Mark 6. 1. *See text of topic.*

A—CONCLUDED.

Luke 4. 16 And he came to Nazareth, where he had been brought up: and, as his custom was, he went into the synagogue on the sabbath day, and stood up for to read.

Luke 4. 23 And he said unto them, Ye will surely say unto me this proverb, Physician, heal thyself: whatsoever we have heard done in Capernaum, do also here in thy country.

B

Matt. 13. 54. *See text of topic.*
Luke 4. 16. *See under A.*

§ 75. JESUS AGAIN AT NAZARETH AND AGAIN REJECTED

MATTHEW — Chap. 13.

Whence hath this *man* this wisdom, and *these* mighty works?

55 [c]Is not this the carpenter's son? is not his mother called Mary? and [d]his brethren, [e]James, and Joses, and Simon, and Judas?

56 And his sisters, are they not all with us? Whence then hath this *man* all these things?

57 And they [f]were offended in him. But Jesus said unto them, [g]A prophet is not without honour, save in his own country, and in his own house.

58 And [h]he did not many mighty works there because of their unbelief.

(p. 240.)

C

Isa. 53. 2 For he shall grow up before him as a tender plant, and as a root out of a dry ground: he hath no form nor comeliness; and when we shall see him, *there is* no beauty that we should desire him.

MARK — Chap. 6.

[i]From whence hath this *man* these things? and what wisdom *is* this which is given unto him, that even such mighty works are wrought by his hands?

3 Is not [k]this the carpenter, the son of Mary, [l]the brother of James, and Joses, and of Juda, and Simon? and are not his sisters here with us? And they [m]were offended at him.

4 But Jesus said unto them, [n]A prophet is not without honour, but in his own country, and among his own kin, and in his own house.

5 [o]And he could there do no mighty work, save that he laid his hands upon a few sick folk, and healed *them*.

6 And he marvelled because of their unbelief. And he went round about the villages, teaching.

§ 76. JESUS MAKES A THIRD TOUR THROUGHOUT

MATTHEW — 9: 35–38.

35 [a]And Jesus went about all the cities and villages, [b]teaching in their synagogues, and preaching the gospel of the kingdom, and healing every sickness and every disease among the people.

36 [c]But when he saw the multitudes, he was moved with compassion on them, because they [1]fainted, and were scattered abroad, [d]as sheep having no shepherd.

37 Then saith he unto his disciples, [e]The harvest truly *is* plenteous, but the labourers *are* few;

38 [f]Pray ye therefore the Lord of the harvest, that he will send forth labourers into his harvest.

MARK — 6: 6.

6 And he marvelled because of their unbelief. And he went round about the villages, teaching.

A

Mark 6. 6. *See text of topic.*

Luke 13. 22 And he went through the cities and villages, teaching, and journeying toward Jerusalem.

B

Matt. 4. 23 And Jesus went about all Galilee, teaching in their synagogues, and preaching the gospel of the kingdom, and healing all manner of sickness and all manner of disease among the people.

C

Mark 6. 34 And Jesus, when he came out, saw much people, and was moved with compassion toward them, because they were as sheep not having a shepherd: and he began to teach them many things.

1

Or, *were tired and lay down.*

(CONCLUDED). TIME, AUTUMN, A. D. 28; PLACE, NAZARETH.

C—CONCLUDED.

Mark 6. 3. *See text of topic.*

Luke 3. 23 And Jesus himself began to be about thirty years of age, being (as was supposed) the son of Joseph, which was *the son* of Heli,

John 6. 42 And they said, Is not this Jesus, the son of Joseph, whose father and mother we know? how is it then that he saith, I came down from heaven?

D

Matt.12. 46 While he yet talked to the people, behold, *his* mother and his brethren stood without, desiring to speak with him.

E

Mark 15. 40 There were also women looking on afar off: among whom was Mary Magdalene, and Mary the mother of James the less and of Joses, and Salome;

F

Ps. 22. 6 But I *am* a worm, and no man; a reproach of men, and despised of the people.

Matt.11. 6 And blessed is *he*, whosoever shall not be offended in me.

Mark 6. 3, 4. *See text of topic.*

G

Luke 4. 24 And he said, Verily I say unto

G—CONCLUDED.

you, No prophet is accepted in his own country.

H

Mark 6. 5, 6. *See text of topic.*

Heb. 3. 19 So we see that they could not enter in because of unbelief.

Heb. 4. 2 For unto us was the gospel preached, as well as unto them: but the word preached did not profit them, not being mixed with faith in them that heard *it.*

I

John 6. 42. *See under C.*

K

Isa. 53. 2. *See under C.*

I Cor. 1. 23 But we preach Christ crucified, unto the Jews a stumblingblock, and unto the Greeks foolishness:

L

Matt. 12. 46. *See under D.*

Gal. 1. 19 But other of the apostles saw I none, save James the Lord's brother.

M

Matt. 11. 6. *See under F.*

N

Matt. 13. 57. *See text of topic.*

O

Gen. 19. 22 Haste thee, escape thither; for I cannot do anything till thou be come thither. Therefore the name of the city was called Zoar.

GALILEE. TIME, WINTER, A. D. 29.

D

Num.27. 17 Which may go out before them, and which may go in before them, and which may lead them out, and which may bring them in; that the congregation of the LORD be not as sheep which have no shepherd.

I Ki. 22. 17 And he said, I saw all Israel scattered upon the hills, as sheep that have not a shepherd: and the LORD said, These have no master: let them return every man to his house in peace.

Eze. 34. 5 And they were scattered, because *there is* no shepherd: and they became meat to all the beasts of the field, when they were scattered.

Zech.10. 2 For the idols have spoken vanity, and the diviners have seen a lie, and have told false dreams; they comfort in vain: therefore they went their way as a flock, they were troubled, because *there was* no shepherd.

E

Luke 10. 2 Therefore said he unto them, The harvest truly *is* great, but the labourers *are* few: pray ye therefore the

E—CONCLUDED.

Lord of the harvest, that he would send forth labourers into his harvest.

John 4. 35 Say not ye, There are yet four months, and *then* cometh harvest? behold, I say unto you, Lift up your eyes, and look on the fields; for they are white already to harvest.

F

Acts 13. 2 As they ministered to the Lord, and fasted, the Holy Ghost said, Separate me Barnabas and Saul for the work whereunto I have called them.

Acts 20. 28 Take heed therefore unto yourselves, and to all the flock, over the which the Holy Ghost hath made you overseers, to feed the church of God, which he hath purchased with his own blood.

Eph. 4. 11 And he gave some, apostles; and some, prophets; and some, evangelists; and some, pastors and teachers;

II Thes.3. 1 Finally, brethren, pray for us, that the word of the Lord may have *free* course, and be glorified, even as *it is* with you:

§ 77. THE TWELVE INSTRUCTED AND SENT FORTH.

MATTHEW 10: 1, 5–42.

1 And [a]when he had called unto *him* his twelve disciples, he gave them power [1]*against* unclean spirits, to cast them out, and to heal all manner of sickness and all manner of disease. p. 122.

* * * * *

5 These twelve Jesus sent forth, and commanded them, saying, [b]Go not into the way of the Gentiles, and into *any* city of [c]the Samaritans enter ye not:

6 [d]But go rather to the [e]lost sheep of the house of Israel.

7 [f]And as ye go, preach, saying, [g]The kingdom of heaven is at hand.

8 Heal the sick, cleanse the lepers, raise the dead, cast out devils: [h]freely ye have received, freely give.

9 [i][2]Provide neither gold, nor silver, [k]nor brass in your purses;

10 Nor scrip for *your* journey, neither two coats, neither shoes, nor yet [3]staves: [l]for the workman is worthy of his meat.

A

Mark 3. 13 And he goeth up into a mountain, and calleth *unto him* whom he would: and they came unto him.

14 And he ordained twelve, that they should be with him, and that he might send them forth to preach,

Mark 6. 7. *See text of topic.*

Luke 6. 13 And when it was day, he called *unto him* his disciples: and of them he chose twelve, whom also he named apostles;

Luke 9. 1. *See text of topic.*

1

Or, *over.*

B

Matt. 4. 15 The land of Zabulon, and the land of Nephthalim, *by* the way of the sea, beyond Jordan, Galilee of the Gentiles;

Acts 11. 1 And the apostles and brethren that were in Judæa heard that the Gentiles had also received the word of God.

MARK 6: 7–13.

7 [m]And he called *unto him* the twelve, and began to send them forth by two and two; and gave them power over unclean spirits;

8 And commanded them that they should take nothing for *their* journey, save a staff only; no scrip, no bread, no [4]money in *their* purse:

9 But [n]*be* shod with sandals, and not put on two coats.

C

John 4. 9 Then saith the woman of Samaria unto him, How is it that thou, being a Jew, askest drink of me, which am a woman of Samaria? for the Jews have no dealings with the Samaritans.

D

Matt. 15. 24 But he answered and said, I am not sent but unto the lost sheep of the house of Israel.

E

Ps. 119. 176 I have gone astray like a lost sheep: seek thy servant; for I do not forget thy commandments.

Isa. 53. 6 All we like sheep have gone astray; we have turned every one to his own way; and the LORD hath laid on him the iniquity of us all.

Jer. 50. 6 My people hath been lost sheep: their shepherds have caused them to go astray, they have turned them away *on* the mountains: they have gone from mountain to hill, they have forgotten their resting place.

Jer. 50. 17 Israel *is* a scattered sheep; the lions have driven *him* away: first the king of Assyria hath devoured him; and last this Nebuchadrezzar king of Babylon hath broken his bones.

Eze. 34. 5 And they were scattered, because *there is* no shepherd: and they became meat to all the beasts of the field, when they were scattered.

6 My sheep wandered through all the mountains, and upon every high hill: yea, my flock was scattered upon all the face of the earth, and none did search or seek *after them.*

Eze. 34. 15 I will feed my flock, and I will cause them to lie down, saith the Lord GOD.

16 I will seek that which was lost, and bring again that which was driven away, and will bind up *that which was*

TIME, WINTER, A. D. 29; PLACE, GALILEE.

9: 1–6.

1 Then [o]he called his twelve disciples together, and gave them [p]power and authority over all devils, and to cure diseases.

2 And [q]he sent them to preach the kingdom of God, and to heal the sick.

3 [r]And he said unto them, Take nothing for *your* journey, neither staves, nor scrip, neither bread, neither money; neither have two coats apiece.

E—CONCLUDED.

broken, and will strenghten that which was sick: but I will destroy the fat and the strong; I will feed them with judgment.

I Pet. 2. 25 For ye were as sheep going astray; but are now returned unto the Shepherd and Bishop of your souls.

F

Luke 9. 2. *See text of topic.*

G

Matt. 3. 2 And saying, Repent ye: for the kingdom of heaven is at hand.

Matt. 4. 17 From that time Jesus began to preach, and to say, Repent: for the kingdom of heaven is at hand.

Luke 10. 9 And heal the sick that are therein, and say unto them, The kingdom of God is come nigh unto you.

H

Acts 8. 18 And when Simon saw that through laying on of the apostles' hands the Holy Ghost was given, he offered them money.

Acts 8. 20 But Peter said unto him, Thy money perish with thee, because thou hast thought that the gift of God may be purchased with money,

I

Mark 6. 8 and Luke 9. 3. *See text of topic.*

Luke 10. 4 Carry neither purse, nor scrip, nor shoes: and salute no man by the way.

Luke 22. 35 And he said unto them, When I sent you without purse, and scrip, and shoes, lacked ye anything? And they said, Nothing.

2

Or, *get.*

K

Mark 6. 8. *See text of topic.*

3

Gr., *a staff.*

L

Luke 10. 7 And in the same house remain, eating and drinking such things as they give: for the labourer is worthy of his hire. Go not from house to house.

I Cor. 9. 7 Who goeth a warfare any time at his own charges? who planteth a vineyard, and eateth not of the fruit thereof? or who feedeth a flock, and eateth not of the milk of the flock?

I Tim. 5. 18 For the Scripture saith, Thou shalt not muzzle the ox that treadeth out the corn. And, The labourer *is* worthy of his reward.

M

Matt. 10. 1. *See text of topic.*
Mark 3. 13. *See under A.*
Luke 9. 1. *See text of topic.*

4

The word in the original signifies *a piece of brass money in value somewhat less than a farthing,* but here it is taken in general for *money.*

Matt. 10. 9 and Luke 9. 3. *See text of topic.*

N

Acts 12. 8 And the angel said unto him, Gird thyself, and bind on thy sandals: and so he did. And he saith unto him, Cast thy garment about thee, and follow me.

O

Matt. 10. 1. *See text of topic.*
Mark 3. 13. *See under A.*
Mark 6. 7. *See text of topic.*

P

John 14. 12 Verily, verily, I say unto you, He that believeth on me, the works that I do shall he do also; and greater *works* than these shall he do; because I go unto my Father.

Acts 3. 6 Then Peter said, Silver and gold have I none; but such as I have give I thee: In the name of Jesus Christ of Nazareth rise up and walk.

Q

Matt. 10. 7, 8. *See text of topic.*
Mark 6. 12. *See text of topic.*

Luke 10. 1 After these things the Lord appointed other seventy also, and sent them two and two before his face into every city and place, whither he himself would come.

Luke 10. 9. *See under G.*

Tit. 1. 9 Holding fast the faithful word as he hath been taught, that he may be able by sound doctrine both to exhort and to convince the gainsayers.

R

Ps. 37. 3 Trust in the LORD, and do good; *so* shalt thou dwell in the land, and verily thou shalt be fed.

Matt. 10. 9 and Mark 6. 8. *See text of topic.*
Luke 10. 4 and Luke 22. 35. *See under I.*

§ 77. THE TWELVE INSTRUCTED AND SENT FORTH

CHAP. 10.

11 [s]And into whatsoever city or town ye shall enter, inquire who in it is worthy; and there abide till ye go thence.

12 And when ye come into a house, salute it.

13 [t]And if the house be worthy, let your peace come upon it: [u]but if it be not worthy, let your peace return to you.

14 [x]And whosoever shall not receive you, nor hear your words, when ye depart out of that house or city, [y]shake off the dust of your feet.

15 Verily I say unto you, [z]It shall be more tolerable for the land of Sodom and Gomorrah in the day of judgment, than for that city.

16 [a]Behold, I send you forth as sheep in the midst of wolves: [b]be ye therefore wise as serpents, and [c5]harmless as doves.

17 But beware of men: for [d]they will deliver you up to the councils, and [e]they will scourge you in their synagogues;

18 And [f]ye shall be brought before governors and kings for my sake, for a testimony against them and the Gentiles.

19 [g]But when they deliver you up, take no thought how or what ye shall speak: for [h]it shall be given you in that same hour what ye shall speak.

S

Luke 10. 8 And into whatsoever city ye enter, and they receive you, eat such things as are set before you:

T

Luke 10. 5 And into whatsoever house ye enter, first say, Peace *be* to this house.

CHAP. 6.

10 [i]And he said unto them, In what place soever ye enter into a house, there abide till ye depart from that place.

11 [k]And whosoever shall not receive you, nor hear you, when ye depart thence, [l]shake off the dust under your feet for a testimony against them. [m]Verily I say unto you, It shall be more tolerable for Sodom and Gomorrah in the day of judgment, than for that city. (p. 240.)

U

Ps. 35. 13 But as for me, when they were sick, my clothing *was* sackcloth: I humbled my soul with fasting; and my prayer returned into mine own bosom.

X

Mark 6. 11. *See text of topic.*

Luke 10. 10 But into whatsoever city ye enter, and they receive you not, go your ways out into the streets of the same, and say,

11 Even the very dust of your city, which cleaveth on us, we do wipe off against you: notwithstanding, be ye sure of this, that the kingdom of God is come nigh unto you.

Luke 9. 5. *See text of topic.*

Y

Neh. 5. 13 Also I shook my lap, and said, So God shake out every man from his house, and from his labour, that performeth not this promise, even thus be he shaken out, and emptied. And all the congregation said, Amen, and praised the LORD. And the people did according to this promise.

Acts 13. 51 But they shook off the dust of their feet against them, and came unto Iconium.

Acts 18. 6 And when they opposed themselves, and blasphemed, he shook *his* raiment, and said unto them, Your blood *be* upon your own heads; I *am* clean; from henceforth I will go unto the Gentiles.

Z

Matt. 11. 22 But I say unto you, It shall be more tolerable for Tyre and Sidon at the day of judgment, than for you.

(Continued). Time, Winter, A. D. 29; Place, Galilee.

Chap. 9.

4 [n]And whatsoever house ye enter into, there abide, and thence depart.

5 [o]And whosoever will not receive you, when ye go out of that city, shake off the very dust from [p]your feet for a testimony against them. (p. 241.)

Z—Concluded.

Matt.11. 24 But I say unto you, That it shall be more tolerable for the land of Sodom in the day of judgment, than for thee.

A

Luke 10. 3 Go your ways: behold, I send you forth as lambs among wolves.

B

Rom.16. 19 For your obedience is come abroad unto all *men*. I am glad therefore on your behalf: but yet I would have you wise unto that which is good, and simple concerning evil.

Eph. 5. 15 See then that ye walk circumspectly, not as fools, but as wise.

C

I Cor.14. 20 Brethren, be not children in understanding: howbeit in malice be ye children, but in understanding be men.

Phil. 2. 15 That ye may be blameless and harmless, the sons of God, without rebuke, in the midst of a crooked and perverse nation, among whom ye shine as lights in the world;

5
Or, *simple*.

D

Matt.24. 9 Then shall they deliver you up to be afflicted, and shall kill you: and ye shall be hated of all nations for my name's sake.

Mark 13. 9 But take heed to yourselves: for they shall deliver you up to councils; and in the synagogues ye shall be beaten: and ye shall be brought before rulers and kings for my sake, for a testimony against them.

Luke 12. 11 And when they bring you unto the synagogues, and *unto* magistrates, and powers, take ye no thought how or what thing ye shall answer, or what ye shall say:

Luke 21. 12 But before all these, they shall lay their hands on you, and persecute *you*, delivering *you* up to the synagogues, and into prisons, being brought before kings and rulers for my name's sake.

E

Acts 5. 40 And to him they agreed; and when they had called the apostles, and beaten *them*, they commanded that they should not speak in the name of Jesus, and let them go.

F

Acts 12. 1 Now about that time Herod the king stretched forth *his* hands to vex certain of the church.

Acts 24. 10 Then Paul, after that the governor had beckoned unto him to speak, answered, Forasmuch as I know that thou hast been of many years a judge unto this nation, I do the more cheerfully answer for myself:

Acts 25. 7 And when he was come, the Jews which came down from Jerusalem stood round about, and laid many and grievous complaints against Paul, which they could not prove.

Acts 25. 23 And on the morrow, when Agrippa was come, and Bernice, with great pomp, and was entered into the place of hearing, with the chief captains, and principal men of the city, at Festus' commandment Paul was brought forth.

II Tim.4. 16 At my first answer no man stood with me, but all *men* forsook me: *I pray God* that it may not be laid to their charge.

G

Mark 13. 11 But when they shall lead *you*, and deliver you up, take no thought beforehand what ye shall speak, neither do ye premeditate: but whatsoever shall be given you in that hour, that speak ye: for it is not ye that speak, but the Holy Ghost.

Luke 12. 11. *See under D.*

H

Ex. 4. 12 Now therefore go, and I will be with thy mouth, and teach thee what thou shalt say.

Jer. 1. 7 But the Lord said unto me, Say not, I *am* a child: for thou shalt go to all that I shall send thee, and whatsoever I command thee thou shalt speak.

I

Matt. 10. 11 and Luke 9. 4. *See text of topic.*
Luke 10. 8. *See under S.*

K

Matt. 10. 14. *See text of topic.*
Luke 10. 10. *See under X.*

L

Acts 13. 51 and Acts 18. 6. *See under Y.*

M

Heb. 10. 31 *It is* a fearful thing to fall into the hands of a living God.

For N, O and P see next page (236).

§ 77. THE TWELVE INSTRUCTED AND SENT FORTH

CHAP. 10.

20 [q]For it is not ye that speak, but
the Spirit of your Father which speaketh in you.

21 [r]And the brother shall deliver up
the brother to death, and the father
the child: and the children shall rise
up against *their* parents, and cause
them to be put to death.

22 And [s]ye shall be hated of all *men*
for my name's sake: [t]but he that endureth to the end shall be saved.

23 But [u]when they persecute you in
this city, flee ye into another: for
verily I say unto you, Ye shall not
have gone over the cities of Israel,
[x]till the Son of man be come.

24 [y]The disciple is not above *his*
master, nor the servant above his lord.

25 It is enough for the disciple that
he be as his master, and the servant as
his lord. If [z]they have called the
master of the house [6]Beelzebub, how
much more *shall they call* them of his
household?

26 Fear them not therefore: [a]for
there is nothing covered, that shall not
be revealed; and hid, that shall not be
known.

27 What I tell you in darkness, *that*
speak ye in light: and what ye hear
in the ear, *that* preach ye upon the
housetops.

28 [b]And fear not them which kill
the body, but are not able to kill the
soul: but rather fear him which is able
to destroy both soul and body in hell.

29 Are not two sparrows sold for a
farthing? and one of them shall not
fall on the ground without your Father.

[CHAP. 6.]

N

Matt. 10. 11 and Mark 6. 10. *See text of topic.*

O

Matt. 10. 14. *See text of topic.*

P

Acts 13. 51. *See under Y, page 234.*

Q

II Sa.23. 2 The Spirit of the LORD spake by me, and his word *was* in my tongue.

Acts 4. 8 Then Peter, filled with the Holy Ghost, said unto them, Ye rulers of the people, and elders of Israel,

Acts 6. 10 And they were not able to resist the wisdom and the spirit by which he spake.

II Tim.4. 17 Notwithstanding the Lord stood with me, and strengthened me; that by me the preaching might be fully known, and *that* all the Gentiles might hear: and I was delivered out of the mouth of the lion.

R

Mic. 7. 6 For the son dishonoureth the father, the daughter riseth up against her mother, the daughter in law against her mother in law; a man's enemies *are* the men of his own house.

Matt. 10. 35, 36. *See text of topic.*

Luke 21. 16 And ye shall be betrayed both by parents, and brethren, and kinsfolks, and friends; and *some* of you shall they cause to be put to death.

S

Luke 21. 17 And ye shall be hated of all *men* for my name's sake.

T

Dan. 12. 12 Blessed *is* he that waiteth, and cometh to the thousand three hundred and five and thirty days.

13 But go thou thy way till the end *be*: for thou shalt rest, and stand in thy lot at the end of the days.

Matt.24. 13 But he that shall endure unto the end, the same shall be saved.

Mark 13. 13 And ye shall be hated of all *men* for my name's sake: but he that shall endure unto the end, the same shall be saved.

Gal. 6. 9 And let us not be weary in well doing: for in due season we shall reap, if we faint not.

U

Matt. 2. 13 And when they were departed, behold, the angel of the Lord appeareth to Joseph in a dream, saying, Arise, and take the young child and his mother, and flee into Egypt, and be thou there until I bring thee word

(Continued). Time, Winter, A. D. 29; Place, Galilee.

[Chap. 9.]

U—Concluded.

for Herod will seek the young child to destroy him.

Matt. 4. 12 Now when Jesus had heard that John was cast into prison, he departed into Galilee;

Matt.12. 15 But when Jesus knew *it*, he withdrew himself from thence: and great multitudes followed him, and he healed them all:

Acts 8. 1 And Saul was consenting unto his death. And at that time there was a great persecution against the church which was at Jerusalem; and they were all scattered abroad throughout the regions of Judæa and Samaria, except the apostles.

Acts 9. 25 Then the disciples took him by night, and let *him* down by the wall in a basket.

Acts 14. 6 They were ware of *it*, and fled unto Lystra and Derbe, cities of Lycaonia, and unto the region that lieth round about:

X

Matt.16. 28 Verily I say unto you, There be some standing here, which shall not taste of death, till they see the Son of man coming in his kingdom.

Acts 2. 1 And when the day of Pentecost was fully come, they were all with one accord in one place.

Y

Luke 6. 40 The disciple is not above his master: but every one that is perfect shall be as his master.

John 13. 16 Verily, verily, I say unto you, The servant is not greater than his lord; neither he that is sent greater than he that sent him.

John 15. 20 Remember the word that I said unto you, The servant is not greater than his lord. If they have persecuted me, they will also persecute you; if they have kept my saying, they will keep yours also.

Z

Matt.12. 24 But when the Pharisees heard *it*, they said, This *fellow* doth not cast out devils, but by Beelzebub the prince of the devils.

Mark 3. 22 And the scribes which came down from Jerusalem said, He hath Beelzebub, and by the prince of the devils casteth he out devils.

Luke 11. 15 But some of them said, He casteth out devils through Beelzebub the chief of the devils.

Z—Concluded.

John 8. 48 Then answered the Jews, and said unto him, Say we not well that thou art a Samaritan, and hast a devil?

John 8. 52 Then said the Jews unto him, Now we know that thou hast a devil. Abraham is dead, and the prophets; and thou sayest, If a man keep my saying, he shall never taste of death.

6

Gr., *Beelzebul.*

A

Mark 4. 22 For there is nothing hid, which shall not be manifested; neither was any thing kept secret, but that it should come abroad.

Luke 8. 17 For nothing is secret, that shall not be made manifest; neither *any thing* hid, that shall not be known and come abroad.

Luke 12. 2 For there is nothing covered, that shall not be revealed; neither hid, that shall not be known.

3 Therefore, whatsoever ye have spoken in darkness shall be heard in the light; and that which ye have spoken in the ear in closets shall be proclaimed upon the housetops.

B

Isa. 8. 12 Say ye not, A confederacy, to all *them to* whom this people shall say, A confederacy; neither fear ye their fear, nor be afraid.

13 Sanctify the Lord of hosts himself; and *let* him *be* your fear, and *let* him *be* your dread.

Isa. 51. 7 Hearken unto me, ye that know righteousness, the people in whose heart *is* my law; fear ye not the reproach of men, neither be ye afraid of their revilings.

8 For the moth shall eat them up like a garment, and the worm shall eat them like wool: but my righteousness shall be for ever, and my salvation from generation to generation.

Luke 12. 4 And I say unto you my friends, Be not afraid of them that kill the body, and after that have no more that they can do.

Acts. 21. 13 Then Paul answered, What mean ye to weep and to break mine heart? for I am ready not to be bound only, but also to die at Jerusalem for the name of the Lord Jesus.

I Pet. 3. 14 But and if ye suffer for righteousness' sake, happy *are ye:* and be not afraid of their terror, neither be troubled;

§ 77. THE TWELVE INSTRUCTED AND SENT FORTH

Chap. 10.

30 [c]But the very hairs of your head are all numbered.

31 Fear ye not therefore, ye are of more value than many sparrows.

32 [d]Whosoever therefore shall confess me before men, [e]him will I confess also before my Father which is in heaven.

33 [f]But whosoever shall deny me before men, him will I also deny before my Father which is in heaven.

34 [g]Think not that I am come to send peace on earth: I came not to send peace, but a sword.

35 For I am come to set a man at variance [h]against his father, and the daughter against her mother, and the daughter in law against her mother in law.

36 [i]And a man's foes *shall be* they of his own household.

37 [k]He that loveth father or mother more than me is not worthy of me: and he that loveth son or daughter more than me is not worthy of me.

38 [l]And he that taketh not his cross, and followeth after me, is not worthy of me.

39 [m]He that findeth his life shall lose it: and he that loseth his life for my sake shall find it.

40 [n]He that receiveth you receiveth me; and he that receiveth me receiveth him that sent me.

41 [o]He that receiveth a prophet in the name of a prophet shall receive a prophet's reward; and he that receiveth a righteous man in the name of a righteous man shall receive a righteous man's reward.

[Chap. 6.]

C

I Sa. 14. 45 And the people said unto Saul, Shall Jonathan die, who hath wrought this great salvation in Israel? God forbid: *as* the Lord liveth, there shall not one hair of his head fall to the ground; for he hath wrought with God this day. So the people rescued Jonathan, that he died not.

II Sa. 14. 11 Then said she, I pray thee, let the king remember the Lord thy God, that thou wouldest not suffer the revengers of blood to destroy any more, lest they destroy my son. And he said, *As* the Lord liveth, there shall not one hair of thy son fall to the earth.

Luke 21. 18 But there shall not a hair of your head perish.

Acts 27. 34 Wherefore I pray you to take *some* meat; for this is for your health: for there shall not a hair fall from the head of any of you.

D

Luke 12. 8 Also I say unto you, Whosoever shall confess me before men, him shall the Son of man also confess before the angels of God:

Rom. 10. 9 That if thou shalt confess with thy mouth the Lord Jesus, and shalt believe in thine heart that God hath raised him from the dead, thou shalt be saved.

10 For with the heart man believeth unto righteousness; and with the mouth confession is made unto salvation.

E

Rev. 3. 5 He that overcometh, the same shall be clothed in white raiment; and I will not blot out his name out of the book of life, but I will confess his name before my Father, and before his angels.

F

Mark 8. 38 Whosoever therefore shall be ashamed of me and of my words, in this adulterous and sinful generation, of him also shall the Son of man be ashamed, when he cometh in the glory of his Father with the holy angels.

Luke 9. 26 For whosoever shall be ashamed of me and of my words, of him shall the Son of man be ashamed, when he shall come in his own glory, and *in his* Father's, and of the holy angels.

(CONTINUED). TIME, WINTER, A. D. 29; PLACE, GALILEE.

[CHAP. 9.]

F—CONCLUDED.

II Tim. 2. 12 If we suffer, we shall also reign with *him:* if we deny *him,* he also will deny us:

G

Luke 12. 49 I am come to send fire on the earth; and what will I, if it be already kindled?

Luke 12. 51 Suppose ye that I am come to give peace on earth? I tell you, Nay; but rather division:

52 For from henceforth there shall be five in one house divided, three against two, and two against three.

53 The father shall be divided against the son, and the son against the father; the mother against the daughter, and the daughter against the mother; the mother in law against her daughter in law, and the daughter in law against her mother in law.

H

Mic. 7. 6. *See under R, page 236.*

I

Ps. 41. 9 Yea, mine own familiar friend, in whom I trusted, which did eat of my bread, hath lifted up *his* heel against me.

Ps. 55. 13 But *it was* thou, a man mine equal, my guide, and mine acquaintance.

Mic. 7. 6. *See under R, page 236.*

John 13. 18 I speak not of you all: I know whom I have chosen: but that the Scripture may be fulfilled, He that eateth bread with me hath lifted up his heel against me.

K

Luke 14. 26 If any *man* come to me, and hate not his father, and mother, and wife, and children, and brethren, and sisters, yea, and his own life also, he cannot be my disciple.

L

Matt. 16. 24 Then said Jesus unto his disciples, If any *man* will come after me, let him deny himself, and take up his cross, and follow me.

Mark 8. 34 And when he had called the people *unto him* with his disciples also, he said unto them, Whosoever will come after me, let him deny himself, and take up his cross, and follow me.

Luke 9. 23 And he said to *them* all, If any *man* will come after me, let him deny himself, and take up his cross daily, and follow me.

Luke 14. 27 And whosoever doth not bear his

L—CONCLUDED.

cross, and come after me, cannot be my disciple.

M

Matt. 16. 25 For whosoever will save his life shall lose it: and whosoever will lose his life for my sake shall find it.

Luke 17. 33 Whosoever shall seek to save his life shall lose it; and whosoever shall lose his life shall preserve it.

John 12. 25 He that loveth his life shall lose it; and he that hateth his life in this world shall keep it unto life eternal.

N

Matt. 18. 5 And whoso shall receive one such little child in my name receiveth me.

Luke 9. 48 And said unto them, Whosoever shall receive this child in my name receiveth me; and whosoever shall receive me, receiveth him that sent me: for he that is least among you all, the same shall be great.

Luke 10. 16 He that heareth you heareth me; and he that despiseth you despiseth me; and he that despiseth me despiseth him that sent me.

John 12. 44 Jesus cried and said, He that believeth on me, believeth not on me, but on him that sent me.

John 13. 20 Verily, verily, I say unto you, He that receiveth whomsoever I send receiveth me; and he that receiveth me receiveth him that sent me.

Gal. 4. 14 And my temptation which was in my flesh ye despised not, nor rejected; but received me as an angel of God, *even* as Christ Jesus.

I Thes. 4. 8 He therefore that despiseth, despiseth not man, but God, who hath also given unto us his Holy Spirit.

O

I Ki. 17. 10 So he arose and went to Zarephath. And when he came to the gate of the city, behold, the widow woman *was* there gathering of sticks: and he called to her, and said, Fetch me, I pray thee, a little water in a vessel, that I may drink.

I Ki. 18. 4 For it was *so,* when Jezebel cut off the prophets of the LORD, that Obadiah took a hundred prophets, and hid them by fifty in a cave, and fed them with bread and water.)

II Ki. 4. 8 And it fell on a day, that Elisha passed to Shunem, where *was* a great woman; and she constrained him to eat bread. And *so* it was, *that* as oft as he passed by, he turned in thither to eat bread.

§ 77. THE TWELVE INSTRUCTED AND SENT FORTH

CHAP. 10.

42 [p]And whosoever shall give to drink unto one of these little ones a cup of cold *water* only in the name of a disciple, verily I say unto you, [q]he shall in no wise lose his reward.

CHAP. 11.

1 And it came to pass, when Jesus had made an end of commanding his twelve disciples, he departed thence to teach and to preach in their cities. p. 154.

P

Matt.18. 5 And whoso shall receive one such little child in my name receiveth me.

CHAP. 6.

12 And they went out, and preached that men should repent.

13 And they cast out many devils, [r]and anointed with oil many that were sick, and healed *them*.

P—CONTINUED.

Matt.18. 6 But whoso shall offend one of these little ones which believe in me, it were better for him that a millstone were hanged about his neck, and *that* he were drowned in the depth of the sea.

Matt.25. 40 And the King shall answer and say unto them, Verily I say unto you, Inasmuch as ye have done *it* unto one of the least of these my brethren, ye have done *it* unto me.

§ 78. HEROD'S OPINION OF JESUS.

14 : 1, 2.

1 At that time [a]Herod the tetrarch heard of the fame of Jesus,

2 And said unto his servants, [b]This is John the Baptist; he is risen from the dead; and therefore mighty works [1]do show forth themselves in him. p. 78.

A

Mark 6. 14 and Luke 9. 7. *See text of topic.*

Acts 4. 27 For of a truth against thy holy child Jesus, whom thou hast anointed, both Herod, and Pontius Pilate, with the Gentiles, and the people of Israel, were gathered together,

B

Matt.11. 11 Verily I say unto you, Among them that are born of women there hath not risen a greater than John the Baptist: notwithstanding, he that is least in the kingdom of heaven is greater than he.

Matt.16. 14 And they said, Some *say that thou art* John the Baptist; some, Elias; and others, Jeremias, or one of the prophets.

Mark 8. 28 And they answered, John the Baptist: but some *say*, Elias; and others, One of the prophets.

John 10. 41 And many resorted unto him, and said, John did no miracle: but all things that John spake of this man were true.

1

Or, *are wrought by him.*

6 : 14–16.

14 [c]And king Herod heard *of him;* (for his name was spread abroad;) and he said, That John the Baptist was risen from the dead, and therefore mighty works do show forth themselves in him.

15 [d]Others said, That it is Elias. And others said, That it is a prophet, or as one of the prophets.

16 [e]But when Herod heard *thereof*, he said, It is John, whom I beheaded: he is risen from the dead. (p. 78.)

C

Matt. 14. 1 and Luke 9. 7. *See text of topic.*

D

Matt. 16. 14. *See under B.*

Matt.17. 10 And his disciples asked him, saying, Why then say the scribes that Elias must first come?

11 And Jesus answered and said unto them, Elias truly shall first come, and restore all things.

Luke 1. 17 And he shall go before him in the spirit and power of Elias, to turn the hearts of the fathers to the children, and the disobedient to the wisdom of the just: to make ready a people prepared for the Lord.

John 1. 20 And he confessed, and denied not; but confessed, I am not the Christ.

(CONCLUDED). TIME, WINTER, A. D. 29; PLACE, GALILEE.

CHAP. 9.

6 [s]And they departed, and went through the towns, preaching the gospel, and healing every where.

P—CONCLUDED.

Mark 9. 41 For whosoever shall give you a cup of water to drink in my name, because ye belong to Christ, verily I say unto you, he shall not lose his reward.

Heb. 6. 10 For God *is* not unrighteous to forget your work and labour of love, which ye have showed toward his name, in that ye have ministered to the saints, and do minister.

Q

Prov.24. 14 So *shall* the knowledge of wisdom *be* unto thy soul: when thou hast found *it*, then there shall be a reward, and thy expectation shall not be cut off.

Q—CONCLUDED.

Luke 6. 35 But love ye your enemies, and do good, and lend, hoping for nothing again; and your reward shall be great, and ye shall be the children of the Highest: for he is kind unto the unthankful and *to* the evil.

II Cor.9. 6 But this *I say*, He which soweth sparingly shall reap also sparingly; and he which soweth bountifully shall reap also bountifully.

R

Jas. 5. 14 Is any sick among you? let him call for the elders of the church; and let them pray over him, anointing him with oil in the name of the Lord:

S

Mark 6. 12. *See text of topic.*

TIME, WINTER, A. D. 29; PLACE, GALILEE, PERÆA.

9: 7–9.

7 [f]Now Herod the tetrarch heard of all that was done by him: and he was perplexed, because that it was said of some, that John was risen from the dead;

8 And of some, that Elias had appeared; and of others, that one of the old prophets was risen again.

9 And Herod said, John have I beheaded; but who is this, of whom I hear such things? [g]And he desired to see him. (p. 245.)

D—CONCLUDED.

John 1. 21 And they asked him, What then? Art thou Elias? And he saith, I am not. Art thou that Prophet? And he answered, No.

John 1. 25 And they asked him, and said unto him, Why baptizest thou then, if thou be not that Christ, nor Elias, neither that Prophet?

E

Ps. 53. 5 There were they in great fear, *where* no fear was: for God hath scattered the bones of him that encampeth *against* thee: thou hast put *them* to shame, because God hath despised them.

Matt. 14. 2. *See text of topic.*

E—CONCLUDED.

Luke 3. 19 But Herod the tetrarch, being reproved by him for Herodias his brother Philip's wife, and for all the evils which Herod had done,

Rev. 11. 10 And they that dwell upon the earth shall rejoice over them, and make merry, and shall send gifts one to another; because these two prophets tormented them that dwelt on the earth.

11 And after three days and a half the Spirit of life from God entered into them, and they stood upon their feet; and great fear fell upon them which saw them.

12 And they heard a great voice from heaven saying unto them, Come up hither. And they ascended up to heaven in a cloud; and their enemies beheld them.

13 And the same hour was there a great earthquake, and the tenth part of the city fell, and in the earthquake were slain of men seven thousand: and the remnant were affrighted, and gave glory to the God of heaven.

F

Matt. 14. 1 and Mark 6. 14. *See text of topic.*

G

Luke 23. 8 And when Herod saw Jesus, he was exceeding glad: for he was desirous to see him of a long *season*, because he had heard many things of him; and he hoped to have seen some miracle done by him.

§ 79. THE FATE OF JOHN THE BAPTIST.

14 : 6–12.

6 But when Herod's [a]birthday was kept, the daughter of Herodias danced [1]before them, and pleased Herod.

7 Whereupon he promised with an oath to give her whatsoever she would ask.

8 And she, being before instructed of her mother, said, Give me here John Baptist's head in a charger.

9 And the king was sorry: [b]nevertheless for the oath's sake, and them which sat with him at meat, he commanded *it* to be given *her*.

10 And he sent, and beheaded John in the prison.

11 And his head was brought in a charger, and given to the damsel: and she brought *it* to her mother.

12 And his disciples came, and took up the body, and buried it, and went and told Jesus.

A

Gen. 40. 20 And it came to pass the third day, *which was* Pharaoh's birthday, that he made a feast unto all his servants: and he lifted up the head of the chief butler and of the chief baker among his servants.

1

Gr., *in the midst.*

B

Tit. 1. 16 They profess that they know God; but in works they deny *him*, being abominable, and disobedient, and unto every good work reprobate.

C

Matt. 14. 6. *See text of topic.*

D

Gen. 40. 20. *See under A.*
Esth. 1. 3 In the third year of his reign, he made a feast unto all his princes and his servants; the power of Persia and Media, the nobles and princes of the provinces, *being* before him:
4 When he showed the riches of his glorious kingdom and the honour of his excellent majesty many days, *even* a hundred and fourscore days.

6 : 21–29.

21 [c]And when a convenient day was come, that Herod [d]on his birthday made a supper to his lords, high captains, and chief *estates* of Galilee;

22 And when [e]the daughter of the said Herodias came in, and danced, and pleased Herod and them that sat with him, the king said unto the damsel, Ask of me whatsoever thou wilt, and I will give *it* thee.

23 And he sware unto her, [f]Whatsoever thou shalt ask of me, I will give *it* thee, unto the half of my kingdom.

24 And she went forth, and said unto her mother, What shall I ask? And she said, the [g]head of John the Baptist.

25 And she came in straightway with haste unto the king, and asked, saying, I will that thou give me by and by in a charger the head of John the Baptist.

26 [h]And the king was exceeding sorry; *yet* for his oath's sake, and for their sakes which sat with him, he would not reject her.

27 And immediately the king sent [2]an executioner, and commanded his head to be brought: and he went and beheaded him in the prison,

28 And brought his head in a charger, and gave it to the damsel; and the damsel gave it to her mother.

29 And when his disciples heard *of it*, they came and [i]took up his corpse, and laid it in a tomb.

D—Continued.

Esth. 1. 5 And when these days were expired, the king made a feast unto all the people that were present in Shushan the palace, both unto great and small, seven days, in the court of the garden of the king's palace;

TIME, WINTER, A.D. 29; PLACE, MACHÆRUS IN PERÆA.

D—CONCLUDED.

Esth. 1. 6 *Where were* white, green, and blue *hangings*, fastened with cords of fine linen and purple to silver rings and pillars of marble: the beds *were of* gold and silver, upon a pavement of red, and blue, and white, and black marble.

7 And they gave *them* drink in vessels of gold, (the vessels being diverse one from another,) and royal wine in abundance, according to the state of the king.

Esth. 2. 18 Then the king made a great feast unto all his princes and his servants, *even* Esther's feast; and he made a release to the provinces, and gave gifts, according to the state of the king.

Prov.31. 4 *It is* not for kings, O Lemuel, *it is* not for kings to drink wine; nor for princes strong drink:

5 Lest they drink, and forget the law, and pervert the judgment of any of the afflicted.

Dan. 5. 1 Belshazzar the king made a great feast to a thousand of his lords, and drank wine before the thousand.

2 Belshazzar, while he tasted the wine, commanded to bring the golden and silver vessels which his father Nebuchadnezzar had taken out of the temple which *was* in Jerusalem; that the king and his princes, his wives and his concubines, might drink therein.

3 Then they brought the golden vessels that were taken out of the temple of the house of God which *was* at Jerusalem; and the king and his princes, his wives and his concubines, drank in them.

4 They drank wine, and praised the gods of gold, and of silver, of brass, of iron, of wood, and of stone.

Hos. 7. 5 In the day of our king, the princes have made *him* sick with bottles of wine; he stretched out his hand with scorners.

E

Esth. 1. 10 On the seventh day, when the heart of the king was merry with wine, he commanded Mehuman, Biztha, Harbona, Bigtha, and Abagtha, Zethar, and Carcas, the seven chamberlains that served in the presence of Ahasuerus the king,

11 To bring Vashti the queen before the king with the crown royal, to show the people and the princes her beauty: for she *was* fair to look on.

F

Esth. 5. 3 Then said the king unto her, What wilt thou, queen Esther? and what *is* thy request? it shall be even given thee to the half of the kingdom.

Esth. 5. 6 And the king said unto Esther at the banquet of wine, What *is* thy petition? and it shall be granted thee: and what *is* thy request? even to the half of the kingdom it shall be performed.

Esth. 7. 2 And the king said again unto Esther on the second day at the banquet of wine, What *is* thy petition, queen Esther? and it shall be granted thee: and what *is* thy request? and it shall be performed, *even* to the half of the kingdom.

Prov. 6. 2 Thou art snared with the words of thy mouth, thou art taken with the words of thy mouth.

G

Job 31. 31 If the men of my tabernacle said not, Oh that we had of his flesh! we cannot be satisfied.

Ps. 37. 12 The wicked plotteth against the just, and gnasheth upon him with his teeth.

Prov.12. 10 A righteous *man* regardeth the life of his beast: but the tender mercies of the wicked *are* cruel.

Prov.27. 3 A stone *is* heavy, and the sand weighty; but a fool's wrath *is* heavier than them both.

4 Wrath *is* cruel, and anger *is* outrageous; but who *is* able to stand before envy?

Acts. 23. 12 And when it was day, certain of the Jews banded together, and bound themselves under a curse, saying that they would neither eat nor drink till they had killed Paul.

13 And they were more than forty which had made this conspiracy.

H

Matt. 14. 9. *See text of topic.*

2

Or, *one of his guard.*

I

IIChr.24. 16 And they buried him in the city of David among the kings, because he had done good in Israel, both toward God, and toward his house.

Matt.27. 60 And laid it in his own new tomb, which he had hewn out in the rock: and he rolled a great stone to the door of the sepulchre, and departed.

Acts 8. 2 And devout men carried Stephen *to his burial*, and made great lamentation over him.

§ 80. THE TWELVE RETURN. FIVE THOUSAND ARE FED.

14: 13–21.

13 [a]When Jesus heard of it he departed thence by ship into a desert place apart: and when the people had heard *thereof*, they followed him on foot out of the cities.

14 And Jesus went forth, and saw a great multitude, and [b]was moved with compassion toward them, and he healed their sick.

15 [c]And when it was evening, his disciples came to him, saying, This is a desert place, and the time is now past; send the multitude away, that they may go into the villages, and buy themselves victuals.

16 But Jesus said unto them, They need not depart; [d]give ye them to eat.

A

Matt.10. 23 But when they persecute you in this city, flee ye into another: for verily I say unto you, Ye shall not have gone over the cities of Israel, till the Son of man be come.

Matt.12. 15 But when Jesus knew *it*, he withdrew himself from thence: and great multitudes followed him, and he healed them all;

Mark 6. 32, Luke 9. 10 and John 6. 1. *See text of topic.*

B

Matt. 9. 36 But when he saw the multitudes, he was moved with compassion on them, because they fainted, and were scattered abroad, as sheep having no shepherd.

Mark 6. 34. *See text of topic.*

Heb. 2. 17 Wherefore in all things it behooved him to be made like unto *his* brethren, that he might be a merciful and faithful high priest in things *pertaining* to God, to make reconciliation for the sins of the people.

Heb. 4. 15 For we have not a high priest which cannot be touched with the feeling of our infirmities; but was in all points tempted like as *we are, yet* without sin.

C

Mark 6. 35, Luke 9. 12 and John 6. 5. *See text of topic.*

6: 30–44.

30 [e]And the apostles gathered themselves together unto Jesus, and told him all things, both what they had done, and what they had taught.

31 [f]And he said unto them, Come ye yourselves apart into a desert place, and rest a while: for [g]there were many coming and going, and they had no leisure so much as to eat.

32 [h]And they departed into a desert place by ship privately.

33 And the people saw them departing, and many knew him, and ran afoot thither out of all cities, and outwent them, and came together unto him.

34 [i]And Jesus, when he came out, saw much people, and was moved with compassion toward them, because they were as sheep not having a shepherd: and [k]he began to teach them many things.

35 [l]And when the day was now far spent, his disciples came unto him, and said, This is a desert place, and now the time *is* far passed:

36 Send them away, that they may go into the country round about, and into the villages, and buy themselves bread: for they have nothing to eat.

37 He answered and said unto them, Give ye them to eat.

D

II Ki. 4. 42 And there came a man from Baal-shalisha, and brought the man of God bread of the first-fruits, twenty loaves of barley, and full ears of corn in the husk thereof. And he said, Give unto the people, that they may eat.

43 And his servitor said, What, should I set this before a hundred

TIME, SPRING, A. D. 29; PLACE, NORTHEAST COAST OF THE LAKE OF GALILEE.

9: 10–17.

10 [m]And the apostles, when they were
returned, told him all that they had
done. [n]And he took them, and went
aside privately into a desert place belonging to the city called Bethsaida.

11 And the people, when they knew
it, followed him: and he received
them, and spake unto them of the
kingdom of God, and healed them
that had need of healing.

12 [o]And when the day began to wear
away, then came the twelve, and said
unto him, Send the multitude away,
that they may go into the towns and
country round about, and lodge, and
get victuals: for we are here in a desert
place.

13 But he said unto them, [p]Give ye
them to eat.

D—CONCLUDED.

men? He said again, Give the people, that they may eat: for thus saith the LORD, They shall eat, and shall leave *thereof.*

E

Luke 9. 10. *See text of topic.*

F

Matt. 14. 13. *See text of topic.*

G

Mark 3. 20 And the multitude cometh together again, so that they could not so much as eat bread.

H

Matt. 14. 13. *See text of topic.*

I

Matt. 9. 36. *See under B.* Matt. 14. 14. *See text of topic.*

K

Isa. 54. 13 And all thy children *shall be* taught of the LORD; and great *shall be* the peace of thy children.

Isa. 61. 1 The Spirit of the Lord GOD *is* upon me; because the LORD hath anointed me to preach good tidings unto the meek; he hath sent me to bind up the brokenhearted, to proclaim liberty to the captives, and the opening of the prison to *them that are* bound:

Luke 9. 11. *See text of topic.*

6: 1–14.

1 After [q]these things Jesus went over
the sea of Galilee, which is *the sea* of
Tiberias.

2 And a great multitude followed
him, because they saw his miracles
which he did on them that were
diseased.

3 And Jesus went up into a mountain, and there he sat with his disciples.

4 [r]And the passover, a feast of the
Jews, was nigh.

5 [s]When Jesus then lifted up *his*
eyes, and saw a great company come
unto him, he saith unto Philip, Whence
shall we buy bread, that these may
eat?

6 And this he said to prove him:
for he himself knew what he would
do.

L

Matt. 14. 15 and Luke 9. 12. *See text of topic.*

M

Mark 6. 30. *See text of topic.*

N

Matt. 14. 13. *See text of topic.*

O

Matt. 14. 15, Mark 6. 35 and John 6. 1, 5. *See text of topic.*

P

II Ki. 4. 42, 43. *See under D.*

Q

Matt. 14. 15, Mark 6. 35 and Luke 9. 10, 12. *See text of topic.*

R

Lev. 23. 5 In the fourteenth *day* of the first month at even *is* the LORD'S passover.

Lev. 23. 7 In the first day ye shall have a holy convocation: ye shall do no servile work therein.

Num. 28. 16 And in the fourteenth day of the first month *is* the passover of the LORD.

John 2. 13 And the Jews' passover was at hand, and Jesus went up to Jerusalem,

John 5. 1 After this there was a feast of the Jews; and Jesus went up to Jerusalem.

S

Matt. 14. 14, Mark 6. 35 and Luke 9. 12. *See text of topic.*

§ 80. THE TWELVE RETURN. FIVE THOUSAND ARE FED (CONCLUDED).

CHAP. 14.

17 And they say unto him, We have here but five loaves, and two fishes.

18 He said, Bring them hither to me.

19 And he commanded the multitude to sit down on the grass, and took the five loaves, and the two fishes, and looking up to heaven, [t]he blessed, and brake, and gave the loaves to *his* disciples, and the disciples to the multitude.

20 And they did all eat, and were filled: and they took up of the fragments that remained twelve baskets full.

21 And they that had eaten were about five thousand men, beside women and children.

T

Matt.15. 36 And he took the seven loaves and the fishes, and gave thanks, and brake *them*, and gave to his disciples, and the disciples to the multitude.

U

Num.11. 13 Whence should I have flesh to give unto all this people? for they weep unto me, saying, Give us flesh, that we may eat.

Num.11. 22 Shall the flocks and the herds be slain for them, to suffice them? or shall all the fish of the sea be gathered together for them, to suffice them?

X

Matt. 14. 17. *See text of topic.*

Matt.15. 34 And Jesus saith unto them, How many loaves have ye? And they said, Seven, and a few little fishes.

Y

Matt.26. 26 And as they were eating, Jesus took bread, and blessed *it*, and brake *it*, and gave *it* to the disciples, and said, Take, eat; this is my body.

Z

Num. 11. 22. *See under U.*

Ps. 78. 19 Yea, they spake against God; they said, Can God furnish a table in the wilderness?

20 Behold, he smote the rock, that the waters gushed out, and the streams overflowed; can he give bread also? can he provide flesh for his people?

CHAP. 6.

And they say unto him, [u]Shall we go and buy two hundred pennyworth of bread, and give them to eat?

38 He saith unto them, How many loaves have ye? go and see. And when they knew, they say, [x]Five, and two fishes.

39 And he commanded them to make all sit down by companies upon the green grass.

40 And they sat down in ranks, by hundreds, and by fifties.

41 And when he had taken the five loaves and the two fishes, he looked up to heaven,[y]and blessed, and brake the loaves, and gave *them* to his disciples to set before them; and the two fishes divided he among them all.

42 And they did all eat, and were filled.

43 And they took up twelve baskets full of the fragments, and of the fishes.

44 And they that did eat of the loaves were about five thousand men.

A

Ps. 145. 15 The eyes of all wait upon thee; and thou givest them their meat in due season.

16 Thou openest thine hand, and satisfiest the desire of every living thing.

B

Num.11. 21 And Moses said, The people, among whom I *am*, *are* six hundred thousand footmen; and thou hast said, I will give them flesh, that they may eat a whole month.

Num. 11. 22. *See under U.*

C

II Ki. 4. 43. *See under D, page 244.*

D

Ex. 23. 25 And ye shall serve the LORD your God, and he shall bless thy bread, and thy water; and I will take sickness away from the midst of thee.

TIME, SPRING, A. D. 29; PLACE, NORTHEAST COAST OF THE LAKE OF GALILEE.

CHAP. 9.

And they said, [z]We have no more but five loaves and two fishes; except we should go and buy meat for all this people.

14 For they were about five thousand men. And he said to his disciples, Make them sit down by fifties in a company.

15 And they did so, and made them all sit down.

16 Then he took the five loaves and the two fishes, and looking up to heaven, he blessed them, and brake, and gave to the disciples to set before the multitude.

17 And they [a]did eat, and were all filled; and there was taken up of fragments that remained to them twelve baskets. (p. 277.)

E

Gen. 49. 10 The sceptre shall not depart from Judah, nor a lawgiver from between his feet, until Shiloh come; and unto him *shall* the gathering of the people *be*.

Deut.18. 15 The LORD thy God will raise up unto thee a Prophet from the midst of thee, of thy brethren, like unto me; unto him ye shall hearken:

Deut.18. 18 I will raise them up a Prophet from among their brethren, like unto thee, and will put my words in his mouth; and he shall speak unto them all that I shall command him.

Isa. 35. 5 Then the eyes of the blind shall be opened, and the ears of the deaf shall be unstopped.

Matt.11. 3 And said unto him, Art thou he that should come, or do we look for another?

John 1. 21 And they asked him, What then? Art thou Elias? And he saith, I am not. Art thou that Prophet? And he answered, No.

John 4. 19 The woman saith unto him, Sir, I perceive that thou art a prophet.

John 4. 25 The woman saith unto him, I know that Messias cometh, which is

CHAP. 6.

7 Philip answered him, [b]Two hundred pennyworth of bread is not sufficient for them, that every one of them may take a little.

8 One of his disciples, Andrew, Simon Peter's brother, saith unto him,

9 There is a lad here, which hath five barley loaves, and two small fishes: [c]but what are they among so many?

10 And Jesus said, Make the men sit down. Now there was much grass in the place. So the men sat down, in number about five thousand.

11 And Jesus took the loaves; and when he had [d]given thanks, he distributed to the disciples, and the disciples to them that were set down; and likewise of the fishes as much as they would.

12 When they were filled, he said unto his disciples, Gather up the fragments that remain, that nothing be lost.

13 Therefore they gathered *them* together, and filled twelve baskets with the fragments of the five barley loaves, which remained over and above unto them that had eaten.

14 Then those men, when they had seen the miracle that Jesus did, said, This is of a truth [e]that Prophet that should come into the world.

E—CONCLUDED.

called Christ: when he is come, he will tell us all things.

John 7. 40 Many of the people therefore, when they heard this saying, said, Of a truth this is the Prophet.

§ 81. JESUS WALKS UPON THE WATER. TIME, SPRING, A. D. 29;

14: 22–33.

22 And straightway Jesus constrained his disciples to get into a ship, and to go before him unto the other side, while he sent the multitudes away.

23 [a]And when he had sent the multitudes away, he went up into a mountain apart to pray: [b]and when the evening was come, he was there alone.

24 But the ship was now in the midst of the sea, tossed with waves: for the wind was contrary.

25 And in the fourth watch of the night Jesus went unto them, walking on the sea.

26 And when the disciples saw him [c]walking on the sea, they were troubled, saying, It is a spirit, and they cried out for fear.

27 But straightway Jesus spake unto them, saying, Be of good cheer; [d]it is I; be not afraid.

28 And Peter answered him and said, Lord, if it be thou, bid me come unto thee on the water.

29 And he said, Come. And when Peter was come down out of the ship, he walked on the water, to go to Jesus.

30 But when he saw the wind [1]boisterous, he was afraid; and beginning to sink, he cried, saying, Lord, save me.

31 And immediately Jesus stretched forth *his* hand, and caught him, and said unto him, O thou of little faith, wherefore [e]didst thou doubt?

32 And when they were come into the ship, the [f]wind ceased.

A

Mark 6. 46. *See text of topic.*

6: 45–52.

45 [g]And straightway he constrained his disciples to get into the ship, and to go to the other side before [2]unto Bethsaida, while he sent away the people.

46 And when he had sent them away, he departed into a mountain to pray.

47 [h]And when even was come, the ship was in the midst of the sea, and he alone on the land.

48 And he saw them toiling in rowing; for the wind was contrary unto them: and about the fourth watch of the night he cometh unto them, walking upon the sea, and [i]would have passed by them.

49 But when they saw him walking upon the sea, they supposed it had been a spirit, and cried out:

50 For they all saw him, and were troubled. And immediately he talked with them, and saith unto them, Be of good cheer: it is I; be not afraid.

51 And he went up unto them into the ship; and the wind ceased: and they were sore amazed in themselves beyond measure, and wondered.

52 For [k]they considered not *the miracle* of the loaves; for their [l]heart was hardened.

B

John 6. 16. *See text of topic.*

C

Job 9. 8 Which alone spreadeth out the heavens, and treadeth upon the waves of the sea;

D

Isa. 41. 4 Who hath wrought and done *it*, calling the generations from the beginning? I the LORD, the first, and with the last; I *am* he.

Isa. 41. 10 Fear thou not: for I *am* with thee: be not dismayed; for I *am* thy God: I will strengthen thee; yea, I

PLACE, LAKE OF GALILEE: ALSO CALLED SEA OF GALILEE, AND SEA OF TIBERIUS.

D—CONCLUDED.

will help thee; yea, I will uphold thee with the right hand of my righteousness.

Isa. 41. 14 Fear not, thou worm Jacob, *and* ye men of Israel; I will help thee, saith the LORD, and thy Redeemer, the Holy One of Israel.

Isa. 51. 12 I, *even* I, *am* he that comforteth you: who *art* thou, that thou shouldest be afraid of a man *that* shall die, and of the son of man *which* shall be made *as* grass:

1

Or, *strong.*

E

Jas. 1. 6 But let him ask in faith, nothing wavering: for he that wavereth is like a wave of the sea driven with the wind and tossed.

F

Ps. 107. 29 He maketh the storm a calm, so that the waves thereof are still.

30 Then are they glad because they be quiet; so he bringeth them unto their desired haven.

G

Matt. 14. 22 and John 6. 17. *See text of topic.*

2

Or, *over against Bethsaida.*

H

Matt. 14. 23 and John 6. 16, 17. *See text of topic.*

I

Luke 24. 28 And they drew nigh unto the village, whither they went: and he made as though he would have gone further.

K

Mark 8. 17 And when Jesus knew *it*, he saith unto them, Why reason ye, because ye have no bread? perceive ye not yet, neither understand? have ye your heart yet hardened?

18 Having eyes, see ye not? and having ears, hear ye not? and do ye not remember?

L

Isa. 63. 17 O LORD, why hast thou made us to err from thy ways, *and* hardened our heart from thy fear? Return for thy servants' sake, the tribes of thine inheritance.

Jer. 17. 9 The heart *is* deceitful above all *things*, and desperately wicked: who can know it?

Mark 3. 5 And when he had looked round about on them with anger, being grieved for the hardness of their hearts, he saith unto the man, Stretch forth thine hand. And he stretched *it* out: and his hand was restored whole as the other.

6: 15–21.

15 When Jesus therefore perceived
that they would come and take him
by force, to make him a king, he departed again into a mountain himself
alone.

16 [m]And when even was *now* come,
his disciples went down unto the sea,

17 And entered into a ship, and
went over the sea toward Capernaum.
And it was now dark, and Jesus was
not come to them.

18 And the sea arose by reason of a
great wind that blew.

19 So when they had rowed about
five and twenty or thirty furlongs,
they see Jesus walking on the sea, and
drawing nigh unto the ship: and they
were afraid.

20 But he saith unto them, It is I;
be not afraid.

21 Then they willingly received him
into the ship:

L—CONCLUDED.

Mark 16. 14 Afterward he appeared unto the eleven as they sat at meat, and upbraided them with their unbelief and hardness of heart, because they believed not them which had seen him after he was risen.

Heb. 3. 13 But exhort one another daily, while it is called To day; lest any of you be hardened through the deceitfulness of sin.

M

Matt. 14. 23 and Mark 6. 47. *See text of topic.*

N

Ps. 2. 7 I will declare the decree: the LORD hath said unto me, Thou *art* my Son; this day have I begotten thee.

Matt. 16. 16 And Simon Peter answered and said, Thou art the Christ, the Son of the living God.

Matt. 26. 63 But Jesus held his peace. And the high priest answered and said unto him, I adjure thee by the living

For N concluded see following pages (250, 251).

§ 81. JESUS WALKS UPON THE WATER (CONCLUDED). TIME, SPRING, A. D. 29;

CHAP. 14.

33 Then they that were in the ship came and worshipped him, saying, Of a truth [n]thou art the Son of God.

N—CONTINUED. See preceding page (249).

God, that thou tell us whether thou be the Christ, the Son of God.

Mark 1. 1 The beginning of the gospel of Jesus Christ, the Son of God;

[CHAP. 6.]

N—CONTINUED.

Luke 4. 41 And devils also came out of many, crying out, and saying, Thou art Christ the Son of God. And he rebuking *them* suffered them not to speak: for they knew that he was Christ.

John 1. 49 Nathanael answered and saith unto him, Rabbi, thou art the Son of

§ 82. MANY MIRACLES OF HEALING IN THE LAND

14: 34–36.

34 [a]And when they were gone over, they came into the land of Gennesaret.

35 And when the men of that place had knowledge of him, they sent out into all that country round about, and brought unto him all that were diseased;

36 And besought him that they might only touch the hem of his garment: and [b]as many as touched were made perfectly whole. (p. 260.)

A

Mark 6. 53. *See text of topic.*

B

Matt. 9. 20 And, behold, a woman which was diseased with an issue of blood twelve years, came behind *him*, and touched the hem of his garment:

Mark 3. 10 For he had healed many; insomuch that they pressed upon him for

6: 53–56.

53 [c]And when they had passed over, they came into the land of Gennesaret, and drew to the shore.

54 And when they were come out of the ship, straightway they knew him,

55 And ran through that whole region round about, and began to carry about in beds those that were sick, where they heard he was.

56 And whithersoever he entered, into villages, or cities, or country, they laid the sick in the streets, and besought him that [d]they might touch if it were but the [e]border of his garment: and as many as touched [1]him were made whole. (p. 260.)

§ 83. DISCOURSE TO THE MULTITUDE IN THE SYNAGOGUE.

A

Matt. 14. 21 And they that had eaten were about five thousand men, beside women and children.

22 And straightway Jesus constrained his disciples to get into a ship, and to go before him unto the other side, while he sent the multitudes away.

23 And when he had sent the multitudes away, he went up into a mountain apart to pray: and when the evening was come, he was there alone.

Mark 6. 44 And they that did eat of the loaves were about five thousand men.

45 And straightway he constrained

A—CONCLUDED.

his disciples to get into the ship, and to go to the other side before unto Bethsaida, while he sent away the people.

46 And when he had sent them away, he departed into a mountain to pray.

John 6. 16 And when even was *now* come, his disciples went down unto the sea,

17 And entered into a ship, and went over the sea toward Capernaum. And it was now dark, and Jesus was not come to them.

1

Or, *work not.*

PLACE, LAKE OF GALILEE: ALSO CALLED SEA OF GALILEE, AND SEA OF TIBERIUS.

N—CONTINUED.

God; thou art the King of Israel.

John 6. 69 And we believe and are sure that thou art that Christ, the Son of the living God.

John 11. 27 She saith unto him, Yea, Lord: I believe that thou art the Christ, the Son of God, which should come into the world.

Acts 8. 37 And Philip said, If thou believest with all thine heart, thou mayest.

CHAP. 6.

and immediately the ship was at the land whither they went.

N—CONCLUDED.

And he answered and said, I believe that Jesus Christ is the Son of God.

Rom. 1. 4 And declared *to be* the Son of God with power, according to the Spirit of holiness, by the resurrection from the dead:

OF GENNESARET. TIME, SPRING, A. D. 29; PLACE, GENNESARET.

B—CONCLUDED.

to touch him, as many as had plagues.

Luke 6. 19 And the whole multitude sought to touch him: for there went virtue out of him, and healed *them* all.

Acts 19. 12 So that from his body were brought unto the sick handkerchiefs or aprons, and the diseases departed from them, and the evil spirits went out of them.

C

Matt. 14. 34. *See text of topic.*

D

Matt. 9. 20. *See under B.*

Mark 5. 27 When she had heard of Jesus, came in the press behind, and touched his garment.

28 For she said, If I may touch but his clothes, I shall be whole.

Acts 5. 15 Insomuch that they brought forth the sick into the streets, and laid *them* on beds and couches, that at the least the shadow of Peter passing by might overshadow some of them.

Acts 19. 12. *See under B.*

E

Num. 15. 38 Speak unto the children of Israel, and bid them that they make them fringes in the borders of their garments, throughout their generations, and that they put upon the fringe of the borders a ribband of blue:

39 And it shall be unto you for a fringe, that ye may look upon it, and remember all the commandments of the LORD, and do them; and that ye seek not after your own heart and your own eyes, after which ye use to go a whoring:

40 That ye may remember, and do all my commandments, and be holy unto your God.

41 I *am* the LORD your God, which brought you out of the land of Egypt, to be your God: I *am* the LORD your God.

Deut. 22. 12 Thou shalt make thee fringes upon the four quarters of thy vesture, wherewith thou coverest *thyself.*

1

Or, *it.*

TIME, SPRING, A. D. 29; PLACE, CAPERNAUM.

B

Eccl. 6. 7 All the labour of man *is* for his mouth, and yet the appetite is not filled.

John 4. 14 But whosoever drinketh of the water that I shall give him shall never thirst; but the water that I shall give him shall be in him a well of water springing up into everlasting life.

John 6. 54. *See text of topic.*

Rom. 6. 23 For the wages of sin *is* death; but the gift of God *is* eternal life through Jesus Christ our Lord.

Heb. 4. 11 Let us labour therefore to enter into that rest, lest any man fall after the same example of unbelief.

6 : 22–65.

22 [a]The day following, when the people, which stood on the other side of the sea, saw that there was none other boat there, save that one whereinto his disciples were entered, and that Jesus went not with his disciples into the boat, but *that* his disciples were gone away alone;

23 Howbeit there came other boats

§ 83. DISCOURSE TO THE MULTITUDE IN THE SYNAGOGUE

For 1 and B see preceding pages (250, 251).

C

I Sa. 2. 9 He will keep the feet of his saints, and the wicked shall be silent in darkness; for by strength shall no man prevail.

Ps. 89. 48 What man *is he that* liveth, and shall not see death? shall he deliver his soul from the hand of the grave? Selah.

Luke 2. 25 And, behold there was a man in Jerusalem, whose name *was* Simeon; and the same man *was* just and devout, waiting for the consolation of Israel: and the Holy Ghost was upon him.

26 And it was revealed unto him by the Holy Ghost, that he should not see death, before he had seen the Lord's Christ.

John 3. 14 And as Moses lifted up the serpent in the wilderness, even so must the Son of man be lifted up:

15 That whosoever believeth in him should not perish, but have eternal life.

John 4. 14 But whosoever drinketh of the water that I shall give him shall never thirst; but the water that I shall give him shall be in him a well of water springing up into everlasting life.

John 5. 39 Search the Scriptures; for in them ye think ye have eternal life: and they are they which testify of me.

40 And ye will not come to me, that ye might have life.

John 8. 51 Verily, verily, I say unto you, If a man keep my saying, he shall never see death.

John 10. 28 And I give unto them eternal life; and they shall never perish, neither shall any *man* pluck them out of my hand.

John 11. 26 And whosoever liveth and believeth in me shall never die. Believest thou this?

John 20. 31 But these are written, that ye might believe that Jesus is the Christ, the Son of God; and that believing ye might have life through his name.

Rom. 5. 21 That as sin hath reigned unto death, even so might grace reign through righteousness unto eternal life by Jesus Christ our Lord.

I Tim. 1. 16 Howbeit for this cause I obtained mercy, that in me first Jesus Christ might show forth all longsuffering, for a pattern to them which should hereafter believe on him to life everlasting.

I Jno. 1. 2 (For the life was manifested, and

C—Concluded.

we have seen *it*, and bear witness, and show unto you that eternal life, which was with the Father, and was manifested unto us;)

3 That which we have seen and heard declare we unto you, that ye also may have fellowship with us: and truly our fellowship *is* with the Father, and with his Son Jesus Christ.

I Jno. 2. 24 Let that therefore abide in you, which ye have heard from the beginning. If that which ye have heard from the beginning shall remain in you, ye also shall continue in the Son, and in the Father.

25 And this is the promise that he hath promised us, *even* eternal life.

Also see under C, page 256.

Jude 20 But ye, beloved, building up yourselves on your most holy faith, praying in the Holy Ghost,

21 Keep yourselves in the love of God, looking for the mercy of our Lord Jesus Christ unto eternal life.

D

Matt. 3. 17 And lo a voice from heaven, saying, This is my beloved Son, in whom I am well pleased.

Matt. 17. 5 While he yet spake, behold, a bright cloud overshadowed them: and behold a voice out of the cloud, which said, This is my beloved Son, in whom I am well pleased; hear ye him.

Mark 1. 11 And there came a voice from heaven, *saying*, Thou art my beloved Son, in whom I am well pleased.

Mark 9. 7 And there was a cloud that overshadowed them: and a voice came out of the cloud, saying, This is my beloved Son: hear him.

Luke 3. 22 And the Holy Ghost descended in a bodily shape like a dove upon him, and a voice came from heaven, which said, Thou art my beloved Son; in thee I am well pleased.

Luke 9. 35 And there came a voice out of the cloud, saying, This is my beloved Son: hear him.

John 1. 33 And I knew him not: but he that sent me to baptize with water, the same said unto me, Upon whom thou shalt see the Spirit descending, and remaining on him, the same is he which baptiseth with the Holy Ghost.

John 5. 37 And the Father himself, which hath sent me, hath borne witness of me. Ye have neither heard his voice at any time, nor seen his shape.

(CONTINUED). TIME, SPRING, A. D. 29; PLACE, CAPERNAUM.

D—CONCLUDED.

John 8. 18 I am one that bear witness of myself, and the Father that sent me beareth witness of me.

Acts 2. 22 Ye men of Israel, hear these words; Jesus of Nazareth, a man approved of God among you by miracles and wonders and signs, which God did by him in the midst of you, as ye yourselves also know:

II Pet.1. 17 For he received from God the Father honour and glory, when there came such a voice to him from the excellent glory, This is my beloved Son, in whom I am well pleased.

E

I Jno. 3. 23 And this is his commandment, That we should believe on the name of his Son Jesus Christ, and love one another, as he gave us commandment.

F

Matt.12. 38 Then certain of the scribes and of the Pharisees answered, saying, Master, we would see a sign from thee.

Matt.16. 1 The Pharisees also with the Sadducees came, and tempting desired him that he would show them a sign from heaven.

Mark 8. 11 And the Pharisees came forth, and began to question with him, seeking of him a sign from heaven, tempting him.

I Cor. 1. 22 For the Jews require a sign, and the Greeks seek after wisdom:

G

Ex. 16. 15 And when the children of Israel saw *it*, they said one to another, It *is* manna: for they wist not what it *was*. And Moses said unto them, This *is* the bread which the LORD hath given you to eat.

Num.11. 7 And the manna *was* as coriander seed, and the colour thereof as the colour of bdellium.

Neh. 9. 15 And gavest them bread from heaven for their hunger, and broughtest forth water for them out of the rock for their thirst, and promisedst them that they should go in to possess the land which thou hadst sworn to give them.

I Cor.10. 3 And did all eat the same spiritual meat;

H

Ps. 78. 24 And had rained down manna upon them to eat, and had given them of the corn of heaven.

25 •Man did eat angels' food: he sent them meat to the full.

CHAP. 6.

from Tiberias nigh unto the place where they did eat bread, after that the Lord had given thanks:

24 When the people therefore saw that Jesus was not there, neither his disciples, they also took shipping, and came to Capernaum, seeking for Jesus.

25 And when they had found him on the other side of the sea, they said unto him, Rabbi, when camest thou hither?

26 Jesus answered them and said, Verily, verily, I say unto you, Ye seek me, not because ye saw the miracles, but because ye did eat of the loaves, and were filled.

27 [1]Labour not for the meat which perisheth, but [b]for that meat which endureth unto [c]everlasting life, which the Son of man shall give unto you: [d]for him hath God the Father sealed.

28 Then said they unto him, What shall we do, that we might work the works of God?

29 Jesus answered and said unto them, [e]This is the work of God, that ye believe on him whom he hath sent.

30 They said therefore unto him, [f]What sign showest thou then, that we may see, and believe thee? what dost thou work?

31 [g]Our fathers did eat manna in the desert; as it is written, [h]He gave them bread from heaven to eat.

32 Then Jesus said unto them, Verily, verily, I say unto you, Moses gave you not that bread from heaven; but my Father giveth you the true bread from heaven.

§ 83. DISCOURSE TO THE MULTITUDE IN THE SYNAGOGUE

I

John 4. 15 The woman saith unto him, Sir, give me this water, that I thirst not, neither come hither to draw.

16 Jesus saith unto her, Go, call thy husband, and come hither.

K

John 6. 48, 58. *See text of topic.*

I Cor.10. 16 The cup of blessing which we bless, is it not the communion of the blood of Christ? The bread which we break, is it not the communion of the body of Christ?

17 For we *being* many are one bread, *and* one body: for we are all partakers of that one bread.

18 Behold Israel after the flesh: are not they which eat of the sacrifices partakers of the altar?

I Cor.11. 23 For I have received of the Lord that which also I delivered unto you, That the Lord Jesus, the *same* night in which he was betrayed, took bread:

24 And when he had given thanks, he brake *it*, and said, Take, eat; this is my body, which is broken for you: this do in remembrance of me.

25 After the same manner also *he took* the cup, when he had supped, saying, This cup is the new testament in my blood: this do ye, as oft as ye drink *it*, in remembrance of me.

26 For as often as ye eat this bread, and drink this cup, ye do show the Lord's death till he come.

27 Wherefore whosoever shall eat this bread, and drink *this* cup of the Lord, unworthily, shall be guilty of the body and blood of the Lord.

28 But let a man examine himself, and so let him eat of *that* bread, and drink of *that* cup.

29 For he that eateth and drinketh unworthily, eateth and drinketh damnation to himself, not discerning the Lord's body.

30 For this cause many *are* weak and sickly among you, and many sleep.

L

John 4. 14 But whosoever drinketh of the water that I shall give him shall never thirst; but the water that I shall give him shall be in him a well of water springing up into everlasting life.

John 7. 37 In the last day, that great *day* of the feast, Jesus stood and cried, saying, If any man thirst, let him come unto me, and drink.

M

Isa. 49. 10 They shall not hunger nor thirst; neither shall the heat nor sun smite them: for he that hath mercy on them shall lead them, even by the springs of water shall he guide them.

Rev. 7. 16 They shall hunger no more, neither thirst any more; neither shall the sun light on them, nor any heat.

17 For the Lamb which is in the midst of the throne shall feed them, and shall lead them unto living fountains of waters: and God shall wipe away all tears from their eyes.

N

John 6. 26, 64. *See text of topic.*

O

John 6. 45. *See text of topic.*

P

Matt.24. 24 For there shall arise false Christs, and false prophets, and shall show great signs and wonders; insomuch that, if *it were* possible, they shall deceive the very elect.

John 10. 28 And I give unto them eternal life; and they shall never perish, neither shall any *man* pluck them out of my hand.

29 My Father, which gave *them* me, is greater than all; and no *man* is able to pluck *them* out of my Father's hand.

II Tim.2. 19 Nevertheless the foundation of God standeth sure, having this seal, The Lord knoweth them that are his. And, Let every one that nameth the name of Christ depart from iniquity.

I Jno. 2. 19 They went out from us, but they were not of us; for if they had been of us, they would *no doubt* have continued with us: but *they went out*, that they might be made manifest that they were not all of us.

Q

Matt.26. 39 And he went a little further, and fell on his face, and prayed, saying, O my Father, if it be possible, let this cup pass from me: nevertheless, not as I will, but as thou *wilt*.

John 5. 30 I can of mine own self do nothing: as I hear, I judge: and my judgment is just; because I seek not mine own will, but the will of the Father which hath sent me.

Heb. 5. 8 Though he were a Son, yet learned he obedience by the things which he suffered;

R

John 4. 34 Jesus saith unto them, My meat is to do the will of him that sent me, and to finish his work.

(CONTINUED). TIME, SPRING, A. D. 29; PLACE, CAPERNAUM.

S

John 10. 28. *See under P.*

John 17. 12 While I was with them in the world, I kept them in thy name: those that thou gavest me I have kept, and none of them is lost, but the son of perdition; that the Scripture might be fulfilled.

John 18. 9 That the saying might be fulfilled, which he spake, Of them which thou gavest me have I lost none.

Col. 3. 3 For ye are dead, and your life is hid with Christ in God.

T

Isa. 45. 22 Look unto me, and be ye saved, all the ends of the earth: for I *am* God, and *there is* none else.

Isa. 53. 2 For he shall grow up before him as a tender plant, and as a root out of a dry ground: he hath no form nor comeliness; and when we shall see him, *there is* no beauty that we should desire him.

John 3. 15 That whosoever believeth in him should not perish, but have eternal life.

16 For God so loved the world, that he gave his only begotten Son, that whosoever believeth in him should not perish, but have everlasting life.

John 4. 14. *See under L.*

John 6. 27, 41, 54. *See text of topic.*

II Cor.4. 6 For God, who commanded the light to shine out of darkness, hath shined in our hearts, to *give* the light of the knowledge of the glory of God in the face of Jesus Christ.

U

Matt.13. 55 Is not this the carpenter's son? is not his mother called Mary? and his brethren, James, and Joses, and Simon, and Judas?

Mark 6. 3 Is not this the carpenter, the son of Mary, the brother of James, and Joses, and of Juda, and Simon? and are not his sisters here with us? And they were offended at him.

Luke 4. 22 And all bare him witness, and wondered at the gracious words which proceeded out of his mouth. And they said, Is not this Joseph's son?

Rom. 1. 3 Concerning his Son Jesus Christ our Lord, which was made of the seed of David according to the flesh;

4 And declared *to be* the Son of God with power, according to the Spirit of holiness, by the resurrection from the dead:

Rom. 9. 5 Whose *are* the fathers, and of whom as concerning the flesh Christ

CHAP. 6.

33 For the bread of God is he which cometh down from heaven, and giveth life unto the world.

34 [i]Then said they unto him, Lord, evermore give us this bread.

35 And Jesus said unto them, [k]I am the bread of life: [l]he that cometh to me shall [m]never hunger; and he that believeth on me shall never thirst.

36 [n]But I said unto you, That ye also have seen me, and believe not.

37 [o]All that the Father giveth me shall come to me; and [p]him that cometh to me I will in no wise cast out.

38 For I came down from heaven, [q]not to do mine own will, [r]but the will of him that sent me.

39 And this is the Father's will which hath sent me, [s]that of all which he hath given me I should lose nothing, but should raise it up again at the last day.

40 And this is the will of him that sent me, [t]that every one which seeth the Son, and believeth on him, may have everlasting life: and I will raise him up at the last day.

41 The Jews then murmured at him, because he said, I am the bread which came down from heaven.

42 And they said, [u]Is not this Jesus, the son of Joseph, whose father and mother we know? how is it then that he saith, I came down from heaven?

43 Jesus therefore answered and said unto them, Murmur not among yourselves.

U—CONCLUDED.

came, who is over all, God blessed for ever. Amen.

§ 83. DISCOURSE TO THE MULTITUDE IN THE SYNAGOGUE

X

Song 1. 4 Draw me, we will run after thee: the King hath brought me into his chambers: we will be glad and rejoice in thee, we will remember thy love more than wine: the upright love thee.

John 6. 65. *See text of topic.*

Y

Isa. 54. 13 And all thy children *shall be* taught of the LORD; and great *shall be* the peace of thy children.

Jer. 31. 34 And they shall teach no more every man his neighbour, and every man his brother, saying, Know the LORD: for they shall all know me, from the least of them unto the greatest of them, saith the LORD: for I will forgive their iniquity, and I will remember their sin no more.

Mic. 4. 2 And many nations shall come, and say, Come, and let us go up to the mountain of the LORD, and to the house of the God of Jacob; and he will teach us of his ways, and we will walk in his paths: for the law shall go forth of Zion, and the word of the LORD from Jerusalem.

Heb. 8. 10 For this *is* the covenant that I will make with the house of Israel after those days, saith the LORD; I will put my laws into their mind, and write them in their hearts: and I will be to them a God, and they shall be to me a people:

Heb. 10. 16 This *is* the covenant that I will make with them after those days, saith the Lord; I will put my laws into their hearts, and in their minds will I write them;

Z

John 6. 37. *See text of topic.*

A

John 1. 18 No man hath seen God at any time; the only begotten Son, which is in the bosom of the Father, he hath declared *him.*

John 5. 37 And the Father himself, which hath sent me, hath borne witness of me. Ye have neither heard his voice at any time, nor seen his shape.

B

Matt. 11. 27 All things are delivered unto me of my Father: and no man knoweth the Son, but the Father; neither knoweth any man the Father, save the Son, and *he* to whomsoever the Son will reveal *him.*

Luke 10. 22 All things are delivered to me of my Father: and no man knoweth who the Son is, but the Father; and who the Father is, but the Son, and *he* to whom the Son will reveal *him.*

B—CONCLUDED.

John 1. 18. *See under A.*

John 7. 29 But I know him; for I am from him, and he hath sent me.

John 8. 19 Then said they unto him, Where is thy Father? Jesus answered, Ye neither know me, nor my Father: if ye had known me, ye should have known my Father also.

II Cor. 4. 6 For God, who commanded the light to shine out of darkness, hath shined in our hearts, to *give* the light of the knowledge of the glory of God in the face of Jesus Christ.

C

John 3. 16. *See under T, page 255.*

John 3. 18 He that believeth on him is not condemned: but he that believeth not is condemned already, because he hath not believed in the name of the only begotten Son of God.

John 3. 36 He that believeth on the Son hath everlasting life: and he that believeth not the Son shall not see life; but the wrath of God abideth on him.

John 6. 40 and John 6. 47. *See text of topic.*

I Jno. 5. 9 If we receive the witness of men, the witness of God is greater: for this is the witness of God which he hath testified of his Son.

10 He that believeth on the Son of God hath the witness in himself: he that believeth not God hath made him a liar; because he believeth not the record that God gave of his Son.

11 And this is the record, that God hath given to us eternal life, and this life is in his Son.

12 He that hath the Son hath life; *and* he that hath not the Son of God hath not life.

13 These things have I written unto you that believe on the name of the Son of God; that ye may know that ye have eternal life, and that ye may believe on the name of the Son of God.

I Jno. 5. 20 And we know that the Son of God is come, and hath given us an understanding, that we may know him that is true; and we are in him that is true, *even* in his Son Jesus Christ. This is the true God, and eternal life.

Also see under C, page 252.

D

John 6. 33, 35. *See text of topic.*

E

John 6. 31. *See text of topic.*

(CONTINUED). TIME, SPRING, A. D. 29; PLACE, CAPERNAUM.

F

John 6. 51, 58. *See text of topic.*

G

John 3. 13 And no man hath ascended up to heaven, but he that came down from heaven, *even* the Son of man which is in heaven.

H

Heb. 10. 5 Wherefore, when he cometh into the world, he saith, Sacrifice and offering thou wouldest not, but a body hast thou prepared me:

Heb. 10. 10 By the which will we are sanctified through the offering of the body of Jesus Christ once *for all.*

I

John 7. 43 So there was a division among the people because of him.

John 9. 16 Therefore said some of the Pharisees, This man is not of God, because he keepeth not the sabbath day. Others said, How can a man that is a sinner do such miracles? And there was a division among them.

John 10. 19 There was a division therefore again among the Jews for these sayings.

K

John 3. 9 Nicodemus answered and said unto him, How can these things be?

L

Matt. 26. 26 And as they were eating, Jesus took bread, and blessed *it*, and brake *it*, and gave *it* to the disciples, and said, Take, eat; this is my body.

Matt. 26. 28 For this is my blood of the new testament, which is shed for many for the remission of sins.

M

John 4. 14. *See under L, page 254.*

John 6. 27, 40, 63. *See text of topic.*

N

Ps. 90. 1 Lord, thou hast been our dwelling-place in all generations.

John 15. 4 Abide in me, and I in you. As the branch cannot bear fruit of itself, except it abide in the vine; no more can ye, except ye abide in me.

5 I am the vine, ye *are* the branches. He that abideth in me, and I in him, the same bringeth forth much fruit; for without me ye can do nothing.

I Cor. 6. 17 But he that is joined unto the Lord is one spirit.

18 Flee fornication. Every sin that a man doeth is without the body; but he that committeth fornication sinneth against his own body.

19 What! know ye not that your body is the temple of the Holy Ghost

For N concluded see next page (258).

CHAP. 6.

44 [x]No man can come to me, except the Father which hath sent me draw him: and I will raise him up at the last day.

45 [y]It is written in the prophets, And they shall be all taught of God. [z]Every man therefore that hath heard, and hath learned of the Father, cometh unto me.

46 [a]Not that any man hath seen the Father, [b]save he which is of God, he hath seen the Father.

47 Verily, verily, I say unto you, [c]He that believeth on me hath everlasting life.

48 [d]I am that bread of life.

49 [e]Your fathers did eat manna in the wilderness, and are dead.

50 [f]This is the bread which cometh down from heaven, that a man may eat thereof, and not die.

51 I am the living bread [g]which came down from heaven: if any man eat of this bread, he shall live for ever: [h]and the bread that I will give is my flesh, which I will give for the life of the world.

52 The Jews therefore [i]strove among themselves, saying, [k]How can this man give us *his* flesh to eat?

53 Then Jesus said unto them, Verily, verily, I say unto you, Except [l]ye eat the flesh of the Son of man, and drink his blood, ye have no life in you.

54 [m]Whoso eateth my flesh, and drinketh my blood, hath eternal life; and I will raise him up at the last day.

55 For my flesh is meat indeed, and my blood is drink indeed.

§ 83. DISCOURSE TO THE MULTITUDE IN THE SYNAGOGUE

N—Concluded. See preceding page (257).
which is in you, which ye have of God, and ye are not your own?

20 For ye are bought with a price: therefore glorify God in your body, and in your spirit, which are God's.

Eph. 3. 17 That Christ may dwell in your hearts by faith; that ye, being rooted and grounded in love,

I Jno. 2. 5 But whoso keepeth his word, in him verily is the love of God perfected: hereby know we that we are in him.

I Jno. 2. 24. *See under C, page 252*

I Jno. 2. 27 But the anointing which ye have received of him abideth in you, and ye need not that any man teach you: but as the same anointing teacheth you of all things, and is truth, and is no lie, and even as it hath taught you, ye shall abide in him.

I Jno. 3. 24 And he that keepeth his commandments dwelleth in him, and he in him. And hereby we know that he abideth in us, by the Spirit which he hath given us.

I Jno. 4. 15 Whosoever shall confess that Jesus is the Son of God, God dwelleth in him, and he in God.

16 And we have known and believed the love that God hath to us. God is love; and he that dwelleth in love dwelleth in God, and God in him.

I Jno. 5. 20. *See under C, page 256.*

O

John 6. 49, 50, 51. *See text of topic.*

P

Matt.11. 6 And blessed is *he*, whosoever shall not be offended in me.

John 6. 66 From that *time* many of his disciples went back, and walked no more with him.

Q

Mark 16. 19 So then, after the Lord had spoken unto them, he was received up into heaven, and sat on the right hand of God.

John 3. 13. *See under G, page 257.*

Acts 1. 9 And when he had spoken these things, while they beheld, he was taken up; and a cloud received him out of their sight.

Eph. 4. 8 Wherefore he saith, When he ascended up on high, he led captivity captive, and gave gifts unto men.

R

Gen. 2. 7 And the Lord God formed man *of* the dust of the ground, and breathed into his nostrils the breath of life; and man became a living soul.

Rom. 8. 2 For the law of the Spirit of life in Christ Jesus hath made me free from the law of sin and death.

I Cor.15. 45 And so it is written, The first man Adam was made a living soul; the last Adam *was made* a quickening spirit.

II Cor.3. 6 Who also hath made us able ministers of the new testament; not of the letter, but of the spirit: for the letter killeth, but the spirit giveth life.

Gal. 5. 25 If we live in the Spirit, let us also walk in the Spirit.

I Pet. 3. 18 For Christ also hath once suffered for sins, the just for the unjust, that he might bring us to God, being put to death in the flesh, but quickened by the Spirit:

S

I Tim.4. 8 For bodily exercise profiteth little: but godliness is profitable unto all things, having promise of the life that now is, and of that which is to come.

Heb. 13. 9 Be not carried about with divers and strange doctrines: for *it is* a good thing that the heart be established with grace; not with meats, which have not profited them that have been occupied therein.

I Pet. 3. 21 The like figure whereunto *even* baptism doth also now save us, (not the putting away of the filth of the flesh, but the answer of a good conscience toward God,) by the resurrection of Jesus Christ:

T

Deut.32. 46 And he said unto them, Set your hearts unto all the words which I testify among you this day, which ye shall command your children to observe to do, all the words of this law.

47 For it *is* not a vain thing for you; because it *is* your life: and through

§ 84. MANY DISCIPLES TURN BACK. PETER'S PROFESSION

A

John 6. 59, 60. *See text of § 83, page 259.*

B

Zeph. 1. 6 And them that are turned back from the Lord; and *those* that have not sought the Lord, nor inquired for him.

B—Continued.

Luke 9. 62 And Jesus said unto him, No man, having put his hand to the plough, and looking back, is fit for the kingdom of God.

Heb. 6. 4 For *it is* impossible for those who

(CONCLUDED). TIME, SPRING, A. D. 29; PLACE, CAPERNAUM.

T—CONCLUDED.

this thing ye shall prolong *your* days in the land, whither ye go over Jordan to possess it.

Ps. 19. 7 The law of the LORD *is* perfect, converting the soul: the testimony of the LORD *is* sure, making wise the simple.

8 The statutes of the LORD *are* right, rejoicing the heart: the commandment of the LORD *is* pure, enlightening the eyes.

9 The fear of the LORD *is* clean, enduring for ever: the judgments of the LORD *are* true *and* righteous altogether.

10 More to be desired *are they* than gold, yea, than much fine gold: sweeter also than honey and the honeycomb.

Rom. 10. 8 But what saith it? The word is nigh thee, *even* in thy mouth, and in thy heart: that is, the word of faith, which we preach;

9 That if thou shalt confess with thy mouth the Lord Jesus, and shalt believe in thine heart that God hath raised him from the dead, thou shalt be saved.

U

John 5. 36. *See text of topic.*

X

John 2. 24 But Jesus did not commit himself unto them, because he knew all *men*,

25 And needed not that any should testify of man; for he knew what was in man.

John 13. 11 For he knew who should betray him; therefore said he, Ye are not all clean.

Acts 15. 18 Known unto God are all his works from the beginning of the world.

19 Wherefore my sentence is, that we trouble not them, which from among the Gentiles are turned to God:

20 But that we write unto them, that they abstain from pollutions of idols, and *from* fornication, and *from* things strangled, and *from* blood.

Y

John 6. 44, 45. *See text of topic.*

CHAP. 6.

56 He that eateth my flesh, and
drinketh my blood, [n]dwelleth in me,
and I in him.

57 As the living Father hath sent
me, and I live by the Father; so he
that eateth me, even he shall live by me.

58 [o]This is that bread which came
down from heaven: not as your
fathers did eat manna, and are dead:
he that eateth of this bread shall live
for ever.

59 These things said he in the synagogue, as he taught in Capernaum.

60 [p]Many therefore of his disciples,
when they had heard *this*, said, This is
a hard saying; who can hear it?

61 When Jesus knew in himself that
his disciples murmured at it, he said
unto them, Doth this offend you?

62 [q]*What* and if ye shall see the Son
of man ascend up where he was before?

63 [r]It is the Spirit that quickeneth;
the [s]flesh profiteth nothing: [t]the words
that I speak unto you, *they* are spirit,
and *they* are life.

64 But [u]there are some of you that
believe not. For [x]Jesus knew from
the beginning who they were that believed not, and who should betray him.

65 And he said, Therefore [y]said I
unto you, that no man can come unto
me, except it were given unto him of
my Father.

OF FAITH. TIME, SPRING, A. D. 29; PLACE, CAPERNAUM.

B—CONTINUED.

were once enlightened, and have tasted of the heavenly gift, and were made partakers of the Holy Ghost,

5 And have tasted the good word of

For B concluded see next page (260).

6: 66–71; 7: 1.

66 [a]From that *time* many of his disciples went [b]back, and walked no
more with him.

§ 84. MANY DISCIPLES TURN BACK. PETER'S PROFESSION

B—CONCLUDED.

See preceding pages (258, 259).

God, and the powers of the world to come,

6 If they shall fall away, to renew them again unto repentance; seeing they crucify to themselves the Son of God afresh, and put *him* to an open shame.

Heb. 10. 38 Now the just shall live by faith: but if *any man* draw back, my soul shall have no pleasure in him.

I Jno. 2. 18 Little children, it is the last time: and as ye have heard that antichrist shall come, even now are there many antichrists; whereby we know that it is the last time.

19 They went out from us, but they were not of us; for if they had been of us, they would *no doubt* have continued with us: but *they went out*, that they might be made manifest that they were not all of us.

C

John 5. 24 Verily, verily, I say unto you, He that heareth my word, and believeth on him that sent me, hath everlasting life, and shall not come into condemnation; but is passed from death unto life.

John 20. 31 But these are written, that ye might believe that Jesus is the Christ, the Son of God; and that believing ye might have life through his name.

Acts 4. 12 Neither is there salvation in any other: for there is none other name

C—CONCLUDED.

under heaven given among men, whereby we must be saved.

Acts 5. 19 But the angel of the Lord by night opened the prison doors, and brought them forth, and said,

20 Go, stand and speak in the temple to the people all the words of this life.

Acts 7. 38 This is he, that was in the church in the wilderness with the angel which spake to him in the mount Sina, and *with* our fathers, who received the lively oracles to give unto us:

I Jno. 5. 11 And this is the record, that God hath given to us eternal life, and this life is in his Son.

12 He that hath the Son hath life; *and* he that hath not the Son of God hath not life.

13 These things have I written unto you that believe on the name of the Son of God; that ye may know that ye have eternal life, and that ye may believe on the name of the Son of God.

D

Matt. 16. 16 And Simon Peter answered and said, Thou art the Christ, the Son of the living God.

17 And Jesus answered and said unto him, Blessed art thou, Simon Barjona: for flesh and blood hath not revealed *it* unto thee, but my Father which is in heaven.

Mark 8. 29 And he saith unto them, But

§ 85. *THE THIRD PASSOVER. UNWASHEN HANDS. PHARASAIC

15: 1–20.

1 Then [a]came to Jesus scribes and Pharisees, which were of Jerusalem, saying,

*

John 6. 4 And the passover, a feast of the Jews, was nigh.

(John 6. 4. *See text of § 80.*)

It seems that Jesus did not attend this passover. (April A. D. 29.)

A

Mark 7. 1. *See text of topic.*

B

Matt. 15. 1. *See text of topic.*

1

Or, *common.*

Acts 10. 14 But Peter said, Not so, Lord; for I have never eaten anything that is common or unclean.

15 And the voice *spake* unto him

7: 1–23.

1 Then [b]came together unto him the Pharisees, and certain of the scribes, which came from Jerusalem.

2 And when they saw some of his disciples eat bread with [1]defiled, that is to say, with unwashen hands, [c]they found fault.

3 For the Pharisees, and all the Jews, [d]except they wash *their* hands [2]oft, eat not, holding the [e]tradition of the elders.

4 And *when they come* from the market, except they wash, they eat not.

OF FAITH (CONCLUDED). TIME, SPRING, A. D. 29; PLACE, CAPERNAUM.

D—CONCLUDED.

whom say ye that I am? And Peter answereth and saith unto him, Thou art the Christ.

Luke 9. 20 He said unto them, But whom say ye that I am? Peter answering said, The Christ of God.

John 1. 49 Nathanael answered and saith unto him, Rabbi, thou art the Son of God; thou art the King of Israel.

50 Jesus answered and said unto him, Because I said unto thee, I saw thee under the fig tree, believest thou? thou shalt see greater things than these.

John 11. 27 She saith unto him, Yea, Lord: I believe that thou art the Christ, the Son of God, which should come into the world.

E

Luke 6. 13 And when it was day, he called *unto him* his disciples: and of them he chose twelve, whom also he named apostles;

F

John 13. 27 And after the sop Satan entered into him. Then said Jesus unto him, That thou doest, do quickly.

G

John 5. 16 And therefore did the Jews persecute Jesus, and sought to slay him, because he had done these things on the sabbath day.

17 But Jesus answered them, My Father worketh hitherto, and I work.

18 Therefore the Jews sought the

CHAP. 6.

67 Then said Jesus unto the twelve,
Will ye also go away?

68 Then Simon Peter answered him,
Lord, to whom shall we go? thou hast
[c]the words of eternal life.

69 [d]And we believe and are sure that
thou art that Christ, the Son of the
living God.

70 Jesus answered them, [e]Have not
I chosen you twelve, [f]and one of you
is a devil?

71 He spake of Judas Iscariot *the*
son of Simon: for he it was that
should betray him, being one of the
twelve.

CHAP. 7.

1 After these things Jesus walked in
Galilee: for he would not walk in
Jewry, [g]because the Jews sought to
kill him. (p. 309.)

G—CONCLUDED.

more to kill him, because he not only had broken the sabbath, but said also that God was his Father, making himself equal with God.

TRADITIONS. TIME, APRIL, A. D. 29; PLACE, JERUSALEM, CAPERNAUM.

1—CONCLUDED.

again the second time, What God hath cleansed, *that* call not thou common.

Acts 10. 28 And he said unto them, Ye know how that it is an unlawful thing for a man that is a Jew to keep company, or come unto one of another nation; but God hath showed me that I should not call any man common or unclean.

C

Dan. 6. 4 Then the presidents and princes sought to find occasion against Daniel concerning the kingdom; but they could find none occasion nor fault; forasmuch as he *was* faithful, neither was there any error or fault found in him.

5 Then said these men, We shall not find any occasion against this Daniel, except we find *it* against him concerning the law of his God.

D

Job 9. 30 If I wash myself with snow water, and make my hands never so clean;

31 Yet shalt thou plunge me in the ditch, and mine own clothes shall abhor me.

Jer. 4. 14 O Jerusalem, wash thine heart from wickedness, that thou mayest be saved. How long shall thy vain thoughts lodge within thee?

Heb. 9. 10 *Which stood* only in meats and drinks, and divers washings, and carnal ordinances, imposed *on them* until the time of reformation.

2

Or, *diligently*, in original, *with the fist.*

E

Gal. 1. 14 And profited in the Jews' religion above many my equals in mine own nation, being more exceedingly zealous of the traditions of my fathers.

§ 85. THE THIRD PASSOVER. UNWASHEN HANDS. PHARASAIC

CHAP. 15.

2 [f]Why do thy disciples transgress [g]the tradition of the elders? for they wash not their hands when they eat bread.

3 But he answered and said unto them, Why do ye also transgress the commandment of God by your tradition?

4 For God commanded, saying, [h]Honour thy father and mother: and, [i]He that curseth father or mother, let him die the death.

5 But ye say, Whosoever shall [k]say to *his* father or *his* mother, *It is* a gift, by whatsoever thou mightest be profited by me;

6 And honour not his father or his mother, *he shall be free.* Thus have ye made the commandment of God of none effect by your tradition.

7 *Ye* [l]hypocrites, well did Esaias prophesy of you, saying,

8 [m]This people draweth nigh unto me with their mouth, and honoureth me with *their* lips; but their heart is far from me.

9 But in vain they do worship me, [n]teaching *for* doctrines the commandments of men.

E—CONCLUDED. See preceding page (261).

Col. 2. 8 Beware lest any man spoil you through philosophy and vain deceit, after the tradition of men, after the rudiments of the world, and not after Christ.

I Pet. 1. 18 Forasmuch as ye know that ye were not redeemed with corruptible things, *as* silver and gold, from your vain conversation *received* by tradition from your fathers;

F

Mark 7. 5. *See text of topic.*

G

Gal. 1. 14 and Col. 2. 8. *See under E, pages 261, 262.*

CHAP. 7.

And many other things there be, which they have received to hold, *as* the washing of cups, and [3]pots, brazen vessels, and of [4]tables.

5 [o]Then the Pharisees and scribes asked him, Why walk not thy disciples according to the tradition of the elders, but eat bread with unwashen hands?

6 He answered and said unto them, Well hath Esaias prophesied of you hypocrites, as it is written, [p]This people honoureth me with *their* lips, but their heart is far from me.

7 Howbeit in vain do they worship me, teaching *for* doctrines the commandments of men.

8 For laying aside the commandment of God, ye hold the tradition of men, *as* the washing of pots and cups: and many other such like things ye do.

9 And he said unto them, Full well ye [5]reject the commandment of God, that ye may keep your own tradition.

10 For Moses said, [q]Honour thy father and thy mother; and, [r]Whoso curseth father or mother, let him die the death:

11 But ye say, If a man shall say to his father or mother, *It is* [s]Corban, that is to say, a gift, by whatsoever thou mightest be profited by me; *he shall be free.*

12 And ye suffer him no more to do aught for his father or his mother;

13 Making the word of God of none effect through your tradition, which ye have delivered: and many such like things do ye.

TRADITIONS (CONTINUED). TIME, APRIL, A. D. 29; PLACE, JERUSALEM, CAPERNAUM.

H

Ex. 20. 12 Honour thy father and thy mother: that thy days may be long upon the land which the LORD thy God giveth thee.

Lev. 19. 3 Ye shall fear every man his mother, and his father, and keep my sabbaths: I *am* the LORD your God.

Deut. 5. 16 Honour thy father and thy mother, as the LORD thy God hath commanded thee; that thy days may be prolonged, and that it may go well with thee, in the land which the LORD thy God giveth thee.

Prov.23. 22 Hearken unto thy father that begat thee, and despise not thy mother when she is old.

Eph. 6. 2 Honour thy father and mother, which is the first commandment with promise;
3 That it may be well with thee, and thou mayest live long on the earth.

I

Ex. 21. 17 And he that curseth his father, or his mother, shall surely be put to death.

Lev. 20. 9 For every one that curseth his father or his mother shall be surely put to death: he hath cursed his father or his mother; his blood *shall be* upon him.

Deut.27. 16 Cursed *be* he that setteth light by his father or his mother: and all the people shall say, Amen.

Prov.20. 20 Whoso curseth his father or his mother, his lamp shall be put out in obscure darkness.

Prov.30. 17 The eye *that* mocketh at *his* father, and despiseth to obey *his* mother, the ravens of the valley shall pick it out, and the young eagles shall eat it.

K

Mark 7. 11, 12. *See text of topic.*

L

Mark 7. 6. *See text of topic.*

M

Isa. 29. 13 Wherefore the Lord said, Forasmuch as this people draw near *me* with their mouth, and with their lips do honour me, but have removed their heart far from me, and their fear toward me is taught by the precept of men:

Eze. 33. 31 And they come unto thee as the people cometh, and they sit before thee *as* my people, and they hear thy words, but they will not do them: for with their mouth they show much love, *but* their heart goeth after their covetousness.

N

Isa. 29. 13. *See under M.*

Prov.30. 5 Every word of God *is* pure: he *is* a shield unto them that put their trust in him.
6 Add thou not unto his words, lest he reprove thee, and thou be found a liar.

Col. 2. 18 Let no man beguile you of your reward in a voluntary humility and worshipping of angels, intruding into those things which he hath not seen, vainly puffed up by his fleshly mind,
19 And not holding the Head, from which all the body by joints and bands having nourishment ministered, and knit together, increaseth with the increase of God.

I Tim. 1. 6 From which some having swerved have turned aside unto vain jangling;
7 Desiring to be teachers of the law; understanding neither what they say, nor whereof they affirm.

I Tim. 4. 1 Now the Spirit speaketh expressly, that in the latter times some shall depart form the faith, giving heed to seducing spirits, and doctrines of devils;

Tit. 1. 14 Not giving heed to Jewish fables, and commandments of men, that turn from the truth.

3

Sextarius is about a pint and a half.

4

Or, *beds.*

O

Matt. 15. 2. *See text of topic.*

P

Isa. 29. 13. *See under M.*
Matt. 15. 8. *See text of topic.*

5

Or, *frustrate.*

Isa. 24. 5 The earth also is defiled under the inhabitants thereof; because they have transgressed the laws, changed the ordinance, broken the everlasting covenant.

Tit. 1. 14. *See under N.*

Q

Ex. 20. 12, Deut. 5. 16. *See under H.*
Matt. 15. 4. *See text of topic.*

R

Ex. 21. 17, Lev. 20. 9 and Prov. 20. 20. *See under I.*

S

Matt. 15. 5. *See text of topic.*

Matt.23. 18 And, Whosoever shall swear by the altar, it is nothing; but whosoever sweareth by the gift that is upon it, he is guilty.

I Tim.5. 8 But if any provide not for his own, and specially for those of his own house, he hath denied the faith, and is worse than an infidel.

§ 85. THE THIRD PASSOVER. UNWASHEN HANDS. PHARASAIC

CHAP. 15.

10 [t]And he called the multitude, and said unto them, Hear, and understand:

11 [u]Not that which goeth into the mouth defileth a man; but that which cometh out of the mouth, this defileth a man.

12 Then came his disciples, and said unto him, Knowest thou that the Pharisees were offended, after they heard this saying?

13 But he answered and said, [x]Every plant, which my heavenly Father hath not planted, shall be rooted up.

14 [y]Let them alone: [z]they be blind leaders of the blind. And if the blind lead the blind, both shall fall into the ditch.

15 [a]Then answered Peter and said unto him, Declare unto us this parable.

16 And Jesus said, [b]Are ye also yet without understanding?

17 Do not ye yet understand, that [c]whatsoever entereth in at the mouth goeth into the belly, and is cast out into the draught?

18 But [d]those things which proceed out of the mouth come forth from the heart; and they defile the man.

19 [e]For out of the heart proceed evil thoughts, murders, adulteries, fornications, thefts, false witness, blasphemies:

20 These are *the things* which defile a man: but to eat with unwashen hands defileth not a man.

CHAP. 7.

14 [f]And when he had called all the people *unto him*, he said unto them, Hearken unto me every one *of you*, and understand:

15 There is [g]nothing from without a man, that entering into him can defile him: but the things which come out of him, those are they that defile the man.

16 [h]If any man have ears to hear, let him hear.

17 [i]And when he was entered into the house from the people, his disciples asked him concerning the parable.

18 And he saith unto them, Are ye so without understanding also? Do ye not perceive, that whatsoever thing from without entereth into the man, *it* cannot defile him;

19 Because it entereth not into his heart, but into the belly, and goeth out into the draught, purging all meats?

20 And he said, That which cometh out of the man, that defileth the man.

21 [k]For from within, out of the heart of men, proceed evil thoughts, adulteries, fornications, murders,

22 Thefts, [6]covetousness, wickedness, deceit, lasciviousness, an evil eye, blasphemy, pride, foolishness:

23 All these evil things come from within, and defile the man.

T

Mark 7. 14. *See text of topic.*

U

Acts 10. 14 But Peter said, Not so, Lord; for I have never eaten any thing that is common or unclean.

15 And the voice *spake* unto him again the second time, What God hath cleansed *that* call not thou common.

U—CONTINUED.

Rom.14. 14 I know, and am persuaded by the Lord Jesus, that *there is* nothing unclean of itself: but to him that esteemeth any thing to be unclean, to him *it is* unclean.

TRADITIONS (CONCLUDED). TIME, APRIL, A. D. 29; PLACE, JERUSALEM, CAPERNAUM.

U—CONCLUDED.

Rom.14. 17 For the kingdom of God is not meat and drink; but righteousness, and peace, and joy in the Holy Ghost.

Rom.14. 20 For meat destroy not the work of God. All things indeed *are* pure; but *it is* evil for that man who eateth with offence.

I Tim.4. 4 For every creature of God *is* good, and nothing to be refused, if it be received with thanksgiving:

Tit. 1. 15 Unto the pure all things *are* pure: but unto them that are defiled and unbelieving *is* nothing pure; but even their mind and conscience is defiled.

X

John 15. 2 Every branch in me that beareth not fruit he taketh away: and every *branch* that beareth fruit, he purgeth it, that it may bring forth more fruit.

Y

Ps. 81. 12 So I gave them up unto their own hearts' lust: *and* they walked in their own counsels.

Hos. 4. 17 Ephraim *is* joined to idols: let him alone.

Rev. 22. 11 He that is unjust, let him be unjust still: and he which is filthy, let him be filthy still: and he that is righteous, let him be righteous still: and he that is holy, let him be holy still.

Z

Isa. 9. 16 For the leaders of this people cause *them* to err; and *they that are* led of them *are* destroyed.

Mal. 2. 8 But ye are departed out of the way; ye have caused many to stumble at the law; ye have corrupted the covenant of Levi, saith the LORD of hosts.

Matt.23. 16 Woe unto you, *ye* blind guides, which say, Whosoever shall swear by the temple, it is nothing; but whosoever shall swear by the gold of the temple, he is a debtor!

Luke 6. 39 And he spake a parable unto them; Can the blind lead the blind? shall they not both fall into the ditch?

A

Mark 7. 17. *See text of topic.*

B

Matt.16. 9 Do ye not yet understand, neither remember the five loaves of the five thousand, and how many baskets ye took up?

Mark 7. 18. *See text of topic.*

C

I Cor. 6. 13 Meats for the belly, and the belly for meats: but God shall destroy both it and them. Now the body *is* not for fornication, but for the Lord; and the Lord for the body.

D

Prov.16. 27 An ungodly man diggeth up evil: and in his lips *there is* as a burning fire.

Jas. 3. 6 And the tongue *is* a fire, a world of iniquity: so is the tongue among our members, that it defileth the whole body, and setteth on fire the course of nature; and it is set on fire of hell.

E

Gen. 6. 5 And GOD saw that the wickedness of man *was* great in the earth, and *that* every imagination of the thoughts of his heart *was* only evil continually.

Prov. 4. 23 Keep thy heart with all diligence; for out of it *are* the issues of life.

Prov. 6. 14 Frowardness *is* in his heart, he deviseth mischief continually; he soweth discord.

Jer. 17. 9 The heart *is* deceitful above all *things*, and desperately wicked: who can know it?

Mark 7. 20, 21. *See text of topic.*

F

Matt. 15. 10. *See text of topic.*

G

Acts 10. 14, 15 and Rom. 14. 17. *See under U.*

I Cor. 8. 8 But meat commendeth us not to God: for neither, if we eat, are we the better; neither, if we eat not, are we the worse.

Tit. 1. 15. *See under U.*

H

Matt.11. 15 He that hath ears to hear, let him hear.

I

Matt. 15. 15. *See text of topic.*

K

Gen. 6. 5. *See under E.* Matt. 15. 19. *See text of topic.*

Gal. 5. 19 Now the works of the flesh are manifest, which are *these*, Adultery, fornication, uncleanness, lasciviousness,

20 Idolatry, witchcraft, hatred, variance, emulations, wrath, strife, seditions, heresies,

21 Envyings, murders, drunkenness, revellings, and such like: of the which I tell you before, as I have also told *you* in time past, that they which do such things shall not inherit the kingdom of God.

6

Gr., *covetousnesses, wickednesses.*

§ 86. THE DAUGHTER OF A SYROPHŒNICIAN

15: 21–28.

21 [a] Then Jesus went thence, and departed into the coasts of Tyre and Sidon.

22 And, behold, a woman of Canaan came out of the same coasts, and cried unto him, saying, Have mercy on me, O Lord, *thou* Son of David; my daughter is grievously vexed with a devil.

23 But he answered her not a word. And his disciples came and besought him, saying, Send her away; for she crieth after us.

24 But he answered and said, [b] I am not sent but unto the lost sheep of the house of Israel.

25 Then came she and worshipped him, saying, Lord, help me.

26 But he answered and said, It is not meet to take the children's bread, and to cast *it* to [c] dogs.

27 And she said, Truth, Lord: yet the dogs eat of the crumbs which fall from their masters' table.

28 Then Jesus answered and said unto her, O woman, great *is* thy faith: be it unto thee even as thou wilt. And her daughter was made whole from that very hour.

A

Mark 7. 24. *See text of topic.*

B

Isa. 53. 6 All we like sheep have gone astray; we have turned every one to his own way; and the LORD hath laid on him the iniquity of us all.

Jer. 50. 6 My people hath been lost sheep; their shepherds have caused them to go astray, they have turned them away *on* the mountains: they have gone from mountain to hill, they have forgotten their resting-place.

7: 24–30.

24 [d] And from thence he arose, and went into the borders of Tyre and Sidon, and entered into a house, and would have no man know *it:* but he could not be hid.

25 For a *certain* woman, whose young daughter had an unclean spirit, heard of him, and came and fell at his feet:

26 The woman was a [1] Greek, a Syrophœnician by nation; and she besought him that he would cast forth the devil out of her daughter.

27 But Jesus said unto her, Let [e] the children first be filled: for it is not meet to take the children's bread, and to cast *it* unto the dogs.

28 And she answered and said unto him, Yes, Lord: [f] yet the dogs under the table eat of the children's crumbs.

29 And he said unto her, For this saying go thy way; the devil is gone out of thy daughter.

30 And when she was come to her house, she found [g] the devil gone out, and her daughter laid upon the bed.

B—CONTINUED.

Jer. 50. 7 All that found them have devoured them; and their adversaries said, We offend not, because they have sinned against the LORD, the habitation of justice, even the LORD, the hope of their fathers.

8 Remove out of the midst of Babylon, and go forth out of the land of the Chaldeans, and be as the he-goats before the flocks.

Eze. 34. 5 And they were scattered, because *there is* no shepherd: and they became meat to all the beasts of the field, when they were scattered.

6 My sheep wandered through all the mountains, and upon every high hill: yea, my flock was scattered upon all

WOMAN HEALED. TIME, SUMMER, A. D. 29; PLACE, PHŒNICIA.

B—CONCLUDED.

the face of the earth, and none did search or seek *after them.*

Matt. 10. 5 These twelve Jesus sent forth, and commanded them, saying, Go not into the way of the Gentiles, and into *any* city of the Samaritans enter ye not:

6 But go rather to the lost sheep of the house of Israel.

Acts 3. 25 Ye are the children of the prophets, and of the covenant which God made with our fathers, saying unto Abraham, And in thy seed shall all the kindreds of the earth be blessed.

26 Unto you first God, having raised up his Son Jesus, sent him to bless you, in turning away every one of you from his iniquities.

Acts 13. 46 Then Paul and Barnabas waxed bold, and said, It was necessary that the word of God should first have been spoken to you: but seeing ye put it from you, and judge yourselves unworthy of everlasting life, lo, we turn to the Gentiles.

Rom. 15. 8 Now I say that Jesus Christ was a minister of the circumcision for the truth of God, to confirm the promises *made* unto the fathers:

C

Isa. 56. 9 All ye beasts of the field, come to devour, *yea*, all ye beasts in the forest.

10 His watchmen *are* blind: they are all ignorant, they *are* all dumb dogs, they cannot bark; sleeping, lying down, loving to slumber.

Matt. 7. 6 Give not that which is holy unto the dogs, neither cast ye your pearls before swine, lest they trample them under their feet, and turn again and rend you.

Eph. 2. 12 That at that time ye were without Christ, being aliens from the commonwealth of Israel, and strangers from the covenants of promise, having no hope, and without God in the world:

Phil. 3. 2 Beware of dogs, beware of evil workers, beware of the concision.

Rev. 22. 15 For without *are* dogs, and sorcerers, and whoremongers, and murderers, and idolaters, and whosoever loveth and maketh a lie.

D

Matt. 15. 21. *See text of topic.*

1

Or, *Gentile.*

E

Matt. 10. 5, 6. *See under B.*
Acts. 13. 46. *See under B.*

Rom. 9. 4 Who are Israelites; to whom *pertaineth* the adoption, and the glory, and the covenants, and the giving of the law, and the service *of God*, and the promises;

Rom. 15. 8. *See under B.*

F

Acts 11. 17 Forasmuch then as God gave them the like gift as *he did* unto us, who believed on the Lord Jesus Christ, what was I, that I could withstand God?

18 When they heard these things, they held their peace, and glorified God, saying, Then hath God also to the Gentiles granted repentance unto life.

Acts 22. 21 And he said unto me, Depart: for I will send thee far hence unto the Gentiles.

Rom. 3. 29 *Is he* the God of the Jews only? *is he* not also of the Gentiles? Yes, of the Gentiles also:

Rom. 10. 12 For there is no difference between the Jew and the Greek: for the same Lord over all is rich unto all that call upon him.

Gal. 3. 28 There is neither Jew nor Greek, there is neither bond nor free, there is neither male nor female: for ye are all one in Christ Jesus.

29 And if ye *be* Christ's, then are ye Abraham's seed, and heirs according to the promise.

Col. 3. 11 Where there is neither Greek nor Jew, circumcision nor uncircumcision, Barbarian, Scythian, bond *nor* free: but Christ *is* all, and in all.

G

Matt. 9. 29 Then touched he their eyes, saying, According to your faith be it unto you.

Mark 9. 23 Jesus said unto him, If thou canst believe, all things *are* possible to him that believeth.

Luke 17. 6 And the Lord said, If ye had faith as a grain of mustard seed, ye might say unto this sycamine tree, Be thou plucked up by the root, and be thou planted in the sea; and it should obey you.

I Jno. 3. 8 He that committeth sin is of the devil; for the devil sinneth from the beginning. For this purpose the Son of God was manifested, that he might destroy the works of the devil.

§ 87. A DEAF AND DUMB MAN AND MANY OTHERS HEALED.

15 : 29–31.

29 [a]And Jesus departed from thence, and came nigh [b]unto the sea of Galilee; and went up into a mountain, and sat down there.

30 [c]And great multitudes came unto him, having with them *those that were* lame, blind, dumb, maimed, and many others, and cast them down at Jesus' feet; and he healed them:

31 Insomuch that the multitude wondered, when they saw the dumb to speak, the maimed to be whole, the lame to walk, and the blind to see: and [d]they glorified the [e]God of Israel.

A

Mark 7. 31. *See text of topic.*

B

Matt. 4. 18 And Jesus, walking by the sea of Galilee, saw two brethren, Simon called Peter, and Andrew his brother, casting a net into the sea: for they were fishers.

C

Isa. 35. 5 Then the eyes of the blind shall be opened, and the ears of the deaf shall be unstopped.

6 Then shall the lame *man* leap as a hart, and the tongue of the dumb sing: for in the wilderness shall waters break out, and streams in the desert.

Matt.11. 5 The blind receive their sight, and the lame walk, the lepers are cleansed, and the deaf hear, the dead are raised up, and the poor have the gospel preached to them.

Luke 7. 22 Then Jesus answering said unto them, Go your way, and tell John what things ye have seen and heard; how that the blind see, the lame walk, the lepers are cleansed, the deaf hear, the dead are raised, to the poor the gospel is preached.

Acts 2. 22 Ye men of Israel, hear these words; Jesus of Nazareth, a man approved of God among you by miracles and wonders and signs, which God did by him in the midst of you, as ye yourselves also know:

Acts 5. 15 Insomuch that they brought forth the sick into the streets, and laid *them* on beds and couches, that at the least

7 : 31–37.

31 [f]And again, departing from the coasts of Tyre and Sidon, he came unto the sea of Galilee, through the midst of the coasts of Decapolis.

32 And [g]they bring unto him one that was deaf, and had an impediment in his speech; and they beseech him to put his hand upon him.

33 And he took him aside from the multitude, and put his fingers into his ears, and [h]he spit, and touched his tongue;

34 And [i]looking up to heaven, [k]he sighed, and saith unto him, Ephphatha, that is, Be opened.

35 [l]And straightway his ears were opened, and the string of his tongue was loosed, and he spake plain.

36 And [m]he charged them that they should tell no man: but the more he charged them, so much the more a great deal they published *it*;

37 And [n]were beyond measure astonished, saying, He hath done all things well: he [o]maketh both the deaf to hear, and the dumb to speak.

C—Concluded.

the shadow of Peter passing by might overshadow some of them.

16 There came also a multitude *out* of the cities round about unto Jerusalem, bringing sick folks, and them which were vexed with unclean spirits: and they were healed every one.

Acts 19. 11 And God wrought special miracles by the hands of Paul:

12 So that from his body were brought unto the sick handkerchiefs or aprons, and the diseases departed from them, and the evil spirits went out of them.

D

Ps. 50. 15 And call upon me in the day of trouble: I will deliver thee, and thou shalt glorify me.

Ps. 50. 23 Whoso offereth praise glorifieth

TIME, SUMMER, A. D. 29; PLACE, THE DECAPOLIS.

D—CONCLUDED.

me: and to him that ordereth *his* conversation *aright* will I show the salvation of God.

Mark 2. 12 And immediately he arose, took up the bed, and went forth before them all; insomuch that they were all amazed, and glorified God, saying, We never saw it on this fashion.

John 9. 24 Then again called they the man that was blind, and said unto him, Give God the praise: we know that this man is a sinner.

E

Gen. 32. 28 And he said, Thy name shall be called no more Jacob, but Israel: for as a prince hast thou power with God and with men, and hast prevailed.

Ex. 24. 10 And they saw the God of Israel: and *there was* under his feet as it were a paved work of a sapphire stone, and as it were the body of heaven in *his* clearness.

F

Matt. 15. 29. *See text of topic.*

G

Matt. 9. 32 As they went out, behold, they brought to him a dumb man possessed with a devil.

Luke 11. 14 And he was casting out a devil, and it was dumb. And it came to pass, when the devil was gone out, the dumb spake; and the people wondered.

H

Mark 8. 23 And he took the blind man by the hand, and led him out of the town; and when he had spit on his eyes, and put his hands upon him, he asked him if he saw aught.

John 9. 6 When he had thus spoken he spat on the ground, and made clay of the spittle, and he anointed the eyes of the blind man with the clay,

I

Mark 6. 41 And when he had taken the five loaves and the two fishes, he looked up to heaven, and blessed, and brake the loaves, and gave *them* to his disciples to set before them; and the two fishes divided he among them all.

John 11. 41 Then they took away the stone *from the place* where the dead was laid. And Jesus lifted up *his* eyes, and said, Father, I thank thee that thou hast heard me.

John 17. 1 These words spake Jesus, and lifted up his eyes to heaven, and said, Father, the hour is come; glorify thy Son, that thy Son also may glorify thee:

K

John 11. 33 When Jesus therefore saw her weeping, and the Jews also weeping which came with her, he groaned in the spirit, and was troubled,

John 11. 38 Jesus therefore again groaning in himself cometh to the grave. It was a cave, and a stone lay upon it.

L

Isa. 35. 5, 6 and Matt. 11. 5. *See under C.*

M

Isa. 42. 2 He shall not cry, nor lift up, nor cause his voice to be heard in the street.

Mark 5. 43 And he charged them straitly that no man should know it; and commanded that something should be given her to eat.

Mark 8. 26 And he sent him away to his house, saying, Neither go into the town, nor tell *it* to any in the town.

N

Ps. 139. 14 I will praise thee; for I am fearfully *and* wonderfully made: marvellous *are* thy works; and *that* my soul knoweth right well.

Acts. 3. 9 And all the people saw him walking and praising God:

10 And they knew that it was he which sat for alms at the Beautiful gate of the temple: and they were filled with wonder and amazement at that which had happened unto him.

11 And as the lame man which was healed held Peter and John, all the people ran together unto them in the porch that is called Solomon's, greatly wondering.

12 And when Peter saw *it*, he answered unto the people, Ye men of Israel, why marvel ye at this? or why look ye so earnestly on us, as though by our own power or holiness we had made this man to walk?

13 The God of Abraham, and of Isaac, and of Jacob, the God of our fathers, hath glorified his Son Jesus; whom ye delivered up, and denied him in the presence of Pilate, when he was determined to let *him* go.

O

Ex. 4. 10 And Moses said unto the LORD, O my Lord, I *am* not eloquent, neither heretofore, nor since thou hast spoken unto thy servant; but I *am* slow of speech, and of a slow tongue.

11 And the LORD said unto him, Who hath made man's mouth? or who maketh the dumb, or deaf, or the seeing, or the blind? have not I the LORD?

§ 88. FEEDING OF THE FOUR THOUSAND.

MATTHEW 15: 32–39.

32 [a] Then Jesus called his disciples *unto him*, and said, I [b] have compassion on the multitude, because they continue with me now three days, and have nothing to eat: and I will not send them away fasting, lest they faint in the way.

33 [c] And his disciples say unto him, Whence should we have so much bread in the wilderness, as to fill so great a multitude?

34 And Jesus saith unto them, How many loaves have ye? And they said, Seven, and a few little fishes.

35 And he commanded the multitude to sit down on the ground.

36 And [d] he took the seven loaves and the fishes, and [e] gave thanks, and brake *them*, and gave to his disciples, and the disciples to the multitude.

37 And they did all eat, and were filled: and they took up of the broken *meat* that was left seven baskets full.

38 And they that did eat were four thousand men, beside women and children.

39 [f] And he sent away the multitude, and took ship, and came into the coasts of Magdala.

A

Mark 8. 1. *See text of topic.*

B

Ps. 103. 13 Like as a father pitieth *his* children, *so* the LORD pitieth them that fear him.

Mic. 7. 18 Who *is* a God like unto thee, that pardoneth iniquity, and passeth by the transgression of the remnant of his heritage? he retaineth not his anger for ever, because he delighteth *in* mercy.

MARK 8: 1–10.

1 In those days [g] the multitude being very great, and having nothing to eat, Jesus called his disciples *unto him*, and saith unto them,

2 I have [h] compassion on the multitude, because they have now been with me three days, and have nothing to eat:

3 And if I send them away fasting to their own houses, they will faint by the way: for divers of them came from far.

4 And his disciples answered him, [i] From whence can a man satisfy these *men* with bread here in the wilderness?

5 [k] And he asked them, how many loaves have ye? And they said, Seven.

6 And he commanded the people to sit down on the ground: and he took the seven loaves, and [l] gave thanks, and brake, and gave to his disciples to set before *them;* and they did set *them* before the people.

7 And they had a few small fishes: and [m] he blessed, and commanded to set them also before *them.*

8 So they did eat, and were filled: and they took up of the broken *meat* that was left seven baskets.

9 And they that had eaten were about four thousand: and he sent them away.

10 [n] And straightway he entered into a ship with his disciples, and came into the parts of Dalmanutha.

B—CONCLUDED.

Heb. 2. 17 Wherefore in all things it behooved him to be made like unto *his* brethren, that he might be a merciful and faithful high priest in things *pertaining* to God, to make reconciliation for the sins of the people.

Time, Summer, A. D. 29; Place, The Decapolis.

C

Num. 11. 21 And Moses said, The people, among whom I *am, are* six hundred thousand footmen; and thou hast said, I will give them flesh, that they may eat a whole month.

22 Shall the flocks and the herds be slain for them, to suffice them? or shall all the fish of the sea be gathered together for them, to suffice them?

II Ki. 4. 42 And there came a man from Baal-shalisha and brought the man of God bread of the first-fruits, twenty loaves of barley, and full ears of corn in the husk thereof. And he said, Give unto the people, that they may eat.

43 And his servitor said, What, should I set this before a hundred men? He said again, Give the people, that they may eat: for thus saith the Lord, They shall eat, and shall leave *thereof.*

44 So he set *it* before them, and they did eat, and left *thereof,* according to the word of the Lord.

Ps. 24. 1 The earth *is* the Lord's, and the fulness thereof; the world, and they that dwell therein:

Ps. 78. 19 Yea, they spake against God; they said, Can God furnish a table in the wilderness?

20 Behold, he smote the rock, that the waters gushed out, and the streams overflowed; can he give bread also? can he provide flesh for his people?

Mark 8. 4. *See text of topic.*

D

Matt. 14. 19 And he commanded the multitude to sit down on the grass, and took the five loaves, and the two fishes, and looking up to heaven, he blessed, and brake, and gave the loaves to *his* disciples, and the disciples to the multitude.

E

Deut. 8. 10 When thou hast eaten and art full, then thou shalt bless the Lord thy God for the good land which he hath given thee.

I Sa. 9. 13 As soon as ye be come into the city, ye shall straightway find him, before he go up to the high place to eat: for the people will not eat until he come, because he doth bless the sacrifice; *and* afterwards they eat that be bidden. Now therefore get you up; for about this time ye shall find him.

E—Concluded.

Luke 22. 19 And he took bread, and gave thanks, and brake *it,* and gave unto them, saying, This is my body which is given for you: this do in remembrance of me.

F

Mark. 8. 10. *See text of topic.*

G

Matt. 15. 32. *See text of topic.*

H

Ps. 145. 9 The Lord *is* good to all: and his tender mercies *are* over all his works.

Heb. 2. 17. *See under B.*

Heb. 4. 15 For we have not a high priest which cannot be touched with the feeling of our infirmities; but was in all points tempted like as *we are, yet* without sin.

I

Num. 11. 21, 22. *See under C.*
II Ki. 4. 42, 43. *See under C.*

II Ki. 7. 1 Then Elisha said, Hear ye the word of the Lord; Thus saith the Lord, To-morrow about this time *shall* a measure of fine flour *be sold* for a shekel, and two measures of barley for a shekel, in the gate of Samaria.

2 Then a lord on whose hand the king leaned answered the man of God, and said, Behold, *if* the Lord would make windows in heaven, might this thing be? And he said, Behold, thou shalt see *it* with thine eyes, but shalt not eat thereof.

K

Matt. 15. 34. *See text of topic.*

Mark 6. 38 He saith unto them, How many loaves have ye? go and see. And when they knew, they say, Five, and two fishes.

L

Deut. 8. 10. *See under E.*

I Tim. 4. 4 For every creature of God *is* good, and nothing to be refused, if it be received with thanksgiving:

5 For it is sanctified by the word of God and prayer.

M

Matt. 14. 19. *See under D.*

Mark 6. 41 And when he had taken the five loaves and the two fishes, he looked up to heaven, and blessed, and brake the loaves, and gave *them* to his disciples to set before them; and the two fishes divided he among them all.

N

Matt. 15. 39. *See text of topic.*

§ 89. THE PHARISEES AND SADDUCEES AGAIN REQUIRE A SIGN.

MATTHEW 16 : 1–4.

1 The [a]Pharisees also with the Sadducees came, and tempting desired him that he would show them a sign from heaven.

2 He answered and said unto them, When it is evening, ye say, *It will be* fair weather: for the sky is red.

3 And in the morning, *It will be* foul weather to day: for the sky is red and lowering. O *ye* hypocrites, ye can discern the face of the sky; but can ye not *discern* the [b]signs of the times?

4 [c]A wicked and adulterous generation seeketh after a sign; and there shall no sign be given unto it, but the sign of the prophet Jonas. And he left them, and departed.

MARK 8 : 11–13.

11 [d]And the Pharisees came forth, and began to question with him, seeking of him a sign from heaven, tempting him.

12 And he sighed deeply in his spirit, and saith, Why doth this generation seek after a sign? verily I say unto you, There shall no sign be given unto this generation.

13 And he left them, and entering into the ship again departed to the other side.

A

Matt.12. 38 Then certain of the scribes and of the Pharisees answered, saying, Master, we would see a sign from thee.

Mark 8. 11. *See text of topic.*

Luke 11. 16 And others, tempting *him*, sought of him a sign from heaven.

Luke 12. 54 And he said also to the people,

§ 90. DISCIPLES CAUTIONED AGAINST THE LEAVEN OF THE PHARISEES.

MATTHEW 16 : 5–12.

5 And [a]when his disciples were come to the other side, they had forgotten to take bread.

6 Then Jesus said unto them, [b]Take heed and beware of the leaven of the Pharisees and of the Sadducees.

7 And they reasoned among themselves, saying, *It is* because we have taken no bread.

8 *Which* when Jesus perceived, he said unto them, O ye of little faith, why reason ye among yourselves, because ye have brought no bread?

A

Mark 8. 14. *See text of topic.*

B

Luke 12. 1 In the mean time, when there were gathered together an innumerable multitude of people, insomuch that they trode one upon another, he began to say unto his disciples first of

MARK 8 : 14–21.

14 [c]Now *the disciples* had forgotten to take bread, neither had they in the ship with them more than one loaf.

15 [d]And he charged them, saying, Take heed, beware of the leaven of the Pharisees, and *of* the leaven of Herod.

16 And they reasoned among themselves, saying, *It is* [e]because we have no bread.

17 And when Jesus knew *it*, he saith unto them, Why reason ye, because ye have no bread? [f]perceive ye not yet, neither understand? have ye your heart yet hardened?

18 [g]Having eyes, see ye not? and having ears, hear ye not? and do ye not remember?

B—CONCLUDED.

all, Beware ye of the leaven of the Pharisees, which is hypocrisy.

[SEE § 52.] TIME, SUMMER, A. D. 29; PLACE, NEAR MAGDALA.

A—CONCLUDED.

When ye see a cloud rise out of the west, straightway ye say, There cometh a shower; and so it is.
55 And when *ye see* the south wind blow, ye say, There will be heat; and it cometh to pass.
56 *Ye* hypocrites, ye can discern the face of the sky and of the earth; but how is it that ye do not discern this time?

I Cor. 1. 22 For the Jews require a sign, and the Greeks seek after wisdom:

B

Gen. 49. 10 The sceptre shall not depart from Judah, nor a lawgiver from between his feet, until Shiloh come; and unto him *shall* the gathering of the people *be*.

Isa. 7. 14 Therefore the Lord himself shall give you a sign; Behold, a virgin shall conceive, and bare a son, and shall call his name Immanuel.

Dan. 9. 24 Seventy weeks are determined upon thy people, and upon thy holy city, to finish the transgression, and to make an end of sins, and to make

B—CONCLUDED.

reconciliation for iniquity, and to bring in everlasting righteousness, and to seal up the vision and prophecy, and to anoint the Most Holy.

Mic. 5. 2 But thou, Beth-lehem Ephratah, *though* thou be little among the thousands of Judah, *yet* out of thee shall he come forth unto me *that is* to be ruler in Israel; whose goings forth *have been* from of old, from everlasting.

Mal. 3. 1 Behold, I will send my messenger, and he shall prepare the way before me: and the Lord, whom ye seek, shall suddenly come to his temple, even the messenger of the covenant, whom ye delight in: behold, he shall come, saith the LORD of hosts.

C

Matt. 12. 39 But he answered and said unto them, An evil and adulterous generation seeketh after a sign; and there shall no sign be given to it, but the sign of the prophet Jonas:

D

Matt. 12. 38. *Under A.* Matt. 16. 1. *See text of topic.*

TIME, SUMMER, A. D. 29; PLACE, NORTHEAST COAST OF THE LAKE OF GALILEE.

C

Matt. 16. 5. *See text of topic.*

D

Matt. 16. 6. *See text of topic.* Luke 12. 1. *Under B.*

I Cor. 5. 6 Your glorying *is* not good. Know ye not that a little leaven leaveneth the whole lump?
7 Purge out therefore the old leaven, that ye may be a new lump, as ye are unleavened. For even Christ our passover is sacrificed for us:
8 Therefore let us keep the feast, not with old leaven, neither with the leaven of malice and wickedness; but with the unleavened *bread* of sincerity and truth.

E

Matt. 16. 7. *See text of topic.*

F

Mark 6. 52 For they considered not *the miracle* of the loaves; for their heart was hardened.

G

Deut. 29. 4 Yet the LORD hath not given you a heart to perceive, and eyes to see, and ears to hear, unto this day.
5 And I have led you forty years in the wilderness: your clothes are not waxen old upon you, and thy shoe is not waxen old upon thy foot.

G—CONCLUDED.

Deut. 29. 6 Ye have not eaten bread, neither have ye drunk wine or strong drink: that ye might know that I *am* the LORD your God.

Ps. 69. 23 Let their eyes be darkened, that they see not; and make their loins continually to shake.

Ps. 115. 5 They have mouths, but they speak not: eyes have they, but they see not:
6 They have ears, but they hear not: noses have they, but they smell not:
7 They have hands, but they handle not: feet have they, but they walk not: neither speak they through their throat.
8 They that make them are like unto them, *so is* every one that trusteth in them.

Isa. 42. 18 Hear, ye deaf; and look, ye blind, that ye may see.

Isa. 44. 18 They have not known nor understood: for he hath shut their eyes, that they cannot see; *and* their hearts, that they cannot understand.

Jer. 5. 21 Hear now this, O foolish people, and without understanding; which have eyes, and see not; which have ears and hear not:

§ 90. DISCIPLES CAUTIONED AGAINST THE LEAVEN OF THE PHARISEES

CHAP. 16.

9 [h]Do ye not yet understand, neither remember the five loaves of the five thousand, and how many baskets ye took up?

10 [i]Neither the seven loaves of the four thousand, and how many baskets ye took up?

11 How is it that ye do not understand that I spake *it* not to you concerning bread, that ye should beware of the leaven of the Pharisees and of the Sadducees?

12 Then understood they how that he bade *them* not beware of the leaven of bread, [k]but of the doctrine of the Pharisees and of the Sadducees.

CHAP. 8.

19 [l]When I brake the five loaves among five thousand, how many baskets full of fragments took ye up? They say unto him, Twelve.

20 And [m]when the seven among four thousand, how many baskets full of fragments took ye up? And they said, Seven.

21 And he said unto them, How is it that [n]ye do not understand?

H

Matt. 14. 17 And they say unto him, We have here but five loaves, and two fishes.

John 6. 9 There is a lad here, which hath five barley loaves, and two small fishes: but what are they among so many?

§ 91. A BLIND MAN HEALED.

8 : 22–26.

22 And he cometh to Bethsaida; and they bring a blind man unto him, and besought him to touch him.

23 And he took the blind man [a]by the hand, and led him out of the town; and when [b]he had spit on his eyes, and put his hands upon him, he asked him if he saw aught.

24 And he looked up, and said, [c]I see men as trees, walking.

25 After that he put *his* hands again upon his eyes, and made him look up; and he was restored, [d]and saw every man clearly.

26 And he sent him away to his house, saying, Neither go into the town, [e]nor tell *it* to any in the town.

A

Isa. 51. 18 *There is* none to guide her among all the sons *whom* she hath brought forth; neither *is there any* that taketh her by the hand of all the sons *that* she hath brought up.

Jer. 31. 32 Not according to the covenant that I made with their fathers, in the day *that* I took them by the hand to bring them out of the land of Egypt; which my covenant they brake, although I was a husband unto them, saith the LORD:

B

Mark 7. 33 And he took him aside from the multitude, and put his fingers into his ears, and he spit, and touched his tongue;

John 9. 6 When he had thus spoken, he spat on the ground, and made clay of the spittle, and he anointed the eyes of the blind man with the clay,

7 And said unto him, Go, wash in the pool of Siloam, (which is by interpretation, Sent.) He went his way therefore, and washed, and came seeing.

Rev. 3. 18 I counsel thee to buy of me gold tried in the fire, that thou mayest be rich; and white raiment, that thou mayest be clothed, and *that* the shame of thy nakedness do not appear; and

B—CONCLUDED.

anoint thine eyes with eyesalve, that thou mayest see.

C

Judg. 9. 36 And when Gaal saw the people, he said to Zebul, Behold, there come

(CONCL'D). TIME, SUMMER, A.D. 29; PLACE, NORTHEAST COAST OF THE LAKE OF GALILEE.

I

Matt.15. 34 And Jesus saith unto them, How many loaves have ye? And they said, Seven, and a few little fishes.

K

Matt.15. 7 *Ye* hypocrites, well did Esaias prophesy of you, saying,
8 This people draweth nigh unto me with their mouth, and honoureth me with *their* lips; but their heart is far from me.
9 But in vain they do worship me, teaching *for* doctrines the commandments of men.

Acts 23. 8 For the Sadducees say that there is no resurrection, neither angel, nor spirit: but the Pharisees confess both.

L

Matt.14. 20 And they did all eat, and were filled: and they took up of the fragments that remained twelve baskets full.

Mark 6. 43 And they took up twelve baskets full of the fragments, and of the fishes.

Luke 9. 17 And they did eat, and were all

L—CONCLUDED.

filled: and there was taken up of fragments that remained to them twelve baskets.

John 6. 13 Therefore they gathered *them* together, and filled twelve baskets with the fragments of the five barley loaves, which remained over and above unto them that had eaten.

M

Matt.15. 37 And they did all eat, and were filled: and they took up of the broken *meat* that was left seven baskets full.

Mark 8. 8 So they did eat, and were filled: and they took up of the broken *meat* that was left seven baskets.

N

Ps. 94. 8 Understand, ye brutish among the people: and *ye* fools, when will ye be wise?

Mark 6. 52. *See under F, page 273.*
Mark 8. 17. *See text of topic.*

I Cor.15. 34 Awake to righteousness, and sin not; for some have not the knowledge of God: I speak *this* to your shame.

TIME, SUMMER, A. D. 29; PLACE, BETHSAIDA (JULIUS).

C—CONCLUDED.

people down from the top of the mountains. And Zebul said unto him, Thou seest the shadow of the mountains as *if they were* men.

Isa. 29. 18 And in that day shall the deaf hear the words of the book, and the eyes of the blind shall see out of obscurity, and out of darkness.

Isa. 32. 3 And the eyes of them that see shall not be dim, and the ears of them that hear shall hearken.

I Cor.13. 9 For ye know in part, and we prophesy in part.
10 But when that which is perfect is come, then that which is in part shall be done away.
11 When I was a child, I spake as a child, I understood as a child, I thought as a child: but when I became a man, I put away childish things.
12 For now we see through a glass, darkly; but then face to face: now I know in part; but then shall I know even as also I am known.

D

Prov. 4. 18 But the path of the just *is* as the shining light, that shineth more and more unto the perfect day.

Phil. 1. 6 Being confident of this very thing, that he which hath begun a good

D—CONCLUDED.

work in you will perform *it* until the day of Jesus Christ:

I Pet. 2. 9 But ye *are* a chosen generation, a royal priesthood, a holy nation, a peculiar people; that ye should show forth the praises of him who hath called you out of darkness into his marvellous light:

II Pet.3. 18 But grow in grace, and *in* the knowledge of our Lord and Saviour Jesus Christ. To him *be* glory both now and for ever. Amen.

E

Matt. 8. 4 And Jesus saith unto him, See thou tell no man; but go thy way, show thyself to the priest, and offer the gift that Moses commanded, for a testimony unto them.

Matt. 9. 30 And their eyes were opened; and Jesus straitly charged them, saying, See *that* no man know *it*.

Matt.12. 16 And charged them that they should not make him known.

Mark 5. 43 And he charged them straitly that no man should know it; and commanded that something should be given her to eat.

Mark 7. 36 And he charged them that they should tell no man: but the more he charged them, so much the more a a great deal they published *it;*

§ 92. PETER AND THE REST AGAIN PROFESS THEIR FAITH IN CHRIST.

16: 13–20.

13 When Jesus came into the coasts of Cæsarea Philippi, he asked his disciples, saying, [a]Whom do men say that I, the Son of man, am?

14 And they said, [b]Some *say that thou art* John the Baptist; some, [c]Elias; and others, Jeremias, or one of the prophets.

15 He saith unto them, But whom say ye that I am?

16 And Simon Peter answered and said, [d]Thou art the Christ, the Son of the living God.

17 And Jesus answered and said unto him, Blessed art thou, Simon Barjona: [e]for flesh and blood hath not revealed *it* unto thee, but [f]my Father which is in heaven.

18 And I say also unto thee, That [g]thou art Peter, and [h]upon this rock I will build my church; and [i]the gates of hell shall not prevail against it.

A

Dan. 7. 13 I saw in the night visions, and, behold, *one* like the Son of man came with the clouds of heaven, and came to the Ancient of days, and they brought him near before him.

Mark 8. 27 and Luke 9. 18. *See text of topic.*

Rom. 1. 3 Concerning his Son Jesus Christ our Lord, which was made of the seed of David according to the flesh;

4 And declared *to be* the Son of God with power, according to the Spirit of holiness, by the resurrection from the dead:

B

Matt.14. 2 And said unto his servants, This is John the Baptist; he is risen from the dead; and therefore mighty works do show forth themselves in him.

Luke 9. 7 Now Herod the tetrarch heard of all that was done by him: and he was perplexed, because that it was said of some, that John was risen from the dead;

8 And of some, that Elias had ap-

8 : 27–30.

27 And Jesus went out, and his disciples, into the towns of Cæsarea Philippi: and by the way he asked his disciples, saying unto them, Whom do men say that I am?

28 And they answered, [k]John the Baptist: but some *say*, Elias; and others, One of the prophets.

29 And he saith unto them, But whom say ye that I am? And Peter answereth and saith unto him, [l]Thou art the Christ.

B—Concluded.

peared; and of others, that one of the old prophets was risen again.

9 And Herod said, John have I beheaded; but who is this, of whom I hear such things? And he desired to see him.

C

Mal. 4. 5 Behold, I will send you Elijah the prophet before the coming of the great and dreadful day of the Lord:

D

Ps. 2. 7 I will declare the decree: the Lord hath said unto me, Thou *art* my Son; this day have I begotten thee.

Matt.14. 33 Then they that were in the ship came and worshipped him, saying, Of a truth thou art the Son of God.

Mark 8. 29 and Luke 9. 20. *See text of topic.*

John 6. 68 Then Simon Peter answered him, Lord, to whom shall we go? thou hast the words of eternal life.

69 And we believe and are sure that thou art that Christ, the Son of the living God.

John 11. 27 She saith unto him, Yea, Lord: I believe that thou art the Christ, the Son of God, which should come into the world.

Acts 8. 37 And Philip said, If thou believest with all thine heart, thou mayest. And he answered and said, I believe that Jesus Christ is the Son of God.

Acts 9. 20 And straightway he preached Christ in the synagogues, that he is the Son of God.

Heb. 1. 2 Hath in these last days spoken unto us by *his* Son, whom he hath appointed heir of all things, by whom also he made the worlds;

[SEE § 84.] TIME, SUMMER, A. D. 29; PLACE, REGION OF CÆSAREA PHILIPPI.

9: 18–21.

18 [m]And it came to pass, as he was alone praying, his disciples were with him; and he asked them, saying, Whom say the people that I am?

19 They answering said, [n]John the Baptist; but some *say*, Elias; and others *say*, that one of the old prophets is risen again.

20 He said unto them, [o]But whom say ye that I am? Peter answering said, The Christ of God.

D—CONCLUDED.

Heb. 1. 5 For unto which of the angels said he at any time, Thou art my Son, this day have I begotten thee? And again, I will be to him a Father, and he shall be to me a Son?

I Jno. 4. 14 And we have seen and do testify that the Father sent the Son *to be* the Saviour of the world.

15 Whosoever shall confess that Jesus is the Son of God, God dwelleth in him, and he in God.

I Jno. 5. 5 Who is he that overcometh the world, but he that believeth that Jesus is the Son of God?

E

Eph. 2. 8 For by grace are ye saved through faith; and that not of yourselves: *it is* the gift of God:

F

Isa. 54. 13 And all thy children *shall be* taught of the LORD; and great *shall be* the peace of thy children.

I Cor. 2. 10 But God hath revealed *them* unto us by his Spirit: for the Spirit searcheth all things, yea, the deep things of God.

Gal. 1. 16 To reveal his son in me, that I might preach him among the heathen; immediately I conferred not with flesh and blood:

Eph. 1. 17 That the God of our Lord Jesus Christ, the Father of glory, may give unto you the spirit of wisdom and revelation in the knowledge of him:

18 The eyes of your understanding being enlightened; that ye may know what is the hope of his calling, and what the riches of the glory of his inheritance in the saints.

I Jno. 4. 15 Whosoever shall confess that Jesus is the Son of God, God dwelleth in him, and he in God.

G

John 1. 42 And he brought him to Jesus. And when Jesus beheld him, he said, Thou art Simon the son of Jona: thou shalt be called Cephas, which is by interpretation, A stone.

H

Isa. 28. 16 Therefore thus saith the Lord GOD, Behold, I lay in Zion for a foundation a stone, a tried stone, a precious corner *stone*, a sure foundation: he that believeth shall not make haste.

I Cor. 3. 11 For other foundation can no man lay than that is laid, which is Jesus Christ.

Eph. 2. 20 And are built upon the foundation of the apostles and prophets, Jesus Christ himself being the chief corner *stone;*

Rev. 21. 14 And the wall of the city had twelve foundations, and in them the names of the twelve apostles of the Lamb.

I

Job 38. 17 Have the gates of death been opened unto thee? or hast thou seen the doors of the shadow of death?

Ps. 9. 13 Have mercy upon me, O LORD; consider my trouble *which I suffer* of them that hate me, thou that liftest me up from the gates of death:

Ps. 107. 18 Their soul abhorreth all manner of meat; and they draw near unto the gates of death.

Ps. 125. 1 They that trust in the LORD *shall be* as mount Zion, *which* cannot be removed, *but* abideth for ever.

Isa. 38. 10 I said in the cutting off of my days, I shall go to the gates of the grave: I am deprived of the residue of my years.

Isa. 54. 17 No weapon that is formed against thee shall prosper; and every tongue *that* shall rise against thee in judgment thou shalt condemn. This *is* the heritage of the servants of the LORD, and their righteousness *is* of me, saith the LORD.

K

Matt. 14. 2. *See under B.*

L

Matt. 16. 16. *See text of topic.*
John 6. 69, John 11. 27, Acts 8. 37 and Acts 9. 20. *See under D.*

M

Matt. 16. 13 and Mark 8. 27. *See text of topic.*

N

Matt. 14. 2 and Luke 9. 7, 8. *See under B.*

O

Matt. 16. 16. *See text of topic.*
John 6. 69, I Jno. 4. 14, 15 and I Jno. 5. 5. *See under D.*

§ 92. PETER AND THE REST AGAIN PROFESS THEIR FAITH IN CHRIST

MATTHEW — CHAP. 16.

19 [p]And I will give unto thee the keys of the kingdom of heaven: and whatsoever thou shalt bind on earth shall be bound in heaven; and whatsoever thou shalt loose on earth shall be loosed in heaven.

20 [q]Then charged he his disciples that they should tell no man that he was Jesus the Christ.

MARK — CHAP. 8.

30 [r]And he charged them that they should tell no man of him.

P

Isa. 22. 22 And the key of the house of David will I lay upon his shoulder; so he shall open, and none shall shut; and he shall shut, and none shall open.

Matt. 18. 18 Verily I say unto you, Whatsoever ye shall bind on earth shall be bound in heaven; and whatsoever ye shall loose on earth shall be loosed in heaven.

§ 93. JESUS FORETELLS HIS DEATH AND RESURRECTION.

MATTHEW — 16: 21–28.

21 From that time forth began Jesus [a]to show unto his disciples, how that he must go unto Jerusalem, and suffer many things of the elders and chief priests and scribes, and be killed, and be raised again the third day.

22 Then Peter took him, and began to rebuke him, saying, [1]Be it far from thee, Lord: this shall not be unto thee.

23 But he turned, and said unto Peter, Get thee behind me, [b]Satan: [c]thou art an offence unto me: for thou savourest not the things that be of God, but those that be of men.

24 [d]Then said Jesus unto his disciples, If any *man* will come after me, let him deny himself, and take up his cross, and follow me.

A

Luke 9. 22. *See text of topic.*

Luke 18. 31 Then he took *unto him* the twelve, and said unto them, Behold, we go up to Jerusalem, and all things that are written by the prophets concerning the Son of man shall be accomplished.

Luke 24. 6 He is not here, but is risen: remember how he spake unto you when he was yet in Galilee,

7 Saying, The Son of man must be delivered into the hands of sinful men,

MARK — 8: 31–38; 9: 1.

31 And [e]he began to teach them, that the Son of man must suffer many things, and be rejected of the elders, and *of* the chief priests, and scribes, and be killed, and after three days rise again.

32 And he spake that saying openly. And Peter took him, and began to rebuke him.

33 But when he had turned about and looked on his disciples, he rebuked Peter, saying, Get thee behind me, Satan: for thou savourest not the things that be of God, but the things that be of men.

34 And when he had called the people *unto him* with his disciples also, he said unto them, [f]Whosoever will come after me, let him deny himself, and take up his cross, and follow me.

A—CONCLUDED.

and be crucified, and the third day rise again.

1

Gr., *pity thyself.*

B

II Sa. 19. 22 And David said, What have I to do with you, ye sons of Zeruiah, that ye should this day be adversaries unto me? shall there any man be put

(CONCL'D). [SEE § 84.] TIME, SUMMER, A. D. 29; PLACE, REGION OF CÆSAREA PHILIPPI.

CHAP. 9.

21 [s]And he straitly charged them, and commanded *them* to tell no man that thing;

P—CONTINUED.

John 20. 23 Whosesoever sins ye remit, they are remitted unto them; *and* whosesoever *sins* ye retain, they are retained.

I Cor. 5. 4 In the name of our Lord Jesus Christ, when ye are gathered together, and my spirit, with the power of our Lord Jesus Christ,

5 To deliver such a one unto Satan

P—CONCLUDED.

for the destruction of the flesh, that the spirit may be saved in the day of the Lord Jesus.

Q

Matt. 17. 9 And as they came down from the mountain, Jesus charged them, saying, Tell the vision to no man, until the Son of man be risen again from the dead.

Mark 8. 30 and Luke 9. 21. *See text of topic.*

R

Matt. 16. 20. *See text of topic.*

S

Matt. 16. 20. *See text of topic.*

TIME, SUMMER, A. D. 29; PLACE, REGION OF CÆSAREA PHILIPPI.

9: 22–27.

22 Saying, [g]The Son of man must suffer many things, and be rejected of the elders and chief priests and scribes, and be slain, and be raised the third day.

23 [h]And he said to *them* all, If any *man* will come after me, let him deny himself, and take up his cross daily, and follow me.

B—CONCLUDED.

to death this day in Israel? for do not I know that I *am* this day king over Israel?

C

Rom. 8. 7 Because the carnal mind is enmity against God: for it is not subject to the law of God, neither indeed can be.

D

Matt. 10. 38 And he that taketh not his cross, and followeth after me, is not worthy of me.

Mark 8. 34 and Luke 9. 23. *See text of topic.*

Luke 14. 27 And whosoever doth not bear his cross, and come after me, cannot be my disciple.

I Thes. 3. 3 That no man should be moved by these afflictions: for yourselves know that we are appointed thereunto.

II Tim. 3. 12 Yea, and all that will live godly in Christ Jesus shall suffer persecution.

E

Matt. 16. 21. *See text of topic.*

Matt. 17. 22 And while they abode in Galilee, Jesus said unto them, The Son of man shall be betrayed into the hands of men:

Luke 9. 22. *See text of topic.*

F

Matt. 5. 29 And if thy right eye offend thee, pluck it out, and cast *it* from thee: for it is profitable for thee that one of thy members should perish, and not *that* thy whole body should be cast into hell.

30 And if thy right hand offend thee, cut it off, and cast *it* from thee: for it is profitable for thee that one of thy members should perish, and not *that* thy whole body should be cast into hell.

Matt. 6. 13 And lead us not into temptation, but deliver us from evil: For thine is the kingdom, and the power, and the glory for ever. Amen.

14 For if ye forgive men their trespasses, your heavenly Father will also forgive you:

Matt. 10. 38 and Luke 14. 27. *See under D.*

Luke 13. 24 Strive to enter in at the strait gate: for many, I say unto you, will seek to enter in, and shall not be able.

Rom. 15. 1 We then that are strong ought to bear the imfirmities of the weak, and not to please ourselves.

2 Let every one of us please *his* neighbour for *his* good to edification.

3 For even Christ pleased not himself; but, as it is written, The reproaches of them that reproached thee fell on me.

Gal. 5. 24 And they that are Christ's have crucified the flesh with the affections and lusts.

Gal. 6. 14 But God forbid that I should glory, save in the cross of our Lord Jesus Christ, by whom the world is crucified unto me, and I unto the world.

G

Matt. 16. 21. *See text of topic.* Matt. 17. 22. *Under E.*

H

Matt. 10. 38 and Luke 14. 27. *See under D.*

§ 93. JESUS FORETELLS HIS DEATH AND RESURRECTION

CHAP. 16.

25 For [i]whosoever will save his life shall lose it: and whosoever will lose his life for my sake shall find it.

26 For what is a man profited, if he shall gain the whole world, and lose his own soul? or [k]what shall a man give in exchange for his soul?

27 For [l]the Son of man shall come in the glory of his Father [m]with his angels; [n]and then he shall reward every man according to his works.

28 Verily I say unto you, [o]There be some standing here, which shall not taste of death, till they see the Son of man coming in his kingdom.

I

Luke 17. 33 Whosoever shall seek to save his life shall lose it; and whosoever shall lose his life shall preserve it.

John 12. 25 He that loveth his life shall lose it; and he that hateth his life in this world shall keep it unto life eternal.

K

Ps. 49. 7 None *of them* can by any means redeem his brother, nor give to God a ransom for him:

8 (For the redemption of their soul *is* precious, and it ceaseth for ever:)

L

Matt. 26. 64 Jesus saith unto him, Thou hast said: nevertheless I say unto you, Hereafter shall ye see the Son of man sitting on the right hand of power, and coming in the clouds of heaven.

Mark 8. 38 and Luke 9. 26. *See text of topic.*

M

Dan. 7. 10 A fiery stream issued and came forth from before him: thousand thousands ministered unto him, and ten thousand times ten thousand stood before him: the judgment was set, and the books were opened.

Zech. 14. 5 And ye shall flee *to* the valley of the mountains; for the valley of the mountains shall reach unto Azal: yea, ye shall flee, like as ye fled from before the earthquake in the days of Uzziah king of Judah: and the LORD my God shall come, *and* all the saints with thee.

Matt. 25. 31 When the Son of man shall come

CHAP. 8.

35 For [p]whosoever will save his life shall lose it; but whosoever shall lose his life for my sake and the gospel's, the same shall save it.

36 For what shall it profit a man, if he shall gain the whole world, and lose his own soul?

37 Or what shall a man give in exchange for his soul?

38 [q]Whosoever therefore [r]shall be ashamed of me and of my words, in this adulterous and sinful generation, of him also shall the Son of man be ashamed, when he cometh in the glory of his Father with the holy angels.

CHAP. 9.

1 And he said unto them, [s]Verily I say unto you, That there be some of them that stand here, which shall not taste of death, till they have seen [t]the kingdom of God come with power.

M—CONCLUDED.

in his glory, and all the holy angels with him, then shall he sit upon the throne of his glory:

Jude 14 And Enoch also, the seventh from Adam, prophesied of these, saying, Behold, the Lord cometh with ten thousand of his saints,

N

Job 34. 11 For the work of a man shall he render unto him, and cause every man to find according to *his* ways.

Ps. 62. 12 Also unto thee, O Lord, *belongeth* mercy: for thou renderest to every man according to his work.

Prov. 24. 12 If thou sayest, Behold, we knew it not; doth not he that pondereth the heart consider *it?* and he that keepeth thy soul, doth *not* he know *it?* and shall *not* he render to *every* man according to his works?

Jer. 17. 10 I the LORD search the heart, *I* try the reins, even to give every man according to his ways, *and* according to the fruit of his doings.

Jer. 32. 19 Great in counsel, and mighty in work: for thine eyes *are* open upon

CHAP. 9.

24 For whosoever will save his life shall lose it: but whosoever will lose his life for my sake, the same shall save it.

25 [u]For what is a man advantaged, if he gain the whole world, and lose himself, or be cast away?

26 [x]For whosoever shall be ashamed of me and of my words, of him shall the Son of man be ashamed, when he shall come in his own glory, and *in his* Father's, and of the holy angels.

27 [y]But I tell you of a truth, there be some standing here, which shall not taste of death, till they see the kingdom of God.

N—CONCLUDED.

all the ways of the sons of men, to give every one according to his ways, and according to the fruit of his doings:

Rom. 2. 6 Who will render to every man according to his deeds:

I Cor. 3. 8 Now he that planteth and he that watereth are one: and every man shall receive his own reward according to his own labour.

II Cor.5. 10 For we must all appear before the judgment seat of Christ; that every one may receive the things *done* in *his* body, according to that he hath done, whether *it be* good or bad.

I Pet. 1. 17 And if ye call on the Father, who without respect of persons judgeth according to every man's work, pass the time of your sojourning *here* in fear:

Rev. 2. 23 And I will kill her children with death; and all the churches shall know that I am he which searcheth the reins and hearts: and I will give unto every one of you according to your works.

Rev. 22. 12 And, Behold, I come quickly; and my reward *is* with me, to give every man according as his work shall be.

O

Mark 9. 1 And he said unto them, Verily I say unto you, That there be some of them that stand here, which shall not

O—CONCLUDED.

taste of death, till they have seen the kingdom of God come with power.

Luke 9. 27. *See text of topic.*

P

John 12. 25. *See under I.*

Rev. 12. 11 And they overcame him by the blood of the Lamb, and by the word of their testimony; and they loved not their lives unto the death.

Q

Matt.10. 33 But whosoever shall deny me before men, him will I also deny before my Father which is in heaven.

Luke 9. 26. *See text of topic.*

Luke 12. 9 But he that denieth me before men shall be denied before the angels of God.

R

Rom. 1. 16 For I am not ashamed of the gospel of Christ: for it is the power of God unto salvation to every one that believeth; to the Jew first, and also to the Greek.

II Tim.1. 8 Be not thou therefore ashamed of the testimony of our Lord, nor of me his prisoner: but be thou partaker of the afflictions of the gospel according to the power of God;

II Tim.2. 12 If we suffer, we shall also reign with *him:* if we deny *him*, he also will deny us:

I Jno. 2. 23 Whosoever denieth the Son, the same hath not the Father: [*but*] *he that acknowledgeth the Son hath the Father also.*

S

Matt. 16. 28 and Luke 9. 27. *See text of topic.*

T

Matt. 25. 31. *See under M.*

Luke 22. 18 For I say unto you, I will not drink of the fruit of the vine, until the kingdom of God shall come.

Luke 22. 30 That ye may eat and drink at my table in my kingdom, and sit on thrones judging the twelve tribes of Israel.

Acts 1. 6 When they therefore were come together, they asked of him, saying, Lord, wilt thou at this time restore again the kingdom to Israel?

7 And he said unto them, It is not for you to know the times or the seasons, which the Father hath put in his own power.

U

Matt. 16. 26 and Mark 8. 36. *See text of topic.*

X

Matt. 10. 33. *Under Q.* II Tim. 2. 12. *See under R.*

Y

Matt. 16. 28 and Mark 9. 1. *See text of topic.*

§ 94. THE TRANSFIGURATION.

17: 1–9.

1 And [a] after six days Jesus taketh Peter, James, and John his brother, and bringeth them up into a high mountain apart,

2 And was transfigured before them: and his face did shine as the sun, and his raiment was white as the light.

3 And, behold, there appeared unto them Moses [b] and Elias talking with him.

4 Then answered Peter, and said unto Jesus, Lord, it is good for us to be here: if thou wilt, let us make here three tabernacles; one for thee, and one for Moses, and one for Elias.

A

Mark 9. 2. *See text of topic.*
Luke 9. 28. *See text of topic.*

B

Rom. 3. 21 But now the righteousness of God without the law is manifested, being witnessed by the law and the prophets;

C

Ps. 2. 6 Yet have I set my King upon my holy hill of Zion.

Matt. 17. 1. *See text of topic.*
Luke 9. 28. *See text of topic.*

D

Dan. 7. 9 I beheld till the thrones were cast down, and the Ancient of days did sit, whose garment *was* white as snow, and the hair of his head like the pure wool: his throne *was like* the fiery flame, *and* his wheels *as* burning fire.

Matt. 28. 3 His countenance was like lightning, and his raiment white as snow.

Acts 10. 30 And Cornelius said, Four days ago I was fasting until this hour; and at the ninth hour I prayed in my house, and, behold, a man stood before me in bright clothing,

Rev. 7. 9 After this I beheld, and, lo, a great multitude, which no man could number, of all nations, and kindreds, and people, and tongues, stood before the throne, and before the Lamb, clothed with white robes, and palms in their hands;

9: 2–10.

2 [c] And after six days Jesus taketh *with him* Peter, and James, and John, and leadeth them up into a high mountain apart by themselves: and he was transfigured before them.

3 And his raiment became shining, exceeding [d] white as snow; so as no fuller on earth can white them.

4 And there appeared unto them Elias with Moses: and they were talking with Jesus.

5 And Peter answered and said to Jesus, Master, it is good for us to be here: and let us make three tabernacles; one for thee, and one for Moses, and one for Elias.

6 For he wist not what to say; for they were sore afraid.

D—Concluded.

Rev. 7. 14 And I said unto him, Sir, thou knowest. And he said to me, These are they which came out of great tribulation, and have washed their robes, and made them white in the blood of the Lamb.

E

Matt. 17. 1. *See text of topic.*
Mark 9. 2. *See text of topic.*

1

Or, *things.*

F

Ex. 34. 29 And it came to pass when Moses came down from mount Sinai with the two tables of testimony in Moses' hand, when he came down from the mount, that Moses wist not that the skin of his face shone while he talked with him.

Ex. 34. 35 And the children of Israel saw the face of Moses, that the skin of Moses' face shone: and Moses put the veil upon his face again, until he went in to speak with Him.

Isa. 33. 17 Thine eyes shall see the King in his beauty: they shall behold the land that is very far off.

Matt. 17. 2. *See text of topic.*

TIME, SUMMER, A. D. 29; PLACE, REGION OF CÆSAREA PHILIPPI.

9: 28–36.

28 [e] And it came to pass about an eight days after these [1] sayings, he took Peter and John and James, and went up into a mountain to pray.

29 And as he prayed, the [f] fashion of his countenance was altered, and his raiment *was* white *and* glistering.

30 And, behold, there talked with him two men, which were Moses and [g] Elias:

31 Who appeared in [h] glory, and spake of his decease which he should accomplish at Jerusalem.

32 But Peter and they that were with him [i] were heavy with sleep: and when they were awake, they saw his glory, and the two men that stood with him.

33 And it came to pass, as they departed from him, Peter said unto Jesus, Master, it is good for us to be here: and let us make three tabernacles; one for thee, and one for Moses, and one for Elias: not knowing what he said.

F—CONTINUED.

Matt. 28. 3. *See under D.*
Mark 9. 3. *See text of topic.*

John 1. 14 And the Word was made flesh, and dwelt among us, (and we beheld his glory, the glory as of the only begotten of the Father,) full of grace and truth.

Acts 6. 15 And all that sat in the council, looking steadfastly on him, saw his face as it had been the face of an angel.

II Cor. 3. 7 But if the ministration of death, written *and* engraven in stones, was glorious, so that the children of Israel could not steadfastly behold the face of Moses for the glory of his countenance; which *glory* was to be done away;

F—CONCLUDED.

II Cor. 3. 8 How shall not the ministration of the spirit be rather glorious?

9 For if the ministration of condemnation *be* glory, much more doth the ministration of righteousness exceed in glory.

10 For even that which was made glorious had no glory in this respect, by reason of the glory that excelleth.

11 For if that which is done away *was* glorious, much more that which remaineth *is* glorious.

G

II Ki. 2. 11 And it came to pass, as they still went on, and talked, that, behold, *there appeared* a chariot of fire, and horses of fire, and parted them both asunder; and Elijah went up by a whirlwind into heaven.

Matt. 17. 3, 4. *See text of topic.*
Mark 9. 4, 5. *See text of topic.*

John 1. 17 For the law was given by Moses, *but* grace and truth came by Jesus Christ.

H

Phil. 3. 21 Who shall change our vile body, that it may be fashioned like unto his glorious body, according to the working whereby he is able even to subdue all things unto himself.

Col. 3. 4 When Christ, *who is* our life, shall appear, then shall ye also appear with him in glory.

I

Dan. 8. 18 Now as he was speaking with me, I was in a deep sleep on my face toward the ground: but he touched me, and set me upright.

Dan. 10. 9 Yet heard I the voice of his words: and when I heard the voice of his words, then was I in a deep sleep on my face, and my face toward the ground.

Matt. 26. 40 And he cometh unto the disciples, and findeth them asleep, and saith unto Peter, What, could ye not watch with me one hour?

41 Watch and pray, that ye enter not into temptation: the spirit indeed *is* willing, but the flesh *is* weak.

42 He went away again the second time, and prayed, saying, O my Father, if this cup may not pass away from me, except I drink it, thy will be done.

43 And he came and found them asleep again: for their eyes were heavy.

§ 94. THE TRANSFIGURATION (CONCLUDED).

CHAP. 17.

5 [k] While he yet spake, behold, a bright cloud overshadowed them: and behold a voice out of the cloud, which said, [l] This is my beloved Son, [m] in whom I am well pleased; [n] hear ye him.

6 [o] And when the disciples heard *it*, they fell on their face, and were sore afraid.

7 And Jesus came and [p] touched them, and said, Arise, and be not afraid.

8 And when they had lifted up their eyes, they saw no man, save Jesus only.

9 And as they came down from the mountain, [q] Jesus charged them, saying, Tell the vision to no man, until the Son of man be risen again from the dead.

K

Ps. 18. 10 And he rode upon a cherub, and did fly: yea, he did fly upon the wings of the wind.

11 He made darkness his secret place; his pavilion round about him *were* dark waters *and* thick clouds of the skies.

Acts 1. 9 And when he had spoken these things, while they beheld, he was taken up; and a cloud received him out of their sight.

II Pet.1. 17 For he received from God the Father honour and glory, when there came such a voice to him from the excellent glory, This is my beloved Son, in whom I am well pleased.

Rev. 1. 7 Behold, he cometh with clouds; and every eye shall see him, and they *also* which pierced him: and all kindreds of the earth shall wail because of him. Even so. Amen.

L

Matt. 3. 17 And lo a voice from heaven, saying, This is my beloved Son, in whom I am well pleased.

Mark 1. 11 And there came a voice from heaven, *saying*, Thou art my beloved Son, in whom I am well pleased.

CHAP. 9.

7 And there was [r] a cloud that overshadowed them: and a voice came out of the cloud, saying, This is my beloved Son: hear [s] him.

8 And suddenly, when they had looked round about, they saw no man any more, save Jesus only with themselves.

9 [t] And as they came down from the mountain, he charged them that they should tell no man what things they had seen, till the Son of man were risen from the dead.

10 And they kept that saying with themselves, questioning one with another what the rising from the dead should mean.

L—CONCLUDED.

Luke 3. 22 And the Holy Ghost descended in a bodily shape like a dove upon him, and a voice came from heaven, which said, Thou art my beloved Son; in thee I am well pleased.

M

Isa.42. 1 Behold my servant, whom I uphold; mine elect, *in whom* my soul delighteth; I have put my Spirit upon him: he shall bring forth judgment to the Gentiles.

N

Deut.18. 15 The LORD thy God will raise up unto thee a Prophet from the midst of thee, of thy brethren, like unto me; unto him ye shall hearken;

Deut.18. 19 And it shall come to pass, *that* whosoever will not hearken unto my words which he shall speak in my name, I will require *it* of him.

Acts 3. 22 For Moses truly said unto the fathers, A Prophet shall the Lord your God raise up unto you of your brethren, like unto me; him shall ye hear in all things whatsoever he shall say unto you.

23 And it shall come to pass, *that* every soul, which will not hear that Prophet, shall be destroyed from among the people.

TIME, SUMMER, A. D. 29; PLACE, REGION OF CÆSAREA PHILIPPI.

CHAP. 9.

34 While he thus spake, there came a cloud, and overshadowed them: and they feared as they entered into the cloud.

35 And there came a voice out of the cloud, saying, [u] This is my beloved Son: hear [x] him.

36 And when the voice was past, Jesus was found alone, [y] And they kept *it* close, and told no man in those days any of those things which they had seen.

N—CONCLUDED.

Heb. 12. 25 See that ye refuse not him that speaketh: for if they escaped not who refused him that spake on earth, much more *shall not* we *escape*, if we turn away from him that *speaketh* from heaven;

O

II Pet.1. 18 And this voice which came from heaven we heard, when we were with him in the holy mount.

P

Dan. 8. 18. *See under I.*

Dan. 9. 21 Yea, while I *was* speaking in prayer, even the man Gabriel, whom I had seen in the vision at the beginning, being caused to fly swiftly, touched me about the time of the evening oblation.

Dan. 10. 10 And, behold, a hand touched me, which set me upon my knees and *upon* the palms of my hands.

Dan. 10. 18 Then there came again and touched me *one* like the appearance of a man, and he strengthened me,

Q

Matt.16. 20 Then charged he his disciples that they should tell no man that he was Jesus the Christ.

Mark 8. 30 And he charged them that they should tell no man of him.

Mark 9. 9. *See text of topic.*

R

Ex. 40. 34 Then a cloud covered the tent of the congregation, and the glory of the LORD filled the tabernacle.

35 And Moses was not able to enter into the tent of the congregation, be-

R—CONCLUDED.

cause the cloud abode thereon, and the glory of the LORD filled the tabernacle.

Isa. 42. 1. *See under M.*

II Pet. 1. 17. *See under K.*

S

Heb. 1. 1 God, who at sundry times and in divers manners spake in time past unto the fathers by the prophets,

2 Hath in these last days spoken unto us by *his* son, whom he hath appointed heir of all things, by whom also he made the worlds;

Heb. 2. 3 How shall we escape, if we neglect so great salvation; which at the first began to be spoken by the Lord, and was confirmed unto us by them that heard *him;*

Heb. 12. 25 See that ye refuse not him that speaketh: for if they escaped not who refused him that spake on earth, much more *shall not* we *escape*, if we turn away from him that *speaketh* from heaven:

26 Whose voice then shook the earth: but now he hath promised, saying, Yet once more I shake not the earth only, but also heaven.

T

Matt. 17. 9. *See text of topic.*

U

Matt. 3. 17. *See under L.*

II Pet.1. 16 For we have not followed cunningly devised fables, when we made known unto you the power and coming of our Lord Jesus Christ, but were eye-witnesses of his majesty.

II Pet. 1. 17. *See under K.*

X

Ex. 23. 20 Behold, I send an Angel before thee, to keep thee in the way, and to bring thee into the place which I have prepared.

21 Beware of him, and obey his voice, provoke him not; for he will not pardon your transgressions: for my name *is* in him.

Deut. 18. 15. *See under N.*

Deut.18. 18 I will raise them up a Prophet from among their brethren, like unto thee, and will put my words in his mouth; and he shall speak unto them all that I shall command him.

Acts 3. 22. *See under N.*

Y

Matt. 17. 9. *See text of topic.*

§ 95. DISCOURSE WITH THE THREE DISCIPLES AFTER THE TRANS-

Matthew 17: 10–13.

10 And his disciples asked him, saying, [a]Why then say the scribes that Elias must first come?

11 And Jesus answered and said unto them, Elias truly shall first come, and [b]restore all things.

12 [c]But I say unto you, That Elias is come already, and they knew him not, but [d]have done unto him whatsoever they listed. Likewise [e]shall also the Son of man suffer of them.

13 [f]Then the disciples understood that he spake unto them of John the Baptist.

A

Mal. 4. 5 Behold, I will send you Elijah the prophet before the coming of the great and dreadful day of the LORD:
6 And he shall turn the heart of the fathers to the children, and the heart of the children to their fathers, lest I come and smite the earth with a curse.

Matt.11. 14 And if ye will receive *it*, this is Elias, which was for to come.

Matt.27. 47 Some of them that stood there, when they heard *that*, said, This *man* calleth for Elias.

Mark 9: 11–13.

11 And they asked him, saying, Why say the scribes [g]that Elias must first come?

12 And he answered and told them, Elias verily cometh first, and restoreth all things; and [h]how it is written of the Son of man, that he must suffer many things, and [i]be set at nought.

13 But I say unto you, That [k]Elias is indeed come, and they have done unto him whatsoever they listed, as it is written of him.

A—CONCLUDED.

Matt.27. 49 The rest said, Let be, let us see whether Elias will come to save him.

Mark 9. 11. *See text of topic.*

B

Mal. 4. 6. *See under A.*

Luke 1. 16 And many of the children of Israel shall he turn to the Lord their God.
17 And he shall go before him in the spirit and power of Elias, to turn the hearts of the fathers to the children, and the disobedient to the wisdom of the just; to make ready a people prepared for the Lord.

§ 96. JESUS HEALS A LUNATIC WHOM THE DISCIPLES COULD NOT HEAL.

Matthew 17: 14–21.

14 [a]And when they were come to the multitude, there came to him a *certain* man, kneeling down to him, and saying,

15 Lord, have mercy on my son; for he is lunatic, and sore vexed:

A

Mark 1. 40 And there came a leper to him, beseeching him, and kneeling down to him, and saying unto him, If thou wilt, thou canst make me clean.

Mark 9. 14 and Luke 9. 37. *See text of topic.*

Mark 10. 17 And when he was gone forth into the way, there came one running, and kneeled to him, and asked him, Good Master, what shall I do that I may inherit eternal life?

Mark 9: 14–29.

14 [b]And when he came to *his* disciples, he saw a great multitude about them, and the scribes questioning with them.

15 And straightway all the people, when they beheld him, were greatly amazed, and running to *him* saluted him.

16 And he asked the scribes, What question ye [1]with them?

17 And [c]one of the multitude answered and said, Master, I have brought unto thee my son, which hath a dumb spirit;

FIGURATION. TIME, SUMMER, A. D. 29; PLACE, REGION OF CÆSAREA PHILIPPI.

B—CONCLUDED.

Acts 3. 21 Whom the heaven must receive until the times of restitution of all things, which God hath spoken by the mouth of all his holy prophets since the world began.

C

Matt. 11. 14. *See under A.* Mark 9. 12, 13. *See text of topic.*

D

Matt.14. 3 For Herod had laid hold on John, and bound him, and put *him* in prison for Herodias' sake, his brother Philip's wife.

Matt.14. 10 And he sent, and beheaded John in the prison.

E

Matt.16. 21 From that time forth began Jesus to show unto his disciples, how that he must go unto Jerusalem, and suffer many things of the elders and chief priests and scribes, and be killed, and be raised again the third day.

F

Matt. 11. 14. *See under A.*

G

Mal. 4. 5. *Under A.* Matt. 17. 10. *See text of topic.*

H

Ps. 22. 6 But I *am* a worm, and no man; a reproach of men, and despised of the people.

Isa. 53. 2 For he shall grow up before him as a tender plant, and as a root out of

H—CONCLUDED.

a dry ground: he hath no form nor comeliness; and when we shall see him, *there is* no beauty that we should desire him.

3 He is despised and rejected of men; a man of sorrows, and acquainted with grief: and we hid as it were *our* faces from him; he was despised, and we esteemed him not.

Dan. 9. 26 And after threescore and two weeks shall Messiah be cut off, but not for himself: and the people of the prince that shall come shall destroy the city and the sanctuary; and the end thereof *shall be* with a flood, and unto the end of the war desolations are determined.

Zech.13. 7 Awake, O Sword, against my Shepherd, and against the man *that is* my fellow, saith the LORD of hosts: smite the Shepherd, and the sheep shall be scattered: and I will turn mine hand upon the little ones.

I

Luke 23. 11 And Herod with his men of war set him at nought, and mocked *him*, and arrayed him in a gorgeous robe, and sent him again to Pilate.

Phil. 2. 7 But made himself of no reputation, and took upon him the form of a servant, and was made in the likeness of men:

K

Matt. 11. 14. *Under A.* Luke 1. 17. *Under B.*

TIME, SUMMER, A. D. 29; PLACE, REGION OF CÆSAREA PHILIPPI.

9: 37–42.

37 [d]And it came to pass, that on the next day, when they were come down from the hill, much people met him.

38 And, behold, a man of the company cried out, saying, Master, I beseech thee, look upon my son; [e]for he is mine only child.

A—CONCLUDED.

Acts 10. 25 And as Peter was coming in, Cornelius met him, and fell down at his feet, and worshipped *him*.

26 But Peter took him up, saying, Stand up; I myself also am a man.

27 And as he talked with him, he went in, and found many that were come together.

B

Matt. 17. 14 and Luke 9. 37. *See text of topic.*

1

Or, *among yourselves?*

C

Matt. 17. 14 and Luke 9. 38. *See text of topic.*

D

Matt. 17. 14 and Mark 9. 14, 17. *See text of topic.*

Mark 5. 23 And besought him greatly, saying, My little daughter lieth at the point of death: *I pray thee,* come and lay thy hands on her, that she may be healed; and she shall live.

Mark 7. 26 The woman was a Greek, a Syrophœnician by nation; and she besought him that he would cast forth the devil out of her daughter.

Mark 10. 13 And they brought young children to him, that he should touch them; and *his* disciples rebuked those that brought *them*.

For E see next page (288).

§ 96. JESUS HEALS A LUNATIC WHOM THE DISCIPLES COULD NOT HEAL

Chap. 17.

for ofttimes he falleth into the fire, and oft into the water.

16 And I brought him to thy disciples, and they could not cure him.

17 Then Jesus answered and said, O faithless and perverse generation, how long shall I be with you? how long shall I suffer you? bring him hither to me.

18 And Jesus rebuked the devil; and he departed out of him: and the child was cured from that very hour.

19 Then came the disciples to Jesus apart, and said, Why could not we cast him out?

E

Gen. 44. 20 And we said unto my lord, We have a father, an old man, and a child of his old age, a little one; and his brother is dead, and he alone is left of his mother, and his father loveth him.

2

Or, *dasheth him.*

F

Mark 1. 26 And when the unclean spirit had torn him, and cried with a loud voice, he came out of him.

Luke 9. 42. *See text of topic.*

G

II Chr.20. 20 And they rose early in the morning, and went forth into the wilderness of Tekoa: and as they went forth, Jehoshaphat stood and said, Hear me, O Judah, and ye inhabitants of Jerusalem; Believe in the Lord your God, so shall ye be established; believe his prophets, so shall ye prosper.

Matt. 17. 20. *See text of topic.*

Mark 11. 23 For verily I say unto you, That whosoever shall say unto this mountain, Be thou removed, and be thou cast into the sea; and shall not doubt in his heart, but shall believe that those things which he saith shall come to pass; he shall have whatsoever he saith.

Luke 17. 6. *See under I, page 291.*

John 11. 40 Jesus saith unto her, Said I not unto thee, that, if thou wouldest believe, thou shouldest see the glory of God?

Chap. 9.

18 And wheresoever he taketh him, he [2]teareth him; and he foameth, and gnasheth with his teeth, and pineth away: and I spake to thy disciples that they should cast him out; and they could not.

19 He answereth him, and saith, O faithless generation, how long shall I be with you? how long shall I suffer you? bring him unto me.

20 And they brought him unto him: and [f]when he saw him, straightway the spirit tare him; and he fell on the ground, and wallowed foaming.

21 And he asked his father, How long is it ago since this came unto him? And he said, Of a child.

22 And ofttimes it hath cast him into the fire, and into the waters, to destroy him: but if thou canst do any thing, have compassion on us, and help us.

23 Jesus said unto him, [g]If thou canst believe, all things *are* possible to him that believeth.

24 And straightway the father of the child cried out, and said with tears, Lord, I believe; help thou mine unbelief.

25 When Jesus saw that the people came running together, he rebuked the foul spirit, saying unto him, *Thou* dumb and deaf spirit, I charge thee, come out of him, and enter no more into him.

26 And *the spirit* cried, and rent him sore, and came out of him: and he was as one dead; insomuch that many said, He is dead.

(CONTINUED). TIME, SUMMER, A. D. 29; PLACE, REGION OF CÆSAREA PHILIPPI.

CHAP. 9.

39 And, lo, a spirit taketh him, and he suddenly crieth out; and it teareth him that he foameth again, and bruising him, hardly departeth from him.

40 And I besought thy disciples to cast him out; and they could not.

41 And Jesus answering said, [h]O faithless and perverse generation, how long shall I be with you, and suffer you? Bring thy son hither.

42 And as he was yet a coming, the devil threw him down, and tare *him*. And Jesus rebuked the unclean spirit, and healed the child, and delivered him again to his father.

G—CONCLUDED.

Acts 14. 8 And there sat a certain man at Lystra, impotent in his feet, being a cripple from his mother's womb, who never had walked:

9 The same heard Paul speak: who steadfastly beholding him, and perceiving that he had faith to be healed,

10 Said with a loud voice, Stand upright on thy feet. And he leaped and walked.

H

Num.14. 11 And the LORD said unto Moses, How long will this people provoke me? and how long will it be ere they believe me, for all the signs which I have showed among them?

12 I will smite them with the pestilence, and disinherit them, and will make of thee a greater nation and mightier than they.

Deut.32. 18 Of the Rock *that* begat thee thou art unmindful, and hast forgotten God that formed thee.

19 And when the LORD saw *it*, he abhorred *them*, because of the provoking of his sons, and of his daughters.

20 And he said, I will hide my face from them, I will see what their end *shall be*: for they *are* a very froward generation, children in whom *is* no faith.

21 They have moved me to jealousy with *that which is* not God; they have provoked me to anger with their vanities: and I will move them to

H—CONCLUDED.

jealousy with *those which are* not a people; I will provoke them to anger with a foolish nation.

22 For a fire is kindled in mine anger, and shall burn unto the lowest hell, and shall consume the earth with her increase, and set on fire the foundations of the mountains.

23 I will heap mischiefs upon them; I will spend mine arrows upon them.

24 *They shall be* burnt with hunger, and devoured with burning heat, and with bitter destruction: I will also send the teeth of beasts upon them, with the poison of serpents of the dust.

25 The sword without, and terror within, shall destroy both the young man and the virgin, the suckling *also* with the man of gray hairs.

26 I said, I would scatter them into corners, I would make the remembrance of them to cease from among men:

27 Were it not that I feared the wrath of the enemy, lest their adversaries should behave themselves strangely, *and* lest they should say, Our hand *is* high, and the LORD hath not done all this.

28 For they *are* a nation void of counsel, neither *is there any* understanding in them.

29 O that they were wise, *that* they understood this, *that* they would consider their latter end!

Ps. 78. 8 And might not be as their fathers, a stubborn and rebellious generation; a generation *that* set not their heart aright, and whose spirit was not steadfast with God.

9 The children of Ephraim, *being* armed, *and* carrying bows, turned back in the day of battle.

10 They kept not the covenant of God and refused to walk in his law;

Acts 2. 40 And with many other words did he testify and exhort, saying, Save yourselves from this untoward generation.

Heb. 3. 10 Wherefore I was grieved with that generation, and said, They do alway err in *their* heart; and they have not known my ways.

11 So I sware in my wrath, They shall not enter into my rest.

12 Take heed, brethren, lest there be in any of you an evil heart of unbelief, in departing from the living God.

§ 96. JESUS HEALS A LUNATIC WHOM THE DISCIPLES COULD NOT HEAL

CHAP. 17.

20 And Jesus said unto them, Because of your unbelief: for verily I say unto you, [i]If ye have faith as a grain of mustard seed, ye shall say unto this mountain, Remove hence to yonder place; and it shall remove: and nothing shall be impossible unto you.

21 Howbeit this kind goeth not out but by prayer and fasting.

CHAP. 9.

27 But Jesus took him by the hand, and lifted him up; and he arose.

28 [k]And when he was come into the house, his disciples asked him privately, Why could not we cast him out?

29 And he said unto them, This kind can come forth by nothing, but by prayer and fasting.

§ 97. JESUS AGAIN FORETELLS HIS OWN DEATH AND RESURRECTION.

17 : 22, 23.

22 [a]And while they abode in Galilee, Jesus said unto them, The Son of man shall be betrayed into the hands of men:

23 And they shall kill him, and the third day he shall be raised again. And they were exceeding sorry.

A

Matt.16. 21 From that time forth began Jesus to show unto his disciples, how that he must go unto Jerusalem, and suffer many things of the elders and chief priests and scribes, and be killed, and be raised again the third day.

Matt.20. 17 And Jesus going up to Jerusalem took the twelve disciples apart in the way, and said unto them,

Mark 8. 31 And he began to teach them, that the Son of man must suffer many things, and be rejected of the elders, and *of* the chief priests, and scribes, and be killed, and after three days rise again.

Mark 9. 30, 31. *See text of topic.*

Mark 10. 33 *Saying*, Behold, we go up to Jerusalem; and the Son of man shall be delivered unto the chief priests, and unto the scribes; and they shall condemn him to death, and shall deliver him to the Gentiles:

Luke 9. 22 Saying, The Son of man must suffer many things, and be rejected of the elders and chief priests and scribes, and be slain, and be raised the third day.

Luke 9. 44. *See text of topic.*

Luke 18. 31 Then he took *unto him* the twelve,

9 : 30–32.

30 And they departed thence, and passed through Galilee; and he would not that any man should know *it*.

31 [b]For he taught his disciples, and said unto them, The Son of man is delivered into the hands of men, and they shall kill him; and after that he is killed, he shall rise the third day.

32 But they understood not that saying, and were afraid to ask him. p. 294.

A—CONCLUDED.

and said unto them, Behold, we go up to Jerusalem, and all things that are written by the prophets concerning the Son of man shall be accomplished.

Luke 24. 6 He is not here, but is risen: remember how he spake unto you when he was yet in Galilee,

7 Saying, The Son of man must be delivered into the hands of sinful men, and be crucified, and the third day rise again.

B

Matt. 17. 22 and Luke 9. 44. *See text of topic.*

C

Isa. 32. 9 Rise up, ye women that are at ease; hear my voice, ye careless daughters; give ear unto my speech.

10 Many days and years shall ye be troubled, ye careless women: for the vintage shall fail, the gathering shall not come.

I Thes. 3. 3 That no man should be moved by these afflictions: for yourselves know that we are appointed thereunto.

4 For verily, when we were with

(Concluded). Time, Summer, A. D. 29; Place, Region of Cæsarea Philippi.

[Chap. 9.]

I

Matt.21. 21 Jesus answered and said unto them, Verily I say unto you, If ye have faith, and doubt not, ye shall not only do this *which is done* to the fig tree, but also if ye shall say unto this mountain, Be thou removed, and be thou cast into the sea; it shall be done.

Mark 9. 23. *See text of topic.*

Mark 11. 23. *See under G, page 288.*

Luke 17. 6 And the Lord said, If ye had faith as a grain of mustard seed, ye might say unto this sycamine tree, Be thou

I—Concluded.

plucked up by the root, and be thou planted in the sea; and it should obey you.

I Cor.12. 9 To another faith by the same Spirit; to another the gifts of healing by the same Spirit;

I Cor.13. 2 And though I have *the gift of* prophecy, and understand all mysteries, and all knowledge; and though I have all faith, so that I could remove mountains, and have not charity, I am nothing.

K

Matt. 17. 19. *See text of topic.*

[See § 93.] Time, Autumn, A. D. 29; Place, Galilee.

9 : 43–45.

43 And they were all amazed at the
mighty power of God. But while they
wondered every one at all things which
Jesus did, he said unto his disciples,
44 [c]Let these sayings sink down into
your ears: [d]for the Son of man shall
be delivered into the hands of men.
45 [e]But they understood not this
saying, and it was hid from them,
that they perceived it not: and they
feared to ask him of that saying. p. 295.

C—Concluded.

you, we told you before that we should suffer tribulation; even as it came to pass, and ye know.

Heb. 2. 1 Therefore we ought to give the more earnest heed to the things which we have heard, lest at any time we should let *them* slip.

D

Matt. 17. 22. *See text of topic.*

Acts 2. 23 Him, being delivered by the determinate counsel and foreknowledge of God, ye have taken, and by wicked hands have crucified and slain:

24 Whom God hath raised up, having loosed the pains of death: because it was not possible that he should be holden of it.

Acts 3. 13 The God of Abraham, and of Isaac, and of Jacob, the God of our fathers, hath glorified his Son Jesus; whom ye delivered up, and denied him in the presence of Pilate, when he was determined to let *him* go.

D—Concluded.

Acts 3. 14 But ye denied the Holy One and the Just, and desired a murderer to be granted unto you;

15 And killed the Prince of life, whom God hath raised from the dead; whereof we are witnesses.

Acts 4. 27 For a truth against thy holy child Jesus, whom thou hast anointed, both Herod and Pontius Pilate, with the Gentiles, and the people of Israel, were gathered together,

28 For to do whatsoever thy hand and thy counsel determined before to be done.

29 And now, Lord, behold their threatenings: and grant unto thy servants, that with all boldness they may speak thy word,

E

Mark 9. 32. *See text of topic.*

Luke 2. 50 And they understood not the saying which he spake unto them.

Luke 18. 34 And they understood none of these things: and this saying was hid from them, neither knew they the things which were spoken.

John 14. 4 And wither I go ye know, and the way ye know.

5 Thomas saith unto him, Lord, we know not whither thou goest; and how can we know the way?

II Cor.3. 14 But their minds were blinded: for until this day remaineth the same vail untaken away in the reading of the old testament; which *vail* is done away in Christ.

15 But even unto this day, when Moses is read, the vail is upon their heart.

16 Nevertheless, when it shall turn to the Lord, the vail shall be taken away.

§ 98. THE FISH CAUGHT FOR THE TRIBUTE MONEY.

17: 24–27.

24 And [a]when they were come to Capernaum, they that received [1]tribute *money* came to Peter, and said, Doth not your master pay tribute?

25 He saith, [b]Yes. And when he was come into the house, Jesus prevented him, saying, What thinkest thou, Simon? of whom do the kings of the earth take custom or tribute? [c]of their own children, or of strangers?

26 Peter saith unto him, Of strangers. Jesus saith unto him, Then are the children free.

27 Notwithstanding, [d]lest we should offend them, go thou to the sea, and cast a hook, [e]and take up the fish that first cometh up; and when thou hast opened his mouth, thou shalt find [2]a piece of money: that [f]take, and give unto them for me and thee.

A

Mark 9. 33 And he came to Capernaum: and being in the house he asked them, What was it that ye disputed among yourselves by the way?

1

Called in the original, *didrachma*, being in value fifteen pence; in American money, *thirty cents*.

Ex. 30. 11 And the LORD spake unto Moses, saying,

12 When thou takest the sum of the children of Israel after their number, then shall they give every man a ransom for his soul unto the LORD, when thou numberest them; that there be no plague among them, when *thou* numberest them.

13 This they shall give, every one that passeth among them that are numbered, half a shekel after the shekel of the sanctuary: (a shekel *is* twenty gerahs:) a half shekel *shall be* the offering of the LORD.

14 Every one that passeth among them that are numbered, from twenty years old and above, shall give an offering unto the LORD.

15 The rich shall not give more,

1—CONCLUDED.

and the poor shall not give less, than half a shekel, when *they* give an offering unto the LORD, to make an atonement for your souls.

Ex. 38. 26 A bekah for every man, *that is* half a shekel, after the shekel of the sanctuary, for every one that went to be numbered, from twenty years old and upward, for six hundred thousand and three thousand and five hundred and fifty *men*.

B

Rom.13. 6 For, for this cause pay ye tribute also: for they are God's ministers, attending continually upon this very thing.

7 Render therefore to all their dues: tribute to whom tribute *is due;* custom to whom custom; fear to whom fear; honour to whom honour.

8 Owe no man anything, but to love one another: for he that loveth another hath fulfilled the law.

C

I Sa. 17. 25 And the men of Israel said, Have ye seen this man that is come up? surely to defy Israel is he come up: and it shall be, *that* the man who killeth him, the king will enrich him with great riches, and will give him his daughter, and make his father's house free in Israel.

D

Mark 12. 17 And Jesus answering said unto them, Render to Cæsar the things that are Cæsar's, and to God the things that are God's. And they marvelled at him.

Rom.14. 21 *It is* good neither to eat flesh, nor to drink wine, nor *any thing* whereby thy brother stumbleth, or is offended, or is made weak.

22 Hast thou faith? have *it* to thyself before God. Happy *is* he that condemneth not himself in that thing which he alloweth.

23 And he that doubteth is damned if he eat, because *he eateth* not of faith: for whatsoever *is* not of faith is sin.

Rom.15. 1 We then that are strong ought to bear the infirmities of the weak, and not to please ourselves.

2 Let every one of us please *his* neighbour for *his* good to edification.

3 For even Christ pleased not himself; but, as it is written, The reproaches of them that reproached thee fell on me.

I Cor. 8. 9 But take heed lest by any means

TIME, AUTUMN, A. D. 29; PLACE, CAPERNAUM.

D—CONCLUDED.

this liberty of yours become a stumblingblock to them that are weak.

I Cor. 8. 13 Wherefore, if meat make my brother to offend, I will eat no flesh while the world standeth, lest I make my brother to offend.

I Cor. 9. 19 For though I be free from all *men*, yet have I made myself servant unto all, that I might gain the more.

20 And unto the Jews I became as a Jew, that I might gain the Jews; to them that are under the law, as under the law, that I might gain them that are under the law;

21 To them that are without law, as without law, (being not without law to God, but under the law to Christ,) that I might gain them that are without law.

22 To the weak became I as weak, that I might gain the weak: I am made all things to all *men*, that I might by all means save some.

I Cor.10. 32 Give none offence, neither to the Jews, nor to the Gentiles, nor to the church of God:

33 Even as I please all *men* in all *things*, not seeking mine own profit, but the *profit* of many, that they may be saved.

II Cor.6. 3 Giving no offence in any thing, that the ministry be not blamed:

4 But in all *things* approving ourselves as the ministers of God, in much patience, in afflictions, in necessities, in distresses.

IThes.5. 22 Abstain from all appearance of evil.

23 And the very God of peace sanctify you wholly; and *I pray God* your whole spirit and soul and body be preserved blameless unto the coming of our Lord Jesus Christ.

Tit. 2. 7 In all things showing thyself a pattern of good works: in doctrine *showing* uncorruptness, gravity, sincerity,

8 Sound speech, that cannot be condemned; that he that is of the contrary part may be ashamed, having no evil thing to say of you.

E

Gen. 1. 28 And God blessed them, and God said unto them, Be fruitful, and multiply, and replenish the earth, and subdue it: and have dominion over the fish of the sea, and over the fowl of the air, and over every living thing that moveth upon the earth.

E—CONCLUDED.

I Ki. 17. 4 And it shall be, *that* thou shalt drink of the brook; and I have commanded the ravens to feed thee there.

Ps. 8. 4 What is man, that thou art mindful of him? and the son of man, that thou visitest him?

5 For thou hast made him a little lower than the angels, and hast crowned him with glory and honour.

6 Thou madest him to have dominion over the works of thy hands; thou hast put all *things* under his feet:

7 All sheep and oxen, yea, and the beasts of the field;

8 The fowl of the air, and the fish of the sea, *and whatsoever* passeth through the paths of the seas.

9 O LORD our Lord, how excellent *is* thy name in all the earth!

Jon. 1. 17 Now the LORD had prepared a great fish to swallow up Jonah. And Jonah was in the belly of the fish three days and three nights.

Jon. 2. 10 And the LORD spake unto the fish, and it vomited out Jonah upon the dry *land*.

Heb. 2. 6 But one in a certain place testified, saying, What is man, that thou art mindful of him? or the son of man, that thou visitest him?

7 Thou madest him a little lower than the angels; thou crownedst him with glory and honour, and didst set him over the works of thy hands:

8 Thou hast put all things in subjection under his feet. For in that he put all in subjection under him, he left nothing *that is* not put under him. But now we see not yet all things put under him.

9 But we see Jesus, who was made a little lower than the angels for the suffering of death, crowned with glory and honour; that he by the grace of God should taste death for every man.

2

Or, *a stater*. It is half an ounce of silver, in value 2s. 6d. after 5s. the ounce; in American money, *sixty cents*.

F

II Cor.8. 9 For ye know the grace of our Lord Jesus Christ, that, though he was rich, yet for your sakes he became poor, that ye through his poverty might be rich.

Jas. 2. 5 Hearken my beloved brethren, Hath not God chosen the poor of this world rich in faith, and heirs of the kingdom which he hath promised to them that love him?

§ 99. THE LITTLE CHILD.

18: 1–5.

1 At [a] the same time came the disciples unto Jesus, saying, Who is the greatest in the kingdom of heaven?

2 And Jesus called a little child unto him, and set him in the midst of them,

3 And said, Verily I say unto you, [b] Except ye be converted, and become as little children, ye shall not enter into the kingdom of heaven.

4 [c] Whosoever therefore shall humble himself as this little child, the same is greatest in the kingdom of heaven.

5 And [d] whoso shall receive one such little child in my name receiveth me.

A

Mark 9. 33. *See text of topic.*
Luke 9. 46. *See text of topic.*
Luke 22. 24 And there was also a strife among them, which of them should be accounted the greatest.

B

Ps. 131. 1 LORD, my heart is not haughty, nor mine eyes lofty: neither do I exercise myself in great matters, or in things too high for me.
2 Surely I have behaved and quieted myself, as a child that is weaned of his mother: my soul *is* even as a weaned child.
Matt. 19. 14 But Jesus said, Suffer little children, and forbid them not, to come unto me; for of such is the kingdom of heaven.
Mark 10. 14 But when Jesus saw *it*, he was much displeased, and said unto them, Suffer the little children to come unto me, and forbid them not; for of such is the kingdom of God.
Luke 18. 16 But Jesus called them *unto him*, and said, Suffer little children to come unto me, and forbid them not: for of such is the kingdom of God.
I Cor. 14. 20 Brethren, be not children in understanding: howbeit in malice be ye children, but in understanding be men.
I Pet. 2. 2 As new born babes, desire the sincere milk of the word, that ye may grow thereby:

9: 33–37.

33 [e] And he came to Capernaum: and being in the house he asked them, What was it that ye disputed among yourselves by the way?

34 But they held their peace: [f] for by the way they had disputed among themselves, who *should be* the greatest.

35 And he sat down, and called the twelve, and saith unto them, [g] if any man desire to be first, *the same* shall be last of all, and servant of all.

36 And [h] he took a child, and set him in the midst of them: and when he had taken him in his arms, he said unto them,

37 Whosoever shall receive one of such children in my name, receiveth me; and [i] whosoever shall receive me, receiveth not me, but him that sent me.

C

Isa. 57. 15 For thus saith the high and lofty One that inhabiteth eternity, whose name *is* Holy; I dwell in the high and holy *place*, with him also *that is* of a contrite and humble spirit, to revive the spirit of the humble, and to revive the heart of the contrite ones.
Matt. 20. 27 And whosoever will be chief among you, let him be your servant:
Matt. 23. 11 But he that is greatest among you shall be your servant.
Luke 14. 11 For whosoever exalteth himself shall be abased; and he that humbleth himself shall be exalted.
I Pet. 5. 5 Likewise, ye younger, submit yourselves unto the elder. Yea, all *of you* be subject one to another, and be clothed with humility: for God resisteth the proud, and giveth grace to the humble.

D

Matt. 10. 42 And whosoever shall give to drink unto one of these little ones a cup of cold *water* only in the name of a disciple, verily I say unto you, he shall in no wise lose his reward.
Luke 9. 48. *See text of topic.*

TIME, AUTUMN, A. D. 29; PLACE, CAPERNAUM.

9: 46–48.

46 [k] Then there arose a reasoning
among them, which of them should be
greatest.
47 And Jesus, [l] perceiving the thought
of their heart, took a child, and set him
by him,
48 And said unto them, [m] Whosoever
shall receive this child in my name receiveth me; and whosoever shall receive
me receiveth him that sent me: [n] for
he that is least among you all, the same
shall be great.

E

Matt. 18. 1. *See text of topic.*
Luke 9. 46. *See text of topic.*
Luke 22. 24. *See under A.*

F

Prov. 13. 10 Only by pride cometh contention: but with the well-advised *is* wisdom.

Matt. 20. 21 And he said unto her, What wilt thou? She saith unto him, Grant that these my two sons may sit, the one on thy right hand, and the other on the left, in thy kingdom.

Matt. 20. 24 And when the ten heard *it*, they were moved with indignation against the two brethren.

Luke 22. 24. *See under A.*

Rom. 12. 10 *Be* kindly affectioned one to another with brotherly love; in honour preferring one another;

I Pet. 5. 3 Neither as being lords over *God's* heritage, but being ensamples to the flock.

III Jno. 9 I wrote unto the church: but Diotrephes, who loveth to have the pre-eminence among them, receiveth us not.

G

Prov. 22. 4 By humility *and* the fear of the LORD *are* riches, and honour, and life.

Matt. 20. 26 But it shall not be so among you: but whosoever will be great among you, let him be your minister;

Matt. 20. 27. *See under C.*

Mark. 10. 43 But so shall it not be among you: but whosoever will be great among you, shall be your minister:

H

Matt. 18. 2. *See text of topic.*

H—CONCLUDED.

Matt. 19. 14 But Jesus said, Suffer little children, and forbid them not, to come unto me; for of such is the kingdom of heaven.

15 And he laid *his* hands on them, and departed thence.

Mark 10. 16 And he took them up in his arms, put *his* hands upon them, and blessed them.

I

Matt. 10. 40 He that receiveth you receiveth me; and he that receiveth me receiveth him that sent me.

Luke 9. 48. *See text of topic.*

Luke 10. 16 He that heareth you heareth me; and he that despiseth you despiseth me; and he that despiseth me despiseth him that sent me.

K

Matt. 18. 1. *See text of topic.*
Mark 9. 34. *See text of topic.*

L

John 2. 25 And needed not that any should testify of man; for he knew what was in man.

John 16. 30 Now are we sure that thou knowest all things, and needest not that any man should ask thee: by this we believe that thou camest forth from God.

Heb. 4. 13 Neither is there any creature that is not manifest in his sight: but all things *are* naked and opened unto the eyes of him with whom we have to do.

M

Matt. 10. 40. *See under I.*
Matt. 18. 5. *See text of topic.*
Mark. 9. 37. *See text of topic.*

John 12. 44 Jesus cried and said, He that believeth on me, believeth not on me, but on him that sent me.

John 13. 20 Verily, verily, I say unto you, He that receiveth whomsoever I send receiveth me; and he that receiveth me receiveth him that sent me.

N

Job 22. 29 When *men* are cast down, then thou shalt say, *There is* lifting up; and he shall save the humble person.

Matt. 23. 11. *See under C.*

Matt. 23. 12 And whosoever shall exalt himself shall be abased; and he that shall humble himself shall be exalted.

Jas. 4. 6 But he giveth more grace. Wherefore he saith, God resisteth the proud, but giveth grace unto the humble.

§ 100. ONE CASTING OUT DEVILS IN JESUS' NAME.

A

Num.11. 28 And Joshua the son of Nun, the servant of Moses, *one* of his young men, answered and said, My lord Moses, forbid them.

Luke 9. 49. *See text of topic.*

B

I Cor.12. 3 Wherefore I give you to understand, that no man speaking by the Spirit of God calleth Jesus accursed: and *that* no man can say that Jesus is the Lord, but by the Holy Ghost.

C

Matt.12. 30 He that is not with me is against me; and he that gathereth not with me scattereth abroad.

D

Matt.10. 42 And whosoever shall give to drink unto one of these little ones a cup of cold *water* only in the name of a disciple, verily I say unto you, he shall in no wise lose his reward.

Matt.25. 40 And the King shall answer and say unto them, Verily I say unto you, Inasmuch as ye have done *it* unto one

9 : 38–41.

38 [a]And John answered him, saying,
Master, we saw one casting out devils
in thy name, and he followeth not us;
and we forbade him, because he followeth not us.
39 But Jesus said, Forbid him not:
[b]for there is no man which shall do a
miracle in my name, that can lightly
speak evil of me.
40 For [c]he that is not against us is
on our part.
41 [d]For whosoever shall give you a
cup of water to drink in my name,
because ye belong to Christ, verily I
say unto you, he shall not lose his
reward.

§ 101. OFFENCES. SALTED WITH FIRE.

18 : 6–9.

6 [a]But whoso shall offend one of
these little ones which believe in me,
it were better for him that a millstone
were hanged about his neck, and *that*
he were drowned in the depth of the
sea.
7 Woe unto the world because of
offences: [b]for it must needs be that
offences come; but [c]woe to that man
by whom the offence cometh!
8 [d]Wherefore if thy hand or thy foot
offend thee, cut them off, and cast *them*
from thee: it is better for thee to enter
into life halt or maimed, rather than
having two hands or two feet to be
cast into everlasting fire.

A

Mark 9. 42. *See text of topic.*

Luke 17. 1 Then said he unto the disciples, It is impossible but that offences will come: but woe *unto him*, through whom they come!

9 : 42–49.

42 [e]And whosoever shall offend one
of *these* little ones that believe in me,
it is better for him that a millstone
were hanged about his neck, and he
were cast into the sea.
43 [f]And if thy hand [1]offend thee,
cut it off: it is better for thee to enter
into life maimed, than having two
hands to go into hell, into the fire that
never shall be quenched:
44 [g]Where their worm dieth not,
and the fire is not quenched.
45 And if thy foot offend thee, cut it
off: it is better for thee to enter halt
into life, than having two feet to be
cast into hell, into the fire that never
shall be quenched:
46 Where their worm dieth not, and
the fire is not quenched.

TIME, AUTUMN, A. D. 29; PLACE, CAPERNAUM.

9: 49, 50.

49 [e]And John answered and said, Master, we saw one casting out devils in thy name; and we forbade him, because he followeth not with us.

50 And Jesus said unto him, Forbid *him* not: for [f]he that is not against us is for us. (p. 311.)

D—CONTINUED.

of the least of these my brethren ye, have done *it* unto me.

John 19. 25 Now there stood by the cross of Jesus his mother, and his mother's sister, Mary the *wife* of Cleophas, and Mary Magdalene.

26 When Jesus therefore saw his mother, and the disciples standing by, whom he loved, he saith unto his mother, Woman, behold thy son!

27 Then saith he to the disciple, Behold thy mother! And from that hour that disciple took her unto his own *home*.

D—CONCLUDED.

Rom. 8. 9 But ye are not in the flesh, but in the Spirit, if so be that the Spirit of God dwell in you. Now if any man have not the Spirit of Christ, he is none of his.

Rom.14. 15 But if thy brother be grieved with *thy* meat, now walkest thou not charitably. Destroy not him with thy meat, for whom Christ died.

I Cor. 3. 23 And ye are Christ's; and Christ *is* God's.

Heb. 6. 10 For God *is* not unrighteous to forget your work and labour of love, which ye have showed toward his name, in that ye have ministered to the saints, and do minister.

E

Num. 11. 28. *Under A.* Mark 9. 38. *See text of topic.*

F

Matt. 12. 30. *See under C.*

Luke 11. 23 He that is not with me is against me; and he that gathereth not with me scattereth.

TIME, AUTUMN, A. D. 29; PLACE, CAPERNAUM.

A—CONCLUDED.

Luke 17. 2 It were better for him that a millstone were hanged about his neck, and he cast into the sea, than that he should offend one of these little ones.

B

Luke 17. 1. *See under A.*

I Cor.11. 19 For there must be also heresies among you, that they which are approved may be made manifest among you.

C

Matt.26. 24 The Son of man goeth as it is written of him: but woe unto that man by whom the Son of man is betrayed! it had been good for that man if he had not been born.

D

Matt. 5. 29 And if thy right eye offend thee, pluck it out, and cast *it* from thee: for it is profitable for thee that one of thy members should perish, and not *that* thy whole body should be cast into hell.

30 And if thy right hand offend thee, cut it off, and cast *it* from thee: for it is profitable for thee that one of thy members should perish, and not *that* thy whole body should be cast into hell.

Mark 9. 43, 45. *See text of topic.*

E

Matt. 18. 6. *See text of topic.* Luke 17. 1. *Under A.*

F

Deut.13. 6 If thy brother, the son of thy mother, or thy son, or thy daughter, or the wife of thy bosom, or thy friend, which *is* as thine own soul, entice thee secretly, saying, Let us go and serve other gods, which thou hast not known, thou, nor thy fathers;

7 *Namely*, of the gods of the people which *are* round about you, nigh unto thee, or far off from thee, from the *one* end of the earth even unto the *other* end of the earth;

8 Thou shalt not consent unto him, nor hearken unto him; neither shall thine eye pity him, neither shalt thou spare, neither shalt thou conceal him:

9 But thou shalt surely kill him; thine hand shall be first upon him to put him to death, and afterwards the hand of all the people.

10 And thou shalt stone him with stones, that he die; because he hath sought to thrust thee away from the LORD thy God, which brought thee out of the land of Egypt, from the house of bondage.

Matt. 5. 29. *Under D.* Matt. 18. 8. *See text of topic.*

For F concluded, 1 and G see following pages (298, 299).

§ 101. OFFENCES. SALTED WITH FIRE (CONCLUDED).

CHAP. 18.

9 And if thine eye offend thee, pluck it out, and cast *it* from thee: it is better for thee to enter into life with one eye, rather than having two eyes to be cast into hell fire.

F—CONCLUDED. See preceding page (297).

Col. 3. 5 Mortify therefore your members which are upon the earth; fornication, uncleanness, inordinate affection, evil concupiscence, and covetousness, which is idolatry:

Heb. 12. 1 Wherefore, seeing we also are compassed about with so great a cloud of witnesses, let us lay aside every weight, and the sin which doth so easily beset *us*, and let us run with patience the race that is set before us,

1 Or, *cause thee to offend.*

G

Isa. 66. 24 And they shall go forth, and look

CHAP. 9.

47 And if thine eye [2]offend thee,
[h]pluck it out: it is better for thee to enter into the kingdom of God with one eye, than having two eyes to be cast into hell fire:

48 Where their worm dieth not, and the fire is not quenched.

49 For every one shall be salted with fire, [i]and every sacrifice shall be salted with salt.

50 [k]Salt *is* good: but if the salt have lost his saltness, wherewith will ye season it? [l]Have salt in yourselves, and [m]have peace one with another. (p. 366.)

G—CONTINUED.

upon the carcasses of the men that have transgressed against me: for

§ 102. THE PARABLE OF THE LOST SHEEP.

18: 10–14.

10 [a]Take heed that ye despise not one of these little ones; for I say unto you, That in heaven their angels do always [b]behold the face of my Father which is in heaven.

11 [c]For the Son of man is come to save that which was lost.

12 [d]How think ye? if a man have a hundred sheep, and one of them be gone astray, doth he not leave the ninety and nine, and goeth into the mountains, and seeketh that [e]which is gone astray?

13 And if so be that he find it, verily I say unto you, he rejoiceth [f]more of that *sheep*, than of the ninety and nine which went not astray.

14 Even so it is not the will of your Father which is in heaven, that one of these little ones should perish.

A

Ps. 34. 7 The angel of the LORD encampeth round about them that fear him, and delivereth them.

Zech. 13. 7 Awake, O sword, against my Shepherd, and against the man *that is* my fellow, saith the LORD of hosts: smite the Shepherd, and the sheep shall be scattered: and I will turn mine hand upon the little ones.

Heb. 1. 14 Are they not all ministering spirits, sent forth to minister for them who shall be heirs of salvation?

B

Esth. 1. 14 And the next unto him *was* Carshena, Shethar, Admatha, Tarshish, Meres, Marsena, *and* Memucan, the seven princes of Persia and Media, which saw the king's face, *and* which sat the first in the kingdom,)

Luke 1. 19 And the angel answering said unto him, I am Gabriel, that stand in the presence of God; and am sent to speak unto thee, and to show thee these glad tidings.

C

Luke 9. 56 For the Son of man is not come to destroy men's lives, but to save *them*. And they went to another village.

Luke 19. 10 For the Son of man is come to

TIME, AUTUMN, A. D. 29; PLACE, CAPERNAUM.

G—CONCLUDED.

their worm shall not die, neither shall their fire be quenched; and they shall be an abhorring unto all flesh.

II Thes. 1. 9 Who shall be punished with everlasting destruction from the presence of the Lord, and from the glory of his power;

2

Or, *cause thee to offend.*

H

Rom. 8. 13 For if ye live after the flesh, ye shall die: but if ye through the Spirit do mortify the deeds of the body, ye shall live.

Gal. 5. 24 And they that are Christ's have crucified the flesh with the affections and lusts.

I

Lev. 2. 13 And every oblation of thy meat offering shalt thou season with salt; neither shalt thou suffer the salt of the covenant of thy God to be lacking from thy meat offering: with all thine offerings thou shalt offer salt.

Eze. 43. 24 And thou shalt offer them before

I—CONCLUDED.

the LORD, and the priests shall cast salt upon them, and they shall offer them up *for* a burnt offering unto the LORD.

K

Luke 14. 34 Salt *is* good: but if the salt have lost his savour, wherewith shall it be seasoned?

L

Eph. 4. 29 Let no corrupt communication proceed out of your mouth, but that which is good to the use of edifying, that it may minister grace unto the hearers.

Col. 4. 6 Let your speech *be* always with grace, seasoned with salt, that ye may know how ye ought to answer every man.

M

Rom. 12. 18 If it be possible, as much as lieth in you, live peaceably with all men.

Rom. 14. 19 Let us therefore follow after the things which make for peace, and things wherewith one may edify another.

TIME, AUTUMN, A. D. 29; PLACE, CAPERNAUM.

C—CONCLUDED.

seek and to save that which was lost.

John 3. 17 For God sent not his Son into the world to condemn the world; but that the world through him might be saved.

John 12. 47 And if any man hear my words, and believe not, I judge him not: for I came not to judge the world, but to save the world.

D

Luke 15. 4 What man of you, having a hundred sheep, if he lose one of them, doth not leave the ninety and nine in the wilderness, and go after that which is lost, until he find it?

5 And when he hath found *it*, he layeth *it* on his shoulders, rejoicing.

6 And when he cometh home, he calleth together *his* friends and neighbours, saying unto them, Rejoice with me; for I have found my sheep which was lost.

7 I say unto you, that likewise joy shall be in heaven over one sinner that repenteth, more than over ninety and nine just persons, which need no repentance.

I Pet. 2. 25 For ye were as sheep going astray; but are now returned unto the Shepherd and Bishop of your souls.

E

I Pet. 2. 10 Which in time past *were* not a people, but *are* now the people of God: which had not obtained mercy, but now have obtained mercy.

F

Ps. 147. 11 The LORD taketh pleasure in them that fear him, in those that hope in his mercy.

Isa. 62. 5 For as a young man marrieth a virgin, *so* shall thy sons marry thee: and *as* the bridegroom rejoiceth over the bride, *so* shall thy God rejoice over thee.

Jer. 32. 38 And they shall be my people, and I will be their God:

39 And I will give them one heart, and one way, that they may fear me for ever, for the good of them, and of their children after them:

40 And I will make an everlasting covenant with them, that I will not turn away from them, to do them good; but I will put my fear in their hearts, that they shall not depart from me.

41 Yea, I will rejoice over them to do them good, and I will plant them in this land assuredly with my whole heart and with my whole soul.

Luke 5. 32 I came not to call the righteous, but sinners to repentance.

18 : 15–20.

15 Moreover [a]if thy brother shall trespass against thee, go and tell him his fault between thee and him alone: if he shall hear thee, [b]thou hast gained thy brother.

16 But if he will not hear *thee, then* take with thee one or two more, that in [c]the mouth of two or three witnesses every word may be established.

17 And if he shall neglect to hear them, tell *it* unto the church: but if he neglect to hear [d]the church, let him be unto thee as a [e]heathen man and a publican.

18 Verily I say unto you, [f]Whatsoever ye shall bind on earth shall be bound in heaven; and whatsoever ye shall loose on earth shall be loosed in heaven.

19 [g]Again I say unto you, That if two of you shall agree on earth as touching any thing that they shall ask, [h]it shall be done for them of my Father which is in heaven.

20 For where two or three are gathered together in my name, [i]there am I in the midst of them.

A

Lev. 19. 17 Thou shalt not hate thy brother in thine heart: thou shalt in any wise rebuke thy neighbour, and not suffer sin upon him.

Luke 17. 3 Take heed to yourselves: If thy brother trespass against thee, rebuke him; and if he repent, forgive him.

B

Jas. 5. 20 Let him know, that he which converteth the sinner from the error of his way shall save a soul from death, and shall hide a multitude of sins.

I Pet. 3. 1 Likewise, ye wives, *be* in subjection to your own husbands; that, if any obey not the word, they also may

§ 103. FORGIVENESS OF INJURIES.

B—Concluded.

without the word be won by the conversation of the wives;

2 While they behold your chaste conversation *coupled* with fear.

C

Deut. 17. 6 At the mouth of two witnesses, or three witnesses, shall he that is worthy of death be put to death; *but* at the mouth of one witness he shall not be put to death.

Deut. 19. 15 One witness shall not rise up against a man for any iniquity, or for any sin, in any sin that he sinneth: at the mouth of two witnesses, or at the mouth of three witnesses, shall the matter be established.

John 8. 17 It is also written in your law, that the testimony of two men is true.

II Cor. 13. 1 This *is* the third *time* I am coming to you. In the mouth of two or three witnesses shall every word be established.

Heb. 10. 28 He that despised Moses' law died without mercy under two or three witnesses:

D

I Tim. 5. 19 Against an elder receive not an accusation, but before two or three witnesses.

20 Them that sin rebuke before all, that others also may fear.

E

Rom. 16. 17 Now I beseech you, brethren, mark them which cause divisions and offences contrary to the doctrine which ye have learned; and avoid them.

I Cor. 5. 9 I wrote unto you in an epistle not to company with fornicators:

II Thes. 3. 6 Now we command you, brethren, in the name of our Lord Jesus Christ, that ye withdraw yourselves from every brother that walketh disorderly, and not after the tradition which he received of us.

II Thes. 3. 14 And if any man obey not our word by this epistle, note that man, and have no company with him, that he may be ashamed.

II Jno. 10 If there come any unto you, and bring not this doctrine, receive him not into *your* house, neither bid him God speed:

F

Matt. 16. 19 And I will give unto thee the keys of the kingdom of heaven: and whatsoever thou shalt bind on earth shall be bound in heaven; and whatsoever thou shalt loose on earth shall be loosed in heaven.

TIME, AUTUMN, A. D. 29; PLACE, CAPERNAUM.

F—CONCLUDED.

John 20. 23 Whosesoever sins ye remit, they are remitted unto them; *and* whosesoever *sins* ye retain, they are retained.

Acts 15. 25 It seemed good unto us, being assembled with one accord, to send chosen men unto you with our beloved Barnabas and Paul,

26 Men that have hazarded their lives for the name of our Lord Jesus Christ.

27 We have sent therefore Judas and Silas, who shall also tell *you* the same things by mouth.

28 For it seemed good to the Holy Ghost, and to us, to lay upon you no greater burden than these necessary things;

29 That ye abstain from meats offered to idols, and from blood, and from things strangled, and from fornication: from which if ye keep yourselves, ye shall do well. Fare ye well.

30 So when they were dismissed, they came to Antioch: and when they had gathered the multitude together, they delivered the epistle:

31 *Which* when they had read, they rejoiced for the consolation.

I Cor. 5. 4 In the name of our Lord Jesus Christ, when ye are gathered together, and my spirit, with the power of our Lord Jesus Christ,

5 To deliver such a one unto Satan for the destruction of the flesh, that the spirit may be saved in the day of the Lord Jesus.

G

Matt. 5. 24 Leave there thy gift before the altar, and go thy way; first be reconciled to thy brother, and then come and offer thy gift.

H

Jas. 5. 16 Confess *your* faults one to another, and pray one for another, that ye may be healed. The effectual fervent prayer of a righteous man availeth much.

I Jno. 3. 22 And whatsoever we ask, we receive of him, because we keep his commandments, and do those things that are pleasing in his sight.

I Jno. 5. 14 And this is the confidence that we have in him, that, if we ask any thing according to his will, he heareth us:

I

Eze. 48. 35 *It was* round about eighteen thousand *measures:* and the name of the city from *that* day *shall be,* The LORD *is* there.

I—CONCLUDED.

Zech. 2. 1 I lifted up mine eyes again, and looked, and behold a man with a measuring line in his hand.

2 Then said I, Whither goest thou? And he said unto me, To measure Jerusalem, to see what *is* the breadth thereof, and what *is* the length thereof.

3 And, behold, the angel that talked with me went forth, and another angel went out to meet him,

4 And said unto him, Run, speak to this young man, saying, Jerusalem shall be inhabited *as* towns without walls for the multitude of men and cattle therein:

5 For I, saith the LORD, will be unto her a wall of fire round about, and will be the glory in the midst of her.

Matt. 28. 20 Teaching them to observe all things whatsoever I have commanded you: and, lo, I am with you alway, *even* unto the end of the world. Amen.

Rev. 1. 10 I was in the Spirit on the Lord's day, and heard behind me a great voice, as of a trumpet.

11 Saying, I am Alpha and Omega, the first and the last: and, What thou seest, write in a book, and send *it* unto the seven churches which are in Asia; unto Ephesus, and unto Smyrna, and unto Pergamos, and unto Thyatira, and unto Sardis, and unto Philadelphia, and unto Laodicea.

12 And I turned to see the voice that spake with me. And being turned, I saw seven golden candlesticks;

13 And in the midst of the seven candlesticks *one* like unto the Son of man, clothed with a garment down to the foot, and girt about the paps with a golden girdle.

Rev. 1. 20 The mystery of the seven stars which thou sawest in my right hand, and the seven golden candlesticks. The seven stars are the angels of the seven churches: and the seven candlesticks which thou sawest are the seven churches.

Rev. 2. 1 Unto the angel of the church of Ephesus write; These things saith he that holdeth the seven stars in his right hand, who walketh in the midst of the seven golden candlesticks;

Rev. 21. 3 And I heard a great voice out of heaven saying, Behold, the tabernacle of God *is* with men, and he will dwell with them, and they shall be his people, and God himself shall be with them, *and be* their God.

§ 104. THE PARABLE OF THE UNMERCIFUL SERVANT.

18: 21–35.

21 Then came Peter to him, and said, Lord, how oft shall my brother sin against me, and I forgive him? [a]till seven times?

22 Jesus saith unto him, I say not unto thee, Until seven times: [b]but, Until seventy times seven.

23 Therefore is the kingdom of heaven likened unto a certain king, which would take account of his servants.

24 And when he had begun to reckon, one was brought unto him, which owed him ten thousand [1]talents.

25 But forasmuch as he had not to pay, his lord commanded him [c]to be sold, and his wife, and children, and all that he had, and payment to be made.

26 The servant therefore fell down, and [2]worshipped him, saying, Lord, have patience with me, and I will pay thee all.

27 Then the lord of that servant was moved with compassion, and loosed him, and forgave him the debt.

28 But the same servant went out, and found one of his fellow servants, which owed him a hundred [3]pence: and he laid hands on him, and took *him* by the throat, saying, Pay me that thou owest.

29 And his fellow servant fell down at his feet, and besought him, saying, Have patience with me, and I will pay thee all.

30 And he would not: but went and cast him into prison, till he should pay the debt.

A

Luke 17. 4 And if he trespass against thee seven times in a day, and seven times in a day turn again to thee, saying, I repent; thou shalt forgive him.

B

Matt. 6. 14 For if ye forgive men their trespasses, your heavenly Father will also forgive you:

Mark 11. 25 And when ye stand praying, forgive, if ye have aught against any; that your Father also which is in heaven may forgive you your trespasses.

Col. 3. 13 Forbearing one another, and forgiving one another, if any man have a quarrel against any: even as Christ forgave you, so also *do* ye.

1

A talent is 750 ounces of silver, which after five shillings the ounce is 187l 10s.; in American money, *$1,440*, or ten thousand talents, *$14,400,000*.

C

Lev. 25. 35 And if thy brother be waxen poor, and fallen in decay with thee; then thou shalt relieve him: *yea, though he be* a stranger, or a sojourner; that he may live with thee.

36 Take thou no usury of him, or increase: but fear thy God; that thy brother may live with thee.

37 Thou shalt not give him thy money upon usury, nor lend him thy victuals for increase.

38 I *am* the LORD your God, which brought you forth out of the land of Egypt, to give you the land of Canaan, *and* to be your God.

39 And if thy brother *that dwelleth* by thee be waxen poor, and be sold unto thee; thou shalt not compel him to serve as a bondservant:

40 *But* as a hired servant, *and* as a sojourner, he shall be with thee, *and* shall serve thee unto the year of jubilee:

41 And *then* shall he depart from thee, *both* he and his children with him, and shall return unto his own family, and unto the possession of his fathers shall he return.

42 For they *are* my servants, which I brought forth out of the land of Egypt: they shall not be sold as bondmen.

43 Thou shalt not rule over him with rigour; but shalt fear thy God.

44 Both thy bondmen, and thy bondmaids, which thou shalt have, *shall be* of the heathen that are round about

Time, Autumn, A. D. 29; Place, Capernaum.

C—Continued.

you; of them shall ye buy bondmen and bondmaids.

45 Moreover, of the children of the strangers that do sojourn among you, of them shall ye buy, and of their families that *are* with you, which they begat in your land: and they shall be your possession.

46 And ye shall take them as an inheritance for your children after you, to inherit *them for* a possession; they shall be your bondmen forever: but over your brethren the children of Israel, ye shall not rule one over another with rigour.

47 And if a sojourner or stranger wax rich by thee, and thy brother *that dwelleth* by him wax poor, and sell himself unto the stranger *or* sojourner by thee, or to the stock of the stranger's family:

48 After that he is sold he may be redeemed again; one of his brethren may redeem him:

49 Either his uncle, or his uncle's son, may redeem him, or *any* that is nigh of kin unto him of his family may redeem him; or if he be able, he may redeem himself.

50 And he shall reckon with him that bought him from the year that he was sold to him unto the year of jubilee: and the price of his sale shall be according unto the number of years, according to the time of a hired servant shall it be with him.

51 If *there be* yet many years *behind*, according unto them he shall give again the price of his redemption out of the money that he was bought for.

52 And if there remain but few years unto the year of jubilee, then he shall count with him, *and* according unto his years shall he give him again the price of his redemption.

53 *And* as a yearly hired servant shall he be with him: *and the other* shall not rule with rigour over him in thy sight.

54 And if he be not redeemed in these *years*, then he shall go out in the year of jubilee, *both* he, and his children with him.

55 For unto me the children of Israel *are* servants; they *are* my servants whom I brought forth out of the land of Egypt: I *am* the Lord your God.

II Ki. 4. 1 Now there cried a certain woman

C—Concluded.

of the wives of the sons of the prophets unto Elisha, saying, Thy servant my husband is dead; and thou knowest that thy servant did fear the Lord: and the creditor is come to take unto him my two sons to be bondmen.

Neh. 5. 1 And there was a great cry of the people and of their wives against their brethren the Jews.

2 For there were that said, We, our sons, and our daughters, *are* many: therefore we take up corn *for them*, that we may eat, and live.

3 *Some* also there were that said, We have mortgaged our lands, vineyards, and houses, that we might buy corn, because of the dearth.

4 There were also that said, We have borrowed money for the king's tribute, *and that upon* our lands and vineyards.

5 Yet now our flesh *is* as the flesh of our brethren, our children as their children: and, lo, we bring into bondage our sons and our daughters to be servants, and *some* of our daughters are brought into bondage *already:* neither *is it* in our power *to redeem them;* for other men have our lands and vineyards.

6 And I was very angry when I heard their cry and these words.

7 Then I consulted with myself, and I rebuked the nobles, and the rulers, and said unto them, Ye exact usury, every one of his brother. And I set a great assembly against them.

8 And I said unto them, We, after our ability, have redeemed our brethren the Jews, which were sold unto the heathen; and will ye even sell your brethren? or shall they be sold unto us? Then held they their peace, and found nothing *to answer*.

Jer. 34. 14 At the end of seven years let ye go every man his brother a Hebrew, which hath been sold unto thee; and when he hath served thee six years, thou shalt let him go free from thee: but your fathers hearkened not unto me, neither inclined their ear.

2

Or, *besought him.*

3

The Roman penny is the eighth part of an ounce which after five shillings the ounce is seven pence half penny.

Matt.20. 2 And when he had agreed with the labourers for a penny a day, he sent them into his vineyard.

§ 104. THE PARABLE OF THE UNMERCIFUL SERVANT

CHAP. 18.

31 So when his fellow servants saw what was done, they were very sorry, and came and told unto their lord all that was done.

32 Then his lord, after that he had called him, said unto him, O thou wicked servant, I forgave thee all that debt, because thou desiredst me:

33 Shouldest [d]not thou also have had compassion on thy fellow servant, even as I had pity on thee?

34 And his lord was wroth, [e]and delivered him to the tormentors, till he should pay all that was due unto him.

35 [f]So likewise shall my heavenly Father do also unto you, if ye [g]from your hearts forgive not every one his brother their trespasses. (p. 366.)

D

Eph. 4. 31 Let all bitterness, and wrath, and anger, and clamour, and evil speaking, be put away from you, with all malice:

32 And be ye kind one to another,

D—CONCLUDED.

tenderhearted, forgiving one another, even as God for Christ's sake hath forgiven you.

Eph. 5. 1 Be ye therefore followers of God, as dear children;

Col. 3. 12 Put on therefore, as the elect of God, holy and beloved, bowels of mercies, kindness, humbleness of mind, meekness, longsuffering;

13 Forbearing one another, and forgiving one another, if any man have a quarrel against any: even as Christ forgave you, so also *do* ye.

E

II Thes. 1. 8 In flaming fire taking vengeance on them that know not God, and that obey not the gospel of our Lord Jesus Christ:

9 Who shall be punished with everlasting destruction from the presence of the Lord, and from the glory of his power;

Rev. 14. 10 The same shall drink of the wine of the wrath of God, which is poured out without mixture into the cup of his indignation; and he shall be tormented with fire and brimstone in the presence of the holy angels, and in the presence of the Lamb:

§ 105. THE SEVENTY INSTRUCTED AND SENT OUT.

A

Matt. 10. 1 And when he had called unto *him* his twelve disciples, he gave them power *against* unclean spirits, to cast them out, and to heal all manner of sickness and all manner of disease.

Mark 6. 7 And he called *unto him* the twelve, and began to send them forth by two and two; and gave them power over unclean spirits;

Luke 9. 1 Then he called his twelve disciples together, and gave them power and authority over all devils, and to cure diseases.

2 And he sent them to preach the kingdom of God, and to heal the sick.

B

Matt. 9. 37 Then saith he unto his disciples, The harvest truly *is* plenteous, but the labourers *are* few;

38 Pray ye therefore the Lord of the harvest, that he will send forth labourers into his harvest.

John 4. 35 Say not ye, There are yet four months, and *then* cometh harvest? behold, I say unto you, Lift up your

B—CONCLUDED.

eyes, and look on the fields; for they are white already to harvest.

C

II Thes. 3. 1 Finally, brethren, pray for us, that the word of the Lord may have *free* course, and be glorified, even as *it is* with you:

D

Jer. 3. 14 Turn, O backsliding children, saith the LORD; for I am married unto you: and I will take you one of a city, and two of a family, and I will bring you to Zion:

15 And I will give you pastors according to mine heart, which shall feed you with knowledge and understanding.

I Cor. 12. 28 And God hath set some in the church, first apostles, secondarily prophets, thirdly teachers, after that miracles, then gifts of healings, helps, governments, diversities of tongues.

E

Matt. 10. 16 Behold, I send you forth as sheep in the midst of wolves: be ye there-

(Concluded). Time, Autumn, A. D. 29; Place, Capernaum.

E—Concluded.

Rev. 14. 11 And the smoke of their torment ascendeth up for ever and ever: and they have no rest day nor night, who worship the beast and his image, and whosoever receiveth the mark of his name.

F

Prov. 21. 13 Whoso stoppeth his ears at the cry of the poor, he also shall cry himself, but shall not be heard.

14 A gift in secret pacifieth anger: and a reward in the bosom, strong wrath.

Matt. 6. 12 And forgive us our debts, as we forgive our debtors.

Mark 11. 26 But if ye do not forgive, neither will your Father which is in heaven forgive your trespasses.

Jas. 2. 13 For he shall have judgment without mercy, that hath showed no mercy; and mercy rejoiceth against judgment.

G

Prov. 21. 2 Every way of a man *is* right in his own eyes: but the Lord pondereth the hearts.

Jer. 3. 10 And yet for all this her treacherous sister Judah hath not turned unto me with her whole heart, but feignedly, saith the Lord.

G—Concluded.

Jer. 3. 11 And the Lord said unto me, The backsliding Israel hath justified herself more than treacherous Judah.

Zech. 7. 12 Yea, they made their hearts *as* an adamant stone, lest they should hear the law, and the words which the Lord of hosts hath sent in his Spirit by the former prophets: therefore came a great wrath from the Lord of hosts.

Luke 16. 15 And he said unto them, Ye are they which justify yourselves before men; but God knoweth your hearts: for that which is highly esteemed among men is abomination in the sight of God.

Jas. 3. 14 But if ye have bitter envying and strife in your hearts, glory not, and lie not against the truth.

Jas. 4. 8 Draw nigh to God, and he will draw nigh to you. Cleanse *your* hands, *ye* sinners; and purify *your* hearts, *ye* doubleminded.

Rev. 2. 23 And I will kill her children with death; and all the churches shall know that I am he which searcheth the reins and hearts: and I will give unto every one of you according to your works.

Time, Autumn, A. D. 29; Place, Capernaum.

10: 1–16.

1 After these things the Lord appointed other seventy also, and [a]sent them two and two before his face into every city and place, whither he himself would come.

2 Therefore said he unto them, [b]The harvest truly *is* great, but the labourers *are* few: [c]pray ye therefore the [d]Lord of the harvest, that he would send forth labourers into his harvest.

3 Go your ways: [e]behold, I send you forth as lambs among wolves.

4 [f]Carry neither purse, nor scrip, nor shoes: and [g]salute no man by the way.

E—Concluded.

fore wise as serpents, and harmless as doves.

F

Matt. 10. 9 Provide neither gold, nor silver, nor brass in your purses;

10 Nor scrip for *your* journey, neither two coats, neither shoes, nor yet staves: for the workman is worthy of his meat.

Mark 6. 8 And commanded them that they should take nothing for *their* journey, save a staff only; no scrip, no bread, no money in *their* purse:

Luke 9. 3 And he said unto them, Take nothing for *your* journey, neither staves, nor scrip, neither bread, neither money; neither have two coats apiece.

G

II Ki. 4. 29 Then he said to Gehazi, Gird up thy loins, and take my staff in thine hand, and go thy way: if thou meet any man, salute him not; and if any salute thee, answer him not again: and lay my staff upon the face of the child.

H

Matt. 10. 12 And when ye come into a house, salute it.

§ 105. THE SEVENTY INSTRUCTED AND SENT OUT

For H see preceding page (305).

I

Matt.10. 11 And into whatsoever city or town ye shall enter, inquire who in it is worthy; and there abide till ye go thence.

Luke 9. 4 And whatsoever house ye enter into, there abide, and thence depart.

K

I Cor.10. 27 If any of them that believe not bid you *to a feast*, and ye be disposed to go; whatsoever is set before you, eat, asking no question for conscience' sake.

L

Matt. 10. 10. *See under F, page 305.*

I Cor. 9. 4 Have we not power to eat and to drink?

5 Have we not power to lead about a sister, a wife, as well as other apostles, and *as* the brethren of the Lord, and Cephas?

6 Or I only and Barnabas, have not we power to forbear working?

I Tim. 5. 17 Let the elders that rule well be counted worthy of double honour, especially they who labour in the word and doctrine.

18 For the Scripture saith, Thou shalt not muzzle the ox that treadeth out the corn. And, The labourer *is* worthy of his reward.

M

Eph. 5. 15 See then that ye walk circumspectly, not as fools, but as wise,

16 Redeeming the time, because the days are evil.

N

Luke 9. 2. *See under A, page 304.*

O

Isa. 2. 1 The word that Isaiah the son of Amoz saw concerning Judah and Jerusalem.

2 And it shall come to pass in the last days, *that* the mountain of the LORD'S house shall be established in the top of the mountains, and shall be exalted above the hills; and all nations shall flow unto it.

Matt. 3. 2 And saying, Repent ye: for the kingdom of heaven is at hand.

Matt. 4. 17 From that time Jesus began to preach, and to say, Repent: for the kingdom of heaven is at hand.

Matt.10. 7 And as ye go, preach, saying, The kingdom of heaven is at hand.

Luke 10. 11. *See text of topic.*

Rom.10. 8 But what saith it? The word is nigh thee, *even* in thy mouth, and in thy heart: that is, the word of faith, which we preach;

P

Matt.10. 14 And whosoever shall not receive you, nor hear your words, when ye depart out of that house or city, shake off the dust of your feet.

Luke 9. 5 And whosoever will not receive you, when ye go out of that city, shake off the very dust from your feet for a testimony against them.

Acts 13. 51 But they shook off the dust of their feet against them, and came unto Iconium.

Acts 18. 6 And when they opposed themselves, and blasphemed, he shook *his* raiment, and said unto them, Your blood *be* upon your own heads; I *am* clean: from henceforth I will go unto the Gentiles.

Q

Matt.10. 15 Verily I say unto you, It shall be more tolerable for the land of Sodom and Gomorrah in the day of judgment, than for that city.

Mark 6. 11 And whosoever shall not receive you, nor hear you, when ye depart thence, shake off the dust under your feet for a testimony against them. Verily I say unto you, It shall be more tolerable for Sodom and Gomorrah in the day of judgment, than for that city.

Heb. 10. 26 For if we sin wilfully after that we have received the knowledge of the truth, there remaineth no more sacrifice for sins,

27 But a certain fearful looking for of judgment and fiery indignation, which shall devour the adversaries.

28 He that despised Moses' law died without mercy under two or three witnesses:

29 Of how much sorer punishment, suppose ye, shall he be thought worthy, who hath trodden under foot the Son of God, and hath counted the blood of the covenant, wherewith he was sanctified, an unholy thing, and hath done despite unto the Spirit of grace?

30 For we know him that hath said, Vengeance *belongeth* unto me, I will recompense, saith the Lord. And again, The Lord shall judge his people.

31 *It is* a fearful thing to fall into the hands of the living God.

R

Matt.11. 21 Woe unto thee, Chorazin! woe unto thee, Bethsaida! for if the mighty works, which were done in

(CONTINUED). TIME, AUTUMN, A. D. 29; PLACE, CAPERNAUM.

CHAP. 10.

5 [h]And into whatsoever house ye enter, first say, Peace *be* to this house.

6 And if the son of peace be there, your peace shall rest upon it: if not, it shall turn to you again.

7 [i]And in the same house remain, [k]eating and drinking such things as they give: for [l]the labourer is worthy of his hire. Go not from [m]house to house.

8 And into whatsoever city ye enter, and they receive you, eat such things as are set before you:

9 [n]And heal the sick that are therein, and say unto them, [o]The kingdom of God is come nigh unto you.

10 But into whatsoever city ye enter, and they receive you not, go your ways out into the streets of the same, and say,

11 [p]Even the very dust of your city, which cleaveth on us, we do wipe off against you: notwithstanding, be ye sure of this, that the kingdom of God is come nigh unto you.

12 But I say unto you, that [q]it shall be more tolerable in that day for Sodom, than for that city.

13 [r]Woe unto thee, Chorazin! woe unto thee, Bethsaida! [s]for if the mighty works had been done in Tyre and Sidon, which have been done in you, they had a great while ago [t]repented, sitting in sackcloth and ashes.

14 But it shall be more tolerable for Tyre and Sidon at the judgment, than for you.

15 [u]And thou, Capernaum, which art [x]exalted to heaven, [y]shalt be thrust down to hell.

R—CONCLUDED.

you, had been done in Tyre and Sidon, they would have repented long ago in sackcloth and ashes.

S

Eze. 3. 6 Not to many people of a strange speech and of a hard language, whose words thou canst not understand. Surely, had I sent thee to them, they would have hearkened unto thee.

T

Jon. 3. 5 So the people of Nineveh believed God, and proclaimed a fast, and put on sackcloth, from the greatest of them even to the least of them.

U

Matt.11. 22 But I say unto you, It shall be more tolerable for Tyre and Sidon at the day of judgment, than for you.

23 And thou, Capernaum, which art exalted unto heaven, shalt be brought down to hell: for if the mighty works, which have been done in thee, had been done in Sodom, it would have remained until this day.

X

Gen. 11. 4 And they said, Go to, let us build us a city, and a tower, whose top *may reach* unto heaven; and let us make us a name, lest we be scattered abroad upon the face of the whole earth.

Deut. 1. 28 Whither shall we go up? our brethren have discouraged our heart, saying, The people *is* greater and taller than we; the cities *are* great and walled up to heaven; and moreover we have seen the sons of the Anakim there.

Isa. 14. 13 For thou hast said in thine heart, I will ascend into heaven, I will exalt my throne above the stars of God: I will sit also upon the mount of the congregation, in the sides of the north:

Jer. 51. 53 Though Babylon should mount up to heaven, and though she should fortify the height of her strength, *yet* from me shall spoilers come unto her, saith the LORD.

Y

Isa. 5. 14 Therefore hell hath enlarged herself, and opened her mouth without measure: and their glory, and their multitude, and their pomp, and he that rejoiceth, shall descend into it.

15 And the mean man shall be brought down, and the mighty man shall be humbled, and the eyes of the lofty shall be humbled:

For Y concluded see following pages (308, 309).

§ 105. THE SEVENTY INSTRUCTED AND SENT OUT

Y—CONTINUED. See preceding page (307).

Isa. 5. 16 But the LORD of hosts shall be exalted in judgment, and God that is holy shall be sanctified in righteousness.
17 Then shall the lambs feed after their manner, and the waste places of the fat ones shall strangers eat,
18 Woe unto them that draw iniquity with cords of vanity, and sin as it were with a cart rope:
19 That say, Let him make speed, *and* hasten his work, that we may see *it:* and let the council of the Holy One of Israel draw nigh and come, that we may know *it!*

Y—CONTINUED.

Isa. 14. 15 Yet thou shalt be brought down to hell, to the sides of the pit.
Eze. 26. 20 When I shall bring thee down with them that descend into the pit, with the people of old time, and shall set thee in the low parts of the earth, in places desolate of old, with them that go down to the pit, that thou be not inhabited; and I shall set glory in the land of the living;
Eze. 32. 18 Son of man, wail for the multitude of Egypt, and cast them down, *even* her, and the daughters of the famous nations, unto the nether parts

§ 106. JESUS GOES UP TO THE FEAST OF THE TABERNACLES.

A

Lev. 23. 34 Speak unto the children of Israel, saying, The fifteenth day of this seventh month *shall be* the feast of tabernacles *for* seven days unto the LORD.

B

Matt.12. 46 While he yet talked to the people, behold, *his* mother and his brethren stood without, desiring to speak with him.
Mark 3. 31 There came then his brethren and his mother, and, standing without, sent unto him, calling him.
Acts 1. 14 These all continued with one accord in prayer and supplication, with the women, and Mary the mother of Jesus, and with his brethren.

C

Mark 3. 21 And when his friends heard *of it,* they went out to lay hold on him: for they said, He is beside himself.

D

Eccl. 3. 8 A time to love, and a time to hate; a time of war, and a time of peace.
John 2. 4 Jesus saith unto her, Woman, what have I to do with thee? mine hour is not yet come.
John 7. 8. *See text of topic.*
John 7. 30 Then they sought to take him: but no man laid hands on him, because his hour was not yet come.
John 8. 20 These words spake Jesus in the treasury, as he taught in the temple: and no man laid hands on him; for his hour was not yet come.

E

John 15. 19 If ye were of the world, the world would love his own; but because ye are not of the world, but I have chosen you out of the world, therefore the world hateth you.

F

I Ki. 21. 20 And Ahab said to Elijah, Hast thou found me, O mine enemy? And he answered, I have found *thee:* because thou hast sold thyself to work evil in the sight of the LORD.
I Ki. 22. 8 And the king of Israel said unto Jehoshaphat, *There is* yet one man, Micaiah the son of Imlah, by whom we may inquire of the LORD: but I hate him; for he doth not prophesy good concerning me, but evil. And Jehoshaphat said, Let not the king say so.
Prov. 9. 7 He that reproveth a scorner getteth to himself shame: and he that rebuketh a wicked *man getteth* himself a blot.
8 Reprove not a scorner, lest he hate thee: rebuke a wise man, and he will love thee.
Prov.15. 12 A scorner loveth not one that reproveth him: neither will he go unto the wise.
Isa. 29. 20 For the terrible one is brought to nought, and the scorner is consumed, and all that watch for iniquity are cut off:
21 That make a man an offender for a word, and lay a snare for him that reproveth in the gate, and turn aside the just for a thing of nought.
Jer. 20. 8 For since I spake, I cried out, I cried violence and spoil; because the word of the LORD was made a reproach unto me, and a derision, daily.
Amos 7. 7 Thus he showed me: and, behold, the Lord stood upon a wall *made* by a plumbline, with a plumbline in his hand.
8 And the LORD said unto me, Amos, what seest thou? And I said, A plumb-

(CONCLUDED). TIME, AUTUMN, A. D. 29; PLACE, CAPERNAUM.

CHAP. 10.

16 [z]He that heareth you heareth me; and [a]he that despiseth you despiseth me; [b]and he that despiseth me despiseth him that sent me. (p. 341.)

Y—CONCLUDED.

of the earth, with them that go down into the pit.

Eze. 32. 20 They shall fall in the midst of *them that are* slain by the sword: she is delivered to the sword: draw her and all her multitudes.

Z

John 13. 20 Verily, verily, I say unto you, He that receiveth whomsoever I send receiveth me; and he that receiveth me receiveth him that sent me.

A

I Thes. 4. 8 He therefore that despiseth, despiseth not man, but God, who hath also given unto us his Holy Spirit.

B

John 5. 23 That all *men* should honour the Son, even as they honour the Father. He that honoureth not the Son honoureth not the Father which hath sent him.

FINAL DEPARTURE FROM GALILEE. TIME, AUTUMN, A. D. 29.

F—CONCLUDED.

line. Then said the Lord, Behold, I will set a plumbline in the midst of my people Israel: I will not again pass by them any more:

9 And the high places of Isaac shall be desolate, and the sanctuaries of Israel shall be laid waste; and I will rise against the house of Jeroboam with the sword.

10 Then Amaziah the priest of Beth-el sent to Jeroboam king of Israel, saying, Amos hath conspired against thee in the midst of the house of Israel: the land is not able to bear all his words.

11 For thus Amos saith, Jeroboam shall die by the sword, and Israel shall surely be led away captive out of their own land.

12 Also Amaziah said unto Amos, O thou seer, go, flee thee away into the land of Judah, and there eat bread, and prophesy there:

13 But prophesy not again any more at Beth-el: for it *is* the king's chapel, and it *is* the king's court.

Mal. 5. 5 And I will come near to you to judgment; and I will be a swift witness against the sorcerers, and against the adulterers, and against false swearers, and against those that oppress the hireling in *his* wages, the widow, and the fatherless, and that turn aside the stranger *from his right*, and fear not me, saith the LORD of hosts.

John 3. 19 And this is the condemnation, that light is come into the world, and men loved darkness rather than light, because their deeds were evil.

G

John 7. 6. *See text of topic.* John 8. 20. *Under D.*

7: 2–10.

2 [a]Now the Jews' feast of tabernacles was at hand.

3 [b]His brethren therefore said unto him, Depart hence, and go into Judæa, that thy disciples also may see the works that thou doest.

4 For *there is* no man *that* doeth any thing in secret, and he himself seeketh to be known openly. If thou do these things, show thyself to the world.

5 For [c]neither did his brethren believe in him.

6 Then Jesus said unto them, [d]My time is not yet come: but your time is always ready.

7 [e]The world cannot hate you; but me it hateth, [f]because I testify of it, that the works thereof are evil.

8 Go ye up unto this feast: I go not up yet unto this feast; [g]for my time is not yet full come.

9 When he had said these words unto them, he abode *still* in Galilee.

10 But when his brethren were gone up, then went he also up unto the feast, not openly, but as it were in secret. (p. 313.)

§ 107. JAMES AND JOHN ASK WHETHER TO COMMAND FIRE

A

Mark 16. 19 So then, after the Lord had
spoken unto them, he was received up
into heaven, and sat on the right
hand of God.

Acts 1. 1 The former treatise have I made,
O Theophilus, of all that Jesus began
both to do and teach,
2 Until the day in which he was
taken up, after that he through the
Holy Ghost had given commandments
unto the apostles whom he had
chosen:

B

John 4. 4 And he must needs go through
Samaria.

John 4. 9 Then saith the woman of Samaria
unto him, How is it that thou, being
a Jew, askest drink of me, which am
a woman of Samaria? for the Jews
have no dealings with the Samaritans.

C

II Ki. 1. 9 Then the king sent unto him a
captain of fifty with his fifty. And he
went up to him: and, behold, he sat
on the top of a hill. And he spake
unto him, Thou man of God, the king
hath said, Come down.
10 And Elijah answered and said to
the captain of fifty, If I *be* a man of
God, then let fire come down from
heaven, and consume thee and thy
fifty. And there came down fire from
heaven, and consumed him and his
fifty.
11 Again also he sent unto him an-

C—Concluded.

other captain of fifty with his fifty.
And he answered and said unto him,
O man of God, thus hath the king
said, Come down quickly.
12 And Elijah answered and said
unto them, If I *be* a man of God, let
fire come down from heaven, and consume thee and thy fifty. And the fire
of God came down from heaven, and
consumed him and his fifty.
13 And he sent again a captain of
the third fifty with his fifty. And the
third captain of fifty went up, and came
and fell on his knees before Elijah, and
besought him, and said unto him, O
man of God, I pray thee, let my life,
and the life of these fifty thy servants,
be precious in thy sight.
14 Behold, there came fire down
from heaven, and burnt up the two
captains of the former fifties with their
fifties: therefore let my life now be
precious in thy sight.

D

Num. 20. 10 And Moses and Aaron gathered
the congregation together before the
rock, and he said unto them, Hear
now, ye rebels; must we fetch you
water out of this rock?
11 And Moses lifted up his hand,
and with his rod he smote the rock
twice: and the water came out
abundantly, and the congregation
drank, and their beasts *also*.
12 And the LORD spake unto Moses

§ 108. TEN LEPERS CLEANSED BY JESUS.

A

Luke 9. 51 And it came to pass, when the
time was come that he should be received up, he steadfastly set his face
to go to Jerusalem,
52 And sent messengers before his
face: and they went, and entered into
a village of the Samaritans, to make
ready for him.

John 4. 4 And he must needs go through
Samaria.

B

Lev. 13. 46 All the days wherein the plague
shall be in him he shall be defiled; he
is unclean: he shall dwell alone;
without the camp *shall* his habitation
be.

II Ki. 5. 1 Now Naaman, captain of the host
of the king of Syria, was a great man
with his master, and honourable, because by him the LORD had given

B—Concluded.

deliverance unto Syria: he was also a
mighty man in valour, *but he was* a
leper.
2 And the Syrians had gone out by
companies, and had brought away
captive out of the land of Israel a
little maid; and she waited on Naaman's wife.
3 And she said unto her mistress,
Would God my lord *were* with the
prophet that *is* in Samaria! for he
would recover him of his leprosy.

C

Lev. 13. 2 When a man shall have in the
skin of his flesh a rising, a scab, or
bright spot, and it be in the skin of
his flesh *like* the plague of leprosy;
then he shall be brought unto Aaron
the priest, or unto one of his sons the
priests:

FROM HEAVEN. TIME, AUTUMN, A. D. 29; PLACE, SAMARIA.

9: 51–56.

51 And it came to pass, when the time was come that [a]he should be received up, he steadfastly set his face to go to Jerusalem,

52 And sent messengers before his face: and they went, and entered into a village of the Samaritans, to make ready for him.

53 And [b]they did not receive him, because his face was as though he would go to Jerusalem.

54 And when his disciples James and John saw *this*, they said, Lord, wilt thou that we command fire to come down from heaven, and consume them, even as [c]Elias did?

55 But he turned, and rebuked them, and said, Ye know not what [d]manner of spirit ye are of.

56 For [e]the Son of man is not come to destroy men's lives, but to save *them*. And they went to another village. (p. 213.)

D—CONCLUDED.

and Aaron, Because ye believed me not, to sanctify me in the eyes of the children of Israel, therefore ye shall not bring this congregation into the land which I have given them.

Rom.10. 2 For I bear them record that they have a zeal of God, but not according to knowledge.

3 For they, being ignorant of God's righteousness, and going about to establish their own righteousness, have not submitted themselves unto the righteousness of God.

E

Matt.18. 11 For the Son of man is come to save that which was lost.

Luke 19. 10 For the Son of man is come to seek and to save that which was lost.

John 3. 17 For God sent not his Son into the world to condemn the world; but that the world through him might be saved.

John 10. 10 The thief cometh not, but for to steal, and to kill, and to destroy: I am come that they might have life, and that they might have *it* more abundantly.

John 12. 27 Now is my soul troubled; and what shall I say? Father, save me from this hour: but for this cause came I unto this hour.

John 12. 47 And if any man hear my words, and believe not, I judge him not: for I came not to judge the world, but to save the world.

TIME, AUTUMN, A. D. 29; PLACE, SAMARIA.

17: 11–19.

11 And it came to pass, [a]as he went to Jerusalem, that he passed through the midst of Samaria and Galilee.

12 And as he entered into a certain village, there met him ten men that were lepers, [b]which stood afar off:

13 And they lifted up *their* voices, and said, Jesus, Master, have mercy on us.

14 And when he saw *them*, he said unto them, [c]Go show yourselves unto the priests. And it came to pass, that, as they went, they were cleansed.

C—CONCLUDED.

Lev. 14. 2 This shall be the law of the leper in the day of his cleansing: He shall be brought unto the priest:

Matt. 8. 4 And Jesus saith unto him, See thou tell no man; but go thy way, show thyself to the priest, and offer the gift that Moses commanded, for a testimony unto them.

Luke 5. 14 And he charged him to tell no man: but go, and show thyself to the priest, and offer for thy cleansing, according as Moses commanded, for a testimony unto them.

D

Ps. 103. 1 Bless the LORD, O my soul: and all that is within me, *bless* his holy name.

Ps. 116 12 What shall I render unto the LORD *for* all his benefits toward me?

For D concluded see next page (312).

§ 108. TEN LEPERS CLEANSED BY JESUS

D—CONCLUDED. See preceding page (311).

Ps. 116. 13 I will take the cup of salvation,
and call upon the name of the LORD.
14 I will pay my vows unto the LORD
now in the presence of all his people.
15 Precious in the sight of the LORD
is the death of his saints.

E

II Ki.17. 22 For the children of Israel walked
in all the sins of Jeroboam which he
did; they departed not from them;
23 Until the LORD removed Israel
out of his sight, as he had said by all
his servants the prophets. So was
Israel carried away out of their own
land to Assyria unto this day.
24 And the king of Assyria brought
men from Babylon, and from Cuthah,
and from Ava, and from Hamath, and
from Sepharvaim, and placed *them* in
the cities of Samaria instead of the
children of Israel: and they possessed Samaria, and dwelt in the
cities thereof.
25 And *so* it was at the beginning of
their dwelling there, *that* they feared
not the LORD: therefore the LORD
sent lions among them, which slew
some of them.
26 Wherefore they spake to the king
of Assyria, saying, The nations which
thou hast removed, and placed in the
cities of Samaria, know not the manner of the God of the land: therefore
he hath sent lions among them, and,
behold, they slay them, because they
know not the manner of the God of
the land.

John 8. 48 Then answered the Jews, and
said unto him, Say we not well that
thou art a Samaritan, and hast a devil?

F

Matt. 9. 22 But Jesus turned him about, and
when he saw her, he said, Daughter,

§ 109. JESUS TEACHES AT THE FEAST OF THE TABERNACLE.

A

John 11. 56 Then sought they for Jesus, and
spake among themselves, as they
stood in the temple, What think ye,
that he will not come to the feast?

B

John 9. 15 Then again the Pharisees also
asked him how he had received his
sight. He said unto them, He put
clay upon mine eyes, and I washed,
and do see.
16 Therefore said some of the Pharisees, This man is not of God, because
he keepeth not the sabbath day.
Others said, How can a man that is a
sinner do such miracles? And there
was a division among them.

John 10. 19 There was a division therefore
again among the Jews for these sayings.

C

John 7. 40. *See text of topic.*

Matt.21. 46 But when they sought to lay
hands on him, they feared the multitude, because they took him for a
prophet.

Luke 7. 16 And there came a fear on all:
and they glorified God, saying, That a
great prophet is risen up among us;
and, That God hath visited his people.

John 6. 14 Then those men, when they had
seen the miracle that Jesus did, said,
This is of a truth that Prophet that
should come into the world.

D

John 9. 22 These *words* spake his parents,
because they feared the Jews: for the
Jews had agreed already, that if any
man did confess that he was Christ, he
should be put out of the synagogue.

John 12. 42 Nevertheless among the chief
rulers also many believed on him;
but because of the Pharisees they did
not confess *him*, lest they should be
put out of the synagogue:

John 19. 38 And after this Joseph of Arimathea, being a disciple of Jesus, but
secretly for fear of the Jews, besought
Pilate that he might take away the
body of Jesus: and Pilate gave *him*
leave. He came therefore, and took
the body of Jesus.

E

Matt.13. 54 And when he was come into his
own country, he taught them in their
synagogue, insomuch that they were
astonished, and said, Whence hath
this *man* this wisdom, and *these*
mighty works?

Mark 6. 2. *See text of* § 75.

Luke 4. 22 And all bare him witness, and
wondered at the gracious words which
proceeded out of his mouth. And
they said, Is not this Joseph's son?

Acts 2. 7 And they were all amazed and
marvelled, saying one to another, Behold, are not all these which speak
Galileans?

(CONCLUDED). TIME, AUTUMN, A. D. 29; PLACE, SAMARIA.

CHAP. 17.

15 And one of them, when he saw
that he was healed, turned back, and
with a loud voice [d]glorified God,
16 And fell down on *his* face at his
feet, giving him thanks: and he was a
[e]Samaritan.
17 And Jesus answering said, Were
there not ten cleansed? but where *are*
the nine?
18 There are not found that returned
to give glory to God, save this stranger.
19 [f]And he said unto him, Arise,
go thy way: thy faith hath made
thee whole. (p. 397.)

F—CONCLUDED.

be of good comfort; thy faith hath made thee whole. And the woman was made whole from that hour.

Mark 5. 34 And he said unto her, Daughter, thy faith hath made thee whole; go in peace, and be whole of thy plague.

Mark 10. 52 And Jesus said unto him, Go thy way; thy faith hath made thee whole. And immediately he received his sight, and followed Jesus in the way.

Luke 7. 50 And he said to the woman, Thy faith hath saved thee; go in peace.

Luke 8. 48 And he said unto her, Daughter, be of good comfort: thy faith hath made thee whole; go in peace.

Luke 18. 42 And Jesus said unto him, Receive thy sight: thy faith hath saved thee.

John 4. 50 Jesus saith unto him, Go thy way; thy son liveth. And the man believed the word that Jesus had spoken unto him, and he went his way

TIME, OCTOBER, A. D. 29; PLACE, JERUSALEM.

7: 11–52.

11 Then [a]the Jews sought him at
the feast, and said, Where is he?
12 And [b]there was much murmuring
among the people concerning him: for
[c]some said, He is a good man: others
said, Nay; but he deceiveth the
people.
13 Howbeit no man spake openly of
him [d]for fear of the Jews.
14 Now about the midst of the feast
Jesus went up into the temple, and
taught.
15 [e]And the Jews marvelled, saying,
How knoweth this man [1]letters, having
never learned?
16 Jesus answered them, and said,
[f]My doctrine is not mine, but his that
sent me.

1 Or, *learning.*

F

John 3. 11 Verily, verily, I say unto thee, We speak that we do know, and testify that we have seen; and ye receive not our witness.

John 3. 31 He that cometh from above is above all: he that is of the earth is earthly, and speaketh of the earth: he that cometh from heaven is above all.

John 8. 28 Then said Jesus unto them, When ye have lifted up the Son of man, then shall ye know that I am *he*, and *that* I do nothing of myself; but as my Father hath taught me, I speak these things.

John 12. 49 For I have not spoken of myself; but the Father which sent me, he gave me a commandment, what I should say, and what I should speak.

50 And I know that his commandment is life everlasting: whatsoever I speak therefore, even as the Father said unto me, so I speak.

John 14. 10 Believest thou not that I am in the Father, and the Father in me? the words that I speak unto you I speak not of myself: but the Father that dwelleth in me, he doeth the works.

John 14. 24 He that loveth me not keepeth not my sayings: and the word which ye hear is not mine, but the Father's which sent me.

F—CONCLUDED.

John 17. 8 For I have given unto them the words which thou gavest me; and they have received *them*, and have known surely that I came out from thee, and they have believed that thou didst send me.

§ 109. JESUS TEACHES AT THE FEAST OF THE TABERNACLE

G

Hos. 6. 1 Come, and let us return unto the LORD: for he hath torn, and he will heal us; he hath smitten, and he will bind us up.

2 After two days will he revive us: in the third day he will raise us up, and we shall live in his sight.

3 Then shall we know, *if* we follow on to know the LORD: his going forth is prepared as the morning; and he shall come unto us as the rain, as the latter *and* former rain unto the earth.

John 8. 43 Why do ye not understand my speech? *even* because ye cannot hear my word.

H

John 5. 41 I receive not honour from men.

John 8. 50 And I seek not mine own glory: there is one that seeketh and judgeth.

I Cor.10. 31 Whether therefore ye eat, or drink, or whatsoever ye do, do all to the glory of God.

32 Give none offence, neither to the Jews, nor to the Gentiles, nor to the church of God:

33 Even as I please all *men* in all *things*, not seeking mine own profit, but the *profit* of many, that they may be saved.

Phil. 2. 3 *Let* nothing *be done* through strife or vainglory; but in lowliness of mind let each esteem other better than themselves.

4 Look not every man on his own things, but every man also on the things of others.

5 Let this mind be in you, which was also in Christ Jesus:

I

Ex. 24. 3 And Moses came and told the people all the words of the LORD, and all the judgments: and all the people answered with one voice, and said, All the words which the LORD hath said will we do.

Deut.33. 4 Moses commanded us a law, *even* the inheritance of the congregation of Jacob.

John 1. 17 For the law was given by Moses, *but* grace and truth came by Jesus Christ.

Acts 7. 38 This is he, that was in the church in the wilderness with the angel which spake to him in the mount Sina, and *with* our fathers: who received the lively oracles to give unto us:

K

Matt.12. 14 Then the Pharisees went out, and held a council against him, how they might destroy him.

K—CONCLUDED.

Mark 3. 6 And the Pharisees went forth, and straightway took council with the Herodians against him, how they might destroy him.

John 5. 16 And therefore did the Jews persecute Jesus, and sought to slay him, because he had done these things on the sabbath day.

John 5. 18 Therefore the Jews sought the more to kill him, because he not only had broken the sabbath, but said also that God was his Father, making himself equal with God.

John 10. 31 Then the Jews took up stones again to stone him.

John 10. 39 Therefore they sought again to take him; but he escaped out of their hand,

John 11. 53 Then from that day forth they took counsel together for to put him to death.

L

John 8. 48 Then answered the Jews, and said unto him, Say we not well that thou art a Samaritan, and hast a devil?

John 8. 52 Then said the Jews unto him, Now we know that thou hast a devil. Abraham is dead, and the prophets; and thou sayest, If a man keep my saying, he shall never taste of death.

John 10. 20 And many of them said, He hath a devil, and is mad; why hear ye him?

M

Lev. 12. 3 And in the eighth day the flesh of his foreskin shall be circumcised.

N

Gen. 17. 10 This *is* my covenant, which ye shall keep, between me and you and thy seed after thee; Every man child among you shall be circumcised.

2

Or, *without breaking the law of Moses.*

O

John 5. 8 Jesus saith unto him, Rise, take up thy bed, and walk.

9 And immediately the man was made whole, and took up his bed, and walked: and on the same day was the sabbath.

John 5. 16. *See under K.*

P

Deut. 1. 16 And I charged your judges at that time, saying, Hear *the causes* between your brethren, and judge righteously between *every* man and his brother, and the stranger *that is* with him.

(CONTINUED). TIME, OCTOBER, A. D. 29; PLACE, JERUSALEM.

P—CONCLUDED.

Deut. 1. 17 Ye shall not respect persons in judgment; *but* ye shall hear the small as well as the great; ye shall not be afraid of the face of man; for the judgment *is* God's: and the cause that is too hard for you, bring *it* unto me, and I will hear it.

Deut. 16. 18 Judges and officers shalt thou make thee in all thy gates, which the LORD thy God giveth thee, throughout thy tribes: and they shall judge the people with just judgment.

19 Thou shalt not wrest judgment; thou shalt not respect persons, neither take a gift: for a gift doth blind the eyes of the wise, and pervert the words of the righteous.

20 That which is altogether just shalt thou follow, that thou mayest live, and inherit the land which the LORD thy God giveth thee.

Ps. 58. 1 Do ye indeed speak righteousness, O congregation? do ye judge uprightly, O ye sons of men?

2 Yea, in heart ye work wickedness; ye weigh the violence of your hands in the earth.

Ps. 82. 2 How long will ye judge unjustly, and accept the persons of the wicked? Selah.

Ps. 94. 20 Shall the throne of iniquity have fellowship with thee, which frameth mischief by a law?

Prov. 17. 15 He that justifieth the wicked, and he that condemneth the just, even they both *are* abomination to the LORD.

Prov. 24. 23 These *things* also *belong* to the wise. *It is* not good to have respect of persons in judgment.

John 8. 15 Ye judge after the flesh; I judge no man.

Jas. 2. 1 My brethren, have not the faith of our Lord Jesus Christ, *the Lord* of glory, with respect of persons.

2 For if there come unto your assembly a man with a gold ring, in goodly apparel, and there come in also a poor man in vile raiment;

3 And ye have respect to him that weareth the gay clothing, and say unto him, Sit thou here in a good place; and say to the poor, Stand thou there, or sit here under my footstool:

4 Are ye not then partial in yourselves, and are become judges of evil thoughts?

Jas. 2. 9 But if ye have respect to persons, ye commit sin, and are convinced of the law as transgressors.

CHAP. 7.

17 [g]If any man will do his will, he shall know of the doctrine, whether it be of God, or *whether* I speak of myself.

18 [h]He that speaketh of himself seeketh his own glory: but he that seeketh his glory that sent him, the same is true, and no unrighteousness is in him.

19 [i]Did not Moses give you the law, and *yet* none of you keepeth the law? [k]Why go ye about to kill me?

20 The people answered and said, [l]Thou hast a devil: who goeth about to kill thee?

21 Jesus answered and said unto them, I have done one work, and ye all marvel.

22 [m]Moses therefore gave unto you circumcision; (not because it is of Moses, [n]but of the fathers;) and ye on the sabbath day circumcise a man.

23 If a man on the sabbath day receive circumcision, [2]that the law of Moses should not be broken; are ye angry at me, because [o]I have made a man every whit whole on the sabbath day?

24 [p]Judge not according to the appearance, but judge righteous judgment.

25 Then said some of them of Jerusalem, Is not this he, whom they seek to kill?

26 But, lo, he speaketh boldly, and they say nothing unto him. [q]Do the rulers know indeed that this is the very Christ?

Q

John 7. 48. *See text of topic.*

§ 109. JESUS TEACHES AT THE FEAST OF THE TABERNACLE

R

Matt.13. 55 Is not this the carpenter's son? is not his mother called Mary? and his brethren, James, and Joses, and Simon, and Judas?
56 And his sisters, are they not all with us? Whence then hath this *man* all these things?

Mark 6. 3 Is not this the carpenter, the son of Mary, the brother of James, and Joses, and of Juda, and Simon? and are not his sisters here with us? And they were offended at him.

Luke 4. 22. *See under E, page 312.*

S

John 8. 14 Jesus answered and said unto them, Though I bear record of myself, *yet* my record is true: for I know whence I came, and whither I go; but ye cannot tell whence I come, and whither I go.

T

John 5. 43 I am come in my Father's name, and ye receive me not: if another shall come in his own name, him ye will receive.

John 8. 42 Jesus said unto them, If God were your Father, ye would love me: for I proceeded forth and came from God; neither came I of myself, but he sent me.

U

John 5. 32 There is another that beareth witness of me; and I know that the witness which he witnesseth of me is true.

John 8. 26 I have many things to say and to judge of you: but he that sent me is true; and I speak to the world those things which I have heard of him.
27 They understood not that he spake to them of the Father.

Rom. 3. 4 God forbid: yea, let God be true, but every man a liar; as it is written, That thou mightest be justified in thy sayings, and mightest overcome when thou art judged.

X

Ps. 9. 10 And they that know thy name will put their trust in thee: for thou, LORD, hast not forsaken them that seek thee.

John 1. 18 No man hath seen God at any time; the only begotten Son, which is in the bosom of the Father, he hath declared *him*.

John 8. 55 Yet ye have not known him; but I know him: and if I should say, I know him not, I shall be a liar like unto you: but I know him, and keep his saying.

Y

Matt.11. 27 All things are delivered unto me of my Father: and no man knoweth the Son, but the Father; neither knoweth any man the Father, save the Son, and *he* to whomsoever the Son will reveal *him*.

John 10. 15 As the Father knoweth me, even so know I the Father: and I lay down my life for the sheep.

Z

Mark 11. 18 And the scribes and chief priests heard *it*, and sought how they might destroy him: for they feared him, because all the people was astonished at his doctrine.

Luke 19. 47 And he taught daily in the temple. But the chief priests and the scribes and the chief of the people sought to destroy him,

Luke 20. 19 And the chief priests and the scribes the same hour sought to lay hands on him; and they feared the people: for they perceived that he had spoken this parable against them.

John 7. 19. *See text of topic.*

John 8. 37 I know that ye are Abraham's seed; but ye seek to kill me, because my word hath no place in you.

A

John 7. 44. *See text of topic.*

John 8. 20 These words spake Jesus in the treasury, as he taught in the temple: and no man laid hands on him; for his hour was not yet come.

B

Matt.12. 23 And all the people were amazed, and said, Is not this the Son of David?

John 3. 1 There was a man of the Pharisees, named Nicodemus, a ruler of the Jews:
2 The same came to Jesus by night, and said unto him, Rabbi, we know that thou art a teacher come from God: for no man can do these miracles that thou doest, except God be with him.

John 8. 30 As he spake these words, many believed on him.

C

John 13. 33 Little children, yet a little while I am with you. Ye shall seek me; and as I said unto the Jews, Whither I go, ye cannot come; so now I say to you.

John 16. 16 A little while, and ye shall not see me: and again, a little while, and ye shall see me, because I go to the Father.

(CONTINUED). TIME, OCTOBER, A. D. 29; PLACE, JERUSALEM.

D

Prov. 1. 24 Because I have called, and ye refused; I have stretched out my hand, and no man regarded;

25 But ye have set at naught all my counsel, and would none of my reproof:

26 I also will laugh at your calamity; I will mock when your fear cometh;

27 When your fear cometh as desolation, and your destruction cometh as a whirlwind; when distress and anguish cometh upon you.

Hos. 5. 6 They shall go with their flocks and with their herds to seek the LORD; but they shall not find *him;* he hath withdrawn himself from them.

John 8. 21 Then said Jesus again unto them, I go my way, and ye shall seek me, and shall die in your sins: whither I go, ye cannot come.

John 13. 33. *See under C.*

E

Isa. 11. 12 And he shall set up an ensign for the nations, and shall assemble the outcasts of Israel, and gather together the dispersed of Judah from the four corners of the earth.

Jas. 1. 1 James, a servant of God and of the Lord Jesus Christ, to the twelve tribes which are scattered abroad, greeting.

I Pet. 1. 1 Peter, an apostle of Jesus Christ, to the strangers scattered throughout Pontus, Galatia, Cappadocia, Asia, and Bithynia.

3

Or, *Greeks.*

F

Ps. 67. 1 God be merciful unto us, and bless us; *and* cause his face to shine upon us; Selah.

2 That thy way may be known upon earth, thy saving health among all nations.

Ps. 98. 2 The LORD hath made known his salvation: his righteousness hath he openly showed in the sight of the heathen.

3 He hath remembered his mercy and his truth toward the house of Israel: all the ends of the earth have seen the salvation of our God.

Isa. 11. 10 And in that day there shall be a root of Jesse, which shall stand for an ensign of the people; to it shall the Gentiles seek: and his rest shall be glorious.

Eph. 3. 8 Unto me, who am less than the least of all saints, is this grace given,

CHAP. 7.

27 [r]Howbeit we know this man
whence he is: but when Christ cometh, no man knoweth whence he is.

28 Then cried Jesus in the temple
as he taught, saying, [s]Ye both know me, and ye know whence I am: and [t]I am not come of myself, but he that sent me [u]is true, [x]whom ye know not.

29 But [y]I know him; for I am from
him, and he hath sent me.

30 Then [z]they sought to take him:
but [a]no man laid hands on him, because his hour was not yet come.

31 And [b]many of the people believed
on him, and said, When Christ cometh, will he do more miracles than these which this *man* hath done?

32 The Pharisees heard that the
people murmured such things concerning him; and the Pharisees and the chief priests sent officers to take him.

33 Then said Jesus unto them, [c]Yet
a little while am I with you, and *then* I go unto him that sent me.

34 Ye [d]shall seek me, and shall not
find *me:* and where I am, *thither* ye cannot come.

35 Then said the Jews among them-
selves, Whither will he go, that we shall not find him? will he go unto the [e]dispersed among the [3]Gentiles, and [f]teach the Gentiles?

36 What *manner of* saying is this
that he said, Ye shall seek me, and shall not find *me:* and where I am, *thither* ye cannot come?

F—CONCLUDED.

that I should preach among the Gentiles the unsearchable riches of Christ;

§ 109. JESUS TEACHES AT THE FEAST OF THE TABERNACLE

G

Lev. 23. 36 Seven days ye shall offer an offering made by fire unto the LORD; on the eighth day shall be a holy convocation unto you, and ye shall offer an offering made by fire unto the LORD: it *is* a solemn assembly; *and* ye shall do no servile work *therein.*

H

Isa. 55. 1 Ho, every one that thirsteth, come ye to the waters, and he that hath no money; come ye, buy, and eat; yea, come, buy wine and milk without money and without price.

John 6. 35 And Jesus said unto them, I am the bread of life: he that cometh to me shall never hunger; and he that believeth on me shall never thirst.

Rev. 22. 17 And the Spirit and the bride say, Come. And let him that heareth say, Come. And let him that is athirst come. And whosoever will, let him take the water of life freely.

I

Deut.18. 15 The LORD thy God will raise up unto thee a Prophet from the midst of thee, of thy brethren, like unto me; unto him ye shall hearken;

K

Prov.18. 4 The words of a man's mouth *are as* deep waters, *and* the wellspring of wisdom *as* a flowing brook.

Isa. 12. 3 Therefore with joy shall ye draw water out of the wells of salvation.

Isa. 44. 3 For I will pour water upon him that is thirsty, and floods upon the dry ground: I will pour my Spirit upon thy seed, and my blessing upon thine offspring:

John 4. 14 But whosoever drinketh of the water that I shall give him shall never thirst; but the water that I shall give him shall be in him a well of water springing up into everlasting life.

L

Prov. 1. 23 Turn you at my reproof: behold, I will pour out my spirit unto you, I will make known my words unto you.

Isa. 32. 15 Until the Spirit be poured upon us from on high, and the wilderness be a fruitful field, and the fruitful field be counted for a forest.

Isa. 44. 3. *See under K.*

Joel 2. 28 And it shall come to pass afterward, *that* I will pour out my Spirit upon all flesh; and your sons and your daughters shall prophesy, your old men shall dream dreams, your young men shall see visions:

L—CONCLUDED.

John 16. 7 Nevertheless I tell you the truth; It is expedient for you that I go away: for if I go not away, the Comforter will not come unto you; but if I depart, I will send him unto you.

Acts 2. 17 And it shall come to pass in the last days, saith God, I will pour out of my Spirit upon all flesh: and your sons and your daughters shall prophesy, and your young men shall see visions, and your old men shall dream dreams:

Acts 2. 33 Therefore being by the right hand of God exalted, and having received of the Father the promise of the Holy Ghost, he hath shed forth this, which ye now see and hear.

Acts 2. 38 Then Peter said unto them, Repent, and be baptized every one of you in the name of Jesus Christ for the remission of sins, and ye shall receive the gift of the Holy Ghost.

M

John 12. 16 These things understood not his disciples at the first: but when Jesus was glorified, then remembered they that these things were written of him, and *that* they had done these things unto him.

John 16. 7. *See under L.*

N

Deut.18. 18 I will raise them up a Prophet from among their brethren, like unto thee, and will put my words in his mouth; and he shall speak unto them all that I shall command him.

John 1. 21 And they asked him, What then? Art thou Elias? And he saith, I am not. Art thou that Prophet? And he answered, No.

John 6. 14 Then those men, when they had seen the miracle that Jesus did, said, This is of a truth that Prophet that should come into the world.

O

John 4. 42 And said unto the woman, Now we believe, not because of thy saying: for we have heard *him* ourselves, and know that this is indeed the Christ, the Saviour of the world.

John 6. 69 And we believe and are sure that thou art that Christ, the Son of the living God.

P

John 7. 52. *See text of topic.*

John 1. 46 And Nathanael said unto him, Can there any good thing come out of Nazareth? Philip saith unto him, Come and see.

(CONTINUED). TIME, OCTOBER, A. D. 29; PLACE, JERUSALEM.

Q

Ps. 132. 11 The LORD hath sworn *in* truth unto David; he will not turn from it; Of the fruit of thy body will I set upon thy throne.

Isa. 11. 1 And there shall come forth a rod out of the stem of Jesse, and a Branch shall grow out of his roots:

2 And the Spirit of the LORD shall rest upon him, the spirit of wisdom and understanding, the spirit of counsel and might, the spirit of knowledge and of the fear of the LORD;

Jer. 23. 5 Behold, the days come, saith the LORD, that I will raise unto David a righteous Branch, and a King shall reign and prosper, and shall execute judgment and justice in the earth.

Mic. 5. 2 But thou, Beth-lehem Ephratah, *though* thou be little among the thousands of Judah, *yet* out of thee shall he come forth unto me *that is* to be ruler in Israel; whose goings forth *have been* from of old, from everlasting.

Matt. 2. 5 And they said unto him, In Bethlehem of Judæa: for thus it is written by the prophet.

Luke 2. 4 And Joseph also went up from Galilee, out of the city of Nazareth, into Judæa, unto the city of David, which is called Bethlehem, (because he was of the house and lineage of David.)

Luke 2. 11 For unto you is born this day in the city of David a Saviour, which is Christ the Lord.

R

I Sa. 16. 1 And the LORD said unto Samuel, How long wilt thou mourn for Saul, seeing I have rejected him from reigning over Israel? fill thine horn with oil, and go, I will send thee to Jesse the Beth-lehemite: for I have provided me a king among his sons.

I Sa. 16. 4 And Samuel did that which the LORD spake, and came to Beth-lehem. And the elders of the town trembled at his coming, and said, Comest thou peaceably?

S

John 7. 12. *See text of topic.*

John 9. 16 Therefore said some of the Pharisees, This man is not of God, because he keepeth not the sabbath day. Others said, How can a man that is a sinner do such miracles? And there was a division among them.

John 10. 19 There was a division therefore again among the Jews for these sayings.

CHAP. 7.

37 [g]In the last day, that great *day* of
the feast, Jesus stood and cried, saying, [h]If any man thirst, let him come unto me, and drink.

38 [i]He that believeth on me, as the Scripture hath said, [k]out of his belly shall flow rivers of living water.

39 [l](But this spake he of the Spirit, which they that believe on him should receive: for the Holy Ghost was not yet *given;* because that Jesus was not yet [m]glorified.)

40 Many of the people therefore, when they heard this saying, said, Of a truth this is [n]the Prophet.

41 Others said, [o]This is the Christ. But some said, Shall Christ come [p]out of Galilee?

42 [q]Hath not the Scripture said, That Christ cometh of the seed of David, and out of the town of Bethlehem, [r]where David was?

43 So [s]there was a division among the people because of him.

44 And [t]some of them would have taken him; but no man laid hands on him.

45 Then came the officers to the chief priests and Pharisees; and they said unto them, Why have ye not brought him?

46 The officers answered, [u]Never man spake like this man.

47 Then answered them the Pharisees, Are ye also deceived?

T

John 7. 30. *See text of topic.*

U

Matt. 7. 29 For he taught them as *one* having authority, and not as the scribes.

§ 109. JESUS TEACHES AT THE FEAST OF THE TABERNACLE

X

John 12. 42 Nevertheless among the chief rulers also many believed on him; but because of the Pharisees they did not confess *him*, lest they should be put out of the synagogue:

Acts 6. 7 And the word of God increased; and the number of the disciples multiplied in Jerusalem greatly; and a great company of the priests were obedient to the faith.

I Cor. 1. 20 Where *is* the wise? where *is* the scribe? where *is* the disputer of this world? hath not God made foolish the wisdom of this world?

I Cor. 1. 26 For ye see your calling, brethren, how that not many wise men after the flesh, not many mighty, not many noble, *are called:*

I Cor. 2. 8 Which none of the princes of this world knew: for had they known *it*, they would not have crucified the Lord of glory.

Y

John 3. 2. *See under B, page 316.*

4

Gr., *to him.*

Z

Deut. 1. 17. *See under P, page 315.*

Deut.17. 8 If there arise a matter too hard for thee in judgment, between blood and blood, between plea and plea, and between stroke and stroke, *being* matters of controversy within thy gates: then shalt thou arise, and get thee up into the place which the LORD thy God shall choose;

Deut.19. 15 One witness shall not rise up against a man for any iniquity, or for any sin, in any sin that he sinneth: at the mouth of two witnesses, or at the mouth of three witnesses, shall the matter be established.

Prov.18. 13 He that answereth a matter before he heareth *it*, it *is* folly and shame unto him.

A

I Ki. 17. 1 And Elijah the Tishbite, *who was* of the inhabitants of Gilead, said unto Ahab, *As* the LORD God of Israel liv-

§ 110. THE WOMAN TAKEN IN ADULTERY.

A

Lev. 20. 10 And the man that committeth adultery with *another* man's wife, *even he* that committeth adultery with his neighbour's wife, the adulterer and the adulteress shall surely be put to death.

Deut.22. 22 If a man be found lying with a woman married to a husband, then they shall both of them die, *both* the man that lay with the woman, and the woman: so shalt thou put away evil from Israel.

Job 31. 9 If mine heart have been deceived by a woman, or *if* I have laid wait at my neighbour's door;

10 *Then* let my wife grind unto another, and let others bow down upon her.

11 For this *is* a heinous crime; yea, it *is* an iniquity *to be punished by* the judges.

12 For it *is* a fire *that* consumeth to destruction, and would root out all mine increase.

Mal. 3. 5 And I will come near to you to judgment; and I will be a swift witness against the sorcerers, and against the adulterers, and against false swearers, and against those that oppress the hireling in *his* wages, the widow, and the fatherless, and that turn aside the stranger *from his right*, and fear not me, saith the LORD of hosts.

B

Gen. 49. 9 Judah *is* a lion's whelp: from the prey, my son, thou art gone up: he stooped down, he couched as a lion, and as an old lion; who shall rouse him up?

Jer. 17. 13 O LORD, the hope of Israel, all that forsake thee shall be ashamed, *and* they that depart from me shall be written in the earth, because they have forsaken the LORD, the fountain of living waters.

Dan. 5. 5 In the same hour came forth fingers of a man's hand, and wrote over against the candlestick upon the plaster of the wall of the king's palace: and the king saw the part of the hand that wrote.

C

Ps. 38. 12 They also that seek after my life lay snares *for me;* and they that seek my hurt, speak mischievous things.

13 But I, as a deaf *man*, heard not; and *I was* as a dumb man *that* openeth not his mouth.

14 Thus I was as a man that heareth not, and in whose mouth *are* no reproofs.

15 For in thee, O LORD, do I hope: thou wilt hear. O Lord my God.

Ps. 39. 1 I said, I will take heed to my ways, that I sin not with my tongue:

(CONCLUDED). TIME, OCTOBER, A. D. 29; PLACE, JERUSALEM.

A—CONCLUDED.

eth, before whom I stand, there shall not be dew nor rain these years, but according to my word.

II Ki.14. 25 He restored the coast of Israel from the entering of Hamath unto the sea of the plain, according to the word of the LORD God of Israel, which he spake by the hand of his servant Jonah, the son of Amittai, the prophet, which *was* of Gath-hepher.

Isa. 9. 1 Nevertheless the dimness *shall* not *be* such as *was* in her vexation, when at the first he lightly afflicted the land of Zebulun, and the land of Naphtali, and afterward did more grievously afflict *her by* the way of the sea, beyond Jordan, in Galilee of the nations.

2 The people that walked in darkness have seen a great light: they that dwell in the land of the shadow of death, upon them hath the light shined.

John 1. 46. *See under P, page 318.*
John 7. 41. *See text of topic.*

CHAP. 7.

48 [x]Have any of the rulers or of the Pharisees believed on him?

49 But this people who knoweth not the law are cursed.

50 Nicodemus saith unto them, [y](he that came [h]to Jesus by night, being one of them,)

51 [z]Doth our law judge *any* man, before it hear him, and know what he doeth?

52 They answered and said unto him, Art thou also of Galilee? Search, and look: for [a]out of Galilee ariseth no prophet.

53 And every man went unto his own house.

TIME, OCTOBER, A. D. 29; PLACE, JERUSALEM.

C—CONCLUDED.

I will keep my mouth with a bridle, while the wicked is before me.

2 I was dumb with silence, I held my peace, *even* from good; and my sorrow was stirred.

Prov.26. 17 He that passeth by, *and* meddleth with strife *belonging* not to him, *is like* one that taketh a dog by the ears.

Eccl. 3. 7 A time to rend, and a time to sew; a time to keep silence, and a time to speak;

Amos 5. 10 They hate him that rebuketh in the gate, and they abhor him that speaketh uprightly.

Amos 5. 13 Therefore the prudent shall keep silence in that time; for it *is* an evil time.

Matt. 10. 16 Behold, I send you forth as sheep in the midst of wolves: be ye therefore wise as serpents, and harmless as doves.

Matt.15. 23 But he answered her not a word. And his disciples came and besought him, saying, Send her away; for she crieth after us.

Matt.26. 62 And the high priest arose, and said unto him, Answerest thou nothing? what *is it which* these witness against thee?

63 But Jesus held his peace. And the high priest answered and said unto him, I adjure thee by the living God, that thou tell us whether thou be the Christ, the Son of God.

8: 1–11.

1 Jesus went unto the mount of Olives.

2 And early in the morning he came again into the temple, and all the people came unto him; and he sat down, and taught them.

3 And the scribes and Pharisees brought unto him a woman taken in adultery; and when they had set her in the midst,

4 They say unto him, Master, this woman was taken in adultery, in the very act.

5 [a]Now Moses in the law commanded us, that such should be stoned: but what sayest thou?

6 This they said, tempting him, that they might have to accuse him. [b]But Jesus stooped down, and with *his* finger wrote on the ground, [c]*as though he heard them not.*

§ 110. THE WOMAN TAKEN IN ADULTERY

D

Deut.17. 6 At the mouth of two witnesses, or three witnesses, shall he that is worthy of death be put to death; *but* at the mouth of one witness he shall not be put to death.

7 The hands of the witnesses shall be first upon him to put him to death, and afterward the hands of all the people. So thou shalt put the evil away from among you.

Job 5. 12 He disappointeth the devices of the crafty, so that their hands cannot perform *their* enterprise.

Ps. 50. 16 But unto the wicked God saith, What hast thou to do to declare my statutes, or *that* thou shouldest take my covenant in thy mouth?

Rom. 2. 1 Therefore thou art inexcusable, O man, whosoever thou art that judgest: for wherein thou judgest another, thou condemnest thyself; for thou that judgest doest the same things.

2 But we are sure that the judgment of God is according to truth against them which commit such things.

3 And thinkest thou this, O man, that judgest them which do such things, and doest the same, that thou shalt escape the judgment of God?

Rom. 2. 21 Thou therefore which teachest

D—Concluded.

another, teachest thou not thyself? thou that preachest a man should not steal, dost thou steal?

22 Thou that sayest a man should not commit adultery, dost thou commit adultery? thou that abhorrest idols, dost thou commit sacrilege?

23 Thou that makest thy boast of the law, through breaking the law dishonourest thou God?

24 For the name of God is blasphemed among the Gentiles through you, as it is written.

25 For circumcision verily profiteth, if thou keep the law: but if thou be a breaker of the law, thy circumcision is made uncircumcision.

E

Gen. 42. 21 And they said one to another, We *are* verily guilty concerning our brother, in that we saw the anguish of his soul, when he besought us, and we would not hear; therefore is this distress come upon us.

22 And Reuben answered them, saying, Spake I not unto you, saying, Do not sin against the child; and ye would not hear? therefore, behold, also his blood is required.

I Ki. 2. 44 The king said moreover to Shimei,

§ 111. PUBLIC TEACHING. DISPUTE WITH THE PHARISEES. SECOND

A

Isa. 42. 6 I the Lord have called thee in righteousness, and will hold thine hand, and will keep thee, and give thee for a covenant of the people, for a light of the Gentiles;

7 To open the blind eyes, to bring out the prisoners from the prison, *and* them that sit in darkness out of the prison house.

Isa. 49. 6 And he said, It is a light thing that thou shouldest be my servant to raise up the tribes of Jacob, and to restore the preserved of Israel: I will also give thee for a light to the Gentiles, that thou mayest be my salvation unto the end of the earth.

Hos. 6. 3 Then shall we know, *if* we follow on to know the Lord: his going forth is prepared as the morning; and he shall come unto us as the rain, as the latter *and* former rain unto the earth.

Matt. 4. 16 The people which sat in darkness saw great light; and to them which sat in the region and shadow of death light is sprung up.

Luke 2. 32 A light to lighten the Gentiles, and the glory of thy people Israel.

John 1. 4 In him was life; and the life was the light of men.

5 And the light shineth in darkness; and the darkness comprehended it not.

John 1. 9 *That* was the true Light, which lighteth every man that cometh into the world.

John 3. 19 And this is the condemnation, that light is come into the world, and men loved darkness rather than light, because their deeds were evil.

John 9. 5 As long as I am in the world, I am the light of the world.

John 12. 35 Then Jesus said unto them, Yet a little while is the light with you. Walk while ye have the light, lest darkness come upon you: for he that walketh in darkness knoweth not whither he goeth.

36 While ye have light, believe in the light, that ye may be the children of light. These things spake Jesus, and departed, and did hide himself from them.

(CONCLUDED). TIME, OCTOBER, A. D. 29; PLACE, JERUSALEM.

E—CONCLUDED.

Thou knowest all the wickedness which thine heart is privy to, that thou didst to David my father; therefore the LORD shall return thy wickedness upon thine own head:

Ps. 50. 21 These *things* hast thou done, and I kept silence; thou thoughtest that I was altogether *such a one* as thyself: *but* I will reprove thee, and set *them* in order before thine eyes.

Eccl. 7. 22 For oftentimes also thine own heart knoweth that thou thyself likewise hast cursed others.

F

Luke 3. 17 Whose fan *is* in his hand, and he will thoroughly purge his floor, and will gather the wheat into his garner; but the chaff he will burn with fire unquenchable.

Luke 9. 56 For the Son of man is not come to destroy men's lives, but to save *them.* And they went to another village.

Luke 12. 14 And he said unto him, Man, who made me a judge or a divider over you?

G

John 5. 14 Afterward Jesus findeth him in the temple, and saith unto him, Behold, thou art made whole: sin no more, lest a worse thing come unto thee.

CHAP. 8.

7 So when they continued asking him, he lifted up himself, and said unto them, [d]He that is without sin among you, let him first cast a stone at her.

8 And again he stooped down, and wrote on the ground.

9 And they which heard *it,* [e]being convicted by *their own* conscience, went out one by one, beginning at the eldest, *even* unto the last: and Jesus was left alone, and the woman standing in the midst.

10 When Jesus had lifted up himself, and saw none but the woman, he said unto her, Woman, where are those thine accusers? hath no man condemned thee?

11 She said, No man, Lord. And Jesus said unto her, [f]Neither do I condemn thee: go, and [g]sin no more.

ATTEMPT TO STONE JESUS. TIME, OCTOBER, A. D. 29; PLACE, JERUSALEM.

A—CONCLUDED.

John 12. 46 I am come a light into the world, that whosoever believeth on me should not abide in darkness.

B

John 5. 31 If I bear witness of myself, my witness is not true.

John 5. 39 Search the scriptures; for in them ye think ye have eternal life: and they are they which testify of me.

40 And ye will not come to me, that ye might have life.

C

John 7. 28 Then cried Jesus in the temple as he taught, saying, Ye both know me, and ye know whence I am: and I am not come of myself, but he that sent me is true, whom ye know not.

John 9. 29 We know that God spake unto Moses: *as for* this *fellow,* we know not from whence he is.

D

1 Sa. 16. 7 But the LORD said unto Samuel, Look not on his countenance, or on the height of his stature; because I have refused him: for *the LORD*

8: 12–59.

12 Then spake Jesus again unto them, saying, [a]I am the light of the world: he that followeth me shall not walk in darkness, but shall have the light of life.

13 The Pharisees therefore said unto him, [b]Thou bearest record of thyself; thy record is not true.

14 Jesus answered and said unto them, Though I bear record of myself, *yet* my record is true: for I know whence I came, and whither I go; but [c]ye cannot tell whence I come, and whither I go.

D—CONTINUED.

seeth not as man seeth; for man looketh on the outward appearance, but the LORD looketh on the heart.

For D concluded see next page (324).

§ 111. PUBLIC TEACHING. DISPUTE WITH THE PHARISEES. SECOND AT-

D—CONCLUDED. See preceding page (323).

Amos 5. 7 Ye who turn judgment to wormwood, and leave off righteousness in the earth,

John 7. 24 Judge not according to the appearance, but judge righteous judgment.

Rom. 2. 1 Therefore thou art inexcusable, O man, whosoever thou art that judgest: for wherein thou judgest another, thou condemnest thyself; for thou that judgest doest the same things.

I Cor. 2. 15 But he that is spiritual judgeth all things, yet he himself is judged of no man.

Jas. 2. 4 Are ye not then partial in yourselves, and are become judges of evil thoughts?

E

Luke 9. 56 For the Son of man is not come to destroy men's lives, but to save *them*. And they went to another village.

Luke 12. 14 And he said unto him, Man, who made me a judge or a divider over you?

John 3. 17 For God sent not his Son into the world to condemn the world; but that the world through him might be saved.

John 12. 47 And if any man hear my words, and believe not, I judge him not: for I came not to judge the world, but to save the world.

John 18. 36 Jesus answered, My kingdom is not of this world: if my kingdom were of this world, then would my servants fight, that I should not be delivered to the Jews: but now is my kingdom not from hence.

F

John 8. 29. *See text of topic.*

John 16. 32 Behold, the hour cometh, yea, is now come, that ye shall be scattered, every man to his own, and shall leave me alone: and yet I am not alone, because the Father is with me.

G

Deut. 17. 6 At the mouth of two witnesses, or three witnesses, shall he that is worthy of death be put to death; *but* at the mouth of one witness he shall not be put to death.

Deut. 19. 15 One witness shall not rise up against a man for any iniquity, or for any sin, in any sin that he sinneth: at the mouth of two witnesses, or at the mouth of three witnesses, shall the matter be established.

Matt. 18. 16 But if he will not hear *thee*, *then* take with thee one or two more, that

G—CONCLUDED.

in the mouth of two or three witnesses every word may be established.

II Cor. 13. 1 This *is* the third *time* I am coming to you. In the mouth of two or three witnesses shall every word be established.

Heb. 10. 28 He that despised Moses' law died without mercy under two or three witnesses:

H

John 5. 37 And the Father himself, which hath sent me, hath borne witness of me. Ye have neither heard his voice at any time, nor seen his shape.

II Pet. 1. 17 For he received from God the Father honour and glory, when there came such a voice to him from the excellent glory, This is my beloved Son, in whom I am well pleased.

I

John 8. 55. *See text of topic.*

John 16. 3 And these things will they do unto you, because they have not known the Father, nor me.

K

John 14. 7 If ye had known me, ye should have known my Father also: and from henceforth ye know him, and have seen him.

L

Mark 12. 41 And Jesus sat over against the treasury, and beheld how the people cast money into the treasury: and many that were rich cast in much.

M

John 7. 30 Then they sought to take him: but no man laid hands on him, because his hour was not yet come.

N

John 7. 8 Go ye up unto this feast: I go not up yet unto this feast; for my time is not yet full come.

O

John 7. 34 Ye shall seek me, and shall not find *me*: and where I am, *thither* ye cannot come.

John 13. 33 Little children, yet a little while I am with you. Ye shall seek me; and as I said unto the Jews, Whither I go, ye cannot come; so now I say to you.

P

John 8. 24. *See text of topic.*

Q

John 3. 31 He that cometh from above is above all: he that is of the earth is earthly, and speaketh of the earth: he that cometh from heaven is above all.

TEMPT TO STONE JESUS (CONTINUED).

R

John 15. 19 If ye were of the world, the world would love his own; but because ye are not of the world, but I have chosen you out of the world, therefore the world hateth you.

John 17. 16 They are not of the world, even as I am not of the world.

I Jno. 4. 5 They are of the world: therefore speak they of the world, and the world heareth them.

I Jno. 5. 19 *And* we know that we are of God, and the whole world lieth in wickedness.

S

John 8. 21. *See text of topic.*

T

Mark 16. 16 He that believeth and is baptized shall be saved; but he that believeth not shall be damned.

John 12. 48 He that rejecteth me, and receiveth not my words, hath one that judgeth him: the word that I have spoken, the same shall judge him in the last day.

Acts 4. 12 Neither is there salvation in any other: for there is none other name under heaven given among men, whereby we must be saved.

II Thes. 1. 8 In flaming fire taking vengeance on them that know not God, and that obey not the gospel of our Lord Jesus Christ:

9 Who shall be punished with everlasting destruction from the presence of the Lord, and from the glory of his power;

Heb. 2. 3 How shall we escape, if we neglect so great salvation; which at the first began to be spoken by the Lord, and was confirmed unto us by them that heard *him;*

Heb. 10. 26 For if we sin wilfully after that we have received the knowledge of the truth, there remaineth no more sacrifice for sins,

27 But a certain fearful looking for of judgment and fiery indignation, which shall devour the adversaries.

28 He that despised Moses' law died without mercy under two or three witnesses:

29 Of how much sorer punishment, suppose ye, shall he be thought worthy, who hath trodden under foot the Son of God, and hath counted the blood of the covenant, wherewith he was sanctified, an unholy thing, and hath done despite unto the Spirit of grace?

TIME, OCTOBER, A.D. 29; PLACE, JERUSALEM.

CHAP. 8.

15 [d]Ye judge after the flesh; [e]I judge no man.

16 And yet if I judge, my judgment is true: for [f]I am not alone, but I and the Father that sent me.

17 [g]It is also written in your law, that the testimony of two men is true.

18 I am one that bear witness of myself, and [h]the Father that sent me beareth witness of me.

19 Then said they unto him, Where is thy Father? Jesus answered, [i]Ye neither know me, nor my Father: [k]if ye had known me, ye should have known my Father also.

20 These words spake Jesus in [l]the treasury, as he taught in the temple: and [m]no man laid hands on him; for [n]his hour was not yet come.

21 Then said Jesus again unto them, I go my way, and [o]ye shall seek me, and [p]shall die in your sins: whither I go, ye cannot come.

22 Then said the Jews, Will he kill himself? because he saith, Whither I go, ye cannot come.

23 And he said unto them, [q]Ye are from beneath; I am from above; [r]ye are of this world; I am not of this world.

24 [s]I said therefore unto you, that ye shall die in your sins: [t]for if ye believe not that I am *he,* ye shall die in your sins.

25 Then said they unto him, Who art thou? And Jesus saith unto them, Even *the same* that I said unto you from the beginning.

§ 111. PUBLIC TEACHING. DISPUTE WITH THE PHARISEES. SECOND ATTEMPT TO ARREST JESUS—CONCLUDED.

U

John 7. 28 Then cried Jesus in the temple as he taught, saying, Ye both know me, and ye know whence I am: and I am not come of myself, but he that sent me is true, whom ye know not.

29 But I know him; for I am from him, and he hath sent me.

X

John 3. 32 And what he hath seen and heard, that he testifieth; and no man receiveth his testimony.

John 15. 15 Henceforth I call you not servants; for the servant knoweth not what his lord doeth: but I have called you friends; for all things that I have heard of my Father I have made known unto you.

Y

Num. 21. 9 And Moses made a serpent of brass, and put it upon a pole; and it came to pass, that if a serpent had bitten any man, when he beheld the serpent of brass, he lived.

II Ki. 18. 4 He removed the high places, and brake the images, and cut down the groves, and brake in pieces the brazen serpent that Moses had made: for unto those days the children of Israel did burn incense to it: and he called it Nehushtan.

Luke 18. 32 For he shall be delivered unto the Gentiles, and shall be mocked, and spitefully entreated, and spitted on:

33 And they shall scourge *him*, and put him to death; and the third day he shall rise again.

John 3. 14 And as Moses lifted up the serpent in the wilderness, even so must the Son of man be lifted up:

John 12. 32 And I, if I be lifted up from the earth, will draw all *men* unto me.

John 12. 34 The people answered him, We have heard out of the law that Christ abideth for ever: and how sayest thou, The Son of man must be lifted up? who is this Son of man?

Rom. 5. 18 Therefore, as by the offence of one *judgment came* upon all men to condemnation; even so by the righteousness of one *the free gift came* upon all men unto justification of life.

19 For as by one man's disobedience many were made sinners, so by the obedience of one shall many be made righteous.

Phil. 2. 7 But made himself of no reputation, and took upon him the form of a servant, and was made in the likeness of men:

8 And being found in fashion as a man, he humbled himself, and became obedient unto death, even the death of the cross.

9 Wherefore God also hath highly exalted him, and given him a name which is above every name:

Heb. 2. 9 But we see Jesus, who was made a little lower than the angels for the suffering of death, crowned with glory and honour; that he by the grace of God should taste death for every man.

Z

Rom. 1. 4 And declared *to be* the Son of God with power, according to the Spirit of holiness, by the resurrection from the dead:

A

John 5. 19 Then answered Jesus and said unto them, Verily, verily, I say unto you, The Son can do nothing of himself, but what he seeth the Father do: for what things soever he doeth, these also doeth the Son likewise.

John 5. 30 I can of mine own self do nothing: as I hear, I judge: and my judgment is just; because I seek not mine own will, but the will of the Father which hath sent me.

B

John 3. 11 Verily, verily, I say unto thee, We speak that we do know, and testify that we have seen; and ye receive not our witness.

C

John 14. 10 Believest thou not that I am in the Father, and the Father in me? the words that I speak unto you I speak not of myself: but the Father that dwelleth in me, he doeth the works.

11 Believe me that I *am* in the Father, and the Father in me: or else believe me for the very works' sake.

D

John 8. 16. *See text of topic.*

E

Isa. 42. 1 Behold my servant, whom I uphold; mine elect, *in whom* my soul delighteth; I have put my Spirit upon him: he shall bring forth judgment to the Gentiles.

John 4. 34 Jesus saith unto them, My meat is to do the will of him that sent me, and to finish his work.

John 5. 30. *See under A.*

John 6. 38 For I came down from heaven, not to do mine own will, but the will of him that sent me.

TEMPT TO STONE JESUS (CONTINUED).

F

John 7. 31 And many of the people believed on him, and said, When Christ cometh, will he do more miracles than these which this *man* hath done?

John 10. 42 And many believed on him there.

John 11. 45 Then many of the Jews which came to Mary, and had seen the things which Jesus did, believed on him.

G

Rom. 6. 14 For sin shall not have dominion over you: for ye are not under the law, but under grace.

Rom. 6. 18 Being then made free from sin, ye became the servants of righteousness.

Rom. 6. 22 But now being made free from sin, and become servants to God, ye have your fruit unto holiness, and the end everlasting life.

Rom. 8. 2 For the law of the spirit of life in Christ Jesus hath made me free from the law of sin and death.

Jas. 1. 25 But whoso looketh into the perfect law of liberty, and continueth *therein*, he being not a forgetful hearer, but a doer of the work, this man shall be blessed in his deed.

Jas. 2. 12 So speak ye, and so do, as they that shall be judged by the law of liberty.

H

Lev. 25. 42 For they *are* my servants, which I brought forth out of the land of Egypt: they shall not be sold as bondmen.

Matt. 3. 9 And think not to say within yourselves, We have Abraham to *our* father: for I say unto you, that God is able of these stones to raise up children unto Abraham.

John 8. 39. *See text of topic.*

I

Rom. 6. 16 Know ye not, that to whom ye yield yourselves servants to obey, his servants ye are to whom ye obey; whether of sin unto death, or of obedience unto righteousness?

Rom. 6. 20 For when ye were the servants of sin, ye were free from righteousness.

Tit. 3. 3 For we ourselves also were sometime foolish, disobedient, deceived, serving divers lusts and pleasures, living in malice and envy, hateful, *and* hating one another.

II Pet. 2. 19 While they promise them liberty, they themselves are the servants of corruption: for of whom a man is overcome, of the same is he brought in bondage.

TIME, OCTOBER, A.D. 29; PLACE, JERUSALEM.

CHAP. 8.

26 I have many things to say and to
judge of you: but [u]he that sent me is
true; and [x]I speak to the world
those things which I have heard of
him.
27 They understood not that he
spake to them of the Father.
28 Then said Jesus unto them, When
ye have [y]lifted up the Son of man,
[z]then shall ye know that I am *he*, and
[a]*that* I do nothing of myself; but [b]as
my Father hath taught me, I speak
these things.
29 And [c]he that sent me is with me:
[d]the Father hath not left me alone;
[e]for I do always those things that
please him.
30 As he spake these words, [f]many
believed on him.
31 Then said Jesus to those Jews
which believed on him, If ye continue
in my word, *then* are ye my disciples
indeed;
32 And ye shall know the truth,
and [g]the truth shall make you free.
33 They answered him, [h]We be
Abraham's seed, and were never in
bondage to any man: how sayest
thou, Ye shall be made free?
34 Jesus answered them, Verily, verily, I say unto you, [i]Whosoever committeth sin is the servant of sin.
35 And [k]the servant abideth not in
the house for ever: *but* the Son
abideth ever.

K

Gal. 4. 30 Nevertheless what saith the Scripture? Cast out the bondwoman and her son: for the son of the bondwoman shall not be heir with the son of the free woman.

§ 111 PUBLIC TEACHING. DISPUTE WITH THE PHARISEES. SECOND AT-N—Concluded.

L

Isa. 49. 24 Shall the prey be taken from the mighty, or the lawful captive delivered?

Luke 4. 18 The Spirit of the Lord *is* upon me, because he hath anointed me to preach the gospel to the poor; he hath sent me to heal the broken-hearted, to preach deliverance to the captives, and recovering of sight to the blind, to set at liberty them that are bruised,

Rom. 8. 2 For the law of the Spirit of life in Christ Jesus hath made me free from the law of sin and death.

II Cor.3. 17 Now the Lord is that Spirit: and where the Spirit of the Lord *is*, there *is* liberty.

Gal. 5. 1 Stand fast therefore in the liberty wherewith Christ hath made us free, and be not entangled again with the yoke of bondage.

Rev. 1. 5 And from Jesus Christ, *who is* the faithful witness, *and* the first-begotten of the dead, and the prince of the kings of the earth. Unto him that loved us, and washed us from our sins in his own blood,

Rev. 5. 9 And they sung a new song, saying, Thou art worthy to take the book, and to open the seals thereof: for thou wast slain, and hast redeemed us to God by thy blood out of every kindred, and tongue, and people, and nation;

M

John 8. 40. *See text of topic.*

John 7. 19 Did not Moses give you the law, and *yet* none of you keepeth the law? Why go ye about to kill me?

N

John 3. 32. *See under X, page 326.*

John 5. 19 Then answered Jesus and said unto them, Verily, verily, I say unto you, The Son can do nothing of himself, but what he seeth the Father do: for what things soever he doeth, these also doeth the Son likewise.

John 5. 30 I can of my own self do nothing: as I hear, I judge: and my judgment is just; because I seek not mine own will, but the will of the Father which hath sent me.

John 12. 49 For I have not spoken of myself; but the Father which sent me, he gave me a commandment, what I should say, and what I should speak.

John 14. 10 Believest thou not that I am in the Father, and the Father in me? the words that I speak unto you I speak not of myself: but the Father that dwelleth in me, he doeth the works.

John 14. 24 He that loveth me not keepeth not my sayings: and the word which ye hear is not mine, but the Father's which sent me.

O

Matt. 3. 9. *See under H, page 327.*
John 8. 33. *See text of topic.*

P

Rom. 2. 28 For he is not a Jew, which is one outwardly; neither *is that* circumcision, which is outward in the flesh:

Rom. 9. 7 Neither, because they are the seed of Abraham, *are they* all children: but, In Isaac shall thy seed be called.

Gal. 3. 7 Know ye therefore that they which are of faith, the same are the children of Abraham.

Gal. 3. 29 And if ye *be* Christ's, then are ye Abraham's seed, and heirs according to the promise.

Q

John 8. 37. *See text of topic.*

R

John 8. 26. *See text of topic.*

S

Isa. 63. 16 Doubtless thou *art* our Father, though Abraham be ignorant of us, and Israel acknowledge us not: thou, O Lord, *art* our Father, our Redeemer; thy name *is* from everlasting.

Isa. 64. 8 But now, O Lord, thou *art* our Father; we *are* the clay, and thou our potter; and we all *are* the work of thy hand.

Mal. 1. 6 A son honoureth *his* father, and a servant his master: if then I *be* a father, where *is* mine honour? and if I *be* a master, where *is* my fear? saith the Lord of hosts unto you, O priests, that despise my name. And ye say, Wherein have we despised thy name?

T

I Jno. 4. 19 We love him, because he first loved us.

I Jno. 5. 1 Whosoever believeth that Jesus is the Christ is born of God: and every one that loveth him that begat loveth him also that is begotten of him.

U

John 1. 14 And the Word was made flesh, and dwelt among us, (and we beheld his glory, the glory as of the only begotten of the Father,) full of grace and truth.

John 3. 16. *See under E, page 330.*

John 16. 27 For the Father himself loveth

TEMPT TO STONE JESUS (CONTINUED).

U—CONCLUDED.

you, because ye have loved me, and have believed that I came out from God.

John 17. 8 For I have given unto them the words which thou gavest me; and they have received *them*, and have known surely that I came out from thee, and they have believed that thou didst send me.

John 17. 25 O righteous Father, the world hath not known thee: but I have known thee, and these have known that thou hast sent me.

Gal. 4. 4 But when the fulness of the time was come, God sent forth his Son, made of a woman, made under the law,

X

John 5. 43 I am come in my Father's name, and ye receive me not: if another shall come in his own name, him ye will receive.

John 7. 28. *See under U, page 326.*

John 7. 29 But I know him; for I am from him, and he hath sent me.

Y

John 7. 17 If any man will do his will, he shall know of the doctrine, whether it be of God, or *whether* I speak of myself.

Z

Gen. 3. 1 Now the serpent was more subtile than any beast of the field which the LORD God had made. And he said unto the woman, Yea, hath God said, Ye shall not eat of every tree of the garden?

Matt.13. 38 The field is the world; the good seed are the children of the kingdom; but the tares are the children of the wicked one;

II Cor. 11. 3 But I fear, lest by any means, as the serpent beguiled Eve through his subtilty, so your minds should be corrupted from the simplicity that is in Christ.

I Jno. 3. 8 He that committeth sin is of the devil; for the devil sinneth from the beginning. For this purpose the Son of God was manifested, that he might destroy the works of the devil.

A

II Pet.2. 4 For if God spared not the angels that sinned, but cast *them* down to hell, and delivered *them* into chains of darkness, to be reserved unto judgment;

Jude 6 And the angels which kept not their first estate, but left their own habitation, he hath reserved in ever-

TIME, OCTOBER, A.D. 29; PLACE, JERUSALEM.

CHAP. 8.

36 [l]If the Son therefore shall make
you free, ye shall be free indeed.
37 I know that ye are Abraham's
seed; but [m]ye seek to kill me, because
my word hath no place in you.
38 [n]I speak that which I have seen
with my Father: and ye do that which
ye have seen with your father.
39 They answered and said unto
him, [o]Abraham is our father. Jesus
saith unto them, [p]If ye were Abraham's children, ye would do the works
of Abraham.
40 [q]But now ye seek to kill me, a
man that hath told you the truth,
[r]which I have heard of God: this did
not Abraham.
41 Ye do the deeds of your father.
Then said they to him, [s]We be not
born of fornication; we have one
Father, *even* God.
42 Jesus said unto them, [t]If God
were your Father, ye would love me:
[u]for I proceeded forth and came from
God; [x]neither came I of myself, but
he sent me.
43 [y]Why do ye not understand my
speech? *even* because ye cannot hear
my word.
44 [z]Ye are of *your* father the devil,
and the lusts of your father ye will
do: he was a murderer from the beginning, [a]and abode not in the truth, because there is no truth in him. When
he speaketh a lie, he speaketh of his
own: for he is a liar, and the father
of it.

A—CONCLUDED.

lasting chains under darkness unto the judgment of the great day.

§ 111. PUBLIC TEACHING. DISPUTE WITH THE PHARISEES. SECOND AT-E—CONCLUDED.

B

John 10. 26 But ye believe not, because ye are not of my sheep, as I said unto you.
27 My sheep hear my voice, and I know them, and they follow me:

I Jno. 4. 6 We are of God: he that knoweth God heareth us; he that is not of God heareth not us. Hereby know we the spirit of truth, and the spirit of error.

C

John 7. 20 The people answered and said, Thou hast a devil: who goeth about to kill thee?

John 8. 52. *See text of topic.*

John 10. 20 And many of them said, He hath a devil, and is mad; why hear ye him?

D

John 5. 41 I receive not honour from men.

John 7. 18 He that speaketh of himself seeketh his own glory: but he that seeketh his glory that sent him, the same is true, and no unrighteousness is in him.

E

Isa. 53. 11 He shall see of the travail of his soul, *and* shall be satisfied: by his knowledge shall my righteous servant justify many; for he shall bear their iniquities.

Matt. 19. 29 And every one that hath forsaken houses, or brethren, or sisters, or father, or mother, or wife, or children, or lands, for my name's sake, shall receive an hundredfold, and shall inherit everlasting life.

John 1. 12 But as many as received him, to them gave he power to become the sons of God, *even* to them that believe on his name:

John 3. 15 That whosoever believeth in him should not perish, but have eternal life.
16 For God so loved the world, that he gave his only begotten Son, that whosoever believeth in him should not perish, but have everlasting life.

John 3. 36 He that believeth on the Son hath everlasting life: and he that believeth not the Son shall not see life; but the wrath of God abideth on him.

John 4. 14 But whosoever drinketh of the water that I shall give him shall never thirst; but the water that I shall give him shall be in him a well of water springing up into everlasting life.

John 5. 24 Verily, verily, I say unto you, He that heareth my word, and believeth on him that sent me, hath everlasting life, and shall not come into condemnation; but is passed from death unto life.

John 6. 27 Labour not for the meat which perisheth, but for that meat which endureth unto everlasting life, which the Son of man shall give unto you: for him hath God the Father sealed.

John 6. 40 And this is the will of him that sent me, that every one which seeth the Son, and believeth on him, may have everlasting life: and I will raise him up at the last day.

John 6. 47 Verily, verily, I say unto you, He that believeth on me hath everlasting life.

John 10. 27 My sheep hear my voice, and I know them, and they follow me:
28 And I give unto them eternal life; and they shall never perish,

John 11. 25 Jesus said unto her, I am the resurrection, and the life: he that believeth in me, though he were dead, yet shall he live:
26 And whosoever liveth and believeth in me shall never die. Believest thou this?

John 12. 50 And I know that his commandment is life everlasting: whatsoever I speak therefore, even as the Father said unto me, so I speak.

John 17. 3 And this is life eternal, that they might know thee the only true God and Jesus Christ, whom thou hast sent.

John 20. 31 But these are written, that ye might believe that Jesus is the Christ, the Son of God; and that believing ye might have life through his name.

Acts 13. 39 And by him all that believe are justified from all things, from which ye could not be justified by the law of Moses.

Rom. 3. 28 Therefore we conclude that a man is justified by faith without the deeds of the law.

Rom. 6. 22 But now being made free from sin, and become servants to God, ye have your fruit unto holiness, and the end everlasting life.
23 For the wages of sin *is* death; but the gift of God *is* eternal life through Jesus Christ our LORD.

Rom. 8. 13 For if ye live after the flesh, ye shall die: but if ye through the Spirit do mortify the deeds of the body, ye shall live,
14 For as many as are led by the

TEMPT TO STONE JESUS (CONTINUED). TIME, OCTOBER, A.D. 29; PLACE, JERUSALEM.

E—CONCLUDED.

Spirit of God, they are the sons of God.

Gal. 6. 8 For he that soweth to his flesh shall of the flesh reap corruption; but he that soweth to the Spirit shall of the Spirit reap life everlasting.

I Tim.1. 16 Howbeit for this cause I obtained mercy, that in me first Jesus Christ might show forth all longsuffering, for a pattern to them which should hereafter believe on him to life everlasting.

I Jno. 2. 25 And this is the promise that he hath promised us, *even* eternal life.

I Jno. 4. 9 In this was manifested the love of God toward us, because that God sent his only begotten Son into the world, that we might live through him.

I Jno. 5. 11 And this is the record, that God hath given to us eternal life, and this life is in his Son.

12 He that hath the Son hath life: *and* he that hath not the Son of God hath not life.

13 These things have I written unto you that believe on the name of the Son of God; that ye may know that ye have eternal life, and that ye may believe on the name of the Son of God.

F

Zech. 1. 5 Your fathers, where *are* they? and the prophets, do they live for ever?

Heb. 11. 13 These all died in faith, not having received the promises, but having seen them afar off, and were persuaded of *them*, and embraced *them*, and confessed that they were strangers and pilgrims on the earth.

G

Prov.25. 27 *It is* not good to eat much honey: so *for men* to search their own glory *is not* glory.

John 5. 31 If I bear witness of myself, my witness is not true.

H

John 5. 41. *See under D.*

John 16. 14 He shall glorify me: for he shall receive of mine, and shall show *it* unto you.

John 17. 1 These words spake Jesus, and lifted up his eyes to heaven, and said, Father, the hour is come; glorify thy Son, that thy Son also may glorify thee:

Acts 3. 13 The God of Abraham, and of Isaac, and of Jacob, the God of our fathers, hath glorified his Son Jesus; whom ye delivered up, and denied him in the presence of Pilate, when he was determined to let *him* go.

CHAP. 8.

45 And because I tell *you* the truth,
ye believe me not.

46 Which of you convinceth me of
sin? And if I say the truth, why do
ye not believe me?

47 [b]He that is of God heareth God's
words: ye therefore hear *them* not,
because ye are not of God.

48 Then answered the Jews, and said
unto him, Say we not well that thou
art a Samaritan, and [c]hast a devil?

49 Jesus answered, I have not a
devil; but I honour my Father, and
ye do dishonour me.

50 And [d]I seek not mine own glory:
there is one that seeketh and judgeth.

51 Verily, verily, I say unto you,
[e]If a man keep my saying, he shall
never see death.

52 Then said the Jews unto him,
Now we know that thou hast a devil.
[f]Abraham is dead, and the prophets;
and thou sayest, If a man keep my
saying, he shall never taste of death.

53 Art thou greater than our father
Abraham, which is dead? and the
prophets are dead: whom makest thou
thyself?

54 Jesus answered, [g]If I honour myself,
my honour is nothing: [h]it is my
Father that honoureth me; of whom
ye say, that he is your God:

55 Yet [i]ye have not known him; but
I know him: and if I should say, I
know him not, I shall be a liar like
unto you: but I know him, and keep
his saying.

I

John 7. 28, 29. *See under U, page 326.*

§ 111. PUBLIC TEACHING. DISPUTE WITH THE PHARISEES. SECOND AT-

K

Gen. 22. 18 And in thy seed shall all the nations of the earth be blessed; because thou hast obeyed my voice.

Luke 2. 28 Then took he him up in his arms, and blessed God, and said,

29 Lord, now lettest thou thy servant depart in peace, according to thy word:

30 For mine eyes have seen thy salvation,

Luke 10. 24 For I tell you, that many prophets and kings have desired to see those things which ye see, and have not seen *them;* and to hear those things which ye hear, and have not heard *them.*

Gal. 3. 8 And the Scripture, foreseeing that God would justify the heathen through faith, preached before the gospel unto Abraham, *saying,* In thee shall all nations be blessed.

Gal. 3. 16 Now to Abraham and his seed were the promises made. He saith not, And to seeds, as of many; but as of one, And to thy seed, which is Christ.

L

Heb. 11. 13 These all died in faith, not having received the promises, but having seen them afar off, and were persuaded of *them,* and embraced *them,* and confessed that they were strangers and pilgrims on the earth.

M

Ex. 3. 14 And God said unto Moses, I AM THAT I AM: and he said, Thus shalt thou say unto the children of Israel, I AM hath sent me unto you.

Isa. 9. 6 For unto us a child is born, unto us a son is given: and the government shall be upon his shoulder: and his name shall be called Wonderful, Counsellor, The mighty God, the everlasting Father, the Prince of Peace.

Isa. 43. 13 Yea, before the day *was* I *am* he; and *there is* none that can deliver out of my hand: I will work, and who shall let it?

Isa. 44. 6 Thus saith the LORD the King of Israel, and his Redeemer the LORD of hosts; I *am* the first, and I *am* the last; and besides me *there is* no God.

Mic. 5. 2 But thou, Beth-lehem Ephratah, *though* thou be little among the thou-

§ 112. A LAWYER INSTRUCTED. THE PARABLE OF THE

A

Matt. 19. 16 And, behold, one came and said unto him, Good Master, what good thing shall I do, that I may have eternal life?

Matt. 22. 35 Then one of them, *which was* a lawyer, asked *him a question,* tempting him, and saying,

Acts 16. 30 And brought them out, and said Sirs, what must I do to be saved?

31 And they said, Believe on the Lord Jesus Christ, and thou shalt be saved, and thy house.

B

Deut. 6. 5 And thou shalt love the LORD thy God with all thine heart, and with all thy soul, and with all thy might.

Matt. 22. 37 Jesus said unto him, Thou shalt love the Lord thy God with all thy heart, and with all thy soul, and with all thy mind.

38 This is the first and great commandment.

39 And the second *is* like unto it, Thou shalt love thy neighbour as thyself.

40 On these two commandments hang all the law and the prophets.

Mark 12. 30 And thou shalt love the Lord thy God with all thy heart, and with all thy soul, and with all thy mind, and with all thy strength: this *is* the first commandment.

31 And the second *is* like, *namely* this, Thou shalt love thy neighbour as thyself. There is none other commandment greater than these.

C

Lev. 19. 18 Thou shalt not avenge, nor bear any grudge against the children of thy people, but thou shalt love thy neighbour as thyself: I *am* the LORD.

Matt. 19. 19 Honour thy father and *thy* mother: and, Thou shalt love thy neighbour as thyself.

Gal. 5. 13 For brethren, ye have been called unto liberty; only *use* not liberty for an occasion to the flesh, but by love serve one another.

D

Lev. 18. 5 Ye shall therefore keep my statutes, and my judgments: which if a man do, he shall live in them: I *am* the LORD.

Neh. 9. 29 And testifiedst against them, that thou mightest bring them again unto thy law: yet they dealt proudly, and hearkened not unto thy commandments, but sinned against thy judg-

TEMPT TO STONE JESUS (CONCLUDED). TIME, OCTOBER, A.D. 29; PLACE, JERUSALEM.

M—CONCLUDED.

sands of Judah, *yet* out of thee shall he come forth unto me *that is* to be ruler in Israel; whose goings forth *have been* from of old, from everlasting.

John 17. 5 And now, O Father, glorify thou me with thine own self with the glory which I had with thee before the world was.

John 17. 24 Father, I will that they also, whom thou hast given me, be with me where I am; that they may behold my glory, which thou hast given me: for thou lovedst me before the foundation of the world.

Col. 1. 17 And he is before all things, and by him all things consist:

Heb. 13. 8 Jesus Christ the same yesterday, and to day, and for ever.

Rev. 1. 8 I am Alpha and Omega, the beginning and the ending, saith the Lord, which is, and which was, and which is to come, the Almighty.

N

John 10. 31 Then the Jews took up stones again to stone him.

John 10. 39 Therefore they sought again to

CHAP. 8.

56 Your father Abraham [k]rejoiced to see my day: [l]and he saw *it*, and was glad.

57 Then said the Jews unto him, Thou art not yet fifty years old, and hast thou seen Abraham?

58 Jesus said unto them, Verily, verily, I say unto you, Before Abraham was, [m]I am.

59 Then [n]took they up stones to cast at him: but Jesus hid himself, and went out of the temple, [o]going through the midst of them, and so passed by.

N—CONCLUDED. (p. 343.)

take him; but he escaped out of their hand,

John 11. 8 *His* disciples say unto him, Master, the Jews of late sought to stone thee; and goest thou thither again?

O

Luke 4. 30 But he, passing through the midst of them, went his way,

GOOD SAMARITAN. TIME, NOVEMBER, A. D. 29; PLACE, JERUSALEM.

10 : 25–37.

25 [a]And, behold, a certain lawyer stood up, and tempted him, saying, Master, what shall I do to inherit eternal life?

26 He said unto him, What is written in the law? how readest thou?

27 And he answering said, [b]Thou shalt love the Lord thy God with all thy heart, and with all thy soul, and with all thy strength, and with all thy mind; and [c]thy neighbour as thyself.

28 And he said unto him, Thou hast answered right: this do, and [d]thou shalt live.

D—CONTINUED.

ments, (which if a man do, he shall live in them;) and withdrew the shoulder, and hardened their neck, and would not hear.

Eze. 20. 11 And I gave them my statutes, and showed them my judgments,

D—CONCLUDED.

which *if* a man do, he shall even live in them.

Eze. 20. 13 But the house of Israel rebelled against me in the wilderness: they walked not in my statutes, and they despised my judgments, which *if* a man do, he shall even live in them; and my sabbaths they greatly polluted: then I said, I would pour out my fury upon them in the wilderness, to consume them.

Eze. 20. 21 Notwithstanding, the children rebelled against me: they walked not in my statutes, neither kept my judgments to do them, which *if* a man do, he shall even live in them; they polluted my sabbaths: then I said, I would pour out my fury upon them, to accomplish my anger against them in the wilderness.

Rom. 10. 5 For Moses describeth the righteousness which is of the law, That the man which doeth those things shall live by them.

Matt. 19. 17 And he said unto him, Why callest thou me good? *there is* none good but one, *that is* God: but if thou wilt enter into life, keep the commandments.

§ 112. A LAWYER INSTRUCTED. THE PARABLE OF THE GOOD

E

Lev. 19. 33 And if a stranger sojourn with
thee in your land, ye shall not vex
him.
34 *But* the stranger that dwelleth
with you shall be unto you as one
born among you, and thou shalt love
him as thyself; for ye were strangers
in the land of Egypt: I *am* the LORD
your God.
Luke 16. 15 And he said unto them, Ye are
they which justify yourselves before
men; but God knoweth your hearts:
for that which is highly esteemed
among men is abomination in the
sight of God.
Luke 18. 9 And he spake this parable unto
certain which trusted in themselves
that they were righteous, and despised
others:

F

Jer. 5. 30 A wonderful and horrible thing
is committed in the land;
31 The prophets prophesy falsely,
and the priests bear rule by their
means; and my people love *to have it*
so: and what will ye do in the end
thereof?
Hos. 5. 1 Hear ye this, O priests; and heark-
en, ye house of Israel; and give ye
ear, O house of the king: for judgment *is* toward you, because ye have
been a snare on Mizpah, and a net
spread upon Tabor.
Mal. 1. 10 Who *is there* even among you that
would shut the doors *for nought?*
neither do ye kindle *fire* on mine altar
for nought. I have no pleasure in
you, saith the LORD of hosts, neither
will I accept an offering at your hand.

G

Ps. 38. 10 My heart panteth, my strength
faileth me: as for the light of mine
eyes, it also is gone from me.
11 My lovers and my friends stand
aloof from my sore; and my kinsmen
stand afar off.
Ps. 69. 20 Reproach hath broken my heart;
and I am full of heaviness: and I
looked *for some* to take pity, but *there*
was none; and for comforters, but I
found none.
Ps. 142. 4 I looked on *my* right hand, and
beheld, but *there was* no man that
would know me: refuge failed me; no
man cared for my soul.
Prov. 21. 13 Whoso stoppeth his ears at the
cry of the poor, he also shall cry himself, but shall not be heard.
Prov. 24. 11 If thou forbear to deliver *them*

G—CONCLUDED.

that are drawn unto death, and *those*
that are ready to be slain;
12 If thou sayest, Behold, we knew
it not; doth not he that pondereth the
heart consider *it?* and he that keepeth
thy soul, doth *not* he know *it?* and
shall *not* he render to *every* man according to his works?
Jas. 2. 13 For he shall have judgment without mercy, that hath showed no mercy; and mercy rejoiceth against judgment.
14 What *doth it* profit, my brethren,
though a man say he hath faith, and
have not works? can faith save him?
15 If a brother or sister be naked,
and destitute of daily food,
16 And one of you say unto them,
Depart in peace, be *ye* warmed and
filled; notwithstanding ye give them
not those things which are needful to
the body; what *doth it* profit?
I Jno. 3. 16 Hereby perceive we the love *of*
God, because he laid down his life for
us: and we ought to lay down *our*
lives for the brethren.
17 But whoso hath this world's good,
and seeth his brother have need, and
shutteth up his bowels *of compassion*
from him, how dwelleth the love of
God in him?
18 My little children, let us not love
in word, neither in tongue; but in
deed and in truth.

H

Prov. 27. 10 Thine own friend, and thy father's friend, forsake not; neither go
into thy brother's house in the day of
thy calamity: *for* better *is* a neighbour
that is near than a brother far off.
Jer. 38. 12 And Ebed-melech the Ethiopian
said unto Jeremiah, Put now *these* old
cast clouts and rotten rags under thine
armholes under the cords. And Jeremiah did so.
13 So they drew up Jeremiah with
cords, and took him up out of the
dungeon: and Jeremiah remained in
the court of the prison.
Luke 17. 16 And fell down on *his* face at his
feet, giving him thanks: and he was
a Samaritan.
17 And Jesus answering said, Were
there not ten cleansed? but where *are*
the nine?
18 There are not found that returned
to give glory to God, save this
stranger.
John 4. 9 Then saith the woman of Samaria

SAMARITAN (CONCLUDED). TIME, NOVEMBER, A. D. 29; PLACE, JERUSALEM.

CHAP. 10.

29 But he, willing to [e]justify himself, said unto Jesus, And who is my neighbour?

30 And Jesus answering said, A certain *man* went down from Jerusalem to Jericho, and fell among thieves, which stripped him of his raiment, and wounded *him*, and departed, leaving *him* half dead.

31 And by chance there came down a certain [f]priest that way; and when he saw him, [g]he passed by on the other side.

32 And likewise a Levite, when he was at the place, came and looked *on him*, and passed by on the other side.

33 But a certain [h]Samaritan, as he journeyed, came where he was; and when he saw him, he had compassion *on him*,

34 [i]And went to *him*, and bound up his wounds, pouring in oil and wine, and set him on his own beast, and brought him to an inn, and took care of him.

35 And on the morrow when he departed, he took out two pence, and gave *them* to the host, and said unto him, Take care of him: and whatsoever thou spendest more, when I come again, I will repay thee.

36 Which now of these three, [k]thinkest thou, was neighbour unto him that fell among the thieves?

37 And he said, [l]He that showed mercy on him. Then said Jesus unto him, [m]Go, and do thou likewise.

H—CONTINUED.

unto him, How is it that thou, being a Jew, askest drink of me, which am a

H—CONCLUDED.

woman of Samaria? for the Jews have no dealings with the Samaritans.

I

Prov.24. 17 Rejoice not when thine enemy falleth, and let not thine heart be glad when he stumbleth:

Prov.25. 21 If thine enemy be hungry, give him bread to eat; and if he be thirsty, give him water to drink:

22 For thou shalt heap coals of fire upon his head, and the LORD shall reward thee.

Matt. 5. 44 But I say unto you, Love your enemies, bless them that curse you, do good to them that hate you, and pray for them which despitefully use you, and persecute you;

45 That ye may be the children of your Father which is in heaven: for he maketh his sun to rise on the evil and on the good, and sendeth rain on the just and on the unjust.

Rom.12. 20 Therefore if thine enemy hunger, feed him; if he thirst, give him drink: for in so doing thou shalt heap coals of fire on his head.

21 Be not overcome of evil, but overcome evil with good.

I Thes.5. 15 See that none render evil for evil unto any *man*; but ever follow that which is good, both among yourselves, and to all *men*.

K

Luke 7. 42 And when they had nothing to pay, he frankly forgave them both. Tell me therefore, which of them will love him most?

L

Prov.14. 21 He that despiseth his neighbour sinneth: but he that hath mercy on the poor, happy *is* he.

M

John 13. 15 For I have given you an example that ye should do as I have done to you.

16 Verily, verily, I say unto you, The servant is not greater than his lord; neither he that is sent greater than he that sent him.

17 If ye know these things, happy are ye if ye do them.

I Pet. 2. 21 For even hereunto were ye called: because Christ also suffered for us, leaving us an example, that ye should follow his steps:

I Jno. 3. 23 And this is his commandment, That we should believe on the name of his Son Jesus Christ, and love one another, as he gave us commandment.

§ 113. JESUS IN THE HOUSE OF MARTHA AND MARY.

A

John 11. 1 Now a certain *man* was sick, *named* Lazarus, of Bethany, the town of Mary and her sister Martha.

John 12. 2 There they made him a supper; and Martha served: but Lazarus was one of them that sat at the table with him.

3 Then took Mary a pound of ointment of spikenard, very costly, and anointed the feet of Jesus, and wiped his feet with her hair: and the house was filled with the odour of the ointment.

B

I Cor. 7. 32 But I would have you without carefulness. He that is unmarried careth for the things that belong to the Lord, how he may please the Lord:

33 But he that is married careth for the things that are of the world, how he may please *his* wife.

34 There is difference *also* between a wife and a virgin. The unmarried woman careth for the things of the Lord, that she may be holy both in body and in spirit: but she that is married careth for the things of the world, how she may please *her* husband.

B—Concluded.

I Cor. 7. 35 And this I speak for your own profit; not that I may cast a snare upon you, but for that which is comely, and that ye may attend upon the Lord without distraction.

C

Deut. 33. 3 Yea, he loved the people; all his saints *are* in thy hand: and they sat down at thy feet; *every one* shall receive of thy words.

Luke 8. 35 Then they went out to see what was done; and came to Jesus, and found the man, out of whom the devils were departed, sitting at the feet of Jesus, clothed, and in his right mind: and they were afraid.

Acts 22. 3 I am verily a man *which am* a Jew, born in Tarsus, *a city* in Cilicia, yet brought up in this city at the feet of Gamaliel, *and* taught according to the perfect manner of the law of the fathers, and was zealous toward God, as ye all are this day.

D

Matt. 6. 31 Therefore take no thought saying, What shall we eat? or What shall we drink? or, Wherewithal shall we be clothed?

Luke 12. 29 And seek not ye what ye shall

§ 114. THE DISCIPLES AGAIN TAUGHT HOW TO PRAY.

A

II Cor. 3. 5 Not that we are sufficient of ourselves to think any thing as of ourselves; but our sufficiency *is* of God:

B

Isa. 63. 16 Doubtless thou *art* our Father, though Abraham be ignorant of us, and Israel acknowledge us not: thou, O Lord, *art* our Father, our Redeemer; thy name *is* from everlasting.

Matt. 6. 9 After this manner therefore pray ye: Our Father which art in heaven, Hallowed be thy name.

10 Thy kingdom come. Thy will be done in earth, as *it is* in heaven.

11 Give us this day our daily bread.

12 And forgive us our debts, as we forgive our debtors.

13 And lead us not into temptation, but deliver us from evil: For thine is the kingdom, and the power, and the glory, for ever. Amen.

C

Isa. 2. 3 And many people shall go and say, Come ye, and let us go up to the mountain of the Lord, to the house of the God of Jacob; and he will teach

C—Concluded.

us of his ways, and we will walk in his paths: for out of Zion shall go forth the law, and the word of the Lord from Jerusalem.

Isa. 11. 8 And the sucking child shall play on the hole of the asp, and the weaned child shall put his hand on the cockatrice' den.

9 They shall not hurt nor destroy in all my holy mountain: for the earth shall be full of the knowledge of the Lord, as the waters cover the sea.

Dan. 7. 14 And there was given him dominion, and glory, and a kingdom, that all people, nations, and languages, should serve him: his dominion *is* an everlasting dominion, which shall not pass away, and his kingdom *that* which shall not be destroyed.

Rev. 19. 6 And I heard as it were the voice of a great multitude, and as the voice of many waters, and as the voice of mighty thunderings, saying, Alleluia: for the Lord God omnipotent reigneth.

1 Or, *for the day.*

TIME, NOVEMBER, A. D. 29; PLACE, BETHANY.

10: 38–42.

38 Now it came to pass, as they went, that he entered into a certain village: and a certain woman named [a]Martha received him into her house.

39 And she had a sister called Mary, [b]which also [c]sat at Jesus' feet, and heard his word.

40 But Martha was [d]cumbered about much serving, and came to him, and said, Lord, [e]dost thou not care that my sister hath left me to serve alone? bid her therefore that she help me.

41 And Jesus answered and said unto her, Martha, Martha, thou art careful and troubled about many things:

42 But [f]one thing is needful; and Mary hath chosen that good part, which shall not be taken away from her.

D—CONCLUDED.

eat, or what ye shall drink, neither be ye of doubtful mind.

John 6. 27 Labour not for the meat which perisheth, but for that meat which endureth unto everlasting life, which the Son of man shall give unto you: for him hath God the Father sealed.

E

Eccl. 6. 11 Seeing there be many things that increase vanity, what *is* man the better?

Matt. 6. 30 Wherefore, if God so clothe the grass of the field, which to day is, and to morrow is cast into the oven, *shall he* not much more *clothe* you, O ye of little faith?

I Pet. 5. 7 Casting all your care upon him; for he careth for you.

F

Deut.30. 19 I call heaven and earth to record this day against you, *that* I have set before you life and death, blessing and cursing: therefore choose life, that both thou and thy seed may live:

Ps. 27. 4 One *thing* have I desired of the LORD, that will I seek after; that I may dwell in the house of the LORD all the days of my life, to behold the beauty of the LORD, and to inquire in his temple.

TIME, NOVEMBER, A. D. 29; PLACE, NEAR JERUSALEM.

11: 1–4.

1 And it came to pass, that, as he was praying in a certain place, when he ceased, one of his disciples said unto him, Lord, [a]teach us to pray, as John also taught his disciples.

2 And he said unto them, When ye pray, say, [b]Our Father which art in heaven, Hallowed be thy name. [c]Thy kingdom come. Thy will be done, as in heaven, so in earth.

3 Give us [1]day by day our daily bread.

4 And forgive us our sins; [d]for we also forgive every one that is indebted to us. And [e]lead us not into temptation; but deliver us from evil.

D

Eph. 4. 32 And be ye kind one to another, tenderhearted, forgiving one another, even as God for Christ's sake hath forgiven you.

E

Matt.26. 41 Watch and pray, that ye enter not into temptation: the spirit indeed *is* willing, but the flesh *is* weak.

I Cor.10. 13 There hath no temptation taken you but such as is common to man: but God *is* faithful, who will not suffer you to be tempted above that ye are able; but will with the temptation also make a way to escape, that ye may be able to bear *it*.

II Cor.12. 8 For this thing I besought the Lord thrice, that it might depart from me.

Jas. 1. 13 Let no man say when he is tempted, I am tempted of God: for God cannot be tempted with evil, neither tempteth he any man:

Rev. 3. 10 Because thou hast kept the word of my patience, I also will keep thee from the hour of temptation, which shall come upon all the world, to try them that dwell upon the earth.

§ 115. PRAYER EFFECTUAL.

1
Or, *out of his way.*

A

Gal. 6. 17 From henceforth let no man trouble me: for I bear in my body the marks of the Lord Jesus.

B

Matt.15. 22 And, behold, a woman of Canaan came out of the same coasts, and cried unto him, saying, Have mercy on me, O Lord, *thou* son of David; my daughter is grievously vexed with a devil.

23 But he answered her not a word. And his disciples came and besought him, saying, Send her away; for she crieth after us.

24 But he answered and said, I am not sent but unto the lost sheep of the house of Israel.

25 Then came she and worshipped him, saying, Lord, help me.

26 But he answered and said, It is not meet to take the children's bread, and to cast *it* to dogs.

27 And she said, Truth, Lord: yet the dogs eat of the crumbs which fall from their masters' table.

28 Then Jesus answered and said unto her, O woman, great *is* thy faith: be it unto thee even as thou wilt. And her daughter was made whole from that very hour.

Luke 18. 1 And he spake a parable unto them *to this end,* that men ought always to pray, and not to faint;

2 Saying, There was in a city a judge, which feared not God, neither regarded man:

3 And there was a widow in that city; and she came unto him, saying, Avenge me of mine adversary.

4 And he would not for a while: but afterward he said within himself, Though I fear not God, nor regard man;

5 Yet because this widow troubleth me, I will avenge her, lest by her continual coming she weary me.

6 And the Lord said, Hear what the unjust judge saith.

7 And shall not God avenge his own elect, which cry day and night unto him, though he bear long with them?

8 I tell you that he will avenge them speedily. Nevertheless, when the Son of man cometh, shall he find faith on the earth?

Rom.15. 30 Now I beseech you, brethren, for the Lord Jesus Christ's sake, and for the love of the Spirit, that ye strive

B—Concluded.

together with me in *your* prayers to God for me;

C

Matt. 7. 7 Ask, and it shall be given you; seek, and ye shall find; knock, and it shall be opened unto you:

8 For every one that asketh receiveth; and he that seeketh findeth; and to him that knocketh it shall be opened.

9 Or what man is there of you, whom if his son ask bread, will he give him a stone?

10 Or if he ask a fish, will he give him a serpent?

11 If ye then, being evil, know how to give good gifts unto your children, how much more shall your Father which is in heaven give good things to them that ask him?

Matt.21. 22 And all things, whatsoever ye shall ask in prayer, believing, ye shall receive.

Mark 11. 24 Therefore I say unto you, What things soever ye desire, when ye pray, believe that ye receive *them,* and ye shall have *them.*

John 15. 7 If ye abide in me, and my words abide in you, ye shall ask what ye will, and it shall be done unto you.

Jas. 1. 5 If any of you lack wisdom, let him ask of God, that giveth to all *men* liberally, and upbraideth not; and it shall be given him.

6 But let him ask in faith, nothing wavering: for he that wavereth is like a wave of the sea driven with the wind and tossed.

I Jno. 3. 22 And whatsoever we ask, we receive of him, because we keep his commandments, and do those things that are pleasing in his sight.

I Jno. 5. 14 And this is the confidence that we have in him, that, if we ask any thing according to his will, he heareth us:

15 And if we know that he hear us, whatsoever we ask, we know that we have the petitions that we desired of him.

D

Isa. 49. 15 Can a woman forget her sucking child, that she should not have compassion on the son of her womb? yea, they may forget, yet will I not forget thee.

16 Behold, I have graven thee upon the palms of *my* hands; thy walls *are* continually before me.

Matt. 7. 9. *See under C.*

Time, November, A. D. 29; Place, Near Jerusalem.

11 : 5–13.

5 And he said unto them, Which of you shall have a friend, and shall go unto him at midnight, and say unto him, Friend, lend me three loaves;

6 For a friend of mine [1]in his journey is come to me, and I have nothing to set before him?

7 And he from within shall answer and say, [a]Trouble me not: the door is now shut, and my children are with me in bed; I cannot rise and give thee.

8 I say unto you, [b]Though he will not rise and give him, because he is his friend, yet because of his importunity he will rise and give him as many as he needeth.

9 [c]And I say unto you, Ask, and it shall be given you; seek, and ye shall find; knock, and it shall be opened unto you.

10 For every one that asketh receiveth; and he that seeketh findeth; and to him that knocketh it shall be opened.

11 [d]If a son shall ask bread of any of you that is a father, will he give him a stone? or if *he ask* a fish, will he for a fish give him a serpent?

12 Or if he shall ask an egg, will he [2]offer him a [e]scorpion?

13 If ye then, being evil, know how to give good gifts unto your children; how much more shall [f]*your* heavenly Father give the Holy Spirit to them that ask him? (p. 167.)

2

Gr., *give.*

E

Eze. 2. 6 And thou, son of man, be not

E—Concluded.

afraid of them, neither be afraid of their words, though briers and thorns *be* with thee, and thou dost dwell among scorpions: be not afraid of their words, nor be dismayed at their looks, though they *be* a rebellious house.

Luke 10. 19 Behold, I give unto you power to tread on serpents and scorpions, and over all the power of the enemy: and nothing shall by any means hurt you.

Rev. 9. 10 And they had tails like unto scorpions, and there were stings in their tails: and their power *was* to hurt men five months.

F

Prov. 1. 23 Turn you at my reproof: behold, I will pour out my spirit unto you, I will make known my words unto you.

Isa. 44. 3 For I will pour water upon him that is thirsty, and floods upon the dry ground: I will pour my Spirit upon thy seed, and my blessing upon thine offspring:

4 And they shall spring up *as* among the grass, as willows by the water-courses.

5 One shall say, I *am* the Lord's; and another shall call *himself* by the name of Jacob; and another shall subscribe *with* his hand unto the Lord, and surname *himself* by the name of Israel.

Joel 2. 28 And it shall come to pass afterward, *that* I will pour out my Spirit upon all flesh; and your sons and your daughters shall prophesy, your old men shall dream dreams, your young men shall see visions:

Matt. 7. 11. *See under C.*

John 4. 10 Jesus answered and said unto her, If thou knewest the gift of God, and who it is that saith to thee, Give me to drink; thou wouldest have asked of him, and he would have given thee living water.

Eph. 5. 18 And be not drunk with wine, wherein is excess; but be filled with the Spirit;

Tit. 3. 4 But after that the kindness and love of God our Saviour toward man appeared,

5 Not by works of righteousness which we have done, but according to his mercy he saved us, by the washing of regeneration, and renewing of the Holy Ghost;

Jas. 1. 5 *See under C.*

A

Luke 10. 1 After these things the Lord appointed other seventy also, and sent them two and two before his face into every city and place, whither he himself would come.

B

John 12. 31 Now is the judgment of this world: now shall the prince of this world be cast out.

John 16. 11 Of judgment, because the prince of this world is judged.

I Jno. 3. 8 He that committeth sin is of the devil; for the devil sinneth from the beginning. For this purpose the Son of God was manifested, that he might destroy the works of the devil.

Rev. 9. 1 And the fifth angel sounded, and I saw a star fall from heaven unto the earth: and to him was given the key of the bottomless pit.

Rev. 12. 8 And prevailed not; neither was their place found any more in heaven.

9 And the great dragon was cast out, that old serpent, called the Devil, and Satan, which deceiveth the whole world: he was cast out into the earth, and his angels were cast out with him.

C

Mark 16. 18 They shall take up serpents; and if they drink any deadly thing, it shall not hurt them; they shall lay hands on the sick, and they shall recover.

Acts 28. 5 And he shook off the beast into the fire, and felt no harm.

D

Ex. 32. 32 Yet now, if thou wilt forgive their sin—; and if not, blot me, I pray thee, out of thy book which thou hast written.

Ps. 69. 28 Let them be blotted out of the book of the living, and not be written with the righteous.

Isa. 4. 3 And it shall come to pass, *that he that is* left in Zion, and *he that* remaineth in Jerusalem, shall be called holy, *even* every one that is written among the living in Jerusalem:

Dan. 12. 1 And at that time shall Michael stand up, the great prince which standeth for the children of thy people: and there shall be a time of trouble, such as never was since there was a nation *even* to that same time: and at that time thy people shall be delivered, every one that shall be found written in the book.

Phil. 4. 3 And I entreat thee also, true yokefellow, help those women which

§ 116. THE SEVENTY RETURN.

D—Concluded.

laboured with me in the gospel, with Clement also, and *with* other my fellow labourers, whose names *are* in the book of life.

Heb. 12. 23 To the general assembly and church of the first-born, which are written in heaven, and to God the Judge of all, and to the spirits of just men made perfect.

Rev. 13. 8 And all that dwell upon the earth shall worship him, whose names are not written in the book of life of the Lamb slain from the foundation of the world.

Rev. 20. 12 And I saw the dead, small and great, stand before God; and the books were opened: and another book was opened, which is *the book* of life: and the dead were judged out of those things which were written in the books, according to their works.

Rev. 21. 27 And there shall in no wise enter into it any thing that defileth, neither *whatsoever* worketh abomination, or *maketh* a lie: but they which are written in the Lamb's book of life.

E

Job 5. 12 He disappointeth the devices of the crafty, so that their hands cannot perform *their* enterprise.

13 He taketh the wise in their own craftiness: and the counsel of the froward is carried headlong.

14 They meet with darkness in the daytime, and grope in the noonday as in the night.

Isa. 29. 14 Therefore, behold, I will proceed to do a marvellous work among this people, *even* a marvellous work and a wonder: for the wisdom of their wise *men* shall perish, and the understanding of their prudent *men* shall be hid.

Matt. 11. 25 At that time Jesus answered and said, I thank thee, O Father, Lord of heaven and earth, because thou hast hid these things from the wise and prudent, and hast revealed them unto babes.

26 Even so, Father; for so it seemed good in thy sight.

I Cor. 1. 19 For it is written, I will destroy the wisdom of the wise, and will bring to nothing the understanding of the prudent.

I Cor. 2. 6 Howbeit we speak wisdom among them that are perfect: yet not the wisdom of this world, nor of the princes of this world, that come to nought:

TIME, NOVEMBER, A. D. 29; PLACE, JERUSALEM.

10 : 17–24.

17 And [a]the seventy returned again
with joy, saying, Lord, even the devils
are subject unto us through thy name.
18 And he said unto them, [b]I beheld
Satan as lightning fall from heaven.
19 Behold, [c]I give unto you power
to tread on serpents and scorpions, and
over all the power of the enemy; and
nothing shall by any means hurt you.
20 Notwithstanding, in this rejoice
not, that the spirits are subject unto
you; but rather rejoice, because [d]your
names are written in heaven.
21 [e]In that hour Jesus rejoiced in
spirit, and said, I thank thee, O Father,
Lord of heaven and earth, that thou
hast hid these things from the wise and
prudent, and hast revealed them unto
babes: even so, Father; for so it
seemed good in thy sight.
22 [f1]All things are delivered to me
of my Father: and [g]no man knoweth
who the Son is, but the Father; and
who the Father is, but the Son, and *he*
to whom the Son will reveal *him.*
23 And he turned him unto *his* disciples,
and said privately, [h]Blessed *are*
the eyes which see the things that ye
see:
24 For I tell you, [i]that many prophets
and kings have desired to see
those things which ye see, and have
not seen *them;* and to hear those things
which ye hear, and have not heard
them.

(p. 333.)

E—CONTINUED.

I Cor. 2. 7 But we speak the wisdom of God in a mystery, *even* the hidden *wisdom,* which God ordained before the world unto our glory;

I Cor. 3. 18 Let no man deceive himself. If any man among you seemeth to be wise in this world, let him become a fool, that he may be wise.

E—CONCLUDED.

19 For the wisdom of this world is foolishness with God: for it is written, He taketh the wise in their own craftiness.

20 And again, the Lord knoweth the thoughts of the wise, that they are vain.

II Cor. 4. 3 But if our gospel be hid, it is hid to them that are lost:

Col. 2. 2 That their hearts might be comforted, being knit together in love, and unto all riches of the full assurance of understanding, to the acknowledgment of the mystery of God, and of the Father, and of Christ:

3 In whom are hid all the treasures of wisdom and knowledge.

F

Matt. 28. 18 And Jesus came and spake unto them, saying, All power is given unto me in heaven and in earth.

John 3. 35 The Father loveth the Son, and hath given all things into his hand.

John 5. 27 And hath given him authority to execute judgment also, because he is the Son of man.

John 17. 2 As thou hast given him power over all flesh, that he should give eternal life to as many as thou hast given him.

Phil. 2. 9 Wherefore God also hath highly exalted him, and given him a name which is above every name:

1

Many ancient copies add these words, *And turning to his disciples he said,*

G

John 1. 18 No man hath seen God at any time; the only begotten Son, which is in the bosom of the Father, he hath declared *him.*

John 6. 44 No man can come to me, except the Father which hath sent me draw him: and I will raise him up at the last day.

John 6. 46 Not that any man hath seen the Father, save he which is of God, he hath seen the Father.

H

Matt. 13. 16 But blessed *are* your eyes, for they see: and your ears, for they hear.

I

I Pet. 1. 10 Of which salvation the prophets have inquired and searched diligently, who prophesied of the grace *that should come* unto you:

§ 117. A MAN BORN BLIND HEALED ON THE SABBATH.

A

Matt.10. 38 And he that taketh not his cross, and followeth after me, is not worthy of me.

John 9. 34. *See text of topic.*

B

Job 1. 8 And the LORD said unto Satan, Hast thou considered my servant Job, that *there is* none like him in the earth, a perfect and an upright man, one that feareth God, and escheweth evil?

9 Then Satan answered the LORD, and said, Doth Job fear God for nought?

10 Hast not thou made a hedge about him, and about his house, and about all that he hath on every side? thou hast blessed the work of his hands, and his substance is increased in the land.

11 But put forth thine hand now, and touch all that he hath, and he will curse thee to thy face.

12 And the LORD said unto Satan, Behold, all that he hath *is* in thy power; only upon himself put not forth thine hand. So Satan went forth from the presence of the LORD.

Job 3. 2 And Job spake, and said,

3 Let the day perish wherein I was born, and the night *in which* it was said, There is a man child conceived.

4 Let the day be darkness; let not God regard it from above, neither let the light shine upon it.

Job 3. 6 *As for* that night, let darkness seize upon it; let it not be joined unto the days of the year; let it not come into the number of the months.

Job 22. 5 *Is* not thy wickedness great? and thine iniquities infinite?

6 For thou hast taken a pledge from thy brother for nought, and stripped the naked of their clothing.

7 Thou hast not given water to the weary to drink, and thou hast withholden bread from the hungry.

8 But *as for* the mighty man, he had the earth; and the honourable man dwelt in it.

9 Thou hast sent widows away empty, and the arms of the fatherless have been broken.

10 Therefore snares *are* round about thee, and sudden fear troubleth thee;

11 Or darkness, *that* thou canst not see; and abundance of waters cover thee.

Job 32. 3 Also against his three friends was his wrath kindled, because they had

B—CONCLUDED.

found no answer, and *yet* had condemned Job.

Eccl. 9. 1 For all this I considered in my heart even to declare all this, that the righteous, and the wise, and their works, *are* in the hand of God: no man knoweth either love or hatred *by* all *that is* before them.

2 All *things come* alike to all: *there is* one event to the righteous, and to the wicked; to the good and to the clean, and to the unclean; to him that sacrificeth, and to him that sacrificeth not: as *is* the good, so *is* the sinner; *and* he that sweareth, as *he* that feareth an oath.

Acts 28. 4 And when the barbarians saw the *venomous* beast hang on his hand they said among themselves, No doubt this man is a murderer, whom, though he hath escaped the sea, yet vengeance suffereth not to live.

5 And he shook off the beast into the fire, and felt no harm.

6 Howbeit they looked when he should have swollen, or fallen down dead suddenly: but after they had looked a great while, and saw no harm come to him, they changed their minds, and said that he was a god.

C

John 11. 4 When Jesus heard *that*, he said, This sickness is not unto death, but for the glory of God, that the Son of God might be glorified thereby.

D

John 4. 34 Jesus saith unto them, My meat is to do the will of him that sent me, and to finish his work.

John 5. 19 Then answered Jesus and said unto them, Verily, verily, I say unto you, The Son can do nothing of himself, but what he seeth the Father do: for what things soever he doeth, these also doeth the Son likewise.

John 5. 36 But I have greater witness than *that* of John: for the works which the Father hath given me to finish, the same works that I do, bear witness of me, that the Father hath sent me.

John 11. 9 Jesus answered, Are there not twelve hours in the day? If any man walk in the day, he stumbleth not, because he seeth the light of this world.

John 12. 35 Then Jesus said unto them, Yet a little while is the light with you. Walk while ye have the light, lest darkness come upon you: for he that

TIME, NOVEMBER, A. D. 29; PLACE, JERUSALEM.

D—CONCLUDED.

walketh in darkness knoweth not whither he goeth.

John 17. 4 I have glorified thee on the earth: I have finished the work which thou gavest me to do.

E

John 1. 5 And the light shineth in darkness; and the darkness comprehended it not.

John 1. 9 *That* was the true Light, which lighteth every man that cometh into the world.

John 3. 19 And this is the condemnation, that light is come into the world, and men loved darkness rather than light, because their deeds were evil.

John 8. 12 Then spake Jesus again unto them, saying, I am the light of the world: he that followeth me shall not walk in darkness, but shall have the light of life.

John 12. 35. *See under D.*

John 12. 46 I am come a light into the world, that whosoever believeth on me should not abide in darkness.

F

Mark 7. 33 And he took him aside from the multitude, and put his fingers into his ears, and he spit, and touched his tongue;

Mark 8. 23 And he took the blind man by the hand, and led him out of the town; and when he had spit on his eyes, and put his hands upon him, he asked him if he saw aught.

1

Or, *spread the clay upon the eyes of the blind man.*

G

Neh. 3. 15 But the gate of the fountain repaired Shallun the son of Col-hozeh, the ruler of part of Mizpah; he built it, and covered it, and set up the doors thereof, the locks thereof, and the bars thereof, and the wall of the pool of Siloah by the king's garden, and unto the stairs that go down from the city of David.

Isa. 8. 6 Forasmuch as this people refuseth the waters of Shiloah that go softly, and rejoice in Rezin and Remaliah's son;

H

II Ki. 5. 14 Then went he down, and dipped himself seven times in Jordan, according to the saying of the man of God: and his flesh came again like unto the flesh of a little child, and he was clean.

I

John 9. 6, 7. *See text of topic.*

9 : 1–41.

1 And as *Jesus* passed by, he saw a man which was blind from *his* birth.

2 And his disciples asked him, saying, Master, [a]who did sin, this man, or his parents, that he was born blind?

3 Jesus answered, [b]Neither hath this man sinned, nor his parents: [c]but that the works of God should be made manifest in him.

4 [d]I must work the works of him that sent me, while it is day: the night cometh, when no man can work.

5 As long as [e]I am in the world, I am the light of the world.

6 When he had thus spoken, [f]he spat on the ground, and made clay of the spittle, and he [1]anointed the eyes of the blind man with the clay,

7 And said unto him, Go, wash [g]in the pool of Siloam, (which is by interpretation, Sent.) [h]He went his way therefore, and washed, and came seeing.

8 The neighbours therefore, and they which before had seen him that he was blind, said, Is not this he that sat and begged?

9 Some said, This is he: others *said*, He is like him: *but* he said, I am *he*.

10 Therefore said they unto him, How were thine eyes opened?

11 He answered and said, [i]A man that is called Jesus made clay, and anointed mine eyes, and said unto me, Go to the pool of Siloam, and wash: and I went and washed, and I received sight.

12 Then said they unto him, Where is he? He said, I know not.

§ 117. A MAN BORN BLIND HEALED ON THE SABBATH

K

John 3. 2 The same came to Jesus by night, and said unto him, Rabbi, we know that thou art a teacher come from God: for no man can do these miracles that thou doest, except God be with him.

John 9. 33. *See text of topic.*

L

John 7. 12 And there was much murmuring among the people concerning him: for some said, He is a good man: others said, Nay; but he deceiveth the people.

John 7. 43 So there was a division among the people because of him.

John 10. 19 There was a division therefore again among the Jews for these sayings.

M

Deut.18. 15 The LORD thy God will raise up unto thee a Prophet from the midst of thee, of thy brethren, like unto me; unto him ye shall hearken;

John 4. 19 The woman saith unto him, Sir, I perceive that thou art a prophet.

John 6. 14 Then those men, when they had seen the miracle that Jesus did, said, This is of a truth that Prophet that should come into the world.

N

Gen. 19. 14 And Lot went out, and spake unto his sons in law, which married his daughters, and said, Up, get you out of this place; for the LORD will destroy this city. But he seemed as one that mocked unto his sons in law.

Isa. 26. 11 LORD, *when* thy hand is lifted up, they will not see: *but* they shall see, and be ashamed for *their* envy at the people; yea, the fire of thine enemies shall devour them.

Isa. 53. 1 Who hath believed our report? and to whom is the arm of the LORD revealed?

Luke 16. 31 And he said unto him, If they hear not Moses and the prophets, neither will they be persuaded, though one rose from the dead.

Heb. 3. 15 While it is said, To day if ye will hear his voice, harden not your hearts, as in the provocation.

16 For some, when they had heard, did provoke: howbeit not all that came out of Egypt by Moses.

17 But with whom was he grieved forty years? *was it* not with them that had sinned, whose carcasses fell in the wilderness?

18 And to whom sware he that they

N—CONCLUDED.

should not enter into his rest, but to them that believed not?

19 So we see that they could not enter in because of unbelief.

Heb. 4. 11 Let us labour therefore to enter into that rest, lest any man fall after the same example of unbelief.

O

Ps. 27. 1 The LORD *is* my light and my salvation; whom shall I fear? the LORD *is* the strength of my life; of whom shall I be afraid?

2 When the wicked, *even* mine enemies and my foes, came upon me to eat up my flesh, they stumbled and fell.

Prov.29. 25 The fear of man bringeth a snare: but whoso putteth his trust in the LORD shall be safe.

Isa. 51. 7 Hearken unto me, ye that know righteousness, the people in whose heart *is* my law; fear ye not the reproach of men, neither be ye afraid of their revilings.

Isa. 51. 12 I, *even* I, *am* he that comforteth you: who *art* thou, that thou shouldest be afraid of a man *that* shall die, and of the son of man *which* shall be made *as* grass;

Isa. 57. 11 And of whom hast thou been afraid or feared, that thou hast lied, and hast not remembered me, nor laid *it* to thy heart? have not I held my peace even of old, and thou fearest me not?

Luke 12. 4 And again he sent unto them another servant: and at him they cast stones, and wounded *him* in the head, and sent *him* away shamefully handled.

5 And again he sent another; and him they killed, and many others; beating some, and killing some.

6 Having yet therefore one son, his well beloved, he sent him also last unto them, saying, They will reverence my son.

7 But those husbandmen said among themselves, This is the heir; come, let us kill him, and the inheritance shall be ours.

8 And they took him, and killed *him*, and cast *him* out of the vineyard.

9 What shall therefore the lord of the vineyard do? he will come and destroy the husbandmen, and will give the vineyard unto others.

John 7. 13 Howbeit no man spake openly of him for fear of the Jews.

(CONTINUED). TIME, NOVEMBER, A. D. 29; PLACE, JERUSALEM.

O—CONCLUDED.

John 12. 42 Nevertheless among the chief rulers also many believed on him; but because of the Pharisees they did not confess *him*, lest they should be put out of the synagogue:

John 19. 38 And after this Joseph of Arimathea, being a disciple of Jesus, but secretly for fear of the Jews, besought Pilate that he might take away the body of Jesus: and Pilate gave *him* leave. He came therefore, and took the body of Jesus.

Acts 5. 13 And of the rest durst no man join himself to them: but the people magnified them.

Gal. 2. 11 But when Peter was come to Antioch, I withstood him to the face, because he was to be blamed.

12 For before that certain came from James, he did eat with the Gentiles: but when they were come, he withdrew and separated himself, fearing them which were of the circumcision.

13 And the other Jews dissembled likewise with him; insomuch that Barnabas also was carried away with their dissimulation.

Rev. 21. 7 He that overcometh shall inherit all things; and I will be his God, and he shall be my son.

8 But the fearful, and unbelieving, and the abominable, and murderers, and whoremongers, and sorcerers, and idolaters, and all liars, shall have their part in the lake which burneth with fire and brimstone: which is the second death.

P

Luke 6. 22 Blessed are ye, when men shall hate you, and when they shall separate you *from their company*, and shall reproach *you*, and cast out your name as evil, for the Son of man's sake.

John 9. 34. *See text of topic.*

John 16. 2 They shall put you out of the synagogues: yea, the time cometh, that whosoever killeth you will think that he doeth God service.

Acts 4. 18 And they called them, and commanded them not to speak at all nor teach in the name of Jesus.

Acts 5. 39 But if it be of God, ye cannot overthrow it; lest haply ye be found even to fight against God.

40 And to him they agreed: and when they had called the apostles, and beaten *them*, they commanded that they should not speak in the name of Jesus, and let them go.

CHAP. 9.

13 They brought to the Pharisees him that aforetime was blind.

14 And it was the sabbath day when Jesus made the clay, and opened his eyes.

15 Then again the Pharisees also asked him how he had received his sight. He said unto them, He put clay upon mine eyes, and I washed, and do see.

16 Therefore said some of the Pharisees, This man is not of God, because he keepeth not the sabbath day. Others said, [k]How can a man that is a sinner do such miracles? [l]And there was a division among them.

17 They say unto the blind man again, What sayest thou of him, that he hath opened thine eyes? He said, [m]He is a prophet.

18 [n]But the Jews did not believe concerning him, that he had been blind, and received his sight, until they called the parents of him that had received his sight.

19 And they asked them, saying, Is this your son, who ye say was born blind? how then doth he now see?

20 His parents answered them and said, We know that this is our son, and that he was born blind:

21 But by what means he now seeth, we know not; or who hath opened his eyes, we know not: he is of age; ask him: he shall speak for himself.

22 These *words* spake his parents, [o]because they feared the Jews: for the Jews had agreed already, that if any man did confess that he was Christ, he [p]should be put out of the synagogue.

§ 117. A MAN BORN BLIND HEALED ON THE SABBATH

Q

Josh. 7. 19 And Joshua said unto Achan, My son, give, I pray thee, glory to the LORD God of Israel, and make confession unto him; and tell me now what thou hast done; hide *it* not from me.

I Sa. 6. 5 Wherefore ye shall make images of your emerods, and images of your mice that mar the land; and ye shall give glory unto the God of Israel: peradventure he will lighten his hand from off you, and from off your gods, and from off your land.

R

John 9. 16. *See text of topic.*

S

John 8. 14 Jesus answered and said unto them, Though I bear record of myself, *yet* my record is true: for I know whence I came, and whither I go; but ye cannot tell whence I come, and whither I go.

T

John 3. 10 Jesus answered and said unto him, Art thou a master of Israel, and knowest not these things?

U

Job 27. 9 Will God hear his cry when trouble cometh upon him?

Job 35. 12 There they cry, but none giveth answer, because of the pride of evil men.

Ps. 18. 41 They cried, but *there was* none to save *them: even* unto the LORD, but he answered them not.

Ps. 34. 15 The eyes of the LORD *are* upon the righteous, and his ears *are open* unto their cry.

Ps. 66. 18 If I regard iniquity in my heart, the Lord will not hear *me:*

Prov. 1. 28 Then shall they call upon me, but I will not answer; they shall seek me early, but they shall not find me:

Prov.15. 29 The LORD *is* far from the wicked: but he heareth the prayer of the righteous.

Prov.28. 9 He that turneth away his ear from hearing the law, even his prayer *shall be* abomination.

Isa. 1. 15 And when ye spread forth your hands, I will hide mine eyes from you; yea, when ye make many prayers, I will not hear: your hands are full of blood.

Jer. 11. 11 Therefore thus saith the LORD, Behold, I will bring evil upon them, which they shall not be able to escape; and though they shall cry unto me, I will not hearken unto them.

U—CONCLUDED.

Jer. 14. 12 When they fast, I will not hear their cry; and when they offer burnt offering and an oblation, I will not accept them: but I will consume them by the sword, and by the famine, and by the pestilence.

Eze. 8. 18 Therefore will I also deal in fury: mine eye shall not spare, neither will I have pity: and though they cry in mine ears with a loud voice, *yet* will I not hear them.

Mic. 3. 4 Then shall they cry unto the LORD, but he will not hear them: he will even hide his face from them at that time, as they have behaved themselves ill in their doings.

Zech. 7. 13 Therefore it is come to pass, *that* as he cried, and they would not hear; so they cried, and I would not hear, saith the LORD of hosts:

X

Gen. 18. 23 And Abraham drew near, and said, Wilt thou also destroy the righteous with the wicked?

24 Peradventure there be fifty righteous within the city: wilt thou also destroy and not spare the place for the fifty righteous that *are* therein?

25 That be far from thee to do after this manner, to slay the righteous with the wicked; and that the righteous should be as the wicked, that be far from thee: Shall not the Judge of all the earth do right?

26 And the LORD said, If I find in Sodom fifty righteous within the city, then I will spare all the place for their sakes.

27 And Abraham answered and said, Behold now, I have taken upon me to speak unto the Lord, which *am but* dust and ashes:

28 Peradventure there shall lack five of the fifty righteous: wilt thou destroy all the city for *lack of* five? And he said, If I find there forty and five, I will not destroy *it.*

29 And he spake unto him yet again, and said, Peradventure there shall be forty found there. And he said, I will not do *it* for forty's sake.

30 And he said *unto him,* Oh let not the Lord be angry, and I will speak: Peradventure there shall thirty be found there. And he said, I will not do *it,* if I find thirty there.

31 And he said, Behold now, I have taken upon me to speak unto the Lord: Peradventure there shall be

(CONTINUED). TIME, NOVEMBER, A. D. 29; PLACE, JERUSALEM.

X—CONCLUDED.

twenty found there. And he said, I
will not destroy *it* for twenty's sake.
32 And he said, Oh let not the Lord
be angry, and I will speak yet but this
once: Peradventure ten shall be found
there. And he said, I will not destroy it for ten's sake.
33 And the LORD went his way, as
soon as he had left communing with
Abraham: and Abraham returned
unto his place.

Gen. 19. 29 And it came to pass, when God destroyed the cities of the plain, that God remembered Abraham, and sent Lot out of the midst of the overthrow, when he overthrew the cities in the which Lot dwelt.

Gen. 20. 7 Now therefore restore the man *his* wife; for he *is* a prophet, and he shall pray for thee, and thou shalt live: and if thou restore *her* not, know thou that thou shalt surely die, thou, and all that *are* thine.

I Ki. 18. 36 And it came to pass at *the time of* the offering of the *evening* sacrifice,
that Elijah the prophet came near,
and said, LORD God of Abraham,
Isaac, and of Israel, let it be known
this day that thou *art* God in Israel,
and *that* I *am* thy servant, and *that*
I have done all these things at thy
word.
37 Hear me, O LORD, hear me, that
this people may know that thou *art*
the LORD God, and *that* thou hast
turned their heart back again.
38 Then the fire of the LORD fell,
and consumed the burnt sacrifice, and
the wood, and the stones, and the
dust, and licked up the water that *was*
in the trench.

II Chr. 32. 20 And for this *cause* Hezekiah the
king, and the prophet Isaiah the son
of Amoz, prayed and cried to heaven.
21 And the LORD sent an angel,
which cut off all the mighty men of
valour, and the leaders and captains
in the camp of the king of Assyria.
So he returned with shame of face to
his own land. And when he was
come into the house of his God, they
that came forth of his own bowels slew
him there with the sword.

Y

John 9. 16. *See text of topic.*

Z

John 9. 2. *See text of topic.*

2

Or, *excommunicate him*

CHAP. 9.

23 Therefore said his parents, He is
of age; ask him.
24 Then again called they the man
that was blind, and said unto him,
[q]Give God the praise: [r]we know that
this man is a sinner.
25 He answered and said, Whether
he be a sinner *or no*, I know not: one
thing I know, that, whereas I was
blind, now I see.
26 Then said they to him again,
What did he to thee? how opened he
thine eyes?
27 He answered them, I have told
you already, and ye did not hear:
wherefore would ye hear *it* again?
will ye also be his disciples?
28 Then they reviled him, and said,
Thou art his disciple; but we are
Moses' disciples.
29 We know that God spake unto
Moses: *as for* this *fellow*, [s]we know not
from whence he is.
30 The man answered and said unto
them, [t]Why herein is a marvellous
thing, that ye know not from whence
he is, and *yet* he hath opened mine eyes.
31 Now we know that [u]God heareth
not sinners: but if any man be a worshipper of God, and doeth his will,
[x]him he heareth.
32 Since the world began was it not
heard that any man opened the eyes of
one that was born blind.
33 [y]If this man were not of God, he
could do nothing.
34 They answered and said unto him,
[z]Thou wast altogether born in sins, and
dost thou teach us? And they [2]cast
him out.

§ 117. A MAN BORN BLIND HEALED ON THE SABBATH

A

Matt.14. 33 Then they that were in the ship came and worshipped him, saying, Of a truth thou art the Son of God.

Matt.16. 16 And Simon Peter answered and said, Thou art the Christ, the Son of the living God.

Mark 1. 1 The beginning of the gospel of Jesus Christ, the Son of God;

John 10. 36 Say ye of him, whom the Father hath sanctified, and sent into the world, Thou blasphemest; because I said, I am the Son of God?

I Jno. 5. 13 These things have I written unto you that believe on the name of the Son of God; that ye may know that ye have eternal life, and that ye may believe on the name of the Son of God.

B

John 4. 26 Jesus saith unto her, I that speak unto thee am *he*.

C

Jer. 1. 9 Then the LORD put forth his hand, and touched my mouth. And the LORD said unto me, Behold, I have put my words in thy mouth.

10 See, I have this day set thee over the nations and over the kingdoms, to root out, and to pull down, and to destroy, and to throw down, to build, and to plant.

Luke 2. 34 And Simeon blessed them, and said unto Mary his mother, Behold, this *child* is set for the fall and rising

C—CONCLUDED.

again of many in Israel; and for a sign which shall be spoken against;

John 3. 17 For God sent not his Son into the world to condemn the world; but that the world through him might be saved.

John 5. 22 For the Father judgeth no man, but hath committed all judgment unto the Son:

John 5. 27 And hath given him authority to execute judgment also, because he is the Son of man.

John 12. 47 And if any man hear my words, and believe not, I judge him not: for I came not to judge the world, but to save the world.

II Cor.2. 16 To the one *we are* the savour of death unto death; and to the other the savour of life unto life. And who *is* sufficient for these things?

D

Isa. 6. 9 And he said, Go, and tell this people, Hear ye indeed, but understand not; and see ye indeed, but perceive not.

10 Make the heart of this people fat, and make their ears heavy, and shut their eyes; lest they see with their eyes, and hear with their ears, and understand with their heart, and convert, and be healed.

Isa. 42. 20 Seeing many things, but thou observest not; opening the ears, but he heareth not.

§ 118. THE GOOD SHEPHERD: DISCOURSE SUBSEQUENT TO THE HEALING

A

Isa. 56. 10 His watchmen *are* blind: they are all ignorant, they *are* all dumb dogs, they cannot bark; sleeping, lying down, loving to slumber.

Jer. 23. 21 I have not sent these prophets, yet they ran: I have not spoken to them, yet they prophesied.

Matt. 7. 15 Beware of false prophets, which come to you in sheep's clothing, but inwardly they are ravening wolves.

Heb. 5. 4 And no man taketh this honour unto himself, but he that is called of God, as *was* Aaron.

B

Ps. 23. 1 The LORD *is* my shepherd; I shall not want.

Eccl. 12. 11 The words of the wise *are* as goads, and as nails fastened *by* the masters of assemblies, *which* are given from one shepherd.

Isa. 61. 1 The Spirit of the Lord GOD *is* upon me; because the LORD hath anointed me to preach good tidings unto the meek; he hath sent me to bind up the brokenhearted, to proclaim liberty to the captives, and the opening of the prison to *them that are* bound:

B—CONTINUED.

Zech.11. 3 *There is* a voice of the howling of the shepherds; for their glory is spoiled: a voice of the roaring of young lions; for the pride of Jordan is spoiled.

4 Thus saith the LORD my God; Feed the flock of the slaughter;

5 Whose possessors slay them, and hold themselves not guilty: and they that sell them say, Blessed *be* the LORD; for I am rich: and their own shepherds pity them not.

Acts 20. 28 Take heed therefore unto yourselves, and to all the flock, over the which the Holy Ghost hath made you

(CONCLUDED). TIME, NOVEMBER, A. D. 29; PLACE, JERUSALEM.

D—CONCLUDED.

Isa. 44. 18 They have not known nor understood: for he hath shut their eyes, that they cannot see; *and* their hearts, that they cannot understand.

Matt.13. 13 Therefore speak I to them in parables: because they seeing see not; and hearing they hear not, neither do they understand.

Rom.11. 8 (According as it is written, God hath given them the spirit of slumber, eyes that they should not see, and ears that they should not hear;) unto this day.

9 And David saith, Let their table be made a snare, and a trap, and a stumblingblock, and a recompense unto them:

10 Let their eyes be darkened, that they may not see, and bow down their back alway.

E

Rom. 2. 19 And art confident that thou thyself art a guide of the blind, a light of them which are in darkness.

F

John 15. 22 If I had not come and spoken unto them, they had not had sin; but now they have no cloak for their sin.

John 15. 24 If I had not done among them the works which none other man did, they had not had sin: but now have they both seen and hated both me and my Father.

CHAP. 9.

35 Jesus heard that they had cast
him out; and when he had found him,
he said unto him, Dost thou believe on
[a]the Son of God?

36 He answered and said, Who is
he, Lord, that I might believe on him?

37 And Jesus said unto him, Thou
hast both seen him, and [b]it is he that
talketh with thee.

38 And he said, Lord, I believe.
And he worshipped him.

39 And Jesus said, [c]For judgment I
am come into this world, [d]that they
which see not might see; and that they
which see might be made blind.

40 And *some* of the Pharisees which
were with him heard these words [e]and
said unto him, Are we blind also?

41 Jesus said unto them, [f]If ye were
blind, ye should have no sin: but now
ye say, We see; therefore your sin
remaineth.

OF THE BLIND MAN. TIME, NOVEMBER, A. D. 29; PLACE, JERUSALEM.

B—CONCLUDED.

overseers, to feed the church of God, which he hath purchased with his own blood.

I Cor.12. 28 And God hath set some in the church, first apostles, secondarily prophets, thirdly teachers, after that miracles, then gifts of healings, helps, governments, diversities of tongues.

C

I Cor.16. 9 For a great door and effectual is opened unto me, and *there are* many adversaries.

Col. 4. 3 Withal praying also for us, that God would open unto us a door of utterance, to speak the mystery of Christ, for which I am also in bonds:

I Pet. 1. 12 Unto whom it was revealed, that not unto themselves, but unto us they did minister the things, which are now reported unto you by them that have preached the gospel unto you

10: 1–21.

1 Verily, verily, I say unto you, [a]He
that entereth not by the door into the
sheepfold, but climbeth up some other
way, the same is a thief and a robber.

2 But he that [b]entereth in by the
door is the shepherd of the sheep.

3 To him the [c]porter openeth; and
the sheep hear his voice: and he calleth his own sheep by name, and leadeth them out.

4 And when he putteth forth his own
sheep, he goeth before them, and the
sheep follow him: for they know his voice.

C—CONCLUDED.

with the Holy Ghost sent down from heaven; which things the angels desire to look into.

§ 118. THE GOOD SHEPHERD: DISCOURSE SUBSEQUENT TO THE HEALING

D

Prov.19. 27 Cease, my son, to hear the instruction *that causeth* to err from the words of knowledge.

Mark 4. 24 And he said unto them, Take heed what ye hear. With what measure ye mete, it shall be measured to you; and unto you that hear shall more be given.

Gal. 1. 8 But though we, or an angel from heaven, preach any other gospel unto you than that which we have preached unto you, let him be accursed.

Eph. 4. 14 That we *henceforth* be no more children, tossed to and fro, and carried about with every wind of doctrine, by the sleight of men, *and* cunning craftiness, whereby they lie in wait to deceive;

E

Eph. 2. 18 For through him we both have access by one Spirit unto the Father.

Heb. 10. 19 Having therefore, brethren, boldness to enter into the holiest by the blood of Jesus,

F

Jer. 23. 1 Woe be unto the pastors that destroy and scatter the sheep of my pasture! saith the LORD.

Jer. 50. 6 My people hath been lost sheep: their shepherds have caused them to go astray, they have turned them away *on* the mountains: they have gone from mountain to hill, they have forgotten their resting place.

Eze.22. 25 *There is* a conspiracy of her prophets in the midst thereof, like a roaring lion ravening the prey: they have devoured souls; they have taken the treasure and precious things; they have made her many widows in the midst thereof.

Zech. 11. 4, 5. *See under B, page 348.*

Zech.11. 6 For I will no more pity the inhabitants of the land, saith the LORD: but, lo, I will deliver the men every one into his neighbour's hand, and into the hand of his king: and they shall smite the land, and out of their hand I will not deliver *them.*

G

John 14. 6 Jesus saith unto him, I am the way, the truth, and the life: no man cometh unto the Father, but by me.

Eph. 2. 18. *See under E.*

H

Acts 20. 29 For I know this, that after my departing shall grievous wolves enter in among you, not sparing the flock.

II Pet.2. 1 But there were false prophets also among the people, even as there shall

H—CONCLUDED.

be false teachers among you, who privily shall bring in damnable heresies, even denying the Lord that bought them, and bring upon themselves swift destruction.

I

Matt.18. 11 For the Son of man is come to save that which was lost.

John 3. 17 For God sent not his Son into the world to condemn the world; but that the world through him might be saved.

John 5. 45 Do not think that I will accuse you to the Father: there is *one* that accuseth you, *even* Moses, in whom ye trust.

John 8. 15 Ye judge after the flesh; I judge no man.

John 12. 47 And if any man hear my words, and believe not, I judge him not: for I came not to judge the world, but to save the world.

I Jno.4. 14 And we have seen and do testify that the Father sent the Son *to be* the Saviour of the world.

K

Isa. 40. 11 He shall feed his flock like a shepherd: he shall gather the lambs with his arm, and carry *them* in his bosom, *and* shall gently lead those that are with young.

Eze. 34. 12 As a shepherd seeketh out his flock in the day that he is among his sheep *that are* scattered; so will I seek out my sheep, and will deliver them out of all places where they have been scattered in the cloudy and dark day.

Eze. 34. 23 And I will set up one Shepherd over them, and he shall feed them, *even* my servant David; he shall feed them, and he shall be their shepherd.

Eze. 37. 24 And David my servant *shall be* king over them; and they all shall have one shepherd: they shall also walk in my judgments, and observe my statutes, and do them.

Heb. 13. 20 Now the God of peace, that brought again from the dead our Lord Jesus, that great Shepherd of the sheep, through the blood of the everlasting covenant,

I Pet. 2. 25 For ye were as sheep going astray; but are now returned unto the Shepherd and Bishop of your souls.

I Pet. 5. 4 And when the chief Shepherd shall appear, ye shall receive a crown of glory that fadeth not away.

OF THE BLIND MAN (CONTINUED). TIME, NOVEMBER, A. D. 29: PLACE, JERUSALEM

L

Zech.11. 16 For, lo, I will raise up a shepherd in the land, *which* shall not visit those that be cut off, neither shall seek the young one, nor heal that that is broken, nor feed that that standeth still: but he shall eat the flesh of the fat, and tear their claws in pieces.

17 Woe to the idol shepherd that leaveth the flock! the sword *shall be* upon his arm, and upon his right eye: his arm shall be clean dried up, and his right eye shall be utterly darkened.

II Tim.4. 10 For Demas hath forsaken me, having loved this present world, and is departed unto Thessalonica; Crescens to Galatia, Titus unto Dalmatia.

M

II Tim.2. 19 Nevertheless the foundation of God standeth sure, having this seal, The Lord knoweth them that are his. And, Let every one that nameth the name of Christ depart from iniquity.

Eph. 1. 17 That the God of our Lord Jesus Christ, the Father of glory, may give unto you the spirit of wisdom and revelation in the knowledge of him:

Phil. 3. 10 That I may know him, and the power of his resurrection, and the fellowship of his sufferings, being made conformable unto his death:

I Jno. 5. 20 And we know that the Son of God is come, and hath given us an understanding, that we may know him that is true; and we are in him that is true, *even* in his Son Jesus Christ. This is the true God, and eternal life.

N

Matt.11. 27 All things are delivered unto me of my Father: and no man knoweth the Son, but the Father; neither knoweth any man the Father, save the Son, and *he* to whomsoever the Son will reveal *him*.

O

Matt.20. 28 Even as the Son of man came not to be ministered unto, but to minister, and to give his life a ransom for many.

John 15. 13 Greater love hath no man than this, that a man lay down his life for his friends.

Gal. 1. 4 Who gave himself for our sins, that he might deliver us from this present evil world, according to the will of God and our Father:

Eph. 5. 2 And walk in love, as Christ also hath loved us, and hath given himself for us an offering and a sacrifice to God for a sweetsmelling savour.

CHAP. 10.

5 And a [d]stranger will they not follow, but will flee from him; for they know not the voice of strangers.

6 This parable spake Jesus unto them; but they understood not what things they were which he spake unto them.

7 Then said Jesus unto them again, Verily, verily, I say unto you, I am the [e]door of the sheep.

8 All that [f]ever came before me are thieves and robbers: but the sheep did not hear them.

9 [g]I am the door: by me if any man enter in, he shall be saved, and shall go in and out, and find pasture.

10 The [h]thief cometh not, but for to steal, and to kill, and to destroy: [i]I am come that they might have life, and that they might have *it* more abundantly.

11 [k]I am the good shepherd: the good shepherd giveth his life for the sheep.

12 But he that is a hireling, and not the shepherd, whose own the sheep are not, seeth the wolf coming, and [l]leaveth the sheep, and fleeth; and the wolf catcheth them, and scattereth the sheep.

13 The hireling fleeth, because he is a hireling, and careth not for the sheep.

14 I am the good shepherd, and [m]know my *sheep*, and am known of mine.

15 [n]As the Father knoweth me, even so know I the Father: and [o]I lay down my life for the sheep.

§ 118. THE GOOD SHEPHERD: DISCOURSE SUBSEQUENT TO THE HEALING

P

Isa. 56. 8 The Lord GOD which gathereth the outcasts of Israel saith, Yet will I gather *others* to him, besides those that are gathered unto him.

Isa. 60. 3 And the Gentiles shall come to thy light, and kings to the brightness of thy rising.

Zech. 2. 11 And many nations shall be joined to the LORD in that day, and shall be my people: and I will dwell in the midst of thee, and thou shalt know that the LORD of hosts hath sent me unto thee.

Q

Eccl. 12. 11 The words of the wise *are* as goads, and as nails fastened *by* the masters of assemblies, *which* are given from one shepherd.

Eze. 34. 23 And I will set up one Shepherd over them, and he shall feed them, *even* my servant David; he shall feed them, and he shall be their shepherd.

Eze. 37. 22 And I will make them one nation in the land upon the mountains of Israel; and one king shall be king to them all: and they shall be no more two nations, neither shall they be divided into two kingdoms any more at all:

Eph. 2. 14 For he is our peace, who hath made both one, and hath broken down the middle wall of partition *between us:*

Heb. 13. 20 Now the God of peace, that brought again from the dead our Lord Jesus, that great Shepherd of the sheep, through the blood of the everlasting covenant,

I Pet. 2. 25. *See under K, page 350.*

R

Isa. 53. 7 He was oppressed, and he was afflicted, yet he opened not his mouth: he is brought as a lamb to the slaughter, and as a sheep before her shearers is dumb, so he openeth not his mouth.

8 He was taken from prison and from judgment: and who shall declare his generation? for he was cut off out of the land of the living: for the transgression of my people was he stricken.

Isa. 53. 12 Therefore will I divide him *a portion* with the great, and he shall divide the spoil with the strong; because he hath poured out his soul unto death: and he was numbered with the transgressors; and he bare the sin of many, and made intercession for the transgressors.

Heb. 2. 9 But we see Jesus, who was made a little lower than the angels for the suffering of death, crowned with glory and honour; that he by the grace of God should taste death for every man.

S

John 2. 19 Jesus answered and said unto them, Destroy this temple, and in three days I will raise it up.

T

John 6. 38 For I came down from heaven, not to do mine own will, but the will of him that sent me.

John 15. 10 If ye keep my commandments, ye shall abide in my love; even as I have kept my Father's commandments, and abide in his love.

Acts 2. 24 Whom God hath raised up, having loosed the pains of death: because

§ 119. JESUS AT THE FEAST OF THE DEDICATION.

A

Acts 3. 11 And as the lame man which was healed held Peter and John, all the people ran together unto them in the porch that is called Solomon's, greatly wondering.

Acts 5. 12 And by the hands of the apostles were many signs and wonders wrought among the people; (and they were all with one accord in Solomon's porch.

B

I Ki. 18. 21 And Elijah came unto all the people, and said, How long halt ye between two opinions? if the LORD *be* God, follow him: but if Baal, *then* follow him. And the people answered him not a word.

Matt. 11. 2 Now when John had heard in the

B—CONCLUDED.

prison the works of Christ, he sent two of his disciples,

3 And said unto him, Art thou he that should come, or do we look for another?

Luke 3. 15 And as the people were in expectation, and all men mused in their hearts of John, whether he were the Christ, or not;

1

Or, *hold us in suspense?*

C

Luke 22. 67 Art thou the Christ? tell us. And he said unto them, If I tell you, ye will not believe:

68 And if I also ask *you*, ye will not answer me, nor let *me* go.

OF THE BLIND MAN (CONCLUDED). TIME, NOVEMBER, A. D. 29; PLACE, JERUSALEM.

T—CONCLUDED.

it was not possible that he should be holden of it.

Acts 2. 32 This Jesus hath God raised up, whereof we all are witnesses.

U

John 7. 43 So there was a division among the people because of him.

John 9. 16 Therefore said some of the Pharisees, This man is not of God, because he keepeth not the sabbath day. Others said, How can a man that is a sinner do such miracles? And there was a division among them.

X

John 7. 20 The people answered and said, Thou hast a devil: who goeth about to kill thee?

John 8. 48 Then answered the Jews, and said unto him, Say we not well that thou art a Samaritan, and hast a devil?

John 8. 52 Then said the Jews unto him, Now we know that thou hast a devil. Abraham is dead, and the prophets; and thou sayest, If a man keep my saying, he shall never taste of death.

Y

Ex. 4. 11 And the LORD said unto him, Who hath made man's mouth? or who maketh the dumb, or deaf, or the seeing, or the blind? have not I the LORD?

Ps. 94. 9 He that planted the ear, shall he not hear? he that formed the eye, shall he not see?

Ps. 146. 8 The LORD openeth *the eyes of* the blind: the LORD raiseth them that are bowed down: the LORD loveth the righteous:

CHAP. 10.

16 And [p]other sheep I have, which are not of this fold: them also I must bring, and they shall hear my voice: [q]and there shall be one fold, *and* one shepherd.

17 Therefore doth my Father love me, [r]because I lay down my life, that I might take it again.

18 No man taketh it from me, but I lay it down of myself. I [s]have power to lay it down, and I have power to take it again. [t]This commandment have I received of my Father.

19 [u]There was a division therefore again among the Jews for these sayings.

20 And many of them said, [x]He hath a devil, and is mad; why hear ye him?

21 Others said, These are not the words of him that hath a devil. [y]Can a devil [z]open the eyes of the blind?

Z

John 9. 6, 7. *See text of* § *117.*

John 9. 32, 33. *See text of* § *117.*

TIME, DECEMBER, A. D. 29; PLACE, JERUSALEM.

C—CONTINUED.

Luke 22. 69 Hereafter shall the Son of man sit on the right hand of the power of God.

70 Then said they all, Art thou then the Son of God? And he said unto them, ye say that I am.

John 1. 19 And this is the record of John, when the Jews sent priests and Levites from Jerusalem to ask him, Who art thou?

John 8. 25 Then said they unto him, Who art thou? And Jesus saith unto them, Even *the same* that I said unto you from the beginning.

John 9. 22 These *words* spake his parents, because they feared the Jews: for the Jews had agreed already, that if any man

10: 22–39.

22 And it was at Jerusalem the feast of the dedication, and it was winter.

23 And Jesus walked in the temple [a]in Solomon's porch.

24 Then came the Jews round about him, and said unto him, [b]How long dost thou [1]make us to doubt? [c]If thou be the Christ, tell us plainly.

C—CONCLUDED.

did confess that he was Christ, he should be put out of the synagogue.

II Cor. 3. 12 Seeing then that we have such hope, we use great plainness of speech:

§ 119. JESUS AT THE FEAST OF THE DEDICATION

D

John 3. 2 The same came to Jesus by night, and said unto him, Rabbi, we know that thou art a teacher come from God: for no man can do these miracles that thou doest, except God be with him.

John 5. 36 But I have greater witness than *that* of John: for the works which the Father hath given me to finish, the same works that I do, bear witness of me, that the Father hath sent me.

John 10. 38. *See text of topic.*

E

John 8. 47 He that is of God heareth God's words: ye therefore hear *them* not, because ye are not of God.

I Jno. 4. 6 We are of God: he that knoweth God heareth us; he that is not of God heareth not us. Hereby know we the spirit of truth, and the spirit of error.

F

John 10. 4 And when he putteth forth his own sheep, he goeth before them, and the sheep follow him: for they know his voice.

John 10. 14 I am the good shepherd, and know my *sheep*, and am known of mine.

Heb. 3. 7 Wherefore as the Holy Ghost saith, To day if ye will hear his voice,

8 Harden not your hearts, as in the provocation, in the day of temptation in the wilderness:

Rev. 3. 20 Behold, I stand at the door, and knock: if any man hear my voice, and open the door, I will come in to him, and will sup with him, and he with me.

G

John 6. 37 All that the Father giveth me shall come to me; and him that cometh to me I will in no wise cast out.

John 17. 11 And now I am no more in the world, but these are in the world, and I come to thee. Holy Father, keep through thine own name those whom thou hast given me, that they may be one, as we *are*.

12 While I was with them in the world, I kept them in thy name: those that thou gavest me I have kept, and none of them is lost, but the son of perdition; that the Scripture might be fulfilled.

John 18. 9 That the saying might be fulfilled, which he spake, Of them which thou gavest me have I lost none.

H

John 17. 2 As thou hast given him power

H—Concluded.

over all flesh, that he should give eternal life to as many as thou hast given him.

John 17. 6 I have manifested thy name unto the men which thou gavest me out of the world: thine they were, and thou gavest them me; and they have kept thy word.

7 Now they have known that all things whatsoever thou hast given me are of thee.

8 For I have given unto them the words which thou gavest me; and they have received *them*, and have known surely that I came out from thee, and they have believed that thou didst send me.

9 I pray for them: I pray not for the world, but for them which thou hast given me; for they are thine.

10 And all mine are thine, and thine are mine; and I am glorified in them.

John 17. 11, 12. *See under G.*

I

John 8. 59 Then took they up stones to cast at him: but Jesus hid himself, and went out of the temple, going through the midst of them, and so passed by.

K

John 5. 18 Therefore the Jews sought the more to kill him, because he not only had broken the sabbath, but said also that God was his Father, making himself equal with God.

L

Ex. 22. 28 Thou shalt not revile the gods, nor curse the ruler of thy people.

Ps. 82. 1 God standeth in the congregation of the mighty; he judgeth among the gods.

Ps. 82. 6 I have said, Ye *are* gods; and all of you *are* children of the Most High.

Ps. 138. 1 I will praise thee with my whole heart: before the gods will I sing praise unto thee.

Isa. 56. 5 Even unto them will I give in mine house and within my walls a place and a name better than of sons and of daughters: I will give them an everlasting name, that shall not be cut off.

John 1. 12 But as many as received him, to them gave he power to become the sons of God, *even* to them that believe on his name:

Rom. 8. 14 For as many as are led by the Spirit of God, they are the sons of God.

(CONTINUED). TIME, DECEMBER, A. D. 29; PLACE, JERUSALEM.

M

Matt. 5. 18 For verily I say unto you, Till heaven and earth pass, one jot or one tittle shall in no wise pass from the law, till all be fulfilled.

Acts 1. 16 Men *and* brethren, this scripture must needs have been fulfilled, which the Holy Ghost by the mouth of David spake before concerning Judas, which was guide to them that took Jesus.

Rom.13. 1 Let every soul be subject unto the higher powers. For there is no power but of God: the powers that be are ordained of God.

N

John 6. 27 Labour not for the meat which perisheth, but for that meat which endureth unto everlasting life, which the Son of man shall give unto you: for him hath God the Father sealed.

O

John 3. 17 For God sent not his Son into the world to condemn the world; but that the world through him might be saved.

John 5. 30 I can of mine own self do nothing: as I hear, I judge: and my judgment is just; because I seek not mine own will, but the will of the Father which hath sent me.

John 5. 36. *See under D.*

John 5. 37 And the Father himself, which hath sent me, hath borne witness of me. Ye have neither heard his voice at any time, nor seen his shape.

John 8. 42 Jesus said unto them, If God were your Father, ye would love me: for I proceeded forth and came from God; neither came I of myself, but he sent me.

P

John 5. 17 But Jesus answered them, My Father worketh hitherto, and I work.

John 5. 18. *See under K.*

John 10. 30. *See text of topic.*

John 18. 8 Jesus answered, I have told you that I am *he:* if therefore ye seek me, let these go their way:

Q

Luke 1. 35 And the angel answered and said unto her, The Holy Ghost shall come upon thee, and the power of the Highest shall overshadow thee: therefore also that holy thing which shall be born of thee shall be called the Son of God.

John 9. 35 Jesus heard that they had cast him out; and when he had found him, he said unto him, Dost thou believe on the Son of God?

CHAP. 10.

25 Jesus answered them, I told you, and ye believed not: [d]the works that I do in my Father's name, they bear witness of me.

26 But [e]ye believe not, because ye are not of my sheep, as I said unto you.

27 [f]My sheep hear my voice, and I know them, and they follow me:

28 And I give unto them eternal life; and [g]they shall never perish, neither shall any *man* pluck them out of my hand.

29 My Father, [h]which gave *them* me, is greater than all; and no *man* is able to pluck *them* out of my Father's hand.

30 I and *my* Father are one.

31 Then [i]the Jews took up stones again to stone him.

32 Jesus answered them, Many good works have I showed you from my Father; for which of those works do ye stone me?

33 The Jews answered him, saying, For a good work we stone thee not; but for blasphemy; and because that thou, being a man, [k]makest thyself God.

34 Jesus answered them, [l]Is it not written in your law, I said, Ye are gods?

35 If he called them gods, [m]unto whom the word of God came, and the Scripture cannot be broken;

36 Say ye of him, [n]whom the Father hath sanctified, and [o]sent into the world, Thou blasphemest; [p]because I said, I am [q]the Son of God?

§ 119. JESUS AT THE FEAST OF THE DEDICATION

R

John 15. 24 If I had not done among them the works which none other man did, they had not had sin: but now have they both seen and hated both me and my Father.

S

John 5. 36. *See under D, page 354.*

John 14. 10 Believest thou not that I am in the Father, and the Father in me? the words that I speak unto you I speak not of myself: but the Father that dwelleth in me, he doeth the works.

11 Believe me that I *am* in the

S—Concluded.

Father, and the Father in me: or else believe me for the very works' sake.

T

John 10. 30. *See text of topic.*
John 14. 10, 11. *See under S.*

John 14. 20 At that day ye shall know that I *am* in my Father, and ye in me, and I in you.

John 17. 12. *See under G, page 354.*

U

Luke 4. 29 And rose up, and thrust him out of the city, and led him unto the brow of the hill whereon their city

§ 120. HE RETIRES BEYOND JORDAN.

A

John 1. 28 These things were done in Bethabara beyond Jordan, where John was baptizing.

John 3. 26 And they came unto John, and said unto him, Rabbi, he that was with thee beyond Jordan, to whom thou barest witness, behold, the same baptizeth, and all *men* come to him.

John 11. 54 Jesus therefore walked no more openly among the Jews; but went thence unto a country near to the wilderness, into a city called Ephraim, and there continued with his disciples.

B

Matt. 14. 2 And said unto his servants, This is John the Baptist; he is risen from the dead; and therefore mighty works do show forth themselves in him.

C

Matt. 3. 11 I indeed baptize you with water unto repentance: but he that cometh after me is mightier than I, whose shoes I am not worthy to bear: he shall baptize you with the Holy Ghost, and *with* fire:

12 Whose fan *is* in his hand, and he will thoroughly purge his floor,

§ 121. THE RAISING OF LAZARUS.

A

Luke 10. 38 Now it came to pass, as they went, that he entered into a certain village: and a certain woman named Martha received him into her house.

39 And she had a sister called Mary, which also sat at Jesus' feet, and heard his word.

B

Matt. 26. 7 There came unto him a woman having an alabaster box of very precious ointment, and poured it on his head, as he sat *at meat.*

Mark 14. 3 And being in Bethany, in the house of Simon the leper, as he sat at meat, there came a woman having an alabaster box of ointment of spikenard very precious; and she brake the box, and poured *it* on his head.

Luke 7. 37 And, behold, a woman in the city, which was a sinner, when she knew that *Jesus* sat at meat in the Pharisee's house, brought an alabaster box of ointment,

John 12. 3 Then took Mary a pound of oint-

B—Concluded.

ment of spikenard, very costly, and anointed the feet of Jesus, and wiped his feet with her hair: and the house was filled with the odour of the ointment.

C

Gen. 22. 2 And he said, take now thy son, thine only *son* Isaac, whom thou lovest, and get thee into the land of Moriah; and offer him there for a burnt offering upon one of the mountains which I will tell thee of.

Ps. 16. 3 *But* to the saints that *are* in the earth, and *to* the excellent, in whom *is* all my delight.

Phil. 2. 26 For he longed after you all, and was full of heaviness, because that ye had heard that he had been sick.

27 For indeed he was sick nigh unto death: but God had mercy on him; and not on him only, but on me also, lest I should have sorrow upon sorrow.

Heb. 12. 6 For whom the Lord loveth he chasteneth, and scourgeth every son whom he receiveth.

(CONCLUDED). TIME, DECEMBER, A. D. 29; PLACE, JERUSALEM.

U—CONCLUDED.

was built, that they might cast him down headlong.

30 But he passing through the midst of them went his way,

John 7. 30 Then they sought to take him: but no man laid hands on him, because his hour was not yet come.

John 7. 44 And some of them would have taken him; but no man laid hands on him.

John 8. 59 Then took they up stones to cast at him: but Jesus hid himself, and went out of the temple, going through the midst of them, and so passed by.

CHAP. 10.

37 [r]If I do not the works of my Father, believe me not.

38 But if I do, though ye believe not me, [s]believe the works; [t]that ye may know, and believe, that the Father *is* in me, and I in him.

39 [u]Therefore they sought again to take him; but he escaped out of their hand,

TIME, DECEMBER, A. D. 29; PLACE, BETHANY BEYOND JORDAN [BETHABARA].

C—CONCLUDED.

and gather his wheat into the garner; but he will burn up the chaff with unquenchable fire.

John 3. 30 He must increase, but I *must* decrease.

D

John 4. 41 And many more believed because of his own word;

John 8. 30 As he spake these words, many believed on him.

John 11. 45 Then many of the Jews which came to Mary, and had seen the things which Jesus did, believed on him.

10: 40–42.

40 And went away again beyond Jordan into the place [a]where John at first baptized; and there he abode.

41 And many resorted unto him, and said, [b]John did no miracle: [c]but all things that John spake of this man were true.

42 [d]And many believed on him there.

TIME, JANUARY–FEBRUARY, A. D. 30; PLACE, BETHANY.

C—CONCLUDED.

Heb. 12. 7 If ye endure chastening, God dealeth with you as with sons; for what son is he whom the father chasteneth not?

Rev. 3. 19 As many as I love, I rebuke and chasten: be zealous therefore, and repent.

D

John 9. 3 Jesus answered, Neither hath this man sinned, nor his parents: but that the works of God should be made manifest in him.

John 11. 40. *See text of topic.*

Phil. 1. 20 According to my earnest expectation and *my* hope, that in nothing I shall be ashamed, but *that* with all boldness, as always, *so* now also Christ shall be magnified in my body, whether *it be* by life, or by death.

I Pet. 1. 21 Who by him do believe in God, that raised him up from the dead, and gave him glory; that your faith and hope might be in God.

11: 1–44.

1 Now a certain *man* was sick, *named* Lazarus, of Bethany, the town of [a]Mary and her sister Martha.

2 [b](It was *that* Mary which anointed the Lord with ointment, and wiped his feet with her hair, whose brother Lazarus was sick.)

3 Therefore his sisters sent unto him, saying, Lord, behold, [c]he whom thou lovest is sick.

4 When Jesus heard *that*, he said, This sickness is not unto death, [d]but for the glory of God, that the Son of God might be glorified thereby.

5 Now Jesus loved Martha, and her sister, and Lazarus.

§ 121. THE RAISING OF LAZARUS (Continued).

E

John 10. 40 And went away again beyond Jordan into the place where John at first baptized; and there he abode.

F

Ps. 11. 1 In the Lord put I my trust; how say ye to my soul, Flee *as* a bird to your mountain?

2 For, lo, the wicked bend *their* bow, they make ready their arrow upon the string, that they may privily shoot at the upright in heart.

John 10. 31 Then the Jews took up stones again to stone him.

Acts 20. 24 But none of these things move me, neither count I my life dear unto myself, so that I might finish my course with joy, and the ministry, which I have received of the Lord Jesus, to testify the gospel of the grace of God.

Acts 21. 12 And when we heard these things, both we, and they of that place, besought him not to go up to Jerusalem.

13 Then Paul answered, What mean ye to weep and to break mine heart? for I am ready not to be bound only, but also to die at Jerusalem for the name of the Lord Jesus.

G

Jer. 13. 16 Give glory to the Lord your God, before he cause darkness, and before your feet stumble upon the dark mountains, and, while ye look for light, he turn it into the shadow of death, *and* make *it* gross darkness.

Jer. 31 9 They shall come with weeping, and with supplications will I lead them: I will cause them to walk by the rivers of waters in a straight way, wherein they shall not stumble: for I am a father to Israel, and Ephraim *is* my first-born.

John 9. 4 I must work the works of him that sent me, while it is day: the night cometh, when no man can work.

John 12. 35 Then Jesus said unto them, Yet a little while is the light with you. Walk while ye have the light, lest darkness come upon you: for he that walketh in darkness knoweth not whither he goeth.

Eph. 5. 8 For ye were sometimes darkness, but now *are ye* light in the Lord: walk as children of light:

H

Ps. 27. 2 When the wicked, *even* mine enemies and my foes, came upon me to eat up my flesh, they stumbled and fell.

Prov. 4. 18 But the path of the just *is* as the

H—Concluded.

shining light, that shineth more and more unto the perfect day.

19 The way of the wicked *is* as darkness: they know not at what they stumble.

Eccl. 2. 14 The wise man's eyes *are* in his head; but the fool walketh in darkness: and I myself perceived also that one event happeneth to them all.

Jer. 13. 16. *See under G.*

Jer. 20. 11 But the Lord *is* with me as a mighty terrible one: therefore my persecutors shall stumble, and they shall not prevail: they shall be greatly ashamed; for they shall not prosper: *their* everlasting confusion shall never be forgotten.

John 8. 12 Then spake Jesus again unto them, saying, I am the light of the world: he that followeth me shall not walk in darkness, but shall have the light of life.

John 12. 35. *See under G.*

Eph. 5. 14 Wherefore he saith, Awake thou that sleepest, and arise from the dead, and Christ shall give thee light.

15 See then that ye walk circumspectly, not as fools, but as wise,

I Jno. 2. 10 He that loveth his brother abideth in the light, and there is none occasion of stumbling in him.

11 But he that hateth his brother is in darkness, and walketh in darkness, and knoweth not whither he goeth, because that darkness hath blinded his eyes.

I

Ex. 33. 11 And the Lord spake unto Moses face to face, as a man speaketh unto his friend. And he turned again into the camp; but his servant Joshua, the son of Nun, a young man, departed not out of the tabernacle.

II Chr. 20. 7 *Art* not thou our God, *who* didst drive out the inhabitants of this land before thy people Israel, and gavest it to the seed of Abraham thy friend for ever?

Isa. 41. 8 But thou, Israel, *art* my servant, Jacob whom I have chosen, the seed of Abraham my friend.

Jas. 2. 23 And the Scripture was fulfilled which saith, Abraham believed God, and it was imputed unto him for righteousness: and he was called the Friend of God.

K

Deut. 31. 16 And the Lord said unto Moses, Behold, thou shalt sleep with thy

TIME, JANUARY–FEBRUARY, A. D. 30; PLACE, BETHANY.

K—CONCLUDED.

fathers; and this people will rise up, and go a whoring after the gods of the strangers of the land, whither they go *to be* among them, and will forsake me, and break my covenant which I have made with them.

Dan. 12. 2 And many of them that sleep in the dust of the earth shall awake, some to everlasting life, and some to shame *and* everlasting contempt.

Matt. 9. 24 He said unto them, Give place: for the maid is not dead, but sleepeth. And they laughed him to scorn.

Acts 7. 60 And he kneeled down, and cried with a loud voice, Lord, lay not this sin to their charge. And when he had said this, he fell asleep.

I Cor.15. 18 Then they also which are fallen asleep in Christ are perished.

I Cor.15. 51 Behold, I show you a mystery; We shall not all sleep, but we shall all be changed,

L

Gen. 26. 24 And the LORD appeared unto him the same night, and said, I *am* the God of Abraham thy father: fear not, for I *am* with thee, and will bless thee, and multiply thy seed for my servant Abraham's sake.

Gen. 39. 5 And it came to pass from the time *that* he had made him overseer in his house, and over all that he had, that the LORD blessed the Egyptian's house for Joseph's sake; and the blessing of the LORD was upon all that he had in the house, and in the field.

Ps. 105. 14 He suffered no man to do them wrong: yea, he reproved kings for their sakes;

Isa. 54. 15 Behold, they shall surely gather together, *but* not by me: whosoever shall gather together against thee shall fall for thy sake.

Isa. 65. 8 Thus saith the LORD, As the new wine is found in the cluster, and *one* saith, Destroy it not; for a blessing *is* in it: so will I do for my servants' sake, that I may not destroy them all.

John 12. 30 Jesus answered and said, This voice came not because of me, but for your sakes.

II Cor.4. 15 For all things *are* for your sakes, that the abundant grace might through the thanksgiving of many redound to the glory of God.

II Tim.2. 10 Therefore I endure all things for the elect's sakes, that they may also obtain the salvation which is in Christ Jesus with eternal glory.

CHAP. 11.

6 When he had heard therefore that he was sick, [e]he abode two days still in the same place where he was.

7 Then after that saith he to *his* disciples, Let us go into Judæa again.

8 *His* disciples say unto him, Master, [f]the Jews of late sought to stone thee; and goest thou thither again?

9 Jesus answered, Are there not twelve hours in the day? [g]If any man walk in the day, he stumbleth not, because he seeth the light of this world.

10 [h]But if a man walk in the night, he stumbleth, because there is no light in him.

11 These things said he: and after that he saith unto them, Our [i]friend Lazarus [k]sleepeth; but I go, that I may awake him out of sleep.

12 Then said his disciples, Lord, if he sleep, he shall do well.

13 Howbeit Jesus spake of his death: but they thought that he had spoken of taking of rest in sleep.

14 Then said Jesus unto them plainly, Lazarus is dead.

15 And I am glad [l]for your sakes that I was not there, to the intent ye may believe: nevertheless let us go unto him.

16 Then said Thomas, which is called Didymus, unto his fellow disciples, Let us also go, that we may die with him.

17 Then when Jesus came, he found that he had *lain* in the grave four days already.

18 Now Bethany was nigh unto Jerusalem, about fifteen furlongs off:

§ 121. THE RAISING OF LAZARUS (Continued).

M

John 9. 31 Now we know that God heareth not sinners: but if any man be a worshipper of God, and doeth his will, him he heareth.

N

Ps. 17. 13 Arise, O Lord, disappoint him, cast him down: deliver my soul from the wicked, *which is* thy sword:

14 From men *which are* thy hand, O Lord, from men of the world, *which have* their portion in *this* life, and whose belly thou fillest with thy hid *treasure:* they are full of children, and leave the rest of their *substance* to their babes.

15 As for me, I will behold thy face in righteousness: I shall be satisfied, when I awake, with thy likeness.

Ps. 49. 14 Like sheep they are laid in the grave; death shall feed on them; and the upright shall have dominion over them in the morning; and their beauty shall consume in the grave from their dwelling.

15 But God will redeem my soul from the power of the grave: for he shall receive me. Selah.

Isa. 25. 8 He will swallow up death in victory; and the Lord God will wipe away tears from off all faces; and the rebuke of his people shall he take away from off all the earth: for the Lord hath spoken *it.*

Isa. 26. 19 Thy dead *men* shall live, *together with* my dead body shall they arise. Awake and sing, ye that dwell in dust: for thy dew *is as* the dew of herbs, and the earth shall cast out the dead.

Eze. 37. 1-10. *The valley of dry bones.*

Dan. 12. 2 And many of them that sleep in the dust of the earth shall awake, some to everlasting life, and some to shame *and* everlasting contempt.

3 And they that be wise shall shine as the brightness of the firmament; and they that turn many to righteousness, as the stars for ever and ever.

Hos. 6. 2 After two days will he revive us: in the third day he will raise us up, and we shall live in his sight.

Hos. 13. 14 I will ransom them from the power of the grave; I will redeem them from death: O death, I will be thy plagues; O grave, I will be thy destruction: repentance shall be hid from mine eyes.

Luke 14. 14 And thou shalt be blessed; for they cannot recompense thee: for thou

N—Concluded.

shalt be recompensed at the resurrection of the just.

John 5. 29 And shall come forth; they that have done good, unto the resurrection of life; and they that have done evil, unto the resurrection of damnation.

Acts 17. 31 Because he hath appointed a day, in the which he will judge the world in righteousness by *that* man whom he hath ordained; *whereof* he hath given assurance unto all *men,* in that he hath raised him from the dead.

Acts 23. 7 And when he had so said, there arose a dissension between the Pharisees and the Sadducees: and the multitude was divided.

Acts 24. 15 And have hope toward God, which they themselves also allow, that there shall be a resurrection of the dead, both of the just and unjust.

I Thes. 4. 14 For if we believe that Jesus died and rose again, even so them also which sleep in Jesus will God bring with him.

Heb. 11. 35 Women received their dead raised to life again: and others were tortured not accepting deliverance; that they might obtain a better resurrection:

O

John 5. 21 For as the Father raiseth up the dead, and quickeneth *them;* even so the Son quickeneth whom he will.

John 6. 39 And this is the Father's will which hath sent me, that of all which he hath given me I should lose nothing, but should raise it up again at the last day.

40 And this is the will of him that sent me, that every one which seeth the Son, and believeth on him, may have everlasting life: and I will raise him up at the last day.

John 6. 44 No man can come to me, except the Father which hath sent me draw him: and I will raise him up at the last day.

P

Ps. 36. 9 For with thee *is* the fountain of life: in thy light shall we see light.

John 1. 4 In him was life; and the life was the light of men.

John 6. 35 And Jesus said unto them, I am the bread of life: he that cometh to me shall never hunger; and he that believeth on me shall never thirst.

John 14. 6 Jesus saith unto him, I am the way, the truth, and the life: no man cometh unto the Father, but by me.

Col. 3. 4 When Christ, *who is* our life shall

TIME, JANUARY–FEBRUARY, A. D. 30; PLACE, BETHANY.

P—CONCLUDED.

appear, then shall ye also appear with him in glory.

I Jno. 1. 1 That which was from the beginning, which we have heard, which we have seen with our eyes, which we have looked upon, and our hands have handled, of the Word of life;

2 (For the life was manifested, and we have seen *it*, and bear witness, and show unto you that eternal life, which was with the Father, and was manifested unto us;)

I Jno. 5. 11 And this is the record, that God hath given to us eternal life, and this life is in his Son.

Q

John 3. 36 He that believeth on the Son hath everlasting life: and he that believeth not the Son shall not see life; but the wrath of God abideth on him.

I Jno. 5. 10 He that believeth on the Son of God hath the witness in himself: he that believeth not God hath made him a liar; because he believeth not the record that God gave of his Son.

I Jno. 5. 11. *See under P.*

I Jno. 5. 12 He that hath the Son hath life; *and* he that hath not the Son of God hath not life.

13 These things have I written unto you that believe on the name of the Son of God; that ye may know that ye have eternal life, and that ye may believe on the name of the Son of God.

R

Matt. 16. 16 And Simon Peter answered and said, Thou art the Christ, the Son of the living God.

John 4. 42 And said unto the woman, Now we believe, not because of thy saying: for we have heard *him* ourselves, and know that this is indeed the Christ, the Saviour of the world.

John 6. 14 Then those men, when they had seen the miracle that Jesus did, said, This is of a truth that Prophet that should come into the world.

John 6. 69 And we believe and are sure that thou art that Christ, the Son of the living God.

Acts 8. 37 And Philip said, If thou believest with all thine heart, thou mayest. And he answered and said, I believe that Jesus Christ is the Son of God.

I Jno. 5. 1 Whosoever believeth that Jesus is the Christ is born of God: and every one that loveth him that begat loveth him also that is begotten of him.

CHAP. 11.

19 And many of the Jews came to Martha and Mary, to comfort them concerning their brother.

20 Then Martha, as soon as she heard that Jesus was coming, went and met him: but Mary sat *still* in the house.

21 Then said Martha unto Jesus, Lord, if thou hadst been here, my brother had not died.

22 But I know, that even now, [m]whatsoever thou wilt ask of God, God will give *it* thee.

23 Jesus saith unto her, Thy brother shall rise again.

24 Martha saith unto him, [n]I know that he shall rise again in the resurrection at the last day.

25 [o]Jesus said unto her, I am the resurrection, and the [p]life: [q]he that believeth in me, though he were dead, yet shall he live:

26 And whosoever liveth and believeth in me shall never die. Believest thou this?

27 She saith unto him, Yea, Lord: [r]I believe that thou art the Christ, the Son of God, which should come into the world.

28 And when she had so said, she went her way, and called Mary her sister secretly, saying, The Master is come, and calleth for thee.

29 As soon as she heard *that*, she arose quickly, and came unto him.

30 Now Jesus was not yet come into the town, but was in that place where Martha met him.

§ 121. THE RAISING OF LAZARUS (CONTINUED).

S

John 11. 19. *See text of topic.*

T

John 11. 21. *See text of topic.*

U

Mark 3. 5 And when he had looked round about on them with anger, being grieved for the hardness of their hearts, he saith unto the man, Stretch forth thine hand. And he stretched *it* out: and his hand was restored whole as the other.

John 12. 27 Now is my soul troubled; and what shall I say? Father, save me from this hour: but for this cause came I unto this hour.

1

Gr., *he troubled himself.*

X

Isa. 53. 3 He is despised and rejected of men; a man of sorrows, and acquainted with grief: and we hid as it were *our* faces from him; he was despised, and we esteemed him not.

Luke 19. 41 And when he was come near, he beheld the city, and wept over it,

John 14. 21 He that hath my commandments, and keepeth them, he it is that loveth me: and he that loveth me shall be loved of my Father, and I will love him, and will manifest myself to him.

John 15. 10 If ye keep my commandments, ye shall abide in my love; even as I have kept my Father's commandments, and abide in his love.

Heb. 2. 17 Wherefore in all things it behooved him to be made like unto *his* brethren, that he might be a merciful and faithful high priest in things *pertaining* to God, to make reconciliation for the sins of the people.

18 For in that he himself hath suffered being tempted, he is able to succour them that are tempted.

Heb. 4. 15 For we have not an high priest which cannot be touched with the feeling of our infirmities; but was in all points tempted like as *we are, yet* without sin.

Y

II Cor. 8. 8 I speak not by commandment, but by occasion of the forwardness of others, and to prove the sincerity of your love.

9 For ye know the grace of our Lord Jesus Christ, that, though he was rich, yet for your sakes he became poor, that ye through his poverty might be rich.

Eph. 5. 2 And walk in love, as Christ also

Y—CONCLUDED.

hath loved us, and hath given himself for us an offering and a sacrifice to God for a sweetsmelling savour.

Eph. 5. 25 Husbands, love your wives, even as Christ also loved the church, and gave himself for it:

I Jno. 3. 1 Behold, what manner of love the Father hath bestowed upon us, that we should be called the sons of God: therefore the world knoweth us not because it knew him not.

I Jno. 4. 8 He that loveth not, knoweth not God; for God is love.

9 In this was manifested the love of God toward us, because that God sent his only begotten Son into the world, that we might live through him.

10 Herein is love, not that we loved God, but that he loved us, and sent his Son *to be* the propitiation for our sins.

11 Beloved, if God so loved us, we ought also to love one another.

12 No man hath seen God at any time. If we love one another, God dwelleth in us, and his love is perfected in us.

Rev. 1. 5 And from Jesus Christ, *who is* the faithful witness, *and* the first-begotten of the dead, and the prince of the kings of the earth. Unto him that loved us, and washed us from our sins in his own blood.

Z

Ps. 78. 19 Yea, they spake against God; they said, Can God furnish a table in the wilderness?

20 Behold, he smote the rock, that the waters gushed out, and the streams overflowed; can he give bread also? can he provide flesh for his people?

John 9. 6 When he had thus spoken, he spat on the ground, and made clay of the spittle, and he anointed the eyes of the blind man with the clay,

A

Eze. 9. 4 And the LORD said unto him, Go through the midst of the city, through the midst of Jerusalem, and set a mark upon the foreheads of the men that sigh and that cry for all the abominations that be done in the midst thereof.

Eze. 21. 6 Sigh therefore, thou son of man, with the breaking of *thy* loins; and with bitterness sigh before their eyes.

Mark 8. 12 And he sighed deeply in his spirit, and saith, Why doth this generation seek after a sign? verily I

TIME, JANUARY–FEBRUARY, A. D. 30; PLACE, BETHANY.

A—CONCLUDED.

say unto you, There shall no sign be given unto this generation.

B

Gen. 23. 19 And after this, Abraham buried Sarah his wife in the cave of the field of Machpelah before Mamre: the same *is* Hebron in the land of Canaan.

Gen. 49. 29 And he charged them, and said unto them, I am to be gathered unto my people: bury me with my fathers in the cave that *is* in the field of Ephron the Hittite,

30 In the cave that *is* in the field of Machpelah, which *is* before Mamre, in the land of Canaan, which Abraham bought with the field of Ephron the Hittite for a possession of a burying-place.

31 There they buried Abraham and Sarah his wife; there they buried Isaac and Rebekah his wife; and there I buried Leah.

Isa. 22. 16 What hast thou here, and whom hast thou here, that thou hast hewed thee out a sepulchre here, *as* he that heweth him out a sepulchre on high, *and* that graveth a habitation for himself in a rock?

C

II Chr. 20. 20 And they rose early in the morning, and went forth into the wilderness of Tekoa: and as they went forth, Jehoshaphat stood and said, Hear me, O Judah, and ye inhabitants of Jerusalem; Believe in the LORD your God, so shall ye be established; believe his prophets, so shall ye prosper.

Rom. 4. 20 He staggered not at the promise of God through unbelief; but was strong in faith, giving glory to God;

21 And being fully persuaded, that what he had promised, he was able also to perform.

D

Ps. 63. 2 To see thy power and thy glory, so *as* I have seen thee in the sanctuary.

Ps. 90. 16 Let thy work appear unto thy servants, and thy glory unto their children.

John 11. 4. *See text of topic.*
John 11. 23. *See text of topic.*

II Cor. 3. 18 But we all, with open face beholding as in a glass the glory of the Lord, are changed into the same image from glory to glory, *even* as by the Spirit of the Lord.

II Cor. 4. 6 For God, who commanded the light to shine out of darkness, hath shined in our hearts, to *give* the light

CHAP. 11.

31 [s]The Jews then which were with her in the house, and comforted her, when they saw Mary, that she rose up hastily and went out, followed her, saying, She goeth unto the grave to weep there.

32 Then when Mary was come where Jesus was, and saw him, she fell down at his feet, saying unto him, [t]Lord, if thou hadst been here, my brother had not died.

33 When Jesus therefore saw her weeping, and the Jews also weeping which came with her, [u]he groaned in the spirit, and [1]was troubled,

34 And said, Where have ye laid him? They say unto him, Lord, come and see.

35 [x]Jesus wept.

36 Then said the Jews, [y]Behold how he loved him!

37 And some of them said, [z]Could not this man, which opened the eyes of the blind, have caused that even this man should not have died?

38 Jesus therefore again [a]groaning in himself cometh to the grave. [b]It was a cave, and a stone lay upon it.

39 Jesus said, Take ye away the stone. Martha, the sister of him that was dead, saith unto him, Lord, by this time he stinketh: for he hath been *dead* four days.

40 Jesus saith unto her, [c]Said I not unto thee, that, if thou wouldest believe, thou shouldest [d]see the glory of God?

D—CONCLUDED.

of the knowledge of the glory of God in the face of Jesus Christ.

§ 121. THE RAISING OF LAZARUS (CONCLUDED).

E

John 17. 1 These words spake Jesus, and lifted up his eyes to heaven, and said, Father, the hour is come; glorify thy Son, that thy Son also may glorify thee:
2 As thou hast given him power over all flesh, that he should give eternal life to as many as thou hast given him.
Matt. 11. 25 At that time Jesus answered and said, I thank thee, O Father, Lord of heaven and earth, because thou hast hid these things from the wise and prudent, and hast revealed them unto babes.

F

John 12. 30 Jesus answered and said, This voice came not because of me, but for your sakes.

G

Hos. 13. 14 I will ransom them from the power of the grave; I will redeem them from death: O death, I will be thy plagues: O grave, I will be thy destruction: repentance shall be hid from mine eyes.
John 10. 28 And I give unto them eternal life; and they shall never perish, neither shall any *man* pluck them out of my hand.

G—CONCLUDED.

John 10. 29 My Father, which gave *them* me, is greater than all; and no *man* is able to pluck *them* out of my Father's hand.
Acts 20. 9 And there sat in a window a certain young man named Eutychus, being fallen into a deep sleep: and as Paul was long preaching, he sunk down with sleep, and fell down from the third loft, and was taken up dead.
10 And Paul went down, and fell on him and embracing *him* said, Trouble not yourselves; for his life is in him.
11 When he therefore was come up again, and had broken bread, and eaten, and talked a long while, even till break of day, so he departed.
12 And they brought the young man alive, and were not a little comforted.
Rev. 1. 18 *I am* he that liveth, and was dead; and, behold, I am alive for evermore, Amen; and have the keys of hell and of death.

H

Deut. 32. 39 See now that I, *even* I, *am* he, and *there is* no god with me: I kill, and I make alive; I wound, and I heal:

§ 122. THE COUNSEL OF CAIAPHAS AGAINST JESUS. HE RETIRES FROM

A

John 2. 23 Now when he was in Jerusalem at the passover, in the feast *day*, many believed in his name, when they saw the miracles which he did.
John 10. 42 And many believed on him there.
John 12. 11 Because that by reason of him many of the Jews went away, and believed on Jesus.
John 12. 18 For this cause the people also met him, for that they heard that he had done this miracle.

B

Ps. 2. 2 The kings of the earth set themselves, and the rulers take counsel together, against the LORD, and against his Anointed, *saying*,
Matt. 26. 3 Then assembled together the chief priests, and the scribes, and the elders of the people, unto the palace of the high priest, who was called Caiaphas.
Mark 14. 1 After two days was *the feast of* the passover, and of unleavened bread: and the chief priests and the scribes sought how they might take him by craft, and put *him* to death.
Luke 22. 2 And the chief priests and scribes sought how they might kill him; for they feared the people.

C

John 12. 19 The Pharisees therefore said among themselves, Perceive ye how ye prevail nothing? behold, the world is gone after him.
Acts 4. 16 Saying, What shall we do to these men? for that indeed a notable miracle hath been done by them *is* manifest to all them that dwell in Jerusalem; and we cannot deny *it*.

D

Deut. 28. 49 The LORD shall bring a nation against thee from far, from the end of the earth, *as swift* as the eagle flieth; a nation whose tongue thou shalt not understand;
50 A nation of fierce countenance, which shall not regard the person of the old, nor show favour to the young:
51 And he shall eat the fruit of thy cattle, and the fruit of thy land, until thou be destroyed: which *also* shall not leave thee *either* corn, wine, or oil, *or* the increase of thy kine, or flocks of thy sheep, until he have destroyed thee.
Dan. 9. 26 And after threescore and two weeks shall Messiah be cut off, but not for himself: and the people of the

TIME, JANUARY–FEBRUARY, A. D. 30; PLACE, BETHANY.

H—CONCLUDED.

neither *is there any* that can deliver out of my hand.

I Sa. 2. 6 The LORD killeth, and maketh alive: he bringeth down to the grave, and bringeth up.

Ps. 33. 9 For he spake, and it was *done;* he commanded, and it stood fast.

Luke 7. 14 And he came and touched the bier: and they that bare *him* stood still. And he said, Young man, I say unto thee, Arise.

Luke 8. 54 And he put them all out, and took her by the hand, and called, saying, Maid, arise.

Acts 3. 15 And killed the Prince of life, whom God hath raised from the dead; whereof we are witnesses.

Acts 9. 40 But Peter put them all forth, and kneeled down, and prayed; and turning *him* to the body said, Tabitha, arise. And she opened her eyes: and when she saw Peter, she sat up.

I

John 20. 7 And the napkin, that was about his head, not lying with the linen clothes, but wrapped together in a place by itself.

CHAP. 11.

41 Then they took away the stone *from the place* where the dead was laid. [e]And Jesus lifted up *his* eyes, and said, Father, I thank thee that thou hast heard me.

42 And I knew that thou hearest me always: but [f]because of the people which stand by I said *it*, that they may believe that thou hast sent me.

43 [g]And when he thus had spoken, he cried with a loud voice, [h]Lazarus, come forth.

44 And he that was dead came forth, bound hand and foot with graveclothes; and [i]his face was bound about with a napkin. Jesus saith unto them, Loose him, and let him go.

JERUSALEM. TIME, JANUARY–FEBRUARY, A. D. 30; PLACE, JERUSALEM, EPHRAIM.

D—CONCLUDED.

prince that shall come shall destroy the city and the sanctuary; and the end thereof *shall be* with a flood, and unto the end of the war desolations are determined.

Zech. 14. 1 Behold, the day of the LORD cometh, and thy spoil shall be divided in the midst of thee.

2 For I will gather all nations against Jerusalem to battle; and the city shall be taken, and the houses rifled, and the women ravished; and half of the city shall go forth into captivity, and the residue of the people shall not be cut off from the city.

E

Luke 3. 2 Annas and Caiaphas being the high priests, the word of God came unto John the son of Zacharias in the wilderness.

John 18. 14 Now Caiaphas was he, which gave counsel to the Jews, that it was expedient that one man should die for the people.

Acts 4. 6 And Annas the high priest, and Caiaphas, and John, and Alexander, and as many as were of the kindred of the high priest, were gathered together at Jerusalem.

11: 45–54.

45 Then many of the Jews which came to Mary, [a]and had seen the things which Jesus did, believed on him.

46 But some of them went their ways to the Pharisees, and told them what things Jesus had done.

47 [b]Then gathered the chief priests and the Pharisees a council, and said, [c]What do we? for this man doeth many miracles.

48 If we let him thus alone, all *men* will believe on him; [d]and the Romans shall come and take away both our place and nation.

49 And one of them, *named* [e]Caiaphas, being the high priest that same year, said unto them, Ye know nothing at all,

§ 122. THE COUNSEL OF CAIAPHAS AGAINST JESUS. HE RETIRES FROM JERU-

F

John 16. 7 Nevertheless I tell you the truth; It is expedient for you that I go away: for if I go not away, the Comforter will not come unto you; but if I depart, I will send him unto you.

John 18. 14. *See under E, page 365.*

John 19. 12 And from thenceforth Pilate sought to release him: but the Jews cried out, saying, If thou let this man go, thou art not Cæsar's friend: whosoever maketh himself a king speaketh against Cæsar.

G

Isa. 49. 6 And he said, It is a light thing that thou shouldest be my servant to raise up the tribes of Jacob, and to restore the preserved of Israel: I will also give thee for a light to the Gentiles, that thou mayest be my salvation unto the end of the earth.

I Jno. 2. 2 And he is the propitiation for our sins: and not for ours only, but also for *the sins of* the whole world.

H

John 10. 16 And other sheep I have, which are not of this fold: them also I must bring, and they shall hear my voice; and there shall be one fold, *and* one shepherd.

Acts 13. 47 For so hath the Lord commanded us, *saying,* I have set thee to be a

H—Concluded.

light of the Gentiles, that thou shouldest be for salvation unto the ends of the earth.

Gal. 3. 28 There is neither Jew nor Greek, there is neither bond nor free, there is neither male nor female: for ye are all one in Christ Jesus.

Eph. 2. 14 For he is our peace, who hath made both one, and hath broken down the middle wall of partition *between us;*

15 Having abolished in his flesh the enmity, *even* the law of commandments *contained* in ordinances; for to make in himself of twain one new man, *so* making peace;

16 And that he might reconcile both unto God in one body by the cross, having slain the enmity thereby:

17 And came and preached peace to you which were afar off, and to them that were nigh.

Eph. 3. 6 That the Gentiles should be fellow heirs, and of the same body, and partakers of his promise in Christ by the gospel:

I

Hos. 1. 10 Yet the number of the children of Israel shall be as the sand of the sea, which cannot be measured nor numbered; and it shall come to pass, *that* in the place where it was said

§ 123. JESUS BEYOND JORDAN. A WOMAN HEALED ON THE SABBATH

19 : 1, 2.

1 And it came to pass, [a]*that* when Jesus had finished these sayings, he departed from Galilee, and came into the coasts of Judæa beyond Jordan;

2 [b]And great multitudes followed him; and he healed them there. p. 402.

A

Mark 10. 1. *See text of topic.*

John 10. 40 And went away again beyond Jordan into the place where John at first baptized; and there he abode.

B

Matt. 12. 14 Then the Pharisees went out, and held a council against him, how they might destroy him.

15 But when Jesus knew *it,* he withdrew himself from thence: and great multitudes followed him, and he healed them all;

10 : 1.

1 And [c]he arose from thence, and cometh into the coasts of Judæa by the farther side of Jordan: and the people resort unto him again; and, as he was wont, he taught them again. (p. 402.)

C

Matt. 19. 1. *See text of topic.* John 10. 40. *Under A.*

John 11. 7 Then after that saith he to *his* disciples, Let us go into Judæa again.

D

Ps. 103. 1 Bless the LORD, O my soul: and all that is within me, *bless* his holy name.

2 Bless the LORD, O my soul, and forget not all his benefits:

3 Who forgiveth all thine iniquities; who healeth all thy diseases;

4 Who redeemeth thy life from destruction; who crowneth thee with loving-kindness and tender mercies;

5 Who satisfieth thy mouth with good

SALEM (CONCL'D). TIME, JANUARY–FEBRUARY, A. D. 30; PLACE, JERUSALEM, EPHRAIM.

I—CONCLUDED.

unto them, Ye *are* not my people, *there* it shall be said unto them, Ye *are* the sons of the living God.

Acts 18. 8 And Crispus, the chief ruler of the synagogue, believed on the Lord with all his house; and many of the Corinthians hearing believed, and were baptized.

9 Then spake the Lord to Paul in the night by a vision, Be not afraid, but speak, and hold not thy peace:

10 For I am with thee, and no man shall set on thee to hurt thee: for I have much people in this city.

K

John 4. 1 When therefore the Lord knew how the Pharisees had heard that Jesus made and baptized more disciples than John,

John 4. 3 He left Judæa, and departed again into Galilee.

John 7. 1 After these things Jesus walked in Galilee: for he would not walk in Jewry, because the Jews sought to kill him.

L

II Chr. 13. 19 And Abijah pursued after Jeroboam, and took cities from him, Beth-el with the towns thereof, and Jeshanah with the towns thereof, and Ephrain with the towns thereof.

CHAP. 11.

50 [f]Nor consider that it is expedient
for us, that one man should die for the
people, and that the whole nation perish not.

51 And this spake he not of himself:
but being high priest that year, he
prophesied that Jesus should die for
that nation;

52 And [g]not for that nation only,
[h]but that also he should gather together
in one [i]the children of God that were
scattered abroad.

53 Then from that day forth they
took counsel together for to put him to
death.

54 Jesus [k]therefore walked no more
openly among the Jews; but went
thence unto a country near to the wilderness, into a city called [l]Ephraim,
and there continued with his disciples.

(p. 429.)

TIME, JANUARY–FEBRUARY, A. D. 30; PLACE, VALLEY OF JORDAN, PERÆA.

13 : 10–17.

10 And he was teaching in one of the
synagogues on the sabbath.

11 And, behold, there was a woman
which had a spirit of infirmity eighteen
years, and was bowed together, and
could in no wise lift up *herself*.

12 And when Jesus saw her, he
called *her to him*, and said unto her,
Woman, thou art loosed from thine
infirmity.

13 [d]And he laid *his* hands on her:
and immediately she was made straight,
and glorified God.

D—CONTINUED.

things; so that thy youth is renewed like the eagle's.

Ps. 107. 19 Then they cry unto the LORD in their trouble, *and* he saveth them out of their distresses.

D—CONCLUDED.

Ps. 107. 20 He sent his word, and healed them, and delivered *them* from their destructions.

21 O that *men* would praise the LORD *for* his goodness, and *for* his wonderful works to the children of men!

22 And let them sacrifice the sacrifices of thanksgiving, and declare his works with rejoicing.

Mark 16. 18 They shall take up serpents; and if they drink any deadly thing, it shall not hurt them; they shall lay hands on the sick, and they shall recover.

Acts 9. 17 And Ananias went his way, and entered into the house; and putting his hands on him said, Brother Saul, the Lord, *even* Jesus, that appeared unto thee in the way as thou camest, hath sent me, that thou mightest receive thy sight, and be filled with the Holy Ghost.

§ 123. JESUS BEYOND JORDAN. A WOMAN HEALED ON THE SABBATH

[Chap. 19.]

E

Rom.10. 1 Brethren, my heart's desire and
prayer to God for Israel is, that they
might be saved.
2 For I bear them record that they
have a zeal of God, but not according
to knowledge.
3 For they, being ignorant of God's
righteousness, and going about to establish their own righteousness, have
not submitted themselves unto the
righteousness of God.
4 For Christ *is* the end of the law
for righteousness to every one that
believeth.

F

Ex. 20. 8 Remember the sabbath day, to
keep it holy.
9 Six days shalt thou labour, and do
all thy work:

G

Job 34. 30 That the hypocrite reign not, lest
the people be ensnared.
Prov.11. 9 A hypocrite with *his* mouth destroyeth his neighbour: but through
knowledge shall the just be delivered.
Isa. 29. 20 For the terrible one is brought to
nought, and the scorner is consumed,
and all that watch for iniquity are
cut off:
Matt. 6. 5 And when thou prayest, thou shalt

[Chap. 10.]

G—Continued.

not be as the hypocrites *are:* for they
love to pray standing in the synagogues and in the corners of the
streets, that they may be seen of men.
Verily I say unto you, They have
their reward.
Acts 8. 20 But Peter said unto him, Thy
money perish with thee, because thou
hast thought that the gift of God may
be purchased with money.
21 Thou hast neither part nor lot in
this matter: for thy heart is not right
in the sight of God.
22 Repent therefore of this thy wickedness, and pray God, if perhaps the
thought of thine heart may be forgiven thee.
23 For I perceive that thou art in
the gall of bitterness, and *in* the bond
of iniquity.
24 Then answered Simon, and said,
Pray ye to the Lord for me, that none
of these things which ye have spoken
come upon me.
Acts 13. 8 But Elymas the sorcerer (for so is
his name by interpretation) withstood
them, seeking to turn away the deputy
from the faith.
9 Then Saul, (who also *is called*
Paul,) filled with the Holy Ghost, set
his eyes on him,

§ 124. PARABLE OF THE GRAIN OF MUSTARD SEED REPEATED.

A

Lam. 2. 13 What thing shall I take to witness for thee? what thing shall I liken
to thee, O daughter of Jerusalem?
what shall I equal to thee, that I may
comfort thee, O virgin daughter of
Zion? for thy breach *is* great like the
sea: who can heal thee?
Matt.13. 31 Another parable put he forth unto them, saying, The kingdom of
heaven is like to a grain of mustard
seed, which a man took, and sowed
in his field;

A—Continued.

Matt.13. 32 Which indeed is the least of all
seeds: but when it is grown, it is the
greatest among herbs, and becometh a
tree, so that the birds of the air come
and lodge in the branches thereof.
Mark 4. 30 And he said, Whereunto shall
we liken the kingdom of God? or with
what comparison shall we compare it?
31 *It is* like a grain of mustard seed,
which, when it is sown in the earth,
is less than all the seeds that be in
the earth:

§ 125. PARABLE OF THE LEAVEN HID IN THE MEAL REPEATED.

A

Matt.13. 33 Another parable spake he unto
them; The kingdom of heaven is like
unto leaven, which a woman took, and
hid in three measures of meal, till the
whole was leavened.

B

Job 17. 9 The righteous also shall hold on
his way, and he that hath clean hands

B—Continued.

shall be stronger and stronger.
Prov. 4. 18 But the path of the just *is* as the
shining light, that shineth more and
more unto the perfect day.
Hos. 6. 3 Then shall we know, *if* we follow
on to know the Lord: his going
forth is prepared as the morning; and
he shall come unto us as the rain, as

(CONCL'D). TIME, JANUARY–FEBRUARY, A. D. 30; PLACE, VALLEY OF JORDAN, PERÆA.

CHAP. 13.

14 And the ruler of the synagogue answered with indignation, because that Jesus had healed on the sabbath day, and said unto the people, [e]There are six days in which men ought to work: in them therefore come and be healed, and [f]not on the sabbath day.

15 The Lord then answered him, and said, [g]*Thou* hypocrite, [h]doth not each one of you on the sabbath loose his ox or *his* ass from the stall, and lead *him* away to watering?

16 And ought not this woman, [i]being a daughter of Abraham, whom Satan hath bound, lo, these eighteen years, be loosed from this bond on the sabbath day?

17 And when he had said these things, all his adversaries were ashamed: and all the people rejoiced for all the glorious things that were done by him.

G—CONCLUDED.

Acts 13. 10 And said, O full of all subtilty and all mischief, *thou* child of the devil, *thou* enemy of all righteousness, wilt thou not cease to pervert the right ways of the Lord?

H

Matt. 12. 10 And, behold, there was a man which had *his* hand withered. And they asked him, saying, Is it lawful to heal on the sabbath days? that they might accuse him.

Mark 3. 2 And they watched him, whether he would heal him on the sabbath day; that they might accuse him.

Luke 6. 7 And the scribes and Pharisees watched him, whether he would heal on the sabbath day; that they might find an accusation against him.

Luke 14. 3 And Jesus answering spake unto the lawyers and Pharisees, saying, Is it lawful to heal on the sabbath day?

Luke 14. 5 And answered them, saying, Which of you shall have an ass or an ox fallen into a pit, and will not straightway pull him out on the sabbath day?

I

Luke 19. 9 And Jesus said unto him, This day is salvation come to this house, forasmuch as he also is a son of Abraham.

[SEE § 63.] TIME, JANUARY–FEBRUARY, A. D. 30; PLACE, PERÆA.

13: 18, 19.

18 [a]Then said he, Unto what is the kingdom of God like? and whereunto shall I resemble it?

19 It is like a grain of mustard seed, which a man took, and cast into his garden; [b]and it grew, and waxed a great tree; and the fowls of the air lodged in the branches of it.

A—CONCLUDED.

Mark 4. 32 But when it is sown, it groweth up, and becometh greater than all herbs, and shooteth out great branches; so that the fowls of the air may lodge under the shadow of it.

B

Ps. 72. 16 There shall be a handful of corn in the earth upon the top of the mountains; the fruit thereof shall shake like Lebanon: and *they* of the city shall flourish like grass of the earth.

[SEE § 64.] TIME, JANUARY–FEBRUARY, A. D. 30; PLACE, PERÆA.

13: 20, 21.

20 And again he said, Whereunto shall I liken the kingdom of God?

21 [a]It is like leaven, which a woman took and hid in three measures of meal, [b]till the whole was leavened.

B—CONCLUDED.

the latter *and* former rain unto the earth.

I Cor. 5. 6 Your glorying *is* not good. Know ye not that a little leaven leaveneth the whole lump?

Phil. 1. 6 Being confident of this very thing, that he which hath begun a good work in you will perform *it* until the day of Jesus Christ:

§ 126. JOURNEYING TOWARD JERUSALEM AND TEACHING

A

Matt. 9. 35 And Jesus went about all the cities and villages, teaching in their synagogues, and preaching the gospel of the kingdom, and healing every sickness and every disease among the people.

Mark 6. 6 And he marvelled because of their unbelief. And he went round about the villages, teaching.

1

Strive as in agony.

B

Gen. 32. 24 And Jacob was left alone; and there wrestled a man with him until the breaking of the day.

25 And when he saw that he prevailed not against him, he touched the hollow of his thigh; and the hollow of Jacob's thigh was out of joint, as he wrestled with him.

26 And he said, Let me go, for the day breaketh. And he said, I will not let thee go, except thou bless me.

John 6. 27 Labour not for the meat which perisheth, but for that meat which endureth unto everlasting life, which the Son of man shall give unto you: for him hath God the Father sealed.

I Cor. 9. 24 Know ye not that they which run in a race run all, but one receiveth the prize? So run. that ye may obtain.

25 And every man that striveth for the mastery is temperate in all things. Now they *do it* to obtain a corruptible crown; but we an incorruptible.

26 I therefore so run, not as uncertainly; so fight I, not as one that beateth the air:

27 But I keep under my body, and bring *it* into subjection: lest that by any means, when I have preached to others, I myself should be a castaway.

Phil. 2. 12 Wherefore, my beloved, as ye have always obeyed, not as in my presence only, but now much more in my absence, work out your own salvation with fear and trembling:

13 For it is God which worketh in you both to will and to do of *his* good pleasure.

Col. 1. 29 Whereunto I also labour, striving according to his working, which worketh in me mightily.

Heb. 4. 11 Let us labour therefore to enter into that rest, lest any man fall after the same example of unbelief.

II Pet.1. 10 Wherefore the rather, brethren, give diligence to make your calling

B—Concluded.

and election sure: for if ye do these things, ye shall never fall:

C

Matt. 7. 13 Enter ye in at the strait gate: for wide *is* the gate, and broad *is* the way, that leadeth to destruction, and many there be which go in thereat:

D

John 7. 34 Ye shall seek me, and shall not find *me:* and where I am, *thither* ye cannot come.

John 8. 21 Then said Jesus again unto them, I go my way, and ye shall seek me, and shall die in your sins: whither I go, ye cannot come.

John 13. 33 Little children, yet a little while I am with you. Ye shall seek me; and as I said unto the Jews, Whither I go, ye cannot come; so now I say to you.

Rom. 9. 31 But Israel, which followed after the law of righteousness, hath not attained to the law of righteousness.

Rom.10. 2 For I bear them record that they have a zeal of God, but not according to knowledge.

3 For they, being ignorant of God's righteousness, and going about to establish their own righteousness, have not submitted themselves unto the righteousness of God.

E

Ps. 52. 6 The righteous also shall see, and fear, and shall laugh at him:

Prov. 1. 25 But ye have set at nought all my counsel, and would none of my reproof:

Isa. 55. 6 Seek ye the Lord while he may be found, call ye upon him while he is near:

F

Matt.25. 10 And while they went to buy, the bridegroom came; and they that were ready went in with him to the marriage: and the door was shut.

G

Luke 6. 46 And why call ye me, Lord, Lord, and do not the things which I say?

I Jno. 1. 6 If we say that we have fellowship with him, and walk in darkness, we lie, and do not the truth:

I Jno. 2. 4 He that saith, I know him, and keepeth not his commandments, is a liar, and the truth is not in him.

H

Matt. 7. 23 And then will I profess unto them, I never knew you: depart from me, ye that work iniquity.

Matt.25. 12 But he answered and said, Verily I say unto you, I know you not.

ON THE WAY. Time, February–March, A. D. 30; Place, Peræa.

13: 22–30.

22 [a]And he went through the cities
and villages, teaching, and journeying
toward Jerusalem.
23 Then said one unto him, Lord,
are there few that be saved? And he
said unto them,
24 [1b]Strive to enter in at the strait
gate: for [c]many, I say unto you, will
[d]seek to enter in, and [e]shall not be able.
25 When once the master of the
house is risen up, and [f]hath shut to
the door, and ye begin to stand without,
and to knock at the door, saying,
[g]Lord, Lord, open unto us; and he
shall answer and say unto you, [h]I
know you not whence ye are:
26 Then shall ye begin to say, [i]We
have eaten and drunk in thy presence,
and thou hast taught in our streets.
27 [k]But he shall say, I tell you, I
know you not whence ye are; [l]depart
from me, all *ye* workers of iniquity.
28 [m]There shall be weeping and
gnashing of teeth, [n]when ye shall see
Abraham, and Isaac, and Jacob, and
all the prophets, in the kingdom of
God, and you *yourselves* thrust out.
29 And they shall come from the
east, and *from* the west, and from the
north, and *from* the south, and shall
sit down in the kingdom of God.
30 [o]And, behold, there are last which
shall be first; and there are first which
shall be last.

I

Isa. 58. 2 Yet they seek me daily, and delight to know my ways, as a nation that did righteousness, and forsook not the ordinance of their God: they ask of me the ordinances of justice; they take delight in approaching to God.

I—Concluded.

II Tim. 3. 5 Having a form of godliness, but denying the power thereof: from such turn away.

Tit. 1. 16 They profess that they know God; but in works they deny *him*, being abominable, and disobedient, and unto every good work reprobate.

K

Matt. 7. 23. *See under H.*

Matt. 25. 41 Then shall he say also unto them on the left hand, Depart from me, ye cursed, into everlasting fire, prepared for the devil and his angels:

Luke 13. 25. *See text of topic.*

L

Ps. 6. 8 Depart from me, all ye workers of iniquity; for the Lord hath heard the voice of my weeping.

Matt. 25. 41. *See under K.*

M

Matt. 8. 12 But the children of the kingdom shall be cast out into outer darkness: there shall be weeping and gnashing of teeth.

Matt. 13. 42 And shall cast them into a furnace of fire: there shall be wailing and gnashing of teeth.

Matt. 24. 51 And shall cut him asunder, and appoint *him* his portion with the hypocrites: there shall be weeping and gnashing of teeth.

N

Gen. 28. 14 And thy seed shall be as the dust of the earth; and thou shalt spread abroad to the west, and to the east, and to the north, and to the south: and in thee and in thy seed shall all the families of the earth be blessed.

Isa. 54. 2 Enlarge the place of thy tent, and let them stretch forth the curtains of thine habitations: spare not, lengthen thy cords, and strengthen thy stakes;
3 For thou shalt break forth on the right hand and on the left; and thy seed shall inherit the Gentiles, and make the desolate cities to be inhabited.

Matt. 8. 11 And I say unto you, That many shall come from the east and west, and shall sit down with Abraham, and Isaac, and Jacob, in the kingdom of heaven:

O

Matt. 19. 30 But many *that are* first shall be last; and the last *shall be* first.

Matt. 20. 16 So the last shall be first, and the first last: for many be called, but few chosen.

Mark 10. 31 But many *that are* first shall be last; and the last first.

§ 127. JESUS IS WARNED AGAINST HEROD.

A

Ps. 11. 1 In the LORD put I my trust: how
say ye to my soul, Flee *as* a bird to
your mountain?
2 For, lo, the wicked bend *their* bow,
they make ready their arrow upon the
string, that they may privily shoot at
the upright in heart.

Amos 7. 12 Also Amaziah said unto Amos, O
thou seer, go, flee thee away into the
land of Judah, and there eat bread,
and prophesy there:
13 But prophesy not again any more
at Beth-el: for it *is* the king's chapel,
and it *is* the king's court.

B

Eze. 13. 3 Thus saith the Lord GOD; Woe unto the foolish prophets, that follow their
own spirit, and have seen nothing!
4 O Israel, thy prophets are like the
foxes in the deserts.

B—CONCLUDED.

Zeph. 3. 3 Her princes within her *are* roaring
lions; her judges *are* evening wolves;
they gnaw not the bones till the morrow.

Mic. 3. 1 And I said, Hear, I pray you, O
heads of Jacob, and ye princes of the
house of Israel; *Is it* not for you to
know judgment?
2 Who hate the good, and love the
evil; who pluck off their skin from
off them, and their flesh from off their
bones:

C

Mark 6. 14 And king Herod heard *of him;*
(for his name was spread abroad:)
and he said, That John the Baptist
was risen from the dead, and therefore
mighty works do show forth themselves in him.

Luke 9. 7 Now Herod the tetrarch heard of
all that was done by him: and he was

§ 128. PROPHECY AGAINST JERUSALEM.

A

Matt. 23. 37 O Jerusalem, Jerusalem, *thou* that
killest the prophets, and stonest them
which are sent unto thee, how often
would I have gathered thy children
together, even as a hen gathereth her
chickens under *her* wings, and ye
would not!
38 Behold, your house is left unto
you desolate.
39 For I say unto you, Ye shall not
see me henceforth, till ye shall say,
Blessed *is* he that cometh in the name
of the Lord.

B

Deut. 32. 11 As an eagle stirreth up her nest,
fluttereth over her young, spreadeth
abroad her wings, taketh them, beareth them on her wings:
12 *So* the LORD alone did lead him,
and *there was* no strange god with him.

Ruth 2. 12 The LORD recompense thy work,
and a full reward be given thee of the
LORD God of Israel, under whose
wings thou art come to trust.

Ps. 17. 8 Keep me as the apple of the eye;
hide me under the shadow of thy wings,

Ps. 57. 1 Be merciful unto me, O God, be
merciful unto me: for my soul trusteth
in thee: yea, in the shadow of thy
wings will I make my refuge, until
these calamities be overpast.

Ps. 91. 4 He shall cover thee with his feathers, and under his wings shalt thou
trust: his truth *shall be thy* shield and
buckler.

C

Lev. 26. 31 And I will make your cities
waste, and bring your sanctuaries unto desolation, and I will not smell the
savour of your sweet odours.
32 And I will bring the land into
desolation: and your enemies which
dwell therein shall be astonished at it.

Ps. 69. 25 Let their habitation be desolate;
and let none dwell in their tents.

Ps. 69. 29 But I *am* poor and sorrowful: let
thy salvation, O God, set me up on high.

Isa. 1. 7 Your country *is* desolate, your
cities *are* burned with fire: your land,
strangers devour it in your presence,
and *it is* desolate, as overthrown by
strangers.
8 And the daughter of Zion is left as a
cottage in a vineyard, as a lodge in a
garden of cucumbers, as a besieged city.

Dan. 9. 27 And he shall confirm the covenant
with many for one week: and in the
midst of the week he shall cause the
sacrifice and the oblation to cease, and
for the overspreading of abominations
he shall make *it* desolate, even until
the consummation, and that determined shall be poured upon the
desolate.

Mic. 3. 12 Therefore shall Zion for your
sake be ploughed *as* a field, and Jerusalem shall become heaps, and the
mountain of the house as the high
places of the forest.

D

Prov. 1. 24 Because I have called, and ye re-

TIME, FEBRUARY–MARCH, A. D. 30; PLACE, PERÆA.

13 : 31–33.

31 The same day there came certain of the Pharisees, saying unto him, [a]Get thee out, and depart hence; for Herod will kill thee.

32 And he said unto them, Go ye, and tell that [b]fox, [c]Behold, I cast out devils, and I do cures to day and to morrow, and the third *day* [d]I shall be perfected.

33 Nevertheless I must walk to day, and to morrow, and the *day* following: for it cannot be that a prophet perish out of Jerusalem.

C—CONCLUDED.

perplexed, because that it was said of some, that John was risen from the dead:

John 10. 32 Jesus answered them, Many good works have I showed you from my Father; for which of those works do ye stone me?

D

John 19. 30 When Jesus therefore had received the vinegar, he said, It is finished: and he bowed his head, and gave up the ghost.

Heb. 2. 10 For it became him, for whom *are* all things, and by whom *are* all things, in bringing many sons unto glory, to make the captain of their salvation perfect through sufferings.

Heb. 5. 9 And being made perfect, he became the author of eternal salvation unto all them that obey him:

TIME, FEBRUARY–MARCH, A. D. 30; PLACE, PERÆA.

13 : 34–35.

34 [a]O Jerusalem, Jerusalem, which killest the prophets, and stonest them that are sent unto thee; how often would [b]I have gathered thy children together, as a hen *doth gather* her brood under *her* wings, and ye would not!

35 Behold, [c]your house is left unto you desolate: and verily I say unto you, Ye shall [d]not see me, until *the time* come when ye shall say, [e]Blessed *is* he that cometh in the name of the Lord.

D—CONTINUED.

fused; I have stretched out my hand, and no man regarded;

25 But ye have set at nought all my counsel, and would none of my reproof:

26 I also will laugh at your calamity; I will mock when your fear cometh;

27 When your fear cometh as desolation, and your destruction cometh as a whirlwind; when distress and anguish cometh upon you.

28 Then shall they call upon me, but I will not answer; they shall seek me early, but they shall not find me:

29 For that they hated knowledge, and did not choose the fear of the LORD:

D—CONCLUDED.

Prov. 1. 30 They would none of my counsel: they despised all my reproof.

John 8. 21 Then said Jesus again unto them, I go my way, and ye shall seek me, and shall die in your sins: whither I go, ye cannot come.

John 8. 24 I said therefore unto you, that ye shall die in your sins: for if ye believe not that I am *he*, ye shall die in your sins.

E

Ps. 118. 26 Blessed *be* he that cometh in the name of the LORD: we have blessed you out of the house of the LORD.

Matt. 21. 9 And the multitudes that went before, and that followed, cried, saying, Hosanna to the Son of David: Blessed *is* he that cometh in the name of the LORD: Hosanna in the highest.

Mark 11. 10 Blessed *be* the kingdom of our father David, that cometh in the name of the Lord: Hosanna in the highest.

Luke 19. 38 Saying, Blessed *be* the King that cometh in the name of the Lord: peace in heaven, and glory in the highest.

John 12. 12 On the next day much people that were come to the feast, when they heard that Jesus was coming to Jerusalem,

13 Took branches of palm trees, and went forth to meet him, and cried, Hosanna: Blessed *is* the King of Israel that cometh in the name of the Lord.

§ 129. JESUS HEALS A MAN OF DROPSY ON THE SABBATH WHILE

A

Luke 7. 34 The Son of man is come eating and drinking; and ye say, Behold a gluttonous man, and a winebibber, a friend of publicans and sinners!
35 But wisdom is justified of all her children.
36 And one of the Pharisees desired him that he would eat with him. And he went into the Pharisee's house, and sat down to meat.
Luke 11. 37 And as he spake, a certain Pharisee besought him to dine with him: and he went in, and sat down to meat.

B

I Cor. 9. 19 For though I be free from all *men*, yet have I made myself servant unto all, that I might gain the more.
20 And unto the Jews I became as a Jew, that I might gain the Jews; to them that are under the law, as under the law, that I might gain them that are under the law;
21 To them that are without law, as without law, (being not without law to God, but under the law to Christ,) that I might gain them that are without law.
22 To the weak became I as weak, that I might gain the weak: I am made all things to all *men*, that I might by all means save some.
23 And this I do for the gospel's sake, that I might be partaker thereof with *you*.

C

Ps. 37. 32 The wicked watcheth the righteous, and seeketh to slay him.
Ps. 41. 6 And if he come to see *me*, he speaketh vanity: his heart gathereth iniquity to itself; *when* he goeth abroad, he telleth *it*.
Ps. 62. 3 How long will ye imagine mischief against a man? ye shall be slain all of you: as a bowing wall *shall ye be, and as* a tottering fence.
4 They only consult to cast *him* down from his excellency: they delight in lies: they bless with their mouth, but they curse inwardly. Selah.
Ps. 64. 5 They encourage themselves *in* an evil matter: they commune of laying snares privily; they say, Who shall see them?
6 They search out iniquities; they accomplish a diligent search: both the inward *thought* of every one *of them*, and the heart, *is* deep.
Prov. 23. 7 For as he thinketh in his heart, so *is* he: Eat and drink, saith he to thee: but his heart *is* not with thee.

§ 130. DISCOURSE ON CHOOSING CHIEF ROOMS SPOKEN AT THE

A

Esth. 6. 6 So Haman came in. And the king said unto him, What shall be done unto the man whom the king delighteth to honour? Now Haman thought in his heart, To whom would the king delight to do honour more than to myself?
7 And Haman answered the king, For the man whom the king delighteth to honour,
8 Let the royal apparel be brought which the king *useth* to wear, and the horse that the king rideth upon, and the crown royal which is set upon his head:
9 And let this apparel and horse be delivered to the hand of one of the king's most noble princes, that they may array the man *withal* whom the king delighteth to honour, and bring him on horseback through the street of the city, and proclaim before him, Thus shall it be done to the man whom the king delighteth to honour.
10 Then the king said to Haman, Make haste, *and* take the apparel and the horse, as thou hast said, and do even so to Mordecai the Jew, that sitteth at the king's gate: let nothing fail of all that thou hast spoken.
11 Then took Haman the apparel and the horse, and arrayed Mordecai, and brought him on horseback through the street of the city, and proclaimed before him, Thus shall it be done unto the man whom the king delighteth to honour.
12 And Mordecai came again to the king's gate. But Haman hasted to his house mourning, and having his head covered.
Prov. 3. 35 The wise shall inherit glory: but shame shall be the promotion of fools.
Prov. 11. 2 *When* pride cometh, then cometh shame: but with the lowly *is* wisdom.
Prov. 16. 18 Pride *goeth* before destruction, and a haughty spirit before a fall.
Eze. 28. 7 Behold, therefore I will bring strangers upon thee, the terrible of the nations: and they shall draw their

DINING WITH A PHARISEE. TIME, FEBRUARY–MARCH, A. D. 30; PLACE, PERÆA.

14: 1–6.

1 And it came to pass, [a]as he went
into the house of one of the chief
Pharisees [b]to eat bread on the sabbath
day, that [c]they watched him.
2 And, behold, there was a certain
man before him which had the dropsy.
3 And Jesus answering spake unto
the lawyers and Pharisees, saying, [d]Is
it lawful to heal on the sabbath day?
4 And they held their peace. And
he took *him*, and healed him, and let
him go;
5 And answered them, saying, [e]Which
of you shall have an ass or an ox fallen
into a pit, and will not straightway
pull him out on the sabbath day?
6 And they could not answer him
again to these things.

C—CONTINUED.

Isa. 29. 20 For the terrible one is brought to nought, and the scorner is consumed,

C—CONCLUDED.

and all that watch for iniquity are cut off:

21 That make a man an offender for a word, and lay a snare for him that reproveth in the gate, and turn aside the just for a thing of nought.

Mark 3. 2 And they watched him, whether he would heal him on the sabbath day; that they might accuse him.

D

Matt.12. 10 And, behold, there was a man which had *his* hand withered. And they asked him, saying, Is it lawful to heal on the sabbath days? that they might accuse him.

E

Ex. 23. 5 If thou see the ass of him that hateth thee lying under his burden, and wouldest forbear to help him, thou shalt surely help with him.

Deut.22. 4 Thou shalt not see thy brother's ass or his ox fall down by the way, and hide thyself from them: thou shalt surely help him to lift *them* up again.

Luke 13. 15 The Lord then answered him, and said, *Thou* hypocrite, doth not each one of you on the sabbath loose his ox or *his* ass from the stall, and lead *him* away to watering?

PHARISEE'S TABLE. TIME, FEBRUARY–MARCH, A. D. 30; PLACE, PERÆA.

14: 7–14.

7 And he put forth a parable to those
which were bidden, when he marked
how they chose out the chief rooms;
saying unto them,
8 When thou art bidden of any
man to a wedding, sit not down in the
highest room; lest a more honourable
man than thou be bidden of him;
9 And he that bade thee and him
come and say to thee, Give this man
place; and [a]thou begin with shame to
take the lowest room.
10 [b]But when thou art bidden, go
and sit down in the lowest room; that
when he that bade thee cometh, he
may say unto thee, Friend, go up
higher: then shalt thou have worship

A—CONCLUDED.

swords against the beauty of thy wisdom, and they shall defile thy brightness.

8 They shall bring thee down to the pit, and thou shalt die the deaths of *them that are* slain in the midst of the seas.

B

I Sa. 15. 17 And Samuel said, When thou *wast* little in thine own sight, *wast* thou not *made* the head of the tribes of Israel, and the LORD anointed thee king over Israel?

Prov.15. 33 The fear of the LORD *is* the instruction of wisdom; and before honour *is* humility.

Prov.18. 12 Before destruction the heart of man is haughty; and before honour *is* humility.

Prov.25. 6 Put not forth thyself in the presence of the king, and stand not in the place of great *men*:

7 For better *it is* that it be said unto thee, Come up hither; than that thou shouldest be put lower in the presence of the prince whom thine eyes have seen.

§ 130. DISCOURSE ON CHOOSING CHIEF ROOMS SPOKEN AT THE PHARI-

C

Job 22. 29 When *men* are cast down, then thou shalt say, *There is* lifting up; and he shall save the humble person.

Prov.16. 18 Pride *goeth* before destruction, and a haughty spirit before a fall.

Ps. 18. 27 For thou wilt save the afflicted people; but wilt bring down high looks.

Prov.29. 23 A man's pride shall bring him low: but honour shall uphold the humble in spirit.

Matt.23. 12 And whosoever shall exalt himself shall be abased; and he that shall humble himself shall be exalted.

Luke 18. 14 I tell you, this man went down to his house justified *rather* than the other: for every one that exalteth himself shall be abased; and he that humbleth himself shall be exalted.

Jas. 4. 6 But he giveth more grace. Wherefore he saith, God resisteth the proud, but giveth grace unto the humble.

I Pet. 5. 5 Likewise, ye younger, submit yourselves unto the elder. Yea, all *of you* be subject one to another, and be clothed with humility: for God resisteth the proud, and giveth grace to the humble.

D

Neh. 8. 10 Then he said unto them, Go your way, eat the fat, and drink the sweet,

D—Continued.

and send portions unto them for whom nothing is prepared: for *this* day *is* holy unto our Lord: neither be ye sorry; for the joy of the Lord is your strength.

Neh. 8. 12 And all the people went their way to eat, and to drink, and to send portions, and to make great mirth, because they had understood the words that were declared unto them.

Job 31. 13 If I did despise the cause of my manservant or of my maidservant, when they contended with me;

14 What then shall I do when God riseth up? and when he visiteth, what shall I answer him?

15 Did not he that made me in the womb make him? and did not one fashion us in the womb?

16 If I have withheld the poor from *their* desire, or have caused the eyes of the widow to fail;

17 Or have eaten my morsel myself alone, and the fatherless hath not eaten thereof;

18 (For from my youth he was brought up with me, as *with* a father, and I have guided her from my mother's womb;)

19 If I have seen any perish for

§ 131. THE PARABLE OF THE GREAT SUPPER SPOKEN AT THE

A

Rev. 19. 9 And he saith unto me, Write, Blessed *are* they which are called unto the marriage supper of the Lamb. And he saith unto me, These are the true sayings of God.

B

Matt.22. 1 And Jesus answered and spake unto them again by parables, and said,

2 The kingdom of heaven is like unto a certain king, which made a marriage for his son,

3 And sent forth his servants to call them that were bidden to the wedding: and they would not come.

4 Again, he sent forth other servants, saying, Tell them which are bidden, Behold, I have prepared my dinner: my oxen and *my* fatlings *are* killed, and all things *are* ready: come unto the marriage.

5 But they made light of *it*, and went their ways, one to his farm, another to his merchandise:

6 And the remnant took his servants,

B—Concluded.

and entreated *them* spitefully, and slew *them*.

7 But when the king heard *thereof*, he was wroth: and he sent forth his armies, and destroyed those murderers, and burned up their city.

8 Then saith he to his servants, The wedding is ready, but they which were bidden were not worthy.

9 Go ye therefore into the highways, and as many as ye shall find, bid to the marriage.

10 So those servants went out into the highways, and gathered together all as many as they found, both bad and good: and the wedding was furnished with guests.

C

Prov. 9. 2 She hath killed her beasts; she hath mingled her wine; she hath also furnished her table.

Prov. 9. 5 Come, eat of my bread, and drink of the wine *which* I have mingled.

D

Matt. 6. 24 No man can serve two masters:

SEE'S TABLE (CONCLUDED). TIME, FEBRUARY–MARCH, A. D. 30; PLACE, PERÆA.

CHAP. 14.

in the presence of them that sit at meat with thee.

11 [c]For whosoever exalteth himself shall be abased; and he that humbleth himself shall be exalted.

12 Then said he also to him that bade him, When thou makest a dinner or a supper, call not thy friends, nor thy brethren, neither thy kinsmen, nor *thy* rich neighbours; lest they also bid thee again, and a recompense be made thee.

13 But when thou makest a feast, call [d]the poor, the maimed, the lame, the blind:

14 And [e]thou shalt be blessed; for they cannot recompense thee: for thou shalt be recompensed at the resurrection of the just.

D—CONCLUDED.

want of clothing, or any poor without covering;

20 If his loins have not blessed me, and *if* he were *not* warmed with the fleece of my sheep;

21 If I have lifted up my hand against the fatherless, when I saw my help in the gate:

22 *Then* let mine arm fall from my shoulder blade, and mine arm be broken from the bone.

23 For destruction *from* God *was* a terror to me, and by reason of his highness I could not endure.

E

Prov.19. 17 He that hath pity upon the poor lendeth unto the LORD; and that which he hath given will he pay him again.

Matt. 6. 4 That thine alms may be in secret: and thy Father which seeth in secret himself shall reward thee openly.

Phil. 4. 18 But I have all, and abound: I am full, having received of Epaphroditus the things *which were sent* from you, an odour of a sweet smell, a sacrifice acceptable, well pleasing to God.

19 But my God shall supply all your need according to his riches in glory by Christ Jesus.

PHARISEE'S TABLE. TIME, FEBRUARY–MARCH, A. D. 30; PLACE, PERÆA.

14: 15–24.

15 And when one of them that sat at meat with him heard these things, he said unto him, [a]Blessed *is* he that shall eat bread in the kingdom of God.

16 [b]Then said he unto him, A certain man made a great supper, and bade many:

17 And sent his servant at supper time to say to them that were bidden, [c]Come; for all things are now ready.

18 [d]And they all with one *consent* began to make excuse. The first said unto him, I have bought a piece of ground, and I must needs go and see it: I pray thee have me excused.

D—CONCLUDED.

for either he will hate the one, and love the other; or else he will hold to the one, and despise the other. Ye cannot serve God and mammon.

Matt.13. 22 He also that received seed among the thorns is he that heareth the word; and the care of this world, and the deceitfulness of riches, choke the word, and he becometh unfruitful.

Luke 8. 14 And that which fell among thorns are they, which, when they have heard, go forth, and are choked with cares and riches and pleasures of *this* life, and bring no fruit to perfection.

John 5. 40 And ye will not come to me, that ye might have life.

I Tim. 6 9 But they that will be rich fall into temptation and a snare, and *into* many foolish and hurtful lusts, which drown men in destruction and perdition.

10 For the love of money is the root of all evil: which while some coveted after, they have erred from the faith, and pierced themselves through with many sorrows.

§ 131. THE PARABLE OF THE GREAT SUPPER SPOKEN AT THE PHARI-

E

Prov. 1. 20–22. *See under G.*

Prov. 8. 1 Doth not wisdom cry? and understanding put forth her voice?

2 She standeth in the top of high places, by the way in the places of the paths.

3 She crieth at the gates, at the entry of the city, at the coming in at the doors:

4 Unto you, O men, I call; and my voice *is* to the sons of man.

Prov. 9. 3 She hath sent forth her maidens: she crieth upon the highest places of the city,

4 Whoso *is* simple, let him turn in hither: *as for* him that wanteth understanding, she saith to him,

Jer. 5. 1 Run ye to and fro through the streets of Jerusalem, and see now, and know, and seek in the broad places thereof, if ye can find a man, if there be *any* that executeth judgment, that seeketh the truth; and I will pardon it.

Matt. 21. 31 Whether of them twain did the will of *his* father? They say unto him, The first. Jesus saith unto them, Verily I say unto you, that the publicans and the harlots go into the kingdom of God before you.

Matt. 28. 18 And Jesus came and spake unto them, saying, All power is given unto me in heaven and in earth.

19 Go ye therefore, and teach all nations, baptizing them in the name of the Father, and of the Son, and of the Holy Ghost:

Acts 13. 46 Then Paul and Barnabas waxed bold, and said, It was necessary that the word of God should first have

E—Concluded.

been spoken to you: but seeing ye put it from you, and judge yourselves unworthy of everlasting life, lo, we turn to the Gentiles.

Jas. 2. 5 Hearken, my beloved brethren, Hath not God chosen the poor of this world rich in faith, and heirs of the kingdom which he hath promised to them that love him?

Rev. 22. 17 And the Spirit and the bride say, Come. And let him that heareth say, Come. And let him that is athirst come. And whosoever will, let him take the water of life freely.

F

Isa. 11. 10 And in that day there shall be a root of Jesse, which shall stand for an ensign of the people; to it shall the Gentiles seek: and his rest shall be glorious.

Isa. 19. 24 In that day shall Israel be the third with Egypt and with Assyria, *even* a blessing in the midst of the land:

25 Whom the Lord of hosts shall bless, saying, Blessed *be* Egypt my people, and Assyria the work of my hands, and Israel mine inheritance.

Isa. 66. 19 And I will set a sign among them, and I will send those that escape of them unto the nations, *to* Tarshish, Pul, and Lud, that draw the bow, *to* Tubal and Javan, *to* the isles afar off, that have not heard my fame, neither have seen my glory; and they shall declare my glory among the Gentiles.

20 And they shall bring all your brethren *for* an offering unto the Lord out of all nations upon horses, and in chariots, and in litters, and upon

§ 132. WHAT IS REQUIRED OF TRUE DISCIPLES.

A

Deut. 13. 6 If thy brother, the son of thy mother, or thy son, or thy daughter, or the wife of thy bosom, or thy friend, which *is* as thine own soul, entice thee secretly, saying, Let us go and serve other gods, which thou hast not known, thou, nor thy fathers;

Deut. 33. 9 Who said unto his father and to his mother, I have not seen him; neither did he acknowledge his brethren, nor knew his own children: for they have observed thy word, and kept thy covenant.

Matt. 10. 37 He that loveth father or mother more than me is not worthy of me: and he that loveth son or daughter

A—Concluded.

more than me is not worthy of me.

38 And he that taketh not his cross, and followeth after me, is not worthy of me.

B

Ex. 21. 15 And he that smiteth his father, or his mother, shall be surely put to death.

Eccl. 2. 17 Therefore I hated life; because the work that is wrought under the sun *is* grievous unto me: for all *is* vanity and vexation of spirit.

18 Yea, I hated all my labour which I had taken under the sun: because I should leave it unto the man that shall be after me.

19 And who knoweth whether he

SEE'S TABLE (CONCLUDED). TIME, FEBRUARY–MARCH, A. D. 30; PLACE, PERÆA.

CHAP. 14.

19 And another said, I have bought five yoke of oxen, and I go to prove them: I pray thee have me excused.

20 And another said, I have married a wife, and therefore I cannot come.

21 So that servant came, and showed his lord these things. Then the master of the house being angry said to his servant, [e]Go out quickly into the streets and lanes of the city, and bring in hither the poor, and the maimed, and the halt, and the blind.

22 And the servant said, Lord, it is done as thou hast commanded, and yet there is room.

23 And the lord said unto the servant, [f]Go out into the highways and hedges, and [g]compel *them* to come in, that my house may be filled.

24 For I say unto you, [h]That none of those men which were bidden shall taste of my supper.

F—CONTINUED.

mules, and upon swift beasts, to my holy mountain Jerusalem, saith the LORD, as the children of Israel bring an offering in a clean vessel into the house of the LORD.

F—CONCLUDED.

Isa. 66. 21 And I will also take of them for priests *and* for Levites, saith the LORD.

G

Prov. 1. 20 Wisdom crieth without; she uttereth her voice in the streets:

21 She crieth in the chief place of concourse, in the openings of the gates: in the city she uttereth her words, *saying*,

22 How long, ye simple ones, will ye love simplicity? and the scorners delight in their scorning, and fools hate knowledge?

II Cor. 5. 20 Now then we are ambassadors for Christ, as though God did beseech *you* by us: we pray *you* in Christ's stead, be ye reconciled to God.

H

Matt. 8. 11 And I say unto you, That many shall come from the east and west, and shall sit down with Abraham, and Isaac, and Jacob, in the kingdom of heaven:

12 But the children of the kingdom shall be cast out into outer darkness: there shall be weeping and gnashing of teeth.

13 And Jesus said unto the centurion, Go thy way; and as thou hast believed, *so* be it done unto thee. And his servant was healed in the selfsame hour.

Matt. 21. 43 Therefore say I unto you, The kingdom of God shall be taken from you, and given to a nation bringing forth the fruits thereof.

Matt. 22. 8. *See under B, page 376.*

Acts 13. 46. *See under E.*

Heb. 3. 19 So we see that they could not enter in because of unbelief.

TIME, FEBRUARY–MARCH, A. D. 30; PLACE, PERÆA.

14: 25–35.

25 And there went great multitudes with him: and he turned, and said unto them,

26 [a]If any *man* come to me, [b]and hate not his father, and mother, and wife, and children, and brethren, and sisters; [c]yea, and his own life also, he cannot be my disciple.

B—CONTINUED.

shall be a wise *man* or a fool? yet shall he have rule over all my labour wherein I have laboured, and wherein I

B—CONCLUDED.

have showed myself wise under the sun. This *is* also vanity.

Mal. 1. 2 I have loved you, saith the LORD. Yet ye say, Wherein hast thou loved us? *Was* not Esau Jacob's brother? saith the LORD: yet I loved Jacob,

3 And I hated Esau, and laid his mountains and his heritage waste for the dragons of the wilderness.

Rom. 9. 13 As it is written, Jacob have I loved, but Esau have I hated.

C

Rev. 12. 11 And they overcame him by the blood of the Lamb, and by the word of their testimony; and they loved not their lives unto the death.

§ 132. WHAT IS REQUIRED OF TRUE DISCIPLES

D

Matt.16. 24 Then said Jesus unto his disciples, If any *man* will come after me, let him deny himself, and take up his cross, and follow me.

Mark 8. 34 And when he had called the people *unto him* with his disciples also, he said unto them, Whosoever will come after me, let him deny himself, and take up his cross, and follow me.

Luke 9. 23 And he said to *them* all, If any *man* will come after me, let him deny himself, and take up his cross daily, and follow me.

II Tim.3. 12 Yea, and all that will live godly in Christ Jesus shall suffer persecution.

E

Gen. 11. 4 And they said, Go to, let us build us a city, and a tower, whose top *may reach* unto heaven; and let us make us a name, lest we be scattered abroad upon the face of the whole earth.

5 And the LORD came down to see the city and the tower, which the children of men builded.

6 And the LORD said, Behold, the people *is* one, and they have all one language; and this they begin to do: and now nothing will be restrained from them, which they have imagined to do.

7 Go to, let us go down, and there confound their language, that they may not understand one another's speech.

8 So the LORD scattered them abroad from thence upon the face of all the earth: and they left off to build the city.

9 Therefore is the name of it called Babel; because the LORD did there confound the language of all the earth: and from thence did the LORD scatter them abroad upon the face of all the earth.

Prov.24. 27 Prepare thy work without, and make it fit for thyself in the field: and afterwards build thine house.

F

Josh. 24. 19 And Joshua said unto the people, Ye cannot serve the LORD: for he *is* a holy God; he *is* a jealous God; he will not forgive your transgressions nor your sins.

20 If ye forsake the LORD, and serve strange gods, then he will turn and do you hurt, and consume you, after that he hath done you good.

21 And the people said unto Joshua, Nay; but we will serve the LORD.

22 And Joshua said unto the people, Ye *are* witnesses against yourselves that ye have chosen you the LORD, to serve him. And they said, *We are* witnesses.

23 Now therefore put away, *said he*, the strange gods which *are* among you, and incline your heart unto the LORD God of Israel.

24 And the people said unto Joshua, The LORD our God will we serve, and his voice will we obey.

Acts 21. 13 Then Paul answered, What mean ye to weep and to break mine heart? for I am ready not to be bound only, but also to die at Jerusalem for the name of the Lord Jesus.

I Thes.3. 4 For verily, when we were with you, we told you before that we should suffer tribulation; even as it came to pass, and ye know.

5 For this cause, when I could no longer forbear, I sent to know your faith, lest by some means the tempter have tempted you, and our labour be in vain.

II Pet.1. 13 Yea, I think it meet, as long as I am in this tabernacle, to stir you up by putting *you* in remembrance;

14 Knowing that shortly I must put off *this* my tabernacle, even as our Lord Jesus Christ hath showed me.

G

Matt. 7. 27 And the rain descended, and the floods came, and the winds blew, and beat upon that house; and it fell: and great was the fall of it.

§ 133. PARABLE OF THE LOST SHEEP SPOKEN A SECOND TIME.

A

Matt. 9. 10 And it came to pass, as Jesus sat at meat in the house, behold, many publicans and sinners came and sat down with him and his disciples.

B

Eze. 18. 21 But if the wicked will turn from all his sins that he hath committed, and keep all my statutes, and do that which is lawful and right, he shall

B—CONTINUED.

surely live, he shall not die.

22 All his transgressions that he hath committed, they shall not be mentioned unto him: in his righteousness that he hath done he shall live.

23 Have I any pleasure at all that the wicked should die? saith the Lord GOD: *and* not that he should return from his ways, and live?

(CONCLUDED). TIME, FEBRUARY–MARCH, A. D. 30; PLACE, PERÆA.

CHAP. 14.

27 And [d]whosoever doth not bear his cross, and come after me, cannot be my disciple.

28 For [e]which of you, intending to build a tower, sitteth not down first, and [f]counteth the cost, whether he have *sufficient* to finish *it?*

29 Lest haply, after he hath laid the foundation, and is not able to finish *it*, all that behold *it*, begin to mock him,

30 Saying, [g]This man began to build, and was not able to finish.

31 Or what king, going to make war against another king, sitteth not down first, and consulteth whether he be able with ten thousand to meet him that cometh against him with twenty thousand?

32 Or else, while the other is yet a great way off, he sendeth an [h]ambassage, and desireth conditions of peace.

33 So likewise, whosoever [i]he be of you that forsaketh not all that he hath, he cannot be my disciple.

34 [k]Salt *is* good: but if the salt have lost his savour, wherewith shall it be seasoned?

35 It is neither fit for the land, nor yet for the dunghill; *but* men cast it out. He that hath ears to hear, let him hear.

G—CONCLUDED.

Acts 1. 18 Now this man purchased a field with the reward of iniquity; and falling headlong, he burst asunder in the midst, and all his bowels gushed out.

19 And it was known unto all the dwellers at Jerusalem; insomuch as that field is called, in their proper tongue, Aceldama, that is to say, The field of blood.

I Cor. 3. 11 For other foundation can no man lay than that is laid, which is Jesus Christ.

H

Job 22. 21 Acquaint now thyself with him, and be at peace: thereby good shall come unto thee.

II Cor.6. 2 (For he saith, I have heard thee in a time accepted, and in the day of salvation have I succoured thee: behold, now *is* the accepted time; behold, now *is* the day of salvation.)

I

Matt.19. 27 Then answered Peter and said unto him, Behold, we have forsaken all, and followed thee; what shall we have therefore?

28 And Jesus said unto them, Verily I say unto you, That ye which have followed me, in the regeneration when the Son of man shall sit in the throne of his glory, ye also shall sit upon twelve thrones, judging the twelve tribes of Israel.

K

Matt. 5. 13 Ye are the salt of the earth: but if the salt have lost his savour, wherewith shall it be salted? it is thenceforth good for nothing, but to be cast out, and to be trodden under foot of men.

Mark 9. 49 For every one shall be salted with fire, and every sacrifice shall be salted with salt.

50 Salt *is* good: but if the salt have lost his saltness, wherewith will ye season it? Have salt in yourselves and have peace one with another.

[SEE § 102.] TIME, FEBRUARY–MARCH, A. D. 30; PLACE, PERÆA.

15: 1–7.

1 Then [a]drew near unto him all the publicans and [b]sinners for to hear him.

2 And the Pharisees and scribes murmured, saying, This man receiveth sinners, [c]and eateth with them.

B—CONCLUDED.

I Tim.1. 15 This *is* a faithful saying, and worthy of all acceptation, that Christ Jesus came into the world to save sinners; of whom I am chief.

C

Acts 11. 3 Saying, Thou wentest in to men uncircumcised, and didst eat with them.

For C concluded see next page (382).

§ 133. PARABLE OF THE LOST SHEEP SPOKEN A SECOND TIME

C—CONCLUDED. See preceding page (381).

Gal. 2. 12 For before that certain came from James, he did eat with the Gentiles: but when they were come, he withdrew and separated himself, fearing them which were of the circumcision.

D

Matt. 18. 10 Take heed that ye despise not one of these little ones; for I say unto you, That in heaven their angels do always behold the face of my Father which is in heaven.

11 For the Son of man is come to save that which was lost.

12 How think ye? if a man have a hundred sheep, and one of them be gone astray, doth he not leave the ninety and nine, and goeth into the mountains, and seeketh that which is gone astray?

13 And if so be that he find it, verily I say unto you, he rejoiceth more of that *sheep*, than of the ninety and nine which went not astray.

14 Even so it is not the will of your Father which is in heaven, that one of these little ones should perish.

John 10. 11 I am the good shepherd: the good shepherd giveth his life for the sheep.

E

I Pet. 2. 25 For ye were as sheep going astray; but are now returned unto the Shepherd and Bishop of your souls.

F

John 15. 14 Ye are my friends, if ye do whatsoever I command you.

Acts 11. 23 Who, when he came, and had seen the grace of God, was glad, and exhorted them all, that with purpose of heart they would cleave unto the Lord.

Acts 15. 3 And being brought on their way by the church, they passed through Phenice and Samaria, declaring the conversion of the Gentiles: and they caused great joy unto all the brethren.

Phil. 1. 3 I thank my God upon every remembrance of you,

4 Always in every prayer of mine for you all making request with joy,

Phil. 2. 17 Yea, and if I be offered upon the sacrifice and service of your faith, I joy, and rejoice with you all.

I Thes. 2. 19 For what *is* our hope, or joy, or crown of rejoicing? *Are* not even ye in the presence of our Lord Jesus Christ at his coming?

I Thes. 3. 9 For what thanks can we render to God again for you, for all the joy

§ 134. THE PARABLE OF THE PIECE OF MONEY.

1

Drachma, here translated, *a piece of silver*, is the eighth part of an ounce and is equal to the Roman penny; in American money, *15 cents*.

A

Matt. 18. 12. *See under D, § 133.*

John 10. 14 I am the good shepherd, and know my *sheep*, and am known of mine.

15 As the Father knoweth me, even so know I the Father: and I lay down my life for the sheep.

B

Isa. 56. 8 The Lord GOD which gathereth the outcasts of Israel saith, Yet will I gather *others* to him, beside those that are gathered unto him.

Eze. 34. 12 As a shepherd seeketh out his flock in the day that he is among his sheep *that are* scattered; so will I seek out my sheep, and will deliver them out of all places where they have been scattered in the cloudy and dark day.

John 10. 16 And other sheep I have, which are not of this fold: them also I must bring, and they shall hear my voice; and there shall be one fold, *and* one shepherd.

B—CONCLUDED.

John 11. 52 And not for that nation only, but that also he should gather together in one the children of God that were scattered abroad.

Eph. 2. 17 And came and preached peace to you which were afar off and to them that were nigh.

I Pet. 2. 25. *See under, E § 133.*

C

Matt. 18. 13. *See under D, § 133.*

D

Eze. 18. 23 Have I any pleasure at all that the wicked should die? saith the Lord GOD: *and* not that he should return from his ways, and live?

Eze. 18. 32 For I have no pleasure in the death of him that dieth, saith the Lord GOD: wherefore turn *yourselves*, and live ye.

Eze. 33. 11 Say unto them, *As* I live, saith the Lord GOD, I have no pleasure in the death of the wicked; but that the wicked turn from his way and live: turn ye, turn ye from your evil ways; for why will ye die, O house of Israel?

(CONCLUDED). [SEE § 102.] TIME, FEBRUARY-MARCH, A. D. 30; PLACE, PERÆA.

CHAP. 15.

3 And he spake this parable unto
them, saying,
4 [d]What man of you, having a hundred sheep, if he [e]lose one of them,
doth not leave the ninety and nine in the wilderness, and go after that which is lost, until he find it?
5 And when he hath found *it*, he layeth *it* on his shoulders, rejoicing.
6 And when he cometh home, he calleth together [f]*his* friends and neighbours, saying unto them, Rejoice with me; for I have found my sheep [g]which was lost.
7 I say unto you, that likewise joy shall be in heaven over one sinner that repenteth, [h]more than over ninety and nine just persons, which need no repentance.

F—CONCLUDED.

wherewith we joy for your sakes before our God;

G

I Pet. 2. 9 But ye *are* a chosen generation, a royal priesthood, a holy nation, a peculiar people; that ye should show forth the praises of him who hath called you out of darkness into his marvellous light:
10 Which in time past *were* not a people, but *are* now the people of God: which had not obtained mercy, but now have obtained mercy.

I Pet. 2. 25. *See under E.*

H

Prov.30. 12 *There is* a generation *that are* pure in their own eyes, and *yet* is not washed from their filthiness.

Luke 5. 32 I came not to call the righteous, but sinners to repentance.

Luke 18. 13 And the publican, standing afar off, would not lift up so much as *his* eyes unto heaven, but smote upon his breast, saying, God be merciful to me a sinner.
14 I tell you, this man went down to his house justified *rather* than the other: for every one that exalteth himself shall be abased; and he that humbleth himself shall be exalted.

TIME, FEBRUARY-MARCH, A. D. 30; PLACE, PERÆA.

15: 8–10.

8 Either what woman having [1]ten pieces of silver, [a]if she lose one piece, doth not light a candle, and sweep the house, [b]and seek diligently till she find *it?*
9 [c]And when she hath found *it*, she calleth *her* friends and *her* neighbours together, saying, Rejoice with me; for I have found the piece which I had lost.
10 Likewise, I say unto you, [d]there is joy in the presence of the angels of God over [e]one sinner that repenteth.

D—CONTINUED.

Matt. 18. 10, 11. *See under D, § 133.*

Luke 2. 10 And the angel said unto them, Fear not: for, behold, I bring you good tidings of great joy, which shall be to all people.
11 For unto you is born this day in the city of David a Saviour, which is Christ the Lord.
12 And this *shall be* a sign unto you; Ye shall find the babe wrapped in

D—CONCLUDED.

swaddling clothes, lying in a manger.
13 And suddenly there was with the angel a multitude of the heavenly host praising God, and saying,
14 Glory to God in the highest, and on earth peace, good will toward men.

Heb. 1. 14 Are they not all ministering spirits, sent forth to minister for them who shall be heirs of salvation?

E

Acts 11. 18 When they heard these things, they held their peace, and glorified God, saying, Then hath God also to the Gentiles granted repentance unto life.

II Cor.7. 10 For godly sorrow worketh repentance to salvation not to be repented of: but the sorrow of the world worketh death.

Phile. 15 For perhaps he therefore departed for a season, that thou shouldest receive him for ever;
16 Not now as a servant, but above a servant, a brother beloved, specially to me, but how much more unto thee, both in the flesh, and in the Lord?

§ 135. THE PARABLE OF THE PRODIGAL SON.

A

Mark 12. 44 For all *they* did cast in of their abundance; but she of her want did cast in all that she had, *even* all her living.

B

Rom. 1. 21 Because that, when they knew God, they glorified *him* not as God, neither were thankful; but became vain in their imaginations, and their foolish heart was darkened.

Tit. 3. 3 For we ourselves also were sometimes foolish, disobedient, deceived, serving divers lusts and pleasures, living in malice and envy, hateful, *and* hating one another.

C

Prov. 5. 8 Remove thy way far from her, and come not nigh the door of her house:

9 Lest thou give thine honour unto others, and thy years unto the cruel:

10 Lest strangers be filled with thy wealth; and thy labours *be* in the house of a stranger;

11 And thou mourn at the last, when thy flesh and thy body are consumed,

12 And say, How have I hated instruction, and my heart despised reproof;

13 And have not obeyed the voice of my teachers, nor inclined mine ear to them that instructed me!

14 I was almost in all evil in the midst of the congregation and assembly.

Prov. 6. 20 My son, keep thy father's commandment, and forsake not the law of thy mother:

Eccl. 11. 9 Rejoice, O young man, in thy youth; and let thy heart cheer thee in the days of thy youth, and walk in the ways of thine heart, and in the sight of thine eyes: but know thou, that for all these *things* God will bring thee into judgment.

10 Therefore remove sorrow from thy heart, and put away evil from thy flesh: for childhood and youth *are* vanity.

Rom. 13. 13 Let us walk honestly, as in the day; not in rioting and drunkenness, not in chambering and wantonness, not in strife and envying:

14 But put ye on the Lord Jesus Christ, and make not provision for the flesh, to *fulfil* the lusts *thereof.*

D

Isa. 1. 5 Why should ye be stricken any more? ye will revolt more and more: the whole head is sick, and the whole heart faint.

D—Concluded.

Isa. 1. 9 Except the Lord of hosts had left unto us a very small remnant, we should have been as Sodom, *and* we should have been like unto Gomorrah.

II Tim. 2. 25 In meekness instructing those that oppose themselves; if God peradventure will give them repentance to the acknowledging of the truth;

26 And *that* they may recover themselves out of the snare of the devil, who are taken captive by him at his will.

E

Mal. 2. 9 Therefore have I also made you comtemptible and base before all the people, according as ye have not kept my ways, but have been partial in the law.

Rom. 1. 24 Wherefore God also gave them up to uncleanness, through the lusts of their own hearts, to dishonour their own bodies between themselves:

25 Who changed the truth of God into a lie, and worshipped and served the creature more than the Creator, who is blessed for ever. Amen.

26 For this cause God gave them up unto vile affections: for even their women did change the natural use into that which is against nature:

F

Isa. 44. 20 He feedeth on ashes: a deceived heart hath turned him aside, that he cannot deliver his soul, nor say, *Is there* not a lie in my right hand?

Rom. 6. 19 I speak after the manner of men because of the infirmity of your flesh: for as ye have yielded your members servants to uncleanness and to iniquity unto iniquity; even so now yield your members servants to righteousness unto holiness.

20 For when ye were the servants of sin, ye were free from righteousness.

21 What fruit had ye then in those things whereof ye are now ashamed? for the end of those things *is* death.

G

Ps. 32. 5 I acknowledged my sin unto thee, and mine iniquity have I not hid. I said, I will confess my transgressions unto the Lord; and thou forgavest the iniquity of my sin. Selah.

Jer. 50. 4 In those days, and in that time, saith the Lord, the children of Israel shall come, they and the children of Judah together, going and weeping: they shall go, and seek the Lord their God.

TIME, FEBRUARY–MARCH, A. D. 30; PLACE, PERÆA.

15 : 11–32.

11 And he said, A certain man had two sons:

12 And the younger of them said to *his* father, Father, give me the portion of goods that falleth *to me.* And he divided unto them [a]*his* living.

13 And not many days after the younger son gathered all together, and took his journey into [b]a far country, [c]and there wasted his substance with riotous living.

14 And when he had spent all, there arose a mighty famine in that land; and he began to be in want.

15 [d]And he went and joined himself to a citizen of that country; and he sent him into his fields [e]to feed swine.

16 And [f]he would fain have filled his belly with the husks that the swine did eat: and no man gave unto him.

17 And when he came to himself, he said, How many hired servants of my father's have bread enough and to spare, and I perish with hunger!

18 I [g]will arise and go to my father, and will say unto him, Father, [h]I have sinned against heaven, and before thee,

19 And am no more worthy to be called thy son: make me as one of thy hired servants.

20 And he arose, and came to his father. But [i]when he was yet a great way off, his father saw him, and had compassion, and ran, and fell on his neck, and kissed him.

21 And the son said unto him, Father, I have sinned against heaven, [k]and in thy sight, and am no more worthy to be called thy son.

G—CONCLUDED.

Jer. 50. 5 They shall ask the way to Zion with their faces thitherward, *saying,* Come, and let us join ourselves to the LORD in a perpetual covenant *that* shall not be forgotten.

Lam. 3. 37 Who *is* he *that* saith, and it cometh to pass, *when* the Lord commandeth *it* not?

38 Out of the mouth of the Most High proceedeth not evil and good?

39 Wherefore doth a living man complain, a man for the punishment of his sins?

40 Let us search and try our ways, and turn again to the LORD.

41 Let us lift up our heart with *our* hands unto God in the heavens.

H

Luke 18. 13 And the publican, standing afar off, would not lift up so much as *his* eyes unto heaven, but smote upon his breast, saying, God be merciful to me a sinner.

I

Isa. 49. 13 Sing, O heavens; and be joyful, O earth; and break forth into singing, O mountains: for the LORD hath comforted his people, and will have mercy upon his afflicted.

14 But Zion said, The LORD hath forsaken me, and my Lord hath forgotten me.

15 Can a woman forget her sucking child, that she should not have compassion on the son of her womb? yea, they may forget, yet will I not forget thee.

16 Behold, I have graven thee upon the palms of *my* hands; thy walls *are* continually before me.

17 Thy children shall make haste; thy destroyers and they that made thee waste shall go forth of thee.

Acts 2. 39 For the promise is unto you, and to your children, and to all that are afar off, *even* as many as the Lord our God shall call.

Eph. 2. 13 But now, in Christ Jesus, ye who sometime were far off are made nigh by the blood of Christ.

Eph. 2. 17 And came and preached peace to you which were afar off, and to them that were nigh.

K

Ps. 51. 4 Against thee, thee only, have I sinned, and done *this* evil in thy sight: that thou mightest be justified when thou speakest, *and* be clear when thou judgest.

§ 135. THE PARABLE OF THE PRODIGAL SON

L

Matt.22. 11 And when the king came in to see the guests, he saw there a man which had not on a wedding garment:

12 And he saith unto him, Friend, how camest thou in hither not having a wedding garment? And he was speechless.

Gal. 3. 27 For as many of you as have been baptized into Christ have put on Christ.

Rev. 19. 7 Let us be glad and rejoice, and give honour to him: for the marriage of the Lamb is come, and his wife hath made herself ready.

8 And to her was granted that she should be arrayed in fine linen, clean and white: for the fine linen is the righteousness of saints.

M

Luke 15. 32. *See text of topic.*

Eph. 2. 1 And you *hath he quickened*, who were dead in trespasses and sins:

Eph. 5. 14 Wherefore he saith, Awake thou that sleepest, and arise from the dead, and Christ shall give thee light.

Col. 1. 12 Giving thanks unto the Father, which hath made us meet to be partakers of the inheritance of the saints in light:

13 Who hath delivered us from the power of darkness, and hath translated *us* into the kingdom of his dear Son:

Col. 2. 13 And you, being dead in your sins and the uncircumcision of your flesh, hath he quickened together with him, having forgiven you all trespasses;

Jude 12 These are spots in your feasts of charity, when they feast with you, feeding themselves without fear: clouds *they are* without water, carried about of winds; trees whose fruit withereth, without fruit, twice dead, plucked up by the roots;

Rev. 3. 1 And unto the angel of the church in Sardis write; These things saith he that hath the seven Spirits of God, and the seven stars; I know thy works, that thou hast a name that thou livest, and art dead.

N

Isa. 35. 8 And a highway shall be there, and a way, and it shall be called The way of holiness; the unclean shall not pass over it; but it *shall be* for those: the wayfaring men, though fools, shall not err *therein.*

9 No lion shall be there, nor *any* ravenous beast shall go up thereon, it shall not be found there; but the redeemed shall walk *there:*

N—Concluded.

Isa. 35. 10 And the ransomed of the Lord shall return, and come to Zion with songs and everlasting joy upon their heads: they shall obtain joy and gladness, and sorrow and sighing shall flee away.

O

Ex. 15. 20 And Miriam the prophetess, the sister of Aaron, took a timbrel in her hand; and all the women went out after her with timbrels and with dances.

Eccl. 3. 4 A time to weep, and a time to laugh; a time to mourn, and a time to dance;

Jer. 31. 4 Again I will build thee, and thou shalt be built, O virgin of Israel: thou shalt again be adorned with thy tabrets, and shalt go forth in the dances of them that make merry.

P

Acts 11. 1 And the apostles and brethren that were in Judæa heard that the Gentiles had also received the word of God.

2 And when Peter was come up to Jerusalem, they that were of the circumcision contended with him,

3 Saying, Thou wentest in to men uncircumcised, and didst eat with them.

Q

I Sa. 15. 13 And Samuel came to Saul: and Saul said unto him, Blessed *be* thou of the Lord: I have performed the commandment of the Lord.

14 And Samuel said, What *meaneth* then this bleating of the sheep in mine ears, and the lowing of the oxen which I hear?

Isa. 58. 1 Cry aloud, spare not, lift up thy voice like a trumpet, and show my people their transgression, and the house of Jacob their sins.

2 Yet they seek me daily, and delight to know my ways, as a nation that did righteousness, and forsook not the ordinance of their God: they ask of me the ordinances of justice; they take delight in approaching to God.

Isa. 65. 5 Which say, Stand by thyself, come not near to me; for I am holier than thou. These *are* a smoke in my nose, a fire that burneth all the day.

Zech. 7. 3 *And* to speak unto the priests which *were* in the house of the Lord of hosts, and to the prophets, saying, Should I weep in the fifth month, separating myself, as I have done these so many years?

(CONCLUDED). TIME, FEBRUARY-MARCH, A. D. 30; PLACE, PERÆA.

CHAP. 15.

22 But the father said to his servants, Bring forth the [l]best robe, and put *it* on him; and put a ring on his hand, and shoes on *his* feet:

23 And bring hither the fatted calf, and kill *it;* and let us eat, and be merry:

24 [m]For this my son was dead, and is alive again; he was lost, and is found. And they [n]began to be merry.

25 Now his elder son was in the field: [o]and as he came and drew nigh to the house, he heard music and dancing.

26 And he called one of the servants, and asked what these things meant.

27 And he said unto him, Thy brother is come; and thy father hath killed the fatted calf, because he hath received him safe and sound.

28 [p]And he was angry, and would not go in: therefore came his father out, and entreated him.

29 And he answering said to *his* father, [q]Lo, these many years do I serve thee, neither transgressed I at any time thy commandment; and [r]yet thou never gavest me a kid, that I might make merry with my friends:

30 But as soon as this thy son was come, which hath devoured thy living with harlots, thou hast killed for him the fatted calf.

31 And he said unto him, Son, thou art ever with me, and all that I have is thine.

32 It [s]was meet that we should make merry, and be glad: [t]for this thy brother was dead, and is alive again; and was lost, and is found.

Q—CONCLUDED.

Matt.20. 12 Saying, These last have wrought *but* one hour, and thou hast made them equal unto us, which have borne the burden and heat of the day.

Rom. 3. 20 Therefore by the deeds of the law there shall no flesh be justified in his sight: for by the law *is* the knowledge of sin.

I Jno. 1. 8 He that loveth not, knoweth not God; for God is love.

I Jno. 4. 9 In this was manifested the love of God toward us, because that God sent his only begotten Son into the world, that we might live through him.

10 Herein is love, not that we loved God, but that he loved us, and sent his Son *to be* the propitiation for our sins.

Rev. 3. 17 Because thou sayest, I am rich, and increased with goods, and have need of nothing; and knowest not that thou art wretched, and miserable, and poor, and blind, and naked:

R

Mal. 3. 14 Ye have said, It *is* vain to serve God: and what profit *is it* that we have kept his ordinance, and that we have walked mournfully before the LORD of hosts?

Matt.20. 10 But when the first came, they supposed that they should have received more; and they likewise received every man a penny.

11 And when they had received *it*, they murmured against the goodman of the house,

Matt. 20. 12. *See under Q.*

S

Rom.15. 8 Now I say that Jesus Christ was a minister of the circumcision for the truth of God, to confirm the promises *made* unto the fathers:

9 And that the Gentiles might glorify God for *his* mercy; as it is written, For this cause I will confess to thee among the Gentiles, and sing unto thy name.

10 And again he saith, Rejoice, ye Gentiles, with his people.

11 And again, Praise the Lord, all ye Gentiles; and laud him, all ye people.

12 And again, Esaias saith, There shall be a root of Jesse, and he that shall rise to reign over the Gentiles; in him shall the Gentiles trust.

T

Luke 15. 24. *See text of topic.*

§ 136. THE PARABLE OF THE UNJUST STEWARD.

A

Ps. 24. 1 The earth *is* the LORD's, and the fulness thereof; the world, and they that dwell therein.

B

Gen. 15. 2 And Abram said, Lord GOD, what wilt thou give me, seeing I go childless, and the steward of my house *is* this Eliezer of Damascus?

Gen. 43. 19 And they came near to the steward of Joseph's house, and they communed with him at the door of the house.

Luke 12. 42 And the Lord said, Who then is that faithful and wise steward, whom *his* lord shall make ruler over his household, to give *them their* portion of meat in due season?

I Cor. 4. 1 Let a man so account of us, as of the ministers of Christ, and stewards of the mysteries of God.

2 Moreover it is required in stewards, that a man be found faithful.

Tit. 1. 7 For a bishop must be blameless, as the steward of God; not selfwilled, not soon angry, not given to wine, no striker, not given to filthy lucre:

I Pet. 4. 10 As every man hath received the gift, *even so* minister the same one to another, as good stewards of the manifold grace of God.

C

Prov.18. 9 He also that is slothful in his work is brother to him that is a great waster.

Hos. 2. 8 For she did not know that I gave her corn, and wine, and oil, and multiplied her silver and gold, *which* they prepared for Baal.

Luke 15. 13. *See text of § 135, page 385.*

Jas. 4. 3 Ye ask, and receive not, because ye ask amiss, that ye may consume *it* upon your lusts.

D

Eccl. 12. 14 For God shall bring every work into judgment, with every secret thing, whether *it be* good, or whether *it be* evil.

Matt.12. 36 But I say unto you, That every idle word that men shall speak, they shall give account thereof in the day of judgment.

Rom.14. 12 So then every one of us shall give account of himself to God.

I Cor. 4. 5 Therefore judge nothing before the time, until the Lord come, who both will bring to light the hidden things of darkness, and will make manifest the counsels of the hearts: and then shall every man have praise of God.

E

Prov. 13. 4 The soul of the sluggard desireth, and *hath* nothing: but the soul of the diligent shall be made fat.

Prov.29. 21 He that delicately bringeth up his servant from a child shall have him become *his* son at the length.

II Thes. 3. 11 For we hear that there are some which walk among you disorderly, working not at all, but are busybodies.

F

Prov.30. 8 Remove far from me vanity and lies; give me neither poverty nor riches; feed me with food convenient for me:

9 Lest I be full, and deny *thee*, and say, Who *is* the LORD? or lest I be poor, and steal, and take the name of my God *in vain*.

Jer. 4. 22 For my people *is* foolish, they have not known me; they *are* sottish children, and they have none understanding: they *are* wise to do evil, but to do good they have no knowledge.

1

The word *Batus* in the original contains nine gallons three quarts.

Eze. 45. 10 Ye shall have just balances, and a just ephah, and a just bath.

11 The ephah and the bath shall be of one measure, that the bath may contain the tenth part of a homer, and the ephah the tenth part of a homer: the measure thereof shall be after the homer.

Eze. 45. 14 Concerning the ordinance of oil, the bath of oil, *ye shall offer* the tenth part of a bath out of the cor, *which is* a homer of ten baths; for ten baths *are* a homer:

2

The word here interpreted *a measure* in the original contains about fourteen bushels and a pottle.

G

Gen. 3. 1 Now the serpent was more subtile than any beast of the field which the LORD God had made. And he said unto the woman, Yea, hath God said, Ye shall not eat of every tree of the garden?

Ex. 1. 10 Come on, let us deal wisely with them; lest they multiply, and it come to pass, that, when there falleth out any war, they join also unto our enemies, and fight against us, and *so* get them up out of the land.

II Ki.10. 19 Now therefore call unto me all the prophets of Baal, all his servants, and all his priests; let none be wanting: for I have a great sacrifice *to do* to

TIME, FEBRUARY–MARCH, A. D. 30; PLACE, PERÆA.

16: 1–13.

1 And he said also unto his disciples, There was a certain [a]rich man, which had a [b]steward; and the same was accused unto him that he had [c]wasted his goods.

2 And he called him, and said unto him, How is it that I hear this of thee? [d]give an account of thy stewardship; for thou mayest be no longer steward.

3 Then the steward said within himself, What shall I do? for my lord taketh away from me the stewardship: [e]I cannot dig; to beg I am ashamed.

4 [f]I am resolved what to do that, when I am put out of the stewardship, they may receive me into their houses.

5 So he called every one of his lord's debtors *unto him*, and said unto the first, How much owest thou unto my lord?

6 And he said, A hundred [1]measures of oil. And he said unto him, Take thy bill, and sit down quickly, and write fifty.

7 Then said he to another, And how much owest thou? And he said, A hundred [2]measures of wheat. And he said unto him, Take thy bill, and write fourscore.

8 And the lord commended the unjust steward, because [g]he had done wisely: for the children of this world are in their generation wiser than [h]the children of light.

9 And I say unto you, [i]Make to yourselves friends of the mammon of unrighteousness; that, when ye fail, they may receive you into everlasting habitations.

G—CONCLUDED.

Baal; whosoever shall be wanting, he shall not live. But Jehu did *it* in subtilty, to the intent that he might destroy the worshippers of Baal.

Prov. 6. 6 Go to the ant, thou sluggard; consider her ways, and be wise:

7 Which having no guide, overseer, or ruler,

8 Provideth her meat in the summer, *and* gathereth her food in the harvest.

H

John 12. 36 While ye have light, believe in the light, that ye may be the children of light. These things spake Jesus, and departed, and did hide himself from them.

Eph. 5. 8 For ye were sometime darkness, but now *are ye* light in the Lord: walk as children of light.

I Thes. 5. 5 Ye are all the children of light, and the children of the day: we are not of the night, nor of darkness.

I Pet. 2. 9 But ye *are* a chosen generation, a royal priesthood, a holy nation, a peculiar people; that ye should show forth the praises of him who hath called you out of darkness into his marvellous light:

I

Dan. 4. 27 Wherefore, O king, let my counsel be acceptable unto thee, and break off thy sins by righteousness, and thine iniquities by showing mercy to the poor; if it may be a lengthening of thy tranquillity.

Matt. 6. 19 Lay not up for yourselves treasures upon earth, where moth and rust doth corrupt, and where thieves break through and steal:

Matt. 19. 21 Jesus said unto him, If thou wilt be perfect, go *and* sell that thou hast, and give to the poor, and thou shalt have treasure in heaven: and come *and* follow me.

Luke 11. 41 But rather give alms of such things as ye have: and, behold, all things are clean unto you.

I Tim. 6. 17 Charge them that are rich in this world, that they be not highminded, nor trust in uncertain riches, but in the living God, who giveth us richly all things to enjoy;

18 That they do good, that they be rich in good works, ready to distribute, willing to communicate:

19 Laying up in store for themselves a good foundation against the time to come, that they may lay hold on eternal life.

§ 136. THE PARABLE OF THE UNJUST STEWARD

K

Matt.25. 21 His lord said unto him, Well done, *thou* good and faithful servant: thou hast been faithful over a few things, I will make thee ruler over many things: enter thou into the joy of thy lord.

Luke 19. 17 And he said unto him, Well, thou good servant: because thou hast been faithful in a very little, have thou authority over ten cities.

Heb. 3. 2 Who was faithful to him that appointed him, as also Moses *was faithful* in all his house.

3

Or, *riches.*

L

Prov. 8. 18 Riches and honour *are* with me; *yea*, durable riches and righteousness.
19 My fruit *is* better than gold, yea, than fine gold; and my revenue than choice silver.
20 I lead in the way of righteousness, in the midst of the paths of judgment:
21 That I may cause those that love me to inherit substance; and I will fill their treasures.

Eph. 3. 8 Unto me, who am less than the least of all saints, is this grace given, that I should preach among the Gentiles the unsearchable riches of Christ;

Jas. 2. 5 Hearken, my beloved brethren,

L—CONCLUDED.

Hath not God chosen the poor of this world rich in faith, and heirs of the kingdom which he hath promised to them that love him?

Rev. 3. 18 I counsel thee to buy of me gold tried in the fire, that thou mayest be rich; and white raiment, that thou mayest be clothed, and *that* the shame of thy nakedness do not appear; and anoint thine eyes with eyesalve, that thou mayest see.

M

Josh. 24. 15 And if it seem evil unto you to serve the LORD, choose you this day whom ye will serve; whether the gods which your fathers served that *were* on the other side of the flood, or the gods of the Amorites, in whose land ye dwell: but as for me and my house, we will serve the LORD.

Matt. 6. 24 No man can serve two masters: for either he will hate the one, and love the other; or else he will hold to the one, and despise the other. Ye cannot serve God and mammon.

Rom. 6. 16 Know ye not, that to whom ye yield yourselves servants to obey, his servants ye are to whom ye obey; whether of sin unto death, or of obedience unto righteousness?

§ 137. THE PHARISEES REPROVED. PARABLE OF THE RICH MAN

A

Matt.23. 14 Woe unto you, scribes and Pharisees, hypocrites! for ye devour widows' houses, and for a pretence make long prayer: therefore ye shall receive the greater damnation.

B

Luke 10. 29 But he, willing to justify himself, said unto Jesus, And who is my neighbour?

C

Ps. 7. 9 Oh let the wickedness of the wicked come to an end; but establish the just: for the righteous God trieth the hearts and reins.

Jer. 17. 10 I the LORD search the heart, *I* try the reins, even to give every man according to his ways, *and* according to the fruit of his doings.

D

I Sa. 16. 7 But the LORD said unto Samuel, Look not on his countenance, or on the height of his stature; because I have refused him: for *the LORD seeth* not as man seeth; for man looketh on the outward appearance, but the LORD looketh on the heart.

D—CONCLUDED.

Jas. 4. 4 Ye adulterers and adulteresses, know ye not that the friendship of the world is enmity with God? whosoever therefore will be a friend of the world is the enemy of God.

E

Matt. 4. 17 From that time Jesus began to preach, and to say, Repent: for the kingdom of heaven is at hand.

Matt.11. 12 And from the days of John the Baptist until now the kingdom of heaven suffereth violence, and the violent take it by force.
13 For all the prophets and the law prophesied until John.

Luke 7. 29 And all the people that heard *him*, and the publicans, justified God, being baptized with the baptism of John.

F

Ps. 102. 25 Of old hast thou laid the foundation of the earth: and the heavens *are* the work of thy hands.
26 They shall perish, but thou shalt endure: yea, all of them shall wax

(CONCLUDED). TIME, FEBRUARY-MARCH, A. D. 30; PLACE, PERÆA.

CHAP. 16.

10 [k]He that is faithful in that which is least is faithful also in much: and he that is unjust in the least is unjust also in much.

11 If therefore ye have not been faithful in the unrighteous [3]mammon, who will commit to your trust the [l]true *riches?*

12 And if ye have not been faithful in that which is another man's, who shall give you that which is your own?

13 [m]No servant can serve two masters: for either he will hate the one, and love the other; or else he will hold to the one, and despise the other. Ye cannot serve God and mammon.

M—CONTINUED.

Rom. 6. 17 But God be thanked, that ye were the servants of sin, but ye have obeyed from the heart that form of doctrine which was delivered you.

18 Being then made free from sin, ye became the servants of righteousness.

M—CONCLUDED.

Rom. 6. 19 I speak after the manner of men because of the infirmity of your flesh: for as ye have yielded your members servants to uncleanness and to iniquity unto iniquity; even so now yield your members servants to righteousness unto holiness.

20 For when ye were the servants of sin, ye were free from righteousness.

21 What fruit had ye then in those things whereof ye are now ashamed? for the end of those things *is* death.

22 But now being made free from sin, and become servants to God, ye have your fruit unto holiness, and the end everlasting life.

Rom. 8. 6 For to be carnally minded *is* death; but to be spiritually minded *is* life and peace.

7 Because the carnal mind *is* enmity against God: for it is not subject to the law of God, neither indeed can be.

I Jno. 2. 15 Love not the world, neither the things *that are* in the world. If any man love the world, the love of the Father is not in him.

16 For all that *is* in the world, the lust of the flesh, and the lust of the eyes, and the pride of life, is not of the Father, but is of the world.

AND LAZARUS. TIME, FEBRUARY-MARCH, A. D. 30; PLACE, PERÆA.

16: 14–31.

14 And the Pharisees also, [a]who were covetous, heard all these things: and they derided him.

15 And he said unto them, Ye are they which [b]justify yourselves before men; but [c]God knoweth your hearts: for [d]that which is highly esteemed among men is abomination in the sight of God.

16 [e]The law and the prophets *were* until John: since that time the kingdom of God is preached, and every man presseth into it.

17 [f]And it is easier for heaven and earth to pass, than one tittle of the law to fail.

F—CONCLUDED.

old like a garment; as a vesture shalt thou change them, and they shall be changed:

27 But thou *art* the same, and thy years shall have no end.

Isa. 40. 8 The grass withereth, the flower fadeth: but the word of our God shall stand for ever.

Isa. 51. 6 Lift up your eyes to the heavens, and look upon the earth beneath: for the heavens shall vanish away like smoke, and the earth shall wax old like a garment, and they that dwell therein shall die in like manner: but my salvation shall be for ever, and my righteousness shall not be abolished.

Matt. 5. 18 For verily I say unto you, Till heaven and earth pass, one jot or one tittle shall in no wise pass from the law, till all be fulfilled.

I Pet. 1. 25 But the word of the Lord endureth for ever. And this is the word which by the gospel is preached unto you.

§ 137. THE PHARISEES REPROVED. PARABLE OF THE RICH MAN AND

G

Matt. 5. 32 But I say unto you, That whosoever shall put away his wife, saving for the cause of fornication, causeth her to commit adultery: and whosoever shall marry her that is divorced committeth adultery.

Matt. 19. 9 And I say unto you, Whosoever shall put away his wife, except *it be* for fornication, and shall marry another, committeth adultery: and whoso marrieth her which is put away doth commit adultery.

Mark 10. 11 And he saith unto them, Whosoever shall put away his wife, and marry another, committeth adultery against her.

12 And if a woman shall put away her husband, and be married to another, she committeth adultery.

I. Cor. 7. 10 And unto the married I command, *yet* not I, but the Lord, Let not the wife depart from *her* husband:

11 But and if she depart, let her remain unmarried, or be reconciled to *her* husband: and let not the husband put away *his* wife.

H

Job 21. 11 They send forth their little ones like a flock, and their children dance.

12 They take the timbrel and harp, and rejoice at the sound of the organ.

13 They spend their days in wealth, and in a moment go down to the grave.

14 Therefore they say unto God, Depart from us; for we desire not the knowledge of thy ways.

15 What *is* the Almighty, that we should serve him? and what profit should we have, if we pray unto him?

Ps. 73. 2 But as for me, my feet were almost gone; my steps had well nigh slipped.

3 For I was envious at the foolish, *when* I saw the prosperity of the wicked.

4 For *there are* no bands in their death: but their strength *is* firm.

5 They *are* not in trouble *as other* men; neither are they plagued like *other* men.

6 Therefore pride compasseth them about as a chain; violence covereth them *as* a garment.

7 Their eyes stand out with fatness: they have more than heart could wish.

8 They are corrupt, and speak wickedly *concerning* oppression; they speak loftily.

H—Concluded.

Ps. 73. 9 They set their mouth against the heavens, and their tongue walketh through the earth.

10 Therefore his people return hither: and waters of a full *cup* are wrung out to them.

11 And they say, How doth God know? and is there knowledge in the Most High?

12 Behold, these *are* the ungodly, who prosper in the world; they increase *in* riches.

13 Verily I have cleansed my heart *in* vain, and washed my hands in innocency.

Ps. 73. 27 For, lo, they that are far from thee shall perish: thou hast destroyed all them that go a whoring from thee.

28 But *it is* good for me to draw near to God: I have put my trust in the Lord God, that I may declare all thy works.

I

Heb. 11. 36 And others had trial of *cruel* mockings and scourgings, yea, moreover of bonds and imprisonment:

37 They were stoned, they were sawn asunder, were tempted, were slain with the sword: they wandered about in sheepskins and goatskins; being destitute, afflicted, tormented;

38 Of whom the world was not worthy: they wandered in deserts, and *in* mountains, and *in* dens and caves of the earth.

K

Heb. 1. 13 But to which of the angels said he at any time, Sit on my right hand, until I make thine enemies thy footstool?

14 Are they not all ministering spirits, sent forth to minister for them who shall be heirs of salvation?

Jas. 2. 5 Hearken, my beloved brethren, Hath not God chosen the poor of this world rich in faith, and heirs of the kingdom which he hath promised to them that love him?

L

Zech. 14. 12 And this shall be the plague wherewith the Lord will smite all the people that have fought against Jerusalem; Their flesh shall consume away while they stand upon their feet, and their eyes shall consume away in their holes, and their tongue shall consume away in their mouth.

13 And it shall come to pass in that day, *that* a great tumult from the

LAZARUS (CONTINUED). TIME, FEBRUARY–MARCH, A. D. 30; PLACE, PERÆA.

CHAP. 16.

18 [g]Whosoever putteth away his wife, and marrieth another, committeth adultery: and whosoever marrieth her that is put away from *her* husband committeth adultery.

19 [h]There was a certain rich man, which was clothed in purple and fine linen, and fared sumptuously every day:

20 And there was a certain beggar named Lazarus, which was laid at his gate, [i]full of sores,

21 And desiring to be fed with the crumbs which fell from the rich man's table: moreover the dogs came and licked his sores.

22 And it came to pass, that the beggar died, and [k]was carried by the angels into Abraham's bosom: the rich man also died, and was buried;

23 And in hell he lifted up his eyes, being in torments, and seeth Abraham afar off, and Lazarus in his bosom.

24 And he cried and said, Father Abraham, have mercy on me, and send Lazarus, that he may dip the tip of his finger in water, and [l]cool my tongue; for I am [m]tormented in this flame.

25 But Abraham said, Son, [n]remember that thou in thy lifetime receivedst thy good things, and likewise Lazarus evil things: but now he is comforted, and thou art tormented.

26 And beside all this, between us and you there is [o]a great gulf fixed: so that they which would pass from hence to you cannot; neither can they pass to us, that *would come* from thence.

L—CONCLUDED.

LORD shall be among them; and they shall lay hold every one on the hand of his neighbour, and his hand shall rise up against the hand of his neighbour.

M

Isa. 66. 23 And it shall come to pass, *that* from one new moon to another, and from one sabbath to another, shall all flesh come to worship before me, saith the LORD.

24 And they shall go forth, and look upon the carcasses of the men that have transgressed against me: for their worm shall not die, neither shall their fire be quenched; and they shall be an abhorring unto all flesh.

Mark 9. 43 And if thy hand offend thee, cut it off: it is better for thee to enter into life maimed, than having two hands to go into hell, into the fire that never shall be quenched:

44 Where their worm dieth not, and the fire is not quenched.

45 And if thy foot offend thee, cut it off: it is better for thee to enter halt into life, than having two feet to be cast into hell, into the fire that never shall be quenched:

46 Where their worm dieth not, and the fire is not quenched.

47 And if thine eye offend thee, pluck it out: it is better for thee to enter into the kingdom of God with one eye, than having two eyes to be cast into hell fire:

48 Where their worm dieth not, and the fire is not quenched.

II Thes. 1. 8 In flaming fire taking vengeance on them that know not God, and that obey not the gospel of our Lord Jesus Christ:

Heb. 10. 31 *It is* a fearful thing to fall into the hands of the living God.

N

Job 21. 12, 13. *See under H.*

Luke 6. 24 But woe unto you that are rich! for ye have received your consolation.

Jas. 1. 11 For the sun is no sooner risen with a burning heat, but it withereth the grass, and the flower thereof falleth, and the grace of the fashion of it perisheth: so also shall the rich man fade away in his ways.

O

II Thes. 1. 9 Who shall be punished with everlasting destruction from the presence of the Lord, and from the glory of his power;

§ 137. THE PHARISEES REPROVED. PARABLE OF THE RICH MAN AND

P

Isa. 8. 19 And when they shall say unto you, Seek unto them that have familiar spirits, and unto wizards that peep and that mutter: should not a people seek unto their God? for the living to the dead?

20 To the law and to the testimony: if they speak not according to this word, *it is* because *there is* no light in them.

21 And they shall pass through it, hardly bestead and hungry: and it shall come to pass, that when they shall be hungry, they shall fret themselves, and curse their king and their God, and look upward.

22 And they shall look unto the earth; and behold trouble and darkness, dimness of anguish; and *they shall be* driven to darkness.

Isa. 34. 16 Seek ye out of the book of the LORD, and read: no one of these shall fail, none shall want her mate: for my mouth it hath commanded, and

P—CONTINUED.

his spirit it hath gathered them.

John 5. 39 Search the Scriptures; for in them ye think ye have eternal life: and they are they which testify of me.

John 5. 45 Do not think that I will accuse you to the Father: there is *one* that accuseth you, *even* Moses, in whom ye trust.

Acts 15. 21 For Moses of old time hath in every city them that preach him, being read in the synagogues every sabbath day.

Acts 17. 11 These were more noble than those in Thessalonica, in that they received the word with all readiness of mind, and searched the Scriptures daily, whether those things were so.

12 Therefore many of them believed; also of honourable women which were Greeks, and of men, not a few.

II Tim.3. 15 And that from a child thou hast known the holy Scriptures, which are able to make thee wise unto salvation

§ 138. JESUS INCULCATES FORBEARANCE, FAITH AND

A

Matt.18. 6 But whoso shall offend one of these little ones which believe in me, it were better for him that a millstone were hanged about his neck, and *that* he were drowned in the depth of the sea.

7 Woe unto the world because of offences! for it must needs be that offences come; but woe to that man by whom the offence cometh!

Mark 9. 42 And whosoever shall offend one of *these* little ones that believe in me, it is better for him that a millstone were hanged about his neck, and he were cast into the sea.

I Cor.11. 19 For there must be also heresies among you, that they which are approved may be made manifest among you.

B

II Thes.1. 6 Seeing *it is* a righteous thing with God to recompense tribulation to them that trouble you;

Rev. 2. 14 But I have a few things against thee, because thou hast there them that hold the doctrine of Balaam, who taught Balak to cast a stumblingblock before the children of Israel, to eat things sacrificed unto idols, and to commit fornication.

15 So hast thou also them that hold

B—CONCLUDED.

the doctrine of the Nicolaitans, which thing I hate.

C

Matt.18. 15 Moreover if thy brother shall trespass against thee, go and tell him his fault between thee and him alone: if he shall hear thee, thou hast gained thy brother.

Matt.18. 21 Then came Peter to him, and said, Lord, how oft shall my brother sin against me, and I forgive him? till seven times?

D

Lev. 19. 17 Thou shalt not hate thy brother in thine heart: thou shalt in any wise rebuke thy neighbour, and not suffer sin upon him.

Prov.17. 10 A reproof entereth more into a wise man than a hundred stripes into a fool.

Jas. 5. 19 Brethren, if any of you do err from the truth, and one convert him;

20 Let him know, that he which converteth the sinner from the error of his way shall save a soul from death, and shall hide a multitude of sins.

E

I Cor.13. 4 Charity suffereth long, *and* is kind; charity envieth not; charity vaunteth not itself, is not puffed up,

LAZARUS (Concluded). Time, February–March, A. D. 30; Place, Peræa.

Chap. 16.

27 Then he said, I pray thee therefore, father, that thou wouldest send him to my father's house:

28 For I have five brethren; that he may testify unto them, lest they also come into this place of torment.

29 Abraham saith unto him, [p]They have Moses and the prophets; let them hear them.

30 And he said, Nay, father Abraham: but if one went unto them from the dead, they will repent.

31 And he said unto him, If they hear not Moses and the prophets, [q]neither will they be persuaded, though one rose from the dead.

P—Concluded.

through faith which is in Christ Jesus.

16 All Scripture *is* given by inspiration of God, and *is* profitable for doctrine, for reproof, for correction, for instruction in righteousness:

17 That the man of God may be perfect, thoroughly furnished unto all good works.

Q

John 12. 9 Much people of the Jews therefore knew that he was there: and they came not for Jesus' sake only, but that they might see Lazarus also, whom he had raised from the dead.

10 But the chief priests consulted that they might put Lazarus also to death;

11 Because that by reason of him many of the Jews went away, and believed on Jesus.

12 On the next day much people that were come to the feast, when they heard that Jesus was coming to Jerusalem,

HUMILITY. Time, February–March, A. D. 30; Place, Peræa.

17: 1–10.

1 Then said he unto the disciples, [a]It is impossible but that offences will come: but [b]woe *unto him,* through whom they come!

2 It were better for him that a millstone were hanged about his neck, and he cast into the sea, than that he should offend one of these little ones.

3 Take heed to yourselves: [c]If thy brother trespass against thee, [d]rebuke him; and if he repent, forgive him.

4 [e]And if he trespass against thee seven times in a day, and seven times in a day turn again to thee, saying, I repent; thou shalt forgive him.

5 And the apostles said unto the Lord, Increase our faith.

6 [f]And the Lord said, If ye had faith as a grain of mustard seed, ye might say unto this sycamine tree, Be

E—Concluded.

Col. 3. 12 Put on therefore, as the elect of God, holy and beloved, bowels of mercies, kindness, humbleness of mind, meekness, longsuffering;

F

Matt. 17. 20 And Jesus said unto them, Because of your unbelief: for verily I say unto you, If ye have faith as a grain of mustard seed, ye shall say unto this mountain, Remove hence to yonder place; and it shall remove: and nothing shall be impossible unto you.

Matt. 21. 21 Jesus answered and said unto them, Verily I say unto you, If ye have faith, and doubt not, ye shall not only do this *which is done* to the fig tree, but also if ye shall say unto this mountain, Be thou removed, and be thou cast into the sea; it shall be done.

Mark 9. 23 Jesus said unto him, If thou canst believe, all things *are* possible to him that believeth.

Mark 11. 23 For verily I say unto you, That whosoever shall say unto this mountain, Be thou removed, and be thou cast into the sea; and shall not doubt in his heart, but shall believe that those things which he saith shall come to pass; he shall have whatsoever he saith.

§ 138. JESUS INCULCATES FORBEARANCE, FAITH AND HUMILITY

G

Gen. 43. 16 And when Joseph saw Benjamin with them, he said to the ruler of his house, Bring *these* men home, and slay, and make ready; for *these* men shall dine with me at noon.

II Sa.12. 20 Then David arose from the earth, and washed, and anointed *himself*, and changed his apparel, and came into the house of the LORD, and worshipped: then he came to his own house; and when he required, they set bread before him, and he did eat.

H

Luke 12. 37 Blessed *are* those servants, whom the lord when he cometh shall find watching: verily I say unto you, that he shall gird himself, and make them to sit down to meat, and will come forth and serve them.

I

I Chr.29. 15 For we *are* strangers before thee, and sojourners, as *were* all our fathers: our days on the earth *are* as a shadow, and *there is* none abiding.

16 O LORD our God, all this store that we have prepared to build thee a house for thine holy name *cometh* of thine hand, and *is* all thine own.

Job 22. 2 Can a man be profitable unto God, as he that is wise may be profitable unto himself?

3 *Is it* any pleasure to the Almighty, that thou art righteous? or *is it* gain *to him*, that thou makest thy ways perfect?

I—CONTINUED.

Job 35. 6 If thou sinnest, what doest thou against him? or *if* thy transgressions be multiplied, what doest thou unto him?

7 If thou be righteous, what givest thou him? or what receiveth he of thine hand?

Ps. 16. 2 *O my soul*, thou hast said unto the LORD, Thou *art* my Lord: my goodness *extendeth* not to thee;

Isa. 6. 5 Then said I, Woe *is* me! for I am undone; because I *am* a man of unclean lips, and I dwell in the midst of a people of unclean lips: for mine eyes have seen the King, the LORD of hosts.

Isa. 64. 6 But we are all as an unclean *thing*, and all our righteousnesses *are* as filthy rags; and we all do fade as a leaf; and our iniquities, like the wind, have taken us away.

Matt.25. 30 And cast ye the unprofitable servant into outer darkness: there shall be weeping and gnashing of teeth.

Rom. 3. 12 They are all gone out of the way, they are together become unprofitable; there is none that doeth good, no, not one.

Rom.11. 35 Or who hath first given to him,

§ 139. HOW THE KINGDOM OF GOD WILL COME.

1

Or, *with outward show.*

A

Luke 17. 23. *See text of topic.*

John 18. 36 Jesus answered, My kingdom is not of this world: if my kingdom were of this world, then would my servants fight, that I should not be delivered to the Jews: but now is my kingdom not from hence.

B

Ex. 29. 45 And I will dwell among the children of Israel, and will be their God.

Lev. 26. 12 And I will walk among you, and will be your God, and ye shall be my people.

Jer. 31. 33 But this *shall be* the covenant that I will make with the house of Israel; After those days, saith the LORD, I will put my law in their inward parts, and write it in their hearts; and will be their God, and they shall be my people.

Jer. 32. 38 And they shall be my people, and I will be their God:

B—CONCLUDED.

Eze. 11. 20 That they may walk in my statutes, and keep mine ordinances, and do them: and they shall be my people, and I will be their God.

Rom.14. 17 For the kingdom of God is not meat and drink; but righteousness, and peace, and joy in the Holy Ghost.

2

Or, *among you.*

Matt.12. 28 But if I cast out devils by the Spirit of God, then the kingdom of God is come unto you.

John 1. 26 John answered them, saying, I baptize with water: but there standeth one among you, whom ye know not;

C

Matt. 9. 15 And Jesus said unto them, Can the children of the bridechamber mourn, as long as the bridegroom is with them? but the days will come, when the bridegroom shall be taken from them, and then shall they fast.

Luke 5. 35 But the days will come, when the bridegroom shall be taken away from

(CONCLUDED). TIME, FEBRUARY–MARCH, A. D. 30; PLACE, PERÆA.

CHAP. 17.

thou plucked up by the root, and be thou planted in the sea; and it should obey you.

7 But which of you, having a servant ploughing or feeding cattle, will say unto him by and by, when he is come from the field, Go and sit down to meat?

8 And will not rather say unto him, [g]Make ready wherewith I may sup, and gird thyself, [h]and serve me, till I have eaten and drunken; and afterward thou shalt eat and drink?

9 Doth he thank that servant because he did the things that were commanded him? I trow not.

10 [i]So likewise ye, when ye shall have done all those things which are commanded you, say, We are unprofitable servants: we have done that which was our duty to do. (p. 311.)

I—CONCLUDED.

and it shall be recompensed unto him again?

I Cor. 9. 16 For though I preach the gospel, I have nothing to glory of: for necessity is laid upon me; yea, woe is unto me, if I preach not the gospel!

17 For if I do this thing willingly, I have a reward: but if against my will, a dispensation *of the gospel* is committed unto me.

I Cor. 15. 9 For I am the least of the apostles, that am not meet to be called an apostle, because I persecuted the church of God.

10 But by the grace of God I am what I am: and his grace which *was bestowed* upon me was not in vain; but I laboured more abundantly than they all: yet not I, but the grace of God which was with me.

Phile. 11 Which in time past was to thee unprofitable, but now profitable to thee and to me:

I Pet. 5. 5 Likewise, ye younger, submit yourselves unto the elder. Yea, all *of you* be subject one to another, and be clothed with humility: for God resisteth the proud, and giveth grace to the humble.

6 Humble yourselves therefore under the mighty hand of God, that he may exalt you in due time:

TIME, FEBRUARY–MARCH, A. D. 30; PLACE, PERÆA.

17 : 20–37.

20 And when he was demanded of the Pharisees, when the kingdom of God should come, he answered them and said, The kingdom of God cometh not [1]with observation:

21 [a]Neither shall they say, Lo here! or, lo there! for, behold, [b]the kingdom of God is [2]within you.

22 And he said unto the disciples, [c]The days will come, when ye shall desire to see one of the days of the Son of man, and ye shall not see *it*.

23 [d]And they shall say to you, See here; or, see there: go not after *them*, nor follow *them*.

C—CONCLUDED.

them, and then shall they fast in those days.

John 17. 12 While I was with them in the world, I kept them in thy name: those that thou gavest me I have kept, and none of them is lost, but the son of perdition; that the Scripture might be fulfilled.

D

Matt. 24. 23 Then if any man shall say unto you, Lo, here *is* Christ, or there; believe *it* not.

Mark 13. 21 And then if any man shall say to you, Lo, here *is* Christ; or, lo, *he is* there; believe *him* not:

Luke 21. 8 And he said, Take heed that ye be not deceived: for many shall come in my name, saying, I am *Christ;* and the time draweth near: go ye not therefore after them.

I Jno. 4. 1 Beloved, believe not every spirit, but try the spirits whether they are of God: because many false prophets are gone out into the world.

§ 139. HOW THE KINGDOM OF GOD WILL COME

E

Zech. 9. 14 And the LORD shall be seen over them, and his arrow shall go forth as the lightning: and the Lord GOD shall blow the trumpet, and shall go with whirlwinds of the south.

Matt.24. 27 For as the lightning cometh out of the east, and shineth even unto the west; so shall also the coming of the Son of man be.

I Tim.6. 15 Which in his times he shall show, *who is* the blessed and only Potentate, the King of kings, and Lord of lords;

F

Mark 8. 31 And he began to teach them, that the Son of man must suffer many things, and be rejected of the elders, and *of* the chief priests, and scribes, and be killed, and after three days rise again.

Mark 9. 31 For he taught his disciples, and said unto them, The Son of man is delivered into the hands of men, and they shall kill him; and after that he is killed, he shall rise the third day.

Mark 10. 33 *Saying*, Behold, we go up to Jerusalem; and the Son of man shall be delivered unto the chief priests, and unto the scribes; and they shall condemn him to death, and shall deliver him to the Gentiles:

Luke 9. 22 Saying, The Son of man must suffer many things, and be rejected of the elders and chief priests and scribes, and be slain, and be raised the third day.

G

Gen. 6. *Read entire chapter.*

Deut. 6. 10 And it shall be, when the LORD thy God shall have brought thee into the land which he sware unto thy fathers, to Abraham, to Isaac, and to Jacob, to give thee great and goodly cities, which thou buildest not,

11 And houses full of all good *things*, which thou filledst not, and wells digged, which thou diggedst not, vineyards and olive trees, which thou plantedst not; when thou shalt have eaten and be full;

12 *Then* beware lest thou forget the LORD, which brought thee forth out of the land of Egypt, from the house of bondage.

Matt.24. 37 But as the days of Noe *were*, so shall also the coming of the Son of man be.

38 For as in the days that were before the flood they were eating and drinking, marrying and giving in

G—CONCLUDED.

marriage, until the day that Noe entered into the ark,

39 And knew not until the flood came, and took them all away; so shall also the coming of the Son of man be.

H

Gen. 19. *Read entire chapter.*

I

Gen. 19. 16 And while he lingered, the men laid hold upon his hand, and upon the hand of his wife, and upon the hand of his two daughters; the LORD being merciful unto him: and they brought him forth, and set him without the city.

Gen. 19. 23 The sun was risen upon the earth when Lot entered into Zoar.

24 Then the LORD rained upon Sodom and upon Gomorrah brimstone and fire from the LORD out of heaven;

25 And he overthrew those cities, and all the plain, and all the inhabitants of the cities, and that which grew upon the ground.

K

Matt.24. 3 And as he sat upon the mount of Olives, the disciples came unto him privately, saying, Tell us, when shall these things be? and what *shall be* the sign of thy coming, and of the end of the world?

Matt. 24. 27. *See under E.*

Matt.24. 28 For wheresoever the carcass is, there will the eagles be gathered together.

29 Immediately after the tribulation of those days shall the sun be darkened, and the moon shall not give her light, and the stars shall fall from heaven, and the powers of the heavens shall be shaken:

30 And then shall appear the sign of the Son of man in heaven: and then shall all the tribes of the earth mourn, and they shall see the Son of man coming in the clouds of heaven with power and great glory.

II Thes.1. 7 And to you who are troubled rest with us, when the Lord Jesus shall be revealed from heaven with his mighty angels.

L

Matt.24. 17 Let him which is on the housetop not come down to take anything out of his house:

Mark13. 15 And let him that is on the housetop not go down into the house, neither enter *therein*, to take anything out of his house:

(CONTINUED). TIME, FEBRUARY–MARCH, A. D. 30; PLACE, PERÆA.

CHAP. 17.

24 [e]For as the lightning, that lighteneth out of the one *part* under heaven, shineth unto the other *part* under heaven; so shall also the Son of man be in his day.

25 [f]But first must he suffer many things, and be rejected of this generation.

26 [g]And as it was in the days of Noe, so shall it be also in the days of the Son of man.

27 They did eat, they drank, they married wives, they were given in marriage, until the day that Noe entered into the ark, and the flood came, and destroyed them all.

28 [h]Likewise also as it was in the days of Lot; they did eat, they drank, they bought, they sold, they planted, they builded;

29 But [i]the same day that Lot went out of Sodom it rained fire and brimstone from heaven, and destroyed *them* all.

30 Even thus shall it be in the day when the Son of man [k]is revealed.

31 In that day, he [l]which shall be upon the housetop, and his stuff in the house, let him not come down to take it away: and he that is in the field, let him likewise not return back.

32 [m]Remember Lot's wife.

33 [n]Whosoever shall seek to save his life shall lose it; and whosoever shall lose his life shall preserve it.

34 [o]I tell you, in that night there shall be two *men* in one bed; the one shall be taken, and the other shall be left.

M

Gen. 19. 17 And it came to pass, when they had brought them forth abroad, that he said, Escape for thy life; look not behind thee, neither stay thou in all the plain; escape to the mountain, lest thou be consumed.

Gen. 19. 26 But his wife looked back from behind him, and she became a pillar of salt.

I Cor.10. 12 Wherefore let him that thinketh he standeth take heed lest he fall.

Heb. 10. 38 Now the just shall live by faith: but if *any man* draw back, my soul shall have no pleasure in him.

39 But we are not of them who draw back into perdition; but of them that believe to the saving of the soul.

II Pet.2. 22 But it is happened unto them according to the true proverb, The dog *is* turned to his own vomit again; and, The sow that was washed to her wallowing in the mire.

N

Matt.10. 39 He that findeth his life shall lose it: and he that loseth his life for my sake shall find it.

Matt.16. 25 For whosoever will save his life shall lose it: and whosoever will lose his life for my sake shall find it.

Mark 8. 35 For whosoever will save his life shall lose it; but whosoever shall lose his life for my sake and the gospel's, the same shall save it.

Luke 9. 24 For whosoever will save his life shall lose it, but whosoever will lose his life for my sake, the same shall save it.

John 12. 25 He that loveth his life shall lose it; and he that hateth his life in this world shall keep it unto life eternal.

O

Matt.24. 40 Then shall two be in the field; the one shall be taken, and the other left.

41 Two *women shall be* grinding at the mill; the one shall be taken, and the other left.

Rom.11. 5 Even so then at this present time also there is a remnant according to the election of grace.

I Thes.4. 17 Then we which are alive *and* remain shall be caught up together with them in the clouds, to meet the Lord in the air: and so shall we ever be with the Lord.

II Pet.2. 9 The Lord knoweth how to deliver the godly out of temptations, and to reserve the unjust unto the day of judgment to be punished:

§ 139. HOW THE KINGDOM OF GOD WILL COME

3

This 36th verse is wanting in most of the Greek copies.

P

Job 39. 27 Doth the eagle mount up at thy command, and make her nest on high?

Job 39. 29 From thence she seeketh the prey, *and* her eyes behold afar off.

30 Her young ones also suck up blood: and where the slain *are* there, *is* she.

Amos 9. 1 I saw the Lord standing upon the altar: and he said, Smite the lintel of the door, that the posts may shake: and cut them in the head, all of them; and I will slay the last of them with the sword: he that fleeth of them shall not flee away, and he that escapeth of them shall not be delivered.

2 Though they dig into hell, thence shall mine hand take them; though

P—CONTINUED.

they climb up to heaven, thence will I bring them down:

3 And though they hide themselves in the top of Carmel, I will search and take them out thence; and though they be hid from my sight in the bottom of the sea, thence I will command the serpent, and he shall bite them:

Zech.13. 8 And it shall come to pass, *that* in all the land, saith the LORD, two parts therein shall be cut off *and* die; but the third shall be left therein.

9 And I will bring the third part through the fire, and will refine them as silver is refined, and will try them as gold is tried: they shall call on my name, and I will hear them: I will say, It *is* my people: and they shall say, The LORD *is* my God.

§ 140. THE PARABLE OF THE IMPORTUNATE WIDOW AND

A

Luke 11. 5 And he said unto them, Which of you shall have a friend, and shall go unto him at midnight, and say unto him, Friend, lend me three loaves;

Luke 21. 36 Watch ye therefore, and pray always, that ye may be accounted worthy to escape all these things that shall come to pass, and to stand before the Son of man.

Rom.12. 12 Rejoicing in hope; patient in tribulation; continuing instant in prayer;

Eph. 6. 18 Praying always with all prayer and supplication in the Spirit, and watching thereunto with all perseverance and supplication for all saints;

Col. 4. 2 Continue in prayer, and watch in the same with thanksgiving;

I Thes.5. 17 Pray without ceasing.

B

Ex. 18. 21 Moreover thou shalt provide out of all the people able men, such as fear God, men of truth, hating covetousness; and place *such* over them, *to be* rulers of thousands, *and* rulers of hundreds, rulers of fifties, and rulers of tens:

22 And let them judge the people at all seasons: and it shall be, *that* every great matter they shall bring unto thee, but every small matter they shall judge: so shall it be easier for thyself, and they shall bear *the burden* with thee.

Job 29. 7 When I went out to the gate through the city, *when* I prepared my seat in the street!

B—CONCLUDED.

Job 29. 8 The young men saw me, and hid themselves: and the aged arose, *and* stood up.

9 The princes refrained talking, and laid *their* hand on their mouth.

10 The nobles held their peace, and their tongue cleaved to the roof of their mouth.

11 When the ear heard *me*, then it blessed me; and when the eye saw *me*, it gave witness to me:

12 Because I delivered the poor that cried, and the fatherless, and *him that had* none to help him.

13 The blessing of him that was ready to perish came upon me: and I caused the widow's heart to sing for joy.

14 I put on righteousness, and it clothed me: my judgment *was* as a robe and a diadem.

15 I was eyes to the blind, and feet *was* I to the lame.

16 I *was* a father to the poor: and the cause *which* I knew not I searched out.

17 And I brake the jaws of the wicked, and plucked the spoil out of his teeth.

C

Luke 11. 8 I say unto you, Though he will not rise and give him, because he is his friend, yet because of his importunity he will rise and give him as many as he needeth.

D

Ps. 9. 8 And he shall judge the world in righteousness, he shall minister judgment to the people in uprightness.

(CONCLUDED). TIME, FEBRUARY-MARCH, A. D. 30; PLACE, PERÆA.

CHAP. 17.

35 Two *women* shall be grinding together; the one shall be taken, and the other left.

36 [s]Two *men* shall be in the field; the one shall be taken, and the other left.

37 And they answered and said unto him, [p]Where, Lord? And he said unto them, Wheresoever the body *is*, thither will the eagles be gathered together.

P—CONTINUED.

Zech.14. 2 For I will gather all nations against

P—CONCLUDED.

Jerusalem to battle; and the city shall be taken, and the houses rifled, and the women ravished; and half of the city shall go forth into captivity, and the residue of the people shall not be cut off from the city.

Matt. 24. 28. *See under K, page 398.*

Rev. 19. 17 And I saw an angel standing in the sun; and he cried with a loud voice, saying to all the fowls that fly in the midst of heaven, Come and gather yourselves together unto the supper of the great God;

18 That ye may eat the flesh of kings, and the flesh of captains, and the flesh of mighty men, and the flesh of horses, and of them that sit on them, and the flesh of all *men, both* free and bond, both small and great.

UNJUST JUDGE. TIME, FEBRUARY-MARCH, A. D. 30; PLACE, PERÆA.

18: 1–8.

1 And he spake a parable unto them *to this end,* that men ought [a]always to pray, and not to faint;

2 Saying, There was in a city [b]a judge, which feared not God, neither regarded man:

3 And there was a widow in that city; and she came unto him, saying, Avenge me of mine adversary.

4 And he would not for a while: but afterward he said within himself, Though I fear not God, nor regard man;

5 [c]Yet because this widow troubleth me, I will avenge her, lest by her continual coming she weary me.

6 And the Lord said, Hear what the unjust judge saith.

7 [d]And shall not God avenge his own elect, which cry day and night unto him, though he bear long with them?

8 I tell you [e]that he will avenge them speedily. Nevertheless, when the Son of man cometh, shall he find faith on the earth?

D—CONCLUDED.

II Thes.1. 6 Seeing *it is* a righteous thing with God to recompense tribulation to them that trouble you;

Rev. 6. 10 And they cried with a loud voice, saying, How long, O Lord, holy and true, dost thou not judge and avenge our blood on them that dwell on the earth?

Rev. 18. 20 Rejoice over her, *thou* heaven, and *ye* holy apostles and prophets; for God hath avenged you on her.

E

I Thes.5. 1 But of the times and the seasons, brethren, ye have no need that I write unto you.

2 For yourselves know perfectly that the day of the Lord so cometh as a thief in the night.

3 For when they shall say, Peace and safety; then sudden destruction cometh upon them, as travail upon a woman with child; and they shall not escape.

Heb. 10. 37 For yet a little while, and he that shall come will come, and will not tarry.

II Pet. 3. 8 But, beloved, be not ignorant of this one thing, that one day *is* with the Lord as a thousand years, and a thousand years as one day.

9 The Lord is not slack concerning his promise, as some men count slackness; but is longsuffering to us-ward, not willing that any should perish, but that all should come to repentance.

§ 141. THE PARABLE OF THE PHARISEE AND THE PUBLICAN.

A

Luke 10. 29 But he, willing to justify himself, said unto Jesus, And who is my neighbour?

Luke 16. 15 And he said unto them, Ye are they which justify yourselves before men; but God knoweth your hearts: for that which is highly esteemed among men is abomination in the sight of God.

John 9. 28 Then they reviled him, and said, Thou art his disciple; but we are Moses' disciples.

29 We know that God spake unto Moses: *as for* this *fellow*, we know not from whence he is.

30 The man answered and said unto them, Why herein is a marvellous thing, that ye know not from whence he is, and *yet* he hath opened mine eyes.

31 Now we know that God heareth not sinners: but if any man be a worshipper of God, and doeth his will, him he heareth.

32 Since the world began was it not heard that any man opened the eyes of one that was born blind.

33 If this man were not of God, he could do nothing.

34 They answered and said unto him, Thou wast altogether born in sins, and dost thou teach us? And they cast him out.

Rom. 10. 3 For they being ignorant of God's righteousness, and going about to establish their own righteousness, have not submitted themselves unto the righteousness of God.

Phil. 3. 9 And be found in him, not having mine own righteousness, which is of the law, but that which is through the faith of Christ, the righteousness which is of God by faith:

A—Concluded.

I Tim. 1. 13 Who was before a blasphemer, and a persecutor, and injurious: but I obtained mercy, because I did *it* ignorantly in unbelief.

1

Or, *as being righteous.*

B

Ps. 135. 2 Ye that stand in the house of the Lord, in the courts of the house of our God,

C

Isa. 1. 15 And when ye spread forth your hands, I will hide mine eyes from you; yea, when ye make many prayers, I will not hear: your hands are full of blood.

Isa. 58. 2 Yet they seek me daily, and delight to know my ways, as a nation that did righteousness, and forsook not the ordinance of their God: they ask of me the ordinances of justice; they take delight in approaching to God.

Rev. 3. 17 Because thou sayest, I am rich, and increased with goods, and have need of nothing; and knowest not that thou art wretched, and miserable, and poor, and blind, and naked:

D

Hab. 2. 4 Behold, his soul *which* is lifted up is not upright in him: but the just shall live by his faith.

Rom. 1. 17 For therein is the righteousness of God revealed from faith to faith: as it is written, The just shall live by faith.

§ 142. PRECEPTS OF JESUS RESPECTING DIVORCE.

MATTHEW 19 : 3–12.

3 The Pharisees also came unto him, tempting him, and saying unto him, [a]Is it lawful for a man to put away his wife for every cause?

A

Mal. 2. 14 Yet ye say, Wherefore? Because the Lord hath been witness between thee and the wife of thy youth, against whom thou hast dealt treacherously: yet *is* she thy companion, and the wife of thy covenant.

15 And did not he make one? Yet had he the residue of the Spirit. And wherefore one? That he might seek a godly seed. Therefore take heed to your spirit, and let none deal treacherously against the wife of his youth.

16 For the Lord, the God of Israel, saith that he hateth putting away: for *one* covereth violence with his garment, saith the Lord of hosts: there-

MARK 10 : 2–12.

2 [b]And the Pharisees came to him, and asked him, Is it lawful for a man to put away *his* wife? tempting him.

3 And he answered and said unto them, What did Moses command you?

4 And they said, [c]Moses suffered to write a bill of divorcement, and to put *her* away.

TIME, FEBRUARY–MARCH, A. D. 30; PLACE, PERÆA.

18: 9–14.

9 And he spake this parable unto certain [a]which trusted in themselves [1]that they were righteous, and despised others:

10 Two men went up into the temple to pray; the one a Pharisee, and the other a publican.

11 The Pharisee [b]stood and prayed thus with himself, [c]God, I thank thee, that I am not as other men *are*, extortioners, unjust, adulterers, or even as this publican.

12 I fast twice in the week, I give tithes of all that I possess.

13 And the publican, [d]standing afar off, would not lift up so much as *his* eyes unto heaven, but smote upon his breast, saying, [e]God be merciful to me a sinner.

14 I tell you, this man went down to his house justified *rather* than the other: [f]for every one that exalteth himself shall be abased; and he that humbleth himself shall be exalted. p. 407.

D—CONCLUDED.

Rom. 4. 3 For what saith the scripture? Abraham believed God, and it was counted unto him for righteousness.

Gal. 3. 11 But that no man is justified by the law in the sight of God, *it is* evident: for, The just shall live by faith.

Heb. 10. 38 Now the just shall live by faith: but if *any man* draw back, my soul shall have no pleasure in him.

E

Ps. 40. 12 For innumerable evils have compassed me about: mine iniquities have taken hold upon me, so that I am not able to look up; they are more than the hairs of mine head: therefore my heart faileth me.

F

Job 22. 29 When *men* are cast down, then thou shalt say, *There is* lifting up; and he shall save the humble person.

Matt.23. 12 And whosoever shall exalt himself shall be abased; and he that shall humble himself shall be exalted.

Luke 14. 11 For whosoever exalteth himself shall be abased; and he that humbleth himself shall be exalted.

Jas. 4. 6 But he giveth more grace. Wherefore he saith, God resisteth the proud, but giveth grace unto the humble.

I Pet. 5. 5 Likewise, ye younger, submit yourselves unto he elder. Yea, all *of you* be subject one to another, and be clothed with humility: for God resisteth the proud, and giveth grace to the humble.

6 Humble yourselves therefore under the mighty hand of God, that he may exalt you in due time:

TIME, FEBRUARY–MARCH, A. D. 30; PLACE, PERÆA.

A—CONCLUDED.

fore take heed to your spirit, that ye deal not treacherously.

17 Ye have wearied the LORD with your words. Yet ye say, Wherein have we wearied *him?* When ye say, Every one that doeth evil *is* good in the sight of the LORD, and he delighteth in them; or, Where *is* the God of judgment?

B

John 27. 32 The Pharisees heard that the people murmured such things concerning him; and the Pharisees and the chief priests sent officers to take him.

C

Deut.24. 1 When a man hath taken a wife, and married her, and it come to pass that she find no favour in his eyes,

C—CONCLUDED.

because he hath found some uncleanness in her: then let him write her a bill of divorcement, and give *it* in her hand, and send her out of his house.

Matt 5. 31 It hath been said, Whosoever shall put away his wife, let him give her a writing of divorcement:

Matt. 19. 7. *See text of topic.*

D

Gen. 1. 27 So God created man in his *own* image, in the image of God created he him; male and female created he them.

Gen. 5. 2 Male and female created he them; and blessed them, and called their name Adam, in the day when they were created.

Mal. 2. 15. *See under A.*

§ 142. PRECEPTS OF JESUS RESPECTING DIVORCE

CHAP. 19.

4 And he answered and said unto them, Have ye not read, [d]that he which made *them* at the beginning made them male and female,

5 And said, [e]For this cause shall a man leave father and mother, and shall cleave to his wife: and [f]they twain shall be one flesh?

6 Wherefore they are no more twain, but one flesh. What therefore God hath joined together, let not man put asunder.

7 They say unto him, [g]Why did Moses then command to give a writing of divorcement, and to put her away?

8 He saith unto them, Moses because of the hardness of your hearts suffered you to put away your wives: [h]but from the beginning it was not so.

9 [i]And I say unto you, Whosoever shall put away his wife, except *it be* for fornication, and shall marry another, committeth adultery: and whoso marrieth her which is put away doth commit adultery.

10 His disciples say unto him, [k]If the case of the man be so with *his* wife, it is not good to marry.

11 But he said unto them, [l]All *men* cannot receive this saying, save *they* to whom it is given.

12 For there are some eunuchs, which were so born from *their* mother's womb: and there are some eunuchs, which were made eunuchs of men: and [m]there be eunuchs, which have made themselves eunuchs for the kingdom of heaven's sake. He that is able to receive *it*, let him receive *it*.

CHAP. 10.

5 And Jesus answered and said unto them, For [n]the hardness of your heart he wrote you this precept.

6 But from the beginning of the creation [o]God made them male and female.

7 [p]For this cause shall a man leave his father and mother, and cleave to his wife;

8 And they twain shall be one flesh: so then they are no more twain, but one flesh.

9 What therefore God hath joined together, let not man put asunder.

10 And in the house his disciples asked him again of the same *matter*.

11 And he saith unto them, [q]Whosoever shall put away his wife, and marry another, committeth adultery against her.

12 And if a woman shall put away her husband, and be married to another, she committeth adultery.

For D see preceding page (403).

E

Gen. 2. 24 Therefore shall a man leave his father and his mother, and shall cleave unto his wife: and they shall be one flesh.

Mark 10. 5-9. *See text of topic.*

Eph. 5. 31 For this cause shall a man leave his father and mother, and shall be joined unto his wife, and they two shall be one flesh.

F

I Cor. 6. 16 What! know ye not that he which is joined to a harlot is one body? for two, saith he, shall be one flesh.

I Cor. 7. 2 Nevertheless, *to avoid* fornication, let every man have his own wife, and let every woman have her own husband.

G

Deut. 24. 1. *See under C, page 403.*
Matt. 5. 31. *See under C, page 403.*

(CONCLUDED). TIME, FEBRUARY–MARCH, A. D. 30; PLACE, PERÆA.

H

Jer. 6. 16 Thus saith the LORD, Stand ye in the ways, and see, and ask for the old paths, where *is* the good way, and walk therein, and ye shall find rest for your souls. But they said, We will not walk *therein*.

I

Matt. 5. 32 But I say unto you, That whosoever shall put away his wife, saving for the cause of fornication, causeth her to commit adultery: and whosoever shall marry her that is divorced committeth adultery.

Mark 10. 11. *See text of topic.*

Luke 16. 18 Whosoever putteth away his wife, and marrieth another, committeth adultery: and whosoever marrieth her that is put away from *her* husband committeth adultery.

I Cor. 7. 10 And unto the married I command, *yet* not I, but the Lord, Let not the wife depart from *her* husband:

11 But and if she depart, let her remain unmarried, or be reconciled to *her* husband: and let not the husband put away *his* wife.

K

Prov. 21. 19 *It is* better to dwell in the wilderness, than with a contentious and an angry woman.

L

I Cor. 7. 2. *See under F.*

I Cor. 7. 7 For I would that all men were even as I myself. But every man hath his proper gift of God, one after this manner, and another after that.

I Cor. 7. 9 But if they cannot contain, let them marry: for it is better to marry than to burn.

I Cor. 7. 17 But as God hath distributed to every man, as the Lord hath called every one, so let him walk. And so ordain I in all churches.

M

I Cor. 7. 32 But I would have you without carefulness. He that is unmarried careth for the things that belong to the Lord, how he may please the Lord:

33 But he that is married careth for the things that are of the world, how he may please *his* wife.

34 There is difference *also* between a wife and a virgin. The unmarried woman careth for the things of the Lord, that she may be holy both in body and in spirit; but she that is married careth for the things of the world, how she may please *her* husband.

I Cor. 9. 5 Have we not power to lead about a

M—CONCLUDED.

sister, a wife, as well as other apostles, and *as* the brethren of the Lord, and Cephas?

I Cor. 9. 15 But I have used none of these things: neither have I written these things, that it should be so done unto me: for *it were* better for me to die, than that any man should make my glorying void.

N

Deut. 9. 6 Understand therefore, that the LORD thy God giveth thee not this good land to possess it for thy righteousness; for thou *art* a stiffnecked people.

Deut. 31. 27 For I know thy rebellion, and thy stiff neck: behold, while I am yet alive with you this day, ye have been rebellious against the LORD; and how much more after my death?

Neh. 9. 16 But they and our fathers dealt proudly, and hardened their necks, and hearkened not to thy commandments,

Neh. 9. 26 Nevertheless they were disobedient, and rebelled against thee, and cast thy law behind their backs, and slew thy prophets which testified against them to turn them to thee, and they wrought great provocations.

Acts 13. 18 And about the time of forty years suffered he their manners in the wilderness.

Heb. 3. 7 Wherefore as the Holy Ghost saith, To day if ye will hear his voice,

8 Harden not your hearts, as in the provocation, in the day of temptation in the wilderness:

9 When your fathers tempted me, proved me, and saw my works forty years.

10 Wherefore I was grieved with that generation, and said, They do alway err in *their* heart; and they have not known my ways.

O

Gen. 1. 27 and Gen. 5. 2. *See under D, page 403.*

P

Gen. 2. 24. *See under E.*

I Cor. 6. 16. *Under F.* Eph. 5. 31. *Under E.*

Q

Matt. 5. 32. *See under I.*

Matt. 19. 9. *See text of topic.* Luke 16. 18. *Under I.*

Rom. 7. 3 So then if, while *her* husband liveth, she be married to another man, she shall be called an adulteress: but if her husband be dead, she is free from that law; so that she is no adulteress, though she be married to another man.

I Cor. 7. 10, 11. *See under I.*

§ 143. JESUS RECEIVES AND BLESSES LITTLE CHILDREN

19: 13–15.

13 [a]Then were there brought unto him little children, that he should put *his* hands on them, and pray: and the disciples rebuked them.

14 But Jesus said, Suffer little children, and forbid them not, to come unto me; for [b]of such is the kingdom of heaven.

15 And he laid *his* hands on them, and departed thence.

A

Mark 10. 13 and Luke 18. 15. *See text of topic.*

B

Matt.18. 3 And said, Verily I say unto you, Except ye be converted, and become as little children, ye shall not enter into the kingdom of heaven.

I Pet. 2. 1 Wherefore laying aside all malice, and all guile, and hypocrisies, and envies, and all evil speakings,

2 As newborn babes, desire the sincere milk of the word, that ye may grow thereby:

C

Matt. 19. 13 and Luke 18. 15. *See text of topic.*

D

Ex. 10. 9 And Moses said, We will go with our young and with our old, with our sons and with our daughters, with our flocks and with our herds will we go; for we *must hold* a feast unto the LORD.

10 And he said unto them, Let the LORD be so with you, as I will let you go, and your little ones: look *to it:* for evil *is* before you.

11 Not so: go now ye *that are* men, and serve the LORD; for that ye did desire. And they were driven out from Pharaoh's presence.

Deut.31. 12 Gather the people together, men, and women, and children, and thy stranger that *is* within thy gates, that they may hear, and that they may learn, and fear the LORD your God, and observe to do all the words of this law:

13 And *that* their children, which have not known *any thing*, may hear and learn to fear the LORD your God, as long as ye live in the land whither ye go over Jordan to possess it.

Joel 2. 16 Gather the people, sanctify the congregation, assemble the elders,

10: 13–16.

13 [c]And they brought young children to him, that he should touch them; and *his* [d]disciples rebuked those that brought *them.*

14 But when Jesus saw *it,* he was much displeased, and said unto them, [e]Suffer the little children to come unto me, and forbid them not; [f]for of such is the kingdom of God.

15 Verily I say unto you, [g]Whosoever shall not receive the kingdom of God as a little child, he shall not enter therein.

16 And he [h]took them up in his arms, put *his* hands upon them, and blessed them.

D—CONCLUDED.

gather the children, and those that suck the breasts: let the bridegroom go forth of his chamber, and the bride out of her closet.

Mark 9. 38 And John answered him, saying, Master, we saw one casting out devils in thy name, and he followeth not us; and we forbade him, because he followeth not us.

39 But Jesus said, Forbid him not: for there is no man which shall do a miracle in my name, that can lightly speak evil of me.

E

Ps. 78. 1 Give ear, O my people, *to* my law: incline your ears to the words of my mouth.

2 I will open my mouth in a parable: I will utter dark sayings of old:

3 Which we have heard and known, and our fathers have told us.

4 We will not hide *them* from their children, showing to the generation to come the praises of the LORD, and his strength, and his wonderful works that he hath done.

5 For he established a testimony in Jacob, and appointed a law in Israel, which he commanded our fathers, that they should make them known to their children:

6 That the generation to come might know *them, even* the children *which*

TIME, FEBRUARY–MARCH, A. D. 30; PLACE, PERÆA.

18: 15–17.

15 [i]And they brought unto him also infants, that he would touch them: but when *his* disciples saw *it*, they rebuked them.

16 But Jesus called them *unto him*, and said, [k]Suffer little children to come unto me, and forbid them not: for [l]of such is the kingdom of God.

17 [m]Verily I say unto you, Whosoever shall not receive the kingdom of God as a little child shall in no wise enter therein.

E—CONCLUDED.

should be born; *who* should arise and declare *them* to their children:

7 That they might set their hope in God, and not forget the works of God, but keep his commandments:

8 And might not be as their fathers, a stubborn and rebellious generation; a generation *that* set not their heart aright, and whose spirit was not steadfast with God.

F

I Cor.14. 20 Brethren, be not children in understanding: howbeit in malice be ye children, but in understanding be men.

I Pet. 2. 2. *See under B.*

G

Matt. 18. 3. *See under B.*

H

Isa. 40. 11 He shall feed his flock like a shepherd: he shall gather the lambs with his arm, and carry *them* in his bosom, *and* shall gently lead those that are with young.

I

Matt. 19. 13 and Mark 10. 13. *See text of topic.*

K

Gen. 45. 9 Haste ye, and go up to my father, and say unto him, Thus saith thy son Joseph, God hath made me lord of all Egypt: come down unto me, tarry not:

10 And thou shalt dwell in the land of Goshen, and thou shalt be near unto me, thou, and thy children, and thy children's children, and thy flocks, and thy herds, and all that thou hast:

11 And there will I nourish thee; for yet *there are* five years of famine; lest thou, and thy household, and all that thou hast, come to poverty.

Gen. 47. 12 And Joseph nourished his father,

K—CONCLUDED.

and his brethren, and all his father's household, with bread, according to *their* families.

Deut.29. 10 Ye stand this day all of you before the LORD your God; your captains of your tribes, your elders, and your officers, *with* all the men of Israel,

11 Your little ones, your wives, and thy stranger that *is* in thy camp, from the hewer of thy wood unto the drawer of thy water:

II Chr.20. 13 And all Judah stood before the LORD, with their little ones, their wives, and their children.

Jer. 32. 38 And they shall be my people, and I will be their God:

39 And I will give them one heart, and one way, that they may fear me for ever, for the good of them, and of their children after them:

40 And I will make an everlasting covenant with them, that I will not turn away from them, to do them good; but I will put my fear in their hearts, that they shall not depart from me.

41 Yea, I will rejoice over them to do them good, and I will plant them in this land assuredly with my whole heart and with my whole soul.

42 For thus saith the LORD; Like as I have brought all this great evil upon this people, so will I bring upon them all the good that I have promised them.

Acts 2. 39 For the promise is unto you, and to your children, and to all that are afar off, *even* as many as the Lord our God shall call.

I Cor. 7. 14 For the unbelieving husband is sanctified by the wife, and the unbelieving wife is sanctified by the husband: else were your children unclean; but now are they holy.

L

I Cor. 14. 20. *Under F.* I Pet 2. 2. *Under B.*

M

Ps. 131. 1 LORD, my heart is not haughty, nor mine eyes lofty: neither do I exercise myself in great matters, or in things too high for me.

2 Surely I have behaved and quieted myself, as a child that is weaned of his mother: my soul *is* even as a weaned child.

Mark 10. 15. *See text of topic.*

I Pet. 1. 14 As obedient children, not fashioning yourselves according to the former lusts in your ignorance:

§ 144. THE RICH YOUNG MAN.

19: 16–26.

16 [a] And, behold, one came and said unto him, [b] Good Master, what good thing shall I do, that I may have eternal life?

17 And he said unto him, Why callest thou me good? *there is* none good but one, *that is*, God: but if thou wilt enter into life, keep the commandments.

18 He saith unto him, Which? Jesus said, [c] Thou shalt do no murder, Thou shalt not commit adultery, Thou shalt not steal, Thou shalt not bear false witness,

19 [d] Honour thy father and *thy* mother: and, [e] Thou shalt love thy neighbour as thyself.

20 The young man saith unto him, All these things have I kept from my youth up: what lack I yet?

21 Jesus said unto him, If thou wilt be perfect, [f] go *and* sell that thou hast, and give to the poor, and thou shalt have treasure in heaven: and come *and* follow me.

A

Mark 10. 17. *See text of topic.*
Luke 18. 18. *See text of topic.*

B

Luke10. 25 And, behold, a certain lawyer stood up, and tempted him, saying, Master, what shall I do to inherit eternal life?

C

Ex. 20. 13 Thou shalt not kill.
Deut. 5. 17 Thou shalt not kill.

D

Matt.15. 4 For God commanded, saying, Honour thy father and mother: and, he that curseth father or mother, let him die the death.

E

Lev. 19. 18 Thou shalt not avenge, nor bear any grudge against the children of thy people, but thou shalt love thy neighbour as thyself: I *am* the Lord.

10: 17–27.

17 [g] And when he was gone forth into the way, there came one running, and kneeled to him, and asked him, Good Master, what shall I do that I may inherit eternal life?

18 And Jesus said unto him, Why callest thou me good? *there is* none good but one, *that is*, God.

19 Thou knowest the commandments, [h] Do not commit adultery, Do not kill, Do not steal, Do not bear false witness, Defraud not, Honour thy father and mother.

20 And he answered and said unto him, Master, all these have I observed from my youth.

21 Then Jesus beholding him loved him, and said unto him, One thing thou lackest: go thy way, sell [i] whatsoever thou hast, and give to the poor, and thou shalt have [k] treasure in heaven: and come, take up the cross, and follow me.

E—Concluded.

Matt.22. 39 And the second *is* like unto it, Thou shalt love thy neighbour as thyself.

Rom.13. 9 For this, Thou shalt not commit adultery, Thou shalt not kill, Thou shalt not steal, Thou shalt not bear false witness, Thou shalt not covet; and if *there be* any other commandment, it is briefly comprehended in this saying, namely, Thou shalt love thy neighbour as thyself.

Gal. 5. 14 For all the law is fulfilled in one word, *even* in this, Thou shalt love thy neighbour as thyself.

Jas. 2. 8 If ye fulfil the royal law according to the Scripture, Thou shalt love thy neighbour as thyself, ye do well:

F

Matt. 6. 20 But lay up for yourselves treasures in heaven, where neither moth nor rust doth corrupt, and where thieves do not break through nor steal.

TIME, FEBRUARY–MARCH, A. D. 30; PLACE, PERÆA.

18: 18–27.

18 [l] And a certain ruler asked him, saying, Good Master, what shall I do to inherit eternal life?

19 And Jesus said unto him, Why callest thou me good? none *is* good, save one, *that is*, God.

20 Thou knowest the commandments, [m] Do not commit adultery, Do not kill, Do not steal, Do not bear false witness, [n] Honour thy father and thy mother.

21 And he said, All these have I kept from my youth up.

22 Now when Jesus heard these things, he said unto him, Yet lackest thou one thing: [o] sell all that thou hast, and distribute unto the poor, and thou shalt have treasure in heaven: and come, follow me.

F—CONTINUED.

Luke12. 33 Sell that ye have, and give alms; provide yourselves bags which wax not old, a treasure in the heavens that faileth not, where no thief approacheth, neither moth corrupteth.

Luke16. 9 And I say unto you, Make to yourselves friends of the mammon of unrighteousness; that, when ye fail, they may receive you into everlasting habitations.

Acts 2. 44 And all that believed were together, and had all things common;

45 And sold their possessions and goods, and parted them to all *men*, as every man had need.

Acts 4. 34 Neither was there any among them that lacked: for as many as were possessors of lands or houses sold them, and brought the prices of the things that were sold,

35 And laid *them* down at the apostles' feet: and distribution was made unto every man according as he had need.

I Tim. 6. 18 That they do good, that they be rich in good works, ready to distribute, willing to communicate;

F—CONCLUDED.

I Tim. 6. 19 Laying up in store for themselves a good foundation against the time to come, that they may lay hold on eternal life.

G

Matt. 19. 16. *See text of topic.*
Luke 18. 18. *See text of topic.*

H

Ex. 20. 1–17. *The Ten Commandments.*
Rom. 13. 9. *See under E.*

I

Acts 2. 44. *See under F.*
I Tim. 6. 18. *See under F.*

K

Matt. 6. 19 Lay not up for yourselves treasures upon earth, where moth and rust doth corrupt, and where thieves break through and steal:

Matt. 6. 20. *See under F.*
Matt. 19. 21. *See text of topic.*
Luke 12. 33. *See under F.*
Luke 16. 9. *See under F.*

L

Matt. 19. 16. *See text of topic.*
Mark 10. 17. *See text of topic.*

M

Ex. 20. 12 Honour thy father and thy mother: that thy days may be long upon the land which the LORD thy God giveth thee.

13 Thou shalt not kill.

14 Thou shalt not commit adultery.

15 Thou shalt not steal.

16 Thou shalt not bear false witness against thy neighbour.

Deut. 5. 16 Honour thy father and thy mother, as the LORD thy God hath commanded thee; that thy days may be prolonged, and that it may go well with thee, in the land which the LORD thy God giveth thee.

17 Thou shalt not kill.

18 Neither shalt thou commit adultery.

19 Neither shalt thou steal.

20 Neither shalt thou bear false witness against thy neighbour.

Rom. 13. 9. *See under E.*

N

Eph. 6. 1 Children, obey your parents in the Lord: for this is right.

2 Honour thy father and mother; which is the first commandment with promise;

Col. 3. 20 Children, obey *your* parents in all things: for this is well-pleasing unto the Lord.

O

Matt. 6. 19, 20. *See under K. and F.*
Matt. 19. 21. *See text of topic.*
I Tim. 6. 19. *See under F.*

§ 144. THE RICH YOUNG MAN (Concluded).

MATTHEW — Chap. 19.

22 But when the young man heard that saying, he went away sorrowful: for he had great possessions.

23 Then said Jesus unto his disciples, Verily I say unto you, That [p] a rich man shall hardly enter into the kingdom of heaven.

24 And again I say unto you, It is easier for a camel to go through the eye of a needle, than for a rich man to enter into the kingdom of God.

25 When his disciples heard *it*, they were exceedingly amazed, saying, [q] Who then can be saved?

26 But Jesus beheld *them*, and said unto them, With men this is impossible; but [r] with God all things are possible.

P

Matt.13. 22 He also that received seed among the thorns is he that heareth the word; and the care of this world, and the deceitfulness of riches, choke the word, and he becometh unfruitful.

Mark 10. 24. *See text of topic.*

Acts 10. 34 Then Peter opened *his* mouth, and said, Of a truth I perceive that God is no respecter of persons:

I Cor. 1. 26 For ye see your calling, brethren, how that not many wise men after the flesh, not many mighty, not many noble, *are called.*

I Tim.6. 9 But they that will be rich fall into temptation and a snare, and *into* many foolish and hurtful lusts, which drown men in destruction and perdition.

10 For the love of money is the root of all evil: which while some coveted after, they have erred from the faith, and pierced themselves through with many sorrows.

Q

Luke13. 23 Then said one unto him, Lord, are there few that be saved? And he said unto them,

24 Strive to enter in at the strait gate: for many, I say unto you, will seek to enter in, and shall not be able.

MARK — Chap. 10.

22 And he was sad at that saying, and went away grieved: for he had great possessions.

23 [s] And Jesus looked round about, and saith unto his disciples, How hardly shall they that have riches enter into the kingdom of God!

24 And the disciples were astonished at his words. But Jesus answereth again, and saith unto them, Children, how hard is it for them [t] that trust in riches to enter into the kingdom of God!

25 It is easier for a camel to go through the eye of a needle, than for a rich man to enter into the kingdom of God.

26 And they were astonished out of measure, saying among themselves, Who then can be saved?

27 And Jesus looking upon them saith, With men *it is* impossible, but not with God: for [u] with God all things are possible.

Q—Concluded.

Rom.10. 9 That if thou shalt confess with thy mouth the Lord Jesus, and shalt believe in thine heart that God hath raised him from the dead, thou shalt be saved.

Rom.10. 13 For whosoever shall call upon the name of the Lord shall be saved.

Rom.11. 5 Even so then at this present time also there is a remnant according to the election of grace.

Rom.11. 7 What then? Israel hath not obtained that which he seeketh for; but the election hath obtained it, and the rest were blinded.

R

Gen. 18. 14 Is anything too hard for the Lord? At the time appointed I will return unto thee, according to the time of life, and Sarah shall have a son.

TIME, FEBRUARY–MARCH, A. D. 30; PLACE, PERÆA.

CHAP. 18.

23 And when he heard this, he was
very sorrowful: for he was very rich.
24 And when Jesus saw that he was
very sorrowful, he said, [x] How hardly
shall they that have riches enter into
the kingdom of God!
25 For it is easier for a camel to go
through a needle's eye, than for a rich
man to enter into the kingdom of God.
26 And they that heard *it* said, Who
then can be saved?
27 And he said, [y] The things which
are impossible with men are possible
with God.

R—CONCLUDED.

Job 42. 2 I know that thou canst do every *thing*, and *that* no thought can be withholden from thee.

Jer. 32. 17 Ah Lord God! behold, thou hast made the heaven and the earth by thy great power and stretched-out arm, *and* there is nothing too hard for thee:

Zech. 8. 6 Thus saith the LORD of hosts: If it be marvellous in the eyes of the remnant of this people in these days, should it also be marvellous in mine eyes? saith the LORD of hosts.

Luke 1. 37 For with God nothing shall be impossible.

Luke 18. 27. *See text of topic.*

S

Matt. 19. 23. *See text of topic.*
Luke 18. 24. *See text of topic.*
I Cor. 1. 26. *See under P.*

Jas. 2. 5 Hearken, my beloved brethren, Hath not God chosen the poor of this world rich in faith, and heirs of the kingdom which he hath promised to them that love him?

Jas. 4. 4 Ye adulterers and adulteresses, know ye not that the friendship of the world is enmity with God? whosoever therefore will be a friend of the world is the enemy of God.

T

Job 31. 24 If I have made gold my hope, or have said to the fine gold, *Thou art* my confidence;

T—CONCLUDED.

Job 31 25 If I rejoiced because my wealth *was* great, and because mine hand had gotten much;

Ps. 52. 7 Lo, *this is* the man *that* made not God his strength; but trusted in the abundance of his riches, *and* strengthened himself in his wickedness.

Ps. 62. 10 Trust not in oppression, and become not vain in robbery: if riches increase, set not your heart *upon them.*

John 5. 44 How can ye believe, which receive honour one of another, and seek not the honour that *cometh* from God only?

I Tim.6. 17 Charge them that are rich in this world, that they be not high-minded, nor trust in uncertain riches, but in the living God, who giveth us richly all things to enjoy;

Jas. 5. 1 Go to now, *ye* rich men, weep and howl for your miseries that shall come upon *you.*
2 Your riches are corrupted, and your garments are moth-eaten.
3 Your gold and silver is cankered; and the rust of them shall be a witness against you, and shall eat your flesh as it were fire. Ye have heaped treasure together for the last days.

Rev. 3. 17 Because thou sayest, I am rich, and increased with goods, and have need of nothing; and knowest not that thou art wretched, and miserable, and poor, and blind, and naked:

U

Jer. 32. 17. *See under R.*
Matt. 19. 26. *See text of topic.*
Luke 1. 37. *See under R.*

Heb. 7. 25 Wherefore he is able also to save them to the uttermost that come unto God by him, seeing he ever liveth to make intercession for them.

X

Prov.11. 28 He that trusteth in his riches shall fall: but the righteous shall flourish as a branch.

Matt. 19. 23. *See text of topic.*
Mark 10. 23. *See text of topic.*
I Tim. 6. 9. *See under P.*

Y

Jer. 32. 17. *See under R.*
Zech. 8. 6. *See under R.*
Matt. 19. 26. *See text of topic.*

Mark14. 36 And he said, Abba, Father, all things *are* possible unto thee; take away this cup from me: nevertheless, not what I will, but what thou wilt.

Luke 1. 37. *See under R.*

§ 145. PROMISES TO DISCIPLES.

19: 27–30.

27 [a]Then answered Peter and said unto him, Behold, [b]we have forsaken all, and followed thee; what shall we have therefore?

28 And Jesus said unto them, Verily I say unto you, That ye which have followed me, [c]in the regeneration when the Son of man shall sit in the throne of his glory, [d]ye also shall sit upon twelve thrones, judging the twelve tribes of Israel.

29 [e]And every one that hath forsaken houses, or brethren, or sisters, or father, or mother, or wife, or children, or lands, for my name's sake, shall receive a hundredfold, and shall inherit everlasting life.

30 [f]But many *that are* first shall be last; and the last *shall be* first.

A

Mark 10. 28 and Luke 18. 28. *See text of topic.*

B

Deut.33. 9 Who said unto his father and to his mother, I have not seen him; neither did he acknowledge his brethren, nor knew his own children: for they have observed thy word, and kept thy covenant.

Matt. 4. 20 And they straightway left *their* nets, and followed him.

10: 28–31.

28 Then Peter began to say unto him, Lo, we have left all, and have followed thee.

29 And Jesus answered and said, Verily I say unto you, There is no man that hath left house, or brethren, or sisters, or father, or mother, or wife, or children, or lands, for my sake, and the gospel's,

30 [g]But he shall receive a hundredfold now in this time, houses, and brethren, and sisters, and mothers, and children, and lands, [h]with persecutions; and in the world to come eternal life.

31 But many *that are* first shall be last; and the last first. (p. 417.)

B—Concluded.

Luke 5. 11 And when they had brought their ships to land, they forsook all, and followed him.

C

II Cor.5. 17 Therefore if any man *be* in Christ, *he is* a new creature: old things are passed away; behold, all things are become new.

D

Matt.20. 21 And he said unto her, What wilt thou? She saith unto him, Grant that these my two sons may sit, the

§ 146. THE PARABLE OF THE LABOURERS IN THE VINEYARD.

20: 1–16.

1 For the kingdom of heaven is like unto [a]a man *that is* a householder, which went out early in the morning to hire [b]labourers into his vineyard.

2 And when he had agreed with the labourers for a [1]penny a day, he sent them into his vineyard.

3 And he went out about the third hour, and saw others [c]standing idle in the marketplace,

4 And said unto them: Go ye also

A

Song 8. 11 Solomon had a vineyard at Baal-hamon; he let out the vineyard unto keepers; every one for the fruit thereof was to bring a thousand *pieces* of silver.

12 My vineyard, which *is* mine, *is* before me: thou, O Solomon, *must have* a thousand, and those that keep the fruit thereof two hundred.

Isa. 5. 1 Now will I sing to my well beloved a song of my beloved touching his vineyard. My well beloved hath a vineyard in a very fruitfull hill:

2 And he fenced it, and gathered out the stones thereof, and planted it with the choicest vine, and built a tower in the midst of it, and also made a wine-

TIME, FEBRUARY–MARCH, A. D. 30; PLACE, PERÆA.

18 : 28–30.

28 Then Peter said, Lo, we have left all, and followed thee.

29 And he said unto them, Verily I say unto you, There is no man that hath left house, or parents, or brethren, or wife, or children, for the kingdom of God's sake,

30 [i]Who shall not receive manifold more in this present time, and [k]in the world to come life everlasting. (p. 417.)

D—CONCLUDED.

one on thy right hand, and the other on the left, in thy kingdom.

Luke 22. 28 Ye are they which have continued with me in my temptations.

29 And I appoint unto you a kingdom, as my Father hath appointed unto me:

30 That ye may eat and drink at my table in my kingdom, and sit on thrones judging the twelve tribes of Israel.

I Cor. 6. 2 Do ye not know that the saints shall judge the world? and if the world shall be judged by you, are ye unworthy to judge the smallest matters?

3 Know we not that we shall judge angels? how much more things that pertain to this life?

Rev. 2. 26 And he that overcometh, and keepeth my works unto the end, to him will I give power over the nations:

E

Mark 10. 29, 30 and Luke 18. 29, 30. *See text of topic.*

F

Matt. 20. 16. *See text of* § 146.
Matt. 21. 31, 32. *See text of* § 160.
Mark 10. 31. *See text of topic.*
Luke 13. 30 And, behold, there are last which shall be first; and there are first which shall be last.

G

II Chr. 25. 9 And Amaziah said to the man of God, But what shall we do for the hundred talents which I have given to the army of Israel? And the man of God answered, The LORD is able to give thee much more than this.

Luke 18. 30. *See text of topic.*

H

Acts 14. 22 Confirming the souls of the disciples, *and* exhorting them to continue in the faith, and that we must through much tribulation enter into the kingdom of God

I Thes. 3. 3 That no man should be moved by these afflictions: for yourselves know that we are appointed thereunto.

II Tim. 3. 12 Yea, and all that will live godly in Christ Jesus shall suffer persecution.

Heb. 12. 6 For whom the Lord loveth he chasteneth, and scourgeth every son whom he receiveth.

I

Job 42. 10 And the LORD turned the captivity of Job, when he prayed for his friends: also the LORD gave Job twice as much as he had before.

K

Rev. 3. 21 To him that overcometh will I grant to sit with me in my throne, even as I also overcame, and am set down with my Father in his throne.

TIME, FEBRUARY–MARCH, A. D. 30; PLACE, PERÆA.

A—CONCLUDED.

press therein: and he looked that it should bring forth grapes, and it brought forth wild grapes.

Matt. 9. 37 Then saith he unto his disciples, The harvest truly *is* plenteous, but the labourers *are* few;

38 Pray ye therefore the Lord of the harvest, that he will send forth labourers into his harvest.

B

Mark 13. 34 *For the Son of man is* as a man taking a far journey, who left his house, and gave authority to his servants, and to every man his work, and commanded the porter to watch.

I Cor. 15. 58 Therefore, my beloved brethren,

B—CONTINUED.

be ye steadfast, unmoveable, always abounding in the work of the Lord, forasmuch as ye know that your labour is not in vain in the Lord.

Heb. 13. 21 Make you perfect in every good work to do his will, working in you that which is well pleasing in his sight, through Jesus Christ; to whom *be* glory for ever and ever. Amen.

II Pet. 1. 5 And besides this, giving all diligence, add to your faith virtue; and to virtue, knowledge;

6 And to knowledge, temperance; and to temperance, patience; and to patience, godliness;

7 And to godliness, brotherly kind-

For B concluded, 1 and C see next page (414).

§ 146. THE PARABLE OF THE LABOURERS IN THE VINEYARD

CHAP. 20.

into the vineyard, and whatsoever is right I will give you. And they went their way.

5 Again he went out about the sixth and ninth hour, and did likewise.

6 And about the eleventh hour he went out, and found others standing idle, and saith unto them, [d]Why stand ye here all the day idle?

7 They say unto him, [e]Because no man hath hired us. He saith unto them, Go ye also into the vineyard; and whatsoever is right, *that* shall ye receive.

8 So when [f]even was come, the lord of the vineyard saith unto his steward, Call the labourers, and give them *their* hire, beginning from the last unto the first.

9 And when they came that *were hired* about the eleventh hour, [g]they received every man a penny.

10 But when the first came, they supposed that they should have received more; and they likewise received every man a penny.

11 And when they had received *it*, they murmured against the goodman of the house,

12 Saying, These last have [2]wrought *but* one hour, and thou hast made them equal unto us, which have borne the burden and heat of the day.

13 But he answered one of them, and said, Friend, I do thee no wrong: didst not thou agree with me for a penny?

14 Take *that* thine *is*, and go thy way: I will give unto this last, even as unto thee.

B—CONCLUDED. See preceding page (413).
ness; and to brotherly kindness, charity.

8 For if these things be in you, and abound, they make *you that ye shall* neither *be* barren nor unfruitful in the knowledge of our Lord Jesus Christ.

9 But he that lacketh these things is blind, and cannot see afar off, and hath forgotten that he was purged from his old sins.

10 Wherefore the rather, brethren, give diligence to make your calling and election sure: for if ye do these things, ye shall never fall:

1

The Roman penny is the eighth part of an ounce, which after five shillings the ounce is seven pence half penny; in American money, *15 cents.*

C

Prov.19. 15 Slothfulness casteth into a deep sleep; and an idle soul shall suffer hunger.

Eze. 16. 49 Behold, this was the iniquity of thy sister Sodom, pride, fulness of bread, and abundance of idleness was in her and in her daughters, neither did she strengthen the hand of the poor and needy.

D

Acts 17. 17 Therefore disputed he in the synagogue with the Jews, and with the devout persons, and in the market daily with them that met with him.

18 Then certain philosophers of the Epicureans, and of the Stoics, encountered him. And some said, What will this babbler say? other some, He seemeth to be a setter forth of strange gods: because he preached unto them Jesus, and the resurrection.

19 And they took him, and brought him unto Areopagus, saying, May we know what this new doctrine, whereof thou speakest, *is?*

20 For thou bringest certain strange things to our ears: we would know therefore what these things mean.

21 (For all the Athenians, and strangers which were there, spent their time in nothing else, but either to tell or to hear some new thing.)

I Tim.5. 13 And withal they learn *to be* idle, wandering about from house to house; and not only idle, but tattlers also and busybodies, speaking things which they ought not.

Heb. 6. 12 That ye be not slothful, but followers of them who through faith and patience inherit the promises.

(CONTINUED). TIME, FEBRUARY-MARCH, A. D. 30; PLACE, PERÆA.

E

Eph. 6. 8 Knowing that whatsoever good thing any man doeth, the same shall he receive of the Lord, whether *he be* bond or free.

F

Matt.13. 39 The enemy that sowed them is the devil; the harvest is the end of the world; and the reapers are the angels.
40 As therefore the tares are gathered and burned in the fire; so shall it be in the end of this world.

Matt.25. 19 After a long time the lord of those servants cometh, and reckoneth with them.
20 And so he that had received five talents came and brought other five talents, saying, Lord, thou deliveredst unto me five talents: behold, I have gained beside them five talents more.

Acts 17. 29 Forasmuch then as we are the offspring of God, we ought not to think that the Godhead is like unto gold, or silver, or stone, graven by art and man's device.
30 And the times of this ignorance God winked at; but now commandeth all men every where to repent:
31 Because he hath appointed a day, in the which he will judge the world in righteousness by *that* man whom he hath ordained; *whereof* he hath given assurance unto all *men*, in that he hath raised him from the dead.

Rom. 2. 6 Who will render to every man according to his deeds:
7 To them who by patient continuance in well doing seek for glory and honour and immortality, eternal life:
8 But unto them that are contentious, and do not obey the truth, but obey unrighteousness, indignation and wrath,
9 Tribulation and anguish, upon every soul of man that doeth evil; of the Jew first, and also of the Gentile;
10 But glory, honour, and peace, to every man that worketh good; to the Jew first, and also to the Gentile:

II Cor.5. 10 For we must all appear before the judgment seat of Christ; that every one may receive the things *done* in *his* body, according to that he hath done, whether *it be* good or bad.

1 Thes.4. 16 For the Lord himself shall descend from heaven with a shout, with the voice of the archangel, and with the trump of God: and the dead in Christ shall rise first:

Heb. 9. 28 So Christ was once offered to bear the sins of many; and unto them that

F—CONCLUDED.

look for him shall he appear the second time without sin unto salvation.

Rev. 20. 11 And I saw a great white throne, and him that sat on it, from whose face the earth and the heaven fled away; and there was found no place for them.
12 And I saw the dead, small and great, stand before God; and the books were opened: and another book was opened, which is *the book* of life: and the dead were judged out of those things which were written in the books, according to their works.

G

Luke 23. 40 But the other answering rebuked him, saying, Dost not thou fear God, seeing thou art in the same condemnation?

Rom. 4. 3 For what saith the Scripture? Abraham believed God, and it was counted unto him for righteousness.
4 Now to him that worketh is the reward not reckoned of grace, but of debt.
5 But to him that worketh not, but believeth on him that justifieth the ungodly, his faith is counted for righteousness.
6 Even as David also describeth the blessedness of the man, unto whom God imputeth righteousness without works,

Eph. 1. 6 To the praise of the glory of his grace, wherein he hath made us accepted in the beloved:
7 In whom we have redemption through his blood, the forgiveness of sins, according to the riches of his grace;
8 Wherein he hath abounded toward us in all wisdom and prudence;

2

Or, *have continued one hour only.*

H

Rom. 9. 21 Hath not the potter power over the clay, of the same lump to make one vessel unto honour, and another into dishonour?

I

Deut.15. 9 Beware that there be not a thought in thy wicked heart, saying, The seventh year, the year of release, is at hand; and thine eye be evil against thy poor brother, and thou givest him nought; and he cry unto the LORD against thee, and it be sin unto thee.
10 Thou shalt surely give him, and

For I concluded see next page (416).

§ 146. THE PARABLE OF THE LABOURERS IN THE VINEYARD

CHAP. 20.

15 [h]Is it not lawful for me to do what
I will with mine own? [i]Is thine eye
evil, because I am good?

16 [k]So the last shall be first, and the
first last: [l]for many be called, but few
chosen.

I—CONTINUED. See preceding page (415).

thine heart shall not be grieved when thou givest unto him: because that for this thing the LORD thy God shall bless thee in all thy works, and in all that thou puttest thine hand unto.

11 For the poor shall never cease out of the land: therefore I command thee, saying, Thou shalt open thine hand wide unto thy brother, to thy poor, and to thy needy, in thy land.

§ 147. JESUS FORETELLS HIS DEATH AND RESURRECTION

20: 17–19.

17 [a]And Jesus going up to Jerusalem, took the twelve disciples apart in
the way, and said unto them,

18 [b]Behold, We go up to Jerusalem;
and the Son of man shall be betrayed
unto the chief priests and unto the
scribes, and they shall condemn him to
death,

19 [c]And shall deliver him to the
Gentiles to mock, and to scourge, and
to crucify *him:* and the third day he
shall rise again.

A

Mark 10. 32 and Luke 18. 31. *See text of topic.*

John 12. 12 On the next day much people that were come to the feast, when they heard that Jesus was coming to Jerusalem,

B

Ps. 2. 1 Why do the heathen rage, and the people imagine a vain thing?

2 The kings of the earth set themselves, and the rulers take counsel together, against the LORD, and against his Anointed, *saying,*

3 Let us break their bands asunder, and cast away their cords from us.

Matt. 16. 21 From that time forth began Jesus to show unto his disciples, how that he must go unto Jerusalem, and suffer many things of the elders and chief priests and scribes, and be killed, and be raised again the third day.

Matt. 17. 22 And while they abode in Galilee, Jesus said unto them, The Son of man shall be betrayed into the hands of men:

23 And they shall kill him, and the third day he shall be raised again. And they were exceeding sorry.

10: 32–34.

32 [d]And they were in the way going
up to Jerusalem; and Jesus went before them: and they were amazed; and
as they followed, they were afraid.
[e]And he took again the twelve, and
began to tell them what things should
happen unto him,

33 *Saying,* Behold, we go up to Jerusalem; and the Son of man shall be
delivered unto the chief priests, and
unto the scribes; and they shall condemn him to death, and shall deliver
him to the Gentiles:

34 And they shall mock him, and
shall scourge him, and shall spit upon
him, and shall kill him; and the third
day he shall rise again.

B—CONCLUDED.

Acts 2. 23 Him, being delivered by the determinate counsel and foreknowledge of God, ye have taken, and by wicked hands have crucified and slain:

Acts 4. 27 For of a truth against thy holy child Jesus, whom thou hast anointed, both Herod, and Pontius Pilate, with the Gentiles, and the people of Israel, were gathered together.

28 For to do whatsoever thy hand and thy counsel determined before to be done.

C

Matt. 27. 2 And when they had bound him, they led *him* away, and delivered him to Pontius Pilate the governor.

Mark 15. 1 And straightway in the morning the chief priests held a consultation with the elders and scribes and the

(CONCLUDED). TIME, FEBRUARY–MARCH, A. D. 30; PLACE, PERÆA.

I—CONTINUED.

Prov.23. 6 Eat thou not the bread of *him that hath* an evil eye, neither desire thou his dainty meats:

Jon. 3. 10 And God saw their works, that they turned from their evil way; and God repented of the evil, that he had said that he would do unto them; and he did *it* not.

Jon. 4. 1 But it displeased Jonah exceedingly, and he was very angry.

I—CONCLUDED.

Matt. 6. 23 But if thine eye be evil, thy whole body shall be full of darkness. If therefore the light that is in thee be darkness, how great *is* that darkness!

K

Matt.19. 30 But many *that are* first shall be last; and the last *shall be* first.

L

Matt.22. 14 For many are called, but few *are* chosen.

A THIRD TIME. [SEE § 93, § 97.] TIME, MARCH, A. D. 30; PLACE, PERÆA.

18: 31–34.

31 [f]Then he took *unto him* the twelve,
and said unto them, Behold, we go up
to Jerusalem, and all things [g]that are
written by the prophets concerning the
Son of man shall be accomplished.

32 For [h]he shall be delivered unto
the Gentiles, and shall be mocked, and
spitefully entreated, and spitted on:

33 And they shall scourge *him*, and
put him to death; and the third day
he shall rise again.

34 [i]And they understood none of
these things: and this saying was hid
from them, neither knew they the
things which were spoken. (p. 423.)

C—CONCLUDED.

whole council, and bound Jesus, and carried *him* away, and delivered *him* to Pilate.

Mark 15. 17 And they clothed him with purple, and platted a crown of thorns, and put it about his *head*,

18 And began to salute him, Hail, King of the Jews!

19 And they smote him on the head with a reed, and did spit upon him, and bowing *their* knees worshipped him.

20 And when they had mocked him, they took off the purple from him, and put his own clothes on him, and led him out to crucify him.

Luke 23. 1 And the whole multitude of them arose, and led him unto Pilate.

John 18. 28, etc. *See text of § 196.*

D

John 10. 4 And when he putteth forth his own sheep, he goeth before them, and the sheep follow him: for they know his voice.

E

Mark 8. 31 And he began to teach them, that the Son of man must suffer many things, and be rejected of the elders, and *of* the chief priests, and scribes, and be killed, and after three days rise again.

Mark 9. 31 For he taught his disciples, and said unto them, The Son of man is delivered into the hands of men, and they shall kill him; and after that he is killed, he shall rise the third day.

Luke 9. 22 Saying, The Son of man must suffer many things, and be rejected of the elders and chief priests and scribes, and be slain, and be raised the third day.

Luke 18. 31. *See text of topic.*

John 10. 17 Therefore doth my Father love me, because I lay down my life, that I might take it again.

F

Matt. 16. 21, 22. *See under B.*

Matt. 20. 17, and Mark 10. 32. *See text of topic.*

G

Ps. 22 and Isa. 53. *Read entire chapters.*

H

Matt. 27. 2 And when they had bound him, they led *him* away, and delivered him to Pontius Pilate the governor.

Luke 23. 1 and John 18. 28. *See under C.*

I

Mark 9. 32 But they understood not that saying, and were afraid to ask him.

Luke 2. 50 And they understood not the saying which he spake unto them.

Luke 9. 45 But they understood not this saying, and it was hid from them, that they perceived it not: and they feared to ask him of that saying.

John 10. 6 This parable spake Jesus unto them; but they understood not what things they were which he spake unto them.

John 12. 16 These things understood not his disciples at the first: but when Jesus was glorified, then remembered they that these things were written of him, and *that* they had done these things unto him.

§ 148. REQUEST OF JAMES AND JOHN.

20 : 20–28.

20 [a]Then came [b]to him the mother of [c]Zebedee's children with her sons, worshipping *him*, and desiring a certain thing of him.

21 And he said unto her, What wilt thou? She saith unto him, Grant that these my two sons [d]may sit, the one on thy right hand, and the other on the left, in thy kingdom.

22 But Jesus answered and said, Ye know not what ye ask. Are ye able to drink of [e]the cup that I shall drink of, and to be baptized with [f]the baptism that I am baptized with? They say unto him, We are able.

23 And he saith unto them, [g]Ye shall drink indeed of my cup, and be baptized with the baptism that I am baptized with: but to sit on my right hand, and on my left, is not mine to [h]give, but *it shall be given to them* for whom it is prepared of my Father.

24 [i]And when the ten heard *it*, they were moved with indignation against the two brethren.

25 But Jesus called them *unto him*, and said, Ye know that the princes of the Gentiles exercise dominion over them, and they that are great exercise authority upon them.

26 But [k]it shall not be so among you: but [l]whosoever will be great among you, let him be your minister;

A

Mark 10. 35. *See text of topic.*

B

Matt.27. 56 Among which was Mary Magdalene, and Mary the mother of James and Joses, and the mother of Zebedee's children.

Mark 15. 40 There were also women looking on afar off: among whom was Mary

10 : 35–45.

35 [m]And James and John, the sons of Zebedee, come unto him, saying, Master, we would that thou shouldest do for us whatsoever we shall desire.

36 And he said unto them, What would ye that I should do for you?

37 They said unto him, Grant unto us that we may sit, one on thy right hand, and the other on thy left hand, in thy glory.

38 But Jesus said unto them, Ye know not what ye ask: can ye drink of the cup that I drink of? and be baptized with the baptism that I am baptized with?

39 And they said unto him, We can. And Jesus said unto them, [n]Ye shall indeed drink of the cup that I drink of; and with the baptism that I am baptized withal shall ye be baptized:

40 But to sit on my right hand and on my left hand is not mine to give; but *it shall be given* [o]*to them* for whom it is prepared.

41 [p]And when the ten heard *it*, they began to be much displeased with James and John.

42 But Jesus called them *to him*, and saith unto them, [q]Ye know that they which [1r]are accounted to rule over the Gentiles exercise lordship over them; and their great ones exercise authority upon them.

43 But so shall it not be among you: but whosoever will be great among you, shall be your minister:

B—Concluded.

Magdalene, and Mary the mother of James the less and of Joses, and Salome;

TIME, MARCH, A. D. 30; PLACE, PERÆA.

C

Matt. 4. 21 And going on from thence, he saw other two brethren, James *the son* of Zebedee, and John his brother, in a ship with Zebedee their father, mending their nets; and he called them.

D

Matt.19. 28 And Jesus said unto them, Verily I say unto you, That ye which have followed me, in the regeneration when the Son of man shall sit in the throne of his glory, ye also shall sit upon twelve thrones, judging the twelve tribes of Israel.

Jas. 4. 3 Ye ask, and receive not, because ye ask amiss, that ye may consume *it* upon your lusts.

E

Matt.26. 39 And he went a little further, and fell on his face, and prayed, saying, O my Father, if it be possible, let this cup pass from me: nevertheless, not as I will, but as thou *wilt*.

Matt.26. 42 He went away again the second time, and prayed, saying, O my Father, if this cup may not pass away from me, except I drink it, thy will be done.

Mark 14. 36 And he said, Abba, Father, all things *are* possible unto thee; take away this cup from me: nevertheless, not what I will, but what thou wilt.

Luke 22. 42 Saying, Father, if thou be willing, remove this cup from me: nevertheless, not my will, but thine, be done.

John 18. 11 Then said Jesus unto Peter, Put up thy sword into the sheath: the cup which my Father hath given me, shall I not drink it?

F

Luke 12. 50 But I have a baptism to be baptized with; and how am I straitened till it be accomplished!

G

Acts 12. 2 And he killed James the brother of John with the sword.

Rom. 8. 17 And if children, then heirs; heirs of God, and joint heirs with Christ; if so be that we suffer with *him*, that we may be also glorified together.

II Cor.1. 7 And our hope of you *is* steadfast, knowing, that as ye are partakers of the sufferings, so *shall ye be* also of the consolation.

Rev. 1. 9 I John, who also am your brother, and companion in tribulation, and in the kingdom and patience of Jesus Christ, was in the isle that is called Patmos, for the word of God, and for the testimony of Jesus Christ.

H

Matt.25. 34 Then shall the King say unto them on his right hand, Come, ye blessed of my Father, inherit the kingdom prepared for you from the foundation of the world:

I

Mark 10. 43. *See text of topic.*

Luke 22. 24 And there was also a strife among them, which of them should be accounted the greatest.

25 And he said unto them, The kings of the Gentiles exercise lordship over them; and they that exercise authority upon them are called benefactors.

K

I Pet. 5. 2 Feed the flock of God which is among you, taking the oversight *thereof*, not by constraint, but willingly; not for filthy lucre, but of a ready mind;

3 Neither as being lords over *God's* heritage, but being ensamples to the flock.

L

Matt.23. 11 But he that is greatest among you shall be your servant.

Mark 9. 35 And he sat down, and called the twelve, and saith unto them, If any man desire to be first, *the same* shall be last of all, and servant of all.

Mark 10. 43. *See text of topic.*

M

Matt. 20. 20. *See text of topic.*

N

Acts 12. 2 and Rev. 1. 9. *See under G.*

O

Jas. 4. 3. *See under D.*

P

Matt. 20. 24. *See text of topic.*

Q

Luke 22. 25. *See under I.*

1

Or, *think good.*

R

Matt. 20. 26, 28. *See text of topic.* Mark 9. 35. *Under L.*

Luke 9. 48 And said unto them, Whosoever shall receive this child in my name receiveth me; and whosoever shall receive me, receiveth him that sent me: for he that is least among you all, the same shall be great.

S

Matt.18. 4 Whosoever therefore shall humble himself as this little child, the same is greatest in the kingdom of heaven.

T

John 13. 4 He riseth from supper, and laid aside his garments, and took a towel, and girded himself.

§ 148. REQUEST OF JAMES AND JOHN

CHAP. 20.

27 [s]And whosoever will be chief among you, let him be your servant:

28 [t]Even as the [u]Son of man came not to be ministered unto, [x]but to minister, and [y]to give his life a ransom [z]for many.

For S and T see preceding page (419).

U

Phil. 2. 7 But made himself of no reputation, and took upon him the form of a servant, and was made in the likeness of men:

X

Luke 22. 27 For whether *is* greater, he that sitteth at meat, or he that serveth? *is* not he that sitteth at meat? but I am among you as he that serveth.

John 13. 14 If I then, *your* Lord and Master, have washed your feet; ye also ought to wash one another's feet.

Y

Job 33. 24 Then he is gracious unto him, and saith, Deliver him from going down to the pit: I have found a ransom.

25 His flesh shall be fresher than a child's: he shall return to the days of his youth:

Ps. 49. 6 They that trust in their wealth, and boast themselves in the multitude of their riches;

7 None *of them* can by any means redeem his brother, nor give to God a ransom for him:

Isa. 53. 5 But he *was* wounded for our transgressions, *he was* bruised for our iniquities: the chastisement of our peace *was* upon him; and with his stripes we are healed.

6 All we like sheep have gone astray; we have turned every one to his own way; and the LORD hath laid on him the iniquity of us all.

7 He was oppressed, and he was afflicted, yet he opened not his mouth: he is brought as a lamb to the slaughter, and as a sheep before her shearers is dumb, so he openeth not his mouth.

8 He was taken from prison and from judgment: and who shall declare his generation? for he was cut off out of the land of the living: for the transgression of my people was he stricken.

9 And he made his grave with the wicked, and with the rich in his death;

CHAP. 10.

44 And whosoever of you will be the chiefest, shall be servant of all.

45 For even [a]the Son of man came not to be ministered unto, but to minister, and [b]to give his life a ransom for many.

Y—CONTINUED.

because he had done no violence, neither *was any* deceit in his mouth.

10 Yet it pleased the LORD to bruise him; he hath put *him* to grief: when thou shalt make his soul an offering for sin, he shall see *his* seed, he shall prolong *his* days, and the pleasure of the LORD shall prosper in his hand.

11 He shall see of the travail of his soul, *and* shall be satisfied: by his knowledge shall my righteous servant justify many; for he shall bear their iniquities.

Dan. 9. 24 Seventy weeks are determined upon thy people and upon thy holy city, to finish the transgression, and to make an end of sins, and to make reconciliation for iniquity, and to bring in everlasting righteousness, and to seal up the vision and prophecy, and to anoint the Most Holy.

25 Know therefore and understand, *that* from the going forth of the commandment to restore and to build Jerusalem, unto the Messiah the Prince, *shall be* seven weeks, and threescore and two weeks: the street shall be built again, and the wall, even in troublous times.

26 And after threescore and two weeks shall Messiah be cut off, but not for himself: and the people of the prince that shall come shall destroy the city and the sanctuary; and the end thereof *shall be* with a flood, and unto the end of the war desolations are determined.

John 10. 15 As the Father knoweth me, even so know I the Father: and I lay down my life for the sheep.

John 11. 50 Nor consider that it is expedient for us, that one man should die for the people, and that the whole nation perish not.

51 And this spake he not of himself: but being high priest that year, he prophesied that Jesus should die for that nation;

(CONCLUDED). TIME, MARCH, A. D. 30; PLACE, PERÆA.

Y—CONTINUED.

John 11. 52 And not for that nation only, but that also he should gather together in one the children of God that were scattered abroad.

Rom. 3. 24 Being justified freely by his grace through the redemption that is in Christ Jesus:

25 Whom God hath set forth *to be* a propitiation through faith in his blood, to declare his righteousness for the remission of sins that are past, through the forbearance of God;

26 To declare, *I say*, at this time his righteousness: that he might be just, and the justifier of him which believeth in Jesus.

Gal. 3. 13 Christ hath redeemed us from the curse of the law, being made a curse for us: for it is written, Cursed *is* every one that hangeth on a tree:

Eph. 1. 7 In whom we have redemption through his blood, the forgiveness of sins, according to the riches of his grace;

Eph. 5. 1 Be ye therefore followers of God, as dear children;

2 And walk in love, as Christ also hath loved us, and hath given himself for us an offering and a sacrifice to God for a sweetsmelling savour.

I Tim. 2. 6 Who gave himself a ransom for all, to be testified in due time.

Tit. 2. 14 Who gave himself for us, that he might redeem us from all iniquity, and purify unto himself a peculiar people, zealous of good works.

Heb. 9. 28 So Christ was once offered to bear the sins of many; and unto them that look for him shall he appear the second time without sin unto salvation.

I Pet. 1. 18 Forasmuch as ye know that ye were not redeemed with corruptible things, *as* silver and gold, from your vain conversation *received* by tradition from your fathers;

19 But with the precious blood of Christ, as of a lamb without blemish and without spot:

I Pet. 2. 24 Who his own self bare our sins in his own body on the tree, that we, being dead to sins, should live unto righteousness: by whose stripes ye were healed.

I Pet. 3. 18 For Christ also hath once suffered for sins, the just for the unjust, that he might bring us to God, being put to death in the flesh, but quickened by the Spirit:

Y—CONCLUDED.

Rev. 1. 5 And from Jesus Christ, *who is* the faithful witness, *and* the first-begotten of the dead, and the prince of the kings of the earth. Unto him that loved us, and washed us from our sins in his own blood.

Rev. 5. 8 And when he had taken the book, the four beasts and four *and* twenty elders fell down before the Lamb, having every one of them harps, and golden vials full of odours, which are the prayers of saints.

9 And they sang a new song, saying, Thou art worthy to take the book, and to open the seals thereof: for thou wast slain, and hast redeemed us to God by thy blood out of every kindred, and tongue, and people, and nation;

Z

Matt. 26. 28 For this is my blood of the new testament, which is shed for many for the remission of sins.

Mark 14. 24 And he said unto them, This is my blood of the new testament, which is shed for many.

Rom. 5. 15 But not as the offense, so also *is* the free gift: for if through the offense of one many be dead, much more the grace of God, and the gift by grace, *which is* by one man, Jesus Christ, hath abounded unto many.

16 And not as *it was* by one that sinned, *so is* the gift: for the judgment *was* by one to condemnation, but the free gift *is* of many offenses unto justification.

17 For if by one man's offense death reigned by one; much more they which receive abundance of grace and of the gift of righteousness shall reign in life by one, Jesus Christ.)

Rom. 5. 19 For as by one man's disobedience many were made sinners, so by the obedience of one shall many be made righteous.

Heb. 9. 28. *See under Y.*

I Jno. 2. 2 And he is the propitiation for our sins: and not for ours only, but also for *the sins of* the whole world.

A

John 13. 14. *See under X.*
Phil. 2. 7. *See under U.*

Heb. 5. 8 Though he were a Son, yet learned he obedience by the things which he suffered;

B

Matt. 20. 28. *See text of topic.*
I Tim. 2. 6, Tit. 2. 14, Isa. 53. 10 and Dan. 9. 26. *See under Y.*

§ 149. THE HEALING OF TWO BLIND MEN.

20 : 29–34.

29 [a]And as they departed from Jericho, a great multitude followed him.

30 And, behold, [b]two blind men sitting by the way side, when they heard that Jesus passed by, cried out, saying, Have mercy on us, O Lord, *thou* Son of David.

31 And the multitude rebuked them, because they should hold their peace: but they cried the more, saying, Have mercy on us, O Lord, *thou* Son of David.

32 And Jesus stood still, and called them, and said, What will ye that I shall do unto you?

33 They say unto him, Lord, that our eyes may be opened.

34 So Jesus had [c]compassion *on them*, and touched their eyes: and immediately their eyes received sight, and they followed him. (p. 432.)

A

Mark 10. 46 and Luke 18. 35. *See text of topic.*

B

Matt. 9. 27 And when Jesus departed thence, two blind men followed him, crying, and saying, *Thou* Son of David, have mercy on us.

C

Ps. 145. 8 The LORD *is* gracious, and full of compassion; slow to anger, and of great mercy.

Heb. 4. 15 For we have not an high priest which cannot be touched with the feeling of our infirmities; but was in all points tempted like as *we are, yet* without sin.

D

Matt. 20. 29 and Luke 18. 35. *See text of topic.*

E

Isa. 11. 1 And there shall come forth a rod out of the stem of Jesse, and a Branch shall grow out of his roots:

Jer. 23. 5 Behold, the days come, saith the LORD, that I will raise unto David a righteous Branch, and a King shall reign and prosper, and shall execute judgment and justice in the earth.

10: 46–52.

46 [d]And they came to Jericho: and as he went out of Jericho with his disciples and a great number of people, blind Bartimeus, the son of Timeus, sat by the highway side begging.

47 And when he heard that it was Jesus of Nazareth, he began to cry out, and say, Jesus, *thou* [e]Son of David, have mercy on me.

48 And many charged him that he should hold his peace: but he cried the more a great deal, *Thou* Son of David, have mercy on me.

49 And Jesus stood still, and commanded him to be called. And they call the blind man, saying unto him, Be of good comfort, rise; he calleth thee.

50 And he, casting away his garment, rose, and came to Jesus.

51 And Jesus answered and said unto him, What wilt thou that I should do unto thee? The blind man said unto him, Lord, that I might receive my sight.

52 And Jesus said unto him, Go thy way; [f]thy faith hath [1]made thee whole. And immediately he [g]received his sight, and followed Jesus in the way. (p. 432.)

E—CONCLUDED.

Jer. 23. 6 In his days Judah shall be saved, and Israel shall dwell safely: and this *is* his name whereby he shall be called, THE LORD OUR RIGHTEOUSNESS.

Rom. 1. 3 Concerning his Son Jesus Christ our Lord, which was made of the seed of David according to the flesh;

Rev. 22. 16 I Jesus have sent mine angel to testify unto you these things in the churches. I am the root and the offspring of David, *and* the bright and morning star.

TIME, MARCH, A. D. 30; PLACE, NEAR JERICHO.

18: 35–43; 19: 1.

35 [h]And it came to pass, that as he was come nigh unto Jericho, a certain blind man sat by the way side begging:

36 And hearing the multitude pass by, he asked what it meant.

37 And they told him, that Jesus of Nazareth passeth by.

38 And he cried, saying, Jesus, *thou* Son of David, have mercy on me.

39 And they which went before rebuked him, that he should hold his peace: but he cried so much the more, *Thou* Son of David, have mercy on me.

40 And Jesus [i]stood, and commanded him to be brought unto him: and when he was come near, he asked him,

41 Saying, What wilt thou that I shall do unto thee? And he said, Lord, that I may receive my sight.

42 And Jesus said unto him, Receive thy sight: [k]thy faith hath saved thee.

43 And immediately he [l]received his sight, and followed him, [m]glorifying God: and all the people, when they saw *it*, gave praise unto God.

CHAP. 19.

1 And *Jesus* entered and passed through [n]Jericho.

F

Matt. 9. 22 But Jesus turned him about, and when he saw her, he said, Daughter, be of good comfort; thy faith hath made thee whole. And the woman was made whole from that hour.

Mark 5. 34 And he said unto her, Daughter, thy faith hath made thee whole; go in peace, and be whole of thy plague.

1

Or, *saved thee.*

G

Isa. 35. 5 Then the eyes of the blind shall be opened, and the ears of the deaf shall be unstopped.

H

Matt. 20. 29 and Mark 10. 46. *See text of topic.*

I

Heb. 2. 17 Wherefore in all things it behooved him to be made like unto *his* brethren, that he might be a merciful and faithful high priest in things *pertaining* to God, to make reconciliation.

Heb. 5. 2 Who can have compassion on the ignorant, and on them that are out of the way; for that he himself also is compassed with infirmity.

K

Luke 17. 19 And he said unto him, Arise, go thy way: thy faith hath made thee whole.

L

Ps. 33. 9 For he spake, and it was *done;* he commanded, and it stood fast.

Isa. 35. 5. *See under G.*

M

Ps. 103. 1 Bless the LORD, O my soul: and all that is within me, *bless* his holy name.

2 Bless the LORD, O my soul, and forget not all his benefits:

Ps. 107. 8 Oh that *men* would praise the LORD *for* his goodness, and *for* his wonderful works to the children of men!

Ps. 107. 15 Oh that *men* would praise the LORD *for* his goodness, and *for* his wonderful works to the children of men!

Ps. 107. 31 Oh that *men* would praise the LORD *for* his goodness, and *for* his wonderful works to the children of men!

32 Let them exalt him also in the congregation of the people, and praise him in the assembly of the elders.

Luke 5. 26 And they were all amazed, and they glorified God, and were filled with fear, saying, We have seen strange things to day.

Acts 4. 21 So when they had further threatened them, they let them go, finding nothing how they might punish them, because of the people: for all *men* glorified God for that which was done.

Acts 11. 18 When they heard these things, they held their peace, and glorified God, saying, Then hath God also to the Gentiles granted repentance unto life.

N

I Ki. 16. 34 In his days did Hiel the Beth-elite build Jericho: he laid the foundation thereof in Abiram his firstborn, and set up the gates thereof in his youngest *son* Segub, according to the word of the LORD, which he spake by Joshua the son of Nun.

§ 150. VISIT TO ZACCHEUS.

A

I Ki. 10. 27 And the king made silver *to be* in Jerusalem as stones, and cedars made he *to be* as the sycamore trees that *are* in the vale, for abundance.

I Chr.27. 28 And over the olive trees and the sycamore trees that *were* in the low plains *was* Baal-hanan, the Gederite: and over the cellars of oil *was* Joash:

Isa. 9. 10 The bricks are fallen down, but we will build with hewn stones: the sycamores are cut down, but we will change *them into* cedars.

Amos 7. 14 Then answered Amos, and said to Amaziah, I *was* no prophet, neither *was* I a prophet's son; but I *was* a herdman, and a gatherer of sycamore fruit:

B

Ps. 139. 1 O LORD, thou hast searched me, and known *me*.

2 Thou knowest my downsitting and mine uprising; thou understandest my thought afar off.

3 Thou compassest my path and my lying down, and art acquainted *with* all my ways.

Eze. 16. 6 And when I passed by thee, and saw thee polluted in thine own blood, I said unto thee *when thou wast* in thy blood, Live; yea, I said unto thee *when thou wast* in thy blood, Live.

John 1. 48 Nathanael saith unto him, Whence knowest thou me? Jesus answered and said unto him, Before that Philip called thee, when thou wast under the fig tree, I saw thee.

C

Eccl. 9. 10 Whatsoever thy hand findeth to do, do *it* with thy might; for *there is* no work, nor device, nor knowledge, nor wisdom, in the grave, whither thou goest.

II Cor.6. 1 We then, *as* workers together *with him*, beseech *you* also that ye receive not the grace of God in vain.

D

Gen. 18. 1 And the LORD appeared unto him in the plains of Mamre: and he sat in the tent door in the heat of the day;

2 And he lifted up his eyes and looked, and, lo, three men stood by him: and when he saw *them*, he ran to meet them from the tent door, and bowed himself toward the ground,

3 And said, my Lord, if now I have found favour in thy sight, pass not away, I pray thee, from thy servant:

4 Let a little water, I pray you, be fetched, and wash your feet, and rest yourselves under the tree:

D—CONCLUDED.

Gen. 18. 5 And I will fetch a morsel of bread, and comfort ye your hearts; after that ye shall pass on: for therefore are ye come to your servant. And they said, So do, as thou hast said.

Gen. 19. 1 And there came two angels to Sodom at even; and Lot sat in the gate of Sodom: and Lot seeing *them* rose up to meet them; and he bowed himself with his face toward the ground;

2 And he said, Behold now, my lords, turn in, I pray you, into your servant's house, and tarry all night, and wash your feet, and ye shall rise up early, and go on your ways. And they said, Nay; but we will abide in the street all night.

3 And he pressed upon them greatly; and they turned in unto him, and entered into his house; and he made them a feast, and did bake unleavened bread, and they did eat.

Ps. 101. 2 I will behave myself wisely in a perfect way. O when wilt thou come unto me? I will walk within my house with a perfect heart.

3 I will set no wicked thing before mine eyes: I hate the work of them that turn aside; *it* shall not cleave to me.

John 14. 23 Jesus answered and said unto him, If a man love me, he will keep my words: and my Father will love him, and we will come unto him, and make our abode with him.

Eph. 3. 17 That Christ may dwell in your hearts by faith; that ye, being rooted and grounded in love,

E

Matt. 9. 11 And when the Pharisees saw *it*, they said unto his disciples, Why eateth your master with publicans and sinners?

Luke 5. 30 But their scribes and Pharisees murmured against his disciples, saying, Why do ye eat and drink with publicans and sinners?

F

Luke 3. 14 And the soldiers likewise demanded of him, saying, And what shall we do? And he said unto them, Do violence to no man, neither accuse *any* falsely; and be content with your wages.

G

Ex. 22. 1 If a man shall steal an ox, or a sheep, and kill it, or sell it; he shall restore five oxen for an ox, and four sheep for a sheep.

TIME, MARCH, A. D. 30; PLACE, JERICHO.

19: 2–10.

2 And, behold, *there was* a man
named Zaccheus, which was the chief
among the publicans, and he was rich.
3 And he sought to see Jesus who he
was; and could not for the press, because he was little of stature.
4 And he ran before, and climbed up
into [a]a sycamore tree to see him: for
he was to pass that *way*.
5 And when Jesus came to the
place, [b]he looked up, and saw him, and
said unto him, Zaccheus, [c]make haste,
and come down; [d]for to day I must
abide at thy house.
6 And he made haste, and came
down, and received him joyfully.
7 And when they saw *it*, they all
murmured, saying, [e]That he was gone
to be guest with a man that is a sinner.
8 And Zaccheus stood, and said unto
the Lord; Behold, Lord, the half of
my goods I give to the poor; and if I
have taken any thing from any man
by [f]false accusation, [g]I restore *him*
fourfold.
9 And Jesus said unto him, This day
is salvation come to this house, forasmuch as [h]he also is [i]a son of Abraham.
10 [k]For the Son of man is come to
seek and to save that which was lost.

G—CONCLUDED.

I Sa. 12. 3 Behold, here I *am:* witness against me before the LORD, and before his anointed: whose ox have I taken? or whose ass have I taken? or whom have I defrauded? whom have I oppressed? or of whose hand have I received *any* bribe to blind mine eyes therewith? and I will restore it you.

II Sa. 12. 6 And he shall restore the lamb fourfold, because he did this thing, and because he had no pity.

H

Rom. 4. 11 And he received the sign of circumcision, a seal of the righteousness of the faith which *he had yet* being uncircumcised: that he might be the father of all them that believe, though they be not circumcised; that righteousness might be imputed unto them also:

12 And the father of circumcision to them who are not of the circumcision only, but who also walk in the steps of that faith of our father Abraham, which *he had* being *yet* uncircumcised.

Rom. 4. 16 Therefore *it is* of faith, that *it might be* by grace; to the end the promise might be sure to all the seed; not to that only which is of the law, but to that also which is of the faith of Abraham; who is the father of us all.

Gal. 3. 7 Know ye therefore that they which are of faith, the same are the children of Abraham.

I

Luke 13. 16 And ought not this woman, being a daughter of Abraham, whom Satan hath bound, lo, these eighteen years, be loosed from this bond on the sabbath day?

K

Eze. 34. 16 I will seek that which was lost, and bring again that which was driven away, and will bind up *that which was* broken, and will strengthen that which was sick: but I will destroy the fat and the strong; I will feed them with judgment.

Matt. 1. 21 And she shall bring forth a son, and thou shalt call his name JESUS: for he shall save his people from their sins.

Matt. 9. 12 But when Jesus heard *that*, he said unto them, They that be whole need not a physician, but they that are sick.

13 But go ye and learn what *that* meaneth, I will have mercy, and not sacrifice: for I am not come to call the righteous, but sinners to repentance.

Matt. 10. 6 But go rather to the lost sheep of the house of Israel.

Matt. 15. 24 But he answered and said, I am not sent but unto the lost sheep of the house of Israel.

Matt. 18. 11 For the Son of man is come to save that which was lost.

I Tim. 1. 15 This *is* a faithful saying, and worthy of all acceptation, that Christ Jesus came into the world to save sinners; of whom I am chief.

§ 151. THE PARABLE OF THE TEN POUNDS.

A

Acts 1. 6 When they therefore were come together, they asked of him, saying, Lord, wilt thou at this time restore again the kingdom to Israel?

B

Matt.25. 14 For *the kingdom of heaven is* as a man travelling into a far country, *who* called his own servants, and delivered unto them his goods.

15 And unto one he gave five talents, to another two, and to another one; to every man according to his several ability; and straightway took his journey.

16 Then he that had received the five talents went and traded with the same, and made *them* other five talents.

17 And likewise he that *had received* two, he also gained other two.

18 But he that had received one went and digged in the earth, and hid his lord's money.

19 After a long time the lord of those servants cometh, and reckoneth with them.

20 And so he that had received five talents came and brought other five talents, saying, Lord, thou deliveredst unto me five talents: behold, I have gained beside them five talents more.

21 His lord said unto him, Well done, *thou* good and faithful servant: thou hast been faithful over a few things, I will make thee ruler over many things: enter thou into the joy of thy lord.

22 He also that had received two talents came and said, Lord, thou deliveredst unto me two talents: behold, I have gained two other talents beside them.

23 His lord said unto him, Well done, good and faithful servant; thou hast been faithful over a few things, I will make thee ruler over many things: enter thou into the joy of thy lord.

24 Then he which had received the one talent came and said, Lord, I knew thee that thou art a hard man, reaping where thou hast not sown, and gathering where thou hast not strewed:

25 And I was afraid, and went and hid thy talent in the earth: lo, *there* thou hast *that is* thine.

26 His lord answered and said unto him, *Thou* wicked and slothful servant, thou knewest that I reap where I

B—Concluded.

sowed not, and gather where I have not strewed:

27 Thou oughtest therefore to have put my money to the exchangers, and *then* at my coming I should have received mine own with usury.

28 Take therefore the talent from him, and give *it* unto him which hath ten talents.

29 For unto every one that hath shall be given, and he shall have abundance: but from him that hath not shall be taken away even that which he hath.

30 And cast ye the unprofitable servant into outer darkness: there shall be weeping and gnashing of teeth.

Mark 13. 34 *For the Son of man is* as a man taking a far journey, who left his house, and gave authority to his servants, and to every man his work, and commanded the porter to watch.

C

Acts 1. 11 Which also said, Ye men of Galilee, why stand ye gazing up into heaven? this same Jesus, which is taken up from you into heaven, shall so come in like manner as ye have seen him go into heaven.

Acts 17. 31 Because he hath appointed a day, in the which he will judge the world in righteousness by *that* man whom he hath ordained; *whereof* he hath given assurance unto all *men*, in that he hath raised him from the dead.

Heb. 9. 28 So Christ was once offered to bear the sins of many; and unto them that look for him shall he appear the second time without sin unto salvation.

Rev. 1. 7 Behold, he cometh with clouds; and every eye shall see him, and they *also* which pierced him: and all kindreds of the earth shall wail because of him. Even so, Amen.

1

Mina, here translated a pound is twelve ounces and a half, which according to five shillings the ounce is three pounds two shillings and sixpence; in American money, *$15.00*.

D

I Sa. 8. 7 And the Lord said unto Samuel, Hearken unto the voice of the people in all that they say unto thee: for they have not rejected thee, but they have rejected me, that I should not reign over them.

Isa. 49. 7 Thus saith the Lord, the Redeemer of Israel, *and* his Holy One,

TIME, MARCH, A. D. 30; PLACE, JERICHO.

19: 11–28.

11 And as they heard these things, he added and spake a parable, because he was nigh to Jerusalem, and because [a]they thought that the kingdom of God should immediately appear.

12 [b]He said therefore, A certain nobleman went into a far country to receive for himself a kingdom, [c]and to return.

13 And he called his ten servants, and delivered them ten [1]pounds, and said unto them, Occupy till I come.

14 [d]But his citizens hated him, and sent a message after him, saying, We will not have this *man* to reign over us.

15 And it came to pass, that when he was returned, having received the kingdom, then he commanded these servants to be called unto him, to whom he had given the [2]money, that he might know how much every man had gained by trading.

16 Then came the first, saying, Lord, thy pound hath gained ten pounds.

17 [e]And he said unto him, Well, thou good servant: because thou hast been faithful in a very little, have thou authority over ten cities.

18 And the second came, saying, Lord, thy pound hath gained five pounds.

19 And he said likewise to him, Be thou also over five cities.

20 And another came, saying, Lord, behold, *here is* thy pound, which I have kept laid up in a napkin:

D—CONTINUED.

to him whom man despiseth, to him whom the nation abhorreth, to a servant of rulers, Kings shall see and arise,

D—CONCLUDED.

princes also shall worship, because of the LORD that is faithful, *and* the Holy One of Israel, and he shall choose thee.

John 1. 11 He came unto his own, and his own received him not.

Acts 3. 14 But ye denied the Holy One and the Just, and desired a murderer to be granted unto you;

15 And killed the Prince of life, whom God hath raised from the dead; whereof we are witnesses.

Acts 4. 27 For of a truth against thy holy child Jesus, whom thou hast anointed, both Herod, and Pontius Pilate, with the Gentiles, and the people of Israel, were gathered together,

28 For to do whatsoever thy hand and thy council determined before to be done.

2

Greek, *silver*.

E

Gen. 39. 4 And Joseph found grace in his sight, and he served him: and he made him overseer over his house, and all *that* he had he put into his hand.

I Sa. 2. 30 Wherefore the LORD God of Israel saith, I said indeed *that* thy house, and the house of thy father, should walk before me for ever: but now the LORD saith, Be it far from me; for them that honour me I will honour, and they that despise me shall be lightly esteemed.

Matt. 25. 21. *See under B.*

Luke 16. 10 He that is faithful in that which is least is faithful also in much: and he that is unjust in the least is unjust also in much.

Luke 22. 30 That ye may eat and drink at my table in my kingdom, and sit on thrones judging the twelve tribes of Israel.

Rom. 2. 29 But he *is* a Jew, which is one inwardly; and circumcision *is that* of the heart, in the spirit, *and* not in the letter; whose praise *is* not of men, but of God.

Rev. 2. 26 And he that overcometh, and keepeth my works unto the end, to him will I give power over the nations:

27 And he shall rule them with a rod of iron; as the vessels of a potter shall they be broken to shivers: even as I received of my Father.

28 And I will give him the morning star.

29 He that hath an ear, let him hear what the Spirit saith unto the churches.

§ 151. THE PARABLE OF THE TEN POUNDS

F

Rev. 21. 8 But the fearful, and unbelieving, and the abominable, and murderers, and whoremongers, and sorcerers, and idolaters, and all liars, shall have their part in the lake which burneth with fire and brimstone: which is the second death.

G

I Sa. 6. 19 And he smote the men of Beth-shemesh, because they had looked into the ark of the LORD, even he smote of the people fifty thousand and three-score and ten men: and the people lamented, because the LORD had smitten *many* of the people with a great slaughter.

20 And the men of Beth-shemesh said, Who is able to stand before this holy LORD God? and to whom shall he go up from us?

21 And they sent messengers to the inhabitants of Kirjath-jearim, saying, The Philistines have brought again the ark of the LORD; come ye down, *and* fetch it up to you.

II Sa. 6. 9 And David was afraid of the LORD that day, and said, How shall the ark of the LORD come to me?

10 So David would not remove the ark of the LORD unto him into the city of David: but David carried it aside into the house of Obed-edom the Gittite.

11 And the ark of the LORD continued in the house of Obed-edom the Gittite three months: and the LORD blessed Obed-edom, and all his household.

Job 21. 14 Therefore they say unto God, Depart from us; for we desire not the knowledge of thy ways.

15 What *is* the Almighty, that we should serve him? and what profit should we have, if we pray unto him?

Eze. 18. 25 Yet ye say, The way of the Lord is not equal. Hear now, O house of

G—CONCLUDED.

Israel; Is not my way equal? are not your ways unequal?

26 When a righteous *man* turneth away from his righteousness, and committeth iniquity, and dieth in them; for his iniquity that he hath done shall he die.

27 Again, when the wicked *man* turneth away from his wickedness that he hath committed, and doeth that which is lawful and right, he shall save his soul alive.

28 Because he considereth, and turneth away from all his transgressions that he hath committed, he shall surely live, he shall not die.

29 Yet saith the house of Israel, The way of the Lord is not equal. O house of Israel, are not my ways equal? are not your ways unequal?

Mal. 3. 14 Ye have said, It *is* vain to serve God: and what profit *is it* that we have kept his ordinance, and that we have walked mournfully before the LORD of hosts?

15 And now we call the proud happy; yea, they that work wickedness are set up; yea, *they that* tempt God are even delivered.

Matt. 25. 24. *See under B, page 426.*

Rom. 8. 6 For to be carnally minded *is* death; but to be spiritually minded *is* life and peace.

7 Because the carnal mind *is* enmity against God: for it is not subject to the law of God, neither indeed can be.

Jude 15 To execute judgment upon all, and to convince all that are ungodly among them of all their ungodly deeds which they have ungodly committed, and of all their hard *speeches* which ungodly sinners have spoken against him.

H

II Sa. 1. 16 And David said unto him, Thy

§ 152. JESUS ARRIVES AT BETHANY SIX DAYS BEFORE THE

A

John 2. 13 And the Jews' passover was at hand, and Jesus went up to Jerusalem.

John 5. 1 After this there was a feast of the Jews; and Jesus went up to Jerusalem.

John 6. 4 And the passover, a feast of the Jews, was nigh.

B

Ex. 19. 10 And the LORD said unto Moses,

B—CONTINUED.

Go unto the people, and sanctify them to day and to morrow, and let them wash their clothes,

11 And be ready against the third day: for the third day the LORD will come down in the sight of all the people upon mount Sinai.

I Sa. 16. 5 And he said, Peaceably: I am come to sacrifice unto the LORD. sanctify yourselves, and come with me

(CONCLUDED). TIME, MARCH, A. D. 30; PLACE, JERICHO.

CHAP. 19.

21 [f]For I feared thee, because thou
art [g]an austere man: thou takest up
that thou layedst not down, and reapest
that thou didst not sow.

22 And he saith unto him, [h]Out of
thine own mouth will I judge thee,
thou wicked servant. [i]Thou knewest
that I was an austere man, taking up
that I laid not down, and reaping that
I did not sow:

23 Wherefore then gavest not thou
my money into the bank, that at my
coming I might have required mine
own with usury?

24 And he said unto them that stood
by, Take from him the pound, and
give *it* to him that hath ten pounds.

25 (And they said unto him, Lord,
he hath ten pounds.)

26 For I say unto you, [k]That unto
every one which hath shall be given;
and from him that hath not, even that
he hath shall be taken away from him.

27 But those mine enemies, which
would not that I should reign over
them, bring hither, and slay *them* before me.

28 And when he had thus spoken,
[l]he went before, ascending up to Jerusalem. (p. 433.)

H—CONCLUDED.

blood *be* upon thy head; for thy mouth hath testified against thee, saying, I have slain the LORD's anointed.

Job 15. 6 Thine own mouth condemneth thee, and not I: yea, thine own lips testify against thee.

Matt.12. 37 For by thy words thou shalt be justified, and by thy words thou shalt be condemned.

Tit. 3. 10 A man that is a heretic, after the first and second admonition, reject;

11 Knowing that he that is such is subverted, and sinneth, being condemned of himself.

I

Matt. 25. 26. *See under B, page 426.*

K

Matt.13. 12 For whosoever hath, to him shall be given, and he shall have more abundance; but whosoever hath not, from him shall be taken away even that he hath.

Matt 25. 29. *See under B, page 426.*

Mark 4. 25 For he that hath, to him shall be given; and he that hath not, from him shall be taken even that which he hath.

Luke 8. 18 Take heed therefore how ye hear: for whosoever hath, to him shall be given; and whosoever hath not, from him shall be taken even that which he seemeth to have.

John 15. 1 I am the true vine, and my Father is the husbandman.

2 Every branch in me that beareth not fruit he taketh away: and every *branch* that beareth fruit, he purgeth it, that it may bring forth more fruit.

L

Mark 10. 32 And they were in the way going up to Jerusalem; and Jesus went before them: and they were amazed; and as they followed, they were afraid. And he took again the twelve, and began to tell them what things should happen unto him,

PASSOVER. TIME, FRIDAY EVENING, MARCH 31 [NISAN 8], A. D. 30.

B—CONCLUDED.

to the sacrifice. And he sanctified Jesse and his sons, and called them to the sacrifice.

Jas. 4. 8 Draw nigh to God, and he will draw nigh to you. Cleanse *your* hands, *ye* sinners; and purify *your* hearts, *ye* doubleminded.

C

John 7. 11 Then the Jews sought him at the feast, and said, Where is he?

11: 55–57; 12: 1.

55 [a]And the Jews' passover was nigh
at hand: and many went out of the
country up to Jerusalem before the
passover, to [b]purify themselves.

56 [c]Then sought they for Jesus, and
spake among themselves, as they stood

§ 152. JESUS ARRIVES AT BETHANY SIX DAYS BEFORE THE PASSOVER

D

Ps. 109. 4 For my love they are my adversaries: but I *give myself unto* prayer.
5 And they have rewarded me evil for good, and hatred for my love.

John 5. 16 And therefore did the Jews persecute Jesus, and sought to slay him, because he had done these things on the sabbath day.
17 But Jesus answered them, My Father worketh hitherto, and I work.
18 Therefore the Jews sought the more to kill him, because he not only had broken the sabbath, but said also that God was his Father, making himself equal with God.

John 8. 59 Then took they up stones to cast at him: but Jesus hid himself, and

D—Concluded.

went out of the temple, going through the midst of them, and so passed by.

John 9. 22 These *words* spake his parents, because they feared the Jews: for the Jews had agreed already, that if any man did confess that he was Christ, he should be put out of the synagogue.

John 10. 39 Therefore they sought again to take him; but he escaped out of their hand.

E

Matt. 21. 17 And he left them, and went out of the city into Bethany; and he lodged there.

Mark 11. 11 And Jesus entered into Jerusalem, and into the temple: and when he had looked round about upon all

§ 153. THE SUPPER AND ANOINTING BY MARY. HOSTILITY OF THE CHIEF

26 : 6–13.

6 [a]Now when Jesus was in [b]Bethany, in the house of Simon the leper,

7 There came unto him a woman having an alabaster box of very precious ointment, and poured it on his head, as he sat at meat.

8 [c]But when his disciples saw *it*, they had indignation, saying, To what purpose *is* this waste?

9 For this ointment might have been sold for much, and given to the poor.

A

Mark 14. 3 and John 12. 3. *See text of topic.*
John 11. 1, 2. *See under E, § 152.*

B

Matt. 21. 17. *See under E, § 152.*

C

John 12. 4. *See text of topic.*

D

Matt. 26. 6. *See text of topic.*

Luke 7. 36 And one of the Pharisees desired him that he would eat with him. And he went into the Pharisee's house, and sat down to meat.
37 And, behold, a woman in the city, which was a sinner, when she knew that *Jesus* sat at meat in the Pharisee's house, brought an alabaster box of ointment,
38 And stood at his feet behind *him* weeping, and began to wash his feet with tears, and did wipe *them* with the

14 : 3–9.

3 [d]And being in Bethany, in the house of Simon the leper, as he sat at meat, there came a woman having an alabaster box of ointment of [1]spikenard very precious; and she brake the box, and poured *it* on his head.

4 And there were some that had indignation within themselves, and said, Why was this waste of the ointment made?

5 For it might have been sold for more than three hundred [2]pence, and have been given to the poor. And they murmured against her.

D—Concluded.

hairs of her head, and kissed his feet, and anointed *them* with the ointment.

John 12. 1. *See text of § 152.*
John 12. 3. *See text of topic.*

1

Or, *pure nard*, or, *liquid nard.*

2

The Roman penny is the eighth part of an ounce which after five shillings the ounce is seven pence half penny; in American money, *fifteen cents*, or three hundred pence, *$45.00.*

E

Matt. 26. 6 and Mark 14. 3. *See text of topic.*

F

Luke 10. 38 Now it came to pass, as they went, that he entered into a certain

(CONCLUDED). TIME, FRIDAY EVENING, MARCH 31 [NISAN 8], A. D. 30.

E—CONCLUDED.

things, and now the eventide was come, he went out unto Bethany with the twelve.

Luke 24. 50 And he led them out as far as to Bethany, and he lifted up his hands, and blessed them.

John 11. 1 Now a certain *man* was sick, *named* Lazarus, of Bethany, the town of Mary and her sister Martha.

2 (It was *that* Mary which anointed the Lord with ointment, and wiped his feet with her hair, whose brother Lazarus was sick.)

John 11. 43 And when he thus had spoken, he cried with a loud voice, Lazarus, come forth.

CHAP. 11.

in the temple, What think ye, that he will not come to the feast?

57 Now both the chief priests and the Pharisees [d]had given a commandment, that, if any man knew where he were, he should show *it*, that they might take him.

CHAP. 12.

1 Then Jesus six days before the passover came to [e]Bethany, where Lazarus was which had been dead, whom he raised from the dead.

PRIESTS. TIME, SATURDAY [SABBATH], APRIL 1 [NISAN 9], A. D. 30; PLACE, BETHANY.

F—CONCLUDED.

village: and a certain woman named Martha received him into her house.

39 And she had a sister called Mary, which also sat at Jesus' feet, and heard his word.

John 11. 2. *See under E, § 152.*

G

Ps. 50. 16 But unto the wicked God saith, What hast thou to do to declare my statutes, or *that* thou shouldest take my covenant in thy mouth?

17 Seeing thou hatest instruction, and castest my words behind thee.

18 When thou sawest a thief, then thou consentedst with him, and hast been partaker with adulterers.

19 Thou givest thy mouth to evil, and thy tongue frameth deceit.

20 Thou sittest *and* speakest against thy brother; thou slanderest thine own mother's son.

21 These *things* hast thou done, and I kept silence; thou thoughtest that I was altogether *such a one* as thyself: *but* I will reprove thee, and set *them* in order before thine eyes.

22 Now consider this, ye that forget God, lest I tear *you* in pieces, and *there be* none to deliver.

Prov. 26. 24 He that hateth dissembleth with his lips, and layeth up deceit within him;

25 When he speaketh fair, believe him not: for *there are* seven abominations in his heart.

John 13. 29 For some *of them* thought, because Judas had the bag, that Jesus had said unto him, Buy *those things* that

12: 2–11.

2 [e]There they made him a supper; and Martha served: but Lazarus was one of them that sat at the table with him.

3 Then took [f]Mary a pound of ointment of spikenard, very costly, and anointed the feet of Jesus, and wiped his feet with her hair: and the house was filled with the odour of the ointment.

4 Then saith one of his disciples, Judas Iscariot, Simon's *son*, which should betray him,

5 Why was not this ointment sold for three hundred pence, and given to the poor?

6 [g]This he said, not that he cared for the poor; but because he was a thief, and had the bag, and bare what was put therein.

G—CONCLUDED.

we have need of against the feast; or, that he should give something to the poor.

I Cor. 6. 10 Nor thieves, nor covetous, nor drunkards, nor revilers, nor extortioners, shall inherit the kingdom of God.

§ 153. THE SUPPER AND ANOINTING BY MARY. HOSTILITY OF THE CHIEF

CHAP. 26.

10 When Jesus understood *it*, he said unto them, Why trouble ye the woman? for she hath wrought a good work upon me.

11 [h]For ye have the poor always with you; but [i]me ye have not always.

12 For in that she hath poured this ointment on my body, she did *it* for my burial.

13 Verily I say unto you, [k]Wheresoever this gospel shall be preached in the whole world, *there* shall also this, that this woman hath done, be told for a memorial of her. (p. 506.)

H

Deut.15. 11 For the poor shall never cease out of the land: therefore I command thee, saying, Thou shalt open thine hand wide unto thy brother, to thy poor, and to thy needy, in thy land.

John 12. 8. *See text of topic.*

I

Matt.18. 20 For where two or three are gathered together in my name, there am I in the midst of them.

Matt.28. 20 Teaching them to observe all things whatsoever I have commanded you: and, lo, I am with you alway, *even* unto the end of the world. Amen.

John 13. 33 Little children, yet a little while

CHAP. 14.

6 And Jesus said, Let her alone; why trouble ye her? she hath wrought a good work on me.

7 For [l]ye have the poor with you always, and whensoever ye will ye may do them good: but me ye have not always.

8 She hath done what she could: she is come aforehand to anoint my body to the burying.

9 Verily I say unto you, Wheresoever this gospel shall be preached throughout the whole world, *this* also that she hath done shall be spoken of for a memorial of her. (p. 506.)

I—CONTINUED.

I am with you. Ye shall seek me; and as I said unto the Jews, Whither I go, ye cannot come; so now I say to you.

John 14. 19 Yet a little while, and the world seeth me no more; but ye see me: because I live, ye shall live also.

John 16. 5 But now I go my way to him that sent me; and none of you asketh me, Whither goest thou?

John 16. 28 I came forth from the Father, and am come into the world: again, I leave the world, and go to the Father.

§ 154. OUR LORD'S PUBLIC ENTRY INTO JERUSALEM.

First Day of the Week of our

21: 1–11, 17.

1 And [a]when they drew nigh unto Jerusalem, and were come to Bethphage, unto [b]the mount of Olives, then sent Jesus two disciples,

A

Mark 11. 1 and Luke 19. 29. *See text of topic.*

B

Zech.14. 4 And his feet shall stand in that day upon the mount of Olives, which *is* before Jerusalem on the east, and the mount of Olives shall cleave in the midst thereof toward the east and toward the west, *and there shall be* a very great valley; and half of the mountain shall remove toward the north, and half of it toward the south.

11: 1–11.

1 And [c]when they came nigh to Jerusalem, unto Bethphage and Bethany, at the mount of [d]Olives, he sendeth forth two of his disciples,

C

Matt. 21. 1 and Luke 19, 29. *See text of topic.*

D

Acts 1. 12 Then returned they unto Jerusalem from the mount called Olivet, which is from Jerusalem a sabbath day's journey.

E

Matt. 21. 1 and Mark 11. 1. *See text of topic.*

F

Matt. 21. 8, Mark 11. 8 and Luke 19. 35, 36, etc. *See text of topic.*

PRIESTS (CONCL'D). TIME, SAT. [SABBATH], APR. 1 [NISAN 9], A. D. 30; PLACE, BETHANY.

I—CONCLUDED.

John 17. 11 And now I am no more in the world, but these are in the world, and I come to thee. Holy Father, keep through thine own name those whom thou hast given me, that they may be one, as we *are*.

K

Mark 13. 10 And the gospel must first be published among all nations.

Rom. 1. 8 First, I thank my God through Jesus Christ for you all, that your faith is spoken of throughout the whole world.

L

Deut. 15. 11. *See under H.*

M

Deut. 15. 11. *See under H.*
Matt. 26. 11 and Mark 14. 7. *See text of topic.*

N

John 11. 43 And when he thus had spoken, he cried with a loud voice, Lazarus, come forth.

44 And he that was dead came forth, bound hand and foot with graveclothes; and his face was bound about with a napkin. Jesus saith unto them, Loose him, and let him go.

O

Prov. 1. 16 For their feet run to evil, and make haste to shed blood.

Prov. 4. 14 Enter not into the path of the wicked, and go not in the way of evil *men*.

15 Avoid it, pass not by it, turn from it, and pass away.

16 For they sleep not, except they have done mischief; and their sleep is taken away, unless they cause *some* to fall.

CHAP. 12.

7 Then said Jesus, Let her alone: against the day of my burying hath she kept this.

8 For [m]the poor always ye have with you; but me ye have not always.

9 Much people of the Jews therefore knew that he was there: and they came not for Jesus' sake only, but that they might see Lazarus also, [n]whom he had raised from the dead.

10 [o]But the chief priests consulted that they might put Lazarus also to death;

11 [p]Because that by reason of him many of the Jews went away, and believed on Jesus.

O—CONCLUDED.

Luke 16. 31 And he said unto him, If they hear not Moses and the prophets, neither will they be persuaded, though one rose from the dead.

P

Mark 15. 10 For he knew that the chief priests had delivered him for envy.

John 11. 45 Then many of the Jews which came to Mary, and had seen the things which Jesus did, believed on him.

John 12. 18 For this cause the people also met him, for that they heard that he had done this miracle.

TIME, SUNDAY, APRIL 2 [NISAN 10], A. D. 30; PLACE, BETHANY, JERUSALEM.
Lord's Fourth and Last Passover.

19: 29–44.

29 [e]And it came to pass, when he was come nigh to Bethphage and Bethany, at the mount called *the mount* of Olives, he sent two of his disciples,

G

Ps. 24. 1 The earth *is* the LORD'S, and the fulness thereof; the world, and they that dwell therein.

H

II Cor. 8. 9 For ye know the grace of our Lord Jesus Christ, that, though he was rich, yet for your sakes he became poor, that ye through his poverty might be rich.

I

I Ki. 1. 33 The king also said unto them,

12: 12–19.

12 [f]On the next day much people that were come to the feast, when they heard that Jesus was coming to Jerusalem,

I—CONTINUED.

Take with you the servants of your lord, and cause Solomon my son to ride upon mine own mule, and bring him down to Gihon:

Isa. 62. 11 Behold, the LORD hath proclaimed unto the end of the world, Say ye to the daughter of Zion, Behold, thy salvation cometh; behold, his reward *is* with him, and his work before him.

For I concluded see next page (434).

§ 154. OUR LORD'S PUBLIC ENTRY INTO JERUSALEM (CONTINUED).
First Day of the Week of our

CHAP. 21.

2 Saying unto them, Go into the village over against you, and straightway ye shall find an ass tied, and a colt with her: loose *them*, and bring *them* unto me.

3 And if any *man* say aught unto you, ye shall say, The [g]Lord hath [h]need of them; and straightway he will send them.

4 All this was done, that it might be fulfilled which was spoken by the prophet, saying,

5 [i]Tell ye the daughter of Sion, Behold, thy King cometh unto thee, meek, and sitting upon an ass, and a colt the foal of an ass.

6 [k]And the disciples went, and did as Jesus commanded them,

7 And brought the ass, and the colt, and [l]put on them their clothes, and they set *him* thereon.

8 And a very great multitude spread their garments in the way; [m]others cut down branches from the trees, and strewed *them* in the way.

9 And the multitudes that went before, and that followed, cried, saying, [n]Hosanna to the Son of David:

For G, H and I see preceding page (433).

I—CONCLUDED.

Zech. 9. 9 Rejoice greatly, O daughter of Zion; shout, O daughter of Jerusalem: behold, thy King cometh unto thee: he *is* just, and having salvation; lowly, and riding upon an ass, and upon a colt the foal of an ass.

John 12. 15. *See text of topic.*

K

Mark 11. 4. *See text of topic.*

L

II Ki. 9. 13 Then they hasted, and took every man his garment, and put *it* under him on the top of the stairs, and blew with trumpets, saying, Jehu is king.

CHAP. 11.

2 And saith unto them, Go your way into the village over against you: and as soon as ye be entered into it, ye shall find a colt tied, whereon never man sat; loose him, and bring *him.*

3 And if any man say unto you, Why do ye this? say ye that the [o]Lord hath need of him; and straightway he will send him hither.

4 And they went their way, and found the colt tied by the door without in a place where two ways met; and they loose him.

5 And certain of them that stood there said unto them, What do ye, loosing the colt?

6 And they said unto them even as Jesus had commanded: and they let them go.

7 And they brought the colt to Jesus, and cast their garments on him; and he [p]sat upon him.

8 [q]And many spread their garments in the way; and others cut down branches off the trees, and strewed *them* in the way.

9 And they that went before, and they that followed, cried, saying, [r]Hosanna:

M

Lev. 23. 40 And ye shall take you on the first day the boughs of goodly trees, branches of palm trees, and the boughs of thick trees, and willows of the brook; and ye shall rejoice before the LORD your God seven days.

John 12. 13. *See text of topic.*

N

Ps. 118. 25 Save now, I beseech thee, O LORD: O LORD, I beseech thee, send now prosperity.

26 Blessed *be* he that cometh in the name of the LORD: we have blessed you out of the house of the LORD.

TIME, SUNDAY, APRIL 2 [NISAN 10], A. D. 30; PLACE, BETHANY, JERUSALEM.
Lord's Fourth and Last Passover.

CHAP. 19.

30 Saying, Go ye into the village
over against *you;* in the which at your
entering ye shall find a colt tied,
whereon yet never man sat: loose
him, and bring *him hither.*
31 And if any man ask you, Why
do ye loose *him?* thus shall ye say unto him, Because the [s]Lord hath need
of him.
32 And they that were sent went
their way, and found even as he had
said unto them.
33 And as they were loosing the colt,
the owners thereof said unto them,
Why loose ye the colt?
34 And they said, The Lord hath
need of him.
35 And they brought him to Jesus:
[t]and they cast their garments upon the
colt, and they set Jesus thereon.
36 [u]And as he went, they spread
their clothes in the way.
37 And when he was come nigh,
even now at the descent of the mount
of Olives, the whole multitude of the
disciples began to rejoice and praise
God with a loud voice for all the
mighty works that they had seen:

O

Acts 10. 36 The word which *God* sent unto the children of Israel, preaching peace by Jesus Christ: (he is Lord of all:)

Heb. 1. 2 Hath in these last days spoken unto us by *his* Son, whom he hath appointed heir of all things, by whom also he made the worlds;

P

I Ki. 1. 33 and Zech. 9. 9. *See under I.*

Q

Matt. 21. 8. *See text of topic.*

R

Ps. 118. 26. *Under N.* Isa. 62. 11. *Under I.*

S

Acts 10. 36. *See under O.*

CHAP. 12.

13 Took branches of palm trees, and
went forth to meet him, and cried,
[x]Hosanna: Blessed *is* the King of
Israel that cometh in the name of the
Lord.
14 [y]And Jesus, when he had found a
young ass, sat thereon; as it is written,
15 [z]Fear not, daughter of Sion: behold, thy king cometh, sitting on an
ass's colt.

T

II Ki. 9. 13. *See under L.*
Matt. 21. 7, Mark 11. 7 and John 12. 14. *See text of topic.*

U

Matt. 21. 8. *See text of topic.*

X

Ps. 72. 17 His name shall endure for ever: his name shall be continued as long as the sun: and *men* shall be blessed in him: all nations shall call him blessed.

Ps. 118. 25, 26. *See under N.*

Y

Matt. 21. 2, Mark 11. 2, and Luke 19. 30. *See text of topic.*

Z

Isa. 62. 11 and Zech 9. 9. *See under I.*

A

Matt.23. 39 For I say unto you, Ye shall not see me henceforth, till ye shall say, Blessed *is* he that cometh in the name of the Lord.

B

Luke 19. 45 And he went into the temple, and began to cast out them that sold therein, and them that bought;

John 2. 13 And the Jews' passover was at hand, and Jesus went up to Jerusalem,
14 And found in the temple those that sold oxen and sheep and doves, and the changers of money sitting:

C

Matt. 2. 23 And he came and dwelt in a city called Nazareth: that it might be fulfilled which was spoken by the prophets, He shall be called a Nazarene.

Luke 7. 16 And there came a fear on all: and they glorified God, saying, That a great prophet is risen up among us; and, That God hath visited his people.

John 6. 14 Then those men, when they had seen the miracle that Jesus did, said, This is of a truth that Prophet that should come into the world.

For C concluded see next page (436).

§ 154. OUR LORD'S PUBLIC ENTRY INTO JERUSALEM (Concluded).

First Day of tne Week of our

Chap. 21.

[a]Blessed *is* he that cometh in the name of the Lord; Hosanna in the highest.

10 [b]And when he was come into Jerusalem, all the city was moved, saying, Who is this?

11 And the multitude said, This is Jesus [c]the prophet of Nazareth of Galilee. (p. 438.)

* * * * *

17 And he left them, and went out of the city into [d]Bethany; and he lodged there.

For A, B and C see preceding page (435).

C—Concluded.

John 9. 17 They say unto the blind man again, What sayest thou of him, that he hath opened thine eyes? He said, He is a prophet.

D

Mark 11. 11. *See text of topic.*
John 11. 18 Now Bethany was nigh unto Jerusalem, about fifteen furlongs off:

E

Ps. 148. 1 Praise ye the Lord. Praise ye the Lord from the heavens: praise him in the heights.

F

Matt. 21. 12 And Jesus went into the temple of God, and cast out all them that sold and bought in the temple, and overthrew the tables of the money changers, and the seats of them that sold doves,

G

Ps. 118. 26. *See under N, page 434.*
Luke 13. 35. *See text of § 128.*
I Tim. 1. 17 Now unto the King eternal, immortal, invisible, the only wise God, *be* honour and glory for ever and ever. Amen.

H

Luke 2. 14 Glory to God in the highest, and on earth peace, good will toward men.
Eph. 2. 14 For he is our peace, who hath made both one, and hath broken down the middle wall of partition *between us:*

I

Hab. 2. 11 For the stone shall cry out of the wall, and the beam out of the timber shall answer it.

K

John 11. 35 Jesus wept.

Chap. 11.

Blessed *is* he that cometh in the name of the Lord:

10 Blessed *be* the kingdom of our father David, that cometh in the name of the Lord: [e]Hosanna in the highest.

11 [f]And Jesus entered into Jerusalem, and into the temple: and when he had looked round about upon all things, and now the eventide was come, he went out unto Bethany with the twelve.

L

Isa. 29. 3 And I will camp against thee round about, and will lay siege against thee with a mount, and I will raise forts against thee.
4 And thou shalt be brought down, *and* shalt speak out of the ground, and thy speech shall be low out of the dust, and thy voice shall be, as of one that hath a familiar spirit, out of the ground, and thy speech shall whisper out of the dust.
Jer. 6. 3 The shepherds with their flocks shall come unto her; they shall pitch *their* tents against her round about; they shall feed every one in his place.
Jer. 6. 6 For thus hath the Lord of hosts said, Hew ye down trees, and cast a mount against Jerusalem: this *is* the city to be visited; she *is* wholly oppression in the midst of her.
Luke 21. 20 And when ye shall see Jerusalem compassed with armies, then know that the desolation thereof is nigh.

M

I Ki. 9. 7 Then will I cut off Israel out of the land which I have given them; and this house, which I have hallowed for my name, will I cast out of my sight; and Israel shall be a proverb and a byword among all people:
8 And at this house, *which* is high, every one that passeth by it shall be astonished, and shall hiss; and they shall say, Why hath the Lord done thus unto this land, and to this house?
Mic. 3. 12 Therefore shall Zion for your sake be ploughed *as* a field, and Jerusalem shall become heaps, and the mountain of the house as the high places of the forest.

TIME, SUNDAY, APRIL 2 [NISAN 10], A. D. 30; PLACE, BETHANY, JERUSALEM.
Lord's Fourth and Last Passover.

CHAP. 19.

38 Saying, [g]Blessed *be* the King that
cometh in the name of the Lord:
[h]peace in heaven, and glory in the
highest.

39 And some of the Pharisees from
among the multitude said unto him,
Master, rebuke thy disciples.

40 And he answered and said unto
them, I tell you that, if these should
hold their peace, [i]the stones would immediately cry out.

41 ¶ And when he was come near
he beheld the city, and [k]wept over it,

42 Saying, If thou hadst known,
even thou, at least in this thy day, the
things *which belong* unto thy peace!
but now they are hid from thine eyes.

43 For the days shall come upon thee,
that thine enemies shall [l]cast a trench
about thee, and compass thee round,
and keep thee in on every side,

44 And [m]shall lay thee even with the
ground, and thy children within thee;
and [n]they shall not leave in thee one
stone upon another; [o]because thou
knewest not the time of thy visitation.

N

Matt.24. 2 And Jesus said unto them, See ye not all these things? verily I say unto you, There shall not be left here one stone upon another, that shall not be thrown down.

Mark 13. 2 And Jesus answering said unto him, Seest thou these great buildings? there shall not be left one stone upon another, that shall not be thrown down.

Luke 21. 6 *As for* these things which ye behold, the days will come, in the which there shall not be left one stone upon another, that shall not be thrown down,

O

Dan. 9. 24. *See under C, page 52.*

Luke 1. 68 Blessed *be* the Lord God of Israel; for he hath visited and redeemed his people.

CHAP. 12.

16 These things [p]understood not his
disciples at the first: [q]but when Jesus
was glorified, [r]then remembered they
that these things were written of him,
and *that* they had done these things
unto him.

17 The people therefore that was with
him when he called Lazarus out of his
grave, and raised him from the dead,
bare record.

18 [s]For this cause the people also met
him, for that they heard that he had
done this miracle.

19 The Pharisees therefore said
among themselves, [t]Perceive ye how
ye prevail nothing? behold, the world
is gone after him. (p. 473.)

O—CONCLUDED.

Luke 1. 78 Through the tender mercy of our God; whereby the dayspring from on high hath visited us,

I Pet. 2. 12 Having your conversation honest among the Gentiles: that, whereas they speak against you as evil doers, they may by *your* good works, which they shall behold, glorify God in the day of visitation.

P

Luke 18. 34 And they understood none of these things: and this saying was hid from them, neither knew they the things which were spoken.

Q

John 7. 39 (But this spake he of the Spirit, which they that believe on him should receive: for the Holy Ghost was not yet *given;* because that Jesus was not yet glorified.)

Heb. 1. 3 Who being the brightness of *his* glory, and the express image of his person, and upholding all things by the word of his power, when he had by himself purged our sins, sat down on the right hand of the Majesty on high;

R

John 14. 26. *See text of § 188.*

S

John 12. 11. *See text of § 153.*

T

John 11. 47, 48. *See text of § 122, page 365.*

§ 155. THE BARREN FIG TREE CURSED. TIME, MONDAY MORNING, Second Day of the Week of our

Matthew 21 : 18, 19.

18 [a]Now in the morning, as he returned into the city, he hungered.

19 [b]And when he saw [1]a fig tree in the way, he came to it, and found nothing thereon, but leaves only, and said unto it, [c]Let no fruit grow on thee henceforward forever. And presently the fig tree withered away. (p. 440.)

A
Mark 11. 12. *See text of topic.*

B
Mark 11. 13. *See text of topic.*

1
Greek, *one fig tree.*

C
Mark 11. 14. *See text of topic.*
Luke 19. 42-44. *See text of § 154.*

Mark 11 : 12–14.

12 [d]And on the morrow, when they were come from Bethany, he was hungry:

13 [e]And seeing a fig tree afar off having leaves, he came, if haply he might find any thing thereon: and when he came to it, he found nothing but leaves; for the time of figs was not *yet*.

14 And Jesus answered and said unto it, No man eat fruit of thee hereafter for ever. And his disciples heard *it*.

§ 156. THE SECOND CLEANSING OF THE TEMPLE. [See § 21.] Second Day of the Week of our

Matthew 21 : 12–16.

12 [a]And Jesus went into the temple of God, and cast out all them that sold and bought in the temple, and overthrew the tables of the [b]money changers, and the seats of them that sold doves,

13 And said unto them, It is written, [c]My house shall be called the house of prayer; [d]but ye have made it a den of thieves.

14 And the [e]blind and the lame came to him in the temple; and he healed them.

15 And when the chief priests and scribes saw the wonderful things that he did, and the children crying in the temple, and saying, Hosanna to the [f]Son of David; they were sore displeased,

16 And said unto him, Hearest thou what these say? And Jesus saith unto them, Yea; have ye never read, [g]Out of the mouth of babes and sucklings thou hast perfected praise? (p. 436.)

Mark 11 : 15–19.

15 [h]And they come to Jerusalem: and Jesus went into the temple, and began to cast out them that sold and bought in the temple, and overthrew the tables of the money changers, and the seats of them that sold doves;

16 And would not suffer that any man should carry *any* vessel through the temple.

17 And he taught, saying unto them, Is it not written, [i]My house shall be called [1]of all nations the house of prayer? but [k]ye have made it a den of thieves.

18 And [l]the scribes and chief priests heard *it*, and sought how they might destroy him: for they feared him, because [m]all the people was astonished at his doctrine.

19 And when even was come, he went out of the city.

A
Mark 11. 15. *See text of topic.*
Luke 19. 45-48. *See text of topic.*
John 2. 13-17. *See text of § 21, page 69.*

April 3 [Nisan 11], A. D. 30; Place, On the Way to Jerusalem.
Lord's Fourth and Last Passover.

C—Continued.

Heb. 6. 7 For the earth which drinketh in the rain that cometh oft upon it, and bringeth forth herbs meet for them by whom it is dressed, receiveth blessing from God:

8 But that which beareth thorns and briers *is* rejected, and *is* nigh unto cursing; whose end *is* to be burned.

II Pet.2. 20 For if after they have escaped the pollutions of the world through the knowledge of the Lord and Saviour Jesus Christ, they are again entangled therein, and overcome, the latter end is worse with them than the beginning.

21 For it had been better for them not to have known the way of righteousness, than, after they have known *it*, to turn from the holy commandment delivered unto them.

22 But it is happened unto them according to the true proverb, The dog *is* turned to his own vomit again; and, The sow that was washed to her wallowing in the mire.

Rev. 22. 11 He that is unjust, let him be unjust still: and he which is filthy, let him be filthy still: and he that is righteous, let him be righteous still: and he that is holy, let him be holy still.

D

Matt. 21. 18. *See text of topic.*

E

Matt. 21. 19. *See text of topic.*

Time, Monday, April 3 [Nisan 11], A. D. 30; Place, Jerusalem.
Lord's Fourth and Last Passover.

19: 45–48; 21: 37, 38.

45 And he went into the temple, and began to cast out them [n]that sold therein, and them that bought;

46 Saying unto them, It is written, My house is the house of prayer; but ye have made it a den of thieves.

47 And he taught daily in the temple. But the chief priests and the scribes and the chief of the people sought to destroy him,

48 And could not find what they might do: for all the people were very attentive to hear him. (p. 443.)

Chap. 21.

37 And in the daytime he was teaching in the temple; and [o]at night he went out and abode in the mount that is called *the mount* of Olives.

B

Deut.14. 25 Then shalt thou turn *it* into money, and bind up the money in thine hand, and shalt go unto the place which the Lord thy God shall choose:

C

Isa. 56. 7 Even them will I bring to my holy mountain, and make them joyful in my house of prayer: their burnt offerings and their sacrifices *shall be* accepted upon mine altar; for mine house shall be called a house of prayer for all people.

D

Jer. 7. 11 Is this house, which is called by my name, become a den of robbers in your eyes? Behold, even I have seen *it*, saith the Lord.

Mark 11. 17 and Luke 19. 46. *See text of topic.*

E

Isa. 35. 5 Then the eyes of the blind shall be opened, and the ears of the deaf shall be unstopped.

F

Isa. 11. 1 And there shall come forth a rod out of the stem of Jesse, and a Branch shall grow out of his roots:

G

Ps. 8. 2 Out of the mouth of babes and sucklings hast thou ordained strength because of thine enemies, that thou mightest still the enemy and the avenger.

H

Matt. 21. 12 and Luke 19. 45. *See text of topic.*

I

Isa. 56. 7. *See under C.*

Zech. 2. 11 And many nations shall be joined to the Lord in that day, and shall be my people: and I will dwell in the midst of thee, and thou shalt know that the Lord of hosts hath sent me unto thee.

1

Or, *an house of prayer for all nations?*

For K, L, M, N and O see following pages (440, 441).

§ 156. THE SECOND CLEANSING OF THE TEMPLE (CONCLUDED).
Second Day of the Week of our

[CHAP. 21.]

K

Jer. 7. 11. *See under D.*

L

Matt.21. 45 And when the chief priests and Pharisees had heard his parables, they perceived that he spake of them.

46 But when they sought to lay hands on him, they feared the multitude,

[CHAP. 11.]

L—CONCLUDED.

because they took him for a prophet.

M

Luke 4. 32 And they were astonished at his doctrine: for his word was with power.

N

John 8. 2 And early in the morning he came again into the temple, and all the peo-

§ 157. THE BARREN FIG TREE WITHERS AWAY. TIME, TUESDAY
Third Day of the Week of our

21 : 20–22.

20 [a]And when the disciples saw *it*,
they marvelled, saying, How soon is
the fig tree withered away!

21 Jesus answered and said unto
them, Verily I say unto you, [b]If ye
have faith, and [c]doubt not, ye shall
not only do this *which is done* to the
fig tree, [d]but also if ye shall say unto
this mountain, Be thou removed, and
be thou cast into the sea; it shall be
done.

22 And [e]all things, whatsoever ye
shall ask in prayer, believing, ye shall
receive.

A

Mark 11. 20. *See text of topic.*

B

Matt.17. 20 And Jesus said unto them, Because of your unbelief. for verily I say unto you, If ye have faith as a grain of mustard seed, ye shall say unto this mountain, Remove hence to yonder place; and it shall remove: and nothing shall be impossible unto you.

11 : 20–24.

20 [f]And in the morning, as they
passed by, they saw the fig tree dried
up from the roots.

21 And Peter calling to remembrance
saith unto him, Master, behold, the fig
tree which thou cursedst is withered
away.

22 And Jesus answering saith unto
them, [1]Have faith in God.

23 For [g]verily I say unto you, That
whosoever shall say unto this mountain,
Be thou removed, and be thou cast into
the sea; and shall not doubt in his
heart, but shall believe that those
things which he saith shall come to
pass; he shall have whatsoever he
saith.

24 Therefore I say unto you, [h]What
things soever ye desire, when ye pray,
believe that ye receive *them*, and ye
shall have *them*.

§ 158. PRAY AND FORGIVE. TIME, TUESDAY MORNING,
Third Day of the Week of our

A

Zech. 3. 1 And he showed me Joshua the high priest standing before the angel of the LORD, and Satan standing at his right hand to resist him.

B

Matt. 6. 14 For if ye forgive men their trespasses, your heavenly Father will also forgive you:

15 But if ye forgive not men their trespasses, neither will your Father forgive your trespasses.

11 : 25, 26.

25 And when ye [a]stand praying,
[b]forgive, if ye have aught against any;
that your Father also which is in
heaven may forgive you your trespasses.

26 But [c]if ye do not forgive, neither
will your Father which is in heaven
forgive your trespasses.

[SEE § 21]. TIME, MONDAY, APRIL 3 [NISAN 11], A. D. 30; PLACE, JERUSALEM.
Lord's Fourth and Last Passover.

CHAP. 21.

38 And all the people came early in the morning to him *p*in the temple, for to hear him. (p. 507.)

N—CONCLUDED.

ple came unto him; and he sat down, and taught them.

O

Luke 22. 39 And he came out, and went, as he was wont, to the mount of Olives; and his disciples also followed him.

P

Hag. 2. 7 And I will shake all nations, and the Desire of all nations shall come: and I will fill this house with glory, saith the LORD of hosts.

MORNING, APRIL 4 [NISAN 12], A. D. 30; PLACE, BETWEEN BETHANY AND JERUSALEM.
Lord's Fourth and Last Passover.

C

Jas. 1. 6 But let him ask in faith, nothing wavering: for he that wavereth is like a wave of the sea driven with the wind and tossed.

D

I Cor. 13. 2 And though I have *the gift of* prophecy, and understand all mysteries, and all knowledge; and though I have all faith, so that I could remove mountains, and have not charity, I am nothing.

E

Matt. 7. 7 Ask, and it shall be given you, seek, and ye shall find; knock, and it shall be opened unto you:

Luke 11. 9 And I say unto you, Ask, and it shall be given you; seek, and ye shall find; knock, and it shall be opened unto you.

Jas. 5. 16 Confess *your* faults one to another, and pray one for another, that ye may be healed. The effectual fervent prayer of a righteous man availeth much.

I Jno. 3. 22 And whatsoever we ask, we receive of him, because we keep his commandments, and do those things that are pleasing in his sight.

I Jno. 5. 14 And this is the confidence that we have in him, that, if we ask any thing according to his will, he heareth us:

F

Matt. 21. 19 And when he saw a fig tree in the way, he came to it, and found nothing thereon, but leaves only, and said unto it, Let no fruit grow on thee henceforward for ever. And presently the fig tree withered away.

I

Or, *have the faith of God.*

G

Matt. 17. 20. *Under B.* Matt. 21. 21. *Text of topic.*
I Cor. 13. 2. *See under D.*

H

Matt. 18. 19 Again I say unto you, That if two of you shall agree on earth as touching any thing that they shall ask, it shall be done for them of my Father which is in heaven.

Matt. 21. 22. *See text of topic.* Luke 11. 9. *Under E.*

John 14. 13 And whatsoever ye shall ask in my name, that will I do, that the Father may be glorified in the Son.

14 If ye shall ask any thing in my name, I will do *it.*

John 15. 7 If ye abide in me, and my words abide in you, ye shall ask what ye will, and it shall be done unto you.

John 16. 24 Hitherto have ye asked nothing in my name: ask, and ye shall receive, that your joy may be full.

Jas. 1. 5 If any of you lack wisdom, let him ask of God, that giveth to all *men* liberally, and upbraideth not; and it shall be given him.

APRIL 4 [NISAN 12], A. D. 30; PLACE, ON THE WAY TO JERUSALEM.
Lord's Fourth and Last Passover.

B—CONTINUED.

Eph. 4. 31 Let all bitterness, and wrath, and anger, and clamour, and evil speaking, be put away from you, with all malice:

32 And be ye kind one to another, tenderhearted, forgiving one another, even as God for Christ's sake hath forgiven you.

Col. 3. 13 Forbearing one another, and forgiving one another, if any man have

B—CONCLUDED.

a quarrel against any: even as Christ forgave you, so also *do* ye.

Jas. 2. 13 For he shall have judgment without mercy, that hath showed no mercy; and mercy rejoiceth against judgment.

C

Matt. 18. 35 So likewise shall my heavenly Father do also unto you, if ye from your hearts forgive not every one his brother their trespasses.

§ 159. CHRIST'S AUTHORITY QUESTIONED.
Third Day of the Week of our

21 : 23–27.

23 [a]And when he was come into the temple, the chief priests and the elders of the people came unto him as he was teaching, and [b]said, By what authority doest thou these things? and who gave thee this authority?

24 And [c]Jesus answered and said unto them, I also will ask you one thing, which if ye tell me, I in like wise will tell you by what authority I do these things.

25 The baptism of John, whence was it? from heaven, or of men? And they reasoned with themselves, saying, If we shall say, From heaven; he will say unto us, Why did ye not then believe him?

26 But if we shall say, Of men; we fear the people; [d]for all hold John as a prophet.

27 And they answered Jesus, and said, We cannot tell. And he said unto them, Neither tell I you by what authority I do these things.

A

Mark 11. 27 and Luke 20. 1. *See text of topic.*

B

Ex. 2. 14 And he said, Who made thee a prince and a judge over us? intendest thou to kill me, as thou killedst the Egyptian? And Moses feared, and said, Surely this thing is known.

Acts 4. 7 And when they had set them in the midst, they asked, By what power, or by what name, have ye done this?

Acts 7. 27 But he that did his neighbour wrong thrust him away, saying, Who made thee a ruler and a judge over us?

C

Job 5. 13 He taketh the wise in their own craftiness: and the counsel of the froward is carried headlong.

D

Matt.14. 5 And when he would have put him to death, he feared the multitude, because they counted him as a prophet.

11 : 27–33.

27 And they come again to Jerusalem: and [e]as he was walking in the temple, there come to him the chief priests, and the scribes, and the elders,

28 And say unto him, By what authority doest thou these things? and who gave thee this authority to do these things?

29 And Jesus answered and said unto them, I will also ask of you one [1]question, and answer me, and I will tell you by what authority I do these things.

30 The baptism of John, was *it* from heaven, or of men? answer me.

31 And they reasoned with themselves, saying, If we shall say, From heaven; he will say, Why then did ye not believe him?

32 But if we shall say, Of men; they feared the people: for [f]all *men* counted John, that he was a prophet indeed.

33 And they answered and said unto Jesus, We cannot tell. And Jesus answering saith unto them, [g]Neither do I tell you by what authority I do these things.

D—Concluded.

Mark 6. 20 For Herod feared John, knowing that he was a just man and a holy, and observed him; and when he heard him, he did many things, and heard him gladly.

Luke 20. 6. *See text of topic.*

E

Matt. 21. 23 and Luke 20. 1. *See text of topic.*

1

Or, *thing.*

F

Matt. 3. 5 Then went out to him Jerusalem, and all Judæa, and all the region round about Jordan.

Matt. 14. 5 and Mark 6. 20. *See under D.*

TIME, TUESDAY, APRIL 4 [NISAN 12], A. D. 30; PLACE, JERUSALEM.
Lord's Fourth and Last Passover.

20 : 1-8.

1 And [h]it came to pass, *that* on one of those days, as he taught the people in the temple, and preached the gospel, the chief priests and the scribes came upon *him* with the elders,

2 And spake unto him, saying, Tell us, [i]by what authority doest thou these things? or who is he that gave thee this authority?

3 And he answered and said unto them, I will also ask you one thing; and answer me:

4 The baptism of John, was it from heaven, or of men?

5 And they reasoned with themselves, saying, If we shall say, From heaven; he will say, Why then believed ye him not?

6 But and if we say, Of men; all the people will stone us: [k]for they be persuaded that John was a prophet.

7 And they answered, [l]that they could not tell whence *it was*.

8 And Jesus said unto them, [m]Neither tell I you by what authority I do these things.

G

Job 5. 13. *See under C.*

Ps. 9. 15 The heathen are sunk down in the pit *that* they made: in the net which they hid is their own foot taken.

Prov. 26. 4 Answer not a fool according to his folly, lest thou also be like unto him.

H

Matt. 21. 23. *See text of topic.*

I

Acts 4. 7 and Acts 7. 27. *See under B.*

K

Matt. 14. 5. *Under D.* Matt. 21. 26. *Text of topic.*

Luke 7. 29 And all the people that heard *him*, and the publicans, justified God, being baptized with the baptism of John.

L

Isa. 26. 11 LORD, *when* thy hand is lifted up, they will not see: *but* they shall see,

L—CONCLUDED.

and be ashamed for *their* envy at the people; yea, the fire of thine enemies shall devour them.

Isa. 29. 9 Stay yourselves, and wonder; cry ye out, and cry: they are drunken, but not with wine; they stagger, but not with strong drink.

10 For the LORD hath poured out upon you the spirit of deep sleep, and hath closed your eyes: the prophets and your rulers, the seers hath he covered.

11 And the vision of all is become unto you as the words of a book that is sealed, which *men* deliver to one that is learned, saying, Read this, I pray thee: and he saith, I cannot; for it *is* sealed:

12 And the book is delivered to him that is not learned, saying, Read this, I pray thee: and he saith, I am not learned.

Isa. 41. 28 For I beheld, and *there was* no man; even among them, and *there was* no counsellor, that, when I asked of them, could answer a word.

Isa. 42. 19 Who *is* blind, but my servant? or deaf, as my messenger *that* I sent? who *is* blind as *he that is* perfect, and blind as the LORD's servant?

20 Seeing many things, but thou observest not; opening the ears, but he heareth not.

Jer. 8. 7 Yea, the stork in the heaven knoweth her appointed times; and the turtle and the crane and the swallow observe the time of their coming; but my people know not the judgment of the LORD.

8 How do ye say, We *are* wise, and the law of the LORD *is* with us? Lo, certainly in vain made he *it;* the pen of the scribes *is* in vain.

9 The wise *men* are ashamed, they are dismayed and taken: lo, they have rejected the word of the LORD; and what wisdom *is* in them?

II Tim. 3. 8 Now as Jannes and Jambres withstood Moses, so do these also resist the truth: men of corrupt minds, reprobate concerning the faith.

M

Job 24. 13 They are of those that rebel against the light; they know not the ways thereof, nor abide in the paths thereof.

II Cor. 4. 3 But if our gospel be hid, it is hid to them that are lost:

§ 160. THE PARABLE OF THE TWO SONS.

Third Day of the Week of our

21: 28–32.

28 But what think ye? A *certain* man had two sons; and he came to the first, and said, Son, go work to day in my vineyard.

29 He answered and said, [a]I will not; but afterward [b]he repented, and went.

30 And he came to the second, and said likewise. And he answered and said, I *go*, sir; and went not.

31 Whether of them twain did the will of *his* father? They say unto him, The first. Jesus saith unto them, [c]Verily I say unto you, That the publicans and the harlots go into the kingdom of God before you.

32 For [d]John came unto you in the way of righteousness, and ye believed him not; [e]but the publicans and the harlots believed him: and ye, when ye had seen *it*, repented not afterward, that ye might believe him.

A

Jer. 44. 16 *As for* the word that thou hast spoken unto us in the name of the LORD, we will not hearken unto thee.

A—CONCLUDED.

Eph. 4. 17 This I say therefore, and testify in the Lord, that ye henceforth walk not as other Gentiles walk, in the vanity of their mind,

18 Having the understanding darkened, being alienated from the life of God through the ignorance that is in them, because of the blindness of their heart:

19 Who being past feeling have given themselves over unto lasciviousness, to work all uncleanness with greediness.

B

II Chr. 33. 10 And the LORD spake to Manasseh, and to his people: but they would not hearken.

11 Wherefore the LORD brought upon them the captains of the host of the king of Assyria, which took Manasseh among the thorns, and bound him with fetters, and carried him to Babylon.

12 And when he was in affliction, he besought the LORD his God, and humbled himself greatly before the God of his fathers,

13 And prayed unto him: and he was entreated of him, and heard his supplication, and brought him again to Jerusalem into his kingdom. Then Manasseh knew that the LORD he *was* God.

Isa. 1. 16 Wash ye, make you clean; put away the evil of your doings from before mine eyes; cease to do evil;

§ 161. THE PARABLE OF THE WICKED HUSBANDMEN.

Third Day of the Week of our

21: 33–46.

33 Hear another parable: There was a certain householder, [a]which planted a vineyard, and hedged it round about, and digged a winepress in it, and built a tower, and let it out to husbandmen, and [b]went into a far country:

A

Ps. 80. 9 Thou preparedst *room* before it, and didst cause it to take deep root, and it filled the land.

Song 8. 11 Solomon had a vineyard at Baal-hamon; he let out the vineyard unto keepers; every one for the fruit thereof was to bring a thousand *pieces* of silver.

12: 1–12.

1 And [c]he began to speak unto them by parables. A *certain* man planted a vineyard, and set a hedge about *it*, and digged *a place for* the winefat, and built a tower, and let it out to husbandmen, and went into a far country.

A—CONTINUED.

Isa. 5. 1 Now will I sing to my well beloved a song of my beloved touching his vineyard. My well beloved hath a vineyard in a very fruitful hill:

Jer. 2. 21 Yet I had planted thee a noble vine, wholly a right seed: how then art thou turned into the degenerate plant of a strange vine unto me?

TIME, TUESDAY, APRIL 4 [NISAN 12], A. D. 30; PLACE, JERUSALEM.
Lord's Fourth and Last Passover.

B—CONTINUED.

Isa. 1. 17 Learn to do well; seek judgment, relieve the oppressed, judge the fatherless, plead for the widow.
18 Come now, and let us reason together, saith the LORD: though your sins be as scarlet, they shall be as white as snow; though they be red like crimson, they shall be as wool.
19 If ye be willing and obedient, ye shall eat the good of the land:

Isa. 55. 6 Seek ye the LORD while he may be found, call ye upon him while he is near:
7 Let the wicked forsake his way, and the unrighteous man his thoughts: and let him return unto the LORD, and he will have mercy upon him; and to our God, for he will abundantly pardon.

Eze. 18. 26 When a righteous *man* turneth away from his righteousness, and committeth iniquity, and dieth in them; for his iniquity that he hath done shall he die.
27 Again, when the wicked *man* turneth away from his wickedness that he hath committed, and doeth that which is lawful and right, he shall save his soul alive.
28 Because he considereth, and turneth away from all his transgressions that he hath committed, he shall surely live, he shall not die.
29 Yet saith the house of Israel, The way of the Lord is not equal. O house of Israel, are not my ways equal? are not your ways unequal?

B—CONCLUDED.

Jon. 3. 2 Arise, go unto Nineveh, that great city, and preach unto it the preaching that I bid thee.

Jon. 3. 8 But let man and beast be covered with sackcloth, and cry mightily unto God: yea, let them turn every one from his evil way, and from the violence that *is* in their hands.
9 Who can tell *if* God will turn and repent, and turn away from his fierce anger, that we perish not?
10 And God saw their works, that they turned from their evil way; and God repented of the evil, that he had said that he would do unto them; and he did *it* not.

Eph. 2. 1 And you *hath he quickened*, who were dead in trespasses and sins;

C

Luke 7. 29 And all the people that heard *him*, and the publicans, justified God, being baptized with the baptism of John.

Luke 7. 50 And he said to the woman, Thy faith hath saved thee; go in peace.

D

Matt. 3. 1 In those days came John the Baptist, preaching in the wilderness of Judæa,
2 And saying, Repent ye: for the kingdom of heaven is at hand.

E

Luke 3. 12 Then came also publicans to be baptized, and said unto him, Master, what shall we do?
13 And he said unto them, Exact no more than that which is appointed you.

TIME, TUESDAY, APRIL 4 [NISAN 12], A. D. 30; PLACE, JERUSALEM.
Lord's Fourth and Last Passover.

20: 9–19.

9 Then began he to speak to the people this parable; [d]A certain man planted a vineyard, and let it forth to husbandmen, and went into a far country for a long time.

A—CONCLUDED.

Hos. 4. 1 Hear the word of the LORD, ye children of Israel: for the LORD hath a controversy with the inhabitants of the land, because *there is* no truth, nor mercy, nor knowledge of God in the land.

Mark 12. 1 and Luke 20. 9. *See text of topic.*

B

Matt. 25. 14 For *the kingdom of heaven is* as a man traveling into a far country, *who* called his own servants, and delivered unto them his goods.
15 And unto one he gave five talents, to another two, and to another one; to every man according to his several ability; and straightway took his journey.

C

Matt. 21. 33 and Luke 20. 9. *See text of topic.*

D

Matt. 21. 33 and Mark 12. 1. *See text of topic.*

E

Song 8. 11. *See under A.*

Song 8. 12 My vineyard, which *is* mine, *is* before me: thou, O Solomon, *must have* a thousand, and those that keep the fruit thereof two hundred.

§ 161. THE PARABLE OF THE WICKED HUSBANDMEN

Third Day of the Week of our

CHAP. 21.

34 And when the time of the fruit drew near, he sent his servants to the husbandmen, [e]that they might receive the fruits of it.

35 [f]And the husbandmen took his servants, and beat one, and killed another, and stoned another.

36 Again, he sent other servants more than the first: and they did unto them likewise.

37 But last of all he [g]sent unto them his son, saying, They will reverence my son.

38 But when the husbandmen saw the son, they said among themselves, [h]This is the heir; [i]come, let us kill him, and let us seize on his inheritance.

39 [k]And they caught him, and cast *him* out of the vineyard, and slew *him*.

40 When the lord therefore of the vineyard cometh, what will he do unto those husbandmen?

For E see preceding page (445).

F

II Chr.24. 21 And they conspired against him, and stoned him with stones at the commandment of the king in the court of the house of the LORD.

II Chr.36. 16 But they mocked the messengers of God, and despised his words, and misused his prophets until the wrath of the LORD arose against his people, till *there was* no remedy.

Neh. 9. 26 Nevertheless they were disobedient, and rebelled against thee, and cast thy law behind their backs, and slew thy prophets which testified against them to turn them to thee, and they wrought great provocations.

Matt. 5. 12 Rejoice, and be exceeding glad: for great *is* your reward in heaven: for so persecuted they the prophets which were before you.

Matt.23. 34 Wherefore, behold, I send unto you prophets, and wise men, and scribes: and *some* of them ye shall kill and crucify; and *some* of them shall

CHAP. 12.

2 And at the season he sent to the husbandmen a servant, that he might receive from the husbandmen of the fruit of the vineyard.

3 And they caught *him*, and beat him, and sent *him* away empty.

4 And again he sent unto them another servant; and at him they cast stones, and wounded *him* in the head, and sent *him* away shamefully handled.

5 And again he sent another; and him they killed, and many others; beating some, and [l]killing some.

6 Having yet therefore one son, [m]his well beloved, he sent him also last unto them, saying, They will reverence my son.

7 But those husbandmen said among themselves, This is the [n]heir; come, let us kill him, and the inheritance shall be ours.

8 And they took him, and [o]killed *him*, and cast *him* out of the vineyard.

9 What shall therefore the lord of the vineyard do?

F—CONTINUED.

ye scourge in your synagogues, and persecute *them* from city to city:

Matt.23. 37 O Jerusalem, Jerusalem, *thou* that killest the prophets, and stonest them which are sent unto thee, how often would I have gathered thy children together, even as a hen gathereth her chickens under *her* wings, and ye would not!

Acts 7. 52 Which of the prophets have not your fathers persecuted? and they have slain them which showed before of the coming of the Just One; of whom ye have been now the betrayers and murderers:

I Thes.2. 15 Who both killed the Lord Jesus, and their own prophets, and have persecuted us; and they please not God, and are contrary to all men:

(CONTINUED). TIME, TUESDAY, APRIL 4 [NISAN 12], A. D. 30; PLACE, JERUSALEM.
Lord's Fourth and Last Passover.

CHAP. 20.

10 And at the season *p*he sent a servant to the husbandmen, that they should give him of the fruit of the vineyard: but the husbandmen beat him, and sent *him* away empty.

11 And again he sent another servant: and they beat him also, and entreated *him* shamefully, and sent *him* away empty.

12 And again he sent a third: and they wounded him also, and cast *him* out.

13 Then said the lord of the vineyard, What shall I do? I will send my beloved son: it may be they will reverence *him* when they see him.

14 But when the husbandmen saw him, they reasoned among themselves, saying, This is the heir: come, let us kill him, that the inheritance may be ours.

15 So they cast him out of the vineyard, and killed *him*. What therefore shall the lord of the vineyard do unto them?

F—CONCLUDED.

Heb. 11. 37 They were stoned, they were sawn asunder, were tempted, were slain with the sword: they wandered about in sheepskins and goatskins; being destitute, afflicted, tormented;

G

Gal. 4. 4 But when the fulness of the time was come, God sent forth his Son, made of a woman, made under the law,

H

Ps. 2. 8 Ask of me, and I shall give *thee* the heathen *for* thine inheritance, and the uttermost parts of the earth *for* thy possession.

Heb. 1. 2 Hath in these last days spoken unto us by *his* Son, whom he hath appointed heir of all things, by whom also he made the worlds;

I

Ps. 2. 2 The kings of the earth set themselves, and the rulers take counsel together, against the LORD, and against his Anointed, *saying*,

I—CONCLUDED.

Matt.26. 3 Then assembled together the chief priests, and the scribes, and the elders of the people, unto the palace of the high priest, who was called Caiaphas.

Matt.27. 1 When the morning was come, all the chief priests and elders of the people took counsel against Jesus to put him to death:

John 11. 53 Then from that day forth they took counsel together for to put him to death.

Acts 4. 27 For of a truth against thy holy child Jesus, whom thou hast anointed, both Herod, and Pontius Pilate, with the Gentiles, and the people of Israel, were gathered together,

K

Matt.26. 50 And Jesus said unto him, Friend, wherefore art thou come? Then came they, and laid hands on Jesus, and took him.

Matt. 26. 51, etc. *See text of* § *193.*

Mark 14. 46 And they laid their hands on him, and took him.

Mark 14. 47, etc. *See text of* § *193.*

Luke 22. 54 Then took they him, and led *him*, and brought him into the high priest's house. And Peter followed afar off.

Luke 22. 55, etc. *See text of* § *194.*

John 18. 12 Then the band and the captain and officers of the Jews took Jesus, and bound him,

13 And led him away to Annas first; for he was father in law to Caiaphas, which was the high priest that same year.

Acts 2. 23 Him, being delivered by the determinate counsel and foreknowledge of God, ye have taken, and by wicked hands have crucified and slain:

L

II Chr. 36. 16, Neh. 9. 26, Acts 7. 52 and I Thes. 2. 15. *See under F.*

M

Rom. 8. 3 For what the law could not do, in that it was weak through the flesh, God sending his own Son in the likeness of sinful flesh, and for sin, condemned sin in the flesh:

Gal. 4. 4. *See under G.*

N

Ps. 2. 8 and Heb. 1. 2. *See under H.*

O

Acts 2. 23. *See under K.*

P

II Chr. 36. 15 And the LORD God of their fathers sent to them by his messengers, rising up betimes, and sending; because he had compassion on his people, and on his dwellingplace:

II Chr. 36. 16. *See under F.*

§ 161. THE PARABLE OF THE WICKED HUSBANDMEN

Third Day of the Week of our

CHAP. 21.

41 [q]They say unto him, [r]He will miserably destroy those wicked men, [s]and will let out *his* vineyard unto other husbandmen, which shall render him the fruits in their seasons.

42 Jesus saith unto them, [t]Did ye never read in the Scriptures, The stone which the builders rejected, the same is become the head of the corner: this is the Lord's doing, and it is [u]marvellous in our eyes?

43 Therefore say I unto you, [x]The kingdom of God shall be taken from you, and given to a nation bringing forth the fruits thereof.

44 And whosoever [y]shall fall on this stone shall be broken: but on whomsoever it shall fall, [z]it will grind him to powder.

45 And when the chief priests and Pharisees had heard his parables, they perceived that he spake of them.

46 But when they sought to lay hands on him, they feared the multitude, because [a]they took him for a prophet.

Q

Luke 20. 16. *See text of topic.*

R

Deut. 4. 26 I call heaven and earth to witness against you this day, that ye shall soon utterly perish from off the land whereunto ye go over Jordan to possess it; ye shall not prolong *your* days upon it, but shall utterly be destroyed.

Luke 21. 24. *See text of § 173.*

Heb. 2. 3 How shall we escape, if we neglect so great salvation; which at the first began to be spoken by the Lord, and was confirmed unto us by them that heard *him;*

S

Acts 13. 46 Then Paul and Barnabas waxed bold, and said, It was necessary that the word of God should first have

CHAP. 12.

he will come and destroy the husbandmen, and will give the vineyard unto others.

10 And have ye not read this Scripture: The stone which the builders rejected is become the head of the corner:

11 This was the Lord's doing, and it is marvellous in our eyes?

12 [b]And they sought to lay hold on him, but feared the people; for they knew that he had spoken the parable against them: and they left him, and went their way. (p. 454.)

S—CONCLUDED.

been spoken to you: but seeing ye put it from you, and judge yourselves unworthy of everlasting life, lo, we turn to the Gentiles.

Acts 15. 7 And when there had been much disputing, Peter rose up, and said unto them, Men *and* brethren, ye know how that a good while ago God made choice among us, that the Gentiles by my mouth should hear the word of the gospel, and believe.

Acts 18. 6 And when they opposed themselves, and blasphemed, he shook *his* raiment, and said unto them, Your blood *be* upon your own heads; I *am* clean: from henceforth I will go unto the Gentiles.

Acts 28. 28 Be it known therefore unto you, that the salvation of God is sent unto the Gentiles, and *that* they will hear it.

Rom. 9. 1 I say the truth in Christ, I lie not, my conscience also bearing me witness in the Holy Ghost,

2 That I have great heaviness and continual sorrow in my heart.

Rom. 9. 3, etc. *Read entire chapter.*

Rom. 10. 2, etc. *Read entire chapter.*

Rom. 11. 1 I say then, Hath God cast away his people? God forbid. For I also am an Israelite, of the seed of Abraham, *of* the tribe of Benjamin.

Rom. 11. 2, etc. *Read entire chapter.*

T

Ps. 118. 22 The stone *which* the builders refused is become the head *stone* of the corner.

(CONCLUDED). TIME, TUESDAY, APRIL 4 [NISAN 12], A. D. 30; PLACE, JERUSALEM.
Lord's Fourth and Last Passover.

CHAP. 20.

16 He shall come and destroy these husbandmen, and shall give the vineyard to others. And when they heard *it*, they said, God forbid.

17 And he beheld them, and said, What is this then that is written, The stone which the builders rejected, the same is become the head of the corner?

18 Whosoever shall fall upon that stone shall be broken; but on whomsoever it shall fall, it will grind him to powder.

19 And the chief priests and the scribes the same hour sought to lay hands on him; and they feared the people: for they perceived that he had spoken this parable against them.

T—CONCLUDED. (p. 455.)

Isa. 28. 16 Therefore thus saith the Lord GOD, Behold, I lay in Zion for a foundation a stone, a tried stone, a precious corner *stone*, a sure foundation: he that believeth shall not make haste.

Mark 12. 10 and Luke 20. 17. *See text of topic.*

Acts 4. 11 This is the stone which was set at nought of you builders, which is become the head of the corner.

Eph. 2. 20 And are built upon the foundation of the apostles and prophets, Jesus Christ himself being the chief corner *stone:*

I Pet. 2. 6 Wherefore also it is contained in the Scripture, Behold, I lay in Sion a chief corner stone, elect, precious: and he that believeth on him shall not be confounded.

7 Unto you therefore which believe *he is* precious: but unto them which be disobedient, the stone which the builders disallowed, the same is made the head of the corner.

U

I Tim.3. 16 And without controversy great is the mystery of godliness: God was manifest in the flesh, justified in the Spirit, seen of angels, preached unto the Gentiles, believed on in the world, received up into glory.

X

Matt. 8. 12 But the children of the kingdom shall be cast out into outer darkness: there shall be weeping and gnashing of teeth.

Y

Isa. 8. 14 And he shall be for a sanctuary; but for a stone of stumbling and for a rock of offence to both the houses of Israel, for a gin and for a snare to the inhabitants of Jerusalem.

15 And many among them shall stumble, and fall, and be broken, and be snared, and be taken.

Zech.12. 3 And in that day will I make Jerusalem a burdensome stone for all people: all that burden themselves with it shall be cut in pieces, though all the people of the earth be gathered together against it.

Luke 20. 18. *See text of topic.*

Rom. 9. 33 As it is written, Behold, I lay in Sion a stumbling stone and rock of offence: and whosoever believeth on him shall not be ashamed.

I Pet. 2. 8 And a stone of stumbling, and a rock of offence, *even to them* which stumble at the word, being disobedient: whereunto also they were appointed.

Z

Isa. 60. 12 For the nation and kingdom that will not serve thee shall perish; yea, *those* nations shall be utterly wasted.

Dan. 2. 44 And in the days of these kings shall the God of heaven set up a kingdom, which shall never be destroyed: and the kingdom shall not be left to other people, *but* it shall break in pieces and consume all these kingdoms, and it shall stand for ever.

A

Matt. 21. 11. *See text of § 154.*

Luke 7. 16 And there came a fear on all: and they glorified God, saying, That a great prophet is risen up among us; and, That God hath visited his people.

John 7. 40 Many of the people therefore, when they heard this saying, said, Of a truth this is the Prophet.

B

Matt. 21. 45, 46. *See text of topic.*

Mark 11. 18 And the scribes and chief priests heard *it*, and sought how they might destroy him: for they feared him, because all the people was astonished at his doctrine.

John 7. 25 Then said some of them of Jerusalem, Is not this he, whom they seek to kill?

John 7. 30 Then they sought to take him: but no man laid hands on him, because his hour was not yet come.

John 7. 44 And some of them would have taken him; but no man laid hands on him.

§ 162. THE PARABLE OF THE WEDDING GARMENT.

Third Day of the Week of our

22: 1–14.

1 And Jesus answered and [a]spake unto them again by parables, and said,

2 The kingdom of heaven is like unto a certain king, which made a marriage for his son,

3 And [b]sent forth his servants to call them that were bidden to the wedding: [c]and they would not come.

4 Again, he sent forth other servants, saying, Tell them which are bidden, Behold, I have prepared my dinner: [d]my oxen and *my* fatlings *are* killed, and all things *are* ready: come unto the marriage.

5 But they [e]made light of *it*, and went their ways, one to his farm, another to his merchandise:

6 And [f]the remnant took his servants, and entreated *them* spitefully, and slew *them*.

7 But when the king heard *thereof*, he was wroth: and he sent forth [g]his armies, and destroyed those murderers, and burned up their city.

A

Luke 14. 16 Then said he unto him, a certain man made a great supper, and bade many:

17 And sent his servant at supper time to say to them that were bidden, Come; for all things are now ready.

18 And they all with one *consent* began to make excuse. The first said unto him, I have bought a piece of ground, and I must needs go and see it: I pray thee have me excused.

19 And another said, I have bought five yoke of oxen, and I go to prove them: I pray thee have me excused.

20 And another said, I have married a wife, and therefore I cannot come.

21 So that servant came, and showed his lord these things. Then the master of the house being angry said to his servant, Go out quickly into the streets and lanes of the city, and bring

A—Concluded.

in hither the poor, and the maimed, and the halt, and the blind.

22 And the servant said, Lord, it is done as thou hast commanded, and yet there is room.

23 And the lord said unto the servant, Go out into the highways and hedges, and compel *them* to come in, that my house may be filled.

24 For I say unto you, That none of those men which were bidden shall taste of my supper.

Rev. 19. 7 Let us be glad and rejoice, and give honour to him: for the marriage of the Lamb is come, and his wife hath made herself ready.

8 And to her was granted that she should be arrayed in fine linen, clean and white: for the fine linen is the righteousness of saints.

9 And he saith unto me, Write, Blessed *are* they which are called unto the marriage supper of the Lamb. And he saith unto me, These are the true sayings of God.

B

Ps. 68. 11 The Lord gave the word: great *was* the company of those that published *it*.

Isa. 55. 1 Ho, every one that thirsteth, come ye to the waters, and he that hath no money; come ye, buy, and eat; yea, come, buy wine and milk without money and without price.

2 Wherefore do ye spend money for *that which is* not bread? and your labour for *that which* satisfieth not? hearken diligently unto me, and eat ye *that which is* good, and let your soul delight itself in fatness.

Jer. 25. 4 And the Lord hath sent unto you all his servants the prophets, rising early and sending *them;* but ye have not hearkened, nor inclined your ear to hear.

Jer. 35. 15 I have sent also unto you all my servants the prophets, rising up early and sending *them*, saying, Return ye now every man from his evil way, and amend your doings, and go not after other gods to serve them, and ye shall dwell in the land which I have given to you and to your fathers: but ye have not inclined your ear, nor hearkened unto me.

Matt. 10. 5 These twelve Jesus sent forth, and commanded them, saying, Go not into the way of the Gentiles, and into *any*

TIME, TUESDAY, APRIL 4 [NISAN 12], A. D. 30; PLACE, JERUSALEM.
Lord's Fourth and Last Passover.

B—CONCLUDED.

city of the Samaritans enter ye not:
6 But go rather to the lost sheep of
the house of Israel.
7 And as ye go, preach, saying, The
kingdom of heaven is at hand.
Mark16. 15 And he said unto them, Go ye
into all the world, and preach the gospel to every creature.
Rev. 22. 17 And the Spirit and the bride say,
Come. And let him that heareth say,
Come. And let him that is athirst
come. And whosoever will, let him
take the water of life freely.

C

Prov. 1. 24 Because I have called, and ye refused; I have stretched out my hand,
and no man regarded;
25 But ye have set at nought all my
counsel, and would none of my reproof:
26 I also will laugh at your calamity;
I will mock when your fear cometh;
27 When your fear cometh as desolation, and your destruction cometh as
a whirlwind; when distress and anguish cometh upon you.
28 Then shall they call upon me,
but I will not answer; they shall seek
me early, but they shall not find me:
29 For that they hated knowledge,
and did not choose the fear of the LORD:
30 They would none of my counsel:
they despised all my reproof.
31 Therefore shall they eat of the
fruit of their own way, and be filled
with their own devices.
32 For the turning away of the
simple shall slay them, and the prosperity of fools shall destroy them.
Isa. 30. 15 For thus saith the Lord GOD, the
Holy One of Israel; In returning and
rest shall ye be saved; in quietness
and in confidence shall be your
strength: and ye would not.
Jer. 6. 16 Thus saith the LORD, Stand ye
in the ways, and see, and ask for the
old paths, where *is* the good way, and
walk therein, and ye shall find rest
for your souls. But they said, We
will not walk *therein*.
17 Also I set watchmen over you,
saying, Hearken to the sound of the
trumpet. But they said, We will not
hearken.
Hos. 11. 2 *As* they called them, so they went
from them: they sacrificed unto Baalim, and burned incense to graven
images.

C—CONCLUDED.

Hos. 11. 7 And my people are bent to backsliding from me: though they called
them to the Most High, none at all
would exalt *him*.

D

Prov. 9. 1 Wisdom hath builded her house,
she hath hewn out her seven pillars:
2 She hath killed her beasts; she
hath mingled her wine; she hath also
furnished her table.
3 She hath sent forth her maidens:
she crieth upon the highest places of
the city,
4 Whoso *is* simple, let him turn in
hither: *as for* him that wanteth understanding, she saith to him,
5 Come, eat of my bread, and drink
of the wine *which* I have mingled.
6 Forsake the foolish, and live; and
go in the way of understanding.

E

Ps. 81. 11 But my people would not hearken
to my voice; and Israel would none
of me.
12 So I gave them up unto their
own heart's lust: *and* they walked in
their own counsels.
Ps. 106. 24 Yea, they despised the pleasant
land, they believed not his word:
25 But murmured in their tents, *and*
hearkened not unto the voice of the
LORD.

F

I Thes. 2. 14 For ye, brethren, became followers of the churches of God which in
Judæa are in Christ Jesus: for ye also
have suffered like things of your own
countrymen, even as they *have* of the
Jews:
15 Who both killed the Lord Jesus,
and their own prophets, and have persecuted us; and they please not God,
and are contrary to all men:
16 Forbidding us to speak to the
Gentiles that they might be saved, to
fill up their sins always: for the wrath
is come upon them to the uttermost.

G

Dan. 9. 26 And after threescore and two
weeks shall Messiah be cut off, but
not for himself: and the people of the
prince that shall come shall destroy
the city and the sanctuary; and the
end thereof *shall be* with a flood, and
unto the end of the war desolations
are determined.
Luke 19. 27 But those mine enemies, which
would not that I should reign over

§ 162. THE PARABLE OF THE WEDDING GARMENT (CONCLUDED).
Third Day of the Week of our

CHAP. 22.

8 Then saith he to his servants, The wedding is ready, but they which were bidden were not [h]worthy.

9 [i]Go ye therefore into the highways, and as many as ye shall find, bid to the marriage.

10 So those servants went out into the highways, and [k]gathered together all as many as they found, both bad and good: [l]and the wedding was furnished with guests.

11 And [m]when the king came in to see the guests, he saw there a man [n]which had not on a wedding garment:

12 And he saith unto him, Friend, how camest thou in hither not having a wedding garment? And he [o]was speechless.

13 Then said the king to the servants, Bind him hand and foot, and take him away, and cast *him* [p]into outer darkness; there shall be weeping and gnashing of teeth.

14 [q]For many are called, but few *are* chosen.

G—CONCLUDED.

them, bring hither, and slay *them* before me.

H

Matt.10. 11 And into whatsoever city or town ye shall enter, inquire who in it is worthy; and there abide till ye go thence.

Matt.10. 13 And if the house be worthy, let your peace come upon it: but if it be not worthy, let your peace return to you.

Acts 13. 46 Then Paul and Barnabus waxed bold, and said, It was necessary that the word of God should first have been spoken to you: but seeing ye put it from you, and judge yourselves unworthy of everlasting life, lo, we turn to the Gentiles.

I

Prov. 1. 20 Wisdom crieth without; she uttereth her voice in the streets:

21 She crieth in the chief place of concourse, in the openings of the gates: in the city she uttereth her words, *saying*,

I—CONCLUDED.

Prov. 1. 22 How long, ye simple ones, will ye love simplicity? and the scorners delight in their scorning, and fools hate knowledge?

23 Turn you at my reproof: behold, I will pour out my spirit unto you, I will make known my words unto you.

Prov. 8. 1 Doth not wisdom cry? and understanding put forth her voice?

2 She standeth in the top of high places, by the way in the places of the paths.

3 She crieth at the gates, at the entry of the city, at the coming in at the doors:

4 Unto you, O men, I call; and my voice *is* to the sons of man.

5 O ye simple, understand wisdom: and, ye fools, be ye of an understanding heart.

Isa. 55. 7 Let the wicked forsake his way, and the unrighteous man his thoughts: and let him return unto the LORD, and he will have mercy upon him; and to our God, for he will abundantly pardon.

Acts 13. 34 And as concerning that he raised him up from the dead, *now* no more to return to corruption, he said on this wise, I will give you the sure mercies of David.

Eph. 3. 8 Unto me, who am less than the least of all saints, is this grace given, that I should preach among the Gentiles the unsearchable riches of Christ:

K

Matt.13. 38 The field is the world; the good seed are the children of the kingdom; but the tares are the children of the wicked one;

Matt.13. 47 Again, the kingdom of heaven is like unto a net, that was cast into the sea, and gathered of every kind:

L

Matt.25. 10 And while they went to buy, the bridegroom came; and they that were ready went in with him to the marriage: and the door was shut.

Rev. 5. 9 And they sung a new song, saying, Thou art worthy to take the book, and to open the seals thereof: for thou wast slain, and hast redeemed us to God by thy blood out of every kindred, and tongue, and people, and nation;

Rev. 7. 9 After this I beheld, and, lo, a great multitude, which no man could number, of all nations, and kindreds, and

TIME, TUESDAY, APRIL 4 [NISAN 12], A. D. 30; PLACE, JERUSALEM.
Lord's Fourth and Last Passover.

L—CONCLUDED.

people, and tongues, stood before the throne, and before the Lamb, clothed with white robes, and palms in their hands:

Rev. 19. 6 And I heard as it were the voice of a great multitude, and as the voice of many waters, and as the voice of mighty thunderings, saying, Alleluia: for the Lord God omnipotent reigneth.

Rev. 19. 7, 8, 9. *See under A, page 450.*

M

Zeph. 1. 12 And it shall come to pass at that time, *that* I will search Jerusalem with candles, and punish the men that are settled on their lees: that say in their heart, The LORD will not do good, neither will he do evil.

Matt. 13. 30 Let both grow together until the harvest: and in the time of harvest I will say to the reapers, Gather ye together first the tares, and bind them in bundles to burn them: but gather the wheat into my barn.

I Cor. 4. 5 Therefore judge nothing before the time, until the Lord come, who both will bring to light the hidden things of darkness, and will make manifest the counsels of the hearts: and then shall every man have praise of God.

Heb. 4. 12 For the word of God *is* quick, and powerful, and sharper than any twoedged sword, piercing even to the dividing asunder of soul and spirit, and of the joints and marrow, and *is* a discerner of the thoughts and intents of the heart.

13 Neither is there any creature that is not manifest in his sight: but all things *are* naked and opened unto the eyes of him with whom we have to do.

Rev. 2. 23 And I will kill her children with death; and all the churches shall know that I am he which searcheth the reins and hearts: and I will give unto every one of you according to your works.

N

II Cor. 5. 3 If so be that being clothed we shall not be found naked.

Eph. 4. 24 And that ye put on the new man, which after God is created in righteousness and true holiness.

Col. 3. 10 And have put on the new *man*, which is renewed in knowledge after the image of him that created him:

Col. 3. 12 Put on therefore, as the elect of God, holy and beloved, bowels of mercies, kindness, humbleness of mind, meekness, longsuffering:

N—CONCLUDED.

Rev. 3. 4 Thou hast a few names even in Sardis which have not defiled their garments; and they shall walk with me in white: for they are worthy.

Rev. 16. 15 Behold, I come as a thief. Blessed *is* he that watcheth, and keepeth his garments, lest he walk naked, and they see his shame.

Rev. 19. 8. *See under A, page 450.*

O

Rom. 3. 19 Now we know that what things soever the law saith, it saith to them who are under the law: that every mouth may be stopped, and all the world may become guilty before God.

P

Ps. 37. 12 The wicked plotteth against the just, and gnasheth upon him with his teeth.

Matt. 8. 12 But the children of the kingdom shall be cast out into outer darkness: there shall be weeping and gnashing of teeth.

Matt. 24. 51 And shall cut him asunder, and appoint *him* his portion with the hypocrites: there shall be weeping and gnashing of teeth.

II Thes. 1. 9 Who shall be punished with everlasting destruction from the presence of the Lord, and from the glory of his power;

II Pet. 2. 4 For if God spared not the angels that sinned, but cast *them* down to hell, and delivered *them* into chains of darkness, to be reserved unto judgment;

II Pet. 2. 17 These are wells without water, clouds that are carried with a tempest; to whom the mist of darkness is reserved for ever.

Jude 6 And the angels which kept not their first estate, but left their own habitation, he hath reserved in everlasting chains under darkness unto the judgment of the great day.

Jude 12 These are spots in your feasts of charity, when they feast with you, feeding themselves without fear: clouds *they are* without water, carried about of winds; trees whose fruit withereth, without fruit, twice dead, plucked up by the roots;

13 Raging waves of the sea, foaming out their own shame; wandering stars, to whom is reserved the blackness of darkness for ever.

Q

Matt. 20. 16 So the last shall be first, and the first last: for many be called, but few chosen.

§ 163. THE TRIBUTE MONEY.

Third Day of the Week

22: 15–22.

15 [a] Then went the Pharisees, and took counsel how they might entangle him in *his* talk.

16 And they sent out unto him their disciples with the Herodians, saying, Master, we know that thou art true, and teachest the way of God in truth, neither carest thou for any *man:* for thou regardest not the person of men.

17 Tell us therefore, What thinkest thou? Is it lawful to give tribute unto Cæsar, or not?

18 But Jesus perceived their wickedness, and said, Why tempt ye me, *ye* hypocrites?

19 Show me the tribute money. And they brought unto him a [1] penny.

20 And he saith unto them, Whose *is* this image and [2] superscription?

21 They say unto him, Cæsar's. Then saith he unto them, [b] Render therefore unto Cæsar the things which are Cæsar's; and unto God the things that are God's.

22 When they had heard *these words,* they [c] marvelled, and left him, and went their way.

A

Mark 12. 13. *See text of topic.*
Luke 20. 20. *See text of topic.*

1

In value seven pence half penny, or about fifteen cents.

Matt.20. 2 And when he had agreed with the labourers for a penny a day, he sent them into his vineyard.

2

Or, *inscription.*

B

Matt.17. 25 He saith, Yes. And when he was come into the house, Jesus prevented him, saying, What thinkest thou, Simon? of whom do the kings of the earth take custom or tribute? of their own children, or of strangers?

12: 13–17.

13 [d] And they send unto him certain of the Pharisees and of the Herodians, to catch him in *his* words.

14 And when they were come, they say unto him, Master, we know that thou art true, and carest for no man; for thou regardest not the person of men, but teachest the way of God in truth: Is it lawful to give tribute to Cæsar, or not?

15 Shall we give, or shall we not give? But he, knowing their hypocrisy, said unto them, Why tempt ye me? bring me a [3] penny, that I may see *it.*

16 And they brought *it.* And he saith unto them, Whose *is* this image and superscription? And they said unto him, Cæsar's.

17 And Jesus answering said unto them, Render to Cæsar the things that are Cæsar's, and to God the things that are God's. And they marvelled at him.

B—Continued.

Matt.17. 26 Peter saith unto him, Of strangers. Jesus saith unto him, Then are the children free.

27 Notwithstanding, lest we should offend them, go thou to the sea, and cast a hook, and take up the fish that first cometh up; and when thou hast opened his mouth, thou shalt find a piece of money: that take, and give unto them for me and thee.

Rom.13. 6 For, for this cause pay ye tribute also: for they are God's ministers, attending continually upon this very thing.

7 Render therefore to all their dues: tribute to whom tribute *is due;* custom to whom custom; fear to whom fear; honour to whom honour.

I Pet. 2. 13 Submit yourselves to every ordinance of man for the Lord's sake: whether it be to the king, as supreme;

TIME, TUESDAY, APRIL 4 [NISAN 12], A. D. 30; PLACE, JERUSALEM.

of our Lord's Fourth and Last Passover.

20: 20–26.

20 [e] And they watched *him*, and sent forth spies, which should feign themselves just men, that they might take hold of his words, that so they might deliver him unto the power and authority of the governor.

21 And they asked him, saying, [f] Master, we know that thou sayest and teachest rightly, neither acceptest thou the person *of any*, but teachest the way of God [4] truly:

22 Is it lawful for us to give tribute unto Cæsar, or no?

23 But he perceived their craftiness, and said unto them, Why tempt ye me?

24 Show me a [5] penny. Whose image and superscription hath it? They answered and said, Cæsar's.

25 And he said unto them, Render therefore unto Cæsar the things which be Cæsar's, and unto God the things which be God's.

26 And they could not take hold of his words before the people: and they marvelled at his answer, and held their peace.

B—CONCLUDED.

I Pet. 2. 14 Or unto governors, as unto them that are sent by him for the punishment of evil doers, and for the praise of them that do well.

15 For so is the will of God, that with well doing ye may put to silence the ignorance of foolish men:

16 As free, and not using *your* liberty for a cloak of maliciousness, but as the servants of God.

17 Honour all *men*. Love the brotherhood. Fear God. Honour the king.

C

Job 5. 13 He taketh the wise in their own craftiness: and the counsel of the froward is carried headlong.

D

Matt. 22. 15. *See text of topic.*
Luke 20. 20. *See text of topic.*

3

See under 1 (A).

Matt. 18. 28 But the same servant went out, and found one of his fellow servants, which owed him a hundred pence: and he laid hands on him, and took *him* by the throat, saying, Pay me that thou owest.

E

Ps. 37. 32 The wicked watcheth the righteous, and seeketh to slay him.

33 The LORD will not leave him in his hand, nor condemn him when he is judged.

Jer. 11. 19 But I *was* like a lamb *or* an ox *that* is brought to the slaughter; and I knew not that they had devised devices against me, *saying*, Let us destroy the tree with the fruit thereof, and let us cut him off from the land of the living, that his name may be no more remembered.

Matt. 22. 15. *See text of topic.*

Rom. 3. 14 Whose mouth *is* full of cursing and bitterness:

15 Their feet *are* swift to shed blood:

16 Destruction and misery *are* in their ways:

F

Ps. 12. 2 They speak vanity every one with his neighbour: *with* flattering lips *and* with a double heart do they speak.

Ps. 55. 21 *The words* of his mouth were smoother than butter, but war *was* in in his heart: his words were softer than oil, yet *were* they drawn swords.

Matt. 26. 49 And forthwith he came to Jesus, and said, Hail, Master; and kissed him.

50 And Jesus said unto him, Friend, wherefore art thou come? Then came they, and laid hands on Jesus, and took him.

John 3. 2 The same came to Jesus by night, and said unto him, Rabbi, we know that thou art a teacher come from God: for no man can do these miracles that thou doest, except God be with him.

4

Or, *of a truth.*

5

Matt. 18. 28. *See under 3 (D).*

§ 164. THE SADDUCEES AND THE RESURRECTION.

Third Day of the Week of our

22: 23–33.

23 [a]The same day came to him the
[b]Sadducees, [c]which say that there is no
resurrection, and asked him,
24 Saying, Master, [d]Moses said, If a
man die, having no children, his
brother shall marry his wife, and raise
up seed unto his brother.
25 Now there were with us seven
brethren: and the first, when he had
married a wife, deceased, and, having
no issue, left his wife unto his brother:
26 Likewise the second also, and the
third, unto the [1]seventh.
27 And last of all the woman died also.
28 Therefore in the resurrection,
whose wife shall she be of the seven?
for they all had her.
29 Jesus answered and said unto
them, Ye do err, [e]not knowing the
Scriptures, nor the power of God.

A

Mark 12. 18 and Luke 20. 27. *See text of topic.*

B

Matt. 3. 7 But when he saw many of the Pharisees and Sadducees come to his baptism, he said unto them, O generation of vipers, who hath warned you to flee from the wrath to come?

Matt.16. 6 Then Jesus said unto them, Take heed and beware of the leaven of the Pharisees and of the Sadducees.

Acts 4. 1 And as they spake unto the people, the priests, and the captain of the temple, and the Sadducees, came upon them,

Acts 5. 17 Then the high priest rose up, and all they that were with him, (which is the sect of the Sadducees,) and were filled with indignation,

Acts 23. 6 But when Paul perceived that the one part were Sadducees, and the other Pharisees, he cried out in the council, Men *and* brethren, I am a Pharisee, the son of a Pharisee: of the hope and resurrection of the dead I am called in question.

7 And when he had so said, there arose a dissension between the Pharisees and the Sadducees: and the multitude was divided.

12: 18–27.

18 [f]Then come unto him the Sadducees, [g]which say there is no resurrection; and they asked him, saying,
19 Master, [h]Moses wrote unto us, If
a man's brother die, and leave *his* wife
behind him, and leave no children, that
his brother should take his wife, and
raise up seed unto his brother.
20 Now there were seven brethren:
and the first took a wife, and dying left
no seed.
21 And the second took her, and
died, neither left he any seed: and the
third likewise.
22 And the seven had her, and left
no seed: last of all the woman died also.
23 In the resurrection therefore,
when they shall rise, whose wife shall
she be of them? for the seven had her
to wife.
24 And Jesus answering said unto
them, Do ye not therefore err, because
ye know not the [i]Scriptures, neither
the [k]power of God?

B—CONCLUDED.

8 For the Sadducees say that there is no resurrection, neither angel, nor spirit: but the Pharisees confess both.

C

I Cor.15. 12 Now if Christ be preached that he rose from the dead, how say some among you that there is no resurrection of the dead?

13 But if there be no resurrection of the dead, then is Christ not risen:

14 And if Christ be not risen, then *is* our preaching vain, and your faith *is* also vain.

IITim.2. 17 And their word will eat as doth a canker: of whom is Hymeneus and Philetus;

18 Who concerning the truth have erred, saying that the resurrection is past already; and overthrow the faith of some.

TIME, TUESDAY, APRIL 4 [NISAN 12], A. D. 30; PLACE, JERUSALEM.
Lord's Fourth and Last Passover.

20 : 27–40.

27 [l]Then came to *him* certain of the Sadducees, [m]which deny that there is any resurrection; and they asked him,

28 Saying, Master, [n]Moses wrote unto us, If any man's brother die, having a wife, and he die without children, that his brother should take his wife, and raise up seed unto his brother.

29 There were therefore seven brethren: and the first took a wife, and died without children.

30 And the second took her to wife, and he died childless.

31 And the third took her; and in like manner the seven also: and they left no children, and died.

32 Last of all the woman died also.

33 Therefore in the resurrection whose wife of them is she? for seven had her to wife.

34 And Jesus answering said unto them, The children of this world marry, and are given in marriage:

D

Gen. 38. 8 And Judah said unto Onan, Go in unto thy brother's wife, and marry her, and raise up seed to thy brother.

Deut. 25. 5 If brethren dwell together, and one of them die, and have no child, the wife of the dead shall not marry without unto a stranger: her husband's brother shall go in unto her, and take her to him to wife, and perform the duty of a husband's brother unto her.

Ruth 1. 11 And Naomi said, Turn again, my daughters: why will ye go with me? *are* there yet *any more* sons in my womb, that they may be your husbands?

1

Gr., *seven.*

E

John 20. 9 For as yet they knew not the Scripture, that he must rise again from the dead.

F

Matt. 22. 23 and Luke 20. 27. *See text of topic.*

G

Acts 23. 8. *Under B.* I Cor. 15. 12. *Under C.*

H

Deut. 25. 5 and Gen. 38. 8. *See under D.*

I

Rom. 4. 17 (As it is written, I have made thee a father of many nations,) before him whom he believed, *even* God, who quickeneth the dead, and calleth those things which be not as though they were:

K

Gen. 18. 14 Is anything too hard for the LORD? At the time appointed I will return unto thee, according to the time of life, and Sarah shall have a son.

Jer. 32. 17 Ah Lord GOD! behold, thou hast made the heaven and the earth by thy great power and stretched-out arm, *and* there is nothing too hard for thee:

Dan. 12. 2 And many of them that sleep in the dust of the earth shall awake, some to everlasting life, and some to shame *and* everlasting contempt.

Mark 10. 27 And Jesus looking upon them saith, With men *it is* impossible, but not with God: for with God all things are possible.

Luke 1. 37 For with God nothing shall be impossible.

Eph. 1. 19 And what *is* the exceeding greatness of his power to us-ward who believe, according to the working of his mighty power,

20 Which he wrought in Christ, when he raised him from the dead, and set *him* at his own right hand in the heavenly *places*,

21 Far above all principality, and power, and might, and dominion, and every name that is named, not only in this world, but also in that which is to come:

22 And hath put all *things* under his feet, and gave him *to be* the head over all *things* to the church,

Phil. 3. 21 Who shall change our vile body, that it may be fashioned like unto his glorious body, according to the working whereby he is able even to subdue all things unto himself.

L

Matt. 22. 23 and Mark 12. 18. *See text of topic.*

M

Acts 23. 8. *See under B.*

Acts 26. 8 Why should it be thought a thing incredible with you, that God should raise the dead?

N

Gen. 38. 8 and Deut. 25. 5. *See under D.*

§ 164. THE SADDUCEES AND THE RESURRECTION (CONCLUDED).
Third Day of the Week of our

CHAP. 22.

30 For in the resurrection they neither marry, nor are given [o]in marriage, but [p]are as the angels of God in heaven.

31 But as touching the resurrection of the dead, have ye not read that which was spoken unto you by God, saying,

32 [q]I am the God of Abraham, and the God of Isaac, and the God of Jacob? God is not the God of the dead, but of the living.

33 And when the multitude heard *this*, [r]they were astonished at his doctrine.

O

I Cor.7. 29 But this I say, brethren, the time *is* short: it remaineth, that both they that have wives be as though they had none;
30 And they that weep, as though they wept not; and they that rejoice, as though they rejoiced not; and they that buy, as though they possessed not;
31 And they that use this world, as not abusing *it:* for the fashion of this world passeth away.

P

Ps. 103. 20 Bless the LORD, ye his angels, that excel in strength, that do his commandments, hearkening unto the voice of his word.

Zech. 3. 7 Thus saith the LORD of hosts; If thou wilt walk in my ways, and if thou wilt keep my charge, then thou shalt also judge my house, and shalt also keep my courts, and I will give thee places to walk among these that stand by.

Matt.18. 10 Take heed that ye despise not one of these little ones; for I say unto you, That in heaven their angels do always behold the face of my Father which is in heaven.

I Cor. 7. 29. *See under O.*

I Jno. 3. 1 Behold, what manner of love the Father hath bestowed upon us, that we should be called the sons of God: therefore the world knoweth us not, because it knew him not.

CHAP. 12.

25 For when they shall rise from the dead, they neither marry, nor are given in marriage; but [s]are as the angels which are in heaven.

26 And as touching the dead, that they rise; have ye not read in the book of Moses, how in the bush God spake unto him, saying, [t]I *am* the God of Abraham, and the God of Isaac, and the God of Jacob?

27 He is not the God of the dead, but the God of the living: ye therefore do greatly err.

P—CONCLUDED.

I Jno. 3. 2 Beloved, now are we the sons of God, and it doth not yet appear what we shall be: but we know that, when he shall appear, we shall be like him; for we shall see him as he is.

Rev. 5. 9 And they sung a new song, saying, Thou art worthy to take the book, and to open the seals thereof: for thou wast slain, and hast redeemed us to God by thy blood out of every kindred, and tongue, and people, and nation;
10 And hast made us unto our God kings and priests: and we shall reign on the earth.
11 And I beheld, and I heard the voice of many angels round about the throne, and the beasts, and the elders: and the number of them was ten thousand times ten thousand, and thousands of thousands;

Rev. 19. 10 And I fell at his feet to worship him. And he said unto me, See *thou do it* not: I am thy fellow servant, and of thy brethren that have the testimony of Jesus: worship God: for the testimony of Jesus is the spirit of prophecy.

Q

Ex. 3. 6 Moreover he said, I *am* the God of thy father, the God of Abraham, the God of Isaac, and the God of Jacob. And Moses hid his face; for he was afraid to look upon God.

Ex. 3. 16 Go, and gather the elders of Israel together, and say unto them, The LORD God of your fathers, the God of

TIME, TUESDAY, APRIL 4 [NISAN 12], A. D. 30; PLACE, JERUSALEM.
Lord's Fourth and Last Passover.

CHAP. 20.

35 But they which shall be accounted worthy to obtain that world, and the resurrection from the dead, neither marry, nor are given in marriage:

36 Neither can they die any more: for [u]they are equal unto the angels; and are the children of God, [x]being the children of the resurrection.

37 Now that the dead are raised, [y]even Moses showed at the bush, when he calleth the Lord the God of Abraham, and the God of Isaac, and the God of Jacob.

38 For [z]he is not a God of the dead, but of the living: for [a]all live unto him.

39 Then certain of the scribes answering said, Master, Thou hast well said.

40 And after that they durst not ask him any *question at all.* (p. 463.)

Q—CONCLUDED.

Abraham, of Isaac, and of Jacob, appeared unto me, saying, I have surely visited you, and *seen* that which is done to you in Egypt:

Mark 12. 26 and Luke 20. 37. *See text of topic.*

Acts 7. 32 *Saying,* I *am* the God of thy fathers, the God of Abraham, and the God of Isaac, and the God of Jacob. Then Moses trembled, and durst not behold.

Heb. 11. 16 But now they desire a better *country,* that is, a heavenly: wherefore God is not ashamed to be called their God: for he hath prepared for them a city.

R

Matt. 7. 28 And it came to pass, when Jesus had ended these sayings, the people were astonished at his doctrine:

29 For he taught them as *one* having authority, and not as the scribes.

S

I Cor.15. 42 So also *is* the resurrection of the dead. It is sown in corruption, it is raised in incorruption:

I Cor.15. 49 And as we have borne the image of the earthy, we shall also bear the image of the heavenly.

S—CONCLUDED.

I Cor.15. 52 In a moment, in the twinkling of an eye, at the last trump: for the trumpet shall sound, and the dead shall be raised incorruptible, and we shall be changed.

I John 3. 2. *See under P.*

T

Ex. 3. 6. *See under Q.*

II Thes.1. 4 So that we ourselves glory in you in the churches of God, for your patience and faith in all your persecutions and tribulations that ye endure:

5 *Which is* a manifest token of the righteous judgment of God, that ye may be counted worthy of the kingdom of God, for which ye also suffer:

Rev. 3. 4 Thou hast a few names even in Sardis which have not defiled their garments; and they shall walk with me in white: for they are worthy.

U

I Cor. 15. 42, 49, 52. *Under S.* I Jno. 3. 2. *Under P.*

X

Rom. 8. 23 And not only *they,* but ourselves also, which have the first-fruits of the Spirit, even we ourselves groan within ourselves, waiting for the adoption, *to wit,* the redemption of our body.

Y

Ex. 3. 6 and Acts 7. 32. *See under Q.*

Z

Ex. 3. 7 And the LORD said, I have surely seen the affliction of my people which *are* in Egypt, and have heard their cry by reason of their taskmasters; for I know their sorrows;

Ex. 4. 5 That they may believe that the LORD God of their fathers, the God of Abraham, the God of Isaac, and the God of Jacob, hath appeared unto thee.

John 11. 25 Jesus said unto her, I am the resurrection, and the life: he that believeth in me, though he were dead, yet shall he live:

Rom. 4. 17. *See under I, page 457.*

Col. 3. 2 For ye are dead, and your life is hid with Christ in God.

4 When Christ, *who is* our life, shall appear, then shall ye also appear with him in glory.

A

Rom. 6. 10 For in that he died, he died unto sin once: but in that he liveth, he liveth unto God.

11 Likewise reckon ye also yourselves to be dead indeed unto sin, but alive unto God through Jesus Christ our Lord.

§ 165. THE TWO GREAT COMMANDMENTS.

Third Day of the Week

22: 34–40.

34 [a] But when the Pharisees had heard that he had put the Sadducees to silence, they were gathered together.

35 Then one of them, *which was* [b] a lawyer, asked *him a question*, tempting him, and saying,

36 Master, which *is* the great commandment in the law?

37 Jesus said unto him, [c] Thou shalt love the Lord thy God with all thy heart, and with all thy soul, and with all thy mind.

38 This is the first and great commandment.

39 And the second *is* like unto it, [d] Thou shalt love thy neighbour as thyself.

40 [e] On these two commandments hang all the law and the prophets.

A

Mark 12. 28. *See text of topic.*

B

Luke10. 25 And, behold, a certain lawyer stood up, and tempted him, saying, Master, what shall I do to inherit eternal life?

C

Deut. 6. 5 And thou shalt love the LORD thy God with all thine heart, and with all thy soul, and with all thy might.

Deut.10. 12 And now, Israel, what doth the LORD thy God require of thee, but to fear the LORD thy God, to walk in all his ways, and to love him, and to serve the LORD thy God with all thy heart and with all thy soul.

Deut.30. 6 And the LORD thy God will circumcise thine heart, and the heart of thy seed, to love the LORD thy God with all thine heart, and with all thy soul, that thou mayest live.

Prov.23. 26 My son, give me thine heart, and let thine eyes observe my ways.

Luke10. 27 And he answering said, Thou shalt love the Lord thy God with all thy heart, and with all thy soul, and with all thy strength, and with all thy mind; and thy neighbour as thyself.

12: 28–34.

28 [f] And one of the scribes came, and having heard them reasoning together, and perceiving that he had answered them well, asked him, Which is the first commandment of all?

29 And Jesus answered him, The first of all the commandments *is*, [g] Hear, O Israel; The Lord our God is one Lord:

30 And thou shalt love the Lord thy God with all thy heart, and with all thy soul, and with all thy mind, and with all thy strength: this *is* the first commandment.

31 And the second *is* like, *namely* this, [h] Thou shalt love thy neighbour as thyself. There is none other commandment greater than these.

32 And the scribe said unto him, Well, Master, thou hast said the truth: for there is one God; [i] and there is none other but he:

33 And to love him with all the heart, and with all the understanding, and with all the soul, and with all the strength, and to love *his* neighbour as himself, [k] is more than all whole burnt offerings and sacrifices.

34 And when Jesus saw that he answered discreetly, he said unto him, Thou art not far from the kingdom of God. [l] And no man after that durst ask him *any question.*

D

Lev. 19. 18 Thou shalt not avenge, nor bear any grudge against the children of thy people, but thou shalt love thy neighbour as thyself: I *am* the LORD.

TIME, TUESDAY, APRIL 4 [NISAN 12], A. D. 30; PLACE, JERUSALEM.

of our Lord's Fourth and Last Passover.

D—CONCLUDED.

Matt.19. 19 Honor thy father and *thy* mother: and, Thou shalt love thy neighbour as thyself.

Mark 12. 31. *See text of topic.*
Luke 10. 27. *See under C.*

Rom.13. 9 For this, Thou shalt not commit adultery, Thou shalt not kill, Thou shalt not steal, Thou shalt not bear false witness, Thou shalt not covet; and if *there be* any other commandment, it is briefly comprehended in this saying, namely, Thou shalt love thy neighbour as thyself.

Gal. 5. 14 For all the law is fulfilled in one word, *even* in this: Thou shalt love thy neighbour as thyself.

Jas. 2. 8 If ye fulfil the royal law according to the Scripture, Thou shalt love thy neighbour as thyself, ye do well:

E

Matt. 7. 12 Therefore all things whatsoever ye would that men should do to you, do ye even so to them: for this is the law and the prophets.

I Tim.1. 5 Now the end of the commandment is charity out of a pure heart, and *of* a good conscience, and *of* faith unfeigned:

F

Matt. 22. 35. *See text of topic.*

G

Deut. 6. 4 Hear, O Israel: The LORD our God *is* one LORD:

Luke 10. 27. *See under C.*

H

Lev. 19. 18. *See under D.*

Matt. 7. 12 Therefore all things whatsoever ye would that men should do to you, do ye even so to them: for this is the law and the prophets.

Matt. 22. 39. *See text of topic.*
Rom. 13. 9. *See under D.*

I Cor.13. 1 Though I speak with the tongues of men and of angels, and have not charity, I am become *as* sounding brass, or a tinkling cymbal.

Gal. 5. 14. *See under D.*
Jas. 2. 8. *See under D.*

I Jno. 3. 18 My little children, let us not love in word, neither in tongue; but in deed and in truth.

I

Deut. 4. 39 Know therefore this day, and consider *it* in thine heart, that the LORD he *is* God in heaven above, and upon the earth beneath: *there is* none else.

I—CONCLUDED.

Isa. 45. 6 That they may know from the rising of the sun, and from the west, that *there is* none besides me. I *am* the LORD, and *there is* none else.

Isa. 45. 22 Look unto me, and be ye saved, all the ends of the earth: for I *am* God, and *there is* none else.

Isa. 46. 9 Remember the former things of old: for I *am* God, and *there is* none else; *I am* God, and *there is* none like me.

K

I Sa. 15. 22 And Samuel said, Hath the Lord *as great* delight in burnt offerings and sacrifices, as in obeying the voice of the LORD? Behold, to obey *is* better than sacrifice, *and* to hearken than the fat of rams.

Hos. 6. 6 For I desired mercy, and not sacrifice; and the knowledge of God more than burnt offerings.

Mic. 6. 6 Wherewith shall I come before the LORD, *and* bow myself before the high God? shall I come before him with burnt offerings, with calves of a year old?

7 Will the LORD be pleased with thousands of rams, *or* with ten thousands of rivers of oil? shall I give my first-born *for* my transgression, the fruit of my body *for* the sin of my soul?

8 He hath showed thee, O man, what *is* good; and what doth the LORD require of thee, but to do justly, and to love mercy, and to walk humbly with thy God?

Matt. 9. 13 But go ye and learn what *that* meaneth, I will have mercy, and not sacrifice: for I am not come to call the righteous, but sinners to repentance.

L

Matt.22. 46 And no man was able to answer him a word, neither durst any *man* from that day forth ask him any more *questions*.

Col. 4. 6 Let your speech *be* always with grace, seasoned with salt, that ye may know how ye ought to answer every man.

Tit. 1. 10 For there are many unruly and vain talkers and deceivers, specially they of the circumcision:

11 Whose mouths must be stopped, who subvert whole houses, teaching things which they ought not, for filthy lucre's sake.

§ 166. DAVID'S SON AND DAVID'S LORD.

Third Day of the Week of our

22: 41–45.

41 [a]While the Pharisees were gathered together, Jesus asked them,

42 Saying, What think ye of Christ? whose son is he? They say unto him, *The son* of David.

43 He saith unto them, How then doth David [b]in spirit call him Lord, saying,

44 [c]The LORD said unto my Lord, Sit thou on my right hand, till I make thine enemies thy footstool?

45 If David then call him Lord, how is he his son?

46 [d]And no man was able to answer him a word, [e]neither durst any *man* from that day forth ask him any more *questions*.

A

Mark 12. 35 and Luke 20. 41. *See text of topic.*

B

II Sa.23. 2 The Spirit of the LORD spake by me, and his word *was* in my tongue.

Acts 2. 30 Therefore being a prophet, and knowing that God had sworn with an oath to him, that of the fruit of his loins, according to the flesh, he would raise up Christ to sit on his throne;

12: 35–37.

35 [f]And Jesus answered and said, while he taught in the temple, How say the scribes that Christ is the son of David?

36 For David himself said [g]by the Holy Ghost, [h]The LORD said to my Lord, Sit thou on my right hand, till I make thine enemies thy footstool.

37 David therefore himself calleth him Lord; and whence is he *then* his son? And the common people heard him gladly.

B—CONCLUDED.

II Pet.1. 21 For the prophecy came not in old time by the will of man: but holy men of God spake *as they were* moved by the Holy Ghost.

C

Ps. 110. 1 The LORD said unto my Lord, Sit thou at my right hand, until I make thine enemies thy footstool.

John 20. 28 And Thomas answered and said unto him, My Lord and my God.

Acts 2. 34 For David is not ascended into the heavens: but he saith himself, The LORD said unto my Lord, Sit thou on my right hand,

35 Until I make thy foes thy footstool.

§ 167. WARNINGS AGAINST THE SCRIBES AND PHARISEES AND THE EIGHT

Third Day of the Week of our

23: 1–36.

1 Then spake Jesus to the multitude, and to his disciples,

2 Saying, [a]The scribes and the Pharisees sit in Moses' seat:

3 All therefore whatsoever they bid you observe, *that* observe and do; but do not ye after their works: for [b]they say, and do not.

A

Neh. 8. 4 And Ezra the scribe stood upon a pulpit of wood, which they had made for the purpose; and beside him stood Mattithiah, and Shema, and Anaiah, Urijah, and Hilkiah, and Maaseiah, on his right hand; and on his left hand,

12: 38–40.

38 And [c]he said unto them in his doctrine, [d]Beware of the scribes, which love to go in long clothing, and [e]*love* salutations in the marketplaces,

39 And the chief seats in the synagogues, and the uppermost rooms at feasts:

A—CONTINUED.

Pedaiah, and Mishael, and Malchiah, and Hashum, and Hashbadana, Zechariah, *and* Meshullam.

Neh. 8. 8 So they read in the book in the law of God distinctly, and gave the sense and caused *them* to understand the reading.

TIME, TUESDAY, APRIL 4 [NISAN 12], A. D. 30; PLACE, JERUSALEM.
Lord's Fourth and Last Passover.

20: 41–44.

41 And he said unto them, [i]How say
they that Christ is David's son?
42 And David himself saith in the
book of Psalms, The LORD said unto
my Lord, Sit thou on my right hand,
43 Till I make thine enemies thy
footstool.
44 David therefore calleth him Lord,
how is he then his son?

C—CONTINUED.

Acts 7. 49 Heaven *is* my throne, and earth *is* my footstool: what house will ye build me? saith the Lord: or what *is* the place of my rest?

I Cor.15. 25 For he must reign, till he hath put all enemies under his feet.

Phil. 3. 8 Yea doubtless, and I count all things *but* loss for the excellency of the knowledge of Christ Jesus my Lord: for whom I have suffered the loss of all things, and do count them *but* dung, that I may win Christ,

Heb. 1. 13 But to which of the angels said he at any time, Sit on my right hand, until I make thine enemies thy footstool?

Heb. 10. 12 But this man, after he had offered one sacrifice for sins for ever, sat down on the right hand of God;
13 From henceforth expecting till his enemies be made his footstool.

Heb. 12. 2 Looking unto Jesus the author and

C—CONCLUDED

finisher of *our* faith; who for the joy that was set before him endured the cross, despising the shame, and is set down at the right hand of the throne of God.

D

Luke 14. 6 And they could not answer him again to these things.

E

Mark 12. 34 And when Jesus saw that he answered discreetly, he said unto him, Thou art not far from the kingdom of God. And no man after that durst ask him *any question.*

Luke 20. 40 And after that they durst not ask him any *question at all.*

F

Matt. 22. 41 and Luke 20. 41. *See text of topic.*

G

II Sam. 23. 2. *See under B.*

II Tim.3. 16 All Scripture *is* given by inspiration of God, and *is* profitable for doctrine, for reproof, for correction, for instruction in righteousness:

II Pet. 1. 21. *See under B.*

H

Ps. 110. 1 and I Cor. 15. 25. *See under C.*

I

Rom. 1. 3 Concerning his Son Jesus Christ our Lord, which was made of the seed of David according to the flesh;

Rev. 22. 16 I Jesus have sent mine angel to testify unto you these things in the churches. I am the root and the offspring of David, *and* the bright and morning star.

WOES. TIME, TUESDAY, APRIL 4 [NISAN 12], A. D. 30; PLACE, JERUSALEM.
Lord's Fourth and Last Passover.

20: 45–47.

45 [f]Then in the audience of all the
people he said unto his disciples,
46 [g]Beware of the scribes, which desire to walk in long robes, and [h]love
greetings in the markets, and the highest seats in the synagogues, and the
chief rooms at feasts;

A—CONCLUDED.

Mal. 2. 7 For the priest's lips should keep knowledge, and they should seek the law at his mouth: for he *is* the messenger of the LORD of hosts.

Mark 12. 38 and Luke 20. 46. *See text of topic.*

B

Rom. 2. 19 And art confident that thou thyself art a guide of the blind, a light of them which are in darkness,

C

Mark 4. 2 And he taught them many things by parables, and said unto them in his doctrine,

D

Matt. 23. 1 and Luke 20. 46. *See text of topic.*

E

Luke 11. 43 Woe unto you, Pharisees! for ye love the uppermost seats in the synagogues, and greetings in the markets.

Luke 14. 8 When thou art bidden of any *man* to a wedding, sit not down in the highest room; lest a more honourable man than thou be bidden of him:

F

Matt. 23. 1 and Mark 12. 38. *See text of topic.*

G

Matt. 23. 5. *See text of topic.*

H

Luke 11. 43. *See under E.*

§ 167. WARNINGS AGAINST THE SCRIBES AND PHARISEES AND THE EIGHT
Third Day of the Week of our

CHAP. 23.

4 [i]For they bind heavy burdens and grievous to be borne, and lay *them* on men's shoulders; but they *themselves* will not move them with one of their fingers.

5 But [k]all their works they do for to be seen of men: [l]they make broad their phylacteries, and enlarge the borders of their garments,

6 [m]And love the uppermost rooms at feasts, and the chief seats in the synagogues,

7 And greetings in the markets, and to be called of men, Rabbi, Rabbi.

8 [n]But be not ye called Rabbi: for one is your Master, *even* Christ; and all ye are brethren.

9 And call no *man* your father upon the earth: [o]for one is your Father, which is in heaven.

10 Neither be ye called masters: for one is your Master, *even* Christ.

11 But [p]he that is greatest among you shall be your servant.

12 [q]And whosoever shall exalt himself shall be abased; and he that shall humble himself shall be exalted.

13 But [r]woe unto you, scribes and Pharisees, hypocrites! for ye shut up the kingdom of heaven against men: for ye neither go in *yourselves*, neither suffer ye them that are entering to go in.

14 Woe unto you, scribes and Pharisees, hypocrites! [s]for ye devour widows' houses, and for a pretence make long prayer: therefore ye shall receive the greater damnation.

CHAP. 12.

40 Which devour widows' houses, and for a pretence make long prayers: these shall receive greater damnation.
(p. 470.)

I

Luke 11. 46 And he said, Woe unto you also, *ye* lawyers! for ye lade men with burdens grievous to be borne, and ye yourselves touch not the burdens with one of your fingers.

Acts 15. 10 Now therefore why tempt ye God, to put a yoke upon the neck of the disciples, which neither our fathers nor we were able to bear?

Gal. 6. 13 For neither they themselves who are circumcised keep the law; but desire to have you circumcised, that they may glory in your flesh.

K

Matt. 6. 1 Take heed that ye do not your alms before men, to be seen of them: otherwise ye have no reward of your Father which is in heaven.

2 Therefore when thou doest *thine* alms, do not sound a trumpet before thee, as the hypocrites do in the synagogues and in the streets, that they may have glory of men. Verily I say unto you, They have their reward.

Matt. 6. 5 And when thou prayest, thou shalt not be as the hypocrites *are*: for they love to pray standing in the synagogues and in the corners of the streets, that they may be seen of men. Verily I say unto you, They have their reward.

Matt. 6. 16 Moreover when ye fast, be not as the hypocrites, of a sad countenance: for they disfigure their faces, that they may appear unto men to fast. Verily I say unto you, They have their reward.

L

Num. 15. 38 Speak unto the children of Israel, and bid them that they make them fringes in the borders of their garments, throughout their generations, and that they put upon the fringe of the borders a ribband of blue:

Deut. 6. 8 And thou shalt bind them for a sign upon thine hand, and they shall be as frontlets between thine eyes.

Deut. 22. 12 Thou shalt make thee fringes upon the four quarters of thy vesture, wherewith thou coverest *thyself*.

Prov. 3. 3 Let not mercy and truth forsake thee: bind them about thy neck; write them upon the table of thine heart:

WOES (Continued). Time, Tuesday, April 4 [Nisan 12], A. D. 30; Place, Jerusalem.
Lord's Fourth and Last Passover.

Chap. 20.

47 ᵗWhich devour widows' houses, and for a show make long prayers: the same shall receive greater damnation.

(p. 471.)

M

Mark 12. 38, 39. *See text of topic.*
Luke 11. 43. *See under E, page 463.*
Luke 20. 46. *See text of topic.*

III Jno. 9 I wrote unto the church: but Diotrephes, who loveth to have the preeminence among them, receiveth us not.

N

II Cor. 1. 24 Not for that we have dominion over your faith, but are helpers of your joy: for by faith ye stand.

Jas. 3. 1 My brethren, be not many masters, knowing that we shall receive the greater condemnation.

I Pet. 5. 3 Neither as being lords over *God's* heritage, but being ensamples to the flock.

O

Mal. 1. 6 A son honoureth *his* father, and a servant his master: if then I *be* a father, where *is* mine honour? and if I *be* a master, where *is* my fear? saith the LORD of hosts unto you, O priests, that despise my name. And ye say, Wherein have we despised thy name?

P

Matt. 20. 26 But it shall not be so among you: but whosoever will be great among you, let him be your minister;
27 And whosoever will be chief among you, let him be your servant:
28 Even as the Son of man came not to be ministered unto, but to minister, and to give his life a ransom for many.

Mark 10. 43 But so shall it not be among you: but whosoever will be great among you, shall be your minister:
44 And whosoever of you will be the chiefest, shall be servant of all.
45 For even the Son of man came not to be ministered unto, but to minister, and to give his life a ransom for many.

John 13. 14 If I then, *your* Lord and Master, have washed your feet; ye also ought to wash one another's feet.
15 For I have given you an example, that ye should do as I have done to you.

Q

Job 22. 29 When *men* are cast down, then thou shalt say, *There is* lifting up; and he shall save the humble person.

Q—Concluded.

Prov. 15. 33 The fear of the LORD *is* the instruction of wisdom; and before honour *is* humility.

Prov. 29. 23 A man's pride shall bring him low: but honour shall uphold the humble in spirit.

Dan. 4. 37 Now I Nebuchadnezzar praise and extol and honour the King of heaven, all whose works *are* truth, and his ways judgment: and those that walk in pride he is able to abase.

Luke 14. 11 For whosoever exalteth himself shall be abased; and he that humbleth himself shall be exalted.

Luke 18. 14 I tell you, this man went down to his house justified *rather* than the other: for every one that exalteth himself shall be abased; and he that humbleth himself shall be exalted.

Jas. 4. 6 But he giveth more grace. Wherefore he saith, God resisteth the proud, but giveth grace unto the humble.

I Pet. 5. 5 Likewise, ye younger, submit yourselves unto the elder. Yea, all *of you* be subject one to another, and be clothed with humility: for God resisteth the proud, and giveth grace to the humble.

R

Luke 11. 52 Woe unto you, lawyers! for ye have taken away the key of knowledge: ye entered not in yourselves, and them that were entering in ye hindered.

S

Eze. 22. 25 *There is* a conspiracy of her prophets in the midst thereof, like a roaring lion ravening the prey: they have devoured souls; they have taken the treasure and precious things; they have made her many widows in the midst thereof.

Mark 12. 40 Which devour widows' houses and for a pretence make long prayers: these shall receive greater damnation.

Luke 20. 47 Which devour widows' houses, and for a show make long prayers: the same shall receive greater damnation.

II Tim. 3. 6 For of this sort are they which creep into houses, and lead captive silly women laden with sins, led away with divers lusts,

Tit. 1. 11 Whose mouths must be stopped, who subvert whole houses, teaching things which they ought not, for filthy lucre's sake.

T

Matt. 23. 14. *See text of topic.*

§ 167. WARNINGS AGAINST THE SCRIBES AND PHARISEES AND THE EIGHT
Third Day of the Week of our

CHAP. 23.

15 Woe unto you, scribes and Pharisees, hypocrites! for ye compass sea and land to make one proselyte; and when he is made, ye make him twofold more the child of hell than yourselves.

16 Woe unto you, [u]ye blind guides, which say, [x]Whosoever shall swear by the temple, it is nothing; but whosoever shall swear by the gold of the temple, he is a debtor!

17 [y]*Ye* fools and blind: for whether is greater, the gold, [z]or the temple that sanctifieth the gold?

18 And, Whosoever shall swear by the altar, it is nothing; but whosoever sweareth by the gift that is upon it, he is [1]guilty.

19 *Ye* fools and blind: for whether *is* greater, the gift, or [a]the altar that sanctifieth the gift?

20 Whoso therefore shall swear by the altar, sweareth by it, and by all things thereon.

21 And whoso shall swear by the temple, sweareth by it, and by [b]him that dwelleth therein.

22 And he that shall swear by heaven, sweareth by [c]the throne of God, and by him that sitteth thereon.

23 Woe unto you, scribes and Pharisees, hypocrites! [d]for ye pay tithe of mint and [2]anise and cummin, and [e]have omitted the weightier *matters* of the law, judgment, mercy, and faith: these ought ye to have done, and not to leave the other undone.

24 *Ye* blind guides, which strain at a gnat, and swallow a camel.

25 Woe unto you, scribes and Phari-

[CHAP. 12.]

U

Isa. 56. 10 His watchmen *are* blind: they are all ignorant, they *are* all dumb dogs, they cannot bark; sleeping, lying down, loving to slumber.

Matt. 15. 14 Let them alone: they be blind leaders of the blind. And if the blind lead the blind, both shall fall into the ditch.

Matt. 23. 24. *See text of topic.*

X

Matt. 5. 33 Again, ye have heard that it hath been said by them of old time, Thou shalt not forswear thyself, but shalt perform unto the Lord thine oaths;

34 But I say unto you, Swear not at all; neither by heaven; for it is God's throne:

Y

Ps. 94. 8 Understand, ye brutish among the people: and *ye* fools, when will ye be wise?

Z

Ex. 30. 26 And thou shalt anoint the tabernacle of the congregation therewith, and the ark of the testimony,

27 And the table and all his vessels, and the candlestick and his vessels, and the altar of incense,

28 And the altar of burnt offering with all his vessels, and the laver and his foot.

29 And thou shalt sanctify them, that they may be most holy: whatsoever toucheth them shall be holy.

Num. 16. 38 The censers of these sinners against their own souls, let them make them broad plates *for* a covering of the altar: for they offered them before the LORD, therefore they are hallowed: and they shall be a sign unto the children of Israel.

39 And Eleazar the priest took the brazen censers, wherewith they that were burnt had offered; and they were made broad *plates for* a covering of the altar:

1

Or, *debtor*, or *bound.*

A

Ex. 29. 37 Seven days thou shalt make an atonement for the altar, and sanctify it; and it shall be an altar most holy: whatsoever toucheth the altar shall be holy.

B

I Ki. 8. 13 I have surely built thee a house to dwell in, a settled place for thee to abide in for ever.

WOES (CONTINUED). TIME, TUESDAY, APRIL 4 [NISAN 12], A. D. 30; PLACE, JERUSALEM.
Lord's Fourth and Last Passover.

[CHAP. 20.]

B—CONCLUDED.

I Ki. 8. 27 But will God indeed dwell on the earth? behold, the heaven and heaven of heavens cannot contain thee; how much less this house that I have builded?

II Chr.6. 2 But I have built a house of habitation for thee, and a place for thy dwelling for ever.

II Chr.7. 1 Now when Solomon had made an end of praying, the fire came down from heaven, and consumed the burnt offering and the sacrifices; and the glory of the LORD filled the house.

2 And the priests could not enter into the house of the LORD, because the glory of the LORD had filled the LORD'S house.

Ps. 26. 8 LORD, I have loved the habitation of thy house, and the place where thine honour dwelleth.

Ps. 132. 13 For the LORD hath chosen Zion; he hath desired *it* for his habitation.

14 This *is* my rest for ever: here will I dwell; for I have desired it.

Eph. 2. 22 In whom ye also are builded together for a habitation of God through the Spirit.

Col. 2. 9 For in him dwelleth all the fulness of the Godhead bodily.

C

Ps. 11. 4 The LORD *is* in his holy temple, the LORD'S throne *is* in heaven: his eyes behold, his eyelids try, the children of men.

Isa. 66. 1 Thus saith the LORD, The heaven *is* my throne, and the earth *is* my footstool: where *is* the house that ye build unto me? and where *is* the place of my rest?

Matt. 5. 34. *See under X.*

Acts 7. 49 Heaven *is* my throne, and earth *is* my footstool: what house will ye build me? saith the Lord: or what *is* the place of my rest?

Rev. 4. 2 And immediately I was in the Spirit: and, behold, a throne was set in heaven, and *one* sat on the throne.

3 And he that sat was to look upon like a jasper and a sardine stone: and *there was* a rainbow round about the throne, in sight like unto an emerald.

D

Luke 11. 42 But woe unto you, Pharisees! for ye tithe mint and rue and all manner of herbs, and pass over judgment and the love of God: these ought ye to have done, and not to leave the other undone.

2

DILL (*Gr. anethon*), a plant bearing pungent and aromatic seeds.

E

I Sa. 15. 22 And Samuel said, Hath the LORD *as great* delight in burnt offerings and sacrifices, as in obeying the voice of the LORD? Behold, to obey *is* better than sacrifice, *and* to hearken than the fat of rams.

Prov.15. 8 The sacrifice of the wicked *is* an abomination to the LORD: but the prayer of the upright *is* his delight.

Prov.21. 3 To do justice and judgment *is* more acceptable to the LORD than sacrifice.

Isa. 1. 14 Your new moons and your appointed feasts my soul hateth: they are a trouble unto me; I am weary to bear *them*.

15 And when ye spread forth your hands, I will hide mine eyes from you; yea, when ye make many prayers, I will not hear: your hands are full of blood.

16 Wash ye, make you clean; put away the evil of your doings from before mine eyes; cease to do evil:

17 Learn to do well; seek judgment, relieve the oppressed, judge the fatherless, plead for the widow.

Jer. 22. 15 Shalt thou reign, because thou closest *thyself* in cedar? did not thy father eat and drink, and do judgment and justice, *and* then *it was* well with him?

16 He judged the cause of the poor and needy; then *it was* well *with him*: *was* not this to know me? saith the LORD.

Hos. 6. 6 For I desired mercy, and not sacrifice; and the knowledge of God more than burnt offerings.

Mic. 6. 8 He hath showed thee, O man, what *is* good; and what doth the LORD require of thee, but to do justly, and to love mercy, and to walk humbly with thy God?

Matt. 9. 13 But go ye and learn what *that* meaneth, I will have mercy, and not sacrifice: for I am not come to call the righteous, but sinners to repentance.

Matt.12. 7 But if ye had known what *this* meaneth, I will have mercy, and not sacrifice, ye would not have condemned the guiltless.

Gal. 5. 22 But the fruit of the Spirit is love, joy, peace, longsuffering, gentleness, goodness, faith.

23 Meekness, temperance: against such there is no law.

§ 167. WARNINGS AGAINST THE SCRIBES AND PHARISEES AND THE EIGHT
Third Day of the Week of our

CHAP. 23.

sees, hypocrites! [f]for ye make clean the outside of the cup and of the platter, but within they are full of extortion and excess.

26 *Thou* blind Pharisee, [g]cleanse first that *which is* within the cup and platter, that the outside of them may be clean also.

27 Woe unto you, scribes and Pharisees, hypocrites! [h]for ye are like unto whited sepulchres, which indeed appear beautiful outward, but are within full of dead *men's* bones, and of all uncleanness.

28 [i]Even so ye also outwardly appear righteous unto men, but within ye are full of hypocrisy and iniquity.

29 [k]Woe unto you, scribes and Pharisees, hypocrites! because ye build the tombs of the prophets, and garnish the sepulchres of the righteous,

30 And say, If we had been in the days of our fathers, we would not have been partakers with them in the blood of the prophets.

31 Wherefore ye be witnesses unto yourselves, that [l]ye are the children of them which killed the prophets.

32 [m]Fill ye up then the measure of your fathers.

33 *Ye* serpents, *ye* [n]generation of vipers, how can ye escape the damnation of hell?

34 [o]Wherefore, behold, I send unto you prophets, and wise men, and scribes: and [p]*some* of them ye shall kill and crucify; and [q]*some* of them shall ye scourge in your synagogues, and persecute *them* from city to city:

[CHAP. 12.]

F

Matt. 7. 4 Or how wilt thou say to thy brother, Let me pull out the mote out of thine eye; and, behold, a beam *is* in thine own eye?

Luke 11. 39 And the Lord said unto him, Now do ye Pharisees make clean the outside of the cup and the platter; but your inward part is full of ravening and wickedness.

Tit. 1. 15 Unto the pure all things *are* pure: but unto them that are defiled and unbelieving *is* nothing pure; but even their mind and conscience is defiled.

G

Isa. 55. 7 Let the wicked forsake his way, and the unrighteous man his thoughts: and let him return unto the LORD, and he will have mercy upon him; and to our God, for he will abundantly pardon.

Jer. 4. 14 O Jerusalem, wash thine heart from wickedness, that thou mayest be saved. How long shall thy vain thoughts lodge within thee?

Eze. 18. 31 Cast away from you all your transgressions, whereby ye have transgressed; and make you a new heart and a new spirit: for why will ye die, O house of Israel?

32 For I have no pleasure in the death of him that dieth, saith the Lord GOD: wherefore turn *yourselves*, and live ye.

Luke 6. 45 A good man out of the good treasure of his heart bringeth forth that which is good; and an evil man out of the evil treasure of his heart bringeth forth that which is evil: for of the abundance of the heart his mouth speaketh.

II Cor. 7. 1 Having therefore these promises, dearly beloved, let us cleanse ourselves from all filthiness of the flesh and spirit, perfecting holiness in the fear of God.

Heb. 10. 22 Let us draw near with a true heart in full assurance of faith, having our hearts sprinkled from an evil conscience, and our bodies washed with pure water.

Jas. 4. 8 Draw nigh to God, and he will draw nigh to you. Cleanse *your* hands, *ye* sinners; and purify *your* hearts, *ye* doubleminded.

H

Luke 11. 44 Woe unto you, scribes and Pharisees, hypocrites! for ye are as graves

WOES (CONTINUED). TIME, TUESDAY, APRIL 4 [NISAN 12], A. D. 30; PLACE, JERUSALEM.
Lord's Fourth and Last Passover.

[CHAP. 20.]

H—CONCLUDED.

which appear not, and the men that walk over *them* are not aware *of them*.

Acts 23. 3 Then said Paul unto him, God shall smite thee, *thou* whited wall: for sittest thou to judge me after the law, and commandest me to be smitten contrary to the law?

I

I Sa. 16. 7 But the LORD said unto Samuel, Look not on his countenance, or on the height of his stature; because I have refused him: for *the LORD seeth* not as man seeth; for man looketh on the outward appearance, but the LORD looketh on the heart.

Ps. 5. 6 Thou shalt destroy them that speak leasing: the LORD will abhor the bloody and deceitful man.

Jer. 17. 9 The heart *is* deceitful above all *things*, and desperately wicked: who can know it?

10 I the LORD search the heart, *I* try the reins, even to give every man according to his ways, *and* according to the fruit of his doings.

Luke 16. 15 And he said unto them, Ye are they which justify yourselves before men; but God knoweth your hearts: for that which is highly esteemed among men is abomination in the sight of God.

Heb. 4. 12 For the word of God *is* quick, and powerful, and sharper than any twoedged sword, piercing even to the dividing asunder of soul and spirit, and of the joints and marrow, and *is* a discerner of the thoughts and intents of the heart.

K

Luke 11. 47 Woe unto you! for ye build the sepulchres of the prophets, and your fathers killed them.

L

Acts 7. 51 Ye stiffnecked and uncircumcised in heart and ears, ye do always resist the Holy Ghost: as your fathers *did*, so *do* ye.

52 Which of the prophets have not your fathers persecuted? and they have slain them which showed before of the coming of the Just One; of whom ye have been now the betrayers and murderers:

I Thes.2. 15 Who both killed the Lord Jesus, and their own prophets, and have persecuted us; and they please not God, and are contrary to all men:

M

Gen. 15. 16 But in the fourth generation they shall come hither again: for the iniquity of the Amorites *is* not yet full.

I Thes.2. 16 Forbidding us to speak to the Gentiles that they might be saved, to fill up their sins always: for the wrath is come upon them to the uttermost.

N

Ps. 58. 4 Their poison *is* like the poison of a serpent: *they are* like the deaf adder *that* stoppeth her ear;

Matt. 3. 7 But when he saw many of the Pharisees and Sadducees come to his baptism, he said unto them, O generation of vipers, who hath warned you to flee from the wrath to come?

Matt.12. 34 O generation of vipers, how can ye, being evil, speak good things? for out of the abundance of the heart the mouth speaketh.

O

Matt.21. 34 And when the time of the fruit drew near, he sent his servants to the husbandmen, that they might receive the fruits of it.

35 And the husbandmen took his servants, and beat one, and killed another, and stoned another.

Luke 11. 49 Therefore also said the wisdom of God, I will send them prophets and apostles, and *some* of them they shall slay and persecute:

P

Acts 7. 58 And cast *him* out of the city, and stoned *him*: and the witnesses laid down their clothes at a young man's feet, whose name was Saul.

59 And they stoned Stephen, calling upon *God*, and saying, Lord Jesus, receive my spirit.

Acts 22. 19 And I said, Lord, they know that I imprisoned and beat in every synagogue them that believed on thee:

Q

Matt.10. 17 But beware of men: for they will deliver you up to the councils, and they will scourge you in their synagogues;

Acts 5. 40 And to him they agreed: and when they had called the apostles, and beaten *them*, they commanded that they should not speak in the name of Jesus, and let them go.

II Cor.11. 24 Of the Jews five times received I forty *stripes* save one.

25 Thrice was I beaten with rods, once was I stoned, thrice I suffered shipwreck, a night and a day I have been in the deep;

§ 167. WARNINGS AGAINST THE SCRIBES AND PHARISEES AND THE EIGHT

Third Day of the Week of our

CHAP. 23.

35 [r]That upon you may come all the
righteous blood shed upon the earth,
[s]from the blood of righteous Abel unto
[t]the blood of Zacharias son of Barachias, whom ye slew between the temple
and the altar.
36 Verily I say unto you, All these
things shall come upon this generation.

R

Gen. 9. 5 And surely your blood of your lives will I require: at the hand of every beast will I require it, and at the hand of man; at the hand of every man's brother will I require the life of man.

6 Whoso sheddeth man's blood, by man shall his blood be shed: for in the image of God made he man.

[CHAP. 12.]

R—CONTINUED.

Num.35. 33 So ye shall not pollute the land wherein ye *are:* for blood it defileth the land: and the land cannot be cleansed of the blood that is shed therein, but by the blood of him that shed it.

Isa. 26. 21 For, behold, the LORD cometh out of his place to punish the inhabitants of the earth for their iniquity: the earth also shall disclose her blood, and shall no more cover her slain.

Jer. 2. 30 In vain have I smitten your children; they received no correction: your own sword hath devoured your prophets, like a destroying lion.

Jer. 2. 34 Also in thy skirts is found the blood of the souls of the poor innocents: I have not found it by secret search, but upon all these.

§ 168. JESUS LAMENTS OVER JERUSALEM.

Third Day of the Week of our

23: 37–39.

37 [a]O Jerusalem, Jerusalem, *thou*
that killest the prophets, [b]and stonest
them which are sent unto thee, how
often would I [c]have gathered thy children together, even as a hen gathereth
her chickens [d]under *her* wings, and ye
would not!
38 Behold, your house is left unto
you desolate.
39 For I say unto you, [e]Ye shall not
see me henceforth, till ye shall say,
[f]Blessed *is* he that cometh in the name
of the Lord.

(p. 480.)

A

Luke 13. 34 O Jerusalem, Jerusalem, which killest the prophets, and stonest them that are sent unto thee; how often would I have gathered thy children together, as a hen *doth gather* her brood under *her* wings, and ye would not!

Rev. 11. 8 And their dead bodies *shall lie* in the street of the great city, which spirtually is called Sodom and Egypt, where also our Lord was crucified.

B

II Chr. 24. 21. *See under T, § 167, page 471.*

II Chr.36. 15 And the LORD God of their fathers sent to them by his messengers, rising up betimes, and sending; because he had compassion on his people, and on his dwellingplace:

16 But they mocked the messengers

§ 169. THE POOR WIDOW'S TWO MITES.

Third Day of the Week of our

A

Luke 21. 1. *See text of topic.*

John 8. 20 These words spake Jesus in the treasury, as he taught in the temple: and no man laid hands on him; for his hour was not yet come.

1

A piece of brass money.

Matt.10. 9 Provide neither gold, nor silver, nor brass in your purses:

B

II Ki.12. 9 But Jehoiada the priest took a

12: 41–44.

41 [a]And Jesus sat over against the
treasury, and beheld how the people
cast [1]money [b]into the treasury: and
many that were rich cast in much.
42 And there came a certain poor
widow, and she threw in two [2]mites
which make a farthing.

WOES (CONCLUDED). TIME, TUESDAY, APRIL 4 [NISAN 12], A. D. 30; PLACE, JERUSALEM.
Lord's Fourth and Last Passover.

[CHAP. 20.]

R—CONCLUDED.

Jer. 26. 15 But know ye for certain, that if ye put me to death, ye shall surely bring innocent blood upon yourselves, and upon this city, and upon the inhabitants thereof: for of a truth the LORD hath sent me unto you to speak all these words in your ears.

Jer. 26. 23 And they fetched forth Urijah out of Egypt, and brought him unto Jehoiakim the king; who slew him with the sword, and cast his dead body into the graves of the common people.

Rev. 18. 24 And in her was found the blood of prophets, and of saints, and of all that were slain upon the earth.

S

Gen. 4. 8 And Cain talked with Abel his brother: and it came to pass, when

S—CONCLUDED.

they were in the field, that Cain rose up against Abel his brother, and slew him.

I Jno. 3. 12 Not as Cain, *who* was of that wicked one, and slew his brother. And wherefore slew he him? Because his own works were evil, and his brother's righteous.

T

II Chr.24. 20 And the Spirit of God came upon Zechariah the son of Jehoiada the priest, which stood above the people, and said unto them, Thus saith God, Why transgress ye the commandments of the LORD, that ye cannot prosper? because ye have forsaken the LORD, he hath also forsaken you.

21 And they conspired against him, and stoned him with stones at the commandment of the king in the court of the house of the LORD.

TIME, TUESDAY, APRIL 4 [NISAN 12], A. D. 30; PLACE, JERUSALEM.
Lord's Fourth and Last Passover.

B—CONCLUDED.

of God, and despised his words, and misused his prophets, until the wrath of the LORD arose against his people, till *there was* no remedy.

C

Deut.32. 11 As an eagle stirreth up her nest, fluttereth over her young, spreadeth abroad her wings, taketh them, beareth them on her wings:

12 *So* the LORD alone did lead him, and *there was* no strange God with him.

D

Ruth 2. 12 The LORD recompense thy work, and a full reward be given thee of the LORD God of Israel, under whose wings thou art come to trust.

Ps. 17. 8 Keep me as the apple of the eye, hide me under the shadow of thy wings,

D—CONCLUDED.

Ps. 36. 7 How excellent *is* thy loving-kindness, O God! therefore the children of men put their trust under the shadow of thy wings.

Ps. 91. 4 He shall cover thee with his feathers, and under his wings shalt thou trust: his trust *shall be thy* shield and buckler.

E

Prov. 1. 26 I also will laugh at your calamity; I will mock when your fear cometh;

27 When your fear cometh as desolation, and your destruction cometh as a whirlwind; when distress and anguish cometh upon you.

28 Then shall they call upon me, but I will not answer; they shall seek me early, but they shall not find me:

TIME, TUESDAY, APRIL 4 [NISAN 12], A. D. 30; PLACE, JERUSALEM.
Lord's Fourth and Last Passover.

21: 1–4.

1 And he looked up, [c]and saw the rich men casting their gifts into the treasury.

2 And he saw also a certain poor widow casting in thither two mites.

B—CONTINUED.

chest, and bored a hole in the lid of it, and set it beside the altar, on the

B—CONCLUDED.

right side as one cometh into the house of the LORD: and the priests that kept the door put therein all the money *that was* brought into the house of the LORD.

2

It is the seventh part of one piece of that brass money.

C

Mark 12. 41. *See text of topic.*

§ 169. THE POOR WIDOW'S TWO MITES (CONCLUDED).

Third Day of the Week of our

D

II Cor.8. 12 For if there be first a willing mind, *it is* accepted according to that a man hath, *and* not according to that he hath not.

E

Deut.24. 6 No man shall take the nether or the upper millstone to pledge: for he taketh *a man's* life to pledge.

I Jno. 3. 17 But whoso hath this world's good, and seeth his brother have need, and shutteth up his bowels *of compassion* from him, how dwelleth the love of God in him?

F

Prov. 3. 9 Honour the LORD with thy sub-

CHAP. 12.

43 And he called *unto him* his disciples, and saith unto them, Verily I say unto you, [d]That this poor widow hath cast more in, than all they which have cast into the treasury:

44 For all *they* did cast in of their abundance; but she of her want did cast in all that she had, [e]*even* all her living.

(p. 480.)

§ 170. CERTAIN GREEKS DESIRE TO SEE JESUS.

Third Day of the Week of our

A

Acts 17. 4 And some of them believed, and consorted with Paul and Silas; and of the devout Greeks a great multitude, and of the chief women not a few.

B

I Ki. 8. 41 Moreover concerning a stranger, that *is* not of thy people Israel, but cometh out of a far country for thy name's sake;

42 (For they shall hear of thy great name, and of thy strong hand, and of thy stretched out arm;) when he shall come and pray toward this house:

Acts 8. 27 And he arose and went: and, behold, a man of Ethiopia, a eunuch of great authority under Candace queen of the Ethiopians, who had the charge of all her treasure, and had come to Jerusalem for to worship,

C

John 1. 44 Now Philip was of Bethsaida, the city of Andrew and Peter.

D

John 13. 32 If God be glorified in him, God shall also glorify him in himself, and shall straightway glorify him.

John 17. 1 These words spake Jesus, and lifted up his eyes to heaven, and said, Father, the hour is come; glorify thy Son, that thy Son also may glorify thee:

E

1 Cor.15. 36 *Thou* fool, that which thou sowest is not quickened, except it die:

37 And that which thou sowest, thou sowest not that body that shall be, but bare grain, it may chance of wheat, or of some other *grain:*

Heb. 2. 10 For it became him, for whom *are* all things, and by whom *are* all things, in bringing many sons unto glory, to make the captain of their salvation perfect through sufferings.

E—CONCLUDED.

I Jno. 4. 14 And we have seen and do testify that the Father sent the Son *to be* the Saviour of the world.

F

John 12. 32 And I, if I be lifted up from the earth, will draw all *men* unto me.

33 This he said, signifying what death he should die.

Heb. 2. 9 But we see Jesus, who was made a little lower than the angels for the suffering of death, crowned with glory and honour; that he by the grace of God should taste death for every man.

Heb. 2. 10. *See under E.*

Rev. 7. 13 And one of the elders answered, saying unto me, What are these which are arrayed in white robes? and whence came they?

14 And I said unto him, Sir, thou knowest. And he said to me, These are they which came out of great tribulation, and have washed their robes, and made them white in the blood of the Lamb.

G

Matt.10. 39 He that findeth his life shall lose it: and he that loseth his life for my sake shall find it.

Matt.16. 25 For whosoever will save his life shall lose it: and whosoever will lose his life for my sake shall find it.

Mark 8. 35 For whosoever will save his life shall lose it; but whosoever shall lose his life for my sake and the gospel's, the same shall save it.

TIME, TUESDAY, APRIL 4 [NISAN 12], A. D. 30; PLACE, JERUSALEM.
Lord's Fourth and Last Passover.

CHAP. 21.

3 And he said, Of a truth I say unto you, [f]that this poor widow hath cast in more than they all:

4 For all these have of their abundance cast in unto the offerings of God: but she of her penury hath cast in all the living that she had. (p. 481.)

F—CONTINUED.

stance, and with the first-fruits of all thine increase:

Prov.11. 24 There is that scattereth, and yet increaseth; and *there is* that withholdeth more than is meet, but *it tendeth* to poverty.

F—CONCLUDED.

25 The liberal soul shall be made fat: and he that watereth shall be watered also himself.

II Cor. 8. 12. *See under D.*

II Cor.9. 6 But this *I say*, He which soweth sparingly shall reap also sparingly; and he which soweth bountifully shall reap also bountifully.

7 Every man according as he purposeth in his heart, *so let him give;* not grudgingly, or of necessity: for God loveth a cheerful giver.

TIME, TUESDAY, APRIL 4 [NISAN 12], A. D. 30; PLACE, JERUSALEM.
Lord's Fourth and Last Passover.

G—CONCLUDED.

Luke 9. 24 For whosoever will save his life shall lose it: but whosoever will lose his life for my sake, the same shall save it.

25 For what is a man advantaged, if he gain the whole world, and lose himself, or be cast away?

Luke 17. 33 Whosoever shall seek to save his life shall lose it; and whosoever shall lose his life shall preserve it.

Acts 20. 24 But none of these things move me, neither count I my life dear unto myself, so that I might finish my course with joy, and the ministry, which I have received of the Lord Jesus, to testify the gospel of the grace of God.

Acts 21. 13 Then Paul answered, What mean ye to weep and to break mine heart? for I am ready not to be bound only, but also to die at Jerusalem for the name of the Lord Jesus.

Heb. 11. 35 Women received their dead raised to life again: and others were tortured, not excepting deliverance; that they might obtain a better resurrection:

Rev. 12 11 And they overcame him by the blood of the Lamb, and by the word of their testimony; and they loved not their lives unto the death.

H

John 14. 3 And if I go and prepare a place for you, I will come again, and receive you unto myself; that where I am, *there* ye may be also.

John 17. 24 Father, I will that they also, whom thou hast given me, be with me where I am; that they may behold my glory, which thou hast given me:

12: 20–36.

20 And there [a]were certain Greeks among them [b]that came up to worship at the feast:

21 The same came therefore to Philip, [c]which was of Bethsaida of Galilee, and desired him, saying, Sir, we would see Jesus.

22 Philip cometh and telleth Andrew: and again Andrew and Philip tell Jesus.

23 And Jesus answered them, saying, [d]The hour is come, that the Son of man should be glorified.

24 Verily, verily, I say unto you, [e]Except a corn of wheat fall into the ground and die, it abideth alone: but [f]if it die, it bringeth forth much fruit.

25 [g]He that loveth his life shall lose it; and he that hateth his life in this world shall keep it unto life eternal.

26 If any man serve me, let him follow me; and [h]where I am, there shall also my servant be: if any man serve me, him will *my* Father honour.

H—CONCLUDED.

for thou lovedst me before the foundation of the world.

I Thes.4. 17 Then we which are alive *and* remain shall be caught up together with them in the clouds, to meet the Lord in the air: and so shall we ever be with the Lord.

§ 170. CERTAIN GREEKS DESIRE TO SEE JESUS (Continued).

Third Day of the Week of our

I

Ps. 69. 1 Save me, O God; for the waters are come in unto *my* soul.

2 I sink in deep mire, where *there is* no standing: I am come into deep waters, where the floods overflow me.

3 I am weary of my crying: my throat is dried: mine eyes fail while I wait for my God.

Ps. 88. 2 Let my prayer come before thee: incline thine ear unto my cry;

3 For my soul is full of troubles: and my life draweth nigh unto the grave.

Matt.26. 38 Then saith he unto them, My soul is exceeding sorrowful, even unto death: tarry ye here, and watch with me.

39 And he went a little further, and fell on his face, and prayed, saying, O my Father, if it be possible, let this cup pass from me: nevertheless, not as I will, but as thou *wilt*.

Luke 12. 50 But I have a baptism to be baptized with; and how am I straitened till it be accomplished!

John 13. 21 When Jesus had thus said, he was troubled in spirit, and testified, and said, Verily, verily, I say unto you, that one of you shall betray me.

K

Luke 23. 53 When I was daily with you in the temple, ye stretched forth no hands against me: but this is your hour, and the power of darkness.

John 18. 37 Pilate therefore said unto him, Art thou a king then? Jesus answered, Thou sayest that I am a king. To this end was I born, and for this cause came I into the world, that I should bear witness unto the truth. Every one that is of the truth heareth my voice.

L

Isa. 49. 7 Thus saith the Lord, the Redeemer of Israel, *and* his Holy One, to him whom man despiseth, to him whom the nation abhorreth, to a servant of rulers, Kings shall see and arise, princes also shall worship, because of the Lord that is faithful, *and* the Holy One of Israel, and he shall choose thee.

Matt. 3. 17 And lo a voice from heaven, saying, This is my beloved Son, in whom I am well pleased.

Eph. 2. 7 That in the ages to come he might show the exceeding riches of his grace, in *his* kindness toward us, through Christ Jesus.

L—Concluded.

Eph. 3. 10 To the intent that now unto the principalities and powers in heavenly *places* might be known by the church the manifold wisdom of God,

II Pet. 1. 17 For he received from God the Father honour and glory, when there came such a voice to him from the excellent glory, This is my beloved Son, in whom I am well pleased.

M

John 11. 42 And I knew that thou hearest me always: but because of the people which stand by I said *it*, that they may believe that thou hast sent me.

N

Matt. 12. 29 Or else, how can one enter into a strong man's house, and spoil his goods, except he first bind the strong man? and then he will spoil his house.

Luke 10. 18 And he said unto them, I beheld Satan as lightning fall from heaven.

John 14. 30 Hereafter I will not talk much with you: for the prince of this world cometh, and hath nothing in me.

John 16. 11 Of judgment, because the prince of this world is judged.

Acts 26. 18 To open their eyes, *and* to turn *them* from darkness to light, and *from* the power of Satan unto God, that they may receive forgiveness of sins, and inheritance among them which are sanctified by faith that is in me.

II Cor. 4. 4 In whom the god of this world hath blinded the minds of them which believe not, lest the light of the glorious gospel of Christ, who is the image of God, should shine unto them.

Eph. 2. 2 Wherein in time past ye walked according to the course of this world, according to the prince of the power of the air, the spirit that now worketh in the children of disobedience:

Eph. 6. 12 For we wrestle not against flesh and blood, but against principalities, against powers, against the rulers of the darkness of this world, against spiritual wickedness in high *places*.

I Jno. 3. 8 He that committeth sin is of the devil; for the devil sinneth from the beginning. For this purpose the Son of God was manifested, that he might destroy the works of the devil.

O

John 3. 14 And as Moses lifted up the serpent in the wilderness, even so must the Son of man be lifted up:

15 That whosoever believeth in him should not perish, but have eternal life.

TIME, TUESDAY, APRIL 4 [NISAN 12], A. D. 30; PLACE, JERUSALEM.
Lord's Fourth and Last Passover.

O—CONCLUDED.

John 8. 28 Then said Jesus unto them, When ye have lifted up the Son of man, then shall ye know that I am *he*, and *that* I do nothing of myself; but as my Father hath taught me, I speak these things.

P

Rom. 5. 18 Therefore, as by the offence of one *judgment came* upon all men to condemnation; even so by the righteousness of one *the free gift came* upon all men unto justification of life.

Heb. 2. 9 But we see Jesus, who was made a little lower than the angels for the suffering of death, crowned with glory and honour; that he by the grace of God should taste death for every man.

Q

John 18. 32 That the saying of Jesus might be fulfilled, which he spake, signifying what death he should die.

R

II Sa. 7. 13 He shall build a house for my name, and I will stablish the throne of his kingdom for ever.

Ps. 89. 36 His seed shall endure for ever, and his throne as the sun before me.

37 It shall be established for ever as the moon, and *as* a faithful witness in heaven. Selah.

Ps. 110. 4 The LORD hath sworn, and will not repent, Thou *art* a priest for ever after the order of Melchizedek.

Isa. 9. 7 Of the increase of *his* government and peace *there shall be* no end, upon the throne of David, and upon his kingdom, to order it, and to establish it with judgment and with justice from henceforth even for ever. The zeal of the LORD of hosts will perform this.

Isa. 53. 8 He was taken from prison and from judgment: and who shall declare his generation? for he was cut off out of the land of the living: for the transgression of my people was he stricken.

Eze. 37. 25 And they shall dwell in the land that I have given unto Jacob my servant, wherein your fathers have dwelt; and they shall dwell therein, *even* they, and their children, and their children's children for ever: and my servant David *shall be* their prince for ever.

Dan. 2. 44 And in the days of these kings shall the God of heaven set up a kingdom, which shall never be destroyed: and the kingdom shall not be left to other people, *but* it shall break in

CHAP. 12.

27 [i]Now is my soul troubled; and what shall I say? Father, save me from this hour: [k]but for this cause came I unto this hour.

28 Father, glorify thy name. Then came there a voice from [l]heaven, *saying*, I have both glorified *it*, and will glorify *it* again.

29 The people therefore that stood by, and heard *it*, said that it thundered: others said, An angel spake to him.

30 Jesus answered and said, [m]This voice came not because of me, but for your sakes.

31 Now is the judgment of this world: now shall the [n]prince of this world be cast out.

32 And I, [o]if I be lifted up from the earth, will draw [p]all *men* unto me.

33 [q]This he said, signifying what death he should die.

34 The people answered him, [r]We have heard out of the law that Christ abideth for ever: and how sayest thou, The Son of man must be lifted up? who is this Son of man?

R—CONCLUDED.

pieces and consume all these kingdoms, and it shall stand for ever.

Dan. 7. 14 And there was given him dominion, and glory, and a kingdom, that all people, nations, and languages, should serve him: his dominion *is* an everlasting dominion, which shall not pass away, and his kingdom *that* which shall not be destroyed.

Dan. 7. 27 And the kingdom and dominion, and the greatness of the kingdom under the whole heaven, shall be given to the people of the saints of the Most High, whose kingdom *is* an everlasting kingdom, and all dominions shall serve and obey him.

Mic. 4. 7 And I will make her that halted a remnant, and her that was cast far off a strong nation: and the LORD shall reign over them in mount Zion from henceforth, even for ever.

§ 170. CERTAIN GREEKS DESIRE TO SEE JESUS (Concluded).

Third Day of the Week of our

S

Isa 42. 6 I the Lord have called thee in righteousness, and will hold thine hand, and will keep thee, and give thee for a covenant of the people, for a light of the Gentiles;

John 1. 9 *That* was the true Light, which lighteth every man that cometh into the world.

John 8. 12 Then spake Jesus again unto them, saying, I am the light of the world: he that followeth me shall not walk in darkness, but shall have the light of life.

John 9. 5 As long as I am in the world, I am the light of the world.

John 12. 46 I am come a light into the world, that whosoever believeth on me should not abide in darkness.

T

Isa. 2. 5 O house of Jacob, come ye, and let us walk in the light of the Lord.

Jer. 13. 15 Hear ye, and give ear; be not proud: for the Lord hath spoken.

T—Concluded.

Jer. 13. 16 Give glory to the Lord your God, before he cause darkness, and before your feet stumble upon the dark mountains, and, while ye look for light, he turn it into the shadow of death, *and* make *it* gross darkness.

Eph. 5. 8 For ye were sometime darkness, but now *are ye* light in the Lord: walk as children of light;

U

Ps. 27. 2 When the wicked, *even* mine enemies and my foes, came upon me to eat up my flesh, they stumbled and fell.

Jer. 20. 11 But the Lord *is* with me as a mighty terrible one: therefore my persecutors shall stumble, and they shall not prevail: they shall be greatly ashamed; for they shall not prosper: *their* everlasting confusion shall never be forgotten.

John 11. 10 But if a man walk in the night, he stumbleth, because there is no light in him.

§ 171. REFLECTIONS OF OUR LORD UPON THE UNBELIEF OF THE JEWS.

Third Day of the Week of our

A

Isa. 53. 1 Who hath believed our report? and to whom is the arm of the Lord revealed?

Rom. 10. 16 But they have not all obeyed the gospel. For Esaias saith, Lord, who hath believed our report?

B

Ps. 44. 3 For they got not the land in possession by their own sword, neither did their own arm save them: but thy right hand, and thine arm, and the light of thy countenance, because thou hadst a favour unto them.

Isa. 40. 10 Behold, the Lord God will come with strong *hand*, and his arm shall rule for him: behold, his reward *is* with him, and his work before him.

Isa. 51. 5 My righteousness *is* near; my salvation is gone forth, and mine arms shall judge the people; the isles shall wait upon me, and on mine arm shall they trust.

Isa. 51. 9 Awake, awake, put on strength, O arm of the Lord; awake, as in the ancient days, in the generations of old. *Art* thou not it that hath cut Rahab, *and* wounded the dragon?

I Cor. 1. 24 But unto them which are called, both Jews and Greeks, Christ the power of God, and the wisdom of God.

Eph. 1. 17 That the God of our Lord Jesus

B—Concluded.

Christ, the Father of glory, may give unto you the spirit of wisdom and revelation in the knowledge of him:

18 The eyes of your understanding being enlightened; that ye may know what is the hope of his calling, and what the riches of the glory of his inheritance in the saints,

19 And what *is* the exceeding greatness of his power to us-ward who believe, according to the working of his mighty power,

C

Isa. 6. 9 And he said, Go, and tell this people, Hear ye indeed, but understand not; and see ye indeed, but perceive not.

10 Make the heart of this people fat, and make their ears heavy, and shut their eyes; lest they see with their eyes, and hear with their ears, and understand with their heart, and convert, and be healed.

Matt. 13. 14 And in them is fulfilled the prophecy of Esaias, which saith, By hearing ye shall hear, and shall not understand; and seeing ye shall see, and shall not perceive:

Rom. 11. 8 (According as it is written, God hath given them the spirit of slumber, eyes that they should not see, and

TIME, TUESDAY, APRIL 4 [NISAN 12], A. D. 30; PLACE, JERUSALEM.
Lord's Fourth and Last Passover.

U—CONCLUDED.

1 Jno. 2. 11 But he that hateth his brother is in darkness, and walketh in darkness, and knoweth not whither he goeth, because that darkness hath blinded his eyes.

X

Luke 16. 8 And the lord commended the unjust steward, because he had done wisely: for the children of this world are in their generation wiser than the children of light.

I Thes. 5. 5 Ye are all the children of light, and the children of the day: we are not of the night, nor of darkness.

I Jno. 2. 9 He that saith he is in the light, and hateth his brother, is in darkness even until now.

10 He that loveth his brother abideth in the light, and there is none occasion of stumbling in him.

Y

John 8. 59 Then took they up stones to cast at him: but Jesus hid himself, and went out of the temple, going through the midst of them, and so passed by.

CHAP. 12.

35 Then Jesus said unto them, Yet a
little while [s]is the light with you.
[t]Walk while ye have the light, lest
darkness come upon you: for [u]he that
walketh in darkness knoweth not
whither he goeth.

36 While ye have light, believe in
the light, that ye may be [x]the children
of light. [y]These things spake Jesus,
and departed, and did hide himself
from them.

Y—CONCLUDED.

went out of the temple, going through the midst of them, and so passed by.

John 11. 54 Jesus therefore walked no more openly among the Jews; but went thence unto a country near to the wilderness, into a city called Ephraim, and there continued with his disciples.

TIME, TUESDAY, APRIL 4 [NISAN 12], A. D. 30; PLACE, JERUSALEM.
Lord's Fourth and Last Passover.

C—CONCLUDED.

ears that they should not hear;) unto this day.

9 And David saith, Let their table be made a snare, and a trap, and a stumblingblock, and a recompense unto them:

10 Let their eyes be darkened, that they may not see, and bow down their back alway.

11 I say then, Have they stumbled that they should fall? God forbid: but *rather* through their fall salvation *is come* unto the Gentiles, for to provoke them to jealousy.

D

Isa. 6. 1 In the year that king Uzziah died I saw also the Lord sitting upon a throne, high and lifted up, and his train filled the temple.

Heb. 11. 13 These all died in faith, not having received the promises, but having seen them afar off, and were persuaded of *them*, and embraced *them*, and confessed that they were strangers and pilgrims on the earth.

E

John 7. 13 Howbeit no man spake openly of him for fear of the Jews.

John 9. 22 These *words* spake his parents, because they feared the Jews; for the

For E concluded see next page (478).

12: 37–50.

37 But though he had done so many
miracles before them, yet they believed
not on him:

38 That the saying of Esaias the
prophet might be fulfilled, which he
spake, [a]Lord, who hath believed our
report? [b]and to whom hath the arm of
the Lord been revealed?

39 Therefore they could not believe,
because that Esaias said again,

40 [c]He hath blinded their eyes, and
hardened their heart; that they should
not see with *their* eyes, nor understand
with *their* heart, and be converted, and
I should heal them.

41 [d]These things said Esaias, when
he saw his glory, and spake of him.

42 Nevertheless among the chief
rulers also many believed on him; but
[e]because of the Pharisees they did not

§ 171. REFLECTIONS OF OUR LORD UPON THE UNBELIEF OF THE JEWS

Third Day of the Week of our

E—CONCLUDED. See preceding page (477).

Jews had agreed already, that if any man did confess that he was Christ, he should be put out of the synagogue.

Acts 5. 41 And they departed from the presence of the council, rejoicing that they were counted worthy to suffer shame for his name.

F

Gen. 11. 4 And they said, Go to, let us build us a city, and a tower, whose top *may reach* unto heaven; and let us make us a name, lest we be scattered abroad upon the face of the whole earth.

Matt.23. 5 But all their works they do for to be seen of men: they make broad their phylacteries, and enlarge the borders of their garments,

Luke 16. 15 And he said unto them, Ye are they which justify yourselves before men; but God knoweth your hearts: for that which is highly esteemed among men is abomination in the sight of God.

John 5. 41 I receive not honour from men.

John 5. 44 How can ye believe, which receive honour one of another, and seek not the honour that *cometh* from God only?

I Thes.2. 6 Nor of men sought we glory, neither of you, nor *yet* of others, when we might have been burdensome, as the apostles of Christ.

Jas. 2. 1 My brethren, have not the faith of our Lord Jesus Christ, *the Lord* of glory, with respect of persons.

2 For if there come unto your assembly a man with a gold ring, in goodly apparel, and there come in also a poor man in vile raiment;

3 And ye have respect to him that weareth the gay clothing, and say unto him, Sit thou here in a good place; and say to the poor, Stand thou there, or sit here under my footstool:

4 Are ye not then partial in yourselves, and are become judges of evil thoughts?

G

Mark 9. 37 Whosoever shall receive one of such children in my name, receiveth me; and whosoever shall receive me, receiveth not me, but him that sent me.

1 Pet. 1. 21 Who by him do believe in God, that raised him up from the dead, and gave him glory; that your faith and hope might be in God.

H

John 14. 9 Jesus saith unto him, Have I been so long time with you, and yet hast thou not known me, Philip? he that hath seen me hath seen the Father; and how sayest thou *then*, show us the Father?

II Cor.4. 6 For God, who commanded the light to shine out of darkness, hath shined in our hearts, to *give* the light of the knowledge of the glory of God in the face of Jesus Christ.

I

John 3. 19 And this is the condemnation, that light is come into the world, and men loved darkness rather than light, because their deeds were evil.

John 8. 12 Then spake Jesus again unto them, saying, I am the light of the world: he that followeth me shall not walk in darkness, but shall have the light of life.

John 9. 5 As long as I am in the world, I am the light of the world.

John 9. 39 And Jesus said, For judgment I am come into this world, that they which see not might see; and that they which see might be made blind.

John 12. 35 Then Jesus said unto them, Yet a little while is the light with you. Walk while ye have the light, lest darkness come upon you: for he that walketh in darkness knoweth not whither he goeth.

36 While ye have light, believe in the light, that ye may be the children of light. These things spake Jesus, and departed, and did hide himself from them.

K

John 5. 45 Do not think that I will accuse you to the Father: there is *one* that accuseth you, *even* Moses, in whom ye trust.

John 8. 15 Ye judge after the flesh; I judge no man.

John 8. 26 I have many things to say and to judge of you: but he that sent me is true; and I speak to the world those things which I have heard of him.

L

Luke 9. 56 For the Son of man is not come to destroy men's lives, but to save *them*. And they went to another village.

Luke 19. 10 For the Son of man is come to seek and to save that which was lost.

John 3. 17 For God sent not his Son into the world to condemn the world; but that the world through him might be saved.

(CONCLUDED). TIME, TUESDAY, APRIL 4 [NISAN 12], A. D. 30; PLACE, JERUSALEM.
Lord's Fourth and Last Passover.

L—CONCLUDED.

I Jno. 4. 14 And we have seen and do testify that the Father sent the Son *to be* the Saviour of the world.

M

Luke 10. 16 He that heareth you heareth me; and he that despiseth you despiseth me; and he that despiseth me despiseth him that sent me.

N

Deut. 18. 19 And it shall come to pass, *that* whosoever will not hearken unto my words which he shall speak in my name, I will require *it* of him.

Mark 16. 16 He that believeth and is baptized shall be saved; but he that believeth not shall be damned.

John 3. 18 He that believeth on him is not condemned: but he that believeth not is condemned already, because he hath not believed in the name of the only begotten Son of God.

II Cor. 2. 15 For we are unto God a sweet savour of Christ, in them that are saved, and in them that perish:

16 To the one *we are* the savour of death unto death; and to the other the savour of life unto life. And who *is* sufficient for these things?

II Thes. 1. 8 In flaming fire taking vengeance on them that know not God, and that obey not the gospel of our Lord Jesus Christ:

O

John 8. 38 I speak that which I have seen with my Father: and ye do that which ye have seen with your father.

John 14. 10 Believest thou not that I am in the Father, and the Father in me? The words that I speak unto you I speak not of myself: but the Father that dwelleth in me, he doeth the works.

P

Deut. 18. 18 I will raise them up a Prophet from among their brethren, like unto thee, and will put my words in his mouth; and he shall speak unto them all that I shall command him.

John 17. 8 For I have given unto them the words which thou gavest me; and they have received *them*, and have known surely that I came out from thee, and they have believed that thou didst send me.

Rev. 1. 1 The revelation of Jesus Christ, which God gave unto him, to show unto his servants things which must shortly come to pass; and he sent and

CHAP. 12.

confess *him*, lest they should be put out
of the synagogue:
43 [f]For they loved the praise of men
more than the praise of God.
44 Jesus cried and said, [g]He that
believeth on me, believeth not on me,
but on him that sent me.
45 And [h]he that seeth me seeth him
that sent me.
46 [i]I am come a light into the world,
that whosoever believeth on me should
not abide in darkness.
47 And if any man hear my words,
and believe not, [k]I judge him not: for
[l]I came not to judge the world, but to
save the world.
48 [m]He that rejecteth me, and receiveth not my words, hath one that
judgeth him: [n]the word that I have
spoken, the same shall judge him in
the last day.
49 For [o]I have not spoken of myself;
but the Father which sent me, he gave
me a commandment, [p]what I should
say, and what I should speak.
50 And I know that [q]his commandment is life everlasting: whatsoever I
speak therefore, even as the Father
said unto me, so I speak. (p. 513.)

P—CONCLUDED.

signified *it* by his angel unto his servant John:

Q

John 6. 63 It is the Spirit that quickeneth; the flesh profiteth nothing: the words that I speak unto you, *they* are spirit, and *they* are life.

John 6. 68 Then Simon Peter answered him, Lord, to whom shall we go? thou hast the words of eternal life.

John 17. 3 And this is life eternal, that they might know thee the only true God, and Jesus Christ, whom thou hast sent.

§ 172. DESTRUCTION OF THE TEMPLE AND PERSECUTION FORETOLD.

Third Day of the Week of our

MATTHEW 24: 1–14.

1 And [a]Jesus went out, and departed from the temple: and his disciples came to *him* for to show him the buildings of the temple.

2 And Jesus said unto them, See ye not all these things? verily I say unto you, [b]There shall not be left here one stone upon another, that shall not be thrown down.

3 And as he sat upon the mount of Olives, [c]the disciples came unto him privately, saying, [d]Tell us, when shall these things be? and what *shall be* the sign of thy coming, and of the end of the world?

4 And Jesus answered and said unto them, [e]Take heed that no man deceive you.

5 For [f]many shall come in my name, saying, I am Christ; [g]and shall deceive many.

A

Mark 13. 1 and Luke 21. 5. *See text of topic.*

B

I Ki. 9. 7 Then will I cut off Israel out of the land which I have given them; and this house, which I have hallowed for my name, will I cast out of my sight; and Israel shall be a proverb and a byword among all people:

Jer. 5. 10 Go ye up upon her walls, and destroy; but make not a full end: take away her battlements; for they *are* not the LORD'S.

Jer. 26. 18 Micah the Morasthite prophesied in the days of Hezekiah king of Judah, and spake to all the people of Judah, saying, Thus saith the LORD of hosts; Zion shall be ploughed *like* a field, and Jerusalem shall become heaps, and the mountain of the house as the high places of a forest.

Mic. 3. 12 Therefore shall Zion for your sake be ploughed *as* a field, and Jerusalem shall become heaps, and the mountain of the house as the high places of the forest.

MARK 13: 1–13.

1 And [h]as he went out of the temple, one of his disciples saith unto him, Master, see what manner of stones and what buildings *are here!*

2 And Jesus answering said unto him, Seest thou these great buildings? [i]there shall not be left one stone upon another, that shall not be thrown down.

3 And as he sat upon the mount of Olives, over against the temple, Peter and James and John and Andrew asked him privately,

4 [k]Tell us, when shall these things be? and what *shall be* the sign when all these things shall be fulfilled?

5 And Jesus answering them began to say, [l]Take heed lest any *man* deceive you:

6 For many shall come in my name, saying, I am *Christ;* and shall deceive many.

B—CONCLUDED.

Luke 19. 44 And shall lay thee even with the ground, and thy children within thee; and they shall not leave in thee one stone upon another; because thou knewest not the time of thy visitation.

C

Mark 13. 3. *See text of topic.*

D

John 21. 21 Peter seeing him saith to Jesus, Lord, and what *shall* this man *do?*

22 Jesus saith unto him, If I will that he tarry till I come, what *is that* to thee? follow thou me.

Acts 1. 7 And he said unto them, It is not for you to know the times or the seasons, which the Father hath put in his own power.

I Thes. 5. 1 But of the times and the seasons, brethren, ye have no need that I write unto you.

E

Eph. 5. 6 Let no man deceive you with vain words: for because of these things cometh the wrath of God upon the children of disobedience.

TIME, TUESDAY, APRIL 4 [NISAN 12], A. D. 30; PLACE, JERUSALEM, MOUNT OF OLIVES.
Lord's Fourth and Last Passover.

21 : 5–19.

5 [m]And as some spake of the temple,
how it was adorned with goodly stones
and gifts, he said,

6 *As for* these things which ye behold,
the days will come, in the which [n]there
shall not be left one stone upon another,
that shall not be thrown down,

7 And they asked him, saying, Master,
but when shall these things be?
and what sign *will there be* when these
things shall come to pass?

8 And he said, Take heed that ye be
not deceived: for many shall come in
my name, saying, I am *Christ:* [o]and
the time draweth near: go ye not therefore
after them.

E—CONCLUDED.

Col. 2. 8 Beware lest any man spoil you through philosophy and vain deceit, after the tradition of men, after the rudiments of the world, and not after Christ.

Col. 2. 18 Let no man beguile you of your reward in a voluntary humility and worshipping of angels, intruding into those things which he hath not seen, vainly puffed up by his fleshly mind,

II Thes.2. 3 Let no man deceive you by any means: for *that day shall not come,* except there come a falling away first, and that man of sin be revealed, the son of perdition;

I. Jno.4. 1 Beloved, believe not every spirit, but try the spirits whether they are of God: because many false prophets are gone out into the world.

F

Jer. 14. 14 Then the LORD said unto me, The prophets prophesy lies in my name: I sent them not, neither have I commanded them, neither spake unto them: they prophesy unto you a false vision and divination, and a thing of nought, and the deceit of their heart.

Jer. 23. 21 I have not sent these prophets, yet they ran: I have not spoken to them, yet they prophesied.

Jer. 23. 25 I have heard what the prophets said, that prophesy lies in my name, saying, I have dreamed, I have dreamed.

Matt.24. 24 For there shall arise false Christs, and false prophets, and shall show great signs and wonders; insomuch that, if *it were* possible, they shall deceive the very elect.

F—CONCLUDED.

John 5. 43 I am come in my Father's name, and ye receive me not: if another shall come in his own name, him ye will receive.

G

Matt. 24. 11. *See text of topic.*

Acts 5. 36 For before these days rose up Theudas, boasting himself to be somebody; to whom a number of men, about four hundred, joined themselves: who was slain; and all, as many as obeyed him, were scattered, and brought to nought.

37 After this man rose up Judas of Galilee in the days of the taxing, and drew away much people after him: he also perished; and all, *even* as many as obeyed him, were dispersed.

Acts 8. 9 But there was a certain man, called Simon, which beforetime in the same city used sorcery, and bewitched the people of Samaria, giving out that himself was some great one:

10 To whom they all gave heed, from the least to the greatest, saying, This man is the great power of God.

II Pet.2. 1 But there were false prophets also among the people, even as there shall be false teachers among you, who privily shall bring in damnable heresies, even denying the Lord that bought them, and bring upon themselves swift destruction.

H

Matt. 24. 1 and Luke 21. 5. *See text of topic.*

I

Luke 19. 44. *See under B.*

K

Matt. 24. 3 and Luke 21. 7. *See text of topic.*

L

Jer. 29. 8 For thus saith the LORD of hosts, the God of Israel; Let not your prophets and your diviners, that *be* in the midst of you, deceive you, neither hearken to your dreams which ye cause to be dreamed.

Eph. 5. 6. *Under E.* II Thes. 2. 3. *Under E.*

M

Matt. 24. 1 and Mark 13. 1. *See text of topic.*

N

I Ki. 9. 7. *See under B.*

O

Matt. 3. 2 And saying, Repent ye: for the kingdom of heaven is at hand.

Matt. 4. 17 From that time Jesus began to preach, and to say, Repent: for the kingdom of heaven is at hand.

§172. DESTRUCTION OF THE TEMPLE AND PERSECUTION FORETOLD (CONT'D)
Third Day of the Week of ou

CHAP. 24.

6 [p]And ye shall hear of wars and rumours of wars: see that ye be not troubled: for all *these things* must come to pass, but the end is not yet.

7 For [q]nation shall rise against nation, and kingdom against kingdom: and there shall be famines, and pestilences, and earthquakes, in divers places.

8 All these *are* the beginning of sorrows.

P

Mark 13. 7 and Luke 21. 9. *See text of topic.*

Q

II Chr.15. 6 And nation was destroyed of nation, and city of city: for God did vex them with all adversity.

Isa. 19. 2 And I will set the Egyptians against the Egyptians: and they shall fight every one against his brother, and every one against his neighbour; city against city, *and* kingdom against kingdom.

Hag. 2. 22 And I will overthrow the throne of kingdoms, and I will destroy the strength of the kingdoms of the heathen; and I will overthrow the chariots, and those that ride in them; and the horses and their riders shall come down, every one by the sword of his brother.

Zech.14. 13 And it shall come to pass in that day, *that* a great tumult from the LORD shall be among them; and they shall lay hold every one on the hand of his neighbour, and his hand shall rise up against the hand of his neighbour.

R

Jer. 4. 27 For thus hath the LORD said, The whole land shall be desolate; yet will I not make a full end.

Jer. 5. 10. *See under B, page 480.*

S

Matt. 24. 8. *See text of topic.*

1

The import of the word in the original is, *the pains of a woman in travail.*

T

Matt. 10. 17. *See under H, page 484.*

Matt.10. 18 And ye shall be brought before governors and kings for my sake, for a testimony against them and the Gentiles.

Matt. 24. 9. *See text of topic.*
Rev. 2. 10. *See under H, page 484.*

CHAP. 13.

7 And when ye shall hear of wars and rumours of wars, be ye not troubled: for *such things* must needs be; [r]but the end *shall* not *be* yet.

8 For nation shall rise against nation, and kingdom against kingdom: and there shall be earthquakes in divers places, and there shall be famines and troubles: [s]these *are* the beginnings of [1]sorrows.

9 But [t]take heed to yourselves: for they shall deliver you up to councils; and in the synagogues ye shall be beaten: and ye shall be brought before rulers and kings for my sake, for a testimony against them. (p. 484.)

* * * * *

11 [u]But when they shall lead *you*, and deliver you up, take no thought beforehand what ye shall speak, neither do ye premeditate: but whatsoever shall be given you in that hour, that speak ye: for it is not ye that speak [x]but the Holy Ghost.

U

Ex. 24. 12 And the LORD said unto Moses, Come up to me into the mount, and be there: and I will give thee tables of stone, and a law, and commandments which I have written; that thou mayest teach them.

Matt.10. 19 But when they deliver you up, take no thought how or what ye shall speak: for it shall be given you in that same hour what ye shall speak.

Luke 12. 11 And when they bring you unto the synagogues, and *unto* magistrates, and powers, take ye no thought how or what thing ye shall answer, or what ye shall say:

Luke 21. 14, 15. *See text of topic.*

X

Acts 2. 4 And they were all filled with the Holy Ghost, and began to speak with other tongues, as the Spirit gave them utterance.

TIME, TUESDAY, APRIL 4 [NISAN 12], A. D. 30; PLACE, JERUSALEM, MOUNT OF OLIVES.
Lord's Fourth and Last Passover.

CHAP. 21.

9 [y]But when ye shall hear of wars and commotions, be not terrified: for these things must first come to pass; but the end *is* not by and by.

10 [z]Then said he unto them, Nation shall rise against nation, and kingdom against kingdom:

11 And great earthquakes shall be in divers places, and famines, and pestilences; and fearful sights and great signs shall there be from heaven.

12 [a]But before all these, they shall lay their hands on you, and persecute *you*, delivering *you* up to the synagogues, and [b]into prisons, [c]being brought before kings and rulers [d]for my name's sake.

13 And [e]it shall turn to you for a testimony.

14 [f]Settle *it* therefore in your hearts, not to meditate before what ye shall answer:

15 For I will give you a mouth and wisdom, [g]which all your adversaries shall not be able to gainsay nor resist.

X—CONCLUDED.

Acts 4. 8 Then Peter, filled with the Holy Ghost, said unto them, Ye rulers of the people, and elders of Israel,

Acts 4. 31 And when they had prayed, the place was shaken where they were assembled together; and they were all filled with the Holy Ghost, and they spake the word of God with boldness.

Y

Matt. 24. 6 and Mark 13. 7. *See text of topic.*

Z

Matt. 24. 7. *See text of topic.*

A

Mark 13. 9. *See text of topic.*

I Thes 2 14 For ye, brethren, became followers of the churches of God which in Judæa are in Christ Jesus: for ye also have suffered like things of your own countrymen, even as they *have* of the Jews:

A—CONCLUDED.

I Thes.2. 15 Who both killed the Lord Jesus, and their own prophets, and have persecuted us; and they please not God, and are contrary to all men:

I Pet. 4. 12 Beloved, think it not strange concerning the fiery trial which is to try you, as though some strange thing happened unto you:

13 But rejoice, inasmuch as ye are partakers of Christ's sufferings; that, when his glory shall be revealed, ye may be glad also with exceeding joy.

14 If ye be reproached for the name of Christ, happy *are ye;* for the Spirit of glory and of God resteth upon you: on their part he is evil spoken of, but on your part he is glorified.

Rev. 2. 10. *See under H, page 484.*

B

Acts 4. 3. *See under H, page 484.*

Acts 5. 18 And laid their hands on the apostles, and put them in the common prison.

Acts 12. 4 And when he had apprehended him, he put *him* in prison, and delivered *him* to four quaternions of soldiers to keep him; intending after Easter to bring him forth to the people.

Acts 16. 24 Who, having received such a charge, thrust them into the inner prison, and made their feet fast in the stocks.

C

Acts 25. 23 And on the morrow, when Agrippa was come, and Bernice, with great pomp, and was entered into the place of hearing, with the chief captains, and principal men of the city, at Festus' commandment Paul was brought forth.

D

I Pet. 2. 13 Submit yourselves to every ordinance of man for the Lord's sake: whether it be to the king, as supreme;

E

Phil. 1. 28 And in nothing terrified by your adversaries: which is to them an evident token of perdition, but to you of salvation, and that of God.

II Thes.1. 5 *Which is* a manifest token of the righteous judgment of God, that ye may be counted worthy of the kingdom of God, for which ye also suffer:

F

Matt. 10. 19. *See under U.*
Mark. 13. 11. *Text of topic.* Luke 12. 11. *Under U.*

G

Acts 6. 10 And they were not able to resist the wisdom and the spirit by which he spake.

§ 172. DESTRUCTION OF THE TEMPLE AND PERSECUTION FORETOLD (CONCL'D).

Third Day of the Week of our

CHAP. 24.

9 [h]Then shall they deliver you up to be afflicted, and shall kill you: and ye shall be hated of all nations for my name's sake.

10 And then shall many [i]be offended, and shall betray one another, and shall hate one another.

11 And [k]many false prophets shall rise, and [l]shall deceive many.

12 And because iniquity shall abound, the love of many shall wax cold.

13 [m]But he that shall endure unto the end, the same shall be saved.

14 And this [n]gospel of the kingdom [o]shall be preached in all the world for a witness unto all nations; and then shall the end come.

H

Matt.10. 17 But beware of men: for they will deliver you up to the councils, and they will scourge you in their synagogues;

Mark 13. 9 and Luke 21. 12. *See text of topic.*

John 15. 20 Remember the word that I said unto you, The servant is not greater than his lord. If they have persecuted me, they will also persecute you; if they have kept my saying, they will keep yours also.

John 16. 2 They shall put you out of the synagogues: yea, the time cometh, that whosoever killeth you will think that he doeth God service.

Acts 4. 2 Being grieved that they taught the people, and preached through Jesus the resurrection from the dead.

3 And they laid hands on them, and put *them* in hold unto the next day: for it was now eventide.

Acts 7. 59 And they stoned Stephen, calling upon *God*, and saying, Lord Jesus, receive my spirit.

Acts 12. 1 Now about that time Herod the king stretched forth *his* hands to vex certain of the church.

2 And he killed James the brother of John with the sword.

I Pet. 4. 16 Yet if *any man suffer* as a Christian, let him not be ashamed; but let him glorify God on this behalf.

CHAP. 13.

12 Now [p]the brother shall betray the brother to death, and the father the son; and children shall rise up against *their* parents, and shall cause them to be put to death.

13 [q]And ye shall be hated of all *men* for my name's sake: but [r]he that shall endure unto the end, [s]the same shall be saved. (p. 486.)

* * * * *

10 And the gospel must first be published among all nations. (p. 482.)

H—CONCLUDED.

Rev. 2. 10 Fear none of those things which thou shalt suffer: behold, the devil shall cast *some* of you into prison, that ye may be tried; and ye shall have tribulation ten days: be thou faithful unto death, and I will give thee a crown of life.

Rev. 2. 13 I know thy works, and where thou dwellest, *even* where Satan's seat *is:* and thou holdest fast my name, and hast not denied my faith, even in those days wherein Antipas *was* my faithful martyr, who was slain among you, where Satan dwelleth.

I

Matt.11. 6 And blessed is *he*, whosoever shall not be offended in me.

Matt.13. 57 And they were offended in him. But Jesus said unto them, A prophet is not without honour, save in his own country, and in his own house.

II Tim.1. 15 This thou knowest, that all they which are in Asia be turned away from me, of whom are Phygellus and Hermogenes.

II Tim.4. 10 For Demas hath forsaken me, having loved this present world, and is departed unto Thessalonica; Crescens to Galatia, Titus unto Dalmatia.

II Tim.4. 16 At my first answer no man stood with me, but all *men* forsook me: *I pray God* that it may not be laid to their charge.

K

Matt. 7. 15 Beware of false prophets, which come to you in sheep's clothing, but inwardly they are ravening wolves.

Acts 20. 29 For I know this, that after my departing shall grievous wolves enter in among you, not sparing the flock.

TIME, TUESDAY, APRIL 4 [NISAN 12], A. D. 30; PLACE, JERUSALEM, MOUNT OF OLIVES.
Lord's Fourth and Last Passover.

CHAP. 21.

16 [t]And ye shall be betrayed both by parents, and brethren, and kinsfolks, and friends; and [u]*some* of you shall they cause to be put to death.

17 And [x]ye shall be hated of all *men* for my name's sake.

18 [y]But there shall not a hair of your head perish.

19 In your patience possess ye your souls.

K—CONCLUDED.

II Cor.11. 13 For such *are* false apostles, deceitful workers, transforming themselves into the apostles of Christ.

II Pet.2. 1 But there were false prophets also among the people, even as there shall be false teachers among you, who privily shall bring in damnable heresies, even denying the Lord that bought them, and bring upon themselves swift destruction.

L

Matt. 24. 5. *See text of topic.*
Matt. 24. 24. *See under F, page 481.*

I Tim.4. 1 Now the Spirit speaketh expressly, that in the latter times some shall depart from the faith, giving heed to seducing spirits, and doctrines of devils;

M

Matt.10. 22 And ye shall be hated of all *men* for my name's sake: but he that endureth to the end shall be saved.

Mark 13. 13. *See text of topic.*

Heb. 3 6 But Christ as a son over his own house; whose house are we, if we hold fast the confidence and the rejoicing of the hope firm unto the end.

Heb. 3. 14 For we are made partakers of Christ, if we hold the beginning of our confidence steadfast unto the end;

Rev. 2. 10. *See under H.*

N

Matt. 4. 23 And Jesus went about all Galilee, teaching in their synagogues, and preaching the gospel of the kingdom, and healing all manner of sickness and all manner of disease among the people.

Matt. 9. 35 And Jesus went about all the cities and villages, teaching in their synagogues, and preaching the gospel of the kingdom, and healing every sickness and every disease among the people.

O

Rom.10. 18 But I say, Have they not heard?

O—CONCLUDED.

Yes verily, their sound went into all the earth, and their words unto the ends of the world.

Col. 1. 6 Which is come unto you, as *it is* in all the world; and bringeth forth fruit, as *it doth* also in you, since the day ye heard *of it*, and knew the grace of God in truth:

Col. 1. 23 If ye continue in the faith grounded and settled, and *be* not moved away from the hope of the gospel, which ye have heard, *and* which was preached to every creature which is under heaven; whereof I Paul am made a minister:

P

Matt. 13. 57. *Under I.* Luke 21. 16. *Text of topic.*

Q

Mic. 7. 6 For the son dishonoureth the father, the daughter riseth up against her mother, the daughter in law against her mother in law; a man's enemies *are* the men of his own house.

Matt.10. 21 And the brother shall deliver up the brother to death, and the father the child: and the children shall rise up against *their* parents, and cause them to be put to death.

Matt. 24. 10 and Luke 21. 16. *See text of topic.*

R

Matt. 24. 13 and Luke 21. 19. *See text of topic.*

S

Dan. 12. 12 Blessed *is* he that waiteth, and cometh to the thousand three hundred and five and thirty days.

Matt. 10. 22. *See under M.*
Matt. 24. 13. *Text of topic.* Heb. 3. 6, 14. *See under M.*

Rev. 2. 7 He that hath an ear, let him hear what the Spirit saith unto the churches; To him that overcometh will I give to eat of the tree of life, which is in the midst of the paradise of God.

Rev. 2. 10. *See under H.*

Rev. 3. 10 Because thou hast kept the word of my patience, I also will keep thee from the hour of temptation, which shall come upon all the world, to try them that dwell upon the earth.

T

Mic. 7. 6. *Under Q.* Mark 13. 12. *Text of topic.*

U

Acts 7. 59 and Acts 12. 2. *See under H.*

X

Matt. 10. 22. *See under M.*

II Tim.3. 12 Yea, and all that will live godly in Christ Jesus shall suffer persecution.

Y

Matt.10. 30 But the very hairs of your head are all numbered.

§ 173. SIGNS OF COMING DESTRUCTION.
Third Day of the Week of our

24: 15–42.

15 [a]When ye therefore shall see the abomination of desolation, spoken of by [b]Daniel the prophet, stand in the holy place, [c](whoso readeth, let him understand,)

16 Then let them which be in Judæa flee into the mountains:

17 Let him which is on the housetop not come down to take anything out of his house:

18 Neither let him which is in the field return back to take his clothes.

19 And [d]woe unto them that are with child, and to them that give suck in those days!

20 But pray ye that your flight be not in the winter, neither on the sabbath day:

21 For [e]then shall be great tribulation, such as was not since the beginning of the world to this time, no, nor ever shall be.

22 And except those days should be shortened, there should no flesh be saved: [f]but for the elect's sake those days shall be shortened.

A

Mark 13. 14 and Luke 21. 20. *See text of topic.*

B

Dan. 9. 27 And he shall confirm the covenant with many for one week: and in the midst of the week he shall cause the sacrifice and the oblation to cease, and for the overspreading of abominations he shall make *it* desolate, even until the consummation, and that determined shall be poured upon the desolate.

Dan. 12. 11 And from the time *that* the daily *sacrifice* shall be taken away, and the abomination that maketh desolate set up, *there shall be* a thousand two hundred and ninety days.

C

Dan. 9. 23 At the beginning of thy supplications the commandment came forth,

13: 14–37.

14 [g]But when ye shall see the abomination of desolation, [h]spoken of by Daniel the prophet, standing where it ought not, (let him that readeth understand,) then [i]let them that be in Judæa flee to the mountains:

15 And let him that is on the housetop not go down into the house, neither enter *therein*, to take any thing out of his house:

16 And let him that is in the field not turn back again for to take up his garment.

17 [k]But woe to them that are with child, and to them that give suck in those days!

18 And pray ye that your flight be not in the winter.

19 [l]For *in* those days shall be affliction, such as was not from the beginning of the creation which God created unto this time, neither shall be.

20 And except that the Lord had shortened those days, no flesh should be saved: but for the elect's sake, whom he hath chosen, he hath shortened the days.

C—Concluded.

and I am come to show *thee;* for thou *art* greatly beloved: therefore understand the matter, and consider the vision.

Dan. 9. 25 Know therefore and understand, *that* from the going forth of the commandment to restore and to build Jerusalem, unto the Messiah the Prince, *shall be* seven weeks, and threescore and two weeks: the street shall be built again, and the wall, even in troublous times.

D

Luke 23. 29 For, behold, the days are coming, in the which they shall say, Blessed *are* the barren, and the wombs that never bare, and the paps which never gave suck.

TIME, TUESDAY, APRIL 4 [NISAN 12], A. D. 30; PLACE, MOUNT OF OLIVES.
Lord's Fourth and Last Passover.

21: 20–36.

20 [m]And when ye shall see Jerusalem compassed with armies, then know that the desolation thereof is nigh.

21 Then let them which are in Judæa flee to the mountains; and let them which are in the midst of it depart out; and let not them that are in the countries enter thereinto.

22 For these be the days of vengeance, [n]that all things which are written may be fulfilled.

23 [o]But woe unto them that are with child, and to them that give suck, in those days! for there shall be great distress in the land, and wrath upon this people.

24 And they shall fall by the edge of the sword, and shall be led away captive into all nations: and Jerusalem shall be trodden down of the Gentiles, [p]until the times of the Gentiles be fulfilled.

E

Dan. 9. 26 And after threescore and two weeks shall Messiah be cut off, but not for himself: and the people of the prince that shall come shall destroy the city and the sanctuary; and the end thereof *shall be* with a flood, and unto the end of the war desolations are determined.

Dan. 12. 1 And at that time shall Michael stand up, the great prince which standeth for the children of thy people: and there shall be a time of trouble, such as never was since there was a nation *even* to that same time: and at that time thy people shall be delivered, every one that shall be found written in the book.

Joel 2. 2 A day of darkness and of gloominess, a day of clouds and of thick darkness, as the morning spread upon the mountains: a great people and a strong; there hath not been ever the like, neither shall be any more after it, *even* to the years of many generations.

F

Isa. 65. 8 Thus saith the LORD, As the new wine is found in the cluster, and *one* saith, Destroy it not; for a blessing *is* in it: so will I do for my servants' sake, that I may not destroy them all.

9 And I will bring forth a seed out of Jacob, and out of Judah an inheritor of my mountains: and mine elect shall inherit it, and my servants shall dwell there.

Zech.14. 2 For I will gather all nations against Jerusalem to battle; and the city shall be taken, and the houses rifled, and the women ravished; and half of the city shall go forth into captivity, and the residue of the people shall not be cut off from the city.

3 Then shall the LORD go forth, and fight against those nations, as when he fought in the day of battle.

G

Matt. 24. 15. *See text of topic.*

H

Dan. 9. 27. *See under B.*

I

Luke 21. 21. *See text of topic.*

K

Luke 21. 23. *Text of topic.* Luke 23. 29. *Under D.*

L

Deut.28. 15 But it shall come to pass, if thou wilt not hearken unto the voice of the LORD thy God, to observe to do all his commandments and his statutes which I command thee this day; that all these curses shall come upon thee, and overtake thee:

Dan. 9. 26, Dan. 12. 1 and Joel 2. 2. *See under E.*
Matt. 24. 21. *See text of topic.*

M

Matt. 24. 15 and Mark 13. 14. *See text of topic.*

N

Dan. 9. 26. *Under E.* Dan. 9. 27. *Under B.*
Zech.11. 1 Open thy doors, O Lebanon, that the fire may devour thy cedars

O

Matt. 24. 19. *See text of topic.*

P

Dan. 9. 27. *See under B.*
Dan 12. 7. And I heard the man clothed in linen, which *was* upon the waters of the river, when he held up his right hand and his left hand unto heaven, and sware by him that liveth for ever, that *it shall be* for a time, times, and a half; and when he shall have accomplished to scatter the power of the holy people, all these *things* shall be finished.

Rom.11. 25 For I would not, brethren, that ye should be ignorant of this mystery,

For P concluded see next page (488).

§ 173. SIGNS OF COMING DESTRUCTION (CONTINUED).
Third Day of the Week of our

CHAP. 24.

23 [q]Then if any man shall say unto you, Lo, here *is* Christ, or there; believe *it* not.

24 For [r]there shall arise false Christs, and false prophets, and shall show great signs and wonders; insomuch that, [s]if *it were* possible, they shall deceive the very elect.

25 Behold, I have told you before.

26 Wherefore if they shall say unto you, Behold, he is in the desert; go not forth: behold, *he is* in the secret chambers; believe *it* not.

27 [t]For as the lightning cometh out of the east, and shineth even unto the west; so shall also the coming of the Son of man be.

28 [u]For wheresoever the carcass is, there will the eagles be gathered together.

29 [x]Immediately after the tribulation of those days [y]shall the sun be darkened, and the moon shall not give her light, and the stars shall fall from heaven, and the powers of the heavens shall be shaken:

P—CONCLUDED. See preceding page (487). lest ye should be wise in your own conceits, that blindness in part is happened to Israel, until the fulness of the Gentiles be come in.

Q

Mark 13. 21. *See text of topic.*
Luke 17. 23 And they shall say to you, See here; or, see there: go not after *them*, nor follow *them*.
Luke 21. 8. *See text of § 172.*

R

Deut. 13. 1 If there arise among you a prophet, or a dreamer of dreams, and giveth thee a sign or a wonder,
Matt. 24. 5 For many shall come in my name, saying, I am Christ; and shall deceive many.
Matt. 24. 11 And many false prophets shall rise, and shall deceive many.

CHAP. 13.

21 [z]And then if any man shall say to you, Lo, here *is* Christ; or, lo, *he is* there; believe *him* not:

22 For false Christs and false prophets shall rise, and shall show signs and wonders, to seduce, if *it were* possible, even the elect.

23 But [a]take ye heed: behold, I have foretold you all things.

24 [b]But in those days, after that tribulation, the sun shall be darkened, and the moon shall not give her light,

25 And the stars of heaven shall fall, and the powers that are in heaven shall be shaken.

R—CONCLUDED.

II Thes. 2. 9 *Even him*, whose coming is after the working of Satan with all power and signs and lying wonders,
10 And with all deceivableness of unrighteousness in them that perish; because they received not the love of the truth, that they might be saved.
11 And for this cause God shall send them strong delusion, that they should believe a lie:
Rev. 13. 13 And he doeth great wonders, so that he maketh fire come down from heaven on the earth in the sight of men,

S

John 6. 37 All that the Father giveth me shall come to me; and him that cometh to me I will in no wise cast out.
John 10. 28 And I give unto them eternal life; and they shall never perish, neither shall any *man* pluck them out of my hand.
29 My Father, which gave *them* me, is greater than all; and no *man* is able to pluck *them* out of my Father's hand.
Rom. 8. 28 And we know that all things work together for good to them that love God, to them who are the called according to *his* purpose.
29 For whom he did foreknow, he also did predestinate *to be* conformed to the image of his Son, that he might be the first-born among many brethren.
30 Moreover, whom he did predesti-

TIME, TUESDAY, APRIL 4 [NISAN 12], A. D. 30; PLACE, MOUNT OF OLIVES.
Lord's Fourth and Last Passover.

CHAP. 21.

25 [c]And there shall be signs in the sun, and in the moon, and in the stars; and upon the earth distress of nations, with perplexity; the sea and the waves roaring;

26 Men's hearts failing them for fear, and for looking after those things which are coming on the earth: [d]for the powers of heaven shall be shaken.

S—CONCLUDED.

nate, them he also called: and whom he called, them he also justified: and whom he justified, them he also glorified.

II Tim. 2. 19 Nevertheless the foundation of God standeth sure, having this seal, The Lord knoweth them that are his. And, Let every one that nameth the name of Christ depart from iniquity.

I Pet. 1. 5 Who are kept by the power of God through faith unto salvation ready to be revealed in the last time.

T

Luke 17. 24 For as the lightning, that lighteneth out of the one *part* under heaven, shineth unto the other *part* under heaven; so shall also the Son of man be in his day.

U

Job 39. 30 Her young ones also suck up blood: and where the slain *are*, there *is* she.

Luke 17. 37 And they answered and said unto him, Where, Lord? And he said unto them, Wheresoever the body *is*, thither will the eagles be gathered together.

X

Dan. 7. 11 I beheld then, because of the voice of the great words which the horn spake: I beheld *even* till the beast was slain, and his body destroyed, and given to the burning flame.

12 As concerning the rest of the beasts, they had their dominion taken away: yet their lives were prolonged for a season and time.

Y

Isa. 13. 10 For the stars of heaven and the constellations thereof shall not give their light: the sun shall be darkened in his going forth, and the moon shall not cause her light to shine.

Y—CONCLUDED.

Eze. 32. 7 And when I shall put thee out, I will cover the heaven, and make the stars thereof dark; I will cover the sun with a cloud, and the moon shall not give her light.

Joel 2. 10 The earth shall quake before them; the heavens shall tremble: the sun and the moon shall be dark, and the stars shall withdraw their shining:

Joel 2. 31 The sun shall be turned into darkness, and the moon into blood, before the great and the terrible day of the LORD come.

Joel 3. 15 The sun and the moon shall be darkened, and the stars shall withdraw their shining.

Amos 5. 20 *Shall* not the day of the LORD *be* darkness, and not light? even very dark, and no brightness in it?

Amos 8. 9 And it shall come to pass in that day, saith the Lord GOD, that I will cause the sun to go down at noon, and I will darken the earth in the clear day:

Mark 13. 24 and Luke 21. 25. *See text of topic.*

Acts 2. 20 The sun shall be turned into darkness, and the moon into blood, before that great and notable day of the Lord come:

Rev. 6. 12 And I beheld when he had opened the sixth seal, and, lo, there was a great earthquake; and the sun became black as sackcloth of hair, and the moon became as blood:

Z

Matt. 24. 23. *See text of topic.*
Luke 17. 23 and Luke 21. 8. *See under Q.*

A

II Pet. 3. 17 Ye therefore, beloved, seeing ye know *these things* before, beware lest ye also, being led away with the error of the wicked, fall from your own steadfastness.

B

Dan. 7. 10 A fiery stream issued and came forth from before him: thousand thousands ministered unto him, and ten thousand times ten thousand stood before him: the judgment was set, and the books were opened.

Zeph. 1. 15 That day *is* a day of wrath, a day of trouble and distress, a day of wasteness and desolation, a day of darkness and gloominess, a day of clouds and thick darkness.

Matt. 24. 29, etc., and Luke 21. 25. *See text of topic.*

C

Matt. 24. 29 and Mark 13. 24. *See text of topic.*
II Pet. 3. 10. *See under S, page 492.*

For C concluded and D see next page (490).

§ 173. SIGNS OF COMING DESTRUCTION (CONTINUED).
Third Day of the Week of our

CHAP. 24.

30 [e]And then shall appear the sign of the Son of man in heaven; [f]and then shall all the tribes of the earth mourn, [g]and they shall see the Son of man coming in the clouds of heaven with power and great glory.

31 [h]And he shall send his angels [1]with a great sound of a trumpet, and they shall gather together his elect from the four winds, from one end of heaven to the other.

32 Now learn a [i]parable of the fig tree; When his branch is yet tender, and putteth forth leaves, ye know that summer *is* nigh:

33 So likewise ye, when ye shall see all these things, know [k]that it is near, *even* at the doors.

34 Verily I say unto you, [l]This generation shall not pass, till all these things be fulfilled.

35 [m]Heaven and earth shall pass away, but my words shall not pass away.

C—CONCLUDED. See preceding page (489).

II Pet.3. 12 Looking for and hasting unto the coming of the day of God, wherein the heavens being on fire shall be dissolved, and the elements shall melt with fervent heat?

D

Matt. 24. 29. *See text of topic.*

E

Dan. 7. 13 I saw in the night visions, and, behold, *one* like the Son of man came with the clouds of heaven, and came to the Ancient of days, and they brought him near before him.

F

Zech.12. 12 And the land shall mourn, every family apart; the family of the house of David apart, and their wives apart; the family of the house of Nathan apart, and their wives apart:

G

Matt.16. 27 For the Son of man shall come

CHAP. 13.

26 [n]And then shall they see the Son of man coming in the clouds with great power and glory.

27 And then shall he send his angels, and shall gather together his elect from the four winds, from the uttermost part of the earth to the uttermost part of heaven.

28 [o]Now learn a parable of the fig tree: When her branch is yet tender, and putteth forth leaves, ye know that summer is near:

29 So ye in like manner, when ye shall see these things come to pass, know that it is nigh, *even* at the doors.

30 Verily I say unto you, that this generation shall not pass, till all these things be done.

31 Heaven and earth shall pass away: but [p]my words shall not pass away.

G—CONCLUDED.

in the glory of his Father with his angels; and then he shall reward every man according to his works.

Mark 13. 26. *See text of topic.*

Rev. 1. 7 Behold, he cometh with clouds; and every eye shall see him, and they *also* which pierced him: and all kindreds of the earth shall wail because of him. Even so. Amen.

H

Matt.13. 41 The Son of man shall send forth his angels, and they shall gather out of his kingdom all things that offend, and them which do iniquity

I Cor.15. 52 In a moment, in the twinkling of an eye, at the last trump: for the trumpet shall sound, and the dead shall be raised incorruptible, and we shall be changed.

I Thes.4. 16 For the Lord himself shall descend from heaven with a shout, with the voice of the archangel, and with the trump of God: and the dead in Christ shall rise first:

1

Or, *with a trumpet, and a great voice.*

I

Mark 13. 28, 29 and Luke 21. 29. *See text of topic.*

TIME, TUESDAY, APRIL 4 [NISAN 12], A. D. 30; PLACE, MOUNT OF OLIVES.
Lord's Fourth and Last Passover.

CHAP. 21.

27 And then shall they see the Son of man [q]coming in a cloud with power and great glory.

28 And when these things begin to come to pass, then look up, and lift up your heads; for [r]your redemption draweth nigh.

29 And he spake to them a parable; Behold the fig tree, and all the trees;

30 When they now shoot forth, ye see and know of your own selves that summer is now nigh at hand.

31 So likewise ye, when ye see these things come to pass, know ye that the kingdom of God is nigh at hand.

32 Verily I say unto you, This generation shall not pass away, till all be fulfilled.

33 Heaven and earth shall pass away; but my words shall not pass away.

K

Jas. 5. 9 Grudge not one against another, brethren, lest ye be condemned: behold, the judge standeth before the door.

L

Matt. 16. 28 Verily I say unto you, There be some standing here, which shall not taste of death, till they see the Son of man coming in his kingdom.

Matt. 23. 36 Verily I say unto you, All these things shall come upon this generation.

Mark 13. 30 and Luke 21. 32. *See text of topic.*

M

Ps. 102. 26 They shall perish, but thou shalt endure: yea, all of them shall wax old like a garment; as a vesture shalt thou change them, and they shall be changed:

Isa. 51. 6 Lift up your eyes to the heavens, and look upon the earth beneath: for the heavens shall vanish away like smoke, and the earth shall wax old like a garment, and they that dwell therein shall die in like manner: but my salvation shall be for ever, and my righteousness shall not be abolished.

Jer. 31. 35 Thus saith the LORD, which giveth the sun for a light by day, *and* the ordinances of the moon and of the stars for a light by night, which divideth the sea when the waves thereof roar; The LORD of hosts *is* his name:

M—CONCLUDED.

36 If those ordinances depart from before me, saith the LORD, *then* the seed of Israel also shall cease from being a nation before me for ever.

Matt. 5. 18 For verily I say unto you, Till heaven and earth pass, one jot or one tittle shall in no wise pass from the law, till all be fulfilled.

Mark 13. 31 and Luke 21. 33. *See text of topic.*

Heb. 1. 11 They shall perish, but thou remainest: and they all shall wax old as doth a garment;

N

Dan. 7. 13. *See under E.*

Dan. 7. 14 And there was given him dominion, and glory, and a kingdom, that all people, nations, and languages, should serve him: his dominion *is* an everlasting dominion, which shall not pass away, and his kingdom *that* which shall not be destroyed.

Matt. 16. 27. *See under G.*

Matt. 24. 30. *See text of topic.*

Mark 14. 62 And Jesus said, I am: and ye shall see the Son of man sitting on the right hand of power, and coming in the clouds of heaven.

Acts 1. 11 Which also said, Ye men of Galilee, why stand ye gazing up into heaven? this same Jesus, which is taken up from you into heaven, shall so come in like manner as ye have seen him go into heaven.

I Thes. 4. 16. *See under H.*

II Thes. 1. 7 And to you who are troubled rest with us, when the Lord Jesus shall be revealed from heaven with his mighty angels,

II Thes. 1. 10 When he shall come to be glorified in his saints, and to be admired in all them that believe (because our testimony among you was believed) in that day.

Rev. 1. 7. *See under G.*

O

Matt. 24. 32 and Luke 21. 29, etc. *See text of topic.*

P

Ps. 102. 26. *See under M.*

Isa. 40. 8 The grass withereth, the flower fadeth: but the word of our God shall stand for ever.

Isa. 51. 6 *See under M.*

Q

Matt. 24. 30. *See text of topic.*

Acts 1. 11. *Under N.* Rev. 1. 7. *Under G.*

For Q concluded and R see next page (492).

§ 173. SIGNS OF COMING DESTRUCTION (CONCLUDED).
Third Day of the Week of our

CHAP. 24.

36 [s]But of that day and hour knoweth no *man*, no, not the angels of heaven, [t]but my Father only.

37 But as the days of Noe *were*, so shall also the coming of the Son of man be.

38 [u]For as in the days that were before the flood they were eating and drinking, marrying and giving in marriage, until the day that Noe entered into the ark,

39 And knew not until the flood came, and took them all away; so shall also the coming of the Son of man be.

40 [x]Then shall two be in the field; the one shall be taken, and the other left.

41 Two *women shall be* grinding at the mill; the one shall be taken, and the other left.

42 [y]Watch therefore; for ye know not what hour your Lord doth come.

Q—CONCLUDED.

Rev. 14. 14 And I looked, and behold a white cloud, and upon the cloud *one* sat like unto the Son of man, having on his head a golden crown, and in his hand a sharp sickle.

R

Rom. 8. 19 For the earnest expectation of the creature waiteth for the manifestation of the sons of God.

Rom. 8. 23 And not only *they*, but ourselves also, which have the first-fruits of the Spirit, even we ourselves groan within ourselves, waiting for the adoption, *to wit*, the redemption of our body.

S

Mark 13. 32. *See text of topic.*

Acts 1. 7 And he said unto them, It is not for you to know the times or the seasons, which the Father hath put in his own power.

I Thes.5. 2 For yourselves know perfectly that the day of the Lord so cometh as a thief in the night.

CHAP. 13.

32 But of that day and *that* hour knoweth no man, no, not the angels which are in heaven, neither the Son, but the Father.

33 [z]Take ye heed, watch and pray: for ye know not when the time is.

34 [a]*For the Son of man is* as a man taking a far journey, who left his house, and gave authority to his servants, and to every man his work, and commanded the porter to watch.

35 [b]Watch ye therefore: for ye know not when the master of the house cometh, at even, or at midnight, or at the cockcrowing, or in the morning:

36 Lest coming suddenly he find you sleeping.

37 And what I say unto you I say unto all, Watch. (p. 506.)

S—CONCLUDED.

II Pet.3. 10 But the day of the Lord will come as a thief in the night; in the which the heavens shall pass away with a great noise, and the elements shall melt with fervent heat, the earth also and the works that are therein shall be burned up.

T

Zech.14. 7 But it shall be one day which shall be known to the LORD, not day, nor night: but it shall come to pass, *that* at evening time it shall be light.

U

Gen. 6. 3 And the LORD said, My Spirit shall not always strive with man, for that he also *is* flesh: yet his days shall be a hundred and twenty years.

4 There were giants in the earth in those days; and also after that, when the sons of God came in unto the daughters of men, and they bare *children* to them, the same *became* mighty men which *were* of old, men of renown.

5 And GOD saw that the wickedness of man *was* great in the earth, and *that* every imagination of the thoughts of his heart *was* only evil continually.

Gen. 7. 5 And Noah did according unto all that the LORD commanded him.

TIME, TUESDAY, APRIL 4 [NISAN 12], A. D. 30; PLACE, MOUNT OF OLIVES.
Lord's Fourth and Last Passover.

CHAP. 21.

34 And [c]take heed to yourselves, lest
at any time your hearts be overcharged
with surfeiting, and drunkenness, and
cares of this life, and *so* that day come
upon you unawares.
35 For [d]as a snare shall it come on
all them that dwell on the face of the
whole earth.
36 [e]Watch ye therefore, and [f]pray
always, that ye may be accounted
worthy to escape all these things that
shall come to pass, and [g]to stand before
the Son of man. (p. 439.)

U—CONCLUDED.

Luke 17. 26 And as it was in the days of Noe, so shall it be also in the days of the Son of man.

I Pet. 3. 20 Which sometime were disobedient, when once the longsuffering of God waited in the days of Noah, while the ark was a preparing, wherein few, that is, eight souls were saved by water.

X

Luke 17. 34 I tell you, in that night there shall be two *men* in one bed; the one shall be taken, and the other shall be left.

35 Two *women* shall be grinding together; the one shall be taken, and the other left.

36 Two *men* shall be in the field; the one shall be taken, and the other left.

Y

Matt. 25. 13 Watch therefore; for ye know neither the day nor the hour wherein the Son of man cometh.

Mark 13. 33, etc., and Luke 21. 36. *See text of topic.*

Rom. 13. 11 And that, knowing the time, that now *it is* high time to awake out of sleep: for now *is* our salvation nearer than when we believed.

I Cor. 16. 13 Watch ye, stand fast in the faith, quit you like men, be strong.

I Thes. 5. 6 Therefore let us not sleep, as *do* others; but let us watch and be sober.

I Pet. 4. 7 But the end of all things is at hand: be ye therefore sober, and watch unto prayer.

I Pet. 5. 8 Be sober, be vigilant; because your adversary, the devil, as a roaring lion, walketh about, seeking whom he may devour:

Rev. 3. 2 Be watchful, and strengthen the things which remain, that are ready to die: for I have not found thy works perfect before God.

Y—CONCLUDED.

Rev. 3. 3 Remember therefore how thou hast received and heard, and hold fast, and repent. If therefore thou shalt not watch, I will come on thee as a thief, and thou shalt not know what hour I will come upon thee.

Rev. 16. 15 Behold, I come as a thief. Blessed *is* he that watcheth, and keepeth his garments, lest he walk naked, and they see his shame.

Z

Matt. 24. 42. *Text of topic.* Matt. 25. 13. *Under Y.*

Luke 12. 40 Be ye therefore ready also: for the Son of man cometh at an hour when ye think not.

Luke 21. 34. *See text of topic.*
I Thes. 5. 6 and Rom. 13. 11. *See under Y.*

A

Matt. 24. 45 Who then is a faithful and wise servant, whom his lord hath made ruler over his household, to give them meat in due season?

Matt. 25. 14 For *the kingdom of heaven is* as a man traveling into a far country, *who* called his own servants, and delivered unto them his goods.

B

Matt. 24. 42. *See text of topic.*

Matt. 24. 44 Therefore be ye also ready: for in such an hour as ye think not the Son of man cometh.

II Pet. 3. *Read entire chapter.* Rev. 3. 3. *Under Y.*

C

Rom. 13. 13 Let us walk honestly, as in the day; not in rioting and drunkenness, not in chambering and wantonness, not in strife and envying:

I Thes. 5. 6 and I Pet. 4. 7. *See under Y.*

D

I Thes. 5. 2 and II Pet. 3. 10. *See under S.*
Rev. 3. 3 and Rev. 16. 15. *See under Y.*

E

Matt. 24. 42. *See text of topic.*
Matt. 25. 13. *Under Y.* Mark. 13. 33. *Text of topic.*

F

Luke 18. 1 And he spake a parable unto them *to this end*, that men ought always to pray, and not to faint;

G

Ps. 1. 5 Therefore the ungodly shall not stand in the judgment, nor sinners in the congregation of the righteous.

Eph. 6. 13 Wherefore take unto you the whole armour of God, that ye may be able to withstand in the evil day, and having done all, to stand.

I Jno. 2. 28 And now, little children, abide in him; that, when he shall appear, we may have confidence, and not be ashamed before him at his coming.

§ 174. EXHORTATION TO WATCHFULNESS.
Third Day of the Week of our

24: 43–51.

43 [a]But know this, that if the goodman of the house had known in what
watch the thief would come, he would
have watched, and would not have suffered his house to be broken up.

44 [b]Therefore be ye also ready: for
in such an hour as ye think not the
Son of man cometh.

45 [c]Who then is a faithful and wise
servant, whom his lord hath made ruler
over his household, to give them meat
in due season?

46 [d]Blessed *is* that servant, whom his
lord when he cometh shall find so doing.

47 Verily I say unto you, That [e]he
shall make him ruler over all his goods.

48 But and if that evil servant shall
say in his heart, [f]My lord delayeth his
coming;

49 And shall begin to smite *his* fellow
servants, and to eat and drink with the
drunken;

50 The lord of that servant shall
come in a day when he looketh not for
him, and in an hour that he is not
aware of,

51 And shall [1]cut him asunder, and
appoint *him* [g]his portion with the hypocrites: [h]there shall be weeping and
gnashing of teeth.

A

Luke 12. 39 And this know, that if the goodman of the house had known what hour the thief would come, he would have watched, and not have suffered his house to be broken through.

I Thes. 5. 2 For yourselves know perfectly that the day of the Lord so cometh as a thief in the night.

I Pet. 3. 10 But the day of the Lord will come as a thief in the night; in the which the heavens shall pass away with a great noise, and the elements

A—Concluded.

shall melt with fervent heat, the earth also and the works that are therein shall be burned up.

Rev. 3. 3 Remember therefore how thou hast received and heard, and hold fast, and repent. If therefore thou shalt not watch, I will come on thee as a thief, and thou shalt not know what hour I will come upon thee.

Rev. 16. 15 Behold, I come as a thief. Blessed *is* he that watcheth, and keepeth his garments, lest he walk naked, and they see his shame.

B

Matt. 25. 13 Watch therefore; for ye know neither the day nor the hour wherein the Son of man cometh.

Phil. 4. 5 Let your moderation be known unto all men. The Lord *is* at hand.

I Thes. 5. 6 Therefore let us not sleep, as *do* others; but let us watch and be sober.

Jas. 5. 9 Grudge not one against another, brethren, lest ye be condemned: behold, the judge standeth before the door.

C

Luke 12. 42 And the Lord said, Who then is that faithful and wise steward, whom *his* lord shall make ruler over his household, to give *them their* portion of meat in due season?

Acts 20. 28 Take heed therefore unto yourselves, and to all the flock, over the which the Holy Ghost hath made you overseers, to feed the church of God, which he hath purchased with his own blood.

I Cor. 4. 2 Moreover it is required in stewards, that a man be found faithful.

I Tim. 1. 12 And I thank Christ Jesus our Lord, who hath enabled me, for that he counted me faithful, putting me into the ministry:

II Tim. 2. 2 And the things that thou hast heard of me among many witnesses, the same commit thou to faithful men, who shall be able to teach others also.

Heb. 3. 5 And Moses verily *was* faithful in all his house as a servant, for a testimony of those things which were to be spoken after;

D

I Tim. 4. 7 But refuse profane and old wives' fables, and exercise thyself *rather* unto godliness.

8 For bodily exercise profiteth little: but godliness is profitable unto all things, having promise of the life that now is, and of that which is to come.

Rev. 16. 15. *See under A.*

Time, Tuesday, April 4 [Nisan 12], A. D. 30; Place, Mount of Olives.
Lord's Fourth and Last Passover.

E

Dan. 12. 3 And they that be wise shall shine as the brightness of the firmament; and they that turn many to righteousness, as the stars for ever and ever.

Matt.25. 21 His lord said unto him, Well done, *thou* good and faithful servant: thou hast been faithful over a few things, I will make thee ruler over many things: enter thou into the joy of thy lord.

Matt.25. 23 His lord said unto him, Well done, good and faithful servant; thou hast been faithful over a few things, I will make thee ruler over many things: enter thou into the joy of thy lord.

Luke 12. 37 Blessed *are* those servants, whom the lord when he cometh shall find watching: verily I say unto you, that he shall gird himself, and make them to sit down to meat, and will come forth and serve them.

Luke 19. 17 And he said unto him, Well, thou good servant: because thou hast been faithful in a very little, have thou authority over ten cities.

Luke 22. 29 And I appoint unto you a kingdom, as my Father hath appointed unto me;

30 That ye may eat and drink at my table in my kingdom, and sit on thrones judging the twelve tribes of Israel.

John 12. 26 If any man serve me, let him follow me; and where I am, there shall also my servant be: if any man serve me, him will *my* Father honour.

II Tim.2. 12 If we suffer, we shall also reign with *him:* if we deny *him,* he also will deny us:

I Pet. 5. 4 And when the chief Shepherd shall appear, ye shall receive a crown of glory that fadeth not away.

Rev. 3. 21 To him that overcometh will I grant to sit with me in my throne, even as I also overcame, and am set down with my Father in his throne.

Rev. 21. 7 He that overcometh shall inherit all things; and I will be his God, and he shall be my son.

F

Eccl. 8. 11 Because sentence against an evil work is not executed speedily, therefore the heart of the sons of men is fully set in them to do evil.

Eze. 12. 21 And the word of the Lord came unto me, saying,

22 Son of man, what *is* that proverb *that* ye have in the land of Israel, saying, The days are prolonged, and every vision faileth?

F—Concluded.

Eze. 12. 23 Tell them therefore, Thus saith the Lord God; I will make this proverb to cease, and they shall no more use it as a proverb in Israel; but say unto them, The days are at hand, and the effect of every vision.

Eze. 12. 26 Again the word of the Lord came to me, saying,

27 Son of man, behold, *they of* the house of Israel say, The vision that he seeth *is* for many days *to come,* and he prophesieth of the times *that are* far off.

28 Therefore say unto them, Thus saith the Lord God; There shall none of my words be prolonged any more, but the word which I have spoken shall be done, saith the Lord God.

II Pet.3. 3 Knowing this first, that there shall come in the last days scoffers, walking after their own lusts,

4 And saying, Where is the promise of his coming? for since the fathers fell asleep, all things continue as *they were* from the beginning of the creation.

5 For this they willingly are ignorant of, that by the word of God the heavens were of old, and the earth standing out of the water and in the water:

1 Or, *cut him off.*

G

Job 20. 29 This *is* the portion of a wicked man from God, and the heritage appointed unto him by God.

Ps. 11. 6 Upon the wicked he shall rain snares, fire and brimstone, and a horrible tempest: *this shall be* the portion of their cup.

Isa. 33. 14 The sinners in Zion are afraid; fearfulness hath surprised the hypocrites. Who among us shall dwell with the devouring fire? who among us shall dwell with everlasting burnings?

H

Matt. 8. 12 But the children of the kingdom shall be cast out into outer darkness: there shall be weeping and gnashing of teeth.

Matt.25. 30 And cast ye the unprofitable servant into outer darkness: there shall be weeping and gnashing of teeth.

Luke 13. 28 There shall be weeping and gnashing of teeth, when ye shall see Abraham, and Isaac, and Jacob, and all the prophets, in the kingdom of God, and you *yourselves* thrust out.

§ 175. THE PARABLE OF THE TEN VIRGINS.

Third Day of the Week of our

25: 1-13.

1 Then shall the kingdom of heaven be likened unto ten virgins, which took their lamps, and went forth to meet [a]the bridegroom.

2 [b]And five of them were wise, and five *were* foolish.

3 They that *were* foolish took their lamps, and took [c]no oil with them:

4 But the wise took oil in their vessels with their lamps.

5 While the bridegroom tarried, [d]they all slumbered and slept.

6 And at midnight [e]there was a cry made, Behold, the bridegroom cometh; go ye out to meet him.

7 Then all those virgins arose, and [f]trimmed their lamps.

8 And the foolish said unto the wise, Give us of your oil; for our lamps are [1]gone out.

9 But the wise answered, saying, *Not so;* lest there be not enough for us and you: but go ye rather to them that sell, and buy for yourselves.

10 And while they went to buy, the bridegroom came; and they that were ready went in with him to the marriage: and the [g]door was shut.

11 Afterward came also the other virgins, saying, [h]Lord, Lord, open to us.

12 But he answered and said, Verily I say unto you, [i]I know you not.

13 [k]Watch therefore; for ye know neither the day nor the hour wherein the Son of man cometh.

A

Eph. 5. 29 For no man ever yet hated his own flesh; but nourisheth and cherisheth it, even as the Lord the church:
30 For we are members of his body, of his flesh, and of his bones.

A—Concluded.

Rev. 19. 7 Let us be glad and rejoice, and give honour to him: for the marriage of the Lamb is come, and his wife hath made herself ready.

Rev. 21. 2 And I John saw the holy city, new Jerusalem, coming down from God out of heaven, prepared as a bride adorned for her husband.

Rev. 21. 9 And there came unto me one of the seven angels which had the seven vials full of the seven last plagues, and talked with me, saying, Come hither, I will show thee the bride, the Lamb's wife.

B

Matt.13. 47 Again, the kingdom of heaven is like unto a net, that was cast into the sea, and gathered of every kind:

Matt.22. 10 So those servants went out into the highways, and gathered together all as many as they found, both bad and good: and the wedding was furnished with guests.

I Cor.10. 5 But with many of them God was not well pleased: for they were overthrown in the wilderness.

I Jno. 2. 19 They went out from us, but they were not of us; for if they had been of us, they would *no doubt* have continued with us: but *they went out,* that they might be made manifest that they were not all of us.

C

II Tim.3. 5 Having a form of godliness, but denying the power thereof: from such turn away.

Tit. 1. 16 They profess that they know God; but in works they deny *him,* being abominable, and disobedient, and unto every good work reprobate.

D

Mark 14. 37 And he cometh, and findeth them sleeping, and saith unto Peter, Simon, sleepest thou? couldest not thou watch one hour?

Rom.13. 11 And that, knowing the time, that now *it is* high time to awake out of sleep: for now *is* our salvation nearer than when we believed.

Eph. 5. 14 Wherefore he saith, Awake thou that sleepest, and arise from the dead, and Christ shall give thee light.

I Thes.5. 6 Therefore let us not sleep, as *do* others; but let us watch and be sober.

E

Matt.24. 31 And he shall send his angels with a great sound of a trumpet, and they shall gather together his elect from the

Time, Tuesday, April 4 [Nisan 12], A. D. 30; Place, Mount of Olives.
Lord's Fourth and Last Passover.

E—Concluded

four winds, from one end of heaven to the other.

I Thes.4. 16 For the Lord himself shall descend from heaven with a shout, with the voice of the archangel, and with the trump of God: and the dead in Christ shall rise first:

F

Luke 12. 35 Let your loins be girded about, and *your* lights burning;

II Pet.3. 14 Wherefore, beloved, seeing that ye look for such things, be diligent that ye may be found of him in peace, without spot, and blameless.

Rev. 2. 5 Remember therefore from whence thou art fallen, and repent, and do the first works; or else I will come unto thee quickly, and will remove thy candlestick out of his place, except thou repent.

1

Or, *going out.*

G

Luke 13. 25 When once the master of the house is risen up, and hath shut to the door, and ye begin to stand without, and to knock at the door, saying, Lord, Lord, open unto us; and he shall answer and say unto you, I know you not whence ye are:

Heb. 3. 18 And to whom sware he that they should not enter into his rest, but to them that believed not?

19 So we see that they could not enter in because of unbelief.

H

Matt. 7. 21 Not every one that saith unto me, Lord, Lord, shall enter into the kingdom of heaven; but he that doeth the will of my Father which is in heaven.

22 Many will say to me in that day, Lord, Lord, have we not prophesied in thy name? and in thy name have cast out devils? and in thy name done many wonderful works?

23 And then will I profess unto them, I never knew you: depart from me, ye that work iniquity.

Heb. 12. 16 Lest there *be* any fornicator, or profane person, as Esau, who for one morsel of meat sold his birthright.

17 For ye know how that afterward, when he would have inherited the blessing, he was rejected: for he found no place of repentance, though he sought it carefully with tears.

I

Ps. 5. 5 The foolish shall not stand in thy

I—Concluded.

sight: thou hatest all workers of iniquity.

Hab. 1. 13 *Thou art* of purer eyes than to behold evil, and canst not look on iniquity: wherefore lookest thou upon them that deal treacherously, *and* holdest thy tongue when the wicked devoureth *the man that is* more righteous than he?

John 9. 31 Now we know that God heareth not sinners: but if any man be a worshipper of God, and doeth his will, him he heareth.

K

Matt.24. 42 Watch therefore; for ye know not what hour your Lord doth come.

43 But know this, that if the goodman of the house had known in what watch the thief would come, he would have watched, and would not have suffered his house to be broken up.

44 Therefore be ye also ready: for in such an hour as ye think not the Son of man cometh.

Mark 13. 33 Take ye heed, watch and pray: for ye know not when the time is.

Mark 13. 35 Watch ye therefore: for ye know not when the master of the house cometh, at even, or at midnight, or at the cock crowing, or in the morning:

36 Lest coming suddenly he find you sleeping.

37 And what I say unto you I say unto all, Watch.

Luke 21. 36 Watch ye therefore, and pray always, that ye may be accounted worthy to escape all these things that shall come to pass, and to stand before the Son of man.

I Cor.16. 13 Watch ye, stand fast in the faith, quit you like men, be strong.

14 Let all your things be done with charity.

I Thes. 5. 6. *See under D.*

II Tim.4. 5 But watch thou in all things, endure afflictions, do the work of an evangelist, make full proof of thy ministry.

I Pet. 4. 7 But the end of all things is at hand: be ye therefore sober, and watch unto prayer.

I Pet. 5. 8 Be sober, be vigilant; because your adversary the devil, as a roaring lion, walketh about, seeking whom he may devour:

Rev. 16. 15 Behold, I come as a thief. Blessed *is* he that watcheth, and keepeth his garments, lest he walk naked, and they see his shame.

§ 176. THE PARABLE OF THE FIVE TALENTS.
Third Day of the Week of our

25: 14–30.

14 [a]For *the kingdom of heaven is* [b]as a man traveling into a far country, *who* called his own servants, and delivered unto them his goods.

15 And unto one he gave five talents, to another two, and to another one; [c]to every man according to his several ability; and straightway took his journey.

16 Then he that had received the five talents went and traded with the same, and made *them* [d]other five talents.

17 And likewise he that *had received* two, he also gained other two.

18 But he that had received one went and digged in the earth, and [e]hid his lord's money.

19 After a long time the lord of those servants cometh, and reckoneth with them.

20 And so he that had received five talents came and brought other five talents, saying, Lord, thou deliveredst unto me five talents: behold, I have gained beside them five talents more.

21 His lord said unto him, Well done, *thou* good and faithful servant: thou hast been faithful over a few things, [f]I will make thee ruler over many things: enter thou into the [g]joy of thy lord.

22 He also that had received two talents came and said, Lord, thou deliveredst unto me two talents: behold, I have gained two other talents beside them.

A

Luke 19. 11 And as they heard these things, he added and spake a parable, because he was nigh to Jerusalem, and because they thought that the kingdom of God should immediately appear.

B

Matt. 21. 33 Hear another parable: There was a certain householder, which planted a vineyard, and hedged it round about, and digged a winepress in it, and built a tower, and let it out to husbandmen, and went into a far country:

Luke 19. 12 He said therefore, A certain nobleman went into a far country to receive for himself a kingdom, and to return.

C

Luke 19. 13 And he called his ten servants, and delivered them ten pounds, and said unto them, Occupy till I come.

14 But his citizens hated him, and sent a message after him, saying, We will not have this *man* to reign over us.

Rom. 12. 6 Having then gifts differing according to the grace that is given to us, whether prophecy, *let us prophesy* according to the proportion of faith;

I Cor. 12. 7 But the manifestation of the Spirit is given to every man to profit withal.

I Cor. 12. 11 But all these worketh that one and the selfsame Spirit, dividing to every man severally as he will.

I Cor. 12. 29 *Are* all apostles? *are* all prophets? *are* all teachers? *are* all workers of miracles?

Eph. 4. 11 And he gave some, apostles; and some, prophets; and some, evangelists; and some, pastors and teachers;

D

Prov. 3. 13 Happy *is* the man *that* findeth wisdom, and the man *that* getteth understanding:

14 For the merchandise of it *is* better than the merchandise of silver, and the gain thereof than fine gold.

15 She *is* more precious than rubies: and all the things thou canst desire are not to be compared unto her.

16 Length of days *is* in her right hand; *and* in her left hand riches and honour.

17 Her ways *are* ways of pleasantness, and all her paths *are* peace.

18 She *is* a tree of life to them that lay hold upon her: and happy *is every one* that retaineth her.

19 The LORD by wisdom hath founded the earth; by understanding hath he established the heavens.

20 By his knowledge the depths are broken up, and the clouds drop down the dew.

I Pet. 4. 10 As every man hath received the gift, *even so* minister the same one to

TIME, TUESDAY, APRIL 4 [NISAN 12], A. D. 30; PLACE, MOUNT OF OLIVES.
Lord's Fourth and Last Passover.

D—CONCLUDED.

another, as good stewards of the manifold grace of God.
11 If any man speak, *let him speak* as
the oracles of God; if any man minister, *let him do it* as of the ability which
God giveth; that God in all things
may be glorified through Jesus Christ:
to whom be praise and dominion for
ever and ever. Amen.

E

Prov.18. 9 He also that is slothful in his work
is brother to him that is a great waster.
Prov.26. 13 The slothful *man* saith, *There is* a
lion in the way; a lion *is* in the streets.
14 *As* the door turneth upon his
hinges, so *doth* the slothful upon his bed.
15 The slothful hideth his hand in
his bosom; it grieveth him to bring it
again to his mouth.
16 The sluggard *is* wiser in his own
conceit than seven men that can render a reason.
Hag. 1. 2 Thus speaketh the LORD of hosts,
saying, This people say, The time is not
come, the time that the LORD's house
should be built.
3 Then came the word of the LORD
by Haggai the prophet, saying,
4 *Is it* time for you, O ye, to dwell in
your ceiled houses, and this house *lie*
waste?
5 Now therefore thus saith the LORD
of hosts; Consider your ways.
Mal. 1. 10 Who *is there* even among you that
would shut the doors *for nought?* neither do ye kindle *fire* on mine altar for
nought. I have no pleasure in you,
saith the LORD of hosts, neither will I
accept an offering at your hand.
Luke 19. 20 And another came, saying, Lord,
behold, *here is* thy pound, which I have
kept laid up in a napkin:
Phil. 2. 21 For all seek their own, not the
things which are Jesus Christ's.
Heb. 6. 12 That ye be not slothful, but followers of them who through faith and
patience inherit the promises.
II Pet.1. 8 For if these things be in you, and
abound, they make *you that ye shall*
neither *be* barren nor unfruitful in the
knowledge of our Lord Jesus Christ.

F

Matt.24. 47 Verily I say unto you, That he
shall make him ruler over all his
goods.
Matt.25. 34 Then shall the King say unto
them on his right hand, Come, ye
blessed of my Father, inherit the kingdom prepared for you from the
foundation of the world:

F—CONCLUDED.

Matt.25. 46 And these shall go away into
everlasting punishment: but the righteous into life eternal.
Luke 12. 44 Of a truth I say unto you, that
he will make him ruler over all that
he hath.
Luke 22. 29 And I appoint unto you a kingdom, as my Father hath appointed
unto me;
30 That ye may eat and drink at my
table in my kingdom, and sit on
thrones judging the twelve tribes of
Israel.

G

Ps. 16. 10 For thou wilt not leave my soul
in hell; neither wilt thou suffer thine
Holy One to see corruption.
11 Thou wilt show me the path of
life: in thy presence *is* fulness of joy;
at thy right hand *there are* pleasures
for evermore.
John 17. 24 Father, I will that they also,
whom thou hast given me, be with me
where I am; that they may behold
my glory, which thou hast given me:
for thou lovedst me before the foundation of the world.
Acts 2. 25 For David speaketh concerning
him, I foresaw the Lord always before my face; for he is on my right
hand, that I should not be moved:
26 Therefore did my heart rejoice,
and my tongue was glad; moreover
also my flesh shall rest in hope:
27 Because thou wilt not leave my
soul in hell, neither wilt thou suffer
thine Holy One to see corruption.
28 Thou hast made known to me
the ways of life; thou shalt make me
full of joy with thy countenance.
Phil. 1. 23 For I am in a strait betwixt two,
having a desire to depart, and to be
with Christ; which is far better:
II Tim.2. 12 If we suffer, we shall also reign
with *him:* if we deny *him*, he also will
deny us:
Heb. 12. 2 Looking unto Jesus the author
and finisher of *our* faith; who for the
joy that was set before him endured
the cross, despising the shame, and is
set down at the right hand of the
throne of God.
I Pet. 1. 8 Whom having not seen, ye love;
in whom, though now ye see *him* not,
yet believing, ye rejoice with joy unspeakable and full of glory:

§ 176. THE PARABLE OF THE FIVE TALENTS (CONCLUDED).
Third Day of the Week of our

CHAP. 25.

23 His lord said unto him, [h]Well done, good and faithful servant; thou hast been faithful over a few things, I will make thee ruler over many things: enter thou into the joy of thy lord.

24 Then he which had received the one talent came and said, [i]Lord, I knew thee that thou art a hard man, reaping where thou hast not sown, and gathering where thou hast not strewed:

25 And I was afraid, and went and hid thy talent in the earth: lo, *there* thou hast *that is* thine.

26 His lord answered and said unto him, *Thou* wicked and slothful servant, thou knewest that I reap where I sowed not, and gather where I have not strewed:

27 Thou oughtest therefore to have put my money to the exchangers, and *then* at my coming I should have received mine own with usury.

28 Take therefore the talent from him, and give *it* unto him which hath ten talents.

29 [k]For unto every one that hath shall be given, and he shall have abundance: but from him that hath not shall be taken away even that which he hath.

30 And cast ye the unprofitable servant [l]into outer darkness: there shall be weeping and gnashing of teeth.

H

Matt. 25. 21. *See text of topic.*
Mark 12. 41 And Jesus sat over against the treasury, and beheld how the people cast money into the treasury: and many that were rich cast in much.
42 And there came a certain poor widow, and she threw in two mites, which make a farthing.

H—CONCLUDED.

Mark 12. 43 And he called *unto him* his disciples, and saith unto them, Verily I say unto you, That this poor widow hath cast more in, than all they which have cast into the treasury:
44 For all *they* did cast in of their abundance; but she of her want did cast in all that she had, *even* all her living.
Luke 19. 19 And he said likewise to him, Be thou also over five cities.
20 And another came, saying, Lord, behold, *here is* thy pound, which I have kept laid up in a napkin:
21 For I feared thee, because thou art an austere man: thou takest up that thou layedst not down, and reapest that thou didst not sow.
22 And he saith unto him, Out of thine own mouth will I judge thee, *thou* wicked servant. Thou knewest that I was an austere man, taking up that I laid not down, and reaping that I did not sow:
23 Wherefore then gavest not thou my money into the bank, that at my coming I might have required mine own with usury?
24 And he said unto them that stood by, Take from him the pound, and give *it* to him that hath ten pounds.
25 (And they said unto him, Lord, he hath ten pounds.)
26 For I say unto you, That unto every one which hath shall be given; and from him that hath not, even that he hath shall be taken away from him.
27 But those mine enemies, which would not that I should reign over them, bring hither, and slay *them* before me.

I

Job 21. 14 Therefore they say unto God, Depart from us; for we desire not the knowledge of thy ways.
15 What *is* the Almighty, that we should serve him? and what profit should we have, if we pray unto him?
Isa. 58. 3 Wherefore have we fasted, *say they*, and thou seest not? *wherefore* have we afflicted our soul, and thou takest no knowledge? Behold, in the day of your fast ye find pleasure, and exact all your labours.
Jer. 44. 16 *As for* the word that thou hast spoken unto us in the name of the LORD, we will not hearken unto thee.
17 But we will certainly do whatso-

TIME, TUESDAY, APRIL 4 [NISAN 12], A. D. 30; PLACE, MOUNT OF OLIVES.
Lord's Fourth and Last Passover.

I—CONTINUED.

ever thing goeth forth out of our own mouth, to burn incense unto the queen of heaven, and to pour out drink offerings unto her, as we have done, we, and our fathers, our kings, and our princes, in the cities of Judah, and in the streets of Jerusalem: for *then* had we plenty of victuals, and were well, and saw no evil.

18 But since we left off to burn incense to the queen of heaven, and to pour out drink offerings unto her, we have wanted all *things*, and have been consumed by the sword and by the famine.

Eze. 18. 25 Yet ye say, The way of the Lord is not equal. Hear now, O house of Israel; Is not my way equal? are not your ways unequal?

26 When a righteous *man* turneth away from his righteousness, and committeth iniquity, and dieth in them; for his iniquity that he hath done shall he die.

27 Again, when the wicked *man* turneth away from his wickedness that he hath committed, and doeth that which is lawful and right, he shall save his soul alive.

28 Because he considereth, and turneth away from all his transgressions that he hath committed, he shall surely live, he shall not die.

29 Yet saith the house of Israel, The way of the Lord is not equal. O house of Israel, are not my ways equal? are not your ways unequal?

30 Therefore I will judge you, O house of Israel, every one according to his ways, saith the Lord GOD. Repent, and turn *yourselves* from all your transgressions; so iniquity shall not be your ruin.

Mal. 1. 12 But ye have profaned it, in that ye say, The table of the LORD *is* polluted; and the fruit thereof, *even* his meat, *is* contemptible.

13 Ye said also, Behold, what a weariness *is it!* and ye have snuffed at it, saith the LORD of hosts; and ye brought *that which was* torn, and the lame, and the sick; thus ye brought an offering: should I accept this of your hand? saith the LORD.

Mal. 3. 14 Ye have said, It *is* vain to serve God: and what profit *is it* that we have kept his ordinance, and that we have

I—CONCLUDED.

walked mournfully before the LORD of hosts?

15 And now we call the proud happy; yea, they that work wickedness are set up; yea, *they that* tempt God are even delivered.

Rom. 8. 7 Because the carnal mind *is* enmity against God: for it is not subject to the law of God, neither indeed can be.

Rom. 9. 20 Nay but, O man, who art thou that repliest against God? Shall the thing formed say to him that formed *it*, Why hast thou made me thus?

K

Lam. 1. 6 And from the daughter of Zion all her beauty is departed: her princes are become like harts *that* find no pasture, and they are gone without strength before the pursuer.

Matt.13. 12. For whosoever hath, to him shall be given, and he shall have more abundance: but whosoever hath not, from him shall be taken away even that he hath.

Mark 4. 25 For he that hath, to him shall be given; and he that hath not, from him shall be taken even that which he hath.

Luke 8. 18 Take heed therefore how ye hear: for whosoever hath, to him shall be given; and whosoever hath not, from him shall be taken even that which he seemeth to have.

Luke19. 26 For I say unto you, That unto every one which hath shall be given: and from him that hath not, even that he hath shall be taken away from him.

John 15. 2 Every branch in me that beareth not fruit he taketh away: and every *branch* that beareth fruit, he purgeth it, that it may bring forth more fruit.

I Cor.15. 10 But by the grace of God I am what I am: and his grace which *was bestowed* upon me was not in vain; but I laboured more abundantly than they all: yet not I, but the grace of God which was with me.

L

Matt. 8. 12 But the children of the kingdom shall be cast out into outer darkness: there shall be weeping and gnashing of teeth.

Matt.13. 42 And shall cast them into a furnace of fire: there shall be wailing and gnashing of teeth.

Matt.24. 51 And shall cut him asunder, and appoint *him* his portion with the hypocrites: there shall be weeping and gnashing of teeth.

§ 177. SCENES OF THE JUDGMENT DAY.
Third Day of the Week of our

25 : 31–46.

31 [a]When the Son of man shall come in his glory, and all the holy angels with him, then shall he sit upon the throne of his glory:

32 And [b]before him shall be gathered all nations: and [c]he shall separate them one from another, as a shepherd divideth *his* sheep from the goats:

33 And he shall set the sheep on his right hand, but the goats on the left.

34 Then shall the King say unto them on his right hand, Come, ye blessed of my Father, [d]inherit the kingdom [e]prepared for you from the foundation of the world:

35 [f]For I was a hungered, and ye gave me meat: I was thirsty, and ye gave me drink: [g]I was a stranger, and ye took me in:

36 [h]Naked, and ye clothed me: I was sick, and ye visited me: [i]I was in prison, and ye came unto me.

37 Then shall the righteous answer him, saying, Lord, when saw we thee a hungered, and fed *thee?* or thirsty, and gave *thee* drink?

A

Zech.14. 5 And ye shall flee *to* the valley of the mountains; for the valley of the mountains shall reach unto Azal: yea, ye shall flee, like as ye fled from before the earthquake in the days of Uzziah king of Judah: and the LORD my God shall come, *and* all the saints with thee.

Matt.16. 27 For the Son of man shall come in the glory of his Father with his angels; and then he shall reward every man according to his works.

Matt.19. 28 And Jesus said unto them, Verily I say unto you, That ye which have followed me, in the regeneration when the Son of man shall sit in the throne of his glory, ye also shall sit upon twelve thrones, judging the twelve tribes of Israel.

A—CONCLUDED.

Mark 8. 38 Whosoever therefore shall be ashamed of me and of my words, in this adulterous and sinful generation, of him also shall the Son of man be ashamed, when he cometh in the glory of his Father with the holy angels.

Acts 1. 11 Which also said, Ye men of Galilee, why stand ye gazing up into heaven? this same Jesus, which is taken up from you into heaven, shall so come in like manner as ye have seen him go into heaven.

I Thes.4. 16 For the Lord himself shall descend from heaven with a shout, with the voice of the archangel, and with the trump of God: and the dead in Christ shall rise first:

II Thes.1. 7 And to you who are troubled rest with us, when the Lord Jesus shall be revealed from heaven with his mighty angels,

Phil. 2. 9 Wherefore God also hath highly exalted him, and given him a name which is above every name:

10 That at the name of Jesus every knee should bow, of *things* in heaven, and *things* in earth, and *things* under the earth:

Heb. 9. 28 So Christ was once offered to bear the sins of many; and unto them that look for him shall he appear the second time without sin unto salvation.

Jude 14 And Enoch also, the seventh from Adam, prophesied of these, saying, Behold, the Lord cometh with ten thousand of his saints.

Rev. 1 7 Behold, he cometh with clouds; and every eye shall see him, and they *also* which pierced him: and all kindreds of the earth shall wail because of him. Even so, Amen.

B

Rom.14. 10 But why dost thou judge thy brother? or why dost thou set at nought thy brother? for we shall all stand before the judgment seat of Christ.

II Cor. 5. 10 For we must all appear before the judgment seat of Christ; that every one may receive the things *done* in *his* body, according to that he hath done, whether *it be* good or bad.

Rev. 20. 12 And I saw the dead, small and great, stand before God; and the books were opened: and another book was opened, which is *the book* of life: and the dead were judged out of those things which were written in the books, according to their works.

TIME. TUESDAY, APRIL 4 [NISAN 12], A. D. 30; PLACE, MOUNT OF OLIVES.
Lord's Fourth and Last Passover.

C

Eze. 20. 38 And I will purge out from among you the rebels, and them that transgress against me: I will bring them forth out of the country where they sojourn, and they shall not enter into the land of Israel: and ye shall know that I *am* the LORD.

Eze. 34. 17 And *as for* you, O my flock, thus saith the Lord GOD; Behold, I judge between cattle and cattle, between the rams and the he goats.

Eze. 34. 20 Therefore thus saith the Lord GOD unto them; Behold, I, *even* I, will judge between the fat cattle and between the lean cattle.

Matt.13. 49 So shall it be at the end of the world: the angels shall come forth, and sever the wicked from among the just,

I Cor. 4. 5 Therefore judge nothing before the time, until the Lord come, who both will bring to light the hidden things of darkness, and will make manifest the counsels of the hearts: and then shall every man have praise of God.

D

Rom. 8. 17 And if children, then heirs; heirs of God, and joint heirs with Christ; if so be that we suffer with *him*, that we may be also glorified together.

I Pet. 1. 4 To an inheritance incorruptible and undefiled, and that fadeth not away, reserved in heaven for you.

I Pet. 1. 9 Receiving the end of your faith, *even* the salvation of *your* souls.

I Pet. 3. 9 Not rendering evil for evil, or railing for railing: but contrariwise blessing; knowing that ye are thereunto called, that ye should inherit a blessing.

Rev. 21. 7 He that overcometh shall inherit all things; and I will be his God, and he shall be my son.

E

Matt.20. 23 And he saith unto them, Ye shall drink indeed of my cup, and be baptized with the baptism that I am baptized with: but to sit on my right hand, and on my left, is not mine to give, but *it shall be given to them* for whom it is prepared of my Father.

Mark10. 40 But to sit on my right hand and on my left hand is not mine to give; but *it shall be given to them* for whom it is prepared.

I Cor. 2. 9 But as it is written, Eye hath not seen, nor ear heard, neither have entered into the heart of man, the things which God hath prepared for them that love him.

E—CONCLUDED.

Heb. 11. 16 But now they desire a better *country*, that is, a heavenly: wherefore God is not ashamed to be called their God: for he hath prepared for them a city.

F

Deut.15. 7 If there be among you a poor man of one of thy brethren within any of thy gates in thy land which the LORD thy God giveth thee, thou shalt not harden thine heart, nor shut thine hand from thy poor brother:

8 But thou shalt open thine hand wide unto him, and shalt surely lend him sufficient for his need, *in that* which he wanteth.

Job 29. 13 The blessing of him that was ready to perish came upon me: and I caused the widow's heart to sing for joy.

14 I put on righteousness, and it clothed me: my judgment *was* as a robe and a diadem.

15 I was eyes to the blind, and feet *was* I to the lame.

16 I *was* a father to the poor: and the cause *which* I knew not I searched out.

Ps. 112. 5 A good man showeth favour, and lendeth: he will guide his affairs with discretion.

Prov. 3. 9 Honour the LORD with thy substance, and with the first-fruits of all thine increase:

10 So shall thy barns be filled with plenty, and thy presses shall burst out with new wine.

Isa. 58. 7 *Is it* not to deal thy bread to the hungry, and that thou bring the poor that are cast out to thy house? when thou seest the naked, that thou cover him; and that thou hide not thyself from thine own flesh?

Eze. 18. 7 And hath not oppressed any, *but* hath restored to the debtor his pledge, hath spoiled none by violence, hath given his bread to the hungry, and hath covered the naked with a garment;

II Tim.1. 16 The Lord give mercy unto the house of Onesiphorus; for he oft refreshed me, and was not ashamed of my chain:

Jas. 1. 27 Pure religion and undefiled before God and the Father is this, To visit the fatherless and widows in their affliction, *and* to keep himself unspotted from the world.

For G, H, and I see next page (504).

§ 177. SCENES OF THE JUDGMENT DAY (CONCLUDED).
Third Day of the Week of our

CHAP. 25.

38 When saw we thee a stranger, and took *thee* in? or naked, and clothed *thee?*

39 Or when saw we thee sick, or in prison, and came unto thee?

40 And the King shall answer and say unto them, Verily I say unto you, [k]Inasmuch as ye have done *it* unto one of the least of these my brethren, ye have done *it* unto me.

41 Then shall he say also unto them on the left hand, [l]Depart from me, ye cursed, [m]into everlasting fire, prepared for [n]the devil and his angels:

42 For I was a hungered, and ye gave me no meat: I was thirsty, and ye gave me no drink:

43 I was a stranger, and ye took me not in: naked, and ye clothed me not: sick, and in prison, and ye visited me not.

44 Then shall they also answer him, saying, Lord, when saw we thee a hungered, or athirst, or a stranger, or naked, or sick, or in prison, and did not minister unto thee?

45 Then shall he answer them, saying, Verily I say unto you, [o]Inasmuch as ye did *it* not to one of the least of these, ye did *it* not to me.

46 And [p]these shall go away into everlasting punishment: but the [q]righteous into life eternal.

G

Heb. 13. 2 Be not forgetful to entertain strangers: for thereby some have entertained angels unawares.

III Jno. 5 Beloved, thou doest faithfully whatsoever thou doest to the brethren, and to strangers;

H

Jas. 2. 15 If a brother or sister be naked, and destitute of daily food,

H—CONCLUDED.

Jas. 2. 16 And one of you say unto them, Depart in peace, be *ye* warmed and filled; notwithstanding ye give them not those things which are needful to the body; what *doth it* profit?

17 Even so faith, if it hat hnot works, is dead, being alone.

I

II Tim. 1. 16. *See under F, page 503.*

K

II Sa. 9. 1 And David said, Is there yet any that is left of the house of Saul, that I may show him kindness for Jonathan's sake?

II Sa. 9. 7 And David said unto him, Fear not: for I will surely show thee kindness for Jonathan thy father's sake, and will restore thee all the land of Saul thy father; and thou shalt eat bread at my table continually.

Prov. 14. 31 He that oppresseth the poor reproacheth his Maker: but he that honoureth him hath mercy on the poor.

Prov. 19. 17 He that hath pity upon the poor lendeth unto the LORD; and that which he hath given will he pay him again.

Matt. 10. 42 And whosoever shall give to drink unto one of these little ones a cup of cold *water* only in the name of a disciple, verily I say unto you, he shall in no wise lose his reward.

Mark 9. 41 For whosoever shall give you a cup of water to drink in my name, because ye belong to Christ, verily I say unto you, he shall not lose his reward.

Heb. 6. 10 For God *is* not unrighteous to forget your work and labour of love, which ye have showed toward his name, in that ye have ministered to the saints, and do minister.

L

Ps. 6. 8 Depart from me, all ye workers of iniquity; for the LORD hath heard the voice of my weeping.

Matt. 7. 23 And then will I profess unto them, I never knew you: depart from me, ye that work iniquity.

Luke 13. 27 But he shall say, I tell you, I know you not whence ye are; depart from me, all *ye* workers of iniquity.

M

Matt. 13. 40 As therefore the tares are gathered and burned in the fire; so shall it be in the end of this world.

Matt. 13. 42 And shall cast them into a furnace of fire: there shall be wailing and gnashing of teeth.

TIME, TUESDAY, APRIL 4 [NISAN 12], A. D. 30; PLACE, MOUNT OF OLIVES.
Lord's Fourth and Last Passover.

N

Ps. 9. 17 The wicked shall be turned into hell, *and* all the nations that forget God.

II Pet.2. 4 For if God spared not the angels that sinned, but cast *them* down to hell, and delivered *them* into chains of darkness, to be reserved unto judgment;

Jude 6 And the angels which kept not their first estate, but left their own habitation, he hath reserved in everlasting chains under darkness unto the judgment of the great day.

O

Gen. 12. 3 And I will bless them that bless thee, and curse him that curseth thee: and in thee shall all families of the earth be blessed.

Num.24. 9 He couched, he lay down as a lion, and as a great lion: who shall stir him up? Blessed *is* he that blesseth thee, and cursed *is* he that curseth thee.

Ps. 105. 14 He suffered no man to do them wrong: yea, he reproved kings for their sakes;

15 *Saying*, Touch not mine anointed, and do my prophets no harm.

Prov. 14. 31. *See under K.*

Prov.17. 5 Whoso mocketh the poor reproacheth his Maker: *and* he that is glad at calamities shall not be unpunished.

Zech. 2. 8 For thus saith the LORD of hosts; After the glory hath he sent me unto the nations which spoiled you: for he that toucheth you, toucheth the apple of his eye.

Acts 9. 5 And he said, Who art thou, Lord? And the Lord said, I am Jesus whom thou persecutest: *it is* hard for thee to kick against the pricks.

P

Dan. 12. 2 And many of them that sleep in the dust of the earth shall awake, some to everlasting life, and some to shame *and* everlasting contempt.

John 5. 29 And shall come forth; they that have done good, unto the resurrection of life; and they that have done evil, unto the resurrection of damnation.

Rom. 2. 7 To them who by patient continuance in well doing seek for glory and honour and immortality, eternal life:

II Thes.1. 9 Who shall be punished with everlasting destruction from the presence of the Lord, and from the glory of his power;

Rev. 14. 11 And the smoke of their torment ascendeth up for ever and ever: and they have no rest day nor night, who

P—CONCLUDED.

worship the beast and his image, and whosoever receiveth the mark of his name.

Rev. 20. 10 And the devil that deceived them was cast into the lake of fire and brimstone, where the beast and the false prophet *are*, and shall be tormented day and night for ever and ever.

Rev. 20. 15 And whosoever was not found written in the book of life was cast into the lake of fire.

Q

Ps. 16. 10 For thou wilt not leave my soul in hell; neither wilt thou suffer thine Holy One to see corruption.

11 Thou wilt show me the path of life: in thy presence *is* fulness of joy; at thy right hand *there are* pleasures for evermore.

Rom. 2. 7. *See under P.*

Rom. 2. 8 But unto them that are contentious, and do not obey the truth, but obey unrighteousness, indignation and wrath,

9 Tribulation and anguish, upon every soul of man that doeth evil; of the Jew first, and also of the Gentile;

10 But glory, honour, and peace, to every man that worketh good; to the Jew first, and also to the Gentile:

11 For there is no respect of persons with God.

Rom. 5. 21 That as sin hath reigned unto death, even so might grace reign through righteousness unto eternal life by Jesus Christ our Lord.

Rom. 6. 23 For the wages of sin *is* death; but the gift of God *is* eternal life through Jesus Christ our Lord.

I Jno. 2. 25 And this is the promise that he hath promised us, *even* eternal life.

I Jno. 5. 11 And this is the record, that God hath given to us eternal life, and this life is in his Son.

12 He that hath the Son hath life; *and* he that hath not the Son of God hath not life.

Jude 21 Keep yourselves in the love of God, looking for the mercy of our Lord Jesus Christ unto eternal life.

Rev. 3. 21 To him that overcometh will I grant to sit with me in my throne, even as I also overcame, and am set down with my Father in his throne.

Rev. 7. 15 Therefore are they before the throne of God, and serve him day and night in his temple: and he that sitteth on the throne shall dwell among them.

§ 178. THE RULERS CONSPIRE AGAINST JESUS.

Third Day of the Week of our

MATTHEW 26 : 1–5.

1 And it came to pass, when Jesus had finished all these sayings, he said unto his disciples,

2 [a]Ye know that after two days is *the feast of* the passover, and the Son of man is betrayed to be crucified.

3 [b]Then assembled together the chief priests, and the scribes, and the elders of the people, unto the palace of the high priest, who was called Caiaphas,

4 And consulted that they might take Jesus by subtilty, and kill *him.*

5 But they said, Not on the feast *day,* lest there be an uproar among the people. (p. 430.)

A

Mark 14. 1 and Luke 22. 1. *See text of topic.*

John 13. 1 Now before the feast of the passover, when Jesus knew that his hour was come that he should depart out of this world unto the Father, having loved his own which were in the world, he loved them unto the end.

MARK 14 : 1, 2.

1 After [c]two days was *the feast of* the passover, and of unleavened bread: and the chief priests and the scribes sought how they might take him by craft, and put *him* to death.

2 But they said, Not on the feast *day,* lest there be an uproar of the people.

A—Concluded. (p. 430.)

B

Ps. 2. 2 The kings of the earth set themselves, and the rulers take counsel together, against the LORD, and against his Anointed, *saying,*

Ps. 94. 20 Shall the throne of iniquity have fellowship with thee, which frameth mischief by a law?

§ 179. *JUDAS ISCARIOT COVENANTS TO BETRAY JESUS.

Evening Introducing the Fourth Day of the Week

MATTHEW 26 : 14–16.

14 [a]Then one of the twelve, called [b]Judas Iscariot, went unto the chief priests,

15 And said *unto them,* [c]What will ye give me, and I will deliver him unto you? And they covenanted with him for [d]thirty pieces of silver.

16 And from that time he sought opportunity to betray him.

*

It is probable that Judas bargained for the betrayal on Tuesday evening, and that Wednesday was spent by Jesus and his disciples in quiet at Bethany.

A

Mark 14. 10 and Luke 22. 3. *See text of topic.*

John 13. 2 And supper being ended, the devil having now put into the heart of Judas Iscariot, Simon's *son,* to betray him;

John 13. 30 He then, having received the sop, went immediately out; and it was night.

B

Matt. 10. 4 Simon the Canaanite, and Judas Iscariot, who also betrayed him.

MARK 14 : 10, 11.

10 And Judas Iscariot, one of the twelve, went unto the chief priests, to betray him unto them.

11 And when they heard *it,* they were glad, and promised to give him [e]money. And he sought how he might conveniently betray him.

C

Judg. 16. 5 And the lords of the Philistines came up unto her, and said unto her, Entice him, and see wherein his great strength *lieth,* and by what *means* we may prevail against him, that we may bind him to afflict him: and we will give thee every one of us eleven hundred *pieces* of silver.

Judg. 18. 19 And they said unto him, Hold thy peace, lay thine hand upon thy mouth, and go with us, and be to us a father and a priest: *is it* better for thee to be a priest unto the house of one man, or that thou be a priest unto a tribe and a family in Israel?

20 And the priest's heart was glad, and he took the ephod, and the tera-

TIME, TUESDAY, APRIL 4 [NISAN 12], A. D. 30; PLACE, JERUSALEM.
Lord's Fourth and Last Passover.

22: 1, 2.

1 Now [d]the feast of unleavened bread drew nigh, which is called the passover.

2 [e]And the chief priests and scribes sought how they might kill him; for they feared the people.

B—CONTINUED.

Ps. 94. 21 They gather themselves together against the soul of the righteous, and condemn the innocent blood.

Jer. 11. 19 But I *was* like a lamb *or* an ox *that* is brought to the slaughter; and I knew not that they had devised devices against me, *saying*, Let us destroy the tree with the fruit thereof, and let us cut him off from the land of the living, that his name may be no more remembered.

John 11. 47 Then gathered the chief priests and the Pharisees a council, and said, What do we? for this man doeth many miracles.

Acts 4. 25 Who by the mouth of thy servant

B—CONCLUDED.

David hast said, Why did the heathen rage, and the people imagine vain things?

26 The kings of the earth stood up, and the rulers were gathered together against the Lord, and against his Christ.

27 For of a truth against thy holy child Jesus, whom thou hast anointed both Herod, and Pontius Pilate, with the Gentiles, and the people of Israel were gathered together.

28 For to do whatsoever thy hand and thy counsel determined before to be done.

C

Ex. 12. *The Passover instituted. Read entire chapter.*

Matt. 26. 2 and Luke 22. 1. *See text of topic.*

John 11. 55 And the Jews' passover was nigh at hand: and many went out of the country up to Jerusalem before the passover, to purify themselves.

John 13. 1. *See under A.*

D

Matt. 26. 2 and Mark 14. 1. *See text of topic.*

E

Ps. 2. 2 and John 11. 47. *See under B.*

TIME, TUESDAY, APRIL 4 [NISAN 12], A. D. 30; PLACE, JERUSALEM.
of our Lord's Fourth and Last Passover.

22: 3–6.

3 [f]Then entered Satan into Judas surnamed Iscariot, being of the number of the twelve.

4 And he went his way, and communed with the chief priests and captains, how he might betray him unto them.

5 And they were glad, and covenanted to give him money.

6 And he promised, and sought opportunity to betray him unto them in the absence of the multitude.

C—CONCLUDED.

phim, and the graven image, and went in the midst of the people.

D

Zech. 11. 12 And I said unto them, If ye think good, give *me* my price; and if not, forbear. So they weighed for my price, thirty *pieces* of silver.

13 And the LORD said unto me, Cast it unto the potter: a goodly price that I was prized at of them. And I took

D—CONCLUDED.

the thirty *pieces* of silver, and cast them to the potter in the house of the LORD.

Matt. 27. 3 Then Judas, which had betrayed him, when he saw that he was condemned, repented himself, and brought again the thirty pieces of silver to the chief priests and elders.

E

Zech. 11. 12. *See under C.*

I Tim. 6. 10 For the love of money is the root of all evil; which while some coveted after, they have erred from the faith, and pierced themselves through with many sorrows.

Jude 11 Woe unto them: for they have gone in the way of Cain, and ran greedily after the error of Balaam for reward, and perished in the gainsaying of Core.

F

Matt. 26. 14, and Mark 14. 10. *See text of topic.*

John 13. 2. *See under A.*

John 13. 27 And after the sop Satan entered into him. Then said Jesus unto him, That thou doest, do quickly.

Acts 5. 3 But Peter said, Ananias, why hath Satan filled thine heart to lie to the Holy Ghost, and to keep back *part* of the price of the land?

§ 180. PREPARATION FOR THE PASSOVER.

Fifth Day of the Week of our

MATTHEW 26 : 17–19.

17 [a]Now the first *day* of the *feast of* unleavened bread the disciples came to Jesus, saying unto him, Where wilt thou that we prepare for thee to eat the passover?

18 And he said, Go into the city to such a man, and say unto him, The Master saith, My time is at hand; I will keep the passover at thy house with my disciples.

19 And the disciples did as Jesus had appointed them; and they made ready the passover.

A

Ex. 12. 6 And ye shall keep it up until the fourteenth day of the same month: and the whole assembly of the congregation of Israel shall kill it in the evening.

Ex. 12. 18 In the first *month*, on the fourteenth day of the month at even, ye shall eat unleavened bread, until the one and twentieth day of the month at even.

Lev. 23. 5 In the fourteenth *day* of the first month at even *is* the LORD's passover.
6 And on the fifteenth day of the same month *is* the feast of unleavened bread unto the LORD: seven days ye must eat unleavened bread.

Num. 28. 16 And in the fourteenth day of the first month *is* the passover of the LORD.
17 And in the fifteenth day of this month *is* the feast: seven days shall unleavened bread be eaten.
18 In the first day *shall be* a holy convocation; ye shall do no manner of servile work *therein:*

Mark 14. 12 and Luke 22. 7. *See text of topic.*

B

Matt. 26. 17 and Luke 22. 7. *See text of topic.*

1

Or, *sacrificed.*

C

Matt. 8. 9 For I am a man under authority, having soldiers under me: and I say to this *man*, Go, and he goeth; and to another, Come, and he cometh; and to my servant, Do this, and he doeth *it*.

Mark 11. 2 And saith unto them, Go your way into the village over against you: and as soon as ye be entered into it, ye shall find a colt tied, whereon never man sat; loose him, and bring *him*.

MARK 14: 12–16.

12 [b]And the first day of unleavened bread, when they [1]killed the passover, his disciples said unto him, Where wilt thou that we go and prepare that thou mayest eat the passover?

13 And he sendeth forth two of his disciples, and saith unto them, [c]Go ye into the city, and there shall meet you a man bearing a pitcher of water: follow him.

14 And wheresoever he shall go in, say ye to the goodman of the house, The Master saith, Where is the guest-chamber, where I shall eat [d]the passover with my disciples?

15 And [e]he will show you a large upper room furnished *and* prepared: there make ready for us.

16 And his disciples went forth, and came into the city, and found as he had said unto them: and they made ready the passover.

C—CONCLUDED.

Mark 11. 3 And if any man say unto you, Why do ye this? say ye that the Lord hath need of him; and straightway he will send him hither.

Luke 19. 30 Saying, Go ye into the village over against *you;* in the which at your entering ye shall find a colt tied, whereon yet never man sat: loose him, and bring *him hither*.
31 And if any man ask you, Why do ye loose *him?* thus shall ye say unto him, Because the Lord hath need of him.

D

Ex. 12. 6 and Lev. 23. 5. *See under A.*

E

John 2. 24 But Jesus did not commit himself unto them, because he knew all *men*,
25 And needed not that any should testify of man: for he knew what was in man.

II Tim. 2. 19 Nevertheless the foundation of God standeth sure, having this seal, The Lord knoweth them that are his. And, Let every one that nameth the name of Christ depart from iniquity.

TIME, THURSDAY, APRIL 6 [NISAN 14], A. D. 30; PLACE, BETHANY. JERUSALEM.
Lord's Fourth and Last Passover.

22: 7-13.

7 *f* Then came the day of unleavened bread, when the passover must be killed.

8 And he sent Peter and John, saying, Go and prepare us the passover, that we may eat.

9 And they said unto him, Where wilt thou that we prepare?

10 And he said unto them, *g* Behold, when ye are entered into the city, there shall a man meet you, bearing a pitcher of water; follow him into the house where he entereth in.

11 And ye shall say unto the goodman of the house, The Master saith unto thee, *h* Where is the guestchamber, where I shall eat the passover with my disciples?

12 And he shall show you a *i* large upper room furnished: there make ready.

13 And they went, and found as he had said unto them: and they made ready the passover.

E—CONCLUDED.

Heb. 4. 13 Neither is there any creature that is not manifest in his sight: but all things *are* naked and opened unto the eyes of him with whom we have to do.

F

Matt. 26. 17, and Mark 14. 12. *See text of topic.*

G

I Sa. 10. 2 When thou art departed from me to day, then thou shalt find two men by Rachel's sepulchre in the border of Benjamin at Zelzah; and they will say unto thee, The asses which thou wentest to seek are found: and, lo, thy father hath left the care of the asses, and sorroweth for you, saying, What shall I do for my son?

3 Then shalt thou go on forward from thence, and thou shalt come to the plain of Tabor, and there shall meet thee three men going up to God to Beth-el, one carrying three kids, and another carrying three loaves of bread, and another carrying a bottle of wine:

G—CONCLUDED.

I Sa. 10. 4 And they will salute thee, and give thee two *loaves* of bread; which thou shalt receive of their hands.

5 After that thou shalt come to the hill of God, where *is* the garrison of the Philistines: and it shall come to pass, when thou art come thither to the city, that thou shalt meet a company of prophets coming down from the high place with a psaltery, and a tabret, and a pipe, and a harp, before them; and they shall prophesy:

6 And the Spirit of the LORD will come upon thee, and thou shalt prophesy with them, and shalt be turned into another man.

7 And let it be, when these signs are come unto thee, *that* thou do as occasion serve thee: for God *is* with thee.

John 16. 4 But these things have I told you, that when the time shall come, ye may remember that I told you of them. And these things I said not unto you at the beginning, because I was with you.

Acts 8. 26 And the angel of the Lord spake unto Philip, saying, Arise, and go toward the south, unto the way that goeth down from Jerusalem unto Gaza, which is desert.

27 And he arose and went: and, behold, a man of Ethiopia, a eunuch of great authority under Candace queen of the Ethiopians, who had the charge of all her treasure, and had come to Jerusalem for to worship,

28 Was returning, and sitting in his chariot read Esaias the prophet.

29 Then the Spirit said unto Philip, Go near, and join thyself to this chariot.

H

Rev. 3. 20 Behold, I stand at the door, and knock: if any man hear my voice, and open the door, I will come in to him, and will sup with him, and he with me.

I

Acts 1. 13 And when they were come in, they went up into an upper room, where abode both Peter, and James, and John, and Andrew, Philip, and Thomas, Bartholomew, and Matthew, James *the son* of Alpheus, and Simon Zelotes, and Judas *the brother* of James.

Acts 20. 8 And there were many lights in the upper chamber, where they were gathered together.

§ 181. THE PASSOVER MEAL. CONTENTION AMONG THE TWELVE.

Evening Introducing the Sixth Day of the

26: 20.

20 [a]Now when the even was come, he sat down with the twelve. (p. 516.)

A

Mark 14. 17 and Luke 22. 14. *See text of topic.*

B

Matt. 26. 20. *See text of topic.*

C

Matt. 26. 20 and Mark 14. 17. *See text of topic.*

1

Or, *I have heartily desired.*

D

Luke 14. 15 And when one of them that sat at meat with him heard these things, he said unto him, Blessed *is* he that shall eat bread in the kingdom of God.

Acts 10. 40 Him God raised up the third day, and showed him openly;

41 Not to all the people, but unto witnesses chosen before of God, *even* to us, who did eat and drink with him after he rose from the dead.

Rev. 19. 9 And he saith unto me, Write, Blessed *are* they which are called unto the marriage supper of the Lamb. And he saith unto me, These are the true sayings of God.

E

Matt. 26. 29 But I say unto you, I will not drink henceforth of this fruit of the vine, until that day when I drink it new with you in my Father's kingdom.

Mark 14. 25 Verily I say unto you, I will drink no more of the fruit of the vine, until that day that I drink it new in the kingdom of God.

F

Mark 9. 34 But they held their peace: for by the way they had disputed among themselves, who *should be* the greatest.

Luke 9. 46 Then there arose a reasoning among them, which of them should be greatest.

G

Matt. 20. 25 But Jesus called them *unto him*, and said, Ye know that the princes of the Gentiles exercise dominion over them, and they that are great exercise authority upon them.

Mark 10. 42 But Jesus called them *to him*, and saith unto them, Ye know that they which are accounted to rule over the Gentiles exercise lordship over them; and their great ones exercise authority upon them.

H

Matt. 20. 26 But it shall not be so among you: but whosoever will be great among you, let him be your minister;

14: 17.

17 [b]And in the evening he cometh with the twelve. (p. 516.)

H—Concluded.

Jas. 4. 6 But he giveth more grace. Wherefore he saith, God resisteth the proud, but giveth grace unto the humble.

I Pet. 5. 3 Neither as being lords over *God's* heritage, but being ensamples to the flock.

I

Luke 9. 48 And said unto them, Whosoever shall receive this child in my name receiveth me; and whosoever shall receive me, receiveth him that sent me: for he that is least among you all, the same shall be great.

K

Luke 12. 37 Blessed *are* those servants, whom the lord when he cometh shall find watching: verily I say unto you, that he shall gird himself, and make them to sit down to meat, and will come forth and serve them.

II Cor. 8. 9 For ye know the grace of our Lord Jesus Christ, that, though he was rich, yet for your sakes he became poor, that ye through his poverty might be rich.

L

Matt. 20. 28 Even as the Son of man came not to be ministered unto, but to minister, and to give his life a ransom for many.

John 13. 13 Ye call me master and Lord: and ye say well; for *so* I am.

14 If I then, *your* Lord and Master, have washed your feet; ye also ought to wash one another's feet.

Phil. 2. 7 But made himself of no reputation, and took upon him the form of a servant, and was made in the likeness of men:

M

Heb. 4. 15 For we have not a high priest which cannot be touched with the feeling of our infirmities, but was in all points tempted like as *we are, yet* without sin.

N

Matt. 24. 46 Blessed *is* that servant, whom his lord when he cometh shall find so doing.

47 Verily I say unto you, That he shall make him ruler over all his goods.

Luke 12. 32 Fear not, little flock; for it is your Father's good pleasure to give you the kingdom.

TIME, THURSDAY EVENING, APRIL 6 [NISAN 14], A. D. 30; PLACE, JERUSALEM.
Week of our Lord's Fourth and Last Passover.

22: 14–18, 24–30.

14 [c]And when the hour was come, he sat down, and the twelve apostles with him.

15 And he said unto them, [1]With desire I have desired to eat this passover with you before I suffer:

16 For I say unto you, I will not any more eat thereof, [d]until it be fulfilled in the kingdom of God.

17 And he took the cup, and gave thanks, and said, Take this, and divide *it* among yourselves:

18 For [e]I say unto you, I will not drink of the fruit of the vine, until the kingdom of God shall come. (p. 521.)

* * * * *

24 [f]And there was also a strife among them, which of them should be accounted the greatest.

25 [g]And he said unto them, The kings of the Gentiles exercise lordship over them; and they that exercise authority upon them are called benefactors.

26 [h]But ye *shall* not *be* so: [i]but he that is greatest among you, let him be as the younger; and he that is chief, as he that doth serve.

27 [k]For whether *is* greater, he that sitteth at meat, or he that serveth? *is* not he that sitteth at meat? but [l]I am among you as he that serveth.

28 Ye are they which have continued with me in [m]my temptations.

29 And [n]I appoint unto you a kingdom, as my Father hath appointed unto me;

30 That [o]ye may eat and drink at my table in my kingdom, [p]and sit on thrones judging the twelve tribes of Israel. (p. 523.)

N—CONCLUDED.

II Cor. 1. 7 And our hope of you *is* steadfast, knowing, that as ye are partakers of the sufferings, so *shall ye be* also of the consolation.

II Tim. 2. 12 If we suffer, we shall also reign with *him:* if we deny *him,* he also will deny us:

Jas. 2. 5 Hearken, my beloved brethren, Hath not God chosen the poor of this world rich in faith, and heirs of the kingdom which he hath promised to them that love him?

I Pet. 5. 4 And when the chief Shepherd shall appear, ye shall receive a crown of glory that fadeth not away.

O

Matt. 8. 11 And I say unto you, That many shall come from the east and west, and shall sit down with Abraham, and Isaac, and Jacob, in the kingdom of heaven:

Luke 14. 15 and Rev. 19. 9. *See under D.*

P

Ps. 49. 14 Like sheep they are laid in the grave; death shall feed on them; and the upright shall have dominion over them in the morning; and their beauty shall consume in the grave from their dwelling.

Matt. 19. 28 And Jesus said unto them, Verily I say unto you, That ye which have followed me, in the regeneration when the Son of man shall sit in the throne of his glory, ye also shall sit upon twelve thrones, judging the twelve tribes of Israel.

I Cor. 6. 1 Dare any of you, having a matter against another, go to law before the unjust, and not before the saints?

2 Do ye not know that the saints shall judge the world? and if the world shall be judged by you, are ye unworthy to judge the smallest matters?

3 Know ye not that we shall judge angels? how much more things that pertain to this life?

4 If then ye have judgments of things pertaining to this life, set them to judge who are least esteemed in the church.

5 I speak to your shame. Is it so, that there is not a wise man among you? no, not one that shall be able to judge between his brethren?

Rev. 3. 21 To him that overcometh will I grant to sit with me in my throne, even as I also overcame, and am set down with my Father in his throne.

§ 182. JESUS WASHES THE DISCIPLES' FEET.

Evening Introducing the Sixth Day of the

A

Matt.26. 2 Ye know that after two days is *the feast of* the passover, and the Son of man is betrayed to be crucified.

B

John 12. 23 And Jesus answered them, saying, The hour is come, that the Son of man should be glorified.

John 17. 1 These words spake Jesus, and lifted up his eyes to heaven, and said, Father, the hour is come; glorify thy Son, that thy Son also may glorify thee:

John 17. 11 And now I am no more in the world, but these are in the world, and I come to thee. Holy Father, keep through thine own name those whom thou hast given me, that they may be one, as we *are*.

C

Luke 22. 3 Then entered Satan into Judas surnamed Iscariot, being of the number of the twelve.

John 13. 27 And after the sop Satan entered into him. Then said Jesus unto him, That thou doest, do quickly.

D

Matt.11. 27 All things are delivered unto me of my Father: and no man knoweth the Son, but the Father; neither knoweth any man the Father, save the Son, and *he* to whomsoever the Son will reveal *him*.

Matt.28. 18 And Jesus came and spake unto them, saying, All power is given unto me in heaven and in earth.

John 3. 35 The Father loveth the Son, and hath given all things into his hand.

John 17. 2 As thou hast given him power over all flesh, that he should give eternal life to as many as thou hast given him.

Acts 2. 36 Therefore let all the house of Israel know assuredly, that God hath made that same Jesus, whom ye have crucified, both Lord and Christ.

I Cor.15. 27 For he hath put all things under his feet. But when he saith, All things are put under *him, it is* manifest that he is excepted, which did put all things under him.

Heb. 2. 8 Thou hast put all things in subjection under his feet. For in that he put all in subjection under him, he left nothing *that is* not put under him. But now we see not yet all things put under him.

E

John 8. 42 Jesus said unto them, If God were your Father, ye would love me: for I proceeded forth and came from

E—Concluded.

God; neither came I of myself, but he sent me.

John 16. 28 I came forth from the Father, and am come into the world: again, I leave the world, and go to the Father.

F

Luke 22. 27 For whether *is* greater, he that sitteth at meat, or he that serveth? *is* not he that sitteth at meat? but I am among you as he that serveth.

Phil. 2. 7 But made himself of no reputation, and took upon him the form of a servant, and was made in the likeness of men:

8 And being found in fashion as a man, he humbled himself, and became obedient unto death, even the death of the cross.

1

Greek, *he*.

G

Matt. 3. 14 But John forbade him, saying, I have need to be baptized of thee, and comest thou to me?

H

John 13. 12. *See text of topic.*

I

Eze. 36. 25 Then will I sprinkle clean water upon you, and ye shall be clean: from all your filthiness, and from all your idols, will I cleanse you.

26 A new heart also will I give you, and a new spirit will I put within you: and I will take away the stony heart out of your flesh, and I will give you a heart of flesh.

27 And I will put my Spirit within you, and cause you to walk in my statutes, and ye shall keep my judgments, and do *them*.

John 3. 5 Jesus answered, Verily, verily, I say unto thee, Except a man be born of water and *of* the Spirit, he cannot enter into the kingdom of God.

Acts 2. 38 Then Peter said unto them, Repent, and be baptized every one of you in the name of Jesus Christ for the remission of sins, and ye shall receive the gift of the Holy Ghost.

I Cor. 6. 11 And such were some of you: but ye are washed, but ye are sanctified, but ye are justified in the name of the Lord Jesus, and by the Spirit of our God.

Eph. 5. 26 That he might sanctify and cleanse it with the washing of water by the word,

Tit. 3. 4 But after that the kindness and

TIME, THURSDAY EVENING, APRIL 6 [NISAN 14], A. D. 30; PLACE, JERUSALEM.
Week of our Lord's Fourth and Last Passover.

I—CONCLUDED.

love of God our Saviour toward man appeared,

5 Not by works of righteousnesss which we have done, but according to his mercy he saved us, by the washing of regeneration, and renewing of the Holy Ghost;

Heb. 10. 22 Let us draw near with a true heart in full assurance of faith, having our hearts sprinkled from an evil conscience, and our bodies washed with pure water.

K

Eccl. 7. 20 For *there is* not a just man upon earth, that doeth good, and sinneth not.

Matt. 6. 12 And forgive us our debts, as we forgive our debtors.

Rom. 7. 20 Now if I do that I would not, it is no more I that do it, but sin that dwelleth in me.

21 I find then a law, that, when I would do good, evil is present with me.

22 For I delight in the law of God after the inward man:

23 But I see another law in my members, warring against the law of my mind, and bringing me into captivity to the law of sin which is in my members.

II Cor. 7. 1 Having therefore these promises, dearly beloved, let us cleanse ourselves from all filthiness of the flesh and spirit, perfecting holiness in the fear of God.

Eph. 4. 22 That ye put off concerning the former conversation the old man, which is corrupt according to the deceitful lusts;

23 And be renewed in the spirit of your mind:

24 And that ye put on the new man, which after God is created in righteousness and true holiness.

Eph. 5. 26 That he might sanctify and cleanse it with the washing of water by the word.

I Thes. 5. 21 Prove all things; hold fast that which is good.

22 Abstain from all appearance of evil.

23 And the very God of peace sanctify you wholly, and *I pray God* your whole spirit and soul and body be preserved blameless unto the coming of our Lord Jesus Christ.

I Jno. 1. 9 If we confess our sins, he is faithful and just to forgive us *our* sins, and to cleanse us from all unrighteousness.

13: 1–20.

1 Now [a]before the feast of the passover, when Jesus knew that [b]his hour was come that he should depart out of this world unto the Father, having loved his own which were in the world, he loved them unto the end.

2 And supper being ended, [c]the devil having now put into the heart of Judas Iscariot, Simon's *son*, to betray him;

3 Jesus knowing [d]that the Father had given all things into his hands, and [e]that he was come from God, and went to God;

4 [f]He riseth from supper, and laid aside his garments, and took a towel, and girded himself.

5 After that he poureth water into a basin, and began to wash the disciples' feet, and to wipe *them* with the towel wherewith he was girded.

6 Then cometh he to Simon Peter: and [1]Peter saith unto him, Lord, [g]dost thou wash my feet?

7 Jesus answered and said unto him, What I do thou knowest not now; [h]but thou shalt know hereafter.

8 Peter saith unto him, Thou shalt never wash my feet. Jesus answered him, [i]If I wash thee not, thou hast no part with me.

9 Simon Peter saith unto him, Lord, not my feet only, but also *my* hands and *my* head.

10 Jesus saith to him, [k]He that is washed needeth not save to wash *his* feet, but is clean every whit: and [l]ye are clean, but not all.

L

John 15. 3 Now ye are clean through the word which I have spoken unto you.

§ 182. JESUS WASHES THE DISCIPLES' FEET (CONCLUDED).
Evening Introducing the Sixth Day of the

M

John 6. 64 But there are some of you that believe not. For Jesus knew from the beginning who they were that believed not, and who should betray him.

N

Matt. 23. 8 But be not ye called Rabbi: for one is your Master, *even* Christ; and all ye are brethren.

Matt. 23. 10 Neither be ye called masters: for one is your Master, *even* Christ.

Luke 6. 46 And why call ye me, Lord, Lord, and do not the things which I say?

I Cor. 8. 6 But to us *there is but* one God, the Father, of whom *are* all things, and we in him; and one Lord Jesus Christ, by whom *are* all things, and we by him.

I Cor. 12. 3 Wherefore I give you to understand, that no man speaking by the Spirit of God calleth Jesus accursed: and *that* no man can say that Jesus is the Lord, but by the Holy Ghost.

Phil. 2. 11 And *that* every tongue should confess that Jesus Christ *is* Lord, to the glory of God the Father.

O

Luke 22. 27. *See under F, page 512.*

P

Rom. 12. 10 *Be* kindly affectioned one to another with brotherly love; in honour preferring one another;

Gal. 6. 1 Brethren, if a man be overtaken in a fault, ye which are spiritual, restore such a one in the spirit of meekness; considering thyself, lest thou also be tempted.

2 Bear ye one another's burdens, and so fulfill the law of Christ.

I Pet. 5. 5 Likewise, ye younger, submit yourselves unto the elder. Yea, all *of you* be subject one to another, and be clothed with humility: for God resisteth the proud, and giveth grace to the humble.

6 Humble yourselves therefore under the mighty hand of God, that he may exalt you in due time:

7 Casting all your care upon him; for he careth for you.

Q

Matt. 11. 29 Take my yoke upon you, and learn of me; for I am meek and lowly in heart: and ye shall find rest unto your souls.

Phil. 2. 5 Let this mind be in you, which was also in Christ Jesus:

I Pet. 2. 21 For even hereunto were ye called: because Christ also suffered for us,

Q—CONCLUDED.

leaving us an example, that ye should follow his steps:

I Jno. 2. 6 He that saith he abideth in him ought himself also so to walk, even as he walked.

R

Matt. 10. 24 The disciple is not above *his* master, nor the servant above his lord.

Luke 6. 40 The disciple is not above his master: but every one that is perfect shall be as his master.

John 15. 20 Remember the word that I said unto you, The servant is not greater than his lord. If they have persecuted me, they will also persecute you; if they have kept my saying, they will keep yours also.

S

Jas. 1. 25 But whoso looketh into the perfect law of liberty, and continueth *therein*, he being not a forgetful hearer, but a doer of the work, this man shall be blessed in his deed.

T

Gen. 6. 22 Thus did Noah; according to all that God commanded him, so did he.

Ex. 40. 16 Thus did Moses: according to all that the LORD commanded him, so did he.

Ps. 19. 11 Moreover by them is thy servant warned: *and* in keeping of them *there is* great reward.

Ps. 119. 1 Blessed *are* the undefiled in the way, who walk in the law of the LORD.

2 Blessed *are* they that keep his testimonies, *and that* seek him with the whole heart.

3 They also do no iniquity: they walk in his ways.

4 Thou hast commanded *us* to keep thy precepts diligently.

5 O that my ways were directed to keep thy statutes!

Eze. 36. 27 And I will put my Spirit within you, and cause you to walk in my statutes, and ye shall keep my judgments, and do *them.*

Matt. 7. 24 Therefore whosoever heareth these sayings of mine, and doeth them, I will liken him unto a wise man, which built his house upon a rock:

25 And the rain descended, and the floods came, and the winds blew, and beat upon that house; and it fell not: for it was founded upon a rock.

Gal. 5. 6 For in Jesus Christ neither circumcision availeth anything, nor uncircumcision; but faith which worketh by love.

TIME, THURSDAY EVENING, APRIL 6 [NISAN 14], A. D. 30; PLACE, JERUSALEM.
Week of our Lord's Fourth and Last Passover.

T—CONCLUDED.

Heb. 11. 7 By faith Noah, being warned of God of things not seen as yet, moved with fear, prepared an ark to the saving of his house; by the which he condemned the world, and became heir of the righteousness which is by faith.

8 By faith Abraham, when he was called to go out into a place which he should after receive for an inheritance, obeyed; and he went out, not knowing whither he went.

Jas. 2. 20 But wilt thou know, O vain man, that faith without works is dead?

21 Was not Abraham our father justified by works, when he had offered Isaac his son upon the altar?

22 Seest thou how faith wrought with his works, and by works was faith made perfect?

23 And the Scripture was fulfilled which saith, Abraham believed God, and it was imputed unto him for righteousness: and he was called the Friend of God.

24 Ye see then how that by works a man is justified, and not by faith only.

U

II Tim. 2. 19 Nevertheless the foundation of God standeth sure, having this seal, The Lord knoweth them that are his. And, Let every one that nameth the name of Christ depart from iniquity.

X

Ps. 41. 9 Yea, mine own familiar friend, in whom I trusted, which did eat of my bread, hath lifted up *his* heel against me.

Matt. 26. 23 And he answered and said, He that dippeth *his* hand with me in the dish, the same shall betray me.

John 13. 21. *See text of* § *183.*

2

Or, *From henceforth.*

Y

John 14. 29 And now I have told you before it come to pass, that, when it is come to pass, ye might believe.

John 16. 4 But these things have I told you that when the time shall come, ye may remember that I told you of them. And these things I said not unto you at the beginning, because I was with you.

Z

Matt. 10. 40 He that receiveth you receiveth me; and he that receiveth me receiveth him that sent me.

Matt. 25. 40 And the King shall answer and

CHAP. 13.

11 For [m]he knew who should betray him; therefore said he, Ye are not all clean.

12 So after he had washed their feet, and had taken his garments, and was set down again, he said unto them, Know ye what I have done to you?

13 [n]Ye call me Master and Lord: and ye say well; for *so* I am.

14 [o]If I then, *your* Lord and Master, have washed your feet; [p]ye also ought to wash one another's feet.

15 For [q]I have given you an example, that ye should do as I have done to you.

16 [r]Verily, verily, I say unto you, The servant is not greater than his lord; neither he that is sent greater than he that sent him.

17 [s]If ye know these things, [t]happy are ye if ye do them.

18 I speak not of you all: [u]I know whom I have chosen: but that the Scripture may be fulfilled, [x]He that eateth bread with me hath lifted up his heel against me.

19 [2]Now [y]I tell you before it come, that, when it is come to pass, ye may believe that I am *he.*

20 [z]Verily, verily, I say unto you, He that receiveth whomsoever I send receiveth me; and he that receiveth me receiveth him that sent me.

Z—CONCLUDED.

say unto them, Verily I say unto you, Inasmuch as ye have done *it* unto one of the least of these my brethren, ye have done *it* unto me.

Luke 10. 16 He that heareth you heareth me; and he that despiseth you despiseth me; and he that despiseth me despiseth him that sent me.

§ 183. THE TRAITOR MADE KNOWN. JUDAS WITHDRAWS.

Evening Introducing the Sixth Day of the

26 : 21–25.

21 And as they did eat, he said, Verily I say unto you, that one of you shall betray me.

22 And they were exceeding sorrowful, and began every one of them to say unto him, Lord is it I?

23 And he answered and said, [a]He that dippeth *his* hand with me in the dish, the same shall betray me.

24 The Son of man goeth [b]as it is written of him: but [c]woe unto that man by whom the Son of man is betrayed! it had been good for that man if he had not been born.

14: 18–21.

18 And as they sat and did eat, Jesus said, Verily I say unto you, One of you which eateth with me shall betray me.

19 And they began to be sorrowful, and to say unto him one by one, *Is* it I? and another *said*, *Is* it I?

20 And he answered and said unto them, *It is* one of the twelve, that dippeth with me in the dish.

21 [d]The Son of man indeed goeth, as it is written of him: but woe to that man by whom the Son of man is betrayed! good were it for that man if he had never been born. (p. 520.)

A

Ps. 41. 9 Yea, mine own familiar friend, in whom I trusted, which did eat of my bread, hath lifted up *his* heel against me.

Luke 22. 21. *Text of topic.* John 13. 18. *Text of § 182.*

B

Ps. 22. 1 My God, my God, why hast thou forsaken me? *why art thou so* far from helping me, *and from* the words of my roaring?

Ps. 22. *Read entire chapter.*

Isa. 53. 1 Who hath believed our report? and to whom is the arm of the LORD revealed?

Isa. 53. *Read entire chapter.*

Dan. 9. 26. *See under G, page 451.*

Mark 9. 12 And he answered and told them, Elias verily cometh first, and restoreth all things; and how it is written of the Son of man, that he must suffer many things, and be set at nought.

Luke 24. 25 Then he said unto them, O fools, and slow of heart to believe all that the prophets have spoken:

26 Ought not Christ to have suffered these things, and to enter into his glory?

Luke 24. 46 And said unto them, Thus it is written, and thus it behooved Christ to suffer, and to rise from the dead the third day:

Acts 17. 2 And Paul, as his manner was, went in unto them, and three sabbath days reasoned with them out of the Scriptures,

B—CONCLUDED.

Acts 17. 3 Opening and alleging, that Christ must needs have suffered, and risen again from the dead; and that this Jesus, whom I preach unto you, is Christ.

4 And some of them believed, and consorted with Paul and Silas; and of the devout Greeks a great multitude, and of the chief women not a few.

Acts 26. 22 Having therefore obtained help of God, I continue unto this day, witnessing both to small and great, saying none other things than those which the prophets and Moses did say should come:

23 That Christ should suffer, *and* that he should be the first that should rise from the dead, and should show light unto the people, and to the Gentiles.

I Cor. 15. 3 For I delivered unto you first of all that which I also received, how that Christ died for our sins according to the Scriptures:

C

Matt. 18. 7 Woe unto the world because of offences! for it must needs be that offences come; but woe to that man by whom the offence cometh!

Matt. 27. 3 Then Judas, which had betrayed him, when he saw that he was condemned, repented himself, and brought again the thirty pieces of silver to the chief priests and elders.

Matt. 27. 4, 5. *See text of § 201.*

TIME, THURSDAY EVENING, APRIL 6 [NISAN 14], A. D. 30; PLACE, JERUSALEM.
Week of our Lord's Fourth and Last Passover.

22 : 21–23.

21 [e]But, behold, the hand of him that
betrayeth me *is* with me on the table.
22 [f]And truly the Son of man goeth,
[g]as it was determined: but woe unto
that man by whom he is betrayed!
23 [h]And they began to inquire among
themselves, which of them it was that
should do this thing. (p. 511.)

C—CONCLUDED.

Mark 14. 21. *See text of topic.*
John 17. 12 While I was with them in the world, I kept them in thy name: those that thou gavest me I have kept, and none of them is lost, but the son of perdition; that the Scripture might be fulfilled.

D

Gen. 3. 15 And I will put enmity between thee and the woman, and between thy seed and her seed; it shall bruise thy head, and thou shalt bruise his heel.
Dan. 9. 24. *See under Y, page 420.*
Zech. 13. 7 Awake, O sword, against my Shepherd, and against the man *that is* my fellow, saith the LORD of hosts: smite the Shepherd, and the sheep shall be scattered: and I will turn mine hand upon the little ones.
Matt 26. 24 and Luke 22 22. *See text of topic.*

E

Ps. 41. 9. *See under A.*
Matt. 26. 21, 23 and Mark 14. 18. *See text of topic.*

F

Matt. 26. 24. *See text of topic.*

G

Acts 2. 23 Him, being delivered by the determinate counsel and foreknowledge of God, ye have taken, and by wicked hands have crucified and slain:
Acts 4. 27 For of a truth against thy holy child Jesus, whom thou hast anointed, both Herod, and Pontius Pilate, with the Gentiles, and the people of Israel, were gathered together,
28 For to do whatsoever thy hand and thy counsel determined before to be done.

H

Matt. 26. 22 and John 13. 22, 25. *See text of topic.*

I

Matt. 26. 21 and Luke 22. 21. *See text of topic.*

K

John 12. 27 Now is my soul troubled; and what shall I say? Father, save me from this hour: but for this cause came I unto this hour.

13: 21–35.

21 [i]When Jesus had thus said, [k]he
was troubled in spirit, and testified,
and said, Verily, verily, I say unto you,
[l]that one of you shall betray me.
22 Then the disciples looked one on
another, doubting of whom he spake.
23 Now [m]there was leaning on Jesus'
bosom one of his disciples, whom Jesus
loved.
24 Simon Peter therefore beckoned
to him, that he should ask who it
should be of whom he spake.
25 He then lying on Jesus' breast
saith unto him, Lord, who is it?

L

Acts 1. 17 For he was numbered with us, and had obtained part of this ministry.
I Jno. 2. 19 They went out from us, but they were not of us; for if they had been of us, they would *no doubt* have continued with us: but *they went out*, that they might be made manifest that they were not all of us.

M

John 19. 26 When Jesus therefore saw his mother, and the disciple standing by, whom he loved, he saith unto his mother, Woman, behold thy son!
John 20. 2 Then she runneth, and cometh to Simon Peter, and to the other disciple, whom Jesus loved, and saith unto them, They have taken away the Lord out of the sepulchre, and we know not where they have laid him.
John 21. 7 Therefore that disciple whom Jesus loved saith unto Peter, It is the Lord. Now when Simon Peter heard that it was the Lord, he girt *his* fisher's coat *unto him*, (for he was naked,) and did cast himself into the sea.
John 21. 20 Then Peter, turning about, seeth the disciple whom Jesus loved following; which also leaned on his breast at supper, and said, Lord, which is he that betrayeth thee?
John 21. 24 This is the disciple which testifieth of these things, and wrote these things: and we know that his testimony is true.

§ 183. THE TRAITOR MADE KNOWN. JUDAS WITHDRAWS (CONCLUDED).
Evening Introducing the Sixth Day of the

CHAP. 26.

25 Then Judas, which betrayed him, answered and said, Master, is it I? He said unto him, Thou hast said.

1

Or, *morsel.*

Ex. 12. 8 And they shall eat the flesh in that night, roast with fire, and unleavened bread; *and* with bitter *herbs* they shall eat it.

9 Eat not of it raw, nor sodden at all with water, but roast *with* fire; his head with his legs, and with the purtenance thereof.

N

Luke 22. 3 Then entered Satan into Judas surnamed Iscariot, being of the number of the twelve.

John 6. 70 Jesus answered them, Have not I chosen you twelve, and one of you is a devil?

O

Prov. 1. 16 For their feet run to evil, and make haste to shed blood.

Eccl. 9. 3 This *is* an evil among all *things* that are done under the sun, that *there is* one event unto all: yea, also the heart of the sons of men is full of evil, and madness *is* in their heart while they live, and after that *they go* to the dead.

Jer. 2. 24 A wild ass used to the wilderness, *that* snuffeth up the wind at her pleasure; in her occasion who can turn her away? all they that seek her will not weary themselves; in her month they shall find her.

25 Withhold thy foot from being unshod, and thy throat from thirst: but thou saidst, There is no hope: no; for I have loved strangers, and after them will I go.

Dan. 2. 15 He answered and said unto Arioch the king's captain, Why *is* the decree *so* hasty from the king? Then Arioch made the thing known to Daniel.

Jas. 1. 13 Let no man say when he is tempted, I am tempted of God: for God cannot be tempted with evil, neither tempteth he any man:

14 But every man is tempted, when he is drawn away of his own lust, and enticed.

15 Then when lust hath conceived, it bringeth forth sin; and sin, when it is finished, bringeth forth death.

P

Ps. 109. 6 Set thou a wicked man over him:

[CHAP. 14.]

P—CONCLUDED.

and let Satan stand at his right hand.

John 12. 6 This he said, not that he cared for the poor; but because he was a thief, and had the bag, and bare what was put therein.

Q

John 12. 23 And Jesus answered them, saying, The hour is come, that the Son of man should be glorified.

R

John 14. 13 And whatsoever ye shall ask in my name, that will I do, that the Father may be glorified in the Son.

I Pet. 4. 11 If any man speak, *let him speak* as the oracles of God; if any man minister, *let him do it* as of the ability which God giveth; that God in all things may be glorified through Jesus Christ: to whom be praise and dominion for ever and ever. Amen.

S

John 17. 1 These words spake Jesus, and lifted up his eyes to heaven, and said, Father, the hour is come; glorify thy Son, that thy Son also may glorify thee:

John 17. 4 I have glorified thee on the earth: I have finished the work which thou gavest me to do.

5 And now, O Father, glorify thou me with thine own self with the glory which I had with thee before the world was.

6 I have manifested thy name unto the men which thou gavest me out of the world: thine they were, and thou gavest them me; and they have kept thy word.

T

John 12. 23. *See under Q.*

U

Gal. 4. 19 My little children, of whom I travail in birth again until Christ be formed in you,

I Jno. 2. 1 My little children, these things write I unto you, that ye sin not. And if any man sin, we have an advocate with the Father, Jesus Christ the righteous:

I Jno. 4. 4 Ye are of God, little children, and have overcome them: because greater is he that is in you, than he that is in the world.

X

John 7. 34 Ye shall seek me, and shall not find *me:* and where I am, *thither* ye cannot come.

TIME, THURSDAY EVENING, APRIL 6 [NISAN 14], A. D. 30; PLACE, JERUSALEM.
Week of our Lord's Fourth and Last Passover.

[CHAP. 22.]

X—CONCLUDED.

John 8. 21 Then said Jesus again unto them, I go my way, and ye shall seek me, and shall die in your sins: whither I go, ye cannot come.

Y

Lev. 19. 18 Thou shalt not avenge, nor bear any grudge against the children of thy people, but thou shalt love thy neighbor as thyself: I *am* the LORD.

John 15. 12 This is my commandment, That ye love one another, as I have loved you.

John 15. 17 These things I command you, that ye love one another.

Eph. 5. 2 And walk in love, as Christ also hath loved us, and hath given himself for us an offering and a sacrifice to God for a sweetsmelling savour.

I Thes. 4. 9 But as touching brotherly love ye need not that I write unto you for ye yourselves are taught of God to love one another.

Jas. 2. 8 If ye fulfil the royal law according to the Scripture, Thou shalt love thy neighbour as thyself, ye do well:

I Pet. 1. 22 Seeing ye have purified your souls in obeying the truth through the Spirit unto unfeigned love of the brethren, *see that ye* love one another with a pure heart fervently:

I Jno. 2. 7 Brethren, I write no new commandment unto you, but an old commandment which ye had from the beginning. The old commandment is the word which ye have heard from the beginning.

8 Again, a new commandment I write unto you, which thing is true in him and in you: because the darkness is past, and the true light now shineth.

I Jno. 3. 11 For this is the message that ye heard from the beginning, that we should love one another.

I Jno. 3. 23 And this is his commandment, That we should believe on the name of his Son Jesus Christ, and love one another, as he gave us commandment.

I Jno. 4. 21 And this commandment have we from him, That he who loveth God love his brother also.

Z

I Jno. 2. 5 But whoso keepeth his word, in him verily is the love of God perfected: hereby know we that we are in him.

I Jno. 4. 20 If a man say, I love God, and

CHAP. 13.

26 Jesus answered, He it is, to whom I shall give a sop, when I have dipped *it*. And when he had dipped the [1]sop, he gave *it* to Judas Iscariot, *the son* of Simon.

27 [n]And after the sop Satan entered into him. Then said Jesus unto him, [o]That thou doest, do quickly.

28 Now no man at the table knew for what intent he spake this unto him.

29 For some *of them* thought, because [p]Judas had the bag, that Jesus had said unto him, Buy *those things* that we have need of against the feast; or, that he should give something to the poor.

30 He then, having received the sop, went immediately out; and it was night.

31 Therefore, when he was gone out, Jesus said, [q]Now is the Son of man glorified, and [r]God is glorified in him.

32 [s]If God be glorified in him, God shall also glorify him in himself, and [t]shall straightway glorify him.

33 [u]Little children, yet a little while I am with you. Ye shall seek me; [x]and as I said unto the Jews, Whither I go, ye cannot come; so now I say to you.

34 [y]A new commandment I give unto you, That ye love one another; as I have loved you, that ye also love one another.

35 [z]By this shall all *men* know that ye are my disciples, if ye have [a]love one to another.

(p. 523.)

Z—CONCLUDED.

hateth his brother, he is a liar: for he that loveth not his brother whom he hath seen, how can he love God whom he hath not seen?

A

Acts 2. 46 And they, continuing daily with one accord in the temple, and breaking bread from house to house, did eat their meat with gladness and singleness of heart.

§ 184. THE LORD'S SUPPER INSTITUTED.
Evening Introducing the Sixth Day of the

26 : 26–29.

26 [a]And as they were eating, [b]Jesus
took bread, and [1]blessed *it*, and brake
it, and gave *it* to the disciples, and said,
Take, eat; [c]this is my body.

27 And he took the cup, and gave
thanks, and gave *it* to them, saying,
[d]Drink ye all of it;

28 For [e]this is my blood [f]of the New
Testament, which is shed [g]for many for
the remission of sins.

29 But [h]I say unto you, I will not
drink henceforth of this fruit of the
vine, [i]until that day when I drink it
new with you in my Father's kingdom.
(p. 548.)

A

Mark 14. 22 and Luke 22. 19. *See text of topic.*

B

I Cor.11. 23 For I have received of the Lord that which also I delivered unto you, That the Lord Jesus, the *same* night in which he was betrayed, took bread:
24 And when he had given thanks, he brake *it*, and said, Take, eat; this is my body, which is broken for you: this do in remembrance of me.
25 After the same manner also *he took* the cup, when he had supped, saying, This cup is the new testament in my blood: this do ye, as oft as ye drink *it*, in remembrance of me.

1

Many Greek copies have, *gave thanks.*

Mark 6. 41 And when he had taken the five loaves and the two fishes, he looked up to heaven, and blessed, and brake the loaves, and gave *them* to his disciples to set before them; and the two fishes divided he among them all.

C

I Cor.10. 3 And did all eat the same spiritual meat;
4 And did all drink the same spiritual drink; for they drank of that spiritual Rock that followed them: and that Rock was Christ.

I Cor.10. 16 The cup of blessing which we bless, is it not the communion of the blood of Christ? The bread which we break, is it not the communion of the body of Christ?

14: 22–25.

22 [k]And as they did eat, Jesus took
bread, and blessed, and brake *it*, and
gave to them, and said, Take, eat;
[l]this is my body.

23 And he took the cup, and when
he had given thanks, he gave *it* to them:
and they all drank of it.

24 And he said unto them, [m]This is
my blood of the new testament, which
is shed for many.

25 Verily I say unto you, I will drink
no more of the fruit of the vine, until
that day that I drink it new in the
kingdom of God. (p. 548.)

D

Mark 14. 23. *See text of topic.*

E

Ex. 24. 8 And Moses took the blood, and sprinkled *it* on the people, and said, Behold the blood of the covenant, which the LORD hath made with you concerning all these words.

Lev. 17. 11 For the life of the flesh *is* in the blood; and I have given it to you upon the altar to make an atonement for your souls: for it *is* the blood *that* maketh an atonement for the soul.

F

Jer. 31. 31 Behold, the days come, saith the LORD, that I will make a new covenant with the house of Israel, and with the house of Judah:

G

Matt.20. 28 Even as the Son of man came not to be ministered unto, but to minister, and to give his life a ransom for many.

Rom. 5. 15 But not as the offence, so also *is* the free gift: for if through the offence of one many be dead, much more the grace of God, and the gift by grace, *which is* by one man, Jesus Christ, hath abounded unto many.

Heb. 9. 22 And almost all things are by the law purged with blood; and without shedding of blood is no remission.

H

Mark 14. 25. *See text of topic.*

Luke 22. 18 For I say unto you, I will not drink of the fruit of the vine, until the kingdom of God shall come.

TIME, THURSDAY EVENING, APRIL 6 [NISAN 14], A. D. 30; PLACE, JERUSALEM.
Week of our Lord's Fourth and Last Passover.

22: 19, 20.

19 [n]And he took bread, and gave
thanks, and brake *it*, and gave unto
them, saying, This is my body which is
given for you: [o]this do in remembrance
of me.

20 Likewise also the cup after supper, saying, [p]This cup *is* the new testament in my blood, which is shed for you.

(p. 517.)

I

Acts 10. 41 Not to all the people, but unto witnesses chosen before of God, *even* to us, who did eat and drink with him after he rose from the dead.

K

Matt. 26. 26 and Luke 22. 19. *See text of topic.*
I Cor. 11. 23. *See under B.*

L

I Cor. 10. 4, 16. *See under C.*

M

John 6. 53 Then Jesus said unto them, Verily, verily, I say unto you, Except ye eat the flesh of the Son of man, and drink his blood, ye have no life in you.

I Cor. 11. 25 After the same manner also *he took* the cup, when he had supped, saying, This cup is the new testament in my blood: this do ye, as oft as ye drink *it*, in remembrance of me.

Heb. 9. 13 For if the blood of bulls and of goats, and the ashes of a heifer sprinkling the unclean, sanctifieth to the purifying of the flesh;

14 How much more shall the blood of Christ, who through the eternal Spirit offered himself without spot to God, purge your conscience from dead works to serve the living God?

N

Matt. 26. 26 and Mark 14. 22. *See text of topic.*

O

Ps. 78. 4 We will not hide *them* from their children, showing to the generation to come the praises of the LORD, and his strength, and his wonderful works that he hath done.

5 For he established a testimony in Jacob, and appointed a law in Israel, which he commanded our fathers, that they should make them known to their children:

6 That the generation to come might know *them*, *even* the children *which* should be born; *who* should arise and declare *them* to their children:

O—CONCLUDED.

Ps. 111. 4 He hath made his wonderful works to be remembered: the LORD *is* gracious and full of compassion.

Song 1. 4 Draw me, we will run after thee: the King hath brought me into his chambers: we will be glad and rejoice in thee, we will remember thy love more than wine: the upright love thee.

I Cor. 11. 24. *See under B.*

P

I Cor 10. 16. *Under C.* I Cor. 11. 25. *Under B.*

Heb. 8. 6 But now hath he obtained a more excellent ministry, by how much also he is the mediator of a better covenant, which was established upon better promises.

7 For if that first *covenant* had been faultless, then should no place have been sought for the second.

8 For finding fault with them, he saith, Behold, the days come, saith the Lord, when I will make a new covenant with the house of Israel and with the house of Judah:

9 Not according to the covenant that I made with their fathers in the day when I took them by the hand to lead them out of the land of Egypt; because they continued not in my covenant, and I regarded them not, saith the Lord.

10 For this *is* the covenant that I will make with the house of Israel after those days, saith the Lord; I will put my laws into their mind, and write them in their hearts: and I will be to them a God, and they shall be to me a people:

11 And they shall not teach every man his neighbour, and every man his brother, saying, Know the Lord: for all shall know me, from the least to the greatest.

12 For I will be merciful to their unrighteousness, and their sins and their iniquities will I remember no more.

13 In that he saith, A new *covenant*, he hath made the first old. Now that which decayeth and waxeth old *is* ready to vanish away.

Heb. 9. 17 For a testament *is* of force after men are dead: otherwise it is of no strength at all while the testator liveth.

Heb. 12. 24 And to Jesus the mediator of the new covenant, and to the blood of sprinkling, that speaketh better things than *that of* Abel.

§ 185. PETER'S FALL FORETOLD.
Evening Introducing the Sixth Day of the

26: 31–35.

31 Then saith Jesus unto them, [a]All
ye shall [b]be offended because of me this
night: for it is written, [c]I will smite
the Shepherd, and the sheep of the
flock shall be scattered abroad.

32 But after I am risen again, [d]I will
go before you into Galilee.

33 Peter answered and said unto him,
Though all *men* shall be offended because of thee, *yet* will I never be offended.

34 Jesus said unto him, Verily I say
unto thee, That this night, before the
cock crow, thou shalt deny me thrice.

35 Peter said unto him, Though I
should die with thee, yet will I not
deny thee. Likewise also said all the
disciples. (p. 548.)

A

Mark 14. 27. *See text of topic.*

John 16. 32 Behold, the hour cometh, yea, is now come, that ye shall be scattered, every man to his own, and shall leave me alone: and yet I am not alone, because the Father is with me.

B

Matt. 11. 6 And blessed is *he*, whosoever shall not be offended in me.

C

Zech. 13. 7 Awake, O sword, against my Shepherd, and against the man *that is* my fellow, saith the LORD of hosts: smite the Shepherd, and the sheep shall be scattered: and I will turn mine hand upon the little ones.

D

Matt. 28. 7 And go quickly, and tell his disciples that he is risen from the dead; and, behold, he goeth before you into Galilee; there shall ye see him: lo, I have told you.

Matt. 28. 10 Then said Jesus unto them, Be not afraid: go tell my brethren that they go into Galilee, and there shall they see me.

Matt. 28. 16 Then the eleven disciples went away into Galilee, into a mountain where Jesus had appointed them,

Mark 14. 28. *See text of topic.*

14: 27–31.

27 And Jesus saith unto them, All ye
shall be offended because of me this
night: for it is written, [e]I will smite
the Shepherd, and the sheep shall be
scattered.

28 But [f]after that I am risen, I will
go before you into Galilee.

29 But Peter said unto him, Although
all shall be offended, yet *will* not I.

30 And Jesus saith unto him, Verily
I say unto thee, That this day, *even* in
this night, before the cock crow twice,
thou shalt deny me thrice.

31 But he spake the more vehemently,
If I should die with thee, I will not deny
thee in any wise. Likewise also said
they all. (p. 548.)

D—CONCLUDED.

Mark 16. 7 But go your way, tell his disciples and Peter that he goeth before you into Galilee: there shall ye see him, as he said unto you.

E

Dan. 9. 26. *See under G, page 451.*
Zech. 13. 7. *See under C.*

F

Mark 16. 7. *See under D.*

G

I Pet. 5. 8 Be sober, be vigilant; because your adversary the devil, as a roaring lion, walketh about, seeking whom he may devour:

H

Amos 9. 9 For, lo, I will command, and I will sift the house of Israel among all nations, like as *corn* is sifted in a sieve, yet shall not the least grain fall upon the earth.

I

John 17. 9 I pray for them: I pray not for the world, but for them which thou hast given me; for they are thine.

John 17. 11 And now I am no more in the world, but these are in the world, and I come to thee. Holy Father, keep through thine own name those whom thou hast given me, that they may be one, as we *are*.

John 17. 15 I pray not that thou shouldest take them out of the world, but that thou shouldest keep them from the evil.

TIME, THURSDAY EVENING, APRIL 6 [NISAN 14] A. D. 30; PLACE, JERUSALEM.
Week of our Lord's Fourth and Last Passover.

22: 31–38.

31 And the Lord said, Simon, Simon, behold, [g]Satan hath desired *to have* you, that he may [h]sift *you* as wheat:

32 But [i]I have prayed for thee, that thy faith fail not: [k]and when thou art converted, strengthen thy brethren.

33 And he said unto him, Lord, I am ready to go with thee, both into prison, and to death.

34 And he said, I tell thee, Peter, the cock shall not crow this day, before that thou shalt thrice deny that thou knowest me.

35 [l]And he said unto them, When I sent you without purse, and scrip, and shoes, lacked ye anything? And they said, Nothing.

36 Then said he unto them, But now, he that hath a purse, let him take *it*, and likewise *his* scrip: and he that hath no sword, let him sell his garment, and buy one.

37 For I say unto you, that this that is written must yet be accomplished in me, [m]And he was reckoned among the transgressors: for the things concerning me have an end.

38 And they said, Lord, behold, here *are* two swords. And he said unto them, It is enough. (p. 549.)

K

Ps. 51. 13 *Then* will I teach transgressors thy ways; and sinners shall be converted unto thee.

John 21. 15 So when they had dined, Jesus saith to Simon Peter, Simon, *son* of Jonas, lovest thou me more than these? He saith unto him, Yea, Lord; thou knowest that I love thee. He saith unto him, Feed my lambs.

16 He saith to him again the second time, Simon, *son* of Jonas, lovest thou

13: 36–38.

36 Simon Peter said unto him, Lord, whither goest thou? Jesus answered him, Whither I go, thou canst not follow me now; but [n]thou shalt follow me afterwards.

37 Peter said unto him, Lord, why cannot I follow thee now? I will lay down my life for thy sake.

38 Jesus answered him, Wilt thou lay down thy life for my sake? Verily, verily, I say unto thee, The cock shall not crow, till thou hast denied me thrice.

K—CONCLUDED.

me? He saith unto him, Yea, Lord; thou knowest that I love thee. He saith unto him, Feed my sheep.

17 He saith unto him the third time, Simon, *son* of Jonas, lovest thou me? Peter was grieved because he said unto him the third time, Lovest thou me? And he said unto him, Lord, thou knowest all things; thou knowest that I love thee. Jesus saith unto him, Feed my sheep.

John 21. 22 Jesus saith unto him, If I will that he tarry till I come, what *is that* to thee? follow thou me.

L

Matt. 10. 9 Provide neither gold, nor silver, nor brass in your purses;

Luke 9. 3 And he said unto them, Take nothing for *your* journey, neither staves, nor scrip, neither bread, neither money; neither have two coats apiece.

Luke 10. 4 Carry neither purse, nor scrip, nor shoes; and salute no man by the way.

M

Isa. 53. 12 Therefore will I divide him *a portion* with the great, and he shall divide the spoil with the strong; because he hath poured out his soul unto death: and he was numbered with the transgressors; and he bare the sin of many, and made intercession for the transgressors.

Mark 15. 28 And the Scripture was fulfilled, which saith, And he was numbered with the transgressors.

N

John 21. 18. *See text of § 221.*

II Pet. 1. 14 Knowing that shortly I must put off *this* my tabernacle, even as our Lord Jesus Christ hath showed me.

§ 186. JESUS COMFORTS HIS DISCIPLES.
Evening Introducing the Sixth Day of the

A

John 14. 27. *See text of topic.*

John 16. 22 And ye now therefore have sorrow: but I will see you again, and your heart shall rejoice, and your joy no man taketh from you.

23 And in that day ye shall ask me nothing. Verily, verily, I say unto you, Whatsoever ye shall ask the Father in my name, he will give *it* you.

B

II Cor 5. 1 For we know that, if our earthly house of *this* tabernacle were dissolved, we have a building of God, a house not made with hands, eternal in the heavens.

Heb. 11. 10 For he looked for a city which hath foundations, whose builder and maker *is* God.

Heb. 11. 14 For they that say such things declare plainly that they seek a country.

15 And truly, if they had been mindful of that *country* from whence they came out, they might have had opportunity to have returned.

16 But now they desire a better *country*, that is, a heavenly: wherefore God is not ashamed to be called their God: for he hath prepared for them a city.

Heb. 13. 14 For here have we no continuing city, but we seek one to come.

Rev. 3. 12 Him that overcometh will I make a pillar in the temple of my God, and he shall go no more out: and I will write upon him the name of my God, and the name of the city of my God, *which is* new Jerusalem, which cometh down out of heaven from my God: and *I will write upon him* my new name.

C

John 13. 33 Little children, yet a little while I am with you. Ye shall seek me; and as I said unto the Jews, Whither I go, ye cannot come: so now I say to you.

John 13. 36 Simon Peter said unto him, Lord, whither goest thou? Jesus answered him, Whither I go, thou canst not follow me now; but thou shalt follow me afterwards.

Heb. 6. 19 Which *hope* we have as an anchor of the soul, both sure and steadfast, and which entereth into that within the vail:

20 Whither the forerunner is for us

C—Concluded.

entered, *even* Jesus, made a high priest for ever after the order of Melchisedec.

D

John 14. 18, 28. *See text of topic.*

Acts 1. 11 Which also said, Ye men of Galilee, why stand ye gazing up into heaven? this same Jesus, which is taken up from you into heaven, shall so come in like manner as ye have seen him go into heaven.

E

John 12. 26 If any man serve me, let him follow me; and where I am, there shall also my servant be: if any man serve me, him will *my* Father honour.

John 17. 24 Father, I will that they also, whom thou hast given me, be with me where I am; that they may behold my glory, which thou hast given me: for thou lovedst me before the foundation of the world.

I Thes. 4. 17 Then we which are alive *and* remain shall be caught up together with them in the clouds, to meet the Lord in the air: and so shall we ever be with the Lord.

F

Heb. 9. 8 The Holy Ghost this signifying, that the way into the holiest of all was not yet made manifest, while as the first tabernacle was yet standing:

G

John 1. 17 For the law was given by Moses, *but* grace and truth came by Jesus Christ.

John 8. 32 And ye shall know the truth, and the truth shall make you free.

H

John 1. 4 In him was life; and the life was the light of men.

John 11. 25 Jesus said unto her, I am the resurrection, and the life: he that believeth in me, though he were dead, yet shall he live:

I

John 10. 9 I am the door: by me if any man enter in, he shall be saved, and shall go in and out, and find pasture.

K

John 8. 19 Then said they unto him, Where is thy Father? Jesus answered, Ye neither know me, nor my Father: if ye had known me, ye should have known my Father also.

L

John 12. 45 And he that seeth me seeth him that sent me.

TIME, THURSDAY EVENING, APRIL 6 [NISAN 14], A. D. 30; PLACE, JERUSALEM.
Week of our Lord's Fourth and Last Passover.

L—CONCLUDED.

Col. 1. 15 Who is the image of the invisible God, the first-born of every creature:

Heb. 1. 3 Who being the brightness of *his* glory, and the express image of his person, and upholding all things by the word of his power, when he had by himself purged our sins, sat down on the right hand of the Majesty on high;

M

John 14. 20. *See text of topic.*

John 10. 38 But if I do, though ye believe not me, believe the works; that ye may know, and believe, that the Father *is* in me, and I in him.

John 17. 21 That they all may be one; as thou, Father, *art* in me, and I in thee, that they also may be one in us: that the world may believe that thou hast sent me.

John 17. 23 I in them, and thou in me, that they may be made perfect in one; and that the world may know that thou hast sent me, and hast loved them, as thou hast loved me.

N

John 5. 19 Then answered Jesus and said unto them, Verily, verily, I say unto you, The Son can do nothing of himself, but what he seeth the Father do: for what things soever he doeth, these also doeth the Son likewise.

John 7. 16 Jesus answered them, and said, My doctrine is not mine, but his that sent me.

John 8. 28 Then said Jesus unto them, When ye have lifted up the Son of man, then shall ye know that I am *he*, and *that* I do nothing of myself; but as my Father hath taught me, I speak these things.

John 12. 49 For I have not spoken of myself; but the Father which sent me, he gave me a commandment, what I should say, and what I should speak.

O

John 5. 36 But I have greater witness than *that* of John: for the works which the Father hath given me to finish, the same works that I do, bear witness of me, that the Father hath sent me.

John 10. 38. *See under M.*

Acts. 2. 22 Ye men of Israel, hear these words; Jesus of Nazareth, a man approved of God among you by miracles and wonders and signs, which God did by him in the midst of you, as ye yourselves also know:

14: 1–31.

1 Let [a]not your heart be troubled: ye believe in God, believe also in me.

2 [b]In my Father's house are many mansions: if *it were* not *so*, I would have told you. [c]I go to prepare a place for you.

3 And if I go and prepare a place for you, [d]I will come again, and receive you unto myself; that [e]where I am, *there* ye may be also.

4 And whither I go ye know, and the way ye know.

5 Thomas saith unto him, Lord we know not whither thou goest; and how can we know the way?

6 Jesus saith unto him, I am [f]the way, [g]the truth, and [h]the life: no man cometh unto the Father, [i]but by me.

7 [k]If ye had known me, ye should have known my Father also: and from henceforth ye know him, and have seen him.

8 Philip saith unto him, Lord, show us the Father, and it sufficeth us.

9 Jesus saith unto him, Have I been so long time with you, and yet hast thou not known me, Philip? [l]he that hath seen me hath seen the Father; and how sayest thou *then*, Show us the Father?

10 Believest thou not that [m]I am in the Father, and the Father in me? the words that [n]I speak unto you I speak not of myself: but the Father that dwelleth in me, he doeth the works.

11 Believe me that I *am* in the Father, and the Father in me: [o]or else believe me for the very works' sake.

§ 186. JESUS COMFORTS HIS DISCIPLES (Continued).
Evening Introducing the Sixth Day of the

P

Matt.21. 21 Jesus answered and said unto them, Verily I say unto you, If ye have faith, and doubt not, ye shall not only do this *which is done* to the fig tree, but also if ye shall say unto this mountain, Be thou removed, and be thou cast into the sea; it shall be done.

Mark 16. 17 And these signs shall follow them that believe; In my name shall they cast out devils; they shall speak with new tongues;

Luke 10. 17 And the seventy returned again with joy, saying, Lord, even the devils are subject unto us through thy name.

I Cor.12. 10 To another the working of miracles; to another prophecy; to another discerning of spirits; to another *divers* kinds of tongues; to another the interpretation of tongues:

Q

Matt. 7. 7 Ask, and it shall be given you; seek, and ye shall find; knock, and it shall be opened unto you:

Matt.21. 22 And all things, whatsoever ye shall ask in prayer, believing, ye shall receive.

Mark 11. 24 Therefore I say unto you, What things soever ye desire, when ye pray, believe that ye receive *them*, and ye shall have *them*.

Luke 11. 9 And I say unto you, Ask, and it shall be given you; seek, and ye shall find; knock, and it shall be opened unto you.

John 15. 7 If ye abide in me, and my words abide in you, ye shall ask what ye will, and it shall be done unto you.

John 15. 16 Ye have not chosen me, but I have chosen you, and ordained you, that ye should go and bring forth fruit, and *that* your fruit should remain; that whatsoever ye shall ask of the Father in my name, he may give it you.

John 16. 23 And in that day ye shall ask me nothing. Verily, verily, I say unto you, Whatsoever ye shall ask the Father in my name, he will give *it* you.

24 Hitherto have ye asked nothing in my name: ask, and ye shall receive, that your joy may be full.

Jas. 1. 5 If any of you lack wisdom, let him ask of God, that giveth to all *men* liberally, and upbraideth not; and it shall be given him.

I Jno. 3. 22 And whatsoever we ask, we receive of him, because we keep his commandments, and do those things that are pleasing in his sight.

Q—Concluded.

I Jno. 5. 14 And this is the confidence that we have in him, that, if we ask any thing according to his will, he heareth us:

R

John 14. 21, 23. *See text of topic.*

John 15. 10 If ye keep my commandments, ye shall abide in my love; even as I have kept my Father's commandments, and abide in his love.

John 15. 14 Ye are my friends, if ye do whatsoever I command you.

I Jno. 5. 3 For this is the love of God, that we keep his commandments: and his commandments are not grievous.

S

John 15. 26 But when the Comforter is come, whom I will send unto you from the Father, *even* the Spirit of truth, which proceedeth from the Father, he shall testify of me:

John 16. 7 Nevertheless I tell you the truth; It is expedient for you that I go away: for if I go not away, the Comforter will not come unto you; but if I depart, I will send him unto you.

Rom. 8. 15 For ye have not received the spirit of bondage again to fear; but ye have received the Spirit of adoption, whereby we cry, Abba, Father.

Rom. 8. 26 Likewise the Spirit also helpeth our infirmities: for we know not what we should pray for as we ought: but the Spirit itself maketh intercession for us with groanings which cannot be uttered.

T

John 15. 26. *See under S.*

John 16. 13 Howbeit when he, the Spirit of truth, is come, he will guide you into all truth: for he shall not speak of himself; but whatsoever he shall hear, *that* shall he speak: and he will shew you things to come.

I Jno. 2. 27 But the anointing which ye have received of him abideth in you, and ye need not that any man teach you: but as the same anointing teacheth you of all things, and is truth, and is no lie, and even as it hath taught you, ye shall abide in him.

I Jno. 4. 6 We are of God: he that knoweth God heareth us; he that is not of God heareth not us. Hereby know we the spirit of truth, and the spirit of error.

TIME, THURSDAY EVENING, APRIL 6 [NISAN 14], A. D. 30; PLACE, JERUSALEM.
Week of our Lord's Fourth and Last Passover.

U

Rom. 8. 7 Because the carnal mind *is* enmity against God: for it is not subject to the law of God, neither indeed can be.

I Cor. 2. 14 But the natural man receiveth not the things of the Spirit of God: for they are foolishness unto him: neither can he know *them*, because they are spiritually discerned.

X

I Jno. 2. 27. *See under T.*

Y

Matt. 28. 20 Teaching them to observe all things whatsoever I have commanded you: and, lo, I am with you alway, *even* unto the end of the world. Amen.

1

Or, *orphans.*

Z

John 14. 3, 28. *See text of topic.*

A

John 16. 16 A little while, and ye shall not see me: and again, a little while, and ye shall see me, because I go to the Father.

B

I Cor. 15. 20 But now is Christ risen from the dead, *and* become the first-fruits of them that slept.

II Cor. 4. 10 Always bearing about in the body the dying of the Lord Jesus, that the life also of Jesus might be made manifest in our body.

C

John 14. 10. *See text of topic.*
John 10. 38 and John 17. 21. *See under M, page 525.*
John 17. 23. *See under M, page 525.*

John 17. 26 And I have declared unto them thy name, and will declare *it;* that the love wherewith thou hast loved me may be in them, and I in them.

D

John 14. 15, 23. *See text of topic.*

I Jno. 2. 5 But whoso keepeth his word, in him verily is the love of God perfected: hereby know we that we are in him.

I Jno. 5. 3. *See under R.*

E

Luke 6. 16 And Judas *the brother* of James, and Judas Iscariot, which also was the traitor.

F

John 14. 15. *See text of topic.*

G

Ps. 91. 1 He that dwelleth in the secret place of the Most High shall abide under the shadow of the Almighty.

Rom. 8. 9 But ye are not in the flesh, but in the Spirit, if so be that the Spirit of God dwell in you. Now if any man

CHAP. 14.

12 [p]Verily, verily, I say unto you, He
that believeth on me, the works that I
do shall he do also; and greater *works*
than these shall he do; because I go
unto my Father.
13 [q]And whatsoever ye shall ask in
my name, that will I do, that the Father
may be glorified in the Son.
14 If ye shall ask any thing in my
name, I will do *it*.
15 [r]If ye love me, keep my commandments.
16 And I will pray the Father, and
[s]he shall give you another Comforter,
that he may abide with you for ever;
17 *Even* [t]the Spirit of truth; [u]whom
the world cannot receive, because it
seeth him not, neither knoweth him:
but ye know him; for he dwelleth with
you, [x]and shall be in you.
18 [y]I will not leave you [1]comfortless:
I [z]will come to you.
19 Yet a little while, and the world
seeth me no more; [a]but ye see me:
[b]because I live, ye shall live also.
20 [c]At that day ye shall know that I
am in my Father, and ye in me, and
I in you.
21 [d]He that hath my commandments,
and keepeth them, he it is that loveth
me: and he that loveth me shall be
loved of my Father, and I will love
him, and will manifest myself to him.
22 [e]Judas saith unto him, not Iscariot,
Lord, how is it that thou wilt manifest
thyself unto us, and not unto the world?

G—CONTINUED.

have not the Spirit of Christ, he is none of his.

For G concluded see next page (528).

§ 186. JESUS COMFORTS HIS DISCIPLES (Concluded).
Evening Introducing the Sixth Day of the

For F and G see preceding page (527).

G—Concluded.

Rom. 8. 10 And if Christ *be* in you, the body *is* dead because of sin; but the Spirit *is* life because of righteousness.

11 But if the Spirit of him that raised up Jesus from the dead dwell in you, he that raised up Christ from the dead shall also quicken your mortal bodies by his Spirit that dwelleth in you.

I Jno. 2. 24 Let that therefore abide in you, which ye have heard from the beginning. If that which ye have heard from the beginning shall remain in you, ye also shall continue in the Son, and in the Father.

I Jno. 4. 16 And we have known and believed the love that God hath to us. God is love; and he that dwelleth in love dwelleth in God, and God in him.

Rev. 3. 20 Behold, I stand at the door, and knock: if any man hear my voice, and open the door, I will come in to him, and will sup with him, and he with me.

H

John 5. 19. *See under N, page 525.*

John 5. 38 And ye have not his word abiding in you: for whom he hath sent, him ye believe not.

John 7. 16, John 8. 28 and John 12. 49. *See under N, page 525.*

John 14. 10. *See text of topic.*

I

Luke 24. 49 And, behold, I send the promise of my Father upon you: but tarry ye in the city of Jerusalem, until ye be endued with power from on high.

John 14. 16. *See text of topic.*

John 15. 26 and John 16. 7. *See under S, page 526.*

Rom. 5. 5 And hope maketh not ashamed; because the love of God is shed abroad in our hearts by the Holy Ghost which is given unto us.

K

John 2. 22 When therefore he was risen from the dead, his disciples remembered that he had said this unto them; and they believed the Scripture, and the word which Jesus had said.

John 12. 16 These things understood not his disciples at the first: but when Jesus was glorified, then remembered they that these things were written of him, and *that* they had done these things unto him.

John 16. 13. *See under T, page 526.*

I Jno. 2. 20 But ye have an unction from the Holy One, and ye know all things.

I Jno. 2. 27. *See under T, page 526,*

L

Phil. 4. 7 And the peace of God, which passeth all understanding, shall keep your hearts and minds through Christ Jesus.

Col. 3. 15 And let the peace of God rule in your hearts, to the which also ye are called in one body; and be ye thankful.

M

John 14. 1. *See text of topic.*

N

John 14. 3, 18. *See text of topic.*

O

John 14. 12. *See text of topic.*

John 16. 16. *See under A, page 527.*

John 20. 17 Jesus saith unto her, Touch me not; for I am not yet ascended to my Father: but go to my brethren, and say unto them, I ascend unto my Father, and your Father; and *to* my God, and your God.

P

Isa. 9. 6 For unto us a child is born, unto us a son is given: and the government shall be upon his shoulder: and his name shall be called Wonderful, Counsellor, The mighty God, The everlasting Father, The Prince of Peace.

Isa. 42. 1 Behold my servant, whom I uphold; mine elect, *in whom* my soul delighteth; I have put my Spirit upon him: he shall bring forth judgment to the Gentiles.

Isa. 49. 1 Listen, O isles, unto me; and hearken, ye people, from far; The Lord hath called me from the womb; from the bowels of my mother hath he made mention of my name.

2 And he hath made my mouth like a sharp sword; in the shadow of his hand hath he hid me, and made me a polished shaft; in his quiver hath he hid me;

3 And said unto me, Thou *art* my servant, O Israel, in whom I will be glorified.

4 Then I said, I have laboured in vain, I have spent my strength for nought, and in vain: *yet* surely my judgment *is* with the Lord, and my work with my God.

5 And now, saith the Lord that formed me from the womb *to be* his servant, to bring Jacob again to him, Though Israel be not gathered, yet shall I be glorious in the eyes of the Lord, and my God shall be my strength.

6 And he said. It is a light thing

TIME, THURSDAY EVENING, APRIL 6 [NISAN 14], A. D. 30; PLACE, JERUSALEM.
Week of our Lord's Fourth and Last Passover.

P—CONCLUDED.

that thou shouldest be my servant to raise up the tribes of Jacob, and to restore the preserved of Israel: I will also give thee for a light to the Gentiles, that thou mayest be my salvation unto the end of the earth.

John 5. 18 Therefore the Jews sought the more to kill him, because he not only had broken the sabbath, but said also that God was his Father, making himself equal with God.

John 10. 30 I and *my* Father are one.

Gal. 4. 4 But when the fulness of the time was come, God sent forth his Son, made of a woman, made under the law,

Phil. 2. 6 Who, being in the form of God, thought it not robbery to be equal with God:

I Jno. 5. 7 For there are three that bear record in heaven, the Father, the Word, and the Holy Ghost: and these three are one.

Q

John 13. 19 Now I tell you before it come, that, when it is come to pass, ye may believe that I am *he*.

John 16. 4 But these things have I told you, that when the time shall come, ye may remember that I told you of them. And these things I said not unto you at the beginning, because I was with you.

R

John 12. 31 Now is the judgment of this world: now shall the prince of this world be cast out.

John 16. 11 Of judgment, because the prince of this world is judged.

S

II Cor. 5. 21 For he hath made him *to be* sin for us, who knew no sin; that we might be made the righteousness of God in him.

I Jno. 3. 5 And ye know that he was manifested to take away our sins; and in him is no sin.

T

John 10. 18 No man taketh it from me, but I lay it down of myself. I have power to lay it down, and I have power to take it again. This commandment have I received of my Father.

Phil. 2. 8 And being found in fashion as a man, he humbled himself, and became obedient unto death, even the death of the cross.

Heb. 5. 8 Though he were a Son, yet learned

CHAP. 14.

23 Jesus answered and said unto him, [f]If a man love me, he will keep my words: and my Father will love him, [g]and we will come unto him, and make our abode with him.

24 He that loveth me not keepeth not my sayings: [h]and the word which ye hear is not mine, but the Father's which sent me.

25 These things have I spoken unto you, being *yet* present with you.

26 But [i]the Comforter, *which is* the Holy Ghost, whom the Father will send in my name, [k]he shall teach you all things, and bring all things to your remembrance, whatsoever I have said unto you.

27 [l]Peace I leave with you, my peace I give unto you: not as the world giveth, give I unto you. [m]Let not your heart be troubled, neither let it be afraid.

28 Ye have heard how [n]I said unto you, I go away, and come *again* unto you. If ye loved me, ye would rejoice, because I said, [o]I go unto the Father: for [p]my Father is greater than I.

29 And [q]now I have told you before it come to pass, that, when it is come to pass, ye might believe.

30 Hereafter I will not talk much with you: [r]for the prince of this world cometh, and [s]hath nothing in me.

31 But that the world may know that I love the Father, and [t]as the Father gave me commandment, even so I do. Arise, let us go hence.

T—CONCLUDED.

he obedience by the things which he suffered;

§ 187. THE VINE AND THE BRANCHES.
Evening Introducing the Sixth Day of the

A

Matt. 15. 13 But he answered and said, Every plant, which my heavenly Father hath not planted, shall be rooted up.

I Cor. 13. 1 Though I speak with the tongues of men and of angels, and have not charity, I am become *as* sounding brass, or a tinkling cymbal.

Heb. 6. 7 For the earth which drinketh in the rain that cometh oft upon it, and bringeth forth herbs meet for them by whom it is dressed, receiveth blessing from God:

8 But that which beareth thorns and briers *is* rejected, and *is* nigh unto cursing; whose end *is* to be burned.

B

John 13. 10 Jesus saith to him, He that is washed needeth not save to wash *his* feet, but is clean every whit: and ye are clean, but not all.

John 17. 17 Sanctify them through thy truth: thy word is truth.

Eph. 5. 26 That he might sanctify and cleanse it with the washing of water by the word,

I Pet. 1. 22 Seeing ye have purified your souls in obeying the truth through the Spirit unto unfeigned love of the brethren, *see that ye* love one another with a pure heart fervently:

C

Col. 1. 23 If ye continue in the faith grounded and settled, and *be* not moved away from the hope of the gospel, which ye have heard, *and* which was preached to every creature which is under heaven; whereof I Paul am made a minister;

I Jno. 2. 6 He that saith he abideth in him ought himself also so to walk, even as he walked.

D

Hos. 14. 8 Ephraim *shall say,* What have I to do any more with idols? I have heard *him,* and observed him: I *am* like a green fir tree. From me is thy fruit found.

Phil. 1. 11 Being filled with the fruits of righteousness, which are by Jesus Christ, unto the glory and praise of God.

Phil. 4. 13 I can do all things through Christ which strengtheneth me.

1

Or, *severed from me.*

Acts 4. 12 Neither is there salvation in any other: for there is none other name under heaven given among men, whereby we must be saved.

E

Matt. 3. 10 And now also the axe is laid unto the root of the trees: therefore every tree which bringeth not forth good fruit is hewn down, and cast into the fire.

Matt. 7. 19 Every tree that bringeth not forth good fruit is hewn down, and cast into the fire.

Heb. 6. 4 For *it is* impossible for those who were once enlightened, and have tasted of the heavenly gift, and were made partakers of the Holy Ghost,

5 And have tasted the good word of God, and the powers of the world to come,

6 If they shall fall away, to renew them again unto repentance; seeing they crucify to themselves the Son of God afresh, and put *him* to an open shame.

F

John 14. 13 And whatsoever ye shall ask in my name, that will I do, that the Father may be glorified in the Son.

14 If ye shall ask anything in my name, I will do *it.*

John 15. 16 Ye have not chosen me, but I have chosen you, and ordained you, that ye should go and bring forth fruit, and *that* your fruit should remain; that whatsoever ye shall ask of the Father in my name, he may give it you.

John 16. 23 And in that day ye shall ask me nothing. Verily, verily, I say unto you, Whatsoever ye shall ask the Father in my name, he will give *it* you.

G

Isa. 60. 21 Thy people also *shall be* all righteous: they shall inherit the land for ever, the branch of my planting, the work of my hands, that I may be glorified.

Hag. 1. 8 Go up to the mountain, and bring wood, and build the house; and I will take pleasure in it, and I will be glorified, saith the LORD.

Matt. 5. 16 Let your light so shine before men, that they may see your good works, and glorify your Father which is in heaven.

Phil. 1. 11. *See under D.*

H

John 8. 31 Then said Jesus to those Jews which believed on him, If ye continue in my word, *then* are ye my disciples indeed;

TIME, THURSDAY EVENING, APRIL 6 [NISAN 14], A. D. 30; PLACE, JERUSALEM.
Week of our Lord's Fourth and Last Passover.

H—CONCLUDED.

John 13. 35 By this shall all *men* know that ye are my disciples, if ye have love one to another.

I

John 14. 15 If ye love me, keep my commandments.

John 14. 21 He that hath my commandments, and keepeth them, he it is that loveth me: and he that loveth me shall be loved of my Father, and I will love him, and will manifest myself to him.

22 Judas saith unto him, not Iscariot, Lord, how is it that thou wilt manifest thyself unto us, and not unto the world?

23 Jesus answered and said unto him, If a man love me, he will keep my words: and my Father will love him, and we will come unto him, and make our abode with him.

I Cor. 7. 19 Circumcision is nothing, and uncircumcision is nothing, but the keeping of the commandments of God.

I Thes. 4. 1 Furthermore then we beseech you, brethren, and exhort *you* by the Lord Jesus, that as ye have received of us how ye ought to walk and to please God, *so* ye would abound more and more.

2 For ye know what commandments we gave you by the Lord Jesus.

II Pet. 2. 21 For it had been better for them not to have known the way of righteousness, than, after they have known *it*, to turn from the holy commandment delivered unto them.

K

John 16. 24 Hitherto have ye asked nothing in my name: ask, and ye shall receive, that your joy may be full.

John 17. 13 And now come I to thee; and these things I speak in the world, that they might have my joy fulfilled in themselves.

Rom. 15. 13 Now the God of hope fill you with all joy and peace in believing, that ye may abound in hope, through the power of the Holy Ghost.

II Cor. 1. 24 Not for that we have dominion over your faith, but are helpers of your joy: for by faith ye stand.

Eph. 5. 18 And be not drunk with wine, wherein is excess; but be filled with the Spirit;

Phil. 1. 25 And having this confidence, I know that I shall abide and continue with you all for your furtherance and joy of faith;

15: 1–11.

1 I am the true vine, and my Father is the husbandman.

2 [a]Every branch in me that beareth not fruit he taketh away: and every *branch* that beareth fruit, he purgeth it, that it may bring forth more fruit.

3 [b]Now ye are clean through the word which I have spoken unto you.

4 [c]Abide in me, and I in you. As the branch cannot bear fruit of itself, except it abide in the vine; no more can ye, except ye abide in me.

5 I am the vine, ye *are* the branches. He that abideth in me, and I in him, the same bringeth forth much [d]fruit; for [1]without me ye can do nothing.

6 If a man abide not in me, [e]he is cast forth as a branch, and is withered; and men gather them, and cast *them* into the fire, and they are burned.

7 If ye abide in me, and my words abide in you, [f]ye shall ask what ye will, and it shall be done unto you.

8 [g]Herein is my Father glorified, that ye bear much fruit; [h]so shall ye be my disciples.

9 As the Father hath loved me, so have I loved you: continue ye in my love.

10 [i]If ye keep my commandments, ye shall abide in my love; even as I have kept my Father's commandments, and abide in his love.

11 These things have I spoken unto you, that my joy might remain in you, and [k]*that* your joy might be full.

K—CONCLUDED.

I Jno. 1. 4 And these things write we unto you, that your joy may be full.

§ 188. MUTUAL LOVE. THE DISCIPLES HATED BY THE WORLD.
Evening Introducing the Sixth Day of the

A

John 13. 34 A new commandment I give unto you, That ye love one another; as I have loved you, that ye also love one another.

I Thes. 4. 9 But as touching brotherly love ye need not that I write unto you: for ye yourselves are taught of God to love one another.

1 Pet. 4. 8 And above all things have fervent charity among yourselves: for charity shall cover the multitude of sins.

I Jno. 3. 11 For this is the message that ye heard from the beginning, that we should love one another.

I Jno. 4. 21 And this commandment have we from him, That he who loveth God love his brother also.

B

John 10. 11 I am the good shepherd: the good shepherd giveth his life for the sheep.

John 10. 15 As the Father knoweth me, even so know I the Father: and I lay down my life for the sheep.

Rom. 5. 7 For scarcely for a righteous man will one die: yet peradventure for a good man some would even dare to die.
8 But God commendeth his love toward us, in that, while we were yet sinners, Christ died for us.

Eph. 5. 2 And walk in love, as Christ also hath loved us, and hath given himself for us an offering and a sacrifice to God for a sweetsmelling savour.

I Jno. 3. 16 Hereby perceive we the love *of God*, because he laid down his life for us: and we ought to lay down *our* lives for the brethren.

C

Matt. 12 50 For whosoever shall do the will of my Father which is in heaven, the same is my brother, and sister, and mother.

John 14. 15 If ye love me, keep my commandments.

John 14. 23 Jesus answered and said unto him, If a man love me, he will keep my words: and my Father will love him, and we will come unto him, and make our abode with him.

D

Gen. 18. 17 And the LORD said, Shall I hide from Abraham that thing which I do;
18 Seeing that Abraham shall surely become a great and mighty nation, and all the nations of the earth shall be blessed in him?

John 17. 26 And I have declared unto them thy name, and will declare *it;* that

D—CONCLUDED.

the love wherewith thou hast loved me may be in them, and I in them.

Acts 20. 27 For I have not shunned to declare unto you all the counsel of God.

E

John 6. 70 Jesus answered them, Have not I chosen you twelve, and one of you is a devil?

John 13. 18 I speak not of you all: I know whom I have chosen: but that the Scripture may be fulfilled, He that eateth bread with me hath lifted up his heel against me.

I Jno. 4. 10 Herein is love, not that we loved God, but that he loved us, and sent his Son *to be* the propitiation for our sins.

I Jno. 4. 19 We love him, because he first loved us.

F

Matt. 28. 19 Go ye therefore, and teach all nations, baptizing them in the name of the Father, and of the Son, and of the Holy Ghost:

Mark 16. 15 And he said unto them, Go ye into all the world, and preach the gospel to every creature.

Col. 1. 6 Which is come unto you, as *it is* in all the world; and bringeth forth fruit, as *it doth* also in you, since the day ye heard *of it,* and knew the grace of God in truth:

G

Matt. 21. 22 And all things, whatsoever ye shall ask in prayer, believing, ye shall receive.

John 14. 13 And whatsoever ye shall ask in my name, that will I do, that the Father may be glorified in the Son.

John 15. 7 If ye abide in me, and my words abide in you, ye shall ask what ye will, and it shall be done unto you.

H

John 15. 12. *See text of topic.*

I Pet. 2. 17 Honour all *men.* Love the brotherhood. Fear God. Honour the king.

I

I Jno. 3. 1 Behold, what manner of love the Father hath bestowed upon us, that we should be called the sons of God: therefore the world knoweth us not, because it knew him not.

I Jno. 3. 13 Marvel not, my brethren, if the world hate you.

K

Luke 6. 32 For if ye love them which love you, what thank have ye? for sinners also love those that love them.

TIME, THURSDAY EVENING, APRIL 6 [NISAN 14], A. D. 30; PLACE, JERUSALEM.
Week of our Lord's Fourth and Last Passover.

K—CONCLUDED.

I Jno. 4. 5 They are of the world: therefore speak they of the world, and the world heareth them.

L

John 17. 14 I have given them thy word; and the world hath hated them, because they are not of the world, even as I am not of the world.

M

Matt. 10. 24 The disciple is not above *his* master, nor the servant above his lord.

Luke 6. 40 The disciple is not above his master: but every one that is perfect shall be as his master.

John 13. 16 Verily, verily, I say unto you, The servant is not greater than his lord; neither he that is sent greater than he that sent him.

N

Isa. 53. 1 Who hath believed our report? and to whom is the arm of the LORD revealed?

2 For he shall grow up before him as a tender plant, and as a root out of a dry ground: he hath no form nor comliness; and when we shall see him, *there is* no beauty that we should desire him.

3 He is despised and rejected of men; a man of sorrows, and acquainted with grief: and we hid as it were *our* faces from him; he was despised, and we esteemed him not.

Eze. 3. 7 But the house of Israel will not hearken unto thee; for they will not hearken unto me: for all the house of Israel *are* impudent and hardhearted.

O

Matt. 10. 32 And ye shall be hated of all *men* for my name's sake: but he that endureth to the end shall be saved.

Matt. 24. 9 Then shall they deliver you up to be afflicted, and shall kill you: and ye shall be hated of all nations for my name's sake.

John 16. 3 And these things will they do unto you, because they have not known the Father, nor me.

P

John 9. 41 Jesus said unto them, If ye were blind, ye should have no sin: but now ye say, We see; therefore your sin remaineth.

Q

Rom. 1. 20 For the invisible things of him from the creation of the world are clearly seen, being understood by the

For Q concluded see next page (534).

15: 12–27.

12 [a]This is my commandment, That ye love one another, as I have loved you.

13 [b]Greater love hath no man than this, that a man lay down his life for his friends.

14 [c]Ye are my friends, if ye do whatsoever I command you.

15 Henceforth I call you not servants; for the servant knoweth not what his lord doeth: but I have called you friends; [d]for all things that I have heard of my Father I have made known unto you.

16 [e]Ye have not chosen me, but I have chosen you, and [f]ordained you, that ye should go and bring forth fruit, and *that* your fruit should remain; that [g]whatsoever ye shall ask of the Father in my name, he may give it you.

17 [h]These things I command you, that ye love one another.

18 [i]If the world hate you, ye know that it hated me before *it hated* you.

19 [k]If ye were of the world, the world would love his own; but [l]because ye are not of the world, but I have chosen you out of the world, therefore the world hateth you.

20 Remember the word that I said unto you, [m]The servant is not greater than his lord. If they have persecuted me, they will also persecute you; [n]if they have kept my saying, they will keep yours also.

21 But [o]all these things will they do unto you for my name's sake, because they know not him that sent me.

§ 188. MUTUAL LOVE. THE DISCIPLES HATED BY THE WORLD (Concluded) Evening Introducing the Sixth Day of the

For P and Q see preceding page (533).

Q—Concluded.

things that are made, *even* his eternal power and Godhead; so that they are without excuse:

Jas. 4. 17 Therefore to him that knoweth to do good, and doeth *it* not, to him it is sin.

1

Or, *excuse*.

R

John 3. 2 The same came to Jesus by night, and said unto him, Rabbi, we know that thou art a teacher come from God: for no man can do these miracles that thou doest, except God be with him.

John 7. 31 And many of the people believed on him, and said, When Christ cometh, will he do more miracles than these which this *man* hath done?

John 9. 32 Since the world began was it not heard that any man opened the eyes of one that was born blind.

S

Ps. 35. 19 Let not them that are mine enemies wrongfully rejoice over me: *neither* let them wink with the eye that hate me without a cause.

Ps. 69. 4 They that hate me without a cause are more than the hairs of mine head: they that would destroy me, *being* mine enemies wrongfully, are mighty: then I restored *that* which I took not away.

T

Luke 24. 49 And, behold, I send the promise of my Father upon you: but tarry ye in the city of Jerusalem, until ye be endued with power from on high.

John 14. 17 *Even* the Spirit of truth; whom the world cannot receive, because it seeth him not, neither knoweth him: but ye know him; for he dwelleth with you, and shall be in you.

John 14. 26 But the Comforter, *which is* the Holy Ghost, whom the Father will send in my name, he shall teach you all things, and bring all things to your remembrance, whatsoever I have said unto you.

John 16. 7 Nevertheless I tell you the truth; It is expedient for you that I go away: for if I go not away, the Comforter will not come unto you; but if I depart, I will send him unto you.

John 16. 13 Howbeit when he, the Spirit of truth, is come, he will guide you into all truth: for he shall not speak of himself; but whatsoever he shall hear, *that* shall he speak: and he will show you things to come.

Acts 2. 33 Therefore being by the right hand of God exalted, and having received of the Father the promise of the Holy Ghost, he hath shed forth this, which ye now see and hear.

U

Luke 24. 48 And ye are witnesses of these things.

§ 189. PERSECUTION FORETOLD. FURTHER PROMISE OF THE HOLY SPIRIT Evening Introducing the Sixth Day of the

A

Matt. 11. 6 And blessed is *he*, whosoever shall not be offended in me.

Matt. 24. 10 And then shall many be offended, and shall betray one another, and shall hate one another.

Matt. 26. 31 Then saith Jesus unto them, All ye shall be offended because of me this night: for it is written, I will smite the Shepherd, and the sheep of the flock shall be scattered abroad.

B

John 9. 22 These *words* spake his parents, because they feared the Jews: for the Jews had agreed already, that if any man did confess that he was Christ, he should be put out of the synagogue.

John 9. 34 They answered and said unto him, Thou wast altogether born in sins, and dost thou teach us? And they cast him out.

B—Concluded.

John 12. 42 Nevertheless among the chief rulers also many believed on him; but because of the Pharisees they did not confess *him*, lest they should be put out of the synagogue:

C

Acts 8. 1 And Saul was consenting unto his death. And at that time there was a great persecution against the church which was at Jerusalem; and they were all scattered abroad throughout the regions of Judæa and Samaria, except the apostles.

Acts 9. 1 And Saul, yet breathing out threatenings and slaughter against the disciples of the Lord, went unto the high priest,

D

John 15. 21 But all these things will they do unto you for my name's sake, be-

TIME, THURSDAY EVENING, APRIL 6 [NISAN 14], A. D. 30; PLACE, JERUSALEM.
Week of our Lord's Fourth and Last Passover.

U—CONCLUDED.

Acts 2. 32 This Jesus hath God raised up, whereof we all are witnesses.

Acts 4. 20 For we cannot but speak the things which we have seen and heard.

Acts 4. 33 And with great power gave the apostles witness of the resurrection of the Lord Jesus: and great grace was upon them all.

Acts 5. 32 And we are his witnesses of these things; and *so is* also the Holy Ghost, whom God hath given to them that obey him.

Acts 10. 39 And we are witnesses of all things which he did both in the land of the Jews, and in Jerusalem; whom they slew and hanged on a tree:

Acts 13. 31 And he was seen many days of them which came up with him from Galilee to Jerusalem, who are his witnesses unto the people.

I Pet. 5. 1 The elders which are among you I exhort, who am also an elder, and a witness of the sufferings of Christ, and also a partaker of the glory that shall be revealed:

II Pet.1. 16 For we have not followed cunningly devised fables, when we made known unto you the power and coming of our Lord Jesus Christ, but were eyewitnesses of his majesty.

X

Luke 1. 2 Even as they delivered them unto us, which from the beginning were eyewitnesses, and ministers of the word;

CHAP. 15.

22 [p]If I had not come and spoken unto them, they had not had sin; [q]but now they have no [1]cloak for their sin.

23 He that hateth me hateth my Father also.

24 If I had not done among them [r]the works which none other man did, they had not had sin: but now have they both seen and hated both me and my Father.

25 But *this cometh to pass*, that the word might be fulfilled that is written in their law, [s]They hated me without a cause.

26 [t]But when the Comforter is come, whom I will send unto you from the Father, *even* the Spirit of truth, which proceedeth from the Father, he shall testify of me:

27 And [u]ye also shall bear witness, because [x]ye have been with me from the beginning.

TIME, THURSDAY EVENING, APRIL 6 [NISAN 14], A. D. 30; PLACE, JERUSALEM.
Week of our Lord's Fourth and Last Passover.

D—CONCLUDED.

cause they know not him that sent me.

Rom.10. 2 For I bear them record that they have a zeal of God, but not according to knowledge.

I Cor. 2. 8 Which none of the princes of this world knew: for had they known *it*, they would not have crucified the Lord of glory.

I Tim.1. 13 Who was before a blasphemer, and a persecutor, and injurious; but I obtained mercy, because I did *it* ignorantly in unbelief.

E

John 13. 19 Now I tell you before it come, that, when it is come to pass, ye may believe that I am *he*.

John 14. 29 And now I have told you before it come to pass, that, when it is come to pass, ye might believe.

For F see next page (536).

16: 1–16.

1 These things have I spoken unto you, that ye [a]should not be offended.

2 [b]They shall put you out of the synagogues: yea, the time cometh, [c]that whosoever killeth you will think that he doeth God service.

3 And [d]these things will they do unto you, because they have not known the Father, nor me.

4 But [e]these things have I told you, that when the time shall come, ye may remember that I told you of them. And [f]these things I said not unto you at the beginning, because I was with you.

§ 189. PERSECUTION FORETOLD. FURTHER PROMISE OF THE HOLY SPIRIT.

Evening Introducing the Sixth Day of the

F

Matt. 9. 15 And Jesus said unto them, Can the children of the bridechamber mourn, as long as the bridegroom is with them? but the days will come, when the bridegroom shall be taken from them, and then shall they fast.

G

John 7. 33 Then said Jesus unto them, Yet a little while am I with you, and *then* I go unto him that sent me.

John 13. 3 Jesus knowing that the Father had given all things into his hands, and that he was come from God, and went to God;

John 14. 28 Ye have heard how I said unto you, I go away, and come *again* unto you. If ye loved me, ye would rejoice, because I said, I go unto the Father: for my Father is greater than I.

John 16. 10, 16. *See text of topic.*

H

John 14. 1 Let not your heart be troubled: ye believe in God, believe also in me.

John 16. 22 And ye now therefore have sorrow: but I will see you again, and your heart shall rejoice, and your joy no man taketh from you.

I

John 7. 39 (But this spake he of the Spirit, which they that believe on him should receive: for the Holy Ghost was not yet *given;* because that Jesus was not yet glorified.)

John 14. 16 And I will pray the Father, and he shall give you another Comforter, that he may abide with you for ever;

John 14. 26 But the Comforter, *which is* the Holy Ghost, whom the Father will send in my name, he shall teach you all things, and bring all things to your remembrance, whatsoever I have said unto you.

John 15. 26 But when the Comforter is come, whom I will send unto you from the Father, *even* the Spirit of truth, which proceedeth from the Father, he shall testify of me:

K

Acts 2. 33 Therefore being by the right hand of God exalted, and having received of the Father the promise of the Holy Ghost, he hath shed forth this, which ye now see and hear.

Eph. 4. 8 Wherefore he saith, When he ascended up on high, he led captivity captive, and gave gifts unto men.

1

Or, *convince.*

L

Acts 2. 22 Ye men of Israel, hear these words; Jesus of Nazareth, a man approved of God among you by miracles and wonders and signs, which God did by him in the midst of you, as ye yourselves also know:

Acts 3. 15 And killed the Prince of life, whom God hath raised from the dead; whereof we are witnesses.

M

John 3. 14 And as Moses lifted up the serpent in the wilderness, even so must the Son of man be lifted up:

John 5. 32 There is another that beareth witness of me; and I know that the witness which he witnesseth of me is true.

N

Acts 26. 18 To open their eyes, *and* to turn *them* from darkness to light, and *from* the power of Satan unto God, that they may receive forgiveness of sins, and inheritance among them which are sanctified by faith that is in me.

O

Luke 10. 18 And he said unto them, I beheld Satan as lightning fall from heaven.

John 12. 31 Now is the judgment of this world: now shall the prince of this world be cast out.

Eph. 2. 2 Wherein in time past ye walked according to the course of this world, according to the prince of the power of the air, the spirit that now worketh in the children of disobedience:

Col. 2. 15 *And* having spoiled principalities and powers, he made a show of them openly, triumphing over them in it.

Heb. 2. 14 Forasmuch then as the children are partakers of flesh and blood, he also himself likewise took part of the same; that through death he might destroy him that had the power of death, that is, the devil;

P

Mark 4. 33 And with many such parables spake he the word unto them, as they were able to hear *it.*

I Cor. 3. 2 I have fed you with milk, and not with meat: for hitherto ye were not able *to bear it,* neither yet now are ye able.

Heb. 5. 12 For when for the time ye ought to be teachers, ye have need that one teach you again which *be* the first principles of the oracles of God; and are become such as have need of milk, and not of strong meat.

(CONCL'D). TIME, THURSDAY EVENING, APRIL 6 [NISAN 14], A. D. 30; PLACE, JERUSALEM.
Week of our Lord's Fourth and Last Passover.

Q

John 14. 17 *Even* the Spirit of truth; whom the world cannot receive, because it seeth him not, neither knoweth him: but ye know him; for he dwelleth with you, and shall be in you.

John 15. 26. *See text of § 188.*

I Jno. 4. 6 We are of God: he that knoweth God heareth us; he that is not of God heareth not us. Hereby know we the spirit of truth, and the spirit of error.

R

John 14. 26. *See text of § 186.*

I Jno. 2. 20 But ye have an unction from the Holy One, and ye know all things.

I Jno. 2. 27 But the anointing which ye have received of him abideth in you, and ye need not that any man teach you: but as the same anointing teacheth you of all things, and is truth, and is no lie, and even as it hath taught you, ye shall abide in him.

S

I Tim. 4. 1 Now the Spirit speaketh expressly, that in the latter times some shall depart from the faith, giving heed to seducing spirits, and doctrines of devils;

T

Matt. 11. 27 All things are delivered unto me of my Father: and no man knoweth the Son, but the Father; neither knoweth any man the Father, save the Son, and *he* to whomsover the Son will reveal *him*.

John 3. 35 The Father loveth the Son, and hath given all things into his hand.

John 13. 3 Jesus knowing that the Father had given all things into his hands, and that he was come from God, and went to God;

John 17. 10 And all mine are thine, and thine are mine; and I am glorified in them.

Col. 1. 19 For it pleased *the Father* that in him should all fulness dwell;

U

John 7. 33. *See under G.*

John 13. 33 Little children, yet a little while I am with you. Ye shall seek me; and as I said unto the Jews, Whither I go, ye cannot come; so now I say to you.

John 14. 19 Yet a little while, and the world seeth me no more; but ye see me: because I live, ye shall live also.

John 16. 10. *See text of topic.*

X

John 13. 3. *See under G.*

John 16. 28 I came forth from the Father, and am come into the world: again, I leave the world, and go to the Father.

CHAP. 16.

5 But now [g]I go my way to him that
sent me: and none of you asketh me,
Whither goest thou?

6 But because I have said these things
unto you, [h]sorrow hath filled your heart.

7 Nevertheless I tell you the truth;
It is expedient for you that I go away:
for if I go not away, [i]the Comforter
will not come unto you; but [k]if I depart,
I will send him unto you.

8 And when he is come, he will [1]re-
prove the world of sin, and of righteousness, and of judgment:

9 [l]Of sin, because they believe not on
me;

10 Of righteousness, [m]because I go to
my Father, and ye see me no more;

11 [n]Of judgment, because the [o]prince
of this world is judged.

12 I have yet many things to say unto
you, [p]but ye cannot bear them now.

13 Howbeit when he, [q]the Spirit of
truth, is come, [r]he will guide you into
all truth: for he shall not speak of
himself; but whatsoever he shall hear,
that shall he speak: and he will [s]show
you things to come.

14 He shall glorify me: for he shall
receive of mine, and shall show *it* unto
you.

15 [t]All things that the Father hath
are mine: therefore said I, that he shall
take of mine, and shall show *it* unto
you.

16 [u]A little while, and ye shall not
see me: and again, a little while, and
ye shall see me, [x]because I go to the
Father.

§ 190. PRAYER IN THE NAME OF CHRIST.

Evening Introducing the Sixth Day of the

A

Ps. 30. 11 Thou hast turned for me my mourning into dancing: thou hast put off my sackcloth, and girded me with gladness;

Ps. 40. 1 I waited patiently for the LORD; and he inclined unto me, and heard my cry.

2 He brought me up also out of a horrible pit, out of the miry clay, and set my feet upon a rock, *and* established my goings.

3 And he hath put a new song in my mouth, *even* praise unto our God: many shall see *it*, and fear, and shall trust in the LORD.

Ps. 97. 11 Light is sown for the righteous, and gladness for the upright in heart.

Ps. 126. 5 They that sow in tears shall reap in joy.

6 He that goeth forth and weepeth, bearing precious seed, shall doubtless come again with rejoicing, bringing his sheaves *with him*.

Isa. 12. 1 And in that day thou shalt say, O LORD, I will praise thee: though thou wast angry with me, thine anger is turned away, and thou comfortedst me.

Isa. 25. 8 He will swallow up death in victory; and the Lord GOD will wipe away tears from off all faces; and the rebuke of his people shall he take away from off all the earth: for the LORD hath spoken *it*.

9 And it shall be said in that day, Lo, this *is* our God; we have waited for him, and he will save us: this *is* the LORD; we have waited for him, we will be glad and rejoice in his salvation.

Isa. 61. 3 To appoint unto them that mourn in Zion, to give unto them beauty for ashes, the oil of joy for mourning, the garment of praise for the spirit of heaviness; that they might be called Trees of righteousness, The planting of the LORD, that he might be glorified.

Isa. 66. 5 Hear the word of the LORD, ye that tremble at his word; Your brethren that hated you, that cast you out for my name's sake, said, Let the LORD be glorified: but he shall appear to your joy, and they shall be ashamed.

Jer. 31. 9 They shall come with weeping, and with supplications will I lead them: I will cause them to walk by the rivers of waters in a straight way, wherein they shall not stumble: for I am a father to Israel, and Ephraim *is* my first-born.

A—CONTINUED.

Jer. 31. 10 Hear the word of the LORD, O ye nations, and declare *it* in the isles afar off, and say, He that scattered Israel will gather him, and keep him, as a shepherd *doth* his flock.

11 For the LORD hath redeemed Jacob, and ransomed him from the hand of *him that was* stronger than he.

12 Therefore they shall come and sing in the height of Zion, and shall flow together to the goodness of the LORD, for wheat, and for wine, and for oil, and for the young of the flock and of the herd: and their soul shall be as a watered garden; and they shall not sorrow any more at all.

13 Then shall the virgin rejoice in the dance, both young men and old together: for I will turn their mourning into joy, and will comfort them, and make them rejoice from their sorrow.

14 And I will satiate the soul of the priests with fatness, and my people shall be satisfied with my goodness, saith the LORD.

Jer. 31. 25 For I have satiated the weary soul, and I have replenished every sorrowful soul.

Matt. 5. 4 Blessed *are* they that mourn: for they shall be comforted.

Acts 2. 47 Praising God, and having favour with all the people. And the Lord added to the church daily such as should be saved.

Acts 5. 41 And they departed from the presence of the council, rejoicing that they were counted worthy to suffer shame for his name.

Rom. 5. 2 By whom also we have access by faith into this grace wherein we stand, and rejoice in hope of the glory of God.

3 And not only *so*, but we glory in tribulations also; knowing that tribulation worketh patience;

Rom. 5. 11 And not only *so*, but we also joy in God through our Lord Jesus Christ, by whom we have now received the atonement.

II Cor. 6. 10 As sorrowful, yet alway rejoicing; as poor, yet making many rich; as having nothing, and *yet* possessing all things.

Gal. 5. 22 But the fruit of the Spirit is love, joy, peace, longsuffering, gentleness, goodness, faith,

I Thes. 1. 6 And ye became followers of us, and of the Lord, having received the word

TIME, THURSDAY EVENING, APRIL 6 [NISAN 14], A. D. 30; PLACE, JERUSALEM.
Week of our Lord's Fourth and Last Passover.

A—CONCLUDED.

in much affliction, with joy of the Holy Ghost:

B

Isa. 26. 17 Like as a woman with child, *that* draweth near the time of her delivery, is in pain, *and* crieth out in her pangs; so have we been in thy sight, O LORD.

Hos. 13. 13 The sorrows of a travailing woman shall come upon him: he *is* an unwise son; for he should not stay long in *the place of* the breaking forth of children.

14 I will ransom them from the power of the grave; I will redeem them from death: O death, I will be thy plagues; O grave, I will be thy destruction: repentance shall be hid from mine eyes.

C

John 16. 6 But because I have said these things unto you, sorrow hath filled your heart.

D

Luke 24. 41 And while they yet believed not for joy, and wondered, he said unto them, Have ye here any meat?

Luke 24. 52 And they worshipped him, and returned to Jerusalem with great joy;

John 14. 1 Let not your heart be troubled: ye believe in God, believe also in me.

John 14. 27 Peace I leave with you, my peace I give unto you: not as the world giveth, give I unto you. Let not your heart be troubled, neither let it be afraid.

John 20. 20 And when he had so said, he showed unto them *his* hands and his side. Then were the disciples glad, when they saw the Lord.

Acts 2. 46 And they, continuing daily with one accord in the temple, and breaking bread from house to house, did eat their meat with gladness and singleness of heart,

Acts 13. 52 And the disciples were filled with joy, and with the Holy Ghost.

I Pet. 1. 8 Whom having not seen, ye love; in whom, though now ye see *him* not, yet believing, ye rejoice with joy unspeakable and full of glory:

E

Matt. 7. 7 Ask, and it shall be given you; seek, and ye shall find; knock, and it shall be opened unto you:

John 14. 13 And whatsoever ye shall ask in my name, that will I do, that the Father may be glorified in the Son.

John 15. 16 Ye have not chosen me, but I

16: 17–33.

17 Then said *some* of his disciples
among themselves, What is this that he
saith unto us, A little while, and ye
shall not see me: and again, a little
while, and ye shall see me: and, Because I go to the Father?

18 They said therefore, What is this
that he saith, A little while? we cannot
tell what he saith.

19 Now Jesus knew that they were
desirous to ask him, and said unto them,
Do ye inquire among yourselves of
that I said, A little while, and ye shall
not see me: and again, a little while,
and ye shall see me?

20 Verily, verily, I say unto you,
That ye shall weep and lament, but the
world shall rejoice; and ye shall be
sorrowful, but [a]your sorrow shall be
turned into joy.

21 [b]A woman when she is in travail
hath sorrow, because her hour is come;
but as soon as she is delivered of the
child, she remembereth no more the
anguish, for joy that a man is born into
the world.

22 [c]And ye now therefore have sorrow: but I will see you again, and
[d]your heart shall rejoice, and your joy
no man taketh from you.

23 And in that day ye shall ask me
nothing. [e]Verily, verily, I say unto
you, Whatsoever ye shall ask the
Father in my name, he will give *it* you.

E—CONCLUDED

have chosen you, and ordained you, that ye should go and bring forth fruit, and *that* your fruit should remain; that whatsoever ye shall ask of the Father in my name, he may give it you.

§ 190. PRAYER IN THE NAME OF CHRIST (CONCLUDED).

Evening Introducing the Sixth Day of the

F

John 15. 11 These things have I spoken unto you, that my joy might remain in you, and *that* your joy might be full.

I Jno. 1. 4 And these things write we unto you, that your joy may be full.

II Jno. 12 Having many things to write unto you, I would not *write* with paper and ink: but I trust to come unto you, and speak face to face, that our joy may be full.

1

Or, *parables.*

Prov. 1. 6 To understand a proverb, and the interpretation; the words of the wise, and their dark sayings.

G

John 16. 23. *See text of topic.*

H

John 14. 21 He that hath my commandments, and keepeth them, he it is that loveth me: and he that loveth me shall be loved of my Father, and I will love him, and will manifest myself to him.

22 Judas saith unto him, not Iscariot, Lord, how is it that thou wilt manifest thyself unto us, and not unto the world?

23 Jesus answered and said unto him, If a man love me, he will keep my words: and my Father will love him, and we will come unto him, and make our abode with him.

Heb. 12. 6 For whom the Lord loveth he chasteneth, and scourgeth every son whom he receiveth.

Jude 20 But ye, beloved, building up yourselves on your most holy faith, praying in the Holy Ghost,

21 Keep yourselves in the love of God, looking for the mercy of our Lord Jesus Christ unto eternal life.

I

John 3. 13 And no man hath ascended up to heaven, but he that came down from heaven, *even* the Son of man which is in heaven.

John 16. 30. *See text of topic.*

John 17. 8 For I have given unto them the words which thou gavest me; and they have received *them*, and have known surely that I came out from thee, and they have believed that thou didst send me.

K

John 13. 3 Jesus knowing that the Father had given all things into his hands, and that he was come from God, and went to God;

2

Or, *parable.*

L

John 21. 17 He saith unto him the third time, Simon, *son* of Jonas, lovest thou me? Peter was grieved because he said unto him the third time, Lovest thou me? And he said unto him, Lord, thou knowest all things; thou knowest that I love thee. Jesus saith unto him, Feed my sheep.

M

John 16. 27. *Text of topic.* John 17. 8. *Under I.*

N

Matt. 26. 31 Then saith Jesus unto them, All ye shall be offended because of me this night: for it is written, I will smite the Shepherd, and the sheep of the flock shall be scattered abroad.

Mark 14. 27 And Jesus saith unto them, All ye shall be offended because of me this night: for it is written, I will smite the Shepherd, and the sheep shall be scattered.

O

John 20. 10 Then the disciples went away again unto their own home.

3

Or, *his own home.*

P

John 8. 29 And he that sent me is with me: the Father hath not left me alone; for I do always those things that please him.

John 14. 10 Believest thou not that I am in the Father, and the Father in me? the words that I speak unto you I speak not of myself: but the Father that dwelleth in me, he doeth the works.

11 Believe me that I *am* in the Father, and the Father in me: or else believe me for the very works' sake.

Q

Isa. 9. 6 For unto us a child is born, unto us a son is given: and the government shall be upon his shoulder: and his name shall be called Wonderful, Counsellor, The mighty God, The everlasting Father, The Prince of Peace.

John 14. 27. *See under D, page 539.*

Rom. 5. 1 Therefore being justified by faith, we have peace with God through our Lord Jesus Christ:

Eph. 2. 14 For he is our peace, who hath made both one, and hath broken down the middle wall of partition *between us;*

Col. 1. 20 And, having made peace through the blood of his cross, by him to reconcile all things unto himself; by him, *I say*, whether *they be* things in earth, or things in heaven.

TIME, THURSDAY EVENING, APRIL 6 [NISAN 14], A. D. 30; PLACE, JERUSALEM.
Week of our Lord's Fourth and Last Passover.

R

John 15. 19 If ye were of the world, the world would love his own; but because ye are not of the world, but I have chosen you out of the world, therefore the world hateth you.

20 Remember the word that I said unto you, The servant is not greater than his lord. If they have persecuted me, they will also persecute you; if they have kept my saying, they will keep yours also.

21 But all these things they will do unto you for my name's sake, because they know not him that sent me.

Acts 14. 22 Confirming the souls of the disciples, *and* exhorting them to continue in the faith, and that we must through much tribulation enter into the kingdom of God.

II Tim.3. 12 Yea, and all that will live godly in Christ Jesus shall suffer persecution.

Heb. 12. 6 For whom the Lord loveth he chasteneth, and scourgeth every son whom he receiveth.

Rev. 3. 19 As many as I love, I rebuke and chasten: be zealous therefore, and repent.

S

John 14. 1. *See under D, page 539.*

T

Isa. 49. 24 Shall the prey be taken from the mighty, or the lawful captive delivered?

25 But thus saith the LORD, Even the captives of the mighty shall be taken away, and the prey of the terrible shall be delivered: for I will contend with him that contendeth with thee, and I will save thy children.

Rom. 8. 37 Nay, in all these things we are more than conquerors through him that loved us.

I Cor.15. 27 For he hath put all things under his feet. But when he saith, All things are put under *him, it is* manifest that he is excepted, which did put all things under him.

Gal. 6. 14 But God forbid that I should glory, save in the cross of our Lord Jesus Christ, by whom the world is crucified unto me, and I unto the world.

I Jno. 4. 4 Ye are of God, little children, and have overcome them: because greater is he that is in you, than he that is in the world.

I Jno. 5. 4 For whatsoever is born of God overcometh the world: and this is the victory that overcometh the world, *even* our faith.

CHAP. 16.

24 Hitherto have ye asked nothing
in my name: ask, and ye shall receive,
[f]that your joy may be full.

25 These things have I spoken unto
you in proverbs: but the time cometh,
when I shall no more speak unto you
in [1]proverbs, but I shall show you
plainly of the Father.

26 [g]At that day ye shall ask in my
name: and I say not unto you, that I
will pray the Father for you:

27 [h]For the Father himself loveth
you, because ye have loved me, and
[i]have believed that I came out from God.

28 [k]I came forth from the Father,
and am come into the world: again, I
leave the world, and go to the Father.

29 His disciples said unto him, Lo,
now speakest thou plainly, and speakest
no [2]proverb.

30 Now are we sure that [l]thou knowest
all things, and needest not that any man
should ask thee: by this [m]we believe
that thou camest forth from God.

31 Jesus answered them, Do ye now
believe?

32 [n]Behold, the hour cometh, yea, is
now come, that ye shall be scattered,
[o]every man to [3]his own, and shall leave
me alone: and [p]yet I am not alone,
because the Father is with me.

33 These things I have spoken unto
you, that [q]in me ye might have peace.
[r]In the world ye shall have tribulation:
[s]but be of good cheer; [t]I have overcome the world.

T—CONCLUDED.

§ 191. CHRIST'S LAST PRAYER WITH HIS DISCIPLES.
Evening Introducing the Sixth Day of the

A

John 12. 23 And Jesus answered them, saying, The hour is come, that the Son of man should be glorified.

John 13. 32 If God be glorified in him, God shall also glorify him in himself, and shall straightway glorify him.

B

Dan. 7. 14 And there was given him dominion, and glory, and a kingdom, that all people, nations, and languages, should serve him: his dominion *is* an everlasting dominion, which shall not pass away, and his kingdom *that* which shall not be destroyed.

Matt. 11. 27 All things are delivered unto me of my Father: and no man knoweth the Son, but the Father; neither knoweth any man the Father, save the Son, and *he* to whomsoever the Son will reveal *him*.

Matt. 28 18 And Jesus came and spake unto them, saying, All power is given unto me in heaven and in earth.

John 3. 35 The Father loveth the Son, and hath given all things into his hand.

John 5. 27 And hath given him authority to execute judgment also, because he is the Son of man.

I Cor. 15. 25 For he must reign, till he hath put all enemies under his feet.

I Cor. 15. 27 For he hath put all things under his feet. But when he saith, All things are put under *him*, *it is* manifest that he is excepted, which did put all things under him.

Phil. 2. 10 That at the name of Jesus every knee should bow, of *things* in heaven, and *things* in earth, and *things* under the earth;

Heb. 2. 8 Thou hast put all things in subjection under his feet. For in that he put all in subjection under him, he left nothing *that is* not put under him. But now we see not yet all things put under him.

C

John 17 6, 9, 24. *See text of topic.*

John 6. 37 All that the Father giveth me shall come to me; and him that cometh to me I will in no wise cast out.

D

Isa. 53. 11 He shall see of the travail of his soul, *and* shall be satisfied: by his knowledge shall my righteous servant justify many; for he shall bear their iniquities.

Jer. 9. 24 But let him that glorieth glory in this, that he understandeth and

D—CONCLUDED.

knoweth me, that I *am* the LORD which exercise loving-kindness, judgment, and righteousness, in the earth: for in these *things* I delight, saith the LORD.

E

I Cor. 8. 4 As concerning therefore the eating of those things that are offered in sacrifice unto idols, we know that an idol *is* nothing in the world, and that *there is* none other God but one.

I Thes. 1. 9 For they themselves show of us what manner of entering in we had unto you, and how ye turned to God from idols to serve the living and true God;

F

John 3. 34 For he whom God hath sent speaketh the words of God: for God giveth not the Spirit by measure *unto him*.

John 5. 36 But I have greater witness than *that* of John: for the works which the Father hath given me to finish, the same works that I do, bear witness of me, that the Father hath sent me.

37 And the Father himself, which hath sent me, hath borne witness of me. Ye have neither heard his voice at any time, nor seen his shape.

John 6. 29 Jesus answered and said unto them, This is the work of God, that ye believe on him whom he hath sent.

John 6. 57 As the living Father hath sent me, and I live by the Father; so he that eateth me, even he shall live by me.

John 7. 29 But I know him; for I am from him, and he hath sent me.

John 10. 36 Say ye of him, whom the Father hath sanctified, and sent into the world, Thou blasphemest; because I said, I am the Son of God?

John 11. 42 And I knew that thou hearest me always: but because of the people which stand by I said *it*, that they may believe that thou hast sent me.

G

John 13. 31 Therefore, when he was gone out, Jesus said, Now is the Son of man glorified, and God is glorified in him.

John 14. 13 And whatsoever ye shall ask in my name, that will I do, that the Father may be glorified in the Son.

H

John 4. 34 Jesus saith unto them, My meat is to do the will of him that sent me, and to finish his work.

John 5. 36. *See under F.*

TIME, THURSDAY EVENING, APRIL 6 [NISAN 14], A. D. 30; PLACE, JERUSALEM.
Week of our Lord's Fourth and Last Passover.

H—CONCLUDED.

John 9. 3 Jesus answered, Neither hath this man sinned, nor his parents: but that the works of God should be made manifest in him.

John 19. 30 When Jesus therefore had received the vinegar, he said, It is finished: and he bowed his head, and gave up the ghost.

I

John 14. 31 But that the world may know that I love the Father; and as the Father gave me commandment, even so I do. Arise, let us go hence.

John 15. 10 If ye keep my commandments, ye shall abide in my love; even as I have kept my Father's commandments, and abide in his love.

K

John 1. 1 In the beginning was the Word, and the Word was with God, and the Word was God.

2 The same was in the beginning with God.

John 10. 30 I and *my* Father are one.

John 14. 9 Jesus saith unto him, Have I been so long time with you, and yet hast thou not known me, Philip? he that hath seen me hath seen the Father; and how sayest thou *then*, Show us the Father?

Phil. 2. 6 Who, being in the form of God, thought it not robbery to be equal with God:

Col. 1. 15 Who is the image of the invisible God, the first-born of every creature:

Col. 1. 17 And he is before all things, and by him all things consist:

Heb. 1. 3 Who being the brightness of *his* glory, and the express image of his person, and upholding all things by the word of his power, when he had by himself purged our sins, sat down on the right hand of the Majesty on high;

Heb. 1. 10 And, Thou, Lord, in the beginning hast laid the foundation of the earth; and the heavens are the works of thine hands.

Rev. 13. 8 And all that dwell upon the earth shall worship him, whose names are not written in the book of life of the Lamb slain from the foundation of the world.

L

Ps. 22. 22 I will declare thy name unto my brethren: in the midst of the congregation will I praise thee.

John 17. 26. *See text of topic.*

17: 1–26.

1 These words spake Jesus, and lifted
up his eyes to heaven, and said, Father,
[a]the hour is come; glorify thy Son, that
thy Son also may glorify thee:
2 [b]As thou hast given him power over
all flesh, that he should give eternal
life to [c]as many as thou hast given him.
3 And [d]this is life eternal, that they
might know thee [e]the only true God,
and Jesus Christ, [f]whom thou hast sent.
4 [g]I have glorified thee on the earth:
[h]I have finished the work [i]which thou
gavest me to do.
5 And now, O Father, glorify thou
me with thine own self with the glory
[k]which I had with thee before the world
was.
6 [l]I have manifested thy name unto
the men [m]which thou gavest me out of
the world: thine they were, and thou
gavest them me; and they have kept
thy word.
7 Now they have known that all
things whatsoever thou hast given me
are of thee.

M

John 6. 37 All that the Father giveth me shall come to me; and him that cometh to me I will in no wise cast out.

John 6. 39 And this is the Father's will which hath sent me, that of all which he hath given me I should lose nothing, but should raise it up again at the last day.

John 10. 29 My Father, which gave *them* me, is greater than all; and no *man* is able to pluck *them* out of my Father's hand.

John 15. 19 If ye were of the world, the world would love his own; but because ye are not of the world, but I have chosen you out of the world, therefore the world hateth you.

John 17, 2, 9, 11. *See text of topic.*

§ 191. CHRIST'S LAST PRAYER WITH HIS DISCIPLES (CONTINUED).
Evening Introducing the Sixth Day of the

N

John 8. 28 Then said Jesus unto them, When ye have lifted up the Son of man, then shall ye know that I am *he*, and *that* I do nothing of myself; but as my Father hath taught me, I speak these things.

John 12. 49 For I have not spoken of myself; but the Father which sent me, he gave me a commandment, what I should say, and what I should speak.

John 14. 10 Believest thou not that I am in the Father, and the Father in me? the words that I speak unto you I speak not of myself: but the Father that dwelleth in me, he doeth the works.

O

John 16. 27 For the Father himself loveth you, because ye have loved me, and have believed that I came out from God.

John 16. 30 Now are we sure that thou knowest all things, and needest not that any man should ask thee: by this we believe that thou camest forth from God.

John 17. 25. *See text of topic.*

P

I Jno. 5. 19 *And* we know that we are of God, and the whole world lieth in wickedness.

Q

Rom. 8. 30 Moreover, whom he did predestinate, them he also called: and whom he called, them he also justified: and whom he justified, them he also glorified.

R

John 16. 15 All things that the Father hath are mine: therefore said I, that he shall take of mine, and shall show *it* unto you.

S

John 13. 1 Now before the feast of the passover, when Jesus knew that his hour was come that he should depart out of this world unto the Father, having loved his own which were in the world, he loved them unto the end.

John 16. 28 I came forth from the Father, and am come into the world: again, I leave the world, and go to the Father.

T

I Pet. 1. 5 Who are kept by the power of God through faith unto salvation ready to be revealed in the last time.

Jude 1 Jude, the servant of Jesus Christ, and brother of James, to them that are sanctified by God the Father, and preserved in Jesus Christ, *and* called:

U

John 17. 21, etc. *See text of topic.*

X

John 10. 30. *See under K, page 543.*

Y

John 6. 39 And this is the Father's will which hath sent me, that of all which he hath given me I should lose nothing, but should raise it up again at the last day.

John 10. 28 And I give unto them eternal life; and they shall never perish, neither shall any *man* pluck them out of my hand.

Heb. 2. 13 And again, I will put my trust in him. And again, Behold I and the children which God hath given me.

Z

John 18. 9 That the saying might be fulfilled, which he spake, Of them which thou gavest me have I lost none.

I Jno. 2. 19 They went out from us, but they were not of us; for if they had been of us, they would *no doubt* have continued with us: but *they went out*, that they might be made manifest that they were not all of us.

A

John 6. 70 Jesus answered them, Have not I chosen you twelve, and one of you is a devil?

John 13. 18 I speak not of you all: I know whom I have chosen: but that the Scripture may be fulfilled, He that eateth bread with me hath lifted up his heel against me.

B

Ps. 69. 25 Let their habitation be desolate; *and* let none dwell in their tents.

Ps. 109. 8 Let his days be few; *and* let another take his office.

Acts. 1. 20 For it is written in the book of Psalms, Let his habitation be desolate, and let no man dwell therein: and, His bishoprick let another take.

C

John 17. 8. *See text of topic.*

D

John 15. 18 If the world hate you, ye know that it hated me before *it hated* you.
19 If ye were of the world, the world would love his own; but because ye are not of the world, but I have chosen you out of the world, therefore the world hateth you.

I Jno. 3. 13 Marvel not, my brethren, if the world hate you.

TIME, THURSDAY EVENING, APRIL 6 [NISAN 14], A. D. 30; PLACE, JERUSALEM.
Week of our Lord's Fourth and Last Passover.

E

John 8. 23 And he said unto them, Ye are from beneath; I am from above: ye are of this world; I am not of this world.

John 17. 16. *See text of topic.*

F

Ps. 30. 9 What profit *is there* in my blood, when I go down to the pit? Shall the dust praise thee? shall it declare thy truth?

Eccl. 9. 10 Whatsoever thy hand findeth to do, do *it* with thy might; for *there is* no work, nor device, nor knowledge, nor wisdom, in the grave, whither thou goest.

Isa. 38. 18 For the grave cannot praise thee, death cannot celebrate thee: they that go down into the pit cannot hope for thy truth.

19 The living, the living, he shall praise thee, as I *do* this day: the father to the children shall make known thy truth.

Isa. 57. 1 The righteous perisheth, and no man layeth *it* to heart: and merciful men *are* taken away, none considering that the righteous is taken away from the evil *to come.*

Phil. 1. 21 For to me to live *is* Christ, and to die *is* gain.

22 But if I live in the flesh, this *is* the fruit of my labour: yet what I shall choose I wot not.

G

Gen. 48. 16 The Angel which redeemed me from all evil, bless the lads; and let my name be named on them, and the name of my fathers Abraham and Isaac; and let them grow into a multitude in the midst of the earth.

Matt. 6. 13 And lead us not into temptation, but deliver us from evil: For thine is the kingdom, and the power, and the glory, for ever. Amen.

II Cor. 13. 4 For though he was crucified through weakness, yet ye liveth by the power of God. For we also are weak in him, but we shall live with him by the power of God toward you.

Gal. 1. 4 Who gave himself for our sins, that he might deliver us from this present evil world, according to the will of God and our Father:

II Thes. 3. 3 But the Lord is faithful, who shall stablish you, and keep *you* from evil.

I Jno. 5. 18 We know that whosoever is born of God sinneth not; but he that is be-

CHAP. 17.

8 For I have given unto them the
words [n]which thou gavest me; and they
have received *them,* [o]and have known
surely that I came out from thee, and
they have believed that thou didst send
me.

9 I pray for them: [p]I pray not for
the world, but for them which thou
hast given me; for they are thine.

10 And [q]all mine are thine, and [r]thine
are mine; and I am glorified in them.

11 [s]And now I am no more in the
world, but these are in the world, and
I come to thee. Holy Father, [t]keep
through thine own name those whom
thou hast given me, [u]that they may be
one, [x]as we *are.*

12 While I was with them in the
world, [y]I kept them in thy name: those
that thou gavest me I have kept, and
[z]none of them is lost, [a]but the son of
perdition: [b]that the Scripture might be
fulfilled.

13 And now come I to thee; and
these things I speak in the world, that
they might have my joy fulfilled in
themselves.

14 [c]I have given them thy word;
[d]and the world hath hated them, because they are not of the world, [e]even
as I am not of the world.

15 I pray not that thou shouldest
[f]take them out of the world, but [g]that
thou shouldest keep them from the evil.

16 [h]They are not of the world, even
as I am not of the world.

G—CONCLUDED.

gotten of God keepeth himself, and that wicked one toucheth him not.

H

John 17. 14. *See text of topic.*

§ 191. CHRIST'S LAST PRAYER WITH HIS DISCIPLES (Concluded). Evening Introducing the Sixth Day of the

I

John 15. 3 Now ye are clean through the word which I have spoken unto you.

Acts 15. 9 And put no difference between us and them, purifying their hearts by faith.

Eph. 5. 26 That he might sanctify and cleanse it with the washing of water by the word.

I Pet. 1. 22 Seeing ye have purified your souls in obeying the truth through the Spirit unto unfeigned love of the brethren, *see that ye* love one another with a pure heart fervently:

K

II Sa. 7. 28 And now, O Lord God, thou *art* that God, and thy words be true, and thou hast promised this goodness unto thy servant:

Ps. 119. 142 Thy righteousness *is* an everlasting righteousness, and thy law *is* the truth.

Ps. 119. 151 Thou *art* near, O Lord; and all thy commandments *are* truth.

John 8. 40 But now ye seek to kill me, a man that hath told you the truth, which I have heard of God: this did not Abraham.

L

John 20. 21 Then said Jesus to them again, Peace *be* unto you: as *my* Father hath sent me, even so send I you.

M

I Cor. 1. 2 Unto the church of God which is at Corinth, to them that are sanctified in Christ Jesus, called *to be* saints, with all that in every place call upon the name of Jesus Christ our Lord, both theirs and ours:

I Cor. 1. 30 But of him are ye in Christ Jesus, who of God is made unto us wisdom, and righteousness, and sanctification, and redemption:

I Thes. 4. 7 For God hath not called us unto uncleanness, but unto holiness.

Heb. 10. 10 By the which will we are sanctified through the offering of the body of Jesus Christ once *for all*.

1

Or, *truly sanctified.*

N

Acts 2. 41 Then they that gladly received his word were baptized: and the same day there were added *unto them* about three thousand souls.

Acts 4. 4 Howbeit many of them which heard the word believed; and the number of the men was about five thousand.

O

John 10. 16 And other sheep I have, which are not of this fold: them also I must bring, and they shall hear my voice; and there shall be one fold, *and* one shepherd.

John 17. 11, 22, 23. *See text of topic.*

Rom. 12. 5 So we, *being* many, are one body in Christ, and every one members one of another.

I Cor. 1. 10 Now I beseech you, brethren, by the name of our Lord Jesus Christ, that ye all speak the same thing, and *that* there be no divisions among you; but *that* ye be perfectly joined together in the same mind and in the same judgment.

Gal. 3. 28 There is neither Jew nor Greek, there is neither bond nor free, there is neither male nor female: for ye are all one in Christ Jesus.

P

John 10. 38 But if I do, though ye believe not me, believe the works: that ye may know, and believe, that the Father *is* in me, and I in him.

John 14. 11 Believe me that I *am* in the Father, and the Father in me: or else believe me for the very works' sake.

Phil. 2. 6 Who, being in the form of God, thought it not robbery to be equal with God:

I Jno. 5. 7 For there are three that bear record in heaven, the Father, the Word, and the Holy Ghost: and these three are one.

Q

John 14. 20 At that day ye shall know that I *am* in my Father, and ye in me, and I in you.

I Jno. 1. 3 That which we have seen and heard declare we unto you, that ye also may have fellowship with us: and truly our fellowship *is* with the Father, and with his Son Jesus Christ.

I Jno. 3. 24 And he that keepeth his commandments dwelleth in him, and he in him. And hereby we know that he abideth in us, by the Spirit which he hath given us.

R

Col. 3. 14 And above all these things *put on* charity, which is the bond of perfectness.

Heb. 12. 23 To the general assembly and church of the first-born, which are written in heaven, and to God the Judge of all, and to the spirits of just men made perfect.

TIME, THURSDAY EVENING, APRIL 6 [NISAN 14], A. D. 30; PLACE, JERUSALEM.
Week of our Lord's Fourth and Last Passover.

S

John 12. 26 If any man serve me, let him follow me; and where I am, there shall also my servant be: if any man serve me, him will *my* Father honour.

John 14. 3 And if I go and prepare a place for you, I will come again, and receive you unto myself; that where I am, *there* ye may be also.

I Thes. 4. 17 Then we which are alive *and* remain shall be caught up together with them in the clouds, to meet the Lord in the air: and so shall we ever be with the Lord.

T

John 17. 5. *See text of topic.*

U

John 15. 21 But all these things will they do unto you for my name's sake, because they know not him that sent me.

John 16. 3 And these things will they do unto you, because they have not known the Father, nor me.

X

John 7. 29. *See under F, page 542.*

John 8. 55 Yet ye have not known him; but I know him: and if I should say, I know him not, I shall be a liar like unto you: but I know him, and keep his saying.

John 10. 15 As the Father knoweth me, even so know I the Father: and I lay down my life for the sheep.

Y

John 17. 8. *Text of topic.* John 16. 27. *Under O, p. 544.*

Z

John 15. 15 Henceforth I call you not servants; for the servant knoweth not what his lord doeth: but I have called you friends; for all things that I have heard of my Father I have made known unto you.

John 17. 6. *See text of topic.*

A

John 15. 9 As the Father hath loved me, so have I loved you: continue ye in my love.

Eph. 1. 6 To the praise of the glory of his grace, wherein he hath made us accepted in the beloved:

Eph. 1. 22 And hath put all *things* under his feet, and gave him *to be* the head over all *things* to the church,

23 Which is his body, the fulness of him that filleth all in all.

Eph. 2. 4 But God, who is rich in mercy, for his great love wherewith he loved us,

5 Even when we were dead in sins, hath quickened us together with Christ, (by grace ye are saved;)

CHAP. 17.

17 [i]Sanctify them through thy truth: [k]thy word is truth.

18 [l]As thou hast sent me into the world, even so have I also sent them into the world.

19 And [m]for their sakes I sanctify myself, that they also might be [1]sanctified through the truth.

20 Neither pray I for these alone, but for them [n]also which shall believe on me through their word;

21 [o]That they all may be one; as [p]thou, Father, *art* in me, and I in thee, [q]that they also may be one in us: that the world may believe that thou hast sent me.

22 And the glory which thou gavest me I have given them; that they may be one, even as we are one:

23 I in them, and thou in me, [r]that they may be made perfect in one; and that the world may know that thou hast sent me, and hast loved them, as thou hast loved me.

24 [s]Father, I will that they also, whom thou hast given me, be with me where I am; that they may behold my glory, which thou hast given me: [t]for thou lovedst me before the foundation of the world.

25 O righteous Father, [u]the world hath not known thee: but [x]I have known thee, and [y]these have known that thou hast sent me.

26 [z]And I have declared unto them thy name, and will declare *it;* that the love [a]wherewith thou hast loved me may be in them, and I in them.

§ 192. THE AGONY IN THE GARDEN OF GETHSEMANE.

Evening Introducing the Sixth Day of the

26: 30, 36–46.

30 And when they had sung a hymn, they went out into the mount of Olives.

* * * * * p. 522.

36 [a]Then cometh Jesus with them unto a place called Gethsemane, and saith unto the disciples, Sit ye here, while I go and pray yonder.

37 And he took with him Peter and [b]the two sons of Zebedee, and began to be sorrowful and very heavy.

38 Then saith he unto them, [c]My soul is exceeding sorrowful, even unto death: tarry ye here, and [d]watch with me.

39 And he went a little further, and fell on his face, and [e]prayed, saying, [f]O my Father, if it be possible, [g]let this cup pass from me: nevertheless, [h]not as I will, but as thou *wilt*.

40 And he cometh unto the disciples, and findeth them asleep, and saith unto Peter, What, could ye not watch with me one hour?

A

Mark 14. 32, 35. *See text of topic.*
Luke 22. 39 and John 18. 1. *See text of topic.*

B

Matt. 4. 21 And going on from thence, he saw other two brethren, James *the son* of Zebedee, and John his brother, in a ship with Zebedee their father, mending their nets; and he called them.

C

John 12. 27 Now is my soul troubled; and what shall I say? Father, save me from this hour: but for this cause came I unto this hour.

D

I Pet. 5. 8 Be sober, be vigilant; because your adversary the devil, as a roaring lion, walketh about, seeking whom he may devour:

E

Mark 14. 36 and Luke 22. 42. *See text of topic.*
Heb. 5. 7 Who in the days of his flesh, when he had offered up prayers and supplications with strong crying and tears

14: 26, 32–42.

26 And when they had sung a hymn, they went out into the mount of Olives.

* * * * * p. 522.

32 [i]And they came to a place which was named Gethsemane: and he saith to his disciples, Sit ye here, while [k]I shall pray.

33 And he taketh with him Peter and James and John, and began to be sore amazed, and to be very heavy;

34 And saith unto them, [l]My soul is exceeding sorrowful unto death: tarry ye here, and watch.

35 And he went forward a little, and fell on the ground, and prayed that, if it were possible, the hour might pass from him.

36 And he said, [m]Abba, Father, [n]all things *are* possible unto thee; take away this cup from me: [o]nevertheless, not what I will, but what thou wilt.

37 And he cometh, and findeth them sleeping, and saith unto Peter, Simon, sleepest thou? couldest not thou watch one hour?

E—Concluded.

unto him that was able to save him from death, and was heard in that he feared;

8 Though he were a Son, yet learned he obedience by the things which he suffered;

F

John 11. 41 Then they took away the stone *from the place* where the dead was laid. And Jesus lifted up *his* eyes, and said, Father, I thank thee that thou hast heard me.

G

Matt. 20. 22 But Jesus answered and said, Ye know not what ye ask. Are ye able to drink of the cup that I shall drink of, and to be baptized with the baptism that I am baptized with? They say unto him, We are able.

TIME, THURSDAY, MIDNIGHT, APRIL 6 [NISAN 14], A. D. 30; PLACE, MOUNT OF OLIVES.
Week of our Lord's Fourth and Last Passover.

22: 39–46.

39 [p]And he came out, and [q]went, as
he was wont, to the mount of Olives;
and his disciples also followed him.
40 [r]And when he was at the place, he
said unto them, Pray that ye enter not
into temptation.
41 [s]And he was withdrawn from them
about a stone's cast, and kneeled down,
and prayed,
42 Saying, Father, if thou be [1]willing,
remove this cup from me: nevertheless,
[t]not my will, but thine, be done.
43 And there appeared [u]an angel
unto him from heaven, strengthening
him.
44 [x]And being in an agony he prayed
more earnestly: and his sweat was as
it were great drops of blood falling
down to the ground.
45 And when he rose up from prayer,
and was come to his disciples, he found
them sleeping for sorrow,

H

John 5. 30 I can of mine own self do nothing: as I hear, I judge: and my judgment is just; because I seek not mine own will, but the will of the Father which hath sent me.

John 6. 38 For I came down from heaven, not to do mine own will, but the will of him that sent me.

Phil. 2. 8 And being found in fashion as a man, he humbled himself, and became obedient unto death, even the death of the cross.

I

Matt. 26. 36 and Luke 22. 39. *See text of topic.*

K

Heb. 5. 7. *See under E.*

L

John 12. 27. *See under C.*

M

Rom. 8. 15 For ye have not received the spirit of bondage again to fear; but ye have received the Spirit of adoption, whereby we cry, Abba, Father.

18: 1, 2.

1 When Jesus had spoken these
words, [y]he went forth with his disciples
over the [z]brook Cedron, where was a
garden, into the which he entered, and
his disciples.
2 And Judas also, which betrayed
him, knew the place: [a]for Jesus ofttimes
resorted thither with his disciples.

M—CONCLUDED. (p. 553.)

Gal. 4. 6 And because ye are sons, God hath sent forth the Spirit of his Son into your hearts, crying, Abba, Father.

N

Heb. 5. 7. *See under E.*

O

John 5. 30 and John 6. 38. *See under H.*

P

Matt. 26. 36. *See text of topic.*

Q

Luke 21. 37 And in the daytime he was teaching in the temple; and at night he went out, and abode in the mount that is called *the mount* of Olives.

R

Matt. 6. 13 And lead us not into temptation, but deliver us from evil: For thine is the kingdom, and the power, and the glory, for ever. Amen.

Matt. 26. 41 and Mark 14. 38. *See text of topic.*
Luke 22. 46. *See text of topic.*

S

Matt. 26. 39 and Mark 16. 35. *See text of topic*

1

Gr., *willing to remove.*

T

John 5. 30 and John 6. 38. *See under H.*

U

Matt. 4. 11 Then the devil leaveth him, and, behold, angels came and ministered unto him.

X

John 12. 27. *Under C.* Heb. 5. 7. *Under E.*

Y

Matt. 26. 36. *See text of topic.*
Mark 14. 32 and Luke 22. 39. *See text of topic.*

Z

II Sa. 15. 23 And all the country wept with a loud voice, and all the people passed over: the king also himself passed over the brook Kidron, and all the people passed over, toward the way of the wilderness.

A

Luke 21. 37. *Under Q.* Luke 22. 39. *Text of topic.*

§ 192. THE AGONY IN THE GARDEN OF GETHSEMANE (CONCLUDED).
Evening Introducing the Sixth Day of the

CHAP. 26.

41 [b]Watch and pray, that ye enter not into temptation: [c]the spirit indeed *is* willing, but the flesh *is* weak.

42 He went away again the second time, and prayed, saying, O my Father, if this cup may not pass away from me, except I drink it, thy will be done.

43 And he came and found them asleep again: for their eyes were heavy.

44 And he left them, and went away again, and prayed the third time, saying the same words.

45 Then cometh he to his disciples, and saith unto them, Sleep on now, and take *your* rest: behold, the hour is at hand, and the Son of man is betrayed into the hands of sinners.

46 Rise, let us be going: behold, he is at hand that doth betray me.

B

Mark 13. 33 Take ye heed, watch and pray for ye know not when the time is.

Mark 14. 38 and Luke 22. 40, 46. *See text of topic.*

Eph. 6. 18 Praying always with all prayer and supplication in the Spirit, and watching thereunto with all perseverance and supplication for all saints;

C

Ps. 119. 4 Thou hast commanded *us* to keep thy precepts diligently.

5 O that my ways were directed to keep thy statutes!

Ps. 119. 24 Thy testimonies also *are* my delight, *and* my counsellors.

25 My soul cleaveth unto the dust: quicken thou me according to thy word.

Ps. 119. 32 I will run the way of thy commandments, when thou shalt enlarge my heart.

Ps. 119. 35 Make me to go in the path of thy commandments; for therein do I delight.

36 Incline my heart unto thy testimonies, and not to covetousness.

37 Turn away mine eyes from beholding vanity; *and* quicken thou me in thy way.

Ps. 119. 115 Depart from me, ye evil doers:

CHAP. 14.

38 Watch ye and pray, lest ye enter into temptation. [d]The spirit truly *is* ready, but the flesh *is* weak.

39 And again he went away, and prayed, and spake the same words.

40 And when he returned, he found them asleep again, (for their eyes were heavy,) neither wist they what to answer him.

41 And he cometh the third time, and saith unto them, Sleep on now, and take *your* rest: it is enough, [e]the hour is come; behold, the Son of man is betrayed into the hands of sinners.

42 [f]Rise up, let us go; lo, he that betrayeth me is at hand.

C—CONTINUED.

for I will keep the commandments of my God.

Ps. 119. 117 Hold thou me up, and I shall be safe: and I will have respect unto thy statutes continually.

Ps. 119. 173 Let thine hand help me; for I have chosen thy precepts.

174 I have longed for thy salvation, O LORD; and thy law *is* my delight.

Isa. 26. 8 Yea, in the way of thy judgments, O LORD, have we waited for thee; the desire of *our* soul *is* to thy name, and to the remembrance of thee.

9 With my soul have I desired thee in the night; yea, with my spirit within me will I seek thee early: for when thy judgments *are* in the earth, the inhabitants of the world will learn righteousness.

Rom. 7. 18 For I know that in me (that is, in my flesh,) dwelleth no good thing: for to will is present with me; but *how* to perform that which is good I find not.

19 For the good that I would, I do not: but the evil which I would not, that I do.

20 Now if I do that I would not, it is no more I that do it, but sin that dwelleth in me.

21 I find then a law, that, when I would do good, evil is present with me.

22 For I delight in the law of God after the inward man:

TIME, THURSDAY, MIDNIGHT, APRIL 6 [NISAN 14], A. D. 30; PLACE, MOUNT OF OLIVES.
Week of our Lord's Fourth and Last Passover.

CHAP. 22.

46 And said unto them, [g]Why sleep ye? rise and pray, lest ye enter into temptation.

C—CONCLUDED.

Rom. 7. 23 But I see another law in my members, warring against the law of my mind, and bringing me into captivity to the law of sin which is in my members.

24 O wretched man that I am! who shall deliver me from the body of this death?

25 I thank God through Jesus Christ our Lord. So then with the mind I myself serve the law of God; but with the flesh the law of sin.

Rom. 8. 3 For what the law could not do, in that it was weak through the flesh, God sending his own Son in the likeness of sinful flesh, and for sin, condemned sin in the flesh:

I Cor. 9. 27 But I keep under my body, and bring *it* into subjection: lest that by any means, when I have preached to others, I myself should be a castaway.

Gal. 5. 16 *This* I say then, Walk in the Spirit, and ye shall not fulfil the lust of the flesh.

17 For the flesh lusteth against the Spirit, and the Spirit against the flesh: and these are contrary the one to the other; so that ye cannot do the things that ye would.

Gal. 5. 24 And they that are Christ's have crucified the flesh with the affections and lusts.

Phil. 2. 12 Wherefore, my beloved, as ye have always obeyed, not as in my presence only, but now much more in my absence, work out your own salvation with fear and trembling:

13 For it is God which worketh in you both to will and to do of *his* good pleasure.

Phil. 3. 12 Not as though I had already attained, either were already perfect: but I follow after, if that I may apprehend that for which also I am apprehended of Christ Jesus.

13 Brethren, I count not myself to have apprehended: but *this* one thing *I do*, forgetting those things which are behind, and reaching forth unto those things which are before,

14 I press toward the mark for the prize of the high calling of God in Christ Jesus.

[CHAP. 18.]

D

Rom. 7. 23. *See under C.*

E

John 13. 1 Now before the feast of the passover, when Jesus knew that his hour was come that he should depart out of this world unto the Father, having loved his own which were in the world, he loved them unto the end.

F

Matt. 26. 46 and John 18. 1, 2. *See text of topic.*

G

Prov. 6. 4 Give not sleep to thine eyes, nor slumber to thine eyelids.

5 Deliver thyself as a roe from the hand *of the hunter*, and as a bird from the hand of the fowler.

6 Go to the ant, thou sluggard; consider her ways, and be wise:

7 Which having no guide, overseer, or ruler,

8 Provideth her meat in the summer, *and* gathereth her food in the harvest.

9 How long wilt thou sleep, O sluggard? when wilt thou arise out of thy sleep?

10 *Yet* a little sleep, a little slumber, a little folding of the hands to sleep:

11 So shall thy poverty come as one that travelleth, and thy want as an armed man.

Jon. 1. 6 So the shipmaster came to him, and said unto him, What meanest thou, O sleeper? arise, call upon thy God, if so be that God will think upon us, that we perish not.

Luke 21. 34 And take heed to yourselves, lest at any time your hearts be overcharged with surfeiting, and drunkenness, and cares of this life, and so that day come upon you unawares.

35 For as a snare shall it come on all them that dwell on the face of the whole earth.

36 Watch ye therefore, and pray always, that ye may be accounted worthy to escape all these things that shall come to pass, and to stand before the Son of man.

Luke 22. 40. *See text of topic.*

I Pet. 4. 7 But the end of all things is at hand: be ye therefore sober, and watch unto prayer.

Rev. 16. 15 Behold, I come as a thief. Blessed *is* he that watcheth, and keepeth his garments, lest he walk naked, and they see his shame.

§ 193. JESUS BETRAYED AND MADE PRISONER.
Evening Introducing the Sixth Day of the

26: 47–56.

47 [a]And while he yet spake, lo, Judas,
one of the twelve, came, and with him a
great multitude with swords and staves,
from the chief priests and elders of the
people.

48 Now he that betrayed him gave
them a sign, saying, [b]Whomsoever I
shall kiss, that same is he; hold him
fast.

49 And forthwith he came to Jesus,
and said, Hail, Master; and kissed
him.

A

Mark 14. 43 and Luke 22. 47. *See text of topic.*

Acts 1. 16 Men *and* brethren, this Scripture must needs have been fulfilled, which the Holy Ghost by the mouth of David spake before concerning Judas, which was guide to them that took Jesus.

B

II Sa. 3. 27 And when Abner was returned to Hebron, Joab took him aside in the gate to speak with him quietly, and smote him there under the fifth *rib*, that he died, for the blood of Asahel his brother.

II Sa. 20. 9 And Joab said to Amasa, *Art* thou in health, my brother? And Joab took Amasa by the beard with the right hand to kiss him.

10 But Amasa took no heed to the sword that *was* in Joab's hand: so he smote him therewith in the fifth *rib*, and shed out his bowels to the ground, and struck him not again; and he died. So Joab and Abishai his brother pursued after Sheba the son of Bichri.

Ps. 28. 3 Draw me not away with the wicked, and with the workers of iniquity, which speak peace to their neighbours, but mischief *is* in their hearts.

Ps. 55. 20 He hath put forth his hands against such as be at peace with him: he hath broken his covenant.

21 *The words* of his mouth were smoother than butter, but war *was* in his heart: his words were softer than oil, yet *were* they drawn swords.

C

Matt. 17. 22 And while they abode in Galilee, Jesus said unto them, The Son of man

14: 43–52.

43 And immediately, while he yet
spake, cometh Judas, one of the twelve,
and with him a great multitude with
swords and staves, from the chief
priests and the scribes and the elders.

44 And he that betrayed him had
given them a token, saying, Whomsoever I shall kiss, that same is he; take
him, and lead *him* away safely.

45 And as soon as he was come, he
goeth straightway to him, and saith,
Master, Master; and kissed him.

C—CONCLUDED.

shall be betrayed into the hands of men:

23 And they shall kill him, and the third day he shall be raised again. And they were exceeding sorry.

Mark 10. 33 *Saying*, Behold, we go up to Jerusalem; and the Son of man shall be delivered unto the chief priests, and unto the scribes; and they shall condemn him to death, and shall deliver him to the Gentiles:

34 And they shall mock him, and shall scourge him, and shall spit upon him, and shall kill him; and the third day he shall rise again.

John 10. 17 Therefore doth my Father love me, because I lay down my life, that I might take it again.

18 No man taketh it from me, but I lay it down of myself. I have power to lay it down, and I have power to take it again. This commandment have I received of my Father.

John 19. 28 After this, Jesus knowing that all things were now accomplished, that the Scripture might be fulfilled, saith, I thirst.

Acts 2. 28 Thou hast made known to me the ways of life; thou shalt make me full of joy with thy countenance.

D

Ps. 34. 7 The angel of the LORD encampeth round about them that fear him, and delivereth them.

Matt. 6. 34 Take therefore no thought for the morrow: for the morrow shall take thought for the things of itself. Sufficient unto the day *is* the evil thereof.

TIME, THURSDAY, MIDNIGHT, APRIL 6 [NISAN 14], A. D. 30; PLACE, MOUNT OF OLIVES.
Week of our Lord's Fourth and Last Passover.

22: 47–53.

47 And while he yet spake, behold a multitude, and he that was called Judas, one of the twelve, went before them, and drew near unto Jesus to kiss him.

48 But Jesus said unto him, Judas, betrayest thou the Son of man with a kiss?

D—CONCLUDED.

John 10. 28 And I give unto them eternal life; and they shall never perish, neither shall any *man* pluck them out of my hand.

Phil. 4. 6 Be careful for nothing; but in every thing by prayer and supplication with thanksgiving let your requests be made known unto God.

7 And the peace of God, which passeth all understanding, shall keep your hearts and minds through Christ Jesus.

I Pet. 5. 7 Casting all your care upon him; for he careth for you.

E

John 17. 12 While I was with them in the world, I kept them in thy name: those that thou gavest me I have kept, and none of them is lost, but the son of perdition; that the Scripture might be fulfilled.

Jude 1 Jude, the servant of Jesus Christ, and brother of James, to them that are sanctified by God the Father, and preserved in Jesus Christ, *and* called:

F

Ps 41. 9 Yea, mine own familiar friend, in whom I trusted, which did eat of my bread, hath lifted up *his* heel against me.

Ps. 55. 13 But *it was* thou, a man mine equal, my guide, and mine acquaintance.

14 We took sweet counsel together, *and* walked unto the house of God in company.

G

John 18. 10. *See text of topic.*

H

I Cor. 4. 12 And labour, working with our own hands: being reviled, we bless; being persecuted, we suffer it:

13 Being defamed, we entreat: we are made as the filth of the world, *and are* the offscouring of all things unto this day.

I

Gen. 9. 6 Whoso sheddeth man's blood, by man shall his blood be shed: for in the image of God made he man.

18: 3–12.

3 Judas then, having received a band *of men* and officers from the chief priests and Pharisees, cometh thither with lanterns and torches and weapons.

4 Jesus therefore, [c]knowing all things that should come upon him, went forth, and said unto them, Whom seek ye?

5 They answered him, Jesus of Nazareth. Jesus saith unto them, I am *he*. And Judas also, which betrayed him, stood with them.

6 As soon then as he had said unto them, I am *he*, they went backward, and fell to the ground.

7 Then asked he them again, Whom seek ye? And they said, Jesus of Nazareth.

8 Jesus answered, I have told you that I am *he*: if therefore ye seek me, [d]let these go their way:

9 That the saying might be fulfilled, which he spake, [e]Of them which thou gavest me, have I lost none.

I—CONCLUDED.

Rev. 13. 10 He that leadeth into captivity shall go into captivity: he that killeth with the sword must be killed with the sword. Here is the patience and the faith of the saints.

K

II Ki. 6. 17 And Elisha prayed, and said, LORD, I pray thee, open his eyes, that he may see. And the LORD opened the eyes of the young man; and he saw: and, behold, the mountain *was* full of horses and chariots of fire round about Elisha.

Ps. 91. 11 For he shall give his angels charge over thee, to keep thee in all thy ways.

Dan. 7. 10 A fiery stream issued and came forth from before him: thousand thousands ministered unto him, and ten thousand times ten thousand stood before him: the judgment was set, and the books were opened.

§ 193. JESUS BETRAYED AND MADE PRISONER (CONCLUDED).
Evening Introducing the Sixth Day of the

CHAP. 26.

50 And Jesus said unto him, [f]Friend, wherefore art thou come? Then came they, and laid hands on Jesus, and took him.

51 And, behold, [g]one of them which were with Jesus stretched out *his* hand, and drew his sword, and struck a servant of the high priest, and smote off his ear.

52 Then said Jesus unto him, [h]Put up again thy sword into his place: [i]for all they that take the sword shall perish with the sword.

53 Thinkest thou that I cannot now pray to my Father, and he shall presently give me [k]more than twelve legions of angels?

54 But how then shall the Scriptures be fulfilled, [l]that thus it must be?

55 In that same hour said Jesus to the multitudes, Are ye come out as against a thief with swords and staves for to take me? I sat daily with you teaching in the temple, and ye laid no hold on me.

56 But all this was done, that the [m]Scriptures of the prophets might be fulfilled. Then [n]all the disciples forsook him, and fled.

For F, G, H, I and K see preceding page (553).

L

Isa. 53. 7 He was oppressed, and he was afflicted, yet he opened not his mouth: he is brought as a lamb to the slaughter, and as a sheep before her shearers is dumb, so he openeth not his mouth.

8 He was taken from prison and from judgment: and who shall declare his generation? for he was cut off out of the land of the living: for the transgression of my people was he stricken.

CHAP. 14.

46 And they laid their hands on him, and took him.

47 And one of them that stood by drew a sword, and smote a servant of the high priest, and cut off his ear.

48 [o]And Jesus answered and said unto them, Are ye come out, as against a thief, with swords and *with* staves to take me?

49 I was daily with you in the temple teaching, and ye took me not: but [p]the Scriptures must be fulfilled.

50 [q]And they all forsook him, and fled.

51 And there followed him a certain young man, having a linen cloth cast about *his* naked *body;* and the young men laid hold on him:

52 And he left the linen cloth, and fled from them naked.

L—CONTINUED.

Isa. 53. 9 And he made his grave with the wicked, and with the rich in his death; because he had done no violence, neither *was any* deceit in his mouth.

Dan. 9. 26 And after threescore and two weeks shall Messiah be cut off, but not for himself: and the people of the prince that shall come shall destroy the city and the scantuary; and the end thereof *shall be* with a flood, and unto the end of the war desolations are determined.

Matt.26. 24 The Son of man goeth as it is written of him: but woe unto that man by whom the Son of man is betrayed! it had been good for that man if he had not been born.

Luke 24. 44 And he said unto them, These *are* the words which I spake unto you, while I was yet with you, that all things must be fulfilled, which were written in the law of Moses, and *in* the prophets, and *in* the psalms, concerning me.

45 Then opened he their understanding, that they might understand the Scriptures,

46 And said unto them, Thus it is

TIME, THURSDAY, MIDNIGHT, APRIL 6 [NISAN 14], A. D. 30; PLACE, MOUNT OF OLIVES.
Week of our Lord's Fourth and Last Passover.

CHAP. 22.

49 When they which were about him saw what would follow, they said unto him, Lord, shall we smite with the sword?

50 And one of them smote the servant of the high priest, and cut off his right ear.

51 And Jesus answered and said, Suffer ye thus far. And he touched his ear, and healed him.

52 [r]Then Jesus said unto the chief priests, and captains of the temple, and the elders, which were come to him, Be ye come out, as against a thief, with swords and staves?

53 When I was daily with you in the temple, ye stretched forth no hands against me: [s]but this is your hour, and the power of darkness.

L—CONCLUDED.

written, and thus it behooved Christ to suffer, and to rise from the dead the third day:

M

Lam. 4. 20 The breath of our nostrils, the anointed of the LORD, was taken in their pits, of whom we said, Under his shadow we shall live among the heathen.

Matt. 26. 54. *See text of topic.*

N

John 18. 15 And Simon Peter followed Jesus, and *so did* another disciple: that disciple was known unto the high priest, and went in with Jesus into the palace of the high priest.

O

Matt. 26. 55 and Luke 22. 52. *See text of topic.*

P

Ps. 22. 6 But I *am* a worm, and no man; a reproach of men, and despised of the people.

Is. 53. 7, etc. *See under L.*

Luke 22. 37 For I say unto you, that this that is written must yet be accomplished in me, And he was reckoned among the transgressors: for the things concerning me have no end.

Luke 24. 44. *See under L.*

CHAP. 18.

10 Then Simon Peter having a sword drew it, and smote the high priest's servant, and cut off his right ear. The servant's name was Malchus.

11 Then said Jesus unto Peter, Put up thy sword into the sheath: [t]the cup which my Father hath given me, shall I not drink it?

12 Then the band and the captain and officers of the Jews took Jesus, and bound him,

Q

Ps. 88. 8 Thou hast put away mine acquaintance far from me; thou hast made me an abomination unto them: *I am* shut up, and I cannot come forth.

Mark 14. 27 And Jesus saith unto them, All ye shall be offended because of me this night: for it is written, I will smite the Shepherd, and the sheep shall be scattered.

R

Matt. 26. 55 and Mark 14. 48. *See text of topic.*

S

Gen. 3. 15 And I will put enmity between thee and the woman, and between thy seed and her seed; it shall bruise thy head, and thou shalt bruise his heel.

John 12. 27 Now is my soul troubled; and what shall I say? Father, save me from this hour: but for this cause came I unto this hour.

Acts 2. 23 Him, being delivered by the determinate counsel and foreknowledge of God, ye have taken, and by wicked hands have crucified and slain:

T

Matt. 20. 22 But Jesus answered and said, Ye know not what ye ask. Are ye able to drink of the cup that I shall drink of, and to be baptized with the baptism that I am baptized with? They say unto him, We are able.

Matt. 26. 39 And he went a little further, and fell on his face, and prayed, saying, O my Father, if it be possible, let this cup pass from me: nevertheless, not as I will, but as thou *wilt.*

Matt. 26. 42 He went away again the second time, and prayed, saying, O my Father, if this cup may not pass away from me, except I drink it, thy will be done.

§ 194. JESUS BEFORE ANNAS AND CAIAPHAS. PETER'S DENIAL.

Night Introducing the Sixth Day of the Week

26: 57, 58, 69–75.

57 [a]And they that had laid hold on Jesus led *him* away to Caiaphas the high priest, where the scribes and the elders were assembled.

58 But Peter followed him afar off unto the high priest's palace, and went in, and sat with the servants, to see the end. (p. 560.)

* * * * *

69 [b]Now Peter sat without in the palace: and a damsel came unto him, saying, Thou also wast with Jesus of Galilee.

70 [c]But he denied before *them* all, saying, I know not what thou sayest.

71 And when he was gone out into the porch, another *maid* saw him, and said unto them that were there, This *fellow* was also with Jesus of Nazareth.

72 And again he denied with an oath, I do not know the man.

A

Ps. 56. 5 Every day they wrest my words: all their thoughts *are* against me for evil.
6 They gather themselves together, they hide themselves, they mark my steps, when they wait for my soul.

Mark 14. 53 and Luke 22. 54. *See text of topic.*

John 18. 12 Then the band and the captain and the officers of the Jews took Jesus, and bound him,

B

Mark 14. 66, Luke 22. 55 and John 18. 16, 17, 25. *See text of topic.*

C

Ps. 119. 115 Depart from me, ye evil doers: for I will keep the commandments of my God.
116 Uphold me according unto thy word, that I may live: and let me not be ashamed of my hope.
117 Hold thou me up, and I shall be safe: and I will have respect unto thy statutes continually.

Prov. 28. 26 He that trusteth in his own heart is a fool: but whoso walketh wisely, he shall be delivered.

Prov. 29. 23 A man's pride shall bring him

14: 53, 54, 66–72.

53 And they led Jesus away to the high priest: and with him were assembled all the chief priests and the elders and the scribes.

54 And Peter followed him afar off, even into the palace of the high priest: and he sat with the servants, and warmed himself at the fire. (p. 560.)

* * * * *

66 And as Peter was beneath in the palace, there cometh one of the maids of the high priest:

67 And when she saw Peter warming himself, she looked upon him, and said, And thou also wast with Jesus of Nazareth.

68 But he denied, saying, I know not, neither understand I what thou sayest. And he went out into the porch; and the cock crew.

69 And a maid saw him again, and began to say to them that stood by, This is *one* of them.

70 And he denied it again.

C—Continued.

low: but honour shall uphold the humble in spirit.
24 Whoso is partner with a thief hateth his own soul: he heareth cursing, and bewrayeth *it* not.
25 The fear of man bringeth a snare: but whoso putteth his trust in the LORD shall be safe.

Isa. 57. 11 And of whom hast thou been afraid or feared, that thou hast lied, and hast not remembered me, nor laid *it* to thy heart? have not I held my peace even of old, and thou fearest me not?

Jer. 17. 9 The heart *is* deceitful above all *things*, and desperately wicked: who can know it?

Luke 22. 60. *See text of topic.*

Rom. 11. 20 Well; because of unbelief they were broken off, and thou standest by faith. Be not highminded, but fear:

TIME, FRIDAY, 1–5 A. M., APRIL 7 [NISAN 15], A. D. 30; PLACE, JERUSALEM.
of our Lord's Fourth and Last Passover.

22: 54–62.

54 [d]Then took they him, and led *him*,
and brought him into the high priest's
house. And Peter followed afar off.
55 And when they had kindled a fire
in the midst of the hall, and were set
down together, Peter sat down among
them.
56 But a certain maid beheld him as
he sat by the fire, and earnestly looked
upon him, and said, This man was also
with him.
57 And he denied him, saying, Woman, I know him not.
58 And after a little while another
saw him, and said, Thou art also of
them. And Peter said, Man, I am not.

C—CONCLUDED.

I Cor.10. 12 Wherefore let him that thinketh he standeth take heed lest he fall.

D

Matt. 26. 57. *See text of topic.*

Acts 8. 32 The place of the Scripture which he read was this, He was led as a sheep to the slaughter; and like a lamb dumb before his shearer, so opened he not his mouth:

E

Luke 3. 2 Annas and Caiaphas being the high priests, the word of God came unto John the son of Zacharias in the wilderness.

Acts 4. 6 And Annas the high priest, and Caiaphas, and John, and Alexander, and as many as were of the kindred of the high priest, were gathered together at Jerusalem.

1

And Annas sent Christ bound unto Caiaphas the high priest.

John 18. 24. *See text of § 195.*

F

John 11. 49 And one of them, *named* Caiaphas, being the high priest that same year, said unto them, Ye know nothing at all,
50 Nor consider that it is expedient for us, that one man should die for the people, and that the whole nation perish not.
51 And this spake he not of him-

18: 13–18, 25–27.

13 And led him away to [e]Annas first:
for he was father in law to Caiaphas,
which was the high priest that same
year.[1]
14 [f]Now Caiaphas was he, which gave
counsel to the Jews, that it was expedient that one man should die for the
people.
15 And Simon Peter followed Jesus,
and *so did* another disciple: that disciple was known unto the high priest,
and went in with Jesus into the palace
of the high priest.
16 But Peter stood at the door without. Then went out that other disciple,
which was known unto the high priest,
and spake unto her that kept the door,
and brought in Peter.
17 Then saith the damsel that kept
the door unto Peter, Art not thou also
one of this man's disciples? He saith,
I am not.
18 And the servants and officers stood
there, who had made a fire of coals, for
it was cold; and they warmed themselves: and Peter stood with them, and
warmed himself. (p. 561.)

* * * * *

25 And Simon Peter stood and
warmed himself. They said therefore
unto him, Art not thou also *one* of his
disciples? He denied *it*, and said, I
am not.

F—CONCLUDED.

self: but being high priest that year, he prophesied that Jesus should die for that nation;
52 And not for that nation only, but that also he should gather together in one the children of God that were scattered abroad.

§ 191. JESUS BEFORE ANNAS AND CAIAPHAS. PETER'S DENIAL (Con-
Night Introducing the Sixth Day of the Week

Chap. 26.

73 And after a while came unto *him* they that stood by, and said to Peter, Surely thou also art *one* of them; for thy speech bewrayeth thee.

74 Then [g]began he to curse and to swear, *saying*, I know not the man. And immediately the cock crew.

75 And Peter remembered the word of Jesus, which said unto him, [h]Before the cock crow, thou shalt deny me thrice. And he went out, and [i]wept bitterly. (p. 564.)

Chap. 14.

And a little after, they that stood by said again to Peter, Surely thou art *one* of them: [k]for thou art a Galilean, and thy speech agreeth *thereto*.

71 [l]But he began to curse and to swear, *saying*, I know not this man of whom ye speak.

72 And the second time the cock crew. And Peter called to mind the word that Jesus said unto him, Before the cock crow twice, thou shalt deny me thrice. And [2]when he thought thereon, he wept. (p. 564.)

G

Ex. 20. 7 Thou shalt not take the name of the Lord thy God in vain: for the Lord will not hold him guiltless that taketh his name in vain.

Judg. 17. 2 And he said unto his mother, The eleven hundred *shekels* of silver that were taken from thee, about which thou cursedst, and spakest of also in mine ears, behold, the silver *is* with me; I took it. And his mother said, Blessed *be thou* of the Lord, my son.

H

Matt. 26. 34 Jesus said unto him, Verily I say unto thee, That this night, before the cock crow, thou shalt deny me thrice.

Mark 14. 30 And Jesus saith unto him, Verily I say unto thee, That this day, *even* in this night, before the cock crow twice, thou shalt deny me thrice.

Luke 22. 61, 62. *See text of topic.*

John 13. 38 Jesus answered him, Wilt thou lay down thy life for my sake? Verily, verily, I say unto thee, The cock shall not crow, till thou hast denied me thrice.

I

II Sa. 12. 13 And David said unto Nathan, I have sinned against the Lord. And Nathan said unto David, The Lord also hath put away thy sin; thou shalt not die.

I Ki. 8. 47 *Yet* if they shall bethink themselves in the land whither they were carried captives, and repent, and make supplication unto thee in the land of them that carried them captives, saying, We have sinned, and have done perversely, we have committed wickedness;

I—Continued.

I Ki. 8. 48 And *so* return unto thee with all their heart, and with all their soul, in the land of their enemies, which led them away captive, and pray unto thee toward their land, which thou gavest unto their fathers, the city which thou hast chosen, and the house which I have built for thy name:

49 Then hear thou their prayer and their supplication in heaven thy dwellingplace, and maintain their cause,

50 And forgive thy people that have sinned against thee, and all their transgressions wherein they have transgressed against thee, and give them compassion before them who carried them captive, that they may have compassion on them:

Job 33. 27 He looketh upon men, and *if any* say, I have sinned, and perverted *that which was* right, and it profited me not;

28 He will deliver his soul from going into the pit, and his life shall see the light.

29 Lo, all these *things* worketh God oftentimes with man,

30 To bring back his soul from the pit, to be enlightened with the light of the living.

Zech. 12. 10 And I will pour upon the house of David, and upon the inhabitants of Jerusalem, the spirit of grace and of supplications: and they shall look upon me whom they have pierced, and they shall mourn for him, as one

CLUDED). TIME, FRIDAY, 1-5 A. M., APRIL 7 [NISAN 15], A. D. 30; PLACE, JERUSALEM.
of our Lord's Fourth and Last Passover.

CHAP. 22.

59 And about the space of one hour after another confidently affirmed, saying, Of a truth this *fellow* also was with him; for he is a Galilean.

60 And Peter said, Man, I know not what thou sayest. And immediately, while he yet spake, the cock crew.

61 And the Lord turned, and looked upon Peter. And Peter remembered the word of the Lord, how he had said unto him, Before the cock crow, thou shalt deny me thrice.

62 And Peter went out, and [m]wept bitterly. (p. 563.)

I—CONCLUDED.

mourneth for *his* only *son*, and shall be in bitterness for him, as one that is in bitterness for *his* first-born.

II Cor.7. 10 For godly sorrow worketh repentance to salvation not to be repented of: but the sorrow of the world worketh death.

Gal. 6. 1 Brethren, if a man be overtaken in a fault, ye which are spiritual, restore such a one in the spirit of meekness; considering thyself, lest thou also be tempted.

K

Judg.12. 5. And the Gileadites took the passages of Jordan before the Ephraimites: and it was *so*, that when those Ephraimites which were escaped said, Let me go over, that the men of Gilead said unto him, *Art* thou an Ephraimite? If he said, Nay;

6 Then said they unto him, Say now Shibboleth: and he said Sibboleth: for he could not frame to pronounce *it* right. Then they took him and slew him at the passages of Jordan: and there fell at that time of the Ephraimites forty and two thousand.

Acts 2. 7 And they were all amazed and marvelled, saying one to another, Behold, are not all these which speak Galileans?

L

II Ki. 8. 13 And Hazael said, But what, *is* thy servant a dog, that he should do this great thing? And Elisha answered,

CHAP. 18.

26 One of the servants of the high priest, being *his* kinsman whose ear Peter cut off, saith, Did not I see thee in the garden with him?

27 Peter then denied again; and immediately the cock crew. (p. 565.)

L—CONCLUDED.

The LORD hath showed me that thou *shalt be* king over Syria.

II Ki. 8. 15 And it came to pass on the morrow, that he took a thick cloth, and dipped *it* in water, and spread *it* on his face, so that he died: and Hazael reigned in his stead.

II Ki.10. 32 In those days the LORD began to cut Israel short: and Hazael smote them in all the coasts of Israel:

2

Or, *he wept abundantly*, or, *he began to weep.*

Eze. 7. 16 But they that escape of them shall escape, and shall be on the mountains like doves of the valleys, all of them mourning, every one for his iniquity.

Zech. 12. 10 and II Cor. 7. 10. *See under I.*

M

Ps. 38. 18 For I will declare mine iniquity; I will be sorry for my sin.

Ps. 126. 5 They that sow in tears shall reap in joy.

6 He that goeth forth and weepeth, bearing precious seed, shall doubtless come again with rejoicing, bringing his sheaves *with him.*

Ps. 130. 1 Out of the depths have I cried unto thee, O LORD.

2 Lord, hear my voice: let thine ears be attentive to the voice of my supplications.

3 If thou, LORD, shouldest mark iniquities, O Lord, who shall stand?

4 But *there is* forgiveness with thee, that thou mayest be feared.

Ps. 143. 3 For the enemy hath persecuted my soul; he hath smitten my life down to the ground; he hath made me to dwell in darkness, as those that have been long dead.

4 Therefore is my spirit overwhelmed within me; my heart within me is desolate.

Isa. 66. 2 For all those *things* hath mine hand made, and all those *things* have been, saith the LORD: but to this *man* will I look, *even* to *him that is* poor and of a contrite spirit, and trembleth at my word.

§ 195. JESUS BEFORE CAIAPHAS AND THE SANHEDRIN.

Morning of the Sixth Day of the Week

MATTHEW 26 : 59–68.

59 Now the chief priests, and elders, and all the council, sought false witness against Jesus, to put him to death;

60 But found none: yea, though [a]many false witnesses came, *yet* found they none. At the last came [b]two false witnesses,

61 And said, This *fellow* said, [c]I am able to destroy the temple of God, and to build it in three days.

62 [d]And the high priest arose, and said unto him, Answerest thou nothing? what *is it which* these witness against thee?

A

I Ki. 21. 9 And she wrote in the letters, saying, Proclaim a fast, and set Naboth on high among the people:
10 And set two men, sons of Belial, before him, to bear witness against him, saying, Thou didst blaspheme God and the king. And *then* carry him out, and stone him, that he may die.

Ps. 27. 12 Deliver me not over unto the will of mine enemies: for false witnesses are risen up against me, and such as breathe out cruelty.

Ps. 35. 11 False witnesses did rise up; they laid to my charge *things* that I knew not.

Ps. 55. 11 Wickedness *is* in the midst thereof: deceit and guile depart not from her streets.

Mark 14. 55. *See text of topic.*

Acts 6. 13 And set up false witnesses, which said, This man ceaseth not to speak blasphemous words against this holy place, and the law:

B

Deut.19. 15 One witness shall not rise up against a man for any iniquity, or for any sin, in any sin that he sinneth: at the mouth of two witnesses, or at the mouth of three witnesses, shall the matter be established.

C

Matt.27. 40 And saying, Thou that destroyest the temple, and buildest *it* in three days, save thyself. If thou be the Son of God, come down from the cross.

MARK 14: 55–65.

55 And the chief priests and all the council sought for witness against Jesus to put him to death; and [e]found none.

56 For many bare [f]false witness against him, but their witness agreed not together.

57 And there arose certain, and bare false witness against him, saying,

58 We heard him say, [g]I will destroy this temple that is made with hands, and within three days I will build another made without hands.

59 But neither so did their witness agree together.

60 And the high priest stood up in the midst, and asked Jesus, saying, Answerest thou nothing? what *is it which* these witness against thee?

C—Concluded.

John 2. 19 Jesus answered and said unto them, Destroy this temple, and in three days I will raise it up.

D

Mark 14. 60. *See text of topic.*

E

Dan. 6. 4 Then the presidents and princes sought to find occasion against Daniel concerning the kingdom; but they could find none occasion nor fault; forasmuch as he *was* faithful, neither was there any error or fault found in him.

I Pet. 3. 16 Having a good conscience; that, whereas they speak evil of you, as of evil doers, they may be ashamed that falsely accuse your good conversation in Christ.

F

Prov. 6. 19 A false witness *that* speaketh lies, and he that soweth discord among brethren.

Prov.19. 5 A false witness shall not be unpunished; and *he that* speaketh lies shall not escape.

G

Mark 15. 29 And they that passed by railed on him, wagging their heads, and saying, Ah, thou that destroyest the temple, and buildest *it* in three days,

John 2. 19. *See under C.*

TIME, FRIDAY, 1–5 A. M., APRIL 7 [NISAN 15], A. D. 30; PLACE, JERUSALEM.
of our Lord's Fourth and Last Passover.

[22: 63–71.]

H

Matt.26. 55 In that same hour said Jesus to the multitudes, Are ye come out as against a thief with swords and staves for to take me? I sat daily with you teaching in the temple, and ye laid no hold on me.

Luke 4. 15 And he taught in their synagogues, being glorified of all.

John 7. 14 Now about the midst of the feast Jesus went up into the temple, and taught.

John 7. 26 But, lo, he speaketh boldly, and they say nothing unto him. Do the rulers know indeed that this is the very Christ?

John 7. 28 Then cried Jesus in the temple as he taught, saying, Ye both know me, and ye know whence I am: and I am not come of myself, but he that sent me is true, whom ye know not.

John 8. 2 And early in the morning he came again into the temple, and all the people came unto him; and he sat down, and taught them.

I

Isa. 50. 6 I gave my back to the smiters, and my cheeks to them that plucked off the hair: I hid not my face from shame and spitting.

Jer. 20. 2 Then Pashur smote Jeremiah the prophet, and put him in the stocks that *were* in the high gate of Benjamin, which *was* by the house of the LORD.

Mic. 5. 1 Now gather thyself in troops, O daughter of troops: he hath laid siege against us: they shall smite the judge of Israel with a rod upon the cheek.

Acts 23. 2 And the high priest Ananias commanded them that stood by him to smite him on the mouth.

K

I Pet. 2. 23 Who, when he was reviled, reviled not again; when he suffered, he threatened not; but committed *himself* to him that judgeth righteously:

L

Isa. 53. 7 He was oppressed, and he was afflicted, yet he opened not his mouth: he is brought as a lamb to the slaughter, and as a sheep before her shearers is dumb, so he openeth not his mouth.

Matt.17. 12 But I say unto you, That Elias is come already, and they knew him not, but have done unto him whatsoever they listed. Likewise shall also the the Son of man suffer of them.

18: 19–24.

19 The high priest then asked Jesus of his disciples, and of his doctrine.

20 Jesus answered him, [h]I spake openly to the world; I ever taught in the synagogue, and in the temple, whither the Jews always resort; and in secret have I said nothing.

21 Why askest thou me? ask them which heard me, what I have said unto them: behold, they know what I said.

22 And when he had thus spoken, one of the officers which stood by [i]struck Jesus with the palm of his hand, saying, Answerest thou the high priest so?

23 Jesus answered him, [k]If I have spoken evil, bear witness of the evil: but if well, why smitest thou me?

24 Now Annas had sent him bound unto Caiaphas the high priest. (p. 557.)

M

Lev. 5. 1 And if a soul sin, and hear the voice of swearing, and *is* a witness, whether he hath seen or known *of it;* if he do not utter *it*, then he shall bear his iniquity.

I Sa. 14. 24 And the men of Israel were distressed that day: for Saul had adjured the people, saying, Cursed *be* the man that eateth *any* food until evening, that I may be avenged on mine enemies. So none of the people tasted *any* food.

N

Dan. 7. 13 I saw in the night visions, and, behold, *one* like the Son of man came with the clouds of heaven, and came to the Ancient of days, and they brought him near before him.

Matt.16. 27 For the Son of man shall come in the glory of his Father with his angels; and then he shall reward every man according to his works.

Matt.24. 30 And then shall appear the sign of the Son of man in heaven: and then shall all the tribes of the earth mourn, and they shall see the Son of man coming in the clouds of heaven with power and great glory.

For N concluded see next page (562).

§ 195. JESUS BEFORE CAIAPHAS AND THE SANHEDRIN (Concluded).
Morning of the Sixth Day of the Week

Chap. 26.

63 But [l]Jesus held his peace. And the high priest answered and said unto him, [m]I adjure thee by the living God, that thou tell us whether thou be the Christ, the Son of God.

64 Jesus saith unto him, Thou hast said: nevertheless I say unto you, [n]Hereafter shall ye see the Son of man [o]sitting on the right hand of power, and coming in the clouds of heaven.

65 [p]Then the high priest rent his clothes, saying, He hath spoken blasphemy; what further need have we of witnesses? behold, now ye have heard his blasphemy.

66 What think ye? They answered and said, [q]He is guilty of death.

67 [r]Then did they spit in his face, and buffeted him; and others smote *him* with [1]the palms of their hands,

68 Saying, [s]Prophesy unto us, thou Christ, Who is he that smote thee? p. 556

For L, M and N see preceding page (561).

N—Continued.

Matt.25. 31 When the Son of man shall come in his glory, and all the holy angels with him, then shall he sit upon the throne of his glory:

Luke 21. 27 And then shall they see the Son of man coming in a cloud with power and great glory.

John 1. 51 And he saith unto him, Verily, verily, I say unto you, Hereafter ye shall see heaven open, and the angels of God ascending and descending upon the Son of man.

Rom.14. 10 But why dost thou judge thy brother? or why dost thou set at nought thy brother? for we shall all stand before the judgment seat of Christ.

I Thes.4. 16 For the Lord himself shall descend from heaven with a shout, with the voice of the archangel, and with the trump of God: and the dead in Christ shall rise first:

Rev. 1. 7 Behold, he cometh with clouds;

Chap. 14.

61 But [l]he held his peace, and answered nothing. Again the high priest asked him, and said unto him, Art thou the Christ, the Son of the Blessed?

62 And Jesus said, I am: and ye shall see the Son of man sitting on the right hand of power, and coming in the clouds of heaven.

63 Then the high priest rent his clothes, and saith, What need we any further witnesses?

64 Ye have heard the blasphemy: what think ye? And they all condemned him to be guilty of death.

65 And some began to spit on him, and to cover his face, and to buffet him, and to say unto him, Prophesy: and the servants did strike him with the palms of their hands. (p. 556.)

N—Concluded.

and every eye shall see him, and they *also* which pierced him: and all kindreds of the earth shall wail because of him. Even so, Amen.

O

Ps.110.1. The Lord said unto my Lord, Sit thou at my right hand, until I make thine enemies thy footstool.

Acts 7. 55 But he, being full of the Holy Ghost, looked up steadfastly into heaven, and saw the glory of God, and Jesus standing on the right hand of God,

P

II Ki.18. 37 Then came Eliakim the son of Hilkiah, which *was* over the household, and Shebna the scribe, and Joah the son of Asaph the recorder, to Hezekiah with *their* clothes rent, and told him the words of Rab-shakeh.

II Ki.19. 1 And it came to pass, when king Hezekiah heard *it*, that he rent his clothes, and covered himself with sackcloth, and went into the house of the Lord.

Q

Lev. 24. 16 And he that blasphemeth the name of the Lord, he shall surely be put to

TIME, FRIDAY, 1–5 A. M., APRIL 7 [NISAN 15], A. D. 30; PLACE, JERUSALEM.
of our Lord's Fourth and Last Passover.

CHAP. 22.

63 And the men that held Jesus mocked him, and smote *him*.

64 And when they had blindfolded him, they struck him on the face, and asked him, saying, Prophesy, who is it that smote thee?

65 And many other things blasphemously spake they against him.

66 [u]And as soon as it was day, [x]the elders of the people and the chief priests and the scribes came together, and led him into their council, saying,

67 Art thou the Christ? tell us. And he said unto them, If I tell you, ye will not believe:

68 And if I also ask *you*, ye will not answer me, nor let *me* go.

69 [y]Hereafter shall the Son of man sit on the right hand of the power of God.

70 Then said they all, Art thou then the Son of God? And he said unto them, Ye say that I am.

71 And they said, What need we any further witness? for we ourselves have heard of his own mouth.

Q—CONCLUDED.

death, *and* all the congregation shall certainly stone him: as well the stranger, as he that is born in the land, when he blasphemeth the name *of the LORD*, shall be put to death.

John 19. 7 The Jews answered him, We have a law, and by our law he ought to die, because he made himself the Son of God.

R

Isa. 50. 6. *See under I, page 561.*

Isa. 53. 3 He is despised and rejected of men; a man of sorrows, and acquainted with grief: and we hid as it were *our* faces from him; he was despised, and we esteemed him not.

Matt. 27. 30 And they spit upon him, and took the reed, and smote him on the head.

1
Or, *rods*.

[CHAP. 18.]

S

Luke 22. 63. *See text of topic.*

John 19. 3 And said, Hail, King of the Jews! and they smote him with their hands.

T

Isa. 53. 7. *See under L, page 561.*

I Pet. 2. 23. *See under K, page 561.*

U

Matt. 27. 1, 2. *See text of § 196.*

X

Ps. 2. 1 Why do the heathen rage, and the people imagine a vain thing?

Ps. 22. 12 Many bulls have compassed me: strong *bulls* of Bashan have beset me round.

Ps. 22. 16 For dogs have compassed me: the assembly of the wicked have inclosed me: they pierced my hands and my feet.

Acts 4. 26 The kings of the earth stood up, and the rulers were gathered together against the Lord, and against his Christ.

Acts 22. 5 As also the high priest doth bear me witness, and all the estate of the elders: from whom also I received letters unto the brethren, and went to Damascus, to bring them which were there bound unto Jerusalem, for to be punished.

Y

Ps. 110. 1. *Under O.* Dan. 7. 13. *Under N, page 561.*

Dan. 7. 14 And there was given him dominion, and glory, and a kingdom, that all people, nations, and languages, should serve him: his dominion *is* an everlasting dominion, which shall not pass away, and his kingdom *that* which shall not be destroyed.

Matt. 26. 64 and Mark 14. 62. *See text of topic.*

Acts 3. 21 Whom the heaven must receive until the times of restitution of all things, which God hath spoken by the mouth of all his holy prophets since the world began.

I Thes. 4. 16. *See under N.*

Heb. 1. 3 Who being the brightness of *his* glory, and the express image of his person, and upholding all things by the word of his power, when he had by himself purged our sins, sat down on the right hand of the Majesty on high;

Heb. 8. 1. Now of the things which we have spoken *this is* the sum; We have such a high priest, who is set on the right hand of the throne of the Majesty in the heavens;

Rev. 1. 7. *See under N.*

§ 196. THE SANHEDRIN LEAD JESUS AWAY TO PILATE.

Sixth Day of the Week of our

27: 1, 2, 11–14.

1 When the morning was come, [a]all the chief priests and elders of the people took counsel against Jesus to put him to death:

2 And when they had bound him, they led *him* away, and [b]delivered him to [c]Pontius Pilate the governor. p. 578.

A

Ps. 2. 2 The kings of the earth set themselves, and the rulers take counsel together, against the LORD, and against his anointed, *saying*,

Mark. 15. 1. *See text of topic.*

Luke 22. 66 And as soon as it was day, the elders of the people and the chief priests and the scribes came together, and led him into their council, saying,

Luke 23. 1 and John 18. 28. *See text of topic.*

B

Matt.20. 19 And shall deliver him to the Gentiles to mock, and to scourge, and to crucify *him:* and the third day he shall rise again.

Acts 3. 13 The God of Abraham, and of Isaac, and of Jacob, the God of our fathers, hath glorified his Son Jesus; whom ye delivered up, and denied him in the presence of Pilate, when he was determined to let *him* go.

C

Mark 15. 1 and Luke 23. 1. *See text of topic.*

D

Ps. 2. 2. *Under A.* Matt. 27. 1. *See text of topic.*
Luke 22. 66. *Under A.* Luke 23. 1. *Text of topic.*
John 18. 28. *Text of topic.* Acts 3. 13. *Under B.*

Acts 4. 25 Who by the mouth of thy servant David hast said, Why did the heathen rage, and the people imagine vain things?

26 The kings of the earth stood up, and the rulers were gathered together against the Lord, and against his Christ.

E

Matt. 27. 2, Mark 15. 1, and John 18. 28. *See text of topic.*

F

Dan. 3. 12 There are certain Jews whom thou hast set over the affairs of the province of Babylon, Shadrach, Meshach, and Abed-nego; these men, O king, have not regarded thee: they serve not thy gods, nor worship the golden image which thou hast set up.

Acts 17. 7 Whom Jason hath received: and these all do contrary to the decrees of

15: 1–5.

1 And [d]straightway in the morning the chief priests held a consultation with the elders and scribes and the whole council, and bound Jesus, and carried *him* away, and delivered *him* to Pilate.

F—CONCLUDED.

Cæsar, saying that there is another king, *one* Jesus.

Acts 24. 5 For we have found this man *a* pestilent *fellow*, and a mover of sedition among all the Jews throughout the world, and a ringleader of the sect of the Nazarenes:

G

Matt.17. 27 Notwithstanding, lest we should offend them, go thou to the sea, and cast a hook, and take up the fish that first cometh up; and when thou hast opened his mouth, thou shalt find a piece of money: that take, and give unto them for me and thee.

Matt.22. 21 They say unto him, Cæsar's. Then saith he unto them, Render therefore unto Cæsar the things which are Cæsar's; and unto God the things that are God's.

Mark 12. 17 And Jesus answering said unto them, Render to Cæsar the things that are Cæsar's, and to God the things that are God's. And they marvelled at him.

H

John 19. 12 And from thenceforth Pilate sought to release him: but the Jews cried out, saying, If thou let this man go, thou art not Cæsar's friend: whosoever maketh himself a king speaketh against Cæsar.

I

Matt. 27. 2 and Mark 15. 1. *See text of topic.*
Luke 23. 1. *Text of topic.* Acts 3. 13. *Under B.*

1

Or, *Pilate's house.*

Matt.27. 27 Then the soldiers of the governor took Jesus into the common hall, and gathered unto him the whole band *of soldiers.*

K

Acts 10. 28 And he said unto them, Ye know how that it is an unlawful thing for a man that is a Jew to keep company, or come unto one of another nation; but God hath showed me that I should not call any man common or unclean.

Acts 11. 3 Saying, Thou wentest in to men uncircumcised, and didst eat with them.

TIME, FRIDAY, 1–5 A. M., APRIL 7 [NISAN 15], A. D. 30; PLACE, JERUSALEM.
Lord's Fourth and Last Passover.

23: 1–5.

1 And [e]the whole multitude of them arose, and led him unto Pilate.

2 And they began to accuse him, [f]saying, We found this *fellow* perverting the nation, and [g]forbidding to give tribute to Cæsar, saying [h]that he himself is Christ a king.

L

Deut.16. 2 Thou shalt therefore sacrifice the passover unto the LORD thy God, of the flock and the herd, in the place which the LORD shall choose to place his name there.

Eze. 45. 21 In the first *month*, in the fourteenth day of the month, ye shall have the passover, a feast of seven days; unleavened bread shall be eaten.

John 19. 14 And it was the preparation of the passover, and about the sixth hour: and he saith unto the Jews, Behold your King!

M

Gen. 49. 10 The sceptre shall not depart from Judah, nor a lawgiver from between his feet, until Shiloh come; and unto him *shall* the gathering of the people *be*.

Eze. 21. 26 Thus saith the Lord GOD; Remove the diadem, and take off the crown: this *shall* not *be* the same: exalt *him that is* low, and abase *him that is* high.

27 I will overturn, overturn, overturn it: and it shall be no *more*, until he come whose right it is; and I will give it *him*.

Hos. 3. 3 And I said unto her, Thou shalt abide for me many days; thou shalt not play the harlot, and thou shalt not be for *another* man: so *will* I also *be* for thee.

4 For the children of Israel shall abide many days without a king, and without a prince, and without a sacrifice, and without an image, and without an ephod, and *without* teraphim:

5 Afterward shall the children of Israel return, and seek the LORD their God, and David their king; and shall fear the LORD and his goodness in the latter days.

N

Matt. 20. 19 And shall deliver him to the Gentiles to mock, and to scourge, and

18: 28–38.

28 [i]Then led they Jesus from Caiaphas unto [1]the hall of judgment: and it was early; [k]and they themselves went not into the judgment hall, lest they should be defiled; but that they might eat the [l]passover.

29 Pilate then went out unto them, and said, What accusation bring ye against this man?

30 They answered and said unto him, If he were not a malefactor, we would not have delivered him up unto thee.

31 Then said Pilate unto them, Take ye him, and judge him according to your law. The Jews therefore said unto him, It [m]is not lawful for us to put any man to death:

32 [n]That the saying of Jesus might be fulfilled, which he spake, signifying what death he should die.

N—CONCLUDED.

to crucify *him:* and the third day he shall rise again.

John 12. 32 And I, if I be lifted up from the earth, will draw all *men* unto me.

33 This he said, signifying what death he should die.

Acts 7. 59 And they stoned Stephen, calling upon *God*, and saying, Lord Jesus, receive my spirit.

O

Mark 15. 2, Luke 23. 3 and John 18. 33. *See text of topic.*

P

John 18. 37. *See text of topic.*

I Tim. 6. 13 I give thee charge in the sight of God, who quickeneth all things, and *before* Christ Jesus, who before Pontius Pilate witnessed a good confession;

Q

Isa. 53. 7 He was oppressed, and he was afflicted, yet he opened not his mouth: he is brought as a lamb to the slaughter, and as a sheep before her shearers is dumb, so he openeth not his mouth.

8 He was taken from prison and from judgment: and who shall declare

For Q concluded see next page (566).

§ 196. THE SANHEDRIN LEAD JESUS AWAY TO PILATE (CONCLUDED).

Sixth Day of the Week of our

CHAP. 27.

11 And Jesus stood before the governor: [o]and the governor asked him,
saying, Art thou the King of the Jews?
And Jesus said unto him, [p]Thou sayest.
12 And when he was accused of the
chief priests and elders, [q]he answered
nothing.
13 Then said Pilate unto him, [r]Hear-
est thou not how many things they
witness against thee?
14 And he answered him to never a
word; insomuch that the governor
marvelled greatly.

For O, P and Q see preceding page (565).

Q—CONCLUDED.

his generation? for he was cut off out of the land of the living: for the transgression of my people was he stricken.

Matt.26. 63 But Jesus held his peace. And the high priest answered and said unto him, I adjure thee by the living God, that thou tell us whether thou be the Christ, the Son of God.

John 19. 9 And went again into the judgment hall, and saith unto Jesus, Whence art thou? But Jesus gave him no answer.

R

Matt.26. 62 And the high priest arose, and said unto him, Answerest thou nothing? what *is it which* these witness against thee?

John 19. 10 Then saith Pilate unto him, Speakest thou not unto me? knowest thou not that I have power to crucify thee, and have power to release thee?

Acts 22. 24 The chief captain commanded him to be brought into the castle, and bade that he should be examined by scourging; that he might know wherefore they cried so against him.

S

Matt. 27. 11. *See text of topic.*

John 19. 19 And Pilate wrote a title, and put *it* on the cross. And the writing was, JESUS OF NAZARETH THE KING OF THE JEWS.

20 This title then read many of the Jews; for the place where Jesus was crucified was nigh to the city: and it was written in Hebrew, *and* Greek, *and* Latin.

CHAP. 15.

2 [s]And Pilate asked him, Art thou
the King of the Jews? And he answering said unto him, Thou sayest *it*.
3 And the chief priests accused him
of many things; but he answered
nothing.
4 [t]And Pilate asked him again, saying, Answerest thou nothing? behold
how many things they witness against
thee.
5 [u]But Jesus yet answered nothing;
so that Pilate marvelled.

T

I Pet. 2. 23 Who, when he was reviled, reviled not again; when he suffered, he threatened not; but committed *himself* to him that judgeth righteously:

U

Isa. 53. 7. *See under Q, page 565.*
John 19. 9. *See text of § 200.*

X

John 18. 38. *See text of topic.*

Y

Matt. 27. 11 and Mark 15. 2. *See text of topic.*

Z

Isa. 9. 6 For unto us a child is born, unto us a son is given: and the government shall be upon his shoulder: and his name shall be called Wonderful, Counsellor, The mighty God, The everlasting Father, The Prince of Peace.

Dan. 2. 44 And in the days of these kings shall the God of heaven set up a kingdom, which shall never be destroyed: and the kingdom shall not be left to other people, *but* it shall break in pieces and consume all these kingdoms, and it shall stand for ever.

Dan. 7. 14 And there was given him dominion, and glory, and a kingdom, that all people, nations, and languages, should serve him: his dominion *is* an everlasting dominion, which shall not pass away, and his kingdom *that* which shall not be destroyed.

Luke 12. 14 And he said unto him, Man, who made me a judge or a divider over you?

Luke 17. 20 And when he was demanded of the Pharisees, when the kingdom of God should come, he answered them

TIME, FRIDAY, 1–5 A. M., APRIL 7 [NISAN 15], A. D. 30; PLACE, JERUSALEM.
Lord's Fourth and Last Passover.

CHAP. 23.

3 And Pilate asked him, saying, Art thou the King of the Jews? And he answered him and said, Thou sayest *it*.

4 Then said Pilate to the chief priests and *to* the people, [x]I find no fault in this man.

5 And they were the more fierce, saying, He stirreth up the people, teaching throughout all Jewry, beginning from Galilee to this place.

Z—CONCLUDED.

and said, The kingdom of God cometh not with observation:

21 Neither shall they say, Lo here! or, lo there! for, behold, the kingdom of God is within you.

John 6. 15 When Jesus therefore perceived that they would come and take him by force, to make him a king, he departed again into a mountain himself alone.

John 8. 15 Ye judge after the flesh; I judge no man.

A

Matt.26. 64 Jesus saith unto him, Thou hast said: nevertheless I say unto you, Hereafter shall ye see the Son of man sitting on the right hand of power, and coming in the clouds of heaven.

B

Isa. 55. 4 Behold, I have given him *for* a witness to the people, a leader and commander to the people.

I Tim. 6. 13. *See under P, page 565.*

Rev. 1. 5 And from Jesus Christ, *who is* the faithful witness, *and* the first-begotten of the dead, and the prince of the kings of the earth. Unto him that loved us, and washed us from our sins in his own blood,

Rev. 3. 14 And unto the angel of the church of the Laodiceans write; These things saith the Amen, the faithful and true witness, the beginning of the creation of God;

C

John 8. 47 He that is of God heareth God's words: ye therefore hear *them* not, because ye are not of God.

I Jno. 4. 6 We are of God: he that knoweth God heareth us; he that is not of God heareth not us. Hereby know we the spirit of truth, and the spirit of error.

CHAP. 18.

33 [y]Then Pilate entered into the judgment hall again, and called Jesus, and said unto him, Art thou the King of the Jews?

34 Jesus answered him, Sayest thou this thing of thyself, or did others tell it thee of me?

35 Pilate answered, Am I a Jew? Thine own nation and the chief priests have delivered thee unto me: what hast thou done?

36 [z]Jesus answered, My kingdom is not of this world: if my kingdom were of this world, then would my servants fight, that I should not be delivered to the Jews: but now is my kingdom not from hence.

37 [a]Pilate therefore said unto him, Art thou a king then? Jesus answered, Thou sayest that I am a king. To this end was I born, and for this cause came I into the world, that I should [b]bear witness unto the truth. Every one that [c]is of the truth heareth my voice.

38 Pilate saith unto him, What is truth? And when he had said this, he went out again unto the Jews, and saith unto them, [d]I find in him no fault *at all*.

D

Matt.27. 24 When Pilate saw that he could prevail nothing, but *that* rather a tumult was made, he took water, and washed *his* hands before the multitude, saying, I am innocent of the blood of this just person: see ye *to it*.

II Cor.5. 21 For he hath made him *to be* sin for us, who knew no sin; that we might be made the righteousness of God in him.

I Pet. 1. 19 But with the precious blood of Christ, as of a lamb without blemish and without spot:

I Pet. 2. 22 Who did no sin, neither was guile found in his mouth:

§ 197. JESUS BEFORE HEROD.
Sixth Day of the Week of our

A

Luke 3. 1 Now in the fifteenth year of the reign of Tiberius Cæsar, Pontius Pilate being governor of Judæa, and Herod being tetrarch of Galilee, and his brother Philip tetrarch of Iturea and of the region of Trachonitis, and Lysanias the tetrarch of Abilene,

Luke 13. 31 The same day there came certain of the Pharisees, saying unto him, Get thee out, and depart hence: for Herod will kill thee.

B

Luke 9. 9 And Herod said, John have I beheaded; but who is this, of whom I hear such things? And he desired to see him.

C

Matt.14. 1 At that time Herod the tetrarch heard of the fame of Jesus.

Mark 6. 14 And king Herod heard *of him;* (for his name was spread abroad;) and he said, That John the Baptist was risen from the dead, and therefore mighty works do show forth themselves in him.

D

Ps. 22. 6 But I *am* a worm, and no man; a reproach of men, and despised of the people.

Ps. 69. 19 Thou hast known my reproach, and my shame, and my dishonour: mine adversaries *are* all before thee.

20 Reproach hath broken my heart; and I am full of heaviness: and I looked *for some* to take pity, but *there was* none; and for comforters, but I found none.

Isa. 49. 7 Thus saith the LORD, the Redeemer of Israel, *and* his Holy One to him whom man despiseth, to him whom the nation abhorreth, to a servant of rulers, Kings shall see and arise, princes also shall worship, because of the LORD that is faithful, *and* the Holy One of Israel, and he shall choose thee.

D—CONCLUDED.

Isa. 53. 3 He is despised and rejected of men; a man of sorrows, and acquainted with grief: and we hid as it were *our* faces from him; he was despised, and we esteemed him not.

Matt.27. 27 Then the soldiers of the governor took Jesus into the common hall, and gathered unto him the whole band *of soldiers.*

28 And they stripped him, and put on him a scarlet robe.

29 And when they had platted a crown of thorns, they put *it* upon his head, and a reed in his right hand: and they bowed the knee before him, and mocked him, saying, Hail, King of the Jews!

30 And they spit upon him, and took the reed, and smote him on the head.

Mark 9. 12 And he answered and told them, Elias verily cometh first, and restoreth all things; and how it is written of the Son of man, that he must suffer many things, and be set at nought.

John 19. 5 Then came Jesus forth, wearing the crown of thorns, and the purple robe. And *Pilate* saith unto them, Behold the man!

§ 198. PILATE SEEKS TO RELEASE JESUS. BARABBAS DEMANDED.
Sixth Day of the Week of our

27: 15–25.

15 [a]Now at *that* feast the governor was wont to release unto the people a prisoner, whom they would.

A

Matt.26. 5 But they said, Not on the feast *day*, lest there be an uproar among the people.

Mark 15. 6, Luke 23. 17 and John 18. 39. *See text of topic.*

B

Matt. 27. 23 and Mark 15. 14. *See text of topic.*

John 18. 38 Pilate saith unto him, What is truth? And when he had said this, he went out again unto the Jews, and saith unto them, I find in him no fault *at all.*

15: 6–14.

6 Now at *that* feast he released unto them one prisoner, whomsoever they desired.

B—CONCLUDED.

John 19. 4 Pilate therefore went forth again, and saith unto them, Behold, I bring him forth to you, that ye may know that I find no fault in him..

C

Luke 23. 1 And the whole multitude of them arose, and led him unto Pilate.

2 And they began to accuse him, saying, We found this *fellow* perverting the nation, and forbidding to give tribute to Cæsar, saying that he himself is Christ a king.

TIME, FRIDAY, 5–6 A. M., APRIL 7 [NISAN 15], A. D. 30; PLACE, JERUSALEM.
Lord's Fourth and Last Passover.

23: 6–12.

6 When Pilate heard of Galilee, he asked whether the man were a Galilean.

7 And as soon as he knew that he belonged unto [a]Herod's jurisdiction, he sent him to Herod, who himself also was at Jerusalem at that time.

8 And when Herod saw Jesus, he was exceeding glad: for [b]he was desirous to see him of a long *season*, because [c]he had heard many things of him; and he hoped to have seen some miracle done by him.

9 Then he questioned with him in many words; but he answered him nothing.

10 And the chief priests and scribes stood and vehemently accused him.

11 [d]And Herod with his men of war set him at naught, and mocked *him*, and arrayed him in a gorgeous robe, and sent him again to Pilate.

12 And the same day [e]Pilate and Herod were made friends together; for before they were at enmity between themselves.

E

Ps. 83. 4 They have said, Come, and let us cut them off from *being* a nation; that the name of Israel may be no more in remembrance.
5 For they have consulted together with one consent: they are confederate against thee:

Acts 4. 25 Who by the mouth of thy servant David hast said, Why did the heathen rage, and the people imagine vain things?
26 The kings of the earth stood up, and the rulers were gathered together against the Lord, and against his Christ.
27 For of a truth against thy holy child Jesus, whom thou hast anointed, both Herod, and Pontius Pilate, with the Gentiles, and the people of Israel, were gathered together,
28 For to do whatsoever thy hand and thy council determined before to be done.

Jas. 4. 4 Ye adulterers and adulteresses, know ye not that the friendship of the world is enmity with God? whosoever therefore will be a friend of the world is the enemy of God.

Rev. 17. 13 These have one mind, and shall give their power and strength unto the beast.
14 These shall make war with the Lamb, and the Lamb shall overcome them: for he is Lord of lords, and King of kings: and they that are with him *are* called, and chosen, and faithful.

TIME, FRIDAY, 6–9 A. M., APRIL 7 [NISAN 15], A. D. 30; PLACE, JERUSALEM.
Lord's Fourth and Last Passover.

23: 13–23.

13 [b]And Pilate, when he had called together the chief priests and the rulers and the people,

14 Said unto them, [c]Ye have brought this man unto me, as one that perverteth the people; and, behold, [d]I, having examined *him* before you, have found no fault in this man touching those things whereof ye accuse him:

15 No, nor yet Herod: for I sent you to him; and, lo, nothing worthy of death is done unto him.

18: 39, 40.

39 But ye have a custom, that I should release unto you one at the passover:

D

Dan. 6. 4 Then the presidents and princes sought to find occasion against Daniel concerning the kingdom; but they could find none occasion nor fault; forasmuch as he *was* faithful, neither was there any error or fault found in him.

Luke 23. 4 Then said Pilate to the chief priests and *to* the people, I find no fault in this man.

Acts 13. 28 And though they found no cause of death *in him*, yet desired they Pilate that he should be slain.

§ 198. PILATE SEEKS TO RELEASE JESUS. BARABBAS DEMANDED (CON-
Sixth Day of the Week of our

CHAP. 27.

16 And they had then a notable prisoner, [e]called Barabbas.

17 Therefore when they were gathered together, Pilate said unto them, Whom will ye that I release unto you? Barabbas, or Jesus which is called Christ?

18 For he knew that for [f]envy they had delivered him.

19 When he was set down on the judgment seat, his wife sent unto him, saying, Have thou nothing to do with that just man: for I have suffered many things this day in a [g]dream because of him.

20 [h]But the chief priests and elders persuaded the multitude that they should ask Barabbas, and destroy Jesus.

21 The governor answered and said unto them, Whether of the twain will ye that I release unto you? They said, Barabbas.

22 Pilate saith unto them, What shall I do then with Jesus which is called Christ? *They* all say unto him, Let him be crucified.

23 And the governor said, Why, what evil hath he done? But they cried out the more, saying, Let him be crucified.

24 When Pilate saw that he could prevail nothing, but *that* rather a tumult was made, he [i]took water, and washed *his* hands before the multitude, saying, I am innocent of the blood of this just person: see ye *to it*.

25 Then answered all the people, and said, [k]His blood *be* on us, and on our children.

E

Mark 15. 7 and John 18. 40. *See text of topic*

CHAP. 15.

7 And there was *one* named Barabbas, *which lay* bound with them that had made insurrection with him, who had committed murder in the insurrection.

8 And the multitude crying aloud began to desire *him to do* as he had ever done unto them.

9 But Pilate answered them, saying, Will ye that I release unto you the King of the Jews?

10 For he knew that the chief priests had delivered him for [l]envy.

11 But [m]the chief priests moved the people, that he should rather release Barabbas unto them.

12 And Pilate answered and said again unto them, What will ye then that I shall do *unto him* whom ye call [n]the King of the Jews?

13 And they cried out again, Crucify him.

14 Then Pilate said unto them, Why, what evil hath he done? And they cried out the more exceedingly, Crucify him.

F

Acts 7. 9 And the patriarchs, moved with envy, sold Joseph into Egypt: but God was with him,

G

Job 33. 15 In a dream, in a vision of the night, when deep sleep falleth upon men, in slumberings upon the bed;

H

Mark 15. 11, Luke 23. 18 and John 18. 40. *See text of topic.*

Acts 3. 14 But ye denied the Holy One and the Just, and desired a murderer to be granted unto you;

I

Deut. 21. 6 And all the elders of that city, *that are* next unto the slain *man*, shall wash their hands over the heifer that is beheaded in the valley:

K

Deut. 19. 10 That innocent blood be not shed

CLUDED). TIME, FRIDAY, 6–9 A. M., APRIL 7 [NISAN 15], A. D. 30; PLACE, JERUSALEM.
Lord's Fourth and Last Passover.

CHAP. 23.

16 [o]I will therefore chastise him, and release *him*.

17 (For of necessity he must release one unto them at the feast.)

18 And they cried out all at once, saying, [p]Away with this *man*, and release unto us Barabbas:

19 (Who for a certain sedition made in the city, and for murder, was cast into prison.)

20 Pilate therefore, willing to release Jesus, spake again to them.

21 But they cried, saying, Crucify *him*, crucify him.

22 And he said unto them the third time, Why, what evil hath he done? I have found no cause of death in him: I will therefore chastise him, and let *him* go.

23 And they were instant with loud voices, requiring that he might be crucified: and the voices of them and of the chief priests prevailed.

K—CONTINUED.

in thy land, which the LORD thy God giveth thee *for* an inheritance, and *so* blood be upon thee.

Josh. 2. 19 And it shall be, *that* whosoever shall go out of the doors of thy house into the street, his blood *shall be* upon his head, and we *will be* guiltless: and whosoever shall be with thee in the house, his blood *shall be* on our head, if *any* hand be upon him.

II Sa. 1. 16 And David said unto him, Thy blood *be* upon thy head; for thy mouth hath testified against thee, saying, I have slain the LORD's anointed.

I Ki. 2. 32 And the LORD shall return his blood upon his own head, who fell upon two men more righteous and better than he, and slew them with the sword, my father David not knowing *thereof, to wit*, Abner the son of Ner, captain of the host of Israel, and

CHAP. 18.

will ye therefore that I release unto you the King of the Jews?

40 Then cried they all again, saying, Not this man, but Barabbas. Now Barabbas was a robber.

K—CONCLUDED.

Amasa the son of Jether, captain of the host of Judah.

Acts 5. 28 Saying, Did not we straightly command you that ye should not teach in this name? and, behold, ye have filled Jerusalem with your doctrine, and intend to bring this man's blood upon us.

L

Prov. 27. 4 Wrath *is* cruel, and anger *is* outrageous; but who *is* able to stand before envy?

Eccl. 4. 4 Again, I considered all travail, and every right work, that for this a man is envied of his neighbour. This *is* also vanity and vexation of spirit.

Acts 7. 9. *See under F.*

I Jno. 3. 12 Not as Cain, *who* was of that wicked one, and slew his brother. And wherefore slew he him? Because his own works were evil, and his brother's righteous.

M

Matt. 27. 20. *Text of topic.* Acts 3. 14. *Under H.*

N

Ps. 2. 6 Yet have I set my king upon my holy hill of Zion.

7 I will declare the decree: the LORD hath said unto me, Thou *art* my Son; this day have I begotten thee.

Mic. 5. 2 But thou, Beth-lehem Ephratah, *though* thou be little among the thousands of Judah, *yet* out of thee shall he come forth unto me *that is* to be ruler in Israel; whose goings forth *have been* from of old, from everlasting.

O

Isa. 53. 5 But he *was* wounded for our transgressions, *he was* bruised for our iniquities: the chastisement of our peace *was* upon him: and with his stripes we are healed.

Matt. 27. 26 Then released he Barabbas unto them: and when he had scourged Jesus, he delivered *him* to be crucified.

John 19. 1 Then Pilate therefore took Jesus, and scourged *him*.

P

Acts 21. 36 For the multitude of the people followed after, crying, Away with him.

§ 199. BARABBAS RELEASED. JESUS DELIVERED UP TO DEATH

Sixth Day of the Week of our

27: 26–30.

26 Then released he Barabbas unto them: and when [a]he had scourged Jesus, he delivered *him* to be crucified.

27 [b]Then the soldiers of the governor took Jesus into the [1]common hall, and gathered unto him the whole band *of soldiers.*

28 And they stripped him, and [c]put on him a scarlet robe.

29 [d]And when they had platted a crown of thorns, they put *it* upon his head, and a reed in his right hand: and they bowed the knee before him, and mocked him, saying, Hail, King of the Jews!

30 And [e]they spit upon him, and took the reed, and [f]smote him on the head.

(p. 580.)

A

Isa. 53. 5 But he *was* wounded for our transgressions, *he was* bruised for our iniquities: the chastisement of our peace *was* upon him; and with his stripes we are healed.

Mark 15. 15. *See text of topic.*

Luke 23. 16 I will therefore chastise him, and release *him.*

Luke 23. 24, 25 and John 19. 1. *See text of topic.*

John 19. 16 Then delivered he him therefore unto them to be crucified. And they took Jesus, and led *him* away.

B

Mark 15. 16 and John 19. 2. *See text of topic.*

1

Or, *governor's house.*

C

Luke 23. 11 And Herod with his men of war set him at nought, and mocked *him,* and arrayed him in a gorgeous robe, and sent him again to Pilate.

D

Ps. 22. 6 But I *am* a worm, and no man; a reproach of men, and despised of the people.

Ps. 35. 15 But in mine adversity they rejoiced, and gathered themselves together: *yea,* the abjects gathered themselves together against me, and I knew *it* not; they did tear *me,* and ceased not:

16 With hypocritical mockers in

15: 15–19.

15 [g]And *so* Pilate, willing to content the people, released Barabbas unto them, and delivered Jesus, when he had scourged *him,* to be crucified.

16 And the soldiers led him away into the hall, called Pretorium; and they call together the whole band.

17 And they clothed him with purple, and platted a crown of thorns, and put it about his *head,*

18 And began to salute him, Hail, King of the Jews!

19 And they smote him on the head with a reed, and did spit upon him, and bowing *their* knees worshipped him.

(p. 580.)

D—Concluded.

feasts, they gnashed upon me with their teeth.

Ps. 69. 7 Because for thy sake I have borne reproach; shame hath covered my face.

Ps. 69. 19 Thou hast known my reproach, and my shame, and my dishonour: mine adversaries *are* all before thee.

Isa. 53. 3 He is despised and rejected of men; a man of sorrows, and acquainted with grief: and we hid as it were *our* faces from him; he was despised, and we esteemed him not.

Jer. 20. 7 O Lord, Thou hast deceived me, and I was deceived: thou art stronger than I, and hast prevailed: I am in derision daily, every one mocketh me.

Heb. 12. 2 Looking unto Jesus the author and finisher of *our* faith; who for the joy that was set before him endured the cross, despising the shame, and is set down at the right hand of the throne of God.

3 For consider him that endured such contradiction of sinners against himself, lest ye be wearied and faint in your minds.

E

Job 30. 8 *They were* children of fools, yea, children of base men: they were viler than the earth.

9 And now am I their song, yea, I am their byword.

10 They abhor me, they flee far

TIME, FRIDAY, 6–9 A. M., APRIL 7 [NISAN 15], A. D. 30; PLACE, JERUSALEM.
Lord's Fourth and Last Passover.

23: 24, 25.

24 And Pilate [2]gave sentence that it should be as they required.

25 And he released unto them him that for sedition and murder was cast into prison, [h]whom they had desired: but he delivered Jesus to their will.

19: 1–3.

1 Then [i]Pilate therefore took Jesus, and scourged *him*.

2 And the soldiers platted a crown of thorns, and put *it* on his head, and they put on him a purple robe,

3 And said, Hail, King of the Jews! and they smote him with their hands.

E—CONCLUDED. (p. 581.)

from me, and spare not to spit in my face.

Isa. 50. 5 The Lord GOD hath opened mine ear, and I was not rebellious, neither turned away back.

6 I gave my back to the smiters, and my cheeks to them that plucked off the hair: I hid not my face from shame and spitting.

Isa. 52. 14 As many were astonied at thee; his visage was so marred more than any man, and his form more than the sons of men:

Isa. 53. 7 He was oppressed, and he was afflicted, yet he opened not his mouth: he is brought as a lamb to the slaughter, and as a sheep before her shearers is dumb, so he openeth not his mouth.

Matt.26. 67 Then did they spit in his face, and buffeted him; and others smote *him* with the palms of their hands,

F

Jer. 20. 2 Then Pashur smote Jeremiah the prophet, and put him in the stocks that *were* in the high gate of Benjamin, which *was* by the house of the LORD.

Mic. 5. 1 Now gather thyself in troops, O daughter of troops: he hath laid siege against us: they shall smite the judge of Israel with a rod upon the cheek.

G

Prov.29. 25 The fear of man bringeth a snare: but whoso putteth his trust in the LORD shall be safe.

Matt. 27. 26 and John 19. 1. *See text of topic.*
John 19. 16. *See under A.*

2

Or, *assented.*

Ex. 23. 2 Thou shalt not follow a multitude to *do* evil; neither shalt thou speak in a cause to decline after many to wrest *judgment;*

Prov.17. 15 He that justifieth the wicked, and he that condemneth the just, even they both *are* abomination to the LORD.

H

I Sa. 12. 13 Now therefore, behold the king

H—CONCLUDED.

whom ye have chosen, *and* whom ye have desired! and, behold, the LORD hath set a king over you.

Acts 3. 14 But ye denied the Holy One and the Just, and desired a murderer to be granted unto you;

I

Ps. 129. 3 The ploughers ploughed upon my back: they made long their furrows.

Isa. 50. 6. *See under E.*

Matt.20. 19 And shall deliver him to the Gentiles to mock, and to scourge, and to crucify *him:* and the third day he shall rise again.

Matt. 27. 26 and Mark 15. 15. *See text of topic.*

Luke 18. 33 And they shall scourge *him*, and put him to death; and the third day he shall rise again.

Acts 16. 22 And the multitude rose up together against them; and the magistrates rent off their clothes, and commanded to beat *them.*

23 And when they had laid many stripes upon them, they cast *them* into prison, charging the jailer to keep them safely:

Acts 22. 24 The chief captain commanded him to be brought into the castle, and bade that he should be examined by scourging; that he might know wherefore they cried so against him.

25 And as they bound him with thongs, Paul said unto the centurion that stood by, Is it lawful for you to scourge a man that is a Roman, and uncondemned?

II Cor.11. 24 Of the Jews five times received I forty *stripes* save one.

Heb. 11. 36 And others had trial of *cruel* mockings and scourgings, yea, moreover of bonds and imprisonment:

I Pet. 2. 24 Who his own self bare our sins in his own body on the tree, that we, being dead to sins, should live unto righteousness: by whose stripes ye were healed.

§ 200. PILATE AGAIN SEEKS TO RELEASE JESUS.

Sixth Day of the Week of our

A

John 18. 38 Pilate saith unto him, What is truth? And when he had said this, he went out again unto the Jews, and saith unto them, I find in him no fault *at all*.

John 19. 6. *See text of topic*

II Cor. 5. 21 For he hath made him *to be* sin for us, who knew no sin; that we might be made the righteousness of God in him.

B

Isa. 7. 14 Therefore the Lord himself shall give you a sign; Behold, a virgin shall conceive, and bear a son, and shall call his name Immanuel.

Isa. 40. 9 O Zion, that bringest good tidings, get thee up into the high mountain; O Jerusalem, that bringest good tidings, lift up thy voice with strength; lift *it* up, be not afraid; say unto the cities of Judah, Behold your God!

Isa. 43. 1 But now thus saith the LORD that created thee, O Jacob, and he that formed thee, O Israel, Fear not: for I have redeemed thee, I have called *thee* by thy name; thou *art* mine.

Lam. 1. 12 *Is it* nothing to you, all ye that pass by? behold, and see if there be any sorrow like unto my sorrow, which is done unto me, wherewith the LORD hath afflicted *me* in the day of his fierce anger.

Heb. 12. 2 Looking unto Jesus the author and finisher of *our* faith; who for the joy that was set before him endured the cross, despising the shame, and is set down at the right hand of the throne of God.

C

Acts 3. 13 The God of Abraham, and of Isaac, and of Jacob, the God of our fathers, hath glorified his Son Jesus; whom ye delivered up, and denied him in the presence of Pilate, when he was determined to let *him* go.

D

Lev. 24. 16 And he that blasphemeth the name of the LORD, he shall surely be put to death, *and* all the congregation shall certainly stone him: as well the stranger, as he that is born in the land, when he blasphemeth the name *of the LORD*, shall be put to death.

Deut. 18. 20 But the prophet, which shall presume to speak a word in my name, which I have not commanded him to speak, or that shall speak in the name of other gods, even that prophet shall die.

E

Matt. 26. 65 Then the high priest rent his clothes, saying, He hath spoken blasphemy; what further need have we of witnesses? behold, now ye have heard his blasphemy.

John 5. 18 Therefore the Jews sought the more to kill him, because he not only had broken the sabbath, but said also that God was his Father, making himself equal with God.

John 10. 33 The Jews answered him, saying, For a good work we stone thee not; but for blasphemy; and because that thou, being a man, makest thyself God.

F

Acts 14. 11 And when the people saw what Paul had done, they lifted up their voices, saying in the speech of Lycaonia, The gods are come down to us in the likeness of men.

12 And they called Barnabas, Jupiter; and Paul, Mercurius, because he was the chief speaker.

13 Then the priest of Jupiter, which was before their city, brought oxen and garlands unto the gates, and would have done sacrifice with the people.

14 *Which* when the apostles, Barnabas and Paul, heard *of*, they rent their clothes, and ran in among the people, crying out,

15 And saying, Sirs, why do ye these things? We also are men of like passions with you, and preach unto you that ye should turn from these vanities unto the living God, which made heaven, and earth, and the sea, and all things that are therein:

16 Who in times past suffered all nations to walk in their own ways:

17 Nevertheless he left not himself without witness, in that he did good, and gave us rain from heaven, and fruitful seasons, filling our hearts with food and gladness.

18 And with these sayings scarce restrained they the people, that they had not done sacrifice unto them.

19 And there came thither *certain* Jews from Antioch and Iconium, who persuaded the people, and, having stoned Paul, drew *him* out of the city, supposing he had been dead.

G

Isa. 53. 5 But he *was* wounded for our transgressions, *he was* bruised for our iniquities: the chastisement of our peace

TIME, FRIDAY, 6–9 A. M., APRIL 7 [NISAN 15], A. D. 30; PLACE, JERUSALEM.
Lord's Fourth and Last Passover.

G—CONCLUDED.

was upon him; and with his stripes we are healed.

6 All we like sheep have gone astray; we have turned every one to his own way; and the LORD hath laid on him the iniquity of us all.

7 He was oppressed, and he was afflicted, yet he opened not his mouth: he is brought as a lamb to the slaughter, and as a sheep before her shearers is dumb, so he openeth not his mouth.

Matt.27. 12 And when he was accused of the chief priests and elders, he answered nothing.

13 Then said Pilate unto him, Hearest thou not how many things they witness against thee?

14 And he answered him to never a word; insomuch that the governor marvelled greatly.

H

Gen. 45. 7 And God sent me before you to preserve you a posterity in the earth, and to save your lives by a great deliverance.

8 So now *it was* not you *that* sent me hither, but God: and he hath made me a father to Pharaoh, and lord of all his house, and a ruler throughout all the land of Egypt.

I Chr.29. 11 Thine, O LORD, *is* the greatness, and the power, and the glory, and the victory, and the majesty: for all *that is* in the heaven and in the earth *is thine;* thine *is* the kingdom, O LORD, and thou art exalted as head above all.

Dan. 5. 21 And he was driven from the sons of men; and his heart was made like the beasts, and his dwelling *was* with the wild asses: they fed him with grass like oxen, and his body was wet with the dew of heaven; till he knew that the most high God ruled in the kingdom of men, and *that* he appointeth over it whomsoever he will.

Luke 22. 53 When I was daily with you in the temple, ye stretched forth no hands against me: but this is your hour, and the power of darkness.

John 7. 30 Then they sought to take him: but no man laid hands on him, because his hour was not yet come.

Acts 2. 22 Ye men of Israel, hear these words; Jesus of Nazareth, a man approved of God among you by miracles and wonders and signs, which God did by him in the midst of you, as ye yourselves also know:

19: 4–16.

4 Pilate therefore went forth again, and saith unto them, Behold, I bring him forth to you, [a]that ye may know that I find no fault in him.

5 Then came Jesus forth, wearing the crown of thorns, and the purple robe. And *Pilate* saith unto them, [b]Behold the man!

6 [c]When the chief priests therefore and officers saw him, they cried out, saying, Crucify *him,* crucify *him.* Pilate saith unto them, Take ye him, and crucify *him:* for I find no fault in him.

7 The Jews answered him, [d]We have a law, and by our law he ought to die, because [e]he made himself the Son of God.

8 When Pilate therefore [f]heard that saying, he was the more afraid;

9 And went again into the judgment hall, and saith unto Jesus, Whence art thou? [g]But Jesus gave him no answer.

10 Then saith Pilate unto him, Speakest thou not unto me? knowest thou not that I have power to crucify thee, and have power to release thee?

11 Jesus answered, [h]Thou couldest have no power *at all* against me, except it were given thee from above: therefore he that delivered me unto thee hath the greater sin.

H—CONCLUDED.

Acts 2. 23 Him, being delivered by the determinate counsel and foreknowledge of God, ye have taken, and by wicked hands have crucified and slain:

Acts 4. 28 For to do whatsoever thy hand and thy counsel determined before to be done.

Rom.11. 36 For of him, and through him, and to him, *are* all things: to whom *be* glory for ever. Amen.

§ 200. PILATE AGAIN SEEKS TO RELEASE JESUS (Concluded).

Sixth Day of the Week of our

I

Mark 6. 16 But when Herod heard *thereof*, he said, It is John, whom I beheaded: he is risen from the dead.

17 For Herod himself had sent forth and laid hold upon John, and bound him in prison for Herodias' sake, his brother Philip's wife; for he had married her.

18 For John had said unto Herod, It is not lawful for thee to have thy brother's wife.

19 Therefore Herodias had a quarrel against him, and would have killed him; but she could not:

20 For Herod feared John, knowing that he was a just man and a holy, and observed him; and when he heard him, he did many things, and heard him gladly.

21 And when a convenient day was come, that Herod on his birthday made a supper to his lords, high captains, and chief *estates* of Galilee;

22 And when the daughter of the said Herodias came in, and danced, and pleased Herod and them that sat with him, the king said unto the damsel, Ask of me whatsoever thou wilt, and I will give *it* thee.

23 And he sware unto her, Whatsoever thou shalt ask of me, I will give *it* thee, unto the half of my kingdom.

24 And she went forth, and said unto her mother, What shall I ask? And she said, The head of John the Baptist.

25 And she came in straightway with haste unto the king, and asked, saying, I will that thou give me by and by in a charger the head of John the Baptist.

26 And the king was exceeding sorry; *yet* for his oath's sake, and for their sakes which sat with him, he would not reject her.

Acts 24. 24 And after certain days, when Felix came with his wife Drusilla, which was a Jewess, he sent for Paul, and heard him concerning the faith in Christ.

25 And as he reasoned of righteousness, temperance, and judgment to come, Felix trembled, and answered, Go thy way for this time; when I have a convenient season, I will call for thee.

26 He hoped also that money should have been given him of Paul, that he might loose him: wherefore he sent for him the oftener, and communed with him.

I—Concluded.

Acts 24. 27 But after two years Porcius Festus came into Felix' room: and Felix, willing to show the Jews a pleasure, left Paul bound.

K

Luke 23. 2 And they began to accuse him, saying, We found this *fellow* perverting the nation, and forbidding to give tribute to Cæsar, saying that he himself is Christ a king.

Acts 17. 6 And when they found them not, they drew Jason and certain brethren unto the rulers of the city, crying, These that have turned the world upside down are come hither also;

7 Whom Jason hath received: and these all do contrary to the decrees of Cæsar, saying that there is another king, *one* Jesus.

L

Prov. 29. 25 The fear of man bringeth a snare: but whoso putteth his trust in the LORD shall be safe.

Isa. 51. 12 I, *even* I, *am* he that comforteth you: who *art* thou, that thou shouldest be afraid of a man *that* shall die, and of the son of man *which* shall be made *as* grass;

13 And forgettest the LORD thy Maker, that hath stretched forth the heavens, and laid the foundations of the earth; and hast feared continually every day because of the fury of the oppressor, as if he were ready to destroy? and where *is* the fury of the oppressor?

Isa. 57. 11 And of whom hast thou been afraid or feared, that thou hast lied, and hast not remembered me, nor laid *it* to thy heart? have not I held my peace even of old, and thou fearest me not?

Luke 12. 5 But I will forewarn you whom ye shall fear: Fear him, which after he hath killed hath power to cast into hell; yea, I say unto you, Fear him.

Acts 4. 19 But Peter and John answered and said unto them, Whether it be right in the sight of God to hearken unto you more than unto God, judge ye.

M

Ps. 58. 1 Do ye indeed speak righteousness, O congregation? do ye judge uprightly, O ye sons of men?

2 Yea, in heart ye work wickedness; ye weigh the violence of your hands in the earth.

TIME, FRIDAY, 6–9 A. M., APRIL 7 [NISAN 15], A. D. 30; PLACE, JERUSALEM.
Lord's Fourth and Last Passover.

M—CONCLUDED.

Ps. 82. 5 They know not, neither will they understand; they walk on in darkness: all the foundations of the earth are out of course.

6 I have said, Ye *are* gods; and all of you *are* children of the Most High.

7 But ye shall die like men, and fall like one of the princes.

Ps. 94. 20 Shall the throne of iniquity have fellowship with thee, which frameth mischief by a law?

21 They gather themselves together against the soul of the righteous, and condemn the innocent blood.

Eccl. 5. 8 If thou seest the oppression of the poor, and violent perverting of judgment and justice in a province, marvel not at the matter: for *he that is* higher than the highest regardeth; and *there be* higher than they.

Amos 5. 7 Ye who turn judgment to wormwood, and leave off righteousness in the earth.

8 *Seek him* that maketh the seven stars and Orion, and turneth the shadow of death into the morning, and maketh the day dark with night: that calleth for the waters of the sea, and poureth them out upon the face of the earth: The LORD *is* his name:

1
Meaning, *elevated.*

N

Matt.27. 62 Now the next day, that followed the day of the preparation, the chief priests and Pharisees came together unto Pilate,

O

John 19. 6 When the chief priests therefore and officers saw him, they cried out, saying, Crucify *him*, crucify *him*. Pilate saith unto them, Take ye him, and crucify *him:* for I find no fault in him.

Acts 22. 22 And they gave him audience unto this word, and *then* lifted up their voices, and said, Away with such a *fellow* from the earth: for it is not fit that he should live.

P

Gen. 49. 10 The sceptre shall not depart from Judah, nor a lawgiver from between his feet, until Shiloh come; and unto him *shall* the gathering of the people *be*.

Eze. 21. 25 And thou, profane wicked prince of Israel, whose day is come, when iniquity *shall have* an end,

CHAP. 19.

12 And [i]from thenceforth Pilate sought to release him: but the Jews cried out, saying, [k]If thou let this man go, thou art not Cæsar's friend: whosoever maketh himself a king speaketh against Cæsar.

13 When Pilate therefore [l]heard that saying, he brought Jesus forth, and [m]sat down in the judgment seat in a place that is called the Pavement, but in the Hebrew, [1]Gabbatha.

14 And [n]it was the preparation of the passover, and about the sixth hour: and he saith unto the Jews, Behold your King!

15 But they cried out, [o]Away with *him*, away with *him*, crucify him. Pilate saith unto them, Shall I crucify your King? The chief priests answered, [p]We have no king but Cæsar.

16 [q]Then delivered he him therefore unto them to be crucified. And they took Jesus, and led *him* away. (p. 581.)

P—CONCLUDED.

Eze. 21. 26 Thus saith the Lord GOD; Remove the diadem, and take off the crown: this *shall* not *be* the same: exalt *him that is* low, and abase *him that is* high.

27 I will overturn, overturn, overturn it: and it shall be no *more*, until he come whose right it is; and I will give it *him*.

Q

Matt.27. 26 Then released he Barabbas unto them: and when he had scourged Jesus, he delivered *him* to be crucified.

Matt.27. 31 And after that they had mocked him, they took the robe off from him, and put his own raiment on him, and led him away to crucify *him*.

Mark 15. 15 And *so* Pilate, willing to content the people, released Barabbas unto them, and delivered Jesus, when he had scourged *him*, to be crucified.

Luke 23. 24 And Pilate gave sentence that it should be as they required.

§ 201. JUDAS REPENTS AND HANGS HIMSELF.
Sixth Day of the Week of our

27 : 3–10.

3 Then [a]Judas, which had betrayed him, when he saw that he was condemned, repented himself, and brought again the thirty pieces of silver to the chief priests and elders,

4 Saying, [b]I have sinned in that I have betrayed the innocent blood. And they said, What *is that* to us? see thou *to that*.

5 And he cast down the pieces of silver in the temple, [c]and departed, and went and hanged himself.

6 And the chief priests took the silver pieces, and said, It is not lawful for to put them into the treasury, because it is the price of blood.

7 And they took counsel, and bought with them the potter's field, to bury strangers in.

8 Wherefore [d]that field was called, The field of blood, [e]unto this day.

9 Then was fulfilled that which was spoken by Jeremy the prophet, saying, [f]And they took the [g]thirty pieces of silver, the price of him that was valued, [1]whom they of the children of Israel did value;

10 And gave them for the potter's field, as the Lord appointed me. p. 566.

A

Job 20. 4 Knowest thou *not* this of old, since man was placed upon earth,
5 That the triumphing of the wicked *is* short, and the joy of the hypocrite *but* for a moment?
6 Though his excellency mount up to the heavens, and his head reach unto the clouds;
7 *Yet* he shall perish for ever like his own dung: they which have seen him, shall say, Where *is* he?
8 He shall fly away as a dream, and shall not be found: yea, he shall be

A—CONCLUDED.

chased away as a vision of the night.
9 The eye also *which* saw him shall *see him* no more; neither shall his place any more behold him.
10 His children shall seek to please the poor, and his hands shall restore their goods.
11 His bones are full *of the sin* of his youth, which shall lie down with him in the dust.

Matt.26. 14 Then one of the twelve, called Judas Iscariot, went unto the chief priests,
15 And said *unto them*, What will ye give me, and I will deliver him unto you? And they covenanted with him for thirty pieces of silver.
16 And from that time he sought opportunity to betray him.

II Cor.7. 10 For godly sorrow worketh repentance to salvation not to be repented of: but the sorrow of the world worketh death.

B

Gen. 42. 21 And they said one to another, We *are* verily guilty concerning our brother, in that we saw the anguish of his soul, when he besought us, and we would not hear; therefore is this distress come upon us.
22 And Reuben answered them, saying, Spake I not unto you, saying, Do not sin against the child; and ye would not hear? therefore, behold, also his blood is required.

Ex. 9. 27 And Pharaoh sent, and called for Moses and Aaron, and said unto them, I have sinned this time: the LORD *is* righteous, and I and my people *are* wicked.

Ex. 10. 16 Then Pharaoh called for Moses and Aaron in haste; and he said, I have sinned against the LORD your God, and against you.
17 Now therefore forgive, I pray thee, my sin only this once, and entreat the LORD your God, that he may take away from me this death only.

Job 20. 15 He hath swallowed down riches, and he shall vomit them up again: God shall cast them out of his belly.
16 He shall suck the poison of asps: the viper's tongue shall slay him.
17 He shall not see the rivers, the floods, the brooks of honey and butter.
18 That which he laboured for shall he restore, and shall not swallow *it* down: according to *his* substance *shall*

TIME, FRIDAY, APRIL 7 [NISAN 15], A. D. 30; PLACE, JERUSALEM.
Lord's Fourth and Last Passover.

B—CONCLUDED.

the restitution *be*, and he shall not rejoice *therein*.
19 Because he hath oppressed *and*
hath forsaken the poor; *because* he
hath violently taken away a house
which he builded not;
20 Surely he shall not feel quietness
in his belly, he shall not save of that
which he desired.
21 There shall none of his meat be
left; therefore shall no man look for
his goods.
22 In the fulness of his sufficiency he
shall be in straits: every hand of the
wicked shall come upon him.
23 *When* he is about to fill his belly,
God shall cast the fury of his wrath
upon him, and shall rain *it* upon him
while he is eating.
24 He shall flee from the iron weapon, *and* the bow of steel shall strike
him through.
25 It is drawn, and cometh out of
the body; yea, the glittering sword
cometh out of his gall: terrors *are* upon him.
26 All darkness *shall be* hid in his
secret places: a fire not blown shall
consume him; it shall go ill with him
that is left in his tabernacle.
27 The heaven shall reveal his iniquity; and the earth shall rise up
against him.
28 The increase of his house shall
depart, *and his goods* shall flow away
in the day of his wrath.
29 This *is* the portion of a wicked
man from God, and the heritage appointed unto him by God.

C

II Sa.17. 23 And when Ahithophel saw that
his counsel was not followed, he saddled *his* ass, and arose, and gat him
home to his house, to his city, and
put his household in order, and
hanged himself, and died, and was
buried in the sepulchre of his father.
Job 2. 9 Then said his wife unto him, Dost
thou still retain thine integrity? curse
God, and die.
Job 7. 15 So that my soul chooseth strangling, *and* death rather than my life.
Acts 1. 18 Now this man purchased a field
with the reward of iniquity; and falling headlong, he burst asunder in the
midst, and all his bowels gushed out.

D

Acts 1. 19 And it was known unto all the

D—CONCLUDED.

dwellers at Jerusalem; insomuch as
that field is called, in their proper
tongue, Aceldama, that is to say, The
field of blood.

E

Josh. 4. 9 And Joshua set up twelve stones
in the midst of Jordan, in the place
where the feet of the priests which
bare the ark of the covenant stood:
and they are there unto this day.
Matt.28. 15 So they took the money, and did
as they were taught: and this saying
is commonly reported among the Jews
until this day.

F

Zech.11. 12 And I said unto them, If ye think
good, give *me* my price; and if not,
forbear. So they weighed for my
price thirty *pieces* of silver.
13 And the LORD said unto me, Cast
it unto the potter: a goodly price that
I was prized at of them. And I took
the thirty *pieces* of silver, and cast
them to the potter in the house of the
LORD.

G

Ex. 21. 32 If the ox shall push a manservant
or a maidservant; he shall give unto
their master thirty shekels of silver,
and the ox shall be stoned.
Lev. 27. 2 Speak unto the children of Israel,
and say unto them, When a man shall
make a singular vow, the persons *shall
be* for the LORD by thy estimation.
3 And thy estimation shall be of the
male from twenty years old even unto sixty years old, even thy estimation
shall be fifty shekels of silver, after
the shekel of the sanctuary.
4 And if it *be* a female, then thy
estimation shall be thirty shekels.
5 And if *it be* from five years old
even unto twenty years old, then thy
estimation shall be of the male twenty
shekels, and for the female ten shekels.
6 And if *it be* from a month old even
unto five years old, then thy estimation shall be of the male five shekels
of silver, and for the female thy estimation *shall be* three shekels of silver.
7 And if *it be* from sixty years old
and above; if *it be* a male, then thy
estimation shall be fifteen shekels, and
for the female ten shekels.
Deut.24. 6 No man shall take the nether or
the upper millstone to pledge: for he
taketh *a man's* life to pledge.

1

Or, *whom they bought of the children of Israel.*

§ 202. ON THE WAY TO GOLGOTHA.
Sixth Day of the Week of our

27: 31–34.

31 And after that they had mocked him, they took the robe off from him, and put his own raiment on him, [a]and led him away to crucify *him*.

32 [b]And as they came out, [c]they found a man of Cyrene, Simon by name: him they compelled to bear his cross.

33 [d]And when they were come unto a place called Golgotha, that is to say, a place of a skull,

34 [e]They gave him vinegar to drink mingled with gall: and when he had tasted *thereof*, he would not drink.

A

Isa. 53. 7 He was oppressed, and he was afflicted, yet he opened not his mouth: he is brought as a lamb to the slaughter, and as a sheep before her shearers is dumb, so he openeth not his mouth.

B

Num. 15. 35 And the LORD said unto Moses, The man shall be surely put to death: all the congregation shall stone him with stones without the camp.

I Ki. 21. 13 And there came in two men, children of Belial, and sat before him: and the men of Belial witnessed against him, *even* against Naboth, in the presence of the people, saying, Naboth did blaspheme God and the king. Then they carried him forth out of the city, and stoned him with stones, that he died.

14 Then they sent to Jezebel, saying, Naboth is stoned, and is dead.

Acts 7. 57 Then they cried out with a loud voice, and stopped their ears, and ran upon him with one accord,

58 And cast *him* out of the city, and stoned *him:* and the witnesses laid down their clothes at a young man's feet, whose name was Saul.

Heb. 13. 12 Wherefore Jesus also, that he might sanctify the people with his own blood, suffered without the gate.

C

Mark 15. 21 and Luke 23. 26. *See text of topic.*

D

Mark 15. 22. *See text of topic.*

Luke 23. 33 And when they were come to the place, which is called Calvary, there they crucified him, and the malefac-

15: 20–23.

20 And when they had mocked him, they took off the purple from him, and put his own clothes on him, and led him out to crucify him.

21 And they compel one Simon a Cyrenian, who passed by, coming out of the country, the father of Alexander [f]and Rufus, to bear his cross.

22 [g]And they bring him unto the place Golgotha, which is, being interpreted, The place of a skull.

23 And they gave him to drink wine mingled with myrrh: but he received *it* not.

D—CONCLUDED.

tors, one on the right hand and the other on the left.

John 19. 17. *See text of topic.*

E

Ps. 69. 21 They gave me also gall for my meat; and in my thirst they gave me vinegar to drink.

Matt. 27. 48 And straightway one of them ran, and took a sponge, and filled *it* with vinegar, and put *it* on a reed, and gave him to drink.

F

Rom. 16. 13 Salute Rufus chosen in the Lord, and his mother and mine.

G

Matt. 27. 33. *Text of topic.* Luke 23. 33. *Under D.*

H

Matt. 24. 19 And woe unto them that are with child, and to them that give suck in those days!

Luke 21. 23 But woe unto them that are with child, and to them that give suck, in those days! for there shall be great distress in the land, and wrath upon this people.

I

Isa. 2. 19 And they shall go into the holes of the rocks, and into the caves of the earth, for fear of the LORD, and for the glory of his majesty, when he ariseth to shake terribly the earth.

Hos. 10. 8 The high places also of Aven, the sin of Israel, shall be destroyed: the thorn and the thistle shall come up on their altars; and they shall say to the mountains, Cover us; and to the hills, Fall on us.

TIME, FRIDAY, 6–9 A. M., APRIL 7 [NISAN 15], A. D. 30; PLACE, JERUSALEM.
Lord's Fourth and Last Passover.

23: 26–32.

26 And as they led him away, they laid hold upon one Simon, a Cyrenian, coming out of the country, and on him they laid the cross, that he might bear *it* after Jesus.

27 And there followed him a great company of people, and of women, which also bewailed and lamented him.

28 But Jesus turning unto them said, Daughters of Jerusalem, weep not for me, but weep for yourselves, and for your children.

29 [h]For, behold, the days are coming, in the which they shall say, Blessed *are* the barren, and the wombs that never bare, and the paps which never gave suck.

30 [i]Then shall they begin to say to the mountains, Fall on us; and to the hills, Cover us.

31 [k]For if they do these things in a green tree, what shall be done in the dry?

32 [l]And there were also two others, malefactors, led with him to be put to death.

I—CONCLUDED.

Rev. 6. 16 And said to the mountains and rocks, Fall on us, and hide us from the face of him that sitteth on the throne, and from the wrath of the Lamb:

Rev. 9. 6 And in those days shall men seek death, and shall not find it; and shall desire to die, and death shall flee from them.

K

Prov.11. 31 Behold, the righteous shall be recompensed in the earth: much more the wicked and the sinner.

Jer. 25. 29 For, lo, I begin to bring evil on the city which is called by my name, and should ye be utterly unpunished? Ye shall not be unpunished: for I will call for a sword upon all the inhabitants of the earth, saith the LORD of hosts.

19: 17.

17 [m]And he bearing his cross went forth into a place called *the place* of a skull, which is called in the Hebrew Golgotha:

K—CONCLUDED.

Eze. 20. 47 And say to the forest of the south, Hear the word of the LORD; Thus saith the Lord GOD; Behold, I will kindle a fire in thee, and it shall devour every green tree in thee, and every dry tree: the flaming flame shall not be quenched, and all faces from the south to the north shall be burned therein.

Eze. 21. 3 And say to the land of Israel, Thus saith the LORD; Behold, I *am* against thee, and will draw forth my sword out of his sheath, and will cut off from thee the righteous and the wicked.

4 Seeing then that I will cut off from thee the righteous and the wicked, therefore shall my sword go forth out of his sheath against all flesh from the south to the north:

Heb. 6. 8 But that which beareth thorns and briers *is* rejected, and *is* nigh unto cursing; whose end *is* to be burned.

I Pet. 4. 17 For the time *is come* that judgment must begin at the house of God: and if *it* first *begin* at us, what shall the end *be* of them that obey not the gospel of God?

18 And if the righteous scarcely be saved, where shall the ungodly and the sinner appear?

L

Ps. 22. 16 For dogs have compassed me: the assembly of the wicked have inclosed me: they pierced my hands and my feet.

Isa. 53. 12 Therefore will I divide him *a portion* with the great, and he shall divide the spoil with the strong; because he hath poured out his soul unto death: and he was numbered with the transgressors; and he bare the sin of many, and made intercession for the transgressors.

Matt.27. 38 Then were there two thieves crucified with him; one on the right hand, and another on the left.

M

Num.15. 36 And all the congregation brought him without the camp, and stoned him with stones, and he died; as the LORD commanded Moses.

·Heb. 13. 12. *See under B.*

§ 203. THE CRUCIFIXION.
Sixth Day of the Week of our

27 : 35–38.

35 [a]And they crucified him, and parted his garments, casting lots: that it might be fulfilled which was spoken by the prophet, [b]They parted my garments among them, and upon my vesture did they cast lots.

36 [c]And sitting down they watched him there;

37 [d]And set up over his head his accusation written, THIS IS JESUS THE KING OF THE JEWS.

38 [e]Then were there two thieves crucified with him; one on the right hand, and another on the left.

A

Mark 15. 24 and Luke 23. 34. *See text of topic.*

B

Ps. 22. 18 They part my garments among them, and cast lots upon my vesture.

John 19. 24. *See text of topic.*

C

Matt.27. 54 Now when the centurion, and they that were with him, watching Jesus, saw the earthquake, and those things that were done, they feared greatly, saying, Truly this was the Son of God.

D

Mark 15. 26 and Luke 23. 38. *See text of topic.*
John 19. 19. *See text of topic.*

E

Isa. 53. 12 Therefore will I divide him *a portion* with the great, and he shall divide the spoil with the strong; because he hath poured out his soul unto death: and he was numbered with the transgressors; and he bare the sin of many, and made intercession for the transgressors.

Mark 15. 27. *See text of topic.*

Luke 23. 32 And there were also two others, malefactors, led with him to be put to death.

Luke 23. 33 and John 19. 18. *See text of topic.*

F

Ps. 22. 18. *See under B.*
Luke 23. 34 and John 19. 23. *See text of topic.*

G

Matt.27. 45 Now from the sixth hour there was darkness over all the land unto the ninth hour.

15: 24–28.

24 And when they had crucified him, [f]they parted his garments, casting lots upon them, what every man should take.

25 And [g]it was the third hour, and they crucified him.

26 And [h]the superscription of his accusation was written over, THE KING OF THE JEWS.

27 And [i]with him they crucify two thieves; the one on his right hand, and the other on his left.

28 And the Scripture was fulfilled, which saith, [k]And he was numbered with the transgressors.

G—Concluded.

Luke 23. 44 And it was about the sixth hour, and there was a darkness over all the earth until the ninth hour.

John 19. 14 And it was the preparation of the passover, and about the sixth hour: and he saith unto the Jews, Behold your King!

H

Deut.23. 5 Nevertheless, the Lord thy God would not hearken unto Balaam; but the Lord thy God turned the curse into a blessing unto thee, because the Lord thy God loved thee.

Matt. 27. 37 and John 19. 19. *See text of topic.*

I

Matt. 27. 38. *See text of topic.*

K

Isa. 53. 12. *See under E.*

Luke 22. 37 For I say unto you, that this that is written must yet be accomplished in me, And he was reckoned among the transgressors: for the things concerning me have an end.

L

Matt.27. 33 And when they were come unto a place called Golgotha, that is to say, a place of a skull,

Mark 15. 22 And they bring him unto the place Golgotha, which is, being interpreted, The place of a skull.

John 19. 17 And he bearing his cross went forth into a place called *the place* of a skull, which is called in the Hebrew Golgotha:

John 19. 18. *See text of topic.*

TIME, FRIDAY, 9–12 A. M., APRIL 7 [NISAN 15], A. D. 30; PLACE, JERUSALEM.
Lord's Fourth and Last Passover.

23: 33, 34, 38.

33 And [l]when they were come to the place, which is called [1]Calvary, there they crucified him, and the malefactors, one on the right hand, and the other on the left.

34 Then said Jesus, Father, [m]forgive them; for [n]they know not what they do. And [o]they parted his raiment, and cast lots. (p. 585.)

* * * * *

38 And a superscription also was written over him in letters of Greek, and Latin, and Hebrew, THIS IS THE KING OF THE JEWS. (p. 585.)

1 Or, *The place of a skull.*

Heb. 13. 12 Wherefore Jesus also, that he might sanctify the people with his own blood, suffered without the gate.

M

Matt. 5. 44 But I say unto you, Love your enemies, bless them that curse you, do good to them that hate you, and pray for them which despitefully use you, and persecute you;

Acts 7. 60 And he kneeled down, and cried with a loud voice, Lord, lay not this sin to their charge. And when he had said this, he fell asleep.

I Cor. 4. 12 And labour, working with our own hands: being reviled, we bless; being persecuted, we suffer it:

N

Acts 3. 17 And now, brethren, I wot that through ignorance ye did *it*, as *did* also your rulers.

O

Matt. 27. 35, Mark 15. 24 and John 19. 23. *See text of topic.*

P

Deut.21. 22 And if a man have committed a sin worthy of death, and he be to be put to death, and thou hang him on a tree:

23 His body shall not remain all night upon the tree, but thou shalt in any wise bury him that day; (for he that is hanged *is* accursed of God;) that thy land be not defiled, which the LORD thy God giveth thee *for* an inheritance.

Isa. 53. 12. *See under E.*

Dan. 9. 26 And after threescore and two weeks shall Messiah be cut off, but not

19: 18–24.

18 Where [p]they crucified him, and two others with him, on either side one, and Jesus in the midst.

19 And Pilate wrote a title, and put *it* on the cross. And the writing was, JESUS OF NAZARETH THE KING OF THE JEWS.

20 This title then read many of the Jews; for the place where Jesus was crucified was nigh to the city: and it was written in Hebrew, *and* Greek, *and* Latin.

21 Then said the chief priests of the Jews to Pilate, Write not, The King of the Jews; but that he said, I am King of the Jews.

22 Pilate answered, What I have written I have written.

23 Then the soldiers, when they had crucified Jesus, took his garments, and made four parts, to every soldier a part; and also *his* coat: now the coat was without seam, [2]woven from the top throughout.

24 They said therefore among themselves, Let us not rend it, but cast lots for it, whose it shall be: that the Scripture might be fulfilled, which saith, They parted my raiment among them, and for my vesture they did cast lots. These things therefore the soldiers did. (p. 587.)

P—CONCLUDED.

for himself: and the people of the prince that shall come shall destroy the city and the sanctuary; and the end thereof *shall be* with a flood, and unto the end of the war desolations are determined.

Gal. 3. 13 Christ hath redeemed us from the curse of the law, being made a curse for us: for it is written, Cursed *is* every one that hangeth on a tree:

2 Or, *wrought.*

§ 204. MOCKED ON THE CROSS.
Sixth Day of the Week of our

27: 39–44.

39 And [a]they that passed by reviled him, wagging their heads,

40 And saying, [b]Thou that destroyest the temple, and buildest *it* in three days, save thyself. [c]If thou be the Son of God, come down from the cross.

41 Likewise also the chief priests mocking *him*, with the scribes and elders, said,

42 He saved others; himself he cannot save. If he be the King of Israel, let him now come down from the cross, and we will believe him.

43 [d]He trusted in God; let him deliver him now, if he will have him: for he said, I am the Son of God.

44 [e]The thieves also, which were crucified with him, cast the same in his teeth. (p. 588.)

15: 29–32.

29 And [f]they that passed by railed on him, wagging their heads, and saying, Ah, [g]thou that destroyest the temple, and buildest *it* in three days,

30 Save thyself, and come down from the cross.

31 Likewise also the chief priests mocking said among themselves with the scribes, He saved others; himself he cannot save.

32 Let Christ the King of Israel descend now from the cross, that we may see and believe. And [h]they that were crucified with him reviled him.

A

Ps. 22. 7 All they that see me laugh me to scorn: they shoot out the lip, they shake the head, *saying*,

Ps. 31. 11 I was a reproach among all mine enemies, but especially among my neighbours, and a fear to mine acquaintance: they that did see me without fled from me.

12 I am forgotten as a dead man out of mind: I am like a broken vessel.

13 For I have heard the slander of many: fear *was* on every side: while they took counsel together against me, they devised to take away my life.

Ps. 35. 17 Lord, how long wilt thou look on? rescue my soul from their destructions, my darling from the lions.

18 I will give thee thanks in the great congregation: I will praise thee among much people.

19 Let not them that are mine enemies wrongfully rejoice over me: *neither* let them wink with the eye that hate me without a cause.

20 For they speak not peace: but they devise deceitful matters against *them that are* quiet in the land.

21 Yea, they opened their mouth

A—Continued. (p. 588.)

wide against me, *and* said, Aha, aha, our eye hath seen *it*.

Ps. 109. 25 I became also a reproach unto them: *when* they looked upon me they shaked their heads.

Lam. 1. 12 *Is it* nothing to you, all ye that pass by? behold, and see if there be any sorrow like unto my sorrow, which is done unto me, wherewith the Lord hath afflicted *me* in the day of his fierce anger.

Lam. 2. 15 All that pass by clap *their* hands at thee; they hiss and wag their head at the daughter of Jerusalem, *saying*, *Is* this the city that *men* call The perfection of beauty, The joy of the whole earth?

16 All thine enemies have opened their mouth against thee: they hiss and gnash the teeth: they say, We have swallowed *her* up: certainly this *is* the day that we looked for; we have found, we have seen *it*.

17 The Lord hath done *that* which he had devised; he hath fulfilled his word that he had commanded in the days of old: he hath thrown down, and hath not pitied: and he hath caused *thine* enemy to rejoice over thee, he hath set up the horn of thine adversaries.

Mark 15. 29 and Luke 23. 35. *See text of topic.*

I Pet. 2. 22 Who did no sin, neither was guile found in his mouth:

23 Who, when he was reviled, reviled not again: when he suffered, he

TIME, FRIDAY, 12 M.–3 P. M., APRIL 7 [NISAN 15], A. D. 30; PLACE, JERUSALEM.
Lord's Fourth and Last Passover.

23: 35–37, 39.

35 [i]And the people stood beholding. And the rulers also with them derided *him*, saying, He saved others; let him save himself, if he be Christ, the chosen of God.

36 And the soldiers also mocked him, coming to him, and offering him vinegar,

37 And saying, If thou be the King of the Jews, save thyself. (p. 583.)

* * * * *

39 And one of the malefactors which were hanged railed on him, saying, If thou be Christ, save thyself and us.

A—CONCLUDED.

threatened not; but committed *himself* to him that judgeth righteously:
24 Who his own self bare our sins in his own body on the tree, that we, being dead to sins, should live unto righteousness: by whose stripes ye were healed.

B

Matt.26. 61 And said, This *fellow* said, I am able to destroy the temple of God, and to build it in three days.

John 2. 19 Jesus answered and said unto them, Destroy this temple, and in three days I will raise it up.

C

Matt.26. 63 But Jesus held his peace. And the high priest answered and said unto him, I adjure thee by the living God, that thou tell us whether thou be the Christ, the Son of God.

D

Ps. 22. 8 He trusted on the LORD *that* he would deliver him: let him deliver him, seeing he delighted in him.

E

Ps. 42. 10 *As* with a sword in my bones, mine enemies reproach me; while they say daily unto me, Where *is* thy God?

Ps. 71. 11 Saying, God hath forsaken him: persecute and take him; for *there is* none to deliver *him*.

Isa. 36. 13 Then Rabshakeh stood, and cried with a loud voice in the Jews' language, and said, Hear ye the words of the great king, the king of Assyria.

E—CONCLUDED.

Isa. 36. 14 Thus saith the king, Let not Hezekiah deceive you: for he shall not be able to deliver you.
15 Neither let Hezekiah make you trust in the LORD, saying, The LORD will surely deliver us: this city shall not be delivered into the hand of the king of Assyria.
16 Hearken not to Hezekiah: for thus saith the king of Assyria, Make *an agreement* with me *by* a present, and come out to me: and eat ye every one of his vine, and every one of his fig tree, and drink ye every one the waters of his own cistern;
17 Until I come and take you away to a land like your own land, a land of corn and wine, a land of bread and vineyards.
18 *Beware* lest Hezekiah persuade you, saying, The LORD will deliver us. Hath any of the gods of the nations delivered his land out of the hand of the king of Assyria?

Isa. 37. 10 Thus shall ye speak to Hezekiah king of Judah, saying, Let not thy God, in whom thou trustest, deceive thee, saying, Jerusalem shall not be given into the hand of the king of Assyria.

Mark 15. 32. *See text of topic.*
Luke 23. 39. *See text of topic.*

F

Ps. 22. 7. *See under A.*

G

Mark 14. 58 We heard him say, I will destroy this temple that is made with hands, and within three days I will build another made without hands.

John 2. 19. *See under B.*

H

Matt. 27. 44 and Luke 23. 39. *See text of topic.*

Heb. 12. 3 For consider him that endured such contradiction of sinners against himself, lest ye be wearied and faint in your minds.

I

Ps. 22. 17 I may tell all my bones: they look *and* stare upon me.

Zech. 12. 10 And I will pour upon the house of David, and upon the inhabitants of Jerusalem, the spirit of grace and of supplications: and they shall look upon me whom they have pierced, and they shall mourn for him, as one mourneth for *his* only *son*, and shall be in bitterness for him, as one that is in bitterness for *his* first-born.

§ 205. THE PENITENT THIEF.
Sixth Day of the Week of our

A

Eph. 5. 11 And have no fellowship with the unfruitful works of darkness, but rather reprove *them.*

B

Heb. 1. 3 Who being the brightness of *his* glory, and the express image of his person, and upholding all things by the word of his power, when he had by himself purged our sins, sat down on the right hand of the Majesty on high;

4 Being made so much better than the angels, as he hath by inheritance obtained a more excellent name than they.

Heb. 8. 1 Now of the things which we have spoken *this is* the sum: We have such a high priest, who is set on the right hand of the throne of the Majesty in the heavens;

2 A minister of the sanctuary, and of the true tabernacle, which the Lord pitched, and not man.

C

Eze. 33. 10 Therefore, O thou son of man,

C—CONTINUED.

speak unto the house of Israel; Thus ye speak, saying, If our transgressions and our sins *be* upon us, and we pine away in them, how should we then live?

11 Say unto them, *As* I live, saith the Lord GOD, I have no pleasure in the death of the wicked; but that the wicked turn from his way and live: turn ye, turn ye from your evil ways; for why will ye die, O house of Israel?

12 Therefore, thou son of man, say unto the children of thy people, The righteousness of the righteous shall not deliver him in the day of his transgression: as for the wickedness of the wicked, he shall not fall thereby in the day that he turneth from his wickedness; neither shall the righteous be able to live for his *righteousness* in the day that he sinneth.

13 When I shall say to the righteous, *that* he shall surely live; if he trust to his own righteousness, and commit iniquity, all his righteousnesses shall not

§ 206. THE MOTHER OF JESUS AT THE CROSS.
Sixth Day of the Week of our

A

Matt. 27. 55 And many women were there beholding afar off, which followed Jesus from Galilee, ministering unto him:

Mark 15. 40 There were also women looking on afar off: among whom was Mary Magdalene, and Mary the mother of James the less and of Joses, and Salome;

Luke 2. 35 (Yea, a sword shall pierce through thy own soul also;) that the thoughts of many hearts may be revealed.

Luke 23. 49 And all his acquaintance, and the women that followed him from Galilee, stood afar off, beholding these things.

1

Or, *Clopas.*

B

Luke 24. 18 And the one of them, whose name was Cleopas, answering said unto him, Art thou only a stranger in Jerusalem, and hast not known the things which are come to pass there in these days?

C

John 13. 23 Now there was leaning on Jesus' bosom one of his disciples, whom Jesus loved.

John 20. 2 Then she runneth, and cometh to Simon Peter, and to the other disciple,

C—CONCLUDED.

whom Jesus loved, and saith unto them, They have taken away the Lord out of the sepulchre, and we know not where they have laid him.

John 21. 7 Therefore that disciple whom Jesus loved saith unto Peter, It is the Lord. Now when Simon Peter heard that it was the Lord, he girt *his* fisher's coat *unto him,* (for he was naked,) and did cast himself into the sea.

John 21. 20 Then Peter, turning about, seeth the disciple whom Jesus loved following; which also leaned on his breast at supper, and said, Lord, which is he that betrayeth thee?

John 21. 23 Then went this saying abroad among the brethren, that that disciple should not die: yet Jesus said not unto him, He shall not die; but, If I will that he tarry till I come, what *is that* to thee?

24 This is the disciple which testifieth of these things, and wrote these things: and we know that his testimony is true.

D

John 2. 4 Jesus saith unto her, Woman, what have I to do with thee? mine hour is not yet come.

TIME, FRIDAY, 12 M.–3 P. M., APRIL 7 [NISAN 15], A. D. 30; PLACE, JERUSALEM.
Lord's Fourth and Last Passover.

23: 40–43.

40 But the other answering [a]rebuked him, saying, Dost not thou fear God, seeing thou art in the same condemnation?

41 And we indeed justly; for we receive the due reward of our deeds: but this man hath done nothing amiss.

42 And he said unto Jesus, Lord, remember me when thou comest into [b]thy kingdom.

43 And Jesus said unto him, [c]Verily I say unto thee, To day shalt thou be with me in [d]paradise.

C—CONTINUED.

be remembered; but for his iniquity that he hath committed, he shall die for it.

14 Again, when I say unto the wicked, Thou shalt surely die; if he turn from his sin, and do that which is lawful and right;

C—CONCLUDED.

Eze. 33. 15 *If* the wicked restore the pledge, give again that he had robbed, walk in the statutes of life, without committing iniquity; he shall surely live, he shall not die.

16 None of his sins that he hath committed shall be mentioned unto him: he hath done that which is lawful and right; he shall surely live.

17 Yet the children of thy people say, The way of the Lord is not equal: but as for them, their way is not equal.

18 When the righteous turneth from his righteousness, and committeth iniquity, he shall even die thereby.

19 But if the wicked turn from his wickedness, and do that which is lawful and right, he shall live thereby.

D

Rev. 2. 7 He that hath an ear, let him hear what the Spirit saith unto the churches; To him that overcometh will I give to eat of the tree of life, which is in the midst of the paradise of God.

TIME, FRIDAY, 12 M.–3 P. M., APRIL 7 [NISAN 15], A. D. 30; PLACE, JERUSALEM.
Lord's Fourth and Last Passover.

E

Gen. 45. 8 So now *it was* not you *that* sent me hither, but God: and he hath made me a father to Pharaoh, and lord of all his house, and a ruler throughout all the land of Egypt.

Gen. 47. 11 And Joseph placed his father and his brethren, and gave them a possession in the land of Egypt, in the best of the land, in the land of Rameses, as Pharaoh had commanded.

12 And Joseph nourished his father, and his brethren, and all his father's household, with bread, according to *their* families.

John 1. 11 He came unto his own, and his own received him not.

12 But as many as received him, to them gave he power to become the sons of God, *even* to them that believe on his name:

John 16. 32 Behold, the hour cometh, yea, is now come, that ye shall be scattered, every man to his own, and shall leave me alone: and yet I am not alone, because the Father is with me.

I Tim. 5. 2 The elder women as mothers; the younger as sisters, with all purity.

3 Honour widows that are widows indeed.

19: 25–27.

25 [a]Now there stood by the cross of Jesus his mother, and his mother's sister, Mary the *wife* of [1b]Cleophas, and Mary Magdalene.

26 When Jesus therefore saw his mother, and [c]the disciple standing by, whom he loved, he saith unto his mother, [d]Woman, behold thy son!

27 Then saith he to the disciple, [e]Behold thy mother! And from that hour that disciple took her unto his own *home*.

E—CONCLUDED.

I Tim. 5. 4 But if any widow have children or nephews, let them learn first to show piety at home, and to requite their parents: for that is good and acceptable before God.

I Jno. 3. 18 My little children, let us not love in word, neither in tongue; but in deed and in truth.

19 And hereby we know that we are of the truth, and shall assure our hearts before him.

§ 207. DARKNESS PREVAILS. CHRIST EXPIRES ON THE CROSS.

Sixth Day of the Week of our

27: 45–50.

45 [a]Now from the sixth hour there was darkness over all the land unto the ninth hour.

46 And about the ninth hour [b]Jesus cried with a loud voice, saying, Eli, Eli, lama sabachthani? that is to say, [c]My God, my God, why hast thou forsaken me?

47 Some of them that stood there, when they heard *that,* said, This *man* calleth for Elias.

48 And straightway one of them ran, and took a sponge, [d]and filled *it* with vinegar, and put *it* on a reed, and gave him to drink.

49 The rest said, Let be, let us see whether Elias will come to save him.

50 [e]Jesus, when he had cried again with a loud voice, yielded up the ghost.

A

Isa. 50. 3 I clothe the heavens with blackness, and I make sackcloth their covering.

Amos 8. 9 And it shall come to pass in that day, saith the Lord GOD, that I will cause the sun to go down at noon, and I will darken the earth in a clear day:

Mark 15. 33 and Luke 23. 44. *See text of topic.*

Rev. 8. 12 And the fourth angel sounded, and the third part of the sun was smitten, and the third part of the moon, and the third part of the stars; so as the third part of them was darkened, and the day shown not for a third part of it, and the night likewise.

B

Heb. 5. 7 Who in the days of his flesh, when he had offered up prayers and supplications with strong crying and tears unto him that was able to save him from death, and was heard in that he feared;

C

Ps. 22. 1 My God, my God, why hast thou forsaken me? *why art thou so* far from helping me, *and from* the words of my roaring?

15: 33–37.

33 And when the sixth hour was come, there was darkness over the whole land until the ninth hour.

34 And at the ninth hour Jesus cried with a loud voice, saying, Eloi, Eloi, lama sabachthani? which is, being interpreted, My God, my God, why hast thou forsaken me?

35 And some of them that stood by, when they heard *it,* said, Behold, he calleth Elias.

36 And one ran and filled a sponge full of vinegar, and put *it* on a reed, and gave him to drink, saying, Let alone; let us see whether Elias will come to take him down.

37 And Jesus cried with a loud voice, and gave up the ghost.

C—CONCLUDED.

Ps. 77. 1 I cried unto God with my voice, *even* unto God with my voice; and he gave ear unto me.

Isa. 53. 10 Yet it pleased the LORD to bruise him; he hath put *him* to grief: when thou shalt make his soul an offering for sin, he shall see *his* seed, he shall prolong *his* days, and the pleasure of the LORD shall prosper in his hand.

D

Ps. 69. 21 They gave me also gall for my meat; and in my thirst they gave me vinegar to drink.

Luke 23. 36 And the soldiers also mocked him, coming to him, and offering him vinegar,

E

Mark 15. 37 and Luke 23. 46. *See text of topic.*

John 10. 11 I am the good shepherd; the good shepherd giveth his life for the sheep.

1

Or, *land.*

F

Ps. 31. 5 Into thine hand I commit my spirit: thou hast redeemed me, O LORD God of truth.

I Pet. 2. 23 Who, when he was reviled, reviled not again; when he suffered, he threatened not; but committeth *himself* to him that judgeth righteously:

TIME, FRIDAY, 12 M.–3 P. M., APRIL 7 [NISAN 15], A. D. 30; PLACE, JERUSALEM.
Lord's Fourth and Last Passover.

23: 44, 46.

44 And it was about the sixth hour, and there was a darkness over all the [l]earth until the ninth hour. (p. 591.)

* * * * *

46 And when Jesus had cried with a loud voice, he said, [f]Father, into thy hands I commend my spirit: [g]and having said thus, he gave up the ghost. (p. 591.)

G

Phil. 2. 8 And being found in fashion as a man, he humbled himself, and became obedient unto death, even the death of the cross.

H

Gen. 3. 15 And I will put enmity between thee and the woman, and between thy seed and her seed; it shall bruise thy head, and thou shalt bruise his heel.

Ps. 2. 1 Why do the heathen rage, and the people imagine a vain thing?

2 The kings of the earth set themselves, and the rulers take counsel together, against the LORD, and against his Anointed, *saying*,

3 Let us break their bands asunder, and cast away their cords from us.

Ps. 22. 1. *See under C.*

Isa. 53. 1 Who hath believed our report? and to whom is the arm of the LORD revealed?

Isa. 53. 2, etc. *Read entire chapter.*

I

Ex. 12. 22 And ye shall take a bunch of hyssop, and dip *it*, in the blood that *is* in the bason, and strike the lintel and the two side posts with the blood that *is* in the bason; and none of you shall go out at the door of his house until the morning.

Num. 19. 18 And a clean person shall take hyssop, and dip *it* in the water, and sprinkle *it* upon the tent, and upon all the vessels, and upon the persons that were there, and upon him that touched a bone, or one slain, or one dead, or a grave:

K

Gen. 3. 15. *See under H.*

Isa. 42. 21 The LORD is well pleased for his righteousness' sake; he will magnify the law, and make *it* honourable.

Dan. 9. 24 Seventy weeks are determined upon thy people, and upon thy holy city, to finish the transgression, and to make an end of sins, and to make

19: 28–30.

28 After this, Jesus knowing that [h]all things were now accomplished, that the Scripture might be fulfilled, saith, I thirst.

29 Now there was set a vessel full of vinegar: and [i]they filled a sponge with vinegar, and put *it* upon hyssop, and put *it* to his mouth.

30 When Jesus therefore had received the vinegar, he said, [k]It is finished: and he bowed his head, and [l]gave up the ghost. (p. 593.)

K—CONCLUDED.

reconciliation for iniquity, and to bring in everlasting righteousness, and to seal up the vision and prophecy, and to anoint the Most Holy.

John 17. 4 I have glorified thee on the earth: I have finished the work which thou gavest me to do.

Rom. 10. 4 For Christ *is* the end of the law for righteousness to every one that believeth.

Heb. 10. 1 For the law having a shadow of good things to come, *and* not the very image of the things, can never with those sacrifices, which they offered year by year continually, make the comers thereunto perfect.

2 For then would they not have ceased to be offered? because that the worshippers once purged should have had no more conscience of sins.

3 But in those *sacrifices there is* a remembrance again *made* of sins every year.

4 For *it is* not possible that the blood of bulls and of goats should take away sins.

5 Wherefore, when he cometh into the world, he saith, Sacrifice and offering thou wouldest not, but a body hast thou prepared me:

6 In burnt offerings and *sacrifices* for sin thou hast had no pleasure.

L

I Thes. 5. 9 For God hath not appointed us to wrath, but to obtain salvation by our Lord Jesus Christ,

10 Who died for us, that, whether we wake or sleep, we should live together with him.

§ 208. THE VAIL OF THE TEMPLE RENT, AND TOMBS OPENED.

Sixth Day of the Week of our

27 : 51–56.

51 And, behold, [a]the vail of the temple was rent in twain from the top to the bottom; and [b]the earth did quake, and the rocks rent;

52 And the graves were opened; [c]and many bodies of the saints which slept arose,

53 And came out of the graves after his resurrection, and went into the holy city, and appeared unto many.

54 [d]Now when the centurion, and they that were with him, watching Jesus, saw the earthquake, and those things that were done, they feared greatly, saying, Truly this was the Son of God.

55 And many women were there beholding afar off, [e]which followed Jesus from Galilee, ministering unto him:

56 [f]Among which was Mary Magdalene, and Mary the mother of James and Joses, and the mother of Zebedee's children.

A

Ex. 26. 31 And thou shalt make a vail *of* blue, and purple, and scarlet, and fine twined linen of cunning work: with cherubim shall it be made.

II Chr.3. 14 And he made the vail *of* blue, and purple, and crimson, and fine linen, and wrought cherubim thereon.

Mark 15. 38 and Luke 23. 45. *See text of topic.*

Eph. 2. 14 For he is our peace, who hath made both one, and hath broken down the middle wall of partition *between us;*

15 Having abolished in his flesh the enmity, *even* the law of commandments *contained* in ordinances; for to make in himself of twain one new man, *so* making peace;

Heb. 6. 19 Which *hope* we have as an anchor of the soul, both sure and steadfast, and which entereth into that within the vail;

20 Whither the forerunner is for us entered, *even* Jesus, made a high

15: 38–41.

38 And the vail of the temple was rent in twain from the top to the bottom.

39 And when the centurion, which stood over against him, saw that he so cried out, and gave up the ghost, he said, Truly this man was the Son of God.

40 There were also women looking on [g]afar off: among whom was Mary Magdalene, and Mary the mother of James the less and of Joses, and Salome;

41 Who also, when he was in Galilee, followed him, and ministered unto him; and many other women which came up with him unto Jerusalem.

A—Concluded.

priest for ever after the order of Melchisedec.

Heb. 10. 19 Having therefore, brethren, boldness to enter into the holiest by the blood of Jesus,

20 By a new and living way, which he hath consecrated for us, through the vail, that is to say, his flesh;

B

Ex. 19. 18 And mount Sinai was altogether on a smoke, because the Lord descended upon it in fire: and the smoke thereof ascended as the smoke of a furnace, and the whole mount quaked greatly.

Ps. 18. 6 In my distress I called upon the Lord, and cried unto my God: he heard my voice out of his temple, and my cry came before him, *even* into his ears.

7 Then the earth shook and trembled; the foundations also of the hills moved and were shaken, because he was wroth.

C

Ps. 68. 20 *He that is* our God *is* the God of salvation; and unto God the Lord *belong* the issues from death.

Isa. 25. 8 He will swallow up death in victory; and the Lord God will wipe away tears from off all faces; and the rebuke of his people shall he take away from off all the earth: for the Lord hath spoken *it.*

Isa. 26. 19 Thy dead *men* shall live, *together*

TIME, FRIDAY, 12 M.–3 P. M., APRIL 7 [NISAN 15], A. D. 30; PLACE, JERUSALEM.
Lord's Fourth and Last Passover.

23: 45, 47–49.

45 And the sun was darkened, and [h]the vail of the temple was rent in the midst. (p. 589.)

* * * * *

47 Now when the centurion saw what was done, he glorified God, saying, Certainly this was a righteous man.

48 And all the people that came together to that sight, beholding the things which were done, smote their breasts, and returned.

49 [i]And all his acquaintance, and the women that followed him from Galilee, stood afar off, beholding these things.

C—CONCLUDED.

with my dead body shall they arise. Awake and sing, ye that dwell in dust: for thy dew *is as* the dew of herbs, and the earth shall cast out the dead.

Dan. 12. 2 And many of them that sleep in the dust of the earth shall awake, some to everlasting life, and some to shame *and* everlasting contempt.

Hos. 13. 14 I will ransom them from the power of the grave; I will redeem them from death: O death, I will be thy plagues; O grave, I will be thy destruction: repentance shall be hid from mine eyes.

I Cor.15. 51 Behold, I show you a mystery; We shall not all sleep, but we shall all be changed,

I Thes.5. 10 Who died for us, that, whether we wake or sleep, we should live together with him.

D

Ex. 20. 18 And all the people saw the thunderings, and the lightnings, and the noise of the trumpet, and the mountain smoking: and when the people saw *it*, they removed, and stood afar off.

Matt.27. 36 And sitting down they watched him there;

Mark 15. 39 and Luke 23. 47. *See text of topic.*

E

Luke 8. 2 And certain women, which had been healed of evil spirits and infirmities, Mary called Magdalene, out of whom went seven devils,

3 And Joanna the wife of Chuza Herod's steward, and Susanna, and

E—CONCLUDED

many others, which ministered unto him of their substance.

F

Mark 15. 40. *See text of topic.*

G

Ps. 38. 11 My lovers and my friends stand aloof from my sore: and my kinsmen stand afar off.

H

Matt. 27. 51 and Mark 15. 38. *See text of topic.*

II Cor.3. 14 But their minds were blinded: for until this day remaineth the same vail untaken away in the reading of the old testament; which *vail* is done away in Christ.

Eph. 2. 14 and Heb. 6. 19. *See under A.*

I

Job 19. 13 He hath put my brethren far from me, and mine acquaintance are verily estranged from me.

14 My kinsfolk have failed, and my familiar friends have forgotten me.

15 They that dwell in mine house, and my maids, count me for a stranger: I am an alien in their sight.

16 I called my servant, and he gave *me* no answer; I entreated him with my mouth.

17 My breath is strange to my wife, though I entreated for the children's *sake* of mine own body.

18 Yea, young children despised me; I arose, and they spake against me.

19 All my inward friends abhorred me: and they whom I loved are turned against me.

20 My bone cleaveth to my skin and to my flesh, and I am escaped with the skin of my teeth.

21 Have pity upon me, have pity upon me, O ye my friends; for the hand of God hath touched me.

22 Why do ye persecute me as God, and are not satisfied with my flesh?

Ps. 38. 11. *See under G.*

Ps. 88. 18 Lover and friend hast thou put far from me, *and* mine acquaintance into darkness.

Ps. 142. 4 I looked on *my* right hand, and beheld, but *there was* no man that would know me: refuge failed me; no man cared for my soul.

Matt. 27. 55 and Mark 15. 40. *See text of topic.*

John 19. 25 Now there stood by the cross of Jesus his mother, and his mother's sister, Mary the *wife* of Cleophas, and Mary Magdalene.

§ 209. THE SIDE PIERCED.
Sixth Day of the Week of our

A

Mark 15. 42 And now when the even was come, because it was the preparation, that is, the day before the sabbath,

43 Joseph of Arimathea, an honourable counsellor, which also waited for the kingdom of God, came, and went in boldly unto Pilate, and craved the body of Jesus.

John 19. 42 There laid they Jesus therefore because of the Jews' preparation *day;* for the sepulchre was nigh at hand.

B

Deut. 21. 23 His body shall not remain all night upon the tree, but thou shalt in any wise bury him that day; (for he that is hanged *is* accursed of God;) that thy land be not defiled, which the LORD thy God giveth thee *for* an inheritance.

C

Ex. 12. 18 In the first *month*, on the fourteenth day of the month at even, ye shall eat unleavened bread, until the one and twentieth day of the month at even.

Num. 28. 17 And in the fifteenth day of this month *is* the feast: seven days shall unleavened bread be eaten.

18 In the first day *shall be* a holy convocation; ye shall do no manner of servile work *therein:*

D

I Jno. 5. 6 This is he that came by water and blood, *even* Jesus Christ; not by water only, but by water and blood. And it is the Spirit that beareth witness, because the Spirit is truth.

D—CONCLUDED.

I Jno. 5. 7 For there are three that bear record in heaven, the Father, the Word, and the Holy Ghost: and these three are one.

8 And there are three that bear witness in earth, the spirit, and the water, and the blood: and these three agree in one.

E

John 17. 21 That they all may be one; as thou, Father, *art* in me, and I in thee, that they also may be one in us: that the world may believe that thou hast sent me.

22 And the glory which thou gavest me I have given them; that they may be one, even as we are one:

23 I in them, and thou in me, that they may be made perfect in one; and that the world may know that thou hast sent me, and hast loved them, as thou hast loved me.

John 20. 31 But these are written, that ye might believe that Jesus is the Christ, the Son of God; and that believing ye might have life through his name.

John 21. 24 This is the disciple which testifieth of these things, and wrote these things: and we know that his testimony is true.

Acts 10. 39 And we are witnesses of all things which he did both in the land of the Jews, and in Jerusalem; whom they slew and hanged on a tree:

Rom. 15. 4 For whatsoever things were written aforetime were written for our

§ 210. TAKEN DOWN FROM THE CROSS AND LAID IN THE TOMB.
Sixth Day of the Week of our

27: 57–61.

57 [a]When the even was come, there came a rich man of Arimathea, named Joseph, who also himself was Jesus' disciple:

58 He went to Pilate, and begged the body of Jesus.

A

Mark 15. 42, 43, Luke 23. 50 and John 19. 33. *See text of topic.*

B

Luke 2. 25 And, behold, there was a man in Jerusalem, whose name *was* Simeon; and the same man *was* just and devout, waiting for the consolation of Israel: and the Holy Ghost was upon him.

15: 42–47.

42 And now when the even was come, because it was the preparation, that is, the day before the sabbath,

43 Joseph of Arimathea, an honourable counsellor, which also [b]waited for the kingdom of God, came, and went in boldly unto Pilate, and craved the body of Jesus.

B—CONCLUDED.

Luke 2. 38 And she coming in that instant gave thanks likewise unto the Lord, and spake of him to all them that looked for redemption in Jerusalem.

TIME, FRIDAY, 3–6 P. M., APRIL 7 [NISAN 15], A. D. 30; PLACE, JERUSALEM.
Lord's Fourth and Last Passover.

E—CONCLUDED.

learning, that we through patience and comfort of the Scriptures might have hope.

F

Ex. 12. 46 In one house shall it be eaten; thou shalt not carry forth aught of the flesh abroad out of the house; neither shall ye break a bone thereof.

Num. 9. 12 They shall leave none of it unto the morning, nor break any bone of it: according to all the ordinances of the passover they shall keep it.

Ps. 34. 20 He keepeth all his bones: not one of them is broken.

G

Ps. 22. 16 For dogs have compassed me: the assembly of the wicked have inclosed me: they pierced my hands and my feet.

17 I may tell all my bones: they look *and* stare upon me.

Zech.12. 10 And I will pour upon the house of David, and upon the inhabitants of Jerusalem, the spirit of grace and of supplications: and they shall look upon me whom they have pierced, and they shall mourn for him, as one mourneth for *his* only *son*, and shall be in bitterness for him, as one that is in bitterness for *his* first-born.

Rev. 1. 7 Behold, he cometh with clouds; and every eye shall see him, and they *also* which pierced him: and all kindreds of the earth shall wail because of him. Even so, Amen.

19: 31–37.

31 The Jews therefore, [a]because it
was the preparation, [b]that the bodies
should not remain upon the cross on the
sabbath day, (for that sabbath day was
a [c]high day,) besought Pilate that their
legs might be broken, and *that* they
might be taken away.
32 Then came the soldiers, and brake
the legs of the first, and of the other
which was crucified with him.
33 But when they came to Jesus, and
saw that he was dead already, they
brake not his legs:
34 But one of the soldiers with a
spear pierced his side, and forthwith
[d]came there out blood and water.
35 And he that saw *it* bare record,
and his record is true; [e]and he knoweth
that he saith true, that ye might believe.
36 For these things were done, [f]that
the Scripture should be fulfilled, A bone
of him shall not be broken.
37 And again another Scripture saith,
[g]They shall look on him whom they
pierced.

TIME, FRIDAY, 3–6 P. M., APRIL 7 [NISAN 15], A. D. 30; PLACE, JERUSALEM.
Lord's Fourth and Last Passover.

23: 50–56.

50 And, behold, *there was* a man
named Joseph, a counsellor; *and he
was* a good man, and a just:
51 (The same [c]had not consented to
the counsel and deed of them:) *he was*
of Arimathea, a city of the Jews; [d]who
also himself waited for the kingdom of
God.
52 This *man* went unto Pilate, and
begged the body of Jesus.

19: 38–42.

38 And after this Joseph of Arimathea, being a disciple of Jesus, but
secretly [e]for fear of the Jews, besought
Pilate that he might take away the
body of Jesus:

C

I Tim.5. 22 Lay hands suddenly on no man, neither be partaker of other men's sins: keep thyself pure.

D

Gen. 49. 18 I have waited for thy salvation, O LORD.

Mark 15. 43. *Text of topic.* Luke 2. 25, 38. *Under B.*

For E see next page (594).

§ 210. TAKEN DOWN FROM THE CROSS AND LAID IN THE TOMB (CON-
Sixth Day of the Week of our

CHAP. 27.

Then Pilate commanded the body to be delivered.

59 And when Joseph had taken the body, he wrapped it in a clean linen cloth,

60 And [f] laid it in his own new tomb, which he had hewn out in the rock: and he rolled a great stone to the door of the sepulchre, and departed.

61 And there was Mary Magdalene, and the other Mary, sitting over against the sepulchre.

E

John 9. 22 These *words* spake his parents, because they feared the Jews: for the Jews had agreed already, that if any man did confess that he was Christ, he should be put out of the synagogue.

John 12. 42 Nevertheless among the chief rulers also many believed on him; but because of the Pharisees they did not confess *him*, lest they should be put out of the synagogue:

F

Isa. 53. 9 And he made his grave with the wicked, and with the rich in his death; because he had done no violence, neither *was any* deceit in his mouth.

G

Isa. 53. 9. *Under F.* Matt. 27. 59, 60. *Text of topic.* Luke 23, 53 and John 19. 40. *See text of topic.*

H

Matt. 27. 59 and Mark 15. 46. *See text of topic.*

I

Isa. 53. 9. *See under F.*

K

Matt. 27. 62 Now the next day, that followed the day of the preparation, the chief priests and Pharisees came together unto Pilate,

L

Luke 8. 2 And certain women, which had been healed of evil spirits and infirmities, Mary called Magdalene, out of whom went seven devils,

M

Mark 15. 47. *See text of topic.*

N

II Chr. 16. 14 And they buried him in his own sepulchres, which he had made for himself in the city of David, and laid him in the bed which was filled with

CHAP. 15.

44 And Pilate marvelled if he were already dead: and calling *unto him* the centurion, he asked him whether he had been any while dead.

45 And when he knew *it* of the centurion, he gave the body to Joseph.

46 [g] And he bought fine linen, and took him down, and wrapped him in the linen, and laid him in a sepulchre which was hewn out of a rock, and rolled a stone unto the door of the sepulchre.

47 And Mary Magdalene and Mary *the mother* of Joses beheld where he was laid.

N—CONCLUDED.

sweet odours and divers kinds *of spices* prepared by the apothecaries' art: and they made a very great burning for him.

Mark 16. 1 And when the sabbath was past, Mary Magdalene, and Mary the *mother* of James, and Salome, had bought sweet spices, that they might come and anoint him.

O

Ex. 20. 10 But the seventh day *is* the sabbath of the LORD thy God: *in it* thou shalt not do any work, thou, nor thy son, nor thy daughter, thy manservant, nor thy maidservant, nor thy cattle, nor thy stranger that *is* within thy gates:

Isa. 56. 2 Blessed *is* the man *that* doeth this, and the son of man *that* layeth hold on it; that keepeth the sabbath from polluting it, and keepeth his hand from doing any evil.

Isa. 56. 6 Also the sons of the stranger, that join themselves to the LORD, to serve him, and to love the name of the LORD, to be his servants, every one that keepeth the sabbath from polluting it, and taketh hold of my covenant;

Isa. 58. 13 If thou turn away thy foot from the sabbath, *from* doing thy pleasure on my holy day; and call the sabbath a delight, the holy of the LORD, honourable; and shalt honour him, not

CLUDED). TIME, FRIDAY, 3–6 P. M., APRIL 7 [NISAN 15], A. D. 30: PLACE, JERUSALEM.
Lord's Fourth and Last Passover.

CHAP. 23.

53 [h]And he took it down, and wrapped
it in linen, and laid it in a [i]sepulchre
that was hewn in stone, wherein never
man before was laid.
54 And that day was [k]the preparation, and the sabbath drew on.
55 And the women also, [l]which came
with him from Galilee, followed after,
and [m]beheld the sepulchre, and how his
body was laid.
56 And they returned, and [n]prepared
spices and ointments; and rested the
sabbath day [o]according to the commandment.

CHAP. 19.

And Pilate gave *him* leave. He came
therefore, and took the body of Jesus.
39 And there came also [p]Nicodemus,
(which at the first came to Jesus by
night,) and brought a [q]mixture of
myrrh and aloes, about a hundred
pound *weight*.
40 Then took they the body of Jesus,
and [r]wound it in linen clothes with the
spices, as the manner of the Jews is to
bury.
41 Now in the place where he was
crucified there was a garden; and in
the garden a [s]new sepulchre, wherein
was never man yet laid.
42 [t]There laid they Jesus therefore
[u]because of the Jews' preparation *day;*
for the sepulchre was nigh at hand.

O—CONCLUDED.

doing thine own ways, nor finding thine own pleasure, nor speaking *thine own* words:

Jer. 17. 24 And it shall come to pass, if ye diligently hearken unto me, saith the LORD, to bring in no burden through the gates of this city on the sabbath day, but hallow the sabbath day, to do no work therein:

P

John 3. 1 There was a man of the Pharisees, named Nicodemus, a ruler of the Jews:

2 The same came to Jesus by night, and said unto him, Rabbi, we know that thou art a teacher come from God: for no man can do these miracles that thou doest, except God be with him.

John 7. 50 Nicodemus saith unto them, (he that came to Jesus by night, being one of them,)

51 Doth our law judge *any* man, before it hear him, and know what he doeth?

John 9. 22 and John 12. 42. *See under E.*

Q

II Chr. 16. 13 And Asa slept with his fathers, and died in the one and fortieth year of his reign.

II Chr. 16. 14. *See under N.*

Song 4. 6 Until the day break, and the shadows flee away, I will get me to the mountain of myrrh, and to the hill of frankincense.

Song 4. 14 Spikenard and saffron; calamus

Q—CONCLUDED.

and cinnamon, with all trees of frankincense; myrrh and aloes, with all the chief spices:

Luke 23. 56. *See text of topic.*

R

Acts 5. 6 And the young men arose, wound him up, and carried *him* out, and buried *him*.

S

Luke 23. 53. *See text of topic.*

T

Ps. 22. 15 My strength is dried up like a potsherd; and my tongue cleaveth to my jaws; and thou hast brought me into the dust of death.

Isa. 22. 16 What hast thou here, and whom hast thou here, that thou hast hewed thee out a sepulchre here, *as* he that heweth him out a sepulchre on high, *and* that graveth a habitation for himself in a rock?

Isa. 53. 9. *See under F.*

U

John 19. 31 The Jews therefore, because it was the preparation, that the bodies should not remain upon the cross on the sabbath day, (for that sabbath day was a high day,) besought Pilate that their legs might be broken, and *that* they might be taken away.

§ 211. THE GUARD AT THE SEPULCHRE.

Seventh Day of the Week of our

27 : 62–66.

62 Now the next day, that followed the day of the preparation, the [a]chief priests and Pharisees came together unto Pilate,

63 Saying, Sir, we remember that that deceiver said, while he was yet alive, [b]After three days I will rise again.

64 Command therefore that the sepulchre be made sure until the third day, lest his disciples come by night, and steal him away, and say unto the people, He is risen from the dead: so the last error shall be worse than the first.

65 Pilate said unto them, Ye have a watch: go your way, [c]make *it* as sure as ye can.

66 So they went, and made the sepulchre sure, [d]sealing the stone, and setting a watch.

A

Ps. 2. 1 Why do the heathen rage, and the people imagine a vain thing?

A—Concluded.

Ps. 2. 2 The kings of the earth set themselves, and the rulers take counsel together, against the Lord, and against his Anointed, *saying*,

3 Let us break their bands asunder, and cast away their cords from us.

4 He that sitteth in the heavens shall laugh: the Lord shall have them in derision.

5 Then shall he speak unto them in his wrath, and vex them in his sore displeasure.

6 Yet have I set my King upon my holy hill of Zion.

Acts 4. 26 The kings of the earth stood up, and the rulers were gathered together against the Lord, and against his Christ.

27 For of a truth against thy holy child Jesus, whom thou hast anointed, both Herod, and Pontius Pilate, with the Gentiles, and the people of Israel, were gathered together,

28 For to do whatsoever thy hand and thy counsel determined before to be done.

B

Matt.16. 21 From that time forth began Jesus to show unto his disciples, how that he must go unto Jerusalem, and suffer many things of the elders and chief

§ 212. MORNING OF THE RESURRECTION. WOMEN VISIT THE TOMB.

First Day of the Week following our

28: 1–4.

1 In the [a]end of the sabbath, as it began to dawn toward the first *day* of the week, came Mary Magdalene [b]and the other Mary to see the sepulchre.

2 And, behold, there [1]was a great earthquake: for [c]the angel of the Lord descended from heaven, and came and rolled back the stone from the door, and sat upon it.

3 [d]His countenance was like lightning, and his raiment white as snow:

4 And for fear of him the keepers did shake, and became as dead *men*.

A

Mark 16. 1, Luke 24. 1 and John 20. 1. *See text of topic.*

16 : 1–4.

1 And when the sabbath was past, Mary Magdalene, and Mary the *mother* of James, and Salome, [e]had bought sweet spices, that they might come and anoint him.

2 And very early in the morning, the first *day* of the week, they came unto the sepulchre at the rising of the sun.

3 And they said among themselves, Who shall roll us away the stone from the door of the sepulchre?

B

Matt.27. 56 Among which was Mary Magdalene, and Mary the mother of James and Joses, and the mother of Zebedee's children.

1

Or, *had been.*

TIME, SATURDAY [SABBATH], APRIL 8 [NISAN 16], A. D., 30; PLACE, JERUSALEM.
Lord's Fourth and Last Passover.

B—CONTINUED.

priests and scribes, and be killed, and be raised again the third day.

Matt.17. 23 And they shall kill him, and the third day he shall be raised again. And they were exceeding sorry.

Matt.20. 19 And shall deliver him to the Gentiles to mock, and to scourge, and to crucify *him:* and the third day he shall rise again.

Matt.26. 61 And said, This *fellow* said, I am able to destroy the temple of God, and to build it in three days.

Mark 8. 31 And he began to teach them, that the Son of man must suffer many things, and be rejected of the elders, and *of* the chief priests, and scribes, and be killed, and after three days rise again.

Mark 10. 34 And they shall mock him, and shall scourge him, and shall spit upon him, and shall kill him; and the third day he shall rise again.

Luke 9. 22 Saying, The Son of man must suffer many things, and be rejected of the elders and chief priests and scribes, and be slain, and be raised the third day.

Luke 18. 32 For he shall be delivered unto the Gentiles, and shall be mocked, and spitefully entreated, and spitted on:

B—CONCLUDED.

Luke 18. 33 And they shall scourge *him,* and put him to death; and the third day he shall rise again.

Luke 24. 6 He is not here, but is risen: remember how he spake unto you when he was yet in Galilee,

7 Saying, The Son of man must be delivered into the hands of sinful men, and be crucified, and the third day rise again.

John 2. 19 Jesus answered and said unto them, Destroy this temple, and in three days I will raise it up.

C

Ps. 76. 10 Surely the wrath of man shall praise thee: the remainder of wrath shalt thou restrain.

Prov.21. 30 *There is* no wisdom nor understanding nor counsel against the LORD.

D

Dan. 6. 17 And a stone was brought, and laid upon the mouth of the den; and the king sealed it with his own signet, and with the signet of his lords; that the purpose might not be changed concerning Daniel.

II Tim.2. 19 Nevertheless the foundation of God standeth sure, having this seal, The Lord knoweth them that are his. And, Let every one that nameth the name of Christ depart from iniquity.

TIME, SUNDAY MORNING, APRIL 9 [NISAN 17], A. D. 30; PLACE, JERUSALEM.
Lord's Fourth and Last Passover.

24: 1–3.

1 Now upon the first *day* of the week, very early in the morning, they came unto the sepulchre, bringing the spices which they had prepared, and certain *others* with them.

C

Mark 16. 5 And entering into the sepulchre, they saw a young man sitting on the right side, clothed in a long white garment; and they were affrighted.

Luke 24. 4 And it came to pass, as they were much perplexed thereabout, behold, two men stood by them in shining garments:

John 20. 12 And seeth two angels in white sitting, the one at the head, and the other at the feet, where the body of Jesus had lain.

D

Ps. 104. 4 Who maketh his angels spirits; his ministers a flaming fire:

20: 1, 2.

1 The first *day* of the week cometh Mary Magdalene early, when it was yet dark, unto the sepulchre,

D—CONCLUDED.

Dan. 10. 6 His body also *was* like the beryl, and his face as the appearance of lightning, and his eyes as lamps of fire, and his arms and his feet like in colour to polished brass, and the voice of his words like the voice of a multitude.

Rev. 10. 1 And I saw another mighty angel come down from heaven, clothed with a cloud: and a rainbow *was* upon his head, and his face *was* as it were the sun, and his feet as pillars of fire:

E

Luke 23. 56 And they returned, and prepared spices and ointments; and rested the sabbath day according to the commandment.

§ 212. MORNING OF THE RESURRECTION. WOMEN VISIT THE TOMB (Con-
First Day of the Week following our

[Chap. 28.]

F

Matt 28. 2 and Mark 16. 4. *See text of topic.*

G

Mark 16. 5, 6. *See text of* § 213.

Luke 24. 23 And when they found not his body, they came, saying, that they had also seen a vision of angels, which said that he was alive.

John 20. 6 Then cometh Simon Peter following him, and went into the sepulchre, and seeth the linen clothes lie,

7 And the napkin, that was about his head, not lying with the linen clothes, but wrapped together in a place by itself.

Chap. 16.

4 And when they looked, they saw that the stone was rolled away: for it was very great.

H

John 13. 23 Now there was leaning on Jesus' bosom one of his disciples, whom Jesus loved.

John 19. 26 When Jesus therefore saw his mother, and the disciple standing by, whom he loved, he saith unto his mother, Woman, behold thy son!

John 21. 7 Therefore that disciple whom Jesus loved saith unto Peter, It is the Lord. Now when Simon Peter heard

§ 213. VISION OF ANGELS IN THE TOMB.
First Day of the Week following our

28: 5–7.

5 And the angel answered and said unto the women, [a]Fear not ye: for I know that ye seek Jesus, which was crucified.

6 [b]He is not here: for he is risen, as he said. Come, see the place where the Lord lay.

7 And go quickly, and tell his disciples that he is risen from the dead; and, behold, [c]he goeth before you into Galilee; there shall ye see him: lo, I have told you.

A

Rev. 1. 17 And when I saw him, I fell at his feet as dead. And he laid his right hand upon me, saying unto me, Fear not; I am the first and the last:

B

Matt. 12. 40 For as Jonas was three days and three nights in the whale's belly; so shall the Son of man be three days and three nights in the heart of the earth.

Matt. 16. 21 From that time forth began Jesus to show unto his disciples, how that he must go unto Jerusalem, and suffer many things of the elders and chief priests and scribes, and be killed, and be raised again the third day.

Matt. 17. 23 And they shall kill him, and the third day he shall be raised again. And they were exceedingly sorry.

16: 5–7.

5 [d]And entering into the sepulchre, they saw a young man sitting on the right side, clothed in a long white garment; and they were affrighted.

6 [e]And he saith unto them, Be not affrighted: ye seek Jesus of Nazareth, which was crucified: he is [f]risen; he is not here: behold the place where they laid him.

7 But go your way, tell his disciples and Peter that he goeth before you into Galilee: there shall ye see him, [g]as he said unto you.

B—Concluded.

Matt. 20. 19 And shall deliver him to the Gentiles to mock, and to scourge, and to crucify *him:* and the third day he shall rise again.

C

Matt. 26. 32 But after I am risen again, I will go before you into Galilee.

Mark 16. 7. *See text of topic.*

D

Luke 24. 3. *See text of* § 212.

John 20. 11 But Mary stood without at the sepulchre weeping: and as she wept, she stooped down, *and looked* into the sepulchre,

12 And seeth two angels in white sitting, the one at the head, and the other at the feet, where the body of Jesus had lain.

CLUDED). TIME, SUNDAY MORNING, APRIL 9 [NISAN 17], A. D. 30; PLACE, JERUSALEM.
Lord's Fourth and Last Passover.

CHAP. 24.

2 [f]And they found the stone rolled
away from the sepulchre.

3 [g]And they entered in, and found not
the body of the Lord Jesus.

H—CONTINUED.

that it was the Lord, he girt *his* fisher's coat *unto him*, (for he was naked,) and did cast himself into the sea.

John 21. 20 Then Peter, turning about, seeth the disciple whom Jesus loved following; which also leaned on his breast at supper, and said, Lord, which is he that betrayeth thee?

CHAP. 20.

and seeth the stone taken away from
the sepulchre.

2 Then she runneth, and cometh to
Simon Peter, and to the [h]other disciple,
whom Jesus loved, and saith unto them,
They have taken away the Lord out of
the sepulchre, and we know not where
they have laid him.

H—CONCLUDED.

John 21. 24 This is the disciple which testifieth of these things, and wrote these things: and we know that his testimony is true.

TIME, SUNDAY MORNING, APRIL 9 [NISAN 17], A. D. 30; PLACE, JERUSALEM.
Lord's Fourth and Last Passover.

24: 4–8.

4 And it came to pass, as they were
much perplexed thereabout, [h]behold,
two men stood by them in shining garments:

5 And as they were afraid, and bowed
down *their* faces to the earth, they said
unto them, Why seek ye [1]the living
among the dead?

6 He is not here, but is risen: [i]remember how he spake unto you when
he was yet in Galilee,

7 Saying, The Son of man must be
delivered into the hands of sinful men,
and be crucified, and the third day rise
again.

8 And [k]they remembered his words.

E

Matt. 28. 5, 6, 7. *See text of topic.*

F

John 2. 19 Jesus answered and said unto them, Destroy this temple, and in three days I will raise it up.

G

Matt. 26. 32. *See under C.*

Mark 14. 28 But after that I am risen, I will go before you into Galilee.

H

Gen. 18. 2 And he lift up his eyes and looked, and, lo, three men stood by him: and when he saw *them*, he ran to meet them from the tent door, and bowed himself toward the ground.

John 20. 12. *See under D.*

Acts 1. 10 And while they looked steadfastly toward heaven as he went up, behold, two men stood by them in white apparel;

1

Or, *him that liveth.*

Heb. 7. 8 And here men that die receive tithes; but there he *receiveth them*, of whom it is witnessed that he liveth.

I

Matt. 16. 21 and Matt. 17. 23. *See under B.*

Mark 8. 31 And he began to teach them, that the Son of man must suffer many things, and be rejected of the elders, and *of* the chief priests, and scribes, and be killed, and after three days rise again.

Mark 9. 31 For he taught his disciples, and said unto them, The Son of man is delivered into the hands of men, and they shall kill him; and after that he is killed, he shall rise the third day.

Luke 9. 22 Saying, The Son of man must suffer many things, and be rejected of the elders and chief priests and scribes, and be slain, and be raised the third day.

K

John 2. 22 When therefore he was risen from the dead, his disciples remembered that he had said this unto them; and they believed the Scripture, and the word which Jesus had said.

§ 214. THE WOMEN RETURN TO THE CITY. JESUS MEETS THEM.

First Day of the Week following our

28: 8–10.

8 And they departed quickly from
the sepulchre with fear and great joy;
and did run to bring his disciples word.
9 And as they went to tell his disciples, behold, [a]Jesus met them, saying,
All hail. And they came and held him
by the feet, and worshipped him.
10 Then said Jesus unto them, Be not
afraid: go tell [b]my brethren that they
go into Galilee, and there shall they
see me. (p. 604.)

A

Mark 16. 9 and John 20. 14. *See text of* § 216.

16: 8.

8 And they went out quickly, and
fled from the sepulchre; for they trembled and were amazed: neither said
they any thing to any *man;* for they
were afraid.

B

John 20. 17. *See text of* § 216.

Rom. 8. 29 For whom he did foreknow, he also did predestinate *to be* conformed to the image of his Son, that he might be the first-born among many brethren.

Heb. 2. 11 For both he that sanctifieth and they who are sanctified *are* all of one: for which cause he is not ashamed to call them brethren,

§ 215. PETER AND JOHN RUN TO THE TOMB.

First Day of the Week following our

A

John 20. 3, 6. *See text of topic.*

B

Luke 24. 12. *See text of topic.*

C

John 19. 40 Then took they the body of Jesus, and wound it in linen clothes with the spices, as the manner of the Jews is to bury.

D

John 11. 44 And he that was dead came forth, bound hand and foot with grave-clothes; and his face was bound about with a napkin. Jesus saith unto them, Loose him, and let him go.

E

Ps. 16. 10 For thou wilt not leave my soul in hell; neither wilt thou suffer thine Holy One to see corruption.

Ps. 22. 15 My strength is dried up like a potsherd; and my tongue cleaveth to my jaws; and thou hast brought me into the dust of death.

Ps. 22. 23 Ye that fear the LORD, praise him; all ye the seed of Jacob, glorify him; and fear him, all ye the seed of Israel.

24 For he hath not despised nor abhorred the affliction of the afflicted; neither hath he hid his face from him; but when he cried unto him, he heard.

25 My praise *shall be* of thee in the great congregation: I will pay my vows before them that fear him.

26 The meek shall eat and be satisfied: they shall praise the LORD that seek him: your heart shall live for ever.

E—CONTINUED.

Ps. 22. 27 All the ends of the world shall remember and turn unto the LORD: and all the kindreds of the nations shall worship before thee.

28 For the kingdom *is* the LORD'S: and he *is* the governor among the nations.

29 All *they that be* fat upon earth shall eat and worship: all they that go down to the dust shall bow before him: and none can keep alive his own soul.

Isa. 26. 19 Thy dead *men* shall live, *together with* my dead body shall they arise. Awake and sing, ye that dwell in dust: for thy dew *is as* the dew of herbs, and the earth shall cast out the dead.

Hos. 13. 14 I will ransom them from the power of the grave; I will redeem them from death: O death, I will be thy plagues; O grave, I will be thy destruction: repentance shall be hid from mine eyes.

Matt. 16. 21 From that time forth began Jesus to show unto his disciples, how that he must go unto Jerusalem, and suffer many things of the elders and chief priests and scribes, and be killed, and be raised again the third day.

Acts 2. 25 For David speaketh concerning him, I foresaw the Lord always before my face; for he is on my right hand, that I should not be moved:

26 Therefore did my heart rejoice, and my tongue was glad; moreover also my flesh shall rest in hope:

TIME, SUNDAY A. M., APRIL 9 [NISAN 17], A. D. 30; PLACE, JERUSALEM.
Lord's Fourth and Last Passover.

24: 9–11.

9 [c]And returned from the sepulchre, and told all these things unto the eleven, and to all the rest.

10 It was Mary Magdalene, and [d]Joanna, and Mary *the mother* of James, and other *women that were* with them, which told these things unto the apostles.

11 [e]And their words seem to them as idle tales, and they believed them not.

C

Matt. 28. 8. *See text of topic.*
Mark 16. 10 *And* she went and told them that

C—CONCLUDED.

had been with him, as they mourned and wept.

D

Luke 8. 2 And certain women, which had been healed of evil spirits and infirmities, Mary called Magdalene, out of whom went seven devils,
3 And Joanna the wife of Chuza Herod's steward, and Susanna, and many others, which ministered unto him of their substance.

E

Mark 16. 11 And they, when they had heard that he was alive, and had been seen of her, believed not.
Luke 24. 25 Then he said unto them, O fools, and slow of heart to believe all that the prophets have spoken:

TIME, SUNDAY A. M., APRIL 9 [NISAN 17], A. D. 30; PLACE, JERUSALEM.
Lord's Fourth and Last Passover.

24: 12.

12 [a]Then arose Peter, and ran unto the sepulchre; and stooping down, he beheld the linen clothes laid by themselves, and departed, wondering in himself at that which was come to pass.

(p. 605.)

E—CONCLUDED.

Acts 2. 27 Because thou wilt not leave my soul in hell, neither wilt thou suffer thine Holy One to see corruption.
28 Thou hast made known to me the ways of life; thou shalt make me full of joy with thy countenance.
29 Men *and* brethren, let me freely speak unto you of the patriarch David, that he is both dead and buried, and his sepulchre is with us unto this day.
30 Therefore being a prophet, and knowing that God had sworn with an oath to him, that of the fruit of his loins, according to the flesh, he would raise up Christ to sit on his throne;
31 He, seeing this before, spake of the resurrection of Christ, that his soul was not left in hell, neither his flesh did see corruption.
Acts 13. 34 And as concerning that he raised him up from the dead, *now* no more to return to corruption, he said on this wise, I will give you the sure mercies of David.
35 Wherefore he saith also in another *psalm*, Thou shalt not suffer thine Holy One to see corruption.

20: 3–10.

3 [b]Peter therefore went forth, and that other disciple, and came to the sepulchre.

4 So they ran both together, and the other disciple did outrun Peter, and came first to the sepulchre.

5 And he stooping down, *and looking in,* saw [c]the linen clothes lying; yet went he not in.

6 Then cometh Simon Peter following him, and went into the sepulchre, and seeth the linen clothes lie,

7 And [d]the napkin, that was about his head, not lying with the linen clothes, but wrapped together in a place by itself.

8 Then went in also that other disciple, which came first to the sepulchre, and he saw, and believed.

9 For as yet they knew not the [e]Scripture, that he must rise again from the dead.

10 Then the disciples went away again unto their own home.

§ 216. OUR LORD IS SEEN BY MARY MAGDALENE AT THE TOMB.

First Day of the Week following our

A

John 20. 14. *See text of topic.*

B

Luke 8. 2 And certain women, which had been healed of evil spirits and infirmities, Mary called Magdalene, out of whom went seven devils,

C

Luke 24. 10 It was Mary Magdalene, and Joanna, and Mary *the mother* of James, and other *women that were* with them, which told these things unto the apostles.

John 20. 18. *See text of topic.*

D

Luke 24. 11 And their words seemed to them as idle tales, and they believed them not.

E

Mark 16. 5 And entering into the sepulchre, they saw a young man sitting on the right side, clothed in a long white garment; and they were affrighted.

F

I Sa. 1. 8 Then said Elkanah her husband to her, Hannah, why weepest thou? and why eatest thou not? and why is thy heart grieved? *am* not I better to thee than ten sons?

Eccl. 3. 4 A time to weep, and a time to laugh; a time to mourn, and a time to dance;

Jer. 31. 16 Thus saith the LORD; Refrain thy voice from weeping, and thine eyes from tears: for thy work shall be rewarded, saith the LORD; and they shall come again from the land of the enemy.

Acts 21. 13 Then Paul answered, What mean ye to weep and to break mine heart? for I am ready not to be bound only, but also to die at Jerusalem for the name of the Lord Jesus.

G

Song 3. 1 By night on my bed I sought him whom my soul loveth: I sought him, but I found him not.

2 I will rise now, and go about the city in the streets, and in the broad ways I will seek him whom my soul loveth: I sought him, but I found him not.

3 The watchmen that go about the city found me: *to whom I said*, Saw ye him whom my soul loveth?

4 *It was* but a little that I passed from them, but I found him whom my soul loveth: I held him, and would not let him go, until I had

16: 9–11.

9 Now when *Jesus* was risen early the
first *day* of the week, [a]he appeared first
to Mary Magdalene, [b]out of whom he
had cast seven devils.

10 [c]*And* she went and told them that
had been with him, as they mourned
and wept.

11 [d]And they, when they had heard
that he was alive, and had been seen of
her, believed not.

G—CONCLUDED.

brought him into my mother's house, and into the chamber of her that conceived me.

Matt. 28. 9 And as they went to tell his disciples, behold, Jesus met them, saying, All hail. And they came and held him by the feet, and worshipped him.

Mark. 16. 9. *See text of topic.*

H

Luke 24. 16 But their eyes were holden that they should not know him.

Luke 24. 32 And they said one to another, Did not our heart burn within us, while he talked with us by the way, and while he opened to us the Scriptures?

John 21. 4 But when the morning was now come, Jesus stood on the shore; but the disciples knew not that it was Jesus.

I

Song 2. 8 The voice of my beloved! behold, he cometh leaping upon the mountains, skipping upon the hills.

Matt. 23. 8 But be not ye called Rabbi: for one is your Master, *even* Christ; and all ye are brethren.

9 And call no *man* your father upon the earth: for one is your Father, which is in heaven.

10 Neither be ye called masters: for one is your Master, *even* Christ.

John 3. 2 The same came to Jesus by night, and said unto him, Rabbi, we know that thou art a teacher come from God: for no man can do these miracles that thou doest, except God be with him.

K

Ps. 22. 22 I will declare thy name unto my brethren: in the midst of the congregation will I praise thee.

Matt. 28. 10 Then said Jesus unto them, Be

TIME, SUNDAY A. M., APRIL 9 [NISAN 17], A. D. 30; PLACE, JERUSALEM.
Lord's Fourth and Last Passover.

K—CONCLUDED.

not afraid: go tell my brethren that they go into Galilee, and there shall they see me.

Rom. 8. 29 For whom he did foreknow, he also did predestinate *to be* conformed to the image of his Son, that he might be the first-born among many brethren.

Heb. 2. 11 For both he that sanctifieth and they who are sanctified *are* all of one: for which cause he is not ashamed to call them brethren,

12 Saying, I will declare thy name unto my brethren, in the midst of the church will I sing praise unto thee.

L

John 16. 28 I came forth from the Father, and am come into the world: again, I leave the world, and go to the Father.

I Pet. 1. 3 Blessed *be* the God and Father of our Lord Jesus Christ, which according to his abundant mercy hath begotten us again unto a lively hope by the resurrection of Jesus Christ from the dead,

M

Eph. 1. 16 Cease not to give thanks for you, making mention of you in my prayers;

17 That the God of our Lord Jesus Christ, the Father of glory, may give unto you the spirit of wisdom and revelation in the knowledge of him:

N

Gen. 17. 7 And I will establish my covenant between me and thee and thy seed after thee in their generations, for an everlasting covenant, to be a God unto thee and to thy seed after thee.

8 And I will give unto thee, and to thy seed after thee, the land wherein thou art a stranger, all the land of Canaan, for an everlasting possession; and I will be their God.

Ps. 43. 4 Then will I go unto the altar of God, unto God my exceeding joy: yea, upon the harp will I praise thee, O God my God.

Isa. 41. 10 Fear thou not; for I *am* with thee: be not dismayed; for I *am* thy God: I will strengthen thee; yea, I will help thee; yea, I will uphold thee with the right hand of my righteousness.

Jer. 31. 33 But this *shall be* the covenant that I will make with the house of Israel; After those days, saith the LORD, I will put my law in their inward parts, and write it in their hearts; and will be their God, and they shall be my people.

20: 11–18.

11 [e]But Mary stood without at the sepulchre weeping: and as she wept, she stooped down, *and looked* into the sepulchre,

12 And seeth two angels in white sitting, the one at the head, and the other at the feet, where the body of Jesus had lain.

13 And they say unto her, [f]Woman, why weepest thou? She saith unto them, Because they have taken away my Lord, and I know not where they have laid him.

14 [g]And when she had thus said, she turned herself back, and saw Jesus standing, and [h]knew not that it was Jesus.

15 Jesus saith unto her, Woman, why weepest thou? whom seekest thou? She, supposing him to be the gardener, saith unto him, Sir, if thou have borne him hence, tell me where thou hast laid him, and I will take him away.

16 Jesus saith unto her, Mary. She turned herself, and saith unto him, [i]Rabboni; which is to say, Master.

17 Jesus saith unto her, Touch me not; for I am not yet ascended to my Father: but go to [k]my brethren, and say unto them, [l]I ascend unto my Father, and your Father; and *to* [m]my God, and [n]your God.

18 [o]Mary Magdalene came and told the disciples that she had seen the Lord, and *that* he had spoken these things unto her.

O

Matt. 28. 10. *Under K.*
Luke 24. 10. *Under C.*

§ 217. REPORT OF THE GUARD.
First Day of the Week following our

28: 11–15.

11 Now when they were going, behold, [a]some of the watch came into the city, and showed unto the chief priests all the things that were done.

12 [b]And when they were assembled with the elders, and had taken counsel, [c]they gave large money unto the soldiers,

13 [d]Saying, Say ye, His disciples came by night, and stole him *away* while we slept.

14 And if this come to the governor's ears, we will persuade him, and secure you.

15 [e]So they took the money, and did as they were taught: and this saying is commonly reported among the Jews until this day. (p. 616.)

A

Jer. 51. 12 Set up the standard upon the walls of Babylon, make the watch strong, set up the watchmen, prepare the ambushes: for the LORD hath both devised and done that which he spake against the inhabitants of Babylon.

Matt.27. 65 Pilate said unto them, Ye have a watch: go your way, make *it* as sure as ye can.

A—CONCLUDED.

Matt.27. 66 So they went, and made the sepulchre sure, sealing the stone, and setting a watch.

Matt.28. 4 And for fear of him the keepers did shake, and became as dead *men.*

B

Isa. 8. 9 Associate yourselves, O ye people, and ye shall be broken in pieces; and give ear, all ye of far countries: gird yourselves, and ye shall be broken in pieces; gird yourselves, and ye shall be broken in pieces.

10 Take counsel together, and it shall come to nought; speak the word, and it shall not stand: for God *is* with us.

11 For the LORD spake thus to me with a strong hand, and instructed me that I should not walk in the way of this people, saying,

12 Say ye not, A confederacy, to all *them to* whom this people shall say, A confederacy; neither fear ye their fear, nor be afraid.

C

I Sa. 9. 7 Then said Saul to his servant, But, behold, *if* we go, what shall we bring the man? for the bread is spent in our vessels, and *there is* not a present to bring to the man of God: what have we?

8 And the servant answered Saul again, and said, Behold, I have here at hand the fourth part of a shekel of silver: *that* will I give to the man of God, to tell us our way.

Isa. 56. 11 Yea, *they are* greedy dogs *which*

§ 218. *JESUS APPEARS TO TWO DISCIPLES ON THE WAY TO EMMAUS.
First Day of the Week following our

*

JESUS APPEARS TO PETER.

Probably about the time Cleopas and his companion left Jerusalem for Emmaus, or shortly afterwards, Jesus appeared to Peter (Cephas). This appearance of our Lord is mentioned only by Luke, 24:34 (*See text of topic*) and by Paul in his first epistle to the Corinthians.

1 Cor.15. 4 And that he was buried, and that he rose again the third day according to the Scriptures:

5 And that he was seen of Cephas, then of the twelve:

A

Luke 24. 13. *See text of topic.*

B

Mark 16. 12. *See text of topic.*

C

Deut. 6. 7 And thou shalt teach them dili-

16: 12, 13.

12 After that he appeared in another form [a]unto two of them, as they walked, and went into the country.

C—CONTINUED.

gently unto thy children, and shalt talk of them when thou sittest in thine house, and when thou walkest by the way, and when thou liest down, and when thou risest up.

8 And thou shalt bind them for a sign upon thine hand, and they shall be as frontlets between thine eyes.

I Sa. 23. 16 And Jonathan Saul's son arose, and went to David into the wood, and strengthened his hand in God.

TIME, SUNDAY A. M., APRIL 9 [NISAN 17], A. D. 30; PLACE, JERUSALEM.
Lord's Fourth and Last Passover.

C—CONCLUDED.

can never have enough, and they *are* shepherds *that* cannot understand: they all look to their own way, every one for his gain, from his quarter.

12 Come ye, *say they*, I will fetch wine, and we will fill ourselves with strong drink; and to morrow shall be as this day, *and* much more abundant.

Mic. 3. 11 The heads thereof judge for reward, and the priests thereof teach for hire, and the prophets thereof divine for money: yet will they lean upon the LORD, and say, *Is* not the LORD among us? none evil can come upon us.

Rom.16. 18 For they that are such serve not our Lord Jesus Christ, but their own belly; and by good words and fair speeches deceive the hearts of the simple.

I Tim.6. 9 But they that will be rich fall into temptation and a snare, and *into* many foolish and hurtful lusts, which drown men in destruction and perdition.

10 For the love of money is the root of all evil: which while some coveted after, they have erred from the faith, and pierced themselves through with many sorrows.

D

Neh. 4. 3 Now Tobiah the Ammonite *was* by him, and he said, Even that which they build, if a fox go up, he shall even break down their stone wall.

Neh. 4. 8 And conspired all of them together to come *and* to fight against Jerusalem, and to hinder it.

D—CONCLUDED.

Job 5. 12 He disappointeth the devices of the crafty, so that their hands cannot perform *their* enterprise.

13 He taketh the wise in their own craftiness: and the counsel of the froward is carried headlong.

14 They meet with darkness in the daytime, and grope in the noonday as in the night.

Ps. 33. 10 The LORD bringeth the counsel of the heathen to nought: he maketh the devices of the people of none effect.

11 The counsel of the LORD standeth for ever, the thoughts of his heart to all generations.

E

Num.22. 37 And Balak said unto Balaam, Did I not earnestly send unto thee to call thee? wherefore camest thou not unto me? am I not able indeed to promote thee to honour?

Num.22. 40 And Balak offered oxen and sheep, and sent to Balaam, and to the princes that *were* with him.

41 And it came to pass on the morrow, that Balak took Balaam, and brought him up into the high places of Baal, that thence he might see the utmost *part* of the people.

Matt. 4. 8 Again, the devil taketh him up into an exceeding high mountain, and showeth him all the kingdoms of the world, and the glory of them;

9 And saith unto him, All these things will I give thee, if thou wilt fall down and worship me.

TIME, SUNDAY P. M., APRIL 9 [NISAN 17], A. D. 30; PLACE, JERUSALEM. EMMAUS.
Lord's Fourth and Last Passover.

24: 13-35.

13 [b]And, behold, two of them went that same day to a village called Emmaus, which was from Jerusalem *about* threescore furlongs.

14 And they [c]talked together of all these things which had happened.

C—CONTINUED.

Ps. 66. 16 Come *and* hear, all ye that fear God, and I will declare what he hath done for my soul.

Ps. 119. 63 I *am* a companion of all *them* that fear thee, and of them that keep thy precepts.

C—CONCLUDED.

Prov.13. 20 He that walketh with wise *men* shall be wise: but a companion of fools shall be destroyed.

Dan. 2. 17 Then Daniel went to his house, and made the thing known to Hananiah, Mishael, and Azariah, his companions:

Mal. 3. 16 Then they that feared the LORD spake often one to another: and the LORD hearkened, and heard *it*, and a book of remembrance was written before him for them that feared the LORD, and that thought upon his name.

Luke 2. 38 And she coming in that instant gave thanks likewise unto the Lord, and spake of him to all them that looked for redemption in Jerusalem.

§ 218. JESUS APPEARS TO TWO DISCIPLES ON THE WAY TO EMMAUS

First Day of the Week following our

D

Matt.18. 20 For where two or three are gathered together in my name, there am I in the midst of them.

Luke 24. 36 And as they thus spake, Jesus himself stood in the midst of them, and saith unto them, Peace *be* unto you.

John 14. 18 I will not leave you comfortless: I will come to you.

19 Yet a little while, and the world seeth me no more; but ye see me: because I live, ye shall live also.

John 16. 22 And ye now therefore have sorrow: but I will see you again, and your heart shall rejoice, and your joy no man taketh from you.

E

II Ki. 6. 18 And when they came down to him, Elisha prayed unto the LORD, and said, Smite this people, I pray thee, with blindness. And he smote them with blindness according to the word of Elisha.

19 And Elisha said unto them, This *is* not the way, neither *is* this the city: follow me, and I will bring you to the man whom ye seek. But he led them to Samaria.

20 And it came to pass, when they were come into Samaria, that Elisha said, LORD, open the eyes of these *men*, that they may see. And the LORD opened their eyes, and they saw; and, behold, *they were* in the midst of Samaria.

John 20. 14 And when she had thus said, she turned herself back and saw Jesus standing, and knew not that it was Jesus.

John 21. 4 But when the morning was now come, Jesus stood on the shore; but the disciples knew not that it was Jesus.

F

Eze. 9. 4 And the LORD said unto him, Go through the midst of the city, through the midst of Jerusalem, and set a mark upon the foreheads of the men that sigh and that cry for all the abominations that be done in the midst thereof.

5 And to the others he said in mine hearing, Go ye after him through the city, and smite: let not your eye spare, neither have ye pity:

6 Slay utterly old *and* young, both maids, and little children, and women: but come not near any man upon whom *is* the mark; and begin at my sanctu-

CHAP. 16.

13 And they went and told *it* unto the residue: neither believed they them.

F—CONCLUDED. (p. 610.)

ary. Then they began at the ancient men which *were* before the house.

G

John 19. 25 Now there stood by the cross of Jesus his mother, and his mother's sister, Mary the *wife* of Cleophas, and Mary Magdalene.

H

Matt.21. 11 And the multitude said, This is Jesus the prophet of Nazareth of Galilee.

Luke 7. 16 And there came a fear on all: and they glorified God, saying, That a great prophet is risen up among us; and, That God hath visited his people.

John 3. 2 The same came to Jesus by night, and said unto him, Rabbi, we know that thou art a teacher come from God: for no man can do these miracles that thou doest, except God be with him.

John 4. 19 The woman saith unto him, Sir, I perceive that thou art a prophet.

John 6. 14 Then those men, when they had seen the miracle that Jesus did, said, This is of a truth that Prophet that should come into the world.

Acts 2. 22 Ye men of Israel, hear these words; Jesus of Nazareth, a man approved of God among you by miracles and wonders and signs, which God did by him in the midst of you, as ye yourselves also know:

Acts 10. 37 That word, *I say*, ye know, which was published throughout all Judæa, and began from Galilee, after the baptism which John preached;

38 How God anointed Jesus of Nazareth with the Holy Ghost and with power: who went about doing good, and healing all that were oppressed of the devil; for God was with him.

I

Acts 7. 22 And Moses was learned in all the wisdom of the Egyptians, and was mighty in words and in deeds.

K

Luke 23. 1 And the whole multitude of them arose, and led him unto Pilate.

Acts 13. 27 For they that dwell at Jerusalem, and their rulers, because they knew him not, nor yet the voices of the prophets which are read every sabbath

(CONTINUED). TIME, SUNDAY P. M., APRIL 9 [NISAN 17], A. D. 30; PLACE, JERUSALEM.
Lord's Fourth and Last Passover.

CHAP. 24.

15 And it came to pass, that, while they communed *together* and reasoned, [d]Jesus himself drew near, and went with them.

16 But [e]their eyes were holden that they should not know him.

17 And he said unto them, What manner of communications *are* these that ye have one to another, as ye walk, and [f]are sad?

18 And the one of them, [g]whose name was Cleopas, answering said unto him, Art thou only a stranger in Jerusalem, and hast not known the things which are come to pass there in these days?

19 And he said unto them, What things? And they said unto him, Concerning Jesus of Nazareth, [h]which was a prophet [i]mighty in deed and word before God and all the people:

20 [k]And how the chief priests and our rulers delivered him to be condemned to death, and have crucified him.

21 But we trusted [l]that it had been he which should have redeemed Israel: and beside all this, to day is the third day since these things were done.

22 Yea, and [m]certain women also of our company made us astonished, which were early at the sepulchre;

23 And when they found not his body, they came, saying, that they had also seen a vision of angels, which said that he was alive.

24 And [n]certain of them which were with us went to the sepulchre, and found *it* even so as the women had said: but him they saw not.

K—CONCLUDED.

day, they have fulfilled *them* in condemning *him*.

28 And though they found no cause of death *in him*, yet desired they Pilate that he should be slain.

L

Ps. 130. 7 Let Israel hope in the LORD: for with the LORD *there is* mercy, and with him *is* plenteous redemption.

8 And he shall redeem Israel from all his iniquities.

Isa. 59. 20 And the Redeemer shall come to Zion, and unto them that turn from transgression in Jacob, saith the LORD.

Luke 1. 68 Blessed *be* the Lord God of Israel; for he hath visited and redeemed his people.

Luke 2. 38 And she coming in that instant gave thanks likewise unto the Lord, and spake of him to all them that looked for redemption in Jerusalem.

Acts 1. 6 When they therefore were come together, they asked of him, saying, Lord, wilt thou at this time restore again the kingdom to Israel?

Rev. 5. 9 And they sung a new song, saying, Thou art worthy to take the book, and to open the seals thereof: for thou wast slain, and hast redeemed us to God by thy blood out of every kindred, and tongue, and people, and nation;

M

Luke 24. 9 And returned from the sepulchre, and told all these things unto the eleven, and to all the rest.

10 It was Mary Magdalene, and Joanna, and Mary *the mother* of James, and other *women that were* with them, which told these things unto the apostles.

Matt. 28. 8 And they departed quickly from the sepulchre with fear and great joy; and did run to bring his disciples word.

Mark 16. 10 *And* she went and told them that had been with him, as they mourned and wept.

John 20. 18 Mary Magdalene came and told the disciples that she had seen the Lord, and *that* he had spoken these things unto her.

N

Luke 24. 12 Then arose Peter, and ran unto the sepulchre; and stooping down, he beheld the linen clothes laid by themselves, and departed, wondering in himself at that which was come to pass.

§ 218. JESUS APPEARS TO TWO DISCIPLES ON THE WAY TO EMMAUS

First Day of the Week following our

O

Luke 24. 46 And said unto them, Thus it is written, and thus it behooved Christ to suffer, and to rise from the dead the third day:

Acts 17. 3 Opening and alleging, that Christ must needs have suffered, and risen again from the dead; and that this Jesus, whom I preach unto you, is Christ.

I Pet. 1. 11 Searching what, or what manner of time the Spirit of Christ which was in them did signify, when it testified beforehand the sufferings of Christ, and the glory that should follow.

P

Luke 24. 45. *See text of* § 219.

Q

Gen. 3. 15 And I will put enmity between thee and the woman, and between thy seed and her seed; it shall bruise thy head, and thou shalt bruise his heel.

Gen. 22. 18 And in thy seed shall all the nations of the earth be blessed; because thou hast obeyed my voice.

Gen. 26. 4 And I will make thy seed to multiply as the stars of heaven, and will give unto thy seed all these countries; and in thy seed shall all the nations of the earth be blessed:

Gen. 49. 10 The sceptre shall not depart from Judah, nor a lawgiver from between his feet, until Shiloh come; and unto him *shall* the gathering of the people *be*.

Num. 21. 9 And Moses made a serpent of brass, and put it upon a pole; and it came to pass, that if a serpent had bitten any man, when he beheld the serpent of brass, he lived.

Deut. 18. 15 The LORD thy God will raise up unto thee a Prophet from the midst of thee, of thy brethren, like unto me; unto him ye shall hearken;

R

Ps. 16. 9 Therefore my heart is glad, and my glory rejoiceth: my flesh also shall rest in hope.

10 For thou wilt not leave my soul in hell; neither wilt thou suffer thine Holy One to see corruption.

Ps. 132. 11 The LORD hath sworn *in* truth unto David; he will not turn from it; Of the fruit of thy body will I set upon thy throne.

Isa. 7. 14 Therefore the Lord himself shall give you a sign; Behold, a virgin shall conceive, and bare a son, and shall call his name Immanuel.

Isa. 9. 6 For unto us a child is born, unto

[CHAP. 16.]

R—CONTINUED.

us a son is given: and the government shall be upon his shoulder: and his name shall be called Wonderful, Counsellor, The mighty God, The everlasting Father, The Prince of Peace.

Isa. 40. 10 Behold, the Lord GOD will come with strong *hand*, and his arm shall rule for him: behold, his reward *is* with him, and his work before him.

11 He shall feed his flock like a shepherd: he shall gather the lambs with his arm, and carry *them* in his bosom, *and* shall gently lead those that are with young.

Isa. 50. 6 I gave my back to the smiters, and my cheeks to them that plucked off the hair: I hid not my face from shame and spitting.

Jer. 23. 5 Behold, the days come, saith the LORD, that I will raise unto David a righteous Branch, and a King shall reign and prosper, and shall execute judgment and justice in the earth.

Jer. 33. 14 Behold, the days come, saith the LORD, that I will perform that good thing which I have promised unto the house of Israel and to the house of Judah.

15 In those days, and at that time, will I cause the Branch of righteousness to grow up unto David; and he shall execute judgment and righteousness in the land.

Eze. 34. 23 And I will set up one Shepherd over them, and he shall feed them, *even* my servant David; he shall feed them, and he shall be their shepherd.

Eze. 37. 25 And they shall dwell in the land that I have given unto Jacob my servant, wherein your fathers have dwelt; and they shall dwell therein, *even* they, and their children, and their children's children for ever: and my servant David *shall be* their prince for ever.

Dan. 9. 24 Seventy weeks are determined upon thy people and upon thy holy city, to finish the transgression, and to make an end of sins, and to make reconciliation for iniquity, and to bring in everlasting righteousness, and to seal up the vision and prophecy, and to anoint the Most Holy.

Mic. 7. 20 Thou wilt perform the truth to Jacob, *and* the mercy to Abraham, which thou hast sworn unto our fathers from the days of old.

(CONCLUDED) TIME, SUNDAY P. M., APRIL 9 [NISAN 17], A. D. 30; PLACE, JERUSALEM.
Lord's Fourth and Last Passover.

CHAP. 24.

25 Then he said unto them, O fools, and slow of heart to believe all that the prophets have spoken:

26 [o]Ought not Christ to have suffered these things, and to enter into his glory?

27 [p]And beginning at [q]Moses and [r]all the prophets, he expounded unto them in all the Scriptures the things concerning himself.

28 And they drew nigh unto the village, whither they went: and [s]he made as though he would have gone further.

29 But [t]they constrained him, saying, Abide with us; for it is toward evening, and the day is far spent. And he went in to tarry with them.

30 And it came to pass, as he sat at meat with them, [u]he took bread, and blessed *it*, and brake, and gave to them.

31 And their eyes were opened, and they knew him; and he [1]vanished out of their sight.

32 And they said one to another, Did not our heart burn within us, while he talked with us by the way, and while he opened to us the Scriptures?

33 And they rose up the same hour, and returned to Jerusalem, and found the eleven gathered together, and them that were with them,

34 Saying, The Lord is risen indeed, and [x]hath appeared to Simon.

35 And they told what things *were done* in the way, and how he was known of them in breaking of bread.

R—CONTINUED.

Mal. 3. 1 Behold, I will send my messenger, and he shall prepare the way before me: and the Lord, whom ye seek, shall suddenly come to his temple,

R—CONCLUDED.

even the messenger of the covenant whom ye delight in: behold, he shall come, saith the LORD of hosts.

Mal. 4. 2 But unto you that fear my name shall the Sun of righteousness arise with healing in his wings; and ye shall go forth, and grow up as calves of the stall.

John 1. 45 Philip findeth Nathanael, and saith unto him, We have found him, of whom Moses in the law, and the prophets, did write, Jesus of Nazareth, the son of Joseph.

S

Gen. 32. 26 And he said, Let me go, for the day breaketh. And he said, I will not let thee go, except thou bless me.

Gen. 42. 7 And Joseph saw his brethren, and he knew them, but made himself strange unto them, and spake roughly unto them; and he said unto them, Whence come ye? And they said, From the land of Canaan to buy food.

Mark 6. 48 And he saw them toiling in rowing; for the wind was contrary unto them: and about the fourth watch of the night he cometh unto them, walking upon the sea, and would have passed by them.

T

Gen. 19. 3 And he pressed upon them greatly; and they turned in unto him, and entered into his house; and he made them a feast, and did bake unleavened bread, and they did eat.

Acts 16. 15 And when she was baptized, and her household, she besought *us*, saying, If ye have judged me to be faithful to the Lord, come into my house, and abide *there*. And she constrained us.

U

Matt. 14. 19 And he commanded the multitude to sit down on the grass, and took the five loaves, and the two fishes, and looking up to heaven, he blessed, and brake, and gave the loaves to *his* disciples, and the disciples to the multitude.

1

Or, *ceased to be seen of them.*

Luke 4. 30 But he, passing through the midst of them, went his way,

John 8. 59 Then took they up stones to cast at him: but Jesus hid himself, and went out of the temple, going through the midst of them, and so passed by.

X

I Cor. 15. 5. *See under *, page 605.*

§ 219. JESUS APPEARS IN THE MIDST OF THE APOSTLES, THOMAS BEING

Evening following the First Day (i. e., introducing the Second Day)

A

Luke 24. 36 and John 20. 19. *See text of topic.*

I Cor.15. 5 And that he was seen of Cephas, then of the twelve:

1

Or, *together.*

B

Job 4. *Read entire chapter.*

Mark 6. 49 But when they saw him walking upon the sea, they supposed it had been a spirit, and cried out:

C

Gen. 45. 26 And told him, saying, Joseph *is* yet alive, and he *is* governor over all the land of Egypt. And Jacob's heart fainted, for he believed them not.

D

John 21. 5 Then Jesus saith unto them, Children, have ye any meat? They answered him, No.

E

Acts 10. 41 Not to all the people, but unto witnesses chosen before of God, *even* to us, who did eat and drink with him after he rose from the dead.

F

Matt.16. 21 From that time forth began Jesus to show unto his disciples, how that he must go unto Jerusalem, and suffer many things of the elders and chief priests and scribes, and be killed, and be raised again the third day.

Matt.17. 22 And while they abode in Galilee, Jesus said unto them, The Son of man shall be betrayed into the hands of men:

Matt.20. 18 Behold, we go up to Jerusalem; and the Son of man shall be betrayed unto the chief priests and unto the scribes, and they shall condemn him to death.

Mark 8. 31 And he began to teach them, that the Son of man must suffer many things, and be rejected of the elders, and *of* the chief priests, and scribes, and be killed, and after three days rise again

Luke 9. 22 Saying, The Son of man must suffer many things, and be rejected of the elders and chief priests and scribes, and be slain, and be raised the third day.

Luke 18. 31 Then he took *unto him* the twelve, and said unto them, Behold, we go up to Jerusalem, and all things that are written by the prophets concerning the Son of man shall be accomplished.

Luke 24. 6 He is not here, but is risen: remember how he spake unto you when he was yet in Galilee.

16: 14–18.

14 [a]Afterward he appeared unto the eleven as they sat [1]at meat, and upbraided them with their unbelief and hardness of heart, because they believed not them which had seen him after he was risen.

G

Acts 16. 14 And a certain woman named Lydia, a seller of purple, of the city of Thyatira, which worshipped God, heard *us:* whose heart the Lord opened, that she attended unto the things which were spoken of Paul.

II Cor.4. 6 For God, who commanded the light to shine out of darkness, hath shined in our hearts, to *give* the light of the knowledge of the glory of God in the face of Jesus Christ.

H

Ps. 22. *Read entire chapter.*

Isa. 50. 6 I gave my back to the smiters, and my cheeks to them that plucked off the hair: I hid not my face from shame and spitting.

Isa. 53. 1 Who hath believed our report? and to whom is the arm of the LORD revealed?

2 For he shall grow up before him as a tender plant, and as a root out of a dry ground: he hath no form nor comeliness; and when we shall see him, *there is* no beauty that we should desire him.

3 He is despised and rejected of men; a man of sorrows, and acquainted with grief: and we hid as it were *our* faces from him; he was despised, and we esteemed him not.

4 Surely he hath borne our griefs, and carried our sorrows: yet we did esteem him stricken, smitten of God, and afflicted.

5 But he *was* wounded for our transgressions, *he was* bruised for our iniquities: the chastisement of our peace *was* upon him; and with his stripes we are healed.

Luke 24. 26 Ought not Christ to have suffered these things, and to enter into his glory?

Acts 17. 3 Opening and alleging, that Christ must needs have suffered, and risen again from the dead; and that this Jesus, whom I preach unto you, is Christ.

ABSENT. Time, Sunday Evening, April 9 [Nisan 17], A. D. 30; Place, Jerusalem.
of the Week succeeding our Lord's Fourth and Last Passover.

24: 36–49.

36 And as they thus spake, Jesus himself stood in the midst of them, and saith unto them, Peace *be* unto you.

37 But they were terrified and affrighted, and supposed that they had seen [b]a spirit.

38 And he said unto them, Why are ye troubled? and why do thoughts arise in your hearts?

39 Behold my hands and my feet, that it is I myself: handle me, and see; for a spirit hath not flesh and bones, as ye see me have.

40 And when he had thus spoken, he showed them *his* hands and *his* feet.

41 And while they yet believed not [c]for joy, and wondered, he said unto them, [d]Have ye here any meat?

42 And they gave him a piece of a broiled fish, and of a honeycomb.

43 [e]And he took *it*, and did eat before them.

44 And he said unto them, [f]These *are* the words which I spake unto you, while I was yet with you, that all things must be fulfilled, which were written in the law of Moses, and *in* the prophets, and *in* the psalms, concerning me.

45 Then [g]opened he their understanding, that they might understand the Scriptures,

46 And said unto them, [h]Thus it is written, and thus it behooved Christ to suffer, and to rise from the dead the third day:

47 And that repentance and [i]remission of sins should be preached in his name [k]among all nations, beginning at Jerusalem.

20: 19–23.

19 Then the same day at evening, being the first *day* of the week, when the doors were shut where the disciples were assembled for fear of the Jews, came Jesus and stood in the midst, and saith unto them, Peace *be* unto you.

20 And when he had so said, he [l]showed unto them *his* hands and his side. [m]Then were the disciples glad, when they saw the Lord.

I

Dan. 9. 24 Seventy weeks are determined upon thy people, and upon thy holy city, to finish the transgression, and to make an end of sins, and to make reconciliation for iniquity, and to bring in everlasting righteousness, and to seal up the vision and prophecy, and to anoint the Most Holy.

Acts 13. 38 Be it known unto you therefore, men *and* brethren, that through this man is preached unto you the forgiveness of sins:

Acts 13. 46 Then Paul and Barnabas waxed bold, and said, It was necessary that the word of God should first have been spoken to you: but seeing ye put it from you, and judge yourselves unworthy of everlasting life, lo, we turn to the Gentiles.

I Jno. 2. 12 I write unto you, little children, because your sins are forgiven you for his name's sake.

K

Gen. 12. 3 And I will bless them that bless thee, and curse him that curseth thee: and in thee shall all families of the earth be blessed.

Ps. 22. 27 All the ends of the world shall remember and turn unto the Lord: and all the kindreds of the nations shall worship before thee.

Isa. 49. 6 And he said, It is a light thing that thou shouldest be my servant to raise up the tribes of Jacob, and to restore the preserved of Israel: I will also give thee for a light to the Gentiles, that thou mayest be my salvation unto the end of the earth.

Isa. 49. 22 Thus saith the Lord God, Behold, I will lift up mine hand to the Gentiles, and set up my standard to the

For K concluded, L and M see next page (612).

§ 219. JESUS APPEARS IN THE MIDST OF THE APOSTLES, THOMAS ABSENT

Evening following the First Day (i. e., introducing the Second Day)

K—CONCLUDED. See preceding page (611).

people: and they shall bring thy sons in *their* arms, and thy daughters shall be carried upon *their* shoulders.

Jer. 31. 34 And they shall teach no more every man his neighbour, and every man his brother, saying, Know the LORD: for they shall all know me, from the least of them unto the greatest of them, saith the LORD: for I will forgive their iniquity, and I will remember their sin no more.

Hos. 2. 23 And I will sow her unto me in the earth; and I will have mercy upon her that had not obtained mercy; and I will say to *them which were* not my people, Thou *art* my people; and they shall say, *Thou art* my God.

Mic. 4. 2 And many nations shall come, and say, Come, and let us go up to the mountain of the LORD, and to the house of the God of Jacob; and he will teach us of his ways, and we will walk in his paths: for the law shall go forth of Zion, and the word of the LORD from Jerusalem.

Mal. 1. 11 For, from the rising of the sun even unto the going down of the same, my name *shall be* great among the Gentiles; and in every place incense *shall be* offered unto my name, and a pure offering: for my name *shall be* great among the heathen, saith the LORD of hosts.

Gal. 3. 28 There is neither Jew nor Greek, there is neither bond nor free, there is neither male nor female: for ye are all one in Christ Jesus.

L

I Jno. 1 1 That which was from the beginning, which we have heard, which we have seen with our eyes, which we have looked upon, and our hands have handled, of the Word of life:

M

John 16. 22 And ye now therefore have sorrow: but I will see you again, and your heart shall rejoice, and your joy no man taketh from you.

N

Matt.28. 19 Go ye therefore, and teach all nations, baptizing them in the name of the Father, and of the Son, and of the Holy Ghost:

John 15. 16 Ye have not chosen me, but I have chosen you, and ordained you, that ye should go and bring forth fruit, and *that* your fruit should remain; that whatsoever ye shall ask of

CHAP. 16.

15 [n]And he said unto them, Go ye into all the world, [o]and preach the gospel to every creature.

16 [p]He that believeth and is baptized shall be saved; [q]but he that believeth not shall be damned.

17 And these signs shall follow them that believe; [r]In my name shall they cast out devils; [s]they shall speak with new tongues;

N—CONCLUDED.

the Father in my name, he may give it you.

O

Col. 1. 23 If ye continue in the faith grounded and settled, and *be* not moved away from the hope of the gospel, which ye have heard, *and* which was preached to every creature which is under heaven; whereof I Paul am made a minister;

P

John 3. 18 He that believeth on him is not condemned: but he that believeth not is condemned already, because he hath not believed in the name of the only begotten Son of God.

John 3. 36 He that believeth on the Son hath everlasting life: and he that believeth not the Son shall not see life; but the wrath of God abideth on him.

Acts 2. 38 Then Peter said unto them, Repent, and be baptized every one of you in the name of Jesus Christ for the remission of sins, and ye shall receive the gift of the Holy Ghost.

Acts 16. 30 And brought them out, and said, Sirs, what must I do to be saved?

31 And they said, Believe on the Lord Jesus Christ, and thou shalt be saved, and thy house.

32 And they spake unto him the word of the Lord, and to all that were in his house.

Rom.10. 9 That if thou shalt confess with thy mouth the Lord Jesus, and shalt believe in thine heart that God hath raised him from the dead, thou shalt be saved.

I Pet. 3. 21 The like figure whereunto *even* baptism doth also now save us, (not the putting away of the filth of the flesh, but the answer of a good con-

(CONTINUED). TIME, SUNDAY EVENING, APRIL 9 [NISAN 17], A. D. 30; PLACE, JERUSALEM.
of the Week succeeding our Lord's Fourth and Last Passover.

CHAP. 24.

48 And [t]ye are witnesses of these things.

49 [u]And, behold, I send the promise of my Father upon you: but tarry ye in the city of Jerusalem, until ye be endued with power from on high.

(p. 625.)

P—CONCLUDED.

science toward God,) by the resurrection of Jesus Christ:

Q

John 12. 48 He that rejecteth me, and receiveth not my words, hath one that judgeth him: the word that I have spoken, the same shall judge him in the last day.

R

Luke 10. 17 And the seventy returned again with joy, saying, Lord, even the devils are subject unto us through thy name.

Acts 5. 16 There came also a multitude *out* of the cities round about unto Jerusalem, bringing sick folks, and them which were vexed with unclean spirits: and they were healed every one.

Acts 8. 7 For unclean spirits, crying with loud voice, came out of many that were possessed *with them:* and many taken with palsies, and that were lame, were healed.

Acts 16. 18 And this did she many days. But Paul, being grieved, turned and said to the spirit, I command thee in the name of Jesus Christ to come out of her. And he came out the same hour.

Acts 19. 12 So that from his body were brought unto the sick handkerchiefs or aprons, and the diseases departed from them, and the evil spirits went out of them.

S

Acts 2. 4 And they were all filled with the Holy Ghost, and began to speak with other tongues, as the Spirit gave them utterance.

Acts 10. 46 For they heard them speak with tongues, and magnify God. Then answered Peter,

Acts 19. 6 And when Paul had laid *his* hands upon them, the Holy Ghost came on them; and they spake with tongues, and prophesied.

I Cor. 12. 10 To another the working of miracles; to another prophecy; to another discerning of spirits; to another *divers* kinds of tongues; to another the interpretation of tongues:

CHAP. 20.

21 Then said Jesus to them again, Peace *be* unto you: [x]as *my* Father hath sent me, even so send I you.

S—CONCLUDED.

I Cor. 12. 28 And God hath set some in the church, first apostles, secondarily prophets, thirdly teachers, after that miracles, then gifts of healings, helps, governments, diversities of tongues.

T

John 15. 27 And ye also shall bear witness, because ye have been with me from the beginning.

Acts 1. 8 But ye shall receive power, after that the Holy Ghost is come upon you: and ye shall be witnesses unto me both in Jerusalem, and in all Judæa, and in Samaria, and unto the uttermost part of the earth.

Acts 1. 22 Beginning from the baptism of John, unto that same day that he was taken up from us, must one be ordained to be a witness with us of his resurrection.

Acts 2. 32 This Jesus hath God raised up, whereof we all are witnesses.

Acts 3. 15 And killed the Prince of life, whom God hath raised from the dead; whereof we are witnesses.

U

Isa. 44. 3 For I will pour water upon him that is thirsty, and floods upon the dry ground: I will pour my Spirit upon thy seed, and my blessing upon thine offspring:

Joel 2. 28 And it shall come to pass afterward, *that* I will pour out my Spirit upon all flesh; and your sons and your daughters shall prophesy, your old men shall dream dreams, your young men shall see visions:

John 14. 16 And I will pray the Father, and he shall give you another Comforter, that he may abide with you for ever;

John 14. 26 But the Comforter, *which is* the Holy Ghost, whom the Father will send in my name, he shall teach you all things, and bring all things to your remembrance, whatsoever I have said unto you.

John 15. 26 But when the Comforter is come, whom I will send unto you from the Father, *even* the Spirit of truth, which proceedeth from the Father, he shall testify of me:

For U conclu'd and X see following pages (614, 615).

§ 219. JESUS APPEARS IN THE MIDST OF THE APOSTLES, THOMAS ABSENT

Evening following the First Day (i. e., introducing the Second Day)

U—Concluded. See preceding page (613).

John 16. 7 Nevertheless I tell you the truth; It is expedient for you that I go away: for if I go not away, the Comforter will not come unto you; but if I depart, I will send him unto you.

Acts 1. 4 And, being assembled together with *them*, commanded them that they should not depart from Jerusalem, but wait for the promise of the Father, which, *saith he*, ye have heard of me.

Acts 2. 1 And when the day of Pentecost was fully come, they were all with one accord in one place.

2 And suddenly there came a sound from heaven as of a rushing mighty wind, and it filled all the house where they were sitting.

3 And there appeared unto them cloven tongues like as of fire, and it sat upon each of them.

4 And they were all filled with the Holy Ghost, and began to speak with other tongues, as the Spirit gave them utterance.

X

Isa. 11. 2 And the Spirit of the LORD shall rest upon him, the spirit of wisdom and understanding, the spirit of counsel and might, the spirit of knowledge and of the fear of the LORD:

CHAP. 16.

18 [y]They shall take up serpents; and if they drink any deadly thing, it shall not hurt them; [z]they shall lay hands on the sick, and they shall recover.
(p. 624.)

X—Continued.

Isa. 61. 1 The Spirit of the Lord GOD *is* upon me; because the LORD hath anointed me to preach good tidings unto the meek; he hath sent me to bind up the brokenhearted, to proclaim liberty to the captives, and the opening of the prison to *them that are* bound;

Matt. 28. 18 And Jesus came and spake unto them, saying, All power is given unto me in heaven and in earth.

John 17. 18 As thou hast sent me into the world, even so have I also sent them into the world.

19 And for their sakes I sanctify myself, that they also might be sanctified through the truth.

II Tim. 2. 2 And the things that thou hast heard of me among many witnesses, the same commit thou to faithful men, who shall be able to teach others also.

Heb. 3. 1 Wherefore, holy brethren, partakers of the heavenly calling, consider

§ 220. JESUS APPEARS IN THE MIDST OF THE APOSTLES, THOMAS

Evening following the First Day (i. e., introducing the Second

A

Matt. 10. 3 Philip, and Bartholomew; Thomas, and Matthew the publican; James *the son* of Alpheus, and Lebbeus, whose surname was Thaddeus;

John 11. 16 Then said Thomas, which is called Didymus, unto his fellow disciples, Let us also go, that we may die with him.

B

Isa. 9. 7 Of the increase of *his* government and peace *there shall be* no end, upon the throne of David, and upon his kingdom, to order it, and to establish it with judgment and with justice from henceforth even for ever. The zeal of the LORD of hosts will perform this.

Mic. 5. 5 And this *man* shall be the peace, when the Assyrian shall come into our land: and when he shall tread in our palaces, then shall we raise against him seven shepherds, and eight principal men.

6 And they shall waste the land of Assyria with the sword, and the land

B—Concluded.

of Nimrod in the entrances thereof: thus shall he deliver *us* from the Assyrian, when he cometh into our land, and when he treadeth within our borders.

7 And the remnant of Jacob shall be in the midst of many people as a dew from the LORD, as the showers upon the grass, that tarrieth not for man, nor waiteth for the sons of men.

Col. 1. 20 And, having made peace through the blood of his cross, by him to reconcile all things unto himself; by him, *I say*, whether *they be* things in earth, or things in heaven.

C

Ps. 78. 37 For their heart was not right with him, neither were they steadfast in his covenant.

38 But he, *being* full of compassion, forgave *their* iniquity, and destroyed *them* not: yea, many a time turned he his anger away, and did not stir up all his wrath

(CONCLUDED). TIME, SUNDAY EVENING, APRIL 9 [NISAN 17], A. D. 30; PLACE, JERUSALEM.
of the Week succeeding our Lord's Fourth and Last Passover.

[CHAP. 24.]

X—CONCLUDED.

the Apostle and High Priest of our profession, Christ Jesus;

Y

Luke 10. 19 Behold, I give unto you power to tread on serpents and scorpions, and over all the power of the enemy; and nothing shall by any means hurt you.

Acts 28. 5 And he shook off the beast into the fire, and felt no harm.

Z

Acts 5. 15 Insomuch that they brought forth the sick into the streets, and laid *them* on beds and couches, that at the least the shadow of Peter passing by might overshadow some of them.

Acts 5. 16. *See under R, page 613.*

Acts 9. 17 And Ananias went his way, and entered into the house; and putting his hands on him said, Brother Saul, the Lord, *even* Jesus, that appeared unto thee in the way as thou camest, hath sent me, that thou mightest receive thy sight, and be filled with the Holy Ghost.

Acts 28. 8 And it came to pass, that the father of Publius lay sick of a fever and of a bloody flux: to whom Paul entered in, and prayed, and laid his hands on him, and healed him.

CHAP. 20.

22 And when he had said this, he
breathed on *them*, and saith unto them,
Receive ye the Holy Ghost:

23 [a]Whosesoever sins ye remit, they
are remitted unto them; *and* whosesoever *sins* ye retain, they are retained.

Z—CONCLUDED.

Jas. 5. 14 Is any sick among you? let him call for the elders of the church; and let them pray over him, anointing him with oil in the name of the Lord:

15 And the prayer of faith shall save the sick, and the Lord shall raise him up; and if he have committed sins, they shall be forgiven him.

A

Matt.16. 19 And I will give unto thee the keys of the kingdom of heaven: and whatsoever thou shalt bind on earth shall be bound in heaven; and whatsoever thou shalt loose on earth shall be loosed in heaven.

Matt.18. 18 Verily I say unto you, Whatsoever ye shall bind on earth shall be bound in heaven; and whatsoever ye shall loose on earth shall be loosed in heaven.

BEING PRESENT. TIME, SUNDAY EVENING, APRIL 16, A. D. 30; PLACE, JERUSALEM.
Day) of the Week; Seven Days after the Resurrection.

C—CONCLUDED.

Ps. 103. 13 Like as a father pitieth *his* children, *so* the LORD pitieth them that fear him.

14 For he knoweth our frame; he remembereth that we *are* dust.

I Jno. 1. 1 That which was from the beginning, which we have heard, which we have seen with our eyes, which we have looked upon, and our hands have handled, of the Word of life;

D

Ps. 45. 6 Thy throne, O God, *is* for ever and ever: the sceptre of thy kingdom *is* a right sceptre.

7 Thou lovest righteousness, and hatest wickedness: therefore God, thy God, hath anointed thee with the oil of gladness above thy fellows.

8 All thy garments *smell* of myrrh, and aloes, *and* cassia, out of the ivory palaces, whereby they have made thee glad.

9 King's daughters *were* among thy

For D concluded see following pages (616, 617).

20: 24–29.

24 [a]But Thomas, one of the twelve, called Didymus, was not with them when Jesus came.

25 The other disciples therefore said unto him, We have seen the Lord. But he said unto them, Except I shall see in his hands the print of the nails, and put my finger into the print of the nails, and thrust my hand into his side, I will not believe.

26 And after eight days again his disciples were within, and Thomas with them: *then* came Jesus, the doors being shut, and stood in the midst, and said, [b]Peace *be* unto you.

§ 220. JESUS APPEARS IN THE MIDST OF THE APOSTLES, THOMAS BEING

Evening following the First Day (i. e., introducing the Second

For C and D see preceding pages (614, 615).

D—CONTINUED.

honourable women: upon thy right hand did stand the queen in gold of Ophir.

10 Hearken, O daughter, and consider, and incline thine ear; forget also thine own people, and thy father's house;

11 So shall the King greatly desire thy beauty: for he *is* thy Lord; and worship thou him.

Ps. 73. 26 My flesh and my heart faileth: *but* God *is* the strength of my heart, and my portion for ever.

27 For, lo, they that are far from thee shall perish: thou hast destroyed all them that go a whoring from thee.

28 But *it is* good for me to draw near to God: I have put my trust in the Lord GOD, that I may declare all thy works.

Ps. 91. 2 I will say of the LORD, *He is* my

D—CONTINUED.

refuge and my fortress: my God; in him will I trust.

Ps. 102. 24 I said, O my God, take me not away in the midst of my days: thy years *are* throughout all generations.

25 Of old hast thou laid the foundation of the earth: and the heavens *are* the work of thy hands.

26 They shall perish, but thou shalt endure: yea, all of them shall wax old like a garment; as a vesture shalt thou change them, and they shall be changed:

27 But thou *art* the same, and thy years shall have no end.

28 The children of thy servants shall continue, and their seed shall be established before thee.

Ps. 118. 27 God *is* the LORD, which hath showed us light: bind the sacrifice with cords, *even* unto the horns of the altar.

§ 221. JESUS APPEARS TO SEVEN APOSTLES AT THE SEA OF TIBERIAS.

28 : 16.

16 Then the eleven disciples went away into Galilee, into a mountain where Jesus had appointed them. p. 622.

A

John 1. 45 Philip findeth Nathanael and saith unto him, We have found him, of whom Moses in the law, and the prophets, did write, Jesus of Nazareth, the son of Joseph.

B

Matt. 4. 21 And going on from thence, he saw other two brethren, James *the son* of Zebedee, and John his brother, in a ship with Zebedee their father, mending their nets; and he called them.

C

II Ki. 6. 1 And the sons of the prophets said unto Elisha, Behold now, the place where we dwell with thee is too strait for us.

2 Let us go, we pray thee, unto Jordan, and take thence every man a beam, and let us make us a place there, where we may dwell. And he answered, Go ye.

3 And one said, Be content, I pray thee, and go with thy servants. And he answered, I will go.

4 So he went with them. And when they came to Jordan, they cut down wood.

C—CONTINUED.

II Ki. 6. 5 But as one was felling a beam, the axe head fell into the water: and he cried, and said, Alas, master! for it was borrowed.

6 And the man of God said, Where fell it? And he showed him the place. And he cut down a stick, and cast *it* in thither; and the iron did swim.

7 Therefore said he, Take *it* up to thee. And he put out his hand, and took it.

Luke 5. 10 And so *was* also James, and John, the sons of Zebedee, which were partners with Simon. And Jesus said unto Simon, Fear not; from henceforth thou shalt catch men.

11 And when they had brought their ships to land, they forsook all, and followed him.

Acts 18. 3 And because he was of the same craft, he abode with them, and wrought: (for by their occupation they were tentmakers.)

Acts 20. 34 Yea, ye yourselves know, that these hands have ministered unto my necessities, and to them that were with me.

I Cor. 9. 6 Or I only and Barnabas, have not we power to forbear working?

I Thes. 2. 9 For ye remember, brethren, our labour and travail: for labouring night and day, because we would not

PRESENT (CONCL'D). TIME, SUNDAY EVENING, APRIL 16, A. D. 30; PLACE, JERUSALEM.
Day) of the Week; Seven Days after the Resurrection.

D—CONCLUDED.

Ps. 118. 28 Thou *art* my God, and I will praise thee: *thou art* my God, I will exalt thee.

Luke 1. 46 And Mary said, My soul doth magnify the Lord,

47 And my spirit hath rejoiced in God my Saviour.

I Tim.1. 17 Now unto the King eternal, immortal, invisible, the only wise God, *be* honour and glory for ever and ever. Amen.

E

II Cor.5. 7 (For we walk by faith, not by sight:)

8 We are confident, *I say*, and willing rather to be absent from the body, and to be present with the Lord.

9 Wherefore we labour, that, whether present or absent, we may be accepted of him.

I Pet. 1. 8 Whom having not seen, ye love; in whom, though now ye see *him* not,

E—CONCLUDED.

yet believing, ye rejoice with joy unspeakable and full of glory:

Heb. 11. *Read entire chapter.*

CHAP. 20.

27 Then saith he to Thomas, Reach
hither thy finger, and behold my hands;
and [c]reach hither thy hand, and thrust
it into my side; and be not faithless,
but believing.

28 And Thomas answered and said
unto him, [d]My Lord and My God.

29 Jesus saith unto him, Thomas, because thou hast seen me, thou hast
believed: [e]blessed *are* they that have
not seen, and *yet* have believed. (p. 625.)

TIME, APRIL–MAY, A. D. 30; PLACE, GALILEE.

C—CONCLUDED.

be chargeable unto any of you, we preached unto you the gospel of God.

II Thes.3. 7 For yourselves know how ye ought to follow us: for we behaved not ourselves disorderly among you;

8 Neither did we eat any man's bread for nought; but wrought with labour and travail night and day, that we might not be chargeable to any of you:

9 Not because we have not power, but to make ourselves an ensample unto you to follow us.

D

John 20. 14 And when she had thus said, she turned herself back, and saw Jesus standing, and knew not that it was Jesus.

E

Luke 24. 41 And while they yet believed not for joy, and wondered, he said unto them, Have ye here any meat?

1

Or, *Sirs.*

F

Ps. 37. 3 Trust in the LORD, and do good; *so* shalt thou dwell in the land, and verily thou shalt be fed.

Phil. 4. 11 Not that I speak in respect of want: for I have learned, in whatsoever state I am, *therewith* to be content.

12 I know both how to be abased,

For F concluded and G see next page (618).

21: 1–24.

1 After these things Jesus showed
himself again to the disciples at the sea
of Tiberias; and on this wise showed
he *himself*.

2 There were together Simon Peter,
and Thomas called Didymus, and [a]Na-
thanael of Cana in Galilee, and [b]the
sons of Zebedee, and two other of his
disciples.

3 Simon Peter saith unto them, [c]I go
a fishing. They say unto him, We also
go with thee. They went forth, and
entered into a ship immediately; and
that night they caught nothing.

4 But when the morning was now
come, Jesus stood on the shore; but the
disciples [d]knew not that it was Jesus.

5 Then [e]Jesus saith unto them, [1]Chil-
dren, [f]have ye any meat? They
answered him, No.

6 And he said unto them, [g]Cast the
net on the right side of the ship, and

§ 221. JESUS APPEARS TO SEVEN APOSTLES AT THE SEA OF TIBERIAS

[CHAP. 28.]

F—CONCLUDED. See preceding page (617).

and I know how to abound: every where and in all things I am instructed both to be full and to be hungry, both to abound and to suffer need.

G

Luke 5. 4 Now when he had left speaking,
he said unto Simon, Launch out into
the deep, and let down your nets for a
draught.
5 And Simon answering said unto
him, Master, we have toiled all the
night, and have taken nothing: nevertheless at thy word I will let down the
net.
6 And when they had this done, they
inclosed a great multitude of fishes:
and their net brake.
7 And they beckoned unto *their* partners, which were in the other ship,
that they should come and help them.
And they came, and filled both the
ships, so that they began to sink.

H

Ps. 8. 3 When I consider thy heavens, the
work of thy fingers, the moon and he
stars, which thou hast ordained;
4 What is man, that thou art mindful of him? and the son of man, that
thou visitest him?
5 For thou hast made him a little
lower than the angels, and hast crowned him with glory and honour.
6 Thou madest him to have dominion
over the works of thy hands; thou
hast put all *things* under his feet:
7 All sheep and oxen, yea, and the
beasts of the field;
8 The fowl of the air, and the fish
of the sea, *and whatsoever* passeth
through the paths of the seas.

Heb. 2. 6 But one in a certain place testified,
saying, What is man, that thou art
mindful of him? or the son of man,
that thou visitest him?
7 Thou madest him a little lower
than the angels; thou crownedst him
with glory and honour, and didst set
him over the works of thy hands:
8 Thou hast put all things in subjection under his feet. For in that he
put all in subjection under him, he
left nothing *that is* not put under him.
But now we see not yet all things put
under him.
9 But we see Jesus, who was made a
little lower than the angels for the
suffering of death, crowned with glory

H—CONCLUDED.

and honour; that he by the grace of God should taste death for every man.

I

John 13. 23 Now there was leaning on Jesus' bosom one of his disciples, whom Jesus loved.

John 20. 2 Then she runneth, and cometh to Simon Peter, and to the other disciple, whom Jesus loved, and saith unto them, They have taken away the Lord out of the sepulchre, and we know not where they have laid him.

K

Song 8. 7 Many waters cannot quench love, neither can the floods drown it: if a man would give all the substance of his house for love, it would utterly be contemned.

L

I Ki. 19. 6 And he looked, and, behold, *there was* a cake baken on the coals, and a cruse of water at his head. And he did eat and drink, and laid him down again.

M

Acts 10. 41 Not to all the people, but unto witnesses chosen before of God, *even* to us, who did eat and drink with him after he rose from the dead.

N

John 20. 19 Then the same day at evening being the first *day* of the week, when the doors were shut where the disciples were assembled for fear of the Jews, came Jesus and stood in the midst, and saith unto them, Peace *be* unto you.

John 20. 26 And after eight days again his disciples were within, and Thomas with them: *then* came Jesus, the doors being shut, and stood in the midst, and said, Peace *be* unto you.

O

Matt. 26. 33 Peter answered and said unto him, Though all *men* shall be offended because of thee, *yet* will I never be offended.

P

II Ki. 20. 3 I beseech thee, O LORD, remember now how I have walked before thee in truth and with a perfect heart, and have done *that which is* good in thy sight. And Hezekiah wept sore.

Q

Ps. 78. 70 He chose David also his servant,
and took him from the sheepfolds:
71 From following the ewes great
with young he brought him to feed Jacob his people, and Israel his inheritance.

(CONTINUED). TIME, APRIL–MAY, A. D. 30; PLACE, GALILEE.

Q—CONTINUED.

Ps. 78. 72 So he fed them according to the integrity of his heart; and guided them by the skilfulness of his hands.

Jer. 3. 15 And I will give you pastors according to mine heart, which shall feed you with knowledge and understanding.

Jer. 23. 4 And I will set up shepherds over them which shall feed them: and they shall fear no more, nor be dismayed, neither shall they be lacking, saith the LORD.

Eze. 34. 2 Son of man, prophesy against the shepherds of Israel, prophesy, and say unto them, Thus saith the Lord GOD unto the shepherds; Woe *be* to the shepherds of Israel that do feed themselves! should not the shepherds feed the flocks?

3 Ye eat the fat, and ye clothe you with the wool, ye kill them that are fed: *but* ye feed not the flock.

4 The diseased have ye not strengthened, neither have ye healed that which was sick, neither have ye bound up *that which was* broken, neither have ye brought again that which was driven away, neither have ye sought that which was lost; but with force and with cruelty have ye ruled them.

5 And they were scattered, because *there is* no shepherd: and they became meat to all the beasts of the field, when they were scattered.

6 My sheep wandered through all the mountains, and upon every high hill: yea, my flock was scattered upon all the face of the earth, and none did search or seek *after them.*

7 Therefore, ye shepherds, hear the word of the LORD;

8 *As* I live, saith the Lord GOD, surely because my flock became a prey, and my flock became meat to every beast of the field, because *there was* no shepherd, neither did my shepherds search for my flock, but the shepherds fed themselves, and fed not my flock;

9 Therefore, O ye shepherds, hear the word of the LORD;

10 Thus saith the Lord GOD; Behold, I *am* against the shepherds; and I will require my flock at their hand, and cause them to cease from feeding the flock; neither shall the shepherds feed themselves any more; for I will deliver my flock from their mouth, that they may not be meat for them.

For Q concluded see next page (620).

CHAP. 21.

ye shall find. [h]They cast therefore, and now they were not able to draw it for the multitude of fishes.

7 Therefore [i]that disciple whom Jesus loved saith unto Peter, It is the Lord. Now when Simon Peter heard that it was the Lord, he girt *his* fisher's coat *unto him,* (for he was naked,) and [k]did cast himself into the sea.

8 And the other disciples came in a little ship, (for they were not far from land, but as it were two hundred cubits,) dragging the net with fishes.

9 As soon then as they were come to land, they saw a [l]fire of coals there, and fish laid thereon, and bread.

10 Jesus saith unto them, Bring of the fish which ye have now caught.

11 Simon Peter went up, and drew the net to land full of great fishes, a hundred and fifty and three: and for all there were so many, yet was not the net broken.

12 Jesus saith unto them, [m]Come *and* dine. And none of the disciples durst ask him, Who art thou? knowing that it was the Lord.

13 Jesus then cometh, and taketh bread, and giveth them, and fish likewise.

14 This is now [n]the third time that Jesus showed himself to his disciples, after that he was risen from the dead.

15 So when they had dined, Jesus saith to Simon Peter, Simon, *son* of Jonas, lovest thou me [o]more than these? He saith unto him, Yea, Lord; [p]thou knowest that I love thee. He saith unto him, [q]Feed my lambs.

§ 221. JESUS APPEARS TO SEVEN APOSTLES AT THE SEA OF TIBERIAS

[Chap. 28.]

Q—Concluded.

See preceding pages (618, 619).

Eze. 34. 23 And I will set up one Shepherd over them, and he shall feed them, *even* my servant David; he shall feed them, and he shall be their shepherd.

Acts 20. 28 Take heed therefore unto yourselves, and to all the flock, over the which the Holy Ghost hath made you overseers, to feed the church of God, which he hath purchased with his own blood.

I Tim.4. 15 Meditate upon these things; give thyself wholly to them; that thy profiting may appear to all.

16 Take heed unto thyself, and unto the doctrine; continue in them: for in doing this thou shalt both save thyself, and them that hear thee.

Heb. 13. 20 Now the God of peace, that brought again from the dead our Lord Jesus, that great Shepherd of the sheep, through the blood of the everlasting covenant,

I Pet. 2. 25 For ye were as sheep going astray; but are now returned unto the Shepherd and Bishop of your souls.

I Pet. 5. 1 The elders which are among you I exhort, who am also an elder, and a witness of the sufferings of Christ, and also a partaker of the glory that shall be revealed:

2 Feed the flock of God which is among you, taking the oversight *thereof*, not by constraint, but willingly; not for filthy lucre, but of a ready mind;

3 Neither as being lords over *God's* heritage, but being ensamples to the flock.

4 And when the chief Shepherd shall appear, ye shall receive a crown of glory that fadeth not away.

R

John 13. 38 Jesus answered him, Wilt thou lay down thy life for my sake? Verily, verily, I say unto thee, The cock shall not crow, till thou hast denied me thrice.

S

John 2. 24 But Jesus did dot commit himself unto them, because he knew all *men*,

25 And needed not that any should testify of man; for he knew what was in man.

John 16. 30 Now are we sure that thou knowest all things, and needest not that any man should ask thee: by this we believe that thou camest forth from God.

Acts 1. 24 And they prayed, and said, Thou,

S—Concluded.

Lord, which knowest the hearts of all *men*, show whether of these two thou hast chosen,

I Thes.2. 4 But as we were allowed of God to be put in trust with the gospel, even so we speak; not as pleasing men, but God, which trieth our hearts.

T

Ps. 95. 7 For he *is* our God; and we *are* the people of his pasture, and the sheep of his hand. To day if ye will hear his voice,

Ps. 100. 3 Know ye that the Lord he *is* God: *it is* he *that* hath made us, and not we ourselves; *we are* his people, and the sheep of his pasture.

Zech.13. 7 Awake, O sword, against my Shepherd, and against the man *that is* my fellow, saith the Lord of hosts: smite the Shepherd, and the sheep shall be scattered: and I will turn mine hand upon the little ones.

U

John 13. 36 Simon Peter said unto him, Lord, whither goest thou? Jesus answered him, Whither I go, thou canst not follow me now; but thou shalt follow me afterwards.

Acts 12. 3 And because he saw it pleased the Jews, he proceeded further to take Peter also. (Then were the days of unleavened bread.)

4 And when he had apprehended him, he put *him* in prison, and delivered *him* to four quaternions of soldiers to keep him; intending after Easter to bring him forth to the people.

X

Phil. 1. 20 According to my earnest expectation and *my* hope, that in nothing I shall be ashamed, but *that* with all boldness, as always, *so* now also Christ shall be magnified in my body, whether *it be* by life, or by death.

I Pet. 4. 11 If any man speak, *let him speak* as the oracles of God; if any man minister, *let him do it* as of the ability which God giveth; that God in all things may be glorified through Jesus Christ: to whom be praise and dominion for ever and ever. Amen.

12 Beloved, think it not strange concerning the fiery trial which is to try you, as though some strange thing happened unto you:

13 But rejoice, inasmuch as ye are partakers of Christ's sufferings; that, when his glory shall be revealed, ye may be glad also with exceeding joy.

CONTINUED). TIME, APRIL–MAY, A. D. 30; PLACE, GALILEE.

X—CONCLUDED.

I Pet. 4. 14 If ye be reproached for the name of Christ, happy *are ye;* for the Spirit of glory and of God resteth upon you: on their part he is evil spoken of, but on your part he is glorified.

II Pet.1. 14 Knowing that shortly I must put off *this* my tabernacle, even as our Lord Jesus Christ hath showed me.

Y

John 13. 23 and John 20. 2. *See under I, page 618.*

John 13. 25 He then lying on Jesus' breast saith unto him, Lord, who is it?

Z

Acts 1. 6 When they therefore were come together, they asked of him, saying, Lord, wilt thou at this time restore again the kingdom to Israel?

A

Matt.16. 27 For the Son of man shall come in the glory of his Father with his angels; and then he shall reward every man according to his works.

28 Verily I say unto you, There be some standing here, which shall not taste of death, till they see the Son of man coming in his kingdom.

Matt.25. 31 When the Son of man shall come in his glory, and all the holy angels with him, then shall he sit upon the throne of his glory:

I Cor. 4. 5 Therefore judge nothing before the time, until the Lord come, who both will bring to light the hidden things of darkness, and will make manifest the counsels of the hearts: and then shall every man have praise of God.

I Cor.11. 26 For as often as ye eat this bread, and drink this cup, ye do show the Lord's death till he come.

Rev. 2. 25 But that which ye have *already,* hold fast till I come.

Rev. 3. 11 Behold, I come quickly: hold that fast which thou hast, that no man take thy crown.

Rev. 22. 7 Behold, I come quickly: blessed *is* he that keepeth the sayings of the prophecy of this book.

Rev. 22. 20 He which testifieth these things saith, Surely I come quickly: Amen. Even so, come, Lord Jesus.

B

Deut.29. 29 The secret *things belong* unto the LORD our God: but those *things which are* revealed *belong* unto us and to our children for ever, that *we* may do all the words of this law.

Job 28. 28 And unto man he said, Behold, the fear of the Lord, that *is* wisdom;

For b concluded see next page (622).

CHAP. 21.

16 He saith to him again the second
time, Simon, *son* of Jonas, lovest thou
me? He saith unto him, Yea, Lord;
thou knowest that I love thee. He
saith unto him, Feed my sheep.

17 He saith unto him the [r]third time,
Simon, *son* of Jonas, lovest thou me?
Peter was grieved because he said unto
him the third time, Lovest thou me?
And he said unto him, Lord, [s]thou
knowest all things; thou knowest that
I love thee. Jesus saith unto him,
Feed [t]my sheep.

18 [u]Verily, verily, I say unto thee,
When thou wast young, thou girdedst
thyself, and walkedst whither thou
wouldest: but when thou shalt be old,
thou shalt stretch forth thy hands, and
another shall gird thee, and carry *thee*
whither thou wouldest not.

19 This spake he, [x]signifying by what
death he should glorify God. And
when he had spoken this, he saith unto
him, Follow me.

20 Then Peter, turning about, seeth
the disciple [y]whom Jesus loved following; which also leaned on his breast at
supper, and said, Lord, which is he that
betrayeth thee?

21 Peter seeing him saith to Jesus,
Lord, and [z]what *shall* this man *do?*

22 Jesus saith unto him, If I will
that he tarry [a]till I come, what *is that*
to thee? follow thou me.

23 Then went this saying abroad
among the brethren, that that disciple
should not die: yet Jesus said not unto
him, He shall not die; but, If I will
that he tarry till I come, what [b]*is that*
to thee?

§ 221. JESUS APPEARS TO SEVEN APOSTLES AT THE SEA OF TIBERIAS

[CHAP. 28].

B—CONTINUED. See preceding page (621.)

and to depart from evil *is* understanding.

Job 33. 13 Why dost thou strive against him: for he giveth not account of any of his matters.

Dan. 4. 35 And all the inhabitants of the earth *are* reputed as nothing: and he doeth according to his will in the army

B—CONCLUDED.

of heaven, and *among* the inhabitants of the earth: and none can stay his hand, or say unto him, What doest thou?

C

John 19. 35 And he that saw *it* bare record, and his record is true; and he knoweth that he saith true, that ye might believe.

I Jno. 1. 1 That which was from the begin-

§ 222. JESUS MEETS THE APOSTLES AND ABOVE FIVE HUNDRED DISCIPLES

28: 16–20.

16 Then the eleven disciples went away into Galilee, into a mountain [a]where Jesus had appointed them.

17 And when they saw him, they worshipped him: but some doubted.

18 And Jesus came and spake unto them, saying, [b]All power is given unto me in heaven and in earth.

19 [c]Go ye therefore, and [d1]teach all nations, baptizing them in the name of the Father, and of the Son, and of the Holy Ghost:

20 [e]Teaching them to observe all things whatsoever I have commanded you: and, lo, I am with you alway, *even* unto the end of the world. Amen.

A

Matt. 26. 32 But after I am risen again, I will go before you into Galilee.

Matt. 28. 7 And go quickly, and tell his disciples that he is risen from the dead; and, behold, he goeth before you into Galilee; there shall ye see him: lo, I have told you.

B

I Cor. 15. 6 After that, he was seen of above

B—CONTINUED.

five hundred brethren at once; of whom the greater part remain unto this present, but some are fallen asleep.

Luke 10. 22 All things are delivered to me of my Father: and no man knoweth who the Son is, but the Father; and who the Father is, but the Son, and *he* to whom the Son will reveal *him*.

John 5. 22 For the Father judgeth no man, but hath committed all judgment unto the Son:

John 13. 3 Jesus knowing that the Father had given all things into his hands, and that he was come from God, and went to God;

John 17. 2 As thou hast given him power over all flesh, that he should give eternal life to as many as thou hast given him.

Acts 2. 36 Therefore let all the house of Israel know assuredly, that God hath made that same Jesus, whom ye have crucified, both Lord and Christ.

Rom. 14. 9 For to this end Christ both died, and rose, and revived, that he might be Lord both of the dead and living.

I Cor. 15. 27 For he hath put all things under his feet. But when he saith, All things are put under *him, it is* manifest that he is excepted, which did put all things under him.

Eph. 1. 10 That in the dispensation of the fulness of times he might gather together in one all things in Christ, both which are in heaven, and which are on earth; *even* in him:

§ 223. OUR LORD APPEARS TO JAMES, AND THEN TO ALL THE

This appearance to the Apostles is not mentioned in the Four Gospels, but is referred to

Acts. 1. 1 The former treatise have I made, O Theophilus, of all that Jesus began both to do and teach,

2 Until the day in which he was taken up, after that he through the Holy Ghost had given commandments unto the apostles whom he had chosen:

3 To whom also he showed himself alive after his passion by many infallible proofs, being seen of them forty days, and speaking of the things pertaining to the kingdom of God:

4 And, being assembled together with *them*, commanded them that they should not depart from Jerusalem, but wait for the promise of the Father, which, *saith he*, ye have heard of me.

5 For John truly baptized with wa-

(CONCLUDED). TIME, APRIL–MAY, A. D. 30; PLACE, GALILEE.

C—CONTINUED.

ning, which we have heard, which we have seen with our eyes, which we have looked upon, and our hands have handled, of the Word of life;
2 (For the life was manifested, and we have seen *it*, and bear witness, and show unto you that eternal life, which was with the Father, and was manifested unto us;)

CHAP. 21.

24 This is the disciple which testifieth of these things, and wrote these things: and [c]we know that his testimony is true.

C—CONCLUDED.

III Jno. 12 Demetrius hath good report of all *men*, and of the truth itself: yea, and we *also* bear record; and ye know that our record is true.

ON A MOUNTAIN IN GALILEE. TIME, APRIL–MAY, A. D. 30; PLACE, GALILEE.

B—CONCLUDED.

Eph. 1. 21 Far above all principality, and power, and might, and dominion, and every name that is named, not only in this world, but also in that which is to come:

Phil 2. 9 Wherefore God also hath highly exalted him, and given him a name which is above every name:
10 That at the name of Jesus every knee should bow, of *things* in heaven, and *things* in earth, and *things* under the earth;

Heb. 1. 2 Hath in these last days spoken unto us by *his* Son, whom he hath appointed heir of all things, by whom also he made the worlds;

Heb. 2. 8 Thou has put all things in subjection under his feet. For in that he put all in subjection under him, he left nothing *that is* not put under him. But now we see not yet all things put under him.

I Pet. 3. 22 Who is gone into heaven, and is on the right hand of God; angels and authorities and powers being made subject unto him.

Rev. 17. 14 These shall make war with the Lamb, and the Lamb shall overcome them: for he is Lord of lords, and King of kings: and they that are with him *are* called, and chosen, and faithful.

C

Mark 16. 15 And he said unto them, Go ye into all the world, and preach the gospel to every creature.

D

Isa. 52. 10 The LORD hath made bare his holy arm in the eyes of all the nations; and all the ends of the earth shall see the salvation of our God.

Luke 24. 47 And that repentance and remission of sins should be preached in his name among all nations, beginning at Jerusalem.

Acts 2. 38 Then Peter said unto them, Repent, and be baptized every one of you in the name of Jesus Christ for the remission of sins, and ye shall receive the gift of the Holy Ghost.
39 For the promise is unto you, and to your children, and to all that are afar off, *even* as many as the Lord our God shall call.

Rom. 10. 18 But I say, Have they not heard? Yes verily, their sound went into all the earth, and their words unto the ends of the world.

Col. 1. 23 If ye continue in the faith grounded and settled, and *be* not moved away from the hope of the gospel, which ye have heard, *and* which was preached to every creature which is under heaven; whereof I Paul am made a minister;

1

Or, *make disciples*, or, *Christians of all nations*.

E

Acts 2. 42 And they continued steadfastly in the apostles' doctrine and fellowship, and in breaking of bread, and in prayers.

APOSTLES. TIME, THURSDAY, MAY 18, A. D. 30; PLACE, JERUSALEM.
by Luke in the Acts of the Apostles, and by Paul in his First Epistle to the Corinthians.

ter; but ye shall be baptized with the Holy Ghost not many days hence.
6 When they therefore were come together, they asked of him, saying, Lord, wilt thou at this time restore again the kingdom to Israel?
7 And he said unto them, It is not for you to know the times or the seasons, which the Father hath put in his own power.
8 But ye shall receive power, after that the Holy Ghost is come upon you: and ye shall be witnesses unto me both in Jerusalem, and in all Judæa, and in Samaria, and unto the uttermost part of the earth.

I Cor. 15. 7 After that, he was seen of James; then of all the apostles.

§ 224. THE ASCENSION OF OUR LORD.

16 : 19, 20.

19 So then, [a]after the Lord had spoken unto them, he was [b]received up into heaven, and [c]sat on the right hand of God.

20 And they went forth, and preached every where, the Lord working with *them,* [d]and confirming the word with signs following. Amen.

A

Acts 1. 2 Until the day in which he was taken up, after that he through the Holy Ghost had given commandments unto the apostles whom he had chosen:

3 To whom also he showed himself alive after his passion by many infallible proofs, being seen of them forty days, and speaking of the things pertaining to the kingdom of God:

Acts 1. 9 And when he had spoken these things, while they beheld, he was taken up; and a cloud received him out of their sight.

10 And while they looked steadfastly toward heaven as he went up, behold, two men stood by them in white apparel;

11 Which also said, Ye men of Galilee, why stand ye gazing up into heaven? this same Jesus, which is taken up from you into heaven, shall so come in like manner as ye have seen him go into heaven.

B

Luke 24. 51. *See text of topic.*

C

Ps. 110. 1 The LORD said unto my Lord, Sit thou at my right hand, until I make thine enemies thy footstool.

Acts 7. 55 But he, being full of the Holy Ghost, looked up steadfastly into heaven, and saw the glory of God, and Jesus standing on the right hand of God,

C—CONCLUDED.

Rev. 3. 21 To him that overcometh will I grant to sit with me in my throne, even as I also overcame, and am set down with my Father in his throne.

D

Acts 5. 12 And by the hands of the apostles were many signs and wonders wrought among the people; (and they were all with one accord in Solomon's porch.

Acts 14. 3 Long time therefore abode they speaking boldly in the Lord, which gave testimony unto the word of his grace, and granted signs and wonders to be done by their hands.

Rom. 15. 19 Through mighty signs and wonders, by the power of the Spirit of God; so that from Jerusalem, and round about unto Illyricum, I have fully preached the gospel of Christ.

§ 225. CONCLUSION OF

A

Luke 1. 4 That thou mightest know the certainty of those things, wherein thou hast been instructed.

Rom. 15. 4 For whatsoever things were written aforetime were written for our learning, that we through patience and comfort of the Scriptures might have hope.

B

Matt. 11. 27 All things are delivered unto me of my Father: and no man knoweth the Son, but the Father; neither knoweth any man the Father, save the Son, and *he* to whomsoever the Son will reveal *him.*

John 3. 15 That whosoever believeth in him should not perish, but have eternal life.

16 For God so loved the world, that he gave his only begotten Son, that whosoever believeth in him should not perish, but have everlasting life.

John 5. 24 Verily, verily, I say unto you, He that heareth my word, and be-

B—CONCLUDED.

lieveth on him that sent me, hath everlasting life, and shall not come into condemnation; but is passed from death unto life.

I Pet. 1. 8 Whom having not seen, ye love; in whom, though now ye see *him* not, yet believing, ye rejoice with joy unspeakable and full of glory:

9 Receiving the end of your faith, *even* the salvation of *your* souls.

C

Dan. 7. 14 And there was given him dominion, and glory, and a kingdom, that all people, nations, and languages, should serve him: his dominion *is* an everlasting dominion, which shall not pass away, and his kingdom *that* which shall not be destroyed.

Luke 1. 32 He shall be great, and shall be called the Son of the Highest; and the Lord God shall give unto him the throne of his father David:

TIME, THURSDAY, MAY 18, A. D. 30; PLACE, BETHANY.

24: 50–53.

50 And he led them out [e]as far as to Bethany, and he lifted up his hands, and blessed them.

51 [f]And it came to pass, while he blessed them, he was parted from them, and carried up into heaven.

52 [g]And they worshipped him, and returned to Jerusalem with great joy:

53 And were continually [h]in the temple, praising and blessing God. Amen.

D—CONCLUDED.

I Cor. 2. 4 And my speech and my preaching *was* not with enticing words of man's wisdom, but in demonstration of the Spirit and of power:

5 That your faith should not stand in the wisdom of men, but in the power of God.

Heb. 2. 4 God also bearing *them* witness, both with signs and wonders, and with divers miracles, and gifts of the Holy Ghost, according to his own will?

E

Acts 1. 12 Then returned they unto Jerusalem from the mount called Olivet, which is from Jerusalem a sabbath day's journey.

F

II Ki. 2. 11 And it came to pass, as they still went on, and talked, that, behold, *there appeared* a chariot of fire, and horses of fire, and parted them both asunder; and Elijah went up by a whirlwind into heaven.

Mark 16. 19. *See text of topic.*

John 20. 17 Jesus saith unto her, Touch me not; for I am not yet ascended to my Father: but go to my brethren, and say unto them, I ascend unto my Father, and your Father; and *to* my God, and your God.

Acts 1. 9. *See under A.*

Eph. 4. 8 Wherefore he saith, When he ascended up on high, he led captivity captive, and gave gifts unto men.

G

Matt. 28. 9 And as they went to tell his disciples, behold, Jesus met them, saying, All hail. And they came and held him by the feet, and worshipped him.

Matt. 28. 17 And when they saw him, they worshipped him: but some doubted.

H

Acts 2. 46 And they, continuing daily with one accord in the temple, and breaking bread from house to house, did eat their meat with gladness and singleness of heart.

Acts 5. 42 And daily in the temple, and in every house, they ceased not to teach and preach Jesus Christ.

JOHN'S GOSPEL.

20: 30, 31; 21: 25.

30 And many other signs truly did Jesus in the presence of his disciples, which are not written in this book:

31 [a]But these are written, that ye might believe that Jesus is the Christ, the Son of God; [b]and that believing ye might have life through his [c]name.

(p. 617.)

CHAP. 21.

25 [d]And there are also many other things which Jesus did, the which, if they should be written every one, [e]I suppose that even the world itself could not contain the books that should be written. Amen.

D

Job 26. 14 Lo, these *are* parts of his ways; but how little a portion is heard of him? but the thunder of his power who can understand?

Ps. 40. 5 Many, O LORD my God, *are* thy wonderful works *which* thou hast done, and thy thoughts *which are* to us-ward: they cannot be reckoned up in order unto thee: *if* I would declare and speak *of them*, they are more than can be numbered.

Ps. 71. 15 My mouth shall show forth thy righteousness *and* thy salvation all the day; for I know not the numbers *thereof.*

E

Amos 7. 10 Then Amaziah the priest of Beth-el sent to Jeroboam king of Israel, saying, Amos hath conspired against thee in the midst of the house of Israel: the land is not able to bear all his words.

THE ACTS OF

§ 226. INTRODUCTION.

1: 1–3.

1 The former treatise have I made, O [a]Theophilus, [b]of all that Jesus began both to do and teach,

2 Until [c]the day in which he was taken up, after that he through the Holy Ghost had given [d]commandments unto the apostles whom he had chosen:

3 [e]To whom also he shewed himself alive after his passion by many infallible proofs, being seen of them forty days, and [f]speaking of the things pertaining to the kingdom of God:

A

Luke 1. 3 It seemed good to me also, having had perfect understanding of all things from the very first, to write unto thee in order, most excellent Theophilus,

B

Matt. 4. 23 And Jesus went about all Galilee, teaching in their synagogues, and preaching the gospel of the kingdom, and healing all manner of sickness and all manner of disease among the people.

Matt. 11. 5 The blind receive their sight, and the lame walk, the lepers are cleansed,

B—Concluded.

and the deaf hear, the dead are raised up, and the poor have the gospel preached to them.

C

Mark 16. 19 So then after the Lord had spoken unto them, he was received up into heaven, and sat on the right hand of God.

Luke 9. 51 And it came to pass, when the time was come that he should be received up, he steadfastly set his face to go to Jerusalem.

Luke 24. 51 And it came to pass, while he blessed them, he was parted from them, and carried up into heaven.

I Tim. 3. 16 And without controversy great is the mystery of godliness: God was manifest in the flesh, justified in the Spirit, seen of angels, preached unto the Gentiles, believed on in the world, received up into glory.

D

Matt. 28. 19 Go ye therefore, and teach all nations, baptizing them in the name of the Father, and of the Son, and of the Holy Ghost:

Mark 16. 15 And he said unto them, Go ye into all the world, and preach the gospel to every creature.

John 20. 21 Then said Jesus to them again, Peace *be* unto you: as *my* Father hath sent me, even so send I you.

§ 227. THE PROMISE OF THE HOLY SPIRIT AND THE COMMISSION.

1: 4–8.

4 And, [1]being [a]assembled together with *them*, commanded them that they should not depart from Jerusalem, but wait for the promise of the Father, [b]which, *saith he*, ye have heard of me.

5 For John [c]truly baptized with water; [d]but ye shall be baptized with the Holy Ghost not many days hence.

6 When they therefore were come together, they asked of him, saying,

1

Or, *eating together with them.*

A

Luke 24. 41 And while they yet believed not for joy, and wondered, he said unto them, Have ye here any meat?

42 And they gave him a piece of a broiled fish, and of a honeycomb.

43 And he took *it*, and did eat before them.

Luke 24. 49 And, behold, I send the promise of my Father upon you: but tarry ye in the city of Jerusalem, until ye be endued with power from on high.

B

John 7. 39 (But this spake he of the Spirit, which they that believe on him should

THE APOSTLES.

Very probably written by Luke at Rome about A. D. 63.

D—CONCLUDED.

Acts 10. 41 Not to all the people, but unto witnesses chosen before of God, *even* to us, who did eat and drink with him after he rose from the dead.

42 And he commanded us to preach unto the people, and to testify that it is he which was ordained of God *to be* the Judge of quick and dead.

E

Mark 16. 14 Afterward he appeared unto the eleven as they sat at meat, and upbraided them with their unbelief and hardness of heart, because they believed not them which had seen him after he was risen.

Luke 24. 36 And as they thus spake, Jesus himself stood in the midst of them, and saith unto them, Peace *be* unto you.

John 20. 19 Then the same day at evening, being the first *day* of the week, when the doors were shut where the disciples were assembled for fear of the Jews, came Jesus and stood in the midst, and saith unto them, Peace *be* unto you.

John 20. 26 And after eight days again his disciples were within, and Thomas with them: *then* came Jesus, the doors being shut, and stood in the midst, and said, Peace *be* unto you.

John 21. 1 After these things Jesus shewed himself again to the disciples at the

E—CONCLUDED.

sea of Tiberias; and on this wise shewed he *himself*.

John 21. 14 This is now the third time that Jesus shewed himself to his disciples, after that he was risen from the dead.

I Cor. 15. 5 And that he was seen of Cephas, then of the twelve:

F

Dan. 2. 44 And in the days of these kings shall the God of heaven set up a kingdom, which shall never be destroyed: and the kingdom shall not be left to other people, *but* it shall break in pieces and consume all these kingdoms, and it shall stand for ever

Matt. 3. 2 And saying, Repent ye: for the kingdom of heaven is at hand.

Matt. 21. 43 Therefore say I unto you, The kingdom of God shall be taken from you, and given to a nation bringing forth the fruits thereof.

Luke 17. 20 And when he was demanded of the Pharisees, when the kingdom of God should come, he answered them and said, The kingdom of God cometh not with observation:

21 Neither shall they say, Lo here! or, lo there! for, behold, the kingdom of God is within you.

Rom. 14. 17 For the kingdom of God is not meat and drink; but righteousness, and peace, and joy in the Holy Ghost.

TIME, SUNDAY EVENING, APRIL 9, A. D. 30; PLACE, JERUSALEM.

B—CONCLUDED.

receive: for the Holy Ghost was not yet *given;* because that Jesus was not yet glorified.)

John 14. *Read entire chapter.*

John 15. 26 But when the Comforter is come, whom I will send unto you from the Father, *even* the Spirit of truth, which proceedeth from the Father, he shall testify of me:

John 16. *Read entire chapter.*

C

Matt. 3. 11 I indeed baptize you with water unto repentance: but he that cometh after me is mightier than I, whose shoes I am not worthy to bear: he shall baptize you with the Holy Ghost, and *with* fire:

C—CONCLUDED.

Acts 11. 16 Then remembered I the word of the Lord, how that he said, John indeed baptized with water; but ye shall be baptized with the Holy Ghost.

Acts 19. 4 Then said Paul, John verily baptized with the baptism of repentance, saying unto the people, that they should believe on him which should come after him, that is, on Christ Jesus.

D

Joel 2. 28 And it shall come to pass afterward, *that* I will pour out my Spirit upon all flesh; and your sons and your daughters shall prophesy, your old men shall dream dreams, your young men shall see visions:

For D concluded see next page (628).

§ 227. THE PROMISE OF THE HOLY SPIRIT AND THE COMMISSION

CHAP. I.

Lord, wilt thou at this time [f]restore
again the kingdom to Israel?
7 And he said unto them, [g]It is not
for you to know the times or the seasons, which the Father hath put in
his own power.
8 [h]But ye shall receive [2]power,
[i]after that the Holy Ghost is come
upon you: and [k]ye shall be witnesses
unto me both in Jerusalem, and in
all Judea, and in Samaria, and unto
the uttermost part of the earth.

D—CONCLUDED.

Joel 2. 29 And also upon the servants and upon the handmaids in those days will I pour out my Spirit.

Acts 2. 4 And they were all filled with the Holy Ghost, and began to speak with other tongues, as the Spirit gave them utterance.

Acts 11. 15 And as I began to speak, the Holy Ghost fell on them, as on us at the beginning.

E

Matt. 24. 3 And as he sat upon the mount of Olives, the disciples came unto him privately, saying, Tell us, when shall these things be? and what *shall be* the sign of thy coming, and of the end of the world?

F

Gen. 49. 10 The sceptre shall not depart from Judah, nor a lawgiver from between his feet, until Shiloh come; and unto him *shall* the gathering of the people *be*.

Isa. 1. 26 And I will restore thy judges as at the first, and thy counsellors as at the beginning: afterward thou shalt be called, The city of righteousness, the faithful city.

Jer. 23. 5 Behold, the days come, saith the LORD, that I will raise unto David a righteous Branch, and a King shall reign and prosper, and shall execute judgment and justice in the earth.

Eze. 37. 24 And David my servant *shall be* king over them; and they all shall have one shepherd: they shall also walk in my judgments, and observe my statutes, and do them.

25 And they shall dwell in the land that I have given unto Jacob my servant, wherein your fathers have dwelt; and they shall dwell therein, *even* they, and their children, and their children's children for ever: and my servant David *shall be* their prince for ever.

Dan. 7. 27 And the kingdom and dominion, and the greatness of the kingdom under the whole heaven, shall be given to the people of the saints of the Most High, whose kingdom *is* an everlasting kingdom, and all dominions shall serve and obey him.

§ 228. THE ASCENSION. THE RETURN TO JERUSALEM.

1: 9–14.

9 And [a]when he had spoken these
things, while they beheld, he was
taken up; and [b]a cloud received him
out of their sight.

10 And while they looked steadfastly toward heaven as he went up,
behold, two men stood by them [c]in
white apparel;

11 Which also said, Ye men of
Galilee, why stand ye gazing up into
heaven? this same Jesus, which is
taken up from you into heaven,
[d]shall so come in like manner as ye
have seen him go into heaven.

A

Luke 24. 51 And it came to pass, while he blessed them, he was parted from them, and carried up into heaven.

John 6. 62 *What* and if ye shall see the Son of man ascend up where he was before?

B

Acts 1. 2 Until the day in which he was taken up, after that he through the Holy Ghost had given commandments unto the apostles whom he had chosen.

C

Matt. 28. 3 His countenance was like lightning, and his raiment white as snow:

Mark 16. 5 And entering into the sepulchre, they saw a young man sitting on the right side, clothed in a long white garment; and they were affrighted.

(CONCLUDED). TIME, SUNDAY EVENING, APRIL 9; PLACE, JERUSALEM.

F—CONCLUDED.

Amos 9. 11 In that day will I raise up the tabernacle of David that is fallen, and close up the breaches thereof; and I will raise up his ruins, and I will build it as in the days of old:

G

Matt. 24. 36 But of that day and hour knoweth no *man*, no, not the angels of heaven, but my Father only.

Mark 13. 32 But of that day and *that* hour knoweth no man, no, not the angels which are in heaven, neither the Son, but the Father.

I Thes. 5. 1 But of the times and the seasons, brethren, ye have no need that I write unto you.

2 For yourselves know perfectly that the day of the Lord so cometh as a thief in the night.

H

Acts 2. 1 And when the day of Pentecost was fully come, they were all with one accord in one place.

Acts 2. 4. *See under D.*

2

Or, *the power of the Holy Ghost coming upon you.*

I

Luke 24. 49 And behold, I send the promise of my Father upon you: but tarry ye in the city of Jerusalem, until ye be endued with power from on high.

K

Ps. 98. 2 The LORD hath made known his salvation: his righteousness hath he openly shewed in the sight of the heathen.

3 He hath remembered his mercy and his truth toward the house of Israel: all the ends of the earth have seen the salvation of our God,

Isa. 52. 10 The LORD hath made bare his holy arm in the eyes of all the nations; and all the ends of the earth shall see the salvation of our God.

Matt. 28. 19 Go ye therefore, and teach all nations, baptizing them in the name of the Father, and of the Son, and of the Holy Ghost:

Luke 24. 47 And that repentance and remission of sins should be preached in his name among all nations, beginning at Jerusalem.

48 And ye are witnesses of these things.

John 15. 27 And ye also shall bear witness, because ye have been with me from the beginning.

Acts 1. 22 Beginning from the baptism of John, unto that same day that he was taken up from us, must one be ordained to be a witness with us of his resurrection.

Rom. 10. 18 But I say, Have they not heard? Yes verily, their sound went into all the earth, and their words unto the ends of the world.

TIME, MAY 18, A. D. 30; PLACE, BETHANY.

C—CONCLUDED.

Luke 24. 4 And it came to pass, as they were much perplexed thereabout, behold, two men stood by them in shining garments:

John 20. 12 And seeth two angels in white sitting, the one at the head, and the other at the feet, where the body of Jesus had lain.

Acts 10. 3 He saw in a vision evidently, about the ninth hour of the day, an angel of God coming in to him, and saying unto him, Cornelius.

Acts . 30 And Cornelius said, Four days ago I was fasting until this hour; and at the ninth hour I prayed in my house, and, behold, a man stood before me in bright clothing,

D

Dan. 7. 13 I saw in the night visions, and, behold, *one* like the Son of man came with the clouds of heaven, and came to the Ancient of days, and they brought him near before him.

Zech. 14. 5 And ye shall flee *to* the valley of the mountains; for the valley of the mountains shall reach unto Azal: yea, ye shall flee, like as ye fled from before the earthquake in the days of Uzziah king of Judah: and the LORD my God shall come, *and* all the saints with thee.

Matt. 16. 27 For the Son of man shall come in the glory of his Father with his angels; and then he shall reward every man according to his works.

For D continued see next page (630).

§ 228. THE ASCENSION. THE RETURN TO JERUSALEM

CHAP. I.

12 Then [e]returned they unto Jerusalem from the mount called Olivet,
which is from Jerusalem a sabbath
day's journey.

13 And when they were come in,
they went up [f]into an upper room,
where abode both [g]Peter, and James,
and John, and Andrew, Philip, and
Thomas, Bartholomew, and Matthew, James *the son* of Alpheus, and
[h]Simon Zelotes, and [i]Judas *the
brother* of James.

14 These [k]all continued with one
accord in prayer and supplication,
with [l]the women, and Mary the
mother of Jesus, and with [m]his
brethren.

D—CONTINUED.

Matt. 19. 28 And Jesus said unto them, Verily I say unto you, That ye which have followed me, in the regeneration when the Son of man shall sit in the throne of his glory, ye also shall sit upon twelve thrones, judging the twelve tribes of Israel.

Matt. 24. 30 And then shall appear the sign of the Son of man in heaven: and then shall all the tribes of the earth mourn, and they shall see the Son of man coming in the clouds of heaven with power and great glory.

Matt. 25. 31 When the Son of man shall come in his glory, and all the holy angels with him, then shall he sit upon the throne of his glory:

Matt. 26. 64 Jesus saith unto him, Thou hast said: nevertheless I say unto you, Hereafter shall ye see the Son of man sitting on the right hand of power, and coming in the clouds of heaven.

D—CONTINUED.

Mark 8. 38 Whosoever therefore shall be ashamed of me and of my words in this adulterous and sinful generation; of him also shall the Son of man be ashamed, when he cometh in the glory of his Father with the holy angels.

Mark 13. 26 And then shall they see the Son of man coming in the clouds with great power and glory.

Mark 14. 62 And Jesus said, I am: and ye shall see the Son of man sitting on the right hand of power, and coming in the clouds of heaven.

Luke 21. 27 And then shall they see the Son of man coming in a cloud with power and great glory.

Luke 22. 69 Hereafter shall the Son of man sit on the right hand of the power of God.

John 14. 3 And if I go and prepare a place for you, I will come again, and receive you unto myself; that where I am, *there* ye may be also.

I Thes. 1. 10 And to wait for his Son from heaven, whom he raised from the dead, *even* Jesus, which delivered us from the wrath to come.

I Thes. 4. 16 For the Lord himself shall descend from heaven with a shout, with the voice of the archangel, and with the trump of God: and the dead in Christ shall rise first:

II Thes. 1. 7 And to you who are troubled rest with us, when the Lord Jesus shall be revealed from heaven with his mighty angels,

8 In flaming fire taking vengeance on them that know not God, and that obey not the gospel of our Lord Jesus Christ:

9 Who shall be punished with everlasting destruction from the presence of the Lord, and from the glory of his power;

10 When he shall come to be glorified in his saints, and to be admired in all them that believe (because our testimony among you was believed) in that day.

§ 229. THE APPOINTMENT OF MATTHIAS IN JUDAS' STEAD.

1: 15–26.

15 And in those days [a]Peter stood
up in the midst of the disciples, and
said, (the number of names together
were about a hundred and twenty,)

A

Ps. 51. 13 *Then* will I teach transgressors thy ways: and sinners shall be converted unto thee.

Luke 22. 32 But I have prayed for thee, that thy faith fail not: and when thou art converted strengthen thy brethren.

(CONCLUDED). TIME, MAY 18, A. D. 30; PLACE, BETHANY.

D—CONCLUDED.

Jude 14 And Enoch also, the seventh from Adam, prophesied of these, saying, Behold, the Lord cometh with ten thousand of his saints.

Rev. 1. 7 Behold, he cometh with clouds; and every eye shall see him, and they *also* which pierced him: and all kindreds of the earth shall wail because of him. Even so, Amen.

E

Luke 24. 52 And they worshipped him, and returned to Jerusalem with great joy:

F

Acts 9. 37 And it came to pass in those days, that she was sick, and died: whom when they had washed, they laid *her* in an upper chamber.

Acts 9. 39 Then Peter arose and went with them. When he was come, they brought him into the upper chamber: and all the widows stood by him weeping, and shewing the coats and garments which Dorcas made, while she was with him.

G

Matt. 10. 2 Now the names of the twelve apostles are these: The first Simon, who is called Peter, and Andrew his brother; James *the son* of Zebedee, and John his brother;

3 Philip, and Bartholomew; Thomas, and Matthew the publican; James *the son* of Alpheus, and Lebbeus, whose surname was Thaddeus;

4 Simon the Canaanite, and Judas Iscariot, who also betrayed him.

H

Luke 6. 15 Matthew and Thomas, James the *son* of Alpheus, and Simon called Zelotes.

I

Luke 6. 16 And Judas *the brother* of James, and Judas Iscariot, which also was the traitor.

Jude 1 Jude, the servant of Jesus Christ, and brother of James, to them that are sanctified by God the Father, and preserved in Jesus Christ, *and* called:

K

Acts 2. 1 And when the day of Pentecost was fully come, they were all with one accord in one place.

Acts 2. 46 And they, continuing daily with one accord in the temple, and breaking bread from house to house, did eat their meat with gladness and singleness of heart.

L

Luke 23. 49 And all his acquaintance, and the women that followed him from Galilee, stood afar off, beholding these things.

Luke 23. 55 And the women also, which came with him from Galilee, followed after, and beheld the sepulchre, and how his body was laid.

Luke 24. 10 It was Mary Magdalene, and Joanna, and Mary *the mother* of James, and other *women that were* with them, which told these things unto the apostles.

M

Matt. 13. 55 Is not this the carpenter's son? is not his mother called Mary? and his brethren, James, and Joses, and Simon, and Judas?

56 And his sisters, are they not all with us? Whence then hath this *man* all these things?

Mark 3. 31 There came then his brethren and his mother, and, standing without, sent unto him, calling him.

32 And the multitude sat about him, and they said unto him, Behold, thy mother and thy brethren without seek for thee.

33 And he answered them, saying, Who is my mother, or my brethren?

34 And he looked round about on them, which sat about him, and said, Behold my mother and my brethren!

35 For whosoever shall do the will of God, the same is my brother, and my sister, and mother.

Mark 6. 3 Is not this the carpenter, the son of Mary, the brother of James, and Joses, and of Juda, and Simon? and are not his sisters here with us? And they were offended at him.

TIME, DURING THE 10 DAYS BEFORE PENTECOST; PLACE, JERUSALEM.

B

Ps. 41. 9 Yea, mine own familiar friend, in whom I trusted, which did eat of my bread, hath lifted up *his* heel against me.

Ps. 55. 12 For *it was* not an enemy *that* reproached me; then I could have borne

B—CONTINUED.

it: neither *was it* he that hated me *that* did magnify *himself* against me; then I would have hid myself from him:

Ps. 55. 13 But *it was* thou, a man mine equal, my guide, and mine acquaintance.

§ 229. THE APPOINTMENT OF MATTHIAS IN JUDAS' STEAD

CHAP. I.

16 Men *and* brethren, this Scripture must needs have been fulfilled,
[b]which the Holy Ghost by the mouth
of David spake before concerning
Judas, [c]which was guide to them that
took Jesus.

17 For [d]he was numbered with us,
and had obtained part of this [e]min-
istry.

18 Now [f]this man purchased a field
with the [g]reward of iniquity; and falling headlong, he burst asunder in the
midst, and all his bowels gushed out.

19 And it was known unto all the
dwellers at Jerusalem; insomuch as
that field is called in their proper
tongue, Aceldama, that is to say,
The field of blood.

20 For it is written in the book of
Psalms, [h]Let his habitation be desolate, and let no man dwell therein:
and,[i]His [1]bishoprick let another take.

21 Wherefore of these men [k]which
have companied with us all the time
that the Lord Jesus went in and out
among us,

22 [l]Beginning from the baptism of
John, unto that same day that [m]he
was taken up from us, must one be
ordained [n]to be a witness with us of
his resurrection.

23 And they appointed two, Joseph
called [o]Barsabas, who was surnamed
Justus, and Matthias.

24 And they prayed, and said,
Thou, Lord, [p]which knowest the
hearts of all *men*, shew whether of
these two thou has chosen,

25 That he may take part of this
ministry and apostleship, from which
Judas by transgression fell, that he
might go to his own place.

B—CONCLUDED. See preceding page (631).

Ps. 55. 14 We took sweet counsel together *and* walked unto the house of God in company.

15 Let death seize upon them, *and* let them go down quick into hell: for wickedness *is* in their dwelling, *and* among them.

John 13. 18 I speak not of you all: I know whom I have chosen: but that the Scripture may be fulfilled, He that eateth bread with me hath lifted up his heel against me.

C

Matt. 26. 47 And while he yet spake, lo, Judas, one of the twelve, came, and with him a great multitude with swords and staves, from the chief priests and elders of the people.

Luke 22. 47 And while he yet spake, behold a multitude, and he that was called Judas, one of the twelve, went before them, and drew near unto Jesus to kiss him.

John 18. 3 Judas then, having received a band *of men* and officers from the chief priests and Pharisees, cometh thither with lanterns and torches and weapons.

D

Matt. 10. 4 Simon the Canaanite, and Judas Iscariot, who also betrayed him.

Luke 6. 16 And Judas *the brother* of James, and Judas Iscariot, which also was the traitor.

E

Acts 1. 25. *See text of topic.*

Acts 12. 25 And Barnabas and Saul returned from Jerusalem, when they had fulfilled *their* ministry, and took with them John, whose surname was Mark.

Acts 20. 24 But none of these things move me, neither count I my life dear unto myself, so that I might finish my course with joy, and the ministry, which I have received of the Lord Jesus, to testify the gospel of the grace of God.

Acts 21. 19 And when he had saluted them, he declared particularly what things God had wrought among the Gentiles by his ministry.

II Cor. 4. 1 Therefore, seeing we have this ministry, as we have received mercy, we faint not;

II Cor. 5. 18 And all things *are* of God, who hath reconciled us to himself by Jesus Christ, and hath given to us the ministry of reconciliation;

Eph. 4. 11 And he gave some, apostles; and some, prophets; and some, evangelists; and some, pastors and teachers;

(CONTINUED). TIME, DURING THE 10 DAYS BEFORE PENTECOST; PLACE, JERUSALEM.

E—CONCLUDED.

12 For the perfecting of the saints, for the work of the ministry, for the edifying of the body of Christ:

F

Matt. 27. 5 And he cast down the pieces of silver in the temple, and departed, and went and hanged himself.

Matt. 27. 7 And they took counsel, and bought with them the potter's field, to bury strangers in.

8 Wherefore that field was called, The field of blood, unto this day.

9 Then was fulfilled that which was spoken by Jeremy the prophet, saying, And they took the thirty pieces of silver, the price of him that was valued, whom they of the children of Israel did value;

10 And gave them for the potter's field, as the Lord appointed me.

G

Num. 22. 7 And the elders of Moab and the elders of Midian departed with the rewards of divination in their hand; and they came unto Balaam, and spake unto him the words of Balak.

Matt. 26. 15 And said *unto them*, What will ye give me, and I will deliver him unto you? And they covenanted with him for thirty pieces of silver.

II Pet. 2. 15 Which have forsaken the right way, and are gone astray, following the way of Balaam *the son* of Bosor, who loved the wages of unrighteousness:

H

Ps. 69. 25 Let their habitation be desolate; *and* let none dwell in their tents.

I

Ps. 109. 8 Let his days be few; *and* let another take his office.

1

Or, *office*, or, *charge*.

K

Luke 10. 1 After these things the Lord appointed other seventy also, and sent them two and two before his face into every city and place, whither he himself would come.

2 Therefore said he unto them, The harvest truly *is* great, but the labourers *are* few: pray ye therefore the Lord of the harvest, that he would send forth labourers into his harvest.

L

Mark 1. 1 The beginning of the gospel of Jesus Christ, the Son of God:

M

Acts 1. 9 And when he had spoken these things, while they beheld, he was taken up; and a cloud received him out of their sight.

N

John 15. 27 And ye also shall bear witness, because ye have been with me from the beginning.

Acts 1. 8 But ye shall receive power, after that the Holy Ghost is come upon you: and ye shall be witnesses unto me both in Jerusalem, and in all Judea, and in Samaria, and unto the uttermost part of the earth.

O

Acts 15. 22 Then pleased it the apostles and elders, with the whole church, to send chosen men of their own company to Antioch with Paul and Barnabas; *namely*, Judas surnamed Barsabas, and Silas, chief men among the brethren:

P

I Sa. 16. 7 But the LORD said unto Samuel, Look not on his countenance, or on the height of his stature; because I have refused him: for *the LORD seeth* not as man seeth; for man looketh on the outward appearance, but the LORD looketh on the heart.

I Ch. 28. 9 And thou, Solomon my son, know thou the God of thy father, and serve him with a perfect heart and with a willing mind: for the LORD searcheth all hearts, and understandeth all the imaginations of the thoughts: if thou seek him, he will be found of thee; but if thou forsake him, he will cast thee off for ever.

Ps. 44. 21 Shall not God search this out? for he knoweth the secrets of the heart.

Jer. 11. 20 But, O LORD of hosts, that judgest righteously, that triest the reins and the heart, let me see thy vengeance on them: for unto thee have I revealed my cause.

Jer. 17. 10 I the LORD search the heart, *I* try the reins, even to give every man according to his ways, *and* according to the fruit of his doings.

Acts 15. 8 And God, which knoweth the hearts, bare them witness, giving them the Holy Ghost, even as *he did* unto us;

Rev. 2. 23 And I will kill her children with death; and all the churches shall know that I am he which searcheth the reins and hearts: and I will give unto every one of you according to your works.

§ 229. THE APPOINTMENT OF MATTHIAS IN JUDAS' STEAD

CHAP. 1.

¶ 26 And [q]they gave forth their lots; and the lot fell upon Matthias; and he was numbered with the eleven apostles.

Q

Lev. 16. 8 And Aaron shall cast lots upon the two goats; one lot for the LORD, and the other lot for the scapegoat.

Acts 13. 19 And when he had destroyed seven nations in the land of Chanaan, he divided their land to them by lot.

§ 230. THE DAY OF PENTECOST.

2: 1–13.

1 And when [a]the day of Pentecost was fully come, [b]they were all with one accord in one place.

2 [c]And suddenly there came a sound from heaven as of a rushing mighty wind, and it filled all the house where they were sitting.

3 And there appeared unto them cloven tongues like as of fire, and it sat upon each of them.

4 And [d]they were all filled with the Holy Ghost, and began [e]to speak with other tongues, as the Spirit gave them utterance.

5 And there were dwelling at Jerusalem Jews, and devout men, out of every nation under heaven.

6 Now [1]when this was noised abroad, the multitude came together, and were [2]confounded, because that every man heard them speak in his own language.

CHAP. 2.

7 And they were all amazed and marvelled, saying one to another, Behold, are not all these which speak [f]Galileans?

8 And how hear we every man in our own tongue, wherein we were born?

9 Parthians, and Medes, and Elamites, and the dwellers in Mesopotamia, and in Judea, and Cappadocia, in Pontus and Asia,

10 Phrygia, and Pamphylia, in Egypt, and in the parts of Libya about Cyrene, and strangers of Rome, Jews and proselytes,

11 Cretes and Arabians, we do hear them speak in our tongues the wonderful works of God.

12 And they were all amazed, and were in doubt, saying one to another, What meaneth this?

13 Others mocking said, [g]These men are full of new wine.

A

Lev. 23. 15 And ye shall count unto you from the morrow after the sabbath, from the day that ye brought the sheaf of the wave offering; seven sabbaths shall be complete:

16 Even unto the morrow after the seventh sabbath shall ye number fifty days; and ye shall offer a new meat offering unto the LORD.

Deut. 16. 9 Seven weeks shalt thou number unto thee: begin to number the seven weeks from *such time as* thou beginnest *to put* the sickle to the corn.

B

Acts 1. 14. *See text of topic § 228, and under K, page 631.*

C

Ps. 18. 10 And he rode upon a cherub, and did fly: yea, he did fly upon the wings of the wind.

Ps 104. 3 Who layeth the beams of his chambers in the waters: who maketh the clouds his chariot: who walketh upon the wings of the wind:

Eze. 37. 9 Then said he unto me, Prophesy unto the wind, prophesy, son of man, and say to the wind, Thus saith the Lord GOD; Come from the four winds, O breath, and breathe upon these slain, that they may live.

10 So I prophesied as he commanded me, and the breath came into them,

(CONCLUDED). TIME, DURING THE 10 DAYS BEFORE PENTECOST; PLACE, JERUSALEM.

Q—CONTINUED.

Josh. 18. 10 And Joshua cast lots for them in Shiloh before the Lord: and there Joshua divided the land unto the children of Israel according to their divisions.

I Sa. 14. 41 Therefore Saul said unto the LORD God of Israel, Give a perfect *lot*. And Saul and Jonathan were taken: but the people escaped.

Q—CONCLUDED.

I Sa. 14. 42 And Saul said, Cast *lots* between me and Jonathan my son. And Jonathan was taken.

TIME, MAY 28, A. D. 30; PLACE, JERUSALEM.

C—CONCLUDED.

and they lived, and stood up upon their feet, an exceeding great army.

Acts 4. 31 And when they had prayed, the place was shaken where they were assembled together; and they were all filled with the Holy Ghost, and they spake the word of God with boldness.

D

Luke 1. 15 For he shall be great in the sight of the Lord, and shall drink neither wine nor strong drink; and he shall be filled with the Holy Ghost, even from his mother's womb.

Luke 1. 41 And it came to pass, that, when Elisabeth heard the salutation of Mary, the babe leaped in her womb: and Elisabeth was filled with the Holy Ghost:

Acts 1. 5 For John truly baptized with water; but ye shall be baptized with the Holy Ghost not many days hence.

E

Mark 16. 17 And these signs shall follow them that believe; in my name shall they cast out devils; they shall speak with new tongues;

Acts 10. 46 For they heard them speak with tongues, and magnify God. Then answered Peter,

Acts 19. 6 And when Paul had laid *his* hands upon them, the Holy Ghost came on them; and they spake with tongues, and prophesied.

I Cor. 12. 10 To another the working of miracles; to another prophecy; to another discerning of spirits; to another *divers* kinds of tongues; to another the interpretation of tongues:

I Cor. 12. 28 And God hath set some in the church, first apostles, secondarily prophets, thirdly teachers, after that miracles, then gifts of healings, helps, governments, diversities of tongues.

I Cor. 12. 30 Have all the gifts of healing? do all speak with tongues? do all interpret?

E—CONCLUDED.

I Cor. 13. 1 Though I speak with the tongues of men and of angels, and have not charity, I am become *as* sounding brass, or a tinkling cymbal.

I Cor. 14. 2 For he that speaketh in an *unknown* tongue speaketh not unto men, but unto God: for no man understandeth *him;* howbeit in the spirit he speaketh mysteries.

1

Gr, *when this voice was made.*

2

Or, *troubled in mind.*

F

Acts 1. 11 Which also said, Ye men of Galilee, why stand ye gazing up into heaven? this same Jesus, which is taken up from you into heaven, shall so come in like manner as ye have seen him go into heaven.

G

I Sa. 1. 14 And Eli said unto her, How long wilt thou be drunken? put away thy wine from thee.

15 And Hannah answered and said, No, my Lord, I *am* a woman of a sorrowful spirit: I have drunk neither wine nor strong drink, but have poured out my soul before the LORD.

Zech. 9. 15 The LORD of hosts shall defend them; and they shall devour, and subdue with sling stones; and they shall drink, *and* make a noise as through wine; and they shall be filled like bowls, *and* as the corners of the altar.

16 And the LORD their God shall save them in that day as the flock of his people: for *they shall be as* the stones of a crown, lifted up as an ensign upon his land.

17 For how great *is* his goodness, and how great *is* his beauty! corn shall make the young men cheerful, and new wine the maids.

§ 231. PETER'S ADDRESS.

2: 14-36.

14 But Peter, standing up with the eleven, lifted up his voice, and said unto them, Ye men of Judea, and all *ye* that dwell at Jerusalem, be this known unto you, and hearken to my words:

15 For these are not drunken, as ye suppose, [a]seeing it is *but* the third hour of the day.

16 But this is that which was spoken by the prophet Joel;

17 [b]And it shall come to pass in the last days, saith God, I will pour out of my Spirit upon all flesh: [c]and your sons and your daughters shall prophesy, and your young men shall see visions, and your old men shall dream dreams:

18 And on my servants and on my handmaidens I will pour out in those days of my Spirit; and they shall prophesy:

19 And [d]I will shew wonders in heaven above, and signs in the earth beneath; blood, and fire, and vapour of smoke:

20 [e]The sun shall be turned into darkness, and the moon into blood, before that great and notable day of the Lord come:

21 And it shall come to pass, *that* [f]whosoever shall call on the name of the Lord shall be saved.

22 Ye men of Israel, hear these words; Jesus of Nazareth, a man approved of God among you [g]by miracles and wonders and signs, which God did by him in the midst of you, as ye yourselves also know:

23 Him, [h]being delivered by the determinate counsel and foreknowl-

A

I Thes. 5. 7 For they that sleep sleep in the night; and they that be drunken are drunken in the night.

B

Isa. 44. 3 For I will pour water upon him that is thirsty, and floods upon the dry ground: I will pour my Spirit upon thy seed, and my blessing upon thine offspring:

Eze. 11. 19 And I will give them one heart, and I will put a new spirit within you; and I will take the stony heart out of their flesh, and will give them a heart of flesh:

Eze. 36. 27 And I will put my Spirit within you, and cause you to walk in my statutes, and ye shall keep my judgments, and do *them*.

Joel 2. 28 And it shall come to pass afterward, *that* I will pour out my Spirit upon all flesh; and your sons and your daughters shall prophesy, your old men shall dream dreams, your young men shall see visions:

29 And also upon the servants and upon the handmaids in those days will I pour out my Spirit.

Zech. 12. 10 And I will pour upon the house of David, and upon the inhabitants of Jerusalem, the spirit of grace and of supplications: and they shall look upon me whom they have pierced, and they shall mourn for him, as one mourneth for *his* only *son*, and shall be in bitterness for him, as one that is in bitterness for *his* firstborn.

Acts 10. 45 And they of the circumcision which believed were astonished, as many as came with Peter, because that on the Gentiles also was poured out the gift of the Holy Ghost.

Rom. 11. 25 For I would not, brethren, that ye should be ignorant of this mystery, lest ye should be wise in your own conceits; that blindness in part is happened to Israel, until the fulness of the Gentiles be come in.

26 And so all Israel shall be saved: as it is written, There shall come out of Sion the Deliverer, and shall turn away ungodliness from Jacob:

C

Acts 2. 4. *See e, E. § 230, page 634.*

Mark 16. 17 And these signs shall follow them that believe; In my name shall they cast out devils; they shall speak with new tongues.

Acts 21. 9 And the same man had four daughters, virgins, which did prophesy.

TIME, MAY 28, A. D. 30; PLACE, JERUSALEM.

C—CONCLUDED.

Acts 21. 10 And as we tarried *there* many days, there came down from Judea a certain prophet, named Agabus.

D

Joel 2. 30 And I will show wonders in the heavens and in the earth, blood, and fire, and pillars of smoke.

31 The sun shall be turned into darkness, and the moon into blood, before the great and terrible day of the LORD come.

E

Matt. 24. 29 Immediately after the tribulation of those days shall the sun be darkened, and the moon shall not give her light, and the stars shall fall from heaven, and the powers of the heavens shall be shaken:

Mark 13. 24 But in those days, after that tribulation, the sun shall be darkened, and the moon shall not give her light.

Luke 21. 25 And there shall be signs in the sun, and in the moon, and in the stars; and upon the earth distress of nations, with perplexity; the sea and the waves roaring;

F

Joel 2. 32 And it shall come to pass, *that* whosoever shall call on the name of the LORD shall be delivered: for in mount Zion and in Jerusalem shall be deliverance as the LORD hath said, and the remnant whom the LORD shall call.

Ps. 86. 5 For thou, Lord, *art* good, and ready to forgive; and plenteous in mercy unto all them that call upon thee.

Ps. 145. 18 The LORD *is* nigh unto all them that call upon him, to all that call upon him in truth.

Jer. 33. 3 Call unto me, and I will answer thee, and shew thee great and mighty things, which thou knowest not.

Rom. 10. 13 For whosoever shall call upon the name of the Lord shall be saved.

Heb. 4. 16 Let us therefore come boldly unto the throne of grace, that we may obtain mercy, and find grace to help in time of need.

Rev. 22. 17 And the Spirit and the bride say, Come. And let him that heareth say, Come. And let him that is athirst come. And whosoever will, let him take the water of life freely.

G

John 3. 2 The same came to Jesus by night, and said unto him, Rabbi, we know that thou art a teacher come from God:

G—CONCLUDED.

for no man can do these miracles that thou doest, except God be with him.

John 14. 10 Believest thou not that I am in the Father, and the Father in me? the words that I speak unto you I speak not of myself: but the Father that dwelleth in me, he doeth the works.

11 Believe me that I *am* in the Father, and the Father in me: or else believe me for the very works' sake.

Acts 10. 38 How God anointed Jesus of Nazareth with the Holy Ghost and with power: who went about doing good, and healing all that were oppressed of the devil; for God was with him.

Heb. 2. 4 God also bearing *them* witness, both with signs and wonders, and with divers miracles, and gifts of the Holy Ghost, according to his own will?

H

Matt. 26. 24 The Son of man goeth as it is written of him: but woe unto that man by whom the Son of man is betrayed! it had been good for that man if he had not been born.

Luke 22. 22 And truly the Son of man goeth, as it was determined: but woe unto that man by whom he is betrayed!

Luke 24. 44 And he said unto them, These *are* the words which I spake unto you, while I was yet with you, that all things must be fulfilled, which were written in the law of Moses, and *in* the prophets, and *in* the psalms, concerning me.

Acts 3. 18 But those things, which God before had shewed by the mouth of all his prophets, that Christ should suffer, he hath so fulfilled.

Acts 4. 28 For to do whatsoever thy hand and thy counsel determined before to be done.

I

Acts 5. 30 The God of our fathers raised up Jesus, whom ye slew and hanged on a tree.

K

For Gospel account, see §§ 211-213, etc., page 596.

Acts 3. 15 And killed the Prince of life, whom God hath raised from the dead; whereof we are witnesses.

Acts 4. 10 Be it known unto you all, and to all the people of Israel, that by the name of Jesus Christ of Nazareth, whom ye crucified, whom God raised from the dead, *even* by him doth this man stand here before you whole.

For K concluded, see next page (638).

CHAP. 2.

edge of God, [i]ye have taken, and by wicked hands have crucified and slain:

24 [k]Whom God hath raised up, having loosed the pains of death: [l]because it was not possible that he should be holden of it.

25 For David speaketh concerning him, [m]I foresaw the Lord always before my face, for he is on my right hand, that I should not be moved:

26 Therefore did my heart rejoice, and my tongue was glad; moreover also my flesh shall rest in hope:

27 Because thou wilt not leave my soul in hell, neither wilt thou suffer thine Holy One to see corruption.

28 Thou hast made known to me the ways of life; thou shalt make me full of joy with thy countenance.

29 Men *and* brethren, [l]let me freely speak unto you [n]of the patriarch David, that he is both dead and buried, and his sepulchre is with us unto this day.

30 Therefore [o]being a prophet, and knowing that God had sworn [p]with an oath to him, that [q]of the fruit of his loins, according to the flesh, he would raise up Christ to sit on his throne;

31 He seeing this before, spake of the resurrection of Christ, [r]that his soul was not left in hell, neither his flesh did see corruption.

32 This [s]Jesus hath God raised up, whereof [t]we all are witnesses.

33 Therefore [u]being by the right hand of God exalted, and [x]having received of the Father the promise of the Holy Ghost, he [y]hath shed forth this, which ye now see and hear.

§ 231. PETER'S ADDRESS (CONTINUED).

For I and K see preceding page (637).

K—CONCLUDED.

Acts 10. 40 Him God raised up the third day, and shewed him openly;

Acts 13. 30 But God raised him from the dead:

Acts 13. 34 And as concerning that he raised him up from the dead, *now* no more to return to corruption, he said on this wise, I will give you the sure mercies of David.

Acts 17. 31 Because he hath appointed a day, in the which he will judge the world in righteousness by *that* man whom he hath ordained; *whereof* he hath given assurance unto all *men*, in that he hath raised him from the dead.

Rom. 4. 24 But for us also, to whom it shall be imputed, if we believe on him that raised up Jesus our Lord from the dead:

Rom. 8. 11 But if the Spirit of him that raised up Jesus from the dead dwell in you, he that raised up Christ from the dead shall also quicken your mortal bodies by his Spirit that dwelleth in you.

I Cor. 6. 14 And God hath both raised up the Lord, and will also raise up us by his own power.

I Cor. 15. 15 Yea, and we are found false witness of God; because we have testified of God that he raised up Christ: whom he raised not up, if so be that the dead rise not.

II Cor. 4. 14 Knowing that he which raised up the Lord Jesus shall raise up us also by Jesus, and shall present *us* with you.

Gal. 1. 1 Paul, an apostle, (not of men, neither by man, but by Jesus Christ, and God the Father, who raised him from the dead;)

Eph. 1. 20 Which he wrought in Christ, when he raised him from the dead, and set *him* at his own right hand in the heavenly *places*.

Col. 2. 12 Buried with him in baptism, wherein also ye are risen with *him* through the faith of the operation of God, who hath raised him from the dead.

I Thes. 1. 10 And to wait for his Son from heaven, whom he raised from the dead, *even* Jesus, which delivered us from the wrath to come.

Heb. 13. 20 Now the God of peace, that brought again from the dead our Lord Jesus, that great Shepherd of the sheep, through the blood of the everlasting covenant,

I Pet. 1. 21 Who by him do believe in God, that raised him up from the dead, and gave him glory; that your faith and hope might be in God.

TIME, MAY 28, A. D. 30; PLACE, JERUSALEM.

Y

Acts 10. 45 And they of the circumcision which believed were astonished, as many as came with Peter, because that on the Gentiles also was poured out the gift of the Holy Ghost.

Eph. 4. 8 Wherefore he saith, When he ascended up on high, he led captivity captive, and gave gifts unto men.

Z

Ps. 110. 1 The LORD said unto my Lord, Sit thou at my right hand, until I make thine enemies thy footstool.

Matt. 22. 44 The LORD said unto my Lord, Sit thou on my right hand, till I make thine enemies thy footstool?

Z—CONCLUDED.

1 Cor. 15. 25 For he must reign, till he hath put all enemies under his feet.

Eph. 1. 20. *See under K, page 638.*

Heb. 1. 13 But to which of the angels said he at any time, Sit on my right hand, until I make thine enemies thy footstool?

A

Zech. 13. 1 In that day there shall be a fountain opened to the house of David and to the inhabitants of Jerusalem for sin and for uncleanness.

B

Acts 5. 31 Him hath God exalted with his right hand *to be* a Prince and a Saviour, for to give repentance to Israel, and forgiveness of sins.

TIME, MAY 28, A. D. 30; PLACE, JERUSALEM.

B—CONCLUDED.

Hos. 12. 6 Therefore turn thou to thy God: keep mercy and judgment, and wait on thy God continually.

Joel 2. 12 Therefore also now, saith the LORD, turn ye *even* to me with all your heart, and with fasting, and with weeping, and with mourning:

13 And rend your heart, and not your garments, and turn unto the LORD your God: for he *is* gracious and merciful, slow to anger, and of great kindness, and repenteth him of the evil.

Matt. 3. 2 And saying, Repent ye: for the kingdom of heaven is at hand.

Matt. 4. 17 From that time Jesus began to preach, and to say, Repent: for the kingdom of heaven is at hand.

Luke 24. 47 And that repentance and remission of sins should be preached in his name among all nations, beginning at Jerusalem.

Acts 3. 19 Repent ye therefore, and be converted, that your sins may be blotted out, when the times of refreshing shall come from the presence of the Lord;

Acts 17. 30 And the times of this ignorance God winked at; but now commandeth all men every where to repent.

Acts 20. 21 Testifying both to the Jews, and also to the Greeks repentance toward God, and faith toward our Lord Jesus Christ.

Acts 26. 20 But showed first unto them of Damascus, and at Jerusalem, and throughout all the coasts of Judea, and *then* to the Gentiles, that they should repent and turn to God, and do works meet for repentance.

C

Joel 2. 28 And it shall come to pass afterward, *that* I will pour out my Spirit upon all flesh; and your sons and your daughters shall prophesy, your old men shall dream dreams, your young men shall see visions:

Acts 3. 25 Ye are the children of the prophets, and of the covenant which God made with our fathers, saying unto Abraham, And in thy seed shall all the kindreds of the earth be blessed.

D

Acts 10. 45. *See under Y, § 231.*

Isa. 60. 3 And the Gentiles shall come to thy light, and kings to the brightness of thy rising.

Acts 11. 15 And as I began to speak, the Holy Ghost fell on them, as on us at the beginning.

Acts 11. 18 When they heard these things, they held their peace, and glorified God, saying, Then hath God also to the Gentiles granted repentance unto life.

Acts 14. 27 And when they were come, and had gathered the church together, they rehearsed all that God had done with them, and how he had opened the door of faith unto the Gentiles.

Eph. 2. 13 But now, in Christ Jesus, ye who sometimes were far off are made nigh by the blood of Christ.

E

Acts 1. 14 These all continued with one accord in prayer and supplication, with the women, and Mary the mother of Jesus, and with his brethren.

For E concluded see next page (642).

§ 232. THREE THOUSAND ADDED. THEIR COMMON ACCORD TOGETHER

CHAP. 2.

43 And fear came upon every soul: and [f]many wonders and signs were done by the apostles.

44 And all that believed were together, and [g]had all things common;

45 And sold their possessions and goods, and [h]parted them to all *men*, as every man had need.

46 And they, [i]continuing daily with one accord [k]in the temple, [l]and breaking bread [1]from house to house, did eat their meat with gladness and singleness of heart,

47 Praising God, and [m]having favour with all the people. And [n]the Lord added to the church daily such as should be saved.

E—CONCLUDED.

Acts 2. 46. *See text of topic.*

Rom. 12. 12 Rejoicing in hope; patient in tribulation; continuing instant in prayer;

Eph. 6. 18 Praying always with all prayer and supplication in the Spirit, and watching thereunto with all perseverance and supplication for all saints;

Col. 4. 2 Continue in prayer, and watch in the same with thanksgiving;

Heb. 10. 25 Not forsaking the assembling of ourselves together, as the manner of some *is;* but exhorting *one another:* and so much the more, as ye see the day approaching.

F

Mark 16. 17 And these signs shall follow them that believe; In my name shall they cast out devils; they shall speak with new tongues;

Acts 4. 33 And with great power gave the apostles witness of the resurrection of the Lord Jesus: and great grace was upon them all.

Acts 5. 12 And by the hands of the apostles were many signs and wonders wrought

§ 233. PETER AND JOHN RESTORE THE LAME MAN.

3: 1–11.

1 Now Peter and John went up together [a]into the temple at the hour of prayer, [b]*being* the ninth *hour.*

2 And a [c]certain man lame from his mother's womb was carried, whom they laid daily at the gate of the temple which is called Beautiful, [d]to ask alms of them that entered into the temple;

3 Who, seeing Peter and John about to go into the temple, asked an alms.

4 And Peter, fastening his eyes upon him with John, said, Look on us.

5 And he gave heed unto them, expecting to receive something of them.

6 Then Peter said, Silver and gold have I none; but such as I have give I thee: [e]In the name of Jesus Christ of Nazareth rise up and walk.

CHAP. 3.

7 And he took him by the right hand, and lifted *him* up: and immediately his feet and ankle bones received strength.

8 And he [f]leaping up stood, and walked, and entered with them into the temple, walking, and leaping, and praising God.

9 And [g]all the people saw him walking and praising God.

10 And they knew that it was he which [h]sat for alms at the Beautiful gate of the temple: and they were filled with wonder and amazement at that which had happened unto him.

11 And as the lame man which was healed held Peter and John, all the people ran together unto them in the porch that [i]is called Solomon's, greatly wondering.

(CONCLUDED). TIME, MAY 28, A. D. 30; PLACE, JERUSALEM.

F—CONCLUDED.

among the people; (and they were all with one accord in Solomon's porch.

Acts 5. 15 Insomuch that they brought forth the sick into the streets, and laid *them* on beds and couches, that at the least the shadow of Peter passing by might overshadow some of them.

G

Acts 4. 32 And the multitude of them that believed were of one heart and of one soul: neither said any *of them* that aught of the things which he possessed was his own; but they had all things common.

H

Isa. 58. 7 *Is it* not to deal thy bread to the hungry, and that thou bring the poor that are cast out to thy house? when thou seest the naked, that thou cover him; and that thou hide not thyself from thine own flesh?

I

Acts 1. 14. *See text of topic, § 228, page 630.*

K

Luke 24 53 And were continually in the temple, praising and blessing God. Amen.

K—CONCLUDED.

Acts 5. 42 And daily in the temple, and in every house, they ceased not to teach and preach Jesus Christ.

L

Acts 20. 7 And upon the first *day* of the week, when the disciples came together to break bread, Paul preached unto them, ready to depart on the morrow; and continued his speech until midnight.

1

Or, *at home.*

M

Luke 2. 52 And Jesus increased in wisdom and stature, and in favour with God and man.

Acts 4. 33. *See under F.*

Rom. 14. 18 For he that in these things serveth Christ *is* acceptable to God, and approved of men.

N

Acts 5. 14 And believers were the more added to the Lord, multitudes both of men and women;)

Acts 11. 24 For he was a good man, and full of the Holy Ghost and of faith: and much people was added unto the Lord.

TIME, A. D. 30; PLACE, JERUSALEM.

A

Acts 2. 46. *See text of topic, § 232.*

B

Ps. 55. 17 Evening, and morning, and at noon, will I pray, and cry aloud: and he shall hear my voice.

C

Acts 14. 8 And there sat a certain man at Lystra, impotent in his feet, being a cripple from his mother's womb, who never had walked:

D

John 9. 8 The neighbours therefore, and they which before had seen him that he was blind, said, Is not this he that sat and begged?

E

Acts 3. 16 And his name, through faith in his name, hath made this man strong, whom ye see and know: yea, the faith which is by him hath given him this perfect soundness in the presence of you all.

Acts 4. 10 Be it known unto you all, and to all the people of Israel, that by the name of Jesus Christ of Nazareth, whom ye crucified, whom God raised from the dead, *even* by him doth this man stand here before you whole.

E—CONCLUDED.

Acts 16. 18 And this did she many days. But Paul, being grieved, turned and said to the spirit, I command thee in the name of Jesus Christ to come out of her. And he came out the same hour.

F

Isa. 35. 6 Then shall the lame *man* leap as a hart, and the tongue of the dumb sing: for in the wilderness shall waters break out, and streams in the desert.

G

Acts 4. 16 Saying, What shall we do to these men? for that indeed a notable miracle hath been done by them *is* manifest to all them that dwell in Jerusalem; and we cannot deny *it.*

Acts 4. 21 So when they had further threatened them, they let them go, finding nothing how they might punish them, because of the people: for all *men* glorified God for that which was done.

H

John 9. 8. *See under D.*

I

John 10. 23 And Jesus walked in the temple in Solomon's porch.

Acts 5. 12. *See under F, § 232.*

§ 234. PETER'S SECOND ADDRESS.

3:12–26.

12 And when Peter saw *it*, he answered unto the people, Ye men of
Israel, why marvel ye at this? or why
look ye so earnestly on us, as though
by our [a]own power or holiness we
had made this man to walk?

13 The God of Abraham, and of
Isaac, and of Jacob, the God of our
fathers, [b]hath glorified his Son Jesus;
whom ye delivered up, and [c]denied
him in the presence of Pilate, when
he was determined to let *him* go.

14 But ye denied the [d]Holy One
and [e]the Just, and desired a murderer to be granted unto you;

15 And killed the [1]Prince of life,
[f]whom God hath raised from the
dead; whereof [g]we are witnesses.

16 And [h]his name, through faith in
his name, hath made this man strong,
whom ye see and know: yea, the faith
which is by him hath given him this
perfect soundness in the presence of
you all.

17 And now, brethren, I wot that
[i]through ignorance ye did *it*, as *did*
also your rulers.

18 But [k]those things, which God
before had shewed [l]by the mouth of
all his prophets, that Christ should
suffer, he hath so fulfilled.

19 [m]Repent ye therefore, and be
converted, that your sins may be
blotted out, when the [n]times of refreshing shall come from the presence
of the Lord;

A

II Cor. 3. 5 Not that we are sufficient of ourselves to think any thing as of ourselves; but our sufficiency *is* of God:

A—Concluded.

Phil. 2. 13 For it is God which worketh in you both to will and to do of *his* good pleasure.

B

John 17. 1 These words spake Jesus, and lifted up his eyes to heaven, and said, Father, the hour is come; glorify thy Son, that thy Son also may glorify thee:

Phil. 2. 9 Wherefore God also hath highly exalted him, and given him a name which is above every name:

Heb. 2. 9 But we see Jesus, who was made a little lower than the angels for the suffering of death, crowned with glory and honour; that he by the grace of God should taste death for every man.

C

Gospel Accounts See §§ 196-200, page 564.

Acts 7. 52 Which of the prophets have not your fathers persecuted? and they have slain them which shewed before of the coming of the Just One; of whom ye have been now the betrayers and murderers:

Acts 13. 28 And though they found no cause of death *in him*, yet desired they Pilate that he should be slain.

D

Ps. 16. 10 For thou wilt not leave my soul in hell; neither wilt thou suffer thine Holy One to see corruption.

Mark 1. 24 Saying, Let *us* alone; what have we to do with thee, thou Jesus of Nazareth? art thou come to destroy us? I know thee who thou art, the Holy One of God.

Luke 1. 35 And the angel answered and said unto her, The Holy Ghost shall come upon thee, and the power of the Highest shall overshadow thee: therefore also that holy thing which shall be born of thee shall be called the Son of God.

E

Acts 7. 52. *See under C.*

Acts 22. 14 And he said, The God of our fathers hath chosen thee, that thou shouldest know his will, and see that Just One, and shouldest hear the voice of his mouth.

1

Or, *Author.*

John 1. 4 In him was life; and the life was the light of men.

Heb. 5. 9 And being made perfect, he became the author of eternal salvation unto all them that obey him;

I John 5. 11 And this is the record, that God hath given to us eternal life, and this life is in his Son.

TIME, A. D. 30; PLACE, JERUSALEM.

F

Gospel Accounts, §§ 212, 213, page 598.

Acts 2. 24 Whom God hath raised up, having loosed the pains of death: because it was not possible that he should be holden of it.

Eph. 1. 20 Which he wrought in Christ, when he raised him from the dead, and set *him* at his own right hand in the heavenly *places*,

G

Acts 2. 32 This Jesus hath God raised up, whereof we all are witnesses.

See under K, page 629.

H

Matt. 9. 22 But Jesus turned him about, and when he saw her, he said, daughter, be of good comfort; thy faith hath made thee whole. And the woman was made whole from that hour.

Luke 7. 50 And he said to the woman, Thy faith hath saved thee; go in peace.

Luke 10. 17 And the seventy returned again with joy, saying, Lord, even the devils are subject unto us through thy name.

I Pet. 1. 21 Who by him do believe in God, that raised him up from the dead, and gave him glory; that your faith and hope might be in God.

I

Num. 15 26 And it shall be forgiven all the congregation of the children of Israel, and the stranger that sojourneth among them; seeing all the people *were* in ignorance.

Luke 23 4 Then said Pilate to the chief priests and *to* the people, I find no fault in this man.

John 16. 3 And these things will they do unto you, because they have not known the Father, nor me.

Acts 13. 27 For they that dwell at Jerusalem, and their rulers, because they knew him not, nor yet the voices of the prophets which are read every sabbath day, they have fulfilled *them* in condemning *him*.

I Cor. 2 8 Which none of the princes of this world knew: for had they known *it*, they would not have crucified the Lord of glory.

I Tim. 1. 13 Who was before a blasphemer, and a persecutor, and injurious: but I obtained mercy, because I did *it* ignorantly in unbelief.

K

Luke 24. 44 And he said unto them, These *are* the words which I spake unto you, while I was yet with you, that all things must be fulfilled, which were written in the law of Moses, and *in* the prophets, and *in* the psalms, concerning me.

Acts 26. 22 Having therefore obtained help of God, I continue unto this day, witnessing both to small and great, saying none other things than those which the prophets and Moses did say should come:

L

Ps. 22. *Read entire chapter.*

Isa. 50. 6 I gave my back to the smiters, and my cheeks to them that plucked off the hair: I hid not my face from shame and spitting.

Isa. 53. *Read entire chapter.*

I Pet. 1. 10 Of which salvation the prophets have inquired and searched diligently, who prophesied of the grace *that should come* unto you:

11 Searching what, or what manner of time the Spirit of Christ which was in them did signify, when it testified beforehand the sufferings of Christ, and the glory that should follow

M

Ps. 51. 13 *Then* will I teach transgressors thy ways; and sinners shall be converted unto thee.

Isa. 1 16 Wash ye, make you clean; put away the evil of your doings from before mine eyes; cease to do evil:

17 Learn to do well; seek judgment, relieve the oppressed, judge the fatherless, plead for the widow.

18 Come now, and let us reason together, saith the LORD: though your sins be as scarlet, they shall be as white as snow; though they be red like crimson, they shall be as wool.

Isa. 55. 6 Seek ye the LORD while he may be found, call ye upon him while he is near:

7 Let the wicked forsake his way, and the unrighteous man his thoughts: and let him return unto the LORD, and he will have mercy upon him; and to our God, for he will abundantly pardon.

II Tim. 2. 25 In meekness instructing those that oppose themselves; if God peradventure will give them repentance to the acknowledging of the truth;

For M concluded and N, see next page (646).

§ 234. PETER'S SECOND ADDRESS (CONCLUDED).

CHAP. 3.

20 And [o]he shall send Jesus Christ, which before was preached unto you:

21 [p]Whom the heaven must receive until the times of [q]restitution of all things, [r]which God hath spoken by the mouth of all his holy prophets since the world began.

22 For Moses truly said unto the fathers, [s]A Prophet shall the Lord your God raise up unto you of your brethren, like unto me; him shall ye hear in all things whatsoever he shall say unto you.

23 And it shall come to pass, *that* every soul, which will not hear that Prophet, shall be destroyed from among the people.

24 Yea, and all the prophets from Samuel and those that follow after, as many as have spoken, have likewise foretold of these days.

25 [t]Ye are the children of the prophets, and of the covenant which God made with our fathers, saying unto Abraham, [u]And in thy seed shall all the kindreds of the earth be blessed.

26 [x]Unto you first God, having raised up his Son Jesus, [y]sent him to bless you, in [z]turning away every one of you from his iniquities.

M—CONCLUDED.

See under B, page 640.

N

Ps. 72 and 79. *Read entire chapters.*

Isa. 2. 2 And it shall come to pass in the last days, *that* the mountain of the LORD'S house shall be established in the top of the mountains, and shall be exalted above the hills; and all nations shall flow unto it.

N—CONCLUDED.

Isa. 2. 3 And many people shall go and say, Come ye, and let us go up to the mountain of the LORD, to the house of the God of Jacob; and he will teach us of his ways, and we will walk in his paths: for out of Zion shall go forth the law, and the word of the LORD from Jerusalem.

Read Isaiah 49, 51 and 66.

Jer. 32. 37 Behold, I will gather them out of all countries, whither I have driven them in mine anger, and in my fury, and in great wrath; and I will bring them again unto this place, and I will cause them to dwell safely:

Jer. 32. 41 Yea, I will rejoice over them to do them good, and I will plant them in this land assuredly with my whole heart and with my whole soul.

Eze. 34. 25 And I will make with them a covenant of peace, and will cause the evil beasts to cease out of the land: and they shall dwell safely in the wilderness, and sleep in the woods.

26 And I will make them and the places round about my hill a blessing; and I will cause the shower to come down in his season; there shall be showers of blessing.

27 And the tree of the field shall yield her fruit, and the earth shall yield her increase, and they shall be safe in their land, and shall know that I *am* the LORD, when I have broken the bands of their yoke, and delivered them out of the hand of those that served themselves of them.

O

Acts 1. 11 Which also said, Ye men of Galilee, why stand ye gazing up into heaven? this same Jesus, which is taken up from you into heaven, shall so come in like manner as ye have seen him go into heaven.

IIThes. 2. 2 That ye be not soon shaken in mind, or be troubled, neither by spirit, nor by word, nor by letter as from us, as that the day of Christ is at hand.

IIThes. 2. 8 And then shall that Wicked be revealed, whom the Lord shall consume with the spirit of his mouth, and shall destroy with the brightness of his coming:

Heb. 9. 28 So Christ was once offered to bear the sins of many: and unto them that look for him shall he appear the second time without sin unto salvation.

TIME, A. D. 30; PLACE, JERUSALEM.

O—CONCLUDED.

Rev. 1. 7 Behold, he cometh with clouds; and every eye shall see him, and they *also* which pierced him: and all kindreds of the earth shall wail because of him. Even so, Amen.

Rev. 19. 11-16. *See text of* § *597*.

P

Acts 1. 11. *See under O.*

Heb. 8. 1 Now of the things which we have spoken *this is* the sum: We have such a high priest, who is set on the right hand of the throne of the Majesty in the heavens;

Q

Matt. 17. 11 And Jesus answered and said unto them, Elias truly shall first come, and restore all things.

R

Luke 1. 70 As he spake by the mouth of his holy prophets, which have been since the world began:

S

Deut. 18. 15 The LORD thy God will raise up unto thee a Prophet from the midst of thee, of thy brethren, like unto me; unto him ye shall hearken;

Deut. 18. 18 I will raise them up a Prophet from among their brethren, like unto thee, and will put my words in his mouth; and he shall speak unto them all that I shall command him.

Acts 7. 37 This is that Moses, which said unto the children of Israel, A Prophet shall the Lord your God raise up unto you of your brethren, like unto me; him shall ye hear.

T

Acts 2. 39 For the promise is unto you and your children, and to all that are afar off, *even* as many as the Lord our God shall call.

Rom. 9. 4 Who are Israelites; to whom *pertaineth* the adoption, and the glory, and the covenants, and the giving of the law, and the service *of God*, and the promises;

Rom. 9. 8 That is, They which are the children of the flesh, these *are* not the children of God: but the children of the promise are counted for the seed.

Gal. 3. 26 For ye are all the children of God by faith in Christ Jesus.

U

Gen. 12. 3 And I will bless them that bless thee, and curse him that curseth thee: and in thee shall all families of the earth be blessed.

Gen. 18. 18 Seeing that Abraham shall surely become a great and mighty nation, and all the nations of the earth shall be blessed in him?

Gen. 22. 18 And in thy seed shall all the nations of the earth be blessed; because thou hast obeyed my voice.

Gen. 26. 4 And I will make thy seed to multiply as the stars of heaven, and will give unto thy seed all these countries; and in thy seed shall all the nations of the earth be blessed:

Gen. 28. 14 And thy seed shall be as the dust of the earth; and thou shalt spread abroad to the west, and to the east, and to the north, and to the south: and in thee and in thy seed shall all the families of the earth be blessed.

Gal. 3. 8 And the Scripture, foreseeing that God would justify the heathen through faith, preached before the gospel unto Abraham, *saying*, In thee shall all nations be blessed.

X

Matt. 10. 5 These twelve Jesus sent forth, and commanded them, saying, Go not into the way of the Gentiles, and into *any* city of the Samaritans enter ye not:

Matt. 15. 24 But he answered and said, I am not sent but unto the lost sheep of the house of Israel.

Luke 24. 47 And that repentance and remission of sins should be preached in his name among all nations, beginning at Jerusalem.

Acts 13. 46 Then Paul and Barnabas waxed bold, and said, It was necessary that the word of God should first have been spoken to you: but seeing ye put it from you, and judge yourselves unworthy of everlasting life, lo, we turn to the Gentiles.

Y

Luke 2. 11 For unto you is born this day in the city of David a Saviour; which is Christ the Lord.

Acts 3. 22. *See Text of Topic.*

Z

Matt. 1. 21 And she shall bring forth a son, and thou shalt call his name JESUS: for he shall save his people from their sins.

§ 235. PETER AND JOHN IMPRISONED AND TRIED.

4: 1–7.

1 And as they spake unto the people, the priests, and the [1]captain of
the temple, and the [a]Sadducees,
came upon them,
2 Being [b]grieved that they taught
the people, and [c]preached through
Jesus the resurrection from the dead.
3 And they laid hands on them,
and put *them* in hold unto the next
day: for it was now eventide.
4 Howbeit many of them which
heard the word believed; and the
number of the men was about five
thousand.
5 And it came to pass on the morrow, that their rulers, and elders,
and scribes,
6 And Annas [d]the high priest, and
Caiaphas, and John, and Alexander,
and as many as were of the kindred
of the high priest, were gathered to-
gethered at Jerusalem.
7 And when they had set them in
the midst, they asked, [e]By what
power, or by what name, have ye
done this?

1
Or, *ruler*.

1—Concluded.

Luke 22. 4 And he went his way, and communed with the chief priests and captains, how he might betray him unto them

Acts 5. 24 Now when the high priest and the captain of the temple and the chief priests heard these things, they doubted of them whereunto this would grow.

A

Matt. 16. 12 Then understood they how that he bade *them* not beware of the leaven of bread, but of the doctrine of the Pharisees and of the Sadducees.

Matt. 22. 23 The same day came to him the Sadducees, which say that there is no resurrection, and asked him,

Acts 23. 6 But when Paul perceived that the one part were Sadducees, and the other Pharisees, he cried out in the council, Men *and* brethren, I am a Pharisee, the son of a Pharisee: of the hope and resurrection of the dead I am called in question.

7 And when he had so said, there arose a dissension between the Pharisees and the Sadducees: and the multitude was divided.

8 For the Sadducees say that there is no resurrection, neither angel, nor spirit: but the Pharisees confess both.

B

Neh. 2. 10 When Sanballat the Horonite, and Tobiah the servant, the Ammonite, heard *of it*, it grieved them exceedingly that there was come a man to seek the welfare of the children of Israel.

John 11. 47 Then gathered the chief priests and the Pharisees a council, and said, What do we? for this man doeth many miracles,

§ 236. PETER'S DEFENSE BEFORE THE SANHEDRIM.

4: 8–12.

8 Then Peter, [a]filled with the Holy
Ghost, said unto them, Ye rulers of
the people, and elders of Israel,
9 If we this day be examined of
the good deed done to the impotent
man, by what means he is made
whole;

Chap. 4.

10 Be it known unto you all, and
to all the people of Israel, [b]that by
the name of Jesus Christ of Nazareth, whom ye crucified, [c]whom God
raised from the dead, *even* by him
doth this man stand here before you
whole.

TIME, A. D. 30; PLACE, JERUSALEM.

B—CONCLUDED.

John 11. 48 If we let him thus alone, all *men* will believe on him; and the Romans shall come and take away both our place and nation.

Acts 5. 17 Then the high priest rose up, and all they that were with him, (which is the sect of the Sadducees,) and were filled with indignation,

Acts 13. 45 But when the Jews saw the multitudes, they were filled with envy, and spake against those things which were spoken by Paul, contradicting and blaspheming.

Acts 19. 23 And the same time there arose no small stir about that way.

C

Acts 10. 40 Him God raised up the third day, and shewed him openly;
41 Not to all the people, but unto witnesses chosen before of God, *even* to us, who did eat and drink with him after he rose from the dead.

Acts 17. 31 Because he hath appointed a day, in the which he will judge the world in righteousness by *that* man whom he hath ordained; *whereof* he hath given assurance unto all *men*, in that he hath raised him from the dead.

Acts 26. 23 That Christ should suffer, *and* that he should be the first that should rise from the dead, and should shew light unto the people, and to the Gentiles.

Rom. 8. 11 But if the Spirit of him that raised up Jesus from the dead dwell in you, he that raised up Christ from the dead shall also quicken your mortal bodies by his Spirit that dwelleth in you.

I Cor. 15. 12 Now if Christ be preached that he rose from the dead, how say some among you that there is no resurrection of the dead?

C—CONCLUDED.

I Cor. 15. 20 But now is Christ risen from the dead, *and* become the first-fruits of them that slept.

II Cor. 4. 14 Knowing that he which raised up the Lord Jesus shall raise up us also by Jesus, and shall present *us* with you.

I Thes. 4. 16 For the Lord himself shall descend from heaven with a shout, with the voice of the archangel, and with the trump of God: and the dead in Christ shall rise first:

D

Luke 3. 2 Annas and Caiaphas being the high priests, the word of God came unto John the son of Zacharias in the wilderness.

John 11. 49 And one of them, *named* Caiaphas, being the high priest that same year, said unto them, Ye know nothing at all.

John 18. 13 And led him away to Annas first; for he was father in law to Caiaphas, which was the high priest that same year.

E

Ex. 2. 14 And he said, Who made thee a prince and a judge over us? intendest thou to kill me, as thou killedst the Egyptian? And Moses feared, and said, Surely this thing is known.

Matt. 21. 23 And when he was come into the temple, the chief priests and the elders of the people came unto him as he was teaching, and said, By what authority doest thou these things? and who gave thee this authority?

Acts 7. 27 But he that did his neighbor wrong thrust him away, saying, Who made thee a ruler and a judge over us?

TIME, A. D. 30; PLACE, JERUSALEM.

A

Luke 12. 11 And when they bring you unto the synagogues, and *unto* magistrates, and powers, take ye no thought how or what thing ye shall answer, or what ye shall say:
12 For the Holy Ghost shall teach you in the same hour what ye ought to say.

Acts 7. 55 But he, being full of the Holy Ghost, looked up steadfastly into heaven, and saw the glory of God, and

A—CONCLUDED.

Jesus standing on the right hand of God.

B

Acts 3. 6 Then Peter said, Silver and gold have I none; but such as I have give I thee: In the name of Jesus Christ of Nazareth rise up and walk.

Acts 3. 16 And his name, through faith in his name, hath made this man strong, whom ye see and know: yea, the faith

For B concluded and C, see next page (650).

§ 236. PETER'S DEFENSE BEFORE THE SANHEDRIM

CHAP. 4.

11 [d]This is the stone which was set at nought of you builders, which is become the head of the corner.

12 Neither is there [e]salvation in any other: for there is none other name under heaven given among men, whereby we must be saved.

B—CONCLUDED.

which is by him hath given him this perfect soundness in the presence of you all.

C

Acts 2. 24 Whom God hath raised up, having loosed the pains of death: because it was not possible that he should be holden of it.

D

Ps. 118. 22 The stone *which* the builders refused is become the head *stone* of the corner.

Isa. 28. 16 Therefore thus saith the Lord GOD, Behold, I lay in Zion for a foundation a stone, a tried stone, a precious corner *stone*, a sure foundation: he that believeth shall not make haste.

Matt. 21. 42 Jesus saith unto them, Did ye never read in the Scriptures, The stone which the builders rejected, the same is become the head of the corner: this is the Lord's doing, and it is marvellous in our eyes?

E

Ps. 40. 17 But I *am* poor and needy; *yet* the Lord thinketh upon me: thou *art* my help and my deliverer: make no tarrying, O my God.

§ 237. THE APOSTLES RELEASED.

4: 13–22.

13 Now when they saw the boldness of Peter and John, and perceived that they were [a]unlearned and ignorant men, they marvelled; and [b]they took knowledge of them, that they had been with Jesus.

14 And beholding the man which was healed [c]standing with them, they could say nothing against it.

15 But when they had commanded them to go aside out of the council, they conferred among themselves,

16 Saying, [d]What shall we do to these men? for that indeed a notable miracle hath been done by them *is* manifest to all them that dwell in Jerusalem; and we cannot deny *it*.

17 But that it spread no further among the people, let us straitly threaten them, that they speak henceforth to no man in this name.

18 And [e]they called them, and commanded them not to speak at all nor teach in the name of Jesus.

A

Matt. 4. 19 And he saith unto them, Follow me, and I will make you fishers of men.

20 And they straightway left *their* nets, and followed him.

Matt. 11. 25 At that time Jesus answered and said, I thank thee, O Father, Lord of heaven and earth, because thou hast hid these things from the wise and prudent, and hast revealed them unto babes.

John 7. 15 And the Jews marvelled, saying, How knoweth this man letters, having never learned?

John 7. 49 But this people who knoweth not the law are cursed.

Acts 2. 7 And they were all amazed and marvelled, saying one to another, Behold, are not all these which speak Galileans?

8 And how hear we every man in our own tongue, wherein we were born?

I Cor. 1. 27 But God hath chosen the foolish things of the world to confound the wise; and God hath chosen the weak things of the world to confound the things which are mighty.

B

Matt. 26. 71 And when he was gone out into the porch, another *maid* saw him, and said unto them that were there, This *fellow* was also with Jesus of Nazareth.

(CONCLUDED). TIME, A. D. 30; PLACE, JERUSALEM.

E—CONTINUED.

Matt. 1. 21 And she shall bring forth a son, and thou shalt call his name JESUS: for he shall save his people from their sins.

Mark 16. 16 He that believeth and is baptized shall be saved; but he that believeth not shall be damned.

John 14. 6 Jesus saith unto him, I am the way, the truth, and the life: no man cometh unto the Father, but by me.

Acts 10. 43 To him give all the prophets witness, that through his name whosoever believeth in him shall receive remission of sins.

Rom. 3. 24 Being justified freely by his grace through the redemption that is in Christ Jesus:

1 Cor. 3. 11 For other foundation can no man lay than that is laid, which is Jesus Christ.

E—CONCLUDED.

1 Tim. 2. 5 For *there is* one God, and one mediator between God and men, the man Christ Jesus;
6 Who gave himself a ransom for all, to be testified in due time.

Heb. 12. 25 See that ye refuse not him that speaketh: for if they escaped not who refused him that spake on earth, much more *shall not* we *escape*, if we turn away from him that *speaketh* from heaven:

1 Jno. 5. 12 He that hath the Son hath life; *and* he that hath not the Son of God hath not life.

Rev. 12. 10 And I heard a loud voice saying in heaven, Now is come salvation, and strength, and the kingdom of God, and the power of Christ: for the accuser of our brethren is cast down, which accused them before our God day and night.

TIME, A. D. 30; PLACE, JERUSALEM.

B—CONCLUDED.

Matt. 26. 73 And after a while came unto *him* they that stood by, and said to Peter, Surely thou also art *one* of them; for thy speech bewrayeth thee.

Luke 22. 56 But a certain maid beheld him as he sat by the fire, and earnestly looked upon him, and said, This man was also with him.

Luke 22. 58 And after a little while another saw him, and said, Thou art also of them. And Peter said, Man, I am not.

John 18. 16 But Peter stood at the door without. Then went out that other disciple, which was known unto the high priest, and spake unto her that kept the door, and brought in Peter.
17 Then saith the damsel that kept the door unto Peter, Art not thou also *one* of this man's disciples? He saith, I am not.

C

Acts 3. 11 And as the lame man which was healed held Peter and John, all the people ran together unto them in the porch that is called Solomon's, greatly wondering.

D

John 11. 47 Then gathered the chief priests and Pharisees a council, and said, What do we? for this man doeth many miracles.

E

Acts 5. 40 And to him they agreed: and when they had called the apostles, and beaten *them*, they commanded that they should not speak in the name of Jesus, and let them go.

F

Acts 5. 29 Then Peter and the *other* apostles answered and said, We ought to obey God rather than men.

Gal. 1. 10 For do I now persuade men, or God? or do I seek to please men? for if I yet pleased men, I should not be the servant of Christ.

G

Jer. 20. 9 Then I said, I will not make mention of him, nor speak any more in his name. But *his word* was in mine heart as a burning fire shut up in my bones, and I was weary with forbearing, and I could not *stay*.

Acts 1. 8 But ye shall receive power, after that the Holy Ghost is come upon you: and ye shall be witnesses unto me both in Jerusalem, and in all Judea, and in Samaria, and unto the uttermost part of the earth.

Acts 2. 32 This Jesus hath God raised up, whereof we all are witnesses.

H

Acts 22. 15 For thou shalt be his witness unto all men of what thou hast seen and heard.

§ 237. THE APOSTLES RELEASED (CONCLUDED).

CHAP. 4.

19 But Peter and John answered and said unto them, [f]Whether it be right in the sight of God to hearken unto you more than unto God, judge ye.

20 For [g]we cannot but speak the things which we [h]have seen and heard.

21 So when they had further threatened them, they let them go, finding nothing how they might punish them, [i]because of the people: for all *men* glorified God for [k]that which was done.

22 For the man was above forty years old, on whom this miracle of healing was shewed.

For F, G, and H, see preceding page (651).

H—CONTINUED.

I John 1. 1 That which was from the beginning, which we have heard, which we have seen with our eyes, which we have

§ 238. THE REPORT TO THE BRETHREN. THEIR PRAYER.

4:23-31.

23 And being let go, [a]they went to their own company, and reported all that the chief priests and elders had said unto them.

24 And when they heard that, they lifted up their voice to God with one accord, and said, Lord, [b]thou *art* God, which hast made heaven, and earth, and the sea, and all that in them is;

25 Who by the mouth of thy servant David hast said, [c]Why did the heathen rage, and the people imagine vain things?

26 The kings of the earth stood up, and the rulers were gathered together against the Lord, and against his Christ.

27 For of a truth against [d]thy holy child Jesus, [e]whom thou hast anointed, both Herod, and Pontius Pilate, with the Gentiles, and the people of Israel, [f]were gathered together,

28 For [g]to do whatsoever thy hand and thy counsel determined before to be done

A

Acts 2. 44 And all that believed were together, and had all things common;

Acts 2. 46 And they, continuing daily with one accord in the temple, and breaking bread from house to house, did eat their meat with gladness and singleness of heart,

Acts 12. 12 And when he had considered *the thing*, he came to the house of Mary the mother of John, whose surname was Mark; where many were gathered together praying.

B

Ex. 20. 11 For *in* six days the LORD made heaven and earth, the sea, and all that in them *is*, and rested the seventh day: wherefore the LORD blessed the sabbath day, and hallowed it.

II Ki. 19. 15 And Hezekiah prayed before the LORD, and said, O LORD God of Israel which dwellest *between* the cherubim, thou art the God, *even* thou alone, of all the kingdoms of the earth; thou hast made heaven and earth.

Jer. 32. 17 Ah Lord GOD! behold, thou hast made the heaven and the earth by thy great power and stretched out arm, *and* there is nothing too hard for thee:

C

Ps. 2. 1 Why do the heathen rage, and the people imagine a vain thing?

D

Luke 1. 35 And the angel answered and said unto her, The Holy Ghost shall come upon thee, and the power of the Highest shall overshadow thee: therefore

TIME, A. D. 30; PLACE, JERUSALEM.

H—CONCLUDED.

looked upon, and our hands have handled, of the Word of life;

I John 1. 3 That which we have seen and heard declare we unto you, that ye also may have fellowship with us: and truly our fellowship *is* with the Father, and with his Son Jesus Christ.

I

Matt. 21. 26 But if we shall say, Of men; we fear the people; for all hold John as a prophet.

Luke 20. 6 But and if we say, Of men; all the people will stone us: for they be persuaded that John was a prophet.

I—CONCLUDED.

Luke 20. 19 And the chief priests and the scribes the same hour sought to lay hands on him; and they feared the people: for they perceived that he had spoken this parable against them.

Luke 22. 2 And the chief priests and scribes sought how they might kill him: for they feared the people.

K

Acts 3. 7 And he took him by the right hand, and lifted *him* up: and immediately his feet and ankle bones received strength.

TIME, A. D. 30–36; PLACE, JERUSALEM.

D—CONCLUDED.

also that holy thing which shall be born of thee shall be called the Son of God.

Heb. 7. 26 For such a high priest became us, *who is* holy, harmless, undefiled, separate from sinners, and made higher than the heavens;

E

Isa. 61. 1 The Spirit of the Lord GOD *is* upon me; because the LORD hath anointed me to preach good tidings unto the meek; he hath sent me to bind up the broken hearted, to proclaim liberty to the captives, and the opening of the prison to *them that are* bound;

John 10. 36 Say ye of him, whom the Father hath sanctified, and sent into the world, Thou blasphemest; because I said, I am the Son of God?

F

Matt. 26. 3 Then assembled together the chief priests, and the scribes, and the elders of the people, unto the palace of the high priest, who was called Caiaphas,
4 And consulted that they might take Jesus by subtilty, and kill *him*.

Luke 22. 2. *See under I, § 237.*

Luke 22. 3 Then entered Satan into Judas surnamed Iscariot, being of the number of the twelve.

4 And he went his way, and communed with the chief priests and captains, how he might betray him unto them.

Luke 23. 1 And the whole multitude of them arose, and led him unto Pilate.

F—CONCLUDED.

Luke 23. 8 And when Herod saw Jesus, he was exceeding glad: for he was desirous to see him of a long *season*, because he had heard many things of him; and he hoped to have seen some miracle done by him.

Luke 23. 24 And Pilate gave sentence that it should be as they required.

G

Acts 2. 23 Him, being delivered by the determinate counsel and foreknowledge of God, ye have taken, and by wicked hands have crucified and slain:

Acts 3. 18 But those things, which God before had shewed by the mouth of all his prophets, that Christ should suffer, he hath so fulfilled

H

Isa. 58. 1 Cry aloud, spare not, lift up thy voice like a trumpet, and shew my people their transgressions, and the house of Jacob their sins.

Eze. 2. 6 And thou, son of man, be not afraid of them, neither be afraid of their words, though briers and thorns *be* with thee, and thou dost dwell among scorpions: be not afraid of their words, nor be dismayed at their looks, though they *be* a rebellious house.

Acts 4. 13 Now when they saw the boldness of Peter and John, and perceived that they were unlearned and ignorant men, they marvelled; and they took knowledge of them, that they had been with Jesus.

Acts 4. 31. *See text of topic.*

§ 238. THE REPORT TO THE BRETHREN. THEIR PRAYER

CHAP. 4.

29 And now, Lord, behold their
threatenings: and grant unto thy
servants, [h]that with all boldness they
may speak thy word,

30 By stretching forth thine hand
to heal; [i]and that signs and wonders
may be done [k]by the name of thy
holy child Jesus.

31 And when they had prayed, [l]the
place was shaken where they were
assembled together; and they were
all filled with the Holy Ghost, and
they spake the word of God with
boldness.

H—CONTINUED. See preceding page (653).

Acts 9. 27 But Barnabas took him, and brought *him* to the apostles, and declared unto them how he had seen the Lord in the way, and that he had spoken to him, and how he had preached boldly at Damascus in the name of Jesus.

Acts 14. 3 Long time therefore abode they speaking boldly in the Lord, which gave testimony unto the word of his grace and granted signs and wonders to be done by their hands.

Acts 19. 8 And he went into the synagogue, and spake boldly for the space of three months, disputing and persuading the things concerning the kingdom of God.

Acts 26. 26 For the king knoweth of these things, before whom also I speak freely: for I am persuaded that none of these things are hidden from him; for this thing was not done in a corner.

§ 239. THE CHARACTER OF THE EARLY CHURCH.

4:32–37.

32 And the multitude of them that
believed [a]were of one heart and of one
soul: [b]neither said any *of them* that
aught of the things which he possessed was his own; but they had all
things common.

33 And with [c]great power gave the
apostles [d]witness of the resurrection
of the Lord Jesus: and [e]great grace
was upon them all.

34 Neither [f]was there any among
them that lacked: [g]for as many as
were possessors of lands or houses
sold them, and brought the prices
of the things that were sold,

35 And [h]laid *them* down at the
apostles' feet: and [i]distribution was
made unto every man according as
he had need.

36 And Joses, who by the apostles
was surnamed Barnabas, (which is,

A

Acts 5. 12. *See under I, § 238.*

Rom. 15. 5 Now the God of patience and consolation grant you to be like-minded one toward another according to Christ Jesus:

6 That ye may with one mind *and* one mouth glorify God, even the Father of our Lord Jesus Christ.

II Cor. 13. 11 Finally, brethren, farewell. Be perfect, be of good comfort, be of one mind, live in peace; and the God of love and peace shall be with you.

Phil. 1. 27 Only let your conversation be as it becometh the gospel of Christ: that whether I come and see you, or else be absent, I may hear of your affairs, that ye stand fast in one spirit, with one mind striving together for the faith of the gospel;

Phil. 2. 2 Fulfil ye my joy, that ye be like-minded, having the same love, *being* of one accord, of one mind.

I Pet. 3. 8 Finally, *be ye* all of one mind, having compassion one of another; love as brethren, *be* pitiful, *be* courteous:

B

Acts 2. 44 And all that believed were together, and had all things common;

(CONCLUDED). TIME, A. D. 30–36; PLACE, JERUSALEM.

H—CONCLUDED.

Acts 28. 31 Preaching the kingdom of God, and teaching those things which concern the Lord Jesus Christ, with all confidence, no man forbidding him.

Eph. 6. 18 Praying always with all prayer and supplication in the Spirit, and watching thereunto with all perseverance and supplication for all saints;

19 And for me, that utterance may be given unto me, that I may open my mouth boldly, to make known the mystery of the gospel,

I Thes. 2. 2 But even after that we had suffered before, and were shamefully entreated, as ye know, at Philippi, we were bold in our God to speak unto you the gospel of God with much contention.

I

Acts 2. 43 And fear came upon every soul: and many wonders and signs were done by the apostles.

I—CONCLUDED.

Acts 5. 12 And by the hands of the apostles were many signs and wonders wrought among the people; (and they were all with one accord in Solomon's porch.

K

Acts 3. 6. *See e. E.* § *233, page 642.*

L

Acts 2. 2 And suddenly there came a sound from heaven as of a rushing mighty wind, and it filled all the house where they were sitting.

Acts 2. 4 And they were all filled with the Holy Ghost, and began to speak with other tongues, as the Spirit gave them utterance.

Acts 16. 26 And suddenly there was a great earthquake, so that the foundations of the prison were shaken: and immediately all the doors were opened, and every one's bands were loosed.

TIME, A. D. 30–36; PLACE, JERUSALEM.

C

Acts 1. 8 But ye shall receive power, after that the Holy Ghost is come upon you: and ye shall be winesses unto me both in Jerusalem, and in all Judea, and in Samaria, and unto the uttermost part of the earth.

D

Acts 1. 22 Beginning from the baptism of John, unto that same day that he was taken up from us, must one be ordained to be a witness with us of his resurrection.

E

John 1. 16 And of his fulness have all we received, and grace for grace.

F

Jas. 1. 27 Pure religion and undefiled before God and the Father is this, To visit the fatherless and widows in their affliction, *and* to keep himself unspotted from the world.

1 Jno. 3. 17 But whoso hath this world's good, and seeth his brother have need, and shutteth up his bowels *of compassion* from him, how dwelleth the love of God in him?

G

Acts 2. 45 And sold their possessions and goods, and parted them to all *men*, as every man had need.

H

Acts 4. 37. *See text of topic.*

Acts 5. 2 And kept back *part* of the price, his wife also being privy *to it*, and brought a certain part, and laid *it* at the apostles' feet.

I

Acts 2. 45. *See under G.*

Acts 6. 1 And in those days, when the number of the disciples was multiplied, there arose a murmuring of the Grecians against the Hebrews, because their widows were neglected in the daily ministration.

K

Prov. 3. 9 Honour the Lord with thy substance, and with the firstfruits of all thine increase:

Prov. 11. 25 The liberal soul shall be made fat: and he that watereth shall be watered also himself.

Matt. 19. 29 And every one that hath forsaken houses, or brethren, or sisters, or father, or mother, or wife, or children, or lands, for my name's sake, shall receive a hundredfold, and shall inherit everlasting life.

Luke 12. 33 Sell that ye have, and give alms; provide yourselves bags which wax not old, a treasure in the heavens that faileth not, where no thief approacheth, neither moth corrupteth.

§ 239. THE CHARACTER OF THE EARLY CHURCH

CHAP. 4.

being interpreted, The son of consolation,) a Levite, *and* of the country of Cyprus,

37 Having land, sold *it*, and [k]brought the money, and laid *it* at the apostles' feet.

K—CONTINUED. See preceding page (655).

MARK 10. 29 And Jesus answered and said, Verily I say unto you, There is no man that hath left house, or brethren, or sisters, or father, or mother, or wife, or children, or lands, for my sake, and the gospel's,

30 But he shall receive a hundredfold now in this time, houses, and brethren,

§ 240. ANANIAS AND SAPPHIRA.

5: 1-11.

1 But a certain man named Ananias, with Sapphira his wife, sold a possession,

2 And [a]kept back *part* of the price, his wife also being privy *to it*, and brought a certain part, and laid *it* at the apostles' feet.

3 [b]But Peter said, Ananias, why hath Satan filled thine heart [1]to lie to the Holy Ghost, and [c]to keep back *part* of the price of the land?

4 While it remained, was it not thine own? and after it was sold, was it not in thine own power? why hast thou conceived this thing in thine heart? [d]thou hast not lied unto men, but unto God.

5 And Ananias hearing these words [e]fell down, and gave up the ghost: and great fear came on all them that heard these things.

6 And the young men arose, [f]wound him up, and carried *him* out, and buried *him*.

7 And it was about the space of three hours after, when his wife, not knowing what was done, came in.

8 And Peter answered unto her, Tell me whether ye sold the land for so much? And she said, Yea, for so much.

CHAP. 5.

9 Then Peter said unto her, How is it that ye have agreed together [g]to tempt the Spirit of the Lord? behold, the feet of them which have buried thy husband *are* at the door, and shall carry thee out.

10 Then fell she down straightway at his feet, and yielded up the ghost: and the young men came in, and found her dead, and, carrying *her* forth, buried *her* by her husband.

11 And [h]great fear came upon all the church, and upon as many as heard these things.

A

Josh. 7. 1 But the children of Israel committed a trespass in the accursed thing: for Achan, the son of Carmi, the son of Zabdi, the son of Zerah, of the tribe of Judah, took of the accursed thing: and the anger of the LORD was kindled against the children of Israel.

II Ki. 5. 20 But Gehazi, the servant of Elisha the man of God, said, Behold, my master hath spared Naaman this Syrian, in not receiving at his hands that which he brought: but, *as* the LORD liveth, I will run after him, and take somewhat of him.

Mal. 3. 8 Will a man rob God? Yet ye have robbed me. But ye say, Wherein have we robbed thee? In tithes and offerings.

B

Luke 22. 3 Then entered Satan into Judas surnamed Iscariot, being of the number of the twelve.

1
Or, to deceive.

(CONCLUDED). TIME, A. D. 30–36; PLACE, JERUSALEM.

K—CONTINUED.

and sisters, and mothers, and children, and lands, with persecutions; and in the world to come eternal life.

Acts 4. 34, 35. *See text of topic.*

Acts 5. 1, 2. *See text of topic, § 240.*

IICor.8. 2 How that in a great trial of affliction, the abundance of their joy and their deep poverty abounded unto the

K—CONCLUDED.

riches of their liberality.

IICor.8. 3 For to *their* power, I bear record, yea, and beyond *their* power *they were* willing of themselves;

4 Praying us with much entreaty that we would receive the gift, and *take upon us* the fellowship of the ministering to the saints.

TIME, A. D. 30–36; PLACE, JERUSALEM.

1—CONCLUDED.

Ps. 94. 9 He that planted the ear, shall he not hear? he that formed the eye, shall he not see?

Acts 5. 9. *See text of Topic.*

C

Num.30. 2 If a man vow a vow unto the LORD, or swear an oath to bind his soul with a bond; he shall not break his word, he shall do according to all that proceedeth out of his mouth.

Deut.23. 21 When thou shalt vow a vow unto the LORD thy God, thou shalt not slack to pay it: for the LORD thy God will surely require it of thee; and it would be sin in thee.

Prov.20 25 *It is* a snare to the man *who* devoureth *that which is* holy, and after vows to make inquiry.

Eccl. 5. 4 When thou vowest a vow unto God, defer not to pay it; for *he hath* no pleasure in fools: pay that which thou hast vowed.

D

Ex. 16 8 And Moses said, *This shall be*, when the LORD shall give you in the evening flesh to eat, and in the morning bread to the full; for that the LORD heareth your murmurings which ye murmur against him: and what *are* we? your murmurings *are* not against us, but against the LORD.

Num.16. 11 For which cause *both* thou and all thy company *are* gathered together against the LORD: and what *is* Aaron, that ye murmur against him?

ISam.8. 7 And the LORD said unto Samuel, Hearken unto the voice of the people in all that they say unto thee: for they have not rejected thee, but they have rejected me, that I should not reign over them.

Ps. 139. 4 For *there is* not a word in my tongue, *but*, lo, O LORD, thou knowest it altogether.

D—CONCLUDED.

Ps. 139. 5 Thou hast beset me behind and before, and laid thine hand upon me.

6 *Such* knowledge *is* too wonderful for me; it is high, I cannot *attain* unto it.

7 Whither shall I go from thy Spirit? or whither shall I flee from thy presence?

Luke 10. 16 He that heareth you heareth me; and he that despiseth you despiseth me; and he that despiseth me despiseth him that sent me.

E

Num.14. 37 Even those men that did bring up the evil report upon the land, died by the plague before the LORD.

Num.16. 32 And the earth opened her mouth, and swallowed them up, and their houses, and all the men that *appertained* unto Korah, and all *their* goods.

II Ki. 1. 14 Behold, there came fire down from heaven, and burnt up the two captains of the former fifties with their fifties: therefore let my life now be precious in thy sight.

F

John 19. 40 Then took they the body of Jesus, and wound it in linen clothes, with the spices, as the manner of the Jews is to bury.

G

Ps. 50. 18 When thou sawest a thief, then thou consentedst with him, and hast been partaker with adulterers.

H

Acts 5. 5. *See text of Topic.*

Acts 2. 43 And fear came upon every soul: and many wonders and signs were done by the apostles.

Acts 19. 17 And this was known to all the Jews and Greeks also dwelling at Ephesus; and fear fell on them all, and the name of the Lord Jesus was magnified.

§ 241. SIGNS AND WONDERS WROUGHT.

5 : 12–16.

12 And [a]by the hands of the apostles were many signs and wonders wrought among the people; (and they were all with one accord in Solomon's porch.

13 And [b]of the rest durst no man join himself to them: [c]but the people magnified them.

14 And believers were the more added to the Lord, multitudes both of men and women;)

15 Insomuch that they brought forth the sick [1]into the streets, and laid *them* on beds and couches, [d]that at the least the shadow of Peter passing by might overshadow some of them.

16 There came also a multitude *out* of the cities round about unto Jerusalem, bringing sick folks, and them which were vexed with unclean spirits: [e]and they were healed every one.

A

Mark 16. 17 And these signs shall follow them that believe; In my name shall they cast out devils; they shall speak with new tongues;

Acts 2. 43 And fear came upon every soul: and many wonders and signs were done by the apostles.

Acts 4. 30 By stretching forth thine hand to heal; and that signs and wonders may be done by the name of thy holy child Jesus.

Acts 14. 3 Long time therefore abode they speaking boldly in the Lord, which gave testimony unto the word of his grace, and granted signs and wonders to be done by their hands.

Acts 19. 11 And God wrought special miracles by the hands of Paul:

Rom. 15. 19 Through mighty signs and wonders, by the power of the Spirit of God; so that from Jerusalem, and round about unto Illyricum, I have fully preached the gospel of Christ.

I Cor. 2. 4 And my speech and my preaching *was* not with enticing words of man's wisdom, but in demonstration of the Spirit and of power:

II Cor. 12. 12 Truly the signs of an apostle were wrought among you in all patience, in signs, and wonders, and mighty deeds.

§ 242. SECOND IMPRISONMENT. MIRACULOUS DELIVERY. TRIAL.

5 : 17–32.

17 Then [a]the high priest rose up, and all they that were with him, (which is the sect of the Sadducees,) and were filled with [1]indignation,

18 And [b]laid their hands on the apostles, and put them in the common [c]prison.

19 But [d]the angel of the Lord by night opened the prison doors, and brought them forth, and said,

20 Go, stand and speak in the temple to the people [e]all the words of this life.

21 And when they heard *that*, they entered into the temple early in the morning, and taught. [f]But the high

A

Acts 4. 1 And as they spake unto the people, the priests, and the captain of the temple, and the Sadducees, came upon them,

2 Being grieved that they taught the people, and preached through Jesus the resurrection from the dead.

Acts 4. 6 And Annas the high priest, and Caiaphas, and John, and Alexander, and as many as were of the kindred of the high priest, were gathered together at Jerusalem.

1

Or, *envy*.

B

Luke 21. 12 But before all these, they shall lay their hands on you, and persecute *you*, delivering *you* up to the synagogues, and into prisons, being brought before kings and rulers for my name's sake.

TIME, A. D. 30–36; PLACE, JERUSALEM.

A—CONCLUDED.

Heb. 2. 4 God also bearing *them* witness, both with signs and wonders, and with divers miracles, and gifts of the Holy Ghost, according to his own will?

B

John 9. 22 These *words* spake his parents, because they feared the Jews: for the Jews had agreed already, that if any man did confess that he was Christ, he should be put out of the synagogue.

John 12. 42 Nevertheless among the chief rulers also many believed on him; but because of the Pharisees they did not confess *him*, lest they should be put out of the synagogue:

John 19. 38 And after this Joseph of Arimathea, being a disciple of Jesus, but secretly for fear of the Jews, besought Pilate that he might take the body of Jesus: and Pilate gave *him* leave. He came therefore, and took the body of Jesus.

C

Acts 2. 47 Praising God, and having favour with all the people. And the Lord added to the church daily such as should be saved.

Acts 4. 21 So when they had further threatened them, they let them go, finding nothing how they might punish them, because of the people: for all *men*

C—CONCLUDED.

glorified God for that which was done.

1

Or, *in every street.*

D

Matt. 9. 21 For she said within herself, If I may but touch his garment, I shall be whole.

Matt. 14. 36 And besought him that they might only touch the hem of his garment: and as many as touched were made perfectly whole.

Acts 19. 12 So that from his body were brought unto the sick handkerchiefs or aprons, and the diseases departed from them, and the evil spirits went out of them.

E

Mark 16. 17. *See under A.*

18 They shall take up serpents; and if they drink any deadly thing, it shall not hurt them; they shall lay hands on the sick, and they shall recover.

Jas. 5. 15 And the prayer of faith shall save the sick, and the Lord shall raise him up; and if he have committed sins, they shall be forgiven him.

16 Confess *your* faults one to another, and pray one for another, that ye may be healed. The effectual fervent prayer of a righteous man availeth much.

TIME, A. D. 30–36; PLACE, JERUSALEM.

C

Acts 12. 5 Peter therefore was kept in prison: but prayer was made without ceasing of the church unto God for him.

Acts 16. 23 And when they had laid many stripes upon them, they cast *them* into prison, charging the jailer to keep them safely:

D

Ps. 34. 7 The angel of the LORD encampeth round about them that fear him, and delivereth them.

Acts 12. 7 And, behold, the angel of the Lord came upon *him*, and a light shined in the prison: and he smote Peter on the side, and raised him up, saying, Arise up quickly. And his chains fell off from *his* hands.

Acts 16. 26 And suddenly there was a great earthquake, so that the foundations of the prison were shaken: and immediately all the doors were opened, and every one's bands were loosed.

D—CONCLUDED.

Heb. 1. 14 Are they not all ministering spirits, sent forth to minister for them who shall be heirs of salvation?

E

Ex. 24. 3 And Moses came and told the people all the words of the LORD, and all the judgments: and all the people answered with one voice, and said, All the words which the LORD hath said will we do.

John 6. 63 It is the Spirit that quickeneth; the flesh profiteth nothing: the words that I speak unto you, *they* are spirit, and *they* are life.

John 6. 68 Then Simon Peter answered him, Lord, to whom shall we go? thou hast the words of eternal life.

1 Jno. 5. 11 And this is the record, that God hath given to us eternal life, and this life is in his Son.

For F see next page (660).

§ 242. SECOND IMPRISONMENT. MIRACULOUS DELIVERY. TRIAL

CHAP. 5.

priest came, and they that were with him, and called the council together, and all the senate of the children of Israel, and sent to the prison to have them brought.

22 But when the officers came, and found them not in the prison, they returned, and told,

23 Saying, The prison truly found we shut with all safety, and the keepers standing without before the doors: but when we had opened, we found no man within.

24 Now when the high priest and the [g]captain of the temple and the chief priests heard these things, they doubted of them whereunto this would grow.

25 Then came one and told them, saying, Behold, the men whom ye put in prison are standing in the temple, and teaching the people.

26 Then went the captain with the officers, and brought them without violence: [h]for they feared the people, lest they should have been stoned.

27 And when they had brought them, they set *them* before the council: and the high priest asked them,

28 Saying, [i]Did not we straitly command you that ye should not teach in this name? and, behold, ye have filled Jerusalem with your doctrine, [k]and intend to bring this man's [l]blood upon us.

29 Then Peter and the *other* apostles answered and said, [m]We ought to obey God rather than men.

30 The [n]God of our fathers raised up Jesus, whom ye slew and [o]hanged on a tree.

F

Acts 4. 5 And it came to pass on the morrow, that their rulers, and elders, and scribes,

6 And Annas the high priest, and Caiaphas, and John, and Alexander, and as many as were of the kindred of the high priest, were gathered together at Jerusalem.

G

Luke 22. 4 And he went his way, and communed with the chief priests and captains, how he might betray him unto them.

Acts 4. 1 And as they spake unto the people, the priests, and the captain of the temple, and the Sadducees, came upon them.

H

Matt. 21. 26 But if we shall say, Of men; we fear the people; for all hold John as a prophet.

I

Acts 4. 18 And they called them, and commanded them not to speak at all nor teach in the name of Jesus.

K

Acts 2. 23 Him, being delivered by the determinate counsel and foreknowledge of God, ye have taken, and by wicked hands have crucified and slain:

Acts 2. 36 Therefore let all the house of Israel know assuredly, that God hath made that same Jesus, whom ye have crucified, both Lord and Christ.

Acts 3. 15 And killed the Prince of life, whom God hath raised from the dead; whereof we are witnesses.

Acts 7. 52 Which of the prophets have not your fathers persecuted? and they have slain them which shewed before of the coming of the Just One; of whom ye have been now the betrayers and murderers:

L

Matt. 23. 35 That upon you may come all the righteous blood shed upon the earth, from the blood of righteous Abel unto the blood of Zacharias son of Barachias, whom ye slew between the temple and the altar.

Matt. 27. 25 Then answered all the people, and said, His blood *be* on us, and on our children.

M

Gen. 3. 17 And unto Adam he said, Because thou hast hearkened unto the voice of

(CONTINUED). TIME, A. D. 30–36; PLACE, JERUSALEM.

M—CONCLUDED.

thy wife, and hast eaten of the tree, of which I commanded thee, saying, Thou shalt not eat of it: cursed *is* the ground for thy sake; in sorrow shalt thou eat *of* it all the days of thy life;

I Sa. 15. 22 And Samuel said, Hath the LORD *as great* delight in burnt offerings and sacrifices, as in obeying the voice of the LORD? Behold, to obey *is* better than sacrifice, *and* to hearken than the fat of rams.

I Sa. 15. 24 And Saul said unto Samuel, I have sinned: for I have transgressed the commandment of the LORD, and thy words: because I feared the people, and obeyed their voice.

Mark 7. 7 Howbeit in vain do they worship me, teaching *for* doctrines the commandments of men.

8 For laying aside the commandment of God, ye hold the tradition of men, *as* the washing of pots and cups: and many other such like things ye do.

9 And he said unto them, Full well ye reject the commandment of God, that ye may keep your own tradition.

Acts 4. 19 But Peter and John answered and said unto them, Whether it be right in the sight of God to hearken unto you more than unto God, judge ye.

Gal. 1. 10 For do I now persuade men, or God? or do I seek to please men? for if I yet pleased men, I should not be the servant of Christ.

N

Acts 2. 24. *See k, K, §231, page 638.*

O

Acts 10. 39 And we are witnesses of all things which he did both in the land of the Jews, and in Jerusalem; whom they slew and hanged on a tree:

Acts 13. 29 And when they had fulfilled all that was written of him, they took *him* down from the tree, and laid *him* in a sepulchre.

Gal. 3. 13 Christ hath redeemed us from the curse of the law, being made a curse for us: for it is written, Cursed is every one that hangeth on a tree:

I Pet. 2. 24 Who his own self bare our sins in his own body on the tree, that we, being dead to sins, should live unto righteousness: by whose stripes ye are healed.

P

Acts 2. 33 Therefore being by the right hand of God exalted, and having received

P—CONCLUDED.

of the Father the promise of the Holy Ghost, he hath shed forth this which ye now see and hear.

Acts 2. 36 Therefore let all the house of Israel know assuredly, that God hath made that same Jesus, whom ye have crucified, both Lord and Christ.

Phil. 2. 9 Wherefore God also hath highly exalted him, and given him a name which is above every name:

Heb. 2. 10 For it became him, for whom *are* all things, and by whom *are* all things, in bringing many sons unto glory, to make the captain of their salvation perfect through sufferings.

Heb. 12. 2 Looking unto Jesus the author and finisher of *our* faith; who for the joy that was set before him endured the cross, despising the shame, and is set down at the right hand of the throne of God.

Q

Isa. 9. 6 For unto us a child is born, unto us a son is given: and the government shall be upon his shoulder: and his name shall be called Wonderful, Counsellor, The mighty God, The everlasting Father, The Prince of Peace.

Eze. 34. 24 And I the LORD will be their God, and my servant David a prince among them: I the LORD have spoken *it*.

Acts 3. 15. *See under K.*

Rev. 1. 5 And from Jesus Christ, *who is* the faithful witness, *and* the first begotten of the dead, and the prince of the kings of the earth. Unto him that loved us, and washed us from our sins in his own blood,

R

Matt. 1. 21 And she shall bring forth a son, and thou shalt call his name JESUS: for he shall save his people from their sins.

John 4. 42 And said unto the woman, Now we believe, not because of thy saying: for we have heard *him* ourselves, and know that this is indeed the Christ, the Saviour of the world.

Acts 4. 12 Neither is there salvation in any other: for there is none other name under heaven given among men, whereby we must be saved.

Acts 13. 23 Of this man's seed hath God, according to *his* promise, raised unto Israel a Saviour, Jesus:

Heb. 7. 25 Wherefore he is able also to save them to the uttermost that come unto God by him, seeing he ever liveth to make intercession for them.

§ 242. SECOND IMPRISONMENT. MIRACULOUS DELIVERY. TRIAL

CHAP. 5.

31 [p]Him hath God exalted with his
right hand *to be* a [q]Prince and a
[r]Saviour, for [s]to give repentance to
Israel, and forgiveness of sins.

32 [t]And we are his witnesses of
these things; and *so is* also the Holy
Ghost, [u]whom God hath given to
them that obey him.

For P, Q, and R, see preceding page (661).

S

Luke 24. 47 And that repentance and remission of sins should be preached in his name among all nations, beginning at Jerusalem.

Acts 3. 26 Unto you first God, having raised up his Son Jesus, sent him to bless you, in turning away every one of you from his iniquities.

Acts 13. 38 Be it known unto you therefore, men *and* brethren, that through this man is preached unto you the forgiveness of sins:

§ 243. GAMALIEL'S COUNSEL. APOSTLES BEATEN AND RELEASED.

5: 33–42.

33 When [a]they heard *that,* they
were cut *to the heart,* and took counsel to slay them.

34 Then stood there up one in the
council, a Pharisee, named [b]Gama-
liel, a doctor of the law, had in reputation among all the people, and
commanded to put the apostles forth
a little space;

35 And said unto them, Ye men of
Israel, take heed to yourselves what
ye intend to do as touching these
men.

36 For before these days rose up
Theudas, boasting himself to be
somebody; to whom a number of
men, about four hundred, joined
themselves: who was slain; and all,
as many as [1]obeyed him, were scattered, and brought to nought.

37 After this man rose up Judas of
Galilee in the days of the taxing,
and drew away much people after
him: he also perished; and all, *even*
as many as obeyed him, were dispersed.

38 And now I say unto you, Refrain
from these men, and let them alone:

CHAP. 5.

for [c]if this counsel or this work be
of men, it will come to nought:

39 [d]But if it be of God, ye cannot
overthrow it; lest haply ye be found
even [e]to fight against God,

40 And to him they agreed: and
when they had called the apostles,
[f]and beaten *them,* they commanded
that they should not speak in the
name of Jesus, and let them go.

41 And they departed from the
presence of the council, [g]rejoicing
that they were counted worthy to
suffer shame for his name.

42 And daily in the temple, and in
every house, they ceased not to teach
and preach Jesus Christ.

A

Acts 7. 54 When they heard these things, they were cut to the heart, and they gnashed on him with *their* teeth.

B

Acts 22. 3 I am verily a man *which am* a Jew, born in Tarsus, *a city* in Cilicia, yet brought up in this city at the feet of Gamaliel, *and* taught according to the perfect manner of the law of the fathers, and was zealous toward God, as ye all are this day.

1

Or, *believed.*

(CONCLUDED). TIME, A. D. 30–36; PLACE, JERUSALEM.

S—CONCLUDED.

Eph. 1. 7 In whom we have redemption through his blood, the forgiveness of sins, according to the riches of his grace;

Col 1. 14 In whom we have redemption through his blood, *even* the forgiveness of sins:

T

John 15. 26 But when the Comforter is come, whom I will send unto you from the Father, *even* the Spirit of truth, which proceedeth from the Father, he shall testify of me:

T—CONCLUDED.

John 15. 27 And ye also shall bear witness, because ye have been with me from the beginning.

U

Acts 2. 4 And they were all filled with the Holy Ghost, and began to speak with other tongues, as the Spirit gave them utterance.

Acts 10. 44 While Peter yet spake these words, the Holy Ghost fell on all them which heard the word.

TIME, A. D. 30–36; PLACE, JERUSALEM.

C

Prov. 21. 30 *There is* no wisdom nor understanding nor counsel against the LORD.

Isa. 8. 10 Take counsel together, and it shall come to nought; speak the word, and it shall not stand: for God *is* with us.

Matt. 15. 13 But he answered and said, Every plant, which my heavenly Father hath not planted, shall be rooted up.

D

Luke 21. 15 For I will give you a mouth and wisdom, which all your adversaries shall not be able to gainsay nor resist.

I Cor. 1. 25 Because the foolishness of God is wiser than men; and the weakness of God is stronger than men.

E

Acts 7. 51 Ye stiffnecked and uncircumcised in heart and ears, ye do always resist the Holy Ghost: as your fathers *did*, so *do* ye.

Acts 9. 5 And he said, Who art thou, Lord? And the Lord said, I am Jesus whom thou persecutest: *it is* hard for thee to kick against the pricks.

Acts 23. 9 And there arose a great cry, and the scribes *that were* of the Pharisees' part arose, and strove, saying, We find no evil in this man: but if a spirit or an angel hath spoken to him, let us not fight against God.

F

Matt. 10. 17 But beware of men: for they will deliver you up to the councils, and they will scourge you in their synagogues;

Matt. 23. 34 Wherefore, behold, I send unto you prophets, and wise men, and scribes; and *some* of them ye shall kill

F—CONCLUDED.

and crucify; and *some* of them shall ye scourge in your synagogues, and persecute *them* from city to city:

Mark 13. 9 But take heed to yourselves: for they shall deliver you up to councils; and in the synagogues ye shall be beaten: and ye shall be brought before rulers and kings for my sake, for a testimony against them.

G

Matt. 5. 12 Rejoice, and be exceeding glad: for great *is* your reward in heaven: for so persecuted they the prophets which were before you.

Rom. 5. 3 And not only *so*, but we glory in tribulations also; knowing that tribulation worketh patience;

II Cor. 12. 10 Therefore I take pleasure in infirmities, in reproaches, in necessities, in persecutions, in distresses for Christ's sake: for when I am weak, then am I strong.

Phil. 1. 29 For unto you it is given in the behalf of Christ, not only to believe on him, but also to suffer for his sake;

Heb. 10. 34 For ye had compassion of me in my bonds, and took joyfully the spoiling of your goods, knowing in yourselves that ye have in heaven a better and an enduring substance.

Jas. 1. 2 My brethren, count it all joy when ye fall into divers temptations;

I. Pet. 4. 12 Beloved, think it not strange concerning the fiery trial which is to try you, as though some strange thing happened unto you:

13 But rejoice, inasmuch as ye are partakers of Christ's sufferings; that, when his glory shall be revealed, ye may be glad also with exceeding joy.

§ 244. SEVEN APPOINTED OVER THE DAILY MINISTRATION.

6:1–7.

1 And in those days, [a]when the number of the disciples was multiplied, there arose a murmuring of the [b]Grecians against the Hebrews, because their widows were neglected [c]in the daily ministration.

2 Then the twelve called the multitude of the disciples *unto them*, and said, [d]It is not reason that we should leave the word of God, and serve tables.

3 Wherefore, brethren, [e]look ye out among you seven men [f]of honest report, full of the Holy Ghost and wisdom, whom we may appoint over this business.

4 But we [g]will give ourselves continually to prayer, and to the ministry of the word.

5 And the saying pleased the whole multitude: and they chose Stephen, [h]a man full of faith and of the Holy Ghost, and [i]Philip, and Prochorus, and Nicanor, and Timon, and Parmenas, and Nicolas a proselyte of Antioch;

6 Whom they set before the apostles: and [k]when they had prayed, [l]they laid *their* hands on them.

7 And [m]the word of God increased; and the number of the disciples multiplied in Jerusalem greatly; and a great company [n]of the priests were obedient to the faith.

A

Acts 2. 41 Then they that gladly received his word were baptized: and the same day there were added *unto them* about three thousand souls.

Acts 4. 4 Howbeit many of them which heard the word believed; and the number of the men was about five thousand.

Acts 5. 14 And believers were the more added to the Lord, multitudes both of men and women;)

B

Acts 9. 29 And he spake boldly in the name of the Lord Jesus, and disputed against the Grecians: but they went about to slay him.

Acts 11. 20 And some of them were men of Cyprus and Cyrene, which, when they were come to Antioch, spake unto the Grecians, preaching the Lord Jesus.

C

Acts 4. 35 And laid *them* down at the apostles' feet: and distribution was made unto every man according as he had need.

D

Ex. 18. 17 And Moses' father in law said unto him, The thing that thou doest *is* not good.

Ex. 18. 20 And thou shalt teach them ordinances and laws, and shalt shew them the way wherein they must walk, and the work that they must do.

E

Ex. 18. 21 Moreover thou shalt provide out of all the people able men, such as fear God, men of truth, hating covetousness; and place *such* over them, *to be* rulers of thousands, *and* rulers of hundreds, rulers of fifties, and rulers of tens:

Acts 1. 22 Beginning from the baptism of John, unto that same day that he was taken up from us, must one be ordained to be a witness with us of his resurrection.

§ 245. STEPHEN'S MINISTRY, PERSECUTION AND TRIAL.

6:8–15.

8 And Stephen, full of faith and power, did great wonders and miracles among the people.

9 Then there arose certain of the synagogue, which is called *the synagogue* of the Libertines, and Cyrenians, and Alexandrians, and of them of Cilicia and of Asia, disputing with Stephen.

CHAP.

TIME, A. D. 30–36; PLACE, JERUSALEM.

F

Deut. 1. 13 Take you wise men, and understanding, and known among your tribes, and I will make them rulers over you.

Acts 16. 1 Then came he to Derbe and Lystra: and, behold, a certain disciple was there, named Timotheus, the son of a certain woman, which was a Jewess, and believed; but his father *was* a Greek:

2 Which was well reported of by the brethren that were at Lystra and Iconium.

I Tim.3. 2 A bishop then must be blameless, the husband of one wife, vigilant, sober, of good behaviour, given to hospitality, apt to teach;

G

Acts 2. 42 And they continued steadfastly in the apostles' doctrine and fellowship, and in breaking of bread, and in prayers.

I Tim.4. 15 Meditate upon these things; give thyself wholly to them; that thy profiting may appear to all.

H

Acts 11 24 For he was a good man and full of the Holy Ghost and of faith: and much people was added unto the Lord.

I

Acts 8. 5 Then Philip went down to the city of Samaria, and preached Christ unto them.

Acts 8. 26 And the angel of the Lord spake unto Philip, saying, Arise, and go toward the south, unto the way that goeth down from Jerusalem unto Gaza, which is desert.

Acts 21. 8 And the next *day* we that were of Paul's company departed, and came unto Cesarea; and we entered into the house of Philip the evangelist, which was *one* of the seven; and abode with him.

K

Acts 1. 24 And they prayed, and said, Thou Lord, which knowest the hearts of all

K—CONCLUDED.

men, shew whether of these two thou hast chosen,

Acts 13. 3 And when they had fasted and prayed, and laid *their* hands on them, they sent *them* away.

L

Acts 8. 17 Then laid they *their* hands on them, and they received the Holy Ghost.

Acts 9. 17 And Ananias went his way, and entered into the house; and putting his hands on him said, Brother Saul, the Lord, *even* Jesus, that appeared unto thee in the way as thou camest, hath sent me, that thou mightest receive thy sight, and be filled with the Holy Ghost.

Acts 13. 3. *See under K.*

I Tim.4. 14 Neglect not the gift that is in thee, which was given thee by prophecy, with the laying on of the hands of the presbytery.

I Tim.5. 22 Lay hands suddenly on no man, neither be partaker of other men's sins: keep thyself pure.

IITim.1. 6 Wherefore I put thee in remembrance, that thou stir up the gift of God, which is in thee by the putting on of my hands.

M

Acts 12. 24 But the word of God grew and multiplied.

Acts 19. 20 So mightily grew the word of God and prevailed.

Col. 1. 6 Which is come unto you, as *it is* in all the world; and bringeth forth fruit, as *it doth* also in you, since the day ye heard *of it*, and knew the grace of God in truth:

N

Ps. 132. 16 I will also clothe her priests with salvation: and her saints shall shout aloud for joy.

John 12. 42 Nevertheless among the chief rulers also many believed on him; but because of the Pharisees they did not confess *him*, lest they should be put out of the synagogue:

TIME, A. D. 36; PLACE, JERUSALEM.

A

Isa. 54. 17 No weapon that is formed against thee shall prosper; and every tongue *that* shall rise against thee in judgment thou shalt condemn. This *is* the heritage of the servants of the LORD, and their righteousness *is* of me, saith the LORD.

A—CONCLUDED.

Luke 21. 15 For I will give you a mouth and wisdom, which all your adversaries shall not be able to gainsay nor resist.

Acts 5. 39 But if it be of God, ye cannot overthrow it; lest haply ye be found even to fight against God.

§ 245. STEPHEN'S MINISTRY, PERSECUTION AND TRIAL

CHAP. 6.

10 And [a]they were not able to resist the wisdom and the spirit by which he spake.

11 Then [b]they suborned men, which said, We have heard him speak blasphemous words against Moses, and *against* God.

12 And they stirred up the people, and the elders, and the scribes, and came upon *him*, and caught him, and brought *him* to the council,

CHAP. 6.

13 And set up false witnesses, which said, This man ceaseth not to speak blasphemous words against this holy place, and the law:

14 For [c]we have heard him say, that this Jesus of Nazareth shall [d]destroy this place, and shall change the [1]customs which Moses delivered us.

15 And all that sat in the council, looking steadfastly on him, saw his face as it had been the face of an angel.

§ 246. STEPHEN'S DEFENSE AND MARTYRDOM.

7: 1-60.

1 Then said the high priest, Are these things so?

2 And he said, [a]Men, brethren, and fathers, hearken; The God of glory appeared unto our father Abraham, when he was in Mesopotamia, before he dwelt in Charran,

3 And said unto him, [b]Get thee out of thy country, and from thy kindred, and come into the land which I shall shew thee.

4 Then [c]came he out of the land of the Chaldeans, and dwelt in Charran: and from thence, when his father was dead, he removed him into this land, wherein ye now dwell.

5 And he gave him none inheritance in it, no, not *so much as* to set his foot on: [d]yet he promised that he would give it to him for a possession, and to his seed after him, when *as yet* he had no child.

6 And God spake on this wise, [e]That his seed should sojourn in a strange land; and that they should bring them into bondage, and entreat *them* evil [f]four hundred years.

CHAP. 7.

7 And the nation to whom they shall be in bondage will I judge, said God: and after that shall they come forth, and [g]serve me in this place.

8 And [h]he gave them the covenant of circumcision: [i]and so *Abraham* begat Isaac, and circumcised him the eighth day; and Isaac *begat* Jacob; and Jacob *begat* the twelve patriarchs.

A

Acts 22. 1 Men, brethren, and fathers, hear ye my defence *which I make* now unto you.

B

Gen. 12. 1 Now the LORD had said unto Abram, Get thee out of thy country, and from thy kindred, and from thy father's house, unto a land that I will shew thee:

C

Gen. 12. 4 So Abram departed, as the LORD had spoken unto him; and Lot went with him: and Abram *was* seventy and five years old when he departed out of Haran.

5 And Abram took Sarai his wife, and Lot his brother's son, and all their substance that they had gathered, and the souls that they had gotten in Haran; and they went forth to go into the land of Canaan; and into the land of Canaan they came.

(CONCLUDED). TIME, A. D. 36; PLACE, JERUSALEM.

For A see preceeding page.

B

I Ki. 21. 10 And set two men, sons of Belial, before him, to bear witness against him, saying, Thou didst plaspheme God and the king. And *then* carry him out, and stone him, that he may die.

Matt. 26. 59 Now the chief priests, and elders, and all the council, sought false witness against Jesus, to put him to death;

60 But found none: yea, though many false witnesses came, *yet* found they none. At the last came two false witnesses,

C

John 2. 19 Jesus answered and said unto them, Destroy this temple, and in three days I will raise it up.

C—CONCLUDED.

Acts 25. 8 While he answered for himself, Neither against the law of the Jews, neither against the temple, nor yet against Cæsar, have I offended any-thing at all.

D

Mic. 3. 12 Therefore shall Zion for your sake be ploughed *as* a field, and Jerusalem shall become heaps, and the mountain of the house as the high places of the forest.

Zech. 11. 1 Open thy doors, O Lebanon, that the fire may devour thy cedars.

1

Or, *Rites.*

TIME, A. D. 36; PLACE, JERUSALEM.

D

Gen. 12. 7 And the LORD appeared unto Abram, and said, Unto thy seed will I give this land: and there builded he an altar unto the LORD, who appeared unto him.

Gen 13. 15 For all the land which thou seest, to thee will I give it, and to thy seed for ever.

Gen. 15. 4 So Abram departed, as the LORD had spoken unto him; and Lot went with him: And Abram *was* seventy and five years old when he departed out of Haran.

Gen. 15. 18 In that same day the LORD made a covenant with Abram, saying, Unto thy seed have I given this land, from the river of Egypt unto the great river, the river Euphrates:

Gen. 17. 8 And I will give unto thee, and to thy seed after thee, the land wherein thou art a stranger, all the land of Canaan, for an everlasting possession; and I will be their God.

Gen. 26. 3 Sojourn in this land, and I will be with thee, and will bless thee; for unto thee, and unto thy seed, I will give all these countries, and I will perform the oath which I sware unto Abraham thy father;

E

Gen. 15. 13 And he said unto Abram, Know of a surety that thy seed shall be a stranger in a land *that is* not theirs, and shall serve them; and they shall afflict them four hundred years;

Gen 15. 16 But in the fourth generation they shall come hither again: for the iniquity of the Amorites *is* not yet full.

F

Ex. 12. 40 Now the sojourning of the children of Israel, who dwelt in Egypt, *was* four hundred and thirty years.

Gal. 3. 17 And this I say, *that* the covenant, that was confirmed before of God in Christ, the law, which was four hundred and thirty years after, cannot disannul, that it should make the promise of none effect.

G

Ex. 3. 12 And he said, Certainly I will be with thee; and this *shall be* a token unto thee, that I have sent thee: When thou hast brought forth the people out of Egypt, ye shall serve God upon this mountain.

H

Gen. 17. 9 And God said unto Abraham, Thou shalt keep my covenant therefore, thou, and thy seed after thee in their generations.

10 This *is* my covenant, which ye shall keep, between me and you and thy seed after thee; Every man child among you shall be circumcised.

11 And ye shall circumcise the flesh of your foreskin; and it shall be a token of the covenant betwixt me and you.

Rom. 4. 11 And he received the sign of circumcision, a seal of the righteousness of the faith which *he had yet* being uncircumcised: that he might be the father of all them that believe, though they be not circumcised; that righteousness might be imputed unto them also:

For I see next page (668).

§ 246. STEPHEN'S DEFENSE AND MARTYRDOM

CHAP. 7.

9 And [k]the patriarchs, moved with envy, sold Joseph into Egypt: but [l]God was with him,

10 And delivered him out of all his afflictions, and [m]gave him favour and wisdom in the sight of Pharaoh king of Egypt; and he made him governor over Egypt and all his house.

11 Now [n]there came a dearth over all the land of Egypt and Chanaan, and great affliction: and our fathers found no sustenance.

12 But [o]when Jacob heard that there was corn in Egypt, he sent out our fathers first.

13 And at the second *time* Joseph [p]was made known to his brethren; and Joseph's kindred was made known unto Pharaoh.

14 Then [q]sent Joseph, and called his father Jacob to *him*, and all his kindred, threescore and fifteen souls.

15 So Jacob [r]went down into Egypt, and died, he, and our fathers,

16 And [s]were carried over into Sychem, and laid in [t]the sepulchre that Abraham bought for a sum of money of the sons of Emmor, *the father* of Sychem.

17 But [u]when the time of the promise drew nigh, which God had sworn to Abraham, [x]the people grew and multiplied in Egypt,

18 Till another king arose, which knew not Joseph.

19 The same dealt subtilly with our kindred, and evil entreated our fathers, [y]so that they cast out their young children, to the end they might not live.

CHAP. 7.

20 In which time [z]Moses was born, and was [1]exceeding fair, and nourished up in his father's house three months:

21 And [a]when he was cast out, Pharaoh's daughter took him up, and nourished him for her own son.

22 And Moses was learned in all the wisdom of the Egyptians, and was [b]mighty in words and in deeds.

I

Gen. 21. 2 For Sarah conceived, and bare Abraham a son in his old age, at the set time of which God had spoken to him.

3 And Abraham called the name of his son that was born unto him, which Sarah bare to him, Isaac.

K

Gen. 37. 4 And when his brethren saw that their father loved him more than all his brethren, they hated him, and could not speak peaceably unto him.

Gen. 37. 11 And his brethren envied him; but his father observed the saying.

Gen. 37. 28 Then there passed by Midianites merchantmen; and they drew and lifted up Joseph out of the pit, and sold Joseph to the Ishmaelites for twenty *pieces* of silver: and they brought Joseph into Egypt.

Ps. 105. 17 He sent a man before them, *even* Joseph, *who* was sold for a servant:

L

Gen. 39. 2 And the LORD was with Joseph and he was a prosperous man; and he was in the house of his master the Egyptian.

Gen. 39. 21 But the LORD was with Joseph, and shewed him mercy, and gave him favour in the sight of the keeper of the prison.

M

Gen. 41. 37 And the thing was good in the eyes of Pharaoh, and in the eyes of all his servants.

Gen. 42. 6 And Joseph *was* the governor over the land, *and* he *it was* that sold to all the people of the land: and Joseph's brethren came, and bowed down themselves before him *with* their faces to the earth.

(CONTINUED). TIME, A. D. 36; PLACE, JERUSALEM.

N

Gen. 41. 54 And the seven years of dearth began to come, according as Joseph had said: and the dearth was in all lands; but in all the land of Egypt there was bread.

O

Gen. 42. 1 Now when Jacob saw that there was corn in Egypt, Jacob said unto his sons, Why do ye look one upon another?

P

Gen. 45. 4 And Joseph said unto his brethren, Come near to me, I pray you. And And they came near. And he said, I *am* Joseph your brother, whom ye sold into Egypt.

Gen. 45. 16 And the fame thereof was heard in Pharaoh's house, saying, Joseph's brethren are come: and it pleased Pharaoh well, and his servants.

Q

Gen. 45. 9 Haste ye, and go up to my father, and say unto him, Thus saith thy son Joseph, God hath made me lord of all Egypt: come down unto me, tarry not:

Gen. 45. 27 And they told him all the words of Joseph, which he had said unto them: and when he saw the wagons which Joseph had sent to carry him, the spirit of Jacob their father revived.

Gen. 46. 27 And the sons of Joseph, which were born him in Egypt, *were* two souls: all the souls of the house of Jacob, which came into Egypt, *were* threescore and ten.

Deut. 10. 22 Thy fathers went down into Egypt with threescore and ten persons; and now the LORD thy God hath made thee as the stars of heaven for multitude.

R

Gen. 46. 5 And Jacob rose up from Beer-sheba: and the sons of Israel carried Jacob their father, and their little ones and their wives, in the wagons which Pharaoh had sent to carry him.

Gen. 49. 33 And when Jacob had made an end of commanding his sons, he gathered up his feet into the bed, and yielded up the ghost, and was gathered unto his people.

Ex. 1. 6 And Joseph died, and all his brethren, and all that generation.

S

Ex. 13. 19 And Moses took the bones of Joseph with him: for he had straitly sworn the children of Israel, saying,

S—CONCLUDED.

God will surely visit you; and ye shall carry up my bones away hence with you.

Josh. 24. 32 And the bones of Joseph, which the children of Israel brought up out of Egypt, buried they in Shechem, in a parcel of ground which Jacob bought of the sons of Hamor the father of Shechem for a hundred pieces of silver; and it became the inheritance of the children of Joseph.

T

Gen. 23. 15 My lord, hearken unto me: the land *is worth* four hundred shekels of silver; what *is* that betwixt me and thee? bury therefore thy dead.

Gen. 33. 19 And he bought a parcel of a field, where he had spread his tent, at the hand of the children of Hamor, Shechem's father, for a hundred pieces of money.

U

Gen. 15. 18 In that same day the LORD made a covenant with Abram, saying, Unto thy seed have I given this land, from the river of Egypt unto the great river, the river Euphrates:

X

Ex. 1. 7 And the children of Israel were fruitful, and increased abundantly, and multiplied, and waxed exceeding mighty; and the land was filled with them.

Ps. 105. 24 And he increased his people greatly; and made them stronger than their enemies.

Y

Ex. 1. 22 And Pharaoh charged all his people, saying, Every son that is born ye shall cast into the river, and every daughter ye shall save alive.

Z

Ex. 2. 2 And the woman conceived, and bare a son: and when she saw him that he *was a* goodly *child*, she hid him three months.

Heb. 11. 23 By faith Moses, when he was born, was hid three months of his parents, because they saw *he was* a proper child; and they were not afraid of the king's commandment.

1

Or, *fair to God.*

A

Ex. 2. 8 And Pharaoh's daughter said to her, Go. And the maid went and called the child's mother.

For A concluded and B see next page (670).

§ 246. STEPHEN'S DEFENSE AND MARTYRDOM

CHAP. 7.

23 And [c]when he was full forty years old, it came into his heart to visit his brethren the children of Israel.

24 And seeing one *of them* suffer wrong, he defended *him,* and avenged him that was oppressed, and smote the Egyptian:

25 [2]For he supposed his brethren would have understood how that God by his hand would deliver them; but they understood not.

26 And [d]the next day he shewed himself unto them as they strove, and would have set them at one again, saying, Sirs, ye are brethren; why do ye wrong one to another?

27 But he that did his neighbour wrong thrust him away saying, [e]Who made thee a ruler and a judge over us?

28 Wilt thou kill me, as thou didst the Egyptian yesterday?

29 Then [f]fled Moses at this saying, and was a stranger in the land of Madian, [g]where he begat two sons.

30 And when forty years were expired, there appeared to him in the wilderness of mount Sina an [h]angel of the Lord in a flame of fire in a bush.

31 When Moses saw *it,* he wondered at the sight: and as he drew near to behold *it,* the voice of the Lord came unto him,

32 *Saying,* [i]I *am* the God of thy fathers, the God of Abraham, and the God of Isaac, and the God of Jacob. Them Moses trembled, and durst not behold.

CHAP. 7.

33 Then said the Lord to him, [k]Put off thy shoes from thy feet: for the place where thou standest is holy ground.

34 I [l]have seen, I have seen the affliction of my people which is in Egypt, and I have heard their groaning, and am come down to deliver them. And now come, I will send thee into Egypt.

35 This Moses whom they refused, saying, Who made thee a ruler and a judge? the same did God send *to be* a ruler and a deliverer [m]by the hand of the angel which appear to him in the bush.

A—CONCLUDED.

Ex. 2. 9 And Pharaoh's daughter said unto her, Take this child away, and nurse it for me, and I will give *thee* thy wages. And the woman took the child, and nursed it.

10 And the child grew, and she brought him unto Pharaoh's daughter, and he became her son. And she called his name Moses: and she said, Because I drew him out of the water.

B

Luke 24. 19 And he said unto them, What things? And they said unto him, Concerning Jesus of Nazareth, which was a prophet mighty in deed and word before God and all the people:

C

Ex. 2. 11 And it came to pass in those days, when Moses was grown, that he went out unto his brethren, and looked on their burdens: and he spied an Egyptian smiting a Hebrew, one of his brethren.

2

Or, *Now.*

D

Ex. 2. 13 And when he went out the second day, behold, two men of the Hebrews strove together: and he said to him that did the wrong, Wherefore smitest thou thy fellow?

(CONTINUED). TIME, A. D. 36; PLACE JERUSALEM.

E

Luke 12. 14 And he said unto him, Man, who made me a judge or a divider over you?

Acts 4. 11 This is the stone which was set at nought of you builders, which is become the head of the corner.

F

Ex. 2. 15 Now when Pharaoh heard this thing, he sought to slay Moses. But Moses fled from the face of Pharaoh, and dwelt in the land of Midian: and he sat down by a well.

G

Ex. 2. 22 And she bare *him* a son, and he called his name Gershom: for he said, I have been a stranger in a strange land.

Ex. 4. 20 And Moses took his wife and his sons, and set them upon an ass, and he returned to the land of Egypt: and Moses took the rod of God in his hand.

Ex. 18. 3 And her two sons; of which the name of the one *was* Gershom; for he said, I have been an alien in a strange land:

4 And the name of the other *was* Eliezer; for the God of my father, *said he*, *was* mine help, and delivered me from the sword of Pharaoh:

H

Gen. 48. 16 The Angel which redeemed me from all evil, bless the lads; and let my name be named on them, and the name of my fathers Abraham and Isaac; and let them grow into a multitude in the midst of the earth.

Ex. 3. 2 And the Angel of the LORD appeared unto him in a flame of fire out of the midst of a bush: and he looked, and, behold, the bush burned with fire, and the bush *was* not consumed.

Isa. 63. 9 In all their affliction he was afflicted, and the Angel of his presence saved them: in his love and in his pity he redeemed them; and he bare them, and carried them all the days of old.

John 1. 14 And the Word was made flesh, and dwelt among us, (and we beheld his glory, the glory as of the only begotten of the Father,) full of grace and truth.

Tit. 2. 13 Looking for that blessed hope, and the glorious appearing of the great God and our Saviour Jesus Christ:

I

Matt. 22. 32 I am the God of Abraham, and the God of Isaac, and the God of Jacob? God is not the God of the dead, but of the living.

Heb. 11. 16 But now they desire a better *country*, that is, a heavenly: wherefore God is not ashamed to be called their God: for he hath prepared for them a city.

K

Ex. 3. 5 And he said, Draw not nigh hither: put off thy shoes from off thy feet; for the place whereon thou standest *is* holy ground.

Josh. 5. 15 And the captain of the LORD'S host said unto Joshua, Loose thy shoe from off thy foot; for the place whereon thou standest *is* holy. And Joshua did so.

Eccl. 5. 1 Keep thy foot when thou goest to the house of God, and be more ready to hear, than to give the sacrifice of fools: for they consider not that they do evil.

L

Ex. 3. 7 And the LORD said, I have surely seen the affliction of my people which *are* in Egypt, and have heard their cry by reason of their taskmasters; for I know their sorrows;

M

Ex. 14. 19 And the Angel of God, which went before the camp of Israel, removed and went behind them; and the pillar of the cloud went from before their face, and stood behind them:

Num. 20. 16 And when we cried unto the LORD, he heard our voice, and sent an angel, and hath brought us forth out of Egypt: and, behold, we *are* in Kadesh, a city in the uttermost of thy border.

N

Ex. 12. 41 And it came to pass at the end of the four hundred and thirty years, even the selfsame day it came to pass, that all the hosts of the LORD went out from the land of Egypt.

Ex. 33. 1 And the LORD said unto Moses, Depart, *and* go up hence, thou and the people which thou hast brought up out of the land of Egypt, unto the land which I sware unto Abraham, to Isaac, and to Jacob, saying, Unto thy seed will I give it:

§ 246. STEPHEN'S DEFENSE AND MARTYRDOM

CHAP. 7.

36 He [n]brought them out, after that
he had [o]shewed wonders and signs in
the land of Egypt, and in the Red
sea, and in the wilderness forty years.

37 This is that Moses, which said
unto the children of Israel, [p]A Prophet shall the Lord your God raise up
unto you of your brethren, [3]like unto
me; [q]him shall ye hear.

38 This [r]is he, that was in the
church in the wilderness with the [s]an-
gel which spake to him in the mount
Sina, and *with* our fathers: [t]who received the lively [u]oracles to give
unto us:

39 To whom our fathers would not
obey, but thrust *him* from them, and
in their hearts turned back again
into Egypt,

40 Saying [x]unto Aaron, Make us
gods to go before us: for *as for* this
Moses, which brought us out of the
land of Egypt, we wot not what is
become of him.

41 And [y]they made a calf in those
days, and offered sacrifice unto the
idol, and rejoiced in the works of
their own hands.

42 Then [z]God turned, and gave
them up to worship [a]the host of
heaven; as it is written in the book
of the prophets, [b]O ye house of Israel, have ye offered to me slain
beasts and sacrifices *by the space of*
forty years in the wilderness?

43 Yea, ye took up the tabernacle
of Moloch, and the star of your god
Remphan, figures which ye made to
worship them: and I will carry you
away beyond Babylon.

44 Our fathers had the tabernacle of

For N, see preceding page, 671.

O

Ex. 7, 8, 9, 10, 11, and 14. *Read entire chapters.*

Ex. 16. 35 And the children of Israel did eat manna forty years, until they came to a land inhabited; they did eat manna, until they came unto the borders of the land of Canaan.

Ps. 105. 27 They shewed his signs among them, and wonders in the land of Ham.

P

Deut. 18. 15, 18, *See S, § 234, page 647.*

3

Or, *as myself.*

Q

Matt. 17. 5 While he yet spake, behold, a bright cloud overshadowed them: and behold a voice out of the cloud, which said, This is my beloved Son, in whom I am well pleased; hear ye him.

Mark 9. 7 And there was a cloud that overshadowed them: and a voice came out of the cloud, saying, This is my beloved Son: hear him.

Luke 9. 35 And there came a voice out of the cloud, saying, This is my beloved Son: hear him.

John 8. 47 He that is of God heareth God's words: ye therefore hear *them* not, because ye are not of God.

Acts 3. 22 For Moses truly said unto the fathers, A Prophet shall the Lord your God raise up unto you of your brethren, like unto me; him shall ye hear in all things whatsoever he shall say unto you.

R

Ex. 19. 3 And Moses went up unto God, and the LORD called unto him out of the mountain, saying, Thus shalt thou say to the house of Jacob, and tell the children of Israel;

Ex. 19. 17 And Moses brought forth the people out of the camp to meet with God; and they stood at the nether part of the mount.

S

See under H, page 671.

Gal. 3. 19 Wherefore then *serveth* the law? It was added because of transgressions, till the seed should come to whom the promise was made; *and it was* ordained by angels in the hand of a mediator.

Heb. 2. 2 For if the word spoken by angels was steadfast, and every transgression and disobedience received a just recompense of reward;

(CONTINUED). TIME, A. D. 36; PLACE, JERUSALEM.

T

Ex. 21. 1 Now these *are* the judgments which thou shalt set before them.

Lev. 1. 1 And the LORD called unto Moses, and spake unto him out of the tabernacle of the congregation, saying,

Deut. 5. 27 Go thou near, and hear all that the LORD our God shall say; and speak thou unto us all that the LORD our God shall speak unto thee; and we will hear *it*, and do *it*.

Deut. 5. 31 But as for thee, stand thou here by me, and I will speak unto thee all the commandments, and the statutes, and the judgments, which thou shalt teach them, that they may do *them* in the land which I give them to possess it.

Deut. 33. 4 Moses commanded us a law, *even* the inheritance of the congregation of Jacob.

John 1. 17 For the law was given by Moses, *but* grace and truth came by Jesus Christ.

U

Rom. 3. 2 Much every way: chiefly, because that unto them were committed the oracles of God.

Rom. 9. 4 Who are Israelites; to whom *pertaineth* the adoption, and the glory, and the covenants, and the giving of the law, and the service *of God*, and the promises;

X

Ex. 32. 1 And when the people saw that Moses delayed to come down out of the mount, the people gathered themselves together unto Aaron, and said unto him, Up, make us gods, which shall go before us; for *as for* this Moses, the man that brought us up out of the land of Egypt, we wot not what is become of him.

Y

Deut 9. 16 And I looked, and, behold, ye had sinned against the LORD your God, *and* had made you a molten calf: ye had turned aside quickly out of the way which the LORD had commanded you.

Ps. 106. 19 They made a calf in Horeb, and worshipped the molten image.

20 Thus they changed their glory into the similitude of an ox that eateth grass.

Z

Ps 81. 11 But my people would not hearken to my voice; and Israel would none of me.

Z—CONCLUDED.

Ps. 81. 12 So I gave them up unto their own hearts' lust: *and* they walked in their own counsels.

Eze. 20. 25 Wherefore I gave them also statutes *that were* not good, and judgments whereby they should not live;

Eze. 20. 39 As for you, O house of Israel, thus saith the Lord GOD; Go ye, serve ye every one his idols, and hereafter *also*, if ye will not hearken unto me: but pollute ye my holy name no more with your gifts, and with your idols.

Rom. 1. 24 Wherefore God also gave them up to uncleanness, through the lusts of their own hearts, to dishonor their own bodies between themselves:

IIThes. 2. 11 And for this cause God shall send them strong delusion, that they should believe a lie:

A

Deut. 4. 19 And lest thou lift up thine eyes unto heaven, and when thou seest the sun, and the moon, and the stars, *even* all the host of heaven, shouldest be driven to worship them, and serve them, which the LORD thy God hath divided unto all nations under the whole heaven.

Deut. 17. 3 And hath gone and served other gods, and worshipped them, either the sun, or moon, or any of the host of heaven, which I have not commanded;

IIKi. 17. 16 And they left all the commandments of the LORD their God, and made them molten images, *even* two calves, and made a grove, and worshipped all the host of heaven, and served Baal.

Jer. 19. 13 And the houses of Jerusalem, and the houses of the kings of Judah, shall be defiled as the place of Tophet, because of all the houses upon whose roofs they have burned incense unto all the host of heaven, and have poured out drink offerings unto other gods.

B

Amos 5. 25 Have ye offered unto me sacrifices and offerings in the wilderness forty years, O house of Israel?

26 But ye have borne the tabernacle of your Moloch and Chiun your images, the star of your god, which ye made to yourselves.

4
Or, *who spake*.

§ 246. STEPHEN'S DEFENSE AND MARTYRDOM

CHAP. 7.

witness in the wilderness, as he had
appointed, [4]speaking unto Moses,
[c]that he should make it according to
the fashion that he had seen.

45 [d]Which also our fathers [5]that
came after brought in with [6]Jesus
into the possession of the Gentiles,
[e]whom God drave out before the face
of our fathers, unto the days of David;

46 Who [f]found favour before God,
and desired [g]to find a tabernacle for
the God of Jacob.

47 But [h]Solomon built him a house.

48 Howbeit the [i]Most High dwelleth not in temples made with hands;
as saith the prophet,

49 [k]Heaven *is* my throne, and earth
is my footstool: what house will ye
build me? saith the Lord: or what
is the place of my rest?

50 Hath not my hand made all
these things?

51 Ye [l]stiffnecked and [m]uncircum-
cised in heart and ears, ye do always resist the Holy Ghost: as your
fathers *did*, so *do* ye.

52 [n]Which of the prophets have not
your fathers persecuted? and they
have slain them which shewed before
of the coming of the Just One; of
whom ye have been now the betrayers and murderers:

53 Who [o]have received the law by
the disposition of angels, and have
not kept *it*.

54 When [p]they heard these things,
they were cut to the heart, and they
gnashed on him with *their* teeth.

55 But he, [q]being full of the Holy

For 4, see preceding page, 673.

C

Ex. 25. 9 According to all that I shew thee, *after* the pattern of the tabernacle, and the pattern of all the instruments thereof, even so shall ye make *it*.

Ex. 25. 40 And look that thou make *them* after their pattern, which was shewed thee in the mount.

Ex. 26. 30 And thou shalt rear up the tabernacle according to the fashion thereof which was shewed thee in the mount.

Heb. 8. 5 Who serve unto the example and shadow of heavenly things, as Moses was admonished of God when he was about to make the tabernacle: for, See, saith he, *that* thou make all things according to the pattern shewed to thee in the mount.

D

Josh. 3. 14 And it came to pass, when the people removed from their tents, to pass over Jordon, and the priests bearing the ark of the covenant before the people;

Josh. 4. 11 And it came to pass, when all the people were clean passed over, that the ark of the LORD passed over, and the priests, in the presence of the people.

5
Or, *having received.*

6
That is, *Joshua.*

E

Neh. 9. 24 So the children went in and possessed the land, and thou subduedst before them the inhabitants of the land, the Canaanites, and gavest them into their hands, with their kings, and the people of the land, that they might do with them as they would.

Ps. 44. 2 *How* thou didst drive out the heathen with thy hand, and plantedst them; *how* thou didst afflict the people, and cast them out.

Ps. 78. 55 He cast out the heathen also before them, and divided them an inheritance by line, and made the tribes of Israel to dwell in their tents.

Acts 13. 19 And when he had destroyed seven nations in the land of Chanaan, he divided their land to them by lot.

F

I Sa. 16. 1 And the LORD said unto Samuel, How long wilt thou mourn for Saul, seeing I have rejected him from reigning over Israel? fill thine horn with oil, and go, I will send thee to Jesse the Beth-lehemite: for I have provided me a king among his sons.

(CONTINUED). TIME, A. D. 36; PLACE, JERUSALEM.

F—CONCLUDED.

II Sa. 7. 1 And it came to pass, when the king sat in his house, and the LORD had given him rest round about from all his enemies;

Ps. 89. 20 I have found David my servant; with my holy oil have I anointed him:

Acts 13. 22 And when he had removed him, he raised up unto them David to be their king; to whom also he gave testimony, and said, I have found David the *son* of Jesse, a man after mine own heart, which shall fulfill all my will.

G

I Ki. 8. 17 And it was in the heart of David my father to build a house for the name of the LORD God of Israel.

I Chr. 22. 7 And David said to Solomon, My son, as for me, it was in my mind to build a house unto the name of the LORD my God:

Ps. 132. 4 I will not give sleep to mine eyes, *or* slumber to mine eyelids,
5 Until I find out a place for the LORD, a habitation for the mighty *God* of Jacob.

H

I Ki. 6. 1 And it came to pass in the four hundred and eightieth year after the children of Israel were come out of the land of Egypt, in the fourth year of Solomon's reign over Israel, in the month Zif, which *is* the second month, that he began to build the house of the LORD.

I Ki. 8. 20 And the LORD hath performed his word that he spake, and I am risen up in the room of David my father, and sit on the throne of Israel as the LORD promised, and have built a house for the name of the LORD God of Israel.

I Ch. 17. 12 He shall build me a house, and I will stablish his throne for ever.

II Ch. 3. 1 Then Solomon began to build the house of the LORD at Jerusalem in mount Moriah, where *the LORD* appeared unto David his father, in the place that David had prepared in the threshingfloor of Ornan the Jebusite.

I

I Ki. 8. 27 But will God indeed dwell on the earth? behold, the heaven and heaven of heavens cannot contain thee; how much less this house that I have builded?

II Ch. 2. 6 But who is able to build him a house, seeing the heaven and heaven

I—CONCLUDED.

of heavens cannot contain him? who *am* I then, that I should build him a house, save only to burn sacrifice before him?

II Ch. 6. 18 But will God in very deed dwell with men on earth? Behold, heaven and the heaven of heavens cannot contain thee; how much less this house which I have built!

Acts 17. 24 God that made the world and all things therein, seeing that he is Lord of heaven and earth, dwelleth not in temples made with hands;

K

Isa. 66. 1 Thus saith the LORD, The heaven *is* my throne, and the earth *is* my footstool: where *is* the house that ye build unto me? and where *is* the place of my rest?

Matt. 5. 34 But I say unto you, Swear not at all; neither by heaven; for it is God's throne:
35 Nor by the earth; for it is his footstool: neither by Jerusalem; for it is the city of the great King.

Matt. 23. 22 And he that shall swear by heaven, sweareth by the throne of God, and by him that sitteth thereon.

L

Ex. 32. 9 And the LORD said unto Moses, I have seen this people, and, behold, it *is* a stiffnecked people:

Ex. 33. 3 Unto a land flowing with milk and honey: for I will not go up in the midst of thee; for thou *art* a stiffnecked people: lest I consume thee in the way.

Isa. 48. 4 Because I knew that thou *art* obstinate, and thy neck *is* an iron sinew, and thy brow brass;

M

Deut. 10. 16 Circumcise therefore the foreskin of your heart, and be no more stiffnecked.

Jer. 4. 4 Circumcise yourselves to the LORD, and take away the foreskins of your heart, ye men of Judah and inhabitants of Jerusalem; lest my fury come forth like fire, and burn that none can quench *it*, because of the evil of your doings.

Eze. 44. 9 Thus saith the Lord GOD; No stranger, uncircumcised in heart, nor uncircumcised in flesh, shall enter into my sanctuary, of any stranger that *is* among the children of Israel.

For N, O, P, Q, *see next page, 676.*

§ 246. STEPHEN'S DEFENSE AND MARTYRDOM

CHAP. 7.

Ghost, looked up stedfastly into
heaven, and saw the glory of God,
and Jesus standing on the right hand
of God,

56 And said, [r]Behold, I see the heavens opened, and the [s]Son of man
standing on the right hand of God.

57 Then they cried out with a loud
voice, and stopped their ears, and
ran upon him with one accord,

58 And [t]cast *him* out of the city,
and stoned *him:* and [u]the witnesses
laid down their clothes at a young
man's feet, whose name was Saul.

59 And they stoned Stephen, [x]call-
ing upon *God,* and saying, Lord Jesus, [y]receive my spirit.

60 And he [z]kneeled down, and cried
with a loud voice, Lord, [a]lay not
this sin to their charge. And when
he had said this, he fell asleep.

N

IICh.36. 16 But they mocked the messengers of God, and despised his words, and misused his prophets, until the wrath of the LORD arose against his people, till *there was* no remedy.

Matt.21. 35 And the husbandmen took his servants, and beat one, and killed another, and stoned another.

Matt.23. 34 Wherefore, behold, I send unto you prophets, and wise men, and scribes: and *some* of them ye shall kill and crucify; and *some* of them shall ye

N—CONCLUDED

scourge in your synagogues, and persecute *them* from city to city:

Matt.23. 37 O Jerusalem, Jerusalem, *thou* that killest the prophets, and stonest them which are sent unto thee, how often would I have gathered thy children together, even as a hen gathereth her chickens under *her* wings, and ye would not!

IThes.2. 15 Who both killed the Lord Jesus, and their own prophets, and have persecuted us; and they please not God, and are contrary to all men:

O

Ex. 20. 1 And God spake all these words, saying,

See under S and T, page 672.

P

Acts 5. 33 When they heard *that,* they were cut *to the heart,* and took counsel to slay them.

Q

Acts 6. 5 And the saying pleased the whole multitude: and they chose Stephen, a man full of faith and of the Holy Ghost, and Philip, and Prochorus, and Nicanor, and Timon, and Parmenas, and Nicolas a proselyte of Antioch;

R

Eze. 1. 1 Now it came to pass in the thirtieth year, in the fourth *month,* in the fifth *day* of the month, as I *was* among the captives by the river of Chebar, *that* the heavens were opened, and I saw visions of God.

Matt. 3. 16 And Jesus, when he was baptized, went up straightway out of the water: and, lo, the heavens were opened unto him, and he saw the Spirit of God descending like a dove, and lighting upon him:

Acts 10. 11 And saw heaven opened, and a certain vessel descending unto him, as it had been a great sheet knit at the four corners, and let down to the earth:

§ 247. SAUL PERSECUTING THE CHURCH. STEPHEN'S BURIAL.

8: 1–4.

CHAP. 8.

1 And [a]Saul was consenting unto
his death. And at that time there
was a great persecution against the
church which was at Jerusalem; and
[b]they were all scattered abroad
throughout the regions of Judea and
Samaria, except the apostles.

2 And devout men carried Stephen

(CONCLUDED). TIME, A. D. 36. PLACE, JERUSALEM.

S

Dan. 7. 13 I saw in the night visions, and, behold, *one* like the Son of man came with the clouds of heaven, and came to the Ancient of days, and they brought him near before him.

T

I Ki. 21. 13 And there came in two men, children of Belial, and sat before him: and the men of Belial witnessed against him, *even* against Naboth, in the presence of the people, saying, Naboth did blaspheme God and the king. Then they carried him forth out of the city, and stoned him with stones, that he died.

Luke 4. 29 And rose up, and thrust him out of the city, and led him unto the brow of the hill whereon their city was built, that they might cast him down headlong.

Heb 13. 12 Wherefore Jesus also, that he might sanctify the people with his own blood, suffered without the gate.

U

Deut. 13. 9 But thou shalt surely kill him; thine hand shall be first upon him to put him to death, and afterwards the hand of all the people.

10 And thou shalt stone him with stones, that he die; because he hath sought to thrust thee away from the LORD thy God, which brought thee out of the land of Egypt, from the house of bondage.

Deut. 17. 7 The hands of the witnesses shall be first upon him to put him to death, and afterward the hands of all the people. So thou shalt put the evil away from among you.

Acts 22 20 And when the blood of thy martyr Stephen was shed, I also was standing by, and consenting unto his death, and kept the raiment of them that slew him.

X

Acts 9. 14 And here he hath authority from the chief priests to bind all that call on thy name.

Y

Ps. 31. 5 Into thine hand I commit my spirit: thou hast redeemed me, O LORD God of truth.

Luke 23. 46 And when Jesus had cried with a loud voice, he said, Father, into thy hands I commend my spirit: and having said thus, he gave up the ghost.

Z

Acts 9. 40 But Peter put them all forth, and kneeled down, and prayed; and turning *him* to the body said, Tabitha, arise. And she opened her eyes: and when she saw Peter, she sat up.

Acts 20. 36 And when he had thus spoken, he kneeled down, and prayed with them all.

Acts 21. 5 And when we had accomplished those days, we departed and went our way; and they all brought us on our way, with wives and children, till *we were* out of the city: and we kneeled down on the shore, and prayed.

A

Matt. 5. 44 But I say unto you, Love your enemies, bless them that curse you, do good to them that hate you, and pray for them which despitefully use you, and persecute you;

Luke 6. 28 Bless them that curse you, and pray for them which despitefully use you.

Luke 23. 34 Then said Jesus, Father, forgive them; for they know not what they do. And they parted his raiment, and cast lots.

Rom. 12. 14 Bless them which persecute you: bless, and curse not.

Rom. 12. 20 Therefore if thine enemy hunger, feed him; if he thirst, give him drink: for in so doing thou shalt heap coals of fire on his head.

TIME A. D. 36, 37; PLACE, JERUSALEM.

A

Acts 7. 58. *See text of topic, § 246 under U.*

Act. 20 19 Serving the LORD with all humility of mind, and with many tears and temptations which befell me by the lying in wait of the Jews:

B

Acts. 11. 19 Now they which were scattered abroad upon the persecution that arose about Stephen travelled as far as Phenice, and Cyprus, and Antioch, preaching the word to none but unto the Jews only.

§ 247. SAUL PERSECUTING THE CHURCH. STEPHEN'S BURIAL.

CHAP. 8.

to his burial, and [e]made great lamentation over him.

3 As for Saul, [d]he made havoc of the church, entering into every house, and haling men and women committed *them* to prison.

4 Therefore [e]they that were scattered abroad went every where preaching the word.

C

Gen. 23. 2 And Sarah died in Kirjath-arba; the same *is* Hebron in the land of Canaan: and Abraham came to mourn for Sarah, and to weep for her.

Gen. 50. 10 And they came to the threshing-floor of Atad, which *is* beyond Jordan; and there they mourned with a great

C—CONCLUDED.

and very sore lamentation: and he made a mourning for his father seven days.

II Sa. 3. 31 And David said to Joab, and to all the people that *were* with him, Rend your clothes, and gird you with sackcloth, and mourn before Abner. And king David *himself* followed the bier.

D

Acts 7. 58 And cast *him* out of the city, and stoned *him:* and the witnesses laid down their clothes at a young man's feet, whose name was Saul.

Acts 9. 1 And Saul, yet breathing out threatenings and slaughter against the disciples of the Lord, went unto the high priest,

Acts 9. 13 Then Ananias answered, Lord, I have heard by many of this man, how much evil he hath done to thy saints at Jerusalem:

§ 248 PHILIP PREACHING AT SAMARIA. SIMON THE SORCERER.

8: 5–13.

5 Then [a]Philip went down to the city of Samaria, and preached Christ unto them.

6 And the people with one accord gave heed unto those things which Philip spake, hearing and seeing the miracles which he did.

7 For [b]unclean spirits, crying with loud voice, came out of many that were possessed *with them:* and many taken with palsies, and that were lame, were healed.

8 And there was great joy in that city.

9 But there was a certain man, called Simon, which beforetime in the same city used [c]sorcery, and bewitched the people of Samaria, giving out that himself was some great one:

10 To whom they all gave heed,

CHAP. 8.

from the least to the greatest, saying, This man is the great power of God.

11 And to him they had regard, because that of long time he had bewitched them with sorceries.

12 But when they believed Philip preaching the things concerning the kingdom of God, and the name of Jesus Christ, they were baptized, both men and women.

13 Then Simon himself believed also: and when he was baptized, he continued with Philip, and wondered, beholding the [1]miracles and signs which were done.

A

Acts 6. 5 And the saying pleased the whole multitude: and they chose Stephen, a man full of faith and of the Holy Ghost, and Philip, and Prochorus, and Nicanor, and Timon, and Parmenas, and Nicolas a proselyte of Antioch:

(CONCLUDED). TIME, A. D. 36, 37; PLACE, JERUSALEM.

D—CONTINUED.

Acts 9. 21 But all that heard *him* were amazed, and said; Is not this he that destroyed them which called on this name in Jerusalem, and came hither for that intent, that he might bring them bound unto the chief priests?

Acts 22. 4 And I persecuted this way unto the death, binding and delivering into prisons both men and women.

Acts 26. 10 Which thing I also did in Jerusalem: and many of the saints did I shut up in prison, having received authority from the chief priests; and when they were put to death, I gave my voice against *them*.

11 And I punished them oft in every synagogue, and compelled *them* to blaspheme; and being exceedingly mad against them, I persecuted *them* even unto strange cities.

I Cor. 15. 9 For I am the least of the apostles, that am not meet to be called an apostle, because I persecuted the church of God.

D—CONCLUDED.

Gal. 1. 13 For ye have heard of my conversation in time past in the Jews' religion, how that beyond measure I persecuted the church of God, and wasted it:

Phil. 3. 6 Concerning zeal, persecuting the church; touching the righteousness which is in the law, blameless.

I Tim. 1. 13 Who was before a blasphemer and a persecutor, and injurious: but I obtained mercy, because I did *it* ignorantly in unbelief.

E

Matt. 10. 23 But when they persecute you in this city, flee ye into another: for verily I say unto you, Ye shall not have gone over the cities of Israel, till the Son of man be come.

Acts 14. 6 They were ware of *it*, and fled unto Lystra and Derbe, cities of Lycaonia, and unto the region that lieth round about:

TIME, A. D. 36, 37; PLACE, SAMARIA.

A—CONCLUDED.

Acts 21. 8 And the next *day* we that were of Paul's company departed, and came unto Cesarea; and we entered into the house of Philip the evangelist, which was *one* of the seven; and abode with him.

B

Mark 16. 17 And these signs shall follow them that believe; In my name shall they cast out devils; they shall speak with new tongues;

C

Ex. 7. 11 Then Pharaoh also called the wise men and the sorcerers: now the magicians of Egypt, they also did in like manner with their enchantments.

Ex. 8. 18 And the magicians did so with their enchantments to bring forth lice, but they could not: so there were lice upon man, and upon beast.

19 Then the magicians said unto Pharaoh, This *is* the finger of God: and Pharaoh's heart was hardened, and he hearkened not unto them; as the LORD had said.

Ex. 9. 11 And the magicians could not stand before Moses because of the boils; for the boil was upon the magicians, and upon all the Egyptians.

Lev. 20. 6 And the soul that turneth after such as have familiar spirits, and after wizards, to go a whoring after them, I will even set my face against that soul, and will cut him off from among his people.

C—CONCLUDED.

Deut. 18. 10 There shall not be found among you *any one* that maketh his son or his daughter to pass through the fire, *or* that useth divination, *or* an observer of times, or an enchanter, or a witch,

11 Or a charmer, or a consulter with familiar spirits, or a wizard, or a necromancer.

12 For all that do these things *are* an abomination unto the LORD: and because of these abominations the LORD thy God doth drive them out from before thee.

Acts 13. 6 And when they had gone through the isle unto Paphos, they found a certain sorcerer, a false prophet, a Jew, whose name *was* Bar-jesus:

Rev. 13. 13 And he doeth great wonders, so that he maketh fire come down from heaven on the earth in the sight of men,

Rev. 22. 15 For without *are* dogs, and sorcerers, and whoremongers, and murderers, and idolaters, and whosoever loveth and maketh a lie.

1

Gr, *Signs and great miracles.*

§ 249. PETER AND JOHN SENT TO SAMARIA. SIMON REBUKED.

8: 14–25.

14 Now when the apostles which were at Jerusalem heard that Samaria had received the word of God, they sent unto them Peter and John:

15 Who, when they were come down, prayed for them, [a]that they might receive the Holy Ghost:

16 (For [b]as yet he was fallen upon none of them: only they [c]were baptized in the name of the Lord Jesus.)

17 Then [d]laid they *their* hands on them, and they received the Holy Ghost.

18 And when Simon saw that through laying on of the apostles' hands the Holy Ghost was given, he offered them money,

19 Saying, Give me also this power, that on whomsoever I lay hands, he may receive the Holy Ghost.

20 But Peter said unto him, Thy money perish with thee, because [e]thou hast thought that the [f]gift of God may be purchased with money.

21 Thou hast neither part nor lot in this matter: for thy [g]heart is not right in the sight of God.

22 Repent therefore of this thy wickedness, and pray God, [h]if perhaps the thought of thine heart may be forgiven thee.

23 For I perceive that thou art in [i]the gall of bitterness, and *in* the bond of iniquity.

24 Then answered Simon, and said, [k]Pray ye to the Lord for me, that none of these things which ye have spoken come upon me.

25 And they, when they had testified and preached the word of the Lord, returned to Jerusalem, and preached the gospel in many villages of the Samaritans.

CHAP. 8.

A

Acts 2. 38 Then Peter said unto them, Repent, and be baptized every one of you in the name of Jesus Christ for the remission of sins, and ye shall receive the gift of the Holy Ghost.

B

Acts 19. 2 He said unto them, Have ye received the Holy Ghost since ye believed? And they said unto him, We have not so much as heard whether there be any Holy Ghost.

C

Matt. 28. 19 Go ye therefore, and teach all nations, baptizing them in the name of the Father, and of the Son, and of the Holy Ghost:

Acts 2. 38. *See under A.*

Acts 10. 48 And he commanded them to be baptized in the name of the Lord. Then prayed they him to tarry certain days.

Acts 19. 5 When they heard *this*, they were baptized in the name of the Lord Jesus.

D

Num. 8. 10 And thou shalt bring the Levites before the LORD: and the children of Israel shall put their hands upon the Levites:

Acts 6. 6 Whom they set before the apostles: and when they had prayed, they laid *their* hands on them.

Acts 19. 6 And when Paul had laid *his* hands upon them, the Holy Ghost came on them; and they spake with tongues, and prophesied.

Heb 6. 2 Of the doctrine of baptisms, and of laying on of hands, and of resurrection of the dead, and of eternal judgment.

E

II Ki. 5 25 But he went in, and stood before his master. And Elisha said unto him, Whence *comest thou*, Gehazi? And he said, Thy servant went no whither.

26 And he said unto him, Went not mine heart *with thee*, when the man turned again from his chariot to meet thee? *Is it* a time to receive money, and to receive garments, and oliveyards, and vineyards, and sheep, and

TIME, A. D. 36, 37; PLACE, SAMARIA.

E—CONCLUDED.

oxen, and menservants, and maidservants?

Matt. 10. 8 Heal the sick, cleanse the lepers, raise the dead, cast out devils: freely ye have received, freely give.

F

Acts 2. 38. *See under A.*

Acts 10. 45 And they of the circumcision which believed were astonished, as many as came with Peter, because that on the Gentiles also was poured out the gift of the Holy Ghost.

Acts 11. 17 Forasmuch then as God gave them the like gift as *he did* unto us, who believed on the Lord Jesus Christ; what was I, that I could withstand God?

G

Job 15. 12 Why doth thine heart carry thee away? and what do thy eyes wink at,

Prov. 6. 16 These six *things* doth the LORD hate; yea, seven *are* an abomination unto him:

Prov. 6. 18 A heart that deviseth wicked imaginations, feet that be swift in running to mischief,

Prov. 11. 20 They that are of a froward heart *are* abomination to the LORD: but *such as are* upright in *their* way *are* his delight.

Prov. 12. 20 Deceit *is* in the heart of them that imagine evil: but to the counsellors of peace *is* joy.

Isa. 44. 20 He feedeth on ashes: a deceived heart hath turned him aside, that he cannot deliver his soul, nor say, *Is there* not a lie in my right hand?

Jer. 17. 9 The heart *is* deceitful above all *things*, and desperately wicked: who can know it?

Rom. 8. 7 Because the carnal mind *is* enmity against God: for it is not subject to the law of God, neither indeed can be.

II Tim. 3. 5 Having a form of godliness, but denying the power thereof: from such turn away.

H

Dan. 4. 27 Wherefore, O king, let my counsel be acceptable unto thee, and break off thy sins by righteousness, and thine iniquities by shewing mercy to the poor; if it may be a lengthening of thy tranquillity.

II Tim. 2. 25 In meekness instructing those that oppose themselves; if God peradventure will give them repentance to the acknowledging of the truth;

I

Job 20. 14 *Yet* his meat in his bowels is turned, *it is* the gall of asps within him.

I—CONCLUDED.

Jer. 4. 18 Thy way and thy doings have procured these *things* unto thee; this *is* thy wickedness, because it is bitter, because it reacheth unto thine heart.

Lam. 3. 5 He hath builded against me, and compassed *me* with gall and travel.

Heb. 12. 15 Looking diligently lest any man fail of the grace of God; lest any root of bitterness springing up trouble *you*, and thereby many be defiled;

K

Gen. 20. 7 Now therefore restore the man *his* wife; for he *is* a prophet, and he shall pray for thee, and thou shalt live: and if thou restore *her* not, know thou that thou shalt surely die, thou, and all that *are* thine.

Gen. 20. 17 So Abraham prayed unto God: and God healed Abimelech, and his wife, and his maidservants; and they bare *children*.

Ex. 8. 8 Then Pharaoh called for Moses and Aaron, and said, Entreat the LORD, that he may take away the frogs from me, and from my people; and I will let the people go, that they may do sacrifice unto the LORD.

Num. 21. 7 Therefore the people came to Moses, and said, We have sinned, for we have spoken against the LORD, and against thee; pray unto the LORD, that he take away the serpents from us. And Moses prayed for the people.

I Ki. 13. 6 And the king answered and said unto the man of God, Entreat now the face of the LORD thy God, and pray for me, that my hand may be restored me again. And the man of God besought the LORD, and the king's hand was restored him again, and became as *it was* before.

Job 42. 8 Therefore take unto you now seven bullocks and seven rams, and go to my servant Job, and offer up for yourselves a burnt offering; and my servant Job shall pray for you: for him will I accept: lest I deal with you *after your* folly, in that ye have not spoken of me *the thing which is* right, like my servant Job.

Jer. 14. 11 Then said the LORD unto me, Pray not for this people for *their* good.

Jas. 5. 16 Confess *your* faults one to another, and pray one for another, that ye may be healed. The effectual fervent prayer of a righteous man availeth much.

§ 250. PHILIP AND THE EUNUCH.

8: 26–40.

26 And the angel of the Lord spake unto Philip, saying, Arise, and go toward the south, unto the way that goeth down from Jerusalem unto Gaza, which is desert.

27 And he arose and went: and, behold, a [a]man of Ethiopia, [b]a eunuch of great authority under Candace queen of the Ethiopians, who had the charge of all her treasure, and [c]had come to Jerusalem for to worship,

28 Was returning, and sitting in his chariot read Esaias the prophet.

29 Then [d]the Spirit said unto Philip, Go near, and join thyself to this chariot.

30 And Philip ran thither to *him*, and heard him read the prophet Esaias, and said, Understandest thou what thou readest?

31 And he said, How can I, except some man should guide me? And he desired Philip that he would come up and sit with him.

32 The place of the Scripture which he read was this, [e]He was led as a sheep to the slaughter; and like a lamb dumb before his shearer, so opened he not his mouth:

33 In his humiliation his judgment was taken away: and who shall declare his generation? for his life is taken from the earth.

34 And the eunuch answered Philip, and said, I pray thee, of whom speaketh the prophet this? of himself, or of some other man?

35 Then Philip opened his mouth,

CHAP. 8.

and began [f]at the same Scripture, and preached unto him Jesus.

36 And as they went on *their* way, they came unto a certain water: and the eunuch said, See, *here is* water; [g]what doth hinder me to be baptized?

37 And Philip said, [h]If thou believest with all thine heart, thou mayest. And he answered and said, [i]I believe that Jesus Christ is the Son of God.

38 And he commanded the chariot to stand still: and they went down both into the water, both Philip and the eunuch; and he baptized him.

39 And when they were come up out of the water, the [k]Spirit of the Lord caught away Philip, that the eunuch saw him no more: and he went on his way rejoicing.

40 But Philip was found at Azotus: and passing through he preached in all the cities, till he came to Cesarea.

A

Zeph. 3. 10 From beyond the rivers of Ethiopia my suppliants, *even* the daughter of my dispersed, shall bring mine offering.

B

Isa. 56. 4 For thus saith the LORD unto the eunuchs that keep my sabbaths, and choose *the things* that please me, and take hold of my covenant;

5 Even unto them will I give in mine house and within my walls a place and a name better than of sons and of daughters: I will give them an everlasting name, that shall not be cut off.

Jer. 38. 7 Now when Ebed-melech the Ethiopian, one of the eunuchs which was in the king's house, heard that they had put Jeremiah in the dungeon; the king then sitting in the gate of Benjamin;

Jer. 38. 12 And Ebed-melech the Ethiopian said unto Jeremiah, Put now *these* old cast clouts and rotten rags under thine

TIME, A. D. 36, 37; PLACE, WAY TO GAZA.

B—CONCLUDED.

armholes under the cords. And Jeremiah did so.

Matt. 19. 12 For there are some eunuchs, which were so born from *their* mother's womb: and there are some eunuchs, which were made eunuchs of men: and there be eunuchs, which have made themselves eunuchs for the kingdom of heaven's sake. He that is able to receive *it*, let him receive *it*.

C

II Chr. 6. 32 Moreover concerning the stranger, which is not of thy people Israel, but is come from a far country for thy great name's sake, and thy mighty hand, and thy stretched out arm; if they come and pray in this house;

D

Acts 10. 19 While Peter thought on the vision, the Spirit said unto him, Behold, three men seek thee.

Acts 11. 12 And the Spirit bade me go with them, nothing doubting. Moreover these six brethren accompanied me, and we entered into the man's house:

Acts 13. 2 As they ministered to the Lord, and fasted, the Holy Ghost said, Separate me Barnabas and Saul for the work whereunto I have called them.

Acts 16. 6 Now when they had gone througout Phrygia and the region of Galatia, and were forbidden of the Holy Ghost to preach the word in Asia.

7 After they were come to Mysia they assayed to go into Bithynia: but the Spirit suffered them not.

E

Isa. 53. 7 He was oppressed, and he was afflicted, yet he opened not his mouth: he is brought as a lamb to the slaughter, and as a sheep before her shearers is dumb, so he openeth not his mouth.

F

Luke 24. 27 And beginning at Moses and all the prophets, he expounded unto them in all the Scriptures the things concerning himself.

Acts 18. 28 For he mightily convinced the Jews, *and that* publicly, shewing by the Scriptures that Jesus was Christ.

G

Acts 10. 47 Can any man forbid water, that these should not be baptized, which have received the Holy Ghost as well as we?

H

Matt. 28. 19 Go ye therefore, and teach all nations, baptizing them in the name of the Father, and of the Son, and of the Holy Ghost:

Mark 16. 16 He that believeth and is baptized shall be saved; but he that believeth not shall be damned.

Rom. 10. 13 For whosoever shall call upon the name of the Lord shall be saved.

I

Matt. 16. 16 And Simon Peter answered and said, Thou art the Christ, the Son of the living God.

John 6. 69 And we believe and are sure that thou art that Christ, the Son of the living God.

John 9. 38 And he said, Lord, I believe. And he worshipped him.

John 11. 27 She saith unto him, Yea, Lord: I believe that thou art the Christ, the Son of God, which should come into the world.

Acts 9. 20 And straightway he preached Christ in the Synagogues, that he is the Son of God.

I Jno. 4. 15 Whosoever shall confess that Jesus is the Son of God, God dwelleth in him, and he in God.

I Jno. 5. 5 Who is he that overcometh the world, but he that believeth that Jesus is the Son of God?

K

I Ki. 18. 12 And it shall come to pass, *as soon as* I am gone from thee, that the Spirit of the LORD shall carry thee whither I know not; and *so* when I come and tell Ahab, and he cannot find thee, he shall slay me: but I thy servant fear the LORD from my youth.

II Ki. 2. 16 And tney said unto him, Behold now, there be with thy servants fifty strong men; let them go, we pray thee and seek thy master: lest peradventure the Spirit of the LORD hath taken him up, and cast him upon some mountain, or into some valley. And he said, Ye shall not send.

Eze. 3. 12 Then the spirit took me up, and I heard behind me a voice of a great rushing, *saying*, Blessed *be* the glory of the LORD from his place.

Eze. 3. 14 So the spirit lifted me up, and took me away, and I went in bitterness, in the heat of my spirit; but the hand of the LORD was strong upon me.

§ 251. SAUL'S CONVERSION. ANANIAS. SAUL PREACHING.

9: 1–22.

1 And [a]Saul, yet breathing out threatenings and slaughter against the disciples of the Lord, went unto the high priest,

2 And desired of him letters to Damascus to the synagogues, that if he found any [1]of this way, whether they were men or women, he might bring them bound unto Jerusalem.

3 And [b]as he journeyed, he came near Damascus: and suddenly there shined round about him a light from heaven:

4 And he fell to the earth, and heard a voice saying unto him, Saul, Saul, [c]why persecutest thou me?

5 And he said, Who art thou, Lord? And the Lord said, I am Jesus whom thou persecutest: [d]*it is* hard for thee to kick against the pricks.

6 And he trembling and astonished said, Lord, [e]what wilt thou have me to do? And the Lord *said* unto him, Arise, and go into the city, and it shall be told thee what thou must do.

7 And [f]the men which journeyed with him stood speechless, hearing a voice, but seeing no man.

8 And Saul arose from the earth; and when his eyes were opened, he saw no man: but they led him by the hand, and brought *him* into Damascus.

9 And he was three days without sight, and neither did eat nor drink.

10 And there was a certain disciple at Damascus, [g]named Ananias; and to him said the Lord in a vision, Ananias. And he said, Behold, I *am here*, Lord.

Chap. 9.

11 And the Lord *said* unto him, Arise, and go into the street which is called Straight, and inquire in the house of Judas for *one* called Saul, of [h]Tarsus: for, behold, he prayeth,

12 And hath seen in a vision a man named Ananias coming in, and putting *his* hand on him, that he might receive his sight.

13 Then Ananias answered, Lord, I have heard by many of this man, [i]how much evil he hath done to thy saints at Jerusalem:

14 And here he hath authority from the chief priests to bind all [k]that call on thy name.

15 But the Lord said unto him, Go thy way: for [l]he is a chosen vessel unto me, to bear my name before [m]the Gentiles, and [n]kings, and the children of Israel:

A

Acts 8. 3 As for Saul, he made havoc of the church, entering into every house, and haling men and women committed *them* to prison.

Gal. 1. 13 For ye have heard of my conversation in time past in the Jews' religion, how that beyond measure I persecuted the church of God, and wasted it:

1Tim. 1. 13 Who was before a blasphemer, and a persecutor, and injurious: but I obtained mercy, because I did *it* ignorantly in unbelief.

1

Gr., *of the way:*

Acts 19. 9 But when divers were hardened, and believed not, but spake evil of that way before the multitude, he departed from them, and separated the disciples, disputing daily in the school of one Tyrannus.

Acts 19. 23 And the same time there arose no small stir about that way.

TIME, A. D. 37; PLACE, DAMASCUS.

B

Acts 22. 6 And it came to pass, that, as I made my journey, and was come nigh unto Damascus about noon, suddenly there shone from heaven a great light round about me.

Acts 26. 12 Whereupon as I went to Damascus with authority and commission from the chief priests,

13 At midday, O king, I saw in the way a light from heaven, above the brightness of the sun, shining round about me and them which journeyed with me.

I Cor. 15. 8 And last of all he was seen of me also, as of one born out of due time.

C

Matt. 25. 40 And the King shall answer and say unto them, Verily I say unto you, Inasmuch as ye have done *it* unto one of the least of these my brethren, ye have done *it* unto me.

I Cor. 12. 12 For as the body is one, and hath many members, and all the members of that one body, being many, are one body: so also *is* Christ.

D

Acts 5. 39 But if it be of God, ye cannot overthrow it; lest haply ye be found even to fight against God.

E

Luke 3. 10 And the people asked him, saying, What shall we do then?

Acts 2. 37 Now when they heard *this*, they were pricked in their heart, and said unto Peter and to the rest of the apostles, Men *and* brethren, what shall we do?

Acts 16. 30 And brought them out, and said, Sirs, what must I do to be saved?

F

Dan. 10. 7 And I Daniel alone saw the vision: for the men that were with me saw not the vision; but a great quaking fell upon them, so that they fled to hide themselves.

Acts 22. 9 And they that were with me saw indeed the light, and were afraid; but they heard not the voice of him that spake to me.

Acts 26. 13. *See under B.*

G

Acts 22. 12 And one Ananias, a devout man according to the law, having a good report of all the Jews which dwelt *there*,

H

Acts 21. 39 But Paul said, I am a man *which am* a Jew of Tarsus, *a city* in Cilicia, a citizen of no mean city: and, I beseech thee, suffer me to speak unto the people.

Acts 22. 3 I am verily a man *which am* a Jew, born in Tarsus, *a city* in Cilicia, yet brought up in this city at the feet of Gamaliel, *and* taught according to the perfect manner of the law of the fathers, and was zealous toward God, as ye all are this day.

I

Acts 9. 1. *See text of topic.*

I. Tim. 1. 13. *See under A.*

K

Acts 9. 21. *See text of topic, page 686.*

Acts 7. 59 And they stoned Stephen, calling upon *God*, and saying, Lord Jesus, receive my Spirit.

Acts 22. 16 And now why tarriest thou? arise, and be baptized, and wash away thy sins, calling on the name of the Lord.

I. Cor. 1. 2 Unto the church of God which is at Corinth, to them that are sanctified in Christ Jesus, called *to be* saints, with all that in every place call upon the name of Jesus Christ our Lord, both theirs and ours:

II Tim. 2. 22 Flee also youthful lusts: but follow righteousness, faith, charity, peace, with them that call on the Lord out of a pure heart.

L

Acts 13. 2 As they ministered to the Lord, and fasted, the Holy Ghost said, Separate me Barnabas and Saul for the work whereunto I have called them.

Acts 22. 21 And he said unto me, Depart: for I will send thee far hence unto the Gentiles.

Acts 26. 17 Delivering thee from the people, and *from* the Gentiles, unto whom now I send thee,

Rom. 1. 1 Paul, a servant of Jesus Christ, called *to be* an apostle, separated unto the gospel of God,

I Cor. 15. 10 But by the grace of God I am what I am: and his grace which *was bestowed* upon me was not in vain; but I laboured more abundantly than they all: yet not I, but the grace of God which was with me.

Gal. 1. 15 But when it pleased God, who separated me from my mother's womb, and called *me* by his grace,

For L concluded, M and N, see next page (686).

§ 251. SAUL'S CONVERSION. ANANIAS. SAUL PREACHING

CHAP. 9.

16 For I will shew him how great things he must [o]suffer for my name's sake.

17 And Ananias went his way, and entered into the house; and [p]putting his hands on him said, Brother Saul, the Lord, *even* Jesus, that appeared unto thee in the way as thou camest, hath sent me, that thou mightest receive thy sight, and [q]be filled with the Holy Ghost.

18 And immediately there fell from his eyes as it had been scales: and he received sight forthwith, and arose, and was baptized.

19 And when he had received meat, he was strengthened. [r]Then was Saul certain days with the disciples which were at Damascus.

20 And straightway he preached Christ in the synagogues, [s]that he is the Son of God.

21 But all that heard *him* were amazed, and said; [t]Is not this he that destroyed them which called on this name in Jerusalem, and came hither for that intent, that he might bring them bound unto the chief priests?

22 But Saul increased the more in strength, [u]and confounded the Jews which dwelt at Damascus, proving that this is very Christ.

L—CONCLUDED.

Eph. 3. 7 Whereof I was made a minister, according to the gift of the grace of God given unto me by the effectual working of his power.

8 Unto me, who am less than the least of all saints, is this grace given, that I should preach among the Gentiles the unsearchable riches of Christ;

I. Tim. 2. 7 Whereunto I am ordained a preacher, and an apostle, (I speak the truth in Christ, *and* lie not,) a teacher of the Gentiles in faith and verity.

II Tim. 1. 11 Whereunto I am appointed a preacher, and an apostle, and a teacher of the Gentiles.

M

Rom 1. 5 By whom we have received grace and apostleship, for obedience to the faith among all nations, for his name:

Rom 11. 13 For I speak to you Gentiles, inasmuch as I am the apostle of the Gentiles, I magnify mine office:

Gal. 2. 7 But contrariwise, when they saw that the gospel of the uncircumcision was committed unto me, as *the gospel* of the circumcision *was* unto Peter;

8 (For he that wrought effectually in Peter to the apostleship of the circumcision, the same was mighty in me toward the Gentiles;)

N

Acts 25. 22 Then Agrippa said unto Festus, I would also hear the man myself. To morrow, said he, thou shalt hear him.

23 And on the morrow, when Agrippa was come, and Bernice, with great pomp, and was entered into the place of hearing, with the chief captains, and principal men of the city, at Festus' commandment Paul was brought forth.

Acts 26. 1 Then Agrippa said unto Paul, Thou art permitted to speak for thyself. Then Paul stretched forth the hand, and answered for himself:

§ 252. SAUL PERSECUTED. HIS ESCAPE. AT JERUSALEM.

9: 23-31.

23 And after that many days were fulfilled, the [a]Jews took counsel to kill him:

24 But [b]their laying wait was known

A

Acts 23. 12 And when it was day, certain of the Jews banded together, and bound themselves under a curse, saying that they would neither eat nor drink till they had killed Paul.

Acts 25. 3 And desired favour against him,

(CONCLUDED). TIME, A. D. 37; PLACE, DAMASCUS.

O

Acts 20. 23 Save that the Holy Ghost witnesseth in every city, saying that bonds and afflictions abide me.

IICor.11. 23 Are they ministers of Christ? (I speak as a fool,) I *am* more; in labours more abundant, in stripes above measure, in prisons more frequent, in deaths oft

IICor.11. 27 In weariness and painfulness, in watchings often, in hunger and thirst, in fastings often, in cold and nakedness.

IITim.1. 12 For the which cause I also suffer these things: nevertheless I am not ashamed; for I know whom I have believed, and am persuaded that he is able to keep that which I have committed unto him against that day.

P

Acts 8. 17. See d, D, § 249, page 680.

Q

Acts 2. 4 And they were all filled with the Holy Ghost, and began to speak with other tongues, as the Spirit gave them utterance.

Acts 4. 8 Then Peter, filled with the Holy Ghost, said unto them, Ye rulers of the people, and elders of Israel,

Acts 4. 31 And when they had prayed, the place was shaken where they were assembled together; and they were all filled with the Holy Ghost, and they spake the word of God with boldness.

Acts 6. 8 And Stephen, full of faith and power, did great wonders and miracles among the people.

Acts 8. 17 Then laid they *their* hands on them, and they received the Holy Ghost.

Acts 11. 24 For he was a good man, and full of the Holy Ghost and of faith: and much people was added unto the Lord.

Acts 13. 52 And the disciples were filled with joy, and with the Holy Ghost.

Rom.15. 13 Now the God of hope fill you with all joy and peace in believing, that ye may abound in hope, through the power of the Holy Ghost.

Q—CONCLUDED.

Eph. 3. 19 And to know the love of Christ, which passeth knowledge, that ye might be filled with all the fulness of God.

Eph. 5. 18 And be not drunk with wine, wherein is excess; but be filled with the Spirit;

R

Acts 26. 20 But shewed first unto them of Damascus, and at Jerusalem, and throughout all the coasts of Judea, and *then* to the Gentiles, that they should repent and turn to God, and do works meet for repentance.

Gal 1. 17 Neither went I up to Jerusalem to them which were apostles before me; but I went into Arabia, and returned again unto Damascus.

18 Then after three years I went up to Jerusalem to see Peter, and abode with him fifteen days.

S

Acts 8. 37 And Philip said, If thou believest with all thine heart, thou mayest. And he answered and said, I believe that Jesus Christ is the Son of God.

T

Acts 8. 3 As for Saul, he made havoc of the church, entering into every house, and haling men and women committed *them* to prison.

Acts 9 1 *See text of topic, page 684.*

Gal. 1. 13 For ye have heard of my conversation in time past in the Jews' religion, how that beyond measure I persecuted the church of God, and wasted it:

Gal. 1. 23 But they had heard only, That he which persecuted us in times past now preacheth the faith which once he destroyed.

U

Acts 18. 28 For he mightily convinced the Jews, *and that* publicly, shewing by the Scriptures that Jesus was Christ.

TIME, A. D. 37-(AFTER MANY DAYS); PLACE, JERUSALEM.

A—CONTINUED

that he would send for him to Jerusalem, laying wait in the way to kill him.

IICor.11. 26 *In* journeyings often, *in* perils of waters, *in* perils of robbers, *in* perils by *mine own* countrymen, *in* perils by the heathen, *in* perils in the city, *in*

A—CONCLUDED.

perils in the wilderness, *in* perils in the sea, *in* perils among false brethren;

B

IICor.11. 32 In Damascus the governor under Aretas the king kept the city of the

For B concluded, see next page (688).

§ 252. SAUL PERSECUTED. HIS ESCAPE. AT JERUSALEM

CHAP. 9.

of Saul. And they watched the gates day and night to kill him.

25 Then the disciples took him by night, and [c]let *him* down by the wall in a basket.

26 And [d]when Saul was come to Jerusalem, he assayed to join himself to the disciples: but they were all afraid of him, and believed not that he was a disciple.

27 But [e]Barnabas took him, and brought *him* to the apostles, and declared unto them how he had seen the Lord in the way, and that he had spoken to him, [f]and how he had preached boldly at Damascus in the name of Jesus.

28 And [g]he was with them coming in and going out at Jerusalem.

29 And he spake [h]boldly in the name of the Lord Jesus, and disputed against the [i]Grecians: but they went about to slay him.

30 *Which* when the brethren knew, they brought him down to Cesarea, and sent him forth to Tarsus.

CHAP. 9.

31 Then had the churches [k]rest throughout all Judea and Galilee and Samaria, and were edified; and walking in the fear of the Lord, and in the comfort of the Holy Ghost, were multiplied.

B—CONCLUDED.

Damascenes with a garrison, desirous to apprehend me;

C

Josh. 2. 15 Then she let them down by a cord through the window: for her house *was* upon the town wall, and she dwelt upon the wall.

I Sa. 19. 12 So Michal let David down through a window: and he went, and fled, and escaped.

D

Acts 22. 17 And it came to pass, that, when I was come again to Jerusalem, even while I prayed in the temple, I was in a trance;

Gal. 1. 17 Neither went I up to Jerusalem to them which were apostles before me; but I went into Arabia, and returned again unto Damascus.

18 Then after three years I went up to Jerusalem to see Peter, and abode with him fifteen days.

E

Acts 4. 36 And Joses, who by the apostles was surnamed Barnabas, (which is, being interpreted, The son of consolation,) a Levite, *and* of the country of Cyprus.

§ 253. PETER'S MISSIONARY TOUR. ÆNEAS HEALED. DORCAS RAISED.

9: 32–43.

32 And it came to pass, as Peter passed [a]throughout all *quarters*, he came down also to the saints which dwelt at Lydda.

33 And there he found a certain man named Æneas, which had kept his bed eight years, and was sick of the palsy.

34 And Peter said unto him, Æneas, [b]Jesus Christ maketh thee whole:

A

Acts 8. 14 Now when the apostles which were at Jerusalem heard that Samaria had received the word of God, they sent unto them Peter and John:

B

Acts 3. 6 Then Peter said, Silver and gold have I none; but such as I have give I thee: In the name of Jesus Christ of Nazareth rise up and walk.

Acts 3. 16 And his name, through faith in his name, hath made this man strong, whom ye see and know: yea, the faith which is by him hath given him this perfect soundness in the presence of you all.

(CONCLUDED). TIME, A. D. 37–(AFTER MANY DAYS); PLACE, DAMASCUS.

E—CONCLUDED.

Acts 13. 2 As they ministered to the Lord, and fasted, the Holy Ghost said, Separate me Barnabas and Saul, for the work whereunto I have called them,

F

Acts 9. 20. and 22. *See text of § 251, page 686.*

G

Gal 1. 18. *See under D.*

H

Eph. 6. 19 And for me, that utterance may be given unto me, that I may open my mouth boldly, to make known the mystery of the gospel.

I

Acts 6. 1 And in those days, when the number of the disciples was multiplied, there arose a murmuring of the Grecians against the Hebrews, because their widows were neglected in daily ministration.

Acts 11. 20 And some of them were men of Cyprus and Cyrene, which, when they were come to Antioch, spake unto the Grecians, preaching the Lord Jesus.

K

Deut. 12. 10 But *when* ye go over Jordan, and dwell in the land which the LORD your God giveth you to inherit, and *when* he giveth you rest from all your enemies round about, so that ye dwell in safety;

Josh. 21. 44 And the LORD gave them rest round about, according to all that he sware unto their fathers: and there stood not a man of all their enemies before them; the LORD delivered all their enemies into their hand.

K—CONCLUDED.

Judg. 3. 30 So Moab was subdued that day under the hand of Israel. And the land had rest fourscore years.

IChr. 22. 9 Behold, a son shall be born to thee, who shall be a man of rest: and I will give him rest from all his enemies round about; for his name shall be Solomon, and I will give peace and quietness unto Israel in his days

Ps. 94. 13 That thou mayest give him rest from the days of adversity, until the pit be digged for the wicked.

Prov. 16. 7 When a man's ways please the LORD, he maketh even his enemies to be at peace with him.

Isa. 11. 10 And in that day there shall be a root of Jesse, which shall stand for an ensign of the people; to it shall the Gentiles seek; and his rest shall be glorious.

Zech. 9. 1 The burden of the word of the LORD in the land of Hadrach, and Damascus *shall be* the rest thereof: when the eyes of man, as of all the tribes of Isarel, *shall be* toward the LORD.

Heb. 4. 9 There remaineth therefore a rest to the people of God.

10 For he that is entered into his rest, he also hath ceased from his own works, as God *did* from his.

11 Let us labour therefore to enter into that rest, lest any man fall after the same example of unbelief.

Rev. 21. 4 And God shall wipe away all tears from their eyes; and there shall be no more death, neither sorrow, nor crying, neither shall there be any more pain: for the former things are passed away.

TIME, A. D. 40; PLACE, LYDDA, JOPPA.

B—CONCLUDED.

Acts 4. 10 Be it known unto you all, and to all the people of Israel, that by the name of Jesus Christ of Nazareth, whom ye crucified, whom God raised from the dead, *even* by him doth this man stand here before you whole.

C

IChr. 5. 16 And they dwelt in Gilead in Bashan, and in her towns, and in all the suburbs of Sharon, upon their borders.

D

Acts 11. 21 And the hand of the Lord was with them: and a great number believed, and turned unto the Lord.

1

Or, *Doe*, or, *Roe*.

E

Prov. 31. 31 Give her of the fruit of her hands; and let her own works praise her in the gates.

John 15. 8 Herein is my Father glorified, that ye bear much fruit; so shall ye be my disciples.

Eph. 2. 10 For we are his workmanship, created in Christ Jesus unto good works, which God hath before ordained that we should walk in them.

Phil. 1. 11 Being filled with the fruits of righteousness, which are by Jesus Christ, unto the glory and praise of God.

§ 253. PETER'S MISSIONARY TOUR. ÆNEAS HEALED. DORCAS RAISED

CHAP. 9.

arise, and make thy bed. And he arose immediately.

35 And all that dwelt at Lydda and [c]Saron saw him, and [d]turned to the Lord.

36 Now there was at Joppa a certain disciple named Tabitha, which by interpretation is called [1]Dorcas: this woman was full [e]of good works and almsdeeds which she did.

37 And it came to pass in those days, that she was sick, and died: whom when they had washed, they laid *her* in an [f]upper chamber.

38 And forasmuch as Lydda was nigh to Joppa, and the disciples had heard that Peter was there, they sent unto him two men, desiring *him* that he would not [2]delay to come to them.

39 Then Peter arose and went with them. When he was come, they brought him into the upper chamber: and all the widows stood by him weeping, and shewing the coats and garments which Dorcas made, while [g]she was with them.

40 But Peter [h]put them all forth, and kneeled down,[i]and prayed; and turning *him* to the body [k]said, Tabitha, arise. And she opened her eyes: and when she saw Peter, she sat up.

CHAP. 9.

41 And he gave her *his* hand, and lifted her up; and when he had called the saints and widows, he presented her alive.

42 And it was known throughout all Joppa; and [l]many believed in the Lord.

43 And it came to pass, that he tarried many days in Joppa with one [m]Simon a tanner.

For C, D, 1 and E, see preceding page (689).

E—CONTINUED.

Col. 1. 10 That ye might walk worthy of the Lord unto all pleasing, being fruitful in every good work, and increasing in the knowledge of God;

1 Thes. 4. 11 And that ye study to be quiet, and to do your own business, and to work with your own hands, as we commanded you:

1 Tim. 2. 9 In like manner also, that women adorn themselves in modest apparel, with shamefacedness and sobriety; not with braided hair, or gold, or pearls, or costly array;

10 But (which becometh women professing godliness) with good works.

1 Tim. 5. 10 Well reported of for good works; if she have brought up children, if she have lodged strangers, if she have washed the saints' feet, if she have relieved the afflicted, if she have diligently followed every good work.

Tit. 2. 7 In all things shewing thyself a pattern of good works: in doctrine *shewing* uncorruptness, gravity, sincerity,

Tit. 2. 14 Who gave himself for us, that he might redeem us from all iniquity, and purify unto himself a peculiar people, zealous of good works.

§ 254. THE CONVERSION OF CORNELIUS, A GENTILE.

10: 1-48.

1 There was a certain man in Cesarea called Cornelius, a centurion of the band called the Italian *band*,

2 [a]*A* devout *man*, and one that [b]feared

A

Acts 8. 2 And devout men carried Stephen *to his burial*, and made great lamentation over him.

Acts 10. 22 And they said, Cornelius the centurion, a just man, and one that feareth God, and of good report among all

(CONCLUDED). TIME, A. D. 40; PLACE, LYDDA, JOPPA.

E—CONCLUDED.

Tit 3. 8 *This is* a faithful saying, and these things I will that thou affirm constantly, that they which have believed in God might be careful to maintain good works. These things are good and profitable unto men.

Heb. 13. 21 Make you perfect in every good work to do his will, working in you that which is well pleasing in his sight, through Jesus Christ; to whom *be* glory for ever and ever. Amen.

Jas. 1. 27 Pure religion and undefiled before God and the Father is this, To visit the fatherless and widows in their affliction, *and* to keep himself unspotted from the world.

F

Acts 1. 13 And when they were come in, they went up into an upper room, where abode both Peter, and James, and John, and Andrew, Philip, and Thomas, Bartholomew, and Matthew, James *the son* of Alpheus, and Simon Zelotes, and Judas *the brother* of James.

2

Or, *be grieved.*

G

Eccl. 9. 10 Whatsoever thy hand findeth to do, do *it* with thy might; for *there is* no work, nor device, nor knowledge, nor wisdom, in the grave, whither thou goest.

H

Matt. 9. 25 But when the people were put forth, he went in, and took her by the hand, and the maid arose.

I

I Ki. 17. 21 And he stretched himself upon the child three times, and cried unto the LORD, and said, O LORD my God, I pray thee, let this child's soul come into him again.

22 And the LORD heard the voice of Elijah; and the soul of the child came into him again, and he revived.

I—CONCLUDED.

II Ki. 4. 33 He went in therefore, and shut the door upon them twain, and prayed unto the LORD.

34 And he went up, and lay upon the child, and put his mouth upon his mouth, and his eyes upon his eyes, and his hands upon his hands: and he stretched himself upon the child; and the flesh of the child waxed warm.

K

Mark 5. 41 And he took the damsel by the hand, and said unto her, Talitha cumi; which is, being interpreted, Damsel, (I say unto thee,) arise.

42 And straightway the damsel arose, and walked; for she was *of the age* of twelve years. And they were astonished with a great astonishment.

L

John 2. 23 Now when he was in Jerusalem at the passover, in the feast *day*, many believed in his name, when they saw the miracles which he did.

John 10. 42 And many believed on him there.

John 11. 44 And he that was dead came forth, bound hand and foot with graveclothes: and his face was bound about with a napkin. Jesus said unto them, Loose him, and let him go.

John 11. 45 Then many of the Jews which came to Mary, and had seen the things which Jesus did, believed on him.

John 12. 11 Because that by reason of him many of the Jews went away, and believed on Jesus.

Acts 4. 4 Howbeit many of them which heard the word believed; and the number of the men was about five thousand.

M

Acts 10. 6 He lodgeth with one Simon a tanner, whose house is by the sea side: he shall tell thee what thou oughtest to do.

TIME, A. D. 40; PLACE, CESAREA.

A—CONTINUED.

the nation of the Jews, was warned from God by a holy angel to send for thee into his house, and to hear words of thee.

Acts 22. 12 And one Ananias, a devout man according to the law, having a good report of all the Jews which dwelt *there*,

B

Eccl. 7. 18 *It is* good that thou shouldest take hold of this; yea, also from this withdraw not thine hand: for he that feareth God shall come forth of them all.

For B concluded, see next page (692).

§ 254. THE CONVERSION OF CORNELIUS, A GENTILE (CONTINUED).

CHAP. 10.

God with all his house, which gave much alms to the people, and [c]prayed to God always.

3 He saw in a vision evidently, about the ninth hour of the day, an [d]angel of God coming in to him, and saying unto him, Cornelius.

4 And when he looked on him, he was afraid and said, What is it, Lord? And he said unto him, Thy prayers and thine alms [e]are come up for a memorial before God.

5 And now send men to Joppa, and call for *one* Simon, whose surname is Peter:

6 He lodgeth with one [f]Simon a tanner, whose house is by the sea side: [g]he shall tell thee what thou oughtest to do.

7 And when the angel which spake unto Cornelius was departed, he called two of his household servants, and a devout soldier of them that waited on him continually;

8 And when he had declared all *these* things unto them, he sent them to Joppa.

9 On the morrow, as they went on their journey, and drew nigh unto the city, [h]Peter went up upon the housetop to pray about the sixth hour:

10 And he became very hungry, and would have eaten: but while they made ready, he fell into a trance,

11 And [i]saw heaven opened, and a certain vessel descending unto him, as it had been a great sheet knit at the four corners, and let down to the earth:

CHAP. 10.

12 Wherein were all manner of four-footed beasts of the earth, and wild beasts, and creeping things, and fowls of the air.

13 And there came a voice to him, Rise, Peter; kill, and eat.

14 But Peter said, Not so, Lord; for I have never eaten any thing that is [k]common or unclean.

15 And the voice *spake* unto him again the second time, [l]What God hath cleansed, *that* call not thou common.

16 This was done thrice: and the vessel was received up again into heaven.

17 Now while Peter doubted in himself what this vision which he had seen should mean, behold, the men which were sent from Cornelius had made inquiry for Simon's house, and stood before the gate,

18 And called, and asked whether Simon, which was surnamed Peter, were lodged there.

B—CONCLUDED.

Acts 10. 35 But in every nation he that feareth him, and worketh righteousness, is accepted with him.

C

Ps. 25. 5 Lead me in thy truth, and teach me: for thou *art* the God of my salvation; on thee do I wait all the day.

Ps. 55. 17 Evening, and morning, and at noon, will I pray, and cry aloud: and he shall hear my voice.

Ps. 88. 1 O LORD God of my salvation, I have cried day *and* night before thee:

Ps. 119. 2 Blessed *are* they that keep his testimonies, *and that* seek him with the whole heart.

D

Heb. 1. 13 But to which of the angels said he at any time, Sit on my right hand, until I make thine enemies thy footstool?

14 Are they not all ministering spirits, sent forth to minister for them who shall be heirs of salvation?

TIME, A. D. 40; PLACE, CESAREA.

E

Ps. 102. 17 He will regard the prayer of the destitute, and not despise their prayer.

Prov. 15. 8 The sacrifice of the wicked *is* an abomination to the LORD: but the prayer of the upright *is* his delight.

Prov. 15. 29 The LORD *is* far from the wicked: but he heareth the prayer of the righteous.

Phil. 4. 18 But I have all, and abound: I am full, having received of Epaphroditus the things *which were sent* from you, an odour of a sweet smell, a sacrifice acceptable, well pleasing to God.

Heb. 13. 16 But to do good and to communicate forget not: for with such sacrifices God is well pleased.

Jas 5. 16 Confess *your* faults one to another, and pray one for another, that ye may be healed. The effectual fervent prayer of a righteous man availeth much.

I Pet. 3. 12 For the eyes of the Lord *are* over the righteous, and his ears *are open* unto their prayers: but the face of the Lord *is* against them that do evil.

F

Acts 9. 43 And it came to pass, that he tarried many days in Joppa with one Simon a tanner.

G

Acts 11. 14 Who shall tell thee words, whereby thou and all thy house shall be saved.

H

Ps. 55. 17. *See under C.*

Acts 11. 5 I was in the city of Joppa praying: and in a trance I saw a vision, A certain vessel descend, as it had been a great sheet, let down from heaven by four corners; and it came even to me:

I

Eze. 1. 1 Now it came to pass in the thirtieth year, in the fourth *month*, in the fifth *day* of the month, as I *was* among the captives by the river of Chebar, *that* the heavens were opened, and I saw visions of God.

Mark 1. 10 And straightway coming up out of the water, he saw the heavens opened, and the Spirit like a dove descending upon him:

Acts 7. 56 And said, Behold, I see the heavens opened, and the Son of man standing on the right hand of God.

Rev. 19. 11 And I saw heaven opened, and behold a white horse; and he that sat upon him *was* called Faithful and True, and in righteousness he doth judge and make war.

I—CONCLUDED.

K

Lev. 11. 4 Nevertheless, these shall ye not eat of them that chew the cud, or of them that divide the hoof: *as* the camel, because he cheweth the cud, but divideth not the hoof; he *is* unclean unto you.

Lev. 20. 25 Ye shall therefore put difference between clean beasts and unclean, and between unclean fowls and clean: and ye shall not make your souls abominable by beast, or by fowl, or by any manner of living thing that creepeth on the ground, which I have separated from you as unclean.

Deut. 14. 3 Thou shalt not eat any abominable thing.

Eze. 4. 14 Then said I, Ah Lord GOD! behold, my soul hath not been polluted: for from my youth up even till now have I not eaten of that which dieth of itself, or is torn in pieces; neither came there abominable flesh into my mouth.

L

Matt. 15. 11 Not that which goeth into the mouth defileth a man; but that which cometh out of the mouth, this defileth a man.

Acts 10. 28 And he said unto them, Ye know how that it is an unlawful thing for a man that is a Jew to keep company, or come unto one of another nation; but God hath shewed me that I should not call any man common or unclean.

Rom. 14. 14 I know, and am persuaded by the Lord Jesus, that *there is* nothing unclean of itself: but to him that esteemeth any thing to be unclean, to him *it is* unclean.

Rom. 14. 17 For the kingdom of God is not meat and drink; but righteousness, and peace, and joy in the Holy Ghost.

Rom. 14. 20 For meat destroy not the work of God. All things indeed *are* pure; but *it is* evil for that man who eateth with offence.

I Cor. 10. 25 Whatsoever is sold in the shambles, *that* eat, asking no question for conscience' sake:

I Tim. 4. 4 For every creature of God *is* good, and nothing to be refused, if it be received with thanksgiving:

Tit. 1. 15 Unto the pure all things *are* pure: but unto them that are defiled and unbelieving *is* nothing pure; but even their mind and conscience is defiled.

§ 254. THE CONVERSION OF CORNELIUS (CONTINUED).

CHAP. 10.

19 While Peter thought on the vision, the [m]Spirit said unto him, Behold, three men seek thee.
20 [n]Arise therefore, and get thee
down, and go with them, doubting
nothing: for I have sent them.
21 Then Peter went down to the
men which were sent unto him from
Cornelius; and said, Behold, I am
he whom ye seek: what *is* the cause
wherefore ye are come?
22 And they said, Cornelius the
centurian, a just man, and one that
feareth God, and of [o]good report
among all the nation of the Jews,
was warned from God by a holy
angel to send for thee into his house,
[p]and to hear words of thee.
23 Then called he them in, and
lodged *them*. And on the morrow
Peter went away with them, and
[q]certain brethren from Joppa accompanied him.
24 And the morrow after they entered into Cesarea. And Cornelius
waited for them, and had called together his kinsmen and near friends.
25 And as Peter was coming in,
Cornelius met him, and fell down at
his feet, and worshipped *him*.
26 But Peter took him up, saying,
[r]Stand up; I myself also am a man.
27 And as he talked with him, he
went in, and found many that were
come together.
28 And he said unto them, Ye
know how that [s]it is an unlawful thing
for a man that is a Jew to keep company, or come unto one of another
nation; but [t]God hath shewed me
that I should not call any man common or unclean.
29 Therefore came I *unto you* without gainsaying, as soon as I was sent
for: I ask therefore for what intent
ye have sent for me?
30 And Cornelius said, Four days
ago I was fasting until this hour;
and at the ninth hour I prayed in
my house, and, behold, [u]a man stood
before me [x]in bright clothing,

M

John 16. 13 Howbeit when he, the Spirit of truth, is come, he will guide you into all truth: for he shall not speak of himself; but whatsoever he shall hear, *that* shall he speak: and he will shew you things to come.

Acts 11. 12 And the Spirit bade me go with them, nothing doubting. Moreover these six brethren accompanied me, and we entered into the man's house:

Acts 16. 6 Now when they had gone throughout Phrygia and the region of Galatia, and were forbidden of the Holy Ghost to preach the word in Asia.

Acts 21. 4 And finding disciples, we tarried there seven days: who said to Paul through the Spirit, that he should not go up to Jerusalem.

1 Jno. 2. 27 But the anointing which ye have received of him abideth in you, and ye need not that any man teach you: but as the same anointing teacheth you of all things, and is truth, and is no lie, and even as it hath taught you, ye shall abide in him.

N

Matt. 28. 19 Go ye therefore, and teach all nations, baptizing them in the name of the Father, and of the Son, and of the Holy Ghost:

Mark 16. 15 And he said unto them, Go ye into all the world, and preach the gospel to every creature.

Acts 15. 7 And when there had been much disputing, Peter rose up, and said unto them, Men *and* brethren, ye know how that a good while ago God made choice among us, that the Gentiles by my mouth should hear the word of the gospel, and believe.

TIME, A. D. 40; PLACE, CESAREA.

O

Acts 22. 12 And one Ananias, a devout man according to the law, having a good report of all the Jews which dwelt *there*,

Heb. 11. 1 Now faith is the substance of things hoped for, the evidence of things not seen.

2 For by it the elders obtained a good report.

P

John 6. 63 It is the Spirit that quickeneth; the flesh profiteth nothing: the words that I speak unto you, *they* are spirit, and *they* are life.

John 6. 68 Then Simon Peter answered him, Lord, to whom shall we go? thou hast the words of eternal life.

John 17. 8 For I have given unto them the words which thou gavest me; and they have received *them*, and have known surely that I came out from thee, and they have believed that thou didst send me.

John 17. 20 Neither pray I for these alone, but for them also which shall believe on me through their word;

Acts 10. 33 Immediately therefore I sent to thee; and thou hast well done that thou art come. Now therefore are we all here present before God, to hear all things that are commanded thee of God.

Acts 11. 14 Who shall tell thee words, whereby thou and all thy house shall be saved.

II Pet. 3. 2 That ye may be mindful of the words which were spoken before by the holy prophets, and of the commandment of us the apostles of the Lord and Saviour:

Q

Acts 10. 45. *See text of topic, page 698.*

Acts 11. 12. *See under M.*

R

Ex. 34. 14 For thou shalt worship no other god; for the LORD, whose name *is* Jealous, *is* a jealous God.

Ps. 81. 9 There shall no strange god be in thee; neither shalt thou worship any strange god.

Acts 14. 15 And saying, Sirs, why do ye these things? We also are men of like passions with you, and preach unto you that ye should turn from these vanities unto the living God, which made heaven, and earth, and the sea, and all things that are therein:

Rev. 22. 9 Then saith he unto me, See *thou do it* not: for I am thy fellow servant,

R—CONCLUDED.

and of thy brethren the prophets, and of them which keep the sayings of this book: worship God.

S

John 4. 9 Then saith the woman of Samaria unto him, How is it that thou, being a Jew, askest drink of me, which am a woman of Samaria? for the Jews have no dealings with the Samaritans.

John 18. 28 Then led they Jesus from Caiaphas unto the hall of judgment: and it was early; and they themselves went not into the judgment hall, lest they should be defiled; but that they might eat the passover.

Acts 11. 3 Saying, Thou wentest in to men uncircumcised, and didst eat with them.

Gal. 2. 12 For before that certain came from James, he did eat with the Gentiles: but when they were come, he withdrew and separated himself, fearing them which were of the circumcision.

T

Isa. 65. 5 Which say, Stand by thyself, come not near to me; for I am holier than thou. These *are* a smoke in my nose, a fire that burneth all the day.

Acts 11. 9 But the voice answered me again from heaven, What God hath cleansed, *that* call not thou common.

Acts 15. 8 And God, which knoweth the hearts, bear them witness, giving them the Holy Ghost, even as *he did* unto us;

9 And put no difference between us and them, purifying their hearts by faith.

Eph. 3. 6 That the Gentiles should be fellow heirs, and of the same body, and partakers of his promise in Christ by the gospel:

U

Acts 1. 10 And while they looked steadfastly toward heaven as he went up, behold, two men stood by them in white apparel;

X

Matt. 28. 3 His countenance was like lightning, and his raiment white as snow:

Mark 16. 5 And entering into the sepulchre, they saw a young man sitting on the right side, clothed in a long white garment; and they were affrighted.

Luke 24. 4 And it came to pass, as they were much perplexed thereabout, behold, two men stood by them in shining garments:

§ 254. THE CONVERSION OF CORNELIUS (CONTINUED),

CHAP. 10.

31 And said, Cornelius, [y]thy prayer is heard, [z]and thine alms are had in remembrance in the sight of God.

32 Send therefore to Joppa, and call hither Simon, whose surname is Peter; he is lodged in the house of *one* Simon a tanner by the sea side: who, when he cometh, shall speak unto thee.

33 Immediately therefore I sent to thee; and thou hast well done that thou art come. [a]Now therefore are we all here present before God, to hear all things that are commanded thee of God.

34 Then Peter opened *his* mouth, and said, [b]Of a truth I perceive that God is no respecter of persons:

35 But [c]in every nation he that feareth him, and worketh righteousness, is accepted with him.

36 The word which *God* sent unto the children of Israel, [d]preaching peace by Jesus Christ: ([e]he is Lord of all:)

37 That word, *I say*, ye know, which was published throughout all Judea, and [f]began from Galilee, after the baptism which John preached;

38 How [g]God anointed Jesus of Nazareth with the Holy Ghost and with power: who went about doing good, and healing all that were oppressed of the devil; [h]for God was with him.

39 And [i]we are witnesses of all things which he did both in the land of the Jews, and in Jerusalem; [k]whom they slew and hanged on a tree:

Y

Dan. 10. 12 Then said he unto me, Fear not, Daniel: for from the first day that thou didst set thine heart to understand, and to chasten thyself before thy God, thy words were heard, and I am come for thy words.

Acts 10. 4 And when he looked on him, he was afraid, and said, What is it, Lord? And he said unto him, Thy prayers and thine alms are come up for a memorial before God.

Z

Matt. 6. 4 That thine alms may be in secret: and thy Father which seeth in secret himself shall reward thee openly.

Matt. 10. 42 And whosoever shall give to drink unto one of these little ones a cup of cold *water* only in the name of a disciple, verily I say unto you, he shall in no wise lose his reward.

Heb. 6. 10 For God *is* not unrighteous to forget your work and labour of love, which ye have shewed toward his name, in that ye have ministered to the saints, and do minister.

A

Deut. 5. 27 Go thou near, and hear all that the LORD our God shall say; and speak thou unto us all that the LORD our God shall speak unto thee; and we will hear *it*, and do *it*.

B

Deut. 10. 17 For the LORD your God *is* God of gods, and Lord of lords, a great God, a mighty, and a terrible, which regardeth not persons, nor taketh reward;

II Chr. 19. 7 Wherefore now let the fear of the LORD be upon you; take heed and do *it*: for *there is* no iniquity with the LORD our God, nor respect of persons, nor taking of gifts.

Job 34. 19 *How much less to him* that accepteth not the persons of princes, nor regardeth the rich more than the poor? for they all *are* the work of his hands.

Rom. 2. 11 For there is no respect of persons with God.

Gal. 2. 6 But of these who seemed to be somewhat, whatsoever they were, it maketh no matter to me: God accepteth no man's person: for they who seemed *to be somewhat* in conference added nothing to me:

Eph. 6. 9 And, ye masters, do the same things unto them, forbearing threatening: knowing that your Master also is in heaven; neither is there respect of persons with him.

TIME, A. D. 40; PLACE, CESAREA.

B—CONCLUDED.

Eph. 6. 10 Finally, my brethren, be strong in the Lord, and in the power of his might.

Col. 3. 11 Where there is neither Greek nor Jew, circumcision nor uncircumcision, Barbarian, Scythian, bond *nor* free: but Christ *is* all, and in all.

Col. 3. 25 But he that doeth wrong shall receive for the wrong which he hath done: and there is no respect of persons.

I Pet. 1. 17 And if ye call on the Father, who without respect of persons judgeth according to every man's work, pass the time of your sojourning *here* in fear:

C

Acts 15. 9 And put no difference between us and them, purifying their hearts by faith.

Rom. 2. 13 (For not the hearers of the law *are* just before God, but the doers of the law shall be justified.

Rom. 3. 22 Even the righteousness of God *which is* by faith of Jesus Christ unto all and upon all them that believe; for there is no difference:

Rom. 10. 12 For there is no difference between the Jew and the Greek: for the same Lord over all is rich unto all that call upon him.

I. Cor. 12 13 For by one Spirit are we all baptized into one body, whether *we be* Jews or Gentiles, whether *we be* bond or free; and have been all made to drink into one Spirit.

Gal. 3. 28 There is neither Jew nor Greek, there is neither bond nor free, there is neither male nor female: for ye are all one in Christ Jesus.

Eph. 2. 13 But now, in Christ Jesus, ye who sometime were far off are made nigh by the blood of Christ.

Eph. 2. 18 For through him we both have access by one Spirit unto the Father.

Eph. 3. 6 That the Gentiles should be fellow heirs, and of the same body, and partakers of his promise in Christ by the gospel:

D

Isa. 57. 19 I create the fruit of the lips; Peace, peace to *him that is* far off, and to *him that is* near, saith the LORD; and I will heal him.

Eph. 2. 14 For he is our peace, who hath made both one, and hath broken down the middle wall of partition *between us*:

D—CONCLUDED.

Eph. 2. 15 Having abolished in his flesh the enmity, *even* the law of commandments *contained* in ordinances; for to make in himself of twain one new man, *so* making peace;

16 And that he might reconcile both unto God in one body by the cross, having slain the enmity thereby:

17 And came and preached peace to you which were afar off, and to them that were nigh.

Col. 1. 20 And, having made peace through the blood of his cross, by him to reconcile all things unto himself; by him, *I say*, whether *they be* things in earth, or things in heaven.

E

Ps. 24. 10 Who is this King of glory? The LORD of hosts, he *is* the King of glory. Selah.

Dan. 7. 14 And there was given him dominion, and glory, and a kingdom, that all people, nations, and languages, should serve him: his dominion *is* an everlasting dominion, which shall not pass away, and his kingdom *that* which shall not be destroyed.

Rom. 10. 12. *See under C.*

Matt. 28. 18. *See b B, §222 page 622.*

F

Luke 4. 14 And Jesus returned in the power of the Spirit into Galilee: and there went out a fame of him through all the region round about.

G

Luke 4. 18 The Spirit of the Lord *is* upon me, because he hath anointed me to preach the gospel to the poor; he hath sent me to heal the brokenhearted, to preach deliverance to the captives, and recovering of sight to the blind, to set at liberty them that are bruised,

Acts 2. 22. *See g, G, § 231, page 636.*

Acts 4. 27 For of a truth against thy holy child Jesus, whom thou hast anointed, both Herod, and Pontius Pilate, with the Gentiles, and the people of Israel, were gathered together,

Heb. 1. 9 Thou hast loved righteousness, and hated iniquity; therefore God, *even* thy God, hath anointed thee with the oil of gladness above thy fellows.

H

John 1. 1 In the beginning was the Word, and the Word was with God, and the Word was God.

For H concluded, I, and K, see next page (698).

§ 254. THE CONVERSION OF CORNELIUS (CONCLUDED).

CHAP. 10.

40 [l]Him God raised up the third day, and shewed him openly;

41 [m]Not to all the people, but unto witnesses chosen before of God, *even* to us, [n]who did eat and drink with him after he rose from the dead.

42 And he [o]commanded us to preach unto the people, and to testify [p]that it is he which was ordained of God *to be* the Judge of quick and dead.

43 To [q]him give all the prophets witness, that through his name [r]whosoever believeth in him shall receive remission of sins.

44 While Peter yet spake these words, the [s]Holy Ghost fell on all them which heard the word.

45 And [t]they of the circumcision which believed were astonished, as many as came with Peter, [u]because that on the Gentiles also was poured out the gift of the Holy Ghost.

46 For they heard them speak with tongues, and magnify God. Then answered Peter,

47 Can any man forbid water, that these should not be baptized, which have received the Holy Ghost [x]as well as we?

48 And he commanded them to be baptized in the name of the Lord. Then prayed they him to tarry certain days.

H—CONCLUDED.

John 3. 2 The same came to Jesus by night, and said unto him, Rabbi, we know that thou art a teacher come from God: for no man can do these miracles that thou doest, except God be with him.

Col. 2. 9 For in him dwelleth all the fulness of the Godhead bodily.

I

Acts 5. 32. *See t, T, §242, page 662.*

K

Acts 2. 23. *See i, I, §231, page 638.*

L

Acts 2. 24. *See k, K, § 231, page 638.*

M

Matt. 13. 11 He answered and said unto them, Because it is given unto you to know the mysteries of the kingdom of heaven, but to them it is not given.

John 14. 17 *Even* the Spirit of truth; whom the world cannot receive, because it seeth him not, neither knoweth him: but ye know him; for he dwelleth with you, and shall be in you.

John 14. 22 Judas saith unto him, not Iscariot, Lord, how is it that thou wilt manifest thyself unto us, and not unto the world?

23 Jesus answered and said unto him, If a man love me, he will keep my words: and my Father will love him, and we will come unto him, and make our abode with him

24 He that loveth me not keepeth not my sayings: and the word which ye hear is not mine, but the Father's which sent me.

N

Luke 24. 30 And it came to pass, as he sat at meat with them, he took bread, and and blessed *it*, and brake, and gave to them.

Luke 24. 43 And he took *it*, and did eat before them.

O

Matt. 28. 19 Go ye therefore, and teach all nations, baptizing them in the name of the Father, and of the Son, and of the Holy Ghost:

20 Teaching them to observe all things whatsoever I have commanded you: and, lo, I am with you alway, *even* unto the end of the world. Amen.

Acts 1. 8 But ye shall receive power, after that the Holy Ghost is come upon you: and ye shall be witnesses unto me both in Jerusalem, and in all Judea, and in Samaria, and unto the uttermost part of the earth.

P

Matt. 25, *Study §177, Page 502.*

John 5. 22 For the Father judgeth no man, but hath committed all judgment unto the Son:

John 5. 27 And hath given him authority to execute judgment also, because he is the Son of man.

TIME. A. D. 40; PLACE, CESAREA.

P—CONCLUDED.

Acts 17. 31 Because he hath appointed a day, in the which he will judge the world in righteousness by *that* man whom he hath ordained; *whereof* he hath given assurance unto all *men*, in that he hath raised him from the dead.

IICor. 5. 10 For we must all appear before the judgment seat of Christ; that every one may receive the things *done* in *his* body, according to that he hath done, whether *it be* good or bad.

IITim. 4. 1 I charge *thee* therefore before God, and the Lord Jesus Christ, who shall judge the quick and the dead at his appearing and his kingdom;

I Pet. 4. 5 Who shall give account to him that is ready to judge the quick and the dead.

Q

Isa. 53. 11 He shall see of the travail of his soul, *and* shall be satisfied: by his knowledge shall my righteous servant justify many; for he shall bear their iniquities.

Jer. 31. 34 And they shall teach no more every man his neighbor, and every man his brother, saying, Know the LORD: for they shall all know me, from the least of them unto the greatest of them, saith the LORD: for I will forgive their iniquity, and I will remember their sin no more.

Da. 9. 24 Seventy weeks are determined upon thy people and upon thy holy city, to finish the transgression, and to make an end of sins, and to make reconciliation for iniquity, and to bring in everlasting righteousness, and to seal up the vision and prophecy, and to anoint the Most Holy.

Mic. 7. 18 Who *is* a God like unto thee, that pardoneth iniquity, and passeth by the transgression of the remnant of his heritage? he retaineth not his anger for ever, because he delighteth *in* mercy.

Zech. 13. 1 In that day there shall be a fountain opened to the house of David and to the inhabitants of Jerusalem for sin and for uncleanness.

Mal. 4. 2 But unto you that fear my name shall the Sun of righteousness arise with healing in his wings; and ye shall go forth, and grow up as calves of the stall.

R

Acts 15. 9 And put no difference between us and them, purifying their hearts by faith.

R—CONCLUDED.

Acts 26. 18 To open their eyes, *and* to turn *them* from darkness to light, and *from* the power of Satan unto God, that they may receive forgiveness of sins, and inheritance among them which are sanctified by faith that is in me.

Rom. 10. 11 For the Scripture saith, Whosoever believeth on him shall not be ashamed.

Gal. 3. 22 But the Scripture hath concluded all under sin, that the promise by faith of Jesus Christ might be given to them that believe.

S

Acts 2. 4 And they were all filled with the Holy Ghost, and began to speak with other tongues, as the Spirit gave them utterance.

Acts 4. 31 And when they had prayed, the place was shaken where they were assembled together; and they were all filled with the Holy Ghost, and they spake the word of God with boldness.

Acts 8. 17 Then laid they *their* hands on them, and they received the Holy Ghost.

18 And when Simon saw that through laying on of the apostles' hands the Holy Ghost was given, he offered them money,

T

Acts 10. 23 Then called he them in, and lodged *them*. And on the morrow Peter went away with them, and certain brethren from Joppa accompanied him.

U

Acts 11. 18 When they heard these things, they held their peace, and glorified God, saying, Then hath God also to the Gentiles granted repentance unto life.

Gal. 3. 14 That the blessing of Abraham might come on the Gentiles through Jesus Christ; that we might receive the promise of the Spirit through faith.

X

Acts 11. 17 Forasmuch then as God gave them the like gift as *he did* unto us, who believed on the Lord Jesus Christ, what was I, that I could withstand God?

Acts 15. 8 And God, which knoweth the hearts, bare them witness, giving them the Holy Ghost, even as *he did* unto us;

9 And put no difference between us and them, purifying their hearts by faith.

Rom. 10. 12 For there is no difference between the Jew and the Greek: for the same Lord over all is rich unto all that call upon him.

§ 255. PETER ACCUSED AT JERUSALEM. HIS DEFENSE.

11:1–18.

1 And the apostles and brethren that were in Judea heard that the Gentiles had also received the word of God.

2 And when Peter was come up to Jerusalem, [a]they that were of the circumcision contended with him,

3 Saying, [b]Thou wentest in to men uncircumcised, and didst eat with them.

4 But Peter rehearsed *the matter* from the beginning, and [c]expounded *it* by order unto them, saying,

5 [d]I was in the city of Joppa praying: and [e]in a trance I saw a vision, A certain vessel descend, as it had been a great sheet, let down from heaven by four corners; and it came even to me:

6 Upon the which when I had fastened mine eyes, I considered, and saw four-footed beasts of the earth, and wild beasts, and creeping things, and fowls of the air.

7 And I heard a voice saying unto me, Arise, Peter; slay and eat.

8 But I said, Not so, Lord: for [f]nothing common or unclean hath at any time entered into my mouth.

9 But the voice answered me again from heaven, What God hath cleansed, *that* call not thou common.

10 And this was done three times: and all were drawn up again into heaven.

11 And, behold, immediately there were three men already come unto the house where I was, sent from Cesarea unto me.

CHAP. 11.

12 And [g]the Spirit bade me go with them, nothing doubting. Moreover these [h]six brethren accompanied me, and we entered into the man's house:

13 And he [i]shewed us how he had seen an angel in his house, which stood and said unto him, Send men to Joppa, and call for Simon, whose surname is Peter;

14 Who shall tell thee [k]words, whereby thou and all thy house shall be saved.

15 And as I began to speak, the Holy Ghost fell on them, [l]as on us at the beginning.

16 Then remembered I the word of the Lord, how that he said, [m]John indeed baptized with water; but ye shall be baptized with the Holy Ghost.

17 [n]Forasmuch then as God gave them the like gift as *he did* unto us, who believed on the Lord Jesus Christ, what was I, that I could withstand God?

18 When they heard these things, they held their peace, and glorified God, saying, Then hath God also to the Gentiles granted repentance unto life.

A

Acts 10. 45 And they of the circumcision which believed were astonished, as many as came with Peter, because that on the Gentiles also was poured out the gift of the Holy Ghost.

Gal. 2. 12 For before that certain came from James, he did eat with the Gentiles: but when they were come, he withdrew and separated himself, fearing them which were of the circumcision.

13 And the other Jews dissembled likewise with him; insomuch that Barnabas also was carried away with their dissimulation.

TIME, A. D. 40, 41; PLACE, JERUSALEM.

B

Luke 15. 2 And the Pharisees and scribes murmured, saying, This man receiveth sinners, and eateth with them.

Acts 10. 28 And he said unto them, Ye know how that it is an unlawful thing for a man that is a Jew to keep company, or come unto one of another nation; but God hath shewed me that I should not call any man common or unclean.

C

Luke 1. 3 It seemed good to me also, having had perfect understanding of all things from the very first, to write unto thee in order, most excellent Theophilus,

Acts 14 27 And when they were come, and had gathered the church together, they rehearsed all that God had done with them, and how he had opened the door of faith unto the Gentiles.

D

Acts 10 8 And when he had declared all *these* things unto them, he sent them to Joppa.

9 On the morrow, as they went on their journey, and drew nigh unto the city, Peter went up upon the housetop to pray about the sixth hour:

E

Acts 22 17 And it came to pass, that, when I was come again to Jerusalem, even while I prayed in the temple, I was in a trance;

IICor. 12 1 It is not expedient for me doubtless to glory. I will come to visions and revelations of the Lord.

F

Lev. 11 46 This *is* the law of the beasts, and of the fowl, and of every living creature that moveth in the waters, and of every creature that creepeth upon the earth:

47 To make a difference between the unclean and the clean, and between the beast that may be eaten and the beast that may not be eaten.

Eze. 4. 14 Then said I, Ah Lord GOD! behold, my soul hath not been polluted: for from my youth up even till now have I not eaten of that which dieth of itself, or is torn in pieces; neither came there abominable flesh into my mouth.

Mark 7 2 And when they saw some of his disciples eat bread with defiled, that is to say, with unwashen, hands, they found fault.

3 For the Pharisees, and all the Jews, except they wash *their* hands oft, eat not, holding the tradition of the elders.

F—CONCLUDED.

Mark 7. 4 And *when they come* from the market, except they wash, they eat not. And many other things there be, which they have received to hold, *as* the washing of cups, and pots, brazen vessels, and of tables.

G

Acts 10. 19. *See m, M, § 254, page 694.*

H

Acts 10. 23 Then called he them in, and lodged *them*. And on the morrow Peter went away with them: and certain brethren from Joppa accompanied him.

I

Acts 10. 30 And Cornelius said, Four days ago I was fasting until this hour; and at the ninth hour I prayed in my house, and, behold, a man stood before me in bright clothing,

K

Ps. 19. 7 The law of the LORD *is* perfect, converting the soul: the testimony of the LORD *is* sure, making wise the simple.

Ps. 119. 11 Thy word have I hid in mine heart, that I might not sin against thee.

John 12. 50 And I know that his commandment is life everlasting: whatsoever I speak therefore, even as the Father said unto me, so I speak.

John 15. 3 Now ye are clean through the word which I have spoken unto you.

Acts 10. 22. *See p, P, § 254, page 694.*

Rom. 1. 16 For I am not ashamed of the gospel of Christ: for it is the power of God unto salvation to every one that believeth; to the Jew first, and also to the Greek.

Rom. 10. 8 But what saith it? The word is nigh thee, *even* in thy mouth, and in thy heart: that is, the word of faith, which we preach;

9 That if thou shalt confess with thy mouth the Lord Jesus, and shalt believe in thine heart that God hath raised him from the dead, thou shalt be saved.

10 For with the heart man believeth unto righteousness; and with the mouth confession is made unto salvation.

L

Acts 2. 4 And they were all filled with the Holy Ghost, and began to speak with other tongues, as the Spirit gave them utterance.

M

Matt. 3. 11. *See h, H, § 14, page 50.*

N

Acts 10. 47. *See x, X, § 254, page 698.*

§ 256. BARNABAS SENT TO ANTIOCH. SAUL BROUGHT THITHER.

11 : 19–26.

19 Now [a]they which were scattered abroad upon the persecution that arose about Stephen travelled as far as Phenice, and Cyprus, and Antioch, preaching the word to none but unto the Jews only.

20 And some of them were men of Cyprus and Cyrene, which, when they were come to Antioch, spake unto [b]the Grecians, preaching the Lord Jesus.

21 And [c]the hand of the Lord was with them: and a great number believed, and [d]turned unto the Lord.

22 Then tidings of these things came unto the ears of the church which was in Jerusalem: and they sent forth [e]Barnabas, that he should go as far as Antioch.

23 Who, when he came, and had seen the grace of God, was glad, and [f]exhorted them all, that with purpose of heart they would [g]cleave unto the Lord.

24 For he was a good man, and [h]full of the Holy Ghost and of faith: and much people was added unto the Lord.

25 [i]Then departed Barnabas to Tarsus, for to seek Saul:

CHAP. 11.

26 And when he had found him, he brought him unto Antioch. And it came to pass, that a whole year they assembled themselves [1]with the church, and taught much people. And the disciples were called Christians first in Antioch.

A

Acts 8. 1 And Saul was consenting unto his death. And at that time there was a great persecution against the church which was at Jerusalem; and they were all scattered abroad throughout the regions of Judea and Samaria, except the apostles.

B

Acts 6. 1 And in those days, when the number of the disciples was multiplied, there arose a murmuring of the Grecians against the Hebrews, because their widows were neglected in the daily ministration.

Acts 9. 29 And he spake boldly in the name of the Lord Jesus, and disputed against the Grecians: but they went about to slay him.

C

IIChr 30. 12 Also in Judah the hand of God was to give them one heart to do the commandment of the king and of the princes, by the word of the LORD.

Isa. 53. 1 Who hath believed our report? and to whom is the arm of the LORD revealed?

Isa. 59. 1 Behold, the LORD's hand is not shortened, that it cannot save; neither his ear heavy, that it cannot hear:

Luke 1. 66 And all they that heard *them* laid *them* up in their hearts, saying, What manner of child shall this be! And the hand of the Lord was with him.

§ 257. FAMINE. SAUL AND BARNABAS SENT TO JERUSALEM.

11 : 27–30.

27 And in these days came [a]prophets from Jerusalem unto Antioch,

28 And there stood up one of them named [b]Agabus, and signified by the Spirit that there should be great dearth throughout all the world:

A

Acts 2. 17 And it shall come to pass in the last days, saith God, I will pour out of my Spirit upon all flesh: and your sons and your daughters shall prophesy, and your young men shall see visions, and your old men shall dream dreams;

Acts 13. 1 Now there were in the church that was at Antioch certain prophets and teachers; as Barnabas, and Simeon

TIME, A. D. 41–44; PLACE, ANTIOCH.

C—CONCLUDED.

Acts 2. 47 Praising God, and having favour with all the people. And the Lord added to the church daily such as should be saved.

D

Acts 9. 35 And all that dwelt at Lydda and Saron saw him, and turned to the Lord.

Acts 15. 19 Wherefore my sentence is, that we trouble not them, which from among the Gentiles are turned to God:

E

Acts 4. 36 And Joses, who by the apostles was surnamed Barnabas, (which is, being interpreted, The son of consolation,) a Levite, *and* of the country of Cyprus,

37 Having land, sold *it*, and brought the money and laid *it* at the apostles' feet.

Acts 9. 27 But Barnabas took him, and brought *him* to the apostles, and declared unto them how he had seen the Lord in the way, and that he had spoken to him, and how he had preached boldly at Damascus in the name of Jesus.

Acts 13. 1. *See under A, § 257.*

Acts 13. 2 As they ministered to the Lord, and fasted, the Holy Ghost said, Separate me Barnabas and Saul for the work whereunto I have called them.

3 And when they had fasted and prayed, and laid *their* hands on them, they sent *them* away.

Acts 15. 2 When therefore Paul and Barnabas had no small dissension and disputation with them, they determined that Paul and Barnabas, and certain other of them, should go up to Jerusalem unto the apostles and elders about this question.

Acts 15. 39 And the contention was so sharp between them, that they departed asunder one from the other: and so

E—CONCLUDED.

Barnabas took Mark, and sailed unto Cyprus;

F

Acts 13. 43 Now when the congregation was broken up, many of the Jews and religious proselytes followed Paul and Barnabas; who, speaking to them, persuaded them to continue in the grace of God.

Acts 14. 22 Confirming the souls of the disciples, *and* exhorting them to continue in the faith, and that we must through much tribulation enter into the kingdom of God.

G

Deut. 10. 20 Thou shalt fear the LORD thy God; him shalt thou serve, and to him shalt thou cleave, and swear by his name.

I. Cor. 15. 58 Therefore, my beloved brethren, be ye steadfast, unmoveable, always abounding in the work of the Lord, forasmuch as ye know that your labour is not in vain in the Lord.

Gal. 2. 19 For I through the law am dead to the law, that I might live unto God.

Col. 2. 6 As ye have therefore received Christ Jesus the Lord, *so* walk ye in him:

H

Acts 6. 5 And the saying pleased the whole multitude: and they chose Stephen, a man full of faith and of the Holy Ghost, and Philip, and Prochorus, and Nicanor, and Timon, and Parmenas, and Nicolas a proselyte of Antioch;

I

Acts 9. 27. *See under E.*

Acts 9. 30 *Which* when the brethren knew, they brought him down to Cesarea, and sent him forth to Tarsus.

1

Or, *in the church.*

TIME, A. D. 45; PLACE, JERUSALEM.

A—CONTINUED.

that was called Niger, and Lucius of Cyrene, and Manaen, which had been brought up with Herod the tetrarch, and[1] Saul.

Acts 15. 32 And Judas and Silas, being prophets also themselves, exhorted the brethren with many words, and confirmed *them*.

Acts 21. 9 And the same man had four daughters, virgins, which did prophesy.

A—CONCLUDED.

I. Cor. 12. 28 And God hath set some in the church, first apostles, secondarily prophets, thirdly teachers, after that miracles, then gifts of healings, helps, governments, diversities of tongues.

Eph. 4. 11 And he gave some, apostles; and some, prophets; and some, evangelists; and some, pastors and teachers;

For B see next page (704).

§ 257. FAMINE. SAUL AND BARNABAS SENT TO JERUSALEM.

CHAP. 11.

which came to pass in the days of Claudius Cæsar.

29 Then the disciples, every man according to his ability, determined to send [c]relief unto the brethren which dwelt in Judea:

30 Which also [d]they did, and sent it to the elders by the hands of Barnabas and Saul.

B

Acts 21. 10 And as we tarried *there* many days, there came down from Judea a certain prophet, named Agabus.

C

Eccl. 11. 1 Cast thy bread upon the waters: for thou shalt find it after many days.
2 Give a portion to seven, and also to eight; for thou knowest not what evil shall be upon the earth.

Rom. 15. 26 For it hath pleased them of Macedonia and Achaia to make a certain contribution for the poor saints which are at Jerusalem.

§ 258. HEROD KILLS JAMES AND IMPRISONS PETER.

12 : 1–19.

1 Now about that time Herod the the king [1]stretched forth *his* hands [a]to vex certain of the church.

2 And he killed James [b]the brother of John with the sword.

3 And because he saw it pleased the Jews, he proceeded further to take Peter also. (Then were [c]the days of unleavened bread.)

4 And [d]when he had apprehended him, he put *him* in prison, and delivered *him* to four quaternions of soldiers to keep him; intending after Easter to bring him forth to the people.

5 Peter therefore was kept in prison: but [2]prayer was made without ceasing of the church unto God for him.

6 And when Herod would have brought him forth, the same night Peter was sleeping between two soldiers, bound with two chains: and the keepers before the door kept the prison.

7 And, behold, [e]the angel of the Lord came upon *him*, and a light

CHAP. 12.

shined in the prison: and he smote Peter on the side, and raised him up, saying, Arise up quickly. [f]And his chains fell off from *his* hands.

8 And the angel said unto him, Gird thyself, and bind on thy sandals: and so he did. And he said unto him, Cast thy garment about thee, and follow me.

9 And he went out, and followed him; and [g]wist not that it was true which was done by the angel; but thought [h]he saw a vision.

1

Or, *began*

A

Matt. 10. 17 But beware of men: for they will deliver you up to the councils, and they will scourge you in their synagogues;

B

Matt. 4. 21 And going on from thence, he saw other two brethren, James *the son* of Zebedee, and John his brother, in a ship with Zebedee their father, mending their nets; and he called them,

Matt. 20. 23 And he said unto them, Ye shall drink indeed of my cup, and be baptized with the baptism that I am baptized with: but to sit on my right hand, and on my left, is not mine to give, but *it shall be given to them* for whom it is prepared of my Father.

CONCLUDED. TIME, A. D. 45; PLACE, JERUSALEM.

C—CONCLUDED.

ICor.16. 1 Now concerning the collection for
the saints, as I have given order to the
churches of Galatia, even so do ye.

Gal. 2. 10 Only *they would* that we should
remember the poor; the same which I
also was forward to do.

D

Acts 12. 25 And Barnabas and Saul returned
from Jerusalem, when they had fulfilled *their* ministry, and took with
them John, whose surname was Mark.

ICor.16. 3 And when I come, whomsoever ye
shall approve by *your* letters, them

D—CONCLUDED.

will I send to bring your liberality unto
Jerusalem.

4 And if it be meet that I go also,
they shall go with me.

IICor.8. 4 Praying us with much entreaty that
we would receive the gift, and *take
upon us* the fellowship of the ministering to the saints.

IICor.8. And not *that* only, but who was also
chosen of the churches to travel with
us with this grace, which is administered by us to the glory of the same
Lord, and *declaration of* your ready
mind;

TIME, A. D. 44; PLACE, JERUSALEM.

C

Ex. 12. 14 And this day shall be unto you for
a memorial; and ye shall keep it a feast
to the LORD throughout your generations: ye shall keep it a feast by an ordinance for ever.

Ex. 12. 15 Seven days shall ye eat unleavened
bread; even the first day ye shall put
away leaven out of your houses: for
whosoever eateth leavened bread from
the first day until the seventh day, that
soul shall be cut off from Israel.

Ex. 23. 15 Thou shalt keep the feast of unleavened bread: (thou shalt eat unleavened bread seven days, as I commanded thee, in the time appointed of
the month Abib; for in it thou camest
out from Egypt: and none shall appear
before me empty:)

D

John 21. 18 Verily, verily, I say unto thee,
When thou wast young, thou girdedst
thyself, and walkedst whither thou
wouldest: but when thou shalt be old,
thou shalt stretch forth thy hands, and
another shall gird thee, and carry *thee*
whither thou wouldest not.

2

Or, instant and earnest prayer was made,

Isa. 62. 6 I have set watchmen upon thy walls,
O Jerusalem, *which* shall never hold
their peace day nor night: ye that make
mention of the LORD, keep not silence,

7 And give him no rest, till he establish, and till he make Jerusalem a
praise in the earth.

IICor.1. 11 Ye also helping together by prayer
for us, that for the gift *bestowed* upon
us by the means of many persons thanks
may be given by many on our behalf.

2—CONCLUDED.

Eph. 6. 18 Praying always with all prayer
and supplication in the Spirit, and
watching thereunto with all perseverance and supplication for all saints;

IThes.5. 17 Pray without ceasing.

Jas. 5. 16 Confess *your* faults one to another,
and pray one for another, that ye may
be healed. The effectual fervent prayer
of a righteous man availeth much.

E

Ps. 37. 32 The wicked watcheth the righteous, and seeketh to slay him.

33 The LORD will not leave him in
his hand, nor condemn him when he is
judged.

Acts 5. 19 But the angel of the Lord by night
opened the prison doors, and brought
them forth, and said,

F

Acts 16. 26 And suddenly there was a great
earthquake, so that the foundations of
the prison were shaken: and immediately all the doors were opened, and
every one's bands were loosed.

G

Ps. 126. 1 When the LORD turned again the
captivity of Zion, we were like them
that dream.

H

Acts 10. 3 He saw in a vision evidently, about
the ninth hour of the day, an angel of
God coming in to him, and saying unto
him, Cornelius.

Acts 10. 17 Now while Peter doubted in himself what this vision he had seen should
mean, behold, the men which were
sent from Cornelius had made inquiry for Simon's house, and stood before the gate.

For H concluded, see next page (706).

§ 258. HERODS KILLS JAMES AND IMPRISONS PETER

CHAP. 12.

10 When they were past the first and second ward, they came unto the iron gate that leadeth unto the city; [i]which opened to them of his own accord: and they went out, and passed on through one street; and forthwith the angel departed from him.

11 And when Peter was come to himself, he said, Now I know of a surety, that [k]the Lord hath sent his angel, and [l]hath delivered me out of the hand of Herod, and *from* all the expectation of the people of the Jews.

12 And when he had considered *the thing*, [m]he came to the house of Mary the mother of [n]John, whose surname was Mark; where many were gathered together praying.

13 And as Peter knocked at the door of the gate, a damsel came [1]to hearken, named Rhoda.

14 And when she knew Peter's voice, she opened not the gate for gladness, but ran in, and told how Peter stood before the gate.

15 And they said unto her, Thou art mad. But she constantly affirmed that it was even so. Then said they, [o]It is his angel.

16 But Peter continued knocking: and when they had opened *the door*, and saw him, they were astonished.

17 But he, [p]beckoning unto them with the hand to hold their peace, [q]declared unto them how the Lord had brought him out of the prison. And he said, Go shew these things unto James, and to the brethren.

CHAP. 12.

And he departed, and went into another place.

18 Now as soon as it was day, there was no small stir among the soldiers, what was become of Peter.

19 And when Herod had sought for him, and found him not, he examined the keepers and commanded that *they* should be put to death. And he went down from Judea to Cesarea, and *there* abode.

H—CONCLUDED.

Acts 11. 5 I was in the city of Joppa praying: and in a trance I saw a vision, A certain vessel descend, as it had been a great sheet, let down from heaven by four corners; and it came even to me:

I

Acts 16. 26. *See under F, page 705.*

Isa. 45. 1 Thus saith the LORD to his anointed, to Cyrus, whose right hand I have holden, to subdue nations before him; and I will loose the loins of kings, to open before him the twoleaved gates; and the gates shall not be shut;

2 I will go before thee, and make the crooked places straight: I will break in pieces the gates of brass, and cut in sunder the bars of iron:

Rev. 3, 7 And to the angel of the church in Philadelphia write: These things saith he that is holy, he that is true, he that hath the key of David, he that openeth, and no man shutteth; and shutteth, and no man openeth;

K

Ps. 34. 7 The angel of the LORD encampeth round about them that fear him, and delivereth them.

Dan. 3. 28 *Then* Nebuchadnezzar spake, and said, Blessed *be* the God of Shadrach, Meshach, and Abed-nego, who hath sent his angel, and delivered his servants that trusted in him, and have changed the king's word, and yielded their bodies, that they might not serve nor worship any god, except their own God.

Dan. 6. 22 My God hath sent his angel, and hath shut the lions' mouths, that they have not hurt me: forasmuch as before

(CONCLUDED). TIME, A. D. 44; PLACE, JERUSALEM.

K—CONCLUDED.

him innocency was found in me; and also before thee, O King, have I done no hurt.

Heb. 1. 14 Are they not all ministering spirits, sent forth to minister unto them who shall be heirs of salvation?

L

Job 5. 19 He shall deliver thee in six troubles: yea, in seven shall no evil touch thee.

Ps. 33. 18 Behold, the eye of the LORD *is* upon them that fear him, upon them that hope in his mercy;

19 To deliver their soul from death, and to keep them alive in famine.

Ps. 33. 22 The LORD redeemeth the soul of his servants: and none of hem that trust in him shall be desolate.

Ps. 41. 2 The LORD will preserve him, and keep him alive; *and* he shall be blessed upon the earth: and thou wilt not deliver him unto the will of his enemies.

Ps. 97. 10 Ye that love the LORD, hate evil: he preserveth the souls of his saints; he delivereth them out of the hand of the wicked.

Ps. 109. 31 For he shall stand at the right hand of the poor, to save *him* from those that condemn his soul.

IICor. 1. 8 For we would not, brethren, have you ignorant of our trouble which came to us in Asia, that we were pressed out of measure, above strength, insomuch that we despaired even of life:

9 But we had the sentence of death in ourselves, that we should not trust in ourselves, but in God which raiseth the dead:

10 Who delivered us from so great a death, and doth deliver; in whom we trust that he will yet deliver *us;*

IIPet. 2. 9 The Lord knoweth how to deliver the godly out of temptations, and to reserve the unjust unto the day of judgment to be punished:

M

Acts 4. 23 And being let go, they went to their own company, and reported all that the chief priests and elders had said unto them.

N

Acts 13. 5 And when they were at Salamis, they preached the word of God in the synagogues of the Jews: and they had also John to *their* minister.

Acts 13. 13 Now when Paul and his company loosed from Paphos, they came to Per-

N—CONCLUDED.

ga in Pamphylia: and John departing from them returned to Jerusalem.

Acts 15. 37 And Barnabas determined to take with them John, whose surname was Mark.

38 But Paul thought not good to take him with them, who departed from them from Pamphylia, and went not with them to the work.

Col. 4. 10 Aristarchus my fellow prisoner saluteth you, and Marcus, sister's son to Barnabas, (touching whom ye received commandments: if he come unto you, receive him;)

IITim. 4. 11 Only Luke is with me. Take Mark, and bring him with thee: for he is profitable to me for the ministry.

Phile. 24 Marcus, Aristarchus, Demas, Lucas, my fellow labourers.

1

Or, *to ask who was there.*

O

Gen. 48. 16 The Angel which redeemed me from all evil, bless the lads; and let my name be named on them, and the name of my fathers Abraham and Isaac; and let them grow into a multitude in the midst of the earth.

Matt. 18. 10 Take heed that ye despise not one of these little ones; for I say unto you, That in heaven their angels do always behold the face of my father which is in heaven.

P

Acts 13. 16 Then Paul stood up, and beckoning with *his* hand said, Men of Israel, and ye that fear God, give audience.

Acts 19. 33 And they drew Alexander out of the multitude, the Jews putting him forward. And Alexander beckoned with the hand, and would have made his defence unto the people.

Acts 21. 40 And when he had given him license, Paul stood on the stairs, and beckoned with the hand unto the people. And when there was made a great silence, he spake unto *them* in the Hebrew tongue, saying,

Q

Ps. 66. 16 Come *and* hear, all ye that fear God, and I will declare what he hath done for my soul.

Ps. 102. 20 To hear the groaning of the prisoner; to loose those that are appointed to death;

21 To declare the name of the LORD in Zion, and his praise in Jerusalem;

§ 259. THE DEATH OF HEROD. BARNABAS AND SAUL RETURN.

12 : 20–25.

20 And Herod [1]was highly displeased with them of Tyre and Sidon: but they came with one accord to him, and, having made Blastus [2]the king's chamberlain their friend, desired peace; because [a]their country was nourished by the king's *country*.

21 And upon a set day Herod, arrayed in royal apparel, sat upon his throne, and made an oration unto them.

22 And the people gave a shout, *saying*, [b]*It is* the voice of a god, and not of a man.

23 And immediately the angel of the Lord [c]smote him, because [d]he gave not God the glory: and he was eaten of worms, and gave up the ghost.

24 But [e]the word of God grew and multiplied.

25 And Barnabas and Saul returned from Jerusalem, when they had fulfilled *their* [3]ministry, and [f]took with them John, whose surname was Mark.

1

Or, *bare an hostile mind, intending war.*

2

Gr. *that was over the king's bedchamber.*

A

1 Ki. 5. 9 My servants shall bring *them* down from Lebanon unto the sea; and I will convey them by sea in floats unto the place that thou shalt appoint me, and will cause them to be discharged there, and thou shalt receive *them:* and thou shalt accomplish my desire, in giving food for my household.

10 So Hiram gave Solomon cedar trees and fir trees *according to* all his desire.

11 And Solomon gave Hiram twenty thousand measures of wheat *for* food to his household, and twenty measures of pure oil: thus gave Solomon to Hiram year by year.

Eze. 27. 17 Judah, and the land of Israel, they *were* thy merchants: they traded in thy market wheat of Minnith, and Pannag, and honey, and oil, and balm.

B

Acts 14. 11 And when the people saw what Paul had done, they lifted up their voices, saying in the speech of Lycaonia, The gods are come down to us in the likeness of men.

12 And they called Barnabas, Jupiter; and Paul, Mercurius, because he was the chief speaker.

§ 260. BARNABAS AND SAUL SEPARATED AS MINISTERS TO THE

13 : 1–3.

1 Now there were [a]in the church that was at Antioch certain prophets and teachers; as [b]Barnabas, and Simeon that was called Niger, and [c]Lucius of Cyrene, and Manaen, [1]which had been brought up with Herod the tetrarch, and Saul.

2 As they ministered to the Lord, and fasted, the Holy Ghost said, [d]Separate me Barnabas and Saul for the work [e]whereunto I have called them.

3 [f]And when they had fasted and prayed, and laid *their* hands on them, they sent *them* away.

A

Acts 11. 27 And in these days came prophets from Jerusalem unto Antioch.

Acts 14. 26 And thence sailed to Antioch, from whence they had been recommended to the grace of God for the work which they fulfilled.

Acts 15. 35 Paul also and Barnabas continued in Antioch, teaching and preaching the word of the Lord, with many others also.

B

Acts 11. 22. *See e, E,* § *256, page 702.*

C

Rom. 16. 21 Timotheus my workfellow, and Lucius, and Jason, and Sosipater, my kinsmen, salute you.

1

Or, *Herod's fosterbrother.*

TIME, A. D. 44—45; PLACE, CESAREA.

B—CONCLUDED.

Jude 16 These are murmurers, complainers, walking after their own lusts; and their mouth speaketh great swelling *words*, having men's persons in admiration because of advantage.

C

Lev. 10. 2 And there went out fire from the LORD, and devoured them, and they died before the LORD.

3 Then Moses said unto Aaron, This *is it* that the LORD spake, saying, I will be sanctified in them that come nigh me, and before all the people I will be glorified. And Aaron held his peace.

I Sa. 25. 38 And it came to pass about ten days *after*, that the LORD smote Nabal, that he died.

D

Deut. 28. 58 If thou wilt not observe to do all the words of this law that are written in this book, that thou mayest fear this glorious and fearful name, THE LORD THY GOD;

59 Then the LORD will make thy plagues wonderful, and the plagues of thy seed, *even* great plagues, and of long continuance, and sore sicknesses, and of long continuance.

Ps. 115. 1 Not unto us, O LORD, not unto us, but unto thy name give glory, for thy mercy, *and* for thy truth's sake.

D—CONCLUDED.

Isa. 42. 8 I *am* the LORD; that *is* my name: and my glory will I not give to another, neither my praise to graven images.

Isa. 48. 11 For mine own sake, *even* for mine own sake, will I do *it*: for how should *my name* be polluted? and I will not give my glory unto another.

I Cor. 1. 29 That no flesh should glory in his presence.

E

Isa. 55. 11 So shall my word be that goeth forth out of my mouth: it shall not return unto me void, but it shall accomplish that which I please, and it shall prosper *in the thing* whereto I sent it.

Acts 6. 7 And the word of God increased; and the number of the disciples multiplied in Jerusalem greatly; and a great company of the priests were obedient to the faith.

Acts 19. 20 So mightily grew the word of God and prevailed.

3

Or, *charge.*

Acts 11. 29 Then the disciples, every man according to his ability, determined to send relief unto the brethren which dwelt in Judea:

30 Which also they did, and sent it to the elders by the hands of Barnabas and Saul.

F

Acts 12, 12. *See n, N, § 258, page 706.*

GENTILES. TIME, A. D. 48; PLACE, ANTIOCH.

D

Num. 8. 14 Thus shalt thou separate the Levites from among the children of Israel: and the Levites shall be mine.

Acts 9 15. *See l, L, § 251, page 684.*

Gal. 2. 9 And when James, Cephas, and John, who seemed to be pillars, perceived the grace that was given unto me, they gave to me and Barnabas the right hands of fellowship; that we *should go* unto the heathen, and they unto the circumcision.

E

Matt. 9. 38 Pray ye therefore the Lord of the harvest, that he will send forth labourers into his harvest.

Acts 14. 26. *See under A.*

Rom. 10. 15 And how shall they preach, except they be sent? as it is written, How beautiful are the feet of them that

E—CONCLUDED.

preach the gospel of peace, and bring glad tidings of good things!

Eph. 3. 7. *See L, § 251, page 686.*

II Tim. 1. 11 Whereunto I am appointed a preacher, and an apostle, and a teacher of the Gentiles.

Heb. 5. 4 And no man taketh this honour unto himself, but he that is called of God, as *was* Aaron.

F

Acts 6. 6 Whom they set before the apostles: and when they had prayed, they laid *their* hands on them.

Acts 8. 17 Then laid they *their* hands on them, and they received the Holy Ghost.

Acts 8. 17. *See d, D, § 249, page 680*

§ 261. PAUL'S FIRST MISSIONARY JOURNEY WITH BARNABAS.

13 : 4–13.

4 So they, being sent forth by the Holy Ghost, departed unto Seleucia; and from thence they sailed to [a]Cyprus.

5 And when they were at Salamis, they preached the word of God in the synagogues of the Jews: and they had also [b]John to *their* minister.

6 And when they had gone through the isle unto Paphos, they found [c]a certain sorcerer, a false prophet, a Jew, whose name *was* Bar-jesus:

7 Which was with the deputy of the country, Sergius Paulus, a prudent man; who called for Barnabas and Saul, and desired to hear the word of God.

8 But Elymas [d]the sorcerer (for so is his name by interpretation) withstood them, seeking to turn away the deputy from the faith.

9 Then Saul, (who also *is called* Paul,) [e]filled with the Holy Ghost, set his eyes on him,

10 And said, O full of all subtilty and all mischief, [f]*thou* child of the devil, *thou* enemy of all righteousness, wilt thou not cease to pervert the right ways of the Lord?

11 And now, behold, [g]the hand of the Lord *is* upon thee, and thou shalt be blind, not seeing the sun for

Chap. 13.

a season. And immediately there fell on him a mist and a darkness; and he went about seeking some to lead him by the hand.

12 Then the deputy, when he saw what was done, believed, being astonished at the doctrine of the Lord.

13 Now when Paul and his company loosed from Paphos, they came to Perga in Pamphylia: and [h]John departing from them returned to Jerusalem.

A

Acts 4. 36 And Joses, who by the apostles was surnamed Barnabas, (which is, being interpreted, The son of consolation,) a Levite, *and* of the country of Cyprus,

B

Acts 12. 12. *See n, N, § 258, page 706.*

C

Ex. 22. 18 Thou shalt not suffer a witch to live.

Lev. 20. 6 And the soul that turneth after such as have familiar spirits, and after wizards, to go a whoring after them, I will even set my face against that soul, and will cut him off from among his people.

Deut. 18. 10 There shall not be found among you *any one* that maketh his son or his daughter to pass through the fire, *or* that useth divination, *or* an observer of times, or an enchanter, or a witch,

11 Or a charmer, or a consulter with familiar spirits, or a wizard, or a necromancer.

12 For all that do these things *are* an abomination unto the Lord: and because of these abominations the Lord thy God doth drive them out from before thee.

§ 262. PAUL'S SERMON AT ANTIOCH IN PISIDIA.

13 : 14–43.

14 But when they departed from Perga, they came to Antioch in Pisidia, and [a]went into the synagogue on the sabbath day, and sat down.

Chap. 13.

15 And [b]after the reading of the law

A

Acts 16. 13 And on the sabbath we went out of the city by a river side, where prayer was wont to be made; and we

IN CYPRESS. TIME, A. D. 48–49; PLACE, ANTIOCH TO CYPRESS.

C—CONCLUDED.

I Chr. 10. 13 So Saul died for his transgression which he committed against the LORD, *even* against the word of the LORD, which he kept not, also for asking *counsel* of *one that had* a familiar spirit, to inquire *of it:*

Isa. 8. 19 And when they shall say unto you, Seek unto them that have familiar spirits, and unto wizards that peep and that mutter: should not a people seek unto their God? for the living to the dead?

20 To the law and to the testimony: if they speak not according to this word, *it is* because *there is* no light in them.

D

Ex. 7. 11 Then Pharaoh also called the wise men and the sorcerers: now the magicians of Egypt, they also did in like manner with their enchantments.

I Ki. 22. 24 But Zedekiah the son of Chenaanah went near, and smote Micaiah on the cheek, and said, Which way went the Spirit of the LORD from me to speak unto thee?

II Tim. 3. 8 Now as Jannes and Jambres withstood Moses, so do these also resist the truth: men of corrupt minds, reprobate concerning the faith.

II Tim. 4. 14 Alexander the coppersmith did me much evil: the Lord reward him according to his works:

15 Of whom be thou ware also; for he hath greatly withstood our words.

E

Mic. 3. 8 But truly I am full of power by the Spirit of the LORD, and of judgment, and of might, to declare unto Jacob his transgression, and to Israel his sin.

Acts 2. 4 And they were all filled with the Holy Ghost, and began to speak with other tongues, as the Spirit gave them utterance.

Acts 4. 8 Then Peter, filled with the Holy Ghost, said unto them, Ye rulers of

E—CONCLUDED.

the people, and elders of Israel.

Acts 4. 31 And when they had prayed, the place was shaken where they were assembled together; and they were all filled with the Holy Ghost, and they spake the word of God with boldness.

Acts 7. 55 But he, being full of the Holy Ghost, looked up steadfastly into heaven, and saw the glory of God, and Jesus standing on the right hand of God,

F

Matt. 13. 38 The field is the world; the good seed are the children of the kingdom; but the tares are the children of the wicked *one;*

John 8. 44 Ye are of *your* father the devil, and the lusts of your father ye will do. he was a murderer from the beginning, and abode not in the truth, because there is no truth in him. When he speaketh a lie, he speaketh of his own: for he is a liar, and the father of it.

I Jno. 3. 8 He that committeth sin is of the devil; for the devil sinneth from the beginning. For this purpose the Son of God was manifested, that he might destroy the works of the devil.

G

Ex. 9. 3 Behold, the hand of the LORD is upon thy cattle which *is* in the field, upon the horses, upon the asses, upon the camels, upon the oxen, and upon the sheep: *there shall be* a very grievous murrain.

I. Sa. 5. 6 But the hand of the LORD was heavy upon them of Ashdod, and he destroyed them, and smote them with emerods, *even* Ashdod and the coasts thereof.

H

Acts 15. 38 But Paul thought not good to take him with them, who departed from them from Pamphylia, and went not with them to the work.

TIME, A. D. 48–49; PLACE, ANTIOCH IN PISIDIA.

A—CONTINUED.

sat down, and spake unto the women which resorted *thither*.

Acts 17. 2 And Paul, as his manner was, went in unto them, and three sabbath days reasoned with them out of the Scriptures.

A—CONCLUDED.

Acts 19. 8 And he went into the synagogue, and spake boldly for the space of three months, disputing and persuading the things concerning the kingdom of God.

For B see next page (712).

§ 262. PAUL'S SERMON AT ANTIOCH IN PISIDIA

CHAP. 13.

and the prophets, the rulers of the
synagogue sent unto them, saying,
Ye men *and* brethren, if ye have [c]any
word of exhortation for the people,
say on.
16 Then Paul stood up, and [d]beck-
oning with *his* hand said, Men of
Israel, and [e]ye that fear God, give
audience.
17 The God of this people of Israel [f]chose our fathers, and exalted
the people [g]when they dwelt as strangers in the land of Egypt, [h]and with
a high arm brought he them out of it.
18 And [i]about the time of forty
years [l]suffered he their manners in
the wilderness.
19 And when [k]he had destroyed
seven nations in the land of Chanaan,
[l]he divided their land to them by lot.
20 And after that [m]he gave *unto*
them judges about the space of four
hundred and fifty years, until Samuel the prophet.
21 [n]And afterward they desired a
king: and God gave unto them Saul
the son of Cis, a man of the tribe of
Benjamin, by the space of forty
years.
22 And [o]when he had removed him,
[p]he raised up unto them David to be
their king; to whom also he gave testimony, and said, [q]I have found David
the *son* of Jesse, [r]a man after mine
own heart, which shall fulfil all my
will.
23 [s]Of this man's seed hath God, according [t]to *his* promise, raised unto
Israel [u]a Saviour, Jesus:
24 [x]When John had first preached
before his coming the baptism of repentance to all the people of Israel.

B

Luke 4. 16 And he came to Nazareth, where he had been brought up: and, as his custom was, he went into the synagogue on the sabbath day, and stood up for to read.

Acts 13. 27 For they that dwell at Jerusalem, and their rulers, because they knew him not, nor yet the voices of the prophets which are read every sabbath day, they have fulfilled *them* in condemning *him*.

C

Heb. 13. 22 And I beseech you, brethren, suffer the word of exhortation: for I have written a letter unto you in few words.

D

Acts 12. 17. *See p. P, § 258, page 706.*

E

Acts 10. 2 A devout *man*, and one that feared God with all his house, which gave much alms to the people, and prayed to God always.

Acts 10. 35 But in every nation he that feareth him, and worketh righteousness, is accepted with him.

Acts 13. 26 Men *and* brethren, children of the stock of Abraham, and whosoever among you feareth God, to you is the word of this salvation sent.

F

Gen. 12. 1 Now the LORD had said unto Abram, Get thee out of thy country, and from thy kindred, and from thy father's house, unto a land that I will shew thee:

2 And I will make of thee a great nation, and I will bless thee, and make thy name great; and thou shalt be a blessing:

Deut. 4. 37 And because he loved thy fathers, therefore he chose their seed after them, and brought thee out in his sight with his mighty power out of Egypt;

Deut. 7. 6 For thou *art* a holy people unto the LORD thy God: the LORD thy God hath chosen thee to be a special people unto himself, above all people that *are* upon the face of the earth.

7 The LORD did not set his love upon you, nor choose you, because ye were more in number than any people; for ye *were* the fewest of all people:

G

Ex. 1. 1 Now these *are* the names of the children of Israel, which came into Egypt; every man and his household came with Jacob.

(CONTINUED). TIME, A. D. 48-49; PLACE, ANTIOCH IN PISIDIA.

G—CONCLUDED.

Ps. 105. 23 Israel also came into Egypt; and Jacob sojourned in the land of Ham.
24 And he increased his people greatly; and made them stronger than their enemies.

Acts 7. 17 But when the time of the promise drew nigh, which God had sworn to Abraham, the people grew and multiplied in Egypt,

H

Ex. 6. 6 Wherefore say unto the children of Israel, I *am* the LORD, and I will bring you out from under the burdens of the Egyptians, and I will rid you out of their bondage, and I will redeem you with a stretched out arm, and with great judgments:

Ex. 13. 14 And it shall be when thy son asketh thee in time to come, saying, What *is* this? that thou shalt say unto him, By strength of hand the LORD brought us out from Egypt, from the house of bondage:

I

Ex. 16. 35 And the children of Israel did eat manna forty years, until they came to a land inhabited: they did eat manna, until they came unto the borders of the land of Canaan.

1

etropophoresen, perhaps for *etrophophoresen, bore*, or, *fed them, as a nurse beareth*, or, *feedeth her child*, according to the LXX and so Chrysostom.

Ex. 19. 4 Ye have seen what I did unto the Egyptians, and *how* I bare you on eagles' wings, and brought you unto myself.

Deut. 1. 31 And in the wilderness, where thou hast seen how that the LORD thy God bare thee, as a man doth bear his son, in all the way that ye went, until ye came into this place.

K

Deut. 7. 1 When the LORD thy God shall bring thee into the land whither thou goest to possess it, and hath cast out many nations before thee, the Hittites, and the Girgashites, and the Amorites, and the Canaanites, and the Perizzites, and the Hivites, and the Jebusites, seven nations greater and mightier than thou;

L

Josh. 1. 1 Now after the death of Moses the servant of the LORD, it came to pass, that the LORD spake unto Joshua the son of Nun, Moses' minister, saying,

L—CONCLUDED.

Josh. 1. 2 Moses my servant is dead; now therefore arise, go over this Jordan, thou and all this people, unto the land which I do give to them, *even* to the children of Israel.

Ps. 78. 55 He cast out the heathen also before them, and divided them an inheritance by line, and made the tribes of Israel to dwell in their tents.

M

Judg. 2. 16 Nevertheless the LORD raised up judges, which delivered them out of the hand of those that spoiled them.

I Sa. 3. 20 And all Israel from Dan even to Beer-sheba knew that Samuel *was* established *to be* a prophet of the LORD.

N

I Sa. 8. 5 And said unto him, Behold, thou art old, and thy sons walk not in thy ways: now make us a king to judge us like all the nations.

I Sa. 10. 1 Then Samuel took a vial of oil, and poured *it* upon his head, and kissed him, and said, *Is it* not because the LORD hath anointed thee *to be* captain over his inheritance?

O

I Sa. 15. 26 And Samuel said unto Saul, I will not return with thee: for thou hast rejected the word of the LORD, and the LORD hath rejected thee from being king over Israel.

I Sa. 16. 1 And the LORD said unto Samuel, How long wilt thou mourn for Saul, seeing I have rejected him from reigning over Israel? fill thine horn with oil, and go, I will send thee to Jesse the Beth-lehemite: for I have provided me a king among his sons.

P

I Sa. 16. 13 Then Samuel took the horn of oil, and anointed him in the midst of his brethren: and the Spirit of the LORD came upon David from that day forward. So Samuel rose up, and went to Ramah.

II Sa. 2. 4 And the men of Judah came, and there they anointed David king over the house of Judah. And they told David, saying, *That* the men of Jabesh-gilead *were they* that buried Saul.

II Sa. 5. 3 So all the elders of Israel came to the king to Hebron; and king David made a league with them in Hebron before the LORD: and they anointed David king over Israel.

For Q, R, S, T, U and X see next page (714).

§ 262. PAUL'S SERMON AT ANTIOCH IN PISIDIA

CHAP. 13.

25 And as John fulfilled his course, he said, [y]Whom think ye that I am? I am not *he*. But, behold, there cometh one after me, whose shoes of *his* feet I am not worthy to loose.

26 Men *and* brethren, children of the stock of Abraham, and whosoever among you feareth God, [z]to you is the word of this salvation sent.

27 For they that dwell at Jerusalem, and their rulers, [a]because they knew him not, nor yet the voices of the prophets [b]which are read every sabbath day, they have fulfilled *them* in condemning *him*.

28 [c]And though they found no cause of death *in him*, [d]yet desired they Pilate that he should be slain.

29 [e]And when they had fulfilled all that was written of him, [f]they took *him* down from the tree, and laid *him* in a sepulchre.

30 [g]But God raised him from the dead:

31 And [h]he was seen many days of them which came up with him [i]from Galilee to Jerusalem, [k]who are his witnesses unto the people.

32 And we declare unto you glad tidings, [l]how that the promise which was made unto the fathers,

33 God hath fulfilled the same unto us their children, in that he hath raised up Jesus again; as it is also written in the second psalm, [m]Thou art my Son, this day have I begotten thee.

34 And as concerning that he raised him up from the dead *now* no more to return to corruption, he said on this wise, [n]I will give you the sure [2]mercies of David.

Q

Ps. 89. 20 I have found David my servant; with my holy oil have I anointed him:

R

I Sa. 13. 14 But now thy kingdom shall not continue; the LORD hath sought him a man after his own heart, and the LORD hath commanded him *to be* captain over his people, because thou hast not kept *that* which the LORD commanded thee.

Acts 7. 46 Who found favour before God, and desired to find a tabernacle for the God of Jacob.

S

Isa. 11. 1 And there shall come forth a rod out of the stem of Jesse, and a Branch shall grow out of his roots:

Luke 1. 32 He shall be great, and shall be called the Son of the Highest; and the Lord God shall give unto him the throne of his father David:

Luke 1. 69 And hath raised up a horn of salvation for us in the house of his servant David;

Acts 2. 30 Therefore being a prophet, and knowing that God had sworn with an oath to him, that of the fruit of his loins, according to the flesh, he would raise up Christ to sit on his throne;

Rom. 1. 3 Concerning his son Jesus Christ our Lord, which was made of the seed of David according to the flesh;

T

II Sa. 7. 12 And when thy days be fulfilled, and thou shalt sleep with thy fathers, I will set up thy seed after thee, which shall proceed out of thy bowels, and I will establish his kingdom.

Ps. 132. 11 The LORD hath sworn *in* truth unto David; he will not turn from it; Of the fruit of thy body will I set upon thy throne.

U

Matt. 1. 21 And she shall bring forth a son, and thou shalt call his name JESUS: for he shall save his people from their sins.

Rom. 11. 26 And so all Israel shall be saved: as it is written, There shall come out of Sion the Deliverer, and shall turn away ungodliness from Jacob:

X

Matt. 3. 1 In those days came John the Baptist, preaching in the wilderness of Judea.

Luke 3. 3 And he came into all the country about Jordan, preaching the baptism of repentance for the remission of sins;

(CONTINUED). TIME, A. D. 48–49; PLACE, ANTIOCH IN PISIDIA.

Y

Mark 1. 7 And preached, saying, There cometh one mightier than I after me, the latchet of whose shoes I am not worthy to stoop down and unloose.

John 1. 20 And he confessed, and denied not; but confessed, I am not the Christ.

Z

Matt. 10. 6 But go rather to the lost sheep of the house of Israel.

Luke 24. 47 And that repentance and remission of sins should be preached in his name among all nations, beginning at Jerusalem.

Acts 3. 26 Unto you first God, having raised up his Son Jesus, sent him to bless you, in turning away every one of you from his iniquities.

A

Luke 23. 34 Then said Jesus, Father, forgive them; for they know not what they do. And they parted his raiment, and cast lots.

Acts 3. 17 And now, brethren, I wot that through ignorance ye did *it*, as *did* also your rulers.

I Cor. 2. 8 Which none of the princes of this world knew: for had they known *it*, they would not have crucified the Lord of glory.

B

Luke 24. 44 And he said unto them, These *are* the words which I spake unto you, while I was yet with you, that all things must be fulfilled, which were written in the law of Moses, and *in* the prophets, and *in* the psalms, concerning me.

Acts 26. 22 Having therefore obtained help of God, I continue unto this day, witnessing both to small and great, saying none other things than those which the prophets and Moses did say should come:

C

Matt. 27. 24 When Pilate saw that he could prevail nothing, but *that* rather a tumult was made, he took water, and washed *his* hands before the multitude, saying, I am innocent of the blood of this just person: see ye *to it*.

Mark 15. 14 Then Pilate said unto them, Why, what evil hath he done? And they cried out the more exceedingly, Crucify him.

Luke 23. 22 And he said unto them the third time, Why, what evil hath he done?

C—CONCLUDED.

I have found no cause of death in him: I will therefore chastise him, and let *him* go.

John 19. 6 When the chief priests therefore and officers saw him, they cried out, saying, Crucify *him*, crucify *him*. Pilate saith unto them, Take ye him, and crucify *him*: for I find no fault in him.

D

Acts 3. 13 The God of Abraham, and of Isaac, and of Jacob, the God of our fathers, hath glorified his Son Jesus; whom ye delivered up, and denied him in the presence of Pilate, when he was determined to let *him* go.

14 But ye denied the Holy One and the Just, and desired a murderer to be granted unto you;

E

Luke 18. 31 Then he took *unto him* the twelve, and said unto them, Behold, we go up to Jerusalem, and all things that are written by the prophets concerning the Son of man shall be accomplished.

Luke 24. 44. *See under B.*

John 19. 36 For these things were done, that the Scripture should be fulfilled, A bone of him shall not be broken.

F

Matt. 27. 59 And when Joseph had taken the body, he wrapped it in a clean linen cloth,

Mark 15. 46 And he bought fine linen, and took him down, and wrapped him in the linen, and laid him in a sepulchre which was hewn out of a rock, and rolled a stone unto the door of the sepulchre.

Luke 23. 53 And he took it down, and wrapped it in linen, and laid it in a sepulchre that was hewn in stone, wherein never man before was laid.

John 19. 38 And after this Joseph of Arimathea, being a disciple of Jesus, but secretly for fear of the Jews, besought Pilate that he might take away the body of Jesus: and Pilate gave *him* leave. He came therefore, and took the body of Jesus.

G

Acts 2. 24. *See k, K, § 231, page 631.*

H

Matt. 28. 16 Then the eleven disciples went away into Galilee, into a mountain where Jesus had appointed them.

For H concluded, I, K, L, M, N and Z, see next page (716).

§ 262. PAUL'S SERMON AT ANTIOCH IN PISIDIA

CHAP. 13.

35 Wherefore he saith also in another *psalm*, [o]Thou shalt not suffer thine Holy One to see corruption.

36 For David, [3]after he had served his own generation by the will of God, [p]fell on sleep, and was laid unto his fathers, and saw corruption:

37 But he, whom God raised again, saw no corruption.

38 Be it known unto you therefore, men *and* brethren, [q]that through this man is preached unto you the forgiveness of sins:

39 And [r]by him all that believe are justified from all things, from which ye could not be justified by the law of Moses.

40 Beware therefore, lest that come upon you, which is spoken of [s]in the prophets;

41 Behold, ye despisers, and wonder, and perish: for I work a work in your days, a work which ye shall in no wise believe, though a man declare it unto you.

42 And when the Jews were gone out of the synagogue, the Gentiles besought that these words might be preached to them [4]the next sabbath.

43 Now when the congregation was broken up, many of the Jews and religious proselytes followed Paul and Barnabas; who, speaking to them, [t]persuaded them to continue in [u]the grace of God.

H—CONCLUDED.

Acts 1. 3. *See e, E, § 226, page 626.*

Matt. 28. 17 And when they saw him, they worshipped him: but some doubted.

I

Acts 1. 11 Which also said, Ye men of Galilee, why stand ye gazing up into heaven? this same Jesus, which is taken up from you into heaven, shall so come in like manner as ye have seen him go into heaven.

K

Acts 1. 8. *See k, K, § 227, page 628.*

L

Gen. 3. 15 And I will put enmity between thee and the woman, and between thy seed and her seed; it shall bruise thy head, and thou shalt bruise his heel.

Gen. 12. 3 And I will bless them that bless thee, and curse him that curseth thee: and in thee shall all families of the earth be blessed.

Gen. 22. 18 And in thy seed shall all the nations of the earth be blessed; because thou hast obeyed my voice.

Gen. 26. 4 And I will make thy seed to multiply as the stars of heaven, and will give unto thy seed all these countries; and in thy seed shall all the nations of the earth be blessed:

Gen. 49. 10 The sceptre shall not depart from Judah, nor a lawgiver from between his feet, until Shiloh come; and unto him *shall* the gathering of the people *be*.

Deut. 18. 18 I will raise them up a Prophet from among their brethren, like unto thee, and will put my words in his mouth; and he shall speak unto them all that I shall command him.

Rom. 4. 13 For the promise, that he should be the heir of the world, *was* not to Abraham, or to his seed, through the law, but through the righteousness of faith.

Gal. 3. 16 Now to Abraham and his seed were the promises made. He saith not, And to seeds, as of many; but as of one, And to thy seed, which is Christ.

M

Ps. 2. 7 I will declare the decree: the LORD hath said unto me, Thou *art* my Son; This day have I begotten thee.

Heb. 1. 5 For unto which of the angels said he at any time, Thou art my Son, this day have I begotten thee? And again, I will be to him a Father, and he shall be to me a Son?

Heb. 5. 5 So also Christ glorified not himself to be made a high priest; but he said unto him, Thou art my Son, to day have I begotten thee.

(CONCLUDED). TIME, A. D. 48—49; PLACE, ANTIOCH IN PISIDIA.

N

Isa. 55. 3 Incline your ear, and come unto me: hear, and your soul shall live; and I will make an everlasting covenant with you, *even* the sure mercies of David.

2

ta osia, holy, or, *just things:* which word the LXX both in the place of Isa. 55. 3 and in many others, use for that which is in the Hebrew, *mercies.*

O

Ps. 16. 10 For thou wilt not leave my soul in hell; neither wilt thou suffer thine Holy One to see corruption.

Acts 2. 31 He, seeing this before, spake of the resurrection of Christ, that his soul was not left in hell, neither his flesh did see corruption.

3

Or, *after he had in his own age served the will of God,*

Ps. 78. 72 So he fed them according to the integrity of his heart; and guided them by the skilfulness of his hands.

Acts 13. 22 And when he had removed him, he raised up unto them David to be their king; to whom also he gave testimony, and said, I have found David the *son* of Jesse, a man after mine own heart, which shall fulfil all my will.

P

I Ki. 2. 10 So David slept with his fathers, and was buried in the city of David.

Acts 2. 29 Men *and* brethren, let me freely speak unto you of the patriarch David, that he is both dead and buried, and his sepulchre is with us unto this day.

Q

Jer. 31. 34 And they shall teach no more every man his neighbour, and every man his brother, saying, Know the LORD: for they shall all know me, from the least of them unto the greatest of them, saith the LORD; for I will forgive their iniquity, and I will remember their sin no more.

Da. 9. 24 Seventy weeks are determined upon thy people and upon thy holy city, to finish the transgression, and to make an end of sins, and to make reconciliation for iniquity, and to bring in everlasting righteousness, and to seal up the vision and prophecy, and to anoint the Most Holy.

I Jno. 2. 12 I write unto you, little children, because your sins are forgiven you for his name's sake.

R

Isa. 53. 11 He shall see of the travail of his soul, *and* shall be satisfied: by his knowledge shall my righteous servant justify many; for he shall bear their iniquities.

Hab. 2. 4 Behold, his soul *which* is lifted up is not upright in him: but the just shall live by his faith.

Rom. 3. 28 Therefore we conclude that a man is justified by faith without the deeds of the law.

Rom. 8. 3 For what the law could not do, in that it was weak through the flesh, God sending his own Son in the likeness of sinful flesh, and for sin, condemned sin in the flesh:

Heb. 7. 19 For the law made nothing perfect, but the bringing in of a better hope *did;* by the which we draw nigh unto God.

S

Isa. 29. 14 Therefore, behold, I will proceed to do a marvellous work among this people, *even* a marvellous work and a wonder: for the wisdom of their wise *men* shall perish, and the understanding of their prudent *men* shall be hid.

Hab. 1. 5 Behold ye among the heathen, and regard, and wonder marvellously: for *I* will work a work in your days, *which* ye will not believe, though it be told *you.*

4

Gr. *in the week between,* or, *in the sabbath between*

T

Acts 11. 23 Who, when he came, and had seen the grace of God, was glad, and exhorted them all, that with purpose of heart they would cleave unto the Lord.

Acts 14. 22 Confirming the souls of the disciples, *and* exhorting them to continue in the faith, and that we must through much tribulation enter into the kingdom of God.

U

Tit. 2. 11 For the grace of God that bringeth salvation hath appeared to all men,

Heb. 12. 15 Looking diligently lest any man fail of the grace of God; lest any root of bitterness springing up trouble *you,* and thereby many be defiled:

I Pet. 5. 12 By Silvanus, a faithful brother unto you, as I suppose, I have written briefly, exhorting, and testifying that this is the true grace of God wherein ye stand.

§ 263. ENVIOUS JEWS PERSECUTE PAUL AND BARNABAS.

13 : 44–52.

44 And the next sabbath day came almost the whole city together to hear the word of God.

45 But when the Jews saw the multitudes, they were filled with envy, and [a]spake against those things which were spoken by Paul, contradicting and blaspheming.

46 Then Paul and Barnabas waxed bold, and said, [b]It was necessary that the word of God should first have been spoken to you: but [c]seeing ye put it from you, and judge yourselves unworthy of everlasting life, lo, [d]we turn to the Gentiles.

47 For so hath the Lord commanded us, *saying*, [e]I have set thee to be a light of the Gentiles, that thou shouldest be for salvation unto the ends of the earth.

48 And when the Gentiles heard this, they were glad, and glorified the word of the Lord: [f]and as many as were ordained to eternal life believed.

49 And the word of the Lord was published throughout all the region.

50 But the Jews stirred up the devout and honourable women, and the chief men of the city, and [g]raised persecution against Paul and Barnabas, and expelled them out of their coasts.

51 But [h]they shook off the dust of their feet against them, and came unto Iconium.

52 And the disciples [i]were filled with joy, and with the Holy Ghost.

A

Acts 18. 6 And when they opposed themselves, and blasphemed, he shook *his* raiment, and said unto them, Your blood *be* upon your own heads; I *am* clean: from henceforth I will go unto the Gentiles.

A—CONCLUDED.

I Pet. 4. 4 Wherein they think it strange that ye run not with *them* to the same excess of riot, speaking evil of *you:*

Jude 10 But these speak evil of those things which they know not: but what they know naturally, as brute beasts, in those things they corrupt themselves.

B

Matt. 10. 6 But go rather to the lost sheep of the house of Israel.

Acts 3. 26 Unto you first God, having raised up his Son Jesus, sent him to bless you, in turning away every one of you from his iniquities.

Acts 13. 26 Men *and* brethren, children of the stock of Abraham, and whosoever among you feareth God, to you is the word of this salvation sent.

Rom. 1. 16 For I am not ashamed of the gospel of Christ: for it is the power of God unto salvation to every one that believeth; to the Jew first, and also to the Greek.

C

Ex. 32. 9 And the LORD said unto Moses, I have seen this people, and, behold, it *is* a stiffnecked people:

Deut. 32 20 And he said, I will hide my face from them, I will see what their end *shall be:* for they *are* a very froward generation, children in whom *is* no faith.

D

Deut. 32. 21 They have moved me to jealousy with *that which is* not God; they have provoked me to anger with their vanities: and I will move them to jealousy with *those which are* not a people; I will provoke them to anger with a foolish nation.

Isa. 55. 5 Behold, thou shalt call a nation *that* thou knowest not, and nations *that* knew not thee shall run unto thee, because of the LORD thy God, and for the Holy One of Israel; for he hath glorified thee.

Matt. 21. 43 Therefore say I unto you, The kingdom of God shall be taken from you, and given to a nation bringing forth the fruits thereof.

Acts 28. 28 Be it known therefore unto you, that the salvation of God is sent unto the Gentiles, and *that* they will hear it.

Rom. 10. 19. But I say, Did not Israel know? First Moses saith, I will provoke you to jealousy by *them that are* no people, *and* by a foolish nation I will anger you.

TIME, A. D. 48–49; PLACE, ANTIOCH IN PISIDIA.

E

Isa. 42. 6 I the LORD have called thee in righteousness, and will hold thine hand, and will keep thee, and give thee for a covenant of the people, for a light of the Gentiles;

Isa. 49. 6 And he said, It is a light thing that thou shouldest be my servant to raise up the tribes of Jacob, and to restore the preserved of Israel: I will also give thee for a light to the Gentiles, that thou mayest be my salvation unto the end of the earth.

Luke 2. 32 A light to lighten the Gentiles, and the glory of thy people Israel.

F

Isa. 41. 9 *Thou* whom I have taken from the ends of the earth, and called thee from the chief men thereof, and said unto thee, Thou *art* my servant; I have chosen thee, and not cast thee away.

Acts 2. 47 Praising God, and having favour with all the people. And the Lord added to the church daily such as should be saved.

Rom. 1. 6 Among whom are ye also the called of Jesus Christ:

Rom. 8. 30 Moreover, whom he did predestinate, them he also called: and whom he called, them he also justified: and whom he justified, them he also glorified.

Rom. 9. 23 And that he might make known the riches of his glory on the vessels of mercy, which he had afore prepared unto glory.

Rom. 11. 7 What then? Israel hath not obtained that which he seeketh for; but the election hath obtained it, and the rest were blinded.

Eph. 1. 5 Having predestinated us unto the adoption of children by Jesus Christ to himself, according to the good pleasure of his will,

Eph. 1. 11 In whom also we have obtained an inheritance, being predestinated according to the purpose of him who worketh all things after the counsel of his own will:

Eph. 2. 10 For we are his workmanship, created in Christ Jesus unto good works, which God hath before ordained that we should walk in them.

II Thes. 2. 13 But we are bound to give thanks alway to God for you, brethren beloved of the Lord, because God hath from the beginning chosen you to salvation through sanctification of the Spirit and belief of the truth:

F—CONCLUDED

Heb. 9. 15 And for this cause he is the mediator of the new testament, that by means of death, for the redemption of the transgressions *that were* under the first testament, they which are called might receive the promise of eternal inheritance.

II Pet. 1. 10 Wherefore the rather, brethren, give diligence to make your calling and election sure: for if ye do these things, ye shall never fall:

Rev. 17. 14 These shall make war with the Lamb, and the Lamb shall overcome them: for he is Lord of lords, and King of kings: and they that are with him *are* called, and chosen, and faithful.

G

II Tim. 3. 11 Persecutions, afflictions, which came unto me at Antioch, at Iconium, at Lystra; what persecutions I endured: but out of *them* all the Lord delivered me.

H

Matt. 10. 14 And whosoever shall not receive you, nor hear your words, when ye depart out of that house or city, shake off the dust of your feet.

Mark 6. 11 And whosoever shall not receive you, nor hear you, when ye depart thence, shake off the dust under your feet for a testimony against them. Verily I say unto you, It shall be more tolerable for Sodom and Gomorrah in the day of judgment, than for that city.

Luke 9. 5 And whosoever will not receive you, when ye go out of that city, shake off the very dust from your feet for a testimony against them.

Acts 18. 6. *See under A.*

I

Matt. 5. 12 Rejoice, and be exceeding glad: for great *is* your reward in heaven: for so persecuted they the prophets which were before you.

John 16. 22. *See d, D, § 190, page 539.*

Acts 2. 46 And they, continuing daily with one accord in the temple, and breaking bread from house to house, did eat their meat with gladness and singleness of heart,

I Thes. 1. 6 And ye became followers of us, and of the Lord, having received the word in much affliction, with joy of the Holy Ghost:

I. Pet. 1. 8 Whom having not seen, ye love; in whom, though now ye see *him* not, yet believing, ye rejoice with joy unspeakable and full of glory:

§ 264. THEY COME TO ICONIUM, ARE PERSECUTED AND FLEE

14:1–7.

And it came to pass in Iconium, that they went both together into the synagogue of the Jews, and so spake, that a great multitude both of the Jews and also of the Greeks believed.

2 But [a]the unbelieving Jews stirred up the Gentiles, and made their minds evil affected against the brethren.

3 Long time therefore abode they speaking boldly in the Lord, [b]which gave testimony unto the word of his grace, and [c]granted signs and wonders to be done by their hands.

4 But the multitude of the city was divided: and part held with the Jews, and part with the apostles.

5 And when there was an assault made both of the Gentiles, and also of the Jews with their rulers, to [d]use *them* despitefully, and to stone them,

6 They were ware of *it*, and [e]fled unto Lystra and Derbe, cities of Lycaonia, and unto the region that lieth round about:

7 And there they preached the gospel.

A

Mark 15. 10 For he knew that the chief priests had delivered him for envy.

11 But the chief priests moved the people, that he should rather release Barabbas unto them.

Acts 13. 45 But when the Jews saw the multitudes, they were filled with envy, and spake against those things which were spoken by Paul, contradicting and blaspheming.

Acts 13. 50 But the Jews stirred up the devout and honourable women, and the chief men of the city, and raised persecution against Paul and Barnabas, and expelled them out of their coasts.

Acts 14. 19 And there came thither *certain* Jews from Antioch and Iconium, who persuaded the people, and, having stoned Paul, drew *him* out of the city, supposing he had been dead.

Acts 17. 5 But the Jews which believed not, moved with envy, took unto them certain lewd fellows of the baser sort, and gathered a company, and set all the city on an uproar, and assaulted the house of Jason, and sought to bring them out to the people.

Acts 17. 13 But when the Jews of Thessalonica had knowledge that the word of God was preached of Paul at Berea, they came thither also, and stirred up the people.

Acts 18. 12 And when Gallio was the deputy of Achaia, the Jews made insurrection with one accord against Paul, and brought him to the judgment seat,

§ 265. PAUL HEALS THE MAN WITH IMPOTENT FEET

14:8–18

8 And [a]there sat a certain man at Lystra, impotent in his feet, being a cripple from his mother's womb, who never had walked:

9 The same heard Paul speak: who steadfastly beholding him, and [b]perceiving that he had faith to be healed,

10 Said with a loud voice, [c]Stand upright on thy feet. And he leaped and walked.

A

John 5. 5 And a certain man was there, which had an infirmity thirty and eight years.

Acts 3. 2 And a certain man lame from his mother's womb was carried, whom they laid daily at the gate of the temple which is called Beautiful, to ask alms of them that entered into the temple;

B

Matt. 8. 10 When Jesus heard *it*, he marvelled, and said to them that followed, Verily I say unto you, I have not found so great faith, no, not in Israel.

Matt. 9. 22 But Jesus turned him about, and when he saw her, he said, Daughter,

TO LYSTRA. Time, A. D. 48–49.

A—Concluded.

Acts 21. 27 And when the seven days were almost ended, the Jews which were of Asia, when they saw him in the temple, stirred up all the people, and laid hands on him,

I Thes. 2. 15 Who both killed the Lord Jesus, and their own prophets, and have persecuted us; and they please not God, and are contrary to all men:

B

Mark 16. 20 And they went forth, and preached every where, the Lord working with *them*, and confirming the word with signs following. Amen.

Acts 2. 22 Ye men of Israel, hear these words; Jesus of Nazareth, a man approved of God among you by miracles and wonders and signs, which God did by him in the midst of you, as ye yourselves also know:

Acts 5. 32 And we are his witnesses of these things; and *so is* also the Holy Ghost, whom God hath given to them that obey him.

Rom. 15. 19 Through mighty signs and wonders, by the power of the Spirit of God; so that from Jerusalem, and round about unto Illyricum, I have fully preached the gospel of Christ.

Heb. 2. 4 God also bearing *them* witness, both with signs and wonders, and with divers miracles, and gifts of the Holy Ghost, according to his own will?

C

Acts 4. 29 And now, Lord, behold their threatenings: and grant unto thy servants, that with all boldness they may speak thy word,

C—Concluded.

Acts 4. 30 By stretching forth thine hand to heal; and that signs and wonders may be done by the name of thy holy child Jesus.

Acts 5. 12 And by the hands of the apostles were many signs and wonders wrought among the people; (and they were all with one accord in Solomon's porch.

Acts 19. 11 And God wrought special miracles by the hands of Paul:

12 So that from his body were brought unto the sick handkerchiefs or aprons, and the diseases departed from them, and the evil spirits went out of them.

D

Ps. 34. 19 Many *are* the afflictions of the righteous: but the Lord delivereth him out of them all.

I Thes. 2. 14 For ye, brethren, became followers of the churches of God which in Judea are in Christ Jesus: for ye also have suffered like things of your own countrymen, even as they *have* of the Jews:

I Thes. 2. 15. *See under A.*

II Tim. 3. 11 Persecutions, afflictions, which came unto me at Antioch, at Iconium, at Lystra; what persecutions I endured: but out of *them* all the Lord delivered me.

E

Matt. 10. 23 But when they persecute you in this city, flee ye into another: for verily I say unto you, Ye shall not have gone over the cities of Israel, till the Son of man be come.

AT LYSTRA. Time, A. D. 48–49.

B—Continued.

be of good comfort; thy faith hath made thee whole. And the woman was made whole from that hour.

Matt. 9. 28 And when he was come into the house, the blind men came to him: and Jesus saith unto them, Believe ye that I am able to do this? They said unto him, Yea, Lord.

29 Then touched he their eyes, saying, According to your faith be it unto you.

Mark 5. 34 And he said unto her, Daughter, thy faith hath made thee whole; go in peace, and be whole of thy plague.

B—Concluded.

Mark 10. 52 And Jesus said unto him, Go thy way; thy faith hath made thee whole. And immediately he received his sight, and followed Jesus in the way.

Luke 7. 50 And he said to the woman, Thy faith hath saved thee; go in peace.

Luke 8. 48 And he said unto her, Daughter, be of good comfort: thy faith hath made thee whole; go in peace.

Luke 17. 19 And he said unto him, Arise, go thy way: thy faith hath made thee whole.

Luke 18. 42 And Jesus said unto him, Receive thy sight: thy faith hath saved thee.

For C, see next page (722).

§ 265. PAUL HEALS THE MAN WITH IMPOTENT FEET AT LYSTRA

CHAP. 14.

11 And when the people saw what Paul had done, they lifted up their voices, saying in the speech of Lycaonia, [d]The gods are come down to us in the likeness of men.

12 And they called Barnabas, Jupiter; and Paul, Mercurius, because he was the chief speaker.

13 Then the priest of Jupiter, which was before their city, brought oxen and garlands into the gates, [e]and would have done sacrifice with the people.

14 *Which* when the apostles, Barnabas and Paul, heard *of*, [f]they rent their clothes, and ran in among the people, crying out,

15 And saying, Sirs, [g]why do ye these things? [h]We also are men of like passions with you, and preach unto you that ye should turn from [i]these vanities [k]unto the living God, [l]which made heaven, and earth, and the sea, and all things that are therein:

16 [m]Who in times past suffered all nations to walk in their own ways.

17 Nevertheless [n]he left not himself without witness, in that he did good, and [o]gave us rain from heaven, and fruitful seasons, filling our hearts with food and gladness.

CHAP. 14.

18 And with these sayings scarce restrained they the people, that they had not done sacrifice unto them.

C

Isa. 35. 6 Then shall the lame *man* leap as a hart, and the tongue of the dumb sing: for in the wilderness shall waters break out, and streams in the desert.

John 5. 8 Jesus saith unto him, Rise, take up thy bed, and walk.

9 And immediately the man was made whole, and took up his bed, and walked: and on the same day was the sabbath.

D

Acts 8. 10 To whom they all gave heed, from the least to the greatest, saying, This man is the great power of God.

Acts 12. 22 And the people gave a shout, *saying*, *It is* the voice of a god, and not of a man.

Acts 28. 6 Howbeit they looked when he should have swollen, or fallen down dead suddenly: but after they had looked a great while, and saw no harm come to him, they changed their minds, and said that he was a god.

E

Da. 2. 46 Then the king Nebuchadnezzar fell upon his face, and worshipped Daniel, and commanded that they should offer an oblation and sweet odours unto him.

Acts 10. 25 And as Peter was coming in, Cornelius met him, and fell down at his feet, and worshipped *him*.

F

Matt. 26. 65 Then the high priest rent his clothes, saying, He hath spoken blasphemy; what further need have we of witnesses? behold, now ye have heard his blasphemy.

G

Acts. 10. 26 But Peter took him up, saying, Stand up; I myself also am a man.

§ 266. PAUL STONED. THEY GO TO DERBE. THE RETURN.

14 : 19–28

19 And [a]there came thither *certain* Jews from Antioch and Iconium, who persuaded the people, [b]and, having stoned Paul, drew *him* out of the city, supposing he had been dead.

A

Acts 13. 45 But when the Jews saw the multitudes, they were filled with envy, and spake against those things which were spoken by Paul, contradicting and blaspheming.

B

IICor. 1. 8 For we would brethren, have

(CONCLUDED). TIME, A. D. 48–49.

H

Jas. 5. 17 Elias was a man subject to like passions as we are, and he prayed earnestly that it might not rain: and it rained not on the earth by the space of three years and six months.

Rev. 22. 9 Then saith he unto me, See *thou do it* not: for I am thy fellow servant, and of thy brethren the prophets, and of them which keep the sayings of this book: worship God.

I

I Sa. 12. 21 And turn ye not aside: for *then should ye go* after vain *things*, which cannot profit nor deliver; for they *are* vain.

I Ki. 16. 13 For all the sins of Baasha, and the sins of Elah his son, by which they sinned, and by which they made Israel to sin, in provoking the LORD God of Israel to anger with their vanities.

I Cor. 8. 4 As concerning therefore the eating of those things that are offered in sacrifice unto idols, we know that an idol *is* nothing in the world, and that *there is* none other God but one.

K

I Thess. 1. 9 For they themselves shew of us what manner of entering in we had unto you, and how ye turned to God from idols to serve the living and true God;

L

Gen. 1. 1 In the beginning God created the heaven and the earth.

Ps. 33. 6. By the word of the LORD were the heavens made; and all the host of them by the breath of his mouth.

Ps. 146. 6 Which made heaven, and earth, the sea, and all that therein *is*: which keepeth truth forever:

M

Ps. 81. 12 So I gave them up unto their own hearts' lust: *and* they walked in their own counsels.

Acts 17. 30 And the times of this ignorance God winked at; but now commandeth all men every where to repent:

M—CONCLUDED.

I Pet. 4. 3 For the time past of *our* life may suffice us to have wrought the will of the Gentiles, when we walked in lasciviousness, lusts, excess of wine, revelings, banquetings, and abominable idolatries:

N

Acts 17. 27 That they should seek the Lord, if haply they might feel after him, and find him, though he be not far from every one of us:

Rom. 1. 20 For the invisible things of him from the creation of the world are clearly seen, being understood by the things that are made, *even* his eternal power and Godhead; so that they are without excuse:

O

Lev. 26. 4 Then I will give you rain in due season, and the land shall yield her increase, and the trees of the field shall yield their fruit.

Deut. 11. 14 That I will give *you* the rain in your land in his due season, the first rain and the latter rain, that thou mayest gather in thy corn, and thy wine, and thine oil.

Job 5. 10 Who giveth rain upon the earth, and sendeth waters upon the fields:

Ps. 65. 10 Thou waterest the ridges thereof abundantly: thou settlest the furrows thereof: thou makest it soft with showers: thou blessest the springing thereof.

Ps. 68. 9 Thou, O God, didst send a plentiful rain, whereby thou didst confirm thine inheritence, when it was weary.

Ps. 147. 8 Who covereth the heaven with clouds, who prepareth rain for the earth, who maketh grass to grow upon mountains.

Matt. 5. 45 That ye may be the children of your Father which is in heaven; for he maketh his sun to rise on the evil and on the good, and sendeth rain on the just and on the unjust.

TIME, A. D. 48–49; PLACE, LYSTRA, DERBE.

B—CONTINUED.

you ignorant of our trouble which came to us in Asia, that we were pressed out of measure above strength, insomuch that we despaired even of life:

II Cor. 11. 25 Thrice was I beaten with rods, once was I stoned, thrice I suffered

B—CONCLUDED.

shipwreck, a night and a day I have been in the deep;

II Tim. 3. 11 Persecutions, afflictions, which came unto me at Antioch, at Iconium, at Lystra; what persecutions I endured: but out of *them* all the Lord delivered me.

§ 266. PAUL STONED. THEY GO TO DERBE, THE RETURN

CHAP. 14.

20 Howbeit, as the disciples stood round about him, he rose up, and came into the city: and the next day he departed with Barnabas to Derbe.

21 And when they had preached the gospel to that city, [c]and [1]had taught many, they returned again to Lystra, and *to* Iconium, and Antioch,

22 Confirming the souls of the disciples, *and* [d]exhorting them to continue in the faith, and that [e]we must through much tribulation enter into the kingdom of God.

23 And when they had [f]ordained them elders in every church, and had prayed with fasting, they commended them to the Lord, on whom they believed.

24 And after they had passed throughout Pisidia, they came to Pamphylia.

25 And when they had preached the word in Perga, they went down into Attalia:

26 And thence sailed to Antioch, [g]from whence they had been recommended to the grace of God for the work which they fulfilled.

27 And when they were come, and had gathered the church together, [h]they rehearsed all that God had done with them, and how he had [i]opened the door of faith unto the Gentiles.

28 And there they abode long time with the disciples.

C

Matt. 28. 19 Go ye therefore, and teach all nations, baptizing them in the name of the Father, and of the Son, and of the Holy Ghost:

1

Gr. *Had made many disciples.*

D

Acts 11. 23 Who, when he came, and had seen the grace of God, was glad, and exhorted them all, that with purpose of heart they would cleave unto the Lord.

Acts 13. 43 Now when the congregation was broken up, many of the Jews and religious proselytes followed Paul and Barnabas; who, speaking to them, persuaded them to continue in the grace of God.

E

Matt. 10. 21 And the brother shall deliver up the brother to death, and the father the child: and the children shall rise up against *their* parents, and cause them to be put to death.

22 And ye shall be hated of all *men* for my name's sake: but he that endureth to the end shall be saved.

23 But when they persecute you in this city, flee ye into another: for verily I say unto you, Ye shall not have gone over the cities of Israel, till the Son of man be come.

Matt. 16. 24 Then said Jesus unto his disciples, If any *man* will come after me, let him deny himself, and take up his cross, and follow me.

Luke 22. 28 Ye are they which have continued with me in my temptations.

29 And I appoint unto you a kingdom, as my Father hath appointed unto me;

30 That ye may eat and drink at my table in my kingdom, and sit on thrones judging the twelves tribes of Israel.

Luke 24. 26 Ought not Christ to have suffered these things, and to enter into his glory?

John 15. 18 If the world hate you, ye know that it hated me before *it hated* you.

John 16. 1 These things have I spoken unto you, that ye should not be offended.

2 They shall put you out of the synagogues: yea, the time cometh, that whosoever killeth you will think that he doeth God service.

John 16. 33 These things I have spoken unto you, that in me ye might have peace. In the world ye shall have tribulation: but be of good cheer: I have overcome the world.

Rom. 8. 17 And if children, then heirs; heirs of God, and joint heirs with Christ; if so be that we suffer with *him*, that we may be also glorified together.

(CONCLUDED). TIME, A. D. 48-49; PLACE, LYSTRA, DERBE.

E—CONCLUDED.

I Thes. 3. 4 For verily, when we were with you, we told you before that we should suffer tribulation; even as it came to pass, and ye know.

II Tim. 1. 8 Be not thou therefore ashamed of the testimony of our Lord, nor of me his prisoner: but be thou partaker of the afflictions of the gospel according to the power of God:

II Tim. 2. 11 *It is* a faithful saying: For if we be dead with *him*, we shall also live with *him*:

12 If we suffer, we shall also reign with *him*: if we deny *him*, he also will deny us:

II Tim. 3. 12 Yea, and all that will live godly in Christ Jesus shall suffer persecution.

I Pet. 4. 12 Beloved, think it not strange concerning the fiery trial which is to try you, as though some strange thing happened unto you:

13 But rejoice, inasmuch as ye are partakers of Christ's sufferings; that, when his glory shall be revealed, ye may be glad also with exceeding joy.

14 If ye be reproached for the name of Christ, happy *are ye*; for the Spirit of glory and of God resteth upon you: on their part he is evil spoken of, but on your part he is glorified.

15 But let none of you suffer as a murderer, or *as* a thief, or *as* an evil doer, or as a busybody in other men's matters.

16 Yet if *any man suffer* as a Christian, let him not be ashamed; but let him glorify God on this behalf.

Rev. 2. 10 Fear none of those things which thou shalt suffer: behold, the devil shall cast *some* of you into prison, that ye may be tried; and ye shall have tribulation ten days: be thou faithful unto death, and I will give thee a crown of life.

Rev. 7. 14 And I said unto him, Sir, thou knowest. And he said to me, These are they which came out of great tribulation, and have washed their robes, and made them white in the blood of the Lamb.

F

Tit. 1. 5 For this cause left I thee in Crete, that thou shouldest set in order the things that are wanting, and ordain elders in every city, as I had appointed thee:

I Pet. 5. 5 Likewise, ye younger, submit yourselves unto the elder. Yea, all *of you*

F—CONCLUDED.

be subject one to another, and be clothed with humility: for God resisteth the proud, and giveth grace to the humble.

G

Acts 13. 1 Now there were in the church that was at Antioch certain prophets and teachers; as Barnabas, and Simeon that was called Niger, and Lucius of Cyrene, and Manaen, which had been brought up with Herod the tetrarch, and Saul.

Acts 13. 3 And when they had fasted and prayed, and laid *their* hands on them, they sent *them* away.

Acts 15. 40 And Paul chose Silas, and departed, being recommended by the brethren unto the grace of God.

H

Acts 15. 4 And when they were come to Jerusalem, they were received of the church, and *of* the apostles and elders, and they declared all things that God had done with them.

Acts 15. 12 Then all the multitude kept silence, and gave audience to Barnabas and Paul, declaring what miracles and wonders God had wrought among the Gentiles by them.

Acts 21. 19 And when he had saluted them, he declared particularly what things God had wrought among the Gentiles by his ministry.

Rom. 15. 18 For I will not dare to speak of any of those things which Christ hath not wrought by me, to make the Gentiles obedient, by word and deed,

19 Through mighty signs and wonders, by the power of the Spirit of God; so that from Jerusalem, and round about unto Illyricum, I have fully preached the gospel of Christ.

I

I Cor. 16. 9 For a great door and effectual is opened unto me, and *there are* many adversaries.

II Cor. 2. 12 Furthermore, when I came to Troas to *preach* Christ's gospel, and a door was opened unto me of the Lord,

Col. 4. 3 Withal praying also for us, that God would open unto us a door of utterance, to speak the mystery of Christ, for which I am also in bonds:

Rev. 3. 8 I know thy works: behold, I have set before thee an open door, and no man can shut it: for thou hast a little strength, and hast kept my word, and hast not denied my name.

§ 267. DISSENSION CONCERNING CIRCUMCISION.

15: 1–5.

1 And [a]certain men which came down from Judea taught the brethren, *and said,* [b]Except ye be circumcised [c]after the manner of Moses, ye cannot be saved.

2 When therefore [d]Paul and Barnabas had no small dissension and disputation with them, they determined that Paul and Barnabas, and certain other of them, should go up to Jerusalem unto the apostles and elders about this question.

3 And [e]being brought on their way by the church, they passed through Phenice and Samaria, [f]declaring the conversion of the Gentiles: and they caused great joy unto all the brethren.

4 And when they were come to Jerusalem, they were received of

Chap. 15.

the church, and *of* the apostles and elders, and they declared all things that God had done with them.

5 But there [1]rose up certain of the sect of the Pharisees which believed, saying, [g]That it was needful to circumcise them, and to command *them* to keep the law of Moses.

A

Gal. 2. 12 For before that certain came from James, he did eat with the Gentiles: but when they were come, he withdrew and separated himself, fearing them which were of the circumcision.

B

John 7. 22 Moses therefore gave unto you circumcision; (not because it is of Moses, but of the fathers;) and ye on the sabbath day circumcise a man.

Gal. 5. 2. Behold, I Paul say unto you, that if ye be circumcised, Christ shall profit you nothing.

Phil. 3. 2 Beware of dogs, beware of evil workers, beware of the concision.

§ 268. THE COUNCIL AT JERUSALEM.

15: 6–21.

6 And the [a]apostles and elders came together for to consider of this matter.

7 And when there had been much disputing, Peter rose up, and said unto them, Men *and* brethren, [b]ye know how that a good while ago God made choice among us, that the Gentiles by my mouth should hear the word of the gospel and believe.

8 And God, [c]which knoweth the hearts, bare them witness, [d]giving them the Holy Ghost, even as *he did* unto us;

9 And [e]put no difference between us and them, [f]purifying their hearts by faith.

A

Prov. 15. 22 Without counsel purposes are disappointed; but in the multitude of counsellors they are established.

Acts 6. 2 Then the twelve called the multitude of the disciples *unto them*, and said, It is not reason that we should leave the word of God, and serve tables.

Acts 21. 18 And the *day* following Paul went in with us unto James; and all the elders were present.

B

Acts 10. 20 Arise therefore, and get thee down, and go with them, doubting nothing: for I have sent them.

Acts 11. 12 And the Spirit bade me go with them, nothing doubting. Moreover these six brethren accompanied me, and we entered into the man's house:

C

1 Sa. 16. 7 But the LORD said unto Samuel, Look not on his countenance, or on

THEY GO TO JERUSALEM. TIME, A. D. 50.

B—CONCLUDED.

Col. 2. 8 Beware lest any man spoil you through philosophy and vain deceit, after the tradition of men, after the rudiments of the world, and not after Christ.

Col. 2. 11 In whom also ye are circumcised with the circumcision made without hands, in putting off the body of the sins of the flesh by the circumcision of Christ :

Col. 2. 16 Let no man therefore judge you in meat, or in drink, or in respect of a holy day, or of the new moon, or of the sabbath *days :*

17 Which are a shadow of things to come ; but the body *is* of Christ.

C

Gen. 17. 10 This *is* my covenant, which ye shall keep, between me and you and thy seed after thee ; Every man child among you shall be circumcised.

Lev. 12. 3 And in the eighth day the flesh of his foreskin shall be circumcised.

D

Gal. 2. 1 Then fourteen years after I went up again to Jerusalem with Barnabas, and took Titus with *me* also.

E

Rom. 15. 24 Whensoever I take my journey into Spain, I will come to you : for I

E CONCLUDED.

trust to see you in my journey, and to be brought on my way thitherward by you, if first I be somewhat filled with your *company.*

I Cor. 16. 6 And it may be that I will abide, yea, and winter with you, that ye may bring me on my journey whithersoever I go.

I Cor. 16. 11 Let no man therefore despise him : but conduct him forth in peace, that he may come unto me : for I look for him with the brethren.

F

Acts 14. 27. *See h, H, § 266, page 724.*

1

Or, rose up, said they, *certain.*

G

I Cor. 7. 18 Is any man called being circumcised ? let him not become uncircumcised. Is any called in uncircumcision ? let him not be circumcised.

19 Circumcision is nothing, and uncircumcision is nothing, but the keeping of the commandments of God.

Gal. 5. 2. *See under B.*

3 For I testify again to every man that is circumcised, that he is a debtor to do the whole law.

4 Christ is become of no effect unto you, whosoever of you are justified by the law ; ye are fallen from grace.

TIME, A. D. 50.

C—CONCLUDED.

the height of his stature ; because I have refused him : for *the LORD seeth* not as man seeth ; for man looketh on the outward appearance, but the LORD looketh on the heart.

I Ki. 8. 39 Then hear thou in heaven thy dwellingplace, and forgive, and do, and give to every man according to his ways, whose heart thou knowest ; (for thou, *even* thou only, knowest the hearts of all the children of men;)

I Chr. 28. 9 And thou, Solomon my son, know thou the God of thy father, and serve him with a perfect heart and with a willing mind : for the LORD searcheth all hearts, and understandeth all the imaginations of the thoughts : if thou seek him, he will be found of thee ; but if thou forsake him, he will cast thee off for ever.

Ps. 44. 21 Shall not God search this out ? for he knoweth the secrets of the heart.

C—CONCLUDED.

Ps. 139. 1 O LORD, thou hast searched me, and known *me.*

2 Thou knowest my downsitting and mine uprising ; thou understandest my thought afar off.

Jer. 11. 20 But, O LORD of hosts, that judgest righteously, that triest the reins and the heart, let me see thy vengeance on them : for unto thee have I revealed my cause.

Heb. 4. 13 Neither is there any creature that is not manifest in his sight : but all things *are* naked and opened unto the eyes of him with whom we have to do.

Rev. 2. 23 And I will kill her children with death ; and all the churches shall know that I am he which searcheth the reins and hearts : and I will give unto every one of you according to your works.

For D, E, and F, see next page (728).

§ 268. THE COUNCIL AT JERUSALEM

CHAP. 15.

10 Now therefore why tempt ye God, [g]to put a yoke upon the neck of the disciples, which neither our fathers nor we were able to bear?

11 But [h]we believe that through the grace of the Lord Jesus Christ we shall be saved, even as they.

12 Then all the multitude kept silence, and gave audience to Barnabas and Paul, declaring what miracles and wonders God had [i]wrought among the Gentiles by them.

13 And after they had held their peace, [k]James answered, saying, Men *and* brethren, hearken unto me:

14 [l]Simeon hath declared how God at the first did visit the Gentiles, to take out of them a people for his name.

15 And to this agree the [m]words of the prophets; as it is written,

16 [n]After this I will return, and will build again the tabernacle of David, which is fallen down; and I will build again the ruins thereof, and I will set it up:

17 That the residue of men might seek after the Lord, and all the Gentiles, upon whom my name is called, saith the Lord, who doeth all these things.

18 [o]Known unto God are all his works from the beginning of the world.

19 Wherefore [p]my sentence is, that we trouble not them, which from among the Gentiles [q]are turned to God:

D

Acts 10. 44 While Peter yet spake these words, the Holy Ghost fell on all them which heard the word.

E

Rom. 10. 11 For the Scripture saith, Whosoever believeth on him shall not be ashamed.

F

Acts 10. 15 And the voice *spake* unto him again the second time, What God hath cleansed, *that* call not thou common.

Acts 10. 28 And he said unto them, Ye know how that it is an unlawful thing for a man that is a Jew to keep company, or come unto one of another nation; but God hath shewed me that I should not call any man common or unclean.

Acts 10. 43 To him give all the prophets witness, that through his name whosoever believeth in him shall receive remission of sins.

I Cor. 1. 2 Unto the church of God which is at Corinth, to them that are sanctified in Christ Jesus, called *to be* saints, with all that in every place call upon the name of Jesus Christ our Lord, both theirs and ours:

Heb. 9. 13 For if the blood of bulls and of goats, and the ashes of a heifer sprinkling the unclean, sanctifieth to the purifying of the flesh:

14 How much more shall the blood of Christ, who through the eternal Spirit offered himself without spot to God, purge your conscience from dead works to serve the living God?

I Pet. 1. 22 Seeing ye have purified your souls in obeying the truth through the Spirit unto unfeigned love of the brethren, *see that ye* love one another with a pure heart fervently:

G

Matt. 23. 4 For they bind heavy burdens and grievous to be borne, and lay *them* on men's shoulders; but they *themselves* will not move them with one of their fingers.

Gal. 5. 1 Stand fast therefore in the liberty wherewith Christ hath made us free, and be not entangled again with the yoke of bondage.

H

Rom. 3. 24 Being justified freely by his grace through the redemption that is in Christ Jesus:

Eph. 1. 7 In whom we have redemption through his blood, the forgiveness of sins, according to the riches of his grace;

Eph. 2. 8 For by grace are ye saved through faith; and that not of yourselves; *it is* the gift of God:

(CONTINUED). TIME, A. D. 50.

H—CONCLUDED.

Tit. 2. 11 For the grace of God that bringeth salvation hath appeared to all men,

Tit. 3. 4 But after that the kindness and love of God our Saviour toward man appeared,
5 Not by works of righteousness which we have done, but according to his mercy he saved us, by the washing of regeneration, and renewing of the Holy Ghost;

I

Acts 14. 27. *See h. H § 266, page 724.*

K

Acts 12. 17 But he, beckoning unto them with the hand to hold their peace, declared unto them how the Lord had brought him out of the prison. And he said, Go shew these things unto James, and to the brethren. And he departed, and went into another place.

L

Acts 15. 7 *See text of topic, page 726.*

M

Isa 11. 10 And in that day there shall be a root of Jesse, which shall stand for an ensign of the people; to it shall the Gentiles seek: and his rest shall be glorious.

N

Amos 9. 11 In that day will I raise the tabernacle of David which is fallen, and close up the breaches thereof; and I will raise up his ruins, and I will build it as in the days of old:
12 That they may possess the remnant of Edom, and of all the heathen, which are called by my name, saith the LORD that doeth this.

O

Num. 23. 19 God *is* not a man, that he should lie; neither the son of man, that he should repent: hath he said, and shall he not do *it?* or hath he spoken, and shall he not make it good?

Isa. 46. 10 Declaring the end from the beginning, and from ancient times *the things* that are not *yet* done, saying, My counsel shall stand, and I will do all my pleasure:

P

Acts 15. 28 For it seemed good to the Holy Ghost, and to us, to lay upon you on greater burden than these necessary things;

Q

I Thes. 1. 9 For they themselves shew of us what manner of entering in we had unto you, and how ye turned to God from idols to serve the living and true God:

R

Gen. 35. 2 Then Jacob said unto his household, and to all that *were* with him, Put away the strange gods that *are* among you, and be clean, and change your garments:

Ex. 20. 3 Thou shalt have no other gods before me.

Ex. 20. 23 Ye shall not make with me gods of silver, neither shall ye make unto you gods of gold.

Eze. 20. 30 Wherefore say unto the house of Israel, Thus saith the Lord GOD; Are ye polluted after the manner of your fathers? and commit ye whoredom after their abominations?

I Cor. 10. 20 But *I say*, that the things which the Gentiles sacrifice, they sacrifice to devils, and not to God: and I would not that ye should have fellowship with devils.

I Cor. 10. 28 But if any man say unto you, This is offered in sacrifice unto idols, eat not for his sake that shewed it, and for conscience sake: for the earth *is* the Lord's, and the fulness thereof:

Rev. 2. 20 Notwithstanding I have a few things against thee, because thou sufferest that woman Jezebel, which calleth herself a prophetess, to teach and to seduce my servants to commit fornication, and to eat things sacrificed unto idols.

S

I Cor. 6. 9 Know ye not that the unrighteous shall not inherit the kingdom of God? Be not deceived: neither fornicators, nor idoloters, nor adulterers, nor effeminate, nor abusers of themselves with mankind,

I Cor. 6. 18 Flee fornication. Every sin that a man doeth is without the body; but he that committeth fornication sinneth against his own body.

Gal. 5. 19 Now the works of the flesh are manifest, which are *these;* Adultery, fornication, uncleanness, lasciviousness,

Eph. 5. 3 But fornication, and all uncleanness, or covetousness, let it not be once named among you, as becometh saints:

§ 268. THE COUNCIL AT JERUSALEM

CHAP. 15.

20 But that we write unto them, that they abstain [r]from pollutions of idols, and [s]*from* fornication, and *from* things strangled, and [t]*from* blood.

21 For Moses of old time hath in every city them that preach him, [u]being read in the synagogues every sabbath day.

For R and S, see preceding page (729).

S—CONTINUED.

Col. 3. 5 Mortify therefore your members

S—CONCLUDED.

which are upon the earth; fornication, uncleanness, inordinate affection, evil concupiscence, and covetousness, which is idolatry:

1 Thes. 4. 3 For this is the will of God, *even* your sanctification, that ye should abstain from fornication:

1 Pet. 4. 3 For the time past of *our* life may suffice us to have wrought the will of the Gentiles, when we walked in lasciviousness, lusts, excess of wine, revelings, banquetings, and abominable idolatries:

§ 269. A DEPUTATION SENT TO ANTIOCH WITH A LETTER.

15: 22–35.

22 Then pleased it the apostles and elders, with the whole church, to send chosen men of their own company to Antioch with Paul and Barnabas; *namely*, Judas surnamed [a]Barsabas, and Silas, chief men among the brethren:

23 And they wrote *letters* by them after this manner: The apostles and elders and brethren *send* greeting unto the brethren which are of the Gentiles in Antioch and Syria and Cilicia:

24 Forasmuch as we have heard, that [b]certain which went out from us have troubled you with words, subverting your souls, saying, *Ye must* be circumcised, and keep the law; to whom we gave no *such* commandment:

25 It seemed good unto us, being assembled with one accord, to send chosen men unto you with our beloved Barnabas and Paul,

26 [c]Men that have hazarded their lives for the name of our Lord Jesus Christ.

27 We have sent therefore Judas and Silas, who shall also tell *you* the same things by [1]mouth.

28 For it seemed good to [d]the Holy Ghost, and to us, to lay upon

CHAP. 15.

you no greater [e]burden than these necessary things;

29 [f]That ye abstain from meats offered to idols, and [g]from blood, and from things strangled, and from fornication: from which if ye keep yourselves, ye shall do well. Fare ye well.

30 So when they were dismissed, they came to Antioch: and when they had gathered the multitude together, they delivered the epistle:

31 *Which* when they had read, they rejoiced for the [2]consolation.

32 And Judas and Silas, being prophets also themselves, [h]exhorted the brethren with many words, and confirmed *them*.

33 And after they had tarried *there* a space, they were let [i]go in peace from the brethren unto the apostles.

A

Acts 1. 23 And they appointed two, Joseph called Barsabas, who was surnamed Justus, and Matthias.

B

Acts 15. 1 And certain men which came down from Judea taught the brethren, *and said*, Except ye be circumcised after the manner of Moses, ye cannot be saved.

Gal. 2. 4 And that because of false brethren unawares brought in, who came in

(CONCLUDED). TIME, A. D. 50.

T

Gen. 9. 4 But flesh with the life thereof, *which is* the blood thereof, shall ye not eat.

Lev. 3. 17 *It shall be* a perpetual statute for your generations throughout all your dwellings, that ye eat neither fat nor blood.

Deut. 12. 16 Only ye shall not eat the blood; ye shall pour it upon the earth as water.

Deut. 12. 23 Only be sure that thou eat not the blood: for the blood *is* the life:

T—CONCLUDED.

and thou mayest not eat the life with the flesh.

U

Acts 13. 15 And after the reading of the law and the prophets, the rulers of the synagogue sent unto them, saying, *Ye* men *and* brethren, if ye have any word of exhortation for the people, say on.

Acts 13. 27 For they that dwell at Jerusalem, and their rulers, because they knew him not, nor yet the voices of the prophets which are read every sabbath day, they have fulfilled *them* in condemning *him*.

TIME, A. D. 50; PLACE, JERUSALEM.

B—CONCLUDED.

privily to spy out our liberty which we have in Christ Jesus, that they might bring us into bondage:

Gal. 5. 12 I would they were even cut off which trouble you.

Tit. 1. 10 For there are many unruly and vain talkers and deceivers, specially they of the circumcision:

C

Acts 13. 50 But the Jews stirred up the devout and honourable women, and the chief men of the city, and raised persecution against Paul and Barnabas, and expelled them out of their coasts.

Acts 14. 19 And there came thither *certain* Jews from Antioch and Iconium, who persuaded the people, and, having stoned Paul, drew *him* out of the city, supposing he had been dead.

ICor. 15. 30 And why stand we in jeopardy every hour.

IICor. 11. 23 Are they ministers of Christ? (I speak as a fool,) I *am* more; in labours more abundant, in stripes above measure, in prisons more frequent, in deaths oft.

IICor. 11. 26 *In* journeyings often, *in* perils of waters, *in* perils of robbers, *in* perils by *mine own* countrymen, *in* perils by the heathen, *in* perils in the city, *in* perils in the wilderness, *in* perils in the sea, *in* perils among false brethren;

1

Gr. *word.*

D

John 16. 13 Howbeit when he, the Spirit of truth, is come, he will guide you into all truth: for he shall not speak of himself: but whatsoever he shall hear, *that* shall he speak: and he will shew you things to come.

E

Rev. 2. 24 But unto you I say, and unto the rest in Thyatira, as many as have not this doctrine, and which have not known the depths of Satan, as they speak; I will put upon you none other burden.

F

Acts 15. 20. *See text of topic § 268, page 730.*

Acts 21. 25 As touching the Gentiles which believe, we have written *and* concluded that they observe no such thing, save only that they keep themselves from *things* offered to idols, and from blood, and from strangled, and from fornication.

Rev. 2. 14 But I have a few things against thee, because thou hast there them that hold the doctrine of Balaam, who taught Balak to cast a stumblingblock before the children of Israel, to eat things sacrificed unto idols, and to commit fornication.

Rev. 2. 20 Notwithstanding I have a few things against thee, because thou sufferest that woman Jezebel, which calleth herself a prophetess, to teach and to seduce my servants to commit fornication, and to eat things sacrificed unto idols.

G

Lev. 17. 14 For *it is* the life of all flesh; the blood of it *is* for the life thereof: therefore I said unto the children of Israel, Ye shall eat the blood of no manner of flesh; for the life of all flesh *is* the blood thereof: whosoever eateth it shall be cut off.

Acts 15. 20. *See t, T, § 268, page 630.*

For 2, H and I, see next page (732).

§ 269. A DEPUTATION SENT TO ANTIOCH WITH A LETTER

CHAP. 15.

34 Notwithstanding it pleased Silas to abide there still.

35 [k]Paul also and Barnabas continued in Antioch, teaching and preaching the word of the Lord, with many others also.

2

Or, *exhortation.*

H

Acts 14. 22 Confirming the souls of the disciples, *and* exhorting them to continue in the faith, and that we must through much tribulation enter into the kingdom of God.

Acts 18. 28 For he mightily convinced the Jews, *and that* publicly, shewing by

§ 270. THE SECOND MISSIONARY JOURNEY. PAUL AND

15: 36–41.

36 And some days after, Paul said unto Barnabas, Let us go again and visit our brethren [a]in every city where we have preached the word of the Lord, *and see* how they do.

37 And Barnabas determined to take with them [b]John, whose surname was Mark.

38 But Paul thought not good to take him with them, [c]who departed from them from Pamphylia, and went not with them to the work.

39 And the [d]contention was so sharp between them, that they departed asunder one from the other: and so Barnabas took Mark, and sailed unto Cyprus;

40 And Paul chose Silas, and departed, [e]being recommended by the brethren unto the grace of God.

41 And he went through Syria and Cilicia, [f]confirming the churches.

A

Acts 13. 4 So they, being sent forth by the Holy Ghost, departed unto Seleucia; and from thence they sailed to Cyprus.

Acts 13. 13 Now when Paul and his company loosed from Paphos, they came to Perga in Pamphylia: and John departing from them returned to Jerusalem.

14 But when they departed from Perga, they came to Antioch in Pisidia, and went into the synagogue on the sabbath day, and sat down.

Acts 13. 51 But they shook off the dust of their feet against them, and came unto Iconium.

Acts 14. 6 They were ware of *it*, and fled unto Lystra and Derbe, cities of Lycaonia, and unto the region that lieth round about:

Acts 14. 24 And after they had passed throughout Pisidia, they came to Pamphylia.

25 And when they had preached the word in Perga, they went down into Attalia:

B

Acts 12. 12 And when he had considered *the thing*, he came to the house of Mary the mother of John, whose surname was Mark; where many were gathered together praying.

Acts 12. 25 And Barnabas and Saul returned from Jerusalem, when they had ful-

§ 271. THE INCEPTION OF TIMOTHY.

16: 1–5.

1 Then came he to [a]Derbe and Lystra: and, behold, a certain disciple was there, [b]named Timotheus, [c]the son of a certain woman,

A

Acts 14. 6. *See under A* § 270.

B

Acts 19. 22 So he sent unto Macedonia two of them that ministered unto him, Timotheus and Erastus; but he himself stayed in Asia for a season.

(CONCLUDED). TIME, A. D. 50; PLACE, JERUSALEM.

H—CONCLUDED.

the Scriptures that Jesus was Christ.

I

I Cor. 16. 11 Let no man therefore despise him: but conduct him forth in peace, that he may come unto me: for I look for him with the brethren.

Heb. 11. 31 By faith the harlot Rahab perished not with them that believed not, when she had received the spies with peace.

K

Acts 13. 1 Now there were in the church that was at Antioch certain prophets and teachers; as Barnabas, and Simeon that was called Niger, and Lucius of Cyrene, and Manaen, which had been brought up with Herod the tetrarch, and Saul.

Acts 14. 28 And there they abode long time with the disciples.

BARNABAS SEPARATE. TIME, A. D. 51; PLACE, FROM ANTIOCH.

B—CONCLUDED.

filled *their* ministry, and took with them John, whose surname was Mark.

Acts 13. 5 And when they were at Salamis, they preached the word of God in the synagogues of the Jews: and they had also John to *their* minister.

Col. 4. 10 Aristarchus my fellow prisoner saluteth you, and Marcus, sister's son to Barnabas, (touching whom ye received commandments; if he come unto you, receive him;)

II Tim. 4. 11 Only Luke is with me. Take Mark, and bring him with thee: for he is profitable to me for the ministry.

Phile. 24 Marcus, Aristarchus, Demas, Lucas, my fellow labourers.

C

Ps. 78. 9 The children of Ephraim, *being* armed, *and* carrying bows, turned back in the day of battle.

10 They kept not the covenant of God, and refused to walk in his law;

Prov. 25. 19 Confidence in an unfaithful man in time of trouble *is like* a broken tooth, and a foot out of joint.

Luke 9. 61 And another also said, Lord, I will follow thee; but let me first go bid them farewell, which are at home at my house.

Acts 13. 13. *See under A.*

Jas. 1. 8 A doubleminded man *is* unstable in all his ways.

D

Ps. 106. 33 Because they provoked his spirit, so that he spake unadvisedly with his lips.

Ps. 119. 96 I have seen an end of all perfection: *but* thy commandment *is* exceeding broad.

Eccl. 7. 20 For *there is* not a just man upon earth, that doeth good, and sinneth not.

Rom. 7. 21 I find then a law, that, when I would do good, evil is present with me.

Jas. 3. 2 For in many things we offend all. If any man offend not in word, the same *is* a perfect man, *and* able also to bridle the whole body.

Jas. 3. 5 Even so the tongue is a little member, and boasteth great things. Behold, how great a matter a little fire kindleth!

6 And the tongue *is* a fire, a world of iniquity: so is the tongue among our members, that it defileth the whole body, and setteth on fire the course of nature; and it is set on fire of hell.

E

Acts 14. 26 And thence sailed to Antioch, from whence they had been recommended to the grace of God for the work which they fulfilled.

F

Acts 16. 5 And so were the churches established in the faith, and increased in number daily.

TIME, A. D. 51; PLACE, LYSTRA.

B—CONTINUED.

Rom. 16. 21 Timotheus my workfellow, and Lucius, and Jason, and Sosipater, my kinsmen, salute you.

I Cor. 4. 17 For this cause have I sent unto you Timotheus, who is my beloved son, and faithful in the Lord, who

B—CONTINUED.

shall bring you into remembrance of my ways which be in Christ, as I teach everywhere in every church.

Phil. 2. 19 But I trust in the Lord Jesus to send Timotheus shortly unto you,

For B concluded and C, see next page (739).

§ 271. THE INCEPTION OF TIMOTHY (CONCLUDED).

CHAP. 16.

which was a Jewess, and believed; but his father *was* a Greek:

2 Which [d]was well reported of by the brethren that were at Lystra and Iconium.

3 Him would Paul have to go forth with him; and [e]took and circumcised him [f]because of the Jews which were in those quarters: for they knew all that his father was a Greek.

4 And as they went through the cities, they delivered them the decrees for to keep, [g]that were ordained of the apostles and elders which were at Jerusalem.

5 And [h]so were the churches established in the faith, and increased in number daily.

B—CONCLUDED.

that I also may be of good comfort, when I know your state.

IThes. 3. 2 And sent Timotheus, our brother, and minister of God, and our fellow labourer in the gospel of Christ, to establish you, and to comfort you concerning your faith:

I Tim. 1. 2 Unto Timothy, *my* own son in the faith: Grace, mercy, *and* peace, from God our Father, and Jesus Christ our Lord.

IITim. 1. 2 To Timothy, *my* dearly beloved son: Grace, mercy, *and* peace, from God the Father and Christ Jesus our Lord.

Heb. 13. 23 Know ye that *our* brother Timothy is set at liberty; with whom, if he come shortly, I will see you.

C

IITim. 1. 5 When I call to remembrance the unfeigned faith that is in thee, which dwelt first in thy grandmother Lois, and thy mother Eunice; and I am persuaded that in thee also.

D

Acts 6. 3 Wherefore, brethren, look ye out among you seven men of honest re-

§ 272. THE CALL INTO MACEDONIA.

16: 6–10.

6 Now when they had gone throughout Phrygia and the region of Galatia, and were forbidden of the [a]Holy Ghost to preach the word in [b]Asia,

7 After they were come to Mysia, they assayed to go into Bithynia: but the Spirit suffered them not.

8 And they passing by Mysia [c]came down to Troas.

9 And a vision appeared to Paul in the night; There stood a man of Macedonia, and prayed him, saying, [d]Come over into Macedonia and help us.

10 And after he had seen the vision, immediately we endeavoured to go into Macedonia, assuredly gathering that the Lord had called us for to preach the gospel unto them.

A

Acts 10. 19. *See m, M,* § 254, *page* 694.

B

Acts 19. 10 And this continued by the space of two years; so that all they which dwelt in Asia heard the word of the Lord Jesus, both Jews and Greeks.

Acts 19. 26 Moreover ye see and hear, that not alone at Ephesus, but almost throughout all Asia, this Paul hath persuaded and turned away much people, saying that they be no gods, which are made with hands.

Acts 20. 4 And there accompanied him into Asia Sopater of Berea; and of the Thessalonians, Aristarchus and Secundus; and Gaius of Derbe, and Timotheus; and of Asia, Tychicus and Trophimus.

Acts 20. 16 For Paul had determined to sail by Ephesus, because he would not spend the time in Asia: for he hasted, if it were possible for him, to be at Jerusalem the day of Pentecost.

IICor. 1. 8 For we would not, brethren, have you ignorant of our trouble which came to us in Asia, that we were pressed out of measure, above

TIME, A. D. 51; PLACE, LYSTRA.

D—CONCLUDED.

port, full of the Holy Ghost and wisdom, whom we may appoint over this business.

I Tim. 3. 7 Moreover he must have a good report of them which are without; lest he fall into reproach and the snare of the devil.

I Tim. 5. 10 Well reported of for good works; if she have brought up children, if she have lodged strangers, if she have washed the saints' feet, if she have relieved the afflicted, if she have diligently followed every good work.

II Tim. 3. 15 And that from a child thou hast known the holy Scriptures, which are able to make thee wise unto salvation through faith which is in Christ Jesus.

Heb. 11. 1 Now faith is the substance of things hoped for, the evidence of things not seen.

2 For by it the elders obtained a good report.

E

Gal. 2. 3 But neither Titus, who was with me, being a Greek, was compelled to be circumcised:

E—CONCLUDED.

Gal. 5. 3 For I testify again to every man that is circumcised, that he is a debtor to do the whole law.

F

I Cor. 9. 20 And unto the Jews I became as a Jew, that I might gain the Jews; to them that are under the law, as under the law, that I might gain them that are under the law;

G

Acts 15. 28 For it seemed good to the Holy Ghost, and to us, to lay upon you no greater burden than these necessary things;

29 That ye abstain from meats offered to idols, and from blood, and from things strangled, and from fornication: from which if ye keep yourselves, ye shall do well. Fare ye well.

H

Acts 15. 41 And he went through Syria and Cilicia, confirming the churches.

TIME, A. D. 52; PLACE, TROAS.

B—CONCLUDED.

strength, insomuch that we despaired even of life:

II Tim. 1. 15 This thou knowest, that all they which are in Asia be turned away from me; of whom are Phygellus and Hermogenes.

I Pet. 1. 1 Peter, an apostle of Jesus Christ, to the strangers scattered throughout Pontus, Galatia, Cappadocia, Asia, and Bithynia,

Rev. 1. 4 John to the seven churches which are in Asia: Grace *be* unto you, and peace, from him which is, and which was, and which is to come; and from the seven Spirits which are before his throne;

C

Acts 20. 5 These going before tarried for us at Troas.

II Cor. 2. 12 Furthermore, when I came to Troas to *preach* Christ's gospel, and a door was opened unto me of the Lord,

II Tim. 4. 13 The cloak that I left at Troas with Carpus, when thou comest, bring *with thee*, and the books, *but* especially the parchments.

D

Acts 8. 26 And the angel of the Lord spake unto Philip, saying, Arise, and go toward the south, unto the way that goeth down from Jerusalem unto Gaza, which is desert.

Acts 9. 38 And forasmuch as Lydda was nigh to Joppa, and the disciples had heard that Peter was there, they sent unto him two men, desiring *him* that he would not delay to come to them.

Acts 10. 33 Immediately therefore I sent to thee: and thou hast well done that thou art come. Now therefore are we all here present before God, to hear all things that are commanded thee of God.

Rom. 10. 14 How then shall they call on him in whom they have not believed? and how shall they believe in him of whom they have not heard? and how shall they hear without a preacher?

15 And how shall they preach, except they be sent? as it is written, How beautiful are the feet of them that preach the gospel of peace, and bring glad tidings of good things!

§ 273. THE CONVERSION OF LYDIA AT PHILIPPI.

16: 11–15.

11 Therefore loosing from Troas, we came with a straight course to Samothracia, and the next *day* to Neapolis ;

12 And from thence to [a]Philippi, which is [1]the chief city of that part of Macedonia, *and* a colony : and we were in that city abiding certain days.

13 And on the [2]sabbath we went out of the city by a river side, [b]where prayer was wont to be made; and we sat down, and spake unto the women which resorted *thither*.

14 And a certain woman named Lydia, a seller of purple, of the city of Thyatira, which worshipped God, heard *us* : [c]whose heart the Lord opened, that she attended unto the things that were spoken of Paul.

15 And when she was baptized, and her household, she besought *us*, saying, If ye have judged me to be faithful to the Lord, [d]come into my house and abide *there*. And she constrained us.

A

Phil. 1. 1 Paul and Timotheus, the servants of Jesus Christ, to all the saints in Christ Jesus which are at Philippi, with the bishops and deacons :

1Thes. 2. 2 But even after that we had suffered before, and were shamefully entreated, as ye know, at Philippi, we were bold in our God to speak unto you the gospel of God with much contention.

1
Or, *the first.*

2
Gr. *sabbath day.*

B

Acts 21. 5 And when we had accomplished those days, we departed and went our way; and they all brought us on our way, with wives and children, till *we were* out of the city: and we kneeled down on the shore, and prayed.

C

Ps. 110. 3 Thy people *shall be* willing in the day of thy power, in the beauties of holiness from the womb of the morning: thou hast the dew of thy youth.

Isa. 50. 5 The Lord GOD hath opened mine ear and I was not rebellious, neither turned away back.

Luke 24. 45 Then opened he their understanding, that they might understand the Scriptures.

John 6. 44 No man can come to me, except the Father which hath sent me draw him : and I will raise him up at the last day.

§ 274. PAUL CLEANSES A DAMSEL HAVING A SPIRIT OF

16: 16–18.

16 And it came to pass, as we went to prayer, a certain damsel [a]possessed with a spirit of [1]divination met us, which brought her masters [b]much gain by soothsaying:

17 The same followed Paul and us, and cried, saying, These men are the servants of the most high God, which shew unto us [c]the way of salvation.

18 And this did she many days. But Paul, [d]being grieved, turned and said to the Spirit, I command

CHAP. 16.

thee in the name of Jesus Christ to come out of her. [e]And he came out the same hour.

A

1 Sa. 28. 7 Then said Saul unto his servants, seek me a woman that hath a familiar spirit, that I may go to her, and inquire of her. And his servants said to him, Behold, *there is* a woman that hath a familiar spirit at En-dor.

1
Or, *of Python.*

B

Acts 19. 24 For a certain *man* named Demetrius, a silversmith, which made silver shrines for Diana, brought no small gain unto the craftsmen;

TIME, A. D. 52; PLACE, PHILIPPI.

C—CONTINUED.

John 6. 45 It is written in the prophets, And they shall be all taught of God. Every man therefore that hath heard, and hath learned of the Father, cometh unto me.

Rom. 9. 16 So then *it is* not of him that willeth, nor of him that runneth, but of God that sheweth mercy.

I Cor. 3. 6 I have planted, Apollos watered; but God gave the increase.

7 So then neither is he that planteth anything, neither he that watereth; but God that giveth the increase.

II Cor. 3. 14 But their minds were blinded: for until this day remaineth the same vail untaken away in the reading of the old testament; which *vail* is done away in Christ.

15 But even unto this day, when Moses is read, the vail is upon their heart.

16 Nevertheless, when it shall turn to the Lord, the vail shall be taken away.

II Cor. 4. 4 In whom the God of this world hath blinded the minds of them which believe not, lest the light of the glorious gospel of Christ, who is the image of God, should shine unto them.

5 For we preach not ourselves, but Christ Jesus the Lord; and ourselves your servants for Jesus' sake.

6 For God, who commanded the light to shine out of darkness, hath shined in our hearts, to *give* the light

C—CONCLUDED.

of the knowledge of the glory of God in the face of Jesus Christ.

Eph. 1. 17 That the God of our Lord Jesus Christ, the Father of glory, may give unto you the spirit of wisdom and revelation in the knowledge of him:

18 The eyes of your understanding being enlightened; that ye may know what is the hope of his calling, and what the riches of the glory of his inheritance in the saints.

Phil. 2. 13 For it is God which worketh in you both to will and to do of *his* good pleasure.

Jas. 1. 17 Every good gift and every perfect gift is from above, and cometh down from the Father of lights, with whom is no variableness, neither shadow of turning.

D

Gen. 18. 4 Let a little water, I pray you, be fetched, and wash your feet, and rest yourselves under the tree:

Judg. 19. 20 And the old man said, Peace *be* with thee; howsoever, *let* all thy wants *lie* upon me; only lodge not in the street.

Matt. 10. 41 He that receiveth a prophet in the name of a prophet shall receive a prophet's reward; and he that receiveth a righteous man in the name of a righteous man shall receive a righteous man's reward.

Heb. 13. 2 Be not forgetful to entertain strangers: for thereby some have entertained angels unawares.

DIVINATION. TIME, A. D. 52; PLACE, PHILIPPI.

B—CONCLUDED.

I Tim. 6. 10 For the love of money is the root of all evil: which while some coveted after, they have erred from the faith, and pierced themselves through with many sorrows.

II Pet. 2. 3 And through covetousness shall they with feigned words make merchandise of you: whose judgment now of a long time lingereth not, and their damnation slumbereth not.

C

Matt. 7. 14 Because strait *is* the gate and narrow *is* the way, which leadeth unto life, and few there be that find it.

Luke 1. 79 To give light to them that sit in darkness and *in* the shadow of death, to guide our feet into the way of peace.

C—CONCLUDED.

Luke 20. 21 And they asked him, saying, Master, we know that thou sayest and teachest rightly, neither acceptest thou the person *of any*, but teachest the way of God truly:

D

Mark 1. 25 And Jesus rebuked him, saying, Hold thy peace, and come out of him.

Mark 1. 34 And he healed many that were sick of divers diseases, and cast out many devils; and suffered not the devils to speak, because they knew him.

E

Mark 16. 17 And these signs shall follow them that believe; In my name shall they cast out devils; they shall speak with new tongues;

§ 275. PAUL AND SILAS IMPRISONED. CONVERSION OF

16: 19-34.

19 And [a]when her masters saw that
the hope of their gains was gone,
[b]they caught Paul and Silas, and
[c]drew *them* into the [1]marketplace
unto the rulers,
20 And brought them to the magistrates, saying, These men, being Jews,
[d]do exceedingly trouble our city,
21 And teach customs, which are
not lawful for us to receive, neither
to observe, being Romans.
22 And the multitude rose up together against them; and [e]the magistrates rent off their clothes, and
commanded to beat *them*.
23 And when they had laid many
stripes upon them, they cast *them*
into prison, charging the jailer to
keep them safely:
24 Who, having received such a
charge, thrust them into the inner
prison, and [f]made their feet fast in
the stocks.
25 And [g]at midnight Paul and Silas
prayed, and sang praises unto God:
and the prisoners heard them.
26 And [h]suddenly there was a great
earthquake, so that the foundations
of the prison were shaken: and immediately all the doors were opened,
[i]and every one's bands were loosed.
27 And the keeper of the prison
awaking out of his sleep, and seeing
the prison doors open, he drew out his
sword, and would have killed himself,
supposing that the prisoners had
been fled.
28 But Paul cried with a loud
voice, saying, Do thyself no harm:
for we are all here.

CHAP. 16.

29 Then he called for a light, and
sprang in, and came trembling, and
fell down before Paul and Silas,
30 And brought them out, and said,
[k]Sirs, what must I do to be saved?
31 And they said, [l]Believe on the
Lord Jesus Christ, and thou shalt
be saved, and thy house.
32 And they spake unto him the
word of the Lord, and to all that
were in his house.
33 And he took them the same
hour of the night, and washed *their*
stripes; and was baptized, he and
all his, straightway.
34 And when he had brought them
into his house, [m]he set meat before
them, and rejoiced, believing in
God with all his house.

A

Acts 19. 25 Whom he called together with the workmen of like occupation, and said, Sirs, ye know that by this craft we have our wealth.

Phil. 3. 19 Whose end *is* destruction, whose God *is their* belly, and *whose* glory *is* in their shame, who mind earthly things.)

B

II Cor. 6. 5 In stripes, in imprisonments, in tumults, in labors, in watchings, in fastings;

C

Matt. 10. 18 And ye shall be brought before governors and kings for my sake, for a testimony against them and the Gentiles.

1

Or, *court*.

D

I Ki. 18. 17 And it came to pass, when Ahab saw Elijah, that Ahab said unto him, *Art* thou he that troubleth Israel?

Acts 17. 6 And when they found them not, they drew Jason and certain brethren unto the rulers of the city, crying, These that have turned the world upside down are come hither also;

THE PHILIPPIAN JAILER. TIME, A. D. 52; PLACE, PHILIPPI.

E

Matt. 10. 17 But beware of men: for they will deliver you up to the councils, and they will scourge you in their synagogues;

IICor. 11. 23 Are they ministers of Christ? (I speak as a fool,) I *am* more; in labours more abundant, in stripes above measure, in prisons more frequent, in deaths oft.

IThes. 2. 2 But even after that we had suffered before, and were shamefully entreated, as ye know, at Philippi, we were bold in our God to speak unto you the gospel of God with much contention.

Heb. 11. 36 And others had trial of *cruel* mockings and scourgings, yea, moreover of bonds and imprisonment:

F

IIChr. 16. 10 Then Asa was wroth, with the seer, and put him in a prison house; for *he was* in a rage with him because of this *thing*. And Asa oppressed *some* of the people at the same time.

Job 13. 27 Thou puttest my feet also in the stocks, and lookest narrowly unto all my paths; thou settest a print upon the heels of my feet.

Job 33. 11 He putteth my feet in the stocks, he marketh all my paths.

Ps. 105. 18 Whose feet they hurt with fetters; he was laid in iron:

Jer. 20. 2 Then Pashur smote Jeremiah the prophet, and put him in the stocks that *were* in the high gate of Benjamin, which *was* by the house of the LORD.

G

Job 35. 10 But none saith, Where *is* God my maker, who giveth songs in the night;

Ps. 22. 2 O my God, I cry in the daytime, but thou hearest not; and in the night season, and am not silent.

Ps. 42. 8 *Yet* the LORD will command his loving kindness in the daytime, and in the night his song *shall be* with me, *and* my prayer unto the God of my life.

Ps. 77. 6 I call to remembrance my song in the night; I commune with mine own heart: and my spirit made diligent search.

Ps. 119. 55 I have remembered thy name, O LORD, in the night, and have kept thy law.

Ps. 119. 62 At midnight I will rise up to give thanks unto thee because of thy righteous judgments.

Isa. 30. 29 Ye shall have a song, as in the night *when* a holy solemnity is kept; and gladness of heart, as when one goeth with a pipe to come into the mountain of the LORD, to the Mighty One of Israel.

G—CONCLUUED.

H

Acts 4. 31 And when they had prayed, the place was shaken where they were assembled together; and they were all filled with the Holy Ghost, and they spake the word of God with boldness.

I

Ps. 79. 11 Let the sighing of the prisoner come before thee; according to the greatness of thy power preserve thou those that are appointed to die;

Ps. 102. 19 For he hath looked down from the height of his sanctuary; from heaven did the Lord behold the earth:

20 To hear the groaning of the prisoner; to loose those that are appointed to death;

Acts 5. 19 But the angel of the Lord by night opened the prison doors, and brought them forth, and said,

Acts 12. 7 And, behold, the angel of the Lord came upon *him*, and a light shined in the prison; and he smote Peter on the side, and raised him up, saying, Arise up quickly. And his chains fell off from *his* hands.

K

Luke 3. 10 And the people asked him, saying, What shall we do then?

Acts 2. 37 Now when they heard *this*, they were pricked in their heart, and said unto Peter and to the rest of the apostles, Men *and* brethren, what shall we do?

Acts 9. 6 And he trembling and astonished said, Lord, what wilt thou have me to do? And the Lord *said* unto him, Arise, and go into the city, and it shall be told thee what thou must do.

L

Isa. 45. 22 Look unto me, and be ye saved, all the ends of the earth: for I *am* God, and *there is* none else.

John 6. 47. *See c, C,* § 83, *page* 257.

M

Luke 5. 29 And Levi made him a great feast in his own house: and there was a great company of publicans and of others that sat down with them.

Luke 19. 6 And he made haste, and came down, and received him joyfully.

§ 276. PAUL AND SILAS ARE RELEASED AND DEPART.

16: 35–40.

35 And when it was day, the magistrates sent the serjeants, saying,
[a]Let those men go.
36 And the keeper of the prison
told this saying to Paul, The magistrates have sent to let you go: now
therefore depart, and go in peace.
37 But Paul said unto them, [b]They
have beaten us openly uncondemned,
being Romans, and have cast *us* into
prison; and now do they thrust us
out privily? nay verily; but let them

CHAP. 16.

come themselves and fetch us out.
38 And the serjeants told these
words unto the magistrates: and
they feared, when they heard that
they were Romans.
39 And they came and besought
them, and brought *them* out, [c]and desired *them* to depart out of the city.
40 And they went out of the prison,
and entered into *the house of* Lydia:
and when they had seen the brethren,
[d]they comforted them, and departed.

§ 277. THEY COME TO THESSALONICA.

17: 1–9.

1 Now when they had passed
through Amphipolis and Apollonia,
they came to Thessalonica, where
was a synagogue of the Jews:
2 And Paul, as his manner was,
[a]went in unto them, and three sabbath days reasoned with them out
of the Scriptures,
3 Opening and alleging, [b]that
Christ must needs have suffered, and
risen again from the dead; and that
this Jesus, [1]whom I preach unto you,
is Christ.
4 And [c]some of them believed, and
consorted with Paul and [d]Silas; and
of the devout Greeks a great multitude, and of the chief women not a
few.
5 But the Jews which believed not,
moved with envy, took unto them
certain lewd fellows of the baser
sort, and gathered a company, and
set all the city in an uproar, and assaulted the house of [e]Jason, and

CHAP. 17.

sought to bring them out to the people.
6 And when they found them not,
they drew Jason and certain brethren unto the rulers of the city, crying, These[f] that have turned the world
upside down are come hither also;
7 Whom Jason hath received: and
these all do contrary to the decrees
of Cæsar, [g]saying that there is another king, *one* Jesus.
8 And they troubled the people
and the rulers of the city, when they
heard these things.
9 And when they had taken secu-
rity of Jason, and of the other, they
let them go.

A

Luke 4. 16 And he came to Nazareth, where he had been brought up: and, as his custom was, he went into the synagogue on the sabbath day, and stood up for to read.

Acts 9. 20 And straightway he preached Christ in the synagogues, that he is the Son of God.

TIME, A. D. 52; PLACE, PHILIPPI.

A

Acts 4. 21 So when they had further threatened them, they let them go, finding nothing how they might punish them, because of the people: for all *men* glorified God for that which was done.

Acts 5. 40 And to him they agreed: and when they had called the apostles, and beaten *them*, they commanded that they should not speak in the name of Jesus, and let them go.

B

Prov. 28. 1 The wicked flee when no man pursueth : but the righteous are bold as a lion.

Acts 22. 25 And as they bound him with thongs, Paul said unto the centurion that stood by, Is it lawful for you to

B—CONCLUDED.

scourge a man that is a Roman, and uncondemned ?

C

Matt. 8. 34 And, behold, the whole city came out to meet Jesus: and when they saw him, they besought *him* that he would depart out of their coasts.

D

II Cor. 1. 3 Blessed *be* God, even the Father of our Lord Jesus Christ, the Father of mercies, and the God of all comfort;

4 Who comforteth us in all our tribulation, that we may be able to comfort them which are in any trouble, by the comfort wherewith we ourselves are comforted of God.

THE UPROAR. TIME, A. D. 52.

A—CONCLUDED.

Acts 13. 5 And when they were at Salamis, they preached the word of God in the synagogues of the Jews: and they had also John to *their* minister.

Acts 14. 1 And it came to pass in Iconium, that they went both together into the synagogue of the Jews, and so spake, that a great multitude both of the Jews and also of the Greeks believed.

B

Luke 24. 26 Ought not Christ to have suffered these things, and to enter into his glory ?

Luke 24. 46 And said unto them, Thus it is written, and thus it behooved Christ to suffer, and to rise from the dead the third day:

Acts 18. 28 For he mightily convinced the Jews, *and that* publicly, shewing by the Scriptures that Jesus was Christ.

Gal. 3. 1 O foolish Galatians, who hath bewitched you, that ye should not obey the truth, before whose eyes Jesus Christ hath been evidently set forth, crucified among you ?

1

Or, *whom,* said he, *I preach.*

C

Acts 28. 24 And some believed the things which were spoken, and some believed not.

D

Acts 15. 22 Then pleased it the apostles and elders, with the whole church, to send

D—CONCLUDED.

chosen men of their own company to Antioch with Paui and Barnabas; *namely*, Judas surnamed Barsabas, and Silas, chief men among the brethren :

Acts 15. 27 We have sent therefore Judas and Silas, who shall also tell *you* the same things by mouth.

Acts 15. 32 And Judas and Silas, being prophets also themselves, exhorted the brethren with many words, and confirmed *them*.

Acts 15. 40 And Paul chose Silas, and departed, being recommended by the brethren unto the grace of God.

E

Rom. 16. 21 Timotheus my workfellow, and Lucius, and Jason, and Sosipater, my kinsmen, salute you.

F

Acts 16. 20 And brought them to the magistrates, saying, These men, being Jews, do exceedingly trouble our city,

G

Luke 23. 2 And they began to accuse him, saying, We found this *fellow* perverting the nation, and forbidding to give tribute to Cæsar, saying that he himself is Christ a king.

John 19. 12 And from thenceforth Pilate sought to release him: but the Jews cried out, saying, If thou let this man go, thou art not Cæsar's friend: whosoever maketh himself a king speaketh against Cæsar.

§ 278. PAUL LEAVES SILAS AND TIMOTHY AT BEREA.

17: 10-15.

10 And [a]the brethren immediately sent away Paul and Silas by night unto Berea; who coming *thither* went into the synagogue of the Jews.

11 These were more noble than those in Thessalonica, in that they [b]received the word with all readiness of mind, and [c]searched the Scriptures daily, whether those things were so.

12 Therefore many of them believed; also of honourable women which were Greeks, and of men not a few.

13 But when the Jews of Thessalonica had knowledge that the word of God was preached of Paul at Berea, they came thither also, and stirred up the people.

14 And then immediately the brethren sent away Paul to go as it were to the sea: but Silas and Timotheus abode there still.

15 And they that conducted Paul brought him unto Athens: and receiving a commandment unto Silas and Timotheus for to come to him with all speed, they departed.

§ 279. PAUL ENCOUNTERED BY THE PHILOSOPHERS.

17: 16–34.

16 Now while Paul waited for them at Athens, his [a]spirit was stirred in him, when he saw the city [1]wholly given to idolatry.

17 Therefore disputed he in the synagogue with the Jews, and with the devout persons, and in the market daily with them that met with him.

18 Then certain [b]philosophers of the Epicureans, and of the Stoics, encountered him. And some said, What will this [2]babbler say? other some, He seemeth to be a setter forth of strange gods: because he preached unto them Jesus and the ressurrection.

19 And they took him, and brought him unto [3]Areopagus, saying, May we know what this [c]new doctrine, whereof thou speakest, *is?*

20 For [d]thou bringest certain strange things to our ears: we would know therefore what these things mean.

21 (For all the Athenians, and strangers which were there [e]spent their time in nothing else, but either to tell or to hear some new thing.)

A

Ex. 32. 19 And it came to pass, as soon as he came nigh unto the camp, that he saw the calf, and the dancing: and Moses' anger waxed hot, and he cast the tables out of his hands, and brake them beneath the mount.

20 And he took the calf which they had made, and burnt *it* in the fire, and ground *it* to powder, and strewed *it* upon the water, and made the children of Israel drink *of it.*

1 Ki. 19. 10 And he said, I have been very jealous for the LORD God of hosts: for the children of Israel have forsaken thy covenant, thrown down thine altars, and slain thy prophets with the sword; and I, *even* I only, am left; and they seek my life, to take it away.

Job 32. 2 Then was kindled the wrath of Elihu the son of Barachel the Buzite, of the kindred of Ram; against Job was his wrath kindled, because he justified himself rather than God.

3 Also against his three friends was his wrath kindled, because they had

BROUGHT TO ATHENS. TIME, A. D. 52.

A

Acts 17. 14. *See Text of Topic.*

Acts 9. 25 Then the disciples took him by night, and let *him* down by the wall in a basket.

B

Job 23. 12 Neither have I gone back from the commandment of his lips; I have esteemed the words of his mouth more than my necessary *food*.

Prov. 2. 4 If thou seekest her as silver, and searchest for her as *for* hid treasures;

5 Then shalt thou understand the fear of the LORD, and find the knowledge of God.

C

Ps. 1. 2 But his delight *is* in the law of the LORD; and in his law doth he meditate day and night.

Ps. 119. 97 O how love I thy law! it *is* my meditation all the day.

C—CONCLUDED.

Ps. 119. 147 I prevented the dawning of the morning, and cried; I hoped in thy word.

148 Mine eyes prevent the *night* watches, that I might meditate in thy word.

Isa. 34. 16 Seek ye out of the book of the LORD, and read: no one of these shall fail, none shall want her mate; for my mouth it hath commanded, and his spirit it hath gathered them.

Luke 16. 29 Abraham saith unto him, They have Moses and the prophets; let them hear them.

IIPet. 1. 19 We have also a more sure word of prophecy; whereunto ye do well that ye take heed, as unto a light that shineth in a dark place, until the day dawn, and the daystar arise in your hearts:

HIS ADDRESS. TIME, A. D. 52; PLACE, ATHENS.

A—CONCLUDED.

found no answer, and *yet* had condemned Job.

Ps. 69. 9 For the zeal of thine house hath eaten me up; and the reproaches of them that reproached thee are fallen upon me.

Ps. 119. 136 Rivers of waters run down mine eyes, because they keep not thy law.

Ps. 119. 158 I beheld the transgressors, and was grieved: because they kept not thy word.

John 2. 15 And when he had made a scourge of small cords, he drove them all out of the temple, and the sheep, and the oxen; and poured out the changers' money, and overthrew the tables;

IIPet. 2. 8 (For that righteous man dwelling among them, in seeing and hearing, vexed *his* righteous soul from day to day with *their* unlawful deeds:)

1

Or, *full of idols.*

B

Col. 2. 8 Beware lest any man spoil you through philosophy and vain deceit, after the tradition of men, after the rudiments of the world, and not after Christ.

2

Or, *base fellow.*

3

Or, *Mars' hill.* It was the highest court in Athens.

C

John 13. 34 A new commandment I give unto you, That ye love one another; as I have loved you, that ye also love one another.

I Jno. 2. 8 Again, a new commandment I write unto you, which thing is true in him and in you: because the darkness is past, and the true light now shineth.

D

Hos. 8. 12 I have written to him the great things of my law, *but* they were counted as a strange thing.

E

Eph. 5. 16 Redeeming the time, because the days are evil.

Col. 4. 5 Walk in wisdom toward them that are without, redeeming the time.

IIThes. 3. 11 For we hear that there are some which walk among you disorderly, working not at all, but are busybodies.

12 Now them that are such we command and exhort by our Lord Jesus Christ, that with quietness they work, and eat their own bread.

I Tim. 5. 13 And withal they learn *to be* idle, wandering about from house to house; and not only idle, but tattlers also and busybodies, speaking things which they ought not.

For E concluded see next page (744).

§ 279. PAUL ENCOUNTERED BY THE PHILOSOPHERS.

CHAP. 17.

22 Then Paul stood in the midst
of [4]Mars' hill, and said, *Ye* men of
Athens, I perceive that in all things
ye are [f]too superstitious.

23 For as I passed by, and beheld
your [5]devotions, I found an altar
with this inscription, TO THE UN-
KNOWN GOD. Whom therefore
ye ignorantly worship, him declare
I unto you.

24 God [g]that made the world and
all things therein, seeing that [h]he is
Lord of heaven and earth, [i]dwelleth
not in temples made with hands;

25 Neither is worshipped with
men's hands, [k]as though he needed
any thing, seeing [l]he giveth to all
life, and breath, and all things;

26 And hath made of one blood all
nations of men for to dwell on all the
face of the earth, and hath determined the times before appointed,
and [m]the bounds of their habitation;

27 That [n]they should seek the
Lord, if haply they might feel after
him, and find him, [o]though he be not
far from every one of us:

28 For [p]in him we live, and move,
and have our being; as certain also
of your own poets have said, For
we are also his offspring.

29 Forasmuch then as we are the
offspring of God, [q]we ought not to
think that the Godhead is like unto
gold, or silver, or stone, graven by
art and man's device.

30 And [r]the times of this ignorance
God winked at; but [s]now commandeth all men everywhere to repent:

E—CONCLUDED.

II Tim. 2. 16 But shun profane *and* vain babblings; for they will increase unto more ungodliness.

17 And their word will eat as doth a canker: of whom is Hymeneus and Philetus;

4

Or, *the court of the Areopagites.*

F

Jer. 10. 2 Thus saith the LORD, Learn not the way of the heathen, and be not dismayed at the signs of heaven; for the heathen are dismayed at them.

3 For the customs of the people *are* vain; for *one* cutteth a tree out of the forest, the work of the hands of the workman, with the axe.

Jer. 50. 38 A drought *is* upon her waters; and they shall be dried up: for it *is* the land of the graven images, and they are mad upon *their* idols.

Acts 17. 16. *See text of topic, page 742.*

5

Or, *God's that ye worship,*

Gal. 4. 8 Howbeit then, when ye knew not God, ye did service unto them which by nature are no gods.

G

Ps. 146. 5 Happy *is he* that *hath* the God of Jacob for his help, whose hope *is* in the LORD his God.

6 Which made heaven, and earth, the sea, and all that therein *is*: which keepeth truth forever:

Isa. 40. 12 Who hath measured the waters in the hollow of his hand, and meted out heaven with the span, and comprehended the dust of the earth in a measure, and weighed the mountains in scales, and the hills in a balance?

Jer. 10. 11 Thus shall ye say unto them, The gods that have not made the heavens and the earth, *even* they shall perish from the earth, and from under these heavens.

12 He hath made the earth by his power, he hath established the world by his wisdom, and hath stretched out the heavens by his discretion.

H

Matt. 11. 25 At that time Jesus answered and said, I thank thee, O Father, Lord of heaven and earth, because thou hast hid these things from the wise and prudent, and hast revealed them unto babes.

HIS ADDRESS (CONTINUED). TIME, A. D. 52; PLACE, ATHENS.

I

Acts. 7. 48 Howbeit the Most High dwelleth not in temples made with hands; as saith the prophet,

K

Ps. 50. 8 I will not reprove thee for thy sacrifices or thy burnt offerings, *to have been* continually before me.

Ps. 50. 12 If I were hungry, I would not tell thee: for the world *is* mine, and the fulness thereof.

L

Gen. 2. 7 And the LORD God formed man *of* the dust of the ground, and breathed into his nostrils the breath of life; and man became a living soul.

Job 12. 10 In whose hand *is* the soul of every living thing, and the breath of all mankind.

Job 33. 4 The Spirit of God hath made me, and the breath of the Almighty hath given me life.

Isa. 42. 5 Thus saith God the LORD, he that created the heavens, and stretched them out; he that spread forth the earth, and that which cometh out of it; he that giveth breath unto the people upon it, and spirit to them that walk therein;

Isa. 57. 16 For I will not contend for ever, neither will I be always wroth: for the spirit should fail before me, and the souls *which* I have made.

Zech. 12. 1 The burden of the word of the LORD for Israel, saith the LORD, which stretcheth forth the heavens, and layeth the foundation of the earth, and formeth the spirit of man within him.

M

Deut. 32. 8 When the Most High divided to the nations their inheritance, when he separated the sons of Adam, he set the bounds of the people according to the number of the children of Israel.

N

Ps. 19. 1 The heavens declare the glory of God; and the firmament sheweth his handywork.

2 Day unto day uttereth speech, and night unto night sheweth knowledge.

3 *There is* no speech nor language, *where* their voice is not heard.

4 Their line is gone out through all the earth, and their words to the end of the world. In them hath he set a tabernacle for the sun,

5 Which *is* as a bridegroom coming out of his chamber, *and* rejoiceth as a strong man to run a race.

N—CONCLUDED.

Ps. 19. 6 His going forth *is* from the end of the heaven, and his circuit unto the ends of it: and there is nothing hid from the heat thereof.

Rom. 1. 20 For the invisible things of him from the creation of the world are clearly seen, being understood by the things that are made, *even* his eternal power and Godhead; so that they are without excuse:

O

Jer. 23. 24 Can any hide himself in secret places that I shall not see him? saith the LORD. Do not I fill heaven and earth? saith the LORD.

Acts 14. 17 Nevertheless he left not himself without witness, in that he did good, and gave us rain from heaven, and fruitful seasons, filling our hearts with food and gladness.

P

Col. 1. 17 And he is before all things, and by him all things consist.

Heb. 1. 3 Who being the brightness of *his* glory, and the express image of his person, and upholding all things by the word of his power, when he had by himself purged our sins, sat down on the right hand of the Majesty on high;

Q

Isa. 40. 18 To whom then will ye liken God? or what likeness will ye compare unto him?

R

Acts 14. 16 Who in times past suffered all nations to walk in their own ways.

Rom. 3. 25 Whom God hath set forth *to be* a propitiation through faith in his blood, to declare his righteousness for the remission of sins that are past, through the forbearance of God;

S

Luke 24. 47 And that repentance and remission of sins should be preached in his name among all nations, beginning at Jerusalem.

Tit. 2. 11 For the grace of God that bringeth salvation hath appeared to all men,

12 Teaching us that, denying ungodliness and worldly lusts, we should live soberly, righteously, and godly, in this present world;

I Pet. 1. 14 As obedient children, not fashioning yourselves according to the former lusts in your ignorance:

For S concluded see page (747).

§ 279. PAUL ENCOUNTERED BY THE PHILOSOPHERS.

CHAP. 17.

31 Because he hath appointed a day, in the which [t]he will judge the world in righteousness by *that* man whom he hath ordained; *whereof* he hath [6]given assurance unto all *men*, in that [u]he hath raised him from the dead.

32 And when they heard of the resurrection of the dead, some mocked:

CHAP. 17.

and others said, We will hear thee again of this *matter*.

33 So Paul departed from among them.

34 Howbeit certain men clave unto him, and believed; among the which *was* Dionysius the Areopagite, and a woman named Damaris, and others with them.

§ 280. PAUL AT CORINTH. JOINED BY SILAS AND

The *First Epistle to the Thessalonians* was

18: 1–11.

1 After these things Paul departed from Athens, and came to Corinth;

2 And found a certain Jew named [a]Aquila, born in Pontus, lately come from Italy, with his wife Priscilla; (because that Claudius had commanded all Jews to depart from Rome:) and came unto them.

3 And because he was of the same craft, he abode with them, [b]and wrought; for by their occupation they were tentmakers.

4 And [c]he reasoned in the synagogue every sabbath, and persuaded the Jews and the Greeks.

5 And [d]when Silas and Timotheus were come from Macedonia, Paul was [e]pressed in the spirit, and testified to the Jews *that* Jesus [1]*was* Christ.

6 And [f]when they opposed themselves, and blasphemed, [g]he shook *his* raiment, and said unto them, [h]Your blood *be* upon your own heads; [i]I *am* clean: [k]from henceforth I will go unto the Gentiles.

7 And he departed thence, and entered into a certain *man's* house,

A

Rom.16. 3 Greet Priscilla and Aquila, my helpers in Christ Jesus:

ICor.16. 19 The churches of Asia salute you. Aquila and Priscilla salute you much in the Lord, with the church that is in their house.

IITim.4. 19 Salute Prisca and Aquila, and the household of Onesiphorus.

B

Acts 20. 34 Yea, ye yourselves know, that these hands have ministered unto my necessities, and to them that were with me.

I Cor. 4. 12 and labour, working with our own hands: being reviled, we bless; being persecuted, we suffer it :

I Cor. 9. 6 Or I only and Barnabas, have not we power to forbear working?

IICor.11. 9 And when I was present with you, and wanted, I was chargeable to no man: for that which was lacking to me the brethren which came from Macedonia supplied: and in all *things* I have kept myself from being burdensome unto you, and *so* will I keep *myself*.

IThes.2. 9 For ye remember, brethren, our labour and travail: for labouring night and day, because we would not be chargeable unto any of you, we preached unto you the gospel of God.

IIThes.3. 8 Neither did we eat any man's bread for nought; but wrought with labour and travail night and day, that we might not be chargeable to any of you :

9 Not because we have not power, but to make ourselves an ensample unto you to follow us,

HIS ADDRESS (CONCLUDED). TIME, A. D. 52; PLACE, ATHENS.

S—CONCLUDED.

I Pet. 4. 3 For the time past of *our* life may suffice us to have wrought the will of the Gentiles, when we walked in lasciviousness, lusts, excess of wine, revellings, banquetings, and abominable idolatries :

T

Acts 10. 42 And he commanded us to preach unto the people, and to testify that it is he which was ordained of God *to be* the Judge of quick and dead.

Rom. 2. 16 In the day when God shall judge the secrets of men by Jesus Christ according to my gospel.

T—CONCLUDED.

Rom. 14. 10 But why dost thou judge thy brother? or why dost thou set at nought thy brother? for we shall all stand before the judgment seat of Christ.

Rom. 14. 12 So then every one of us shall give account of himself to God.

6

Or, *offered faith.*

U

Acts 2. 24 Whom God hath raised up, having loosed the pains of death; because it was not possible that he should be holden of it.

TIMOTHY. HE MINISTERS. TIME, A. D. 52-53.

written at this time from Corinth.

C

Acts 17. 2 And Paul, as his manner was, went in unto them, and three sabbath days reasoned with them out of the Scriptures,

D

Acts 17. 14 And then immediately the brethren sent away Paul to go as it were to the sea; but Silas and Timotheus abode there still.

15 And they that conducted Paul brought him unto Athens: and receiving a commandment unto Silas and Timotheus for to come to him with all speed, they departed.

E

Job 32. 18 For I am full of matter, the spirit within me constraineth me.

Acts 17. 3 Opening and alleging, that Christ must needs have suffered and risen again from the dead; and that this Jesus, whom I preach unto you, is Christ.

Acts 18. 28 For he mightily convinced the Jews, *and that* publicly, shewing by the Scriptures that Jesus was Christ.

1

Or, is *the Christ*

F

Acts 13. 45 But when the Jews saw the multitudes, they were filled with envy, and spake against those things which were spoken by Paul, contradicting and blaspheming.

II Tim. 2. 25 In meekness instructing those that oppose themselves; if God peradventure will give them repentance to the acknowledging of the truth ;

I Pet. 4. 4 Wherein they think it strange that

F—CONCLUDED.

ye run not with *them* to the same excess of riot, speaking evil of *you:*

G

Neh. 5. 13 Also I shook my lap, and said, So God shake out every man from his house, and from his labour, that performeth not this promise, even thus be he shaken out, and emptied. And all the congregation said, Amen, and praised the LORD. And the people did according to this promise.

Matt. 10. 14 And whosoever shall not receive you, nor hear your words, when ye depart out of that house or city, shake off the dust of your feet.

Acts 13. 51 But they shook off the dust of their feet against them, and came unto Iconium.

H

Lev. 20. 9 For every one that curseth his father or his mother shall be surely put to death: he hath cursed his father or his mother; his blood *shall be* upon him.

II Sa. 1. 16 And David said unto him, Thy blood *be* upon thy head; for thy mouth hath testified against thee, saying, I have slain the LORD'S anointed.

Eze. 18. 13 Hath given forth upon usury, and hath taken increase: shall he then live? he shall not live: he hath done all these abominations; he shall surely die; his blood shall be upon him.

Eze. 33. 4 Then whosoever heareth the sound of the trumpet, and taketh not warning; if the sword come, and take him away, his blood be upon his own head.

For I and K see next page (748).

§ 280. PAUL AT CORINTH. JOINED BY SILAS AND TIMOTHY.

CHAP. 18.

named Justus, *one* that worshipped
God, whose house joined hard to the
synagogue.
8 And [l]Crispus, the chief ruler of
the synagogue, believed on the Lord
with all his house; and many of the
Corinthians hearing believed, and
were baptized.
9 Then [m]spake the Lord to Paul in
the night by a vision, Be not afraid,
but speak, and hold not thy peace:
10 For [n]I am with thee, and no man
shall set on thee to hurt thee: for I
have much people in this city.
11 And he [2]continued *there* a year
and six months, teaching the word
of God among them.

I

Eze. 3. 19 Yet if thou warn the wicked, and he turn not from his wickedness, nor from his wicked way, he shall die in his iniquity; but thou hast delivered thy soul.

Eze. 33. 9 Nevertheless, if thou warn the wicked of his way to turn from it; if he do not turn from his way, he shall die in his iniquity; but thou hast delivered thy soul.

Acts 20. 26 Wherefore I take you to record this day, that I *am* pure from the blood of all *men*.

K

Acts 13. 46. *See d, D,* § 263, *page* 718.

L

I Cor. 1. 14 I thank God that I baptized none of you, but Crispus and Gaius;

M

Acts 23. 11 And the night following the Lord stood by him, and said, Be of good cheer, Paul: for as thou hast testified of me in Jerusalem, so must thou bear witness also at Rome.

§ 281. PAUL AND SOSTHENES BEFORE THE JUDGMENT

The *Second Epistle to the Thessalonians* was

18: 12–17.

12 And when Gallio was the deputy of Achaia, the Jews made insurrection with one accord against Paul,
and brought him to the judgment
seat,
13 Saying, This *fellow* persuadeth
men to worship God contrary to the
law.
14 And when Paul was now about to
open *his* mouth, Gallio said unto the
Jews, [a]If it were a matter of wrong or
wicked lewdness, O *ye* Jews, [b]reason

CHAP. 18.

would that I should bear with you:
15 [c]But if it be a question of words
and names, and *of* your law, look
ye *to it;* for I will be no judge of
such *matters*.
16 And he drave them from the
judgment seat.
17 Then all the Greeks took Sosthenes, the chief ruler of the synagogue, and beat *him* before the
judgment seat. And Gallio [d]cared
for none of those things.

§ 282. PAUL SAILS INTO SYRIA, COMES TO EPHESUS, GOES TO JERUSALEM

18: 18–22.

18 And Paul *after this* tarried *there*
yet a good while, and then took his
leave of the brethren, and sailed
thence into Syria, and with him Pris-

CHAP. 18.

cilla and Aquila; having [a]shorn *his*
head in [b]Cenchrea: for he had a vow.
19 And he came to Ephesus, and left
them there: but he himself entered

HE MINISTERS (CONCLUDED). TIME, A. D. 52–53.

N

Ex. 4. 12 Now therefore go, and I will be with thy mouth, and teach thee what thou shalt say.

Josh. 1. 5 There shall not any man be able to stand before thee all the days of thy life: as I was with Moses, *so* I will be with thee: I will not fail thee, nor forsake thee.

Judg. 2. 18 And when the LORD raised them up judges, then the LORD was with the judge, and delivered them out of the hand of their enemies all the days of the judge: for it repented the LORD because of their groanings by reason of them that oppressed them and vexed them.

Isa. 8. 10 Take counsel together, and it shall come to nought; speak the word, and it shall not stand: for God *is* with us.

Isa. 41. 10 Fear thou not; for I *am* with thee: be not dismayed; for I *am* thy God: I will strengthen thee: yea, I will help thee: yea, I will uphold thee with the right hand of my righteousness.

N—CONCLUDED.

Isa. 41. 13 For I the LORD thy God will hold thy right hand, saying unto thee, Fear not; I will help thee.

Isa. 43. 2 When thou passest through the waters, I *will be* with thee: and through the rivers, they shall not overflow thee: when thou walkest through the fire, thou shalt not be burned; neither shall the flame kindle upon thee.

Isa. 43. 5 Fear not: for I *am* with thee: I will bring thy seed from the east, and gather thee from the west;

Jer. 1. 19 And they shall fight against thee; but they shall not prevail against thee; for I *am* with thee, saith the LORD, to deliver thee.

Matt. 28. 20 Teaching them to observe all things whatsoever I have commanded you: and lo, I am with you alway, *even* unto the end of the world. Amen.

Rom. 8. 31 What shall we then say to these things? If God *be* for us, who *can be* against us?

2

Gr. *sat* there.

SEAT OF GALLIO. TIME, A. D. 53; PLACE, CORINTH.

written about this time from Corinth.

A

Acts 23. 29 Whom I perceived to be accused of questions of their law, but to have nothing laid to his charge worthy of death or of bonds.

Acts 25. 11 For if I be an offender, or have committed anything worthy of death, I refuse not to die: but if there be none of these things whereof these accuse me, no man may deliver me unto them. I appeal unto Cæsar.

Acts 25. 19 But had certain questions against him of their own superstition, and of one Jesus, which was dead, whom Paul affirmed to be alive.

B

Rom 13. 3 For rulers are not a terror to good works, but to the evil. Wilt thou then not be afraid of the power? do

B—CONCLUDED.

that which is good, and thou shalt have praise of the same:

C

II Tim. 2. 23 But foolish and unlearned questions avoid, knowing that they do gender strifes.

D

Amos 6. 6 That drink wine in bowls, and anoint themselves with the chief ointments: but they are not grieved for the affliction of Joseph.

Acts 17. 32 And when they heard of the resurrection of the dead, some mocked; and others said, We will hear thee again of this *matter*.

I Cor. 1. 23 But we preach Christ crucified, unto the Jews a stumblingblock, and unto the Greeks foolishness;

AND RETURNS TO ANTIOCH. TIME, SPRING AND SUMMER, A. D. 54.

A

Num. 6. 18 And the Nazarite shall shave the head of his separation *at* the door of the tabernacle of the congregation, and shall take the hair of the head of his separation, and put *it* in the fire which *is* under the sacrifice of peace offerings.

A—CONTINUED.

Acts 21. 24 Them take, and purify thyself with them, and be at charges with them, that they may shave *their* heads: and all may know that those things, whereof they were informed concerning thee, are nothing;

For A concluded and B see next page (750).

§ 282. PAUL SAILS TO SYRIA, COMES TO EPHESUS, GOES TO JERUSALEM

CHAP. 18.

into the synagogue, and reasoned
with the Jews.
20 When they desired *him* to tarry
longer time with them, he consented
not;
21 But bade them farewell, saying,
[c]I must by all means keep this feast
that cometh in Jerusalem: but I will
return again unto you, [d]if God will.
And he sailed from Ephesus.

CHAP. 18.

22 And when he had landed at Cesarea, and gone up, and saluted the church, he went down to Antioch.

A—CONCLUDED.

but *that* thou thyself also walkest orderly, and keepest the law.

B

Rom. 16. 1 I commend unto you Phebe our sister, which is a servant of the church which is at Cenchrea:

§ 283. PAUL'S THIRD MISSIONARY TOUR.

18: 23.

23 And after he had spent some
time *there*, he departed, and went
over *all* the country of [a]Galatia and
Phrygia in order, [b]strengthening all
the disciples.

A

Gal. 1. 2 And all the brethren which are with me, unto the churches of Galatia:

B

Deut. 3. 28 But charge Joshua, and encourage him, and strengthen him: for he shall go over before this people, and he shall cause them to inherit the land which thou shalt see.

B—CONTINUED.

Ezra 1. 6 And all they that *were* about them strengthened their hands with vessels of silver, with gold, with goods, and with beasts, and with precious things, besides all *that* was willingly offered.

Isa. 35. 3 Strengthen ye the weak hands, and confirm the feeble knees.
4 Say to them *that are* of a fearful heart, Be strong, fear not: behold, your God will come *with* vengeance, *even* God *with* a recompense; he will come and save you.

Da. 11. 1 Also I in the first year of Darius the Mede, *even* I, stood to confirm and to strengthen him.

Luke 22. 32 But I have prayed for thee, that thy faith fail not: and when thou art converted, strengthen thy brethren.

§ 284. APOLLOS' MINISTRY AT EPHESUS.

18: 24–28.

24 And [a]a certain Jew named Apollos, born at Alexandria, an eloquent
man, *and* mighty in the Scriptures,
came to Ephesus.
25 This man was instructed in the
way of the Lord; and being [b]fervent
in the spirit, he spake and taught diligently the things of the Lord, [c]know-
ing only the baptism of John.
26 And he began to speak boldly in
the synagogue: whom when Aquila
and Priscilla had heard, they took

CHAP. 18.

him unto *them*, and expounded unto
him the way of God more perfectly.
27 And when he was disposed to
pass into Achaia, the brethren wrote,
exhorting the disciples to receive
him: who, when he was come, [d]helped
them much which had believed
through grace:
28 For he mightily convinced the
Jews, *and that* publicly, [e]shewing
by the Scriptures that Jesus [1]was
Christ.

AND RETURNS TO ANTIOCH (CONCLUDED). TIME, SPRING AND SUMMER, A. D. 54.

C

Acts 19. 21 After these things were ended, Paul purposed in the spirit, when he passed through Macedonia and Achaia, to go to Jerusalem, saying, After I have been there, I must also see Rome.

Acts 20. 16 For Paul had determined to sail by Ephesus, because he would not spend the time in Asia: for he hasted, if it were possible for him, to be at Jerusalem the day of Pentecost.

D

Prov. 19. 21 *There are* many devices in a man's heart; nevertheless the counsel of the LORD, that shall stand.

D—CONCLUDED.

Acts 21. 14 And when he would not be persuaded, we ceased, saying, The will of the Lord be done.

I Cor. 4. 19 But I will come to you shortly, if the Lord will, and will know, not the speech of them which are puffed up, but the power.

Phil. 2. 24 But I trust in the Lord that I also myself shall come shortly.

Heb. 6. 3 And this will we do, if God permit.

Jas. 4. 15 For that ye *ought* to say, If the Lord will, we shall live, and do this, or that.

TIME, AUTUMN, A. D. 54; PLACE, FROM ANTIOCH.

B—CONTINUED.

Luke 22. 43 And there appeared an angel unto him from heaven, strengthening him.

Acts 14. 22 Confirming the souls of the disciples, *and* exhorting them to continue in the faith, and that we must through much tribulation enter into the kingdom of God.

Acts 15. 32 And Judas and Silas, being prophets also themselves, exhorted the brethren with many words, and confirmed *them*.

Acts 15. 41 And he went through Syria and Cilicia, confirming the churches.

Acts 16. 40 And they went out of the prison, and entered into *the house of* Lydia: and when they had seen the brethren, they comforted them, and departed.

B—CONCLUDED.

I Thes. 3. 2 And sent Timotheus, our brother, and minister of God, and our fellow labourer in the gospel of Christ, to establish you, and to comfort you concerning your faith:

I Thes. 4. 18 Wherefore comfort one another with these words.

I Thes. 5. 14 Now we exhort you, brethren, warn them that are unruly, comfort the feebleminded, support the weak, be patient toward all *men*.

Heb. 12. 12 Wherefore lift up the hands which hang down, and the feeble knees;
13 And make straight paths for your feet, lest that which is lame be turned out of the way; but let it rather be healed.

TIME, A. D. 53–55.

A

I Cor. 1. 12 Now this I say, that every one of you saith, I am of Paul; and I of Apollos; and I of Cephas; and I of Christ.

I Cor. 3. 5 Who then is Paul, and who *is* Apollos, but ministers by whom ye believed, even as the Lord gave to every man?
6 I have planted, Apollos watered; but God gave the increase.

Tit. 3. 13 Bring Zenas the lawyer and Apollos on their journey diligently, that nothing be wanting unto them.

B

Rom. 12. 11 Not slothful in business; fervent in spirit; serving the Lord;

C

Acts 19. 3 And he said unto them, Unto what then were ye baptized? And they said, Unto John's baptism.

D

I Cor. 3. 6. *See under A.*

II Cor. 1. 24 Not for that we have dominion over your faith, but are helpers of your joy: for by faith ye stand.

E

Acts 9. 22 But Saul increased the more in strength, and confounded the Jews which dwelt at Damascus, proving that this is very Christ.

Acts 17. 3 Opening and alleging, that Christ must needs have suffered, and risen again from the dead; and that this Jesus, whom I preach unto you, is Christ.

1

Or, *is the Christ*.

§ 285. PAUL INSTRUCTS DISCIPLES AT EPHESUS.

19: 1–7.

1 And it came to pass, that, while [a]Apollos was at Corinth, Paul having passed through the upper coasts came to Ephesus: and finding certain disciples,

2 He said unto them, Have ye received the Holy Ghost since ye believed? And they said unto him, [b]We have not so much as heard whether there be any Holy Ghost.

3 And he said unto them, Unto what then were ye baptized? And they said, [c]Unto John's baptism.

4 Then said Paul, [d]John verily baptized with the baptism of repentance, saying unto the people, that they should believe on him which should come after him, that is on Christ Jesus.

CHAP. 19.

5 When they heard *this*, they were baptized in the name of the Lord Jesus.

6 And when Paul had [e]laid *his* hands upon them, the Holy Ghost came on them; and [f]they spake with tongues, and prophesied.

7 And all the men were about twelve.

A

I Cor. 1. 12. *See a, A, § 284, page 750.*

B

I Sa. 3. 7 Now Samuel did not yet know the LORD, neither was the word of the LORD yet revealed unto him.

John 7. 39 (But this spake he of the Spirit, which they that believe on him should receive: for the Holy Ghost was not yet *given*; because that Jesus was not yet glorified.)

Acts 8. 16 (For as yet he was fallen on none of them: only they were baptized in the name of the Lord Jesus.)

§ 286. PAUL DISPUTING AND WORKING MIRACLES.

19: 8–20.

8 And [a]he went into the synagogue, and spake boldly for the space of three months, disputing and persuading the things [b]concerning the kingdom of God.

9 But [c]when divers were hardened, and believed not, but spake evil [d]of that way before the multitude, he departed from them, and separated the disciples, disputing daily in the school of one Tyrannus.

10 And [e]this continued by the space of two years; so that all they which dwelt in Asia heard the word of the Lord Jesus, both Jews and Greeks.

11 And [f]God wrought special miracles by the hands of Paul:

12 So [g]that from his body were brought unto the sick handkerchiefs

A

Acts 17. 2 And Paul, as his manner was, went in unto them, and three sabbath days reasoned with them out of the Scriptures,

Acts 18. 4 And he reasoned in the synagogue every sabbath, and persuaded the Jews and the Greeks.

B

Acts 1. 3 To whom also he shewed himself alive after his passion by many infallible proofs, being seen of them forty days, and speaking of the things pertaining to the kingdom of God:

Acts 28. 23 And when they had appointed him a day, there came many to him into *his* lodging; to whom he expounded and testified the kingdom of God, persuading them concerning Jesus, both out of the law of Moses, and *out of* the prophets, from morning till evening.

C

Rom. 11. 7 What then? Israel hath not obtained that which he seeketh for; but the election hath obtained it, and the rest were blinded.

TIME, A. D. 55.

B—CONCLUDED.

I Cor. 6. 19 What? know ye not that your body is the temple of the Holy Ghost *which is* in you, which ye have of God, and ye are not your own?

I Cor. 12. 1 Now concerning spiritual *gifts*, brethren, I would not have you ignorant.

C

Acts 18. 25 This man was instructed in the way of the Lord; and being fervent in the spirit, he spake and taught diligently the things of the Lord, knowing only the baptism of John.

D

Matt. 3. 11 I indeed baptize you with water unto repentance: but he that cometh after me is mightier than I, whose shoes I am not worthy to bear: he shall baptize you with the Holy Ghost, and with fire:

John 1. 15 John bare witness of him, and cried, saying, This was he of whom I spake, He that cometh after me is preferred before me: for he was before me.

D—CONCLUDED.

John 1. 27 He it is, who coming after me is preferred before me, whose shoe's latchet I am not worthy to unloose.

John 1. 30 This is he of whom I said, After me cometh a man which is preferred before me: for he was before me.

Acts 1. 5 For John truly baptized with water; but ye shall be baptized with the Holy Ghost not many days hence.

Acts 11. 16 Then remembered I the word of the Lord, how that he said, John indeed baptized with water; but ye shall be baptized with the Holy Ghost.

Acts 13. 24 When John had first preached before his coming the baptism of repentance to all the people of Israel.

25 And as John fulfilled his course, he said, Whom think ye that I am? I am not *he*. But, behold, there cometh one after me, whose shoes of *his* feet I am not worthy to loose.

E

Acts 6. 6. *See l, L, § 244, page 664.*

F

Acts 2. 4. *See e, E, § 230, page 634.*

BOOKS BURNED. TIME, A. D. 56; PLACE, EPHESUS.

C—CONCLUDED.

II Tim. 1. 15 This thou knowest, that all they which are in Asia be turned away from me; of whom are Phygellus and Hermogenes.

Heb. 3. 13 But exhort one another daily, while it is called To-day; lest any of you be hardened through the deceitfulness of sin.

II Pet. 2. 2 And many shall follow their pernicious ways; by reason of whom the way of truth shall be evil spoken of.

Jude 10 But these speak evil of those things which they know not: but what they know naturally, as brute beasts, in those things they corrupt themselves.

D

Acts 9. 2 And desired of him letters to Damascus to the synagogues, that if he found any of this way, whether they were men or women, he might bring them bound unto Jerusalem.

Acts 19. 23 And the same time there arose no small stir about that way.

Acts 22. 4 And I persecuted this way unto the death, binding and delivering into prisons both men and women.

Acts 24. 14 But this I confess unto thee, that after the way which they call heresy,

D—CONCLUDED.

so worship I the God of my fathers, believing all things which are written in the law and in the prophets:

E

Acts 20. 31 Therefore watch, and remember, that by the space of three years I ceased not to warn every one night and day with tears.

F

Mark 16. 20 And they went forth, and preached every where, the Lord working with *them*, and confirming the word with signs following. Amen.

Acts 14. 3 Long time therefore abode they speaking boldly in the Lord, which gave testimony unto the word of his grace, and granted signs and wonders to be done by their hands.

G

II Ki. 4. 29 Then he said to Gehazi, Gird up thy loins, and take my staff in thine hand, and go thy way: if thou meet any man, salute him not; and if any salute thee, answer him not again: and lay my staff upon the face of the child.

For G concluded see next page (754).

§ 286. PAUL DISPUTING AND WORKING MIRACLES.

CHAP. 19.

or aprons, and the diseases departed from them, and the evil spirits went out of them.

13 Then [h]certain of the vagabond Jews, exorcists, [i]took upon them to call over them which had evil spirits the name of the Lord Jesus, saying, We adjure you by Jesus whom Paul preacheth.

14 And there were seven sons of *one* Sceva, a Jew, *and* chief of the priests, which did so.

15 And the evil spirit answered and said, [k]Jesus I know, and Paul I know; but who are ye?

16 And the man in whom the evil spirit was leaped on them, and overcame them, and prevailed against them, so that they fled out of that house naked and wounded.

17 And this was known to all the Jews and Greeks also dwelling at Ephesus; and [l]fear fell on them all, and the name of the Lord Jesus was magnified.

CHAP. 19.

18 And many that believed came, and [m]confessed, and shewed their deeds.

19 Many of them also which used curious arts brought their books together, and burned them before all *men*: and they counted the price of them, and found *it* fifty thousand *pieces* of silver.

20 So [n]mightily grew the word of God and prevailed.

G—CONCLUDED.

II Ki. 13. 21 And it came to pass, as they were burying a man, that, behold, they spied a band *of men;* and they cast the man into the sepulchre of Elisha: and when the man was let down, and touched the bones of Elisha, he revived, and stood up on his feet.

Acts 5. 15 Insomuch that they brought forth the sick into the streets, and laid *them* on beds and couches, that at the least the shadow of Peter passing by might overshadow some of them.

H

Matt. 12. 27 And if I by Beelzebub cast out devils, by whom do your children cast *them* out? therefore they shall be your judges.

§ 287. PAUL'S PURPOSE. TIMOTHY AND ERASTUS SENT TO MACEDONIA.

The *First Epistle to the Corinthians* was written about

19: 21, 22.

21 [a]After these things were ended, Paul [b]purposed in the spirit, when he had passed through Macedonia and Achaia, to go to Jerusalem, saying, After I have been there, [c]I must also see Rome.

22 So he sent into Macedonia two of [d]them that ministered unto him, Timotheus and [e]Erastus; but he himself stayed in Asia for a season.

A

Rom. 15. 25 But now I go unto Jerusalem to minister unto the saints.

Gal. 2. 1 Then fourteen years after I went up again to Jerusalem with Barnabas, and took Titus with *me* also.

A—CONCLUDED.

Gal. 2. 2 And I went up by revelation, and communicated unto them that gospel which I preach among the Gentiles, but privately to them which were of reputation, lest by any means I should run, or had run, in vain.

B

Acts 20. 22 And now, behold, I go bound in the spirit unto Jerusalem, not knowing the things that shall befall me there:

C

Acts 18. 21 But bade them farewell, saying, I must by all means keep this feast that cometh in Jerusalem: but I will return again unto you, if God will. And he sailed from Ephesus.

Acts 23. 11 And the night following the Lord stood by him, and said, Be of good cheer, Paul: for as thou hast testified

BOOKS BURNED (CONCLUDED). TIME, A. D. 56; PLACE, EPHESUS.

I

Mark 9. 38 And John answered him, saying, Master, we saw one casting out devils in thy name, and he followeth not us: and we forbade him, because he followeth not us.

Luke 9. 49 And John answered and said, Master, we saw one casting out devils in thy name; and we forbade him, because he followeth not with us.

K

Matt. 8. 29 And, behold, they cried out, saying, What have we to do with thee, Jesus, thou Son of God? art thou come hither to torment us before the time?

Mark 1. 24 Saying, Let *us* alone; what have we to do with thee, thou Jesus of Nazareth? art thou come to destroy us? I know thee who thou art, the Holy One of God.

Mark 5. 7 And cried with a loud voice, and said, What have I to do with thee, Jesus, *thou* Son of the most high God? I adjure thee by God, that thou torment me not.

Acts 16. 17 The same followed Paul and us, and cried, saying, These men are the servants of the most high God, which shew unto us the way of salvation.

Jas. 2. 19 Thou believest that there is one God; thou doest well: the devils also believe, and tremble.

L

Luke 1. 65 And fear came on all that dwelt round about them: and all these sayings were noised abroad throughout all the hill country of Judea.

Luke 7. 16 And there came a fear on all: and they glorified God, saying, That a great prophet is risen up among us; and, that God hath visited his people.

Acts 2. 43 And fear came upon every soul: and many wonders and signs were done by the apostles.

Acts 5. 5 And Ananias hearing these words fell down, and gave up the ghost: and great fear came on all them that heard these things.

Acts 5. 11 And great fear came upon all the church, and upon as many as heard these things.

M

Jer. 3. 13 Only acknowledge thine iniquity, that thou has transgressed against the LORD thy God, and hast scattered thy ways to the strangers under every green tree, and ye have not obeyed my voice, saith the LORD.

Matt. 3. 6 And were baptized of him in Jordan, confessing their sins.

N

Acts 6. 7. *See m, M, § 244, page 664.*

IIThes. 3. 1 Finally, brethren, pray for us, that the word of the Lord may have *free* course, and be glorified, even as *it is* with you:

HE TARRIES IN ASIA. TIME, A. D. 57; PLACE, EPHESUS.

this time (Easter, Spring of A. D. 57) from Ephesus.

C—CONTINUED.

of me in Jerusalem, so must thou bear witness also at Rome.

Rom. 15. 23 But now having no more place in these parts, and having a great desire these many years to come unto you;

24 Whensoever I take my journey into Spain, I will come to you: for I trust to see you in my journey, and to be brought on my way thitherward by you, if first I be somewhat filled with your *company*.

25 But now I go unto Jerusalem to minister unto the saints.

26 For it hath pleased them of Macedonia and Achaia to make a certain contribution for the poor saints which are at Jerusalem.

27 It hath pleased them verily; and their debtors they are. For if the Gentiles have been made partakers of

C—CONCLUDED.

their spiritual things, their duty is also to minister unto them in carnal things.

Rom. 15. 28 When therefore I have performed this, and have sealed to them this fruit, I will come by you into Spain.

D

Acts 13. 5 And when they were at Salamis, they preached the word of God in the synagogues of the Jews: and they had also John to *their* minister.

E

Rom. 16. 23 Gaius mine host, and of the whole church, saluteth you. Erastus the chamberlain of the city saluteth you, and Quartus a brother.

IITim. 4. 20 Erastus abode at Corinth: but Trophimus have I left at Miletum sick.

§ 288. THE UPROAR AT EPHESUS.

19: 23–41.

23 And the same time there arose no small stir about that way.

24 For a certain *man* named Demetrius, a silversmith, which made silver shrines for Diana, brought [a]no small gain unto the craftsmen;

25 Whom he called together with the workmen of like occupation, and said, Sirs, ye know that by this craft we have our wealth.

26 Moreover ye see and hear, that not alone at Ephesus, but almost throughout all Asia, this Paul hath persuaded and turned away much people, saying that [b]they be no gods, which are made with hands:

27 So that not only this our craft is in danger to be set at nought; but also that the temple of the great goddess Diana should be despised, and her magnificence should be destroyed, whom all Asia and the world worshippeth.

28 And when they heard *these sayings*, they were full of wrath, and cried out, saying, [c]Great *is* Diana of the Ephesians.

29 And the whole city was filled with confusion: and having caught [d]Gaius and [e]Aristarchus, men of Macedonia, Paul's companions in travel, they rushed with one accord into the theatre.

30 And when Paul would have entered in unto the people, the disciples suffered him not.

31 And certain of the chief of Asia, which were his friends, sent unto him, desiring *him* that he would not adventure himself into the theatre.

CHAP. 19.

32 Some therefore cried one thing, and some another: for the assembly was confused; and the more part knew not wherefore they were come together.

33 And they drew Alexander out of the multitude, the Jews putting him forward. And [f]Alexander beckoned with the hand, and would have made his defence unto the people.

34 But when they knew that he was a Jew, all with one voice about the space of two hours cried out, Great *is* Diana of the Ephesians.

35 And when the townclerk had appeased the people, he said, *Ye* men of Ephesus, what man is there that knoweth not how that the city of the Ephesians is [1]a worshipper of the great goddess Diana, and of the *image* which fell down from Jupiter?

36 Seeing then that these things cannot be spoken against, ye ought to be quiet, and to do nothing rashly.

37 For ye have brought hither these men, which are neither robbers of churches, nor yet blasphemers of your goddess.

38 Wherefore if Demetrius, and the craftsmen which are with him, have a matter against any man, [2]the law is open, and there are deputies: let them implead one another.

39 But if ye inquire any thing concerning other matters, it shall be determined in a [3]lawful assembly.

40 For we are in danger to be called into question for this day's uproar, there being no cause whereby we may give an account of this concourse.

41 And [g]when he had thus spoken, he dismissed the assembly.

TIME, A. D. 57.

A

Acts 16. 16 And it came to pass, as we went to prayer, a certain damsel possessed with a spirit of divination met us, which brought her masters much gain by soothsaying:

Acts 16. 19 And when her masters saw that the hope of their gains was gone, they caught Paul and Silas, and drew *them* into the marketplace unto the rulers.

B

I Chr. 16. 26 For all the gods of the people *are* idols: but the LORD made the heavens.

Ps. 115. 4 Their idols *are* silver and gold, the work of men's hands.

Isa. 44. 9 They that make a graven image *are* all of them vanity; and their delectable things shall not profit; and they *are* their own witnesses; they see not, nor know; that they may be ashamed.

Isa. 46. 5 To whom will ye liken me, and make *me* equal, and compare me, that we may be like?

6 They lavish gold out of the bag, and weigh silver in the balance, *and* hire a goldsmith; and he maketh it a god: they fall down, yea, they worship.

7 They bear him upon the shoulder, they carry him, and set him in his place, and he standeth; from his place shall he not remove: yea, *one* shall cry unto him, yet can he not answer, nor save him out of his trouble.

Jer. 6. 30 Reprobate silver shall *men* call them, because the LORD hath rejected them.

Jer. 10. 3 For the customs of the people *are* vain: for *one* cutteth a tree out of the forest, the work of the hands of the workman, with the ax.

4 They deck it with silver and with gold; they fasten it with nails and with hammers, that it move not.

5 They *are* upright as the palm tree, but speak not: they must needs be borne, because they cannot go. Be not afraid of them; for they cannot do evil, neither also *is it* in them to do good.

Acts 17. 29 Forasmuch then as we are the offspring of God, we ought not to think that the Godhead is like unto gold, or silver, or stone, graven by art and man's device.

I Cor 8. 4 As concerning therefore the eating of those things that are offered in sacrifice unto idols, we know that an idol *is* nothing in the world, and that *there is* none other God but one.

C

Jer. 50. 38 A drought *is* upon her waters; and they shall be dried up: for it *is* the land of graven images, and they are mad upon *their* idols.

Rev. 13. 4 And they worshipped the dragon which gave power unto the beast: and they worshipped the beast, saying, Who *is* like unto the beast? who is able to make war with him?

D

Rom. 16. 23 Gaius mine host, and of the whole church, saluteth you. Erastus the chamberlain of the city saluteth you, and Quartus a brother.

I Cor. 1. 14 I thank God that I baptized none of you, but Crispus and Gaius.

E

Acts 20. 4 And there accompanied him into Asia Sopater of Berea; and of the Thessalonians, Aristarchus and Secundus: and Gaius of Derbe, and Timotheus; and of Asia, Tychicus and Trophimus.

Acts 27. 2 And entering into a ship of Adramyttium, we launched, meaning to sail by the coasts of Asia; *one* Aristarchus, a Macedonian of Thessalonica, being with us.

Col. 4. 10 Aristarchus my fellow prisoner saluteth you, and Marcus, sister's son to Barnabas, (touching whom ye received commandments: if he come unto you, receive him;)

Phile 24 Marcus, Aristarchus, Demas, Lucas, my fellow labourers.

F

I Tim. 1. 20 Of whom is Hymeneus and Alexander; whom I have delivered unto Satan, that they may learn not to blaspheme.

II Tim. 4. 14 Alexander the coppersmith did me much evil: the Lord reward him according to his works:

1

Gr. *the temple keeper.*

2

Or, *the court days are kept.*

3

Or, *ordinary.*

G

Prov. 15. 1 A Soft answer turneth away wrath: but grievous words stir up anger.

2 The tongue of the wise useth knowledge aright: but the mouth of fools poureth out foolishness.

Eccl. 9. 17 The words of wise *men are* heard in quiet more than the cry of him that ruleth among fools.

§ 289. PAUL DEPARTS INTO MACEDONIA. VISITS CORINTH.

The *Second Epistle to the Corinthians* was probably written (Autumn, A. D. 57)

20: 1–6.

1 And after the uproar was ceased, Paul called unto *him* the disciples, and embraced *them*, and [a]departed for to go into Macedonia.

2 And when he had gone over those parts, and had given them much exhortation, he came into Greece,

3 And *there* abode three months, And [b]when the Jews laid wait for him, as he was about to sail into Syria, he purposed to return through Macedonia.

4 And there accompanied him into Asia Sopater of Berea; and of the Thessalonians, [c]Aristarchus and Secundus; and [d]Gaius of Derbe, [e]and Timotheus; and of Asia, [f]Tychicus and [g]Trophimus.

5 These going before tarried for us at Troas.

6 And we sailed away from Philippi after [h]the days of unleavened bread, and came unto them [i]to Troas in five days; where we abode seven days.

A

I Cor. 16. 5 Now I will come unto you, when I shall pass through Macedonia: for I do pass through Macedonia.

II Cor. 7. 5 For, when we were come into Macedonia, our flesh had no rest, but we were troubled on every side; without *were* fightings, within *were* fears.

I Tim. 1. 3 As I besought thee to abide still at Ephesus, when I went into Macedonia, that thou mightest charge some that they teach no other doctrine,

B

Acts 9. 23 And after that many days were fulfilled, the Jews took counsel to kill him:

Acts 23. 12 And when it was day, certain of the Jews banded together, and bound themselves under a curse, saying that they would neither eat nor drink till they had killed Paul.

Acts 25. 3 And desired favour against him, that he would send for him to Jerusalem, laying wait in the way to kill him.

II Cor. 11. 26 *In* journeyings often, *in* perils of waters, *in* perils of robbers, *in* perils by *mine own* countrymen, *in* perils by the heathen, *in* perils in the city, *in* perils in the wilderness, *in* perils in the sea, *in* perils among false brethren;

C

Acts 19. 29. *See e, E, § 288, page 756.*

D

Acts 19. 29. *See d, D, § 288, page 756.*

§ 290. PAUL PREACHES LONG. EUTYCHUS FALLS FROM

The chronological order of this event is probably not clear

20: 7–12.

7 And upon [a]the first *day* of the week, when the disciples came together [b]to break bread, Paul preached unto them, ready to depart on the morrow; and continued his speech until midnight.

8 And there were many lights in [c]the upper chamber, where they were gathered together.

9 And there sat in a window a certain young man named Eutychus, being fallen into a deep sleep: and as Paul was long preaching, he sunk

A

John 20. 1 The first *day* of the week cometh Mary Magdalene early, when it was yet dark, unto the sepulchre, and seeth the stone taken away from the sepulchre.

I Cor. 16. 2 Upon the first *day* of the week let every one of you lay by him in store, as *God* hath prospered him, that there be no gatherings when I come.

Rev. 1. 10 I was in the spirit on the Lord's day, and heard behind me a great voice, as of a trumpet,

B

Luke 22. 19 And he took bread, and gave thanks, and brake *it*, and gave unto them, saying, This is my body which is given for you: this do in remembrance of me.

THEN COMES TO TROAS. TIME, SUMMER, A. D. 57–SPRING, A. D. 58.
from Macedonia. *Galatians* probably (Winter, A. D. 57) from Corinth.

E

Acts 16. 1. *See b, B, § 271, page 732.*

F

Eph. 6. 21 But that ye also may know my affairs, *and* how I do, Tychicus, a beloved brother and faithful minister in the Lord, shall make known to you all things:

Col. 4. 7 All my state shall Tychicus declare unto you, *who is* a beloved brother, and a faithful minister and fellow servant in the Lord:

IITim.4. 12 And Tychicus have I sent to Ephesus.

Tit. 3. 12 When I shall send Artemas unto thee, or Tychicus, be diligent to come unto me to Nicopolis: for I have determined there to winter.

G

Acts 21. 29 (For they had seen before with him in the city, Trophimus an Ephesian, whom they supposed that Paul had brought into the temple.)

IITim.4. 20 Erastus abode at Corinth: but Trophimus have I left at Miletum sick.

H

Ex. 12. 14 And this day shall be unto you for a memorial; and ye shall keep it a feast to the LORD throughout your generations: ye shall keep it a feast by an ordinance forever.

15 Seven days shall ye eat unleavened bread; even the first day ye shall put away leaven out of your houses:

H—CONCLUDED.

for whosoever eateth leavened bread from the first day until the seventh day, that soul shall be cut off from Israel.

Ex. 23. 15 Thou shalt keep the feast of unleavened bread: (thou shalt eat unleavened bread seven days, as I commanded thee, in the time appointed of the month Abib; for in it thou camest out from Egypt: and none shall appear before me empty:)

Acts 12. 3 And because he saw it pleased the Jews, he proceeded further to take Peter also. (Then were the days of unleavened bread.)

I Cor.5. 7 Purge out therefore the old leaven, that ye may be a new lump, as ye are unleavened. For even Christ our passover is sacrificed for us:

8 Therefore let us keep the feast, not with old leaven, neither with the leaven of malice and wickedness; but with the unleavened *bread* of sincerity and truth.

I

Acts 16. 8 And they passing by Mysia came down to Troas.

IICor.2. 12 Furthermore, when I came to Troas to *preach* Christ's gospel, and a door was opened unto me of the Lord,

IITim.4. 13 The cloak that I left at Troas with Carpus, when thou comest, bring *with thee*, and the books, *but* especially the parchments.

A WINDOW. TIME, SPRING, A. D. 57; PLACE, TROAS.
Visit to Troas probably occurred before his visit to Macedonia and Greece.

B—CONTINUED.

Luke 24. 35 And they told what things *were done* in the way, and how he was known of them in breaking of bread.

Acts 2. 42 And they continued steadfastly in the apostles' doctrine and fellowship, and in breaking of bread, and in prayers.

Acts 2. 46 And they, continuing daily with one accord in the temple, and breaking bread from house to house, did eat their meat with gladness and singleness of heart.

Acts 20. 11 When he therefore was come up again, and had broken bread, and eaten, and talked a long while, even till break of day, so he departed.

ICor.10. 16 The cup of blessing which we bless, is it not the communion of the blood of Christ? The bread which

B—CONCLUDED.

we break, is it not the communion of the body of Christ?

ICor.11. 23 For I have received of the Lord that which also I delivered unto you, That the Lord Jesus, the *same* night in which he was betrayed, took bread:

C

Luke22. 12 And he shall shew you a large upper room furnished: there make ready.

Acts 1. 13 And when they were come in, they went up into an upper room, where abode both Peter, and James, and John, and Andrew, Philip, and Thomas, Bartholomew, and Matthew, James *the son* of Alpheus, and Simon Zelotes, and Judas *the brother* of James.

§ 290. PAUL PREACHES LONG. EUTYCHUS FALLS FROM

CHAP. 20.

down with sleep, and fell down from
the third loft, and was taken up
dead.
10 And Paul went down, and [d]fell
on him, and embracing *him* said,
[e]Trouble not yourselves; for his life
is in him.
11 When he therefore was come up

CHAP. 20.

again, and had broken bread, and
eaten, and talked a long while, even
till break of day, so he departed.
12 And they brought the young man
alive, and were not a little comforted.

D

1 Ki. 17. 21 And he stretched himself upon the child three times, and cried unto

§ 291. PAUL'S JOURNEY TO MILETUS, WHITHER HE

The *Epistle to the Romans* was probably written from Corinth,

20: 13–17.

13 And we went before to ship, and
sailed unto Assos, there intending
to take in Paul: for so had he appointed, minding himself to go afoot.
14 And when he met with us at
Assos, we took him in, and came to
Mitylene.
15 And we sailed thence, and came
the next *day* over against Chios; and
the next *day* we arrived at Samos,

CHAP. 20.

and tarried at Trogyllium; and the
next *day* we came to Miletus.
16 For Paul had determined to sail
by Ephesus, because he would not
spend the time in Asia: for [a]he hasted, if it were possible for him, [b]to be
at Jerusalem [c]the day of Pentecost.
17 And from Miletus he sent to
Ephesus, and called the elders of
the church.

§ 292. PAUL'S ADDRESS AND FAREWELL TO THE EPHESIAN ELDERS.

20: 18–38.

18 And when they were come to
him, he said unto them, Ye know,
[a]from the first day that I came into
Asia, after what manner I have been
with you at all seasons,
19 Serving the Lord with all humility of mind, and with many tears, and
temptations, which befell me [b]by
the lying in wait of the Jews:
20 *And* how [c]I kept back nothing
that was profitable *unto you*, but have
shewed you, and have taught you
publicly, and from house to house,
21 [d]Testifying both to the Jews, and
also to the Greeks, [e]repentance to-

CHAP. 20.

ward God, and faith toward our
Lord Jesus Christ.
22 And now, behold, [f]I go bound in
the spirit unto Jerusalem, not knowing the things that shall befall me
there:

A

Acts 18. 19 And he came to Ephesus, and left them there: but he himself entered into the synagogue, and reasoned with the Jews.

Acts 19. 1 And it came to pass, that, while Apollos was at Corinth, Paul having passed through the upper coasts came to Ephesus: and finding certain disciples,

Acts 19. 10 And this continued by the space of two years; so that all they which dwelt in Asia heard the word of the Lord Jesus, both Jews and Greeks.

A WINDOW (CONCLUDED). TIME, SPRING, A. D. 57; PLACE, TROAS.

D—CONTINUED.

the LORD, and said, O LORD my God, I pray thee, let this child's soul come into him again.

I Ki. 17. 22 And the LORD heard the voice of Elijah; and the soul of the child came into him again, and he revived.

II Ki. 4. 34 And he went up, and lay upon the child, and put his mouth upon his mouth, and his eyes upon his eyes, and his hands upon his hands: and he stretched himself upon the child; and the flesh of the child waxed warm.

D—CONCLUDED.

II Ki. 4. 35 Then he returned, and walked in the house to and fro; and went up, and stretched himself upon him: and the child sneezed seven times, and the child opened his eyes.

E

Matt. 9. 24 He said unto them, Give place: for the maid is not dead, but sleepeth. And they laughed him to scorn.

Mark 5. 39 And when he was come in, he saith unto them, Why make ye this ado, and weep? the damsel is not dead, but sleepeth.

CALLS THE ELDERS. TIME, SPRING, A. D. 58.

(Spring, A. D. 58) then journeying by Philippi to Miletus.

A

Acts 18. 21 But bade them farewell, saying, I must by all means keep this feast that cometh in Jerusalem: but I will return again unto you, if God will. And he sailed from Ephesus.

Acts 19. 21 After these things were ended, Paul purposed in the spirit, when he had passed through Macedonia and Achaia, to go to Jerusalem, saying, After I have been there, I must also see Rome.

Acts 21. 4 And finding disciples, we tarried there seven days: who said to Paul through the Spirit, that he should not go up to Jerusalem.

A—CONCLUDED.

Acts 21. 12 And when we heard these things, both we, and they of that place, besought him not to go up to Jerusalem.

Acts 21. 15 And after those days we took up our carriages, and went up to Jerusalem.

B

Acts 24. 17 Now after many years I came to bring alms to my nation, and offerings.

C

Acts 2. 1 And when the day of Pentecost was fully come, they were all with one accord in one place.

I Cor. 16. 8 But I will tarry at Ephesus until Pentecost.

HIS DEPARTURE. TIME, SPRING, A. D. 58; PLACE, MILETUS.

B

Acts 20. 3 And *there* abode three months. And when the Jews laid wait for him, as he was about to sail into Syria, he purposed to return through Macedonia.

C

Acts 20. 27. *See text of topic, page 762.*

D

Acts 18. 5 And when Silas and Timotheus were come from Macedonia, Paul was pressed in the spirit, and testified to the Jews *that* Jesus *was* Christ.

E

Mark 1. 15 And saying, The time is fulfilled, and the kingdom of God is at hand: repent ye, and believe the gospel.

Luke 24. 47 And that repentance and remission of sins should be preached in his name among all nations, beginning at Jerusalem.

E—CONCLUDED.

Acts 2. 38 Then Peter said unto them, Repent, and be baptized every one of you in the name of Jesus Christ for the remission of sins, and ye shall receive the gift of the Holy Ghost.

F

Acts 19. 21. *See under A § 291.*

Acts 21. 13 Then Paul answered, What mean ye to weep and to break mine heart? for I am ready not to be bound only, but also to die at Jerusalem for the name of the Lord Jesus.

G

Acts 21. 4. *See under A, § 293, page 764.*

Acts 21. 11 And when he was come unto us, he took Paul's girdle, and bound his own hands and feet, and said, Thus saith the Holy Ghost, So shall the Jews at Jerusalem bind the man that owneth this girdle, and shall deliver *him* into the hands of the Gentiles.

For G concluded see next page (762).

§ 292. PAUL'S ADDRESS AND FAREWELL TO THE EPHESIAN ELDERS.

CHAP. 20.

23 Save that the [g]Holy Ghost witnesseth in every city, saying that bonds and afflictions [1]abide me.

24 But [h]none of these things move me, neither count I my life dear unto myself, [i]so that I might finish my course with joy, [k]and the ministry, [l]which I have received of the Lord Jesus, to testify the gospel of the grace of God.

25 And now, behold, [m]I know that ye all, among whom I have gone preaching the kingdom of God, shall see my face no more.

26 Wherefore I take you to record this day, that I *am* [n]pure from the blood of all *men*.

27 For [o]I have not shunned to declare unto you all [p]the counsel of God.

28 [q]Take heed therefore unto yourselves, and to all the flock, over the which the Holy Ghost [r]hath made you overseers, to feed the church of God, [s]which he hath purchased [t]with his own blood.

29 For I know this, that after my departing [u]shall grievous wolves enter in among you not sparing the flock.

30 Also [x]of your own selves shall men arise, speaking perverse things, to draw away disciples after them.

31 Therefore watch, and remember, that [y] by the space of three years I ceased not to warn every one night and day with tears.

32 And now, brethren, I commend you to God, and [z]to the word of his grace, which is able [a]to build you up,

For G see preceding page (761).

G—CONCLUDED.

I Thes. 3. 3 That no man should be moved by these afflictions: for yourselves know that we are appointed thereunto.

1

Or, *wait for me.*

H

Acts 21. 13 Then Paul answered, What mean ye to weep and to break mine heart? for I am ready not to be bound only, but also to die at Jerusalem for the name of the Lord Jesus.

Rom. 8. 35 Who shall separate us from the love of Christ? *shall* tribulation, or distress, or persecution, or famine, or nakedness, or peril, or sword?

II Cor. 4. 16 For which cause we faint not; but though our outward man perish, yet the inward *man* is renewed day by day.

I

II Tim. 4. 7 I have fought a good fight, I have finished *my* course, I have kept the faith:

K

Acts 1. 17 Eor he was numbered with us, and had obtained part of this ministry.

II Cor. 4. 1 Therefore, seeing we have this ministry, as we have received mercy, we faint not;

L

Gal. 1. 1 Paul, an apostle, (not of men, neither by man, but by Jesus Christ, and God the Father, who raised him from the dead;)

Tit. 1. 3 But hath in due times manifested his word through preaching, which is committed unto me according to the commandment of God our Saviour;

M

Acts 20. 38. *See text of topic, page 764.*

Rom. 15. 23 But now having no more place in these parts, and having a great desire these many years to come unto you;

N

Acts 18. 6 And when they opposed themselves, and blasphemed, he shook *his* raiment, and said unto them, Your blood *be* upon your own heads; I *am* clean: from henceforth I will go unto the Gentiles.

II Cor. 7. 2 Receive us; we have wronged no man, we have corrupted no man, we have defrauded no man.

HIS DEPARTURE (CONTINUED). TIME, SPRING, A. D. 58; PLACE, MILETUS.

O

Acts 20. 20. *See text of topic, page 760.*

P

Luke 7. 30 But the Pharisees and lawyers rejected the counsel of God against themselves, being not baptized of him.

John 15. 15 Henceforth I call you not servants; for the servant knoweth not what his lord doeth: but I have called you friends; for all things that I have heard of my father I have made known unto you.

Eph. 1. 11 In whom also we have obtained an inheritance, being predestinated according to the purpose of him who worketh all things after the counsel of his own will:

Q

Luke 21. 34 And take heed to yourselves, lest at any time your hearts be overcharged with surfeiting, and drunkenness, and cares of this life, and *so* that day come upon you unawares.

Col. 4. 17 And say to Archippus, Take heed to the ministry which thou hast received in the Lord, that thou fulfil it.

I Tim. 4. 16 Take heed unto thyself, and unto the doctrine; continue in them: for in doing this thou shalt both save thyself, and them that hear thee.

Heb. 12. 15 Looking diligently lest any man fail of the grace of God; lest any root of bitterness springing up trouble *you*, and thereby many be defiled;

I Pet. 5. 2 Feed the flock of God which is among you, taking the oversight *thereof*, not by constraint, but willingly; not for filthy lucre, but of a ready mind;

R

I Cor. 12. 28 And God hath set some in the church, first apostles, secondarily prophets, thirdly teachers, after that miracles, then gifts of healings, helps, governments, diversities of tongues.

S

Ps. 74. 2 Remember thy congregation, *which* thou hast purchased of old; the rod of thine inheritance, *which* thou hast redeemed; this mount Zion, wherein thou hast dwelt.

Isa. 53. 12 Therefore will I divide him *a portion* with the great, and he shall divide the spoil with the strong; because he hath poured out his soul unto death: and he was numbered with the transgressors; and he bare the sin of many, and made intercession for the transgressors.

S—CONCLUDED.

Eph. 1. 7 In whom we have redemption through his blood, the forgiveness of sins, according to the riches of his grace;

Eph. 1. 14 Which is the earnest of our inheritance until the redemption of the purchased possession, unto the praise of his glory.

Col. 1. 14 In whom we have redemption through his blood, *even* the forgiveness of sins:

Heb. 9. 12 Neither by the blood of goats and calves, but by his own blood he entered in once into the holy place, having obtained eternal redemption *for us*.

I Pet. 1. 19 But with the precious blood of Christ, as of a lamb without blemish and without spot:

Rev. 5. 9 And they sung a new song, saying, Thou art worthy to take the book, and to open the seals thereof: for thou wast slain, and hast redeemed us to God by thy blood out of every kindred, and tongue, and people, and nation;

T

Heb. 9. 14 How much more shall the blood of Christ, who through the eternal Spirit offered himself without spot to God, purge your conscience from dead works to serve the living God?

U

Matt. 7. 15 Beware of false prophets, which come to you in sheep's clothing, but inwardly they are ravening wolves.

II Pet. 2. 1 But there were false prophets also among the people, even as there shall be false teachers among you, who privily shall bring in damnable heresies, even denying the Lord that bought them, and bring upon themselves swift destruction.

X

I Tim. 1. 20 Of whom is Hymeneus and Alexander; whom I have delivered unto Satan, that they may learn not to blaspheme.

I Jno. 2. 19 They went out from us, but they were not of us; for if they had been of us, they would *no doubt* have continued with us: but *they went out*, that they might be made manifest that they were not all of us.

For X concluded, Y, Z and A, see next page (764).

§ 292. PAUL'S ADDRESS AND FAREWELL TO THE EPHESIAN ELDERS.

CHAP. 20.

and to give you [b]an inheritance
among all them which are sanctified.
33 [c]I have coveted no man's silver,
or gold, or apparel.
34 Yea, ye yourselves know, [d]that
these hands have ministered unto
my necessities, and to them that
were with me.
35 I have shewed you all things,
[e]how that so labouring ye ought to
support the weak, and to remember
the words of the Lord Jesus, how he
said, [f]It is more blessed to give than
to receive.
36 And when he had thus spoken,
he [g]kneeled down, and prayed with
them all.
37 And they all wept sore, and [h]fell
on Paul's neck, and kissed him,
38 Sorrowing most of all for the
words [i]which he spake, that they
should see his face no more. And
they accompanied him unto the
ship.

X—CONCLUDED.

Jude 4 For there are certain men crept in unawares, who were before of old ordained to this condemnation, ungodly men, turning the grace of our God into lasciviousness, and denying the only Lord God, and our Lord Jesus Christ.

Y

Acts 19. 10 And this continued by the space of two years; so that all they which dwelt in Asia heard the word of the Lord Jesus, both Jews and Greeks.

Z

Heb. 13. 9 Be not carried about with divers and strange doctrines. For *it is* a good thing that the heart be established with grace; not with meats, which have not profited them that have been occupied therein.

A

Acts 9. 31 Then had the churches rest throughout all Judea and Galilee and Samaria, and were edified; and walking in the fear of the Lord, and in the comfort of the Holy Ghost, were multiplied.

B

Acts 26. 18 To open their eyes, *and* to turn *them* from darkness to light, and *from* the power of Satan unto God, that they may receive forgiveness of sins, and inheritance among them which are sanctified by faith that is in me.

Eph. 1. 18 The eyes of your understanding being enlightened; that ye may know what is the hope of his calling, and what the riches of the glory of his inheritance in the saints,

Col. 1. 12 Giving thanks unto the Father, which hath made us meet to be partakers of the inheritance of the saints in light;

Col. 3. 24 Knowing that of the Lord ye shall receive the reward of the inheritance: for ye serve the Lord Christ.

Heb. 9. 15 And for this cause he is the mediator of the new testament, that by means of death, for the redemption of the transgressions *that were* under the first testament, they which are called might receive the promise of eternal inheritance.

§ 293. THEY COME TO TYRE AND PTOLEMAIS.

21: 1–7.

1 And it came to pass, that after
we were gotten from them, and had
launched, we came with a straight
course unto Coos, and the *day* following unto Rhodes, and from
thence unto Patara:

CHAP. 21.

2 And finding a ship sailing over
unto Phenicia, we went aboard, and
set forth.
3 Now when we had discovered Cyprus, we left it on the left hand, and
sailed into Syria, and landed at

HIS DEPARTURE (CONCLUDED). TIME, SPRING, A. D. 58; PLACE, MILETUS.

B—CONCLUDED.

I Pet. 1. 4 To an inheritance incorruptible, and undefiled, and that fadeth not away, reserved in heaven for you,

C

I Sa. 12. 3 Behold, here I *am:* witness against me before the LORD, and before his anointed: whose ox have I taken? or whose ass have I taken? or whom have I defrauded? whom have I oppressed? or of whose hand have I received *any* bribe to blind mine eyes therewith? and I will restore it you.

I Cor. 9. 12 If others be partakers of *this* power over you, *are* not we rather? Nevertheless we have not used this power; but suffer all things, lest we should hinder the gospel of Christ.

II Cor. 11. 9 And when I was present with you, and wanted, I was chargeable to no man: for that which was lacking to me the brethren which came from Macedonia supplied: and in all *things* I have kept myself from being burdensome unto you, *so* will I keep *myself*.

II Cor. 12. 17 Did I make a gain of you by any of them whom I sent unto you?

D

Acts 18. 3. *See b, B, § 280, page 746.*

E

Rom. 15. 1 We then that are strong ought to bear the infirmities of the weak, and not to please ourselves.

I Cor. 9. 12. *See under C.*

Eph. 4. 28 Let him that stole steal no more: but rather let him labour, working with *his* hands the thing which is good, that he may have to give to him that needeth.

I Thes. 4. 11 And that ye study to be quiet, and to do your own business, and to work with your own hands, as we commanded you;

E—CONCLUDED.

I Thes. 5. 14 Now we exhort you, brethren, warn them that are unruly, comfort the feebleminded, support the weak, be patient toward all *men*.

II Thes. 3. 8 Neither did we eat any man's bread for nought; but wrought with labour and travail night and day, that we might not be chargeable to any of you:

F

Matt. 10. 8 Heal the sick, cleanse the lepers, raise the dead, cast out devils: freely ye have received, freely give.

Luke 14. 13 But when thou makest a feast, call the poor, the maimed, the lame, the blind:

14 And thou shalt be blessed; for they cannot recompense thee: for thou shalt be recompensed at the resurrection of the just.

Heb. 13. 1 Let brotherly love continue.

2 Be not forgetful to entertain strangers: for thereby some have entertained angels unawares.

3 Remember them that are in bonds, as bound with them; *and* them which suffer adversity, as being yourselves also in the body.

G

Acts 7. 60. *See z, Z, § 246, page 676.*

H

Gen. 29. 11 And Jacob kissed Rachel, and lifted up his voice, and wept.

Gen. 33. 4 And Esau ran to meet him, and embraced him, and fell on his neck, and kissed him: and they wept.

Gen. 45. 14 And he fell upon his brother Benjamin's neck, and wept; and Benjamin wept upon his neck.

Gen. 46. 29 And Joseph made ready his chariot, and went up to meet Israel his father, to Goshen, and presented himself unto him; and he fell on his neck, and wept on his neck a good while.

I

Acts 20. 25. *See text of topic, page 762.*

TIME, SUMMER, A. D. 58.

CHAP. 21.

Tyre: for there the ship was to unlade her burden.

4 And finding disciples, we tarried there seven days: [a]who said to Paul through the Spirit, that he should not go up to Jerusalem.

A

Acts 20. 22 And now, behold, I go bound in the spirit unto Jerusalem, not knowing the things that shall befall me there:

23 Save that the Holy Ghost witnesseth in every city, saying that bonds and afflictions abide me.

Acts 21. 12 And when we heard these things, both we, and they of that place, besought him not to go up to Jerusalem.

§ 293. THEY COME TO TYRE AND PTOLEMAIS

CHAP. 21.

5 And when we had accomplished those days, we departed and went our way; [b]and they all brought us on our way, with wives and children, till *we were* out of the city: and [c]we kneeled down on the shore, and prayed.

CHAP. 21.

6 And when we had taken our leave one of another, we took ship; and they returned home again.

7 And when we had finished *our* course from Tyre, we came to Ptolemais, and [d]saluted the brethren, and abode with them one day.

§ 294. THEY COME TO THE HOUSE OF PHILIP THE EVANGELIST

21: 8–14.

8 And the next *day* we that were of Paul's company departed, and came unto Cesarea; and we entered into the house of Philip [a]the evangelist, [b]which was *one* of the seven; and abode with him.

9 And the same man had four daughters, [c]virgins, which did prophesy.

10 And as we tarried *there* many days, there came down from Judea a certain prophet, named [d]Agabus.

11 And when he was come unto us, he [e]took Paul's girdle, and bound his own hands and feet, and said, Thus saith the Holy Ghost, [f]So shall the Jews at Jerusalem bind the man that owneth this girdle, and shall deliver *him* into the hands of the Gentiles.

12 And when we heard these things, both we, and they of that place, besought him not to go up to Jerusalem.

13 Then Paul answered, [g]What mean ye to weep and to break mine heart? for [h]I am ready not to be bound only, but also to die at Jerusalem for the name of the Lord Jesus.

14 And when he would not be persuaded, we ceased, saying, [i]The will of the Lord be done.

A

Eph. 4. 11 And he gave some, apostles; and some, prophets; and some, evangelists; and some, pastors and teachers;

IITim.4. 11 Only Luke is with me. Take Mark, and bring him with thee: for he is profitable to me for the ministry.

B

Acts 6. 5 And the saying pleased the whole multitude: and they chose Stephen, a man full of faith and of the Holy Ghost, and Philip, and Prochorus, and Nicanor, and Timon, and Parmenas, and Nicolas a proselyte of Antioch:

Acts 8. 26 And the angel of the Lord spake unto Philip, saying, Arise, and go toward the south, unto the way that goeth down from Jerusalem unto Gaza, which is desert.

Acts 8. 40 But Philip was found at Azotus: and passing through he preached in all the cities, till he came to Cesarea.

C

Ex. 15. 20 And Miriam the prophetess, the sister of Aaron, took a timbrel in her hand; and all the women went out after her with timbrels and with dances.

Joel 2. 28 And it shall come to pass afterward, *that* I will pour out my Spirit upon all flesh; and your sons and your daughters shall prophesy, your old men shall dream dreams, your young men shall see visions:

D

Acts 11. 28 And there stood up one of them named Agabus, and signified by the Spirit that there should be great dearth throughout all the world: which came to pass in the days of Claudius Cæsar.

(CONCLUDED). TIME, SUMMER, A. D. 58.

B

Acts 15. 3 And being brought on their way by the church, they passed through Phenice and Samaria, declaring the conversion of the Gentiles: and they caused great joy unto all the brethren.

Acts 20. 38 Sorrowing most of all for the words which he spake, that they should see his face no more. And they accompanied him unto the ship.

C

Acts 20. 36 And when he had thus spoken, he

C—CONCLUDED.

kneeled down, and prayed with them all.

D

I Sa. 10. 4 And they will salute thee, and give thee two *loaves* of bread; which thou shalt receive of their hands.

I Sa. 13. 10 And it came to pass, that as soon as he had made an end of offering the burnt offering, behold, Samuel came; and Saul went out to meet him, that he might salute him.

IN CESAREA. TIME, SUMMER, A. D. 58.

E

I Sa. 15. 27 And as Samuel turned about to go away, he laid hold upon the skirt of his mantle, and it rent.

28 And Samuel said unto him, The LORD hath rent the kingdom of Israel from thee this day, and hath given it to a neighbour of thine, *that is* better than thou.

I Ki. 11. 30 And Ahijah caught the new gargarment that *was* on him, and rent it *in* twelve pieces:

31 And he said to Jeroboam, Take thee ten pieces: for thus saith the LORD, the God of Israel, Behold, I will rend the kingdom out of the hand of Solomon, and will give ten tribes to thee.

Jer. 13. 6 And it came to pass after many days, that the LORD said unto me, Arise, go to Euphrates, and take the girdle from thence, which I commanded thee to hide there.

Jer. 19. 10 Then shalt thou break the bottle in the sight of the men that go with thee,

11 And shalt say unto them, Thus saith the LORD of hosts; Even so will I break this people and this city, as *one* breaketh a potter's vessel, that cannot be made whole again: and they shall bury *them* in Tophet, till *there be* no place to bury.

Hos. 12. 10 I have also spoken by the prophets, and I have multiplied visions, and used similitudes, by the ministry of the prophets.

F

Acts 20. 23 Save that the Holy Ghost witnesseth in every city, saying that bonds and afflictions abide me.

Acts 21. 33 Then the chief captain came near, and took him, and commanded *him* to be bound with two chains; and de-

F---CONCLUDED.

manded who he was, and what he had done.

G

Acts 20. 24 But none of these things move me, neither count I my life dear unto myself, so that I might finish my course with joy, and the ministry, which I have received of the Lord Jesus, to testify the gospel of the grace of God.

H

Rom. 8. 35 Who shall separate us from the love of Christ? *shall* tribulation, or distress, or persecution, or famine, or nakedness, or peril, or sword?

II Cor. 4. 10 Always bearing about in the body the dying of the Lord Jesus, that the life also of Jesus might be made manifest in our body.

Col. 1. 24 Who now rejoice in my sufferings for you, and fill up that which is behind of the afflictions of Christ in my flesh, for his body's sake, which is the church:

II Tim. 4. 6 For I am now ready to be offered, and the time of my departure is at hand.

I

Matt. 26. 42 He went away again the second time, and prayed, saying, O my Father, if this cup may not pass away from me, except I drink it, thy will be done.

Luke 11. 2 And he said unto them, When ye pray, say, Our Father which art in heaven, Hallowed be thy name. Thy kingdom come. Thy will be done, as in heaven, so in earth.

Luke 22. 42 Saying, Father, if thou be willing, remove this cup from me: nevertheless, not my will, but thine, be done.

§ 295. PAUL'S RECEPTION BY JAMES AND THE ELDERS

21: 15-26.

15 And after those days we took up our carriages, and went up to Jerusalem.

16 There went with us also *certain* of the disciples of Cesarea, and brought with them one Mnason of Cyprus, [a]an old disciple, with whom we should lodge.

17 And [b]when we were come to Jerusalem, the brethren received us gladly.

18 And the *day* following Paul went in with us unto [c]James; and all the elders were present.

19 And when he had saluted them, [d]he declared particularly what things God had wrought among the Gentiles [e]by his ministry.

20 And when they heard *it*, they glorified the Lord, and said unto him, Thou seest, brother, how many thousands of Jews there are which believe; and they are all [f]zealous of the law:

21 And they are informed of thee, that thou teachest all the Jews which are among the Gentiles to forsake

CHAP. 21.

Moses, saying that they ought not to circumcise *their* children, neither to walk after the customs.

22 What is it therefore? the multitude must needs come together: for they will hear that thou art come.

23 Do therefore this that we say to thee: We have four men which have a vow on them;

24 Them take, and purify thyself with them, and be at charges with them, that they may [g]shave *their* heads: and all may know that those things, whereof they were informed concerning thee, are nothing; but *that* thou thyself also walkest orderly, and keepest the law.

25 As touching the Gentiles which believe, [h]we have written *and* concluded that they observe no such thing, save only that they keep themselves from *things* offered to idols, and from blood, and from strangled, and from fornication.

26 Then Paul took the men, and the next day purifying himself with them [i]entered into the temple, [k]to signify the accomplishment of the days of purification, until that an offering should be offered for every one of them.

§ 296. PAUL SEIZED IN AN UPROAR AND BOUND. HIS APPEAL TO

21: 27-40.

27 And when the seven days were almost ended, [a]the Jews which were of Asia, when they saw him in the temple, stirred up all the people, and [b]laid hands on him,

28 Crying out, Men of Israel, help: This is the man, [c]that teacheth all *men* every where against the people, and the law, and this place: and

A

Acts 24. 18. *See under I, § 295.*

B

Mark 10. 30 But he shall receive a hundredfold now in this time, houses, and brethren, and sisters, and mothers, and children, and lands, with persecutions; and in the world to come eternal life.

Acts 26. 21 For these causes the Jews caught me in the temple, and went about to kill *me*.

Rom. 8. 35 Who shall separate us from the love of Christ? *shall* tribulation, or distress, or persecution, or famine, or nakedness, or peril, or sword?

HIS PURIFICATION. TIME, SUMMER, A. D. 58; PLACE, JERUSALEM.

A

Rom. 16. 7 Salute Andronicus and Junia, my kinsmen, and my fellow prisoners, who are of note among the apostles, who also were in Christ before me.

B

Acts 15. 4 And when they were come to Jerusalem, they were received of the church, and *of* the apostles and elders, and they declared all things that God had done with them.

C

Acts 15. 13 And after they had held their peace, James answered, saying, Men *and* brethren, hearken unto me:

Gal. 1. 19 But other of the apostles saw I none, save James the Lord's brother.

D

Acts 15. 4. *See under B.*

Rom. 15. 18 For I will not dare to speak of any of those things which Christ hath not wrought by me, to make the Gentiles obedient, by word and deed,

19 Through mighty signs and wonders, by the power of the Spirit of God; so that from Jerusalem, and round about unto Illyricum, I have fully preached the gospel of Christ.

E

Acts 20. 24 But none of these things move me, neither count I my life dear unto myself, so that I might finish my course with joy, and the ministry, which I have received of the Lord Jesus, to testify the gospel of the grace of God.

F

Acts 22. 3 I am verily a man *which am* a Jew, born in Tarsus, *a city* in Cilicia, yet brought up in this city at the feet of Gamaliel, *and* taught according to the perfect manner of the law of the

F—CONCLUDED.

fathers, and was zealous toward God, as ye all are this day.

Rom. 10. 2 For I bear them record that they have a zeal of God, but not according to knowledge.

Gal. 1. 14 And profited in the Jews' religion above many my equals in mine own nation, being more exceedingly zealous of the traditions of my fathers.

G

Num. 6. 5 All the days of the vow of his separation there shall no razor come upon his head: until the days be fulfilled, in the which he separateth *himself* unto the LORD, he shall be holy, *and* shall let the locks of the hair of his head grow.

Num. 6. 18 And the Nazarite shall shave the head of his separation *at* the door of the tabernacle of the congregation, and shall take the hair of the head of his separation, and put *it* in the fire which *is* under the sacrifice of the peace offerings.

H

Acts 15. 20 But that we write unto them, that they abstain from pollutions of idols, and *from* fornication, and *from* things strangled, and *from* blood.

Acts 15. 29 That ye abstain from meats offered to idols, and from blood, and from things strangled, and from fornication: from which if ye keep yourselves, ye shall do well. Fare ye well.

I

Acts 24. 18 Whereupon certain Jews from Asia found me purified in the temple, neither with multitude, nor with tumult.

K

Num. 6. 18. *See under G.*

THE CHIEF CAPTAIN. TIME, SUMMER, A. D. 58; PLACE, JERUSALEM.

B—CONTINUED.

II Cor. 4. 9 Persecuted, but not forsaken; cast down, but not destroyed;

II Cor. 12. 10 Therefore I take pleasure in infirmities, in reproaches, in necessities, in persecutions, in distresses for Christ's sake: for when I am weak, then am I strong.

I Thes. 2. 14 For ye, brethren, became followers of the churches of God which in Judea are in Christ Jesus: for ye also have suffered like things of your own countrymen, even as they *have* of the Jews:

15 Who both killed the Lord Jesus,

B—CONCLUDED.

and their own prophets, and have persecuted us; and they please not God, and are contrary to all men:

I Thes. 2. 16 Forbidding us to speak to the Gentiles that they might be saved, to fill up their sins alway: for the wrath is come upon them to the uttermost.

II Tim. 3. 12 Yea, and all that will live godly in Christ Jesus shall suffer persecution.

C

Matt. 5. 11 Blessed are ye, when *men* shall revile you, and persecute *you*, and shall say all manner of evil against

For C concluded see next page 770.

§ 296. PAUL SEIZED IN AN UPROAR AND BOUND. HE APPEALS TO THE

CHAP. 21.

further brought Greeks also into the temple, and hath polluted this holy place.

29 (For they had seen before with him in the city, [d]Trophimus an Ephesian, whom they supposed that Paul had brought into the temple.)

30 And [e]all the city was moved, and the people ran together: and they took Paul, and drew him out of the temple: and forthwith the doors were shut.

31 And as they went [f]about to kill him, tidings came unto the chief captain of the band, that all Jerusalem was in an uproar.

32 [g]Who immediately took soldiers and centurions, and ran down unto them: and when they saw the chief captain and the soldiers, they left beating of Paul.

33 Then the chief captain came near, and took him, and [h]commanded *him* to be bound with two chains; and demanded who he was, and what he had done.

34 And some cried one thing, some another, among the multitude: and when he could not know the certainty for the tumult, he commanded him to be carried into the castle.

35 And when he came upon the stairs, so it was, that he was borne of the soldiers for the violence of the people.

36 For the multitude of the people followed after, crying, [i]Away with him.

37 And as Paul was to be led into the castle, he said unto the chief captain, May I speak unto thee? Who said, Canst thou speak Greek?

CHAP. 21.

38 [k]Art not thou that [l]Egyptian, which before these days madest an uproar, and leddest out into the wilderness four thousand men that were murderers?

39 But Paul said, [l]I am a man *which am* a Jew of Tarsus, *a city* in Cilicia, a citizen of no mean city: and, I beseech thee, [m]suffer me to speak unto the people.

40 And when he had given him license, Paul stood on the stairs, and [n]beckoned with the hand unto the people. And when there was made a great silence, he spake unto *them* in the Hebrew tongue, saying,

C—CONTINUED.

you falsely, for my sake.

Luke 6. 22 Blessed are ye, when men shall hate you, and when they shall separate you *from their company*, and shall reproach *you*, and cast out your name as evil, for the Son of man's sake.

Luke 11. 49 Therefore also said the wisdom of God, I will send them prophets and apostles, and *some* of them they shall slay and persecute:

Luke 21. 12 But before all these, they shall lay their hands on you, and persecute *you*, delivering *you* up to the synagogues, and into prisons, being brought before kings and rulers for my name's sake.

13 And it shall turn to you for a testimony.

John 15. 20 Remember the word that I said unto you, The servant is not greater than his lord. If they have persecuted me, they will also persecute you; if they have kept my saying, they will keep yours also.

Acts 6. 13 And set up false witnesses, which said, This man ceaseth not to speak blasphemous words against this holy place, and the law:

Acts 16. 20 And brought them to the magistrates, saying, These men, being Jews, do exceedingly trouble our city,

Acts 17. 6 And when they found them not, they drew Jason and certain brethren unto the rulers of the city, crying, These that have turned the world upside down are come hither also;

CHIEF CAPTAIN (CONCLUDED). TIME, SUMMER, A. D. 58; PLACE, JERUSALEM.

C—CONCLUDED.

Acts 24. 5 For we have found this man *a* pestilent *fellow*, and a mover of sedition among all the Jews throughout the world, and a ringleader of the sect of the Nazarenes:
6 Who also hath gone about to profane the temple: whom we took, and would have judged according to our law.

I Cor. 4. 12 And labour, working with our own hands: being reviled, we bless; being persecuted, we suffer it:

I Pet. 2. 12 Having your conversation honest among the Gentiles: that, whereas they speak against you as evildoers, they may by *your* good works, which they shall behold, glorify God in the day of visitation.

D

Acts 20. 4 And there accompanied him into Asia Sopater of Berea; and of the Thessalonians, Aristarchus and Secundus; and Gaius of Derbe, and Timotheus; and of Asia, Tychicus and Trophimus.

II Tim. 4. 20 Erastus abode at Corinth: but Trophimus have I left at Miletum sick.

E

Acts 26. 21. *See under B.*

F

II Cor. 11. 23 Are they ministers of Christ? (I speak as a fool,) I *am* more; in labours more abundant, in stripes above measure, in prisons more frequent, in deaths oft.

G

Acts 23. 27 This man was taken of the Jews, and should have been killed of them: then came I with an army, and rescued him, having understood that he was a Roman.

Acts 24. 7 But the chief captain Lysias came *upon us*, and with great violence took *him* away out of our hands,

H

Acts 20. 23 Save that the Holy Ghost witnesseth in every city, saying that bonds and afflictions abide me.

Acts 21. 11 And when he was come unto us, he took Paul's girdle, and bound his own hands and feet, and said, Thus saith the Holy Ghost, So shall the Jews at Jerusalem bind the man that owneth this girdle, and shall deliver *him* into the hands of the Gentiles.

I

Luke 23. 18 And they cried out all at once, saying, Away with this *man*, and release unto us Barabbas:

John 19. 15 But they cried out, Away with *him*, away with *him*, crucify him.

I—CONCLUDED.

Pilate saith unto them, Shall I crucify your King? The chief priests answered, We have no king but Caesar.

Acts 22. 22 And they gave him audience unto this word, and *then* lifted up their voices, and said, Away with such a *fellow* from the earth: for it is not fit that he should live.

K

Acts 5. 36 For before these days rose up Theudas, boasting himself to be somebody; to whom a number of men, about four hundred, joined themselves: who was slain; and all, as many as obeyed him, were scattered, and brought to nought.
37 After this man rose up Judas of Galilee in the days of the taxing, and drew away much people after him: he also perished; and all, *even* as many as obeyed him, were dispersed.

1

This Egyptian rose A. D. 55.

L

Acts 9. 11 And the Lord *said* unto him, Arise, and go into the street which is called Straight, and inquire in the house of Judas for *one* called Saul, of Tarsus: for, behold, he prayeth,

Acts 22. 3 I am verily a man *which am* a Jew, born in Tarsus, *a city* in Cilicia, yet brought up in this city at the feet of Gamaliel, *and* taught according to the perfect manner of the law of the fathers, and was zealous toward God, as ye all are this day.

II Cor. 11. 22 Are they Hebrews? so *am* I. Are they Israelites? so *am* I. Are they the seed of Abraham? so *am* I.

Phil. 3. 5 Circumcised the eighth day, of the stock of Israel, *of* the tribe of Benjamin, a Hebrew of the Hebrews; as touching the law, a Pharisee:

M

I Pet. 3. 15 But sanctify the Lord God in your hearts: and *be* ready always to *give* an answer to every man that asketh you a reason of the hope that is in you, with meekness and fear:

I Pet. 4. 16 Yet if *any man suffer* as a Christian, let him not be ashamed; but let him glorify God on this behalf.

N

Acts 12. 17 But he, beckoning unto them with the hand to hold their peace, declared unto them how the Lord had brought him out of the prison. And he said, Go shew these things unto James, and to the brethren. And he departed, and went into another place.

§ 297. PAUL MAKES HIS DEFENSE BEFORE THE

22 : 1-21.

1 Men, [a]brethren, and fathers, hear
ye my defence *which I make* now
unto you.
2 (And when they heard that he
spake in the Hebrew tongue to them;
they kept the more silence: and he
saith,)
3 [b]I am verily a man *which am* a
Jew, born in Tarsus, *a city* in Cilicia, yet brought up in this city [c]at
the feet of [d]Gamaliel, *and* taught [e]according to the perfect manner of the
law of the fathers, and [f]was zealous
toward God, [g]as ye all are this day.
4 [h]And I persecuted this way unto
the death, binding and delivering
into prisons both men and women.
5 As also the high priest doth bear
me witness, and [i]all the estate of the
elders: [k]from whom also I received
letters unto the brethren, and went
to Damascus, to bring them which
were there bound unto Jerusalem,
for to be punished.
6 And [l]it came to pass, that, as I
made my journey, and was come
nigh unto Damascus about noon,
suddenly there shone from heaven
a great light round about me.
7 And I fell unto the ground, and
heard a voice saying unto me, Saul,
Saul, why persecutest thou me?
8 And I answered, Who art thou,
Lord? And he said unto me, I am
Jesus of Nazareth, whom thou persecutest.
9 And [m]they that were with me saw
indeed the light, and were afraid;
but they heard not the voice of him
that spake to me.
10 And I said, What shall I do,
Lord? And the Lord said unto me,

CHAP. 22.

Arise, and go into Damascus; and
there it shall be told thee of all
things which are appointed for thee
to do.
11 And when I could not see for
the glory of that light, being led by
the hand of them that were with me,
I came into Damascus.
12 And [n]one Ananias, a devout
man according to the law, [o]having a
good report of all the [p]Jews which
dwelt *there*,
13 Came unto me, and stood, and
said unto me, Brother Saul, receive
thy sight. And the same hour I
looked up upon him.
14 And he said, [q]The God of our
fathers [r]hath chosen thee that thou

A

Acts 7. 2 And he said, Men, brethren, and fathers, hearken; The God of glory appeared unto our father Abraham, when he was in Mesopotamia, before he dwelt in Charran,

B

Acts 21. 39. *See l, L, § 276, page 770.*

C

Deut. 33. 3 Yea, he loved the people; all his saints *are* in thy hand: and they sat down at thy feet; *every one* shall receive of thy words.

II Ki. 4. 38 And Elisha came again to Gilgal: and *there was* a dearth in the land; and the sons of the prophets *were* sitting before him: and he said unto his servant, Set on the great pot, and seethe pottage for the sons of the prophets.

Luke 8. 35 Then they went out to see what was done; and came to Jesus, and found the man, out of whom the devils were departed, sitting at the feet of Jesus, clothed, and in his right mind: and they were afraid.

Luke 10. 39 And she had a sister called Mary, which also sat at Jesus' feet, and heard his word.

D

Acts 5. 34 Then stood there up one in the council, a Pharisee, named Gamaliel, a doctor of the law, had in reputation among all the people, and commanded to put the apostles forth a little space;

PEOPLE. TIME, SUMMER, A. D. 58; PLACE, JERUSALEM.

E

Acts 26. 5 Which knew me from the beginning, if they would testify, that after the most straitest sect of our religion I lived a Pharisee.

F

Gal. 1. 14 And profited in the Jews' religion above many my equals in mine own nation, being more exceedingly zealous of the traditions of my fathers.

G

Acts 21. 20 And when they heard *it*, they glorified the Lord, and said unto him, Thou seest, brother, how many thousands of Jews there are which believe; and they are all zealous of the law:

Rom. 10. 2 For I bear them record that they have a zeal of God, but not according to knowledge.

H

Acts 8. 3 As for Saul, he made havoc of the church, entering into every house, and haling men and women committed *them* to prison.

I Tim. 1. 13 Who was before a blasphemer, and a persecutor, and injurious: but I obtained mercy, because I did *it* ignorantly in unbelief:

I

Luke 22. 66 And as soon as it was day, the elders of the people and the chief priests and the scribes came together, and led him into their council, saying,

Acts 4. 5 And it came to pass on the morrow, that their rulers, and elders, and scribes,

K

Acts 9. 2 And desired of him letters to Damascus to the synagogues, that if he found any of this way, whether they were men or women, he might bring them bound unto Jerusalem.

Acts 26. 10 Which thing I also did in Jerusalem: and many of the saints did I shut up in prison, having received authority from the chief priests; and when they were put to death, I gave my voice against *them*.

Acts 26. 12 Whereupon as I went to Damascus with authority and commission from the chief priests,

L

Acts 9. 3 And as he journeyed, he came near Damascus: and suddenly there shined round about him a light from heaven:

Acts 26. 12. *See under K.*

Acts 26. 13 At midday, O king, I saw in the way a light from heaven, above the brightness of the sun, shining round about me and them which journeyed with me.

M

Da. 10. 7 And I Daniel alone saw the vision: for the men that were with me saw not the vision; but a great quaking fell upon them, so they fled to hide themselves.

Acts 9. 7 And the men which journeyed with him stood speechless, hearing a voice, but seeing no man.

N

Acts 9. 17 And Ananias went his way, and entered into the house; and putting his hands on him said, Brother Saul, the Lord, *even* Jesus, that appeared unto thee in the way as thou camest, hath sent me, that thou mightest receive thy sight, and be filled with the Holy Ghost.

O

Acts 10. 22 And they said, Cornelius the centurion, a just man, and one that feareth God, and of good report among all the nation of the Jews, was warned from God by a holy angel to send for thee into his house, and to hear words of thee.

P

I. Tim. 3. 7 Moreover he must have a good report of them which are without; lest he fall into reproach and the snare of the devil.

Q

Acts 3. 13 The God of Abraham, and of Isaac, and of Jacob, the God of our fathers, hath glorified his Son Jesus; whom ye delivered up, and denied him in the presence of Pilate, when he was determined to let *him* go.

Acts 5. 30 The God of our fathers raised up Jesus, whom ye slew and hanged on a tree.

R

Acts 9. 15 But the Lord said unto him, Go thy way: for he is a chosen vessel unto me, to bear my name before the Gentiles, and kings, and the children of Israel:

Acts 26. 16 But rise, and stand upon thy feet: for I have appeared unto thee for this purpose, to make thee a minister and a witness both of these things which thou hast seen, and of those things in the which I will appear unto thee;

§ 297. PAUL MAKES HIS DEFENSE BEFORE THE PEOPLE

CHAP. 22.

shouldest know his will, and [t]see
[t]that Just One, and [u]shouldest hear
the voice of his mouth.

15 [x]For thou shalt be his witness
unto all men of [y]what thou hast seen
and heard.

16 And now why tarriest thou?
arise, and be baptized, [z]and wash
away thy sins, [a]calling on the name
of the Lord.

17 And [b]it came to pass, that, when
I was come again to Jerusalem, even
while I prayed in the temple, I was
in a trance;

18 And [c]saw him saying unto me,
[d]Make haste, and get thee quickly
out of Jerusalem: for they will not
receive thy testimony concerning
me.

19 And I said, Lord, [e]they know
that I imprisoned and [f]beat in every
synagogue them that believed on
thee:

20 And [g]when the blood of thy
martyr Stephen was shed, I also was
standing by, and [h]consenting unto
his death, and kept the raiment of
them that slew him.

21 And he said unto me, Depart:
[i]for I will send thee far hence unto
the Gentiles.

S

I Cor. 9. 1 Am I not an apostle? am I not free? have I not seen Jesus Christ our Lord? are not ye my work in the Lord?

I Cor. 15. 8 And last of all he was seen of me also, as of one born out of due time.

T

Acts 3. 14 But ye denied the Holy One and the Just, and desired a murderer to be granted unto you;

Acts 7. 52 Which of the prophets have not your fathers persecuted? and they have slain them which shewed before of the coming of the Just One; of whom ye have been now the betrayers and murderers:

U

I Cor. 11. 23 For I have received of the Lord that which also I delivered unto you, That the Lord Jesus, the *same* night in which he was betrayed, took bread:

Gal. 1. 12 For I neither received it of man, neither was I taught *it*, but by the revelation of Jesus Christ.

X

Acts 23. 11 And the night following the Lord stood by him, and said, Be of good cheer, Paul: for as thou hast testified of me in Jerusalem, so must thou bear witness also at Rome.

Y

Acts 4. 20 For we cannot but speak the things which we have seen and heard.

Acts 26. 16 But rise, and stand upon thy feet: for I have appeared unto thee for this purpose, to make thee a minister and a witness both of these things which thou hast seen, and of those things in the which I will appear unto thee;

Z

Acts 2. 38 Then Peter said unto them, Repent, and be baptized every one of you in the name of Jesus Christ, for the remission of sins, and ye shall receive the gift of the Holy Ghost.

Heb. 10. 22 Let us draw near with a true heart in full assurance of faith, having our hearts sprinkled from an evil conscience, and our bodies washed with pure water.

A

Acts 9. 14 And here he hath authority from the chief priests to bind all that call on thy name.

§ 298. UPROAR RENEWED. PAUL ASSERTS ROMAN

22:22-30.

22 And they gave him audience
unto this word, and *then* lifted up
their voices, and said, [a]Away with

CHAP. 22.

such a *fellow* from the earth: for it
is not [b]fit that he should live.

23 And as they cried out, and cast

(CONCLUDED). TIME, SUMMER, A. D. 58; PLACE, JERUSALEM.

A—CONCLUDED.

Rom. 10. 13 For whosoever shall call upon the name of the Lord shall be saved.

B

Acts 9. 26 And when Saul was come to Jerusalem, he assayed to join himself to the disciples: but they were all afraid of him, and believed not that he was a disciple.

II Cor. 12. 2 I knew a man in Christ above fourteen years ago, (whether in the body, I cannot tell; or whether out of the body, I cannot tell: God knoweth;) such a one caught up to the third heaven.

C

Acts 22. 14. *See text of topic.*

D

Matt. 10. 14 And whosoever shall not receive you, nor hear your words, when ye depart out of that house or city, shake off the dust of your feet.

E

Acts 8. 3 As for Saul, he made havoc of the church, entering into every house, and haling men and women committed *them* to prison.

Acts 22. 4 And I persecuted this way unto the death, binding and delivering into prisons both men and women.

F

Matt. 10. 17 But beware of men: for they will deliver you up to the councils, and they will scourge you in their synagogues;

G

Acts 7. 58 And cast *him* out of the city, and stoned *him*: and the witnesses laid down their clothes at a young man's feet, whose name was Saul.

H

Luke 11. 48 Truly ye bear witness that ye allow the deeds of your fathers: for they indeed killed them, and ye build their sepulchres.

Acts 8. 1 And Saul was consenting unto his death. And at that time there was a

H—CONCLUDED.

great persecution against the church which was at Jerusalem; and they were all scattered abroad throughout the regions of Judea and Samaria, except the apostles.

Rom. 1. 32 Who, knowing the judgment of God, that they which commit such things are worthy of death, not only do the same, but have pleasure in them that do them.

I

Acts 9. 15. *See m, M, § 251, page 684.*

Acts 26. 17 Delivering thee from the people, and *from* the Gentiles, unto whom now I send thee,

18 To open their eyes, *and* to turn *them* from darkness to light, and *from* the power of Satan unto God, that they may receive forgiveness of sins, and inheritance among them which are sanctified by faith that is in me.

Rom. 15. 16 That I should be the minister of Jesus Christ to the Gentiles, ministering the gospel of God, that the offering up of the Gentiles might be acceptable, being sanctified by the Holy Ghost.

Gal. 1. 15 But when it pleased God, who separated me from my mother's womb, and called *me* by his grace,

16 To reveal his Son in me, that I might preach him among the heathen; immediately I conferred not with flesh and blood:

Eph. 3. 7 Whereof I was made a minister, according to the gift of the grace of God given unto me by the effectual working of his power.

8 Unto me, who am less than the least of all saints, is this grace given, that I should preach among the Gentiles the unsearchable riches of Christ;

I Tim. 2. 7 Whereunto I am ordained a preacher, and an apostle, (I speak the truth in Christ, *and* lie not;) a teacher of the Gentiles in faith and verity.

II Tim. 1. 11 Whereunto I am appointed a preacher, and an apostle, and a teacher of the Gentiles.

CITIZENSHIP. TIME, SUMMER, A. D. 58; PLACE, JERUSALEM.

A

Acts 21. 36. *See i, I, § 296, page 770.*

B

Acts 25. 24 And Festus said, King Agrippa, and all men which are here present

B—CONCLUDED.

with us, ye see this man, about whom all the multitude of the Jews have dealt with me, both at Jerusalem, and *also* here, crying that he ought not to live any longer.

§ 298. UPROAR RENEWED. PAUL ASSERTS ROMAN CITIZENSHIP

CHAP. 22.

off *their* clothes, and threw dust into
the air,
24 The chief captain commanded
him to be brought into the castle,
and bade that he [c]should be examined
by scourging; that he might know
wherefore they cried so against him.
25 And as they bound him with
thongs, Paul said unto the centurion
that stood by, [d]Is it lawful for you
to scourge a man that is a Roman,
and uncondemned?
26 When the centurion heard *that*,
he went and told the chief captain,
saying, Take heed what thou doest;
for this man is a Roman.
27 Then the chief captain came,
and said unto him, Tell me, art thou
a Roman? He said, Yea.
28 And the chief captain answered,
With a great sum obtained I this
freedom. And Paul said, But I was
free born.
29 Then straightway they departed
from him which should have [1]examined him; and [e]the chief captain also
was afraid, after he knew that he
was a Roman, and because he had
bound him.
30 On the morrow, because he would
have known the certainty wherefore
he was accused of the Jews, he loosed
him from *his* bands, and [f]commanded the chief priests and all their
council to appear, and brought Paul
down, and set him before them.

§ 299. PAUL'S DEFENSE BEFORE THE COUNCIL. THE LORD'S

23: 1-11.

1 And Paul, earnestly beholding
the council, said, Men *and* brethren,
[a]I have lived in all good conscience
before God until this day.
2 And the high priest Ananias commanded them that stood by him [b]to
smite him on the mouth.
3 Then said Paul unto him, God
shall smite thee, *thou* whited wall:
for sittest thou to judge me after the
law, [c]and commandest me to be
smitten contrary to the law?
4 And they that stood by said, Revilest thou God's high priest?
5 Then said Paul, [d]I wist not, breth
ren, that he was the high priest: for
it is written, [e]Thou shalt not speak
evil of the ruler of thy people.

A

Acts 24. 16 And herein do I exercise myself, to have always a conscience void of offence toward God, and *toward* men.

I Cor. 4. 4 For I know nothing by myself; yet am I not hereby justified; but he that judgeth me is the Lord.

II Cor. 1. 12 For our rejoicing is this, the testimony of our conscience, that in simplicity and Godly sincerity, not with fleshly wisdom, but by the grace of God, we have had our conversation in the world, and more abundantly to you-ward.

II Cor. 4. 2 But have renounced the hidden things of dishonesty, not walking in craftiness, nor handling the word of God deceitfully; but, by manifestation of the truth, commending ourselves to every man's conscience in the sight of God.

II Tim. 1. 3 I thank God, whom I serve from *my* forefathers with pure conscience, that without ceasing I have remembrance of thee in my prayers night and day;

Heb. 13. 18 Pray for us: for we trust we have a good conscience, in all things willing to live honestly.

(CONCLUDED). TIME, SUMMER, A. D. 58; PLACE, JERUSALEM.

C

John 19. 1 Then Pilate therefore took Jesus, and scourged *him*.

Acts 16. 22 And the multitude rose up together against them; and the magistrates rent off their clothes, and commanded to beat *them*.

23 And when they had laid many stripes upon them, they cast *them* into prison, charging the jailer to keep them safely:

Heb. 11. 36 And others had trials of *cruel* mockings and scourgings, yea, moreover of bonds and imprisonment:

D

Acts 16. 37 But Paul said unto them, They have beaten us openly uncondemned, being Romans, and have cast *us* into prison; and now do they thrust us out privily? nay verily; but let them come themselves and fetch us out.

Acts 25. 16 To whom I answered, It is not the manner of the Romans to deliver any man to die, before that he which is accused have the accusers face to face, and have license to answer for himself concerning the crime laid against him.

1

Or, *tortured him*,

Acts 22. 24. *See text of topic.*

Heb. 11. 35 Women received their dead raised to life again: and others were tortured, not accepting deliverance; that they might obtain a better resurrection:

E

Acts 16. 38 And the serjeants told these words unto the magistrates; and they feared, when they heard that they were Romans.

39 And they came and besought them, and brought *them* out, and desired *them* to depart out of the city.

F

Matt. 10. 17 But beware of men: for they will deliver you up to the councils, and they will scourge you in their synagogues;

Luke 21. 12 But before all these, they shall lay their hands on you, and persecute *you*, delivering *you* up to the synagogues, and into prisons, being brought before kings and rulers for my name's sake.

MESSAGE OF CHEER. TIME, SUMMER, A. D. 58; PLACE, JERUSALEM.

A—CONCLUDED.

I Pet. 3. 16 Having a good conscience; that, whereas they speak evil of you, as of evil doers, they may be ashamed that falsely accuse your good conversation in Christ.

B

I Ki. 22. 24 But Zedekiah the son of Chenaanah went near, and smote Micaiah on the cheek, and said, Which way went the Spirit of the LORD from me to speak unto thee?

Jer. 20. 2 Then Pashur smote Jeremiah the prophet, and put him in the stocks that *were* in the high gate of Benjamin, which *was* by the house of the LORD.

Mich. 5. 1 Now gather thyself in troops, O daughter of troops: he hath laid siege against us: they shall smite the judge of Israel with a rod upon the cheek.

Matt. 26. 67 Then did they spit in his face, and buffeted him; and others smote *him* with the palms of their hands,

John 18. 22 And when he had thus spoken, one of the officers which stood by struck Jesus with the palm of his hand,

B—CONCLUDED.

saying, Answerest thou the high priest so?

C

Lev. 19. 35 Ye shall do no unrighteousness in judgment, in meteyard, in weight, or in measure.

Deut. 25. 1 If there be a controversy between men, and they come unto judgment, that *the judges* may judge them; then they shall justify the righteous, and condemn the wicked.

2 And it shall be, if the wicked man *be* worthy to be beaten, that the judge shall cause him to lie down, and to be beaten before his face, according to his fault, by a certain number.

John 7. 51 Doth our law judge *any* man, before it hear him, and know what he doeth?

D

Acts 24. 17 Now after many years I came to bring alms to my nation, and offerings.

E

Ex. 22. 28 Thou shalt not revile the gods, nor curse the ruler of thy people.

For E. concluded see next page (778.)

§ 299. PAUL'S DEFENSE BEFORE THE COUNCIL. THE LORD'S MESSAGE

CHAP. 23.

6 But when Paul perceived that the one part were Sadducees, and the other Pharisees, he cried out in the council, Men *and* brethren, [f]I am a Pharisee, the son of a Pharisee: [g]of the hope and resurrection of the dead I am called in question.

7 And when he had so said, there arose a dissension between the Pharisees and the Sadducees: and the multitude was divided.

8 [h]For the Sadducees say that there is no resurrection, neither angel, nor spirit: but the Pharisees confess both.

9 And there arose a great cry: and the scribes *that were* of the Pharisees' part arose, and strove, saying, [i]We find no evil in this man: but [k]if a spirit or an angel hath spoken to him, [l]let us not fight against God.

10 And when there arose a great dissension, the chief captain, fearing lest Paul should have been pulled in pieces of them, commanded the soldiers to go down, and to take him by force from among them, and to bring *him* into the castle.

CHAP. 23.

11 And [m]the night following the Lord stood by him, and said, Be of good cheer, Paul: for as thou hast testified of me in Jerusalem, so must thou bear witness also at Rome.

E—CONCLUDED.

Eccl. 10. 20 Curse not the king, no not in thy thought; and curse not the rich in thy bedchamber: for a bird of the air shall carry the voice, and that which hath wings shall tell the matter.

IIPet. 2. 10 But chiefly them that walk after the flesh in the lust of uncleanness, and despise government. Presumptuous *are they*, selfwilled, they are not afraid to speak evil of dignities.

Jude 8 Likewise also these *filthy* dreamers defile the flesh, despise dominion, and speak evil of dignities.

F

Acts 26. 5 Which knew me from the beginning, if they would testify, that after the most straitest sect of our religion I lived a Pharisee.

Phil. 3. 5 Circumcised the eighth day, of the stock of Israel, *of* the tribe of Benjamin, a Hebrew of the Hebrews; as touching the law, a Pharisee;

G

Acts 24. 15 And have hope toward God, which they themselves also allow, that there shall be a resurrection of the dead, both of the just and unjust.

Acts 24. 21 Except it be for this one voice, that I cried standing among them, Touching the resurrection of the dead I am called in question by you this day.

§ 300. A CONSPIRACY. IT IS REVEALED. CHIEF CAPTAIN'S

23: 12-30.

12 And when it was day, [a]certain of the Jews banded together, and bound themselves [1]under a curse, saying that they would neither eat nor drink till they had killed Paul.

13 And they were more than forty which had made this conspiracy.

14 And they came to the chief priests and elders, and said, We have

CHAP. 23.

bound ourselves under a great curse, that we will eat nothing until we have slain Paul.

15 Now therefore ye with the council signify to to the chief captain that he bring him down unto you to morrow, as though ye would inquire something more perfectly concerning him: and we, or ever he come near, are ready to kill him.

OF CHEER (CONCLUDED). TIME, SUMMER, A. D. 58; PLACE, JERUSALEM.

G—CONCLUDED.

Acts 26. 6 And now I stand and am judged for the hope of the promise made of God unto our fathers:

H

Matt. 22. 23 The same day came to him the Sadducees, which say that there is no resurrection, and asked him,

Mark 12. 18 Then come unto him the Sadducees, which say there is no resurrection; and they asked him, saying,

Luke 20. 27 Then came to *him* certain of the Sadducees, which deny that there is any resurrection; and they asked him,

I

Acts 25. 25 But when I found that he had committed nothing worthy of death, and that he himself hath appealed to Augustus, I have determined to send him.

Acts 26. 31 And when they were gone aside, they talked between themselves, saying, This man doeth nothing worthy of death or of bonds.

K

Acts 22. 17 And it came to pass, that, when I was come again to Jerusalem, even while I prayed in the temple, I was in a trance;

18 And saw him saying unto me, Make haste, and get thee quickly out of Jerusalem: for they will not receive thy testimony concerning me.

L

Acts 5. 39 But if it be of God, ye cannot overthrow it; lest haply ye be found even to fight against God.

Acts 9. 4 And he fell to the earth, and heard a voice saying unto him, Saul, Saul, why persecutest thou me?

L—CONCLUDED.

5 And he said, Who art thou, Lord? And the Lord said, I am Jesus whom thou persecutest: *it is* hard for thee to kick against the pricks.

Acts 11. 17 Forasmuch then as God gave them the like gift as *he did* unto us, who believed on the Lord Jesus Christ; what was I, that I could withstand God?

M

Ps. 46. 1 God *is* our refuge and strength, a very present help in trouble.

2 Therefore will not we fear, though the earth be removed, and though the mountains be carried into the midst of the sea;

Isa. 41. 10 Fear thou not; for I *am* with thee: be not dismayed; for I *am* thy God: I will strengthen thee; yea, I will help thee; yea, I will uphold thee with the right hand of my righteousness.

Isa. 43. 2 When thou passest through the waters, I *will be* with thee; and through the rivers, they shall not overflow thee: when thou walkest through the fire, thou shalt not be burned; neither shall the flame kindle upon thee.

Acts 2. 25 For David speaketh concerning him, I foresaw the Lord always before my face, for he is on my right hand, that I should not be moved:

Acts 18. 9 Then spake the Lord to Paul in the night by a vision, Be not afraid, but speak, and hold not thy peace:

Acts 27. 23 For there stood by me this night the angel of God, whose I am, and whom I serve.

LETTER TO FELIX. TIME, SUMMER, A. D. 58; PLACE, JERUSALEM.

A

Ps. 64. 2 Hide me from the secret counsel of the wicked; from the insurrection of the workers of iniquity:

3 Who whet their tongue like a sword, *and* bend *their bows to shoot* their arrows, *even* bitter words:

4 That they may shoot in secret at the perfect; suddenly do they shoot at him, and fear not.

5 They encourage themselves *in* an evil matter: They commune of laying snares privily; they say, Who shall see them?

6 They search out iniquities; they

A—CONTINUED.

accomplish a diligent search: both the inward *thought* of every one *of them*, and the heart, *is* deep.

Isa. 8. 9 Associate yourselves, O ye people, and ye shall be broken in pieces; and give ear, all ye of far countries: gird yourselves, and ye shall be broken in pieces; gird yourselves, and ye shall be broken in pieces.

10 Take counsel together, and it shall come to nought; speak the word, and it shall not stand: for God *is* with us.

For A concluded and 1 see next page (780).

§ 300. A CONSPIRACY. IT IS REVEALED. CHIEF CAPTAIN'S

CHAP. 23.

16 And [b]when Paul's sister's son heard of their lying in wait, he went and entered into the castle, and told Paul.

17 Then Paul called one of the centurions unto *him*, and said, Bring this young man unto the chief captain: for he hath a certain thing to tell him.

18 So he took him, and brought *him* to the chief captain, and said, Paul the prisoner called me unto *him*, and prayed me to bring this young man unto thee, who hath something to say unto thee.

19 Then the chief captain took him by the hand, and went *with him* aside privately, and asked *him*, What is that thou hast to tell me?

20 And he said, [c]The Jews have agreed to desire thee that thou wouldest bring down Paul to morrow into the council, [d]as though they would inquire some what of him more perfectly.

21 But do not thou yield unto them: [e]for there lie in wait for him of them more than forty men, which have bound themselves with an oath, that they will neither eat nor drink till they have killed him: and now are they ready, looking for a promise from thee.

22 So the chief captain *then* let the young man depart, and charged *him*, *See thou* tell no man that thou hast shewed these things to me.

23 And he called unto *him* two centurions, saying, Make ready two hundred soldiers to go to Cesarea, and horsemen threescore and ten, and spearmen two hundred, at the third hour of the night;

24 And provide *them*[f] beasts, that they my set Paul on, and bring *him* safe unto Felix the governor.

25 And he wrote a letter after this manner:

26 Claudius Lysias unto the most excellent governor Felix *sendeth* greeting.

27 [g]This man was taken of the Jews, and should have been killed of them: then came I with an army, and rescused him, having understood that he was a Roman.

28 And[h] when I would have known the cause wherefore they accused him, I brought him forth into their council:

29 Whom I preceived to be accused [i]of questions of their law, [k]but to have nothing laid to his charge worthy of death or of bonds.

30 And when it was told me how that the Jews laid wait for the man, I sent straightway to thee, [l]and gave commandment to his accusers also to say before thee what *they had* against him. Farewell.

A—CONCLUDED.

Matt. 26. 4 And consulted that they might take Jesus by subtility, and kill *him*.

Acts 23. 21 and 30. *See text of topic.*

Acts 25. 3 And desired favor against him, that he would send for him to Jerusalem, laying wait in the way to kill him.

1

Or, *with an oath of execration.*

1 Sa. 3. 17 And he said, What *is* the thing that *the LORD* hath said unto thee? I pray thee hide *it* not from me: God do so to thee, and more also, if thou hide *any* thing from me of all the things that he said unto thee.

LETTER TO FELIX (CONCLUDED). TIME, SUMMER, A. D. 58; PLACE, JERUSALEM.

1—CONCLUDED.

I Sa. 20. 13 The LORD do so and much more to Jonathan: but if it please my father *to do* thee evil, then I will show it thee, and send thee away, that thou mayest go in peace: and the LORD be with thee, as he hath been with my father.

I Sa. 25. 22 So and more also do God unto the enemies of David, if I leave of all that *pertain* to him by the morning light any that pisseth against the wall.

II Sa. 3. 9 So do God to Abner, and more also, except, as the LORD hath sworn to David, even so I do to him;

I Ki. 2. 23 Then king Solomon sware by the LORD, saying, God do so to me, and more also, if Adonijah have not spoken this word against his own life.

I Ki. 19. 2 Then Jezebel sent a messenger unto Elijah, saying, So let the gods do *to me*, and more also, if I make not thy life as the life of one of them by to morrow about this time.

B

Job. 5. 13 He taketh the wise in their own craftiness: and the counsel of the froward is carried headlong.

Prov. 21. 30 *There is* no wisdom nor understanding nor counsel against the LORD.

Lam. 3. 37 Who *is* he *that* saith, and it cometh to pass, *when* the Lord commandeth *it* not?

C

Acts 23. 12. *See text of topic.*

D

Ps. 12. 2 They speak vanity every one with his neighbour: *with* flattering lips, *and* with a double heart do they speak.

Da. 6. 5 Then said these men, We shall not find any occasion against this Daniel, except we find *it* against him concerning the law of his God.

6 Then these presidents and princes assembled together to the king, and said thus unto him, King Darius, live for ever.

7 All the presidents of the kingdom, the governors, and the princes, the counsellors, and the captains, have consulted together to establish a royal statute, and to make a firm decree, that whosoever shall ask a petition of any God or man for thirty days, save of thee, O King, he shall be cast into the den of lions.

E

IICor. 11. 26 *In* journeyings often, *in* perils of waters, *in* perils of robbers, *in* perils by *mine own* countrymen, *in* perils by the heathen, *in* perils in the city, *in* perils in the wilderness, *in* perils in the sea, *in* perils among false brethren;

IICor. 11. 32 In Damascus the governor under Aretas the king kept the city of the Damascenes with a garrison, desirous to apprehend me:

33 And through a window in a basket was I let down by the wall, and escaped his hand.

F

Neh. 2. 12 And I arose in the night, I and some few men with me; neither told I *any* man what my God had put in my heart to do at Jerusalem: neither *was there any* beast with me, save the beast that I rode upon.

Esth. 8. 10 And he wrote in the king Ahasuerus' name, and sealed *it* with the king's ring, and sent letters by posts on horseback, *and* riders on mules, camels, *and* young dromedaries:

G

Acts 21. 33 Then the chief captain came near, and took him, and commanded *him* to be bound with two chains: and demanded who he was, and what he had done.

Acts 24. 7 But the chief captain Lysias came *upon us*, and with great violence took *him* away out of our hands,

H

Acts 22. 30 On the morrow, because he would have known the certainty wherefore he was accused of the Jews, he loosed him from *his* bands, and commanded the chief priests and all their council to appear, and brought Paul down, and set him before them.

I

Acts 18. 15 But if it be a question of words and names, and *of* your law, look ye *to it;* for I will be no judge of such *matters*.

Acts 25. 19 But had certain questions against him of their own superstition, and of one Jesus, which was dead, whom Paul affirmed to be alive.

K

Acts 26. 31 And when they were gone aside, they talked between themselves, saying, This man doeth nothing worthy of death or of bonds.

L

Acts 24. 8 Commanding his accusers to come unto thee: by examining of whom thyself mayest take knowledge of all these things, whereof we accuse him.

23: 31–35.

31 Then the soldiers, [a]as it was
commanded them, took Paul, and
brought *him* by night to Antipatris.
32 On the morrow they left the
horsemen to go with him, and returned to the castle:
33 Who, when they came to Cesarea, and delivered the epistle to the
governor, presented Paul also before
him.
34 And when the governor had read
the letter, he asked of what province

§ 301. PAUL IS TAKEN BEFORE THE

CHAP. 23.

he was. And when he understood
that *he was* of [b]Cilicia;
35 [c]I will hear thee, said he, when
thine accusers are also come. And
he commanded him to be kept in
[d]Herod's judgment hall.

A

Luke 7. 8 For I also am a man set under authority, having under me soldiers, and I say unto one, Go, and he goeth; and to another, Come, and he cometh; and to my servant, Do this, and he doeth *it*.

24: 1-9.

1 And after [a]five days [b]Ananias the
high priest descended with the elders, and *with* a certain orator *named*
Tertullus, who informed the governor against Paul.
2 And when he was called forth,
Tertullus began to accuse *him*, saying, [c]Seeing that by thee we enjoy
great quietness, and that very worthy
deeds are done unto this nation by
thy providence,
3 We accept *it* always, and in all
places, most noble Felix, with all
thankfulness.
4 Notwithstanding, that I be not
further tedious unto thee, I pray
thee that thou wouldest hear us of
thy clemency a few words.
5 For [d]we have found this man *a*
pestilent *fellow*, and a mover of sedition among all the Jews throughout the world, and a ringleader of
the sect of the Nazarenes:
6 [e]Who also hath gone about to
profane the temple: whom we took,
and would [f]have judged according to
our law.

§ 302. PAUL ACCUSED BEFORE FELIX.

CHAP. 24.

7 But [g]the chief captain Lysias
came *upon us*, and with great violence took *him* away out of our
hands,
8 [h]Commanding his accusers to
come unto thee: by examining of
whom thyself mayest take knowledge
of all these things, whereof we accuse
him.
9 And the Jews also assented, saying that these things were so.

A

Acts 21. 27 And when the seven days were almost ended, the Jews which were of Asia, when they saw him in the temple, stirred up all the people, and laid hands on him,

Acts 24. 11. *See text of topic § 303, page 784.*

B

Acts 23. 2 And the high priest Ananias commanded them that stood by him to smite him on the mouth.

Acts 23. 30 And when it was told me how that the Jews laid wait for the man, I sent straightway for thee, and gave commandment to his accusers also to say before thee what *they had* against him. Farewell.

Acts 23. 35. *See text of topic § 301.*

Acts 25. 2 Then the high priest and the chief of the Jews informed him against Paul, and besought him,

GOVERNOR AT CESAREA. TIME, A. D. 56.

A—CONCLUDED.

IITim. 2. 4 No man that warreth entangleth himself with the affairs of *this* life; that he may please him who hath chosen him to be a soldier.

B

Acts 21. 39 But Paul said, I am a man *which am* a Jew of Tarsus, *a city* in Cilica, a citizen of no mean city: and I beseech thee, suffer me to speak unto the people.

C

Acts 24. 1. *See text of topic, § 302*

Acts 22. 25 And as they bound him with thongs, Paul said unto the centurion that stood by, Is it lawful for you to scourge a man that is a Roman, and uncondemned?

26 When the ceuturion heard *that*,

C—CONCLUDED.

he went and told the chief captain, saying, Take heed what thou doest: for this man is a Roman.

27 Then the chief captain came, and said unto him, Tell me, art thou a Roman? He said, Yea.

Acts 25. 16 To whom I answered, It is not the manner of the Romans to deliver any man to die, before that he which is accused have the accusers face to face, and have license to answer for himself concerning the crime laid against him.

D

Matt. 27. 27 Then the soldiers of the governor took Jesus into the common hall, and gathered unto him the whole band *of soldiers*.

TIME, A. D. 59; PLACE, CESAREA.

C

Ps. 5. 9 For *there is* no faithfulness in their mouth; their inward part *is* very wickedness; their throat *is* an open sepulchre; they flatter with their tongue.

Ps. 10. 3 For the wicked boasteth of his heart's desire, and blesseth the covetous, *whom* the LORD abhorreth.

Ps. 12. 2 They speak vanity every one with his neighbour: *with* flattering lips, *and* with a double heart do they speak.

Ps. 28. 3 Draw me not away with the wicked, and with the workers of iniquity, which speak peace to their neighbours, but mischief *is* in their hearts.

Prov. 26. 28 A lying tongue hateth *those that are* afflicted by it; and a flattering mouth worketh ruin.

Prov. 29. 5 A man that flattereth his neighbour spreadeth a net for his feet.

Jude 16 These are murmurers, complainers, walking after their own lusts; and their mouth speaketh great swelling *words*, having men's persons in admiration because of advantage.

D

Luke 23. 2 And they began to accuse him, saying, We found this *fellow* perverting the nation, and forbidding to give tribute to Cæsar, saying that he himself is Christ a king.

Acts 6. 13 And set up false witnesses, which said, This man ceaseth not to speak blasphemous words against this holy place, and the law:

Acts 16. 20 And brought them to the magistrates, saying, These men, being Jews, do exceedingly trouble our city,

D—CONCLUDED.

Acts 17. 6 And when they found them not, they drew Jason and certain brethren unto the rulers of the city, crying, These that have turned the world upside down are come hither also;

7 Whom Jason hath received: and these all do contrary to the decrees of Cæsar, saying that there is another king, *one* Jesus.

I Pet. 2. 12 Having your conversation honest among the Gentiles: that, whereas they speak against you as evil doers, they may by *your* good works, which they shall behold, glorify God in the day of visitation.

E

Acts 21. 28 Crying out, Men of Israel, help: This is the man, that teacheth all *men* every where against the people, and the law, and this place; and further brought Greeks also into the temple, and hath polluted this holy place.

F

John 18. 31 Then said Pilate unto them, Take ye him, and judge him according to your law. The Jews therefore said unto him, It is not lawful for us to put any man to death:

G

Acts 21. 31 And as they went about to kill him, tidings came unto the chief captain of the band, that all Jerusalem was in an uproar:

H

Acts 23. 3c. *See under B.*

§ 303. PAUL'S DEFENSE BEFORE FELIX.

24:10-21.

10 Then Paul, after that the governor had beckoned unto him to speak, answered, Forasmuch as I know that thou hast been of many years a judge unto this nation, I do the more cheerfully answer for myself:

11 Because that thou mayest understand, that there are yet but twelve days since I went up to Jerusalem [a]for to worship.

12 And [b]they neither found me in the temple disputing with any man, neither raising up the people, neither in the synagogues, nor in the city:

13 Neither can they prove the things whereof they now accuse me.

14 But this I confess unto thee, that after the [c]way which they call heresy, so worship I the [d]God of my fathers, believing all things which are written in [e]the law and in the prophets:

15 And [f]have hope toward God, which they themselves also allow, [g]that there shall be a resurrection of the dead, both of the just and unjust.

16 And [h]herein do I exercise myself, to have always a conscience void of offence toward God, and *toward* men.

17 Now after many years [i]I came to bring alms to my nation, and offerings.

18 [k]Whereupon certain Jews from Asia found me purified in the temple, neither with multitude, nor with tumult.

19 [l]Who ought to have been here before thee, and object, if they had aught against me.

20 Or else let these same *here* say, if they have found any evil doing in

A

Acts 21. 26 Then Paul took the men, and the next day purifying himself with them entered into the temple, to signify the accomplishment of the days of purification, until that an offering should be offered for every one of them.

Acts 24. 17. *See text of topic.*

B

Acts 25. 8 While he answered for himself, Neither against the law of the Jews, neither against the temple, nor yet against Cæsar, have I offended any thing at all.

Acts 28. 17 And it came to pass, that after three days Paul called the chief of the Jews together: and when they were come together, he said unto them, Men *and* brethren, though I have committed nothing against the people, or customs of our fathers, yet was I delivered prisoner from Jerusalem into the hands of the Romans.

C

Ps. 119. 46 I will speak of thy testimonies also before kings, and will not be ashamed.

Amos 8. 14 They that swear by the sin of Samaria, and say, Thy God, O Dan, liveth; and, The manner of Beer-sheba liveth; even they shall fall, and never rise up again.

Mic. 4. 5 For all people will walk every one in the name of his god, and we will walk in the name of the LORD our God for ever and ever.

Acts 9. 2 And desired of him letters to Damascus to the synagogues, that if he found any of this way, whether they were men or women, he might bring them bound unto Jerusalem.

D

IITim. 1. 3 I thank God, whom I serve from *my* forefathers with pure conscience, that without ceasing I have remembrance of thee in my prayers night and day;

E

Acts 26. 22 Having therefore obtained help of God, I continue unto this day, witnessing both to small and great, saying none other things than those which the prophets and Moses did say should come.

Acts 28. 23 And when they had appointed him a day, there came many to him into *his* lodging; to whom he expounded and testified the kingdom of God, persuading them concerning Jesus, both out of the law of Moses,

Time, A. D. 59; Place, Cesarea.

E—Concluded.

and *out of* the prophets, from morning till evening.

IICor. 1. 20 For all the promises of God in him *are* yea, and in him Amen, unto the glory of God by us.

F

Acts 23. 6 But when Paul perceived that the one part were Sadducees, and the other Pharisees, he cried out in the council, Men *and* brethren, I am a Pharisee, the Son of a Pharisee: of the hope and resurrection of the dead I am called in question.

Acts 26. 6 And now I stand and am judged for the hope of the promise made of God unto our fathers:

7 Unto which *promise* our twelve tribes, instantly serving *God* day and night, hope to come. For which hope's sake, king Agrippa, I am accused of the Jews.

Acts 28. 20 For this cause therefore have I called for you, to see *you*, and to speak with *you*: because that for the hope of Israel I am bound with this chain.

G

Job 19. 25 For I know *that* my Redeemer liveth, and *that* he shall stand at the latter *day* upon the earth:

26 And *though* after my skin *worms* destroy this *body*, yet in my flesh shall I see God:

Isa. 26. 19 Thy dead *men* shall live, *together with* my dead body shall they arise. Awake and sing, ye that dwell in dust: for thy dew *is as* the dew of herbs, and the earth shall cast out the dead.

Eze. 37. *Read entire chapter.*

Da. 12. 2 And many of them that sleep in the dust of the earth shall awake, some to everlasting life, and some to shame *and* everlasting contempt.

John 5. 28 Marvel not at this: for the hour is coming, in the which all that are in the graves shall hear his voice,

29 And shall come forth; they that have done good, unto the resurrection of life; and they that have done evil, unto the resurrection of damnation.

John 11. 23 Jesus saith unto her, Thy brother shall rise again.

24 Martha saith unto him, I know that he shall rise again in the resurrection at the last day.

ICor. 15. 12 Now if Christ be preached that he rose from the dead, how say some among you that there is no resurrection of the dead?

G—Concluded.

ICor. 15. 13 But if there be no resurrection of the dead, then is Christ not risen:

14 And if Christ be not risen, then *is* our preaching vain, and your faith *is* also vain.

ICor. 15. 53 For this corruptible must put on incorruption, and this mortal *must* put on immortality.

IThes. 4. 14 For if we believe that Jesus died and rose again, even so them also which sleep in Jesus will God bring with him.

Rev. 20. 6 Blessed and holy *is* he that hath part in the first resurrection: on such the second death hath no power, but they shall be priests of God and of Christ, and shall reign with him a thousand years.

Rev. 20. 12 And I saw the dead, small and great, stand before God; and the books were opened: and another book was opened, which is *the book* of life: and the dead were judged out of those things which were written in the books, according to their works.

H

Acts 23. 1 And Paul, earnestly beholding the council, said, Men *and* brethren, I have lived in all good conscience before God until this day.

I

Acts 11. 29 Then the disciples, every man according to his ability, determined to send relief unto the brethren which dwelt in Judea:

30 Which also they did, and sent it to the elders by the hands of Barnabas and Saul.

Acts 20. 16 For Paul had determined to sail by Ephesus, because he would not spend the time in Asia: for he hasted, if it were possible for him, to be at Jerusalem the day of Pentecost.

Rom. 15. 25 But now I go unto Jerusalem to minister unto the saints.

IICor. 8. 5 And *this they did*, not as we hoped, but first gave their own selves to the Lord, and unto us by the will of God.

Gal. 2. 10 Only *they would* that we should remember the poor; the same which I also was forward to do.

K

Acts 21. 26. *See under A.*

Acts 21. 27 And when the seven days were almost ended, the Jews which were of Asia, when they saw him in the temple, stirred up all the people, and laid hands on him,

For K concluded and L, see next page (786).

§ 303. PAUL'S DEFENSE BEFORE FELIX

CHAP. 24.

me, while I stood before the council,
21 Except it be for this one voice,
that I cried standing among them,
[m]Touching the resurrection of the
dead I am called in question by you
this day.

K—CONCLUDED.

Acts 26. 21 For these causes the Jews caught me in the temple, and went about to kill *me*.

L

Acts 23. 30 And when it was told me how that the Jews laid wait for the man, I sent straightway to thee, and gave commandment to his accusers also to say before thee what *they had* against him. Farewell.

§ 304. FELIX AND DRUSILLA HEAR PAUL. HE IS RETAINED

24 : 22-27.

22 And when Felix heard these
things, having more perfect knowledge of *that* way, he deferred them,
and said, When [a]Lysias the chief
captain shall come down, I will know
the uttermost of your matter.
23 And he commanded a centurion
to keep Paul, and to let *him* have liberty and [b]that he should forbid none
of his acquaintance to minister or
come unto him.
24 And after certain days, when
Felix came with his wife Drusilla,
which was a Jewess, he sent for Paul,
and heard him concerning the faith
in Christ.

CHAP. 24.

25 And as he reasoned of righteousness, temperance, and judgment to
come, Felix trembled, and answered,
Go thy way for this time; [c]when I
have a convenient season, I will call
for thee.
26 He hoped also that [d]money
should have been given him of Paul,
that he might loose him: wherefore
he sent for him the oftener, and communed with him.
27 But after two years Porcius Festus came into Felix' room: and
Felix, [e]willing to shew the Jews a
pleasure, left Paul bound.

§ 305. FESTUS VISITS JERUSALEM. JEWS SEEK

25 : 1-6.

1 Now when Festus was come into
the province, after three days he ascended from Cesarea to Jerusalem.
2 Then[a] the high priest and the
chief of the Jews informed him
against Paul, and besought him,
3 And desired favour against him,
that he would send for him to Jerusalem, laying[b] wait in the way to kill
him.
4 But Festus answered, that Paul

CHAP. 25.

should be kept at Cesarea, and that he
himself would depart shortly *thither*.
5 Let them therefore, said he, which
among you are able, go down with
me, and accuse this man, [c]if there be
any wickedness in him.
6 And when he had tarried among
them [1]more than ten days, he went
down unto Cesarea; and the next
day sitting on the judgment seat
commanded Paul to be brought.

(Concluded). Time, A. D. 59; Place, Cesarea.

L—Concluded.

Acts 25. 16 To whom I answered, it is not the manner of the Romans to deliver any man to die, before that he which is accused have the accusers face to face, and have license to answer for himself concerning the crime laid against him.

M

Acts 23. 6 But when Paul perceived that the one part were Sadducees, and the other

M—Concluded.

Pharisees, he cried out in the council, Men *and* brethren, I am a Pharisee, the son of a Pharisee: of the hope and resurrection of the dead I am called in question.

Acts 28. 20 For this cause therefore have I called for you, to see *you*, and to speak with *you:* because that for the hope of Israel I am bound with this chain

FOR A BRIBE. Time, A. D. 59; Place, Cesarea.

A

Acts 24. 7 But the chief captain Lysias came *upon us*, and with great violence took *him* away out of our hands,

B

Acts 27. 3 And the next *day* we touched at Sidon. And Julius courteously entreated Paul, and gave *him* liberty to go unto his friends to refresh himself.

Acts 28. 16 And when we came to Rome, the centurion delivered the prisoners to the captain of the guard: but Paul was suffered to dwell by himself with a soldier that kept him.

C

II Cor 6. 2 (For he saith, I have heard thee in a time accepted, and in the day of salvation have I succoured thee: behold, now *is* the accepted time; behold, now *is* the day of salvation.)

Heb. 3. 7 Wherefore (as the Holy Ghost saith, To day if ye will hear his voice,

8 Harden not your hearts, as in the provocation, in the day of temptation in the wilderness:

D

Ex. 23. 2 Thou shalt not follow a multitude to *do* evil; neither shalt thou speak in a cause to decline after many to wrest *judgment:*

Ps. 26. 10 In whose hands *is* mischief, and their right hand is full of bribes.

I Tim. 6. 10 For the love of money is the root of all evil: which while some coveted after, they have erred from the faith, and pierced themselves through with many sorrows.

E

Acts 12. 3 And because he saw it pleased the Jews, he proceeded further to take Peter also. (Then were the days of unleaven bread.)

Acts 25. 9 But Festus, willing to do the Jews a pleasure, answered Paul, and said, Wilt thou go up to Jerusalem, and there be judged of these things before me?

Acts 25. 14 And when they had been there many days, Festus declared Paul' cause unto the king, saying, There i a certain man left in bonds by Felix s

FAVOUR AGAINST PAUL. Time, A. D. 59.

A

Acts 24. 1 And after five days Ananias the high priest descended with the elders, and *with* a certain orator *named* Tertullus, who informed the governor against Paul.

Acts 25. 15 *See text of topic* § 307, *page* 788

B

Acts 23. 12 And when it was day, certain of the Jews banded together, and bound themselves under a curse, saying that they would neither eat nor drink till they had killed Paul.

Acts 23. 15 Now therefore ye with the council signify to the chief captain that he bring him down unto you to morrow, as though ye would inquire something

B—Concluded.

more perfectly concerning him: and we, or ever he come near, are ready to kill him.

C

Acts 18. 14 And when Paul was now about to open *his* mouth, Gallio said unto the Jews, If it were a matter of wrong or wicked lewdness, O *ye* Jews, reason would that I should bear with you:

Acts 25. 18 Against whom when the accusers stood up, they brought none accusation of such things as I supposed:

1

Or, As some copies read, ***no more than eight or ten days,***

§ 306. PAUL'S DEFENSE BEFORE FESTUS. HE APPEALS

25: 7–12.

7 And when he was come, the Jews which came down from Jerusalem stood round about, [a]and laid many and grievous complaints against Paul, which they could not prove.

8 While he answered for himself, [b]Neither against the law of the Jews, neither against the temple, nor yet against Cæsar, have I offended any thing at all.

9 But Festus, [c]willing to do the Jews a pleasure, answered Paul, and said, [d]Wilt thou go up to Jerusalem, and there be judged of these things before me?

10 Then said Paul, I stand at Cæsar's judgment seat, where I ought to be judged: to the Jews have I done no wrong, as thou very well knowest.

11 For [e]if I be an offender, or have committed any thing worthy of death, I refuse not to die: but if there be none of these things whereof these accuse me, no man may deliver me unto them. [f]I appeal unto Cæsar.

12 Then Festus, when he had conferred with the council, answered,

CHAP. 25.

Hast thou appealed unto Cæsar? unto Cæsar shalt thou go.

A

Esth. 3. 8 And Haman said unto king Ahasuerus, There is a certain people scattered abroad and dispersed among the people in all the provinces of thy kingdom; and their laws *are* diverse from all people; neither keep they the king's laws: therefore it *is* not for the king's profit to suffer them.

Ps. 27. 12 Deliver me not over unto the will of mine enemies: for false witnesses are risen up against me, and such as breathe out cruelty.

Ps. 35. 11 False witnesses did rise up; they laid to my charge *things* that I knew not.

Mark 15. 3 And the chief priests accused him of many things: but he answered nothing.

Luke 23. 2 And they began to accuse him, saying, We found this *fellow* perverting the nation, and forbidding to give tribute to Cæsar, saying that he himself is Christ a king.

Luke 23. 10 And the chief priests and scribes stood and vehemently accused him.

Acts 24. 5 For we have found this man *a* pestilent *fellow*, and a mover of sedition among all the Jews throughout the world, and a ringleader of the sect of the Nazarenes:

Acts 24. 13 Neither can they prove the things whereof they now accuse me.

B

Acts 6. 13 And set up false witnesses, which said, This man ceaseth not to speak blasphemous words against this holy place, and the law:

§ 307. AGRIPPA VISITS FESTUS UNTO WHOM PAUL'S CAUSE IS

25: 13–22.

13 And after certain days king Agrippa and Bernice came unto Cesarea to salute Festus.

14 And when they had been there many days, Festus declared Paul's cause unto the king, saying, [a]There is a certain man left in bonds by Felix:

15 [b]About whom, when I was at

CHAP. 25.

Jerusalem, the chief priests and the elders of the Jews informed *me*, desiring *to have* judgment against him.

16 [c]To whom I answered, It is not the manner of the Romans to deliver any man to die, before that he which is accused have the accusers face to face, [d]and have license to answer for

UNTO CÆSAR. TIME, A. D. 59; PLACE, CÆSAREA.

B—CONCLUDED.

Acts 23. 1 And Paul, earnestly beholding the council, said, Men *and* brethren, I have lived in all good conscience before God until this day.

2 And the high priest Ananias commanded them that stood by him to smite him on the mouth.

Acts 24. 12 And they neither found me in the temple disputing with any man, neither raising up the people, neither in the synagogues, nor in the city:

Acts 28. 17 And it came to pass, that after three days Paul called the chief of the Jews together: and when they were come together, he said unto them, Men *and* brethren, though I have committed nothing against the people, or customs of our fathers, yet was I delivered prisoner from Jerusalem into the hands of the Romans.

C

Deut. 27. 19 Cursed *be* he that perverteth the judgment of the stranger, fatherless, and widow. And all the people shall say, Amen.

II Ch. 19. 6 And said to the judges, Take heed what ye do: for ye judge not for man, but for the LORD, who *is* with you in the judgment.

Prov. 29. 25 The fear of man bringeth a snare: but whoso putteth his trust in the LORD shall be safe.

Mark 15. 15 And *so* Pilate, willing to content the people, released Barabbas unto them, and delivered Jesus, when he had scourged *him*, to be crucified.

Acts 12. 3 And because he saw it pleased the Jews, he proceeded further to take Peter also. (Then were the days of unleavened bread.)

Acts 24. 27 But after two years Porcius Festus came into Felix' room: and Felix,

C—CONCLUDED.

willing to shew the Jews a pleasure, left Paul bound.

D

Acts 25. 20 And because I doubted of such manner of questions, I asked *him* whether he would go to Jerusalem, and there be judged of these matters.

E

Acts 18. 14 And when Paul was now about to open *his* mouth, Gallio said unto the Jews, If it were a matter of wrong or wicked lewdness, O *ye* Jews, reason would that I should bear with you:

Acts 23. 29 Whom I perceived to be accused of questions of their law, but to have nothing laid to his charge worthy of death or of bonds.

Acts 26. 31 And when they were gone aside, they talked between themselves, saying, This man doeth nothing worthy of death or of bonds.

F

Prov. 14. 8 The wisdom of the prudent *is* to understand his way: but the folly of fools *is* deceit.

Prov. 21. 22 A wise *man* scaleth the city of the mighty, and casteth down the strength of the confidence thereof.

Eccl. 9. 18 Wisdom *is* better than weapons of war: but one sinner destroyeth much good.

Matt. 10. 16 Behold, I send you forth as sheep in the midst of wolves: be ye therefore wise as serpents, and harmless as doves.

Acts 26. 32 Then said Agrippa unto Festus, This man might have been set at liberty, if he had not appealed unto Cæsar.

Acts 28. 19 But when the Jews spake against *it*, I was constrained to appeal unto Cæsar; not that I had aught to accuse my nation of.

DECLARED. TIME, A. D. 59; PLACE, CESAREA

A

Acts 24. 27 But after two years Porcius Festus came into Felix' room: and Felix, willing to shew the Jews a pleasure, left Paul bound.

B

Acts 25. 1 Now when Festus was come into the province, after three days he ascended from Cesarea to Jerusalem.

2 Then the high priest and the chief of the Jews informed him against Paul, and besought him

C

Acts 25. 4 But Festus answered, that Paul should be kept at Cesarea, and that he himself would depart shortly *thither*.

5 Let them therefore, said he, which among you are able, go down with *me*, and accuse this man, if there be any wickedness in him.

D

Deut. 19. 17 Then both the men, between whom the controversy *is*, shall stand before

For D concluded see next page (790).

§ 307. AGRIPPA VISITS FESTUS UNTO WHOM PAUL'S CAUSE

CHAP. 25.

himself concerning the crime laid against him.

17 Therefore, when they were come hither, [e]without any delay on the morrow I sat on the judgment seat, and commanded the man to be brought forth.

18 Against whom when the accusers stood up, they brought none accusation of such things as I supposed:

19 But [f]had certain questions against him of their own superstition, and of one Jesus, which was dead, whom Paul affirmed to be alive.

20 And because [1]I doubted of such manner of questions, I asked *him* whether he would go to Jerusalem, and there be judged of these matters.

21 But when Paul had appealed to be reserved unto the [2]hearing of Augustus, I commanded him to be kept till I might send him to Cæsar.

22 Then [g]Agrippa said unto Festus, I would also hear the man myself. To morrow, said he, thou shalt hear him.

D—CONTINUED.

the LORD, before the priests and the judges, which shall be in those days;

Deut. 19. 18 And the judges shall make diligent inquisition: and, behold, *if* the witness *be* a false witness, *and* hath testified falsely against his brother;

§ 308. PAUL IS PRESENTED BEFORE AGRIPPA FOR A

25:23–27.

23 And on the morrow, when Agrippa was come, and Bernice, with great pomp, and was entered into the place of hearing, with the chief captains, and principal men of the city, at Festus' commandment Paul was brought forth.

24 And Festus said, King Agrippa, and all men which are here present with us, ye see this man, about whom

CHAP. 25.

[a]all the multitude of the Jews have dealt with me, both at Jerusalem, and *also* here, crying that he ought [b]not to live any longer.

25 But when I found that [c]he had committed nothing worthy of death, and [d]that he himself hath appealed to Augustus, I have determined to send him.

26 Of whom I have no certain thing

§ 309. PAUL'S DEFENSE BEFORE AGRIPPA.

26: 1–23.

1 Then Agrippa said unto Paul, Thou art permitted to speak for thyself. Then Paul stretched forth the hand, and answered for himself:

2 I think myself happy, king Agrippa, because I shall answer for myself this day before thee touching all the

CHAP. 26.

things whereof I am accused of the Jews:

3 Especially *because I know* thee to be [a]expert in all customs and questions which are among the Jews: wherefore I beseech thee to hear me patiently.

IS DECLARED (CONCLUDED.) TIME, A. D. 59; PLACE, CESAREA.

D—CONCLUDED.

Prov. 18. 13 He that answereth a matter before he heareth *it*, it *is* folly and shame unto him.

Prov. 18. 17 *He that is* first in his own cause *seemeth* just; but his neighbour cometh and searcheth him.

John 7. 51 Doth our law judge *any* man, before it hear him, and know what he doeth?

E

Acts 25. 6 And when he had tarried among them more than ten days, he went down unto Cesarea; and the next day sitting on the judgment seat commanded Paul to be brought.

F

Acts 18. 15 But if it be a question of words and names, and *of* your law, look ye *to it;* for I will be no judge of such *matters*.

Acts 23. 29 Whom I perceived to be accused of questions of their law, but to have nothing laid to his charge worthy of death or of bonds.

F—CONCLUDED.

1 Cor. 1. 18 For the preaching of the cross is to them that perish foolishness; but unto us which are saved, it is the power of God.

I Cor. 2. 14 But the natural man receiveth not the things of the Spirit of God: for they are foolishness unto him: neither can he know *them*, because they are spiritually discerned.

1

Or, *I was doubtful how to enquire hereof.*

2

Or, *judgment.*

G

Matt. 10. 18 And ye shall be brought before governors and kings for my sake, for a testimony against them and the Gentiles.

Acts 9. 15 But the Lord said unto him, Go thy way: for he is a chosen vessel unto me, to bear my name before the Gentiles, and kings, and the children of Israel:

HEARING. TIME, A. D. 59; PLACE, CESAREA.

CHAP. 25.

to write unto my lord. Wherefore I
have brought him forth before you,
and specially before thee, O king
Agrippa, that, after examination had,
I might have somewhat to write.
27 For it seemeth to me unreasonable to send a prisoner, and not
withal to signify the crimes *laid*
against him.

A

Acts 25. 15. *See b, B, §307, page 788.*

Acts 25. 7. *See a, A, § 306, page 788.*

B

Acts 22. 22 And they gave him audience unto this word, and *then* lifted up their voices, and said, Away with such a *fellow* from the earth: for it is not fit that he should live.

C

Acts 23. 9. *See text of topic, § 299, page 778.*

Acts 23. 29. *See text of topic, § 300, page 780.*

D

Acts 25. 11 and 12. *See text of topic, § 306, page 788.*

TIME, A. D. 59; PLACE, CESAREA.

A

Deut. 17. 18 And it shall be, when he sitteth upon the throne of his kingdom, that he shall write him a copy of this law in a book out of *that which is* before the priests the Levites:

19 And it shall be with him, and he shall read therein all the days of his life: that he may learn to fear the LORD his God, to keep all the words of this law and these statutes, to do them:

B

II Tim. 3. 10 But thou hast fully known my doctrine, manner of life, purpose, faith, longsuffering, charity, patience,

C

Acts 22. 3. *See f, F, and G, § 299, page 772.*

Gal. 1. 13 For ye have heard of my conversation in time past in the Jews' religion, how that beyond measure I persecuted the church of God, and wasted it:

§ 309. PAUL'S DEFENSE BEFORE AGRIPPA

CHAP. 26.

4 [b]My manner of life from my youth,
which was at the first among mine
own nation at Jerusalem, know all
the Jews;

5 Which knew me from the beginning, if they would testify, that after
[c]the most straitest sect of our religion I lived a Pharisee.

6 And now I stand and am judged
for the hope of the [d]promise made
of God unto our fathers:

7 Unto which *promise* our twelve
tribes, instantly serving *God* [1e]day
and night, [f]hope to come. For which
hope's sake, king Agrippa, I am accused of the Jews.

8 Why should it be thought a thing
incredible with you, that God should
raise the dead?

9 [g]I verily thought with myself, that
I ought to do many things contrary
to the name of Jesus of Nazareth.

10 [h]Which thing I also did in Jerusalem: and many of the saints did I
shut up in prison, having received
authority [i]from the chief priests; and
when they were put to death, I gave
my voice against *them*.

11 And [k]I punished them oft in
every synagogue, and compelled *them*
to blaspheme; and being exceedingly mad against them, I persecuted
them even unto strange cities.

12 [l]Whereupon as I went to Damascus with authority and commission from the chief priests,

13 At midday, O king, I saw in the
way a light from heaven, above the
brightness of the sun, shining round
about me and them which journeyed
with me.

14 And when we were all fallen to

See preceding page for B and C.

D

Gen. 3. 15 etc. *See under L. page 716.*

II Sa. 7. 12 And when thy days be fulfilled, and thou shalt sleep with thy fathers, I will set up thy seed after thee, which shall proceed out of thy bowels, and I will establish his kingdom.

Isa. 4. 2 In that day shall the branch of the LORD be beautiful and glorious, and the fruit of the earth *shall be* excellent and comely for them that are escaped of Israel.

Isa. 9. 6 For unto us a child is born, unto us a son is given: and the government shall be upon his shoulder: and his name shall be called Wonderful, Counsellor, The Mighty God, The everlasting Father, The Prince of Peace.

Isa. 40. 10 Behold, the Lord GOD will come with strong *hand*, and his arm shall rule for him: behold, his reward *is* with him, and his work before him.

Jer. 23. 5 Behold, the days come, saith the LORD, that I will raise unto David a righteous Branch, and a King shall reign and prosper, and shall execute judgment and justice in the earth.

Jer. 33. 14 Behold, the days come, saith the LORD, that I will perform that good thing which I have promised unto the house of Israel and to the house of Judah.

Eze. 34. 23 And I will set up one Shepherd over them, and he shall feed them, *even* my servant David; he shall feed them, and he shall be their shepherd.

Eze. 37. 12 Therefore prophesy and say unto them, Thus saith the Lord GOD; Behold, O my people, I will open your graves, and cause you to come up out of your graves, and bring you into the land of Israel.

Da. 12. 2 etc. *See under G. page 784.*

Mal. 4. 2 But unto you that fear my name shall the Sun of righteousness arise with healing in his wings; and ye shall go forth, and grow up as calves of the stall.

1

Gr. *night and day.*

E

Luke 2. 37 And she *was* a widow of about fourscore and four years, which departed not from the temple, but served *God* with fastings and prayers night and day.

I Thes. 3. 10 Night and day praying exceedingly that we might see your face, and

(CONTINUED). TIME, A. D. 59; PLACE, CESAREA.

E—CONCLUDED.

might perfect that which is lacking in your faith?

I Tim. 5. 5 Now she that is a widow indeed, and desolate, trusteth in God, and continueth in supplications and prayers night and day.

F

Phil. 3. 11 If by any means I might attain unto the resurrection of the dead.

G

John 16. 2 They shall put you out of the synagogues: yea, the time cometh, that whosoever killeth you will think that he doeth God service.

Rom. 10. 2 For I bear them record that they have a zeal of God, but not according to knowledge.

Phil. 3. 6 Concerning zeal, persecuting the church; touching the righteousness which is in the law, blameless.

I Tim. 1. 13 Who was before a blasphemer, and a persecutor, and injurious: but I obtained mercy, because I did *it* ignorantly in unbelief.

H

Acts 8. 3 As for Saul, he made havoc of the church, entering into every house, and haling men and women committed *them* to prison.

Gal. 1. 13 For ye have heard of my conversation in time past in the Jews' religion, how that beyond measure I persecuted the church of God, and wasted it:

I

Acts 9. 14 And here he hath authority from the chief priests to bind all that call on thy name.

Acts 9. 21 But all that heard *him* were amazed, and said; Is not this he that destroyed them which called on this name in Jerusalem, and came hither for that intent, that he might bring them bound unto the chief priests?

Acts 22. 5 As also the high priest doth bear me witness, and all the estate of the elders: from whom also I received letters unto the brethren, and went to Damascus, to bring them which were there bound unto Jerusalem, for to be punished.

K

Acts 22. 19 And I said, Lord, they know that I imprisoned and beat in every synagogue them that believed on thee:

L

Acts 9. 3 And as he journeyed, he came near Damascus: and suddenly there

L—CONCLUDED.

shined round about him a light from heaven;

Acts 22. 6 And it came to pass, that as I made my journey, and was come nigh unto Damascus, about noon, suddenly there shone from heaven a great light round about me.

M

Acts 9. 15 etc. *See under L. and M, page 684.*

Acts 22. 15 For thou shalt be his witness unto all men of what thou hast seen and heard.

N

Acts 22. 21 And he said unto me, Depart: for I will send thee far hence unto the Gentiles.

O

Isa. 35. 5 Then the eyes of the blind shall be opened, and the ears of the deaf shall be unstopped.

Isa. 42. 7 To open the blind eyes, to bring out the prisoners from the prison, *and* them that sit in darkness out of the prison house.

Luke 1. 79 To give light to them that sit in darkness and *in* the shadow of death, to guide our feet into the way of peace.

John 8. 12 Then spake Jesus again unto them, saying, I am the light of the world: he that followeth me shall not walk in darkness, but shall have the light of life.

II Cor. 4. 4 In whom the god of this world hath blinded the minds of them which believe not, lest the light of the glorious gospel of Christ, who is the image of God, should shine unto them.

Eph. 1. 18 The eyes of your understanding being enlightened; that ye may know what is the hope of his calling, and what the riches of the glory of his inheritance in the saints,

I Thes. 5. 5 Ye are all the children of light, and the children of the day: we are not of the night, nor of darkness.

P

II Cor. 6. 14 Be ye not unequally yoked together with unbelievers: for what fellowship hath righteousness with unrighteousness? and what communion hath light with darkness?

Eph. 4. 18 Having the understanding darkened, being alienated from the life of God through the ignorance that is in them, because of the blindness of their heart:

Eph. 5. 8 For ye were sometimes darkness, but now *are ye* light in the Lord: walk as children of light:

§ 309. PAUL'S DEFENSE BEFORE AGRIPPA

CHAP. 26.

the earth, I heard a voice speaking unto me, and saying in the Hebrew tongue, Saul, Saul, why persecutest thou me? *it is* hard for thee to kick against the pricks.

15 And I said, Who art thou, Lord? And he said, I am Jesus whom thou persecutest.

16 But rise, and stand upon thy feet: for I have appeared unto thee for this purpose, [m]to make thee a minister and a witness both of these things which thou hast seen, and of those things in the which I will appear unto thee;

17 Delivering thee from the people, and *from* the Gentiles, [n]unto whom now I send thee,

18 [o]To open their eyes, *and* [p]to turn *them* from darkness to light, and *from* the power of Satan unto God, [q]that they may receive forgiveness of sins, and [r]inheritance among them which are [s]sanctified by faith that is in me.

19 Whereupon, O king Agrippa, I was not disobedient unto the heavenly vision:

20 But [t]shewed first unto them of Damascus, and at Jerusalem, and throughout all the coasts of Judea, and *then* to the Gentiles, that they should repent and turn to God, and do [u]works meet for repentance.

21 For these causes [x]the Jews caught me in the temple, and went about to kill *me*.

22 Having therefore obtained help of God, I continue unto this day, witnessing both to small and great, saying none other things than those

CHAP. 26.

[y]which the prophets and [z]Moses did say should come:

23 [a]That Christ should suffer, *and* [b]that he should be the first that should rise from the dead, and [c]should shew light unto the people, and to the Gentiles.

For M, N, O and P, see preceding page (797).

P—CONCLUDED.

Col. 1. 13 Who hath delivered us from the power of darkness, and hath translated *us* into the kingdom of his dear Son:

1 Pet. 2. 9 But ye *are* a chosen generation, a royal priesthood, a holy nation, a peculiar people; that ye should shew forth the praises of him who hath called you out of darkness into his marvellous light:

1 Pet. 2. 25 For ye were as sheep going astray; but are now returned unto the Shepherd and Bishop of your souls.

Q

Ps. 32. 1 Blessed *is he whose* transgression *is* forgiven, *whose* sin *is* covered.

2 Blessed *is* the man unto whom the LORD imputeth not iniquity, and in whose spirit *there is* no guile.

Luke 1. 77 To give knowledge of salvation unto his people by the remission of their sins,

Acts 5. 31. *See q, Q, § 242, page 662.*

R

Acts 20. 32. *See b, B, § 292, page 764.*

S

John 17. 17 Sanctify them through thy truth; thy word is truth.

Acts 20. 32 And now, brethren, I commend you to God, and to the word of his grace, which is able to build you up, and to give you an inheritance among all them which are sanctified.

1 Cor. 1. 2 Unto the church of God which is at Corinth, to them that are sanctified in Christ Jesus, called *to be* saints, with all that in every place call upon the name of Jesus Christ our Lord, both theirs and ours:

1 Cor. 1. 30 But of him are ye in Christ Jesus, who of God is made unto us wisdom, and righteousness, and sanctification, and redemption:

1 Cor. 6. 11 And such were some of you: but ye are washed, but ye are sanctified, but ye are justified in the name of the Lord Jesus, and by the Spirit of our God.

(CONCLUDED). TIME, A. D. 59; PLACE, CESAREA.

S—CONCLUDED.

Eph. 5. 26 That he might sanctify and cleanse it with the washing of water by the word,

IIThes.2. 13 But we are bound to give thanks alway to God for you, brethren beloved of the Lord, because God hath from the beginning chosen you to salvation through sanctification of the Spirit and belief of the truth:

Tit. 3. 5 Not by works of righteousness which we have done, but according to his mercy he saved us, by the washing of regeneration, and renewing of the Holy Ghost;

6 Which he shed on us abundantly through Jesus Christ our Saviour;

Heb. 2. 11 For both he that sanctifieth and they who are sanctified *are* all of one; for which cause he is not ashamed to call them brethren,

Heb. 10. 10 By the which will we are sanctified through the offering of the body of Jesus Christ once *for all.*

Heb. 10. 14 For by one offering he hath perfected for ever them that are sanctified.

Heb. 13. 12 Wherefore Jesus also, that he might sanctify the people with his own blood, suffered without the gate.

I Pet. 1. 22 Seeing ye have purified your souls in obeying the truth through the Spirit unto unfeigned love of the brethren, *see that ye* love one another with a pure heart fervently:

Jude 1 Jude, the servant of Jesus Christ, and brother of James, to them that are sanctified by God the Father, and preserved in Jesus Christ, *and* called:

T

Acts 9. 20 And straightway he preached Christ in the synagogues, that he is the Son of God.

Acts 11. 26 And when he had found him, he brought him unto Antioch. And it came to pass, that a whole year they assembled themselves with the church, and taught much people. And the disciples were called Christians first in Antioch.

U

Matt. 3. 8 Bring forth therefore fruits meet for repentance:

X

Acts 21. 30 And all the city was moved, and the people ran together: and they took Paul, and drew him out of the temple: and forthwith the doors were shut.

31 And as they went about to kill

X—CONCLUDED.

him, tidings came unto the chief captain of the band, that all Jerusalem was in an uproar.

Y

Luke 24. 27 And beginning at Moses and all the prophets, he expounded unto them in all the Scriptures the things concerning himself.

Luke 24. 44 And he said unto them, These *are* the words which I spake unto you, while I was yet with you, that all things must be fulfilled which were written in the law of Moses, and *in* the prophets, and *in* the psalms, concerning me.

Acts 24. 14 But this I confess unto thee, that after the way which they call heresy, so worship I the God of my fathers, believing all things which are written in the law and in the prophets:

Acts 28. 23 And when they had appointed him a day, there came many to him into *his* lodging; to whom he expounded and testified the kingdom of God, persuading them concerning Jesus, both out of the law of Moses, and *out of* the prophets, from morning till evening.

Rom. 3. 21 But now the righteousness of God without the law is manifested, being witnessed by the law and the prophets;

Z

John 5. 46 For had ye believed Moses, ye would have believed me: for he wrote of me.

A

Luke 24. 26 Ought not Christ to have suffered these things, and to enter into his glory?

Luke 24. 46 And said unto them, Thus it is written, and thus it behooved Christ to suffer, and to rise from the dead the third day:

B

ICor.15. 20 But now is Christ risen from the dead, *and* become the firstfruits of them that slept.

Col. 1. 18 And he is the head of the body, the church: who is the beginning, the firstborn from the dead; that in all *things* he might have the preeminence.

Rev. 1. 5 And from Jesus Christ, *who is* the faithful witness, *and* the first-begotten of the dead, and the prince of the kings of the earth. Unto him that loved us, and washed us from our sins in his own blood

C

Luke 2. 32 A light to lighten the Gentiles, and the glory of thy people Israel.

§ 310. FESTUS INTERRUPTS PAUL. AGRIPPA RENDERS

26 : 24-32.

24 And as he thus spake for himself, Festus said with a loud voice, Paul, [a]thou art beside thyself; much learning doth make thee mad.

25 But he said, I am not mad, most noble Festus; but speak forth the words of truth and soberness.

26 For the king knoweth of these things, before whom also I speak freely: for I am persuaded that none of these things are hidden from him; for [b]this thing was not done in a corner.

27 King Agrippa, believest thou the prophets? I know that thou believest.

28 Then Agrippa said unto Paul, [c]Almost thou persuadest me to be a Christian.

29 And Paul said, [d]I would to God, that not only thou, but also all that hear me this day, were both almost, and altogether such as I am, except these bonds.

30 And when he had thus spoken, the king rose up, and the governor, and Bernice, and they that sat with them:

31 And when they were gone aside, they talked between themselves, saying, [e]This man doeth nothing worthy of death or of bonds.

Chap. 26.

32 Then said Agrippa unto Festus, This man might have been set at liberty, [f]if he had not appealed unto Cæsar.

A

II Ki. 9. 11 Then Jehu came forth to the servants of his lord: and *one* said unto him, *Is* all well? wherefore came this mad *fellow* to thee? And he said unto them, Ye know the man, and his communication.

John 10. 20 And many of them said, He hath a devil, and is mad; why hear ye him?

I Cor. 1. 23 But we preach Christ crucified, unto the Jews a stumbling block, and unto the Greeks foolishness;

I Cor. 2. 13 Which things also we speak, not in the words which man's wisdom teacheth, but which the Holy Ghost teacheth; comparing spiritual things with spiritual.

14 But the natural man receiveth not the things of the Spirit of God: for they are foolishness unto him: neither can he know *them*, because they are spiritually discerned.

I Cor. 4. 10 We *are* fools for Christ's sake, but ye *are* wise in Christ; we *are* weak, but ye *are* strong; ye *are* honourable, but we *are* despised.

B

Isa. 30. 20 And *though* the Lord give you the bread of adversity, and the water of affliction, yet shall not thy teachers be removed into a corner any more, but thine eyes shall see thy teachers:

Matt. 26. 5 But they said, Not on the feast *day*, lest there be an uproar among the people.

Acts. 2. 6 Now when this was noised abroad, the multitude came together, and were confounded, because that every man heard them speak in his own language.

§ 311. THE VOYAGE TO ROME. THEY COME TO

27 : 1-8.

1 And when [a]it was determined that we should sail into Italy, they delivered Paul and certain other prisoners unto *one* named Julius, a centurion of Augustus' band.

2 And entering into a ship of Adramyttium, we launched, meaning to sail by the coasts of Asia; *one* [b]Aristarchus, a Macedonian of Thessalonica, being with us.

Chap. 27.

3 And the next *day* we touched at Sidon. And Julius [c]courteously entreat-

AN OPINION. TIME, A. D., 59; PLACE, CESAREA.

B—CONCLUDED.

Acts 4. 16 Saying, What shall we do to these men? for that indeed a notable miracle hath been done by them *is* manifest to all them that dwell in Jerusalem; and we cannot deny *it*.

Acts 5. 19 But the angel of the Lord by night opened the prison doors, and brought them forth, and said,

20 Go, stand and speak in the temple to the people all the words of this life.

21 And when they heard *that*, they entered into the temple early in the morning, and taught. But the high priest came, and they that were with him, and called the council together, and all the senate of the children of Israel, and sent to the prison to have them brought.

C

Eze. 33. 31 And they come unto thee as the people cometh, and they sit before thee *as* my people, and they hear thy words, but they will not do them: for with their mouth they shew much love, *but* their heart goeth after their covetousness.

Mark. 6. 20 For Herod feared John, knowing that he was a just man and a holy, and observed him; and when he heard him, he did many things, and heard him gladly.

Mark 10. 17 And when he was gone forth into the way, there came one running, and kneeled to him, and asked him, Good Master, what shall I do that I may inherit eternal life?

Mark 10. 21 Then Jesus beholding him loved him, and said unto him, One thing thou lackest: go thy way, sell whatsoever thou hast, and give to the poor, and thou shalt have treasure in heaven: and come, take up the cross, and follow me.

22 And he was sad at that saying, and and went away grieved: for he had great possessions.

C—CONCLUDED.

II Cor. 4. 2 But have renounced the hidden things of dishonesty, not walking in craftiness, nor handling the word of God deceitfully; but, by manifestation of the truth, commending ourselves to every man's conscience in the sight of God.

3 But if our gospel be hid, it is hid to them that are lost:

Jas. 1. 23 For if any be a hearer of the word, and not a doer, he is like unto a man beholding his natural face in a glass:

24 For he beholdeth himself, and goeth his way, and straightway forgetteth what manner of man he was.

D

I Cor 7. 7 For I would that all men were even as I myself. But every man hath his proper gift of God, one after this manner, and another after that.

E

Luke 23. 4 Then said Pilate to the chief priests and *to* the people, I find no fault in this man.

Acts 23. 9 And there arose a great cry: and the scribes *that were* of the Pharisees' part arose, and strove, saying, We find no evil in this man: but if a spirit or an angel hath spoken to him, let us not fight against God.

Acts 23. 29 Whom I perceived to be accused of questions of their law, but to have nothing laid to his charge worthy of death or of bonds.

Acts 25. 25 But when I found that he had committed nothing worthy of death, and that he himself hath appealed to Augustus, I have determined to send him.

F

Acts 25. 11. *See f, F,* § 306, *page* 788.

FAIR HAVENS. TIME, PROBABLY AUGUST, A. D. 60.

A

Acts 25. 12 Then Festus, when he had conferred with the council, answered, Hast thou appealed unto Cæsar? unto Cæsar shalt thou go.

Acts 25. 25. *See under E,* § 310.

B

Acts 19. 29. *See e. E.* § 288, *page* 756.

C

Prov. 16. 7 When a man's ways please the LORD, he maketh even his enemies to be at peace with him.

Acts 24. 23 And he commanded a centurion to keep Paul, and to let *him* have liberty, and that he should forbid none

For C continued see page (798).

§311, THE VOYAGE TO ROME. THEY COME TO FAIR

CHAP. 27.

ed Paul, and gave *him* liberty to go
unto his friends to refresh himself.
4 And when we had launched from
thence, we sailed unto Cyprus, because [d]the winds were contrary.
5 And when we had sailed over the
sea of Cilicia and Pamphylia, we
came to Myra, *a city* of Lycia.
6 And there the centurian found a
ship of Alexandria sailing into Italy;
and he put us therein.

CHAP. 27.

7 And when we had sailed slowly
many days, and scarce were come
over against Cnidus, the wind not
suffering us, we sailed under [1]Crete,
over against Salmone;
8 And, hardly passing it, came unto a
place which is called the Fair Havens;
nigh whereunto was the city *of* Lasea.

C—CONTINUED.

of his acquaintance to minister or come unto him.

§ 312. DISREGARDING PAUL'S ADMONITION, THE VOYAGE IS

27:9–26.

9 Now when much time was spent,
and when sailing was now dangerous,
[a]because the fast was now already
past, Paul admonished *them*,
10 And said unto them, Sirs, I perceive that this voyage will be with
[1]hurt and much damage, not only of
the lading and ship, but also of our
lives.
11 Nevertheless the centurion believed the master and the owner of
the ship, more than those things
which were spoken by Paul.
12 And because the haven was not
commodious to winter in, the more
part advised to depart thence also, if
by any means they might attain to
Phenice, *and there* to winter, *which is*
a haven of Crete, and lieth toward
the southwest and northwest.
13 And when the south wind blew
softly, supposing that they had obtained *their* purpose, loosing *thence*,
they sailed close by Crete.
14 But not long after there [2]arose
against it a tempestuous wind, called
Euroclydon.

CHAP. 27.

15 And when the ship was caught,
and could not bear up into the wind,
we let *her* drive.
16 And running under a certain island which is called Clauda, we had
much work to come by the boat:
17 Which when they had taken up,
they used helps, undergirding the
ship; and, fearing lest they should
fall into the quicksands, strake sail,
and so were driven.
18 And we being exceedingly tossed
with a tempest, the next *day* they
lightened the ship;
19 And the third *day* [b]we cast out
with our own hands the tackling of
the ship.
20 And when neither sun nor stars
in many days appeared, and no small
tempest lay on *us*, all hope that we
should be saved was then taken away.
21 But after long abstinence, Paul
stood forth in the midst of them, and
said, Sirs, ye should have hearkened
unto me, and not have loosed from
Crete, and to have gained this harm
and loss.

HAVENS (CONCLUDED). TIME, PROBABLY AUGUST, A. D. 60

C—CONCLUDED.

Acts 28. 16 And when we came to Rome, the centurion delivered the prisoners to the captain of the guard: but Paul was suffered to dwell by himself with a soldier that kept him.

Acts 28. 31 Preaching the kingdom of God, and teaching those things which concern the Lord Jesus Christ, with all confidence, no man forbidding him.

D

Matt. 14. 24 But the ship was now in the midst of the sea, tossed with waves: for the wind was contrary.

Mark 6. 48 And he saw them toiling in rowing; for the wind was contrary unto them: and about the fourth watch of the night he cometh unto them, walking upon the sea, and would have passed by them.

1

Or, *Candy*,—a large island in the Mediterranean.

Tit. 1. 5 For this cause left I thee in Crete, that thou shouldest set in order the things that are wanting, and ordain elders in every city, as I had appointed thee:

Tit. 1. 12 One of themselves, *even* a prophet of their own, said, The Cretians *are* alway liars, evil beasts, slow bellies.

CONTINUED. THE STORM. TIME, WINTER, A. D. 60.

CHAP. 27.

22 And now I exhort you to be of good cheer: for there shall be no loss of *any man's* life among you, but of the ship.

23 [c]For there stood by me this night the angel of God, whose I am, and [d]whom I serve,

24 Saying, Fear not, Paul; thou must be brought before Cæsar: and, lo, God hath given them that sail with thee.

25 Wherefore, sirs, be of good cheer: [e]for I believe God, that it shall be even as it was told me.

26 Howbeit [f]we must be cast upon a certain island.

A

The fast was on the tenth day of the seventh month.

Lev. 23. 27 Also on the tenth *day* of this seventh month *there shall be* a day of atonement: it shall be a holy convocation unto you; and ye shall afflict your souls, and offer an offering made by fire unto the LORD.

1

Or, *injury*.

2

Or, *beat*.

B

Jonah 1. 5 Then the mariners were afraid, and cried every man unto his god, and cast forth the wares that *were* in the ship into the sea, to lighten *it* of them. But Jonah was gone down into the sides of the ship; and he lay, and was fast asleep.

B—CONCLUDED.

C

Acts 23. 11. *See m, M, § 299, page 778.*

D

Da. 6. 16 Then the king commanded, and they brought Daniel, and cast *him* into the den of lions. *Now* the king spake and said unto Daniel, Thy God whom thou servest continually, he will deliver thee.

Rom. 1. 9 For God is my witness, whom I serve with my spirit in the gospel of his Son, that without ceasing I make mention of you always in my prayers;

II Tim. 1. 3 I thank God, whom I serve from *my* forefathers with pure conscience, that without ceasing I have remembrance of thee in my prayers night and day;

E

Rom. 4. 20 He staggered not at the promise of God through unbelief; but was strong in faith, giving glory to God;

21 And being fully persuaded that, what he had promised, he was able also to perform.

II Tim. 1. 12 For the which cause I also suffer these things: nevertheless I am not ashamed; for I know whom I have believed, and am persuaded that he is able to keep that which I have committed unto him against that day.

F

Acts 28. 1 And when they were escaped, then they knew that the island was called Melita.

§ 313. THE SHIPWRECK AND ESCAPE TO LAND.

27: 27-44.

27 But when the fourteenth night was come, as we were driven up and down in Adria, about midnight the shipmen deemed that they drew near to some country;

28 And sounded, and found *it* twenty fathoms: and when they had gone a little further, they sounded again, and found *it* fifteen fathoms.

29 Then fearing lest we should have fallen upon rocks, they cast four anchors out of the stern, and wished for the day.

30 And as the shipmen were about to flee out of the ship, when they had let down the boat into the sea, under colour as though they would have cast anchors out of the foreship,

31 Paul said to the centurion and to the soldiers, Except these abide in the ship, ye cannot be saved.

32 Then the soldiers cut off the ropes of the boat, and let her fall off.

33 And while the day was coming on, Paul besought *them* all to take meat, saying, This day is the fourteenth day that ye have tarried and continued fasting, having taken nothing.

34 Wherefore I pray you to take *some* meat; for this is for your health: for [a]there shall not an hair fall from the head of any of you.

35 And when he had thus spoken, he took bread, [b]and gave thanks to God in presence of them all; and when he had broken *it*, he began to eat.

36 Then were they all of good cheer, and they also took *some* meat.

CHAP. 27.

37 And we were in all in the ship two hundred threescore and sixteen [c]souls.

38 And when they had eaten enough, they lightened the ship, and [d]cast out the wheat into the sea.

39 And when it was day, they knew not the land: but they discovered a certain creek with a shore, into the which they were minded, if it were possible, to thrust in the ship.

40 And when they had [1]taken up the anchors, they committed *themselves* unto the sea, and loosed the rudder bands, and hoised up the mainsail to the wind, and made toward shore.

41 And falling into a place where two seas met, [e]they ran the ship aground; and the forepart stuck fast, and remained unmoveable, but the hinder part was broken with the violence of the waves.

42 And the soldiers' counsel [f]was to kill the prisoners, lest any of them should swim out, and escape.

43 But the centurion, [g]willing to save Paul, kept them from *their* purpose; and commanded that they which could swim should cast *themselves* first *into the sea*, and get to land:

44 And the rest, some on boards, and some on *broken pieces* of the ship. And so it came to pass, [h]that they escaped all safe to land.

A

I Ki. 1. 52 And Solomon said, If he will shew himself a worthy man, there shall not a hair of him fall to the earth: but if wickedness shall be found in him, he shall die.

Matt. 10. 30 But the very hairs of your head are all numbered.

Luke 12. 7 But even the very hairs of your head are all numbered. Fear not therefore: ye are of more value than many sparrows.

Luke 21. 18 But there shall not a hair of your head perish.

TIME, WINTER, A. D. 60; PLACE, MEDITERRANEAN SEA, NEAR MELITA (MALTA).

B

Deut. 8. 10 When thou hast eaten and art full, then thou shalt bless the LORD thy God for the good land which he hath given thee.

I Sa. 9. 13 As soon as ye be come into the city, ye shall straightway find him, before he go up to the high place to eat: for the people will not eat until he come, because he doth bless the sacrifice; *and* afterwards they eat that be bidden. Now therefore get you up; for about this time ye shall find him.

Matt. 15. 36 And he took the seven loaves and the fishes, and gave thanks, and brake *them*, and gave to his disciples, and the disciples to the multitude.

Mark 8. 6 And he commanded the people to sit down on the ground: and he took the seven loaves, and gave thanks, and brake, and gave to his disciples to set before *them;* and they did set *them* before the people.

John 6. 11 And Jesus took the loaves; and when he had given thanks, he distributed to the disciples, and the disciples to them that were set down; and likewise of the fishes as much as they would.

I Tim. 4. 3 Forbidding to marry, *and commanding* to abstain from meats, which God hath created to be received with thanksgiving of them which believe and know the truth.

4 For every creature of God *is* good, and nothing to be refused, if it be received with thanksgiving:

C

Acts 2. 41 Then they that gladly received his word were baptized: and the same day there were added *unto them* about three thousand souls.

Acts 7. 14 Then sent Joseph, and called his father Jacob to *him*, and all his kindred, threescore and fifteen souls.

Rom. 13. 1 Let every soul be subject unto the higher powers. For there is no power but of God: the powers that be are ordained of God.

I Pet. 3. 20 Which sometime were disobedient, when once the longsuffering of God waited in the days of Noah, while the ark was a preparing, wherein few, that is, eight souls were saved by water.

D

Job 2. 4 And Satan answered the LORD, and said, Skin for skin, yea, all that a man hath will he give for his life.

D—CONCLUDED.

Jonah 1. 5 Then the mariners were afraid, and cried every man unto his god, and cast forth the wares that *were* in the ship into the sea, to lighten *it* of them. But Jonah was gone down into the sides of the ship; and he lay, and was fast asleep.

1

Or, *Cut the anchors, they left them in the sea*, etc.

E

II Cor. 11. 25 Thrice was I beaten with rods, once was I stoned, thrice I suffered shipwreck, a night and a day have I been in the deep:

F

Prov. 1. 16 For their feet run to evil, and make haste to shed blood.

Prov. 12. 10 A righteous *man* regardeth the life of his beast: but the tender mercies of the wicked *are* cruel.

Isa. 59. 7 Their feet run to evil, and they make haste to shed innocent blood: their thoughts *are* thoughts of iniquity; wasting and destruction *are* in their paths.

Rom. 3. 15 Their feet *are* swift to shed blood:

G

Ps. 34. 17 *The righteous* cry, and the LORD heareth, and delivereth them out of all their troubles.

Ps. 34. 19 Many *are* the afflictions of the righteous: but the LORD delivereth him out of them all.

Prov. 16. 7 When a man's ways please the the LORD, he maketh even his enemies to be at peace with him.

Jer. 38. 10 Then the king commanded Ebed-melech the Ethiopian, saying, Take from hence thirty men with thee, and take up Jeremiah the prophet out of the dungeon, before he die.

Acts 23. 10 And when there arose a great dissension, the chief captain, fearing lest Paul should have been pulled in pieces of them, commanded the soldiers to go down, and to take him by force from among them, and to bring *him* into the castle.

II Pet. 2. 9 The Lord knoweth how to deliver the godly out of temptations, and to reserve the unjust unto the day of judgment to be punished:

H

Ps. 107. 29 He maketh the storm a calm, so that the waves thereof are still.

30 Then are they glad because they be quiet; so he bringeth them unto their desired haven.

§ 314. THEY ARE CAST UPON THE ISLAND OF

28 : 1–6.

1 And when they were escaped, then they knew that the [a]island was called Melita.

2 And the [b]barbarous people shewed us no little kindness: for they kindled a fire, and received us every one, because of the present rain, and because of the cold.

3 And when Paul had gathered a bundle of sticks, and laid *them* on the fire, there came a viper out of the heat, and fastened on his hand.

4 And when the barbarians saw the *venomous* beast hang on his hand, they said among themselves, [c]No doubt this man is a murderer, whom, though he hath escaped the sea, yet vengeance suffereth not to live.

5 And he shook off the beast into the fire, and [d]felt no harm.

6 Howbeit they looked when he should have swollen, or fallen down dead suddenly: but after they had looked a great while, and saw no harm come to him, they changed their minds, and [e]said that he was a god.

CHAP. 28.

A

Acts 27. 26 Howbeit we must be cast upon a certain island.

Acts 27. 44 And the rest, some on boards, and some on *broken pieces* of the ship. And so it came to pass, that they escaped all safe to land.

§ 315. PAUL HEALS PUBLIUS AND OTHERS. THEY CONTINUE

28 : 7–16.

7 In the same quarters were possessions of the chief man of the island, whose name was Publius; who received us, and lodged us three days courteously.

8 And it came to pass, that the father of Publius lay sick of a fever and of a bloody flux: to whom Paul entered in, and [a]prayed, and [b]laid his hands on him, and healed him.

9 So when this was done, others also, which had diseases in the island, came, and were healed:

10 Who also honoured us with many [c]honours; and when we departed, they laded *us* with such things as were necessary.

11 And after three months we departed in a ship of Alexandria, which had wintered in the isle, whose sign was Castor and Pollux.

CHAP. 28.

12 And landing at Syracuse, we tarried *there* three days.

13 And from thence we fetched a compass, and came to Rhegium: and after one day the south wind blew, and we came the next day to Puteoli:

14 Where we found brethren, and were desired to tarry with them seven days: and so we went toward Rome.

15 And from thence, when the brethren heard of us, they came to meet us as far as Appii Forum, and the Three Taverns; whom when Paul saw, he thanked God, and took courage.

16 And when we came to Rome, the centurion delivered the prisoners to the captain of the guard: but [d]Paul was suffered to dwell by himself with a soldier that kept him.

A

1 Ki. 17. 20 And he cried unto the LORD, and said, O LORD my God, hast thou also brought evil upon the widow with whom I sojourn, by slaying her son?

MELITA. THE VIPER. TIME, WINTER, A. D. 60.

B

Acts 27. 3 And the next *day* we touched at Sidon. And Julius courteously entreated Paul, and gave *him* liberty to go unto his friends to refresh himself.

Rom. 1. 14 I am debtor both to the Greeks, and to the Barbarians; both to the wise, and to the unwise.

I Cor. 14. 11 Therefore if I know not the meaning of the voice, I shall be unto him that speaketh a barbarian, and he that speaketh *shall be* a barbarian unto me.

Col. 3. 11 Where there is neither Greek nor Jew, circumcision nor uncircumcision, Barbarian, Scythian, bond *nor* free; but Christ *is* all, and in all.

Heb. 13. 1 Let brotherly love continue.

2 Be not forgetful to entertain strangers: for thereby some have entertained angels unawares.

C

Luke 13. 2 And Jesus answering said unto them, Suppose ye that these Galileans were sinners above all the Galileans, because they suffered such things?

C—CONCLUDED.

John 9. 2 And his disciples asked him, saying, Master, who did sin, this man, or his parents, that he was born blind?

D

Ps. 91. 13 Thou shalt tread upon the lion and adder: the young lion and the dragon shalt thou trample under feet.

Mark 16. 18 They shall take up serpents; and if they drink any deadly thing, it shall not hurt them; they shall lay hands on the sick, and they shall recover.

Luke 10. 19 Behold, I give unto you power to tread on serpents and scorpions, and over all the power of the enemy: and nothing shall by any means hurt you.

E

Acts 14. 11. *See d, D, § 265, page 722.*

THE VOYAGE TO ROME. TIME, A. D. 61; PLACE, MELITA AND ROME.

A—CONCLUDED.

I Ki. 17. 21 And he stretched himself upon the child three times, and cried unto the LORD, and said, O LORD my God, I pray unto thee, let this child's soul come into him again.

22 And the LORD heard the voice of Elijah: and the soul of the child came into him again, and he revived.

Jas. 5. 14 Is any sick among you? let him call for the elders of the church; and let them pray over him, anointing him with oil in the name of the Lord:

15 And the prayer of faith shall save the sick, and the Lord shall raise him up; and if he have committed sins, they shall be forgiven him.

16 Confess *your* faults one to another, and pray one for another, that ye may be healed. The effectual fervent prayer of a righteous man availeth much.

Acts 9. 40 But Peter put them all forth, and kneeled down, and prayed; and turning *him* to the body said, Tabitha, arise. And she opened her eyes: and when she saw Peter, she sat up.

B

Mark 6. 5 And he could there do no mighty work, save that he laid his hands upon a few sick folk, and healed *them*.

Mark 7. 32 And they bring unto him one that was deaf, and had an impediment in his speech; and they beseech him to put his hand upon him.

B—CONCLUDED.

Mark 16. 18. *See under D, § 314.*

Luke 4. 40 Now when the sun was setting, all they that had any sick with divers diseases brought them unto him; and he laid his hands on every one of them, and healed them.

Acts 19. 11 And God wrought special miracles by the hands of Paul:

12 So that from his body were brought unto the sick handkerchiefs or aprons, and the diseases departed from them, and the evil spirits went out of them.

I Cor. 12. 9 To another faith by the same Spirit; to another the gifts of healing by the same Spirit;

I Cor. 12. 28 And God hath set some in the church, first apostles, secondarily prophets, thirdly teachers, after that miracles, then gifts of healings, helps, governments, diversities of tongues.

C

I Tim. 5. 17 Let the elders that rule well be counted worthy of double honour, especially they who labour in the word and doctrine.

D

Acts 27. 3. *See c, C, § 311, page 796.*

§ 316. PAUL TESTIFIES OF THE KINGDOM TO THE JEWS.

While at Rome (Spring, A. D. 62) the following epistles were written:

28 : 17–31.

17 And it came to pass, that after three days Paul called the chief of the Jews together: and when they were come together, he said unto them, Men *and* brethren, [a]though I have committed nothing against the people, or customs of our fathers, yet [b]was I delivered prisoner from Jerusalem into the hands of the Romans.

18 Who, [c]when they had examined me, would have let *me* go, because there was no cause of death in me.

19 But when the Jews spake against *it*, [d]I was constrained to appeal unto Cæsar; not that I had aught to accuse my nation of.

20 For this cause therefore have I called for you, to see *you*, and to speak with *you:* because that [e]for the hope of Israel I am bound with [f]this chain.

21 And they said unto him, We neither received letters out of Judea concerning thee, neither any of the brethren that came shewed or spake any harm of thee.

22 But we desire to hear of thee what thou thinkest: for as concerning this sect, we know that every where [g]it is spoken against.

23 And when they had appointed him a day, there came many to him into *his* lodging; [h]to whom he expounded and testified the kingdom of God, persuading them concerning Jesus, [i]both out of the law of Moses, and *out of* the prophets, from morning till evening.

24 And [k]some believed the things which were spoken, and some believed not.

CHAP. 28.

25 And when they agreed not among themselves, they departed, after that Paul had spoken one word, Well spake the Holy Ghost by Esaias the prophet unto our fathers,

A

Acts 24. 12 And they neither found me in the temple disputing with any man, neither raising up the people, neither in the synagogues, nor in the city:

13 Neither can they prove the things whereof they now accuse me.

Acts 25. 8 While he answered for himself, Neither against the law of the Jews, neither against the temple, nor yet against Cæsar, have I offended any thing at all.

B

Acts 21. 33 Then the chief captain came near, and took him, and commanded *him* to be bound with two chains; and demanded who he was, and what he had done.

C

Acts 22. 24 The chief captain commanded him to be brought into the castle, and bade that he should be examined by scourging; that he might know whereof they cried so against him.

Acts 24. 10 Then Paul, after that the governor had beckoned unto him to speak, answered, Forasmuch as I know that thou hast been of many years a judge unto this nation, I do the more cheerfully answer for myself;

Acts 25. 8. *See under A.*

Acts 26. 31 And when they were gone aside, they talked between themselves, saying, This man doeth nothing worthy of death, or of bonds.

D

Acts 25. 11 For if I be an offender, or have committed any thing worthy of death, I refuse not to die: but if there be none of these things whereof these accuse me, no man may deliver me unto them. I appeal unto Cæsar.

E

Acts 26. 6 And now I stand and am judged for the hope of the promise made of God unto our fathers:

7 Unto which *promise* our twelve tribes, instantly serving *God* day and night, hope to come. For which hope's

HE IS RETAINED TWO YEARS. TIME, SPRING, A. D. 61–63; PLACE, ROME.

Philemon, Colossians and *Ephesians.* To the *Philippians,* Autumn, A. D. 62.

E—CONCLUDED.

sake, king Agrippa, I am accused of
the Jews.

F

Acts 26. 29 And Paul said, I would to God,
that not only thou, but also all that
hear me this day, were both almost,
and altogether such as I am, except
these bonds.

Eph. 3. 1 For this cause I Paul, the prisoner
of Jesus Christ for you Gentiles,

Eph. 4. 1 I therefore, the prisoner of the
Lord, beseech you that ye walk worthy
of the vocation wherewith ye are called,

Eph. 6. 20 For which I am an ambassador in
bonds: that therein I may speak
boldly, as I ought to speak.

IITim 1. 16 The Lord give mercy unto the
house of Onesiphorus; for he oft refreshed
me, and was not ashamed of
my chain:

IITim 2. 9 Wherein I suffer trouble, as an evil
doer, *even* unto bonds; but the word of
God is not bound.

Phile. 10 I beseech thee for my son Onesimus,
whom I have begotten in my
bonds:

Phile. 13 Whom I would have retained with
me, that in thy stead he might have
ministered unto me in the bonds of the
gospel:

G

Luke 2. 34 And Simeon blessed them, and
said unto Mary his mother, Behold,
this *child* is set for the fall and rising
again of many in Israel; and for a sign
which shall be spoken against;

Acts 24. 5 For we have found this man *a* pestilent
fellow, and a mover of sedition
among all the Jews throughout the
world, and a ringleader of the sect of
the Nazarenes:

Acts 24. 14 But this I confess unto thee, that
after the way which they call heresy,
so worship I the God of my fathers,
believing all things which are written
in the law and in the prophets:

I Pet. 2. 12 Having your conversation honest
among the Gentiles: that, whereas
they speak against you as evil doers,
they may by *your* good works, which
they shall behold, glorify God in the
day of visitation.

I Pet. 4. 14 If ye be reproached for the name
of Christ, happy *are ye*: for the Spirit
of glory and of God resteth upon you:
on their part he is evil spoken of, but
on your part he is glorified.

H

Luke 24. 27 And beginning at Moses and all
the prophets, he expounded unto them
in all the Scriptures the things concerning
himself.

Acts 17. 3 Opening and alleging, that Christ
must needs have suffered, and risen
again from the dead; and that this
Jesus, whom I preach unto you, is
Christ.

Acts 19. 8 And he went into the synagogue,
and spake boldly for the space of three
months, disputing and persuading the
things concerning the kingdom of God.

I

Acts 26. 6. *See d, D, § 309, page 792.*

K

Acts 14. 4 But the multitude of the city was
divided: and part held with the Jews,
and part with the apostles.

Acts 17. 4 And some of them believed, and
consorted with Paul and Silas; and of
the devout Greeks a great multitude,
and of the chief women not a few.

Acts 19. 9 But when divers were hardened,
and believed not, but spake evil of that
way before the multitude, he departed
from them, and separated the disciples,
disputing daily in the school of one
Tyrannus.

L

Isa. 6. 9 And he said, Go, and tell this people,
Hear ye indeed, but understand
not; and see ye indeed, but perceive
not.

Jer. 5. 21 Hear now this, O foolish people,
and without understanding; which have
eyes, and see not; which have ears
and hear not:

Eze. 12. 2 Son of man, thou dwellest in the
midst of a rebellious house, which
have eyes to see, and see not; they
have ears to hear, and hear not: for
they *are* a rebellious house.

Matt. 13. 14 And in them is fulfilled the
prophecy of Esaias, which saith, By
hearing ye shall hear, and shall not
understand; and seeing ye shall see,
and shall not perceive:

15 For this people's heart is waxed
gross, and *their* ears are dull of hearing,
and their eyes they have closed;
lest at any time they should see with
their eyes, and hear with *their* ears,
and should understand with *their*
heart, and should be converted, and I
should heal them.

§ 316. PAUL TESTIFIES OF THE KINGDOM TO THE JEWS.

CHAP. 28.

26 Saying, [l]Go unto this people, and say, Hearing ye shall hear, and shall not understand; and seeing ye shall see, and not perceive:

27 For the heart of this people is waxed gross, and their ears are dull of hearing, and their eyes have they closed; lest they should see with *their* eyes, and hear with *their* ears, and understand with *their* heart, and should be converted, and I should heal them.

28 Be it known therefore unto you, that [m]the salvation of God is sent [n]unto the Gentiles, and *that* they will hear it.

29 And when he had said these words, the Jews departed, and had great reasoning among themselves.

30 And Paul dwelt two whole years in his own hired house, and received all that came in unto him,

31 [o]Preaching the kingdom of God, and teaching those things which concern the Lord Jesus Christ, with all confidence, no man forbidding him.

For L, see preceding page (805).

L—CONTINUED.

Mark 4. 12 That seeing they may see, and not perceive; and hearing they may hear, and not understand; lest at any time they should be converted, and *their* sins should be forgiven them.

Luke 8. 10 And he said, Unto you it is given to know the mysteries of the kingdom of God: but to others in parables; that seeing they might not see, and hearing they might not understand.

L—CONCLUDED.

John 12. 37 But though he had done so many miracles before them, yet they believed not on him.

38 That the saying of Esaias the prophet might be fulfilled, which he spake, Lord, who hath believed our report? and to whom hath the arm of the Lord been revealed?

39 Therefore they could not believe, because that Esaias said again,

40 He hath blinded their eyes, and hardened their heart; that they should not see with *their* eyes, nor understand with *their* heart, and be converted, and I should heal them.

Rom. 11. 8 (According as it is written, God hath given them the spirit of slumber, eyes that they should not see, and ears that they should not hear;) unto this day.

M

Ps. 98. 2 The LORD hath made known his salvation: his righteousness hath he openly shewed in the sight of the heathen.

3 He hath remembered his mercy and his truth toward the house of Israel: all the ends of the earth have seen the salvation of our God.

Isa. 49. 6 And he said, It is a light thing that thou shouldest be my servant to raise up the tribes of Jacob, and to restore the preserved of Israel: I will also give thee for a light to the Gentiles, that thou mayest be my salvation unto the end of the earth.

Isa. 52. 10 The LORD hath made bare his holy arm in the eyes of all the nations; and all the ends of the earth shall see the salvation of our God.

Lam. 3. 26 *It is* good that *a man* should both hope and quietly wait for the salvation of the LORD.

Luke 2. 30 For mine eyes have seen thy salvation,

31 Which thou hast prepared before the face of all people;

32 A light to lighten the Gentiles, and the glory of thy people Israel.

Luke 3. 6 And all flesh shall see the salvation of God.

* A. D. 63 Paul was acquitted. He goes to Macedonia, then to Asia Minor. If he
66 he is found in Asia Minor again (Ephesus), and a year later (Summer A. D. 67) in Mace-
67) he writes his *Epistle to Titus* from Ephesus. The Winter was spent in Nicopolis. In the
Timothy. He was probably executed shortly before the death of Nero, which occurred about
Paul's, can not be clearly thus authenticated.

HE IS RETAINED TWO YEARS (CONCLUDED). TIME, SPRING, A. D. 61–63.*

N

Matt. 21. 41 They say unto him, He will miserably destroy those wicked men, and will let out *his* vineyard unto other husbandmen, which shall render him the fruits in their seasons.

42 Jesus saith unto them, Did ye never read in the Scriptures, The stone which the builders rejected, the same is become the head of the corner: this is the Lord's doing, and it is marvellous in our eyes?

43 Therefore say I unto you, The kingdom of God shall be taken from you, and given to a nation bringing forth the fruits thereof.

Acts 11. 18 When they heard these things, they held their peace, and glorified God, saying, Then hath God also to the Gentiles granted repentance unto life.

Acts 13. 46 Then Paul and Barnabas waxed bold, and said, It was necessary that the word of God should first have been spoken to you: but seeing ye put it from you, and judge yourselves unworthy of everlasting life, lo, we turn to the Gentiles.

47 For so hath the Lord commanded us, *saying*, I have set thee to be a light of the Gentiles, that thou shouldest be for salvation unto the ends of the earth.

Acts 14. 27 And when they were come, and had gathered the church together, they rehearsed all that God had done with them, and how he had opened the door of faith unto the Gentiles.

Acts 18. 6 And when they opposed themselves, and blasphemed, he shook *his* raiment, and said unto them, Your blood *be* upon your own heads; I *am* clean: from henceforth I will go unto the Gentiles.

Acts 22. 21 And he said unto me, Depart: for I will send thee far hence unto the Gentiles.

Acts 26. 17 Delivering thee from the people, and *from* the Gentiles, unto whom now I send thee.

18 To open their eyes, *and* to turn *them* from darkness to light, and *from* the power of Satan unto God, that they may receive forgiveness of sins, and inheritance among them which are sanctified by faith that is in me.

N—CONCLUDED.

Rom. 11. 11 I say then, Have they stumbled that they should fall? God forbid: but *rather* through their fall salvation *is come* unto the Gentiles, for to provoke them to jealousy.

Rom. 15. 8 Now I say that Jesus Christ was a minister of the circumcision for the truth of God, to confirm the promises *made* unto the fathers:

9 And that the Gentiles might glorify God for *his* mercy; as it is written, For this cause I will confess to thee among the Gentiles, and sing unto thy name.

10 And again he saith, Rejoice, ye Gentiles, with his people.

11 And again, Praise the Lord, all ye Gentiles; and laud him, all ye people.

12 And again, Esaias saith, There shall be a root of Jesse, and he that shall rise to reign over the Gentiles; in him shall the Gentiles trust.

13 Now the God of hope fill you with all joy and peace in believing, that ye may abound in hope, through the power of the Holy Ghost.

14 And I myself also am persuaded of you, my brethren, that ye also are full of goodness, filled with all knowledge, able also to admonish one another.

O

Luke 16. 16 The law and the prophets *were* until John: since that time the kingdom of God is preached, and every man presseth into it.

Acts 8. 12 But when they believed Philip preaching the things concerning the kingdom of God, and the name of Jesus Christ, they were baptized, both men and women.

Acts 20. 25 And now, behold, I know that ye all, among whom I have gone preaching the kingdom of God, shall see my face no more.

Eph. 6. 19 And for me, that utterance may be given unto me, that I may open my mouth boldly, to make known the mystery of the gospel,

ever visited Spain, it probably occurred at this time, A. D. 64–65. In the Summer of A. D.
donia, from whence he writes his *First Epistle to Timothy*. The same year (Autumn, A. D.
Spring of A. D. 68 he is again a prisoner at Rome, whence he writes his *Second Epistle to*
the middle of June, A. D. 68. The *Epistle to the Hebrews*, so commonly thought of as one of

§ 317. THE

The epistle to the *Romans* was probably written

1:1–7.

1 Paul, a servant of Jesus Christ, [a]called *to be* an apostle, [b]separated unto the gospel of God,

2 ([c]Which he had promised afore [d]by his prophets in the holy Scriptures,)

3 Concerning his son Jesus Christ our Lord, [e]which was [f]made of the seed of David according to the flesh;

4 And [1g]declared *to be* the Son of God with power, according [h]to the Spirit of holiness, by the resurrection from the dead:

5 By whom [i]we have received grace and apostleship, [2]for [k]obedience to the faith among all nations, for his name:

6 Among whom are ye also the called of Jesus Christ:

7 To all that be in Rome, beloved of God, [l]called *to be* saints: [m]Grace to you, and peace, from God our Father and the Lord Jesus Christ.

A

Acts 22. 21. *See i, I, § 297, page 774.*

I Cor. 1. 1 Paul, called *to be* an apostle of Jesus Christ through the will of God, and Sosthenes *our* brother,

Gal. 1. 1 Paul, an apostle, (not of men, neither by man, but by Jesus Christ, and God the Father, who raised him from the dead;)

Gal. 1. 15 But when it pleased God, who separated me from my mother's womb, and called *me* by his grace,

A—Concluded.

I Tim. 1. 11 According to the glorious gospel of the blessed God, which was committed to my trust.

Rom. 1. 5. *See text of topic.*

B

Acts 9. 15 But the Lord said unto him, Go thy way: for he is a chosen vessel unto me, to bear my name before the Gentiles, and kings, and the children of Israel:

Acts 13. 2 As they ministered to the Lord, and fasted, the Holy Ghost said, Separate me Barnabas and Saul for the work whereunto I have called them.

C

Acts 26. 6. *See d, D, § 309, page 792.*

Tit. 1. 2 In hope of eternal life, which God, that cannot lie, promised before the world began;

D

Rom. 3. 21 But now the righteousness of God without the law is manifested, being witnessed by the law and the prophets;

Rom. 16. 26 But now is made manifest, and by the Scriptures of the prophets, according to the commandment of the everlasting God, made known to all nations for the obedience of faith:

Gal. 3. 8 And the Scripture, foreseeing that God would justify the heathen through faith, preached before the gospel unto Abraham, *saying*, In thee shall all nations be blessed.

E

Matt. 1. 6 And Jesse begat David the king; and David the king begat Solomon of her *that had been the wife* of Urias;

Matt. 1. 16 And Jacob begat Joseph the husband of Mary, of whom was born Jesus, who is called Christ.

Acts 2. 30. *See q, Q, § 231, page 638.*

§ 318. PAUL'S PURPOSE TO VISIT ROME TO PREACH THE

1:8–17.

8 First, [a]I thank my God through Jesus Christ for you all, that [b]your faith is spoken of throughout the whole world.

9 For [c]God is my witness, [d]whom I serve [1]with my spirit in the gospel of his Son, that without ceasing I make

A

I Cor. 1. 4 I thank my God always on your behalf, for the grace of God which is given you by Jesus Christ;

Phil. 1. 3 I thank my God upon every remembrance of you,

Col. 1. 3 We give thanks to God and the Father of our Lord Jesus Christ, praying always for you,

4 Since we heard of your faith in

TO THE ROMANS.

SALUTATION.

from Corinth in the Spring of A. D. 58.

F

John 1. 14 And the word was made flesh, and dwelt among us, (and we beheld his glory, the glory as of the only begotten of the Father,) full of grace and truth.

Gal. 4. 4 But when the fulness of the time was come, God sent forth his Son, made of a woman, made under the law,

1

Gr. *determined.*

G

Acts 13. 33 God hath fulfilled the same unto us their children, in that he hath raised up Jesus again; as it is also written in the second psalm, Thou art my Son, this day have I begotten thee.

H

Heb. 9. 14 How much more shall the blood of Christ, who through the eternal Spirit offered himself without spot to God, purge your conscience from dead works to serve the living God?

I Pet. 3. 18 For Christ also hath once suffered for sins, the just for the unjust, that he might bring us to God, being put to death in the flesh, but quickened by the Spirit:

I

Rom. 12. 3 For I say, through the grace given unto me, to every man that is among you, not to think *of himself* more highly than he ought to think; but to think soberly, according as God hath dealt to every man the measure of faith.

Rom. 15. 15 Nevertheless, brethren, I have written the more boldly unto you in some sort, as putting you in mind, because of the grace that is given to me of God,

I Cor. 15. 10 But by the grace of God I am what I am: and his grace which *was bestowed* upon me was not in vain; but I laboured more abundantly than they all: yet not I, but the grace of God which was with me.

I—CONCLUDED.

Gal. 1. 15. *See under A.*

Gal. 2. 9 And when James, Cephas, and John, who seemed to be pillars, perceived the grace that was given unto me, they gave to me and Barnabas the right hands of fellowship; that we *should go* unto the heathen, and they unto the circumcision.

Eph. 3. 8 Unto me, who am less than the least of all saints, is this grace given, that I should preach among the Gentiles the unsearchable riches of Christ;

2

Or, *to the obedience of faith.*

K

Acts 6. 7 And the word of God increased; and the number of the disciples multiplied in Jerusalem greatly; and a great company of the priests were obedient to the faith.

Rom. 16. 26. *See under D.*

L

Rom. 9. 24 Even us, whom he hath called, not of the Jews only, but also of the Gentiles?

I Cor. 1. 2 Unto the church of God which is at Corinth, to them that are sanctified in Christ Jesus, called *to be* saints, with all that in every place call upon the name of Jesus Christ our Lord, both theirs and ours:

I Thes. 4. 7 For God hath not called us unto uncleanness, but unto holiness.

M

I Cor. 1. 3 Grace *be* unto you, and peace, from God our Father, and *from* the Lord Jesus Christ,

II Cor. 1. 2 Grace *be* to you, and peace, from God our Father, and *from* the Lord Jesus Christ.

Gal. 1. 3 Grace *be* to you, and peace, from God the Father, and *from* our Lord Jesus Christ,

GOSPEL WHEREIN THE RIGHTEOUSNESS OF GOD IS REVEALED.

A—CONCLUDED.

Christ Jesus, and of the love *which ye have* to all the saints,

I Thes. 1. 2 We give thanks to God always for you all, making mention of you in our prayers;

Phile. 4 I thank my God, making mention of thee always in my prayers,

B

Rom. 16. 19 For your obedience is come abroad unto all *men.* I am glad therefore on

B—CONCLUDED.

your behalf: but yet I would have you wise unto that which is good, and simple concerning evil.

I Thes. 1. 8 For from you sounded out the word of the Lord not only in Macedonia and Achaia, but also in every place your faith to Godward is spread abroad; so that we need not to speak any thing.

For C, D and 1 see next page (810).

§ 318. PAUL'S PURPOSE TO VISIT ROME TO PREACH THE GOSPEL

CHAP. 1.

mention of you always in my prayers;
10 Making request, if by any means
now at length I might have a prosperous journey [e]by the will of God
to come unto you.
11 For I long to see you, that [f]I may
impart unto you some spiritual gift,
to the end ye may be established;
12 That is, that I may be comforted together [2]with you by [g]the
mutual faith both of you and me.
13 Now I would not have you ignorant, brethren, that oftentimes I purposed to come unto you, (but [h]was
let hitherto,) that I might have some
[i]fruit[2]among you also, even as among
other Gentiles.
14 [k]I am debtor both to the Greeks,
and to the Barbarians; both to the
wise, and to the unwise.
15 So, as much as in me is, I am
ready to preach the gospel to you
that are at Rome also.
16 For [l]I am not ashamed of the
gospel of Christ: for [m]it is the power
of God unto salvation to every one
that believeth; [n]to the Jew first, and
also to the Greek.
17 For [o]therein is the righteousness
of God revealed from faith to faith:
as it is written, [p]The just shall live
by faith.

C

Rom. 9. 1 I say the truth in Christ, I lie not, my conscience also bearing me witness in the Holy Ghost,

II Cor. 1. 23 Moreover I call God for a record upon my soul, that to spare you I came not as yet unto Corinth.

Phil. 1. 8 For God is my record, how greatly I long after you all in the bowels of Jesus Christ.

I Thes. 2. 5 For neither at any time used we flattering words, as ye know, nor a cloak of covetousness; God *is* witness:

D

Acts 27. 23. *See d, D, § 312, page 799.*

1

Or, *in my spirit*

E

Jas. 4. 15 For that ye *ought* to say, If the Lord will, we shall live, and do this, or that.

F

Rom. 15. 29 And I am sure that, when I come unto you, I shall come in the fulness of the blessing of the gospel of Christ.

2

Or, *in you.*

G

Tit. 1. 4 To Titus, *mine* own son after the common faith: Grace, mercy, *and* peace, from God the Father and the Lord Jesus Christ our Saviour.

II Pet. 1. 1 Simon Peter, a servant and an apostle of Jesus Christ, to them that have obtained like precious faith with us through the righteousness of God and our Saviour Jesus Christ:

H

Acts 16. 7 After they were come to Mysia, they assayed to go into Bithynia: but the Spirit suffered them not.

I Thes. 2 18 Wherefore we would have come unto you, even I Paul, once and again; but Satan hindered us.

I

Phil. 4. 17 Not because I desire a gift: but I desire fruit that may abound to your account.

K

I Cor. 9. 16 For though I preach the gospel, I have nothing to glory of: for necessity is laid upon me; yea, woe is unto me, if I preach not the gospel!

L

Ps. 40. 9 I have preached righteousness in the great congregation: lo, I have not refrained my lips, O LORD, thou knowest.

10 I have not hid thy righteousness within my heart; I have declared thy faithfulness and thy salvation: I have not concealed thy lovingkindness and thy truth from the great congregation.

Mark 8. 38 Whosoever therefore shall be ashamed of me and of my words, in this adulterous and sinful generation; of him also shall the Son of man be ashamed, when he cometh in the glory of his Father with the holy angels.

II Tim. 1. 8 Be not thou therefore ashamed of the testimony of our Lord, nor of me his prisoner: but be thou partaker of the afflictions of the gospel according to the power of God;

WHEREIN THE RIGHTEOUSNESS OF GOD IS REVEALED (CONCLUDED).

M

Jer. 23. 29 *Is* not my word like as a fire? saith the LORD; and like a hammer *that* breaketh the rock in pieces?

I Cor. 1. 18 For the preaching of the cross is to them that perish, foolishness; but unto us which are saved, it is the power of God.

I Cor. 2. 4 And my speech and my preaching *was* not with enticing words of man's wisdom, but in demonstration of the Spirit and of power:

I Cor. 15. 2 By which also ye are saved, if ye keep in memory what I preached unto you, unless ye have believed in vain.

Col. 1. 5 For the hope which is laid up for you in heaven, whereof ye heard before in the word of the truth of the gospel;

6 Which is come unto you, as *it is* in all the world; and bringeth forth fruit, as *it doth* also in you, since the day ye heard *of it*, and knew the grace of God in truth:

I Thes. 1. 5 For our gospel came not unto you in word only, but also in power, and in the Holy Ghost, and in much assurance; as ye know what manner of men we were among you for your sake.

I Thes. 2. 13 For this cause also thank we God without ceasing, because, when ye received the word of God which ye heard of us, ye received *it* not *as* the word of men, but, as it is in truth, the word of God, which effectually worketh also in you that believe.

Heb. 4. 12 For the word of God *is* quick, and powerful, and sharper than any two-edged sword, piercing even to the dividing asunder of soul and spirit, and of the joints and marrow, and *is* a discerner of the thoughts and intents of the heart.

N

Luke 2. 30 For mine eyes have seen thy salvation,

31 Which thou has prepared before the face of all people;

32 A light to lighten the Gentiles, and the glory of thy people Israel.

Luke 24. 47 And that repentance and remission of sins should be preached in his name among all nations, beginning at Jerusalem.

Acts 3. 26 Unto you first God, having raised up his Son Jesus, sent him to bless you, in turning away every one of you from his iniquities.

N—CONCLUDED.

Acts 13. 26 Men *and* brethren, children of the stock of Abraham, and whosoever among you feareth God, to you is the word of this salvation sent.

Acts 13. 46 Then Paul and Barnabas waxed bold, and said, It was necessary that the word of God should first have been spoken to you: but seeing ye put it from you, and judge yourselves unworthy of everlasting life, lo, we turn to the Gentiles:

Rom. 2. 9 Tribulation and anguish, upon every soul of man that doeth evil, of the Jew first, and also of the Gentile:

O

Isa. 46. 13 I bring near my righteousness; it shall not be far off, and my salvation shall not tarry: and I will place salvation in Zion for Israel my glory.

Isa. 51. 8 For the moth shall eat them up like a garment, and the worms shall eat them like wool: but my righteousness shall be forever, and my salvation from generation to generation.

Rom. 3. 21 But now the righteousness of God without the law is manifested, being witnessed by the law and the prophets;

P

Hab. 2. 4 Behold, his soul *which* is lifted up is not upright in him: but the just shall live by his faith.

John 3. 36 He that believeth on the Son hath everlasting life: and he that believeth not the Son shall not see life; but the wrath of God abideth on him.

Gal. 3. 11 But that no man is justified by the law in the sight of God, *it is* evident: for, The just shall live by faith.

Phil. 3. 9 And be found in him, not having mine own righteousness, which is of the law, but that which is through the faith of Christ, the righteousness which is of God by faith:

Heb. 10. 38 Now the just shall live by faith: but if *any man* draw back, my soul shall have no pleasure in him.

Heb. 11. 6 But without faith *it is* impossible to please *him*: for he that cometh to God must believe that he is, and *that* he is a rewarder of them that diligently seek him.

7 By faith Noah, being warned of God of things not seen as yet, moved with fear, prepared an ark to the saving of his house; by the which he condemned the world, and became heir of the righteousness which is by faith.

§ 319. GENTILES WILFULLY VIOLATING THE KNOWLEDGE OF GOD

1: 18-32.

18 For [a]the wrath of God is revealed from heaven against all ungodliness and unrighteousness of men, who hold the truth in unrighteousness;

19 Because [b]that which may be known of God is manifest [1]in them; [c]for God hath shewed *it* unto them.

20 For [d]the invisible things of him from the creation of the world are clearly seen, being understood by the things that are made, *even* his eternal power and Godhead; [2]so that they are without excuse:

21 Because that, when they knew God, they glorified *him* not as God, neither were thankful; but [e]became vain in their imaginations, and their foolish heart was darkened.

22 [f]Professing themselves to be wise, they became fools,

23 And changed the glory of the uncorruptible [g]God into an image made like to corruptible man, and to birds, and fourfooted beasts, and creeping things.

24 [h]Wherefore God also gave them up to uncleanness, through the lusts of their own hearts, [i]to dishonour their own bodies [k]between themselves:

25 Who changed [l]the truth of God [m]into a lie, and worshipped and served the creature [3]more than the Creator, who is blessed for ever. Amen.

26 For this cause God gave them up unto [n]vile affections: for even their women did change the natural use into that which is against nature:

27 And likewise also the men, leaving the natural use of the woman, burned in their lust one toward an-

A

Acts 17. 30 And the time of this ignorance God winked at; but now commandeth all men every where to repent:

Eph. 5. 6 Let no man deceive you with vain words: for because of these things cometh the wrath of God upon the children of disobedience.

Col. 3. 6 For which things' sake the wrath of God cometh on the children of disobedience:

B

Ps. 19. 1 The heavens declare the glory of God; and the firmament sheweth his handywork.

2 Day unto day uttereth speech, and night unto night showeth knowledge.

3 *There is* no speech nor language, *where* their voice is not heard.

4 Their line is gone out through all the earth, and their words to the end of the world. In them hath he set a tabernacle for the sun,

Isa. 40. 26 Lift up your eyes on high, and behold who hath created these *things*, that bringeth out their host by number: he calleth them all by names by the greatness of his might, for that *he is* strong in power; not one faileth.

Acts 14. 17 Nevertheless he left not himself without witness, in that he did good, and gave us rain from heaven, and fruitful seasons, filling our hearts with food and gladness.

Acts 17. 27 That they should seek the Lord, if haply they might feel after him, and find him, though he be not far from every one of us:

28 For in him we live, and move, and have our being; as certain also of your own poets have said, For we are also his offspring.

1

Or, *to them.*

C

John 1. 9 *That* was the true Light, which lighteth every man that cometh into the world.

D

Ps. 19. 1, etc. *See under B.*

2

Or, *that they may be.*

E

Gen. 6. 5 And GOD saw that the wickedness of man *was* great in the earth, and *that* every imagination of the thoughts of his heart *was* only evil continually.

MANIFESTED TO THEM, WERE GIVEN OVER TO REPROBATE MINDS.

E—CONCLUDED.

II Ki. 17. 15 And they rejected his statutes, and his covenant that he made with their fathers, and his testimonies which he testified against them; and they followed vanity, and became vain, and went after the heathen that *were* round about them, *concerning* whom the LORD had charged them, that they should not do like them.

Ps. 81. 12 So I gave them up unto their own hearts' lust: *and* they walked in their own counsels.

Eccl. 7. 29 Lo, this only have I found, that God hath made man upright; but they have sought out many inventions.

Jer. 2. 5 Thus saith the LORD, What iniquity have your fathers found in me, that they are gone far from me, and have walked after vanity, and are become vain?

Eph. 4. 17 This I say therefore, and testify in the Lord, that ye henceforth walk not as other Gentiles walk, in the vanity of their mind.

18 Having the understanding darkened, being alienated from the life of God through the ignorance that is in them, because of the blindness of their heart:

I Pet. 1. 18 Forasmuch as ye know that ye were not redeemed with corruptible things, *as* silver and gold, from your vain conversation *received* by tradition from your fathers;

F

Jer. 10. 14 Every man is brutish in *his* knowledge: every founder is confounded by the graven image: for his molten image *is* falsehood, and *there is* no breath in them.

G

Deut. 4. 16 Lest ye corrupt *yourselves*, and make you a graven image, the similitude of any figure, the likeness of male or female.

Ps. 106. 20 Thus they changed their glory into the similitude of an ox that eateth grass.

Isa. 40. 18 To whom then will ye liken God? or what likeness will ye compare unto him?

19 The workman melteth a graven image, and the goldsmith spreadeth it over with gold, and casteth silver chains.

20 He that *is* so impoverished that he hath no oblation chooseth a tree *that* will not rot; he seeketh unto him a

G—CONCLUDED.

cunning workman to prepare a graven image, *that* shall not be moved.

Jer. 2. 11 Hath a nation changed *their* gods, which *are* yet no gods? but my people have changed their glory for *that which* doth not profit.

Eze. 8. 10 So I went in and saw; and behold every form of creeping things, and abominable beasts, and all the idols of the house of Israel, portrayed upon the wall round about.

Acts 17. 29 Forasmuch then as we are the offspring of God, we ought not to think that the Godhead is like unto gold, or silver, or stone, graven by art and man's device.

H

Ps. 81. 12. *See under E.*

Acts 7. 42 Then God turned, and gave them up to worship the host of heaven; as it is written in the book of the prophets, O ye house of Israel, have ye offered to me slain beasts and sacrifices *by the space of* forty years in the wilderness?

Eph. 4. 18. *See under E.*

Eph. 4. 19 Who being past feeling have given themselves over unto lasciviousness, to work all uncleanness with greediness.

II Thes. 2. 11 And for this cause God shall send them strong delusion, that they should believe a lie:

12 That they all might be damned who believed not the truth; but had pleasure in unrighteousness.

I

I Cor. 6. 18 Flee fornication. Every sin that a man doeth is without the body; but he that committeth fornication sinneth against his own body.

I Thes. 4. 4 That every one of you should know how to possess his vessel in sanctification and honour;

I Pet. 4. 3 For the time past of *our* life may suffice us to have wrought the will of the Gentiles, when we walked in lasciviousness, lusts, excess of wine, revellings, banquetings, and abominable idolatries:

K

Lev. 18. 22 Thou shalt not lie with mankind, as with womankind: it *is* abomination.

L

I Thes. 1. 9 For they themselves shew of us what manner of entering in we had unto you, and how ye turned to God from idols to serve the living and true God;

For L concluded, M, 3 and N, see next page (814.)

§ 319. GENTILES WILFULLY VIOLATING THE KNOWLEDGE OF GOD MANI-

CHAP. I.

other; men with men working that which is unseemly, and receiving in themselves that recompense of their error which was meet.

28 And even as they did not like [4]to retain God in *their* knowledge, God gave them over to [5]a reprobate mind, to do those things [o]which are not convenient;

29 Being filled with all unrighteousness, fornication, wickedness, covetousness, maliciousness; full of envy, murder, debate, deceit, malignity; whisperers,

30 Backbiters, haters of God, despiteful, proud, boasters, inventors of evil things, disobedient to parents,

31 Without understanding, cov-

CHAP. I.

enant-breakers, [6]without natural affection, implacable, unmerciful:

32 Who, knowing the judgment of God, that they which commit such things are worthy of death, not only do the same, but [7p]have pleasure in them that do them.

L—CONCLUDED.

I Jno. 5. 20 And we know that the Son of God is come, and hath given us an understanding, that we may know him that is true, and we are in him that is true, *even* in his Son Jesus Christ. This is the true God, and eternal life.

M

Isa. 44. 20 He feedeth on ashes: a deceived heart hath turned him aside, that he cannot deliver his soul, nor say, *Is there* not a lie in my right hand?

Jer. 10. 14 Every man is brutish in *his* knowledge: every founder is confounded by the graven image: for his molten image *is* falsehood, and *there is* no breath in them.

§ 320. JUDGING OTHERS WE CONDEMN SELVES. SINNING WITHOUT

2 : 1–16.

1 Therefore thou art [a]inexcusable, O man, whosoever thou art that judgest: [b]for wherein thou judgest another, thou condemnest thyself; for thou that judgest doest the same things.

2 But we are sure that the judgment of God is according to truth against them which commit such things.

3 And thinkest thou this, O man, that judgest them which do such things, and doest the same, that thou shalt escape the judgment of God?

4 Or despisest thou [c]the riches of his goodness and [d]forbearance and [e]longsuffering; [f]not knowing that the goodness of God leadeth thee to repentance?

A

Rom. 1. 20 For the invisible things of him from the creation of the world are clearly seen, being understood by the things that are made, *even* his eternal power and Godhead; so that they are without excuse:

B

IISa. 12. 5 And David's anger was greatly kindled against the man; and he said to Nathan, *As* the LORD liveth, the man that hath done this *thing* shall surely die:

6 And he shall restore the lamb fourfold, because he did this thing, and because he had no pity.

7 And Nathan said to David, Thou *art* the man. Thus saith the LORD God of Israel, I anointed thee king over Israel, and I delivered thee out of the hand of Saul;

Ps. 50. 19 Thou givest thy mouth to evil, and thy tongue frameth deceit.

20 Thou sittest *and* speakest against thy brother; thou slanderest thine own mother's son.

FESTED TO THEM, WERE GIVEN OVER TO REPROBATE MINDS (CONCLUDED).

M—CONCLUDED.

Jer. 13. 25 This *is* thy lot, the portion of thy measures from me, saith the LORD; because thou hast forgotten me, and trusted in falsehood.

Amos 2. 4 Thus saith the LORD; For three transgressions of Judah, and for four, I will not turn away *the punishment* thereof; because they have despised the law of the LORD, and have not kept his commandments, and their lies caused them to err, after the which their fathers have walked:

3

Or, *rather.*

N

Lev. 18. 22. *See under K, page 813.*

23 Neither shalt thou lie with any beast to defile thyself therewith: neither shall any woman stand before a beast to lie down thereto: it *is* confusion.

Eph. 5. 12 For it is a shame even to speak of those things which are done of them in secret.

Jude 10 But these speak evil of those things which they know not: but what they know naturally, as brute beasts, in those things they corrupt themselsve.

4

Or, *to acknowledge.*

5

Or, *a mind void of judgment.*

O

Eph. 5. 4 Neither filthiness, nor foolish talking, nor jesting, which are not convenient: but rather giving of thanks.

Phile. 8 Wherefore, though I might be much bold in Christ to enjoin thee that which is convenient,

6

Or, *unsociable.*

7

Or, *consent with them.*

P

Ps. 50. 18 When thou sawest a thief, then thou consentedst with him, and hast been partaker with adulterers.

Hos. 7. 3 They make the king glad with their wickedness, and the princes with their lies.

Mark 14. 11 And when they heard *it*, they were glad, and promised to give him money. And he sought how he might conveniently betray him.

LAW, WE PERISH WITHOUT. SINNING UNDER LAW, ARE JUDGED THEREBY.

B—CONCLUDED.

Ps. 50. 21 These *things* has thou done, and I kept silence; thou thoughtest that I was altogether *such a one* as thyself: *but* I will reprove thee, and set *them* in order before thine eyes.

Matt. 7. 1 Judge not that ye be not judged.

2 For with what judgment ye judge, ye shall be judged: and with what measure ye mete, it shall be measured to you again.

John 8. 9 And they which heard *it*, being convicted by *their own* conscience, went out one by one, beginning at the eldest, *even* unto the last: and Jesus was left alone, and the woman standing in the midst.

Jas. 4. 11 Speak not evil one of another, brethren. He that speaketh evil of *his* brother, and judgeth his brother, speaketh evil of the law, and judgeth the law: but if thou judge the law, thou art not a doer of the law, but a judge.

C

Rom. 9. 23 And that he might make known the riches of his glory on the vessels

C—CONCLUDED.

of mercy, which he had afore prepared unto glory,

Eph. 1. 7 In whom we have redemption through his blood, the forgiveness of sins, according to the riches of his grace;

Eph. 2. 4 But God, who is rich in mercy, for his great love wherewith he loved us,

Eph. 2. 7 That in the ages to come he might shew the exceeding riches of his grace, in *his* kindness toward us, through Christ Jesus.

D

Rom. 3. 25 Whom God hath set forth *to be* a propitiation through faith in his blood, to declare his righteousness for the remission of sins that are past, through the forbearance of God;

E

Ex. 34. 6 And the LORD passed by before him, and proclaimed, The LORD, The LORD God, merciful and gracious, long-suffering, and abundant in goodness and truth,

For E concluded and F see next page (816).

§ 320. JUDGING OTHERS WE CONDEMN SELVES. SINNING WITHOUT LAW,

CHAP. 2.

5 But, after thy hardness and impenitent heart, [g]treasurest up unto thyself wrath against the day of wrath and revelation of the righteous judgment of God;

6 [h]Who will render to every man according to his deeds:

7 To them who by patient continuance in well doing seek for glory and honour and immortality, eternal life:

8 But unto them that are contentious, and [i]do not obey the truth, but obey unrighteousness, indignation and wrath,

9 Tribulation and anguish, upon every soul of man that doeth evil; of the Jew [k]first, and also of the [1]Gentile;

10 [l]But glory, honour, and peace, to every man that worketh good; to the Jew first, and also to the [1]Gentile:

11 For [m]there is no respect of persons with God.

12 For as many as have sinned without law shall also perish without law; and as many as have sinned in the law shall be judged by the law;

E—CONCLUDED.

Num. 14. 18 The LORD *is* longsuffering, and of great mercy, forgiving iniquity and transgression, and by no means clearing *the guilty*, visiting the iniquity of the fathers upon the children unto the third and fourth *generation.*

Ps. 86. 15 But thou, O LORD, *art* a God full of compassion, and gracious, longsuffering, and plenteous in mercy and truth.

I Tim. 1. 16 Howbeit for this cause I obtained mercy, that in me first Jesus Christ might shew forth all longsuffering, for a pattern to them which should hereafter believe on him to life everlasting.

I Pet. 3. 20 Which sometime were disobedient, when once the longsuffering of God waited in the days of Noah, while the ark was a preparing, wherein few, that is, eight souls were saved by water.

F

Isa. 30. 18 And therefore will the LORD wait, that he may be gracious unto you, and therefore will he be exalted, that he may have mercy upon you: for the LORD *is* a God of judgment: blessed *are* all they that wait for him.

II Pet. 3. 9 The Lord is not slack concerning his promise, as some men count slackness; but is longsuffering to us-ward, not willing that any should perish, but that all should come to repentance.

II Pet. 3. 15 And account *that* the longsuffering of our Lord *is* salvation; even as our beloved brother Paul also according to the wisdom given unto him hath written unto you;

G

Deut 32. 34 *Is* not this laid up in store with me, *and* sealed up among my treasures?

Jas. 5. 3 Your gold and silver is cankered; and the rust of them shall be a witness against you, and shall eat your flesh as it were fire. Ye have heaped treasure together for the last days.

H

Job. 34. 11 For the work of a man shall he render unto him, and cause every man to find according to *his* ways.

Ps. 62. 12 Also unto thee, O Lord, *belongeth* mercy: for thou renderest to every man according to his work.

Prov. 24. 12 If thou sayest, Behold, we knew it not; doth not he that pondereth the heart consider *it?* and he that keepeth thy soul, doth *not* he know *it?* and shall *not* he render to *every* man according to his works?

Jer. 17. 10 I the LORD search the heart, *I* try the reins, even to give every man according to his ways, *and* according to the fruit of his doings.

Jer. 32. 19 Great in counsel, and mighty in work: for thine eyes *are* open upon all the ways of the sons of men: to give every one according to his ways, and according to the fruit of his doings:

Matt. 16. 27 For the Son of man shall come in the glory of his Father with his angels; and then he shall reward every man according to his works.

Rom. 14. 12 So then every one of us shall give account of himself to God.

I Cor. 3. 8 Now he that planteth and he that watereth are one: and every man shall receive his own reward according to his own labour.

WE PERISH WITHOUT. SINNING UNDER LAW, ARE JUDGED THEREBY (CONT'D).

H—CONCLUDED.

II Cor. 5. 10 For we must all appear before the judgment seat of Christ; that every one may receive the things *done* in *his* body, according to that he hath done, whether *it be* good or bad.

Rev. 2. 20 Notwithstanding I have a few things against thee, because thou sufferest that woman Jezebel, which calleth herself a prophetess, to teach and to seduce my servants to commit fornication, and to eat things sacrificed unto idols.

Rev. 20. 12 And I saw the dead, small and great, stand before God; and the books were opened: and another book was opened, which is *the book* of life: and the dead were judged out of those things which were written in the books, according to their works.

Rev. 22. 12 And, behold, I come quickly; and my reward *is* with me, to give every man according as his work shall be.

I

Job 24. 13 They are of those that rebel against the light; they know not the ways thereof, nor abide in the paths thereof.

Isa. 3. 11 Woe unto the wicked! *it shall be* ill *with him:* for the reward of his hands shall be given him.

Rom. 1. 18 For the wrath of God is revealed from heaven against all ungodliness and unrighteousness of men, who hold the truth in unrighteousness;

II Thes. 1. 8 In flaming fire taking vengeance on them that know not God, and that obey not the gospel of our Lord Jesus Christ:

K

Amos 3. 2 You only have I known of all the families of the earth: therefore I will punish you for all your iniquities.

Luke 12. 47 And that servant, which knew his lord's will, and prepared not *himself*, neither did according to his will, shall be beaten with many *stripes*.

48 But he that knew not, and did commit things worthy of stripes, shall be beaten with few *stripes*. For unto whomsoever much is given, of him shall be much required; and to whom men have committed much, of him they will ask the more.

1

Gr. *Greek.*

L

I Pet. 1. 7 That the trial of your faith, being much more precious than of gold that

L—CONCLUDED.

perisheth, though it be tried with fire, might be found unto praise and honour and glory at the appearing of Jesus Christ:

M

Deut 10. 17 For the LORD your God *is* God of gods, and Lord of lords, a great God, a mighty, and a terrible, which regardeth not persons, nor taketh reward:

II Chr. 19. 7 Wherefore now let the fear of the LORD be upon you; take heed and do *it:* for *there is* no iniquity with the LORD our God, nor respect of persons, nor taking of gifts.

Job 34. 19 *How much less to him* that accepeth not the persons of princes, nor regardeth the rich more than the poor? for they all *are* the work of his hands.

Matt 22. 16 And they sent out unto him their disciples with the Herodians, saying, Master, we know that thou ar true, and teachest the way of God in truth, neither carest thou for any *man:* for thou regardest not the person of men.

Luke 20. 21 And they asked him, saying, Master, we know that thou sayest and teachest rightly, neither acceptest thou the person *of any*, but teachest the way of God truly:

Acts 10. 34 Then Peter opened *his* mouth, and said, Of a truth I perceive that God is no respecter of persons:

Gal. 2. 6 But of these who seemed to be somewhat, (whatsoever they were, it maketh no matter to me: God accepteth no man's person:) for they who seemed *to be somewhat* in conference added nothing to me:

Eph. 6. 9 And, ye masters, do the same things unto them, forbearing threatening: knowing that your Master also is in heaven; neither is there respect of persons with him.

Col. 3. 25 But he that doeth wrong shall receive for the wrong which he hath done: and there is no respect of persons.

I Pet. 1. 17 And if ye call on the Father, who without respect of persons judgeth according to every man's work, pass the time of your sojourning *here* in fear:

N

Matt. 7. 21 Not every one that saith unto me, Lord, Lord, shall enter into the kingdom of heaven; but he that doeth the will of my Father which is in heaven.

§ 320. JUDGING OTHERS WE CONDEMN SELVES. SINNING WITHOUT LAW,

CHAP. 2.

13 (For [n]not the hearers of the law *are* just before God, but the doers of the law shall be justified.

14 For when the Gentiles, which have not the law, do by nature the things contained in the law, these, having not the law, are a law unto themselves:

15 Which shew the work of the law written in their hearts, [2]their conscience also bearing witness, and *their* thoughts [3]the mean while accusing or else excusing one another;)

CHAP. 2.

16 [o]In the day when God shall judge the secrets of men [p]by Jesus Christ [q]according to my gospel.

N—CONCLUDED. See preceding page (817).

Jas. 1. 22 But be ye doers of the word, and not hearers only, deceiving your own selves.

23 For if any be a hearer of the word, and not a doer, he is like unto a man beholding his natural face in a glass:

Jas. 1. 25 But whoso looketh into the perfect law of liberty, and continueth *therein*, he being not a forgetful hearer, but a doer of the work, this man shall be blessed in his deed.

1 Jno. 3. 7 Little children, let no man deceive you: he that doeth righteousness is righteous, even as he is righteous.

§ 321. JEWS REST UPON THE LAW. BREAKING IT, CIRCUMCISION IS

2: 17-29.

17 Behold, [a]thou art called a Jew, and [b]restest in the law, [c]and makest thy boast of God,

18 And [d]knowest *his* will, and [1e]approvest the things that are more excellent, being instructed out of the law;

19 And [f]art confident that thou thyself art a guide of the blind, a light of them which are in darkness,

20 An instructor of the foolish, a teacher of babes, [g]which hast the form of knowledge and of the truth in the law.

21 [h]Thou therefore which teachest another, teachest thou not thyself? thou that preachest a man should not steal, dost thou steal?

22 Thou that sayest a man should not commit adultery, dost thou commit adultery? thou that abhorrest idols, [i]dost thou commit sacrilege?

23 Thou that makest thy boast of

A

John 8. 33 They answered him, We be Abraham's seed, and were never in bondage to any man: how sayest thou, Ye shall be made free?

Rom. 9. 6 Not as though the word of God hath taken none effect. For they *are* not all Israel, which are of Israel:

7 Neither, because they are the seed of Abraham, *are they* all children: but, In Isaac shall thy seed be called.

II Cor. 11. 22 Are they Hebrews? so *am* I. Are they Israelites? so *am* I. Are they the seed of Abraham? so *am* I.

B

Mic. 3. 11 The heads thereof judge for reward, and the priests thereof teach for hire, and the prophets thereof divine for money: yet will they lean upon the LORD, and say, *Is* not the LORD among us? none evil can come upon us.

Rom. 9. 4 Who are Israelites; to whom *pertaineth* the adoption, and the glory, and the covenants, and the giving of the law, and the service *of God*, and the promises;

C

Isa. 45. 25 In the LORD shall all the seed of Israel be justified, and shall glory.

Isa. 48. 2 For they call themselves of the holy city, and stay themselves upon the God of Isarel: The LORD of hosts *is* his name.

WE PERISH WITHOUT. SINNING UNDER LAW, ARE JUDGED THEREBY (CONC'D).

2

Or, *the conscience witnessing with them.*

3

Or, *between themselves.*

O

Eccl. 12. 14 For God shall bring every work into judgment, with every secret thing, whether *it be* good, or whether *it be* evil.

Matt. 25. 31 When the Son of man shall come in his glory, and all the holy angels with him, then shall he sit upon the throne of his glory:

John 12. 48 He that rejecteth me, and receiveth not my words, hath one that judgeth him: the word that I have spoken, the same shall judge him in the last day.

Rom. 3. 6 God forbid: for then how shall God judge the world?

O—CONCLUDED.

I Cor. 4. 5 Therefore judge nothing before the time, until the Lord come, who both will bring to light the hidden things of darkness, and will make manifest the counsels of the hearts: and then shall every man have praise of God.

Rev. 20. 12. *See under H, page 817.*

P

Acts 10. 42. *See p, P, §254, page 698.*

Q

Rom. 16. 25 Now to him that is of power to stablish you according to my gospel, and the preaching of Jesus Christ, according to the revelation of the mystery, which was kept secret since the world began,

II Tim. 2. 8 Remember that Jesus Christ of the seed of David was raised from the dead, according to my gospel:

PROFITLESS. CIRCUMCISION IS OF THE HEART, IN THE SPIRIT.

C—CONCLUDED.

John 8. 41 Ye do the deeds of your father. Then said they to him, We be not born of fornication; we have one father, *even* God.

D

Deut. 4. 8 And what nation *is there so* great, that hath statutes and judgments *so* righteous as all this law, which I set before you this day?

Ps. 147. 19 He sheweth his word unto Jacob, his statutes and his judgments unto Israel.

20 He hath not dealt so with any nation: and *as for his* judgments, they have not known them. Praise ye the LORD.

1

Or, *triest the things that differ,*

E

Phil. 1. 10 That ye may approve things that are excellent; that ye may be sincere and without offence till the day of Christ;

F

Matt. 15. 14 Let them alone: they be blind leaders of the blind. And if the blind lead the blind, both shall fall into the ditch.

Matt. 23. 16 Woe unto you, *ye* blind guides, which say, Whosoever shall swear by the temple, it is nothing; but whosoever shall swear by the gold of the temple, he is a debtor!

F—CONCLUDED.

Matt. 23. 17 *Ye* fools and blind: for whether is greater, the gold, or the temple that sanctifieth the gold?

Matt. 23. 19 *Ye* fools and blind: for whether *is* greater, the gift, or the altar that sanctifieth the gift?

Matt. 23. 24 *Ye* blind guides, which strain at a gnat, and swallow a camel.

John 9. 34 They answered and said nnto him, Thou wast altogether born in sins, and dost thou teach us? And they cast him out.

John 9. 40 And *some* of the Pharisees which were with him heard these words, and said unto him, Are we blind also?

41 Jesus said unto them, If ye were blind, ye should have no sin: but now ye say, We see; therefore your sin remaineth.

G

Rom. 6. 17 But God be thanked, that ye were the servants of sin, but ye have obeyed from the heart that form of doctrine which was delivered you.

II Tim. 1. 13 Hold fast the form of sound words, which thou hast heard of me, in faith and love which is in Cnrist Jesus.

II Tim. 3. 5 Having a form of godliness, but denying the power thereof: from such turn away.

For G concluded, H and I, see next page (820).

§ 321. JEWS REST UPON THE LAW. BREAKING IT, CIRCUMCISION IS PROFIT-

CHAP. 2.

the law, through breaking the law dishonourest thou God?

24 For the name of God is blasphemed among the Gentiles through you, as it is [k]written.

25 [l]For circumcision verily profiteth, if thou keep the law: but if thou be a breaker of the law, thy circumcision is made uncircumcision.

26 Therefore, [m]if the uncircumcision keep the righteousness of the law, shall not his uncircumcision be counted for circumcision?

27 And shall not uncircumcision which is by nature, if it fulfil the law, [n]judge thee, who by the letter and circumcision dost transgress the law?

28 For [o]he is not a Jew, which is one outwardly; neither *is that* circumcision, which is outward in the flesh:

29 But he *is* a Jew, [p]which is one inwardly; and [q]circumcision *is that* of the heart, [r]in the spirit, *and* not in the letter; whose praise *is* not of men, but of God.

G—CONCLUDED.

Tit. 1. 16 They profess that they know God; but in works they deny *him*, being abominable, and disobedient, and unto every good work reprobate.

H

Ps. 50. 16 But unto the wicked God saith, What hast thou to do to declare my statutes, or *that* thou shouldest take my covenant in thy mouth?

Matt. 23. 3 All therefore whatsoever they bid you observe, *that* observe and do; but do not ye after their works: for they say, and do not.

I

Mal. 3. 8 Will a man rob God? Yet ye have robbed me. But ye say, Wherein have we robbed thee? In tithes and offerings.

K

IISa. 12. 14 Howbeit, because by this deed thou hast given great occasion to the enemies of the LORD to blaspheme, the child also *that is* born unto thee shall surely die.

Eze. 36. 20 And when they entered unto the heathen, whither they went, they profaned my holy name, when they said to them, These *are* the people of the LORD, and are gone forth out of his land.

L

Gal. 5. 3 For I testify again to every man that is circumcised, that he is a debtor to do the whole law.

M

Acts. 10. 34 Then Peter opened *his* mouth, and said, Of a truth I perceive that God is no respecter of persons:

35 But in every nation he that feareth him, and worketh righteousness, is accepted with him.

N

Matt. 12. 41 The men of Nineveh shall rise in judgment with this generation, and shall condemn it: because they repented at the preaching of Jonas; and behold, a greater than Jonas *is* here

§ 322. THOUGH ENTRUSTED WITH THE ORACLES THE JEWS WERE FAITHLESS. GOD WAS

3: 1–8.

1 What advantage then hath the Jew? or what profit *is there* of circumcision?

2 Much every way: chiefly, because that [a]unto them were committed the oracles of God.

3 For what if [b]some did not believe?

A

Rom. 2. 18. *See d, D, §321, page 818.*

Rom. 9. 4 Who are Israelites; to whom *pertaineth* the adoption, and the glory, and the covenants, and the giving of the law, and the service *of God*, and the promises;

B

Rom. 10. 16 But they have not all obeyed the gospel. For Esaias saith, Lord, who hath believed our report?

Heb. 4. 2 For unto us was the gospel preached,

LESS. CIRCUMCISION IS OF THE HEART, IN THE SPIRIT (Concluded).

N—Concluded.

Matt. 12. 42 The queen of the south shall rise up in the judgment with this generation, and shall condemn it: for she came from the uttermost parts of the earth to hear the wisdom of Solomon; and, behold, a greater than Solomon *is* here.

O

Matt. 3. 9 And think not to say within yourselves, We have Abraham to *our* father: for I say unto you, that God is able of these stones to raise up children unto Abraham.

John 8. 39 They answered and said unto him, Abraham is our father. Jesus saith unto them, If ye were Abraham's children, ye would do the works of Abraham.

Rom. 9. 6 and 7. *See under A, §321, page 818.*

Gal. 6. 15 For in Christ Jesus neither circumcision availeth any thing, nor uncircumcision, but a new creature.

Rev. 2. 9 I know thy works, and tribulation, and poverty, (but thou art rich) and *I know* the blasphemy of them which say they are Jews, and are not, but *are* the synagogue of Satan.

P

I Sa. 16. 7 But the LORD said unto Samuel, Look not on his countenance, or on the height of his stature; because I have refused him: for *the LORD seeth* not as man seeth; for man looketh on the outward appearance, but the LORD looketh on the heart.

Ps. 45. 13 The King's daughter *is* all glorious within: her clothing *is* of wrought gold.

Matt. 23. 25 Woe unto you, scribes and Pharisees, hypocrites! for ye make clean the outside of the cup and of the platter, but within they are full of extortion and excess.

P—Concluded.

Matt. 23. 26 *Thou* blind Pharisee, cleanse first that *which is* within the cup and platter, that the outside of them may be clean also.

27 Woe unto you scribes and Pharisees, hypocrites! for ye are like unto whited sepulchres, which indeed appear beautiful outward, but are within full of dead *men's* bones, and of all uncleanness.

28 Even so ye also outwardly appear righteous unto men, but within ye are full of hypocrisy and iniquity.

I Pet. 3. 4 But *let it be* the hidden man of the heart, in that which is not corruptible, *even the ornament* of a meek and quiet spirit, which is in the sight of God of great price.

Q

Phil. 3. 3 For we are the circumcision, which worship God in the spirit, and rejoice in Christ Jesus, and have no confidence in the flesh.

Col. 2. 11 In whom also ye are circumcised with the circumcision made without hands, in putting off the body of the sins of the flesh by the circumcision of Christ:

R

John 3. 5 Jesus answered, verily, verily, I say unto thee, Except a man be born of water and *of* the Spirit, he cannot enter into the kingdom of God.

Rom. 7. 6 But now we are delivered from the law, that being dead wherein we were held; that we should serve in newness of spirit, and not *in* the oldness of the letter.

II Cor. 3. 6 Who also hath made us able ministers of the new testament; not of the letter, but of the spirit: for the letter killeth, but the spirit giveth life.

FAITHFUL NEVERTHELESS AND THEREBY ESTABLISHED HIS RIGHTEOUSNESS.

B—Concluded.

as well as unto them: but the word preached did not profit them, not being mixed with faith in them that heard *it*.

C

Num. 23. 19 God *is* not a man, that he should lie; neither the son of man, that he should repent: hath he said, and shall he not *do it?* or hath he spoken, and shall he not make it good?

Rom. 9. 6 Now as though the word of God

C—Concluded.

hath taken none effect. For they *are* not all Israel, which are of Israel:

Rom. 11. 29 For the gifts and calling of God *are* without repentance.

II Tim. 2. 13 If we believe not, *yet* he abideth faithful: he cannot deny himself.

D

Job 40. 8 Wilt thou also disannul my judgment? wilt thou condemn me, that thou mayest be righteous?

§ 322. THOUGH ENTRUSTED WITH THE ORACLES, THE JEWS WERE FAITHLESS. GOD WAS

CHAP. 3.

[c]shall their unbelief make the faith
of God without effect?
4 [d]God forbid: yea, let [e]God be
true, but [f]every man a liar; as it is
written, [g]That thou mightest be justified in thy sayings, and mightest
overcome when thou art judged.
5 But if our unrighteousness commend the righteousness of God,
what shall we say? *Is* God unrighteous who taketh vengeance? ([h]I
speak as a man)
6 God forbid: for then [i]how shall
God judge the world?
7 For if the truth of God hath
more abounded through my lie unto

CHAP. 3.

his glory: why yet am I also judged
as a sinner?
8 And not *rather*, (as we be slanderously reported, and as some
affirm that we say,) [k]Let us do evil,
that good may come? whose damnation is just.

For C and D see preceding page (821).

E

John 3. 33 He that hath received his testimony hath set to his seal that God is true.

F

Ps. 62. 9 Surely men of low degree *are* vanity, *and* men of high degree *are* a lie; to be laid in the balance, they *are* altogether *lighter* than vanity.

§ 323. JEW AND GENTILE ALIKE ARE ALL UNDER SIN.

3:9–18.

9 What then? are we better *than they*? No, in no wise: for we have before [1]proved both Jews and Gentiles, that [a]they are all under sin;

10 As it is written, [b]There is none righteous, no, not one:

11 There is none that understandeth, there is none that seeketh after God.

12 They are all gone out of the way, they are together become unprofitable; there is none that doeth good, no, not one.

13 [c]Their throat *is* an open sepulchre; with their tongues they have used deceit; [d]the poison of asps *is* under their lips:

14 [e]Whose mouth *is* full of cursing and bitterness:

15 [f]Their feet *are* swift to shed blood;

16 Destruction and misery *are* in their ways;

CHAP. 3.

17 And the way of peace have they not known:

18 [g]There is no fear of God before their eyes.

1

Cr. *charged.*

Rom. 1. 28 And even as they did not like to retain God in *their* knowledge, God gave them over to a reprobate mind, to do those things which are not convenient:

Rom. 2. 1. Therefore thou art inexcusable, O man, whosoever thou art that judgest: for wherein thou judgest another, thou condemnest thyself; for thou that judgest doest the same thing.

A

Eccl. 7. 20 For *there is* not a just man upon earth, that doeth good, and sinneth not.

Rom. 3. 23 For all have sinned, and come short of the glory of God;

Gal. 3. 22 But the Scripture hath concluded all under sin, that the promise by faith of Jesus Christ might be given to them that believe.

B

Job 14. 4 Who can bring a clean *thing* out of an unclean? not one.

Job 15. 14 What *is* man, that he should be clean? and *he which is* born of a woman, that he should be righteous?

FAITHFUL NEVERTHELESS AND THEREBY ESTABLISHED HIS RIGHTEOUSNESS (CONCLUDED).

G

Ps. 51. 4 Against thee, thee only, have I sinned, and done *this* evil in thy sight: that thou mightest be justified when thou speakest, *and* be clear when thou judgest.

H

Rom. 6. 19 I speak after the manner of men because of the infirmity of your flesh: for as ye have yielded your members servants to uncleanness and to iniquity unto iniquity; even so now yield your members servants to righteousness unto holiness.

Gal. 3. 15 Brethren, I speak after the manner of men; Though *it* be but a man's covenant, yet *if it be* confirmed, no man disannulleth, or addeth thereto.

I

Gen. 18. 25 That be far from thee to do after this manner, to slay the righteous with the wicked; and that the righteous should be as the wicked, that be far from thee: Shall not the Judge of all the earth do right?

Job 34. 17 Shall even he that hateth right govern? and wilt thou condemn him that is most just?

K

Rom. 5. 20 Moreover the law entered, that the offence might abound. But where sin abounded, grace did much more abound:

Rom. 6. 1 What shall we say then? Shall we continue in sin, that grace may abound?

Rom. 6. 15 What then? shall we sin, because we are not under the law, but under grace? God forbid.

IT IS SO DECLARED IN THE SCRIPTURES.

B—CONCLUDED.

Job 15. 16 How much more abominable and filthy *is* man, which drinketh iniquity like water?

Job 25. 4 How then can man be justified with God? or how can he be clean *that is* born of a woman?

Ps. 14. 1. The fool hath said in his heart, *There is* no God. They are corrupt, they have done abominable works, *there is* none that doeth good.

2 The Lord looked down from heaven upon the children of men, to see if there were any that did understand, *and* seek God.

3 They are all gone aside, they are *all* together become filthy: *there is* none that doeth good, no, not one.

Ps. 53. 1. The fool hath said in his heart, *There is* no God. Corrupt are they, and have done abominable iniquity: *there is* none that doeth good.

Jer. 17. 9 The heart *is* deceitful above all *things*, and desperately wicked: who can know it?

Matt. 15. 19 For out of the heart proceed evil thoughts, murders, adulteries, fornications, thefts, false witness, blasphemies:

Mark 10. 18 And Jesus said unto him, Why callest thou me good? *there is* none good but one, *that is*, God.

C

Ps. 5. 9 For *there is* no faithfulness in their mouth; their inward part *is* very wickedness; their throat *is* an open sepulchre; they flatter with their tongue.

Jer. 5. 16 Their quiver *is* as an open sepulche, they *are* all mighty men.

D

Ps. 140. 3 They have sharpened their tongues like a serpent; adders' poison *is* under their lips. Selah.

E

Ps. 10. 7 His mouth is full of cursing and deceit and fraud: under his tongue *is* mischief and vanity.

F

Prov. 1. 16 For their feet run to evil, and make haste to shed blood.

Prov. 6. 18 A heart that deviseth wicked imaginations, feet that be swift in running to mischief.

Isa. 59. 7 Their feet run to evil, and they make haste to shed innocent blood: their thoughts *are* thoughts of iniquity; wasting and destruction *are* in their paths.

8 The way of peace they know not; and *there is* no judgment in their goings: they have made them crooked paths: whosoever goeth therein shall not know peace.

G

Ps. 36. 1 The transgression of the wicked saith within my heart, *that there is* no fear of God before his eyes.

§ 324. BY THE LAW THERE IS NO JUSTIFCATION, BUT KNOWLEDGE OF SIN. GOD IS THE

3: 19–31.

19 Now we know that what things soever the law saith, it saith to them who are under the law: that [a]every mouth may be stopped, and [b]all the world may become[1]guilty before God.

20 Therefore [c]by the deeds of the law there shall no flesh be justified in his sight: for [d]by the law *is* the knowledge of sin.

21 But now [e]the righteousness of God without the law is manifested, [f]being witnessed by the law [g]and the prophets;

22 Even the righteousness of God *which is* [h]by faith of Jesus Christ unto all and upon all them that believe; for [i]there is no difference:

23 For [k]all have sinned, and come short of the glory of God;

24 Being justified freely [l]by his grace [m]through the redemption that is in Christ Jesus:

25 Whom God hath [2]set forth [n]*to be* a propitiation through faith [o]in his blood, to declare his righteousness [p]for the [3]remission of [q]sins that are past, through the forbearance of God;

A

Job 5. 16 So the poor hath hope, and iniquity stoppeth her mouth.

Ps. 107. 42 The righteous shall see *it*, and rejoice: and all iniquity shall stop her mouth.

Eze. 16. 63 That thou mayest remember, and be confounded, and never open thy mouth any more because of thy shame, when I am pacified toward thee for all that thou hast done, saith the Lord GOD.

Rom. 1. 20 For the invisible things of him from the creation of the world are clearly seen, being understood by the things that are made, *even* his eternal power and Godhead; so that they are without excuse:

B

Rom. 2. 2 But we are sure that the judgment of God is according to truth against them which commit such things.

Rom. 3. 9. *See text of topic, page 822.*

Rom. 3. 23. *See text of topic.*

1

Or, *subject to the judgment of God.*

C

Job 25. 4 How then can man be justified with God? or how can he be clean *that is* born of a woman?

Ps. 130. 3 If thou, LORD, shouldest mark iniquities, O Lord, who shall stand?

Ps. 143. 2 And enter not into judgment with thy servant: for in thy sight shall no man living be justified.

Acts 13. 39 And by him all that believe are justified from all things, from which ye could not be justified by the law of Moses.

Gal. 2. 16 Knowing that a man is not justified by the works of the law, but by the faith of Jesus Christ, even we have believed in Jesus Christ, that we might be justified by the faith of Christ, and not by the works of the law: for by the works of the law shall no flesh be justified.

Gal. 3. 11 But that no man is justified by the law in the sight of God, *it is* evident: for, The just shall live by faith.

Gal. 5. 4 Christ is become of no effect unto you, whosoever of you are justified by the law; ye are fallen from grace.

Eph. 2. 8 For by grace are ye saved through faith; and that not of yourselves: *it is* the gift of God:

9 Not of works, lest any man should boast.

Tit. 3. 5 Not by works of righteousness which we have done, but according to his mercy he saved us, by the washing of regeneration, and renewing of the Holy Ghost;

Jas. 2. 10 For whosoever shall keep the whole law, and yet offend in one *point*, he is guilty of all.

D

Rom. 7. 7 What shall we say then? *Is* the law sin? God forbid. Nay, I had not known sin, but by the law: for I had not known lust, except the law had said, Thou shalt not covet.

Jas. 2. 9 But if ye have respect to persons, ye commit sin, and are convinced of the law as transgressors.

JUSTIFIER OF FAITH IN JESUS. BOASTING IS EXCLUDED. THE LAW IS ESTABLISHED.

E

Acts 15. 11 But we believe that through the grace of the Lord Jesus Christ we shall be saved, even as they.

Rom. 1. 17 For therein is the righteousness of God revealed from faith to faith: as it is written, The just shall live by faith.

Phil. 3. 9 And be found in him, not having mine own righteousness, which is of the law, but that which is through the faith of Christ, the righteousness which is of God by faith:

Heb. 11. 4 By faith Abel offered unto God a more excellent sacrifice than Cain, by which he obtained witness that he was righteous, God testifying of his gifts: and by it he being dead yet speaketh.

II Pet. 1. 1 Simon Peter, a servant and an apostle of Jesus Christ, to them that have obtained like precious faith with us through the righteousness of God and our Saviour Jesus Christ:

F

John 5. 46 For had ye believed Moses, ye would have believed me: for he wrote of me.

Acts 26. 22 Having therefore obtained help of God, I continue unto this day, witnessing both to small and great, saying none other things than those which the prophets and Moses did say should come:

G

Rom. 1. 2 (Which he had promised afore by his prophets in the holy Scriptures,)

I Pet. 1. 10 Of which salvation the prophets have inquired and searched diligently, who prophesied of the grace *that should come* unto you:

H

Rom. 4. *Read entire chapter.*

I

Rom. 10. 12 For there is no difference between the Jew and the Greek: for the same Lord over all is rich unto all that call upon him.

Gal. 3. 28 There is neither Jew nor Greek, there is neither bond nor free, there is neither male nor female: for ye are all one in Christ Jesus.

Col. 3. 11 Where there is neither Greek nor Jew, circumcision nor uncircumcision, Barbarian, Scythian, bond *nor* free: but Christ *is* all, and in all.

K

Rom. 3. 9. *See a, A, § 323, page 322.*

Rom. 11. 32 For God hath concluded them all in unbelief, that he might have mercy upon all.

L

Rom. 4. 16 Therefore *it is* of faith, that *it might be* by grace; to the end the promise might be sure to all the seed; not to that only which is of the law, but to that also which is of the faith of Abraham; who is the father of us all,

Eph. 2. 8. *See under C.*

Tit. 3. 7 That being justified by his grace, we should be made heirs according to the hope of eternal life.

M

Matt. 20. 28 Even as the Son of man came not to be ministered unto, but to minister, and to give his life a ransom for many.

Eph. 1. 7 In whom we have redemption through his blood, the forgiveness of sins, according to the riches of his grace;

Col. 1. 14 In whom we have redemption through his blood, *even* the forgiveness of sins:

I Tim. 2. 6 Who gave himself a ransom for all, to be testified in due time.

Heb. 9. 12 Neither by the blood of goats and calves, but by his own blood he entered in once into the holy place, having obtained eternal redemption *for us.*

I Pet. 1. 18 Forasmuch as ye know that ye were not redeemed with corruptible things, *as* silver and gold, from your vain conversation *received* by tradition from your fathers;

19 But with the precious blood of Christ, as of a lamb without blemish and without spot:

2

Or, *foreordained.*

N

Lev. 16. 15 Then shall he kill the goat of the sin offering, that *is* for the people, and bring his blood within the vail, and do with that blood as he did with the blood of the bullock, and sprinkle it upon the mercy seat, and before the mercy seat:

I Jno. 2. 2 And he is the propitiation for our sins: and not for ours only, but also for *the sins of* the whole world.

I Jno. 4. 10 Herein is love, not that we loved God, but that he loved us, and sent his Son *to be* the propitiation for our sins.

O

Col. 1. 20 And, having made peace through the blood of his cross, by him to reconcile all things unto himself; by him,

For O concluded, P, 3 and Q, see next page (826).

§ 324. By the Law There is no Justification, but Knowledge of Sin. God is the

Chap. 3.

26 To declare, *I say*, at this time
his righteousness: that he might be
just, and the justifier of him which
believeth in Jesus.

27 [r]Where *is* boasting then? It is
excluded. By what law? of works?
Nay: but by the law of faith.

28 Therefore we conclude [s]that a
man is justified by faith without the
deeds of the law.

29 *Is he* the God of the Jews only?
is he not also of the Gentiles? Yes,
of the Gentiles also:

30 Seeing [t]*it is* one God, which shall
justify the circumcision by faith, and
uncircumcision through faith.

Chap. 3.

31 Do we then make void the law
through faith? God forbid: yea,
we establish the law.

O—Concluded.

I say, whether *they be* things in earth, or things in heaven.

P

Acts 13. 38 Be it known unto you therefore, men *and* brethren, that through this man is preached unto you the forgiveness of sins:

Acts 13. 39. *See under C, page 824.*

I Tim. 1. 15 This *is* a faithful saying, and worthy of all acceptation, that Christ Jesus came into the world to save sinners; of whom I am chief.

3

Or, *passing over.*

Q

Acts 17. 30 And the times of this ignorance God winked at; but now commandeth all men every where to repent:

§ 325. JUSTIFICATION BY FAITH FORESHADOWED

4 : 1–25.

1 What shall we say then that
[a]Abraham our father, as pertaining
to the flesh, hath found?

2 For if Abraham were [b]justified by
works, he hath *whereof* to glory; but
not before God.

3 For what saith the Scripture?
[c]Abraham believed God, and it was
counted unto him for righteousness.

4 Now [d]to him that worketh is the
reward not reckoned of grace, but
of debt.

5 But to him that worketh not, but
believeth on him that justifieth the
[e]ungodly, his [f]faith is counted for
righteousness.

6 Even as David also describeth
the blessedness of the man, unto
whom God [g]imputeth righteousness
without works,

A

Isa. 51. 2 Look unto Abraham your father, and unto Sarah *that* bare you: for I called him alone, and blessed him, and increased him.

Matt. 3. 9 And think not to say within yourselves, We have Abraham to *our* father: for I say unto you, that God is able of these stones to raise up children unto Abraham.

John 8. 33 They answered him, We be Abraham's seed, and were never in bondage to any man: how sayest thou, Ye shall be made free?

34 Jesus answered them, Verily, verily, I say unto you, Whosoever committeth sin is the servant of sin.

II Cor. 11. 22 Are they Hebrews? so *am* I. Are they Israelites? so *am* I. Are they the seed of Abraham? so *am* I.

B

Rom. 3. 20 Therefore by the deeds of the law there shall no flesh be justified in his sight: for by the law *is* the knowledge of sin.

Rom. 3. 27, 28. *See text of topic, § 324.*

C

Gen. 15. 6 And he believed in the Lord; and he counted it to him for righteousness.

JUSTIFIER OF FAITH IN JESUS. BOASTING IS EXCLUDED. THE LAW IS ESTABLISHED (CONC'D).

Q—CONCLUDED.

Heb. 9. 15 And for this cause he is the mediator of the new testament, that by means of death, for the redemption of the transgressions *that were* under the first testament, they which are called might receive the promise of eternal inheritance.

R

Rom. 2. 17 Behold, thou art called a Jew, and restest in the law, and makest thy boast of God,

Rom. 2. 23 Thou that makest thy boast of the law, through breaking the law dishonourest thou God ?

Rom. 4. 2 For if Abraham were justified by works, he hath *whereof* to glory; but not before God.

I Cor. 1. 29 That no flesh should glory in his presence.

30 But of him are ye in Christ Jesus, who of God is made unto us wisdom, and righteousness, and sanctification, and redemption:

R—CONCLUDED.

31 That according as it is written, He that glorieth, let him glory in the Lord.

Eph. 2. 9 Not of works, lest any man should boast.

S

Rom. 3. 20, etc. *See under B, § 325.*

Rom. 8. 3 For what the law could not do, in that it was weak through the flesh, God sending his own Son in the likeness of sinful flesh, and for sin, condemned sin in the flesh:

4 That the righteousness of the law might be fulfilled in us, who walk not after the flesh, but after the Spirit.

T

Rom. 10. 12. *See under K.*

Gal. 3. 8 And the Scripture, foreseeing that God would justify the heathen through faith, preached before the gospel unto Abraham, *saying*, In thee shall all nations be blessed.

Gal. 3. 20 Now a mediator is not *a mediator* of one, but God is one.

Gal. 3. 28. *See under I, page 825.*

IN THE RIGHTEOUSNESS OF ABRAHAM'S FAITH.

C—CONCLUDED.

Gal. 3. 6 Even as Abraham believed God, and it was accounted to him for righteousness.

Heb. 11. 8 By faith Abraham, when he was called to go out into a place which he should after receive for an inheritance, obeyed; and he went out, not knowing whither he went.

9 By faith he sojourned in the land of promise, as *in* a strange country, dwelling in tabernacles with Isaac and Jacob, the heirs with him of the same promise:

10 For he looked for a city which hath foundations, whose builder and maker *is* God.

Jas. 2. 23 And the Scripture was fulfilled which saith, Abraham believed God, and it was imputed unto him for righteousness: and he was called the Friend of God.

D

Rom. 11. 6 And if by grace, then *is it* no more of works: otherwise grace is no more grace. But if *it be* of works, then is it no more grace: otherwise work is no more work.

E

Josh. 24. 2 And Joshua said unto all the people, Thus saith the LORD God of Israel, Your fathers dwelt on the other side of the flood in old time, *even* Terah, the father of Abraham, and the father of Nachor: and they served other gods.

Zech. 3. 3 Now Joshua was clothed with filthy garments, and stood before the angel.

4 And he answered and spake unto those that stood before him, saying, Take away the filthy garments from him. And unto him he said, Behold, I have caused thine iniquity to pass from thee, and I will clothe thee with change of raiment.

Acts 13. 39 And by him all that believe are justified from all things, from which ye could not be justified by the law of Moses.

F

Hab. 2. 4 Behold, his soul *which* is lifted up is not upright in him: but the just shall live by his faith.

G

Jer. 23. 6 In his days Judah shall be saved, and Israel shall dwell safely: and this *is* his name whereby he shall be called THE LORD OUR RIGHTEOUSNESS.

For G concluded see next page (828).

§ 325. JUSTIFICATION BY FAITH FORESHADOWED IN THE

CHAP. 4.

7 *Saying*, [h]blessed *are* they whose iniquities are forgiven, and whose sins are covered.

8 Blessed *is* the man to whom the Lord will not impute sin.

9 *Cometh* this blessedness then upon the circumcision *only*, or upon the uncircumcision also? for we say that faith was reckoned to Abraham for righteousness.

10 How was it then reckoned? when he was in circumcision, or in uncircumcision? Not in circumcision, but in uncircumcision.

11 And [i]he received the sign of circumcision, a seal of the righteousness of the faith which *he had yet* being uncircumcised; that [k]he might be the father of all them that believe, though they be not circumcised; that righteousness might be imputed unto them also:

12 And the father of circumcision to them who are not in the circumcision only, but who also walk in the steps of that faith of our father Abraham, which *he had* being *yet* uncircumcised.

13 For the promise, that he should be the [l]heir of the world, *was* not to Abraham, or to his seed, through the law, but through the righteousness of faith.

14 For [m]if they which are of the law *be* heirs, faith is made void, and the promise made of none effect:

15 Because [n]the law worketh wrath: for where no law is, *there is* no transgression,

16 Therefore *it is* of faith, that *it might be* [o]by grace; [p]to the end the promise might be sure to all the seed; not to that only which is of the law, but to that also which is of the faith of Abraham; [q]who is the father of us all,

CHAP. 4.

17 (As it is written, [r]I have made thee a father of many nations,) [1]before him whom he believed, *even* God, [s]who quickeneth the dead, and calleth those [t]things which be not as though they were.

18 Who against hope believed in hope, that he might become the father of many nations, according

G—CONCLUDED.

I Cor. 1. 30 But of him are ye in Christ Jesus, who of God is made unto us wisdom, and righteousness, and sanctification, and redemption:

II Cor. 5. 19 To wit, that God was in Christ, reconciling the world unto himself, not imputing their trespasses unto them; and hath committed unto us the word of reconciliation.

H

Ps. 32. 1 Blessed *is he whose* transgression *is* forgiven, *whose* sin *is* covered.

2 Blessed *is* the man unto whom the LORD imputeth not iniquity, and in whose spirit *there is* no guile.

I

Gen. 17. 10 This *is* my covenant, which ye shall keep, between me and you and thy seed after thee: Every man child among you shall be circumcised.

K

Luke 19. 9 And Jesus said unto him, This day is salvation come to this house, forsomuch as he also is a son of Abraham.

Rom. 4. 12 and 18. *See Text of Topic.*

Rom. 9. 6 Not as though the word of God hath taken none effect. For they *are* not all Israel, which are of Israel;

Gal. 3. 7 Know ye therefore that they which are of faith, the same are the children of Abraham.

L

Gen. 17. 4 As for me, behold, my covenant *is* with thee, and thou shalt be a father of many nations.

5 Neither shall thy name any more be called Abram, but thy name shall be Abraham; for a father of many nations have I made thee.

Gen. 28. 14 And thy seed shall be as the dust of the earth, and thou shalt spread abroad to the west, and to the east, and to the north, and to the south: and in thee and in thy seed shall all the families of the earth be blessed.

RIGHTEOUSNESS OF ABRAHAM'S FAITH (CONTINUED).

L—CONCLUDED.

Ps. 2. 8 Ask of me, and I shall give *thee* the heathen *for* thine inheritance, and the uttermost parts of the earth *for* thy possession.

Ps. 72. 11 Yea, all kings shall fall down before him: all nations shall serve him.

Gal. 3. 29 And if ye *be* Christ's, then are ye Abraham's seed, and heirs according to the promise.

M

Gal. 3. 18 For if the inheritance *be* of the law, *it is* no more of promise: but God gave *it* to Abraham by promise.

N

Rom. 3. 20 Therefore by the deeds of the law there shall no flesh be justified in his sight: for by the law *is* the knowledge of sin.

Rom. 5 13 (For until the law sin was in the world: but sin is not imputed when there is no law.

Rom. 5. 20 Moreover the law entered, that the offence might abound. But where sin abounded, grace did much more abound.

Rom. 7. 8 But sin, taking occasion by the commandment, wrought in me all manner of concupiscence. For without the law sin *was* dead.

Rom. 7. 10 And the commandment, which *was ordained* to life, I found *to be* unto death.

11 For sin, taking occasion by the commandment, deceived me, and by it slew *me*.

I Cor. 15. 56 The sting of death *is* sin; and the strength of sin *is* the law.

II Cor. 3. 7 But if the ministration of death, written *and* engraven in stones, was glorious, so that the children of Israel could not steadfastly behold the face of Moses for the glory of his countenance; which *glory* was to be done away:

II Cor. 3. 9 For if the ministration of condemnation *be* glory, much more doth the ministration of righteousness exceed in glory.

Gal. 3. 10 For as many as are of the works of the law are under the curse: for it is written, Cursed *is* every one that continueth not in all things which are written in the book of the law to do them.

Gal. 3. 19 Wherefore then *serveth* the law? It was added because of transgressions, till the seed should come to whom the promise was made; *and it was* ordain-

N—CONCLUDED.

ed by angels in the hand of a mediator.

I John 3. 4 Whosoever committeth sin transgresseth also the law: for sin is the transgression of the law.

O

Rom. 3. 24. *Study C and L, §324, Page 824.*

P

Gal. 3. 22 But the Scripture hath concluded all under sin, that the promise by faith of Jesus Christ might be given to them that believe.

Q

Isa. 51. 2. *See under A, Page 826.*

R

Gen. 17. 5. *See under L.*

1

Or, *like unto him.*

S

Rom. 8. 11 But if the Spirit of him that raised up Jesus from the dead dwell in you, he that raised up Christ from the dead shall also quicken your mortal bodies by his Spirit that dwelleth in you.

Eph. 2. 1 And you *hath he quickened*, who were dead in trespasses and sins:

Eph. 2. 5 Even when we were dead in sins, hath quickened us together with Christ, (by grace ye are saved;)

T

Rom. 9. 26 And it shall come to pass, *that* in the place where it was said unto them, Ye *are* not my people: there shall they be called the children of the living God.

I Cor. 1. 28 And base things of the world, and things which are despised, hath God chosen, *yea*, and things which are not, to bring to nought things that are:

I Pet. 2. 10 Which in time past *were* not a people, but *are* now the people of God: which had not obtained mercy, but now have obtained mercy.

U

Gen. 15. 5 And he brought him forth abroad, and said, Look now toward heaven, and tell the stars, if thou be able to number them: and he said unto him, So shall thy seed be.

X

Gen. 17. 17 Then Abraham fell upon his face, and laughed, and said in his heart, Shall *a child* be born unto him that is a hundred years old? and shall Sarah, that is ninety years old, bear.

§ 325. JUSTIFICATION BY FAITH FORESHADOWED IN THE

CHAP. 4.

to that which was spoken, [u]So shall
thy seed be.
19 And being not weak in faith,
[x]he considered not his own body now
dead, when he was about a hundred
years old, neither yet the deadness
of Sarah's womb:
20 He staggered not at the promise of God through unbelief; but
was strong in faith, giving glory to
God;
21 And being fully persuaded, that
what he had promised, [y]he was able
also to perform.
22 And therefore it was imputed
to him for righteousness.
23 Now [z]it was not written for his
sake alone, that it was imputed to
him;
24 But for us also, to whom it
shall be imputed, if we believe [a]on
him that raised up Jesus our Lord
from the dead;
25 [b]Who was delivered for our offences, and [c]was raised again for
our justification.

For U and X, see preceding page (829).

X—CONCLUDED.

Gen. 18. 11 Now Abraham and Sarah *were* old *and* well stricken in age; *and* it ceased to be with Sarah after the manner of women.

Heb. 11. 11 Through faith also Sarah herself received strength to conceive seed, and was delivered of a child when she was past age, because she judged him faithful who had promised.

12 Therefore sprang there even of one, and him as good as dead, *so many* as the stars of the sky in multitude, and as the sand which is by the sea shore innumerable.

Y

Ps. 115. 3 But our God *is* in the heavens: he hath done whatsoever he hath pleased.

Luke 1. 37 For with God nothing shall be impossible.

Luke 1. 45 And blessed *is* she that believed: for there shall be a performance of those things which were told her from the Lord.

Heb. 11. 19 Accounting that God *was* able to raise *him* up, even from the dead; from whence also he received him in a figure.

Z

Rom. 15. 4 For whatsoever things were written aforetime were written for our learning, that we through patience and comfort of the Scriptures might have hope.

§ 326. BEING JUSTIFIED WE HAVE PEACE, HOPE OF GLORY,

5: 1–11.

1 Therefore being justified by faith,
[a]we have peace with God through
our Lord Jesus Christ:
2 [b]By whom also we have access
by faith into this grace [c]wherein we
stand, [d]and rejoice in hope of the
glory of God.
3 And not only *so*, but [e]we glory in

A

Isa. 32. 17 And the work of righteousness shall be peace; and the effect of righteousness, quietness and assurance for ever.

John 16. 33 These things I have spoken unto you, that in me ye might have peace. In the world ye shall have tribulation: but be of good cheer; I have overcome the world.

A—CONCLUDED.

Eph. 2. 14 For he is our peace, who hath made both one, and hath broken down the middle wall of partition *between us;*

Col. 1. 20 And, having made peace through the blood of his cross, by him to reconcile all things unto himself; by him, *I say*, whether *they be* things in earth, or things in heaven.

B

John 10. 9 I am the door: by me if any man enter in, he shall be saved, and shall go in and out, and find pasture.

John 14. 6 Jesus saith unto him, I am the way, the truth, and the life: no man cometh unto the Father, but by me.

Eph. 2. 18 For through him we both have access by one Spirit unto the Father.

Eph. 3. 12 In whom we have boldness and access with confidence by the faith of him.

RIGHTEOUSNESS OF ABRAHAM'S FAITH (CONCLUDED).

Z—CONCLUDED.

I Cor. 10. 6 Now these things were our examples, to the intent we should not lust after evil things, as they also lusted.

I Cor. 10. 11 Now all these things happened unto them for ensamples: and they are written for our admonition, upon whom the ends of the world are come.

A

Acts 2. 24 Whom God hath raised up, having loosed the pains of death: because it was not possible that he should be holden of it.

Acts 13. 30 But God raised him from the dead: *Study K, § 231, page 638.*

B

Isa. 53. 5 But he *was* wounded for our transgressions, *he was* bruised for our iniquities: the chastisement of our peace *was* upon him; and with his stripes we are healed.

6 All we like sheep have gone astray; we have turned every one to his own way; and the LORD hath laid on him the iniquity of us all.

Rom. 3. 25 Whom God hath set forth *to be* a propitiation through faith in his blood, to declare his righteousness for the remission of sins that are past, through the forbearance of God;

Rom. 5. 6 For when we were yet without strength, in due time Christ died for the ungodly.

B—CONCLUDED.

Rom. 8. 32 He that spared not his own Son, but delivered him up for us all, how shall he not with him also freely give us all things?

II Cor. 5. 21 For he hath made him *to be* sin for us, who knew no sin; that we might be made the righteousness of God in him.

Gal. 1. 4 Who gave himself for our sins, that he might deliver us from this present evil world, according to the will of God and our Father:

Heb. 9. 28 So Christ was once offered to bear the sins of many; and unto them that look for him shall he appear the second time without sin unto salvation.

I Pet. 2. 24 Who his own self bare our sins in his own body on the tree, that we, being dead to sins, should live unto righteousness: by whose stripes ye were healed.

I Pet. 3. 18 For Christ also hath once suffered for sins, the just for the unjust, that he might bring us to God, being put to death in the flesh, but quickened by the Spirit:

C

I Cor. 15. 17 And if Christ be not raised, your faith *is* vain; ye are yet in your sins.

I Pet. 1. 21 Who by him do believe in God, that raised him up from the dead, and gave him glory; that your faith and hope might be in God.

RECONCILIATION AND SALVATION THROUGH CHRIST.

B—CONCLUDED.

Heb. 10. 19 Having therefore, brethren, boldness to enter into the holiest by the blood of Jesus,

C

I Cor. 15. 1 Moreover, brethren, I declare unto you the gospel which I preached unto you, which also ye have received, and wherein ye stand;

D

Ps. 16. 9 Therefore my heart is glad, and my glory rejoiceth: my flesh also shall rest in hope.

Prov. 14. 32 The wicked is driven away in his wickedness: but the righteous hath hope in his death.

II Thes. 2. 16 Now our Lord Jesus Christ himself, and God, even our Father, which hath loved us, and hath given *us* everlasting consolation and good hope through grace,

D—CONCLUDED.

Heb. 3. 6 But Christ as a son over his own house; whose house are we, if we hold fast the confidence and the rejoicing of the hope firm unto the end.

Heb. 6. 18 That by two immutable things, in which *it was* impossible for God to lie, we might have a strong consolation, who have fled for refuge to lay hold upon the hope set before us:

I Pet. 1. 3 Blessed *be* the God and Father of our Lord Jesus Christ, which according to his abundant mercy hath begotten us again unto a lively hope by the resurrection of Jesus Christ from the dead,

E

Matt. 5. 11 Blessed are ye, when *men* shall revile you, and persecute *you*, and shall say all manner of evil against you falsely, for my sake.

For E concluded see next page.

§ 326. BEING JUSTIFIED WE HAVE PEACE, HOPE OF GLORY,

CHAP. 5.

tribulations also: [f]knowing that tribulation worketh patience;
4 And [g]patience, experience; and
experience, hope:
5 And [h]hope maketh not ashamed;
[i]because the love of God is shed
abroad in our hearts by the Holy
Ghost which is given unto us.
6 For when we were yet without
strength, [1]in due time [k]Christ died
for the ungodly.
7 For scarcely for a righteous man
will one die: yet peradventure for a
good man some would even dare to
die.
8 But [l]God commendeth his love
toward us, in that, while we were
yet sinners, Christ died for us.
9 Much more then, being now justified [m]by his blood, we shall be saved
[n]from wrath through him.
10 For if, when we were enemies,
[o]we were reconciled to God by the
death of his Son; much more, being
reconciled, we shall be saved [p]by
his life.
11 And not only *so*, but we also
[q]joy in God through our Lord Jesus
Christ, by whom we have now received the [2]atonement.

E—CONTINUED.

Matt. 5. 12 Rejoice, and be exceeding glad: for great *is* your reward in heaven: for so persecuted they the prophets which were before you.

Acts 5. 41 And they departed from the presence of the council, rejoicing that they were counted worthy to suffer shame for his name.

IICor.12. 10 Therefore I take pleasure in infirmities, in reproaches, in necessities, in persecutions, in distresses for Christ's sake: for when I am weak, then am I strong.

Phil. 2. 17 Yea, and if I be offered upon the sacrifice and service of your faith, I joy, and rejoice with you all.

Jas. 1. 2 My brethren, count it all joy when ye fall into divers temptations;

E—CONCLUDED.

I Pet. 3. 14 But and if ye suffer for righteousness' sake, happy *are ye:* and be not afraid of their terror, neither be troubled;

F

IICor.4. 17 For our light affliction, which is but for a moment, worketh for us a far more exceeding *and* eternal weight of glory;

Heb. 12. 11 Now no chastening for the present seemeth to be joyous, but grievous: nevertheless, afterward it yieldeth the peaceable fruit of righteousness unto them which are exercised thereby.

Jas. 1. 3 Knowing *this*, that the trying of your faith worketh patience.

G

Jas. 1. 12 Blessed *is* the man that endureth temptation: for when he is tried, he shall receive the crown of life, which the Lord hath promised to them that love him.

H

Phil. 1. 20 According to my earnest expectation and *my* hope, that in nothing I shall be ashamed, but *that* with all boldness, as always, *so* now also Christ shall be magnified in my body, whether *it be* by life, or by death.

IITim.1. 12 For the which cause I also suffer these things: nevertheless I am not ashamed: for I know whom I have believed, and am persuaded that he is able to keep that which I have committed unto him against that day.

I

IICor.1. 22 Who hath also sealed us, and given the earnest of the Spirit in our hearts.

Gal. 4. 6 And because ye are sons, God hath sent forth the Spirit of his Son into your hearts, crying, Abba, Father.

Eph. 1. 13 In whom ye also *trusted*, after that ye heard the word of truth, the gospel of your salvation: in whom also after that ye believed, ye were sealed with that Holy Spirit of promise,

14 Which is the earnest of our inheritance until the redemption of the purchased possession, unto the praise of his glory.

1

Or, *according to the time.*

K

Rom. 4. 25. *See b, B, § 325, page 830.*

L

John 15. 13 Greater love hath no man than this, that a man lay down his life for his friends.

RECONCILIATION AND SALVATION THROUGH CHRIST (CONCLUDED).

L—CONCLUDED.

I Pet. 3. 18 For Christ also hath once suffered for sins, the just for the unjust, that he might bring us to God, being put to death in the flesh, but quickened by the Spirit:

I Jno. 3. 16 Hereby perceive we the love *of God*, because he laid down his life for us: and we ought to lay down *our* lives for the brethren.

I Jno. 4. 9 In this was manifested the love of God toward us, because that God sent his only begotten Son into the world, that we might live through him.

10 Herein is love, not that we loved God, but that he loved us, and sent his Son *to be* the propitiation for our sins.

M

Rom. 3. 24 Being justified freely by his grace through the redemption that is in Christ Jesus:

25 Whom God hath set forth *to be* a propitiation through faith in his blood, to declare his righteousness for the remission of sins that are past, through the forbearance of God;

Rom. 8. 1 *There is* therefore now no condemnation to them which are in Christ Jesus, who walk not after the flesh, but after the Spirit.

Eph. 1. 7 In whom we have redemption through his blood, the forgiveness of sins, according to the riches of his grace;

Eph. 2. 13 But now, in Christ Jesus, ye who sometimes were far off are made nigh by the blood of Christ.

Heb. 9. 14 How much more shall the blood of Christ, who through the eternal Spirit offered himself without spot to God, purge your conscience from dead works to serve the living God?

Heb. 9. 22 And almost all things are by the law purged with blood; and without shedding of blood is no remission.

I Pet. 1. 18 Forasmuch as ye know that ye were not redeemed with corruptible things, *as* silver and gold, from your vain conversation *received* by tradition from your fathers;

19 But with the precious blood of Christ, as of a lamb without blemish and without spot:

I Jno. 1. 7 But if we walk in the light, as he is in the light, we have fellowship one with another, and the blood of Jesus Christ his Son cleanseth us from all sin.

M—CONCLUDED.

Rev. 1. 5 And from Jesus Christ, *who is* the faithful witness, *and* the first-begotten of the dead, and the prince of the kings of the earth. Unto him that loved us, and washed us from our sins in his own blood,

N

I Thes. 1. 10 And to wait for his Son from heaven, whom he raised from the dead, *even* Jesus, which delivered us from the wrath to come.

O

II Cor. 5. 18 And all things *are* of God, who hath reconciled us to himself by Jesus Christ, and hath given to us the ministry of reconciliation;

19 To wit, that God was in Christ, reconciling the world unto himself, not imputing their trespasses unto them; and hath committed unto us the word of reconciliation.

Eph. 2. 16 And that he might reconcile both unto God in one body by the cross, having slain the enmity thereby:

Col. 1. 20 And, having made peace through the blood of his cross, by him to reconcile all things unto himself; by him, *I say*, whether *they be* things in earth, or things in heaven.

21 And you, that were sometime alienated and enemies in *your* mind by wicked works, yet now hath he reconciled

P

John 5. 26 For as the Father hath life in himself; so hath he given to the Son to have life in himself;

John 14. 19 Yet a little while, and the world seeth me no more; but ye see me: because I live, ye shall live also.

II Cor. 4. 10 Always bearing about in the body the dying of the Lord Jesus, that the life also of Jesus might be made manifest in our body.

11 For we which live are alway delivered unto death for Jesus' sake, that the life also of Jesus might be made manifest in our mortal flesh.

Q

Ps. 149. 2 Let Israel rejoice in him that made him: let the children of Zion be joyful in their King.

Hab. 3. 18 Yet I will rejoice in the LORD, I will joy in the God of my salvation.

2 Or, *reconciliation.*

§ 327. Through Adam Many Became Sinners. Through Christ Many Become

5 : 12-21.

12 Wherefore, as [a]by one man sin entered into the world, and [b]death by sin; and so death passed upon all men, [1]for that all have sinned:

13 (For until the law sin was in the world: but [c]sin is not imputed when there is no law.

14 Nevertheless death reigned from Adam to Moses, even over them that had not sinned after the similitude of Adam's transgression, [d]who is the figure of him that was to come.

15 But not as the offence, so also *is* the free gift. For if through the offence of one many be dead, much more the grace of God, and the gift by grace *which is* by one man, Jesus Christ, hath abounded [e]unto many.

16 And not as *it was* by one that sinned, *so is* the gift: for the judgment *was* by one to condemnation, but the free gift *is* of many offences unto justification.

17 For if [2]by one man's offence death reigned by one; much more they which receive abundance of grace and of the gift of righteousness shall reign in life by one, Jesus Christ.)

18 Therefore, as [2]by the offence of one *judgment came* upon all men to

Chap. 5.

condemnation; even so [3]by the righteousness of one *the free gift came* [f]upon all men unto justification of life.

19 For as by one man's disobedience many were made sinners, so by the obedience of one shall many be made righteous.

20 Moreover [g]the law entered, that the offence might abound. But where sin abounded, grace did much [h]more abound:

21 That as sin hath reigned unto death, even so might [i]grace reign through righteousness unto eternal life by Jesus Christ our Lord.

A

Gen. 3. 6 And when the woman saw that the tree *was* good for food, and that it *was* pleasant to the eyes, and a tree to be desired to make *one* wise, she took of the fruit thereof, and did eat, and gave also unto her husband with her; and he did eat.

1 Cor. 15. 21 For since by man *came* death, by man *came* also the resurrection of the dead.

B

Gen. 2. 17 But of the tree of the knowledge of good and evil, thou shalt not eat of it: for in the day that thou eatest thereof thou shalt surely die.

Gen. 3. 19 In the sweat of thy face shalt thou eat bread, till thou return unto the ground; for out of it wast thou taken: for dust thou *art*, and unto dust shalt thou return.

§ 328. CONTINUE NOT IN SIN FOR GRACE. THE FAITHFUL IN CHRIST

6 : 1-14.

1 What shall we say then? [a]Shall we continue in sin, that grace may abound?

2 God forbid. How shall we, that are [b]dead to sin, live any longer therein?

A

Rom. 3. 8 And not *rather*, (as we be slanderously reported, and as some affirm that we say,) Let us do evil, that good may come? whose damnation is just.

Rom. 6. 15. *See text of § 329, page 838.*

B

Rom. 6. 11. *See text of topic, § 328, page 832.*

Rom. 7. 4 Wherefore, my brethren, ye also are become dead to the law by the

RIGHTEOUS. THE LAW ENTERED THAT SIN MIGHT ABOUND, BUT GRACE MUCH MORE.

B—CONCLUDED.

Eze. 18. 4 Behold, all souls are mine; as the soul of the father, so also the soul of the son is mine: the soul that sinneth, it shall die.

Rom. 6. 23 For the wages of sin *is* death; but the gift of God *is* eternal life through Jesus Christ our Lord.

Jas. 1. 15 Then when lust hath conceived, it bringeth forth sin: and sin, when it is finished, bringeth forth death.

1

Or, *in whom.*

C

Rom. 4. 15 Because the law worketh wrath: for where no law is, *there is* no transgression.

I Jno. 3. 4 Whosoever committeth sin transgresseth also the law: for sin is the transgression of the law.

D

I Cor. 15. 21. *See Under A.*

I Cor. 15. 22 For as in Adam all die, even so in Christ shall all be made alive.

I Cor. 15. 45 And so it is written, The first man Adam was made a living soul; the last Adam *was made* a quickening spirit.

E

Isa. 53. 11 He shall see of the travail of his soul, *and* shall be satisfied: by his knowledge shall my righteous servant justify many; for he shall bear their iniquities.

Matt. 20. 28 Even as the Son of man came not to be ministered unto, but to minister, and to give his life a ransom for many.

Matt. 26. 28 For this is my blood of the new testament, which is shed for many for the remission of sins.

2

Or, *by one offence.*

3

Or, *by one righteousness.*

F

John 12. 32 And I, if I be lifted up from the earth, will draw all *men* unto me.

Heb. 2. 9 But we see Jesus, who was made a little lower than the angels for the suffering of death, crowned with glory and honour; that he by the grace of God should taste death for every man.

G

John 15. 22 If I had not come and spoken unto them, they had not had sin: but now they have no cloak for their sin.

Rom. 3. 20. *See d, D, § 324, page 824.*

Gal. 3. 19 Wherefore then *serveth* the law? It was added because of transgressions, till the seed should come to whom the promise was made; *and it was* ordained by angels in the hand of a mediator.

Gal. 3. 24 Wherefore the law was our schoolmaster *to bring us* unto Christ, that we might be justified by faith.

H

Luke 7. 47 Wherefore I say unto thee, Her sins, which are many, are forgiven; for she loved much: but to whom little is forgiven, *the same* loveth little.

I Tim. 1. 14 And the grace of our Lord was exceeding abundant with faith and love which is in Christ Jesus.

John 10. 10 The thief cometh not, but for to steal, and to kill, and to destroy: I am come that they might have life, and that they might have *it* more abundantly.

I

John 1. 16 And of his fulness have all we received, and grace for grace.
17 For the law was given by Moses, *but* grace and truth came by Jesus Christ.

Tit. 2. 11 For the grace of God that bringeth salvation hath appeared to all men,

ARE DEAD UNTO SIN AND DEATH, AND ALIVE UNTO GOD.

B—CONTINUED.

body of Christ; that ye should be married to another, *even* to him who is raised from the dead, that we should bring forth fruit unto God.

Gal. 2. 19 For I through the law am dead to the law, that I might live unto God.

Gal. 6. 14 But God forbid that I should glory, save in the cross of our Lord Jesus Christ, by whom the world is crucified unto me, and I unto the world.

B—CONCLUDED.

Col. 3. 3 For ye are dead, and your life is hid with Christ in God.

I Pet. 2. 24 Who his own self bare our sins in his own body on the tree, that we, being dead to sins, should live unto righteousness: by whose stripes ye were healed.

§ 328. CONTINUE NOT IN SIN FOR GRACE. THE FAITHFUL IN CHRIST

CHAP. 6.

3 Know ye not, that [c]so many of us
as [1]were baptized into Jesus Christ
[d]were baptized into his death?
4 Therefore we are [e]buried with him
by baptism into death: that [f]like as
Christ was raised up from the dead
[g]by the glory of the Father, [h]even so
we also should walk in newness of life.
5 For [i]if we have been planted together in the likeness of his death,
we shall be also *in the likeness* of *his*
resurrection:
6 Knowing this, that [k]our old man
is crucified with *him*, that [l]the body
of sin might be destroyed, that
henceforth we should not serve sin.
7 For [m]he that is dead is [2]freed
from sin.
8 Now [n]if we be dead with Christ,
we believe that we shall also live
with him:
9 Knowing that [o]Christ being raised
from the dead dieth no more; death
hath no more dominion over him.
10 For in that he died, [p]he died
unto sin once: but in that he liveth,
[q]he liveth unto God.
11 Likewise reckon ye also yourselves to be [r]dead indeed unto sin,
but alive unto God through Jesus
Christ our Lord.
12 [s]Let not sin therefore reign in
your mortal body, that ye should
obey it in the lusts thereof.
13 Neither yield ye your [t]members
as [3]instruments of unrighteousness
unto sin: but [u]yield yourselves unto
God, as those that are alive from
the dead, and your members *as* instruments of righteousness unto God.
14 For [x]sin shall not have dominion over you: for ye are not under
the law, but under grace.

C

Gal. 3. 27 For as many of you as have been baptized into Christ have put on Christ.

1

Or, *are.*

D

ICor. 15. 29 Else what shall they do which are baptized for the dead, if the dead rise not at all? why are they then baptized for the dead?

E

Col. 2. 12 Buried with him in baptism, wherein also ye are risen with *him* through the faith of the operation of God, who hath raised him from the dead.

I. Pet. 3. 21 The like figure whereunto *even* baptism doth also now save us, (not the putting away of the filth of the flesh, but the answer of a good conscience toward God,) by the resurrection of Jesus Christ:

F

Rom. 8. 11 But if the Spirit of him that raised up Jesus from the dead dwell in you, he that raised up Christ from the dead shall also quicken your mortal bodies by the Spirit that dwelleth in you.

I. Cor. 6. 14 And God hath both raised up the Lord, and will also raise up us by his own power:

IICor. 13. 4 For though he was crucified through weakness, yet he liveth by the power of God. For we also are weak in him, but we shall live with him by the power of God toward you.

G

John 11. 40 Jesus said unto her, Said I not unto thee, that, if thou wouldest believe, thou shouldest see the glory of God?

H

IICor. 5. 17 Therefore if any man *be* in Christ, *he is* a new creature: old things are passed away; behold, all things are become new.

Gal. 6. 15 For in Christ Jesus neither circumcision availeth any thing, nor uncircumcision, but a new creature.

Eph. 4. 22 That ye put off concerning the former conversation the old man, which is corrupt according to the deceitful lusts;

23 And be renewed in the spirit of your mind;

24 And that ye put on the new man, which after God is created in righteousness and true holiness.

Col. 3. 10 And have put on the new *man*, which is renewed in knowledge after the image of him that created him:

ARE DEAD UNTO SIN AND DEATH, AND ALIVE UNTO GOD (CONCLUDED).

I

Eph. 2. 5 Even when we were dead in sins, hath quickened us together with Christ, (by grace ye are saved;)
6 And hath raised *us* up together, and made *us* sit together in heavenly *places* in Christ Jesus:

Phil. 3. 10 That I may know him, and the power of his resurrection, and the fellowship of his sufferings, being made conformable unto his death;
11 If by any means I might attain unto the resurrection of the dead.

K

Gal. 2. 20 I am crucified with Christ: nevertheless I live; yet not I, but Christ liveth in me: and the life which I now live in the flesh I live by the faith of the Son of God, who loved me, and gave himself for me.

Gal. 5. 24 And they that are Christ's have crucified the flesh with the affections and lusts.

Gal. 6. 14 But God forbid that I should glory, save in the cross of our Lord Jesus Christ, by whom the world is crucified unto me, and I unto the world.

Eph. 4. 22. *See under H.*

Col. 3. 5 Mortify therefore your members which are upon the earth; fornication, uncleanness, inordinate affection, evil concupiscence, and covetousness, which is idolatry:

Col. 3. 8 But now ye also put off all these; anger, wrath, malice, blasphemy, filthy communication out of your mouth.
9 Lie not one to another, seeing that ye have put off the old man with his deeds;

L

Col. 2. 11 In whom also ye are circumcised with the circumcision made without hands, in putting off the body of the sins of the flesh by the circumcision of Christ:

M

I Pet. 4. 1 Forasmuch then as Christ hath suffered for us in the flesh, arm yourselves likewise with the same mind: for he that hath suffered in the flesh hath ceased from sin,

2

Gr, *justified.*

N

IITim. 2. 11 *It is* a faithful saying: For if we be dead with *him*, we shall also live with *him:*

O

Rev. 1. 18 *I am* he that liveth, and was dead; and, behold, I am alive for evermore, Amen; and have the keys of hell and of death.

P

Heb. 9. 27 And as it is appointed unto men once to die, but after this the judgment:
28 So Christ was once offered to bear the sins of many; and unto them that look for him shall he appear the second time without sin unto salvation.

Q

Luke 20. 38 For he is not a God of the dead, but of the living: for all live unto him.

R

Rom. 6. 2. *See text of Topic, § 328, page 834.*

Gal. 2. 19 For I through the law am dead to the law, that I might live unto God.

S

Ps. 19. 13 Keep back thy servant also from presumptuous *sins;* let them not have dominion over me: then shall I be upright, and I shall be innocent from the great transgression.

Ps. 119. 133 Order my steps in thy word: and let not any iniquity have dominion over me.

T

Rom. 7. 5 For when we were in the flesh, the motions of sins, which were by the law, did work in our members to bring forth fruit unto death.

Col. 3. 5. *See under K.*

Jas. 4. 1 From whence *come* wars and fightings among you? *come they* not hence, *even* of your lusts that war in your members?

3

Gr, *arms, or, weapons.*

U

Rom. 12. 1 I beseech you therefore, brethren, by the mercies of God, that ye present your bodies a living sacrifice, holy, acceptable unto God, *which is* your reasonable service.

I Pet. 2. 24. *See under B, page 835.*

I Pet. 4. 2 That he no longer should live the rest of *his* time in the flesh to the lusts of men, but to the will of God.

X

Rom. 7. 4 and 6. *See c, C, § 330, page 840.*

Rom. 8. 2 For the law of the Spirit of life in Christ Jesus hath made me free from the law of sin and death.

§ 329. FREED FROM SIN YE BECAME SERVANTS OF RIGHTEOUS-

6 : 15–23.

15 What then? shall we sin, [a]because we are not under the law, but under grace? God forbid.

16 Know ye not, that [b]to whom ye yield yourselves servants to obey, his servants ye are to whom ye obey; whether of sin unto death, or of obedience unto righteousness?

17 But God be thanked, that ye were the servants of sin, but ye have obeyed from the heart [c]that form of doctrine [1]which was delivered you.

18 Being then [d]made free from sin, ye became the servants of righteousness.

19 I speak after the manner of men because of the infirmity of your flesh: for as ye have yielded your members servants to uncleanness and to iniquity unto iniquity; even so now yield your members servants to righteousness unto holiness.

20 For when ye were [e]the servants of sin, ye were free [2]from righteousness.

21 [f]What fruit had ye then in those things whereof ye are now ashamed? for [g]the end of those things *is* death.

22 But now [h]being made free from sin, and become servants to God, ye have your fruit unto holiness, and the end everlasting life.

CHAP. 6.

23 For [i]the wages of sin *is* death; but [k]the gift of God *is* eternal life through Jesus Christ our Lord.

A

I Cor. 9. 20 And unto the Jews I became as a Jew, that I might gain the Jews; to them that are under the law, as under the law, that I might gain them that are under the law;

B

Josh. 24. 15 And if it seem evil unto you to serve the LORD, choose you this day whom ye will serve; whether the gods which your fathers served that *were* on the other side of the flood, or the gods of the the Amorites, in whose land ye dwell: but as for me and my house, we will serve the LORD.

Matt. 6. 24 No man can serve two masters: for either he will hate the one, and love the other; or else he will hold to the one, and despise the other. Ye cannot serve God and mammon.

John 8. 34 Jesus answered them, Verily, verily, I say unto you, Whosoever committeth sin is the servant of sin.

II Pet. 2. 19 While they promise them liberty, they themselves are the servants of corruption: for of whom a man is overcome, of the same is he brought in bondage.

C

II Tim. 1. 13 Hold fast the form of sound words, which thou hast heard of me, in faith and love which is in Christ Jesus.

1

Gr, *Whereto ye were delivered.*

D

Ps. 116. 16 O LORD, truly I *am* thy servant; I *am* thy servant, *and* the son of thine handmaid: thou hast loosed my bonds.

§ 330. THE DOMINION OF THE LAW AND

7 : 1–6.

1 Know ye not, brethren, (for I speak to them that know the law,) how that the law hath dominion over a man as long as he liveth?

2 For [a]the woman which hath a husband is bound by the law to *her* husband so long as he liveth; but if the husband be dead, she is loosed from the law of *her* husband.

CHAP. 7.

3 So then [b]if, while *her* husband

NESS. THE WAGES OF SIN IS DEATH. GOD'S GIFT IS ETERNAL LIFE.

D—CONCLUDED.

Ps. 119. 32 I will run the way of thy commandments, when thou shalt enlarge my heart.

Ps. 119. 45 And I will walk at liberty: for I seek thy precepts.

Luke 1. 74 That he would grant unto us, that we, being delivered out of the hand of our enemies, might serve him without fear.

75 In holiness and righteousness before him, all the days of our life.

John 8. 32 And ye shall know the truth, and the truth shall make you free.

I Cor. 7. 21 Art thou called *being* a servant? care not for it: but if thou mayest be made free, use *it* rather.

22 For he that is called in the Lord, *being* a servant, is the Lord's freeman: likewise also he that is called, *being* free, is Christ's servant.

Gal. 5. 1 Stand fast therefore in the liberty wherewith Christ hath made us free, and be not entangled again with the yoke of bondage.

I Pet. 2. 16 As free, and not using *your* liberty for a cloak of maliciousness, but as the servants of God.

E

John 8. 34. *See under B.*

2

Gr. *to righteousness.*

F

Rom. 7. 5 For when we were in the flesh, the motions of sins, which were by the law, did work in our members to bring forth fruit unto death.

G

Rom. 1. 32 Who, knowing the judgment of God, that they which commit such things are worthy of death, not only do the same, but have pleasure in them that do them.

H

John 8. 32. *See under D.*

I

Isa. 3. 11 Woe unto the wicked! *it shall be* ill *with him:* for the reward of his hands shall be given him.

Rom. 5. 12. *See b, B, § 327, page 834.*

I Cor. 6. 9 Know ye not that the unrighteous shall not inherit the kingdom of God? Be not deceived: neither fornicators, nor idolaters, nor adulterers, nor effeminate, nor abusers of themselves with mankind.

Gal. 6. 7 Be not deceived; God is not mocked: for whatsoever a man soweth, that shall he also reap.

8 For he that soweth to his flesh shall of flesh reap corruption; but he that soweth to the Spirit shall of the Spirit reap life everlasting.

Rev. 21. 8 But the fearful, and unbelieving, and the abominable, and murderers, and whoremongers, and sorcerers, and idolaters, and all liars, shall have their part in the lake which burneth with fire and brimstone: which is the second death.

K

John 3. 16 For God so loved the world, that he gave his only begotten Son, that whosoever believeth in him should not perish, but have everlasting life.

Rom. 2. 6 Who will render to every man according to his deeds:

7 To them who by patient continuance in well doing seek for glory and honour and immortality, eternal life:

Rom. 5. 17 For if by one man's offence death reigned by one; much more they which receive abundance of grace and of the gift of righteousness shall reign in life by one, Jesus Christ.

Rom. 5. 21 That as sin hath reigned unto death, even so might grace reign through righteousness unto eternal life by Jesus Christ our Lord.

I Pet. 1. 4 To an inheritance incorruptible, and undefiled, and that fadeth not away, reserved in heaven for you.

THE FREEDOM THEREFROM ILLUSTRATED.

A

Gen. 2. 23 And Adam said, This *is* now bone of my bones, and flesh of my flesh: she shall be called Woman, because she was taken out of Man.

24 Therefore shall a man leave his father and his mother, and shall cleave unto his wife: and they shall be one flesh.

A—CONCLUDED.

I Cor. 7. 39 The wife is bound by the law as long as her husband liveth; but if her husband be dead, she is at liberty to be married to whom she will; only in the Lord.

B

Matt. 5. 32 But I say unto you, That who-

For B concldued, see next page (840).

§ 330. THE DOMINION OF THE LAW AND THE

CHAP. 7.

liveth, she be married to another man, she shall be called an adulteress: but if her husband be dead, she is free from that law; so that she is no adulteress, though she be married to another man.

4 Wherefore, my brethren, ye also are become [c]dead to the law by the body of Christ; that ye should be married to another, *even* to him who is raised from the dead, that we should [d]bring forth fruit unto God.

5 For when we were in the flesh, the [1]motions of sins, which were by the law, [e]did work in our members [f]to bring forth fruit unto death.

CHAP. 7.

6 But now we are delivered from the law, [2]that being dead wherein we were held; that we should serve [g]in newness of spirit, and not *in* the oldness of the letter.

B—CONCLUDED.

soever shall put away his wife, saving for the cause of fornication, causeth her to commit adultery: and whosoever shall marry her that is divorced committeth adultery.

C

Rom. 8. 2 For the law of the Spirit of life in Christ Jesus hath made me free from the law of sin and death.

Gal. 2. 19 For I through the law am dead to the law, that I might live unto God.

Gal. 5. 18 But if ye be led of the Spirit, ye are not under the law.

Eph. 2. 15 Having abolished in his flesh the enmity, *even* the law of commandments *contained* in ordinances; for to

§ 331. BY THE LAW IS THE KNOWLEDGE OF SIN. IT IS SPIRITUAL. THE INWARD MAN

7 : 7–25.

7 What shall we say then? *Is* the law sin? God forbid. Nay, [a]I had not known sin, but by the law: for I had not known [1]lust, except the law had said, [b]Thou shalt not covet.

8 But [c]sin, taking occasion by the commandment, wrought in me all manner of concupiscence. For [d]without the law sin *was* dead.

9 For I was alive without the law once: but when the commandment came, sin revived, and I died.

10 And the commandment, [e]which *was ordained* to life, I found *to be* unto death.

11 For sin, taking occasion by the commandment, deceived me, and by it slew *me*.

12 Wherefore the law *is* holy, and the commandment holy, and just, and good.

CHAP. 7.

13 Was then that which is good made death unto me? God forbid. But sin, that it might appear sin, working death in me by that which is good; that sin by the commandment might become exceeding sinful.

14 For we know that the law is spiritual: but I am carnal, [f]sold under sin.

15 For that which I do, I [2]allow not: for [g]what I would, that do I not; but what I hate, that do I.

A

Rom. 3. 20. *See d, D, § 324, page 824.*

1

Or, *concupiscence.*

B

Ex. 20. 17 Thou shalt not covet thy neighbour's house, thou shalt not covet thy neighbour's wife, nor his manservant, nor his maidservant, nor his ox, nor his ass, nor anything that *is* thy neighbour's.

Deut. 5. 21 Neither shalt thou desire thy neighbour's wife, neither shalt thou covet thy neighbour's house, his field,

FREEDOM THEREFROM ILLUSTRATED (CONCLUDED).

C—CONCLUDED.

make in himself of twain one new man, *so* making peace;

Col. 2. 14 Blotting out the handwriting of ordinances that was against us, which was contrary to us, and took it out of the way, nailing it to his cross;

I Pet. 2. 24 Who his own self bare our sins in his own body on the tree, that we, being dead to sins, should live unto righteousness: by whose stripes ye were healed.

D

Gal. 5. 22 But the fruit of the Spirit is love, joy, peace, longsuffering, gentleness, goodness, faith,

1

Gr., *passions.*

E

Rom. 6. 13. *See t, T, § 328, page 836.*

F

Rom. 6. 21 What fruit had ye then in those things whereof ye are now ashamed? for the end of those things *is* death.

F—CONCLUDED.

Gal. 5. 19 Now the works of the flesh are manifest, which are *these*; Adultery, fornication, uncleanness, lasciviousness,

20 Idolatry, witchcraft, hatred, variance, emulations, wrath, strife, seditions, heresies,

21 Envyings, murders, drunkenness, revellings, and such like: of the which I tell you before, as I have also told *you* in time past, that they which do such things shall not inherit the kingdom of God.

Jas. 1. 15 Then when lust hath conceived, it bringeth forth sin; and sin, when it is finished, bringeth forth death.

2

Or, *being dead to that,*

Rom. 6. 2 God forbid. How shall we, that are dead to sin, live any longer therein?

Rom. 7. 4. *See text of topic.*

G

Rom. 2. 29. *See r, R, § 321, page 820.*

DELIGHTS THEREIN. CARNAL MEMBERS WAR AGAINST IT. DELIVERANCE IS IN CHRIST.

B—CONCLUDED.

or his manservant, or his maidservant, his ox, or his ass, or any *thing* that *is* thy neighbour's.

Rom. 13. 9 For this, Thou shalt not commit adultery, Thou shalt not kill, Thou shalt not steal, Thou shalt not bear false witness, Thou shalt not covet; and if *there be* any other commandment, it is briefly comprehended in this saying, namely, Thou shalt love thy neighbour as thyself.

C

Rom. 4. 15 Because the law worketh wrath: for where no law is, *there is* no transgression.

Rom. 5. 20. *See g, G, § 327, page 834.*

D

I Cor. 15. 56 The sting of death *is* sin; and the strength of sin *is* the law.

E

Lev. 18. 5 Ye shall therefore keep my statutes, and my judgments: which if a man do, he shall live in them: I *am* the LORD.

Eze. 20. 11 And I gave them my statutes, and shewed them my judgments, which *if* a man do, he shall even live in them.

Eze. 20. 13 But the house of Israel rebelled against me in the wilderness: they walked not in my statutes, and they

E—CONCLUDED.

despised my judgments, which *if* a man do, he shall even live in them; and my sabbaths they greatly polluted: then I said, I would pour out my fury upon them in the wilderness, to consume them.

II Cor. 3. 7 But if the ministration of death, written *and* engraven in stones, was glorious, so that the children of Israel could not steadfastly behold the face of Moses for the glory of his countenance; which *glory* was to be done away;

F

I Ki. 21. 20 And Ahab said to Elijah, Hast thou found me, O mine enemy? And he answered, I have found *thee*: because thou hast sold thyself to work evil in the sight of the LORD.

I Ki. 21. 25 But there was none like unto Ahab, which did sell himself to work wickedness in the sight of the LORD, whom Jezebel his wife stirred up.

II Ki. 17. 17 And they caused their sons and their daughters to pass through the fire, and used divination and enchantments, and sold themselves to do evil in the sight of the LORD, to provoke him to anger.

For 2 and G, see next page (842).

§ 331. By the Law is the Knowledge of Sin. It is Spiritual. The Inward Man De-

Chap. 7.

16 If then I do that which I would
not, I consent unto the law that *it is*
good.

17 Now then it is no more I that
do it, but sin that dwelleth in me.

18 For I know that [h]in me (that is,
in my flesh,) dwelleth no good thing:
for to will is present with me; but
how to perform that which is good
I find not.

19 For the good that I would, I do
not: but the evil which I would not,
that I do.

20 Now if I do that I would not,
it is no more I that do it, but sin
that dwelleth in me.

21 I find then a law, that, when I
would do good, evil is present with
me.

22 For I [i]delight in the law of God
after [k]the inward man:

23 But [l]I see another law in [m]my
members, warring against the law of
my mind, and bringing me into captivity
to the law of sin which is in
my members.

24 O wretched man that I am!
who shall deliver me from [2]the body
of this death?

25 [n]I thank God through Jesus
Christ our Lord. So then with the
mind I myself serve the law of God;
but with the flesh the law of sin.

2

Gr., *know.*

G

I. Ki. 8. 46 If they sin against thee, (for *there is* no man that sinneth not,) and thou be angry with them, and deliver them to the enemy, so that they carry them away captives unto the land of the enemy, far or near;

Ps. 65. 3 Iniquities prevail against me: *as for* our transgressions, thou shalt purge them away.

Eccl. 7. 20 For *there is* not a just man upon earth, that doeth good, and sinneth not.

§ 332. No Condemnation to Them in Christ. Having Received the Spirit

Chap. 8: 1–17.

1 *THERE is* therefore now no condemnation
to them which are in
Christ Jesus, who [a]walk not after
the flesh, but after the Spirit.

2 [b]For the law of [c]the Spirit of life
in Christ Jesus hath made me free
from [d]the law of sin and death.

3 For [e]what the law could not do,
in that it was weak through the flesh,
[f]God sending his own Son in the
likeness of sinful flesh, and [1]for sin,
condemned sin in the flesh:

4 That the righteousness of the law
might be fulfilled in us, [g]who walk not

A

Rom. 8. 4. *See text of topic.*

Gal. 5. 16 *This* I say then, Walk in the Spirit, and ye shall not fulfil the lust of the flesh.

Gal. 5. 25 If we live in the Spirit, let us also walk in the Spirit.

Tit. 2. 11 For the grace of God that bringeth salvation hath appeared to all men,

12 Teaching us that, denying ungodliness and worldly lusts, we should live soberly, righteously, and godly, in this present world;

B

John 8. 36 If the Son therefore shall make you free, ye shall be free indeed.

Rom. 6. 18. *See d, D, § 329, page 838.*

Gal. 2. 19 For I through the law am dead to the law, that I might live unto God.

C

I Cor. 15. 45 And so it is written, The first man Adam was made a living soul; the last Adam *was made* a quickening spirit.

LIGHTS THEREIN CARNAL MEMBERS WAR AGAINST IT. DELIVERANCE IS IN CHRIST (CON'D).

G—CONCLUDED.

Gal. 5. 17 For the flesh lusteth against the Spirit, and the Spirit against the flesh: and these are contrary the one to the other, so that ye cannot do the things that ye would.

H

Gen. 6. 5 And GOD saw that the wickedness of man *was* great in the earth, and *that* every imagination of the thoughts of his heart *was* only evil continually.

Gen. 8. 21 And the LORD smelled a sweet savour; and the LORD said in his heart, I will not again curse the ground any more for man's sake; for the imagination of man's heart *is* evil from his youth: neither will I again smite any more every thing living, as I have done.

I

Ps. 1. 2 But his delight *is* in the law of the LORD; and in his law doth he meditate day and night.

K

IICor.4. 16 For which cause we faint not; but though our outward man perish, yet the inward *man* is renewed day by day.

Eph. 3. 16 That he would grant you, according to the riches of his glory, to be strengthened with might by his Spirit in the inner man;

Col.3. 9 Lie not one to another, seeing that ye have put off the old man with his deeds;

K—CONCLUDED.

Col. 3. 10 And have put on the new *man*, which is renewed in knowledge after the image of him that created him:

I. Pet.3. 4 But *let it be* the hidden man of the heart, in that which is not corruptible, *even the ornament* of a meek and quiet spirit, which is in the sight of God of great price.

L

Gal. 5. 17. *See under G.*

M

Rom. 6. 13 Neither yield ye your members *as* instruments of unrighteousness unto sin: but yield yourselves unto God, as those that are alive from the dead, and your members *as* instruments of righteousness unto God.

Rom. 6. 19 I speak after the manner of men because of the infirmity of your flesh: for as ye have yielded your members servants to uncleanness and to iniquity unto iniquity; even so now yield your members servants to righteousness unto holiness.

3

Or, *this body of death.*

N

ICor.15. 57 But thanks *be* to God, which giveth us the victory through our Lord Jesus Christ.

OF ADOPTION WE BECOME CHILDREN OF GOD AND JOINT HEIRS WITH CHRIST.

C—CONCLUDED.

IICor.3. 6 Who also hath made us able ministers of the new testament; not of the letter, but of the spirit: for the letter killeth, but the spirit giveth life.

D

Rom. 7. 24, 25. *See text of topic § 331.*

E

Acts 13. 39 And by him all that believe are justified from all things, from which ye could not be justified by the law of Moses.

Rom. 3. 20 Therefore by the deeds of the law there shall no flesh be justified in his sight: for by the law is the knowledge of sin.

Rom. 7. 5-11. *See text of topic, § 330-331, page 840*

Gal. 3. 21 *Is* the law then against the promises of God? God forbid: for if there had been a law given which could have given life, verily righteousness should have been by the law.

E—CONCLUDED.

Heb. 7. 18 For there is verily a disannulling of the commandments going before for the weakness and unprofitableness thereof.

19 For the law made nothing perfect, but the bringing in of a better hope *did;* by the which we draw nigh unto God.

Heb. 10. 1 For the law having a shadow of good things to come, *and* not the very image of the things, can never with those sacrifices, which they offered year by year continually, make the comers thereunto perfect.

2 For then would they not have ceased to be offered? because that the worshippers once purged should have had no more conscience of sins.

F

IICor.5. 21 For he hath made him *to be* sin

For F Concluded, 1 and G, see next page, 844.

§ 332. No Condemnation to Them in Christ. Having Received the Spirit of

Chap. 8.

after the flesh, but after the Spirit.
5 For [h]they that are after the flesh
do mind the things of the flesh ; but
they that are after the Spirit, [i]the
things of the Spirit.
6 For [k2]to be carnally minded *is*
death ; but [3]to be spiritually minded
is life and peace.
7 Because [2l]the carnal mind *is* enmity against God ; for it is not subject to the law of God, [m]neither indeed can be.
8 So then they that are in the flesh
cannot please God.
9 But ye are not in the flesh, but
in the Spirit, if so be that [n]the Spirit
of God dwell in you. Now if any
man have not [o]the Spirit of Christ,
he is none of his.
10 And if Christ *be* in you, the
body *is* dead because of sin ; but the
Spirit *is* life because of righteousness.
11 But if the Spirit of [p]him that
raised up Jesus from the dead dwell
in you, [q]he that raised up Christ
from the dead shall also quicken
your mortal bodies [4]by his Spirit
that dwelleth in you.
12 [r]Therefore, brethren, we are
debtors, not to the flesh, to live after
the flesh.
13 For [s]if ye live after the flesh, ye
shall die : but if ye through the Spirit
do [t]mortify the deeds of the body,
ye shall live.
14 For [u]as many as are led by the
Spirit of God, they are the Sons of
God.
15 For [x]ye have not received the
spirit of bondage again [y]to fear ; but
ye have received the [z]Spirit of adoption, whereby we cry, [a]Abba, Father.
16 [b]The Spirit itself beareth witness

F—Concluded.

for us, who knew no sin; that we might be made the righteousness of God in him.

Gal. 3. 13 Christ hath redeemed us from the curse of the law, being made a curse for us: for it is written, Cursed *is* every one that hangeth on a tree.

1

Or, *by a sacrifice for sin.*

G

Rom. 8. 1. *See a, A, § 332, page 842.*

H

John 3. 6 That which is born of the flesh is flesh; and that which is born of the Spirit is spirit.

I Cor. 2. 14 But the natural man receiveth not the things of the Spirit of God: for they are foolishness unto him: neither can he know *them*, because they are spiritually discerned.

I Cor. 15. 48 As *is* the earthy, such *are* they also that are earthy: and as *is* the heavenly, such *are* they also that are heavenly.

I

Gal. 5. 22 But the fruit of the Spirit is love, joy, peace, longsuffering, gentleness, goodness, faith,

K

Rom. 8. 13. *See text of topic.*

Rom. 6. 21 What fruit had ye then in those things whereof ye are now ashamed ? for the end of those things *is* death.

Gal. 6. 8 For he that soweth to his flesh shall of the flesh reap corruption; but he that soweth to the Spirit shall of the Spirit reap life everlasting.

2

Gr. *the minding of the flesh.*

3

Gr. *the minding of the spirit.*

L

Jas. 4. 4 Ye adulterers and adulteresses, know ye not that the friendship of the world is enmity with God ? whosoever therefore will be a friend of the world is the enemy of God.

M

I Cor. 2. 14. *See under H.*

N

I Cor. 3. 16 Know ye not that ye are the temple of God, and *that* the Spirit of God dwelleth in you ?

I Cor. 6. 19 What ? know ye not that your body is the temple of the Holy Ghost *which is* in you, which ye have of God, and ye are not your own ?

ADOPTION WE BECOME CHILDREN OF GOD AND JOINT HEIRS WITH CHRIST (CONTINUED).

N – CONCLUDED.

IICor. 6. 16 And what agreement hath the temple of God with idols? for ye are the temple of the living God; as God hath said, I will dwell in them, and walk in *them;* and I will be their God, and they shall be my people.

Gal. 4. 6 And because ye are sons, God hath sent forth the Spirit of his Son, into your hearts, crying, Abba, Father.

O

John 3. 34 For he whom God hath sent speaketh the words of God: for God giveth not the Spirit by measure *unto him.*

Gal. 4. 6. *See under N.*

Phil. 1. 19 For I know that this shall turn to my salvation through your prayer, and the supply of the Spirit of Jesus Christ,

I Pet. 1. 11 Searching what, or what manner of time the Spirit of Christ which was in them did signify, when it testified beforehand the sufferings of Christ, and the glory that should follow.

P

Acts 2. 24 Whom God hath raised up, having loosed the pains of death: because it was not possible that he should be holden of it.

Study K, *§ 231, page 638.*

Q

Rom. 6. 4, 5. *See f, F, and i, I, § 328, page 836.*

IICor. 4. 14 Knowing that he which raised up the Lord Jesus shall raise up us also by Jesus, and shall present *us* with you.

4

Or, *because of his spirit.*

R

Rom. 6. 7 For he that is dead is freed from sin.

Rom. 6. 14 For sin shall not have dominion over you: for ye are not under the law, but under grace.

S

Rom. 8. 6. *See text of topic.*
Gal. 6. 8. *See under K.*

T

Eph. 4. 22 That ye put off concerning the former conversation the old man, which is corrupt according to the deceitful lusts;

Col. 3. 5 Mortify therefore your members which are upon the earth; fornication, uncleanness, inordinate affection, evil concupiscence, and covetousness, which is idolatry:

U

Ps. 143. 10 Teach me to do thy will; for thou *art* my God: thy Spirit *is* good; lead me into the land of uprightness.

Prov. 8. 20 I lead in the way of righteousness, in the midst of the paths of judgment:

U—CONCLUDED.

Prov. 8. 21 That I may cause those that love me to inherit substance; and I will fill their treasures.

Isa. 48. 17 Thus saith the LORD, thy Redeemer, the Holy One of Israel; I *am* the LORD thy God which teacheth thee to profit, which leadeth thee by the way *that* thou shouldest go.

Gal. 4. 6. *See under N.*

Gal. 5. 18 But if ye be led of the Spirit, ye are not under the law.

X

I Cor. 2. 12 Now we have received, not the spirit of the world, but the Spirit which is of God; that we might know the things that are freely given to us of God.

Heb. 2. 15 And deliver them, who through fear of death were all their lifetime subject to bondage.

Y

IITim. 1. 7 For God hath not given us the spirit of fear; but of power, and of love, and of a sound mind.

I Jno. 4. 18 There is no fear in love; but perfect love casteth out fear: because fear hath torment. He that feareth is not made perfect in love.

Z

Isa. 56. 5 Even unto them will I give in mine house and within my walls a place and a name better than of sons and of daughters: I will give them an everlasting name, that shall not be cut off.

Gal. 4. 5 To redeem them that were under the law, that we might receive the adoption of sons.

Gal. 4. 6. *See under N,*

A

Mark 14. 36 And he said, Abba, Father, all things *are* possible unto thee; take away this cup from me: nevertheless, not what I will, but what thou wilt.

B

IICor. 1. 22 Who hath also sealed us, and given the earnest of the Spirit in our hearts.

IICor. 5. 5 Now he that hath wrought us for the selfsame thing *is* God, who also hath given unto us the earnest of the Spirit.

Eph. 1. 13 In whom ye also *trusted,* after that ye heard the word of truth, the gospel of your salvation: in whom also, after that ye believed, ye were sealed with that Holy Spirit of promise.

Eph. 4. 30 And grieve not the Holy Spirit of God, whereby ye are sealed unto the day of redemption.

§ 332. No Condemnation to Them in Christ. Having Received the Spirit of

Chap. 8.

with our spirit, that we are the children of God:

17 And if children, then heirs; [c]heirs of God, and joint heirs with Christ; [d]if so be that we suffer with *him*, that we may be also glorified together.

C

Acts 26. 18 To open their eyes, *and* to turn *them* from darkness to light, and *from* the power of Satan unto God, that they may receive forgiveness of sins, and inheritance among them which are sanctified by faith that is in me.

Gal. 4. 7 Wherefore thou art no more a servant, but a son; and if a son, then an heir of God through Christ.

§ 333. ALL CREATION AWAITS REDEMPTION, THE GLORY OF WHICH

8 : 18—25.

18 For I reckon that [a]the sufferings of this present time *are* not worthy *to be compared* with the glory which shall be revealed in us.

19 For [b]the earnest expectation of the creature waiteth for the [c]manifestation of the sons of God.

20 For [d]the creature was made subject to vanity, not willingly, but by reason of him who hath subjected *the same* in hope;

21 Because the creature itself also shall be delivered from the bondage of corruption into the glorious liberty of the children of God.

22 For we know that [1]the whole creation [e]groaneth and travaileth in pain together until now.

23 And not only *they*, but ourselves also, which have [f]the firstfruits of the Spirit, [g]even we ourselves, groan within ourselves [h]waiting for the adoption, *towit*, the [i]redemption of our body.

24 For we are saved by hope: but [k]hope that is seen is not hope: for what a man seeth, why doth he yet hope for?

25 But if we hope for that we see not, *then* do we with patience wait for *it*.

A

IICor.4. 17 For our light affliction, which is but for a moment, worketh for us a far more exceeding *and* eternal weight of glory;

Heb. 11. 25 Choosing rather to suffer affliction with the people of God, than to enjoy the pleasures of sin for a season;

26 Esteeming the reproach of Christ greater riches than the treasures in Egypt: for he had respect unto the recompense of the reward.

Heb. 11. 35 Women received their dead raised to life again: and others were tortured, not accepting deliverance; that they might obtain a better resurrection:

I Pet. 1. 6 Wherein ye greatly rejoice, though now for a season, if need be, ye are in heaviness through manifold temptations:

7 That the trial of your faith, being much more precious than of gold that perisheth, though it be tried with fire, might be found unto praise and honor and glory at the appearing of Jesus Christ:

I Pet. 4. 13 But rejoice, inasmuch as ye are partakers of Christ's sufferings; that, when his glory shall be revealed, ye may be glad also with exceeding joy.

B

IIPet. 3. 13 Nevertheless we, according to his promise, look for new heavens and a new earth, wherein dwelleth righteousness.

C

I Jno.3. 2 Beloved, now are we the sons of God, and it doth not yet appear what we shall be: but we know that, when he shall appear, we shall be like him; for we shall see him as he is.

D

Gen. 3. 18 Thorns also and thistles shall it bring forth to thee; and thou shalt eat the herb of the field;

ADOPTION WE BECOME CHILDREN OF GOD AND JOINT HEIRS WITH CHRIST (CONCLUDED).

D

Acts 14. 22 Confirming the souls of the disciples, *and* exhorting them to continue in the faith, and that we must through much tribulation enter into the kingdom of God.

IICor.4. 11 For we which live are alway delivered unto death for Jesus' sake, that the life also of Jesus might be made manifest in our mortal flesh.

D—CONCLUDED

Phil. 1. 29 For unto you it is given in the behalf of Christ, not only to believe on him, but also to suffer for his sake;

IITim.2. 11 *It is* a faithful saying: For if we be dead with *him*, we shall also live with *him:*

12 If we suffer, we shall also reign with *him:* if we deny *him*, he also will deny us:

WILL GREATLY OVERSHADOW THE PRESENT TRIAL AND SUFFERING.

D—CONCLUDED

19 In the sweat of thy face shalt thou eat bread, till thou return unto the ground; for out of it wast thou taken: for dust thou *art*, and unto dust shalt thou return.

Isa. 24. 5 The earth also is defiled under the inhabitants thereof; because they have transgressed the laws, changed the ordinance, broken the everlasting covenant.

6 Therefore hath the curse devoured the earth, and they that dwell therein are desolate: therefore the inhabitants of the earth are burned, and few men left.

Jer. 12. 4 How long shall the land mourn, and the herbs of every field wither, for the wickedness of them that dwell therein ? the beasts are consumed, and the birds; because they said, He shall not see our last end.

Hos. 4. 3 Therefore shall the land mourn, and every one that dwelleth therein shall languish, with the beasts of the field, and with the fowls of heaven; yea, the fishes of the sea also shall be taken away.

Joel 1. 18 How do the beasts groan! the herds of cattle are perplexed, because they have no pasture; yea, the flocks of sheep are made desolate.

1

Or, *every creature.*

Mark16. 15 And he said unto them, Go ye into all the world, and preach the gospel to every creature.

Col. 1. 23 If ye continue in the faith grounded and settled, and *be* not moved away from the hope of the gospel, which ye have heard, *and* which was preached to every creature which is under heaven; whereof I Paul am made a minister;

E

Jer. 12. 11 They have made it desolate, *and being* desolate it mourneth unto me;

E—CONCLUDED.

the whole land is made desolate, because no man layeth *it* to heart.

F

IICor. 5. 5 Now he that hath wrought us for the selfsame thing *is* God, who also hath given unto us the earnest of the Spirit.

Eph. 1. 14 Which is the earnest of our inheritance until the redemption of the purchased possession, unto the praise of his glory.

G

IICor.5. 2 For in this we groan, earnestly desiring to be clothed upon with our house which is from heaven:

IICor. 5. 4 For we that are in *this* tabernacle do groan, being burdened: not for that we would be unclothed, but clothed upon, that mortality might be swallowed up of life.

H

Luke20. 36 Neither can they die any more: for they are equal unto the angels; and are the children of God, being the children of the resurrection.

Phil. 3. 20 For our conversation is in heaven; from whence also we look for the Saviour, the Lord Jesus Christ:

I

Luke 21. 28 And when these things begin to come to pass, then look up, and lift up your heads; for your redemption draweth nigh.

Eph. 1. 14. *See under* F.

Eph. 4. 30 And grieve not the Holy Spirit of God, whereby ye are sealed unto the day of redemption.

K

IICor. 5. 7 (For we walk by faith, not by sight:)

Heb. 11. 1 Now faith is the substance of things hoped for, the evidence of things not seen.

§ 334. THE SPIRIT HELPS, AND CHRIST INTERCEDES FOR GOD'S ELECT; THERE-

8 : 26–39.

26 Likewise the Spirit also helpeth our infirmities: for [a]we know not what we should pray for as we ought: but [b]the Spirit itself maketh intercession for us with groanings which cannot be uttered.

27 And [c]he that searcheth the hearts knoweth what *is* the mind of the Spirit, [1]because he maketh intercession for the saints [d]according to *the will of* God.

28 And we know that [e]all things work together for good to them that love God, to them [f]who are the called according to *his* purpose.

29 For whom [g]he did foreknow, [h]he also did predestinate [i]*to be* conformed to the image of his Son, [k]that he might be the firstborn among many brethren.

A

Matt. 20. 22 But Jesus answered and said, Ye know not what ye ask. Are ye able to drink of the cup that I shall drink of, and to be baptized with the baptism that I am baptized with? They say unto him, we are able.

Jas. 4. 3 Ye ask, and receive not, because ye ask amiss, that ye may consume *it* upon your lusts.

B

Zech. 12. 10 And I will pour upon the house of David, and upon the inhabitants of Jerusalem, the spirit of grace and of supplications: and they shall look upon me whom they have pierced, and they shall mourn for him, as one mourneth for *his* only *son*, and shall be in bitterness for him, as one that is in bitterness for *his* firstborn.

Eph. 6. 18 Praying always with all prayer and supplication in the Spirit, and watching thereunto with all perseverance and supplication for all saints;

C

Prov. 17. 3 The fining pot *is* for silver, and the furnace for gold: but the LORD trieth the hearts.

Acts 1. 24. *See p, P, § 229, page 632.*

I Thes. 2. 4 But as we were allowed of God to be put in trust with the gospel, even so we speak; not as pleasing men, but God, which trieth our hearts.

1
Or, *that.*

D

Jer. 29. 12 Then shall ye call upon me, and ye shall go and pray unto me, and I will hearken unto you.

13 And ye shall seek me, and find *me*, when ye shall search for me with all your heart,

I Jno. 3. 21 Beloved, if our heart condemn us not, *then* have we confidence toward God.

22 And whatsoever we ask, we receive of him, because we keep his commandments, and do those things that are pleasing in his sight.

I Jno. 5. 14 And this is the confidence that we have in him, that, if we ask any thing according to his will, he heareth us:

15 And if we know that he hear us, whatsoever we ask, we know that we have the petitions that we desired of him.

E

Gen. 50. 20 But as for you, ye thought evil against me; *but* God meant it unto good, to bring to pass, as *it is* this day, to save much people alive.

Deut. 8. 2 And thou shalt remember all the way which the LORD thy God led thee these forty years in the wilderness, to humble thee, *and* to prove thee, to know what *was* in thine heart, whether thou wouldest keep his commandments, or no.

Jer. 24. 5 Thus saith the LORD, the God of Israel; Like these good figs, so will I acknowledge them that are carried away captive of Judah, whom I have sent out of this place into the land of the Chaldeans for *their* good.

6 For I will set mine eyes upon them for good, and I will bring them again to this land: and I will build them, and not pull *them* down; and I will plant them, and not pluck *them* up.

7 And I will give them a heart to know me, that I *am* the LORD; and they shall be my people, and I will be their God: for they shall return unto me with their whole heart.

II Cor. 4. 15 For all things *are* for your sakes, that the abundant grace might through the thanksgiving of many redound to the glory of God.

16 For which cause we faint not; but though our outward man perish, yet the inward *man* is renewed day by day.

17 For our light affliction, which is but for a moment, worketh for us a

fore Nothing Shall be Able to Separate Them from the Love of God.

E—Concluded.

far more exceeding *and* eternal weight of glory;

Heb. 12. 9 Furthermore, we have had fathers of our flesh which corrected *us*, and we gave *them* reverence: shall we not much rather be in subjection unto the Father of spirits, and live?

10 For they verily for a few days chastened *us* after their own pleasure; but he for *our* profit, that *we* might be partakers of his holiness.

11 Now no chastening for the present seemeth to be joyous, but grievous: nevertheless, afterward it yieldeth the peaceable fruit of righteousness unto them which are exercised thereby.

Rev. 3. 19 As many as I love, I rebuke and chasten: be zealous therefore, and repent.

F

Rom. 1. 6 Among whom are ye also the called of Jesus Christ:

Rom. 9. 11 (For *the children* being not yet born, neither having done any good or evil, that the purpose of God according to election might stand, not of works, but of him that calleth:)

Rom. 9. 23 And that he might make known the riches of his glory on the vessels of mercy, which he had afore prepared unto glory,

24 Even us, whom he hath called, not of the Jews only, but also of the Gentiles?

IIThes. 2. 14 Whereunto he called you by our gospel, to the obtaining of the glory of our Lord Jesus Christ.

IITim. 1. 9 Who hath saved us, and called *us* with a holy calling, not according to our works, but according to his own purpose and grace, which was given us in Christ Jesus before the world began;

I Pet. 5. 10 But the God of all grace, who hath called us unto his eternal glory by Christ Jesus, after that ye have suffered a while, make you perfect, stablish, strengthen, settle *you*.

G

Ps. 1. 6 For the Lord knoweth the way of the righteous: but the way of the ungodly shall perish.

Jer. 1. 5 Before I formed thee in the belly I knew thee; and before thou camest forth out of the womb I sanctified thee, *and* I ordained thee a prophet unto the nations.

Rom. 11. 2 God hath not cast away his people which he foreknew. Wot ye not what

G—Concluded.

the Scripture saith of Elias? how he maketh intercession to God against Israel, saying,

IITim. 2. 19 Nevertheless the foundation of God standeth sure, having this seal, The Lord knoweth them that are his. And, Let every one that nameth the name of Christ depart from iniquity.

I Pet. 1. 2 Elect according to the foreknowledge of God the Father, through sanctification of the Spirit, unto obedience and sprinkling of the blood of Jesus Christ: Grace unto you, and peace, be multiplied.

H

Acts 13. 48. *See f, F, § 263, page 718.*

I

John 17. 22 And the glory which thou gavest me I have given them; that they may be one, even as we are one:

IICor. 3. 18 But we all, with open face beholding as in a glass the glory of the Lord, are changed into the same image from glory to glory, *even* as by the Spirit of the Lord.

Phil. 3. 21 Who shall change our vile body, that it may be fashioned like unto his glorious body, according to the working whereby he is able even to subdue all things unto himself.

I Jno. 3. 2 Beloved, now are we the sons of God, and it doth not yet appear what we shall be; but we know that, when he shall appear, we shall be like him; for we shall see him as he is.

K

Col. 1. 15 Who is the image of the invisible God, the firstborn of every creature:

Col. 1. 18 And he is the head of the body, the church: who is the beginning, the firstborn from the dead; that in all *things* he might have the preeminence.

Heb. 1. 6 And again, when he bringeth in the firstbegotten into the world, he saith, And let all the angels of God worship him.

Rev. 1. 5 And from Jesus Christ, *who is* the faithful witness, *and* the firstbegotten of the dead, and the prince of the kings of the earth. Unto him that loved us, and washed us from our sins in his own blood,

L

See under F.

Eph. 4. 4 *There is* one body, and one Spirit, even as ye are called in one hope of your calling;

For L concluded, see next page (850).

§ 334. The Spirit Helps, and Christ Intercedes for God's Elect; Therefore

Chap. 8.

30 Moreover, whom he did predestinate, them he also [l]called: and
whom he called, them he also [m]justi-
fied: and whom he justified, them
he also [n]glorified.

31 What shall we then say to these
things? [o]If God *be* for us, who *can
be* against us?

32 He that spared not his own Son,
but [p] delivered him up for all, how
shall he not with him also freely give
us all things?

33 Who shall lay any thing to the
charge of God's elect? [q]*It is* God
that justifieth.

34 Who *is* he that condemneth? *It
is* Christ that died, yea rather, that
is risen again, [r]who is even at the
right hand of God, [s]who also maketh intercession for us.

35 Who shall separate us from the
love of Christ? *shall* tribulation, or
distress, or persecution, or famine,
or nakedness, or peril, or sword?

36 As it is written, [t]For thy sake
we are killed all the day long; we are
accounted as sheep for the slaughter.

37 Nay, [u]in all these things we are
more than conquerors through him
that loved us.

38 For I am persuaded, that neither
death, nor life, nor angels, nor [x]prin-
cipalities, nor powers, nor things
present, nor things to come,

39 Nor height, nor depth, nor any
other creature, shall be able to separate us from the love of God,
which is in Christ Jesus our Lord.

L—Concluded, See preceding page, 849.

I Pet. 2. 9 But ye *are* a chosen generation, a royal priesthood, a holy nation, a peculiar people; that ye should shew forth the praises of him who hath called you out of darkness into his marvellous light:

M

I Cor. 6. 11 And such were some of you: but ye are washed, but ye are sanctified, but ye are justified in the name of the Lord Jesus, and by the Spirit of our God.

N

John 17. 22. *See under I, page 849.*

Eph. 2. 6 And hath raised *us* up together, and made *us* sit together in heavenly *places* in Christ Jesus:

O

Num. 14. 9 Only rebel not ye against the Lord, neither fear ye the people of the land; for they *are* bread for us: their defence is departed from them, and the Lord *is* with us: fear them not.

I Sa. 14. 6 And Jonathan said to the young man that bare his armour, Come, and let us go over unto the garrison of these uncircumcised: it may be that the Lord will work for us: for *there is* no restraint to the Lord to save by many or by few.

Ps. 27. 1 The Lord *is* my light and my salvation; whom shall I fear? the Lord *is* the strength of my life; of whom shall I be afraid?

2 When the wicked, *even* mine enemies and my foes, came upon me to eat up my flesh, they stumbled and fell.

3 Though a host should encamp against me, my heart shall not fear: though war should rise against me, in this *will* I *be* confident.

Ps. 118. 6 The Lord *is* on my side; I will not fear: what can man do unto me?

Isa. 54. 17 No weapon that is formed against thee shall prosper; and every tongue *that* shall rise against thee in judgment thou shalt condemn. This *is* the heritage of the servants of the Lord, and their righteousness *is* of me, saith the Lord.

Jer. 20. 11 But the Lord *is* with me as a mighty terrible one: therefore my persecutors shall stumble, and they shall not prevail: they shall be greatly ashamed; for they shall not prosper: *their* everlasting confusion shall never be forgotten.

NOTHING SHALL BE ABLE TO SEPARATE THEM FROM THE LOVE OF GOD (CONCLUDED).

O—CONCLUDED.

John 10. 29 My Father, which gave *them* me, is greater than all; and no *man* is able to pluck *them* out of my Father's hand.

P

Rom. 4. 25. *See b, B, § 325, page 830.*

Q

Isa. 50. 8 *He is* near that justifieth me; who will contend with me? let us stand together; who *is* mine adversary? let him come near to me.

9 Behold, the LORD GOD will help me: who *is* he *that* shall condemn me? lo, they all shall wax old as a garment: the moth shall eat them up.

Rev. 12. 10 And I heard a loud voice saying in heaven, Now is come salvation, and strength, and the kingdom of our God, and the power of his Christ: for the accuser of our brethren is cast down, which accused them before our God day and night.

11 And they overcame him by the blood of the lamb, and by the word of their testimony; and they loved not their lives unto the death.

R

Mark 16. 19 So then, after the Lord had spoken unto them, he was received up into heaven, and sat on the right hand of God.

Col. 3. 1 If ye then be risen with Christ, seek those things which are above, where Christ sitteth on the right hand of God.

Heb. 1. 3 Who being the brightness of *his* glory, and the express image of his person, and upholding all things by the word of his power, when he had by himself purged our sins, sat down on the right hand of the Majesty on high;

Heb. 8. 1 Now of the things which we have spoken *this is* the sum: We have such a high priest, who is set on the right hand of the throne of the Majesty in the heavens;

Heb. 12. 2 Looking unto Jesus the author and finisher of *our* faith; who for the joy that was set before him endured the cross, despising the shame, and is set down at the right hand of the throne of God.

I Pet. 3. 22 Who is gone into heaven, and is on the right hand of God; angels and authorities and powers being made subject unto him.

S

Heb. 7. 25 Wherefore he is able also to save them to the uttermost that come unto

S—CONCLUDED

God by him, seeing he ever liveth to make intercession for them.

Heb. 9. 24 For Christ is not entered into the holy places made with hands, *which are* the figures of the true; but into heaven itself, now to appear in the presence of God for us:

T

Ps. 44. 22 Yea, for thy sake are we killed all the day long; we are counted as sheep for the slaughter.

ICor. 15. 30 And why stand we in jeopardy every hour?

31 I protest by your rejoicing which I have in Christ Jesus our Lord, I die daily.

IICor. 4. 11 For we which live are alway delivered unto death for Jesus' sake, that the life also of Jesus might be made manifest in our mortal flesh.

U

ICor. 15. 57 But thanks *be* to God, which giveth us the victory through our Lord Jesus Christ.

IICor. 2. 14 Now thanks *be* unto God, which always causeth us to triumph in Christ, and maketh manifest the savour of his knowledge by us in every place.

I Jno. 4. 4 Ye are of God, little chidren, and have overcome them: because greater is he that is in you, than he that is in the world.

I Jno. 5. 4 For whatsoever is born of God overcometh the world: and this is the victory that overcometh the world, *even* our faith.

Rev. 12. 11. *See under Q.*

X

Eph. 1. 21 Far above all principality, and power, and might, and dominion, and every name that is named, not only in this world, but also in that which is to come:

Eph. 6. 12 For we wrestle not against flesh and blood, but against principalities, against powers, against the rulers of the darkness of this world, against spiritual wickedness in high *places.*

Col. 1. 16 For by him were all things created, that are in heaven, and that are in earth, visible and invisible, whether *they be* thrones, or dominions, or principalities, or powers; all things were created by him, and for him:

Col. 2. 15 *And* having spoiled principalities and powers, he made a shew of them openly, triumphing over them in it.

I Pet. 3. 22. *See under R.*

§ 335. NOT ALL ISRAEL, GOD WORKETH

9 : 1—18.

1 I [a]say the truth in Christ, I lie not, my conscience also bearing me witness in the Holy Ghost,

2 That [b]I have great heaviness and continual sorrow in my heart.

3 For [c]I could wish that myself were [1]accursed from Christ for my brethren, my kinsmen according to the flesh:

4 [d]Who are Israelites; [e]to whom *pertaineth* the adoption, and [f]the glory, and [g]the [2]covenants, and [h]the giving of the law, and [i]the service *of God,* and [k]the promises;

5 [l]Whose *are* the fathers, and [m]of whom as concerning the flesh Christ *came,* [n]who is over all, God blessed for ever. Amen.

6 [o]Not as though the word of God hath taken none effect. [p]For they *are* not all Israel, which are of Israel:

7 [q]Neither, because they are the seed of Abraham, *are they* all children: but, In [r]Isaac shall thy seed be called.

8 That is, They which are the children of the flesh, these *are* not the children of God: but [s]the children of the promise are counted for the seed.

A

Rom. 1. 9 For God is my witness, whom I serve with my spirit in the gospel of his Son, that without ceasing I make mention of you always in my prayers;

IICor. 1. 23 Moreover I call God for a record upon my soul, that to spare you I came not as yet unto Corinth.

IICor. 11. 31 The God and Father of our Lord Jesus Christ, which is blessed for evermore, knoweth that I lie not.

IICor. 12. 19 Again, think ye that we excuse ourselves unto you? we speak before God in Christ; but *we do* all things, dearly beloved, for your edifying.

Gal. 1. 20 Now the things which I write unto you, behold, before God, I lie not.

Phil. 1. 8 For God is my record, how greatly I long after you all in the bowels of Jesus Christ.

A—CONCLUDED.

ITim. 2. 7 Whereunto I am ordained a preacher, and an apostle, (I speak the truth in Christ, *and* lie not;) a teacher of the Gentiles in faith and verity.

B

Rom. 10. 1 Brethren, my heart's desire and prayer to God for Israel is, that they might be saved.

C

Ex. 32. 32 Yet now, if thou wilt forgive their sin—; and if not, blot me, I pray thee, out of thy book which thou hast written.

1

Or, *separated.*

D

Deut. 7. 6 For thou *art* a holy people unto the LORD thy God: the LORD thy God hath chosen thee to be a special people unto himself, above all people that *are* upon the face of the earth.

E

Ex. 4. 22 And thou shalt say unto Pharaoh, Thus saith the LORD, Israel *is* my son, *even* my firstborn:

Deut. 14. 1 Ye *are* the children of the LORD your God: ye shall not cut yourselves, nor make any baldness between your eyes for the dead.

Jer. 31. 9 They shall come with weeping, and with supplications will I lead them: I will cause them to walk by the rivers of waters in a straight way, wherein they shall not stumble: for I am a father to Israel, and Ephraim *is* my firstborn.

F

I Sa. 4. 21 And she named the child I-chabod, saying, The glory is departed from Israel: because the ark of God was taken, and because of her father in law and her husband.

I Ki. 8. 11 So that the priests could not stand to minister because of the cloud: for the glory of the LORD had filled the house of the LORD.

Ps. 63. 2 To see thy power and thy glory, so *as* I have seen thee in the sanctuary.

Ps. 78. 61 And delivered his strength into captivity, and his glory into the enemy's hand.

Ps. 90. 16 Let thy work appear unto thy servants, and thy glory unto their children.

Isa. 60. 19 The sun shall be no more thy light by day; neither for brightness shall the moon give light unto thee:

HIS WILL IN MERCY WITH COMPASSION.

F—CONCLUDED.

but the LORD shall be unto thee an everlasting light, and thy God thy glory.

G

Acts 3. 25 Ye are the children of the prophets, and of the covenant which God made with our fathers, saying unto Abraham, And in thy seed shall all the kindreds of the earth be blessed.

Heb. 8. 8 For finding fault with them, he saith, Behold, the days come, saith the Lord, when I will make a new covenant with the house of Israel and with the house of Judah:

9 Not according to the covenant which I made with their fathers, in the day when I took them by the hand to lead them out of the land of Egypt; because they continued not in my covenant, and I regarded them not, saith the Lord.

10 For this *is* the covenant that I will make with the house of Israel after those days, saith the Lord; I will put my laws into their mind, and write them in their hearts: and I will be to them a God, and they shall be to me a people:

2

Or, *testaments.*

H

Ps. 147. 19 He sheweth his word unto Jacob, his statutes and his judgments unto Israel.

I

Heb. 9. 1 Then verily the first *covenant* had also ordinances of divine service, and a worldly sanctuary.

K

Acts 13. 32 And we declared unto you glad tidings, how that the promise which was made unto the fathers,

Rom. 3. 2 Much every way: chiefly, because that unto them were committed the oracles of God.

Eph. 2. 12 That at that time ye were without Christ, being aliens from the commonwealth of Israel ,and strangers from the covenants of promise, having no hope, and without God in the world:

L

Deut. 10. 15 Only the LORD had a delight in thy fathers to love them, and he chose their seed after them, *even* you above all people, as *it is* this day.

L—CONCLUDED.

Rom. 11. 28 As concerning the gospel, *they are* enemies for your sakes: but as touching the election, *they are* beloved for the father's sakes.

M

Luke 3. 23 And Jesus himself began to be about thirty years of age, being (as was supposed) the son of Joseph, which was *the son* of Heli.

Rom. 1. 3 Concerning his Son Jesus Christ our Lord, which was made of the seed of David according to the flesh;

N

Jer. 23. 6 In his days Judah shall be saved, and Israel shall dwell safely: and this *is* his name whereby he shall be called THE LORD OUR RIGHTEOUSNESS.

John 1. 1 In the beginning was the Word, and the Word was with God, and the Word was God.

Acts 20 28 ¶ Take heed therefore unto yourselves, and to all the flock, over the which the Holy Ghost hath made you overseers, to feed the church of God, which he hath purchased with his own blood.

Heb. 1. 8 But unto the Son *he saith*, Thy throne, O God, *is* for ever and ever: a sceptre of righteousness *is* the sceptre of thy kingdom.

1 Jno. 5. 20 And we know that the Son of God is come, and hath given us an understanding, that we may know him that is true, and we are in him that is true, *even* in his Son Jesus Christ. This is the true God, and eternal life.

O

Rom. 3. 3 *See c, C, §322, page 822.*

P

Rom. 2. 28. *See o, O, §321, page 820.*

Q

Gal. 4. 28 Now we, brethren, as Isaac was, are the children of promise.

R

Gen. 21. 12 ¶ And God said unto Abraham, Let it not be grievous in thy sight because of the lad, and because of thy bondwoman; in all that Sarah hath said unto thee, hearken unto her voice; for in Isaac shall thy seed be called:

Heb. 11. 18 Of whom it was said, That in Isaac shall thy seed be called:

S

Gal. 4. 28. *See under Q.*

§ 335. NOT ALL ISRAEL. GOD WORKETH HIS

CHAP. 9.

9 For this *is* the word of promise, [t]At this time will I come, and Sarah shall have a son.

10 And not only *this;* but when [u]Rebecca also had conceived by one, *even* by our father Isaac;

11 (For *the children* being not yet born, neither having done any good or evil, that the purpose of God according to election might stand, not of works, but of [x]him that calleth ;)

12 It was said unto her, [y]The [3]elder shall serve the [4]younger.

13 As it is written, [z]Jacob have I loved, but Esau have I hated.

14 What shall we say then? [a]*Is there* unrighteousness with God? God forbid.

15 For he saith to Moses, [b]I will have mercy on whom I will have mercy, and I will have compassion on whom I will have compassion.

16 So [c]then *it is* not of him that willeth, nor of him that runneth, but of God that sheweth mercy.

CHAP. 9.

17 For the Scripture saith unto Pharaoh, [d]Even for this same purpose have I raised thee up, that I might shew my power in thee, and that my name might be declared throughout all the earth.

18 Therefore hath he mercy on whom he will *have mercy*, and whom he will he hardeneth.

T

Gen. 18. 10 And he said, I will certainly return unto thee according to the time of life; and, lo, Sarah thy wife shall have a son. And Sarah heard *it* in the tent door, which *was* behind him.

Gen. 18. 14 Is any thing too hard for the LORD? At the time appointed I will return unto thee, according to the time of life, and Sarah shall have a son.

U

Gen. 25. 21 And Isaac entreated the LORD for his wife, because she *was* barren: and the LORD was entreated of him, and Rebekah his wife conceived.

X

Rom. 4. 17 (As it was written, I have made thee a father of many nations,) before him whom he believed, *even* God, who quickeneth the dead, and calleth those things which be not as though they were:

Rom. 8. 28 And we know that all things work together for good to them that love

§ 336. THE CREATURE SHALL NOT REPLY AGAINST THE CREATOR. GENTILES

9: 19–33.

19 Thou wilt say then unto me, Why doth he yet find fault? For [a]who hath resisted his will?

20 Nay but, O man, who art thou that [1]repliest against God? [b]Shall the thing formed say to him that formed *it*, Why hast thou made me thus?

21 Hath not the [c]potter power over the clay, of the same lump to make [d]one vessel unto honour, and another unto dishonour?

CHAP. 9.

22 *What* if God, willing to shew *his* wrath, and to make his power known, endured with much longsuffering [e]the vessels of wrath [2f]fitted to destruction:

23 And that he might make known [g]the riches of his glory on the vessels of mercy, which he had [h]afore prepared unto glory,

A

IICh. 20. 6 And said, O LORD God of our fathers, *art* not thou God in heaven? and rulest *not* thou over all the kingdoms of the heathen? and in thine

WILL IN MERCY WITH COMPASSION (CONCLDUED).

X—CONCLUDED.

God, to them who are the called according to *his* purpose.

Y

Gen. 25. 23 And the LORD said unto her, Two nations *are* in thy womb, and two manner of people shall be separated from thy bowels; and *the one* people shall be stronger than *the other* people; and the elder shall serve the younger.

3

Or, *greater*.

4

Or, *lesser*.

Z

Deut. 21. 15 If a man have two wives, one beloved, and another hated, and they have borne him children, *both* the beloved and the hated; and *if* the firstborn son be hers that was hated:

Prov. 13. 24 He that spareth his rod hateth his son: but he that loveth him chasteneth him betimes.

Mal. 1. 2 I have loved you, saith the LORD. Yet ye say, Wherein hast thou loved us? *Was* not Esau Jacob's brother? saith the LORD: yet I loved Jacob.

3 And I hated Esau, and laid his mountains and his heritage waste for the dragons of the wilderness.

A

Deut. 32. 4 *He is* the Rock, his work *is* perfect: for all his ways *are* judgment: a God of truth and without iniquity, just and right *is* he.

II Ch. 19. 7 Wherefore now let the fear of the LORD be upon you: take heed and do

A—CONCLUDED.

it: for *there is* no iniquity with the LORD our GOD, nor respect of persons, nor taking of gifts.

Job 8. 3 Doth God pervert judgment? or doth the Almighty pervert justice?

Job 34. 10 Therefore hearken unto me, ye men of understanding: far be it from God, *that he should do* wickedness; and *from* the Almighty, *that he should commit* iniquity.

Ps. 92. 15 To shew that the LORD *is* upright: *he is* my rock, and *there is* no unrighteousness in him.

B

Ex. 33. 19 And he said, I will make all my goodness pass before thee, and I will proclaim the name of the LORD before thee; and will be gracious to whom I will be gracious, and will shew mercy on whom I will shew mercy.

Ex. 34. 7 Keeping mercy for thousands, forgiving iniquity and transgression and sin, and that will by no means clear *the guilty;* visiting the iniquity of the fathers upon the children, and upon the children's children, unto the third and to the fourth *generation.*

Rom. 9. 18. *See text of topic.*

C

Ps. 115. 3 But our God *is* in the heavens: he hath done whatsoever he hath pleased.

D

Ex. 9. 16 And in very deed for this *cause* have I raised thee up, for to *shew in* thee my power; and that my name may be declared throughout all the earth.

ATTAIN TO THE RIGHTEOUSNESS OF FAITH AT WHICH THE JEWS STUMBLED.

A—CONCLUDED.

hand *is there not* power and might, so that none is able to withstand thee?

Job 9. 12 Behold, he taketh away, who can hinder him? who will say unto him, What doest thou?

Job 23. 13 But he *is* in one *mind*, and who can turn him? and *what* his soul desireth, even *that* he doeth.

Da. 4. 35 And all the inhabitants of the earth *are* reputed as nothing: and he doeth according to his will in the army of heaven, and *among* the inhabitants of the earth: and none can stay his hand, or say unto him, What doest thou?

1

Or, *answerest again*, or, *disputest with God?*

B

Isa. 29. 16 Surely your turning of things upside down shall be esteemed as the potter's clay: for shall the work say of him that made it, He made me not? or shall the thing framed say of him that framed it, He had no understanding?

Isa. 45. 9 Woe unto him that striveth with his Maker! *Let* the potsherd *strive* with the potsherds of the earth. Shall the clay say to him that fashioneth it, What makest thou? or thy work. He hath no hands?

Isa. 64. 8 But now, O LORD, thou *art* our Father; we *are* the clay, and thou our potter; and we all *are* the work of thy hand.

For C, D, E, 2, F, G and H, see next page (856).

§ 336. THE CREATURE SHALL NOT REPLY AGAINST THE CREATOR. GENTILES ATTAIN

CHAP. 9.

24 Even us, whom he hath called, [i]not of the Jews only, but also of the Gentiles?

25 As he saith also in Osee, [k]I will call them my people, which were not my people; and her beloved, which was not beloved.

26 [l]And it shall come to pass, *that* in the place where it was said unto them, Ye *are* not my people; there shall they be called the children of the living God.

27 Esaias also crieth concerning Israel, [m]Though the number of the children of Israel be as the sand of the sea, [n]a remnant shall be saved:

28 For he will finish [3]the work, and cut *it* short in righteousness: [o]because a short work will the Lord make upon the earth.

29 And as Esaias said before, [p]Except the Lord of Sabaoth had left us a seed, [q]we had been as Sodoma, and been made like unto Gomorrah.

30 What shall we say then? [r]That the Gentiles, which followed not after righteousness, have attained to righteousness, [s]even the righteousness which is of faith.

31 But Israel, [t]which followed after the law of righteousness, [u]hath not attained to the law of righteousness.

32 Wherefore? Because *they sought it* not by faith, but as it were by the works of the law. For [x]they stumbled at that stumblingstone;

33 As it is written, [y]Behold, I lay in Sion a stumblingstone and rock of offense: and [z]whosoever believeth on him shall not be [4]ashamed.

C

Prov. 16. 4 The LORD hath made all *things* for himself: yea, even the wicked for the day of evil.

Jer. 18. 6 O house of Israel, cannot I do with you as this potter? saith the LORD. Behold, as the clay *is* in the potter's hand, so *are* ye in mine hand, O house of Israel.

D

IITim. 2. 20 But in a great house there are not only vessels of gold and of silver, but also of wood and of earth; and some to honour, and some to dishonour.

21 If a man therefore purge himself from these, he shall be a vessel unto honour, sanctified, and meet for the master's use, *and* prepared unto every good work.

E

IThes. 5. 9 For God hath not appointed us to wrath, but to obtain salvation by our Lord Jesus Christ,

2

Or, *made up.*

F

I Pet. 2. 8 And a stone of stumbling, and a rock of offense, *even to them* which stumble at the word, being disobedient: whereunto also they were appointed.

Jude 4 For there are certain men crept in unawares, who were before of old ordained to this condemnation, ungodly men, turning the grace of our God into lasciviousness, and denying the only Lord God, and our Lord Jesus Christ.

G

Rom. 2. 4. *See c, C, § 320, page 814.*

Col. 1. 27 To whom God would make known what *is* the riches of the glory of this mystery among the Gentiles; which is Christ in you, the hope of glory:

H

Rom. 8. 28, etc. *See f, F, § 334, page 848.*

I

Rom. 3. 29 *Is he* the God of the Jews only? *is he* not also of the Gentiles? Yes, of the Gentiles also:

K

Hos. 2. 23 And I will sow her unto me in the earth; and I will have mercy upon her that had not obtained mercy; and I will say to *them which were* not my people, Thou *art* my people; and they shall say, *Thou art* my God.

I Pet. 2. 10 Which in time past *were* not a people, but *are* now the people of God: which had not obtained mercy, but now have obtained mercy.

TO THE RIGHTEOUSNESS OF FAITH AT WHICH THE JEWS STUMBLED (CONCLUDED)

L

Hos. 1. 10 Yet the number of the children of Israel shall be as the sand of the sea, which cannot be measured nor numbered; and it shall come to pass, *that* in the place where it was said unto them, Ye *are* not my people, *there* it shall be said unto them, *Ye are* the sons of the living God.

M

Isa. 10. 22 For though thy people Israel be as the sand of the sea, *yet* a remnant of them shall return: the consumption decreed shall overflow with righteousness.

N

Rom. 11. 5 Even so then at this present time also there is a remnant according to the election of grace.

3

Or, *the account*.

O

Isa. 28. 22 Now therefore be ye not mockers, lest your bands be made strong: for I have heard from the Lord GOD of hosts a consumption, even determined upon the whole earth.

P

Isa. 1. 9 Except the LORD of hosts had left unto us a very small remnant, we should have been as Sodom, *and* we should have been like unto Gomorrah.

Lam. 3. 22 *It is of* the LORD'S mercies that we are not consumed, because his compassions fail not.

Q

Isa. 13. 19 And Babylon, the glory of kingdoms, the beauty of the Chaldees' excellency, shall be as when God overthrew Sodom and Gomorrah.

Jer. 50. 40 As God overthrew Sodom and Gomorrah and the neighbour *cities* thereof, saith the LORD; *so* shall no man abide there, neither shall any son of man dwell therein.

R

Rom. 4. 11 And he received the sign of circumcision, a seal of the righteousness of the faith which *he had yet* being uncircumcised: that he might be the father of all them that believe, though they be not circumcised; that righteousness might be imputed unto them also:

Rom. 10. 20 But Esaias is very bold, and saith, I was found of them that sought me not; I was made manifest unto them that asked not after me.

S

Rom. 1. 17. *See p, P, § 318, page 810.*

T

Rom. 10. 2 For I bear them record that they have a zeal of God, but not according to knowledge.

Rom. 11. 7 What then? Israel hath not obtained that which he seeketh for; but the election hath obtained it, and the rest were blinded.

U

Gal. 5. 4 Christ is become of no effect unto you, whosoever of you are justified by the law; ye are fallen from grace.

X

Luke 2. 34 And Simeon blessed them, and said unto Mary his mother, Behold, this *child* is set for the fall and rising again of many in Israel; and for a sign which shall be spoken against;

I Cor. 1. 23 But we preach Christ crucified, unto the Jews a stumbling block, and unto the Greeks foolishness;

Y

Ps. 118. 22 The stone *which* the builders refused is become the head *stone* of the corner.

Isa. 8. 14 And he shall be for a sanctuary; but for a stone of stumbling and for a rock of offense to both the houses of Israel, for a gin and for a snare to the inhabitants of Jerusalem.

Isa. 28. 16 Therefore thus saith the Lord GOD, Behold, I lay in Zion for a foundation a stone, a tried stone, a precious corner *stone*, a sure foundation: he that believeth shall not make haste.

Matt. 21. 42 Jesus saith unto them, Did ye never read in the Scriptures, The stone which the builders rejected, the same is become the head of the corner: this is the Lord's doing, and it is marvellous in our eyes?

I Pet. 2. 6 Wherefore also it is contained in the Scripture, Behold, I lay in Sion a chief corner stone, elect, precious: and he that believeth on him shall not be confounded.

7 Unto you therefore which believe *he is* precious: but unto them which be disobedient, the stone which the builders disallowed, the same is made the head of the corner,

8 And a stone of stumbling, and a rock of offense, *even to them* which stumble at the word, being disobedient: whereunto also they were appointed.

Z

Rom. 10. 11 For the Scripture saith, Whosoever believeth on him shall not be ashamed.

4

Or, *confounded*.

§ 337. The Jews Though Zealous, Erred in Their Knowledge of God's Right-

10: 1–15.

1 Brethren, my heart's desire and prayer to God for Israel is, that they might be saved.

2 For I bear them record [a]that they have a zeal of God, but not according to knowledge.

3 For they, being ignorant of [b]God's righteousness, and going about to establish their [c]own righteousness, have not submitted themselves unto the righteousness of God.

4 For [d]Christ *is* the end of the law for righteousness to every one that believeth.

5 For Moses describeth the righteousness which is of the law, [e]That the man which doeth those things shall live by them.

6 But the righteousness which is of faith speaketh on this wise, [f]Say not in thine heart, Who shall ascend into heaven? (that is, to bring Christ down *from above:*)

7 Or, Who shall descend into the deep? (that is, to bring up Christ again from the dead.)

8 But what saith it? The [g]word is nigh thee, *even* in thy mouth, and in thy heart: that is, the word of faith, which we preach;

9 That [h]if thou shalt confess with thy mouth the Lord Jesus, and shalt believe in thine heart that God hath raised him from the dead, thou shalt be saved.

10 For [i]with the heart man believeth unto righteousness; and with the mouth confession is made unto salvation.

11 For the Scripture saith, [k]Whosoever believeth on him shall not be ashamed.

12 For [l]there is no difference be-

A

Acts 21. 20. *See f, F, § 295, page 768.*

Gal. 4. 17 They zealously affect you, *but* not well; yea, they would exclude you, that ye might affect them.

B

Rom. 1. 17. *See o, O, § 318, page 810.*

Rom. 9. 30 What shall we say then? That the Gentiles, which followed not after righteousness, have attained to righteousness, even the righteousness which is of faith.

C

Phil. 3. 9 And be found in him, not having mine own righteousness, which is of the law, but that which is through the faith of Christ, the righteousness which is of God by faith:

D

Matt. 5. 17 Think not that I am come to destroy the law, or the prophets: I am not come to destroy, but to fulfil.

Gal. 3. 24 Wherefore the law was our schoolmaster *to bring us* unto Christ, that we might be justified by faith.

Heb. 10. 14 For by one offering he hath perfected for ever them that are sanctified.

E

Lev. 18. 5 Ye shall therefore keep my statutes, and my judgments: which if a man do, he shall live in them: I *am* the LORD.

Neh. 9. 29 And testifiedst against them, that thou mightest bring them again unto thy law: yet they dealt proudly, and hearkened not unto thy commandments, but sinned against thy judgments, (which if a man do, he shall live in them;) and withdrew the shoulder, and hardened their neck, and would not hear.

Eze. 20. 11 And I gave them my statutes, and shewed them my judgments, which *if* a man do, he shall even live in them.

Eze. 20. 13 But the house of Israel rebelled against me in the wilderness: they walked not in my statutes, and they despised my judgments, which *if* a man do, he shall even live in them; and my sabbaths they greatly polluted: then I said, I would pour out my fury upon them in the wilderness, to consume them.

Eze. 20. 21 Notwithstanding the children rebelled against me: they walked not in my statutes, neither kept my judgments to do them, which *if* a man do, he shall even live in them; they polluted my sabbaths: then I said, I would

EOUSNESS, BEHOLDING THE LETTER OF THE LAW RATHER THAN THE SPIRIT THEREOF.

E—CONCLUDED.

pour out my fury upon them, to accomplish my anger against them in the wilderness.

Gal. 3. 12 And the law is not of faith: but, The man that doeth them shall live in them.

F

Deut. 30. 12 It *is* not in heaven, that thou shouldest say, Who shall go up for us to heaven, and bring it unto us, that we may hear it, and do it?

13 Neither *is* it beyond the sea, that thou shouldest say, Who shall go over the sea for us, and bring it unto us, that we may hear it, and do it?

G

Deut. 30. 14 But the word *is* very nigh unto thee, in thy mouth, and in thy heart, that thou mayest do it.

H

Matt. 10. 32 Whosoever therefore shall confess me before men, him will I confess also before my Father which is in heaven.

Luke 12. 8 Also I say unto you, Whosoever shall confess me before men, him shall the Son of man also confess before the angels of God:

Acts 8. 37 And Philip said, If thou believest with all thine heart, thou mayest. And he answered and said, I believe that Jesus Christ is the Son of God.

Phil. 2. 11 And *that* every tongue should confess that Jesus Christ *is* Lord, to the glory of God the Father.

I Jno. 4. 2 Hereby know ye the Spirit of God: Every spirit that confesseth that Jesus Christ is come in the flesh is of God:

3 And every spirit that confesseth not that Jesus Christ is come in the flesh is not of God: and this is that *spirit* of antichrist, whereof ye have heard that it should come; and even now already is it in the world.

II Jno. 7 For many deceivers are entered into the world, who confess not that Jesus Christ is come in the flesh. This is a deceiver and an antichrist.

I

Luke 8. 15 But that on the good ground are they, which in an honest and good heart, having heard the word, keep *it*, and bring forth fruit with patience.

John 1. 12 But as many as received him, to them gave he power to become the sons of God, *even* to them that believe on his name:

I—CONCLUDED.

Heb. 3. 12 Take heed, brethren, lest there be in any of you an evil heart of unbelief, in departing from the living God.

Heb. 10. 22 Let us draw near with a true heart in full assurance of faith, having our hearts sprinkled from an evil conscience, and our bodies washed with pure water.

K

Isa. 28. 16 Therefore thus saith the Lord GOD, Behold, I lay in Zion for a foundation a stone, a tried stone, a precious corner *stone*, a sure foundation: he that believeth shall not make haste.

Isa. 49. 23 And kings shall be thy nursing fathers, and their queens thy nursing mothers: they shall bow down to thee with *their* face toward the earth, and lick up the dust of thy feet; and thou shalt know that I *am* the LORD: for they shall not be ashamed that wait for me.

Jer. 17. 7 Blessed *is* the man that trusteth in the LORD, and whose hope the LORD is.

Rom. 9. 33 As it is written, Behold, I lay in Sion a stumblingstone and rock of offense: and whosoever believeth on him shall not be ashamed.

L

Acts 15. 9 And put no difference between us and them, purifying their hearts by faith.

Rom. 3. 22. *See i, I, § 324, page 824.*

M

Acts 10. 36 The word which *God* sent unto the children of Israel, preaching peace by Jesus Christ: (he is Lord of all:)

Rom. 3. 29 *Is he* the God of the Jews only? *is he* not also of the Gentiles? Yes, of the Gentiles also:

I Tim. 2. 5 For *there is* one God, and one mediator between God and men, the man Christ Jesus;

N

Rom. 2. 4. *See c, C, § 320, page 814.*

O

Acts 2. 21. *See f, F, § 231, page 636.*

P

I Cor. 1. 2 Unto the church of God which is at Corinth, to them that are sanctified in Christ Jesus, called *to be* saints, with all that in every place call upon the name of Jesus Christ our Lord, both theirs and ours:

§ 337. THE JEWS THOUGH ZEALOUS, ERRED IN THEIR KNOWLEDGE OF GOD'S RIGHTEOUS-

CHAP. 10.

tween the Jew and the Greek: for [m]the same Lord over all [n]is rich unto all that call upon him.

13. For [o]whosoever shall call [p]upon the name of the Lord shall be saved.

14 How then shall they call on him in whom they have not believed? and how shall they believe in him of

CHAP. 10.

whom they have not heard? and how shall they hear [q]without a preacher?

15 And how shall they preach, except they be sent? as it is written, [r]How beautiful are the feet of them that preach the gospel of peace, and bring glad tidings of good things!

For M, N, O and P, see preceding page (859).

§ 338. THE GOSPEL WAS PROCLAIMED BY MOSES AND THE

10:16–21.

16 But [a]they have not all obeyed the gospel. For Esaias saith, [b]Lord, who hath believed [1]our [2]report?

17 So then faith *cometh* by hearing, and hearing by the word of God.

18 But I say, Have they not heard? Yes verily, [c]their sound went into all the earth, and their words unto the ends of the world.

19 But I say, Did not Israel know? First Moses saith, [d]I will provoke you to jealousy by *them that are* no people, *and* by a [e]foolish nation I will anger you.

20 But Esaias is very bold, and saith, [f]I was found of them that sought me not; I was made manifest unto them that asked not after me.

CHAP. 10.

21 But to Israel he saith, [g]All day long I have stretched forth my hands unto a disobedient and gainsaying people.

A

Rom. 3. 3. *See b, B, § 322, page 820.*

B

Isa. 53. 1 Who hath believed our report? and to whom is the arm of the LORD revealed?

John 12. 38 That the saying of Esaias the prophet might be fulfilled, which he spake, Lord, who hath believed our report? and to whom hath the arm of the Lord been revealed?

1

Gr. *the hearing of us?*

2

Or, *preaching?*

C

Ps. 19. 4 Their line is gone out through all the earth, and their words to the end of the world. In them hath he set a tabernacle for the sun,

§ 339. ISRAEL IS NOT CAST OFF. BUT FOUND NOT THAT WHICH WAS SOUGHT, BEING

11:1–12.

1 I say then, [a]Hath God cast away his people? God forbid. For [b]I also am an Israelite, of the seed of Abraham, *of* the tribe of Benjamin.

2 God hath not cast away his people which [c]he foreknew. Wot ye not what the Scripture saith [1]of Elias?

A

I Sa. 12. 22 For the LORD will not forsake his people for his great name's sake: because it hath pleased the LORD to make you his people.

II Ki. 23. 27 And the LORD said, I will remove Judah also out of my sight, as I have removed Israel, and will cast off this city Jerusalem which I have chosen, and the house of which I said, My name shall be there.

NESS, BEHOLDING THE LETTER OF THE LAW RATHER THAN THE SPIRIT THEREOF (CON'D).

Q

John 20. 21 Then said Jesus to them again, Peace *be* unto you: as *my* Father hath sent me, even so send I you.

Acts 19. 2 He said unto them, Have ye received the Holy Ghost since ye believed? And they said unto him, We have not so much as heard whether there be any Holy Ghost.

Tit. 1. 3 But hath in due times manifested his word through preaching which is committed unto me according to the commandment of God our Saviour;

R

Isa. 52. 7 How beautiful upon the mountains are the feet of him that bringeth good tidings, that publisheth peace; that bringeth good tidings of good, that publisheth salvation; that saith unto Zion, Thy God reigneth!

Nah. 1. 15 Behold upon the mountains the feet of him that bringeth good tidings, that publisheth peace! O Judah, keep thy solemn feasts, perform thy vows: for the wicked shall no more pass through thee; he is utterly cut off.

PROPHETS. THE DISOBEDIENT JEWS HEARKENED NOT.

C—CONCLUDED.

Matt. 24. 14 And this gospel of the kingdom shall be preached in all the world for a witness unto all nations; and then shall the end come.

Matt. 28. 19 Go ye therefore, and teach all nations, baptizing them in the name of the Father, and of the Son, and of the Holy Ghost:

Mark 16. 15 And he said unto them, Go ye into all the world, and preach the gospel to every creature.

Col. 1. 6 Which is come unto you, as *it is* in all the world: and bringeth forth fruit, as *it doth* also in you, since the day ye heard *of it*, and knew the grace of God in truth:

Col. 1. 23 If ye continue in the faith grounded and settled, and *be* not moved away from the hope of the gospel, which ye have heard, *and* which was preached to every creature which is under heaven; whereof I Paul am made a minister;

D

Deut. 32. 21 They have moved me to jealousy with *that which is* not God; they have provoked me to anger with their vanities: and I will move them to jealousy with *those which are* not a people; I will provoke them to anger with a foolish nation.

D—CONCLUDED.

Rom. 11. 11 I say then, Have they stumbled that they should fall? God forbid: but *rather* through their fall salvation *is come* unto the Gentiles, for to provoke them to jealousy.

E

Tit. 3. 3 For we ourselves also were sometime foolish, disobedient, deceived, serving divers lusts and pleasures, living in malice and envy, hateful, *and* hating one another.

F

Isa. 65. 1 I am sought of *them that* asked not *for me;* I am found of *them that* sought me not: I said, Behold me, behold me, unto a nation *that* was not called by my name.

2 I have spread out my hands all the day unto a rebellious people, which walketh in a way *that was* not good, after their own thoughts:

HARDENED. THE ELECTION OBTAINED IT, AND SALVATION IS COME TO THE GENTILES.

A—CONTINUED.

Ps. 77. 7 Will the Lord cast off for ever? and will he be favourable no more?

8 Is his mercy clean gone for ever? doth *his* promise fail for evermore?

Ps. 89. 31 If they break my statutes, and keep not my commandments;

32 Then will I visit their transgression with the rod, and their iniquity with stripes.

33 Nevertheless my lovingkindness will I not utterly take from him, nor suffer my faithfulness to fail.

A—CONTINUED.

Ps. 89. 34 My covenant will I not break, nor alter the thing that is gone out of my lips.

35 Once have I sworn by my holiness that I will not lie unto David.

36 His seed shall endure for ever, and his throne as the sun before me.

For A concluded, B, C and 1, see next page (862).

§ 339. Israel is Not Cast Off. But Found Not that which was Sought, being

Chap. 11.

how he maketh intercession to God
against Israel, saying,
3 [d]Lord, they have killed thy prophets, and digged down thine altars;
and I am left alone, and they seek
my life.
4 But what saith the answer of God
unto him? [e]I have reserved to myself
seven thousand men, who have not
bowed the knee to *the image of* Baal.
5 [f]Even so then at this present time
also there is a remnant according to
the election of grace.
6 And [g]if by grace, then *is it* no
more of works: otherwise grace is
no more grace. But if *it be* of works,
then is it no more grace: otherwise
work is no more work.
7 What then? [h]Israel hath not obtained that which he seeketh for;
but the election hath obtained it,
and the rest were [2]blinded.
8 (According as it is written, [i]God
hath given them the spirit of [3]slum-
ber, [k]eyes that they should not see,
and ears that they should not hear;)
unto this day.
9 And David saith, [l]Let their table
be made a snare, and a trap, and a
stumblingblock, and a recompense
unto them:
10 Let their eyes be darkened, that
they may not see, and bow down
their back alway.
11 I say then, Have they stumbled
that they should fall? God forbid:
but *rather* through [m]their fall salvation *is come* unto the Gentiles, for
to provoke them to jealousy.

Chap. 11.

12 Now if the fall of them *be* the
riches of the world, and the [4]dimin-
ishing of them the riches of the Gentiles; how much more their [n]fulness?

A—Concluded.

Ps. 89. 37 It shall be established for ever as the moon, and *as* a faithful witness in heaven. Selah.

Ps. 94. 14 For the Lord will not cast off his people, neither will he forsake his inheritance.

Jer. 31. 37 Thus saith the Lord: If heaven above can be measured, and the foundations of the earth searched out beneath, I will also cast off all the seed of Israel for all that they have done, saith the Lord.

B

II Cor 11. 22 Are they Hebrews? so *am* I. Are they Israelites? so *am* I. Are they the seed of Abraham? so *am* I.

Phil. 3. 5 Circumcised the eighth day, of the stock of Israel, *of* the tribe of Benjamin, a Hebrew of the Hebrews; as touching the law, a Pharisee;

C

Rom. 8. 29. *See g, G, § 334, page 848.*

1

Gr. *in Elias?*

D

1 Ki. 19. 10 And he said, I have been very jealous for the Lord God of hosts; for the children of Israel have forsaken thy covenant, thrown down thine altars, and slain thy prophets with the sword; and I, *even* I only, am left; and they seek my life, to take it away.

E

1 Ki. 19. 18 Yet I have left *me* seven thousand in Israel, all the knees which have not bowed unto Baal, and every mouth which hath not kissed him.

F

Rom. 9. 27. *See n, N, § 336, page 856.*

G

Deut. 9. 5 Not for thy righteousness, or for the uprightness of thine heart, dost thou go to possess their land: but for the wickdness of these nations the Lord thy God doth drive them out from before thee, and that he may perform the word which the Lord sware unto thy fathers, Abraham, Isaac, and Jacob.

HARDENED. THE ELECTION OBTAINED IT, AND SALVATION IS COME TO THE GENTILES (CON'D).

G—CONCLUDED.

Rom. 4. 4 Now to him that worketh is the reward not reckoned of grace, but of debt.
5 But to him that worketh not, but believeth on him that justifieth the ungodly, his faith is counted for righteousness.

Gal. 5. 4 Christ is become of no effect unto you, whosoever of you are justified by the law; ye are fallen from grace.

Eph. 2. 8 For by grace are ye saved through faith; and that not of yourselves: *it is* the gift of God:

H

Rom. 9. 31 But Israel, which followed after the law of righteousness, hath not attained to the law of righteousness.

Rom. 10. 3 For they, being ignorant of God's righteousness, and going about to establish their own righteousness, have not submitted themselves unto the righteousness of God.

Gal. 5. 4. *See under G.*

2

Or, *hardened.*

II Cor. 3. 14 But their minds were blinded: for until this day remaineth the same vail untaken away in the reading of the old testament; which *vail* is done away in Christ.

I

Isa. 29. 10 For the LORD hath poured out upon you the spirit of deep sleep, and hath closed your eyes: the prophets and your rulers, the seers hath he covered.

3

s

Or, *remorse.*

K

Isa. 6. 9 And he said, Go, and tell this people, Hear ye indeed, but understand not; and see ye indeed, but perceive not.

Jer. 5. 21 Hear now this, O foolish people, and without understanding; which have eyes, and see not; which have ears, and hear not:

Eze. 12. 2 Son of man, thou dwellest in the midst of a rebellious house, which have eyes to see, and see not; they have ears to hear, and hear not: for they *are* a rebellious house.

Matt. 13. 14 And in them is fulfilled the prophecy of Esaias, which saith, By hearing ye shall hear, and shall not understand; and seeing ye shall see, and shall not perceive:

K—CONCLUDED.

John 12. 40 He hath blinded their eyes, and hardened their heart; that they should not see with *their* eyes, nor understand with *their* heart, and be converted, and I should heal them.

Acts 28. 26 Saying, Go unto this people, and say, Hearing ye shall hear, and shall not understand; and seeing ye shall see, and not perceive:
27 For the heart of this people is waxed gross, and their ears are dull of hearing, and their eyes have they closed; lest they should see with *their* eyes, and hear with *their* ears, and understand with *their* heart, and should be converted, and I should heal them.

L

Ps. 69. 22 Let their table become a snare before them: and *that which should have been* for *their* welfare, *let it become* a trap.
23 Let their eyes be darkened, that they see not; and make their loins continually to shake.

M

Acts 28. 28. *See n, N, § 316, page 806.*

4

Or, *decay,* or, *loss.*

N

Isa. 11. 11 And it shall come to pass in that day, *that* the Lord shall set his hand again the second time to recover the remnant of his people, which shall be left, from Assyria, and from Egypt, and from Pathros, and from Cush, and from Elam, and from Shinar, and from Hamath, and from the islands of the sea.

Isa. 66. 12 For thus saith the LORD, Behold, I will extend peace to her like a river, and the glory of the Gentiles like a flowing stream: then shall ye suck, ye shall be borne upon *her* sides, and be dandled upon *her* knees.

Mic. 4. 2 And many nations shall come, and say, Come, and let us go up to the mountain of the LORD, and to the house of the God of Jacob; and he will teach us of his ways, and we will walk in his paths: for the law shall go forth of Zion, and the word of the LORD from Jerusalem.

Zech. 8. 23 Thus saith the LORD of hosts; In those days *it shall come to pass,* that ten men shall take hold out of all languages of the nations, even shall take hold of the skirt of him that is a Jew, saying, We will go with you; for we have heard *that* God *is* with you.

§ 340. THE SEVERITY OF GOD TOWARD UNBELIEF, AND HIS GOODNESS

11 : 13–24.

13 For I speak to you Gentiles, inasmuch as [a]I am the apostle of the
Gentiles, I magnify mine office :
14 If by any means I may provoke
to emulation *them which are* my flesh,
and [b]might save some of them.
15 For if the casting away of them
be the reconciling of the world, what
shall the receiving *of them be*, but
life from the dead ?
16 For if [c]the firstfruit *be* holy, the
lump *is* also *holy*: and if the root *be*
holy, so *are* the branches.
17 And if [d]some of the branches be
broken off, [e]and thou, being a wild
olive tree, wert graffed [1]in among
them, and with them partakest of the
root and fatness of the olive tree;
18 [f]Boast not against the branches.
But if thou boast, thou bearest not
the root, but the root thee.
19 Thou wilt say then, The branches were broken off, that I might be
graffed in.
20 Well ; because of unbelief they
were broken off, and thou standest
by faith. [g]Be not highminded, [h]but
fear:
21 For if God spared not the natural branches, *take heed* lest he also
spare not thee.

CHAP. 11.

22 Behold therefore the goodness
and severity of God: on them which
fell, severity; but toward thee, goodness, [i]if thou continue in *his* goodness: otherwise [k]thou also shalt be
cut off.
23 And they also, [l]if they abide not
still in unbelief, shall be graffed in:
for God is able to graff them in again.
24 For if thou wert cut out of the
olive tree which is wild by nature,
and wert graffed contrary to nature
into a good olive tree; how much
more shall these, which be the natural *branches*, be graffed into their
own olive tree ?

A

Acts 13. 2 As they ministered to the Lord, and fasted, the Holy Ghost said, Separate me Barnabas and Saul for the work whereunto I have called them.

Acts 22. 21. *See i, I, § 297, page 774.*

B

I Cor. 7. 16 For what knowest thou, O wife, whether thou shalt save *thy* husband ? or how knowest thou, O man, whether thou shalt save *thy* wife ?

I Cor. 9. 22 To the weak became I as weak, that I might gain the weak: I am made all things to all *men*, that I might by all means save some.

I Tim. 4. 16 Take heed unto thyself, and unto the doctrine; continue in them: for in doing this thou shalt both save thyself, and them that hear thee.

Jas. 5. 20 Let him know, that he which converteth the sinner from the error of his

§ 341. THE DELIVERER SHALL COME OUT OF ZION. ALL ISRAEL

11 : 25–36.

25 For I would not, brethren, that
ye should be ignorant of this mystery, lest ye should be [a]wise in your
own conceits, that [b][1]blindness in part
is happened to Israel, [c]until the full-

A

Rom. 12. 16. *See under G, § 340, page 865.*

B

Rom. 11. 7 What then ? Israel hath not obtained that which he seeketh for ; but the election hath obtained it, and the rest were blinded

II Cor. 3. 14 But their minds were blinded: for until this day remaineth the same vail

TOWARD FAITH ARE ILLUSTRATED IN THE FIGURE OF A GRAFT.

B—CONCLUDED.

way shall save a soul from death, and shall hide a multitude of sins.

C

Lev. 23. 10 Speak unto the children of Israel, and say unto them, When ye be come into the land which I give unto you, and shall reap the harvests thereof, then ye shall bring a sheaf of the firstfruits of your harvest unto the priests:

Num. 15. 18 Speak unto the children of Israel, and say unto them, When ye come into the land whither I bring you,

19 Then it shall be, that, when ye eat of the bread of the land, ye shall offer up a heave offering unto the LORD.

20 Ye shall offer up a cake of the first of your dough *for* a heave offering: as *ye do* the heave offering of the threshingfloor, so shall ye heave it.

21 Of the first of your dough ye shall give unto the LORD a heave offering in your generations.

D

Jer. 11. 16 The LORD called thy name, A green olive tree, fair *and* of goodly fruit: with the noise of a great tumult he hath kindled fire upon it, and the branches of it are broken.

E

Acts 2. 39 For the promise is unto you, and to your children, and to all that are afar off, *even* as many as the Lord our God shall call.

Eph. 2. 12 That at that time ye were without Christ, being aliens from the commonwealth of Israel, and strangers from the covenants of promise, having no hope, and without God in the world:

13 But now, in Christ Jesus, ye who sometime were far off are made nigh by the blood of Christ.

1

Or, *for them.*

F

I Cor. 10. 12 Wherefore let him that thinketh he standeth take heed lest he fall.

G

Rom. 12. 16 *Be* of the same mind one toward another. Mind not high things, but condescend to men of low estate. Be not wise in your own conceits.

H

Prov. 28. 14 Happy *is* the man that feareth alway: but he that hardeneth his heart shall fall into mischief.

Isa. 66. 2 For all those *things* hath mine hand made, and all those *things* have been, saith the LORD: but to this *man* will I look, *even* to *him that is* poor and of a contrite spirit, and trembleth at my word.

Phil. 2. 12 Wherefore, my beloved, as ye have always obeyed, not as in my presence only, but now much more in my absence, work out your own salvation with fear and trembling.

I

I Cor. 15. 2 By which also ye are saved, if ye keep in memory what I preached unto you, unless ye have believed in vain.

Heb. 3. 6 But Christ as a son over his own house; whose house are we, if we hold fast the confidence and the rejoicing of the hope firm unto the end.

Heb. 3. 14 For we are made partakers of Christ, if we hold the beginning of our confidence steadfast unto the end;

K

John 15. 2 Every branch in me that beareth not fruit he taketh away: and every *branch* that beareth fruit, he purgeth it, that it may bring forth more fruit.

L

II Cor. 3. 16 Nevertheless, when it shall turn to the Lord, the vail shall be taken away.

SHALL BE SAVED. THE WAYS OF GOD ARE PAST FINDING OUT.

B—CONCLUDED.

untaken away in the reading of the old testament; which *vail* is done away in Christ.

1

Or, *hardness.*

C

Luke 21. 24 And they shall fall by the edge of the sword, and shall be led away captive

C—CONCLUDED.

into all nations: and Jerusalem shall be trodden down of the Gentiles, until the times of the Gentiles be fulfilled.

Acts 15. 16 After this I will return, and will build again the tabernacle of David, which is fallen down; and I will build again the ruins thereof, and I will set it up;

§ 341. THE DELIVERER SHALL COME OUT OF ZION. ALL ISRAEL SHALL

CHAP. 11.

ness of the Gentiles be come in.

26 And so all [d]Israel shall be saved: as it is written, [e]There shall come out of Sion the Deliverer, and shall turn away ungodliness from Jacob:

27 [f]For this *is* my covenant unto them, when I shall take away their sins.

28 As concerning the gospel, *they are* enemies for your sakes: but as touching the election, *they are* [g]beloved for the fathers' sakes.

29 For the gifts and calling of God *are* [h]without repentance.

30 For as ye [i]in times past have not [2]believed God, yet have now obtained mercy through their unbelief:

31 Even so have these also now not [2]believed, that through your mercy they also may obtain mercy.

32 For [k]God hath [3]concluded them all in unbelief, that he might have mercy upon all.

33 O the depth of the riches both of the wisdom and knowledge of God! [l]how unsearchable *are* his judgments, and [m]his ways past finding out!

34 [n]For who hath known the mind of the Lord? or [o]who hath been his counsellor?

35 Or, [p]who hath first given to him, and it shall be recompensed unto him again?

36 For [q]of him, and through him, and to him, *are* all things: [r]to [4]whom *be* glory for ever. Amen.

D

Isa. 45. 17 *But* Israel shall be saved in the LORD with an everlasting salvation: ye shall not be ashamed nor confounded world without end.

D—CONCLUDED.

Isa. 54. 13 And all thy children *shall be* taught of the LORD; and great *shall be* the peace of thy children.

Jer. 3. 23 Truly in vain *is salvation hoped for* from the hills, *and from* the multitude of mountains: truly in the LORD our God *is* the salvation of Israel.

Jer. 31. 34 And they shall teach no more every man his neighbour, and every man his brother, saying, Know the LORD: for they shall all know me, from the least of them unto the greatest of them, saith the LORD: for I will forgive their iniquity, and I will remember their sin no more.

Eze. 34. 22 Therefore will I save my flock, and they shall no more be a prey; and I will judge between cattle and cattle.

Eze. 37. 23 Neither shall they defile themselves any more with their idols, nor with their detestable things, nor with any of their transgressions: but I will save them out of all their dwellingplaces, wherein they have sinned, and will cleanse them: so shall they be my people, and I will be their God.

Eze. 39. 25 Therefore thus saith the Lord GOD; Now will I bring again the captivity of Jacob, and have mercy upon the whole house of Israel, and will be jealous for my holy name;

Mic. 7. 19 He will turn again, he will have compassion upon us; he will subdue our iniquities; and thou wilt cast all their sins into the depths of the sea.

Zeph. 3. 17 The LORD thy God in the midst of thee *is* mighty; he will save, he will rejoice over thee with joy; he will rest in his love, he will joy over thee with singing.

E

Isa. 59. 20 And the Redeemer shall come to Zion, and unto them that turn from transgression in Jacob, saith the LORD.

Ps. 14. 7 Oh that the salvation of Israel *were come* out of Zion! when the LORD bringeth back the captivity of his people, Jacob shall rejoice, *and* Israel shall be glad.

F

Jer. 31. 31 Behold, the days come, saith the LORD, that I will make a new covenant with the house of Israel, and with the house of Judah:

Heb. 8. 8 For finding fault with them, he saith, Behold, the days come, saith the Lord, when I will make a new covenant with the house of Israel and with the house of Judah:

BE SAVED. THE WAYS OF GOD ARE PAST FINDING OUT (CONCLUDED).

F—CONCLUDED.

Heb. 10. 16 This *is* the covenant that I will make with them after those days, saith the Lord; I will put my laws into their hearts, and in their minds will I write them;

G

Deut. 7. 8 But because the LORD loved you, and because he would keep the oath which he had sworn unto your fathers, hath the LORD brought you out with a mighty hand, and redeemed you out of the house of bondmen, from the hand of Pharaoh king of Egypt.

Deut. 9. 5 Not for thy righteousness, or for the uprightness of thine heart, dost thou go to possess their land: but for the wickedness of these nations the LORD thy God doth drive them out from before thee, and that he may perform the word which the LORD sware unto thy fathers, Abraham, Isaac, and Jacob.

Deut. 10. 15 Only the LORD had a delight in thy fathers to love them, and he chose their seed after them, *even* you above all people, as *it is* this day.

H

Num. 23. 19 God *is* not a man, that he should lie; neither the son of man, that he should repent: hath he said, and shall he not do *it?* or hath he spoken, and shall he not make it good?

I

Eph. 2. 2 Wherein in time past ye walked according to the course of this world, according to the prince of the power of the air, the spirit that now worketh in the children of disobedience:

Col. 3. 7 In the which ye also walked sometime, when ye lived in them.

2

Or, *obeyed.*

K

Rom. 3. 9. *See a, A, § 323, page 822.*

3

Or, *shut them all up together.*

L

Ps. 36. 6 Thy righteousness *is* like the great mountains; thy judgments *are* a great deep: O LORD, thou preservest man and beast.

M

Job 11. 7 Canst thou by searching find out God? canst thou find out the Almighty unto perfection?

Ps. 92. 5 O LORD, how great are thy works! *and* thy thoughts are very deep.

N

Job 15. 8 Hast thou heard the secret of God? and dost thou restrain wisdom to thyself?

Isa. 40. 13 Who hath directed the Spirit of the LORD, or *being* his counsellor hath taught him?

Jer. 23. 18 For who hath stood in the counsel of the LORD, and hath perceived and heard his word? who hath marked his word, and heard *it?*

I Cor. 2. 16 For who hath known the mind of the Lord, that he may instruct him? But we have the mind of Christ.

O

Job 36. 23 Who hath enjoined him his way? or who can say, Thou hast wrought iniquity?

P

Job 35. 7 If thou be righteous, what givest thou him? or what receiveth he of thine hand?

Q

I Cor. 8. 6 But to us *there is but* one God, the Father, of whom *are* all things, and we in him; and one Lord Jesus Christ, by whom *are* all things, and we by him.

Col. 1. 16 For by him were all things created, that are in heaven, and that are in earth, visible and invisible, whether *they be* thrones, or dominions, or principalities, or powers: all things were created by him, and for him:

R

Gal. 1. 5 To whom *be* glory for ever and ever. Amen.

II Tim. 4. 18 And the Lord shall deliver me from every evil work, and will preserve *me* unto his heavenly kingdom: to whom *be* glory for ever and ever. Amen.

Heb. 13. 21 Make you perfect in every good work to do his will, working in you that which is well pleasing in his sight, through Jesus Christ; to whom *be* glory for ever and ever. Amen.

II Pet. 3. 18 But grow in grace, and *in* the knowledge of our Lord and Saviour Jesus Christ. To him *be* glory both now and for ever. Amen.

Jude 25 To the only wise God our Saviour, *be* glory and majesty, dominion and power, both now and ever. Amen.

Rev. 1. 6 And hath made us kings and priests unto God and his Father; to him *be* glory and dominion for ever and ever. Amen.

4

Gr. *him.*

§ 342. AN EXHORTATION TO LOVE GOD, THE FAITHFUL

12 : 1–21.

1 I [a]beseech you therefore, brethren, by the mercies of God, that [b]ye
present your bodies [c]a living sacrifice,
holy, acceptable unto God, *which is*
your reasonable service.

2 And [d]be not conformed to this
world : but [e]be ye transformed by the
renewing of your mind, that ye may
[f]prove what *is* that good, and acceptable, and perfect will of God.

3 For I say, [g]through the grace giv-
en unto me, to every man that is
among you, [h]not to think *of himself*
more highly than he ought to think;
but to think [1]soberly, according as
God hath dealt [i]to every man the
measure of faith.

4 For [k]as we have many members
in one body, and all members have
not the same office :

5 So [l]we, *being* many, are one body
in Christ, and every one members
one of another.

6 [m]Having then gifts differing according to the grace that is given to
us, whether [n]prophecy, *let us prophesy*
according to the proportion of faith;

7 Or ministry, *let us wait* on *our*
ministering: or [o]he that teacheth, on
teaching ;

A

IICor.10. 1 Now I Paul myself beseech you by the meekness and gentleness of Christ, who in presence *am* base among you, but being absent am bold toward you:

B

Ps. 50. 14 Offer unto God thanksgiving; and pay thy vows unto the Most High :

Rom. 6. 13 Neither yield ye your members *as* instruments of unrighteousness unto sin : but yield yourselves unto God, as those that are alive from the dead, and your members *as* instruments of righteousness unto God.

Rom. 6. 16 Know ye not, that to whom ye yield yourselves servants to obey, his servants ye are to whom ye obey; whether of sin unto death, or of obedience unto righteousness ?

I Cor. 6. 13 Meats for the belly, and the belly for meats ; but God shall destroy both

B—Concluded.

it and them. Now the body *is* not for fornication, but for the Lord; and the Lord for the body.

I Cor. 6. 20 For ye are bought with a price : therefore glorify God in your body and in your spirit, which are God's.

C

Heb. 10. 20 By a new and living way, which he hath consecrated for us, through the vail, that is to say, his flesh;

D

I Pet. 1. 14 As obedient children, not fashioning yourselves according to the former lusts in your ignorance:

I Jno. 2. 15 Love not the world, neither the things *that are* in the world. If any man love the world, the love of the Father is not in him.

E

Eph. 1. 18 The eyes of your understanding being enlightened; that ye may know what is the hope of his calling, and what the riches of the glory of his inheritance in the saints,

Eph. 4. 23 And be renewed in the spirit of your mind;

Col. 1. 21 And you, that were sometime alienated and enemies in *your* mind by wicked works, yet now hath he reconciled.

22 In the body of his flesh through death, to present you holy and unblameable and unreproveable in his sight:

Col. 3. 10 And have put on the new *man*, which is renewed in knowledge after the image of him that created him:

F

Eph. 5. 10 Proving what is acceptable unto the Lord.

Eph. 5. 17 Wherefore be ye not unwise, but understanding what the will of the Lord *is*.

IThes.4. 3 For this is the will of God, *even* your sanctification, that ye should abstain from fornication :

G

Rom. 1. 5. *See i, I, § 317, page 808.*

H

Prov.25. 27 *It is* not good to eat much honey: so *for men* to search their own glory *is not* glory.

Eccl. 7. 16 Be not righteous over much, neither make thyself over wise ; why shouldest thou destroy thyself ?

1

Gr. *to sobriety.*

I

ICor.12. 7 But the manifestation of the Spirit is given to every man to profit withal.

PERFORMANCE OF DUTY, AND LOVE TOWARD MEN.

I—CONCLUDED.

1Cor.12. 11 But all these worketh that one and the selfsame Spirit, dividing to every man severally as he will.

Eph. 4. 7 But unto every one of us is given grace according to the measure of the gift of Christ.

K

1 Cor.12. 12 For as the body is one, and hath many members, and all the members of that one body, being many, are one body: so also *is* Christ.

Eph. 4. 16 From whom the whole body fitly joined together and compacted by that which every joint supplieth, according to the effectual working in the measure of every part, maketh increase of the body unto the edifying of itself in love.

L

1Cor.10. 17 For we *being* many are one bread, *and* one body: for we are all partakers of that one bread.

1Cor.12. 20 But now *are they* many members, yet but one body.

1Cor.12. 27 Now ye are the body of Christ, and members in particular.

Eph. 1. 23 Which is his body, the fullness of him that filleth all in all.

Eph. 4. 25 Wherefore putting away lying, speak every man truth with his neighbour; for we are members one of another.

M

1Cor.12. 4 Now there are diversities of gifts, but the same Spirit.

1 Pet. 4. 10 As every man hath received the gift, *even so* minister the same one to another, as good stewards of the manifold grace of God.

11 If any man speak, *let him speak* as the oracles of God; if any man minister, *let him do it* as of the ability which God giveth: that God in all things may be glorified through Jesus Christ: to whom be praise and dominion for ever and ever. Amen.

N

Acts 11. 27 And in these days came prophets from Jerusalem unto Antioch.

1Cor.12. 10 To another the working of miracles; to another prophecy; to another discerning of spirits; to another *divers* kinds of tongues; to another the interpretation of tongues:

1Cor.12. 28 And God hath set some in the church, first apostles, secondarily prophets, thirdly teachers, after that miracles, then gifts of healings, helps, governments, diversities of tongues.

N—CONCLUDED.

1Cor.13. 2 And though I have *the gift of* prophecy, and understand all mysteries, and all knowledge; and though I have all faith, so that I could remove mountains, and have not charity, I am nothing.

1Cor.14. 1 Follow after charity, and desire spiritual *gifts*, but rather that ye may prophesy.

1Cor.14. 6 Now, brethren, if I come unto you speaking with tongues, what shall I profit you, except I shall speak to you either by revelation, or by knowledge, or by prophesying, or by doctrine ?

1Cor.14. 29 Let the prophets speak two or three, and let the other judge.

1Cor.14. 31 For ye may all prophesy one by one, that all may learn, and all may be comforted.

O

Acts 13. 1 Now there were in the church that was at Antioch certain prophets and teachers; as Barnabas, and Simeon that was called Niger, and Lucius of Cyrene, and Manaen, which had been brought up with Herod the tetrarch, and Saul.

Gal. 6. 6 Let him that is taught in the word communicate unto him that teacheth in all good things.

Eph. 4. 11 And he gave some apostles; and some, prophets; and some, evangelists; and some, pastors and teachers;

1 Tim.5. 17 Let the elders that rule well be counted worthy of double honour, especially they who labour in the word and doctrine.

P

Acts 15. 32 And Judas and Silas, being prophets also themselves, exhorted the brethren with many words, and confirmed *them*.

1Cor.14. 3 But he that prophesieth speaketh unto men *to* edification, and exhortation, and comfort.

Q

Matt. 6. 1 Take heed that ye do not your alms before men, to be seen of them: otherwise ye have no reward of your Father which is in heaven.

2 Therefore when thou doest *thine* alms, do not sound a trumpet before thee, as the hypocrites do in the synagogues and in the streets, that they may have glory of men. Verily I say unto you, They have their reward.

3 But when thou doest alms, let not thy left hand know what thy right hand doeth :

2
Or, *imparteth*.

§ 342. AN EXHORTATION TO LOVE GOD, THE FAITHFUL PERFORM-

CHAP. 12.

8 Or [p]he that exhorteth, on exhortation: [q]he that [2]giveth, *let him do it*
[3]with simplicity; [r]he that ruleth, with
diligence; he that showeth mercy,
[s]with cheerfulness.
9 [t]*Let* love be without dissimulation. [u]Abhor that which is evil;
cleave to that which is good.
10 [x]*Be* kindly affectioned one to
another [4]with brotherly love; [y]in honour preferring one another;
11 Not slothful in business; fervent
in spirit; serving the Lord;
12 [z]Rejoicing in hope; [a]patient in
tribulation; [b]continuing instant in
prayer;
13 [c]Distributing to the necessity of
saints; [d]given to hospitality.
14 [e]Bless them which persecute you:
bless, and curse not.
15 [f]Rejoice with them that do rejoice, and weep with them that weep.

For P, Q, and 2, see preceding page (869).

3

Or, *liberally.*

R

Acts 20. 28 Take heed therefore unto yourselves, and to all the flock, over the which the Holy Ghost hath made you overseers, to feed the church of God, which he hath purchased with his own blood.

I Tim. 5. 17. *See under O, page 869.*

Heb. 13. 7 Remember them which have the rule over you, who have spoken unto you the word of God: whose faith follow, considering the end of *their* conversation.

Heb. 13. 24 Salute all them that have the rule over you, and all the saints. They of Italy salute you.

I Pet. 5. 2 Feed the flock of God which is among you, taking the oversight *hereof*, not by constraint, but willingly; not for filthy lucre, but of a ready mind;

S

II Cor. 9. 7 Every man according as he purposeth in his heart, *so let him give;* not grudgingly, or of necessity: for God loveth a cheerful giver.

T

I Tim. 1. 5 Now the end of the commandment is charity out of a pure heart, and *of* a good conscience, and *of* faith unfeigned:

I Pet. 1. 22 Seeing ye have purified your souls in obeying the truth through the Spirit unto unfeigned love of the brethren, *see that ye* love one another with a pure heart fervently:

U

Ps. 34. 14 Depart from evil, and do good: seek peace, and pursue it.

Ps. 36. 4 He deviseth mischief upon his bed; he setteth himself in a way *that is* not good; he abhorreth not evil.

Ps. 97. 10 Ye that love the LORD, hate evil: he preserveth the souls of his saints; he delivereth them out of the hand of the wicked.

Amos 5. 15 Hate the evil, and love the good, and establish judgment in the gate: it may be that the LORD God of hosts will be gracious unto the remnant of Joseph.

X

Heb. 13. 1 Let brotherly love coutinue.

I Pet. 1. 22. *See under T.*

I Pet. 2. 17 Honour all *men*. Love the brotherhood. Fear God. Honour the king.

I Pet. 3. 8 Finally, *be ye* all of one mind, having compassion one of another, love as brethren, *be* pitiful, *be* courteous:

II Pet. 1. 7 And to godliness brotherly kindness; and to brotherly kindness charity.

4

Or, *in the love of the brethren.*

Y

Phil. 2. 3 *Let* nothing *be done* through strife or vainglory; but in lowliness of mind let each esteem other better than themselves.

I Pet. 5. 5 Likewise, ye younger, submit yourselves unto the elder. Yea, all *of you* be subject one to another, and be clothed with humility: for God resisteth the proud, and giveth grace to the humble.

Z

Luke 10. 21 In that hour Jesus rejoiced in spirit, and said, I thank thee, O Father, Lord of heaven and earth, that thou hast hid these things from the wise and prudent, and hast revealed them unto babes: even so, Father; for so it seemed good in thy sight.

ANCE OF DUTY, AND LOVE TOWARD MEN (CONTINUED).

Z—CONCLUDED.

Rom. 5. 2 By whom also we have access by faith into this grace wherein we stand, and rejoice in hope of the glory of God.

Rom. 15. 13 Now the God of hope fill you with all joy and peace in believing, that ye may abound in hope, through the power of the Holy Ghost.

Phil. 3. 1 Finally, my brethren, rejoice in the Lord. To write the same things to you, to me indeed *is* not grievous, but for you *it is* safe.

Phil. 4. 4 Rejoice in the Lord alway: *and* again I say, Rejoice.

IThes. 5. 16 Rejoice evermore.

Heb. 3. 6 But Christ as a son over his own house; whose house are we, if we hold fast the confidence and the rejoicing of the hope firm unto the end.

I Pet. 4. 13 But rejoice, inasmuch as ye are partakers of Christ's sufferings; that, when his glory shall be revealed, ye may be glad also with exceeding joy.

A

Luke 21. 19 In your patience possess ye your souls.

ITim. 6. 11 But thou, O man of God, flee these things; and follow after righteousness, godliness, faith, love, patience, meekness.

Heb. 10. 36 For ye have need of patience, that, after ye have done the will of God, ye might receive the promise.

Heb. 12. 1 Wherefore, seeing we also are compassed about with so great a cloud of witnesses, let us lay aside every weight, and the sin which doth so easily beset *us*, and let us run with patience the race that is set before us,

Jas. 1. 4 But let patience have *her* perfect work, that ye may be perfect and entire, wanting nothing.

Jas. 5. 7 Be patient therefore, brethren, unto the coming of the Lord. Behold, the husbandman waiteth for the precious fruit of the earth, and hath long patience for it, until he receive the early and latter rain.

I Pet. 2. 19 For this *is* thankworthy, if a man for conscience toward God endure grief, suffering wrongfully.

20 For what glory *is it*, if, when ye be buffetted for your faults, ye shall take it patiently? but if, when ye do well, and suffer *for it*, ye take it patiently, this *is* acceptable with God.

B

Luke 18. 1 And he spake a parable unto them *to this end*, that men ought always to pray, and not to faint;

B—CONCLUDED.

Acts 2. 42. *See e, E, §232, page 640.*

IThes. 5. 17 Pray without ceasing.

C

ICor. 16. 1 Now concerning the collection for the saints, as I have given order to the churches of Galatia, even so do ye.

IICor. 9. 1 For as touching the ministering to the saints, it is superfluous for me to write to you:

IICor. 9. 12 For the administration of this service not only supplieth the want of the saints, but is abundant also by many thanksgivings unto God;

Heb. 6. 10 For God *is* not unrighteous to forget your work and labour of love, which ye have shewed toward his name, in that ye have ministered to the saints, and do minister.

Heb. 13. 16 But to do good and to communicate forget not: for with such sacrifices God is well pleased.

I Jno. 3. 17 But whoso hath this world's good, and seeth his brother have need, and shutteth up his bowels *of compassion* from him, how dwelleth the love of God in him?

D

I Tim. 3. 2 A bishop then must be blameless, the husband of one wife, vigilant, sober, of good behaviour, given to hospitality, apt to teach;

Tit. 1. 8 But a lover of hospitality, a lover of good men, sober, just, holy, temperate;

Heb. 13. 2 Be not forgetful to entertain strangers: for thereby some have entertained angels unawares.

I Pet. 4. 9 Use hospitality one to another without grudging.

E

Acts 7. 60. *See a, A, §246, page 676.*

ICor. 4. 12 And labour, working with our own hands: being reviled, we bless; being persecuted, we suffer it;

I Pet. 2. 23 Who, when he was reviled, reviled not again; when he suffered, he threatened not; but committed *himself* to him that judgeth righteously:

I Pet. 3. 9 Not rendering evil for evil, or railing for railing: but contrariwise blessing; knowing that ye are thereunto called, that ye should inherit a blessing.

F

ICor. 12. 26 And whether one member suffer, all the members suffer with it; or one member be honoured, all the members rejoice with it.

Phil. 2. 18 For the same cause also do ye joy, and rejoice with me.

§ 342. AN EXHORTATION TO LOVE GOD, THE FAITHFUL

CHAP. 12.

16 [g]*Be* of the same mind one toward another. [h]Mind not high things, but [5]condescend to men of low estate. [i]Be not wise in your own conceits.

17 [k]Recompense to no man evil for evil. [l]Provide things honest in the sight of all men.

18 If it be possible, as much as lieth in you, [m]live peaceably with all men.

19 Dearly beloved, [n]avenge not yourselves, but *rather* give place unto wrath; for it is written, [o]Vengeance *is* mine; I will repay, saith the Lord.

20 [p]Therefore if thine enemy hunger, feed him; if he thirst, give him drink; for in so doing thou shalt heap coals of fire on his head.

21 Be not overcome of evil, but evercome evil with good.

G

Rom. 15. 5 Now the God of patience and consolation grant you to be likeminded one toward another according to Christ Jesus:

G—CONCLUDED.

I Cor. 1. 10 Now I beseech you, brethren, by the name of our Lord Jesus Christ, that ye all speak the same thing, and *that* there be no divisions among you; but *that* ye be perfectly joined together in the same mind and in the same judgment.

Phil. 2. 2 Fulfil ye my joy, that ye be likeminded, having the same love, *being* of one accord, of one mind.

Phil. 3. 16 Nevertheless, whereto we have already attained, let us walk by the same rule, let us mind the same thing.

I Pet. 3. 8. *See under X, page 870.*

H

Ps. 131. 1 Lord, my heart is not haughty, nor mine eyes lofty: neither do I exercise myself in great matters, or in things too high for me.

2 Surely I have behaved and quieted myself, as a child that is weaned of his mother: my soul *is* even as a weaned child.

Jer. 45. 5 And seekest thou great things for thyself? seek *them* not: for, behold, I will bring evil upon all flesh, saith the LORD: but thy life will I give unto thee for a prey in all places whither thou goest.

5

Or, *be contented with mean things.*

I

Prov. 3. 7 Be not wise in thine own eyes: fear the LORD, and depart from evil.

Prov. 26. 12 Seest thou a man wise in his own conceit? *there is* more hope of a fool than of him.

§ 343. AN EXHORTATION TO BE SUBJECT TO THE HIGHER

13: 1–14.

1 Let every soul [a]be subject unto the higher powers. For [b]there is no power but of God: the powers that be are [1]ordained of God.

2 Whosoever therefore resisteth the power, resisteth the ordinance of God: and they that resist shall receive to themselves damnation.

3 For rulers are not a terror to good works, but to the evil. Wilt thou then not be afraid of the power? [c]do

CHAP. 13.

that which is good, and thou shalt have praise of the same:

4 For he is the minister of God to thee for good. But if thou do that which is evil, be afraid; for he beareth not the sword in vain: for he is the minister of God, a revenger to *execute* wrath upon him that doeth evil.

A

Tit. 3. 1 Put them in mind to be subject to principalities and powers, to obey magistrates, to be ready to every good work.

PERFORMANCE OF DUTY, AND LOVE TOWARD MAN (CONCLUDED).

I—CONCLUDED.

Isa. 5. 21 Woe unto *them that are* wise in their own eyes, and prudent in their own sight!

Rom. 11. 25 For I would not, brethren, that ye should be ignorant of this mystery, lest ye should be wise in your own conceits, that blindness in part is happened to Israel, until the fulness of the Gentiles be come in.

K

Prov. 20. 22 Say not thou, I will recompense evil; *but* wait on the LORD, and he shall save thee.

Matt. 5. 39 But I say unto you, That ye resist not evil: but whosoever shall smite thee on thy right cheek, turn to him the other also.

I Thes. 5. 15 See that none render evil for evil unto any *man;* but ever follow that which is good, both among yourselves, and to all *men.*

I Pet. 3. 9. *See under E, page 871.*

L

Rom. 14. 16 Let not then your good be evil spoken of:

II Cor. 8. 21 Providing for honest things, not only in the sight of the Lord, but also in the sight of men.

M

Mark 9. 50 Salt *is* good: but if the salt have lost his saltness, wherewith will ye season it? Have salt in yourselves, and have peace one with another.

Rom. 14. 19 Let us therefore follow after the things which make for peace, and things wherewith one may edify another.

M—CONCLUDED.

Heb. 12. 14 Follow peace with all *men,* and holiness, without which no man shall see the Lord:

N

Lev. 19. 18 Thou shalt not avenge, nor bear any grudge against the children of thy people, but thou shalt love thy neighbour as thyself: I *am* the LORD.

Prov. 24. 29 Say not, I will do so to him as he hath done to me: I will render to the man according to his work.

O

Deut. 32. 35 To me *belongeth* vengeance, and recompense; their foot shall slide in *due* time: for the day of their calamity *is* at hand, and the things that shall come upon them make haste.

Heb. 10. 30 For we know him that hath said, Vengeance *belongeth* unto me, I will recompense, saith the Lord. And again, The Lord shall judge his people.

P

Ex. 23. 4 If thou meet thine enemy's ox or his ass going astray, thou shalt surely bring it back to him again.

Prov. 25. 21 If thine enemy be hungry, give him bread to eat; and if he be thirsty, give him water to drink:

22 For thou shalt heap coals of fire upon his head, and the LORD shall reward thee.

Matt. 5. 44 But I say unto you, Love your enemies, bless them that curse you, do good to them that hate you, and pray for them which despitefully use you, and persecute you;

POWERS, LOVE TO MAN, AND A PURE AND SOBER LIFE.

A—CONCLUDED.

I Pet. 2. 13 Submit yourselves to every ordinance of man for the Lord's sake: whether it be to the king, as supreme;

B

Prov. 8. 15 By me kings reign, and princes decree justice.

16 By me princes rule, and nobles, *even* all the judges of the earth.

Da. 2. 21 And he changeth the times and the seasons: he removeth kings, and setteth up kings: he giveth wisdom unto the wise, and knowledge to them that know understanding:

Da. 4. 32 And they shall drive thee from men, and thy dwelling *shall be* with the beasts of the field: they shall make thee to eat grass as oxen, and seven times shall pass over thee, until thou know that the Most High ruleth in the kingdom of men, and giveth it to whomsoever he will.

John 19. 11 Jesus answered, Thou couldest have no power *at all* against me, except it were given thee from above: therefore he that delivered me unto thee hath the greater sin.

1

Or, *ordered.*

C

I Pet. 2. 14 Or unto governors, as unto them that are sent by him for the punishment of evil doers, and for the praise of them that do well.

For C concluded, see next page (874).

§ 343. AN EXHORTATION TO BE SUBJECT TO THE HIGHER

CHAP. 13.

5 Wherefore [d]*ye* must needs be subject, not only for wrath, [e]but also for conscience' sake.

6 For, for this cause pay ye tribute also: for they are God's ministers, attending continually upon this very thing.

7 [f]Render therefore to all their dues: tribute to whom tribute *is due;* custom to whom custom; fear to whom fear; honour to whom honour.

8 [g]Owe no man any thing, but to love one another: for [h]he that loveth another hath fulfilled the law.

9 For this, [i]Thou shalt not commit adultery, Thou shalt not kill, Thou shalt not steal, Thou shalt not bear false witness, Thou shalt not covet; and if *there be* any other commandment, it is briefly comprehended in this saying, namely, [k]Thou shalt love thy neighbour as thyself.

10 Love worketh no ill to his neighbour: therefore [l]love *is* the fullfiling of the law.

11 And that, knowing the time, that now *it is* high time [m]to awake out of sleep: for now *is* our salvation nearer than when we believed.

12 The night is far spent, the day is at hand: [n]let us therefore cast off the works of darkness, and [o]let us put on the armour of light.

13 [p]Let us walk [z]honestly, as in the day; [q]not in rioting and drunkenness, [r]not in chambering and wantonness, [s]not in strife and envying:

14 But [t]put ye on the Lord Jesus Christ, and [u]make not provision for the flesh, to *fulfil* the lusts *thereof.*

C—CONCLUDED.

1 Pet. 3. 13 And who *is* he that will harm you, if ye be followers of that which is good?

D

Eccl. 8. 2 I *counsel thee* to keep the king's commandment, and *that* in regard of the oath of God.

E

Acts 23. 1. *See a, A, § 299, page 776.*

1 Pet. 2. 19 For this *is* thankworthy, if a man for conscience toward God endure grief, suffering wrongfully.

F

Matt. 22. 21 They say unto him, Cæsar's. Then saith he unto them, Render therefore unto Cæsar the things which are Cæsar's; and unto God the things that are God's.

Mark 12. 17 And Jesus answering said unto them, Render to Cæsar the things that are Cæsar's, and to God the things that are God's. And they marvelled at him.

Luke 20. 25 And he said unto them, Render therefore unto Cæsar the things which be Cæsar's, and unto God the things which be God's.

G

Deut. 24. 14 Thou shalt not oppress a hired servant *that is* poor and needy, *whether he be* of thy brethren, or of thy strangers that *are* in thy land within thy gates:

15 At his day thou shalt give *him* his hire, neither shall the sun go down upon it; for he *is* poor, and setteth his heart upon it: lest he cry against thee unto the LORD, and it be sin unto thee.

Prov. 3. 27 Withhold not good from them to whom it is due, when it is in the power of thine hand to do *it.*

28 Say not unto thy neighbour, Go, and come again, and to morrow I will give; when thou hast it by thee.

H

Matt. 7. 12 Therefore all things whatsoever ye would that men should do to you, do ye even so to them: for this is the law and the prophets.

Rom. 13. 10. *See text of topic.*

Gal. 5. 14 For all the law is fulfilled in one word, *even* in this; Thou shalt love thy neighbour as thyself.

Col. 3. 14 And above all these things *put on* charity, which is the bond of perfectness.

POWERS, LOVE TO MAN, AND A PURE AND SOBER LIFE (CONCLUDED).

H—CONCLUDED.

I Tim. 1. 5 Now the end of the commandment is charity out of a pure heart, and *of* a good conscience, and *of* faith unfeigned:

Jas. 2. 8 If ye fulfil the royal law according to the Scripture, Thou shalt love thy neighbour as thyself, ye do well:

I

Ex. 20. 13 Thou shalt not kill.

Deut. 5. 18 Neither shalt thou commit adultery.

K

Lev. 19. 18 Thou shalt not avenge, nor bear any grudge against the children of thy people, but thou shalt love thy neighbour as thyself: I *am* the LORD.

Matt. 22. 39 And the second *is* like unto it, Thou shalt love thy neighbour as thyself.

Mark 12. 31 And the second *is* like, *namely* this, Thou shalt love thy neighbour as thyself. There is none other commandment greater than these.

Gal. 5. 14 and Jas. 2. 8. *See under H.*

L

Matt. 22. 40 On these two commandments hang all the law and the prophets.

Rom. 13. 8. *See text of topic.*

M

I Cor. 15. 34 Awake to righteousness, and sin not; for some have not the knowledge of God: I speak *this* to your shame.

Eph. 5. 14 Wherefore he saith, Awake thou that sleepest, and arise from the dead, and Christ shall give thee light.

I Thes. 5. 5 Ye are all the children of light, and the children of the day: we are not of the night, nor of darkness.
6 Therefore let us not sleep, as *do* others; but let us watch and be sober.

N

Eph. 5. 11 And have no fellowship with the unfruitful works of darkness, but rather reprove *them*.

Col. 3. 8 But now ye also put off all these; anger, wrath, malice, blasphemy, filthy communication out of your mouth.

O

Eph. 6. 13 Wherefore take unto you the whole armour of God, that ye may be able to withstand in the evil day, and having done all, to stand.

I Thes. 5. 8 But let us, who are of the day, be sober, putting on the breastplate of faith and love; and for a helmet, the hope of salvation.

P

Phil. 4. 8 Finally, brethren, whatsoever things are true, whatsoever things *are* honest, whatsoever things *are* just, whatsoever things *are* pure, whatsoever things *are* lovely, whatsoever things *are* of good report; if *there be* any virtue, and if *there be* any praise, think on these things.

P—CONCLUDED.

I Thes. 4. 12 That ye may walk honestly toward them that are without, and *that* ye may have lack of nothing.

I Pet. 2. 12 Having your conversation honest among the Gentiles: that, whereas they speak against you as evil doers, they may by *your* good works, which they shall behold, glorify God in the day of visitation.

2
Or, *decently.*

Q

Prov. 23. 20 Be not among winebibbers; among riotous eaters of flesh:

Luke 21. 34 And take heed to yourselves, lest at any time your hearts be overcharged with surfeiting, and drunkenness, and cares of this life, and *so* that day come upon you unawares.

I Pet. 4. 3 For the time past of *our* life may suffice us to have wrought the will of the Gentiles, when we walked in lasciviousness, lusts, excess of wine, revellings, banquetings, and abominable idolatries:

R

I Cor. 6. 9 Know ye not that the unrighteous shall not inherit the kingdom of God? Be not deceived: neither fornicators, nor idolaters, nor adulterers, nor effeminate, nor abusers of themselves with mankind,

Eph. 5. 5 For this ye know, that no whoremonger, nor unclean person, nor covetous man, who is an idolater, hath any inheritance in the kingdom of Christ and of God.

S

Jas. 3. 14 But if ye have bitter envying and strife in your hearts, glory not, and lie not against the truth.

T

Gal. 3. 27 For as many of you as have been baptized into Christ have put on Christ.

Eph. 4. 24 And that ye put on the new man, which after God is created in righteousness and true holiness.

Col. 3. 10 And have put on the new *man*, which is renewed in knowledge after the image of him that created him:

U

Gal. 5. 16 *This* I say then, Walk in the Spirit, and ye shall not fulfil the lust of the flesh.

§ 344. ADMONISHED TO BE CHARITABLE, NOT TO JUDGE, PUT NO STUMBLING

14: 1–23.

1 Him that [a]is weak in the faith receive ye, *but* [1]not to doubtful disputations.

2 For one believeth that he [b]may eat all things: another, who is weak, eateth herbs.

3 Let not him that eateth despise him that eateth not; and [c]let not him which eateth not judge him that eateth: for God hath received him.

4 [d]Who art thou that judgest another man's servant? to his own master he standeth or falleth; yea, he shall be holden up: for God is able to make him stand.

5 [e]One man esteemeth one day above another: another esteemeth every day *alike*. Let every man be [2]fully persuaded in his own mind.

6 He that [3]regardeth the day, regardeth *it* unto the Lord; and he that regardeth not the day, to the Lord he doth not regard *it*. He that eateth, eateth to the Lord, for [f]he giveth God thanks; and he that eateth not, to the Lord he eateth not, and giveth God thanks.

7 For [g]none of us liveth to himself, and no man dieth to himself.

8 For whether we live, we live unto the Lord; and whether we die, we die unto the Lord: whether we live therefore, or die, we are the Lord's.

9 For [h]to this end Christ both died, and rose, and revived, that he might be [i]Lord both of the dead and living.

10 But why dost thou judge thy brother? or why dost thou set at nought thy brother? for [k]we shall all

CHAP. 14.

stand before the judgment seat of Christ.

11 For it is written, [l]*As* I live, saith the Lord, every knee shall bow to me, and every tongue shall confess to God.

12 So then [m]every one of us shall give account of himself to God.

13 Let us not therefore judge one another any more: but judge this rather, that [n]no man put a stumblingblock or an occasion to fall in *his* brother's way.

14 I know, and am persuaded by the Lord Jesus, [o]that *there is* nothing [4]unclean of itself: but [p]to him that esteemeth any thing to be [4]unclean, to him *it is* unclean.

15 But if thy brother be grieved with *thy* meat, now walkest thou not [5]charitably. [q]Destroy not him with thy meat, for whom Christ died.

A

Rom. 15. 1 We then that are strong ought to bear the infirmities of the weak, and not to please ourselves.

Rom. 15. 7 Wherefore receive ye one another, as Christ also received us to the glory of God.

1 Cor. 8. 9 But take heed lest by any means this liberty of yours become a stumblingblock to them that are weak.

1 Cor. 8. 11 And through thy knowledge shall the weak brother perish, for whom Christ died?

1 Cor. 9. 22 To the weak became I as weak, that I might gain the weak: I am made all things to all *men*, that I might by all means save some.

1

Or, *not to judge his doubtful thoughts.*

B

Rom. 14. 14. *See text of topic.*

1 Cor. 10. 25 Whatsoever is sold in the shambles, *that* eat, asking no question for conscience' sake:

BLOCKS, BUT TO FOLLOW RIGHTEOUSNESS, JOY, PEACE AND EDIFICATION.

B—Concluded.

I Tim. 4. 4 For every creature of God *is* good, and nothing to be refused, if it be received with thanksgiving:

Tit. 1. 15 Unto the pure all things *are* pure: but unto them that are defiled and unbelieving *is* nothing pure; but even their mind and conscience is defiled.

C

Col. 2. 16 Let no man therefore judge you in meat, or in drink, or in respect of a holyday, or of the new moon, or of the sabbath *days*:

D

Jas. 4. 12 There is one lawgiver, who is able to save and to destroy: who art thou that judgest another?

E

Gal. 4. 10 Ye observe days, and months, and times, and years.

Col. 2. 16. *See under C.*

2

Or, *fully assured.*

3

Or, *observeth.*

F

I Cor. 10. 31 Whether therefore ye eat, or drink, or whatsoever ye do, do all to the glory of God.

I Tim. 4. 3 Forbidding to marry, *and commanding* to abstain from meats, which God hath created to be received with thanksgiving of them which believe and know the truth.

G

I Cor. 6. 19 What! know ye not that your body is the temple of the Holy Ghost *which is* in you, which ye have of God, and ye are not your own?

20 For ye are bought with a price: therefore glorify God in your body, and in your spirit, which are God's.

Gal. 2. 20 I am crucified with Christ: nevertheless I live; yet not I, but Christ liveth in me: and the life which I now live in the flesh I live by the faith of the Son of God, who loved me, and gave himself for me.

I Thes. 5. 10 Who died for us, that, whether we wake or sleep, we should live together with him.

I Pet. 4. 2 That he no longer should live the rest of *his* time in the flesh to the lusts of men, but to the will of God.

H

II Cor. 5. 15 And *that* he died for all, that they which live should not henceforth live unto themselves, but unto him which died for them, and rose again.

I

Acts 10. 36. *See e, E, § 254, page 696.*

K

Acts 10. 42. *See p, P, § 254, page 698.*

Jude. 14 And Enoch also, the seventh from Adam, prophesied of these, saying, Behold, the Lord cometh with ten thousand of his saints,

15 To execute judgment upon all, and to convince all that are ungodly among them of all their ungodly deeds which they have ungodly committed, and of all their hard *speeches* which ungodly sinners have spoken against him.

L

Isa. 45. 23 I have sworn by myself, the word is gone out of my mouth *in* righteousness, and shall not return, That unto me every knee shall bow, every tongue shall swear.

Phil. 2. 10 That at the name of Jesus every knee should bow, of *things* in heaven, and *things* in earth, and *things* under the earth;

M

Matt. 12. 36 But I say unto you, That every idle word that men shall speak, they shall give account thereof in the day of judgment.

Gal. 6. 5 For every man shall bear his own burden.

I Pet. 4. 5 Who shall give account to him that is ready to judge the quick and the dead.

N

I Cor. 8. 9. *See under A.*

I Cor. 8. 13 Wherefore, if meat make my brother to offend, I will eat no flesh while the world standeth, lest I make my brother to offend.

I Cor. 10. 32 Give none offense, neither to the Jews, nor to the Gentiles, nor to the church of God:

O

Acts 10. 15. *See l, L, § 254, page 692.*

4

Gr. *common.*

P

I Cor. 8. 7 Howbeit *there is* not in every man that knowledge: for some with conscience of the idol unto this hour eat *it* as a thing offered unto an idol; and their conscience being weak is defiled.

I Cor. 8. 10 For if any man see thee which hast knowledge sit at meat in the idol's temple, shall not the conscience of him which is weak be emboldened to eat those things which are offered to idols;

For 5 and Q, see next page (878).

§ 344. ADMONISHED TO BE CHARITABLE, NOT TO JUDGE, PUT NO STUMBLING

CHAP. 14.

16 [r]Let not then your good be evil spoken of:

17 [s]For the kingdom of God is not meat and drink; but righteousness, and peace, and joy in the Holy Ghost.

18 For he that in these things serveth Christ [t]*is* acceptable to God, and approved of men.

19 [u]Let us therefore follow after the things which make for peace, and things wherewith [x]one may edify another.

20 [y]For meat destroy not the work of God. All things indeed *are* pure; [z]but *it is* evil for that man who eateth with offence.

CHAP. 14.

21 *It is* good neither to eat [a]flesh, nor to drink wine, nor *any thing* whereby thy brother stumbleth, or is offended, or is made weak.

22 Hast thou faith? have *it* to thyself before God. [b]Happy *is* he that condemneth not himself in that thing which he alloweth.

23 And he that [6]doubteth is damned if he eat, because *he eateth* not of faith: for [c]whatsoever *is* not of faith is sin.

5

Gr. *according to charity.*

Q

I Cor. 8. 11 And through thy knowledge shall the weak brother perish, for whom Christ died?

§ 345. EXHORTATION TO BEAR WITH THE WEAK, PLEASE OUR FELLOW-

15 : 1–13.

1 We [a]then that are strong ought to bear the [b]infirmities of the weak, and not to please ourselves.

2 [c]Let every one of us please *his* neighbour for *his* good [d]to edification.

3 For even Christ pleased not himself; but, as it is written, [f]The reproaches of them that reproached thee fell on me.

4 For [g]whatsoever things were written aforetime were written for our learning, that we through patience and comfort of the Scriptures might have hope.

5 [h]Now the God of patience and consolation grant you to be likeminded one toward another, [1]according to Christ Jesus:

6 That ye may [i]with one mind *and* one mouth glorify God, even the Father of our Lord Jesus Christ.

A

Gal. 6. 1 Brethren, if a man be overtaken in a fault, ye which are spiritual, restore such a one in the spirit of meekness; considering thyself, lest thou also be tempted.

B

Rom. 14. 1. *See a, A, § 344, page 876.*

C

I Cor. 9. 19 For though I be free from all *men*, yet have I made myself servant unto all, that I might gain the more.

I Cor. 9. 22 To the weak became I as weak, that I might gain the weak: I am made all things to all *men*, that I might by all means save some.

I Cor. 10. 24 Let no man seek his own, but every man another's *wealth.*

I Cor. 10. 33 Even as I please all *men* in all *things*, not seeking mine own profit, but the *profit* of many, that they may be saved.

I Cor. 13. 5 Doth not behave itself unseemly, seeketh not her own, is not easily provoked, thinketh no evil;

Phil 2. 4 Look not every man on his own things, but every man also on the things of others.

5 Let this mind be in you, which was also in Christ Jesus:

BLOCKS, BUT TO FOLLOW RIGHTEOUSNESS, JOY, PEACE AND EDIFICATION (CONCLUDED).

R

Rom. 12 17. *See l, L, § 342, page 872.*

S

I Cor. 8. 8 But meat commendeth us not to God: for neither, if we eat, are we the better; neither, if we eat not, are we the worse.

T

II Cor. 8. 21 Providing for honest things, not only in the sight of the Lord, but also in the sight of men.

U

Ps. 34. 14 Depart from evil, and do good; seek peace, and pursue it.

Rom. 12. 18. *See m, M, § 342, page 872.*

X

Rom. 15. 2. *See text of topic, § 345.*

I Cor. 14. 12 Even so ye, forasmuch as ye are zealous of spiritual *gifts*, seek that ye may excel to the edifying of the church.

I Thes. 5. 11 Wherefore comfort yourselves together, and edify one another, even as also ye do.

Y

Rom. 14. 15. *See text of topic, page 876.*

Z

I Cor. 8. 9 But take heed lest by any means this liberty of yours become a stumblingblock to them that are weak.

I. Cor. 8. 10. *See under P, page 877.*

I. Cor. 8. 11. *See under Q.*

12 But when ye sin so against the brethren, and wound their weak conscience, ye sin against Christ.

A

I. Cor. 8. 13. *See under N, page 877.*

B

I Jno. 3. 21 Beloved, if our heart condemn us not, *then* have we confidence toward God.

6

Or, *discerneth and putteth a difference between meats.*

C

Tit. 1. 15 Unto the pure all things *are* pure: but unto them that are defiled and unbelieving *is* nothing pure: but even their mind and conscience is defiled.

MEN UNTO GOOD AS DID CHRIST, AND TO GLORIFY GOD AS IT IS WRITTEN.

D

I Tim. 1. 4 Neither give heed to fables and endless genealogies, which minister questions, rather than godly edifying which is in faith: *so do.*

E

Matt. 26. 39 And he went a little farther, and fell on his face, and prayed, saying, O my father, if it be possible, let this cup pass from me: nevertheless, not as I will, but as thou *wilt.*

John 5. 30 I can of mine own self do nothing: as I hear, I judge: and my judgment is just; because I seek not mine own will, but the will of the Father which hath sent me.

John 6. 38 For I came down from heaven, not to do mine own will, but the will of him that sent me.

F

Ps. 69. 9 For the zeal of thine house hath eaten me up; and the reproaches of them that reproached thee are fallen upon me.

G

Rom. 4. 23 Now it was not written for his sake alone, that it was imputed to him;
24 But for us also, to whom it shall be imputed, if we believe on him that raised up Jesus our Lord from the dead;

G—CONCLUDED.

I Cor. 9. 9 For it is written in the law of Moses, Thou shalt not muzzle the mouth of the ox that treadeth out the corn. Doth God take care for oxen?
10 Or saith he *it* altogether for our sakes? For our sakes, no doubt, *this* is written: that he that plougheth should plough in hope; and that he that thresheth in hope should be partaker of his hope.

I Cor. 10 11 Now all these things happened unto them for ensamples: and they are written for our admonition, upon whom the ends of the world are come.

II Tim. 3. 16 All Scripture *is* given by inspiration of God, and *is* profitable for doctrine, for reproof, for correction, for instruction in righteousness:
17 That the man of God may be perfect, thoroughly furnished unto all good works.

H

Rom. 12. 16. *See g, G, § 342, page 872.*

1

Or, *after the example of.*

I

Acts 4. 32. *See a, A, § 239, page 654.*

K

Rom. 14. 1. *See a, A, § 344, page 876.*

§ 345. EXHORTATION TO BEAR WITH THE WEAK, PLEASE OUR FELLOWMEN

CHAP. 15.

7 Wherefore [k]receive ye one another, [l]as Christ also received us, to the glory of God.

8 Now I say that [m]Jesus Christ was a minister of the circumcision for the truth of God, [n]to confirm the promises *made* unto the fathers:

9 And [o]that the Gentiles might glorify God for *his* mercy; as it is written, [p]For this cause I will confess to thee among the Gentiles, and sing unto thy name.

10 And again he saith, [q]Rejoice, ye Gentiles, with his people.

11 And again, [r]Praise the Lord, all ye Gentiles; and laud him, all ye people.

12 And again, Esaias saith, [s]There shall be a root of Jesse, and he that shall rise to reign over the Gentiles; in him shall the Gentiles trust.

13 Now the God of hope fill you with all [t]joy and peace in believing, that ye may abound in hope, through the power of the Holy Ghost.

For K, see preceding page (879).

L

Rom. 5. 2 By whom also we have access by faith into this grace wherein we stand, and rejoice in hope of the glory of God.

M

Matt. 15. 24 But he answered and said, I am not sent but unto the lost sheep of the house of Israel.

John 1. 11 He came unto his own, and his own received him not.

Acts 3. 25 Ye are the children of the prophets, and of the covenant which God made with our fathers, saying unto Abraham, And in thy seed shall all the kindreds of the earth be blessed.
26 Unto you first God, having raised up his Son Jesus, sent him to bless you, in turning away every one of you from his iniquities.

§ 346. PAUL REMINDS THE ROMANS OF HIS MINISTRY, DECLARES

15 : 14-33

14 And [a] I myself also am persuaded of you, my brethren, that ye also are full of goodness, [b]filled with all knowledge, able also to admonish one another.

15 Nevertheless, brethren, I have written the more boldly unto you in some sort, as putting you in mind, [c]because of the grace that is given to me of God,

16 That [d]I should be the minister of Jesus Christ to the Gentiles, ministering the gospel of God, that the [1e]offering up of the Gentiles might be acceptable, being sanctified by the Holy Ghost.

CHAP. 15.

17 [f]I have therefore whereof I may glory through Jesus Christ in those things which pertain to God.

18 For I will not dare to speak of any of those things which Christ hath not wrought by me, [g]to make the Gentiles obedient, by word and deed,

19 [h]Through mighty signs and wonders, by the power of the Spirit of God; so that from Jerusalem, and round about unto Illyricum, I have fully preached the gospel of Christ.

A

II Pet. 1. 12 Wherefore I will not be negligent to put you always in remembrance of these things, though ye know *them*, and be established in the present truth.

UNTO GOOD AS DID CHRIST, AND TO GLORIFY GOD AS IT IS WRITTEN (CON'D).

M—CONCLUDED.

Acts 13. 46 Then Paul and Barnabas waxed bold, and said, It was necessary that the word of God should first have been spoken to you: but seeing ye put it from you, and judge yourselves unworthy of everlasting life, lo, we turn to the Gentiles.

N

Rom. 3. 3 For what if some did not believe? shall their unbelief make the faith of God without effect?

O

John 10. 16 And other sheep I have, which are not of this fold: them also I must bring, and they shall hear my voice; and there shall be one fold, *and* one shepherd.

Rom. 9. 23 And that he might make known the riches of his glory on the vessels of mercy, which he had afore prepared unto glory.

P

Ps. 18. 49 Therefore will I give thanks unto thee, O LORD, among the heathen, and sing praises unto thy name.

Q

Deut. 32. 43 Rejoice, O ye nations, *with* his people: for he will avenge the blood

Q—CONCLUDED.

of his servants, and will render vengeance to his adversaries, and will be merciful unto his land, *and* to his people.

R

Ps. 117. 1 O praise the LORD, all ye nations: praise him, all ye people.

S

Isa. 11. 1 And there shall come forth a rod out of the stem of Jesse, and a Branch shall grow out of his roots:

Isa. 11. 10 And in that day there shall be a root of Jesse, which shall stand for an ensign of the people; to it shall the Gentiles seek: and his rest shall be glorious.

Rev. 5. 5 And one of the elders saith unto me, Weep not: behold, the Lion of the tribe of Judah, the Root of David, hath prevailed to open the book, and to loose the seven seals thereof.

Rev. 22. 16 I Jesus have sent mine angel to testify unto you these things in the churches. I am the root and the offspring of David, *and* the bright and morning star.

T

Rom. 12. 12. *See z, Z, § 342, page 870.*

HIS PURPOSE TO VISIT THEM, AND SOLICITS THEIR PRAYERS.

A—CONCLUDED.

I Jno. 2. 21 I have not written unto you because ye know not the truth, but because ye know it, and that no lie is of the truth.

B

I Cor. 8. 1 Now as touching things offered unto idols, we know that we all have knowledge. Knowledge puffeth up, but charity edifieth.

I Cor. 8. 7 Howbeit *there is* not in every man that knowledge: for some with conscience of the idol unto this hour eat *it* as a thing offered unto an idol; and their conscience being weak is defiled.

I Cor 8. 10 For if any man see thee which hast knowledge sit at meat in the idol's temple, shall not the conscience of him which is weak be emboldened to eat those things which are offered to idols;

C

Rom. 1. 5. *See i, I, § 317, page 808.*

D

Acts 22. 21. *See i, I, § 297, page 774.*

1

Or, *sacrificing.*

E

Isa. 66. 20 And they shall bring all your brethren *for* an offering unto the LORD out of all nations upon horses, and in chariots, and in litters, and upon mules, and upon swift beasts, to my holy mountain Jerusalem, saith the LORD, as the children of Israel bring an offering in a clean vessel into the house of the LORD.

Phil. 2. 17 Yea, and if I be offered upon the sacrifice and service of your faith, I joy, and rejoice with you all.

F

II Co. 12. 9 And he said unto me, My grace is sufficient for thee: for my strength is made perfect in weakness. Most gladly therefore will I rather glory in my infirmities, that the power of Christ may rest upon me.

Acts 21. 19 And when he had saluted them, he declared particularly what things God hath wrought among the Gentiles by his ministry.

For F concluded, G and H, see next page (882).

§ 346. PAUL REMINDS THE ROMANS OF HIS MINISTRY, DECLARES HIS

CHAP. 15.

20 Yea, so have I strived to preach
the gospel, not where Christ was
named, [i]lest I should build upon
another man's foundation:
21 But as it is written, [k]To whom he
was not spoken of, they shall see:
and they that have not heard shall
understand.
22 For which cause also [l]I have been
[2]much hindered from coming to you.
23 But now having no more place in
these parts, and [m]having a great desire
these many years to come unto you;
24 Whensoever I take my journey
into Spain, I will come to you: for
I trust to see you in my journey, and
to be brought on my way thitherward
by you, if first I be somewhat filled
[3]with your *company*.
25 But now [n]I go unto Jerusalem to
minister unto the saints.
26 For [o]it hath pleased them of
Macedonia and Achaia to make a
certain contribution for the poor
saints which are at Jerusalem.
27 It hath pleased them verily; and
their debtors they are. For [p]if the
Gentiles have been made partakers
of their spiritual things, [q]their duty is
also to minister unto them in carnal
things.
28 When therefore I have performed
this, and have sealed to them [r]this
fruit, I will come by you into Spain.
29 [s]And I am sure that, when I
come unto you, I shall come in the
fulness of the blessing of the gospel
of Christ.
30 Now I beseech you, brethren,
for the Lord Jesus Christ's sake, and

CHAP. 15.

for the love of the Spirit, that ye
strive together with me in *your* prayers to God for me;
31 [t]That I may be delivered from
them that [4]do not believe in Judea;
and that [u]my service which *I have*
for Jerusalem may be accepted of the
saints;
32 [x]That I may come unto you with
joy [y]by the will of God, and may
with you be [z]refreshed.
33 Now [a]the God of peace *be* with
you all. Amen.

F—CONCLUDED.

Gal. 2. 8 (For he that wrought effectually in Peter to the apostleship of the circumcision, the same was mighty in me toward the Gentiles:)

G

Rom. 1. 5 By whom we have received grace and apostleship, for obedience to the faith among all nations, for his name:

Rom. 16. 26 But now is made manifest, and by the Scriptures of the prophets, according to the commandment of the everlasting God, made known to all nations for the obedience of faith:

H

Acts 19. 11 And God wrought special miracles by the hands of Paul:

II Cor. 12. 12 Truly the signs of an apostle were wrought among you in all patience, in signs, and wonders, and mighty deeds.

I

II. Cor. 10. 13 But we will not boast of things without *our* measure but according to the measure of the rule which God hath distributed to us, a measure to reach even unto you.

II Cor. 10. 15 Not boasting of things without *our* measure, *that is*, of other men's labours; but having hope, when your faith is increased, that we shall be enlarged by you according to our rule abundantly,

16 To preach the gospel in the *regions* beyond you, *and* not to boast in another man's line of things made ready to our hand.

K

Isa. 52. 15 So shall he sprinkle many nations; the kings shall shut their mouths at him: for *that* which had not been told them shall they see; and *that* which they had not heard shall they consider.

PURPOSE TO VISIT THEM, AND SOLICITS THEIR PRAYERS (CONCLUDED).

L

Rom. 1. 13. *See h, H, §318, page 810.*

2

Or, *many ways;* or, *often-times.*

M

Acts 19. 21. *See c, C, §287, page 754.*

Rom. 1. 11 For I long to see you, that I may impart unto you some spiritual gift, to the end ye may be established;

Rom. 15. 32. *See text of topic.*

3

Gr. *with you.*

N

Acts 19. 21. *See c, C, §287, page 754.*

O

I Cor. 16. 1 Now concerning the collection for the saints, as I have given order to the churches of Galatia, even so do ye.

2 Upon the first *day* of the week let every one of you lay by him in store, as *God* hath prospered him, that there be no gatherings when I come.

II Cor. 8. 1 Moreover, brethren, we do you to wit of the grace of God bestowed on the churches of Macedonia;

II Cor. 9. 2 For I know the forwardness of your mind, for which I boast of you to them of Macedonia, that Achaia was ready a year ago; and your zeal hath provoked very many.

II Cor. 9. 12 For the administration of this service not only supplieth the want of the saints, but is abundant also by many thanksgivings unto God;

P

Rom. 11. 17 And if some of the branches be broken off, and thou, being a wild olive tree, wert graffed in among them, and with them partakest of the root and fatness of the olive tree;

Q

I Cor. 9. 11 If we have sown unto you spiritual things, *is it* a great thing if we shall reap your carnal things?

Gal. 6. 6 Let him that is taught in the word communicate unto him that teacheth in all good things.

R

Phil. 4. 17 Not because I desire a gift: but I desire fruit that may abound to your account.

S

Rom. 1. 11. *See under N.*

T

II Thes. 3. 2 And that we may be delivered from unreasonable and wicked men: for all *men* have not faith.

4

Or, *are disobedient.*

U

II Cor. 8. 4 Praying us with much entreaty that we would receive the gift, and *take upon us* the fellowship of the ministering to the saints.

X

Rom. 1. 10. *See e, E, § 318, page 810.*

Y

Acts 18. 21. *See d, D, § 282, page 750.*

Z

I Cor. 16. 18 For they have refreshed my spirit and yours: therefore acknowledge ye them that are such.

II Cor. 7. 13 Therefore we were comforted in your comfort: yea, and exceedingly the more joyed we for the joy of Titus, because his spirit was refreshed by you all.

II Tim. 1. 16 The Lord give mercy unto the house of Onesiphorus; for he oft refreshed me, and was not ashamed of my chain:

Phile. 7 For we have great joy and consolation in thy love, because the bowels of the saints are refreshed by thee, brother.

Phile. 20 Yea, brother, let me have joy of thee in the Lord: refresh my bowels in the Lord.

A

Rom. 16. 20 And the God of peace shall bruise Satan under your feet shortly. The grace of our Lord Jesus Christ *be* with you. Amen.

I Cor. 14. 33 For God is not *the author* of confusion, but of peace, as in all churches of the saints.

II Cor. 13. 11 Finally, brethren, farewell. Be perfect, be of good comfort, be of one mind, live in peace; and the God of love and peace shall be with you.

Phil. 4. 9 Those things, which ye have both learned, and received, and heard, and seen in me, do: and the God of peace shall be with you.

I Thes. 5. 23 And the very God of peace sanctify you wholly; and *I pray God* your whole spirit and soul and body be preserved blameless unto the coming of our Lord Jesus Christ.

II Thes. 3. 16 Now the Lord of peace himself give you peace always by all means. The Lord *be* with you all.

Heb. 13. 20 Now the God of peace, that brought again from the dead our Lord Jesus, that great Shepherd of the sheep, through the blood of the everlasting covenant,

§ 347. PAUL COMMENDS PHEBE AND SENDS

16 : 1-27.

1 I commend unto you Phebe our sister, which is a servant of the church which is at [a]Cenchrea:

2 [b]That ye receive her in the Lord, as becometh saints, and that ye assist her in whatsoever business she hath need of you: for she hath been a succourer of many, and of myself also.

3 Greet [c]Priscilla and Auqila, my helpers in Christ Jesus:

4 Who have for my life laid down their own necks: unto whom not only I give thanks, but also all the churches of the Gentiles.

5 Likewise *greet* [d]the church that is in their house. Salute my well beloved Epenetus, who is [e]the firstfruits of Achaia unto Christ.

6 Greet Mary, who bestowed much labour on us.

7 Salute Andronicus and Junia, my kinsmen, and my fellow prisoners, who are of note among the apostles, who also [f]were in Christ before me.

8 Greet Amplias, my beloved in the Lord.

9 Salute Urbane, our helper in Christ, and Stachys my beloved.

10 Salute Apelles approved in Christ. Salute them which are of Aristobulus' [1]*household.*

11 Salute Herodion my kinsman. Greet them that be of the [1]*household* of Narcissus, which are in the Lord.

12 Salute Tryphena and Tryphosa, who labour in the Lord. Salute the beloved Persis, which laboured much in the Lord.

CHAP. 16.

13 Salute Rufus [g]chosen in the Lord, and his mother and mine.

14 Salute Asyncritus, Phlegon, Hermas, Patrobas, Hermes, and the brethren which are with them.

15 Salute Philologus, and Julia, Nereus, and his sister, and Olympas, and all the saints which are with them.

16 [h]Salute one another with a holy kiss. The churches of Christ salute you.

17 Now I beseech you, brethren, mark them [i]which cause divisions and offences contrary to the doctrine which ye have learned; and [k]avoid them.

18 For they that are such serve not our Lord Jesus Christ, but [l]their own belly; and [m]by good words and fair speeches deceive the hearts of the simple.

A

Acts 18. 18 And Paul *after this* tarried *there* yet a good while, and then took his leave of the brethren, and sailed thence into Syria, and with him Priscilla and Aquila; having shorn *his* head in Cenchrea: for he had a vow.

B

Phil. 2. 29 Receive him therefore in the Lord with all gladness; and hold such in reputation:

III Jno. 5 Beloved, thou doest faithfully whatsoever thou doest to the brethren, and to strangers;

6 Which have borne witness of thy charity before the church: whom if thou bring forward on their journey after a godly sort, thou shalt do well:

C

Acts 18. 2 And found a certain Jew named Aquila, born in Pontus, lately come from Italy, with his wife Priscilla; (because that Claudius had commanded all Jews to depart from Rome:) and came unto them.

Acts 18. 26 And he began to speak boldly in the synagogue: whom when Aquila and Priscilla had heard, they took him unto *them*, and expounded unto him the way of God more perfectly.

I Cor. 16. 19. *See under D.*

GREETINGS AND SALUTATIONS TO MANY AT ROME.

D

I Cor. 16. 19 The churches of Asia salute you, Aquila and Priscilla salute you much in the Lord, with the church that is in their house.

Col. 4. 15 Salute the brethren which are in Laodicea, and Nymphas, and the church which is in his house.

Phile. 2 And to *our* beloved Apphia, and Archippus our fellow soldier, and to the church in thy house:

E

I Cor. 16. 15 I beseech you, brethren, (ye know the house of Stephanas, that it is the firstfruits of Achaia, and *that* they have addicted themselves to the ministry of the saints.)

F

Gal. 1. 22 And was unknown by face unto the churches of Judea which were in Christ:

1

Or, *friends.*

G

Eph. 1. 4 According as he hath chosen us in him before the foundation of the world, that we should be holy and without blame before him in love:

II Jno. 1 The elder unto the elect lady and her children, whom I love in the truth; and not I only, but also all they that have known the truth;

H

I Cor. 16. 20 All the brethren greet you. Greet ye one another with a holy kiss.

II Cor. 13. 12 Greet one another with a holy kiss.

I Thes. 5. 26 Greet all the brethren with a holy kiss.

I Pet. 5. 14 Greet ye one another, with a kiss of charity. Peace *be* with you all that are in Christ Jesus. Amen.

I

Acts 15. 1 And certain men which came down from Judea taught the brethren, *and said*, Except ye be circumcised after the manner of Moses, ye cannot be saved.

Acts 15. 5 But there rose up certain of the sect of the Pharisees which believed, saying, That it was needful to circumcise them, and to command *them* to keep the law of Moses.

Acts 15. 24 Forasmuch as we have heard, that certain which went out from us have troubled you with words, subverting your souls, saying, *Ye must* be circumcised, and keep the law: to whom we gave no *such* commandment:

K

I Cor. 5. 9 I wrote unto you in an epistle not to company with fornicators:

I Cor. 5. 11 But now I have written unto you not to keep company, if any man that is called a brother be a fornicator, or covetous, or an idolater, or a railer, or a drunkard, or an extortioner: with such a one no not to eat.

II Thes. 3. 6 Now we command you, brethren, in the name of our Lord Jesus Christ, that ye withdraw yourselves from every brother that walketh disorderly, and not after the tradition which he received of us.

II Thes. 3. 14 And if any man obey not our word by this epistle, note that man, and have no company with him, that he may be ashamed.

II Tim. 3. 5 Having a form of godliness, but denying the power thereof: from such turn away.

Tit. 3. 10 A man that is a heretic, after the first and second admonition, reject;

II Jno. 10 If there come any unto you, and bring not this doctrine, receive him not into *your* house, neither bid him God speed;

L

Phil. 3. 19 Whose end *is* destruction, whose God *is their* belly, and *whose* glory *is* in their shame, who mind earthly things.)

I Tim. 6. 5 Perverse disputings of men of corrupt minds, and destitute of the truth, supposing that gain is godliness; from such withdraw thyself.

M

Col. 2. 4 And this I say, lest any man should beguile you with enticing words.

II Tim. 3 6 For of this sort are they which creep into houses, and lead captive silly women laden with sins, led away with divers lusts,

Tit. 1. 10 For there are many unruly and vain talkers and deceivers, specially they of the circumcision:

N

Rom. 1. 8. *See b, B. § 318, page 808.*

O

Matt. 10. 16 Behold, I send you forth as sheep in the midst of wolves: be ye therefore wise as serpents, and harmless as doves.

I Cor. 14. 20 Brethren, be not children in understanding: howbeit in malice be ye children, but in understanding be men.

2

Or, *harmless.*

§ 347. PAUL COMMENDS PHEBE AND SENDS GREETINGS

CHAP. 16.

19 For [n]your obedience is come
abroad unto all *men*. I am glad therefore on your behalf: but yet I would
have you [o]wise unto that which is
good, and [2]simple concerning evil.
20 And [p]the God of peace [q]shall
[3]bruise Satan under your feet shortly. [r]The grace of our Lord Jesus
Christ *be* with you. Amen.
21 [s]Timotheus my workfellow, and
[t]Lucius, and [u]Jason, and [x]Sosipater,
my kinsmen, salute you.
22 I Tertius, who wrote *this* epistle, salute you in the Lord.
23 [y]Gaius mine host, and of the
whole church, saluteth you. [z]Eras-
tus the chamberlain of the city saluteth you, and Quartus a brother.
24 [a]The grace of our Lord Jesus
Christ *be* with you all. Amen.
25 Now [b]to him that is of power to
establish you [c]according to my gospel, and the preaching of Jesus
Christ, [d]according to the revelation
of the mystery, [e]which was kept secret since the world began,
26 But [f]now is made manifest, and
by the Scriptures of the prophets,
according to the commandments of
the everlasting God, made known to
all nations for [g]the obedience of faith:
27 To [h]God only wise, *be* glory
through Jesus Christ for ever. Amen.

For N, O, and 2, see preceding page (885).

P

Rom. 15. 33. *See a, A, § 346, page 882.*

Q

Gen 3. 15 And I will put enmity between thee and the woman, and between thy seed and her seed; it shall bruise thy head, and thou shalt bruise his heel.

3

Or, *tread.*

R

Rom. 16. 24. *See text of topic.*

ICor. 16. 23 The grace of our Lord Jesus Christ *be* with you.

IICor. 13. 14 The grace of the Lord Jesus Christ, and the love of God, and the communion of the Holy Ghost, *be* with you all. Amen.

Phil. 4. 23 The grace of our Lord Jesus Christ *be* with you all. Amen.

IThes. 5. 28 The grace of our Lord Jesus Christ *be* with you. Amen.

IIThes. 3. 18 The grace of our Lord Jesus Christ *be* with you all. Amen.

Rev. 22. 21 The grace of our Lord Jesus Christ *be* with you all. Amen.

S

Acts 16. 1. *See b, B, § 271, page 732.*

T

Acts 13. 1. *See c, C, § 260, page 708.*

U

Acts 17. 5. *See e, E, § 277, page 740.*

X

Acts 20. 4 And there accompanied him into Asia Sopater of Berea; and of the Thessalonians, Aristarchus and Secundus; and Gaius of Derbe, and Timotheus; and of Asia, Tychicus and Trophimus.

Y

I Cor. 1. 14 I thank God that I baptized none of you, but Crispus and Gaius;

Z

Acts 19. 22. *See e, E, § 287, page 754.*

A

Rom. 16. 20. *See text of topic.*

B

Acts 20. 32 And now, brethren, I commend you to God, and to the word of his grace, which is able to build you up, and to give you an inheritance among all them which are sanctified.

Eph. 3. 20 Now unto him that is able to do exceeding abundantly above all that we ask or think, according to the power that worketh in us,

IThes. 3. 13 To the end he may stablish your hearts unblameable in holiness before God, even our Father, at the coming of our Lord Jesus Christ with all his saints.

IIThes. 2. 16 Now our Lord Jesus Christ himself, and God, even our Father, which hath loved us, and hath given *us* everlasting consolation and good hope through grace,

AND SALUTATIONS TO MANY AT ROME (CONCLUDED).

B—CONCLUDED.

IIThes.2. 17 Comfort your hearts, and stablish you in every good word and work.

IIThes.3. 3 But the Lord is faithful, who shall stablish you, and keep *you* from evil.

I Pet. 5. 10 But the God of all grace, who hath called us unto his eternal glory by Christ Jesus, after that ye have suffered a while, make you perfect, stablish, strengthen, settle *you*.

Jude 24 Now unto him that is able to keep you from falling, and to present *you* faultless before the presence of his glory with exceeding joy,

C

Rom. 2. 16. *See q, Q, § 320, page 818.*

D

Eph. 1. 9 Having made known unto us the mystery of his will, according to his good pleasure which he hath purposed in himself :

Eph. 3. 3 How that by revelation he made known unto me the mystery ; (as I wrote afore in few words;

4 Whereby, when ye read, ye may understand my knowledge in the mystery of Christ)

5 Which in other ages was not made known unto the sons of men, as it is now revealed unto his holy apostles and prophets by the Spirit;

Col. 1. 27 To whom God would make known what *is* the riches of the glory of this mystery among the Gentiles; which is Christ in you, the hope of glory:

I Pet. 1. 10 Of which salvation the prophets have inquired and searched diligently, who prophesied of the grace *that should come* unto you:

11 Searching what, or what manner of time the Spirit of Christ which was in them did signify, when it testified beforehand the sufferings of Christ, and the glory that should follow.

12 Unto whom it was revealed, that not unto themselves, but unto us they did minister the things, which are now reported unto you by them that have preached the gospel unto you with the Holy Ghost sent down from heaven; which things the angels desire to look into.

E

I Cor. 2. 7 But we speak the wisdom of God in a mystery, *even* the hidden *wisdom*, which God ordained before the world unto our glory;

E—CONCLUDED.

Eph. 3. 5. *See under D.*

Eph. 3. 6 That the Gentiles should be fellow heirs, and of the same body, and partakers of his promise in Christ by the gospel:

7 Whereof I was made a minister, according to the gift of the grace of God given unto me by the effectual working of his power.

Eph. 3. 9 And to make all *men* see what *is* the fellowship of the mystery, which from the beginning of the world hath been hid in God, who created all things by Jesus Christ:

10 To the intent that now unto the principalities and powers in heavenly *places* might be known by the church the manifold wisdom of God,

11 According to the eternal purpose which he purposed in Christ Jesus our Lord:

Col. 1. 26 *Even* the mystery which hath been hid from ages and from generations, but now is made manifest to his saints :

F

Eph. 1. 9. *See under D.*

IITim.1. 10 But is now made manifest by the appearing of our Saviour Jesus Christ, who hath abolished death, and hath brought life and immortality to light through the gospel :

Tit. 1. 2 In hope of eternal life, which God, that cannot lie, promised before the world began;

3 But hath in due times manifested his word through preaching, which is committed unto me according to the commandment of God our Saviour;

G

Rom. 1. 5. *See k, K, § 317, page 808.*

Rom. 15. 18. *See g, G, § 346, page 880.*

H

I Tim.1. 17 Now unto the King eternal, immortal, invisible, the only wise God, *be* honour and glory for ever and ever. Amen.

I Tim.6. 16 Who only hath immortality, dwelling in the light which no man can approach unto; whom no man hath seen, nor can see: to whom *be* honour and power everlasting. Amen.

Jude 25 To the only wise God our Saviour, *be* glory and majesty, dominion and power, both now and ever. Amen.

§ 348. THE

1 : 1–3.

1 Paul, [a]called *to be* an apostle of
Jesus Christ [b]through the will of God,
and [c]Sosthenes *our* brother,
2 Unto the church of God which is
at Corinth, [d]to them that [e]are sanctified in Christ Jesus, [f]called *to be*
saints, with all that in every place
[g]call upon the name of Jesus Christ
[h]our Lord, both theirs and ours:
3 [i]Grace *be* unto you, and peace,
from God our Father, and *from* the
Lord Jesus Christ.

A

Rom. 1. 1. *See a, A, § 317, page 808.*

B

I Cor. 1. 1 Paul, called *to be* an apostle of Jesus Christ through the will of God, and Sosthenes *our* brother.

Eph. 1. 1 Paul, an apostle of Jesus Christ by the will of God, to the saints which are at Ephesus, and to the faithful in Christ Jesus:

B—Concluded.

Col. 1. 1 Paul, an apostle of Jesus Christ by the will of God, and Timotheus *our* brother,

C

Acts 18. 17 Then all the Greeks took Sosthenes, the chief ruler of the synagogue, and beat *him* before the judgment seat. And Gallio cared for none of those things.

I Cor. 1. 1. *See under B.*

D

Jude 1 Jude, the servant of Jesus Christ, and brother of James, to them that are sanctified by God the Father, and preserved in Jesus Christ, *and* called:

E

John 17. 15 I pray not that thou shouldest take them out of the world, but that thou shouldest keep them from the evil.
16 They are not of the world, even as I am not of the world.
17 Sanctify them through thy truth: thy word is truth.
18 As thou hast sent me into the world, even so have I also sent them into the world.

§ 349. THANKSGIVING FOR

1 : 4–9.

4 [a]I thank my God always on your
behalf, for the grace of God which
is given you by Jesus Christ;
5 That in everything ye are enriched by him, [b]in all utterance, and
in all knowledge;
6 Even as [c]the testimony of Christ
was confirmed in you:
7 So that ye come behind in no
gift; [d]waiting for the [1]coming of our
Lord Jesus Christ:

A

Rom. 1. 8. *See a, A, § 318, page 808.*

B

I Cor. 12. 8 For to one is given by the Spirit

B—Concluded.

the word of wisdom; to another the word of knowledge by the same Spirit;

II Cor. 8. 7 Therefore, as ye abound in every *thing, in* faith, and utterance, and knowledge, and *in* all diligence, and *in* your love to us, *see* that ye abound in this grace also.

C

I Cor. 2. 1 And I, brethren, when I came to you, came not with excellency of speech or of wisdom, declaring unto you the testimony of God.

II Tim. 1. 8 Be not thou therefore ashamed of the testimony of our Lord, nor of me his prisoner: but be thou partaker of the afflictions of the gospel according to the power of God;

Rev. 1. 2 Who bare record of the word of God, and of the testimony of Jesus Christ, and of all things that he saw.

SALUTATION. Written probably during Spring of A. D. 57 at Ephesus.

E—Concluded.

19 And for their sakes I sanctify myself, that they also might be sanctified through the truth.

20 Neither pray I for these alone, but for them also which shall believe on me through their word;

Heb. 13. 12 Wherefore Jesus also, that he might sanctify the people with his own blood, suffered without the gate.

Acts 15. 9 And put no difference between us and them, purifying their hearts by faith.

F

I Pet. 1. 15 But as he which hath called you is holy, so be ye holy in all manner of conversation;

16 Because it is written, Be ye holy; for I am holy.

Rom. 1. 7. *See l, L, § 317, page 808.*

IITim. 1 9 Who hath saved us, and called *us* with a holy calling, not according to our works, but according to his own purpose and grace, which was given us in Christ Jesus before the world began,

G

Acts 9. 14. *See k, K, § 251, page 864.*

H

Ps. 45. 11 So shall the King greatly desire

H—Concluded.

thy beauty: for he *is* thy Lord; and worship thou him.

Rom. 3. 22 Even the righteousness of God *which is* by faith of Jesus Christ unto all and upon all them that believe: for there is no difference:

Rom. 10. 12 For there is no difference between the Jew and the Greek: for the same Lord over all is rich unto all that call upon him.

I Cor. 8. 6 But to us *there is but* one God, the Father, of whom *are* all things, and we in him; and one Lord Jesus Christ, by whom *are* all things, and we by him.

I

Rom. 1. 7. *See m, M, § 317, page 808.*

Eph. 1. 2 Grace *be* to you, and peace, from God our Father, and *from* the Lord Jesus Christ.

I Pet. 1. 2 Elect according to the foreknowledge of God the Father, through sanctification of the Spirit, unto obedience and sprinkling of the blood of Jesus Christ: Grace unto you, and peace, be multiplied.

GOD'S GRACE TO THEM.

D

Phil. 3. 20 For our conversation is in heaven; from whence also we look for the Saviour, the Lord Jesus Christ:

Tit. 2. 13 Looking for that blessed hope, and the glorious appearing of the great God and our Saviour Jesus Christ;

IIPet. 3. 12 Looking for and hasting unto the coming of the day of God, wherein the heavens being on fire shall be dissolved, and the elements shall melt with fervent heat?

1

Gr. *revelation.*

Luke 17. 30 Even thus shall it be in the day when the Son of man is revealed.

Col. 3. 4 When Christ, *who is* our life, shall appear, then shall ye also appear with him in glory.

IIThes. 1. 7 And to you who are troubled rest with us, when the Lord Jesus shall be

1—Continued.

revealed from heaven with his mighty angels.

I Tim. 6. 14 That thou keep *this* commandment without spot, unrebukeable, until the appearing of our Lord Jesus Christ:

15 Which in his times he shall shew, *who is* the blessed and only Potentate, the King of kings, and Lord of lords;

I Pet. 1. 13 Wherefore gird up the loins of your mind, be sober, and hope to the end for the grace that is to be brought unto you at the revelation of Jesus Christ;

I Pet. 4. 13 But rejoice, inasmuch as ye are partakers of Christ's sufferings; that, when his glory shall be revealed, ye may be glad also with exceeding joy.

I Pet. 5. 4 And when the chief Shepherd shall appear, ye shall receive a crown of glory that fadeth not away.

For 1 concluded see next page (890).

§ 349. THANKSGIVING FOR GOD'S

CHAP. I.

8 [e]Who shall also confirm you unto the end, [f]*that ye may be* blameless in the day of our Lord Jesus Christ.

9 [g]God *is* faithful, by whom ye were called unto [h]the fellowship of his Son Jesus Christ our Lord.

1—CONCLUDED.

IJohn 3. 2 Beloved, now are we the sons of God, and it doth not yet appear what we shall be; but we know that, when he shall appear, we shall be like him; for we shall see him as he is.

E

IThes. 3. 13 To the end he may stablish your hearts unblameable in holiness before God, even our Father, at the coming of our Lord Jesus Christ with all his saints.

E—CONCLUDED.

F

Col. 1. 22 In the body of his flesh through death, to present you holy and unblameable and unreproveable in his sight:

IThes. 5. 23 And the very God of peace sanctify you wholly; and *I pray God* your whole spirit and soul and body be preserved blameless unto the coming of our Lord Jesus Christ.

G

Isa. 49. 7 Thus saith the LORD, the Redeemer of Israel, *and* his Holy One, to him whom man despiseth, to him whom the nation abhorreth, to a servant of

§ 350. A REBUKE FOR THE CONTENTIONS

1 : 10–17.

10 Now I beseech you, brethren, by the name of our Lord Jesus Christ, [a]that ye all speak the same thing, and *that* there be no [1]divisions among you: but *that* ye be perfectly joined together in the same mind and in the same judgment.

11 For it hath been declared unto me of you, my brethren, by them *which are of the house* of Chloe, that there are contentions among you.

12 Now this I say, [b]that every one of you saith, I am of Paul; and I of [c]Apollos; and I of [d]Cephas; and I of Christ.

13 [e]Is Christ divided? was Paul crucified for you? or were ye baptized in the name of Paul?

14 I thank God that I baptized none of you, but [f]Crispus and [g]Gaius;

15 Lest any should say that I had baptized in mine own name.

16 And I baptized also the household of [h]Stephanas: besides, I know

CHAP. I.

not whether I baptized any other.

17 For Christ sent me [i]not to baptize, but to preach the gospel: [k]not with wisdom of [2]words, lest the cross of Christ should be made of none effect.

A

Rom. 12. 16. *See g, G, §342, page 872.*

IICor. 13. 11 Finally, brethren, farewell. Be perfect, be of good comfort, be of one mind, live in peace; and the God of love and peace shall be with you.

1

Gr. *Schisms.*

ICor. 11. 18 For first of all, when ye come together in the church, I hear that there be divisions among you; and I partly believe it.

B

ICor. 3. 4 For while one saith, I am of Paul; and another, I *am* of Apollos; are ye not carnal?

C

Acts 18. 24. *See a, A, §284, page 750.*

D

John 1. 42 And he brought him to Jesus. And when Jesus beheld him, he said, Thou art Simon, the son of Jona: thou shalt be called Cephas, which is by interpretation, A stone.

GRACE TO THEM (CONCLUDED).

G—CONCLUDED.

rulers, Kings shall see and arise, princes also shall worship, because of the LORD that is faithful, *and* the Holy One of Israel, and he shall choose thee.

ICor.10. 13 There hath no temptation taken you but such as is common to man: but God *is* faithful, who will not suffer you to be tempted above that ye are able; but will with the temptation also make a way to escape, that ye may be able to bear *it*.

IThes.5. 24 Faithful *is* he that calleth you, who also will do *it*.

IIThes.3. 3 But the Lord is faithful, who shall stablish you, and keep *you* from evil.

Heb. 10. 23 Let us hold fast the profession of *our* faith without wavering; (for he *is* faithful that promised;)

H

John 15. 4 Abide in me, and I in you. As the branch cannot bear fruit of itself, except it abide in the vine; no more can ye, except ye abide in me.

John 17. 21 That they all may be one; as thou, Father, *art* in me, and I in thee, that they also may be one in us: that the world may believe that thou hast sent me.

I Jno. 1. 3 That which we have seen and heard declare we unto you, that ye also may have fellowship with us: and truly our fellowship *is* with the Father, and with his Son Jesus Christ.

I Jno. 4. 13 Hereby know we that we dwell in him, and he in us, because he hath given us of his Spirit.

AND DIVISIONS AMONG THEM.

E

IICor.11. 4 For if he that cometh preacheth another Jesus, whom we have not preached, or *if* ye receive another spirit, which ye have not received, or another gospel, which ye have not accepted, ye might well bear with *him*.

Eph. 4. 5 One Lord, one faith, one baptism,

F

Acts 18. 8. *See l, L, §280, page 748.*

G

Acts 19. 29. *See d, D, §288, page 756.*

H

1Cor.16. 15 I beseech you, brethren, (ye know the house of Stephanas, that it is the firstfruits of Achaia, and *that* they have addicted themselves to the ministry of the saints,)

ICor.16. 17 I am glad of the coming of Stephanas and Fortunatus and Achaicus: for that which was lacking on your part they have supplied.

I

John 4. 2 (Though Jesus himself baptized not, but his disciples,)

Acts 10. 48 And he commanded them to be baptized in the name of the Lord. Then prayed they him to tarry certain days.

Acts 26. 17 Delivering thee from the people, and *from* the Gentiles, unto whom now I send thee,

18 To open their eyes, *and* to turn *them* from darkness to light, and *from* the power of Satan unto God, that

I—CONCLUDED.

they may receive forgiveness of sins, and inheritance among them which are sanctified by faith that is in me.

K

I Cor. 2. 1 And I, brethren, when I came to you, came not with excellency of speech or of wisdom, declaring unto you the testimony of God.

I Cor. 2. 4 And my speech and my preaching *was* not with enticing words of man's wisdom, but in demonstration of the Spirit and of power:

I Cor 2. 13 Which things also we speak, not in the words which man's wisdom teacheth, but which the Holy Ghost teacheth; comparing spiritual things with spiritual.

IICor.4. 2 But have renounced the hidden things of dishonesty, not walking in craftiness, nor handling the word of God deceitfully; but, by manifestation of the truth, commending ourselves to every man's conscience in the sight of God.

IICor.10. 10 For *his* letters, say they, *are* weighty and powerful; but *his* bodily presence *is* weak, and *his* speech contemptible.

II Pet.1. 16 For we have not followed cunningly devised fables, when we made known unto you the power and coming of our Lord Jesus Christ, but were eyewitnesses of his majesty.

2

Or, *speech*.

§ 351. THE WISDOM OF MAN

1:18–31.

18 For the preaching of the cross
is to [a]them that perish, [b]foolishness;
but unto us which are saved it is
the [c]power of God.

19 For it is written, [d]I will destroy
the wisdom of the wise, and will
bring to nothing the understanding
of the prudent.

20 [e]Where *is* the wise? where *is* the
scribe? where *is* the disputer of this
world? [f]hath not God made foolish
the wisdom of this world?

21 [g]For after that in the wisdom of
God the world by wisdom knew not
God, it pleased God by the foolishness
of preaching to save them that
believe.

22 For the [h]Jews require a sign,
and the Greeks seek after wisdom:

23 But we preach Christ crucified,
[i]unto the Jews a stumblingblock, and
unto the Greeks [k]foolishness;

24 But unto them which are called,
both Jews and Greeks, [l]Christ the
power of God, and [m]the wisdom of
God.

25 Because the foolishness of God
is wiser than men; and the weakness
of God is stronger than men.

26 For ye see your calling, brethren,
how that [n]not many wise men
after the flesh, not many mighty, not
many noble, *are called:*

27 But [o]God hath chosen the foolish
things of the world to confound
the wise; and God hath chosen the
weak things of the world to confound
the things which are mighty;

28 And base things of the world,
and things which are despised, hath
God chosen, *yea*, and [p]things which

A

II Cor. 2. 15 For we are unto God a sweet savour of Christ, in them that are saved, and in them that perish:

B

Acts 17. 18 Then certain philosophers of the Epicureans, and of the Stoics, encountered him. And some said, What will this babbler say? other some, He seemeth to be a setter forth of strange gods: because he preached unto them Jesus, and the resurrection.

I Cor. 2. 14 But the natural man receiveth not the things of the Spirit of God: for they are foolishness unto him: neither can he know *them*, because they are spiritually discerned.

C

Rom. 1. 16. *See m, M, §318, page 810.*

I Cor. 1. 24. *See text of topic.*

D

Job 5. 12 He disappointeth the devices of the crafty, so that their hands cannot perform *their* enterprise.

13 He taketh the wise in their own craftiness: and the counsel of the froward is carried headlong.

Isa. 29. 14 Therefore, behold, I will proceed to do a marvellous work among this people, *even* a marvellous work and a wonder: for the wisdom of their wise *men* shall perish, and the understanding of their prudent *men* shall be hid.

Jer. 8. 9 The wise *men* are ashamed, they are dismayed and taken: lo, they have rejected the word of the LORD; and what wisdom *is* in them?

E

Isa. 33. 18 Thine heart shall meditate terror. Where *is* the scribe? where *is* the receiver? where *is* he that counted the towers?

F

Job 12. 17 He leadeth counsellors away spoiled, and maketh the judges fools.

Job 12. 20 He removeth away the speech of the trusty, and taketh away the understanding of the aged.

Job 12. 24 He taketh away the heart of the chief of the people of the earth, and causeth them to wander in a wilderness *where there is* no way.

Isa. 44. 25 That frustrateth the tokens of the liars, and maketh diviners mad; that turneth wise *men* backward, and maketh their knowledge foolish;

Rom. 1. 22 Professing themselves to be wise, they became fools,

AND THE WISDOM OF GOD.

G

Matt. 11. 25 At that time Jesus answered and said, I thank thee, O Father, Lord of heaven and earth, because thou hast hid these things from the wise and prudent, and hast revealed them unto babes.

Rom. 1. 20 For the invisible things of him from the creation of the world are clearly seen, being understood by the things that are made, *even* his eternal power and Godhead; so that they are without excuse:

21 Because that, when they knew God, they glorified *him* not as God, neither were thankful; but became vain in their imaginations, and their foolish heart was darkened.

Rom. 1. 28 And even as they did not like to retain God in *their* knowledge, God gave them over to a reprobate mind, to do those things which are not convenient;

H

Matt. 12. 38 Then certain of the scribes and of the Pharisees answered, saying, Master, we would see a sign from thee.

Matt. 16. 1 The Pharisees also with the Sadducees came, and tempting desired him that he would shew them a sign from heaven.

Mark 8. 11 And the Pharisees came forth, and began to question with him, seeking of him a sign from heaven, tempting him.

Luke 11. 16 And others, tempting *him*, sought of him a sign from heaven.

John 4. 48 Then said Jesus unto him, Except ye see signs and wonders, ye will not believe.

I

Isa 8. 14 And he shall be for a sanctuary; but for a stone of stumbling and for a rock of offence to both the houses of Israel, for a gin and for a snare to the inhabitants of Jerusalem.

Matt. 11. 6 And blessed is *he*, whosoever shall not be offended in me.

Matt. 13. 57 And they were offended in him. But Jesus said unto them, A prophet is not without honour, save in his own country, and in his own house.

Luke 2. 34 And Simeon blessed them, and said unto Mary his mother, Behold, this *child* is set for the fall and rising again of many in Israel; and for a sign which shall be spoken against;

John 6. 60 Many therefore of his disciples, when they had heard *this*, said, This is a hard saying; who can hear it?

I—CONCLUDED.

John 6. 66 From that *time* many of his disciples went back, and walked no more with him.

Rom. 9. 32 Wherefore? Because *they sought it* not by faith, but as it were by the works of the law. For they stumbled at that stumblingstone;

Gal. 5. 11 And I, brethren, if I yet preach circumcision, why do I yet suffer persecution? then is the offence of the cross ceased.

I Pet. 2. 8 And a stone of stumbling, and a rock of offence, *even to them* which stumble at the word, being disobedient: whereunto also they were appointed.

K

I Cor. 1. 18. *See text of topic.*

L

I Cor. 1. 18. *See text of topic.*

M

Col. 2. 3 In whom are hid all the treasures of wisdom and knowledge.

N

Zeph. 3. 12 I will also leave in the midst of thee an afflicted and poor people, and they shall trust in the name of the LORD.

John 7. 48 Have any of the rulers or of the Pharisees believed on him?

Luke 18. 24 And when Jesus saw that he was very sorrowful, he said: How hardly shall they that have riches enter into the kingdom of God!

25 For it is easier for a camel to go through a needle's eye, than for a rich man to enter into the kingdom of God.

O

Ps. 8. 2 Out of the mouth of babes and sucklings hast thou ordained strength because of thine enemies, that thou mightest still the enemy and the avenger.

Matt. 11. 25. *See under G.*

Matt. 21. 16 And said unto him, Hearest thou what these say? And Jesus saith unto them, Yea; have ye never read, Out of the mouth of babes and sucklings thou hast perfected praise?

Luke 19. 39 And some of the Pharisees from among the multitude said unto him, Master, rebuke thy disciples.

40 And he answered and said unto them, I tell you that, if these should hold their peace, the stones would immediately cry out.

II Cor. 4. 7 But we have this treasure in earthen vessels, that the excellency of

For O concluded and P, see next page

CHAP. 1.

are not, [q]to bring to nought things
that are:

29 [r]That no flesh should glory in
his presence.

30 But of him are ye in Christ Jesus, who of God is made unto us [s]wis-
dom, and [t]righteousness, and [u]sanc-
tification, and [x]redemption:

31 That, according as it is written,
[y]He that glorieth, let him glory in
the Lord.

O—CONTINUED.

the power may be of God, and not of us.

IICor. 10. 4 (For the weapons of our warfare *are* not carnal, but mighty through God to the pulling down of strong holds;)

5 Casting down imaginations, and every high thing that exhalteth itself

§ 351. THE WISDOM OF MAN AND

O—CONCLUDED.

against the knowledge of God, and bringing into captivity every thought to the obedience of Christ;

IICor. 10. 10 For *his* letters, say they, *are* weighty and powerful: but *his* bodily presence *is* weak, and *his* speech contemptible.

Jas. 2. 5 Hearken, my beloved brethren, Hath not God chosen the poor of this world rich in faith, and heirs of the kingdom which he hath promised to them that love him?

P

Rom. 4. 17. *See, t, T, §325, page 828.*

Q

ICor. 2. 6 Howbeit we speak wisdom among them that are perfect: yet not the wisdom of this world, nor of the princes of this world, that come to nought:

R

Rom. 3. 27. *See r, R, §324, page 826.*

S

I Cor. 1. 24. *See Text of Topic, page 892.*

§ 352. PAUL DECLARES HIS PREACHING WAS OF THE SPIRIT

2:1-16.

1 And I, brethren, when I came to
you, [a]came not with excellency of
speech or of wisdom, declaring unto
you the [b]testimony of God.

2 For I determined not to know
any thing among you, [c]save Jesus
Christ, and him crucified.

3 And [d]I was with you [e]in weakness,
and in fear, and in much trembling.

4 And my speech and my preach-
ing [f]*was* not with [1]enticing words of
man's wisdom, [g]but in demonstration
of the Spirit and of power:

5 That your faith should not [2]stand
in the wisdom of men, but [h]in the
power of God.

6 Howbeit we speak wisdom among
them that are [i]perfect: yet not [k]the wisdom of this world, nor of the princes

A

I Cor. 1. 17. *See k, K, §350, page 890.*

B

I Cor. 1. 6. *See c, C, §349, page 888.*

C

Gal. 6. 14 But God forbid that I should glory, save in the cross of our Lord Jesus Christ, by whom the world is crucified unto me, and I unto the world.

Phil. 3. 8 Yea doubtless, and I count all things *but* loss for the excellency of the knowledge of Christ Jesus my Lord: for whom I have suffered the loss of all things, and do count them *but* dung, that I may win Christ,

D

Acts 18. 1 After these things Paul departed from Athens, and came to Corinth;

Acts 18. 6 And when they opposed themselves, and blasphemed, he shook *his* raiment, and said unto them, Your blood *be* upon your own heads; I *am* clean: from henceforth I will go unto the Gentiles.

Acts 18. 12 And when Gallio was the deputy of Achaia, the Jews made insurrection with one accord against Paul, and brought him to the judgment seat,

THE WISDOM OF GOD (CONCLUDED).

T

Isa. 45. 24 Surely, shall *one* say, In the LORD have I righteousness and strength: *even* to him shall *men* come; and all that are incensed against him shall be ashamed.

Jer. 23. 5 Behold, the days come, saith the LORD, that I will raise unto David a righteous Branch, and a King shall reign and prosper, and shall execute judgment and justice in the earth.

6 In his days Judah shall be saved, and Israel shall dwell safely: and this *is* his name whereby he shall be called, THE LORD OUR RIGHTEOUSNESS.

Rom. 4. 25 Who was delivered for our offences, and was raised again for our justification.

IICor. 5. 21 For he hath made him *to be* sin for us, who knew no sin; that we might be made the righteousness of God in him.

Phil. 3. 9 And be found in him, not having mine own righteousness, which is of the law, but that which is through the

T—CONCLUDED.

faith of Christ, the righteousness, which is of God by faith:

U

John 17. 19 And for their sakes I sanctify myself, that they also might be sanctified through the truth.

X

Eph. 1. 7 In whom we have redemption through his blood, the forgiveness of sins, according to the riches of his grace;

Y

Jer. 9. 23 Thus saith the LORD, Let not the wise *man* glory in his wisdom, neither let the mighty *man* glory in his might, let not the rich *man* glory in his riches:

24 But let him that glorieth glory in this, that he understandeth and knoweth me, that I *am* the LORD which exercise lovingkindness, in the earth: for in these *things* I delight, saith the LORD.

IICor. 10. 17 But he that glorieth, let him glory in the Lord.

WITH POWER, WHICH THE NATURAL MAN RECEIVETH NOT.

E

IICor. 4. 7 But we have this treasure in earthen vessels, that the excellency of the power may be of God, and not of us.

IICor. 7. 5 For, when we were come into Macedonia, our flesh had no rest, but we were troubled on every side; without *were* fightings, within were fears.

IICor. 10. 1 Now I Paul myself beseech you by the meekness and gentleness of Christ, who in presence *am* base among you, but being absent am bold toward you:

II Cor. 10. 10. *See under O, § 351.*

IICor. 11. 30 If I must needs glory, I will glory of the things which concern mine infirmities.

IICor. 12. 5 Of such a one will I glory: yet of myself I will not glory, but in mine infirmities.

IICor. 12. 9 And he said unto me, My grace is sufficient for thee: for my strength is made perfect in weakness. Most gladly therefore will I rather glory in my infirmities, that the power of Christ may rest upon me.

Gal. 4. 13 Ye know how through infirmity of the flesh I preached the gospel unto you at the first.

F

I Cor. 1. 17. *See k, K, § 350, page 890.*

1

Or, *persuasible.*

G

Rom. 15. 19 Through mighty signs and wonders, by the power of the Spirit of God; so that from Jerusalem, and round about unto Illyricum, I have fully preached the gospel of Christ.

IThes. 1. 5 For our gospel came not unto you in word only, but also in power, and in the Holy Ghost, and in much assurance; as ye know what manner of men we were among you for your sake.

2

Gr. *be.*

H

II Cor. 4. 7. *See under E.*

IICor. 6. 7 By the word of truth, by the power of God, by the armour of righteousness on the right hand and on the left,

I

Job 1. 1 There was a man in the land of Uz, whose name *was* Job; and that man was perfect and upright, and one that feared God, and eschewed evil.

Ps. 37. 37 Mark the perfect *man*, and behold the upright: for the end of *that* man *is* peace.

Matt. 5. 48 Be ye therefore perfect, even as

For I concluded and K, see next page (896).

§ 352. PAUL DECLARES HIS PREACHING WAS OF THE SPIRIT WITH

CHAP. 2.

of this world, [l]that come to nought:

7 But we speak the wisdom of God in a mystery, *even* the hidden *wisdom*, [m]which God ordained before the world unto our glory:

8 [n]Which none of the princes of this world knew: for [o]had they known *it*, they would not have crucified the Lord of glory.

9 But as it is written, [p]Eye hath not seen, nor ear heard, neither have entered into the heart of man, the things which God hath prepared for them that love him.

10 [q]But God hath revealed *them* unto us by his Spirit: for the Spirit searcheth all things, yea, the deep things of God.

11 For what man knoweth the things of a man, [r]save the spirit of man which is in him? [s]even so the things of God knoweth no man, but the Spirit of God.

12 Now we have received, not the spirit of the world, but [t]the Spirit which is of God; that we might know the things that are freely given to us of God.

13 [u]Which things also we speak, not in the words which man's wisdom teacheth, but which the Holy Ghost teacheth; comparing spiritual things with spiritual.

14 [x]But the natural man receiveth not the things of the Spirit of God: [y]for they are foolishness unto him: [z]neither can he know *them*, because they are spiritually discerned.

15 [a]But he that is spiritual [3]judgeth all things, yet he himself is [4]judged of no man.

CHAP. 2.

16 [b]For who hath known the mind of the Lord, that he [5]may instruct him? [c]But we have the mind of Christ.

I—CONCLUDED.

your Father which is in heaven is perfect.

Matt. 19. 21 Jesus said unto him, If thou wilt be perfect, go *and* sell that thou hast, and give to the poor, and thou shalt have treasure in heaven: and come *and* follow me.

I Cor. 14. 20 Brethren, be not children in understanding: howbeit in malice be ye children, but in understanding be men.

II Cor. 13. 11 Finally, brethren, farewell. Be perfect, be of good comfort, be of one mind, live in peace; and the God of love and peace shall be with you.

Eph. 4. 11 And he gave some, apostles; and some, prophets; and some, evangelists; and some, pastors and teachers;

12 For the perfecting of the saints, for the work of the ministry, for the edifying of the body of Christ:

13 Till we all come in the unity of the faith, and of the knowledge of the Son of God, unto a perfect man, unto the measure of the stature of the fullness of Christ:

Phil. 3. 12 Not as though I had already attained, either were already perfect: but I follow after, if that I may apprehend that for which also I am apprehended of Christ Jesus.

Phil. 3. 15 Let us therefore, as many as be perfect, be thus minded: and if in any thing ye be otherwise minded, God shall reveal even this unto you.

Col. 4. 12 Epaphras, who is *one* of you, a servant of Christ, saluteth you, always labouring fervently for you in prayers, that ye may stand perfect and complete in all the will of God.

Heb. 5. 14 But strong meat belongeth to them that are of full age, *even* those who by reason of use have their senses exercised to discern both good and evil.

Jas. 3. 2 For in many things we offend all. If any man offend not in word, the same *is* a perfect man, *and* able also to bridle the whole body.

I Pet. 5. 10 But the God of all grace, who hath called us unto his eternal glory by Christ Jesus, after that ye have suffered a while, make you perfect, stablish, strengthen, settle *you*.

POWER, WHICH THE NATURAL MAN RECEIVETH NOT (CONCLUDED).

K

I Cor. 3. 19. *See b, B, § 355, page 900.*

L

I Cor. 1. 28. *See q, Q, § 351, page 894.*

M

Rom. 16. 25, 26. *See e, E, § 347, page 886.*

N

Matt. 11. 25 At that time Jesus answered and said, I thank thee, O Father, Lord of heaven and earth, because thou hast hid these things from the wise and prudent, and hast revealed them unto babes.

John 7 48 Have any of the rulers or of the Pharisees believed on him?

II Cor. 3. 14 But their minds were blinded: for until this day remaineth the same vail untaken away in the reading of the old testament; which *vail* is done away in Christ.

O

Acts 13. 27. *See a, A, § 262, page 714.*

P

Isa. 64. 4 For since the beginning of the world *men* have not heard, nor perceived by the ear, neither hath the eye seen, O God, besides thee, *what* he hath prepared for him that waiteth for him.

Q

Matt. 13. 11 He answered and said unto them, Because it is given unto you to know the mysteries of the kingdom of heaven, but to them it is not given.

Matt. 16. 17 And Jesus answered and said unto him, Blessed art thou, Simon Bar-jona: for flesh and blood hath not revealed *it* unto thee, but my Father which is in heaven.

John 14. 26 But the Comforter, *which is* the Holy Ghost, whom the Father will send in my name, he shall teach you all things, and bring all things to your remembrance, whatsoever I have said unto you.

John 16. 13 Howbeit when he, the Spirit of truth, is come, he will guide you into all truth: for he shall not speak of himself; but whatsoever he shall hear, *that* shall he speak: and he will shew you things to come.

Eph. 3. 5 Which in other ages was not made known unto the sons of men, as it is now revealed unto his holy apostles and prophets by the Spirit;

I Jno. 2. 27 But the anointing which ye have received of him abideth in you, and ye need not that any man teach you: but as the same anointing teacheth you of

Q—CONCLUDED.

all things, and is truth, and is no lie, and even as it hath taught you, ye shall abide in him.

R

Prov. 27. 19 As in water face *answereth* to face so the heart of man to man.

Jer. 17. 9 The heart *is* deceitful above all *things*, and desperately wicked: who can know it?

S

Rom. 11. 33 O the depth of the riches both of the wisdom and knowledge of God! how unsearchable *are* his judgments, and his ways past finding out!

34 For who hath known the mind of the Lord? or who hath been his counsellor?

T

Rom. 8. 15. *See z, Z, § 332, page 844.*

U

I Cor. 1. 17. *See k, K, § 350, page 890.*

X

Matt. 16. 23 But he turned, and said unto Peter, Get thee behind me, Satan: thou art an offence unto me: for thou savourest not the things that be of God, but those that be of men.

Y

I Cor. 1. 18. *See b, B, § 351, page 392.*

Z

Rom. 8. 5, 6 and 7. *See h, H, § 332, page 844.*

Jude 19 These be they who separate themselves, sensual, having not the Spirit.

A

Prov. 28. 5 Evil men understand not judgment: but they that seek the LORD understand all *things*.

I Thes. 5. 21 Prove all things; hold fast that which is good.

I Jno. 4. 1 Beloved, believe not every spirit, but try the spirits whether they are of God: because many false prophets are gone out into the world.

3

Or, *discerneth.*

4

Or, *discerned.*

B

Rom. 11. 34. *See n, N, § 341, page 866.*

5

Gr. *shall.*

C

John 15. 15 Henceforth I call you not servants; for the servant knoweth not what his lord doeth: but I have called you friends; for all things that I have heard of my Father I have made known unto you.

§ 353. REBUKE FOR CARNAL WALK AFTER THE

3 : 1–9.

1 And I, brethren, could not speak unto you as unto [a]spiritual, but as unto [b]carnal, *even* as unto babes in Christ.

2 I have fed you with [c]milk, and not with meat: [d]for hitherto ye were not able *to bear it,* neither yet now are ye able.

3 For ye are yet carnal: for [e]whereas *there is* among you envying, and strife, and [1]divisions, are ye not carnal, and walk [2]as men?

4 For while one saith, [f]I am of Paul; and another, I *am* of Apollos; are ye not carnal?

5 Who then is Paul, and who *is* Apollos, but [g]ministers by whom ye believed, [h]even as the Lord gave to every man?

6 [i]I have planted, [k]Apollos watered; but [l]God gave the increase.

7 So then [m]neither is he that planteth any thing, neither he that watereth; but God that giveth the increase.

8 Now he that planteth and he that watereth are one: [n]and every man shall receive his own reward according to his own labour.

9 For [o]we are labourers together with God: ye are God's [3]husbandry, *ye are* God's building.

A

I Cor. 2. 15. *See a, A, § 352, page 896.*

B

I Cor. 2. 14. *See x, X, § 352, page 896.*

C

Heb. 5. 12 For when for the time ye ought to be teachers, ye have need that one teach you again which *be* the first principles of the oracles of God; and are become such as have need of milk, and not of strong meat.

13 For every one that useth milk *is* unskilful in the word of righteousness: for he is a babe.

I Pet. 2. 2 As newborn babes, desire the sincere milk of the word, that ye may grow thereby:

D

John 16. 12 I have yet many things to say unto you, but ye cannot bear them now.

E

I Cor. 1. 11 For it hath been declared unto me of you, my brethren, by them *which are of the house* of Chloe, that there are contentions among you.

I Cor. 11. 18 For first of all, when ye come together in the church, I hear that there be divisions among you; and I partly believe it.

Gal. 5. 20 Idolatry, witchcraft, hatred, variance, emulations, wrath, strife, seditions, heresies,

21 Envyings, murders, drunkenness, revelings, and such like: of the which I tell you before, as I have also told *you* in time past, that they which do such things shall not inherit the kingdom of God.

1

Or, *factions.*

2

Gr. *according to man?*

F

I Cor. 1. 12. *See b, B, § 350, page 890.*

§ 354. CHRIST THE FOUNDATION. EACH

3 : 10-17.

10 [a]According to the grace of God which is given unto me, as a wise masterbuilder, I have laid [b]the foundation and another buildeth thereon. But [c]let every man take heed how he

A

Rom. 1. 5. *See i, I, § 317, page 808.*

B

Rom. 15. 20 Yea, so have I strived to preach the gospel, not where Christ was named, lest I should build upon another man's foundation:

I Cor. 3. 6. *See text of topic, § 353.*

I Cor. 4. 15 For though ye have ten thousand

MANNER OF MEN. WE ARE GOD'S FELLOW-WORKERS.

G

I Cor. 4. 1 Let a man so account of us, as of the ministers of Christ, and stewards of the mysteries of God.

IICor. 3. 3 *Forasmuch as ye are* manifestly declared to be the epistle of Christ ministered by us, written not with ink, but with the Spirit of the living God; not in tables of stone, but in fleshly tables of the heart.

H

Rom. 12. 3 and 6. *See m, M, § 342, page 868.*

I

Acts 18. 4 And he reasoned in the synagogue every sabbath, and persuaded the Jews and the Greeks.

Acts 18. 8 And Crispus, the chief ruler of the synagogue, believed on the Lord with all his house; and many of the Corinthians hearing believed, and were baptized.

Acts 18. 11 And he continued *there* a year and six months, teaching the word of God among them.

K

Acts 18. 24 And a certain Jew named Apollos, born at Alexandria, an eloquent man, *and* mighty in the Scriptures, came to Ephesus.

Acts 18. 27 And when he was disposed to pass into Achaia, the brethren wrote, exhorting the disciples to receive him: who, when he was come, helped them much which had believed through grace:

Acts 19. 1 And it came to pass, that, while Apollos was at Corinth, Paul having passed through the upper coasts came to Ephesus: and finding certain disciples,

L

I Cor. 1. 30 But of him are ye in Christ Jesus, who of God is made unto us wisdom, and righteousness, and sanctification, and redemption:

L—Concluded.

ICor. 15. 10 But by the grace of God I am what I am: and his grace which *was bestowed* upon me was not in vain; but I laboured more abundantly than they all: yet not I, but the grace of God which was with me.

IICor. 3. 5 Not that we are sufficient of ourselves to think any thing as of ourselves; but our sufficiency *is* of God;

M

IICor. 12. 11 I am become a fool in glorying; ye have compelled me: for I ought to have been commended of you: for in nothing am I behind the very chiefest apostles, though I be nothing.

Gal. 6. 3 For if a man think himself to be something, when he is nothing, he deceiveth himself.

N

Rom. 2. 6. *See h, H, § 320, page 816.*

I Cor. 4. 5 Therefore judge nothing before the time, until the Lord come, who both will bring to light the hidden things of darkness, and will make manifest the counsels of the hearts: and then shall every man have praise of God.

Gal. 6. 4 But let every man prove his own work, and then shall he have rejoicing in himself alone, and not in another.
5 For every man shall bear his own burden.

Rev. 2. 23 And I will kill her children with death; and all the churches shall know that I am he which searcheth the reins and hearts: and I will give unto every one of you according to your works.

O

Acts 15. 4 And when they were come to Jerusalem, they were received of the church, and *of* the apostles and elders, and they declared all things that God had done with them.

II Cor. 6. 1 We then, *as* workers together *with him*, beseech *you* also that ye receive not the grace of God in vain.

3

Or, *tillage.*

BUILDER'S WORK THEREON TRIED BY FIRE.

B—Concluded.

instructors in Christ, yet *have ye* not many fathers: for in Christ Jesus I have begotten you through the gospel.

Rev. 21. 14 And the wall of the city had twelve foundations, and in them the names of the twelve apostles of the Lamb.

C

I Pet. 4. 11 If any man speak, *let him speak* as the oracles of God; if any man minister, *let him do it* as of the ability which God giveth; that God in all things may be glorified through Jesus Christ, to whom be praise and dominion for ever and ever. Amen.

§ 354. CHRIST THE FOUNDATION. EACH BUILDER'S

CHAP. 3.

buildeth thereupon.

11 For other foundation can no man lay than [d]that is laid, [e]which is Jesus Christ.

12 Now if any man build upon this foundation gold, silver, precious stones, wood, hay, stubble;

13 [f]Every man's work shall be made manifest: for the day [g]shall declare it, because [h]it [1]shall be revealed by fire; [i]and the fire shall try every man's work of what sort it is.

14 If any man's work abide which he hath built thereupon, [k]he shall receive a reward.

15 If any man's work shall be burned, he shall suffer loss: but he himself shall be saved; [l]yet so as by fire.

16 [m]Know ye not that ye are the temple of God, and *that* the Spirit of God dwelleth in you?

17 If any man [2]defile the temple of God, him shall God destroy; for the temple of God is holy, which *temple* ye are.

D

Isa. 28. 16 Therefore thus saith the Lord GOD, Behold, I lay in Zion for a foundation a stone, a tried stone, a precious corner *stone*, a sure foundation: he that believeth shall not make haste.

Matt. 16. 18 And I say also unto thee, That thou art Peter, and upon this rock I

D—CONCLUDED.

will build my church; and the gates of hell shall not prevail against it.

E

Eph. 2. 20 And are built upon the foundation of the apostles and prophets, Jesus Christ himself being the chief corner *stone;*

F

I Cor. 4. 5 Therefore judge nothing before the time, until the Lord come, who both will bring to light the hidden things of darkness, and will make manifest the counsels of the hearts: and then shall every man have praise of God.

G

I Pet. 1. 7 That the trial of your faith, being much more precious than of gold that perisheth, though it be tried with fire, might be found unto praise and honour and glory at the appearing of Jesus Christ:

I Pet. 4. 12 Beloved, think it not strange concerning the fiery trial which is to try you, as though some strange thing happened unto you:

H

Luke 2. 35 (Yea, a sword shall pierce through thy own soul also,) that the thoughts of many hearts may be revealed.

1

Gr. *is revealed.*

I

Isa. 8. 20 To the law and to the testimony: if they speak not according to this word, *it is* because *there is* no light in them.

Isa. 28. 17 Judgment also will I lay to the line, and righteousness to the plummet: and the hail shall sweep away the refuge of lies, and the waters shall overflow the hiding place.

Jer. 23. 29 *Is* not my word like as a fire? saith the LORD; and like a hammer *that* breaketh the rock in pieces?

Zech. 13. 9 And I will bring the third part through the fire, and will refine them

§ 355. LET NO ONE

3:18–23.

18 [a]Let no man deceive himself. If any man among you seemeth to be wise in this world, let him become a fool, that he may be wise.

CHAP. 3.

19 For [b]the wisdom of this world is foolishness with God. For it is written, [c]He taketh the wise in their own craftiness.

WORK THEREON TRIED BY FIRE (Concluded).

I—Concluded.

as silver is refined, and will try them as gold is tried: they shall call on my name, and I will hear them: I will say, It *is* my people: and they shall say, The LORD *is* my God.

K

Da. 12. 3 And they that be wise shall shine as the brightness of the firmament; and they that turn many to righteousness as the stars for ever and ever.

Matt. 24. 46 Blessed *is* that servant, whom his Lord when he cometh shall find so doing.

47 Verily I say unto you, That he shall make him ruler over all his goods.

Matt. 25. 21 His lord said unto him, Well done, *thou* good and faithful servant: thou hast been faithful over a few things, I will make thee ruler over many things: enter thou into the joy of thy lord.

I Cor. 4. 5. *See under F.*

I Thes. 2. 19 For what *is* our hope, or joy, or crown of rejoicing? *Are* not even ye in the presence of our Lord Jesus Christ at his coming?

II Tim. 4. 7 I have fought a good fight, I have finished *my* course, I have kept the faith:

8 Henceforth there is laid up for me a crown of righteousness, which the Lord, the righteous judge, shall give me at that day: and not to me only, but unto all them also that love his appearing.

Jas. 1. 12 Blessed *is* the man that endureth temptation: for when he is tried, he shall receive the crown of life, which the Lord hath promised to them that love him.

I Pet. 5. 1 The elders which are among you I exhort, who am also an elder, and a witness of the sufferings of Christ, and also a partaker of the glory that shall be revealed:

I Pet. 5. 4 And when the chief Shepherd shall appear, ye shall receive a crown of glory that fadeth not away.

K—Concluded.

Rev. 2. 10 Fear none of those things which thou shalt suffer: behold, the devil shall cast *some* of you into prison, that ye may be tried; and ye shall have tribulation ten days: be thou faithful unto death, and I will give thee a crown of life.

L

Amos 4. 11 I have overthrown *some* of you, as God overthrew Sodom and Gomorrah, and ye were as a firebrand plucked out of the burning: yet have ye not returned unto me, saith the LORD.

I Pet. 4. 18 And if the righteous scarcely be saved, where shall the ungodly and the sinner appear?

Jude 23 And others save with fear, pulling *them* out of the fire; hating even the garment spotted by the flesh.

M

I Cor. 6. 19 What? know ye not that your body is the temple of the Holy Ghost *which is* in you, which ye have of God, and ye are not your own?

II Cor. 6. 16 And what agreement hath the temple of God with idols? for ye are the temple of the living God; as God hath said, I will dwell in them, and walk in *them;* and I will be their God, and they shall be my people.

Eph. 2. 21 In whom all the building fitly framed together groweth unto a holy temple in the Lord:

22 In whom ye also are builded together for a habitation of God through the Spirit.

Heb. 3. 6 But Christ as a son over his own house; whose house are we, if we hold fast the confidence and the rejoicing of the hope firm unto the end.

I Pet. 2. 5 Ye also, as lively stones, are built up a spiritual house, a holy priesthood, to offer up spiritual sacrifices, acceptable to God by Jesus Christ.

2 Or, *destroy.*

GLORY IN MEN.

A

Prov. 3. 7 Be not wise in thine own eyes: fear the LORD, and depart from evil.

Isa. 5. 21 Woe unto *them that are* wise in their own eyes, and prudent in their own sight!

B

I Cor. 1. 20 Where *is* the wise? where *is* the scribe? where *is* the disputer of this world? Hath not God made foolish the wisdom of this world?

I Cor. 2. 1 And I, brethren, when I came to you, came not with excellency of speech

For B concluded and C see next page (902)

§ 355. LET NO ONE GLORY

CHAP. 3.

20 And again, [d]The Lord knoweth the thoughts of the wise, that they are vain.

21 Therefore [e]let no man glory in men. For [f]all things are yours;

22 Whether Paul, or Apollos, or Cephas, or the world, or life, or death, or things present, or things to come; all are yours;

23 And [g]ye are Christ's; and Christ *is* God's.

B—CONTINUED.

or of wisdom, declaring unto you the testimony of God.

B—CONCLUDED.

I Cor. 2. 6 Howbeit we speak wisdom among them that are perfect: yet not the wisdom of this world, nor of the princes of this world, that come to nought:

I Cor. 2. 13 Which things also we speak, not in the words which man's wisdom teacheth, but which the Holy Ghost teacheth; comparing spiritual things with spiritual.

II Cor. 1. 12 For our rejoicing is this, the testimony of our conscience, that in simplicity and godly sincerity, not with fleshly wisdom, but by the grace of God, we have had our conversation in the world, and more abundantly to you-ward.

Jas. 3. 15 This wisdom descendeth not from above, but *is* earthly, sensual, devilish.

§ 356. JUDGE NOTHING BEFORE THE TIME. THE LORD WILL

4: 1–5.

1 Let a man so account of us, as of [a]the ministers of Christ, [b]and stewards of the mysteries of God.

2 Moreover it is required in stewards, that a man be found faithful.

3 But with me it is a very small thing that I should be judged of you, or of man's [1]judgment: yea, I judge not mine own self.

4 For I know nothing by myself; [c]yet am I not hereby justified: but he that judgeth me is the Lord.

5 [d]Therefore judge nothing before the time, until the Lord come, [e]who

CHAP. 4.

both will bring to light the hidden things of darkness, and will make manifest the counsels of the hearts: and then shall every man have praise of God.

A

I Cor. 3. 5. *See g, G, § 353, page 898.*

I Cor. 9. 17 For if I do this thing willingly, I have a reward: but if against my will, a dispensation *of the gospel* is committed unto me.

II Cor. 6. 4 But in all *things* approving ourselves as the ministers of God, in much patience, in afflictions, in necessities, in distresses,

Col. 1. 25 Whereof I am made a minister, according to the dispensation of God

§ 357. ADMONISHED NOT TO BE PUFFED UP AGAINST EACH

4: 6–13.

6 And these things, brethren, [a]I have in a figure transferred to myself and *to* Apollos for your sakes; [b]that ye might learn in us not to think *of men* above that which is written, that no one of you [c]be puffed up for one against another.

CHAP. 4.

7 For who [1]maketh thee to differ *from another?* and [d]what hast thou that thou didst not receive? now if thou didst receive *it*, why dost thou glory, as if thou hadst not received *it?*

A

I Cor. 1. 12. *See b, B, § 350, page 890.*

IN MEN (CONCLUDED).

C

I Cor. 1. 19. *See d, D, § 351, page 892.*

D

Ps. 94. 11 The LORD knoweth the thoughts of man, that they *are* vanity.

E

Jer 9. 23 Thus saith the LORD, Let not the wise *man* glory in his wisdom, neither let the mighty *man* glory in his might, let not the rich *man* glory in his riches:
24 But let him that glorieth glory in this, that he understandeth and knoweth me, that I *am* the LORD which exercise lovingkindness, judgment, and righteousness, in the earth: for in these *things* I delight, saith the LORD.

I Cor. 1. 12 Now this I say, that every one of

E—CONCLUDED.

you saith, I am of Paul; and I of Apollos; and I of Cephas; and I of Christ.

I Cor. 3. 4, 5 and 6. *See text of topic, § 333, page 898.*

F

II Cor. 4. 5 For we preach not ourselves, but Christ Jesus the Lord; and ourselves your servants for Jesus' sake.

II Cor. 4. 15 For all things *are* for your sakes, that the abundant grace might through the thanksgiving of many redound to the glory of God.

G

II Cor. 10. 7 Do ye look on things after the outward appearance? If any man trust to himself that he is Christ's, let him of himself think this again, that, as he *is* Christ's, even so *are* we Christ's.

BRING TO LIGHT HIDDEN THINGS OF DARKNESS WHEN HE COMES.

A—CONCLUDED.

which is given to me for you, to fulfil the word of God;

B

Matt. 24. 45 Who then is a faithful and wise servant, whom his lord hath made ruler over his household, to give them meat in due season?

Luke 12. 42 And the Lord said, Who then is that faithful and wise steward, whom *his* lord shall make ruler over his household, to give *them their* portion of meat in due season?

Tit. 1. 7 For a bishop must be blameless, as the steward of God; not selfwilled, not soon angry, not given to wine, no striker, not given to filthy lucre;

I Pet. 4. 10 As every man hath received the gift, *even so* minister the same one to another, as good stewards of the manifold grace of God.

1

Gr. *day.*

C

Job 9. 2 I know *it is* so of a truth: but how should man be just with God?

Prov. 21. 2 Every way of a man *is* right in his own eyes: but the LORD pondereth the hearts.

Rom. 3. 20. *See c, C, § 324, page 824.*

Rom. 4. 2 For if Abraham were justified by works, he hath *whereof* to glory; but not before God.

D

Rom. 2. 1. *See b, B, § 320, page 814.*

Rom. 2. 16. *See o, O, § 320, page 818.*

E

I Cor. 3. 13 Every man's work shall be made manifest: for the day shall declare it, because it shall be revealed by fire; and the fire shall try every man's work of what sort it is.

OTHER. THE APOSTLES WERE MADE SPECTACLES UNTO THE WORLD.

B

Rom. 12. 3 For I say, through the grace given unto me, to every man that is among you, not to think *of himself* more highly than he ought to think; but to think soberly, according as God hath dealt to every man the measure of faith.

C

I Cor. 3. 21 Therefore let no man glory in men. For all things are yours;

I Cor. 5. 2 And ye are puffed up, and have not rather mourned, that he that hath done

C—CONCLUDED.

this deed might be taken away from among you.

I Cor. 5. 6 Your glorying *is* not good. Know ye not that a little leaven leaveneth the whole lump?

1

Gr. *distinguisheth thee.*

D

John 3. 27 John answered and said, A man

For D concluded, see next page (904).

§ 357. ADMONISHED NOT TO BE PUFFED UP AGAINST EACH OTHER.

CHAP. 4.

8 Now ye are full, [e]now ye are rich, ye have reigned as kings without us: and I would to God ye did reign, that we also might reign with you.

9 For I think that God hath set forth [2]us the apostles last, [f]as it were appointed to death: for [g]we are made a [3]spectacle unto the world, and to angels, and to men.

10 [h]We *are* [i]fools for Christ's sake, but ye *are* wise in Christ; [k]we *are* weak, but ye *are* strong; ye *are* honourable, but we *are* despised.

11 [l]Even unto this present hour we both hunger, and thirst, and [m]are naked, and [n]are buffeted, and have no certain dwellingplace;

12 [o]And labour, working with our own hands: [p]being reviled, we bless; being persecuted, we suffer it:

CHAP. 4.

13 Being defamed, we entreat: [q]we are made as the filth of the world, *and are* the offscouring of all things unto this day.

D—CONCLUDED.

can receive nothing, except it be given him from heaven.

Jas. 1. 17 Every good gift and every perfect gift is from above, and cometh down from the Father of lights, with whom is no variableness, neither shadow of turning.

1 Pet. 4. 10. *See under B, § 356, page 903.*

E

Rev. 3. 17 Because thou sayest, I am rich, and increased with goods, and have need of nothing; and knowest not that thou art wretched, and miserable, and poor, and blind, and naked:

2

Or, *us the last apostles, as.*

F

Rom. 8. 36. *See t, T, § 334, page 850*

II Cor. 6. 9 As unknown, and *yet* well known; as dying, and, behold, we live; as chastened, and not killed;

§ 358. ADMONISHED TO FOLLOW THE

4 : 14–21.

14 I write not these things to shame you, but [a]as my beloved sons I warn *you*.

15 For though ye have ten thousand instructors in Christ, yet *have ye* not many fathers: for [b]in Christ Jesus I have begotten you through the gospel.

16 Wherefore I beseech you, [c]be ye followers of me.

17 For this cause have I sent unto you [d]Timotheus, [e]who is my beloved son, and faithful in the Lord, who shall bring you [f]into remembrance of my ways which be in Christ, as I [g]teach every where [h]in every church.

18 [i]Now some are puffed up, as though I would not come to you.

A

I Thes. 2. 11 As ye know how we exhorted and comforted and charged every one of you, as a father *doth* his children,

B

Acts 18. 11 And he continued *there* a year and six months, teaching the word of God among them.

Rom. 15. 20 Yea, so have I strived to preach the gospel, not where Christ was named, lest I should build upon another man's foundation:

I Cor. 3. 6 I have planted, Apollos watered; but God gave the increase.

Gal. 4. 19 My little children, of whom I travail in birth again until Christ be formed in you,

Phile. 10 I beseech thee for my son Onesimus, whom I have begotten in my bonds:

Jas. 1. 18 Of his own will begat he us with the word of truth, that we should be a kind of firstfruits of his creatures.

C

I Cor. 11. 1 Be ye followers of me, even as I also *am* of Christ.

THE APOSTLES WERE MADE SPECTACLES UNTO THE WORLD (Concluded).

G

Heb. 10. 33 Partly, whilst ye were made a gazingstock both by reproaches and afflictions; and partly, whilst ye became companions of them that were so used.

3

Gr. *theatre.*

H

Acts 26. 24 And as he thus spake for himself, Festus said with a loud voice, Paul, thou art beside thyself; much learning doth make thee mad.

I Cor. 2. 3 And I was with you in weakness, and in fear, and in much trembling.

I

I Cor. 1. 18. *See b, B, §351, page 892.*

I Cor. 3. 18 Let no man deceive himself. If any man among you seemeth to be wise in this world, let him become a fool, that he may be wise.

K

II Cor. 13. 9 For we are glad, when we are weak, and ye are strong: and this also we wish, *even* your perfection.

L

II Cor. 4. 8 *We are* troubled on every side, yet not distressed; *we are* perplexed, but not in despair;

L—Concluded.

II Cor. 11. 27 In weariness and painfulness, in watchings often, in hunger and thirst, in fastings often, in cold and nakedness.

Phil. 4. 12 I know both how to be abased, and I know how to abound: every where and in all things I am instructed both to be full and to be hungry, both to abound and to suffer need.

M

Job 22. 6 For thou hast taken a pledge from thy brother for nought, and stripped the naked of their clothing.

Rom. 8. 35 Who shall separate us from the love of Christ? *shall* tribulation, or distress, or persecution, or famine, or nakedness, or peril, or sword?

N

Acts 23. 2 And the high priest Ananias commanded them that stood by him to smite him on the mouth.

O

Acts 18. 3. *See b, B, § 280, page 746.*

P

Rom. 12. 14. *See e, E, §342, page 870.*

Q

Lam. 3. 45 Thou hast made us *as* the offscouring and refuse in the midst of the people.

APOSTLE IN THE WAYS OF CHRIST.

C—Concluded.

Phil. 3. 17 Brethren, be followers together of me, and mark them which walk so as ye have us for an ensample.

I Thes. 1. 6 And ye became followers of us, and of the Lord, having received the word in much affliction, with joy of the Holy Ghost:

II Thes. 3. 9 Not because we have not power, but to make ourselves an ensample unto you to follow us.

D

Acts 16. 1. *See b, B, §271, page 732.*

E

I Tim. 1. 2 Unto Timothy, *my* own son in the faith: Grace, mercy, *and* peace, from God our Father and Jesus Christ our Lord.

II Tim. 1. 2 To Timothy, *my* dearly beloved son: Grace, mercy, *and* peace, from God the Father and Christ Jesus our Lord.

F

I Cor. 11. 2 Now I praise you, brethren, that ye remember me in all things, and keep the ordinances, as I delivered *them* to you.

G

I Cor. 7. 17 But as God hath distributed to every man, as the Lord hath called every one, so let him walk. And so ordain I in all the churches.

H

I Cor. 14. 33 For God is not *the author* of confusion, but of peace, as in all churches of the saints.

I

I Cor. 5. 2 And ye are puffed up, and have not rather mourned, that he that hath done this deed might be taken away from among you.

K

Acts. 19. 21 After these things were ended, Paul purposed in the spirit, when he had passed through Macedonia and Achaia, to go to Jerusalem, saying, After I have been there, I must also see Rome.

I Cor. 16. 5 Now I will come unto you, when I shall pass through Macedonia: for I do pass through Macedonia.

§ 358. ADMONISHED TO FOLLOW THE APOSTLE

CHAP. 4.

19 But [k]I will come to you shortly, [l]if the Lord will, and will know, not the speech of them which are puffed up, but the power.

20 For [m]the kingdom of God *is* not in word, but in power.

21 What will ye? [n]shall I come unto you with a rod, or in love, and *in* the spirit of meekness?

K—CONCLUDED, See preceding page, 905.

IICor.1. 15 And in this confidence I was minded to come unto you before, that ye might have a second benefit;

IICor.1. 23 Moreover I call God for a record upon my soul, that to spare you I came not as yet unto Corinth.

L

Acts 18. 21. *See d, D, § 282, page 750.*

M

Rom.14. 17 For the kingdom of God is not meat and drink; but righteousness, and peace, and joy in the Holy Ghost.

Rom.15. 19 Through mighty signs and wonders, by the power of the Spirit of

§ 359. FORNICATION REBUKED, AND TOGETHER WITH OTHER

5 : 1–13.

1 It is reported commonly *that there is* fornication among you, and such fornication as is not so much as [a]named among the Gentiles, [b]that one should have his father's wife.

2 [c]And ye are puffed up, and have not rather [d]mourned, [e]that he that hath done this deed might be taken away from among you.

3 [f]For I verily, as absent in body, but present in spirit, have [1]judged already, as though I were present, *concerning* him that hath so done this deed,

4 In the name of our Lord Jesus Christ, when ye are gathered together, and my spirit, with the [g]power of our Lord Jesus Christ,

5 [h]To deliver such a one unto [i]Satan for the destruction of the flesh, that the spirit may be saved in the day of the Lord Jesus.

6 [k]Your glorying *is* not good. Know ye not that [l]a little leaven leaveneth the whole lump?

7 Purge out therefore the old leaven, that ye may be a new lump, as ye are

A

Eph.5. 3 But fornication, and all uncleanness, or covetousness, let it not be once named among you, as becometh saints;

B

Lev. 18. 8 The nakedness of thy father's wife shalt thou not uncover: it *is* thy father's nakedness.

Deut. 22. 30 A man shall not take his father's wife, nor discover his father's skirt.

Deut. 27. 20 Cursed *be* he that lieth with his father's wife; because he uncovereth his father's skirt: and all the people shall say, Amen.

C

I Cor. 4. 18. *See i, I, § 358, page 904.*

D

IICor.7. 7 And not by his coming only, but by the consolation wherewith he was comforted in you, when he told us your earnest desire, your mourning, your fervent mind toward me; so that I rejoiced the more.

E

IICor.7. 12 Wherefore, though I wrote unto you, *I did it* not for his cause that had done the wrong, nor for his cause that suffered wrong, but that our care for you in the sight of God might appear unto you.

F

Col. 2. 5 For though I be absent in the flesh, yet am I with you in the spirit, joying and beholding your order, and the steadfastness of your faith in Christ.

1

Or, *determined.*

IN THE WAYS OF CHRIST (Concluded).

M—Continued.

God; so that from Jerusalem, and round about unto Illyricum, I have fully preached the gospel of Christ.

IICor. 10. 4 (For the weapons of our warfare *are* not carnal, but mighty through God to the pulling down of strong holds;)

5 Casting down imaginations, and every high thing that exalteth itself against the knowledge of God, and bringing into captivity every thought to the obedience of Christ;

IThes. 1. 5 For our gospel came not unto you in word only, but also in power, and in the Holy Ghost, and in much assurance; as ye know what manner of men we were among you for your sake.

N

IICor. 10. 2 But I beseech *you*, that I may not be bold when I am present with that confidence, wherewith I think to be bold against some, which think of us as if we walked according to the flesh.

IICor. 13. 10 Therefore I write these things being absent, lest being present I should use sharpness, according to the power which the Lord hath given me to edification, and not to destruction.

EVIL DOING TO BE ADJUDGED UNWORTHY OF FELLOWSHIP.

G

Matt. 16. 19 And I will give unto thee the keys of the kingdom of heaven: and whatsoever thou shalt bind on earth shall be bound in heaven: and whatsoever thou shalt loose on earth shall be loosed in heaven.

Matt. 18. 18 Verily I say unto you, Whatsoever ye shall bind on earth shall be bound in heaven: and whatsoever ye shall loose on earth shall be loosed in heaven.

John 20. 23 Whosesoever sins ye remit, they are remitted unto them; *and* whosesoever *sins* ye retain, they are retained.

IICor. 2. 10 To whom ye forgive any thing, I *forgive* also; for if I forgave any thing, to whom I forgave *it*, for your sakes *forgave I it* in the person of Christ:

IICor. 13. 3 Since ye seek a proof of Christ speaking in me, which to you-ward is not weak, but is mighty in you.

4 For though he was crucified through weakness, yet he liveth by the power of God. For we also are weak in him, but we shall live with him by the power of God toward you.

H

Job 2. 6 And the Lord said unto Satan, Behold, he *is* in thine hand; but save his life.

Ps. 109. 6 Set thou a wicked man over him: and let Satan stand at his right hand.

IICor. 2. 6 Sufficient to such a man *is* this punishment, which *was inflicted* of many.

IICor. 10. 6 And having in a readiness to revenge all disobedience, when your obedience is fulfilled.

H—Concluded.

II Cor. 13. 10. *See under N § 358.*

I Tim. 1. 20 Of whom is Hymeneus and Alexander; whom I have delivered unto Satan, that they may learn not to blaspheme.

I

Acts 26. 18 To open their eyes, *and* to turn *them* from darkness to light, and *from* the power of Satan unto God, that they may receive forgiveness of sins, and inheritance among them which are sanctified by faith that is in me.

K

I Cor. 3. 21. *See e, E, § 355, page 902.*

I Cor. 4. 19. *See text of topic, § 358.*

Jas. 4. 16 But now ye rejoice in your boastings: all such rejoicing is evil.

L

Matt. 13. 33 Another parable spake he unto them; The kingdom of heaven is like unto leaven, which a woman took, and hid in three measures of meal, till the whole was leavened.

Matt. 16. 6 Then Jesus said unto them, Take heed and beware of the leaven of the Pharisees and of the Sadducees.

Matt. 16. 11 How is it that ye do not understand that I spake *it* not to you concerning bread, that ye should beware of the leaven of the Pharisees and of the Sadducees?

12 Then understood they how that he bade *them* not beware of the leaven of bread, but of the doctrine of the Pharisees and of the Sadducees.

For L concluded, see next page (908).

§ 359. FORNICATION REBUKED, AND TOGETHER WITH OTHER EVIL-

CHAP. 5.

unleavened. For even [m]Christ our
[n]passover [2]is sacrificed for us:
8 Therefore [o]let us keep [3]the feast
[p]not with old leaven, neither [q]with
the leaven of malice and wickedness; but with the unleavened *bread*
of sincerity and truth.
9 I wrote unto you in an epistle
[r]not to company with fornicators:
10 [s]Yet not altogether with the
fornicators [t]of this world, or with
the covetous, or extortioners, or with
idolaters; for then must ye needs go
[u]out of the world.
11 But now I have written unto you
not to keep company, [x]if any man
that is called a brother be a fornicator, or covetous, or an idolater,
or a railer, or a drunkard, or an extortioner; with such a one [y]no not
to eat.
12 For what have I to do to judge
[z]them also that are without? do not
ye judge [a]them that are within?
13 But them that are without God
judgeth. Therefore [b]put away from
among yourselves that wicked person.

L—CONCLUDED.

Luke 13. 21 It is like leaven, which a woman took and hid in three measures of meal, till the whole was leavened.

I Cor. 15. 33 Be not deceived: evil communications corrupt good manners.

Gal. 5. 9 A little leaven leaveneth the whole lump.

II Tim. 2. 17 And their word will eat as doth a canker: of whom is Hymeneus and Philetus;

M

Isa. 53. 7 He was oppressed, and he was afflicted, yet he opened not his mouth: he is brought as a lamb to the slaughter, and as a sheep before her shearers is dumb, so he openeth not his mouth.

John 1. 29 The next day John seeth Jesus coming unto him, and saith, Behold the Lamb of God, which taketh away the sin of the world.

M—CONCLUDED.

I Cor. 15. 3 For I delivered unto you first of all that which I also received, how that Christ died for our sins according to the Scriptures:

I Pet. 1. 19 But with the precious blood of Christ, as of a lamb without blemish and without spot:

Rev. 5. 6 And I beheld, and, lo, in the midst of the throne and of the four beasts, and in the midst of the elders, stood a Lamb as it had been slain, having seven horns and seven eyes, which are the seven Spirits of God sent forth into all the earth.

Rev. 5. 12 Saying with a loud voice, Worthy is the Lamb that was slain to receive power, and riches, and wisdom, and strength, and honour, and glory, and blessing.

N

John 19. 14 And it was the preparation of the passover, and about the sixth hour: and he saith unto the Jews, Behold your King!

2

Or, *is slain.*

O

Ex. 12. 15 Seven days shall ye eat unleavened bread; even the first day ye shall put away leaven out of your houses: for whosoever eateth leavened bread from the first day until the seventh day, that soul shall be cut off from Israel.

Ex. 13. 6 Seven days thou shalt eat unleavened bread, and in the seventh day *shall be* a feast to the LORD.

3

Or, *holyday.*

P

Deut. 16. 3 Thou shalt eat no unleavened bread with it, seven days shalt thou eat unleavened bread therewith, *even* the bread of affliction; for thou camest forth out of the land of Egypt in haste: that thou mayest remember the day when thou camest forth out of the land of Egypt all the days of thy life.

Q

Matt. 16. 6 and 12. *See under L.*

Luke 12. 1 In the mean time, when there were gathered together an innumerable multitude of people, insomuch that they trode one upon another, he began to say unto his disciples first of all, Beware ye of the leaven of the Pharisees, which is hypocrisy,

DOING TO BE ADJUDGED UNWORTHY OF FELLOWSHIP (CONCLUDED).

R

I Cor. 5. 2 and 7. *See text of topic, page 906.*

II Cor. 6. 14 Be ye not unequally yoked together with unbelievers: for what fellowship hath righteousness with unrighteousness? and what communion hath light with darkness?

Eph. 5. 11 And have no fellowship with the unfruitful works of darkness, but rather reprove *them*.

II Thes. 3. 14 And if any man obey not our word by this epistle, note that man, and have no company with him, that he may be ashamed.

S

I Cor. 10. 27 If any of them that believe not bid you *to a feast*, and ye be disposed to go; whatsoever is set before you, eat, asking no questions for conscience' sake.

T

I Cor. 1. 20 Where *is* the wise? where *is* the scribe? where *is* the disputer of this world? hath not God made foolish the wisdom of this world?

Eph. 2. 2 Wherein in time past ye walked according to the course of this world, according to the prince of the power of the air, the spirit that now worketh in the children of disobedience:

U

John 17. 15 I pray not that thou shouldest take them out of the world, but that thou shouldest keep them from the evil.

Phil. 2. 15 That ye may be blameless and harmless, the sons of God, without rebuke, in the midst of a crooked and perverse nation, among whom ye shine as lights in the world;

X

Matt. 18. 17 And if he shall neglect to hear them, tell *it* unto the church: but if he neglect to hear the church, let him be unto thee as a heathen man and a publican.

Rom. 16. 17 Now I beseech you, brethren, mark them which cause divisions and offences contrary to the doctrine which ye have learned: and avoid them.

II Thes. 3 6 Now we command you, brethren, in the name of our Lord Jesus Christ, that ye withdraw yourselves from every brother that walketh disorderly, and not after the tradition which he received of us.

II Thes. 3. 14. *See under R.*

X—CONCLUDED.

II Jno. 10 If there come any unto you, and bring not this doctrine, receive him not into *your* house, neither bid him God speed:

Y

Rom. 16. 17. *See k, K, § 347, page 884.*

Gal. 2. 12 For before that certain came from James, he did eat with the Gentiles: but when they were come, he withdrew and separated himself, fearing them which were of the circumcision.

Z

Mark 4. 11 And he said unto them, Unto you it is given to know the mystery of the kingdom of God: but unto them that are without, all *these* things are done in parables:

Col. 4. 5 Walk in wisdom toward them that are without, redeeming the time.

I Thes. 4. 12 That ye may walk honestly toward them that are without, and *that* ye may have lack of nothing.

I Tim. 3. 7 Moreover he must have a good report of them which are without; lest he fall into reproach and the snare of the devil.

A

I Cor. 6. 1, 2, 3, 4. *See text of topic, § 360, page 910.*

B

Deut. 13. 5 And that prophet, or that dreamer of dreams, shall be put to death; because he hath spoken to turn *you* away from the LORD your God, which brought you out of the land of Egypt, and redeemed you out of the house of bondage, to thrust thee out of the way which the LORD thy God commanded thee to walk in. So shalt thou put the evil away from the midst of thee.

Deut. 17. 7 The hands of the witnesses shall be first upon him to put him to death, and afterward the hands of all the people. So thou shalt put the evil away from among you.

Deut. 21. 21 And all the men of his city shall stone him with stones, that he die: so shalt thou put evil away from among you; and all Israel shall hear, and fear.

Deut. 22. 21 Then they shall bring out the damsel to the door of her father's house, and the men of her city shall stone her with stones that she die; because she hath wrought folly in Israel, to play the whore in her father's house: so shalt thou put evil away from among you.

§ 360. REBUKE FOR GOING TO LAW WITH ONE ANOTHER, AND THAT BEFORE

6 : 1–11.

1 Dare any of you, having a matter against another, go to law before the unjust, and not before the saints?

2 Do ye not know that [a]the saints shall judge the world? and if the world shall be judged by you, are ye unworthy to judge the smallest matters?

3 Know ye not that we shall [b]judge angels? how much more things that pertain to this life?

4 [c]If then ye have judgments of things pertaining to this life, set them to judge who are least esteemed in the church.

5 I speak to your shame. Is it so, that there is not a wise man among you? no, not one that shall be able to judge between his brethren?

6 But brother goeth to law with brother, and that before the unbelievers.

7 Now therefore there is utterly a fault among you, because ye go to law one with another. [d]Why do ye not rather take wrong? Why do ye not rather *suffer yourselves to* be defrauded?

8 Nay, ye do wrong, and defraud, [e]and that *your* brethren.

9 Know ye not that the unrighteous shall not inherit the kingdom of God? Be not deceived: [f]neither fornicators, nor idolators, nor adulterers, nor effeminate, nor abusers of themselves with mankind,

10 Nor thieves, nor covetous, nor drunkards, nor revilers, nor extortioners, shall inherit the kingdom of God.

11 And [g]such were some of you: [h]but ye are washed, but ye are sanctified, but ye are justified in the name of the Lord Jesus, and by the Spirit of our God,

A

Ps. 49. 14 Like sheep they are laid in the grave; death shall feed on them; and the upright shall have dominion over them in the morning; and their beauty shall consume in the grave from their dwelling.

Ps. 149. 5 Let the saints be joyful in glory: let them sing aloud upon their beds.

6 *Let* the high *praises* of God *be* in their mouth, and a twoedged sword in their hand;

7 To execute vengeance upon the heathen *and* punishments upon the people;

8 To bind their kings with chains, and their nobles with fetters of iron;

9 To execute upon them the judgment written: this honour have all his saints. Praise ye the LORD.

Da. 7. 18 But the saints of the Most High shall take the kingdom, and possess the kingdom for ever, even for ever and ever.

Da. 7. 22 Until the Ancient of days came, and judgment was given to the saints of the Most High; and the time came that the saints possessed the kingdom.

Matt. 19. 28 And Jesus said unto them, Verily I say unto you, That ye which have followed me, in the regeneration when the Son of man shall sit in the throne of his glory, ye also shall sit upon twelve thrones, judging the twelve tribes of Israel.

Luke 22. 30 That ye may eat and drink at my table in my kingdom, and sit on thrones judging the twelve tribes of Israel.

Rev. 2. 26 And he that overcometh, and keepeth my works unto the end, to him will I give power over the nations:

Rev. 3. 21 To him that overcometh will I grant to sit with me in my throne, even as I also overcame, and am set down with my Father in his throne.

Rev. 20. 4 And I saw thrones, and they sat upon them, and judgment was given unto them: and *I saw* the souls of them that were beheaded for the witness of Jesus, and for the word of God, and which had not worshipped the beast, neither his image, neither had received *his* mark upon their foreheads, or in their hands; and they lived and reigned with Christ a thousand years.

B

II Pet. 2. 4 For if God spared not the angels that sinned, but cast *them* down to hell, and delivered *them* into chains of darkness, to be reserved unto judgment;

THE UNJUST, WHEREAS SAINTS SHALL JUDGE THE WORLD AND ANGELS.

B—CONCLUDED.

Jude 6 And the angels which kept not their first estate, but left their own habitation, he hath reserved in everlasting chains under darkness unto the judgment of the great day.

C

ICor. 5. 12 For what have I to do to judge them also that are without? do not ye judge them that are within?

D

Prov. 20. 22 Say not thou, I will recompense evil; *but* wait on the LORD, and he shall save thee.

Matt. 5. 39 But I say unto you, That ye resist not evil: but whosoever shall smite thee on thy right cheek, turn to him the other also.

40 And if any man will sue thee at the law, and take away thy coat, let him have *thy* cloak also.

Luke 6. 29 And unto him that smiteth thee on the *one* cheek offer also the other; and him that taketh away thy cloak forbid not *to take thy* coat also.

Rom. 12. 17 Recompense to no man evil for evil. Provide things honest in the sight of all men.

Rom. 12. 19 Dearly beloved, avenge not yourselves, but *rather* give place unto wrath: for it is written, Vengeance *is* mine; I will repay, saith the Lord.

IThes. 5. 15 See that none render evil for evil unto any *man;* but ever follow that which is good, both among yourselves, and to all *men.*

E

IThes 4. 6 That no *man* go beyond and defraud his brother in *any* matter: because that the Lord *is* the avenger of all such, as we also have forewarned you and testified.

F

ICor. 15. 50 Now this I say, brethren, that flesh and blood cannot inherit the kingdom of God; neither doth corruption inherit incorruption.

Gal. 5. 21 Envyings, murders, drunkenness, revellings, and such like: of the which I tell you before, as I have also told *you* in time past, that they which do such things shall not inherit the kingdom of God.

Eph. 5. 5 For this ye know, that no whoremonger, nor unclean person, nor covetous man, who is an idolater, hath any inheritance in the kingdom of Christ and of God.

F—CONCLUDED.

ITim. 1. 9 Knowing this, that the law is not made for a righteous man, but for the lawless and disobedient, for the ungodly and for sinners, for unholy and profane, for murderers of fathers and murderers of mothers, for manslayers,

Heb. 12. 14 Follow peace with all *men*, and holiness, without which no man shall see the Lord:

Heb. 13. 4 Marriage *is* honourable in all, and the bed undefiled: but whoremongers and adulterers God will judge.

Rev. 22. 15 For without *are* dogs, and sorcerers, and whoremongers, and murderers, and idolaters, and whosoever loveth and maketh a lie.

G

ICor. 12. 2 Ye know that ye were Gentiles, carried away unto these dumb idols, even as ye were led.

Eph. 2. 2 Wherein in time past ye walked according to the course of this world, according to the prince of the power of the air, the spirit that now worketh in the children of disobedience:

Eph. 4. 22 That ye put off concerning the former conversation the old man, which is corrupt according to the deceitful lusts;

Eph. 5. 8 For ye were sometimes darkness, but now *are ye* light in the Lord: walk as children of light;

Col. 3. 7 In the which ye also walked sometime, when ye lived in them.

Tit. 3. 3 For we ourselves also were sometimes foolish, disobedient, deceived, serving divers lusts and pleasures, living in malice and envy, hateful, *and* hating one another.

H

John 13. 10 Jesus saith to him, He that is washed needeth not save to wash *his* feet, but is clean every whit: and ye are clean, but not all.

John 15. 3 Now ye are clean through the word which I have spoken unto you.

ICor. 1. 30 But of him are ye in Christ Jesus, who of God is made unto us wisdom, and righteousness, and sanctification, and redemption:

Eph. 5. 26 That he might sanctify and cleanse it with the washing of water by the word,

Heb. 10. 22 Let us draw near with a true heart in full assurance of faith, having our hearts sprinkled from an evil conscience, and our bodies washed with pure water.

§ 361. ALL THINGS ARE LAWFUL, BUT NOT EXPEDIENT. THE BODY

6 : 12-20.

12 [a]All things are lawful unto me, but all things are not [1]expedient: all things are lawful for me, but I will not be brought under the power of any.

13 [b]Meats for the belly, and the belly for meats: but God shall destroy both it and them. Now the body *is* not for fornication, but [c]for the Lord; [d]and the Lord for the body.

14 And [e]God hath both raised up the Lord, and will also raise up us [f]by his own power.

15 Know ye not that [g]your bodies are the members of Christ? shall I then take the members of Christ, and make *them* the members of a harlot? God forbid.

16 What? know ye not that he which is joined to a harlot is one body? for [h]two, saith he, shall be one flesh.

17 [i]But he that is joined unto the Lord is one spirit.

18 [k]Flee fornication. Every sin that a man doeth is without the body; but he that committeth fornication sinneth [l]against his own body.

19 What? [m]know ye not that your body is the temple of the Holy Ghost *which is* in you, which ye have of God, [n]and ye are not your own?

CHAP. 6.

20 For [o]ye are bought with a price: therefore glorify God in your body, and in your spirit, which are God's.

A

ICor.10. 23 All things are lawful for me, but all things are not expedient: all things are lawful for me, but all things edify not.

1

Or, *profitable.*

B

Matt.15. 17 Do not ye yet understand, that whatsoever entereth in at the mouth goeth into the belly, and is cast out into the draught?

Rom.14. 17 For the kingdom of God is not meat and drink; but righteousness, and peace, and joy in the Holy Ghost.

Col. 2. 22 Which all are to perish with the using;) after the commandments and doctrines of men?

23 Which things have indeed a shew of wisdom in will-worship, and humility, and neglecting of the body; not in any honour to the satisfying of the flesh.

C

I Cor. 6. 15, 19 and 20. *See text of topic.*

IThes.4. 3 For this is the will of God, *even* your sanctification, that ye should abstain from fornication:

IThes.4. 7 For God hath not called us unto uncleanness, but unto holiness

D

Eph. 5. 23 For the husband is the head of the wife, even as Christ is the head of the church: and he is the Saviour of the body.

§ 362. ANSWER TO QUESTIONS CONCERNING MARRIAGE, WITH

7 : 1-24.

1 Now concerning the things whereof ye wrote unto me: [a]*It is* good for a man not to touch a woman.

2 Nevertheless, *to avoid* fornication, let every man have his own wife, and let every woman have her own husband.

3 [b]Let the husband render unto the wife due benevolence: and likewise

CHAP. 7.

also the wife unto the husband.

4 The wife hath not power of her own body, but the husband: and likewise also the husband hath not power of his own body, but the wife.

5 [c]Defraud ye not one the other, except *it be* with consent for a time, that ye may give yourselves to fasting and prayer; and come together

IS NOT FOR FORNICATION, IT IS A TEMPLE OF THE HOLY SPIRIT.

E

Rom. 6. 5 For if we have been planted together in the likeness of his death, we shall be also *in the likeness* of *his* resurrection:

Rom. 6. 8 Now if we be dead with Christ, we believe that we shall also live with him:

Rom. 8. 11. *See q, Q, § 332, page 844.*

F

Eph. 1. 19 And what *is* the exceeding greatness of his power to us-ward who believe, according to the working of his mighty power,

20 Which he wrought in Christ, when he raised him from the dead, and set *him* at his own right hand in the heavenly *places*,

G

Rom. 12. 5. *See l, L, § 342, page 868.*

Eph. 5. 30 For we are members of his body, of his flesh, and of his bones.

H

Gen. 2. 24 Therefore shall a man leave his father and his mother, and shall cleave to his wife: and they shall be one flesh.

Matt. 19. 5 And said, For this cause shall a man leave father and mother, and shall cleave to his wife: and they twain shall be one flesh?

Eph. 5. 31 For this cause shall a man leave his father and mother, and shall be joined unto his wife, and they two shall be one flesh.

I

John 17. 21 That they all may be one; as thou, Father, *art* in me, and I in thee, that they also may be one in us: that the world may believe that thou hast sent me.

I—CONCLUDED.

22 And the glory which thou gavest me I have given them; that they may be one, even as we are one:

23 I in them, and thou in me, that they may be made perfect in one; and that the world may know that thou hast sent me, and hast loved them, as thou hast loved me.

Eph. 4. 4 *There is* one body, and one Spirit, even as ye are called in one hope of your calling;

Eph. 5. 30. *See under G.*

K

Rom. 6. 12 and 13. *See t, T, § 328, page 836.*

Heb. 13. 4 Marriage *is* honourable in all, and the bed undefiled: but whoremongers and adulterers God will judge.

L

Rom. 1. 24. *See i, I, § 319, page 812.*

M

I Cor 3. 16. *See m, M, § 354, page 900.*

N

Rom. 14. 7 and 8. *See g, G, § 344, page 886*

O

Acts 20. 28. *See s, S, § 292, page 762.*

I Cor. 7. 23 Ye are bought with a price; be not ye the servants of men.

Gal. 3. 13 Christ hath redeemed us from the curse of the law, being made a curse for us: for it is written, Cursed *is* every one that hangeth on a tree:

II Pet. 2. 1 But there were false prophets also among the people, even as there shall be false teachers among you, who privily shall bring in damnable heresies, even denying the Lord that bought them, and bring upon themselves swift destruction.

SPECIAL REFERENCE TO MIXED MARRIAGES AND TO BONDSERVANTS.

A

I Cor. 7. 8. *See text of topic, page 914.*

I Cor. 7. 26. *See text of topic, § 362, page 916.*

B

Ex. 21. 10 If he take him another *wife*, her food, her raiment, and her duty of marriage, shall he not diminish.

I Pet. 3. 7 Likewise, ye husbands, dwell with *them* according to knowledge, giving honour unto the wife, as unto the weaker vessel, and as being heirs together of the grace of life; that your prayers be not hindered.

C

Ex. 19. 15 And he said unto the people, Be ready against the third day: come not at *your* wives.

I Sa. 21. 4 And the priest answered David, and said, *There is* no common bread under mine hand, but there is hallowed bread: if the young men have kept themselves at least from women.

5 And David answered the priest, and said unto him, Of a truth, women *have been* kept from us about these three days, since I came out, and the

For C concluded, see next page (914).

§ 362. ANSWER TO QUESTIONS CONCERNING MARRIAGE, WITH SPECIAL

Chap. 7.

again, [d]that Satan tempt you not for
your incontinency.
6 But I speak this by permission,
[e]*and* not of commandment.
7 For [f]I would that all men were
[g]even as I myself. But [h]every man
hath his proper gift of God, one after this manner, and another after
that.
8 I say therefore to the unmarried
and widows, [i]It is good for them if
they abide even as I.
9 But [k]if they cannot contain, let
them marry: for it is better to marry
than to burn.
10 And unto the married I com-
mand, [l]*yet* not I, but the Lord, [m]Let
not the wife depart from *her* husband:
11 But and if she depart, let her
remain unmarried, or be reconciled
to *her* husband: and let not the husband put away *his* wife.
12 But to the rest speak I, [n]not the
Lord: If any brother hath a wife that
believeth not, and she be pleased to
dwell with him, let him not put her
away.
13 And the woman which hath a
husband that believeth not, and if he
be pleased to dwell with her, let her
not leave him.
14 For the unbelieving husband is
sanctified by the wife, and the unbelieving wife is sanctified by the
husband: else [o]were your children
unclean; but now are they holy.
15 But if the unbelieving depart,
let him depart. A brother or a sister is not under bondage in such
cases; but God hath called us
[p]to [1]peace.
16 For what knowest thou, O wife,
whether thou shalt [q]save *thy* husband?

Chap. 7.

or [2]how knowest thou, O man, whether thou salt save *thy* wife?
17 But as God hath distributed to
every man, as the Lord hath called
every one, so let him walk. And [r]so
ordain I in all churches.
18 Is any man called being circumcised? let him not become uncircumcised. Is any called in uncircumcision? [s]let him not be circumcised.
19 [t]Circumcision is nothing, and
uncircumcision is nothing, [u]but the
keeping of the commandments of
God.

C—Concluded.

vessels of the young men are holy, and *the bread is* in a manner common, yea, though it were sanctified this day in the vessel.

Joel 2. 16 Gather the people, sanctify the congregation, assemble the elders, gather the children, and those that suck the breasts: let the bridegroom go forth of his chamber, and the bride out of her closet.

Zech. 7. 3 *And* to speak unto the priests which *were* in the house of the Lord of hosts, and to the prophets, saying, Should I weep in the fifth month, separating myself, as I have done these so many years?

D

I Thes. 3. 5 For this cause, when I could no longer forbear, I sent to know your faith, lest by some means the tempter have tempted you, and our labour be in vain.

E

I Cor. 7. 12. *See text of topic.*
I Cor. 7. 25. *See text of topic, §363, page 916.*

II Cor. 8. 8 I speak not by commandment, but by occasion of the forwardness of others, and to prove the sincerity of your love.

II Cor. 11. 17 That which I speak, I speak *it* not after the Lord, but as it were foolishly, in this confidence of boasting.

F

Acts 26. 29 And Paul said, I would to God, that not only thou, but also all that hear me this day, were both almost, and altogether such as I am, except these bonds.

REFERENCE TO MIXED MARRIAGES AND TO BONDSERVANTS (CONTINUED).

G

I Cor. 9. 5 Have we not power to lead about a sister, a wife, as well as other apostles, and *as* the brethren of the Lord, and Cephas?

H

Matt. 19. 12 For there are some eunuchs, which were so born from *their* mother's womb: and there are some eunuchs, which were made eunuchs of men: and there be eunuchs, which have made themselves eunuchs for the kingdom of heaven's sake. He that is able to receive *it*, let him receive *it*.

I Cor. 12. 11 But all these worketh that one and the selfsame Spirit, dividing to every man severally as he will.

I

I Cor. 7. 1. *See text of topic.*

I Cor. 7. 26. *See text of topic of* §*363, page 916.*

K

I Tim. 5. 14 I will therefore that the younger women marry, bear children, guide the house, give none occasion to the adversary to speak reproachfully.

L

I Cor. 7. 12. *See text of topic.*

I Cor. 7. 25 and 40. *See text of topic,* §*363, page 916.*

M

Mal. 2. 14 Yet ye say, Wherefore? Because the LORD hath been witness between thee and the wife of thy youth, against whom thou hast dealt treacherously: yet *is* she thy companion, and the wife of thy covenant.

Mal. 2. 16 For the LORD, the God of Israel, saith that he hateth putting away: for *one* covereth violence with his garment, saith the LORD of hosts: therefore take heed to your spirit, that ye deal not treacherously.

Matt. 5. 32 But I say unto you, That whosoever shall put away his wife, saving for the cause of fornication, causeth her to commit adultery: and whosoever shall marry her that is divorced committeth adultery.

Matt. 19. 6 Wherefore they are no more twain, but one flesh. What therefore God hath joined together, let not man put asunder.

Matt. 19. 9 And I say unto you, Whosoever shall put away his wife, except *it be* for fornication, and shall marry another, committeth adultery: and whoso marrieth her which is put away doth commit adultery.

M—CONCLUDED.

Mark 10. 11 And he saith unto them, Whosoever shall put away his wife, and marry another, committeth adultery against her.

12 And if a woman shall put away her husband, and be married to another, she committeth adultery.

Luke 16. 18 Whosoever putteth away his wife, and marrieth another, committeth adultery: and whosoever marrieth her that is put away from *her* husband committeth adultery.

N

I Cor. 7. 6. *See text of topic.*

O

Mal. 2. 15 And did not he make one? Yet had he the residue of the Spirit. And wherefore one? That he might seek a godly seed. Therefore take heed to your spirit, and let none deal treacherously against the wife of his youth.

P

Rom. 12. 18. *See m, M,* §*342, page 872.*

Rom. 14. 19 Let us therefore follow after the things which make for peace, and things wherewith one may edify another.

I Cor. 14. 33 For God is not *the author* of confusion, but of peace, as in all churches of the saints.

1

Gr., *in peace.*

Q

I Pet. 3. 1 Likewise, ye wives, *be* in subjection to your own husbands; that, if any obey not the word, they also may without the word be won by the conversation of the wives;

2

Gr., *what.*

R

I Cor. 4. 17. *See g, G,* §*358, page 904.*

II Cor. 11. 28 Beside those things that are without, that which cometh upon me daily, the care of all the churches.

S

Acts 15. 5. *See g, C,* §*267, page 726.*

T

Rom. 2. 28 For he is not a Jew, which is one outwardly; neither *is that* circumcision, which is outward in the flesh:

29 But he *is* a Jew, which is one inwardly; and circumcision *is that* of the heart, in the spirit, *and* not in the letter; whose praise *is* not of men, but of God.

For T Concluded and U, see next page (916).

§ 362. ANSWER TO QUESTIONS CONCERNING MARRIAGE, WITH SPECIAL

CHAP. 7.

20 Let every man abide in the same
calling wherein he was called.
21 Art thou called *being* a servant?
care not for it: but if thou mayest
be made free, use *it* rather.
22 For he that is called in the Lord,
being a servant, is [x]the Lord's [3]free-
man: likewise also he that is called,
being free, is [y]Christ's servant.
23 [z]Ye are bought with a price; be
not ye the servants of men.
24 Brethren, [a]let every man, wherein
he is called, therein abide with God.

T—CONCLUDED.

Rom. 3. 30 Seeing *it is* one God, which shall justify the circumcision by faith, and uncircumcision through faith.

Gal. 5. 6 For in Jesus Christ neither circumcision availeth any thing, nor uncircumcision; but faith which worketh by love.

Gal. 6. 15 For in Christ Jesus neither circumcision availeth any thing, nor uncircumcision, but a new creature.

U

John 15. 14 Ye are my friends, if ye do whatsoever I command you.

1 Jno. 2. 3 And hereby we do know that we know him, if we keep his commandments.

1 Jno. 3. 24 And he that keepeth his commandments dwelleth in him, and he in him. And hereby we know that he

§ 363. ANSWER CONCERNING THE

7:25-40.

25 Now concerning virgins [a]I have
no commandment of the Lord: yet
I give my judgment, as one [b]that
hath obtained mercy of the Lord [c]to
be faithful.
26 I suppose therefore that this is
good for the present [1]distress, *I say*,
[d]that *it is* good for a man so to be.
27 Art thou bound unto a wife?
seek not to be loosed. Art thou
loosed from a wife? seek not a wife.
28 But and if thou marry, thou
hast not sinned; and if a virgin
marry, she hath not sinned. Nevertheless
such shall have trouble in the
flesh: but I spare you.
29 But [e]this I say, brethren, the
time *is* short: it remaineth, that both
they that have wives be as though
they had none;
30 And they that weep, as though
they wept not; and they that rejoice,
as though they rejoiced not; and

CHAP. 7.

they that buy, as though they possessed
not;
31 And they that use this world, as
not [f]abusing *it*: for [g]the fashion of
this world passeth away.
32 But I would have you without
carefulness. [h]He that is unmarried
careth for the things [2]that belong
to the Lord, how he may please the
Lord.
33 But he that is married careth
for the things that are of the world,
how he may please *his* wife.
34 There is a difference *also* between
a wife and a virgin. The unmarried
woman [i]careth for the things
of the Lord, that she may be holy
both in body and in spirit: but she
that is married careth for the things
of the world, how she may please
her husband.
35 And this I speak for your own
profit; not that I may cast a snare
upon you, but for that which is
comely, and that ye may attend
upon the Lord without distraction,

REFERENCE TO MIXED MARRIAGES AND TO BONDSERVANTS (CONCLUDED).

U—CONCLUDED.

abideth in us, by the Spirit which he hath given us.

X

John 8. 32 And ye shall know the truth, and the truth shall make you free.

John 8. 36 If the Son therefore shall make you free, ye shall be free indeed.

Rom. 6. 18 Being then made free from sin, ye became the servants of righteousness.

Rom. 6. 22 But now, being made free from sin, and become servants to God, ye have your fruit unto holiness, and the end everlasting life.

Phile. 16 Not now as a servant, but above a servant, a brother beloved, especially to me, but how much more unto thee, both in the flesh, and in the Lord?

3

Gr, *made free.*

Y

I Cor. 9. 21 To them that are without law, as without law, (being not without law to God, but under the law to Christ,) that I might gain them that are without law.

Gal. 5. 13 For, brethren, ye have been called unto liberty; only *use* not liberty for an occasion to the flesh, but by love serve one another.

Eph. 6. 6 Not with eyeservice, as menpleasers; but as the servants of Christ, doing the will of God from the heart;

I Pet. 2. 16 As free, and not using *your* liberty for a cloak of maliciousness, but as the servants of God.

Z

Acts 20. 28. *See s, S, ¿ 292, page 760.*

A

I Co. 7. 20. *See text of topic.*

MARRIAGE OF VIRGIN DAUGHTERS.

A

I Cor. 7. 6. *See e, E, ¿ 362, page 914.*

B

I Tim. 1. 16 Howbeit for this cause I obtained mercy, that in me first Jesus Christ might shew forth all longsuffering, for a pattern to them which should hereafter believe on him to life everlasting.

C

I Cor. 4. 2 Moreover it is required in stewards, that a man be found faithful.

I Tim. 1. 12 And I thank Christ Jesus our Lord, who hath enabled me, for that he counted me faithful, putting me into the ministry;

1

Or, *necessity.*

D

I Cor. 7. 1 and 8. *See text of topic, ¿ 362, page 912.*

E

Rom. 13. 11 And that, knowing the time, that now *it is* high time to awake out of sleep: for now *is* our salvation nearer than when we believed.

I Pet. 4. 7 But the end of all things is at hand: be ye therefore sober, and watch unto prayer.

II Pet. 3. 8 But, beloved, be not ignorant of this one thing, that one day *is* with the Lord as a thousand years, and a thousand years as one day.

9 The Lord is not slack concerning his promise, as some men count slack-

E—CONCLUDED.

ness; but is longsuffering to us-ward, not willing that any should perish, but that all should come to repentance.

F

I Cor. 9. 18 What is my reward then? *Verily* that, when I preach the gospel, I may make the gospel of Christ without charge, that I abuse not my power in the gospel.

G

Ps. 39. 6 Surely every man walketh in a vain shew: surely they are disquieted in vain: he heapeth up *riches*, and knoweth not who shall gather them.

Ps. 73. 20 As a dream when *one* awaketh; *so*, O Lord, when thou awakest, thou shalt despise their image.

Ps. 102. 26 They shall perish, but thou shalt endure: yea, all of them shall wax old like a garment; as a vesture shalt thou change them, and they shall be changed:

Eccl. 1. 4 *One* generation passeth away, and *another* generation cometh: but the earth abideth for ever.

Isa. 51. 6 Lift up your eyes to the heavens, and look upon the earth beneath: for the heavens shall vanish away like smoke, and the earth shall wax old like a garment, and they that dwell therein shall die in like manner: but my salvation shall be for ever, and my righteousness shall not be abolished.

For G concluded, H, 2 and I, see next page (918).

§ 363. ANSWER CONCERNING THE MARRIAGE

CHAP. 7.

36 But if any man think that he behaveth himself uncomely toward his virgin, if she pass the flower of *her* age, and need so require, let him do what he will, he sinneth not: let them marry.

37 Nevertheless he that standeth steadfast in his heart, having no necessity, but hath power over his own will, and hath so decreed in his heart that he will keep his virgin, doeth well.

38 [k]So then he that giveth *her* in marriage doeth well; but he that giveth *her* not in marriage doeth better.

CHAP. 7.

39 [l]The wife is bound by the law as long as her husband liveth; but if her husband be dead, she is at liberty to be married to whom she will; [m]only in the Lord.

40 But she is happier if she so abide, [n]after my judgment: and [o]I think also that I have the Spirit of God.

G—CONTINUED.

Jas. 1. 10 But the rich, in that he is made low: because as the flower of the grass he shall pass away.

Jas. 4. 14 Whereas ye know not what *shall be* on the morrow. For what *is* your life? It is even a vapour, that appeareth for a little time, and then vanisheth away.

§ 364. ANSWER CONCERNING THINGS

8 : 1–13.

1 Now [a]as touching things offered unto idols, we know that we all have [b]knowledge. [c]Knowledge puffeth up, but charity edifieth.

2 And [d]if any man think that he knoweth any thing, he knoweth nothing yet as he ought to know.

3 But if any man love God, [e]the same is known of him.

4 As concerning therefore the eating of those things that are offered in sacrifice unto idols, we know that [f]an idol *is* nothing in the world, [g]and that *there is* none other God but one.

5 For though there be that are [h]called gods, whether in heaven or in earth, (as there be gods many, and lords many,)

6 But [i]to us *there is but* one God, the Father, [k]of whom *are* all things, and we [1]in him; and [l]one Lord Jesus

A

Acts 15. 20. *See r, R, § 268, page 730.*

B

Rom. 14. 14 I know, and am persuaded by the Lord Jesus, that *there is* nothing unclean of itself: but to him that esteemeth any thing to be unclean, to him *it is* unclean.

Rom. 14. 22 Hast thou faith? have *it* to thyself before God. Happy *is* he that condemneth not himself in that thing which he alloweth.

C

Rom. 14. 3 Let not him that eateth despise him that eateth not; and let not him which eateth not judge him that eateth: for God hath received him.

Rom. 14. 10 But why dost thou judge thy brother? or why dost thou set at nought thy brother? for we shall all stand before the judgment seat of Christ.

D

1 Cor. 13. 8 Charity never faileth: but whether *there be* prophecies, they shall fail; whether *there be* tongues, they shall cease; whether *there be* knowledge, it shall vanish away.

9 For we know in part, and we prophesy in part.

1 Cor. 13. 12 For now we see through a glass, darkly; but then face to face: now I know in part; but then shall I know even as also I am known.

OF VIRGIN DAUGHTERS (CONCLUDED).

G—CONCLUDED.

I Pet. 1. 24 For all flesh *is* as grass, and all the glory of man as the flower of grass. The grass withereth, and the flower thereof falleth away;

I Pet. 4. 7. *See under E.*

I Jno. 2. 17 And the world passeth away, and the lust thereof: but he that doeth the will of God abideth for ever.

H

I Tim. 5. 5 Now she that is a widow indeed, and desolate, trusteth in God, and continueth in supplications and prayers night and day.

2

Gr, *of the Lord,* as ver. 34.

I

Luke 10. 40 But Martha was cumbered about much serving, and came to him, and said, Lord, dost thou not care that my sister hath left me to serve alone? bid her therefore that she help me.

K

Heb. 13. 4 Marriage *is* honourable in all, and the bed undefiled: but whoremongers and adulterers God will judge.

L

Rom. 7. 2 For the woman which hath a husband is bound by the law to *her* husband so long as he liveth; but if the husband be dead, she is loosed from the law of *her* husband.

M

II Cor. 6. 14 Be ye not unequally yoked together with unbelievers: for what fellowship hath righteousness with unrighteousness? and what communion hath light with darkness?

N

I Cor. 7. 6. *See e, E, § 362, page 914.*

O

I Thes. 4. 8 He therefore that despiseth, despiseth not man, but God, who hath also given unto us his Holy Spirit.

SACRIFICED TO IDOLS, ESPECIALLY MEATS.

D—CONCLUDED.

Gal. 6. 3 For if a man think himself to be something, when he is nothing, he deceiveth himself.

I Tim. 6. 4 He is proud, knowing nothing, but doting about questions and strifes of words, whereof cometh envy, strife, railings, evil surmisings,

E

Ex. 33. 12 And Moses said unto the LORD, See, thou sayest unto me, Bring up this people: and thou hast not let me know whom thou wilt send with me. Yet thou hast said, I know thee by name, and thou hast also found grace in my sight.

Nah. 1. 7 The LORD *is* good, a strong hold in the day of trouble; and he knoweth them that trust in him.

Matt. 7. 23 And then will I profess unto them, I never knew you: depart from me, ye that work iniquity.

Gal. 4. 9 But now, after that ye have known God, or rather are known of God, how turn ye again to the weak and beggarly elements, whereunto ye desire again to be in bondage?

II Tim. 2. 19 Nevertheless the foundation of God standeth sure, having this seal, The Lord knoweth them that are his. And Let every one that nameth the name of Christ depart from iniquity.

F

Isa. 41. 24 Behold, ye *are* of nothing, and your work of nought: an abomination *is he that* chooseth you.

I Cor. 10. 19 What say I then? that the idol is any thing, or that which is offered in sacrifice to idols is any thing?

G

Deut. 4. 39 Know therefore this day, and consider *it* in thine heart, that the LORD he *is* God in heaven above, and upon the earth beneath: *there is* none else.

Deut. 6. 4 Hear, O Israel: The LORD our God *is* one LORD.

Isa. 44. 8 Fear ye not, neither be afraid: have not I told thee from that time, and have declared *it?* ye *are* even my witnesses. Is there a God besides me? yea, *there is* no God; I know not *any.*

Mark 12. 29 And Jesus answered him, The first of all the commandments *is,* Hear, O Israel; The Lord our God is one Lord:

Eph. 4. 6 One God and Father of all, who *is* above all, and through all, and in you all.

I Tim. 2. 5 For *there is* one God, and one mediator between God and men, the man Christ Jesus;

H

John 10. 34 Jesus answered them, Is it not written in your law, I said, Ye are gods?

For I, K, 1, and L, see next page (920).

§ 364. ANSWER CONCERNING THINGS SACRIFICED

CHAP. 8.

Christ [m]by whom *are* all things, and we by him.

7 Howbeit *there is* not in every man that knowledge: for some [n]with conscience of the idol unto this hour eat *it* as a thing offered unto an idol; and their conscience being weak is [o]defiled.

8 But [p]meat commendeth us not to God: for neither, if we eat, [2]are we the better; neither, if we eat not, [3]are we the worse.

9 But [q]take heed lest by any means this [4]liberty of yours become [r]a stumblingblock to them that are weak.

10 For if any man see thee which hast knowledge sit at meat in the idol's temple, shall not [s]the conscience of him which is weak be [5]emboldened to eat those things which are offered to idols;

11 And [t]through thy knowledge shall the weak brother perish, for whom Christ died?

12 But [u]when ye sin so against the brethren, and wound their weak conscience, ye sin against Christ.

13 Wherefore, [x]if meat make my brother to offend, I will eat no flesh while the world standeth, lest I make my brother to offend.

I

Mal. 2. 10 Have we not all one father? hath not one God created us? why do we deal treacherously every man against his brother by profaning the covenant of our fathers?

I Cor. 8. 4. *See g, G, §364, page 918.*

K

Acts 17. 28 For in him we live, and move, and have our being; as certain also of your own poets have said, For we are also his offspring.

1

Or, *for him.*

L

John 13. 13 Ye call me Master and Lord: and ye say well; for *so* I am.

Acts 2. 36 Therefore let all the house of Israel know assuredly, that God hath made that same Jesus, whom ye have crucified, both Lord and Christ.

I Cor. 12. 3 Wherefore I give you to understand, that no man speaking by the Spirit of God calleth Jesus accursed: and *that* no man can say that Jesus is the Lord, but by the Holy Ghost.

Eph. 4. 5 One Lord, one faith, one baptism.

Phil. 2. 11 And *that* every tongue should confess that Jesus Christ *is* Lord, to the glory of God the Father,

M

John 1. 3. *See e, E, §1, page 5.*

N

I Cor. 10. 28 But if any man say unto you, This is offered in sacrifice unto idols, eat not for his sake that shewed it, and for conscience' sake: for the earth *is* the Lord's, and the fulness thereof:

29 Conscience I say, not thine own, but of the other: for why is my liberty judged of another *man's* conscience?

O

Rom. 14. 14. *See under B, page 918.*

Rom. 14. 23 And he that doubteth is damned if he eat, because *he eateth* not of faith: for whatsoever *is* not of faith is sin.

§ 365. PAUL ASSERTS HIS APOSTLESHIP AND PRIVILEGES THEREIN

9:1–27.

1 [a]Am I not an apostle? am I not free? [b]have I not seen Jesus Christ our Lord? [c]are not ye my work in the Lord?

2 If I be not an apostle unto others, yet doubtless I am to you: for [d]the seal of mine apostleship are ye in the Lord.

A

Acts 9. 15. *See l, L, §251, page 684.*

Acts 13. 2 As they ministered to the Lord, and fasted, the Holy Ghost said, Separate me Barnabas and Saul for the work whereunto I have called them.

Acts 26. 17 Delivering thee from the people, and *from* the Gentiles, unto whom now I send thee,

TO IDOLS, ESPECIALLY MEATS (CONCLUDED).

P

Rom.14. 17 For the kingdom of God is not meat and drink; but righteousness, and peace, and joy in the Holy Ghost.

2

Or, *have we the more.*

3

Or, *have we the less.*

Q

Gal. 5. 13 For, brethren, ye have been called unto liberty; only *use* not liberty for an occasion to the flesh, but by love serve one another.

4

Or, *power.*

R

Rom. 14. 13. *See n, N, §344, page 876.*

Rom.14. 20 For meat destroy not the work of God. All things indeed *are* pure; but *it is* evil for that man who eateth with offence.

S

I Cor. 10. 28. *See under N.*

ICor.10. 32 Give none offence, neither to the Jews, nor to the Gentiles, nor to the church of God:

5

Gr., *edified.*

T

Rom.14. 15 But if thy brother be grieved with *thy* meat, now walkest thou not charitably. Destroy not him with thy meat, for whom Christ died.

Rom.14. 20. *See under R.*

U

Gen. 20. 9 Then Abimelech called Abraham, and said unto him, What hast thou done unto us? and what have I offended thee, that thou hast brought on me and on my kingdom a great sin? thou hast done deeds unto me that ought not to be done.

U—CONCLUDED.

Matt.25. 40 And the King shall answer and say unto them, Verily I say unto you, Inasmuch as ye have done *it* unto one of the least of these my brethren, ye have done *it* unto me.

Matt.25. 45 Then shall he answer them, saying, Verily I say unto you, Inasmuch as ye did *it* not to one of the least of these, ye did *it* not to me.

X

Rom.14. 21 *It is* good neither to eat flesh, nor to drink wine, nor *any thing* whereby thy brother stumbleth, or is offended, or is made weak.

ICor.6. 12 All things are lawful unto me, but all things are not expedient: all things are lawful for me, but I will not be brought under the power of any.

ICor.9. 12 If others be partakers of *this* power over you *are* not we rather? Nevertheless we have not used this power; but suffer all things, lest we should hinder the gospel of Christ.

I Cor.9. 19 For though I be free from all *men*, yet have I made myself servant unto all, that I might gain the more.

ICor.10. 33 Even as I please all *men* in all *things*, not seeking mine own profit, but the *profit* of many, that they may be saved.

ICor.11. 1 Be ye followers of me, even as I also *am* of Christ.

I Cor.13. 5 Doth not behave itself unseemly, seeketh not her own, is not easily provoked, thinketh no evil:

IICor.11. 29 Who is weak, and I am not weak? who is offended, and I burn not?

IIThes.3. 8 Neither did we eat any man's bread for nought; but wrought with labour and travail night and day, that we might not be chargeable to any of you:
9 Not because we have not power, but to make ourselves an ensample unto you to follow us.

THAT HIS ABSTINANCE WAS FOR THE FURTHERANCE OF THE GOSPEL

B

Acts 9. 3 And as he journeyed, he came near Damascus: and suddenly there shined round about him a light from heaven:

Acts 9. 17 And Ananias went his way, and entered into the house; and putting his hands on him said, Brother Saul, the Lord, *even* Jesus, that appeared unto thee in the way as thou camest, hath sent me, that thou mightest receive thy sight, and be filled with the Holy Ghost.

B—CONTINUED.

Acts 18. 9 Then spake the Lord to Paul in the night by a vision, Be not afraid, but speak, and hold not thy peace:

Acts 22. 14. *See s, S, §297, page 774.*

Acts 22. 18 And saw him saying unto me, Make haste, and get thee quickly out of Jerusalem: for they will not receive thy testimony concerning me.

For B Concluded, C and D, see next page (922).

§ 365. PAUL ASSERTS HIS APOSTLESHIP AND PRIVILEGES THEREIN. THAT

CHAP. 9.

3 Mine answer to them that do examine me is this:

4 [e]Have we not power to eat and to drink?

5 Have we not power to lead about a sister, a [1]wife, as well as other apostles, and *as* [f]the brethren of the Lord, and [g]Cephas?

6 Or I only and Barnabas, [h]have not we power to forbear working?

7 Who [i]goeth a warfare any time at his own charges? who [k]planteth a vineyard, and eateth not of the fruit thereof? or who [l]feedeth a flock, and eateth not of the milk of the flock?

8 Say I these things as a man? or saith not the law the same also?

9 For it is written in the law of Moses, [m]Thou shalt not muzzle the mouth of the ox that treadeth out the corn. Doth God take care for oxen?

10 Or saith he *it* altogether for our sakes? For our sakes, no doubt, *this* is written: that [n]he that plougheth should plough in hope; and that he that thresheth in hope should be partaker of his hope.

11 [o]If we have sown unto you spiritual things, *is it* a great thing if we shall reap your carnal things?

12 If others be partakers of *this* power over you, *are* not we rather? [p]Nevertheless we have not used this power; but suffer all things, [q]lest we should hinder the gospel of Christ.

13 [r]Do ye not know that they which minister about holy things [2]live *of the things* of the temple? and they which

B—CONCLUDED.

Acts 23. 11 And the night following the Lord stood by him, and said, Be of good cheer, Paul: for as thou hast testified of me in Jerusalem, so must thou bear witness also at Rome.

C

I Co. 3. 6 I have planted, Apollos watered; but God gave the increase.

I Cor. 4. 15 For though he have ten thousand instructors in Christ, yet *have ye* not many fathers: for in Christ Jesus I have begotten you through the gospel.

D

II Cor. 3. 2 Ye are our epistle written in our hearts, known and read of all men:

II Cor. 12. 12 Truly the signs of an apostle were wrought among you in all patience, in signs, and wonders, and mighty deeds.

E

I Cor. 9. 14. *See text of topic, page 924.*

I Thes. 2. 6 Nor of men sought we glory, neither of you, nor *yet* of others, when we might have been burdensome, as the apostles of Christ.

II Thes. 3. 8 Neither did we eat any man's bread for nought; but wrought with labour and travail night and day, that we might not be chargeable to any of you:

9 Not because we have not power, but to make ourselves an ensample unto you to follow us.

1

Or, *woman.*

F

Matt. 12. 46. *See b, B, § 55, page 176.*

G

Matt. 8. 14 And when Jesus was come into Peter's house, he saw his wife's mother laid, and sick of a fever.

H

I. Cor. 9. 4. *See text of topic.*

I

II Cor. 10. 4 (For the weapons of our warfare *are* not carnal, but mighty through God to the pulling down of strong holds;)

I Tim. 1. 18 This charge I commit unto thee, son Timothy, according to the prophecies which went before on thee, that thou by them mightest war a good warfare;

I Tim. 6. 12 Fight the good fight of faith, lay hold on eternal life, whereunto thou art also called, and hast professed a good profession before many witnesses.

II Tim. 2. 3 Thou therefore endure hardness, as a good soldier of Jesus Christ.

HIS ABSTINENCE WAS FOR THE FURTHERANCE OF THE GOSPEL (Continued).

I—Concluded.

IITim.4. 7 I have fought a good fight, I have finished *my* course, I have kept the faith:

K

Deut.20. 6 And what man *is he* that hath planted a vineyard, and hath not *yet* eaten of it? let him *also* go and return unto his house, lest he die in the battle, and another man eat of it.

Prov.27. 18 Whoso keepeth the fig tree shall eat the fruit thereof: so he that waiteth on his master shall be honoured.

I Cor. 3. 6 I have planted, Apollos watered; but God gave the increase.

7 So then neither is he that planteth anything, neither he that watereth; but God that giveth the increase.

8 Now he that planteth and he that watereth are one: and every man shall receive his own reward according to his own labour.

L

John 21. 15 So when they had dined, Jesus saith to Simon Peter, Simon, *son* of Jonas, lovest thou me more than these? He saith unto him, Yea, Lord; thou knowest that I love thee. He saith unto him, Feed my lambs.

I Pet. 5. 2 Feed the flock of God which is among you, taking the oversight *thereof*, not by constraint, but willingly; not for filthy lucre, but of a ready mind;

M

Deut.25. 4 Thou shalt not muzzle the ox when he treadeth out *the corn*.

I Tim.5. 18 For the Scripture saith, Thou shalt not muzzle the ox that treadeth out the corn. And, The labourer *is* worthy of his reward.

N

IITim.2. 6 The husbandman that laboureth must be first partaker of the fruits.

O

Rom. 15. 27. *See r, R, § 346, page 882.*

P

Acts 20. 33 I have coveted no man's silver, or gold, or apparel.

34 Yea, ye yourselves know, that these hands have ministered unto my necessities, and to them that were with me.

I Cor. 9. 15, 18. *See text of topic, page 924.*

IICor.11. 7 Have I committed an offence in abasing myself that ye might be exalted, because I have preached to you the gospel of God freely?

P—Concluded.

IICor.11. 9 And when I was present with you, and wanted, I was chargeable to no man: for that which was lacking to me the brethren which came from Macedonia supplied: and in all *things* I have kept myself from being burdensome unto you, and *so* will I keep *myself*.

IICor.12. 13 For what is it wherein ye were inferior to other churches, except *it be* that I myself was not burdensome to you? forgive me this wrong.

IThes.2. 6 Nor of men sought we glory, neither of you, nor *yet* of others, when we might have been burdensome, as the apostles of Christ.

Q

IICor.11. 12 But what I do, that I will do, that I may cut off occasion from them which desire occasion; that wherein they glory, they may be found even as we.

R

Lev. 6. 16 And the remainder thereof shall Aaron and his sons eat: with unleavened bread shall it be eaten in the holy place; in the court of the tabernacle of the congregation they shall eat it.

Lev. 6. 26 The priest that offereth it for sin shall eat it: in the holy place shall it be eaten, in the court of the tabernacle of the congregation.

Lev. 7. 6 Every male among the priests shall eat thereof: it shall be eaten in the holy place: it *is* most holy.

Num. 5. 9 And every offering of all the holy things of the children of Israel, which they bring unto the priest, shall be his.

10 And every man's hallowed things shall be his: whatsoever any man giveth the priest, it shall be his.

Num.18. 8 And the Lord spake unto Aaron, Behold, I also have given thee the charge of mine heave offerings of all the hallowed things of the children of Israel; unto thee have I given them by reason of the anointing, and to thy sons, by an ordinance for ever.

2

Or, *feed*.

S

Matt.10. 10 Nor scrip for *your* journey, neither two coats, neither shoes, nor yet staves: for the workman is worthy of his meat.

Luke 10. 7 And in the same house remain, eating and drinking such things as they give: for the labourer is worthy of his hire. Go not from house to house.

§ 365. PAUL ASSERTS HIS APOSTLESHIP AND PRIVILEGES THEREIN. THAT

CHAP. 9.

wait at the altar are partakers with
the altar?
14 Even so [s]hath the Lord ordained
[t]that they which preach the gospel
should live of the gospel.
15 But [u]I have used none of these
things: neither have I written these
things, that it should be so done unto
me: for [x]*it were* better for me to die,
than that any man should make my
glorying void.
16 For though I preach the gospel,
I have nothing to glory of: for [y]ne-
cessity is laid upon me; yea, woe is
unto me, if I preach not the gospel!
17 For if I do this thing willingly,
[z]I have a reward: but if against my
will, [a]a dispensation *of the gospel* is
committed unto me.
18 What is my reward then? *Verily*
that, [b]when I preach the gospel, I
may make the gospel of Christ without charge, that [c]I abuse not my
power in the gospel.
19 For though I be [d]free from all
men, yet have [e]I made myself servant
unto all, [f]that I might gain the more.
20 And [g]unto the Jews I became
as a Jew, that I might gain the Jews;
to them that are under the law, as
under the law, that I might gain
them that are under the law;
21 [h]To [i]them that are without law,
as without law, ([k]being not without
law to God, but under the law to
Christ,) that I might gain them that
are without law.
22 [l]To the weak became I as weak,
that I might gain the weak: [m]I am

For S, see preceding page.

T

Gal. 6. 6 Let him that is taught in the word communicate unto him that teacheth in all good things.

I Tim. 5. 17 Let the elders that rule well be counted worthy of double honour, especially they who labour in the word and doctrine.

U

Acts 18. 3. *See b, B, § 280, page 746.*
I Cor. 9. 12. *See text of topic, § 365, page 922.*

X

II Cor. 11. 10 As the truth of Christ is in me, no man shall stop me of this boasting in the regions of Achaia.

Y

Rom. 1. 14. *See k, K, § 318, page 810.*

Z

I Cor. 3. 14. *See k, K, § 354, page 900.*

A

I Cor. 4. 1. Let a man so account of us, as of the ministers of Christ, and stewards of the mysteries of God.

Gal. 2. 7 But contrawise, when they saw that the gospel of the uncircumcision was committed unto me, as *the gospel* of the circumcision *was* unto Peter;

Eph. 3. 2 If ye have heard of the dispensation of the grace of God which is given me to you-ward:

3 How that by revelation he made known unto me the mystery; (as I wrote afore in few words;

4 Whereby, when ye read, ye may understand my knowledge in the mystery of Christ)

5 Which in other ages was not made known unto the sons of men, as it is now revealed unto his holy apostles and prophets by the spirit;

6 That the Gentiles should be fellow heirs, and of the same body, and partakers of his promise in Christ by the gospel:

7 Whereof I was made a minister, according to the gift of the grace of God, given unto me by the effectual working of his power.

Phil. 1. 17 But the other of love, knowing that I am set for the defence of the gospel.

Col. 1. 25 Whereof I am made a minister, according to the dispensation of God which is given to me for you, to fulfil the word of God;

I Thes. 2. 4 But as we were allowed of God to be put in trust with the gospel, even so we speak; not as pleasing men, but God, which trieth our hearts.

HIS ABSTINENCE WAS FOR THE FURTHERANCE OF THE GOSPEL (CONTINUED).

A—CONCLUDED.

I Tim. 1. 11 According to the glorious gospel of the blessed God, which was committed to my trust.

B

I Cor. 10. 33 Even as I please all *men* in all *things*, not seeking mine own profit, but the *profit* of many, that they may be saved.

II Cor. 4. 5 For we preach not ourselves, but Christ Jesus the Lord; and ourselves your servants for Jesus' sake.

II Cor. 11. 7 Have I committed an offence in abasing myself that ye might be exalted, because I have preached to you the gospel of God freely?

C

I Cor. 7. 31. *See f, F, § 363, page 916.*

D

I Cor. 9. 1. *See text of topic, page 920.*

E

Gal. 5. 13 For, brethren, ye have been called unto liberty; only *use* not liberty for an occasion to the flesh, but by love serve one another.

F

Matt. 18. 15 Moreover if thy brother shall trespass against thee, go and tell him his fault between thee and him alone; if he shall hear thee, thou has gained thy brother.

I. Pet. 3. 1 Likewise ye wives *be* in subjection to your own husbands; that, if any obey not the word, they also may without the word be won by the conversation of the wives;

G

Acts 16. 3 Him would Paul have to go forth with him; and took and circumcised him because of the Jews which were in those quarters: for they knew all that his father was a Greek.

Acts 21. 26 Then Paul took the men, and the next day purifying himself with them entered into the temple, to signify the accomplishment of the days of purification, until that an offering should be offered for every one of them.

H

Gal. 3. 2 This only would I learn of you, Received ye the Spirit by the works of the law, or by the hearing of faith?

I

Rom. 2. 12 For as many as have sinned without law shall also perish without law; and as many as have sinned in the law shall be judged by the law;

Rom. 2. 14 For when the Gentiles, which have not the law, do by nature the things

I—CONCLUDED.

contained in the law, these, having not the law, are a law unto themselves:

K

I Cor. 7. 22 For he that is called in the Lord, *being* a servant, is the Lord's freeman: likewise also he that is called, *being* free, is Christ's servant.

L

Rom. 15. 1 We then that are strong ought to bear the infirmities of the weak, and not to please ourselves.

II Cor. 11. 29 Who is weak, and I am not weak? who is offended, and I burn not?

M

I Cor. 10. 33. *See c, C, § 367, page 932.*

N

Rom. 11. 14. *See b, B, § 340, page 864.*

O

Gal. 2. 2 And I went up by revelation, and communicated unto them that gospel which I preach among the Gentiles, but privately to them which were of reputation, lest by any means I should run, or had run, in vain.

Gal. 5. 7 Ye did run well; who did hinder you that ye should not obey the truth?

Phil. 2. 16 Holding forth the word of life; that I may rejoice in the day of Christ, that I have not run in vain, neither laboured in vain.

Phil. 3. 14 I press toward the mark for the prize of the high calling of God in Christ Jesus.

II Tim. 4. 7 I have fought a good fight, I have finished *my* course, I have kept the faith:

Heb. 12. 1 Wherefore, seeing we also are compassed about with so great a cloud of witnesses, let us lay aside every weight, and the sin which doth so easily beset *us*, and let us run with patience the race that is set before us,

P

Eph. 6. 12 For we wrestle not against flesh and blood, but against principalities, against powers, against the rulers of the darkness of this world, against spiritual wickedness in high *places*.

I Tim. 6. 12 Fight the good fight of faith, lay hold on eternal life, whereunto thou art also called, and hast professed a good profession before many witnesses.

II Tim. 2. 5 And if a man also strive for masteries, *yet* is he not crowned, except he strive lawfully.

II Tim. 4. 7. *See under O.*

Q

I Cor. 3. 14. *See k, K, § 354, page 906.*

§ 365. PAUL ASSERTS HIS APOSTLESHIP AND PRIVILEGES THEREIN. THAT

CHAP. 9.

made all things to all *men*, [n]that I
might by all means save some.
23 And this I do for the gospel's
sake, that I might be partaker thereof
with *you*.
24 Know ye not that they which
run in a race run all, but one receiveth the prize? [o]So run, that ye
may obtain.
25 And every man that [p]striveth
for the mastery is temperate in all

CHAP. 9.

things. Now they *do it* to obtain a
corruptible crown; but we [q]an incorruptible.
26 I therefore so run, [r]not as uncertainly; so fight I, not as one that
beateth the air:
27 [s]But I keep under my body, and
[t]bring *it* into subjection: lest that by
any means, when I have preached
to others, I myself should be [u]a
castaway.

§ 366. FURTHER WARNING IN THE EXAMPLE

10:1–13.

1 Moreover, brethren, I would not
that ye should be ignorant, how that
all our fathers were under [a]the cloud,
and all passed through [b]the sea;
2 And were all baptized unto Moses
in the cloud and in the sea;
3 And did all eat the same [c]spiritual
meat;
4 And did all drink the same [d]spir-
itual drink; for they drank of that
spiritual Rock that [1]followed them:
and that Rock was Christ.
5 But with many of them God was
not well pleased: for they [e]were
overthrown in the wilderness.
6 Now these things were [2]our examples, to the intent that we should
not lust after evil things, as [f]they
also lusted.

A

Ex. 13. 21 And the LORD went before them by day in a pillar of a cloud, to lead them the way; and by night in a pillar of fire, to give them light; to go by day and night:

Num. 14. 14 And they will tell *it* to the inhabitants of this land: *for* they have heard

A—CONCLUDED.

that thou LORD *art* among this people, that thou LORD art seen face to face, and *that* thy cloud standeth over them, and *that* thou goest before them, by daytime in a pillar of a cloud, and in a pillar of fire by night.

Deut. 1. 33 Who went in the way before you, to search you out a place to pitch your tents *in*, in fire by night, to show you by what way ye should go, and in a cloud by day.

Neh. 9. 12 Moreover thou leddest them in the day by a cloudy pillar; and in the night by a pillar of fire, to give them light in the way wherein they should go.

Ps. 78. 14 In the daytime also he led them with a cloud, and all the night with a light of fire.

Ps. 105. 39 He spread a cloud for a covering; and fire to give light in the night.

B

Ex. 14. 22 And the children of Israel went into the midst of the sea upon the dry *ground:* and the waters *were* a wall unto them on their right hand, and on their left.

Josh. 4. 23 For the LORD your God dried up the waters of Jordan from before you, until ye were passed over, as the LORD your God did to the Red sea, which he dried up from before us, until we were gone over:

Ps. 78. 13 He divided the sea, and caused them to pass through; and he made the waters to stand as a heap.

C

Ex. 16. 15 And when the children of Israel

HIS ABSTINENCE WAS FOR THE FURTHERANCE OF THE GOSPEL (CONCLUDED).

For N, O, P and Q, see preceding page (925).

R

II Tim. 2. 5. *See under P, page 925.*

S

Rom. 8. 13. *See t, T, § 332, page 844.*

T

Rom. 6. 18 Being then made free from sin, ye became the servants of righteousness.
19 I speak after the manner of men because of the infirmity of your flesh: for as ye have yielded your members servants to uncleanness and to iniquity unto iniquity; even so now yield your members servants to righteousness unto holiness.

U

Jer. 6. 30 Reprobate silver shall *men* call them, because the LORD hath rejected them.

Luke 9. 25 For what is a man advantaged, if he gain the whole world, and lose himself, or be cast away?

Acts 1. 25 That he may take part of this ministry and apostleship, from which Judas by transgression fell, that he might go to his own place.

IICor. 13. 5 Examine yourselves, whether ye be in the faith; prove your own selves. Know ye not your own selves, how that Jesus Christ is in you, except ye be reprobates?
6 But I trust that ye shall know that we are not reprobates.

OF ISRAEL AGAINST LUSTING AFTER EVIL.

C—CONCLUDED.

saw *it*, they said one to another, It *is* manna: for they wist not what it *was*. And Moses said unto them, This *is* the bread which the LORD hath given you to eat.

Ex. 16. 35 And the children of Israel did eat manna forty years, until they came to a land inhabited: they did eat manna, until they came unto the borders of the land of Canaan.

Neh. 9. 20 Thou gavest also thy good Spirit to instruct them, and withheldest not thy manna from their mouth, and gavest them water for their thirst.

Ps. 78. 24 And had rained down manna upon them to eat, and had given them of the corn of heaven.

D

Ex. 17. 6 Behold, I will stand before thee there upon the rock in Horeb; and thou shalt smite the rock, and there shall come water out of it, that the people may drink. And Moses did so in the sight of the elders of Israel.

Num. 20. 11 And Moses lifted up his hand, and with his rod he smote the rock twice: and the water came out abundantly, and the congregation drank, and their beasts *also*.

Ps. 78. 15 He clave the rocks in the wilderness, and gave *them* drink as *out of* the great depths.

1

Or, *went with them.*

Ps. 105. 41 He opened the rock, and the waters gushed out; they ran in the dry places *like* a river.

E

Num. 14. 32 But *as for* you, your carcasses, they shall fall in this wilderness.
33 And your children shall wander in the wilderness forty years, and bear your whoredoms, until your carcasses be wasted in the wilderness.

Num. 26. 65 For the LORD had said of them, They shall surely die in the wilderness. And there was not left a man of them, save Caleb the son of Jephunneh, and Joshua the son of Nun.

Ps. 106. 26 Therefore he lifted up his hand against them, to overthrow them in the wilderness:

Heb. 3. 17 But with whom was he grieved forty years? *was it* not with them that had sinned, whose carcasses fell in the wilderness?

Jude 5 I will therefore put you in remembrance, though ye once knew this, how that the Lord, having saved the people out of the land of Egypt, afterward destroyed them that believed not.

2

Gr, *our figures.*

F

Num. 11. 4 And the mixed multitude that *was* among them fell a lusting: and the children of Israel also wept again, and said, Who shall give us flesh to eat?

Ps. 106. 14 But lusted exceedingly in the wilderness, and tempted God in the desert.

G

I Cor. 10. 14. *See text of topic, § 367, page 928.*

§ 366. FURTHER WARNING IN THE EXAMPLE OF

CHAP. 10.

7 [g]Neither be ye idolaters, as *were*
some of them; as it is written, [h]The
people sat down to eat and drink,
and rose up to play.

8 [i]Neither let us commit fornication, as some of them committed,
and [k]fell in one day three and twenty
thousand.

9 Neither let us tempt Christ, as
[l]some of them also tempted, and
[m]were destroyed of serpents.

10 Neither murmur ye, as [n]some
of them also murmured, and [o]were
destroyed of [p]the destroyer.

11 Now all these things happened
unto them for [3]ensamples: and [p]they
are written for our admonition, [r]upon
whom the ends of the world are come.

12 Wherefore [s]let him that thinketh
he standeth take heed lest he fall.

13 There hath no temptation taken
you but such as is [4]common to man:
but [t]God *is* faithful, [u]who will not
suffer you to be tempted above that
ye are able; but will with the temptation also [x]make a way to escape,
that ye may be able to bear *it*.

For G, see preceding page (927).

H

Ex. 32. 6 And they rose up early on the morrow, and offered burnt offerings, and brought peace offerings; and the people sat down to eat and to drink, and rose up to play.

I

1 Cor. 6. 18 Flee fornication. Every sin that a man doeth is without the body; but he that committeth fornication sinneth against his own body.

K

Num. 25. 1 And Israel abode in Shittim, and the people began to commit whoredom with the daughters of Moab.

Num. 25. 9 And those that died of the plague were twenty and four thousand.

Ps. 106. 29 Thus they provoked *him* to anger with their inventions: and the plague brake in upon them.

L

Ex. 17. 2 Wherefore the people did chide with Moses, and said, Give us water that we may drink. And Moses said unto them, Why chide ye with me? wherefore do ye tempt the LORD?

Ex. 17. 7 And he called the name of the place Massah, and Meribah, because of the chiding of the children of Israel, and because they tempted the LORD, saying, Is the LORD among us, or not?

Num. 21. 5 And the people spake against God, and against Moses, Wherefore have ye brought us up out of Egypt to die in the wilderness? for *there is* no bread, neither *is there any* water; and our soul loatheth this light bread.

Ps. 78. 18 And they tempted God in their heart by asking meat for their lust.

Ps. 78. 56 Yet they tempted and provoked the most high God, and kept not his testimonies:

Ps. 106. 14 But lusted exceedingly in the wilderness, and tempted God in the desert.

M

Num. 21. 6 And the LORD sent fiery serpents among the people, and they bit the people; and much people of Israel died.

N

Ex. 16. 2 And the whole congregation of the children of Israel murmured against Moses and Aaron in the wilderness:

Ex. 17. 2. *See under L.*

Num. 14. 2 And all the children of Israel murmured against Moses and against

§ 367. ALL FELLOWSHIP WITH IDOLATRY MUST BE RENOUNCED.

10: 14–33.

14 Wherefore, my dearly beloved,
[a]flee from idolatry.

15 I speak as to wise men; judge

CHAP. 10.

ye what I say.

16 [b]The cup of blessing which we
bless, is it not the communion of the

ISRAEL AGAINST LUSTING AFTER EVIL (CONCLUDED).

N—CONCLUDED.

Aaron: and the whole congregation said unto them, Would God that we had died in the land of Egypt! or would God we had died in this wilderness!

Num. 14. 29 Your carcasses shall fall in this wilderness; and all that were numbered of you, according to your whole number, from twenty years old and upward, which have murmured against me,

Num. 16. 41 But on the morrow all the congregation of the children of Israel murmured against Moses and against Aaron, saying, Ye have killed the people of the LORD.

O

Num. 14. 37 Even those men that did bring up the evil report upon the land, died by the plague before the LORD.

Num. 16. 49 Now they that died in the plague were fourteen thousand and seven hundred, besides them that died about the matter of Korah.

P

Ex. 12. 23 For the LORD will pass through to smite the Egyptians; and when he seeth the blood upon the lintel, and on the two side posts, the LORD will pass over the door, and will not suffer the destroyer to come in unto your houses to smite *you*.

II Sa. 24. 16 And when the angel stretched out his hand upon Jerusalem to destroy it, the LORD repented him of the evil, and said to the angel that destroyed the people, It is enough: stay now thine hand. And the angel of the LORD was by the threshingplace of Araunah the Jebusite.

3

Or, *types*.

Q

Rom. 15. 4. *See g, G, § 345, page 878.*

I Cor. 9. 10 Or saith he *it* altogether for our sakes? For our sakes, no doubt, *this* is written: that he that ploweth should plough in hope; and that he that thresheth in hope should be partaker of his hope.

R

I Cor. 7. 29 But this I say, brethren, the time *is* short: it remaineth, that both they that have wives be as though they had none;

Phil. 4. 5 Let your moderation be known unto all men. The Lord *is* at hand.

Heb. 10. 25 Not forsaking the assembling of yourselves together, as the manner of some *is;* but exhorting *one another:* and so much the more, as ye see the day approaching.

Heb. 10. 37 For yet a little while, and he that shall come will come, and will not tarry.

I Jno. 2. 18 Little children, it is the last time: and as ye have heard that antichrist shall come, even now are there many antichrists; whereby we know that it is the last time.

S

Rom. 11. 20 Well; because of unbelief they were broken off, and thou standest by faith. Be not highminded, but fear:

4

Or, *moderate*.

T

I Cor. 1. 9, *See g, G, § 349, page 890.*

U

Ps. 125. 3 For the rod of the wicked shall not rest upon the lot of the righteous; lest the righteous put forth their hands unto iniquity.

II Cor. 1. 10 Who delivered us from so great a death, and doth deliver: in whom we trust that he will yet deliver *us;*

II Pet. 2. 9 The Lord knoweth how to deliver the godly out of temptation, and to reserve the unjust unto the day of judgment to be punished:

X

Jer. 29. 11 For I know the thoughts that I think toward you, saith the LORD, thoughts of peace, and not of evil, to give you an expected end.

Jas. 5. 11 Behold, we count them happy which endure. Ye have heard of the patience of Job, and have seen the end of the Lord; that the Lord is very pitiful, and of tender mercy.

EAT WITHOUT QUESTION, BUT SPARE ANOTHER'S CONSCIENCE.

A

I Cor. 10. 7. *See text of topic § 366.*

II Cor. 6. 17 Wherefore come out from among them, and be ye separate, saith the Lord, and touch not the unclean *thing;* and I will receive you.

A—CONCLUDED.

I Jno. 5. 21 Little children, keep yourselves from idols. Amen.

B

Matt. 26. 26 And as they were eating, Jesus

For B concluded, see next page (930).

§ 367. ALL FELLOWSHIP WITH IDOLATRY MUST BE RENOUNCED. EAT

CHAP. 10.

blood of Christ? [c]The bread which we break, is it not the communion of the body of Christ?

17 For [d]we *being* many are one bread, *and* one body: for we are all partakers of that one bread.

18 Behold [e]Israel [f]after the flesh: [g]are not they which eat of the sacrifices partakers of the altar?

19 What say I then? [h]that the idol is any thing, or that which is offered in sacrifice to idols is any thing?

20 But *I say*, that the things which the Gentiles [i]sacrifice, they sacrifice to devils, and not to God: and I would not that ye should have fellowship with devils.

21 [k]Ye cannot drink the cup of the Lord, and [l]the cup of devils: ye cannot be partakers of the Lord's table, and of the table of devils.

22 Do we [m]provoke the Lord to jealousy? [n]are we stronger than he?

23 [o]All things are lawful for me, but all things are not expedient: all things are lawful for me, but all things edify not.

24 [p]Let no man seek his own, but every man another's *wealth*.

25 [q]Whatsoever is sold in the shambles, *that* eat, asking no question for conscience' sake.

26 For [r]the earth *is* the Lord's, and the fulness thereof.

27 If any of them that believe not bid you *to a feast*, and ye be disposed to go; [s]whatsoever is set before you, eat, asking no question for conscience' sake.

28 But if any man say unto you, This is offered in sacrifice unto idols, eat not [t]for his sake that shewed it, and for conscience' sake: for [u]the earth *is* the Lord's, and the fulness thereof:

CHAP. 10.

29 Conscience, I say, not thine own, but of the other: for [x]why is my liberty judged of another *man's* conscience?

B—CONCLUDED.

took bread, and blessed *it*, and brake *it*, and gave *it* to the disciples, and said, Take, eat; this is my body.

Matt. 26. 27 And he took the cup, and gave thanks, and gave *it* to them, saying, Drink ye all of it;

28 For this is my blood of the new testament, which is shed for many for the remission of sins.

C

Acts 2. 42 And they continued steadfastly in the apostles' doctrine and fellowship, and in breaking of bread, and in prayers.

Acts 2. 46 And they, continuing daily with one accord in the temple, and breaking bread from house to house, did eat their meat with gladness and singleness of heart,

I Cor. 11. 23 For I have received of the Lord that which also I delivered unto you, That the Lord Jesus, the *same* night in which he was betrayed, took bread:

24 And when he had given thanks, he brake *it*, and said, Take, eat; this is my body, which is broken for you: this do in remembrance of me.

D

Rom. 12. 5. *See l, L, § 342, page 868.*

E

Rom. 4. 12 And the father of circumcision to them who are not of the circumcision only, but who also walk in the steps of that faith of our father Abraham, which *he had* being *yet* uncircumcised.

Gal. 6. 16 And as many as walk according to this rule, peace *be* on them, and mercy, and upon the Israel of God.

F

Rom. 4. 1 What shall we say then that Abraham our father, as pertaining to the flesh, hath found?

Rom. 9. 3 For I could wish that myself were accursed from Christ for my brethren, my kinsmen according to the flesh:

Rom. 9. 5 Whose *are* the fathers, and of whom as concerning the flesh Christ *came*, who is over all, God blessed for ever. Amen.

II Cor. 11 18 Seeing that many glory after the flesh, I will glory also.

WITHOUT QUESTION, BUT SPARE ANOTHER'S CONSCIENCE (CONTINUED).

G

Lev. 3. 3 And he shall offer of the sacrifice of the peace offering an offering made by fire unto the LORD; the fat that covereth the inwards, and all the fat that *is* upon the inwards,

Lev. 7. 15 And the flesh of the sacrifice of his peace offerings for thanksgiving shall be eaten the same day that it is offered; he shall not leave any of it until the morning.

H

I Cor. 8. 4. *See f, F, § 364, page 918.*

I

Lev. 17. 7 And they shall no more offer their sacrifices unto devils, after whom they have gone a whoring. This shall be a statute for ever unto them throughout their generations.

Deut. 32. 17 They sacrificed unto devils, not to God; to gods whom they knew not, to new *gods that* came newly up, whom your fathers feared not.

Ps. 106. 37 Yea, they sacrificed their sons and their daughters unto devils.

Rev. 9. 20 And the rest of the men which were not killed by these plagues yet repented not of the works of their hands, that they should not worship devils, and idols of gold, and silver, and brass, and stone, and of wood; which neither can see, nor hear, nor walk:

K

II Cor. 6. 15 And what concord hath Christ with Belial? or what part hath he that believeth with an infidel?

16 And what agreement hath the temple of God with idols? for ye are the temple of the living God; as God hath said, I will dwell in them, and walk in *them;* and I will be their God, and they shall be my people.

L

Deut. 32. 38 Which did eat the fat of their sacrifices, *and* drank the wine of their drink offierings? let them rise up and help you, *and* be your protection.

M

Deut. 32. 21 They have moved me to jealousy with *that which is* not God; they have provoked me to anger with their vanities: and I will move them to jealousy with *those which are* not a people; I will provoke them to anger with a foolish nation.

N

Eze. 22. 14 Can thine heart endure, or can thine hands be strong, in the days that I shall deal with thee? I the LORD have spoken *it*, and will do *it*.

O

I Cor. 6. 12. *See a, A, § 361, page 912.*

P

Rom. 15. 1 and 2. *See c, C, § 345, page 878.*

Q

I Tim. 4. 4 For every creature of God *is* good, and nothing to be refused, if it be received with thanksgiving:

R

Ex. 19. 5 Now therefore, if ye will obey my voice indeed, and keep my covenant, then ye shall be a peculiar treasure unto me above all people: for all the earth *is* mine:

Deut. 10. 14 Behold, the heaven and the heaven of heavens *is* the LORD'S thy God, the earth *also*, with all that therein *is*.

Ps. 24. 1 The earth *is* the LORD'S, and the fulness thereof; the world, and they that dwell therein.

Ps. 50. 12 If I were hungry, I would not tell thee: for the world *is* mine, and the fulness thereof.

S

Luke 10. 7 And in the same house remain, eating and drinking such things as they give: for the labourer is worthy of his hire. Go not from house to house.

T

I Cor. 8. 10. *See s, S. § 364, page 920.*

U

I Cor. 10. 26. *See text of topic.*

X

Rom. 14. 16 Let not then your good be evil spoken of:

1

Or, *thanksgiving.*

Y

Rom. 14. 6. *See f, F, § 344, page 876.*

Z

Col. 3. 17 And whatsoever ye do in word or deed, *do* all in the name of the Lord Jesus, giving thanks to God and the Father by him.

I Pet. 4. 11 If any man speak, *let him speak* as the oracles of God; if any man minister, *let him do it* as of the ability which God giveth; that God in all things may be glorified through Jesus Christ: to whom be praise and dominion for ever and ever. Amen.

A

I Cor. 8. 13. *See x, X, § 364, page 920.*

2

Gr, *Greeks.*

B

Acts 20. 28 Take heed therefore unto yourselves, and to all the flock, over the which the Holy Ghost hath made you

§ 367. ALL FELLOWSHIP WITH IDOLATRY MUST BE RENOUNCED. EAT

CHAP. 10.

30 For if I by [1]grace be a partaker, why am I evil spoken of for that [x]for which I give thanks?

31 [y]Whether therefore ye eat, or drink, or [z]whatsoever ye do, do all to the glory of God.

32 [a]Give none offence, neither to the Jews, nor to the [2]Gentiles, nor to [b]the church of God:

33 Even as [c]I please all *men* in all *things*, [d]not seeking mine own profit, but the *profit* of many, that they may be saved.

For 1, Y, Z, A, 2 and B, see preceding page (931).

§ 368. CONCERNING AUTHORITY AND

11 : 1–16.

1 Be [a]ye followers of me, even as I also *am* of Christ.

2 Now I praise you, brethren, [b]that ye remember me in all things, and [c]keep the [1]ordinances, as I delivered *them* to you.

3 But I would have you know, that [d]the head of every man is Christ; and [e]the head of the woman *is* the man; and [f]the head of Christ *is* God.

4 Every man praying or [g]prophesying, having *his* head covered, dishonoureth his head.

5 But [h]every woman that prayeth or prophesieth with *her* head uncovered dishonoureth her head: for that is even all one as if she were [i]shaven.

6 For if the woman be not covered, let her also be shorn: but if it be [k]a shame for a woman to be shorn or shaven, let her be covered.

7 For a man indeed ought not to cover *his* head, forasmuch as [l]he is the image and glory of God: but the woman is the glory of the man.

8 For [m]the man is not of the woman: but the woman of the man.

A

I Cor. 4. 16. *See c, C, § 358, 904.*

Eph. 5. 1 Be ye therefore followers of God, as dear children;

B

I Cor. 4. 17. *See f, F, § 358, page 904.*

C

I Cor. 7. 17 But as God hath distributed to every man, as the Lord hath called every one, so let him walk. And so ordain I in all churches.

1

Or, *traditions.*

II Thes. 2. 15 Therefore, brethren, stand fast, and hold the traditions which ye have been taught, whether by word, or our epistle.

II Thes. 3. 6 Now we command you, brethren, in the name of our Lord Jesus Christ, that ye withdraw yourselves from every brother that walketh disorderly, and not after the tradition which he received of us.

D

Rom. 14. 9 For to this end Christ both died, and rose, and revived, that he might be Lord both of the dead and living.

Eph. 5. 23 For the husband is the head of the wife, even as Christ is the head of the church: and he is the Saviour of the body.

E

Gen. 3. 16 Unto the woman he said, I will greatly multiply thy sorrow and thy conception; in sorrow thou shalt bring forth children; and thy desire *shall be* to thy husband, and he shall rule over thee.

Eph. 5. 22 Wives, submit yourselves unto your own husbands, as unto the Lord.

Eph. 5. 23. *See under D.*

WITHOUT QUESTION, BUT SPARE ANOTHER'S CONSCIENCE (CONCLUDED).

B—CONCLUDED. See preceding page (931).
overseers, to feed the church of God, which he hath purchased with his own blood.

I Cor. 11. 22 What? have ye not houses to eat and to drink in? or despise ye the church of God, and shame them that have not? What shall I say to you? shall I praise you in this? I praise *you* not:

I Tim. 3. 5 (For if a man know not how to rule his own house, how shall he take care of the church of God?)

C

Rom. 15. 2 Let every one of us please *his* neighbour for his good to edification.

I Cor. 9. 19 For though I be free from all *men*, yet have I made myself servant unto all, that I might gain the more.

I Cor. 9. 22 To the weak became I as weak, that I might gain the weak: I am made all things to all *men*, that I might by all means save some.

D

I Cor. 10. 24. *See text of topic, § 367, page 930.*

ITS SIGNS, THE COVERING OF HEADS.

E—CONCLUDED.

Eph. 5. 24 Therefore as the church is subject unto Christ, so *let* the wives *be* to their own husbands in every thing.

Col. 3. 18 Wives, submit yourselves unto your own husbands, as it is fit in the Lord.

I Tim. 2. 11 Let the woman learn in silence with all subjection.

I Pet. 3. 1 Likewise, ye wives, *be* in subjection to your own husbands; that, if any obey not the word, they also may without the word be won by the conversation of the wives.

I Pet. 3. 5 For after this manner in the old time the holy women also, who trusted in God, adorned themselves, being in subjection unto their own husbands:

6 Even as Sarah obeyed Abraham, calling him lord: whose daughters ye are, as long as ye do well, and are not afraid with any amazement.

F

John 14. 28 Ye have heard how I said unto you, I go away, and come *again* unto you. If ye loved me, ye would rejoice, because I said, I go unto the Father: for my Father is greater than I.

I Cor. 3. 23 And ye are Christ's; and Christ *is* God's

I Cor. 15. 27 For he hath put all things under his feet. But when he saith, All things are put under *him*, *it is* manifest that he is excepted, which did put all things under him.

28 And when all things shall be subdued unto him, then shall the Son also himself be subject unto him that put all things under him, that God may be all in all.

Phil. 2. 7 But made himself of no reputation, and took upon him the form of a servant, and was made in the likeness of men:

F—CONCLUDED.

Phil. 2. 8 And being found in fashion as a man, he humbled himself, and became obedient unto death, even the death of the cross.

9 Wherefore God also hath highly exalted him, and given him a name which is above every name:

G

Rom. 12. 6. *See n, N, § 342, page 868.*

H

Acts 21. 9 And the same man had four daughters, virgins, which did prophesy.

I

Deut. 21. 12 Then thou shalt bring her home to thine house; and she shall shave her head, and pare her nails;

K

Num. 5. 18 And the priest shall set the woman before the LORD, and uncover the woman's head, and put the offering of memorial in her hands, which *is* the jealousy offering: and the priest shall have in his hand the bitter water that causeth the curse:

L

Gen. 1. 26 And God said, Let us make man in our image, after our likeness: and let them have dominion over the fish of the sea, and over the fowl of the air, and over the cattle, and over all the earth, and over every creeping thing that creepeth upon the earth.

27 So God created man in his *own* image, in the image of God created he him; male and female created he them.

Gen. 5. 1 This *is* the book of the generations of Adam. In the day that God created man, in the likeness of God made he him;

Gen. 9. 6 Whoso sheddeth man's blood, by man shall his blood be shed: for in the image of God made he man.

For L concluded and M, see next page (934.)

§ 368. CONCERNING AUTHORITY AND ITS

CHAP. 11.

9 [n]Neither was the man created
for the woman; but the woman for
the man.

10 For this cause ought the woman
[o]to have [2]power on *her* head [p]because
of the angels.

11 Nevertheless [q]neither is the man
without the woman, neither the
woman without the man, in the
Lord.

12 For as the woman *is* of the man,
even so *is* the man also by the
woman; [r]but all things of God.

13 Judge in yourselves: is it comely
that a woman pray unto God uncovered?

14 Doth not even nature itself teach

CHAP. 11.

you, that, if a man have long hair,
it is a shame unto him?

15 But if a woman have long hair,
it is a glory to her: for *her* hair is
given her for a [3]covering.

16 But [s]if any man seem to be contentious, we have no such custom,
neither the [t]churches of God.

L—CONCLUDED.

Jas. 3. 9 Therewith bless we God, even the Father; and therewith curse we men, which are made after the similitude of God.

M

Gen. 2. 21 And the LORD God caused a deep sleep to fall upon Adam, and he slept: and he took one of his ribs, and closed up the flesh instead thereof;

22 And the rib, which the LORD God

§ 369. PAUL CENSURES DIVISIONS, HERESIES AND PROFANATIONS, AND

11:17–34.

17 Now in this that I declare *unto
you* I praise *you* not, that ye come
together not for the better, but for
the worse.

18 For first of all, when ye come
together in the church, [a]I hear that
there be [1]divisions among you; and
I partly believe it.

19 For [b]there must be also [2]heresies
among you, [c]that they which are approved may be made manifest among
you.

20 When ye come together therefore into one place, [3]*this* is not to
eat the Lord's supper.

21 For in eating every one taketh
before *other* his own supper: and
one is hungry, and [d]another is
drunken.

CHAP. 11.

22 What? have ye not houses to
eat and to drink in? or despise ye
[e]the church of God, and [f]shame [4]them
that have not? What shall I say to
you? shall I praise you in this? I
praise *you* not.

23 For [g]I have received of the Lord
that which also I delivered unto you,
[h]That the Lord Jesus the *same* night
in which he was betrayed, took
bread:

24 And when he had given thanks,
he brake *it*, and said, Take, eat:
this is my body, which is broken for
you: this do, [5]in remembrance of me.

25 After the same manner also *he
took* the cup, when he had supped,
saying, This cup is the new testament in my blood: this do ye, as oft
as ye drink *it*, in remembrance of
me.

26 For as often as ye eat this bread,

SIGNS, THE COVERING OF HEADS (Concluded).

M—Concluded.

had taken from man, made he a woman, and brought her unto the man.

N

Gen. 2. 18 And the Lord God said, *It is* not good that the man should be alone; I will make him a help meet for him.

Gen. 2. 21 and 22. *See under M.*

Gen. 2. 23 And Adam said, This *is* now bone of my bones, and flesh of my flesh: she shall be called Woman, because she was taken out of Man.

O

Gen. 24. 65 For she *had* said unto the servant, What man *is* this that walketh in the field to meet us? And the servant *had* said, It *is* my master: therefore she took a vail, and covered herself.

2

That is, *a covering, in sign that she is under the power of her husband.*

P

Eccl. 5. 6 Suffer not thy mouth to cause thy flesh to sin; neither say thou before the angel, that it *was* an error: wherefore should God be angry at thy voice, and destroy the work of thine hands?

Q

Gal. 3. 28 There is neither Jew nor Greek, there is neither bond nor free, there is neither male nor female: for ye are all one in Christ Jesus.

R

Rom. 11. 36 For of him, and through him, and to him, *are* all things: to whom *be* glory for ever. Amen.

3

Or, *veil.*

S

I Tim. 6. 4 He is proud, knowing nothing, but doting about questions and strifes of words, whereof cometh envy, strife, railings, evil surmisings,

T

I Cor. 7. 17 But as God hath distributed to every man, as the Lord hath called every one, so let him walk. And so ordain I in all churches.

I Cor. 14. 33 For God is not *the author* of confusion, but of peace, as in all churches of the saints.

SETS FOURTH THE MANNER AND PURPOSE OF THE LORD'S SUPPER.

A

I Cor. 3. 3. *See e, E, § 353, page 898.*

1

Or, *schisms.*

B

Matt. 18. 7 Woe unto the world because of offences! for it must needs be that offences come; but woe to that man by whom the offence cometh!

Luke 17. 1 Then said he unto the disciples, It is impossible but that offences will come: but woe *unto him*, through whom they come!

Acts 20. 30 Also of your own selves shall men arise, speaking perverse things, to draw away disciples after them.

I Tim. 4. 1 Now the spirit speaketh expressly, that in the latter times some shall depart from the faith, giving heed to seducing spirits, and doctrines of devils;

II Pet. 2. 1 But there were false prophets also among the people, even as there shall be false teachers among you, who privily shall bring in damnable heresies, even denying the Lord that bought them, and bring upon themselves swift destruction.

2 And many shall follow their pernicious ways; by reason of whom the way of truth shall be evil spoken of.

2

Or, *sects.*

C

Deut. 13. 3 Thou shalt not hearken unto the words of that prophet, or that dreamer of dreams: for the Lord your God proveth you, to know whether ye love the Lord your God with all your heart and with all your soul.

Luke 2. 35 (Yea, a sword shall pierce through thy own soul also,) that the thoughts of many hearts may be revealed.

I Jno. 2. 19 They went out from us, but they were not of us; for if they had been of us, they would *no doubt* have continued with us: but *they went out*, that they might be made manifest that they were not all of us.

3

Or, *ye cannot eat.*

D

II Pet. 2. 13 And shall receive the reward of unrighteousness, *as* they that count it pleasure to riot in the daytime. Spots *they are* and blemishes, sporting themselves with their own deceivings while they feast with you;

Jude. 12 These are spots in your feasts of charity, when they feast with you,

For D concluded, E, F, 4, G, H and 5, see next page (936).

§ 369. PAUL CENSURES DIVISIONS, HERESIES AND PROFANATIONS, AND SETS

D—CONCLUDED.

CHAP. 11.

and drink this cup, [6]ye do shew the
Lord's death [i]till he come.

27 [k]Wherefore whosoever shall eat
this bread, and drink *this* cup of the
Lord, unworthily, shall be guilty of
the body and blood of the Lord.

28 But [l]let a man examine himself,
and so let him eat of *that* bread, and
drink of *that* cup.

29 For he that eateth and drinketh
unworthily, eateth and drinketh [7]dam-
nation to himself, not discerning the
Lord's body.

30 For this cause many *are* weak
and sickly among you, and many
sleep.

31 For [m]if we would judge ourselves, we should not be judged.

32 But when we are judged, [n]we are
chastened of the Lord, that we
should not be condemned with the
world.

33 Wherefore, my brethren, when
ye come together to eat, tarry one
for another.

34 And if any man hunger, let him
eat at [o]home; that ye come not together unto [7]condemnation. And
the rest will I [p]set in order when I
come.

feeding themselves without fear: clouds *they are* without water, carried about of winds; trees whose fruit withereth, without fruit, twice dead, plucked up by the roots;

E

I Cor. 10. 32. *See b, B, § 367, page 932.*

F

Jas. 2. 6 But ye have despised the poor. Do not rich men oppress you, and draw you before the judgment seats?

4

Or, *them that are poor?*

G

1 Cor. 15. 3 For I delivered unto you first of all that which I also received, how that Christ died for our sins according to the Scriptures;

Gal. 1. 1 Paul, an apostle, (not of men, neither by man, but by Jesus Christ, and God the Father, who raised him from the dead;)

Gal. 1. 11 But I certify you, brethren, that the gospel which was preached of me is not after man.

12 For I neither received it of man, neither was I taught *it*, but by the revelation of Jesus Christ.

H

Matt. 26. 26 And as they were eating, Jesus took bread, and blessed *it*, and brake *it*, and gave *it* to the disciples, and said, Take, eat; this is my body.

Mark 14. 22 And as they did eat, Jesus took bread, and blessed, and brake *it*, and gave to them, and said, Take, eat: this is my body.

Luke 22. 19 And he took bread, and gave thanks, and brake *it*, and gave unto them, saying, This is my body which is given for you: this do in remembrance of me.

§ 370. THE DIVERSITY OF GIFTS, MINISTRATIONS

12:1–11.

1 Now [a]concerning spiritual *gifts*,
brethren, I would not have you ignorant.

2 Ye know [b]that ye were Gentiles,
carried away unto these [c]dumb idols,
even as ye were led.

3 Wherefore I give you to understand, [d]that no man speaking by the

A

1 Cor. 14. 1 Follow after charity, and desire spiritual *gifts*, but rather that ye may prophesy.

1 Cor. 14. 37 If any man think himself to be a prophet, or spiritual, let him acknowledge that the things that I write unto you are the commandments of the Lord.

B

1 Cor. 6. 11 And such were some of you: but ye are washed, but ye are sanctified, but ye are justified in the name of the

FORTH THE MANNER AND PURPOSE OF THE LORD'S SUPPER (CONCLUDED).

5

Or, *for a remembrance.*

6

Or, *shew ye.*

I

Acts 1. 11. *See d, D, § 228, page 628.*

K

Num. 9. 10 Speak unto the children of Israel, saying, If any man of you or of your posterity shall be unclean by reason of a dead body, or *be* in a journey afar off, yet he shall keep the passover unto the LORD.

Num. 9. 13 But the man that *is* clean, and is not in a journey, and forbeareth to keep the passover, even the same soul shall be cut off from among his people: because he brought not the offering of the LORD in his appointed season, that man shall bear his sin.

John 6. 51 I am the living bread which came down from heaven: if any man eat of this bread, he shall live for ever: and the bread that I will give is my flesh, which I will give for the life of the world.

John 6. 63 It is the spirit that quickeneth; the flesh profiteth nothing: the words that I speak unto you, *they* are spirit, and *they* are life.

64 But there are some of you that believe not. For Jesus knew from the beginning who they were that believed not, and who should betray him.

I Cor. 10. 21 Ye cannot drink the cup of the Lord, and the cup of devils: ye cannot be partakers of the Lord's table, and of the table of devils.

L

II Cor. 13. 5 Examine yourselves, whether ye be in the faith; prove your own selves. Know ye not your own selves, how that Jesus Christ is in you, except ye be reprobates?

L—CONCLUDED

Gal. 6. 4 But let every man prove his own work, and then shall he have rejoicing in himself alone, and not in another.

7

Or, *judgment.*

M

Ps. 32. 5 I acknowledged my sin unto thee, and mine iniquity have I not hid. I said, I will confess my transgressions unto the LORD; and thou forgavest the iniquity of my sin. Selah.

N

Ps. 94. 12 Blessed *is* the man whom thou chastenest, O LORD, and teachest him out of thy law;

Heb. 12. 5 And ye have forgotten the exhortation which speaketh unto you as unto children, My son, despise not thou the chastening of the Lord, nor faint when thou art rebuked of him:

6 For whom the Lord loveth he chasteneth, and scourgeth every son whom he receiveth.

7 If ye endure chastening, God dealeth with you as with sons; for what son is he whom the father chasteneth not?

8 But if ye be without chastisement, whereof all are partakers, then are ye bastards, and not sons.

O

I Cor. 11. 22. *See text of topic, page 934*

P

I Cor. 7. 17 But as God hath distributed to every man, as the Lord hath called every one, so let him walk. And so ordain I in all churches.

Tit. 1. 5 For this cause left I thee in Crete, that thou shouldest set in order the things that are wanting, and ordain elders in every city, as I had appointed thee:

AND WORKINGS IN THE SAME SPIRIT.

B—CONTINUED.

Lord Jesus, and by the Spirit of our God.

Eph. 2. 11 Wherefore remember, that ye *being* in time past Gentiles in the flesh, who are called Uncircumcision by that which is called Circumcision in the flesh made by hands;

12 That at that time ye were without Christ, being aliens from the commonwealth of Israel, and strangers from the covenants of promise, having no hope, and without God in the world:

B—CONTINUED.

I Thes. 1. 9 For they themselves shew of us what manner of entering in we had unto you, and how ye turned to God from idols to serve the living and true God;

Tit. 3. 3 For we ourselves also were sometimes foolish, disobedient, deceived, serving divers lusts and pleasures, living in malice and envy, hateful, *and* hating one another.

For B concluded, C and D, see next page (938).

§ 370. THE DIVERSITY OF GIFTS, MINISTRATIONS

CHAP. 12.

spirit of God calleth Jesus [1]accursed:
and [e]*that* no man can say that Jesus is
the Lord, but by the Holy Ghost.
4 Now [f]there are diversities of gifts,
but the [g]same Spirit.
5 And there are differences of [2]ad-
ministrations, but the same Lord.
6 And there are diversities of operations, but it is the same God
[h]which worketh all in all.
7 [i]But the manifestation of the
Spirit is given to every man to profit
withal.
8 For to one is given by the Spirit
[k]the word of wisdom; to another the
[l]word of knowledge by the same
Spirit;
9 [m]To another faith by the same
Spirit; to another [n]the gifts of healing by the same Spirit;
10 [o]To another the working of miracles; to another [p]prophecy; [q]to another discerning of spirits; to another [r]*divers* kinds of tongues; to another the interpretation of tongues:
11 But all these worketh that one
and the selfsame Spirit, [s]dividing to
every man severally [t]as he will.

B—CONCLUDED.

1 Pet. 4. 3 For the time past of *our* life may suffice us to have wrought the will of the Gentiles, when we walked in lasciviousness, lusts, excess of wine, revellings, banquetings, and abominable idolatries:

C

Ps. 115. 5 They have mouths, but they speak not: eyes have they, but they see not:

D

Mark 9. 39 But Jesus said, Forbid him not: for there is no man which shall do a miracle in my name, that can lightly speak evil of me.

I Jno. 4. 2 Hereby know ye the Spirit of God: Every spirit that confesseth that Jesus

D—CONCLUDED.

Christ is come in the flesh is of God:
3 And every spirit that confesseth not that Jesus Christ is come in the flesh is not of God: and this is that *spirit* of antichrist, whereof ye have heard that it should come; and even now already is it in the world.

1

Or, *anathema.*

E

Matt. 16. 17 And Jesus answered and said unto him, Blessed art thou, Simon Bar-jona: for flesh and blood hath not revealed *it* unto thee, but my Father which is in heaven.

John 15. 26 But when the Comforter is come, whom I will send unto you from the Father, *even* the Spirit of truth, which proceedeth from the Father, he shall testify of me:

II Cor. 3. 5 Not that we are sufficient of ourselves to think any thing as of ourselves; but our sufficiency *is* of God;

F

Rom. 12. 6. *See m, M, § 342, page 868.*

Eph. 4. 11 And he gave some, apostles; and some, prophets; and some, evangelists; and some, pastors and teacher;

Heb. 2. 4 God also bearing *them* witness, both with signs and wonders, and with divers miracles, and gifts of the Holy Ghost, according to his own will?

G

Eph. 4. 4 *There is* one body, and one Spirit, even as ye are called in one hope of your calling;

2

Or, *ministries.*

H

Eph. 1. 23 Which is his body, the fulness of him that filleth all in all.

I

Rom. 12. 6 Having then gifts differing according to the grace that is given to us, whether prophecy, *let us prophesy* according to the proportion of faith;
7 Or ministry *let us wait* on *our* ministering: or he that teacheth, on teaching;
8 Or he that exhorteth, on exhortation: he that giveth, *let him do it* with simplicity; he that ruleth, with diligence; he that sheweth mercy, with cheerfulness.

I Cor. 10. 33 Even as I please all *men* in all *things*, not seeking mine own profit, but the *profit* of many, that they may be saved.

AND WORKINGS IN THE SAME SPIRIT (CONCLUDED).

I—CONCLUDED.

I Cor. 14. 26 How is it then, brethren? when ye come together, every one of you hath a psalm, hath a doctrine, hath a tongue, hath a revelation, hath an interpretation. Let all things be done unto edifying.

II Cor. 12. 19 Again, think ye that we excuse ourselves unto you? we speak before God in Christ: but *we do* all things, dearly beloved, for your edifying.

Eph. 4. 12 For the perfecting of the saints, for the work of the ministry, for the edifying of the body of Christ:

I Pet. 4. 10 As every man hath received the gift, *even so* minister the same one to another, as good stewards of the manifold grace of God.

11 If any man speak, *let him speak* as the oracles of God; if any man minister, *let him do it* as of the ability which God giveth: that God in all things may be glorified through Jesus Christ, to whom be praise and dominion for ever and ever. Amen.

K

I Cor. 2. 6 Howbeit we speak wisdom among them that are perfect: yet not the wisdom of this world, nor of the princes of this world, that come to nought:

7 But we speak the wisdom of God in a mystery, *even* the hidden *wisdom*, which God ordained before the world unto our glory:

L

I Cor. 1. 5. *See b, B, § 349, page 888.*

I Cor. 13. 2 And though I have *the gift of* prophecy, and understand all mysteries, and all knowledge; and though I have all faith, so that I could remove mountains, and have not charity, I am nothing.

M

Matt. 17. 19 Then came the disciples to Jesus apart, and said, Why could not we cast him out?

20 And Jesus said unto them, Because of your unbelief: for verily I say unto you, If ye have faith as a grain of mustard seed, ye shall say unto this mountain, Remove hence to yonder place; and it shall remove: and nothing shall be impossible unto you.

I Cor. 13. 2. *See under L.*

II Cor. 4. 13 We having the same spirit of faith, according as it is written, I believed, and therefore have I spoken; we also believe, and therefore speak;

N

Matt. 10. 8 Heal the sick, cleanse the lepers,

N—CONCLUDED.

raise the dead, cast out devils: freely ye have received, freely give.

Mark 6. 13 And they cast out many devils, and anointed with oil many that were sick, and healed *them*.

Mark 16 18. *See z, Z, § 219, page 614.*

Luke 9. 2 And he sent them to preach the kingdom of God, and to heal the sick.

Luke 10. 9 And heal the sick that are therein, and say unto them, The kingdom of God is come nigh unto you.

Acts 19. 11 And God wrought special miracles by the hands of Paul:

12 So that from his body were brought unto the sick handkerchiefs or aprons, and the diseases departed from them, and the evil spirits went out of them.

Jas. 5. 14 Is any sick among you? let him call for the elders of the church; and let them pray over him, anointing him with oil in the name of the Lord:

15 And the prayer of faith shall save the sick, and the Lord shall raise him up; and if he have committed sins, they shall be forgiven him.

O

Mark 16. 17 And these signs shall follow them that believe; In my name shall they cast out devils; they shall speak with new tongues;

I Cor. 12. 28. *See text of topic, § 371.*

Gal. 3. 5 He therefore that ministereth to you the Spirit, and worketh miracles among you, *doeth he it* by the works of the law, or by the hearing of faith?

P

Rom. 12. 6. *See n, N, § 342, page 868.*

Q

I Cor. 14. 29 Let the prophets speak two or three, and let the other judge.

I Jno. 4. 1 Beloved, believe not every spirit, but try the spirits whether they are of God: because many false prophets are gone out into the world.

R

Acts 2. 4. *See e, E, § 230, page 634.*

S

Rom. 12. 6. *See under I.*

I Cor. 7. 7. *See h, H, § 362, page 914.*

Eph. 4. 7 But unto every one of us is given grace according to the measure of the gift of Christ.

T

Heb. 2. 4 God also bearing *them* witness, both with signs and wonders, and with divers miracles, and gifts of the Holy Ghost, according to his own will?

§ 371. BY THE FIGURE OF THE BODY IT IS SHOWN

12: 12–31.

12 For [a]as the body is one, and hath many members, and all the members of that one body, being many, are one body: [b]so also *is* Christ.

13 For [c]by one Spirit are we all baptized into one body, [d]whether *we be* Jews or [1]Gentiles, whether *we be* bond or free; and [e]have been all made to drink into one Spirit.

14 For the body is not one member, but many.

15 If the foot shall say, Because I am not the hand, I am not of the body; is it therefore not of the body?

16 And if the ear shall say, Because I am not the eye, I am not of the body; is it therefore not of the body?

17 If the whole body *were* an eye, where *were* the hearing? If the whole *were* hearing, where *were* the smelling?

18 But now hath [f]God set the members every one of them in the body, [g]as it hath pleased him.

19 And if they were all one member, where *were* the body?

20 But now *are they* many members, yet but one body.

21 And the eye cannot say unto the hand, I have no need of thee: nor again the head to the feet, I have no need of you.

22 Nay, much more those members of the body, which seem to be more feeble, are necessary:

23 And those *members* of the body, which we think to be less honourable, upon these we [2]bestow more abundant honour; and our uncomely

CHAP. 12.

parts have more abundant comeliness.

24 For our comely *parts* have no need: but God hath tempered the body together, having given more abundant honour to that *part* which lacked:

25 That there should be [3]no schism in the body; but *that* the members should have the same care one for another.

26 And whether one member suffer, all the members suffer with it; or one member be honoured, all the members rejoice with it.

27 Now [h]ye are the body of Christ, and members in particular.

28 And God hath set some in the church, first [i]apostles, secondarily [k]prophets, thirdly teachers, after that [l]miracles, then [m]gifts of healings, [n]helps, [o]governments, [4]diversities of tongues.

29 *Are* all apostles? *are* all prophets? *are* all teachers? *are* all [5]workers of miracles?

30 Have all the gifts of healing? do all speak with tongues? do all interpret?

31 But [p]covet earnestly the best gifts: and yet shew I unto you a more excellent way.

A

Rom. 12. 4. *See k, K, § 342, page 868.*

Eph. 4. 5 One Lord, one faith, one baptism, 6 One God and Father of all, who *is* above all, and through all, and in you all.

B

I Cor. 12. 27. *See text of topic.*

Gal. 3. 16 Now to Abraham and his seed were the promises made. He saith not, And to seeds, as of many; but as of one, And to thy seed, which is Christ.

C

Rom. 6. 5 For if we have been planted together in the likeness of his death, we shall be also *in the likeness* of *his* resurrection:

HOW ALL ARE BAPTIZED INTO THE BODY OF CHRIST.

D

Gal. 3. 28 There is neither Jew nor Greek, there is neither bond nor free, there is neither male nor female: for ye are all one in Christ Jesus.

Eph. 2. 13 But now, in Christ Jesus, ye who sometimes were far off are made nigh by the blood of Christ.

14 For he is our peace, who hath made both one, and hath broken down the middle wall of partition *between us;*

Eph. 2. 16 And that he might reconcile both unto God in one body by the cross, having slain the enmity thereby:

1

Gr. *Greeks.*

E

John 6. 63 It is the Spirit that quickeneth; the flesh profiteth nothing: the words that I speak unto you, *they* are spirit, and *they* are life.

John 7. 37 In the last day, that great *day* of the feast, Jesus stood and cried, saying, If any man thirst, let him come unto me, and drink.

38 He that believeth on me, as the Scripture hath said, out of his belly shall flow rivers of living water.

39 (But this spake he of the Spirit, which they that believe on him should receive: for the Holy Ghost was not yet *given;* because that Jesus was not yet glorified.)

F

I Cor. 12. 28. *See text of topic.*

G

Rom. 12. 3 For I say, through the grace given unto me, to every man that is among you, not to think *of himself* more highly than he ought to think; but to think soberly, according as God hath dealt to every man the measure of faith.

I Cor. 3. 5 Who then is Paul, and who *is* Apollos, but ministers by whom ye believed, even as the Lord gave to every man?

2

Or, *put on.*

3

Or, *division.*

H

Rom. 12. 5. *See l, L, § 342, page 868.*

Eph. 4. 12 For the perfecting of the saints, for the work of the ministry, for the edifying of the body of Christ:

Eph. 5. 23 For the husband is the head of the wife, even as Christ is the head of the church: and he is the Saviour of the body.

H—Concluded.

Eph. 5. 30 For we are members of his body, of his flesh, and of his bones.

Col. 1. 24 Who now rejoice in my sufferings for you, and fill up that which is behind of the afflictions of Christ in my flesh for his body's sake, which is the church:

I

Eph. 2. 20 And are built upon the foundation of the apostles and prophets, Jesus Christ himself being the chief corner *stone;*

Eph. 3. 5 Which in other ages was not made known unto the sons of men, as it is now revealed unto his holy apostles and prophets by the Spirit;

Eph. 4. 11 And he gave some, apostles; and some, prophets; and some, evangelists; and some, pastors and teachers;

K

Acts 13. 1 Now there were in the church that was at Antioch certain prophets and teachers; as Barnabas, and Simeon that was called Niger, and Lucius of Cyrene, and Manaen, which had been brought up with Herod the tetrarch, and Saul.

Rom. 12. 6. *See n, N, § 342, page 868.*

L

I Cor. 12. 10. *See o, O, § 370, page 938*

M

I Cor. 12. 9. *See n, N, § 370, page 938.*

N

Num. 11. 17 And I will come down and talk with thee there: and I will take of the spirit which *is* upon thee, and will put *it* upon them; and they shall bear the burden of the people with thee, that thou bear *it* not thyself alone.

O

Rom. 12. 8. *See, r, R, § 342, page 870.*

Heb. 13. 17 Obey them that have the rule over you, and submit yourselves: for they watch for your souls, as they that must give account, that they may do it with joy, and not with grief: for that *is* unprofitable for you.

4

Or, *kinds.*

I Cor. 12. 10. *See text of topic, § 370, page 938.*

5

Or, *powers.*

P

I Cor. 14. 1 Follow after charity, and desire spiritual *gifts*, but rather that ye may prophesy.

I Cor. 14. 39 Wherefore, brethren, covet to prophesy, and forbid not to speak with tongues.

13:1–13.

1 Though I speak with the tongues
of men [a]and of angels, and have not
[b]charity, I am become *as* sounding
brass, or a tinkling cymbal.

2 And though I have *the gift of*
[c]prophecy, and understand all mysteries, and all knowledge; and though
I have all faith, [d]so that I could remove mountains, and have not charity, I am nothing.

3 And [e]though I bestow all my
goods to feed *the poor*, and though I
give my body to be burned, and have
not charity, it profiteth me nothing.

4 [f]Charity suffereth long, *and* is
kind; charity envieth not; charity
[1]vaunteth not itself, is not puffed up,

5 Doth not behave itself unseemly,
[g]seeketh not her own, is not easily
provoked, thinketh no evil;

6 [h]Rejoiceth not in iniquity, but
[i]rejoiceth [2]in the truth;

7 [k]Beareth all things, believeth all
things, hopeth all things, endureth
all things.

8 Charity never faileth: but whether
there be prophecies, they shall fail;
whether *there be* tongues, they shall
cease; whether *there be* knowledge,
it shall vanish away.

9 [l]For we know in part, and we
prophesy in part.

10 But when that which is perfect
is come, then that which is in part
shall be done away.

11 When I was a child, I spake as
a child, I understood as a child, I
[3]thought as a child: but when I became a man, I put away childish
things.

12 For [m]now we see through a glass,
[4]darkly; but then face to face: now
I know in part; but then shall I
know even as also I am known.

13 And now abideth faith, [n]hope,
charity, these three; but the greatest of these *is* charity.

§ 372. LOVE AND ITS

CHAP. 13.

A

II Cor. 12. 4 How that he was caught up into paradise, and heard unspeakable words, which it is not lawful for a man to utter.

B

Prov. 10. 12 Hatred stirreth up strifes: but love covereth all sins.

Prov. 17. 9 He that covereth a transgression seeketh love; but he that repeateth a matter separateth *very* friends.

Matt. 25. 45 Then shall he answer them, saying, Verily I say unto you, Inasmuch as ye did *it* not to one of the least of these, ye did *it* not to me.

Gal. 5. 6 For in Jesus Christ neither circumcision availeth anything, nor uncircumcision; but faith which worketh by love.

Gal. 5. 22 But the fruit of the Spirit is love, joy, peace, long-suffering, gentleness, goodness, faith,

23 Meekness, temperance: against such there is no law.

I Thes. 4. 9 But as touching brotherly love ye need not that I write unto you: for ye yourselves are taught of God to love one another.

II Thes. 1. 3 We are bound to thank God always for you, brethren, as it is meet, because that your faith groweth exceedingly, and the charity of every one of you all toward each other aboundeth;

I Tim. 1. 5 Now the end of the commandment is charity out of a pure heart, and *of* a good conscience, and *of* faith unfeigned:

I Pet. 4. 8 And above all things have fervent charity among yourselves: for charity shall cover the multitude of sins.

C

I Cor. 12. 8, 9, 10. *See text of topic, § 370, page 938.*
I Cor. 14. 1, 2, etc. *See text of topic, § 373, page 944.*

D

Matt. 17. 20 And Jesus said unto them, Because of your unbelief: for verily I say unto you, If ye have faith as a grain of mustard seed, ye shall say unto this mountain, Remove hence to yonder place; and it shall remove: and nothing shall be impossible unto you.

GREATNESS ABOVE ALL.

D—CONCLUDED.

Mark 11. 23 For verily I say unto you, That whosoever shall say unto this mountain. Be thou removed, and be thou cast into the sea; and shall not doubt in his heart, but shall believe that those things which he saith shall come to pass; he shall have whatsoever he saith.

Luke 17. 6 And the Lord said, If ye had faith as a grain of mustard seed, ye might say unto this sycamine tree, Be thou plucked up by the root, and be thou planted in the sea; and it should obey you.

E

Matt. 6 1 Take heed that ye do not your alms before men, to be seen of them: otherwise ye have no reward of your Father which is in heaven.

2 Therefore when thou doest *thine* alms, do not sound a trumpet before thee, as the hypocrites do in the synagogues and in the streets, that they may have glory of men. Verily I say unto you, They have their reward.

F

Prov. 10. 12; I Pet. 4. 8. *See under B.*

1

Or, *is not rash.*

G

Rom. 15. 1, 2. *See c, C, § 345, page 878.*

Gal. 6. 2 Bear ye one another's burdens, and so fulfil the law of Christ.

I Jno. 3. 16 Hereby perceive we the love *of God*, because he laid down his life for us: and we ought to lay down *our* lives for the brethren.

H

Ps. 10. 3 For the wicked boasteth of his heart's desire, and blesseth the covetous, *whom* the LORD abhorreth.

Rom. 1. 32 Who, knowing the judgment of God, that they which commit such things are worthy of death, not only do the same, but have pleasure in them that do them.

I

II Jno. 4 I rejoiced greatly that I found of thy children walking in truth, as we have received a commandment from the Father.

2

Or, *with the truth.*

K

Rom. 15. 1. *See under G.*

II Tim. 2. 24 And the servant of the Lord must not strive; but be gentle unto all *men*, apt to teach, patient,

L

Job 11. 7 Canst thou by searching find out God? canst thou find out the Almighty unto perfection?

8 *It is* as high as heaven; what canst thou do? deeper than hell; what canst thou know?

Job 26. 14 Lo, these *are* parts of his ways: but how little a portion is heard of him? but the thunder of his power who can understand?

Ps. 40. 5 Many, O LORD my God, *are* thy wonderful works *which* thou hast done, and thy thoughts *which are* to us-ward: they cannot be reckoned up in order unto thee: *if* I would declare and speak *of them*, they are more than can be numbered.

Ps. 139. 6 *Such* knowledge *is* too wonderful for me; it is high, I cannot *attain* unto it.

Prov. 30. 3 I neither learned wisdom, nor have the knowledge of the holy.

3

Or, *reasoned.*

M

II Cor. 3. 18 But we all, with open face beholding as in a glass the glory of the Lord, are changed into the same image from glory to glory, *even* as by the Spirit of the Lord.

II Cor. 5. 7 (For we walk by faith, not by sight:)

Phil. 3. 12 Not as though I had already attained, either were already perfect: but I follow after, if that I may apprehend that for which also I am apprehended of Christ Jesus.

4

Gr. *in a riddle.*

N

Ps. 42. 11 Why art thou cast down, O my soul? and why art thou disquieted within me? hope thou in God: for I shall yet praise him, *who is* the health of my countenance, and my God.

Ps. 146. 5 Happy *is he* that *hath* the God of Jacob for his help, whose hope *is* in the LORD his God:

Lam. 3. 26 *It is* good that *a man* should both hope and quietly wait for the salvation of the LORD.

Rom. 5. 5 And hope maketh not ashamed; because the love of God is shed abroad in our hearts by the Holy Ghost which is given unto us.

Rom. 8. 24. *See k, K, § 333, page 846.*

Heb. 6. 19 Which *hope* we have as an anchor of the soul, both sure and steadfast, and which entereth into that within the vail;

§ 373. INSTRUCTIONS AS TO THE EXERCISE

14 : 1–19.

1 Follow after [a]charity, and [b]desire
spiritual *gifts*, [c]but rather that ye
may prophesy.

2 For he that [d]speaketh in an *unknown* tongue speaketh not unto men,
but unto God: for no man [1]under-
standeth *him;* howbeit in the spirit
he speaketh [e]mysteries.

3 But he that prophesieth speaketh
unto men *to* edification, and exhortation, and comfort.

4 He that speaketh in an *unknown*
tongue edifieth himself; but he that
prophesieth edifieth the church.

5 I would that ye all spake with
tongues, but rather that ye prophesied : for greater *is* he that prophesieth than he that speaketh with
tongues, except he interpret, that
the church may receive edifying.

6 Now, brethren, if I come unto
you speaking with tongues, what shall
I profit you, except I shall speak to
you either by [f]revelation, or by
knowledge, or by prophesying, or by
doctrine?

7 And even things without life giving sound, whether pipe or harp,
except they give a distinction in
the [2]sounds, how shall it be known
what is piped or harped?

8 For if the trumpet [g]give an uncertain sound, who shall prepare
himself to the battle?

9 So likewise ye, except ye utter
by the tongue words [3]easy to be understood, how shall it be known what
is spoken? for ye shall speak [h]into
the air.

10 There are, it may be, so many

CHAP. 14.

kinds of voices in the world, and
none of them *is* without signification.

11 Therefore if I know not the
meaning of the voice, I shall be unto
him that speaketh a barbarian, and
he that speaketh *shall be* a barbarian
unto me.

12 Even so ye, forasmuch as ye are
zealous [4]of spiritual *gifts*, seek that
ye may excel to the edifying of the
church.

13 Wherefore let him that speaketh
in an *unknown* tongue pray that [i]he
may interpret.

14 For if I pray in an *unknown*
tongue, my spirit prayeth, but my
understanding is unfruitful.

15 What is it then? I will pray with
the spirit, and I will pray with the
understanding also: [k]I will sing with
the spirit, and I will sing [l]with the
understanding also.

16 Else, when thou shalt bless with
the spirit, how shall he that occu-
pieth the room of the unlearned say
[m]Amen at thy giving of thanks, seeing
he understandeth not what thou
sayest?

17 For thou verily givest thanks
well, but the other is not edified.

18 I thank my God, I speak with
tongues more than ye all:

19 Yet in the church I had rather
speak five words with my understanding, that *by my voice* I might teach
others also, than ten thousand words
in an *unknown* tongue.

A

Lev. 19. 18 Thou shalt not avenge, nor bear any grudge against the children of thy people, but thou shalt love thy neighbour as thyself: I *am* the LORD.

Matt. 22. 39 And the second *is* like unto it, Thou shalt love thy neighbour as thyself.

Mark 12. 31 And the second *is* like, *namely* this, Thou shalt love thy neighbour as thyself. There is none other commandment greater than these.

OF THE GIFT OF PROPHECY AND OF TONGUES.

A—CONCLUDED.

Rom. 13. 8 Owe no man anything, but to love one another: for he that loveth another hath fulfilled the law.

Rom. 13. 10 Love worketh no ill to his neighbour: therefore love *is* the fulfilling of the law.

I Cor. 13. 1. *See b, B, § 372, page 942.*

Gal. 5. 14 For all the law is fulfilled in one word, *even* in this; Thou shalt love thy neighbour as thyself.

Eph. 5. 2 And walk in love, as Christ also hath loved us, and hath given himself for us an offering and a sacrifice to God for a sweetsmelling savour.

Col. 3. 14 And above all these things *put on* charity, which is the bond of perfectness.

Jas. 2. 8 If ye fulfill the royal law according to the Scripture, Thou shalt love thy neighbour as thyself, ye do well:

B

I Cor. 12. 31 But covet earnestly the best gifts: and yet shew I unto you a more excellent way.

C

Num. 11. 25 And the LORD came down in a cloud, and spake unto him, and took of the spirit that *was* upon him, and gave *it* unto the seventy elders: and it came to pass, *that*, when the spirit rested upon them, they prophesied, and did not cease.

26 But there remained two *of the* men in the camp, the name of the one *was* Eldad, and the name of the other Medad: and the spirit rested upon them; and they *were* of them that were written, but went not out unto the tabernacle: and they prophesied in the camp.

Rom. 12. 6. *See n, N, § 342, page 868.*

D

Acts 2. 4 And they were all filled with the Holy Ghost, and began to speak with other tongues, as the Spirit gave them utterance.

Acts 10. 46 For they heard them speak with tongues, and magnify God. Then answered Peter,

1

Gr. *heareth,*

E

Matt. 13. 11 He answered and said unto them, Because it is given unto you to know the mysteries of the kingdom of heaven, but to them it is not given.

F

I Cor. 14. 26. *See text of topic, § 375, page 946.*

2

Or, *tunes.*

G

Num. 10. 9 And if ye go to war in your land against the enemy that oppresseth you, then ye shall blow an alarm with the trumpets; and ye shall be remembered before the LORD your God, and ye shall be saved from your enemies.

10 Also in the day of your gladness, and in your solemn days, and in the beginnings of your months, ye shall blow with the trumpets over your burnt offerings, and over the sacrifices of your peace offerings; that they may be to you for a memorial before your God: I *am* the LORD your God.

3

Gr, *significant.*

H

I Cor. 9. 26 I therefore so run, not as uncertainly; so fight I, not as one that beateth the air:

4

Gr. *of spirits.*

I

I Cor. 12. 10 To another the working of miracles; to another prophecy; to another discerning of spirits; to another *divers* kinds of tongues; to another the interpretation of tongues:

K

Eph. 5. 19 Speaking to yourselves in psalms and hymns and spiritual songs, singing and making melody in your heart to the Lord;

Col. 3. 16 Let the word of Christ dwell in you richly in all wisdom; teaching and admonishing one another in psalms and hymns and spiritual songs, singing with grace in your hearts to the Lord.

L

Ps. 47. 7 For God *is* the King of all the earth: sing ye praises with understanding.

M

Deut. 27. 14, *read to the end of the chapter.*

Ps. 89. 52 Blessed *be* the LORD for evermore. Amen, and Amen.

Jer. 28. 6 Even the prophet Jeremiah said, Amen: the LORD do so: the LORD perform thy words which thou hast prophesied, to bring again the vessels of the LORD'S house, and all that is carried away captive, from Babylon into this place.

§ 374. TONGUES ARE A SIGN UNTO THE

14 : 20–25.

20 Brethren, [a]be not children in
understanding: howbeit in malice
[b]be ye children, but in understanding
be [1]men.

21 [c]In the law it is [d]written, With
men of other tongues and other lips
will I speak unto this people; and
yet for all that will they not hear
me, saith the Lord.

22 Wherefore tongues are for a
sign, not to them that believe, but
to them that believe not: but prophesying *serveth* not for them that believe not, but for them which believe.

23 If therefore the whole church be
come together into one place, and all
speak with tongues, and there come
in *those that are* unlearned, or unbelievers, [e]will they not say that ye are
mad?

24 But if all prophesy, and there

CHAP. 14.

come in one that believeth not, or
one unlearned, he is convinced of
all, he is judged of all:

25 And thus are the secrets of his
heart made manifest; and so falling
down on *his* face he will worship
God, and report [f]that God is in you
of a truth.

A

Ps. 119. 99 I have more understanding than all my teachers: for thy testimonies *are* my meditation.

Ps. 131. 2 Surely I have behaved and quieted myself, as a child that is weaned of his mother: my soul *is* even as a weaned child.

Rom. 16. 19 For your obedience is come abroad unto all *men*. I am glad therefore on your behalf: but yet I would have you wise unto that which is good, and simple concerning evil.

Eph. 4. 14 That we *henceforth* be no more children, tossed to and fro, and carried about with every wind of doctrine, by the sleight of men, *and* cunning craftiness, whereby they lie in wait to deceive:

15 But speaking the truth in love, may grow up into him in all things, which is the head, *even* Christ:

§ 375. INSTRUCTION AS TO DECENCY AND ORDER IN

14 : 26–40.

26 How is it then, brethren? when
ye come together, every one of you
hath a psalm, [a]hath a doctrine, hath
a tongue, hath a revelation, hath an
interpretation. [b]Let all things be
done unto edifying.

27 If any man speak in an *unknown*
tongue, *let it be* by two, or at the
most *by* three, and *that* by course;
and let one interpret.

28 But if there be no interpreter,
let him keep silence in the church;
and let him speak to himself, and to
God.

29 Let the prophets speak two or

CHAP. 14.

three, and [c]let the other judge.

30 If *any thing* be revealed to another that sitteth by, [d]let the first
hold his peace.

31 For ye may all prophesy one by
one, that all may learn, and all may
be comforted.

32 And [e]the spirits of the prophets
are subject to the prophets.

33 For God is not *the author* of [1]confusion, but of peace, [f]as in all
churches of the saints.

34 [g]Let your women keep silence in
the churches: for it is not permitted
unto them to speak; but [h]*they are*

UNBELIEVING, PROPHECY TO THE BELIEVER.

A—CONCLUDED.

Heb. 6. 1 Therefore leaving the principles of the doctrine of Christ, let us go on unto perfection; not laying again the foundation of repentance from dead works, and of faith toward God,

II Pet. 3. 18 But grow in grace, and *in* the knowledge of our Lord and Saviour Jesus Christ. To him *be* glory both now and forever. Amen.

B

Matt. 18. 3 And said, Verily I say unto you, Except ye be converted, and become as little children, ye shall not enter into the kingdom of heaven.

I Pet. 2. 1 Wherefore laying aside all malice, and all guile, and hypocrisies, and envies, and all evil speakings,

2 As newborn babes, desire the sincere milk of the word, that ye may grow thereby:

1

Gr. *perfect*, or, *of a ripe age.*

I Cor. 2. 6 Howbeit we speak wisdom among them that are perfect: yet not the wisdom of this world, nor of the princes of this world, that come to nought:

C

John 10. 34 Jesus answered them, Is it not written in your law, I said, Ye are gods?

D

Isa. 28. 11 For with stammering lips and another tongue will he speak to this people.

E

John 10. 20 And many of them said, He hath a devil, and is mad; why hear ye him?

Acts 2. 13 Others mocking said, These men are full of new wine.

Acts 26. 24 And as he thus spake for himself, Festus said with a loud voice, Paul, thou art beside thyself; much learning doth make thee mad.

F

Isa. 45. 14 Thus saith the LORD, The labour of Egypt, and merchandise of Ethiopia and of the Sabeans, men of stature, shall come over unto thee, and they shall be thine: they shall come after thee; in chains they shall come over, and they shall fall down unto thee, they shall make supplication unto thee, *saying*, Surely, God *is* in thee; and *there is* none else, *there is* no God.

Zech. 8. 23 Thus saith the LORD of hosts; In those days *it shall come to pass*, that ten men shall take hold out of all languages of the nations, even shall take hold of the skirt of him that is a Jew, saying, We will go with you: for we have heard *that* God *is* with you.

THE CONGREGATION, AND THE SUBJECTION OF WOMEN.

A

I Cor. 12. 8 For to one is given by the Spirit the word of wisdom; to another the word of knowledge by the same Spirit;

9 To another faith by the same Spirit; to another the gifts of healing by the same Spirit;

10 To another the working of miracles; to another prophecy; to another discerning of spirits; to another *divers* kinds of tongues; to another the interpretation of tongues:

I Cor. 14. 6 Now, brethren, if I come unto you speaking with tongues, what shall I profit you, except I shall speak to you either by revelation, or by knowledge, or by prophesying, or by doctrine?

B

Rom. 14. 19 Let us therefore follow after the things which make for peace, and things wherewith one may edify another.

I Cor. 12. 7. *See i, I, § 370, page 938.*

B—CONCLUDED.

I Thes. 5. 11 Wherefore comfort yourselves together, and edify one another, even as also ye do.

C

I Cor. 12. 10. *See under A.*

D

I Thes. 5. 19 Quench not the Spirit:

20 Despise not prophesyings.

E

I Jno. 4. 1 Beloved, believe not every spirit, but try the spirits whether they are of God: because many false prophets are gone out into the world.

1

Gr. *tumult, or unquietness.*

F

I Cor. 11. 16 But if any man seem to be contentious, we have no such custom, neither the churches of God.

For G and H, see next page (948).

§ 375. INSTRUCTION AS TO DECENCY AND ORDER IN THE

CHAP. 14.

commanded to be under obedience,
as also saith the [i]law.
35 And if they will learn any thing,
let them ask their husbands at home:
for it is a shame for women to speak
in the church.
36 What? came the word of God
[k]out from you? or came it unto you
only?
37 [l]If any man think himself to be
a prophet, or spiritual, let him acknowledge that the things that I
write unto you are the commandments of the Lord.

CHAP. 14.

38 But if any man be ignorant, let
him be ignorant.
39 Wherefore, brethren, [m]covet to
prophesy, and forbid not to speak
with tongues.
40 [n]Let all things be done decently
and in order.

G

I Tim. 2. 11 Let the woman learn in silence with all subjection.
12 But I suffer not a woman to teach, nor to usurp authority over the man, but to be in silence.

I Cor. 11. 3. *See e, E, § 368, page 932.*

H

Tit. 2. 5 *To be* discreet, chaste, keepers at home, good, obedient to their own hus-

§ 376. PAUL SETS FORTH BRIEFLY

15 : 1–11.

1 Moreover, brethren, I declare unto you the gospel [a]which I preached
unto you, which also ye have received, and [b]wherein ye stand;
2 [c]By which also ye are saved, if
ye [1]keep in memory [2]what I preached
unto you, unless [d]ye have believed
in vain.
3 For [e]I delivered unto you first of
all that [f]which I also received, how
that Christ died for our sins [g]accord-
ing to the Scriptures;
4 And that he was buried, and that
he rose again the third day [h]accord-
ing to the Scriptures:
5 [i]And that he was seen of Cephas,
then [k]of the twelve:
6 After that, he was seen of above
five hundred brethren at once; of
whom the greater part remain unto
this present, but some are fallen
asleep.

CHAP. 15.

7 After that, he was seen of James;
then [l]of all the apostles.
8 [m]And last of all he was seen of me
also, as of [3]one born out of due time.

A

Gal. 1. 11 But I certify you, brethren, that the gospel which was preached of me is not after man.

B

Rom. 5. 2 By whom also we have access by faith into this grace wherein we stand, and rejoice in hope of the glory of God.

C

Rom. 1. 16. *See m, M, § 318, page 810.*

I Cor. 1. 21 For after that in the wisdom of God the world by wisdom knew not God, it pleased God by the foolishness of preaching to save them that believe.

1

Or, *hold fast.*

2

Gr. *by what speech.*

D

Gal. 3. 4 Have ye suffered so many things in vain? if *it be* yet in vain.

E

I Cor. 11. 2 Now I praise you, brethren, that ye remember me in all things, and keep the ordinances, as I delivered *them* to you.

I Cor. 11. 23. *See g, G, § 369, page 934.*

CONGREGATION, AND THE SUBJECTION OF WOMEN (CONCLUDED).

H—CONCLUDED.

bands, that the word of God be not blasphemed.

I

Gen. 3. 16 Unto the woman he said, I will greatly multiply thy sorrow and thy conception; in sorrow thou shalt bring forth children; and thy desire *shall be* to thy husband, and he shall rule over thee.

K

Isa. 2. 3 And many people shall go and say, Come ye, and let us go up to the mountain of the LORD, to the house of the God of Jacob; and he will teach us of his ways, and we will walk in his paths: for out of Zion shall go forth the law, and the word of the LORD from Jerusalem.

L

Luke 10. 16 He that heareth you heareth me; and he that despiseth you despiseth me; and he that despiseth me despiseth him that sent me.

II Cor. 10. 7 Do ye look on things after the outward appearance? If any man trust to himself that he is Christ's, let him of himself think this again, that, as he *is* Christ's, even so *are* we Christ's.

I Jno. 4. 6 We are of God: he that knoweth God heareth us; he that is not of God heareth not us. Hereby know we the spirit of truth, and the spirit of error.

M

I Cor. 12. 31. *See p, P, § 371, page 940.*

I Thes. 5. 20. *See under D, page 947.*

N

I Cor. 11. 34 And if any man hunger, let him eat at home; that ye come not together unto condemnation. And the rest will I set in order when I come.

THE GOSPEL WHICH HE PREACHED.

F

Gal. 1. 12 For I neither received it of man, neither was I taught *it*, but by the revelation of Jesus Christ.

G

Luke 24. 46. *See h, H, § 219, page 611.*

Acts 3. 18 *See l, L, § 234, page 644.*

Rom. 4. 25. *See b, B, § 325, page 830.*

H

Ps. 16. 10 For thou wilt not leave my soul in hell; neither wilt thou suffer thine Holy One to see corruption.

Isa. 53. 10 Yet it pleased the LORD to bruise him; he hath put *him* to grief: when thou shalt make his soul an offering for sin, he shall see *his* seed, he shall prolong *his* days, and the pleasure of the LORD shall prosper in his hand.

Hos. 6. 2 After two days will he revive us: in the third day he will raise us up, and we shall live in his sight.

Luke 24. 26 Ought not Christ to have suffered these things, and to enter into his glory?

Luke 24. 46 And said unto them, Thus it is written, and thus it behooved Christ to suffer, and to rise from the dead the third day:

I

Luke 24. 34 Saying, the Lord is risen indeed, and hath appeared to Simon.

K

Matt. 28. 16 Then the eleven disciples went away into Galilee, into a mountain where Jesus had appointed them.

K—CONCLUDED.

Matt. 28. 17 And when they saw him, they worshipped him: but some doubted.

Mark 16. 14 Afterward he appeared unto the eleven as they sat at meat, and upbraided them with their unbelief and hardness of heart, because they believed not them which had seen him after he was risen.

Luke 24. 36 And as they thus spake, Jesus himself stood in the midst of them, and saith unto them, Peace *be* unto you.

John 20. 19 Then the same day at evening, being the first *day* of the week, when the doors were shut where the disciples were assembled for fear of the Jews, came Jesus and stood in the midst, and saith unto them, Peace *be* unto you.

John 20. 26 And after eight days again his disciples were within, and Thomas with them: *then* came Jesus, the doors being shut, and stood in the midst, and said, Peace *be* unto you.

Acts 10. 41 Not to all the people, but unto witnesses chosen before of God, *even* to us, who did eat and drink with him after he rose from the dead.

L

Luke 24. 50 And he led them out as far as to Bethany, and he lifted up his hands, and blessed them.

Acts 1. 3 To whom also he shewed himself alive after his passion by many infal-

For L concluded, M and 3, see next page (950).

§ 376. PAUL SETS FORTH BRIEFLY THE GOSPEL

CHAP. 15.

9 For I am [n]the least of the apostles,
that am not meet to be called an
apostle, because [o]I persecuted the
church of God.

10 But [p]by the grace of God I am
what I am: and his grace which *was*
bestowed upon me was not in vain;
but [q]I laboured more abundantly
than they all: [r]yet not I, but the
grace of God which was with me.

11 Therefore whether *it were* I or
they, so we preach, and so ye believed.

L—CONCLUDED.

lible proofs, being seen of them forty days, and speaking of the things pertaining to the kingdom of God:

Acts 1. 4 And, being assembled together with *them*, commanded them that they should not depart from Jerusalem, but wait for the promise of the Father, which, *saith he*, ye have heard of me.

M

I. Cor 9. 1. *See b, B, § 365, page 920.*

3

Or, *an abortive.*

N

Eph. 3. 8 Unto me, who am less than the least of all saints, is this grace given, that I should preach among the Gentiles the unsearchable riches of Christ;

O

Acts 8. 3. *See d, D, § 247, page 678.*

§ 377. THE RESURRECTION OF CHRIST

15:12–19.

12 Now if Christ be preached that
he rose from the dead, how say some
among you that there is no resurrection of the dead?

13 But if there be no resurrection
of the dead, [a]then is Christ not risen:

14 And if Christ be not risen, then
is our preaching vain, and your faith
is also vain.

15 Yea, and we are found false
witnesses of God; because [b]we have
testified of God that he raised up

CHAP. 15.

Christ: whom he raised not up, if so
be that the dead rise not.

16 For if the dead rise not, then is
not Christ raised:

17 And if Christ be not raised, your
faith *is* vain; [c]ye are yet in your
sins.

18 Then they also which are fallen
asleep in Christ are perished.

19 [d]If in this life only we have
hope in Christ, we are of all men
most miserable.

§ 378. THE IMPORTANCE OF THE RESURRECTION

15:20–28.

20 But now [a]is Christ risen from
the dead, *and* become [b]the firstfruits
of them that slept.

21 For [c]since by man *came* death,
[d]by man *came* also the resurrection
of the dead.

CHAP. 15.

22 For as in Adam all die, even so
in Christ shall all be made alive.

23 [e]But every man in his own order: Christ the firstfruits; afterward
they that are Christ's at his coming.

24 Then *cometh* the end, when he

WHICH HE PREACHED (CONCLUDED).

P

Eph. 3. 7 Whereof I was made a minister, according to the gift of the grace of God given unto me by the effectual working of his power.

Eph. 3. 8. *See under N.*

Q

IICor. 11. 23 Are they ministers of Christ? (I speak as a fool) I *am* more; in labours more abundant, in stripes above measure, in prisons more frequent, in deaths oft.

IICor. 12. 11 I am become a fool in glorying; ye have compelled me: for I ought to have been commended of you: for in nothing am I behind the very chiefest apostles, though I be nothing.

R

Matt. 10. 20 For it is not ye that speak, but the Spirit of your Father which speaketh in you.

R—CONCLUDED.

Rom. 15. 18 For I will not dare to speak of any of those things which Christ hath not wrought by me, to make the Gentiles obedient, by word and deed,

19 Through mighty signs and wonders, by the power of the Spirit of God; so that from Jerusalem, and round about unto Illyricum, I have fully preached the gospel of Christ.

II Cor. 3. 5 Not that we are sufficient of ourselves to think any thing as of ourselves; but our sufficiency *is* of God;

Gal. 2. 8 (For he that wrought effectually in Peter to the apostleship of the circumcision, the same was mighty in me toward the Gentiles:)

Eph. 3. 7. *See under P.*

Phil. 2. 13 For it is God which worketh in you both to will and to do of *his* good pleasure.

THE FOUNDATION OF THE FAITH.

A

I Thes. 4. 14 For if we believe that Jesus died and rose again, even so them also which sleep in Jesus will God bring with him.

B

Acts 2. 24 Whom God hath raised up, having loosed the pains of death: because it was not possible that he should be holden of it.

Acts 2. 32 This Jesus hath God raised up, whereof we all are witnesses.

Acts 4. 10 Be it known unto you all, and to all the people of Israel, that by the name of Jesus Christ of Nazareth, whom ye crucified, whom God raised from the dead *even* by him doth this man stand here before you whole.

B—CONCLUDED.

Acts 4. 33 And with great power gave the apostles witness of the resurrection of the Lord Jesus: and great grace was upon them all.

Acts 13. 30 But God raised him from the dead:

C

Rom. 4. 25 Who was delivered for our offences, and was raised again for our justification.

D

John 16. 2 They shall put you out of the synagogues: yea, the time cometh, that whosoever killeth you will think that he doeth God service.

II Tim. 3. 12 Yea, and all that will live godly in Christ Jesus shall suffer persecution.

IN THE ORDER OF DISPENSATION.

A

I Pet. 1. 3 Blessed *be* the God and Father of our Lord Jesus Christ, which according to his abundant mercy hath begotten us again unto a lively hope by the resurrection of Jesus Christ from the dead,

B

Acts 26. 23. *See b, B, § 309, page 794.*

I Cor. 15. 23. *See text of topic.*

C

Rom. 5. 12 and 17. *See a, A, § 327, page 834.*

D

John 11. 25 Jesus said unto her, I am the resurrection, and the life: he that believeth in me, though he were dead, yet shall he live:

Rom. 6. 23 For the wages of sin *is* death; but the gift of God *is* eternal life through Jesus Christ our Lord.

For E, see next page (952).

§ 378. THE IMPORTANCE OF THE RESURRECTION

CHAP. 15.

shall have delivered up [f]the kingdom to God, even the Father; when he shall have put down all rule and all authority and power.

25 For he must reign, till he hath put all enemies under his feet.

26 [g]The last enemy *that* shall be destroyed *is* death.

27 For he [h]hath put all things under his feet. But when he saith, All things are put under *him, it is* manifest that he is excepted, which did put all things under him.

28 [i]And when all things shall be subdued unto him, then [k]shall the Son also himself be subject unto him that put all things under him, that God may be all in all

E

I Cor. 15. 20. *See text of topic, page 950.*

IThes.4. 15 For this we say unto you by the word of the Lord, that we which are alive *and* remain unto the coming of the Lord shall not prevent them which are asleep.

16 For the Lord himself shall descend from heaven with a shout, with the voice of the archangel, and with the trump of God: and the dead in Christ shall rise first:

17 Then we which are alive *and* remain shall be caught up together with them in the clouds, to meet the Lord in the air: and so shall we ever be with the Lord.

F

Da. 7: 14 And there was given him dominion, and glory, and a kingdom, that all people, nations, and languages, should serve him: his dominion *is* an everlasting dominion, which shall not pass away, and his kingdom *that* which shall not be destroyed.

Da. 7. 27 And the kingdom and dominion, and the greatness of the kingdom under the whole heaven, shall be given

§ 379. NO PROFIT IN THE EXERCISE OF

15 :29-34.

29 Else what shall they do which are baptized for the dead, if the dead rise not at all? why are they then baptized for the dead?

30 And [a]why stand we in jeopardy every hour?

31 I protest by [1][b]your rejoicing which I have in Christ Jesus our Lord, [c]I die daily.

32 If [2]after the manner of men [d]I have fought with beasts at Ephesus, what advantageth it me, if the dead rise not? [e]let us eat and drink; for to morrow we die.

33 Be not deceived: [f]evil communications corrupt good manners.

34 [g]Awake to righteousness, and sin not; [h]for some have not the knowledge of God: I speak *this* to your shame.

A

IICor.11. 26 *In* journeyings often, *in* perils of waters, *in* perils of robbers, *in* perils by *mine own* countrymen, *in* perils by the heathen, *in* perils in the city, *in* perils in the wilderness, *in* perils in the sea, *in* perils among false brethren;

Gal. 5. 11 And I, brethren, if I yet preach circumcision, why do I yet suffer persecution? then is the offence of the cross ceased.

1

Some read, *our.*

B

IThes.2. 19 For what *is* our hope, or joy, or crown of rejoicing? *Are* not even ye in the presence of our Lord Jesus Christ at his coming?

C

Rom. 8. 36 As it is written, For thy sake we are killed all the day long; we are accounted as sheep for the slaughter.

I Cor. 4. 9 For I think that God hath set forth us the apostles last, as it were appointed to death; for we are made a

IN THE ORDER OF DISPENSATION (CONCLUDED).

F—CONCLUDED.

to the people of the saints of the Most High, whose kingdom *is* an everlasting kingdom, and all dominions shall serve and obey him.

G

II Tim. 1. 10 But is now made manifest by the appearing of our Saviour Jesus Christ, who hath abolished death, and hath brought life and immortality to light through the gospel:

Rev. 20. 1 And I saw an angel come down from heaven, having the key of the bottomless pit and a great chain in his hand.

2 And he laid hold on the dragon, that old serpent, which is the Devil, and Satan, and bound him a thousand years,

H

Ps. 8. 6 Thou madest him to have dominion over the works of thy hands; thou hast put all *things* under his feet:

Matt. 28. 18 And Jesus came and spake unto them, saying, All power is given unto me in heaven and in earth.

Heb. 2. 8 Thou hast put all things in subjection under his feet. For in that he

H—CONCLUDED.

put all in subjection under him, he left nothing *that is* not put under him. But now we see not yet all things put under him.

I Pet. 3. 22 Who is gone into heaven, and is on the right hand of God; angels and authorities and powers being made subject unto him.

I

Eph. 1. 10 That in the dispensation of the fulness of times he might gather together in one all things in Christ, both which are in heaven, and which are on earth; *even* in him:

Phil. 3. 21 Who shall change our vile body, that it may be fashioned like unto his glorious body, according to the working whereby he is able even to subdue all things unto himself.

K

I Cor. 3. 23 And ye are Christ's; and Christ *is* God's.

I Cor. 11. 3 But I would have you know, that the head of every man is Christ; and the head of the woman *is* the man; and the head of Christ *is* God.

THE FAITH IF THE DEAD ARE NOT RAISED.

C—CONCLUDED.

spectacle unto the world, and to angels, and to men.

2

Or, *to speak after the manner of men.*

D

II Cor. 1. 8 For we would not, brethren, have you ignorant of our trouble which came to us in Asia, that we were pressed out of measure, above strength, insomuch that we despaired even of life:

E

Eccl. 2. 24 *There is* nothing better for a man, *than* that he should eat and drink, and *that* he should make his soul enjoy good in his labour. This also I saw, that it *was* from the hand of God.

Eccl. 11. 9 Rejoice, O young man, in thy youth; and let thy heart cheer thee in the days of thy youth, and walk in the ways of thine heart, and in the sight of thine eyes: but know thou, that for all these *things* God will bring thee into judgment.

Isa. 22. 13 And behold joy and gladness, slaying oxen, and killing sheep, eating

E—CONCLUDED.

flesh, and drinking wine: let us eat and drink; for to morrow we shall die.

Isa. 56. 12 Come ye, *say they*, I will fetch wine, and we will fill ourselves with strong drink; and to morrow shall be as this day, *and* much more abundant.

Luke 12. 19 And I will say to my soul, Soul, thou hast much goods laid up for many years; take thine ease, eat, drink, *and* be merry.

F

I Cor. 5. 6. *See l, L, § 359, page 906.*

G

Rom. 13. 11 And that, knowing the time, that now *it is* high time to awake out of sleep: for now *is* our salvation nearer than when we believed.

Eph. 5. 14 Wherefore he saith, Awake thou that sleepest, and arise from the dead, and Christ shall give thee light.

H

I Thes. 4. 5 Not in the lust of concupiscence, even as the Gentiles which know not God:

§ 380. THE DIVERSE CHARACTER OF NATURAL AND RISEN

15:35–49.

35 But some *man* will say, [a]How
are the dead raised up? and with
what body do they come?
36 *Thou* fool, [b]that which thou sowest is not quickened, except it die:
37 And that which thou sowest,
thou sowest not that body that shall
be, but bare grain, it may chance of
wheat, or some other *grain*:
38 But God giveth it a body as it
hath pleased him, and to every seed
his own body.
39 All flesh *is* not the same flesh:
but *there is* one *kind of* flesh of men,
another flesh of beasts, another of
fishes, *and* another of birds.
40 *There are* also celestial bodies,
and bodies terrestrial: but the glory
of the celestial *is* one, and the *glory*
of the terrestrial *is* another.
41 *There is* one glory of the sun,
and another glory of the moon, and
another glory of the stars: for *one*
star differeth from *another* star in
glory.
42 [c]So also *is* the resurrection of
the dead. It is sown in corruption;
it is raised in incorruption:
43 [d]It is sown in dishonour; it is
raised in glory: it is sown in weakness; it is raised in power.
44 It is sown a natural body; it is
raised a spiritual body. There is a
natural body, and there is a spiritual
body.
45 And so it is written, The first
man Adam [e]was made a living soul;
[f]the last Adam *was made* [g]a quickening spirit.
46 Howbeit that *was* not first which
is spiritual, but that which is natural;
and afterward that which is spiritual.
47 [h]The first man *is* of the earth,
[i]earthy: the second man *is* the Lord
[k]from heaven.
48 As *is* the earthy, such *are* they
also that are earthy: [l]and as *is* the
heavenly, such *are* they also that are
heavenly.
49 And [m]as we have borne the image of the earthy, [n]we shall also bear
the image of the heavenly.

CHAP. 15.

A

Eze. 37. 3 And he said unto me, Son of man, can these bones live? And I answered, O Lord GOD, thou knowest.

Eze. 37. 9 Then said he unto me, Prophesy unto the wind, prophesy, son of man, and say to the wind, Thus saith the Lord GOD; Come from the four winds, O breath, and breathe upon these slain, that they may live.

10 So I prophesied as he commanded me, and the breath came into them, and they lived, and stood up upon their feet, an exceeding great army.

John 11. 43 And when he thus had spoken, he cried with a loud voice, Lazarus, come forth.

44 And he that was dead came forth, bound hand and foot with graveclothes; and his face was bound about with a napkin. Jesus saith unto them, Loose him, and let him go.

§ 381. THE ORDER, MANNER AND VICTORY

15:50–58.

50 Now this I say, brethren, that
[a]flesh and blood cannot inherit the
kingdom of God; neither doth cor-

A

Matt. 16. 17 And Jesus answered and said unto him, Blessed art thou, Simon Bar-jona: for flesh and blood hath not revealed *it* unto thee, but my Father which is in heaven.

BODIES AND THEIR ORDER SET FORTH IN FIGURE AND EXAMPLE.

B

John 12. 24 Verily, verily, I say unto you, Except a corn of wheat fall into the ground and die, it abideth alone: but if it die, it bringeth forth much fruit.

C

Da. 12. 3 And they that be wise shall shine as the brightness of the firmament; and they that turn many to righteousness as the stars for ever and ever.

Matt. 13. 43 Then shall the righteous shine forth as the sun in the kingdom of their Father. Who hath ears to hear, let him hear.

D

Phil. 3. 21 Who shall change our vile body, that it may be fashioned like unto his glorious body, according to the working whereby he is able even to subdue all things unto himself.

E

Gen. 2. 7 And the LORD God formed man *of* the dust of the ground, and breathed into his nostrils the breath of life; and man became a living soul.

F

Rom. 5. 14 Nevertheless death reigned from Adam to Moses, even over them that had not sinned after the similitude of Adam's transgression, who is the figure of him that was to come.

G

John 5. 21 For as the Father raiseth up the dead, and quickeneth *them;* even so the Son quickeneth whom he will.

John 6. 33 For the bread of God is he which cometh down from heaven, and giveth life unto the world.

John 6. 39 And this is the Father's will which hath sent me, that of all which he hath given me I should lose nothing, but should raise it up again at the last day.

40 And this is the will of him that sent me, that every one which seeth the Son, and believeth on him, may have everlasting life: and I will raise him up at the last day.

John 6. 54 Whoso eateth my flesh, and drinketh my blood, hath eternal life; and I

G—CONCLUDED.

will raise him up at the last day.

John 6. 57 As the living Father hath sent me, and I live by the Father: so he that eateth me, even he shall live by me.

Phil. 3. 21. *See under D.*

Col. 3. 4 When Christ, *who is* our life, shall appear, then shall ye also appear with him in glory.

H

John 3. 31 He that cometh from above is above all: he that is of the earth is earthly, and speaketh of the earth: he that cometh from heaven is above all.

I

Gen. 2. 7. *See under E.*

Gen. 3. 19 In the sweat of thy face shalt thou eat bread, till thou return unto the ground; for out of it wast thou taken: for dust thou *art*, and unto dust shalt thou return.

K

John 3. 13 And no man hath ascended up to heaven, but he that came down from heaven, *even* the Son of man which is in heaven.

John 3. 31. *See under H.*

L

Phil. 3. 20 For our conversation is in heaven; from whence also we look for the Saviour, the Lord Jesus Christ:

Phil. 3. 21. *See under D.*

M

Gen. 5. 3 And Adam lived a hundred and thirty years, and begat *a son* in his own likeness, after his image; and called his name Seth:

N

Rom. 8. 29. *See i, I, § 334, page 848.*

II Cor. 4. 10 Always bearing about in the body the dying of the Lord Jesus, that the life also of Jesus might be made manifest in our body.

11 For we which live are alway delivered unto death for Jesus' sake, that the life also of Jesus might be made manifest in our mortal flesh.

OF THE RESURRECTION OF THE SAINTS.

A—CONTINUED.

John 3. 3 Jesus answered and said unto him, Verily, verily, I say unto thee, Except a man be born again, he cannot see the kingdom of God.

4 Nicodemus saith unto him, How can a man be born when he is old? can he enter the second time into his mother's womb, and be born?

John 3. 5 Jesus answered, Verily, verily, I

For A concluded, see next page (936).

§ 381. THE ORDER, MANNER AND VICTORY OF THE

CHAP. 15.

ruption inherit incorruption.
51 Behold, I shew you a mystery;
[b]We shall not all sleep, [c]but we shall
all be changed,
52 In a moment, in the twinkling
of an eye, at the last trump: [d]for
the trumpet shall sound, and the
dead shall be raised incorruptible,
and we shall be changed.
53 For this corruptible must put
on incorruption, and [e]this mortal
must put on immortality.
54 So when this corruptible shall
have put on incorruption, and this
mortal shall have put on immortality, then shall be brought to pass
the saying that is written, [f]Death is
swallowed up in victory.
55 [g]O death, where *is* thy sting?
O [1]grave, where *is* thy victory?
56 The sting of death *is* sin; and
[h]the strength of sin *is* the law.
57 [i]But thanks *be* to God, which
giveth us [k]the victory through our
Lord Jesus Christ.
58 [l]Therefore, my beloved brethren, be ye steadfast, unmoveable,
always abounding in the work of the

CHAP. 15.

Lord, forasmuch as ye know [m]that
your labour is not in vain in the
Lord.

A—CONCLUDED.

say unto thee, Except a man be born of water and *of* the Spirit, he cannot enter into the kingdom of God.

John 3. 6 That which is born of the flesh is flesh; and that which is born of the Spirit is spirit.

II Cor. 5. 1 For we know that, if our earthly house of *this* tabernacle were dissolved, we have a building of God, a house not made with hands, eternal in the heavens.

B

I Thes. 4. 14 For if we believe that Jesus died and rose again, even so them also which sleep in Jesus will God bring with him.

15 For this we say unto you by the word of the Lord, that we which are alive *and* remain unto the coming of the Lord shall not prevent them which are asleep.

16 For the Lord himself shall descend from heaven with a shout, with the voice of the archangel, and with the trump of God: and the dead in Christ shall rise first:

17 Then we which are alive *and* remain shall be caught up together with them in the clouds, to meet the Lord in the air: and so shall we ever be with the Lord.

C

Phil. 3. 21 Who shall change our vile body, that it may be fashioned like unto his glorious body, according to the working whereby he is able even to subdue all things unto himself.

§ 382. CONCERNING THE COLLECTION

16:1–9.

1 Now concerning [a]the collection
for the saints, as I have given order
to the churches of Galatia, even so
do ye.
2 [b]Upon the first *day* of the week
let every one of you lay by him in
store, as *God* hath prospered him,
that there be no gatherings when I
come.

CHAP. 16.

3 And when I come, [c]whomsoever
ye shall approve by *your* letters, them
will I send to bring your [1]liberality
unto Jerusalem.
4 And if it be meet that I go also,
they shall go with me.
5 Now I will come unto you, [d]when
I shall pass through Macedonia: for
I do pass through Macedonia.

RESURRECTION OF THE SAINTS (CONCLUDED).

D

Zech. 9. 14 And the LORD shall be seen over them, and his arrow shall go forth as the lightning: and the Lord GOD shall blow the trumpet, and shall go with whirlwinds of the south.

Matt.24. 31 And he shall send his angels with a great sound of a trumpet, and they shall gather together his elect from the four winds, from one end of heaven to the other.

John 5. 25 Verily, verily, I say unto you, The hour is coming, and now is, when the dead shall hear the voice of the Son of God: and they that hear shall live.

I Thes. 4. 16. *See under B.*

E

II Cor.5. 4 For we that are in *this* tabernacle do groan, being burdened: not for that we would be unclothed, but clothed upon, that mortality might be swallowed up of life.

F

Isa. 25. 8 He will swallow up death in victory; and the Lord GOD will wipe away tears from all faces; and the rebuke of his people shall he take away from off all the earth: for the LORD hath spoken *it*.

Luke 20. 36 Neither can they die any more: for they are equal unto the angels; and are the children of God, being the children of the resurrection:

Heb. 2. 14 Forasmuch then as the children are partakers of flesh and blood, he also himself likewise took part of the same; that through death he might destroy him that had the power of death, that is, the devil;

15 And deliver them who through fear of death were all their lifetime subject to bondage.

F—CONCLUDED.

Rev. 20. 14 And death and hell were cast into the lake of fire. This is the second death.

Rev. 21. 4 And God shall wipe away all tears from their eyes; and there shall be no more death, neither sorrow, nor crying, neither shall there be any more pain: for the former things are passed away.

G

Hos. 13. 14 I will ransom them from the power of the grave; I will redeem them from death: O death, I will be thy plagues; O grave, I will be thy destruction: repentance shall be hid from mine eyes.

1

Or, *hell.*

H

Rom. 4. 15. *See n, N, § 325, page 828.*

I

Rom. 7. 25. *See n, N, § 331, page 842.*

K

I Jno. 5. 4 For whosoever is born of God overcometh the world: and this is the victory that overcometh the world, *even* our faith.

5 Who is he that overcometh the world, but he that believeth that Jesus is the Son of God?

L

II Chr. 15. 7 Be ye strong therefore, and let not your hands be weak: for your work shall be rewarded.

II Pet. 3. 17 Ye therefore, beloved, seeing ye know *these things* before, beware lest ye also, being led away with the error of the wicked, fall from your own steadfastness.

M

Rom. 2. 6. *See h, H, § 320 page 816.*

FOR THE SAINTS AND PAUL'S VISIT.

A

Acts 11. 29. *See c, C, § 257, page 704.*

Acts 24. 17. *See i, I, § 303, page 784.*

B

Acts 20. 7. *See a, A, § 290, page 758.*

C

II Cor.8. 19 And not *that* only, but who was also chosen of the churches to travel with us with this grace, which is administered by us to the glory of the same Lord, and *declaration of* your ready mind:

1

Gr. *gift.*

D

Acts 19. 21 After these things were ended, Paul purposed in the spirit, when he had passed through Macedonia and Achaia, to go to Jerusalem, saying, After I have been there, I must also see Rome.

II Cor. 1. 16 And to pass by you into Macedonia, and to come again out of Macedonia unto you, and of you to be brought on my way toward Judea.

§ 382. CONCERNING THE COLLECTION FOR

CHAP. 16.

6 And it may be that I will abide, yea, and winter with you, that ye may [e]bring me on my journey whithersoever I go.

7 For I will not see you now by the way; but I trust to tarry a while with you, [f]if the Lord permit.

8 But I will tarry at Ephesus until Pentecost.

9 For [g]a great door and effectual is opened unto me, and [h]*there are* many adversaries.

E

Acts 15. 3. *See e, E, § 267, page 726.*

Acts 17. 15 And they that conducted Paul brought him unto Athens: and receiving a commandment unto Silas and Timotheus for to come to him with all speed, they departed.

Acts 21. 5 And when we had accomplished those days, we departed and went our way; and they all brought us on our way, with wives and children, till *we were* out of the city: and we kneeled down on the shore, and prayed.

F

Prov. 19. 21 *There are* many devices in a man's heart; nevertheless the counsel of the LORD, that shall stand.

Jer. 10. 23 O LORD, I know that the way of man *is* not in himself: *it is* not in man that walketh to direct his steps.

§ 383. INSTRUCTIONS CONCERNING TIMOTHY,

16:10–18.

10 Now [a]if Timotheus come, see that he may be with you without fear: for [b]he worketh the work of the Lord, as I also *do*.

11 [c]Let no man therefore despise him: but conduct him forth [d]in peace, that he may come unto me: for I look for him with the brethren.

12 As touching *our* brother [e]Apollos, I greatly desired him to come unto you with the brethren: but his will was not at all to come at this time; but he will come when he shall have convenient time.

13 [f]Watch ye, [g]stand fast in the faith, quit you like men, [h]be strong.

14 [i]Let all your things be done with charity.

15 I beseech you, brethren, (ye know [k]the house of Stephanas, that it is [l]the firstfruits of Achaia, and *that* they have addicted themselves to [m]the ministry of the saints,)

A

Acts 19. 22 So he sent into Macedonia two of them that ministered unto him, Timotheus and Erastus; but he himself stayed in Asia for a season.

B

Rom. 16. 21 Timotheus my workfellow, and Lucius, and Jason, and Sosipater, my kinsmen, salute you.

Phil. 2. 20 For I have no man likeminded, who will naturally care for your state.

Phil. 2. 22 But ye know the proof of him, that, as a son with the father, he hath served with me in the gospel.

I Thes. 3. 2 And sent Timotheus, our brother, and minister of God, and our fellow labourer in the gospel of Christ, to establish you, and to comfort you concerning your faith:

C

I Tim. 4. 12 Let no man despise thy youth; but be thou an example of the believers, in word, in conversation, in charity, in spirit, in faith, in purity.

D

Acts 15. 33 And after they had tarried *there* a space, they were let go in peace from the brethren unto the apostles.

E

Acts 18. 24. *See a, A, § 284, page 750.*

F

Matt. 24. 42. *See y, Y, § 173, page 492.*

THE SAINTS AND PAUL'S VISIT (Concluded).

F—Continued.

Acts 18. 21 But bade them farewell, saying, I must by all means keep this feast that cometh in Jerusalem: but I will return again unto you, if God will. And he sailed from Ephesus.

Acts 21. 14 And when he would not be persuaded, we ceased, saying, The will of the Lord be done.

Rom. 1. 10 Making request, if by any means now at length I might have a prosperous journey by the will of God to come unto you.

I Cor. 4. 19 But I will come to you shortly, if the Lord will, and will know, not the speech of them which are puffed up, but the power.

Phil. 2. 24 But I trust in the Lord that I also myself shall come shortly.

F—Concluded.

Heb. 6. 3 And this will we do, if God permit.

Jas. 4. 15 For that ye *ought* to say, If the Lord will, we shall live, and do this, or that.

G

Acts 14. 27. *See i, I, § 266, page 724.*

H

Acts 19. 9 But when divers were hardened, and believed not, but spake evil of that way before the multitude, he departed from them, and separated the disciples, disputing daily in the school of one Tyrannus.

Phil. 3. 18 (For many walk, of whom I have told you often, and now tell you even weeping, *that they are* the enemies of the cross of Christ:

APOLLOS, STEPHANAS, FORTUNATUS AND ACHAICUS.

G

I Cor. 15. 1 Moreover, brethren, I declare unto you the gospel which I preached unto you, which also ye have received, and wherein ye stand;

II Cor. 1. 24 Not for that we have dominion over your faith, but are helpers of your joy: for by faith ye stand.

Phil. 1. 27 Only let your conversation be as it becometh the gospel of Christ: that whether I come and see you, or else be absent, I may hear of your affairs, that ye stand fast in one spirit, with one mind striving together for the faith of the gospel;

Phil. 4. 1 Therefore, my brethren dearly beloved and longed for, my joy and crown, so stand fast in the Lord, *my* dearly beloved.

Col. 1. 21 And you, that were sometime alienated and enemies in *your* mind by wicked works, yet now hath he reconciled

22 In the body of his flesh through death, to present you holy and unblameable and unreproveable in his sight:

23 If ye continue in the faith grounded and settled, and *be* not moved away from the hope of the gospel, which ye have heard, *and* which was preached to every creature which is under heaven; whereof I Paul am made a minister;

Col. 4. 12 Epaphras, who is *one* of you, a

G—Concluded.

servant of Christ, saluteth you, always labouring fervently for you in prayers, that ye may stand perfect and complete in all the will of God.

Eph. 6. 13 Wherefore take unto you the whole armour of God, that ye may be able to withstand in the evil day, and having done all, to stand.

14 Stand therefore, having your loins girt about with truth, and having on the breastplate of righteousness;

I Thes. 3. 8 For now we live, if ye stand fast in the Lord.

II Thes. 2. 15 Therefore, brethren, stand fast, and hold the traditions which ye have been taught, whether by word or our epistle.

H

Josh. 1. 6 Be strong and of a good courage: for unto this people shalt thou divide for an inheritance the land, which I sware unto their fathers to give them.

7 Only be thou strong and very courageous, that thou mayest observe to do according to all the law, which Moses my servant commanded thee: turn not from it *to* the right hand or *to* the left, that thou mayest prosper whithersoever thou goest.

8 This book of the law shall not depart out of thy mouth; but thou shalt meditate therein day and night, that

For H concluded, I, K, L and M, see next page (960).

§ 383. INSTRUCTIONS CONCERNING TIMOTHY, APOLLOS.

CHAP. 16.

16 [n]That ye submit yourselves unto
such, and to every one that helpeth
with *us*, and [o]laboureth.

17 I am glad of the coming of
Stephanas and Fortunatus and Achaicus: [p]for that which was lacking on
your part they have supplied.

18 [q]For they have refreshed my
spirit and yours: therefore [r]acknowl-
edge ye them that are such.

H—CONTINUED.

thou mayest observe to do according to all that is written therein: for then thou shalt make thy way prosperous, and then thou shalt have good success.

9 Have not I commanded thee? Be strong and of a good courage; be not afraid, neither be thou dismayed: for the LORD thy God *is* with thee whithersoever thou goest.

I Ki. 2. 2 I go the way of all the earth: be thou strong therefore, and shew thyself a man;

3 And keep the charge of the LORD thy God, to walk in his ways, to keep his statutes, and his commandments, and his judgments, and his testimonies, as it is written in the law of

H—CONCLUDED.

Moses, that thou mayest prosper in all that thou doest, and whithersoever thou turnest thyself:

Isa. 35. 3 Strengthen ye the weak hands, and confirm the feeble knees.

4 Say to them *that are* of a fearful heart, Be strong, fear not: behold, your God will come *with* vengeance, *even* God *with* a recompense; he will come and save you.

Da. 11. 32 And such as do wickedly against the covenant shall be corrupt by flatteries: but the people that do know their God shall be strong, and do *exploits*.

Hag. 2. 4 Yet now be strong, O Zerubbabel, saith the LORD; and be strong, O Joshua, son of Josedech, the high priest; and be strong, all ye people of the land, saith the LORD, and work: for I *am* with you, saith the LORD of hosts:

Eph. 6. 10 Finally, my brethren, be strong in the Lord, and in the power of his might.

Col. 1. 11 Strengthened with all might, according to his glorious power, unto all patience and longsuffering with joyfulness;

I

I Cor. 14. 1 Follow after charity, and desire spiritual *gifts*, but rather that ye may prophesy.

§ 384. AN EXHORTATION OF GREETING AND

16: 19–24.

19 The churches of Asia salute you.
Aquila and Priscilla salute you much
in the Lord, [a]with the church that
is in their house.

20 All the brethren greet you.
[b]Greet ye one another with a holy
kiss.

21 [c]The salutation of *me* Paul with
mine own hand.

22 If any man [d]love not the Lord
Jesus Christ, [e]let him be Anathema,
[f]Maran-atha.

23 [g]The grace of our Lord Jesus
Christ *be* with you.

CHAP. 16.

24 My love *be* with you all in
Christ Jesus. Amen.

A

Rom. 16. 5. *See under L, § 383.*

Rom. 16. 16 Salute one another with a holy kiss. The churches of Christ salute you.

Phile. 2 And to *our* beloved Apphia, and Archippus our fellow soldier, and to the church in thy house:

B

Rom. 16. 16. *See under A.*

II Cor. 13. 12 Greet one another with a holy kiss.

I Pet. 5. 14 Greet ye one another with a kiss of charity. Peace *be* with you all that are in Christ Jesus. Amen.

C

Col. 4. 18 The salutation by the hand of me Paul. Remember my bonds. Grace *be* with you. Amen.

STEPHANAS, FORTUNATUS AND ACHAICUS (CONCLUDED).

I—CONCLUDED.

I Pet. 4. 8 And above all things have fervent charity among yourselves: for charity shall cover the multitude of sins.

K

I Cor. 1. 16. *See h, H, § 350, page 890.*

L

Rom. 16. 5 Likewise *greet* the church that is in their house. Salute my well beloved Epenetus, who is the firstfruits of Achaia unto Christ.

M

II Cor. 8. 4 Praying us with much entreaty that we would receive the gift, and *take upon us* the fellowship of the ministering to the saints.

II Cor. 9. 1 For as touching the ministering to the saints, it is superfluous for me to write to you:

Heb. 6. 10 For God is not unrighteous to forget your work and labour of love, which ye have shewed toward his name, in that ye have ministered to the saints, and do minister.

N

Heb. 13. 17 Obey them that have the rule over you, and submit yourselves: for they watch for your soul, as they that must give account, that they may do it with joy, and not with grief: for that *is* unprofitable for you.

O

Heb. 6. 10. *See under M.*

P

II Cor. 11. 9 And when I was present with you, and wanted, I was chargeable to no man: for that which was lacking to me the brethren which came from Macedonia supplied: and in all *things* I have kept myself from being burdensome unto you, and *so* will I keep *myself.*

Phil. 2. 30 Because for the work of Christ he was nigh unto death, not regarding his life, to supply your lack of service toward me.

Phile. 13 Whom I would have retained with me, that in thy stead he might have ministered unto me in the bonds of the gospel:

Q

Col. 4. 8 Whom I have sent unto you for the same purpose, that he might know your estate, and comfort your hearts;

R

Phil. 2. 29 Receive him therefore in the Lord with all gladnesss; and hold such in reputation:

I Thes. 5. 12. And we beseech you, brethren, to know them which labour among you, and are over you in the Lord, and admonish you;

ANATHEMA WITH CONCLUDING SALUTATIONS.

C—CONCLUDED.

II Thes. 3. 17 The salutation of Paul with mine own hand, which is the token in every epistle: so I write.

D

Eph. 6. 24 Grace *be* with all them that love our Lord Jesus Christ in sincerity. Amen.

E

Gal. 1. 8 But though we, or an angel from heaven, preach any other gospel unto you than that which we have preached unto you, let him be accursed.

9 As we said before, so say I now again, If any *man* preach any other gospel unto you than that ye have received, let him be accursed.

F

II Thes. 1. 8 In flaming fire taking vengeance on them that know not God, and that obey not the gospel of our Lord Jesus Christ:

F—CONCLUDED.

9 Who shall be punished with everlasting destruction from the presence of the Lord, and from the glory of his power;

Jude 14 And Enoch also, the seventh from Adam, prophesied of these, saying, Behold, the Lord cometh with ten thousands of his saints,

15 To execute judgment upon all, and to convince all that are ungodly among them of all their ungodly deeds which they have ungodly committed, and of all their hard *speeches* which ungodly sinners have spoken against him.

16 These are murmurers, complainers, walking after their own lusts; and their mouth speaketh great swelling *words*, having men's persons in admiration because of advantage.

G

Rom. 16. 20. *See r, R, § 347, page 886.*

§ 385. THE

1 : 1–2.

1 Paul, [a]an apostle of Jesus Christ by the will of God, and Timothy *our* brother, unto the church of God which is at Corinth, [b]with all the saints which are in all Achaia:

2 [c]Grace *be* to you and peace from God our Father, and *from* the Lord Jesus Christ.

A

I Cor. 1. 1 Paul, called *to be* an apostle of Jesus Christ through the will of God, and Sosthenes *our* brother,

A—CONCLUDED.

Eph. 1. 1 Paul, an apostle of Jesus Christ by the will of God, to the saints which are at Ephesus, and to the faithful in Christ Jesus:

Col. 1. 1 Paul, an apostle of Jesus Christ by the will of God, and Timotheus *our* brother,

I Tim. 1. 1 Paul, an apostle of Jesus Christ by the commandment of God our Saviour, and Lord Jesus Christ, *which is* our hope;

II Tim. 1. 1 Paul, an apostle of Jesus Christ by the will of God, according to the promise of life which is in Christ Jesus,

B

Phil. 1. 1 Paul and Timotheus, the servants of Jesus Christ, to all the saints in

§ 386. PAUL'S THANKSGIVING FOR COMFORT IN AFFLICTION,

1 : 3–14.

3 [a]Blessed *be* God, even the Father of our Lord Jesus Christ, the Father of mercies, and the God of all comfort;

4 Who comforteth us in all our tribulation, that we may be able to comfort them which are in any trouble, by the comfort wherewith we ourselves are comforted of God.

5 For as [b]the sufferings of Christ abound in us, so our consolation also aboundeth by Christ.

6 And whether we be afflicted, [c]*it is* for your consolation and salvation, which [1]is effectual in the enduring of the same sufferings which we also suffer: or whether we be comforted, *it is* for your consolation and salvation.

7 And our hope of you *is* steadfast, knowing, that [d]as ye are partakers of the sufferings, so *shall ye be* also of the consolation.

CHAP. 1.

8 For we would not, brethren, have you ignorant of [e]our trouble which came to us in Asia, that we were pressed out of measure, above strength, insomuch that we despaired even of life:

9 But we had the [2]sentence of death in ourselves, that we should [f]not trust in ourselves, but in God which raiseth the dead:

10 [g]Who delivered us from so great a death, and doth deliver: in whom we trust that he will yet deliver *us;*

A

Eph. 1. 3 Blessed *be* the God and Father of our Lord Jesus Christ, who hath blessed us with all spiritual blessings in heavenly *places* in Christ:

I Pet. 1. 3 Blessed *be* the God and Father of our Lord Jesus Christ, which according to his abundant mercy hath begotten us again unto a lively hope by the resurrection of Jesus Christ from the dead,

TO THE CORINTHIANS.

SALUTATION. **Written probably during Autumn of A. D 57 at Macedonia.**

B—CONCLUDED.

Christ Jesus which are at Philippi, with the bishops and deacons:

Col. 1. 2 To the saints and faithful brethren in Christ which are at Colosse: Grace *be* unto you, and peace, from God our Father and the Lord Jesus Christ.

C

Rom. 1. 7 To all that be in Rome, beloved of God, called *to be* saints: Grace to you, and peace from God our Father, and the Lord Jesus Christ.

I Cor. 1. 3. *See i, L, ¶ 348, page 888.*

Gal. 1. 3 Grace *be* to you, and peace, from God the Father, and *from* our Lord Jesus Christ,

C—CONCLUDED.

Phil. 1. 2 Grace *be* unto you, and peace from God our Father, and *from* the Lord Jesus Christ.

Col. 1. 2. *See under B.*

I Thes. 1. 1 Paul, and Silvanus, and Timotheus, unto the church of the Thessalonians *which is* in God the Father and *in* the Lord Jesus Christ: Grace *be* unto you, and peace, from God our Father, and the Lord Jesus Christ.

II Thes. 1. 2 Grace unto you, and peace, from God our Father and the Lord Jesus Christ.

Phile. 3 Grace to you, and peace, from God our Father and the Lord Jesus Christ.

AND AFFIRMATION OF A HOLY AND SINCERE CONSCIENCE.

B

Acts 9. 4 And he fell to the earth, and heard a voice saying unto him, Saul, Saul, why persecutest thou me?

II Cor. 4. 10 Always bearing about in the body the dying of the Lord Jesus, that the life also of Jesus might be made manifest in our body.

Col. 1. 24 Who now rejoice in my sufferings for you, and fill up that which is behind of the afflictions of Christ in my flesh for his body's sake, which is the church:

C

II Cor. 4. 15 For all things *are* for your sakes, that the abundant grace might through the thanksgiving of many redound to the glory of God.

1

Or, *is wrought.*

D

Rom. 8. 17. *See d, D, ¶ 332, page 846.*

E

Acts 19. 23 And the same time there arose no small stir about that way.

24 For a certain *man* named Demetrius, a silversmith, which made silver shrines for Diana, brought no small gain unto the craftsmen;

Acts 20. 1 And after the uproar was ceased, Paul called unto *him* the disciples, and

E—CONCLUDED.

embraced *them*, and departed for to go into Macedonia.

I Cor. 15. 32 If after the manner of men I have fought with beasts at Ephesus, what advantageth it me, if the dead rise not? let us eat and drink; for to morrow we die.

I Cor. 16. 9 For a great door and effectual is opened unto me, and *there are* many adversaries.

2

Or, *answer.*

F

Jer. 17. 5 Thus saith the LORD; Cursed *be* the man that trusteth in man, and maketh flesh his arm, and whose heart departeth from the LORD.

Jer. 17. 7 Blessed *is* the man that trusteth in the LORD, and whose hope the LORD is.

G

II Pet. 2. 9 The Lord knoweth how to deliver the godly out of temptation, and to reserve the unjust unto the day of judgment to be punished:

H

Rom. 15. 30 Now I beseech you, brethren, for the Lord Jesus Christ's sake, and for the love of the Spirit, that ye strive together with me in *your* prayers to God for me;

§ 386. PAUL'S THANKSGIVING FOR COMFORT IN AFFLICTION, AND

CHAP. I.

11 Ye also [h]helping together by prayer for us, that [i]for the gift *bestowed* upon us by the means of many persons thanks may be given by many on our behalf.

12 For our rejoicing is this, the testimony of our conscience, that in simplicity and [k]godly sincerity, [l]not with fleshly wisdom, but by the grace of God, we have had our conversation in the world, and more abundantly to you-ward.

CHAP. I.

13 For we write none other things unto you, than what ye read or acknowledge; and I trust ye shall acknowledge even to the end;

14 As also ye have acknowledged us in part, that [m]we are your rejoicing, even as [n]ye also *are* ours in the day of the Lord Jesus.

H—CONCLUDED, See preceding page, 963.

Phil. 1. 19 For I know that this shall turn to my salvation through your prayer, and the supply of the Spirit of Jesus Christ,

Phile. 22 But withal prepare me also a lodging: for I trust that through your prayers I shall be given unto you.

§ 387. PAUL ANSWERS WITH REASONS

1 : 15–24; 2 : 1–4.

15 And in this confidence [a]I was minded to come unto you before, that ye might have [b]a second [1]benefit;

16 And to pass by you into Macedonia, and [c]to come again out of Macedonia unto you, and of you to be brought on my way toward Judea.

17 When I therefore was thus minded, did I use lightness? or the things that I purpose, do I purpose [d]according to the flesh, that with me there should be yea yea, and nay nay?

18 But *as* God *is* true, our [2]word toward you was not yea and nay.

19 For [e]the Son of God, Jesus Christ, who was preached among you by us, *even* by me and Silvanus and Timotheus, was not yea and nay, [f]but in him was yea.

20 [g]For all the promises of God in him *are* yea, and in him Amen, unto the glory of God by us.

21 Now he which stablisheth us with you in Christ, and [h]hath anointed us, *is* God·

CHAP. I.

22 Who [i]hath also sealed us, and [k]given the earnest of the Spirit in our hearts.

23 Moreover [l]I call God for a rec-

A

I Cor. 4. 19. *See k, K, § 358, page 906.*

B

Rom. 1. 11 For I long to see you, that I may impart unto you some spiritual gift, to the end ye may be established;

1

Or, *grace.*

C

Rom. 16. 5. *See d, D, § 346, page 884.*

D

IICor. 10. 2 But I beseech *you,* that I may not be bold when I am present with that confidence, wherewith I think to be bold against some, which think of us as if we walked according to the flesh.

2

Or, *preaching.*

E

Mark 1. 1 The beginning of the gospel of Jesus Christ, the Son of God;

Luke 1. 35 And the angel answered and said unto her, The Holy Ghost shall come upon thee, and the power of the Highest shall overshadow thee: therefore also that holy thing which shall be born of thee shall be called the Son of God.

AFFIRMATION OF A HOLY AND SINCERE CONSCIENCE (Concluded).

I

II Cor. 4. 15. *See under* C, *page 963.*

K

II Cor. 2. 17 For we are not as many, which corrupt the word of God: but as of sincerity, but as of God, in the sight of God speak we in Christ.

II Cor. 4. 2 But have renounced the hidden things of dishonesty, not walking in craftiness, nor handling the word of God deceitfully; but by manifestation of the truth commending ourselves to every man's conscience in the sight of God.

L

I Cor. 1. 17. *See k, K, ℥ 350, page 890.*

M

II Cor. 5. 12 For we commend not ourselves again unto you, but give you occasion

M—Concluded.

to glory on our behalf, that ye may have somewhat to *answer* them which glory in appearance, and not in heart.

N

Phil. 2. 16 Holding forth the word of life; that I may rejoice in the day of Christ, that I have not run in vain, neither laboured in vain.

Phil. 4. 1 Therefore, my brethren dearly beloved and longed for, my joy and crown, so stand fast in the Lord, *my* dearly beloved.

I Thes. 2. 19 For what *is* our hope, or joy, or crown of rejoicing? *Are* not even ye in the presence of our Lord Jesus Christ at his coming?
20 For ye are our glory and joy.

FOR DELAYING HIS PURPOSED VISIT.

E—Concluded.

Acts 9. 20 And straightway he preached Christ in the synagogues, that he is the Son of God.

F

Heb. 13. 8 Jesus Christ the same yesterday, and to day, and for ever.

G

Rom. 15. 8 Now I say that Jesus Christ was a minister of the circumcision for the truth of God, to confirm the promises *made* unto the fathers:
9 And that the Gentiles might glorify God for *his* mercy: as it is written, For this cause I will confess to thee among the Gentiles, and sing unto thy name.

H

I Jno. 2. 20 But ye have an unction from the Holy One, and ye know all things.

I Jno. 2. 27 But the anointing which ye have received of him abideth in you, and ye need not that any man teach you: but as the same anointing teacheth you of all things, and is truth, and is no lie, and even as it hath taught you, ye shall abide in him.

I

Eph. 1. 13 In whom ye also *trusted*, after that ye heard the word of truth, the gospel of your salvation: in whom also after that ye believed, ye were sealed with that Holy Spirit of promise,

Eph. 4. 30 And grieve not the Holy Spirit of

I—Concluded.

God, whereby ye are sealed unto the day of redemption.

II Tim. 2. 19 Nevertheless the foundation of God standeth sure, having this seal, The Lord knoweth them that are his. And, Let every one that nameth the name of Christ depart from iniquity.

Rev. 2. 17 He that hath an ear, let him hear what the Spirit saith unto the churches; To him that overcometh will I give to eat of the hidden manna, and will give him a white stone, and in the stone a new name written, which no man knoweth saving he that receiveth *it*.

K

Rom. 8. 23 And not only *they*, but ourselves also, which have the firstfruits of the Spirit, even we ourselves groan within ourselves, waiting for the adoption, *to wit*, the redemption of our body.

II Cor. 5. 5 Now he that hath wrought us for the selfsame thing *is* God, who also hath given unto us the earnest of the Spirit.

Eph. 1. 14 Which is the earnest of our inheritance until the redemption of the purchased possession, unto the praise of his glory.

L

Rom. 1. 9. *See c, C, ℥ 318, page 808.*

II Cor. 11. 31 The God and Father of our Lord Jesus Christ, which is blessed for evermore, knoweth that I lie not.

Gal. 1. 20 Now the things which I write unto you, behold, before God, I lie not.

§ 387. PAUL ANSWERS WITH REASONS FOR

CHAP. 1.

ord upon my soul, [m]that to spare you
I came not as yet unto Corinth.
24 Not for [n]that we have dominion
over your faith, but are helpers of
your joy: for [o]by faith ye stand.

CHAP. 2.

1 But I determined this with myself, [p]that I would not come again
to you in heaviness.
2 For if I make you sorry, who is
he then that maketh me glad, but
the same which is made sorry by me?
3 And I wrote this same unto you,
lest, when I came, [q]I should have
sorrow from them of whom I ought
to rejoice; [r]having confidence in
you all, that my joy is *the joy* of you
all.
4 For out of much affliction and
anguish of heart I wrote unto you

CHAP. 2.

with many tears; [s]not that ye should
be grieved, but that ye might know
the love which I have more abundantly unto you.

M

I Cor. 4. 21 What will ye? shall I come unto you with a rod, or in love, and *in* the spirit of meekness?

II Cor. 2. 3 And I wrote this same unto you, lest when I came, I should have sorrow from them of whom I ought to rejoice; having confidence in you all, that my joy is *the joy* of you all.

II Cor. 12. 20 For I fear, lest, when I come, I shall not find you such as I would, and *that* I shall be found unto you such as ye would not: lest *there be* debates, envyings, wraths, strifes, backbitings, whisperings, swellings, tumults:
21 *And* lest, when I come again, my God will humble me among you, and *that* I shall bewail many which have sinned already, and have not repented of the uncleanness and fornication and lasciviousness which they have committed.

II Cor. 13. 2 I told you before, and foretell you,

§ 388. FORGIVENESS AND

2:5–11.

5 But [a]if any have caused grief, he
hath not [b]grieved me, but in part:
that I may not overcharge you all.
6 Sufficient to such a man *is*
this [1]punishment, which *was inflicted*
[c]of many.
7 [d]So that contrariwise ye *ought*
rather to forgive *him*, and comfort
him, lest perhaps such a one should
be swallowed up with overmuch sorrow.
8 Wherefore I beseech you that ye
would confirm *your* love toward him.
9 For to this end also did I write,
that I might know the proof of you,
whether ye be [e]obedient in all things.

CHAP. 2.

10 To whom ye forgive any thing,
I *forgive* also: for if I forgave any
thing, to whom I forgave *it*, for
your sakes *forgave I it* [2]in the person of Christ;
11 [f]Lest Satan should get an advantage of us: for we are not ignorant of his devices.

A

I Cor. 5. 1 It is reported commonly *that there is* fornication among you, and such fornication as is not so much as named among the Gentiles, that one should have his father's wife.

Gal. 5. 10 I have confidence in you through the Lord, that ye will be none otherwise minded: but he that troubleth you shall bear his judgment, whosoever he be.

DELAYING HIS PURPOSED VISIT (CONCLUDED).

M—CONCLUDED.

as if I were present, the second time; and being absent now I write to them which heretofore have sinned, and to all other, that, if I come again, I will not spare:

IICor.13. 10 Therefore I write these things being absent, lest being present I should use sharpness, according to the power which the Lord hath given me to edification, and not to destruction.

N

I Cor. 3. 5 Who then is Paul, and who *is* Apollos, but ministers by whom ye believed, even as the Lord gave to every man?

I Pet. 5. 3 Neither as being lords over *God's* heritage, but being ensamples to the flock.

O

Rom. 11. 20 Well; because of unbelief they were broken off, and thou standest by faith. Be not highminded, but fear:

I Cor. 15. 1 Moreover, brethren, I declare unto you the gospel which I preached unto you, which also ye have received, and wherein ye stand;

P

II Cor. 1. 23. *See text of topic, m, M.*

Q

I Cor. 12. 21. *See under M.*

R

IICor. 7. 16 I rejoice therefore that I have confidence in you in all *things*.

IICor 8. 22 And we have sent with them our brother, whom we have oftentimes proved diligent in many things, but now much more diligent, upon the great confidence which *I have* in you.

Gal. 5. 10. *See under A, § 388.*

IIThes. 3. 4 And we have confidence in the Lord touching you, that ye both do and will do things which we command you.

S

II Cor. 7. 8 For though I made you sorry with a letter, I do not repent, though I did repent: for I perceive that the same epistle hath made you sorry, though *it were* but for a season,

9 Now I rejoice, not that ye were made sorry, but that ye sorrowed to repentance: for ye were made sorry after a godly manner, that ye might receive damage by us in nothing.

II Cor. 7. 12 Wherefore, though I wrote unto you, *I did it* not for his cause that had done the wrong, nor for his cause that suffered wrong, but that our care for you in the sight of God might appear unto you.

COMFORT FOR THE OFFENDER.

B

Gal. 4. 12 Brethren, I beseech you, be as I *am;* for I *am* as ye *are:* ye have not injured me at all.

1

Or, *censure.*

C

I Cor. 5. 4 In the name of our Lord Jesus Christ, when ye are gathered together, and my spirit, with the power of our Lord Jesus Christ,

5 To deliver such a one unto Satan for the destruction of the flesh, that the spirit may be saved in the day of the Lord Jesus.

I Tim. 5. 20 Them that sin rebuke before all, that others also may fear.

D

Gal. 6. 1 Brethren, if a man be overtaken in a fault, ye which are spiritual, restore such a one in the spirit of meekness; considering thyself, lest thou also be tempted.

Heb. 12. 12 Wherefore lift up the hands which hang down, and the feeble knees;

E

II Cor. 7. 15 And his inward affection is more abundant toward you, whilst he remembereth the obedience of you all, how with fear and trembling ye received him.

IICor. 10. 6 And having in a readiness to revenge all disobedience, when your obedience is fulfilled.

2

Or, *in the sight.*

F

IICor. 11. 3 But I fear, lest by any means, as the serpent beguiled Eve through his subtilty, so your minds should be corrupted from the simplicity that is in Christ.

Eph. 6. 11 Put on the whole armour of God, that ye may be able to stand against the wiles of the devil.

I Pet. 5. 8 Be sober, be vigilant; because your adversary the devil, as a roaring lion, walketh about, seeking whom he may devour:

§ 389. NOT FINDING TITUS AND HAVING NO

2 : 12-17.

12 Furthermore, [a]when I came to
Troas to *preach* Christ's gospel, and
[b]a door was opened unto me of the
Lord,

13 [c]I had no rest in my spirit, because I found not Titus my brother :
but taking my leave of them, I went
from thence into Macedonia.

14 Now thanks *be* unto God, which
always causeth us to triumph in
Christ, and maketh manifest [d]the
savour of his knowledge by us in
every place.

15 For we are unto God a sweet
savour of Christ, [e]in them that are
saved, and [f]in them that perish:

16 [g]To the one *we are* the savour
of death unto death; and to the
other the savour of life unto life.
And [h]who *is* sufficient for these
things?

CHAP. 2.

17 For we are not as many,
which [i1]corrupt the word of God:
but as [k]of sincerity, but as of God, in
the sight of God speak we [2]in Christ.

A

Acts 16. 8 And they passing by Mysia came down to Troas.

Acts 20. 6 And we sailed away from Philippi after the days of unleavened bread, and came unto them to Troas in five days; where we abode seven days.

B

Acts 14. 27. *See i, I, § 266, page 724.*

C

II Cor. 7. 5 For, when we were come into Macedonia, our flesh had no rest, but we were troubled on every side; without *were* fightings, within *were* fears.

6 Nevertheless God, that comforteth those that are cast down, comforted us by the coming of Titus;

D

Song 1. 3 Because of the savour of thy good ointments thy name *is as* ointment poured forth, therefore do the virgins love thee.

§ 390. THE SUFFICIENCY OF THE SPIRIT'S MINIS-

3 : 1–11.

1 Do [a]we begin again to commend
ourselves? or need we, as some
others, [b]epistles of commendation to
you, or *letters* of commendation
from you?

2 [c]Ye are our epistle written in our
hearts, known and read of all men:

3 *Forasmuch as ye are* manifestly
declared to be the epistle of Christ
[d]ministered by us, written not with
ink, but with the spirit of the living
God; not [e]in tables of stone, but [f]in
fleshly tables of the heart.

4 And such trust have we through
Christ to God-ward:

5 [g]Not that we are sufficient of our-

A

II Cor. 5. 12 For we commend not ourselves again unto you, but give you occasion to glory on our behalf, that ye may have somewhat to *answer* them which glory in appearance, and not in heart.

II Cor. 10. 8 For though I should boast somewhat more of our authority, which the Lord hath given us for edification, and not for your destruction, I should not be ashamed.

II Cor. 10. 12 For we dare not make ourselves of the number, or compare ourselves with some that commend themselves: but they measuring themselves by themselves, and comparing themselves among themselves, are not wise.

II Cor. 12. 11 I am become a fool in glorying; ye have compelled me: for I ought to have been commended of you: for in nothing am I behind the very chiefest apostles, though I be nothing.

B

Acts 18. 27 And when he was disposed to pass

RELIEF IN THE SPIRIT, PAUL LEAVES TROAS.

E

I Cor. 1. 18 For the preaching of the cross is to them that perish foolishness; but unto us which are saved, it is the power of God.

F

II Cor. 4. 3 But if our gospel be hid, it is hid to them that are lost:

G

Luke 2. 34 And Simeon blessed them, and said unto Mary his mother, Behold, this *child* is set for the fall and rising again of many in Israel; and for a sign which shall be spoken against;

John 9. 39 And Jesus said, For judgment I am come into this world, that they which see not might see; and that they which see might be made blind.

I Pet. 2. 7 Unto you therefore which believe *he is* precious: but unto them which be disobedient, the stone which the builders disallowed, the same is made the head of the corner,

8 And a stone of stumbling, and a rock of offence, *even to them* which stumble at the word, being disobedient: whereunto also they were appointed.

H

I Cor. 15. 10 But by the grace of God I am what I am: and his grace which *was bestowed* upon me was not in vain; but I laboured more abundantly than they

H—CONCLUDED.

all: yet not I, but the grace of God which was with me.

II Cor. 3. 5 Not that we are sufficient of ourselves to think anything as of ourselves; but our sufficiency *is* of God;

6 Who also hath made us able ministers of the new testament; not of the letter, but of the spirit: for the letter killeth, but the spirit giveth life.

I

II Cor. 4. But have renounced the hidden things of dishonesty, not walking in craftiness, nor handling the word of God deceitfully; but by manifestation of the truth commending ourselves to every man's conscience in the sight of God.

II Cor. 11. 13 For such *are* false apostles, deceitful workers, transforming themselves into the apostles of Christ.

II Pet. 2. 3 And through covetousness shall they with feigned words make merchandise of you: whose judgment now of a long time lingereth not, and their damnation slumbereth not.

1

Or, *deal deceitfully with.*

K

II Cor. 1. 12. *See k, K, § 386, page 964.*

2

Or, *of.*

TRATION, AND THE GLORY OF THE NEW COVENANT.

B—CONCLUDED.

into Achaia, the brethren wrote, exhorting the disciples to receive him: who, when he was come, helped them much which had believed through grace:

C

I Cor. 9. 2. *See d, D, § 365, page 920.*

D

I Cor. 3. 5 Who then is Paul, and who *is* Apollos, but ministers by whom ye believed, even as the Lord gave to every man?

E

Ex. 24. 12 And the LORD said unto Moses, Come up to me into the mount, and be there: and I will give thee tables of stone, and a law, and commandments which I have written; that thou mayest teach them.

Ex. 34. 1 And the LORD said unto Moses, Hew thee two tables of stone like unto the first: and I will write upon *these* tables the words that were in the first tables, which thou brakest.

F

Ps. 40. 8 I delight to do thy will, O my God: yea, thy law *is* within my heart.

Jer. 31. 33 But this *shall be* the covenant that I will make with the house of Israel; After those days, saith the LORD, I will put my law in their inward parts, and write it in their hearts; and will be their God, and they shall be my people.

Eze. 11. 19 And I will give them one heart, and I will put a new spirit within you; and I will take the stony heart out of their flesh, and will give them a heart of flesh:

Eze. 36. 26 A new heart also will I give you: and a new spirit will I put within you: and I will take away the stony heart out of your flesh, and I will give you a heart of flesh.

Heb. 8. 10 For this *is* the covenant that I will make with the house of Israel after those days, saith the Lord; I will put my laws into their mind, and write

For F concluded and G, see next page (970).

§ 390. THE SUFFICIENCY OF THE SPIRIT'S MINISTRATION,

CHAP. 3.

selves to think any thing as of ourselves; but [h]our sufficiency *is* of God;
6 Who also hath made us able [i]min-
isters of the [k]new testament; not [l]of
the letter, but of the spirit: for [m]the
letter killeth, [n]but the spirit [1]giveth
life.
7 But if [o]the ministration of death,
[p]written *and* engraven in stones, was
glorious, [q]so that the children of Israel could not steadfastly behold the
face of Moses for the glory of his
countenance; which *glory* was to be
done away:
8 How shall not [r]the ministration
of the spirit be rather glorious?
9 For if the ministration of condemnation *be* glory, much more doth
the ministration [s]of righteousness exceed in glory.
10 For even that which was made
glorious had no glory in this respect,
by reason of the glory that excelleth.
11 [t]For if that which is done away
was glorious, much more that which
remaineth *is* glorious.

F—CONCLUDED.

them in their hearts: and I will be to them a God, and they shall be to me a people:

G

II Cor. 2. 16. *See h, H, § 389, page 968.*

H

I Cor. 15. 10. *See p, P, § 376, page 950.*

I

I Cor. 4. 1. *See a, A, § 356 page 902.*
I Cor. 9. 17. *See a, A, § 365, page 924.*

K

Jer. 31. 31 Behold, the days come, saith the LORD, that I will make a new covenant with the house of Israel, and with the house of Judah:

Matt. 26. 28 For this is my blood of the new testament, which is shed for many for the remission of sins.

I Cor. 11. 25 After the same manner also *he took* the cup, when he had supped, saying, This cup is the new testament in my blood: this do ye, as oft as ye drink *it*, in remembrance of me.

Heb. 7. 22 By so much was Jesus made a surety of a better testament.

Heb. 8. 6 But now hath he obtained a more excellent ministry, by how much also he is the mediator of a better covenant, which was established upon better promises.

Heb. 8. 8 For finding fault with them, he saith, Behold, the days come, saith the Lord, when I will make a new cove-

§ 391. THE GLORY OF THE

3 : 12-18.

12 Seeing then that we have such
hope, [a]we use great [1]plainness of
speech:
13 And not as Moses, [b]*which* put a
vail over his face, that the children
of Israel could not steadfastly look to
[c]the end of that which is abolished:
14 But [d]their minds were blinded:
for until this day remaineth the same
vail untaken away in the reading of
the old testament; which *vail* is done
away in Christ.
15 But even unto this day, when

CHAP. 3.

Moses is read, the vail is upon their
heart.
16 Nevertheless, [e]when it shall turn
to the Lord, [f]the vail shall be taken
away.
17 Now [g]the Lord is that Spirit:
and where the Spirit of the Lord *is*,
there *is* liberty.
18 But we all, with open face beholding [h]as in a glass [i]the glory of
the Lord, [k]are changed into the same
image from glory to glory, *even* as
[2]by the Spirit of the Lord.

AND THE GLORY OF THE NEW COVENANT (CONCLUDED).

K—CONCLUDED.

nant with the house of Israel and with the house of Judah:

Heb. 9. 15 And for this cause he is the mediator of the new testament, that by means of death, for the redemption of the transgressions *that were* under the first testament, they which are called might receive the promise of eternal inheritance.

Heb. 12. 24 And to Jesus the mediator of the new covenant, and to the blood of sprinkling, that speaketh better things than *that of* Abel.

Heb. 13. 20 Now the God of peace, that brought again from the dead our Lord Jesus, that great Shepherd of the sheep, through the blood of the everlasting covenant,

L

Rom. 2. 29. *See r, R, § 321, page 820.*

M

Rom. 4. 15. *See n, N, § 325, page 828.*

N

Rom. 8. 2 For the law of the Spirit of life in Christ Jesus hath made me free from the law of sin and death.

I Cor. 15. 45. *See g, G, § 380, page 954.*

1

Or, *quickeneth.*

O

Rom. 7. 10 And the commandment, which *was ordained* to life, I found *to be* unto death.

P

Ex. 34. 1. *See under E.*

Deut. 10. 1 At that time the LORD said unto me, Hew thee two tables of stone like unto the first, and come up unto me into the mount, and make thee an ark of wood.

2 And I will write on the tables the words that were in the first tables which thou brakest, and thou shalt put them in the ark.

Q

Ex. 34. 29 And it came to pass, when Moses came down from mount Sinai with the two tables of testimony in Moses' hand, when he came down from the mount, that Moses wist not that the skin of his face shone while he talked with him.

30 And when Aaron and all the children of Israel saw Moses, behold, the skin of his face shone; and they were afraid to come nigh him.

Ex. 34. 35 And the children of Israel saw the face of Moses, that the skin of Moses' face shone: and Moses put the vail upon his face again, until he went in to speak with Him.

R

Gal. 3. 5 He therefore that ministereth to you the Spirit, and worketh miracles among you, *doeth he it* by the works of the law, or by the hearing of faith?

S

Rom. 1. 17. *See o, O, § 318, page 810.*

T

Rom. 5. 20, 21. *See i, I, § 327, page 834.*

NEW COVENANT REFLECTED.

A

II Cor. 7. 4 Great *is* my boldness of speech toward you, great *is* my glorying of you: I am filled with comfort, I am exceeding joyful in all our tribulation.

Eph. 6. 19 And for me, that utterance may be given unto me, that I may open my mouth boldly, to make known the mystery of the gospel,

1

Or, *boldness.*

B

Ex. 34. 35. *See under Q, § 390.*

Ex. 54. 33 And *till* Moses had done speaking with them, he put a vail on his face.

C

Rom. 10. 4. *See d, D, § 337, page 858.*

D

Rom. 11. 7, 8. *See k, K, § 339, page 862.*

E

Rom. 11. 23, 26. *See d, D, § 341, page 866.*

F

Isa. 25. 7 And he will destroy in this mountain the face of the covering cast over all people, and the vail that is spread over all nations.

G

I Cor. 15. 45. *See g, G, § 380, page 954.*

H

I Cor. 13. 12. *See m, M, § 372, page 942.*

I

Rom. 9. 4. *See f, F, § 335, page 852.*

K

Rom. 8. 29. *See i, I, § 334, page 848.*

2

Or, *of the Lord the Spirit.*

§ 392. A VEILED GOSPEL TO UNBELIEVERS, BUT TO BELIEVERS

4 : 1–6.

1 Therefore seeing we have [a]this ministry, [b]as we have received mercy, we faint not;

2 But have renounced the hidden things of [1]dishonesty, not walking in craftiness, [c]nor handling the word of God deceitfully; [d]but by manifestation of the truth [e]commending ourselves to every man's conscience in the sight of God.

3 But if our gospel be hid, [f]it is hid to them that are lost:

4 In whom [g]the god of this world [h]hath blinded the minds of them which believe not, lest [i]the light of the glorious gospel of Christ, [k]who is the image of God, should shine unto them.

5 [l]For we preach not ourselves, but Christ Jesus the Lord; and [m]ourselves your servants for Jesus' sake.

6 For God, [n]who commanded the light to shine out of darkness, [2]hath [o]shined in our hearts, to *give* [p]the light of the knowledge of the glory of God in the face of Jesus Christ.

A

I Cor. 4. 1. *See a, A, § 356, page 902.*

B

I Cor. 7. 25 Now concerning virgins I have no commandment of the Lord: yet I give my judgment, as one that hath obtained mercy of the Lord to be faithful.

I Tim. 1. 13 Who was before a blasphemer, and a persecutor, and injurious: but I obtained mercy, because I did *it* ignorantly in unbelief.

1

Gr. *shame.*

C

II Cor. 2. 17. *See i, I, § 389, page 968.*

I Thes. 2. 3 For our exhortation *was* not of deceit, nor of uncleanness, nor in guile:

I Thes. 2. 5 For neither at any time used we flattering words, as ye know, nor a cloak of covetousness; God *is* witness:

D

II Cor. 6. 4 But in all *things* approving ourselves as the ministers of God, in much patience, in afflictions, in necessities, in distresses,

II Cor. 6. 7 By the word of truth, by the power of God, by the armour of righteousness on the right hand and on the left,

II Cor. 7. 14 For if I have boasted any thing to him of you, I am not ashamed; but as we spake all things to you in truth, even so our boasting, which *I made* before Titus, is found a truth.

E

II Cor. 5. 11 Knowing therefore the terror of the Lord, we persuade men; but we are made manifest unto God; and I trust also are made manifest in your consciences.

§ 393. OUR LIGHT AFFLICTIONS WORK A FAR MORE

4 : 7–18.

7 But we have this treasure in [a]earthen vessels, [b]that the excellency of the power may be of God, and not of us.

8 *We are* [c]troubled on every side, yet not distressed; *we are* perplexed, but [1]not in despair;

9 Persecuted, but not forsaken; [d]cast down, but not destroyed;

10 [e]Always bearing about in the body the dying of the Lord Jesus,

A

II Cor. 5. 1 For we know that if our earthly house of *this* tabernacle were dissolved, we have a building of God, a house not made with hands, eternal in the heavens.

B

I Cor. 2. 5 That your faith should not stand in the wisdom of men, but in the power of God.

II Cor. 12. 9 And he said unto me, My grace is sufficient for thee: for my strength is made perfect in weakness. Most gladly therefore will I rather glory in my infirmities, that the power of Christ may rest upon me.

A LIGHT TO THE KNOWLEDGE OF THE GLORY OF GOD.

F

I Cor. 1. 18. *See a, A, § 351, page 892.*

IIThes. 2. 10 And with all deceivableness of unrighteousness in them that perish; because they received not the love of the truth, that they might be saved.

G

Matt. 4. 8 Again, the devil taketh him up into an exceeding high mountain, and sheweth him all the kingdoms of the world, and the glory of them;

9 And saith unto him, All these things will I give thee, if thou wilt fall down and worship me.

John 12. 31 Now is the judgment of this world: now shall the prince of this world be cast out.

John 14. 30 Hereafter I will not talk much with you: for the prince of this world cometh, and hath nothing in me.

John 16. 11 Of judgment, because the prince of this world is judged.

Eph. 2. 2 Wherein in time past ye walked according to the course of this world, according to the prince of the power of the air, the spirit that now worketh in the children of disobedience:

Eph. 6. 12 For we wrestle not against flesh and blood, but against principalities, against powers, against the rulers of the darkness of this world, against spiritual wickedness in high *places*.

H

Rom. 11. 7, 8. *See k, K, § 339, page 862.*

I

II Cor. 3. 8, 9, 11, 18. *See text of topic, § 390, § 391.*

K

John 14. 9. *See l, L, § 186, page 525.*

L

I Cor. 1. 13 Is Christ divided? was Paul crucified for you? or were ye baptized in the name of Paul?

I Cor. 1. 23 But we preach Christ crucified, unto the Jews a stumbling block, and unto the Greeks foolishness;

I Cor. 10. 33 Even as I please all *men* in all *things*, not seeking mine own profit, but the *profit* of many, that they may be saved.

M

I Cor. 9. 19 For though I be free from all *men*, yet have I made myself servant unto all, that I might gain the more.

II Cor. 1. 24 Not for that we have dominion over your faith, but are helpers of your joy: for by faith ye stand.

N

Gen. 1. 3 And God said, Let there be light: and there was light.

2

Gr. *is he who hath.*

O

II Pet. 1. 19 We have also a more sure word of prophecy; whereunto ye do well that ye take heed, as unto a light that shineth in a dark place, until the day dawn, and the daystar arise in your hearts:

P

II Cor. 4. 4. *See text of topic.*

I Pet. 2. 9 But ye *are* a chosen generation, a royal priesthood, a holy nation, a peculiar people; that ye should shew forth the praises of him who hath called you out of darkness into his marvellous light:

EXCEEDING AND ETERNAL WEIGHT OF GLORY.

C

II Cor. 7. 5 For, when we were come into Macedonia, our flesh had no rest, but we were troubled on every side; without *were* fightings, within *were* fears.

1

Or, *not altogether without help*, or, *means.*

D

Ps. 37. 24 Though he fall, he shall not be utterly cast down: for the LORD upholdeth *him with* his hand.

E

Ps. 44. 22 Yea, for thy sake are we killed all the day long; we are counted as sheep for the slaughter.

E—CONCLUDED.

Rom. 8. 36 As it is written, For thy sake we are killed all the day long; we are accounted as sheep for the slaughter.

I Cor. 15. 31 I protest by your rejoicing which I have in Christ Jesus our Lord, I die daily.

II Cor. 1. 5 For as the sufferings of Christ abound in us, so our consolation also aboundeth by Christ.

II Cor. 1. 9 But we had the sentence of death in ourselves, that we should not trust in ourselves, but in God which raiseth the dead:

For E concluded, see next page (974).

§ 393. OUR LIGHT AFFLICTIONS WORK A FAR MORE

CHAP. 4.

[f]that the life also of Jesus might be
made manifest in our body.

11 For we which live [g]are alway delivered unto death for Jesus' sake,
that the life also of Jesus might be
made manifest in our mortal flesh.

12 So then [h]death worketh in us,
but life in you.

13 We having [i]the same spirit of
faith, according as it is written, [k]I believed, and therefore have I spoken;
we also believe, and therefore speak;

14 Knowing that [l]he which raised
up the Lord Jesus shall raise up us
also by Jesus, and shall present *us*
with you.

15 For [m]all things *are* for your
sakes, that [n]the abundant grace might
through the thanksgiving of many
redound to the glory of God.

16 For which cause we faint not;
but though our outward man perish,
yet [o]the inward *man* is renewed day
by day.

CHAP. 4.

17 For [p]our light affliction, which
is but for a moment, worketh for us
a far more exceeding *and* eternal
weight of glory;

18 [q]While we look not at the things
which are seen, but at the things
which are not seen: for the things
which are seen *are* temporal; but the
things which are not seen *are* eternal.

E—CONCLUDED.

Gal. 6. 17 From henceforth let no man trouble me: for I bear in my body the marks of the Lord Jesus.

Phil. 3. 10 That I may know him, and the power of his resurrection, and the fellowship of his sufferings, being made conformable unto his death;

F

Rom. 8. 17. *See d, D, § 332, page 846.*

I Pet. 4. 13 But rejoice, inasmuch as ye are partakers of Christ's sufferings; that, when his glory shall be revealed, ye may be glad also with exceeding joy.

G

See under E.

H

II Cor. 13. 9 For we are glad, when we are weak, and ye are strong: and this also we wish, *even* your perfection.

§ 394. A MANSION IN HEAVEN. IN THIS BODY WE HAVE THE

5 : 1–10.

1 For we know that if [a]our earthly
house of *this* tabernacle were dissolved, we have a building of God,
a house not made with hands, eternal
in the heavens.

2 For in this [b]we groan, earnestly
desiring to be clothed upon with our
house which is from heaven:

3 If so be that [c]being clothed we
shall not be found naked.

4 For we that are in *this* tabernacle
do groan, being burdened: not for

CHAP. 5.

that we would be unclothed, but
[d]clothed upon, that mortality might
be swallowed up of life.

A

Job 4. 19 How much less *in* them that dwell in houses of clay, whose foundation *is* in the dust, *which* are crushed before the moth?

II Cor. 4. 7 But we have this treasure in earthen vessels, that the excellency of the power may be of God, and not of us.

II Pet. 1. 13 Yea, I think it meet, as long as I am in this tabernacle, to stir you up by putting *you* in remembrance;

14 Knowing that shortly I must put off *this* my tabernacle, even as our Lord Jesus Christ hath shewed me.

EXCEEDING AND ETERNAL WEIGHT OF GLORY (Concluded).

I

Rom. 1. 12. *See g, G, § 318, page 810.*

K

Ps. 116. 10 I believed; therefore have I spoken: I was greatly afflicted;

L

Acts 2. 24. *See k, K, § 231, page 638.*

M

I Cor. 3. 21. *See f, F, § 355, page 902.*

Col. 1. 24 Who now rejoice in my sufferings for you, and fill up that which is behind of the afflictions of Christ in my flesh for his body's sake, which is the church:

II Tim. 2. 10 Therefore I endure all things for the elect's sake, that they may also obtain the salvation which is in Christ Jesus with eternal glory.

N

II Cor. 1. 11 Ye also helping together by prayer for us, that for the gift *bestowed* upon us by the means of many persons thanks may be given by many on our behalf.

II Cor. 8. 19 And not *that* only, but who was also chosen of the churches to travel with us with this grace, which is administered by us to the glory of the same Lord, and *declaration of* your ready mind:

II Cor. 9. 11 Being enriched in every thing to all bountifulness, which causeth through us thanksgiving to God.

12 For the administration of this service not only supplieth the want of the saints, but is abundant also by many thanksgivings unto God;

O

Rom. 7. 22. *See k, K, § 331, page 842.*

P

Ps. 30. 5 For his anger *endureth but* a moment; in his favour *is* life: weeping may endure for a night, but joy *cometh* in the morning.

Isa. 54. 8 In a little wrath I hid my face from thee for a moment: but with everlasting kindness will I have mercy on thee, saith the LORD thy Redeemer.

Matt. 5. 12 Rejoice, and be exceeding glad: for great *is* your reward in heaven: for so persecuted they the prophets which were before you.

Acts 20. 23 Save that the Holy Ghost witnesseth in every city, saying that bonds and afflictions abide me.

Rom. 8. 18 For I reckon that the sufferings of this present time *are* not worthy *to be compared* with the glory which shall be revealed in us.

Rom. 8. 37 Nay, in all these things we are more than conquerors through him that loved us.

I Pet. 1. 6 Wherein ye greatly rejoice, though now for a season, if need be, ye are in heaviness through manifold temptations:

I Pet. 5. 10 But the God of all grace, who hath called us unto his eternal glory by Christ Jesus, after that ye have suffered a while, make you perfect, stablish, strengthen, settle *you*.

Q

Rom. 8. 24. *See k, K, § 333, page 846.*

EARNEST OF THE SPIRIT THAT WE MAY STRIVE TO PLEASE GOD.

B

Rom. 8. 23. *See g, G, § 333, page 846.*

C

Rev. 3. 18 I counsel thee to buy of me gold tried in the fire, that thou mayest be rich; and white raiment, that thou mayest be clothed, and *that* the shame of thy nakedness do not appear; and anoint thine eyes with eyesalve, that thou mayest see.

Rev. 16. 15 Behold, I come as a thief. Blessed *is* he that watcheth, and keepeth his garments, lest he walk naked, and they see his shame.

D

I Cor. 15. 53 For this corruptible must put on incorruption, and this mortal *must* put on immortality.

54 So when this corruptible shall

D—Concluded.

have put on incorruption, and this mortal shall have put on immortality, then shall be brought to pass the saying that is written, Death is swallowed up in victory.

E

Isa. 29. 23 But when he seeth his children, the work of mine hands, in the midst of him, they shall sanctify my name, and sanctify the Holy One of Jacob, and shall fear the God of Israel.

Eph. 2. 10 For we are his workmanship, created in Christ Jesus unto good works, which God hath before ordained that we should walk in them.

F

II Cor. 1. 22. *See k, K, § 387, page 964.*

For F concluded, see next page (976).

§ 394. A MANSION IN HEAVEN. IN THIS BODY WE HAVE THE EARNEST

CHAP. 5.

5 Now [e]he that hath wrought us for the selfsame thing *is* God, who also [f]hath given unto us the earnest of the Spirit.

6 Therefore *we are* always confident, knowing that, whilst we are at home in the body, we are absent from the Lord:

7 (For [g]we walk by faith, not by sight:)

8 We are confident, *I say*, and [h]willing rather to be absent from the body, and to be present with the Lord.

9 Wherefore we [1]labour, that, whether present or absent, we may be accepted of him.

10 [i]For we must all appear before the judgment seat of Christ; [k]that every one may receive the things *done* in *his* body, according to that he hath done, whether *it be* good or bad.

For E and F, see preceding page (975).

F—CONCLUDED.

Eph. 4. 30 And grieve not the Holy Spirit of God, whereby ye are sealed unto the day of redemption.

G

Rom. 8. 24 For we are saved by hope: but hope that is seen is not hope: for what a man seeth, why doth he yet hope for?
25 But if we hope for that we see not, *then* do we with patience wait for *it*.

I Cor. 13. 12 For now we see through a glass, darkly; but then face to face; now I know in part; but then shall I know even as also I am known.

II Cor. 4. 18 While we look not at the things which are seen, but at the things which are not seen: for the things which are seen *are* temporal; but the things which are not seen *are* eternal.

Heb. 11. 1 Now faith is the substance of things hoped for, the evidence of things not seen.

H

Phil. 1. 23 For I am in a strait betwixt two, having a desire to depart, and to be with Christ; which is far better:

1

Or, *endeavour*.

I

Gen. 18. 25 That be far from thee to do after this manner, to slay the righteous with the wicked: and that the righteous

§ 395. ALL THINGS ARE OF GOD WHO GAVE THE

5 : 11–21.

11 Knowing therefore [a]the terror of the Lord, we persuade men; but [b]we are made manifest unto God; and I trust also are made manifest in your consciences.

12 For [c]we commend not ourselves again unto you, but give you occasion [d]to glory on our behalf, that ye may have somewhat to *answer* them which glory [1]in appearance, and not in heart.

13 For [e]whether we be beside ourselves, *it is* to God: or whether we be sober, *it is* for your cause.

CHAP. 5.

14 For the love of Christ constraineth us; because we thus judge, that [f]if one died for all, then were all dead:

15 And *that* he died for all, [g]that they which live should not henceforth live unto themselves, but unto him which died for them, and rose again.

16 [h]Wherefore henceforth know we no man after the flesh: yea, though

A

Heb. 10. 31 *It is* a fearful thing to fall into the hands of the living God.

Jude 23 And others save with fear, pulling *them* out of the fire; hating even the garment spotted by the flesh.

B

II Cor. 4. 2. *See d, D, § 392, page 972.*

OF THE SPIRIT THAT WE MAY STRIVE TO PLEASE GOD (CONCLUDED).

I—CONTINUED.

should be as the wicked, that be far
from thee: Shall not the Judge of all
the earth do right?

Ps. 50. 4 He shall call to the heavens from
above, and to the earth, that he may
judge his people.

5 Gather my saints together unto me;
those that have made a covenant with
me by sacrifice.

6 And the heavens shall declare his
righteousness: for God *is* judge himself. Selah.

Matt.25. 31 When the Son of man shall come
in his glory, and all the holy angels
with him, then shall he sit upon the
throne of his glory:

32 And before him shall be gathered
all nations: and he shall separate them
one from another, as a shepherd divideth *his* sheep from the goats:

Acts 10. 42 And he commanded us to preach
unto the people, and to testify that it
is he which was ordained of God *to be*
the Judge of quick and dead.

Acts 17. 31 Because he hath appointed a day,
in the which he will judge the world
in righteousness by *that* man whom he
hath ordained; *whereof* he hath given
assurance unto all *men*, in that he hath
raised him from the dead.

Rom. 14. 10 But why dost thou judge thy
brother? or why dost thou set at
nought thy brother? for we shall all

I—CONCLUDED.

stand before the judgment seat of
Christ.

I Pet. 4. 5 Who shall give account to him that
is ready to judge the quick and the
dead.

Jude 14 And Enoch also, the seventh from
Adam, prophesied of these, saying, Behold, the Lord cometh with ten thousand of his saints,

15 To execute judgment upon all,
and to convince all that are ungodly
among them of all their ungodly deeds
which they have ungodly committed,
and of all their hard *speeches* which
ungodly sinners have spoken against
him.

K

Rom. 2. 6 Who will render to every man according to his deeds:

Gal. 6. 7 Be not deceived; God is not mocked:
for whatsoever a man soweth, that
shall he also reap.

Eph. 6. 8 Knowing that whatsoever good
thing any man doeth, the same shall
he receive of the Lord, whether *he be*
bond or free.

Col. 3. 24 Knowing that of the Lord ye shall
receive the reward of the inheritance:
for ye serve the Lord Christ.

Rev. 22. 12 And, behold, I come quickly; and
my reward *is* with me, to give every
man according as his work shall be.

MINISTRY OF RECONCILIATION. WE ARE AMBASSADORS.

C

II Cor 3. 1. *See a, A, § 390, page 968.*

D

II Cor. 1. 14. *See m, M, § 386, page 964.*

1

Gr. *in the face.*

E

IICor.11. 1 Would to God ye could bear with
me a little in *my* folly: and indeed
bear with me.

IICor.11. 16 I say again, Let no man think me
a fool; if otherwise, yet as a fool receive me, that I may boast myself a
little.

17 That which I speak, I speak *it* not
after the Lord, but as it were foolishly,
in this confidence of boasting.

IICor.12. 6 For though I would desire to glory,
I shall not be a fool; for I will say the
truth: but *now* I forbear, lest any man
should think of me above that which
he seeth me *to be*, or *that* he heareth
of me.

E—CONCLUDED.

IICor.12. 11 I am become a fool in glorying;
ye have compelled me: for I ought to
have been commended of you: for in
nothing am I behind the very chiefest
apostles, though I be nothing.

F

Rom. 5. 15 But not as the offence, so also *is*
the free gift. For if through the offence
of one many be dead, much more the
grace of God, and the gift by grace,
which is by one man, Jesus Christ,
hath abounded unto many.

G

Rom. 14. 7, 8. *See g, G, § 344, page 876.*

H

Matt.12. 50 For whosoever shall do the will of
my Father which is in heaven, the same
is my brother, and sister, and mother.

John 15. 14 Ye are my friends, if ye do whatsoever I command you.

For H concluded, see next page (978).

§ 395. ALL THINGS ARE OF GOD WHO GAVE THE MINISTRY

CHAP. 5.

we have known Christ after the flesh,
[i]yet now henceforth know we *him* no
more.

17 Therefore if any man *be* in
Christ, *he is* [k]a new creature: [l]old
things are passed away; behold, all
things are become new.

18 And all things *are* of God,[m]who
hath reconciled us to himself by Jesus Christ, and hath given to us the
ministry of reconciliation;

19 To wit, that [n]God was in Christ,
reconciling the world unto himself,
not imputing their trespasses unto
them; and hath [2]committed unto us
the word of reconciliation.

20 Now then we are [o]ambassadors
for Christ, as [p]though God did beseech *you* by us: we pray *you* in
Christ's stead, be ye reconciled to
God.

21 For [q]he hath made him *to be* sin
for us, who knew no sin; that we

CHAP. 5.

might be made [r]the righteousness of
God in him.

H—CONCLUDED.

Gal. 5. 6 For in Jesus Christ neither circumcision availeth any thing, nor uncircumcision; but faith which worketh by love.

Col. 3. 11 Where there is neither Greek nor Jew, circumcision nor uncircumcision, Barbarian, Scythian, bond *nor* free: but Christ *is* all, and in all.

I

John 6. 63 It is the spirit that quickeneth; the flesh profiteth nothing: the words that I speak unto you, *they* are spirit, and *they* are life.

K

Gal. 5. 6. *See under H.*

Gal. 6. 15 For in Christ Jesus neither circumcision availeth any thing, nor uncircumcision, but a new creature.

L

Isa. 43. 18 Remember ye not the former things, neither consider the things of old.

19 Behold, I will do a new thing; now it shall spring forth; shall ye not know it? I will even make a way in the wilderness, *and* rivers in the desert.

Isa. 65. 17 For, behold, I create new heavens and a new earth: and the former shall not be remembered, nor come into mind.

§ 396. WITH AN APPEAL FOR FAITHFULNESS, PAUL

6: 1–13.

1 We then, *as* [a]workers together
with him, [b]beseech *you* also [c]that ye
receive not the grace of God in vain.

2 (For he saith, [d]I have heard thee
in a time accepted, and in the day
of salvation have I succoured thee:
behold, now *is* the accepted time;
behold, now *is* the day of salvation.)

3 [e]Giving no offence in any thing,
that the ministry be not blamed:

4 But in all *things* [1]approving ourselves [f]as the ministers of God, in
much patience, in afflictions, in necessities, in distresses,

CHAP. 6.

5 [g]In stripes, in imprisonments, [2]in
tumults, in labours, in watchings, in
fastings;

6 By pureness, by knowledge, by
longsuffering, by kindness, by the
Holy Ghost, by love unfeigned,

7 [h]By the word of truth, by [i]the
power of God, by [k]the armour of
righteousness on the right hand and
on the left,

A

I Cor. 3. 9. *See o, O, § 353, page 898.*

B

II Cor. 5. 20. *See text of topic, § 395.*

OF RECONCILIATION. WE ARE AMBASSADORS (CONCLUDED).

L—CONCLUDED.

Eph. 2. 15 Having abolished in his flesh the enmity, *even* the law of commandments *contained* in ordinances; for to make in himself of twain one new man, *so* making peace;

Rev. 21. 5 And he that sat upon the throne said, Behold, I make all things new. And he said unto me, Write: for these words are true and faithful.

M

Rom. 5. 10. *See o, O, § 326, page 832.*

N

Rom. 3. 24 Being justified freely by his grace through the redemption that is in Christ Jesus:

25 Whom God hath set forth *to be* a propitiation through faith in his blood, to declare his righteousness for the remission of sins that are past, through the forbearance of God;

2

Gr. *put in us.*

O

Job 33. 23 If there be a messenger with him, an interpreter, one among a thousand, to shew unto man his uprightness;

Mal. 2. 7 For the priest's lips should keep knowledge, and they should seek the law at his mouth: for he *is* the messenger of the LORD of hosts.

II Cor. 3. 6 Who also hath made us able ministers of the new testament; not of the letter, but of the spirit: for the letter killeth, but the spirit giveth life.

O—CONCLUDED.

Eph. 6. 20 For which I am an ambassador in bonds: that therein I may speak boldly, as I ought to speak.

P

II Cor. 6. 1. *See text of topic, § 396.*

Q

Isa. 53. 6 All we like sheep have gone astray; we have turned every one to his own way; and the LORD hath laid on him the iniquity of us all.

Isa. 53. 9 And he made his grave with the wicked, and with the rich in his death; because he had done no violence, neither *was any* deceit in his mouth.

Gal. 3. 13 Christ hath redeemed us from the curse of the law, being made a curse for us: for it is written, Cursed *is* every one that hangeth on a tree:

I Pet. 2. 22 Who did no sin, neither was guile found in his mouth:

I Pet. 2. 24 Who his own self bare our sins in his own body on the tree, that we, being dead to sins, should live unto righteousness: by whose stripes ye were healed.

I Jno. 3. 5 And ye know that he was manifested to take away our sins; and in him is no sin.

R

Rom 1. 17. *See o, O, § 318, page 810.*

Rom. 5. 19 For as by one man's disobedience many were made sinners, so by the obedience of one shall many be made righteous.

SETS FORTH THE CHARACTER OF HIS MINISTRY.

C

Heb. 12. 15 Looking diligently lest any man fail of the grace of God; lest any root of bitterness springing up trouble *you*, and thereby many be defiled;

D

Isa. 49. 8 Thus saith the LORD, In an acceptable time have I heard thee, and in a day of salvation have I helped thee: and I will preserve thee, and give thee for a covenant of the people, to establish the earth, to cause to inherit the desolate heritages;

Isa. 61. 2 To proclaim the acceptable year of the LORD, and the day of vengeance of our God; to comfort all that mourn;

Luke 4. 19 To preach the acceptable year of the Lord.

E

I Cor. 8. 13. *See x, X, § 364, page 920.*

1

Gr. *commending.*

II Cor. 4. 2 But have renounced the hidden things of dishonesty, not walking in craftiness, nor handling the word of God deceitfully; but by manifestation of the truth commending ourselves to every man's conscience in the sight of God.

F

I Cor. 4. 1. *See a, A, § 356, page 902.*

G

II Cor. 11. 23 Are they ministers of Christ? (I speak as a fool,) I *am* more; in labours more abundant, in stripes above measure, in prisons more frequent, in deaths oft.

24 Of the Jews five times received I forty *stripes* save one.

For G concluded, 2, H, I and K, see next page (980).

§ 396. WITH AN APPEAL FOR FAITHFULNESS, PAUL SETS

CHAP. 6.

8 By honour and dishonour, by evil
report and good report: as deceivers,
and *yet* true;
9 As unknown, and [l]*yet* well known;
[m]as dying, and, behold, we live; [n]as
chastened, and not killed;
10 As sorrowful, yet alway rejoicing; as poor, yet making many rich;
as having nothing, and *yet* possessing all things.
11 O *ye* Corinthians, our mouth is
open unto you, [o]our heart is enlarged.
12 Ye are not straitened in us, but
[p]ye are straitened in your own bowels.
13 Now for a recompense in the
same, ([q]I speak as unto *my* children,)
be ye also enlarged.

G—CONCLUDED.

IICor. 11. 25 Thrice was I beaten with rods, once was I stoned, thrice I suffered shipwreck, a night and a day I have been in the deep;

2

Or, *in tossings to and fro.*

H

II Cor. 4. 2. *See d, D, § 392, page 972.*

I

I Cor. 2. 4, 5. *See h, H, § 352, page 894.*

K

IICor. 10. 4 (For the weapons of our warfare *are* not carnal, but mighty through God to the pulling down of strong holds;)

Eph. 6. 11 Put on the whole armour of God, that ye may be able to stand against the wiles of the devil.

Eph. 6. 13 Wherefore take unto you the whole armour of God, that ye may be able to withstand in the evil day, and having done all, to stand.

IITim. 4. 7 I have fought a good fight, I have finished *my* course, I have kept the faith:

§ 397. ADMONISHED NOT TO HAVE FELLOWSHIP WITH UNBELIEVERS,

6: 14–18; 7: 1–4.

14 [a]Be ye not unequally yoked together with unbelievers: for [b]what
fellowship hath righteousness with
unrighteousness? and what communion hath light with darkness?
15 And what concord hath Christ
with Belial? or what part hath he
that believeth with an infidel?
16 And what agreement hath the
temple of God with idols? for [c]ye
are the temple of the living God; as
God hath said, [d]I will dwell in them,
and walk in *them;* and I will be their
God, and they shall be my people.
17 [e]Wherefore come out from among
them, and be ye separate, saith the
Lord, and touch not the unclean
thing; and I will receive you,
18 [f]And will be a Father unto you,
and ye shall be my sons and daughters, saith the Lord Almighty.

A

Deut. 7. 2 And when the LORD thy God shall deliver them before thee; thou shalt smite them, *and* utterly destroy them; thou shalt make no covenant with them, nor shew mercy unto them:

3 Neither shalt thou make marriages with them; thy daughter thou shalt not give unto his son, nor his daughter shalt thou take unto thy son.

I Cor. 5. 9. *See r, R, § 359, page 908.*

I Cor. 7. 39 The wife is bound by the law as long as her husband liveth; but if her husband be dead, she is at liberty to be married to whom she will; only in the Lord.

B

I Sa. 5. 2 When the Philistines took the ark of God, they brought it into the house of Dagon, and set it by Dagon.

3 And when they of Ashdod arose early on the morrow, behold, Dagon *was* fallen upon his face to the earth before the ark of the LORD. And they took Dagon, and set him in his place again.

I Cor. 10. 21. *See k, K, § 367, page 930.*

Eph. 5. 7 Be not ye therefore partakers with them.

FORTH THE CHARACTER OF HIS MINISTRY (CONCLUDED).

L

II Cor. 4. 2 But have renounced the hidden things of dishonesty, not walking in craftiness, nor handling the word of God deceitfully; but by manifestation of the truth, commending ourselves to every man's conscience in the sight of God.

II Cor. 5. 11 Knowing therefore the terror of the Lord, we persuade men; but we are made manifest unto God; and I trust also are made manifest in your consciences.

II Cor. 11. 6 But though *I be* rude in speech, yet not in knowledge; but we have been thoroughly made manifest among you in all things.

M

Rom. 8. 36. *See t, T, § 334, page 850.*

I Cor. 4. 9 For I think that God hath set forth us the apostles last, as it were appointed to death: for we are made a spectacle unto the world, and to angels, and to men.

II Cor. 1. 9 But we had the sentence of death in ourselves, that we should not trust

M—CONCLUDED.

in ourselves, but in God which raiseth the dead:

N

Ps. 118. 18 The LORD hath chastened me sore: but he hath not given me over unto death.

O

II Cor. 7. 3 I speak not *this* to condemn *you:* for I have said before, that ye are in our hearts to die and live with *you.*

P

II Cor. 12. 15 And I will very gladly spend and be spent for you; though the more abundantly I love you, the less I be loved.

Phil. 1. 8 For God is my record, how greatly I long after you all in the bowels of Jesus Christ.

Q

I Cor. 4. 14 I write not these things to shame you, but as my beloved sons I warn *you.*
15 For though ye have ten thousand instructors in Christ, yet *have ye* not many fathers: for in Christ Jesus I have begotten you through the gospel.

TO CLEANSE THEMSELVES AND BE OPEN HEARTED.

B—CONCLUDED.

Eph. 5. 11 And have no fellowship with the unfruitful works of darkness, but rather reprove *them.*

C

I Cor. 3. 16. *See m, M, § 354, page 900.*

D

Ex. 29. 45 And I will dwell among the chil- of Israel, and will be their God.

Lev. 26. 12 And I will walk among you, and will be your God, and ye shall be my people.

Jer. 31. 33 But this *shall be* the covenant that I will make with the house of Israel; After those days, saith the LORD, I will put my law in their inward parts, and write it in their hearts; and will be their God, and they shall be my people.

Jer. 32. 38 And they shall be my people, and I will be their God:

Eze. 11. 20 That they may walk in my statutes, and keep mine ordinances, and do them: and they shall be my people, and I will be their God.

Eze. 36. 28 And ye shall dwell in the land that I gave to your fathers; and ye shall be my people, and I will be your God.

D—CONCLUDED.

Eze. 37. 26 Moreover I will make a covenant of peace with them; it shall be an everlasting covenant with them: and I will place them, and multiply them, and will set my sanctuary in the midst of them for evermore.

Zech. 8. 8 And I will bring them, and they shall dwell in the midst of Jerusalem: and they shall be my people, and I will be their God, in truth and in righteousness.

Zech. 13. 9 And I will bring the third part through the fire, and will refine them as silver is refined, and will try them as gold is tried: they shall call on my name, and I will hear them: I will say, It *is* my people: and they shall say, The LORD *is* my God.

E

Num. 16. 21 Separate yourselves from among this congregation, that I may consume them in a moment.

Num. 16. 26 And he spake unto the congregation, saying, Depart, I pray you, from the tents of these wicked men, and touch nothing of theirs, lest ye be consumed in all their sins.

For E concluded and F, see next page (982).

§ 397. ADMONISHED NOT TO HAVE FELLOWSHIP WITH UNBELIEVERS,

CHAP. 7.

1 Having [g]therefore these promises, dearly beloved, [h]let us cleanse ourselves from all filthiness of the flesh and spirit, perfecting holiness in the fear of God.

2 Receive us; we have wronged no man, we have corrupted no man, [i]we have defrauded no man.

3 I speak not *this* to condemn *you:* for [k]I have said before, that ye are in our hearts to die and live with *you.*

4 [l]Great *is* my boldness of speech toward you, [m]great *is* my glorying of you: [n]I am filled with comfort, I am exceeding joyful in all our tribulation.

E—CONTINUED.

Ezra 6. 21 And the children of Israel, which were come again out of captivity, and all such as had separated themselves unto them from the filthiness of the heathen of the land, to seek the LORD God of Israel, did eat,

E—CONCLUDED.

Ezra 10. 11 Now therefore make confession unto the LORD God of your fathers, and do his pleasure: and separate yourselves from the people of the land, and from the strange wives.

Prov. 9. 6 Forsake the foolish, and live; and go in the way of understanding.

Isa. 52. 11 Depart ye, depart ye, go ye out from thence, touch no unclean *thing;* go ye out of the midst of her; be ye clean, that bear the vessels of the LORD.

Act 2. 40 And with many other words did he testify and exhort, saying, Save yourselves from this untoward generation.

IICor. 7. 1. *See text of topic.*

Rev. 18. 4 And I heard another voice from heaven, saying, Come out of her, my people, that ye be not partakers of her sins, and that ye receive not of her plagues.

F

Jer. 31. 1 At the same time, saith the LORD, will I be the God of all the families of Israel, and they shall be my people.

Jer. 31. 9 They shall come with weeping, and with supplications will I lead them: I will cause them to walk by the rivers of waters in a straight way, wherein they shall not stumble: for I am a father to Israel, and Ephraim *is* my firstborn.

§ 398. PAUL COMFORTED BY THE COMING OF TITUS

7:5–16.

5 For, [a]when we were come into Macedonia, our flesh had no rest, but [b]we were troubled on every side; [c]without *were* fightings, within *were* fears.

6 Nevertheless [d]God, that comforteth those that are cast down, comforted us by the [e]coming of Titus;

7 And not by his coming only, but by the consolation wherewith he was comforted in you, when he told us your earnest desire, your mourning, your fervent mind toward me; so that I rejoiced the more.

CHAP. 7.

8 For though I made you sorry with a letter, I do not repent, [f]though I did repent: for I perceive that the same epistle hath made you sorry, though *it were* but for a season.

9 Now I rejoice, not that ye were made sorry, but that ye sorrowed to repentance: for ye were made sorry [1]after a godly manner, that ye might receive damage by us in nothing.

10 For [g]godly sorrow worketh repentance to salvation not to be repented of: [h]but the sorrow of the world worketh death.

11 For behold this selfsame thing,

TO CLEANSE THEMSELVES AND TO BE OPEN HEARTED (CONCLUDED).

F—CONCLUDED.

Rev. 21. 7 He that overcometh shall inherit all things; and I will be his God, and he shall be my son.

G

II Cor. 6. 17, 18. *See text of topic page 980.*

I Jno. 3. 3 And every man that hath this hope in him purifieth himself, even as he is pure.

H

Ps. 51. 10 Create in me a clean heart, O God; and renew a right spirit within me.

Eze. 36. 25 Then will I sprinkle clean water upon you, and ye shall be clean: from all your filthiness, and from all your idols, will I cleanse you.

26 A new heart also will I give you, and a new spirit will I put within you: and I will take away the stony heart out of your flesh, and I will give you a heart of flesh.

I Jno. 1. 7 But if we walk in the light, as he is in the light, we have fellowship one with another, and the blood of Jesus Christ his Son cleanseth us from all sin.

I Jno. 1. 9 If we confess our sins, he is faithful and just to forgive us *our* sins, and to cleanse us from all unrighteousness.

I

Acts 20. 33. *See c, C, § 292, page 764.*

K

II Cor. 6. 11, 12. *See o, O, § 396, page 980.*

L

II Cor. 3. 12. *See a, A, § 391, page 970.*

M

I Cor. 1. 4 I thank my God always on your behalf, for the grace of God which is given you by Jesus Christ;

II Cor. 1. 14 As also ye have acknowledged us in part, that we are your rejoicing, even as ye also *are* ours in the day of the Lord Jesus.

N

Rom. 5. 3 And not only so, but we glory in tribulations also: knowing that tribulation worketh patience:

II Cor. 1. 4 Who comforteth us in all our tribulation, that we may be able to comfort them which are in any trouble, by the comfort wherewith we ourselves are comforted of God.

II Cor. 6. 7. *See text of topic § 398.*

Phil. 2. 17 Yea, and if I be offered upon the sacrifice and service of your faith, I joy, and rejoice with you all.

Col. 1. 24 Who now rejoice in my sufferings for you, and fill up that which is behind of the afflictions of Christ in my flesh for his body's sake, which is the church:

I Thes. 3. 7 Therefore, brethren, we were comforted over you in all our affliction and distress by your faith:

8 For now we live, if ye stand fast in the Lord.

AND THE GOOD REPORT HE BROUGHT OF THE CORINTHIANS.

A

II Cor. 2. 13 I had no rest in my spirit, because I found not Titus my brother: but taking my leave of them, I went from thence into Macedonia.

B

II Cor. 4. 8 *We are* troubled on every side, yet not distressed; *we are* perplexed, but not in despair;

C

Deut. 32. 25 The sword without, and terror within, shall destroy both the young man and the virgin, the suckling *also* with the man of gray hairs.

D

Isa. 57. 18 I have seen his ways, and will heal him: I will lead him also, and restore comforts unto him and to his mourners.

II Cor. 1. 4. *See under N, § 397.*

II Thes. 2. 16 Now our Lord Jesus Christ himself, and God, even our Father, which

D—CONCLUDED.

hath loved us, and hath given *us* everlasting consolation and good hope through grace,

E

II Cor. 2. 13. *See under A.*

F

II Cor. 2. 4 For out of much affliction and anguish of heart I wrote unto you with many tears; not that ye should be grieved, but that ye might know the love which I have more abundantly unto you.

1

Or, *according to God.*

G

II Sa. 12. 13 And David said unto Nathan, I have sinned against the LORD. And Nathan said unto David, The LORD also hath put away thy sin; thou shalt not die.

For G concluded and H, see next page (984).

§ 398. PAUL COMFORTED BY THE COMING OF TITUS AND THE

CHAP. 7.

that ye sorrowed [i]after a godly sort, what carefulness it wrought in you, yea, *what* clearing of yourselves, yea, *what* indignation, yea, *what* fear, yea, *what* vehement desire, yea, *what* zeal, yea, *what* revenge! In all *things* ye have approved yourselves to be clear in this matter.

12 Wherefore, though I wrote unto you, *I did it* not for his cause that had done the wrong, nor for his cause that suffered wrong, [k]but that our care for you in the sight of God might appear unto you.

13 Therefore we were comforted in your comfort: yea, and exceedingly the more joyed we for the joy of Titus, because his spirit [l]was refreshed by you all.

14 For if I have boasted any thing to him of you, I am not ashamed; but as we spake all things to you in truth, even so our boasting, which *I made* before Titus, is found a truth.

15 And his [1]inward affection is more abundant toward you, whilst he remembereth [m]the obedience of you all, how with fear and trembling ye received him.

16 I rejoice therefore that [n]I have confidence in you in all *things*.

§ 399. PAUL EXHORTS THEM TO THE GRACE

8: 1-15.

1 Moreover, brethren, we do you to wit of the grace of God bestowed on the churches of Macedonia;

2 How that in a great trial of affliction the abundance of their joy and [a]their deep poverty abounded unto the riches of their [1]liberality.

3 For to *their* power, I bear record, yea, and beyond *their* power *they were* willing of themselves;

4 Praying us with much entreaty that we would receive the gift, and *take upon us* [b]the fellowship of the ministering to the saints.

5 And *this they did*, not as we hoped, but first gave their own selves to the Lord, and unto us by the will of God.

6 Insomuch that [c]we desired Titus, that as he had begun, so he would also finish in you the same [2]grace also.

7 Therefore, as [d]ye abound in every thing, *in* faith, and utterance, and knowledge, and *in* all diligence, and *in* your love to us, *see* [e]that ye abound in this grace also.

8 [f]I speak not by commandment, but by occasion of the forwardness of others, and to prove the sincerity of your love.

A

Mark 12. 44 For all *they* did cast in of their abundance; but she of her want did cast in all that she had, *even* all her living.

1

Gr. *simplicity*.

II Cor. 9. 11. *See text of topic, § 401, page 988.*

B

Acts 11. 29 Then the disciples, every man according to his ability, determined to send relief unto the brethren which dwelt in Judea:

Acts 24. 17 Now after many years I came to bring alms to my nation, and offerings.

Rom. 15. 25 But now I go unto Jerusalem to minister unto the saints.

26 For it hath pleased them of Macedonia and Achaia to make a certain contribution for the poor saints which are at Jerusalem.

GOOD REPORT HE BROUGHT OF THE CORINTHIANS (CONCLUDED).

G—CONCLUDED.

Matt.26. 75 And Peter remembered the word of Jesus, which said unto him, Before the cock crow, thou shalt deny me thrice. And he went out, and wept bitterly.

H

Prov.17. 22 A merry heart doeth good *like* a medicine: but a broken spirit drieth the bones.

I

Zech.12. 10 And I will pour upon the house of David, and upon the inhabitants of Jerusalem, the spirit of grace and of supplications: and they shall look upon me whom they have pierced, and they shall mourn for him, as one mourneth for *his* only *son*, and shall be in bitterness for him, as one that is in bitterness for *his* firstborn.

K

II Cor. 2. 4. *See under F.*

L

Rom.15. 32 That I may come unto you with joy by the will of God, and may with you be refreshed.

1

Gr. *bowels.*

M

IICor.2. 9 For to this end also did I write, that I might know the proof of you, whether ye be obedient in all things.

Phil. 2. 12 Wherefore, my beloved, as ye have always obeyed, not as in my presence only, but now much more in my absence, work out your own salvation with fear and trembling;

N

IIThes.3. 4 And we have confidence in the Lord touching you, that ye both do and will do the things which we command you.

Phile. 8 Wherefore, though I might be much bold in Christ to enjoin thee that which is convenient.

Phile. 21 Having confidence in thy obedience I wrote unto thee, knowing that thou wilt also do more than I say.

OF A LIBERAL OFFERING FOR THE POOR SAINTS.

B—CONCLUDED.

I Cor.16. 1 Now concerning the collection for the saints, as I have given order to the churches of Galatia, even so do ye.

I Cor.16. 3 And when I come, whomsoever ye shall approve by *your* letters, them will I send to bring your liberality unto Jerusalem.

4 And if it be meet that I go also, they shall go with me.

II Cor.9. 1 For as touching the ministering to the saints, it is superfluous for me to write to you:

C

II Cor.8. 17 For indeed he accepted the exhortation; but being more forward, of his own accord he went unto you.

IICor.12. 18 I desired Titus, and with *him* I sent a brother. Did Titus make a gain of you? walked we not in the same spirit? *walked we* not in the same steps?

2

Or, *gift.*

D

I Cor. 1. 5 That in everything ye are enriched by him, in all utterance, and *in* all knowledge;

I Cor 12. 13 For by one Spirit are we all baptized into one body, whether *we be* Jews or Gentiles, whether *we be* bond

D—CONCLUDED.

or free; and have been all made to drink into one Spirit.

E

Ps 112. 9 He hath dispersed, he hath given to the poor; his righteousness endureth for ever; his horn shall be exalted with honour.

Prov.22. 9 He that hath a bountiful eye shall be blessed; for he giveth of his bread to the poor.

Prov.28. 27 He that giveth unto the poor shall not lack: but he that hideth his eyes shall have many a curse.

Prov.31. 20 She stretcheth out her hand to the poor; yea, she reacheth forth her hands to the needy.

Luke 18. 22 Now when Jesus heard these things, he said unto him, Yet lackest thou one thing: sell all that thou hast, and distribute unto the poor, and thou shalt have treasure in heaven: and come, follow me.

IICor.9. 8 And God *is* able to make all grace abound toward you; that ye, always having all sufficiency in all *things*, may abound to every good work:

F

I Cor. 7. 6. *See e, E, § 362, page 914.*

G

Luke 9. 58. *See h, H, § 68, page 213.*

For G concluded, see next page (986).

§ 399. PAUL EXHORTS THEM TO THE GRACE OF A

CHAP. 8.

9 For ye know the grace of our Lord
Jesus Christ, [g]that, though he was
rich, yet for your sakes he became
poor, that ye through his poverty
might be rich.

10 And herein [h]I give *my* advice:
for [i]this is expedient for you, who
have begun before, not only to do,
but also to be [3k]forward a year ago.

11 Now therefore perform the doing *of it;* that as *there was* a readiness to will, so *there may be* a performance also out of that which ye
have.

12 For [l]if there be first a willing
mind, *it is* accepted according to that

CHAP. 8.

a man hath, *and* not according to
that he hath not.

13 For *I mean* not that other men
be eased, and ye burdened:

14 But by an equality, *that* now at
this time your abundance *may be a
supply* for their want, that their abundance also may be *a supply* for your
want; that there may be equality:

15 As it is written, [m]He that *had
gathered* much had nothing over; and
he that *had gathered* little had no lack.

G—CONCLUDED. See preceding page (985).

Phil. 2. 7 But made himself of no reputation, and took upon him the form of a servant, and was made in the likeness of men:

§ 400. TITUS AND ANOTHER

8 : 16–24.

16 But thanks *be* to God, which put
the same earnest care into the heart
of Titus for you.

17 For indeed he accepted [a]the exhortation; but being more forward,
of his own accord he went unto you.

18 And we have sent with him [b]the
brother, whose praise *is* in the gospel throughout all the churches;

19 And not *that* only, but who was
also [c]chosen of the churches to travel
with us with this [1]grace, which is administered by us [d]to the glory of the
same Lord, and *declaration of* your
ready mind:

20 Avoiding this, that no man
should blame us in this abundance
which is administered by us:

21 [e]Providing for honest things, not
only in the sight of the Lord, but
also in the sight of men.

CHAP. 8.

22 And we have sent with them our
brother, whom we have oftentimes
proved diligent in many things, but
now much more diligent, upon the
great confidence which [3]*I have* in you.

23 Whether *any do inquire* of Titus,
he is my partner and fellow helper
concerning you: or our brethren *be
inquired of*, *they are* [f]the messengers
of the churches, *and* the glory of
Christ.

24 Wherefore shew ye to them, and
before the churches, the proof of
your love, and of our [g]boasting on
your behalf.

A

II Cor. 8. 6. *See c, C, § 399, page 984.*

B

II Cor. 12. 18 I desired Titus, and with *him* I sent a brother. Did Titus make a gain of you? walked we not in the same spirit? *walked we* not in the same steps?

LIBERAL OFFERING FOR THE POOR SAINTS (CONCLUDED).

H

I Cor. 7. 26 I suppose therefore that this is good for the present distress, *I say*, that *it is* good for a man so to be.

I

Prov. 19. 17 He that hath pity upon the poor lendeth unto the LORD; and that which he hath given will he pay him again.

Matt. 10. 42 And whosoever shall give to drink unto one of these little ones a cup of cold *water* only in the name of a disciple, verily I say unto you, he shall in no wise lose his reward.

I Tim. 6. 18 That they do good, that they be rich in good works, ready to distribute, willing to communicate;

19 Laying up in store for themselves a good foundation against the time to come, that they may lay hold on eternal life.

Heb. 13. 16 But to do good and to communicate forget not: for with such sacrifices God is well pleased.

3

Gr. *willing*.

K

II Cor. 9. 2 For I know the forwardness of your mind, for which I boast of you to them of Macedonia, that Achaia was ready a year ago; and your zeal hath provoked very many.

L

Ex. 25. 2 Speak unto the children of Israel, that they bring me an offering: of every man that giveth it willingly with his heart ye shall take my offering.

Mark 12. 43, 44. *See d, D, § 169, page 472.*

Luke 21. 3. *See f, F, § 169, page 473.*

M

Ex. 16. 18 And when they did mete *it* with an omer, he that gathered much had nothing over, and he that gathered little had no lack; they gathered every man according to his eating.

Luke 22. 35 And he said unto them, When I sent you without purse, and scrip, and shoes, lacked ye any thing? And they said, Nothing.

SENT UNTO THE CORINTHIANS.

C

I Cor. 16. 3 And when I come, whomsoever ye shall approve by *your* letters, them will I send to bring your liberality unto Jerusalem.

4 And if it be meet that I go also, they shall go with me.

1

Or, *gift*.

II Cor. 8. 4, 6, 7. *See text of topic, § 399, page 984.*

II Cor. 9. 8. *See text of topic, § 401.*

D

II Cor. 4. 15 For all things *are* for your sakes, that the abundant grace might through the thanksgiving of many redound to the glory of God.

E

Rom. 12. 17 Recompense to no man evil for evil. Provide things honest in the sight of all men.

Phil. 4. 8 Finally, brethren, whatsoever things are true, whatsoever things *are* honest, whatsoever things *are* just, whatsoever things *are* pure, whatsoever things *are* lovely, whatsoever things *are* of good report; if *there be* any virtue, and if *there be* any praise, think on these things.

Tit. 2. 6 Young men likewise exhort to be soberminded.

E—CONCLUDED.

Tit. 2. 7 In all things shewing thyself a pattern of good works: in doctrine *shewing* uncorruptness, gravity, sincerity,

8 Sound speech, that cannot be condemned; that he that is of the contrary part may be ashamed, having no evil thing to say of you.

I Pet. 2. 12 Having your conversation honest among the Gentiles: that, whereas they speak against you as evil doers, they may by *your* good works, which they shall behold, glorify God in the day of visitation.

3

Or, *he hath*.

F

Phil. 2. 24 But I trust in the Lord that I also myself shall come shortly.

25 Yet I supposed it necessary to send to you Epaphroditus, my brother, and companion in labour, and fellow soldier, but your messenger, and he that ministered to my wants.

G

II Cor. 7. 14 For if I have boasted any thing to him of you, I am not ashamed; but as we spake all things to you in truth, even so our boasting, which *I made* before Titus, is found a truth.

II Cor. 9. 2. *See text of topic, § 401.*

§ 401. PREPARING FOR THE COLLECTION FOR

9 : 1–15.

1 For as touching [a]the ministering to the saints, it is superfluous for me to write to you:

2 For I know [b]the forwardness of your mind, [c]for which I boast of you to them of Macedonia, that [d]Achaia was ready a year ago; and your zeal hath provoked very many.

3 [e]Yet have I sent the brethren, lest our boasting of you should be in vain in this behalf; that, as I said, ye may be ready:

4 Lest haply if they of Macedonia come with me, and find you unprepared, we (that we say not, ye) should be ashamed in this same confident boasting.

5 Therefore I thought it necessary to exhort the brethren, that they would go before unto you, and make up beforehand your [1]bounty, [2]whereof ye had notice before, that the same might be ready, as *a matter of* bounty, and not as *of* covetousness.

6 [f]But this *I say*, He which soweth sparingly shall reap also sparingly; and he which soweth bountifully shall reap also bountifully.

7 Every man according as he purposeth in his heart, *so let him give;* [g]not grudgingly, or of necessity: for [h]God loveth a cheerful giver.

8 [i]And God *is* able to make all grace abound toward you; that ye, always having all sufficiency in all *things*, may abound to every good work:

9 (As it is written, [k]He hath dispersed abroad; he hath given to the poor: his righteousness remaineth for ever.

CHAP. 9.

10 Now he that [l]ministereth seed to the sower both minister bread for *your* food, and multiply your seed sown, and increase the fruits of your [m]righteousness;)

11 Being enriched in every thing to all [3] [4]bountifulness, [n]which causeth through us thanksgiving to God.

12 For the administration of this service not only [o]supplieth the want of the saints, but is abundant also by many thanksgivings unto God;

A

Acts 11. 29. *See c, C, § 257, page 704.*

Acts 24. 17. *See i, I, § 303, page 784.*

II Cor. 8. 4 Praying us with much entreaty that we would receive the gift, and *take upon us* the fellowship of the ministering to the saints.

B

II Cor. 8. 19 And not *that* only, but who was also chosen of the churches to travel with us with this grace, which is administered by us to the glory of the same Lord, and *declaration of* your ready mind:

C

II Cor. 8. 24 Wherefore shew ye to them, and before the churches, the proof of your love, and of our boasting on your behalf.

D

II Cor. 8. 10 And herein I give *my* advice: for this is expedient for you, who have begun before, not only to do, but also to be forward a year ago.

E

II Cor. 8. 6 Insomuch that we desired Titus, that as he had begun, so he would also finish in you the same grace also.

II Cor. 8. 17 For indeed he accepted the exhortation; but being more forward, of his own accord he went unto you.

II Cor. 8. 22 And we have sent with them our brother, whom we have oftentimes proved diligent in many things, but now much more diligent, upon the great confidence which *I have* in you.

1

Gr. *blessing.*

Gen. 33. 11 Take, I pray thee, my blessing that is brought to thee; because God hath dealt graciously with me, and because I have enough. And he urged him, and he took *it*.

THE POOR SAINTS. CONCERNING GIVING.

1—CONCLUDED.

I Sa. 25. 27 And now this blessing which thine handmaid hath brought unto my lord, let it even be given unto the young men that follow my lord.

II Ki. 5. 15 And he returned to the man of God, he and all his company, and came, and stood before him: and he said, Behold, now I know that *there is* no God in all the earth, but in Israel: now therefore, I pray thee, take a blessing of thy servant.

2

Or, *which hath been so much spoken of before.*

F

Ps. 41. 1 Blessed *is* he that considereth the poor: the LORD will deliver him in time of trouble.

2 The LORD will preserve him, and keep him alive; *and* he shall be blessed upon the earth: and thou wilt not deliver him unto the will of his enemies.

3 The LORD will strengthen him upon the bed of languishing: thou wilt make all his bed in his sickness.

Prov. 11. 24 There is that scattereth, and yet increaseth; and *there is* that withholdeth more than is meet, but *it tendeth* to poverty.

Prov. 19. 17 He that hath pity upon the poor lendeth unto the LORD; and that which he hath given will he pay him again.

Prov. 22. 9 He that hath a bountiful eye shall be blessed; for he giveth of his bread to the poor.

Gal. 6. 7 Be not deceived; God is not mocked: for whatsoever a man soweth, that shall he also reap.

Gal. 6. 9 And let us not be weary in well doing: for in due season we shall reap, if we faint not.

G

Deut. 15. 7 If there be among you a poor man of one of thy brethren within any of thy gates in thy land which the LORD thy God giveth thee, thou shalt not harden thine heart, nor shut thine hand from thy poor brother:

H

Ex. 25. 2 Speak unto the children of Israel, that they bring me an offering: of every man that giveth it willingly with his heart ye shall take my offering.

Ex. 35. 5 Take ye from among you an offering unto the LORD: whosoever *is* of a willing heart, let him bring it, an offering of the LORD; gold, and silver, and brass,

H—CONCLUDED.

Prov. 11. 25 The liberal soul shall be made fat: and he that watereth shall be watered also himself.

Rom. 12. 8 Or he that exhorteth, on exhortation: he that giveth, *let him do it* with simplicity; he that ruleth, with diligence; he that sheweth mercy, with cheerfulness.

II Cor. 8. 12 For if there be first a willing mind, *it is* accepted according to that a man hath, *and* not according to that he hath not.

I

Prov. 11. 24. *See under F.*

Prov. 11. 25. *See under H.*

Prov. 28. 27 He that giveth unto the poor shall not lack: but he that hideth his eyes shall have many a curse.

Phil. 4. 19 But my God shall supply all your need according to his riches in glory by Christ Jesus.

K

Ps. 112. 9 He hath dispersed, he hath given to the poor; his righteousness endureth for ever; his horn shall be exalted with honour.

L

Isa. 55. 10 For as the rain cometh down, and the snow from heaven, and returneth not thither, but watereth the earth, and maketh it bring forth and bud, that it may give seed to the sower, and bread to the eater:

M

Hos. 10. 12 Sow to yourselves in righteousness, reap in mercy; break up your fallow ground: for *it is* time to seek the LORD, till he come and rain righteousness upon you.

Matt. 6. 1 Take heed that ye do not your alms before men, to be seen of them: otherwise ye have no reward of your Father which is in heaven.

3

Or, *liberality.*

4

Gr. *simplicity.*

II Cor. 8. 2. *See text of topic, § 399, page 984.*

N

II Cor. 4. 15. *See n, N, § 393, page 974.*

O

II Cor. 8. 14 But by equality, *that* now at this time your abundance *may be a supply* for their want, that their abundance also may be *a supply* for your want; that there may be equality:

15 As it is written, He that *had gathered* much had nothing over; and he that *had gathered* little had no lack.

§ 401. PREPARING FOR THE COLLECTION FOR THE

CHAP. 9.

13 While by the experiment of this ministration they [p]glorify God for your professed subjection unto the gospel of Christ, and for *your* liberal [q]distribution unto them, and unto all *men;*

CHAP. 9.

14 And by their prayer for you, which long after you for the exceeding [r]grace of God in you.

15 Thanks *be* unto God [s]for his unspeakable gift.

§ 402. PAUL DECLARES HIS WALK WAS NOT ACCORDING TO THE

10: 1–18.

1 Now [a]I Paul myself beseech you by the meekness and gentleness of Christ, [b]who [1]in presence *am* base among you, but being absent am bold toward you:

2 But I beseech *you*, [c]that I may not be bold when I am present with that confidence, wherewith I think to be bold against some, which [2]think of us as if we walked according to the flesh.

3 For though we walk in the flesh, we do not war after the flesh:

4 ([d]For the weapons [e]of our warfare *are* not carnal, but [f]mighty [3]through God [g]to the pulling down of strong holds;)

5 [h]Casting down [4]imaginations, and every high thing that exalteth itself against the knowledge of God, and bringing into captivity every thought to the obedience of Christ;

6 [i]And having in a readiness to revenge all disobedience, when [k]your obedience is fulfilled.

7 [l]Do ye look on things after the outward appearance? [m]If any man trust to himself that he is Christ's, let him of himself think this again, that, as he *is* Christ's, even so *are* [n]we Christ's.

CHAP. 10.

8 For though I should boast somewhat more [o]of our authority, which the Lord hath given us for edification, and not for your destruction, [p]I should not be ashamed:

9 That I may not seem as if I would terrify you by letters.

10 For *his* letters, [6]say they, *are* weighty and powerful; but [q]*his* bodily

A

Rom. 12. 1. *See a, A, § 342, page 868*

B

II Cor. 10. 10. *See text of topic.*

IICor.12. 5 Of such a one will I glory: yet of myself I will not glory, but in mine infirmities.

IICor.12. 7 And lest I should be exalted above measure through the abundance of the revelations, there was given to me a thorn in the flesh, the messenger of Satan to buffet me, lest I should be exalted above measure.

IICor.12. 9 And he said unto me, My grace is sufficient for thee: for my strength is made perfect in weakness. Most gladly therefore will I rather glory in my infirmities, that the power of Christ may rest upon me.

1

Or, *in outward appearance.*

C

I Cor. 4. 21 What will ye? shall I come unto you with a rod, or in love, and *in* the spirit of meekness?

IICor.13. 2 I told you before, and foretell you, as if I were present, the second time; and being absent now I write to them which heretofore have sinned, and to all other, that, if I come again, I will not spare:

IICor.13. 10 Therefore I write these things being absent, lest being present I should use sharpness, according to the power

POOR SAINTS. CONCERNING GIVING (CONCLUDED).

P

Matt. 5. 16 Let your light so shine before men, that they may see your good works, and glorify your Father which is in heaven.

Q

Heb. 13. 16 But to do good and to communicate forget not: for with such sacrifices God is well pleased.

R

II Cor. 8. 1 Moreover, brethren, we do you to wit of the grace of God bestowed on the churches of Macedonia;

S

Jas. 1. 17 Every good gift and every perfect gift is from above, and cometh down from the Father of lights, with whom is no variableness, neither shadow of turning.

FLESH, IF HIS WORD WAS POWERFUL HIS DEED WAS THE SAME.

C—CONCLUDED.

which the Lord hath given me to edification, and not to destruction.

2

Or, *reckon.*

D

Eph. 6. 13 Wherefore take unto you the whole armour of God, that ye may be able to withstand in the evil day, and having done all, to stand.

I Thes. 5. 8 But let us, who are of the day, be sober, putting on the breastplate of faith and love; and for a helmet, the hope of salvation.

E

I Cor. 9. 7. *See i, I, § 365, page 922.*

F

Acts 7. 22 And Moses was learned in all the wisdom of the Egyptians, and was mighty in words and in deeds.

I Cor. 2. 4 And my speech and my preaching *was* not with enticing words of man's wisdom, but in demonstration of the Spirit and of power:

II Cor. 6. 7 By the word of truth, by the power of God, by the armour of righteousness on the right hand and on the left,

II Cor. 13. 3 Since ye seek a proof of Christ speaking in me, which to youward is not weak, but is mighty in you.

4 For though he was crucified through weakness, yet he liveth by the power of God. For we also are weak in him, but we shall live with him by the power of God toward you.

3

Or, *to God.*

G

Jer. 1. 10 See, I have this day set thee over the nations and over the kingdoms, to root out, and to pull down, and to destroy, and to throw down, to build, and to plant.

H

I Cor. 1. 19 For it is written, I will destroy the wisdom of the wise, and will bring to nothing the understanding of the prudent.

H—CONCLUDED.

I Cor. 3. 19 For the wisdom of this world is foolishness with God: for it is written, He taketh the wise in their own craftiness.

4

Or, *reasonings.*

I

II Cor. 13. 2, 10. *See under C.*

K

II Cor. 2. 9. *See e, E, § 388, page 966.*

L

John 7. 24 Judge not according to the appearance, but judge righteous judgment.

II Cor. 5. 12 For we commend not ourselves again unto you, but give you occasion to glory on our behalf, that ye may have somewhat to *answer* them which glory in appearance, and not in heart.

II Cor. 11. 18 Seeing that many glory after the flesh, I will glory also.

M

I Cor. 14. 37. *See l, L, § 375, page 948.*

N

Rom. 14. 8 For whether we live, we live unto the Lord; and whether we die, we die unto the Lord: whether we live therefore, or die, we are the Lord's.

I Cor. 3. 23 And ye are Christ's; and Christ *is* God's.

I Cor. 9. 1 Am I not an apostle? am I not free? have I not seen Jesus Christ our Lord? are not ye my work in the Lord?

I Cor. 11. 3 But I would have you know, that the head of every man is Christ; and the head of the woman *is* the man; and the head of Christ *is* God.

II Cor. 11. 23 Are they ministers of Christ? (I speak as a fool) I *am* more; in labours more abundant, in stripes above measure, in prisons more frequent, in deaths oft.

Gal. 3. 29 And if ye *be* Christ's, then are ye Abraham's seed, and heirs according to the promise.

For O, P, 5, and Q, see next page (992).

§ 402. PAUL DECLARES HIS WALK WAS NOT ACCORDING TO THE FLESH,

CHAP. 10.

presence *is* weak, and *his* [r]speech
contemptible.

11 Let such a one think this, that,
such as we are in word by letters
when we are absent, such *will we be*
also in deed when we are present.

12 [s]For we dare not make ourselves
of the number, or compare ourselves
with some that commend themselves:
but they, measuring themselves by
themselves, and comparing themselves among themselves, [6]are not
wise.

13 but we will not boast of things
without *our* measure, but according
to the measure of the [7]rule which
God hath distributed to us, a measure to reach even unto you.

14 For we stretch not ourselves beyond *our measure*, as though we
reached not unto you: [t]for we are
come as far as to you also in *preaching* the gospel of Christ:

15 Not boasting of things without
our measure, *that is*, [u]of other men's
labours; but having hope, when your
faith is increased, that we shall be
[8]enlarged by you according to our
rule abundantly,

16 To preach the gospel in the
regions beyond you, *and* not to boast
in another man's [9]line of things made
ready to our hand.

17 [x]But he that glorieth, let him
glory in the Lord.

18 For [y]not he that commendeth
himself is approved, but [z]whom the
Lord commendeth.

O

II Cor. 13. 10. *See under C.*

P

II Cor. 7. 14 For if I have boasted anything to him of you, I am not ashamed; but as we spake all things to you in truth, even so our boasting, which I *made* before Titus, is found a truth.

II Cor. 12. 6 For though I would desire to glory, I shall not be a fool; for I will say the truth: but *now* I forbear, lest any man should think of me above that which he seeth me *to be*, or *that* he heareth of me.

§ 403. PAUL EXERCISES A JEALOUS WATCH OVER

11 : 1–15.

1 Would to God ye could bear
with me a little in [a]*my* folly: and indeed [1]bear with me.

2 For I am [b]jealous over you with
godly jealousy: for [c]I have espoused
you to one husband, that [d]I may present *you as* a chaste virgin to Christ.

3 But I fear, lest by any means, [e]as
the serpent beguiled Eve through his
subtilty, so your minds [f]should be
corrupted from the simplicity that
is in Christ.

A

II Cor. 5. 13. *See e, E, § 395, page 976.*

1

Or, *ye do bear with me.*

B

Gal. 4. 17 They zealously affect you, *but* not well; yea, they would exclude you, that ye might affect them.

18 But *it is* good to be zealously affected always in *a* good *thing*, and not only when I am present with you.

C

Hos. 2. 19 And I will betroth thee unto me for ever; yea, I will betroth thee unto me in righteousness, and in judgment, and in lovingkindness, and in mercies.

20 I will even betroth thee unto me in faithfulness: and thou shalt know the LORD.

IF HIS WORD WAS POWERFUL HIS DEED WAS THE SAME (CONCLUDED).

5

Gr. *saith he.*

Q

I Cor. 2. 3, 4. *See e, E, § 352, page 894.*

R

I Cor. 1. 17. *See k, K, § 350, page 890.*

II Cor. 11. 6 But though I *be* rude in speech, yet not in knowledge; but we have been thoroughly made manifest among you in all things.

S

II Cor. 3. 1. *See a, A, § 390, page 968.*

6

Or, *Understood* it *not.*

7

Or, *line.*

T

I Cor. 3. 5 Who then is Paul, and who *is* Apollos, but ministers by whom ye believed, even as the Lord gave to every man?

I Cor. 3. 10 According to the grace of God which is given unto me, as a wise masterbuilder, I have laid the foundation, and another buildeth thereon. But let every man take heed how he buildeth thereupon.

I Cor. 4. 15 For though ye have ten thousand instructors in Christ, yet *have ye* not many fathers: for in Christ Jesus I have begotten you through the gospel.

I Cor. 9. 1. Am I not an apostle? am I not free? have I not seen Jesus Christ our Lord? are not ye my work in the Lord?

U

Rom. 15. 20 Yea, so have I strived to preach the gospel, not where Christ was named, lest I should build upon another man's foundation:

8

Or, *magnified in you.*

9

Or, *rule.*

X

Isa. 65. 16 That he who blesseth himself in the earth shall bless himself in the God of truth; and he that sweareth in the earth shall swear by the God of truth; because the former troubles are forgotten, and because they are hid from mine eyes.

I Cor. 1. 31. *See y, Y, § 351, page 894.*

Y

Prov. 27. 2 Let another man praise thee, and not thine own mouth; a stranger, and not thine own lips.

Z

Rom. 2. 29 But he *is* a Jew, which is one inwardly; and circumcision *is that* of the heart, in the spirit, *and* not in the letter; whose praise *is* not of men, but of God.

I Cor. 4. 5 Therefore judge nothing before the time, until the Lord come, who both will bring to light the hidden things of darkness, and will make manifest the counsels of the hearts: and then shall every man have praise of God.

THE GOSPEL AND WARNS AGAINST FALSE APOSTLES.

D

Lev. 21. 13 And he shalt take a wife in her virginity.

14 A widow, or divorced woman, or profane, *or* a harlot, these shall he not take: but he shall take a virgin of his own people to wife.

Col. 1. 28 Whom we preach, warning every man, and teaching every man in all wisdom; that we may present every man perfect in Christ Jesus;

E

Gen. 3. 4 And the serpent said unto the woman, Ye shall not surely die:

John 8. 44 Ye are of *your* father the devil, and the lusts of your father ye will do: he was a murderer from the beginning, and abode not in the truth, because

E—CONCLUDED.

there is no truth in him. When he speaketh a lie, he speaketh of his own: for he is a liar, and the father of it.

F

Matt. 24. 4 And Jesus answered and said unto them, Take heed that no man deceive you.

5 For many shall come in my name, saying, I am Christ; and shall deceive many.

Eph. 4. 14 That we *henceforth* be no more children, tossed to and fro, and carried about with every wind of doctrine, by the sleight of men, *and* cunning craftiness, whereby they lay in wait to deceive;

For F concluded see next page (994)

§ 403. PAUL EXERCISES A JEALOUS WATCH OVER THE

CHAP. 11.

4 For if he that cometh preacheth another Jesus, whom we have not preached, or *if* ye receive another spirit, which ye have not received, or [g]another gospel, which ye have not accepted, ye might well bear [2]with *him*.

5 For I suppose [h]I was not a whit behind the very chiefest apostles.

6 But though [i]*I be* rude in speech, yet not [k]in knowledge; but [l]we have been thoroughly made manifest among you in all things.

7 Have I committed an offence [m]in abasing myself that ye might be exalted, because I have preached to you the gospel of God freely?

8 I robbed other churches, taking wages *of them*, to do you service.

9 And when I was present with you, and wanted, [n]I was chargeable to no man: for that which was lacking to me [o]the brethren which came from Macedonia supplied: and in all *things* I have kept myself [p]from being burdensome unto you, and *so* will I keep *myself*.

10 [q]As the the truth of Christ is in me, [3]no man shall stop me of this boasting in the regions of Achaia.

11 Wherefore? [r]because I love you not? God knoweth.

12 But what I do, that I will do, [s]that I may cut off occasion from them which desire occasion; that wherein they glory, they may be found even as we.

13 [t]For such *are* false apostles, [u]deceitful workers, transforming themselves into the apostles of Christ.

14 And no marvel; for Satan himself is transformed into [x]an angel of light.

F—CONCLUDED.

Eph. 5. 6 Let no man deceive you with vain words: for because of these things cometh the wrath of God upon the children of disobedience.

Col. 2. 4 And this I say, lest any man should beguile you with enticing words.

Col. 2. 8 Beware lest any man spoil you through philosophy and vain deceit, after the tradition of men, after the rudiments of the world, and not after Christ.

Col. 2. 18 Let no man beguile you of your reward in a voluntary humility and worshipping of angels, intruding into those things which he hath not seen, vainly puffed up by his fleshly mind.

I Tim. 1. 3 As I besought thee to abide still at Ephesus, when I went into Macedonia, that thou mightest charge some that they teach no other doctrine,

4 Neither give heed to fables and endless genealogies, which minister questions, rather than godly edifying which is in faith: *so do*.

I Tim. 4. 1 Now the Spirit speaketh expressly, that in the latter times some shall depart from the faith, giving heed to seducing spirits, and doctrines of devils;

2 Speaking lies in hypocrisy; having their conscience seared with a hot iron;

Heb. 13. 9 Be not carried about with divers and strange doctrines. For *it is* a good thing that the heart be established with grace; not with meats, which have not profited them that have been occupied therein.

II Pet. 3. 17 Ye therefore, beloved, seeing ye know *these things* before, beware lest ye also, being led away with the error of the wicked, fall from your own steadfastness.

Jude 4 For there are certain men crept in unawares, who were before of old ordained to this condemnation, ungodly men, turning the grace of our God into lasciviousness, and denying the only Lord God, and our Lord Jesus Christ.

G

Gal. 1. 6 I marvel that ye are so soon removed from him that called you into the grace of Christ unto another gospel:

7 Which is not another; but there be some that trouble you, and would pervert the gospel of Christ.

8 But though we, or an angel from heaven, preach any other gospel unto you than that which we have preached unto you, let him be accursed.

GOSPEL AND WARNS AGAINST FALSE APOSTLES (CONTINUED).

2

Or, *with me.*

H

I Cor. 15. 10. *See q, Q, § 376, page 950.*

Gal. 2. 6 But of those who seemed to be somewhat, (whatsoever they were, it maketh no matter to me: God accepteth no man's person:) for they who seemed *to be somewhat* in conference added nothing to me:

I

I Cor. 1. 17. *See k, K, § 350, page 890.*

K

Eph. 3. 4 Whereby, when ye read, ye may understand my knowledge in the mystery of Christ)

L

II Cor. 4. 2. *See d, D, § 392, page 972.*

IICor.12. 12 Truly the signs of an apostle were wrought among you in all patience, in signs, and wonders, and mighty deeds.

M

Acts 18. 3. *See b, B, § 280, page 746.*

N

Acts 18. 3. *See b, B, § 280, page 746.*

O

Phil. 4. 10 But I rejoiced in the Lord greatly, that now at the last your care of me hath flourished again; wherein ye were also careful, but ye lacked opportunity.

Phil. 4. 15 Now ye Philippians know also, that in the beginning of the gospel, when I departed from Macedonia, no church communicated with me concerning giving and receiving, but ye only.

16 For even in Thessalonica ye sent once and again unto my necessity.

P

IICor.12. 14 Behold, the third time I am ready to come to you; and I will not be burdensome to you: for I seek not yours, but you: for the children ought not to lay up for the parents, but the parents for the children.

IICor.12. 16 But be it so, I did not burden you: nevertheless, being crafty, I caught you with guile.

Q

Rom. 9. 1. *See a, A, § 335, page 852.*

3

Gr. *this boasting shall not be stopped in me.*

I Cor. 9. 15 But I have used none of these things: neither have I written these things, that it should be so done unto me: for *it were* better for me to die, than that any man should make my glorying void.

R

II Cor. 6. 11, 12. *See o, O, § 396, page 980.*

S

I Cor. 9. 12. *See q, Q, § 365, page 922.*

T

Acts 15. 24 Forasmuch as we have heard, that certain which went out from us have troubled you with words, subverting your souls, saying, *Ye must* be circumcised, and keep the law; to whom we gave no *such* commandment:

Rom.16. 18 For they that are such serve not our Lord Jesus Christ, but their own belly; and by good words and fair speeches deceive the hearts of the simple.

Gal. 1. 7 Which is not another; but there be some that trouble you, and would pervert the gospel of Christ.

Gal. 6. 12 As many as desire to make a fair shew in the flesh, the constrain you to be circumcised; only lest they should suffer persecution for the cross of Christ.

Phil. 1. 15 Some indeed preach Christ even of envy and strife; and some also of good will:

II Pet.2. 1 But there were false prophets also among the people, even as there shall be false teachers among you, who privily shall bring in damnable heresies, even denying the Lord that bought them, and bring upon themselves swift destruction.

I Jno. 4. 1 Beloved, believe not every spirit, but try the spirits whether they are of God: because many false prophets are gone out into the world.

Rev. 2. 2 I know thy works, and thy labour, and thy patience, and how thou canst not bear them which are evil: and thou hast tried them which say they are apostles, and are not, and hast found them liars:

U

II Cor.2. 17 For we are not as many, which corrupt the word of God: but as of sincerity, but as of God, in the sight of God speak we in Christ.

Phil. 3. 2 Beware of dogs, beware of evil workers, beware of the concision.

Tit. 1. 10 For there are many unruly and vain talkers and deceivers, specially they of the circumcision:

11 Whose mouths must be stopped, who subvert whole houses, teaching things which they ought not, for filthy lucre's sake.

X

Gal. 1. 8 But though we, or an angel from heaven, preach any other gospel unto you than that which we have preached unto you, let him be accursed.

For X concluded, see next page (996).

§ 403. PAUL EXERCISES A JEALOUS WATCH OVER THE

CHAP. 11.

15 Therefore *it is* no great thing if his ministers also be transformed as the ministers of righteousness; [y]whose end shall be according to their works.

X—CONCLUDED.

Rev. 12 9 And the great dragon was cast out, that old serpent, called the Devil, and Satan, which deceiveth the whole world: he was cast out into the earth, and his angels were cast out with him.

§ 404. PAUL ASSERTS HIS FITNESS AND RECAPITULATES

11 : 16–33.

16 [a]I say again, Let no man think
me a fool; if otherwise, yet as a
fool [1]receive me, that I may boast
myself a little.
17 That which I speak, [b]I speak *it*
not after the Lord, but as it were foolishly, [c]in this confidence of boasting.
18 [d]Seeing that many glory after
the flesh, I will glory also.
19 For ye suffer fools gladly, [e] seeing ye *yourselves* are wise.
20 For ye suffer, [f]if a man bring you
into bondage, if a man devour *you*, if
a man take *of you*, if a man exalt himself, if a man smite you on the face.
21 I speak as concerning reproach,
[g]as though we had been weak. Howbeit, [h]whereinsoever any is bold, (I
speak foolishly,) I am bold also.
22 Are they Hebrews? [i]so *am* I.
Are they Israelites? so *am* I. Are
they the seed of Abraham? so *am* I.
23 Are they ministers of Christ? (I
speak as a fool) I *am* more; [k]in
labours more abundant, [l]in stripes
above measure, in prisions more frequent, [m]in deaths oft.
24 Of the Jews five times received
I [n]forty *stripes* save one.
25 Thrice was I [o]beaten with rods,
[p]once was I stoned, thrice I [q]suffered
shipwreck, a night and a day I have
been in the deep;

CHAP. 11.

26 *In* journeyings often, *in* perils of
waters, *in* perils of robbers, [r]*in* perils
by *mine own* countrymen, [s]*in* perils by
the heathen, *in* perils in the city, *in*
perils in the wilderness, *in* perils in the
sea, *in* perils among false brethren;
27 In weariness and painfulness,
[t]in watchings often, [u]in hunger and
thirst, in fastings often, in cold and
nakedness.
28 Beside those things that are
without, that which cometh upon me
daily, [x]the care of all the churches.
29 [y]Who is weak, and I am not
weak? who is offended, and I burn
not?
30 If I must needs glory, [z]I will
glory of the things which concern
mine infirmities.
31 [a]The God and Father of our Lord
Jesus Christ, [b]which is blessed for
evermore, knoweth that I lie not.

A

II Cor. 5. 13. *See e, E, § 395, page 976.*

1

Or, *suffer*.

B

I Cor. 7. 6. *See e, E, § 362, page 914.*

C

II Cor. 9. 4 Lest haply if they of Macedonia come with me, and find you unprepared, we (that we say not, ye) should be ashamed in this same confident boasting.

D

Phil. 3. 3 For we are the circumcision, which worship God in the spirit, and rejoice

GOSPEL, AND WARNS AGAINST FALSE APOSTLES (CONCLUDED).

Y

Phil. 3. 19 Whose end *is* destruction, whose God *is their* belly, and *whose* glory *is* in their shame, who mind earthly things.)

IIThes.2. 8 And then shall that Wicked be revealed, whom the Lord shall consume with the spirit of his mouth, and shall destroy with the brightness of his coming:

IIThes.2. 9 *Even him*, whose coming is after the working of Satan with all power and signs and lying wonders,

HIS TRIALS, SUFFERINGS AND PERILS FOR THE GOSPEL.

D—CONCLUDED.

in Christ Jesus, and have no confidence in the flesh.

Phil. 3. 4 Though I might also have confidence in the flesh. If any other man thinketh that he hath whereof he might trust in the flesh, I more;

E

I Cor. 4. 10 We *are* fools for Christ's sake, but ye *are* wise in Christ; we *are* weak, but ye *are* strong; ye *are* honorable, but we *are* despised.

F

Gal. 2. 4 And that because of false brethren unawares brought in, who came in privily to spy out our liberty which we have in Christ Jesus, that they might bring us into bondage:

Gal. 4. 9 But now, after that ye have known God, or rather are known of God, how turn ye again to the weak and beggarly elements, whereunto ye desire again to be in bondage?

G

IICor.10. 10 For *his* letters, say they, *are* weighty and powerful; but *his* bodily presence *is* weak, and *his* speech contemptible.

H

Phil. 3 4. *See under D.*

I

Acts 21. 39. *See l, L, § 296, page 770.*

Rom.11. 1 I say then, Hath God cast away his people? God forbid. For I also am an Israelite, of the seed of Abraham, *of* the tribe of Benjamin.

K

I Cor. 15. 10 *See q, Q, § 376, page 950.*

L

Acts 9. 16. *See o, O, § 251, page 686.*

II Cor. 6. 4 5. *See g, G, § 396, page 978.*

M

II Cor. 4 10. *See e, E, § 393, page 972*

N

Deut.25. 3 Forty stripes he may give him, *and* not exceed: lest, *if* he should exceed, and beat him above these with many stripes, then thy brother should seem vile unto thee.

Acts 16. 22 And the multitude rose up together against them: and the magistrates rent off their clothes, and commanded to beat *them*.

P

Acts 14. 19 And there came thither *certain* Jews from Antioch and Iconium, who persuaded the people, and, having stoned Paul, drew *him* out of the city, supposing he had been dead.

Q

Acts 27. 41 And falling into a place where two seas met, they ran the ship aground; and the forepart stuck fast, and remained unmovable, but the hinder part was broken with the violence of the waves.

R

Acts 20. 3. *See b, B, § 289, page 758.*

S

Acts 14. 5 And when there was an assault made both of the Gentiles, and also of the Jews with their rulers, to use *them* despitefully, and to stone them,

Acts 19. 23 And the same time there arose no small stir about that way.

T

Acts 20. 31 Therefore watch, and remember, that by the space of three years I ceased not to warn every one night and day with tears.

IICor.6. 5 In stripes, in imprisonments, in tumults, in labours, in watchings, in fastings;

U

I Cor. 4. 11. *See l, L, § 357, page 904.*

X

Acts 20. 18 And when they were come to him, he said unto them, Ye know, from the first day that I came into Asia, after what manner I have been with you at all seasons,

Acts 20. 20 *And* how I kept back nothing that was profitable *unto you*, but have shewed you, and have taught you publicly, and from house to house,

For X concluded, Y, Z, A and B see next page (998).

§ 404. PAUL ASSERTS HIS FITNESS AND RECAPITULATES HIS

CHAP. 11.

32 [e]In Damascus the governor under Aretas the king kept the city of the Damascenes with a garrison, desirous to apprehend me:

33 And through a window in a basket was I let down by the wall, and escaped his hands.

X—CONCLUDED.

Rom. 1. 14 I am debtor both to the Greeks, and to the Barbarians; both to the wise, and the unwise.

Y

I Cor. 8. 13 Wherefore, if meat make my brother to offend, I will eat no flesh while the world standeth, lest I make my brother to offend.

I Cor. 9. 22. *See l, L, § 365, page 924.*

§ 405. PAUL RECOUNTS VISIONS AND REVELATIONS AND

12 : 1–10.

1 It is not expedient for me doubtless to glory. [1]I will come to visions and revelations of the Lord.

2 I knew a man[a] in Christ above fourteen [2]years ago, (whether in the body, I cannot tell; or whether out of the body, I cannot tell: God knoweth;) such a one [b]caught up to the third heaven.

3 And I knew such a man, (whether in the body, or out of the body, I cannot tell: God knoweth;)

4 How that he was caught up into [c]paradise, and heard unspeakable words, which it is not [3]lawful for a man to utter.

5 Of such a one will I glory: [d]yet of myself I will not glory, but in mine infirmities.

6 For[e] though I would desire to glory, I shall not be a fool; for I will say the truth: but *now* I forbear, lest any man should think of me above that which he seeth me *to be*, or *that* he heareth of me.

7 And lest I should be exalted above measure through the abundance of the revelations, there was given to me a [f]thorn in the flesh, [g]the messenger of Satan to buffet me, lest I should be exalted above measure.

CHAP. 12.

8 [h]For this thing I besought the Lord thrice, that it might depart from me.

9 And he said unto me,[i] My grace is sufficient for thee: for my strength is made perfect in weakness. Most

1

Gr. *For I will come.*

A

Rom. 16. 7 Salute Andronicus and Junia, my kinsmen, and my fellow prisoners, who are of note among the apostles, who also were in Christ before me.

II Cor. 5. 17 Therefore if any man *be* in Christ, *he is* a new creature: old things are passed away; behold, all things are become new.

Gal. 1. 22 And was unknown by face unto the churches of Judea which were in Christ;

2

A. D. 46 at Lystra.

Acts 14. 6 They were ware of *it*, and fled unto Lystra and Derbe, cities of Lycaonia, and unto the region that lieth round about;

B

Acts 22. 17 And it came to pass, that, when I was come again to Jerusalem, even while I prayed in the temple, I was in a trance;

C

Luke 23. 43 And Jesus said unto him, Verily I say unto thee, To-day shalt thou be with me in paradise.

Rev. 2. 7 He that hath an ear, let him hear what the Spirit saith unto the churches; To him that overcometh will I give to eat of the tree of life, which is in the midst of the paradise of God.

TRIALS, SUFFERINGS AND PERILS FOR THE GOSPEL (CONCLUDED).

Z

IICor.12. 5 Of such a one will I glory: yet of myself I will not glory, but in mine infirmities.

IICor.12. 9 And he said unto me, My grace is sufficient for thee: for my strength is made perfect in weakness. Most gladly therefore will I rather glory in my infirmities, that the power of Christ may rest upon me.

10 Therefore I take pleasure in infirmities, in reproaches, in necesities, in persecutions, in distress for Christ's sake: for when I am weak, then am I strong.

A

Rom. 1. 9. *See c, C, § 318, page 808.*

B

Rom. 9. 5 Whose *are* the fathers, and of whom as concerning the flesh Christ *came*, who is over all, God blessed for ever. Amen.

C

Acts 9. 24, 25. *See b, B, § 252, page 686.*

DECLARES THE POWER OF GOD PERFECTED IN WEAKNESS.

3

Or, *possible.*

D

IICor.11. 30 If I must needs glory, I will glory of the things which concern mine infirmities.

E

IICor.10. 8 For though I should boast somewhat more of our authority, which the Lord hath given us for edification, and not for your destruction, I should not be ashamed:

IICor. 11. 16 I say again, Let no man think me a fool; if otherwise, yet as a fool receive me, that I may boast myself a little.

F

Eze. 28. 24 And there shall be no more a pricking brier unto the house of Israel, nor *any* grieving thorn of all *that are* round about them, that despised them; and they shall know that I *am* the Lord God.

Gal. 4. 13 Ye know how through infirmity of the flesh I preached the gospel unto you at the first.

14 And my temptation which was in my flesh ye despised not, nor rejected; but received me as an angel of God, *even* as Christ Jesus.

G

Job. 2. 7 So went Satan forth from the presence of the Lord, and smote Job with sore boils from the sole of his foot unto his crown.

Luke 13. 16 And ought not this woman, being a daughter of Abraham, whom Satan hath bound, lo, these eighteen years, be loosed from this bond on the Sabbath day?

H

Duet. 3. 23 And I besought the Lord at that time, saying.

H—CONCLUDED.

Deut. 3. 24 O Lord God, thou hast begun to shew thy servant thy greatness, and thy mighty hand: for what God *is there* in heaven or in earth, that can do according to thy works, and according to thy might?

25 I pray thee, let me go over, and see the good land that *is* beyond Jordan, that goodly mountain, and Lebanon.

26 But the Lord was wroth with me for your sakes, and would not hear me: and the Lord saith unto me, Let it suffice thee; speak no more unto me of this matter.

27 Get thee up into the top of Pisgah, and lift up thine eyes westward, and northward, and southward, and eastward and behold *it* with thine eyes: for thou shalt not go over this Jordan.

Matt.26. 44 And he left them, and went away again, and prayed the third time, saying the same words.

I

Eccl. 7. 18 *It is* good that thou shouldest take hold of this; yea, also from this withdraw not thine hand: for he that feareth God shall come forth of them all.

Isa. 40. 29 He giveth power to the faint; and and to *them that have* no might he increaseth strength.

Isa. 41. 10 Fear thou not; for I *am* with thee: be not dismayed; for I *am* thy God: I will strengthen thee; yea, I will help thee; yea, I will uphold thee with the right hand of my righteousness.

I.Cor.10. 13 There hath no temptation taken you but such as is common to man: but God *is* faithful, who will not suffer you to be tempted above that ye are able; but will with the temptation also

For I concluded, see next page (1000).

§ 405. PAUL RECOUNTS VISIONS AND REVELATIONS AND DECLARES

CHAP. 12.

gladly therefore [k]will I rather glory
in my infirmities, [l]that the power of
Christ may rest upon me.

10 Therefore [m]I take pleasure in
infirmities, in reproaches, in necessities, in persecutions, in distresses
for Christ's sake: [n]for when I am
weak, then am I strong.

I—CONCLUDED.

make a way to escape, that ye may be able to bear *it*.

Heb. 2. 18 For in that he himself hath suffered being tempted, he is able to succor them that are tempted.

IIPet. 2. 9 The Lord knoweth how to deliver the godly out of temptation, and to reserve the unjust unto the day of judgment to be punished:

K

II Cor. 11. 30. *See under D, page 999.*

§ 406. PAUL SOLICITS ACKNOWLEDGEMENT OF HIS APOSTLESHIP

12 : 11–21.

11 I am become [a]a fool in glorying;
ye have compelled me: for I ought
to have been commended of you: for
[b]in nothing am I behind the very
chiefest apostles, though [c]I be nothing.

12 [d]Truly the signs of an apostle
were wrought among you in all patience, in signs, and wonders, and
mighty deeds.

13 [e]For what is it wherein ye were
inferior to other churches, except *it
be* that [f]I myself was not burdensome
to you? forgive me [g]this wrong.

14 [h]Behold, the third time I am
ready to come to you; and I will
not be burdensome to you; for [i]I
seek not yours, but you: [k]for the
children ought not to lay up for the
parents, but the parents for the children.

15 And [l]I will very gladly spend
and be spent [m]for [1]you; though [n]the
more abundantly I love you, the less
I be loved.

16 But be it so, [o]I did not burden
you: nevertheless, being crafty, I
caught you with guile.

17 [p]Did I make a gain of you by
any of them whom I sent unto you?

CHAP. 12.

18 [q]I desired Titus, and with *him* I
sent a [r]brother. Did Titus make a
gain of you? walked we not in the
same spirit? *walked we* not in the
same steps?

19 [s]Again, think ye that we excuse
ourselves unto you? we speak before
God in Christ: [t]but *we do* all things,
dearly beloved, for your edifying.

20 For I fear, lest, when I come, I

A

II Cor. 5. 13. *See e, E, § 395, page 976.*

B

I Cor. 15. 10. *See q, Q, § 376, page 950.*

Gal. 2. 6 But of these who seemed to be somewhat, whatsoever they were, it maketh no matter to me; God accepteth no man's person: for they who seemed *to be somewhat* in conference added nothing to me:

7 But contrariwise, when they saw that the gospel of the uncircumcision was committed unto me, as *the gospel* of the circumcision *was* unto Peter;

8 (For he that wrought effectually in Peter to the apostleship of the circumcision, the same was mightly in me toward the Gentiles:)

C

I Cor. 3. 7 So then neither is he that planteth anything, neither he that watereth; but God that giveth the increase.

ICor. 15. 8 And last of all he was seen of me also, as of one born out of due time.

9 For I am the least of the apostles, that am not meet to be called an apostle, because I persecuted the church of God.

THE POWER OF GOD PERFECTED IN WEAKNESS (Concluded).

L

I Pet. 4. 14 If ye be reproached for the name of Christ, happy *are ye;* for the Spirit of glory and of God resteth upon you: on their part he is evil spoken of, but on your part he is glorified.

M

Rom. 5. 3. *See e, E, § 326, page 830.*

II Cor. 7. 4 Great *is* my boldness of speech toward you, great *is* my glorying of you: I am filled with comfort, I am exceeding joyful in all our tribulation.

N

Isa. 40. 29 He giveth power to the faint; and to *them that have* no might he increaseth strength.
30 Even the youths shall faint and be weary, and the young men shall utterly fall:
31 But they that wait upon the Lord shall renew *their* strength; they shall mount up with wings as eagles; they shall run, and not be weary; *and* they shall walk, and not faint.

II Cor. 13. 4. *See text of topic, § 407, page 1002.*

AND OFFERS REASONS FOR THE POSTPONEMENT OF HIS VISIT.

C—Concluded.

Eph. 3. 8 Unto me, who am less than the least of all saints, is this grace given, that I should preach among the Gentiles the unsearchable riches of Christ;

D

Rom. 15. 18, 19. *See i, I, § 346, page 880.*

I Cor. 9. 2 If I be not an apostle unto others, yet doubtless I am to you: for the seal of mine apostleship are ye in the Lord.

II Cor. 4. 2. *See d, D, § 392, page 972.*

E

I Cor. 1. 7 So that ye come behind in no gift; waiting for the coming of our Lord Jesus Christ:

F

I Cor. 9. 12. *See p, P, § 365, page 922.*

G

II Cor. 11. 7 Have I committed an offence in abasing myself that ye might be exalted, because I have preached to you the gospel of God freely?

H

II Cor. 13. 1 This *is* the third *time* I am coming to you. In the mouth of two or three witnesses shall every word be established.

I

Acts 20. 33 I have coveted no man's silver, or gold, or apparal.

I Cor. 10. 33 Even as I please all *men* in all *things*, not seeking mine own profit, but the *profit* of many, that they may be saved.

K

I Cor. 4. 14, 15. *See b, B, § 358, page 904.*

L

Phil. 2. 17 Yea, and if I be offered upon the sacrifice and service of your faith, I joy, and rejoice with you all.

L—Concluded.

I Thes. 2. 8 So being affectionately desirous of you, we were willing to have imparted unto you, not the gospel of God only, but also our own souls,[1] because ye were dear unto us.

M

John 10. 11 I am the good shepherd: the good shepherd giveth his life for the sheep.

II Cor. 1. 6 And whether we be afflicted, *it is* for your consolation and salvation, which is effectual in the enduring of the same sufferings which we also suffer: or whether we be comforted, *it is* for your consolation and salvation.

Col. 1. 24 Who now rejoice in my sufferings for you, and fill up that which is behind of the afflictions of Christ in my flesh for his body's sake, which is the church.

II Tim. 2. 10 Therefore I endure all things for the elect's sake, that they may also obtain the salvation which is in Christ Jesus with eternal glory.

1
Gr. *your souls.*

N

II Cor. 6 12, 13. *See p, P, § 396, page 980.*

O

Acts 18. 3. *See b, B, § 280, page 746.*

P

II Cor. 7. 2. *See i, I, § 397, page 982.*

Q

II Cor. 8. 6. *See c, C, § 399, page 984.*

R

II Cor. 8. 16. *See b, B, § 400, page 986.*

S

II Cor. 3. 1. *See a, A. § 390, page 968.*

T

II Cor. 13. 10 Therefore I write these things being absent, lest being present I should use sharpness, according to the power which the Lord hath given me to edification and not to destruction.

§ 406. PAUL SOLICITS ACKNOWLEDGEMENT OF HIS APOSTLESHIP AND

CHAP. 12.

shall not find you such as I would, and *that* [u]I shall be found unto you such as ye would not: lest *there be* debates, envyings, wraths, strifes, backbitings, whisperings, swellings, tumults:

CHAP. 12.

21 *And* lest, when I come again, my God [x]will humble me among you, and *that* I shall bewail many [y]which have sinned already, and have not repented of the uncleanness and [z]fornication and lasciviousness which they have committed.

§ 407. PAUL DECLARES HIS WRITINGS TO

13 : 1–10.

1 This [a]*is* the third *time* I am coming to you. [b]In the mouth of two or three witnesses shall every word be established.

2 [c]I told you before, and foretell you, as if I were present, the second time; and being absent now I write to them [d]which heretofore have sinned, and to all other, that, if I come again, [e]I will not spare:

3 Since ye seek a proof of Christ [f]speaking in me, which to you-ward is not weak, but mighty [g]in you.

4 [h]For though he was crucified through weakness, yet [i]he liveth by the power of God. [k]For we also are weak [1]in him, but we shall live with him by the power of God toward you.

5 [l]Examine yourselves, whether ye be in the faith; prove your own selves. Know ye not your own selves, [m]how that Jesus Christ is in you, except ye be [n]reprobates?

6 But I trust that ye shall know that we are not reprobates.

7 Now I pray God that ye do no evil; not that we should appear approved, but that ye should do that which is honest, though we be as reprobates.

CHAP. 13.

8 [o]For we can do nothing against the truth, but for the truth.

9 For we are glad, [p]when we are weak, and ye are strong: and this also we wish, [q]*even* your perfection.

10 [r]Therefore I write these things being absent, lest being present [s]I should use sharpness, [t]according to the power which the Lord hath given me to edification, and not to destruction.

A

II Cor. 12. 14. *See h, H, § 406, page 1000.*

B

Num. 35. 30 Whoso killeth any person, the murderer shall be put to death by the mouth of witnesses: but one witness shall not testify against any person *to cause him* to die.

Matt. 18. 16. *See c, C, § 103, page 300.*

C

II Cor. 10. 2. *See c, C, § 402, page 990.*

D

II Cor. 12. 21. *See text of topic, § 406.*

E

II Cor. 1. 23. *See m, M, § 387, page 966.*

F

Matt. 10. 20 For it is not ye that speak, but the Spirit of your Father which speaketh in you.

I Cor. 5. 4. *See g, G, § 359, page 906.*

G

I Cor. 9. 2 If I be not an apostle unto others, yet doubtless I am to you: for the seal of mine apostleship are ye in the Lord.

H

Phil. 2. 7 But made himself of no reputation,

OFFERS REASONS FOR THE POSTPONEMENT OF HIS VISIT (CONCLUDED).

U

II Cor. 10. 2. *See c, C, § 402, page 990.*

X

I Cor. 4. 21 What will ye? shall I come unto you with a rod, or in love, and *in* the spirit of meekness?

II Cor. 2. 3 And I wrote this same unto you, lest, when I came, I should have sorrow from them of whom I ought to rejoice; having confidence in you all, that my joy is *the joy* of you all.

Y

II Cor. 13. 2. *See text of topic, § 407.*

Z

I Cor. 5. 1 It is reported commonly *that there is* fornication among you, and such fornication as is not so much as named among the Gentiles, that one should have his father's wife.

I Thes. 4. 3 For this is the will of God, *even* your sanctification, that ye should abstain from fornication:

BE FOR THE PERFECTING OF THE SAINTS.

H—CONCLUDED.

and took upon him the form of a servant, and was made in the likeness of men:

8 And being found in fashion as a man, he humbled himself, and became obedient unto death, even the death of the cross.

I Pet. 3. 18 For Christ also hath once suffered for sins, the just for the unjust, that he might bring us to God, being put to death in the flesh, but quickened by the Spirit:

I

Rom. 6. 4 Therefore we are buried with him by baptism into death: that like as Christ was raised up from the dead by the glory of the Father, even so we also should walk in newness of life.

K

II Cor. 10. 3, 4. *See f, F, § 402, page 990.*

1

Or, *with him.*

L

I Cor. 11. 28. *See l, L, § 369, page 936.*

M

Rom. 8. 10 And if Christ *be* in you, the body *is* dead because of sin; but the Spirit *is* life because of righteousness.

Gal. 4. 19 My little children, of whom I travail in birth again until Christ be formed in you.

Eph. 3. 17 That Christ may dwell in your hearts by faith; that ye, being rooted and grounded in love,

N

I Cor. 9. 27. *See u, U, § 365, page 926.*

O

Prov. 21. 30 *There is* no wisdom nor understanding nor counsel against the LORD.

P

I Cor. 4. 10 We *are* fools for Christ's sake, but ye *are* wise in Christ; we *are* weak, but ye *are* strong; ye *are* honourable, but we *are* despised.

P—CONCLUDED.

II Cor. 11. 30 If I must needs glory, I will glory of the things which concern mine infirmities.

II Cor. 12. 5 Of such a one will I glory: yet of myself I will not glory, but in mine infirmities.

II Cor. 12. 9 And he said unto me, My grace is sufficient for thee: for my strength is made perfect in weakness. Most gladly therefore will I rather glory in my infirmities, that the power of Christ may rest upon me.

Q

Col. 1. 28 Whom we preach, warning every man, and teaching every man in all wisdom; that we may present every man perfect in Christ Jesus:

29 Whereunto I also labour, striving according to his working, which worketh in me mightily.

R

I Cor. 4. 21 What will ye? shall I come unto you with a rod, or in love, and *in* the spirit of meekness?

II Cor. 2. 3 And I wrote this same unto you, lest, when I came, I should have sorrow from them of whom I ought to rejoice; having confidence in you all, that my joy is *the joy* of you all.

II Cor. 10. 2 But I beseech *you*, that I may not be bold when I am present with that confidence, wherewith I think to be bold against some, which think of us as if we walked according to the flesh.

II Cor. 12. 20, 21. *See text of topic, § 406.*

S

Tit. 1. 13 This witness is true. Wherefore rebuke them sharply, that they may be sound in the faith.

T

II Cor. 10. 8 For though I should boast somewhat more of our authority, which the Lord hath given us for edification, and not for your destruction, I should not be ashamed:

§ 408. CONCLUDING ADMONITIONS,

13: 11–14.

11 Finally, brethren, farewell. [a]Be perfect, be of good comfort, [b]be of one mind, live in peace; and the God of love [c]and peace shall be with you.

12 [d]Greet one another with a holy kiss.

CHAP. 13.

13 All the saints salute you.

14 [e]The grace of the Lord Jesus Christ, and the love of God, and [f]the communion of the Holy Ghost, *be* with you all. Amen.

A

Matt. 5. 48. *See n, N, § 43, page 136.*

B

Rom. 12. 16. *See g, G, § 342, page 872.*

PAUL'S EPISTLE TO

§ 409. THE SALUTATION.

1: 1–5.

1 Paul, an apostle, ([a]not of men, neither by man, but [b]by Jesus Christ, and God the Father, [c]who raised him from the dead;)

2 And all the brethren [d]which are with me, [e]unto the churches of Galatia:

3 [f]Grace *be* to you, and peace, from God the Father, and *from* our Lord Jesus Christ,

4 [g]Who gave himself for our sins, that he might deliver us [h]from this present evil world, according to the will of God and our Father:

5 To whom *be* glory for ever and ever. Amen.

A

Gal. 1. 11, 12. *See text of topic, § 411, page 1006.*

B

Acts 9. 6 And he trembling and astonished said, Lord, what wilt thou have me to do? And the Lord *said* unto him, Arise, and go into the city, and it shall be told thee what thou must do.

Acts 22. 10 And I said, what shall I do, Lord? And the Lord said unto me, Arise, and go into Damascus; and there it shall be told thee of all things which are appointed for thee to do.

Acts 22. 15 For thou shalt be his witness unto all men of what thou hast seen and heard.

Acts 22. 21 And he said unto me, Depart: for I will send thee far hence unto the Gentiles.

Acts 26. 16 But rise, and stand upon thy feet: for I have appeared unto thee for this purpose, to make thee a minister and a witness both of these things which thou hast seen, and of those things in the which I will appear unto thee;

Tit. 1. 3 But hath in due times manifested his word through preaching, which is committed unto me according to the commandment of God our Saviour,

§ 410. THE PERVERTING OF THE

1:6–10.

6 I marvel that ye are so soon removed [a]from him that called you into the grace of Christ unto another gospel:

CHAP. 1.

7 [b]Which is not another; but there be some [c]that trouble you, and would pervert the gospel of Christ.

8 But though [d]we, or an angel from

A SALUTATION AND BENEDICTION.

C

Rom. 15. 33. *See b, B, § 346, page 882.*

D

Rom. 16. 16. *See h, H, § 347, page 884.*

E

Rom. 16. 24 The grace of our Lord Jesus Christ *be* with you all. Amen.

F

John 7. 39 (But this spake he of the Spirit, which they that believe on him should receive: for the Holy Ghost was not

F—CONCLUDED.

yet *given:* because that Jesus was not yet glorified.)

Phil. 2. 1 If *there be* therefore any consolation in Christ, if any comfort of love, if any fellowship of the Spirit, if any bowels and mercies,

I Jno. 3. 24 And he that keepeth his commandments dwelleth in him, and he in him. And hereby we know that he abideth in us, by the Spirit which he hath given us.

THE GALATIANS.

Probably written during the winter of A. D. 57, from Corinth.

C

Acts 2. 24. *See k, K, § 231, page 638.*

D

Phil. 2. 22 But ye know the proof of him, that, as a son with the father, he hath served with me in the gospel.

Phil. 4. 21 Salute every saint in Christ Jesus. The brethren which are with me greet you.

E

Acts 16. 6 Now when they had gone throughout Phrygia and the region of Galatia, and were forbidden of the Holy Ghost to preach the word in Asia,

Acts 18. 23 And after he had spent some time *there*, he departed, and went over *all* the country of Galatia and Phrygia in order, strengthening all the disciples.

I Cor. 16. 1 Now concerning the collection for the saints, as I have given order to the churches of Galatia, even so do ye.

F

II Cor. 1. 2. *See c, C, § 385, page 962.*

G

Matt. 20. 28. *See y, Y, § 148, page 420.*
Rom. 4. 25. *See b, B, § 325, page 830.*

H

Isa. 65. 17 For, behold, I create new heavens and a new earth: and the former shall not be remembered, nor come into mind.

John 12. 31 Now is the judgment of this world: now shall the prince of this world be cast out.

John 14. 30 Hereafter I will not talk much with you: for the prince of this world cometh, and hath nothing in me:

John 17. 14 I have given them thy word; and the world hath hated them, because they are not of the world, even as I am not of the world.

John 17. 15 I pray not that thou shouldest take them out of the world, but that thou shouldest keep them from the evil.

Eph. 6. 12 For we wrestle not against flesh and blood, but against principalities, against powers, against the rulers of the darkness of this world, against spiritual wickedness in high *places*.

I Jno. 5. 19 *And* we know that we are of God, and the whole world lieth in wickedness.

GOSPEL AMONG THE GALATIANS.

A

Gal. 5. 8 This persuasion *cometh* not of him that calleth you.

B

II Cor. 11. 4. *See g, G, § 403, page 994.*

C

Acts 15. 24. *See b, B, § 269, page 730.*

C—CONCLUDED.

II Cor. 2. 17. *See i, I, § 389, page 968.*

D

I Cor. 16. 22 If any man love not the Lord Jesus Christ, let him be Anathema, Maran-atha.

§ 410. THE PERVERTING OF THE GOSPEL

CHAP. I.

heaven, preach any other gospel
unto you than that which we have
preached unto you, let him be accursed.

9 As we said before, so say I now
again, If any *man* preach any other
gospel unto you [e]than that ye have
received, let him be accursed.

10 For [f]do I now [g]persuade men,
or God? or [h]do I seek to please men?
for if I yet pleased men, I should not
be the servant of Christ.

E

Deut. 4. 2 Ye shall not add unto the word which I command you, neither shall ye diminish *aught* from it, that ye may keep the commandments of the LORD your God which I command you.

Deut. 12. 32 What things soever I command you, observe to do it; thou shalt not add thereto, nor diminish from it.

Deut. 13. 3 Thou shalt not hearken unto the words of that prophet, or that dreamer of dreams; for the LORD your God proveth you, to know whether ye love the LORD your God with all your heart and with all your soul.

Prov. 30. 6 Add thou not unto his words, lest he reprove thee, and thou be found a liar.

§ 411. PAUL DECLARES HE RECEIVED THE GOSPEL NOT

I : 11–17.

11 [a]But I certify you, brethren,
that the gospel which was preached
of me is not after man.

12 For [b]I neither received it of man,
neither was I taught *it*, but [c]by the
revelation of Jesus Christ.

13 For ye have heard of my conversation in time past in the Jews'
religion, how that [d]beyond measure
I persecuted the church of God, and
wasted it:

14 And profited in the Jews' religion above many my [1]equals in mine
own nation, [e]being more exceedingly
zealous [f]of the tradition of my fathers.

15 But when it pleased God, [g]who
separated me from my mother's
womb, and called *me* by his grace,

16 [h]To reveal his Son in me, that
[i]I might preach him among the
heathen; immediately I conferred
not with [k]flesh and blood:

17 Neither went I up to Jerusalem to
them which were apostles before me;

CHAP. I.

but I went into Arabia, and returned
again unto Damascus.

A

1 Cor. 15. 1 Moreover, brethren, I declare unto you the gospel which I preached unto you, which also ye have received, and wherein ye stand;

B

1 Cor. 15. 1. *See under A.*

1 Cor. 15. 3 For I delivered unto you first of all that which I also received, how that Christ died for our sins according to the Scriptures;

C

Eph. 3. 3 How that by revelation he made known unto me the mystery; (as I wrote afore in few words,

D

Acts 8. 3. *See d, D, § 247, page 678.*

1

Gr. equals in years,

E

Acts 22. 3 I am verily a man *which am* a Jew, born in Tarsus, *a city* in Cilicia, yet brought up in this city at the feet of Gamaliel, *and* taught according to the perfect manner of the law of the fathers, and was zealous towards God, as ye all are this day.

Acts 26. 11 And I punished them oft in every synagogue, and compelled *them* to blaspheme; and being exceedingly mad against them, I persecuted *them* even unto strange cities.

AMONG THE GALATIANS (CONCLUDED).

E—CONCLUDED.

Rev. 22. 18 For I testify unto every man that heareth the words of the prophecy of this book, If any man shall add unto these things, God shall add unto him the plagues that are written in this book.

19 And if any man shall take away from the words of the book of this prophecy, God shall take away his part out of the book of life, and out of the holy city, and *from* the things which are written in this book.

F

I Thes. 2. 4 But as we were allowed of God to be put in trust with the gospel, even so we speak; not as pleasing men, but God, which trieth our hearts.

G

I Sa. 24. 7. So David stayed his servants with these words, and suffered them not to rise against Saul. But Saul rose up out of the cave, and went on *his* way.

Matt. 28. 14 And if this come to the governor's ears, we will persuade him, and secure you.

I Jno. 3. 19 And hereby we know that we are of the truth, and shall assure our hearts before him.

H

I Thes. 2. 4. *See under F.*

Jas. 4. 4 Ye adulterers and adulteresses, know ye not that the friendship of the world is enmity with God? whosoever therefore will be a friend of the world is the enemy of God.

OF MEN, BUT THROUGH REVELATION OF JESUS CHRIST.

E—CONCLUDED.

Phil. 3. 6 Concerning zeal, persecuting the the church; touching the righteousness which is in the law, blameless.

F

Jer. 9. 14 But have walked after the imagination of their own heart, and after Baalim, which their fathers taught them:

Matt. 15. 2 Why do thy disciples transgress the tradition of the elders? for they wash not their hands when they eat bread.

Mark 7. 5 Then the Pharisees and scribes asked him, Why walk not thy disciples according to the tradition of the elders, but eat bread with unwashed hands?

G

Isa. 49. 1 Listen, O isles, unto me; and hearken, ye people, from far; The LORD hath called me from the womb; from the bowels of my mother hath he made mention of my name.

Isa. 49. 5 And now, saith the LORD that formed me from the womb *to be* his servant, to bring Jacob again to him, Though Israel be not gathered, yet shall I be glorious in the eyes of the LORD, and my God shall be my strength.

Jer. 1. 5 Before I formed thee in the belly I knew thee; and before thou camest forth out of the womb I sanctified thee, *and* I ordained thee a prophet unto the nations.

Acts 9. 15. *See l, L, § 251, page 684.*

H

II Cor. 4. 6 For God, who commanded the light to shine out of darkness, hath shined in our hearts, to *give* the light of the knowledge of the glory of God in the face of Jesus Christ.

I

Acts 9. 15 But the Lord said unto him, Go thy way: for he is a chosen vessel unto me, to bear my name before the Gentiles, and kings, and the children of Israel:

Acts 22. 21. *See i, I, § 297, page 774.*

Acts. 26. 17 Delivering thee from the people, and *from* the Gentiles, unto whom now I send thee,

18 To open their eyes, *and* to turn *them* from darkness to light, and *from* the power of Satan unto God, that they may receive forgiveness of sins, and inheritance among them which are santified by faith that is in me.

K

Matt. 16. 17 And Jesus answered and said unto him, Blessed art thou, Simon Barjona: for flesh and blood hath not revealed *it* unto thee, but my Father which is in heaven.

I Cor. 15. 50 Now this I say, brethren, that flesh and blood cannot inherit the kingdom of God; neither doth corruption inherit incorruption.

Eph. 6. 12 For we wrestle not against flesh and blood, but against principalities, against powers, against the rulers of the darkness of this world, against spiritual wickedness in high *places*.

§ 412. PAUL RECOUNTS HIS VISIT

1:18–24.

18 Then after three years [a]I [1]went up to Jerusalem to see Peter, and abode with him fifteen days.

19 But [b]other of the apostles saw I none, save [c]James the Lord's brother.

20 Now the things which I write unto you, [d]behold, before God, I lie not.

21 [e]Afterwards I came into the regions of Syria and Cilicia;

22 And was unknown by face [f]unto the churches of Judea which [g]were in Christ:

CHAP. 1.

23 But they had heard only, That he which persecuted us in times past now preacheth the faith which once he destroyed.

24 And [h]they glorified God in me.

A

Acts 9. 26 And when Saul was come to Jerusalem, he assayed to join himself to the disciples: but they were all afraid of him, and believed not that he was a disciple.

1

Or, *returned.*

§ 413. PAUL RECOUNTS THE DECISION

2:1–10.

1 Then fourteen years after [a]I went up again to Jerusalem with Barnabas, and took Titus with *me* also.

2 And I went up by revelation, [b]and communicated unto them that gospel which I preach among the Gentiles, but [1]privately to them which were of reputation, lest by any means [c]I should run, or had run, in vain.

3 But neither Titus, who was with me, being a Greek, was compelled to be circumcised:

4 And that because of [d]false brethren unawares brought in, who came in privately to spy out our [e]liberty which we have in Christ Jesus, [f]that they might bring us into bondage:

5 To whom we gave place by subjection, no, not for an hour; that [g]the truth of the gospel might continue with you.

6 But of these [h]who seemed to be somewhat, (whatsoever they were, it maketh no matter to me: [i]God accepteth no man's person:) for they who seemed *to be somewhat* [k]in conference added nothing to me:

CHAP. 2.

7 But contrariwise, [l]when they saw that the gospel of the uncircumcision [m]was committed unto me, as *the gospel* of the circumcision *was* unto Peter;

8 (For he that wrought effectually in Peter to the apostleship of the circumcision, [n]the same was mighty in me toward the Gentiles;)

9 And when James, Cephas, and John, who seemed to be [o]pillars, perceived [p]the grace that was given unto me, they gave to me and Barnabas the right hands of fellowship; that we *should go* unto the heathen, and they unto the circumcision.

A

Acts 15. 2. *See d, D, § 267, page 726.*

B

Acts 15. 12 Then all the multitude kept silence, and gave audience to Barnabas and Paul, declaring what miracles and wonders God had wrought among the Gentiles by them.

1

Or, *severally.*

C

Phil. 2. 16 Holding forth the word of life; that I may rejoice in the day of Christ, that I have not run in vain, neither laboured in vain.

TO PETER TO VERIFY HIS PREACHING.

B

I Cor. 9. 5 Have we not power to lead about a sister, a wife, as well as other apostles, and *as* the brethren of the Lord, and Cephas?

C

Matt. 12. 46. *See b, B, § 55, page 176.*

D

Rom. 9. 1. *See a, A, § 335, page 852.*

E

Acts 9. 30 *Which* when the brethren knew, they brought him down to Cesarea, and sent him forth to Tarsus.

F

I Thes. 2. 14 For ye, brethren, became followers of the churches of God which in Judea are in Christ Jesus: for ye also have suffered like things of your own countrymen, even as they *have* of the Jews:

G

Rom. 16. 7 Salute Adronicus and Junia, my kinsmen, and my fellow prisoners, who are of note among the apostles, who also were in Christ before me.

H

Acts 21. 19 And when he had saluted them, he declared particularly what things God had wrought among the Gentiles by his ministry.

20 And when they heard *it*, they glorified the Lord, and said unto him, Thou seest, brother, how many thousands of Jews there are which believe; and they are all zealous of the law:

II Thes. 1. 10 When he shall come to be glorified in his saints, and to be admired in all them that believe(because our testimony among you was believed) in that day.

OF THE COUNCIL HELD AT JERUSALEM.

C—CONCLUDED.

I Thes. 3. 5 For this cause, when I could no longer forbear, I sent to know your faith, lest by some means the tempter have tempted you, and our labor be in vain.

D

Acts 15. 24. *See b, B, § 269, page 730.*

E

Gal. 3. 25 But after that faith is come, we are no longer under a schoolmaster.

Gal. 5. 1 Stand fast therefore in the liberty wherewith Christ hath made us free, and be not entangled again with the yoke of bondage.

Gal. 5. 13 For, brethren, ye have been called unto liberty; only *use* not liberty for an occasion to the flesh, but by love serve one another.

F

II Cor. 11. 20. *See f, F, § 404, page 996.*

G

Gal. 2. 14. *See text of topic § 414, page 1010.*

Gal. 3. 1 O foolish Galatians, who hath bewitched you, that ye should not obey the truth, before whose eyes Jesus Christ hath been evidently set forth, crucified among you?

Gal. 4. 16 Am I therefore become your enemy, because I tell you the truth?

H

Gal. 6. 3 For if a man think himself to be something, when he is nothing, he deceiveth himself.

I

Acts 10. 34. *See b, B, § 254, page 696.*

K

II Cor. 12. 11. *See b, B, § 406, page 1000.*

L

Acts 13. 46 Then Paul and Barnabas waxed bold, and said, It was necessary that the word of God should first have been spoken to you: but seeing ye put it from you, and judge yourselves unworthy of everlasting life, lo, we turn to the Gentiles.

Acts 22. 21. *See i, I, § 297, page 774.*

Rom. 1. 5 By whom we have received grace and apostleship, for obedience to the faith among all nations, for his name:

Rom. 11. 13 For I speak to you Gentiles, inasmuch as I am the apostle of the Gentiles, I magnify mine office:

M

I Thes. 2. 4 But as we were allowed of God to be put in trust with the gospel, even so we speak; not as pleasing men, but God, which trieth our hearts.

N

Acts 22. 21. *See i, I, § 297, page 774.*

I Cor. 15. 10 But by the grace of God I am what I am: and his grace which *was bestowed* upon me was not in vain; but I labored more abundantly than they all: yet not I, but the grace of God which was with me.

Col. 1. 29 Whereunto I also labor, striving according to his working, which worketh in me mightily.

O

Matt. 16. 18 And I say also unto thee, That thou art Peter, and upon this rock I will build my church: and the gates

For O concluded and P, see next page (1010).

§ 413. PAUL RECOUNTS THE DECISION OF

CHAP. 2.

10 Only *they would* that we should remember the poor; [q]the same which I also was forward to do.

O—CONTINUED.

of hell shall not prevail against it.

Eph. 2. 20 And are built upon the foundation of the apostles and prophets, Jesus Christ himself being the chief corner *stone;*

§ 414. PAUL WITHSTOOD

2 : 11–21.

11 [a]But when Peter was come to
Antioch, I withstood him to the face,
because he was to be blamed.
12 For before that certain came
from James, [b]he did eat with the Gentiles: but when they were come, he
withdrew and separated himself, fearing them which were of the circumcision.
13 And the other Jews dissembled
likewise with him; insomuch that
Barnabas also was carried away with
their dissimulation.
14 But when I saw that they walked
not uprightly according to [c]the truth
of the gospel, I said unto Peter [d]be-
fore *them* all, [e]If thou, being a Jew,
livest after the manner of Gentiles,
and not as do the Jews, why compellest thou the Gentiles to live as
do the Jews?
15 [f]We *who are* Jews by nature, and
not [g]sinners of the Gentiles,
16 [h]Knowing that a man is not justified by the works of the law, but by
the faith of Jesus Christ, even we
have believed in Jesus Christ, that
we might be justified [i]by the faith of
Christ, and not by the works of the
law: for [k]by the works of the law
shall no flesh be justified.
17 But if, while we seek to be justified by Christ, we ourselves also

CHAP. 2.

are found [l]sinners, *is* therefore Christ
the minister of sin? God forbid.
18 For if I build again the things
which I destroyed, I make myself a
transgressor.
19 For I [m]through the law am dead
to the law, that I might [n]live unto
God.

A

Acts 15. 35 Paul also and Barnabas continued in Antioch, teaching and preaching the word of the Lord, with many others also.

B

Acts 10. 28 And he said unto them, Ye know how that it is an unlawful thing for a man that is a Jew to keep company, or come unto one of another nation; but God hath shewed me that I should not call any man common or unclean.

Acts 11. 3 Saying, Thou wentest in to men uncircumcised, and didst eat with them.

C

Gal. 2. 5 To whom we gave place by subjection, no, not for an hour; that the truth of the gospel might continue with you.

D

I Tim. 5. 20 Them that sin rebuke before all, that others also may fear.

E

Acts 2. 10. *See s, S, § 254, page 694.*

F

Acts 15. 10 Now therefore why tempt ye God, to put a yoke upon the neck of the disciples, which neither our fathers nor we were able to bear?

11 But we believe that through the grace of the Lord Jesus Christ we shall be saved, even as they.

G

Matt. 9. 11 And when the Pharisees saw *it*, they said unto his disciples, Why eateth

THE COUNCIL HELD AT JERUSALEM (CONCLUDED).

O—CONCLUDED.

Rev. 21. 14 And the wall of the city had twelve foundations, and in them the names of the twelve apostles of the Lamb.

P

Rom. 1. 5. *See i, I, § 317, page 808.*

Q

Acts 24. 17. *See i, I, § 303, page 784.*

I Cor. 16. 1 Now concerning the collection for the saints, as I have given order to the churches of Galatia, even so do ye.

PETER AT ANTIOCH.

G—CONCLUDED.

your master with publicans and sinners.

Eph. 2. 3 Among whom also we all had our conversation in times past in the lusts of our flesh, fulfilling the desires of the flesh and of the mind; and were by nature the children of wrath, even as others.

Eph. 2. 12 That at that time ye were without Christ, being aliens from the commonwealth of Israel, and strangers from the covenants of promise, having no hope, and without God in the world:

H

Acts 13. 38 Be it known unto you therefore, men *and* brethren, that through this man is preached unto you the forgiveness of sins:
39 And by him all that believe are justied from all things, from which ye could not be justified by the law of Moses.

I

Rom. 1. 17. *See p, P, § 318, page 810.*

Rom. 3. 22 Even the righteousness of God *which is* by faith of Jesus Christ unto all and upon all them that believe; for there is no difference:

Rom. 3. 28 Therefore we conclude that a man is justified by faith without the deeds of the law.

Rom. 8. 3 For what the law could not do, in that it was weak through the flesh, God sending his own Son in the likeness of sinful flesh, and for sin, condemned sin in the flesh:

Gal. 3. 24 Wherefore the law was our schoolmaster *to bring us* unto Christ, that we might be justified by faith.

Heb. 7. 18 For there is verily a disannulling of the commandment going before for the weakness and unprofitableness thereof.
19 For the law made nothing perfect, but the bringing in of a better hope *did;* by the which we draw nigh unto God.

K

Rom. 3. 20. *See c, C, § 324, page 824.*

L

I Jno. 3. 8 He that committeth sin is of the devil; for the devil sinneth from the beginning. For this purpose the Son of God was manifested, that he might destroy the works of the devil.
9 Whosoever is born of God doth not commit sin; for his seed remaineth in him: and he cannot sin, because he is born of God.

M

Rom. 7. 4. *See c, C, § 330, page 840.*

N

Rom. 6. 11 Likewise reckon ye also yourselves to be dead indeed unto sin, but alive unto God through Jesus Christ our Lord.

II Cor 5. 15 And *that* he died for all, that they which live should not henceforth live unto themselves, but unto him which died for them, and rose again.

Rom. 14. 7, 8. *See g, G, § 344, page 876.*

Heb. 9. 14 How much more shall the blood of Christ, who through the eternal Spirit offered himself without spot to God, purge your conscience from dead works to serve the living God?

O

Rom. 6. 6. *See k, K, § 328, page 836.*

P

II Cor. 5. 15 And *that* he died for all, that they which live should not henceforth live unto themselves, but unto him which died for them, and rose again.

I Thes. 5. 10 Who died for us, that, whether we wake or sleep, we should live together with him.

I Pet. 4. 2 That he no longer should live the rest of *his* time in the flesh to the lusts of men, but to the will of God.

Q

Gal. 1. 4 Who gave himself for our sins, that he might deliver us from this present evil world, according to the will of God and our Father:

Eph. 5. 2 And walk in love, as Christ also hath loved us, and hath given himself for us an offering and a sacrifice to God for a sweetsmelling savour.

§ 414. PAUL WITHSTOOD PETER

CHAP. 2.

20 I am [o]crucified with Christ: nevertheless I live; yet not I, but Christ liveth in me: and the life which I now live in the flesh [p]I live by the faith of the Son of God, [q]who loved me, and gave himself for me.

CHAP. 2.

21 I do not frustrate the grace of God: for[r] if righteousness *come* by the law, then Christ is dead in vain.

For O, P, and Q, see preceding page (1011).

Q—CONTINUED.

Tit. 2. 14 Who gave himself for us, that he might redeem us from all iniquity, and

§ 415. THE RIGHTEOUS SHALL LIVE BY FAITH

3: 1–14.

1 O foolish Galatians, [a]who hath bewitched you, that ye should not obey the truth,[b] before whose eyes Jesus Christ hath been evidently set forth, crucified among you?

2 This only would I learn of you, Received ye[c] the Spirit by the works of the law[d], or by the hearing of faith?

3 Are ye so foolish? [e]having begun in the Spirit, are ye now made perfect by the [f]flesh?

4 [g]Have ye suffered so many things in vain? if *it be* yet in vain.

5 He therefore [h]that ministereth to you the Spirit, and worketh miracles among you, *doeth he it* by the works of the law, or by the hearing of faith?

6 Even as [1]Abraham believed God, and it was [2]accounted to him for righteousness.

7 Know ye therefore that [k]they which are of faith, the same are the children of Abraham.

8 And the [l]Scripture, foreseeing that God would justify the heathen through faith, preached before the gospel unto Abraham, *saying*, [m]In thee shall all nations be blessed.

CHAP. 3.

9 So then they which be of faith are blessed with faithful Abraham.

10 For as many as are of the works of the law are under the curse: for it is written, [n]Cursed *is* every one that continueth not in all things which are written in the book of the law to do them.

11 But [o]that no man is justified by the law in the sight of God, *it is* evident: for, [p]The just shall live by faith.

12 And [q]the law is not of faith: but, [r]The man that doeth them shall live in them.

A

Gal. 5. 7 Ye did run well; who did hinder, you that ye should not obey the truth?

B

1 Cor. 1. 23 But we preach Christ crucified, unto the Jews a stumblingblock, and unto the Greeks foolishness:

C

Acts 2. 38 Then Peter said unto them, Repent, and be baptized every one of you in the name of Jesus Christ for the remission of sins, and ye shall receive the gift of the Holy Ghost.

Acts 10. 47 Can any man forbid water, that these should not be baptized, which have received the Holy Ghost as well as we?

Acts 15. 8 And God, which knoweth the hearts, bear them witness, giving them the Holy Ghost, even as *he did* unto us;

Eph. 1. 13 In whom ye also *trusted*, after that ye heard the word of truth, the gospel of your salvation: in whom also, after that ye believed, ye were sealed with that Holy Spirit of promise,

AT ANTIOCH (CONCLUDED).

Q—CONCLUDED

purify unto himself a peculiar people, zealous of good works.

R

Rom. 11. 6. *See g, G, § 339, page 862.*

Gal. 3. 21 *Is* the law then against the promise of God? God forbid: for if there had been a law given which could have given life, verily righteousness should have been by the law.

Heb. 7. 11 If therefore perfection were by the

R—CONCLUDED.

Levitical priesthood, (for under it the people received the law,) what further need *was there* that another priest should rise after the order of Melchisedec, and not be called after the order of Aaron?

Gal. 5. 4 Christ is become of no effect unto you, whosoever of you are justified by the law; ye are fallen from grace.

AND NOT BY THE WORKS OF THE LAW.

C—CONCLUDED.

Heb. 6. 4 For *it is* impossible for those who were once enlightened, and have tasted of the heavenly gift, and were made partakers of the Holy Ghost,

D

Rom. 10. 16 But they have not all obeyed the gospel. For Esaias saith, Lord, who who hath believed our report?
17 So then faith *cometh* by hearing, and hearing by the word of God.

E

Gal. 4. 9 But now, after that ye have known God, or rather are known of God, how turn ye again to the weak and beggarly elements, whereunto ye desire again to be in bondage?

F

Heb. 7. 16 Who is made, not after the law of a carnal commandment, but after the power of an endless life.

Heb 9. 10 *Which stood* only in meats and drinks, and divers washings, and carnal ordinances, imposed *on them* until the time of reformation.

G

Heb. 10. 35 Cast not away therefore your confidence, which hath great recompense of reward.
36 For ye have need of patience, that, after ye have done the will of God, ye might receive the promise.

II John 8 Look to yourselves, that we lose not those things which we have wrought, but that we receive a full reward.

1

Or, *so great.*

H

II Cor. 3. 8. *See r, R, § 390, page, 970.*

I

Rom. 4. 3. *See c, C, § 325, page 826.*

2

Or, *imputed.*

R

John 8. 39 They answered and said unto him, Abraham is our father. Jesus saith unto them, If ye were Abraham's children, ye would do the works of Abraham.

Rom. 4. 11. *See k, K, § 325, page 828.*

L

Rom. 9. 17 For the Scripture saith unto Pharaoh, Even for this same purpose have I raised thee up, that I might shew my power in thee, and that my name might be declared throughout all the earth.

Gal. 3. 22. *See text of § 416, page 1014.*

M

Acts 3. 25. *See u, U, § 234, page 646.*

N

Deut. 27. 26 Cursed *be* he that confirmeth not *all* the words of this law to do them: and all the people shall say, Amen.

Jer. 11. 3 And say thou unto them, Thus saith the Lord God of Israel; Cursed *be* the man that obeyeth not the words of this covenant.

O

Rom. 3. 20. *See c, C, § 324, page 824.*

P

Rom. 1. 17. *See p, P, § 318, page 810.*

Q

Rom. 11. 6 And if by grace, then *is it* no more of works: otherwise grace is no more grace. But if *it be* of works, then is it no more grace: otherwise work is no more work.

R

Rom. 10. 5 *See e, E, § 337, page 858.*

S

Matt 20. 28. *See y, Y § 148, page 420.*

II Cor. 5. 21. *See q, Q, § 395, page 975.*

T

Deut. 21. 23 His body shall not remain all night upon the tree, but thou shalt in any wise bury him that day; (for he that is hanged *is* accursed of God;) that

For T concluded, see next page (1014).

§ 415. THE RIGHTEOUS SHALL LIVE BY FAITH

CHAP. 3.

13 [s]Christ hath redeemed us from the curse of the law, being made a curse for us: for it is written,[t]Cursed *is* every one that hangeth on a tree:
14 [u]That the blessing of Abraham might come on the Gentiles through Jesus Christ; that we might receive [x]the promise of the Spirit through faith.

For S and T, see preceeding page, (1013).

T—CONCLUDED.

thy land be not defiled, which the LORD thy God giveth thee *for* an inheritance.

U

Rom. 4. 9 *Cometh* this blessedness then upon the circumcision *only*, or upon the uncircumcision also? for we say that faith was reckoned to Abraham for righteousness.

Rom. 4. 16 Therefore *it is* of faith, that *it might be* by grace; to the end the

§ 416. THE LAW WAS ADDED BECAUSE OF TRANS-

3 : 15–22.

15 Brethren, I speak after the manner of men; [a]Though *it be* but a man's [1]covenant, yet *if it be* confirmed, no man disannulleth, or addeth thereto.

16 Now [b]to Abraham and his seed were the promises made. He saith not, And to seeds, as of many; but as of one, And to thy seed, which is [c]Christ.

17 And this I say, *that* the covenant, that was confirmed before of God in Christ, the law, [d]which was four hundred and thirty years after, cannot disannul, [e]that it should make the promise of none effect.

18 For if [f]the inheritance *be* of the law, *it is* no more of promise: but God gave *it* to Abraham by promise.

19 Wherefore then *serveth* the law? [g]It was added because of transgressions, till [h]the seed should come to whom the promise was made; *and it was* [i]ordained by angels in the hand [k]of a mediator.

20 Now a mediator is not *a mediator* of one, [l]but God is one.

21 *Is* the law then against the promises of God? God forbid: [m]for if there

CHAP. 3.

had been a law given which could have given life, verily righteousness should have been by the law.

22 But [n]the Scripture hath concluded [o]all under sin, [p]that the promise by faith of Jesus Christ might be given to them that believe.

A

Heb. 9. 17 For a testament *is* of force after men are dead: otherwise it is of no strength at all while the testator liveth.

1

Or, *testament*.

B

Gen. 12. 3 And I will bless them that bless thee, and curse him that curseth thee: and in thee shall all families of the earth be blessed.

Gen. 12. 7 And the LORD appeared unto Abram, and said, Unto thy seed will I give this land: and there builded he an altar unto the LORD, who appeared unto him.

Gen. 17. 7 And I will establish my covenant between me and thee and thy seed after thee in their generations, for an everlasting covenant, to be a God unto thee and to thy seed after thee.

C

I Cor. 12. 12. *See a, A, § 371, page 940.*

D

Ex. 12. 40 Now the sojourning of the children of Israel, who dwelt in Egypt, *was* four hundred and thirty years.

41 And it came to pass at the end of the four hundred and thirty years, even the selfsame day it came to pass,

AND NOT BY THE WORKS OF THE LAW (CONCLUDED).

U—CONCLUDED.

promise might be sure to all the seed; not to that only which is of the law, but to that also which is of the faith of Abraham; who is the father of us all,

X

Jer. 31. 33 But this *shall be* the covenant that I will make with the house of Israel; After those days, saith the LORD, I will put my law in their inward parts, and write it in their hearts; and will be their God, and they shall be my people.

X—CONCLUDED.

Jer. 32. 40 And I will make an everlasting covenant with them, that I will not turn away from them, to do them good; but I will put my fear in their hearts, that they shall not depart from me.

Eze. 39. 29 Neither will I hide my face any more from them: for I have poured out my Spirit upon the house of Israel, saith the Lord GOD.

John 7. 39. *See l, L, § 109, page 319.*

Acts 2. 17. *See b, B, § 231, page 636.*

GRESSIONS AND NOT TO DISANNULL THE PROMISES.

D—CONCLUDED.

that all the hosts of the LORD went out from the land of Egypt.

E

Rom. 4. 13. 14. *See m, M, § 325, page 828.*

F

Rom. 8. 17 And if children, then heirs; heirs of God, and joint heirs with Christ; if so be that we suffer with *him*, that we may be also glorified together.

G

John 15. 22 If I had not come and spoken unto them, they had not had sin: but now they have no cloak for their sin.

Rom. 4. 15 Because the law worketh wrath: for where no law is, *there is* no transgression.

Rom. 5. 20 Moreover the law entered, that the offence might abound. But where sin abounded, grace did much more abound:

Rom. 7. 8 But sin, taking occasion by the commandment, wrought in me all manner of concupiscence. For without the law sin *was* dead.

Rom. 7. 13 Was then that which is good made death unto me? God forbid. But sin, that it might appear sin, working death in me by that which is good; that sin by the commandment might become exceeding sinful.

I Tim. 1. 9 Knowing this, that the law is not made for a righteous man, but for the lawless and disobedient, for the ungodly and for sinners, for unholy and profane, for murderers of fathers and murderers of mothers, for manslayers,

H

Gal. 3. 16. *See text of topic.*

I

Acts 7. 38. *See s, S, § 246, page 672.*

I—CONCLUDED.

Acts 7. 53 Who have received the law by the disposition of angels, and have not kept *it*.

K

Ex. 20. 19 And they said unto Moses, Speak thou with us, and we will hear: but let not God speak with us, lest we die.

Ex. 20. 21 And the people stood afar off, and Moses drew near unto the thick darkness where God *was*.

22 And the LORD said unto Moses, Thus thou shalt say unto the children of Israel, Ye have seen that I have talked with you from heaven.

John 1. 17 For the law was given by Moses, *but* grace and truth came by Jesus Christ.

Acts 7. 38 This is he, that was in the church in the wilderness with the angel which spake to him in the mount Sina, and *with* our fathers: who received the lively oracles to give unto us:

I Tim. 2. 5 For *there is* one God, and one mediator between God and men, the man Christ Jesus;

L

Rom. 3. 29. 30. *See t, T, § 324, page 826.*

M

Gal. 2. 21. *See r, R, § 414, page 1012.*

N

Gal. 3. 8. *See text of topic, § 415, page 1012.*

O

Rom. 3. 9. *See a, A, § 323, page 822.*

Rom. 3. 19 Now we know that what things soever the law saith, it saith to them who are under the law: that every mouth may be stopped, and all the world may become guilty before God.

Rom. 11. 32. *See k, K, § 341, page 866.*

P

Rom. 4. 16. *See p, P, § 325, page 828.*

§ 417. THE LAW OUR

3:23–29.

23 But before faith came, we were kept under the law, shut up unto the faith which should afterwards be revealed.

24 Wherefore [a]the law was our schoolmaster *to bring us* unto Christ, [b]that we might be justified by faith.

25 But after that faith is come, we are no longer under a schoolmaster.

26 For ye [c]are all the children of God by faith in Christ Jesus.

27 For [d]as many of you as have been baptized into Christ [e]have put on Christ.

28 [f]There is neither Jew nor Greek, there is neither bond nor free, there is neither male nor female: for ye are all [g]one in Christ Jesus.

29 And [h]if ye *be* Christ's, then are ye Abraham's seed, and [i]heirs according to the promise.

A

Rom. 10. 4. *See d, D, § 337, page 858.*

Col. 2. 17 Which are a shadow of things to come; but the body *is* of Christ.

B

Gal. 2. 16. *See h, H, § 414, page 1010.*

C

Isa. 56. 5 Even unto them will I give in mine house and within my walls a place and a name better than of sons and of daughters: I will give them an everlasting name, that shall not be cut off.

John 1. 12 But as many as received him, to them gave he power to become the sons of God, *even* to them that believe on his name:

John 20. 17 Jesus said unto her, Touch me not; for I am not yet ascended to my Father: but go to my brethren, and say unto them, I ascend unto my Father, and your Father; and *to* my God, and your God.

Rom. 8. 14 For as many as are led by the Spirit of God, they are the sons of God.

15 For ye have not received the spirit of bondage again to fear; but ye have received the Spirit of adoption, whereby we cry, Abba, Father.

16 The Spirit itself beareth witness with our spirit, that we are the children of God:

§ 418. CHILDREN UNDER BONDAGE OF THE LAW

4:1–7.

1 Now I say, *That* the heir, as long as he is a child, differeth nothing from a servant, though he be lord of all;

2 But is under tutors and governors until the time appointed of the father.

3 Even so we, when we were children, [a]were in bondage under the [1]elements of the world:

4 But [b]when the fulness of the time was come, God sent forth his Son, [c]made [d]of a woman, [e]made under the law,

5 [f]To redeem them that were under the law, [g]that we might receive the adoption of sons.

A

IICor. 11. 20 For ye suffer, if a man bring you into bondage, if a man devour *you*, if a man take *of you*, if a man exalt himself, if a man smite you on the face.

Gal. 2. 4 And that because of false brethren unawares brought in, who came in privily to spy out our liberty which we have in Christ Jesus, that they might bring us into bondage:

Gal. 4. 9. *See text of topic, § 419, page 1018.*

Gal. 5. 1 Stand fast therefore in the liberty wherewith Christ hath made us free, and be not entangled again with the yoke of bondage.

Col. 2. 8 Beware lest any man spoil you through philosophy and vain deceit, after the tradition of men, after the rudiments of the world, and not after Christ.

Col. 2. 20 Wherefore if ye be dead with Christ from the rudiments of the world, why, as though living in the world, are ye subject to ordinances,

TUTOR UNTO CHRIST.

C—CONCLUDED.

Rom. 8. 17 And if children, then heirs; heirs of God, and joint heirs with Christ; if so be that we suffer with *him*, that we may be also glorified together.

II Cor. 6. 18 And will be a Father unto you, and ye shall be my sons and daughters, saith the Lord Almighty.

Eph. 1. 5 Having predestinated us unto the adoption of children by Jesus Christ to himself, according to the good pleasure of his will,

Eph. 5. 1 Be ye therefore followers of God, as dear children;

Phil. 2. 15 That ye may be blameless and harmless, the sons of God, without rebuke, in the midst of a crooked and perverse nation, among whom ye shine as lights in the world;

I Jno. 3. 1 Behold, what manner of love the Father hath bestowed upon us, that we should be called the sons of God: therefore the world knoweth us not, because it knew him not.

2 Beloved, now are we the sons of God, and it doth not yet appear what we shall be: but we know that, when he shall appear, we shall be like him; for we shall see him as he is.

Rev. 21. 7 He that overcometh shall inherit all things; and I will be his God, and he shall be my son.

D

Rom. 6. 3. *See c, C, § 328, page 834.*

E

Rom. 13. 14. *See t, T, § 343, page 874.*

F

Rom. 3. 22. *See i, I, § 324, page 824.*
I Cor. 12. 13. *See d, D, § 371, page 940.*

G

John 17. 21. *See o, O, § 191, page 547.*

H

Rom. 9. 7. *See r, R, § 335, page 852.*

I

Acts 26. 18 To open their eyes, *and* to turn *them* from darkness to light, and *from* the power of Satan unto God, that they may receive forgiveness of sins, and inheritance among them which are sanctified by faith that is in me.

Gal. 4. 7 Wherefore thou art no more a servant, but a son; and if a son, then an heir of God through Christ.

Gal. 4. 28 Now we, brethren, as Isaac was, are the children of promise.

Eph. 3. 6 That the Gentiles should be fellow heirs, and of the same body, and partakers of his promise in Christ by the gospel:

Jas. 2. 5 Hearken, my beloved brethren, Hath not God chosen the poor of this world rich in faith, and heirs of the kingdom which he hath promised to them that love him?

ARE SET FREE AND BECOME SONS BY ADOPTION.

A—CONCLUDED.

Heb. 9. 10 *Which stood* only in meats and drinks, and divers washings, and carnal ordinances, imposed *on them* until the time of reformation.

1

Or, *rudiments.*

B

Gen. 49. 10 The sceptre shall not depart from Judah, nor a lawgiver from between his feet, until Shiloh come; and unto him *shall* the gathering of the people *be*.

Mark 1. 15. *See d, D, § 26, page 86.*

C

John 1. 14 And the Word was made flesh, and dwelt among us, (and we beheld his glory, the glory as of the only begotten of the Father,) full of grace and truth.

Rom. 1. 3 Concerning his Son Jesus Christ our Lord, which was made of the seed of David according to the flesh:

Phil. 2. 7 But made himself of no reputation, and took upon him the form of a servant, and was made in the likeness of men:

C—CONCLUDED.

Heb. 2. 14 Forasmuch then as the children are partakers of flesh and blood, he also himself likewise took part of the same; that through death he might destroy him that had the power of death, that is, the devil;

D

Isa. 7. 14 Therefore the Lord himself shall give you a sign; Behold, a virgin shall conceive, and bear a son, and shall call his name Immanuel.

Mic. 5. 3 Therefore will he give them up, until the time *that* she which travaileth hath brought forth: then the remnant of his brethren shall return unto the children of Israel.

Matt. 1. 23 Behold, a virgin shall be with child, and shall bring forth a son, and they shall call his name Emmanuel, which being interpreted is, God with us.

For D concluded, E, F and G, see next page (1018).

§ 418. CHILDREN UNDER BONDAGE OF THE LAW ARE SET

CHAP. 4.

6 And because ye are sons, God hath sent forth [h]the Spirit of his Son into your hearts, crying, Abba, Father.

7 Wherefore thou art no more a servant, but a son; and [i]if a son, then an heir of God through Christ.

D—CONTINUED.

Luke 1. 31 And, behold, thou shalt conceive in thy womb, and bring forth a son, and shalt call his name JESUS.

D—CONCLUDED.

Luke 2. 7 And she brought forth her firstborn son, and wrapped him in swaddling clothes, and laid him in a manger; because there was no room for them in the inn.

E

Matt. 5. 17 Think not that I am come to destroy the law, or the prophets: I am not come to destroy, but to fulfil.

Luke 2. 27 And he came by the Spirit into the temple; and when the parents brought in the child Jesus, to do for him after the custom of the law.

§ 419. PAUL'S ANXIOUS CARE FOR

4:8–20.

8 Howbeit then, [a]when ye knew not God, [b]ye did service unto them which by nature are no gods.

9 But now, [c]after that ye have known God, or rather are known of God, [d]how turn ye [1]again to [e]the weak and beggarly [2]elements, whereunto ye desire again to be in bondage?

10 [f]Ye observe days, and months, and times, and years.

11 I am afraid of you, [g]lest I have bestowed upon you labour in vain.

12 Brethren, I beseech you, be as I *am;* for I *am* as ye *are:* [h]ye have not injured me at all.

13 Ye know how [i]through infirmity of the flesh I preached the gospel unto you [k]at the first.

14 And my temptation which was in my flesh ye despised not, nor rejected; but received me [l]as an angel of God, [m]*even* as Christ Jesus.

15 [3]Where is then the blessedness ye spake of? for I bear you record, that, if *it had been* possible, ye would have plucked out your own eyes, and have given them to me.

CHAP. 4.

16 Am I therefore become your enemy, [n]because I tell you the truth?

17 They [o]zealously affect you, *but* not well; yea, they would exclude [4]you, that ye might affect them.

18 But *it is* good to be zealously affected always in *a* good *thing*, and not only when I am present with you.

19 [p]My little children, of whom I travail in birth again until Christ be formed in you,

20 I desire to be present with you now, and to change my voice; for [5]I stand in doubt of you.

A

Eph. 2. 12 That at that time ye were without Christ, being aliens from the commonwealth of Israel, and strangers from the covenants of promise, having no hope, and without God in the world:

I Thes. 4. 5 Not in the lust of concupiscense, even as the Gentiles which know not God:

B

Rom. 1. 25 Who changed the truth of God into a lie, and worshipped and served the creature more than the Creator, who is blessed forever. Amen.

I Cor. 12. 2. *See b, B, § 370, page 936.*

C

I Cor. 8. 3. *See e, E, § 364, page 918.*

D

Gal. 3. 3 Are ye so foolish? having begun in the Spirit, are ye now made perfect by the flesh?

FREE AND BECOME SONS BY ADOPTION (Concluded).

F

Matt. 20. 28. *See y, Y, § 148, page 420.*

G

Gal. 3. 26. *See, c, C, § 417, page 1016.*

H

Rom. 5. 5. *See, i, I, § 326, page 832.*

Rom. 8. 15 For ye have not received the
spirit of bondage again to fear; but
ye have received the Spirit of adoption, whereby we cry, Abba, Father.

II Cor. 1. 22. *See, k, K, § 387, page 964.*

I

Rom. 8. 16 The Spirit itself beareth witness
with our spirit, that we are the children of God:

I—Concluded.

17 And if children, then heirs; heirs
of God, and joint heirs with Christ; if
so be that we suffer with *him*, that we
may also be glorified together.

Gal. 3. 29. *See, i, I, § 417, page 1016.*

Rev. 21. 7 He that overcometh shall inherit
all things; and I will be his God, and
he shall be my son.

Ps. 16. 5 The Lord *is* the portion of mine
inheritance and of my cup: thou main-
tainest my lot.
6 The lines are fallen unto me in
pleasant *places;* yea, I have a goodly
heritage.

THE BACKSLIDING GALATIANS.

D—Concluded.

Col. 2. 20 Wherefore if ye be dead with
Christ from the rudiments of the world,
why, as though living in the world,
are ye subject to ordinances.

1

Or, *back.*

E

Rom. 8. 3. *See e, E, § 332, page 842.*

2

Or, *rudiments,*

Gal. 4. 3 Even so we, when we were children, were in bondage under the elements of the world:

F

Rom. 14. 5. *See e, E, § 344, page 876.*

G

Gal. 2. 2. *See c, C, § 413, page 1008.*

H

II Cor. 2. 5 But if any have caused grief, he
hath not grieved me, but in part: that
I may not overcharge you all.

I

I Cor. 2. 3. *See e, E, § 352, page 894.*

K

Gal. 1. 6 I marvel that ye are so soon removed from him that called you into
the grace of Christ unto another gospel:

L

II Sa. 19. 27 And he hath slandered thy servant unto my lord the king; but my
lord the king *is* as an angel of God:
do therefore *what is* good in thine
eyes.

Mal. 2. 7 For the priest's lips should keep
knowledge, and they should seek the
law at his mouth: for he *is* the messenger f the Lord of hosts.

L—Concluded.

Lu. 12. 8 Also I say unto you, Whosoever
shall confess me before men, him shall
the Son of man also confess before the
angels of God:

M

Matt. 10. 40. *See n, N, § 77, page 238.*

I Thes. 2. 13 For this cause also thank we God
without ceasing, because, when ye received the word of God which ye heard
of us, ye received *it* not *as* the word
of men, but, as it is in truth, the word
of God, which effectually worketh also
in you that believe.

3

Or, *What was then.*

N

Gal. 2. 5 To whom we gave place by subjection, no, not for an hour; that the
truth of the gospel might continue
with you.

Gal. 2. 14 But when I saw that they walked
not uprightly according to the truth of
the gospel, I said unto Peter before
them all, If thou, being a Jew, livest
after the manner of Gentiles, and not
as do the Jews, why compellest thou
the Gentiles to live as do the Jews?

O

Rom. 10. 2 For I bear them record that they
have a zeal of God, but not according
to knowledge.

II Cor. 11. 2 For I am jealous over you with
Godly jealousy: for I have espoused
you to one husband, that I may present *you as* a chaste virgin to Christ.

4

Or, *us.*

P

Cor. 4. 15. *See b, B, § 358, page 904.*

5

Gr, *am perplexed for you.*

§ 420. THE ALLEGORY OF

4: 21–31; 5: 1.

21 Tell me, ye that desire to be under the law, do ye not hear the law?

22 For it is written, that Abraham had two sons, [a]the one by a bondmaid, [b]the other by a free woman.

23 But he *who was* of the bondwoman [c]was born after the flesh; [d]but he of the free woman *was* by promise.

24 Which things are an allegory; for these are the two [1]covenants; the one from the mount [2e]Sinai, which genderth to bondage, which is Agar.

25 For this Agar is Mount Sinai in Arabia, and [3]answereth to Jerusalem which now is, and is in bondage with her children.

26 But [f]Jerusalem which is above is free, which is the mother of us all.

27 For it is written, [g]Rejoice, *thou* barren that bearest not; break forth and cry, thou that travailest not, for the desolate hath many more children than she which hath a husband.

28 Now we, brethren, as Isaac was, [h]are the children of promise.

29 But as then [i]he that was born after the flesh persecuted him *that was born* after the Spirit, [k]even so *it is* now.

30 Nevertheless what saith [l]the Scripture? [m]Cast out the bondwoman and her son; for [n]the son of the bondwomen shall not be heir with the son of the free woman.

31 So then, brethren, we are not children of the bondwomen, [o]but of the free.

CHAP. 5.

1 Stand fast therefore in [p]the liberty wherewith Christ hath made us free, and be not entangled again [q]with the yoke of bondage.

A

Gen. 16. 15 And Hagar bare Abram a son: and Abram called his son's name, which Hagar bare, Ishmael.

B

Gen. 21. 2 For Sarah conceived, and bare Abraham a son in his old age, at the set time of which God had spoken to him.

C

Rom. 9. 7 Neither, because they are the seed of Abraham, *are they* all children; but, in Isaac shall thy seed be called.

8 That is They which are the children of the flesh, these *are* not the children of God; but the children of the promise are counted for the seed.

D

Gen. 18. 10 And he said, I will certainly return unto thee according to the time of life; and, lo, Sarah thy wife shall have a son. And Sarah heard *it* in the tent door, which *was* behind him.

Gen. 18. 14 Is any thing too hard for the LORD? At the time appointed I will return unto thee, according to the time of life, and Sarah shall have a son.

Gen. 21. 1 And the LORD visited Sarah as he had said, and the LORD did unto Sarah as he had spoken.

Gen. 21. 2. *See under B.*

§ 421. NEITHER CIRCUMCISION AVAILETH

5: 2–15.

2 Behold, I Paul say unto you, that [a]if ye be circumcised, Christ shall profit you nothing.

CHAP. 5.

3 For I testify again to every man that is circumcised, [b]that he is a debtor to do the whole law.

THE TWO COVENANTS.

D—CONCLUDED.

Heb. 11. 11 Through faith also Sarah herself received strength to conceive seed, and was delivered of a child when she was past age, because she judged him faithful who had promised,

1

Or, testament.

2

Gr. Sina,

E

Deut. 33. 2 And he said, The LORD came from Sinai, and rose up from Seir unto them; he shined forth from mount Paran, and he came with ten thousands of saints: from his right hand *went* a fiery law for them.

3

Or, is in the same rank with.

F

Isa. 2. 2 And it shall come to pass in the last days, *that* the mountain of the LORD'S house shall be established in the top of the mountains, and shall be exalted above the hills; and all nations shall flow unto it.

Heb. 12. 22 But ye are come unto mount Sion, and unto the city of the living God, the heavenly Jerusalem, and to an innumerable company of angels,

Rev. 3. 12 Him that overcometh will I make a pillar in the temple of my God, and he shall go no more out: and I will write upon him the name of my God, and the name of the city of my God, *which is* new Jerusalem, which cometh down out of heaven from my God: and *I will write upon him* my new name.

Rev. 21. 2 And I John saw the holy city, new Jerusalem, coming down from God out of heaven, prepared as a bride adorned for her husband.

Rev. 21. 10 And he carried me away in the spirit to a great and high mountain, and showed me that great city, the holy Jerusalem, descending out of heaven from God,

G

Isa. 54. 1 Sing O barren, thou *that* didst not hear; break forth into singing, and cry aloud, thou *that* didst not travail with child: for more *are* the desolate than the children of the married wife, saith the LORD.

H

Acts 3. 25. *See t, T, § 234, page 646.*

I

Gen. 21. 9 And Sarah saw the son of Hagar the Egyptain, which she had borne unto Abraham, mocking.

K

John 15. 19 If ye were of the world, the world would love his own; but because ye are not of the world, but I have chosen you out of the world, therefore the world hateth you.

Gal. 5. 11 And I brethren, if I yet preach circumcision, why do I yet suffer persecution? then is the offence of the cross ceased.

Gal. 6. 12 As many as desire to make a fair show in the flesh, they constrain you to be circumcised; only lest they should suffer persecution for the cross of Christ,

L

Gal. 3. 8. *See l, L, § 415, page 1012.*

M

Gen. 21. 10 Wherefore she said unto Abraham, Cast out this bondwomen and her son: for the son of this bondwomen shall not be heir with my son, *even* with Isaac,

N

John 8. 35 And the servant abideth not in the house for ever: *but* the Son abideth ever,

O

John 8. 36. *See l, L, § 111, page 329.*

P

John 8. 32. *See g, G, § 111, page 327.*

Q

Gal. 4. 3. *See a, A, § 418, page 1016.*

ANYTHING NOR UNCIRCUMCISION.

A

Acts 15. 1. *See b, B, § 267, page 726.*

B

Gal. 3. 10 For as many as are of the works of the law are under the curse: for it is written, Cursed *is* every one that continueth not in all things which are written in the book of the law to do them.

C

Rom 11. 6. *See g, G, § 339, page 862.*

§ 421. NEITHER CIRCUMCISION AVAILETH ANY-

CHAP. 5.

4 [c]Christ is become of no effect
unto you, whosoever of you are justified by the law; [d]ye are fallen from
grace.
5 For we through the Spirit [e]wait
for the hope of righteousness by faith.
6 For [f]in Jesus Christ neither circumcision availeth any thing, nor
uncircumcision; but [g]faith which
worketh by love.
7 Ye [h]did run well; [i1]who did hinder you that ye should not obey the
truth?
8 This persuasion *cometh* not of
him [k]that calleth you.
9 [l]A little leaven leaveneth the
whole lump.
10 [m]I have confidence in you
through the Lord, that ye will be
none otherwise minded: but [n]he that
troubleth you [o]shall bear his judgment, whosoever he be.
11 [p]And I, brethren, if I yet preach
circumcision, [q]why do I yet suffer
persecution? then is [r]the offence of
the cross ceased.
12 [s]I would they were even cut off
[t]which trouble you.
13 For, brethren, ye have been
called unto liberty; only [u]*use* not
liberty for an occasion to the flesh,
but [x]by love serve one another.
14 For [y]all the law is fulfilled in
one word, *even* in this; Thou shalt
love thy neighbour as thyself.
15 But if ye bite and devour one
another, take heed that ye be not
consumed one of another.

C—CONCLUDED. See preceding page.

Gal. 2. 21 I do not frustrate the grace of God: for if righteousness *come* by the law, then Christ is dead in vain.

D

Heb. 12. 15 Looking diligently lest any man fail of the grace of God; lest any root of bitterness springing up trouble *you*, and thereby many be defiled;

E

Rom. 8. 24 For we are saved by hope: but hope that is seen is not hope: for what a man seeth, why doth he yet hope for?
25 But if we hope for that we see not, *then* do we with patience wait for *it*.

IITim. 4. 8 Henceforth there is laid up for me a crown of righteousness, which the Lord, the righteous judge, shall give me at that day: and not to me only, but unto all them also that love his appearing.

F

I Cor. 7. 19. *See t, T, § 362, page 914.*

Col. 3. 11 Where there is neither Greek nor Jew, circumcision nor uncircumcision, Barbarian, Scythian, bond *nor* free: but Christ *is* all, and in all.

G

IThes. 1. 3 Remembering without ceasing your work of faith, and labour of love, and patience of hope in our Lord Jesus Christ, in the sight of God and our Father;

Jas. 2. 18 Yea, a man may say, Thou hast faith, and I have works: shew me thy faith without thy works, and I will shew thee my faith by my works.

Jas. 2. 20 But wilt thou know, O vain man, that faith without works is dead?

Jas. 2. 22 Seest thou how faith wrought with his works, and by works was faith made perfect?

H

I Cor. 9. 24. *See o, O, § 365, page 926.*

§ 422. THE SPIRIT AND THE FLESH

5:16–26.

16 *This* I say then, [a]Walk in the
Spirit, and [1]ye shall not fulfil the
lust of the flesh.
17 For [b]the flesh lusteth against the
Spirit, and the Spirit against the flesh:

A

Rom. 6. 12 Let not sin therefore reign in your mortal body, that ye should obey it in the lusts thereof.

Rom. 8. 1. *See a, A, § 332, page 842.*

Rom. 13. 14 But put ye on the Lord Jesus Christ, and make not provision for the

THING NOR UNCIRCUMCISION (CONCLUDED).

I

Gal. 3. 1 O foolish Galatians, who hath bewitched you, that ye should not obey the truth, before whose eyes Jesus Christ hath been evidently set forth, crucified among you?

1

Or, *who did drive you back.*

K

Gal. 1. 6 I marvel that ye are so soon removed from him that called you into the grace of Christ unto another gospel:

L

I Cor. 5. 6. *See l, L, § 359, page 906.*

M

II Cor. 2. 3. *See r, R, § 387, page 966.*

N

Acts 15. 24. *See b, B, § 269, page 730.*

O

IICor. 10. 6 And having in a readiness to revenge all disobedience, when your obedience is fulfilled.

P

Gal. 6. 12 As many as desire to make a fair shew in the flesh, they constrain you to be circumcised; only lest they should suffer persecution for the cross of Christ.

Q

I Cor. 15. 30 And why stand we in jeopardy every hour?

Gal. 4. 29. *See k, K, § 420, page 1020.*

R

I Cor. 1. 23. *See i, I, § 351, page 892.*

S

Josh. 7. 25 And Joshua said, Why hast thou troubled us? the LORD shall trouble thee this day. And all Israel stoned him with stones, and burned them with fire, after they had stoned them with stones.

Gal. 1. 8 But though we, or an angel from heaven, preach any other gospel unto

S—CONCLUDED.

you than that which we have preached unto you, let him be accursed.

9 As we said before, so say I now again, If any *man* preach any other gospel unto you than that ye have received, let him be accursed.

T

Acts 15. 24. *See b, B, § 269, page 730.*

U

I Cor. 8. 9 But take heed lest by any means this liberty of yours become a stumblingblock to them that are weak.

I Pet. 2. 16 As free, and not using *your* liberty for a cloak of maliciousness, but as the servants of God.

II Pet. 2. 19 While they promise them liberty, they themselves are the servants of corruption: for of whom a man is overcome, of the same is he brought in bondage.

Jude 4 For there are certain men crept in unawares, who were before of old ordained to this condemnation, ungodly men, turning the grace of our God into lasciviousness, and denying the only Lord God, and our Lord Jesus Christ.

X

I Cor. 9. 19 For though I be free from all *men*, yet have I made myself servant unto all, that I might gain the more.

Gal. 6. 2 Bear ye one another's burdens, and so fulfil the law of Christ.

Y

Matt. 7. 12 Therefore all things whatsoever ye would that men should do to you, do ye even so to them: for this is the law and the prophets.

Matt. 22. 39 And the second *is* like unto it, Thou shalt love thy neighbour as thyself.

40 On these two commandments hang all the law and the prophets.

Jas. 2. 8 If ye fulfil the royal law according to the Scripture, Thou shalt love thy neighbour as thyself, ye do well:

DISCERNED AND FOUND CONTRARY.

A—CONCLUDED.

flesh, to *fulfil* the lusts *thereof*.

I Pet. 2. 11 Dearly beloved, I beseech *you* as strangers and pilgrims, abstain from fleshly lusts, which war against the soul;

1

Or, *fulfil not.*

B

Rom. 7. 23 But I see another law in my members, warring against the law of my mind, and bringing me into captivity to the law of sin which is in my members.

For B concluded, see next page (1024).

§ 422. THE SPIRIT AND THE FLESH DIS-

CHAP. 5.

and these are contrary the one to
the other; [c]so that ye cannot do the
things that ye would.
18 But [d]if ye be led of the Spirit,
ye are not under the law.
19 Now [e]the works of the flesh are
manifest, which are *these;* Adultery,
fornication, uncleanness, lasciviousness,
20 Idolatry, witchcraft, hatred,
variance, emulations, wrath, strife,
seditions; heresies,
21 Envyings, murders, drunkenness, revellings, and such like: of
the which I tell you before, as I
have also told *you* in time past, that
[f]they which do such things shall not
inherit the kingdom of God.
22 But [g]the fruit of the Spirit is
love, joy, peace, longsuffering, [h]gen-
tleness, [i]goodness, [k]faith,
23 Meekness, temperance: [l]against
such there is no law.
24 And they that are Christ's [m]have
crucified the flesh with the [2]affec-
tions and lusts.

CHAP. 5.

25 [n]If we live in the Spirit, let us
also walk in the Spirit.
26 [o]Let us not be desirous of vainglory, provoking one another, envying one another.

B—CONCLUDED.

Rom. 8. 6 For to be carnally minded *is* death; but to be spiritually minded *is* life and peace.

7 Because the carnal mind *is* enmity against God: for it is not subject to the law of God, neither indeed can be.

C

Rom. 7. 15, 19. *See g, G., § 331, page 840.*

D

Rom. 6. 14. *See x, X, § 328, page 836.*

E

Mark 7. 21 For from within, out of the heart of men, proceed evil thoughts, adulteries, fornications, murders,

22 Thefts, covetousness, wickedness, deceit, laciviousness, an evil eye, blasphemy, pride, foolishness:

23 All these evil things come from within, and defile the man.

I Cor. 3. 3 For ye are yet carnal: for whereas *there is* among you envying, and strife, and divisions, are ye not carnal, and walk as men?

Eph. 5. 3 But fornication, and all uncleanness, or covetousness, let it not be once named among you, as becometh saints;

4 Neither filthiness, nor foolish talking, nor jesting, which are not convenient: but rather giving of thanks.

§ 423. EXHORTED TO BEAR WITH ONE ANOTHER

6: 1–10.

1 Brethren, [a1]if a man be overtaken
in a fault, ye [b]which are spiritual,
restore such a one [c]in the spirit of
meekness; considering thyself, [d]lest
thou also be tempted.
2 [e]Bear ye one another's burdens,
and so fulfil [f]the law of Christ.
3 For [g]if a man think himself to be
something, when [h]he is nothing, he
deceiveth himself.

A

Rom. 14. 1. *See a, A, § 344, page 876.*

Heb. 12. 13 And make straight paths for your feet, lest that which is lame be turned out of the way; but let it rather be healed.

Jas. 5. 19 Brethren, if any of you do err from the truth, and one convert him;

1

Or, *although.*

B

I Cor. 2. 15. *See a, A, § 352, page 896.*

C

I Cor. 4. 21 What will ye? shall I come unto you with a rod, or in love, and *in* the spirit of meekness?

CERNED AND FOUND CONTRARY (CONCLUDED).

E—CONCLUDED.

Eph. 5. 5 For this ye know, that no whoremonger, nor unclean person, nor covetous man, who is an idolater, hath any inheritance in the kingdom of Christ and of God.

Col. 3. 5 Mortify therefore your members which are upon the earth; fornication, uncleanness, inordinate affection, evil concupiscence, and covetousness, which is idolatry:

Jas. 3. 14 But if ye have bitter envying and strife in your hearts, glory not, and lie not against the truth.
15 This wisdom descendeth not from above, but *is* earthly, sensual, devilish.
16 For where envying and strife *is*, there *is* confusion and every evil work.

F

I Cor. 6. 9. *See f, F, § 360, page 910.*

Col. 3. 6 For which things' sake the wrath of God cometh on the children of disobedience:

G

John 15. 2 Every branch in me that beareth not fruit he taketh away: and every *branch* that beareth fruit, he purgeth it, that it may bring forth more fruit.

Eph. 5. 9 (For the fruit of the Spirit *is* in all goodness and righteousness and truth;)
10 Proving what is acceptable unto the Lord.

Phil. 1. 11 Being filled with the fruits of righteousness, which are by Jesus Christ, unto the glory and praise of God.

H

Col. 3. 12 Put on therefore, as the elect of God, holy and beloved, bowels of mercies, kindness, humbleness of mind, meekness, longsuffering;

Jas. 3. 17 But the wisdom that is from above is first pure, then peaceable, gentle, *and* easy to be entreated, full of mercy and good fruits, without partiality, and without hypocrisy.

I

Rom. 15. 14 And I myself also am persuaded of you, my brethren, that ye also are full of goodness, filled with all knowledge, able also to admonish one another.

K

I Cor. 13. 7 Beareth all things, believeth all things, hopeth all things, endureth all things.

L

I Tim. 1. 9 Knowing this, that the law is not made for a rightous man, but for the lawless and disobedient, for the ungodly and for sinners, for unholy and profane, for murderers of fathers and murderers of mothers, for manslayers.

M

Rom. 6. 6. *See k, K, § 328, page 836.*

2

Or, *passion.*

N

Rom. 8. 4, 5. *See g, G, § 332, page 842.*

Phil. 2. 3 *Let* nothing *be done* through strife or vainglory; but in lowliness of mind let each esteem other better than themselves.

AND NOT TO WEARY IN WELL DOING.

C—CONCLUDED.

II Thes. 3. 15 Yet count *him* not as an enemy, but admonish *him* as a brother.

II Tim. 2. 25 In meekness instructing those that oppose themselves; if God peradventure will give them repentance to the acknowledging of the truth;

D

I Cor. 7. 5 Defraud ye not one the other, except *it be* with consent for a time, that ye may give yourselves to fasting and prayer; and come together again, that Satan tempt you not for your incontinency.

I Cor. 10. 12 Wherefore let him that thinketh he standeth take heed lest he fall.

E

Ex. 23. 5 If thou see the ass of him that hateth thee lying under his burden, and wouldest forbear to help him, thou shalt surely help with him.

Isa. 58. 6 *Is* not this the fast that I have chosen? to loose the bands of wickedness, to undo the heavy burdens, and to let the oppressed go free, and that ye brake every yoke?

Rom. 15. 1 We then that are strong ought to bear the infirmities of the weak, and not to please ourselves.

Gal. 5. 13 For, brethren, ye have been called unto liberty; only *use* not liberty for

For E concluded, F, G and H, see next page (1026).

§ 423. EXHORTED TO BEAR WITH ONE ANOTHER AND

CHAP. 6.

4 But [i]let every man prove his own work, and then shall he have rejoicing in himself alone, and [k]not in another.

5 [l]For every man shall bear his own burden.

6 [m]Let him that is taught in the word communicate unto him that teacheth in all good things.

7 Be not deceived; [n]God is not mocked: for [o]whatsoever a man soweth, that shall he also reap.

8 [p]For he that soweth to his flesh shall of the flesh reap corruption; but he that soweth to the Spirit shall of the Spirit reap life everlasting.

9 And [q]let us not be weary in well doing: for in due season we shall reap, [r]if we faint not.

10 [s]As we have therefore opportunity, [t]let us do good unto all *men*, especially unto them who are of [u]the household of faith.

E - CONCLUDED.

an occasion to the flesh, but by love serve one another.

I Thes. 5. 14 Now we exhort you, brethren, warn them that are unruly, comfort the feebleminded, support the weak, be patient toward all *men*.

F

John 13. 14 If I then, *your* Lord and Master, have washed your feet; ye also ought to wash one another's feet.

15 For I have given you an example, that ye should do as I have done to you.

G

Rom. 12. 3 For I say, through the grace given unto me, to every man that is among you, not to think *of himself* more highly than he ought to think; but to think soberly, according as God hath dealt to every man the measure of faith.

I Cor. 8. 2. *See d, D, § 364, page 918.*

H

II Cor. 3. 5 Not that we are sufficient of ourselves to think any thing as of ourselves; but our sufficiency *is* of God:

II Cor. 12. 11 I am become a fool in glorying; ye have compelled me: for I ought to have been commended of you: for in nothing am I behind the very chiefest apostles, though I be nothing.

I

I Cor. 11. 28. *See l, L, § 369, page 936.*

K

Luke 18. 11 The Pharisee stood and prayed thus with himself, God, I thank thee, that I am not as other men *are*, extortioners, unjust, adulterers, or even as this publican.

L

Rom. 2. 6. *See h, H, § 320, page 816.*

§ 424. GLORY ONLY IN THE CROSS

6:11–18.

11 Ye see how large a letter I have written unto you with mine own hand.

12 As many as desire to make a fair shew in the flesh, [a]they constrain you to be circumcised; [b]only lest they should [c]suffer persecution for the cross of Christ.

13 For neither they themselves who are circumcised keep the law; but desire to have you circumcised, that they may glory in your flesh.

14 [d]But God forbid that I should

A

Gal. 2. 3 But neither Titus, who was with me, being a Greek, was compelled to be circumcised:

Gal. 2. 14 But when I saw that they walked not uprightly according to the truth of the gospel, I said unto Peter before *them* all, If thou, being a Jew, livest after the manner of Gentiles, and not as do the Jews, why compellest thou the Gentiles to live as do the Jews?

B

Phil. 3. 18 (For many walk, of whom I have told you often, and now tell you even weeping, *that they are* the enemies of the cross of Christ:

C

Gal. 5. 11 And I, brethren, if I yet preach circumcision, why do I yet suffer per-

NOT TO WEARY IN WELL DOING (Concluded).

M

Rom. 15. 27. *See r, R, § 346, page 882.*

N

Job 13. 7 Will ye speak wickedly for God? and talk deceitfully for him?

8 Will ye accept his person? will ye contend for God?

9 Is it good that he should search you out? or as one man mocketh another, do ye *so* mock him?

22 Now therefore be ye not mockers, lest your bands be made strong: for I have heard from the Lord GOD of hosts a consumption, even determined upon the whole earth.

O

Luke 16. 25 But Abraham said, Son, remember that thou in thy lifetime receivedst thy good things, and likewise Lazarus evil things: but now he is comforted, and thou art tormented.

Rom. 2. 6 Who will render to every man according to his deeds:

II Cor. 9. 6. *See f, F, § 401, page 988.*

P

Job 4. 8 Even as I have seen, they that plough iniquity, and sow wickedness, reap the same.

Q

I Cor. 15. 58 Therefore, my beloved brethren, be ye steadfast, unmoveable, always abounding in the work of the Lord, forasmuch as ye know that your labour is not in vain in the Lord.

II Thes. 3. 13 But ye, brethren, be not weary in well doing.

R

Matt. 24. 13. *See m, M, § 172, page 484.*

S

John 9. 4 I must work the works of him that sent me, while it is day: the night cometh, when no man can work.

John 12. 35 Then Jesus said unto them, Yet a little while is the light with you. Walk while ye have the light, lest darkness come upon you: for he that walketh in darkness knoweth not whither he goeth.

T

I Thes. 5. 15 See that none render evil for evil unto any *man;* but ever follow that which is good, both among yourselves, and to all *men.*

I Tim. 6. 18 That they do good, that they be rich in good works, ready to distribute, willing to communicate:

Tit. 3. 8 *This is* a faithful saying, and these things I will that thou affirm constantly, that they which have believed in God might be careful to maintain good works. These things are good and profitable unto men.

U

Eph. 2. 19 Now therefore ye are no more strangers and foreigners, but fellow citizens with the saints, and of the household of God;

Heb. 3. 6 But Christ as a son over his own house; whose house are we, if we hold fast the confidence and the rejoicing of the hope firm unto the end.

OF CHRIST; CONCLUSION; BENEDICTION.

C—Concluded.

secution? then is the offence of the cross ceased.

D

Phil. 3. 3 For we are the circumcision, which worship God in the spirit, and rejoice in Christ Jesus, and have no confidence in the flesh.

Phil. 3. 7 But what things were gain to me, those I counted loss for Christ.

8 Yea doubtless, and I count all things *but* loss for the excellency of the knowledge of Christ Jesus my Lord: for whom I have suffered the loss of all things, and do count them *but* dung, that I may win Christ,

1

Or, *whereby.*

E

Rom. 6. 6 Knowing this, that our old man is crucified with *him*, that the body of sin might be destroyed, that henceforth we should not serve sin.

Gal. 2. 20 I am crucified with Christ: nevertheless I live; yet not I, but Christ liveth in me: and the life which I now live in the flesh I live by the faith of the Son of God, who loved me, and gave himself for me.

F

I Cor. 7. 19. *See t, T, § 362, page 914.*

Col. 3. 11 Where there is neither Greek nor Jew, circumcision nor uncircumcision, Barbarian, Scythian, bond *nor* free: but Christ *is* all, and in all.

§ 424. GLORY ONLY IN THE CROSS OF CHRIST;

CHAP. 6.

glory, save in the cross of our Lord
Jesus Christ, [1]by whom the world is
[e]crucified unto me, and I unto the
world.

15 For [f]in Christ Jesus neither circumcision availeth any thing, nor
uncircumcision, but [g]a new creature.

16 [h]And as many as walk [i]according
to this rule, peace *be* on them, and
mercy, and upon [k]the Israel of God.

17 From henceforth let no man
trouble me: for [l]I bear in my body
the marks of the Lord Jesus.

18 Brethren, [m]the grace of our Lord
Jesus Christ *be* with your spirit.
Amen.

For 1, E and F, see preceding page (1027).

G

IICor. 5. 17 Therefore if any man *be* in Christ *he is* a new creature: old things are passed away; behold, all things are become new.

H

Ps. 125. 5 As for such as turn aside unto their crooked ways, the LORD shall lead them forth with the workers of iniquity: *but* peace *shall be* upon Israel.

I

Phil. 3. 18 (For many walk, of whom I have told you often, and now tell you even weeping, *that they are* the enemies of Christ:

K

Rom. 2. 29 But he *is* a Jew, which is one inwardly; and circircumcision *is that* of the heart, in the spirit, *and* not in the letter; whose praise *is* not of men, but of God.

PAUL'S EPISTLE TO

§ 425. THE SALUTATION

1: 1, 2.

1 Paul, an apostle of Jesus Christ
[a]by the will of God, [b]to the saints
which are at Ephesus, [c]and to the
faithful in Christ Jesus:

2 [d]Grace *be* to you, and peace, from
God our Father, and *from* the Lord
Jesus Christ.

A

II Cor. 1. 1 Paul, an apostle of Jesus Christ by the will of God, and Timothy *our* brother, unto the church of God which is at Corinth, which are in all Achaia:

B

Rom. 1. 7 To all that be in Rome, beloved of God, called *to be* saints: Grace to you and peace from God our Father, and the Lord Jesus Christ.

I Cor. 1. 2 Unto the church of God which is at Corinth, to them that are sanctified in

§ 426. THANKSGIVING FOR SONSHIP, REDEMPTION, FORGIVE-

1: 3–14.

3 [a]Blessed *be* the God and Father of
our Lord Jesus Christ, who hath
blessed us with all spiritual blessings
in heavenly [1]*places* in Christ:

4 According as [b]he hath chosen us
in him [c]before the foundation of the

A

II Cor. 1. 3. *See a, A,* § *386, page 962.*

1

Or, Things.

Eph. 6. 12 For we wrestle not against flesh and blood, but against principalities, against powers, against the rulers of the darkness of this world, against spiritual wickedness in high *places*.

B

Rom. 8. 28. *See f, F,* § *334, page 848.*

CONCLUSION; BENEDICTION (CONCLUDED).

K—CONTINUED.

Rom. 4. 12 And the father of circumcision to them who are not of the circumcision only, but who also walk in the steps of that faith of our father Abraham, which *he had* being *yet* uncircumcised.

Rom. 9. 6 Not as though the word of God hath taken none effect. For they *are* not all Israel, which are of Israel:
7 Neither, because they are the seed of Abraham, *are they* all children: but, in Isaac shall thy seed be called.
8 That is, They which are the children of the flesh, these *are* not the children of God: but the children of the promise are counted for the seed.

Gal. 3. 7 Know ye therefore that they which are of faith, the same are the children of Abraham.

Gal. 3. 9 So then they which be of faith are blessed with faithful Abraham.

Gal. 3. 29 And if ye *be* Christ's, then are ye Abraham's seed, and heirs according to the promise.

K—CONCLUDED.

Phil. 3. 3 For we are the circumcision, which worship God in the spirit, and rejoice in Christ Jesus, and have no confidence in the flesh.

L

II Cor. 1. 5. *See b, B, § 386, page 962.*

II Cor. 11.23 Are they ministers of Christ? (I speak as a fool) I *am* more; in labours more abundant, in stripes above measure, in prisons more frequent, in deaths oft.

Gal. 5. 11 And I, brethren, If I yet preach circumcision, why do I yet suffer persecution? then is the offence of the cross ceased.

M

II Tim. 4. 22 The Lord Jesus Christ *be* with thy spirit. Grace *be* with you. Amen.

Phile. 25 The grace of our Lord Jesus Christ *be* with your spirit. Amen.

THE EPHESIANS.

Written probably during Spring of A. D. 62 at Rome.

B—CONCLUDED.

Christ Jesus, called *to be* saints, with all that in every place call upon the name of Jesus Christ our Lord, both theirs and ours:

C

I Cor. 4. 17 For this cause have I sent unto you Timotheus, who is my beloved son, and faithful in the Lord, who shall bring you into remembrance of my ways which be in Christ, as I teach everywhere in every church.

C—CONCLUDED.

Eph. 6. 21 But that ye also may know my affairs, *and* how I do, Tychicus, a beloved brother and faithful minister in the Lord, shall make known to you all things:

Col. 1. 2 To the saints and faithful brethren in Christ which are at Colosse: Grace *be* unto you, and peace, from God our Father and the Lord Jesus Christ.

D

II Cor. 1, 2. *See c, C, § 385, page 962.*

NESS AND KNOWLEDGE OF THE MYSTERY OF THE WILL OF GOD.

B—CONTINUED.

II Thes. 2. 13 But we are bound to give thanks always to God for you, brethren beloved of the Lord, because God hath from the beginning chosen you to salvation through santification of the Spirit and belief of the truth:

Jas. 2. 5 Harken, my beloved brethren, Hath not God chosen the poor of this world rich in faith, and heirs of the

B—CONCLUDED.

kingdom which he hath promised to them that love him?

I Pet. 1. 2 Elect according to the foreknowledge of God the Father, through sanctification of the Spirit, unto obedience and sprinkling of the blood of Jesus Christ: Grace unto you, and peace, be multiplied.

For B, concluded, and C, see next page (1030).

§ 426. THANKSGIVING FOR SONSHIP, REDEMPTION, FORGIVENESS

CHAP. I.

world, that we should [d]be holy and
without blame before him in love:
5 [e]Having predestinated us unto
[f]the adoption of children by Jesus
Christ to himself, [g]according to the
good pleasure of his will,
6 To the praise of the glory of his
grace, [h]wherein he hath made us accepted in [i]the beloved.
7 [k]In whom we have redemption
through his blood, the forgiveness of
sins, according to [l]the riches of his
grace;
8 Wherein he hath abounded toward us in all wisdom and prudence;
9 [m]Having made known unto us the
mystery of his will, according to his
good pleasure [n]which he hath purposed in himself:
10 That in the dispension of [o]the
fulness of times [p]he might gather together in one all things in Christ, both
which are in [1]heaven, and which are
on earth; *even* in him:
11 [q]In whom also we have obtained
an inheritance, [r]being predestinated
according to [s]the purpose of him
who worketh all things after the
counsel of his own will:
12 [t]That we should be to the praise
of his glory, [u]who first [2]trusted in
Christ.
13 In whom ye also *trusted*, after
that ye heard [x]the word of truth, the
gospel of your salvation: in whom
also, after that ye believed, [y]ye were
sealed with that Holy Spirit of
promise,
14 [z]Which is the earnest of our inheritance [a]until the redemption of
[b]the purchased possession, [c]unto the
praise of his glory.

B—CONCLUDED.

I Pet. 2. 9 But ye *are* a chosen generation, a royal priesthood, a holy nation, a peculiar people; that ye should shew forth the praises of him who hath called you out of darkness into his marvelous light:

C

I Pet. 1. 2. *See under B, page 1029.*

I Pet. 1. 20 Who verily was foreordained before the foundation of the world, but was manifest in these last times for you.

D

Luke 1. 75 In holiness and righteousness before him, all the days of our life.

Eph. 5. 27. *See n, N, § 435, page 1052.*

Col. 1. 22 In the body of his flesh through death, to present you holy and unblamable and unreprovable in his sight:

I Thes. 4. 7 For God hath not called us unto uncleanness, but unto holiness.

Tit. 2. 12 Teaching us that, denying ungodliness and worldly lusts, we should live soberly, righteously, and godly, in this present world;

E

Acts 13. 48. *See f, F, § 263, page 718.*

Rom. 8. 29 For whom he did foreknow, he also did predestinate *to be* conformed to the image of his Son, that he might be the firstborn among many brethren.

30 Moreover whom he did predestinate, them he also called: and whom he called, them he also justified: and whom he justified, them he also glorified.

F

Gal. 3. 26. *See c, C, § 417, page 1016.*

Gal. 4. 5 To redeem them that were under the law, that we might receive the adoption of sons.

G

Luke 12. 32. *See c, C, § 57, page 189.*

H

Rom. 3. 24 Being justified freely by his grace through the redemption that is in Christ Jesus:

Rom. 5. 15 But not as the offence, so also *is* the free gift. For if through the offence of one many be dead, much more the grace of God, and the gift by grace, *which is* by one man, Jesus Christ, hath abonnded unto many.

I

Matt. 3. 17. *See g, G, § 15, page 52.*

K

Acts 20. 28. *See s, S, § 292, page 762.*

L

Rom. 2. 4. *See c, C, § 320, page 814.*

Eph. 3. 8 Unto me, who am less than the least of all saints, is this grace given, that I should preach among the Gentiles the unsearchable riches of Christ:

AND KNOWLEDGE OF THE MYSTERY OF THE WILL OF GOD (COUCLUDED).

L—CONCLUDED.

Eph. 3. 16 That he would grant you, according to the riches of his glory, to be strengthened with might by his Spirit in the inner man;

Phil. 4. 19 But my God shall supply all your need according to his riches in glory by Christ Jesus.

M

Rom. 16. 25. *See d, D, § 347, page 886.*

N

Eph 3. 11 According to the eternal purpose which he purposed in Christ Jesus our Lord:

II Tim. 1. 9 Who hath saved us, and called *us* with a holy calling, not according to our works, but according to his own purpose and grace, which was given us in Christ Jesus before the world began,

O

Gal. 4. 4 But when the fullness of the time was come, God sent forth his Son, made of a woman, made under the law,

Heb. 1. 2 Hath in these last days spoken unto us by *his* Son, whom he hath appointed heir of all things, by whom also he made the worlds;

Heb. 9. 10 *Which stood* only in meats and drinks, and divers washings, and carnal ordinances, imposed *on them* until the time of reformation.

I Pet. 1. 20 Who verily was foreordained before the foundation of the world, but was manifest in these last times for you,

P

I Cor. 3. 22 Whether Paul, or Apollos, or Cephas, or the world, or life, or death, or things present, or things to come; all are yours;

23 And ye are Christ's; and Christ *is* God's.

I Cor. 11. 3 But I would have you know, that the head of every man is Christ; and the head of the woman *is* the man; and the head of Christ *is* God.

Eph. 2. 15 Having abolished in his flesh the enmity, *even* the law of commandments *contained* in ordinances; for to make in himself of twain one new man, *so* making peace;

Eph. 3. 15 Of whom the whole family in heaven and earth is named,

Phil. 2. 9 Wherefore God also hath highly exalted him, and given him a name which is above every name:

10 That at the name of Jesus every knee should bow of *things* in heaven, and *things* in earth, and *things* under the earth;

1

Gr. *the heavens.*

Q

Acts 20. 32. *See b, B, § 292, page 764.*

Rom. 8. 17 And if children, then heirs; heirs of God, and joint heirs of Christ; if so be that we suffer with *him*, that we may be also glorified together.

Tit. 3. 7 That being justified by his grace, we should be made heirs according to the hope of eternal life.

Jas. 2. 5 Hearken, my beloved brethren, Hath not God chosen the poor of this world rich in faith, and heirs of the kingdom which he hath promised to them that love him?

I Pet. 1. 4 To an inheritance incorruptible, and undefiled, and that fadeth not away, reserved in heaven for you,

R

Rom. 8. 29. etc. *See under E.*

S

Isa. 46. 10 Declaring the end from the beginning, and from ancient times *the things* that are not *yet* done, saying, My counsel shall stand, and I will do all my pleasure:

11 Calling a ravenous bird from the east, the man that executeth my counsel from a far country: yea, I have spoken *it*, I will also bring it to pass; I have purposed *it*, I will also do it.

Eph. 3. 11. etc. *See under N.*

T

Eph. 1. 6, 14. *See text of topic.*

II Thes. 2. 13. *See under B.*

U

Jas. 1. 18 Of his own will begat he us with the word of truth, that we should be a kind of firstfruits of his creatures.

2

Or, *hoped.*

X

John 1. 17 For the law was given by Moses, *but* grace and truth came by Jesus Christ.

II Cor. 4. 2. *See d, D, § 392, page 972.*

Y

II Cor. 1. 22. *See i, I, § 387, page 964.*

Z

II Cor. 1. 22. *See k, K, § 387, page 964.*

A

Rom. 8. 23. *See i, I, § 333, page 846.*

B

Acts 20. 28. *See s, S, § 292, page 762.*

C

Eph. 1. 6. 12. *See text of topic.*

I Pet. 2. 9. *See under B.*

§ 427. PAUL GIVES THANKS FOR THEIR FAITH

1 : 15–23.

15 Wherefore I also, [a]after I heard
of your faith in the Lord Jesus, and
love unto all the saints,
16 [b]Cease not to give thanks for
you, making mention of you in my
prayers;
17 That [c]the God of our Lord Jesus
Christ, the Father of glory, [d]may give
unto you the spirit of wisdom and
revelation [1]in the knowledge of him:
18 [e]The eyes of your understanding
being enlightened; that ye may know
what is [f]the hope of his calling, and
what the riches of the glory of his
[g]inheritance in the saints,
19 And what *is* the exceeding greatness of his power to us-ward who believe, [h]according to the working [2]of
his mighty power,
20 Which he wrought in Christ,
when [i]he raised him from the dead,
and [k]set *him* at his own right hand
in the heavenly *places*,
21 [l]Far above all [m]principality, and
power, and might, and dominion,
and every name that is named, not
only in this world, but also in that
which is to come:
22 And [n]hath put all *things* under
his feet, and gave him [o]*to be* the
head over all *things* to the church,
23 [p]Which is his body, [q]the fulness
of him [r]that filleth all in all.

A

Col. 1. 4 Since we heard of your faith in Christ Jesus, and of the love *which ye have* to all the saints,

Phile. 5 Hearing of thy love and faith, which thou hast toward the Lord Jesus, and toward all saints;

B

Rom. 1. 8, 9. *See a, A, § 318, page 808.*

C

John 20. 17. *See m, M, § 216, page 603.*

D

Col. 1. 9 For this cause we also, since the day we heard *it*, do not cease to pray for you, and to desire that ye might be filled with the knowledge of his will in all wisdom and spiritual understanding;

1

Or, *for the acknowledgement.*

Col. 2. 2 That their hearts might be comforted, being knit together in love, and unto all riches of the full assurance of understanding, to the acknowledgment of the mystery of God, and of the Father, and of Christ;

E

Acts 26. 18. *See o, O, § 309, page 794.*

F

Eph. 2. 12 That at that time ye were without Christ, being aliens from the commonwealth of Israel, and strangers from the covenants of promise, having no hope, and without God in the world:
13 But now in Christ Jesus ye who sometimes were far off are made nigh by the blood of Christ.

Eph. 4. 4 *There is* one body, and one Spirit, even as ye are called in one hope of your calling;

G

Acts 20. 32. *See b, B, § 292, page 764.*

Eph. 1. 11 In whom also we have obtained an inheritance, being predestinated according to the purpose of him who worketh all things after the counsel of his own will:

§ 428. SAVED BY GRACE

2 : 1–10.

1 And [a]you *hath he quickened*, [b]who
were dead in trespasses and sins;
2 [c]Wherein in time past ye walked

A

John 5. 24 Verily, verily, I say unto you, He that heareth my word, and believeth on him that sent me, hath everlasting life, and shall not come into condemnation; but is passed from death unto life.

AND PRAYS FOR THEIR ENLIGHTENMENT.

H

Eph. 3. 7 Whereof I was made a minister, according to the gift of the grace of God given unto me by the effectual working of his power.

Col. 1. 29 Whereunto I also labour, striving according to his working, which worketh in me mightily.

Col. 2. 12 Buried with him in baptism, wherein also ye are risen with *him* through the faith of the operation of God, who hath raised him from the dead.

2

Gr. *of the might of his power.*

I

Acts 2. 24. *See k, K, § 231, page 638.*

K

Ps. 110. 1 The LORD said unto my Lord, Sit thou at my right hand, until I make thine enemies thy footstool.

Acts 7. 55 But he, being full of the Holy Ghost, looked up steadfastly into heaven, and saw the glory of God, and Jesus standing on the right hand of God,

56 And said, Behold, I see the heavens opened, and the Son of man standing on the right hand of God.

Col. 3. 1 If ye then be risen with Christ, seek those things which are above, where Christ sitteth on the right hand of God.

Heb. 1. 3 Who being the brightness of *his* glory, and the express image of his person, and upholding all things by the word of his power, when he had by himself purged our sins, sat down on the right hand of the Majesty on high;

Heb. 10. 12 But this man, after he had offered one sacrifice for sins for ever, sat down on the right hand of God;

L

Phil. 2. 9 Wherefore God also hath highly exalted him, and given him a name which is above every name:

10 That at the name of Jesus every knee should bow, of *things* in heaven, and *things* in earth, and *things* under the earth;

L—CONCLUDED.

Col. 2. 10 And ye are complete in him, which is the head of all principality and power:

Heb. 1. 4 Being made so much better than the angels, as he hath by inheritance obtained a more excellent name than they.

M

Rom. 8. 38. *See x, X, § 334, page 850.*

N

1 Cor. 15. 27. *See h, H, § 378, page 952.*

O

Eph. 4. 15 But speaking the truth in love, may grow up into him in all things, which is the head, *even* Christ:

16 From whom the whole body fitly joined together and compacted by that which every joint supplieth, according to the effectual working in the measure of every part, maketh increase of the body unto the edifying of itself in love.

Col. 1. 18 And he is the head of the body, the church: who is the beginning, the firstborn from the dead; that in all things he might have the preeminence.

Heb. 2. 7 Thou madest him a little lower than the angels; thou crownedst him with glory and honour, and didst set him over the works of thy hands.

P

Rom. 12. 5. *See l, L, § 342, page 868.*
1 Cor. 12. 27. *See h, H, § 371, page 940.*

Q

Col. 2. 9 For in him dwelleth all the fulness of the godhead bodily.

R

1 Cor. 12. 6 And there are diversities of operations, but it is the same God which worketh all in all.

Eph. 4. 10 He that descended is the same also that ascended up far above all heavens, that he might fill all things.)

Col. 3. 11 Where there is neither Greek nor Jew, circumcision nor uncircumcision, Barbarian, Scythian, bond *nor* free: but Christ *is* all, and in all.

THROUGH FAITH.

A—CONCLUDED.

Col. 2. 13 And you, being dead in your sins and the uncircumcision of your flesh, hath he quickened together with him, having forgiven you all trespasses;

B

Eph. 2. 5. *See text of topic, page 1034.*

Eph. 4. 18 Having the understanding darkened, being alienated from the life of God through the ignorance that

For B concluded and C, see next page (1034)

CHAP. 2.

according to the course of this world,
according to [d]the prince of the power
of the air, the spirit that now worketh in [e]the children of disobedience:
3 [f]Among whom also we all had our
conversation in times past in [g]the
lusts of our flesh, fulfilling [1]the desires of the flesh and of the mind;
and [h]were by nature the children of
wrath, even as others.
4 But God, [i]who is rich in mercy,
for his great love wherewith he loved
us,
5 [k]Even when we were dead in sins,
hath [l]quickened us together with
Christ, ([2]by grace ye are saved;)
6 And hath raised *us* up together,
and made *us* sit together [m]in heavenly *places* in Christ Jesus:
7 That in the ages to come he
might shew the exceeding riches of
his grace, in [n]*his* kindness toward us,
through Christ Jesus.
8 [o]For by grace are ye saved
[p]through faith; and that not of
yourselves: [q]*it is* the Gift of God:
9 [r]Not of works, lest any man should
boast.
10 For we are [s]his workmanship,
created in Christ Jesus unto good
works, [t]which God hath before [3]or-
dained that we should walk in them.

B—CONCLUDED.

is in them, because of the blindness of their heart:

C

I Cor. 6. 11. *See g, G, § 360, page 910.*

I Jno. 5. 19 *And* we know that we are of God, and the whole world lieth in wickedness.

D

Eph. 6. 12 For we wrestle not against flesh and blood, but against principalities, against powers, against the rulers of the darkness of this world, against spiritual wickedness in high *places.*

§ 428. SAVED BY GRACE

E

Eph. 5. 6 Let no man deceive you with vain words: for because of these things cometh the wrath of God upon the children of disobedience.

Col. 3. 6 For which things' sake the wrath of God cometh on the children of disobedience:

F

Tit. 3. 3 For we ourselves also were sometimes foolish, disobedient, deceived, serving divers lusts and pleasures, living in malice and envy, hateful, *and* hating one another.

I Pet. 4. 3 For the time past of *our* life may suffice us to have wrought the will of the Gentiles, when we walked in lasciviousness, lusts, excess of wine, revellings, banquetings, and abominable idolatries:

G

Gal. 5. 16 *This* I say then, Walk in the Spirit, and ye shall not fulfil the lust of the flesh.

1

Gr. *the wills.*

Rom. 5. 12 Wherefore, as by one man sin entered into the world, and death by sin; and so death passed upon all men, for that all have sinned:

Rom. 5. 14 Nevertheless death reigned from Adam to Moses, even over them that had not sinned after the similitude of Adam's transgression, who is the figure of him that was to come.

I

Rom. 2. 4. *See c, C, § 320, page 814.*

K

Rom. 5. 6, 8, 10. *See l, L, § 326, page 832.*

L

Rom. 6. 4 Therefore we are buried with him by baptism into death: that like as Christ was raised up from the dead by the glory of the Father, even so we also should walk in newness of life.

5 For if we have been planted together in the likeness of his death, we shall also be *in the likeness* of *his* resurrection:

2

Or, *by* whose *grace.*

M

Eph. 1. 20 Which he wrought in Christ, when he raised him from the dead, and set *him* at his own right hand in the heavenly *places,*

N

Tit. 3. 4 But after that the kindness and love of God our Saviour toward man appeared,

THROUGH FAITH (CONCLUDED).

O

Rom. 3. 24 Being justified freely by his grace through the redemption that is in Christ Jesus:

Rom. 11. 5, 6. *See g, G, § 339, page 862.*

Eph. 2. 5. *See text of topic.*

IITim.1. 9 Who hath saved us, and called *us* with a holy calling, not according to our works, but according to his own purpose and grace, which was given us in Christ Jesus before the world began:

P

Rom. 4. 16 Therefore *it is* of faith, that *it might be* by grace; to the end the promise might be sure to all the seed; not to that only which is of the law, but to that also which is of the faith of Abraham; who is the father of us all,

Q

Matt.16. 17 And Jesus answered and said unto him, Blessed art thou, Simon Bar-jona: for flesh and blood hath not revealed *it* unto thee, but my Father which is in heaven.

John 6. 44 No man can come to me, except the Father which hath sent me draw him: and I will raise him up at the last day.

Rom.10. 13 For whosoever shall call upon the name of the Lord shall be saved.

14 How then shall they call on him in whom they have not believed? and how shall they believe in him of whom they have not heard? and how shall they hear without a preacher?

Rom.10. 17 So then faith *cometh* by hearing, and hearing by the word of God.

Eph. 1. 19 And what *is* the exceeding greatness of his power to us-ward who believe, according to the working of his mighty power,

Phil. 1. 29 For unto you it is given in the behalf of Christ, not only to believe on him, but also to suffer for his sake;

R

Rom. 3. 20. *See c, C, § 324, page 824.*

Rom. 3. 27 Where *is* boasting then? It is excluded. By what law? of works? Nay: but by the law of faith.

28 Therefore we conclude that a man is justified by faith without the deeds of the law.

Rom. 4. 2 For if Abraham were justified by works, he hath *whereof* to glory; but not before God.

Rom. 9. 11 (For *the children* being not yet born, neither having done any good or evil, that the purpose of God according to election might stand, not of works, but of him that calleth;)

R—CONCLUDED.

Rom.11. 6 And if by grace, then *is it* no more of works: otherwise grace is no more grace. But if *it be* of works, then is it no more grace: otherwise work is no more work.

IITim.1. 9 Who hath saved us, and called *us* with a holy calling, not according to our works, but according to his own purpose and grace, which was given us in Christ Jesus before the world began,

S

Deut.32. 6 Do ye thus requite the LORD, O foolish people and unwise? *is* not he thy father *that* hath bought thee? hath he not made thee, and established thee?

Ps. 100. 3 Know ye that the LORD he *is* God: *it is* he *that* hath made us, and not we ourselves; *we are* his people, and the sheep of his pasture.

Isa. 19. 25 Whom the LORD of hosts shall bless, saying, Blessed *be* Egypt my people, and Assyria the work of my hands, and Israel my inheritance.

Isa. 29. 23 But when he seeth his children, the work of mine hands, in the midst of him, they shall sanctify my name, and sanctify the Holy One of Jacob, and shall fear the God of Israel.

Isa. 44. 21 Remember these, O Jacob and Israel; for thou *art* my servant: I have formed thee; thou *art* my servant: O Israel, thou shalt not be forgotten of me.

John 3. 5 Jesus answered, Verily, verily, I say unto thee, Except a man be born of water and *of* the Spirit, he cannot enter into the kingdom of God.

ICo3. 9 For we are labourers together with God: ye are God's husbandry, *ye are* God's building.

IICor.5. 5 Now he that hath wrought us for the selfsame thing *is* God, who also hath given unto us the earnest of the Spirit.

Eph. 4. 24 And that ye put on the new man, which after God is created in righteousness and true holiness.

Tit. 2. 14 Who gave himself for us, that he might redeem us from all iniquity, and purify unto himself a peculiar people, zealous of good works.

T

Eph. 1. 4. *See b, B, § 426, page 1028.*

?

Or, *prepared.*

§ 429. THE LAW OF COMMANDMENT IN ORDINANCES ABOLISHED:

2: 11–22.

11 Wherefore [a]remember, that ye *being* in time past Gentiles in the flesh, who are called uncircumcision by that which is called [b]the Circumcision in the flesh made by hands;

12 [c]That at that time ye were with out Christ, [d]being aliens from the commonwealth of Israel, and strangers from [e]the covenants of promise, [f]having no hope, [g]and without God in the world:

13 [h]But now in Christ Jesus, ye who sometimes were [i]far off are made nigh by the blood of Christ.

14 For [k]he is our peace, [l]who hath made both one, and hath broken down the middle wall of partition *between us;*

15 [m]Having abolished in his flesh the emnity, *even* the law of commandments *contained* in ordinances; for to make in himself of twain one [n]new man, *so* making peace;

16 And that he might [o]reconcile both unto God in one body by the cross, [p]having slain the enmity [1]thereby:

17 And came [q]and preached peace to you which were afar off, and [r]to them that were nigh.

18 For [s]through him we both have access [t]by one Spirit unto the Father.

19 Now therefore ye are no more strangers and foreigners, but [u]fellow citizens with the saints, and of [x]the household of God;

20 And [y]are built [z]upon the foundation of the [a]apostles and prophets, Jesus Christ himself being [b]the chief corner *stone;*

21 [c]In whom all the building fitly framed together groweth unto [d]a holy temple in the Lord:

22 [e]In whom ye also are builded together for a habitation of God through the Spirit.

A

I Cor. 12. 2. *See b, B, § 370, page 936.*

Eph. 5. 8 For ye were sometime darkness, but now *are ye* light in the Lord: walk as children of light:

Col. 1. 21 And you, that were sometime alienated and enemies in *your* mind by wicked works, yet now hath he reconciled

B

Rom. 2. 28, 29. *See q, Q, § 321, page 820.*

C

Eph. 4. 18 Having the understanding darkened, being alienated from the life of God through the ignorance that is in them, because of the blindness of their heart:

Col. 1. 21. *See under A.*

D

John 10. 16 And other sheep I have, which are not of this fold: them also I must bring, and they shall hear my voice; and there shall be one fold, *and* one shepherd.

E

Rom. 9. 4, 8. *See g, G, § 335, page 852.*

F

I Thes. 4. 13 But I would not have you to be ignorant, brethren, concerning them which are asleep, that ye sorrow not, even as others which have no hope.

G

Gal. 4. 8. *See a, A, § 419, page 1018.*

H

Gal. 3. 28 There is neither Jew nor Greek, there is neither bond nor free, there is neither male nor female: for ye are all one in Christ Jesus.

I

Acts 2. 39. *See d, D, § 232, page 640.*

K

Acts 10. 36. *See d, D, § 254, page 696.*

Rom. 5. 1. *See a, A, § 326, page 830.*

L

John 17. 21. *See o, O, § 191, page 547.*

M

Col. 1. 21. *See under A.*

Col. 1. 22 In the body of his flesh through death, to present you holy and unblameable and unreproveable in his sight:

Col. 2. 14 Blotting out the handwriting of ordinances that was against us, which was contrary to us, and took it out of the way, nailing it to his cross;

Col. 2. 20 Wherefore if ye be dead with Christ from the rudiments of the world, why, as though living in the world, are ye subject to ordinances.

GENTILES, FELLOW-CITIZENS IN THE HOUSEHOLD OF GOD.

M—CONCLUDED.

Heb. 10. 20 By a new and living way, which he hath consecrated for us, through the vail, that is to say, his flesh:

N

II Cor. 5. 17. *See k, K, § 395, page 978.*

Eph. 4. 24 And that ye put on the new man, which after God is created in righteousness and true holiness.

O

Col. 1. 21. *See under A.*

P

Rom. 6. 6 Knowing this, that our old man is crucified with *him*, that the body of sin might be destroyed, that henceforth we should not serve sin.

Rom. 8. 3 For what the law could not do, in that it was weak through the flesh, God sending his own Son in the likeness of sinful flesh, and for sin, condemned sin in the flesh:

Col. 2. 14. *See under M.*

1

Or, *in himself.*

Q

Acts 10. 36. *See d, D, § 254, page 696.*

Rom. 5. 1 Therefore being justified by faith, we have peace with God through our Lord Jesus Christ:

R

Ps. 148. 14 He also exalteth the horn of his people, the praise of all his saints; *even* of the children of Israel, a people near unto him. Praise ye the LORD.

S

Rom. 5. 2. *See b, B, § 326, page 830.*

Heb. 4. 16 Let us therefore come boldly unto the throne of grace, that we may obtain mercy, and find grace to help in time of need.

I Pet. 3. 18 For Christ also hath once suffered for sins, the just for the unjust, that he might bring us to God, being put to death in the flesh, but quickened by the Spirit:

T

I Cor. 12. 13 For by one Spirit are we all baptized into one body, whether *we be* Jews or Gentiles, whether *we be* bond or free; and have been all made to drink into one Spirit.

Eph. 4. 4 *There is* one body, and one Spirit, even as ye are called in one hope of your calling;

U

Phil. 3. 20 For our conversation is in heaven; from whence also we look for the Saviour, the Lord Jesus Christ.

U—CONCLUDED.

Heb. 12. 22 But ye are come unto mount Sion, and unto the city of the living God, the heavenly Jerusalem, and to an innumerable company of angels,

23 To the general assembly and church of the firstborn, which are written in heaven, and to God the Judge of all, and to the spirits of just men made perfect.

X

Gal. 6. 10. *See u, U, § 423, page 1026.*

Eph. 3. 15 Of whom the whole family in heaven and earth is named.

Y

I Cor. 3 9 For we are labourers together with God: ye are God's husbandry, *ye are* God's building.

10 According to the grace of God which is given unto me, as a wise masbuilder, I have laid the foundation, and another buildeth thereon. But let every man take heed how he buildeth thereon.

Eph. 4. 12 For the perfecting of the saints, for the work of the ministry, for the edifying of the body of Christ:

I Pet. 2. 4 To whom coming, *as unto* a living stone, disallowed indeed of men, but chosen of God, *and* precious,

5 Ye also, as lively stones, are built up a spiritual house, a holy priesthood, to offer up spiritual sacrifices, acceptable to God by Jesus Christ.

Z

Matt. 16. 18. *See h, H, § 92, page 276.*

Gal. 2. 9 And when James, Cephas, and John, who seemed to be pillars, perceived the grace that was given unto me, they gave to me and Barnabas the right hands of fellowship; that we *should go* unto the heathen, and they unto the circumcision.

A

I Cor. 12. 28. *See k, K, § 371, page 940.*

Eph. 4. 11 And he gave some, apostles; and some, prophets; and some, evangelists; and some, pastors and teachers;

B

Matt. 21. 42. *See t, T, § 161, page 448.*

C

Eph. 4. 15, 16. *See text of topic, § 432, page 1044.*

D

I Cor. 3. 16, 17. *See m, M, § 354, page 900.*

E

John 17. 23 I in them, and thou in me, that they may be made perfect in one; and that the world may know that thou hast sent me, and hast loved them, as thou hast loved me.

I Pet. 12. 25. *See under Y.*

§ 430. PAUL PROCLAIMS THE MYSTERY REVEALED TO THE

3 : 1–13.

1 For this cause I Paul, [a]the prisoner of Jesus Christ [b]for you Gentiles,
2 If ye have heard of [c]the dispensation of the grace of God [d]which is given me to you-ward:
3 [e]How that [f]by revelation he made known unto me the mystery; ([g]as I wrote [1]afore in few words;
4 Whereby, when ye read, ye may understand my knowledge [h]in the mystery of Christ)
5 [i]Which in other ages was not made known unto the sons of men, [k]as it is now revealed unto his holy apostles and prophets by the Spirit;
6 That the Gentiles [l]should be fellow heirs, and [m]of the same body, and [n]partakers of his promise in Christ by the gospel:
7 [o]Whereof I was made a minister, [p]according to the gift of the grace of God given unto me by [q]the effectual working of his power.
8 Unto me, [r]who am less than the least of all saints, is this grace given, that [s]I should preach among the Gentiles [t]the unsearchable riches of Christ;
9 And to make all *men* see what *is* the fellowship of [u]the mystery, [x]which from the beginning of the world hath been hid in God, [y]who created all things by Jesus Christ:
10 [z]To the intent that now [a]unto the principalities and powers in heavenly *places* [b]might be known by the church the manifold wisdom of God,
11 [c]According to the eternal purpose which he purposed in Christ Jesus our Lord:

A

Acts. 28. 20. *See f, F, § 316, page 804.*

Phil. 1. 7 Even as it is meet for me to think this of you all, because I have you in my heart; inasmuch as both in my bonds, and in the defence and confirmation of the gospel, ye all are partakers of my grace.

A—Concluded.

Phil. 1. 14 And many of the brethren in the Lord, waxing confident by my bonds, are much more bold to speak the word without fear.

Phil. 1. 16 The one preach Christ of contention, not sincerely, supposing to add affliction to my bonds:

Col. 4. 3 Withal praying also for us, that God would open unto us a door of utterance, to speak the mystery of Christ, for which I am also in bonds:

Col. 4. 18 The salutation by the hand of me Paul. Remember my bonds. Grace *be* with you. Amen.

II Tim. 1. 8 Be not thou therefore ashamed of the testimony of our Lord, nor of me his prisoner: but be thou partaker of the afflictions of the gospel according to the power of God;

II Tim. 2. 9 Wherein I suffer trouble, as an evil doer, *even* unto bonds; but the word of God is not bound.

B

Col. 1. 24 Who now rejoice in my sufferings for you, and fill up that which is behind of the afflictions of Christ in my flesh for his body's sake, which is the church:

II Tim. 2. 10 Therefore I endure all things for the elect's sake, that they may also obtain the salvation which is in Christ Jesus with eternal glory.

C

I Cor. 9. 17. *See a, A, § 365, page 921.*

D

Acts. 9. 15. *See l, L, § 251, page 684.*

E

Acts 22. 17, 21. *See b, B, § 297, page 774.*

F

Gal. 1. 12 For I neither received it of man, neither was I taught *it*, but by the revelation of Jesus Christ.

Rom. 16. 25 Now to him that is of power to stablish you according to my gospel, and the preaching of Jesus Christ, according to the revelation of the mystery, which was kept secret since the world began,

G

Eph. 1. 9 Having made known unto us the mystery of his will, according to his good pleasure which he hath purposed in himself:

10 That in the dispensation of the fulness of times he might gather together in one all things in Christ, both which are in heaven, and which are on earth; *even* in him:

APOSTLES, NOW MADE KROWN THROUGHOUT THE CHURCHES.

1

Or, *a little before.*

H

I Cor. 4. 1 Let a man so account of us, as of the ministers of Christ, and stewards of the mysteries of God.

Eph. 6. 19 And for me, that utterance may be given unto me, that I may open my mouth boldly, to make known the mystery of the gospel,

I

Acts 10. 28 And he said unto them, Ye know how that it is an unlawful thing for a man that is a Jew to keep company, or come unto one of another nation; but God hath shewed me that I should not call any man common or unclean.

Rom. 16. 25. *See under F.*

K

Eph. 2. 20 And are built upon the foundation of the apostles and prophets, Jesus Christ himself being the chief corner *stone;*

L

Gal. 3. 28, 29. *See i, I, § 417, page 1016.*

Eph. 2. 14 For he is our peace, who hath made both one, and hath broken down the middle wall of partition *between us;*

M

Eph. 2. 15, 16. *See text of § 429.*

N

Gal. 3. 14 That the blessing of Abraham might come on the Gentiles through Jesus Christ; that we might receive the promise of the Spirit through faith.

O

Acts 22. 21. *See i, I, § 297, page 774.*

Col. 1. 23 If ye continue in the faith grounded and settled, and *be* not moved away from the hope of the gospel, which ye have heard, *and* which was preached to every creature which is under heaven, whereof I Paul am made a minister;

Col. 1. 25 Whereof I am made a minister, according to the dispensation of God which is given to me for you, to fulfil the word of of God:

P

Rom. 1. 5. *See i, I, § 317, page 808.*

Q

Rom. 15. 18, 19. *See i, I, § 346, page 880.*

Eph. 1. 19. *See h, H, § 427, page 1032.*

R

I Cor. 15. 9 For I am the least of the apostles, that am not meet to be called an apostle, because I persecuted the church of God.

S

Acts 22. 21. *See i, I, § 297, page 774.*

T

Eph. 1. 7. *See l, L, § 426, page 1030.*

Col. 1. 27 To whom God would make known what *is* the riches of the glory of this mystery among the Gentiles; which is Christ in you, the hope of glory:

U

Eph. 1. 9. *See m, M, § 426, page 1030.*

Eph. 3. 3. *See text of topic.*

X

Eph. 3. 5. *See text of topic. Read under I.*

Y

John 1. 3. *See e, E, § 1, page 5.*

Z

I Pet. 1. 12 Unto whom it was revealed, that not unto themselves, but unto us they did minister the things, which are now reported unto you by them that have preached the gospel unto you with the Holy Ghost sent down from heaven; which things the angels desire to look into.

A

Rom. 8. 38. *See x, X, § 334, page 850.*

B

I Cor. 2. 7 But we speak the wisdom of God in a mystery, *even* the hidden *wisdom*, which God ordained before the world unto our glory.

I Tim. 3. 16 And without controversy great is the mystery of godliness: God was manifest in the flesh, justified in the Spirit, seen of angels, preached unto the Gentiles, believed on in the world, received up into glory.

C

Eph. 1. 9. *See n, N, § 426, page 1030.*

D

Eph. 2. 18 For through him we both have access by one Spirit unto the Father.

E

Heb. 4. 16 Let us therefore come boldly unto the throne of grace, that we may obtain mercy, and find grace to help in time of need.

F

Acts 14. 22 Confirming the souls of the disciples, *and* exhorting them to continue in the faith, and that we must through much tribulation enter into the kingdom of God.

Phil. 1. 14 And many of the brethren in the

§ 430. PAUL PROCLAIMS THE MYSTERY REVEALED TO THE APOSTLES,

CHAP. 3.

12 In whom we have boldness and
[d]access [e]with confidence by the faith
of him.

13 [f]Wherefore I desire that ye faint

CHAP. 3.

not at my tribulations [g]for you, [h]which
is your glory.

For D, E and F, see preceding page (1039)

F—CONTINUED.

Lord, waxing confident by my bonds,

§ 431. PAUL PRAYS THAT THE SPIRIT OF LOVE AND

3 : 14–21.

14 For this cause I bow my knees
unto the Father of our Lord Jesus
Christ,

15 Of whom [a]the whole family in
heaven and earth is named,

16 That he would grant you, [b]ac-
cording to the riches of his glory, [c]to
be strengthened with might by his
Spirit in [d]the inner man;

17 [e]That Christ may dwell in your
hearts by faith; that ye, [f]being rooted and grounded in love,

18 [g]May be able to comprehend
with all saints [h]what *is* the breadth,
and length, and depth, and height;

19 And to know the love of Christ,
which passeth knowledge, that ye
might be filled [i]with all the fullness
of God.

20 Now [k]unto him that is able to
do exceeding abundantly [l]above all

CHAP. 3.

that we ask or think, [m]according to
the power that worketh in us,

21 [n]Unto him *be* glory in the church
by Christ Jesus throughout all ages,
world without end. Amen.

A

Eph. 1. 10. *See p, P, § 426, page 1030.*

B

Eph. 1. 7. *See l, L, § 426, page 1030.*

Col. 1. 27 To whom God would make known what *is* the riches of the glory of this mystery among the Gentiles; which is Christ in you, the hope of glory:

C

Eph. 6. 10 Finally, my brethren, be strong in the Lord, and in the power of his might.

Col. 1. 11 Strengthened with all might, according to his glorious power, unto all patience and longsuffering with joyfulness;

D

Rom. 7. 22. *See k, K, § 331, page 842.*

E

John 14. 23. *See g, G, § 186, page 529.*

Eph. 2. 22 In whom ye also are builded together for a habitation of God through the Spirit.

§ 432. EXHORTATION TO WALK IN THE UNITY OF THE SPIRIT

4 : 1–16.

1 I therefore, [a]the prisoner [1]of the
Lord, beseech you that ye [b]walk
worthy of the vocation wherewith
ye are called,

2 [c]With all lowliness and meekness,
with longsuffering, forbearing one
another in love;

3 Endeavouring to keep the unity of
the Spirit [d]in the bond of peace.

A

Eph. 3. 1. *See a, A, § 430, page 1038.*

Phile. 1 Paul, a prisoner of Jesus Christ, and Timothy *our* brother, unto Philemon our dearly beloved, and fellow labourer,

Phile. 9 Yet for love's sake I rather beseech *thee*, being such a one as Paul the aged, and now also a prisoner of Jesus Christ.

1

Or, *in the Lord.*

NOW MADE KNOWN THROUGHOUT THE CHURCHES (CONCLUDED).

F—CONCLUDED.

are much more bold to speak the word without fear.

IThes.3. 3 That no man should be moved by these afflictions: for yourselves know that we are appointed thereunto.

G

Eph. 3. 1. *See text of topic.*

H

IICor. 1. 6 And whether we be afflicted, *it is* for your consolation and salvation, which is effectual in the enduring of the same sufferings which we also suffer: or whether we be comforted, *it is* for your consolation and salvation.

POWER MAY DWELL IN THEM. A DOXOLOGY.

F

Col. 1. 23 If ye continue in the faith grounded and settled, and *be* not moved away from the hope of the gospel, which ye have heard, *and* which was preached to every creature which is under heaven; whereof I Paul am made a minister;

Col. 2. 7 Rooted and built up in him, and established in the faith, as ye have been taught, abounding therein with thanksgiving.

G

Eph 1. 18 The eyes of your understanding being enlightened; that ye may know what is the hope of his calling, and what the riches of the glory of his inheritance in the saints,

H

Rom.10 3 For they, being ignorant of God's righteousness, and going about to establish their own righteousness, have not submitted themselves unto the righteousness of God.

Rom 10 11 For the Scripture saith, Whosoever believeth on him shall not be ashamed.

Rom.10 12 For there is no difference between the Jew and the Greek: for the same Lord over all is rich unto all that call upon him.

I

John 1. 16 And of his fulness have all we received, and grace for grace.

Eph. 1. 23 Which is his body, the fulness of him that filleth all in all.

Col. 2. 9 For in him dwelleth all the fulness of the Godhead bodily.

10 And ye are complete in him, which is the head of all principality and power:

K

Rom. 16. 25. *See b, B, § 347, page 886.*

L

Ps. 36. 8 They shall be abundantly satisfied with the fatness of thy house; and thou shalt make them drink of the river of thy pleasures.

9 For with thee *is* the fountain of life: in thy light shall we see light.

I Cor. 2. 9 But as it is written, Eye hath not seen, nor ear heard, neither have entered into the heart of man, the things which God hath prepared for them that love him.

M

Eph. 3. 7 Whereof I was made a minister, according to the gift of the grace of God given unto me by the effectual working of his power.

N

Rom. 11. 36. *See k, K, § 341, page 866.*

ACCORDING TO THE SEVERAL GIFTS UNTO A FULL STATURE.

B

Phil 1. 27 Only let your conversation be as it becometh the gospel of Christ: that whether I come and see you, or else be absent, I may hear of your affairs, that ye stand fast in one spirit, with one mind striving together for the faith of the gospel;

Col 1. 10 That ye might walk worthy of the Lord unto all pleasing, being fruitful in every good work, and increasing in the knowledge of God;

IThes.2 12 That ye would walk worthy of

B—CONCLUDED.

God, who hath called you unto his kingdom and glory.

C

Matt.11. 29 Take my yoke upon you, and learn of me; for I am meek and lowly in heart: and ye shall find rest unto your souls.

Acts 20. 19 Serving the Lord with all humility of mind, and with many tears, and temptations, which befell me by the lying in wait of the Jews:

For C concluded and D, see next page (1042).

§ 432. EXHORTATION TO WALK IN THE UNITY OF THE SPIRIT ACCORD-

CHAP. 4.

4 [e]*There is* one body, and [f]one
Spirit, even as ye are called in one
[g]hope of your calling;
5 [h]One Lord, [i]one faith, [k]one baptism,
6 [l]One God and Father of all, who
is above all, and [m]through all, and
in you all.
7 But [n]unto every one of us is given
grace according to the measure of
the gift of Christ.
8 Wherefore he saith, [o]When he ascended up on high, [p]he led captivity
captive, and gave gifts unto men.
9 [q](Now that he ascended, what is
it but that he also descended first into
the lower parts of the earth?
10 He that descended is the same
also [r]that ascended up far above all
heavens, [s]that he might [2]fill all things.)
11 [t]And he gave some, apostles; and
some, prophets; and some, [u]evange-
lists; and some, [x]pastors and [y]teachers;
12 [z]For the perfecting of the saints,
for the work of the ministry, [a]for the
edifying of [b]the body of Christ:
13 Till we all come [3]in the unity of
the faith, [c]and of the knowledge of
the Son of God, unto [d]a perfect man,
unto the measure of the [4]stature of
the fulness of Christ:
14 That we *henceforth* be no more
[e]children, [f]tossed to and fro, and car-

C—CONCLUDED.

Gal. 5. 22 But the fruit of the Spirit is love, joy, peace, longsuffering, gentleness, goodness, faith,

23 Meekness, temperance: against such there is no law.

Col. 3. 12 Put on therefore, as the elect of God, holy and beloved, bowels of mercies, kindness, humbleness of mind, meekness, longsuffering;

13 Forbearing one another, and forgiving one another, if any man have a quarrel against any: even as Christ forgave you, so also *do* ye.

D

Col. 3. 14 And above all these things *put on* charity, which is the bond of perfectness.

E

Rom. 12. 5 So we *being* many, are one body in Christ, and every one members one of another.

1 Cor. 12. 12 For as the body is one, and hath many members, and all the members of that one body, being many, are one body: so also *is* Christ.

13 For by one Spirit are we all baptized into one body, whether *we be* Jews or Gentiles, whether *we be* bond or free; and have been all made to drink into one Spirit.

14 For the body is not one member, but many.

Eph. 2. 16 And that he might reconcile both unto God in one body by the cross, having slain the enmity thereby:

F

1 Cor. 12. 4 Now there are diversities of gifts, but the same Spirit.

1 Cor. 12. 11 But all these worketh that one and the selfsame Spirit, dividing to every man severally as he will.

G

Eph. 1. 18. *See f, F, § 427, page 1032.*

H

1 Cor. 1. 13 Is Christ divided? was Paul crucified for you? or were ye baptized in the name of Paul?

1 Cor. 8. 6. *See l, L, § 364, page 918.*

1 Cor. 12. 5 And there are differences of administrations, but the same Lord.

I

Eph. 4. 13. *See text of topic.*

Jude 3 Beloved, when I gave all diligence to write unto you of the common salvation, it was needful for me to write unto you, and exhort *you* that ye should earnestly contend for the faith which was once delivered unto the saints.

K

Gal. 3. 27 For as many of you as have been baptized into Christ have put on Christ.

28 There is neither Jew nor Greek, there is neither bond nor free, there is neither male nor female: for ye are all one in Christ Jesus.

L

1 Cor. 8. 6. *See i, I, § 364, page 918.*

1 Cor. 12. 6 And there are diversities of operations, but it is the same God which worketh all in all.

M

Rom. 11. 30. *See q, Q, § 341, page 866.*

N

Rom. 12. 3. *See i, I, § 342, page 868.*

ING TO THE SEVERAL GIFTS UNTO A FULL STATURE (CONTINUED).

O

Ps. 68. 18 Thou hast ascended on high, thou hast led captivity captive: thou hast received gifts for men; yea, *for* the rebellious also, that the LORD God might dwell *among them.*

P

Judg. 5. 12 Awake, awake, Deborah: awake, awake, utter a song: arise, Barak, and lead thy captivity captive, thou son of Abinoam.

Col. 2. 15 *And* having spoiled principalities and powers, he made a shew of them openly, triumphing over them in it.

1

Or, *a multitude of captives.*

Q

John 3. 13. *See l, L, § 22, page 73.*

R

Acts 1. 9 And when he had spoken these things, while they beheld, he was taken up; and a cloud received him out of their sight.

Acts 1. 11 Which also said, Ye men of Galilee, why stand ye gazing up into heaven? this same Jesus, which is taken up from you into heaven, shall so come in like manner as ye have seen him go into heaven.

I Tim. 3. 16 And without controversy great is the mystery of godliness: God was manifest in the flesh, justified in the Spirit, seen of angels, preached unto the Gentiles, believed on in the world, received up into glory.

Heb. 4. 14 Seeing then that we have a great high priest, that is passed into the heavens, Jesus the Son of God, let us hold fast *our* profession.

Heb. 7. 26 For such a high priest became us, *who is* holy, harmless undefiled, separate from sinners, and made higher than the heavens;

Heb. 8. 1 Now of the things which we have spoken *this is* the sum: We have such a high priest, who is set on the right hand of the throne of the Majesty in the heavens;

Heb. 9. 24 For Christ is not entered into the holy places made with hands, *which are* the figures of the true; but into heaven itself, now to appear in the presence of God for us:

S

Acts 2. 33 Therefore being by the right hand of God exalted, and having received of the Father the promise of the Holy Ghost, he hath shed forth this, which ye now see and hear.

2

Or, *fulfil.*

T

I Cor. 12. 28 And God hath set some in the church, first apostles, secondly prophets, thirdly teachers, after that miracles, then gifts of healings, helps, governments, diversities of tongues.

Eph. 2. 20 And are built upon the foundation of the apostles and prophets Jesus Christ himself being the chief corner *stone*;

Eph. 3. 5 Which in other ages was not made known unto the sons of men, as it is now revealed unto his holy apostles and prophets by the Spirit:

Jude 17 But, beloved, remember ye the words which were spoken before of the apostles of our Lord Jesus Christ;

Rev. 18. 20 Rejoice over her, *thou* heaven, and *ye* holy apostles and prophets; for God hath avenged you on her.

Rev. 21. 14 And the wall of the city had twelve foundations, and in them the names of the twelve apostles of the Lamb.

U

Acts 21. 8. *See a, A, § 294, page 766.*

X

Acts 20. 28 Take heed therefore unto yourselves, and to all the flock, over the which the Holy Ghost hath made you overseers, to feed the church of God, which he hath purchased with his own blood.

Y

Rom. 12. 7. *See o, O, § 342, page 868.*

Z

I Cor. 12. 7. *See i, I, § 370, page 938.*

A

I Cor. 14. 26. *See b, B, 375, page 946.*

B

Rom. 12. 5. *See l, L, § 342, page 868.*

3

Or, *into the unity.*

C

Col. 2. 2 That their hearts might be comforted, being knit together in love, and unto all riches of the full assurance of understanding, to the acknowledgement of the mystery of God, and of the Father, and of Christ;

D

I Cor. 14. 20 Brethren, be not children in understanding: howbeit in malice be ye children, but in understanding be men.

For D concluded 4, E and F, see next page (1044).

§ 432. EXHORTATION TO WALK IN THE UNITY OF THE SPIRIT ACCORD-D—CONCLUDED.

CHAP. 4.

ried about with every [g]wind of doctrine, by the sleight of men, *and* cunning craftiness, [h]whereby they lie in wait to deceive;

15 But [i5]speaking the truth in love, [k]may grow up into him in all things, [l]which is the head, *even* Christ:

16 [m]From whom the whole body fitly joined together and compacted by that which every joint supplieth, according to the effectual working in the measure of every part, maketh increase of the body unto the edifying of itself in love.

Col. 1. 28 Whom we preach, warning every man, and teaching every man in all wisdom; that we may present every man perfect in Christ Jesus:

4

Or, *age.*

E

I Cor. 14. 20. *See a, A,* § *374, page 946.*

F

Heb. 13. 9 Be not carried about with divers and strange doctrines. For *it is* a good thing that the heart be established with grace; not with meats, which have not profited them that have been occupied therein.

G

Matt. 11. 7. *See m, M,* § *46, page 156.*

H

Rom. 16. 18. *See m, M,* § *347, page 884.*

§ 433. EXHORTATION TO PUT OFF THE OLD MANNER

4 : 17–32.

17 This I say therefore, and testify in the Lord, that [a]ye henceforth walk not as other Gentiles walk, [b]in the vanity of their mind,

18 [c]Having the understanding darkened, [d]being alienated from the life of God through the ignorance that is in them, because of the [e1]blindness of their heart:

19 [f]Who being past feeling [g]have given themselves over unto lasciviousness, to work all uncleanness with greediness.

20 But ye have not so learned Chrst;

21 [h]If so be that ye have heard him, and have been taught by him, as the truth is in Jesus:

22 That ye [i]put off concerning [k]the former conversation [l]the old man, which is corrupt according to the deceitful lusts;

23 And [m]be renewed in the spirit of your mind;

24 And that ye [n]put on the new man, which after God is [o]created in righteousness and [2]true holiness.

25 Wherefore putting away lying,

CHAP. 4.

[p]speak every man truth with his neighbour: for [q]we are members one of another.

A

I Cor. 6. 11. *See g, G,* § *360, page 910.*
Eph. 2. 1, 3. *See f, F,* § *427, page 1034.*

B

Rom. 1. 21. *See e, E,* § *319, page 812.*

C

Acts 26. 18. *See p, P,* § *309, page 794.*

D

Gal. 4. 8 Howbeit then, when ye knew not God, ye did service unto them which by nature are no gods.

Eph. 2. 12 That at that time ye were without Christ, being aliens from the commonwealth of Israel, and strangers from the covenants of promise, having no hope, and without God in the world:

Col. 1. 21 And you, that were sometime alienated and enemies in *your* mind by wicked works, yet now hath he reconciled.

I Thes. 4. 5 Not in the lust of concupiscence, even as the Gentiles which know not God:

E

Rom. 1. 21. *See e, E,* § *319, page 812.*

1

Or, *hardness.*

F

I Tim. 4. 2 Speaking lies in hypocrisy; having their conscience seared with a hot iron;

ING TO THE SEVERAL GIFTS UNTO A FULL STATURE (Concluded).

H—Concluded.

II Cor. 2. 17. *See i, I, § 389, page 968.*

I

Zech. 8. 16 These *are* the things that ye shall do; Speak ye every man the truth to his neighbour; execute the judgment of truth and peace in your gates:

II Cor. 4. 2 But have renounced the hidden things of dishonesty, not walking in craftiness, nor handling the word of God deceitfully; but by manifestation of the truth commending ourselves to every man's conscience in the sight of God.

Eph. 4. 25 Wherefore putting away lying, speak every man truth with his neighbour: for we are members one of another.

I Jno. 3. 18 My little children, let us not love in word, neither in tongue; but in deed and in truth.

5

Or, *being Sincere.*

K

Eph. 1. 22 And hath put all *things* under his feet, and gave him *to be* the head over all *things* to the church.

Eph. 2. 21 In whom all the building fitly framed together groweth unto a holy temple in the Lord:

L

Col. 1. 18 And he is the head of the body, the church: who is the beginning, the firstborn from the dead; that in all things he might have the preeminence.

M

Col. 2. 19 And not holding the Head, from which all the body by joints and bands having nourishment ministered, and knit together, increaseth with the increase of God.

OF LIFE AND PUT ON THE NEW MAN.

G

Rom. 1. 24, 26. *See h, H, § 319, page 812.*

H

Eph. 1. 13 In whom ye also *trusted*, after that ye heard the word of truth, the gospel of your salvation: in whom also, after that ye believed, ye were sealed with that Holy Spirit of promise,

I

Col. 2. 11 In whom also ye are circumcised with the circumcision made without hands, in putting off the body of the sins of the flesh by the circumcision of Christ:

Col. 3. 8 But now ye also put off all these; anger, wrath, malice, blasphemy, filthy communication out of your mouth.

9 Lie not one to another, seeing that ye have put off the old man with his deeds;

Heb. 12. 1 Wherefore, seeing we also are compassed about with so great a cloud of witnesses, let us lay aside every weight, and the sin which doth so easily beset *us*, and let us run with patience the race that is set before us,

I Pet. 2. 1 Wherefore laying aside all malice, and all guile, and hypocrisies, and envies, and all evil speakings,

K

I Cor. 6. 11. *See g, G, § 360 page 910.*
Eph. 2. 3. *See f, F, § 428, page 1034.*

L

Rom. 6. 6. *See k, K, § 328, page 836.*

M

Rom. 12. 2. *See e, E, § 342, page 868.*

N

Rom. 6. 4 Therefore we are buried with him by baptism into death: that like as Christ was raised up from the dead by the glory of the Father, even so we also should walk in newness of life.

II Cor. 5. 17 Therefore if any man *be* in Christ, *he is* a new creature: old things are passed away; behold, all things are become new.

Gal. 6. 15 For in Christ Jesus neither circumcision availeth any thing, nor uncircumcision, but a new creature.

Eph. 6. 11 Put on the whole armour of God, that ye may be able to stand against the wiles of the devil.

Col. 3. 10 And have put on the new *man*, which is renewed in knowledge after the image of him that created him:

O

Eph. 2. 10 For we are his workmanship, created in Christ Jesus unto good works, which God hath before ordained that we should walk in them.

2

Or, *holiness of truth.*

P

Eph. 4. 15. *See text of topic, § 482.*

Prov. 12. 17 *He that* speaketh truth sheweth forth righteousness: but a false witness deceit.

Q

Rom. 12. 5. *See l, L, § 342, page 868.*

§ 433. EXHORTATION TO PUT OFF THE OLD MANNER

CHAP. 4.

26 [r]Be ye angry, and sin not: let not the sun go down upon your wrath:

27 [s]Neither give place to the devil.

28 Let him that stole steal no more: but rather [t]let him labour, working with *his* hands the thing which is good, that he may have [3]to give [u]to him that needeth.

29 [x]Let no corrupt communication proceed out of your mouth, but [y]that which, is good [4]to the use of edifying, [z]that it may minister grace unto the hearers.

30 And [a]grieve not the Holy Spirit of God, [b]whereby ye are sealed unto the day of [c]redemption.

31 [d]Let all bitterness, and wrath, and anger, and clamour, and [e]evil speaking, be put away from you, [f]with all malice:

32 And [g]be ye kind one to another, tenderhearted, [h]forgiving one another, even as God for Christ's sake hath forgiven you.

R

Ps. 4. 4 Stand in awe, and sin not: commune with your own heart upon your bed, and be still. Selah.

Ps. 37. 8 Cease from anger, and forsake wrath: fret not thyself in any wise to do evil.

Eccl. 7. 9 Be not hasty in thy spirit to be angry: for anger resteth in the bosom of fools.

S

Acts 5. 3 But Peter, said, Ananias, why hath Satan filled thine heart to lie to the Holy Ghost, and to keep back *part* of the price of the land?

IICor.2. 10 To whom ye forgive anything, I *forgive* also: for if I forgave anything, to whom I forgave *it*, for your sakes *forgave I it* in the person of Christ:

11 Lest Satan should get an advantage of us: for we are not ignorant of his devices.

Eph. 6. 11 Put on the whole armour of God, that ye may be able to stand against the wiles of the devil.

Jas. 4. 7 Submit yourself therefore to God. Resist the devil, and he will flee from you.

I Pet. 5. 8 Be sober, be vigilant; because your adversary the devil, as a roaring lion, walketh about, seeking whom he may devour:

9 Whom resist steadfast in the faith knowing that the same afflictions are accomplished in your brethren that are in the world.

T

Acts 20. 35. *See e, E, § 292, page 764.*

IIThes. 3. 11 For we hear that there are some which walk among you disorderly, working not at all, but are busybodies.

12 Now them that are such we command and exhort by our Lord Jesus Christ, that with quietness they work, and eat their own bread.

13 But ye, brethren, be not weary in well doing,

3

Or, *to distribute.*

U

Luke 3. 11 He answereth and saith unto them, He that hath two coats, let him impart to him that hath none; and he that hath meat, let him do likewise.

§ 434. SUNDRY EXHORTA-

5:1-21.

1 Be [a]ye therefore followers of God, as dear children;

2 And [b]walk in love, as [c]Christ also hath loved us, and hath given himself for us an offering and a sacrifice to God [d]for a sweetsmelling savour.

A

Matt. 5. 45 That ye may be the children of your Father which is in heaven: for he maketh his sun to rise on the evil and on the good, and sendeth rain on the just and on the unjust.

Matt. 5. 48 Be ye therefore perfect, even as your Father which is in heaven is perfect.

Luke 6. 36 Be ye therefore merciful, as your

OF LIFE AND PUT ON THE NEW MAN (CONCLUDED).

X

Matt. 12. 36 But I say unto you. That every idle word that men shall speak, they shall give account thereof in the day of judgment.

37 For by thy words thou shalt be justified, and by thy words thou shalt be condemned.

Eph. 5. 4. *See text of topic, § 434.*

Col. 3. 8 But now ye also put off all these; anger, wrath, malice, blasphemy, filthy communication out of your mouth.

Tit. 3. 2 To speak evil of no man, to be no brawlers, *but* gentle, shewing all meekness unto all men.

Jas. 4. 11 Speak not evil one of another, brethren. He that speaketh evil of *his* brother, and judgeth his brother, speaketh evil of the law, and judgeth the law: but if thou judge the law, thou art not a doer of the law, but a judge.

I Pet. 2. 1 Wherefore laying aside all malice, and all guile, and hypocrisies, and envies, and all evil speakings,

Y

Col. 4. 6 Let your speech *be* always with grace, seasoned with salt that ye may know how ye ought to answer every man.

Thes. 5. 11 Wherefore comfort yourselves together, and edify one another, even as also ye do.

4

Or, *to edify profitably.*

Z

Col. 3. 16 Let the Word of Christ dwell in you richly in all wisdom; teaching and admonishing one another in psalms and hymns and spiritual songs, singing with grace in your hearts to the Lord.

A

Isa. 7. 13 And he said, Hear ye now, house of David: *Is it* a small thing for you

A—CONCLUDED.

to weary men, but will ye weary my God also?

Isa. 63. 10 But they rebelled, and vexed his Holy Spirit: therefore he was turned to be their enemy, *and* he fought against them.

Eze. 16. 43 Because thou hast not remembered the days of thy youth, but hast fretted me in all these *things*; behold, therefore I also will recompence thy way upon *thine* head, saith the Lord God: and thou shalt not commit this lewdness above all thine abominations.

I Thes. 5. 19 Quench not the Spirit.

B

II Cor. 1. 22. *See i, I, § 387, page 964.*

C

Rom. 8. 23. *See i, I, § 333, page 846.*

D

Col. 3. 8. *See under X.*

Col. 3. 19 Husbands, love *your* wives, and be not bitter against them.

E

Eph. 4. 29. *See text of topic.*

F

Tit. 3. 3 For we ourselves also were sometime foolish, disobedient, deceived, serving divers lusts and pleasures, living in malice and envy, hateful, *and* hating one another.

G

II Cor. 2. 10. *See under S.*

Col. 3. 12 Put on therefore, as the elect of God, holy and beloved, bowels of mercies, kindness, humbleness of mind, meekness, longsuffering.

13 Forbearing one another, and forgiving one another, if any man have a quarrel against any: even as Christ forgave you, so also *do* ye.

H

Matt. 6. 14. *See h, H, § 43, page 138.*

TIONS AND WARNINGS.

A—CONCLUDED.

Father also is merciful.

B

Jno. 13. 34. *See y, Y, § 183, page 519.*

C

Gal. 1. 4 Who gave himself for our sins, that he might deliver us from this present evil world, according to the will of God and our Father:

Gal. 2. 20 I am crucified with Christ: nevertheless I live; yet not I, but Christ liveth in me: and the life which I now live in the flesh I live by the faith of the Son of God, who loved me, and gave himself for me.

C—CONTINUED.

Heb. 7. 27 Who needeth not daily, as those high priests, to offer up sacrifice, first for his own sins, and then for

For C concluded and D, see next page (1048)

CHAP. 5.

3 But [e]fornication, and all uncleanness, or covetousness, [f]let it not be
once named among you, as becometh saints;
4 [g]Neither filthiness, nor foolish talking, nor jesting, [h]which are not convenient: but rather giving of thanks.
5 For this ye know, that [i]no whoremonger, nor unclean person, nor
covetous man, [k]who is an idolater,
hath any inheritance in the kingdom
of Christ and of God.
6 [l]Let no man deceive you with
vain words: for because of these
things [m]cometh the wrath of God
[n]upon the children of [1]disobedience.
7 Be not ye therefore partakers
with them.
8 [o]For ye were sometimes darkness,
but now [p]*are ye* light in the Lord:
walk as [q]children of light:
9 (For [r]the fruit of the Spirit *is* in
all goodness and righteousness and
truth;)
10 [s]Proving what is acceptable unto the Lord.
11 And [t]have no fellowship with
[u]the unfruitful works of darkness,
but rather [x]reprove *them*.
12 [y]For it is a shame even to speak
of those things which are done of
them in secret.
13 But [z]all things that are [2]reproved
are made manifest by the light: for
whatsoever doth make manifest is
light.

C—CONTINUED.

the people's: for this he did once, when he offered up himself.

Heb. 9. 14 How much more shall the blood of Christ, who through the eternal Spirit offered himself without spot to God, purge your conscience from dead works to serve the living God?

Heb. 9. 26 For then must he often have suffered since the foundation of the world: but now once in the end of the world hath he appeared to put away sin by the sacrifice of himself.

§ 434. SUNDRY EXHORTATIONS

C—CONCLUDED.

Heb. 10. 10 By the which will we are sanctified through the offering of the body of Jesus Christ once *for all*.

Heb. 10. 12 But this man, after he had offered one sacrifice for sins for ever, sat down on the right hand of God;

I John 3. 16 Hereby perceive we the love *of God*, because he laid down his life for us: and we ought to lay down *our* lives for the brethren.

D

Gen. 8. 21 And the LORD smelled a sweet savour; and the LORD said in his heart, I will not again curse the ground any more for man's sake; for the imagination of man's heart *is* evil from his youth; neither will I again smite any more every thing living, as I have done.

Lev. 1. 9 But his inwards and his legs shall he wash in water: and the priest shall burn all on the altar, *to be* a burnt sacrifice, an offering made by fire, of a sweet savour unto the LORD.

II Cor. 2. 15 For we are unto God a sweet savour of Christ, in them that are saved, and in them that perish:

E

Rom. 6. 13 Neither yield ye your members *as* instruments of unrighteousness unto sin: but yield yourselves unto God, as those that are alive from the dead, and your members *as* instruments of righteousness unto God.

II Cor. 12. 21 *And* lest, when I come again, my God will humble me among you, and *that* I shall bewail many which have sinned already, and have not repented of the uncleanness and fornication and lasciviousness which they have committed.

Eph. 4. 19 Who being past feeling have given themselves over unto lasciviousness, to work all uncleanness with greediness.

F

I Cor. 5. 1. *See a, A, § 359, page 906.*

G

Eph. 4. 29. *See x, X, § 433, page 1046.*

H

Rom. 1. 28. *See o, O, § 319, page 814.*

I

I Cor. 6. 9, 10. *See f, F, § 360, page 910.*

K

Col. 3. 5 Mortify therefore your members which are upon the earth; fornication, uncleanness, inordinate affection, evil concupiscence, and covetousness, which is idolatry:

AND WARNINGS (Continued).

K—Concluded.

I Tim. 6. 17 Charge them that are rich in this world, that they be not highminded, nor trust in uncertain riches, but in the living God, who giveth us richly all things to enjoy;

L

Matt. 24. 4. *See e, E, § 172, page 480.*

M

Rom. 1. 18 For the wrath of God is revealed from heaven against all ungodliness and unrighteousness of men, who hold the truth in unrighteousness;

N

Eph. 2. 2. *See e, 1, § 428, page 1034.*

1

Or, *unbelief.*

Col. 3. 6 For which things' sake the wrath of God cometh on the children of disobedience:

O

Isa. 9. 2 The people that walked in darkness have seen a great light: they that dwell in the land of the shadow of death, upon them hath the light shined.

Matt. 4. 16 The people which sat in darkness saw great light; and to them which sat in the region and shadow of death light is sprung up.

Acts. 26. 18. *See p, P, § 309, page 794.*

Rom. 1. 21 Because that, when they knew God, they glorified *him* not as God, neither were thankful; but became vain in their imaginations, and their foolish heart was darkened.

Tit. 3. 3 For we ourselves also were sometimes foolish, disobedient, deceived, serving divers lusts and pleasures, living in malice and envy, hateful, *and* hating one another.

P

Ps. 27. 1 The Lord *is* my light and my salvation; whom shall I fear? the Lord *is* the strength of my life; of whom shall I be afraid?

Ps. 36. 9 For with thee *is* the fountain of life: in thy light shall we see light.

Isa. 2. 5 O house of Jacob, come ye, and let us walk in the light of the Lord.

John 1. 9 *That* was the true Light, which lighteth every man that cometh into the world.

John 8. 12 Then spake Jesus again unto them, saying, I am the light of the world: he that followeth me shall not walk in darkness, but shall have the light of life.

P—Concluded.

John 12. 46 I am come a light into the world, that whosoever believeth on me should not abide in darkness.

II Cor. 4. 6 For God, who commanded the light to shine out of darkness, hath shined in our hearts, to *give* the light of the knowledge of the glory of God in the face of Jesus Christ.

I Thes. 5. 5 Ye are all the children of light, and the children of the day: we are not of the night, nor of darkness.

I Jno. 2. 10 He that loveth his brother abideth in the light, and there is none occasion of stumbling in him.

Q

John 12. 36. *See x, X, § 170, page 477.*

R

Gal. 5. 22. *See g, G, § 422, page 1024.*

S

Rom. 12. 2. *See f, F, § 342, page 868.*

Phil. 1. 10 That ye may approve things that are excellent; that ye may be sincere and without offence till the day of Christ;

I Thes. 5. 21 Prove all things; hold fast that which is good.

I Tim. 2. 3 For this *is* good and acceptable in the sight of God our Saviour;

T

Rom. 16. 17. *See k, K, § 347, page 884.*

U

Rom. 6. 21 What fruit had ye then in those things whereof ye are now ashamed? for the end of those things *is* death.

Rom. 13. 12. *See n, N, § 347, page 884.*

Gal. 6. 8 For he that soweth to his flesh shall of the flesh reap corruption; but but he that soweth to the Spirit shall of the Spirit reap life everlasting.

X

Lev. 19. 17 Thou shalt not hate thy brother in thine heart: thou shalt in any wise rebuke thy neighbour, and not suffer sin upon him.

I Tim. 5. 20 Them that sin rebuke before all, that others also may fear.

Y

Rom. 1. 24 Wherefore God also gave them up to uncleanness through the lusts of their own hearts, to dishonour their own bodies between themselves:

Rom. 1. 26 For this cause God gave them up unto vile affections: for even their women did change the natural use into that which is against nature:

Eph. 5. 3. *See text of topic.*

For Z and 2, see next page (1050).

§ 434. SUNDRY EXHORTATIONS

CHAP. 5.

14 Wherefore [3]he saith, [a]Awake thou that sleepest, and [b]arise from the dead, and Christ shall give thee light.

15 [c]See then that ye walk circumspectly, not as fools, but as wise,

16 [d]Redeeming the time, [e]because the days are evil.

17 [f]Wherefore be ye not unwise, but [g]understanding [h]what the will of the Lord *is*.

18 And [i]be not drunk with wine, wherein is excess; but be filled with the Spirit;

19 Speaking to yourselves [k]in psalms and hymns and spiritual songs, singing and making melody in your heart to the Lord;

20 [l]Giving thanks always for all things unto God and the Father [m]in the name of our Lord Jesus Christ;

21 [n]Submitting yourselves one to another in the fear of God.

Z

John 3. 20, 21. *See u, U, § 22, page 75.*

Heb. 4. 13 Neither is there any creature that is not manifest in his sight: but all things *are* naked and opened unto the eyes of him with whom we have to do.

2

Or, *discovered.*

3

Or, *it.*

A

Rom. 13. 11, 12. *See m, M, § 343, page 874.*

B

Rom. 6. 4 Therefore we are buried with him by baptism into death: that like as Christ was raised up from the dead by the glory of the Father, even so we also should walk in newness of life.

5 For if we have been planted together in the likeness of his death, we shall be also *in the likeness* of *his* resurrection:

Rom. 6. 8 Now if we be dead with Christ, we believe that we shall also live with him:

C

Col. 4. 5 Walk in wisdom toward them that are without, redeeming the time.

D

Gal. 6. 10 As we have therefore opportunity, let us do good unto all *men*, especially unto them who are of the household of faith.

Col. 4. 5. *See under C.*

E

Eccl. 11. 2 Give a portion to seven, and also to eight; for thou knowest not what evil shall be upon the earth.

Eccl. 12. 1 Remember now thy Creator in the days of thy youth, while the evil days come not, nor the years draw nigh, when thou shalt say, I have no pleasure in them;

John 12. 35 Then Jesus said unto them, Yet a little while is the light with you. Walk while ye have the light, lest darkness come upon you: for he that walketh in darkness knoweth not whither he goeth.

Eph. 6. 13 Wherefore take unto you the whole armour of God, that ye may be able to withstand in the evil day, and having done all, to stand.

F

Col. 4. 5. *See under C.*

G

Rom. 12. 2 And be not conformed to this world: but be ye transformed by the renewing of your mind, that ye may prove what *is* that good, and acceptable, and perfect will of God.

H

1Thes. 4. 3 For this is the will of God, *even* your sanctification, that ye should abstain from fornication:

1Thes. 5. 18 In every thing give thanks: for this is the will of God in Christ Jesus concerning you.

I

Deut. 21. 20 And they shall say unto the elders of his city, This our son *is* stubborn and rebellious, he will not obey our voice; *he is* a glutton, and a drunkard.

21 And all the men of his city shall stone him with stones, that he die: so shalt thou put evil away from among you; and all Israel shall hear, and fear.

Prov. 20. 1 Wine *is* a mocker, strong drink *is* raging: and whosoever is deceived thereby is not wise.

Prov. 23. 20 Be not among winebibbers; among riotous eaters of flesh:

AND WARNINGS (CONCLUDED).

I—CONCLUDED.

Prov. 23. 31 Look not thou upon the wine when it is red, when it giveth his colour in the cup, *when* it moveth itself aright.

Isa. 5. 11 Woe unto them that rise up early in the morning, *that* they may follow strong drink; that continue until night, *till* wine inflame them!

Isa. 5. 22 Woe unto *them that are* mighty to drink wine, and men of strength to mingle strong drink:

Luke 21. 34 And take heed to yourselves, lest at any time your hearts be overcharged with surfeiting, and drunkenness, and cares of this life, and *so* that day come upon you unawares.

Rom. 13. 13 Let us walk honestly, as in the day; not in rioting and drunkenness, not in chambering and wantonness, not in strife and envying:

I Cor. 5. 11 But now I have written unto you not to keep company, if any man that is called a brother be a fornicator, or covetous, or an idolater, or a railer, or a drunkard, or an extortioner; with such a one no not to eat.

I Cor. 6. 10 Nor thieves, nor covetous, nor drunkards, nor revilers, nor extortioners, shall inherit the kingdom of God.

Gal. 5. 21 Envyings, murders, drunkenness, revellings, and such like: of the which I tell you before, as I have also told *you* in time past, that they which do such things shall not inherit the kingdom of God.

K

Ps. 95. 2 Let us come before his presence with thanksgiving, and make a joyful noise unto him with psalms.

Ps. 105. 2 Sing unto him, sing psalms unto him: talk ye of all his wondrous works.

Matt. 26. 30 And when they had sung a hymn, they went out into the mount of Olives.

Acts 16. 25 And at midnight Paul and Silas prayed, and sang praises unto God: and the prisoners heard them.

I Cor. 14. 26 How is it then, brethren? when ye come together, every one of you hath a psalm, hath a doctrine; hath a tongue, hath a revelation, hath an interpretation. Let all things be done unto edifying.

Col. 3. 16 Let the word of Christ dwell in you richly in all wisdom; teaching and admonishing one another in psalms and hymns and spiritual songs, singing with grace in your hearts to the Lord.

Jas. 5. 13 Is any among you afflicted? let him pray. Is any merry? let him sing psalms.

L

Ps. 34. 1 I will bless the LORD at all times: his praise *shall* continually *be* in my mouth.

Isa. 63. 7 I will mention the lovingkindnesses of the LORD, *and* the praises of the LORD, according to all that the LORD hath bestowed on us, and the great goodness toward the house of Israel, which he hath bestowed on them according to his mercies, and according to the multitude of his lovingkindnesses.

Col. 3. 17 And whatsoever ye do in word or deed, *do* all in the name of the Lord Jesus, giving thanks to God and the Father by him.

Phil. 4. 6 Be careful for nothing; but in every thing by prayer and supplication with thanksgiving let your requests be made known unto God.

I Thes. 5. 18 In every thing give thanks: for this is the will of God in Christ Jesus concerning you.

II Thes. 1. 3 We are bound to thank God always for you, brethren, as it is meet, because that your faith groweth exceedingly, and the charity of every one of you all toward each other aboundeth;

M

Heb. 13. 15 By him therefore let us offer the sacrifice of praise to God continually, that is, the fruit of *our* lips giving thanks to his name.

I Pet. 2. 5 Ye also, as lively stones, are built up a spiritual house, a holy priesthood, to offer up spiritual sacrifices, acceptable to God by Jesus Christ.

I Pet. 4. 11 If any man speak, *let him speak* as the oracles of God; if any man minister, *let him do it* as of the ability which God giveth: that God in all things may be glorified through Jesus Christ, to whom be praise and dominion for ever and ever. Amen.

N

Phil. 2. 3 *Let* nothing *be done* through strife or vainglory; but in lowliness of mind let each esteem other better than themselves.

I Pet. 2. 13 Submit yourselves to every ordinance of man for the Lord's sake: whether it be to the king, as supreme;

I Pet. 5. 5 Likewise, ye younger, submit yourselves unto the elder. Yea, all *of you* be subject one to another, and be clothed with humility: for God resisteth the proud, and giveth grace to the humble.

§ 435. THE SACRED RELATIONSHIP OF CHRIST AND THE

5 : 22-33.

22 [a]Wives submit yourself unto your own husbands, [b]as unto the Lord.

23 For [c]the husband is the head of the wife, even as [d]Christ is the head of the church: and he is the Saviour of [e]the body.

24 Therefore as the church is subject unto Christ, so *let* the wives *be* to their own husbands [f]in every thing.

25 [g]Husbands, love your wives, even as Christ also loved the church, and [h]gave himself for it;

26 That he might sanctify and cleanse it [i]with the washing of water [k]by the word,

27 [l]That he might present it to himself a glorious church, [m]not having spot, or wrinkle, or any such thing; [n]but that it should be holy and without blemish.

28 So ought men to love their wives as their own bodies. He that loveth his wife loveth himself.

29 For no man ever yet hated his own flesh; but nourisheth and cherisheth it, even as the Lord the church:

30 For [o]we are members of his body, of his flesh, and of his bones.

31 [p]For this cause shall a man leave his father and mother, and shall be joined unto his wife, and they [q]two shall be one flesh.

32 This is a great mystery: but I speak concerning Christ and the church.

33 Nevertheless [r]let every one of you in particular so love his wife even as himself; and the wife *see* that she [s]reverence *her* husband.

A

Gen. 3. 16 Unto the woman he said, I will greatly multiply thy sorrow and thy conception; in sorrow thou shalt bring forth children; and thy desire *shall be*

A—CONCLUDED.

to thy husband, and he shall rule over thee.

I Cor. 14. 34 Let your women keep silence in the churches: for it is not permitted unto them to speak: but *they are commanded* to be under obedience, as also saith the law.

Col. 3. 18 Wives, submit yourselves unto your own husbands, as it is fit in the Lord.

Tit. 2. 5 *To be* discreet, chaste, keepers at home, good, obedient to their own husbands, that the word of God be not blasphemed.

I Pet. 3. 1 Likewise, ye wives, *be* in subjection to your own husbands; that, if any obey not the word, they also may without the word be won by the conversation of the wives;

B

Eph. 6. 5 Servants, be obedient to them that are *your* masters according to the flesh with fear and trembling, in singleness of your heart, as unto Christ:

C

I Cor. 11. 3 But I would have you know, that the head of every man is Christ; and the head of the woman *is* the man; and the head of Christ *is* God.

D

Eph. 1. 22. *See o, O, § 427, page 1032.*

Eph. 4. 15 But speaking the truth in love, may grow up into him in all things, which is the head, *even* Christ:

Col. 1. 18 And he is the head of the body, the church: who is the beginning, the firstborn from the dead; that in all things he might have the preeminence.

E

I Cor. 12. 27. *See h, H, § 371, page 940.*

F

Col. 3. 20 Children, obey *your* parents in all things: for this is well pleasing unto the Lord.

Col. 3. 22 Servants, obey in all things *your* masters according to the flesh; not with eyeservice, as menpleasers; but in singleness of heart, fearing God:

G

Col. 3. 19 Husbands, love *your* wives, and be not bitter against them.

I Pet. 3. 7 Likewise, ye husbands, dwell with *them* according to knowledge, giving honour unto the wife, as unto the weaker vessel, and as being heirs together of the grace of life; that your prayers be not hindered.

CHURCH ILLUSTRATED IN THAT OF HUSBAND AND WIFE.

H

Acts 20. 28 Take heed therefore unto yourselves and to all the flock, over the which the Holy Ghost hath made you overseers, to feed the church of God, which he hath purchased with his own blood.

Gal. 1. 4 Who gave himself for our sins, that he might deliver us from this present evil world, according to the will of God and our Father:

Gal. 2. 20 I am crucified with Christ: nevertheless I live; yet not I, but Christ liveth in me: and the life which I now live in the flesh I live by the faith of the Son of God, who loved me, and gave himself for me.

I

John 3. 5 Jesus answered, Verily, verily, I say unto thee, Except a man be born of water and *of* the Spirit, he cannot enter into the kingdom of God.

Tit. 3. 5 Not by works of righteousness which we would have done, but according to his mercy he saved us, by the washing of regeneration, and renewing of the Holy Ghost;

Heb. 10. 22 Let us draw near with a true heart in full assurance of faith, having our hearts sprinkled from an evil conscience, and our bodies washed with pure water.

1 Jno 5. 6 This is he that came by water and blood, *even* Jesus Christ; not by water only, but by water and blood. And it is the Spirit that beareth witness, because the Spirit is truth.

K

John 15. 3 Now ye are clean through the word which I have spoken unto you.

John 17. 17 Sanctify them through thy truth: thy word of truth.

Jas. 1. 18 Of his own will begat he us with the word of truth, that we should be a kind of firstfruits of his creatures.

1Pet. 1. 22 Seeing ye have purified your souls in obeying the truth through the Spirit unto unfeigned love of the brethren, *see that ye* love one another with a pure heart fervently:

23 Being born again not of corruptible seed, but of incorruptible, by the word of God, which liveth and abideth for ever.

L

2Cor.11. 2 For I am jealous over you with godly jealousy: for I have espoused you to one husband, that I may present *you as* a chaste virgin to Christ.

L—CONCLUDED.

Col. 1. 22 In the body of his flesh through death, to present you holy and unblameable and unreproveable in his sight:

M

Song. 4. 7 Thou *art* all fair, my love; *there is* no spot in thee.

N

Luke 1. 74 That he would grant unto us, that we, being delivered out of the hand of our enemies, might serve him without fear.

75 In holiness and righteousness before him, all the days of our life.

Eph. 2. 10 For we are his workmanship, created in Christ Jesus unto good works, which God hath before ordained that we should walk in them.

Col. 1. 22. *See under L.*

O

Gen. 2. 24 Therefore shall a man leave his father and his mother, and shall cleave unto his wife: and they shall be one flesh.

Rom. 12. 5 So we, *being* many, are one body in Christ, and every one members one of another.

1 Cor. 6. 15 Know ye not that your bodies are the members of Christ? shall I then take the members of Christ and make *them* the members of a harlot? God forbid.

1 Cor. 12. 5 And there are differences of administrations, but the same Lord.

P

Gen. 2. 24. *See under O.*

Matt. 19. 5 And said, For this cause shall a man leave father and mother, and shall cleave to his wife: and they twain shall be one flesh?

Matt. 19. 7 They say unto him, Why did Moses then command to give a writing of divorcement, and to put her away?

8 He saith unto them, Moses because of the hardness of your hearts suffered you to put away your wives: but from the beginning it was not so.

Q

1Cor. 6. 16 What? know ye not that he which is joined to a harlot is one body? for two, saith he, shall be one flesh.

R

Eph. 5. 25. *See text of topic.*
Col. 3. 19. *See under G.*

S

1Pet. 3. 6 Even as Sara obeyed Abraham, calling him lord: whose daughters ye are, as long as ye do well, and are not afraid with any amazement.

§ 436. DUTIES OF CHILDREN, PARENTS,

6 : 1-9.

1 Children, [a]obey your parents in the Lord: for this is right.

2 [b]Honour thy father and mother; which is the first commandment with promise;

3 That it may be well with thee, and thou mayest live long on the earth.

4 And, [c]ye fathers, provoke not your children to wrath: but [d]bring them up in the nurture and admonition of the Lord.

5 [e]Servants, be obedient to them that are *your* masters according to the flesh, [f]with fear and trembling, [g]in singleness of your heart, as unto Christ;

6 [h]Not with eyeservice, as menpleasers; but as the servants of Christ, doing the will of God from the heart;

7 With good will doing service, as to the Lord, and not to men:

8 [i]Knowing that whatsoever good thing any man doeth, the same shall he receive of the Lord, [k]whether *he be* bond or free.

9 And, ye [l]masters, do the same things unto them,[1] [m]forbearing threatening: knowing that[2] [n]your Master also is in heaven; [o]neither is there respect of persons with him.

A

Gen. 28. 7 And that Jacob obeyed his father and his mother, and was gone to Padan-aram;

Lev. 19. 3 Ye shall fear every man his mother, and his father, and keep my sabbaths: I *am* the LORD your God.

Deut. 21. 18 If a man have a stubborn and rebellious son, which will not obey the voice of his father, or the voice of his mother, and *that*, when they have chastened him, will not hearken unto them:

19 Then shall his father and his mother lay hold on him, and bring

A—CONCLUDED.

him out unto the elders of his city, and unto the gate of his place;

Deut. 21. 20 And they shall say unto the elders of his city, This our son *is* stubborn and rebellious, he will not obey our voice; *he is* a glutton, and a drunkard.

21 And all the men of his city shall stone him with stones, that he die: so shalt thou put evil away from among you; and all Israel shall hear, and fear.

Esth. 2. 20 Esther had not *yet* shewed her kindred nor her people; as Mordecai had charged her: for Esther did the commandment of Mordecai, like as when she was brought up with him.

Prov. 1. 8 My son, hear the instruction of thy father, and forsake not the law of thy mother:

Prov. 6. 20 My son, keep thy father's commandment, and forsake not the law of thy mother:

Prov. 23. 22 Hearken unto thy father that begat thee, and despise not thy mother when she is old.

Jer. 35. 14 The words of Jonadab the son of Rechab, that he commanded his sons not to drink wine, are performed; for unto this day they drink none, but obey their father's commandment: notwithstanding I have spoken unto you, rising early and speaking; but ye hearkened not unto me.

Luke 2. 51 And he went down with them, and came to Nazareth, and was subject unto them: but his mother kept all these sayings in her heart.

Col. 3. 20 Children, obey *your* parents in all things: for this is well pleasing unto the Lord.

B

Jer. 35. 18 And Jeremiah said unto the house of the Rechabites, Thus saith the LORD of hosts, the God of Israel; Because ye have obeyed the commandment of Jonadab your father, and kept all his precepts, and done according unto all that he hath commanded you;

Mal. 1. 6 A son honoureth *his* father, and a servant his master: if then I *be* a father, where *is* mine honour? and if I *be* a master, where *is* my fear? saith the LORD of hosts unto you, O priests, that despise my name. And ye say, wherein have we despised thy name?

C

Col. 3. 21 Fathers, provoke not your children *to anger*, lest they be discouraged.

SERVANTS AND MASTERS.

D

Gen. 18. **19 For I know him, that he will command his children and his household after him, and they shall keep the way of the LORD, to do justice and judgment; that the LORD may bring upon Abraham that which he hath spoken of him.**

Deut. 4. 9 Only take heed to thyself, and keep thy soul diligently, lest thou forget the things which thine eyes have seen, and lest they depart from thy heart all the days of thy life: but teach them thy sons, and thy sons' sons.

Deut. 6. 7 And thou shalt teach them diligently unto thy children, and shalt talk of them when thou sittest in thine house, and when thou walkest by the way, and when thou liest down, and when thou risest up.

Deut. 6. 20 *And* when thy son asketh thee in time to come, saying, What *mean* the testimonies, and the statutes, and the judgments, which the LORD our God hath commanded you?

21 Then thou shalt say unto thy son, we were Pharaoh's bondmen in Egypt; and the LORD brought us out of Egypt with a mighty hand:

Ps. 78. 4 We will not hide *them* from their children, shewing to the generation to come the praises of the LORD, and his strength, and his wonderful works that he hath done.

Prov. 19. 18 Chasten thy son while there is hope, and let not thy soul spare for his crying.

Prov. 22. 6 Train up a child in the way he should go: and when he is old he will not depart from it.

Prov. 29. 17 Correct thy son, and he shall give thee rest; yea, he shall give delight unto thy soul.

E

Col. 3. 22 Servants, obey in all things *your* masters according to the flesh; not with eyeservice, as menpleasers; but in singleness of heart, fearing God:

I Tim. 6. 1 Let as many servants as are under the yoke count their own masters worthy of all honour, that the name of God and *his* doctrine be not blasphemed.

Tit. 2. 9 *Exhort* servants to be obedient unto their own masters, *and* to please *them* well in all things; not answering again.

I Pet. 2. 18 Servants, *be* subject to *your* masters with all fear; not only to the good and gentle, but also to the froward.

E—CONCLUDED.

F

II Cor. 7. 15 And his inward affection is more abundant toward you, whilst he remembereth the obedience of you all, how with fear and trembling ye received him.

Phil. 2. 12 Wherefore, my beloved, as ye have always obeyed, not as in my presence only, but now much more in my absence, work out your own salvation with fear and trembling:

G

I Chr. 29. 17 I know also, my God, that thou triest the heart, and hast pleasure in uprightness. As for me, in the uprightness of mine heart I have willingly offered all these things: and now have I seen with joy thy people, which are present here, to offer willingly unto thee.

H

Col. 3. 22. *See under E.*

23 And whatsoever ye do, do *it* heartily, as to the Lord, and not unto men;

I

Rom. 2. 6. *See h, H, § 320, page 816.*

K

Gal. 3. 28 There is neither Jew nor Greek, there is neither bond nor free, there is neither male nor female: for ye are all one in Christ Jesus.

Col. 3. 11 Where there is neither Greek nor Jew, circumcision nor uncircumcision, Barbarian, Scythian, bond *nor* free: but Christ *is* all, and in all.

L

Col. 4. 1 Masters, give unto *your* servants that which is just and equal; knowing that ye also have a Master in heaven.

1

Or, *moderating.*

M

Lev. 25. 43 Thou shalt not rule over him with rigour; but shalt fear thy God.

2

Some read, *both your and their master.*

N

Matt. 22. 10 Neither be ye called masters: for one is your Master, *even* Christ.

John 13. 13. *See n, N, § 182, page 515.*

O

Rom. 2. 11. *See m, M, § 320, page 816.*

Col. 3. 25 But he that doeth wrong shall receive for the wrong which he hath done: and there is no respect of persons.

§ 437. EXHORTATION TO ZEAL IN THE

6 : 10-20.

10 Finally, my brethren, be strong in the Lord, and [a]in the power of his might.

11 [b]Put on the whole armour of God, that ye may be able to stand against the wiles of the devil.

12 For we wrestle not against [1c]flesh and blood, but against [d]principalities, against powers, against [e]the rulers of the darkness of this world, against [2]spiritual wickedness in [3]high *places*.

13 [f]Wherefore take unto you the whole armour of God, that ye may be able to withstand [g]in the evil day, and [4]having done all, to stand.

14 Stand therefore, [h]having your loins girt about with truth, and [i]having on the breastplate of righteousness;

15 [k]And your feet shod with the preparation of the gospel of peace;

16 Above all, taking [l]the shield of faith, wherewith ye shall be able to quench all the fiery darts of the wicked.

17 And [m]take the helmet of salvation, and [n]the sword of the Spirit, which is the word of God:

18 [o]Praying always with all prayer and supplication in the Spirit, and [p]watching thereunto with all perseverance and [q]supplication for all saints;

19 [r]And for me, that utterance may be given unto me, that I may open my mouth [s]boldly, to make known the mystery of the gospel,

CHAP. 6.

20 For which [t]I am an ambassador [u5]in bonds; that [6]therein [x]I may speak boldly, as I ought to speak.

A

Eph. 1. 19. *See h, H, § 427, page 1032.*
Eph. 3. 16. *See t, T, § 431, page 1040.*

B

Rom. 13. 12 The night is far spent, the day is at hand: let us therefore cast off the works of darkness, and let us put on the armour of light.

II. Cor. 6. 7. *See k, K, § 396, page 978.*

I Thes. 5. 8 But let us, who are of the day, be sober, putting on the breastplate of faith and love; and for a helmet, the hope of salvation.

1

Gr. *blood and flesh.*

C

I. Cor. 15. 50. *See a, A, § 381, page 954.*

D

Rom. 8. 38. *See x, X, § 334, page 850.*

E

Luke 22. When I was daily with you in the temple, ye stretched forth no hands against me: but this is your hour, and the power of darkness.

John 12. 31. *See n, N, § 170, page 475.*

Col. 1. 13 Who hath delivered us from the power of darkness, and hath translated *us* into the kingdom of his dear Son:

2

Or, *wicked spirits.*

3

Or, *heavenly.*

Eph. 1. 3 Blessed *be* the God and Father of our Lord Jesus Christ, who hath blessed us with all spiritual blessings in heavenly *places* in Christ:

F

Eph. 6. 11. *See text of topic.*

G

Eph. 5. 16. *See e, E, § 434, page 1050.*

4

Or, *having overcome all.*

§ 438. TYCHICUS SENT AS A MESSENGER.

6 : 21–24.

21 But [a]that ye also may know my affairs, *and* how I do, [b]Tychicus, a beloved brother and faithful minister

A

Phil. 1. 12 But I would ye should understand, brethren, that the things *which happened* unto me have fallen out rather unto the furtherance of the gospel;

Col. 4. 7 All my state shall Tychicus de-

FIGURE OF ARMOURED WARFARE.

H

Isa. 11. 5 And righteousness shall be the girdle of his loins, and faithfulness the girdle of his reins.

Luke 12. 35. *See f, F,* §57, *page 189.*

I

Isa. 59. 17 For he put on righteousness as a breastplate, and a helmet of salvation upon his head; and he put on the garments of vengeance *for* clothing, and was clad with zeal as a cloak.

II Cor. 6. 7. *See k, K,* § *396 page 978.*

K

Rom. 10. 15. *See r, R,* § *337, page 860.*

L

I Jno. 5. 4 For whatsoever is born of God overcometh the world: and this is the victory that overcometh the world, *even* our faith.

M

Isa. 59. 17. *See under I*
I Thes. 5. 8. *See under B.*

N

Heb. 4. 12 For the word of God *is* quick, and powerful, and sharper than any twoedged sword, piercing even to the dividing asunder of soul and spirit, and of the joints and marrow, and *is* a discerner of the thoughts and intents of the heart.

Rev. 1. 16 And he had in his right hand seven stars: and out of his mouth went a sharp twoedged sword: and his countenance *was* as the sun shineth in his strength.

Rev. 2. 16 Repent; or else I will come unto thee quickly, and will fight against them with the sword of my mouth.

Rev. 19. 15 And out of his mouth goeth a sharp sword, that with it he should smite the nations: and he shall rule them with a rod of iron: and he treadeth the winepress of the fierceness and wrath of Almighty God.

O

Luke 18. 1. *See a, A,* § *140, page 401.*

P

Matt. 26. 41. *See b, B,* § *192, page 550.*

Q

Eph. 1. 16 Cease not to give thanks for you, making mention of you in my prayers;

Q—Concluded.

Phil. 1. 4 Always in every prayer of mine for you all making request with joy.

Col. 1. 4 Since we heard of your faith in Christ Jesus, and of the love *which ye have* to all the saints,

I Tim. 2. 1 I exhort therefore, that, first of all, supplications, prayers, intercessions, *and* giving of thanks, be made for all men;

R

Acts 4. 29 And now, Lord, behold their threatenings: and grant unto thy servants, that with all boldness they may speak thy word,

Col. 4. 3 Withal praying also for us, that God would open unto us a door of utterance, to speak the mystery of Christ, for which I am also in bonds:

II Thes. 3. 1 Finally, brethren, pray for us, that the word of the Lord may have *free* course, and be glorified, even as *it is* with you.

S

II Cor. 3. 12. *See a, A,* § *391, page 970.*

T

II Cor. 5. 20. *See o, O,* § *395 page 978.*

U

Acts 28. 20. *See f, F,* § *316, page 804.*

5

Or, *in a chain.*

6

Or, *thereof.*

X

Acts 28. 31 Preaching the kingdom of God, and teaching those things which concern the Lord Jesus Christ, with all confidence, no man forbidding him.

Phil. 1. 20 According to my earnest expectation and *my* hope, that in nothing I shall be ashamed, but *that* with all boldness, as always, *so* now also Christ shall be magnified in my body, whether *it be* by life, or by death.

I Thes. 2. 2 But even after that we had suffered before, and were shamefully entreated, as ye know, at Philippi, we were bold in our God to speak unto you the gospel of God with much contention.

CLOSING BENEDICTION.

A—Concluded.

clare unto you, *who is* a beloved brother, and a faithful minister and fellow servant in the Lord:

B

Acts 20. 4 And there accompanied him into

B—Continued.

Asia Sopater of Berea; and of the Thessalonians, Aristarchus and Secundus; and Gaius of Derba, and Timotheus; and of Asia, Tychicus and Trophimus.

For B concluded, see next page (1058).

§ 438. TYCHICUS SENT AS A MESSENGER.

CHAP. 6.

in the Lord, shall make known to you all things:

22 [c]Whom I have sent unto you for the same purpose, that ye might know our affairs, and *that* he might comfort your hearts.

23 [d]Peace *be* to the brethren, and love with faith, from God the Father and the Lord Jesus Christ.

24 Grace *be* with all them that love our Lord Jesus Christ [e1]in sincerity. Amen.

B—CONCLUDED.

IITim. 4. 12 And Tychicus have I sent to Ephesus.

Tit. 3. 12 When I shall send Artemas unto thee, or Tychicus, be diligent to come unto me to Nicopolis: for I have determined there to winter.

C

Phil. 2. 19 But I trust in the Lord Jesus to send Timotheus shortly unto you, that I also may be of good comfort, when I know your state.

20 For I have no man likeminded, who will naturally care for your state.

Phil. 2. 25 Yet I supposed it necessary to send to you Epaphroditus, my brother, and companion in labour, and fellow soldier, but your messenger, and he that ministered to my wants.

PAUL'S EPISTLE TO

§ 439. THE SALUTATION.

1 : 1, 2.

1 Paul and Timotheus, the servants of Jesus Christ, to all the saints [a]in Christ Jesus which are [b]at Philippi, with the [c]bishops and deacons:

2 [d]Grace *be* unto you, and peace, from God our Father and *from* the Lord Jesus Christ.

A

I Cor. 1. 2 Unto the church of God which is

A—CONCLUDED.

at Corinth, to them that are sanctified in Christ Jesus, called *to be* saints, with all that in every place call upon the name of Jesus Christ our Lord, both theirs and ours:

B

Acts 16. 12 And from thence to Philippi, which is the chief city of that part of Macedonia, *and* a colony: and we were in that city abiding certain days.

13 And on the sabbath we went out of the city by a river side, where prayer

§ 440. PAUL GIVES THANKS FOR FELLOWSHIP AND

1 : 3–11.

3 [a]I thank my God upon every [1]remembrance of you,

4 Always in every prayer of mine for you all making request with joy,

5 [b]For your fellowship in the gospel from the first day until now;

A

Rom. 1. 8, 9. *See a, A, §318, page 808.*

Eph. 1. 15 Wherefore I also, after I heard of your faith in the Lord Jesus, and love unto all the saints,

16 Cease not to give thanks for you, making mention of you in my prayers;

IIThes. 1. 3 We are bound to thank God always for you, brethren, as it is meet, because that your faith groweth ex-

CLOSING BENEDICTION (Concluded).

C—Concluded.

Col. 4. 7 All my state shall Tychicus declare unto you, *who is* a beloved brother, and a faithful minister and fellow servant in the Lord:

Col. 4. 8 Whom I have sent unto you for the same purpose, that he might know your estate, and comfort your hearts;

I Thes. 3. 2 And sent Timotheus, our brother, and minister of God, and our fellow labourer in the gospel of Christ, to establish you, and to comfort you concerning your faith:

D

Gen. 43. 23 And he said, Peace *be* to you, fear not: your God, and the God of your father, hath given you treasure in your sacks: I had your money. And he brought Simeon out unto them.

D—Concluded.

I Sa. 25. 6 And thus shall ye say to him that liveth *in prosperity*, Peace *be* both to thee, and peace *be* to thine house, and peace *be* unto all that thou hast.

I Pet. 5. 14 Greet ye one another with a kiss of charity. Peace *be* with you all that are in Christ Jesus. Amen.

E

Matt. 22. 37. *See c, C, § 165, page 460.*

II Cor. 8. 8 I speak not by commandment, but by occasion of the forwardness of others, and to prove the sincerity of your love.

Tit. 2. 7 In all things shewing thyself a pattern of good works: in doctrine *shewing* uncorruptness, gravity, sincerity,

1

Or, *with incorruption.*

THE PHILIPPIANS.

Written probably during Autumn of A. D. 62, at Rome.

B—Concluded.

was wont to be made; and we sat down, and spake unto the women which resorted *thither*.

C

Acts 1. 20 For it is written in the book of Psalms, Let his habitation be desolate, and let no man dwell therein: and, His bishoprick let another take.

I Tim. 3. 1 This *is* a true saying, If a man desire the office of a bishop, he desireth a good work.

2 A bishop then must be blameless,

C—Concluded.

the husband of one wife, vigilant, sober, of good behaviour, given to hospitality, apt to teach;

Tit. 1. 7 For a bishop must be blameless, as the steward of God; not selfwilled, not soon angry, not given to wine, no striker, not given to filthy lucre;

I Pet. 2. 25 For ye were as sheep going astray; but are now returned unto the Shepherd and Bishop of your souls.

D

Rom. 1. 7. *See m, M, §317, page 808.*

PRAYS THAT FRUIT OF RIGHTEOUSNESS MAY ABOUND.

A—Concluded.

ceedingly, and the charity of every one of you all toward each other aboundeth;

1

Or, *mention.*

B

Rom. 12. 13 Distributing to the necessity of saints; given to hospitality.

Rom. 15. 16 That I should be the minister of Jesus Christ to the Gentiles, ministering the gospel of God, that the offer-

B—Continued.

ing up of the Gentiles might be acceptable, being sanctified by the Holy Ghost.

II Cor. 8. 1 Moreover, brethren, we do you to wit of the grace of God bestowed on the churches of Macedonia;

Phil. 4. 14 Notwithstanding, ye have well done, that ye did communicate with my affliction.

For B concluded, see next page (1060).

§ 440. PAUL GIVES THANKS FOR FELLOWSHIP AND PRAYS

CHAP. I.

6 Being confident of this very thing,
that he which hath begun [c]a good
work in you [2]will perform *it* [d]until
the day of Jesus Christ:
7 Even as it is meet for me to think
this of you all, because [3]I have you
[e]in my heart; inasmuch as both in
[f]my bonds, and in [g]the defence and
confirmation of the gospel, [h]ye all
are [4]partakers of my grace.
8 For [i]God is my record, [k]how
greatly I long after you all in the
bowels of Jesus Christ.
9 And this I pray, [l]that your love
may abound yet more and more in
knowledge and *in* all [5]judgment;
10 That [m]ye may [6]approve things
that [7]are excellent; [n]that ye may be
sincere and without offence [o]till the
day of Christ;
11 Being filled with the fruits of
righteousness, [p]which are by Jesus
Christ, [q]unto the glory and praise of
God.

B—CONTINUED.

Phil. 4. 15 Now ye Philippians know also, that in the beginning of the gospel, when I departed from Macedonia, no

B—CONCLUDED.

church communicated with me as concerning giving and receiving, but ye only.

C

John 6. 29 Jesus answered and said unto them, This is the work of God, that ye believe on him whom he hath sent.

I Thes. 1. 3 Remembering without ceasing your work of faith, and labour of love, and patience of hope in our Lord Jesus Christ, in the sight of God and our Father;

2

Or, *will finish it.*

D

Phil. 1. 10. *See text of topic.*

II Pet. 3. 10 But the day of the Lord will come as a thief in the night; in the which the heavens shall pass away with a great noise, and the elements shall melt with fervent heat, the earth also and the works that are therein shall be burned up.

3

Or, *ye have me in your heart.*

E

II Cor. 6. 11, 12. *See o, O, § 396, page 980.*

F

Eph. 3. 1. *See a, A, § 430, page 1038.*

G

Phil. 1. 17. *See text of topic, § 441.*

I Cor. 9. 17 For if I do this thing willingly, I have a reward: but if against my will, a dispensation *of the gospel* is committed unto me.

§ 441. PAUL DECLARES HIS BONDS

I: 12–30.

12 But I would ye should understand, brethren, that the things *which*
happened unto me have fallen out
rather unto the furtherance of the
gospel;
13 So that my bonds [1]in Christ are
manifest [a]in all [2]the palace, and [3]in
all other *places;*
14 And many of the brethren in
the Lord, waxing confident by my
bonds, are much more bold to speak
the word without fear.
15 Some indeed preach Christ even

CHAP. I.

of envy and [b]strife; and some also
of good will:
16 The one preach Christ of contention, not sincerely, supposing to
add affliction to my bonds:
17 But the other of love, knowing
that I am set for [c]the defence of the
gospel.
18 What then? notwithstanding,
every way, whether in pretence, or
in truth, Christ is preached; and I
therein do rejoice, yea, and will rejoice.
19 For I know that this shall turn

THAT THE FRUIT OF RIGHTEOUSNESS MAY ABOUND (CONCLUDED).

H

Phil. 4. 14 Notwithstanding ye have well done, that ye did communicate with my affliction.

4

Or, *partakers with me of grace.*

I

Rom. 9. 1. *See a, A, § 335, page 852.*

K

Phil. 2. 26 For he longed after you all, and was full of heaviness, because that ye had heard that he had been sick.

Phil. 4. 1 Therefore, my brethren dearly beloved and longed for, my joy and crown, so stand fast in the Lord, *my* dearly beloved.

L

I Thes. 3. 12 And the Lord make you to increase and abound in love one toward another, and toward all *men*, even as we *do* toward you:

II Pet. 3. 18 But grow in grace, and *in* the knowledge of our Lord and Saviour Jesus Christ. To him *be* glory both now and for ever. Amen.

5

Or, *sense.*

M

Eph. 5. 10. *See s, S, § 434, page 1048.*

6

Or, *try.*

7

Or, *differ.*

N

Acts 24. 16 And herein do I exercise myself, to have always a conscience void of offence toward God, and *toward* men.

N—CONCLUDED.

I Thes. 3. 13 To the end he may stablish your hearts unblameable in holiness before God, even our Father, at the coming of our Lord Jesus Christ with all his saints.

I Thes. 5. 23 And the very God of peace sanctify you wholly; and *I pray God* your whole spirit and soul and body be preserved blameless unto the coming of our Lord Jesus Christ.

O

I Cor. 1. 8 Who shall also confirm you unto the end, *that ye may be* blameless in the day of our Lord Jesus Christ.

P

John 15. 4 Abide in me, and I in you. As the branch cannot bear fruit of itself except it abide in the vine; no more can ye, except ye abide in me.

5 I am the vine, ye *are* the branches. He that abideth in me, and I in him, the same bringeth forth much fruit; for without me ye can do nothing.

Eph. 5. 27. *See n, N, § 435, page 1052.*

Col. 1. 6 Which is come unto you, as *it is* in all the world; and bringeth forth fruit, as *it doth* also in you, since the day ye heard *of it*, and knew the grace of God in truth:

Q

John 15. 8 Herein is my Father glorified, that ye bear much fruit; so shall ye be my disciples.

Eph. 1. 12 That we should be to the praise of his glory, who first trusted in Christ

A FURTHERANCE TO THE GOSPEL.

1

Or, *for Christ.*

A

Phil. 4. 22 All the saints salute you, chiefly they that are of Cæsar's household.

2

Or, *Cæsar's court.*

3

Or, *to all others.*

B

Rom. 16. 17 Now I beseech you, brethren, mark them which cause divisions and offences contrary to the doctrine which ye have learned; and avoid them.

18 For they that are such serve not our Lord Jesus Christ, but their own belly; and by good words and fair speeches deceive the hearts of the simple.

B—CONCLUDED.

I Cor. 3. 3 For ye are yet carnal: for whereas *there is* among you envying, and strife, and divisions, are ye not carnal, and walk as men?

4 For while one saith, I am of Paul; and another, I *am* of Apollos; are ye not carnal?

Phil. 2. 3 *Let* nothing *be done* through strife or vainglory; but in lowliness of mind let each esteem other better than themselves.

C

Phil. 1. 7. *See text of topic, § 440.*

I Cor. 9. 16 For though I preach the gospel, I have nothing to glory of: for necessity is laid upon me; yea, woe is unto me, if I preach not the gospel!

For C concluded, see next page (1062).

§ 441. PAUL DECLARES HIS BONDS A

CHAP. I.

to my salvation [d]through your prayer,
and the supply of [e]the Spirit of Jesus
Christ,
20 According to my [f]earnest expectation and *my* hope, that [g]in nothing
I shall be ashamed, but *that* [h]with
all boldness, as always, *so* now also
Christ shall be magnified in my body,
[i]whether *it be* by life, or by death.
21 For to me to live *is* Christ, and
[k]to die *is* gain.
22 But if I live in the flesh, this *is*
the fruit of my labour: yet what I
shall choose I wot not.
23 For [l]I am in a strait betwixt
two, having a desire to [m]depart, and
to be with Christ; which is far better:
24 Nevertheless to abide in the
flesh *is* more needful for you.
25 And [n]having this confidence, I
know that I shall abide and continue
with you all for your furtherance and
joy of faith;
26 That [o]your rejoicing may be
more abundant in Jesus Christ for
me by my coming to you again.
27 Only [p]let your conversation be
as it becometh the gospel of Christ:
that whether I come and see you, or
else be absent, I may hear of your
affairs, [q]that ye stand fast in one
spirit, [r]with one mind [s]striving together for the faith of the gospel;
28 And in nothing [t]terrified by your
adversaries: [u]which is to them an
evident token of perdition, [x]but to
you of salvation, and that of God.
29 For unto you [y]it is given in the
behalf of Christ, not only to believe
on him, but also to suffer for his sake;
30 [z]Having the same conflict [a]which
ye saw in me, and now hear *to be*
in me.

C—CONCLUDED.

I Cor. 9. 17 For if I do this thing willingly, I have a reward: but if against my will, a dispensation *of the gospel* is committed unto me.

D

II Cor. 1. 11 Ye also helping together by prayer for us, that for the gift *bestowed* upon us by the means of many persons thanks may be given by many on our behalf.

E

Rom. 8. 9 But ye are not in the flesh, but in the Spirit, if so be that the Spirit of God dwell in you. Now if any man have not the Spirit of Christ, he is none of his.

F

Rom. 8. 19 For the earnest expectation of the creature waiteth for the manifestation of the sons of God.

G

Rom. 5. 5 And hope maketh not ashamed; because the love of God is shed abroad in our hearts by the Holy Ghost which is given unto us.

§ 442. ADMONISHED TO BE OF ONE MIND AFTER THE PATTERN

2 : 1–18.

1 If *there be* therefore any consolation in Christ, if any comfort of
love, [a]if any fellowship of the Spirit,
if any [b]bowels and mercies,
2 [c]Fulfil ye my joy, [d]that ye be likeminded, having the same love, *being*

A

II Cor. 13. 14. *See f, F, § 408, page 1004.*

B

Phil. 1. 8 For God is my record, how greatly I long after you all in the bowels of Jesus Christ.

Col. 3. 12 Put on therefore, as the elect of God, holy and beloved, bowels of mercies, kindness, humbleness of mind, meekness, longsuffering;

FURTHERANCE TO THE GOSPEL (Concluded).

H

Eph. 6. 19 And for me, that utterance may
be given unto me, that I may open my
mouth boldly, to make known the
mystery of the gospel,
20 For which I am an ambassador in
bonds; that therein I may speak boldly, as I ought to speak.

I

Rom. 14. 7. *See g, G, § 344, page 876.*

K

Rev. 14. 13 And I heard a voice from heaven
saying unto me, Write, Blessed *are* the
dead which die in the Lord from henceforth: Yea, saith the Spirit, that they
may rest from their labours; and their
works do follow them.

L

II Cor. 5. 8 We are confident, *I say*, and willing rather to be absent from the body,
and to be present with the Lord.

M

II Tim. 4. 6 For I am now ready to be offered,
and the time of my departure is at
hand.

N

Phil. 2. 24 But I trust in the Lord that I also
myself shall come shortly.

O

II Cor. 1. 14. *See m, M, § 386, page 964.*

P

Eph. 4. 1. *See b, B, § 432, page 1040.*

Phil. 3. 20 For our conversation is in heaven;
from whence also we look for the Saviour, the Lord Jesus Christ:

Q

Phil. 4. 1 Therefore, my brethren dearly beloved and longed for, my joy and
crown, so stand fast in the Lord, *my*
dearly beloved.

R

Rom. 12. 16. *See g, G, § 342, page 872.*

S

Jude 3 Beloved, when I gave all diligence
to write unto you of the common salvation, it was needful for me to write
unto you, and exhort *you* that ye should
earnestly contend for the faith which
was once delivered unto the saints.

T

Isa. 41. 10 Fear thou not; for I *am* with thee:
be not dismayed; for I *am* thy God: I
will strengthen thee; yea, I will help
thee; yea, I will uphold thee with the
right hand of my righteousness.

Matt. 10. 28 And fear not them which kill the
body, but are not able to kill the soul:
but rather fear him which is able to
destroy both soul and body in hell.

Heb. 13. 5 *Let your* conversation *be* without
covetousness; *and be* content with such
things as ye have: for he hath said, I
will never leave thee, nor forsake thee.
6 So that we may boldly say, The
Lord *is* my helper, and I will not fear
what man shall do unto me.

U

II Thes. 1. 5 *Which is* a manifest token of the
righteous judgment of God, that ye
may be counted worthy of the kingdom of God, for which ye also suffer:
6 Seeing *it is* a righteous thing with
God to recompense tribulation to them
that trouble you;

X

Rom. 8. 17. *See d, D, § 332, page 846.*

Y

Acts 5. 41. *See g, G, § 243, page 662.*

Z

Col. 2. 1 For I would that ye knew what
great conflict I have for you, and *for*
them at Laodicea, and *for* as many as
have not seen my face in the flesh;

A

Acts 16. 19-24. *See e, E, § 275, page 738.*

OF CHRIST. AS LIGHTS HOLD FORTH THE WORD OF LIFE.

C

John 3. 29 He that hath the bride is the bridegroom: but the friend of the bridegroom, which standeth and heareth
him, rejoiceth greatly because of the
bridegroom's voice: this my joy therefore is fulfilled.

D

Rom. 12. 16. *See g, G, § 342, page 872.*

II Cor. 13. 11 Finally, brethren, farewell. Be

D—Concluded.

perfect, be of good comfort, be of one
mind, live in peace; and the God of
love and peace shall be with you.

Phil. 1. 27. *See text of topic, § 441.*

E

Gal. 5. 26 Let us not be desirous of vainglory, provoking one another, envying
one another.

§ 442. ADMONISHED TO BE OF ONE MIND AFTER THE PATTERN OF

CHAP. 2.

of one accord, of one mind.

3 [e]*Let* nothing *be done* through strife or vainglory; but [f]in lowliness of mind let each esteem other better than themselves.

4 [g]Look not every man on his own things, but every man also on the things of others.

5 [h]Let this mind be in you, which was also in Christ Jesus:

6 Who, [i]being in the form of God, [k]thought it not robbery to be equal with God:

7 [l]But made himself of no reputation, and took upon him the form [m]of a servant, and [n]was made in the [1]likeness of men:

8 And being found in fashion as a man, he humbled himself, and [o]became obedient unto death, even the death of the cross.

9 Wherefore God also [p]hath highly exalted him, and [q]given him a name which is above every name:

10 [r]That at the name of Jesus every knee should bow, of *things* in heaven, and *things* in earth, and *things* under the earth;

11 And [s]*that* every tongue should confess that Jesus Christ *is* Lord, to the glory of God the Father.

12 Wherefore, my beloved, [t]as ye have always obeyed, not as in my presence only, but now much more in my absence, [u]work out your own salvation with [x]fear and trembling:

13 For [y]it is God which worketh in you both to will and to do of *his* good pleasure.

E—CONCLUDED. See preceding page (1063).

Phil. 1. 15, 16. *See b, B, § 441, page 1060.*

Jas. 3. 14 But if ye have bitter envying and strife in your hearts, glory not, and lie not against the truth.

F

Rom. 12. 10. *See y, Y, § 342, page 870.*
Eph. 5. 21. *See n, N, § 434, page 1050.*

G

Rom. 15. 1, 2. *See c, C, § 345, page 878.*

H

Matt. 11. 29 Take my yoke upon you, and learn of me; for I am meek and lowly in heart: and ye shall find rest unto your souls.

John 13. 15 For I have given you an example, that ye should do as I have done to you.

I Pet. 2. 21 For even hereunto were ye called: because Christ also suffered for us, leaving us an example, that ye should follow his steps:

I Jno. 2. 6 He that saith he abideth in him ought himself also so to walk, even as he walked.

I

John 1. 1 In the beginning was the Word, and the word was with God, and the Word was God.

2 The same was in the beginning with God.

John 17. 5 And now, O Father, glorify thou me with thine own self with the glory which I had with thee before the world was.

II Cor. 4. 4 In whom the god of this world hath blinded the minds of them which believe not, lest the light of the glorious gospel of Christ, who is the image of God, should shine unto them.

Col. 1. 15 Who is the image of the invisible God, the firstborn of every creature:

Heb. 1. 3 Who being the brightness of *his* glory, and the express image of his person, and upholding all things by the word of his power, when he had by himself purged our sins, sat down on the right hand of the Majesty on high;

K

John 5. 18. *See c, C, § 38, page 109.*

L

Ps. 22. 6 But I *am* a worm, and no man; a reproach of men, and despised of the people.

Isa. 53. 3 He is despised and rejected of men; a man of sorrows, and acquainted with grief: and we hid as it were *our* faces from him; he was despised, and we esteemed him not.

CHRIST. AS LIGHTS HOLD FORTH THE WORD OF LIFE (Continued).

L—Concluded.

Mark 9. 12 And he answered and told them, Elias verily cometh first, and restoreth all things; and how it is written of the Son of man, that he must suffer many things, and be set at nought.

Rom. 15. 3 For even Christ pleased not himself; but, as it is written, The reproaches of them that reproached thee fell on me.

M

Isa. 42. 1 Behold my servant, whom I uphold; mine elect, *in whom* my soul delighteth; I have put my Spirit upon him: he shall bring forth judgment to the Gentiles.

Eze. 34. 23 And I will set up one Shepherd over them, and he shall feed them, *even* my servant David; he shall feed them, and he shall be their shepherd.

Zech. 3. 8 Hear now, O Joshua the high priest, thou, and thy fellows that sit before thee: for they *are* men wondered at: for, behold, I will bring forth my servant the BRANCH.

Matt. 20. 28. *See y, Y, § 148, page 420.*
Luke 22. 27. *See l, L, § 181, page 511.*

N

John 1. 14 And the Word was made flesh, and dwelt among us, (and we beheld his glory, the glory as of the only begotten of the Father,) full of grace and truth.

Rom. 1. 3 Concerning his Son Jesus Christ our Lord, which was made of the seed of David according to the flesh:

Rom. 8. 3 For what the law could not do, in that it was weak through the flesh, God sending his own Son in the likeness of sinful flesh, and for sin, condemned sin in the flesh:

Gal. 4. 4 But when the fullness of the time was come, God sent forth his Son, made of a woman, made under the law,

Heb. 2. 14 Forasmuch then as the children are partakers of flesh and blood, he also himself likewise took part of the same; that through death he might destroy him that had the power of death, that is, the devil;

Heb. 2. 17 Wherefore in all things it behooved him to be made like unto *his* brethren, that he might be a merciful and faithful high priest in things *pertaining* to God, to make reconciliation for the sins of the people.

1
Or, *habit*.

O

Matt. 26. 39 And he went a little further, and fell on his face, and prayed, saying, O my Father, if it be possible, let this cup pass from me: nevertheless not as I will, but as thou *wilt*.

John 10. 18 No man taketh it from me, but I lay it down of myself. I have power to lay it down, and I have power to take it again. This commandment have I received of my Father.

Heb. 5. 8 Though he were a Son, yet learned he obedience by the things which he suffered;

Heb. 12. 2 Looking unto Jesus the author and finisher of *our* faith; who for the joy that was set before him endured the cross, despising the shame, and is set down at the right hand of the throne of God.

P

John 17. 1 These words spake Jesus, and lifted up his eyes to heaven, and said, Father, the hour is come; glorify thy Son, that thy Son also may glorify thee:

2 As thou hast given him power over all flesh, that he should give eternal life to as many as thou hast given him.

John 17. 5 And now, O Father, glorify thou me with thine own self with the glory which I had with thee before the world was.

Acts 2. 33 Therefore being by the right hand of God exhalted, and having received of the Father the promise of the Holy Ghost, he hath shed forth this, which ye now see and hear.

Heb. 2. 9 But we see Jesus, who was made a little lower than the angels for the suffering of death, crowned with glory and honour; that he by the grace of God should taste death for every man.

Q

Eph. 1. 20 Which he wrought in Christ, when he raised him from the dead, and set *him* at his own right hand in the heavenly *places*,

21 For above all principality, and power, and might, and dominion, and every name that is named, not only in this world, but also in that which is to come:

Heb. 1. 4 Being made so much better than the angels, as he hath by inheritance obtained a more excellent name than they.

For R,S,T,U,X, and Y, see next page, (1066).

§ 442. ADMONISHED TO BE OF ONE MIND AFTER THE PATTERN OF S—CONCLUDED.

CHAP. 2.

14 Do all things [z]without murmurings [a]and disputings:

15 That ye may be blameless and [2]harmless, [b]the sons of God, without rebuke, [c]in the midst of [d]a crooked and perverse nation, among whom [3] [e]ye shine as lights in the world;

16 Holding forth the word of life; that [f]I may rejoice in the day of Christ, that [g]I have not run in vain, neither laboured in vain.

17 Yea, and if [h]I be [4]offered upon the sacrifice [i]and service of your faith, [k]I joy, and rejoice with you all.

18 For the same cause do ye joy, and rejoice with me.

R

Rom. 14. 11. *See l, L, § 344, page 876.*
Eph. 1. 10. *See p, P, § 426, page 1030.*

S

John 13. 13. *See n, N, § 182, page 515.*
Acts 2. 36 Therefore let all the house of Israel know assuredly, that God hath made that same Jesus, whom ye have crucified, both Lord and Christ.
Rom. 14. 9 For to this end Christ both died, and rose, and revived, that he might be Lord both of the dead and living.

T

Phil. 1. 5 For your fellowship in the gospel from the first day until now;

U

Prov. 10. 16 The labour of the righteous *tendeth* to life: the fruit of the wicked to sin.
John 6. 27 Labour not for the meat which perisheth, but for that meat which endureth unto everlasting life, which the Son of man shall give unto you: for him hath God the Father sealed.
John 6. 29 Jesus answered and said unto them, This is the work of God, that ye believe on him whom he hath sent.
Heb. 4. 11 Let us labour therefore to enter into that rest, lest any man fall after the same example of unbelief.
II. Pet. 1. 5-8. *Study § 545, page 1270.*

X

Eph. 6. 5. *See f, F, § 436, page 1054.*

Y

Isa. 26. 12 LORD, thou will ordain peace for us: for thou also hast wrought all our works in us.
John 3. 27 John answered and said, A man can receive nothing, except it be given him from heaven.
II Cor. 3. 5 Not that we are sufficient of ourselves to think any thing as of ourselves; but our sufficiency *is* of God:

§ 443. PAUL DECLARES HIS PURPOSE TO SEND

2: 19-30.

19 [1]But I trust in the Lord Jesus to send [a]Timotheus shortly unto you, that I also may be of good comfort, when I know your state.

20 For I have no man [b2]likeminded, who will naturally care for your state.

21 For all [c]seek their own, not the things which are Jesus Christ's.

22 But ye know the proof of him, [d]that, as a son with the father, he hath served with me in the gospel.

23 Him therefore I hope to send presently, so soon as I shall see how it will go with me.

CHAP. 2.

24 But [e]I trust in the Lord that I also myself shall come shortly.

25 Yet I suppose it necessary to send to you [f]Epaphroditus, my brother, and companion in labour, and [g]fellow soldier, [h]but your messenger, and [i]he that ministered to my wants.

26 [k]For he longed after you all, and was full of heaviness, because that ye had heard that he had been sick.

27 For indeed he was sick nigh unto death: but God had mercy on

1 Or, *moreover.*

CHRIST. AS LIGHTS HOLD FORTH THE WORD OF LIFE (CONCLUDED).

Y—CONCLUDED.

Heb 13. 21 Make you perfect in every good work to do his will, working in you that which is well pleasing in his sight, through Jesus Christ; to whom *be* glory for ever and ever. Amen.

Z

I Cor. 10. 10. *See n, N, § 366, page 928.*

I Pet. 4. 9 Use hospitality one to another without grudging.

A

Rom. 14. 1 Him that is weak in the faith receive ye, *but* not to doubtful disputations.

2

Or, *sincere.*

B

Eph. 5. 1. *See a, A, § 434, page 1046.*

C

I Pet. 2. 12 Having your conversation honest among the Gentiles: that, whereas they speak against you as evil doers, they may by *your* good works which they shall behold, glorify God in the day of visitation.

D

Deut. 32. 5 They have corrupted themselves, their spot *is* not *the spot* of his children; *they are* a perverse and crooked generation.

3

Or, *shine ye.*

E

Matt. 5. 14 Ye are the light of the world. A city that is set on a hill cannot be hid.

Matt. 5. 16 Let your light so shine before men, that they may see your good works, and glorify your Father which is in heaven.

Eph. 5. 8. *See p, P, § 434, page 1048.*

F

II Cor. 1. 14. *See n, N, § 386, page 964.*

G

Gal. 2. 2. *See c, C, § 413, page 1008.*

H

II Tim. 4. 6 For I am now ready to be offered, and the time of my departure is at hand.

4

Gr. *poured forth.*

I

Rom. 15. 16 That I should be the minister of Jesus Christ to the Gentiles, ministering the gospel of God, that the offering up of the Gentiles might be acceptable, being sanctified by the Holy Ghost.

K

II Cor. 7. 4 Great *is* my boldness of speech toward you, great *is* my glorying of you: I am filled with comfort, I am exceeding joyful in all our tribulation.

Col. 1. 24 Who now rejoice in my sufferings for you, and fill up that which is behind of the afflictions of Christ in my flesh for his body's sake, which is the church:

TIMOTHY AND EPAPHRODITUS TO THE PHILIPPIANS.

A

Rom. 16. 21 Timotheus my workfellow, and Lucius, and Jason, and Sosipater, my kinsmen, salute you.

I Thes. 3. 2 And sent Timotheus, our brother, and minister of God, and our fellow labourer in the gospel of Christ, to establish you, and to comfort you concerning your faith:

B

John 10. 13 The hireling fleeth, because he is a hireling, and careth not for the sheep.

2

Or, *so dear unto me.*

C

I Cor. 10. 24 Let no man seek his own, but every man another's *wealth.*

II Tim. 3. 2 For men shall be lovers of their own selves, covetous, boasters, proud, blasphemers, disobedient to parents, unthankful, unholy.

C—CONCLUDED.

II Tim. 4. 10 For Demas hath forsaken me, having loved this present world, and is departed unto Thessalonica; Crescens to Galatia, Titus unto Dalmatia.

II Tim. 4. 16 At my first answer no man stood with me, but all *men* forsook me: *I pray God* that it may not be laid to their charge.

D

I Cor. 4. 17. *See e, E, § 358, page 904.*

E

Phil. 1. 25 And having this confidence, I know that I shall abide and continue with you all for your furtherance and joy of faith.

Phile. 22 But withal prepare me also a lodging: for I trust that through your prayers I shall be given unto you.

For F, G, H, I, and K, see next page (1068).

§ 443. PAUL DECLARES HIS PURPOSE TO SEND TIMOTHY

CHAP. 2.

him; and not on him only, but on me also, lest I should have sorrow upon sorrow.

28 I sent him therefore the more carefully, that, when ye see him again, ye may rejoice, and that I may be the less sorrowful.

29 Receive him therefore in the Lord with all gladnesss; and [3l]hold such in reputation:

30 Because for the work of Christ he was nigh unto death, not regarding his life, [m]to supply your lack of service toward me.

F

Phil. 4. 18 But I have all, and abound: I am full, having received of Epaphroditus the things *which were sent* from you, an odour of a sweet smell, a sacrifice acceptable, well pleasing to God.

G

Phile. 2 And to *our* beloved Apphia, and Archippus our fellow soldier, and to the church in thy house:

H

Prov. 25. 13 As the cold of snow in the time of harvest, *so is* a faithful messenger to them that send him: for he refresheth the soul of his masters.

II Cor. 8. 23 Whether *any do inquire* of Titus, *he is* my partner and fellow helper concerning you: or our brethren *be inquired of*, *they are* the messengers of the churches, *and* the glory of Christ.

444. WARNINGS: NO CONFIDENCE IN THE FLESH.

3: 1–16.

1 Finally, my brethren, [a]rejoice in the Lord. [b]To write the same things to you, to me indeed *is* not grievous, but for you *it is* safe.

2 [c]Beware of dogs, beware of [d]evil workers, [e]beware of the concision.

3 For we are the [f]circumcision, [g]which worship God in the spirit, and [h]rejoice in Christ Jesus, and have no confidence in the flesh.

4 Though [i]I might also have confidence in the flesh. If any other man thinketh that he hath whereof he might trust in the flesh, I more:

5 [k]Circumcised the eighth day, [l]of the stock of Israel, [m]*of* the tribe of Benjamin, [n]a Hebrew of the Hebrews; as touching the law, [o]a Pharisee;

6 [p]Concerning zeal, [q]persecuting the church; [r]touching the righteousness which is in the law, [s]blameless.

A

II Cor. 13. 11 Finally, brethren, farewell. Be perfect, be of good comfort, be of one mind, live in peace; and the God of love and peace shall be with you.

Phil. 4. 4 Rejoice in the Lord always: *and* again I say, Rejoice.

I Thes. 5. 16 Rejoice evermore.

B

II Pet. 1. 12 Wherefore I will not be negligent to put you always in remembrance of these things, though ye know *them*, and be established in the present truth.

C

Isa. 56. 10 His watchmen *are* blind: they are all ignorant, they *are* all dumb dogs, they cannot bark; sleeping, lying down, loving to slumber.

11 Yea, *they are* greedy dogs *which* can never have enough, and they *are* shepherds *that* cannot understand: they all look to their own way, every one for his gain, from his quarter.

Gal. 5. 15 But if ye bite and devour one another, take heed that ye be not consumed one of another.

Rev. 22. 15 For without *are* dogs, and sorcerers, and whoremongers, and murderers, and idolaters, and whosoever loveth and maketh a lie.

D

II Cor. 11. 13. *See u, U, § 403, page 994.*

AND EPAPHRODITUS TO THE PHILIPPIANS (CONCLUDED).

I

IICor. 11. 9 And when I was present with you, and wanted, I was chargeable to no man: for that which was lacking to me the brethren which came from Macedonia supplied: and in all *things* I have kept myself from being burdensome unto you, and *so* will I keep *myself*.

Phil. 4. 18. *See under F.*

K

Phil. 1. 8 For God is my record, how greatly I long after you all in the bowels of Jesus Christ.

3

Or, *honor such.*

L

Acts 28. 10 Who also honoured us with many honours; and when we departed, they laded *us* with such things as were necessary.

L—CONCLUDED.

I Cor. 16. 18 For they have refreshed my spirit and yours: therefore acknowledge ye them that are such.

I Thes. 5. 12 And we beseech you, brethren, to know them which labour among you, and are over you in the Lord, and admonish you;

I Tim. 5. 17 Let the elders that rule well be counted worthy of double honour, especially they who labour in the word and doctrine.

M

I Cor. 16. 17 I am glad of the coming of Stephanas and Fortunatus and Achaicus: for that which was lacking on your part they have supplied.

Phil. 4. 10 But I rejoiced in the Lord greatly, that now at the last your care of me hath flourished again; wherein ye were also careful, but ye lacked opportunity.

PAUL SUFFERS THE LOSS OF ALL THINGS FOR CHRIST.

E

Rom. 2. 28 For he is not a Jew, which is one outwardly; neither *is that* circumcision, which is outward in the flesh:

Gal. 5. 1 Stand fast therefore in the liberty wherewith Christ hath made us free, and be not entangled again with the yoke of bondage.

2 Behold, I Paul say unto you, that if ye be circumcised, Christ shall profit you nothing.

F

Deut. 10. 16 Circumcise therefore the foreskin of your heart, and be no more stiffnecked.

Jer. 4. 4 Circumcise yourselves to the LORD, and take away the foreskins of your heart, ye men of Judah and inhabitants of Jerusalem: lest my fury come forth like fire, and burn that none can quench *it*, because of the evil of your doings.

Rom. 2. 29. *See q, Q, § 321, page 820.*

Rom. 4. 11. *See k, K, § 325, page 828.*

G

John 4. 23 But the hour cometh, and now is, when the true worshippers shall worship the Father in spirit and in truth: for the Father seeketh such to worship him.

24 God *is* a Spirit: and they that worship him must worship *him* in spirit and in truth.

Rom. 2. 29. *See r, R, § 321, page 820.*

H

Gal. 6. 14. *See d, D, § 424, page 1026.*

I

II Cor. 11. 18, 21. *See d, D, § 404, page 996.*

K

Gen. 17. 12 And he that is eight days old shall be circumcised among you, every man child in your generations, he that is born in the house, or bought with money of any stranger, which *is* not of thy seed.

L

Acts 21. 39. *See l, L, § 296, page 770.*

M

Rom. 11. 1. *See b, B, § 339, page 860.*

N

IICor. 11. 22 Are they Hebrews? so *am* I. Are they Israelites? so *am* I. Are they the seed of Abraham? so *am* I.

O

Acts 23. 6 But when Paul perceived that the one part were Sadducees, and the other Pharisees, he cried out in the council, Men *and* brethren, I am a Pharisee, the son of a Pharisee: of the hope and resurrection of the dead I am called in question.

Acts 26. 4 My manner of life from my youth, which was at the first among mine own nation at Jerusalem, know all the Jews;

5 Which knew me from the beginning, if they would testify, that after the most straitest sect of our religion I lived a Pharisee.

For P, Q, R, and S, see next page (1070).

§ 444. WARNINGS; NO CONFIDENCE IN THE FLESH; PAUL

CHAP. 3.

7 But [t]what things were gain to me,
those I counted loss for Christ.

8 Yea doubtless, and I count all
things *but* loss [u]for the excellency of
the knowledge of Christ Jesus my
Lord: for whom I have suffered the
loss of all things, and do count them
but dung, that I may win Christ,

9 And be found in him, not having
[x]mine own righteousness, which is of
the law, but [y]that which is through
the faith of Christ, the righteousness
which is of God by faith:

10 That I may know him, and the
power of his resurrection, and [z]the fellowship of his sufferings, being made
conformable unto his death;

11 If by any means I might [a]attain
unto the resurrection of the dead.

12 Not as though I had already [b]at-
tained, either were already [c]perfect:
but I follow after, if that I may apprehend that for which also I am apprehended of Christ Jesus.

13 Brethren, I count not myself to
have apprehended: but *this* one thing
I do, [d]forgetting those things which
are behind, and [e]reaching forth unto
those things which are before,

14 [f]I press toward the mark for the
prize of [g]the high calling of God in
Christ Jesus.

15 Let us therefore, as many as be
[h]perfect, [i]be thus minded: and if in
any thing ye be otherwise minded,
God shall reveal even this unto you.

16 Nevertheless, whereto we have
already attained, [k]let us walk [l]by the
same rule, [m]let us mind the same thing.

P

Gal. 1. 13, 14. *See e, E, § 411, page 1006.*

Q

Acts 8. 3. *See d, D, § 247, page 678.*

R

Rom. 10. 5 For Moses describeth the righteousness which is of the law, That the man which doeth those things shall live by them.

S

Luke 1. 6 And they were both righteous before God, walking in all the commandments and ordinances of the Lord blameless.

T

Matt. 13. 44 Again, the kingdom of heaven is like unto treasure hid in a field; the which when a man hath found, he hideth, and for joy thereof goeth and selleth all that he hath, and buyeth that field.

U

Isa. 53. 11 He shall see of the travail of his soul, *and* shall be satisfied: by his knowledge shall my righteous servant justify many; for he shall bear their iniquities.

Jer. 9. 23 Thus saith the LORD, Let not the wise *man* glory in his wisdom, neither let the mighty *man* glory in his might, let not the rich *man* glory in his riches:

24 But let him that glorieth glory in this, that he understandeth and knoweth me, and that I *am* the LORD which exercise lovingkindness, judgment, and righteousness, in the earth: for in these *things* I delight, saith the LORD.

John 17. 3 And this is life eternal, that they might know thee the only true God, and Jesus Christ, whom thou hast sent.

1 Cor. 2. 2 For I determined not to know any thing among you, save Jesus Christ, and him crucified.

Col. 2. 2 That their hearts might be comforted, being knit together in love, and unto all riches of the full assurance of understanding to the acknowledgement of the mystery of God, and of the Father, and of Christ;

X

Rom. 10. 3 For they, being ignorant of God's righteousness, and going about to establish their own righteousness, have not submitted themselves unto the righteousness of God.

Rom. 10. 5 For Moses describeth the righteousness which is of the law, That the man which doeth those things shall live by them.

SUFFERS LOSS OF ALL THINGS FOR CHRIST (Concluded).

Y

Gal. 2. 16. *See i, I, § 414, page 1010.*
Rom. 3. 21 22. *See e, E, § 324, page 824.*

Z

Rom. 6. 3 Know ye not, that so many of us as were baptized into Jesus Christ were baptized into his death ?

4 Therefore we are buried with him by baptism into death: that like as Christ was raised up from the dead by the glory of the Father, even so we also should walk in newness of life.

5 For if we have been planted together in the likeness of his death, we shall be also *in the likeness* of *his* resurrection:

Rom. 8. 17 And if children, then heirs; heirs of God, and joint heirs with Christ; if so be that we suffer with *him*, that we may be also glorified together.

II Cor. 4. 10, 11. *See e, E, § 393, page 972.*

A

Luke 20. 35 But they which shall be accounted worthy to obtain that world, and the resurrection from the dead, neither marry, nor are given in marriage:

Acts 26. 7 Unto which *promise* our twelve tribes, instantly serving *God* day and night, hope to come. For which hope's sake, king Agrippa, I am accused of the Jews.

B

I Tim. 6. 12 Fight the good fight of faith, lay hold on eternal life, whereunto thou art also called, and hast professed a good profession before many witnesses.

C

Heb. 12. 23 To the general assembly and church of the firstborn, which are written in heaven, and to God the Judge of all, and to the spirits of just men made perfect.

D

Ps. 45. 10 Hearken, O daughter, and consider, and incline thine ear; forget also thine own people, and thy father's house:

Luke 9. 62 And Jesus said unto him, No man, having put his hand to the plough, and looking back, is fit for the kingdom of God.

II Cor. 5. 16 Wherefore henceforth know we no man after the flesh: yea, though we have known Christ after the flesh, yet now henceforth know we *him* no more.

E

I Cor. 9. 24 Know ye not that they which run in a race run all, but one receiveth the prize? So run, that ye may obtain.

I Cor. 9. 26 I therefore so run, not as uncertainly; so fight I, not as one that beateth the air:

Heb. 6. 1 Therefore leaving the principles of the doctrine of Christ, let us go unto perfection; not laying again the foundation of repentance from dead works, and of faith toward God,

F

II Tim. 4. 7 I have fought a good fight, I have finished *my* course, I have kept the faith:

8 Henceforth there is laid up for me a crown of righteousness, which the Lord, the righteous judge, shall give me at that day: and not to me only, but unto all them also that love his appearing.

Heb. 12. 1 Wherefore, seeing we also are compassed about with so great a cloud of witnesses, let us lay aside every weight, and the sin which doth so easily beset *us*, and let us run with patience the race that is set before us.

G

Heb. 3. 1 Wherefore, holy brethren, partakers of the heavenly calling, consider the Apostle and High Priest of our profession, Christ Jesus;

H

I Cor. 2. 6. *See i, I, § 352, page 894.*

I

Gal. 5. 10 I have confidence in you through the Lord, that ye will be none otherwise minded: but he that troubleth you shall bear his judgement, whosoever he be.

K

Rom. 12. 16 *Be* of the same mind one toward another. Mind not high things, but condescend to men of low estate. Be not wise in your own conceits.

Rom. 15. 5 Now the God of patience and consolation grant you to be likeminded one toward another according to Christ Jesus:

L

Gal. 6. 16 And as many as walk according to this rule, peace *be* on them, and mercy, and upon the Israel of God.

M

Phil. 2. 2 Fulfil ye my joy, that ye be likeminded, having the same love, *being* of one accord, of one mind.

§ 445. CONCERNING WALK, CITIZEN-

3:17–21.

17 Brethren, [a]be followers together
of me, and mark them which walk
so as [b]ye have us for an ensample.

18 (For many walk, of whom I
have told you often, and now tell
you even weeping, *that they are* [c]the
enemies of the cross of Christ:

19 [d]Whose end *is* destruction,
[e]whose God *is their* belly, and [f]*whose*
glory *is* in their shame, [g]who mind
earthly things.)

20 For [h]our conversation is in
heaven; [i]from whence also we [k]look
for the Saviour, the Lord Jesus
Christ:

21 [l]Who shall change our vile body,
that it may be fashioned like unto
his glorious body, [m]according to the
working whereby he is able [n]even to
subdue all things unto himself.

A

I Cor. 4. 16. *See c, C, § 358, page 904.*

Phil. 4. 9 Those things, which ye have both learned, and received, and heard, and seen in me, do: and the God of peace shall be with you.

B

I Pet. 5. 3 Neither as being lords over *God's* heritage, but being ensamples to the flock.

C

II Cor. 11.13. *See u, U, § 403, page 994.*

Gal. 1. 7 Which is not another; but there be some that trouble you, and would pervert the gospel of Christ.

C—CONCLUDED.

Gal. 6. 12 As many as desire to make a fair shew in the flesh, they constrain you to be circumcised; only lest they should suffer persecution for the cross of Christ.

Phil. 1. 15 Some indeed preach Christ even of envy and strife; and some also of good will:

16 The one preach Christ of contention, not sincerely, supposing to add affliction to my bonds:

Phil. 3. 2 Beware of dogs, beware of evil workers, beware of the concision.

D

II Cor. 11. 15 Therefore *it is* no great thing if his ministers also be transformed as the ministers of righteousness; whose end shall be according to their works.

II Thes. 1. 9 Who shall be punished with everlasting destruction from the presence of the Lord, and from the glory of his power;

II Thes. 2. 8 And then shall that Wicked be revealed, whom the Lord shall consume with the spirit of his mouth, and shall destroy with the brightness of his coming:

II Thes. 2. 12 That they all might be damned who believed not the truth, but had pleasure in unrighteousness.

Heb. 6. 8 But that which beareth thorns and briers *is* rejected, and *is* nigh unto cursing; whose end *is* to be burned.

II Pet. 2. 1 But there were false prophets also among the people, even as there shall be false teachers among you, who privily shall bring in damnable heresies, even denying the Lord that bought them, and bring upon themselves swift destruction.

II Pet. 2. 12 But these, as natural brute beasts made to be taken and destroyed, speak evil of the things that they understand not; and shall utterly perish in their own corruption;

§ 446. SUNDRY

4:1–9.

1 Therefore, my brethren dearly
beloved and [a]longed for, [b]my joy
and crown, so [c]stand fast in the
Lord, *my* dearly beloved.

2 I beseech Euodias, and beseech
Syntyche, [d]that they be of the same
mind in the Lord.

CHAP. 4.

3 And I entreat thee also, true
yokefellow, help those women which
[e]laboured with me in the gospel,
with Clement also, and *with* other
my fellowlabourers, whose names
are in [f]the book of life.

SHIP AND THE NEW BODY.

D—CONCLUDED.

Jude 13 Raging waves of the sea, foaming out their own shame; wandering stars, to whom is reserved the blackness of darkness for ever.

Rev. 21. 8 But the fearful, and unbelieving, and the abominable, and murderers, and whoremongers, and sorcerers, and idolaters, and all liars, shall have their part in the lake which burneth with fire and brimstone: which is the second death.

E

Rom. 16. 18. *See l, L, § 347, page 884.*

F

Hos. 4. 7 As they were increased, so they sinned against me: *therefore* will I change their glory into shame.

II Cor. 11. 12 But what I do, that I will do, that I may cut off occasion from them which desire occasion; that wherein they glory, they may be found even as we.

Gal. 6. 13 For neither they themselves who are circumcised keep the law; but desire to have you circumcised, that they may glory in your flesh.

G

Rom. 8. 5 For they that are after the flesh do mind the things of the flesh; but they that are after the Spirit, the things of the Spirit.

H

Eph. 2. 6 And hath raised *us* up together, and made *us* sit together in heavenly *places* in Christ Jesus:

Eph. 2. 19 Now therefore ye are no more strangers and foreigners, but fellow citizens with the saints, and of the household of God;

Col. 3. 1 If ye then be risen with Christ, seek those things which are above, where Christ sitteth on the right hand of God.

2 Set your affection on things above, not on things on the earth.

H—CONCLUDED.

Col. 3. 3 For ye are dead, and your life is hid with Christ in God.

4 When Christ, *who is* our life, shall appear, then shall ye also appear with him in glory.

Heb. 12. 22 But ye are come unto mount Sion, and unto the city of the living God, the heavenly Jerusalem, and to an innumerable company of angels.

23 To the general assembly and church of the firstborn, which are written in heaven, and to God the Judge of all, and to the spirits of just men made perfect,

I

Acts 1. 11 *See d, D. § 228, page 628.*

K

I Cor. 1. 7. *See d, D, § 349, page 888.*

L

Ps. 17. 15 As for me, I will behold thy face in righteousness: I shall be satisfied, when I awake, with thy likeness.

I Cor. 15. 43 It is sown in dishonour, it is raised in glory: it is sown in weakness; it is raised in power:

I Cor. 15. 48 As *is* the earthy, such *are* they also that are earthy: and as *is* the heavenly, such *are* they also that are heavenly.

49 And as we have borne the image of the earthy, we shall also bear the image of the heavenly.

I Cor. 15. 51 Behold, I shew you a mystery; We shall not all sleep, but we shall all be changed.

I Jno. 3. 2 Beloved, now are we the sons of God, and it doth not yet appear what we shall be: but we know that, when he shall appear, we shall be like him; for we shall see him as he is.

M

Eph. 1. 19. *See h, H, § 427, page 1032.*

N

I Cor. 15. 26, 27. *See h, H, § 378, page 952.*

EXHORTATIONS.

A

Phil. 1. 8. *See k, K, § 440, page 1060.*

B

II. Cor. 1. 14. *See n, N. § 386, page 964.*

C

Phil. 1. 27 Only let your conversation be as it becometh the gospel of Christ: that whether I come and see you, or else be absent, I may hear of your affairs, that ye stand fast in one spirit, with one mind striving together for the faith

C—CONCLUDED.

of the gospel;

D

Phil. 2. 2 Fulfil ye my joy, that ye be likeminded, having the same love, *being* of one accord, of one mind.

E

Rom. 16. 3 Greet Priscilla and Aquila, my helpers in Christ Jesus:

Phil. 1. 27. *See under C.*

For F see next page (1074).

§ 446. SUNDRY EXHOR-

CHAP. 4.

4 [g]Rejoice in the Lord always: *and*
again I say, Rejoice.

5 Let your moderation be known
unto all men. [h]The Lord *is* at hand.

6 [i]Be careful for nothing; but in every thing by prayer and supplication with thanksgiving let your requests be made known unto God.

7 And [k]the peace of God, which
passeth all understanding, shall keep your hearts and minds through Christ Jesus.

8 Finally, brethren, whatsoever
things are true, whatsover things *are* [1]honest, whatsoever things *are* just, whatsoever things *are* pure, whatsoever things *are* lovely, whatsoever things *are* of good report; if *there be* any virtue, and if *there be* any praise, think on these things.

9 [l]Those things, which ye have both
learned, and received, and heard, and seen in me, do: and [m]the God of peace shall be with you.

F

Ex. 32. 32 Yet now, if thou will forgive their sin—; and if not, blot me, I pray thee, out of thy book which thou hast written.

Ps. 69. 28 Let them be blotted out of the book of the living, and not be written with the righteous.

Da. 12. 1 And at that time shall Michael stand up, the great prince which standeth for the children of thy people: and there shall be a time of trouble, such as never was since there was a nation *even* to that same time: and at that time thy people shall be delivered every one that shall be found written in the book.

Luke 10. 20 Notwithstanding in this rejoice not, that the spirits are subject unto you; but rather rejoice, because your names are written in heaven.

Rev. 3. 5 He that overcometh, the same shall be clothed in white raiment; and I will not blot out his name out of the book of life, but I will confess his name before my Father, and before his angels.

Rev. 13. 8 And all that dwell upon the earth shall worship him, whose names are not written in the book of life of the Lamb slain from the foundation of the world.

Rev. 20. 12 And I saw the dead, small and great, stand before God; and the books were opened: and another book was opened, which is *the book* of life: and the dead were judged out of those things which were written in the books, according to their works.

§ 447. PAUL ACKNOWLEDGES THE GIFT AND FELLOWSHIP

4: 10–23.

10 But I rejoiced in the Lord
greatly, that now at the last [a]your care of me [1]hath flourished again; wherein ye were also careful, but ye lacked opportunity.

11 Not that I speak in respect of
want: for I have learned, in whatsoever state I am, [b]*therewith* to be content.

12 [c]I know both how to be abased,
and I know how to abound: every where and in all things I am instructed

CHAP. 4.

both to be full and to be hungry, both to abound and to suffer need.

13 [d]I can do all things through
Christ which strengthened me.

14 Notwithstanding ye have well
done, that [e]ye did communicate with my affliction.

A

II Cor. 11. 9. *See o, O, § 403, page 994.*

1

Or, *is revived.*

B

Luke 3. 14 And the soldiers likewise demanded of him, saying, And what

TATIONS (CONCLUDED).

F—CONCLUDED.

Rev. 21. 27 And there shall in no wise enter into it any thing that defileth, neither *whatsoever* worketh abomination, or *maketh* a lie: but they which are written in the Lamb's book of Life.

G

Rom. 12. 12. *See z, Z, § 342, page 870.*

H

IIThes. 2. 2 That ye be not soon shaken in mind, or be troubled, neither by spirit, nor by word, nor by letter as from us, as that the day of Christ is at hand.

Heb. 10. 25 Not forsaking the assembling of ourselves together, as the manner of some *is;* but exhorting *one another:* and so much the more, as ye see the day approaching.

Jas. 5. 8 Be ye also, patient; stablish your hearts: for the coming of the Lord draweth nigh.

9 Grudge not one against another, brethren, lest ye be condemned: behold, the judge standeth before the door.

I Pet. 4. 7 But the end of all things is at hand: be ye therefore sober, and watch unto prayer.

IIPet. 3. 8 But, beloved, be not ignorant of this one thing, that one day *is* with the Lord as a thousand years, and a thousand years as one day.

9 The Lord is not slack concerning his promise, as some men count slackness; but is longsuffering to us-ward, not willing that any should perish, but that all should come to repentance.

I

Ps. 55. 22 Cast thy burden upon the LORD, and he shall sustain thee: he shall never suffer the righteous to be moved.

Prov. 16. 3 Commit thy works unto the LORD, and thy thoughts shall be established.

Matt. 6. 25 Therefore I say unto you, Take no thought for your life, what ye shall eat, or what ye shall drink; nor yet for your body, what ye shall put on. Is not the life more than meat, and the body than raiment?

Luke 12. 22 And he said unto his disciples, Therefore I say unto you, Take no thought for your life, what ye shall eat; neither for the body, what ye shall put on.

I Pet. 5. 7 Casting all your care upon him; for he careth for you.

K

John 14. 27 Peace I leave with you, my peace I give unto you: not as the world giveth, give I unto you. Let not your heart be troubled, neither let it be afraid.

Rom. 5. 1 Therefore being justified by faith, we have peace with God through our Lord Jesus Christ:

Col. 3. 15 And let the peace of God rule in your hearts, to the which also ye are called in one body; and be ye thankful.

1

Or, *venerable.*

L

I Cor. 4. 16. *See c, C, § 358, page 904.*

M

Rom. 15. 33. *See b, B, § 346, page 882.*

OF THE PHILIPPIANS. SALUTATION AND BENEDICTION.

B—CONCLUDED.

shall we do? And he said unto them, Do violence to no man, neither accuse *any* falsely; and be content with your wages.

ITim. 6. 6 But godliness with contentment is great gain.

ITim. 6. 8 And having food and raiment let us be therewith content.

Heb. 13. 5 *Let your* conversation *be* without covetousness; *and be* content with such things as ye have: for he hath said, I will never leave thee, nor forsake thee.

6 So that we may boldly say, The Lord *is* my helper, and I will not fear what man shall do unto me.

C

I Cor. 4. 11. *See l, L, § 357, page 904.*

C—CONCLUDED.

IICor. 6. 10 As sorrowful, yet alway rejoicing; as poor, yet making many rich; as having nothing, and *yet* possessing all things.

D

John 15. 5 I am the vine, ye *are* the branches: He that abideth in me, and I in him, the same bringeth forth much fruit: for without me ye can do nothing.

IICor. 3. 4 And such trust have we through Christ to God-ward:

5 Not that we are sufficient of ourselves to think any thing as of ourselves; but our sufficiency *is* of God;

II Cor. 12. 9 And he said unto me, My grace is sufficient for thee: for my strength

For D concluded, and E see next page (1076).

§ 447. PAUL ACKOWLEDGES THE GIFT AND FELLOWSHIP OF THE

CHAP. 4.

15 Now ye Philippians know also, that in the beginning of the gospel, when I departed from Macedonia, no church communicated with me as concerning giving and receiving, but ye only.

16 For even in Thessalonica ye sent once and again unto my necessity.

17 Not because I desire a gift: but I desire [g]fruit that may abound to your account.

18 But [2]I have all, and abound: I am full, having received [h]of Epaphroditus the things *which were sent* from you, [i]an odour of a sweet smell, [k]a sacrifice acceptable, well pleasing to God.

19 But my God [l]shall supply all your need, [m]according to his riches in glory by Christ Jesus.

CHAP. 4.

20 [n]Now unto God and our Father *be* glory for ever and ever. Amen.

21 Salute every saint in Christ Jesus. The brethren [o]which are with me greet you.

22 All the saints salute you, [p]chiefly they that are of Cæsar's household.

23 [q]The grace of our Lord Jesus Christ *be* with you all. Amen.

D—CONCLUDED.

is made perfect in weakness. Most gladly therefore will I rather glory in my infirmities, that the power of Christ may rest upon me.

E

Phil. 1. 7 Even as it is meet for me to think this of you all, because I have you in my heart; inasmuch as both in my bonds, and in the defence and confirmation of the gospel, ye all are partakers of my grace.

F

IICor. 11. 8 I robbed other churches, taking wages *of them*, to do you service.

9 And when I was present with you, and wanted, I was chargeable to no man: for that which was lacking to me the brethren which came from Mace-

PAUL'S EPISTLE TO

§ 448. SALUTATION. THANKSGIVING FOR THEIR FAITH AND LOVE.

1:1–8.

1 Paul, [a]an apostle of Jesus Christ by the will of God, and Timotheus *our* brother,

2 To the saints [b]and faithful brethren in Christ which are at Colosse: [c]Grace *be* unto you, and peace, from God our Father and the Lord Jesus Christ.

3 [d]We give thanks to God and the Father of our Lord Jesus Christ, praying always for you,

CHAP. 1.

4 [e]Since we heard of your faith in Christ Jesus, and of [f]the love *which ye have* to all the saints,

5 For the hope [g]which is laid up for you in heaven, whereof ye heard before in the word of the truth of the gospel;

6 Which is come unto you, [h]as *it is* in all the world; and [i]bringeth forth fruit, as *it doth* also in you,

A

Rom. 1. 1. *See a, A, § 317, page 808.*

PHILIPPIANS. SALUTATION AND BENEDICTION (CONCLUDED).

F—CONCLUDED.

donia supplied: and in all *things* I have kept myself from being burdensome unto you, and *so* will I keep *myself*.

G

Rom. 15. 28 When therefore I have performed this, and have sealed to them this fruit, I will come by you into Spain.

Tit. 3. 14 And let ours also learn to maintain good works for necessary uses, that they be not unfruitful.

2

Or, *I have received all.*

H

Phil. 2. 25 Yet I supposed it necessary to send to you Epaphroditus, my brother, and companion in labour, and fellow soldier, but your messenger, and he that ministered to my wants.

I

Heb. 13. 16 But to do good and to communicate forget not: for with such sacrifices God is well pleased.

K

II Cor. 9. 12 For the administration of this service not only supplieth the want of the saints, but is abundant also by many thanksgivings unto God;

L

Ps. 23. 1 The LORD *is* my shepherd; I shall not want.

L—CONCLUDED.

Prov. 8. 21 That I may cause those that love me to inherit substance; and I will fill their treasures.

II Cor. 9. 8 And God *is* able to make all grace abound toward you; that ye, always having all sufficiency in all *things*, may abound to every good work:

M

Eph. 1. 7 In whom we have redemption through his blood, the forgiveness of sins, according to the riches of his grace;

Eph. 3. 16 That he would grant you, according to the riches of his glory, to be strengthened with might by his Spirit in the inner man;

N

Rom. 16. 27 To God only wise, *be* glory through Jesus Christ for ever. Amen.

Gal. 1. 5 To whom *be* glory for ever and ever. Amen.

O

Gal. 1. 2 And all the brethren which are with me, unto the churches of Galatia:

P

Phil. 1. 13 So that my bonds in Christ are manifest in all the palace, and in all other *places;*

Q

Rom. 16. 24 The grace of our Lord Jesus Christ *be* with you all. Amen.

THE COLOSSIANS.

Probably written during spring of A. D. 62, at Rome.

B

I Cor. 4. 17 For this cause have I sent unto you Timotheus, who is my beloved son, and faithful in the Lord, who shall bring you into remembrance of my ways which be in Christ, as I teach every where in every church.

Eph. 6. 21 But that ye also may know my affairs, *and* how I do, Tychicus, a beloved brother and faithful minister in the Lord, shall make known to you all things:

C

II Cor. 1. 2. *See c, C, § 385, page 962.*

D

Rom. 1. 8. *See a, A, § 318, page 808.*

E

Eph. 1. 15. *See a, A, § 427, page 1032.*

F

Heb. 6. 10 For God *is* not unrighteous to forget your work and labour of love, which ye have shewed toward his name, in that ye have ministered to the saints, and do minister.

G

Matt. 5. 12 Rejoice, and be exceeding glad: for great *is* your reward in heaven: for so persecuted they the prophets which were before you.

II Tim. 4. 8 Henceforth there is laid up for me a crown of righteousness, which the Lord, the righteous judge, shall give me at that day: and not to me only, but unto all them also that love his appearing.

For G concl'd, H and I, see next page (1078).

§ 448. SALUTATION. THANKSGIVING FOR

CHAP. I.

since the day ye heard *of it*, and
knew [k]the grace of God in truth:
7 As ye also learned of [l]Epaphras
our dear fellowservant, who is for
you a faithful minister of Christ;
8 Who also declared unto us your
love in the Spirit.

G—CONCLUDED.

1 Pet. 1. 4 To an inheritance incorruptible, and undefiled, and that fadeth not away, reserved in heaven for you,

H

Rom. 10. 18. *See c, C, § 338, page 860.*

H—CONCLUDED.

Col. 1. 23. *See text of § 449 page 1080.*

I

Mark 4. 8 And other fell on good ground, and did yield fruit that sprang up and increased; and brought forth, some thirty, and some sixty, and some a hundred.

John 15. 16 Ye have not chosen me, but I have chosen you, and ordained you, that ye should go and bring forth fruit, and *that* your fruit should remain: that whatsoever ye shall ask of the Father in my name, he may give it you.

Phil. 1. 11 Being filled with the fruits of righteousness, which are by Jesus Christ, unto the glory and praise of God.

§ 449. PAUL PRAYS FOR THEIR SPIRITUAL GROWTH

1:9–23.

9 [a]For this cause we also, since the
day we heard *it*, do not cease to
pray for you, and to desire [b]that ye
might be filled with [c]the knowledge
of his will [d]in all wisdom and spiritual understanding;
10 [e]That ye might walk worthy of
the Lord [f]unto all pleasing, [g]being
fruitful in every good work, and increasing in the knowledge of God;
11 [h]Strengthened with all might,
according to his glorious power,
[i]unto all patience and longsuffering
[k]with joyfulness;
12 [l]Giving thanks unto the Father,
which hath made us meet to be partakers of [m]the inheritance of the
saints in light:
13 Who hath delivered us from [n]the
power of darkness, [o]and hath translated *us* into the kingdom of [1]his
dear Son:
14 [p]In whom we have redemption
through his blood, *even* the forgiveness of sins:

CHAP. I.

15 [q]Who is the image of the invisible God, [r]the firstborn of every
creature:
16 For [s]by him were all things created, that are in heaven, and that are
in earth, visible and invisible, whether
they be thrones, or [t]dominions, or

A

Eph. 1. 15, 16. *See b, B, § 427 page 1032.*

B

1 Cor. 1. 5 That in every thing ye are enriched by him, in all utterance, and *in* all knowledge;

C

Ps. 143. 10 Teach me to do thy will, for thou *art* my God: thy Spirit *is* good; lead me into the land of uprightness.

Rom. 12. 2 And be not conformed to this world: but be ye transformed by the renewing of your mind, that ye may prove what *is* that good, and acceptable, and perfect will of God.

Eph. 5. 10 Proving what is acceptable unto the Lord.

Eph. 5. 17 Wherefore be ye not unwise, but understanding what the will of the Lord *is*.

Eph. 6. 6 Not with eyeservice, as menpleasers; but as the servants of Christ, doing the will of God from the heart;

D

Eph. 1. 8 Wherein he hath abounded toward us in all wisdom and prudence;

THEIR FAITH AND LOVE (CONCLUDED).

K

II Cor. 6. 1 We then, *as* workers together *with him*, beseech *you* also that ye receive not the grace of God in vain.

Eph. 3. 2 If ye have heard of the dispensation of the grace of God which is given me to you-ward:

Tit. 2. 11 For the grace of God that bringeth salvation hath appeared to all men,

I Pet. 5. 12 By Silvanus, a faithful brother unto you, as I suppose, I have written briefly, exhorting, and testifying that this is the true grace of God wherein ye stand.

L

Phil. 2. 25 Yet I supposed it necessary to send to you Epaphroditus, my brother, and companion in labour, and fellow soldier, but your messenger, and he that ministered to my wants.

L—CONCLUDED.

Phil. 4. 18 But I have all, and abound: I am full, having received of Epaphroditus the things *which were sent* from you, an odour of a sweet smell, a sacrifice acceptable, well pleasing to God.

Col. 4. 12 Epaphras, who is *one* of you, a servant of Christ, saluteth you, always labouring fervently for you in prayers, that ye may stand perfect and complete in all the will of God.

Phile. 23 There salute thee Epaphras, my fellow prisoner in Christ Jesus;

AND GIVES THANKS FOR THE KINGDOM OF THE SON.

E

Eph. 4. 1. *See b, B, § 432 page 1040.*

F

I Thes. 4. 1 Furthermore then we beseech you, brethren, and exhort *you* by the Lord Jesus, that as ye have received of us how ye ought to walk and to please God, *so* ye would abound more and more.

G

Col. 1. 6. *See i, I § 448, page 1076.*

Tit. 3. 1 Put them in mind to be subject to principalities and powers, to obey magistrates, to be ready to every good work,

Heb. 13. 21 Make you perfect in every good work to do his will, working in you that which is well pleasing in his sight, through Jesus Christ; to whom *be* glory for ever and ever. Amen.

H

Eph. 3. 16. *See c, C, § 431, page 1040.*

I

Eph. 4. 2. *See c, C, § 432, page 1040.*

Jas. 1. 4 But let patience have *her* perfect work, that ye may be perfect and entire, wanting nothing.

K

Rom. 5. 3. *See e, E, § 326, page 830.*

L

Eph. 5. 20. *See l, L, § 434, page 1050.*

M

Eph. 1. 11. *See q, Q, § 426, page 1030.*

N

Eph. 6. 12. *See e, E, § 437, page 1056.*

O

Eph. 2. 6 And hath raised *us* up together, and made *us* sit together in heavenly *places* in Christ Jesus:

I Thes. 2. 12 That ye would walk worthy of God, who hath called you unto his kingdom and glory.

II Pet. 1. 11 For so an entrance shall be ministered unto you abundantly into the everlasting kingdom of our Lord and Saviour Jesus Christ.

1

Gr. *the son of his love.*

Matt. 3. 17 And lo a voice from heaven, saying, This is my beloved Son, in whom I am well pleased.

Eph. 1. 6 To the praise of the glory of his grace, wherein he hath made us accepted in the beloved.

P

Eph. 1. 7. *See k, K, § 426, page 1030.*

Q

John 14. 9. *See l, L, § 183, page 525.*

R

Rev. 3. 14 And unto the angel of the church of the Laodiceans write; These things saith the Amen, the faithful and true witness, the beginning of the creation of God;

S

John 1. 3. *See e, E, § 1, page 5.*

T

Rom. 8. 38. *See x, X, § 334, page 850.*

U

Rom. 11. 36. *See q, Q, § 341, page 866.*

§ 449. PAUL PRAYS FOR THEIR SPIRITUAL GROWTH AND

CHAP. I.

principalities, or powers: all things
created [u]by him, and for him:
17 [x]And he is before all things, and
by him all things consist.
18 And [y]he is the head of the body,
the church: who is the beginning,
[z]the firstborn from the dead; that [2]in
all things he might have the preeminence.
19 For it pleased *the Father* that
[a]in him should all fullness dwell;
20 And, [3b]having made peace
through the blood of his cross, [c]by
him to reconcile [d]all things unto
himself; by him, *I say*, whether
they be things in earth, or things in
heaven.
21 And you, [e]that were sometime
alienated and enemies [4]in *your* mind
[f]by wicked works, yet now hath he
reconciled
22 [g]In the body of his flesh through
death, [h]to present you holy and unblameable and unreproveable in his
sight:
23 If ye continue in the faith
[i]grounded and settled, and *be* [k]not
moved away from the hope of the
gospel, which ye have heard, *and*
[l]which was preached [m]to every creature which is under heaven; [n]whereof
I Paul am made a minister;

CHAP. I.

For U see preceding page (1079).

X

John 1. 1 In the beginning was the Word, and the Word was with God, and the Word was God.

John 1. 3 All things were made by him; and without him was not any thing made that was made.

John 17. 5 And now, O Father, glorify thou me with thine own self with the glory which I had with thee before the world was.

I Cor. 8. 6 But to us *there is but* one God, the Father, of whom *are* all things, and we in him; and one Lord Jesus Christ, by whom *are* all things, and we by him.

Y

I Cor. 11. 3 But I would have you know, that the head of every man is Christ; and the head of the woman *is* the man; and the head of Christ *is* God.

Eph. 1. 10 That in the dispensation of the fulness of times he might gather together in one all things in Christ, both which are in heaven, and which are on earth; *even* in him:

Eph. 1. 22 And hath put all *things* under his feet, and gave him *to be* the head over all *things* to the church,

Eph. 4. 15 But speaking the truth in love, may grow up into him in all things, which is the head, *even* Christ:

§ 450. PAUL REJOICES IN HIS MINISTRY

1 : 24–29.

24 [a]Who now rejoice in my sufferings [b]for you, and fill up [c]that which
is behind of the afflictions of Christ
in my flesh [d]for his body's sake,
which is the church:
25 Whereof I am made a minister,
according to [e]the dispensation of
God which is given to me for you, [1]to
fulfil the word of God;
26 *Even* [f]the mystery which hath
been hid from ages and from generations, [g]but now is made manifest to
his saints:

A

Rom. 5. 3. *See e, E, § 326, page 830.*

B

Eph. 3. 1. *See b, B, § 430, page 1038.*

C

II Cor. 1. 5 For as the sufferings of Christ abound in us, so our consolation also aboundeth by Christ.

6 And whether we be afflicted, *it is* for your consolation and salvation, which is effectual in the enduring of the same sufferings which we also suffer: or whether we be comforted, *it is* for your consolation and salvation.

Phil. 3. 10 That I may know him, and the power of his resurrection, and the fellowship of his sufferings, being made conformable unto his death;

II Tim. 1. 8 Be not thou therefore ashamed

GIVES THANKS FOR THE KINGDOM OF THE SON (CONCLUDED).

Y—CONCLUDED.

Eph. 5. 23 For the husband is the head of the wife, even as Christ is the head of the church: and he is the Saviour of the body.

Z

Acts 26. 23. *See b, B, § 309, page 794.*

2

Or, *among all.*

A

John 1. 16 And of his fulness have all we received, and grace for grace.

John 3. 34 For he whom God hath sent speaketh the words of God: for God giveth not the Spirit by measure *unto him.*

Col. 2. 9 For in him dwelleth all the fulness of the Godhead bodily.

Col. 3. 11 Where there is neither Greek nor Jew, circumcision nor uncircumcision, Barbarian, Scythian, bond *nor* free: but Christ *is* all, and in all.

3

Or, *making peace.*

B

Eph. 2. 14-17. *See n, N, § 429, page 1036.*

C

IICor. 5. 18 And all things *are* of God, who hath reconciled us to himself by Jesus Christ, and hath given to us the ministry of reconciliation;

D

Eph. 1. 10 That in the dispensation of the fulness of times he might gather together in one all things in Christ, both which are in heaven, and which are on earth; *even* in him:

E

Eph. 2. 12. *See d, D, § 429, page 1036.*
Eph. 4. 18. *See d, D, § 433, page 1044.*

4

Or, *by,* your *mind in wicked works.*

F

Tit. 1. 15 Unto the pure all things *are* pure: but unto them that are defiled and unbelieving *is* nothing pure; but even their mind and conscience is defiled.
16 They profess that they know God; but in works they deny *him,* being abominable, and disobedient, and unto every good work reprobate.

G

Eph. 2. 15, 16. *See m, M, § 429, page 1036.*

H

Eph. 1. 4. *See d, D, § 426, page 1030.*

I

Eph. 3. 17. *See f, F, § 431, page 1040.*

K

John 15. 6 If a man abide not in me, he is cast forth as a branch, and is withered; and men gather them, and cast *them* into the fire, and they are burned.

L

Rom. 10. 18 But I say, Have they not heard? Yes verily, their sound went into all the earth, and their words unto the ends of the world.

M

Col. 1. 6. *See i, I, § 448, page 1076.*

N

Eph. 3. 7. *See o, O, § 430, page 1038.*

OF THE MYSTERY WITH HIS SUFFERINGS.

C—CONCLUDED.

of the testimony or our Lord, nor of me his prisoner: but be though partaker of the afflictions of the gospel according to the power of God.

IITim. 2. 10 Therefore I endure all things for the elect's sake, that they may also obtain the salvation which is in Christ Jesus with eternal glory.

D

Eph. 1. 23 Which is his body, the fulness of him that filleth all in all.

E

I Cor. 9. 17. *See a, A, § 365, page 924.*

1

Or, *fully to preach the word of God.*

Rom. 15. 19 Through mighty signs and wonders, by the power of the Spirit of God; so that from Jerusalem, and round about unto Illyricum, I have

1—CONCLUDED.

fully preached the gospel of Christ.

F

Rom. 16. 25. *See e, E, § 347, page 886.*

G

Matt. 13. 11 He answered and said unto them, Because it is given unto you to know the mysteries of the kingdom of heaven, but to them it is not given.

IITim. 1. 10 But is now made manifest by the appearing of our Saviour Jesus Christ, who hath abolished death, and hath brought life and immortality to light through the gospel:

H

IICor. 2. 14 Now thanks *be* unto God: which always causeth us to triumph in Christ, and maketh manifest the savour of his knowledge by us in every place.

§ 450. PAUL REJOICES IN HIS MINISTRY OF THE

CHAP. 1.

27 [h]To whom God would make known what *is* [i]the riches of the glory of this mystery among the Gentiles; which is Christ [2]in you, [k]the hope of glory:

28 Whom we preach, [l]warning every man, and teaching every man in all wisdom; [m]that we may present every man perfect in Christ Jesus:

29 [n]Whereunto I also labour, [o]striving [p]according to his working, which worketh in me mightily.

For H, see preceding page (1081).

I

Rom. 9. 23 And that he might make known the riches of his glory on the vessels of mercy, which he had afore prepared unto glory.

Eph. 1. 7 In whom we have redemption through his blood, the forgiveness of sins, according to the riches of his grace;

Eph. 3. 8 Unto me, who am less than the least of all saints, is this grace given, that I should preach among the Gentiles the unsearchable riches of Christ;

2

Or, *among you.*

K

I Tim. 1. 1 Paul an apostle of Jesus Christ by the commandment of God our Saviour, and Lord Jesus Christ, *which is* our hope;

§ 451. PAUL MAKES KNOWN HIS ZEALOUS CONCERN,

2: 1–7.

1 For I would that ye knew what great [1a]conflict I have for you, and *for* them at Laodicea, and *for* as many as have not seen my face in the flesh;

2 [b]That their hearts might be comforted, [c]being knit together in love, and unto all riches of the full assurance of understanding, [d]to the acknowledgement of the mystery of God, and of the Father, and of Christ;

3 [2e]In whom are hid all the treasures of wisdom and knowledge.

4 And this I say, [f]lest any man should beguile you with enticing words.

5 For [g]though I be absent in the flesh, yet am I with you in the spirit, joying and beholding [h]your order, and the [i]steadfastness of your faith in Christ.

6 [k]As ye have therefore received Christ Jesus the Lord, *so* walk ye in him:

7 [l]Rooted and built up in him, and stablished in the faith, as ye have been taught, abounding therein with thanksgiving.

1

Or, *fear*, or, *care.*

A

Phil. 1. 30 Having the same conflict which ye saw in me, and now hear *to be* in me.

Col. 1. 29. *See text of topic* § *450.*

I Thes. 2. 2 But even after that we had suffered before, and were shamefully entreated, as ye know, at Philippi, we were bold in our God to speak unto you the gospel of God with much contention.

B

II Cor. 1. 6 And whether we be afflicted, *it is* for your consolation and salvation, which is effectual in the enduring of the same sufferings which we also suffer: or whether we be comforted, *it is* for your consolation and salvation.

C

Col. 3. 14 And above all these things *put on* charity, which is the bond of perfectness.

D

Phil. 3. 8 Yea doubtless, and I count all things *but* loss for the excellency of the knowledge of Christ Jesus my Lord: for whom I have suffered the loss of all things, and do count them *but* dung, that I may win Christ,

Col. 1. 9 For this cause we also, since the day we heard *it*, do not cease to pray for you, and to desire that ye might be filled with the knowledge of his will in all wisdom and spiritual understanding;

MYSTERY WITH HIS SUFFERINGS (CONCLUDED).

L

Acts 20. 20 *And* how I kept back nothing that was profitable *unto you*, but have shewed you, and have taught you publicly, and from house to house,

Acts 20. 27 For I have not shunned to declare unto you all the counsel of God.

Acts 20. 31 Therefore watch, and remember, that by the space of three years I ceased not to warn every one night and day with tears.

M

II Cor. 11. 2 For I am jealous over you with godly jealousy: for I have espoused you to one husband, that I may present *you as* a chaste virgin to Christ.

Eph. 5. 27 That he might present it to himself a glorious church, not having spot, or wrinkle, or any such thing;

M—CONCLUDED.

but that it should be holy and without blemish.

Col. 1. 22 In the body of his flesh through death, to present you holy and unblameable and unreproveable in his sight:

N

I Cor. 15. 10 But by the grace of God I am what I am: and his grace which *was bestowed* upon me was not in vain; but I laboured more abundantly than they all: yet not I, but the grace of God which was with me.

O

Col. 2. 1. *See text of topic*, § *451*.

P

Eph. 1. 19. *See h, H*, § *427, page 1032.*

GUARDING THEM AGAINST DELUSIONS.

2

Or, *wherein.*

E

I Cor. 1. 24 But unto them which are called, both Jews and Greeks, Christ the power of God, and the wisdom of God.

I Cor. 2. 6 Howbeit we speak wisdom among them that are perfect: yet not the wisdom of this world, nor of the princes of this world, that come to nought:

7 But we speak the wisdom of God in a mystery, *even* the hidden *wisdom*, which God ordained before the world unto our glory;

Eph. 1. 8 Wherein he hath abounded toward us in all wisdom and prudence;

Col. 1. 9. *See under D.*

F

Rom. 16. 18 For they that are such serve not, our Lord Jesus Christ, but their own belly; and by good words and fair speeches deceive the hearts of the simple.

II Cor. 11. 13 For such *are* false apostles, deceitful workers, transforming themselves into the apostles of Christ.

Eph. 4. 14 That we *henceforth* be no more children, tossed to and fro, and carried about with every wind of doctrine, by the sleight of men, *and* cunning craftness, whereby they lie in wait to deceive;

Eph. 5. 6 Let no man deceive you with vain words: for because of these things cometh the wrath of God upon the children of disobedience.

F—CONCLUDED.

Col. 2. 8, 18. *See text of topic*, § *452 and 453.*

G

I Cor. 5. 3. *See f, F*, § *359, page 906.*

H

I Cor. 14. 40 Let all things be done decently and in order.

I

I Pet. 5. 9 Whom resist steadfast in the faith, knowing that the same afflictions are accomplished in your brethren that are in the world.

K

I Thes. 4. 1 Furthermore then we beseech you, brethren, and exhort *you* by the Lord Jesus, that as ye have received of us how ye ought to walk and to please God, *so* ye would abound more and more.

Jude 3 Beloved, when I gave all diligence to write unto you of the common salvation, it was needful for me to write unto you, and exhort *you* that ye should earnestly contend for the faith which was once delivered unto the saints.

L

Eph. 2. 21 In whom all the building fitly framed together groweth unto a holy temple in the Lord:

22 In whom ye also are builded together for a habitation of God through the Spirit.

Eph. 3. 17. *See e, E*, § *431, page 1040.*

§ 452. WARNING AGAINST PHILOSOPHIES AND

2: 8–15.

8 [a]Beware lest any man spoil you through philosophy and vain deceit, after [b]the tradition of men, after the [1c]rudiments of the world, and not after Christ.

9 For [d]in him dwelleth all the fulness of the Godhead bodily.

10 [e]And ye are complete in him, [f]which is the head of all [g]principality and power:

11 In whom also ye are [h]circumcised with the circumcision made without hands, in [i]putting off the body of the sins of the flesh by the circumcision of Christ:

12 [k]Buried with him in baptism, wherein also [l]ye are risen with *him* through [m]the faith of the operation of God, [n]who hath raised him from the dead.

13 [o]And you, being dead in your sins and the uncircumcision, of your flesh hath he quickened together with him, having forgiven you all trespasses;

14 [p]Blotting out the handwriting of ordinances that was against us, which was contrary to us, and took it out of the way, nailing it to his cross;

15 *And* [q]having spoiled [r]principalities and powers, he made a shew of them openly, triumphing over them [2]in it.

A

Jer. 29. 8 For thus saith the LORD of hosts, the God of Israel; Let not your prophets and your diviners, that *be* in the midst of you, deceive you, neither hearken to your dreams which ye cause to be dreamed.

Rom. 16. 17 Now I beseech you, brethren, mark them which cause divisions and offences contrary to the doctrine which ye have learned; and avoid them.

Eph. 5. 6 *Let* no man deceive you with vain words: for because of these things cometh the wrath of God upon the children of disobedience.

A—CONCLUDED.

Heb. 13. 9 Be not carried about with divers and strange doctrines. For *it is* a good thing that the heart be established with grace; not with meats, which have not profited them that have been occupied therein.

Col. 2. 18. *See text of topic,* § 453.

B

Matt. 15. 2 Why do thy disciples transgress the tradition of the elders? for they wash not their hands when they eat bread.

3 But he answered and said unto them, Why do ye also transgress the commandment of God by your tradition?

Mark 7. 5 Then the Pharisees and scribes asked him, Why walk not thy disciples according to the tradition of the elders, but eat bread with unwashen hands?

6 He answered and said unto them, Well hath Esaias prophesied of you hypocrites, as it is written. This people honoureth me with *their* lips, but their heart is far from me.

7 Howbeit in vain do they worship me, teaching *for* doctrines the commandments of men.

Mark 7. 9 And he said unto them, Full well ye reject the commandment of God, that ye may keep your own tradition.

Mark 7 13 Making the word of God of none effect through your tradition, which ye have delivered: and many such like things do ye.

Gal. 1. 14 And profited in the Jews' religion above many my equals in mine own nation, being more exceedingly zealous of the traditions of my fathers.

I Pet. 1. 18 Forasmuch as ye know that ye were not redeemed with corruptible things, *as* silver and gold, from your vain conversation *received* by tradition from your fathers;

1

Or, *elements.*

C

Gal. 4. 3 Even so we, when we were children, were in bondage under the elements of the world:

Gal. 4. 9 But now, after that ye have known God, or rather are known of God, how turn ye again to the weak and beggarly elements, whereunto ye desire again to be in bondage?

Col. 2. 20. *See text of topic,* § 453.

AGAINST EVIL DOCTRINES.

D—CONCLUDED.

not make him that did the service perfect, as pertaining to the conscience;

Heb. 10. 1 For the law having a shadow of good things to come, *and* not the very image of the things, can never with those sacrifices which they offered year by year continually, make the comers thereunto perfect.

E

Col. 2. 4. *See, f, F, § 451, page 1082.*

3

Or, *judge against you.*

4

Gr. *being a voluntary in humility.*

Col. 2. 23. *See text of topic.*

F

Eze. 13. 3 Thus saith the Lord GOD; Woe unto the foolish prophets, that follow their own spirit, and have seen nothing!

I Tim. 1. 7 Desiring to be teachers of the law; understanding neither what they say, nor whereof they affirm.

G

Eph. 4. 15, 16. *See l, L, § 432, page 1044.*

H

Rom. 7. 4. *See c, C, § 330, page 840.*

I

Col. 2. 8 Beware lest any man spoil you through philosophy and vain deceit, after the tradition of men, after the rudiments of the world, and not after Christ.

5

Or, *elements.*

K

Gal. 4. 3 Even so we, when we were children, were in bondage under the elements of the world:

K—CONCLUDED.

Gal. 4. 9 But now, after that ye have known God, or rather are known of God, how turn ye again to the weak and beggarly elements, whereunto ye desire again to be in bondage?

L

Gen. 3. 3 But of the fruit of the tree which *is* in the midst of the garden, God hath said, Ye shall not eat of it, neither shall ye touch it, lest ye die.

Isa. 52. 11 Depart ye, depart ye, go ye out from thence, touch no unclean *thing;* go ye out of the midst of her; be ye clean, that bear the vessels of the LORD.

II Cor. 6. 17 Wherefore come out from among them, and be ye separate, saith the Lord, and touch not the unclean *thing;* and I will receive you,

I Tim. 4. 3 Forbidding to marry, *and commanding* to abstain from meats, which God hath created to be received with thanksgiving of them which believe and know the truth.

M

Matt. 15. 9 But in vain they do worship me, teaching *for* doctrines the commandments of men.

Col. 2. 8. *See b, B, § 452, page 1084.*

Tit. 1. 14 Not giving heed to Jewish fables, and commandments of men, that turn from the truth.

N

I Tim. 4. 8 For bodily exercise profiteth little: but godliness is profitable unto all things, having promise of the life that now is, and of that which is to come.

O

Col. 2. 18. *See text of topic.*

6

Or, *punishing,* or, *not sparing.*

PUT OFF THE OLD, PUT ON THE NEW MAN.

B

Rom. 8. 34. *See r, R, § 334, page 850.*

Eph. 1. 20 Which he wrought in Christ, when he raised him from the dead, and set *him* at his own right hand in the heavenly *places,*

1

Or, *mind.*

C

Rom. 6. 2 God forbid. How shall we, that are dead to sin, live any longer therein?

Gal. 2. 20 I am crucified with Christ: nevertheless I live; yet not I, but Christ liveth in me: and the life which I now live in the flesh I live by the faith of the Son of God, who loved me, and gave himself for me.

C—CONCLUDED.

Col. 2. 25. *See text of topic, § 453.*

D

Rom. 8. 2 For the law of the Spirit of life in Christ Jesus hath made me free from the law of sin and death.

II Cor. 5 7 (For we walk by faith, not by sight:)

§ 454. SET THE MIND ON THINGS ABOVE. PUT

CHAP. 3.

4 [e]When Christ, *who is* [f]our life,
shall appear, then shall ye also appear with him [g]in glory.

5 [h]Mortify therefore [i]your members
which are upon the earth; [k]fornica-
tion, uncleanness, inordinate affection, [l]evil concupiscence, and covetousness, [m]which is idolatry:

6 [n]For which things' sake the wrath
of God cometh on [o]the children of
disobedience:

7 [p]In the which ye also walked
some time, when ye lived in them.

8 [q]But now ye also put off all these;
anger, wrath, malice, blasphemy,
[r]filthy communication out of your
mouth.

9 [s]Lie not one to another, [t]seeing
that ye have put off the old man
with his deeds;

10 And have put on the new *man*,
which [u]is renewed in knowledge [x]after
the image of him that [y]created him:

11 Where there is neither [z]Greek nor
Jew, circumcision nor uncircumcision, Barbarian, Scythian, bond
nor free: [a]but Christ *is* all, and in all.

12 [b]Put on therefore, [c]as the elect of
God, holy and beloved, [d]bowels of
mercies, kindness, humbleness of
mind, meekness, longsuffering;

13 [e]Forbearing one another, and
forgiving one another, if any man
have a [1]quarrel against any: even as
Christ forgave you, so also *do* ye.

14 [f]And above all these things [g]*put
on* charity, which is the [h]bond of
perfectness.

15 And let [i]the peace of God rule
in your hearts, [k]to the which also ye
are called [l]in one body; [m]and be ye
thankful.

16 Let the word of Christ dwell in
you richly in all wisdom; teaching
and admonishing one another [n]in
psalms and hymns and spiritual

CHAP. 3.

songs, singing [o]with grace in your
hearts to the Lord.

17 And [p]whatsoever ye do in word
or deed, *do* all in the name of the
Lord Jesus, [q]giving thanks to God
and the Father by him.

E

I John 3. 2 Beloved, now are we the sons of God, and it doth not yet appear what we shall be: but we know that when he shall appear, we shall be like him; for we shall see him as he is.

F

John 11. 25 Jesus said unto her, I am the resurrection, and the life: he that believeth in me, though he were dead, yet shall he live:

John 14. 6 Jesus saith unto him, I am the way, the truth, and the life: no man cometh unto the Father, but by me:

G

I Cor. 15. 43. *See d, D, § 380, page 954.*

H

Rom. 8. 13. *See t, T, § 332, page 844.*

Gal. 5. 24 And they that are Christ's have crucified the flesh with the affections and lusts.

I

Rom. 6. 13. *See t, T, § 328, page 836.*

K

Eph. 5. 3. *See e, E, § 434, page 1048.*

L

I Thes. 4. 5 Not in the lust of concupiscence, even as the Gentiles which know not God:

M

Eph. 5. 5. *See k, K, § 434, page 1048.*

N

Rom. 1. 18. *See a, A, § 319, page 812.*

O

Eph. 2. 2 Wherein in time past ye walked according to the course of this world, according to the prince of the power of the air, the spirit that now worketh in the children of disobedience:

P

Rom. 6. 19 I speak after the manner of men because of the infirmity of your flesh: for as ye have yielded your members servants to uncleanness and to iniquity unto iniquity; even so now yield your members servants to righteousness unto holiness.

20 For when ye were the servants of sins, ye were free from righteousness.

I Cor. 6. 11. *See g, G, § 360, page 910.*

OFF THE OLD, PUT ON THE NEW MAN (CONCLUDED).

Q

Eph. 4. 22. *See i, I, § 433, page 1044.*

Jas. 1. 21 Wherefore lay apart all filthiness, and superfluity of naughtiness, and receive with meekness the engrafted word, which is able to save your souls.

R

Eph. 4. 29. *See x, X, § 433, page 1046.*

S

Lev. 19. 11 Ye shall not steal, neither deal falsely, neither lie one to another.

Eph. 4. 25 Wherefore putting away lying, speak every man truth with his neighbour: for we are members one of another.

T

Eph. 4. 22. *See i, I, § 433, page 1044.*

U

Rom. 12. 2 And be not conformed to this world: but be ye transformed by the renewing of your mind, that ye may prove what *is* that good, and acceptable, and perfect will of God.

X

Eph. 4. 23 And be renewed in the spirit of your mind;

24 And that ye put on the new man, which after God is created in righteousness and true holiness.

Y

Eph. 2. 10 For we are his workmanship, created in Christ Jesus unto good works, which God hath before ordained that we should walk in them.

Z

Rom. 3. 22. *See i, I, § 324, page 824.*

A

Eph. 1. 23. *See r, R, § 427, page 1032.*

B

Eph. 4. 24. *See under X.*

C

I Thes. 1. 4 Knowing, brethren beloved, your election of God.

I Pet. 1. 2 Elect according to the foreknowledge of God the Father, through sanctification of the Spirit, unto obedience and sprinkling of the blood of Jesus Christ: Grace unto you, and peace, be multiplied.

II Pet. 1. 10 Wherefore the rather, brethren, give diligence to make your calling and election sure: for if ye do these things, ye shall never fall:

D

Gal. 5. 22 But the fruit of the Spirit is love, joy, peace, longsuffering, gentleness, goodness, faith,

D—CONCLUDED.

Eph. 4. 32. *See g, G, § 433, page 1044.*

Phil. 2. 1. *See b, B, § 442, page 1062.*

E

Eph. 4. 2, 3. *See c, C, § 432, page 1040.*

Or, *complaint.*

F

I Pet. 4. 8 And above all things have fervent charity among yourselves: for charity shall cover the multitude of sins.

G

John 13. 34. *See y, Y, § 183, page 519.*

I Cor. 13. *Read entire chapter.*

H

Eph. 4. 3 Endeavoring to keep the unity of the Spirit in the bond of peace.

I

Rom. 14. 17 For the kingdom of God is not meat and drink; but righteousness, and peace, and joy in the Holy Ghost.

Phil. 4. 7 And the peace of God, which passeth all understanding, shall keep your hearts and minds through Christ Jesus.

K

I Cor. 7. 15 But if the unbelieving depart, let him depart. A brother or a sister is not under bondage in such *cases:* but God hath called us to peace.

L

Eph. 2. 16 And that he might reconcile both unto God in one body by the cross, having slain the enmity thereby:

17 And came and preached peace to you which were afar off, and to them that were nigh.

Eph. 4. 4 *There is* one body, and one Spirit, even as ye are called in one hope of your calling;

M

Col. 2. 7 Rooted and built up in him, and stablished in the faith, as ye have been taught, abounding therein with thanksgiving.

Col. 3. 17. *See text of topic.*

N

Eph. 5. 19. *See k, K, § 434, page 1050.*

O

Col. 4. 6 Let your speech *be* alway with grace, seasoned with salt, that ye may know how ye ought to answer every man.

P

I Cor. 10. 31 Whether therefore ye eat, or drink, or whatsoever ye do, do all to the glory of God.

Q

Rom. 1. 8. *See a, A, § 318, page 808.*

Eph. 5. 20. *See l, L, § 434, page 1050.*

§ 455. SUNDRY ADMONITIONS

3 : 18–25 ; 4 : 1–6.

18 [a]Wives, submit yourselves unto
your own husbands, as it is fit in the
Lord.

19 [b]Husbands, love *your* wives, and
be not bitter against them.

20 [c]Children, obey *your* parents [d]in
all things: for this is well pleasing
unto the Lord.

21 [e]Fathers, provoke not your children *to anger*, lest they be discouraged.

22 [f]Servants, obey in all things
your masters [g]according to the flesh;
not with eyeservice, as menpleasers;
but in singleness of heart, fearing
God:

23 [h]And whatsoever ye do, do *it*
heartily, as to the Lord, and not
unto men;

24 [i]Knowing that of the Lord ye
shall receive the reward of the inheritance: [k]for ye serve the Lord
Christ.

25 But he that doeth wrong shall
receive for the wrong which he hath
done: and [l]there is no respect of
persons.

CHAP. 4.

1 Masters, [m]give unto *your* servants
that which is just and equal; knowing that ye also have a Master in
heaven.

CHAP. 4.

2 [n]Continue in prayer, and watch in
the same [o]with thanksgiving;

3 [p]Withal praying also for us, that
God would [q]open unto us a door of
utterance, to speak [r]the mystery of
Christ, [s]for which I am also in
bonds:

4 That I may make it manifest, as
I ought to speak.

5 [t]Walk in wisdom toward them
that are without, [u]redeeming the
time.

6 Let your speech *be* alway [x]with
grace, [y]seasoned with salt, [z]that ye
may know how ye ought to answer
every man.

A

Eph. 5. 22. *See a, A, § 435, page 1052.*

B

Eph. 6. 25, 28, 33. *See g, G, § 435, page 1052.*

C

Eph. 6. 1 Children, obey your parents in the Lord: for this is right.

D

Eph. 5. 24 Therefore as the church is subject unto Christ, so *let* the wives *be* to their own husbands in every thing.

Tit. 2. 9 *Exhort* servants to be obedient unto their own masters, *and* to please *them* well in all things; not answering again;

E

Eph. 6. 9 And, ye masters, do the same things unto them, forbearing threatening: knowing that your Master also is in heaven; neither is there respect of persons with him.

§ 456. TYCHICUS AND ONESIMUS IN THE LORD

4 : 7–18.

7 [a]All my state shall Tychicus declare unto you, *who is* a beloved
brother, and a faithful minister and
fellow servant in the Lord:

8 [b]Whom I have sent unto you for
the same purpose, that he might
know your estate, and comfort your
hearts;

9 With [c]Onesimus, a faithful and

CHAP. 4.

beloved brother, who is *one* of you.
They shall make known unto you all
things which *are done* here.

10 [d]Aristarchus my fellow prisoner
saluteth you, and [e]Marcus, sister's
son to Barnabas, (touching whom ye
received commandments: if he come
unto you, receive him;)

IN THE NEW LIFE.

F

Eph. 6. 5, 6. *See e, E, § 436, page 1054.*

G

Phile. 16 Not now as a servant, but above a servant, a brother beloved, specially to me, but how much more unto thee, both in the flesh, and in the Lord?

H

Eph. 6. 6 Not with eyeservice, as menpleasers; but as the servants of Christ, doing the will of God from the heart;
7 With good will doing service, as to the Lord, and not to men:

I

Eph. 6. 8 Knowing that whatsoever good thing any man doeth, the same shall he receive of the Lord, whether *he be* bond or free.

K

I Cor. 7. 22 For he that is called in the Lord, *being* a servant, is the Lord's freeman: likewise also he that is called, *being* free, is Christ's servant.

L

Rom. 2. 11. *See m, M, § 320, page 816.*

M

Eph. 6. 9. *See under E.*

Lev. 19. 13 Thou shalt not defraud thy neighbour, neither rob *him:* the wages of him that is hired shall not abide with thee all night until the morning.

N

Luke 18. 1. *See a, A, § 140, page 401.*

O

Col. 2. 7 Rooted and built up in him, and stablished in the faith, as ye have been taught, abounding therein with thanksgiving.

Col. 3. 15 And let the peace of God rule in your hearts, to the which also ye are called in one body; and be ye thankful.

P

Eph. 6. 19. *See r, R, § 437, page 1056.*

Q

I Cor. 16. 9 For a great door and effectual is opened unto me, and *there are* many adversaries.

II Cor. 2. 12 Furthermore, when I came to Troas to *preach* Christ's gospel, and a door was opened unto me of the Lord,

R

Rom. 16. 25. *See d, D, § 347, page 886.*

S

Eph. 3. 1. *See a, A, § 430, page 1038.*

T

Eph. 5. 15 See then that ye walk circumspectly, not as fools, but as wise,

I Thes. 4. 12 That ye may walk honestly toward them that are without, and *that* ye may have lack of nothing.

U

Eph. 5. 16 Redeeming the time, because the days are evil.

X

Eccl. 10. 12 The word's of a wise man's mouth *are* gracious; but the lips of a fool will swallow up himself.

Col. 3. 16 Let the word of Christ dwell in you richly in all wisdom; teaching and admonishing one another in psalms and hymns and spiritual songs, singing with grace in your hearts to the Lord.

Y

Mark 9. 50 Salt *is* good: but if the salt have lost his saltness, wherewith will ye season it? Have salt in yourselves, and have peace one with another.

Z

I Pet. 3. 15 But sanctify the Lord God in you hearts: and *be* ready always to *give* an answer to every man that asketh you a reason of the hope that is in you with meekness and fear:

INTRODUCED. SALUTATIONS. BENEDICTION.

A

Eph. 6. 21 But that ye also may know my affairs, *and* how I do, Tychicus, a beloved brother and faithful minister in the Lord, shall make known to you all things:

B

Eph. 6. 22 Whom I have sent unto you for the same purpose, that ye might know our affairs, and *that* he might comfort your hearts.

C

Phile. 10 I beseech thee for my son Onesimus, whom I have begotten in my bonds:

D

Acts. 19. 29. *See e, E, § 288, page 756.*

E

Acts 15. 37 And Barnabas determined to take with them John, whose surname was Mark.

II Tim. 4. 11 Only Luke is with me. Take Mark, and bring him with thee: for he is profitable to me for the ministry.

F

Col. 1. 7. *See l, L, § 448, page 1078.*

1

Or, *striving.*

§ 456. TYCHICUS AND ONESIMUS IN THE LORD

CHAP. 4.

11 And Jesus, which is called Justus, who are of the circumcision. These only *are my* fellow workers unto the kingdom of God, which have been a comfort unto me.

12 [f]Epaphras, who is *one* of you, a servant of Christ, saluteth you, always [19][g]labouring fervently for you in prayers, that ye may stand [h]perfect and [2]complete in all the will of God.

13 For I bear him record, that he hath a great zeal for you, and them *that are* in Laodicea, and them in Hierapolis.

14 [i]Luke, the beloved physician, and [k]Demas, greet you.

15 Salute the brethren which are in Laodicea, and Nymphas, and [l]the church which is in his house.

16 And when [m]this epistle is read among you, cause that it be read also in the church of the Laodiceans; and that ye likewise read the *epistle* from Laodicea.

17 And say to [n]Archippus, Take heed to [o]the ministry which thou hast received in the Lord, that thou fulfil it.

18 The [p]salutation by the hand of me Paul. [q]Remember my bonds. [r]Grace *be* with you. Amen.

For F and 1, see preceding page (1091).

G

Rom. 15. 30 Now I beseech you, brethren, for the Lord Jesus Christ's sake, and for the love of the Spirit, that ye strive together with me in *your* prayers to God for me;

Jas. 5. 16 Confess *your* faults one to another, and pray one for another, that ye may be healed. The effectual fervent prayer of a righteous man availeth much.

H

I Cor. 2. 6. *See i, I, § 352, page 894.*

PAUL'S FIRST EPISTLE

§ 457. SALUTATION, THANKSGIVING AND COMMENDATION

1 : 1–10.

1 Paul, and [a]Silvanus, and Timotheus, unto the church of the [b]Thessalonians *which is* in God the Father, and *in* the Lord Jesus Christ: [c]Grace *be* unto you, and peace, from God our Father, and the Lord Jesus Christ.

2 [d]We give thanks to God always for you all, making mention of you in our prayers;

3 [e]Remembering without ceasing [f]your work of faith, [g]and labour of love, and patience of hope in our Lord Jesus Christ, in the sight of God and our Father;

A

II Cor. 1. 19 For the Son of God, Jesus Christ, who was preached among you by us, *even* by me and Silvanus and Timotheus, was not yea and nay, but in him was yea.

II Thes. 1. 1 Paul, and Silvanus, and Timotheus, unto the church of the Thessalonians in God our Father and the Lord Jesus Christ:

INTRODUCED. SALUTATIONS. BENEDICTION (CONCLUDED).

2

Or, *filled.*

I

II Tim. 4. 11 Only Luke is with me. Take Mark, and bring him with thee: for he is profitable to me for the ministry.

K

II Tim. 4. 10 For Demas hath forsaken me, having loved this present world, and is departed unto Thessalonica; Crescens to Galatia, Titus unto Dalmatia.

Phile. 24 Marcus, Aristarchus, Demas, Lucas, my fellow labourers.

L

Rom. 16. 5 Likewise *greet* the church that is in their house. Salute my well beloved Epenetus, who is the first-fruits of Achaia unto Christ.

I Cor. 16. 19 The churches of Asia salute you. Aquilla and Priscilla salute you much in the Lord, with the church that is in their house.

M

I Thes. 5. 27 I charge you by the Lord, that this epistle be read unto all the holy brethren.

N

Phile. 2 And to *our* beloved Apphia, and Archippus our fellow soldier, and to the church in thy house:

O

I Cor. 4. 1 Let a man so account of us, as of the ministers of Christ, and stewards of the mysteries of God.

2 Moreover it is required in stewards, that a man be found faithful.

I Tim. 4. 6 If thou put the brethren in remembrance of these things, thou shalt be a good minister of Jesus Christ, nourished up in the words of faith and of good doctrine, whereunto thou hast attained.

I Tim. 4. 14 Neglect not the gift that is in thee, which was given thee by prophecy, with the laying on of the hands of the presbytery.

P

I Cor. 16. 21 The salutation of *me* Paul with mine own hand.

Q

Heb. 13. 3 Remember them that are in bonds, as bound with them; *and* them which suffer adversity, as being yourselves also in the body.

II Tim. 1. 8 Be not thou therefore ashamed of the testimony of our Lord, nor of me his prisoner: but be thou partaker of the afflictions of the gospel according to the power of God;

R

Heb. 13. 25 Grace *be* with you all. Amen.

TO THE THESSALONIANS.

FOR FAITH AND LABOR OF LOVE. Written A. D. 52, at Corinth.

A—CONCLUDED.

I Pet. 5. 12 By Silvanus, a faithful brother unto you, as I suppose, I have written briefly, exhorting, and testifying that this is the true grace of God wherein ye stand.

B

Acts 17. 1 Now when they had passed through Amphipolis and Apollonia, they came to Thessalonica, where was a synagogue of the Jews:

C

Eph. 1. 2 Grace *be* to you, and peace, from God our Father, and *from* the Lord Jesus Christ.

D

Rom. 1. 8. *See a, A, § 318, page 808.*

E

I Thes. 2. 13 For this cause also thank we God without ceasing, because, when ye received the word of God which ye heard of us, ye received *it* not *as* the word of men, but as it is in truth, the word of God, which effectually worketh also in you that believe.

F

John 6. 29 Jesus answered and said unto them, This is the work of God, that ye believe on him whom he hath sent.

Gal. 5. 6 For in Jesus Christ neither circumcision availeth any thing, nor uncircumcision; but faith which worketh by love.

For F Concl'd and G, see next page (1094).

§ 457. SALUTATION, THANKSGIVING AND COMMENDATION—CONCLUDED.

CHAP. 1.

4 Knowing, brethren [1]beloved, [h]your election of God.

5 For [i]our gospel came not unto you in word only, but also in power, and [k]in the Holy Ghost, [l]and in much assurance; as [m]ye know what manner of men we were among you for your sake.

6 And [n]ye became followers of us, and of the Lord, having received the word in much affliction, [o]with jóy of the Holy Ghost:

7 So that ye were ensamples to all that believe in Macedonia and Achaia.

8 For from you [p]sounded out the word of the Lord not only in Macedonia and Achaia, but also [q]in every place your faith to God-ward is spread abroad; so that we need not to speak any thing.

9 For they themselves shew of us [r]what manner of entering in we had unto you, and [s]how ye turned to God from idols to serve the living and true God;

10 And [t]to wait for his Son [u]from heaven, [x]whom he raised from the dead, *even* Jesus, which delivered us [y]from the wrath to come.

IThes.3. 6 But now when Timotheus came from you unto us, and brought us good tidings of your faith and charity, and that ye have good remembrance of us always, desiring greatly to see us, as we also *to see* you:

II Thes. 1.3 We are bound to thank God alway for you, brethren, as it is meet, because that your faith groweth exceedingly, and the charity of every one of you all toward each other aboundeth:

II Thes. 1.11 Wherefore also we pray always for you, that our God would count you worthy of *this* calling, and fulfill all the good pleasure of *his* goodness, and the work of faith with power:

G

Rom. 16. 6 Greet Mary, who bestowed much labour on us.

Heb. 6. 10 For God *is* not unrighteous to forget your work and labour of love, which ye have shewed toward his name, in that ye have ministered to the saints, and do minister.

1

Or, *beloved of God, your election.*

H

Col. 3. 12 Put on therefore, as the elect of God, holy and beloved, bowels of mercies, kindness, humbleness of mind, meekness, longsuffering;

Thes. 2. 13 But we are bound to give thanks alway to God for you, brethren beloved of the Lord, because God hath from the beginning chosen you to salvation through sanctification of the Spirit and belief of the truth:

I

Isa. 55. 11 So shall my word be that goeth forth out of my mouth: it shall not return unto me void, but it shall accom-

§ 458. PAUL RECOUNTS THE MANNER OF

2: 1–12.

1 For [a]yourselves, brethren, know our entrance in unto you, that it was not in vain:

2 But even after that we had suffered before, and were shamefully entreated, as ye know, at [b]Philippi, [c]we were bold in our God to speak unto you the gospel of God [d]with much contention.

CHAP. 2.

3 [e]For our exhortation *was* not of deceit, nor of uncleanness, nor in guile:

4 But as [f]we were allowed of God [g]to be put in trust with the gospel,

DATION FOR FAITH AND LABOR OF LOVE (CONCLUDED).

I—CONCLUDED.

plish that which I please, and it shall prosper *in the thing* whereto I sent it.

Mark 16. 20 And they went forth, and preached every where, the Lord working with *them*, and confirming the word with signs following. Amen.

I Cor. 2. 4 And my speech and my preaching *was* not with enticing words of man's wisdom, but in demonstration of the Spirit and of power:

I Cor. 4. 20 For the kingdom of God *is* not in word, but in power.

K

II Cor. 6. 6 By pureness, by knowledge, by longsuffering, by kindness, by the Holy Ghost, by love unfeigned.

L

Col. 2. 2 That their hearts might be comforted being knit together in love, and unto all riches of the full assurance of understanding, to the acknowledgement of the mystery of God, and of the Father and of the Christ;

Heb. 2. 3 How shall we escape, if we neglect so great salvation; which at the first began to be spoken by the Lord, and was confirmed unto us by them that heard *him;*

M

I Thes. 2. 1 For yourselves, brethren, know our entrance in unto you, that it was not in vain:

I Thes. 2. 5 For neither at any time used we flattering words, as ye know, nor a cloak of covetousness; God *is* witness:

I Thes. 2. 10 Ye *are* witnesses, and God *also* how holily and justly and unblameably we behaved ourselves among you that believe:

I Thes. 2. 11 As ye know how we exhorted and comforted and charged every one of you, as a father *doth* his children.

II Thes. 3. 7 For yourselves know how ye

M—CONCLUDED.

ought to follow us: for we behaved not ourselves disorderly among you;

N

I Cor. 4. 16. *See c, C, § 358, page 904.*

O

Acts 5. 41 And they departed from the presence of the council, rejoicing that they were counted worthy to suffer shame for his name.

Heb. 10. 34 For ye had compassion of me in my bonds, and took joyfully the spoiling of your goods, knowing in yourselves that ye have in heaven a better and an enduring substance.

P

Rom. 10. 18 But I say, Have they not heard? Yes verily, their sound went into all the earth, and their words unto the ends of the world.

Q

Rom. 1. 8 First, I thank my God through Jesus Christ for you all, that your faith is spoken of throughout the whole world.

II Thes. 1. 4 So that we ourselves glory in you in the churches of God, for your patience and faith in all your persecutions and tribulations that ye endure:

R

Phil. 4. 9 Those things, which ye have both learned, and received, and heard, and seen in me, do: and the God of peace shall be with you.

S

Gal. 4. 8. *See a, A, § 419, page 1018.*

T

I Cor. 1. 7. *See d, D, § 349, page 888.*

U

Acts 1. 11. *See d, D, § 228, page 628.*

X

Acts 2. 24. *See k, K, § 231, page 638.*

Y

Matt. 3. 7. *See b, B, § 14, page 48.*

THEIR ENTRANCE AND THEIR EXAMPLE.

A

I Thes. 1. 5, 9. *See text of topic, § 457.*

B

Acts 16. 22 And the multitude rose up together against them: and the magistrates rent off their clothes, and commanded to beat *them.*

C

Acts 17. 2 And Paul, as his manner was, went

C—CONCLUDED.

in unto them, and three sabbath days reasoned with them out of the Scriptures.

Acts 17. 3 Opening and alleging, that Christ must needs have suffered, and risen again from the dead; and that this Jesus, whom I preach unto you, is Christ.

For D, E, F, and G, see next page (1096)

§ 458. PAUL RECOUNTS THE MANNER OF THEIR

CHAP. 2.

even so we speak; [h]not as pleasing
men, but God, [i]which trieth our
hearts.
5 For [k]neither at any time used we
flattering words, as ye know, nor a
cloak of covetousness; [l]God *is* witness:
6 [m]Nor of men sought we glory,
neither of you, nor *yet* of others,
when [n]we might have [1]been [o]burdensome [p]as the apostles of Christ.
7 But [q]we were gentle among you,
even as a nurse cherisheth her children:
8 So being affectionately desirous
of you, we were willing [r]to have imparted unto you, not the gospel of
God only, but also [s]our own souls,
because ye were dear unto us.
9 For ye remember, brethren, our
labour and travail: for [t]labouring
night and day, [u]because we would
not be chargeable unto any of you,
we preached unto you the gospel of
God.
10 [x]Ye *are* witnesses, and God *also*,
[y]how holily and justly and unblameably we behaved ourselves among
you that believe:
11 As ye know how we exhorted
and comforted and charged every
one of you, as a father *doth* his children,
12 [z]That ye would walk worthy of
God; [a]who hath called you unto his
kingdom and glory.

D

Jude 3 Beloved, when I gave all diligence to write unto you of the common salvation, it was needful for me to write unto you, and exhort *you* that ye should earnestly contend for the faith which was once delivered unto the saints.

E

II Cor. 7. 2 Receive us; we have wronged no man, we have corrupted no man, we have defrauded no man.

E—CONCLUDED.

I Thes. 1. 5 For our gospel came not unto you in word only, but also in power, and in the Holy Ghost, and in much assurance; as ye know what manner of men we were among you for your sake.

II Pet. 1. 16 For we have not followed cunningly devised fables, when we made known unto you the power and coming of our Lord Jesus Christ, but were eyewitnesses of his majesty.

F

I Cor. 7. 25 Now concerning virgins I have no commandment of the Lord: yet I give my judgment, as one that hath obtained mercy of the Lord to be faithful.

I Tim. 1. 11 According to the glorious gospel of the blessed God, which was committed to my trust.

12 And I thank Christ Jesus our Lord, who hath enabled me, for that he counted me faithful, putting me into the ministry;

G

I Cor. 9. 17 For if I do this thing willingly, I have a reward: but if against my will, a dispensation *of the gospel* is committed unto me.

Gal. 2. 7 But contrariwise, when they saw that the gospel of the uncircumcision was committed unto me, as *the gospel* of the circumcision *was* unto Peter:

Tit. 1. 3 But hath in due times manifested his word through preaching, which is committed unto me according to the commandment of God our Saviour;

H

Gal. 1. 10 For do I now persuade men, or God? or do I seek to please men? for if I yet pleased men, I should not be the servant of Christ.

I

Prov. 17. 3 The fining pot *is* for silver, and the furnace for gold: but the LORD trieth the hearts.

Rom. 8. 27 And he that searcheth the hearts knoweth what *is* the mind of the Spirit, because he maketh intercession for the saints according to *the will of* God.

K

Acts 20. 33 I have coveted no man's silver, or gold, or apparel.

II Cor. 2. 17. *See i, I, § 389, page 968.*

II Cor. 7. 2. *See under E.*

II Cor. 12. 17 Did I make a gain of you by any of them whom I sent unto you?

L

Rom. 1. 9. *See c, C, § 318, page 808.*

ENTRANCE AND THEIR EXAMPLE (CONCLUDED).

M

John 12. 43. *See f, F, § 171, page 479.*
Gal. 1. 10. *See under H.*

N

I Cor. 9. 4 Have we not power to eat and to drink?

I Cor. 9. 6 Or I only and Barnabas, have not we power to forbear working?

I Cor. 9. 12 If others be partakers of *this* power over you, *are* not we rather? Nevertheless we have not used this power; but suffer all things, lest we should hinder the gospel of Christ.

I Cor. 9. 18 What is my reward then? *Verily* that, when I preach the gospel, I may make the gospel of Christ without charge, that I abuse not my power in the gospel.

IICor.10. 1 Now I Paul myself beseech you by the meekness and gentleness of Christ, who in presence *am* base among you, but being absent am bold toward you:
2 But I beseech *you*, that I may not be bold when I am present with that confidence, wherewith I think to be bold against some, which think of us as if we walked according to the flesh.

IICor.10. 10 For *his* letters, say they, *are* weighty and powerful; but *his* bodily presence *is* weak, and *his* speech contemptible.
11 Let such a one think this, that, such as we are in word by letters when we are absent, such *will we be* also in deed when we are present.

IICor.13. 10 Therefore I write these things being absent, lest being present I should use sharpness, according to the power which the Lord hath given me to edification, and not to destruction.

IIThes.3. 9 Not because we have not power, but to make ourselves an ensample unto you to follow us.

Phile. 8 Wherefore, though I might be much bold in Christ to enjoin thee that which is convenient,
9 Yet for love's sake I rather beseech *thee*, being such a one as Paul the aged, and now also a prisoner of Jesus Christ.

1

Or, *used authority.*

O

Acts 18. 3. *See b, B, § 280, page 746.*

P

I Cor. 9. 1, 2. *See a, A, § 365, page 920.*

Q

I Cor. 2. 3. *See e, E, § 352, page 894.*

I Cor. 9. 22 To the weak became I as weak, that I might gain the weak: I am made

Q—CONCLUDED.

all things to all *men*, that I might by all means save some.

IICor.13. 4 For though he was crucified through weakness, yet he liveth by the power of God. For we also are weak in him, but we shall live with him by the power of God toward you.

IITim.2. 24 And the servant of the Lord must not strive; but be gentle unto all *men*, apt to teach, patient,

R

Rom. 1. 11 For I long to see you, that I may impart unto you some spiritual gift, to the end ye may be established;

Rom.15. 29 And I am sure that, when I come unto you, I shall come in the fulness of the blessing of the gospel of Christ.

S

IICor.12. 15 And I will very gladly spend and be spent for you; though the more abundantly I love you, the less I be loved.

T

Acts 18. 3. *See b, B, § 280, page 746.*

U

I Cor. 9. 12. *See p, P, § 365, page 922.*

X

IThes.1. 5 For our gospel came not unto you in word only, but also in power, and in the Holy Ghost, and in much assurance; as ye know what manner of men we were among you for your sake.

Y

II Cor. 7. 2. *See under E.*

IIThes.3. 7 For yourselves know how ye ought to follow us: for we behaved not ourselves disorderly among you;

Z

Eph. 4. 1. *See b, B, § 432, page 1040.*

IThes.4. 1 Furthermore then we beseech you, brethren, and exhort *you* by the Lord Jesus, that as ye have received of us how ye ought to walk and to please God, *so* ye would abound more and more.

A

1 Cor. 1. 9 God *is* faithful, by whom ye were called unto the fellowship of his Son Jesus Christ our Lord.

IIThes.2. 14 Whereunto he called you by our gospel, to the obtaining of the glory of our Lord Jesus Christ.

IITim.1. 9 Who hath saved us, and called *us* with a holy calling, not according to our works, but according to his own purpose and grace, which was given us in Christ Jesus before the world began;

§ 459. THANKSGIVING FOR THEIR FAITHFUL RECEPTION

2 : 13–20.

13 For this cause also thank we God [a]without ceasing, because, when ye received the word of God which ye heard of us, ye received *it* [b]not *as* the word of men, but, as it is in truth, the word of God, which effectually worketh also in you that believe.

14 For ye, brethren, became followers [c]of the churches of God which in Judea are in Christ Jesus: for [d]ye also have suffered like things of your own countrymen, [e]even as they *have* of the Jews:

15 [f]Who both killed the Lord Jesus, and [g]their own prophets, and have [1]persecuted us; and they please not God, [h]and are contrary to all men:

16 [i]Forbidding us to speak to the Gentiles that they might be saved, [k]to fill up their sins alway: [l]for the wrath is come upon them to the uttermost.

17 But we, brethren, being taken from you for a short time [m]in presence, not in heart, endeavoured the more abundantly [n]to see your face with great desire.

18 Wherefore we would have come unto you, even I Paul, once and again; but [o]Satan hindered us.

19 For [p]what *is* our hope, or joy, or [q]crown of [2]rejoicing? *Are* not even ye in the presence of our Lord Jesus Christ [r]at his coming?

20 For ye are our glory and joy.

A

I Thes. 1. 3 Remembering without ceasing your work of faith, and labour of love, and patience of hope in our Lord Jesus Christ, in the sight of God and our Father;

B

Matt. 10. 40 He that receiveth you receiveth me, and he that receiveth me receiveth him that sent me.

Gal. 4. 14 And my temptation which was in my flesh ye despised not, nor rejected; but received me as an angel of God, *even* as Christ Jesus.

B—Concluded.

II Pet. 3. 2 That ye may be mindful of the words which were spoken before by the holy prophets, and of the commandment of us the apostles of the Lord and Saviour:

C

Gal. 1. 22 And was unknown by face unto the churches of Judea which were in Christ:

D

Acts 17. 5 But the Jews which believed not, moved with envy, took unto them certain lewd fellows of the baser sort, and gathered a company, and set all the city on an uproar, and assaulted the house of Jason, and sought to bring them out to the people.

Acts 17. 13 But when the Jews of Thessalonica had knowledge that the word of God was preached of Paul at Berea, they came thither also, and stirred up the people.

E

Heb. 10. 33 Partly, whilst ye were made a gazingstock both by reproaches and afflictions; and partly, whilst ye became companions of them that were so used.

34 For ye had compassion of me in my bonds, and took joyfully the spoiling of your goods, knowing in yourselves that ye have in heaven a better and an enduring substance.

F

Acts 2. 23 Him, being delivered by the determinate counsel and foreknowledge of God, ye have taken, and by wicked hands have crucified and slain:

Acts 3. 15 And killed the Prince of life, whom God hath raised from the dead; whereof we are witnesses.

Acts 5. 30 The God of our fathers raised up Jesus, whom ye slew and hanged on a tree.

Acts 7. 52 Which of the prophets have not your fathers persecuted? and they have slain them which shewed before of the coming of the Just One; of whom ye have been now the betrayers and murderers:

G

Matt. 5. 12. *See s, S, § 43, page 126.*

Luke 13. 33 Nevertheless I must walk to-day, and to-morrow, and the *day* following: for it cannot be that a prophet perish out of Jerusalem.

OF THE WORD. SATAN HINDERS PAUL'S COMING.

G—CONCLUDED.

Luke 13. 34 O Jerusalem, Jerusalem, which killest the prophets, and stonest them that are sent unto thee; how often would I have gathered thy children together as a hen *doth gather* her brood under *her* wings, and ye would not!

1

Or, *chased us out.*

H

Esth. 3. 8 And Haman said unto king Ahasuerus, There is a certain people scattered abroad and dispersed among the people in all the provinces of thy kingdom; and their laws *are* diverse from all people; neither keep they the king's laws: therefore it *is* not for the king's profit to suffer them.

I

Luke 11. 52 Woe unto you, lawyers! for ye have taken away the key of knowledge: ye entered not in yourselves, and them that were entering in ye hindered.

Acts 13. 50 But the Jews stirred up the devout and honourable women, and the chief men of the city, and raised persecution against Paul and Barnabas, and expelled them out of their coasts.

Acts 14. 5 And when there was an assault made both of the Gentiles, and also of the Jews with their rulers, to use *them* despitefully, and to stone them,

Acts 14. 19 And there came thither *certain* Jews from Antioch and Iconium, who persuaded the people, and, having stoned Paul, drew *him* out of the city, supposing he had been dead.

Acts 17. 5. *See under D.*

Acts 18. 12 And when Gallio was the deputy of Achaia, the Jews made insurrection with one accord against Paul, and brought him to the judgment seat.

Acts 19 9 But when divers were hardened, and believed not, but spake evil of that way before the multitude, he departed from them, and separated the disciples, disputing daily in the school of one Tyrannus.

Acts 22. 22 And they gave him audience unto this word, and *then* lifted up their voices, and said, Away with such a *fellow* from the earth: for it is not fit that he should live.

K

Gen. 15. 16 But in the fourth generation they shall come hither again: for the iniquity of the Amorites *is* not yet full.

K—CONCLUDED.

Matt. 23. 32 Fill ye up then the measure of your fathers.

L

Matt. 24. 6 And ye shall hear of wars and rumours of wars: see that ye be not troubled: for all *these things* must come to pass, but the end is not yet.

Matt. 24. 14 And this gospel of the kingdom shall be preached in all the world for a witness unto all nations; and then shall the end come.

M

I Cor. 5. 3. *See f, F, § 359, page 906.*

N

I Thes. 3. 10 Night and day praying exceedingly that we might see your face, and might perfect that which is lacking in your faith?

O

Rom. 1. 13 Now I would not have you ignorant, brethren, that oftentimes I purposed to come unto you, (but was let hitherto,) that I might have some fruit among you also, even as among other Gentiles.

Rom. 15. 22 For which cause also I have been much hindered from coming to you.

P

II Cor. 1. 14. *See n, N, § 386, page 964.*

Q

Prov. 16. 31 The hoary head *is* a crown of glory, *if* it be found in the way of righteousness.

2

Or, *glorying.*

R

I Cor. 15. 23 But every man in his own order: Christ the firstfruits; afterward they that are Christ's at his coming.

I Thes. 3. 13 To the end he may stablish your hearts unblameable in holiness before God, even our Father, at the coming of our Lord Jesus Christ with all his saints.

I Thes. 4. 15 For this we say unto you by the word of the Lord, that we which are alive *and* remain unto the coming of the Lord shall not prevent them which are asleep.

Rev. 1. 7 Behold, he cometh with clouds; and every eye shall see him, and they *also* which pierced him: and all kindreds of the earth shall wail because of him. Even so, Amen.

Rev. 22. 12 And, behold, I come quickly; and my reward *is* with me, to give every man according as his work shall be.

§ 460. TIMOTHY WAS SENT TO ESTABLISH THEM, WHO

3 : 1–13.

1 Wherefore [a]when we could no longer forbear, [b]we thought it good to be left at Athens alone;

2 And sent [c]Timotheus, our brother, and minister of God, and our fellow labourer in the gospel of Christ, to establish you, and to comfort you concerning your faith:

3 [d]That no man should be moved by these afflictions: for yourselves know that [e]we are appointed thereunto.

4 [f]For verily, when we were with you, we told you before that we should suffer tribulation; even as it came to pass, and ye know.

5 For this cause, [g]when I could no longer forbear, I sent to know your faith, [h]lest by some means the tempter have tempted you, and [i]our labour be in vain.

6 [k]But now when Timotheus came from you unto us, and brought us good tidings of your faith and charity, and that ye have good remembrance of us always, desiring greatly to see us, [l]as we also *to see* you:

7 Therefore, brethren, [m]we were comforted over you in all our affliction and distress by your faith:

8 For now we live, if ye [n]stand fast in the Lord.

9 [o]For what thanks can we render to God again for you, for all the joy wherewith we joy for your sakes before our God;

10 [p]Night and day [q]praying exceedingly [r]that we might see your face, [s]and might perfect that which is lacking in your faith?

11 Now God himself and our Father, and our Lord Jesus Christ, [t]direct our way unto you.

CHAP. 3.

12 And the Lord [u]make you to increase and abound in love [x]one toward another, and toward all *men*, even as we *do* toward you:

13 To the end he may [y]stablish your hearts unblameable in holiness before God, even our Father, at the coming of our Lord Jesus Christ [z]with all his saints.

A

I. Thes. 3. 5. *See text of topic.*

B

Acts 17. 15 And they that conducted Paul brought him unto Athens: and receiving a commandment unto Silas and Timotheus for to come to him with all speed, they departed.

C

Acts 16. 1. *See b, B, § 271, page 732.*

I Cor. 16. 10 Now if Timotheus come, see that he may be with you without fear: for he worketh the work of the Lord, as I also *do*.

II Cor. 1. 19 For the Son of God, Jesus Christ, who was preached among you by us, *even* by me and Sylvanus and Timotheus, was not yea and nay, but in him was yea.

D

Eph. 3. 13 Wherefore I desire that ye faint not at my tribulations for you, which is your glory.

E

Acts 9. 16 For I will shew him how great things he must suffer for my name's sake.

Acts 14. 22. *See e, E, § 266, page 724.*

F

Acts 20. 24 But none of these things move me, neither count I my life dear unto myself, so that I might finish my course with joy, and the ministry, which I have received of the Lord Jesus, to testify the gospel of the grace of God.

G

I Thes. 3. 1. *See text of topic.*

H

I Cor. 7. 5 Defraud ye not one the other, except *it be* with consent for a time, that ye may give yourselves to fasting and prayer; and come together again, that Satan tempt you not for your incontinency.

RETURNED WITH A COMFORTING REPORT. A PRAYER.

H—CONCLUDED.

II Cor. 11. 3 But I fear, lest by any means, as the serpent beguiled Eve through his subtility, so your minds should be corrupted from the simplicity that is in Christ.

I

Gal. 2. 2 And I went up by revelation, and communicated unto them that gospel which I preach among the Gentiles, but privately to them which were of reputation, lest by any means I should run, or had run, in vain.

Gal. 4. 11 I am afraid of you, lest I have bestowed upon you labour in vain.

Phil. 2. 16 Holding forth the word of life; that I may rejoice in the day of Christ, that I have not run in vain, neither laboured in vain.

K

Acts 18. 1 After these things Paul departed from Athens, and came to Corinth;

Acts 18. 5 And when Silas and Timotheus were come from Macedonia, Paul was pressed in the spirit, and testified to the Jews *that* Jesus *was* Christ.

L

Phil. 1. 8 For God is my record, how greatly I long after you all in the bowels of Jesus Christ.

M

II Cor. 1. 4 Who comforteth us in all our tribulation, that we may be able to comfort them which are in any trouble, by the comfort wherewith we ourselves are comforted of God.

II Cor. 7. 6 Nevertheless God, that comforteth those that are cast down, comforted us by the coming of Titus;

7 And not by his coming only, but by the consolation wherewith he was comforted in you, when he told us your earnest desire, your mourning, your fervent mind toward me; so that I rejoiced the more.

II Cor. 7. 13 Therefore we were comforted in your comfort: yea, and exceedingly the more joyed we for the joy of Titus, because his spirit was refreshed by you all.

N

Phil. 4. 1 Therefore, my brethren dearly beloved and longed for, my joy and crown, so stand fast in the Lord, *my* dearly beloved.

O

I Thes. 1. 2 We give thanks to God always for you all, making mention of you in our prayers;

P

Acts 26. 7. *See e, E, § 309, page 792.*

Q

Rom. 1. 10 Making request, if by any means now at length I might have a prosperous journey by the will of God to come unto you.

11 For I long to see you, that I may impart unto you some spiritual gift, to the end ye may be established;

Rom. 15. 32 That I may come unto you with joy by the will of God, and may with you be refreshed.

R

I Thes. 2. 17. *See n, N, § 459, page 1098.*

S

I Cor. 2. 6. *See i, I, § 352, page 894.*

1

Or, *guide.*

T

Mark 1. 3 The voice of one crying in the wilderness, Prepare ye the way of the Lord, make his paths straight.

U

I Thes. 4. 10 And indeed ye do it toward all the brethren which are in all Macedonia: but we beseech you, brethren, that ye increase more and more:

X

I Thes. 4. 9 But as touching brotherly love ye need not that I write unto you: for ye yourselves are taught of God to love one another.

I Thes. 5. 15 See that none render evil for evil unto any *man;* but ever follow that which is good, both among yourselves, and to all *men.*

II Pet. 1. 7 And to godliness, brotherly kindness; and to brotherly kindness, charity.

Y

II Thes. 2. 17. *See k, K, § 468, page 1114.*

Z

Zech. 14. 5 And ye shall flee *to* the valley of the mountains; for the valley of the mountains shall reach unto Azal: yea, ye shall flee, like as you fled from before the earthquake in the days of Uzziah king of Judah: and the Lord my God shall come, *and* all the saints with thee.

Jude 14 And Enoch also, the seventh from Adam, prophesied of these, saying, Behold, the Lord cometh with ten thousands of his saints,

§ 461. EXHORTED TO ABSTAIN FROM

4 : 1–8.

1 Furthermore than we [1]beseech you, brethren, and [2]exhort *you* by the Lord Jesus, [a]that as ye have received of us [b]how ye ought to walk [c]and to please God, *so* ye would abound more and more.

2 For ye know what commandments we gave you by the Lord Jesus.

3 For this is [d]the will of God, *even* [e]your sanctification, [f]that ye should abstain from fornication:

4 [g]That every one of you should know how to possess his vessel in sanctification and honour;

5 [h]Not in the lust of concupiscence, [i]even as the Gentiles [k]which know not God:

6 [l]That no *man* go beyond and [3]defraud his brother [4]in *any* matter: because that the Lord [m]*is* the avenger of all such, as we also have forewarned you and testified.

7 For God hath not called us unto uncleanness, [n]but unto holiness.

8 [o]He therefore that [5]despiseth, despiseth not man, but God, [p]who hath also given unto us his Holy Spirit.

1
Or, *request.*

2
Or, *beseech.*

A

Col. 2. 6. *See k, K, § 451, page 1082.*

B

Eph. 4. 1. *See b, B, § 432, page 1040.*

C

Col. 1. 10 That ye might walk worthy of the Lord unto all pleasing, being fruitful in every good work, and increasing in the knowledge of God;

D

Rom. 12. 2. *See f, F, § 342, page 868.*

E

Acts 26. 18. *See s, S, § 309, page 749.*

Eph. 5. 26 That he might sanctify and cleanse it with the washing of water by the word,

27 That he might present it to himself a glorious church, not having spot, or wrinkle, or any such thing; but that it should be holy and without blemish.

F

Acts 15. 20. *See s, S, § 268, page 730.*

G

Rom. 6. 19 I speak after the manner of men because of the infirmity of your flesh: for as ye have yielded your members servants to uncleanness and to iniquity unto iniquity; even so now yield your members servants to righteousness unto holiness.

I Cor. 6. 15 Know ye not that your bodies are the members of Christ? shall I then take the members of Christ, and make *them* the members of a harlot? God forbid.

I Cor. 6. 18 Flee fornication. Every sin that a man doeth is without the body; but

§ 462. EXHORTATION TO INCREASE IN LOVE AND

4 : 9–12.

9 But as touching brotherly love [a]ye need not that I write unto you: for [b]ye yourselves are taught of God [c]to love one another.

10 [d]And indeed ye do it toward all the brethren which are in all Macedonia: but we beseech you, brethren, [e]that ye increase more and more;

A

I Thes. 5. 1 But of the times and the seasons, brethren, ye have no need that I write unto you.

B

Isa. 2. 3 And many people shall go and say, Come ye, and let us go up to the mountain of the LORD, to the house of the God of Jacob; and he will teach us of his ways, and we will walk in his paths: for out of Zion shall go forth the law, and the word of the LORD from Jerusalem.

FORNICATION AND LUSTFUL PASSIONS.

G—CONCLUDED.

he that committeth fornication sinneth against his own body.

H

Rom. 1. 24, 26. *See n, N, § 319, page 812.*
Col. 3. 5. *See l, L, § 454, page 1088.*

I

Eph. 4. 17 This I say therefore, and testify in the Lord, that ye henceforth walk not as other Gentiles walk, in the vanity of their mind,
18 Having the understanding darkened, being alienated from the life of God through the ignorance that is in them, because of the blindness of their heart:

K

I Cor. 15. 34 Awake to righteousness, and sin not; for some have not the knowledge of God: I speak *this* to your shame.
Gal. 4. 8. *See a, A, § 419, page 1018.*

L

Lev. 19. 11 Ye shall not steal, neither deal falsely, neither lie one to another.
Lev. 19 13 Thou shalt not defraud thy neighbour, neither rob *him:* the wages of him that is hired shall not abide with thee all night until the morning.
I Cor. 6. 8 Nay ye do wrong, and defraud, and that *your* brethren.

3

Or, *oppress.* Or, *overreach.*

4

Or, *in the matter.*

M

II Thes. 1. 8 In flaming fire taking vengeance on them that know not God, and that obey not the gospel of our Lord Jesus Christ:

N

Lev. 11. 44 For I *am* the LORD your God: ye shall therefore sanctify yourselves, and

N—CONCLUDED.

ye shall be holy: for I *am* holy: neither shall ye defile yourselves with any manner of creeping thing that creepeth upon the earth.
Lev. 19. 2 Speak unto all the congregation of of the children of Israel, and say unto them, Ye shall be holy: for I the LORD your God *am* holy.
I Cor. 1. 2 Unto the church of God which is at Corinth, to them that are sanctified in Christ Jesus, called *to be* saints, with all that in every place call upon the name of Jesus Christ our Lord, both theirs and ours:
Heb. 12. 14 Follow peace with all *men*, and holiness, without which no man shall see the Lord:
I Pet. 1. 15 But as he which hath called you is holy, so be ye holy in all manner of conversation:
16 Because it is written, Be ye holy; for I am holy.

O

Luke 10. 16 He that heareth you heareth me; and he that despiseth you despiseth me; and he that despiseth me despiseth him that sent me.

5

Or, *rejecteth.*

P

I Cor. 2. 10 But God hath revealed *them* unto us by his Spirit: for the Spirit searcheth all things, yea, the deep things of God.
I Cor. 7. 40 But she is happier if she so abide, after my judgment: and I think also that I have the Spirit of God.
I Jno. 3. 24 And he that keepeth his commandments dwelleth in him, and he in him. And hereby we know that he abideth in us, by the Spirit which he hath given us.

TO BE DILIGENT AND HONEST IN BUSINESS.

B—CONTINUED.

Isa. 54. 13 And all thy children *shall be* taught of the LORD; and great *shall be* the peace of thy children.
Jer. 31. 34 And they shall teach no more every man his neighbour, and every man his brother, saying, Know the LORD: for they shall all know me, from the least of them unto the greatest of them, saith the LORD: for I will forgive their iniquity, and I will remember their sin no more.
John 6. 45 It is written in the prophets, And

B—CONTINUED.

they shall be all taught of God. Every man therefore that hath heard, and hath learned of the Father, cometh unto me.
John 14. 26 But the Comforter, *which is* the Holy Ghost, whom the Father will send in my name, he shall teach you all things, and bring all things to your remembrance, whatsoever I have said unto you.
Eph. 4. 21 If so be that ye have heard him, and have been taught by him, as the truth is in Jesus:

For B concl'd, C, D, and E, see next page, (1104).

§ 462. EXHORTATION TO INCREASE IN LOVE AND TO BE

CHAP. 4.

11 And that ye study to be quiet,
and [f]to do your own business, and
[g]to work with your own hands, as we
commanded you;

12 [h]That ye may walk honestly
toward them that are without, and
that ye may have lack of [1]nothing.

B—CONTINUED.

Heb. 8. 11 And they shall not teach every man his neighbor, and every man his brother, saying, Know the Lord: for all shall know me, from the least to the greatest.

I Jno. 2. 20 But ye have an unction from the Holy One, and ye know all things.

I Jno. 2. 27 But the anointing which ye have received of him abideth in you, and ye

B—CONCLUDED.

need not that any man teach you: but as the same anointing teacheth you of all things, and is truth, and is no lie, and even as it hath taught you, ye shall abide in him.

C

John 13. 34. *See y, Y, § 183, page 519.*

D

IThes. 1. 7 So that ye were ensamples to all that believe in Macedonia and Achaia.

E

IThes. 3. 12 And the Lord make you to increase and abound in love one toward another, and toward all *men*, even as we *do* toward you:

F

Mark 13. 34 *For the Son of man is* as a man taking a far journey, who left his house, and gave authority to his serv-

§ 463. CONCERNING THE SAINTS

4:13–18.

13 But I would not have you to be
ignorant, brethren, concerning them
which are asleep, that ye sorrow
not, [a]even as others [b]which have no
hope.

14 For [c]if we believe that Jesus
died and rose again, even so [d]them
also which sleep in Jesus will God
bring with him.

15 For this we say unto you [e]by
the word of the Lord, that [f]we
which are alive *and* remain unto the
coming of the Lord shall not prevent them which are asleep.

16 For [g]the Lord himself shall descend from heaven with a shout,
with the voice of the archangel, and
with [h]the trump of God: [i]and the
dead in Christ shall rise first:

17 [k]Then we which are alive *and*
remain shall be caught up together
with them [l]in the clouds, to meet the
Lord in the air: and so [m]shall we
ever be with the Lord.

CHAP. 4.

18 [n]Wherefore [1]comfort one another with these words.

A

Lev. 19. 28 Ye shall not make any cuttings in your flesh for the dead, nor print any marks upon you: I *am* the Lord.

Duet. 14. 1 Ye *are* the Children of the LORD your God: ye shall not cut yourselves, nor make any baldness between your eyes for the dead.

B

Eph. 2. 12 That at that time ye were without Christ, being aliens from the commonwealth of Israel, and strangers from the covenants of promise, having no hope, and without God in the world;

C

ICor. 15. 13 But if there be no resurrection of the dead, then is Christ not risen:

D

ICor. 15. 18 Then they also which are fallen asleep in Christ are perished.

ICor. 15. 23 But every man in his own order: Christ the firstfruits; afterward they that are Christ's at his coming.

E

IKi. 13. 17 For it was said to me by the word of the LORD Thou shalt eat no bread nor drink water there, nor turn again to go by the way that thou camest.

DILIGENT AND HONEST IN BUSINESS (CONCLUDED).

F—CONTINUED.

ants, and to every man his work, and commanded the porter to watch.

Luke12. 42 And the Lord said, Who then is that faithful and wise steward, whom *his* lord shall make ruler over his household, to give *them their* portion of meat in due season?

43 Blessed *is* that servant, whom his lord when he cometh shall find so doing.

Rom.12. 6 Having then gifts differing according to the grace that is given to us, whether prophecy, *let us prophesy* according to the proportion of faith;

7 Or ministry, *let us wait* on *our* ministering; or he that teacheth, on teaching;

8 Or he that exhorteth, on exhortation: he that giveth, *let him do it* with simplicity; he that ruleth, with diligence; he that sheweth mercy, with cheerfulness.

F—CONCLUDED.

Rom.12. 11 Not slothful in business; fervent in spirit; serving the Lord;

IIThes. 3. 11 For we hear that there are some which walk among you disorderly, working not at all, but are busybodies.

12 Now them that are such we command and exhort by our Lord Jesus Christ, that with quietness they work, and eat their own bread.

IITim.2 6 The husbandman that laboreth must be first partaker of the fruits.

G

Acts 20. 35. *See e, E, § 292. page 764.*

H

II Cor. 8. 21. *See e, E, § 400, page 986.*

Col. 4. 5. *See t, T, § 455, page 1090.*

1

Or, *of no man.*

AND THE LORD'S COMING.

F

ICor.15. 51 Behold, I shew you a mystery; We shall not all sleep, but we shall all be changed.

G

Matt.24. 30 And then shall appear the sign of the Son of man in heaven: and then shall all the tribes of the earth mourn, and they shall see the Son of man coming in the clouds of heaven with power and great glory.

31 And he shall send his angels with a great sound of a trumpet, and they shall gather together his elect from the four winds, from one end of heaven to the other.

Acts. 1. 11 Which also said, Ye men of Galilee, why stand ye gazing up into heaven? this same Jesus, which is taken up from you into heaven, shall so come in like manner as ye have seen him go into heaven.

IIThes.1. 7 And to you who are troubled rest with us, when the Lord Jesus shall be revealed from heaven with his mighty angels,

H

ICor.15. 52 In a moment, in the twinkling of an eye, at the last trump: for the trumpet shall sound, and the dead shall be raised incorruptible, and we shall be changed.

I

I Cor. 15. 23. *See under D.*

I Cor. 15. 52. *See under H.*

Rev. 20. 5 But the rest of the dead lived not again until the thousand years were finished. This *is* the first resurrection.

6 Blessed and holy *is* he that hath part in the first resurrection: on such the second death hath no power, but they shall be priests of God and of Christ, and shall reign with him a thousand years.

K

I Cor. 15. 51. *See under F.*

L

Acts 1. 9 And when he had spoken these things, while they beheld, he was taken up; and a cloud received him out of their sight.

Rev. 11. 12 And they heard a great voice from heaven saying unto them, Come up hither. And they ascended up to heaven in a cloud; and their enemies beheld them.

M

John 14. 3. *See e, E, § 186, page 525.*

N

IThes.5. 11 Wherefore comfort yourselves together, and edify one another, even as also ye do.

1

Or, ***exhort.***

§ 464. THE UNCERTAINTY OF THE DAY OF THE

5 : 1–11.

1 But of [a]the times and the seasons, brethren, ye have no need that I write unto you.

2 For yourselves know perfectly that [b]the day of the Lord so cometh as a thief in the night.

3 For when they shall say, Peace and safety; then [c]sudden destruction cometh upon them, as travail upon a woman with child; and they shall not escape.

4 [d]But ye, brethren, are not in darkness, that that day should overtake you as a thief.

5 Ye are all [e]the children of light, and the children of the day: we are not of the night, nor of darkness.

6 [f]Therefore let us not sleep, as *do* others; but [g]let us watch and be sober.

7 For [h]they that sleep sleep in the night; and they that be drunken [i]are drunken in the night.

8 But let us, who are of the day, be sober, [k]putting on the breastplate of faith and love; and for a helmet, the hope of salvation.

9 For [l]God hath not appointed us to wrath, [m]but to obtain salvation by our Lord Jesus Christ,

10 [n]Who died for us, that, whether we wake or sleep, we should live together with him.

11 [o]Wherefore [1]comfort yourselves together, and edify one another, even as also ye do.

CHAP. 5.

A

Matt. 24. 3 And as he sat upon the mount of Olives, the disciples came unto him privately, saying, Tell us, when shall these things be? and what *shall be* the sign of thy coming, and of the end of the world?

Matt 24. 36 But of that day and hour knoweth no *man*, no, not the angels of heaven, but my Father only.

Acts 1. 7 And he said unto them, It is not for you to know the times or the seasons, which the Father hath put in his own power.

B

Matt. 24. 43, 44. *See a, A, § 174, page 494.*

C

Ps. 73. 18 Surely thou didst set them in slippery places: thou castedst them down into destruction.

19 How are they *brought* into desolation, as in a moment! they are utterly consumed with terrors.

20 As a dream when *one* awaketh; *so*, O Lord, when thou awakest, thou shalt despise their image.

Prov. 29. 1 He, that being often reproved hardeneth *his* neck, shall suddenly be destroyed, and that without remedy.

§ 465. SUNDRY ADMONITIONS. CONCLUDING

5: 12–28.

12 And we beseech you, brethren, [a]to know them which labour among you, and are over you in the Lord, and admonish you;

13 And to esteem them very highly in love for their work's sake. [b]*And* be at peace among yourselves.

CHAP. 5.

14 Now we [1]exhort you, brethren,

A

Phil. 2. 29. *See l, L, § 443, page 1068.*

Heb. 13. 7 Remember them which have the rule over you, who have spoken unto you the word of God: whose faith follow, considering the end of *their* conversation.

Heb. 13. 17 Obey them that have the rule

LORD'S COMING A MOTIVE TO SOBER WATCHFULNESS.

C—Concluded.

Isa. 13. 6 Howl ye; for the day of the Lord *is* at hand; it shall come as a destruction from the Almighty.

7 Therefore shall all hands be faint, and every man's heart shall melt:

8 And they shall be afraid: pangs and sorrows shall take hold of them; they shall be in pain as a woman that travaileth: they shall be amazed one at another; their faces *shall be as* flames.

9 Behold, the day of the Lord cometh, cruel both with wrath and fierce anger, to lay the land desolate: and he shall destroy the sinners thereof out of it.

Luke 17. 27 They did eat, they drank, they married wives, they were given in marriage, until the day that Noe entered into the ark, and the flood came, and destroyed them all.

28 Likewise also as it was in the days of Lot; they did eat, they drank, they bought, they sold, they planted, they builded;

29 But the same day that Lot went out of Sodom it rained fire and brimstone from heaven, and destroyed *them* all.

IIThes. 1. 9 Who shall be punished with everlasting destruction from the presence of the Lord, and from the glory of his power;

D

Rom. 13. 12, 13. *See p, P, § 343, page 874.*

E

Eph. 5. 8. *See p, P, § 434, page 1048.*

F

Matt. 25. 5 While the bridegroom tarried, they all slumbered and slept.

G

Matt. 25. 13. *See k, K, § 175, page 496.*

H

Luke 21. 34. *See c, C, § 173, page 493.*

I

Acts 2. 15 For these are not drunken, as ye suppose, seeing it is *but* the third hour of the day.

K

Eph. 6. 14, 17. *See i, I, § 437. page 1056.*

L

Rom. 9. 22 *What* if God, willing to shew *his* wrath, and to make his power known, endured with much longsuffering the vessels of wrath fitted to destruction:

IThes. 1. 10 And to wait for his Son from heaven, whom he raised from the dead, *even* Jesus, which delivered us from the wrath to come.

I Pet. 2. 8 And a stone of stumbling, and a rock of offence, *even to them* which stumble at the word, being disobedient: whereunto also they were appointed.

Jude 4 For there are certain men crept in unawares, who were before of old ordained to this condemnation, ungodly men, turning the grace of our God into lasciviousness, and denying the only Lord God, and our Lord Jesus Christ.

M

IIThes. 2. 13 But we are bound to give thanks alway to God for you, brethren beloved of the Lord, because God hath from the beginning chosen you to salvation through sanctification of the Spirit and belief of the truth:

14 Whereunto he called you by our gospel, to the obtaining of the glory of our Lord Jesus Christ.

N

Rom. 14. 7-9. *See n, N, § 344, page 876.*

O

IThes. 4. 18 Wherefore comfort one another with these words.

1

Or, *exhort.*

SALUTATION AND BENEDICTION.

A—Concluded.

over you, and submit yourselves: for they watch for your souls, as they that must give account, that they may do it with joy, and not with grief: for that *is* unprofitable for you.

B

Mark 9. 50 Salt *is* good: but if the salt have lost his saltness, wherewith will ye season it? Have salt in yourselves, and have peace one with another.

1

Or, *beseech.*

C

IIThes. 3. 11 For we hear that there are some which walk among you disorderly, working not at all, but are busybodies.

12 Now them that are such we command and exhort by our Lord Jesus Christ, that with quietness they work, and eat their own bread.

§ 465. SUNDRY ADMONITIONS, CONCLUDING

CHAP. 5.

[c]warn them that are [2]unruly, [d]comfort the feeble-minded, [e]support the weak, [f]be patient toward all *men.*

15 [g]See that none render evil for evil unto any *man;* but ever [h]follow that which is good, both among yourselves, and to all *men.*

16 [i]Rejoice evermore.

17 [k]Pray without ceasing.

18 [l]In everything give thanks: for this is the will of God in Christ Jesus concerning you.

19 [m]Quench not the Spirit.

20 [n]Despise not prophesyings.

21 [o]Prove all things; [p]hold fast that which is good.

22 [q]Abstain from all appearance of evil.

23 And the [r]very God of peace [s]sanctify you wholly; and *I pray God* your whole spirit and soul and body [t]be preserved blameless unto the coming of our Lord Jesus Christ.

24 [u]Faithful *is* he that calleth you, who also will do *it.*

25 Brethren, [x]pray for us.

26 [y]Greet all the brethren with a holy kiss.

27 I [3]charge you by the Lord that [z]this epistle be read unto all the holy brethren.

28 [a]The grace of our Lord Jesus Christ *be* with you. Amen.

For C, see preceding page (1107).

2

Or, *disorderly.*

D

Isa. 35. 3 Strengthen ye the weak hands, and confirm the feeble knees.

4 Say to them *that are* of a fearful heart, Be strong, fear not: behold,

D—CONCLUDED.

your God will come *with* vengeance, *even* God *with* a recompense; he will come and save you.

Isa. 40. 1 Comfort ye, comfort ye my people, saith your God.

2 Speak ye comfortably to Jerusalem, and cry unto her, that her warfare is accomplished, that her iniquity is pardoned: for she hath received of the LORD'S hand double for all her sins.

Heb. 12. 12 Wherefore lift up the hands which hang down, and the feeble knees;

E

Luke 22. 32 But I have prayed for thee, that thy faith fail not: and when thou art converted, strengthen thy brethren.

Rom. 14. 1 Him that is weak in the faith receive ye, *but* not to doubtful disputations.

Rom. 15. 1 We then that are strong ought to bear the infirmities of the weak, and not to please ourselves.

I Cor. 9. 22 To the weak became I as weak, that I might gain the weak: I am made all things to all *men* that I might by all means save some.

I Cor. 12. 22 Nay, much more those members of the body, which seem to be more feeble, are necessary:

23 And those *members* of the body, which we think to be less honourable, upon these we bestow more abundant honour; and our uncomely *parts* have more abundant comliness.

24 For our comely *parts* have no need: but God hath tempered the body together, having given more abundant honour to that *part* which lacked:

F

Eph. 4. 2. *See c, C, § 432, page 1040.*

Rom. 12. 12. *See a, A, § 342, page 870.*

I Cor. 13. 4 Charity suffereth long, *and* is kind; charity envieth not; charity vaunteth not itself, is not puffed up,

II Tim. 2. 24 And the servant of the Lord must not strive; but be gentle unto all *men,* apt to teach, patient;

25 In meekness instructing those that oppose themselves; if God peradventure will give them repentance to the acknowledging of the truth;

G

Lev. 19. 18 Thou shalt not avenge, nor bear any grudge against the children of thy people, but thou shalt love thy neighbor as thyself: I *am* the LORD.

Matt. 5. 39. *See p, P, § 43, page 132.*

SALUTATION AND BENEDICTION (CONCLUDED).

H

Gal. 6. 10 As we have therefore opportunity, let us do good unto all *men*, especially unto them who are of the household of faith.

IThes.3 12 And the Lord make you to increase and abound in love one toward another, and toward all *men*, even as we *do* toward you:

I

IICor.6. 10 As sorrowful, yet alway rejoicing; as poor, yet making many rich; as having nothing, and *yet* possessing all things.

Phil. 4. 4 Rejoice in the Lord alway: *and* again I say, Rejoice.

K

Luke 18. 1. *See a, A, § 140, page 401.*

I Pet. 4. 7 But the end of all things is at hand: be ye therefore sober, and watch unto prayer.

L

Eph. 5. 20 Giving thanks always for all things unto God and the Father in the name of our Lord Jesus Christ;

Col. 3. 17 And whatsoever ye do in word or deed, *do* all in the name of the Lord Jesus, giving thanks to God and the Father by him.

M

Eph. 4. 30 And grieve not the Holy Spirit of God, whereby ye are sealed unto the day of redemption.

I Tim.4. 14 Neglect not the gift that is in thee, which was given thee by prophesy, with the laying on of the hands of the presbytery.

IITim.1. 6 Wherefore I put thee in remembrance, that thou stir up the gift of God, which is in thee by the putting on of my hands.

N

ICor.14. 1 Follow after charity, and desire spiritual *gifts*, but rather that ye may prophesy.

ICor.14. 39 Wherefore, brethren, covet to prophesy, and forbid not to speak with tongues.

O

I Cor. 2. 15. *See a, A, § 352, page 896.*

P

Phil. 4. 8 Finally, brethren, whatsoever things are true whatsoever things *are* honest, whatsoever things *are* just, whatsoever things *are* pure, whatsoever things *are* lovely, whatsoever things *are* of good report; if *there be* any virtue,

P—CONCLUDED.

and if *there be* any praise, think on these things.

Heb. 10. 23 Let us hold fast the profession of *our* faith without wavering; (for he *is* faithful that promised;)

24 And let us consider one another to provoke unto love and to good works:

Q

Ex. 23. 7 Keep thee far from a false matter; and the innocent and righteous slay thou not: for I will not justify the wicked.

IICor. 8. 20 Avoiding this, that no man should blame us in this abundance which is administered by us:

21 Providing for honest things, not only in the sight of the Lord, but also in the sight of men.

IThes.4. 12 That ye may walk honestly toward them that are without, and *that* ye may have lack of nothing.

R

Phil. 4. 9 Those things, which ye have both learned, and received, and heard, and seen in me, do: and the God of peace shall be with you.

S

IThes.3. 13 To the end he may stablish your hearts unblameable in holiness before God, even our Father, at the coming of our Lord Jesus Christ with all his saints.

T

I Cor. 1. 8. *See f, F, § 349, page 890.*

U

I Cor. 1. 9. *See g, G, § 349, page 890.*

X

Eph. 6. 19. *See r, R, § 437, page 1056.*

Col. 4. 3 Withal praying also for us, that God would open unto us a door of utterance, to speak the mystery of Christ, for which I am also in bonds:

Y

Rom. 16. 16. *See h, H, § 347, page 884.*

3

Or, *adjure.*

Z

Col. 4. 16 And when this epistle is read among you, cause that it be read also in the church of the Laodiceans; and that ye likewise read the *epistle* from Laodicea.

A

Rom. 16. 20. *See r, R, § 347, page 886.*

PAUL'S SECOND EPISTLE

§ 466. SALUTATION. THANKSGIVING. HOPE IN THE LORD'S COMING FOR

Written A. D. 53.

1 : 1–12

1 Paul, [a]and Silvanus, and Timotheus, unto the church of the Thessalonians [b]in God our Father and the
Lord Jesus Christ:
2 [c]Grace unto you, and peace, from
God our Father and the Lord Jesus
Christ.
3 [d]We are bound to thank God always for you, brethren, as it is
meet, because that your faith groweth
exceedingly, and the charity of every
one of you all toward each other
aboundeth;
4 So that [e]we ourselves glory in
you in the churches of God [f]for
your patience and faith [g]in all your
persecutions and tribulations that
ye endure:
5 *Which is* [h]a manifest token of
the righteous judgment of God, that
ye may be counted worthy of the
kingdom of God, [i]for which ye also
suffer:
6 [k]Seeing *it is* a righteous thing
with God to recompense tribulation
to them that trouble you;
7 And to you who are troubled
[l]rest with us, [m]when the Lord Jesus
shall be revealed from heaven with
[1]his mighty angels,
8 [n]In flaming fire [2]taking vengeance
on them [o]that know not God, and
[p]that obey not the gospel of our
Lord Jesus Christ:
9 [q]Who shall be punished with
everlasting destruction [r]from the
presence of the Lord, and from the
glory of his power;
10 [s]When he shall come to be
glorified in his saints, and [t]to be admired in all them that believe (because our testimony among you was
believed) in that day.
11 Wherefore also we pray always

CHAP. 1.

for you, that our God would [3u]count
you worthy of *this* calling, and fulfil all the good pleasure of *his* goodness, and [x]the work of faith with
power:
12 [y]That the name of our Lord
Jesus Christ may be glorified in you,
and ye in him, according to the
grace of our God and the Lord
Jesus Christ.

A

II Cor. 1. 19 For the Son of God, Jesus Christ, who was preached among you by us, *even* by me and Silvanus and Timotheus, was not yea and nay, but in him was yea.

B

I Thes. 1. 1 Paul, and Silvanus, and Timotheus, unto the church of the Thessalonians *which is* in God the Father, and *in* the Lord Jesus Christ: Grace *be* unto you, and peace, from God our Father, and the Lord Jesus Christ.

C

I Cor. 1. 3. *See i, I, § 348, page 888.*

D

Phil. 1. 3. *See a, A, § 440, page 1058.*

E

II Cor. 8. 24. *See g, G, § 400, page 986.*

I Thes. 2. 19 For what *is* our hope, or joy, or crown of rejoicing? *Are* not even ye in the presence of our Lord Jesus Christ at his coming?
20 For ye are our glory and joy.

F

I Thes. 1. 3 Remembering without ceasing your work of faith, and labour of love, and patience of hope in our Lord Jesus Christ, in the sight of God and our Father;

G

I Thes. 2. 14 For ye, brethren, became followers of the churches of God which in Judea are in Christ Jesus: for ye also have suffered like things of your own countrymen, even as they *have* of the Jews:

H

Phil. 1. 28 And in nothing terrified by your adversaries: which is to them an evident token of perdition, but to you of salvation, and that of God.

THOSE WHO SUFFER PERSECUTION, AND DESTRUCTION FOR THE UNGODLY.

at Corinth

H—CONCLUDED.

I Pet. 4. 12 Beloved, think it not strange concerning the fiery trial which is to try you, as though some strange thing happened unto you:
13 But rejoice, inasmuch as ye are partakers of Christ's sufferings; that, when his glory shall be revealed, ye may be glad also with exceeding joy.
14 If ye be reproached for the name of Christ, happy *are ye*; for the Spirit of glory and of God resteth upon you: on their part he is evil spoken of, but on your part he is glorified.

I

I Thes. 2. 14. *See under G.*

K

Rev. 6. 10 And they cried with a loud voice, saying, How long, O Lord, holy and true, dost thou not judge and avenge our blood on them that dwell on the earth?

L

Rev. 14. 13 And I heard a voice from heaven saying unto me, Write, Blessed *are* the dead which die in the Lord from henceforth: Yea, saith the Spirit, that they may rest from their labours; and their works do follow them.

M

I Thes. 4. 16. *See g, G, § 463, page 1104.*

Jude 14 And Enoch also, the seventh from Adam, prophesied of these, saying, Behold, the Lord cometh with ten thousand of his saints,

1

Gr. *the angels of his power.*

N

Heb. 10. 27 But a certain fearful looking for of judgment and fiery indignation, which shall devour the adversaries.

II Pet. 3. 7 But the heavens and the earth, which are now, by the same word are kept in store, reserved unto fire against the day of judgment and perdition of ungodly men.

Rev. 21. 8 But the fearful, and unbelieving, and the abominable, and murderers, and whormongers, and sorcerers, and idolaters and all liars, shall have their part in the lake which burneth with fire and brimstone: which is the second death.

2

Or, *yielding.*

O

Ps. 79. 6 Pour out thy wrath upon the heathen that have not known thee, and upon the kingdoms that have not called upon thy name.

I Thes. 4. 5 Not in the lust of concupiscence, even as the Gentiles which know not God:

P

Rom. 2. 8. *See i, I, § 320, page 816.*

Q

Phil. 3. 19. *See d, D, § 445, page 1072.*

R

Gen. 3. 8 And they heard the voice of the LORD God walking in the garden in the cool of the day: and Adam and his wife hid themselves from the presence of the LORD God amongst the trees of the garden.

Gen. 4. 16 And Cain went out from the presence of the LORD, and dwelt in the Land of Nod, on the east of Eden.

Job 21. 14 Therefore they say unto God, Depart from us: for we desire not the knowledge of thy ways.

Job 22. 17 Which said unto God, Depart from us: and what can the Almighty do for them?

Matt. 7. 23 And then will I profess unto them, I never knew you: depart from me, ye that work iniquity.

Matt. 25. 41 Then shall he say also unto them on the left hand, Depart from me, ye cursed, into everlasting fire, prepared for the devil and his angels:

Luke 13. 27 But he shall say, I tell you, I know you not whence ye are; depart from me, all *ye* workers of iniquity.

S

Matt. 25. 31. *See a, A, § 177, page 502.*

T

Ps. 68. 35 O God, *thou art* terrible out of thy holy places: the God of Israel *is* he that giveth strength and power unto *his* people. Blessed *be* God.

3

Or, *vouchsafe.*

U

II Thes. 1. 5. *See text of topic.*

X

I Thes. 1. 3. *See under F.*

Y

I Pet. 1. 7 That the trial of your faith, being much more precious than of gold that perisheth, though it be tried with fire, might be found unto praise and honour and glory at the appearing of Jesus Christ:

I Pet. 4. 14. *See under H.*

2 : 1-12.

1 Now we beseech you, brethren,
[a]by the coming of our Lord Jesus
Christ, [b]and *by* our gathering together unto him,
2 [c]That ye be not soon shaken in
mind, or be troubled, neither by spirit,
nor by word, nor by letter as from us,
as that the day of Christ is at hand.
3 [d]Let no man deceive you by any
mean : for *that day shall not come,*
[e]except there come a falling away
first, and [f]that man of sin be revealed, [g]the son of perdition;
4 Who opposeth and [h]exalteth himself [i]above all that is called God, or
that is worshipped; so that he as
God sitteth in the temple of God,
shewing himself that he is God.
5 Remember ye not, that, when I
was yet with you, I told you these
things?
6 And now ye know what [1]with-
holdeth that he might be revealed in
his time.
7 For [k]the mystery of iniquity doth
already work: only he who now letteth *will let,* until he be taken out of
the way.
8 And then shall that Wicked be
revealed, [l]whom the Lord shall consume [m]with the spirit of his mouth,
and shall destroy [n]with the brightness
of his coming:
9 *Even him,* whose coming is [o]after
the working of Satan with all power
and [p]signs and lying wonders,
10 And with all deceivableness of
unrighteousness in [q]them that perish;
because they received not the love of
the truth, that they might be saved.
11 And [r]for this cause God shall
send them strong delusion, that they
should believe a lie:
12 That they all might be damned
who believed not the truth, [s]but had
pleasure in unrighteousness.

§ 467. CONCERNING THE COMING

A

I Thes. 4. 16. *See g, G, § 463, page 1104.*

B

Matt. 24. 31 And he shall send his angels with a great sound of a trumpet, and they shall gather together his elect from the four winds, from one end of heaven to the other.

Mark 13. 27 And then shall he sends his angels, and shall gather together his elect from the four winds, from the uttermost part of the earth to the uttermost part of heaven.

I Thes. 4. 17 Then we which are alive *and* remain shall be caught up together with them in the clouds, to meet the Lord in the air: and so shall we ever be with the Lord.

C

Matt. 24. 6 And ye shall hear of wars and rumours of wars: see that ye be not troubled: for all *these things* must come to pass, but the end is not yet.

D

Matt. 24. 4. *See e, E, § 172, page 480.*

E

I Tim. 4. 1 Now the Spirit speaketh expressly, that in the latter times some shall depart from the faith, giving heed to seducing spirits, and doctrines of devils;

II Tim. 3. 1 This know also, that in the last days perilous times shall come.

2 For men shall be lovers of their own selves, covetous, boasters, proud, blasphemers, disobedient to parents, unthankful, unholy,

II Tim. 4. 3 For the time will come when they will not endure sound doctrine; but after their own lusts shall they heap to themselves teachers, having itching ears:

4 And they shall turn away *their* ears from the truth, and shall be turned unto fables.

F

Dan. 7. 25 And he shall speak *great* words against the Most High, and shall wear out the saints of the Most High, and think to change times and laws; and they shall be given into his hand until a time and times and the dividing of time.

I Jno. 2. 18 Little children, it is the last time: and as ye have heard that antichrist shall come, even now are there many antichrists; whereby we know that it is the last time.

Rev. 13. 11. *Read to end of chapter.*

OF OUR LORD JESUS CHRIST.

G

John 17. 12. *See a, A, § 191, page 545.*

H

Isa. 14. 13 For thou hast said in thine heart, I will ascend into heaven, I will exalt my throne above the stars of God : I will sit also upon the mount of the congregation, in the sides of the north :

Eze 28. 2 Son of man, say unto the prince of Tyrus, Thus saith the Lord God; Because thine heart *is* lifted up, and thou hast said I *am* a god, I sit *in* the seat of God, in the midst of the seas; yet thou *art* a man, and not God, though thou set thine heart as the heart of God :

Eze. 28. 6 Therefore thus saith the Lord God; Because thou hast set thine heart as the heart of God :

Eze. 28. 9 Wilt thou yet say before him that slayeth thee, I *am* God? but thou *shalt be* a man, and no God, in the hand of him that slayeth thee.

Dan. 7. 25. *Se under F.*

Dan 11. 36 And the king shall do according to his will ; and he shall exalt himself, and magnify himself above every god, and shall speak marvellous things against the God of gods, and shall prosper till the indignation be accomplished ; for that that is determined shall be done.

Rev. 1 3 And he opened his mouth in blasphemy against God, to blaspheme his name, and his tabernacle, and them that dwell in heaven.

I

I Cor. 8. 5 For though there be that are called gods, whether in heaven or in earth, (as there be gods many, and lords many,)

1

Or, *holdeth.*

K

I Jno. 2. 18. *See under F.*

1 Jno. 4. 3 And every spirit that confesseth not that Jesus Christ is come in the flesh is not of God : and this is that *spirit* of antichrist, whereof ye have heard that it should come ; and even now already is it in the world.

L

Dan. 7. 10 A fiery stream issued and came forth from before him; thousand thousands ministered unto him, and ten thousand times ten thousand stood before him : the judgment was set, and the books were opened,

L—Concluded.

Da. 7. 11 I beheld then, because of the voice of the great words which the horn spake : I beheld *even* till the beast was slain, and his body destroyed, and given to the burning flame.

M

Job 4. 9 By the blast of God they perish, and by the breath of his nostrils are they consumed.

Isa. 11. 4 But with righteousness shall he judge the poor, and reprove with equity for the meek of the earth : and he shall smite the earth with the rod of his mouth, and with the breath of his lips shall he slay the wicked.

Hos. 6. 5 Therefore have I hewed *them* by the prophets ; I have slain them by the words of my mouth : and thy judgments *are as* the light *that* goeth forth.

Rev. 2. 16 Repent ; or else I will come unto thee quickly, and will fight against them with the sword of my mouth.

Rev. 19. 15 And out of his mouth goeth a sharp sword, that with it he should smite the nations : and he shall rule them with a rod of iron : and he treadeth the winepress of the fierceness and wrath of Almighty God.

Rev. 19. 21 And the remnant were slain with the sword of him that sat upon the horse, which *sword* proceeded out of his mouth : and all the fowls were filled with their flesh.

N

II Thes. 1.8, 9. *See n, N, § 466, page 1110.*

O

John 8. 41 Ye do the deeds of your father. Then said they to him, We be not born of fornication ; we have one Father, *even* God.

Eph. 2. 2 Wherein in time past ye walked according to the course of this world, according to the prince of the power of the air, the spirit that now worketh in the children of disobedience :

P

Matt. 24. 24. *See r, R, § 173, page 488.*

Q

II Cor. 2. 15. *See f, F, § 389, page 968.*

R

Rom. 1. 24. *See h, H, § 319, page 812.*

S

Rom. 1. 32. *See p, P, § 319, page 814.*

§ 468. EXHORTATION TO STEADFASTNESS

2:13–17.

13 But [a]we are bound to give thanks alway to God for you, brethren beloved of the Lord, because God [b]hath from the beginning chosen you to salvation [c]through sanctification of the Spirit and belief of the truth:

14 Whereunto he called you by our gospel, to [d]the obtaining of the glory of our Lord Jesus Christ.

15 Therefore, brethren, [e]stand fast, and hold [f]the traditions which ye have been taught, whether by word, or our epistle.

16 [g]Now our Lord Jesus Christ himself, and God, even our Father, [h]which hath loved us, and hath given *us* everlasting consolation and [i]good hope through grace,

17 Comfort your hearts, [k]and stablish you in every good word and work.

A

IIThes. 1. 3 Remembering without ceasing your work of faith, and labour of love, and patience of hope in our Lord Jesus Christ, in the sight of God and our Father;

B

I Thes. 1. 4. *See h, H, § 457, page 1094.*

Eph. 1. 4. *See b, B, § 426, page 1028.*

C

Luke 1. 75 In holiness and righteousness before him, all the days of our life.

IPet. 1. 2 Elect according to the foreknowledge of God the Father, through sanctification of the Spirit, unto obedience and sprinkling of the blood of Jesus Christ: Grace unto you, and peace, be multiplied.

D

John 17. 22 And the glory which thou gavest me I have given them; that they may be one, even as we are one:

IThes. 2. 12 That ye would walk worthy of God, who hath called you unto his kingdom and glory.

IPet. 5. 10 But the God of all grace, who hath called us unto his eternal glory by Christ Jesus, after that ye have suffered a while, make you perfect, stablish, strengthen, settle *you*.

§ 469. PAUL SOLICITS THE PRAYERS

3:1–5.

1 Finally, brethren, [a]pray for us, that the word of the Lord [1]may have *free* course, and be glorified, even as *it is* with you:

2 And [b]that we may be delivered from [2]unreasonable and wicked men: for all *men* have not faith.

3 But [d]the Lord is faithful, who shall stablish you, and [e]keep *you* from evil.

4 And [f]we have confidence in the Lord touching you, that ye both do and will do the things which we command you.

5 And [g]the Lord direct your hearts into the love of God, and into [3]the patient waiting for Christ.

A

Eph. 6. 19 And for me that utterance may be given unto me, that I may open my mouth boldly, to make known the mystery of the gospel,

Col. 4. 3 Withal praying also for us, that God would open unto us a door of utterance, to speak the mystery of Christ, for which I am also in bonds:

IThes. 5. 25 Brethren, pray for us.

1

Gr. *may run.*

B

Rom. 15. 31 That I may be delivered from them that do not believe in Judea; and that my service which *I have* for Jerusalem may be accepted of the saints;

2

Gr. *absurd.*

C

Acts 28. 24 And some believed the things which were spoken, and some believed not.

AND OBEDIENCE. A BENEDICTION.

E

ICor.16. 13 Watch ye, stand fast in the faith, quit you like men, be strong.

Phil. 1. 27 Only let your conversation be as it becometh the gospel of Christ: that whether I come and see you, or else be absent, I may hear of your affairs, that ye stand fast in one spirit, with one mind striving together for the faith of the gospel;

Phil. 4. 1 Therefore, my brethren dearly beloved and longed for, my joy and crown, so stand fast in the Lord, *my* dearly beloved.

F

ICor. 11. 2 Now I praise you, brethren, that ye remember me in all things, and keep the ordinances, as I delievered *them* to you.

IIThes.3. 6 Now we command you, brethren, in the name of our Lord Jesus Christ, that ye withdraw yourselves from every brother that walketh disorderly, and not after the tradition which he received of us.

G

IIThes.1. 1 Paul and Silvanus, and Timotheus, unto the church of the Thessalonians in God our Father and the Lord Jesus Christ:

G—Concluded.

IIThes.1. 2 Grace unto you, and peace, from God our Father and the Lord Jesus Christ.

H

IJohn 4. 10 Herein is love, not that we loved God, but that he loved us, and sent his Son *to be* the propitiation for our sins.

Rev. 1. 5 And from Jesus Christ, *who is* the faithful witness, *and* the firstbegotten of the dead, and the prince of the kings of the earth. Unto him that loved us, and washed us from our sins in his own blood,

I

IPet. 1. 3 Blessed *be* the God and Father of our Lord Jesus Christ, which according to his abundent mercy hath begotten us again unto a lively hope by the resurrection of Jesus Christ from the dead,

K

ICor. 1. 8 Who shall also confirm you unto the end, *that ye may be* blameless in the day of our Lord Jesus Christ.

IThes.3. 13 To the end he may stablish your hearts unblameable in holiness before God, even our Father, at the coming of our Lord Jesus Christ with all his saints.

I Pet. 5. 10. *See under D.*

OF THE THESSALONIANS.

C—Concluded.

Rom.10. 16 But they have not all obeyed the gospel. For Esaias saith, Lord, who hath believed our report?

D

ICor. 9 God *is* faithful, by whom ye were called unto the fellowship of his Son Jesus Christ our Lord

IThes.5. 24 Faithful *is* he that calleth you, who also will do *it*.

E

I Chr. 4. 10 And Jabez called on the God of Israel, saying, O that thou wouldest bless me indeed, and enlarge my coast, and that thine hand might be with me, and that thou wouldest keep *me* from evil, that it may not grieve me! And God granted him that which he requested.

John 17. 15 I pray not that thou shouldest take them out of the world, but that thou shouldest keep them from the evil.

IITim.4. 18 And the Lord shall deliver me from every evil work, and will preserve *me* unto his heavenly kingdom: to whom *be* glory for ever and ever. Amen.

E—Concluded.

IIPet.2. 9 The Lord knoweth how to deliver the godly out of temptations, and to reserve the unjust unto the day of judgment to be punished:

F

IICor.7. 16 I rejoice therefore that I have confidence in you in all *things*.

Gal. 5. 10 I have confidence in you through the Lord, that ye will be none otherwise minded, but he that troubleth you shall bear his judgment, whosoever he be.

G

IChr.29. 18 O Lord God of Abraham, Isaac, and of Israel, our fathers, keep this for ever in the imagination of the thoughts of the heart of thy people, and prepare their heart unto thee:

3

Or, *the patience of Christ.*

§ 470. CONCERNING DISORDERLY WALK

3 : 6–15.

6 Now we command you, brethren, in the name of our Lord Jesus Christ, [a]that ye withdraw yourselves from every brother that walketh [b]disorderly, and not after [c]the tradition which he received of us.

7 For yourselves know [d]how ye ought to follow us : for [e]we behaved not ourselves disorderly among you ;

8 Neither did we eat any man's bread for nought ; but [f]wrought with labour and travail night and day, that we might not be chargeable to any of you :

9 [g]Not because we have not power, but to make [h]ourselves an ensample unto you to follow us.

10 For even when we were with you, this we commanded you, [i]that if any would not work, neither should he eat.

11 For we hear that there are some [k]which walk among you disorderly, working not at all, but [l]are busybodies.

12 [m]Now them that are such we command and exhort by our Lord Jesus Christ, [n]that with quietness they work, and eat their own bread.

13 But ye, brethren, [o1]be not weary in well doing.

14 And if any man obey not our

CHAP. 3.

word [2]by this epistle, note that man, and [p]have no company with him, that he may be ashamed.

15 [q]Yet count *him* not as an enemy, but [r]admonish *him* as a brother.

A

Rom. 16. 17. *See k, K, § 347, page 884.*

B

IThes. 4. 11 And that ye study to be quiet, and to do your own business, and to work with your own hands, as we commanded you;

IThes. 5. 14 Now we exhort you, brethren, warn them that are unruly, comfort the feebleminded, support the weak, be patient toward all *men*.

II Thes. 3. 11-14. *See text of topic.*

C

II Thes. 2. 15. *See f, F, § 468, page 1114.*

D

I Cor. 4. 16 Wherefore I beseech you, be ye followers of me.

ICor. 11. 1 Be ye followers of me, even as I also *am* of Christ.

IThes. 1. 6 And ye became followers of us, and of the Lord, having received the word in much affliction, with joy of the Holy Ghost:

7 So that ye were ensamples to all that believe in Macedonia and Achaia.

E

IThes. 2. 10 Ye *are* witnesses, and God *also*, how holily and justly and unblameably we behaved ourselves among you that believe:

F

Acts 18. 3 And because he was of the same craft, he abode with them, and wrought: for by their occupation they were tentmakers.

Acts 20. 34 Yea, ye yourselves know, that these hands have ministered unto my necessities, and to them that were with me.

§ 471. CONCLUDING SALUTATION

3 : 16–18.

16 Now [a]the Lord of peace himself give you peace always by all means. The Lord *be* with you all.

17 [b]The salutation of Paul with mine own hand, [c]which is the token

CHAP. 3.

in every epistle : so I write.

18 The grace of our Lord Jesus Christ *be* with you all. Amen.

A

Rom. 15. 33. *See b, B, § 346, page 882.*

AND DILIGENT WORK FOR BREAD.

F—Concluded.

II Cor. 11. 9 And when I was present with you, and wanted, I was chargeable to no man: for that which was lacking to me the brethren which came from Macedonia supplied: and in all *things* I have kept myself from being burdensome unto you, and *so* will I keep *myself*.

I Thes. 2. 9 For ye remember, brethren, our labour and travail: for labouring night and day, because we would not be chargeable unto any of you, we preached unto you the gospel of God.

G

I Cor. 9. 6 Or I only and Barnabas, have not we power to forbear working?

I Thes. 2. 6 Nor of men sought we glory, neither of you, nor *yet* of others, when we might have been burdensome, as the apostles of Christ.

H

II Thes. 3. 7. *See text of topic.*

I

Gen. 3. 19 In the sweat of thy face shalt thou eat bread, till thou return unto the ground; for out of it wast thou taken: for dust thou *art*, and unto dust shalt thou return.

Prov. 13. 4 The soul of the sluggard desireth, and *hath* nothing: but the soul of the diligent shall be made fat.

Prov. 20. 4 The sluggard will not plough by reason of the cold; *therefore* shall he beg in harvest, and *have* nothing.

Prov. 24. 30 I went by the field of the slothful, and by the vineyard of the man void of understanding;

31 And, lo, it was all grown over with thorns, *and* nettles had covered the face thereof, and the stone wall thereof was broken down.

32 Then I saw, *and* considered *it* well: I looked upon *it*, *and* received instruction.

33 *Yet* a little sleep, a little slumber, a little folding of the hands to sleep;

I—Concluded.

Prov. 24. 34 So shall thy poverty come *as* one that travelleth; and thy want as an armed man.

I Thes. 4. 11. *See f, F, § 462, page 1104.*

K

II Thes. 3. 6. *See text of topic.*

L

I Tim. 5. 13 And withal they learn to be idle, wandering about from house to house; and not only idle, but tattlers also and busybodies, speaking things which they ought not.

I Pet. 4. 15 But let none of you suffer as a murderer, or *as* a thief, or *as* an evildoer, or as a busybody in other men's matters.

M

I Thes. 4. 11. *See f, F, § 462, page 1104.*

N

Eph. 4. 28 Let him that stole steal no more: but rather let him labour, working with *his* hands the thing which is good, that he may have to give to him that needeth.

O

Gal. 6. 9 And let us not be weary in well doing: for in due season we shall reap, if we faint not.

1

Or, *faint not.*

2

Or, *signify that man by an epistle.*

P

II Thes. 3. 6. *See text of topic.*

Q

Lev. 19. 17 Thou shalt not hate thy brother in thine heart: thou shalt in any wise rebuke thy neighbour, and not suffer sin upon him.

18 Thou shalt not avenge, nor bear any grudge against the children of thy people, but thou shalt love thy neighbour as thyself: I *am* the LORD.

R

Tit. 3. 10 A man that is a heretic after the first and second admonition reject;

AND BENEDICTION.

B

I Cor. 16. 21 The salutation of *me* Paul with mine own hand.

C

Josh. 2. 12 Now therefore, I pray you, swear unto me by the LORD, since I have shewed you kindness, that ye will also

C—Concluded.

shew kindness unto my father's house, and give me a true token:

I Sa. 17. 18 And carry these ten cheeses unto the captain of *their* thousand, and look how thy brethren fare, and take their pledge.

PAUL'S FIRST EPISTLE

§ 472. SALUTATION.

1 : 1, 2.

1 Paul, an apostle of Jesus Christ
[a]by the commandment [b]of God our
Saviour, and Lord Jesus Christ,
[c]*which is* our hope;
2 Unto [d]Timothy, [e]*my* own son in
the faith: [f]Grace, mercy, *and* peace,
from God our Father, and Jesus
Christ our Lord.

A

Acts 9. 15. *See l, L, § 251, page 684.*

Gal. 1. 1. *See a, A, § 409, page 1004.*

B

I Tim. 2. 3 For this *is* good and acceptable in the sight of God our Saviour;

I Tim. 4. 10 For therefore we both labour and suffer reproach, because we trust in the living God, who is the Saviour of all men, specially of those that believe.

Tit. 1. 3 But hath in due times manifested his word through preaching, which is

§ 473. TIMOTHY IS REMINDED OF

1 : 3–11.

3 As I besought thee to abide still
at Ephesus, [a]when I went into Macedonia, that thou mightest charge some
[b]that they teach no other doctrine,
4 [c]Neither give heed to fables and
endless genealogies, [d]which minister
questions, rather than godly edifying
which is in faith: *so do.*
5 Now [e]the end of the commandment is charity [f]out of a pure heart,
and *of* a good conscience, and *of*
faith unfeigned:
6 From which some [1]having swerved
have turned aside unto [g]vain jangling;
7 Desiring to be teachers of the law;
[h]understanding neither what they say,
nor whereof they affirm.
8 But we know that [i]the law *is* good,
if a man use it lawfully;
9 [k]Knowing this, that the law is not
made for a righteous man, but for the
lawless and disobedient, for the un-

CHAP. 1.

godly and for sinners, for unholy and
profane, for murderers of fathers and
murderers of mothers, for manslayers,
10 For whoremongers, for them that
defile themselves with mankind, for
menstealers, for liars, for perjured persons, and if there be any other thing
that is contrary [l]to sound doctrine;
11 According to the glorious gospel
of [m]the blessed God, [n]which was committed to my trust.

A

Acts 20. 1, 3. *See a, A, § 289, page 758.*

B

II Cor. 11. 4. *See g, G, § 403, page 994.*

C

I Tim. 4. 7 But refuse profane and old wives' fables, and exercise thyself *rather* unto godliness.

I Tim. 6. 4 He is proud, knowing nothing, but doting about questions and strifes of words, whereof cometh envy, strife, railings, evil surmisings,

I Tim. 6. 20 O Timothy, keep that which is committed to thy trust, avoiding profane *and* vain babblings, and oppositions of science falsely so called;

Written Summer of A. D. 67, in Macedonia.

B—CONCLUDED.

committed unto me according to the commandment of God our Saviour;

Tit. 2. 10 Not purloining, but shewing all good fidelity; that they may adorn the doctrine of God our Saviour in all things.

Tit. 3. 4 But after that the kindness and love of God our Saviour toward man appeared,

Jude 25 To the only wise God our Saviour, *be* glory and majesty, dominion and power, both now and ever. Amen.

C

Col. 1. 27 To whom God would make known what *is* the riches of the glory of this mystery among the Gentiles; which is Christ in you, the hope of glory:

D

Acts 16. 1. *See b, B, § 271, page 732.*

E

Tit. 1. 4 To Titus, *mine* own son after the common faith: Grace, mercy, *and* peace, from God the Father and the Lord Jesus Christ our Saviour.

F

II Cor. 1. 2. *See c, C, § 385, page 962.*

HIS COMMISSION TO THE EPHESIANS.

C—CONCLUDED.

IITim. 2. 14 Of these things put *them* in remembrance, charging *them* before the Lord that they strive not about words to no profit, *but* to the subverting of the hearers.

IITim. 2. 16 But shun profane *and* vain babblings: for they will increase unto more ungodliness.

IITim. 2. 23 But foolish and unlearned questions avoid, knowing that they do gender strifes.

Tit. 1. 14 Not giving heed to Jewish fables, and commandments of men, that turn from the truth.

Tit. 3. 9 But avoid foolish questions, and genealogies, and contentions, and strivings about the law; for they are unprofitable and vain.

D

I Tim. 6. 4. *See under C.*

E

Rom. 13. 8-10. *See h, H, § 343, page 874.*

F

IITim. 2. 22 Flee also youthful lusts: but follow righteousness, faith, charity, peace, with them that call on the Lord out of a pure heart.

1

Or, *not aiming at.*

G

I Tim. 6. 4. *See under C.*

H

Rom. 1. 22 Professing themselves to be wise, they became fools.

I Tim. 6. 4. *See under C.*

I

Rom. 7. 12 Wherefore the law *is* holy, and the commandment holy, and just, and good.

K

Gal. 3. 19. *See g, G, § 416, page 1014.*

Gal. 5. 23 Meekness, temperance: against such there is no law.

L

I Tim. 6. 3 If any man teach otherwise, and consent not to wholesome words, *even* the words of our Lord Jesus Christ, and to the doctrine which is according to godliness;

IITim. 4. 3 For the time will come when they will not endure sound doctrine; but after their own lusts shall they heap to themselves teachers, having itching ears;

Tit. 1. 9 Holding fast the faithful word as he hath been taught, that he may be able by sound doctrine both to exhort and to convince the gainsayers.

Tit. 2. 1 But speak thou the things which become sound doctrine:

M

I Tim. 6. 15 Which in his times he shall shew, *who is* the blessed and only Potentate, the King of kings, and the Lord of lords:

N

I Cor. 9. 17. *See a, A, § 365, page 924.*

§ 474. PAUL GIVES THANKS FOR HIS CALLING AND

I : 12–20.

12 And I thank Christ Jesus our Lord, [a]who hath enabled me, [b]for that he counted me faithful, [c]putting me into the ministry;

13 [d]Who was before a blasphemer, and a persecutor, and injurious: but I obtained mercy, because [e]I did *it* ignorantly in unbelief.

14 [f]And the grace of our Lord was exceeding abundant [g]with faith [h]and love which is in Christ Jesus.

15 [i]This *is* a faithful saying, and worthy of all acceptation, that[k]Christ Jesus came into the world to save sinners; of whom I am chief.

16 Howbeit for this cause [l]I obtained mercy, that in me first Jesus Christ might shew forth all longsuffering, [m]for a pattern to them which should hereafter believe on him to life everlasting.

17 Now unto [n]the King eternal, [o]immortal, [p]invisible, [q]the only wise God, [r]*be* honour and glory for ever and ever. Amen.

18 This charge [s]I commit unto thee, son Timothy, [t]according to the prophecies which went before on thee, that thou by them mightest [u]war a good warfare;

19 [x]Holding faith, and a good conscience; which some having put away, concerning faith [y]have made shipwreck:

20 Of whom is [z]Hymeneus and [a]Alexander; whom I have [b]delivered unto Satan, that they may learn not to [c]blaspheme.

A

II Cor. 12. 9. *See i, I, § 405, page 998.*

B

I Cor. 7. 25. *See c, C, § 363 page 916.*

C

II Cor. 3. 5, 6. *See i, I, § 390, page 970.*

D

Acts 8. 3. *See d, D, § 247, page 678.*

E

Num. 15. 28 And the priest shall make an atonement for the soul that sinneth ignorantly, when he sinneth by ignorance before the LORD, to make an atonement for him; and it shall be forgiven him.

Luke 23. 34 Then said Jesus, Father, forgive them; for they know not what they do. And they parted his raiment, and cast lots.

John 9. 39 And Jesus said, For judgment I am come into this world, that they which see not might see; and that they which see might be made blind.

John 9. 41 Jesus said unto them, If ye were blind, ye should have no sin: but now ye say, We see; therefore your sin remaineth.

Acts 3. 17 And now, brethren, I wot that through ignorance ye did *it*, as *did* also your rulers.

Acts 26. 9 I verily thought with myself, that I ought to do many things contrary to the name of Jesus of Nazareth.

II Pet. 2. 21 For it had been better for them not to have known the way of righteousness, than, after they have known *it*, to turn from the holy commandment delivered unto them.

F

Rom. 1. 5. *See i, I, § 317, page 808.*

G

II Tim. 1. 13 Hold fast the form of sound words, which thou hast heard of me, in faith and love which is in Christ Jesus.

H

Luke 7. 47 Wherefore I say unto thee, Her sins, which are many, are forgiven; for she loved much: but to whom little is forgiven, *the same* loveth little.

I

I Tim. 3. 1 This *is* a true saying, If a man desire the office of a bishop, he desireth a good work.

I Tim. 4. 9 This *is* a faithful saying and worthy of all acceptation.

II Tim. 2. 11 *It is* a faithful saying: For if we be dead with *him*, we shall also live with *him*:

Tit. 3. 8 *This is* a faithful saying, and these things I will that thou affirm con-

CHARGES TIMOTHY TO FULFIL HIS COMMISSION.

I—CONCLUDED.

stantly, that they which have believed in God might be careful to maintain good works. These things are good and profitable unto men.

K

Luke 19. 10. *See k, K, § 150, page 425.*

L

II Cor. 4. 1 Therefore, seeing we have this ministry, as we have received mercy, we faint not;

M

Rom. 15. 4. *See g, G, § 345, page 878.*

N

Ps. 10. 16 The LORD *is* King for ever and ever: the heathen are perished out of his land.

Ps. 145. 13 Thy kingdom *is* an everlasting kingdom, and thy dominion *endureth* throughout all generations.

Da. 7. 14 And there was given him dominion, and glory, and a kingdom, that all people, nations, and languages, should serve him: his dominion *is* an everlasting dominion, which shall not pass away, and his kingdom *that* which shall not be destroyed.

I Tim. 6. 15 Which in his times he shall shew, *who is* the blessed and only Potentate, the King of kings and Lord of lords;
16 Who only hath immortality, dwelling in the light which no man can approach unto; whom no man hath seen, nor can see: to whom *be* honour and power everlasting. Amen.

O

Rom. 1. 23 And changed the glory of the uncorruptible God into an image made like to corruptible man, and to birds, and fourfooted beasts, and creeping things.

Heb. 1. 8 But unto the Son *he saith*, Thy throne, O God, *is* for ever and ever: a sceptre of righteousness *is* the sceptre of thy kingdom.

Heb. 1. 11 They shall perish, but thou remainest: and they all shall wax old as doth a garment;

Rev. 4. 9 And when those beasts give glory and honour and thanks to him that sat on the throne, who liveth for ever and ever,

P

John 1. 18. *See k, K, § 17, page 59.*

Heb. 11. 27 By faith he forsook Egypt, not fearing the wrath of the king: for he endured, as seeing him who is invisble.

Q

Rom. 16. 27. *See h, H, § 347, page 886.*

R

I Chr. 29. 11 Thine, O LORD, *is* the greatness, and the power, and the glory, and the victory, and the majesty: for all *that is* in the heaven and in the earth *is thine;* thine *is* the kingdom, O LORD, and thou art exalted as head above all.

S

I Tim. 6. 13 I give thee charge in the sight of God, who quickeneth all things, and *before* Christ Jesus, who before Pontius Pilate witnessed a good confession:
14 That thou keep *this* commandment without spot, unrebukeable, until the appearing of our Lord Jesus Christ:

I Tim. 6. 20 O Timothy, keep that which is committed to thy trust, avoiding profane *and* vain babblings, and oppositions of science falsely so called:

II Tim. 2. 2 And the things that thou hast heard of me among many witnesses, the same commit thou to faithful men, who shall be able to teach others also.

T

I Tim. 4. 14 Neglect not the gift that is in thee, which was given thee by prophecy, with the laying on of the hands of the presbytery.

U

I Tim. 6. 12 Fight the good fight of faith, lay hold on eternal life, whereunto thou art also called, and hast professed a good profession before many witnesses.

II Tim. 2. 3 Thou therefore endure hardness, as a good soldier of Jesus Christ.

II Tim. 4. 7 I have fought a good fight, I have finished *my* course, I have kept the faith:

X

I Tim. 3. 9 Holding the mystery of the faith in a pure conscience.

Y

I Tim. 6. 9 But they that will be rich fall into temptation and a snare, and *into* many foolish and hurtful lusts, which drown men in destruction and perdition.

Z

II Tim. 2. 17 And their word will eat as doth a canker: of whom is Hymeneus and Philetus;

A

II Tim. 4. 14 Alexander the coppersmith did me much evil: the Lord reward him according to his works:

B

I Cor. 5. 5. *See h, H, § 359, page 906.*

C

Acts 13. 45. *See a, A, § 263, page 718.*

§ 475. EXHORTATION TO PRAY AND GIVE THANKS

2 : 1–15.

1 I [1]exhort therefore, that, first of
all, supplications, prayers, intercessions, *and* giving of thanks, be made
for all men;

2 [a]For kings, and [b]*for* all that are in
[2]authority; that we may lead a quiet
and peaceable life in all godliness
and honesty.

3 For this *is* [c]good and acceptable
in the sight [d]of God our Saviour;

4 [e]Who will have all men to be saved,
[f]and to come unto the knowledge of
the truth.

5 [g]For *there is* one God, and [h]one
mediator between God and men, the
man Christ Jesus;

6 [i]Who gave himself a ransom for
all, [k3]to be testified [l]in due time.

7 [m]Whereunto I am ordained a
preacher, and an apostle, ([n]I speak
the truth in Christ, *and* lie not;) a
teacher of the Gentiles in faith and
verity.

8 I will therefore that men pray
[o]every where, [p]lifting up holy hands,
without wrath and doubting.

9 In like manner also, that [q]women
adorn themselves in modest apparel,
with shamefacedness and sobriety;
not with [4]braided hair, or gold, or
pearls, or costly array;

10 [r]But (which becometh women
professing godliness) with good
works.

11 Let the woman learn in silence
with all subjection.

12 But [s]I suffer not a woman to
teach, [t]nor to usurp authority over
the man, but to be in silence.

13 For [u]Adam was first formed,
then Eve.

14 And [x]Adam was not deceived,
but the woman being deceived was
in the transgression

1

Or, *desire.*

A

Ezra 6. 10 That they may offer sacrifices of sweet savours unto the God of heaven, and pray for the life of the king, and of his sons.

Ps. 72. 1 Give the king thy judgments O God, and thy righteousness unto the king's son.

Jer. 29. 7 And seek the peace of the city whither I have caused you to be carried away captives, and pray unto the Lord for it: for in the peace thereof shall ye have peace.

B

Rom. 13. 1 Let every soul be subject unto the higher powers. For there is no power but of God: the powers that be are ordained of God.

2

Or, *eminent place.*

C

Rom. 12. 2 be not conformed to this world: but be ye transformed by the renewing of your mind, that ye may prove what *is* that good, and acceptable, and perfect will of God.

I Tim. 5. 4 But if any widow have children or nephews, let them learn first to shew piety at home, and to requite their parents: for that is good and acceptable before God.

D

I Tim. 1. 1. *See b, B, § 472, page 1118.*

E

Isa. 45. 22 Look unto me, and be ye saved, all the ends of the earth: for I *am* God, and *there is* none else.

Isa. 55. 1 Ho, every one that thirsteth, come ye to the waters, and he that hath no money; come ye, buy, and eat; yea come, buy wine and milk without money and without price.

Isa. 55. 7 Let the wicked forsake his way, and the unrighteous man his thoughts: and let him return unto the Lord, and he will have mercy upon him; and to our God, for he will abundantly pardon.

Eze. 18. 23 Have I any pleasure at all that the wicked should die? saith the Lord GOD: *and* not that he should return from his ways and live?

Eze. 33. 11 Say unto them, *As* I live, saith the Lord God, I have no pleasure in the death of the wicked; but that the wicked turn from his way and live:

FOR ALL MEN AND RULERS. CONCERNING WOMEN.

E—Concluded.

turn ye, turn ye from your evil ways; for why will ye die, O house of Israel?

John 3. 16 For God so loved the world, that he gave his only begotten Son, that whosoever believeth in him should not perish, but have everlasting life.

17 For God sent not his Son into the world to condemn the world; but that the world through him might be saved.

Tit. 2. 11 For the grace of God that bringeth salvation hath appeared to all men.

II Pet. 3. 9 The Lord is not slack concerning his promise, as some men count slackness; but is longsuffering to us-ward, not willing that any should perish, but that all should come to repentance.

F

John 17. 3 And this is life eternal, that they might know thee the only true God, and Jesus Christ, whom thou hast sent.

II Tim. 2. 25 In meekness instructing those that oppose themselves; if God peradventure will give them repentance to the acknowledging of the truth:

G

Rom. 3. 29 30. *See t, T, § 324, page 826.*

H

Heb. 8. 6 But now hath he obtained a more excellent ministry, by how much also he is the mediator of a better covenant, which was established upon better promises.

I

Matt. 20. 28. *See y, Y, § 148, page 420.*

K

I Cor. 1. 6 Even as the testimony of Christ was confirmed in you:

II Thes. 1. 10 When he shall come to be glorified in his saints, and to be admired in all them that believe (because our testimony among you was believed) in that day.

II Tim. 1. 8 Be not thou therefore ashamed of the testimony of our Lord, nor of me his prisoner: but be thou partaker of the afflicitions of the gospel according to the power of God;

3

Or, *a testimony.*

L

Rom. 5. 6 For when we were yet without strength, in due time Christ died for the ungodly.

Gal. 4. 4 But when the fulness of the time was come, God sent forth his Son, made of a woman, made under the law,

Eph. 1. 10 That in the dispensation of the fulness of times he might gather to-

L—Concluded.

gether in one all things in Christ, both which are in heaven, and which are on earth: *even* in him:

Tit. 1. 3 But hath in due times manifested his word through preaching, which is committed unto me according to the commandment of God our Saviour.

M

Acts 22. 21. *See i, I, § 297, page 774.*

N

Rom. 9. 1. *See a, A, § 335, page 852.*

O

Mal. 4. 11 For, from the rising of the sun even unto the going down of the same my name, *shall be* great among the Gentiles; and in every place incense *shall be* offered unto my name, and a pure offering: for my name *shall be* great among the heathen, saith the Lord of hosts.

John 4. 21 Jesus saith unto her, Women, believe me, the hour cometh, when ye shall neither in this mountain, nor yet at Jerusalem, worship the Father.

P

Ps. 134. 2 Lift up you hands *in* the sanctuary, and bless the Lord,

Isa. 1. 15 And when ye spread forth your hands, I will hide my eyes from you: yea, when ye make many prayers, I will not hear: your hands are full of blood.

Q

I Pet. 3. 3 Whose adorning, let it not be that outward *adorning* of plaiting the hair, and of wearing of gold, or of putting on of apparel:

4

Or, *plaited.*

R

I Pet. 3. 4 But *let it be* the hidden man of heart, in that which is not corruptible, *even the ornament* of a meek and quiet spirit, which is in the sight of God of great price.

S

I Cor. 14. 34 Let your women keep silence in the churches: for it is not permitted unto them to speak; but *they are commanded* to be under obedience, as also saith the law.

T

Eph. 5. 24 Therefore as the church is subject unto Christ, so *let* the wives *be* to their own husbands in every thing.

U

Gen. 1. 27 So God created man in his *own* image, in the image of God created

For U concl'd, and X, see next page (1124).

§ 475. EXHORTATION TO PRAY AND GIVE THANKS FOR ALL U—CONCLUDED.

CHAP. 2.

15 Notwithstanding she shall be saved in childbearing, if they continue in faith and charity and holiness with sobriety.

he him; male and female created he them.

Gen. 2. 18 And the LORD God said, *It is* not good that the man should be alone; I will make him a helpmeet for him.

I Cor. 11. 8, 9. *See m, M, § 368, page 932.*

§ 476. CONCERNING BISHOPS, 3 : 1–13.

CHAP. 3.

1 This [a]*is* a true saying, If a man desire the office of a [b]bishop, he desireth a good [c]work.

2 [d]A bishop then must be blameless, [e]the husband of one wife, vigilant, sober, [1]of good behaviour, given to hospitality, [f]apt to teach;

3 [g2]Not given to wine, [h]no striker, [i]not greedy of filthy lucre; but patient, not a brawler, not covetous;

4 One that ruleth well his own house, [k]having his children in subjection with all gravity;

5 (For if a man know not how to rule his own house, how shall he take care of the church of God?)

6 Not [3]a novice, lest being lifted up with pride [l]he fall into the condemnation of the devil.

7 Moreover he must have a good report [m]of them which are without; lest he fall into reproach [n]and the snare of the devil.

8 Likewise *must* [o]the deacons *be* grave, not doubletongued, [p]not given to much wine, not greedy of filthy lucre;

9 [q]Holding the mystery of the faith in a pure conscience.

10 And let these also first be proved; then let them use the office of a deacon, being *found* blameless.

11 [r]Even so *must their* wives *be* grave, not slanderers, sober, faithful in all things.

12 Let the deacons be the husbands of one wife, ruling their children and their own houses well.

13 For [s]they that have [4]used the office of a deacon well purchase to themselves a good degree, and great boldness in the faith which is in Christ Jesus.

A

I Tim. 1. 15. *See i, I, § 474, page 1120.*

B

Phil. 1. 1 Paul and Timotheus, the servants of Jesus Christ, to all the saints in Christ Jesus which are at Philippi, with the bishops and deacons:

Tit. 1. 7 For a bishop must be blameless, as the steward of God; not selfwilled, not soon angry, not given to wine, no striker, not given to filthy lucre;

I Pet. 2. 25 For ye were as sheep going astray; but are now returned unto the Shepherd and Bishop of your souls.

C

Eph. 4. 12 For the perfecting of the saints, for the work of the ministry, for the edifying of the body of Christ:

13 Till we all come in the unity of the faith, and of the knowledge of the Son of God, unto a perfect man, unto the measure of the stature of the fullness of Christ:

D

Tit. 1. 6 If any be blameless, the husband of one wife, having faithful children, not accused of riot or unruly.

Tit. 1. 7. *See under B.*

MEN AND RULERS. CONCERNING WOMEN (Concluded).

X

Gen. 3. 6 And when the woman saw that the tree *was* good for food, and that it *was* pleasant to the eyes, and a tree to be desired to make *one* wise, she took of the fruit thereof, and did eat, and gave also unto her husband with her;

X—Concluded.

and he did eat.

II Cor. 11. 3 But I fear, lest by any means, as the serpent beguiled Eve through his subtility, so your minds should be corrupted from the simplicity that is in Christ.

DEACONS AND WOMEN.

E

I Tim. 5. 9 Let not a widow be taken into the number under threescore years old, having been the wife of one man.

1

Or, *modest.*

F

II Tim. 2. 24 And the servant of the Lord must not strive; but be gentle unto all *men*, apt to teach, patient,

G

I Tim. 3. 8. *See text of topic.*
Tit. 1. 7. *See under B,*

2

Or, *not ready to quarrel, and offer wrong, as one in wine.*

H

II Tim. 2. 24. *See under F.*

I

I Pet. 5. 2 Feed the flock of God which is among you, taking the oversight *thereof*, not by constraint, but willingly; not for filthy lucre, but of a ready mind;

K

Tit. 1. 6. *See under D.*

3

Or, *one newly come to the faith.*

L

Isa. 14. 12 How art thou fallen from heaven, O Lucifer, son of the morning! *how* art thou cut down to the ground, which didst weaken the nations!

M

Acts 22. 12 And one Ananias, a devout man according to the law, having a good report of all the Jews which dwell *there*,

I Cor. 5. 12 For what have I to do to judge them also that are without? do not ye judge them that are within?

Col. 4. 5 Walk in wisdom toward them that are without, redeeming the time.

I Thes. 4. 12 That ye may walk honestly toward them that are without, and *that* ye may have lack of nothing,

N

I Tim. 6. 9 But they that will be rich fall into temptation and a snare, and *into* many foolish and hurtful lusts, which drown men in destruction and perdition.

II Tim. 2. 26 And *that* they may recover themselves out of the snare of the devil, who are taken captive by him at his will.

O

Acts 6. 3 Wherefore, brethren, look ye out among you seven men of honest report, full of the Holy Ghost and wisdom, whom we may appoint over this business.

Acts 10. 2 *A* devout *man*, and one that feared God with all his house, which gave much alms to the people, and prayed ot God alway.

P

Lev. 10. 9 Do not drink wine nor strong drink, thou, nor thy sons with thee, when ye go into the tabernacle of the congregation, lest ye die: *it shall be* a statute for ever throughout your generations:

Eze. 44. 21 Neither shall any priest drink wine, when they enter into the inner court.

I Tim. 3. 3. *See text of topic.*

Q

I Tim. 1. 5 Now the end of the commandment is charity out of a pure heart, and *of* a good conscience, and *of* faith unfeigned:

I Tim. 1. 19 Holding faith, and a good conscience; which some having put away, concerning faith have made shipwreck:

R

Tit. 2. 3 The aged women likewise, that *they be* in behaviour as becometh holiness, not false accusers, not given to much wine, teachers of good things;

S

Matt. 25. 21. *See g, G, § 176, page 498.*

4

Or, *ministered,*

§ 477. PAUL SETS FORTH HIS PURPOSE

3: 14–16.

14 These things write I unto thee, hoping to come unto thee shortly:

15 But if I tarry long, that thou mayest know how thou oughtest to behave thyself [a]in the house of God, which is the church of the living God, the piller and [1]ground of the truth.

16 And without controversy great is the mystery of godliness: [b]God was [2]manifest in the flesh, [c]justified in the Spirit, [d]seen of angels, [e]preached unto the Gentiles, [f]believed on in the world, [g]received up into the glory.

A

Eph. 2. 21 In whom all the building filthy framed together groweth unto a holy temple in the Lord:

22 In whom ye also are builded together for a habitation of God through the Spirit.

IITim. 2. 20 But in a great house there are not only vessels of gold and of silver, but also of wood and of earth; and some to honour, and some to dishonour.

1

Or, *stay*.

B

Isa. 9. 6 For unto us a child is born, unto us a son is given: and the government shall be upon his shoulder: and his name shall be called Wonderful, Counsellor, The mighty God, The everlasting Father, The Prince of Peace.

John 1. 14 And the Word was made flesh, and dwelt among us, (and we beheld his glory, the glory as of the only begotten of the Father,) full of grace and truth.

Jno. 1. 2 (For the life was manifested, and we have seen *it*, and bear witness, and shew unto you that eternal life, which was with the Father, and was manifested unto us;)

2

Gr. *manifested.*

C

Matt. 3. 16 And Jesus, when he was baptized, went up straightway out of the water: and, lo, the heavens were opened unto him, and he saw the Spirit of God descending like a dove, and lighting upon him:

John 1. 32 And John bare record, saying, I saw the Spirit descending from heaven like a dove, and it abode upon him.

§ 478. CONCERNING FALSE TEACHING IN THE

4: 1–16.

1 Now the Spirit [a]speaketh expressly, that [b]in the latter times some shall depart from the faith, giving heed [c]to seducing spirits, [d]and doctrines of devils;

2 [e]Speaking lies in hypocrisy; having their conscience seared with a hot iron:

A

John 16. 13 Howbeit when he, the Spirit of truth, is come, he will guide you into all truth: for he shall not speak of himself; but whatsoever he shall hear, *that* shall he speak: and he will shew you things to come.

B

IIThes. 2. 3 Let no man deceive you by any means: for *that day shall not come*, except there come a falling away first,

B—Concluded.

and that man of sin be revealed, the son of perdition;

IITim. 3. 1 This know also, that in the last days perilous times shall come.

IIPet. 3. 3 Knowing this first, that there shall come in the last days scoffers, walking after their own lusts,

IJno. 2. 18 Little children, it is the last time: and as ye have heard that antichrist shall come, even now are there many antichrists; whereby we know that it is the last time.

Jude 4 For there are certain men crept in unawares, who were before of old ordained to this condemnation, ungodly men, turning the grace of our God into lasciviousness, and denying the only Lord God, and our Lord Jesus Christ.

Jude 18 How that they told you there should be mockers in the last time, who should walk after their own ungodly lusts,

IN WRITING THIS EPISTLE.

C—CONCLUDED.

33 And I knew him not: but he that sent me to baptize with water, the same said unto me, Upon whom thou shalt see the Spirit descending, and remaining on him, the same is he which baptizeth with the Holy Ghost.

John 15. 26 But when the Comforter is come, whom I will send unto you from the Father, *even* the Spirit of truth, which proceedeth from the Father, he shall test fy of me

Rom. 1. 4 And declared *to be* the Son of God with power, according to the Spirit of holiness, by the resurrection from the dead:

I Pet. 3. 18 For Christ also hath once, suffered for sins, the just for the unjust, that he might bring us to God, being put to death in the flesh, but quickened by the Spirit:

I John 5. 6 This is he that came by water and blood, *even* Jesus Christ; not by water only, but by water and blood. And it is the Spirit that beareth witness, because the Spirit is truth.

D

Luke 24. 4. *See h, H, § 213, page 599.*

Eph. 3. 10 To the intent that now unto the principalities and powers in heavenly *places* might be known by the church the manifold wisdom of God.

D—CONCLUDED.

I Pet. 1. 12 Unto whom it was revealed, that not unto themselves, but unto us they did minister the things which are now reported unto you by them that have preached the gospel unto you with the Holy Ghost sent down from heaven; which things the angels desire to look into.

E

Acts 9. 15. *See l, L, § 251, page 684.*

Col. 1. 27, 28. *See l, L, § 450, page 1082.*

I Tim. 2. 7 Whereunto I am ordained a preacher, and an apostle, (I speak the truth in Christ, *and* lie not;) a teacher of the Gentiles in faith and verity.

F

Col. 1. 6 Which is come unto you, as *it is* in all the world; and bringeth forth fruit, as *it doth* also in you, since the day ye heard *of it*, and knew the grace of God in truth:

Col. 1. 23 If ye continue in the faith grounded and settled and *be* not moved away from the hope of the gospel, which ye have heard, *and* which was preached to every creature which is under heaven; whereof I Paul am made a minister;

G

Luke 24. 51. *See f, F, § 224, page 625.*

LATTER TIMES. SUNDRY EXHORTATIONS.

C

II Tim. 3. 13 But evil men and seducers shall wax worse and worse, deceiving, and being deceived.

II Pet. 2. 1 But there were false prophets also among the people, even as there shall be false teachers among you, who privily shall bring in damnable heresies, even denying the Lord that bought them, and bring upon themselves swift destruction.

Rev. 16. 14 For they are the spirits of devils, working miracles, *which* go forth unto the kings of the earth and of the whole world, to gather them to the battle of that great day of God Almighty.

D

Da. 11. 35 And *some* of them of understanding shall fall, to try them, and to purge, and to make *them* white, *even* to the time of the end: because *it is* yet for a time appointed.

Da. 11. 37 Neither shall he regard the God of his fathers, nor the desire of wo-

D—CONCLUDED.

men, nor regard any god: for he shall magnify himself above all.

Da. 11. 38 But in his estate shall he honour the God of forces: and a god whom his fathers knew not shall he honour with gold, and silver, and with precious stones, and pleasant things.

Rev. 9. 20 And the rest of the men which were not killed by these plagues yet repented not of the works of their hands, that they should not worship devils, and idols of gold, and silver, and brass, and stone, and of wood: which neither can see, nor hear, nor walk:

E

Matt. 7. 15. *See u, U, § 43, page 146.*

F

Eph. 4. 19. *See f, F, § 433, page 1044.*

G

I Cor. 7. 28 But and if thou marry, thou hast not sinned; and if a virgin

§ 478. CONCERNING FALSE TEACHING IN THE

CHAP. 4.

3 [g]Forbidding to marry, [h]*and commanding* to abstain from meats, which God hath created [i]to be received [k]with thanksgiving of them which believe and know the truth.

4 For [l]every creature of God *is* good, and nothing to be refused, if it be received with thanksgiving:

5 For it is sanctified by the word of God and prayer.

6 If thou put the brethren in remembrance of these things, thou shalt be a good minister of Jesus Christ, [m]nourished up in the words of faith and of good doctrine, whereunto thou hast attained.

7 But [n]refuse profane and old wives' fables, and [o]exercise thyself *rather* unto godliness.

8 For bodily exercise profiteth [1]little: but [p]godliness is profitable unto all things, [q]having promise of the life that now is, and of that which is to come.

9 [r]This *is* a faithful saying and worthy of all acceptation.

10 For therefore [s]we both labour and suffer reproach, because we [t]trust in the living God, [u]who is the Saviour of all men, especially of those that believe.

11 [x]These things command and teach.

12 [y]Let no man despise thy youth; but [z]be thou an example of the believers, in word, in conversation, in charity, in spirit, in faith, in purity.

13 Till I come, give attendance to reading, to exhortation, to doctrine.

14 [a]Neglect not the gift that is in thee, which was given thee [b]by prophecy, [c]with the laying on of the hands of the presbytery.

G CONCLUDED, see preceding page (1127).

marry, she hath not sinned. Nevertheless such shall have trouble in the flesh: but I spare you.

I Cor. 7. 36 But if any man think that he behaveth himself uncomely toward his virgin, if she pass the flower of *her* age, and need so require, let him do what he will, he sinneth not: let them marry

I Cor. 7. 38 So then he that giveth *her* in marriage doeth well; but he that giveth *her* not in marriage doeth better.

Heb. 13. 4 Marriage *is* honourable in all, and the bed undefiled: but whoremongers and adulterers God will judge.

H

Rom. 14. 3 Let not him that eateth despise him that eateth not; and let not him which eateth not judge him that eateth: for God hath received him.

Rom. 14. 17 For the kingdom of God is not meat and drink; but righteousness, and peace, and joy in the Holy Ghost.

I Cor. 8. 8 But meat commendeth us not to God: for neither, if we eat, are we the better; neither, if we eat not, are we the worse.

I

Gen. 1. 29 And God said, Behold, I have given you every herb bearing seed, which *is* upon the face of all the earth, and every tree, in the which *is* the fruit of a tree yielding seed; to you it shall be for meat.

Gen. 9. 3 Every moving thing that liveth shall be meat for you; even as the green herb have I given you all things.

K

Rom. 14. 6. *See f, F, § 344, page 876.*

L

Acts 10. 15. *See l, L, § 254, page 692.*

M

Jer. 15. 16 Thy words were found, and I did eat them; and thy word was unto me the joy and rejoicing of mine heart: for I am called by thy name, O LORD God of hosts.

II Tim. 3. 14 But continue thou in the things which thou hast learned and hast been assured of, knowing of whom thou hast learned *them*;

15 And that from a child thou hast known the holy scriptures, which are able to make thee wise unto salvation through faith which is in Christ Jesus.

I Pet. 2. 2 As newborn babes, desire the sincere milk of the word, that ye may grow thereby:

LATTER TIMES. SUNDRY EXHORTATIONS (CONTINUED).

N

I Tim. 1. 4. *See c, C, § 473, page 1118.*

IITim.4. 4 And they shall turn away *their* ears from the truth, and shall be turned unto fables.

O

Heb. 5. 14 But strong meat belongeth to them that are of full age, *even* those who by reason of use have their senses exercised to discern both good and evil.

1

Or, *for a little time.*

P

ITim. 6. 6 But godliness with contentment is great gain.

Q

Ps 37. 4 Delight thyself also in the LORD; and he shall give thee the desires of thine heart.

Ps. 84. 11 For the LORD God *is* a sun and shield: the LORD will give grace and glory: no good *thing* will he withhold from them that walk uprightly.

Ps. 112. 2 His seed shall be mighty upon earth: the generation of the upright shall be blessed.

Ps. 145. 19 He will fulfil the desire of them that fear him: he also will hear their cry, and will save them.

Matt. 6. 33 But seek ye first the kingdom of God, and his righteousness; and all these things shall be added unto you.

Matt.19. 29 And every one that hath forsaken houses, or brethren, or sisters, or father, or mother, or wife, or children, or lands, for my name's sake, shall receive a hundredfold, and shall inherit everlasting life.

Rom. 8. 28 And we know that all things work together for good to them that love God, to them who are the called according to *his* purpose.

R

I Tim. 1. 15. *See i, I, § 474, page 1120.*

S

I Cor. 4. 11 Even unto this present hour we both hunger, and thirst, and are naked, and are buffeted, and have no certain dwelling place;

12 And labour, working with our own hands: being reviled, we bless; being persecuted, we suffer it:

T

ITim. 6. 17 Charge them that are rich in this world, that they be not highminded, nor trust in uncertain riches, but in the living God, who giveth us richly all things to enjoy;

U

Ps. 36. 6 Thy righteousness *is* like the great mountains; thy judgments *are* a great deep: O LORD, thou preservest man and beast.

John 1. 29 The next day John seeth Jesus coming unto him, and saith, Behold the Lamb of God, which taketh away the sin of the world.

John 4. 42 And said unto the woman, Now we believe, not because of thy saying: for we have heard *him* ourselves, and know that this is indeed the Christ, the Saviour of the world.

Acts 17. 25 Neither is worshipped with men's hands, as though he needed any thing, seeing he giveth to all life, and breath, and all things;

ITim. 2. 4 Who will have all men to be saved, and to come unto the knowledge of the truth.

Tit. 2. 11 For the grace of God that bringeth salvation hath appeared to all men,

X

ITim. 6. 2 And they that have believing masters, let them not despise *them*, because they are brethren; but rather do *them* service, because they are faithful and beloved, partakers of the benefit. These things teach and exhort.

Y

ICor.16. 11 Let no man therefore despise him: but conduct him forth in peace, that he may come unto me: for I look for him with the brethren.

Tit. 2. 15 These things speak, and exhort, and rebuke with all authority. Let no man despise thee.

Z

Tit. 2. 7 In all things shewing thyself a pattern of good works: in doctrine *shewing* uncorruptness, gravity, sincerity.

I Pet. 5. 3 Neither as being lords over *God's* heritage, but being ensamples to the flock.

A

IITim.1. 6 Wherefore I put thee in remembrance, that thou stir up the gift of God, which is in thee by the putting on of my hands.

B

ITim. 1. 18 This charge I commit unto thee, son Timothy, according to the prophecies which went before on thee, that thou by them mightest war a good warfare;

C

Acts 6. 6. *See l, L, § 244, page 664.*

§ 478. CONCERNING FALSE TEACHING IN THE LATTER

CHAP. 4.

15 [d]Meditate upon these things;
give thyself wholly to them; that thy
profiting may appear [1]to all.
16 [e]Take heed unto thyself, and unto the doctrine; continue in them:
for in doing this [f]thou shalt both save
thyself, and [g]them that hear thee.

D

Josh. 1. 8 This book of the law shall not depart out of thy mouth; but thou shalt meditate therein day and night, that thou mayest observe to do according to all that is written therein: for then thou shalt make thy way prosperous, and then thou shalt have good success.

1

Or, *in all things.*

E

Acts 20. 28. *See q, Q, § 292, page 762.*

§ 479. CONCERNING ADMONISHING

5 : 1–16.

1 Rebuke [a]not an elder, but entreat
him as a father; *and* the younger men
as brethren;
2 The elder women as mothers; the
younger as sisters, with all purity.
3 Honour widows [b]that are widows
indeed.
4 But if any widow have children
or nephews, let them learn first to
shew [1]piety at home, and [c]to requite
parents: [d]for that is good and acceptable before God.
5 [e]Now she that is a widow indeed,
and desolate, trusteth in God, and
[f]continueth in supplications and
prayers [g]night and day.
6 [h]But she that liveth [2]in pleasure
is dead while she liveth.
7 [i]And these things give in charge,
that they may be blameless.
8 But if any provide not for his
own, [k]and specially for those of his
own [3]house, [l]he hath denied the faith,
[m]and is worse than an infidel.
9 Let not a widow be [4]taken into the
number under threescore years old,
[n]having been the wife of one man,
10 Well reported of for good works;
if she have brought up children, if

CHAP. 5.

she have [o]lodged strangers, if she have
[p]washed the saints' feet, if she have
relieved the afflicted, if she have diligently followed every good work.
11 But the younger widows refuse:
for when they have begun to wax wanton against Christ, they will marry;
12 Having damnation, because they
have cast off their first faith.

A

Lev. 19. 32 Thou shalt rise up before the hoary head, and honour the face of the old man, and fear thy God: I *am* the LORD.

B

I Tim. 5. 5, 16. *See text of topic.*

1

Or, *kindness.*

C

Gen. 45. 10 And thou shalt dwell in the land of Goshen, and thou shalt be near unto me, thou, and thy children, and thy children's children, and thy flocks, and thy herds, and all that thou hast:

11 And there will I nourish thee; for yet *there are* five years of famine; lest thou, and thy household, and all that thou hast, come to poverty.

Matt. 15. 4 For God commanded, saying, Honour thy father and mother: and, He that curseth father or mother, let him die the death.

Eph. 6. 1 Children, obey your parents in the Lord: for this is right.

2 Honour thy father and mother; which is the first commandment with promise;

TIMES. SUNDRY EXHORTATIONS (CONCLUDED).

F

Eze. 3. 19 Yet if thou warn the wicked, and he turn not from his wickedness, nor from his wicked way, he shall die in his iniquity; but thou hast delivered thy soul.

20 Again, When a righteous *man* doth turn from his righteousness, and commit iniquity, and I lay a stumblingblock before him, he shall die: because thou hast not given him warning, he shall die in his sin, and his righteousness

F—CONCLUDED.

which he hath done shall not be remembered; but his blood will I require at thine hand.

Eze. 3. 21 Nevertheless, if thou warn the righteous *man*, that the righteous sin not, and he doth not sin, he shall surely live, because he is warned; also thou hast delivered thy soul.

G

Rom. 11. 14. *See b, B, § 340, page 864.*

AND WIDOWS.

D

I Tim. 2. 3 For this *is* good and acceptable in the sight of God our Saviour;

E

I Cor. 7. 32 But I would have you without carefulness. He that is unmarried careth for the things that belong to the Lord, how he may please the Lord:

F

Luke 2. 37 And she *was* a widow of about fourscore and four years, which departed not from the temple, but served *God* with fastings and prayers night and day.

Luke 18. 1 And he spake a parable unto them *to this end* that men ought always to pray, and not to faint;

G

Acts 26. 7. *See e, E, § 309, page 792.*

H

Amos 6. 6 That drink wine in bowls, and anoint themselves with the chief ointments: but they are not grieved for the affliction of Joseph.

Jas. 5. 5 Ye have lived in pleasure on the earth, and been wanton; ye have nourished your hearts, as in a day of slaughter.

2

Or, *delicately.*

I

I Tim. 1. 3 As I besought thee to abide still at Ephesus, when I went into Macedonia, that thou mightest charge some that they teach no other doctrine,

I Tim. 4. 11 These things command and teach.

I Tim. 6. 17 Charge them that are rich in this world, that they be not highminded, nor trust in uncertain riches, but in the living God, who giveth us richly all things to enjoy;

K

Gen. 30. 30 For *it was* little which thou hadst before I *came*, and it is *now* increased

K—CONCLUDED.

unto a multitude; and the LORD hath blessed thee since my coming: and now when shall I provide for mine own house also?

Isa. 58. 7 *Is it* not to deal thy bread to the hungry, and that thou bring the poor that are cast out to thy house? when thou seest the naked, that thou cover him; and that thou hide not thyself from thine own flesh?

Gal. 6. 10 As we have therefore opportunity, let us do good unto all *men*, especially unto them who are of the household of faith.

3

Or, *kindred.*

L

II Tim. 3. 5 Having a form of godliness, but denying the power thereof: from such turn away.

Tit. 1. 16 They profess that they know God; but in works they deny *him*, being abominable, and disobedient, and unto every good work reprobate.

M

Matt. 18. 17 And if he shall neglect to hear them, tell *it* unto the church: but if he neglect to hear the church, let him be unto thee as a heathen man and a publican.

4

Or, *chosen.*

N

Luke 2. 36 And there was one Anna, a prophetess, the daughter of Phanuel, of the tribe of Aser: she was of a great age, and had lived with a husband seven years from her virginity;

I Tim. 3. 2 A bishop then must be blameless, the husband of one wife, vigilant, sober, of good behaviour, given to hospitality, apt to teach;

For O and P, see next page (1132).

§ 479. CONCERNING ADMONISHING

Chap. 5.

13 [q]And withal they learn *to be* idle,
wandering about from house to
house; and not only idle, but tattlers
also and busybodies, speaking things
which they ought not.

14 [r]I will therefore that the younger
women marry, bear children, guide
the house, [s]give none occasion to the
adversary [6]to speak reproachfully.

15 For some are already turned
aside after Satan.

16 If any man or woman that believeth have widows, let them relieve

Chap. 5.

them, and let not the church be charged; that it may relieve [t]them that are widows indeed.

O

Acts 20. 15. *See d, D, § 273, page 736.*

1 Pet. 4. 9 Use hospitality one to another without grudging.

P

Gen. 18. 4 Let a little water, I pray you, be fetched, and wash your feet, and rest yourselves under the tree:

Gen. 19. 2 And he said, Behold now, my lords, turn in, I pray you, into your servant's house, and tarry all night, and wash your feet, and ye shall rise up early, and go on your ways. And they said, Nay; but we will abide in the street all night.

§ 480. CONCERNING ELDERS

5 : 17–25.

17 [a]Let the elders that rule well be
counted worthy of double honour,
especially they who labour in the
word and doctrine.

18 For the Scripture saith, [b]Thou
shalt not muzzle the ox that treadeth
out the corn. And [c]The labourer *is*
worthy of his reward.

19 Against an elder receive not an
accusation, but [1d]before two or three
witnesses.

20 [e]Them that sin rebuke before
all, [f]that others also may fear.

21 [g]I charge *thee* before God, and
the Lord Jesus Christ, and the elect
angels, that thou observe these
things [2]without preferring one before
another, doing nothing by partiality.

22 [h]Lay hands suddenly on no man,
[i]neither be partaker of other men's
sins: keep thyself pure.

23 Drink no longer water, but [k]use

Chap. 5.

a little wine for thy stomach's sake
and thine often infirmities.

24 [l]Some men's sins are open beforehand, going before to judgment;
and some *men* they follow after.

25 Likewise also the good works
of some are manifest beforehand;
and they that are otherwise cannot
be hid.

A

Rom. 12. 8. *See r, R, § 342, page 870.*

1 Cor. 9. 10 Or saith he *it* altogether for our sakes? For our sakes, no doubt, *this* is written: that he that ploweth should plough in hope; and that he that thresheth in hope should be partaker of his hope.

1 Cor. 9. 14 Even so hath the Lord ordained that they which preach the gospel should live of the gospel.

Gal. 6. 6 Let him that is taught in the word communicate unto him that teacheth in all good things.

Phil. 2. 29 Receive him therefore in the Lord with all gladness; and hold such in reputation:

1 Thes. 5. 12, 13. *See a, A, § 465, page 1106.*

B

1 Cor. 9. 9. *See m, M, § 365, page 922.*

AND WIDOWS (CONCLUDED).

P—CONCLUDED.

Luke 7. 38 And stood at his feet behind *him* weeping, and began to wash his feet with tears, and did wipe *them* with the hairs of her head, and kissed his feet, and anointed *them* with the ointment.

Luke 7. 44 And he turned to the woman, and said unto Simon, Seest thou this woman? I entered into thine house, thou gavest me no water for my feet: but she hath washed my feet with tears, and wiped *them* with the hairs of her head.

John 13. 5 After that he poureth water into a basin, and began to wash the disciples' feet, and to wipe *them* with the towel wherewith he was girded.

John 13. 14 If I then, *your* Lord and Master, have washed your feet; ye also ought to wash one another's feet.

Q

II Thes. 3. 11 For we hear that there are some which walk among you disorderly, working not at all, but are busybodies.

R

I Cor. 7. 9 But if they cannot contain, let them marry: for it is better to marry than to burn.

S

I Tim. 6. 1 Let as many servants as are under the yoke count their own masters worthy of all honour, that the name of God and *his* doctrine be not blasphemed.

Tit. 2. 8 Sound speech, that cannot be condemned; that he that is of the contrary part may be ashamed, having no evil thing to say of you.

5

Gr. *for their railing.*

T

I Tim. 5. 3, 5. *See text of topic.*

AND OTHER CHARGES.

C

Lev. 19. 13 Thou shalt not defraud thy neighbour, neither rob *him:* the wages of him that is hired shall not abide with thee all night until the morning.

Deut. 24. 14 Thou shalt not oppress a hired servant *that is* poor and needy, *whether he be* of thy brethren, or of thy strangers that *are* in thy land within thy gates:
15 At his day thou shalt give *him* his hire, neither shall the sun go down upon it; for he *is* poor, and setteth his heart upon it: lest he cry against thee unto the LORD, and it be sin unto thee.

Luke 10. 7. *See l, L, § 105, page 307.*

1

Or, *under.*

D

Deut. 19. 15 One witness shall not rise up against a man for any iniquity, or for any sin, in any sin that he sinneth: at the mouth of two witnesses, or at the mouth of three witnesses, shall the matter be established.

E

Gal. 2. 11 But when Peter was come to Antioch, I withstood him to the face, because he was to be blamed.

Gal. 2. 14 But when I saw that they walked not uprightly according to the truth of the gospel, I said unto Peter before *them* all, If thou, being a Jew, livest after the manner of Gentiles, and not

E—CONCLUDED.

as do the Jews, why compellest thou the Gentiles to live as do the Jews?

Tit. 1. 13 This witness is true. Wherefore rebuke them sharply, that they may be sound in the faith;

F

Deut. 13. 11 And all Israel shall hear, and fear, and shall do no more any such wickedness as this is among you.

G

I Tim. 1. 18. *See s, S, § 474, page 1120.*

2

Or, *without prejudice.*

H

Acts 6. 6. *See l, L, § 244, page 664.*

I

II Jno. 11 For he that biddeth him God speed is partaker of his evil deeds.

K

Ps. 104. 15 And wine *that* maketh glad the heart of man, *and* oil to make *his* face to shine, and bread *which* strengtheneth man's heart.

Prov. 31. 6 Give strong drink unto him that is ready to perish, and wine unto those that be of heavy hearts.

L

Gal. 5. 19 Now the works of the flesh are manifest, which are *these*; Adultery, fornication, uncleanness, lasciviousness,

§ 481. CONCERNING BONDSERVANTS. REBUKE

6 : 1-10.

1 Let as many [a]servants as are under the yoke count their own masters worthy of all honour, [b]that the name of God and *his* doctrine be not blasphemed.

2 And they that have believing masters, [c]let them not despise *them*, because they are brethren; but rather do *them* service, because they are [1]faithful and beloved, partakers of the benefit. [d]These things teach and exhort.

3 If any man [e]teach otherwise, and consent [f]not to wholesome words, *even* the words of our Lord Jesus Christ, [g]and to the doctrine which is according to godliness;

4 He is [2]proud, [h]knowing nothing, but [3]doting about [i]questions and strifes of words, whereof cometh envy, strife, railings, evil surmisings,

5 [k4]Perverse disputings of [l]men of corrupt minds, and destitute of the truth, [m]supposing that gain is godliness: [n]from such withdraw thyself.

6 But [o]godliness with contentment is great gain.

7 For [p]we brought nothing into *this* world, *and it is* certain we can carry nothing out.

8 And [q]having food and raiment, let us be therewith content.

9 But [r]they that will be rich fall into temptation [s]and a snare, and *into* many foolish and hurtful lusts, [t]which drown men in destruction and perdition.

10 [u]For the love of money is the root of all evil: which while some coveted after, they have [5]erred from the faith, and pierced themselves through with many sorrows.

A

Eph. 6. 5. *See e, E, § 430, page 1054.*

B

Isa. 52. 5 Now therefore, what have I here, saith the LORD, that my people is taken away for nought? they that rule over them make them to howl, saith the LORD; and my name continually every day *is* blasphemed.

Rom. 2. 24 For the name of God is blasphemed among the Gentiles through you, as it is written.

Tit. 2. 5 *To be* discreet, chaste, keepers at home, good, obedient to their own husbands, that the word of God be not blasphemed.

Tit. 2. 8 Sound speech, that cannot be condemned; that he that is of the contrary part may be ashamed, having no evil thing to say of you.

C

Col. 4. 1 Masters, give unto *your* servants that which is just and equal; knowing that ye also have a Master in heaven.

1

Or, *believing.*

D

I Tim. 4. 11 These things command and teach.

E

I Tim. 1. 3 As I besought thee to abide still at Ephesus, when I went into Macedonia, that thou mightest charge some that they teach no other doctrine,

F

I Tim. 1. 10. *See l, L, § 473, page 1118.*

G

Tit. 1. 1 Paul, a servant of God, and an apostle of Jesus Christ, according to the faith of God's elect, and the acknowledging of the truth which is after godliness;

2

Or, *a fool.*

H

I Cor. 8. 2. *See d, D, § 364, page 918.*

I Tim. 1. 7 Desiring to be teachers of the law; understanding neither what they say, nor whereof they affirm.

3

Or, *sick.*

I

I Tim. 1. 4 Neither give heed to fables and endless genealogies, which minister questions, rather than godly edifying which is in faith: *so do.*

II Tim. 2. 23 But foolish and unlearned questions avoid, knowing that they do gender strifes.

TO FALSE AND COVETOUS TEACHERS.

I—CONCLUDED.

Tit. 3. 9 But avoid foolish questions and genealogies, and contentions, and strivings about the law; for they are unprofitable and vain.

K

I Cor. 11. 16 But if any man seem to be contentious, we have no such custom, neither the churches of God.

I Tim. 1. 6 From which some having swerved have turned aside unto vain jangling;

4

Or, *gallings one of another.*

L

II Tim. 3. 8 Now as Jannes and Jambres withstood Moses, so do these also resist the truth: men of corrupt minds, reprobate concerning the faith.

M

Tit. 1. 11 Whose mouths must be stopped, who subvert whole houses, teaching things which they ought not, for filthy lucre's sake.

II Pet. 2. 3 And through covetousness shall they with feigned words make merchandise of you: whose judgment now of a long time lingereth not, and their damnation slumbereth not.

N

Rom. 16. 17. *See k, K, § 347, page 884.*

O

Ps. 37. 16 A little that a righteous man hath *is* better than the riches of many wicked.

Prov. 15. 16 Better *is* little with the fear of the LORD than great treasure and trouble therewith.

Prov. 16. 8 Better *is* a little with righteousness than great revenues without right.

Heb. 13. 5 *Let your* conversation *be* without covetousness; *and be* content with such things as ye have: for he hath said, I will never leave thee, nor forsake thee.

P

Job 1. 21 And said, Naked came I out of my mother's womb, and naked shall I return thither: the LORD gave, and the LORD hath taken away; blessed be the name of the LORD.

Ps. 49. 17 For when he dieth he shall carry nothing away; his glory shall not descend after him.

Prov. 27. 24 For riches *are* not for ever: and doth the crown *endure* to every generation?

Eccl. 5. 15 As he came forth of his mother's womb, naked shall he return to go as he came, and shall take nothing of his labour, which he may carry away in his hand.

P—CONCLUDED.

Eccl. 5. 16 And this also *is* a sore evil, *that* in all points as he came, so shall he go: and what profit hath he that hath laboured for the wind?

Luke 12. 20 But God said unto him, *Thou* fool, this night thy soul shall be required of thee: then whose shall those things be, which thou hast provided?

Q

Gen. 28. 20. And Jacob vowed a vow, saying, If God will be with me, and will keep me in this way that I go, and will give me bread to eat, and raiment to put on,

Heb. 13. 5. *See under O.*

R

Prov. 1. 19 So *are* the ways of every one that is greedy of gain; *which* taketh away the life of the owners thereof.

Prov. 15. 27 He that is greedy of gain troubleth his own house; but he that hateth gifts shall live.

Prov. 20. 21 An inheritance *may be* gotten hastily at the beginning; but the end thereof shall not be blessed.

Prov. 28. 20 A faithful man shall abound with blessings: but he that maketh haste to be rich shall not be innocent.

Matt. 13. 22. *See h, H, § 59, page 200.*

Jas. 5. 1 Go to now, *ye* rich men, weep and howl for your miseries that shall come upon *you.*

S

Deut. 7. 25 The graven images of their gods shall ye burn with fire: thou shalt not desire the silver or gold *that is* on them, nor take *it* unto thee, lest thou be snared therein: for it *is* an abomination to the LORD thy God.

I Tim. 3. 7 Moreover he must have a good report of them which are without; lest he fall into reproach and the snare of the devil.

T

I Tim. 1. 19 Holding faith, and a good conscience; which some have put away concerning faith have made shipwreck:

U

Ex. 23. 8 And thou shalt take no gift: for the gift blindeth the wise, and perverteth the words of the righteous.

Deut. 16. 19 Thou shalt not wrest judgment; thou shalt not respect persons, neither take a gift: for a gift doth blind the eyes of the wise, and pervert the words of the righteous.

5

Or, *been seduced.*

6: 11–16.

11 [a]But thou, [b]O man of God, flee these things; and follow after righteousness, godliness, faith, love, patience, meekness.

12 [c]Fight the good fight of faith, [d]lay hold on eternal life, whereunto thou art also called, [e]and hast professed a good profession before many witnesses.

13 [f]I give thee charge in the sight of God, [g]who quickeneth all things, and *before* Christ Jesus, [h]who before Pontius Pilate witnessed a good [1]confession;

14 That thou keep *this* commandment without spot, unrebukeable, [i]until the appearing of our Lord Jesus Christ:

15 Which in his times he shall shew, *who is* [k]the blessed and only Potentate, [l]the King of kings, and Lord of lords;

16 [m]Who only hath immortality, dwelling in the light which no man can approach unto; [n]whom no man hath seen, nor can see: [o]to whom *be* honour and power everlasting. Amen.

§ 482. PAUL CHARGES TIMOTHY

A

IITim. 2. 22 Flee also youthful lusts: but follow righteousness, faith, charity, peace, with them that call on the Lord out of a pure heart.

B

Deut. 33. 1 And this *is* the blessing, wherewith Moses the man of God blessed the children of Israel before his death.

IITim. 3. 17 That the man of God may be perfect, thoroughly furnished unto all good works.

C

I Cor. 9. 25, 26. *See p, P, § 365, page 926.*

ITim. 1 18 This charge I commit unto thee, son Timothy, according to the prophecies which went before on thee, that thou by them mightest war a good warfare;

D

Phil. 3. 12 Not as though I had already attained, either were already perfect: but I follow after, if that I may apprehend that for which also I am apprehended of Christ Jesus.

Phil. 3. 14 I press toward the mark for the prize of the high calling of God in Christ Jesus.

I Tim. 6. 19. *See text of topic, § 483.*

E

Heb. 13. 23 Know ye that *our* brother Timothy is set at liberty; with whom, if he come shortly, I will see you.

F

I Tim. 1. 18. *See s, S, § 474, page 1120.*

6: 17–19.

17 Charge them that are rich in this world, that they be not highminded, [a]nor trust in [1b]uncertain riches, but in the [c]living God, [d]who giveth us richly all things to enjoy;

18 That they do good, that [e]they be rich in goods works, [f]ready to distribute, [2g]willing to communicate;

19 [h]Laying up in store for themselves a good foundation against the time to come, that they may [i]lay hold on eternal life.

§ 483. A CHARGE

A

Matt. 6. 20. *See n, N, § 43, page 140.*

1

Gr. *uncertainty of riches.*

B

Prov. 23. 5 Wilt thou set thine eyes upon that which is not? for *riches* certainly make themselves wings; they fly away as an eagle toward heaven.

C

IThes. 1. 9 For they themselves shew of us what manner of entering in we had unto you, and how ye turned to God from idols to serve the living and true God;

I Tim. 3. 15 But if I tarry long, thou mayest know how thou oughest to behave thyself in the house of God, which is the church of the living God, the pillar and ground of the truth.

TO FIGHT A GOOD FIGHT.

F—Concluded.

ITim. 5. 21 I charge *thee* before God, and the Lord Jesus Christ, and the elect angels, that thou observe these things without preferring one before another, doing nothing by partiality.

G

Deut. 32. 39 See now that I, *even* I, *am* he, and *there is* no god with me: I kill, and I make alive; I wound, and I heal; neither *is there any* that can deliver out of my hand.

I Sa. 2. 6 The LORD killeth, and maketh alive: he bringeth down to the grave, and bringeth up.

John 5. 21 For as the Father raiseth up the dead, and quickeneth *them;* even so the Son quickeneth whom he will.

H

Study § *196, page 566.*

1

Or, *profession.*

I

Phil. 1. 6 Being confident of this very thing, that he which hath begun a good work in you will perform *it* until the day of Jesus Christ;

Phil. 1. 10 That ye may approve things that are excellent; that ye may be sincere and without offense till the day of Christ;

IThes. 3. 13 To the end he may stablish your hearts unblameable in holiness before God, even our Father, at the coming of our Lord Jesus Christ with all his saints.

K

I Tim. 1. 11, 17. *See n, N,* § *474, page 1120.*

L

Rev. 17. 14 These shall make war with the Lamb, and the Lamb shall overcome them: for he is Lord of lords, and King of kings: and they that are with him *are* called, and chosen, and faithful.

Rev. 19. 16 And he hath on *his* vesture and on his thigh a name written, KING OF KINGS, AND LORD OF LORDS.

M

Deut. 32. 40 For I lift up my hand to heaven, and say, I live for ever.

Ps. 90. 2 Before the mountains were brought forth, or ever thou hadst formed the earth and the world, even from everlasting to everlasting, thou *art* God.

John 5. 26 For as the Father hath life in himself; so hath he given to the Son to have life in himself;

ITim. 1. 17 Now unto the King eternal, immortal, invisible, the only wise God, *be* honour and glory for ever and ever. Amen.

Heb. 13. 8 Jesus Christ the same yesterday, and to-day, and for ever.

Rev. 1. 18 *I am* he that liveth, and was dead; and, behold, I am alive for evermore, Amen; and have the keys of hell and of death.

N

John 1. 18. *See h, H,* § *17, page 59.*

O

Rom. 11. 36. *See r, R,* § *341, page 866.*

TO THE RICH.

C—Concluded.

I Tim. 4. 10 For therefore we both labour and suffer reproach, because we trust in the living God, who is the Saviour of all men, especially of those that believe.

D

Acts 14. 17 Nevertheless he left not himself without witness, in that he did good, and gave us rain from heaven, and fruitful seasons, filling our hearts with food and gladness.

Acts 17. 25 Neither is worshiped with men's hands, as though he needed any thing, seeing he giveth to all life, and breath, and all things;

E

Matt. 19. 21. *See f, F,* § *144, page 408.*
Luke 12. 21. *See r, R,* § *57, page 187.*

F

Rom. 12. 13 Distributing to the necessity of saints; given to hospitality.

2

Or, *sociable.*

G

Gal. 6. 6 Let him that is taught in the word communicate unto him that teacheth in all good things.

Heb. 13. 16 But to do good and to communicate forget not: for with such sacrifices God is well pleased.

H

Matt. 6. 20. *See n, N,* § *43, page 140.*

I

I Tim. 6. 12. *See text of topic,* § 4

§ 484. CONCLUDING CHARGE

6:20, 21.

20 O Timothy, [a]keep that which is committed to thy trust, [b]avoiding profane *and* vain babblings, and oppositions of science falsely so called:
21 Which some professing [c]have erred concerning the faith. Grace *be* with thee. Amen.

A

IITim. 1. 14 That good thing which was committed unto thee keep by the Holy Ghost which dwelleth in us.

A—CONCLUDED.

Tit. 1. 9 Holding fast the faithful word as he hath been taught, that he may be able by sound doctrine both to exhort and convince the gainsayers.

Rev. 3. 3 Remember therefore how thou hast received and heard, and hold fast, and repent. If therefore thou shalt not watch, I will come on thee as a thief, and thou shalt not know what hour I will come upon thee.

B

ITim. 1. 4 Neither give heed to fables and endless genealogies, which minister questions, rather than godly edifying

PAUL'S SECOND

§ 485. SALUTATION.

1:1, 2.

1 Paul, [a]an Apostle of Jesus Christ by the will of God, according to [b]the promise of life which is in Christ Jesus,
2 [c]To Timothy, *my* dearly beloved son: Grace, mercy, *and* peace, from God the Father and Christ Jesus our Lord.

A

I Cor. 1. 1 Paul, called *to be* an apostle of Jesus Christ through the will of God, and Sosthenes *our* brother,

IICor. 1. 1 Paul, an apostle of Jesus Christ by the will of God, and Timothy *our* brother, unto the church of God which is at Corinth, with all the saints which are in all Achaia:

B

John 5. 24 Verily, verily, I say unto you, He that heareth my word, and believeth on him that sent me, hath

§ 486. TIMOTHY'S FAITH. HE IS EXHORTED TO SUFFER

1:3–14.

3 [a]I thank God, [b]whom I serve from *my* forefathers with pure conscience, that [c]without ceasing I have remembrance of thee in my prayers night and day;
4 [d]Greatly desiring to see thee, being mindful of thy tears, that I may be filled with joy;
5 When I call to remembrance [e]the unfeigned faith that is in thee, which dwelt first in thy grandmother Lois, and [f]thy mother Eunice; and I am persuaded that in thee also.

A

Rom. 1. 8. *See a, A, § 318, page 808.*

Eph. 1. 16 Cease not to give thanks for you, making mention of you in my prayers;

B

Acts 22. 3 I am verily a man *which am* a Jew, born in Tarsus, *a city* in Cilicia, yet brought up in this city at the feet of Gamaliel, *and* taught according to the perfect manner of the law of the fathers, and was zealous toward God, as ye all are this day.

Acts 23. 1 And Paul, earnestly beholding the council, said, Men *and* brethren, I have lived in all good conscience before God until this day.

Acts 24. 14 But this I confess unto thee, that after the way which they call heresy, so worship I the God of my fathers,

AND BENEDICTION.

B—CONTINUED.

which is in faith : *so do.*

I Tim. 1. 6 From which some having swerved have turned aside unto vain jangling;

I Tim. 4. 7 But refuse profane and old wives' fables, and exercise thyself *rather* unto godliness.

II Tim. 2. 14 Of these things put *them* in remembrance, charging *them* before the Lord that they strive not about words to no profit, *but* to the subverting of the hearers.

II Tim. 2. 16 But shun profane *and* vain babblings: for they will increase unto more ungodliness.

B—CONCLUDED.

II Tim. 2. 23 But foolish and unlearned questions avoid, knowing that they do gender strifes.

C

I Tim. 1. 6. *See under B.*

I Tim. 1. 19 Holding faith, and a good conscience; which some having put away, concerning faith have made shipwreck:

II Tim. 2. 18 Who concerning the truth have erred, saying that the resurrection is passed already; and overthrow the faith of some.

EPISTLE TO TIMOTHY.

Written Spring of A. D. 68, at Rome.

B—CONTINUED.

everlasting life, and shall not come into condemnation; but is passed from death unto life.

John 5. 39 Search the Scriptures; for in them ye think ye have eternal life: and they are they which testify of me.
40 And ye will not come to me, that ye might have life.

John 6. 40 And this is the will of him that sent me, that every one which seeth the Son, and believeth on him, may have everlasting life: and I will raise

B—CONCLUDED.

him up at the last day.

John 8. 51. *See c, C, § 111, page 331.*

John 10. 28 And I give unto them eternal life; and they shall never perish, neither shall any *man* pluck them out of my hand.

C

I Tim. 1. 2 Unto Timothy, *my* own son in the faith: Grace, mercy, *and* peace, from God our Father and Jesus Christ our Lord.

WITH THE GOSPEL IN THE HOPE OF ETERNAL LIFE.

B—CONCLUDED.

believing all things which are written in the law and in the prophets:

Acts 27. 23 For there stood by me this night the angel of God, whose I am, and whom I serve,

Rom. 1. 9 For God is my witness, whom I serve with my spirit in the gospel of his Son, that without ceasing I make mention of you always in my prayers;

Gal. 1. 14 And profited in the Jews' religion above many my equals in mine own nation, being more exceedingly zealous of the traditions of my fathers.

C

I Thes. 1. 2 We give thanks to God always for you all, making mention of you in our prayers;

C—CONCLUDED.

I Thes. 3. 10 Night and day praying exceedingly that we might see your face, and might perfect that which is lacking in your faith?

D

II Tim. 4. 9 Do thy diligence to come shortly unto me:

II Tim. 4. 21 Do thy diligence to come before winter. Eubulus greeteth thee, and Pudens, and Linus, and Claudia, and all the brethren.

E

I Tim. 1. 5 Now the end of the commandment is charity out of a pure heart, and *of* a good conscience, and *of* faith unfeigned:

For E concl'd, and F, see next page (1140).

§ 486. TIMOTHY'S FAITH; HE IS EXHORTED TO SUFFER WITH E—CONCLUDED.

CHAP. I.

6 Wherefore I put thee in remembrance, [g]that thou stir up the gift of God, which is in thee by the putting on of my hands.

7 For [h]God hath not given us the spirit of fear; [i]but of power, and of love, and of a sound mind.

8 [k]Be not thou therefore ashamed of the [l]testimony of our Lord, nor of me [m]his prisoner: [n]but be thou partaker of the afflictions of the gospel according to the power of God;

9 [o]Who hath saved us, and [p]called *us* with a holy calling, [q]not according to our works but [r]according to his own purpose and grace, which was given us in Christ Jesus before the world began,

10 [t]But is now made manifest by the appearing of our Saviour Jesus Christ, [u]who hath abolished death, and hath brought life and immortality to light through the gospel:

11 [x]Whereunto I am appointed a preacher, and an apostle, and a teacher of the Gentiles.

12 [y]For the which cause I also suffer these things: nevertheless I am not ashamed: [z]for I know whom I have [1]believed, and am persuaded that he is able to keep that which I have committed unto him [a]against that day.

13 [b]Hold fast the [c]form of [d]sound words, [e]which thou hast heard of me, [f]in faith and love which is in Christ Jesus.

14 [g]That good thing which was committed unto thee keep by the Holy Ghost [h]which dwelleth in us.

I Tim. 4. 6 If thou put the brethren in remembrance of these things, thou shalt be a good minister of Jesus Christ, nourished up in the words of faith and of good doctrine, whereunto thou hast attained.

F

Acts 16. 1 Then came he to Derbe and Lystra: and, behold, a certain disciple was there, named Timotheus, the son of a certain woman, which was a Jewess, and believed; but his father *was* a Greek:

G

I Thes. 5. 19. *See m, M, § 465, page 1108.*

H

Rom. 8. 15 For ye have not received the spirit of bondage again to fear; but ye have received the Spirit of adoption, whereby we cry, Abba, Father.

I

Luke 24. 49. *See u, U, § 219, page 613.*

Acts 1. 8 But ye shall receive power, after that the Holy Ghost is come upon you: and ye shall be witnesses unto me both in Jerusalem, and in all Judea, and in Samaria, and unto the uttermost part of the earth.

K

Rom. 1. 16. *See l, L, § 318, page 810.*

L

I Tim. 2. 6. *See k, K, § 475, page 1122.*

Rev. 1. 2 Who bare record of the word of God, and of the testimony of Jesus Christ, and of all things that he saw.

M

Eph. 3. 1. *See a, A, § 430, page 1038.*

N

Col. 1. 24. *See c, C, § 450, page 1080.*

O

I Tim. 1. 1. *See b, B, § 472, page 1118.*

P

I Thes. 4. 7 For God hath not called us unto uncleanness, but unto holiness.

Heb. 3. 1 Wherefore, holy brethren, partakers of the heavenly calling, consider the the apostle and High Priest of our profession, Christ Jesus;

Q

Rom. 3. 20. *See c, C, § 324, page 824.*

R

Rom. 8. 28 And we know that all things work together for good to them that love God, to them who are the called according to *his* purpose.

S

Rom. 16. 25 Now to him that is of power to stablish you according to my gospel,

THE GOSPEL, IN THE HOPE OF ETERNAL LIFE (CONCLUDED).

S—CONCLUDED.

and the preaching of Jesus Christ, according to the revelation of the mystery, which was kept secret since the world began,

Eph. 1. 4 According as he hath chosen us in him before the foundation of the world, that he should be holy and without blame before him in love:

Eph. 3. 11 According to the eternal purpose which he purposed in Christ Jesus our Lord:

Tit. 1. 2 In hope of eternal life, which God, that cannot life, promised before the world began;

I Pet 1. 20 Who verily was foreordained before the foundation of the world, but was manifest in these last times for you,

T

Rom. 16. 26. *See f, F, § 317, page 886.*

Col. 1. 26 *Even* the mystery which hath been hid from ages and from generations, but now is made manifest to his saints:

U

I Cor 15. 54 So when this corruptible shall have put on incorruption, and this mortal shall have put on immortality, then shall be brought to pass the saying that is written, Death is swallowed up in victory.

55 O death, where *is* thy sting? O grave where *is* thy victory?

Heb. 2. 14 Forasmuch then as the children are partakers of flesh and blood, he also himself likewise took part of the same; that through death he might destroy him that had the power of death, that is, the devil;

X

Acts 9. 15. *See l, L, § 251, page 684.*

Y

Eph. 3. 1 For this cause I Paul, the prisoner of Jesus Christ for you Gentiles,

IITim.2. 9 Wherein I suffer trouble, as an evil doer, *even* unto bonds; but the word of God is not bound.

Z

Ps. 9. 10 And they that know thy name will put their trust in thee: for thou, LORD, hast not forsaken them that seek thee.

Ps. 56. 9 When I cry *unto thee*, then shall mine enemies turn back: this I know, for God *is* for me.

Phil 3. 8 Yea doubtless, and I count all things, *but* loss for the excellency of the knowledge of Christ Jesus my Lord: for whom I have suffered the loss of all things, and do count them *but* dung, that I may win Christ,

Z—CONCLUDED.

Phil. 3. 9 And be found in him, not having mine own righteousness, which is of the law, but that which is through the faith of Christ, the righteousness which is of God by faith:

IPet 4. 19 Wherefore, let them that suffer according to the will of God commit the keeping of their souls *to him* in well doing, as unto a faithful Creator.

1

Or, *trusted.*

A

II Tim. 1. 18. *See text of topic, § 487.*

IITim.4. 8 Henceforth there is laid up for me a crown of righteousness, which the Lord, the righteous judge, shall give me at that day: and not to me only, but unto all them also that love his appearing.

B

IITim.3. 14 But continue thou in the things which thou hast learned and hast been assured of, knowing of whom thou hast learned *them*;

Tit. 1. 9 Holding fast the faithful word as he hath been taught, that he may be able by sound doctrine both to exhort and to convince the gainsayers.

Heb. 10. 23 Let us hold fast the profession of *our* faith without wavering; (for he *is* faithful that promised;)

Rev. 2. 25 But that which ye have *already* hold fast till I come.

C

Rom. 6. 17 But God be thanked, that ye were the servants of sin, but ye have obeyed from the heart that form of doctrine which was delievered you.

D

I Tim. 1. 10. *See l, L, § 473, page 1118.*

E

IITim.2. 2 And the things that thou hast heard of me among many witnesses, the same commit thou to faithful men, who shall be able to teach others also.

F

I Tim. 1. 14 And the grace of our Lord was exceeding abundant with faith and love which is in Christ Jesus.

G

I Tim. 6. 20. *See a, A, § 484, page 1138.*

H

Rom. 8. 11 But if the Spirit of him that raised up Jesus from the dead dwell in you, he that raised up Christ from the dead shall also quicken your mortal bodies by his Spirit that dwelleth in you.

§ 487. PAUL IS ABANDONED BY ALL IN ASIA.

1 : 15–18.

15 This thou knowest, that [a]all they which are in Asia be [b]turned away from me; of whom are Phygellus and Hermogenes.

16 The Lord [c]give mercy unto [d]the house of Onesiphorus; [e]for he oft refreshed me, and [f]was not ashamed of [g]my chain:

17 But, when he was in Rome, he sought me out very diligently, and found *me*.

18 The Lord grant unto him [h]that he may find mercy of the Lord [i]in that day: and in how many things he [k]ministered unto me at Ephesus, thou knowest very well.

A

Acts 19. 10 And this continued by the space of two years; so that all they which dwelt in Asia heard the word of the Lord Jesus, both Jews and Greeks.

B

IITim.4. 10 For Demas hath forsaken me, having loved this present world, and is departed unto Thessalonica; Crescens to Galatia, Titus unto Dalmatia.

IITim.4. 16 At my first answer no man stood with me, but all *men* forsook me: *I pray God* that it may not be laid to their charge.

C

Matt. 5. 7 Blessed *are* the merciful: for they shall obtain mercy.

D

IITim.4. 19 Salute Prisca and Aquila, and the household of Onesiphorus.

E

Phile. 7 For we have great joy and consolation in thy love, because the bowels of the saints are refreshed by thee, brother.

§ 488. SUNDRY INSTRUCTIONS IN DUTY

2 : 1–13.

1 Thou therefore, [a]my son, [b]be strong in the grace that is in Christ Jesus.

2 [c]And the things that thou hast heard of me [1]among many witnesses, [d]the same commit thou to faithful men, who shall be [e]able to teach others also.

3 [f]Thou therefore endure hardness, [g]as a good soldier of Jesus Christ.

4 [h]No man that warreth entangleth himself with the affairs of *this* life; that he may please him who hath chosen him to be a soldier.

5 And [i]if a man also strive for masteries, *yet* is he not crowned, except he strive lawfully.

6 [k2]The husbandman that laboureth must be first partaker of the fruits.

7 Consider what I say; and the Lord give thee understanding in all things.

A

I Tim. 1. 2 Unto Timothy, *my* own son in the faith: Grace, mercy, *and* peace, from God our Father and Jesus Christ our Lord.

IITim.1. 2 To Timothy, *my* dearly beloved son: Grace, mercy, *and* peace, from God the Father and Christ Jesus our Lord.

B

Eph. 6. 10 Finally, my brethren, be strong in the Lord, and in the power of his might.

C

IITim.1. 13 Hold fast the form of sound words, which thou hast heard of me, in faith and love which is in Christ Jesus.

IITim.3. 10 But thou hast fully known my doctrine, manner of life, purpose, faith, longsuffering, charity, patience.

IITim. 3. 14 But continue thou in the things which thou hast learned and hast been assured of, knowing of whom thou hast learned *them;*

1

Or, *by*.

D

I Tim. 1. 18 This charge I commit unto thee, son Timothy, according to the prophe-

ONESIPHORUS IS GRATEFULLY REMEMBERED.

F

IITim.1. 8 Be not thou therefore ashamed of the testimony of our Lord, nor of me his prisoner: but be thou partaker of the afflictions of the gospel according to the power of God;

G

Acts 28. 20 For this cause therefore have I called for you, to see *you*, and to speak with *you*: because that for the hope of Israel I am bound with this chain.

Eph. 6. 20 For which I am an ambassador in bonds; that therein I may speak boldly, as I ought to speak.

H

Matt.25. 37 Then shall the righteous answer him, saying, Lord, when saw we thee a hungered, and fed *thee?* or thirsty, and gave *thee* drink?

38 When saw we thee a stranger, and took *thee* in? or naked, and clothed *thee?*

39 Or when saw we thee sick, or in prison, and came unto thee?

H—CONCLUDED.

Matt.25. 40 And the King shall answer and say unto them, Verily I say unto you, Inasmuch as ye have done *it* unto one of the least of these my brethren, ye have done *it* unto me.

I

IITim.1. 12 For the which cause I also suffer these things: nevertheless I am not ashamed: for I know whom I have believed, and am persuaded that he is able to keep that which I have committed unto him against that day.

IIThes.1. 10 When he shall come to be glorified in his saints, and to be admired in all them that believe (because our testimony among you was believed) in that day.

K

Heb. 6. 10 For God *is* not unrighteous to forget your work and labour of love, which ye have shewed toward his name, in that ye have ministered to the saints, and do minister.

AND EXHORTATIONS IN THE GOSPEL.

D—CONCLUDED.

cies which went before on thee, that thou by them mightest war a good warfare;

E

I Tim. 3. 2 A bishop then must be blameless, the husband of one wife, vigilant, sober, of good behaviour, given to hospitality, apt to teach;

Tit. 1. 9 Holding fast the faithful word as he hath been taught, that he may be able by sound doctrine both to exhort and convince the gainsayers.

F

Col. 1. 24. *See c, C, § 450, page 1080.*

IITim.4. 5 But watch thou in all things, endure afflictions, do the work of an evangelist, make full proof of thy ministry.

G

I Tim. 1. 18. *See u, U, § 474, page 1120.*

H

I Cor. 9. 25 And every man that striveth for the mastery is temperate in all things. Now they *do it* to obtain a corruptible crown; but we an incorruptible.

I

I Cor. 9. 25, 26. *See p, P, § 365, page 926.*

K

I Cor. 9. 10 Or saith he *it* altogether for our sakes? For our sakes, no doubt, *this* is written: that he that plougheth should plough in hope; and that he that thresheth in hope should be partaker of his hope.

2

Or, *the husbandman, labouring first, must be partaker of the fruits.*

L

Acts 2. 30 Therefore being a prophet, and knowing that God hath sworn with an oath to him, that of the fruit of his loins, according to the flesh, he would raise up Christ to sit on his throne;

Acts 13. 23 Of this man's seed hath God according to *his* promise, raised unto Israel a Saviour, Jesus:

Rom. 1. 3 Concerning his Son Jesus Christ our Lord, which was made of the seed of David according to the flesh:

4 And declared *to be* the Son of God with power, according to the Spirit of holiness, by the resurrection from the dead:

M

ICor.15. 1 Moreover, brethren, I declare unto you the gospel which I preached unto you, which also ye have received, and wherein ye stand:

§ 488. SUNDRY INSTRUCTIONS IN DUTY AND

CHAP. 2.

8 Remember that Jesus Christ [l]of
the seed of David [m]was raised from
the dead, [n]according to my gospel:
9 [o]Wherein I suffer trouble, as an
evil doer, [p]*even* unto bonds; [q]but the
word of God is not bound.
10 Therefore [r]I endure all things
for the elect's sakes, [s]that they may
also obtain the salvation which is in
Christ Jesus with eternal glory.
11 [t]*It is* a faithful saying: For [u]if
we be dead with *him*, we shall also
live with *him*:
12 [x]If we suffer, we shall also reign
with *him*: [y]if we deny *him*, he also
will deny us:
13 [z]If we believe not, *yet* he abideth faithful: he cannot deny himself.

For L and M, see preceding page (1143)

M—CONCLUDED.

I Cor. 15. 4 And that he was buried, and that he arose again the third day according to the Scriptures:

I Cor. 15. 20 But now is Christ risen from the dead, *and* become the first fruits of them that slept.

N

Rom. 2. 16 In the day when God shall judge the secrets of men by Jesus Christ according to my gospel.

O

Acts 9. 16 For I will shew him how great things he must suffer for my name's sake.

II Tim. 1. 12 For the which cause I also suffer these things: nevertheless I am not ashamed: for I know whom I have believed, and am persuaded that he is able to keep that which I have committed unto him against that day.

P

Eph. 3. 1. *See a, A, § 430, page 1038.*

Q

Acts 28. 31 Preaching the kingdom of God, and teaching those things which concern the Lord Jesus Christ with all confidence, no man forbidding him.

§ 489. SUNDRY INSTRUCTIONS AS TO STRIFE,

2:14–26.

14 Of these things put *them* in re
membrance, [a]charging *them* before
the Lord [b]that they strive not about
words to no profit, *but* to the subverting of the hearers.
15 [c]Study to shew thyself approved
unto God, a workman that needeth
not to be ashamed, [d]rightly dividing
the word of truth.
16 But [e]shun profane *and* vain babblings: for they will increase unto
more ungodliness.
17 And their word will eat as doth
a [1]canker: of whom is [f]Hymeneus
and Philetus;
18 Who [g]concerning the truth have
erred, [h]saying that the resurrection

A

I Tim. 5. 21 I charge *thee* before God, and the Lord Jesus Christ, and the elect angels, that thou observe these things without preferring one before another, doing nothing by partiality.

I Tim. 6. 13 I give thee charge in the sight of God, who quickeneth all things, and *before* Christ Jesus, who before Pontius Pilate witnessed a good confession;

II Tim. 4. 1 I charge *thee* therefore before God, and the Lord Jesus Christ, who shall judge the quick and the dead at his appearing and his kingdom;

B

I Tim. 1. 4. *See c, C, § 473, page 1118.*

C

II Pet. 1. 10 Wherefore the rather, brethren, give diligence to make your calling and election sure: for if ye do these things, ye shall never fall:

D

Matt. 13. 52 Then said he unto them, Therefore every scribe *which is* instructed

EXHORTATIONS IN THE GOSPEL (Concluded).

Q—Concluded.

Eph. 6. 19 And for me, that utterance may be given unto me, that I may open my mouth boldly, to make known the mystery of the gospel.

20 For which I am an ambassador in bonds; that therein I may speak boldly, as I ought to speak.

Phil. 1. 13 So that my bonds in Christ are manifest in all the palace, and in all other *places;*

14 And many of the brethren in the Lord, waxing confident by my bonds, are much more bold to speak the word without fear.

R

Col. 1. 24. *See c, C, § 450, page 1080.*

S

II Cor. 1. 6 And whether we be afflicted, *it is* for your consolation and salvation, which is effectual in the enduring of the same sufferings which we also suffer: or whether we be comforted, *it is* for your consolation and salvation.

T

I Tim. 1. 15. *See i, I, § 474, page 1120.*

U

Rom. 6. 5 For if we have been planted together in the likeness of his death, we

U—Concluded.

shall be also *in the likeness* of *his* resurrection:

Rom. 6. 8 Now if we be dead with Christ, we believe that we shall also live with him:

II Cor. 4. 10 Always bearing about in the body the dying of the Lord Jesus, that the life also of Jesus might be made manifest in our body.

X

II Cor. 4. 10. *See f, F, § 393, page 972.*

Y

Matt. 10. 33. *See f, F, § 77, page 238.*

Luke 12. 9 But he that denieth me before men shall be denied before the angels of God.

Z

Num. 23. 19 God *is* not a man, that he should lie; neither the son of man, that he should repent: hath he said, and shall he not do *it?* or hath he spoken, and shall he not make it good?

Rom. 3. 3 For what if some did not believe shall their unbelief make the faith of God without effect?

Rom. 9. 6 Not as though the word of God hath taken none effect. For they *are* not all Israel, which are of Israel:

UNGODLINESS, ERROR AND PERSONAL CONDUCT.

D—Continued.

unto the kingdom of heaven is like unto a man *that is* a householder, which bringeth forth out of his treasure *things* new and old.

Mark 4. 33 And with many such parables spake he the word unto them, as they were able to hear *it.*

Luke 12. 42 And the Lord said, Who then is that faithful and wise steward, whom *his* lord shall make ruler over his household, to give *them their* portion of meat in due season?

Acts 20. 20 *And* how I kept back nothing that was profitable *unto you*, but have shewed you, and have taught you publicly, and from house to house,

Acts 20. 27 For I have not shunned to declare unto you all the counsel of God.

I Cor. 3. 1 And I, brethren, could not speak unto you as unto spiritual, but as unto carnal, *even* as unto babes in Christ.

2 I have fed you with milk, and not with meat: for hitherto ye were not able *to bear it,* neither yet now are ye able.

D—Concluded.

II Cor. 4. 1 Therefore, seeing we have this ministry, as we have received mercy, we faint not;

2 But have renounced the hidden things of dishonesty, not walking in craftiness, nor handling the word of God deceitfully; but by manifestation of the truth commending ourselves to every man's conscience in the sight of God.

Heb. 5. 12 For when for the time ye ought to be teachers, ye have need that one teach you again which *be* the first principles of the oracles of God; and are become such as have need of milk, and not of strong meat.

13 For every one that useth milk *is* unskilful in the word of righteousness: for he is a babe.

14 But strong meat belongeth to them that are of full age, *even* those who by reason of use have their senses exercised to discern both good and evil.

For E, I, F, G and H, see next page (1146).

§ 489. SUNDRY INSTRUCTIONS AS TO STRIFE, UNGOD-

CHAP. 2.

is past already; and overthrow the faith of some.

19 Nevertheless [i]the foundation of God standeth [2]sure, having this seal, The Lord [k]knoweth them that are his. And, Let every one that nameth the name of Christ depart from iniquity.

20 [l]But in a great house there are not only vessels of gold and of silver, but also of wood and of earth; [m]and some to honour, and some to dishonour.

21 [n]If a man therefore purge himself from these, he shall be a vessel unto honour, sanctified, and meet for the master's use, *and* [o]prepared unto every good work.

22 Flee also youthful lusts: but [p]follow righteousness, faith, charity, peace, with them that [q]call on the Lord [r]out of a pure heart.

23 But [s]foolish and unlearned questions avoid, knowing that they do gender strifes.

24 And [t]the servant of the Lord must not strive; but be gentle unto all *men*, [u]apt to teach, [3]patient,

25 [x]In meekness instructing those that oppose themselves; [y]if God peradventure will give them repentance to the acknowledging of the truth;

26 And *that* they may [4]recover themselves [z]out of the snare of the devil, who are [5]taken captive by him at his will.

CHAP. 2.

E

I Tim. 1. 4. *See* c, *C*, § *473, page 1118.*

1

Or, *gangrene.*

F

I Tim. 1. 20 Of whom is Hymeneus and Alexander; whom I have delivered unto Satan, that they may learn not to blaspheme.

G

I Tim. 6. 21 Which some professing have erred concerning the faith. Grace *be* with thee. Amen.

H

I Cor. 15. 12 Now if Christ be preached that he rose from the dead, how say some among you that there is no resurrection of the dead?

I

Prov. 10. 25 As the whirlwind passeth, so *is* the wicked no *more*: but the righteous *is* an everlasting foundation.

Matt. 24. 24. *See s, S,* § *173, page 488.*

2

Or, *steady.*

K

Num. 16. 5 And he spake unto Korah and unto all his company, saying, Even to morrow the LORD will shew who *are* his, and *who is* holy; and will cause *him* to come near unto him: even *him*

§ 490. THE PERILOUS CHARACTER OF THE LAST DAYS.

3: 1–17.

1 This know also, that [a]in the last days perilous times shall come.

2 For men shall be [b]lovers of their own selves, [c]covetous, boasters, [d]proud, [e]blasphemers, [f]disobedient to parents, unthankful, unholy,

3 [g]Without natural affection, truce-

A

I Tim. 4. 1. *See b, B,* § *478, page 1126.*

II Tim. 4. 3 For the time will come when they will not endure sound doctrine; but after their own lusts shall they heap to themselves teachers, having itching ears;

B

Phil. 2. 21 For all seek their own, not the things which are Jesus Christ's.

LINESS, ERROR, AND PERSONAL CONDUCT (CONCLUDED).

K—CONCLUDED.

whom he hath chosen will he cause to come near unto him.

I Cor. 8. 3 But if any man love God, the same is known of him.

Nah. 1. 7 The LORD *is* good, a strong hold in the day of trouble; and he knoweth them that trust in him.

John 10. 14. *See m, M, § 118, page 351.*

L

I Tim. 3. 15. *See a, A, § 477, page 1126.*

M

Rom. 9. 21 Hath not the potter power over the clay, of the same lump to make one vessel unto honour, and another unto dishonour?

N

Isa. 52. 11 Depart ye, depart ye, go ye out from thence, touch no unclean *thing;* go ye out of the midst of her; be ye clean, that bear the vessels of the LORD.

Jer. 15. 19 Therefore thus saith the LORD, If thou return, then will I bring thee again, *and* thou shalt stand before me: and if thou take forth the precious from the vile, thou shalt be as my mouth: let them return unto thee; but return not thou unto them.

O

II Tim. 3. 17 That the man of God may be perfect, thoroughly furnished unto all good works.

Tit. 3. 1 Put them in mind to be subject to principalities and powers, to obey magistrates, to be ready to every good work,

P

I Tim. 6. 11 But thou, O man of God, flee these things; and follow after righteousness, godliness, faith, love, patience, meekness.

Q

Acts 9. 14. *See k, K, § 251, page 684.*

R

I Tim. 1. 5 Now the end of the commandment is charity out of a pure heart, and *of* a good conscience, and *of* faith unfeigned:

I Tim. 4. 12 Let no man despise thy youth; but be thou an example of the believers, in word, in conversation, in charity, in spirit, in faith, in purity.

S

I Tim. 1. 4. *See c, C, § 473, page 1118.*

T

Tit. 3. 2 To speak evil of no man, to be no brawlers, *but* gentle, shewing all meekness unto all men.

U

I Tim. 3. 2 A bishop then must be blameless, the husband of one wife, vigilant, sober, of good behaviour, given to hospitality, apt to teach;

3

Or, *forbearing.*

X

Gal. 6. 1. *See c, C, § 423, page 1024.*

I Tim. 6. 11. *See under P.*

I Pet. 3. 15 But sanctify the Lord God in your hearts: and *be* ready always to *give* an answer to every man that asketh you a reason of the hope that is in you with meekness and fear:

Y

Acts 8. 22 Repent therefore of this thy wickedness, and pray God, if perhaps the thought of thine heart may be forgiven thee.

4

Gr. awake.

Z

I Tim. 3. 7. *See u, U, § 476, page 1124.*

5

Gr. taken alive.

TIMOTHY EXHORTED TO STEADFASTNESS.

C

II Pet. 2. 3 And through covetousness shall they with feigned words make merchandise of you: whose judgment now of a long time lingereth not, and their damnation slumbereth not.

D

I Tim. 6. 4 He is proud, knowing nothing, but doting about questions and strifes of words, whereof cometh envy, strife, railings, evil surmisings,

E

I Tim. 1. 20. *See under F, § 489.*

II Pet. 2. 12 But these, as natural brute beasts, made to be taken and destroyed, speak evil of the things that they understand not; and shall utterly perish in their own corruption;

Rev. 13. 5 And there was given unto him a mouth speaking great things and blasphemies; and power was given unto him to continue forty *and* two months.

For F and G, see next page (1148).

§ 490. THE PERILOUS CHARACTER OF THE LAST DAYS.

CHAP. 3.

breakers, [1]false accusers, [h]inconti-
nent, fierce, despisers of those that
are good,
4 [i]Traitors, heady, highminded,
[k]lovers of pleasure more than lovers
of God;
5 Having a form of godliness, but
[l]denying the power thereof: [m]from
such turn away.
6 For [n]of this sort are they which
creep into houses, and lead captive
silly women laden with sins, led
away with divers lusts,
7 Ever learning, and never able
[o]to come to the knowledge of the
truth.
8 [p]Now as Jannes and Jambres
withstood Moses, so do these also
resist the truth: [q]men of corrupt
minds, [r2]reprobate concerning the
faith.
9 But they shall proceed no further: for their folly shall be manifest unto all *men*, [s]as theirs also was.
10 [t]But [3]thou hast fully known my
doctrine, manner of life, purpose,
faith, longsuffering, charity, patience,
11 Persecutions, afflictions, which
came unto me [u]at Antioch, [x]at
Iconium, [y]at Lystra; what persecutions I endured: but [z]out of *them*
all the Lord delivered me.
12 Yea, and [a]all that will live
godly in Christ Jesus shall suffer
persecution.
13 [b]But evil men and seducers shall
wax worse and worse, deceiving, and
being deceived.
14 But [c]continue thou in the things
which thou hast learned and hast
been assured of, knowing of whom
thou hast learned *them;*
15 And that from a child thou hast
known [d]the holy Scriptures, which

F

Rom. 1. 30 Backbiters, haters of God, despiteful, proud, boasters, inventors of evil things, disobedient to parents,

G

Rom. 1. 31 Without understanding, covenant-breakers, without natural affection, implacable, unmerciful:

1

Or, *make bates.*

Tit. 2. 3 The aged women likewise, that *they be* in behaviour as becometh holiness, not false accusers, not given to much wine, teachers of good things;

H

IIPet. 3. 3 Knowing this first, that there shall come in the last days scoffers, walking after their own lusts,

I

IIPet. 2. 10 But chiefly them that walk after the flesh in the lust of uncleanness, and despise government. Presumptuous *are they*, selfwilled, they are not afraid to speak evil of dignities.

K

Phil. 3. 19 Whose end *is* destruction, whose God *is their* belly, and *whose* glory *is* in their shame, who mind earthly things.)

IIPet. 2. 13 And shall receive the reward of unrighteousness, *as* they that count it pleasure to riot in the daytime. Spots *they are* and blemishes, sporting themselves with their own deceivings while they feast with you;

Jude 4 For there are certain men crept in unawares, who were before of old ordained to this condemnation, ungodly men, turning the grace of our God into lasciviousness, and denying the only Lord God, and our Lord Jesus Christ.

Jude 19 These be they who separate themselves, sensual, having not the Spirit.

L

I Tim. 5. 8. *See l, L, § 479, page 1130.*

M

Rom. 16. 17. *See k, K, § 347, page 884.*

N

Matt. 23. 14 Woe unto you, scribes and Pharisees, hypocrites! for ye devour widows' houses, and for a pretence make long prayer: therefore ye shall receive the greater damnation.

Tit. 1. 11 Whose mouths must be stopped, who subvert whole houses, teaching things which they ought not, for filthy lucre's sake.

TIMOTHY EXHORTED TO STEADFASTNESS (CONTINUED).

O

ITim. 2. 4 Who will have all men to be saved, and to come unto the knowledge of the truth.

P

Ex. 7. 11 Then Pharaoh also called the wise men and the sorcerers: now the magicians of Egypt, they also did in like manner with their enchantments.

Q

ITim. 6. 5 Perverse disputings of men of corrupt minds, and destitute of the truth, supposing that gain is godliness: from such withdraw thyself.

R

Rom. 1. 28 And even as they did not like to retain God in *their* knowledge, God gave them over to a reprobate mind, to do those things which are not convenient;

IICor. 13. 5 Examine yourselves, whether ye be in the faith; prove your own selves. Know ye not your own selves, how that Jesus Christ is in you, except ye be reprobates?

Tit. 1. 16 They profess that they know God; but in works they deny *him*, being abominable, and disobedient, and unto every good work reprobate.

2

Or, *of no judgment.*

S

Ex. 7. 12 For they cast down every man his rod, and they became serpents: but Aaron's rod swallowed up their rods.

Ex. 8. 18 And the magicians did so with their enchantments to bring forth lice; but they could not: so there were lice upon man, and upon beast.

Ex. 9. 11 And the magicians could not stand before Moses because of the boils; for the boil was upon the magicians, and upon all the Egyptians.

T

Phil. 2. 22 But ye know the proof of him, that, as a son with the father, he hath served with me in the gospel.

ITim. 4. 6 If thou put the brethren in remembrance of these things, thou shalt be a good minister of Jesus Christ, nourished up in the words of faith and of good doctrine, whereunto thou hast attained.

3

Or, *thou hast been a diligent follower of.*

U

Acts 13. 45 But when the Jews saw the multitudes, they were filled with envy,

U—CONCLUDED.

and spake against those things which were spoken by Paul, contradicting and blaspheming.

Acts 13. 50 But the Jews stirred up the devout and honourable women, and the chief men of the city, and raised persecution against Paul and Barnabas, and expelled them out of their coasts.

X

Acts 14. 2 But the unbelieving Jews stirred up the Gentiles, and made their minds evil affected against the brethren.

Acts 14. 5 And when there was an assault made both of the Gentiles, and also of the Jews with their rulers, to use *them* despitefully, and to stone them,

Y

Acts 14. 19 And there came thither *certain* Jews from Antioch and Iconium, who persuaded the people, and, having stoned Paul, drew *him* out of the city, supposing he had been dead.

Z

Ps. 34. 19 Many *are* the afflictions of the righteous: but the LORD delivereth him out of them all.

IICor. 1. 10 Who delivered us from so great a death, and doth deliver: in whom we trust that he will yet deliver *us;*

IITim. 4. 17 Notwithstanding the Lord stood with me, and strengthened me; that by me the preaching might be fully known, and *that* all the Gentiles might hear: and I was delivered out of the mouth of the lion.

A

Ps. 34. 19. *See under Z.*

Matt. 16. 24 Then said Jesus unto his disciples, If any *man* will come after me, let him deny himself, and take up his cross, and follow me.

John 17. 14 I have given them thy word; and the world hath hated them, because they are not of the world, even as I am not of the world.

Acts 14. 22. *See e, E, § 266, page 724.*

ICor. 15. 19 If in this life only we have hope in Christ, we are of all men most miserable.

IThes. 3. 3 That no man should be moved by these afflictions: for yourselves know that we are appointed thereunto.

B

Rom. 1. 24. *See h, H, § 319, page 812.*

II Thes. 2. 11 And for this cause God shall send them strong delusion, that they should believe a lie:

For C and D, see next page (1150).

§ 490. THE PERILOUS CHARACTER OF THE LAST DAYS.

CHAP. 3.

are able to make thee wise unto salvation through faith which is in Christ Jesus.

16 [e]All Scripture *is* given by inspiration of God, [f]and *is* profitable for doctrine, for reproof, for correction, for instruction in righteousness:

17 [g]That the man of God may be perfect, [4h]thoroughly furnished unto all good works.

CHAP. 3.

C

II Tim. 1. 13. *See b, B, § 486, page 1140.*

D

John 5. 39. *See d, D, § 38, page 115.*

E

Luke 1. 70 As he spake by the mouth of his holy prophets, which have been since the world began :

§ 491. A SOLEMN CHARGE TO FULFIL

4: 1–8.

1 I [a]charge *thee* therefore before God, and the Lord Jesus Christ, [b]who shall judge the quick and the dead at his appearing and his kingdom ;

2 Preach the word ; be instant in season out of season ; reprove, [c]rebuke, [d]exhort with all longsuffering and doctrine.

3 [e]For the time will come when they will not endure [f]sound doctrine; [g]but after their own lusts shall they heap to themselves teachers, having itching ears ;

4 And they shall turn away *their* ears from the truth, and [h]shall be turned unto fables.

5 But watch thou in all things, [i]endure afflictions, do the work of [k]an evangelist, [l]make full proof of thy ministry.

6 For [l]I am now ready to be offered, and the time of [m]my departure is at hand.

7 [n]I have fought a good fight, I have finished *my* course, I have kept the faith :

8 Henceforth there is laid up for me [o]a crown of righteousness, which the Lord, the righteous judge, shall give me [p]at that day : and not to me only, but unto all them also that love his appearing.

A

I Tim. 5. 21 I Charge *thee* before God, and the Lord Jesus Christ, and the elect angels, that thou observe these things without perferring one before another, doing nothing by partiality.

I Tim. 6. 13 I give thee charge in the sight of God, who quickeneth all things, and *before* Christ Jesus, who before Pontius Pilate witnessed a good confession;

II Tim. 2. 14 Of these things put *them* in remembrance, charging *them* before the Lord that they strive not about words to no profit, *but* to the subverting of the hearers.

B

Acts. 10. 42 And he commanded us to preach unto the people, and to testify that it is he which was ordained of God *to be* the Judge of quick and dead.

C

I Tim. 5. 20 Them that sin rebuke before all, that others also may fear.

Tit. 1. 13 This witness is true. Wherefore rebuke them sharply, that they may be sound in the faith;

Tit. 2. 15 These things speak, and exhort, and rebuke with all authority. Let no man despise thee.

D

I Tim. 4. 13 Till I come, give attendance to reading, to exhortation to doctrine.

E

II Tim. 3. 1 This know also, that in the last days perilous times shall come.

F

I Tim. 1. 10 For whoremongers, for them that defile themselves with mankind, for menstealers, for liars, for perjured persons, and if there be any other thing that is contrary to sound doctrine;

TIMOTHY EXHORTED TO STEADFASTNESS (Concluded).

E—Concluded.

IIPet. 1. 21 For the prophecy came not in old time by the will of man: but holy men of God spake *as they were* moved by the Holy Ghost.

F

Rom. 15. 4 For whatsoever things were written aforetime were written for our learning, that we through patience and comfort of the Scriptures might have hope.

G

ITim. 6. 11 But thou, O man of God, flee these things; and follow after righteousness, godliness, faith, love, patience, meekness.

4

Or, *perfected.*

H

IITim. 2. 21 If a man therefore purge himself from these, he shall be a vessel unto honour, sanctified, and meet for the master's use, *and* prepared unto every good work.

FAITHFUL MINISTRY.

G

IITim. 3. 6 For of this sort are they which creep into houses and lead captive silly women laden with sins, led away with divers lusts,

H

I Tim. 1. 4. *See c, C, § 473, page 1118.*

I

IITim. 1. 8 Be not thou therefore ashamed of the testimony of our Lord, nor of me his prisoner: but be thou partaker of the afflictions of the gospel according to the power of God;

IITim. 2. 3 Thou therefore endure hardness, as a good soldier of Jesus Christ.

K

Acts. 21. 8 And the next *day* we that were of Paul's company departed, and came unto Cæsarea, and we entered into the house of Philip the evangelist, which was *one* of the seven; and abode with him.

Eph. 4. 11 And he gave some, apostles; and some, prophets; and some, evangelists; and some, pastors and teachers;

I Tim. 4. 12 Let no man despise thy youth; but be thou an example of the believers, in word, in conversation, in charity, in spirit, in faith, in purity.

I Tim. 4. 15 Meditate upon these things; give thyself wholly to them; that thy profiting may appear to all.

1

Or, *fulfilled.*

Rom. 15. 19 Through mighty signs and wonders, by the power of the Spirit of God; so that from Jerusalem, and round about Illyricum, I have fully preached the gospel of Christ.

Col. 1. 25 Whereof I am made a minister, according to the dispensation of God which is given to me for you, to fulfil the word of God;

L

Phil. 2. 17 Yea, and if I be offered upon the sacrifice and service of your faith, I joy, and rejoice with you all.

M

Phil. 1. 23 For I am in a strait betwixt two, having a desire to depart, and to be with Christ; which is far better:

IIPet. 1. 14 Knowing that shortly I must put off *this* my tabernacle, even as our Lord Jesus Christ hath shewed me.

N

1 Cor. 9. 24, 25. *See o, O, § 365, page 926.*

O

Prov. 4. 9 She shall give to thine head an ornament of grace: a crown of glory shall she deliver to thee.

I Cor. 9. 25 And every man that striveth for the mastery is temperate in all things. Now they *do it* to obtain a corruptible crown; but we an incorruptible.

Jas. 1. 12 Blessed *is* the man that endureth temptation: for when he is tried, he shall receive the crown of life, which the Lord hath promised to them that love him.

I Pet 5. 4 And when the chief Shepherd shall appear, ye shall receive a crown of glory that fadeth not away.

Rev. 2. 10 Fear none of those things which thou shalt suffer: behold, the devil shall cast *some* of you into prison, that ye may be tried; and ye shall have tribulation ten days: be thou faithful unto death, and I will give thee a crown of life.

Rev. 4. 4 And round about the throne *were* four and twenty seats: and upon the seats I saw four and twenty elders sitting, clothed in white raiment; and they had on their heads crowns of gold.

P

II Tim. 1. 12. *See a, A, § 486, page 1140.*

§ 492. TIMOTHY REQUIRED TO COME TO

4 : 9–18.

9 Do thy diligence to come shortly
unto me:
10 For [a]Demas hath forsaken me,
[b]having loved this present world, and
is departed unto Thessalonica; Crescens to Galatia, Titus unto Dalmatia.
11 Only [c]Luke is with me. Take
[d]Mark, and bring him with thee: for
he is profitable to me for the ministry.
12 And [e]Tychicus have I sent to
Ephesus.
13 The cloak that I left at Troas
with Carpus, when thou comest,
bring *with thee*, and the books, *but*
especially the parchments.
14 [f]Alexander the coppersmith did
me much evil: the [g]Lord reward him
according to his works:
15 Of whom be thou ware also;
for he hath greatly withstood [1]our
words.
16 At my first answer no man stood
with me, [h]but all *men* forsook me:
[i]*I pray God* that it may not be laid
to their charge.
17 [k]Notwithstanding the Lord stood
with me, and strengthened me; [l]that

CHAP. 4.

by me the preaching might be fully
known, and *that* all the Gentiles
might hear: and I was delivered
[m]out of the mouth of the lion.
18 [n]And the Lord shall deliver me
from every evil work, and will preserve *me* unto his heavenly kingdom:
[o]to whom *be* glory for ever and ever.
Amen.

A

Col. 4. 14. *See k, K, § 456, page 1092.*

B

1 Jno. 2. 15 Love not the world, neither the things *that are* in the world. If any man love the world, the love of the Father is not in him.

C

Col. 4. 14. *See i, I, § 456, page 1092.*

D

Acts 12. 25 And Barnabas and Saul returned from Jerusalem, when they had fulfilled *their* ministry, and took with them John, whose surname was Mark.

Acts 15. 27 And Barnabas determined to take with them John, whose surname was Mark.

Col. 4. 10 Aristarchus my fellow prisoner saluteth you, and Marcus, sister's son to Barnabas, (touching whom ye received commandments: if he come unto you, receive him;)

E

Acts 20. 4 And there accompanied him into Asia Sopater of Berea; and of the

§ 493. CONCLUDING SALUTATIONS

4 : 19–22.

19 Salute [a]Prisca and Aquila, and
[b]the household of Onesiphorus.
20 [c]Erastus abode at Corinth: but
[d]Trophimus have I left at Miletum
sick.
21 [e]Do thy diligence to come before winter. Eubulus greeteth thee,
and Pudens, and Linus, and Claudia,
and all the brethren.

CHAP. 4.

22 [f]The Lord Jesus Christ *be* with
thy spirit. Grace *be* with you. Amen.

A

Acts 18. 2 And found a certain Jew named Aquila, born in Pontus, lately come from Italy, with his wife Priscilla; (because that Claudius had commanded all Jews to depart from Rome:) and came unto them.

Rom. 16. 3 Greet Priscilla and Aquila, my helpers in Christ Jesus:

ROME. CONCERNING PAUL'S TRIAL.

E—CONCLUDED.

Thessalonians, Aristarchus and Secundus; and Gaius of Derbe, and Timotheus; and of Asia, Tychicus and Trophimus.

Eph. 6. 21 But that ye also may know my affairs, *and* how I do, Tychicus, a beloved brother and faithful minister in the Lord, shall make known to you all things:

Col. 4. 7 All my state shall Tychicus declare unto you, *who is* a beloved brother, and a faithful minister and fellow servant in the Lord:

Tit. 3. 12 When I shall send Artemas unto thee, or Tychicus, be diligent to come unto me to Nicopolis: for I have determined there to winter.

F

Acts 19. 33 And they drew Alexander out of the multitude, the Jews putting him forward. And Alexander beckoned with the hand, and would have made his defence unto the people.

I Tim. 1. 20 Of whom is Hymeneus and Alexander; whom I have delivered unto Satan, that they may learn not to blaspheme.

G

II Sa. 3. 39 And I *am* this day weak, though anointed king; and these men the sons of Zeruiah *be* too hard for me: the LORD shall reward the doer of evil according to his wickedness.

Ps. 28. 4 Give them according to their deeds, and according to the wickedness of their endeavours: give them after the work of their hands; render to them their desert.

Rev. 18. 6 Reward her even as she rewarded you, and double unto her double according to her works: in the cup which she hath filled, fill to her double.

1

Or, *our preachings.*

H

II Tim. 1. 15. *See b, B, § 487, page 1142.*

I

Acts 7. 60 And he kneeled down, and cried with a loud voice, Lord, lay not this sin to their charge. And when he had said this, he fell asleep.

K

Matt. 10. 19 But when they deliver you up, take no thought how or what ye shall speak: for it shall be given you in that same hour what ye shall speak.

Acts 23. 11 And the night following the Lord stood by him, and said, Be of good cheer, Paul: for as thou hast testified of me in Jerusalem, so must thou bear witness also at Rome.

Acts 27. 23 For there stood by me this night the angel of God, whose I am, and whom I serve.

L

Acts 9. 15. *See l, L, § 251, page 684.*

M

Ps. 22. 21 Save me from the lion's mouth: for thou hast heard me from the horns of the unicorns.

II Pet. 2. 9 The Lord knoweth how to deliver the godly out of temptations, and to reserve the unjust unto the day of judgment to be punished:

N

Ps. 121. 7 The LORD shall preserve thee from all evil: he shall preserve thy soul.

O

Rom. 11. 36. *See r, R, § 341, page 866.*

AND BENEDICTION.

B

II Tim. 1. 16 The Lord give mercy unto the the house of Onesiphorus; for he oft refreshed me, and was not ashamed of my chain:

C

Acts 19. 22 So he sent into Macedonia two of them that ministered unto him, Timotheus and Erastus; but he himself stayed in Asia for a season.

Rom 16. 23 Gaius mine host, and of the whole church, saluteth you. Erastus the chamberlain of the city saluteth you, and Quartus a brother.

D

Acts 20. 4. *See under E, § 492.*

Acts 21. 29 (For they had seen before with him in the city Trophimus an Ephesian, whom they supposed that Paul had brought into the temple.)

E

II Tim. 4. 9. *See text of topic, § 492.*

F

Gal. 6. 18 Brethren, the grace of our Lord Jesus Christ *be* with your spirit. Amen,

Phile. 25 The grace of our Lord Jesus Christ *be* with your spirit. Amen.

§ 494. SALUTATION.

1 : 1–4.

1 Paul, a servant of God, and an
apostle of Jesus Christ, according to
the faith of God's elect, [a]and the
acknowledging of the truth [b]which is
after godliness;
2 [1c]In hope of eternal life, which
God, [d]that cannot lie, promised [e]be-
fore the world began;
3 [f]But hath in due times manifested
his word through preaching, [g]which
is committed unto me [h]according
to the commandment of God our
Saviour;
4 To [i]Titus, [k]*mine* own son after
[l]the common faith: [m]Grace, mercy,
and peace, from God the Father and
the Lord Jesus Christ our Saviour.

A

II Tim. 2. 25 In meekness instructing those that oppose themselves; if God peradventure will give them repentance to the acknowledging of the truth;

B

I Tim. 3. 16 And without controversy great is the mystery of godliness: God was manifest in the flesh, justified in the Spirit, seen of angels, preached unto the Gentiles, believed on in the world, received up into glory.

I Tim. 6. 3 If any man teach otherwise, and consent not to wholesome words, *even* the words of our Lord Jesus Christ, and to the doctrine which is according to godliness;

1

Or, For.

C

II Tim. 1. 1. *See b, B, § 485, page 1138.*

Tit. 3. 7 That being justified by his grace, we should be made heirs according to the hope of eternal life.

D

Num. 23. 19 God *is* not a man, that he should lie; neither the son of man, that he should repent: hath he said, and shall he not do *it?* or hath he spoken, and shall he not make it good?

I Sa. 15. 29 And also the Strength of Israel will not lie nor repent: for he *is* not a man, that he should repent.

Ps. 89. 35 Once have I sworn by my holiness that I will not lie unto David.

§ 495. PAUL'S CHARGE TO TITUS IN

1 : 5–9.

5 For this cause left I thee in
Crete, that thou shouldest [a]set in
order the things that are [1]wanting,
and [b]ordain elders in every city, as
I had appointed thee:
6 [c]If any be blameless, [d]the husband
of one wife, [e]having faithful children
not accused of riot or unruly.
7 For a bishop must be blameless,
as [f]the steward of God; not selfwilled, not soon angry, [g]not given
to wine, no striker, [h]not given to
filthy lucre;

A

I Cor. 11. 34 And if any man hunger, let him eat at home; that ye come not together unto condemnation. And the rest will I set in order when I come.

1

Or, *left undone.*

B

Acts 14. 23. *See f, F, § 266, page 724.*

II Tim. 2. 2 And the things that thou hast heard of me among many witnesses, the same commit thou to faithful men, who shall be able to teach others also.

C

I Tim. 3. 2. *See d, D, § 476, page 1124.*

D

I Tim. 3. 12 Let the deacons be the husbands of one wife, ruling their children and their own houses well.

TO TITUS.

Written probably during Autumn of A. D. 67, at Ephesus.

D—CONCLUDED.

Hab. 2. 3 For the vision *is* yet for an appointed time, but at the end it shall speak, and not lie: though it tarry, wait for it; because it will surely come, it will not tarry.

Mal. 3. 6 For I *am* the LORD, I change not; therefore ye sons of Jacob are not consumed.

Luke 21. 33 Heaven and earth shall pass away: but my words shall not pass away.

Rom. 11. 29 For the gifts and calling of God *are* without repentance.

Heb. 6. 18 That by two immutable things, in which *it was* impossible for God to lie, we might have a strong consolation, who have fled for refuge to lay hold upon the hope set before us:

E

II Tim. 1. 9. *See s, S, § 486, page 1140.*

F

II Tim. 1. 10. *See t, T, § 486, page 1140.*

G

I Cor. 1. 17. *See a, A, § 365, page 924.*

H

Acts 9. 15. *See l, L, § 251, page 684.*

I

II Cor. 2. 13 I had no rest in my spirit, because I found not Titus my brother: but taking my leave of them, I went from thence into Macedonia.

I—CONCLUDED.

II Cor. 7. 13 Therefore we were comforted in your comfort: yea, and exceedingly the more joyed we for the joy of Titus, because his spirit was refreshed by you all.

II Cor. 8. 6 Insomuch that we desired Titus, that as he had begun, so he would also finish in you the same grace also.

II Cor. 8. 16 But thanks *be* to God, which put the same earnest care into the heart of Titus for you.

II Cor. 8. 23 Whether *any do inquire* of Titus, *he is* my partner and fellow helper concerning you: or our brethren *be inquired of*, *they are* the messengers of the churches, *and* the glory of Christ.

II Cor. 12. 18 I desired Titus, and with *him* I sent a brother. Did Titus make a gain of you? walked we not in the same spirit? *walked we* not in the same steps?

Gal. 2. 3 But neither Titus, who was with me, being a Greek, was compelled to be circumcised:

K

I Tim. 1. 2. *See e, E, § 472. page 1118.*

L

Rom. 1. 12. *See g, G, § 318, page 810.*

M

II Cor. 1. 2. *See c, C, § 385, page 962.*

CRETE. CONCERNING BISHOPS.

E

I Tim. 3. 4 One that ruleth well his own house, having his children in subjection with all gravity;

I Tim. 3. 12. *See under D.*

F

Matt. 24. 45. *See c, C, § 174, page 494.*

G

Lev. 10. 9 Do not drink wine nor strong drink, thou, nor thy sons with thee, when ye go into the tabernacle of the congregation, lest ye die: *it shall be* a statute for ever throughout your generations:

Eph. 5. 18 And be not drunk with wine, wherein is excess; but be filled with the Spirit;

I Tim. 3. 3 Not given to wine, no striker, not greedy of filthy lucre; but patient, not a brawler, not covetous;

G—CONCLUDED.

I Tim. 3. 8 Likewise *must* the deacons *be* grave, not doubletongued, not given to much wine, not greedy of filthy lucre;

H

Isa. 56. 11 Yea, *they are* greedy dogs *which* can never have enough, and they *are* shepherds *that* cannot understand: they all look to their own way, every one for his gain, from his quarter.

I Tim. 3. 3, 8. *See under G.*

I Pet. 5. 2 Feed the flock of God which is among you, taking the oversight *thereof*, not by constraint, but willingly; not for filthy lucre, but of a ready mind;

I

I Tim. 3. 2 A bishop then must be blameless, the husband of one wife, vigilant, sober, of good behaviour, given to hospitality, apt to teach;

§ 495. PAUL'S CHARGE TO TITUS IN CRETE

CHAP. 1.

8 [i]But a lover of hospitality, a lover
of [2]good men, sober, just, holy, temperate;
9 [k]Holding fast [l]the faithful word
[3]as he hath been taught, that he may
be able [m]by sound doctrine both to exhort and to convince the gainsayers.

For I, see preceding p e (1155).

2

Or, *good things*.

K

II Thes. 2. 15 Therefore, brethren, stand fast, and hold the traditions which ye have been taught, whether by word, or our epistle.

II Tim. 1. 13 Hold fast the form of sound words, which thou hast heard of me, in faith and love which is in Christ Jesus.

§ 496. CONCERNING CRETIANS AND

1: 10–16.

10 For [a]there are many unruly and
vain talkers and [b]deceivers, [c]specially
they of the circumcision:
11 Whose mouths must be stopped,
[d]who subvert whole houses, teaching
things which they ought not, [e]for
filthy lucre's sake.
12 [f]One of themselves, *even* a
prophet of their own, said, The Cretians *are* alway liars, evil beasts, slow
bellies.
13 This witness is true. [g]Wherefore rebuke them sharply, that they
may be [h]sound in the faith;
14 [i]Not giving heed to Jewish fables,
and [k]commandments of men, that
turn from the truth.
15 [l]Unto the pure all things *are*
pure: but [m]unto them that are defiled
and unbelieving *is* nothing pure; but
even their mind and conscience is defiled.
16 They profess that they know God;

CHAP. 1.

but [n]in works they deny *him*, being abominable, and disobedient, [o]and unto every good work [1]reprobate.

A

I Tim. 1. 6 From which some having swerved have turned aside unto vain jangling;

B

Rom. 16. 18 For they that are such serve not our Lord Jesus Christ, but their own belly; and by good words and fair speeches deceive the hearts of the simple.

C

Acts 15. 1 And certain men which came down from Judea taught the brethren, *and said*, Except ye be circumcised after the manner of Moses, ye cannot be saved.

D

Matt. 23. 14. *See s, S, § 167, page 464.*

E

I Tim. 6. 5 Perverse disputings of men of corrupt minds, and destitute of the truth, supposing that gain is godliness: from such withdraw thyself.

F

Acts 17. 28 For in him we live, and move, and have our being; as certain also of your own poets have said, For we are also his offspring.

§ 497. INSTRUCTIONS CONCERNING THE AGED, YOUNG

2: 1–15.

1 But speak thou the things which
become [a]sound doctrine:
2 That the aged men be [1]sober,
grave, temperate, [b]sound in faith,
in charity, in patience.

CHAP. 2.

3 [c]The aged women likewise, that
they be in behaviour as becometh [2]holiness, not [3]false accusers, not given

A

I Tim. 1. 10. *See l, L, § 473, page 1118.*

CONCERNING BISHOPS (CONCLUDED).

L

I Tim. 1. 15 This *is* a faithful saying, and worthy of all acceptation, that Christ Jesus came into the world to save sinners; of whom I am chief.

I Tim. 4. 9 This *is* a faithful saying, and worthy of all acceptation.

II Tim. 2. 11 *It is* a faithful saying: For if we be dead with *him*, we shall also live with *him:*

3

Or, *in teaching.*

M

II Tim. 4. 3 For the time will come when they will not endure sound doctrine; but after their own lusts shall they heap to themselves teachers, having itching ears;

Tit. 2. 1 But speak thou the things which become sound doctrine:

FALSE TEACHINGS AMONG THEM.

G

II Cor. 13. 10 Therefore I write these things being absent, lest being present I should use sharpness, according to the power which the Lord hath given me to edification, and not to destruction.

II Tim. 4. 2 Preach the word; be instant in season, out of season; reprove, rebuke, exhort with all longsuffering and doctrine.

H

Tit. 2. 2 That the aged men be sober, grave, temperate, sound in faith, in charity, in patience.

I

I Tim. 1. 4. *See c, C, § 473, page 1118.*

K

Isa. 29. 13 Wherefore the Lord said, Forasmuch as this people draw near *me* with their mouth, and with their lips do honour me, but have removed their heart far from me, and their fear toward me is taught by the precept of men :

Col. 2. 22. *See m, M, § 453, page 1086.*

L

Luke 11. 39 And the Lord said unto him, Now do ye Pharisees make clean the outside of the cup and the platter; but your inward part is full of ravening and wickedness.

40 *Ye* fools, did not he that made that which is without make that which is within also?

L—CONCLUDED.

Luke 11. 41 But rather give alms of such things as ye have; and, behold, all things are clean unto you.

Acts 10. 15. *See l, L, § 254, page 692.*

Rom. 14. 14 I know, and am persuaded by the Lord Jesus, that *there is* nothing unclean of itself: but to him that esteemeth any thing to be unclean, to him *it is* unclean.

I Cor. 6. 12 All things are lawful unto me, but all things are not expedient: all things are lawful for me, but I will not be brought under the power of any.

I Cor. 10. 23 All things are lawful for me, but all things are not expedient: all things are lawful for me, but all things edify not.

24 Let no man seek his own, but every man another's *wealth.*

25 Whatsoever is sold in the shambles, *that* eat, asking no question for conscience sake:

M

Rom. 14. 23 And he that doubteth is damned if he eat, because *he eateth* not of faith: for whatsoever *is* not of faith is sin.

N

I Tim. 5. 8. *See l, L, § 479, page 1130.*

O

II. Tim. 3. 8. *See r, R, § 490, page 1148.*

1

Or, *void of judgment.*

AND SERVANTS. MOTIVE FOR GODLINESS.

1

Or, *vigilant.*

B

Tit. 1. 13. *See text of topic, § 496.*

C

im. 2. 9 In like manner also, that women adorn themselves in modest apparel, with shamefacedness and sobriety; not

C—CONTINUED.

with broided hair, or gold, or pearls, or costly array;

I Tim. 2. 10 But (which becometh women professing godliness) with good works.

I Tim. 3. 11 Even so *must their* wives *be* grave, not slanderers, sober, faithful in all things.

For C, concluded 2 and 3, see next page 1158.

§ 497. INSTRUCTIONS CONCERNING THE AGED, YOUNG AND

CHAP. 2.

to much wine, teachers of good things;

4 That they may teach the young women to be [4]sober, [d]to love their husbands, to love their children,

5 *To be* discreet, chaste, keepers at home, good, [e]obedient to their own husbands, [f]that the word of God be not blasphemed.

6 Young men likewise exhort to be [5]soberminded.

7 [g]In all things shewing thyself a pattern of good works: in doctrine *shewing* uncorruptness, gravity, [h]sincerity,

8 [i]Sound speech, that cannot be condemned; [k]that he that is of the contrary part [l]may be ashamed, having no evil thing to say of you.

9 *Exhort* [m]servants to be obedient unto their own masters, *and* to please *them* well [n]in all *things*; not [6]answering again;

10 Not purloining, but shewing all good fidelity; [o]that they may adorn the doctrine of God our Saviour in all things.

11 For [p]the grace of God [7]that bringeth salvation [q]hath appeared to all men,

12 Teaching us [r]that, denying un-

C—CONCLUDED.

I Pet. 3. 3 Whose adorning let it not be that outward *adorning* of plaiting the hair, and of wearing of gold, or of putting on of apparel;

4 But *let it be* the hidden man of the heart, in that which is not corruptible, *even the ornament* of a meek and quiet spirit, which is in the sight of God of great price.

2

Or, *holy women.*

3

Or, *makebates,*

4

Or, *wise.*

D

I Tim. 5. 14 I will therefore that the younger women marry, bear children, guide the house, give none occasion to the adversary to speak reproachfully.

E

Eph. 5. 22. *See a, A,* § *435, page 1052.*

I Tim. 2. 11 Let the woman learn in silence with all subjection.

F

Rom. 2. 24 For the name of God is blasphemed among the Gentiles through you, as it is written.

I Tim. 6. 1 Let as many servants as are under the yoke count their own masters worthy of all honour, that the name of God and *his* doctrine be not blasphemed.

5

Or, *discreet.*

G

I Tim. 4. 12 Let no man despise thy youth; but be thou an example of the believers, in word, in conversation, in charity, in spirit, in faith, in purity.

I Pet. 5. 3 Neither as being lords over *God's* heritage, but being ensamples to the flock.

H

Eph. 6. 24 Grace *be* with all them that love our Lord Jesus Christ in sincerity. Amen.

I

I Tim. 6. 3 If any man teach otherwise, and consent not to wholesome words, *even* the words of our Lord Jesus Christ, and to the doctrine which is according to godliness;

K

Neh. 5. 9 Also I said, It *is* not good that ye do: ought ye not to walk in the fear of our God because of the reproach of the heathen our enemies?

I Tim. 5. 14. *See under D.*

I Pet. 2. 12 Having your conversation honest among the Gentiles: that, whereas they speak against you as evil doers, they may by *your* good works, which they shall behold, glorify God in the day of visitation.

I Pet. 2. 15 For so is the will of God, that with well doing ye may put to silence the ignorance of foolish men:

I Pet. 3. 16 Having a good conscience; that, whereas they speak evil of you, as of evil doers, they may be ashamed that falsely accuse your good conversation in Christ.

SERVANTS. MOTIVE FOR GODLINESS (CONTINUED).

L

IIThes. 3. 14 And if any man obey not our word by this epistle, note that man, and have no company with him, that he may be ashamed.

M

Eph. 6. 5. *See e, E, § 436, page 1054.*

N

Eph. 5. 24 Therefore as the church is subject unto Christ, so *let* the wives *be* to their own husbands in every thing.

6

Or, *gainsaying.*

O

Matt. 5. 16 Let your light so shine before men, that they may see your good works, and glorify your Father which is in heaven.

Phil. 2. 15 That ye may be blameless and harmless, the sons of God, without rebuke, in the midst of a crooked and perverse nation, among whom ye shine as lights in the world;

P

Rom. 5. 15 But not as the offence, so also *is* the free gift. For if through the offence of one many be dead, much more the grace of God, and the gift by grace, *which is* by one man, Jesus Christ, hath abounded unto many.

Tit. 3. 4 But after that the kindness and love of God our Saviour toward man appeared,

5 Not by works of righteousness which we have done, but according to his mercy he saved us, by the washing of regeneration, and renewing of the Holy Ghost;

6 Which he shed on us abundantly through Jesus Christ our Saviour;

I Pet. 5. 12 By Sylvanus, a faithful brother unto you, as I suppose, I have written briefly, exhorting, and testifying that this is the true grace of God wherein ye stand.

7

Or, *that bringeth salvation to all men, hath appeared.*

Q

Luke 3. 6. *See z, Z, § 14, page 47.*

John 1. 9 *That* was the true Light, which lighteth every man that cometh into the world.

ITim. 2. 4 Who will have all men to be saved, and to come unto the knowledge of the truth.

R

Eph. 1. 4. *See d,D, § 426, page 1030.*

Rom. 6. 19 I speak after the manner of men because of the infirmity of your flesh: for as ye have yielded your members servants to uncleanness and to iniquity unto iniquity; even so now yield your members servants to righteousness unto holiness.

S

IPet. 4. 2 That he no longer should live the rest of *his* time in the flesh to the lusts of men, but the will of God.

I Jno. 2. 16 For all that *is* in the world, the lust of the flesh, and the lust of the eyes, and the pride of life, is not of the Father, but is of the world.

T

I Cor. 1. 7. *See d, D, § 349, page 888.*

U

Acts 24. 15 And have hope toward God, which they themselves also allow, that there shall be a resurrection of the dead, both of the just and unjust.

Col. 1. 5 For the hope which is laid up for you in heaven, whereof ye heard before in the word of the truth of the gospel;

Col. 1. 23 If ye continue in the faith grounded and settled, and *be* not moved away from the hope of the gospel, which ye have heard, *and* which was preached to every creature which is under heaven: whereof I Paul am made a minister;

Tit. 1. 2 In hope of eternal life, which God, that cannot lie, promised before the world began;

Tit. 3. 7 That being justified by his grace, we should be made heirs according to the hope of eternal life.

X

Col. 3. 4 When Christ, *who is* our life, shall appear, then shall ye also appear with him in glory.

IITim. 4. 1 I charge *thee* therefore before God, and the Lord Jesus Christ, who shall judge the quick and the dead at his appearing and his kingdom;

IITim. 4. 8 Henceforth there is laid up for me a crown of righteousness, which the Lord, the righteous judge, shall give me at that day: and not to me only, but unto all them also that love his appearing.

Heb. 9. 28 So Christ was once offered to bear the sins of many; and unto them that look for him shall he appear the second time without sin unto salvation.

§697. INSTRUCTIONS CONCERNING THE AGED, YOUNG AND

CHAP. 2.

godliness [s]and wordly lusts, we should live soberly, righteously, and godly, in this present world ;

13 [t]Looking for that blessed [u]hope, and the glorious [x]appearing of the great God and our Saviour Jesus Christ ;

14 [y]Who gave himself for us, that he might redeem us from all iniquity, [z]and purify unto himself [a]a peculiar people, [b]zealous of good works.

15 These things speak, and [c]exhort, and rebuke with all authority. [d]Let no man despise thee.

For S, T, U, and X, see preceding page (1159).

X—CONCLUDED.

I Pet. 1. 7 That the trial of your faith, being much more precious than of gold that perisheth, though it be tried with fire, might be found unto praise and honour and glory at the appearing of Jesus Christ:

I Jno. 3. 2 Beloved, now are we the sons of God, and it doth not yet appear what we shall be: but we know that, when he shall appear, we shall be like him; for we shall see him as he is.

Y

Matt. 20. 28. *See y, Y, § 148, page 420.*

Z

Heb. 9. 14 How much more shall the blood of Christ, who through the eternal Spirit offered himself without spot to God, purge your conscience from dead works to serve the living God?

§ 498. SUNDRY INSTRUCTIONS AND

3 : 1–11.

1 Put them in mind [a]to be subject to principalities and powers, to obey magistrates, [b]to be ready to every good work,

2 [c]To speak evil of no man, [d]to be no brawlers, *but* [e]gentle, shewing all [f]meekness unto all men.

3 For [g]we ourselves also were sometimes foolish, disobedient, deceived, serving divers lusts and pleasures, living in malice and envy, hateful, *and* hating one another.

4 But after that [h]the kindness and [1]love of [i]God our Saviour toward man appeared,

5 [k]Not by works of righteousness which we have done, but according to his mercy he saved us, by [l]the washing of regeneration, and renewing of the Holy Ghost ;

6 [m]Which he shed on us [2]abundantly through Jesus Christ our Saviour ;

A

Rom. 13. 1. *See a, A, § 343, page 872.*

B

Col. 1. 10. *See g, G, § 448, page 1078.*

C

Eph. 4. 31 Let all bitterness, and wrath, and anger, and clamour, and evil speaking, be put away from you, with all malice:

32 And be ye kind one to another, tenderhearted, forgiving one another, even as God for Christ's sake hath forgiven you.

II Tim. 2. 21 If a man therefore purge himself from these, he shall be a vessel unto honour, sanctified, and meet for the master's use, *and* prepared unto every good work.

D

II Tim. 2. 24 And the servant of the Lord must not strive; but be gentle unto all *men*, apt to teach, patient,

25 In meekness instructing those that oppose themselves; if God peradventure will give them repentance to the acknowledging of the truth;

E

Phil. 4. 5 Let your moderation be known unto all men. The Lord *is* at hand.

F

Eph. 4. 2. *See c, C, § 432, page 1040.*

G

I Cor. 6. 11. *See g, G, § 360, page 910.*

SERVANTS. MOTIVE FOR GODLINESS (CONCLUDED).

A

Deut. 7. 6 For thou *art* a holy people unto the LORD thy God: the LORD thy God hath chosen thee to be a special people unto himself, above all people that *are* upon the face of the earth.

Deut. 14. 2 For thou *art* a holy people unto the LORD thy God, and the LORD hath chosen thee to be a peculiar people unto himself, above all the nations that *are* upon the earth.

Deut. 26. 18 And the LORD hath avouched thee this day to be his peculiar people, as he hath promised thee, and that *thou* shouldest keep all his commandments;

I Pet. 2. 9 But ye *are* a chosen generation, a royal priesthood, a holy nation, a peculiar people; that ye should shew forth the praises of him who hath called you out of darkness into his marvellous light:

B

Eph. 2. 10 For we are his workmanship, created in Christ Jesus unto good works, which God hath before ordained that we should walk in them.

Tit. 3. 8 *This is* a faithful saying, and these things I will that thou affirm constantly, that they which have believed in God might be careful to maintain good works. These things are good and profitable unto men.

C

II Tim. 4. 2 Preach the word; be instant in season, out of season; reprove, rebuke, exhort with all longsuffering and doctrine.

D

I Tim. 4. 12 Let no man despise thy youth; but be thou an example of the believers, in word, in conversation, in charity, in spirit, in faith, in purity.

EXHORTATIONS TO MAINTAIN GOOD WORKS.

G—CONCLUDED.

Col. 1. 21 And you, that were sometime alienated and enemies in *your* mind by wicked works, yet now hath he reconciled.

I Pet. 4. 3 For the time past of *our* life may suffice us to have wrought the will of the Gentiles, when we walked in lasciviousness, lusts, excess of wine, revelings, banquetings, and abominable idolatries:

H

Tit. 2. 11 For the grace of God that bringeth salvation hath appeared to all men,

1

Or, *pity.*

I

I Tim. 1. 1. *See b, B, § 472, page 1118.*

K

Rom. 3. 20. *See c, C, § 324, page 824.*

Rom. 9. 11 (For *the children* being not yet born, neither having done any good or evil, that the purpose of God according to election might stand, not of works, but of him that calleth;)

Rom. 11. 6 And if by grace, then *is it* no more of works: otherwise grace is no more grace. But if *it be* of works, then is it no more grace: otherwise work is no more work.

II Tim. 1. 9 Who hath saved us, and called *us* with a holy calling, not according to our works, but according to his own purpose and grace, which was given us in Christ Jesus before the world began,

L

John 1. 16 And of his fulness have all we received, and grace for grace.

Acts 2. 17. *See b, B, § 231, page 636.*

Acts 2. 33 Therefore being by the right hand of God exalted, and having received of the Father the promise of the Holy Ghost, he hath shed forth this, which ye now see and hear.

Acts 10. 45 And they of the circumcision which believed were astonished, as many as came with Peter, because that on the Gentiles also was poured out the gift of the Holy Ghost.

Rom. 5. 5 And hope maketh not ashamed; because the love of God is shed abroad in our hearts by the Holy Ghost which is given unto us.

M

Rom. 3. 24 Being justified freely by his grace through the redemption that is in Christ Jesus.

Gal. 2. 16 Knowing that a man is not justified by the works of the law, but by the faith of Jesus Christ, even we have believed in Jesus Christ, that we might be justified by the faith of Christ, and not by the works of the law: for by the works of the law shall no flesh be justified.

2

Gr. *richly.*

§ 498. SUNDRY INSTRUCTIONS AND EXHORTATIONS

CHAP. 3.

7 [n]That being justified by his grace, [o]we should be made heirs [p]according to the hope of eternal life.

8 [q]*This is* a faithful saying, and these things I will that thou affirm constantly, that they which have believed in God might be careful [r]to maintain good works. These things are good and profitable unto men.

9 [s]But avoid foolish questions, and genealogies, and contentions, and strivings about the law; [t]for they are unprofitable and vain.

10 A man that is a heretic [u]after the first and second admonition [x]reject;

11 Knowing that he that is such is subverted, and sinneth, [y]being condemned of himself.

N—CONCLUDED, See preceding page (1161).

Tit. 2. 11 For the grace of God that bringeth salvation hath appeared to all men.

O

Rom. 8. 17 And if children, then heirs; heirs with God, and joint heirs with Christ; if so be that we suffer with *him*, that we may be also glorified together.

Rom. 8. 23 And not only *they*, but ourselves also, which have the first fruits of the Spirit, even we ourselves groan within ourselves, waiting for the adoption, *to wit*, the redemption of our body.

P

Tit. 1. 2 In hope of eternal life, which God, that cannot lie, promised before the world began;

Q

I Tim. 1. 15. *See i, I, § 474, page 1120.*

R

Tit. 2. 24 Who gave himself for us, that he might redeem us from all iniquity, and purify unto himself a peculiar people, zealous of good works.

Tit. 3. 1. *See text of topic.*

Tit. 3. 14. *See text of topic, § 499.*

S

I Tim. 1. 4 Neither give heed to fables and endless genealogies, which minister questions, rather than godly edifying which is in faith: *so do.*

II Tim. 2. 23 But foolish and unlearned questions avoid, knowing that they do gender strifes.

Tit. 1. 14 Not giving heed to Jewish fables, and commandments of men, that turn from the truth.

§ 499. CONCERNING TITUS' JOURNEY TO VISIT PAUL.

3:12–15.

12 When I shall send Artemas unto thee, or [a]Tychicus, be diligent to come unto me to Nicopolis: for I have determined there to winter.

13 Bring Zenas the lawyer and [b]Apollos on their journey diligently, that nothing be wanting unto them.

14 And let ours also learn [c]to [1]maintain good works for necessary uses, that they be [d]not unfruitful.

15 All that are with me salute thee. Greet them that love us in the faith. Grace *be* with you all. Amen.

A

Acts 20. 4 And there accompanied him into Asia Sopater of Berea; and of the Thessalonians, Aristarchus and Secundus: and Gaius of Derbe, and Timotheus; and of Asia, Tychicus and Trophimus.

II Tim. 4. 12 And Tychicus have I sent to Ephesus.

B

Acts 18. 24 And a certain Jew named Apollos, born at Alexandria, an eloquent man, *and* mighty in the Scriptures, came to Ephesus.

C

Tit. 3. 8. *See text of topic, § 498.*

1

Or, *profess honest trades.*

Acts 18. 3 And because he was of the same craft, he abode with them, and wrought: for by their occupation they were tentmakers.

TO MAINTAIN GOOD WORKS (CONCLUDED).

T

Job 15. 2 Should a wise man utter vain knowledge, and fill his belly with the east wind?

3 Should he reason with unprofitable talk? or with speeches wherewith he can do no good?

IITim.2. 14 Of these things put *them* in remembrance, charging *them* before the Lord that they strive not about words to no profit, *but* to the subverting of the hearers.

U

IICor 13. 2 I told you before, and foretell you, as if I were present, the second time; and being absent now I write to them which heretofore have sinned, and to all other, that, if I come again, I will not spare:

X

Matt.18. 15 Moreover if thy brother shall tresspass against thee, go and tell him his fault between thee and him alone: if he shall hear thee, thou hast gained thy brother.

16 But if he will not hear *thee*, *then* take with thee one or two more, that in the mouth of two or three witnesses every word may be established.

17 And if he shall neglect to hear them, tell *it* unto the church: but if he neglect to hear the church, let him be unto thee as a heathen man and a publican.

X—CONCLUDED.

Rom.16. 17 Now I beseech you, brethren, mark them which cause divisions and offences contrary to the doctrine which ye have learned; and avoid them.

I Cor.5. 9 I wrote unto you in an epistle not to company with fornicators:

IIThes.3. 6 Now we command you, brethren, in the name of our Lord Jesus Christ, that ye withdraw yourselves from every brother that walketh disorderly, and not after the tradition which he received of us.

IIThes.3. 14 And if any man obey not our word by this epistle, note that man, and have no company with him, that he may be ashamed.

IITim.3. 5 Having a form of godliness, but denying the power thereof: from such turn away.

II Jno. 10 If there come any unto you, and bring not this doctrine, receive him not into *your* house, neither bid him God speed:

Y

Acts 13. 46 Then Paul and Barnabas waxed bold, and said, It was neeessary that the word of God should first have been spoken to you: but seeing ye put it from you, and judge yourselves unworthy of everlasting life, lo, we turn to the Gentiles.

I Jno. 3. 20 For if our heart condemn us, God is greater than our heart, and knoweth all things.

CONCLUDING SALUTATION AND BENEDICTION.

1—CONCLUDED.

Acts 20. 35 I have shewed you all things, how that so labouring ye ought to support the weak, and to remember the words of the Lord Jesus, how he said, It is more blessed to give than to receive.

Eph. 4. 28 Let him that stole steal no more: but rather let him labour, working with *his* hands the thing which is good, that he may have to give to him that needeth.

IThes.2. 9 For ye remember, brethren, our labour and travail: for labouring night and day, because we would not be chargeable unto any of you, we preached unto you the gospel of God.

IIThes.3. 8 Neither did we eat any man's bread for nought; but wrought with labour and travail night and day, that we might not be chargeable to any of you:

D

Rom.15. 28 When therefore I have performed this, and have sealed to them this fruit, I will come by you into Spain.

Phil. 1. 11 Being filled with the fruits of righteousness, which are by Jesus Christ, unto the glory and praise of God.

Phil. 4. 17 Not because I desire a gift: but I desire fruit that may abound to your account.

Col. 1. 10 That ye might walk worthy of the Lord unto all pleasing, being fruitful in every good work, and increasing in the knowledge of God;

IIPet. 1. 8 For if these things be in you, and abound, they make *you that ye shall* neither *be* barren nor unfruitful in the knowledge of our Lord Jesus Christ.

§ 500. SALUTATION.

1–3.

1 Paul, [a]a prisoner of Jesus Christ, and Timothy *our* brother, unto Philemon our dearly beloved, [b]and fellow labourer,

2 And to *our* beloved Apphia, and [c]Archippus [d]our fellow soldier, and and to [e]the church in thy house:

3 [f]Grace to you, and peace, from God our Father and the Lord Jesus Christ.

A

Acts. 26. 29 And Paul said, I would to God, that not only thou, but also all that hear me this day, were both almost and altogether such as I am, except these bonds.

Eph. 3. 1 For this cause I Paul, the prisoner of Jesus Christ for you Gentiles,

A—CONTINUED.

Eph. 4. 1 I therefore, the prisoner of the Lord, beseech you that ye walk worthy of the vocation wherewith ye are called.

Eph. 6. 20 For which I am an ambassador in bonds; that therein I may speak boldly, as I ought to speak.

Phil. 1. 7 Even as it is meet for me to think this of you all, because I have you in my heart; inasmuch as both in my bonds, and in the defence and confirmation of the gospel, ye all are partakers of my grace.

Phil. 1. 14 And many of the brethren in the Lord, waxing confident by my bonds, are much more bold to speak the word without fear.

Phil. 1. 16 The one preach Christ of contention, not sincerely, supposing to add affliction to my bonds:

Col. 4. 3 Withal praying also for us, that God would open unto us a door of ut-

§ 501. PAUL'S THANKFULNESS

4–7.

4 [a]I thank my God, making mention of thee always in my prayers,

5 [b]Hearing of thy love and faith, which thou hast toward the Lord Jesus, and toward all saints;

6 [c]That the communication of thy faith may become effectual by the acknowledging of every good thing which is in you in Christ Jesus.

7 For we have great joy and consolation in thy love, because the bowels of the saints [d]are refreshed by thee, brother.

A

Rom. 1. 8 First, I thank my God through Jesus Christ for you all, that your faith is spoken of thoughout the whole world.

9 For God is my witness, whom I serve with my spirit in the gospel of his Son, that without ceasing I make mention of you always in my prayers;

Eph. 1. 16 Cease not to give thanks for you, making mention of you in my prayers;

Col. 1. 3 We give thanks to God and the Father of our Lord Jesus Christ, praying always for you,

I Thes. 1. 2 We give thanks to God always for you all, making mention of you in our prayers;

II Thes. 1. 3. We are bound to thank God always for you, brethren, as it is meet, because that your faith groweth exceedingly, and the charity of every one of you all toward each other aboundeth;

§ 502. PAUL'S REQUEST OF PHILEMON IN BEHALF OF

8–25.

8 Wherefore, [a]though I might be much bold in Christ to enjoin thee that which is convenient,

9 Yet for love's sake I rather beseech *thee*, being such a one as Paul

A

I Thes. 2. 6 Nor of men sought we glory; neither of you, nor *yet* of others, when we might have been burdensome, as the apostles of Christ.

B

Eph. 3. 1. *See a, A, § 430, page 1038.*

Phile. 1 Paul a prisoner of Jesus Christ, and

TO PHILEMON.

Written probably during Spring of A. D. 62, at Rome.

A—Concluded.

terance, to speak the mystery of Christ, for which I am also in bonds:

Col. 4. 18 The salutation by the hand of me Paul. Remember my bonds. Grace *be* with you. Amen.

II Tim. 1. 8 Be not thou therefore ashamed of the testimony of our Lord, nor of me his prisoner: but be thou partaker of the afflictions of the gospel according to the power of God:

II Tim. 2. 9 Wherein I suffer trouble, as an evil doer, *even* unto bonds; but the Word of God is not bound.

B

Phil. 2. 25 Yet I supposed it necessary to send to you Epaphroditus, my brother, and companion in labour, and fellow soldier, but your messenger, and he that ministered to my wants.

C

Col. 4. 17 And say to Archippus, Take heed

C—Concluded.

to the ministry which thou hast received in the Lord, that thou fulfil it.

D

Phil. 2. 25. *See under B.*

II Tim. 2. 3 Thou therefore endure hardness, as a good soldier of Jesus Christ.

4 No man that warreth entangleth himself with the affairs of *this* life; that he may please him who has chosen him to be a soldier.

E

Rom. 16. 5 Likewise *greet* the church that is in their house. Salute my well beloved Epenetus, who is the first fruits of Achaia unto Christ.

Col. 4. 15 Salute the brethren which are in Laodicea, and Nymphas, and the church which is in his house

F

Eph. 1. 2 Grace *be* to you, and peace, from God our Father, and *from* the Lord Jesus Christ.

AND PRAYER FOR PHILEMON.

B—Concluded.

Col. 1. 4 Since we heard of your faith in Christ Jesus, and of the love *which we have* to all the saints,

C

I Cor. 9. 12 If others be partakers of *this* power over you, *are* not we rather? Nevertheless we have not used this power; but suffer all things, lest we should hinder the gospel of Christ.

13 Do ye not know that they which minister about holy things live *of the things* of the temple? and they which wait at the altar are partakers with the altar?

14 Even so hath the Lord ordained that they which preach the gospel should live of the gospel.

Phil. 1. 9 And this I pray, that your love may abound yet more and more in knowledge and *in* all judgment;

C—Concluded.

10 That ye may approve things that are excellent; that ye may be sincere and without offence till the day of Christ;

11 Being filled with the fruits of righteousness, which are by Jesus Christ, unto the Glory and praise of God.

D

II Cor. 7. 13 Therefore we were comforted in your comfort: yea, and exceedingly the more joyed we for the joy of Titus, because his spirit was refreshed by you all.

II Tim. 1. 16 The Lord give mercy unto the house of Onesiphorus; for he oft refreshed me, and was not ashamed of my chain;

Phile. 20 Yea, brother, let me have joy of thee in the Lord: refresh my bowels in the Lord.

ONESIMUS. CONCLUDING SALUTATION AND BENEDICTION.

B—Concluded.

Timothy *our* brother, unto Philemon our dearly beloved, and fellew labourer,

C

Col. 4. 9 With Onesimus, a faithful and beloved brother, who is *one* of you. They shall make known unto you all things which *are done* here.

D

I Cor. 4. 15 For though ye have ten thousand instructors in Christ, yet *have ye* not many fathers: for in Christ Jesus I have begotten you through the gospel.

Gal. 4. 19 My little children, of whom I travail in birth again until Christ be formed in you.

§ 502. PAUL'S REQUEST OF PHILEMON IN BEHALF OF ONESIMUS.

8–25.

the aged, [b]and now also a prisoner
of Jesus Christ.
10 I beseech thee for my son [c]Onesimus, [d]whom I have begotten in my
bonds:
11 [e]Which in time past was to thee
unprofitable, [f]but now profitable to
thee and to me:
12 Whom I have sent again: thou
therefore receive him, that is, mine
own bowels:
13 Whom I would have retained
with me, [g]that in thy stead he might
have ministered unto me in the bonds
of the gospel:
14 [h]But without thy mind would I
do nothing; [i]that thy benefit should
not be as it were of necessity, but
willingly.
15 [k]For perhaps he therefore departed for a season, that thou shouldest receive him forever;
16 Not now as a servant, but above
a servant, [l]a brother beloved,
specially to me, but how much more
unto thee, [m]both in the flesh, and in
the Lord?
17 If thou count me therefore [n]a
partner, receive him as myself.
18 If he hath wronged thee, or
oweth *thee* aught, put that on mine
account;
19 I Paul have written *it* with mine
own hand, I will repay *it*: albeit I
do not say to thee how thou owest
unto me even thine own self besides.
20 Yea, brother, let me have joy
of thee in the Lord: [o]refresh my
bowels in the Lord.

8–25.

21 [p]Having confidence in thy obedience I wrote unto thee, knowing
that thou wilt also do more than I
say.
22 But withal prepare me also a
lodging: for [q]I trust that [r]through
your prayers I shall be given unto
you.
23 There salute thee [s]Epaphras,
my fellow prisoner in Christ Jesus;
24 [t]Marcus, [u]Aristarchus, [x]Demas,
[y]Lucas, my fellow labourers.
25 The [z]grace of our Lord Jesus
Christ *be* with your spirit. Amen.

For B, C and D, see preceding page (1165).

E

Luke 17. 10 So likewise ye, when ye shall have done all those things which are commanded you, say, We are unprofitable servants: we have done that which was our duty to do.

Rom. 3. 12 They are all gone out of the way, they are together become unprofitable; there is none that doeth good, no, not one.

I Pet. 2. 10 Which in time past *were* not a people, but *are* now the people of God: which had not obtained mercy, but now have obtained mercy.

F

Luke 15. 32 It was meet that we should make merry, and be glad: for this thy brother was dead, and is alive again; and was lost, and is found.

II Tim. 4. 11 Only Luke is with me. Take Mark, and bring him with thee: for he is profitable to me for the ministry,

G

I Cor. 16. 17 I am glad of the coming of Stephanas and Fortunatus and Achaicus: for that which was lacking on your part they have supplied.

Phil. 2. 30 Because for the work of Christ he was nigh unto death, not regarding his life, to supply your lack of service towards me.

H

II Cor. 1. 24 Not for that we have dominion over your faith, but are helpers, of your joy: for by faith ye stand.

CONCLUDING SALUTATION AND BENEDICTION (CONCLUDED).

H—CONCLUDED.

I Pet. 5. 3 Neither as being lords over *God's* heritage, but being ensamples to the flock.

I

IChr.29. 17 I know also, my God, that thou triest the heart, and hast pleasure in uprightness. As for me, in the uprightness of mine heart I have willingly offered all these things: and now have I seen with joy thy people, which are present here, to offer willingly unto thee.

Ps. 110. 3 Thy people *shall* be willing in the day of thy power, in the beauties of holiness from the womb of the morning: thou hast the dew of thy youth.

I Cor. 9. 17 For if I do this thing willingly, I have a reward: but if against my will, dispensation *of the gospel* is committed unto me.

II Cor.8. 12 For if there be first a willing mind *it is* accepted according to that a man hath, *and* not according to that he hath not.

II Cor.9. 7 Every man according as he purposeth in his heart, *so let him give*; not grudgingly, or of necessity: for God loveth a cheerful giver.

I Pet. 5. 2 Feed the flock of God which is among you, taking the oversight *thereof*, not by constraint, but willingly; not for filthy lucre, but of a ready mind;

K

Gen. 45. 5 Now therefore be not grieved, nor angry with yourselves, that ye sold me hither: for God did send one before you to preserve life.

Gen. 45. 8 So now *it was* not you *that* sent me hither: but God and he hath made me a father to Pharaoh, and lord of all his house, and a ruler throughout all the land of Egypt.

L

Matt.23. 8 But be not ye called Rabbi; for one is your Master, *even* Christ; and all ye are brethren.

ITim. 6. 2 And they that have believing masters, let them not despise *them*, because they are brethren; but rather do *them* service, because they are faithful and beloved, partakers of the benefit. These things teach and exhort.

M

Col. 3. 22 Servants, obey in all things *your* master according to the flesh; not with eye service, as men pleasers; but in singleness of heart, fearing God;

N

II Cor.8. 23 Whether *any do enquire* of Titus, *he is* my partner and fellow helper concerning you: or our brethren *be enquired of*, *they are* the messengers of the churches, *and* the glory of Christ.

O

Phile. 7 For we have great joy and consolation in thy love, because the bowels of the saints are refreshed by thee, brother.

P

II Cor.7. 16 I rejoice therefore that I have confidence in you in all *things*.

Q

Phil. 2. 24. *See e, E, § 443, page 1066.*

R

II Cor.1. 11 Ye also helping together by prayer for us, that for the gift *bestowed* upon us by the means of many persons thanks may be given by many on our behalf.

S

Col. 1. 7 As ye also learned of Epaphras our dear fellow servant, who is for you a faithful minister of Christ;

Col. 4. 12 Epaphras, who is *one* of you, a servant of Christ, saluteth you, always labouring fervently for you in prayers, that ye may stand perfect and complete in all the will of God.

T

Acts 12. 12. *See n, N, § 258, page 706.*

U

Acts. 19. 29 And the whole city was filled with confusion: and having caught Gaius and Aristarchus, men of Macedonia, Paul's companions in travel, they rushed with one accord into the theatre.

Acts. 27. 2 And entering into a ship of Adramyttium, we launched, meaning to sail by the coasts of Asia; *one* Aristarchus, a Macedonian of Thessalonica, being with us.

Col. 4. 10 Aristarchus my fellow prisoner saluteth you, and Marcus, sister's son to Barnabas, (touching whom ye received commandments: if he come unto you, receive him;)

X

Col. 4. 14. *See k, K, § 456, page 1092.*

Y

I Tim.4. 11 Only Luke is with me. Take Mark, and bring him with thee: for he is profitable to me for the ministry.

Z

I Tim. 4. 22 The Lord Jesus Christ *be* with thy spirit. Grace *be* with you. Amen.

§ 503. CHRIST BY INHERITANCE IS BETTER THAN ANGELS

I : 1–14.

1 God, who at sundry times and [a]in
divers manners spake in time past
unto the fathers by the prophets,
2 Hath [b]in these last days [c]spoken
unto us by *his* Son, [d]whom he hath
appointed heir of all things, [e]by
whom also he made the worlds;
3 [f]Who being the brightness of *his*
glory, and the express image of his
person, and [g]upholding all things by
the word of his power, [h]when he had
by himself purged our sins, [i]sat down
on the right hand of the Majesty on
high;
4 Being made so much better than
the angels, as [k]he hath by inheritance
obtained a more excellent name than
they.
5 For unto which of the angels said
he at any time, [l]Thou art my Son,
this day have I begotten thee? And
again, [m]I will be to him a Father,
and he shall be to me a Son?
6 [1]And again, when he bringeth in
[n]the firstbegotten into the world, he
saith, [o]And let all the angels of God
worship him.
7 And [2]of the angels he saith, [p]Who
maketh his angels spirits, and his
ministers a flame of fire.
8 But unto the Son *he saith*, [q]Thy
throne, O God, *is* for ever and ever:
a sceptre of [3]righteousness *is* the
sceptre of thy kingdom.

A

Num. 12. 4 And the LORD spake suddenly unto Moses, and unto Aaron, and unto Miriam, Come out ye three unto the

A—CONCLUDED.

tabernacle of the congregation. And they three came out.

5 And the LORD came down in the pillar of the cloud, and stood *in* the door of the tabernacle, and called Aaron and Miriam: and they both came forth.

6 And he said, Hear now my words: If there be a prophet among you, *I* the LORD will make myself known unto him in a vision, *and* will speak unto him in a dream.

7 My servant Moses *is* not so, who *is* faithful in all mine house.

8 With him will I speak mouth to mouth, even apparently, and not in dark speeches; and the similitude of the LORD shall he behold: wherefore then were ye not afraid to speak against my servant Moses?

B

Deut. 4. 29 But if from thence thou shalt seek the LORD thy God, thou shalt find *him*, if thou seek him with all thy heart and with all thy soul.

30 When thou art in tribulation, and all these things are come upon thee, *even* in the latter days, if thou turn to the LORD thy God, and shalt be obedient unto his voice:

Eph. 1. 10. *See o, O, § 426, page 1030.*

C

John 1. 17 For the law was given by Moses, *but* grace and truth came by Jesus Christ.

John 15. 15 Henceforth I call you not servants; for the servant knoweth not what his lord doeth: but I have called you friends; for all things that I have heard of my Father I have made known unto you.

Heb. 2. 3 How shall we escape, if we neglect so great salvation; which at the first began to be spoken by the Lord, and was confirmed unto us by them that heard *him;*

D

Ps. 2. 8 Ask of me, and I shall give *thee* the heathen *for* thine inheritance, and the uttermost parts of the earth *for* thy possession.

Matt. 28. 18. *See b, B, § 222, page 622.*

John 3. 35 The Father loveth the Son, and hath given all things into his hand.

THE HEBREWS.

Author unknown; probably written by Paul A. D. 62–64, at Rome.

D—Concluded.

Rom. 8. 17 And if children, then heirs; heirs of God, and joint heirs with Christ; if so be that we suffer with *him*, that we may be also glorified together.

E

John 1. 3. *See e, E, § 1, page 5.*

F

John 1. 14 And the Word was made flesh, and dwelt among us, (and we beheld his glory, the glory as of the only begotten of the Father,) full of grace and truth.

Phil. 2. 6. *See i, I, § 442, page 1064.*

G

John 1. 4 In him was life; and the life was the light of men.

Col. 1. 17 And he is before all things, and by him all things consist:

Rev. 4. 11 Thou art worthy, O Lord, to receive glory and honour and power: for thou hast created all things, and for thy pleasure they are and were created.

H

Heb. 7. 27 Who needeth not daily, as those high priests, to offer up sacrifice, first for his own sins, and then for the people's: for this he did once, when he offered up himself.

Heb. 9. 12 Neither by the blood of goats and calves, but by his own blood he entered in once into the holy place, having obtained eternal redemption *for us*.

Heb. 9. 14 How much more shall the blood of Christ, who through the eternal Spirit offered himself without spot to God, purge your conscience from dead works to serve the living God?

Heb. 9. 26 For then must he often have suffered since the foundation of the world: but now once in the end of the world hath he appeared to put away sin by the sacrifice of himself.

I

Eph. 1. 20. *See k, K, § 427, page 1032.*

Heb. 8. 1 Now of the things which we have spoken *this is* the sum: We have such a high priest, who is set on the right hand of the throne of the Majesty in the heavens;

Heb. 12. 2 Looking unto Jesus the author and finisher of *our* faith; who for the joy that was set before him endured the cross, despising the shame, and is set

I—Concluded.

down at the right hand of the throne of God.

K

Eph. 1. 21. *See l, L, § 427, page 1032.*

L

Acts 13. 33. *See m, M, § 262, page 714.*

M

II Sa. 7. 14 I will be his father, and he shall be my son. If he commit iniquity, I will chasten him with the rod of men, and with the stripes of the children of men:

I Chr. 22. 10 He shall build a house for my name; and he shall be my son, and I *will be* his father; and I will establish the throne of his kingdom over Israel for ever.

I Chr. 28. 6 And he said unto me, Solomon thy son, he shall build my house and my courts: for I have chosen him *to be* my son, and I will be his father.

Ps. 89. 26 He shall cry unto me, Thou *art* my Father, my God, and the Rock of my salvation.

27 Also I will make him *my* firstborn, higher than the things of the earth.

1

Or, *when he bringeth again.*

N

Rom. 8. 29. *See k, K, § 334, page 848.*

Col. 1. 18 And he is the head of the body, the church: who is the beginning, the firstborn from the dead; that in all things he might have the preeminence.

Rev. 1. 5 And from Jesus Christ, *who is* the faithful witness, *and* the firstbegotten of the dead, and the prince of the kings of the earth. Unto him that loved us, and washed us from our sins in his own blood,

O

Ps. 97. 7 Confounded be all they that serve graven images, that boast themselves of idols: worship him, all *ye* gods.

I Pet. 3. 22 Who is gone into heaven, and is on the right hand of God; angels and authorities and powers being made subject unto him.

2

Gr. *unto.*

P

Ps. 104. 4 Who maketh his angels spirits; his ministers a flaming fire:

For Q and S, see next page (1170).

CHAP. I.

9 Thou hast loved righteousness, and hated iniquity; therefore God, *even* thy God, [r]hath anointed thee with the oil of gladness above thy fellows.

10 And, [s]Thou, Lord, in the beginning hast laid the foundation of the earth; and the heavens are the works of thine hands:

11 [t]They shall perish; but thou remainest; and they all shall wax old as doth a garment;

12 And as a vesture shalt thou fold them up, and they shall be changed: but thou art the same, and thy years shall not fail.

13 But to which of the angels said he at any time, [u]Sit on my right hand, [x]until I make thine enemies thy footstool?

14 [y]Are they not all ministering spirits, sent forth to minister for them who shall be [z]heirs of salvation?

Q

Ps. 45. 6 Thy throne, O God, *is* for ever and ever: the sceptre of thy kingdom *is* a right sceptre.

7 Thou lovest righteousness, and hatest wickedness: therefore God, thy God, hath anointed thee with the oil of gladness above thy fellows.

3

Gr. *righteousness*, or, *straightness*.

R

Isa. 61. 1 The Spirit of the Lord GOD *is* upon me; because the LORD hath anointed me to preach good tidings unto the meek; he hath sent me to bind up the brokenhearted, to proclaim liberty to the captives, and the opening of the prison to *them that are* bound:

Acts 4. 27 For of a truth against thy holy child Jesus, whom thou hast anointed, both Herod, and Pontius Pilate, with

§ 503. CHRIST BY INHERITANCE IS

R—CONCLUDED.

the Gentiles, and the people of Israel were gathered together,

Acts 10. 38 How God anointed Jesus of Nazareth with the Holy Ghost and with power: who went about doing good, and healing all that were oppressed of the devil; for God was with him.

S

Ps. 102. 25 Of old hast thou laid the foundation of the earth: and the heavens *are* the work of thy hands.

26 They shall perish, but thou shalt endure: yea, all of them shall wax old like a garment; as a vesture shalt thou change them, and they shall be changed:

27 But thou *art* the same, and thy years shall have no end.

T

Isa. 34. 4 And all the host of heaven shall be dissolved, and the heavens shall be rolled together as a scroll: and all their host shall fall down, as the leaf falleth off from the vine, and as a falling *fig* from the fig tree.

Matt. 24. 35. *See m, M, § 173, page 490.*

IIPet. 3. 7 But the heavens and the earth, which are now, by the same word are kept in store, reserved unto fire against the day of judgment and perdition of ungodly men.

IIPet. 3. 10 But the day of the Lord will come as a thief in the night; in the which the heavens shall pass away with a great noise, and the elements shall melt with fervent heat, the earth also and the works that are therein shall be burned up.

Rev. 21. 1 And I saw a new heaven and a new earth: for the first heaven and the first earth were passed away; and there was no more sea.

U

Matt. 22. 44. *See c C, § 166, page 462.*

X

Ps. 110. 1 The LORD said unto my Lord, Sit thou at my right hand, until I make thine enemies thy footstool.

2 The LORD shall send the rod of thy strength out of Zion: rule thou in the midst of thine enemies.

3 Thy people *shall be* willing in the day of thy power, in the beauties of holiness from the womb of the morning: thou hast the dew of thy youth.

BETTER THAN ANGELS (CONCLUDED).

X—CONCLUDED.

Ps. 110. 4 The LORD hath sworn, and will not repent, Thou *art* a priest for ever after the order of Melchizedek.

5 The Lord at thy right hand shall strike through kings in the day of his wrath.

6 He shall judge among the heathen, he shall fill *the places* with the dead bodies; he shall wound the heads over many countries.

7 He shall drink of the brook in the way: therefore shall he lift up the head.

Acts 2. 34 For David is not ascended into the heavens: but he saith himself, The LORD said unto my Lord, Sit thou on my right hand,

35 Until I make thy foes thy footstool.

I Cor. 15. 25 For he must reign, till he hath put all enemies under his feet.

Eph. 1. 22 And hath put all *things* under his feet, and gave him *to be* the head over all *things* to the church,

Heb. 10. 13 From henceforth expecting till his enemies be made his footstool.

Y

Gen. 19. 16 And while he lingered, the men laid hold upon his hand, and upon the hand of his wife, and upon the hand of his two daughters; the LORD being merciful unto him: and they brought him forth, and set him without the city.

Gen. 32. 1 And Jacob went on his way, and the angels of God met him.

2 And when Jacob saw them, he said, This *is* God's host: and he called the name of that place Mahanaim.

Gen. 32. 24 And Jacob was left alone; and there wrestled a man with him until the breaking of the day.

Ps. 34. 7 The angels of the LORD encampeth round about them that fear him, and delivereth them.

Ps. 91. 11 For he shall give his angels charge over thee, to keep thee in all thy ways.

Ps. 103. 20 Bless the LORD, ye his angels, that excel in strength, that do his commandments, hearkening unto the voice of his word.

21 Bless ye the LORD all *ye* his hosts; *ye* ministers of his, that do his pleasure.

Da. 3. 28 *Then* Nebuchadnezzar spake, and said, Blessed *be* the God of Shadrack, Meshach, and Abed-ne-go, who hath sent his angel, and delived his servants

Y—CONCLUDED.

that trusted in him, and have changed the king's word, and yielded their bodies, that they might not serve nor worship any god, except their own God.

Da. 7. 10 A fiery stream issued and came forth from before him: thousand thousands ministered unto him, and ten thousand times ten thousand stood before him: the judgment was set, and the books were opened.

Matt. 18. 10 Take heed that ye despise not one of these little ones; for I say unto you, That in heaven their angels do always behold the face of my Father which is in heaven.

Luke 1. 19 And the angel answering said unto him, I am Gabriel, that stand in the presence of God; and am sent to speak unto thee, and to shew thee these glad tidings.

Luke 2. 9 And, lo, the angel of the Lord came upon them, and the glory of the Lord shone round about them: and they were sore afraid.

Luke 2. 13 And suddenly there was with the angel a multitude of the heavenly host praising God, and saying,

Acts 12. 7 And, behold, the angel of the Lord came upon *him*, and a light shined in the prison: and he smote Peter on the side, and raised him up, saying, Arise up quickly. And his chains fell off from *his* hands.

Acts 27. 23 For there stood by me this night the angel of God, whose I am, and whom I serve,

Z

Rom. 8. 17 And if children, then heirs; heirs of God, and joint heirs with Christ; if so be that we suffer with *him*, that we may be also glorified together.

Tit. 3. 7 That being justified by his grace, we should be made heirs according to the hope of eternal life.

Jas. 2. 5 Hearken, my beloved brethren, Hath not God chosen the poor of this world rich in faith, and heirs of the kingdom which he hath promised to them that love him ?

I Pet. 7 Likewise, ye husbands, dwell with *them* according to knowledge, giving honour unto the wife, as unto the weaker vessel, and as being heirs together of the grace of life; that your prayers be not hindered.

§ 504. EXHORTATION TO GIVE THE

2 : 1–4.

1 Therefore we ought to give the more earnest heed to the things which we have heard, lest at any time we should [1]let *them* slip.

2 For if the word [a]spoken by angels was steadfast, and [b]every transgression and disobedience received a just recompense of reward;

3 [c]How shall we escape, if we neglect so great salvation; [d]which at the first began to be spoken by the Lord, and was [e]confirmed unto us by them that heard *him;*

4 [f]God also bearing *them* witness, [g]both with signs and wonders, and with divers miracles, and [2h]gifts of the Holy Ghost, [i]according to his own will?

1

Gr. *run out as leaking vessels.*

A

Deut. 33. 2 And he said, the LORD came from Sinai, and rose up from Seir unto them; he shined forth from mount Paran, and he came with ten thousand of saints: from his right hand *went* a fiery law for them.

A—CONCLUDED.

Acts 7. 53 Who have received the law by the disposition of angels, and have not kept *it.*

Gal. 3. 19 Wherefore then *serveth* the law? It was added because of transgressions, till the seed should come to whom the promise was made; *and it was* ordained by angels in the hand of a mediator.

B

Num. 15. 30 But the soul that doeth *aught* presumptuously, *whether he be* born in the land, or a stranger, the same reproacheth the LORD: and that soul shall be cut off from among his people.

31 Because he hath despised the word of the LORD, and hath broken his commandment, that soul shall utterly be cut off; his iniquity *shall be* upon him.

Deut. 4. 3 Your eyes have seen what the LORD did because of Baal-peor; for all the men that followed Baal-peor, the LORD thy God hath destroyed them from among you.

Deut. 17. 5 Then shalt thou bring forth that man or that woman, which have committed that wicked thing, unto thy gates, *even* that man or that woman, and shalt stone them with stones, till they die.

Deut. 17. 12 And the man that will do presumptuously, and will not hearken unto the priest that standeth to minister there before the LORD thy God, or unto the judge, even that man shall

§ 505. JESUS HUMBLED HIMSELF UNTO

2 : 5–18.

5 For unto the angels hath he not put in subjection [a]the world to come, whereof we speak.

6 But one in a certain place testified, saying, [b]What is man, that thou art mindful of him? or the son of man, that thou visitest him?

7 Thou madest him [1]a little lower than the angels; thou crownedst him with glory and honour, and didst set him over the works of thy hands:

CHAP. 2.

8 [c]Thou hast put all things in subjection under his feet. For in that he put all in subjection under him, he left nothing *that is* not put under him. But now [d]we see not yet all things put under him.

9 But we see Jesus, [e]who was made

A

Heb. 6. 5 And have tasted the good word of God, and the powers of the world to come,

II Pet. 3. 13 Nevertheless we according to his promise, look for new heavens and a new earth, wherein dwelleth righteousness.

MORE EARNEST HEED TO SALVATION.

B—CONCLUDED.

die: and thou shall put away the evil from Israel.

Deut.27. 26 Cursed *be* he that confirmeth not *all* the words of this law to do them. And all the people shall say, Amen.

C

Eze. 17. 15 But he rebelled against him in sending his ambassadors into Egypt, that they might give him horses and much people. Shall he prosper? shall he escape that doeth such *things?* or shall he break the covenant, and be delivered?

Matt.23 33 *Ye* serpents, *ye* generation of vipers, how can ye escape the damnation of hell ?

Rom. 2. 3 And thinkest thou this, O man, that judgest them which do such things, and doest the same that thou shall escape the judgment of God?

I Thes.5. 5 For when they shall say, Peace and safety; then sudden destruction cometh upon them, as travail upon a woman with child; and they shall not escape.

Heb. 4. 1 Let us therefore fear, lest, a promise being left *us* of entering into his rest, any of you should seem to come short of it.

Heb. 4. 11 Let us labour therefore to enter into that rest, lest any man fall after the same example of unbelief.

Heb. 10. 28 He that despised Moses' law died without mercy under two or three witnesses:

C—CONCLUDED.

Heb. 10. 29 Of how much sorer punishment, suppose ye shall he be thought worthy, who hath trodden under foot the Son of God, and hath counted the blood of the covenant, wherewith he was sanctified, an unholy thing, and hath done despite unto the Spirit of grace ?

Heb. 12. 25 See that ye refuse not him that speaketh. For if they escaped not who refused him that spake on earth, much more *shall not* we *escape*, if we turn away from him that *speaketh* from heaven :

I Pet. 4. 17 For the time *is come* that judgment must begin at the house of God: and if *it* first *begin* at us, what shall the end *be* of them that obey not the gospel of God ?

D

Matt. 4. 17. *See a, A, § 26, page 86.*

E

Luke 1. 2. *See a, A, § 2, page 7.*

F

Mark 16. 20. *See d, D, § 224, page 624.*

G

Acts 2. 43. *See f, F, § 232, page 642.*

2

Or, *distributions.*

H

I Cor. 12. 4. *See f, F, § 370, page 938.*

I

Eph. 1. 5 Having predestinated us unto the adoption of children by Jesus Christ to himself, according to the good pleasure of his will,

DEATH AND IS HONORED ABOVE ANGELS.

B

Job 7. 17 What *is* man, that thou shouldest magnify him ? and that thou shouldest set thine heart upon him?

Ps. 8. 4 What is man, that thou art mindful of him ? and the son of man, that thou visitest him ?

Ps. 144. 3 LORD, what *is* man, that thou takest knowledge of him ! *or* the son of man, that thou makest account of him !

1

Or, *a little while inferior to.*

C

Matt. 28. 18. *See b, B, § 222 page 622.*

D

1Cor.15. 24 Then *cometh* the end, when he shall have delivered up the kingdom to

D—CONCLUDED.

God, even the Father; when he shall have put down all rule, and all authority and power.

1Cor.15. 25 For he must reign, till he hath put all enemies under his feet.

E

Phil. 2. 7 But made himself of no reputation, and took upon him the form of a servant, and was made in the likeness of men :

8 And being found in fashion as a man, he humbled himself, and became obedient unto death, even the death of the cross.

9 Wherefore God also hath highly exalted him, and given him a name which is above every name:

§ 505. JESUS HUMBLED HIMSELF UNTO DEATH

CHAP. 2.

a little lower than the angels [2]for the
suffering of death,[f]crowned with glory
and honour; that he by the grace of
God should taste death [g]for every
man.

10 [h]For it became him, [i]for whom
are all things, and by whom *are* all
things, in bringing many sons unto
glory, to make [k]the captain of their
salvation [l]perfect through sufferings.

11 For [m]both he that sanctifieth and
they who are sanctified [n]*are* all of
one: for which cause [o]he is not
ashamed to call them brethren.

12 Saying, [p]I will declare thy name
unto my brethren, in the midst of the
church will I sing praise unto thee.

13 And again, [q]I will put my trust in
him. And again, [r]Behold I and the
children [s]which God hath given me.

14 Forasmuch then as the children
are partakers of flesh and blood, he
[t]also himself likewise took part of
the same; [u]that through death he
might destroy him that had the
power of death, that is, the devil;

15 And deliver them, who [x]through
fear of death were all their lifetime
subject to bondage.

16 For verily [3]he took not on *him*
the nature of angels; but he took on
him the seed of Abraham.

17 Wherefore in all things it behooved him [y]to be made like unto
his brethren, that he might be [z]a
merciful and faithful high priest in
things *pertaining* to God, to make reconciliation for the sins of the people.

18 [a]for in that he himself hath suffered being tempted, he is able to
succour them that are tempted.

2

Or, *by*.

F

Acts 2. 33 Therefore being by the right hand of God exalted, and having received of the Father the promise of the Holy Ghost, he hath shed forth this, which ye now see and hear.

G

John 3. 16 For God so loved the world, that he gave his only begotten Son, that whatsoever believeth in him should not perish, but have everlasting life.

John 12. 32 And I, if I be lifted up from the earth, will draw all *men* unto me.

Rom. 5. 18 Therefore, as by the offence of one *judgment came* upon all men to condemnation; even so by the righteousness of one *the free gift came* upon all men unto justification of life.

Rom. 8. 32 He that spared not his own Son, but delivered him up for us all, how shall he not with him also freely give us all things?

IICor. 5. 15 And *that* he died for all, that they which live should not henceforth live unto themselves, but unto him which died for them, and rose again.

ITim. 2. 6 Who gave himself a ransom for all, to be testified in due time.

IJno. 2. 2 And he is the propitiation for our sins: and not for ours only, but also for *the sins of* the whole world.

Rev. 5. 9 And they sung a new song, saying, Thou art worthy to take the book, and to open the seals thereof: for thou wast slain, and has redeemed us to God by thy blood out of every kindred, and tongue, and people. and nation;

H

Luke 24. 46 And said unto them, Thus it is written, and thus it behooved Christ to suffer, and to rise from the dead the third day:

I

Rom. 11. 36 For of him, and through him, and to him, *are* all things: to whom *be* glory for ever. Amen.

K

Isa. 55. 4 Behold, I have given him *for* a witness to the people, a leader and commander to the people.

Acts 3. 15 And killed the Prince of life, whom God hath raised from the dead; whereof we are witnesses.

Acts 5. 31 Him hath God exalted with his right hand *to be* a Prince and a

AND IS HONORED ABOVE ANGELS (CONCLUDED).

K—CONCLUDED.

Saviour, for to give repentance to Israel, and forgiveness of sin.

Heb. 12. 2 Looking unto Jesus the author and finisher of *our* faith; who for the joy that was set before him endured the cross, despising the shame, and is set down at the right hand of the throne of God.

L

Luke 13. 32 And he said unto them, Go ye, and tell that fox, Behold, I cast out devils, and I do cures to day and to-morrow, and the third *day* I shall be perfected.

Heb. 5. 9 And being made perfect, he became the author of eternal salvation unto all them that obey him;

M

Heb. 10. 10 By the which will we are sanctified through the offering of the body of Jesus Christ once *for all.*

Heb. 10. 14 For by one offering he hath perfected for ever them that are sanctified.

N

Acts 17. 26 And hath made of one blood all nations of men for to dwell on all the face of the earth, and hath determined the times before appointed, and the bounds of their habitation;

O

Matt. 28. 10. *See b, B, § 214, page 600.*

P

Ps. 22. 22 I will declare thy name unto my brethren: in the midst of the congregation will I praise thee.

Ps. 22. 25 My praise *shall be* of thee in the great congregation: I will pay my vows before them that fear him.

Q

Ps. 1 2 The LORD *is* my rock, and my fortress, and my deliverer; my God, my strength, in whom I will trust; my buckler, and the horn of my salvation, *and* my high tower.

Isa. 12. 2 Behold, God *is* my salvation; I will trust, and not be afraid: for the LORD JEHOVAH *is* my strength and *my* song; he also is become my salvation.

R

Isa. 8. 18 Behold, I and the children whom the LORD hath given me *are* for signs and for wonders in Israel from the LORD of hosts, which dwelleth in mount Zion.

S

John 10. 20. *See h, H, § 119, page 355.*

T

John 1. 14 And the Word was made flesh and dwelt among us, (and we behold his glory, the glory as of the only begotten of the Father,) full of grace and truth.

Rom. 8. 3 For what the law could not do, in that it was weak through the flesh, God sending his own Son in the likeness of sinful flesh, and for sin, condemned sin in the flesh:

Phil. 2. 7. *See under E.*

U

I Cor. 15. 54. *See f, F, § 381, page 956.*

Col. 2. 15 *And* having spoiled principalities and powers, he made a shew of them openly, triumphing over them in it.

II Tim. 1. 10. *See u, U, § 486, page 1140.*

X

Luke 1. 74 That he would grant unto us, that we being delivered out of the hand of our enemies might serve him without fear.

Rom. 8. 15. *See y, Y, § 332, page 844.*

3

Gr. *he taketh not hold of angels, but of the seed of Abraham he taketh hold.*

Y

Phil. 2. 7. *See under E.*

Z

Heb. 4. 15 For we have not a high priest which cannot be touched with the feeling of our infirmities; but was in all points tempted like as *we are, yet* without sin.

Heb. 5. 1 For every high priest taken from among men is ordained for men in things *pertaining* to God, that he may offer both gifts and sacrifices for sins:
2 Who can have compassion on the ignorant, and on them that are out of the way; for that he himself also is compassed with infirmity.

A

Heb. 4. 15. *See under Z.*

Heb. 4. 16 Let us therefore come boldly unto the throne of grace, that we may obtain mercy, and find grace to help in time of need.

Heb. 7. 25 Wherefore he is able also to save them to the uttermost that come unto God by him, seeing he ever liveth to make intercession for them.

§ 506. CHRIST JESUS MORE WORTHY THAN MOSES. WARNING

3 : 1–19.

1 Wherefore, holy brethren, partakers of [a]the heavenly calling, consider [b]the Apostle and High Priest of our profession, Christ Jesus;

2 Who was faithful to him that [1]appointed him, as also [c]Moses *was faithful* in all his house.

3 For this *man* was counted worthy of more glory than Moses, inasmuch as [d]he who hath builded the house hath more honour than the house.

4 For every house is builded by some *man;* but [e]he that built all things *is* God.

5 [f]And Moses verily *was* faithful in all his house as [g]a servant, [h]for a testimony of those things which were to be spoken after;

6 But Christ as [i]a son over his own house; [k]whose house are we, [l]if we hold fast the confidence and the rejoicing of the hope firm unto the end.

7 Wherefore (as [m]the Holy Ghost saith, [n]To day if ye will hear his voice,

8 Harden not your hearts, as in the provocation, in the day of temptation in the wilderness:

9 When your fathers tempted me, proved me, and saw my works forty years.

10 Wherefore I was grieved with that generation, and said, They do alway err in *their* heart; and they have not known my ways.

11 So I sware in my wrath, [2]They shall not enter into my rest.)

12 Take heed, brethren, lest there be in any of you an evil heart of unbelief, in departing from the living God.

13 But exhort one another daily, while it is called To day; lest any of you be hardened through the deceitfulness of sin.

A

Rom. 1. 7 To all that be in Rome, beloved of God, called *to be* saints: Grace to you and peace from God our Father, and the Lord Jesus Christ.

I Cor. 1. 2 Unto the church of God which is at Corinth, to them that are sanctified in Christ Jesus, called *to be* saints, with all that in every place call upon the name of Jesus Christ our Lord, both theirs and ours:

Eph. 4. 1 I therefore, the prisoner of the Lord, beseech you that ye walk worthy of the vocation wherewith ye are called,

Phil. 3. 14 I press toward the mark for the prize of the high calling of God in Christ Jesus.

II Thes. 1. 11 Wherefore also we pray always for you, that our God would count you worthy of *this* calling, and fulfil all the good pleasure of *his* goodness, and the work of faith with power:

II Tim. 1. 9 Who hath saved us, and called *us* with a holy calling, not according to our works, but according to his own purpose and grace, which was given us in Christ Jesus before the world began,

II Pet. 1. 10 Wherefore the rather, brethren, give diligence to make your calling and election sure: for if ye do these things, ye shall never fall:

B

Rom. 15. 8 Now I say that Jesus Christ was a minister of the circumcision for the truth of God, to confirm the promises *made* unto the fathers:

Heb. 2. 17 Wherefore in all things it behooved him to be made like unto *his* brethren, that he might be a merciful and faithful high priest in things *pertaining* to God, to make reconciliation for the sins of the people.

Heb. 4. 14 Seeing then that we have a great high priest, that is passed into the heavens, Jesus the Son of God, let us hold fast *our* profession.

Heb. 5. 5 So also Christ glorified not himself to be made a high priest; but he that said unto him, Thou art my Son, to day have I begotten thee.

Heb. 6. 20 Whither the forerunner is for us entered, *even* Jesus, made a high priest for ever after the order of Melchisedec.

Heb. 8. 1 Now of the things which we have spoken *this is* the sum: We have such a high priest, who is set on the right hand of the throne of the Majesty in the heavens;

EXHORTATION FROM ISRAEL WHO ENTERED NOT INTO REST.

B—CONCLUDED.

Heb. 9. 11 But Christ being come a high priest of good things to come, by a greater and more perfect tabernacle, not made with hands, that is to say, not of this building;

Heb. 10. 21 And *having* a high priest over the house of God;

1

Gr. *made.*

I Sa. 12. 6 And Samuel said unto the people, *It is* the LORD that advanced Moses and Aaron, and that brought your fathers up out of the land of Egypt.

C

Num. 12. 7 My servant Moses *is* not so, who *is* faithful in all mine house.

Heb. 3. 5. *See text of topic.*

D

Zech. 6. 12 And speak unto him, saying, Thus speaketh the LORD of hosts, saying, Behold the man whose name *is* The BRANCH; and he shall grow up out of his place, and he shall build the temple of the LORD:

13 Even he shall build the temple of the LORD; and he shall bear the glory, and shall sit and rule upon his throne; and he shall be a priest upon his throne: and the counsel of peace shall be between them both.

Matt. 16. 18 And I say also unto thee, That thou art Peter, and upon this rock I will build my church; and the gates of hell shall not prevail against it.

E

John 1. 3. *See e, E, § 1, page 5.*

Eph. 2. 10. *See s, S, § 428, page 1034.*

F

Heb. 3. 2. *See text of topic.*

G

Ex. 14. 31 And Israel saw that great work which the LORD did upon the Egyptians: and the people feared the Lord, and believed the LORD, and his servant Moses.

Num. 12. 7. *See under C.*

Deut. 3. 24 O Lord GOD, thou hast begun to shew thy servant thy greatness, and thy mighty hand: for what God *is there* in heaven or in earth, that can do according to thy works, and according to thy might?

Josh. 1. 2 Moses my servant is dead; now therefore arise, go over this Jordan, thou, and all this people, unto the land which I do give to them, *even* to the children of Israel.

G—CONCLUDED.

Josh. 8. 31 As Moses the servant of the LORD commanded the children of Israel, as it is written in the book of the law of Moses, an altar of whole stones, over which no man hath lifted up *any* iron: and they offered thereon burnt offerings unto the LORD, and sacrificed peace offerings.

H

Deut. 18. 15 The LORD thy God will raise up unto thee a Prophet from the midst of thee, of thy brethren, like unto me; unto him ye shall hearken:

Deut. 18. 18 I will raise them up a Prophet from among their brethren, like unto thee, and will put my words in his mouth; and he shall speak unto them all that I shall command him.

19 And it shall come to pass, *that* whosoever will not hearken unto my words which he shall speak in my name, I will require *it* of him.

I

Heb. 1. 2 Hath in these last days spoken unto us by *his* Son, whom he hath appointed heir of all things, by whom also he made the worlds;

K

I Cor. 3. 16. *See m, M, § 354, page 900.*

I Tim. 3. 15 But if I tarry long, that thou mayest know how thou oughtest to behave thyself in the house of God, which is the church of the living God, the pillar and ground of the truth.

L

Matt. 24. 13. *See m, M, § 172, page 484.*

Col. 1. 23 If ye continue in the faith grounded and settled, and *be* not moved away from the hope of the gospel, which ye have heard, *and* which was preached to every creature which is under heaven; whereof I Paul am made a minister;

Heb. 6. 11 And we desire that every one of you do shew the same diligence to the full assurance of hope unto the end:

Heb. 10. 35 Cast not away therefore your confidence, which hath great recompense of reward.

M

II Sa. 23. 2 The Spirit of the LORD spake by me, and his word *was* in my tongue.

Acts 1. 16 Men *and* brethren, this Scripture must needs have been fulfilled, which the Holy Ghost by the mouth of David spake before concerning Judas, which was guide to them that took Jesus.

For N and 2, see next page (1178).

§ 506. CHRIST JESUS MORE WORTHY THAN MOSES. WARNING EXHOR-

CHAP. 3.

14 For we are made partakers of Christ, [o]if we hold the beginning of our confidence steadfast unto the end;

15 While it is said, [p]To day if ye will hear his voice, harden not your hearts, as in the provocation.

16 [q]For some, when they had heard, did provoke: howbeit not all that came out of Egypt by Moses.

17 But with whom was he grieved forty years? *was it* not with them that had sinned. [r]whose carcases fell in the wilderness?

18 And [s]to whom sware he that they should not enter into his rest, but to them that believed not?

19 [t]So we see that they could not enter in because of unbelief.

N

Ps. 95. 7 For he *is* our God; and we *are* the people of his pasture, and the sheep of his hand. To-day if ye will hear his voice,

Heb. 3. 15. *See text of topic.*

2

Gr. *if they shall enter.*

O

Rom. 11. 17 And if some of the branches be broken off, and thou, being a wild olive tree, wert graffed in among them, and with them partakest of the root and fatness of the olive tree;

Heb. 3. 6. *See text of topic, page 1176.*

Heb. 12. 10 For they verily for a few days chastened *us* after their own pleasure; but he for *our* profit, that *we* might be partakers of his holiness.

P

Heb. 3. 7. *See text of topic, page 1176.*

Q

Num. 14. 2 And all the children of Israel murmured against Moses and against Aaron: and the whole congregation said unto them, Would God that we had died in the land of Egypt! or would God we had died in this wilderness!

§ 507. CHRIST THE HIGH PRIEST LEADS INTO REST; MOSES AND

4 : 1–16.

1 Let [a]us therefore fear, lest, a promise being left *us* of entering into his rest, any of you should seem to come short of it.

2 For unto us was the gospel preached, as well as unto them: but [1]the word preached did not profit them, [2]not being mixed with faith in them that heard *it*.

3 [b]For we which have believed do enter into rest, as he said, [c]As I have sworn in my wrath, if they shall enter into my rest: althought the works were finished from the foundation of the the world.

4 For he spake in a certain place of the seventh *day* on this wise, [d]And

CHAP. 4.

God did rest the seventh day from all his works.

5 And in this *place* again, If they shall enter into my rest.

6 Seeing therefore it remaineth that some must enter therein, [e]and they to whom [3]it was first preached entered not in because of unbelief:

7 Again, he limiteth a certain day, saying in David, [f]To day, after so long a time; as it is said, To day if ye will hear his voice, harden not your hearts.

8 For if [4]Jesus had given them rest, then would he not afterward have spoken of another day.

9 There remaineth therefore a [5]rest to the people of God.

ATION FROM ISRAEL WHO ENTERED NOT INTO REST (CONCLUDED).

Q—CONTINUED.

Num.14. 4 And they said one to another, Let us make a captain, and let us return into Egypt.

Num.14. 11 And the LORD said unto Moses, How long will this people provoke me? and how long will it be ere they believe me, for all the signs which I have shewed among them?

Num.14. 24 But my servant Caleb, because he had another spirit with him, and hath followed me fully, him will I bring into the land whereinto he went; and his seed shall possess it.

Num.14. 30 Doubtless ye shall not come into the land *concerning* which I sware to make you dwell therein, save Caleb the son of Jephunneh, and Joshua the son of Nun.

Deut. 1. 34 And the LORD heard the voice of your words, and was wroth, and sware, saying,

35 Surely there shall not one of these men of this evil generation see that good land, which I sware to give unto your fathers,

36 Save Caleb the son of Jephunneh; he shall see it, and to him will I give the land that he hath trodden upon, and to his children, because he hath wholly followed the LORD.

Q—CONCLUDED.

Deut. 1. 37 Also the LORD was angry with me for your sakes, saying, Thou also shalt not go in thither.

38 *But* Joshua the son of Nun, which standeth before thee, he shall go in thither: encourage him: for he shall cause Israel to inherit it.

R

Num.14. 22 Because all those men which have seen my glory, and my miracles, which I did in Egypt and in the wilderness, and have tempted me now these ten times, and have not hearkened to my voice;

23 Surely they shall not see the land which I sware unto their fathers, neither shall any of them that provoked me see it:

S

Num. 14. 30. *See under Q.*

Deut. 1. 34, 35. *See under Q.*

T

Heb. 4. 6 Seeing therefore it remaineth that some must enter therein, and they to whom it was first preached entered not in because of unbelief:

JOSHUA COULD NOT; EXHORTATION TO FEAR AND HOLD FAST.

A

Heb. 12. 15 Looking diligently lest any man fail of the grace of God; lest any root of bitterness springing up trouble *you*, and thereby many be defiled;

1

Gr. *the word of hearing.*

2

Or, *because they were not united by faith to.*

B

Heb. 3. 14. *See text of topic,* § *506.*

C

Ps. 95. 11 Unto whom I sware in my wrath that they should not enter into my rest.

Heb. 3. 11 So I sware in my wrath, They should not enter into my rest.)

D

Gen. 2. 2 And on the seventh day God ended his work which he had made; and he rested on the seventh day from all his work which he had made.

Ex. 20. 11 For *in* six days the LORD made heaven and earth, the sea, and all that in them *is*, and rested the seventh day: wherefore the LORD blessed the sabbath day, and hallowed it.

D—CONCLUDED.

Ex. 31. 17 It *is* a sign between me and the children of Israel for ever: for *in* six days the LORD made heaven and earth, and on the seventh day he rested, and was refreshed.

E

Heb. 3. 18, 19. *See text of topic,* § *506.*

3

Or, *the gospel was first preached.*

F

Ps. 95. 7. *See under N,* § *506.*

Heb. 3. 7 Wherefore (as the Holy Ghost saith, To day if ye will hear his voice,

4

That is, *Joshua.*

5

Or, *keeping of a Sabbath.*

G

Heb. 3. 12 Take heed, brethren, lest there be in any of you an evil heart of unbelief, in departing from the living God.

Heb. 3. 18, 19. *See text of topic,* § *506.*

6

Or, *disobedience.*

§ 507. CHRIST THE HIGH PRIEST LEADS INTO REST; MOSES AND JOSHUA

CHAP. 4.

10 For he that is entered into his rest, he also hath ceased from his own works, as God *did* from his.

11 Let us labour therefore to enter into that rest, lest any man fall [g]after the same example of [6]unbelief.

12 For the word of God *is* [h]quick, and powerful, and [i]sharper than any [k]twoedged sword, piercing even to the dividing asunder of soul and spirit, and of the joints and marrow, and *is* [l]a discerner of the thoughts and intents of the heart.

13 [m]Neither is there any creature that is not manifest in his sight: but all things *are* naked [n]and opened unto the eyes of him with whom we have to do.

14 Seeing then that we have [o]a great high priest, [p]that is passed into the heavens, Jesus the Son of God, [q]let us hold fast *our* profession.

15 For [r]we have not a high priest which cannot be touched with the feeling of our infirmities; but [s]was in all points tempted like as *we are*, [t]yet without sin.

CHAP. 4.

-6 [u]Let us therefore come boldly unto the throne of grace, that we may obtain mercy, and find grace to help in time of need.

For G and 6, see preceding page (1179).

H

Isa. 49. 2 And he hath made my mouth like a sharp sword; in the shadow of his hand hath he hid me, and made me a polished shaft; in his quiver hath he hid me;

Jer. 23. 29 *Is* not my word like as a fire? saith the Lord; and like a hammer *that* breaketh the rock in pieces?

IICor. 10. 4 (For the weapons of our warfare *are* not carnal, but mighty through God to the pulling down of strong holds;)

5 Casting down imaginations, and every high thing that exalteth itself against the knowledge of God, and bringing into captivity every thought to the obedience of Christ;

I Pet. 1. 23 Being born again, not of corruptible seed, but of incorruptible, by the word of God, which liveth and abideth for ever.

I

Prov. 5. 4 But her end is bitter as wormwood, sharp as a twoedged sword.

K

Eph. 6. 17. *See n, N, § 437, page 1056.*

L

ICor. 14. 24 But if all prophesy, and there come in one that believeth not, or *one* unlearned, he is convinced of all, he is judged of all:

§ 508. CHRIST A HIGH PRIEST AFTER THE ORDER OF

5: 1-10.

1 For every high priest taken from among men [a]is ordained for men [b]in things *pertaining* to God, [c]that he may offer both gifts and sacrifices for sins:

2 [d]Who [1]can have compassion on the ignorant, and on them that are out of the way; for that [e]he himself also is compassed with infirmity.

3 And [f]by reason hereof he ought, as for the people, so also for himself, to offer for sins.

A

Heb. 8. 3 For every high priest is ordained to offer gifts and sacrifices: wherefore *it is* of necessity that this man have somewhat also to offer.

B

Heb. 2. 17 Wherefore in all things it behooved him to be made like unto *his* brethren, that he might be a merciful and faithful high priest in things *pertaining* to God, to make reconciliation for the sins of the people.

C

Heb. 8. 3. *See under A.*

Heb. 8. 4 For if he were on earth, he should not be a priest, seeing that there are priests that offer gifts according to the law:

COULD NOT; EXHORTATION TO FEAR AND HOLD FAST (CONCLUDED).

L—CONCLUDED.

I Cor. 14. 25 And thus are the secrets of his heart made manifest; and so falling down on his *face* he will worship God, and report that God is in you of a truth.

M

Ps. 33. 13 The Lord looketh from heaven; he beholdeth all the sons of men.

14 From the place of his habitation he looketh upon all the inhabitants of the earth.

Ps. 90. 8 Thou has set our iniquities before thee, our secret *sins* in the light of thy countenance.

Ps. 139. 11 If I say, Surely the darkness shall cover me; even the night shall be light about me.

12 Yea, the darkness hideth not from thee; but the night shineth as the day: the darkness and the light *are* both alike to *thee*.

N

Job 26. 6 Hell *is* naked before him, and destruction hath no covering.

Job 34. 21 For his eyes *are* upon the ways of man, and he seeth all his goings.

Prov. 15. 11 Hell and destruction *are* before the LORD: how much more the hearts of the children of men?

O

Heb. 3. 1. *See b, B, § 506, page 1176.*

P

Heb. 7. 26 For such a high priest became us, *who is* holy, harmless, undefiled, separate from sinners, and made higher than the heavens;

Heb. 9. 12 Neither by the blood of goats and calves, but by his own blood he entered in once into the holy place, having obtained eternal redemption *for us*.

P—CONCLUDED.

Heb. 9. 24 For Christ is not entered into the holy places made with hands, *which are* the figures of the true; but into heaven itself, now to appear in the presence of God for us:

Q

Heb. 10. 23 Let us hold fast the profession of *our* faith without wavering: (for he *is* faithful that promised;)

R

Isa. 53. 3 He is depised and rejected of men; a man of sorrows, and acquainted with grief: and we hid as it were *our* faces from him; he was despised, and we esteemed him not.

Heb. 2. 18. *See a, A, § 505, page 1174.*

S

Luke 22. 28 Ye are they which have continued with me in my temptations.

T

II Cor. 5. 21. *See q, Q, § 395, page 978.*

Heb. 7. 26. *See under P.*

U

Eph. 2. 18 For through him we both have access by one Spirit unto the Father.

Eph. 3. 12 In whom we have boldness and access with confidence by the faith of him:

Heb. 10. 19 Having therefore, brethren, boldness to enter into the holiest by the blood of Jesus,

Heb. 10. 21 And *having* a high priest over the house of God;

22 Let us draw near with a true heart in full assurance of faith, having our hearts sprinkled from an evil conscience, and our bodies washed with pure water.

MELCHISEDEC IS SUPERIOR TO THE LEVITICAL PRIESTHOOD.

C—CONCLUDED.

Heb. 9. 9 Which *was* a figure for the time then present, in which were offered both gifts and sacrifices, that could not make him that did the service perfect, as pertaining to the conscience;

Heb. 10. 11 And every priest standeth daily ministering and offering oftentimes the same sacrifices, which can never take away sins:

Heb. 11. 4 By faith Abel offered unto God a more excellent sacrifice than Cain, by which he obtained witness that he was righteous, God testifying of his gifts: and by it he being dead yet speaketh.

D

Heb. 2. 18. *See a, A, § 505, page 1174.*

1

Or, *can reasonably bear with.*

L

Heb. 7. 28 For the law maketh men high priest which have infirmity; but the word of the oath, which was since the law, *maketh* the Son, who is consecrated for evermore.

F

Lev. 4. 3 If the priest that is anointed do sin according to the sin of the people; then let him bring for his sin, which he hath sinned, a young bullock without blemish unto the LORD for a sin offering.

For F concluded, see next page (1182).

§ 508. CHRIST A HIGH PRIEST AFTER THE ORDER OF MELCHISEDEC

CHAP. 5.

4 [g]And no man taketh this honour unto himself, but he that is called of God, as [h]*was* Aaron.

5 [i]So also Christ glorified not himself to be made a high priest; but he that said unto him, [k]Thou art my Son, to day have I begotten thee.

6 As he said also in another *place*, [l]Thou *art* a priest for ever after the order of Melchisedec.

7 Who in the days of his flesh, when he had [m]offered up prayers and supplications [n]with strong crying and tears unto him [o]that was able to save him from death, and was heard [2p]in that he feared:

8 [q]Though he were a Son, yet learned he [r]obedience by the things which he suffered;

9 And [s]being made perfect, he became the author of eternal salvation unto all them that obey him;

10 Called of God a high priest [t]after the order of Melchisedec.

F—CONTINUED.

Lev. 9. 7 And Moses said unto Aaron, Go unto the altar, and offer thy sin offering, and thy burnt offering, and make an atonement for thyself, and for the people: and offer the offering of the people, and make an atonement for them; as the LORD commanded.

F—CONCLUDED.

Lev. 16. 6 And Aaron shall offer his bullock of the sin offering, which *is* for himself, and make an atonement for himself, and for his house.

Lev. 16. 15 Then shall he kill the goat of the sin offering, that *is* for the people, and bring his blood within the vail, and do with that blood as he did with the blood of the bullock, and sprinkle it upon the mercy seat, and before the mercy seat:

16 And he shall make an atonement for the holy *place*, because of the uncleanness of the children of Israel, and because of their transgressions in all their sins: and so shall he do for the tabernacle of the congregation, that remaineth among them in the midst of their uncleanness.

17 And there shall be no man in the tabernacle of the congregation when he goeth in to make an atonement in the holy *place*, until he come out, and have made an atonement for himself, and for his household, and for all the congregation of Israel.

Heb. 7. 27 Who needeth not daily, as those high priests, to offer up sacrifice, first for his own sins, and then for the people's: for this he did once, when he offered up himself.

Heb. 9. 7 But into the second *went* the high priest alone once every year, not without blood, which he offered for himself, and *for* the errors of the people:

G

II Chr. 26. 18 And they withstood Uzziah the king, and saith unto him, *It appertaineth* not unto thee, Uzziah, to burn incense unto the LORD, but for the priests the sons of Aaron, that are consecrated to burn incense: go out of the sanctuary; for thou hast trespassed; neither *shall it be* for thine honour from the LORD God.

§ 509. BEING DULL THEY UNDERSTOOD NOT. ADMONISHED

5: 11–14; 6: 1–12.

11 Of whom [a]we have many things to say, and hard to be uttered, seeing ye are [b]dull of hearing.

12 For when for the time ye ought to be teachers, ye have need that one teach you again which *be* [c]the first

A

John 16. 12 I have yet many things to say unto you, but ye cannot bear them now.

II Pet. 3. 16 As also in all *his* epistles, speaking in them of these things; in which are some things hard to be understood, which they that are unlearned and unstable wrest, as *they do* also the other Scriptures, unto their own destruction.

IS SUPERIOR TO THE LEVITICAL PRIESTHOOD (CONCLUDED).

G—CONCLUDED.

John 3. 27 John answered and said, A man can receive nothing, except it be given him from heaven.

H

Ex. 28. 1 And take thou unto thee Aaron thy brother, and his sons with him, from among the children of Israel, that he may minister unto me in the priest's office *even* Aaron, Nadab and Abihu, Eleazar and Ithamar, Aaron's sons.

Num. 16. 5 And he spake unto Korah and unto all his company, saying, Even to morrow the LORD will shew who *are* his, and *who is* holy; and will cause *him* to come near unto him: even *him* whom he hath chosen will he cause to come near unto him.

Num. 16. 40 *To be* a memorial unto the children of Israel, that no stranger, which *is* not of the seed of Aaron, come near to offer incense before the LORD; that he be not as Korah, and as his company: as the LORD said to him by the hand of Moses.

I Chr. 23. 13 The sons of Amram; Aaron and Moses: and Aaron was separated, that he should sanctify the most holy things, he and his sons for ever, to burn incense before the LORD, to minister unto him, and to bless in his name for ever.

I

John 8. 54 Jesus answered, If I honour myself, my honour is nothing: it is my Father that honoureth me; of whom ye say, that he is your God:

K

Acts 13. 33. *See m, M, § 262, page 714.*

L

Ps. 110. 4 The LORD hath sworn, and will not repent, Thou *art* a priest for ever after the order of Melchizedek.

L—CONCLUDED.

Heb. 7. 17 For he testifieth, Thou *art* a priest for ever after the order of Melchisedec.

Heb. 7. 21 (For those priests were made without an oath; but this with an oath by him that said unto him, The Lord sware and will not repent, Thou *art* a priest for ever after the order of Melchisedec:)

M

Matt. 26. 39, etc. *Study § 192, page 548.*

N

Matt. 27. 46. *See c, C, § 207, page 588.*

O

Matt. 26. 53. *See k, K, § 193, page 554.*

2

Or, *for his piety.*

P

Matt. 26. 37. *Study § 192, page 548.*

Q

Heb. 3. 6 But Christ as a son over his own house; whose house are we, if we hold fast the confidence and the rejoicing of the hope firm unto the end.

R

Phil. 2. 8 And being found in fashion as a man, he humbled himself, and became obedient unto death, even the death of the cross.

S

Heb. 2. 10. *See l, L, § 505, page 1174.*

Heb. 11. 40 God having provided some better thing for us, that they without us should not be made perfect.

T

Heb. 5. 6. *See text of topic.*

Heb. 6. 20 Whither the forerunner is for us entered, *even* Jesus, made a high priest for ever after the order of Melchisdec.

TO LEAVE THE FIRST PRINCIPLES AND GO ON.

B

Matt. 13. 15. *See t, T, § 39, page 198.*

C

Heb. 6. 1. *See text of topic, page 1184.*

D

I Cor. 3. 1 And I brethren, could not speak unto you as unto spiritual, but as unto carnal, *even* as unto babes in Christ.

2 I have fed you with milk, and not with meat: for hitherto ye were not able *to bear it*, neither yet now are ye able.

D—CONCLUDED.

I Cor. 3. 3 For ye are yet carnal: for whereas *there is* among you envying, and strife, and divisions, are ye not carnal, and walk as men?

1

Gr. *hath no experience.*

§ 509. BEING DULL THEY UNDERSTOOD NOT. ADMONISHED

CHAP. 5.

principles of the oracles of God; and are become such as have need of [d]milk, and not of strong meat.

13 For every one that useth milk [1]*is* unskilful in the word of righteousness: for he is [e]a babe.

14 But strong meat belongeth to them that are [2]of full age, *even* those who by reason [3]of use have their senses exercised [f]to discern both good and evil.

CHAP. 6.

1 Therefore [g]leaving [4]the principles of the doctrines of Christ, let us go on unto perfection; not laying again the foundation of repentance [h]from dead works, and of faith toward God,

2 [i]Of the doctrine of baptisms, [k]and of laying on of hands, [l]and of resurrection of the dead, [m]and of eternal judgment.

3 And this will we do, [n]if God permit.

4 For [o]*it is* impossible for those [p]who were once enlightened, and have tasted of [q]the heavenly gift, and [r]were made partakers of the Holy Ghost,

5 And have tasted the good word of God, and the powers of [s]the world to come,

6 If they shall fall away, to renew them again unto repentance; [t]seeing they crucify to themselves the Son of God afresh, and put *him* to an open shame.

7 For the earth which drinketh in the rain that cometh oft upon it, and bringeth forth herbs meet for them [5]by whom it is dressed, [u]receiveth blessing from God:

8 [x]But that which beareth thorns and briers *is* rejected, and *is* nigh unto cursing; whose end *is* to be burned.

For D and 1, see preceding page (1183).

E

I Cor. 13. 11 When I was a child, I spake as a child, I understood as a child, I thought as a child: but when I became a man, I put away childish things.

I Cor. 14. 20. *See a, A, § 374, page 946.*

I Pet. 2. 2 As newborn babes, desire the sincere milk of the word, that ye may grow thereby:

2

Or, *perfect.*

I Cor. 2. 6 Howbeit we speak wisdom among them that are perfect: yet not the wisdom of this world, nor of the princes of this world, that come to nought:

Eph. 4. 13 Till we all come in the unity of the faith, and of the knowledge of the Son of God, unto a perfect man, unto the measure of the stature of the fulness of Christ:

Phil. 3. 15 Let us therefore, as many as be perfect, be thus minded: and if in any thing ye be otherwise minded, God shall reveal even this unto you.

3

Or, *of an habit;* or, *perfection.*

F

Isa. 7. 15 Butter and honey shall he eat, that he may know to refuse the evil, and choose the good.

I Cor. 2. 14 But the natural man receiveth not the things of the Spirit of God: for they are foolishness unto him: neither can he know *them*, because they are spiritually discerned.

15 But he that is spiritual judgeth all things, yet he himself is judged of no man.

G

Phil. 3. 12 Not as though I had already attained, either were already perfect: but I follow after, if that I may apprehend that for which also I am apprehended of Christ Jesus.

13 Brethren, I count not myself to have apprehended: but *this* one thing *I do*, forgetting those things which are behind, and reaching forth unto those things which are before,

14 I press toward the mark for the prize of the high calling of God in Christ Jesus.

Heb. 5. 12. *See text of topic.*

4

Or, *the word of the beginning of Christ.*

H

Heb. 9. 14 How much more shall the blood of Christ, who through the eternal Spirit offered himself without spot to

TO LEAVE THE FIRST PRINCIPLES AND GO ON (CONTINUED).

H—CONCLUDED.

God, purge your conscience from dead works to serve the living God?

I

Acts 19. 4 Then said Paul, John verily baptized with the baptism of repentance, saying unto the people, that they should believe on him which should come after him, that is, on Christ Jesus.

5 When they heard *this*, they were baptized in the name of the Lord Jesus.

K

Acts 6. 6. *See l, L § 244, page 664.*

L

Acts 2. 24. *See k, K, § 231, page 638.*

M

Acts 24. 25 And as he reasoned of righteousness, temperance, and judgment to come, Felix trembled, and answered, Go thy way for this time; when I have a convenient season, I will call for thee.

Rom. 2. 16. *See o, O, § 320, page 818.*

N

Acts 18. 21. *See d, D, § 282, page 750.*

O

Matt. 5. 13 Ye are the salt of the earth: but if the salt have lost his savour, wherewith shall it be salted? it is thenceforth good for nothing, but to be cast out, and to be trodden under foot of men.

Matt. 12. 31, 32. *See t, T, § 51, page 170.*

John 15. 6 If a man abide not in me, he is cast forth as a branch, and is withered; and men gather them, and cast *them* into the fire, and they are burned.

II Pet. 2. 21 For it had been better for them not to have known the way of righteousness, than, after they have known *it*, to turn from the holy commandment delivered unto them.

22 But it is happened unto them according to the true proverb, The dog *is* turned to his own vomit again; and, The sow that was washed to her wallowing in the mire.

P

Heb. 10. 32 But call to remembrance the former days, in which, after ye were illuminated, ye endured a great fight of afflictions:

Q

John 4. 10 Jesus answered and said unto her, If thou knewest the gift of God, and who it is that saith to thee, Give me to drink; thou wouldest have asked of him, and he would have given thee living water.

Q—CONCLUDED.

John 6. 32 Then Jesus said unto them, Verily, verily, I say unto you, Moses gave you not that bread from heaven; but my Father giveth you the true bread from heaven.

Eph. 2. 8. *See q, Q, § 428, page 1034.*

R

Gal. 3. 2 This only would I learn of you, Received ye the Spirit by the works of the law, or by the hearing of faith?

Gal. 3. 5 He therefore that ministereth to you the Spirit, and worketh miracles among you, *doeth he it* by the works of the law, or by the hearing of faith?

Heb. 2. 4 God also bearing *them* witness, both with signs and wonders, and with divers miracles, and gifts of the Holy Ghost, according to his own will?

S

Heb. 2. 5 For unto the angels hath he not put in subjection the world to come, whereof we speak.

T

Heb. 10. 29 Of how much sorer punishment, suppose ye, shall he be thought worthy, who hath trodden under foot the Son of God, and hath counted the blood of the covenant, wherewith he was sanctified, an unholy thing, and hath done despite unto the Spirit of grace?

5

Or, *for.*

U

Ps. 65. 10 Thou waterest the ridges thereof abundantly: thou settlest the furrows thereof: thou makest it soft with showers: thou blessest the springing thereof.

X

Isa. 5. 6 And I will lay it waste: it shall not be pruned, nor digged; but there shall come up briers and thorns: I will also command the clouds that they rain no rain upon it.

Y

Prov. 14. 31 He that oppresseth the poor reproacheth his Maker: but he that honoureth him hath mercy on the poor.

Matt. 10. 42. *See p, P, § 77, page 240.*

Z

Rom. 3. 4 God forbid: yea, let God be true, but every man a liar; as it is written, That thou mightest be justified in thy saying, and mightest overcome when thou art judged.

II Thes. 1. 6 Seeing *it is* a righteous thing with God to recompense tribulation to them that trouble you:

§ 509. BEING DULL THEY UNDERSTOOD NOT. ADMONISHED

CHAP. 6.

9 But, beloved, we are persuaded better things of you, and things that accompany salvation, though we thus speak.

10 [y]For [z]God *is* not unrighteous to forget [a]your work and labour of love, which ye have shewed toward his name, in that ye have [b]ministered to the saints, and do minister.

11 And we desire that [c]every one of you do shew the same diligence

CHAP. 6.

[d]to the full assurance of hope unto the end:

12 That ye be not slothful, but followers of them who through faith and patience [e]inherit the promises.

For Y and Z, see preceding page (1185).

Z—CONCLUDED.

I Thes. 1. 7 And to you who are troubled rest with us, when the Lord Jesus shall be revealed from heaven with his mighty angels,

A

I Thes. 1. 3 Remembering without ceasing your

§ 510. GOD'S IMMUTABLE OATH IS STRONG ENCOURAGEMENT

6:13–20.

13 For when God made promise to Abraham, because he could swear by no greater, [a]he sware by himself,

14 Saying, Surely blessing I will bless thee, and multiplying I will multiply thee.

15 And so, after he had patiently endured, he obtained the promise.

16 For men verily swear by the greater: and [b]an oath for confirmation *is* to them an end of all strife.

17 Wherein God, willing more abundantly to shew unto [c]the heirs of promise [d]the immutability of his counsel, [1]confirmed *it* by an oath:

18 That by two immutable things, in which *it was* impossible for God to lie, we might have a strong consolation, who have fled for refuge [e]to lay hold upon the hope [f]set before us:

19 Which *hope* we have as an anchor of the soul, both sure and steadfast, [g]and which entereth into that within the vail;

CHAP. 6.

20 [h]Whither the forerunner is for us entered, *even* Jesus, [i]made a high priest for ever after the order of Melchisedec.

A

Gen. 22. 16 And said, By myself have I sworn, saith the LORD, for because thou hast done this thing, and hast not withheld thy son, thine only *son*,

17 That in blessing I will bless thee, and in multiplying I will multiply thy seed as the stars of the heaven, and as the sand which *is* upon the sea shore; and thy seed shall possess the gate of his enemies;

Ps. 105. 9 Which *covenant* he made with Abraham, and his oath unto Isaac;

10 And confirmed the same unto Jacob for a law, *and* to Israel *for* an everlasting covenant:

Isa. 45. 23 I have sworn by myself, the word is gone out of my mouth *in* righteousness, and shall not return, That unto me every knee shall bow, every tongue shall swear.

Jer. 22. 5 But if ye will not hear these words, I swear by myself, saith the LORD, that this house shall become a desolation.

Jer. 49. 13 For I have sworn by myself, saith the LORD, that Bozrah shall become a desolation, a reproach, a waste, and a curse; and all the cities thereof shall be perpetual wastes.

TO LEAVE THE FIRST PRINCIPLES AND GO ON (Concluded).

A—Concluded.

work of faith, and labour of love, and patience of hope in our Lord Jesus Christ, in the sight of God and our Father;

B

Rom. 15. 25 But now I go unto Jerusalem to minister unto the saints.

II Cor. 8. 4. *See b, B, § 399, page 984.*

II Cor. 9. 1 For as touching the ministering to the saints, it is superfluous for me to write to you:

II Cor. 9. 12 For the administration of this service not only supplieth the want of the saints, but is abundant also by many thanksgivings unto God;

II Tim. 1. 18 The Lord grant unto him that he may find mercy of the Lord in that

B—Concluded.

day: and in how many things he ministered unto me at Ephesus, thou knowest very well.

C

Heb. 3. 14. *See o, O, § 506, page 1178.*

D

Col. 2. 2 That their hearts might be comforted, being knit together in love, and unto all riches of the full assurance of understanding, to the acknowledgment of the mystery of God, and of the Father, and of Christ:

E

Heb. 10. 36 For ye have need of patience, that, after ye have done the will of God, ye might receive the promise.

FOR HOPE THROUGH CHRIST OUR HIGH PRIEST.

A—Concluded.

Luke 1. 73 The oath which he sware to our father Abraham,

B

Ex. 22. 11 *Then* shall an oath of the LORD be between them both, that he hath not put his hand unto his neighbour's goods; and the owner of it shall accept *thereof* and he shall not make *it* good.

C

Heb. 11. 9 By faith he sojourned in the land of promise, as *in* a strange country, dwelling in tabernacles with Isaac and Jacob, the heirs with him of the same promise:

D

Rom. 11. 29 For the gifts and calling of God *are* without repentance.

1

Gr. *interposed himself by an oath.*

E

I Tim. 6. 12 Fight the good fight of faith, lay hold on eternal life, whereunto thou art also called, and hast professed a good profession before many witnesses.

F

Heb. 12. 1 Wherefore, seeing we also are compassed about with so great a cloud of witnesses, let us lay aside every weight, and the sin which doth so easily beset *us*, and let us run with patience the race that is set before us,

G

Lev. 16. 15 Then shall he kill the goat of the sin offering, that *is* for the people, and

G—Concluded.

bring his blood within the vail, and do with that blood as he did with the blood of the bullock, and sprinkle it upon the mercy seat, and before the mercy seat:

Heb. 9. 7 But into the second *went* the high priest alone once every year, not without blood, which he offered for himself, and *for* the errors of the people:

H

Heb. 4. 14 Seeing then that we have a great high priest, that is passed into the heavens, Jesus the Son of God, let us hold fast *our* profession.

Heb. 8. 1 Now of the things which we have spoken *this is* the sum: We have such a high priest, who is set on the right hand of the throne of the Majesty in the heavens;

Heb. 9. 24 For Christ is not entered into the holy places made with hands, *which are* the figures of the true; but into heaven itself, now to appear in the presence of God for us:

I

Heb. 3. 1 Wherefore, holy brethren, partakers of the heavenly calling, consider the Apostle and High Priest of our profession, Christ Jesus;

Heb. 5. 6 As he saith also in another *place*, Thou *art* a priest for ever after the order of Melchisedec.

Heb. 5. 10 Called of God a high priest after the order of Melchisedec.

Heb. 7. 17 For he testifieth, Thou *art* a priest for ever after the order of Melchisedec.

§ 511. THE ORDER OF

7:1–3

1 For this [a]Melchisedec, king of [b]Salem, priest of the most high God, who met Abraham returning from the slaughter of the kings, and blessed him;

2 To whom also Abraham gave [c]a tenth part of all; first being by interpretation King of righteousness, and after that also King of Salem, which is, King of peace;

Chap. 7.

3 Without father, without mother, [1]without descent, having neither beginning of days, nor end of life; but made like unto the Son of God; abideth a priest continually.

A

Gen. 14. 18 And Melchizedek king of Salem brought forth bread and wine: and he *was* the priest of the most high God.

19 And he blessed him, and said, Blessed be Abram of the most high God, possessor of heaven and earth:

§ 512. THE ORDER OF MELCHISEDEC IS GREATER

7:4-25.

4 Now consider how great this man *was*, [a]unto whom even the patriarch Abraham gave the tenth of the spoils.

5 And verily [b]they that are of the sons of Levi, who receive the office of the priesthood, have a commandment to take tithes of the people according to the law, that is, of their brethren, though they come out of the loins of Abraham:

6 But he whose [1]descent is not counted from them received tithes of Abaham, [c]and blessed [d]him that had the promises.

7 And without all contradiction the less is blessed of the better.

8 And here men that die receive tithes; but there he *receiveth them*, [e]of whom it is witnessed that he liveth.

9 And as I may so say, Levi also, who receiveth tithes, paid tithes in Abraham.

10 For he was yet in the loins of his father, when Melchisedec met him.

11 [f]If therefore perfection were by the Levitical priesthood, (for under

Chap. 7.

it the people received the law,) what further need *was there* that another priest should rise after the order of Melchisedec, and not be called after the order of Aaron?

12 For the priesthood being changed, there is made of necessity a change also of the law.

13 For he of whom these things are spoken pertaineth to another tribe, of which no man gave attendance at the altar.

14 For *it is* evident that [g]our Lord sprang out of Juda; of which tribe Moses spake nothing concerning priesthood.

15 And it is yet far more evident: for that after the similitude of Melchisedec there ariseth another priest,

16 Who is made, not after the law of a carnal commandment, but after the power of an endless life.

17 For he testifieth, [h]Thou *art* a priest for ever after the order of Melchisedec.

18 For there is verily a disannulling of the commandment going before for [i]the weakness and unprofitableness thereof.

MELCHISEDEC.

A—CONCLUDED.

Gen. 14. 20 And blessed be the most high God, which hath delivered thine enemies into thy hand. And he gave him tithes of all.

B

Ps. 76. 2 In Salem also is his tabernacle, and his dwellingplace in Zion.

C

Gen. 28. 22 And this stone, which I have set *for* a pillar, shall be God's house: and of all that thou shalt give me I will surely give the tenth unto thee.

Lev. 27. 32 And concerning the tithe of the herd, or of the flock, *even* of whatsoever passeth under the rod, the tenth shall be holy unto the LORD.

C—CONCLUDED.

Num. 18. 21 And, behold, I have given the children of Levi all the tenth in Israel for an inheritance, for their service which they serve, *even* the service of the tabernacle of the congregation.

I Sa. 8. 15 And he will take the tenth of your seed, and of your vineyards, and give to his officers, and to his servants.

I Sa. 8. 17 He will take the tenth of your sheep: and ye shall be his servants.

1

Gr. *without pedigree.*

THAN THE LEVITICAL ORDER; IT IS ETERNAL.

A

Gen. 14. 20. *See under A, § 511.*

B

Num. 18. 21. *See under C, § 511.*

Num. 18. 26 Thus speak unto the Levites, and say unto them, When ye take of the children of Israel the tithes which I have given you from them for your inheritance, then ye shall offer up a heave offering of it for the LORD, *even* a tenth *part* of the tithe.

1

Or, *pedigree.*

C

Gen. 14 19. *See under A, § 511.*

D

Rom. 4. 13 For the promise, that he should be the heir of the world, *was* not to Abraham or to his seed, through the law, but through the righteousness of faith.

Rom. 9. 4 Who are Israelites; to whom *pertaineth* the adoption, and the glory, and the covenants, and the giving of the law, and the service *of God*, and the promises;

Gal. 3. 16 Now to Abraham and his seed were the promises made. He saith not, And to seeds, as of many; but as one, And to thy seed, which is Christ.

E

Heb. 5. 6 As he saith also in another *place*, Thou *art* a priest for ever after the order of Melchisedec.

Heb. 6. 20 Whither the forerunner is for us entered, *even* Jesus, made a high priest for ever after the order of Melchisedec.

Rev. 1. 18 *I am* he that liveth, and was dead; and, behold, I am alive for evermore, Amen; and have the keys of hell and of death.

E—CONCLUDED.

F

Gal. 2. 21 I do not frustrate the grace of God: for if righteousness *come* by the law, then Christ is dead in vain,

Heb. 7. 18, 19. *See text of topic.*

Heb. 8. 7 For if that first *covenant* had been faultless, then should no place have been sought for the second.

G

Isa. 11. 1 And there shall come forth a rod out of the stem of Jesse, and a Branch shall grow out of his roots:

Matt. 1. 3 And Judas begat Phares and Zara of Thamar; and Phares begat Esrom; and Esrom begat Aram;

Luke 3. 33 Which was *the son* of Aminadab, which was *the son* of Aram, which was *the son* of Esrom, which was *the son* of Phares, which was *the son* of Juda.

Rom. 1. 3 Concerning his Son Jesus Christ our Lord, which was made of the seed of David according to the flesh;

Rev. 5. 5 And one of the elders saith unto me, Weep not: behold, the Lion of the tribe of Juda, the Root of David, hath prevailed to open the book, and to loose the seven seals thereof.

H

Heb. 5. 6. *See l, L, § 508, page 1182.*
Heb. 6. 20. *See i, I, § 510, page 1186.*

I

Rom. 8. 3. *See e, E, § 332, page 842,*

Gal. 4. 9 But now, after that ye have known God, or rather are known of God how turn ye again to the weak and beggarly elements, whereunto ye desire again to be in bondage?

§ 512. THE ORDER OF MELCHISEDEC IS GREATER THAN

CHAP. 7.

19 For [k]the law made nothing perfect, [2]but the bringing in of [l]a better hope *did;* by the which [m]we draw nigh unto God.

20 And inasmuch as not without an oath *he was made priest:*

21 (For those priests were made [3]without an oath; but this with an oath by him that said unto him,[n]The Lord sware and will not repent, Thou *art* a priest for ever after the order of Melchisedec:)

22 By so much [o]was Jesus made a surety of a better testament.

23 And they truly were many priests, because they were not suffered to continue by reason of death:

24 But this *man,* because he continueth ever, hath an [4]unchangeable priesthood.

25 Wherefore [p]he is able also to save them [5]to the uttermost that come unto God by him, seeing he ever liveth [q]to make intercession for them.

K

Rom. 3. 20, 21, 28. *See c, C, § 324, page 824.*

Heb. 9. 9 Which *was* a figure for the time then present, in which were offered both gifts and sacrifices, that could not make him that did the service perfect, as pertaining to the conscience;

2

Or, *but,* it was *the bringing in,*

Gal. 3. 24 Wherefore the law was our schoolmaster *to bring us* unto Christ, that we might be justified by faith.

L

Heb. 6. 18 That by two immutable things, in which *it was* impossible for God to lie, we might have a strong consolation, who have fled for refuge to lay hold upon the hope set before us:

Heb. 8. 6 But now hath he obtained a more excellent ministry, by how much also he is the mediator of a better covenant, which was established upon better promises.

M

Rom. 5. 2. *See b, B, § 326, page 830.*

3

Or, *without swearing of an oath.*

N

Ps. 110. 4 The LORD hath sworn, and will not repent, Thou *art* a priest for ever after the order of Melchizedek.

O

Heb. 8. 6. *See under L.*

§ 513. CHRIST IS A HOLY HIGH PRIEST.

7 : 26–28.

26 For such a high priest became us, [a]*who is* holy, harmless, undefiled, separate from sinners, [b]and made higher than the heavens;

27 Who needeth not daily, as those high priests, to offer up sacrifice, [c]first for his own sins, and [d]then for the people's: for [e]this he did once, when he offered up himself.

28 For the law maketh [f]men high priests which have infirmity; but the word of the oath, which was since the law, *maketh* the Son, [g]who is [1]consecrated for evermore.

A

Heb. 4. 15 For we have not a high priest which cannot be touched with the feeling of our infirmities; but was in all points tempted like as *we are, yet* without sin.

B

Eph. 1. 20 Which he wrought in Christ, when he raised him from the dead, and set *him* at his own right hand in the heavenly *places,*

Eph. 4. 10 He that descended is the same also that ascended up far above all heavens, that he might fill all things.)

Heb. 8. 1 Now of the things which we have spoken *this is* the sum: We have such a high priest, who is set on the right hand of the throne of the Majesty in the heavens;

THE LEVITICAL ORDER; IT IS ETERNAL (CONCLUDED).

O—CONCLUDED.

Heb. 9. 15 And for this cause he is the mediator of the new testament, that by means of death, for the redemption of the transgressions *that were* under the first testament, they which are called might receive the promise of eternal inheritance.

Heb. 12. 24 And to Jesus the mediator of the new covenant, and to the blood of sprinkling, that speaketh better things than *that of* Abel.

4

Or, *which passeth not from one to another.*

P

Isa. 45. 22 Look unto me, and be ye saved, all the ends of the earth: for I *am* God, and *there is* none else.

Isa. 63. 1 Who *is* this that cometh from Edom, with dyed garments from Bozrah? this *that is* glorious in his apparel, travelling in the greatness of his strength? I that speak in righteousness, mighty to save.

John 10. 29 My Father, which gave *them* me, is greater than all; and no *man* is able to pluck *them* out of my Father's hand.
30 I and *my* Father are one.

Eph. 3. 20 Now unto him that is able to do exceeding abundantly above all that we ask or think, according to the power that worketh in us,
21 Unto him *be* glory in the church by Christ Jesus throughout all ages, world without end. Amen.

P—CONCLUDED.

II Tim. 1. 12 For the which cause I also suffer these things: nevertheless I am not ashamed: for I know whom I have believed, and am persuaded that he is able to keep that which I have committed unto him against that day.

Heb. 2. 18 For in that he himself hath suffered being tempted, he is able to succour them that are tempted.

Jude 24 Now unto him that is able to keep you from falling, and to present *you* faultless before the presence of his glory with exceeding joy,

5

Or, *evermore.*

Q

Rom. 8. 34 Who *is* he that condemneth? *It is* Christ that died, yea rather, that is risen again, who is even at the right hand of God, who also maketh intercession for us.

I Tim. 2. 5 For *there is* one God, and one mediator between God and men, the man Christ Jesus;

Heb. 9. 24 For Christ is not entered into the holy places made with hands, *which are* the figures of the true; but into heaven itself, now to appear in the presence of God for us:

I Jno. 2. 1 My little children, these things write I unto you, that ye sin not. And if any man sin, we have an advocate with the Father, Jesus Christ, the righteous:

HE OFFERED HIMSELF ONCE FOR ALL.

C

Heb. 5. 3. *See f, F, § 508, page 1180.*

D

Lev. 16. 15 Then shall he kill the goat of the sin offering, that *is* for the people, and bring his blood within the vail, and do with that blood as he did with the blood of the bullock, and sprinkle it upon the mercy seat, and before the mercy seat:

E

Rom. 6. 10. *See p, P, § 328, page 836.*

Heb. 9. 12 Neither by the blood of goats and calves, but by his own blood he entered in once into the holy place, having obtained eternal redemption *for us.*

Heb. 10. 12 But this man, after he had offered one sacrifice for sins for ever, sat down on the right hand of God;

F

Heb. 5. 1 For every high priest taken from among men is ordained for men in things *pertaining* to God, that he may offer both gifts and sacrifices for sins:
2 Who can have compassion on the ignorant, and on them that are out of the way; for that he himself also is compassed with infirmity.

G

Heb. 2. 10 For it became him, for whom *are* all things, and by whom *are* all things, in bringing many sons unto glory, to make the captain of their salvation perfect through sufferings.

Heb. 5. 9 And being made perfect, he became the author of eternal salvation unto all them that obey him;

1

Gr. *perfected.*

§ 514. CHRIST OUR HIGH PRIEST IN HEAVEN IS MEDIATOR OF

8 : 1–13.

1 Now of the things which we have spoken *this is* the sum: We have such a high priest, [a]who is set on the right hand of the throne of the Majesty in the heavens;

2 A minister [1]of [b]the sanctuary, and of [c]the true tabernacle, which the Lord pitched, and not man.

3 For [d]every high priest is ordained to offer gifts and sacrifices: wherefore [e]*it is* of necessity that this man have somewhat also to offer.

4 For if he were on earth, he should not be a priest, seeing that [2]there are priests that offer gifts according to the law:

5 Who serve unto the example and shadow of heavenly things, as Moses was admonished of God when he was about to make the tabernacle: [g]for, See, saith he, *that* thou make all things according to the pattern shewed to thee in the mount.

6 But now [h]hath he obtained a more excellent ministry, by how much also he is the mediator of a better [3]covenant, which was established upon better promises.

7 [i]For if that first *covenant* had been faultless, then should no place have been sought for the second.

8 For finding fault with them, he saith, [k]Behold, the days come, saith the Lord, when I will make a new covenant with the house of Israel and with the house of Judah:

9 Not according to the covenant that I made with their fathers, in the day when I took them by the hand

Chap. 8.

to lead them out of the land of Egypt; because they continued not in my covenant, and I regarded them not, saith the Lord.

10 For [l]this *is* the covenant that I will make with the house of Israel after those days, saith the Lord; I will [4]put my laws into their mind, and write them [5]in their hearts: and [m]I will be to them a God, and they shall be to me a people:

11 And [n]they shall not teach every man his neighbour, and every man his brother, saying, Know the Lord: for all shall know me, from the least to the greatest.

12 For I will be merciful to their unrighteousness, [o]and their sins and their iniquities will I remember no more.

13 [p]In that he saith, A new *covenant*, he hath made the first old. Now that which decayeth and waxeth old *is* ready to vanish away.

A

Eph. 1. 20. *See k, K,* *§ 427, page 1032.*

Heb. 12. 2 Looking unto Jesus the author and finisher of *our* faith; who for the joy that was set before him endured the cross, despising the shame, and is set down at the right hand of the throne of God.

1

Or, *of holy things.*

B

Heb. 9. 8 The Holy Ghost this signifying, that the way into the holiest of all was not yet made manifest, while as the first tabernacle was yet standing:

Heb. 9. 12 Neither by the blood of goats and calves, but by his own blood he entered in once into the holy place, having obtained eternal redemption *for us.*

Heb. 9. 24 For Christ is not entered into the holy places made with hands, *which are* the figures of the true; but into heaven itself, now to appear in the presence of God for us:

A NEW COVENANT, FULFILLING SHADOWS AND PROPHECIES.

C

Heb. 9. 11 But Christ being come a high priest of good things to come, by a greater and more perfect tabernacle, not made with hands, that is to say, not of this building;

D

Heb. 5. 1 For every high priest taken from among men is ordained for men in things *pertaining* to God, that he may offer both gifts and sacrifices for sins:

E

Eph. 5. 2 And walk in love, as Christ also hath loved us, and hath given himself for us an offering and a sacrifice to God for a sweetsmelling savour.

Heb. 9. 14 How much more shall the blood of Christ, who through the eternal Spirit offered himself without spot to God, purge your conscience from dead works to serve the living God?

2

Or, *they are priests.*

F

Col. 2. 17. *See d, D, § 453, page 1086.*

Heb. 9. 23 *It was* therefore necessary that the patterns of things in the heavens should be purified with these; but the heavenly things themselves with better sacrifices than these.

Heb. 9. 24. *See under B.*

G

Ex. 25. 40 And look that thou make *them* after their pattern, which was shewed thee in the mount.

Ex. 26. 30 And thou shalt rear up the tabernacle according to the fashion thereof which was shewed thee in the mount.

Ex. 27. 8 Hollow with boards shalt thou make it: as it was shewed thee in the mount, so shall they make *it*.

Acts 7. 44 Our fathers had the tabernacle of witness in the wilderness, as he had appointed, speaking unto Moses, that he should make it according to the fashion that he had seen.

H

II Cor. 3. 6. *See k, K, § 390, page 970.*

3

Or, *testament.*

I

Heb. 7. 11. *See f, F, § 512, page 1188.*

K

Jer. 31. 31 Behold, the days come, saith the LORD, that I will make a new covenant with the house of Israel, and with the house of Judah:

K—CONCLUDED.

Jer. 31. 32 Not according to the covenant that I made with their fathers, in the day *that* I took them by the hand to bring them out of the land of Egypt; which my covenant they brake, although I was a husband unto them, saith the LORD:

33 But this *shall be* the covenant that I will make with the house of Israel; After those days, saith the LORD, I will put my law in their inward parts, and write it in their hearts; and will be their God, and they shall be my people.

34 And they shall teach no more every man his neighbour, and every man his brother, saying, Know the LORD: for they shall all know me, from the least of them unto the greatest of them, saith the LORD: for I will forgive their iniquity, and I will remember their sin no more.

L

Heb. 10 16 This *is* the covenant that I will make with them after those days, saith the Lord, I will put my laws into their hearts, and in their minds will I write them;

4

Gr. *give.*

5

Or, *upon.*

M

Zech. 8. 8 And I will bring them, and they shall dwell in the midst of Jerusalem: and they shall be my people, and I will be their God, in truth and in righteousness.

N

John 6. 45. *See y, Y § 83, page 257.*

I Jno. 2. 27 But the anointing which ye have received of him abideth in you, and ye need not that any man teach you: but as the same anointing teacheth you of all things, and is truth, and is no lie, and even as it hath taught you, ye shall abide in him.

O

Rom. 11. 27 For this *is* my covenant unto them, when I shall take away their sins.

Heb. 10. 17 And their sins and iniquities will I remember no more.

P

II Cor. 5. 17 Therefore if any man *be* in Christ, *he is* a new creature: old things are passed away; behold, all things are become new.

§ 515. THE MINISTRATION OF THE FIRST COVENANT

9 : 1–10.

1 Then verily the first *covenant* had also [1]ordinances of divine service, and [a]a worldly sanctuary.

2 [b]For there was a tabernacle made; the first, [c]wherein *was* [d]the candlestick, and [e]the table, and the shewbread; which is called [2]the sanctuary.

3 [f]And after the second vail, the tabernacle which is called the Holiest of all;

4 Which had the golden censer, and [g]the ark of the covenant overlaid round about with gold, wherein *was* [h]the golden pot that had manna, and [i]Aaron's rod that budded, and [k]the tables of the covenant;

5 And [l]over it the cherubims of glory shadowing the mercy seat; of which we cannot now speak particularly.

6 Now when these things were thus ordained, [m]the priest went always into the first tabernacle, accomplishing the service *of God*.

7 But into the second *went* the high priest alone [n]once every year, not without blood, [o]which he offered for himself, and *for* the errors of the people:

8 [p]The Holy Ghost this signifying, that [q]the way into the holiest of all

1

Or, *ceremonies*.

A

Ex. 25. 8 And let them make me a sanctuary; that I may dwell among them.

B

Ex. 26. 1 Moreover thou shalt make the tabernacle *with* ten curtains *of* fine twined linen, and blue, and purple and scarlet: *with* cherubims of cunning work shalt thou make them.

C

Ex. 26. 35 And thou shalt set the table without the vail, and the candlestick over against the table on the side of the tabernacle toward the south: and thou shalt put the table on the north side.

C—Concluded.

Ex. 40. 4 And thou shalt bring in the table, and set in order the things that are to be set in order upon it; and thou shalt bring in the candlestick, and light the lamps thereof.

D

Ex. 25. 31 And thou shalt make a candlestick *of* pure gold: *of* beaten work shall the candlestick be made: his shaft, and his branches, his bowls, his knops, and his flowers, shall be of the same.

E

Ex. 25. 23 Thou shalt also make a table of shittim wood: two cubits *shall be* the length thereof, and a cubit the breadth thereof, and a cubit and a half the height thereof.

Ex. 25. 30 And thou shalt set upon the table shewbread before me alway.

Lev. 24. 5 And thou shalt take fine flour, and bake twelve cakes thereof: two tenth deals shall be in one cake.

2

Or, *holy*.

F

Ex. 26. 31 And thou shalt make a vail *of* blue, and purple, and scarlet, and fine twined linen of cunning work: with cherubims shall it be made.

Ex. 26. 33 And thou shalt hang up the vail under the taches, that thou mayest bring in thither within the vail the ark of the testimony: and the vail shall divide unto you between the holy *place* and the most holy.

Ex. 40. 3 And thou shalt put therein the ark of the testimony, and cover the ark with the vail.

Ex. 40. 21 And he brought the ark into the tabernacle, and set up the vail of the covering, and covered the ark of the testimony; as the Lord commanded Moses.

Heb. 6. 19 Which *hope* we have as an anchor of the soul, both sure and steadfast, and which entereth into that within the veil.

G

Ex. 25. 10 And they shall make an ark *of* shittim wood: two cubits and a half *shall be* the length thereof, and a cubit and a half the breadth thereof, and a cubit and half the height thereof.

Ex. 26. 33. *See under F.*

Ex. 40. 3, 21. *See under F.*

FAILED TO MAKE THE WORSHIPERS PERFECT.

H

Ex. 16. 33 And Moses said unto Aaron, Take a pot, and put an omer full of manna therein, and lay it up before the LORD, to be kept for your generations.

34 As the LORD commanded Moses, so Aaron laid it up before the Testimony, to be kept.

I

Num. 17. 10 And the LORD said unto Moses, Bring Aaron's rod again before the testimony, to be kept for a token against the rebels; and thou shalt quite take way their murmurings from me, that they die not.

K

Ex. 25. 16 And thou shalt put into the ark the testimony which I shall give thee.

Ex. 25. 21 And thou shalt put the mercy seat above upon the ark: and in the ark thou shalt put the testimony that I shall give thee.

Ex. 34. 29 And it came to pass, when Moses came down from mount Sinai with the two tables of testimony in Moses' hand, when he came down from the mount, that Moses wist not that the skin of his face shone while he talked with him.

Ex. 40. 20 And he took and put the testimony into the ark, and set the staves on the ark, and put the mercy seat above upon the ark:

Deut. 10. 2 And I will write on the tables the words that were in the first tables which thou brakest, and thou shalt put them in the ark.

Deut. 10. 5 And I turned myself and came down from the mount, and put the tables in the ark which I had made; and there they be, as the LORD commanded me.

I Ki. 8. 9 *There was* nothing in the ark save the two tables of stone, which Moses put there at Horeb, when the LORD made *a covenant* with the children of Israel, when they came out of the land of Egypt.

I Ki. 8. 21 And I have set there a place for the ark, wherein *is* the covenant of the LORD, which he made with our fathers, when he brought them out of the land of Egypt.

II Chr. 5. 10 *There was* nothing in the ark save the two tables which Moses put *therein* at Horeb, when the LORD made *a covenant* with the children of Israel, when they came out of Egypt.

L

Ex. 25. 18 And thou shalt make two cherubims *of* gold, *of* beaten work shalt thou make them, in the two ends of the mercy seat.

Ex. 25. 22 And there I will meet with thee, and I will commune with thee, from above the mercy seat, from between the two cherubims which *are* upon the ark of the testimony, of all *things* which I will give thee in commandment unto the children of Israel.

Lev. 16. 2 And the LORD said unto Moses, Speak unto Aaron thy brother, that he come not at all times unto the holy *place* within the vail before the mercy seat, which *is* upon the ark; that he die not: for I will appear in the cloud upon the mercy seat.

I Ki. 8. 6 And the priests brought in the ark of the covenant of the LORD unto his place, into the oracle of the house, to the most holy *place*, *even* under the wings of the cherubims.

7 For the cherubims spread forth *their* two wings over the place of the ark, and the cherubims covered the ark and the staves thereof above.

M

Num. 28. 3 And thou shalt say unto them, This *is* the offering made by fire which ye shall offer unto the LORD; two lambs of the first year without spot day by day, *for* a continual burnt offering.

Da. 8. 11 Yea, he magnified *himself* even to the prince of the host, and by him the daily *sacrifice* was taken away, and the place of his sanctuary was cast down.

N

Ex. 30. 10 And Aaron shall make an atonement upon the horns of it once in a year with the blood of the sin offering of atonements: once in the year shall he make atonement upon it throughout your generations: it *is* most holy unto the LORD.

Lev. 16. 2. *See under L.*

Lev. 16. 11 And Aaron shall bring the bullock of the sin offering, which *is* for himself, and shall make an atonement for himself, and for his house, and shall kill the bullock of the sin offering which *is* for himself:

12 And he shall take a censer full of burning coals of fire from off the altar before the LORD, and his hands full of sweet incense beaten small, and bring *it* within the vail:

For N concluded, O, P and Q, see next page (1196).

§ 515. THE MINISTRATION OF THE FIRST COVENANT

CHAP. 9.

was not yet made manifest, while as
the first tabernacle was yet standing:
9 Which *was* a figure for the time
then present, in which were offered
both gifts and sacrifices, [r]that could
not make him that did the service perfect, as pertaining to the conscience;
10 *Which stood* only in [s]meats and
drinks, and [t]divers washings, [u]and
carnal [3]ordinances, imposed *on them*
until the time of reformation.

N—CONCLUDED.

Lev. 16. 15 Then shall he kill the goat of the sin offering, that *is* for the people, and bring his blood within the vail, and do with that blood as he did with the blood of the bullock, and sprinkle it upon the mercy seat, and before the mercy seat:

Lev. 16. 34 And this shall be an everlasting statute unto you, to make an atonement for the children of Israel for all their sins once a year, And he did as the LORD commanded Moses.

O

Heb. 5. 3. *See f, F, § 508, page 1180.*

§ 516. CHRIST OFFERED HIMSELF FOR SIN AND ENTERED THE HEAVENLIES.

9: 11–28.

11 But Christ being come [a]a high
priest [b]of good things to come, [c]by a
greater and more perfect tabernacle,
not made with hands, that is to say,
not of this building;
12 Neither [d]by the blood of goats
and calves, but [e]by his own blood he
entered in [f]once into the holy place,
[g]having obtained eternal redemption
for us.
13 For if [h]the blood of bulls and of
goats, and [i]the ashes of a heifer
sprinkling the unclean, sanctifieth to
the purifying of the flesh:
14 How much more [k]shall the blood
of Christ, [l]who through the eternal
Spirit [m]offered himself without [1]spot
to God, [n]purge your conscience from
[o]dead works [p]to serve the living God?
15 And for this cause [q]he is the
mediator of the new testament, [r]that
by means of death, for the redemption of the transgressions *that were*
under the first testament, [s]they which
are called might receive the promise
of eternal inheritance.

A

Heb. 3. 1. *See b, B, § 506, page 1176.*

B

Heb. 10. 1 For the law having a shadow of good things to come, *and* not the very image of the things, can never with those sacrifices which they offered year by year continually, make the comers thereunto perfect.

C

Heb. 8. 2 A minister of the sanctuary, and of the true tabernacle, which the Lord pitched, and not man.

D

Heb. 10. 4 For *it is* not possible that the blood of bulls and of goats should take away sins.

E

Acts 20. 28. *See s, S, § 292, page 762.*

F

Zech. 3. 9 For behold the stone that I have laid before Joshua; upon one stone *shall be* seven eyes: behold, I will engrave the graving thereof, saith the LORD of hosts, and I will remove the iniquity of that land in one day.

Heb. 9. 26, 28. *See text of topic, page 1200.*

Heb. 10. 10 By the which will we are sanctified through the offering of the body of Jesus Christ once *for all.*

G

Da. 9. 24 Seventy weeks are determined upon thy people and upon thy holy city, to finish the transgression, and to make an end of sins, and to make reconciliation for iniquity, and to bring in everlasting righteousness, and

FAILED TO MAKE THE WORSHIPERS PERFECT (Concluded).

P

Heb. 10. 19 Having therefore, brethren, boldness to enter into the holiest by the blood of Jesus,

20 By a new and living way, which he hath consecrated for us, through the veil, that is to say, his flesh;

Q

John 14. 6 Jesus saith him, I am the way, the truth, and the life: no man cometh unto the Father, but by me.

R

Rom. 8. 3. *See e, E, § 332, page 842.*

S

Lev. 11. 2 Speak unto the children of Israel, saying, These *are* the beasts which ye

S—Concluded.

shall eat among all the beasts that *are* on the earth.

Col. 2. 16. *See b, B, § 453, page 1086.*

T

Num. 19. 7 Then the priest shall wash his clothes, and he shall bathe his flesh in water, and afterward he shall come into the camp, and the priest shall be unclean until the even.

U

Eph. 2. 15. *See m, M, § 429, page 1036.*

Heb. 7. 16 Who is made, not after the law of a carnal commandment, but after the power of an endless life.

3

Or, *rites*, or, *ceremonies*.

WHENCE HE SHALL APPEAR THE SECOND TIME WITH SALVATION.

G—Concluded.

to seal up the vision and prophecy, and to anoint the Most Holy.

H

Lev. 16. 14 And he shall take of the blood of the bullock, and sprinkle *it* with his finger upon the mercy seat eastward; and before the mercy seat shall he sprinkle of the blood with his finger seven times.

15 Then shall he kill the goat of the sin offering, that *is* for the people, and bring his blood within the vail, and do with that blood as he did with the blood of the bullock, and sprinkle it upon the mercy seat, and before the mercy seat:

16 And he shall make an atonement for the holy *place*, because of the uncleanness of the children of Israel, and because of their transgressions in all their sins: and so shall he do for the tabernacle of the congregation, that remaineth among them in the midst of their uncleanness.

I

Num. 19. 2 This *is* the ordinance of the law which the Lord hath commanded, saying, Speak unto the children of Israel, that they bring thee a red heifer without spot, wherein *is* no blemish, *and* upon which never came yoke:

Num. 19. 17 And for an unclean *person* they shall take of the ashes of the burnt heifer of purification for sin, and running water shall be put thereto in a vessel:

K

I Pet. 1. 19 But with the precious blood of Christ, as of a lamb without blemish and without spot:

I Jno. 1. 7 But if we walk in the light, as he is the light, we have fellowship one with another, and the blood of Jesus Christ his son cleanseth us from all sin.

Rev. 1. 5 And from Jesus Christ, *who is* the faithful witness, *and* the first-begotten of the dead, and the prince of the kings of the earth. Unto him that loved us, and washed us from our sins in his own blood,

L

Rom. 1. 4. *See h, H, § 317, page 808.*

M

Eph. 5. 2. *See c, C, § 434, page 1046.*

1

Or, *fault.*

N

Heb. 1. 3. *See h, H, § 503, page 1168.*

O

Heb. 6. 1. *See h, H, § 509, page 1184.*

P

Luke 1. 74. *See s, S, § 6, page 21.*

I Pet. 4. 2 That he no longer should live the rest of *his* time in the flesh to the lusts of men, but to the will of God.

Q

Heb. 7. 22. *See o, O, § 512, page 1190.*

I Tim. 2. 5 For *there is* one God, and one mediator between God and men, the man Christ Jesus:

For R, and S, see next page (1198).

§ 516. CHRIST OFFERED HIMSELF FOR SIN, ENTERED THE HEAVENLIES,

CHAP. 9.

16 For where a testament *is*, there must also of necessity [2]be the death of the testator.

17 For [t]a testament *is* of force after men are dead: otherwise it is of no strength at all while the testator liveth.

18 [u]Whereupon neither the first *testament* was [3]dedicated without blood.

19 For when Moses had spoken every precept to all the people according to the law, [x]he took the blood of calves and of goats, [y]with water, and [4]scarlet wool, and hyssop, and sprinkled both the book, and all the people,

20 Saying, [z]This *is* the blood of the testament which God hath enjoined unto you.

21 Moreover [a]he sprinkled likewise with blood both the tabernacle, and all the vessels of the ministry.

22 And almost all things are by the law purged with blood; and [b]without shedding of blood is no remission.

23 *It was* therefore necessary that [c]the patterns of things in the heavens should be purified with these; but the heavenly things themselves with better sacrifices than these.

24 For [d]Christ is not entered into the holy places made with hands, *which are* the figures of [e]the true; but into heaven itself, now [f]to appear in the presence of God for us:

25 Nor yet that he should offer himself often, as [g]the high priest entereth into the holy place every year with blood of others;

R

Rom. 4. 25. *See b, B, § 325, page 830.*

S

Heb. 3. 1. *See a, A, § 506, page 1176.*

2

Or, *be brought in.*

T

Gal. 3. 15 Brethren, I speak after the manner of men; Though *it be* but a man's covenant, yet *if it be* confirmed, no man disannulleth, or addeth thereto.

U

Ex. 24. 6 And Moses took half of the blood, and put *it* in basins; and half of the blood he sprinkled on the altar.

3

Or, *purified.*

X

Ex. 24. 5 And he sent young men of the children of Israel which offered burnt offerings, and sacrificed peace offerings of oxen unto the LORD.

Ex. 24. 6. *See under U.*

Ex. 24. 7 And he took the book of the covenant, and read in the audience of the people: and they said, All that the LORD hath said will we do, and be obedient.

8 And Moses took the blood, and sprinkled *it* on the people, and said, Behold the blood of the covenant, which the LORD hath made with you concerning all these words.

Y

Lev. 14. 4 Then shall the priest command to take for him that is to be cleansed two birds alive *and* clean, and cedar wood, and scarlet, and hyssop:

Lev. 14. 6 As for the living bird, he shall take it, and the cedar wood, and the scarlet, and the hyssop, and shall dip them and the living bird in the blood of the bird *that was* killed over the running water:

7 And he shall sprinkle upon him that is to be cleansed from the leprosy seven times, and shall pronounce him clean, and shall let the living bird loose into the open field.

Lev. 14. 49 And he shall take to cleanse the house two birds, and cedar wood, and scarlet, and hyssop:

Lev. 14. 51 And he shall take the cedar wood, and the hyssop, and the scarlet, and the living bird, and dip them in the blood of the slain bird, and in the running water, and sprinkle the house seven times:

WHENCE HE SHALL APPEAR THE SECOND TIME WITH SALVATION (CONTIN'D).

Y—CONCLUDED.

52 And he shall cleanse the house with the blood of the bird, and with the running water, and with the living bird, and with the cedar wood, and with the hyssop, and with the scarlet:

4

Or, *purple.*

Z

Ex. 24. 8 . *See under X.*

Zech. 9. 11 As for thee also, by the blood of thy covenant I have sent forth thy prisoners out of the pit wherein *is* no water.

Matt. 26. 28 For this is my blood of the new testament, which is shed for many for the remission of sins.

A

Ex. 29. 12 And thou shalt take of the blood of the bullock, and put *it* upon the horns of the altar with thy finger, and pour all the blood beside the bottom of the altar.

Ex 29. 36 And thou shalt offer every day a bullock *for* a sin offering for atonement: and thou shalt cleanse the altar, when thou hast made an atonement for it, and thou shalt anoint it, to sanctify it.

Lev. 8. 15 And he slew *it*; and Moses took the blood, and put *it* upon the horns of the altar round about with his finger, and purified the altar, and poured the blood at the bottom of the altar, and sanctified it, to make reconciliation upon it.

Lev. 8. 19 And he killed *it*; and Moses sprinkled the blood upon the altar round about.

Lev. 16. 14, 15, 16. *See under H, page 1197.*

Lev. 16. 18 And he shall go out unto the altar that *is* before the LORD, and make an atonement for it; and shall take of the blood of the bullock and of the blood of the goat, and put *it* upon the horns of the altar round about.

19 And he shall sprinkle of the blood upon it with his finger seven times, and cleanse it, and hallow it from the uncleanness of the children of Israel.

B

Lev. 17. 11 For the life of the flesh *is* in the blood; and I have given it to you upon the altar to make an atonement for your souls: for it *is* the blood *that* maketh an atonement for the soul.

C

Heb. 8. 5. *See f, F, § 514, page 1192.*

D

Heb. 6. 20. *See h, H, § 509, page 1186.*

E

Heb. 8. 2 A minister of the sanctuary, and of the true tabernacle, which the LORD pitched, and not man.

F

Rom. 8. 34. *See s, S, § 334, page 850.*

I Jno. 2. 1 My little children, these things write I unto you, that ye sin not. And if any man sin, we have an advocate with the Father, Jesus Christ the righteous:

G

Heb. 9. 7 But unto the second *went* the high priest alone once every year, not without blood, which he offered for himself, and *for* the errors of the people:

H

Heb. 9. 12. *See text of topic.*

I Pet. 3. 18 For Christ also hath once suffered for sins, the just for the unjust, that he might bring us to God, being put to death in the flesh, but quickened by the Spirit:

I

I Cor. 10. 11 Now all these things happened unto them for ensamples: and they are written for our admonition, upon whom the ends of the world are come.

Eph. 1. 10. *See o, O, § 426, page 1030.*

K

Gen. 3. 19 In the sweat of thy face shalt thou eat bread, till thou return unto the ground; for out of it wast thou taken: for dust thou *art*, and unto dust shalt thou return.

II Sa. 14. 14 For we must needs die, and *are* as water spilt on the ground, which cannot be gathered up again: neither doth God respect *any* person; yet doth he devise means, that his banished be not expelled from him.

Job 14. 10 But man dieth, and wasteth away: yea, man giveth up the ghost, and where *is* he?

Job 30. 23 For I know *that* thou wilt bring me *to* death, and *to* the house appointed for all living.

Ps. 89. 48 What man *is he that* liveth, and shall not see death? shall he deliver his soul from the hand of the grave? Selah.

Eccl. 3. 20 All go unto one place; all are of the dust, and all turn to dust again.

Eccl. 9. 5 For the living know that they shall die: but the dead know not any thing, neither have they any more a reward; for the memory of them is forgotten.

§ 516. CHRIST OFFERED HIMSELF FOR SIN, ENTERED THE HEAVENLIES,

CHAP. 9.

26 For then must he often have
suffered since the foundation of the
world: but now [h]once [i]in the end of
the world hath he appeared to put
away sin by the sacrifice of himself.
27 [k]And as it is appointed unto
men once to die, [l]but after this the
judgment:
28 [m]Christ was once [n]offered to
bear the sins [o]of many; and unto
them that [p]look for him shall he appear
the second time without sin
unto salvation.

For H, I and K, see preceding page (1199).

K—CONCLUDED.

Eccl. 12. 7 Then shall the dust return to the earth as it was: and the spirit shall return unto God who gave it.

Rom. 5. 12 Wherefore as by one man sin entered into the world, and death by sin; and so death passed upon all men, for that all have sinned:

L

Acts 17. 31. *See t, T, § 279, page 746.*

II Cor. 5. 10. *See i, I, § 394, page 976.*

Rev. 20. 12 And I saw the dead, small and great, stand before God; and the books were opened: and another book was opened, which is *the book* of life: and the dead were judged out of those

§ 517. THE LAW HAVING A SHADOW, COULD NOT PERFECT, BUT THE

10:1-18.

1 For the law having [a]a shadow
[b]of good things to come, *and* not the
very image of the things, [c]can never
with those sacrifices, which they offered
year by year continually make
the comers thereunto [d]perfect.
2 For then [1]would they not have
ceased to be offered? because that
the worshippers once purged should
have had no more conscience of
sins.
3 [e]But in those *sacrifices there is*
a remembrance again *made* of sins
every year.
4 For [f]*it is* not possible that the
blood of bulls and of goats should
take away sins.
5 Wherefore, when he cometh into
the world, he saith, [g]Sacrifice and
offering thou wouldest not, but a
body [2]hast thou prepared me:
6 In burnt offerings and *sacrifices*
for sin thou hast had no pleasure.
7 Then said I, Lo, I come (in the

CHAP. 10.

volume of the book it is written of
me,) to do thy will, O God.
8 Above when he said, Sacrifice
and offering and burnt offerings and
offering for sin thou wouldest not,
neither hadst pleasure *therein;* which
are offered by the law;
9 Then said he, Lo, I come to do
thy will, O God. He taketh away
the first, that he may establish the
second.

A

Col. 2. 17. *See d, D, § 453, page 1086.*

Heb. 9. 23 *It was* therefore necessary that the patterns of things in the heavens should be purified with these; but the heavenly things themselves with better sacrifices than these.

B

Heb. 9. 11 But Christ being come a high priest of good things to come, by a greater and more perfect tabernacle, not made with hands, that is to say, not of this building;

C

Heb. 9. 9 Which *was* a figure for the time then present, in which were offered both gifts and sacrifices, that could not make him that did the service perfect, as pertaining to the conscience;

D

Heb. 10. 14. *See text of topic.*

WHENCE HE SHALL APPEAR THE SECOND TIME WITH SALVATION (Conclu'd).

L—Concluded.

things which were written in the books, according to their works.

Rev. 20. 13 And the sea gave up the dead which were in it; and death and hell delivered up the dead which were in them: and they were judged every man according to their works.

M

Rom. 6. 10. *See p, P, § 328, page 836.*
I Pet. 3. 18. *See under H.*

N

1 Pet. 2. 24 Who his own self bare our sins in his own body on the tree, that we, being dead to sins, should live unto righteousness: by whose stripes ye were healed.

I Jno. 3. 5 And ye know that he was manifested to take away our sins; and in him is no sin.

O

Rom. 5. 15. *See e, E, § 327, page 834.*

P

I Cor. 1. 7 So that ye come behind in no gift; waiting for the coming of our Lord Jesus Christ:

Tit. 2. 13 Looking for that blessed hope, and the glorious appearing of the great God and our Saviour Jesus Christ;

II Pet. 3. 12 Looking for and hasting unto the coming of the day of God, wherein the heavens being on fire shall be dissolved, and the elements shall melt with fervent heat?

OFFERING OF THE BODY OF CHRIST BY THE WILL OF GOD SANCTIFIETH.

I

Or, *they would have ceased to be offered, because, etc.*

E

Lev. 16. 21 And Aaron shall lay both his hands upon the head of the live goat, and confess over him all the iniquities of the children of Israel, and all their transgressions in all their sins, putting them upon the head of the goat, and shall send *him* away by the hand of a fit man into the wilderness:

Lev. 16. 34 And this shall be an everlasting statute unto you, to make an atonement for the children of Israel for all their sins once a year. And he did as the Lord commanded Moses.

Heb. 9. 7 But into the second *went* the high priest alone once every year, not without blood, which he offered for himself, and *for* the errors of the people:

F

Mic. 6. 6 Wherewith shall I come before the Lord, *and* bow myself before the high God? shall I come before him with burnt offerings, with calves of a year old?

7 Will the Lord be pleased with thousands of rams, *or* with ten thousands of rivers of oil? shall I give my firstborn *for* my transgression, the fruit of my body *for* the sin of my soul?

Heb. 9. 13 For if the blood of bulls and of goats, and the ashes of a heifer sprinkling the unclean, sanctifieth to the purifying of the flesh;

Heb. 10. 11. *See text of topic.*

G

Ps. 40. 6 Sacrifice and offering thou didst not desire; mine ears hast thou opened: burnt offering and sin offering hast thou not required.

7 Then said I, Lo, I come: in the volume of the book *it is* written of me,

8 I delight to do thy will, O my God: yea, thy law *is* within my heart.

Ps. 50. 8 I will not reprove thee for thy sacrifices or thy burnt offerings, *to have been* continually before me.

9 I will take no bullock out of thy house, *nor* he goats out of thy folds.

10 For every beast of the forest *is* mine, *and* the cattle upon a thousand hills.

11 I know all the fowls of the mountains: and the wild beasts of the field *are* mine.

12 If I were hungry, I would not tell thee: for the world *is* mine, and the fullness thereof.

13 Will I eat the flesh of bulls, or drink the blood of goats?

14 Offer unto God thanksgiving: and pay thy vows unto the Most High:

Isa. 1. 11 To what purpose *is* the multitude of your sacrifices unto me? saith the Lord: I am full of the burnt offerings of rams, and the fat of fed beasts: and I delight not in the blood of bullocks, or of lambs, or of he goats.

Jer. 6. 20 To what purpose cometh there to me incense from Sheba and the sweet cane from a far counry? your burnt

For G concluded and 2, see next page (1202.)

§ 517. THE LAW HAVING A SHADOW, COULD NOT PERFECT, BUT THE

CHAP. 10.

10 [h]By the which will we are sanctified [i]through the offering of the body
of Jesus Christ once *for all.*

11 And every priest standeth [k]daily
ministering and offering oftentimes
the same sacrifices, [l]which can never
take away sins:

12 [m]But this man, after he had offered one sacrifice for sins for ever,
sat down on the right hand of God;

13 From henceforth expecting [n]till
his enemies be made his footstool.

14 For by one offering [o]he hath perfected for ever them that are sanctified.

CHAP. 10.

15 *Whereof* the Holy Ghost also is
a witness to us: for after that he had
said before,

16 [p]This *is* the covenant that I will
make with them after those days,
saith the Lord, I will put my laws
into their hearts, and in their minds
will I write them;

17 [3]And their sins and iniquities
will I remember no more.

18 Now where remission of these *is,*
there is no more offering for sin.

G—CONTINUED.

offerings *are* not acceptable, nor your sacrifices sweet unto me.

Amos 5. 21 I hate, I despise your feast days, and I will not smell in your solemn assemblies.

§ 518. EXHORTATION TO USE THE PRIVILEGES OF THE

10: 19–31.

19 Having therefore, brethren,
[a1]boldness to enter [b]into the holiest
by the blood of Jesus,

20 By [c]a new and living way, which
he hath [2]consecrated for us, [d]through
the vail, that is to say, his flesh;

21 And *having* [e]a high priest over
[f]the house of God;

22 [g]Let us draw near with a true
heart [h]in full assurance of faith,
having our hearts sprinkled [i]from an
evil conscience, and [k]our bodies
washed with pure water.

23 [l]Let us hold fast the profession
of *our* faith without wavering; (for
[m]he *is* faithful that promised;)

24 And let us consider one another
to provoke unto love and to good
works:

25 [n]Not forsaking the assembling of
ourselves together, as the manner of
some *is;* but exhorting *one another:*

A

Rom. 5. 2. *See b, B, § 326, page 830.*

1

Or, *liberty.*

B

Rom. 5. 2 By whom also we have access by faith into this grace wherein we stand, and rejoice in hope of the glory of God.

Eph. 2. 18 For through him we both have access by one Spirit unto the Father.

Heb. 9. 8 The Holy Ghost this signifying, that the way into the holiest of all was not yet made manifest, while as the first tabernacle was yet standing:

C

John 10. 9 I am the door: by me if any man enter in, he shall be saved, and shall go in and out, and find pasture.

John 14. 6 Jesus saith unto him, I am the way, the truth, and the life: no man cometh unto the Father, but by me.

Heb. 9. 8. *See under B.*

2

Or, *new made.*

D

Heb. 9. 3 And after the second veil, the tabernacle which is called the holiest of all;

E

Heb. 3. 1. *See b, B, § 506, page 1176.*

OFFERING OF THE BODY OF CHRIST BY THE WILL OF GOD, ETC. (CONCLU'D).

G—CONCLUDED.

Amos. 5. 22 Though ye offer me burnt offerings and your meat offerings, I will not accept *them:* neither will I regard the peace offerings of your fat beasts.

2

Or, *thou hast fitted me.*

H

John 17. 19. *See m, M, § 191, page 547.*

Heb. 13. 12 Wherefore Jesus also, that he might sanctify the people with his own blood, suffered without the gate.

I

Heb. 9. 12 Neither by the blood of goats and calves, but by his own blood he entered in once into the holy place, having obtained eternal redemption *for us.*

K

Num. 28. 3 And thou shall say unto them, This *is* the offering made by fire which ye shall offer unto the LORD; two lambs of the first year without spot day by day, *for* a continual burnt offering.

K—CONCLUDED.

Heb. 7. 27 Who needeth not daily, as those high priests, to offer up sacrifice, first for his own sins, and then for the people's: for this he did once, when he offered up himself.

L

Heb. 10. 4. *See text of topic.*

M

Col. 3. 1 If ye then be risen with Christ, seek those things which are above, where Christ sitteth on the right hand of God.

Heb. 1. 3. *See h, H, § 503, page 1168.*

N

Heb. 1. 13. *See x, X, § 503, page 1170.*

O

Heb. 10. 1. *See text of topic.*

P

Heb. 8. 8-10. *See k, K, § 514, page 1192.*

3

Some copies have, *Then he said, And their.*

NEW COVENANT. WARNING AGAINST WILFUL SINNING.

F

I Tim. 3. 15 But if I tarry long, that thou mayest know how thou oughtest to behave thyself in the house of God, which is the church of the living God, the pillar and ground of the truth.

G

Heb. 4. 16. *See u, U, § 507, page 1180.*

H

Eph. 3. 12 In whom we have boldness and access with confidence by the faith of him.

Jas. 1. 6 But let him ask in faith, nothing wavering. For he that wavereth is like a wave of the sea driven with the wind and tossed.

I Jno. 3. 21 Beloved, if our heart condemn us not, *then* have we confidence toward God.

I

Heb. 9. 14 How much more shall the blood of Christ, who through the eternal Spirit offered himself without spot to God, purge your conscience from dead works to serve the living God?

K

II Cor. 7. 1. *See h, H, § 397, page 982.*

L

Heb. 4. 14 Seeing then that we have a great high priest, that is passed into the heavens, Jesus the Son of God, let us hold fast *our* profession.

M

I Cor. 1. 9. *See g, G, § 349, page 890.*

Heb. 11. 11 Through faith also Sara herself received strength to conceive seed, and was delivered of a child when she was past age, because she judged him faithful who had promised.

N

Matt. 18. 20 For where two or three are gathered together in my name, there am I in the midst of them.

Acts 2. 1 And when the day of Pentecost was fully come, they were all with one accord in one place.

Acts 2. 42 And they continued steadfastly in the apostles' doctrine and fellowship, and in breaking of bread, and in prayers.

Acts 20. 7 And upon the first *day* of the week, when the disciples came together to break bread, Paul preached unto them, ready to depart on the morrow; and continued his speech until midnight.

Jude 19 These be they who separate themselves, sensual, having not the Spirit.

O

Rom. 13. 11 And that, knowing the time, that now *it is* high time to awake out of sleep: for now *is* our salvation nearer than when we believed.

§ 518. EXHORTATION TO USE THE PRIVILEGES OF THE NEW

CHAP. 10.

and [o]so much the more, as ye see
[p]the day approaching.
26 For [q]if we sin wilfully [r]after that
we have received the knowledge of
the truth, there remaineth no more
sacrifice for sins,
27 But a certain fearful looking for
of judgment and [s]fiery indignation,
which shall devour the adversaries.
28 [t]He that despised Moses' law
died without mercy [u]under two or
three witnesses:
29 [x]Of how much sorer punishment,
suppose ye, shall he be thought
worthy, who hath trodden under foot
the Son of God, and [y]hath counted
the blood of the covenant, wherewith he was sanctified, an unholy
thing, [z]and hath done despite unto
the Spirit of grace?
30 For we know him that hath said,
[a]Vengeance *belongeth* unto me, I will
recompense, saith the Lord. And
again, [b]the Lord shall judge his people.
31 [c]*It is* a fearful thing to fall into
the hands of the living God.

For O, see preceding page (1203).

P

Phil. 4. 5. *See h, H, § 446, page 1074.*

Q

Num. 15. 30 But the soul that doeth *aught* presumptuously, *whether he be* born in the land, or a stranger, the same reproacheth the LORD; and that soul shall be cut off from among his people.

Heb. 6. 4 For *it is* impossible for those who were once enlightened, and have tasted of the heavenly gift, and were made partakers of the Holy Ghost,

I Jno. 5. 16 If any man see his brother sin a sin *which is* not unto death, he shall ask, and he shall give him life for them that sin not unto death. There is a sin unto death: I do not say that he shall pray for it.

R

II Pet. 2. 20 For if after they have escaped the pollutions of the world through the knowledge of the Lord and Saviour Jesus Christ, they are again entangled therein, and overcome, the latter end is worse with them than the beginning.
21 For it had been better for them not to have known the way of righteousness, than, after they have known *it*, to turn from the holy commandment delivered unto them.

S

Eze. 36. 5 Therefore thus saith the Lord GOD; Surely in the fire of my jealousy have I spoken against the residue of the heathen, and against all Idumea, which have appointed my land into their possession with the joy of all *their* heart,

§ 519. EXHORTATION TO TAKE COURAGE AND ENDURE WITH

10:32–39.

32 But [a]call to remembrance the
former days, in which, [b]after ye were
illuminated, ye endured [c]a great fight
of afflictions;
33 Partly, whilst ye were made [d]a
gazingstock both by reproaches and
afflictions; and partly, whilst [e]ye became companions of them that were
so used.
34 For ye had compassion of me
[f]in my bonds, and [g]took joyfully the

A

Gal. 3. 4 Have ye suffered so many things in vain? if *it be* yet in vain.

II Jno. 8 Look to yourselves, that we lose not those things which we have wrought, but that we receive a full reward.

B

II Cor. 4. 6 For God, who commanded the light to shine out of darkness, hath shined in our hearts, to *give* the light of the knowledge of the glory of God in the face of Jesus Christ.

C

Phil. 1. 29 For unto you it is given in the behalf of Christ, not only to believe on him, but also to suffer for his sake;

COVENANT. WARNING AGAINST WILFUL SINNING (CONCLUDED).

S—CONCLUDED.

with despiteful minds, to cast it out for a prey.

Zeph. 1. 18 Neither their silver nor their gold shall be able to deliver them in the day of the LORD'S wrath; but the whole land shall be devoured by the fire of his jealousy: for he shall make even a speedy riddance of all them that dwell in the land.

Zeph. 3. 8 Therefore wait ye upon me, saith the LORD, until the day that I rise up to the prey: for my determination *is* to gather the nations, that I may assemble the kingdoms, to pour upon them mine indignation, *even* all my fierce anger: for all the earth shall be devoured with the fire of my jealousy.

II Thes. 1. 8. *See n, N, § 466, page 1110.*

T

Heb. 2. 2. *See b, B, § 504, page 1172.*

U

Matt. 18. 16. *See c, C, § 103, page 300.*

X

Heb. 2. 3. *See c, C, § 504, page 1172.*

Y

I Cor. 11. 29 For he that eateth and drinketh unworthily, eateth and drinketh damnation to himself, not discerning the Lord's body.

Heb. 13. 20 Now the God of peace, that brought again from the dead our Lord Jesus, that great Shepherd of the sheep, through the blood of the everlasting covenant,

Z

Matt. 12. 31, 32. *See t, T, § 51, page 170.*

Eph. 4. 30 And grieve not the Holy Spirit of God, whereby ye are sealed unto the day of redemption.

A

Rom. 12. 19. *See o, O, § 342, page 872.*

B

Deut. 32. 36 For the LORD shall judge his people, and repent himself for his servants, when he seeth that *their* power is gone, and *there is* none shut up, or left.

Ps. 50. 4 He shall call to the heavens from above, and to the earth, that he may judge his people.

Ps. 135. 14 For the LORD will judge his people, and he will repent himself concerning his servants.

C

Ps. 50. 22 Now consider this, ye that forget God, lest I tear *you* in pieces, and *there be* none to deliver.

Ps. 76. 7 Thou, *even* thou, *art* to be feared: and who may stand in thy sight when once thou art angry?

Ps. 90. 11 Who knoweth the power of thine anger? even according to thy fear: *so is* thy wrath.

Luke 12. 5 But I will forewarn you whom ye shall fear: Fear him, which after he hath killed hath power to cast into hell; yea, I say unto you, Fear him.

Deut. 32. 35 To me *belongeth* vengeance, and recompense; their foot shall slide in *due* time: for the day of their calamity *is* at hand, and the things that shall come upon them make haste.

Rom. 12. 19 Dearly beloved, avenge not yourselves, but *rather* give place unto wrath: for it is written, Vengeance *is* mine; I will repay, saith the Lord.

BOLDNESS, FOR THE LORD WILL COME AND WILL NOT TARRY.

C—CONCLUDED.

Phil. 1. 30 Having the same conflict which ye saw in me, and now hear *to be* in me.

Col. 2. 1 For I would that ye knew what great conflict I have for you, and for them at Laodicea, and *for* as many as have not seen my face in the flesh;

D

Ps. 71. 7 I am as a wonder unto many; but thou *art* my strong refuge.

I Cor. 4. 9 For I think that God hath set forth us the apostles last, as it were appointed to death: for we are made a spectacle unto the world, and to angels, and to men.

Heb. 11. 36 And others had trial of *cruel* mockings and scourgings, yea, moreover of bonds and imprisonment:

E

Phil. 1. 7 Even as it is meet for me to think this of you all, because I have you in my heart; inasmuch as both in my bonds, and in the defence and confirmation of the gospel, ye all are partakers of my grace.

Phil. 4. 14 Notwithstanding ye have well done, that ye did communicate with my affliction.

I Thes. 2. 14 For ye, brethren, became followers of the churches of God which in Judea are in Christ Jesus: for ye also have suffered like things of your own countrymen, even as they *have* of the Jews:

For F and G, see next page (1206).

§ 519. EXHORTATION TO TAKE COURAGE AND ENDURE WITH BOLD-

CHAP. 10.

spoiling of your goods, knowing [1]in
yourselves that [h]ye have in heaven
a better and an enduring substance.
35 Cast not away therefore your
confidence, [i]which hath great recompense of reward.
36 [k]For ye have need of patience,
that after ye have done the will of
God, [l]ye might receive the promise.
37 For [m]yet a little while, and [n]he
that shall come will come, and will
not tarry.
38 Now [o]the just shall live by faith:
but if *any man* draw back, my soul
shall have no pleasure in him.
39 But we are not of them [p]who
draw back unto perdition; but of
them that [q]believe to the saving of
the soul.

F

Phil. 1. 7. *See under E.*

IITim. 1. 16 The Lord give mercy unto the house of Onesiphorus; for he oft refreshed me, and was not ashamed of my chain:

G

Matt. 5. 12. *See r, R, § 43, page 126.*

1

Or, *that ye have in yourselves,* or, *for yourselves.*

H

Matt. 6. 20. *See n, N, § 43, page 140.*

I

Matt. 5. 12 Rejoice, and be exceeding glad: for great *is* your reward in heaven: for so persecuted they the prophets which were before you.

Matt. 10. 32 Whosoever therefore shall confess me before men, him will I confess also before my Father which is in heaven.

K

Luke 21. 19 In your patience possess ye your souls.

Gal. 6. 9 And let us not be weary in well doing: for in due season we shall reap, if we faint not.

Heb. 12. 1 Wherefore seeing we also are com-

§ 520. FAITH, ITS CHARACTER, TRIALS AND

11: 1–40.

1 Now faith is the [1]substance of
things hoped for, the evidence [a]of
things not seen.
2 For [b]by it the elders obtained a
good report.
3 Through faith we understand
that [c]the worlds were framed by the
word of God, so that things which
are seen were not made of things
which do appear.
4 By faith [d]Abel offered unto God
a more excellent sacrifice than Cain,
by which he obtained witness that
he was righteous, God testifying of
his gifts: and by it he being dead
[e2]yet speaketh.
5 By faith [f]Enoch was translated that

CHAP. 11.

he should not see death; and was not
found, because God had translated
him: for before his translation he had
this testimony, that he pleased God.

1

Or, *ground,* or *confidence.*

A

Ps. 27. 13 *I had fainted,* unless I had believed to see the goodness of the LORD in the land of the living.

Rom. 8. 24 For we are saved by hope: but hope that is seen is not hope: for what a man seeth, why doth he yet hope for?
25 But if we hope for that we see not, *then* do we with patience wait for *it.*

IICor. 4. 18 While we look not at the things which are seen, but at the things which are not seen: for the things which are seen *are* temporal; but the things which are not seen *are* eternal.

IICor. 5. 7 (For we walk by faith, not by sight:)

NESS, FOR THE LORD WILL COME AND WILL NOT TARRY (CONCLUDED).

K—CONCLUDED.

passed about with so great a cloud of witnessess, let us lay aside every weight, and the sin which both so easily beset *us*, and let us run with patience the race that is set before us,

L

Eph. 6. 8 Knowing that whatsoever good thing any man doeth, the same shall he receive of the Lord, whether *he be* bond or free.

Col. 3. 24 Knowing that of the Lord ye shall receive the reward of the inheritance: for ye serve the Lord Christ.

Heb. 9. 15 And for this cause he is the mediator of the new testament, that by means of death, for the redemption of the transgressions *that were* under the first testament, they which are called might receive the promise of eternal inheritance.

M

Luke 18. 8. *See e, E,* § *140, page 401.*

N

Hab. 2. 3 For the vision *is* yet for an appointed time, but at the end it shall speak, and not lie: though it tarry, wait for it; because it will surely come, it will not tarry.

N—CONCLUDED.

Hab. 2. 4 Behold, his soul *which* is lifted up is not upright in him: but the just shall live by his faith.

O

Rom. 1. 17. *See p, P,* § *318, page 810.*

P

IIPet. 2. 20 For if after they have escaped the pollutions of the world through the knowledge of the Lord and Savionr Jesus Christ, they are again entangled therein, and overcome, the latter end is worse with them than the beginning.

21 For it had been better for them not to have known the way of righteousness, than, after they have known *it*, to turn from the holy commandment delivered unto them.

Q

Acts 16. 30 And brought them out, and said, Sirs, what must I do to be saved ?

31 And they said, Believe on the Lord Jesus Christ, and thou shalt be saved, and thy house.

IThes. 5. 9 For God hath not appointed us to wrath, but to obtain salvation by our Lord Jesus Christ.

IIThes. 2. 14 Whereunto he called you by our gospel, to the obtaining of the glory of our Lord Jesus Christ;

TRIUMPHS EXEMPLIFIED IN SCRIPTURAL HISTORY.

B

Heb. 11. 39 And these all, having obtained a good report through faith, received not the promise:

C

Gen. 1. 1 In the beginning God created the heaven and the earth.

John 1. 3. *See e, E,* § *1, page 5.*

IIPet. 3. 5 For this they willingly are ignorant of, that by the word of God the heavens were of old, and the earth standing out of the water and in the water:

D

Gen. 4. 4 And Abel, he also brought of the firstlings of his flock and of the fat thereof. And the LORD had respect unto Able and to his offering:

IJno. 3. 12 Not as Cain, *who* was of that wicked one, and slew his brother. And wherefore slew he him ? Because his own works were evil, and his brother's righteous.

E

Gen. 4. 10 And he said, What hast thou done the voice of thy brother's blood

E—CONCLUDED.

crieth unto me from the ground.

Matt. 23. 35 That upon you may come all the righteous blood shed upon the earth, from the blood of righteous Abel unto the blood of Zacharias son of Barachias, whom ye slew between the temple and the altar.

Heb. 12. 24 And to Jesus the mediator of the new covenant, and to the blood of sprinkling, that speaketh better things than *that of* Abel.

2

Or, *is yet spoken of.*

F

Gen. 5. 22 And Enoch walked with God after he begat Methuselah three hundred years, and begat sons and daughters:

23 And all the days of Enoch were three hundred sixty and five years:

24 And Enoch walked with God: and he *was* not; for God took him.

G

Ps. 106. 21 They forgat God their saviour, which had done great things in Egypt:

§ 520. FAITH, ITS CHARACTER, TRIALS AND TRIUMPHS

CHAP. 11.

6 But[g] without faith *it is* impossible to please *him:* for he that cometh to God must believe that he is, and *that* he is a rewarder of them that diligently seek him.

7 By faith [h]Noah, being warned of God of things not seen as yet,[3]moved with fear,[i]prepared an ark to the saving of his house; by the which he condemned the world, and became heir of [k]the righteousness which is by faith.

8 By faith [l]Abraham, when he was called to go out into a place which he should after receive for an inheritance, obeyed; and he went out, not knowing whither he went.

9 By faith he sojourned in the land of promise, as *in* a strange country, [m]dwelling in tabernacles with Isaac and Jacob, [n]the heirs with him of the same promise:

10 For he looked for [o]a city which hath foundations, [p]whose builder and maker *is* God.

11 Through faith also [q]Sara herself received strength to conceive seed, and was delivered of a child when she was past age, because she judged him [r]faithful who had promised.

12 Therefore sprang there even of one, and [s]him as good as dead, [t]*so many* as the stars of the sky in multitude, and as the sand which is by the sea shore innumerable.

13 These all died [4]in faith,[u]not having received the promises, but[x]having seen them afar off, and were persuaded of *them*, and embraced *them*, and [y]confessed that they were strangers and pilgrims on the earth.

CHAP. 11.

14 For they that say such things [z]declare plainly that they seek a country.

15 And truly, if they had been mindful of that *country* from whence they came out, they might have had opportunity to have returned.

16 But now they desire a better *country*, that is, a heavenly: wherefore God is not ashamed [a]to be called their God: for [b]he hath prepared for them a city.

17 By faith [c]Abraham, when he was tried, offered up Isaac: and he that

G—CONCLUDED. See preceding page (1007).

Ps. 106. 24 Yea, they despised the pleasant land, they believed not his word:

John 3. 18 He that believeth on him is not condemned: but he that believeth not is condemned already, because he hath not believed in the name of the only begotten Son of God.

John 3. 36 He that believeth on the Son hath everlasting life: and he that believeth not the Son shall not see life; but the wrath of God abideth on him.

H

Gen. 6. 13 And God said unto Noah, The end of all flesh is come before me; for the earth is filled with violence through them; and, behold, I will destroy them with the earth.

Gen. 6. 22 Thus did Noah; according to all that God commanded him, so did he.

3

Or, *being wary.*

I

1 Pet. 3. 20 Which sometime were disobedient, when once the longsuffering of God waited in the days of Noah, while the ark was a preparing, wherein few, that is, eight souls were saved by water.

K

Rom. 3. 21, 22. *See e, E, § 324, page 824.*

L

Acts 7. 2, 3, 4. *See c, C, § 246, page 666.*

M

Gen. 12. 8 And he removed from thence unto a mountain on the east of Beth-el, and

EXEMPLIFIED IN SCRIPTURAL HISTORY (Continued).

M—Concluded.

pitched his tent, *having* Beth-el on the west, and Hai on the east: and there he builded an altar unto the LORD, and called upon the name of the LORD.

Gen. 13. 3 And he went on his journeys from the south even to Beth-el, unto the place where his tent had been at the beginning, between Beth-el and Hai;

Gen. 13. 18 Then Abram removed *his* tent, and came and dwelt in the plain of Mamre, which *is* in Hebron, and built there an altar unto the LORD.

Gen. 18. 1 And the LORD appeared unto him in the plains of Mamre: and he sat in tent door in the heat of the day;

Gen. 18. 9 And they said unto him, Where *is* Sarah thy wife? And he said Behold, in the tent.

N

Heb. 6. 17 Wherein God, willing more abundantly to shew unto the heirs of promise the immutability of his counsel, confirmed *it* by an oath:

O

Heb. 12. 22 But ye are come unto mount Sion, and unto the city of the living God, the heavenly Jerusalem, and to an innumerable company of angels.

Heb. 13. 14 For here have we no continuing city, but we seek one to come.

P

Heb. 3. 4 For every house is builded by some *man;* but he that built all things *is* God.

Rev. 21. 2 And I John saw the holy city, new Jerusalem, coming down from God out of heaven, prepared as a bride adorned for her husband.

Rev. 21. 10 And he carried me away in the spirit to a great and high mountain, and shewed me that great city, the holy Jerusalem, descending out of heaven from God,

Q

Gen. 17. 19 And God said, Sarah thy wife shall bear thee a son indeed; and thou shalt call his name Isaac: and I will establish my covenant with him for an everlasting covenant, *and* with his seed after him.

Gen. 18. 11 Now Abraham and Sarah *were* old *and* well stricken in age; *and* it ceased to be with Sarah after the manner of women.

Gen. 18. 14 Is any thing too hard for the LORD? At the time appointed I will return unto thee, according to the time of life, and Sarah shall have a son.

Q—Concluded.

Gen. 21. 2 For Sarah conceived, and bare Abraham a son in his old age, at the set time of which God had spoken to him.

R

I Cor. 1. 9. *See g, G, § 349, page 890.*

S

Rom. 4. 19 And being not weak in faith, he considered not his own body now dead, when he was about a hundred years old, neither yet the deadness of Sarah's womb:

T

Gen. 22. 17 That in blessing I will bless thee, and in multiplying I will multiply thy seed as the stars of the heaven, and as the sand which *is* upon the sea shore; and thy seed shall possess the gate of his enemies;

Rom. 4. 18 Who against hope believed in hope, that he might become the father of many nations, according to that which was spoken, So shall thy seed be.

4

Gr. *according to faith.*

U

Heb. 11. 39. *See text of topic.*

X

John 8. 56 Your father Abraham rejoiced to see my day: and he saw *it*, and was glad.

Heb. 11. 27. *See text of topic.*

Y

Gen. 23. 4 I *am* a stranger and a sojourner with you: give me possession of a buryingplace with you, that I may bury my dead out of my sight.

Gen. 47. 9 And Jacob said unto Pharaoh, The days of the years of my pilgrimage *are* a hundred and thirty years: few and evil have the days of the years of my life been, and have not attained unto the days of the years of the life of my fathers in the days of their pilgrimage.

I Chr. 29. 15 For we *are* strangers before thee, and sojourners, as *were* all our fathers: our days on the earth *are* as a shadow, and *there is* none abiding.

Ps. 39. 12 Hear my prayer, O LORD, and give ear unto my cry; hold not thy peace at my tears: for I *am* a stranger with thee, *and* a sojourner, as all my fathers *were*.

Ps. 119. 19 I *am* a stranger in the earth: hide not thy commandments from me.

For Y, concl'd, Z, A, B, and C, see next page (1210).

§ 520. FAITH, ITS CHARACTER, TRIALS AND TRIUMPHS

CHAP. 11.

had received the promises [d]offered up his only begotten *son*,

18 [5]Of whom it was said, [e]That in Isaac shall thy seed be called:

19 Accounting that God [f]*was* able to raise *him* up, even from the dead; from whence also he received him in a figure.

20 By faith [g]Isaac blessed Jacob and Esau concerning things to come.

21 By faith Jacob, when he was a dying, [h]blessed both the sons of Joseph; and [i]worshipped, *leaning* upon the top of his staff.

22 By faith Joseph, when he died, [k]made mention of the departing of the children of Israel; and gave commandment concerning his bones.

23 By faith [l]Moses, when he was born, was hid three months of his parents, because they saw *he was* a proper child; and they were not afraid of the king's [m]commandment.

24 By faith [n]Moses, when he was come to years, refused to be called the son of Pharaoh's daughter;

25 [o]Choosing rather to suffer affliction with the people of God, than to enjoy the pleasures of sin for a season;

26 Esteeming [p]the reproach [7]of Christ greater riches than the treasures in Egypt: for he had respect unto [q]the recompense of the reward.

27 By faith [r]he forsook Egypt, not fearing the wrath of the king: for he endured, as [s]seeing him who is invisible.

28 Through faith [t]he kept the passover, and the sprinkling of blood, lest he that destroyed the firstborn should touch them.

Y—CONCLUDED.

1 Pet. 1. 17 And if ye call on the Father, who without respect of persons judgeth according to every man's work, pass the time of your sojourning *here* in fear:

1 Pet. 2. 11 Dearly beloved, I beseech *you* as strangers and pilgrims, abstain from fleshly lusts, which war against the soul;

Z

Heb. 13. 14. *See under O, page 1209.*

A

Matt. 22. 32. *See q, Q, § 164, page 458.*

B

Phil. 3. 20 For our conversation is in heaven; from whence also we look for the Saviour, the Lord Jesus Christ:

Heb. 13. 14. *See under O, page 1209.*

C

Gen. 22. 1 And it came to pass after these things, that God did tempt Abraham, and said unto him, Abraham: and he said, Behold, *here* I *am*.

Gen. 22. 9 And they came to the place which God had told him of; and Abraham built an altar there, and laid the wood in order, and bound Isaac his son, and laid him on the altar upon the wood.

D

Jas. 2. 21 Was not Abraham our father justified by works, when he had offered Isaac his son upon the altar?

5

Or, *To.*

E

Gen. 21. 12 And God said unto Abraham, Let it not be grievous in thy sight because of the lad, and because of thy bondwoman; in all that Sarah hath said unto thee, hearken unto her voice; for in Isaac shall thy seed be called.

Rom. 9. 7 Neither, because they are the seed of Abraham, *are they* all children: but, In Isaac shall thy seed be called.

F

Rom. 4. 17 (As it is written, I have made thee a father of many nations,) before him whom he believed, *even* God, who quickeneth the dead, and calleth those things which be not as though they were.

Rom. 4. 19 And being not weak in faith, he considered not his own body now dead, when he was about a hundred years old, neither yet the deadness of Sarah's womb:

Rom. 4. 21 And being fully persuaded, that what he had promised, he was able also to perform.

EXEMPLIFIED IN SCRIPTURAL HISTORY (CONTINUED).

G

Gen. 27. 27 And he came near, and kissed him: and he smelled the smell of his raiment, and blessed him, and said, See, the smell of my son *is* as the smell of a field which the LORD hath blessed:

Gen. 27. 39 And Isaac his father answered and said unto him, Behold, thy dwelling shall be the fatness of the earth, and of the dew of heaven from above;

H

Gen. 48. 5 And now thy two sons, Ephraim and Manasseh, which were born unto thee in the land of Egypt, before I came unto thee into Egypt, *are* mine; as Reuben and Simeon, they shall be mine.

Gen. 48. 16 The Angel which redeemed me from all evil, bless the lads; and let my name be named on them, and the name of my fathers Abraham and Isaac; and let them grow into a multitude in the midst of the earth.

Gen. 48. 21 And Israel said unto Joseph, Behold, I die: but God shall be with you, and bring you again unto the land of your fathers.

I

Gen. 47. 31 And he said, Swear unto me. And he sware unto him. And Israel bowed himself upon the bed's head.

K

Gen. 50. 24 And Joseph said unto his brethren, I die: and God will surely visit you, and bring you out of this land unto the land which he sware to Abraham, to Isaac, and to Jacob.

25 And Joseph took an oath of the children of Israel, saying, God will surely visit you, and ye shall carry up my bones from hence.

Ex. 13. 19 And Moses took the bones of Joseph with him: for he had straitly sworn the children of Israel, saying, God will surely visit you; and ye shall carry up my bones away hence with you.

6

Or, *remembered.*

L

Ex. 2. 2 And the woman conceived, and bare a son: and when she saw him that he *was* a goodly *child*, she hid him three months.

Act. 7. 20 In which time Moses was born, and was exceeding fair, and nourished up in his father's house three months:

M

Ex. 1. 16 And he said, When ye do the office of a midwife to the Hebrew women, and see *them* upon the stools, if it *be* a son, then ye shall kill him: but if it *be* a daughter, then she shall live.

M—CONCLUDED.

Ex. 1. 22 And Pharaoh charged all his people, saying, Every son that is born ye shall cast into the river, and every daughter ye shall save alive.

N

Ex. 2. 10 And the child grew, and she brought him unto Pharaoh's daughter, and he became her son. And she called his name Moses: and she said, Because I drew him out of the water.

11 And it came to pass in those days, when Moses was grown, that he went out unto his brethren, and looked on their burdens: and he spied an Egyptian smiting a Hebrew, one of his brethren.

O

Ps. 84. 10 For a day in thy courts *is* better than a thousand. I had rather be a doorkeeper in the house of my God, than to dwell in the tents of wickedness.

P

Heb. 13. 13 Let us go forth therefore unto him without the camp, bearing his reproach.

7

Or, *for Christ.*

Q

Heb. 10. 35 Cast not away therefore your confidence, which hath great recompense of reward.

R

Ex. 10. 28 And Pharaoh said unto him, Get thee from me, take heed to thyself, see my face no more; for in *that* day thou seest my face thou shalt die.

29 And Moses said, Thou has spoken well, I will see thy face again no more.

Ex. 12. 37 And the children of Israel journeyed from Rameses to Succoth, about six hundred thousand on foot *that were* men, beside children.

Ex. 13. 17 And it came to pass, when Pharaoh had let the people go that God led them not *through* the way of the land of the Philistines, although that *was* near; for God said, Lest peradventure the people repent when they see war, and they return to Egypt;

18 But God led the people about, *through* the way of the wilderness of the Red sea: and the children of Israel went up harnessed out of the land of Egypt.

For S and T, see next page (1212).

§ 520. FAITH, ITS CHARACTER, TRIALS AND TRIUMPHS X—CONCLUDED.

CHAP. 11.

29 By faith [u]they passed through the Red sea as by dry *land:* which the Egyptians assaying to do were drowned.

30 By faith [x]the walls of Jericho fell down, after they were compassed about seven days.

31 By faith [y]the harlot Rahab perished not with them [8]that believed not, when [z]she had received the spies with peace.

32 And what shall I more say? for the time would fail me to tell of [a]Gideon, and *of* [b]Barak, and *of* [c]Samson, and *of* [d]Jephthah; *of* [e]David also, and [f]Samuel, and *of* the prophets:

33 Who through faith subdued kingdoms, wrought righteousness, [g]obtained promises, [h]stopped the mouths of lions,

34 [i]Quenched the violence of fire, [k]escaped the edge of the sword, [l]out of weakness were made strong, waxed valiant in fight, [m]turned to flight the armies of the aliens.

S

Heb. 11. 13. *See text of topic.*

T

Ex. 12. 21 Then Moses called for all the elders of Israel, and said unto them, Draw out and take you a lamb according to your families, and kill the passover.

U

Ex. 14. 22 And the children of Israel went into the midst of the sea upon the dry *ground:* and the waters *were* a wall unto them on their right hand, and on their left.

Ex. 14. 29 But the children of Israel walked upon dry *land* in the midst of the sea; and the waters *were* a wall unto them on their right hand, and on their left.

X

Josh 6. 20 So the people shouted when *the priests* blew with the trumpets: and it came to pass, when the people heard the sound of the trumpet, and the people shouted with a great shout, that the wall fell down flat, so that the people went up into the city, every man straight before him, and they took the city.

Y

Josh. 6. 23 And the young men that were spies went in, and brought out Rahab, and her father, and her mother, and her brethren, and all that she had; and they brought out all her kindred, and left them without the camp of Israel.

8

Or, *that were disobedient.*

Z

Josh. 2. 1 And Joshua the son of Nun sent out of Shittim two men to spy secretly, saying, Go view the land, even Jericho. And they went, and came into a harlot's house, named Rahab, and lodged there.

A

Judg 6. 11 And there came an angel of the LORD, and sat under an oak which *was* in Ophrah, that *pertained* unto Joash the Abi-ezrite: and his son Gideon threshed wheat by the winepress, to hide *it* from the Midianites.

B

Judg. 4. 6 And she sent and called Barak the son of Abinoam out of Kedesh-naphtali, and said unto him, Hath not the LORD God of Israel commanded, *saying*, Go and draw toward mount Tabor, and take with thee ten thousand men of the children of Naphtali and of the children of Zebulun?

C

Judg. 13. 24 And the woman bare a son, and called his name Samson: and the child grew, and the LORD blessed him.

D

Judg. 11. 1 Now Jephthah the Gileadite was a mighty man of valour, and he *was* the son of a harlot: and Gilead begat Jephthah.

Judg. 12. 7 And Jephthah judged Israel six years. Then died Jephthah the Gileadite, and was buried in *one of* the cities of Gilead.

E

1 Sa. 16. 1 And the LORD said unto Samuel, How long wilt thou mourn for Saul, seeing I have rejected him from reign-

EXEMPLIFIED IN SCRIPTURAL HISTORY (CONTINUED).

E—CONCLUDED.

ing over Israel? fill thine horn with oil, and go, I will send thee to Jesse the Beth-lehemite: for I have provided me a king among his sons.

I Sa 16. 13 Then Samuel took the horn of oil, and anointed him in the midst of his brethren: and the Spirit of the LORD came upon David from that day forward. So Samuel rose up, and went to Ramah.

I Sa. 17. 45 Then said David to the Philistine, Thou comest to me with a sword, and with a spear, and with a shield: but I come to thee in the name of the LORD of hosts, the God of the armies of Israel, whom thou hast defied.

F

I Sa. 1. 20 Wherefore it came to pass, when the time was come about after Hannah had conceived, that she bare a son, and called his name Samuel, *saying*, Because I have asked him of the LORD.

I Sa. 12. 20 And Samuel said unto the people, Fear not: ye have done all this wickedness: yet turn not aside from following the LORD, but serve the LORD with all your heart;

G

II Sa. 7. 11 And as since the time that I commanded judges *to be* over my people Israel, and have caused thee to rest from all thine enemies. Also the LORD telleth thee that he will make thee a house.

12 And when thy days be fulfilled, and thou shalt sleep with thy fathers, I will set up thy seed after thee, which shall proceed out of thy bowels, and I will establish his kingdom.

13 He shall build a house for my name, and I will stablish the throne of his kingdom for ever.

H

Judg. 14. 5 Then went Samson down, and his father and his mother, to Timnah, and came to the vineyards of Timnah: and, behold, a young lion roared against him.

6 And the Spirit of the LORD came mightily upon him, and he rent him as he would have rent a kid, and *he had* nohing in his hand: but he told not his father or his mother what he had done.

I Sa. 17. 34 And David said unto Saul, Thy servant kept his father's sheep, and there came a lion, and a bear, and took a lamb out of the flock:

H—CONCLUDED.

I Sa. 17. 35 And I went out after him, and smote him, and delivered *it* out of his mouth: and when he arose against me, I caught *him* by his beard, and smote him, and slew him.

Da. 6. 22 My God hath sent his angel, and hath shut the lions' mouths, that they have not hurt me: forasmuch as before him innocency was found in me; and also before thee, O king, have I done no hurt.

I

Da. 3. 25 He answered and said, Lo, I see four men loose, walking in the midst of the fire, and they have no hurt; and the form of the fourth is like the Son of God.

K

I Sa. 20. 1 And David fled from Naioth in Ramah, and came and said before Jonathan, What have I done? what *is* mine iniquity? and what *is* my sin before thy father, that he seeketh my life?

I Ki. 19. 3 And when he saw *that*, he arose and went for his life, and came to Beer-sheba, which *belongeth* to Judah, and left his servant there.

II Ki. 6. 16 And he answered, Fear not: for they that *be* with us *are* more than they that *be* with them.

L

II Ki. 20. 7 And Isaiah said, Take a lump of figs. And they took and laid *it* on the boil, and he recovered.

Job 42. 10 And the LORD turned the captivity of Job, when he prayed for his friends: also the LORD gave Job twice as much as he had before.

Ps. 6. 8 Depart from me, all ye workers of iniquity; for the LORD hath heard the voice of my weeping.

M

Judg. 15. 8 And he smote them hip and thigh with a great slaughter: and he went down and dwelt in the top of the rock Etam.

Judg. 15. 15 And he found a new jawbone of an ass, and put forth his hand, and took it, and slew a thousand men therewith.

1 Sa. 14. 13 And Jonathan climbed up upon his hands and upon his feet, and his armourbearer after him: and they fell before Jonathan; and his armourbearer slew after him.

For M concluded, see next page (1214).

§ 520. FAITH, ITS CHARACTER, TRIALS AND TRIUMPHS

CHAP. 11.

[n]35 Women received their dead raised to life again: and others were [o]tortured, not accepting deliverance; that they might obtain a better resurrection:

36 And others had trial of *cruel* mockings and scourgings, yea, moreover [p]of bonds and imprisonment:

37 [q]They were stoned, they were sawn asunder, were tempted, were slain with the sword: [r]they wandered about [s]in sheepskins and goatskins; being destitute, afflicted, tormented;

38 (Of whom the world was not worthy:) they wandered in deserts, and *in* mountains, and [t]*in* dens and caves of the earth.

39 And these all, [u]having obtained a good report through faith, received not the promise:

40 God having [9]provided [x]some better thing for us, that they without us should not be [y]made perfect.

M—CONTINUED.

I Sa. 17. 51 Therefore David ran, and stood upon the Philistine, and took his sword, and drew it out of the sheath thereof, and slew him, and cut off his head

M—CONCLUDED.

therewith. And when the Philistines saw their champion was dead, they fled.

I Sa. 17. 52 And the men of Israel and of Judah arose, and shouted, and pursued the Philistines, until thou come to the valley, and to the gates of Ekron. And the wounded of the Philistines fell down by the way to Shaaraim, even unto Gath, and unto Ekron.

II Chr. 16. 8 Were not the Ethiopians and the Lubims a huge host, with very many chariots and horsemen? yet, because thou didst rely on the LORD, he delivered them into thine hand.

N

I Ki. 17. 22 And the LORD heard the voice of Elijah: and the soul of the child came into him again, and he revived.

II Ki. 4. 35 Then he returned, and walked in the house to and fro; and went up, and stretched himself upon him: and the child sneezed seven times, and the child opened his eyes.

O

Acts 22. 25 And as they bound him with thongs, Paul said unto the centurion that stood by, Is it lawful for you to scourge a man that is a Roman, and uncondemned?

P

Gen. 39. 20 And Joseph's master took him, and put him into the prison, a place where the king's prisoners *were* bound: and he was there in the prison.

Jer. 20. 2 Then Pashur smote Jeremiah the prophet, and put him in the stocks that *were* in the high gate of Benjamin, which *was* by the house of the LORD.

§ 521. EXHORTATION IN THE FIGURE OF A RACE.

12 : 1–13.

1 Wherefore, seeing we also are compassed about with so great a cloud of witnesses, [a]let us lay aside every weight, and the sin which doth so easily beset *us*, and [b]let us run [c]with patience the race that is set before us,

2 Looking unto Jesus the [1]author and finisher of *our* faith; [d]who for the joy that was set before him endured the cross, despising the shame,

CHAP. 12.

and [e]is set down at the right hand of the throne of God.

3 [f]For consider him that endured such contradiction of sinners against

A

II Cor. 7. 1 Having therefore these promises, dearly beloved, let us cleanse ourselves from all filthiness of the flesh and spirit, perfecting holiness in the fear of God.

Col. 3. 8 But now ye also put off all these; anger, wrath, malice, blasphemy, filthy communication out of your mouth.

EXEMPLIFIED IN SCRIPTURAL HISTORY (CONCLUDED).

P—CONCLUDED.

Jer. 37. 15 Wherefore the princes were wroth with Jeremiah, and smote him, and put him into prison in the house of Jonathan the scribe: for they had made that the prison.

Q

I Ki. 21. 13 And there came in two men, children of Belial, and sat before him: and the men of Belial witnessed against him, *even* against Naboth, in the presence of the people, saying, Naboth did blaspheme God and the king. Then they carried him forth out of the city, and stoned him with stones, that he died.

II Chr. 24. 21 And they conspired against him, and stoned him with stones at the commandment of the king in the court of the house of the LORD.

Acts 7. 58 And cast *him* out of the city, and stoned *him*: and the witnesses laid down their clothes at a young man's feet, whose name was Saul.

Acts 14. 19 And there came thither *certain* Jews from Antioch and Iconium, who persuaded the people, and, having stoned Paul, drew *him* out of the city, supposing he had been dead.

R

II Ki. 1. 8 And they answered him, *He was* a hairy man, and girt with a girdle of leather about his loins. And he said, It *is* Elijah the Tishbite.

Matt. 3. 4 And the same John had his raiment of camel's hair, and a leathern girdle about his loins; and his meat was locusts and wild honey.

S

Zech. 13. 4 And it shall come to pass in that day, *that* the prophets shall be ashamed every one of his vision, when he hath prophesied; neither shall they wear a rough garment to deceive:

T

I Ki. 18. 4 For it was *so* when Jezebel cut off the prophets of the LORD, that Obadiah took a hundred prophets, and hid them by fifty in a cave, and fed them with bread and water.)

I Ki. 19. 9 And he came thither unto a cave, and lodged there; and, behold, the word of the LORD *came* to him, and he said unto him, What doest thou here, Elijah?

U

Heb. 11. 2, 13. *See text of topic.*

9

Or, *foreseen.*

X

Heb. 7. 22. *See o, O, § 512, page 1190.*

Rev. 6. 11 And white robes were given unto every one of them; and it was said unto them, that they should rest yet for a little season, until their fellow servants also and their brethren, that should be killed as they *were*, should be fulfilled.

Y

Heb. 5. 9 And being made perfect, he became the author of eternal salvation unto all them that obey him:

Heb. 12. 23 To the general assembly and church of the firstborn, which are written in heaven, and to God the Judge of all, and to the spirits of just men made perfect,

DESPISE NOT THE CHASTENING OF THE LORD.

A—CONCLUDED.

I Pet. 2. 1 Wherefore laying aside all malice, and all guile, and hypocrisies, and envies, and all evil speakings,

B

Phil. 3. 13, 14. *See e, E, § 444, page 1070.*

C

Rom. 12. 12. *See a, A, § 342, page 870.*

1

Or, *beginner.*

D

Luke 24. 26. *See o, O, § 218, page 609.*

D—CONCLUDED.

Phil. 2. 8 And being found in fashion as a man, he humbled himself, and became obedient unto death, even the death of the cross.

9 Wherefore God also hath highly exalted him, and given him a name which is above every name:

E

Eph. 1. 20. *See k, K, § 427, page 1032.*

I Pet. 3. 22 Who is gone into heaven, and is on the right hand of God; angels and authorities and powers being made subject unto him.

For F, see next page (1216).

§ 521. EXHORTATION IN THE FIGURE OF A RACE.

CHAP. 12.

himself, [g]lest ye be wearied and faint in your minds.

4 [h]Ye have not yet resisted unto blood, striving against sin.

5 And ye have forgotten the exhortation which speaketh unto you as unto children, [i]My son, despise not thou the chastening of the Lord, nor faint when thou art rebuked of him:

6 For [k]whom the Lord loveth he chasteneth, and scourgeth every son whom he receiveth.

7 [l]If ye endure chastening, God dealeth with you as with sons; for what son is he whom the father chasteneth not?

8 But if ye be without chastisement, [m]whereof all are partakers, then are ye bastards, and not sons.

9 Furthermore we have had fathers of our flesh which corrected *us*, and we gave *them* reverence: shall we not much rather be in subjection unto [n]the Father of spirits, and live?

10 For they verily for a few days chastened *us* [2]after their own pleasure; but he for *our* profit, [o]that *we* might be partakers of his holiness.

11 Now no chastening for the present seemeth to be joyous, but grievous: nevertheless, afterward it yieldeth [p]the peaceable fruit of righteousness unto them which are exercised thereby.

12 Wherefore [q]lift up the hands which hang down, and the feeble knees;

13 [r]And make [3]straight paths for your feet, lest that which is lame be turned out of the way; [s]but let it rather be healed.

F

Matt. 10. 24 The disciple is not above *his* master, nor the servant above his lord.

25 It is enough for the disciple that he be as his master, and the servant as his lord. If they have called the master of the house Beelzebub, how much more *shall they call* them of his household?

John 15. 20 Remember the word that I said unto you, The servant is not greater than his lord. If they have persecuted me, they will also persecute you; if they have kept my saying, they will keep yours also.

G

Gal. 6. 9 And let us not be weary in well doing: for in due season we shall reap, if we faint not.

H

1 Cor. 10. 13 There hath no temptation taken you but such as is common to man: but God *is* faithful, who will not suffer you to be tempted above that ye are able; but will with the temptation also make a way to escape, that ye may be able to bear *it*.

Heb. 10. 32 But call to rememberance the former days, in which, after ye were illuminated, ye endured a great fight of afflictions;

33 Partly, whilst ye were made a gazingstock both by reproaches and afflictions; and partly, whilst ye became companions of them that were so used.

34 For ye had compassion of me in my bonds and took joyfully the spoiling of our goods, knowing in yourselves that ye have in heaven a better and an enduring substance.

I

Job 5. 17 Behold, happy *is* the man whom God correcteth: therefore despise not thou the chastening of the Almighty.

Prov. 3. 11 My son, despise not the chastening of the LORD: neither be weary of his correction:

K

Ps. 94. 12 Blessed *is* the man whom thou chastenest, O LORD; and teachest him out of thy law;

Ps. 119. 75 I know, O LORD, that thy judgments *are* right, and *that* thou in faithfulness hast afflicted me.

Prov. 3. 12 For whom the LORD loveth he correcteth; even as a father the son *in whom* he delighteth.

Jas. 1. 12 Blessed *is* the man that endureth temptation: for when he is tried, he shall receive the crown of life, which

DESPISE NOT THE CHASTENING OF THE LORD (CONCLUDED).

K—CONCLUDED.

the LORD hath promised to them that love him.

Rev. 3. 19 As many as I love, I rebuke and chasten: be zealous therefore, and repent.

L

Duet. 8. 5 Thou shalt also consider in thine heart, that, as a man chasteneth his son, *so* the LORD thy God chasteneth thee.

II Sa. 7. 14 I will be his father, and he shall be my son. If he commit iniquity, I will chasten him with the rod of men, and with the stripes of the children of men:

Prov.13. 24 He that spareth his rod hateth his son: but he that loveth him chasteneth him betimes.

Prov.19. 18 Chasten thy son while there is hope, and let not thy soul spare for his crying.

Prov.22. 15 Foolishness *is* bound in the heart of a child; *but* the rod of correction shall drive it far from him.

Prov.23. 13 Withhold not correction from the child: for *if* thou beatest him with the rod, he shall not die.

14 Thou shalt beat him with the rod, and shalt deliver his soul from hell.

Prov.29. 15 The rod and reproof give wisdom: but a child left *to himself* bringeth his mother to shame.

Prov.29. 17 Correct thy son, and he shall give thee rest; yea, he shall give delight unto thy soul.

Acts 14. 22 Confirming the souls of the disciples, *and* exhorting them to continue in the faith, and that we must through much tribulation enter into the kingdom of God.

M

Ps. 73 12 Behold, these *are* the ungodly, who prosper in the world; they increase *in* riches.

I Pet. 5. 9 Whom resist steadfast in the faith, knowing that the same afflictions are accomplished in your brethren that are in the world.

N

Num.16. 22 And they fell upon their faces, and said, O God, the God of the spirits of all flesh, shall one man sin, and wilt thou be wroth with all the congregation?

Num.27. 16 Let the LORD, the God of the spirits of all flesh, set a man over the congregation,

Job 12. 10 In whose hand *is* the soul of every living thing, and the breath of all mankind.

N—CONCLUDED.

Eccl. 12. 7 Then shall the dust return to the earth as it was: and the spirit shall return unto God who gave it.

Isa. 42. 5 Thus saith God the LORD, he that created the heavens, and stretched them out; he that spread forth the earth, and that which cometh out of it; he that giveth breath unto the people upon it, and spirit to them that walk therein:

Isa. 57. 16 For I will not contend for ever, neither will I be always wroth: for the spirit should fail before me, and the souls *which* I have made.

Zech.12. 1 The burden of the word of the LORD for Israel, saith the LORD, which stretcheth forth the heavens, and layeth the foundation of the earth, and formeth the spirit of man within him.

2

Or, *as seemed good*, or, *meet to them*,

O

Lev. 11. 44 For I *am* the LORD your God: ye shall therefore sanctify yourselves, and ye shall be holy; for I *am* holy: neither shall ye defile yourselves with any manner of creeping thing that creepeth upon the earth.

Lev. 19. 2 Speak unto all the congregation of the children of Israel, and say unto them, Ye shall be holy: for I the LORD your God *am* holy.

Eph. 5. 27. *See n, N, § 435, page 1052.*

I Pet. 1. 15 But as he which hath called you is holy, so be ye holy in all manner of conversation;

16 Because it is written, Be ye holy; for I am holy.

P

Jas. 3. 18 And the fruit of righteousness is sown in peace of them that make peace.

Q

Job 4. 3 Behold, thou hast instructed many, and thou hast strenghtened the weak hands.

4 Thy words have upholden him that was falling, and thou hast strengthened the feeble knees.

Isa. 35. 3 Strengthen ye the weak hands, and confirm the feeble knees.

R

Prov. 4. 26 Ponder the path of thy feet, and let all thy ways be established.

27 Turn not to the right hand nor to the left: remove thy foot from evil.

3

Or, *even*.

S

Gal. 6. 1. *See a, A, § 423, page 1024.*

§ 522. EXHORTATION TO FOLLOW PEACE AND

12:14–17.

14 [a]Follow peace with all *men*, and holiness, [b]without which no man shall see the Lord:

15 [c]Looking diligently [d]lest any man [1]fail of the grace of God; [e]lest any root of bitterness springing up trouble *you*, and thereby many be defiled;

16 [f]Lest there *be* any fornicator, or profane person, as Esau, [g]who for one morsel of meat sold his birthright.

17 For ye know how that afterward, [h]when he would have inherited the blessing, he was rejected: [i]for he found no [2]place of repentance, though he sought it carefully with tears.

A

Rom. 14. 19. *See u, U, § 344, page 878.*

IITim. 2. 22 Flee also youthful lusts: but follow righteousness, faith, charity, peace, with them that call on the Lord out of a pure heart.

B

Matt. 5. 8. *See h, H, § 43, page 124.*

C

IICor. 6. 1 We then, *as* workers together *with him*, beseech *you* also that ye receive not the grace of God in vain.

D

Gal. 5. 4 Christ is become of no effect unto you, whosoever of you are justified by the law; ye are fallen from grace.

1

Or, *fall from.*

E

Deut. 29. 18 Lest there should be among you man, or woman, or family, or tribe, whose heart turneth away this day from the LORD our God, to go *and*

§ 523. THE ADMINISTRATION OF THE GOSPEL IS SUPERIOR

12:18–29.

18 For ye are not come unto [a]the mount that might be touched, and that burned with fire, nor unto blackness, and darkness, and tempest,

19 And the sound of a trumpet, and the voice of words; which *voice* they that heard, [b]intreated that the word should not be spoken to them any more:

20 (For they could not endure that which was commanded, [c]And if so much as a beast touch the mountain, it shall be stoned, or thrust through with a dart:

21 [d]And so terrible was the sight, *that* Moses said, I exceedingly fear and quake:)

22 But ye are come [e]unto mount Sion, [f]and unto the city of the living God, the heavenly Jerusalem, [g]and to an innumerable company of angels,

A

Ex. 19. 12 And thou shalt set bounds unto the people round about, saying, Take heed to yourselves, *that ye* go *not* up into the mount, or touch the border of it: whosoever toucheth the mount shall be surely put to death:

Ex. 19. 18 And mount Sinai was altogether on a smoke, because the LORD descended upon it in fire: and the smoke thereof ascended as the smoke of a furnace, and the whole mount quaked greatly.

19 And when the voice of the trumpet sounded long, and waxed louder and louder, Moses spake, and God answered him by a voice.

Deut. 4. 11 And ye came near and stood under the mountain; and the mountain burned with fire unto the midst of heaven, with darkness, clouds, and thick darkness.

Deut. 5. 22 These words the LORD spake unto all your assembly in the mount out of the midst of the fire, of the cloud, and of the thick darkness, with a great voice: and he added no more. And he wrote them in two tables of stone, and delivered them unto me.

Rom. 6. 14 For sin shall not have dominion over you: for ye are not under the law, but under grace.

SANCTIFICATION AND TO SHUN DEFILING ASSOCIATIONS.

E—Concluded.

serve the gods of these nations; lest there should be among you a root that beareth gall and wormwood;

Heb. 3. 12 Take heed, brethren, lest there be in any of you an evil heart of unbelief, in departing from the living God.

F

Acts 15. 20. *See s, S, § 268, page 730.*

G

Gen. 25. 33 And Jacob said, Swear to me this day; and he sware unto him: and he sold his birthright unto Jacob.

H

Gen. 27. 34 And when Esau heard the words of his father, he cried with a great and exceeding bitter cry, and said unto his father, Bless me, *even* me also, O my father.

Gen. 27. 36 And he said, Is not he rightly named Jacob? for he hath supplanted me these two times: he took away my birthright; and, behold, now he hath

H—Concluded.

taken away my blessing. And he said, Hast thou not reserved a blessing for me?

Gen. 27. 38 And Esau said unto his father, Hast thou but one blessing, my father? bless me, *even* me also, O my father. And Esau lifted up his voice, and wept.

I

Heb. 6. 6 If they shall fall away, to renew them again unto repentance; seeing they crucify to themselves the Son of God afresh, and put *him* to an open shame.

Heb. 10. 26 For if we sin wilfully after that we have received the knowledge of the truth, there remaineth no more sacrifice for sins,

27 But a certain fearful looking for of judgment and fiery indignation, which shall devour the adversaries.

2

Or, *way to change his mind.*

TO THAT OF THE LAW. ITS WARNINGS MORE TO BE FEARED.

A—Concluded.

Rom. 8. 15 For ye have not received the spirit of bondage again to fear, but ye have received the Spirit of adoption, whereby we cry, Abba, Father.

IITim. 1. 7 For God hath not given us the spirit of fear; but of power, and of love, and of a sound mind.

B

Ex. 20. 19 And they said unto Moses, Speak thou with us, and we will hear: but let not God speak with us, lest we die.

Deut. 5. 5 (I stood between the Lord and you at that time, to shew you the word of the Lord: for ye were afraid by reason of the fire, and went not up into the monnt;) saying,

Deut. 5. 25 Now therefore why should we die? for this great fire will consume us: if we hear the voice of the Lord our God any more, then we shall die.

Deut. 18. 16 According to all that thou desiredst of the Lord thy God in Horeb in the day of the assembly, saying, Let me not hear again the voice of the Lord my God, neither let me see this great fire any more, that I die not.

C

Ex. 19. 13 There shall not a hand touch it, but he shall surely be stoned, or shot through; whether *it be* beast or man,

C—Concluded.

it shall not live: when the trumpet soundeth long, they shall come up to the mount.

D

Ex. 19. 16 And it came to pass on the third day in the morning, that there were thunders and lightnings, and a thick cloud upon the mount, and the voice of the trumpet exceeding loud; so that all the people that *was* in the camp trembled.

E

Gal. 4. 26. *See f, F, § 420, page 1020.*

F

Phil. 3. 20 For our conversation is in heaven; from whence also we look for the Saviour, the Lord Jesus Christ:

G

Deut. 33. 2 And he said, The Lord came from Sinai, and rose up from Seir unto them; he shined forth from mount Paran, and he came with ten thousands of saints: from his right hand *went* a fiery law for them.

Ps. 68. 17 The chariots of God *are* twenty thousand, *even* thousands of angels: the Lord *is* among them, *as in* Sinai, in the holy *place*.

For G concluded, see next page (1220).

§ 523. THE ADMINISTRATION OF THE GOSPEL IS SUPERIOR TO THAT

CHAP. 12.

23 To the general assembly and church of [h]the firstborn, [i]which are [1]written in heaven, and to God the [k]Judge of all, and to the spirits of just men [l]made perfect,

24 And to Jesus [m]the mediator of the new [2]covenant, and to [n]the blood of sprinkling, that speaketh better things [o]than *that* of Abel.

25 See that ye refuse not him that speaketh. For [p]if they escaped not who refused him that spake on earth, much more *shall not* we *escape*, if we turn away from him that *speaketh* from heaven:

26 [q]Whose voice then shook the earth: but now he hath promised, saying, [r]Yet once more I shake not the earth only, but also heaven.

27 And this *word*, Yet once more, signifieth [s]the removing of those things that [3]are shaken, as of things that are made, that those things which cannot be shaken may remain.

CHAP. 12.

28 Wherefore we receiving a kingdom which cannot be moved, [4]let us have grace, whereby we may serve God acceptably with reverence and godly fear:

29 For [t]our God *is* a consuming fire.

G—CONCLUDED.

H

Ex. 4. 22 And thou shalt say unto Pharaoh, Thus saith the LORD, Israel *is* my son, *even* my firstborn:

Jas. 1. 18 Of his own will begat he us with the word of truth, that we should be a kind of firstfruits of his creatures.

Rev. 14. 4 These are they which were not defiled with women; for they are virgins. These are they which follow the Lamb whithersoever he goeth. These were redeemed from among men, *being* the firstfruits unto God and to the Lamb.

I

Luke 10. 20. *See d, D, § 116, page 341.*

1

Or, *enrolled.*

K

Gen. 18. 25 That be far from thee to do after this manner, to slay the righteous with the wicked; and that the righteous should be as the wicked, that be far from thee: Shall not the Judge of all the earth do right?

§ 524. EXHORTATIONS

13 : 1–6.

1 Let [a]brotherly love continue.

2 [b]Be not forgetful to entertain strangers: for thereby [c]some have entertained angels unawares.

3 [d]Remember them that are in bonds, as bound with them; *and* them which suffer adversity, as being yourselves also in the body.

4 Marriage *is* honourable in all, and the bed undefiled: [e]but whoremongers and adulterers God will judge.

A

Rom. 12. 10. *See x, X, § 342, page 870.*

1 Thes. 4. 9 But as touching brotherly love ye need not that I write unto you: for ye yourselves are taught of God to love one another.

1 Jno. 3. 11 For this is the message that ye heard from the beginning, that we should love one another.

1 Jno. 4. 7 Beloved, let us love one another: for love is of God; and every one that loveth is born of God, and knoweth God.

1 Jno. 4. 20 If a man say, I love God, and hateth his brother, he is a liar: for he that loveth not his brother whom he hath seen, how can he love God whom he hath not seen?

OF THE LAW. ITS WARNINGS MORE TO BE FEARED (Concluded).

K—Concluded.

Ps. 94. 2 Lift up thyself, thou Judge of the earth: render a reward to the proud.

L

Heb. 11. 40. *See y, Y, § 520, page 12[illegible]4.*

M

II Cor. 3. 6. *See k, K, § 390, page 970.*

2

Or, *testament.*

N

Ex. 24. 8 And Moses took the blood, and sprinkled *it* on the people, and said, Behold the blood of the covenant, which the Lord hath made with you concerning all these words.

Heb. 10. 22 Let us draw near with a true heart in full assurance of faith, having our hearts sprinkled from an evil conscience, and our bodies washed with pure water.

I Pet. 1. 2 Elect according to the foreknowledge of God the Father, through sanctification of the Spirit, unto obedience and sprinkling of the blood of Jesus Christ: Grace unto you, and peace, be multiplied.

O

Heb. 11. 4. *See e, E, § 520, page 1206.*

P

Heb. 2. 2, 3. *See c, C, § 504, page 1172.*

Q

Ex. 19. 18. *See under [illegible], page 1218.*

R

Hag. 2. 6 For thus saith the Lord of hosts; Yet once, it *is* a little while, and I will shake the heavens, and the earth, and the sea, and the dry *land;*

S

Matt. 24. 35. *See m, M, § 173, page 490.*

II Pet. 3. 10 But the day of the Lord will come as a thief in the night; in the which the heavens shall pass away with a great noise, and the elements shall melt with fervent heat, the earth also and the works that are therein shall be burned up.

Rev. 21. 1 And I saw a new heaven and a new earth: for the first heaven and the first earth were passed away; and there was no more sea.

3

Or, *may be shaken.*

4

Or, *let us hold fast.*

T

Ex. 24. 17 And the sight of the glory of the Lord *was* like devouring fire on the top of the mount in the eyes of the children of Israel.

Deut. 4. 24 For the Lord thy God *is* a consuming fire, *even* a jealous God.

Deut. 9. 3 Understand therefore this day, that the Lord thy God *is* he which goeth over before thee; *as* a consuming fire shall he destroy them, and he shall bring them down before thy face: so shalt thou drive them out, and destroy them quickly, as the Lord hath said unto thee.

Ps. 50. 3 Our God shall come, and shall not keep silence: a fire shall devour before him, and it shall be very tempestuous round about him.

Ps. 97. 3 A fire goeth before him, and burneth up his enemies round about.

II Thes. 1. 8. *See n, N, § 466, page 1110.*

TO SUNDRY DUTIES.

A—Concluded

I Jno. 4. 21 And this commandment have we from him, That he who loveth God love his brother also.

B

Rom. 12. 13. *See d, D, § 342, page 870.*

C

Gen. 18 3 And said, My Lord, if now I have found favour in thy sight, pass not away, I pray thee, from thy servant:

Gen. 19. 2 And he said, Behold now, my lords, turn in, I pray you, into your servant's house, and tarry all night, and wash your feet, and ye shall rise up early, and go on your ways. And they said, Nay; but we will abide in the street all night.

D

Matt. 25. 36 Naked, and ye clothed me: I was sick, and ye visited me: I was in prison, and ye came unto me.

Rom. 12. 15 Rejoice with them that do rejoice, and weep with them that weep.

I Cor. 12. 26 And whether one member suffer, all the members suffer with it; or one member be honoured, all the members rejoice with it.

Col. 4. 18 The salutation by the hand of me Paul. Remember my bonds. Grace *be* with you. Amen.

I Pet. 3. 8 Finally, *be ye* all of one mind, having compassion one of another; love as brethren, *be* pitiful, *be* courteous:

E

I Cor. 6. 9. *See f, F, § 360, page 910.*

For E, concluded, see next page (1222).

§ 524. EXHORTATIONS TO

CHAP. 13.

5 *Let your* conversation *be* without covetousness; *and* [f]*be* content with such things as ye have: for he hath said,[g]I will never leave thee, nor forsake thee.

6 So that we may boldly say, [h]The Lord *is* my helper, and I will not fear what man shall do unto me.

E—CONCLUDED.

Col. 3. 5 Mortify therefore your members which are upon the earth; fornication, uncleanness, inordinate affection, evil concupiscence, and covetousness, which is idolatry:

6 For which things' sake the wrath of God cometh on the children of disobedience:

F

Matt. 6. 25 Therefore I say unto you, Take no thought for your life, what ye shall eat, or what ye shall drink; nor yet for your body, what ye shall put on. Is not the life more than meat, and the body than raiment?

Matt. 6. 34 Take therefore no thought for the morrow: for the morrow shall take thought for the things of itself. Sufficient unto the day *is* the evil thereof.

Phil. 4. 11. *See b, B, § 447, page 1074.*

G

Gen. 28. 15 And, behold, I *am* with thee, and will keep thee in all *places* whither thou goest, and will bring thee again into this land; for I will not leave thee, until I have done *that* which I have spoken to thee of.

§ 525. EXHORTATION TO REMEMBER THEIR INSTRUCTORS

13:7–17.

7 [a]Remember them which [1]have the rule over you, who have spoken unto you the word of God: [b]whose faith follow, considering the end of *their* conversation.

8 Jesus Christ [c]the same yesterday, and to day, and for ever.

9 [d]Be not carried about with divers and strange doctrines. For *it is* a good thing that the heart be established with grace; [e]not with meats, which have not profited them that have been occupied therein.

10 [f]We have an altar, whereof they have no right to eat which serve the tabernacle.

11 For [g]the bodies of those beasts, whose blood is brought into the sanctuary by the high priest for sin, are burned without the camp.

12 Wherefore Jesus also, that he might sanctify the people with his own blood, [h]suffered without the gate.

A

Heb. 13. 17. *See text of topic.*

1

Or, *are the guides.*

B

Heb. 6. 12 That ye be not slothful, but followers of them who though faith and patience inherit the promises.

C

John 8. 58 Jesus said unto them, Verily, verily, I say unto you, Before Abraham was, I am.

Heb. 1. 12 And as a vesture shalt thou fold them up, and they shalt be changed: but thou art the same, and thy years shall not fail.

Rev. 1. 4 John to the seven churches which are in Asia: Grace *be* unto you, and peace, from him which is, and which was, and which is to come; and from the seven Spirits which are before his throne;

D

Matt. 24. 4. *See e, E, § 172, page 480.*

Eph. 4. 14 That we *henceforth* be no more children, tossed to and fro, and carried about with every wind of doctrine, by the sleight of men, *and* cunning craftiness, whereby they lie in wait to deceive;

E

Col. 2. 16 Let no man therefore judge you in meat, or in drink, or in respect of a holyday, or of the new moon, or of the sabbath *days:*

1 Tim. 4. 3. *See h, H, § 478, page 1128.*

SUNDRY DUTIES (CONCLUDED).

G—CONTINUED.

Deut.31. 6 Be strong and of a good courage, Fear not, nor be afraid of them: for the LORD thy God, he *it is* that doth go with thee: he will not fail thee, nor forsake thee.

Deut.31. 8 And the LORD, he *it is* that doth go before thee; he will be with thee, he will not fail thee, neither forsake thee: fear not, neither be dismayed.

Josh. 1. 5 There shall not any man be able to stand before thee all the days of thy life: as I was with Moses, *so* I will be with thee: I will not fail thee, nor forsake thee.

IChr.28. 20 And David said to Solomon his son, Be strong and of good courage, and do *it:* fear not, nor be dismayed, for the LORD God, *even* my God, *will be* with thee; he will not fail thee, nor forsake thee, until thou hast finished all the work for the service of the house of the LORD.

G—CONCLUDED.

Ps. 37. 25 I have been young, and *now* am old; yet have I not seen the righteous forsaken, nor his seed begging bread.

H

Ps. 27. 1 The LORD *is* my light and my salvation; whom shall I fear? the LORD *is* the strength of my life; of whom shall I be afraid ?

Ps. 56. 4 In God I will praise his word, in God I have put my trust; I will not fear what flesh can do unto me.

Ps. 56. 11 In God have I put my trust: I will not be afraid what man can do unto me.

12 Thy vows *are* upon me, O God: I will render praises unto thee.

Ps. 118. 6 The LORD *is* on my side; I will not fear: what can man do unto me?

AND TO CONTINUE STEADFAST, BEARING REPROACH.

F

I Cor. 9. 13 Do ye not know that they which minister about holy things live *of the things* of the temple? and they which wait at the altar are partakers with the altar?

ICor.10. 18 Behold Israel after the flesh: are not they which eat of the sacrifices partakers of the altar?

G

Ex. 29. 14 But the flesh of the bullock, and his skin, and his dung, shalt thou burn with fire without the camp: it *is* a sin offering.

Lev. 4. 11 And the skin of the bullock, and all his flesh, with his head, and with his legs, and his inwards, and his dung,

12 Even the whole bullock shall he carry forth without the camp unto a clean place, where the ashes are poured out, and burn him on the wood with fire: where the ashes are poured out shall he be burnt.

Lev. 4. 21 And he shall carry forth the bullock without the camp, and burn him as he burned the first bullock: it *is* a sin offering for the congregation.

Lev. 9. 11 And the flesh and the hide he burnt with fire without the camp.

Lev. 16. 27 And the bullock *for* the sin offering, and the goat *for* the sin offering, whose blood was brought in to make atonement in the holy *place*, shall *one* carry forth without the camp; and they shall burn in the fire their skins, and their flesh, and their dung.

G—CONCLUDED.

Num. 19. 3 And ye shall give her unto Eleazar the priest, that he may bring her forth without the camp, and *one* shall slay her before his face:

H

John 19. 17 And he bearing his cross went forth into a place called *the place* of a skull, which is called in the Hebrew Golgotha:

18 Where they crucified him, and two other with him, on either side one, and Jesus in the midst.

Acts. 7. 58 And cast *him* out of the city, and stoned *him:* and the witnesses laid down their clothes at a young man's feet, whose name was Saul.

I

Heb. 11. 26 Esteeming the reproach of Christ greater riches than the treasures in Egypt: for he had respect unto the recompense of the reward.

I Pet. 4. 14 If ye be reproached for the name of Christ, happy *are ye;* for the Spirit of glory and of God resteth upon you: on their part he is evil spoken of, but on your part he is glorified.

K

Mic. 2. 10 Arise ye, and depart; for this *is* not *your* rest: because it is polluted, it shall destroy *you*, even with a sore destruction.

§ 525. EXHORTATION TO REMEMBER THEIR INSTRUCTORS

CHAP. 13.

13 Let us go forth therefore unto him without the camp, bearing [i]his reproach.

14 [k]For here have we no continuing city, but we seek one to come.

15 [l]By him therefore let us offer [m]the sacrifice of praise to God continually, that is, [n]the fruit of *our* lips, [2]giving thanks to his name.

16 [o]But to do good and to communicate forget not: for [p]with such sacrifices God is well pleased.

17 Obey them that [3]have the rule over you, and submit yourselves: for [q]they watch for your souls, as they that must give account, that they may do it with joy, and not with grief: for that *is* unprofitable for you.

For I and K, see preceding page (1223).

K—CONCLUDED.

Phil. 3. 20. *See h, H, § 445, page 1072.*

Heb. 11. 10 For he looked for a city which hath foundations, whose builder and maker *is* God.

Heb. 11. 16 But now they desire a better *country*, that is, a heavenly: wherefore God is not ashamed to be called their God: for he hath prepared for them a city.

L

Eph. 5. 20. *See l, L, § 434, page 1050.*

M

Lev. 7. 12 If he offer it for a thanksgiving, then he shall offer with the sacrifice of thanksgiving unleavened cakes mingled with oil, and unleavened wafers anointed with oil, and cakes mingled with oil, of fine flour, fried.

Ps. 50. 14 Offer unto God thanksgiving; and pay thy vows unto the Most High:

Ps. 50. 23 Whoso offereth praise glorifieth me: and to him that ordereth *his* conversation *aright* will I shew the salvation of God.

Ps. 69. 30 I will praise the name of God with a song, and will magnify him with thanksgiving.

§ 526 SOLICITATION FOR THEIR PRAYERS. CONCERNING

13 : 18–25.

18 [a]Pray for us: for we trust we have [b]a good conscience, in all things willing to live honestly.

19 But I beseech *you* [c]the rather to do this, that I may be restored to you the sooner.

20 Now [d]the God of peace, [e]that brought again from the dead our Lord Jesus, [f]that great Shepherd of the sheep, [g]through the blood of the everlasting [1]covenant,

21 [h]Make you perfect in every good work to do his will, [2i]working in you that which is well pleasing in his sight, through Jesus Christ; [k]to whom *be* glory for ever and ever. Amen.

22 And I beseech you, brethren, suffer the word of exhortation: for [l]I have written a letter unto you in few words.

CHAP. 13.

23 Know ye that [m]*our* brother Timothy [n]is set at liberty; with whom, if he come shortly, I will see you.

24 Salute all them [o]that have the rule over you, and all the saints. They of Italy salute you.

25 [p]Grace *be* with you all. Amen.

A

Eph. 6. 19. *See r, R, § 437, page 1056.*

B

Acts 23. 1. *See a, A, § 299, page 776.*

C

Phile. 22 But withal prepare me also a lodging: for I trust that through your prayers I shall be given unto you.

D

Rom. 15. 33. *See b, B, § 346, page 882.*

E

Acts 2. 24. *See k, K, § 231, page 638.*

F

John 10. 11, 14. *See k, K, § 118, page 351.*

G

Zech. 9. 11 As for thee also, by the blood of thy covenant I have sent forth thy

AND TO CONTINUE STEADFAST, BEARING REPROACH (CONCLUDED).

M—CONCLUDED.

Ps. 69. 31 *This* also shall please the LORD better than an ox *or* bullock that hath horns and hoofs.

Ps. 107. 22 And let them sacrifice the sacrifices of thanksgiving, and declare his works with rejoicing.

Ps. 116. 17 I will offer to thee the sacrifice of thanksgiving, and will call upon the name of the LORD.

N

Hos. 14. 2 Take with you words, and turn to the LORD: say unto him, Take away all iniquity, and receive *us* graciously: so will we render the calves of our lips.

2

Gr. *confessing to.*

O

Rom. 12. 13 Distributing to the necessity of saints; given to hospitality.

P

II Cor. 9. 12 For the administration of this service not only supplieth the want of the saints, but is abundant also by many thanksgivings unto God;

Phil. 4. 18 But I have all, and abound: I am full, having received of Epaphroditus

P—CONCLUDED.

the things *which were sent* from you, an odour of a sweet smell, a sacrifice acceptable, well pleasing to God.

Heb. 6. 10 For God *is* not unrighteous to forget your work and labour of love, which ye have shewed toward his name, in that ye have ministered to the saints, and do minister.

3

Or, *guide.*

Q

Eze. 3. 17 Son of man, I have made thee a watchman unto the house of Israel: therefore hear the word at my mouth, and give them warning from me.

Eze. 33. 2 Son of man, speak to the children of thy people, and say unto them, When I bring the sword upon a land, if the people of the land take a man of their coasts, and set him for their watchman:

Eze. 33. 7 So thou, O son of man, I have set thee a watchman unto the house of Israel; therefore thou shalt hear the word at my mouth, and warn them from me.

Acts 20. 26, 28. *See q, Q, § 292, page 762.*

TIMOTHY. CLOSING SALUTATIONS AND BENEDICTIONS.

G—CONCLUDED.

prisoners out of the pit wherein *is* no water.

Heb. 10. 29 Of how much sorer punishment, suppose ye, shall he be thought worthy, who hath trodden under foot the Son of God, and hath counted the blood of the covenant, wherewith he was sanctified, an unholy thing, and hath done despite unto the Spirit of grace?

1

Or, *testament.*

H

II Thes. 2. 17 Comfort your hearts, and stablish you in every good word and work.

I Pet. 5. 10 But the God of all grace, who hath called us unto his eternal glory by Christ Jesus, after that ye have suffered a while, make you perfect, stablish, strengthen, settle *you.*

2

Or, *doing.*

I

Phil. 2. 13 For it is God which worketh in you both to will and to do of *his* good pleasure.

K

Rom. 11. 36. *See r, R, § 341, page 866.*

L

I Pet. 5. 12 By Silvanus, a faithful brother unto you, as I suppose, I have written briefly, exhorting, and testifying that this is the true grace of God wherein ye stand.

M

I Thes. 3. 2 And sent Timotheus, our brother and minister of God, and our fellow labourer in the gospel of Christ, to establish you, and to comfort you concerning your faith:

N

I Tim. 6. 12 Fight the good fight of faith, lay hold on eternal life, whereunto thou art also called, and hast professed a good profession before many witnesses.

O

Heb. 13. 17. *See text of topic, § 525.*

P

Tit. 3. 15 All that are with me salute thee. Greet them that love us in the faith. Grace *be* with you all. Amen.

THE EPISTLE

§ 527. INTRODUCTORY GREETING.

I : I.

1 [a]James, [b]a servant of God and of the Lord Jesus Christ, [c]to the twelve tribes [d]which are scattered abroad, greeting.

A

Matt. 13. 55 Is not this the carpenter's son? is not his mother called Mary? and his brethren, James, and Joses, and Simon, and Judas?

Mark 6. 3 Is not this the carpenter, the son of Mary, the brother of James, and Joses, and of Juda, and Simon? and are not his sisters here with us? And they were offended at him.

A —CONTINUED.

Mark 15. 40 There were also women looking on afar off: among whom was Mary Magdalene, and Mary the mother of James the less and of Joses, and Salome;

Acts 12. 17 But he, beckoning unto them with the hand to hold their peace, declared unto them how the Lord had brought him out of the prison. And he said, Go shew these things unto James, and to the brethren. And he departed, and went into another place.

Acts 15. 13 And after they had held their peace, James answered, saying, Men *and* brethren, hearken unto me:

Gal. 1. 19 But other of the apostles saw I none, save James the Lord's brother.

§ 528. EXHORTATION TO BEAR TRIAL PATIENTLY, AND TO PRAY FOR

I : 2–18.

2 My brethren, [a]count it all joy [b]when ye fall into divers temptations;

3 [c]Knowing *this*, that the trying of your faith worketh patience.

4 But let patience have *her* perfect work, that ye may be perfect and entire, wanting nothing.

5 [d]If any of you lack wisdom, [e]let him ask of God, that giveth to all *men* liberally, and upbraideth not; and [f]it shall be given him.

6 But [g]let him ask in faith, nothing wavering: for he that wavereth is like a wave of the sea driven with the wind and tossed.

7 For let not that man think that he shall receive any thing of the Lord.

8 [h]A doubleminded man *is* unstable in all his ways.

9 Let the brother of low degree [i]rejoice in that he is exalted:

CHAP. I.

10 But the rich, in that he is made low: because [i]as the flower of the grass he shall pass away.

A

Matt. 5. 12. *See r, R, § 43, page 126.*

Heb. 10. 34 For ye had compassion of me in my bonds, and took joyfully the spoiling of your goods, knowing in yourselves that ye have in heaven a better and an enduring substance.

I Pet. 4. 16 Yet if *any man suffer* as a Christian, let him not be ashamed; but let him glorify God on this behalf.

B

I Pet. 1. 6 Wherein ye greatly rejoice, though now for a season, if need be, ye are in heaviness through manifold temptations:

C

Rom. 5. 3 And not only *so*, but we glory in tribulations also; knowing that tribulation worketh patience;

4 And patience, experience; and experience, hope:

D

I Ki. 3. 9 Give therefore thy servant an understanding heart to judge thy people, that I may discern between good and bad: for who is able to judge this thy so great a people?

OF JAMES.

Writte probably A. D. 62, at Jerusalem.

A—Concluded.

Gal. 2. 9 And when James, Cephas, and John, who seemed to be pillars, perceived the grace that was given unto me, they gave to me and Barnabas the right hands of fellowship; that we *should go* unto the heathen, and they unto the circumcision.

Gal. 2. 12 For before that certain came from James, he did eat with the Gentiles: but when they were come, he withdrew and separated himself, fearing them which were of the circumcision.

Jude 1 Jude, the servant of Jesus Christ, and brother of James, to them that are sanctified by God the Father, and preserved in Jesus Christ, *and* called:

B

Tit. 1. 1 Paul, a servant of God, and an apostle of Jesus Christ, according to the faith of God's elect, and the acknowledging of the truth which is after godliness;

C

Acts 26. 7 Unto which *promise* our twelve tribes, instantly serving *God* day and night, hope to come. For which hope's sake, king Agrippa, I am accused of the Jews.

D

Deut. 32. 26 I said, I would scatter them into corners, I would make the remembrance of them to cease from among men:

John 7. 35. *See e, E, § 109, page 317.*

Acts 11. 19. *See a, A, § 256, page 702.*

WISDOM. GOOD GIFTS COME FROM GOD, EVIL SPRINGS FROM LUST.

D—Concluded.

10 And the speech pleased the Lord, that Solomon had asked this thing.

11 And God said unto him, because thou hast asked this thing, and hast not asked for thyself long life; neither hast asked riches for thyself, nor hast asked the life of thine enemies; but hast asked for thyself understanding to discern judgment;

1 Behold, I have done according to thy word: lo, I have given thee a wise and an understanding heart; so that there was none like thee before thee, neither after thee shall any arise like unto thee.

Prov. 2. 3 Yea, if thou criest after knowledge, *and* liftest up thy voice for understanding;

Prov. 2. 6 For the Lord giveth wisdom: out of his mouth *cometh* knowledge and understanding.

E

Matt. 7. 7. *See k, K, § 43, page 144.*

F

Jer. 29. 12 Then shall ye call upon me, and ye shall go and pray unto me, and I will hearken unto you.

1 Jno. 5 14 And this is the confidence that we have in him, that if we ask any thing according to his will, he heareth us:

15 And if we know that he hear us,

F—Concluded.

whatsoever we ask, we know that we have the petitions that we desired of him.

G

Mark 11. 24 Therefore I say unto you, What things soever ye desire, when ye pray, believe that ye receive *them*, and ye shall have *them*.

1 Tim. 2. 8 I will therefore that men pray every where, lifting up holy hands, without wrath and doubting.

H

Jas. 4. 8 Draw nigh to God, and he will draw nigh to you. Cleanse *your* hands, *ye* sinners; and purify *your* hearts, *ye* doubleminded.

1

Or, *glory.*

I

Job 14. 2 He cometh forth like a flower, and is cut down: he fleeth also as a shadow, and continueth not.

Ps. 37. 2 For they shall soon be cut down like the grass, and wither as the green herb.

Ps. 90. 5 Thou carriest them away as with a flood; they are *as* a sleep: in the morning *they are* like grass *which* groweth up.

For I, concluded see next page (1228).

§ 528. EXHORTATION TO BEAR TRIAL PATIENTLY, AND TO PRAY FOR WIS-

Chap. I.

11 For the sun is no sooner risen with a burning heat, but it withereth the grass, and the flower thereof falleth, and the grace of the fashion of it perisheth: so also shall the rich man fade away in his ways.

12 [k]Blessed *is* the man that endureth temptation: for when he is tried, he shall receive [l]the crown of life, [m]which the Lord hath promised to them that love him.

13 Let no man say when he is tempted, I am tempted of God: for God cannot be tempted with [2]evil neither tempteth he any man:

14 But every man is tempted, when he is drawn away of his own lust, and enticed.

15 Then [n]when lust hath conceived, it bringeth forth sin: and sin, when it is finished, [o]bringeth forth death.

16 Do not err, my beloved brethren.

17 [p]Every good gift and every perfect gift is from above, and cometh down from the Father of lights, [q]with whom is no variableness, neither shadow of turning.

18 [r]Of his own will begat he us with the word of truth, [s]that we should be a kind of [t]firstfruits of his creatures.

I—Concluded.

Ps. 90. 6 In the morning it flourisheth, and groweth up; in the evening it is cut down, and withereth.

Ps. 103. 15 *As for* man, his days *are* as grass: as a flower of the field, so he flourisheth.

Isa. 40. 6 The voice said, Cry. And he said, What shall I cry? All flesh *is* grass, and all the goodliness thereof *is* as the flower of the field:

I Cor. 7. 31. *See g, G, § 363, page 916.*

K

Job 5. 17 Behold, happy *is* the man whom God correcteth: therefore despise not thou the chastening of the Almighty:

Ps. 94. 12 Blessed *is* the man whom thou chastenest, O Lord, and teachest him out of thy law;

Ps. 119. 67 Before I was afflicted I went astray: but now have I kept thy word.

Ps. 119. 71 *It is* good for me that I have been afflicted; that I might learn thy statutes.

Prov. 3. 11 My son, despise not the chastening of the Lord; neither be weary of his correction:

12 For whom the Lord loveth he correcteth; even as a father the son *in whom* he delighteth.

Heb. 6. 15 And so, after he had patiently endured, he obtained the promise.

Heb. 12. 5. *See i, I, § 521, page 1216.*

Jas. 5. 11 Behold, we count them happy which endure. Ye have heard of the patience of Job, and have seen the end of the Lord; that the Lord is very pitiful, and of tender mercy.

Rev. 3. 19 As many as I love, I rebuke and chasten: be zealous therefore, and repent.

L

I Cor. 9. 25 And every man that striveth for the mastery is temperate in all things. Now they *do it* to obtain a corruptible crown; but we an incorruptible.

§ 529. EXHORTATION TO BRIDLE THE TONGUE, PUT AWAY EVIL, RECEIVE

I: 19–27.

19 Wherefore, my beloved brethren, [a]let every man be swift to hear, [b]slow to speak, [c]slow to wrath:

20 For the wrath of man worketh not the righteousness of God.

A

Eccl. 5. 1 Keep thy foot when thou goest to the house of God, and be more ready to hear, than to give the sacrifice of fools: for they consider not that they do evil.

B

Prov. 10. 19 In the multitude of words there wanteth not sin: but he that refraineth his lips *is* wise.

DOM. GOOD GIFTS COME FROM GOD, EVIL SPRINGS FROM LUST (CONCLUDED).

L—CONCLUDED.

IITim. 4. 8 Henceforth there is laid up for me a crown of righteousness, which the Lord, the righteous judge, shall give me at that day: and not to me only, but unto all them also that love his appearing.

I Pet. 5. 4 And when the chief Shepherd shall appear, ye shall receive a crown of glory that fadeth not away.

Rev. 2. 10 Fear none of those things which thou shalt suffer; behold, the devil shall cast *some* of you into prison, that ye may be tried; and ye shall have tribulation ten days: be thou faithful unto death, and I will give thee a crown of life.

Rev. 3. 21 To him that overcometh will I grant to sit with me in my throne, even as I also overcame, and am set down with my Father in his throne.

M

Matt. 10. 22 And ye shall be hated of all *men* for my name's sake: but he that endureth to the end shall be saved.

Matt. 19. 28, 29. *See d, D, § 145, page 412.*

Jas. 2. 5 Hearken my beloved brethren Hath not God chosen the poor of this world rich in faith, and heirs of the kingdom which he hath promised to them that love him?

2

Or, *evils.*

N

Job 15. 35 They conceive mischief, and bring forth vanity, and their belly prepareth deceit.

Ps. 7. 14 Behold, he travaileth with iniquity, and hath conceived mischief, and brought forth falsehood.

O

Rom. 7. 5. *See f, F, § 330, page 840.*

P

John 3. 27 John answered and said, A man can receive nothing, except it be given him from heaven.

P—CONCLUDED.

I Cor. 4. 7 For who maketh thee to differ *from another?* and what hast thou that thou didst not receive? now if thou didst receive *it*, why dost thou glory, as if thou hadst not received *it?*

Q

Num. 23. 19 God *is* not a man, that he should lie; neither the son of man, that he should repent: hath he said, and shall he not do *it?* or hath he spoken, and shall he not make it good?

I Sa. 15. 29 And also the Strength of Israel will not lie or repent: for he *is* not a man, that he should repent.

Ps. 33. 11 The counsel of the LORD standeth for ever, the thoughts of his heart to all generations.

Prov. 19. 21 *There are* many devices in a man's heart; nevertheless the counsel of the LORD, that shall stand.

Mal. 3. 6 For I *am* the LORD, I change not; therefore ye sons of Jacob are not consumed.

Rom. 11. 29 For the gifts and calling of God *are* without repentance.

R

John 1. 13. *See q, Q, § 1, page 7.*

I Cor. 4. 15 For though ye have ten thousand instructors in Christ, yet *have ye* not many fathers: for in Christ Jesus I have begotten you through the gospel.

S

Eph. 1. 12 That we should be to the praise of his glory, who first trusted in Christ.

T

Jer. 2. 3 Israel *was* holiness unto the LORD, *and* the firstfruits of his increase: all that devour him shall offend; evil shall come upon them, saith the LORD.

Rev. 14. 4 These are they which were not defiled with women; for they are virgins. These are they which follow the Lamb whithersoever he goeth. These were redeemed from among men, *being* the firstfruits unto God and to the Lamb.

THE WORD, BE DOERS NOT ONLY HEARERS AND FOLLOW PURE RELIGION.

B—CONCLUDED.

Prov. 17. 27 He that hath knowledge spareth his words: *and* a man of understanding is of an excellent spirit.

Eccl. 5. 2 Be not rash with thy mouth, and let not thine heart be hasty to utter *any* thing before God: for God *is* in heaven, and thou upon earth: therefore let thy words be few.

C

Prov. 14. 17 *He that is* soon angry dealeth foolishly: and a man of wicked devices is hated.

Prov. 16. 32 *He that is* slow to anger *is* better than the mighty; and he that ruleth his spirit than he that taketh a city.

Eccl. 7. 9 Be not hasty in thy spirit to be angry: for anger resteth in the bosom of fools.

§ 529. EXHORTATION TO BRIDLE THE TONGUE, PUT AWAY EVIL, RECEIVE

CHAP. 1.

21 Wherefore [d]lay apart all filthiness and superfluity of naughtiness, and receive with meekness the engrafted word, [e]which is able to save your souls.

22 But [f]be ye doers of the word, and not hearers only, deceiving your own selves.

23 For [g]if any be a hearer of the word, and not a doer, he is like unto a man beholding his natural face in a glass:

24 For he beholdeth himself, and goeth his way, and straightway forgetteth what manner of man he was.

25 But [h]whoso looketh into the perfect [i]law of liberty, and continueth *therein*, he being not a forgetful hearer, but a doer of the work, [k]this man shall be blessed in his [1]deed.

26 If any man among you seem to be religious, and [l]bridleth not his tongue, but deceiveth his own heart, this man's religion *is* vain.

27 [m]Pure religion and undefiled before God and the Father is this, [n]To visit the fatherless and widows in their affliction, [o]*and* to keep himself unspotted from the world.

D

Eph. 4. 22. *See i, I, § 433, page 1044.*

E

Acts 13. 26 Men *and* brethren, children of the stock of Abraham, and whosoever among you feareth God, to you is the word of this salvation sent.

Rom. 1. 16. *See m, M, § 318, page 810.*

Eph. 1. 13 In whom ye also *trusted*, after that ye heard the word of truth, the gospel of your salvation: in whom also after that ye believed, ye were sealed with that Holy Spirit of promise,

Tit. 2. 11 For the grace of God that bringeth salvation hath appeared to all men,

Heb. 2. 3 How shall we escape, if we neglect so great salvation; which at the first began to be spoken by the Lord, and was confirmed unto us by them that heard *him;*

I Pet. 1. 9 Receiving the end of your faith, *even* the salvation of *your* souls.

F

Matt. 7. 21. *See h, H, § 43, page 148.*

G

Luke 6. 47 Whosoever cometh to me, and heareth my sayings, and doeth them, I will shew you to whom he is like:

Luke 11. 28 But he said, Yea, rather, blessed *are* they that hear the word of God, and keep it.

Jas. 2. 14 What *doth it* profit, my brethren, though a man say he hath faith, and have not works? can faith save him?

H

II Cor. 3. 18 But we all, with open face beholding as in a glass the glory of the Lord, are changed into the same image from glory to glory, *even* as by the Spirit of the Lord.

§ 530. A REBUKE TO THOSE WHO PROFESS

2 : 1–13.

1 My brethren, have not the faith of our Lord Jesus Christ, [a]*the Lord* of glory, [b]with respect of persons.

2 For if there come unto your [1]assembly a man with a gold ring, in goodly apparel, and there come in also a poor man in vile raiment;

3 And ye have respect to him that weareth the gay clothing, and say unto

A

I Cor. 2. 8 Which none of the princes of this world knew: for had they known *it*, they would not have crucified the Lord of glory.

B

Lev. 19. 15 Ye shall do no unrighteousness in judgment; thou shalt not respect the personof the poor, nor honour the person of the mighty: *but* in righteousness shalt thou judge thy neighbour.

Deut. 1. 17 Ye shall not respect persons in judgment; *but* ye shall hear the small as well as the great; ye shall not be

THE WORD, BE DOERS NOT ONLY HEARERS AND FOLLOW, ETC. (CONCLUDED).

I

Jas. 2. 12 So speak ye, and so do, as they that shall be judged by the law of liberty.

K

John 13. 17 If ye know these things, happy are ye if ye do them.

1

Or, *doing*.

L

Ps. 34. 13 Keep thy tongue from evil, and thy lips from speaking guile.

Ps. 39. 1 I said, I will take heed to my ways, that I sin not with my tongue: I will keep my mouth with a bridle, while the wicked is before me.

Ps. 141. 3 Set a watch, O LORD, before my mouth; keep the door of my lips.

Prov. 10. 19 In the multitude of words there wanteth not sin: but he that refraineth his lips *is* wise.

Prov. 13. 3 He that keepeth his mouth keepeth his life: *but* he that openeth wide his lips shall have destruction.

Col. 4. 6 Let your speech *be* alway with grace, seasoned with salt, that ye may know how ye ought to answer every man.

I Pet. 3. 10 For he that will love life, and see good days, let him refrain his tongue from evil, and his lips that they speak no guile:

M

Ps. 119. 1 Blessed *are* the undefiled in the way, who walk in the way of the LORD.

Matt. 5. 8 Blessed *are* the pure in heart: for they shall see God.

Luke 1. 6 And they were both righteous before God, walking in all the commandments and ordinances of the Lord blameless.

M—CONCLUDED.

I Tim. 1. 2 Unto Timothy, *my* own son in the faith: Grace, mercy, *and* peace, from God our Father and Jesus Christ our Lord.

N

Isa. 1. 16 Wash ye, make you clean; put away the evil of your doings from before mine eyes; cease to do evil;

17 Learn to do well; seek judgment, relieve the oppressed, judge the fatherless, plead for the widow.

Isa. 58. 6 *Is* not this the fast that I have chosen? to loose the bands of wickedness, to undo the heavy burdens, and to let the oppressed go free, and that ye break every yoke?

7 *Is it* not to deal thy bread to the hungry, and that thou bring the poor that are cast out to thy house? when thou seest the naked, that thou cover him; and that thou hide not thyself from thine own flesh?

Matt. 25. 36 Naked, and ye clothed me: I was sick, and ye visited me: I was in prison, and ye came unto me.

O

Rom. 12. 2 And be not conformed to this world: but be ye transformed by the renewing of your mind, that ye may prove what *is* that good, and acceptable, and perfect will of God.

Jas. 4. 4 Ye adulterers and adulteresses, know ye not that the friendship of the world is enmity with God? whosoever therefore will be a friend of the world is the enemy of God.

I Jno. 5. 18 We know that whosoever is born of God sinneth not; but he that is begotten of God keepeth himself, and that wicked one toucheth him not.

FAITH AND SHOW RESPECT TO PERSONS.

B—CONTINUED.

afraid of the face of man; for the judgement *is* God's: and the cause that is too hard for you, bring *it* unto me, and I will hear it.

Deut. 16. 19 Thou shalt not wrest judgment; thou shalt not respect persons, neither take a gift: for a gift doth blind the eyes of the wise, and pervert the words of the righteous.

Prov. 24. 23 These *things* also *belong* to the wise. *It is* not good to have respect of persons in judgment.

Prov. 28. 21 To have respect of persons *is* not

B—CONCLUDED.

good: for, for a piece of bread *that* man will transgress.

Matt. 22. 16 And they sent out unto him their disciples with the Herodians, saying, Master, we know that thou art true, and teachest the way of God in truth, neither carest thou for any *man:* for thou regardest not the person of men.

Jude. 16 These are murmurers, complainers, walking after their own lusts; and their mouth speaketh great swelling *words*, having men's persons in admiration because of advantage.

For 1, see next page (1232).

§ 530. A REBUKE TO THOSE WHO PROFESS FAITH

CHAP. 2.

him, Sit thou here [2]in a good place; and say to the poor, Stand thou there, or sit here under my footstool:

4 Are ye not then partial in yourselves, and are become judges of evil thoughts?

5 Hearken, my beloved brethren, [c]Hath not God chosen the poor of this world [d]rich in faith, and heirs of [3]the kingdom [e]which he hath promised to them that love him?

6 But [f]ye have despised the poor. Do not rich men oppress you, [g]and draw you before the judgment seats?

7 Do not they blaspheme that worthy name by the which ye are called?

8 If ye fulfill the royal law according to the Scripture, [h]Thou shalt love thy neighbour as thyself, ye do well:

9 But [i]if ye have respect to persons, ye commit sin, and are convinced of the law as transgressors.

10 For whosoever shall keep the whole law, and yet offend in one *point*, [k]he is guilty of all.

11 For [4]he that said, Do not commit adultery, said also, [l]Do not kill. Now if thou commit no adultery, yet if thou kill, thou art become a transgressor of the law.

CHAP. 2.

12 So speak ye, and so do, as they that shall be judged by [m]the law of liberty.

13 For [n]he shall have judgment without [o]mercy, that hath shewed no mercy; and mercy [5]rejoiceth against judgment.

1

Gr. *synagogue*.

2

Or, *well*, or *seemly*.

C

Isa. 14. 32 What shall *one* then answer the messengers of the nation? That the LORD hath founded Zion, and the poor of his people shall trust in it.

Isa. 29. 19 The meek also shall increase *their* joy in the LORD, and the poor among men shall rejoice in the Holy One of Israel.

Zeph. 3. 12 I will also leave in the midst of thee an afflicted and poor people, and they shall trust in the name of the LORD.

John 7. 48 Have any of the rulers or of the Pharisees believed on him?

I Cor. 1. 26 For ye see your calling, brethren, how that not many wise men after the flesh, not many mighty, not many noble, *are called*:

I Cor. 1. 28 And base things of the world, and things which are despised, hath God chosen, *yea*, and things which are not, to bring to nought things that are:

D

Luke 12. 21. *See r, R, § 57, page 187.*

Rev. 2. 9 I know thy works, and tribulation, and poverty, (but thou are rich) and *I know* the blasphemy of them which say they are Jews, and are not, but *are* the synagogue of Satan.

§ 531. FAITH WITHOUT WORKS AND PROFESSIONS

2: 14–26.

14 [a]What *doth it* profit, my brethren, though a man say he hath faith, and have not works? can faith save him?

15 [b]If a brother or sister be naked, and destitute of daily food,

A

Matt. 7. 26 And every one that heareth these sayings of mine, and doeth them not, shall be likened unto a foolish man, which built his house upon the sand:

Jas. 1. 23 For if any be a hearer of the word, and not a doer, he is like unto a man beholding his natural face in a glass:

AND SHOW RESPECT TO PERSONS (CONCLUDED).

3

Or, *that.*

E

Ex. 20. 6 And shewing mercy unto thousands of them that love me, and keep my commandments.

I Sa. 2. 30 Wherefore the LORD God of Israel saith, I said indeed *that* thy house, and the house of thy father, should walk before me for ever: but now the LORD saith, Be it far from me; for them that honour me I will honour, and they that despise me shall be lightly esteemed.

Prov. 8. 17 I love them that love me; and those that seek me early shall find me.

Matt. 5. 3 Blessed *are* the poor in spirit: for theirs is the kingdom of heaven.

Luke 6. 20 And he lifted up his eyes on his disciples, and said, Blessed *be ye* poor: for yours is the kingdom of God.

Luke 12. 32 Fear not, little flock; for it is your Father's good pleasure to give you the kingdom.

I Cor. 2. 9 But as it is written, Eye hath not seen, nor ear heard, neither have entered into the heart of man, the things which God hath prepared for them that love him.

II Tim. 4. 8 Henceforth there is laid up for me a crown of righteousness, which the Lord, the righteous judge, shall give me at that day: and not to me only, but unto all them also that love his appearing.

Jas. 1. 12 Blessed *is* the man that endureth temptation: for when he is tried, he shall receive the crown of life, which the Lord hath promised to them that love him.

F

I Cor. 11. 22 What? have ye not houses to eat and to drink in? or despise ye the church of God, and shame them that have not? What shall I say to you? shall I praise you in this? I praise *you* not.

G

Acts 13. 50 But the Jews stirred up the devout and honourable women, and the chief men of the city, and raised persecution against Paul and Barnabas, and expelled them out of their coasts.

Acts 17. 6 And when they found them not, they drew Jason and certain brethren unto the rulers of the city, crying, These that have turned the world upside down are come hither also;

Acts 18. 12 And when Gallio was the deputy of Achaia, the Jews made insurrection with one accord against Paul, and brought him to the judgment seat.

Jas. 5. 6 Ye have condemned *and* killed the just; *and* he doth not resist you.

H

Matt. 22. 39. *See d, D, § 165, page 460.*

I

Jas. 2. 1 My brethren, have not the faith of our Lord Jesus Christ, *the Lord* of glory, with respect of persons.

K

Gal. 3. 10. *See n, N, § 415, page 1012.*
Matt. 5. 19. *See o, O, § 43, page 128.*

4

Or, *that law which saith.*

L

Ex. 20. 13 Thou shalt not kill.
14 Thou shalt not commit adultery.

M

Jas. 1. 25. *See i, I, § 529, page 1230.*

N

Matt. 18. 35. *See f, F, § 104, page 304.*

O

I Jno. 4. 17 Herein is only our love made perfect, that we may have boldness in the day of judgment: because as he is, so are we in this world.
18 There is no fear in love; but perfect love casteth out fear: because fear hath torment. He that feareth is not made perfect in love.

5

Or, *glorieth.*

WITHOUT DEEDS OF MERCY ARE PROFITLESS.

B

Job 31. 19 If I have seen any perish for want of clothing, or any poor without covering:
20 If his loins have not blessed me, and *if* he were *not* warmed with the fleece of my sheep;
21 If I have lifted up my hand against the fatherless, when I saw my help in the gate.

B—CONTINUED.

Job 31. 22 *Then* let mine arm fall from my shoulder blade, and mine arm be broken from the bone.

Prov. 21. 13 Whoso stoppeth his ears at the cry of the poor, he also shall cry himself, but shall not be heard.

For B, concluded, see next page (1234).

§ 531. FAITH WITHOUT WORKS AND PROFESSIONS WITH-

CHAP. 2.

16 And [c]one of you say unto them, Depart in peace, be *ye* warmed and filled; notwithstanding ye give them not those things which are needful to the body; what *doth it* profit?

17 Even so faith, if it hath not works, is dead, being [1]alone.

18 Yea, a man may say, Thou hast faith, and I have works: shew me thy faith [2]without thy works, [d]and I will shew thee my faith by my works.

19 Thou believest that there is one God; thou doest well: [e]the devils also believe, and tremble.

20 But wilt thou know, O vain man, that faith without works is dead?

21 Was not Abraham our father justified by works, [f]when he had offered Isaac his son upon the altar?

22 [3]Seest thou [g]how faith wrought with his works, and by works was faith made perfect?

23 And the Scripture was fulfilled which saith, [h]Abraham believed God, and it was imputed unto him for righteousness: and [i]he was called the Friend of God.

24 Ye see then how that by works a man is justified, and not by faith only.

25 Likewise also [k]was not Rahab the [l]harlot justified by works, when she had received the messengers, and had sent *them* out another way?

26 For as the body without the [4]spirit is dead, so faith without works is dead also.

B—CONCLUDED.

Luke 3. 11 He answereth and saith unto them, He that hath two coats, let him impart to him that hath none; and he that hath meat, let him do likewise.

C

Matt. 14. 16 But Jesus said unto them, They need not depart; give ye them to eat.

17 And they say unto him, We have here but five loaves, and two fishes.

18 He said, Bring them hither to me.

I Jno. 3. 18 My little children, let us not love in word, neither in tongue; but in deed and in truth.

1

Gr. *by itself.*

2

Some copies read, *by thy works.*

D

Jas. 3. 13 Who *is* a wise man and endued with knowledge among you? let him shew out of a good conversation his works with meekness of wisdom.

E

Matt. 8. 29 And, behold, they cried out, saying, What have we to do with thee, Jesus, thou Son of God? art thou come hither to torment us before the time?

§ 532. THE INIQUITY OF AN UNBRIDLED TONGUE

3 : 1–12.

1 My brethren, [a]be not many masters, [b]knowing that we shall receive the greater [1]condemnation.

2 For [c]in many things we offend all. [d]If any man offend not in word, [e]the same *is* a perfect man, *and* able also to bridle the whole body.

3 Behold, [f]we put bits in the horses'

A

Matt. 23. 8, 14. *See n, N, § 167 page 464.*

Rom. 2. 20 An instructor of the foolish, a teacher of babes, which hast the form of knowledge and of the truth in the law.

21 Thou therefore which teacheth another, teachest thou not thyself? thou that preachest a man should not steal, dost thou steal?

B

Luke 6. 37 Judge not, and ye shall not be judged: condemn not, and ye shall not

OUT DEEDS OF MERCY ARE PROFITLESS (CONCLUDED).

E—CONCLUDED.

Mark 1. 24 Saying, Let *us* alone; what have we to do with thee, thou Jesus of Nazareth? art thou come to destroy us? I know thee who thou art, the Holy One of God.

Mark 5. 7 And cried with a loud voice, and said, What have I to do with thee, Jesus, *thou* Son of the most high God? I adjure thee by God, that thou torment me not.

Luke 4. 34 Saying, Let *us* alone; what have we to do with thee, *thou* Jesus of Nazareth? art thou come to destroy us? I know thee who thou art; the Holy One of God.

Acts 16. 17 The same followed Paul and us, and cried, saying, These men are servants of the most high God, which shew unto us the way of salvation.

Acts 19. 15 And the evil spirit answered and said, Jesus I know, and Paul I know; but who are ye?

F

Gen. 22. 9 And they came to the place which God had told him of; and Abraham built an altar there, and laid the wood in order, and bound Isaac his son, and laid him on the altar upon the wood.

Gen. 22. 12 And he said, Lay not thine hand upon the lad, neither do thou anything unto him: for now I know that thou fearest God, seeing thou hast not withheld thy son, thine only *son*, from me.

3

Or, *thou seest.*

G

Heb. 11. 17 By faith Abraham, when he was tried, offered up Isaac: and he that had received the promises offered up his only begotten *son*,

H

Gen. 15. 6 And he believed in the LORD; and he counted it to him for righteousness.

Rom. 4. 3 For what saith the Scriptures? Abraham believed God, and it was counted unto him for righteousness.

Gal. 3. 6 Even as Abraham believed God, and it was accounted to him for righteousness.

I

IIChr. 20. 7 *Art* not thou our God, *who* didst drive out the inhabitants of this land before thy people Israel, and gavest it to the seed of Abraham thy friend for ever?

Isa. 41. 8 But thou, Israel, *art* my servant, Jacob whom I have chosen, the seed of Abraham my friend.

John 15. 13 Greater love hath no man than this, that a man lay down his life for his friends.

14 Ye are my friends, if ye do whatsoever I command you.

K

Josh. 2. 1 And Joshua the son of Nun sent out of Shittim two men to spy secretly, saying, Go view the land, even Jericho. And they went, and came into a harlot's house, named Rahab, and lodged there.

Heb. 11. 31 By faith the harlot Rahab perished not with them that believed not, when she had received the spies with peace.

L

Matt. 21. 31 Whether of them twain did the will of *his* father? They say unto him, The first. Jesus saith unto them, Verily I say unto you, That the publicans and the harlots go into the kingdom of God before you.

4

Or, *breath.*

ILLUSTRATED BY THE BIT, HELM AND FOUNTAIN.

B—CONCLUDED.

be condemned: forgive, and ye shall be forgiven:

1

Or, *judgment.*

C

I Ki. 8. 46 If they sin against thee, (for *there is* no man that sinneth not,) and thou be angry with them, and deliver them to the enemy, so that they carry them away captives unto the land of the enemy, far or near;

IIChr. 6. 36 If they sin against thee, (for *there*

C—CONTINUED.

is no man which sinneth not,) and thou be angry with them, and deliver them over before *their* enemies, and they carry them away captives unto a land far off or near;

Prov. 20. 9 Who can say, I have made my heart clean, I am pure from my sin?

Eccl. 7. 20 For *there is* not a just man upon earth, that doeth good, and sinneth not.

Isa. 64. 6 But we are all as an unclean *thing*, and all our righteousnesses *are* as filthy

For C concl'd, D, E, and F, see next page (1236).

§ 532. THE INIQUITY OF AN UNBRIDLED TONGUE ILLUS-

CHAP. 3.

mouths, that they may obey us; and we turn about their whole body.

4 Behold also the ships, which though *they be* so great, and *are* driven of fierce winds, yet are they turned about with a very small helm, whithersoever the governor listeth.

5 Even so [g]the tongue is a little member, and [h]boasteth great things. Behold, how great [2]a matter a little fire kindleth!

6 And [i]the tongue *is* a fire, a world of iniquity: so is the tongue among our members, that [k]it defileth the whole body, and setteth on fire the [3]course of nature; and it is set on fire of hell.

7 For every [4]kind of beasts, and of birds, and of serpents, and of things in the sea, is tamed, and hath been tamed of [5]mankind:

8 But the tongue can no man tame; *it is* an unruly evil, [l]full of deadly poison.

9 Therewith bless we God, even the Father; and therewith curse we

CHAP. 3.

men, [m]which are made after the similitude of God.

10 Out of the same mouth proceedeth blessing and cursing. My brethren, these things ought not so to be.

11 Doth a fountain send forth at the same [6]place sweet *water* and bitter?

12 [n]Can the fig tree, my brethren, bear olive berries? either a vine, figs? so *can* no fountain both yield salt water and fresh.

C—CONCLUDED.

rags; and we all do fade as a leaf; and our iniquities, like the wind, have taken us away.

Rom. 3. 10 As it is written, There is none righteous, no, not one:

Rom. 7. 21 I find then a law, that, when I would do good, evil is present with me.

Gal. 3. 22 But the Scripture hath concluded all under sin, that the promise by faith of Jesus Christ might be given to them that believe.

I Jno. 1. 8 If we say that we have no sin, we deceive ourselves, and the truth is not in us.

D

Ps. 34. 13 Keep thy tongue from evil, and thy lips from speaking guile.

Jas. 1. 26 If any man among you seem to be religious, and bridleth not his tongue, but deceiveth his own heart, this man's religion *is* vain.

§ 533. WORLDLY AND HEAVENLY

3 : 13–18.

13 [a]Who *is* a wise man and endued with knowledge among you? let him shew out of a good conversation [b]his works [c]with meekness of wisdom.

14 But if ye have [d]bitter envying and strife in your hearts, [e]glory not, and lie not against the truth.

15 [f]This wisdom descendeth not from above, but *is* earthly, [1]sensual, devilish.

A

Ps. 107. 43 Whoso *is* wise, and will observe these *things*, even they shall understand the lovingkindness of the LORD.

Gal. 6. 4 But let every man prove his own work, and then shall he have rejoicing in himself alone, and not in another.

B

Jas. 2. 18 Yea, a man may say, Thou hast faith, and I have works: shew me thy faith without thy works, and I will shew thee my faith by my works.

C

Jas. 1. 21 Wherefore lay apart all filthiness and superfluity of naughtiness, and re-

TRATED BY THE BIT, HELM AND FOUNTAIN CONCLUDED).

D—CONCLUDED.

I Pet. 3. 10 For he that will love life, and see good days, let him refrain his tongue from evil, and his lips that they speak no guile:

E

Matt. 12. 37 For by thy words thou shalt be justified, and by thy words thou shalt be condemned.

F

Ps. 32. 9 Be ye not as the horse, *or* as the mule, *which* have no understanding: whose mouth must be held in with bit and bridle, lest they came near unto thee.

G

Prov. 12. 18 There is that speaketh like the piercings of a sword: but the tongue of the wise *is* health.

Prov. 15. 2 The tongue of the wise useth knowledge aright: but the mouth of fools poureth out foolishness.

H

Ps. 12. 3 The LORD shall cut off all flattering lips, *and* the tongue that speaketh proud things:

Ps. 73. 8 They are corrupt, and speak wickedly *concerning* oppression: they speak loftily.

9 They set their mouth against the heavens, and their tongue walketh through the earth.

2

Or, *wood.*

I

Prov. 16. 27 An ungodly man diggeth up evil: and in his lips *there is* as a burning fire.

K

Matt. 15. 11, 19. *See e, E, § 85, page 264.*

3

Gr. *wheel.*

4

Gr. *nature.*

5

Gr. *nature of man.*

L

Ps. 140. 3 They have sharpened their tongues like a serpent; adders' poison *is* under their lips. Selah.

Rom. 3. 13 Their throat *is* an open sepulchre; with their tongues they have used deceit; the poison of asps *is* under their lips:

M

Gen. 1. 26 And God said, Let us make man in our image, after our likeness: and let them have dominion over the fish of the sea, and over the fowls of the air, and over the cattle, and over all the earth, and over every creeping thing that creepeth upon the earth.

Gen. 5. 1 This *is* the book of the generations of Adam. In the day that God created man, in the likeness of God made he him;

Gen. 9. 6 Whoso sheddeth man's blood, by man shall his blood be shed: for in the image of God made he man.

I Cor. 11. 7 For a man indeed ought not to cover *his* head, forasmuch as he is the image and glory of God: but the women is the glory of the man.

6

Or, *hole.*

N

Matt. 7. 16 Ye shall know them by their fruits. Do men gather grapes of thorns, or figs of thistles ?

WISDOM DEFINED.

C—CONCLUDED.

ceive with meekness the engrafted word, which is able to save your souls.

D

Rom. 13. 13 Let us walk honestly, as in the day; not in rioting and drunkenness, not in chambering and wantonness, not in strife and envying:

E

Rom. 2. 17 Behold, thou art called a Jew, and restest in the law, and makest thy boast of God,

Rom. 2. 23 Thou that makest thy boast of the law, through breaking the law dishonourest thou God ?

F

Phil. 3. 19 Whose end *is* destruction, whose God *is their* belly, and *whose* glory *is* in their shame, who mind earthly things.)

Jas. 1. 17 Every good gift and every perfect gift is from above, and cometh down from the Father of lights, with whom is no variableness, neither shadow of turning.

1

Or, *natural.*

Jude 19 These be they who separate themselves, sensual, having not the Spirit.

§ 533. WORLDLY AND HEAVENLY

CHAP. 3.

16 For [g]where envying and strife *is*, there *is* [2]confusion and every evil work.

17 But [h]the wisdom that is from above is first pure, then peaceable, gentle, *and* easy to be entreated, full of mercy and good fruits, [3]without partiality, [i]and without hypocrisy.

18 [k]And the fruit of righteousness is sown in peace of them that make peace.

G

1 Cor. 3. 3 For ye are yet carnal: for whereas *there is* among you envying, and strife,

G—CONCLUDED.

and divisions, are ye not carnal, and walk as men?

Gal. 5. 19 Now the works of the flesh are manifest, which are *these*; Adultery, fornication, uncleanness, lasciviousness,

20 Idolatry, witchcraft, hatred, variance, emulations, wrath, strife, seditions, heresies,

2

Gr. *tumult*, or, *unquietness.*

H

1 Cor. 2. 6 Howbeit we speak wisdom among them that are perfect: yet not the wisdom of this world, nor of the princes of this world, that come to nought:

7 But we speak the wisdom of God in a mystery *even* the hidden *wisdom*,

§ 534. SOME SOURCES OF EVIL SET FORTH

4: 1–17.

1 From whence *come* wars and [1]fightings among you? *come they* not hence, *even* of your [2]lusts [a]that war in your members?

2 Ye lust, and have not: ye [3]kill, and desire to have, and cannot obtain: ye fight and war, yet ye have not, because ye ask not.

3 [b]Ye ask, and receive not, [c]because ye ask amiss, that ye may consume *it* upon your [2]lusts.

4 [d]Ye adulterers and adulteresses, know ye not that [e]the friendship of the world is enmity with God? [f]whosoever therefore will be a friend of the world is the enemy of God.

5 Do ye think that the Scripture saith in vain, [g]The spirit that dwelleth in us lusteth [4]to envy?

6 But he giveth more grace. Wherefore he saith, [h]God resisteth the proud, but giveth grace unto the humble.

1

Or, *brawlings.*

2

Or, *pleasures.*

A

Gal. 5. 17. *See b, B, § 422, page 1022.*

1 Pet. 2. 11 Dearly beloved, I beseech *you* as strangers and pilgrims, abstain from fleshly lusts, which war against the soul;

3

Or, *envy.*

B

Job 27. 9 Will God hear his cry when trouble cometh upon him?

Job 35. 12 There they cry, but none giveth answer, because of the pride of evil men.

Ps. 18. 41 They cried, but *there was* none to save *them*: *even* unto the LORD, but he answered them not.

Prov. 1. 28 Then shall they call upon me, but I will not answer; they shall seek me early, but they shall not find me:

Isa. 1. 15 And when ye spread forth your hands, I will hide mine eyes from you: yea, when ye make many prayers, I will not hear: your hands are full of blood.

Jer. 11. 11 Therefore thus saith the LORD, Behold, I will bring evil upon them, which they shall not be able to escape; and though they shall cry unto me, I will not hearken unto them.

WISDOM DEFINED (CONCLUDED).

H—CONCLUDED.

which God ordained before the world unto our glory ;

3

Or, *without wrangling.*

I

Rom. 12. 9 *Let* love be without dissimulation. Abhor that which is evil; cleave to that which is good.

I Pet. 1. 22 Seeing ye have purified your souls in obeying the truth through the Spirit unto unfeigned love of the brethren, *see that ye* love one another with a pure heart fervently:

I Pet. 2. 1 Wherefore laying aside all malice, and all guile, and hypocrisies, and envies, and all evil speakings,

I Jno. 3. 18 My little children, let us not love in word, neither in tongue; but in deed and in truth.

K

Prov. 11. 18 The wicked worketh a deceitful work: but to him that soweth righteousness *shall be* a sure reward.

Hos. 10. 12 Sow to yourselves in righteousness, reap in mercy; break up your fallow ground: for *it is* time to seek the LORD, till he come and rain righteousness upon you.

Matt. 5. 9 Blessed *are* the peacemakers: for they shall be called the children of God.

Phil. 1. 11 Being filled with the fruits of righteousness, which are by Jesus Christ, unto the glory and praise of God.

Heb. 12. 11 Now no chastening for the present seemeth to be joyous, but grievous: nevertheless afterward it yieldeth the peaceable fruit of righteousness unto them which are exercised thereby.

AND SOME REMEDIES EXHORTED.

B—CONCLUDED.

Mic. 3. 4 Then shall they cry unto the LORD, but he will not hear them: he will even hide his face from them at that time, as they have behaved themselves ill in their doings.

Zech. 7. 13 Therefore it is come to pass, *that* as he cried, and they would not hear; so they cried, and I would not hear, saith the LORD of hosts:

C

Ps. 66. 18 If I regard iniquity in my heart, the Lord will not hear *me*:

Mark 10. 38 But Jesus said unto them, Ye know not what ye ask: can ye drink of the cup that I drink of? and be baptized with the baptism that I am baptized with?

I Jno. 3. 22 And whatsoever we ask, we receive of him, because we keep his commandments, and do those things that are pleasing in his sight.

I Jno. 5. 14 And this is the confidence that we have in him, that, if we ask any thing according to his will, he heareth us:

D

Ps. 73. 27 For, lo, they that are far from thee shall perish: thou hast destroyed all them that go a whoring from thee.

E

I Jno. 2. 15 Love not the world, neither the things *that are* in the world. If any man love the world, the love of the Father is not in him.

F

John 17. 14. *See d, D, § 191, page 545.*

Gal. 1. 10 For do I now persuade men, or God? or do I seek to please men? for if I yet pleased men, I should not be the servant of Christ.

G

Gen. 6. 5 And GOD saw that the wickedness of man *was* great in the earth, and *that* every imagination of the thoughts of his heart *was* only evil continually.

Gen. 8. 21 And the LORD smelled a sweet savour; and the LORD said in his heart, I will not again curse the ground any more for man's sake; for the imagination of man's heart *is* evil from his youth; neither will I again smite any more every thing living, as I have done.

Gen. 37. 11 And his brethren envied him; but his father observed the saying.

Num. 11. 29 And Moses said unto him, Enviest thou for my sake? would God that all the LORD'S people were prophets, *and* that the LORD would put his Spirit upon them!

Prov. 21. 10 The soul of the wicked desireth evil: his neighbour findeth no favour in his eyes.

4

Or, *enviously?*

H

Ps. 138. 6 Though the LORD *be* nigh, yet hath he respect unto the lowly: but the proud he knoweth afar off.

For H concluded, see next page (1240).

§ 534. SOME SOURCES OF EVIL SET FORTH

CHAP. 4.

7 Submit yourselves therefore to
God. [i]Resist the devil, and he will
flee from you.

8 [k]Draw nigh to God, and he will
draw nigh to you. [l]Cleanse *your*
hands, *ye* sinners; and [m]purify *your*
hearts, *ye* [n]doubleminded.

9 [o]Be afflicted, and mourn, and
weep: let your laughter be turned to
mourning, and *your* joy to heaviness.

10 [p]Humble yourselves in the sight
of the Lord, and he shall lift you up.

11 [q]Speak not evil one of another,
brethren. He that speaketh evil of
his brother, [r]and judgeth his brother,
speaketh evil of the law, and judgeth
the law: but if thou judge the law,
thou art not a doer of the law, but
a judge.

12 There is one lawgiver, [s]who is
able to save and to destroy: [t]who
art thou that judgest another?

13 [u]Go to now, ye that say, To day
or to morrow we will go into such a
city, and continue there a year, and
buy and sell, and get gain:

CHAP. 4.

14 Whereas ye know not what *shall*
be on the morrow. For what *is* your
life? [5x]It is even a vapour, that appeareth for a little time, and then
vanisheth away.

15 For that ye *ought* to say, [y]If the
Lord will, we shall live, and do this,
or that.

16 But now ye rejoice in your
boastings: [z]all such rejoicing is evil.

17 Therefore [a]to him that knoweth
to do good, and doeth *it* not, to him
it is sin.

H—CONCLUDED.

Prov. 3. 34 Surely he scorneth the scorners: but he giveth grace unto the lowly.

Matt. 23. 12. *See q, Q, § 167, page 464.*

Luke 1. 52 He hath put down the mighty from *their* seats, and exalted them of low degree.

I

Eph. 4. 27. *See s, S, § 433, page 1046.*

K

IIChr. 15. 2 And he went out to meet Asa, and said unto him, Hear ye me, Asa, and all Judah and Benjamin; The LORD *is* with you, while ye be with him; and if ye seek him, he will be found of you; but if ye forsake him, he will forsake you.

§ 535. WARNINGS AND

5 : 1–20.

1 [a]Go to now, *ye* rich men, weep
and howl for your miseries that shall
come upon *you*.

2 Your riches are corrupted, and
[b]your garments are motheaten.

3 Your gold and silver is cankered;
and the rust of them shall be a witness against you, and shall eat your
flesh as it were fire. [c]Ye have heaped
treasure together for the last days.

4 Behold, [d]the hire of the labourers

A

Prov. 11. 28 He that trusteth in his riches shall fall: but the righteous shall flourish as a branch.

Luke 6. 24. *See c, C, § 43, page 127.*

I Tim. 6. 9 But they that will be rich fall into temptation and a snare, and *into* many foolish and hurtful lusts, which drown men in destruction and perdition.

B

Job 13. 28 And he, as a rotten thing, consumeth, as a garment that is motheaten.

Matt. 6. 20. *See n, N, § 43, page 140.*

Jas. 2. 2 For if there come unto your assembly a man with a gold ring, in goodly apparel, and there come in also a poor man in vile raiment;

AND SOME REMEDIES EXHORTED (CONCLUDED).

L

Isa. 1. 16 Wash ye, make you clean; put away the evil of your doings from before mine eyes; cease to do evil;

M

1 Pet. 1. 22 Seeing ye have purified your souls in obeying the truth through the Spirit unto unfeigned love of the brethren, *see that ye* love one another with a pure heart fervently:

1 Jno. 3. 3 And every man that hath this hope in him purifieth himself, even as he is pure.

N

Jas. 1. 8 A double minded man *is* unstable in all his ways.

O

Matt. 5. 4. *See c, C, § 43, page 124.*

P

Matt. 23. 12. *See q, Q, § 167, page 464.*

1 Pet. 5. 6 Humble yourselves therefore under the mighty hand of God, that he may exalt you in due time:

Q

Eph. 4. 29. *See x, X, § 433, page 1046.*

R

Matt. 7. 1. *See x, X, § 43, page 142.*

S

Matt. 10. 28. *See b, B, § 77, page 236.*

T

Rom. 14. 4 Who art thou that judgest another man's servant? to his own master he standeth or falleth. Yea, he shall be holden up: for God is able to make him stand.

T—CONCLUDED.

Rom. 14. 13 Let us not therefore judge one another any more: but judge this rather, that no man put a stumblingblock or an occasion to fall in *his* brother's way.

U

Luke 12. 18-20. *See o, O, § 57, page 185.*

5

Or, *For it is.*

X

Job 7. 7 O remember that my life *is* wind: mine eye shall no more see good.

Ps. 102. 3 For my days are consumed like smoke, and my bones are burned as a hearth.

Jas. 1. 10 But the rich, in that he is made low: because as the flower of the grass he shall pass away.

1 Pet. 1. 24 For all flesh *is* as grass, and all the glory of man as the flower of grass. The grass withereth, and the flower thereof falleth away:

1 Jno. 2. 17 And the world passeth away, and the lust thereof: but he that doeth the will of God abideth for ever.

Y

Acts 18. 21. *See d, D, § 282, page 750.*

Z

1 Cor. 5. 6 Your glorying *is* not good. Know ye not that a little leaven leaveneth the whole lump?

A

Luke 12. 47. *See q, Q, § 57, page 191.*

Rom. 1. 18-32. *Study § 319, page 812.*

Rom. 2. 17-29. *Study § 321, page 818.*

SUNDRY EXHORTATIONS.

C

Rom. 2. 5 But, after thy hardness and impenitent heart, treasurest up unto thyself wrath against the day of wrath and revelation of the righteous judgment of God;

D

Lev. 19. 13 Thou shalt not defraud thy neighbour, neither rob *him:* the wages of him that is hired shall not abide with thee all night until the morning.

Job 24. 10 They cause *him* to go naked without clothing, and they take away the sheaf *from* the hungry;

11 *Which* make oil within their walls, *and* tread *their* winepresses, and suffer thirst.

D—CONCLUDED.

Job 31. 39 If I have eaten the fruits thereof without money, or have caused the owners thereof to lose their life:

Jer. 22. 13 Woe unto him that buildeth his house by unrighteousness, and his chambers by wrong; *that* useth his neighbour's service without wages, and giveth him not for his work;

Mal. 3. 5 And I will come near to you to judgment; and I will be a swift witness against the sorcerers, and against the adulterers, and against false swearers, and against those that oppress the hireling in *his* wages, the widow, and the fatherless, and that turn aside the stranger *from his right,* and fear not me, saith the LORD of hosts.

CHAP. 5.

who have reaped down your fields,
which is of you kept back by fraud,
crieth: and [e]the cries of them which
have reaped are entered into the
ears of the Lord of sabaoth.

5 [f]Ye have lived in pleasure on the
earth, and been wanton; ye have
nourished your hearts, as in a day
of slaughter.

6 [g]Ye have condemned *and* killed
the just; *and* he doth not resist you.

7 [1]Be patient therefore, brethren,
unto the coming of the Lord. Behold, the husbandman waiteth for
the precious fruit of the earth, and
hath long patience for it, until he
receive [h]the early and latter rain.

8 Be ye also patient; stablish your
hearts: [i]for the coming of the Lord
draweth nigh.

9 [k2]Grudge not one against another,
brethren, lest ye be condemned: behold, the judge [l]standeth before the
door.

10 [m]Take, my brethren, the prophets, who have spoken in the name
of the Lord, for an example of suffering affliction, and of patience.

11 Behold, [n]we count them happy
which endure. Ye have heard of
[o]the patience of Job, and have seen
[p]the end of the Lord; that [q]the Lord
is very pitiful, and of tender mercy.

12 But above all things, my brethren, [r]swear not, neither by heaven,
neither by the earth, neither by any
other oath: but let your yea be yea;
and *your* nay, nay; lest ye fall into
condemnation.

13 Is any among you afflicted? let
him pray. Is any merry? [s]let him
sing psalms.

§ 535. WARNINGS AND SUNDRY

CHAP. 5.

14 [t]Is any sick among you? let him
call for the elders of the church; [u]and
let them pray over him, [x]anointing
him with oil in the name of the Lord:

15 And [y]the prayer of faith shall
save the sick, and the Lord shall
raise him up; [z]and if he have committed sins, they shall be forgiven
him.

16 Confess *your* faults one to
another, and pray one for another,

E

Deut. 24. 15 At his day thou shalt give *him* his hire, neither shall the sun go down upon it; for he *is* poor, and setteth his heart upon it: lest he cry against thee unto the LORD, and it be sin unto thee.

F

Amos 6. 1 Woe to them *that are* at ease in Zion, and trust in the mountain of Samaria, *which are* named chief of the nations, to whom the house of Isreal came!

Luke 16. 19, 25. *See h, H, § 137, page 393.*

1 Tim. 5. 6 But she that liveth in pleasure is dead while she liveth.

G

Jas. 2. 6 But ye have despised the poor. Do not rich men oppress you, and draw you before the judgment seats?

1

Or, *be long patient*, or, *Suffer with long patience.*

H

Deut. 11. 14 That I will give *you* the rain of your land in his due season, the first rain and the latter rain, that thou mayest gather in thy corn, and thy wine, and thine oil.

Jer. 5. 24 Neither say they in their heart, Let us now fear the LORD our God, that giveth rain, both the former and the latter, in his season: he reserveth unto us the appointed weeks of the harvest.

Hos. 6. 3 Then shall we know, *if* we follow on to know the LORD: his going forth is prepared as the morning; and he shall come unto us as the rain, as the latter *and* former rain unto the earth.

Zech. 10. 1 Ask ye of the LORD rain in the time of the latter rain; *so* the LORD shall make bright clouds, and give them showers of rain, to every one grass in the field.

I

Phil. 4. 5. *See h, H, § 446, page 1074.*

EXHORTATIONS (CONTINUED).

K

Jas. 4. 11 Speak not evil one of another brethren. He that speaketh evil of *his* brother, and judgeth his brother, speaketh evil of the law, and judgeth the law: but if thou judge the law, thou art not a doer of the law, but a judge.

2

Or, *Groan*, or, *Grieve not*.

L

Matt.24. 33 So likewise ye, when ye shall see all these things, know that it is near, *even* at the doors.

I Cor. 4. 5 Therefore judge nothing before the time, until the LORD come, who both will bring to light the hidden things of darkness, and will make manifest the counsels of the hearts: and then shall every man have praise of God.

M

Matt. 5. 12. *See s, S, § 43, page 126.*

Heb. 11. 35 Women received their dead raised to life again: and others were tortured, not accepting deliverance; that they might obtain a better resurrection:

N

Matt. 5. 10, 11. *See l, L, § 43, page 124.*

O

Job 1. 22 In all this Job sinned not, nor charged God foolishly.

Job 2. 10 But he said unto her, Thou speakest as one of the foolish women speaketh. What? shall we receive good at the hand of God, and shall we not receive evil? In all this did not Job sin with his lips.

P

Job 42. 10 And the LORD turned the captivity of Job, when he prayed for his friends: also the LORD gave Job twice as much as he had before.

Q

Num.14. 18 The LORD *is* longsuffering, and of great mercy, forgiving iniquity and transgression, and by no means clearing *the guilty*, visiting the iniquity of the fathers upon the children unto the third and forth *generation*.

Ps. 103. 8 The LORD *is* merciful and gracious, slow to anger, and plenteous in mercy.

R

Matt. 5. 34. *See k, K, § 43, page 132.*

S

Eph. 5. 19. *See k, K, § 434, page 1050.*

T

Ex. 15. 26 And said, If thou wilt diligently hearken to the voice of the LORD thy God, and wilt do that which is right in his sight, and wilt give ear to his commandments, and keep all his statutes, I will put none of these diseases upon thee, which I have brought upon the Egyptians: for I *am* the LORD that healeth thee.

Ps. 103. 2 Bless the LORD, O my soul, and forget not all his benefits.

3 Who forgiveth all thine iniquities; who healeth all thy diseases;

IIChr.16. 12 And Asa in the thirty and ninth year of his reign was diseased in his feet, until his disease *was* exceeding *great*: yet in his disease he sought not to the LORD, but to the physicians.

13 And Asa slept with his fathers, and died in the one and fortieth year of his reign.

Matt. 8. 17 That it might be fulfilled which was spoken by Esaias the prophet, saying, Himself took our infirmities, and bare *our* sicknesses.

U

I Ki. 17. 21 And he stretched hinself upon the child three times, and cried unto the LORD, and said, O LORD my God, I pray thee, let this child's soul come into him again.

II Ki. 4. 33 He went in therefore, and shut the door upon them twain, and prayed unto the LORD.

II Ki. 5. 11 But Naaman was wroth, and went away, and said, Behold, I thought, He will surely come out to me, and stand and call on the name of the LORD his God, and strike his hand over the place, and recover the leper.

Acts 9. 40 But Peter put them all forth, and kneeled down and prayed; and turning *him* to the body said, Tabitha, arise. And she opened her eyes: and when she saw Peter, she sat up.

Acts 28. 8 And it came to pass, that the father of Publius lay sick of a fever and of a bloody flux: to whom Paul entered in, and prayed, and laid his hands on him, and healed him.

X

Mark 6. 13 And they cast out many devils, and anointed with oil many that were sick, and healed *them*.

Mark16. 18 They shall take up serpents; and if they drink any deadly thing, it shall not hurt them; they shall lay hands on the sick, and they shall recover.

For Y and Z, see next page (1244).

§ 535. WARNINGS AND SUNDRY

Chap. 5.

that ye may be healed. [a]The effectual fervent prayer of a righteous
man availeth much.
17 Elias was a man [b]subject to like
passions as we are, and [c]he prayed
[3]earnestly that it might not rain: [d]and
it rained not on the earth by the
space of three years and six months.
18 And [e]he prayed again, and the
heaven gave rain, and the earth
brought forth her fruit.
19 Brethren, [f]if any of you do err
from the truth, and one convert him;
20 Let him know, that he which
converteth the sinner from the error
of his way [g]shall save a soul from
death, and [h]shall hide a multitude of
sins.

Y

Matt. 17. 20 And Jesus said unto them, Because of your unbelief: for verily I say unto you, If ye have faith as a grain of mustard seed, ye shall say unto this mountain, Remove hence to yonder place; and it shall remove: and nothing shall be impossible unto you.

21 Howbeit this kind goeth not out but by prayer and fasting.

Mark 16. 17 And these signs shall follow them that believe; In my name shall they cast out devils; they shall speak with new tongues;

Mark 16. 18. *See under X.*

1 Cor. 12. 28 And God hath set some in the church, first apostles, secondarily prophets, thirdly teachers, after that miracles, then gifts of healings, helps, governments, diversities of tongues.

1 Cor. 12. 30 Have all the gifts of healing? do all speak with tongues? do all terpret?

Z

Ps. 51. 2 Wash me thoroughly from mine iniquity, and clease me from my sin.

3 For I acknowledge my transgressions: and my sin *is* ever before me.

4 Against thee, thee only, have I sinned, and done *this* evil in thy sight: that thou mightest be justified when

Z—Concluded.

thou speakest, *and* be clear when thou judgest.

Isa. 33. 24 And the inhabitant shall not say, I am sick: the people that dwell therein *shall be* forgiven *their* iniquity.

Matt. 9. 2 And, behold, they brought to him a man sick of the palsy, lying on a bed: and Jesus seeing their faith said unto the sick of the palsy; Son, be of good cheer; thy sins be forgiven thee.

Rom. 5. 11 And not only *so*, but we also joy in God through our Lord Jesus Christ, by whom we have now received the atonement.

Eph. 1. 7 In whom we have redemption through his blood, the forgiveness of sins, according to the riches of his grace;

A

Gen. 20. 17 So Abraham prayed unto God: and God healed Abimelech, and his wife, and his maidservents; and they bare *children*.

Num. 11. 2 And the people cried unto Moses; and when Moses prayed unto the Lord, the fire was quenched.

Deut. 9. 18 And I fell down before the Lord, as at the first, forty days and forty nights: I did neither eat bread nor drink water, because of all your sins which ye sinned, in doing wickedly in the sight of the Lord, to provoke him to anger.

19 For I was afraid of the anger and hot displeasure, wherewith the Lord was wroth against you to destroy you. But the Lord hearkened unto me at that time also.

20 And the Lord was very angry with Aaron to have destroyed him: and I prayed for Aaron also the same time.

Josh. 10. 12 Then spake Joshua to the Lord in the day when the Lord delivered up the Amorites before the children of Israel, and he said in the sight of Israel, Sun, stand thou still uponGibeon; and thou, Moon, in the valley of Ajalon.

1 Sa. 12. 18 So Samuel called upon the Lord; and the Lord sent thunder and rain that day: and all the people greatly feared the Lord and Samuel.

1 Ki. 13. 6 And the king answered and said unto the man of God, Intreat now the face of the Lord thy God, and pray for me, that my hand may be restored me again. And the man of God besought the Lord, and the king's hand was restored him again, and became as *it was* before,

EXHORTATIONS (CONCLUDED).

A—CONCLUDED.

II Ki. 4. 33. *See under U.*

IIKi.19. 15 And Hezekiah prayed before the LORD, and said, O LORD God of Israel, which dwellest *between* the cherubims, thou art the God, *even* thou alone, of all the kingdoms of the earth; thou hast made heaven and earth.

IIKi.19. 20 Then Isaiah the son of Amoz sent to Hezekiah, saying, Thus saith the LORD God of Israel, *That* which thou hast prayed to me against Sennacherib king of Assyria I have heard.

IIKi. 20. 2 Then he turned his face to the wall, and prayed unto the LORD saying,
3 I beseech thee, O LORD, remember now how I have walked before thee in truth and with a perfect heart, and have done *that which is* good in thy sight. And Hezekiah wept sore.
4 And it came to pass, afore Isaiah was gone out into the middle court, that the word of the LORD came to him, saying.
5 Turn again, and tell Hezekiah the captain of my people, Thus saith the LORD, God of David thy father, I have heard thy prayer, I have seen thy tears: behold, I will heal thee: on the third day thou shalt go up unto the house of the LORD.

Ps. 10. 17 LORD, thou hast heard the desire of the humble: thou wilt prepare their heart, thou wilt cause thine ear to hear:

Ps. 34. 15 The eyes of the LORD *are* upon the righteous, and his ears *are open* unto their cry.

Ps 145. 18 The LORD *is* nigh unto all them that call upon him, to all that call upon him in truth.

Prov.15. 29 The LORD *is* far from the wicked: but he heareth the prayer of the righteous,

Prov.28. 9 He that turneth away his ear from hearing the law, even his prayer *shall be* abomination.

John 9. 31 Now we know that God heareth not sinners: but if any man be a worshipper of God, and doeth his will, him he heareth.

I Jno. 3. 22 And whatsoever we ask, we receive of him, because we keep his commandments, and do those things that are pleasing in his sight.

B

Acts 14. 15 And saying, Sirs, why do ye these things? We also are men of like passions with you, and preach unto you

B—CONCLUDED.

that ye should turn from these vanities unto the living God, which made heaven, and earth, and the sea, and all things that are therein:

C

I Ki. 17. 1 And Elijah the Tishbite, *who was* of the inhabitants of Gilead, said unto Ahab, *As* the LORD God of Israel liveth, before whom I stand, there shall not be dew nor rain these years, but according to my word.

3

Or, *in his prayer.*

D

Luke 4. 25 But I tell you of a truth, many widows were in Israel in the days of Elias, when the heaven was shut up three years and six months, when great famine was throughout all the land;

E

I Ki. 18. 42 So Ahab went up to eat and to drink, And Elijah went up to the top of Carmel; and he cast himself down upon the earth, and put his face between his knees,

I Ki. 18. 45 And it came to pass in the mean while, that the heaven was black with clouds and wind, and there was a great rain. And Ahab rode, and went to Jezreel.

F

Matt.18. 15 Moreover if thy brother shall tresspass against thee, go and tell him his fault between thee and him alone: if he shall hear thee, thou hast gained thy brother.

G

Rom.11. 14 If by any means I may provoke to emulation *them which are* my flesh, and might save some of them.

I Cor. 9. 22 To the weak became I as weak, that I might gain the weak: I am made all things to all *men*, that I might by all means save some.

ITim. 4. 16 Take heed unto thyself, and unto the doctrine; continue in them: for in doing this thou shalt both save thyself, and them that hear thee.

H

Prov.10. 12 Hatred stirreth up strifes: but love covereth all sins.

I Pet. 4. 8 And above all things have fervent charity among yourselves: for charity shall cover the multitude of sins.

THE FIRST EPISTLE

§ 536. SALUTATION.

I: 1, 2.

1 Peter, an apostle of Jesus Christ, to the strangers [a]scattered throughout Pontus, Galatia, Cappadocia, Asia, and Bithynia,

2 [b]Elect [c]according to the foreknowledge of God the Father, [d]through sanctification of the Spirit, unto obedience and [e]sprinkling of the blood of Jesus Christ: [f]Grace unto you, and peace, be multiplied.

A

John 7. 35. *See e, E, § 109, page 317.*

Acts 2. 5 And there were dwelling at Jerusalem Jews, devout men, out of every nation under heaven.

Acts 2. 9 Parthians, and Medes, and Elamites, and the dwellers in Mesopotamia, and in Judea, and Cappadocia, in Pontus, and Asia.
10 Phrygia, and Pamphylia, in Egypt, and in the parts of Libya about Cyrene, and strangers of Rome, Jews and proselytes,

B

Eph. 1. 4. *See b, B, § 426, page 1028.*

§ 537. GRATEFUL PRAISE FOR SALVATION FORETOLD AND

I: 3–12.

3 [a]Blessed *be* the God and Father of our Lord Jesus Christ, which [b]according to his [1]abundant mercy [c]hath begotten us again unto a lively hope [d]by the resurrection of Jesus Christ from the dead,

4 To an inheritance incorruptible, and undefiled, [e]and that fadeth not away, [f]reserved in heaven [2]for you,

5 [g]Who are kept by the power of God through faith unto salvation ready to be revealed in the last time.

6 [h]Wherein ye greatly rejoice, though now [i]for a season, if need be, [k]ye are in heaviness through manifold temptations:

7 That [l]the trial of your faith, being much more precious than of gold that perisheth, though [m]it be

A

II Cor. 1. 3 Blessed *be* God, even the Father of our Lord Jesus Christ, the Father of mercies, and the God of all comfort;

A—Concluded.

Eph. 1. 3 Blessed *be* the God and Father of our Lord Jesus Christ, who hath blessed us with all spiritual blessings in heavenly *places* in Christ:

B

Tit. 3. 5 Not by works of righteousness which we have done, but according to his mercy he saved us, by the washing of regeneration, and renewing of the Holy Ghost;

1

Gr. *much.*

C

John 3. 3 Jesus answered and said unto him, Verily, verily, I say unto thee, Except a man be born again, he cannot see the kingdom of God.

John 3. 5 Jesus answered, Verily, verily, I say unto thee, Except a man be born of water and *of* the Spirit, he cannot enter into the kingdom of God.

Jas. 1. 18 Of his own will begat he us with the word of truth, that we should be a kind of firstfruits of his creatures.

D

I Cor. 15. 20 But now is Christ risen from the dead, *and* become the firstfruits of them that slept.

I Thes. 4. 14 For if we believe that Jesus died and rose again, even so them also which sleep in Jesus will God bring with him.

Written probably between A. D. 63 and 67, at Babylon.

C

Rom. 8. 29. *See g, G, § 334, page 848.*

D

II Thes. 2. 13 But we are bound to give thanks alway to God for you, brethren beloved of the Lord, because God hath from the beginning chosen you to salvation through sanctification of the Spirit and belief of the truth:

E

Heb. 10. 22 Let us draw near with a true heart in full assurance of faith, having our hearts sprinkled from an evil conscience, and our bodies washed with pure water.

E—CONCLUDED.

Heb. 12. 24 And to Jesus the mediator of the new covenant, and to the blood of sprinkling, that speaketh better things than *that of* Abel.

F

Rom. 1. 7 To all that be in Rome, beloved of God, called *to be* saints: Grace to you and peace from God our Father, and the Lord Jesus Christ.

IIPet. 1. 2 Grace and peace be multiplied unto you through the knowledge of God, and of Jesus our Lord,

Jude 2 Mercy unto you, and peace, and love, be multiplied.

SOUGHT FOR BY THE PROPHETS AND COMFORT FOR THEIR TRIALS.

D—CONCLUDED.

I Pet 3. 21 The like figure whereunto *even* baptism doth also now save us, (not the putting away of the filth of the flesh, but the answer of a good conscience toward God,) by the resurrection of Jesus Christ:

E

I Pet. 5. 4 And when the chief Shepherd shall appear, ye shall receive a crown of glory that fadeth not away.

F

Col. 1. 5 For the hope which is laid up for you in heaven, whereof ye heard before in the word of the truth of the gospel:

IITim. 4. 8 Henceforth there is laid up for me a crown of righteousness, which the Lord, the righteous judge, shall give me at that day: and not to me only, but unto all them also that love his appearing.

2

Or, *for us.*

G

John 10. 28, 29. *See h, H, § 119, page 355.*

Jude 1 Jude, the servant of Jesus Christ and brother of James, to them that are sanctified by God the Father, and preserved in Jesus Christ, *and* called:

G—CONCLUDED.

Jude 24 Now unto him that is able to keep you from falling, and to present *you* faultless before the presence of his glory with exceeding joy.

H

Matt. 5. 12 Rejoice, and be exceeding glad: for great *is* your reward in heaven: for so persecuted they the prophets which were before you.

Rom. 12. 12. *See z, Z, § 342, page 870.*

IICor. 6. 10 As sorrowful, yet alway rejoicing; as poor, yet making many rich; as having nothing, and *yet* possessing all things.

I

II Cor. 4. 17. *See p, P, § 393, page 974.*

K

Jas. 1. 2 My brethren, count it all joy when ye fall into divers temptations;

L

Jas. 1. 3 Knowing *this*, that the trying of your faith worketh patience.

Jas. 1. 12 Blessed *is* the man that endureth temptation: for when he is tried, he shall receive the crown of life, which the Lord hath promised to them that love him.

For L concluded and M, see next page (1247).

§ 537. GRATEFUL PRAISE FOR SALVATION FORETOLD AND SOUGHT

CHAP. 1.

tried with fire, [n]might be found unto
praise and honour and glory at the
appearing of Jesus Christ:
8 [o]Whom having not seen, ye love;
[p]in whom, though now ye see *him* not,
yet believing, ye rejoice with joy unspeakable and full of glory:
9 Receiving [q]the end of your faith,
even the salvation of *your* souls.
10 [r]Of which salvation the prophets
have inquired and searched diligently, who prophesied of the grace *that*
should come unto you:
11 Searching what, or what manner
of time [s]the Spirit of Christ which
was in them did signify, when it testified beforehand [t]the sufferings of
Christ, and the glory that should
follow.
12 [u]Unto whom it was revealed,
that [x]not unto themselves, but unto
us they did minister the things, which
are now reported unto you by them
that have preached the gospel unto
you with [y]the Holy Ghost sent down
from heaven; [z]which things the angels desire to look into.

L—CONCLUDED.

I Pet. 4. 12 Beloved, think it not strange concerning the fiery trial which is to try you, as though some strange thing happened unto you:

M

Job 23. 10 But he knoweth the way that I take: *when* he hath tried me, I shall come forth as gold.

Ps. 66. 10 For thou, O God, hast proved us: thou hast tried us, as silver is tried.

11 Thou broughtest us into the net; thou laidst affliction upon our loins.

12 Thou hast caused men to ride over our heads; we went through fire and through water: but thou broughtest us out into a wealthy *place*.

M—CONCLUDED.

Prov. 17. 3 The fining pot *is* for silver, and the furnace for gold: but the LORD trieth the hearts.

Isa. 48. 10 Behold, I have refined thee, but not with silver; I have chosen thee in the furnace of affliction.

Jer. 9. 7 Therefore thus saith the LORD of hosts, Behold, I will melt them, and try them; for how shall I do for the daughter of my people?

Zech. 13. 9 And I will bring the third part through the fire, and will refine them as silver is refined, and will try them as gold is tried: they shall call on my name, and I will hear them: I will say, It *is* my people: and they shall say, The LORD *is* my God.

Mal. 3. 3 And he shall sit *as* a refiner and purifier of silver: and he shall purify the sons of Levi, and purge them as gold and silver, that they may offer unto the LORD an offering in righteousness.

I Cor. 3. 13 Every man's work shall be made manifest: for the day shall declare it, because it shall be revealed by fire; and the fire shall try every man's work of what sort it is.

N

Rom. 2. 7 To them who by patient continuance in well doing seek for glory and honour and immortality, eternal life:

Rom. 2. 10 But glory, honour, and peace, to every man that worketh good, to the Jew first, and also to the Gentile:

I Cor. 4. 5 Therefore judge nothing before the time, until the Lord come, who both will bring to light the hidden things of darkness, and will make manifest the counsels of the hearts: and then shall every man have praise of God.

II Thes. 1 5-12. *See h, H, § 466, page 1110.*

O

I Jno. 4. 20 If a man say, I love God, and hateth his brother, he is a liar: for he that loveth not his brother whom he hath seen, how can he love God whom he hath not seen?

P

John 20. 29. *See e, E, § 220, page 617.*

Q

Rom. 6. 22 But now being made free from sin, and become servants to God, ye have your fruit unto holiness, and the end everlasting life.

R

Gen. 49. 10 The sceptre shall not depart from Judah, nor a lawgiver from between

OR BY THE PROPHETS AND COMFORT FOR THEIR TRIALS (CONCLUDED).

R—CONCLUDED.

his feet, until Shiloh come; and unto him *shall* the gathering of the people *be*.

Da. 2. 44 And in the days of these kings shall the God of heaven set up a kingdom, which shall never be destroyed: and the kingdom shall not be left to other people, *but* it shall break in pieces and consume all these kingdoms, and it shall stand forever.

Hag. 2. 7 And I will shake all nations, and the Desire of all nations shall come: and I will fill this house with glory, saith the LORD of hosts.

Zech. 6. 12 And speak unto him, saying, Thus speaketh the LORD of hosts, saying, Behold the man whose name *is* The BRANCH; and he shall grow up out of his place, and he shall build the temple of the LORD:

Matt. 13. 17 For verily I say unto you, That many prophets and righteous *men* have desired to see *those things* which ye see, and have not seen *them;* and to hear *those things* which ye hear, and have not heard *them*.

Luke 10. 24 For I tell you, that many prophets and kings have desired to see those things which ye see, and have not seen *them;* and to hear those things which ye hear, and have not heard *them*.

II Pet. 1. 19 We have also a more sure word of prophecy; whereunto ye do well that ye take heed, as unto a light that shineth in a dark place, until the day dawn, and the daystar arise in your hearts:

20 Knowing this first, that no prophecy of the Scripture is of any private interpretation.

21 For the prophecy came not in old time by the will of man: but holy men of God spake *as they were* moved by the Holy Ghost.

S

Rom. 5. 5 And hope maketh not ashamed; because the love of God is shed abroad in our hearts by the Holy Ghost which is given unto us.

Rom. 8. 9 But ye are not in the flesh, but in the Spirit, if so be that the Spirit of God dwell in you. Now if any man have not the Spirit of Christ, he is none of his.

Gal. 4. 6 And because ye are sons, God hath sent forth the Spirit of his Son into your hearts, crying, Abba, Father.

T

Luke 24. 46. *See h, H, § 219, page 611,*

U

Da. 9. 24 Seventy weeks are determined upon thy people and upon thy holy city, to finish the transgression, and to make an end of sins, and to make reconciliation for iniquity, and to bring in everlasting righteousness, and to seal up the vision and prophecy, and to anoint the Most Holy.

Da. 12. 9 And he said, Go thy way, Daniel: for the words *are* closed up and sealed till the time of the end.

X

Heb. 11. 13 These all died in faith, not having received the promises, but having seen them afar off, and were persuaded of *them*, and embraced *them*, and confessed that they were strangers and pilgrims on the earth.

Heb. 11. 39 And these all, having obtained a good report through faith, received not the promise:

40 God having provided some better thing for us, that they without us should not be made perfect.

Y

Acts 2. 4 And they were all filled with the Holy Ghost, and began to speak with other tongues, as the Spirit gave them utterance.

Z

Ex. 25. 20 And the cherubims shall stretch forth *their* wings on high, covering the mercy seat with their wings, and their faces *shall look* one to another; toward the mercy seat shall the faces of the cherubims be.

Da. 8. 13 Then I heard one saint speaking, and another saint said unto that certain *saint* which spake, How long *shall be* the vision *concerning* the daily *sacrifice*, and the transgression of desolation, to give both the sanctuary and the host to be trodden under foot?

Da. 12. 5 Then I Daniel looked, and, behold, there stood other two, the one on this side of the bank of the river, and the other on that side of the bank of the river.

6 And *one* said to the man clothed in linen, which *was* upon the waters of the river, How long *shall it be to* the end of these wonders?

Luke 15. 10 Likewise, I say unto you, there is joy in the presence of the angels of God over one sinner that repenteth.

Eph. 3. 10 To the intent that now unto the principalities and powers in heavenly *places* might be known by the church the manifold wisdom of God,

§ 538. EXHORTATION TO HOLY LIFE, KNOWING THEIR

1 : 13–25 ; 2 : 1–10.

13 Wherefore [a]gird up the loins of
your mind, [b]be sober, and hope [1]to
the end for the grace that is to be
brought unto you [c]at the revelation
of Jesus Christ;
14 As obedient children, [d]not fashioning yourselves according to the
former lusts [e]in your ignorance:
15 [f]But as he which hath called you
is holy, so be ye holy in all manner
of conversation;
16 Because it is written, [g]Be ye
holy; for I am holy.
17 And if ye call on the Father, [h]who
without respect of persons judgeth
according to every man's work, [i]pass
the time of your [k]sojourning *here* in
fear:
18 Forasmuch as ye know [l]that ye
were not redeemed with corruptible
things, *as* silver and gold, from your
vain conversation [m]*received* by tradition from your fathers;
19 But [n]with the pecious blood of
Christ, [o]as of a lamb without blemish
and without spot:
20 [p]Who verily was foreordained
before the foundation of the world,
but was manifest [q]in these last times
for you,
21 Who by him do believe in God,
[r]that raised him up from the dead,
and [s]gave him glory; that your faith
and hope might be in God.
22 Seeing ye [t]have purified your
souls in obeying the truth through
the Spirit unto unfeigned [u]love of the
brethren, *see that ye* love one another
with a pure heart fervently:
23 [x]Being born again, not of corruptible seed, but of incorruptible,

A

Luke 12. 35. *See f, F, § 57, page 189.*

B

Luke 21. 34 And take heed to yourselves, lest at any time your hearts be overcharged with surfeiting, and drunkenness, and cares of this life, and *so* that day come upon you unawares.

Rom. 13. 13 Let us walk honestly, as in the day; not in rioting and drunkenness, not in chambering and wantonness, not in strife and envying.

I Thes. 5. 6 Therefore let us not sleep, as *do* others; but let us watch and be sober.

I Thes. 5. 8 But let us, who are of the day, be sober, putting on the breastplate of faith and love; and for a helmet, the hope of salvation.

I Pet. 4. 7 But the end of all things is at hand: be ye therefore sober, and watch unto prayer.

8 And above all things have fervent charity among yourselves: for charity shall cover the multitude of sins.

I Pet. 5. 8 Be sober, be vigilant; because your adversary the devil, as a roaring lion, walketh about, seeking whom he may devour:

1

Gr. *perfectly.*

C

I Cor. 1. 7. *See d, D, § 349, page 888.*

D

Rom. 12. 2 And be not conformed to this world: but be ye transformed by the renewing of your mind, that ye may prove what *is* that good, and acceptable, and perfect will of God.

I Pet. 4 2 That he no longer should live the rest of *his* time in the flesh to the lusts of men, but to the will of God.

I Jno. 2. 15 Love not the world, neither the things *that are* in the world. If any man love the world, the love of the Father is not in him.

E

Acts 17. 30 And the times of this ignorance God winked at; but now commandeth all men every where to repent

I Thes. 4. 5 Not in the lust of concupicence, even as the Gentiles which know not God:

F

Eph. 5. 27. *See n, N, § 435, page 1052.*
I Thes. 4. 7. *See n, N, § 461, page 1102.*

G

Lev. 20. 7 Sanctify yourselves therefore, and be ye holy: for I *am* the LORD your God.

I Thes. 4. 7. *See n, N, § 461, page 1102.*

REDEMPTION AND ROYAL PRIESTLY CALLING.

H

Rom. 2. 11. *See m, M, § 320, page 816.*

I

Prov. 14. 16 A wise *man* feareth, and departeth from evil: but the fool rageth, and is confident.

Prov. 28. 14 Happy *is* the man that feareth alway: but he that hardeneth his heart shall fall into mischief.

II Cor. 7. 1 *See under F.*

Eph. 6. 5 Servants, be obedient to them that are *your* masters according to the flesh, with fear and trembling, in singleness of your heart, as unto Christ;

Phil. 2. 12 Wherefore, my beloved, as ye have always obeyed, not as in my presence only, but now much more in my absence, work out your own salvation with fear and trembling.

Heb. 12. 28 Wherefore we receiving a kingdom which cannot be moved, let us have grace, whereby we may serve God acceptably with reverence and godly fear:

K

II Cor. 5. 6 Therefore *we are* always confident, knowing that, whilst we are at home in the body, we are absent from the Lord:

Heb. 11. 13. *See y, Y, § 520, page 1208.*

L

Acts 20. 28. *See s, S, § 292, page 762.*

I Cor. 6. 20 For ye are bought with a price: therefore glorify God in your body, and in your spirit, which are God's.

I Cor. 7. 23 Ye are bought with a price; be not ye the servants of men.

M

Eze. 20. 18 But I said unto their children in the wilderness, Walk ye not in the statutes of your fathers, neither observe their judgments, nor defile yourselves with their idols:

I Pet. 4. 3 For the time past of *our* life may suffice us to have wrought the will of the Gentiles, when we walked in lasciviousness, lusts, excess of wine, revellings, banquetings, and abominable idolatries:

N

Acts 20. 28. *See s, S, § 292, page 762.*

O

Ex. 12. 5 Your lamb shall be without blemish, a male of the first year: ye shall take *it* out from the sheep, or from the goats:

I Cor. 5. 7. *See m, M, § 359, page 908.*

P

Rom. 16. 25. *See e, E, § 347, page 886.*

II Tim. 1. 9. *See s, S, § 486, page 1140.*

Rev. 13. 8 And all that dwell upon the earth shall worship him, whose names are

P—Concluded.

not written in the book of life of the Lamb slain from the foundation of the world.

Q

Gal. 4. 4 But when the fulness of the time was come, God sent forth his Son, made of a woman, made under the law,

Eph. 1. 10 That in the dispensation of the fulness of times he might gather together in one all things in Christ, both which are in heaven, and which are on earth; *even* in him:

Heb. 1. 2 Hath in these last days spoken unto us by *his* Son, whom he hath appointed heir of all things, by whom also he made the worlds;

Heb. 9. 26 For then must he often have suffered since the foundation of the world: but now once in the end of the world hath he appeared to put away sin by the sacrifice of himself.

R

Acts 2. 24. *See k, K, § 231, page 638.*

S

Matt. 28. 18. *See b, B, § 222, page 622.*

Acts 2. 33 Therefore being by the right hand of God exalted, and having received of the Father the promise of the Holy Ghost, he hath shed forth this, which ye now see and hear.

Acts 3. 13 The God of Abraham, and of Isaac, and of Jacob, the God of our fathers, hath glorified his Son Jesus; whom ye delivered up, and denied him in the presence of Pilate, when he was determined to let *him* go.

T

Acts 15. 9 And put no difference between us and them, purifying their hearts by faith.

U

John 13. 34. *See y, Y, § 183, page 519.*

Rom. 12. 9 *Let* love be without dissimulation. Abhor that which is evil; cleave to that which is good.

10 *Be* kindly affectioned one to another with brotherly love; in honour preferring one another;

I Tim. 1. 5 Now the end of the commandment is charity out of a pure heart, and *of* a good conscience, and *of* faith unfeigned:

Heb. 13. 1 Let brotherly love continue.

I Pet. 2. 17 Honour all *men*. Love the brotherhood. Fear God. Honour the king.

I Pet. 3. 8 Finally, *be ye* all of one mind, having compassion one of another, love as brethren, *be* pitiful, *be* courteous:

For U concluded and X, see next page (1252).

§ 538. EXHORTATION TO HOLY LIFE, KNOWING THEIR

CHAP. 1.

[y]by the word of God, which liveth and abideth for ever.

24 [2]For [z]all flesh *is* as grass, and all the glory of man as the flower of grass. The grass withereth, and the flower thereof falleth away:

25 [a]But the word of the Lord endureth for ever. [b]And this is the word which by the gospel is preached unto you.

CHAP. 2.

1 Wherefore [c]laying aside all malice, and all guile, and hypocrisies, and envies, and all evil speakings,

2 [d]As newborn babes, desire the sincere [e]milk of the word, that ye may grow thereby:

3 If so be ye have [f]tasted that the Lord *is* gracious.

4 To whom coming, *as unto* a living stone, [g]disallowed indeed of men, but chosen of God, *and* precious.

5 [h]Ye also, as lively stones, [3]are built up [i]a spiritual house, [k]a holy priesthood, to offer up [l]spiritual sacrifices, [m]acceptable to God by Jesus Christ.

6 Wherefore also it is contained in the Scripture, [n]Behold, I lay in Sion a chief corner stone, elect, precious: and he that believeth on him shall not be confounded.

7 Unto you therefore which believe *he is* [4]precious: but unto them which be disobedient, [o]the stone which the builders disallowed, the same is made the head of the corner,

8 [p]And a stone of stumbling, and a rock of offence, [q]*even to them* which stumble at the word, being disobedient: [r]whereunto also they were appointed.

U—CONCLUDED.

I Pet. 4. 8 And above all things have fervent charity among yourselves: for charity shall cover the multitude of sins.

X

John 1. 13 Which were born, not of blood, nor of the will of the flesh, nor of the will of man, but of God.

John. 3. 5 Jesus answered, Verily, verily, I say unto thee, Except a man be born of water and *of* the Spirit, he cannot enter into the kingdom of God.

Y

Jas. 1. 18 Of his own will begat he us with the word of truth, that we should be a kind of firstfruits of his creatures.

I Jno. 3. 9 Whosoever is born of God doth not commit sin; for his seed remaineth in him: and he cannot sin, because he is born of God.

2

Or, *for that.*

Z

James 1. 10. *See i, I, § 528, page 1226.*

I Cor. 7. 31. *See g, G, § 363, page 916.*

A

Ps. 102. 12 But thou, O LORD, shalt endure for ever; and thy remembrance unto all generations.

Ps. 102. 26 They shall perish, but thou shalt endure: yea, all of them shall wax old like a garment; as a vesture shalt thou change them, and they shall be changed:

Isa. 40. 8 The grass withereth, the flower fadeth: but the word of our God shall stand for ever.

Luke 16. 17 And it is easier for heaven and earth to pass, than one tittle of the law to fail.

B

John 1. 1 In the beginning was the Word, and the Word was with God, and the Word was God.

John 1. 14 And the Word was made flesh, and dwelt among us, (and we beheld his glory, the glory as of the only begotten of the Father,) full of grace and truth.

I Jno. 1. 1 That which was from the beginning, which we have heard, which we have seen with our eyes, which we have looked upon, and our hands have handled, of the Word of life;

I Jno. 1. 3 That which we have seen and heard declare we unto you, that ye also may have followship with us: and truly our fellowship *is* with the Father, and with his Son Jesus Christ.

REDEMPTION AND ROYAL PRIESTLY CALLING (CONTINUED).

C

Eph. 4. 22. *See i, I, § 433, page 1044.*

Jas. 1. 21 Wherefore lay apart all filthiness and superfluity of naughtiness, and receive with meekness the engrafted word, which is able to save your souls.

Jas. 5. 9 Grudge not one against another, brethren, lest ye be condemned: behold, the Judge standeth before the door.

I Pet. 4. 2 That he no longer should live the rest of *his* time in the flesh to the lusts of men, but to the will of God.

D

Matt. 18. 3 And said, Verily I say unto you, Except ye be converted, and become as little children, ye shall not enter into the kingdom of heaven.

Mark 10. 15 Verily I say unto you, Whosoever shall not receive the kingdom of God as a little child, he shall not enter therein.

Rom. 6. 4 Therefore we are buried with him by baptism into death: that like as Christ was raised up from the dead by the glory of the Father, even so we also should walk in newness of life.

1 Cor. 14. 20 Brethren, be not children in understanding: howbeit in malice be ye children, but in understanding be men.

I Pet. 1. 23 Being born again, not of corruptible seed, but of incorruptible, by the word of God, which liveth and abideth for ever.

E

I Cor. 3. 2. *See c, C, § 353, page 898.*

F

Ps. 34. 8 O taste and see that the LORD *is* good: blessed *is* the man *that* trusteth in him.

Heb. 6. 5 And have tasted the good word of God, and the powers of the world to come,

G

Matt. 21. 42. *See t, T, § 161, page 448.*

H

Eph. 2. 21 In whom all the building fitly framed together groweth unto a holy temple in the Lord:

22 In whom ye also are builded together for a habitation of God through the Spirit.

3

Or, *be ye built.*

I

I Cor. 3. 16. *See m, M, § 354, page 900.*

K

Isa. 61. 6 But ye shall be named the Priests of the LORD: *men* shall call you the Ministers of our God: ye shall eat the riches of the Gentiles, and in their glory shall ye boast yourselves.

K—CONCLUDED.

Isa. 66. 21 And I will also take of them for priests *and* for Levites, saith the LORD.

I Pet. 2. 9. *See text of topic.*

L

Rom. 12. 1 I beseech you therefore, brethren, by the mercies of God, that ye present your bodies a living sacrifice, holy, acceptable unto God, *which is* your reasonable service.

Heb. 13. 15, 16. *See m, M, § 525, page 1224.*

M

Phil. 4. 18 But I have all, and abound: I am full, having received of Epaphroditus the things *which were sent* from you, an odour of a sweet smell, a sacrifice acceptable, well pleasing to God.

N

Rom. 9. 33. *See y, Y, § 336, page 856.*

4

Or, *an honour.*

O

Matt. 21. 42. *See t, T, § 161, page 448.*

P

Luke 2. 34. *See m, M, § 10, page 35.*

Q

I Cor. 1. 23 But we preach Christ crucified, unto the Jews a stumblingblock, and unto the Greeks foolishness;

R

Ex. 9. 16 And in very deed for this *cause* have I raised thee up, for to shew *in* thee my power; and that my name may be declared throughout all the earth.

I Thes. 5. 9. *See l, L, § 464, page 1106.*

S

Deut. 10. 15 Only the LORD had a delight in thy fathers to love them, and he chose their seed after them, *even* you above all people, as *it is* this day.

I Pet. 1. 2 Elect according to the foreknowledge of God the Father, through sanctification of the Spirit, unto obedience and sprinkling of the blood of Jesus Christ: Grace unto you, and peace, be multiplied.

T

Ex. 19. 5 Now therefore, if ye will obey my voice indeed, and keep my covenant, then ye shall be a peculiar treasure unto me above all people: for all the earth *is* mine:

6 And ye shall be unto me a kingdom of priests, and a holy nation. These *are* the words which thou shalt speak unto the children of Israel.

§ 538. EXHORTATION TO HOLY LIFE, KNOWING THEIR

CHAP. 2.

9 But ye *are* [s]a chosen generation, [t]a royal priesthood, [u]a holy nation, a [x5]peculiar people; that ye should shew forth the [6]praises of him who hath called you out of [y]darkness into his marvellous light:

10 [z]Which in time past *were* not a people, but *are* now the people of God: which had not obtained mercy, but now have obtained mercy.

For S, and T, see preceding page (1253).

T—CONTINUED.

Isa. 61. 6, and 66. 21. *See under K.*

Rev. 1. 6 And hath made us kings and priests unto God and his Father; to him *be* glory and dominion for ever and ever. Amen.

Rev. 5. 10 And hast made us unto our God kings and priests: and we shall reign on the earth.

Rev. 20. 6 Blessed and holy *is* he that hath part in the first resurrection: on such the second death hath no power, but they shall be priests of God and of Christ, and shall reign with him a thousand years.

T—CONCLUDED.

U

John 17. 19 And for their sakes I sanctify myself, that they also might be sanctified through the truth.

I Cor. 3. 17 If any man defile the temple of God, him shall God destroy; for the temple of God is holy, which *temple* ye are.

IITim. 1. 9 Who hath saved us and called *us* with a holy calling not according to our works, but according to his own purpose and grace, which was given us in Christ Jesus before the world began,

X

Deut. 4. 20 But the LORD hath taken you, and brought you forth out of the iron furnace, *even* out of Egypt, to be unto him a people of inheritance, as *ye are* this day.

Deut. 7. 6 For thou *art* a holy people unto the LORD thy God: the LORD thy God hath chosen thee to be a special people unto himself, above all people that *are* upon the face of the earth.

§ 539. EXHORTATION CONCERNING WORLDLY WALK; SUBJECTION TO

2: 11-25.

11 Dearly beloved, I beseech *you* [a]as strangers and pilgrims, [b]abstain from fleshly lusts, [c]which war against the soul;

12 [d]Having your conversation honest among the Gentiles: that [1]whereas they speak against you as evil doers, [e]they may by *your* good works, which they shall behold, glorify God [f]in the day of visitation.

13 [g]Submit yourselves to every ordinance of man for the Lord's sake: whether it be to the king, as supreme;

14 Or unto governors, as unto them that are sent by him [h]for the punishment of evil doers, and [i]for the praise of them that do well.

CHAP. 2.

15 For so is the will of God, that [k]with well doing ye may put to silence the ignorance of foolish men:

A

Heb. 11. 13. *See y, Y, § 520, page 1208.*

B

Rom. 13. 14 But put ye on the Lord Jesus Christ, and make not provision for the flesh, to *fulfill* the lusts *thereof*.

Gal. 5. 16 *This* I say then, Walk in the Spirit, and ye shall not fulfill the lust of the flesh.

C

Rom. 8. 13 For if ye live after the flesh, ye shall die: but if ye through the Spirit do mortify the deeds of the body, ye shall live.

Jas. 4. 1 From whence *come* wars and fightings among you? *come they* not hence, *even* of your lusts that war in your members?

REDEMPTION AND ROYAL PRIESTLY CALLING (CONCLUDED).

X—CONCLUDED.

Deut. 14. 2 For thou *art* a holy people unto the LORD thy God, and the LORD hath chosen thee to be a peculiar people unto himself, above all the nations that *are* upon the earth.

Deut 26. 18 And the LORD hath avouched thee this day to be his peculiar people, as he hath promised thee, that *thou* shouldest keep all his commandments;
19 And to make thee high above all nations which he hath made, in praise, and in name, and in honour; and that thou mayest be a holy people unto the LORD thy God, as he hath spoken.

Acts 20. 28 Take heed therefore unto yourselves, and to all the flock, over the which the Holy Ghost hath made you overseers, to feed the church of God, which he hath purchased with his own blood.

Eph. 1. 14 Which is the earnest of our inheritance until the redemption of the purchased possession, unto the praise of his glory.

Tit. 2. 14 Who gave himself for us, that he might redeem us from all iniquity, and and purify unto himself a peculiar people, zealous of good works.

5

Or, a purchased people.

6

Or, *virtues.*

Y

Acts 26. 18. *See p, P, § 369, page 794.*
Eph. 5. 8. *See p, P, § 434, page 1048.*

Z

Hos. 1. 9 Then said *God*, Call his name Lo-ammi: for ye *are* not my people, and I will not be your *God*.
10 Yet the number of the children of Israel shall be as the sand of the sea, which cannot be measured nor numbered; and it shall come to pass, *that* in the place where it was said unto them, Ye *are* not my people, *there* it shall be said unto them, *Ye are* the sons of the living God.

Hos. 2. 23 And I will sow her unto me in the earth; and I will have mercy upon her that had not obtained mercy and I will say to *them which were* not my people, Thou *art* my people; and they shall say, *Thou art* my God.

Rom. 9. 25 As he saith also in Osee, I will call them my people, which were not my people; and her beloved, which was not beloved.

AUTHORITIES, TO SERVANTS; AND TO ENDURE SUFFERING BLAMELESS.

D

II Cor. 8. 21. *See e, E, § 400, page 986.*
Tit. 2. 8. *See k, K, § 497, page 1158.*

1

Or, *wherein.*

E

Matt. 5. 16 Let your light so shine before men, that they may see your good works, and glorify your Father which is in heaven.

F

Luke 1. 68 Blessed *be* the Lord God of Israel; for he hath visited and redeemed his people,

Luke 19. 44 And shall lay thee even with the ground, and thy children within thee; and they shall not leave in thee one stone upon another; because thou knewest not the time of thy visitation.

Acts 15. 14 Simeon hath declared how God at the first did visit the Gentiles, to take out of them a people for his name.

G

Matt. 22. 21. *See b, B, § 163, page 454.*

Tit. 3. 1 Put them in mind to be subject to principalities and powers, to obey magistrates, to be ready to every good work,

H

Rom. 13. 4 For he is the minister of God to thee for good. But if thou do that which is evil, be afraid; for he beareth not the sword in vain: for he is the minister of God, a revenger to *execute* wrath upon him that doeth evil.

I

Rom. 13. 3 For rulers are not a terror to good works, but to the evil. Wilt thou then not be afraid of the power? do that which is good, and thou shalt have praise of the same:

K

Tit. 2. 8. *See k, K, § 497, page 1158.*

L

Gal. 5. 1 Stand fast therefore in the liberty wherewith Christ hath made us free, and be not entangled again with the yoke of bondage.

§ 539. EXHORTATION CONNCERNING WORLDLY WALK, SUBJECTION TO

CHAP. 2.

16 [l]As free, and not [2]using *your*
liberty for a cloak of maliciousness,
but as [m]the servants of God.

17 [n3]Honour all *men.* Love the
brotherhood. [o]Fear God. Honour
the king.

18 [p]Servants, *be* subject to *your*
masters with all fear; not only to the
good and gentle, but also to the froward.

19 For this *is* [4q]thankworthy, if a
man for conscience toward God endure grief, suffering wrongfully.

20 For [r]what glory *is it,* if, when
ye be buffeted for your faults, ye
shall take it patiently? but if, when
ye do well, and suffer *for it,* ye take
it patiently, this *is* [4]acceptable with
God.

21 For [s]even hereunto were ye
called: because [t]Christ also suffered
[6]for us, [u]leaving us an example, that
ye should follow his steps:

22 [x]Who did no sin, neither was
guile found in his mouth:

23 [y]Who, when he was reviled, reviled not again; when he suffered,
he threatened not; but [z6]committed
himself to him that judgeth righteously:

24 [a]Who his own self bare our sins
in his own body [7]on the tree, [b]that we,
being dead to sins, should live unto
righteousness: by whose stripes ye
were healed.

CHAP. 2.

25 [c]For ye were as sheep going
astray; but are now returned [d]unto
the Shepherd and Bishop of your
souls.

L—CONCLUDED. See preceding page (1255).

Gal. 5. 13 For, brethern, ye have been called unto liberty; only *use* not liberty for an occasion to the flesh, but by love serve one another.

2

Gr. *having.*

M

I Cor. 7. 22 For he that is called in the Lord, *being* a servant, is the Lord's freeman: likewise also he that is called, *being* free, is Christ's servant.

N

Lev. 19. 32 Thou shalt rise up before the hoary head, and honour the face of the old man, and fear thy God: I *am* the LORD.

Rom. 12. 10. *See x, X, § 342, page 870.*

Phil. 2. 3 *Let* nothing *be done* through strife or vainglory; but in lowliness of mind let each esteem other better than themselves.

3

Or, *esteem.*

O

Ps. 111. 10 The fear of the LORD *is* the beginning of wisdom: a good understanding have all they that do *his commandments:* his praise endureth for ever.

Prov. 1. 7 The fear of the LORD *is* the beginning of knowledge: *but* fools despise wisdom and instruction.

Prov. 23. 17 Let not thine heart envy sinners; but *be thou* in the fear of the LORD all the day long.

Prov. 24. 21 My son, fear thou the LORD and the king: *and* meddle not with them that are given to change:

§ 540. EXHORTATION CONCERNING

3 : 1–7.

1 Likewise, [a]ye wives, *be* in subjection to your own husbands; that, if
any obey not the word, [b]they also
may without the word [c]be won by
the conversation of the wives;

2 [d]While they behold your chaste
conversation *coupled* with fear.

CHAP. 3.

3 [e]Whose adorning, let it not be
that outward *adorning* of plaiting

A

Eph. 5. 22. *See a, A, § 435, page 1052.*

B

I Cor. 7. 16 For what knowest thou, O wife, whether thou shalt save *thy* husband?

AUTHORITIES, TO SERVANTS, AND TO ENDURE SUFFERING, ETC. (CONCL'D).

O—CONCLUDED.

Matt. 22. 21 They say unto him, Cæsar's. Then saith he unto them, Render therefore unto Cæsar the things which are Cæsar's and unto God the things that are God's.

Rom. 13. 7 Render therefore to all their dues: tribute to whom tribute *is due;* custom to whom custom; fear to whom fear; honour to whom honour.

II Cor. 7. 1 Having therefore these promises, dearly beloved, let us cleanse ourselves from all filthiness of the flesh and spirit, perfecting holiness in the fear of God.

Eph. 5. 21 Submitting yourselves one to another in the fear of God.

P

Eph. 6. 5. *See e, E, § 436, page 1054.*

4

Or, *thank.*

Q

Matt. 5. 10 Blessed *are* they which are persecuted for righteousness' sake: for theirs is the kingdom of heaven.

Rom. 13. 5 Wherefore *ye* must needs be subject, not only for wrath, but also for conscience' sake.

I Pet. 3. 14 But and if ye suffer for righteousness' sake, happy *are ye;* and be not afraid of their terror, neither be troubled:

R

I Pet. 3. 14. *See under Q.*

I Pet. 4. 14 If ye be reproached for the name of Christ, happy *are ye;* for the Spirit of glory and of God resteth upon you: on their part he is evil spoken of, but on your part, he is glorified.

15 But let none of you suffer as a murderer, or *as* a thief, or *as* an evil doer, or as a busybody in other men's matters.

S

Acts 14. 22. *See e, E, § 266, page 724.*

T

I Pet. 3. 18 For Christ also hath once suffered for sins, the just for the unjust, that he might bring us to God, being put to death in the flesh, but quickened by the Spirit:

5

Some read, *for you.*

U

John 13. 15. *See q, Q, § 182, page 515.*

X

Luke 23. 41 And we indeed justly; for we receive the due reward of our deeds: but this man hath done nothing amiss.

John 8. 46 Which of you convinceth me of sin? And if I say the truth, why do ye not believe me?

II Cor. 5. 21. *See q, Q, § 395, page 978.*

Heb. 4. 15 For we have not a high priest which cannot be touched with the feeling of our infirmities; but was in all points tempted like as *we are, yet* without sin.

Heb. 7. 26 For such a high priest became us, *who is* holy, harmless, undefiled, separate from sinners, and made higher than the heavens;

Y

Matt. 27. 13. *Study § 204, page 584.*

Z

Luke 23. 46. *See f, F, § 207, page 589.*

6

Or, *committed his cause.*

A

Matt. 20. 28. *See y, Y, § 148, page 420.*

7

Or, *to.*

B

Rom. 6. 2. *See b, B, § 328, page 834.*

C

Matt. 9. 36. *See d, D, § 76, page 230.*

D

John 10. 11. *See k, K, § 118, page 351.*

WIVES AND HUSBANDS.

B—CONCLUDED.

or how knowest thou, O man, whether thou shalt save *thy* wife?

C

I Cor. 9. 19-22. *See f, F, § 365, page 924.*

D

3

I Pet. 2. 12 Having your conversation honest among the Gentiles: that, whereas they speak against you as evil doers, they may by *your* good works, which

D—CONCLUDED.

they shall behold, glorify God in the day of visitation.

E

Isa. 3. 16 Moreover the LORD saith, Because the daughters of Zion are haughty, and walk with stretched forth necks and wanton eyes, walking and mincing *as* they go, and making a tinkling with their feet:

For E concluded, see next page (1258).

§ 540. EXHORTATION CONCERNING

CHAP. 3.

the hair, and of wearing of gold, or of putting on of apparel;

4 But *let it be* [f]the hidden man of the heart, in that which is not corruptible, *even the ornament* of a meek and quiet spirit, which is in the sight of God of great price.

5 For after this manner in the old time the holy women also, who trusted in God, adorned themselves, being in subjection unto their own husbands:

6 Even as Sarah obeyed Abraham, [g]calling him lord: whose [1]daughters ye are, as long as ye do well, and are not afraid with any amazement.

7 [h]Likewise, ye husbands, dwell with *them* according to knowledge, giving honour unto the wife, [i]as unto the weaker vessel, and as being heirs together of the grace of life; [k]that your prayers be not hindered.

E—CONTINUED.

Isa. 3. 17 Therefore the Lord will smite with a scab the crown of the head of the daughters of Zion, and the LORD will discover their secret parts.

18 In that day the Lord will take away the bravery of *their* tinkling ornaments *about their feet*, and *their* cauls, and *their* round tires like the moon.

19 The chains, and the bracelets, and the mufflers,

20 The bonnets, and the ornaments of the legs, and the headbands, and the tablets, and the earrings.

21 The rings, and nose jewels,

22 The changeable suits of apparel, and the mantles, and the wimples, and the crisping pins.

23 The glasses, and the fine linen, and the hoods, and the vails.

24 And it shall come to pass, *that* instead of sweet smell there shall be stink; and instead of a girdle a rent; and instead of well set hair baldness; and instead of a stomacher a girding of sackcloth, *and* burning instead of beauty.

1 Tim. 2. 9 In like manner also, that women adorned themselves in modest apparel, with shamefacedness and sobriety; not with broided hair, or gold, or pearls, or costly array;

§ 541. EXHORTATION CONCERNING SOCIAL RELATIONS, AND

3: 8–22; 4: 1–19.

8 Finally, [a]*be ye* all of one mind, having compassion one of another, [b1]love as brethren, [c]*be* pitiful, *be* courteous:

9 [d]Not rendering evil for evil, or railing for railing: but contrariwise blessing; knowing that ye are thereunto called, [e]that ye should inherit a blessing.

10 For [f]he that will love life, and see good days, [g]let him refrain his tongue from evil, and his lips that they speak no guile:

11 Let him [h]eschew evil, and do good; [i]let him seek peace, and ensue it.

A

Rom. 12. 16. *See g, G, § 342, page 872.*

B

Rom. 12. 10 *Be* kindly affectioned one to another with brotherly love; in honour preferring one another;

Heb. 13. 1 Let brotherly love continue.

1 Pet. 2. 17 Honour all *men*. Love the brotherhood. Fear God, Honour the king.

1

Or, *loving to the brethren.*

C

Eph. 4. 32 And be ye kind one to another, tenderhearted, forgiving one another, even as God for Christ's sake hath forgiven you.

Col. 3. 12 Put on therefore, as the elect of God, holy and beloved, bowels of mercies, kindness, humbleness of mind, meekness, longsuffering;

WIVES AND HUSBANDS (CONCLUDED).

E—CONCLUDED.

Tit. 2. 3 The aged women likewise, that *they be* in behaviour as becometh holiness, not false accusers, not given to much wine, teachers of good things;
4 That they may teach the young women to be sober, to love their children,
5 *To be* discreet, chaste, keepers at home, good, obedient to their own husbands, that the word of God be not blasphemed.

F

Ps. 45. 13 The King's daughter *is* all glorious within: her clothing *is* of wrought gold.

Rom. 7. 22. *See k, K, § 331, page 842.*

G

Gen. 18. 12 Therefore Sarah laughed within herself, saying, After I am waxed old shall I have pleasure, my lord being old also?

1

Gr. *children.*

H

I Cor. 7. 3 Let the husband render unto the wife due benevolence: and likewise also the wife unto the husband.

Eph. 5. 25. *See g, G, " 435, page 1052.*

I

I Cor. 12. 23 And those *members* of the body, which we think to be less honourable, upon these we bestow more abundant honour; and our uncomely *parts* have more abundant comeliness.

I Thes. 4. 4 That every one of you should know how to possess his vessel in sanctification and honour;

K

Job 42. 8 Therefore take unto you now seven bullocks and seven rams, and go to my servant Job, and offer up for yourselves a burnt offering; and my servant Job shall pray for you: for him will I accept: lest I deal with you *after your* folly, in that ye have not spoken of me *the thing which is* right, like my servant Job.

Matt. 5. 23 Therefore if thou bring thy gift to the altar, and there rememberest that thy brother hath aught against thee;
24 Leave there thy gift before the altar, and go thy way; first be reconciled to thy brother, and then come and offer thy gift.

Matt. 18. 19 Again I say unto you, That if two of you shall agree on earth as touching any thing that they shall ask, it shall be done for them of my Father which is in heaven.

SUFFERING AFTER THE PATTERN OF CHRIST. THE END IS AT HAND.

D

Prov. 17. 13 Whoso rewardeth evil for good, evil shall not depart from his house.

Matt. 5. 39. *See p, P, § 43, page 132.*

Rom. 12. 14 Bless them which persecute you: bless, and curse not.

I Cor. 4. 13 Being defamed, we entreat: we are made as the filth of the world, *and are* the offscouring of all things unto this day.

E

Matt. 25. 34 Then shall the King say unto them on his right hand, Come, ye blessed of my Father, inherit the kingdom prepared for you from the foundation of the world:

F

Ps. 34. 12 What man *is he that* desireth life, *and* loveth *many* days, that he may see good?
13 Keep thy tongue from evil, and thy lips from speaking guile.

F—CONCLUDED.

14 Depart from evil, and do good; seek peace, and pursue it.

Ps. 34. 15 The eyes of the LORD *are* upon the righteous, and his ears *are open* unto their cry.
16 The face of the LORD *is* against them that do evil to cut off the remembrance of them from the earth.

G

Jas. 1. 26 If any man among you seem to to be religious, and bridleth not his tongue, but deceiveth his own heart, this man's religion *is* vain.

I Pet. 2. 1 Wherefore laying aside all malice, and all guile, and hypocrisies, and envies, and all evil speakings,

I Pet. 2. 22 Who did no sin, neither was guile found in his mouth:

Rev. 14. 5 And in their mouth was found no guile: for they are without fault before the throne of God.

For H, and I, see next page (1260).

§ 541. EXHORTATION CONCERNING SOCIAL RELATIONS, AND SUFFERING

CHAP. 3.

12 For the eyes of the Lord *are* over the righteous, [k]and his ears *are open* unto his prayers: but the face of the Lord *is* [2]against them that do evil.

13 [l]And who *is* he that will harm you, if ye be followers of that which is good?

14 [m]But and if ye suffer for righteousness' sake, happy *are ye:* and [n]be not afraid of their terror, neither be troubled;

15 But sanctify the Lord God in your hearts: and [o]*be* ready always to *give* an answer to every man that asketh you a reason of the hope that is in you, with meekness and [3]fear:

16 [p]Having a good conscience; [q]that, whereas they speak evil of you, as of evil doers, they may be ashamed that falsely accuse your good conversation in Christ.

17 For *it is* better, if the will of God be so, that ye suffer for well doing, than for evil doing.

18 For Christ also hath [r]once suffered for sins, the just for the unjust, that he might bring us to God, [s]being put to death [t]in the flesh, but [u]quickened by the Spirit:

19 By which also he went and [x]preached unto the spirits [y]in prison;

20 Which sometime were disobedient, [z]when once the longsuffering of God waited in the days of Noah, while [a]the ark was a preparing, [b]wherein few, that is, eight souls were saved by water.

H

Ps. 37. 27 Depart from evil, and do good; and dwell for evermore.

Isa. 1. 16 Wash ye, make you clean; put away the evil of your doings from before mine eyes; cease to do evil;

17 Learn to do well; seek judgment, relieve the oppressed, judge the fatherless, plead for the widow.

H—CONCLUDED.

III Jno. 11 Beloved, follow not that which is evil, but that which is good. He that doeth good is of God: but he that doeth evil hath not seen God.

I

Rom. 12. 18. *See m, M, § 342, page 872.*

K

James 5. 15. *See z, Z, § 535, page 1242.*

John 9. 31. *See x, X, § 117, page 347.*

2

Gr. *upon.*

L

Prov. 16. 7 When a man's ways please the LORD, he maketh even his enemies to be at peace with him.

Rom. 8. 28 And we know that all things work together for good to them that love God, to them who are the called according to *his* purpose.

M

Matt. 5. 10 Blessed *are* they which are persecuted for righteousness' sake: for theirs is the kingdom of heaven.

11 Blessed are ye, when *men* shall revile you, and persecute *you*, and shall say all manner of evil against you falsely, for my sake.

12 Rejoice and be exceeding glad: for great *is* your reward in heaven: for so persecuted they the prophets which were before you.

Jas. 1. 12 Blessed *is* the man that endureth temptation: for when he is tried, he shall receive the crown of life, which the Lord hath promised to them that love him.

I Pet. 2. 19 For this *is* thankworthy, if a man for conscience toward God endure grief, suffering wrongfully.

I Pet. 4. 14 If ye be reproached for the name of Christ, happy *are ye;* for the Spirit of glory and of God resteth upon you: on their part he is evil spoken of, but on your part he is glorified.

N

Isa. 8. 12 Say ye not, A confederacy, to all *them to* whom this people shall say, A confederacy; neither fear ye their fear, nor be afraid.

13 Sanctify the LORD of hosts himself; and *let* him *be* your fear, and *let* him *be* your dread.

Jer. 1. 8 Be not afraid of their faces: for I *am* with thee to deliver thee, saith the LORD.

John 14. 1 Let not your heart be troubled: ye believe in God, believe also in me.

AFTER THE PATTERN OF CHRIST. THE END IS AT HAND (CONTINUED).

N—CONCLUDED.

John 14. 27 Peace I leave with you, my peace I give unto you: not as the world giveth, give I unto you. Let not your heart be troubled, neither let it be afraid.

O

Ps. 119. 46 I will speak of thy testimonies also before kings, and will not be ashamed.

Col. 4. 6 Let your speech *be* always with grace, seasoned with salt, that ye may know how ye ought to answer every man.

II Tim. 2. 25 In meekness instructing those that oppose themselves; if God peradventure will give them repentance to the acknowledging of the truth;

3

Or, *reverence.*

P

Acts 23. 1. *See a, A, § 299, page 776.*

Q

Tit. 2. 8 Sound speech, that cannot be condemned; that he that is of the contrary part may be ashamed, having no evil thing to say of you.

I Pet. 2. 12 Having your conversation honest among the gentiles: that, whereas they speak against you as evildoers, they may by *your* good works, which they shall behold, glorify God in the day of visitation.

R

Rom. 4. 25. *See b, B, § 325, page 830.*

I Pet. 2. 21 For even hereunto were ye called; because Christ also suffered for us, leaving us an example, that ye should follow his steps;

I Pet. 4. 1 Forasmuch then as Christ hath suffered for us in the flesh, arm yourselves likewise with the same mind: for he that hath suffered in the flesh hath ceased from sin;

S

II Cor. 13. 4. *See h, H, § 407, page 1002.*

T

Col. 1. 21 And you, that were sometime alienated and enemies in *your* mind by wicked works, yet now hath he reconciled

22 In the body of his flesh through death, to present you holy and unblameable and unreproveable in his sight:

U

Rom. 6. 4, 5. *Study § 328, page 834.*

X

I Pet. 1. 12 Unto whom it was revealed, that not unto themselves, but unto us they did minister the things, which are now

X—CONCLUDED.

reported unto you by them that have preached the gospel unto you with the Holy Ghost sent down from heaven; which things the angels desire to look into.

I Pet. 4. 6 For, for this cause was the gospel preached also to them that are dead, that they might be judged according to men in the flesh, but live according to God in the spirit.

Y

Isa. 42. 7 To open the blind eyes, to bring out the prisoners from the prison, *and* them that sit in darkness out of the prison house.

Isa. 49. 9 That thou mayest say to the prisoners, Go forth; to them that *are* in darkness, Shew yourselves. They shall feed in the ways, and their pastures *shall be* in all high places.

Isa. 61. 1 The Spirit of the Lord GOD *is* upon me; because the LORD hath anointed me to preach good tidings unto the meek; he hath sent me to bind up the brokenhearted, to proclaim liberty to the captives, and the opening of the prison to *them that are* bound;

Z

Gen. 6. 3 And the LORD said, My Spirit shall not always strive with man, for that he also *is* flesh: yet his days shall be a hundred and twenty years.

Gen. 6. 5 And GOD saw that the wickedness of man *was* great in the earth, and *that* every imagination of the thoughts of his heart *was* only evil continually.

Gen. 6. 13 And God said unto Noah, The end of all flesh is come before me; for the earth is filled with violence through them; and, behold, I will destroy them with the earth.

A

Heb. 11. 7 By faith Noah, being warned of God of things not seen as yet, moved with fear, prepared an ark to the saving of his house; by the which he condemned the world, and became heir of the righteousness which is by faith.

B

Gen. 7. 7 And Noah went in, and his sons, and his wife, and his sons' wives with him, into the ark, because of the waters of the flood.

Gen. 8. 18 And Noah went forth, and his sons, and his wife, and his sons' wives with him:

For B, concluded, see next page (1262).

§ 541. EXHORTATION CONCERNING SOCIAL RELATIONS, AND SUFFERING

CHAP. 3.

21 [c]The like figure whereunto *even*
baptism doth also now save us, (not
the putting away of [d]the filth of the
flesh, [e]but the answer of a good conscience toward God,) [f]by the resurrection of Jesus Christ:
22 Who is gone into heaven, and
[g]is on the right hand of God; [h]angels
and authorities and powers being
made subject unto him.

CHAP. 4.

1 Forasmuch then [i]as Christ hath
suffered for us in the flesh, arm yourselves likewise with the same mind:
for [k]he that hath suffered in the flesh
hath ceased from sin;
2 [l]That he no longer [m]should live the
rest of *his* time in the flesh to the
lusts of men, [n]but to the will of God.
3 [o]For the time past of *our* life may
suffice us [p]to have wrought the will
of the Gentiles, when we walked in
lasciviousness, lusts, excess of wine,
revellings, banquetings, and abominable idolatries:
4 Wherein they think it strange
that ye run not with *them* to the
same excess of riot, [q]speaking evil of
you:
5 Who shall give account to him
that is ready [r]to judge the quick and
the dead.
6 For, for this cause [s]was the gospel preached also to them that are
dead, that they might be judged according to men in the flesh, but live
according to God in the spirit.
7 But [t]the end of all things is at
hand: [u]be ye therefore sober, and
watch unto prayer.
8 [x]And above all things have fervent

B—CONCLUDED.

II Pet. 2. 5 And spared not the old world, but saved Noah the eighth *person*, a preacher of righteousness, bringing in the flood upon the world of the ungodly;

C

Eph. 5. 26 That he might sanctify and cleanse it with the washing of water by the word,

D

Tit. 3. 5 Not by works of righteousness which we have done, but according to his mercy he saved us, by the washing of regeneration, and renewing of the Holy Ghost;

E

Acts 8. 37 And Philip said, If thou believest with all thine heart, thou mayest. And he answered and said, I believe that Jesus Christ is the Son of God.

Rom. 10. 9 That if thou shalt confess with thy mouth the Lord Jesus, and shalt believe in thine heart that God hath raised him from the dead, thou shalt be saved.

10 For with the heart man believeth unto righteousness; and with the mouth confession is made unto salvation.

II Cor. 1. 12 For our rejoicing is this, the testimony of our conscience, that in simplicity and godly sincerity, not with fleshly wisdom, but by the grace of God, we have had our conversation in the world, and more abundantly to you-ward.

F

I Pet. 1. 3 Blessed *be* the God and Father of our Lord Jesus Christ, which according to his abundant mercy hath begotten us again unto a lively hope by the resurrection of Jesus Christ from the dead,

G

Rom. 8. 34 Who *is* he that condemneth? *It is* Christ that died, yea rather, that is risen again, who is even at the right hand of God, who also maketh intercession for us.

Eph. 1. 20. *See k, K, § 427, page 1032.*

H

Rom. 8. 38. *See x, X, § 334, page 850.*

I Cor. 15. 24 Then *cometh* the end, when he shall have delivered up the kingdom to God, even the Father; when he shall have put down all rule and all authority and power.

25 For he must reign, till he hath put all enemies under his feet.

AFTER THE PATTERN OF CHRIST. THE END IS AT HAND (Continued).

I

I Pet. 3. 18. *See r, R, § 541, page 1260.*

K

Rom. 6. 2. *See b, B, § 328, page 834.*

Rom. 6. 7 For he that is dead is freed from sin.

Gal. 5. 24 And they that are Christ's have crucified the flesh with the affections and lusts.

L

Rom. 14. 7 For none of us liveth to himself, and no man dieth to himself.

I Pet. 2. 1 Wherefore laying aside all malice, and all guile, and hypocrisies, and envies, and all evil speakings,

M

Gal. 2. 20 I am crucified with Christ: nevertheless I live; yet not I, but Christ liveth in me: and the life which I now live in the flesh I live by the faith of the Son of God, who loved me, and gave himself for me.

I Pet. 1. 14 As obedient children, not fashioning yourselves according to the former lusts in your ignorance:

N

John 1. 13 Which were born, not of blood, nor of the will of the flesh, nor of the will of man, but of God.

Rom. 6. 11 Likewise reckon ye also yourselves to be dead indeed unto sin, but alive unto God through Jesus Christ our Lord.

Rom. 14. 7, 8. *See g, G, § 344, page 876.*

II Cor. 5. 15 And *that* he died for all, that they which live should not henceforth live unto themselves, but unto him which died for them, and rose again.

Jas. 1. 18 Of his own will begat he us with the word of truth, that we should be a kind of firstfruits of his creatures.

O

Eze. 44. 6 And thou shalt say to the rebellious, *even* to the house of Israel, Thus saith the Lord God; O ye house of Israel, let it suffice you of all your abominations,

Eze. 45. 9 Thus saith the Lord God; Let it suffice you, O princes of Israel: remove violence and spoil, and execute judgment and justice, take away your exactions from my people, saith the Lord God

Rom. 8. 12 Therefore, brethren, we are debtors; not to the flesh, to live after the flesh.

Acts 17. 30. *See s, S, § 279, page 744.*

P

I Cor. 6. 11. *See g, G, § 360, page 910.*

Eph. 4. 17 This I say therefore, and testify in the Lord, that ye henceforth walk

P—Concluded.

not as other Gentiles walk, in the vanity of their mind,

I Thes. 4. 5 Not in the lust of concupiscence, even as the Gentiles which know not God:

I Pet. 1. 14 As obedient children, not fashioning yourselves according to the former lusts in your ignorance:

Q

Acts. 13. 45. *See a, A, § 263, page 718.*

Tit. 2. 8. *See k, K, § 497, page 1158.*

R

II Cor. 5. 10. *See i, I, § 394, page 976.*

Acts 10. 42. *See p, P, § 254, page 698.*

S

I Pet. 3. 19 By which also he went and preached unto the spirits in prison;

T

Matt. 24. 13 But he that shall endure unto the end, the same shall be saved.

14 And this gospel of the kingdom shall be preached in all the world for a witness unto all nations; and then shall the end come.

I Cor. 7. 29. *See c, C, § 363, page 916.*

Phil. 4. 5. *See h, H, § 446, page 1074.*

U

I Pet. 1. 13. *See b, B, § 538, page 1150.*

X

Col. 3. 14 And above all these things *put on* charity, which is the bond of perfectness.

Heb. 13. 1 Let brotherly love continue.

Y

I Cor. 13. 1. *See b, B, § 372, page 942.*

Jas. 5. 20 Let him know, that he which converteth the sinner from the error of his way shall save a soul from death, and shall hide a multitude of sins.

1

Or, *will.*

Z

Rom. 12. 13 Distributing to the necessity of the saints; given to hospitality.

Heb. 13. 2 Be not forgetful to entertain strangers: for thereby some have entertained angels unawares.

A

II Cor. 9. 7 Every man according as he purposeth in his heart, *so let him give;* not grudgingly, or of necessity: for God loveth a cheerful giver.

Phil. 2. 14 Do all things without murmurings and disputings:

Phile. 14 But without thy mind would I do nothing; that thy benefit should not be as it were of necessity, but willingly.

§ 541. EXHORTATION CONCERNING SOCIAL RELATIONS, AND SUFFERING

CHAP. 4.

[1]charity among yourselves: for [y]charity shall cover the multitude of sins.

9 [z]Use hospitality one to another [a]without grudging.

10 [b]As every man hath received the gifts, *even so* minister the same one to another, [c]as good stewards of [d]the manifold grace of God.

11 [e]If any man speak, *let him speak* as the oracles of God: [f]if any man minister, *let him do it* as of the ability which God giveth: that God in all things may be glorified through Jesus Christ, [g]to whom be praise and dominion for ever and ever. Amen.

12 Beloved, think it not strange concerning [h]the fiery trial which is to try you, as though some strange thing happened unto you:

13 [i]But rejoice, inasmuch as [k]ye are partakers of Christ's sufferings; [l]that, when his glory shall be revealed, ye may be glad also with exceeding joy.

14 [m]If ye be reproached for the name of Christ, happy *are ye;* for the Spirit of glory and of God resteth upon you: [n]on their part he is evil spoken of, but on your part he is glorified.

15 But [o]let none of you suffer as a murderer, or *as* a thief, or *as* an evil doer, [p]or as a busybody in other men's matters.

16 Yet if *any man suffer* as a Christian, let him not be ashamed; [q]but let him glorify God on this behalf.

17 For the time *is come* [r]that judgment must begin at the house of God: and if *it* first *begin* at us, [s]what shall the end *be* of them that obey not the gospel of God?

CHAP. 4.

18 [t]And if the righteous scarcely be saved, where shall the ungodly and the sinner appear?

19 Wherefore let them that suffer according to the will of God [u]commit the keeping of their souls *to him* in well doing, as unto a faithful Creator.

For Y, 1, Z and A, see preceding page (1263).

B

Rom. 12. 6 Having then gifts differing according to the grace that is given to us, whether prophecy, *let us prophesy* according to the proportion of faith;

I Cor. 4. 7 For who maketh thee to differ *from another?* and what hast thou that thou didst not receive? now if thou didst receive *it*, why dost thou glory, as if thou hadst not received *it?*

C

Matt. 24. 45. *See c, C, § 174. page 494.*

Tit. 1. 7 For a bishop must be blameless, as the steward of God; not selfwilled, not soon angry, not given to wine, no striker, not given to filthy lucre;

D

I Cor. 12. 4 Now there are diversities of gifts, but the same Spirit.

Eph. 4. 11 And he gave some, apostles; and some, prophets; and some, evangelists; and some, pastors and teachers;

E

Jer. 23. 22 But if they had stood in my counsel, and had caused my people to hear my words, then they should have turned them from their evil way, and from the evil of their doings.

F

Rom. 12. 6-8. *See page 868, also study § 353, page 898.*

G

I Tim. 6. 16 Who only hath immortality, dwelling in the light which no man can approach unto; whom no man hath seen, nor can see: to them *be* honour and power everlasting. Amen.

I Pet. 5. 11 To him *be* glory and dominion forever and ever. Amen.

Rev. 1. 6 And hath made us kings and priests unto God and the Father; to *be* glory and dominion for ever and ever. Amen.

AFTER THE PATTERN OF CHRIST. THE END IS AT HAND (CONCLUDED).

H

I Cor. 3. 13 Every man's work shall be made manifest: for the day shall declare it, because it shall be revealed by fire; and the fire shall try every man s work of what sort it is.

I Pet. 1. 7 That the trial of your faith, being much more precious than of gold that perisheth, though it be tried with fire, might be found unto praise and honour and glory at the appearing of Jesus Christ:

I

Acts 5. 41. *See g, G, § 243, page 662.*

K

II Cor. 4. 10. *See e, E, § 393, page 972.*

Col. 1. 24. *See c, C, § 449, page 1080.*

I Pet. 5. 1 The elders which are among you I exhort, who am also an elder, and a witness of the sufferings of Christ, and also a partaker of the glory that shall be revealed:

I Pet. 5. 10 But the God of all grace, who hath called us unto his eternal glory by Christ Jesus, after that ye have suffered a while, make you perfect, stablish, strengthen, settle *you*.

L

I Pet. 1. 5 Who are kept by the power of God through faith unto salvation ready to be revealed in the last time.

6 Wherein ye greatly rejoice, though now for a season, if need be, ye are in heaviness through manifold temptations:

M

Rom. 5. 3. *See e, E, § 326, page 830.*

Jas. 1. 12 Blessed *is* the man that endureth temptation: for when he is tried, he shall receive the crown of life, which the Lord hath promised to them that love him.

I Pet. 2. 19 For this *is* thankworthy, if a man for conscience toward God endure grief, suffering wrongfully.

20 For what glory *is it*, if, when ye be buffeted for your faults, ye shall take it patiently ? but if, when ye do well, and suffer *for it*, ye take it patiently, this *is* acceptable with God.

N

I Pet. 3. 16. *See q, Q, § 541, page 1260.*

O

I Pet. 2. 20. *See under M.*

P

I Thes. 4. 11 And that ye study to be quiet, and to do your own business, and to work with your own hands, as we commanded you:

P—CONCLUDED.

II Thes. 3. 11 For we hear that there are some which walk among you disorderly, working not at all, but are busybodies.

I Tim. 5. 13 And withal they learn *to be* idle, wandering about from house to house; and not only idle, but tattlers also and busybodies, speaking things which they ought not.

Q

Acts 5. 41. *See g, G, § 243, page 662.*

R

Isa. 10. 12 Wherefore it shall come to pass, *that*, when the Lord hath performed his whole work upon mount Zion and on Jerusalem, I will punish the fruits of the stout heart of the king of Assyria, and the glory of his high looks.

Jer. 25. 29 For, lo, I began to bring evil on the city which is called by my name, and should ye be utterly unpunished ? Ye shall not be unpunished: for I will call for a sword upon all the inhabitants of the earth, saith the LORD of hosts.

Jer. 49. 12 For thus saith the LORD; Behold, they whose judgment *was* not to drink of the cup have assuredly drunken; and *art* thou he *that* shall altogether go unpunished ? thou shall not go unpunished, but thou shalt surely drink *of it*.

Eze. 9. 6 Slay utterly old *and* young, both maids, and little children, and women: but come not near any man upon whom *is* the mark; and begin at my sanctuary. Then they began at the ancient men which *were* before the house.

Mal. 3. 5 And I will come near to you to judgment; and I will be a swift witness against the sorcerers, and against the adulterers, and against false swearers, and against those that oppress the hireling in *his* wages, the widow, and the fatherless, and that turn aside the stranger *from his right*, and fear not me, saith the LORD of hosts.

S

Luke 10. 12, 14. *See q, Q, § 105, page 307.*

T

Luke 23. 31. *See k, K, § 202, page 581.*

U

Ps. 31. 5 Into thine hand I commit my spirit: thou has redeemed me, O LORD God of truth.

Luke 23. 46 And when Jesus had cried with a loud voice, he said, Father, into thy hands I commend my spirit: and having said thus, he gave up the ghost.

II Tim. 1. 12. *See z, Z, § 486, page 1140.*

§ 542. EXHORTATION TO ELDERS, TO BE HUMBLE.

5 : 1–11.

1 The elders which are among you I exhort, who am also [a]an elder, and [b]a witness of the sufferings of Christ, and also [c]a partaker of the glory that shall be revealed :

2 [d]Feed the flock of God [1]which is among you, taking the oversight *thereof*, [e]not by constraint, but willingly ; [f]not for filthy lucre, but of a ready mind ;

3 Neither as [2g]being lords over [h]*God's* heritage, but [i]being ensamples to the flock.

4 And when [k]the chief Shepherd shall appear, ye shall receive [l]a crown of glory [m]that fadeth not away.

5 Likewise, ye younger, submit yourselves unto the elder. Yea, [n]all *of you* be subject one to another, and be clothed with humility: for [o]God resisteth the proud, [p]and giveth grace to the humble.

6 [q]Humble yourselves therefore under the mighty hand of God, that he may exalt you in due time :

7 [r]Casting all your care upon him ; for he careth for you.

8 [s]Be sober, be vigilant; because [t]your adversary the devil, as a roaring lion, walketh about, seeking whom he may devour:

9 [u]Whom resist steadfast in the faith, [x]knowing that the same afflictions are accomplished in your brethren that are in the world.

10 But the God of all grace, [y]who hath called us unto his eternal glory by Christ Jesus, after that ye have suffered [z]a while, [a]make you perfect, [b]stablish, strengthen, settle *you*.

11 [c]To him *be* glory and dominion for ever and ever. Amen.

A

Phile. 9 Yet for love's sake I rather beseech *thee*, being such a one as Paul the aged, and now also a prisoner of Jesus Christ.

B

John 15. 27. *See u, U, § 188, page 535.*

C

Rom. 8. 17, 18. *See a, A, § 333, page 846.*

D

John 21. 15 So when they had dined Jesus saith to Simon Peter, Simon, *son* of Jonas, lovest thou me more than these ? He saith unto him, Yea, Lord; thou knowest that I love thee. He saith unto him, Feed my lambs.

16 He saith to him again the second time, Simon, *son* of Jonas, lovest thou me ? He saith unto him, Yea, Lord; thou knowest that I love thee. He saith unto him, Feed my sheep.

17 He saith unto him the third time, Simon, *son* of Jonas, lovest thou me ? Peter was grieved because he said unto him the third time, Lovest thou me ? And he said unto him, Lord thou knowest all things; thou knowest that I love thee. Jesus said unto him, Feed my sheep.

Acts 20. 28 Take heed therefore unto yourselves, and to all the flock, over the which the Holy Ghost hath made you overseers, to feed the church of God, which he hath purchased with his own blood.

1

Or, *as much as in you is.*

E

I Cor. 9. 17 For if I do this thing willingly, I have a reward: but if against my will a dispensation *of the gospel* is commited unto me.

F

Tit. 1. 7. *See h, H. § 495, page 1154.*

2

Or, *over-ruling.*

G

Eze. 34. 4 The diseased have ye not strengthened, neither have ye healed that which was sick, neither have ye bound up *that which was* broken, neither have ye brought again that which was driven away, neither have ye sought that which was lost; but with force and with cruelty have ye ruled them.

Luke 22. 25, 26. *See g, G, § 181, page 511.*

II Cor. 1. 24 Not for that we have dominion over your faith, but are helpers of your joy: for by faith ye stand.

SOBER, WATCHFUL AND STEADFAST.

H

Ps. 33. 12 Blessed *is* the nation whose God *is* the LORD; *and* the people *whom* he hath chosen for his own inheritance.

Ps. 74. 2 Remember thy congregation, *which* thou hast purchased of old; the rod of thine inheritance, *which* thou hast redeemed; this mount Zion, wherein thou hast dwelt.

I

Phil. 3. 17 Brethren, be followers together of me, and mark them which walk so as ye have us for an example.

II Thes. 3. 9 Not because we have not power, but to make ourselves an example unto you to follow us.

I Tim. 4. 12 Let no man despise thy youth; but be thou an example of the believers, in word, in conversation, in charity, in spirit, in faith, in purity.

Tit. 2. 7 In all things showing thyself a pattern of good works: in doctrine *shewing* uncorruptness, gravity, sincerity.

K

John 10. 11. *See k, K, § 118, page 351.*

L

James 1. 12. *See l, L, § 528, page 1228.*

M

I Pet. 1. 4 To an inheritance incorruptible, and undefiled, and that fadeth not away, reserved in heaven for you,

N

Rom. 12. 10 *Be* kindly affectioned one to another with brotherly love; in honour preferring one another;

Eph. 5. 21. *See n, N, § 434, page 1050.*

O

Jas. 4. 6 But he giveth more grace. Wherefore he saith, God resisteth the proud, but giveth grace unto the humble.

P

Isa. 57. 15 For thus saith the high and lofty One that inhabiteth eternity, whose name *is* Holy; I dwell in the high and holy *place*, with him also *that is* of a contrite and humble spirit, to revive the spirit of the humble, and to revive the heart of the contrite ones.

Isa. 66. 2 For all those *things* hath mine hand made, and all those *things* have been, saith the LORD: but to this *man* will I look, *even* to *him that is* poor and of a contrite spirit, and trembleth at my word.

Q

Matt. 23. 12. *See q, Q, § 167, page 464.*

Jas. 4. 10 Humble yourselves in the sight of the Lord, and he shall lift you up.

R

Ps. 37. 5 Commit thy way unto the LORD; trust also in him; and he shall bring *it* to pass.

Matt. 6. 25. *See r, R, § 43, page 140.*

Heb. 13. 5 *Let your* conversation *be* without covetousness; *and be* content with such things as ye have: for he hath said, I will never leave thee, nor forsake thee.

S

I Pet. 1. 13. *See b, B, § 538, page 1250.*

T

Job 1. 7 And the LORD said unto Satan, Whence comest thou? Then Satan answered the LORD, and said, From going to and fro in the earth, and from walking up and down in it.

Job 2. 2 And the LORD said unto Satan, From whence cometh thou? And Satan answered the LORD, and said, From going to and fro in the earth, and from walking up and down in it.

Luke 22. 31 And the Lord said, Simon, Simon, behold, Satan hath desired *to have* you, that he may sift *you* as wheat:

Rev. 12. 12 Therefore rejoice, *ye* heavens, and ye that dwell in them. Woe to the inhabiters of the earth and of the sea! for the devil is come down unto you, having great wrath, because he knoweth that he hath but a short time.

U

Eph. 4. 27. *See s, S, § 433, page 1046.*

X

Acts 14. 22. *See e, E, § 266, page 724.*

Y

I Cor. 1. 9 God *is* faithful, by whom ye were called unto the fellowship of his Son Jesus Christ our Lord.

I Tim. 6. 12 Fight the good fight of faith, lay hold on eternal life, whereunto thou art also called, and hast professed a good profession before many witnesses.

Z

II Cor. 4. 17. *See p, P, § 393 page 974.*

A

Heb. 13. 21 Make you perfect in every good work to do his will, working in you that which is well pleasing in his sight, through Jesus Christ; to whom *be* glory for ever and ever. Amen.

Jude. 24 Now unto him that is able to keep you from falling, and to present *you* faultless before the presence of his glory with exceeding joy,

B

II Thes. 2. 17. *See k, K, § 468, page 1114.*

C

I Pet. 4. 11. *See g, G, § 541, page 1264.*

§ 543. CONCLUDING SALUTATIONS

5: 12–14.

12 [a]By Silvanus, a faithful brother unto you, as I suppose, I have [b]written briefly, exhorting, and testifying [c]that this is the true grace of God wherein ye stand.

13 The *church that is* at Babylon, elected together with *you*, saluteth you; and *so doth* [d]Marcus my son.

14 [e]Greet ye one another with a kiss of charity. [f]Peace *be* with you all that are in Christ Jesus. Amen.

A

IICor. 1. 19 For the Son of God, Jesus Christ, who was preached among you by us, *even* by me and Silvanus and Timotheus, was not yea and nay, but in him was yea.

B

Heb. 13. 22 And I beseech you, brethren, suffer the word of exhortation: for I have written a letter unto you in few words.

C

Acts 20. 24 But none of these things move me, neither count I my life dear unto myself, so that I might finish my course with joy, and the ministry, which I have received of the Lord Jesus, to testify the gospel of the grace of God.

THE SECOND

§ 544. THE SALUTATION.

1: 1, 2.

1 [1]Simon Peter, a servant and an apostle of Jesus Christ, to them that have obtained [a]like precious faith with us through the righteousness [2]of God and our Saviour Jesus Christ:

2 [b]Grace and peace be multiplied unto you through the knowledge of God, and of Jesus our Lord,

1

Or, *Symeon.*

Acts 15. 14 Simeon hath declared how God at the first did visit the Gentiles, to take out of them a people for his name.

A

Acts 15. 8 And God, which knoweth the hearts, bare them witness, giving them the Holy Ghost, even as *he did* unto us;

9 And put no difference between us and them, purifying their hearts by faith.

Rom. 1. 12 That is, that I may be comforted together with you by the mutual faith both of you and me.

IICor. 4. 13 We having the same spirit of faith, according as it is written, I believed, and therefore have I spoken; we also believe, and therefore speak;

Phil. 1. 29 For unto you it is given in the behalf of Christ, not only to believe on him, but also to suffer for his sake;

30 Having the same conflict which ye saw in me, and now hear *to be* in me.

§ 545. THROUGH THE PROMISES WE BECOME

1: 3–11.

3 According as his divine power hath [a]given unto us all things that *pertain* unto life and godliness, through the knowledge of him [b]that hath called us [1]to glory and virtue:

4 [c]Whereby are given unto us ex-

A

Isa. 53. 11 He shall see of the travail of his soul, *and* shall be satisfied: by his knowledge shall my righteous servant

A—Continued.

justify many; for he shall bear their iniquities.

Jer. 9. 23 Thus saith the Lord, Let not the wise *man* glory in his wisdom, neither let the mighty *man* glory in his might, let not the rich *man* glory in his riches:

24 But let him that glorieth glory in this, that he understandeth and knoweth me, that I *am* the Lord which exercise lovingkindness, judgment, and righteousness, in the earth: for in these *things* I delight, saith the Lord.

John 17. 3. And this is life eternal, that they

AND BENEDICTIONS.

C—Concluded.

ICor.15. 1 Moreover, brethren, I declare unto you the gospel which I preached unto you, which also ye have received, and wherein ye stand:

IIPet.1. 12 Wherefore I will not be negligent to put you always in remembrance of these things, though ye know *them*, and be established in the present truth.

D

Acts 12. 12 And when he had considered *the thing*, he came to the house of Mary the mother of John, whose surname was Mark; where many were gathered together praying.

Acts 12. 25 And Barnabas and Saul returned from Jerusalem, when they had ful-

D—Concluded.

filled *their* ministry, and took with them John, whose surname was Mark.

E

Rom.16. 16 Salute one another with a holy kiss. The churches of Christ salute you.

ICor.16. 20 All the brethren greet you. Greet ye one another with a holy kiss.

II Cor. 13. 12 Greet one another with a holy kiss.

IThes.5. 26 Greet all the brethren with a holy kiss.

F

Eph. 6. 23 Peace *be* to the brethren, and love with faith, from God the Father and the Lord Jesus Christ.

EPISTLE OF PETER.

Written probably A. D. 68, at Rome.

A—Concluded.

Tit. 1. 4 To Titus, *mine* own son after the common faith: Grace, mercy, *and* peace, from God the Father and the Lord Jesus Christ our Saviour.

Tit. 2. 13 Looking for that blessed hope, and the glorious appearing of the great God and our Saviour Jesus Christ:

2

Gr. *of our God and Saviour.*

Isa. 12. 2 Behold, God *is* my salvation; I will trust, and not be afraid: for the Lord JEHOVAH *is* my strength and *my* song; he also is become my salvation.

Luke 1. 47 And my spirit hath rejoiced in God my Saviour.

Eph. 4. 5 One Lord, one faith, one baptism,

B

Dan. 4. 1 Nebuchadnezzar the king, unto all people, nations, and languages, that dwell in all the earth; Peace be multiplied unto you.

Dan. 6. 25 Then King Darius wrote unto all people, nations, and languages, that dwell in all the earth; Peace be multiplied unto you.

I Pet. 1. 2 Elect according to the foreknowledge of God the Father, through sanctification of the Spirit, unto obedience and sprinkling of the blood of Jesus Christ: Grace unto you, and peace, be multiplied.

Jude 2 Mercy unto you, and peace, and love, be multiplied.

PARTAKERS OF THE DIVINE NATURE.

A—Concluded.

might know thee the only true God, and Jesus Christ, whom thou hast sent.

B

Rom. 8. 28. *See f, F, § 334, page 848.*

IThes.2. 12 That ye would walk worthy of God, who hath called you unto his kingdom and glory.

IThes.4. 7 For God hath not called us unto uncleanness, but unto holiness.

II Thes. 2. 14 Whereunto he called you by our gospel, to the obtaining of the glory of our Lord Jesus Christ.

B—Continued.

IITim.1. 9 Who hath saved us, and called *us* with a holy calling, not according to our works, but according to his own purpose and grace, which was given us in Christ Jesus before the world began;

I Pet. 2. 9 But ye *are* a chosen generation, a royal priesthood, a holy nation, a peculiar people; that ye should shew forth the praises of him who hath called you out of darkness into his marvellous light:

For B concluded, 1 and C, see next page (1270).

§ 545. THROUGH THE PROMISES WE BECOME

Chap. 1.

ceeding great and precious promises: that by these ye might be [d]partakers of the divine nature, [e]having escaped the corruption that is in the world through lust.

5 And besides this, [f]giving all diligence, add to your faith virtue; and to virtue, [g]knowledge;

6 And to knowledge temperance; and to temperance patience; and to patience godliness;

7 And to godliness brotherly kindness; and [h]to brotherly kindness charity.

8 For if these things be in you, and abound, they make *you that ye shall* neither *be* [2]barren [i]nor unfruitful in the knowledge of our Lord Jesus Christ.

9 But he that lacketh these things [k]is blind, and cannot see afar off, and hath forgotten that he was [l]purged from his old sins.

10 Wherefore the rather, brethren, give diligence [m]to make your calling and election sure: for if ye do these things, [n]ye shall never fall:

11 For [o]so an entrance shall be ministered unto you abundantly into the everlasting kingdom of our Lord and Saviour Jesus Christ.

B—Continued.

I Pet. 3. 9 Not rendering evil for evil, or railing for railing: but contrariwise bless-

B—Concluded.

ing; knowing that ye are thereunto called, that ye should inherit a blessing.

1

Or, *by*.

C

IICor.7. 1 Having therefore these promises, dearly beloved, let us cleanse ourselves from all filthiness of the flesh and spirit, perfecting holiness in the fear of God.

D

IICor.3. 18 But we all, with open face beholding as in a glass the glory of the Lord, are changed into the same image from glory to glory, *even* as by the Spirit of the Lord.

Eph. 4. 24 And that ye put on the new man, which after God is created in righteousness and true holiness.

Col. 3. 10 And have put on the new *man*, which is renewed in knowledge after the image of him that created him:

Heb. 12. 10 For they verily for a few days chastened *us* after their own pleasure; but he for *our* profit, that *we* might be partakers of his holiness.

I Jno. 3. 2 Beloved, now are we the sons of God, and it doth not yet appear what we shall be: but we know that, when he shall appear, we shall be like him; for we shall see him as he is.

E

IIPet. 2. 18 For when they speak great swelling *words* of vanity, they allure through the lusts of the flesh, *through much* wantonness, those that were clean escaped from them who live in error.

IIPet. 2. 20 For if after they have escaped the pollutions of the world through the knowledge of the Lord and Saviour Jesus Christ, they are again entangled therein, and overcome, the latter end

§ 546. PETER, AN EYE WITNESS OF THE POWER AND MAJESTY OF THE

1: 12–21.

12 Wherefore [a]I will not be negligent to put you always in remembrance of these things, [b]though ye know *them*, and be established in the present truth.

13 Yea, I think it meet, [c]as long as I am in this tabernacle, [d]to stir you up by putting *you* in remembrance;

A

Rom.15. 14 And I myself also am persuaded of you, my brethren, that ye also are full of goodness, filled with all knowledge, able also to admonish one another.

II Pet.2. 15 Nevertheless, brethren, I have written the more boldly unto you in some sort, as putting you in mind, because of the grace that is given to me of God.

Phil. 3. 1 Finally, my brethren, rejoice in the Lord. To write the same things

PARTAKERS OF THE DIVINE NATURE (Concluded).

E—Concluded.

is worse with them than the beginning.

F

IIPet. 3. 18 But grow in grace, and *in* the knowledge of our Lord and Saviour Jesus Christ. To him *be* glory both now and for ever. Amen.

G

Prov. 1. 7 The fear of the Lord *is* the beginning of knowledge: *but* fools despise wisdom and instruction.

Prov. 19. 2 Also, *that* the soul *be* without knowledge, *it is* not good; and he that hasteth with *his* feet sinneth.

Hos. 4. 6 My people are destroyed for lack of knowledge: because thou hast rejected knowledge, I will also reject thee, that thou shalt be no priest to me: seeing thou hast forgotten the law of thy God, I will also forget thy children.

IICor. 6. 6 By pureness, by knowledge, by longsuffering, by kindness, by the Holy Ghost, by love unfeigned,

Phil. 1. 9 And this I pray, that your love may abound yet more and more in knowledge and *in* all judgment;

I Pet. 3. 7 Likewise, ye husbands, dwell with *them* according to knowledge, giving honour unto the wife, as unto the weaker vessel, and as being heirs together of the grace of life; that your prayers be not hindered.

II Pet. 3. 18. *See under F.*

H

I Thes. 3. 12. *See x, X, § 460 page 1100.*

I Jno. 4. 21 And this commandment have we from him, That he who loveth God love his brother also.

2

Gr. idle.

I

John 15. 2 Every branch in me that beareth not fruit he taketh away: and every *branch* that beareth fruit, he purgeth

I—Concluded.

it, that it may bring forth more fruit.

Tit. 3. 14 And let ours also learn to maintain good works for necessary uses, that they be not unfruitful.

K

I Jno. 2. 9 He that saith he is in the light, and hateth his brother, is in darkness even until now.

I Jno. 2. 11 But he that hateth his brother is in darkness, and walketh in darkness, and knoweth not whither he goeth, because that darkness hath blinded his his eyes.

L

Eph. 5. 26 That he might sanctify and cleanse it with the washing of water by the word,

Heb. 9. 14 How much more shall the blood of Christ, who through the eternal Spirit offered himself without spot to God, purge your conscience from dead works to serve the living God?

I Jno. 1. 7 But if we walk in the light, as he is in the light, we have fellowship one with another, and the blood of Jesus Christ his son cleanseth us from all sin.

M

I Jno. 3. 19 And hereby we know that we are of the truth, and shall assure our hearts before him.

Rev. 22. 14 Blessed *are* they that do his commandments, that they may have right to the tree of life, and may enter in through the gates into the city.

N

IIPet. 3. 17 Ye therefore, beloved, seeing ye know *these things* before, beware lest ye also, being led away with the error of the wicked, fall from your own steadfastness.

O

II Tim. 4. 8. *See o, O, § 491, page 1150.*

SON OF GOD, COMMENDS THE MORE SURE WORD OF PROPHECY.

A—Concluded.

to you, to me indeed *is* not grievous, but for you *it is* safe.

I Jno. 2. 21 I have not written unto you because ye know not the truth, but because ye know it, and that no lie is of the truth.

B

I Pet. 5. 12 By Silvanus, a faithful brother unto you, as I suppose, I have written briefly, exhorting, and testifying that this is the true grace of God wherein ye stand.

B—Concluded.

II Pet. 3. 17. *See under N, § 545.*

C

II Cor. 5. 1, 4. *See a, A, § 394, page 974.*

D

IITim. 1. 6 Wherefore I put thee in remembrance that thou stir up the gift of God, which is in thee by the putting on of my hands.

IIPet. 3. 1 This second epistle, beloved, I now write unto you; in *both* which I stir up your pure minds by way of remembrance:

§ 546. PETER, AN EYE WITNESS OF THE POWER AND MAJESTY OF THE

CHAP. 1.

14 [e]Knowing that shortly I must put off *this* my tabernacle, even as [f]our Lord Jesus Christ hath shewed me.

15 Moreover I will endeavour that ye may be able after my decease to have these things always in remembrance.

16 For we have not followed [g]cunningly devised fables, when we made known unto you the power and coming of our Lord Jesus Christ, but [h]were eyewitnesses of his majesty.

17 For he received from God the Father honour and glory, when there came such a voice to him from the excellent glory, [i]This is my beloved Son, in whom I am well pleased.

18 And this voice which came from heaven we heard, when we were with him in [k]the holy mount.

19 We have also a more sure word of prophecy; whereunto ye do well that ye take heed, as unto [m]a light that shineth in a dark place, until [n]the day dawn, and the day star arise in your hearts:

CHAP. 1.

20 Knowing this first, that [o]no prophecy of the Scripture is of any private interpretation.

21 For [p]the prophecy came not [1]in old time by the will of man: [q]but holy men of God spake *as they were* moved by the Holy Ghost.

E

Deut.4. 22 But I must die in this land, I must not go over Jordan: but ye shall go over, and possess that good land.

Deut.31. 14 And the LORD said unto Moses, Behold, thy days approach that thou must die: call Joshua, and present yourselves in the tabernacle of the congregation, that I may give him a charge. And Moses and Joshua went, and presented themselves in the tabernacle of the congregation.

IITim.4. 6 For I am now ready to be offered, and the time of my departure is at hand.

F

John 21. 18 Verily, verily, I say unto thee, When thou wast young, thou girdedst thyself, and walkedst whither thou wouldest: but when thou shalt be old, thou shalt stretch forth thy hands, and another shall gird thee, and carry *thee* whither thou wouldest not.

19 This spake he, signifying by what death he should glorify God. And when he had spoken this, he saith unto him, Follow me.

§ 547. WARNINGS AGAINST

2 : 1—22.

1 But [a]there were false prophets also among the people, even as [b]there shall be false teachers among you, who privily shall bring in damnable heresies, even [c]denying the Lord [d]that bought them, [e]and bring upon themselves swift destruction.

2 And many shall follow their [1]pernicious ways; by reason of whom the way of truth shall be evil spoken of.

A

Deut.13. 1 If there arise among you a prophet, or a dreamer of dreams, and giveth thee a sign or a wonder,

2 And the sign or the wonder come to pass, whereof he spake unto thee, saying, Let us go after other gods, which thou hast not known, and let us serve them;

Deut.13. 6 If thy brother, the son of thy mother, or thy son, or thy daughter, or the wife of thy bosom, or thy friend, which *is* as thine own soul, entice thee secretly, saying, Let us go and serve other gods, which thou hast not known, thou, nor thy fathers;

SON OF GOD, COMMENDS THE MORE SURE WORD OF PROPHECY (CONCLU'D).

G

I Cor. 1. 17. *See k, K, § 350, page 890.*

H

Matt. 17. 1, 2. *Study § 94, page 282.*

I

Luke 9. 35. *See u, U, § 94, page 285.*

K

Ex. 3. 5 And he said, Draw not nigh hither: put off thy shoes from off thy feet; for the place whereon thou standest *is* holy ground.

Josh. 5. 15 And the captain of the LORD's host said unto Joshua, Loose thy shoe from off thy foot; for the place whereon thou standest *is* holy. And Joshua did so.

Matt. 17. 1 And after six days Jesus taketh Peter, James, and John his brother, and bringeth them up into a high mountain apart,

2 And was transfigured before them: and his face did shine as the sun, and his raiment was white as the light.

M

Ps. 119. 105 Thy word *is* a lamp unto my feet, and a light unto my path.

Prov. 6. 23 For the commandment *is* a lamp; and the law *is* light; and reproofs of instruction *are* the way of life:

N

II Cor. 4. 4 In whom the god of this world hath blinded the minds of them which believe not, lest the light of the glorious gospel of Christ, who is the image of God, should shine unto them.

II Cor 4. 6 For God, who commanded the light to shine out of darkness, hath shined in our hearts, to *give* the light

N—CONCLUDED.

of the knowledge of the glory of God in the face of Jesus Christ.

Rev. 2. 28 And I will give him the morning star.

Rev. 22. 16 I Jesus have sent mine angel to testify unto you these things in the churches. I am the root and the offspring of David, *and* the bright and morning star.

O

II Cor. 13. 1. *See b, B, § 407, page 1002.*

P

II Tim. 3. 16 All Scriptnre *is* given by inspiration of God, and *is* profitable for doctrine, for reproof, for correction, for instruction in righteousness:

I Pet. 1. 11 Searching what, or what manner of time the Spirit of Christ which was in them did signify, when it testified beforehand the sufferings of Christ, and the glory that should follow.

1

Or, *at any time.*

Q

II Sa. 23. 2 The Spirit of the LORD spake by me, and his word *was* in my tongue.

Luke 1. 70 As he spake by the mouth of his holy prophets, which have been since the world began:

Acts 1. 16 Men *and* brethren, this Scripture must needs have been fulfilled, which the Holy Ghost by the mouth of David spake before concerning Judas, which was guide to them that took Jesus.

Acts 3. 18 But those things, which God before had shewed by the mouth of all his prophets, that Christ should suffer, he hath so fulfilled.

FALSE TEACHERS.

B

II Cor. 11. 3, 13. *Study § 403, page 992.*

C

Jude 4 For there are certain men crept in unawares, who were before of old ordained to this condemnation, ungodly men, turning the grace of our God into lasciviousness, and denying the only Lord God, and our Lord Jesus Christ.

D

Matt. 20. 28. *See y, Y, § 148, page 420.*
Acts 20. 28. *See s, S, § 292, page 762.*

E

Phil. 3. 19. *See d, D, § 445, page 1072.*

1

Or, *lascivious ways,* as some copies read.

F

Rom. 16. 18 For they that are such serve not our Lord Jesus Christ, but their own belly; and by good words and fair speeches deceive the hearts of the simple.

II Cor. 12. 17 Did I make a gain of you by any of them whom I sent unto you?

18 I desired Titus, and with *him* I sent a brother. Did Titus make a gain of you? walked we not in the same spirit? *walked we* not in the same steps?

I Tim. 6. 5 Perverse disputings of men of corrupt minds, and destitute of the truth, supposing that gain is godliness: from such withdraw thyself.

CHAP. 2.

3 And [f]through covetousness shall they with feigned words [g]make merchandise of you: [h]whose judgment now of a long time lingereth not, and their damnation slumbereth not.

4 For if God spared not [i]the angels [k]that sinned, but [l]cast *them* down to hell, and delivered *them* into chains of darkness, to be reserved unto judgment;

5 And spared not the old world, but saved [m]Noah the eighth *person*, [n]a preacher of righteousness, [o]bringing in the flood upon the world of the ungodly;

6 And [p]turning the cities of Sodom and Gomorrah into ashes condemned *them* with an overthrow, [q]making *them* an ensample unto those that after should live ungodly;

7 And [r]delivered just Lot, vexed with the filthy conversation of the wicked:

8 (For that righteous man dwelling among them, [s]in seeing and hearing, vexed *his* righteous soul from day to day with *their* unlawful deeds;)

9 [t]The Lord knoweth how to deliver the godly out of temptations, and to reserve the unjust unto the day of judgment to be punished:

10 But chiefly [u]them that walk after the flesh in the lust of uncleanness, and despise [2]government. [x]Presumptuous *are they*, selfwilled, they are not afraid to speak evil of dignities.

11 Whereas [y]angels, which are greater in power and might, bring not railing accusation [3]against them before the Lord.

CHAP. 2.

12 But these, [z]as natural brute beasts made to be taken and destroyed, speak evil of the things that they understand not; and shall utterly perish in their own corruption;

F—CONCLUDED. See preceding page (1273.)

Tit. 1. 11 Whose mouths must be stopped, who subvert whole houses, teaching things which they ought not, for filthy lucre's sake.

G

II Cor. 2. 17. *See i I, § 389, page 968.*

H

Deut. 32. 35 To me *belongeth* vengeance, and recompense; their foot shall slide in *due* time: for the day of their calamity *is* at hand, and the things that shall come upon them make haste.

Jude 4. *See under C.*

Jude 15 To execute judgment upon all, and to convince all that are ungodly among them of all their ungodly deeds which they have ungodly committed, and of all their hard *speeches* which ungodly sinners have spoken against him.

I

Job 4. 18 Behold, he put no trust in his servants; and his angels he charged with folly:

Jude 6 And the angels which kept not their first estate, but left their own habitation, he hath reserved in everlasting chains under darkness unto the judgment of the great day.

K

John 8. 44. *See a, A, § 111, page 329.*

L

Luke 8. 31 And they besought him that he would not command them to go out into the deep.

Rev. 20. 2 And he laid hold on the dragon, that old serpent, which is the Devil, and Satan, and bound him a thousand years,

3 And cast him into the bottomless pit, and shut him up, and set a seal upon him, that he should deceive the nations no more, till the thousand years should be fulfilled: and after that he must be loosed a little season.

M

Gen. 7. 1 And the LORD said unto Noah, Come thou and all thy house into the ark; for thee have I seen righteous before me in this generation.

FALSE TEACHERS (CONTINUED).

M—CONCLUDED.

Gen. 7. 7 And Noah went in, and his sons, and his wife, and his sons' wives with him, into the ark, because of the waters of the flood.

Gen. 7. 23 And every living substance was destroyed which was upon the face of the ground, both man, and cattle, and the creeping things, and the fowl of the heaven; and they were destroyed from the earth: and Noah only remained *alive*, and they that *were* with him in the ark.

Heb. 11. 7 By faith Noah, being warned of God of things not seen as yet, moved with fear, prepared an ark to the saving of his house; by the which he condemned the world, and became heir of the righteousness which is by faith.

I Pet. 3. 20 Which sometime were disobedient, when once the longsuffering of God waited in the days of Noah, while the ark was a preparing, wherein few, that is, eight souls were saved by water.

N

I Pet. 3. 19 By which also he went and preached unto the spirits in prison:

O

II Pet. 3. 6 Whereby the world that then was, being overflowed with water, perished:

P

Gen. 19. 24 Then the LORD rained upon Sodom and upon Gomorrah brimstone and fire from the LORD out of heaven;

Deut. 29. 23 *And that* the whole land thereof *is* brimstone, and salt, *and* burning, *that* it is not sown, nor beareth, nor any grass groweth therein, like the overthrow of Sodom, and Gomorrah, Admah and Zeboim, which the LORD overthrew in his anger, and in his wrath:

Jude 7 Even as Sodom and Gomorrah, and the cities about them in like manner, giving themselves over to fornication, and going after strange flesh, are set forth for an example, suffering the vengeance of eternal fire.

Q

Num. 26. 10 And the earth opened her mouth, and swallowed them up together with Korah, when that company died, what time the fire devoured two hundred and fifty men: and they became a sign.

R

Gen. 19. 16 And while he lingered, the men laid hold upon his hand, and upon the hand of his wife, and upon the hand

R—CONCLUDED.

of his two daughters; the LORD being merciful unto him: and they brought him forth, and set him without the city.

S

Ps. 119. 139 My zeal hath consumed me, because mine enemies have forgotten thy words.

Ps. 119. 158 I beheld the transgressors, and was grieved; because they kept not thy word.

Eze. 9. 4 And the LORD said unto him, Go through the midst of the city, through the midst of Jerusalem, and set a mark upon the foreheads of the men that sigh and that cry for all the abominations that be done in the midst thereof.

T

Ps. 34. 15 The eyes of the LORD *are* upon the righteous, and his ears *are open* unto their cry.

Ps. 34. 17 *The righteous* cry, and the LORD heareth, and delivereth them out of all their troubles.

Ps. 34. 19 Many *are* the afflictions of the righteous: but the LORD delivereth him out of them all.

I Cor. 10. 13 There hath no temptation taken you but such as is common to man: but God *is* faithful, who will not suffer you to be tempted above that ye are able; but will with the temptation also make a way to escape, that ye may be able to bear *it*.

U

Jude 4, 8, 10, 16. *Study* § *565*, § *566*, *page 1308*.

2

Or, *dominion*.

X

Jude 8 Likewise also these *filthy* dreamers defile the flesh, despise dominion, and speak evil of dignities.

Y

Jude 9 Yet Michael the archangel, when contending with the devil he disputed about the body of Moses, durst not bring against him a railing accusation, but said, The Lord rebuke thee.

3

Some read, *against themselves*.

Z

Jer. 12. 3 But thou, O LORD, knowest me: thou hast seen me, and tried mine heart toward thee: pull them out like sheep for the slaughter, and prepare them for the day of slaughter.

For Z, concluded, see next page (1276).

§ 547. WARNINGS AGAINST

CHAP. 2.

13 [a]And shall receive the reward of
unrighteousness, *as* they that count
it pleasure [b]to riot in the daytime.
[c]Spots *they are* and blemishes, sporting themselves with their own deceivings while [d]they feast with you;

14 Having eyes full of [4]adultery,
and that cannot cease from sin; be-
guiling unstable souls: [e]a heart they
have exercised with covetous prac-
tices; cursed children:

15 Which have forsaken the right
way, and are gone astray, following
the way of [f]Balaam *the son* of Bosor,
who loved the wages of unrighteousness;

16 But was rebuked for his iniquity: the dumb ass speaking with
man's voice forbade the madness of
the prophet.

17 [g]These are wells without water,
clouds that are carried with a tempest; to whom the mist of darkness
is reserved for ever.

18 For when [h]they speak great
swelling *words* of vanity, they allure
through the lusts of the flesh, *through
much* wantonness, those that [i]were
[5]clean escaped from them who live
in error.

19 While they promise them [k]lib-
erty, they themselves are [l]the servants of corruption: for of whom a
man is overcome, of the same is he
brought in bondage.

20 For [m]if after they [n]have escaped
the pollutions of the world [o]through
the knowledge of the Lord and
Saviour Jesus Christ, they are again
entangled therein, and overcome,
the latter end is worse with them
than the beginning.

CHAP. 2.

21 For [p]it had been better for them
not to have known the way of righteousness, than, after they have
known *it*, to turn from the holy
commandment delivered unto them.

22 But it is happened unto them according to the true proverb, [q]The
dog *is* turned to his own vomit
again; and The sow that was washed
to her wallowing in the mire.

Z—CONCLUDED.

Jude 10 But these speak evil of those things
which they know not: but what they
know naturally, as brute beasts, in
those things they corrupt themselves.

A

Phil. 3. 19. *See d, D, § 445, page 1072.*

B

Rom. 13. 13 Let us walk honestly, as in the
day; not in rioting and drunkenness,
not in chambering and wantonness,
not in strife and envying.

C

Jude 12 These are spots in your feasts of
charity, when they feast with you, feeding themselves without fear: clouds
they are without water, carried about
of winds; trees whose fruit withereth,
without fruit, twice dead, plucked up
by the roots;

D

1 Cor. 11. 20 When ye come together therefore
into one place, *this* is not to eat the
Lord's supper.

21 For in eating every one taketh before *other* his own supper: and one is
hungry, and another is drunken.

4

Gr. *an adulteress.*

E

Jude 11 Woe unto them! for they have
gone in the way of Cain, and ran greedily after the error of Balaam for reward,
and perished in the gainsaying of Core.

F

Num. 22. 5 He sent messengers therefore unto
Balaam the son of Beor to Pethor,
which *is* by the river of the land of the
children of his people, to call him, saying, Behold, there is a people come out
from Egypt: behold, they cover the
face of the earth, and they abide over
against me:

FALSE TEACHERS (Concluded).

F—Concluded.

Num. 22. 7 And the elders of Moab and the elders of Midian departed with the rewards of divination in their hand; and they came unto Balaam, and spake unto him the words of Balak.

Num. 22. 21 And Balaam rose up in the morning, and saddled his ass, and went with the princes of Moab.

22 And God's anger was kindled because he went: and the angel of the LORD stood in the way for an adversary against him. Now he was riding upon his ass, and his two servants *were* with him.

23 And the ass saw the angel of the LORD standing in the way, and his sword drawn in his hand: and the ass turned aside out of the way, and went into the field: and Balaam smote the ass, to turn her into the way.

G

Jude 12. *See under C.*

13 Raging waves of the sea, foaming out their own shame; wandering stars, to whom is reserved the blackness of darkness for ever.

H

Jude 16 These are murmurers, complainers, walking after their own lusts; and their mouth speaketh great swelling *words*, having men's persons in admiration because of advantage.

I

Acts 2. 40 And with many other words did he testify and exhort, saying, Save yourselves from this untoward generation.

II Pet. 1. 4 Whereby are given unto us exceeding great and precious promises: that by these ye might be partakers of the divine nature, having escaped the corruption that is in the world through lust.

II Pet. 2. 20. *See text of topic.*

5

Or, *for a little*, or, *a while*, as some read.

K

Gal. 5. 13. *See u, U, § 421, page 1022.*

L

John 8. 34. *See i, I, § 111, page 327.*

M

Matt. 12. 45 Then goeth he, and taketh with himself seven other spirits more wicked than himself, and they enter in and dwell there: and the last *state* of that man is worse than the first. Even so shall it be also unto this wicked generation.

M—Concluded.

Heb. 6. 4 For *it is* impossible for those who were once enlightened, and have tasted of the heavenly gift, and were made partakers of the Holy Ghost,

5 And have tasted the good word of God, and the powers of the world to come,

6 If they shall fall away, to renew them again unto repentance; seeing they crucify to themselves the Son of God afresh, and put *him* to an open shame.

Heb. 10. 26 For if we sin wilfully after that we have received the knowledge of the truth, there remaineth no more sacrifice for sins,

27 But a certain fearful looking for of judgment and fiery indignation, which shall devour the adversaries.

N

II Pet. 1. 4. *See under I.*

II Pet. 2. 18. *See text of topic.*

O

II Pet. 1. 2 Grace and peace be multiplied unto you through the knowledge of God, and of Jesus our Lord,

P

Num. 15. 30 But the soul that doeth *aught* presumptuously, *whether he be* born in the land, or a stranger, the same reproacheth the LORD; and that soul shall be cut off from among his people.

Luke 12. 47 And that servant, which knew his lord's will, and prepared not *himself*, neither did according to his will, shall be beaten with many *stripes*.

48 But he that knew not, and did commit things worthy of stripes, shall be beaten with few *stripes*. For unto whomsoever much is given, of him shall be much required: and to whom men have committed much, of him they will ask the more.

John 9. 41 Jesus said unto them, If ye were blind, ye should have no sin: but now ye say, We see; therefore your sin remaineth.

John 15. 22 If I had not come and spoken unto them, they had not had sin; but now they have no cloak for their sin.

Acts 17. 30 And the times of this ignorance God winked at; but now commandeth all men every where to repent:

Jas. 4. 17 Therefore to him that knoweth to do good, and doeth *it* not, to him it is sin.

Q

Prov. 26. 11 As a dog returneth to his vomit, *so* a fool returneth to his folly.

3 : 1–18.

1 This second epistle, beloved, I
now write unto you; in *both* which
[a]I stir up your pure minds by way
of remembrance:

2 That ye may be mindful of the
words which were spoken before by
the holy prophets, [b]and of the commandment of us the apostles of the
Lord and Saviour:

3 [c]Knowing this first, that there
shall come in the last days scoffers,
[d]walking after their own lusts,

4 And saying, [e]Where is the promise
of his coming? for since the fathers
fell asleep, all things continue as
they were from the beginning of the
creation.

5 For this they willingly are ignorant of, that [f]by the word of God
the heavens were of old, and the
earth [1g]standing out of the water and
in the water:

6 [h]Whereby the world that then
was, being overflowed with water,
perished:

7 But [i]the heavens and the earth,
which are now, by the same word
are kept in store, reserved unto [k]fire
against the day of judgment and
perdition of ungodly men.

8 But, beloved, be not ignorant of
this one thing, that one day *is* with
the Lord as [l]a thousand years, and
a thousand years as one day.

9 [m]The Lord is not slack concerning his promise, as some men count
slackness; but [n]is longsuffering to
us-ward, [o]not willing that any should
perish, but [p]that all should come to
repentance.

10 But [q]the day of the Lord will
come as a thief in the night; in the
which [r]the heavens shall pass away
with a great noise, and the elements
shall melt with fervent heat, the

§ 548. PETER DEFENDS THE LORD'S

A

II Pet. 1. 13 Yea, I think it meet, as long as I am in this tabernacle, to stir you up by putting *you* in remembrance;

B

Jude 17 But, beloved, remember ye the words which were spoken before of the apostles of our Lord Jesus Christ;

C

I Tim. 4. 1. *See b, B, § 478, page 1126.*

D

II Pet. 2. 10 But chiefly them that walk after the flesh in the lust of uncleanness, and despise government. Presumptuous *are they*, selfwilled, they are not afraid to speak evil of dignities.

E

Gen. 19. 14 And Lot went out, and spake unto his sons in law, which married his daughters, and said, Up, get you out of this place; for the LORD will destroy this city. But he seemed as one that mocked unto his sons in law.

Eccl. 8. 11 Because sentence against an evil work is not executed speedily, therefore the heart of the sons of men is fully set in them to do evil.

Isa. 5. 19 That say, Let him make speed, *and* hasten his work, that we may see *it*: and let the counsel of the Holy One of Israel draw nigh and come, that we may know *it*!

Jer. 17. 15 Behold, they say unto me, Where *is* the word of the LORD? let it come now.

Eze. 12. 22 Son of man, what *is* that proverb *that* ye have in the land of Israel, saying, The days are prolonged, and every vision faileth?

Eze. 12. 27 Son of man, behold, *they of* the house of Israel say, The vision that he seeth *is* for many days *to come*, and he prophesieth of the times *that are* far off.

Matt. 24. 48 But and if that evil servant shall say in his heart, My lord delayeth his coming;

Luke 12. 45 But and if that servant say in his heart, My lord delayeth his coming; and shall begin to beat the menservants and maidens, and to eat and drink, and to be drunken;

F

Gen. 1. 6 And God said, Let there be a firmament in the midst of the waters, and let it divide the waters from the waters.

Gen. 1. 9 And God said, Let the waters under the heaven be gathered together unto one place, and let the dry *land* appear: and it was so.

COMING AGAINST SCOFFERS.

F—CONCLUDED.

John 1. 3. *See e, E, § 1, page 5.*

1

Gr. *consisting.*

G

Ps. 24. 2 For he hath founded it upon the seas, and established it upon the floods.

Ps. 136. 6 To him that stretched out the earth above the waters: for his mercy *endureth* for ever.

Col. 1. 17 And he is before all things and by him all things consist:

H

Gen. 7. 11 In the six hundredth year of Noah's life, in the second month, the seventeenth day of the month, the same day were all the fountains of the great deep broken up, and the windows of heaven were opened.

Gen. 7. 21 And all flesh died that moved upon the earth, both of fowl, and of cattle, and of beast, and of every creeping thing that creepeth upon the earth, and every man:

22 All in whose nostrils *was* the breath of life, of all that *was* in the dry *land*, died.

23 And every living substance was destroyed which was upon the face of the ground, both man, and cattle, and the creeping things, and the fowl of the heaven; and they were destroyed from the earth: and Noah only remained *alive*, and they that *were* with him in the ark.

Matt. 24. 38 For as in the days that were before the flood they were eating and drinking, marrying and giving in marriage, until the day that Noe entered into the ark.

39 And knew not until the flood came, and took them all away; so shall also the coming of the Son of man be.

I

II Pet. 3. 10. *See text of topic.*

K

Matt. 10. 15 Verily I say unto you, It shall be more tolerable for the land of Sodom and Gomorrah in the day of judgment, than for that city.

Matt. 11. 22 But I say unto you, It shall be more tolerable for Tyre and Sidon at the day of judgment, than for you.

Matt. 13. 40 As therefore the tares are gathered and burned in the fire; so shall it be in the end of this world.

Matt. 13. 42 And shall cast them into a furnace of fire; there shall be wailing and gnashing of teeth.

Matt. 25. 41 Then shall he say also unto them

K—CONCLUDED.

on the left hand, Depart from me, ye cursed, into everlasting fire, prepared for the devil and his angels:

II Thes. 1. 8 In flaming fire taking vengeance on them that know not God, and that obey not the gospel of our Lord Jesus Christ:

Heb. 10. 27 But a certain fearful looking for of judgment and fiery indignation, which shall devour the adversaries.

Heb. 12. 29 For our God *is* a consuming fire.

Rev. 20. 14 And death and hell were cast into the lake of fire. This is the second death.

15 And whosoever was not found written in the book of life was cast into the lake of fire.

Rev. 21. 8 But the fearful, and unbelieving, and the abominable, and murderers, and whoremongers, and sorcerers, and idolators, and all liars, shall have their part in the lake which burneth with fire and brimstone: which is the second death.

L

Ps. 90. 4 For a thousand years in thy sight *are but* as yesterday when it is past, and *as* a watch in the night.

M

Heb. 10. 37. *See m, M, § 519, page 1206.*

N

Isa. 30. 18 And therefore will the LORD wait, that he may be gracious unto you, and therefore will he be exalted, that he may have mercy upon you: for the LORD *is* a God of judgment: blessed *are* all they that wait for him.

I Pet. 3. 20 Which sometime were disobedient, when once the longsuffering of God waited in the days of Noah, while the ark was a preparing, wherein few, that is, eight souls were saved by water.

II Pet. 3. 15. *See text of topic.*

O

Eze. 18. 23 Have I any pleasure at all that the wicked should die? saith the Lord GOD: *and* not that he should return from his ways, and live?

Eze. 18. 32 For I have no pleasure in the death of him that dieth, saith the Lord GOD: wherefore turn *yourselves*, and live ye.

Eze. 33. 11 Say unto them, *As* I live, saith the Lord GOD, I have no pleasure in the death of the wicked; but that the wicked turn from his way and live: turn ye, turn ye from your evil ways; for why will ye die, O house of Israel?

For P, Q, and R, see next page (1280).

§ 548. PETER DEFENDS THE LORD'S

CHAP. 3.

earth also and the works that are
therein shall be burned up.

11 *Seeing* then *that* all these things
shall be dissolved, what manner *of*
persons ought ye to be [s]in *all* holy
conversation and godliness,

12 [t]Looking for and [2]hasting unto
the coming of the day of God,
wherein the heavens being on fire
shall [u]be dissolved, and the elements
shall [x]melt with fervent heat?

13 Nevertheless we, according to
his promise, look for [y]new heavens
and a new earth, wherein dwelleth
righteousness.

14 Wherefore, beloved, seeing that
ye look for such things, be diligent
[z]that ye may be found of him in
peace, without spot, and blameless.

15 And account *that* [a]the longsuffering of our Lord *is* salvation;
even as our beloved brother Paul
also according to the wisdom given
unto him hath written unto you;

16 As also in all *his* epistles, [b]speak-
ing in them of these things; in which
are some things hard to be understood, which they that are unlearned
and unstable wrest, as *they do* also
the other Scriptures, unto their own
destruction.

17 Ye therefore, beloved, [c]seeing
ye know *these things* before, [d]beware
lest ye also, being led away with the
error of the wicked, fall from your
own steadfastness.

18 [e]But grow in grace, and *in* the
knowledge of our Lord and Saviour
Jesus Christ. [f]To him *be* glory both
now and forever. Amen.

P

Acts 2. 38. *See b, B, § 232, page 640.*

Rom. 2. 4 Or despisest thou the riches of his goodness and forbearance and long-suffering; not knowing that the goodness of God leadeth thee to repentance?

I Tim. 2. 4 Who will have all men to be saved, and to come unto the knowledge of the truth.

Q

Matt. 24. 43. *See a, A, § 174, page 494.*

R

Ps. 102. 26 They shall perish, but thou shalt endure: yea, all of them shall wax old like a garment; as a vesture shalt thou change them, and they shall be changed:

Isa. 51. 6 Lift up your eyes to the heavens, and look upon the earth beneath; for the heavens shall vanish away like smoke, and the earth shall wax old like a garment, and they that dwell therein shall die in like manner: but my salvation shall be for ever, and my righteousness shall not be abolished.

Matt. 5. 18 For verily I say unto you, Till heaven and earth pass, one jot or one tittle shall in no wise pass from the law, till all be fulfilled.

Matt. 24. 35 Heaven and earth shall pass away, but my words shall not pass away.

Heb. 1. 11 They shall perish; but thou remainest; and they all shall wax old as doth a garment;

Rev. 20. 11 And I saw a great white throne, and him that sat on it, from whose face the earth and the heaven fled away; and there was found no place for them.

Rev. 21. 1 And I saw a new heaven and a new earth: for the first heaven and the first earth were passed away; and there was no more sea.

S

I Pet. 1. 15 But as he which hath called you is holy, so be ye holy in all manner of conversation;

T

I Cor. 1. 7 So that ye come behind in no gift; waiting for the coming of our Lord Jesus Christ:

Tit. 2. 13 Looking for that blessed hope, and the glorious appearing of the great God and our Saviour Jesus Christ;

2.

Or, hasting the coming.

COMING AGAINST SCOFFERS (CONCLUDED).

U

Ps. 50. 3 Our God shall come and shall not keep silence: a fire shall devour before him, and it shall be very tempestuous round about him.

Isa. 34. 4 And all the host of heaven shall be dissolved, and the heavens shall be rolled together as a scroll: and all their host shall fall down, as the leaf falleth off from the vine, and as a falling *fig* from the fig tree.

X

Mic. 1. 4 And the mountains shall be molten under him, and the valleys shall be cleft, as wax before the the fire, *and* as the waters *that are* poured down a steep place.

II Pet. 3. 10. *See text of topic.*

Y

Isa. 65. 17 For, behold, I create new heavens and a new earth; and the former shall not be remembered nor come into mind.

Isa. 66. 22 For as the new heavens and new earth, which I will make, shall remain before me, saith the LORD, so shall your seed and your name remain.

Rev. 21. 1. *See under R.*

Rev. 21. 27 And there shall in no wise enter into it any thing that defileth, neither *whatsoever* worketh abomination, or *maketh* a lie: but they which are written in the Lamb's book of life.

Z

I Cor. 1. 8 Who shall also confirm you unto the end, *that ye may be* blameless in the day of our Lord Jesus Christ.

I Cor. 15. 58 Therefore, my beloved brethren, be ye steadfast, unmoveable always abounding in the work of the Lord, forasmuch as ye know that your labour is not in vain in the Lord.

Phil. 1. 10 That ye may approve things that are excellent; that ye may be sincere and without offence till the day of Christ;

I Thes. 3. 13 To the end he may stablish your hearts unblameable in holiness before God, even our Father, at the coming of our Lord Jesus Christ with all his saints.

I Thes. 5. 23 And the very God of peace sanctify you wholly; and *I pray God* your whole spirit and soul and body be preserved blameless unto the coming of our Lord Jesus Christ.

A

Rom. 2. 4. *See under P.*

I Pet. 3. 20. *See under N, page 1279.*

B

Rom. 8. 19 For the earnest expectation of the creature waiteth for the manifestation of the sons of God.

I Cor. 15. 24 Then *cometh* the end, when he shall have delivered up the kingdom to God, even the Father; when he shall have put down all rule, and all authority and power.

I Thes. 4. 15 For this we say unto you by the word of the Lord, that we which are alive *and* remain unto the coming of the Lord shall not prevent them which are asleep.

C

Mark 13. 23 But take ye heed: behold, I have foretold you all things.

II Pet. 1. 12 Wherefore I will not be negligent to put you always in remembrance of these things, though ye know *them*, and be established in the present truth.

D

Eph. 4. 14 That we *henceforth* be no more children, tossed to and fro, and carried about with every wind of doctrine, by the sleight of men, *and* cunning craftiness, whereby they lie in wait to deceive;

II Pet. 1. 10 Wherefore the rather, brethren, give diligence to make your calling and election sure: for if ye do these things, ye shall never fall:

11 For so an entrance shall be ministered unto you abundantly into the everlasting kingdom of our Lord and Saviour Jesus Christ.

II Pet. 2. 18 For when they speak great swelling *words* of vanity, they allure through the lusts of the flesh, *through much* wantonness, those that were clean escaped from them who live in error.

E

Eph. 4. 15 But speaking the truth in love, may grow up into him in all things, which is the head, *even* Christ:

I Pet. 2. 2 As newborn babes, desire the sincere milk of the word, that ye may grow thereby:

F

Rom. 11. 36. *See r, R, § 341, page 866.*

§ 549. INTRODUCTION.

1 : 1–4.

1 That [a]which was from the beginning, which we have heard, which
we have seen with our eyes, [b]which
we have looked upon, and [c]our hands
have handled, of the Word of life;
2 (For [d]the life [e]was manifested, and
we have seen *it*, [f]and bear witness,
[g]and shew unto you that eternal life,
[h]which was with the Father, and was
manifested unto us;)
3 [i]That which we have seen and
heard declare we unto you, that ye
also may have fellowship with us:
and truly [k]our fellowship *is* with the
Father, and with his Son Jesus Christ.
4 And these things write we unto
you, [l]that your joy may be full.

A

Mic. 5. 2 But thou, Beth-lehem, Ephratah, *though* thou be little among the thousands of Judah, *yet* out of thee shall he come forth unto me *that is* to be ruler in Israel; whose goings forth *have been* from of old, from everlasting.

A—CONCLUDED.

John 1. 1. *See a, A, § 1, page 5.*

I Jno. 2. 13 I write unto you, fathers, because ye have known him *that is* from the beginning. I write unto you, young men, because ye have overcome the wicked one. I write unto you, little children, because ye have known the Father.

B

John 1. 14. *See u, U, § 1, page 7.*

II Pet. 1. 16 For we have not followed cunningly devised fables, when we made known unto you the power and coming of our Lord Jesus Christ, but were eyewitnesses of his majesty.

I Jno. 4. 14 And we have seen and do testify that the Father sent the Son *to be* the Saviour of the world.

C

Luke 24. 39 Behold my hands and my feet, that it is I myself: handle me, and see; for a spirit hath not flesh and bones, as ye see me have.

John 20. 27 Then saith he to Thomas, Reach hither thy finger, and behold my hands; and reach hither thy hand, and thrust *it* into my side: and be not faithless, but believing.

D

Ps. 36. 9 For with thee *is* the fountain of life: in thy light shall we see light.

§ 550. GOD IS LIGHT, AND HAS NO FELLOWSHIP WITH

1: 5–10.

5 [a]This then is the message which
we have heard of him, and declare
unto you, that [b]God is light, and in
him is no darkness at all.
6 [c]If we say that we have fellowship
with him, and walk in darkness, we
lie, and do not the truth:
7 But if we [d]walk in the light, as he
is in the light, we have fellowship
one with another, and [e]the blood of
Jesus Christ his Son cleanseth us
from all sin.

A

I Jno. 3. 11 For this is the message that ye heard from the beginning, that we should love one another.

B

John 8. 12. *See a, A, § 111, page 323.*

I Tim. 6. 16 Who only hath immortality, dwelling in the light which no man can approach unto; whom no man hath seen, nor can see: to whom *be* honour and power everlasting. Amen.

C

II Cor. 6. 14 Be ye not unequally yoked together with unbelievers: for what fellowship hath righteousness with unrighteousness? and what communion hath light with darkness?

Written probably about the close of the first century, at Ephesus.

D—CONCLUDED.

John 1. 4 In him was life; and the life was the light of men.

John 6. 35 And Jesus said unto them, I am the bread of life: he that cometh to me shall never hunger; and he that believeth on me shall never thirst.

John 11. 25. *See p, P, § 121, page 361.*

John 14. 6 Jesus saith unto him, I am the way, the truth, and the life: no man cometh unto the Father, but by me.

Col. 3. 4 When Christ, *who is* our life, shall appear, then shall ye also appear with him in glory.

I Jno. 5. 11 And this is the record, that God hath given to us eternal life, and this life is in his Son.

12 He that hath the Son hath life; *and* he that hath not the Son of God hath not life.

E

Rom. 16. 26 But now is made manifest, and by the Scriptures of the prophets, according to the commandment of the everlasting God, made known to all nations for the obedience of faith:

I Tim. 3. 16 And without controversy great is the mystery of godliness: God was manifest in the flesh, justified in the Spirit, seen of angels, preached unto the Gentiles, believed on in the world, received up into glory.

I Jno. 3. 5 And ye know that he was manifested to take away our sins; and in him is no sin.

F

John 21. 24 This is the disciple which testifieth of these things, and wrote these things: and we know that his testimony is true.

Acts 1. 8. *See k, K, § 227, page 628.*

Acts 2. 32 This Jesus hath God raised up, whereof we all are witnesses.

G

John 17. 3 And this is life eternal, that they might know thee the only true God, and Jesus Christ, whom thou hast sent.

I Jno. 5. 20 And we know that the Son of God is come, and hath given us an understanding, that we may know him that is true; and we are in him that is true, *even* in his Son Jesus Christ. This is the true God, and eternal life.

H

John 1. 1, 2. *See a, A, § 1, page 5.*

I

Acts 4. 20 For we cannot but speak the things which we have seen and heard.

K

I Cor. 1. 9. *See h, H, § 349, page 890.*

I Jno. 2. 24 Let that therefore abide in you, which ye have heard from the beginning. If that which ye have heard from the beginning shall remain in you, ye also shall continue in the Son, and in the Father.

L

John 15. 11. *See k, K, § 187, page 531.*
John 16. 24. *See f, F, § 190, page 541.*

DARKNESS. CONFESSION AND FORGIVENESS OF SINS.

C—CONCLUDED.

I Jno. 2. 4 He that saith, I know him, and keepeth not his commandments, is a liar, and the truth is not in him.

D

John 12. 35 Then Jesus said unto them, Yet a little while is the light with you. Walk while ye have the light, lest darkness come upon you: for he that walketh in darkness knoweth not whither he goeth.

E

I Cor. 6. 11 And such were some of you: but ye are washed, but ye are sanctified, but ye are justified in the name of the Lord Jesus, and by the Spirit of our God.

E—CONTINUED.

Eph. 1. 7 In whom we have redemption through his blood, the forgiveness of sins, according to the riches of his grace;

Heb. 9. 14 How much more shall the blood of Christ, who through the eternal Spirit offered himself without spot to God, purge your conscience from dead works to serve the living God?

I Pet. 1. 19 But with the precious blood of Christ, as of a lamb without blemish and without spot:

I Jno. 2. 2 And he is the propitiation for our sins: and not for ours only, but also for *the sins of* the whole world.

For E concluded, see next page (1284).

§ 550. GOD IS LIGHT, AND HAS NO FELLOWSHIP WITH

CHAP. I.

8 [f]If we say that we have no sin, we deceive ourselves, [g]and the truth is not in us.

9 [h]If we confess our sins, he is faithful and just to forgive us *our* sins, and to [i]cleanse us from all unrighteousness.

10 If we say that we have not sinned, we make him a liar, and his word is not in us.

CHAP. I.

E—CONCLUDED.

Rev. 1 5 And from Jesus Christ, *who is* the faithful witness, *and* the first begotten of the dead, and the prince of the kings of the earth. Unto him that loved us, and washed us from our sins in his own blood,

§ 551. JESUS CHRIST OUR ADVOCATE AND A PROPITIATION.

2: 1–11.

1 My little children, these things write I unto you, that ye sin not. And if any man sin, [a]we have an advocate with the Father, Jesus Christ the righteous:

2 And [b]he is the propitiation for our sins: and not for ours only, but [c]also for *the sins of* the whole world.

3 And hereby we do know that we know him, if we keep his commandments.

4 [d]He that saith, I know him, and keepeth not his commandments, [e]is a liar, and the truth is not in him.

5 But [f]whoso keepeth his word, [g]in him verily is the love of God perfected: [h]hereby know we that we are in him.

6 [i]He that saith he abideth in him [k]ought himself also so to walk, even as he walked.

7 Brethren, [l]I write no new commandment unto you, but an old commandment [m]which ye had from the beginning. The old commandment is the word which ye have heard from the beginning.

8 Again, [n]a new commandment I

A

Rom. 8. 34 Who *is* he that condemneth? *It is* Christ that died, yea rather, that is risen again, who is even at the right hand of God, who also maketh intercession for us.

I Tim. 2. 5 For *there is* one God, and one mediator between God and men, the man Christ Jesus;

Heb. 7. 25 Wherefore he is able also to save them to the uttermost that come unto God by him, seeing he ever liveth to make intercession for them.

Heb. 8. 6 But now hath he obtained a more excellent ministry, by how much also he is the mediator of a better covenant, which was established upon better promises.

Heb. 9. 24 For Christ is not entered into the holy places made with hands, *which are* the figures of the true; but into heaven itself, now to appear in the presence of God for us:

B

Rom. 3. 25 Whom God hath set forth *to be* a propitiation through faith in his blood, to declare his righteousness for the remission of sins that are past, through the forbearance of God;

II Cor. 5. 18 And all things *are* of God, who hath reconciled us to himself by Jesus Christ, and hath given to us the ministry of reconciliation;

I Jno. 1. 7 But if we walk in the light, as he is in the light, we have fellowship one with another, and the blood of Jesus Christ his Son cleanseth us from all sin.

I Jno. 4. 10 Herein is love, not that we loved God, but that he loved us, and sent his Son *to be* the propitiation for our sins.

DARKNESS. CONFESSION AND FORGIVENESS OF SINS (CONCLUDED).

F

Job 9. 2 I know *it is* so of a truth: but how should man be just with God?

Job 15. 14 What *is* man, that he should be clean? and *he which is* born of a woman, that he should be righteous?

Job 25. 4 How then can man be justified with God? or how can he be clean *that is* born of a woman?

Jas. 3. 2. *See c, C, § 532, page 1234.*

G

I Jno. 2. 4 He that saith, I know him, and keepeth not his commandments, is a liar, and the truth is not in him.

H

Ps. 32. 5 I acknowledged my sin unto thee, and mine iniquity have I not hid. I said, I will confess my transgressions unto the LORD; and thou forgavest the iniquity of my sin. Selah.

Prov. 28. 13 He that covereth his sins shall not prosper: but whoso confesseth and forsaketh *them* shall have mercy.

I

Ps. 51. 2 Wash me thoroughly from mine iniquity, and cleanse me from my sin.

I John 1. 7. *See text of topic.*

I Cor. 6. 11. *See under E.*

KEEP HIS WORD, LOVE IS LIGHT, HATE IS DARKNESS.

C

John 1. 29. *See z, Z, § 17, page 61.*

John 4. 42 And said unto the woman, Now we believe, not because of thy saying: for we have heard *him* ourselves, and know that this is indeed the Christ, the Saviour of the world.

John 11. 51, 52. *See h, H, § 122, page 367.*

D

I Jno. 1. 6 If we say that we have fellowship with him, and walk in darkness, we lie, and do not the truth:

I Jno. 4. 20 If a man say, I love God, and hateth his brother, he is a liar: for he that loveth not his brother whom he hath seen, how can he love God whom he hath not seen?

21 And this commandment have we from him, That he who loveth God love his brother also.

E

I John 1. 8. *See text of topic, § 550.*

F

John 14. 21 He that hath my commandments, and keepeth them, he it is that loveth me: and he that loveth me shall be loved of my Father, and I will love him, and will manifest myself to him.

John 14. 23 Jesus answered and said unto him, If a man love me, he will keep my words: and my Father will love him, and we will come unto him, and make our abode with him.

G

I Jno. 4. 12 No man hath seen God at any time. If we love one another, God dwelleth in us, and his love is perfected in us.

H

I Jno. 4. 13 Hereby know we that we dwell in him, and he in us, because he hath given us of his Spirit.

I

John 15. 4 Abide in me, and I in you. As the branch cannot bear fruit of itself, except it abide in the vine; no more can ye, except ye abide in me.

5 I am the vine, ye *are* the branches. He that abideth in me, and I in him, the same bringeth forth much fruit; for without me ye can do nothing.

K

Matt. 11. 29. *See f, F, § 48, page 162.*

L

II Jno. 5 And now I beseech thee, lady, not as though I wrote a new commandment unto thee, but that which we had from the beginning, that we love one another.

M

I Jno. 3. 11 For this is the message that ye heard from the beginning, that we should love one another.

II John 5. *See under L.*

N

John 13. 34 A new commandment I give unto you, That ye love one another; as I have loved you, that ye also love one another.

John 15. 12 This is my commandment, That ye love one another, as I have loved you.

O

Rom. 13. 12 The night is far spent, the day is at hand: let us therefore cast off the works of darkness, and let us put on the armour of light.

Eph. 5. 8 For ye were sometime darkness, but now *are ye* light in the Lord: walk as children of light:

I Thes. 5. 5 Ye are all the children of light, and the children of the day: we are not of the night, nor of darkness.

§ 551. JESUS CHRIST OUR ADVOCATE AND A PROPITIATION.

CHAP. 2.

write unto you, which thing is true in him and in you: [o]because the darkness is past, and [p]the true light now shineth.

9 [q]He that saith he is in the light, and hateth his brother, is in darkness even until now.

10 [r]He that loveth his brother abideth in the light, and [s]there is none [1]occasion of stumbling in him.

CHAP. 2.

11 But he that hateth his brother is in darkness, and [t]walketh in darkness, and knoweth not whither he goeth, because that darkness hath blinded his eyes.

O—CONCLUDED. See preceding page (1285).

I Thes. 5. 8 But let us, who are of the day, be sober, putting on the breastplate of faith and love; and for a helmet, the hope of salvation.

P

John 8. 12. *See a, A, § 111, page 323.*

§ 552. SPECIAL MESSAGES. LOVE NOT THE

2 : 12–29.

12 I write unto you, little children, because [a]your sins are forgiven you for his name's sake.

13 I write unto you, fathers, because ye have known him [b]*that is* from the beginning. I write unto you, young men, because ye have overcome the wicked one. I write unto you, little children, because ye have known the Father.

14 I have written unto you, fathers, because ye have known him *that is* from the beginning. I have written unto you, young men, because [c]ye are strong, and [d]the word of God abideth in you, and ye have overcome the wicked one.

15 [e]Love not the world, neither the things *that are* in the world. [f]If any man love the world, the love of the Father is not in him.

16 For all that *is* in the world, the lust of the flesh, and [g]the lust of the eyes, and the pride of life, is not of the Father, but is of the world.

17 And [h]the world passeth away,

CHAP. 2.

and the lust thereof: but he that doeth the will of God abideth for ever.

18 [i]Little children, [k]it is the last time: and as ye have heard that [l]antichrist shall come, [m]even now are there many antichrists; whereby we know [n]that it is the last time.

19 [o]They went out from us, but they were not of us; for [p]if they had been of us, they would *no doubt* have continued with us: but *they went out*, [q]that they might be made manifest that they were not all of us.

20 But [r]ye have an unction from [s]the Holy One, and [t]ye know all things.

A

Ps. 25. 11 For thy name's sake, O LORD, pardon mine iniquity; for it *is* great.

Luke 24. 47. *See i, I, § 219, page 611.*

Acts 10. 43 To him give all the prophets witness, that through his name whosoever believeth in him shall receive remission of sins.

I Jno. 1. 7 But if we walk in the light, as he is in the light, we have fellowship one with another, and the blood of Jesus Christ his Son cleanseth us from all sin.

KEEP HIS WORD, LOVE IS LIGHT, HATE IS DARKNESS (CONCLUDED).

Q

I Cor. 13. 2 And though I have *the gift of* prophecy, and understand all mysteries, and all knowledge; and though I have all faith, so that I could remove mountains, and have not charity, I am nothing.

II Pet. 1. 9 But he that lacketh these things is blind, and cannot see afar off, and hath forgotten that he was purged from his old sins.

I Jno. 3. 14 We know that we have passed from death unto life, because we love the brethren. He that loveth not *his* brother abideth in death.

15 Whosoever hateth his brother is a murderer: and ye know that no murderer hath eternal life abiding in him.

R

I John 3. 14. *See under Q.*

S

II Pet. 1. 10 Wherefore the rather, brethren, give diligence to make your calling and election sure: for if ye do these things, ye shall never fall:

1

Gr. *scandal.*

T

John 12. 35. *See u, U, § 170, page 477.*

WORLD, IT PASSETH AWAY. ANTICHRIST.

B

I Jno. 1. 1 That which was from the beginning, which we have heard, which we have seen with our eyes, which we have looked upon, and our hands have handled, of the Word of life;

C

Eph. 6. 10 Finally, my brethren, be strong in the Lord, and in the power of his might.

D

John 15. 7 If ye abide in me, and my words abide in you, ye shall ask what ye will, and it shall be done unto you.

E

Rom. 12. 2 And be not conformed to this world: but be ye transformed by the renewing of your mind, that ye may prove what *is* that good, and acceptable, and perfect will of God.

F

Matt. 6. 24. *See q, Q, § 43, page 140.*

G

Ps. 119. 37 Turn away mine eyes from beholding vanity; *and* quicken thou me in thy way.

Eccl. 5. 11 When goods increase, they are increased that eat them: and what good *is there* to the owners thereof, saving the beholding *of them* with their eyes?

H

I Cor. 7. 31. *See g, G, § 363, page 916.*

I

John 21. 5 Then Jesus saith unto them, Children, have ye any meat? They answered him, No.

K

Eph. 1. 10. *See o, O, § 426, page 1030.*

L

II Cor. 11. 3, 13. *Study § 403, page 992.*

M

Matt. 24. 5. *See f, F, § 172, page 480.*

N

I Tim. 4. 1 Now the Spirit speaketh expressly, that in the latter times some shall depart from the faith, giving heed to seducing spirits, and doctrines of devils;

O

Deut. 13. 13 *Certain* men, the children of Belial, are gone out from among you, and have withdrawn the inhabitants of their city, saying, Let us go and serve other gods, which ye have not known;

Ps. 41. 9 Yea, mine own familiar friend, in whom I trusted, which did eat of my bread, hath lifted up *his* heel against me.

Acts 20. 30 Also of your own selves shall men arise, speaking perverse things, to draw away disciples after them.

P

Matt. 24. 24. *See s, S, § 173, page 488.*

Q

I Cor. 11. 19 For there must be also heresies among you, that they which are approved may be made manifest among you.

R

I John 2. 27. *See text of topic.*

II Cor. 1. 21 Now he which stablisheth us with you in Christ, and hath anointed us, *is* God;

Heb. 1. 9 Thou hast loved righteousness, and hated iniquity; therefore God, *even* thy God, hath anointed thee with the oil of gladness above thy fellows.

For S and T see next page (1288).

§ 552. SPECIAL MESSAGES. LOVE NOT THE WORLD,

CHAP. 2.

21 I have not written unto you because ye know not the truth, but because ye know it, and that no lie is of the truth.

22 [u]Who is a liar but he that denieth that Jesus is the Christ? He is anti-christ, that denieth the Father and the Son.

23 [x]Whosoever denieth the Son, the same hath not the Father: [*but*] [y]*he that acknowledgeth the Son hath the Father also.*

24 Let that therefore abide in you, [z]which ye have heard from the beginning. If that which ye have heard from the beginning shall remain in you, [a]ye also shall continue in the Son, and in the Father.

25 [b]And this is the promise that he hath promised us, *even* eternal life.

26 These *things* have I written unto you [c]concerning them that seduce you.

27 But [d]the anointing which ye have received of him abideth in you, and [e]ye need not that any man teach you: but as the same anointing teacheth you of all things, and is truth, and is no lie, and even as it hath taught you, ye shall abide in [1]him.

CHAP. 2.

28 And now, little children, abide in him; that, [f]when he shall appear, we may have confidence, [g]and not be ashamed before him at his coming.

29 [h]If ye know that he is righteous, [2]ye know that [i]every one that doeth righteousness is born of him.

S

Mark 1. 24 Saying, Let *us* alone; what have we to do with thee, thou Jesus of Nazareth? art thou come to destroy us? I know thee who thou art, the Holy One of God.

T

John 14. 26. *See k, K, § 186, page 529.*

U

I Jno. 4. 3 And every spirit that confesseth not that Jesus Christ is come in the flesh is not of God: and this is that *spirit* of antichrist, whereof ye have heard that it should come; and even now already is it in the world.

II Jno. 7 For many deceivers are entered into the world, who confess not that Jesus Christ is come in the flesh. This is a deceiver and an antichrist.

X

John 15. 23 He that hateth me hateth my Father also.

II Jno. 9 Whosoever transgresseth, and abideth not in the doctrine of Christ, hath not God. He that abideth in the doctrine of Christ, he hath both the Father and the Son.

Y

John 14. 7-10. *Study, K, L, and M, § 186, page 525.*

I Jno. 4. 15 Whosoever shall confess that Jesus is the Son of God, God dwelleth in him, and he in God.

§ 553. THE LOVE OF GOD. THE SONS OF GOD AND

3: 1–12.

1 Behold, what manner of love the Father hath bestowed upon us, that [a]we should be called the sons of God: therefore the world knoweth us not, [b]because it knew him not.

A

John 1. 12. *See p, P, § 1, page 7.*

B

John 16. 3. *See d, D, § 189, page 535.*

John 17. 25 O righteous Father, the world hath not known thee: but I have known thee, and these have known that thou hast sent me.

IT PASSETH AWAY. ANTICHRIST (Concluded).

Z

II Jno. 6 And this is love, that we walk after his commandments. This is the commandment, That, as ye have heard from the beginning, ye should walk in it.

A

John 14. 23 Jesus answered and said unto him, If a man love me, he will keep my words: and my Father will love him, and we will come unto him, and make our abode with him.

I Jno. 1. 3 That which we have seen and heard declare we unto you, that ye also may have fellowship with us: and truly our fellowship *is* with the Father, and with his Son Jesus Christ.

B

John 17. 3 And this is life eternal, that they might know thee the only true God, and Jesus Christ, whom thou hast sent.

I Jno. 1. 2 (For the life was manifested, and we have seen *it*, and bear witness, and shew unto you that eternal life, which was with the Father, and was manifested unto us;)

I Jno. 5. 11 And this is the record, that God hath given to us eternal life, and this life is in his Son.

C

I Jno. 3. 7 Little children, let no man deceive you: he that doeth righteousness is righteous, even as he is righteous.

II John 7. *See under U.*

D

I John 2. 20. *See text of topic*

E

Jer. 31. 33 But this *shall be* the covenant that I will make with the house of Israel; After those days, saith the LORD, I will put my law in their inward parts, and write it in their hearts; and will be their God, and they shall be my people.

34 And they shall teach no more every man his neighbour, and every man his brother, saying, Know the LORD: for they shall all know me,

E—Concluded.

from the least of them unto the greatest of them, saith the LORD: for I will forgive their iniquity, and I will remember their sin no more.

John 14. 26 But the Comforter, *which is* the Holy Ghost, whom the Father will send in my name, he shall teach you all things, and bring all things to your remembrance, whatsoever I have said unto you.

John 16. 13 Howbeit when he, the Spirit of truth, is come, he will guide you into all truth: for he shall not speak of himself: but whatsoever he shall hear, *that* shall he speak: and he will shew you things to come.

Heb. 8. 8-11. *See k, K, § 514, page 1192.*

1

Or, *it.*

F

I Jno. 3. 2 Beloved, now are we the sons of God, and it doth not yet appear what we shall be: but we know that, when he shall appear, we shall be like him; for we shall see him as he is.

G

I Jno. 4. 17 Herein is our love made perfect, that we may have boldness in the day of judgment: because as he is, so are we in this world.

H

Acts 22. 14 And he said, The God of our fathers hath chosen thee, that thou shouldest know his will, and see that Just One, and shouldest hear the voice of his mouth.

2

Or, *know ye.*

I

I John 3. 7. *See under C.*

I Jno. 3. 10 In this the children of God are manifest, and the children of the devil: whosoever doeth not righteousness is not of God, neither he that loveth not his brother.

THE SONS OF THE DEVIL ARE MANIFEST IN DEEDS.

C

Gal. 3. 26. *See c C, § 417, page 1016.*

Gal. 4. 6 And because ye are sons, God hath sent forth the Spirit of his Son into your hearts, crying, Abba, Father.

D

Rom. 8. 18 For I reckon that the sufferings of this present time *are* not worthy *to be compared* with the glory which shall be revealed in us.

D—Concluded.

I Cor. 2. 9 But as it is written, Eye hath not seen, nor ear heard, neither have entered into the heart of man, the things which God hath prepared for them that love him.

§ 553. THE LOVE OF GOD. THE SONS OF GOD AND THE

CHAP. 3.

2 Beloved, [c]now are we the sons of God, and [d]it doth not yet appear what we shall be: but we know that, when he shall appear, [e]we shall be like him; for [f]we shall see him as he is.

3 [g]And every man that hath this hope in him purifieth himself, even as he is pure.

4 Whosover committeth sin transgresseth also the law: for [h]sin is the transgression of the law.

5 And ye know [i]that he was manifested [k]to take away our sins; and [l]in him is no sin.

6 Whosoever abideth in him sinneth not: [m]whosoever sinneth hath not seen him, neither known him.

7 Little children, [n]let no man deceive you: [o]he that doeth righteousness is righteous, even as he is righteous.

8 [p]He that committeth sin is of the devil; for the devil sinneth from the beginning. For this purpose the Son of God was manifested, [q]that he might destroy the works of the devil.

9 [r]Whosoever is born of God doth not commit sin; for [s]his seed remaineth in him: and he cannot sin, because he is born of God.

10 In this the children of God are manifest, and the children of the devil: [t]whosoever doeth not righteousness is not of God, [u]neither he that loveth not his brother.

11 For [x]this is the [1]message that ye heard from the beginning, [y]that we should love one another.

12 Not as [z]Cain, *who* was of that wicked one, and slew his brother. And wherefore slew he him? Because his own works were evil, and his brother's righteous.

For C and D, see preceding page (1289).

E

Ps. 17. 15 As for me, I will behold thy face in righteousness: I shall be satisfied, when I awake, with thy likeness.

Rom. 8. 29 For whom he did foreknow, he also did predestinate *to be* conformed to the image of his Son, that he might be the firstborn among many brethren.

I Cor. 15. 49 And as we have borne the image of the earthy, we shall also bear the image of the heavenly.

Phil. 3. 21 Who shall change our vile body, that it may be fashioned like unto his glorious body, according to the working whereby he is able even to subdue all things unto himself.

II Pet. 1. 4 Whereby are given unto us exceeding great and precious promises; that by these ye might be partakers of the divine nature, having escaped the corruption that is in the world through lust.

F

Job 19. 26 And *though* after my skin *worms* destroy this *body*, yet in my flesh shall I see God:

Ps. 16. 11 Thou wilt shew me the path of life: in thy presence *is* fulness of joy; at thy right hand *there are* pleasures for evermore.

Matt. 5. 8 Blessed *are* the pure in heart: for they shall see God.

I Cor. 13. 12 For now we see through a glass, darkly; but then face to face: now I know in part; but then shall I know even as also I am known.

G

I Jno. 4. 17 Herein is our love made perfect, that we may have boldness in the day of judgment: because as he is, so are we in this world.

H

Rom. 4. 15 Because the law worketh wrath: for where no law is, *there is* no transgression.

Rom. 7. 9 For I was alive without the law once: but when the commandment came, sin revived, and I died.

10 And the commandment, which *was ordained* to life, I found *to be* unto death.

11 For sin, taking occassion by the commandment, deceived me, and by it slew *me*.

12 Wherefore the law *is* holy, and the commandment holy, and just, and good.

SONS OF THE DEVIL ARE MANIFEST IN DEEDS (CONCLUDED).

H—CONCLUDED.

Rom. 7. 13 Was then that which is good made death unto me? God forbid. But sin, that it might appear sin, working death in me by that which is good; that sin by the commandment might become exceeding sinful.

I Jno. 5. 17 All unrighteousness is sin: and there is a sin not unto death.

I

I John 1. 2. *See e, E, § 549, page 1282.*

K

Isa. 53. 5 But he *was* wounded for our transgressions, *he was* bruised for our iniquities: the chastisement of our peace *was* upon him; and with his stripes we are healed.

6 All we like sheep have gone astray; we have turned every one to his own way; and the LORD hath laid on him the iniquity of us all.

I Tim. 1. 15 This *is* a faithful saying, and worthy of all acceptation, that Christ Jesus came into the world to save sinners; of whom I am chief.

Heb. 1. 3 Who being the brightness of *his* glory, and the express image of his person, and upholding all things by the word of his power, when he had by himself purged our sins, sat down on the right hand of the Majesty on high;

Heb. 9. 26 For then must he often have suffered since the foundation of the world: but now once in the end of the world hath he appeared to put away sin by the sacrifice of himself.

I Pet. 2. 24 Who his own self bare our sins in his own body on the tree, that we, being dead to sins, should live unto righteousness: by whose stripes ye were healed.

L

I Pet. 2. 22. *See x, X, § 539, page 1256.*

M

I John 2. 4. *See d, D, § 551, page 1284.*

I Jno. 4. 8 He that loveth not, knoweth not God; for God is love.

N

I Jno. 2. 26 These *things* have I written unto you concerning them that seduce you.

O

Eze. 18. 5 But if a man be just, and do that which is lawful and right,

6 *And* hath not eaten upon the mountains, neither hath lifted up his eyes to the idols of the house of Israel, neither hath defiled his neighbor's wife, neither hath come near to a menstruous woman,

O—CONCLUDED.

7 And hath not oppressed any, *but* hath restored to the debtor his pledge, hath spoiled none by violence, hath given his bread to the hungry, and hath covered the naked with a garment;

8 He *that* hath not given forth upon usury, neither hath taken any increase, *that* hath withdrawn his hand from iniquity, hath executed true judgment between man and man,

9 Hath walked in my statutes, and hath kept my judgments, to deal truly; he *is* just, he shall surely live, saith the Lord GOD.

Rom. 2. 13. *See n, N, § 320, page 818.*

P

Matt. 13. 38. *See c, C, § 66, page 208.*

Q

Gen. 3. 15 And I will put enmity between thee and the woman, and between thy seed and her seed; it shall bruise thy head, and thou shalt bruise his heel.

John 16. 11. *See o, O, § 189, page 537.*

R

I Jno. 5. 18 We know that whosoever is born of God sinneth not; but he that is begotten of God keepeth himself, and that wicked one toucheth him not.

S

I Pet. 1. 23 Being born again, not of corruptible seed, but of incorruptible, by the word of God, which liveth and abideth for ever.

T

I Jno. 2. 29 If ye know that he is righteous, ye know that every one that doeth righteousness is born of him.

U

I Jno. 4. 8 He that loveth not knoweth not God; for God is love.

X

I Jno. 1. 5 This then is the message which we have heard of him, and declare unto you, that God is light, and in him is no darkness at all.

I Jno. 2. 7 Brethren, I write no new commandment unto you, but an old commandment which ye had from the beginning. The old commandment is the word which ye have heard from the beginning.

1

Or, *commandment.*

Y

John 13. 34. *See y, Y, § 183, page 519.*

Z

Jude 11. *See m, M, § 566, page 1310.*

§ 554. WE MAY KNOW WE ARE OF THE TRUTH

3: 13–24.

13 Marvel not, my brethren, if [a]the world hate you.

14 [b]We know that we have passed from death unto life, because we love the brethren. [c]He that loveth not *his* brother abideth in death.

15 [d]Whosoever hateth his brother is a murderer: and ye know that [e]no murderer hath eternal life abiding in him.

16 [f]Hereby perceive we the love *of God*, because he laid down his life for us: and we ought to lay down *our* lives for the brethren.

17 But [g]whoso hath this world's good, and seeth his brother have need, and shutteth up his bowels *of compassion* from him, [h]how dwelleth the love of God in him?

18 My little children, [i]let us not love in word, neither in tongue; but in deed and in truth.

19 And hereby we know [k]that we are of the truth, and shall [1]assure our hearts before him.

20 [l]For if our heart condemn us, God is greater than our heart, and knoweth all things.

21 [m]Beloved, if our heart condemn us not, [n]*then* have we confidence toward God.

22 And [o]whatsoever we ask, we receive of him, because we keep his commandments, and do those things that are pleasing in his sight.

23 [p]And this is his commandment, That we should believe on the name of his Son Jesus Christ, [q]and love one another, as he gave us commandment.

CHAP. 3.

24 And [r]he that keepeth his commandments [s]dwelleth in him, and he in him. And [t]hereby we know that he abideth in us, by the Spirit which he hath given us.

A

John 17. 14. *See d, D, § 191, page 545.*

B

I Jno. 2. 10 He that loveth his brother abideth in the light, and there is none occasion of stumbling in him.

C

I John 2. 9, 11. *See q, Q, § 551, page 1286.*

D

Prov. 26. 24 He that hateth dissembleth with his lips, and layeth up deceit within him;

25 When he speaketh fair, believe him not: for *there are* seven abominations in his heart.

26 *Whose* hatred is covered by deceit, his wickedness shall be shewed before the *whole* congregation.

Matt. 5. 21 Ye have heard that it was said by them of old time, Thou shalt not kill; and whosoever shall kill shall be in danger of the judgment:

22 But I say unto you, That whosoever is angry with his brother without a cause shall be in danger of the judgment; and whosoever shall say to his brother, Raca, shall be in danger of the council: but whosoever shall say, Thou fool, shall be in danger of hell fire.

I Jno. 4. 20 If a man say, I love God, and hateth his brother, he is a liar: for he that loveth not his brother whom he hath seen, how can he love God whom he hath not seen?

E

Gal. 5. 21. *See f, F, § 422, page 1024.*

F

IJohn 3. 16 Hereby perceive we the love *of God*, because he laid down his life for us: and we ought to lay down *our* lives for the brethren.

John 15. 13 Greater love hath no man than this, that a man lay down his life for his friends.

Eph. 5. 2 And walk in love, as Christ also hath loved us, and hath given himself for us an offering and a sacrifice to God for a sweetsmelling savour.

Eph. 5. 25 Husbands, love your wives, even as Christ also loved the church, and gave himself for it;

IF WE LIVE IN THE DEED OF THE TRUTH.

G

Duet. 15. 7 If there be among you a poor man of one of thy brethren within any of thy gates in thy land which the LORD thy God giveth thee, thou shalt not harden thine heart, nor shut thine hand from thy poor brother;

Luke 3. 11. *See q, Q, § 14, page 51.*

H

I John 4. 20. *See under D.*

I

Eze. 33. 31 And they come unto thee as the people cometh, and they sit before thee *as* my people, and they hear thy words, but they will not do them: for with their mouth they shew much love, *but* their heart goeth after their covetousness.

Rom. 12. 9 *Let* love be without dissimulation. Abhor that which is evil; cleave to that which is good.

Eph. 4. 15 But speaking the truth in love, may grow up into him in all things, which is the head, *even* Christ:

Jas. 2. 15, 16. *See b, B, § 531, page 1232*

I Pet. 1. 22 Seeing ye have purified your souls in obeying the truth through the Spirit unto unfeigned love of the brethren, *see that ye* love one another with a pure heart fervently:

K

John 18. 37 Pilate therefore said unto him, Art thou a king then? Jesus answered, Thou sayest that I am a king. To this end was I born, and for this cause came I into the world, that I should bear witness unto the truth. Every one that is of the truth heareth my voice.

I Jno. 1. 8 If we say that we have no sin, we deceive ourselves, and the truth is not in us.

1

Gr, *persuade.*

L

I Cor. 4. 4 For I know nothing by myself; yet am I not hereby justified: but he that judgeth me is the Lord.

M

Job 22. 26 For then shalt thou have thy delight in the Almighty, and shalt lift up thy face unto God.

N

Heb. 10. 22 Let us draw near with a true heart in full assurance of faith, having our hearts sprinkled from an evil conscience, and our bodies washed with pure water.

N—CONCLUDED.

I Jno. 2. 28 And now, little children, abide in him; that, when he shall appear, we may have confidence, and not be ashamed before him at his coming.

I Jno. 4. 17 Herein is our love made perfect, that we may have boldness in the day of judgment: because as he is, so are we in this world.

O

Ps. 34. 15 The eyes of the LORD *are* upon the righteous, and his ears *are open* unto their cry.

Ps. 145. 18 The LORD *is* nigh unto all them that call upon him, to all that call upon him in truth.

19 He will fulfill the desire of them that fear him: he also will hear their cry, and will save them.

Prov. 15. 29 The LORD *is* far from the wicked: but he heareth the prayer of the righteous.

Jer. 29. 12 Then shall ye call upon me, and ye shall go and pray unto me, and I will hearken unto you.

Matt. 7. 8. *See k, K, § 43, page 144.*

P

Deut. 18. 15 The LORD thy God will raise up unto thee a Prophet from the midst of thee, of thy brethren, like unto me; unto him ye shall hearken;

Deut. 18. 19 And it shall come to pass, *that* whosoever will not hearken unto my words which he shall speak in my name, I will require *it* of him.

John 6. 29 Jesus answered and said unto them, This is the work of God, that ye believe on him whom he hath sent.

John 14. 1 Let not your heart be troubled: ye believe in God, believe also in me.

Q

John 13. 34. *See y, Y, § 183, page 519.*

R

John 15. 10. *See i, I, § 187, page 531.*

S

John 17. 21. *See o, O, § 191, page 547.*

T

Rom. 8. 9 But ye are not in the flesh, but in the Spirit, if so be that the Spirit of God dwell in you. Now if any man have not the Spirit of Christ, he is none of his.

Rom. 8. 14 For as many as are led by the Spirit of God, they are the sons of God.

I Jno. 4. 18 There is no fear in love; but perfect love casteth out fear: because fear hath torment. He that feareth is not made perfect in love.

4: 1–6.

1 Beloved, [a]believe not every spirit,
but [b]try the spirits whether they are
of God: because [c]many false prophets are gone out into the world.

2 Hereby know ye the Spirit of
God: [d]Every spirit that confesseth
that Jesus Christ is come in the flesh
is of God:

3 And [e]every spirit that confesseth
not that Jesus Christ is come in the
flesh is not of God: and this is that
spirit of antichrist, whereof ye have
heard that it should come; and [f]even
now already is it in the world.

4 [g]Ye are of God, little children,
and have overcome them: because
greater is he that is in you, than [h]he
that is in the world.

5 [i]They are of the world: therefore
speak they of the world, and [k]the
world heareth them.

6 We are of God: [l]he that knoweth
God heareth us; he that is not of
God heareth not us. Hereby know
we [m]the spirit of truth, and the spirit
of error.

§ 555. THE PROOF OF THE SPIRIT OF

A

Jer. 29. 8 For thus saith the LORD of hosts, the God of Israel; Let not your prophets and your diviners, that *be* in the midst of you, deceive you, neither hearken to your dreams which ye cause to be dreamed.

Matt. 24. 4 And Jesus answered and said unto them, Take heed that no man deceive you.

B

I Cor. 14. 29 Let the prophets speak two or three, and let the other judge.

I Thes. 5. 21 Prove all things; hold fast that which is good.

Rev. 2. 2 I know thy works, and thy labour, and thy patience, and how thou canst not bear them which are evil: and thou hast tried them which say they are apostles, and are not, and hast found them liars:

C

Matt. 24. 4. 5. *Study E, F and G, page 480.*

II Cor. 11. 13. *See t, T, § 403, page 994.*

II Jno. 7 For many deceivers are entered into the world, who confess not that Jesus Christ is come in the flesh. This is a deceiver and an antichrist.

D

I Cor. 12. 3 Wherefore I give you to understand, that no man speaking by the Spirit of God calleth Jesus accursed: and *that* no man can say that Jesus is the Lord, but by the Holy Ghost.

I Jno. 5. 1 Whosoever believeth that Jesus is the Christ is born of God: and every

4: 7–21.

7 [a]Beloved, let us love one another:
for love is of God; and every one
that loveth is born of God, and
knoweth God.

8 He that loveth not, [b]knoweth not
God; for [c]God is love.

9 [d]In this was manifested the love of
God toward us, because that God sent
his only begotten Son into the world,
[e]that we might live through him.

10 Herein is love, [f]not that we
loved God, but that he loved us.

§ 556. GOD IS LOVE. GOD LOVES US.

A

I Jno. 3. 10 In this the children of God are manifest, and the children of the devil: whosoever doeth not righteousness is not of God, neither he that loveth not his brother.

11 For this is the message that ye heard from the beginning, that we should love one another.

I Jno. 3. 23 And this is his commandment, That we should believe on the name of his Son Jesus Christ, and love one another, as he gave us commandment.

B

I Jno. 2. 4 He that saith, I know him, and keepeth not his commandments, is a liar, and the truth is not in him.

I Jno. 3. 6 Whosoever abideth in him sinneth not: whosoever sinneth hath not seen him, neither known him.

TRUTH AND THE SPIRIT OF ERROR.

D—CONCLUDED.

one that loveth him that begat loveth him also that is begotten of him.

E

I Jno. 2. 22 Who is a liar but he that denieth that Jesus is the Christ? He is antichrist, that denieth the Father and the Son.

II John 7. *See under C.*

F

II Thes. 2. 7. *See k, K, § 467, page 1112.*

G

I Jno. 5. 4 For whatsoever is born of God overcometh the world: and this is the victory that overcometh the world, *even* our faith.

H

John 12. 31. *See n, N, § 170, page 475.*

I

John 3. 31 He that cometh from above is above all: he that is of the earth is earthly, and speaketh of the earth: he that cometh from heaven is above all.

K

John 15. 19 If ye were of the world, the world would love his own: but because ye are not of the world, but I have chosen you out of the world, therefore the world hateth you.

John 17. 14 I have given them thy word; and the world hath hated them, because they are not of the world, even as I am not of the world.

L

John 8. 47 He that is of God heareth God's words: ye therefore hear *them* not, because ye are not of God.

L—CONCLUDED.

John 10. 27 My sheep hear my voice, and I know them, and they follow me:

I Cor. 14. 37 If any man think himself to be a prophet, or spiritual, let him acknowledge that the things that I write unto you are the commandments of the Lord.

II Cor. 10. 7 Do ye look on things after the outward appearance? If any man trust to himself that he is Christ's, let him of himself think this again, that, as he *is* Christ's, even so *are* we Christ's.

M

Isa. 8. 20 To the law and to the testimony: if they speak not according to this word, *it is* because *there is* no light in them.

John 14. 17 *Even* the spirit of truth; whom the world cannot receive, because it seeth him not, neither knoweth him: but ye know him; for he dwelleth with you, and shall be in you.

John 16. 13 Howbeit when he, the Spirit of truth, is come, he will guide you into all truth: for he shall not speak of himself; but whatsoever he shall hear, *that* shall he speak: and he will shew you things to come.

I Jno. 2. 27 But the anointing which ye have received of him abideth in you, and ye need not that any man teach you: but as the same anointing teacheth you of all things, and is truth, and is no lie, and even as it hath taught you, ye shall abide in him.

WE OUGHT TO LOVE ONE ANOTHER.

C

Ex. 34. 6 And the LORD passed by before him, and proclaimed, The LORD, The LORD God, merciful and gracious, longsuffering, and abundant in goodness and truth,

Ps. 86. 5 For thou, Lord, *art* good, and ready to forgive; and plenteous in mercy unto all them that call upon thee.

Ps. 86. 15 But thou, O Lord, *art* a God full of compassion, and gracious, longsuffering, and plenteous in mercy and truth.

Mic. 7. 18 Who *is* a God like unto thee, that pardoneth iniquity, and passeth by the transgression of the remnant of his heritage? he retaineth not his anger for ever, because he delighteth *in* mercy.

C—CONCLUDED.

II Cor. 13. 11 Finally, brethren, farewell. Be perfect, be of good comfort, be of one mind, live in peace; and the God of love and peace shall be with you.

Eph. 2. 4 But God, who is rich in mercy, for his great love wherewith he loved us,

I John 4. 16. *See text of topic.*

D

Rom. 5. 8 But God commendeth his love toward us, in that, while we were yet sinners, Christ died for us.

Rom. 8. 32 He that spared not his own Son, but delivered him up for us all, how shall he not with him also freely give us all things?

I John 3. 16. *See f, F, § 554, page 1292.*

For E and F, see next page (1296).

§ 556. GOD IS LOVE. GOD LOVES US. WE

CHAP. 4.

and sent his Son [g]*to be* the propitiation for our sins.
11 Beloved, [h]if God so loved us,
we ought also to love one another.
12 [i]No man hath seen God at any
time. If we love one another, God
dwelleth in us, and [k]his love is perfected in us.
13 [l]Hereby know we that we dwell in
him, and he in us, because he hath
given us of his Spirit.
14 And [m]we have seen and do testify
that [n]the Father sent the Son *to be*
the Saviour of the world.
15 [o]Whosoever shall confess that
Jesus is the Son of God, God dwelleth in him, and he in God.
16 And we have known and believed the love that God hath to us.
[p]God is love; and [q]he that dwelleth
in love dwelleth in God, and God in
him.
17 Herein is [1]our love made perfect, that [r]we may have boldness in
the day of judgment: [s]because as he
is, so are we in this world.
18 There is no fear in love; but perfect love casteth out fear: because
fear hath torment. He that feareth
[t]is not made perfect in love.
19 We love him, because he first
loved us.
20 [u]If a man say, I love God, and
hateth his brother, he is a liar: for
he that loveth not his brother whom
he hath seen, how can he love God
[x]whom he hath not seen?
21 And [y]this commandment have
we from him, That he who loveth
God love his brother also.

E

I Jno. 5. 11 And this is the record, that God hath given to us eternal life, and this life is in his Son.

F

John 15. 16 Ye have not chosen me, but I have chosen you, and ordained you, that ye should go and bring forth fruit, and *that* your fruit should remain: that whatsoever ye shall ask of the Father in my name, he may give it you.

Rom. 5. 8 But God commendeth his love toward us, in that, while we were yet sinners, Christ died for us.

Rom. 8. 32 He that spared not his own Son, but delivered him up for us all, how shall he not with him also freely give us all things?

G

I Jno. 2. 2. *See b, B, § 551, page 1284.*

§ 557. THE SPIRIT BEARETH WITNESS. ALL THAT

5: 1–12.

1 Whosoever [a]believeth that [b]Jesus
is the Christ is [c]born of God: [d]and
every one that loveth him that begat
loveth him also that is begotten of
him.
2 By this we know that we love the
children of God, when we love God,
and keep his commandments.
3 [e]For this is the love of God, that

A

John 1. 12. *See p, P, § 1, page 7.*

B

I Jno. 2. 22 Who is a liar but he that denieth that Jesus is the Christ? He is antichrist, that denieth the Father and the Son.

I Jno. 4. 2 Hereby know ye the Spirit of God: Every spirit that confesseth that Jesus Christ is come in the flesh is of God:

I John 4. 15. *See text of topic, § 556.*

C

John 1. 13. *See q, Q, § 1, page 7.*

OUGHT TO LOVE ONE ANOTHER (CONCLUDED).

H

Matt. 18. 33. *See d, D, § 104, page 354.*
John 15. 12. 13. *Study A and B, page 533.*

I

John 1. 18. *See h, H, § 17, page 59.*

K

I Jno. 2. 5 But whoso keepeth his word, in him verily is the love of God perfected: hereby know we that we are in him.

I John 4. 18. *See text of topic.*

L

John 14. 20 At that day ye shall know that I *am* in my Father, and ye in me, and I in you.

I John 3. 24. *See t, T, § 554, page 1292.*

M

John 1. 14. *See u, U, § 1, page 7.*

N

John 3. 17. *See q, Q, § 22, page 73.*

O

Rom. 10. 9. *See h, H, § 337, page 858.*

I Jno. 5. 1 Whosoever believeth that Jesus is the Christ is born of God: and every one that loveth him that begat loveth him also that is begotten of him.

I Jno. 5. 5 Who is he that overcometh the world, but he that believeth that Jesus is the Son of God?

P

I John 4. 8. *See text of topic, Study C.*

Q

I Jno. 3. 24 And he that keepeth his commandments dwelleth in him, and he in him. And hereby we know that he abideth in us, by the Spirit which he hath given us.

I John 4. 12. *See text of topic.*

1

Gr. *love with us.*

R

Jas. 2. 13 For he shall have judgment without mercy, that hath showed no mercy; and mercy rejoiceth against judgment.

I Jno. 2. 28 And now, little children, abide in him; that, when he shall appear, we may have confidence, and not be ashamed before him at his coming.

I Jno. 3. 19 And hereby we know that we are of the truth, and shall assure our hearts before him.

20 For if our heart condemn us, God is greater than our heart, and knoweth all things.

21 Beloved, if our heart condemn us not, *then* have we confidence toward God.

S

Luke 6. 40 The disciple is not above his master: but every one that is perfect shall be as his master.

I Jno. 3. 3 And every man that hath this hope in him purifieth himself, even as he is pure.

T

Jas. 2. 22 Seest thou how faith wrought with his works, and by works was faith made perfect?

I John 4. 12. *See text of topic.*

U

I Jno. 2. 4 He that saith, I know him, and keepeth not his commandments, is a liar, and the truth is not in him.

I Jno. 3. 17 But whoso hath this world's good, and seeth his brother have need, and shutteth up his bowels *of compassion* from him, how dwelleth the love of God in him?

X

John 1. 18. *See h, H, § 17, page 59.*

Y

Matt. 22. 37, 39. *See d, D, § 165, page 460.*
John 13. 34. *See y, Y, § 183, page 519.*

BELIEVE OVERCOME THE WORLD AND HAVE LIFE.

D

John 15. 23 He that hateth me hateth my Father also.

E

John 14. 15 If ye love me, keep my commandments.

John 14. 21 He that hath my commandments, and keepeth them, he it is that loveth me: and he that loveth me shall be loved of my Father, and I will love him, and will manifest myself to him.

John 14. 23 Jesus answered and said unto him, If a man love me, he will keep my

E—CONCLUDED.

words: and my Father will love him, and we will come unto him, and make our abode with him.

John 15. 10 If ye keep my commandments, ye shall abide in my love; even as I have kept my Father's commandments, and abide in his love.

II Jno. 6 And this is love, that we walk after his commandments. This is the commandment, That, as ye have heard from the beginning, ye should walk in it.

§ 557. THE SPIRIT BEARETH WITNESS. ALL THAT BELIEVE

CHAP. 5.

we keep his commadnments: [f]and his commandments are not grievous.

4 For [g]whatsoever is born of God overcometh the world: and this is the victory that overcometh the world, *even* our faith.

5 Who is he that overcometh the world, but [h]he that believeth that Jesus is the Son of God?

6 This is he that came [i]by water and blood, *even* Jesus Christ; not by water only, but by water and blood. [k]And it is the Spirit that beareth witness, because the Spirit is truth.

7 For there are three that bear record in heaven, the Father, [l]the Word, and the Holy Ghost: [m]and these three are one.

8 And there are three that bear witness in earth, the spirit, and the water, and the blood, and these three agree in one.

9 If we receive the [n]witness of men, the witness of God is greater: [o]for this is the witness of God which he hath testified of his Son.

10 He that believeth on the Son of God [p]hath the witness in himself: he that believeth not God [q]hath

CHAP. 5.

made him a liar; because he believeth not the record that God gave of his Son.

11 [r]And this is the record, that God hath given to us eternal life, and [s]this life is in his Son.

12 [t]He that hath the Son hath life; *and* he that hath not the Son of God hath not life.

F

Ps. 119. 45 And I will walk at liberty: for I seek thy precepts.

Prov. 3. 17 Her ways *are* ways of pleasantness, and all her paths *are* peace.

Mic. 6. 8 He hath shewed thee, O man, what *is* good; and what doth the LORD require of thee, but to do justly, and to love mercy, and to walk humbly with thy God?

Matt. 11. 30 For my yoke *is* easy, and my burden is light.

Rom. 7. 12 Wherefore the law *is* holy and the commandment holy, and just, and good.

G

John 16. 33. *See t, T, § 190, page 541.*

H

I Cor. 15. 57 But thanks *be* to God, which giveth us the victory through our Lord Jesus Christ.

I Jno. 4. 15 Whosoever shall confess that Jesus is the Son of God, God dwelleth in him, and he in God.

I

John 19. 34. *See d, D, § 209, page 593*

K

John 15. 26. *See t, T, § 188, page 535.*

I Tim. 3. 16 And without controversy great is the mystery of godliness: God was manifest in the flesh, justified in the Spirit, seen of angels, preached unto the Gentiles, believed on in the world, received up into glory.

§ 558. THESE THINGS ARE WRITTEN UNTO BELIEVERS

5 : 13-21.

13 [a]These things have I written unto you that believe on the name of the Son of God; [b]that ye may know that ye have eternal life, and that ye may believe on the name of the Son of God.

14 And this is the confidence that

CHAP. 5.

we have [1]in him, that, [c]if we ask any thing according to his will, he heareth us:

15 And if we know that he hear us, whatsoever we ask, we know that we have the petitions that we desired of him.

OVERCOME THE WORLD AND HAVE LIFE (Concluded).

L

John 1. 1 In the beginning was the word, and the Word was with God, and the Word was God.

Heb. 4. 12 For the word of God is quick, and powerful, and sharper than any two-edged sword, piercing even to the dividing asunder of soul and spirit, and of the joints and marrow, and *is* a discerner of the thoughts and intents of the heart.

I Jno. 1. 1 That which was from the beginning, which we have heard, which we have seen with our eyes, which we have looked upon, and our hands have handled, of the word of life;

Rev. 19. 13 And he *was* clothed with a vesture dipped in blood: and his name is called The Word of God.

M

Deut. 6. 4 Hear, O Israel: The LORD our God *is* one LORD:

John 10. 30 I and *my* Father are one.

N

John 8. 17. *See g, G, § 111, page 325.*

O

Matt. 3. 16. 17. *Study E and G, page 52.*

P

Rom. 8. 16 The Spirit itself beareth witness with our spirit, that we are the children of God:

Gal. 4. 6 And because ye are sons, God hath sent forth the Spirit of his Son into your hearts, crying, Abba, Father.

Q

John 3. 33 He that hath received his testimony hath set to his seal that God is true.

John 5. 38 And ye have not his word abiding in you: for whom he hath sent, him ye believe not.

Q—Concluded.

I Jno. 1. 10 If we say that we have not sinned, we make him a liar, and his word is not in us.

R

I Jno. 2. 25 And this is the promise that he hath promised us, *even* eternal life.

S

John 1. 4. In him was life; and the life was the light of men.

I Jno. 4. 9 In this was manifested the love of God toward us because that God sent his only begotten Son into the world, that we might live through him.

T

John 3. 36 He that believeth on the Son hath everlasting life: and he that believeth not the Son shall not see life; but the wrath of God abideth on him.

John 5. 24 Verily, verily, I say unto you, He that heareth my word, and believeth on him that sent me, hath everlasting life, and shall not come into condemnation; but is passed from death unto life.

John 6. 40 And this is the will of him that sent me, that every one which seeth the Son, and believeth on him, may have everlasting life: and I will raise him up at the last day.

John 6. 47 Verily, verily, I say unto you, He that believeth on me hath everlasting life.

John 6. 54 Whoso eateth my flesh, and drinketh my blood, hath eternal life; and I will raise him up at the last day.

John 6. 63 It is the Spirit that quickeneth; the flesh that profiteth nothing: the words that I speak unto you, *they* are spirit, and *they* are life.

John 6. 68 Then Simon Peter answered him, Lord, to whom shall we go? thou hast the words of eternal life.

THAT THEY MAY KNOW THEY HAVE ETERNAL LIFE.

A

John 20. 31 But these are written, that ye might believe that Jesus is the Christ, the Son of God; and that believing ye might have life through his name.

B

John 21. 24 This is the disciple which testifieth of these things, and wrote these things: and we know that his testimony is true.

25 And there are also many other

B—Concluded.

things which Jesus did, the which, if they should be written every one, I suppose that even the world itself could not contain the books that should be written. Amen.

I Jno. 1. 2 (For the life was manifested, and we have seen *it*, and bear witness, and shew unto you that eternal life, which was with the Father, and was manifested unto us;)

For I and C, see next page (1300).

§ 558. THESE THINGS ARE WRITTEN UNTO BELIEVERS THAT

CHAP. 5.

16 If any man see his brother sin a sin *which is* not unto death, he shall ask, and [d]he shall give him life for them that sin not unto death. [e]There is a sin unto death: [f]I do not say that he shall pray for it.

17 [g]All unrighteousness is sin: and there is a sin not unto death.

18 We know that [h]whosoever is born of God sinneth not; but he that is begotten of God [i]keepeth himself, and that wicked one toucheth him not.

19 *And* we know that we are of God, and [k]the whole world lieth in wickedness.

20 And we know that the Son of God is come, and [l]hath given us an understanding, [m]that we may know him that is true, and we are in him that is true, *even* in his Son Jesus Christ. [n]This is the true God, [o]and eternal life.

21 Little children, keep [p]yourselves from idols. Amen.

1

Or, *concerning him.*

C

I Jno. 3. 22. *See o, O, § 554, page 1292.*

D

Job 42. 8 Therefore take unto you now seven bullocks and seven rams, and go to my servant Job, and offer up for yourselves a burnt offering; and my servant Job shall pray for you: for him will I accept: lest I deal with you *after your* folly, in that ye have not spoken of me *the thing which is* right, like my servant Job.

James 5. 14, 15. *See t, T, § 535, page 1242.*

E

Matt. 12. 31. *See t, T, § 51, page 170.*

F

Jer. 7. 16 Therefore pray not thou for this people, neither lift up cry nor prayer for them, neither make intercession to me: for I will not hear thee.

Jer. 14. 11 Then said the LORD unto me, Pray not for this people for *their* good.

John 17. 9 I pray for them: I pray not for the world, but for them which thou hast given me; for they are thine.

G

I John 3. 4. *See h, H, § 553, page 1290.*

H

John. 1. 12 But as many as received him, to them gave he power to become the sons of God, *even* to them that believe on his name:

13 Which were born, not of blood, nor of the will of the flesh, nor of the will of man, but of God.

Rom. 8. 14 For as many as are led by the Spirit of God, they are the sons of God.

THE SECOND

§ 559. SALUTATION TO THE ELECT LADY

1–3.

1 The [a]elder unto the elect lady and her children, [b]whom I love in the truth; and not I only, but also all they that have known [c]the truth;

2 For the truth's sake, which dwelleth in us, and shall be with us for ever.

3 [d]Grace [1]be with you, mercy, *and*

A

I Pet. 5. 1 The elders which are among you I exhort, who am also an elder, and a witness of the sufferings of Christ, and also a partaker of the glory that shall be revealed:

B

I Jno. 3. 18 My little children, let us not love in word, neither in tongue; but in deed and in truth.

III Jno. 1 The elder unto the well beloved Gaius, whom I love in the truth.

THEY MAY KNOW THEY HAVE ETERNAL LIFE (CONCLUDED).

H—CONCLUDED.

Rom. 8. 15 For ye have not received the spirit of bondage again to fear; but ye have received the Spirit of adoption, whereby we cry, Abba, Father.

16 The Spirit itself beareth witness with our spirit, that we are the children of God:

I Pet. 1. 23 Being born again, not of corruptible seed, but of incorruptible, by the word of God, which liveth and abideth for ever.

I Jno. 3. 9 Whosoever is born of God doth not commit sin; for his seed remaineth in him: and he cannot sin, because he is born of God.

I

Jas. 1. 27 Pure religion and undefiled before God and the Father is this, To visit the fatherless and widows in their affliction, *and* to keep himself unspotted from the world.

K

Gal. 1. 4 Who gave himself for our sins, that he might deliver us from this present evil world, according to the will of God and our Father:

L

Luke 24. 45 Then opened he their understanding, that they might understand the Scriptures,

M

John 17. 3 And this is life eternal, that they might know thee the only true God, and Jesus Christ, whom thou hast sent.

N

Isa. 9. 6 For unto us a child is born, unto

N—CONCLUDED.

us a son is given: and the government shall be upon his shoulder: and his name shall be called Wonderful, Counsellor, The mighty God, The everlasting Father, The Prince of Peace.

Isa. 44. 6 Thus saith the LORD the King of Israel, and his Redeemer the LORD of hosts; I *am* the first, and I *am* the last; and besides me *there is* no God.

Isa. 54. 5 For thy Maker *is* thine husband; The LORD of hosts *is* his name; and thy Redeemer the Holy One of Israel; The God of the whole earth shall he be called.

John 20. 28 And Thomas answered and said unto him, My Lord and my God.

Rom 9. 5 Whose *are* the fathers, and of whom as concerning the flesh Christ *came*, who is over all, God blessed for ever. Amen.

I Tim. 3. 16 And without controversy great is the mystery of godliness: God was manifest in the flesh, justified in the Spirit, seen of angels, preached unto the Gentiles, believed on in the world, received up into glory.

Tit. 2. 13 Looking for that blessed hope, and the glorious appearing of the great God and our Saviour Jesus Christ;

Heb. 1. 8 But unto the Son *he saith*, Thy throne, O God, *is* for ever and ever: a sceptre of righteousness *is* the sceptre of thy kingdom.

O

I John 5. 11, 13. *See text of topic §§557, 558.*

P

I Cor. 10. 14. *See a, A, § 367, page 928.*

EPISTLE OF JOHN.

Written probably about the close of the first century.

C

John 8. 32 And ye shall know the truth, and the truth shall make you free.

Gal. 2. 5 To whom we gave place by subjection, no, not for an hour; that the truth of the gospel might continue with you.

Gal. 3. 1 O foolish Galatians, who hath bewitched you, that ye should not obey the truth, before whose eyes Jesus Christ hath been evidently set forth, crucified among you?

Gal. 5. 7 Ye did run well; who did hinder

C—CONTINUED.

you that ye should not obey the truth?

Col. 1. 5 For the hope which is laid up for you in heaven, whereof ye heard before in the word of the truth of the gospel;

II Thes. 2. 13 But we are bound to give thanks alway to God for you, brethren beloved of the Lord, because God hath from the beginning chosen you to salvation through sanctification of the Spirit and belief of the truth:

For C concluded, D and 1, see next page (1302).

§ 559. SALUTATION TO THE

1--3.

peace, from God the Father, and
from the Lord Jesus Christ, the Son
of the Father, [e]in truth and love.

C—CONCLUDED.

I Tim. 2. 4 Who will have all men to be saved, and to come unto the knowledge of the truth.

D

II Cor. 1. 2. *See c, C, § 385, page 962.*

§ 560. REJOICING. EXHORTATION TO LOVE AND

4–11.

4 I rejoiced greatly that I found of
thy children [a]walking in truth, as we
have received a commandment from
the Father.
5. And now I beseech thee, lady,
[b]not as though I wrote a new commandment unto thee, but that which
we had from the beginning, [c]that we
love one another.
6 And [d]this is love, that we walk
after his commandments. This is
the commandment, That, [e]as ye have
heard from the beginning, ye should
walk in it.
7 For [f]many deceivers are entered
into the world, [g]who confess not that
Jesus Christ is come in the flesh.
[h]This is a deceiver and an antichrist.
8 [i]Look to yourselves, [k]that we
lose not those things which we have
[1]wrought, but that we receive a full
reward.
9 [l]Whosoever transgresseth, and
abideth not in the doctrine of Christ,
hath not God. He that abideth in
the doctrine of Christ, he hath both
the Father and the Son.
10 If there come any unto you, and
bring not this doctrine, receive him
not into *your* house, [m]neither bid him
God speed:
11 For he that biddeth him God
speed is partaker of his evil deeds.

A

III Jno. 3 For I rejoiced greatly, when the brethren came and testified of the truth that is in thee, even as thou walkest in the truth.

B

I Jno. 2. 7 Brethren, I write no new commandment unto you, but an old commandment which ye had from the beginning. The old commandment is the word which ye have heard from the beginning.
8 Again, a new commandment I write unto you, which thing is true in him and in you: because the darkness is past, and the true light now shineth.

I Jno. 3. 11 For this is the message that ye heard from the beginning, that we should love one another.

C

John 13. 34. *See y, Y, § 183, page 519.*

§ 561. CONCLUDING

12, 13.

12 [a]Having many things to write
unto you, I would not *write* with
paper and ink: but [b]I trust to come
unto you, and speak [1]face to face,
[c]that [2]our joy may be full.
13 [d]The children of thy elect sister
greet thee. Amen.

A

John 16. 12 I have yet many things to say unto you, but ye cannot bear them now.

A—CONCLUDED.

III Jno. 13 I had many things to write, but I will not with ink and pen write unto thee:

B

Rom. 15. 24 Whensoever I take my journey into Spain, I will come to you: for I trust to see you in my journey, and to be brought on my way thitherward by you, if first I be somewhat filled with your *company*.

Rom. 1. 13 Now I would not have you ignorant, brethren, that oftentimes I purposed to come unto you, (but was let

ELECT LADY (CONCLUDED).

D—CONCLUDED.

I Tim. 1. 2 Unto Timothy, *my* own son in the faith: Grace, mercy, *and* peace, from God our Father and Jesus Christ our Lord.

1

Gr. *shall be.*

E

II Jno. 1 The elder unto the elect lady and her children, whom I love in the truth; and not I only, but also all they that have known the truth;

OBEDIENCE. WARNING AGAINST ANTICHRIST.

D

John 14. 15 If ye love me, keep my commandments.

I Jno. 2. 5 But whoso keepeth his word, in him verily is the love of God perfected: hereby know we that we are in him.

I Jno. 5. 3. *See e, E, § 557, page 1296.*

E

I Jno. 2. 24 Let that therefore abide in you, which ye have heard from the beginning. If that which ye have heard from the beginning shall remain in you, ye also shall continue in the Son, and in the Father.

F

Matt. 24. 4, 5. *Study E, F, and G, page 480.*

G

I Jno. 4. 2 Hereby know ye the Spirit of God: Every spirit that confesseth that Jesus Christ is come in the flesh is of God:
3 And every spirit that confesseth not that Jesus Christ is come in the flesh is not of God: and this is that *spirit* of antichrist, whereof ye have heard that it should come; and even now already is it in the world.

H

I Jno. 2. 22 Who is a liar but he that denieth that Jesus is the Christ? He is antichrist, that denieth the Father and the Son.

I John 4. 3. *See under G.*

I

Mark 13. 9 But take heed to yourselves: for they shall deliver you up to councils; and in the synagogues ye shall be beaten: and ye shall be brought before rulers and kings for my sake, for a testimony against them.

K

Gal. 3. 4 Have ye suffered so many things in vain? if *it be* yet in vain.

Heb. 10. 32 But call to remembrance the former days, in which, after ye were illuminated, ye endured a great fight of afflictions;

Heb. 10. 35 Cast not away therefore your confidence, which hath great recompense of reward.

1

Or, *gained*: Some copies read, *which ye have gained, but that ye received &c,*

L

I Jno. 2. 23 Whosoever denieth the Son, the same hath not the Father: [*but*] *he that acknowledgeth the Son hath the Father also.*

M

Rom. 16. 17. *See k, K, § 374, page 884.*

Gal. 1. 8 But though we, or an angel from heaven, preach any other gospel unto you than that which we have preached unto you, let him be accursed.

SALUTATION.

B—CONTINUED.

hitherto,) that I might have some fruit among you also, even as among other Gentiles.

Phile. 22 But withal prepare me also a lodging: for I trust that through your prayers I shall be given unto you.

1

Gr. *mouth to mouth.*

C

John 16. 24 Hitherto have ye asked nothing in my name: ask, and ye shall receive, that your joy may be full.

John 17. 13 And now come I to thee; and these things I speak in the world, that

C—CONCLUDED.

they might have my joy fulfilled in themselves.

Rom. 15. 13 Now the God of hope fill you with all joy and peace in believing, that ye may abound in hope, through the power of the Holy Ghost.

I Jno. 1. 4 And these things write we unto you, that your joy may be full.

2

Or, *your.*

D

I Pet. 5. 13 The *church that is* at Babylon, elected together with *you*, saluteth you; and *so doth* Marcus my son.

§ 562. SALUTATION OF REJOICING UNTO GAIUS.

1–4.

1 The elder unto the well beloved Gaius, [a]whom I love [1]in the truth.

2 Beloved, [2]I wish above all things that [b]thou mayest prosper and be in health, [c]even as thy soul prospereth.

3 For I rejoiced greatly, when the brethren came and testified of the truth that is in thee, even as [d]thou walkest in the truth.

4 [e]I have no greater joy than to hear that [f]my children walk in truth.

A

II Jno. 1 The elder unto the elect lady and her children, whom I love in the truth; and not I only, but also all they that have known the truth;

1

Or, *truly.*

2

Or, *pray.*

B

Ps. 20. 1 The LORD hear thee in the day of trouble; the name of the God of Jacob defend thee;

2 Send thee help from the sanctuary, and strengthen thee out of Zion;

3 Remember all thy offerings, and accept thy burnt sacrifice; Selah.

4 Grant thee according to thine own heart, and fulfill all thy counsel.

5 We will rejoice in thy salvation, and in the name of our God we will set up *our* banners: the LORD fulfill all thy petitions.

C

Col. 1. 4 Since we heard of your faith in Christ Jesus, and of the love *which ye have* to all the saints.

5 For the hope which is laid up for you in heaven, whereof ye heard before in the word of the truth of the gospel;

6 Which is come unto you, as *it is* in all the world; and bringeth forth fruit, as *it doth* also in you, since the day

§ 563. COMMENDATIONS TO

5–8.

5 Beloved, thou doest faithfully whatsoever thou doest to the brethren, and to strangers;

6 Which [a]have borne witness of thy charity before the church: whom if thou bring forward on their journey [1]after a godly sort, thou shalt do well:

7 Because that for his name's sake they went forth, [b]taking nothing of the Gentiles.

8 We therefore ought to receive such, that we might be fellow helpers to the truth.

A

Phile. 5 Hearing of thy love and faith, which thou hast toward the Lord Jesus, and toward all saints;

6 That the communication of thy faith may become effectual by the acknowledging of every good thing which is in you in Christ Jesus.

7 For we have great joy and consolation in thy love, because the bowels of

A—CONCLUDED.

the saints are refreshed by thee, brother.

1

Gr. *worthy of God.*

B

II Ki. 5. 15 And he returned to the man of God, he and all his company, and came, and stood before him: and he said, Behold, now I know that *there is* no God in all the earth, but in Israel: now therefore, I pray thee, take a blessing of thy servant.

16 But he said *As* the LORD liveth, before whom I stand, I will receive none. And he urged him to take *it*; but he refused.

II Ki. 5. 25 But he went in, and stood before his master. And Elisha said unto him, Whence *comest thou*, Gehazi? And he said, Thy servant went no whither.

26 And he said unto him, Went not mine heart *with thee*, when the man turned again from his chariot to meet thee. *Is it* a time to receive money, and to receive garments, and oliveyards, and vineyards, and sheep, and

EPISTLE OF JOHN.

Written probably about the close of the first century.

C—CONCLUDED.

ye heard *of it*, and knew the grace of
God in truth:

IThes. 1. 7 So that ye were ensamples to all
that believe in Macedonia and Achaia.

IThes. 1. 8 For from you sounded out the
word of the Lord not only in Macedonia
and Achaia, but also in every
place your faith to Godward is spread
abroad; so that we need not to speak
any thing.

IThes. 3. 6 But now when Timotheus came
from you unto us, and brought us
good tidings of your faith and charity,
and that ye have good remembrance of
us always, desiring greatly to see us,
as we also *to see* you:
7 Therefore, brethren, we were comforted
over you in all our affliction and
distress by your faith:
8 For now we live, if ye stand fast
in the Lord.
9 For what thanks can we render to
God again for you, for all the joy
wherewith we joy for your sakes before
our God;

D

II Jno. 4 I rejoice greatly that I found of
thy children walking in truth, as we
have received a commandment from
the Father.

E

Prov. 23. 24 The father of the righteous shall
greatly rejoice: and he that begetteth
a wise *child* shall have joy of him.

IThes. 2. 19 For what *is* our hope, or joy, or
crown of rejoicing? *Are* not even ye
in the presence of our Lord Jesus
Christ at his coming?
20 For ye are our glory and joy.

F

I Cor. 4. 15 For though ye have ten thousand
instructors in Christ, yet *have ye* not
many fathers: for in Christ Jesus I have
begotten you through the gospel.

Gal. 4. 19 My little children, of whom I
travail in birth again until Christ be
formed in you.

Phile. 10 I beseech thee for my son Onesimus,
whom I have begotten in my
bonds:

GAIUS FOR HIS HOSPITALITY.

B—CONTINUED.

oxen, and menservants, and maidservants?

II Ki. 5. 27 The leprosy therefore of Naaman
shall cleave unto thee, and unto thy
seed for ever. And he went out from
his presence a leper *as white* as snow.

Neh. 6. 2 That Sanballat and Geshem sent
unto me, saying, Come, let us meet together
in *some one of* the villages in
the plain of Ono. But they thought
to do me mischief.
3 And I sent messengers unto them,
saying, I *am* doing a great work, so
that I cannot come down: why should
the work cease, whilst I leave it, and
come down to you?

I Cor. 9. 12 If others be partakers of *this*
power over you, *are* not we rather?
Nevertheless we have not used this
power; but suffer all things, lest we
should hinder the gospel of Christ.
13 Do ye not know that they which
minister about holy things live *of the
things* of the temple? and they which
wait at the altar are partakers with the
altar?
14 Even so hath the Lord ordained

B—CONCLUDED.

that they which preach the gospel
should live of the gospel.

I Cor. 9. 15 But I have used none of these
things: neither have I written these
things, that it should be so done unto
me: for *it were* better for me to die,
than that any man should make my
glorying void.

I Cor. 9 18 What is my reward then? *Verily*
that, when I preach the gospel, I
may make the gospel of Christ without
charge, that I abuse not my power in
the gospel.

IICo. 11. 7 Have I committed an offence in
abasing myself that ye might be exalted,
because I have preached to you
the gospel of God freely?
8 I robbed other churches, taking
wages *of them*, to do you service.
9 And when I was present with you,
and wanted, I was chargeable to no
man: for that which was lacking to
me the brethren which came from
Macedonia supplied: and in all *things*
I have kept myself from being burdensome
unto you and *so* will I keep *myself*.

§ 564. THE UNCOMMENDABLE CONDUCT OF DIOTREPHES.

9–14

9 I wrote unto the church: but Diotrephes, [a]who loveth to have the preeminence among them, receiveth us not.

10 Wherefore, if I come, I will remember his deeds which he doeth, prating against us with malicious words: and not content therewith, neither doth he himself receive the brethren, and forbiddeth them that would, and casteth *them* out of the church.

11 Beloved, [b]follow not that which is evil, but that which is good. [c]He that doeth good is of God: but he that doeth evil hath not seen God.

12 Demetrius [d]hath good report of all *men*, and of the truth itself: yea,

9–14.

and we *also* bear record; and [e]ye know that our record is true.

13 [f]I had many things to write, but I will not with ink and pen write unto thee:

14 But I trust I shall shortly see thee, and we shall speak [1]face to face. Peace *be* to thee. *Our* friends salute thee. Greet the friends by name.

A

Matt. 23. 4 For they bind heavy burdens and grievous to be borne, and lay *them* on men's shoulders; but they *themselves* will not move them with one of their fingers.

5 But all their works they do for to be seen of men: they make broad their phylacteries, and enlarge the borders of their garments,

6 And love the uppermost rooms at feasts, and the chief seats in the synagogues,

THE EPISTLE

§ 565. SALUTATION AND EXHORTATION

1–4.

1 Jude, the servant of Jesus Christ, and [a]brother of James, to them that are sanctified by God the Father, and [b]preserved in Jesus Christ, *and* [c]called:

2 Mercy unto you, and [d]peace, and love, be multiplied.

3 Beloved, when I gave all diligence to write unto you [e]of the common salvation, it was needful for me to write unto you, and exhort *you* that [f]ye should earnestly con-

A

Luke 6. 16 And Judas *the brother* of James, and Judas Iscariot, which also was the traitor.

A—CONCLUDED.

Acts 13. 13 And when they were come in, they went up into an upper room, where abode both Peter, and James, and John and Andrew, Philip, and Thomas, Bartholomew, and Matthew, James *the son* of Alpheus, and Simon Zelotes, and Judas *the brother* of James.

B

John 17. 11 And now I am no more in the world, but these are in the world, and I come to thee. Holy Father, keep through thine own name those whom thou hast given me, that they may be one, as we *are*.

12 While I was with them in the world, I kept them in thy name: those that thou gavest me I have kept, and none of them is lost, but the son of perdition; that the Scripture might be fulfilled,

DEMETRIUS. CONCLUDING SALUTATION.

A—CONCLUDED.

Matt.23. 7 And greetings in the markets, and to be called of men, Rabbi, Rabbi.

8 But be not ye called Rabbi: for one is your Master, *even* Christ; and all ye are brethren.

B

Ex. 23. 2 Thou shalt not follow a multitude to *do* evil; neither shalt thou speak in a cause to decline after many to wrest *judgment*:

Ps. 37. 27 Depart from evil, and do good; and dwell for evermore.

Prov.12. 11 He that tilleth his land shall be satisfied with bread: but he that followeth vain *persons is* void of understanding.

12 The wicked desireth the net of evil *men*: but the root of the righteous yieldeth *fruit*.

Isa. 1. 16 Wash you, make you clean; put away the evil of your doings from before mine eyes; cease to do evil;

17 Learn to do well; seek judgment, relieve the oppressed, judge the fatherless, plead for the widow.

I Pet. 3. 11 Let him eschew evil, and do good; let him seek peace, and ensue it.

C

I Jno. 2. 29 If ye know that he is righteous, ye know that every one that doeth righteousness is born of him.

I Jno. 3. 6 Whosoever abideth in him sinneth not: whosoever sinneth hath not seen him, neither known him.

I Jno. 3. 9 Whosoever is born of God doth not commit sin; for his seed remaineth in him: and he cannot sin, because he is born of God.

D

I Tim. 3. 7 Moreover he must have a good report of them which are without; lest he fall into reproach and the snare of the devil.

E

John 21. 24 This is the disciple which testifieth of these things, and wrote these things: and we know that his testimony is true.

F

II Jno. 12 Having many things to write unto you, I would not *write* with paper and ink: but I trust to come unto you, and speak face to face, that our joy may be full.

1

Cr. *mouth to mouth.*

OF JUDE.

OF WARNING. Written probably A. D. 65.

B—CONCLUDED.

John 17. 15 I pray not that thou shouldest take them out of the world, but that thou shouldest keep them from the evil.

I Pet. 1. 5 Who are kept by the power of God through faith unto salvation ready to be revealed in the last time.

C

Rom. 8. 28. *See F and L, page 848.*

D

I Pet. 1. 2. *See f, F, § 536, page 1246.*

E

Isa. 45. 22 Look unto me, and be ye saved, all the ends of the earth: for I *am* God, and *there is* none else.

Gal. 3. 28 There is neither Jew nor Greek, there is neither bond nor free, there is neither male nor female: for ye are all one in Christ Jesus.

Tit. 1 4 To Titus, *mine* own son after the common faith: Grace, mercy, *and*

E—CONCLUDED.

peace, from God the Father and the Lord Jesus Christ our Saviour.

F

I Cor. 9. 23 And this I do for the gospel's sake, that I might be partaker thereof with *you*.

24 Know ye not that they which run in a race run all, but one receiveth the prize? So run, that ye may obtain.

25 And every man that striveth for the mastery is temperate in all things. Now they *do it* to obtain a corruptible crown; but we an incorruptible.

26 I therefore so run, not as uncertainly; so fight I, not as one that beateth the air:

27 But I keep under my body, and bring *it* into subjection: lest that by any means, when I have preached to others, I myself should be a castaway.

For F concluded see next page (1308).

§ 565. SALUTATION AND EXHORTATION

1–4.

tend for the faith which was once delivered unto the saints.

4 [g]For there are certain men crept in unawares, [h]who were before of old ordained to this condemnation, ungodly men, [i]turning [k]the grace of our God into lasciviousness, and [l]denying the only Lord God, and our Lord Jesus Christ.

F—CONCLUDED.

I Cor. 9. 24, 27. *See O and P, page 926.*

G

Gal. 2. 4 And that because of false brethren unawares brought in, who came in privily to spy out our liberty which we have in Christ Jesus, that they might bring us into bondage:

II Pet. 2. 1 But there were false prophets also among the people, even as there shall be false teachers among you, who privily shall bring in damnable heresies, even denying the Lord that bought them, and bring upon themselves swift destruction.

H

Rom. 9. 21 Hath not the potter power over the clay, of the same lump to make one vessel unto honour, and another unto dishonour?

22 *What* if God, willing to shew *his*

§ 566. WARNINGS BY SCRIPTURAL EXAMPLE

5–23.

5 I will therefore put you in remembrance, though ye once knew this, [a]how that the Lord, having saved the people out of the land of Egypt, afterward destroyed them that believed not.

6 And [b]the angels which kept not their [1]first estate, but left their own habitation, he hath reserved in everlasting chains under darkness [c]unto the judgment of the great day.

7 Even as [d]Sodom and Gomorrah, and the cities about them in like manner, giving themselves over to fornication, and going after [2]strange flesh, are set forth for an example, suffering the vengeance of eternal fire.

8 [e]Likewise also these *filthy* dreamers defile the flesh, despise dominion, and [f]speak evil of dignities.

9 Yet [g]Michael the archangel, when contending with the devil he disputed about [h]the body of Moses, [i]durst not bring against him a railing accusation, but said, [k]The Lord rebuke thee.

10 [l]But these speak evil of those things which they know not: but what they know naturally, as brute beasts, in those things they corrupt themselves.

A

I Cor. 10. 1-13. *Study § 366, page 726.*

B

John 8. 44 Ye are of *your* father the devil, and the lusts of your father ye will do. He was a murderer from the beginning, and abode not in the truth, because there is no truth in him. When he speaketh a lie, he speaketh of his own: for he is a liar, and the father of it.

II Pet. 2. 4 For if God spared not the angels that sinned, but cast *them* down to hell, and delivered *them* into chains of darkness, to be reserved unto judgment;

1

Gr. *principality.*

C

Rev 20. 10 And the devil that deceived them was cast into the lake of fire and brimstone, where the beast and the false prophet *are*, and shall be tormented day and night for ever and ever.

OF WARNING (CONCLUDED).

H—CONCLUDED.

wrath, and to make his power known, endured with much longsuffering the vessels of wrath fitted to destruction:

I Pet. 2. 8 And a stone of stumbling, and a rock of offence, *even to them* which stumble at the word, being disobedient: whereunto also they were appointed.

I

Rom. 6. 1 What shall we say then? Shall we continue in sin, that grace may abound?
2 God forbid. How shall we, that are dead to sin, live any longer therein?

K

Tit. 2. 11. *See p, P, § 497, page 1158.*

Heb. 12. 15 Looking diligently lest any man fail of the grace of God; lest any

K—CONCLUDED.

root of bitterness springing up trouble *you*, and thereby many be defiled;

L

Tit. 1. 16 They profess that they know God; but in works they deny *him*, being abominable, and disobedient, and unto every good work reprobate.

II Pet. 2. 1. *See under G.*

I Jno. 2. 22 Who is a liar but he that denieth that Jesus is the Christ? He is antichrist, that denieth the Father and the Son.

I Jno. 4. 3 And every spirit that confesseth not that Jesus Christ is come in the flesh is not of God: and this is that *spirit* of antichrist, whereof ye have heard that it should come; and even now already is it in the world.

AGAINST THE UNGODLINESS OF THE LAST DAYS.

D

II Pet. 2. 6. *See p, P, § 547, page 1274.*

2

Gr. *other.*

E

II Pet. 2. 10 But chiefly them that walk after the flesh in the lust of uncleanness, and despise government. Presumptuous *are they*, selfwilled, they are not afraid to speak evil of dignities.

F

Ex. 22. 28 Thou shalt not revile the gods, nor curse the ruler of thy people.

G

Da. 10. 13 But the prince of the kingdom of Persia withstood me one and twenty days: but, lo, Michael, one of the chief princes, came to help me; and I remained there with the kings of Persia.

Da. 12. 1 And at that time shall Michael stand up, the great prince which standeth for the children of thy people: and there shall be a time of trouble, such as never was since there was a nation *even* to that same time: and at that time thy people shall be delivered, every one that shall be found written in the book.

Rev. 12. 7 And there was war in heaven: Michael and his angels fought against the dragon; and the dragon fought and his angels.

H

Deut. 34. 6 And he buried him in a valley in the land of Moab, over against Bethpeor: but no man knoweth of his sepulchre unto this day.

I

II Pet. 2. 11 Whereas angels, which are greater in power and might, bring not railing accusation against them before the Lord.

K

Zech. 3. 2 And the LORD said unto Satan, the LORD rebuke thee, O Satan; even the LORD that hath chosen Jerusalem rebuke thee: *is* not this a brand plucked out of the fire?

L

II Pet. 2. 12 But these, as natural brute beasts made to be taken and destroyed, speak evil of the things that they understand not; and shall utterly perish in their own corruption;

M

Gen. 4. 4 And Abel, he also brought of the firstlings of his flock and of the fat thereof. And the LORD had respect unto Abel and to his offering:
5 But unto Cain and to his offering he had not respect. And Cain was very wroth, and his countenance fell.

Gen. 4. 8 And Cain talked with Abel his brother: and it came to pass, when they were in the field, that Cain rose up against Abel his brother, and slew him.

Heb. 11. 4 By faith Abel offered unto God a more excellent sacrifice than Cain, by which he obtained witness that he was righteous, God testifying of his gifts: and by it he being dead yet speaketh.

§ 566. WARNINGS BY SCRIPTURAL EXAMPLE AGAINST

5–23.

11 Woe unto them! for they have gone in the way [m]of Cain, and [n]ran greedily after the error of Balaam for reward, and perished [o]in the gainsaying of Core.

12 [p]These are spots in your [q]feasts of charity, when they feast with you, feeding themselves without fear: [r]clouds *they are* without water, [s]carried about of winds; trees [t]whose fruit withereth, without fruit, twice dead, [u]plucked up by the roots;

13 [x]Raging waves of the sea, [y]foaming out their own shame; [z]wandering stars, [a]to whom is reserved the blackness of darkness for ever.

14 And Enoch also, [b]the seventh from Adam, prophesied of these, saying, Behold, [c]the Lord cometh with ten thousand of his saints,

15 [d]To execute judgment upon all, and to convince all that are ungodly among them of all their ungodly deeds which they have ungodly committed, and of all their [e]hard *speeches* which ungodly sinners have spoken against him.

16 These are murmurers, complainers, walking after their own lusts; and [f]their mouth speaketh great swelling *words*, [g]having men's persons in admiration because of advantage.

17 [h]But, beloved, remember ye the words which were spoken before of the apostles of our Lord Jesus Christ;

18 How that they told you [i]there should be mockers in the last time, who should walk after their own ungodly lusts.

M—Conclu'd. See preceding page (1309)

I Jno. 3. 12 Not as Cain, *who* was of that wicked one, and slew his brother. And wherefore slew he him? Because his own works were evil, and his brother's righteous.

N

II Pet. 2. 15. *See f, F, § 547, page 1276.*

O

Num. 16. 1 Now Korah, the son of Izhar, the son of Kohath, the son of Levi, and Dathan and Abiram, the sons of Eliab, and On, the son of Peleth, sons of Reuben, took *men:*

2 And they rose up before Moses, with certain of the children of Israel, two hundred and fifty princes of the assembly, famous in the congregation, men of renown:

3 And they gathered themselves together against Moses and against Aaron, and said unto them, *Ye take* too much upon you, seeing all the congregation *are* holy, every one of them, and the LORD *is* among them: wherefore then lift ye up yourselves above the congregation of the LORD?

P

II Pet. 2. 13 And shall receive the reward of unrighteousness *as* they that count it pleasure to riot in the daytime. Spots *they are* and blemishes, sporting themselves with their own deceivings while they feast with you;

Q

I Cor. 11. 21 For in eating every one taketh before *other* his own supper: and one is hungry, and another is drunken.

R

Prov. 25. 14 Whoso boasteth himself of a false gift *is like* clouds and wind without rain.

II Pet. 2. 17 These are wells without water, clouds that are carried with a tempest; to whom the mist of darkness is reserved for ever.

S

Eph. 4. 14 That we *henceforth* be no more children, tossed to and fro, and carried about with every wind of doctrine, by the sleight of men, *and* cunning craftiness, whereby they lie in wait to deceive;

T

John 15. 6. *See e, E, § 187, page 531.*

THE UNGODLINESS OF THE LAST DAYS CONTINUED).

U

Matt. 15. 13 But he answered and said, Every plant, which my heavenly Father hath not planted, shall be rooted up.

X

Isa. 57. 2 He shall enter into peace: they shall rest in their beds, *each one* walking *in* his uprightness.

Y

Phil. 3. 19 Whose end *is* destruction, whose God *is their* belly, and *whose* glory *is* in their shame, who mind earthly things.)

Z

Rev. 8. 10 And the third angel sounded, and there fell a great star from heaven, burning as it were a lamp, and it fell upon the third part of the rivers, and upon the fountains of waters;

11 And the name of the star is called Wormwood: and the third part of the waters became wormwood; and many men died of the waters, because they were made bitter.

A

II Pet. 2. 17. *See under R.*

B

Gen. 5. 18 And Jared lived a hundred sixty and two years, and he begat Enoch:

C

Deut. 33. 2 And he said, The LORD came from Sinai, and rose up from Seir unto them; he shined forth from mount Paran, and he came with ten thousands of saints: from his right hand *went* a fiery law for them.

Da. 7. 10 A fiery stream issued and came forth from before him: thousand thousands ministered unto him, and ten thousand times ten thousand stood before him: the judgment was set, and the books were opened.

Matt. 25. 31. *See a, A, § 177, page 502.*

D

Rev. 20. 13 And the sea gave up the dead which were in it; and death and hell delivered up the dead which were in them: and they were judged every man according to their works.

E

I Sa. 2. 3 Talk no more so exceeding proudly; let *not* arrogancy come out of your mouth: for the LORD *is* a God of knowledge, and by him actions are weighed.

E—CONCLUDED.

Ps. 31. 18 Let the lying lips be put to silence; which speak grievous things proudly and contemptuously against the righteous.

Ps. 73. 9 They set their mouth against the heavens, and their tongue walketh through the earth.

Ps. 94. 4 *How long* shall they utter *and* speak hard things? *and* all the workers of iniquity boast themselves?

Mal. 3. 13 Your words have been stout against me, saith the LORD. Yet ye say, What have we spoken *so much* against thee?

F

II Pet. 2. 18 For when they speak great swelling *words* of vanity, they allure through the lusts of the flesh, *through much* wantonness, those that were clean escaped from them who live in error.

G

Jas. 2. 1, 9. *See b, B, § 530, page 1230.*

H

II Pet. 3. 2 That ye may be mindful of the words which were spoken before by the holy prophets, and of the commandment of us the apostles of the Lord and Saviour:

I

I Tim. 4. 1. *See b, B, § 478, page 1126.*

II Tim. 4. 3 For the time will come when they will not endure sound doctrine; but after their own lusts shall they heap to themselves teachers, having itching ears;

II Pet. 2. 1 But there were false prophets also among the people, even as there shall be false teachers among you, who privily shall bring in damnable heresies, even denying the Lord that bought them, and bring upon themselves swift destruction.

K

Prov. 18. 1 Through desire a man, having separated himself, seeketh *and* intermeddleth with all wisdom.

Eze. 14. 7 For every one of the house of Israel, or of the stranger that sojourneth in Israel, which separateth himself from me, and setteth up his idols in his heart, and putteth the stumbling block of his iniquity before his face, and cometh to a prophet to enquire of him concerning me; I the LORD will answer him by myself:

§ 566. WARNINGS BY SCRIPTURAL EXAMPLE AGAINST

5–23.

19 These be they [k]who separate themselves, [l]sensual, having not the Spirit.

20 But ye, beloved, [m]building up yourselves on your most holy faith, [n]praying in the Holy Ghost,

21 Keep yourselves in the love of God, [o]looking for the mercy of our Lord Jesus Christ unto eternal life.

22 And of some have compassion, making a difference:

23 And others [p]save with fear, [q]pulling *them* out of the fire; hating even [r]the garment spotted by the flesh.

K—CONCLUDED. See preceding page (1311.)

Hos. 4. 14 I will not punish your daughters when they commit whoredom, nor your spouses when they commit adultery: for themselves are separated with whores, and they sacrifice with harlots: therefore the people *that* doth not understand shall fall.

Hos. 9. 10 I found Israel like grapes in the wilderness; I saw your fathers as the first ripe in the fig tree at her first time: *but* they went to Baal-peor, and separated themselves unto *that* shame; and *their* abominations were according as they loved.

Heb. 10. 25 Not forsaking the assembling of ourselves together, as the manner of

K—CONCLUDED.

some *is;* but exhorting *one another:* and so much the more, as ye see the day approaching.

L

1 Cor. 2. 14 But the natural man receiveth not the things of the Spirit of God: for they are foolishness unto him: neither can he know *them*, because they are spiritually discerned.

Jas. 3. 15 This wisdom descendeth not from above, but *is* earthly, sensual, devilish.

M

Col. 2. 7 Rooted and built up in him, and stablished in the faith, as ye have been taught, abounding therein with thanksgiving.

N

Ps. 10. 17 LORD, thou hast heard the desire of the humble: thou wilt prepare their heart, thou wilt cause thine ear to hear:

Zech. 12. 10 And I will pour upon the house of David, and upon the inhabitants of Jerusalem, the spirit of grace and of supplications: and they shall look upon me whom they have pierced, and they shall mourn for him, as one mourneth for *his* only *son*, and shall be in bitterness for him, as one that is in bitterness for *his* firstborn.

Matt. 10. 20 For it is not ye that speak, but the Spirit of your Father which speaketh in you.

Rom. 8. 26 Likewise the Spirit also helpeth our infirmities: for we know not what we should pray for as we ought: but the Spirit itself maketh intercession for us with groanings which cannot be uttered.

Eph. 6. 18 Praying always with all prayer and supplication in the Spirit, and

§ 567. CONCLUDING

24, 25.

24 [a]Now unto him that is able to keep you from falling, and [b]to present *you* faultless before the presence of his glory with exceeding joy,

25 [c]To the only wise God our Saviour, *be* glory and majesty, dominion and power, both now and ever. Amen.

A

Rom. 8. 31 What shall we then say to these things? If God *be* for us, who *can be* against us?

32 He that spared not his own Son, but delivered him up for us all, how shall he not with him also freely give us all things?

Rom. 16. 25 Now to him that is of power to stablish you according to my gospel, and the preaching of Jesus Christ, according to the revelation of the mystery, which was kept secret since the

THE UNGODLINESS OF THE LAST DAYS (CONCLUDED).

N—CONCLUDED.

watching thereunto with all perseverance and supplication for all saints;

O

Job 14. 14 If a man die, shall he live *again?* all the days of my appointed time will I wait, till my change come.

Lam. 3. 25 The LORD *is* good unto them that wait for him, to the soul *that* seeketh him.

26 *It is* good that *a man* should both hope and quietly wait for the salvation of the LORD.

Luke 12. 35 Let your loins be girded about, and *your* lights burning;

36 And ye yourselves like unto men that wait for their lord, when he will return from the wedding; that when he cometh and knocketh, they may open unto him immediately.

37 Blessed *are* those servants, whom the lord when he cometh shall find watching: verily I say unto you, that he shall gird himself, and make them to sit down to meat, and will come forth and serve them.

I Cor. 1. 7 *See d, D, § 349, page 888.*

Tit. 2. 13 Looking for that blessed hope, and the glorious appearing of the great God and our Saviour Jesus Christ;

P

Rom. 11. 14 If by any means I may provoke to emulation *them which are* my flesh, and might save some of them.

I Cor. 7. 16 For what knowest thou, O wife, whether thou shalt save *thy* husband? or how knowest thou, O man, whether thou shalt save *thy* wife?

Cor. 9. 22 To the weak became I as weak, that I might gain the weak: I am made

P—CONCLUDED.

all things to all *men*, that I might by all means save some.

I Tim. 4. 16 Take heed unto thyself, and unto the doctrine; continue in them: for in doing this thou shalt both save thyself, and them that hear thee.

Jas. 5. 20 Let him know, that he which converteth the sinner from the error of his way shall save a soul from death, and shall hide a multitude of sins.

Q

Zech. 3. 2 And the LORD said unto Satan, The LORD rebuke thee, O Satan; even the LORD that hath chosen Jerusalem rebuke thee: *is* not this a brand plucked out of the fire?

I Cor. 3. 15. *See l, L, § 354, page 900.*

R

Isa. 64. 6 But we are all as an unclean *thing*, and all our righteousnesses *are* as filthy rags; and we all do fade as a leaf; and our iniquities, like the wind, have taken us away.

Zech. 3. 4 And he answered and spake unto those that stood before him, saying, Take away the filthy garments from him. And unto him he said, Behold, I have caused thine iniquity to pass from thee, and I will clothe thee with change of raiment.

5 And I said, Let them set a fair mitre upon his head. So they set a fair mitre upon his head, and clothed him with garments. And the angel of the LORD stood by.

Rev. 3. 4 Thou hast a few names even in Sardis which have not defiled their garments; and they shall walk with me in white: for they are worthy.

DOXOLOGY

A—CONCLUDED.

world began.

Eph. 3. 20 Now unto him that is able to do exceeding abundantly above all that we ask or think, according to the power that worketh in us,

B

Col. 1. 22 In the body of his flesh through death, to present you holy and unblameable and unreproveable in his sight:

Rev. 14. 5 And in their mouth was found no guile: for they are without fault be-

B—CONCLUDED.

fore the throne of God.

C

Rom. 11. 33 O the depth of the riches both of the wisdom and knowledge of God! how unsearchable *are* his judgments, and his ways past finding out!

Rom. 16. 27 To God only wise, *be* glory through Jesus Christ for ever. Amen.

I Tim. 1. 17 Now unto the King eternal, immortal, invisible, the only wise God, *be* honour and glory for ever and ever. Amen.

I : 1–3.

1 The [a]Revelation of Jesus Christ, [b]which God gave unto him, [c]to shew unto his servants things which must shortly come to pass; and he sent and [d]signified *it* by his angel unto his servant John:

2 [e]Who bare record of the word of God, and of the testimony of Jesus Christ, and of all things that he saw.

3 [f]Blessed *is* he that readeth, and they that hear the words of this prophecy, and keep those things which are written therein: for [g]the time *is* at hand.

A

Da. 2. 28 But there is a God in heaven that revealeth secrets, and maketh known to the king Nebuchadnezzar what shall be in the latter days.

Amos 3. 7 Surely the Lord GOD will do nothing, but he revealeth his secret unto his servants the prophets.

Rom. 16. 25 Now to him that is of power to stablish you according to my gospel, and the preaching of Jesus Christ, according to the revelation of the

A—CONCLUDED.

mystery, which was kept secret since the world began.

Rom. 16. 26 But now is made manifest, and by the Scriptures of the prophets, according to the commandment of the everlasting God, made known to all nations for the obedience of faith:

B

John 3. 32. *See r, R, § 23, page 77.*

C

Ps. 25. 9 The meek will he guide in judgment: and the meek will he teach his way.

Ps. 25. 14 The secret of the LORD *is* with them that fear him; and he will shew them his covenant.

Prov. 3. 32 For the froward *is* abomination to the LORD: but his secret *is* with the righteous.

Matt. 11. 25 At that time Jesus answered and said, I thank thee, O Father, Lord of heaven and earth, because thou hast hid these things from the wise and prudent, and hast revealed them unto babes.

Luke 8. 10 And he said Unto you, it is given to know the mysteries of the kingdom of God: but to others in parables; that seeing they might not see, and hearing they might not understand.

D

Rev. 22. 16 I Jesus have sent mine angel to testify unto you these things in the

§ 569. SALUTATION OF JOHN

I : 4–8.

4 John to the seven churches which are in Asia: Grace *be* unto you, and peace, from him [a]which is, and [b]which was, and which is to come; [c]and from the seven Spirits which are before his throne;

5 And from Jesus Christ, [d]*who is* the faithful witness, *and* the [e]first begotten of the dead, and [f]the prince of the kings of the earth. Unto him [g]that loved us, [h]and washed us from our sins in his own blood,

A

Ex. 3. 14 And God said unto Moses, I AM THAT I AM: and he said, Thus shalt thou say unto the children of Israel, I AM hath sent me unto you.

John 8. 58. *See m, M, § 111, page 333.*

B

John 1. 1. *See a, A, § 1, page 5.*

C

Zech. 4. 10 For who hath despised the day of small things? for they shall rejoice, and shall see the plummet in the hand of Zerubbabel *with* those seven; they *are* the eyes of the LORD, which run to and fro through the whole earth.

Rev. 3. 1 And unto the angel of the church in Sardis write; These things saith he that hath the seven Spirits of God, and the seven stars; I know thy works,

the Divine, probably A. D. 95-97, on the Island of Patmos.

D—CONCLUDED.

churches. I am the root and the offspring of David, *and* the bright and morning star.

E

I Cor. 1. 6. *See c, C, § 349, page 888.*

F

Prov. 1. 33 But whoso hearkeneth unto me shall dwell safely, and shall be quiet from fear of evil.

Prov. 3. 13 Happy *is* the man *that* findeth wisdom, and the man *that* getteth understanding:

14 For the merchandise of it *is* better than the merchandise of silver, and the gain thereof than fine gold.

15 She *is* more precious than rubies: and all the things thou canst desire are not to be compared unto her.

16 Length of days *is* in her right hand; *and* in her left hand riches and honour.

17 Her ways *are* ways of pleasantness, and all her paths *are* peace.

18 She *is* a tree of life to them that lay hold upon her: and happy *is every one* that retaineth her.

Prov. 8. 32 Now therefore hearken unto me, O ye children: for blessed *are they that* keep my ways.

33 Hear instruction, and be wise, and refuse it not.

34 Blessed *is* the man that heareth me, watching daily at my gates, waiting at the posts of my doors.

F—CONCLUDED.

Prov. 8. 35 For whoso findeth me findeth life, and shall obtain favour of the LORD.

Luke 11. 28 But he said, Yea, rather, blessed *are* they that hear the word of God, and keep it.

John 5. 24 Verily, verily, I say unto you, He that heareth my word, and believeth on him that sent me, hath everlasting life, and shall not come into condemnation; but is passed from death unto life.

Rev. 22. 7 Behold, I come quickly: blessed *is* he that keepeth the sayings of the prophecy of this book.

G

Luke 21. 31 So likewise ye, when ye see these things come to pass, know ye that the kingdom of God is nigh at hand.

Phil. 4. 5 Let your moderation be known unto all men. The Lord *is* at hand.

Jas. 5. 8 Be ye also patient; stablish your hearts: for the coming of the Lord draweth nigh.

9 Grudge not one against another, brethren, lest ye be condemned: behold, the judge standeth before the door.

I Pet. 4. 7 But the end of all things is at hand: be ye therefore sober, and watch unto prayer.

Rev. 22. 10 And he saith unto me, Seal not the sayings of the prophecy of this book: for the time is at hand.

TO THE CHURCHES IN ASIA.

C—CONCLUDED.

that thou hast a name that thou livest, and are dead.

Rev. 4. 5 And out of the throne proceeded lightnings and thunderings and voices: and *there were* seven lamps of fire burning before the throne, which are the seven Spirits of God.

Rev. 5. 6 And I beheld, and, lo, in the midst of the throne and of the four beasts, and in the midst of the elders, stood a Lamb as it had been slain, having seven horns and seven eyes, which are the seven Spirits of God sent forth into all the earth.

D

John 8. 14 Jesus answered and said unto them, Though I bear record of myself, *yet* my record is true: for I know

D—CONCLUDED.

whence I came and whither I go; but ye cannot tell whence I come, and whither I go.

I Tim. 6. 13 I give thee charge in the sight of God, who quickeneth all things, and *before* Christ Jesus, who before Pontius Pilate witnessed a good confession;

Rev. 3. 14 And unto the angel of the church of the Laodiceans write; These things saith the Amen, the faithful and true witness, the beginning of the creation of God;

E

Acts 26. 23. *See b, B, § 309, page 794.*

F

Eph. 1. 20 Which he wrought in Christ, when he raised him from the dead, and set

For F concluded, G and H, see next page (1316).

§ 569. SALUTATION OF JOHN TO THE

CHAP. I.

6 And hath [i]made us kings and priests unto God and his Father; [k]to him *be* glory and dominion for ever and ever. Amen.

7 [l]Behold, he cometh with clouds; and every eye shall see him, and [m]they *also* which pierced him: and all kindreds of the earth shall wail because of him. Even so, Amen.

8 [n]I am Alpha and Omega, the beginning and the ending, saith the Lord, [o]which is, and which was, and which is to come, the Almighty.

F—CONCLUDED.

him at his own right hand in the heavenly *places*,

Rev. 17. 14 These shall make war with the Lamb, and the Lamb shall overcome them: for he is Lord of lords, and King of kings: and they that are with him *are* called, and chosen, and faithful.

Rev. 19. 16 And he hath on *his* vesture and on his thigh a name written, KING OF KINGS, AND LORD OF LORDS.

G

Gal. 2. 20 I am crucified with Christ: nevertheless I live; yet not I, but Christ liveth in me: and the life which I now live in the flesh I live by the faith of the Son of God, who loved me, and gave himself for me.

I Jno. 4. 10. *See f, F, § 556, page 1294.*

H

Heb. 1. 3. *See h, H, § 503, page 1168.*

I John 1. 7. *See e, E, § 550, page 1282.*

I

Ex. 19. 6 And ye shall be unto me a kingdom of priests, and a holy nation. These *are* the words whic.. thou shalt speak unto the children of Israel.

Isa. 61. 6 But ye shall be named the Priests of the LORD: *men* shall call you the Ministers of our God: ye shall eat the riches of the Gentiles, and in their glory shall ye boast yourselves.

Matt. 19. 28. *See d, D, § 145, page 412.*

I Pet. 2. 5 Ye also, as lively stones, are built up a spiritual house, a holy priesthood, to offer up spiritual sacrifices, acceptable to God by Jesus Christ.

I Pet. 2. 9 But ye *are* a chosen generation, a royal priesthood, a holy nation, a peculiar people; that ye should shew forth the praises of him who hath called you out of darkness into his marvelous light:

Rev. 5. 10 And hast made us unto our God kings and priests: and we shall reign on the earth.

§ 570. JOHN'S VISION

1: 9–20.

9 I John, who also am your brother, and [a]companion in tribulation, and [b]in the kingdom and patience of Jesus Christ, was in the isle that is called Patmos, [c]for the word of God, and for the testimony of Jesus Christ.

10 [d]I was in the Spirit on [e]the Lord's day, and heard behind me [f]a great voice, as of a trumpet,

A

Phil. 1. 7 Even as it is meet for me to think this of you all, because I have you in my heart; inasmuch as both in my bonds, and in the defence and confirma-

A—CONCLUDED.

tion of the gospel, ye all are partakers of my grace.

Phil. 4. 14 Notwithstanding ye have well done, that ye did communicate with my affliction.

IITim. 1. 8 Be not thou therefore ashamed of the testimony of our Lord, nor of me his prisoner: but be thou partaker of the afflictions of the gospel according to the power of God;

B

Rom. 8. 17 And if children, then heirs; heirs of God, and joint heirs with Christ; if so be that we suffer with *him*, that we may be also glorified together.

IITim. 2. 12 If we suffer, we shall also reign with *him*: if we deny *him*, he also will deny us:

C

Rev. 1. 2 Who bare record of the word of God, and of the testimony of Jesus

CHURCHES IN ASIA (CONCLUDED).

I—CONCLUDED.

Rev. 20. 6 Blessed and holy *is* he that hath part in the first resurrection: on such the second death hath no power, but they shall be priests of God and of Christ, and shall reign with him a thousand years.

K

Rom. 11. 36. *See r, R, § 341, page 866.*

I Pet. 4. 11 If any man speak, *let him speak* as the oracles of God; if any man minister, *let him do it* as of the ability which God giveth: that God in all things may be glorified through Jesus Christ: to whom be praise and dominion for ever and ever. Amen.

I Pet. 5. 11 To him *be* glory and dominion for ever and ever. Amen.

L

Da. 7. 13 I saw in the night visions, and, behold, *one* like the Son of man came with the clouds of heaven, and came to the Ancient of days, and they brought him near before him.

Matt. 24. 30 And then shall appear the sign of the Son of man in heaven: and then shall all the tribes of the earth mourn, and they shall see the Son of man coming in the clouds of heaven with power and great glory.

Matt. 26. 64 Jesus saith unto him, Thou hast said: nevertheless I say unto you, Hereafter shall ye see the Son of man sitting on the right hand of power, and coming in the clouds of heaven.

L—CONCLUDED.

Acts 1. 11 Which also said, Ye men of Galilee, why stand ye gazing up into heaven? this same Jesus, which is taken up from you into heaven, shall so come in like manner as ye have seen him go into heaven.

M

John 19. 37. *See g, G, § 209, page 593.*

N

Isa. 41. 4 Who hath wrought and done *it*, calling the generations from the beginning? I the LORD, the first, and with the last; I *am* he.

Isa. 44. 6 Thus saith the LORD the King of Israel, and his Redeemer the LORD of hosts; I *am* the first, and I *am* the last; and besides me *there is* no God.

Isa. 48. 12 Hearken unto me, O Jacob and Israel, my called; I *am* he; I *am* the first, I also *am* the last.

Rev. 2. 8 And unto the angel of the church in Smyrna write; These things saith the first and the last, which was dead, and is alive;

Rev. 21. 6 And he said unto me, It is done. I am Alpha and Omega, the beginning and the end. I will give unto him that is athirst of the fountain of the water of life freely.

Rev. 22. 13 I am Alpha and Omega, the beginning and the end, the first and the last.

O

Rev. 1. 4. *See text of topic. Study A.*

OF JESUS CHRIST.

C—CONCLUDED.

Christ, and of all things that he saw.

Rev. 6. 9 And when he had opened the fifth seal, I saw under the altar the souls of them that were slain for the word of God, and for the testimony which they held:

D

Acts 10. 10 And he became very hungry, and would have eaten: but while they made ready, he fell into a trance,

II Cor. 12. 2 I knew a man in Christ above fourteen years ago, (whether in the body, I cannot tell; or whether out of the body, I cannot tell: God knoweth;) such a one caught up to the third heaven.

Rev. 4. 2 And immediately I was in the Spirit: and, behold, a throne was set in heaven, and *one* sat on the throne.

Rev. 17. 3 So he carried me away in the spirit into the wilderness; and I saw a

D—CONCLUDED.

woman sit upon a scarlet coloured beast, full of names of blasphemy, having seven heads and ten horns.

Rev. 21. 10 And he carried me away in the spirit to a great and high mountain, and shewed me that great city, the holy Jerusalem, descending out of heaven from God.

E

John 20. 26 And after eight days again his disciples were within, and Thomas with them: *then* came Jesus, the doors being shut, and stood in the midst, and said, Peace *be* unto you.

Acts 20. 7. *See a A, § 290, page 758.*

F

Rev. 4. 1 After this I looked, and, behold, a door *was* opened in heaven: and the first voice which I heard *was* as

For F concluded, see next page (1318).

CHAP. I.

11 Saying, [g]I am Alpha and Omega, [h]the first and the last: and, What thou seest, write in a book, and send *it* unto the seven churches which are in Asia; unto Ephesus, and unto Smyrna, and unto Pergamos, and unto Thyatira, and unto Sardis, and unto Philadelphia, and unto Laodicea.

12 And I turned to see the voice that spake with me. And being turned, [i]I saw seven golden candlesticks;

13 [k]And in the midst of the seven candlesticks [l]*one* like unto the Son of man, [m]clothed with a garment down to the foot, and [n]girt about the paps with a golden girdle.

14 His head and [o]*his* hairs *were* white like wool, as white as snow; and [p]his eyes *were* as a flame of fire;

15 [q]And his feet like unto fine brass, as if they burned in a furnace; and [r]his voice as the sound of many waters.

16 [s]And he had in his right hand seven stars: and [t]out of his mouth went a sharp twoedged sword: [u]and his countenance *was* as the sun shineth in his strength.

17 And [x]when I saw him, I fell at his feet as dead. And [y]he laid his right hand upon me, saying unto me, Fear not; [z]I am the first and the last:

18 [a]*I am* he that liveth, and was dead; and, behold, [b]I am alive for evermore, Amen; and [c]have the keys of hell and of death.

19 Write [d]the things which thou hast seen, [e]and the things which are, [f]and the things which shall be hereafter;

20 The mystery [g]of the seven stars

§ 570. JOHN'S VISION OF

F—CONCLUDED.

it were of a trumpet talking with me; which said, Come up hither, and I will shew thee things which must be hereafter.

Rev. 10. 8 And the voice which I heard from heaven spake unto me again, and said, Go *and* take the little book which is open in the hand of the angel which standeth upon the sea and upon the earth.

G

Rev. 1. 8. *See n, N, § 569, page 1316.*

H

Rev. 1. 17. *See text of topic.*

I

Ex. 25. 37 And thou shalt make the seven lamps thereof: and they shall light the lamps thereof, that they may give light over against it.

Zech. 4. 2 And said unto me, What seest thou? And I said, I have looked, and behold a candlestick all *of* gold, with a bowl upon the top of it, and his seven lamps thereon, and seven pipes to the seven lamps, which *are* upon the top thereof:

Rev. 1. 20. *See text of topic.*

K

Rev. 2. 1 Unto the angel of the church of Ephesus write; These things saith he that holdeth the seven stars in his right hand, who walketh in the midst of the seven golden candlesticks;

L

Eze. 1. 26 And above the firmament that *was* over their heads *was* the likeness of a throne, as the appearance of a sapphire stone: and upon the likeness of the throne *was* the likeness as the appearance of a man above upon it.

Da. 7. 13 I saw in the night visions, and, behold, *one* like the Son of man came with the clouds of heaven, and came to the Ancient of days, and they brought him near before him.

Da. 10. 16 And, behold, *one* like the similitude of the sons of men touched my lips: then I opened my mouth, and spake, and said unto him that stood before me, O my lord, by the vision my sorrows are turned upon me, and I have retained no strength.

Rev. 14. 14 And I looked, and behold a white cloud, and upon the cloud *one* sat like unto the Son of man, having on his head a golden crown, and in his hand a sharp sickle.

JESUS CHRIST (CONTINUED).

M

Da. 10. 5 Then I lifted up mine eyes, and looked, and behold a certain man clothed in linen, whose loins *were* girded with fine gold of Uphaz:

N

Rev. 15. 6 And the seven angels came out of the temple, having the seven plagues, clothed in pure and white linen, and having their breasts girded with golden girdles.

O

Da. 7. 9 I beheld till the thrones were cast down, and the Ancient of days did sit, whose garment *was* white as snow, and the hair of his head like the pure wool: his throne *was like* the fiery flame, *and* his wheels *as* burning fire.

P

Da. 10. 6 His body also *was* like the beryl, and his face as the appearance of lightning, and his eyes as lamps of fire, and his arms and his feet like in colour to polished brass, and the voice of his words like the voice of a multitude.

Rev. 2. 18 And unto the angel of the church in Thyatira write; These things saith the Son of God, who hath his eyes like unto a flame of fire, and his feet *are* like fine brass;

Rev. 19. 12 His eyes *were* as a flame of fire, and on his head *were* many crowns; and he had a name written, that no man knew, but he himself.

Q

Eze. 1. 7 And their feet *were* straight feet; and the sole of their feet *was* like the sole of a calf's foot: and they sparkled like the colour of burnished brass.

Da. 10. 6. and Rev. 2. 18. *See under P.*

R

Eze. 43. 2 And, behold, the glory of the God of Israel came from the way of the east: and his voice *was* like a noise of many waters: and the earth shined with his glory.

Da. 10. 6. *See under P.*

Rev. 14. 2 And I heard a voice from heaven, as the voice of many waters, and as the voice of a great thunder: and I heard the voice of harpers harping with their harps:

Rev. 19. 6 And I heard as it were the voice of a great multitude, and as the voice of many waters, and as the voice of mighty thunderings, saying, Alleluia: for the Lord God omnipotent reigneth.

S

Rev. 1. 20. *See text of topic.*

Rev. 2. 1. *See under K.*

S—CONCLUDED.

Rev. 3. 1 And unto the angel of the church in Sardis write; These things saith he that hath the seven Spirits of God, and the seven stars; I know thy works, that thou hast a name that thou livest, and art dead.

T

Isa. 49. 2 And he hath made my mouth like a sharp sword; in the shadow of his hand hath he hid me, and made me a polished shaft; in his quiver hath he hid me;

Eph. 6. 17. *See n, N, § 437, page 1056.*

U

Acts 26. 13 At midday, O king, I saw in the way a light from heaven, above the brightness of the sun, shining round about me and them which journeyed with me.

Rev. 10. 1 And I saw another mighty angel come down from heaven, clothed with a cloud: and a rainbow *was* upon his head, and his face *was* as it were the sun, and his feet as pillars of fire:

X

Eze. 1. 28 As the appearance of the bow that is in the cloud in the day of rain, so *was* the appearance of the brightness round about. This *was* the appearance of the likeness of the glory of the LORD. And when I saw *it*, I fell upon my face, and I heard a voice of one that spake.

Y

Da. 8. 18 Now as he was speaking with me, I was in a deep sleep on my face toward the ground: but he touched me, and set me upright.

Da. 10. 10 And, behold, a hand touched me, which set me upon my knees and *upon* the palms of my hands.

Z

Rev. 1. 8. *See n, N, § 569, page 1316.*

A

Rom. 6. 9 Knowing that Christ being raised from the dead dieth no more; death hath no more dominion over him.

B

Rev. 4. 9 And when those beasts give glory and honour and thanks to him that sat on the throne, who liveth for ever and ever,

Rev. 5. 14 And the four beasts said, Amen. And the four *and* twenty elders fell down and worshipped him that liveth for ever and ever.

For C, D, E, F, and G, see next page (1320).

§ 570. JOHN'S VISION OF

CHAP. 1.

which thou sawest in my right hand, and the seven golden candlesticks. The seven stars are [h]the angels of the seven churches: and [i]the seven candlesticks which thou sawest are the seven churches.

C

Ps. 68. 20 *He that is* our God *is* the God of salvation; and unto GOD the Lord *belong* the issues from death.

Rev. 20. 1 And I saw an angel come down from heaven, having the key of the bottomless pit and a great chain in his hand.

D

Rev. 1. 12, etc. *See text of topic.*

§ 571. MESSAGE TO THE ANGEL

2: 1-7.

1 Unto the angel of [a]the church of
Ephesus write; These things saith
[b]he that holdeth the seven stars in
his right hand, [c]who walketh in the
midst of the seven golden candlesticks;
2 [d]I know thy works, and thy
labour, and thy patience, and how
thou canst not bear them which are
evil: and [e]thou hast tried them
[f]which say they are apostles, and
are not, and hast found them liars:
3 And hast borne, and hast
patience, and for my name's sake
hast laboured, and hast [g]not fainted.
4 Nevertheless [h]I have *somewhat*
against thee, because thou hast left
thy first love.
5 Remember therefore from whence
thou art fallen, and repent, and do
the first works; [i]or else I will come
unto thee quickly, and will remove
thy candlestick out of his place,
except thou repent.
6 But this thou hast, that thou
hatest the deeds of [k]the Nicolaitans,
which I also hate.
7 [l]He that hath an ear, let him
hear what the Spirit saith unto the
churches; To him that overcometh

CHAP. 2.

will I give [m]to eat of the tree of life, which is in the midst of the [n]paradise of God.

A

Acts 19. *Read entire chapter, page 752.*

B

Rev. 1. 16, 20. *See text of topic, § 570.*

C

Rev. 1. 13. *See text of topic, § 570.*

D

Ps. 1. 6 For the LORD knoweth the way of the righteous: but the way of the ungodly shall perish.

Rev. 2. 9 I know thy works, and tribulation, and poverty, (but thou art rich) and *I know* the blasphemy of them which say they are Jews, and are not, but *are* the synagogue of Satan.

Rev. 2. 19 I know thy works, and charity, and service, and faith, and thy patience, and thy works; and the last *to be* more than the first.

Rev. 3. 15 I know thy works, that thou art neither cold nor hot: I would thou wert cold or hot.

E

I Jno. 4. 1. *See b, B, § 555, page 1294.*

F

II Cor. 11. 13. *See t, T, § 403, page 994.*

G

Heb. 12. 3, 5. *See g, G, § 521, page 1216.*

H

Jer. 2. 2 Go and cry in the ears of Jerusalem, saying, Thus saith the LORD; I remember thee, the kindness of thy youth, the love of thine espousals, when thou wentest after me in the wilderness, in a land *that was* not sown.

JESUS CHRIST (Concluded).

E

Rev. 2. 1. *See text of topic, § 571.*

F

Rev. 4. 1 After this I looked, and, behold, a door *was* opened in heaven: and the first voice which I heard *was* as it were of a trumpet talking with me; which said, Come up hither, and I will shew thee things which must be hereafter.

G

Rev. 1. 16. *See text of topic.*

H

Mal. 2. 7 For the priest's lips should keep knowledge, and they should seek the law at his mouth: for he *is* the messenger of the Lord of hosts.

Rev. 2. 1. *See text of topic, § 571.*

I

Phil. 2. 15. *See e, E, § 442, page 1066.*

OF THE CHURCH IN EPHESUS.

H—Concluded.

Jer. 2. 3 Israel *was* holiness unto the Lord, *and* the firstfruits of his increase: all that devour him shall offend; evil shall come upon them, saith the Lord.

4 Hear ye the word of the Lord, O house of Jacob, and all the families of the house of Israel:

5 Thus saith the Lord, What iniquity have your fathers found in me, that they are gone far from me, and have walked after vanity, and are become vain?

I

Matt. 21. 41 They say unto him, He will miserably destroy those wicked men, and will let out *his* vineyard unto other husbandmen, which shall render him the fruits in their seasons.

Matt. 21. 43 Therefore say I unto you, The kingdom of God shall be taken from you, and given to a nation bringing forth the fruits thereof.

K

Ps. 26. 5 I have hated the congregation of evil doers; and will not sit with the wicked.

Ps. 139. 22 I hate them with perfect hatred: I count them mine enemies.

23 Search me, O God, and know my heart: try me, and know my thoughts:

II Jno. 9 Whosoever transgresseth, and abideth not in the doctrine of Christ, hath not God. He that abideth in the doctrine of Christ, he hath both the Father and the Son.

Rev. 2. 15 So hast thou also them that hold the doctrine of the Nicolaitans which thing I hate.

L

Matt. 11. 15. *See x, X, § 46, page 158.*

M

Gen. 2. 9 And out of the ground made the Lord God to grow every tree that is

M—Concluded.

pleasant to the sight, and good for food; the tree of life also in the midst of the garden, and the tree of knowledge of good and evil.

Gen. 3. 22 And the Lord God said, Behold, the man is become as one of us, to know good and evil: and now, lest he put forth his hand, and take also of the tree of life, and eat, and live for ever:

23 Therefore the Lord God sent him forth from the garden of Eden, to till the ground from whence he was taken.

24 So he drove out the man; and he placed at the east of the garden of Eden cherubims, and a flaming sword which turned every way, to keep the way of the tree of life.

Prov. 3. 18 She *is* a tree of life to them that lay hold upon her: and happy *is every one* that retaineth her.

Prov. 11. 30 The fruit of the righteous *is* a tree of life; and he that winneth souls *is* wise.

Prov. 13. 12 Hope deferred maketh the heart sick: but *when* the desire cometh, *it is* a tree of life.

Prov. 15. 4 A wholesome tongue *is* a tree of life: but perverseness therein *is* a breach in the spirit.

Rev. 22. 2 In the midst of the street of it, and on either side of the river, *was there* the tree of life, which bare twelve *manner of* fruits, *and* yielded her fruit every month: and the leaves of the tree *were* for the healing of the nations.

Rev. 22. 14 Blessed *are* they that do his commandments, that they may have right to the tree of life, and may enter in through the gates into the city.

N

II Cor. 12. 4. *See c, C, § 405, page 998.*

§ 572. MESSAGE TO THE ANGEL

2 : 8–11.

8 And unto the angel of the church
in Smyrna write; These things saith
[a]the first and the last, which was
dead, and is alive;
9 [b]I know thy works, and tribulation, and poverty, (but thou art
[c]rich) and *I know* the blasphemy of
[d]them which say they are Jews, and
are not, [e]but *are* the synagogue of
Satan.
10 [f]Fear none of those things which
thou shalt suffer: behold, the devil
shall cast *some* of you into prison,
that ye may be tried; and ye shall
have tribulation ten days: [g]be thou
faithful unto death, and I will give
thee [h]a crown of life.

CHAP. 2.

11 [i]He that hath an ear, let him
hear what the Spirit saith unto the
churches; He that overcometh shall
not be hurt of [k]the second death.

A

Rev. 1. 8. *See n, N, § 569, page 1316.*

B

Rev. 2. 2. *See d, D, § 571, page 1320.*

C

Luke 12. 21 So *is* he that layeth up treasure for himself, and is not rich toward God.

ITim.6. 18 That they do good, that they be rich in good works, ready to distribute, willing to communicate;

Jas. 2. 5 Hearken, my beloved brethren, Hath not God chosen the poor of this world rich in faith, and heirs of the kingdom which he hath promised to them that love him?

D

Rom. 2. 28, 29. *See o, O, § 321, page 820.*

§ 573. MESSAGE TO THE ANGEL

2 : 12–17.

12 And to the angel of the church
in Pergamos write; These things saith
[a]he which hath the sharp sword with
two edges;
13 I know thy works, and where
thou dwellest, *even* [b]where Satan's
seat *is:* and thou holdest fast my
name, and has not denied my faith,
even in those days wherein Antipas
was my faithful martyr, who was
slain among you, where Satan
dwelleth.
14 But I have a few things against
thee, because thou hast there them
that hold the doctrine of [c]Balaam,
who taught Balak to cast a stumbling block before the children of
Israel, [d]to eat things sacrificed unto
idols, [e]and to commit fornication.
15 So hast thou also them that
hold the doctrine of [f]the Nicolaitans,
which thing I hate.
16 Repent; or else I will come unto

CHAP. 2.

thee quickly, and [g]will fight against
them with the sword of my mouth.
17 [h]He that hath an ear, let him
hear what the Spirit saith unto
the churches; To him that overcometh will I give [i]to eat of the hidden manna, and will give him a
white stone, and in the stone [k]a new
name written, which no man knoweth saving he that receiveth *it.*

A

Rev. 1. 16. *See t, T, § 570, page 1318.*

B

Rev. 2. 9. *See text of topic, § 572.*

C

Num.24. 14 And now, behold, I go unto my people: come *therefore, and* I will advertise thee what this people shall do to thy people in the latter days.

Num.25. 1 And Israel abode in Shittim, and the people began to commit whoredom with the daughters of Moab.

Num.31. 16 Behold, these caused the children of Israel, through the counsel of Balaam, to commit trespass against the LORD in the matter of Peor, and

OF THE CHURCH IN SMYRNA.

E

Rev. 3. 9 Behold I will make them of the synagogue of Satan, which say they are Jews, and art not, but do lie; behold, I will make them to come and worship before thy feet, and to know that I have loved thee.

F

Isa. 41. 10 Fear thou not; for I *am* with thee: be not dismayed; for I *am* thy God: I will strengthen thee; yea, I will help thee; yea I will uphold thee with the right hand of my righteousness.

Isa. 41. 14 Fear not, thou worm Jacob, *and* ye men of Israel; I will help thee, saith the LORD, and thy Redeemer, the Holy One of Israel.

Matt. 10. 22 And ye shall be hated of all *men* for my name's sake: but he that endureth to the end shall be saved.

G

Matt. 24. 13 But he that shall endure unto the end, the same shall be saved.

Heb. 3 14 For we are made partakers of Christ, if we hold the beginning of

G—CONCLUDED.

our confidence steadfast unto the end;

H

Jas. 1. 12. *See l, L, § 528, page 1228.*

I

Matt. 11. 15. *See x, X, § 46, page 158.*

K

Rev. 20. 6 Blessed and holy *is* he that hath part in the first resurrection: on such the second death hath no power, but they shall be priests of God and of Christ, and shall reign with him a thousand years.

Rev. 20. 14 And death and hell were cast into the lake of fire. This is the second death.

15 And whosoever was not found written in the book of life was cast into the lake of fire.

Rev. 21. 8 But the fearful, and unbelieving, and the abominable, and murderers, and whoremongers, and sorcerers, and idolaters, and all liars, shall have their part in the lake which burneth with fire and brimstone: which is the second death.

OF THE CHURCH IN PERGAMOS.

C—CONCLUDED.

there was a plague among the congregation of the LORD.

II Pet. 2. 15. *See f, F, § 547, page 1276.*

Jude. 11 Woe unto them! for they have gone in the way of Cain, and ran greedily after the error of Balaam for reward, and perished in the gainsaying of Core.

D

Acts 15. 20, 29. *Study R and* F, *page 730.*

E

I Cor. 6. 13. *Study § 361, page 912.*

F

Rev. 2. 6. *See k, K, § 571, page 1320.*

G

II Thes. 2. 8. *See m, M, § 467, page 1112.*

H

Matt. 11. 15. *See x, X, § 46, page 158.*

I

Ps. 25. 14 The secret of the LORD *is* with them that fear him; and he will shew them his covenant.

Ps. 36. 8 They shall be abundantly satisfied with the fatness of thy house; and thou shalt make them drink of the river of thy pleasures.

John 4. 32 But he said unto them, I have meat to eat that ye know not of.

I—CONCLUDED.

John 6. 48 I am the bread of life.

49 Your fathers did eat manna in the wilderness, and are dead.

50 This is the bread which cometh down from heaven, that a man may eat thereof, and not die.

51 I am the living bread which came down from heaven: if any man eat of this bread, he shall live for ever: and the bread that I will give is my flesh, which I will give for the life of the world.

K

Rev. 3. 12 Him that overcometh will I make a pillar in the temple of my God, and he shall go no more out: and I will write upon him the name of my God, and the name of the city of my God, *which is* new Jerusalem, which cometh down out of heaven from my God: and *I will write upon him* my new name.

Rev. 19. 12 His eyes *were* as a flame of fire, and on his head *were* many crowns; and he had a name written, that no man knew, but he himself.

13 And he *was* clothed with a vesture dipped in blood: and his name is called The Word of God.

§ 574. MESSAGE TO THE ANGEL

2 : 18–29.

18 And unto the angel of the church
in Thyatira write ; These things saith
the Son of God, [a]who hath his eyes
like unto a flame of fire, and his feet
are like fine brass ;
19 [b]I know thy works, and charity,
and service, and faith, and thy patience, and thy works ; and the last
to be more than the first.
20 Notwithstanding I have a few
things against thee, because thou
sufferest that woman [c]Jezebel, which
calleth herself a prophetess, to teach
and to seduce my servants [d]to commit
fornication, and to eat things sacrificed unto idols.
21 And I gave her space [e]to repent
of her fornication ; and she repented
not.
22 Behold, I will cast her into a
bed, and them that commit adultery
with her into great tribulation, except they repent of their deeds.
23 And I will kill her children with
death ; and all the churches shall
know that [f]I am he which searcheth
the reins and hearts : and [g]I will
give unto every one of you according to your works.
24 But unto you I say, and unto
the rest in Thyatira, as many as have
not this doctrine, and which have
not known the depths of Satan, as

CHAP. 2.

they speak ; [h]I will put upon you
none other burden.
25 But [i]that which ye have *already*
hold fast till I come.
26 And he that overcometh, and
keepeth [k]my works unto the end, [l]to
him will I give power over the nations :
27 [m]And he shall rule them with a
rod of iron ; as the vessels of a potter shall they be broken to shivers :
even as I received of my Father.
28 And I will give him [n]the morning star.
29 [o]He that hath an ear, let him
hear what the Spirit saith unto the
churches.

A

Rev. 1. 14. *See p, P, § 570, page 1318.*

B

Rev. 2. 2. *See d, D, § 571, page 1320.*

C

I Ki. 16. 31 And it came to pass, as if it had been a light thing for him to walk in the sins of Jeroboam the son of Nebat, that he took to wife Jezebel the daughter of Ethbaal king of the Zidonians, and went and served Baal, and worshipped him.

I Ki. 21. 25 But there was none like unto Ahab, which did sell himself to work wickedness in the sight of the LORD, whom Jezebel his wife stirred up.

II Ki. 9. 7 And thou shalt smite the house of Ahab thy master, that I may avenge the blood of my servants the prophets, and the blood of all the servants of the LORD, at the hand of Jezebel.

§ 575. MESSAGE TO THE ANGEL

3 : 1–6.

1 And unto the angel of the church
in Sardis write ; These things saith
he [a]that hath the seven Spirits of
God, and the seven stars ; [b]I know
thy works, that thou hast a name
that thou livest, and [c]art dead.
2 Be watchful, and strengthen the
things which remain, that are ready

CHAP. 3.

to die : for I have not found thy
works perfect before God.
3 [d]Remember therefore how thou
hast received and heard, and hold
fast, and [e]repent. [f]If therefore thou
shalt not watch, I will come on thee
as a thief, and thou shalt not know
what hour I will come upon thee.

OF THE CHURCH IN THYATIRA.

D

Ex. 34. 15 Lest thou make a covenant with the inhabitants of the land, and they go a whoring after their gods, and do sacrifice unto their gods, and *one* call thee, and thou eat of his sacrifice;

Acts 15. 20, 29. *Study R and F, page 730.*

I Cor. 10. 19 What say I then? that the idol is any thing, or that which is offered in sacrifice to idols is any thing?

20 But *I say*, that the things which the Gentiles sacrifice, they sacrifice to devils, and not to God: and I would not that ye should have fellowship with devils.

E

Rom. 2. 4 Or despisest thou the riches of his goodness and forbearance and long-suffering; not knowing that the goodness of God leadeth thee to repentance?

Rev. 9. 20 And the rest of the men which were not killed by these plagues yet repented not of the works of their hands, that they should not worship devils, and idols of gold, and silver, and brass, and stone, and of wood: which neither can see, nor hear, nor walk:

F

John 2. 23-25. *See i, I, § 21, page 69.*
Acts 1. 24. *See p, P, § 229, page 632.*

G

Rom. 2. 6. *See h, H, § 320, page 816.*

Gal. 6. 5 For every man shall bear his own burden.

H

Acts 15. 28 For it seemed good to the Holy Ghost, and to us, to lay upon you no greater burden than these necessary things;

I

Rev. 3. 11 Behold, I come quickly: hold that fast which thou hast, that no man take thy crown.

K

I Jno. 3. 23. *See p, P, § 554, page 1292.*

L

Matt. 19. 28. *See d, D, § 145, page 412.*

Rev. 3. 21 To him that overcometh will I grant to sit with me in my throne, even as I also overcame, and am set down with my Father in his throne.

Rev. 20. 4 And I saw thrones, and they sat upon them, and judgment was given unto them: and *I saw* the souls of them that were beheaded for the witness of Jesus, and for the word of God, and which had not worshipped the beast, neither his image, neither had received *his* mark upon their foreheads, or in their hands; and they lived and reigned with Christ a thousand years.

M

Ps. 2. 8 Ask of me, and I shall give *thee* the heathen *for* thine inheritance, and the uttermost parts of the earth *for* thy possession.

9 Thou shalt break them with a rod of iron; thou shalt dash them in pieces like a potter's vessel.

Rev. 12. 5 And she brought forth a man child, who was to rule all nations with a rod of iron: and her child was caught up unto God, and *to* his throne.

Rev. 19. 15 And out of his mouth goeth a sharp sword, that with it he should smite the nations: and he shall rule them with a rod of iron: and he treadeth the winepress of the fierceness and wrath of Almighty God.

N

II Pet. 1. 19. *See n, N, § 546, page 1272.*

O

Matt. 11. 15. *See x, X § 46, page 158.*

OF THE CHURCH IN SARDIS.

A

Rev. 1. 4. *See c, C, § 569, page 1314.*

B

Rev. 2. 2. *See d, D, § 571, page 1320.*

C

Eph. 2. 1 And you *hath he quickened*, who were dead in trespasses and sins;

Eph. 2. 5 Even when we were dead in sins, hath quickened us together with Christ, (by grace ye are saved;)

I Tim. 5. 6 But she that liveth in pleasure is dead while she liveth.

D

I Tim. 6. 20. *See a, A, § 484, page 1138.*

E

Rev. 3. 19 As many as I love, I rebuke and chasten: be zealous therefore, and repent.

F

Matt. 24. 42, 43. *Study Y, page 492, and B, page 494.*

G

Acts 1. 15 And in those days Peter stood up in the midst of the disciples, and said, (the number of names together were about a hundred and twenty,)

§ 575. MESSAGE TO THE ANGEL OF

CHAP. 3.

4 Thou hast [g]a few names even in Sardis which have not [h]defiled their garments; and they shall walk with me [i]in white: for they are worthy.

5 He that overcometh, [k]the same shall be clothed in white raiment; and I will not [l]blot out his name out of the [m]book of life, but [n]I will confess his name before my Father, and before his angels.

6 [o]He that hath an ear, let him hear what the Spirit saith unto the churches.

For G, see preceding page (1325).

H

Jude 23 And others save with fear, pulling *them* out of the fire; hating even the garment spotted by the flesh.

I

Rev. 4. 4 And round about the throne *were* four and twenty seats: and upon the seats I saw four and twenty elders sitting, clothed in white raiment; and they had on their heads crowns of gold.

Rev. 6. 11 And white robes were given unto every one of them; and it was said unto them, that they should rest yet for a little season, until their fellow servants also and their brethren, that should be killed as they *were*, should be fulfilled.

Rev. 7. 9 After this I beheld, and, lo, a

§ 576. MESSAGE TO THE ANGEL OF

3 : 7–13.

7 And to the angel of the church in Philadelphia write; These things saith [a]he that is holy, [b]he that is true, he that hath [c]the key of David, [d]he that openeth, and no man shutteth; and [e]shutteth, and no man openeth;

8 [f]I know thy works: behold, I have set before thee [g]an open door, and no man can shut it: for thou hast a little strength, and hast kept my word, and hast not denied my name.

9 Behold, I will make [h]them of the synagogue of Satan, which say they are Jews, and are not, but do lie; behold, [i]I will make them to come and worship before thy feet, and to know that I have loved thee.

10 Because thou hast kept the word of my patience, [k]I also will keep thee from the hour of temptation, which shall come upon all the world, to try them that dwell upon the earth.

11 Behold, [l]I come quickly: [m]hold

A

Isa. 6. 3 And one cried unto another, and said, Holy, holy, holy, *is* the LORD of hosts: the whole earth *is* full of his glory.

Acts 3. 14. *See d, D, § 234, page 644.*

Heb. 7. 26 For such a high priest became us, *who is* holy, harmless, undefiled, separate from sinners, and made higher than the heavens;

B

John 14. 6 Jesus saith unto him, I am the way, the truth, and the life: no man cometh unto the Father, but by me.

1 Jno. 5. 20 And we know that the Son of God is come, and hath given us an understanding, that we may know him that is true; and we are in him that is true, *even* in his Son Jesus Christ. This is the true God, and eternal life.

Rev. 1. 5 And from Jesus Christ, *who is* the faithful witness, *and* the firstbegotten of the dead, and the prince of the kings of the earth. Unto him that loved us, and washed us from our sins in his own blood,

Rev. 6. 10 And they cried with a loud voice, saying, How long, O Lord, holy and true, dost thou not judge and avenge our blood on them that dwell on the earth?

Rev. 19. 11 And I saw heaven opened, and behold a white horse; and he that sat upon him *was* called Faithful and True, and in righteousness he doth judge and make war.

THE CHURCH IN SARDIS (Concluded).

I—Concluded.

great multitude, which no man could number, of all nations, and kindreds, and people, and tongues, stood before the throne, and before the Lamb, clothed with white robes, and palms in their hands;

Rev. 7. 13 And one of the elders answered, saying unto me, What are these which are arrayed in white robes? and whence came they?

K

Rev. 19. 8 And to her was granted that she should be arrayed in fine linen, clean and white: for the fine linen is the righteousness of saints.

L

Ex. 32. 32 Yet now, if thou wilt forgive their sin—: and if not, blot me, I pray thee, out of thy book which thou hast written.

L—Concluded.

Ps. 69. 28 Let them be blotted out of the book of the living, and not be written with the righteous.

M

Phil. 4. 3. *See f, F, § 446, page 1072.*

Rev. 17. 8 The beast that thou sawest was, and is not; and shall ascend out of the bottomless pit, and go into perdition: and they that dwell on the earth shall wonder, whose names were not written in the book of life from the foundation of the world, when they behold the beast that was, and is not, and yet is.

N

Luke 12. 8. *See h, H, § 57, page 183.*

O

Matt. 11. 15. *See x, X, § 46, page 158.*

THE CHURCH IN PHILADELPHIA.

C

Isa. 22. 22 And the key of the house of David will I lay upon his shoulder; so he shall open, and none shall shut; and he shall shut, and none shall open.

Luke 1. 32. *See i, I, § 4, page 15.*

D

Matt. 16. 19 And I will give unto thee the keys of the kingdom of heaven: and whatsoever thou shalt bind on earth shall be bound in heaven: and whatsoever thou shalt loose on earth shall be loosed in heaven.

E

Job 12. 14 Behold, he breaketh down, and it cannot be built again: he shutteth up a man, and there can be no opening.

F

Rev. 2. 2. *See d, D, § 571, page 1320.*

G

Acts 14. 27. *See i, I, § 266, page 724.*

H

Rev. 2. 9 I know thy works, and tribulation, and poverty, (but thou art rich) and *I know* the blasphemy of them which say they are Jews, and are not, but *are* the synagogue of Satan.

I

Isa. 49. 23 And kings shall be thy nursing fathers, and their queens thy nursing mothers: they shall bow down to thee with *their* face toward the earth, and lick up the dust of thy feet; and thou shalt know that I *am* the LORD: for they shall not be ashamed that wait for me.

I—Concluded.

Isa. 60. 14 The sons also of them that afflicted thee shall come bending unto thee; and all they that despised thee shall bow themselves down at the soles of thy feet; and they shall call thee, The city of the LORD, The Zion of the Holy One of Israel.

K

Da. 12. 1 And at that time shall Michael stand up, the great prince which standeth for the children of thy people: and there shall be a time of trouble, such as never was since there was a nation *even* to that same time: and at that time thy people shall be delivered, every one that shall be found written in the book.

Joel 2. 2 A day of darkness and of gloominess, a day of clouds and of thick darkness, as the morning spread upon the mountains: a great people and a strong; there hath not been ever the like, neither shall be any more after it, *even* to the years of many generations.

Matt. 24. 21 For then shall be great tribulation, such as was not since the beginning of the world to this time, no, nor ever shall be.

22 And except those days should be shortened, there should no flesh be saved: but for the elect's sake those days shall be shortened.

II Pet. 2. 9. *See t, T, § 547 page 1274.*

For L and M, see next page (1328).

Chap. 3.

that fast which thou hast, that no man take [n]thy crown.

12 Him that overcometh will I make [o]a pillar in the temple of my God, and he shall go no more out: and [p]I will write upon him the name of my God, and the name of the city of my God, *which is* [q]new Jerusalem, which cometh down out of heaven from my God: and *I will write upon him* my new name.

13 He that hath an ear, let him hear what the Spirit saith unto the churches.

§ 576. MESSAGE TO THE ANGEL OF

L

Phil. 4. 5 Let your moderation be known unto all men. The Lord *is* at hand.

Rev. 1. 3 Blessed *is* he that readeth, and they that hear the words of this prophecy, and keep those things which are written therein: for the time *is* at hand.

Rev. 22. 7 Behold, I come quickly: blessed *is* he that keepeth the sayings of the prophecy of this book.

Rev. 22. 12 And, behold, I come quickly; and my reward *is* with me, to give every man according as his work shall be.

Rev. 22. 20 He which testifieth these things saith, Surely I come quickly. Amen. Even so, come, Lord Jesus.

3 : 14-22.

14 And unto the angel of the church [1]of the Laodiceans write; [a]These things saith the Amen, [b]the faithful and true witness, [c]the beginning of the creation of God;

15 I know thy works, that thou art neither cold nor hot: I would thou wert cold or hot.

16 So then because thou art lukewarm, and neither cold nor hot, I will spew thee out of my mouth.

17 Because thou sayest, [d]I am rich, and increased with goods, and have need of nothing; and knowest not that thou art wretched, and miserable, and poor, and blind, and naked:

18 I counsel thee [e]to buy of me gold tried in the fire, that thou mayest be rich; and [f]white raiment, that thou mayest be clothed, and *that* the shame of thy nakedness do not appear; and anoint thine eyes with eyesalve, that thou mayest see.

19 [g]As many as I love, I rebuke and chasten: be zealous therefore, and repent.

§ 577. MESSAGE TO THE ANGEL

Chap. 3.

20 Behold, [h]I stand at the door, and knock: [i]if any man hear my voice, and open the door, [k]I will come in to him, and will sup with him, and he with me.

21 To him that overcometh [l]will I grant to sit with me in my throne, even as I also overcame, and am set down with my Father in his throne.

22 [m]He that hath an ear, let him hear what the Spirit saith unto the churches.

[1] Or, *in Laodicea.*

A

Isa. 65. 16 That he who blesseth himself in the earth shall bless himself in the God of truth; and he that sweareth in the earth shall swear by the God of truth; because the former troubles are forgotten, and because they are hid from mine eyes.

II Cor. 1. 20 For all the promises of God in him *are* yea, and in him Amen, unto the glory of God by us.

B

Rev. 1. 5. *See d, D, § 569, page 1314.*

Rev. 19. 11 And I saw heaven opened, and behold a white horse; and he that sat upon him *was* called Faithful and True, and in righteousness he doth judge and make war.

THE CHURCH IN PHILADELPHIA (CONCLUDED).

M

Rev. 2. 25 But that which ye have *already*, hold fast till I come.

Rev. 3. 3 Remember therefore how thou hast received and heard, and hold fast, and repent. If therefore thou shalt not watch, I will come on thee as a thief, and thou shalt not know what hour I will come upon thee.

N

Jas. 1 12. *See l, L, § 528, page 12·?.*

O

Jer. 1. 18 For, behold, I have made thee this day a defenced city, and an iron pillar, and brazen walls against the whole land, against the kings of Judah, against the princes thereof, against the priests thereof, and against the people of the land.

O—CONCLUDED.

Gal. 2. 9 And when James, Cephas, and John, who seemed to be pillars, perceived the grace that was given unto me, they gave to me and Barnabas the right hands of fellowship; that we *should go* unto the heathen, and they unto the circumcision.

P

Rev. 2. 17. *See k, K, § 573, page 1·22.*

Rev. 14. 1 And I looked, and, lo, a Lamb stood on the mount Sion, and with him a hundred forty *and* four thousand, having his Father's name written in their foreheads.

Rev. 22. 4 And they shall see his face; and his name *shall be* in their foreheads.

Q

Gal. 4. 26. *See f, F, § 420, page 1020.*

OF THE CHURCH IN LAODICEA·

B—CONCLUDED.

Rev. 22. 6 And he said unto me, These sayings *are* faithful and true: and the Lord God of the holy prophets sent his angel to shew unto his servants the things which must shortly be done.

C

Col. 1. 15 Who is the image of the invisible God, the firstborn of every creature:

D

Hos. 12. 8 And Ephraim said, Yet I am become rich, I have found me out substance: *in* all my labours they shall find none iniquity in me that *were* sin.

I Cor. 4. 8 Now ye are full, now ye are rich, ye have reigned as kings without us: and I would to God ye did reign, that we also might reign with you.

E

Prov. 23. 23 Buy the truth, and sell *it* not; *also* wisdom, and instruction, and understanding.

Isa. 55. 1 Ho, every one that thirsteth, come ye to the waters, and he that hath no money; come ye, buy, and eat; yea, come, buy wine and milk without money and without price.

F

II Cor. 5. 3 If so be that being clothed we shall not be found naked.

Rev. 7. 13 And one of the elders answered, saying unto me, What are these which are arrayed in white robes? and whence came they?

F—CONCLUDED.

Rev. 16. 15 Behold, I come as a thief. Blessed *is* he that watcheth, and keepeth his garments, lest he walk naked, and they see his shame.

Rev. 19. 8 And to her was granted that she should be arrayed in fine linen, clean and white: for the fine linen is the righteousness of saints.

G

Heb. 12. 5, 6. *Study I and K, page 1216.*

H

Song. 5. 2 I sleep, but my heart waketh: *it is* the voice of my beloved that knocketh, *saying*, Open to me, my sister, my love, my dove, my undefiled: for my head is filled with dew, *and* my locks with the drops of the night.

I

Luke 12. 37 Blessed *are* those servants, whom the lord when he cometh shall find watching: verily I say unto you, that he shall gird himself, and make them to sit down to meat, and will come forth and serve them.

K

John 14. 23 Jesus answered and said unto him, If a man love me, he will keep my words: and my Father will love him, and we will come unto him, and make our abode with him.

L

Matt. 19. 28. *See d, D, § 145, page 412.*

M

Matt. 11. 15. *See x, X, § 46, page 158.*

§ 578. THINGS WHICH MUST COME TO

4: 1–11.

1 After this I looked, and, behold, a door *was* opened in heaven: and [a]the first voice which I heard *was* as it were of a trumpet talking with me; which said, [b]Come up hither, [c]and I will shew thee things which must be hereafter.

2 And immediately [d]I was in the Spirit: and, behold, [e]a throne was set in heaven, and *one* sat on the throne.

3 And he that sat was to look upon like a jasper and a sardine stone: [f]and *there was* a rainbow round about the throne, in sight like unto an emerald.

4 [g]And round about the throne *were* four and twenty seats: and upon the seats I saw four and twenty elders sitting, [h]clothed in white raiment; [i]and they had on their heads crowns of gold.

5 And out of the throne proceeded [k]lightnings and thunderings and voices: [l]and *there were* seven lamps of fire burning before the throne, which are [m]the seven Spirits of God.

6 And before the throne *there was* [n]a sea of glass like unto crystal: [o]and in the midst of the throne, and round about the throne, *were* four beasts full of eyes before and behind.

7 And the first beast *was* like a lion, and the second beast like a calf, and the third beast had a face as a man, and the fourth beast *was* like a flying eagle.

8 And the four beasts had each of them six wings about *him;* and *they were* full of eyes within: and they rest not day and night, saying, Holy, holy, holy, Lord God Almighty, which was, and is, and is to come.

A

Rev. 1. 10 I was in the Spirit on the Lord's day, and heard behind me a great voice, as of a trumpet.

B

Rev. 11. 12 And they heard a great voice from heaven saying unto them, Come up hither. And they ascended up to heaven in a cloud; and their enemies beheld them.

C

Rev. 1. 19 Write the things which thou hast seen, and the things which are, and the things which shall be hereafter.

Rev. 22. 6 And he said unto me, These sayings *are* faithful and true: and the Lord God of the holy prophets sent his angel to shew unto his servants the things which must shortly be done.

D

Rev. 1. 10. *See d, D, § 570, page 1316.*

E

Rev. 6. 1. *See under O.*

Jer. 17. 12 A glorious high throne from the beginning *is* the place of our sanctuary.

Eze. 1. 26 And above the firmament that *was* over their heads *was* the likeness of a throne, as the appearance of a sapphire stone: and upon the likeness of the throne *was* the likeness as the appearance of a man above upon it.

Eze. 10. 1 Then I looked, and, behold, in the firmament that was above the head of the cherubims there appeared over the as it were a sapphire stone, as the appearance of the likeness of a throne.

Da. 7. 9 I beheld till the thrones were cast down, and the Ancient of days did sit, whose garment *was* white as snow, and the hair of his head like the pure wool: his throne *was like* the fiery flame, *and* his wheels *as* burning fire.

F

Eze. 1. 28 As the appearance of the bow that is in the cloud in the day of rain, so *was* the appearance of the brightness round about. This *was* the appearance of the likeness of the glory of the LORD. And when I saw *it*, I fell upon my face, and I heard a voice of one that spake.

G

Rev. 11. 16 And the four and twenty elders, which sat before God on their seats, fell upon their faces, and worshipped God,

H

Rev. 3. 4. *See i, I, § 575, page 1326.*

PASS. A VISION OF THE THRONE.

H—CONCLUDED.

Rev. 19. 14 And the armies *which were* in heaven followed him upon white horses, clothed in fine linen, white and clean.

I

Rev. 4. 10. *See text of topic.*

K

Rev. 8. 5 And the angel took the censer, and filled it with fire of the altar, and cast *it* into the earth: and there were voices, and thunderings, and lightnings, and an earthquake.

Rev. 16. 18 And there were voices, and thunders, and lightnings: and there was a great earthquake, such as was not since men were upon the earth, so mighty an earthquake, *and* so great.

L

Gen. 15. 17 And it came to pass, that, when the sun went down, and it was dark, behold a smoking furnace, and a burning lamp that passed between those pieces.

Ex. 37. 23 And he made his seven lamps, and his snuffers, and his snuffdishes, *of* pure gold.

II Chr. 4. 20 Moreover the candlesticks with their lamps, that they should burn after the manner before the oracle, of pure gold;

Zech. 4. 2 And said unto me, what seest thou? And I said, I have looked, and behold a candlestick all *of* gold, with a bowl upon the top of it, and his seven lamps thereon, and seven pipes to the seven lamps, which *are* upon the top thereof:

M

Rev. 1. 4. *See c, C, § 569, page 1314.*

N

Ex. 38. 8 And he made the laver *of* brass, and the foot of it *of* brass, of the lookingglasses of *the women* assembling, which assembled *at* the door of the tabernacle of the congregation.

Rev. 15. 2 And I saw as it were a sea of glass mingled with fire: and them that had gotten the victory over the beast, and over his image, and over his mark, *and* over the number of his name, stand on the sea of glass, having the harps of God.

O

Isa. 6. 1 In the year that king Uzziah died I saw also the Lord sitting upon a throne, high and lifted up, and his train filled the temple.

O—CONTINUED.

Isa. 6. 2 Above it stood the seraphims: each one had six wings; with twain he covered his face, and with twain he covered his feet, and with twain he did fly.

3 And one cried unto another, and said, Holy, holy, holy, *is* the LORD of hosts: the whole earth *is* full of his glory.

Eze. 1. 4 And I looked, and, behold, a whirlwind came out of the north, a great cloud, and a fire infolding itself, and a brightness *was* about it, and out of the midst thereof as the colour of amber, out of the midst of the fire.

5 Also out of the midst thereof *came* the likeness of four living creatures. And this *was* their appearance; they had the likeness of a man.

6 And every one had four faces, and every one had four wings.

7 And their feet *were* straight feet; and the sole of their feet *was* like the sole of a calf's foot: and they sparkled like the colour of burnished brass.

8 And *they had* the hands of a man under their wings on their four sides; and they four had their faces and their wings.

9 Their wings *were* joined one to another; they turned not when they went; they went every one straight forward.

10 As for the likeness of their faces, they four had the face of a man, and the face of a lion, on the right side: and they four had the face of an ox on the left side; they four also had the face of an eagle.

Eze. 10. 12 And their whole body, and their backs, and their hands, and their wings, and the wheels, *were* full of eyes round about, *even* the wheels that they four had.

13 As for the wheels, it was cried unto them in my hearing, O wheel.

14 And every one had four faces: the first face *was* the face of a cherub, and the second face *was* the face of a man, and the third the face of a lion, and the fourth the face of an eagle.

15 And the cherubims were lifted up. This *is* the living creature that I saw by the river of Chebar.

Eze. 10. 20 This *is* the living creature that I saw under the God of Israel by the river of Chebar; and I knew that they *were* the cherubims.

For O concluded, see next page (1332).

§ 578. THINGS WHICH MUST COME TO PASS.

CHAP. 4.

9 And when those beasts give glory and honour and thanks to him that sat on the throne, who liveth for ever and ever,

10 [p]The four and twenty elders fall down before him that sat on the throne, and worship him that liveth for ever and ever, and cast their crowns before the throne, saying,

CHAP. 4.

11 [q]Thou art worthy, O Lord, to receive glory and honour and power: [r]for thou hast created all things, and for thy pleasure they are and were created.

O—CONTINUED.

Eze. 10. 21 Every one had four faces apiece, and every one four wings; and the likeness of the hands of a man *was* under their wings.

Eze. 10. 22 And the likeness of their faces *was* the same faces which I saw by

§ 579. THE SEALED BOOK AND

5 : 1–14.

1 And I saw in the right hand of
him that sat on the throne [a]a book
written within and on the back side,
[b]sealed with seven seals.
2 And I saw a strong angel pro-
claiming with a loud voice, Who is
worthy to open the book, and to
loose the seals thereof?
3 And no man in heaven, nor in
earth, neither under the earth, was
able to open the book, neither to
look thereon.
4 And I wept much, because no
man was found worthy to open and
to read the book, neither to look
thereon.
5 And one of the elders saith unto
me, Weep not: behold, [c]the Lion of
the tribe of Juda, [d]the Root of
David, hath prevailed to open the
book, [e]and to loose the seven seals
thereof.
6 And I beheld, and, lo, in the
midst of the throne and of the four
beasts, and in the midst of the
elders, stood [f]a Lamb as it had been
slain, having seven horns and [g]seven

CHAP. 5.

eyes, which are [h]the seven Spirits of
God sent forth into all the earth.
7 And he came and took the book
out of the right hand [i]of him that
sat upon the throne.
8 And when he had taken the book,
[k]the four beasts and four *and* twenty
elders fell down before the Lamb,
having every one of them [l]harps,
and golden vials full of [1]odours,
[m]which are the prayers of saints.

A

Eze. 2. 9 And when I looked, behold, a hand *was* sent unto me; and, lo, a roll of a book *was* therein;

10 And he spread it before me; and it *was* written within and without: and *there was* written therein lamentations, and mourning, and woe.

B

Isa. 29. 11 And the vision of all is become unto you as the words of a book that is sealed, which *men* deliver to one that is learned, saying, Read this, I pray thee: and he saith, I cannot; for it *is* sealed:

Da. 12. 4 But thou, O Daniel, shut up the words, and seal the book, *even* to the time of the end: many shall run to and fro, and knowledge shall be increased.

C

Gen. 49. 10 The sceptre shall not depart from Judah, nor a lawgiver from between

A VISION OF THE THRONE (Concluded).

O—Concluded.

the river of Chebar, their appearances and themselves: they went every one straight forward.

P

Rev. 5. 8 And when he had taken the book, the four beasts and four *and* twenty elders fell down before the Lamb, having every one of them harps, and golden vials full of odours, which are the prayers of saints.

Rev. 5. 14 And the four beasts said, Amen. And the four *and* twenty elders fell down and worshipped him that liveth for ever and ever.

Q

Ps. 96. 7 Give unto the Lord, O ye kindreds of the people, give unto the Lord glory and strength.

8 Give unto the Lord the glory *due unto* his name: bring an offering, and come into his courts.

Rev. 5. 12 Saying with a loud voice, Worthy is the Lamb that was slain to receive power, and riches, and wisdom, and strength, and honour, and glory, and blessing.

R

John 1. 3. *See e, E, § 1, page 5.*

THE LAMB THAT IS WORTHY.

C—Concluded.

his feet, until Shiloh come; and unto him *shall* the gathering of the people *be*.

Num. 24. 9 He couched, he lay down as a lion, and as a great lion: who shall stir him up? Blessed *is* he that blesseth thee, and cursed *is* he that curseth thee.

Heb. 7. 14 For *it is* evident that our Lord sprang out of Juda; of which tribe Moses spake nothing concerning priesthood.

D

Rom. 15. 12. *See s, S, § 345, page 880.*

E

Rev. 5. 1. *See text of topic.*

Rev. 6. 1 And I saw when the Lamb opened one of the seals, and I heard, as it were the noise of thunder, one of the four beasts saying, Come and see.

F

I Cor. 5. 7. *See m, M, § 359, page 908.*

G

Zech. 3. 9 For behold the stone that I have laid before Joshua; upon one stone *shall be* seven eyes: behold, I will engrave the graving thereof, saith the Lord of hosts, and I will remove the iniquity of that land in one day.

10 In that day, saith the Lord of hosts, shall ye call every man his neighbor under the vine and under the fig tree.

H

Rev. 1. 4. *See c, C, § 569, page 1314.*

I

Rev. 4. 2 And immediately I was in the Spirit: and, behold, a throne was set in heaven, and *one* sat on the throne.

K

Rev. 4. 8 And the four beasts had each of them six wings about *him;* and *they were* full of eyes within: and they rest not day and night, saying, Holy, holy, holy, Lord God Almighty, which was, and is, and is to come.

Rev. 4. 10. *See text of topic, § 578.*

L

Rev. 14. 2 And I heard a voice from heaven, as the voice of many waters, and as the voice of a great thunder: and I heard the voice of harpers harping with their harps:

Rev. 15. 2 And I saw as it were a sea of glass mingled with fire: and them that had gotten the victory over the beast, and over his image, and over his mark, *and* over the number of his name, stand on the sea of glass, having the harps of God.

1

Or, *incense.*

M

Ps. 141. 2 Let my prayer be set forth before thee *as* incense; *and* the lifting up of my hands *as* the evening sacrifice.

Rev. 8. 3 And another angel came and stood at the altar, having a golden censer; and there was given unto him much incense, that he should offer *it* with the prayers of all saints upon the golden altar which was before the throne.

4 And the smoke of the incense, *which came* with the prayers of the saints, ascended up before God out of the angel's hand.

CHAP. 5.

9 And [n]they sung a new song, saying, [o]Thou art worthy to take the
book, and to open the seals thereof:
[p]for thou wast slain, and hast redeemed us to God by thy blood [q]out
of every kindred, and tongue, and
people, and nation;
10 [r]And hast made us unto our God
kings and priests: and we shall
reign on the earth.
11 And I beheld, and I heard the
voice of many angels [s]round about
the throne, and the beasts, and the
elders: and the number of them was
[t]ten thousand times ten thousand,
and thousands of thousands;
12 Saying with a loud voice,
[u]Worthy is the Lamb that was slain
to receive power, and riches, and
wisdom, and strength, and honour,
and glory, and blessing.
13 [x]And every creature which is in
heaven, and on earth, and under the
earth, and such as are in the sea,

§ 579. THE SEALED BOOK AND THE

CHAP. 5.

and all that are in them, heard I
saying, [y]Blessing, and honour, and
glory, and power, *be* unto him [z]that
sitteth upon the throne, and unto
the Lamb for ever and ever.
14 [a]And the four beasts said, Amen.
And the four *and* twenty elders fell
down and worshipped him [b]that liveth for ever and ever.

N

Ps. 40. 3 And he hath put a new song in my mouth, *even* praise unto our God: many shall see *it* and fear, and shall trust in the LORD.

Rev. 14. 3 And they sung as it were a new song before the throne, and before the four beasts, and the elders: and no man could learn that song but the hundred *and* forty *and* four thousand, which were redeemed from the earth.

O

Rev. 4. 11. *See q, Q, § 578, page 1332.*

P

Acts 20. 28. *See s, S, § 292, page 762.*

Q

Rev. 7. 9 After this I beheld, and, lo, a great multitude, which no man could number, of all nations, and kindreds, and people, and tongues, stood before the throne, and before the Lamb, clothed with white robes, and palms in their hands:

6: 1–17.

1 And [a]I saw when the Lamb
opened one of the seals, and I
heard, as it were the noise of thunder, [b]one of the four beasts saying,
Come and see.
2 And I saw, and behold [c]a white
horse: and [d]he that sat on him had
a bow; [e]and a crown was given unto him: and he went forth conquer-
ing, and to conquer.
3 And when he had opened the
second seal, [f]I heard the second
beast say, Come and see.

§ 580. THE LAMB OPENS

A

Rev. 5. 5-7. *See f, F, § 579, page 1332.*

B

Rev. 4. 6, 7. *See o, O, § 578, page 1330*

C

Zech. 1. 8 I saw by night, and behold a man riding upon a red horse, and he stood among the myrtle trees that *were* in the bottom; and behind him *were there* red horses, speckled, and white.

9 Then said I, O my lord, what *are* these? And the angel that talked with me said unto me, I will shew thee what these *be*.

10 And the man that stood among the myrtle trees answered and said, These *are they* whom the LORD hath sent to walk to and fro through the earth.

LAMB THAT IS WORTHY (CONCLUDED).

Q—CONCLUDED.

Rev. 11. 9 And they of the people and kindreds and tongues and nations shall see their dead bodies three days and a half, and shall not suffer their dead bodies to be put in graves.

Rev. 14. 6 And I saw another angel fly in the midst of heaven, having the everlasting gospel to preach unto them that dwell on the earth, and to every nation, and kindred, and tongue, and people,

R

Rev. 1. 5. *See i, I, § 569, page 1316.*

S

Rev. 4. 4 And round about the throne *were* four and twenty seats: and upon the seats I saw four and twenty elders sitting, clothed in white raiment; and they had on their heads crowns of gold.

Rev. 5. 6 And I beheld, and, lo, in the midst of the throne and of the four beasts, and in the midst of the elders, stood a Lamb as it had been slain, having seven horns and seven eyes, which are the seven spirits of God sent forth into all the earth.

T

Ps. 68. 17 The chariots of God *are* twenty thousand, *even* thousands of angels: the Lord *is* among them, *as in* Sinai, in the holy *place*.

Da. 7. 10 A fiery stream issued and came forth from before him: thousand thousands ministered unto him, and ten thousand times ten thousand stood

T—CONCLUDED.

before him: the judgment was set, and the books were opened.

Heb. 12. 22 But ye are come unto mount Sion, and unto the city of the living God, the heavenly Jerusalem, and to an innumerable company of angels.

U

Rev. 4. 11. *See q, Q, § 578, page 1332.*

X

Phil. 2. 10 That at the name of Jesus every knee should bow, of *things* in heaven, and *things* in earth, and *things* under the earth;

Y

Rom. 9. 5 Whose *are* the fathers, and of whom as concerning the flesh Christ *came*, who is over all, God blessed for ever. Amen.

Rom. 11. 36. *See r, R, § 341, page 866.*

Rom. 16. 27. *See h, H, § 347, page 886.*

Z

Rev. 6. 16 And said to the mountains and rocks, Fall on us, and hide us from the face of him that sitteth on the throne, and from the wrath of the Lamb:

Rev. 7. 10 And cried with a loud voice, saying, Salvation to our God which sitteth upon the throne, and unto the Lamb.

A

Rev. 19. 4 And the four and twenty elders and the four beasts fell down and worshiped God that sat on the throne, saying, Amen; Alleluia.

B

Rev. 1. 18. *See b, B, § 570, page 1318.*

SIX SEALS OF THE BOOK.

C—CONTINUED.

Zech. 1. 11 And they answered the angel of the LORD that stood among the myrtle trees, and said, We have walked to and fro through the earth, and, behold, all the earth sitteth still, and is at rest.

Zech. 6. 1 And I turned, and lifted up mine eyes, and looked, and, behold, there came four chariots out from between two mountains; and the mountains *were* mountains of brass.

2 In the first chariot *were* red horses; and in the second chariot black horses;

3 And in the third chariot white horses; and in the fourth chariot grizzled and bay horses.

4 Then I answered and said unto the angel that talked with me, what *are* these, my lord?

C—CONTINUED.

Zech. 6. 5 And the angel answered and said unto me, These *are* the four spirits of the heavens, which go forth from standing before the Lord of all the earth.

6 The black horses which *are* therein go forth into the north country; and the white go forth after them: and the grizzled go forth toward the south country.

7 And the bay went forth, and sought to go that they might walk to and fro through the earth: and he said, Get you hence, walk to and fro through the earth. So they walked to and fro through the earth.

For C concluded, D, E and F, see next page (1336).

CHAP. 6.

4 [g]And there went out another horse *that was* red: and *power* was given to him that sat thereon to take peace from the earth, and that they should kill one another: and there was given unto him a great sword.

5 And when he had opened the third seal, [h]I heard the third beast say, Come and see. And I beheld, and lo [i]a black horse; and he that sat on him had a pair of balances in his hand.

6 And I heard a voice in the midst of the four beasts say, [1]A measure of wheat for a penny, and three measures of barley for a penny; and [k]*see* thou hurt not the oil and the wine.

7 And when he had opened the fourth seal, [l]I heard the voice of the fourth beast say, Come and see.

8 [m]And I looked, and behold a pale horse: and his name that sat on him was Death, and Hell followed with him. And power was given [2]unto them over the fourth part of the earth, [n]to kill with sword, and with hunger, and with death, [o]and with the beasts of the earth.

9 And when he had opened the fifth seal, I saw under [p]the altar [q]the souls of them that were slain [r]for the word of God, and for [s]the testimony which they held:

10 And they cried with a loud voice, saying, [t]How long, O Lord, [u]holy and true, [x]dost thou not judge and avenge our blood on them that dwell on the earth?

§ 580. THE LAMB OPENS SIX

CHAP. 6.

11 And [y]white robes were given unto every one of them; and it was said unto them, [z]that they should rest yet for a little season, until their fellow servants also and their brethren, that should be killed as they *were*, should be fulfilled.

12 And I beheld when he had opened the sixth seal, [a]and, lo, there

C—CONCLUDED.

Rev. 19. 11 And I saw heaven opened, and behold a white horse; and he that sat upon him *was* called Faithful and True, and in righteousness he doth judge and make war.

D

Ps. 45. 4 And in thy majesty ride prosperously, because of truth and meekness *and* righteousness; and thy right hand shall teach thee terrible things.

5 Thine arrows *are* sharp in the heart of the King's enemies; *whereby* the people fall under thee.

E

Zech. 6. 11 Then take silver and gold, and make crowns, and set *them* upon the head of Joshua the son of Josedech, the high priest;

12 And speak unto him, saying, Thus speaketh the LORD of hosts, saying, Behold the man whose name *is* The BRANCH; and he shall grow up out of his place, and he shall build the temple of the LORD:

13 Even he shall build the temple of the LORD; and he shall bear the glory, and shall sit and rule upon his throne; and he shall be a priest upon his throne: and the counsel of peace shall be between them both.

Rev. 14. 14 And I looked, and behold a white cloud, and upon the cloud *one* sat like unto the Son of man, having on his head a golden crown, and in his hand a sharp sickle.

Rev. 19. 12 His eyes *were* as a flame of fire, and on his head *were* many crowns; and he had a name written, that no man knew, but he himself.

F

Rev. 4. 6, 7. *See o, O, § 578, page 1330.*

G

Zech. 6. 2. *See under C, page 1335.*

SEALS OF THE BOOK (Continued).

H

Rev. 4. 6, 7. *See o, O, § 578, page 1330.*

I

Zech. 6. 2. *See under C, page 1335.*

1

The word, *choenix,* signifieth a measure containing one wine quart, and the twelfth part of a quart.

K

Rev. 9. 4 And it was commanded them that they should not hurt the grass of the earth, neither any green thing, neither any tree; but only those men which have not the seal of God in their foreheads.

L

Rev. 4. 6, 7. *See o, O, § 578, page 1330.*

M

Zech. 6. 3. *See under C, page 1335.*

2

Or, *to him.*

N

Eze. 14. 21 For thus saith the Lord God: How much more when I send my four sore judgments upon Jerusalem, the sword, and the famine, and the noisesome beast, and the pestilence, to cut off from it man and beast?

O

Lev. 26. 22 I will also send wild beasts among you, which shall rob you of your children, and destroy your cattle, and make you few in number; and your *high* ways shall be desolate.

P

Rev. 8 3 And another angel came and stood at the altar, having a golden censer; and there was given unto him much incense, that he should offer *it* with the prayers of all saints upon the golden altar which was before the throne.

Rev. 9. 13 And the sixth angel sounded, and I heard a voice from the four horns of the golden altar which is before God,

Rev. 14. 18 And another angel came out from the altar, which had power over fire; and cried with a loud cry to him that had the sharp sickle, saying, Thrust in thy sharp sickle, and gather the clusters of the vine of the earth; for her grapes are fully ripe.

Q

Rev. 20. 4 And I saw thrones, and they sat upon them, and judgment was given unto them: and *I saw* the souls of them that were beheaded for the witness of Jesus, and for the word of God, and which had not worshipped the beast, neither his image, neither had received

Q—Concluded.

his mark upon their foreheads, or in their hands; and they lived and reigned with Christ a thousand years.

R

Rev. 1. 9. *See c, C, § 570, page 1316.*

S

II Tim. 1. 8 Be not thou therefore ashamed of the testimony of our Lord, nor of me his prisoner: but be thou partaker of the afflictions of the gospel according to the power of God;

Rev. 12. 17 And the dragon was wroth with the woman, and went to make war with the remnant of her seed, which keep the commandments of God, and have the testimony of Jesus Christ.

Rev. 19. 10 And I fell at his feet to worship him. And he said unto me, See *thou do it* not: I am thy fellow servant, and of thy brethren that have the testimony of Jesus: worship God: for the testimony of Jesus is the spirit of prophecy.

T

Zech. 1. 12 Then the angel of the Lord answered and said, O Lord of hosts, how long wilt thou not have mercy on Jerusalem and on the cities of Judah, against which thou hast had indignation these threescore and ten years?

U

Rev. 3. 7. *See A and B, § 376, page 1326.*

X

Deut. 32. 41 If I whet my glittering sword, and mine hand take hold on judgment; I will render vengeance to mine enemies, and will reward them that hate me.

42 I will make mine arrows drunk with blood, and my sword shall devour flesh; *and that* with the blood of the slain and of the captives, from the beginning of revenges upon the enemy.

43 Rejoice, O ye nations, *with* his people: for he will avenge the blood of his servants, and will render vengeance to his adversaries, and will be merciful unto his land, *and* to his people.

Rev. 11. 18 And the nations were angry, and thy wrath is come, and the time of the dead, that they should be judged, and that thou shouldest give reward unto thy servants the prophets, and to the saints, and them that fear thy name, small and great; and shouldest destroy them which destroy the earth.

For X concluded, Y, Z and A, see next page (1338).

§ 580. THE LAMB OPENS SIX

CHAP. 6.

was a great earthquake; [b]and the
sun became black as sackcloth of
hair, and the moon became as blood;
13 [c]And the stars of heaven fell
unto the earth, even as a fig tree
casteth her [3]untimely figs, when she
is shaken of a mighty wind.
14 [d]And the heaven departed as a
scroll when it is rolled together; and
[e]every mountain and island were
moved out of their places.
15 And the kings of the earth, and
the great men, and the rich men,
and the chief captains, and the
mighty men, and every bond man,
and every free man, [f]hid themselves
in the dens and in the rocks of the
mountains;
16 [g]And said to the mountains and
rocks, Fall on us, and hide us from
the face of him that sitteth on the
throne, and from the wrath of the
Lamb:
17 [h]For the great day of his wrath
is come; [i]and who shall be able to
stand?

X—CONCLUDED.

Rev. 19. 2 For true and righteous *are* his judgments; for he hath judged the great whore,' which did corrupt the earth with her fornication, and hath avenged the blood of his servants at her hand.

Y

Rev. 3. 4, 5. *See i, I, § 575, page 1326.*

Z

Heb. 11. 40 God having provided some better thing for us that they without us should not be made perfect.

Rev. 14. 13 And I heard a voice from heaven saying unto me, Write, Blessed *are* the dead which die in the Lord from henceforth: Yea, saith the Spirit, that they may rest from their labours; and their works do follow them.

A

Rev. 16. 18 And there were voices, and thunders, and lightnings; and there was a great earthquake, such as was not since men were upon the earth, so mighty an earthquake, *and* so great.

B

Matt. 24. 29. *See y, Y, § 173, page 488.*

C

Rev. 8. 10 And the third angel sounded, and there fell a great star from heaven, burning as it were a lamp, and it fell upon the third part of the rivers, and upon the fountains of waters;

3

Or, *green figs.*

D

Matt. 24. 35. *See m, M, § 173, page 490.*
Heb. 1. 11, 12. *See t, T, § 503, page 1170.*

§ 581. THE SEALED OF ISRAEL. THE MULTITUDE WHICH

7 : 1–17.

CHAP. 7.

1 And after these things I saw four
angels standing on the four corners
of the earth, [a]holding the four winds
of the earth, that the wind should
not blow on the earth, nor on the
sea, nor on any tree.
2 And I saw another angel ascending from the east, having the seal
of the living God: and he cried with
a loud voice to the four angels, to
whom it was given to hurt the earth
and the sea,
3 Saying, [b]Hurt not the earth,
neither the sea, nor the trees, [c]till
we have sealed the servants of our
God [d]in their foreheads.
4 [e]And I heard the number of them
which were sealed: *and there were*
sealed [f]a hundred *and* forty *and* four
thousand of all the tribes of the
children of Israel.

SEALS OF THE BOOK (Concluded).

E

Jer. 3. 23 Truly in vain *is salvation hoped for* from the hills, *and from* the multitude of mountains: truly in the LORD our God *is* the salvation of Israel.

Jer. 4. 24 I beheld the mountains, and, lo, they trembled, and all the hills moved lightly.

Rev. 16. 20 And every island fled away, and the mountains were not found.

F

Isa. 2. 19 And they shall go into the holes of the rocks, and into the caves of the earth, for fear of the LORD, and for the glory of his majesty, when he ariseth to shake terribly the earth.
20 In that day a man shall cast his idols of silver, and his idols of gold, which they made *each one* for himself to worship, to the moles and to the bats;
21 To go into the clefts of the rocks, and into the tops of the ragged rocks, for fear of the LORD, and for the glory of his majesty, when he ariseth to shake terribly the earth.

G

Luke 23. 30. *See i, I, § 202, page 581.*

H

Isa. 13. 6 Howl ye; for the day of the LORD *is* at hand; it shall come as a destruction from the Almighty.
7 Therefore shall all hands be faint, and every man's heart shall melt:
8 And they shall be afraid: pangs and sorrows shall take hold of them; they shall be in pain as a woman that travaileth: they shall be amazed one at another; their faces *shall be as* flames.

H—Concluded.

Isa. 13. 9 Behold the day of the LORD cometh, cruel both with wrath and fierce anger, to lay the land desolate: and he shall destroy the sinners thereof out of it.

Zeph. 1. 14 The great day of the LORD *is* near, *it is* near, and hasteth greatly, *even* the voice of the day of the LORD: the mighty man shall cry there bitterly.
15 That day *is* a day of wrath, a day of trouble and distress, a day of wasteness and desolation, a day of darkness and gloominess, a day of clouds and thick darkness,
16 A day of the trumpet and alarm against the fenced cities, and against the high towers.
17 And I will bring distress upon men, that they shall walk like blind men, because they have sinned against the LORD: and their blood shall be poured out as dust, and their flesh as the dung.
18 Neither their silver nor their gold shall be able to deliver them in the day of the LORD's wrath; but the whole land shall be devoured by the fire of his jealously: for he shall make even a speedy riddance of all them that dwell in the land.

Rev. 16. 14 For they are the spirits of devils, working miracles, *which* go forth unto the kings of the earth and of the whole world, to gather them to the battle of that great day of God Almighty.

I

Ps. 76. 7 Thou, *even* thou, *art* to be feared: and who may stand in thy sight when once thou art angry?

CAME OUT OF MUCH TRIBULATION, BEARING PALMS.

A

Da. 7. 2 Daniel spake and said, I saw in my vision by night, and, behold, the four winds of the heaven strove upon the great sea.

B

Rev. 6. 6 And I heard a voice in the midst of the four beasts say, A measure of wheat for a penny, and three measures of barley for a penny; and *see* thou hurt not the oil and the wine.

Rev. 9. 4 And it was commanded them that they should not hurt the grass of the earth, neither any green thing, neither any tree; but only those men which have not the seal of God in

B—Concluded.

their foreheads.

C

Eze. 9. 4 And the LORD said unto him, Go through the midst of the city, through the midst of Jerusalem, and set a mark upon the foreheads of the men that sigh and that cry for all the abominations that be done in the midst thereof.

Zeph. 2. 3 Seek ye the LORD, all ye meek of the earth, which have wrought his judgment; seek righteousness, seek meekness: it may be ye shall be hid in the day of the LORD's anger.

For C concluded, D, E and F, **see next page** (1340).

§ 581. THE SEALED OF ISRAEL THE MULTITUDE WHICH

CHAP. 7.

5 Of the tribe of Juda *were* sealed
twelve thousand. Of the tribe of
Reuben *were* sealed twelve thousand.
Of the tribe of Gad *were* sealed
twelve thousand.

6 Of the tribe of Aser *were* sealed
twelve thousand. Of the tribe of
Nephthalim *were* sealed twelve thousand. Of the tribe of Manasses *were*
sealed twelve thousand.

7 Of the tribe of Simeon *were* sealed
twelve thousand. Of the tribe of
Levi *were* sealed twelve thousand.
Of the tribe of Issachar *were* sealed
twelve thousand.

8 Of the tribe of Zabulon *were*
sealed twelve thousand. Of the
tribe of Joseph *were* sealed twelve
thousand. Of the tribe of Benjamin *were* sealed twelve thousand.

9 After this I beheld, and, lo, [g]a
great multitude, which no man could
number, [h]of all nations, and kindreds, and people, and tongues,
stood before the throne, and before
the Lamb, [i]clothed with white robes,
and palms in their hands ;

10 And cried with a loud voice,
saying, [k]Salvation to our God [l]which
sitteth upon the throne, and unto
the Lamb.

11 [m]And all the angels stood round
about the throne, and *about* the elders and the four beasts, and fell
before the throne on their faces,
and worshipped God,

12 [n]Saying, Amen : Blessing, and
glory, and wisdom, and thanksgiving, and honour, and power, and

CHAP. 7.

might, *be* unto our God for ever and
ever. Amen.

13 And one of the elders answered,
saying unto me, What are these
which are arrayed in [o]white robes?
and whence came they?

14 And I said unto him, Sir, thou
knowest. And he said to me,
[p]These are they which came out of
great tribulation, and have [q]washed
their robes, and made them white
in the blood of the Lamb.

C—CONCLUDED.

Eph. 4. 30 And grieve not the Holy Spirit of God, whereby ye are sealed unto the day of redemption.

II Tim. 2. 19 Nevertheless the foundation of God standeth sure, having this seal, The Lord knoweth them that are his. And, Let every one that nameth the name of Christ depart from iniquity.

Rev. 14. 1 And I looked, and, lo, a Lamb stood on the mount Sion, and with him a hundred forty *and* four thousand, having his Father's name written in their foreheads.

D

Rev. 22. 4 And they shall see his face; and his name *shall be* in their foreheads.

E

Rev. 9. 16 And the number of the army of the horsemen *were* two hundred thousand thousand : and I heard the number of them.

F

Isa. 4. 2 In that day shall the branch of the LORD be beautiful and glorious, and the fruit of the earth *shall be* excellent and comely for them that are escaped of Israel.

3 And it shall come to pass, *that he that is* left in Zion, and *he that* remaineth in Jerusalem, shall be called holy, *even* every one that is written among the living in Jerusalem :

Rev. 14. 1. *See under C.*

G

Gen. 12. 3 And I will bless them that bless thee, and curse him that curseth thee :

CAME OUT OF GREAT TRIBULATION, BEARING PALMS (CONTINUED).

G—CONCLUDED.

and in thee shall all families of the earth be blessed.

Gen. 49. 10 The sceptre shall not depart from Judah, nor a lawgiver from between his feet, until Shiloh come; and unto him *shall* the gathering of the people *be*.

Luke 21. 24 And they shall fall by the edge of the sword, and shall be led away captive into all nations: and Jerusalem shall be trodden down of the Gentiles, until the times of the Gentiles be fulfilled.

Rom. 11. 25 For I would not, brethren, that ye should be ignorant of this mystery, lest ye should be wise in your own conceits; that blindness in part is happened to Israel, until the fullness of the Gentiles be come in.

H

Rev. 5. 9 And they sung a new song, saying, Thou art worthy to take the book, and to open the seals thereof: for thou wast slain, and hast redeemed us to God by thy blood out of every kindred, and tongue, and people, and nation;

I

Rev. 3. 4, 5. *See i, I,* § 575, *page 1326.*

K

Ps. 3. 8 Salvation *belongeth* unto the LORD: thy blessing *is* upon thy people. Selah.

Isa. 43. 11 I, *even* I, *am* the LORD; and beside me *there is* no saviour.

Jer. 3. 23 Truly in vain *is salvation hoped for* from the hills, *and from* the multitude of mountains: truly in the LORD our God *is* the salvation of Israel.

Hos. 13. 4 Yet I *am* the LORD thy God from the land of Egypt, and thou shalt know no god but me: for *there is* no saviour beside me.

Rev. 19. 1 And after these things I heard a great voice of much people in heaven, saying, Alleluia; Salvation, and glory, and honour, and power, unto the Lord our God:

L

Rev. 5. 13. *See z, Z,* § 579, *page 1334.*

M

Rev. 4. 6 And before the throne *there was* a sea of glass like unto crystal: and in the midst of the throne, and round about the throne *were* four beasts full of eyes before and behind.

N

Rev. 5. 13. *See z, Z,* § 579, *page 1334.*

N—CONCLUDED.

Rev. 5. 14 And the four beasts said, Amen. And the four *and* twenty elders fell down and worshipped him that liveth for ever and ever.

O

Rev. 3. 4, 5. *See i, I,* § 575, *page 1326.*

P

John 16. 33 These things I have spoken unto you, that in me ye might have peace. In the world ye shall have tribulation: but be of good cheer; I have overcome the world.

Q

Isa. 1. 18 Come now, and let us reason together, saith the LORD: though your sins be as scarlet, they shall be as white as snow; though they be red like crimson, they shall be as wool.

I Jno. 1. 7. *See e, E,* § 550, *page 1282.*

R

Ex. 29. 45 And I will dwell among the children of Israel, and will be their God.

I Ki. 6. 13 And I will dwell among the children of Israel, and will not forsake my people Israel.

Ps. 68. 16 Why leap ye, ye high hills? *this is* the hill *which* God desireth to dwell in; yea, the LORD will dwell *in it* for ever.

17 The chariots of God *are* twenty thousand, *even* thousands of angels: the Lord *is* among them *as in* Sinai, in the holy *place*.

18 Thou hast ascended on high, thou hast led captivity captive: thou hast received gifts for men; yea, *for* the rebellious also, that the LORD God might dwell *among them*.

Isa. 4. 5 And the LORD will create upon every dwellingplace of mount Zion, and upon her assemblies, a cloud and smoke by day, and the shining of a flaming fire by night: for upon all the glory *shall be* a defence.

6 And there shall be a tabernacle for a shadow in the daytime from the heat, and for a place of refuge, and for a covert from storm and from rain.

Rev. 21. 3 And I heard a great voice out of heaven saying, Behold, the tabernacle of God *is* with men, and he will dwell with them, and they shall be his people, and God himself shall be with them, *and be* their God.

Rev. 22. 3 And there shall be no more curse: but the throne of God and of the Lamb shall be in it: and his servants shall serve him:

§ 581. THE SEALED OF ISRAEL. THE MULTITUDE WHICH

CHAP. 7.

15 Therefore are they before the throne of God, and serve him day and night in his temple: and he that sitteth on the throne [r]shall dwell among them.

16 [s]They shall hunger no more, neither thirst any more; [t]neither shall the sun light on them, nor any heat.

17 For the Lamb which is in the midst of the throne [u]shall feed them, and shall lead them unto living fountains of waters: [x]and God shall wipe away all tears from their eyes.

For R, see preceding page (1341)

S

Isa. 49. 10 They shall not hunger nor thirst; neither shall the heat nor sun smite them: for he that hath mercy on them shall lead them, even by the springs of water shall he guide them.

§ 582. SEVENTH SEAL OPENED, SEVEN ANGELS

8 : 1–6.

1 And [a]when he had opened the seventh seal, there was silence in heaven about the space of half an hour.

2 [b]And I saw the seven angles which stood before God; [c]and to them were given seven trumpets.

3 And another angel came and stood at the altar, having a golden censer; and there was given unto him much incense, that he should [1]offer *it* with [d]the prayers of all saints upon [e]the golden altar which was before the throne.

4 And [f]the smoke of the incense, *which came* with the prayers of the saints, ascended up before God out of the angel's hand.

5 And the angel took the censer, and filled it with fire of the altar, and cast *it* [2]into the earth: and [g]there were voices, and thunderings, and lightnings, [h]and an earthquake.

6 And the seven angels which had the seven trumpets prepared themselves to sound.

A

Rev. 5. 5 And one of the elders saith unto me, Weep not: behold, the Lion of the tribe of Juda, the Root of David, hath prevailed to open the book, and to loose the seven seals thereof.

A—CONCLUDED.

Rev. 6. 1 And I saw when the Lamb opened one of the seals, and I heard, as it were the noise of thunder, one of the four beasts saying, Come and see.

B

Matt. 18. 10 Take heed that ye despise not one of these little ones; for I say unto you, That in heaven their angels do always behold the face of my Father which is in heaven.

Luke 1. 19 And the angel answering said unto him, I am Gabriel, that stand in the presence of God; and am sent to speak unto thee, and to shew thee these glad tidings.

Heb. 1. 14 Are they not all ministering spirits, sent forth to minister for them who shall be heirs of salvation?

C

II Chr. 29. 25 And he set the Levites in the house of the LORD with cymbals, with psalteries, and with harps, according to the commandment of David, and of Gad the king's seer, and Nathan the prophet: for *so was* the commandment of the LORD by his prophets.

26 And the Levites stood with the instruments of David, and the priests with trumpets.

27 And Hezekiah commanded to offer the burnt offering upon the altar. And when the burnt offering began, the song of the LORD began *also* with the trumpets, and with the instruments *ordained* by David king of Israel.

CAME OUT OF GREAT TRIBULATION, BEARING PALMS (Concluded).

T

Ps. 121. 6 The sun shall not smite thee by day, nor the moon by night.

Rev. 21. 4 And God shall wipe away all tears from their eyes; and there shall be no more death, neither sorrow, nor crying, neither shall there be any more pain: for the former things are passed away.

U

Ps. 23. *Read entire chapter.*

Ps. 36. 8 They shall be abundantly satisfied with the fatness of thy house; and

U—Concluded.

thou shalt make them drink of the river of thy pleasures.

John 10. 9 I am the door: by me if any man enter in, he shall be saved, and shall go in and out, and find pasture.

X

Isa. 25. 8 He will swallow up death in victory; and the Lord God will wipe away tears from off all faces; and the rebuke of his people shall he take away from off all the earth: for the Lord hath spoken *it*.

Rev. 21. 4. *See under T.*

WITH TRUMPETS, AND THE ANGEL OF INCENSE.

C—Concluded.

IIChr. 29. 28 And all the congregation worshipped, and the singers sang, and the trumpeters sounded: *and* all *this continued* until the burnt offering was finished.

1

Or, *add* it *to the prayers.*

D

Num. 16. 47 And Aaron took as Moses commanded, and ran into the midst of the congregation; and, behold, the plague was begun among the people: and he put on incense, and made an atonement for the people.

Mal. 1. 11 For, from the rising of the sun even unto the going down of the same, my name *shall be* great among the Gentiles; and in every place incense *shall be* offered unto my name, and a pure offering: for my name, *shall be* great among the heathen, saith the Lord of hosts.

Rev. 5. 8 And when he had taken the book, the four beasts and four *and* twenty elders fell down before the Lamb, having every one of them harps, and golden vials full of odours, which are the prayers of saints.

E

Ex. 30. 1 And thou shalt make an altar to burn incense upon: *of* shittim wood shalt thou make it.

Rev. 6. 9 And when he had opened the fifth seal, I saw under the altar the souls of them that were slain for the word of God, and for the testimony which they held:

F

Lev. 16. 13 And he shall put the incense upon the fire before the Lord, that the cloud

F—Concluded.

of the incense may cover the mercy seat that *is* upon the testimony, that he die not:

Ps. 141. 2 Let my prayer be set forth before thee *as* incense; *and* the lifting up of my hands *as* the evening sacrifice.

Luke 1. 10 And the whole multitude of the people were praying without at the time of the incense.

Rev. 15. 8 And the temple was filled with smoke from the glory of God, and from his power; and no man was able to enter into the temple, till the seven plagues of the angels were fulfilled.

2

Or, *upon.*

G

Rev. 16. 18 And there were voices, and thunders, and lightnings; and there was a great earthquake, such as was not since men were upon the earth, so mighty an earthquake, *and* so great.

H

II Sa. 22. 8 Then the earth shook and trembled; the foundations of heaven moved and shook, because he was wroth.

I Ki. 19. 11 And he said, Go forth, and stand upon the mount before the Lord. And, behold, the Lord passed by, and a great and strong wind rent the mountains, and brake in pieces the rocks before the Lord; *but* the Lord *was* not in the wind: and after the wind an earthquake; *but* the Lord *was* not in the earthquake:

Acts 4. 31 And when they had prayed, the place was shaken where they had assembled together; and they were all filled with the Holy Ghost, and they spake the word of God with boldness.

§ 583. SIX TRUMPETS SOUNDED

8:7–13; 9:1–21.

7 The first angel sounded, [a]and there followed hail and fire mingled with blood, and they were cast upon the earth: and the third part [b]of trees was burnt up, and all green grass was burnt up.

8 And the second angel sounded, [c]and as it were a great mountain burning with fire was cast into the sea: [d]and the third part of the sea became blood;

9 And the third part of the creatures which were in the sea, and had life, died; and the third part of the ships were destroyed.

10 And the third angel sounded, [e]and there fell a great star from heaven, burning as it were a lamp, [f]and it fell upon the third part of the rivers, and upon the fountains of waters;

11 [g]And the name of the star is called Wormwood: and [h]the third part of the waters became wormwood; and many men died of the waters, because they were made bitter.

12 [i]And the fourth angel sounded, and the third part of the sun was smitten, and the third part of the moon, and the third part of the stars; so as the third part of them was darkened, and the day shone not for a third part of it, and the night likewise.

13 And I beheld, [k]and heard an angel flying through the midst of heaven, saying with a loud voice, [l]Woe, woe, woe, to the inhabiters of the earth by reason of the other voices of the trumpet of the three angels, which are yet to sound!

CHAP. 9.

1 And the fifth angel sounded, [m]and I saw a star fall from heaven unto

A

Ex. 9. 23 And Moses stretched forth his rod toward heaven: and the LORD sent thunder and hail, and the fire ran along upon the ground; and the LORD rained hail upon the land of Egypt.

Josh. 10. 11 And it came to pass, as they fled from before Israel, *and* were in the going down to Beth-horon, that the LORD cast down great stones from heaven upon them unto Azekah, and they died: *they were* more which died with hailstones than *they* whom the children of Israel slew with the sword.

Ps. 11. 6 Upon the wicked he shall rain snares, fire and brimstone, and a horrible tempest: *this shall be* the portion of their cup.

Ps. 18. 12 At the brightness *that was* before him his thick clouds passed, hail *stones* and coals of fire.

13 The LORD also thundered in the heavens, and the Highest gave his voice; hail *stones* and coals of fire.

Ps. 78. 47 He destroyed their vines with hail, and their sycamore trees with frost.

48 He gave up their cattle also to the hail, and their flocks to hot thunderbolts.

Ps. 105. 32 He gave them hail for rain, *and* flaming fire in their land.

Isa. 28. 2 Behold, the Lord hath a mighty and strong one, *which* as a tempest of hail *and* a destroying storm, as a flood of mighty waters overflowing, shall cast down to the earth with the hand.

Isa. 29. 6 Thou shalt be visited of the LORD of hosts with thunder, and with earthquake, and great noise, with storm and tempest, and the flame of devouring fire.

Isa. 30. 30 And the LORD shall cause his glorious voice to be heard, and shall shew the lighting down of his arm, with the indignation of *his* anger, and *with* the flame of a devouring fire, *with* scattering, and tempest, and hailstones.

Isa. 32. 18 And my people shall dwell in a peaceable habitation, and in sure dwellings, and in quiet resting places;

19 When it shall hail, coming down on the forest; and the city shall be low in a low place.

Eze. 13. 13 Therefore thus saith the Lord GOD; I will even rend *it* with a stormy wind in my fury; and there shall be an overflowing shower in mine anger, and great hailstones in *my* fury to consume *it*.

AND THE WOES.

A—CONCLUDED.

Eze. 38. 22 And I will plead against him with pestilence and with blood; and I will rain upon him, and upon his bands, and upon the many people that *are* with him, an overflowing rain, and great hailstones, fire, and brimstone.

Rev. 16. 21 And there fell upon men a great hail out of heaven, *every stone* about the weight of a talent: and men blasphemed God because of the plague of the hail; for the plague thereof was exceeding great.

B

Isa. 2. 13 And upon all the cedars of Lebanon, *that are* high and lifted up, and upon all the oaks of Bashan.

Rev. 9. 4 And it was commanded them that they should not hurt the grass of the earth, neither any green thing, neither any tree; but only those men which have not the seal of God in their foreheads.

C

Jer. 51. 25 Behold, I *am* against thee, O destroying mountain, saith the LORD, which destroyest all the earth: and I will stretch out mine hand upon thee, and roll thee down from the rocks, and will make thee a burnt mountain.

Amos 7. 4 Thus hath the Lord GOD shewed unto me: and, behold, the Lord GOD called to contend by fire, and it devoured the great deep, and did eat up a part.

D

Eze. 14. 19 Or *if* I send a pestilence into that land, and pour out my fury upon it in blood, to cut off from it man and beast:

Rev. 16. 3 And the second angel poured out his vial upon the sea; and it became as the blood of a dead *man:* and every living soul died in the sea.

E

Isa. 14. 12 How art thou fallen from heaven, O Lucifer, son of the morning! *how* art thou cut down to the ground, which didst weaken the nations!

Rev. 9. 1 And the fifth angel sounded, and I saw a star fall from heaven unto the earth: and to him was given the key of the bottomless pit.

F

Rev. 16. 4 And the third angel poured out his vial upon the rivers and fountains of waters; and they became blood.

G

Deut. 29. 18 Lest there should be among you man, or woman, or family, or tribe, whose heart turneth away this day from the LORD our God, to go *and* serve the gods of these nations; lest there should be among you a root that beareth gall and wormwood;

Ruth 1. 20 And she said unto them, Call me not Naomi, call me Mara: for the Almighty hath dealt very bitterly with me.

Amos 5. 7 Ye who turn judgment to wormwood, and leave off righteousness in the earth,

Heb. 12. 15 Looking diligently lest any man fail of the grace of God; lest any root of bitterness springing up trouble *you*, and thereby many be defiled;

H

Ex. 15. 23 And when they came to Marah, they could not drink of the waters of Marah, for they *were* bitter: therefore the name of it was called Marah.

Jer. 9. 15 Therefore thus saith the LORD of hosts, the God of Israel; Behold, I will feed them, *even* this people, with wormwood, and give them water of gall to drink.

Jer. 23. 15 Therefore thus saith the LORD of hosts concerning the prophets; Behold I will feed them with wormwood, and make them drink the water of gall: for from the prophets of Jerusalem is profaneness gone forth into all the land.

I

Matt. 24. 29. *See y, Y, § 173, page 488.*

K

Rev. 14. 6 And I saw another angel fly in the midst of heaven, having the everlasting gospel to preach unto them that dwell on the earth, and to every nation, and kindred, and tongue, and people,

Rev. 19. 17 And I saw an angel standing in the sun; and he cried with a loud voice, saying to all the fowls that fly in the midst of heaven, Come and gather yourselves together unto the supper of the great God;

L

Rev. 9. 12 One woe is past; *and*, behold, there come two woes more hereafter.

Rev. 11. 14 The second woe is past; *and*, behold, the third woe cometh quickly.

M

Luke 10. 18. *See b, B, § 116, page 341.*

Rev. 8. 10. *See text of topic.*

CHAP. 9.

the earth: and to him was given the
key of [n]the bottomless pit.
2 And he opened the bottomless
pit; [o]and there arose a smoke out
of the pit, as the smoke of a great
furnace; and the sun and the air
were darkened by reason of the
smoke of the pit.
3 And there came out of the smoke
[p]locusts upon the earth: and unto
them was given power, [q]as the scorpions of the earth have power.
4 And it was commanded them
[r]that they should not hurt [s]the grass
of the earth, neither any green thing,
neither any tree; but only those
men which have not [t]the seal of God
in their foreheads.
5 And to them it was given that
they should not kill them, [u]but that
they should be tormented five
months: and their torment *was* as
the torment of a scorpion, when he
striketh a man.
6 And in those days [x]shall men
seek death, and shall not find it;
and shall desire to die, and death
shall flee from them.
7 And [y]the shapes of the locusts
were like unto horses prepared unto
battle; [z]and on their heads *were* as
it were crowns like gold, [a]and their
faces *were* as the faces of men.
8 And they had hair as the hair of
women, and [b]their teeth were as *the
teeth* of lions.
9 And they had breastplates, as it
were breastplates of iron; and the
sound of their wings *was* as the
sound of chariots of many horses
running to battle.
10 And they had tails like unto
scorpions, and there were stings in
their tails: [c]and their power *was* to
hurt men five months.

CHAP. 9.

11 [d]And they had a king over them,
which is, [e]the angel of the bottomless pit, whose name in the Hebrew
tongue *is* Abaddon, but in the Greek
tongue hath *his* name [1]Apollyon.
12 [f]One woe is past; *and*, behold,
there come two woes more hereafter.
13 And the sixth angel sounded,
and I heard a voice from the four
horns of the golden altar which is
before God.

N

Luke 8. 31 And they besought him that he would not command them to go out into the deep.

Rom. 10. 7 Or, Who shall descend into the deep? (that is, to bring up Christ again from the dead.)

Rev. 9. 2, 11. *See text of topic.*

Rev. 17. 8 The beast that thou sawest was, and is not; and shall ascend out of the bottomless pit, and go into perdition: and they that dwell on the earth shall wonder, whose names were not written in the book of life from the foundation of the world, when they behold the beast that was, and is not, and yet is.

Rev. 20. 1 And I saw an angel come down from heaven, having the key of the bottomless pit and a great chain in his hand.
2 And he laid hold on the dragon, that old serpent, which is the Devil, and Satan, and bound him a thousand years,
3 And cast him into the bottomless pit, and shut him up, and set a seal upon him, that he should deceive the nations no more, till the thousand years should be fulfilled: and after that he must be loosed a little season.

O

Joel 2. 2. *See under Y.*

P

Ex. 10. 4 Else, if thou refuse to let my people go, behold, to morrow will I bring the locusts into thy coast:

Judg. 7. 12 And the Midianites and the Amalekites and all the children of the east lay along in the valley like grasshoppers for multitude; and their camels *were* without number, as the sand by the sea side for multitude.

AND THE WOES (CONTINUED).

Q

Rev. 9. 10. *See text of topic.*

R

Rev. 6. 6 And I heard a voice in the midst of the four beasts say, A measure of wheat for a penny, and three measures of barley for a penny; and *see* thou hurt not the oil and the wine.

Rev. 7. 3 Saying, Hurt not the earth, neither the sea, nor the trees, till we have sealed the servants of our God in their foreheads.

S

Rev. 8. 7. *See text of topic.*

T

Rev. 7. 3. *See c, C, § 581, page 1338.*

U

Rev. 9. 10. *See text of topic.*

Rev. 11. 7 And when they shall have finished their testimony, the beast that ascendeth out of the bottomless pit shall make war against them, and shall overcome them, and kill them.

X

Job 3. 21 Which long for death, but it *cometh* not; and dig for it more than for hid treasures;

Job 7. 15 So that my soul chooseth strangling, *and* death rather than my life.

Isa. 2. 19 And they shall go into the holes of the rocks, and into the caves of the earth, for fear of the LORD, and for the glory of his majesty, when he ariseth to shake terribly the earth.

Jer. 8. 3 And death shall be chosen rather than life by all the residue of them that remain of this evil family, which remain in all the places whither I have driven them, saith the LORD of hosts.

Rev. 6. 16 And said to the mountains and rocks, Fall on us, and hide us from the face of him that sitteth on the throne, and from the wrath of the Lamb:

Y

Joel 2. 1 Blow ye the trumpet in Zion, and sound an alarm in my holy mountain: let all the inhabitants of the land tremble: for the day of the LORD cometh, for *it is* nigh at hand;

2 A day of darkness and of gloominess, a day of clouds and of thick darkness, as the morning spread upon the mountains: a great people and a strong; there hath not been ever the like, neither shall be any more after it, *even* to the years of many generations.

Y—CONCLUDED.

Joel 2. 3 A fire devoureth before them; and behind them a flame burneth: the land *is* as the garden of Eden before them, and behind them a desolate wilderness; yea, and nothing shall escape them.

4 The appearance of them *is* as the appearance of horses; and as horsemen, so shall they run.

5 Like the noise of chariots on the tops of mountains shall they leap, like the noise of a flame of fire that devoureth the stubble, as a strong people set in battle array.

6 Before their face the people shall be much pained: all faces shall gather blackness.

7 They shall run like mighty men; they shall climb the wall like men of war; and they shall march every one on his ways, and they shall not break their ranks:

8 Neither shall one thrust another; they shall walk every one in his path: and *when* they fall upon the sword, they shall not be wounded.

9 They shall run to and fro in the city; they shall run upon the wall, they shall climb up upon the houses; they shall enter in at the windows like a thief.

10 The earth shall quake before them; the heavens shall tremble: the sun and the moon shall be dark, and the stars shall withdraw their shining:

Z

Nah. 3. 17 Thy crowned *are* as the locusts, and thy captains as the great grasshoppers, which camp in the hedges in the cold day, *but* when the sun ariseth they flee away, and their place is not known where they *are*.

A

Da. 7. 8 I considered the horns, and, behold, there came up among them another little horn, before whom there were three of the first horns plucked up by the roots: and, behold, in this horn *were* eyes like the eyes of man, and a mouth speaking great things.

B

Joel 1. 6 For a nation is come up upon my land, strong, and without number, whose teeth *are* the teeth of a lion, and he hath the cheek teeth of a great lion.

For C, D, E, 1 and F, see next page (1348).

§ 583. SIX TRUMPETS SOUNDED,

CHAP. 9.

14 Saying to the sixth angel which had the trumpet, Loose the four angels which are bound [g]in the great river Euphrates.

15 And the four angels were loosed, which were prepared [2]for an hour, and a day, and a month, and a year, for to slay the third part of men.

16 And [h]the number of the army [i]of the horsemen *were* two hundred thousand thousand: [k]and I heard the number of them.

17 And thus I saw the horses in the vision, and them that sat on them, having breastplates of fire, and of jacinth, and brimstone: [l]and the heads of the horses *were* as the heads of lions; and out of their mouths issued fire and smoke and brimstone.

18 By these three was the third part of men killed, by the fire, and by the smoke, and by the brimstone, which issued out of their mouths.

19 For their power is in their mouth, and in their tails: [m]for their tails *were* like unto serpents, and had heads, and with them they do hurt.

CHAP. 9.

20 And the rest of the men which were not killed by these plagues [n]yet repented not of the works of their hands, that they should not worship [o]devils, [p]and idols of gold, and silver, and brass, and stone, and of wood; which neither can see, nor hear, nor walk:

21 Neither repented they of their murders, [q]nor of their sorceries, nor of their fornication, nor of their thefts.

C

Rev. 9. 5. *See text of topic.*

D

John 12. 31. *See n, N, § 170, page 475.*

E

Rev. 9. 1 *See text of topic.*

1

That is to say, *A destroyer.*

F

Rev. 8. 13. *See text of topic.*

G

Rev. 16. 12 And the sixth angel poured out his vial upon the great river Euphrates; and the water thereof was dried up, that the way of the kings of the east might be prepared.

2

Or, *at.*

H

Ps. 68. 17 The chariots of God *are* twenty thousand, *even* thousands of angels: the Lord *is* among them *as in* Sinai, in the holy *place.*

§ 584. THE

10: 1–11.

1 And I saw another mighty angel come down from heaven, clothed with a cloud: [a]and a rainbow *was* upon his head, and [b]his face *was* as it were the sun, [c]and his feet as pillars of fire:

2 And he had in his hand a little book open: [d]and he set his right

CHAP. 10.

foot upon the sea, and *his* left *foot* on the earth,

3 And cried with a loud voice, as *when* a lion roareth: and when he had cried, [e]seven thunders uttered their voices.

A

Eze. 1. 28 As the appearance of the bow that is in the cloud in the day of rain, so

AND THE WOES (CONCLUDED).

H—CONCLUDED.

Da. 7. 10 A fiery stream issued and came forth from before him: thousand thousands ministered unto him, and ten thousand times ten thousand stood before him: the judgment was set, and the books were opened.

I

Eze. 38. 4 And I will turn thee back, and put hooks into thy jaws, and I will bring thee forth, and all thine army, horses and horsemen, all of them clothed with all sorts *of armour*, *even* a great company *with* bucklers and shields, all of them handling swords:

K

Rev. 7. 4 And I heard the number of them which were sealed: *and there were* sealed a hundred *and* forty *and* four thousand of all the tribes of the children of Israel.

L

I Chr. 12. 8 And of the Gadites there separated themselves unto David into the hold to the wilderness men of might, *and* men of war *fit* for the battle, that could handle shield and buckler, whose faces *were like* the faces of lions, and *were* as swift as the roes upon the mountains;

Isa. 5. 28 Whose arrows *are* sharp, and all their bows bent, their horses' hoofs shall be counted like flint, and their wheels like a whirlwind:

29 Their roaring *shall be* like a lion, they shall roar like young lions: yea, they shall roar, and lay hold of the prey, and shall carry *it* away safe, and none shall deliver *it*.

M

Isa. 9. 13 For the people turneth not unto him that smiteth them, neither do they seek the LORD of hosts.

M—CONCLUDED.

Isa. 9. 14 Therefore the LORD will cut off from Israel head and tail, branch and rush, in one day.

15 The ancient and honourable, he *is* the head; and the prophet that teacheth lies, he *is* the tail.

16 For the leaders of this people cause *them* to err; and *they that are* led of them *are* destroyed.

N

Deut. 31. 29 For I know that after my death ye will utterly corrupt *yourselves*, and turn aside from the way which I have commanded you; and evil will befall you in the latter days; because ye will do evil in the sight of the LORD, to provoke him to anger through the work of your hands.

O

I Cor. 10. 20. *See i, I, § 367, page 930.*

P

Ps. 115. 4 Their idols *are* silver and gold, the work of men's hands.

Ps. 135. 15 The idols of the heathen *are* silver and gold, the work of men's hands.

Da. 5. 23 But hast lifted up thyself against the Lord of heaven; and they have brought the vessels of his house before thee, and thou, and thy lords, thy wives and thy concubines, have drunk wine in them; and thou hast praised the gods of silver, and gold, of brass, iron, wood, and stone, which see not, nor hear, nor know: and the God in whose hand thy breath *is*, and whose *are* all thy ways, hast thou not glorified:

Q

Rev. 22. 15 For without *are* dogs, and sorcerers, and whoremongers, and murderers, and idolaters, and whosoever loveth and maketh a lie.

LITTLE BOOK.

A—CONCLUDED.

was the appearance of the brightness round about. This *was* the appearance of the likeness of the glory of the LORD. And when I saw *it*, I fell upon my face, and I heard a voice of one that spake.

B

Matt. 17. 2 And was transfigured before them: and his face did shine as the sun, and his raiment was white as the light.

Rev. 1. 16 And he had in his right hand seven stars: and out of his mouth went a sharp twoedged sword: and his countenance *was* as the sun shineth in his strength.

B—CONCLUDED.

C

Rev. 1. 15 And his feet like unto fine brass, as if they burned in a furnace; and his voice as the sound of many waters.

D

Matt. 28. 18 And Jesus came and spake unto them, saying, All power is given unto me in heaven and in earth.

For E, see next page (1350).

§ 584. THE LITTLE

CHAP. 10.

4 And when the seven thunders had uttered their voices, I was about to write: and I heard a voice from heaven saying unto me, [f]Seal up those things which the seven thunders uttered, and write them not.

5 And the angel which I saw stand upon the sea and upon the earth [g]lifted up his hand to heaven,

6 And sware by him that liveth for ever and ever, [h]who created heaven, and the things that therein are, and the earth, and the things that therein are, and the sea, and the things which are therein, [i]that there should be time no longer:

7 But [k]in the days of the voice of the seventh angel, when he shall begin to sound, the mystery of God should be finished, as he hath declared to his servants the prophets.

8 And [l]the voice which I heard from heaven spake unto me again, and said, Go *and* take the little book which is open in the hand of the angel which standeth upon the sea and upon the earth.

9 And I went unto the angel, and said unto him, Give me the little book. And he said unto me, [m]Take

CHAP. 10.

it, and eat it up; and it shall make thy belly bitter, but it shall be in thy mouth sweet as honey.

10 And I took the little book out of the angel's hand, and ate it up; and it was in my mouth sweet as honey: and as soon as I had eaten it, my belly was bitter.

11 And he said unto me, [n]Thou must prophesy again before many peoples, and nations, and tongues, and kings.

E

Rev. 8. 5 And the angel took the censer, and filled it with fire of the altar, and cast *it* into the earth: and there were voices, and thunderings, and lightnings, and an earthquake.

F

Da. 8. 26 And the vision of the evening and the morning which was told *is* true: wherefore shut thou up the vision; for it *shall be* for many days.

Da. 12. 4 But thou, O Daniel, shut up the words, and seal the book, *even* to the time of the end: many shall run to and fro, and knowledge shall be increased.

Da. 12. 9 And he said, Go thy way, Daniel: for the words *are* closed up and sealed till the time of the end.

G

Da. 12. 5 Then I Daniel looked, and, behold, there stood other two, the one on this side of the bank of the river, and the other on that side of the bank of the river.

§ 585. THE TWO WITNESSES

11: 1–13.

1 And [a]there was given me a reed like unto a rod: and the angel stood, saying, [b]Rise, and measure the temple of God, and the altar, and them that worship therein.

2 But [c]the court which is without

A

Eze. 40. 3 And he brought me thither, and, behold, *there was* a man, whose appearance *was* like the appearance of brass, with a line of flax in his hand, and a measuring reed; and he stood in the gate.

Zech. 2. 1 I lifted up mine eyes again, and looked, and behold a man with a measuring line in his hand.

Rev. 21. 15 And he that talked with me had

BOOK (CONCLUDED).

G—CONCLUDED.

Da. 12. 6 And *one* said to the man clothed in linen, which *was* upon the waters of the river, How long *shall it be* to the end of these wonders?

7 And I heard the man clothed in linen, which *was* upon the waters of the river, when he held up his right hand and his left hand unto heaven, and sware by him that liveth forever, that *it shall be* for a time, times, and a half; and when he shall have accomplished to scatter the power of the holy people, all these *things* shall be finished.

8 And I heard, but I understood not: then said I, O my Lord, what *shall be* the end of these *things?*

H

Neh. 9. 6 Thou, *even* thou, *art* LORD alone; thou hast made heaven, the heaven of heavens, with all their host, the earth, and all *things* that *are* therein, the seas, and all that *is* therein, and thou preservest them all; and the host of heaven worshippeth thee.

John 1. 3. *ee e, E, § 1, page 5.*

I

Da. 12. 7. *See under G.*

Rev. 12. 12 Therefore rejoice, *ye* heavens, and ye that dwell in them. Woe to the inhabiters of the earth and of the sea! for the devil is come down unto you, having great wrath, because he knoweth that he hath but a short time.

Rev. 16. 17 And the seventh angel poured out his vial into the air; and there came a great voice out of the temple of heaven, from the throne, saying, It is done.

Rev. 21. 6 And he said unto me, It is done. I am Alpha and Omega, the beginning and the end. I will give unto him that is athirst of the fountain of the water of life freely.

K

Rev. 11. 15 And the seventh angel sounded; and there were great voices in heaven, saying, The kingdoms of this world are become *the kingdoms* of our Lord, and of his Christ; and he shall reign for ever and ever.

L

Rev. 10. 4. *See text of topic.*

M

Jer. 15. 16 Thy words were found, and I did eat them: and thy word was unto me the joy and rejoicing of mine heart: for I am called by thy name, O LORD God of hosts.

Eze. 2. 8 But thou, son of man, hear what I say unto thee; Be not thou rebellious like that rebellious house: open thy mouth, and eat that I give thee.

9 And when I looked, behold, a hand *was* sent unto me; and, lo, a roll of a book *was* therein;

10 And he spread it before me; and it *was* written within and without: and *there was* written therein lamentations, and mourning, and woe.

Eze. 3. 1 Moreover he said unto me, Son of man, eat that thou findest; eat this roll, and go speak unto the house of Israel.

2 So I opened my mouth, and he caused me to eat that roll.

3 And he said unto me, Son of man, cause thy belly to eat, and fill thy bowels with this roll that I give thee. Then did I eat *it;* and it was in my mouth as honey for sweetness.

N

Jer. 1. 9 Then the LORD put forth his hand, and touched my mouth. And the LORD said unto me, Behold, I have put my words in thy mouth.

10 See I have this day set thee over the nations and over the kingdoms, to root-out, and to pull down, and to destroy, and to throw down, to build, and to plant.

THAT SHALL PROPHESY.

A—CONCLUDED.

a golden reed to measure the city, and the gates thereof, and the wall thereof.

Eze. 40 and 41. *Read the entire chapters.*

B

Num. 23. 18 And he took up his parable, and said, Rise up, Balak, and hear; hearken unto me, thou son of Zippor:

C

Eze. 40. 17 Then brought he me into the outward court, and, lo, *there were* chambers, and a pavement made for the court round about: thirty chambers *were* upon the pavement.

C—CONCLUDED.

1

Gr. *cast out.*

D

Ps. 79. 1 O God, the heathen are come into

§ 585. THE TWO WITNESSES THAT

CHAP. 11.

the temple [1]leave out, and measure it not; [d]for it is given unto the Gentiles: and the holy city shall they [e]tread under foot [f]forty *and* two months.

3 And [2]I will give *power* unto my two [g]witnesses, [h]and they shall prophesy [i]a thousand two hundred *and* threescore days, clothed in sackcloth.

4 These are the [k]two olive trees, and the [l]two candlesticks standing before the God of the earth.

5 And if any man will hurt them, [m]fire proceedeth out of their mouth, and devoureth their enemies: [n]and if any man will hurt them, he must in this manner be killed.

6 These [o]have power to shut heaven, that it rain not in the days of their prophecy: and [p]have power over waters to turn them to blood, and to smite the earth with all plagues, as often as they will.

7 And when they shall have finished their testimony, [q]the beast that ascendeth [r]out of the bottomless pit [s]shall make war against them, and shall overcome them, and kill them.

For 1 and D, see preceding page (1351).

D—CONCLUDED.

thine inheritance; thy holy temple have they defiled; they have laid Jerusalem on heaps.

Lam. 1. 10 The adversary hath spread out his hand upon all her pleasant things: for she hath seen *that* the heathen entered into her sanctuary, whom thou didst command *that* they should not enter into thy congregation.

Luke 21. 24 And they shall fall by the edge of the sword, and shall be led away captive into all nations: and Jerusalem shall be trodden down of the Gentiles, until the times of the Gentiles be fulfilled.

II Thes. 2. 4 Who opposeth and exalteth himself above all that is called God, or that is worshipped; so that he as God sitteth in the temple of God, shewing himself that he is God.

E

Da. 7. 19 Then I would know the truth of the fourth beast, which was diverse from all the others, exceeding dreadful, whose teeth *were of* iron, and his nails *of* brass; *which* devoured, brake in pieces, and stamped the residue with his feet;

Da. 8. 10 And it waxed great, *even* to the host of heaven; and it cast down *some* of the host and of the stars to the ground, and stamped upon them.

Da. 8. 24 And his power shall be mighty, but not by his own power: and he shall destroy wonderfully, and shall prosper, and practise, and shall destroy the mighty and the holy people.

F

Da. 7. 25 And he shall speak *great* words against the Most High, and shall wear out the saints of the Most High, and think to change times and laws: and they shall be given into his hand until a time and times and the dividing of time.

Rev. 13. 5 And there was given unto him a mouth speaking great things and blasphemies; and power was given unto him to continue forty *and* two months.

2

Or, *I will give unto my two witnesses that they may prophesy.*

G

Rev. 20. 4 And I saw thrones, and they sat upon them, and judgment was given unto them; and *I saw* the souls of them that were beheaded for the witness of Jesus, and for the word of God, and which had not worshipped the beast, neither his image, neither had received *his* mark upon their foreheads, or in their hands; and they lived and reigned with Christ a thousand years.

H

Mal. 4. 5 Behold, I will send you Elijah the prophet before the coming of the great and dreadful day of the LORD:

Rev. 19. 10 And I fell at his feet to worship him. And he said unto me, See *thou do it* not: I am thy fellowservant, and of thy brethren that have the testimony of Jesus: worship God: for the testimony of Jesus is the spirit of prophecy.

I

Rev. 12. 6 And the woman fled into the wilderness, where she hath a place prepared of God, that they should feed her there a thousand two hundred *and* threescore days.

SHALL PROPHESY (CONTINUED).

K

Ps. 52. 8 But I *am* like a green olive tree in the house of God: I trust in the mercy of God for ever and ever.

Jer. 11. 16 The LORD called thy name, A green olive tree, fair, *and* of goodly fruit: with the noise of a great tumult he hath kindled fire upon it, and the branches of it are broken.

Zech. 4. 3 And two olive trees by it, one upon the right *side* of the bowl, and the other upon the left *side* thereof.

Zech. 4. 11 Then answered I, and said unto him, What *are* these two olive trees upon the right *side* of the candlestick and upon the left *side* thereof?

12 And I answered again, and said unto him, What *be these* two olive branches, which through the two golden pipes empty the golden *oil* out of themselves?

13 And he answered me and said, Knowest thou not what these *be?* And I said, No, my lord.

Rom. 11. 17 And if some of the branches be broken off, and thou, being a wild olive tree, were graffed in among them, and with them partakest of the root and fatness of the olive tree;

18 Boast not against the branches. But if thou boast, thou bearest not the root, but the root thee.

Rom. 11. 24 For if thou wert cut out of the olive tree which is wild by nature, and were graffed contrary to nature into a good olive tree; how much more shall these, which be the natural *branches*, be graffed into their own olive tree?

L

Zech. 4. 2 And said unto me, What seest thou? And I said, I have looked, and behold a candlestick all *of* gold, with a bowl upon the top of it, and his seven lamps thereon, and seven pipes to the seven lamps, which *are* upon the top thereof:

M

Num. 16. 35 And there came out a fire from the LORD, and consumed the two hundred and fifty men that offered incense.

II Ki. 1. 10 And Elijah answered and said to the captain of fifty, If I *be* a man of God, then let fire come down from heaven, and consume thee and thy fifty. And there came down fire from heaven, and consumed him and his fifty.

M—CONCLUDED.

II Ki. 1. 12 And Elijah answered and said unto them, If I *be* a man of God, let fire come down from heaven, and consume thee and thy fifty. And the fire of God came down from heaven, and consumed him and his fifty.

Jer. 5. 14 Wherefore thus saith the LORD God of hosts, Because ye speak this word, behold, I will make my words in thy mouth fire, and this people wood, and it shall devour them.

Hos. 6. 5 Therefore have I hewed *them* by the prophets; I have slain them by the words of my mouth: and thy judgments *are as* the light *that* goeth forth.

N

Num. 16. 29 If these men die the common death of all men, or if they be visited after the visitation of all men; *then* the LORD hath not sent me.

O

I Ki. 17. 1 And Elijah the Tishbite, *who was* of the inhabitants of Gilead, said unto Ahab, *As* the LORD God of Israel liveth, before whom I stand, there shall not be dew nor rain these years, but according to my word.

P

Ex. 7. 20 And Moses and Aaron did so, as the LORD commanded; and he lifted up the rod, and smote the waters that *were* in the river, in the sight of Pharaoh, and in the sight of his servants; and all the waters that *were* in the river were turned to blood.

Q

Da. 7 and 8. *Read entire chapters.*

R

Rev. 9. 2 And he opened the bottomless pit; and there arose a smoke out of the pit, as the smoke of a great furnace; and the sun and the air were darkened by reason of the smoke of the pit.

S

Da. 7. 21 I beheld, and the same horn made war with the saints, and prevailed against them;

Zech. 14. 2 For I will gather all nations against Jerusalem to battle; and the city shall be taken, and the houses rifled, and the women ravished; and half of the city shall go forth into captivity, and the residue of the people shall not be cut off from the city.

CHAP. 11.

8 And their dead bodies *shall lie* in the street of [t]the great city, which spiritually is called Sodom and Egypt, [u]where also our Lord was crucified.

9 And [x]they of the people and kindreds and tongues and nations shall see their dead bodies three days and a half, and [y]shall not suffer their dead bodies to be put in graves.

10 And [z]they that dwell upon the earth shall rejoice over them, and make merry, [a]and shall send gifts one to another; because these two prophets tormented them that dwelt on the earth.

11 And after three days and a half [b]the Spirit of life from God entered into them, and they stood upon their feet; and great fear fell upon them which saw them.

12 And they heard a great voice from heaven saying unto them, Come up hither. [c]And they ascended up to heaven [d]in a cloud; and their enemies beheld them.

13 And the same hour [e]was there a great earthquake, [f]and the tenth part of the city fell, and in the earthquake were slain [8]of men seven thousand: and the remnant were affrighted, [g]and gave glory to the God of heaven.

§ 585. THE TWO WITNESSES THAT

T

Isa. 1. 10 Hear the word of the LORD, ye rulers of Sodom; give ear unto the law of our God, ye people of Gomorrah.

Jer. 23. 14 I have seen also in the prophets of Jerusalem a horrible thing: they commit adultery, and walk in lies: they strengthen also the hands of evildoers, that none doth return from his wickedness: they are all of them unto me as Sodom, and the inhabitants thereof as Gomorrah.

Eze. 16. 48 *As* I live, said the Lord GOD, Sodom thy sister hath not done, she nor her daughters, as thou hast done, thou and thy daughters.

U

Luke 13. 33 Nevertheless I must walk to day, and to morrow, and the *day* following: for it cannot be that a prophet perish out of Jerusalem.

34 O Jerusalem, Jerusalem, which killest the prophets, and stonest them that are sent unto thee; how often would I have gathered thy children together, as a hen *doth gather* her brood under *her* wings, and ye would not!

Heb. 13. 12 Wherefore Jesus also, that he might sanctify the people with his own blood, suffered without the gate.

Rev. 18. 24 And in her was found the blood of prophets, and of saints, and of all that were slain upon the earth.

X

Rev. 17. 15 And he saith unto me, The waters which thou sawest, where the whore sitteth, are peoples, and multitudes, and nations, and tongues.

Y

Ps. 79. 2 The dead bodies of thy servants have they given *to be* meat unto the fowls of the heaven, the flesh of thy saints unto the beasts of the earth.

11:14–19.

14 [a]The second woe is past, *and*, behold, the third woe cometh quickly.

15 And [b]the seventh angel sounded; and [c]there were great voices in heaven, saying, [d]The kingdoms of this world are become *the kingdoms*

§ 586. THE SEVENTH

A

Rev. 8. 13 And I beheld, and heard an angel flying through the midst of heaven, saying with a loud voice, Woe, woe, woe, to the inhabiters of the earth by reason of the other voices of the trumpet of the three angels, which are yet to sound!

Rev. 9. 12 One woe is past; *and*, behold, there come two woes more hereafter.

SHALL PROPHESY (CONCLUDED).

Y—CONCLUDED.

Ps. 79. 3 Their blood have they shed like water round about Jerusalem; and *there was* none to bury *them*.

Eccl. 6. 3 If a man beget a hundred *children*, and live many years, so that the days of his years be many, and his soul be not filled with good, and also *that* he have no burial; I say, *that* an untimely birth *is* better than he.

Jer. 7. 33 And the carcasses of this people shall be meat for the fowls of the heaven, and for the beasts of the earth; and none shall fray *them* away.

Z

Judg. 16. 23 Then the lords of the Philistines gathered them together for to offer a great sacrifice unto Dagon their god, and to rejoice: for they said, Our god hath delivered Samson our enemy into our hand.

24 And when the people saw him, they praised their god: for they said, Our god hath delivered into our hands our enemy, and the destroyer of our country, which slew many of us.

A

Esth. 9. 19 Therefore the Jews of the villages, that dwelt in the unwalled towns, made the fourteenth day of the month Adar *a day of* gladness and feasting, and a good day, and of sending portions one to another.

Esth. 9. 22 As the days wherein the Jews rested from their enemies, and the month which was turned unto them from sorrow to joy, and from mourning into a good day: that they should make them days of feasting and joy, and of sending portions one to another, and gifts to the poor.

B

Eze. 37. *Read first half of chapter.*

C

II Ki. 2. 11 And it came to pass, as they still went on, and talked, that, behold, *there appeared* a chariot of fire, and horses of fire, and parted them both asunder; and Elijah went up by a whirlwind into heaven.

Rev. 12. 5 And she brought forth a man child, who was to rule all nations with a rod of iron: and her child was caught up unto God, and *to* his throne.

D

Isa. 60. 8 Who *are* these *that* fly as a cloud, and as the doves to their windows?

Acts 1. 9 And when he had spoken these things, while they beheld, he was taken up; and a cloud received him out of their sight.

E

Rev. 6. 12 And I beheld when he had opened the sixth seal, and, lo, there was a great earthquake; and the sun became black as sackcloth of hair, and the moon became as blood;

F

Rev. 16. 19 And the great city was divided into three parts, and the cities of the nations fell: and great Babylon came in remembrance before God, to give unto her the cup of the wine of the fierceness of his wrath.

3

Gr. *names of men,*

G

Mal. 2. 2 If ye will not hear, and if ye will not lay *it* to heart, to give glory unto my name, saith the LORD of hosts, I will even send a curse upon you, and I will curse your blessings: yea, I have cursed them already, because ye do not lay *it* to heart.

Rev. 14. 7 Saying with a loud voice, Fear God, and give glory to him; for the hour of his judgment is come: and worship him that made heaven, and earth, and the sea, and the fountains of waters.

TRUMPET SOUNDED.

A—CONCLUDED.

Rev. 15. 1 And I saw another sign in heaven, great and marvellous, seven angels having the seven last plagues; for in them is filled up the wrath of God.

B

Isa. 27. 13 And it shall come to pass in that day, *that* the great trumpet shall be blown, and they shall come which were ready to perish in the land of

B—CONCLUDED.

Assyria, and the outcasts in the land of Egypt, and shall worship the LORD in the holy mount at Jerusalem.

Rev. 10. 7 But in the days of the voice of the seventh angel, when he shall begin to sound, the mystery of God should be finished, as he hath declared to his servants the prophets.

For C and D, see next page (1356).

§ 586. THE SEVENTH TRUMPET

CHAP. 11.

of our Lord, and of his Christ;
and [e]he shall reign for ever and ever.
16 And [f]the four and twenty elders, which sat before God on their seats, fell upon their faces, and worshipped God,
17 Saying, We give thee thanks, O Lord God Almighty, [g]which art, and wast, and art to come; because [h]thou hast taken to thee thy great power, and hast reigned.
18 And [i]the nations were angry, [k]and thy wrath is come, [l]and the time of the dead, that they should be judged, and that [m]thou shouldest give reward unto thy servants the prophets, and to the saints, and them that fear thy name, [n]small and great; [o]and shouldest destroy them which [1]destroy the earth.
19 And [p]the temple of God was opened in heaven, and there was seen in his temple the ark of his testament: and [q]there were lightnings, and voices, and thunderings, and an earthquake, [r]and great hail.

C

Rev. 16. 17 And the seventh angel poured out his vial into the air; and there came a great voice out of the temple of heaven, from the throne, saying, It is done.

Rev. 19. 6 And I heard as it were the voice of a great multitude, and as the voice of many waters, and as the voice of mighty thunderings, saying, Alleluia: for the Lord God omnipotent reigneth.

D

Ps. 22. 27 All the ends of the world shall remember and turn unto the LORD: and all the kindreds of the nations shall worship before thee.

28 For the kingdom *is* the LORD'S: and he *is* the governor among the nations.

Ps. 72. 11 Yea, all kings shall fall down before him: all nations shall serve him.

Ps. 86. 9 All nations whom thou hast made shall come and worship before thee, O Lord; and shall glorify thy name.

Isa. 2. 2 And it shall come to pass in the last days, *that* the mountain of the

D—CONCLUDED.

LORD'S house shall be established in the top of the mountains, and shall be exalted above the hills; and all nations shall flow unto it.

Isa. 2. 3 And many people shall go and say, Come ye, and let us go up to the mountain of the LORD, to the house of the God of Jacob; and he will teach us of his ways, and we will walk in his paths: for out of Zion shall go forth the law, and the word of the LORD from Jerusalem.

Isa. 49. 7 Thus saith the LORD, the Redeemer of Israel, *and* his Holy One, to him whom man despiseth, to him whom the nation abhorreth, to a servant of rulers, Kings shall see and arise, princes also shall worship, because of the LORD that is faithful, *and* the Holy One of Israel, and he shall choose thee.

Isa. 60. *Read entire chapter.*

Da. 2. 44 And in the days of these kings shall the God of heaven set up a kingdom, which shall never be destroyed: and the kingdom shall not be left to other people *but* it shall break in pieces and consume all these kingdoms, and it shall stand for ever.

Da. 7. 14 And there was given him dominion, and glory, and a kingdom, that all people, nations, and languages, should serve him: his dominion *is* an everlasting dominion, which shall not pass away, and his kingdom *that* which shall not be destroyed.

Amos 9. 11 In that day will I raise up the tabernacle of David that is fallen, and close up the breaches thereof; and I will raise up his ruins, and I will build it as in the days of old:

12 That they may possess the remnant of Edom, and of all the heathen, which are called by my name, saith the LORD that doeth this.

Zech. 2 11 And many nations shall be joined to the LORD in that day, and shall be my people: and I will dwell in the midst of thee, and thou shalt know that the LORD of hosts hath sent me unto thee.

Zech. 14. 9 And the LORD shall be king over all the earth: in that day shall there be one LORD, and his name one.

E

Ps. 146. 10 The LORD shall reign for ever, *even* thy God, O Zion, unto all generations. Praise ye the LORD.

Da. 2. 44; Da. 7. 14. *See under D.*

SOUNDED (Concluded).

F

Rev. 4. 4 And round about the throne *were* four and twenty seats: and upon the seats I saw four and twenty elders sitting clothed in white raiment; and they had on their heads crowns of gold.

Rev. 5. 8 And when he had taken the book, the four beasts and four *and* twenty elders fell down before the Lamb, having every one of them harps, and golden vials full of odours, which are the prayers of saints.

Rev. 19. 4 And the four and twenty elders and the four beasts fell down and worshipped God that sat on the throne, saying, Amen; Alleluia.

G

John 8. 58. *See m, M, § 111, page 333.*

Rev. 1. 4 John to the seven churches which are in Asia: Grace *be* unto you, and peace, from him which is, and which was, and which is to come; and from the seven Spirits which are before his throne;

Rev. 4. 8 And the four beasts had each of them six wings about *him;* and *they were* full of eyes within: and they rest not day and night, saying, Holy, holy, holy, Lord God Almighty, which was and is, and is to come.

H

Rev. 19. 6. *See under C.*

I

Ps. 2. 1 Why do the heathen rage, and the people imagine a vain thing?

2 The kings of the earth set themselves, and the rulers take counsel together, against the LORD, and against his Anointed, *saying,*

3 Let us break their bands asunder, and cast away their cords from us.

Rev. 11. 2 But the court which is without the temple leave out, and measure it not; for it is given unto the Gentiles: and the holy city shall they tread under foot forty *and* two months.

Rev. 11. 9 And they of the people and kindreds and tongues and nations shall see their dead bodies three days and a half, and shall not suffer their dead bodies to be put in graves.

K

Rev. 6. 17. *See h, H, § 580, page 1338.*

L

Eccl. 3. 17 I said in mine heart, God shall judge the righteous and the wicked: for *there is* a time there for every purpose and for every work.

L—Concluded.

Da. 7. 9 I beheld till the thrones were cast down, and the Ancient of days did sit, whose garment *was* white as snow, and the hair of his head like the pure wool: his throne *was like* the fiery flame, *and* his wheels *as* burning fire.

10 A fiery stream issued and came forth from before him: thousand thousands ministered unto him, and ten thousand times ten thousand stood before him: the judgment was set, and the books were opened.

II. Tim. 4. 1 I charge *thee* therefore before God, and the Lord Jesus Christ, who shall judge the quick and the dead at his appearing and his kingdom;

I Pet. 4. 5 Who shall give account to him that is ready to judge the quick and the dead.

Rev. 6. 10 And they cried with a loud voice, saying, How long, O Lord, holy and true, dost thou not judge and avenge our blood on them that dwell on the earth?

M

I Cor. 3. 14. *See k, K, § 354, page 900.*

N

Rev. 19. 5 And a voice came out of the throne, saying, Praise our God, all ye his servants, and ye that fear him, both small and great.

O

Rev. 13. 10 He that leadeth into captivity shall go into captivity: he that killeth with the sword must be killed with the sword. Here is the patience and the faith of the saints.

Rev. 18. 6 Reward her even as she rewarded you, and double unto her double according to her works: in the cup which she hath filled, fill to her double.

1

Or, *corrupt.*

P

Rev. 15. 5 And after that I looked, and, behold, the temple of the tabernacle of the testimony in heaven was opened:

Rev. 15. 8 And the temple was filled with smoke from the glory of God, and from his power; and no man was able to enter into the temple, till the seven plagues of the seven angels were fullfilled.

Q

Rev. 8. 5. *See g, G, § 582, page 1342.*

R

Rev. 8. 7. *See a, A, § 583, page 1344.*

§ 587. MYSTIC SIGNS, THE WOMAN,

12: 1–6.

1 And there appeared a great [1]wonder in heaven; a [a]woman clothed with the sun, and the moon under her feet, and upon her head a crown of twelve stars:

2 And she being with child cried, [b]travailing in birth, and pained to be delivered.

3 And there appeared another [1]wonder in heaven; and behold [c]a great red dragon, [d]having seven heads and ten horns, and [e]seven crowns upon his heads.

4 And [f]his tail drew the third part [g]of the stars of heaven, [h]and did cast them to the earth: and the dragon stood before [i]the woman which was ready to be delivered, for [k]to devour her child as soon as it was born.

5 And she brought forth a man child, [l]who was to rule all nations with a rod of iron: and [m]her child was caught up unto God, and *to* his throne.

6 And [n]the woman fled into the wilderness, where she hath a place prepared of God, that they should feed her there [o]a thousand two hundred *and* threescore days.

1

Or, *sign.*

A

Isa. 49. 14 But Zion said, The LORD hath forsaken me, and my Lord hath forgotten me.

Isa. 54. 6 For the LORD hath called thee as a woman forsaken and grieved in spirit, and a wife of youth, when thou wast refused, saith thy God.

7 For a small moment have I forsaken thee; but with great mercies will I gather thee.

B

Isa. 66. 7 Before she travailed, she brought forth; before her pain came, she was delivered of a man child.

8 Who had heard such a thing? who hath seen such things? Shall the earth be made to bring forth in one day? *or* shall a nation be born at once? for as soon as Zion travailed, she brought forth her children.

C

Rev. 12. 9. *See text of topic,* § *588.*

Rev. 17. 3 So he carried me away in the spirit into the wilderness: and I saw a woman sit upon a scarlet coloured beast, full of names of blasphemy, having seven heads and ten horns.

D

Rev. 17. 9 And here *is* the mind which hath wisdom. The seven heads are seven mountains, on which the woman sitteth.

10 And there are seven kings: five are fallen, and one is, *and* the other is not yet come; and when he cometh, he must continue a short space.

§ 588. WAR IN HEAVEN. THE RED DRAGON IS CAST

12: 7–17.

7 And there was war in heaven: [a]Michael and his angels fought [b]against the dragon; and the dragon fought and his angels,

8 And prevailed not; neither was their place found any more in heaven.

9 And [c]the great dragon was cast out, [d]that old serpent, called the

A

Jude 9. *See g, G,* § *566, page 1308.*

B

Rev. 12. 3. *See text of topic,* § *587.*

Rev. 20. 2 And he laid hold on the dragon, that old serpent, which is the Devil, and Satan, and bound him a thousand years,

C

Luke 10. 18 And he said unto them, I beheld Satan as lightning fall from heaven.

THE RED DRAGON, THE MAN CHILD.

E

Rev. 13. 1 And I stood upon the sand of the sea, and saw a beast rise up out of the sea, having seven heads and ten horns, and upon his horns ten crowns and upon his heads the name of blasphemy.

F

Da. 8. 9 And out of one of them came forth a little horn, which waxed exceeding great, toward the south, and toward the east, and toward the pleasant *land*.

10 And it waxed great, *even* to the host of heaven; and it cast down *some* of the host and of the stars to the ground, and stamped upon them.

11 Yea, he magnified *himself* even to the prince of the host, and by him the daily *sacrifice* was taken away, and the place of his sanctuary was cast down.

12 And a host was given *him* against the daily *sacrifice* by reason of transgression, and it cast down the truth to the ground; and it practised, and prospered.

Rev. 9. 10 And they had tails like unto scorpions, and there were stings in their tails: and their power *was* to hurt men five months.

Rev. 9. 19 For their power is in their mouth, and in their tails: for their tails *were* like unto serpents, and had heads, and with them they do hurt.

G

Rev. 17. 18 And the woman which thou sawest is that great city, which reigneth over the kings of the earth.

H

Da. 8. 10. *See under F.*

I

Jer. 31. 22 How long wilt thou go about, O thou backsliding daughter? for the

I—CONCLUDED.

LORD hath created a new thing in the earth, A woman shall compass a man.

Rev. 12. 2. *See text of topic.*

K

Ex. 1. 16 And he said, When ye do the office of a midwife to the Hebrew women, and see *them* upon the stools, if it *be* a son, then ye shall kill him: but if it *be* a daughter, then she shall live.

I Pet. 5. 8 Be sober, be vigilant; because your adversary the devil, as a roaring lion, walketh about, seeking whom he may devour:

L

Rev. 2. 27. *See m, M, § 574, page 1324.*

M

Mark 16. 19 So then, after the Lord had spoken unto them, he was received up into heaven, and sat on the right hand of God.

Rev. 11. 12 And they heard a great voice from heaven saying unto them, Come up hither. And they ascended up to heaven in a cloud; and their enemies beheld them.

N

I Ki. 17. 3 Get thee hence, an turn thee eastward, and hide thyself by the brook Cherith, that *is* before Jordan.

4 And it shall be, *that* thou shalt drink of the brook; and I have commanded the ravens to feed thee there.

5 So he went and did according unto the word of the LORD: for he went and dwelt by the brook Cherith, that *is* before Jordan.

Rev. 12. 4. *See text of topic.*

Rev. 12. 14. *See text of § 588, page 1360.*

O

Rev. 11. 3. *See i, I, § 585, page 1352.*

TO THE EARTH; HE PERSECUTES THE WOMAN.

C—CONCLUDED.

John 12. 31 Now is the judgment of this world: now shall the prince of this world be cast out.

D

Gen. 3. 1 Now the serpent was more subtile than any beast of the field which the LORD God had made. And he said unto the woman, Yea, hath God said, Ye shall not eat of every tree of the garden?

Gen. 3. 4 And the serpent said unto the woman, Ye shall not surely die:

D—CONCLUDED.

Gen. 3. 14 And the LORD God said unto the serpent, Because thou hast done this, thou *art* cursed above all cattle, and above every beast of the field; upon thy belly shalt thou go, and dust shalt thou eat all the days of thy life:

Isa. 27. 1 In that day the LORD with his sore and great and strong sword shall punish leviathan the piercing serpent, even leviathan that crooked serpent; and he shall slay the dragon that *is* in the sea.

§ 588. WAR IN HEAVEN. THE RED DRAGON IS CAST TO

CHAP. 12.

Devil, and Satan, [e]which deceiveth
the whole world: [f]he was cast out
into the earth, and his angels were
cast out with him.

10 And I heard a loud voice saying
in heaven, [g]Now is come salvation,
and strength, and the kingdom of
our God, and the power of his
Christ: for the accuser of our brethren is cast down, [h]which accused
them before our God day and night.

11 And [i]they overcame him by the
blood of the Lamb, and by the word
of their testimony; [k]and they loved
not their lives unto the death.

12 Therefore [l]rejoice, *ye* heavens,
and ye that dwell in them. [m]Woe
to the inhabiters of the earth and of
the sea! for the devil is come down
unto you, having great wrath, [n]be-
cause he knoweth that he hath but
a short time.

13 And when the dragon saw that
he was cast unto the earth, he persecuted [o]the woman which brought
forth the man *child*.

14 And [p]to the woman were given
two wings of a great eagle, [q]that she
might fly [r]into the wilderness, into
her place, where she is nourished
[s]for a time, and times, and half a
time, from the face of the serpent.

15 And the serpent [t]cast out of his
mouth water as a flood after the
woman, that he might cause her to
be carried away of the flood.

16 And the earth helped the woman, and the earth opened her
mouth, and swallowed up the flood
which the dragon cast out of his
mouth.

17 And the dragon was wroth with
the woman, [u]and went to make war
with the remnant of her seed, [x]which
keep the commandments of God, and
have [y]the testimony of Jesus Christ.

E

Rev. 20. 3 And cast him into the bottomless pit, and shut him up, and set a seal upon him, that he should deceive the nations no more, till the thousand years should be fulfilled: and after that he must be loosed a little season.

Zech. 3. 1 And he shewed me Joshua the high priest standing before the angel of the LORD, and Satan standing at his right hand to resist him.

F

Eze. 28. 16 By the multitude of thy merchandise they have filled the midst ot thee with violence, and thou hasf sinned: therefore I will cast thee as profane out of the mountain of God: and I will destroy thee, O covering cherub, from the midst of the stones of fire.

17 Thine heart was lifted up because of thy beauty, thou hast corrupted thy wisdom by reason of thy brightness: I will cast thee to the ground, I will lay thee before kings, that they may behold thee.

John 12. 31. *See under C, page 1359.*

G

Rev. 11. 15 And the seventh angel sounded; and there were great voices in heaven, saying, The kingdoms of this world are become *the kingdoms* of our Lord, and of his Christ; and he shall reign for ever and ever.

Rev. 19. 1 And after these things I heard a great voice of much people in heaven, saying, Alleluia; Salvation, and glory, and honour, and power, unto the Lord our God:

H

Job 1. 9 Then Satan answered the LORD, and said, Doth Job fear God for nought?

Job 2. 5 But put forth thine hand now, and touch his bone and his flesh, and he will curse thee to thy face.

Zech. 3. 1. *See under E.*

I

Rom. 8. 32-38. *Study § 334 page 850.*

Rom. 16. 20 And the God of peace shall bruise Satan under your feet shortly. The grace of our Lord Jesus Christ *be* with you. Amen.

K

Luke 14. 26 If any *man* come to me, and hate not his father, and mother, and wife, and children, and brethren, and sisters, yea, and his own life also, he cannot be my disciple.

THE EARTH; HE PERSECUTES THE WOMAN (CONCLUDED).

L

Ps. 96. 10 Say among the heathen *that* the LORD reigneth: the world also shall be established that it shall not be moved: he shall judge the people righteously.
11 Let the heavens rejoice, and let the earth be glad; let the sea roar, and the fulness thereof.
12 Let the field be joyful, and all that *is* therein: then shall all the trees of the wood rejoice
13 Before the LORD: for he cometh, for he cometh to judge the earth: he shall judge the world with righteousness, and the people with his truth.

Rev. 18. 20 Rejoice over her, *thou* heaven, and *ye* holy apostles and prophets; for God hath avenged you on her.

M

Rev. 8. 13 And I beheld, and heard an angel flying through the midst of heaven, saying with a loud voice, Woe, woe, woe, to the inhabiters of the earth by reason of the other voices of the trumpet of the three angels, which are yet to sound!

Rev. 9. 12 One woe is past; *and*, behold, there come two woes more hereafter.

Rev. 11. 14. *See a, A, § 586, page 1354.*

N

Rev. 10. 6 And sware by him that liveth for ever and ever, who created heaven, and the things that therein are, and the earth, and the things that therein are, and the sea, and the things which are therein, that there should be time no longer:

O

Rev. 12. 5 And she brought forth a man child, who was to rule all nations with a rod of iron: and her child was caught up unto God, and *to* his throne.

P

Ex. 19. 4 Ye have seen what I did unto the Egyptians, and *how* I bare you on eagles' wings, and brought you unto myself.

Isa. 40. 31 But they that wait upon the LORD shall renew *their* strength; they shall mount up with wings as eagles; they shall run, and not be weary; *and* they shall walk, and not faint.

Q

Rev. 12. 6. *See n, N, § 587, page 1358.*

R

Rev. 17. 3 So he carried me away in the spirit into the wilderness: and I saw a woman sit upon a scarlet coloured beast, full of names of blasphemy, having seven heads and ten horns.

S

Da. 7. 25 And he shall speak *great* words against the Most High, and shall wear out the saints of the Most High, and think to change times and laws: and they shall be given into his hand until a time and times and the dividing of time.

Da. 12. 7 And I heard the man clothed in linen, which *was* upon the waters of the river, when he held up his right hand and his left hand unto heaven, and sware by him that liveth for ever that *it shall be* for a time, times, and a half; and when he shall have accomplished to scatter the power of the holy people, all these *things* shall be finished.

T

Ps. 18. 4 The sorrows of death compassed me, and the floods of ungodly men made me afraid.

Ps. 93. 3 The floods have lifted up, O LORD, the floods have lifted up their voice; the floods lift up their waves.

Isa. 28. 2 Behold, the Lord hath a mighty and strong one, *which* as a tempest of hail *and* a destroying storm, as a flood of mighty waters overflowing, shall cast down to the earth with the hand.

Isa. 59. 19 So shall they fear the name of the LORD from the west, and his glory from the rising of the sun. When the enemy shall come in like a flood, the Spirit of the LORD shall lift up a standard against him.

U

Gen. 3. 15 And I will put enmity between thee and the woman, and between thy seed and her seed; it shall bruise thy head, and thou shalt bruise his heel.

Rev. 11. 7. *See s, S, § 587, page 1352.*

X

Rev. 14. 12 Here is the patience of the saints: here *are* they that keep the commandments of God, and the faith of Jesus.

Y

I Cor. 1. 6. *See c, C, § 340, page 888.*

I Jno. 5. 10 He that believeth on the Son of God hath the witness in himself: he that believeth not God hath made him a liar; because he believeth not the record that God gave of his Son.

Rev. 19. 10 And I fell at his feet to worship him. And he said unto me, See *thou do it* not: I am thy fellow servant, and of thy brethren that have the testimony of Jesus: for the testimony of Jesus is the spirit of prophecy.

§ 589. MYSTIC SIGN OF THE

13 : 1–10.

1 And I stood upon the sand of
the sea, and saw [a]a beast rise up out
of the sea, [b]having seven heads and
ten horns, and upon his horns ten
crowns, and upon his heads the [1]name
of blasphemy.
2 And [c]the beast which I saw was
like unto a leopard, and [d]his feet
were as *the feet* of a bear, and [e]his
mouth as the mouth of a lion : and
[f]the dragon gave him his power,
[g]and his seat, [h]and great authority.
3 And I saw one of his heads [i]as
it were [2]wounded to death ; and his
deadly wound was healed : and [k]all
the world wondered after the beast.
4 And they worshipped the dragon
which gave power unto the beast :
and they worshipped the beast, saying, [l]Who *is* like unto the beast? who
is able to make war with him?
5 And there was given unto him [m]a
mouth speaking great things and
blasphemies ; and power was given
unto him [3]to continue [n]forty *and* two
months.
6 And he opened his mouth in
blasphemy against God, to blaspheme his name, [o]and his tabernacle, and them that dwell in heaven.
7 And it was given unto him [p]to
make war with the saints, and to
overcome them : and [q]power was
given him over all kindreds, and
tongues, and nations.
8 And all that dwell upon the earth
shall worship him, [r]whose names
are not written in the book of life

CHAP. 13.

of the Lamb slain [s]from the foundation of the world.
9 [t]If any man have an ear, let him
hear.
10 [u]He that leadeth into captivity
shall go into captivity : [x]he that killeth with the sword must be killed
with the sword. [y]Here is the patience and the faith of the saints.

A

Da. 7. 2 Daniel spake and said, I saw in my vision by night, and, behold, the four winds of the heaven strove upon the great sea.

3 And four great beasts came up from the sea, diverse one from another.

B

Rev. 12. 3. *See d, D, § 587, page 1358.*

1

Or, *names.*

C

Jer. 5. 6 Wherefore a lion out of the forest shall slay them, *and* a wolf of the evenings shall spoil them, a leopard shall watch over their cities : every one that goeth out thence shall be torn in pieces : because their transgressions are many, *and* their backslidings are increased.

Da. 7. 6 After this I beheld, and lo another, like a leopard, which had upon the back of it four wings of a fowl ; the beast had also four heads ; and dominion was given to it.

D

Prov. 28. 15 *As* a roaring lion, and a ranging bear ; *so is* a wicked ruler over the poor people.

Da. 7. 5 And behold another beast, a second, like to a bear, and it raised up itself on one side, and *it had* three ribs in the mouth of it between the teeth of it : and they said thus unto it, Arise, devour much flesh.

§ 590. MYSTIC SIGN OF THE

13 : 11–18.

11 And I beheld another beast
[a]coming up out of the earth ; and
he had two horns like a lamb, and
he spake as a dragon.

CHAP. 13.

12 And he exerciseth all the power
of the first beast before him, and
[b]causeth the earth and them which
dwell therein to worship the first

BEAST OUT OF THE SEA.

E

Isa. 5. 29 Their roaring *shall be* like a lion, they shall roar like young lions: yea, they shall roar, and lay hold of the prey, and shall carry *it* away safe, and none shall deliver *it*.

Da. 7. 4 The first *was* like a lion, and had eagle's wings: I beheld till the wings thereof were plucked, and it was lifted up from the earth, and made stand upon the feet as a man, and a man's heart was given to it.

F

Rev. 12. 3. *See c, C, § 587, page 1358.*

G

Rev. 16. 10 And the fifth angel poured out his vial upon the seat of the beast; and his kingdom was full of darkness; and they gnawed their tongues for pain,

H

Rev. 12. 4 And his tail drew the third part of the stars of heaven, and did cast them to the earth: and the dragon stood before the woman which was ready to be delivered, for to devour her child as soon as it was born.

I

Rev. 13. 12, 14. *See text of topic, § 590, page 1364.*

2

Gr. *slain.*

K

Rev. 17. 8 The beast that thou sawest was, and is not; and shall ascend out of the bottomless pit, and go into perdition: and they that dwell on the earth shall wonder, whose names were not written in the book of life from the foundation of the world, when they behold the beast that was, and is not, and yet is.

L

Rev. 18. 18 And cried when they saw the smoke of her burning, saying, What *city is* like unto this great city!

M

Da. 7. 8, 11, 25. *Read entire chapter.*

3

Or, *to make war.*

N

Rev. 11. 2. *See f, F, § 585, page 1352.*

O

John 1. 14 And the word was made flesh, and dwelt among us, (and we beheld his glory, the glory as of the only begotten of the Father,) full of grace and truth.

Col. 2. 9 For in him dwelleth all the fullness of the Godhead bodily.

Heb. 9. 11 But Christ being come a high priest of good things to come, by a greater and more perfect tabernacle, not made with hands, that is to say, not of this building;

P

Rev. 11. 7. *See s, S, § 585, page 1352.*

Q

Rev. 11. 18 And the nations were angry, and thy wrath is come, and the time of the dead, that they should be judged, and that thou shouldest give reward unto thy servants the prophets, and to the saints, and them that fear thy name, small and great; and shouldest destroy them which destroy the earth.

R

Phil. 4. 3. *See f, F, § 446, page 1072.*

S

Rev. 17. 8. *See under K.*

T

Matt. 11. 15. *See x, X, § 46, page 158.*

U

Isa. 33. 1 Woe to thee that spoilest, and thou *wast* not spoiled; and dealest treacherously; and they dealt not treacherously with thee! when thou shalt cease to spoil, thou shalt be spoiled; *and* when thou shalt make an end to deal treacherously, they shall deal treacherously with thee.

X

Matt. 26. 52. *See i, I, § 193, page 554.*

Y

Rev. 14. 12 Here is the patience of the saints: here *are* they that keep the commandments of God, and the faith of Jesus.

BEAST OUT OF THE EARTH.

A

Rev. 11. 7 And when they shall have finished their testimony, the beast that ascendeth out of the bottomless pit shall make war against them, and shall overcome them, and kill them.

Rev. 17. 8. *See under K, § 589.*

B

IIThes. 2. 4 Who opposeth and exalteth himself above all that is called God, or that is worshipped; so that he as God sitteth in the temple of God, shewing himself that he is God.

C

Rev. 13. 3. *See text of topic, § 589.*

CHAP. 13.

beast, [c]whose deadly wound was healed.

13 And [d]he doeth great wonders, [e]so that he maketh fire come down from heaven on the earth in the sight of men.

14 And [f]deceiveth them that dwell on the earth [g]by *the means of* those miracles which he had power to do in the sight of the beast; saying to them that dwell on the earth, that they should make an image to the beast, which had the wound by a sword, and did live.

15 And he had power to give life unto the image of the beast, that the image of the beast should both speak, [h]and cause that as many as would not worship the image of the beast should be killed.

16 And he causeth all, both small and great, rich and poor, free and bond, [i2]to receive a mark in their right hand, or in their foreheads:

17 And that no man might buy or sell, save he that had the mark, or the [k]name of the beast, [l]or the number of his name.

18 [m]Here is wisdom. Let him that hath understanding count the number of the beast: [n]for it is the number of a man; and his number *is* Six hundred threescore *and* six.

§ 590. MYSTIC SIGN OF THE BEAST

For C, see preceding page (1363).

D

Ex. 7. 11 Then Pharaoh also called the wise men and the sorcerers: now the magicians of Egypt, they also did in like manner with their enchantments.

Deut. 13. 1 If there arise among you a prophet, or a dreamer of dreams, and giveth thee a sign or a wonder,

2 And the sign or the wonder come to pass, whereof he spake unto thee, saying, Let us go after other gods, which thou hast not known, and let us serve them;

3 Thou shalt not hearken unto the words of that prophet, or that dreamer of dreams: for the LORD your God proveth you, to know whether ye love the LORD your God with all your heart and with all your soul.

Matt. 24. 24 For there shall arise false Christs, and false prophets, and shall shew great signs and wonders; insomuch that, if *it were* possible, they shall deceive the very elect.

II Thes. 2. 9 *Even him*, whose coming is after the working of Satan with all power and signs and lying wonders,

Rev. 16. 14 For they are the spirits of devils, working miracles, *which* go forth unto the kings of the earth and of the whole world, to gather them to the battle of that great day of God Almighty.

E

I Ki. 18. 38 Then the fire of the LORD fell, and consumed the burnt sacrifice, and the wood, and the stones, and the dust, and licked up the water that *was* in the trench.

II Ki. 1. 10 And Elijah answered and said to the captain of fifty, If I *be* a man of God, then let fire come down from heaven, and consume thee and thy fifty. And there came down fire from heaven, and consumed him and his fifty.

F

Rev. 12. 9. *See e, E, § 588, page 1360.*

Rev. 19. 20 And the beast was taken, and with him the false prophet that

14: 1–5.

1 And I looked, and, lo, [a]a Lamb stood [b]on the mount Sion, and with him [c]a hundred forty *and* four thousand, [d]having his Father's name

§ 591. THE SIGN OF

A

John 1. 29 The next day John seeth Jesus coming unto him, and saith, Behold the Lamb of God, which taketh away the sin of the world.

I Cor. 5. 7. *See m, M, § 359, page 908.*

B

Ps. 132. 13 For the LORD hath chosen Zion;

OUT OF THE EARTH (CONCLUDED).

F—CONCLUDED.

wrought miracles before him, with which
he deceived them that had received
the mark of the beast, and them that
worshipped his image. These both
were cast alive into a lake of fire
burning with brimstone.

G

II Thes 2.10 And with all deceivableness of
unrighteousness in them that perish;
because they received not the love of
the truth, that they might be saved.
11 And for this cause God shall send
them strong delusion, that they should
believe a lie:
12 That they all might be dammed
who believed not the truth, but had
pleasure in unrighteousness.

1

Gr. *breath.*

H

Da. 7. 25 And he shall speak *great* words
against the Most High, and shall wear
out the saints of the Most High, and
think to change times and laws: and
they shall be given into his hand until a time and times and the dividing
of time.

Rev. 16. 2 And the first went, and poured
out his vial upon the earth; and there
fell a noisome and grievous sore upon
the men which had the mark of the
beast, and *upon* them which worshipped his image.

Rev. 19. 20. *e under F.*

Rev. 20. 4 And I saw thrones, and they sat
upon them, and judgment was given
unto them: and I *saw* the souls of
them that were beheaded for the witness of Jesus, and for the word of
God, and which had not worshipped
the beast, neither his image, neither
had received *his* mark upon their foreheads, or in their hands; and they
lived and reigned with Christ a thousand years.

I

Zech. 13. 6 And *one* shall say unto him, What
are these wounds in thine hands?

I—CONCLUDED.

Then he shall answer, *Those* with
which I was a wounded *in* the
house of my friends.

Rev. 14. 9 And the third angel followed them,
saying with a loud voice, If any man
worship the beast and his image, and
receive *his* mark in his forehead, or in
his hand,

Rev. 19. 20 and Rev. 20. 4. *See under H.*

2

Gr. *to give them.*

K

Rev. 14. 11 And the smoke of their torment
ascended up for ever and ever: and
they have no rest day nor night, who
worship the beast and his image, and
whosoever receiveth the mark of his
name.

L

Rev. 15. 2 And I saw as it were a sea of glass
mingled with fire: and them that had
gotten the victory over the beast, and
over his image, and over his mark,
and over the number of his name,
stand on the sea of glass, having the
harps of God.

M

Ps. 107. 43 Whoso *is* wise, and will observe
these *things*, even they shall understand the loving kindness of the LORD.

Da. 12. 10 Many shall be purified, and made
white, and tried; but the wicked shall
do wickedly: and none of the wicked
shall understand; but the wise shall
understand.

Mark. 13.14 But when ye shall see the abomination of desolation, spoken of by
Daniel the prophet, standing where it
ought not, (let him that readeth understand,) then let them that be in
Judea flee to the mountains:

Rev. 17. 9 And here *is* the mind which hath
wisdom. The seven heads are seven
mountains, on which the woman sitteth.

N

Rev. 21. 17 And he measured the wall thereof,
a hundred *and* forty *and* four cubits,
according to the measure of a man,
that is, of the angel.

THE LAMB ON ZION.

B—CONTINUED.

he hath desired *it* for his habitation.
14 This *is* my rest for ever: here will
I dwell; for I have desired it.

Joel. 2. 32 And it shall come to pass, *that*
whosoever shall call on the name of
the LORD shall be delivered: for in

B—CONTINUED.

mount Zion and in Jerusalem shall
be deliverance, as the LORD hath said,
and in the remnant whom the LORD
shall call.

For B concluded, C and D, see next page (1366).

CHAP. 14.

written in their foreheads.
2 And I heard a voice from heaven,
[e]as the voice of many waters, and as
the voice of a great thunder: and I
heard the voice of [f]harpers harping
with their harps:
3 And they sung as it were a new
song before the throne, and before
the four beasts, and the elders: and
no man could learn that song [g]but
the hundred *and* forty *and* four thousand, which were redeemed from
the earth.
4 These are they which were not
defiled with women; [h]for they are
virgins. These are they [i]which follow the Lamb whithersoever he goeth. These [1k]were redeemed from
among men, [l]*being* the firstfruits unto
God and to the Lamb.
5 And [m]in their mouth was found
no guile: for [n]they are without fault
before the throne of God.

§ 591. THE SIGN OF THE

B—CONCLUDED.

Mic. 4. 7 And I will make her that halted a remnant, and her that was cast far off a strong nation: and the LORD shall reign over them in mount Zion from henceforth, even for ever.

C

Rev. 7. 4. *See f, F, § 581, page 1340.*

D

Rev. 7. 3 Saying, Hurt not the earth, neither the sea, nor the trees, till we have sealed the servants of our God in their foreheads.

Rev. 13. 16 And he causeth all, both small and great, rich and poor, free and bond, to receive a mark in their right hand, or in their foreheads:

Rev. 22. 4 And they shall see his face; and his name *shall be* in their foreheads.

E

Rev. 1. 15. *See r, R, § 570, page 1318.*

F

Rev. 5. 8, 9. *See l, L, § 579, page 1332.*

G

Rev. 14. 1. *See text of topic.*

H

Song 1. 3 Because of the saviour of thy good ointments thy name *is as* ointment poured forth, therefore do the virgins love thee.

Song 6. 8 There are threescore queens, and fourscore concubines, and virgins without number.

§ 592. THE SIGN OF THE SON OF MAN ON

14:6–20.

6 And I saw another angel [a]fly in
the midst of heaven, [b]having the
everlasting gospel to preach unto
them that dwell on the earth, [c]and
to every nation, and kindred, and
tongue, and people,
7 Saying with a loud voice, [d]Fear
God, and give glory to him; for the
hour of his judgment is come: [e]and
worship him that made heaven, and
earth, and the sea, and the fountains of waters.
8 And there followed another angel,
saying, [f]Babylon is fallen, is fallen,
[g]that great city, because she made

A

Rev. 8, 13. *See k, K, § 583, page 1344.*

B

II Sa. 23. 5 Although my house *be* not so with God; yet he hath made with me an everlasting covenant, ordered in all *things*, and sure: for *this is* all my salvation, and all *my* desire, although he make *it* not to grow.

Eph. 3. 9 And to make all *men* see what *is* the fellowship of the mystery, which from the beginning of the world hath been hid in God, who created all things by Jesus Christ:

10 To the intent that now unto the principalities and powers in heavenly *places* might be known by the church the manifold wisdom of God,

11 According to the eternal purpose which he proposed in Christ Jesus our Lord:

Tit. 1. 2 In hope of eternal life, which God, that cannot lie, promised before the world began;

LAMB ON ZION (Concluded).

H—Concluded.

II Cor. 11. 2. *See d, D, § 403, page 992.*

I

John 10. 27 My sheep hear my voice, and I know them, and they follow me:

Rev. 3. 4 Thou hast a few names even in Sardis which have not defiled their garments; and they shall walk with me in white: for they are worthy.

Rev. 7. 15 Therefore are they before the throne of God, and serve him day and night in his temple: and he that sitteth on the throne shall dwell among them.

Rev. 7. 17 For the Lamb which is in the midst of the throne shall feed them, and shall lead them unto living fountains of waters: and God shall wipe away all tears from their eyes.

Rev. 17. 14 These shall make war with the Lamb, and the Lamb shall overcome them: for he is Lord of lords, and King of kings: and they that are with him *are* called, and chosen, and faithful.

1

Gr. *were bought.*

K

Acts 20. 28. *See s, S, § 292, page 762.*

L

Jer. 2. 3 Israel *was* holiness unto the LORD, *and* the firstfruits of his increase: all that devour him shall offend; evil shall come upon them, saith the LORD.

L—Concluded.

Amos 6. 1 Woe to them *that are* at ease in Zion, and trust in the mountain of Samaria, *which are* named chief of the nations, to whom the house of Israel came!

I Cor. 16. 15 I beseech you, brethren, (ye know the house of Stephanas, that it is the firstfruits of Achaia, and *that* they have addicted themselves to the ministry of the saints,)

Jas. 1. 18 Of his own will begat he us with the word of truth, that we should be a kind of firstfruits of his creatures.

M

Ps. 32. 2 Blessed *is* the man unto whom the LORD imputeth not iniquity, and in whose spirit *there is* no guile.

Zeph. 3. 13 The remnant of Israel shall not do inquity, nor speak lies; neither shall a deceitful tongue be found in their mouth: for they shall feed and lie down, and none shall make *them* afraid.

N

Eph. 5. 27 That he might present it to himself a glorious church, not having spot, or wrinkle, or any such thing; but that it should be holy and without blemish.

Jude 24 Now unto him that is able to keep you from falling, and to present *you* faultless before the presence of his glory with exceeding joy,

THE CLOUDS COMING TO JUDGE THE EARTH.

C

Rev. 10. 11 And he said unto me, Thou must prophesy again before many peoples, and nations, and tongues, and kings.

Rev. 13. 7 And it was given unto him to make war with the saints, and to overcome them: and power was given him over all kindreds, and tongues, and nations.

D

Rev. 11. 18 And the nations were angry, and thy wrath is come, and the time of the dead, that they should be judged, and that thou shouldest give reward unto thy servants the prophets, and to the saints, and them that fear thy name, small and great; and shouldest destroy them which destroy the earth.

Rev. 15. 4 Who should not fear thee, O Lord, and glorify thy name? for *thou* only *art* holy: for all nations shall come and worship before thee; for thy judgments are made manifest.

E

Neh. 9. 6 Thou, *even* thou, *art* LORD alone; thou hast made heaven, the heaven of heavens, with all their host, the earth, and all *things* that *are* therein, the seas, and all that *is* therein, and thou preservest them all; and the host of heaven worshippeth thee.

Acts 14. 15. *See l, L, § 265, page 722.*

Acts 17. 24. *See g, G, § 279, page 744.*

F

Isa. 21. 9 And, behold, here cometh a chariot of men, *with* a couple of horsemen. And he answered and said, Babylon is fallen, is fallen; and all the graven images of her gods he hath broken unto the ground.

Jer. 51. 8. *Read the entire chapter.*

Rev. 16. 19 And the great city was divided into three parts, and the cities of the nations fell: and great Babylon came

For F concluded and G, see next page (1368).

§ 592. THE SIGN OF THE SON OF MAN ON THE

CHAP. 14.

all nations drink of the wine of the
wrath of her fornication.
9 And the third angel followed
them, saying with a loud voice, [h]If
any man worship the beast and his
image, and receive *his* mark in his
forehead, or in his hand,
10 The same [i]shall drink of the
wine of the wrath of God, which is
[k]poured out without mixture into
[l]the cup of his indignation; and [m]he
shall be tormented with fire and
brimstone in the presence of the
holy angels, and in the presence of
the Lamb:
11 And [n]the smoke of their torment
ascendeth up for ever and ever: and
they have no rest day nor night, who
worship the beast and his image,
and whosoever receiveth the mark
of his name.
12 [o]Here is the patience of the
saints: [p]here *are* they that keep the
commandments of God, and the
faith of Jesus.
13 And I heard a voice from heaven
saying unto me, Write, [q]Blessed *are*
the dead which die in the Lord [1]from
henceforth: Yea, saith the Spirit,
[r]that they may rest from their
labours; and their works do follow
them.
14 And I looked, and behold a
white cloud, and upon the cloud *one*
sat [s]like unto the Son of man, [t]hav-
ing on his head a golden crown, and
in his hand a sharp sickle.
15 And another angel [u]came out of
the temple, crying with a loud voice
to him that sat on the cloud, [x]Thrust
in thy sickle, and reap: for the time
is come for thee to reap; for the
harvest [y]of the earth is [2]ripe.
16 And he that sat on the cloud

F—CONCLUDED.

in remembrance before God, to give unto her the cup of the wine of the fierceness of his wrath.

Rev. 17. 5 And upon her forehead *was* a name written, MYSTERY, BABYLON THE GREAT, THE MOTHER OF HARLOTS AND ABOMINATIONS OF THE EARTH.

Rev. 18. 3. *Read entire chapter.*

G

Rev. 11. 8. *See t, T, § 585, page 1354.*

H

Rev. 13. 14 And deceiveth them that dwell on the earth by *the means of* those miracles which he had power to do in the sight of the beast; saying to them that dwell on the earth, that they should make an image to the beast, which had the wound by a sword, and did live.

15 And he had power to give life unto the image of the beast, that the image of the beast should both speak, and cause that as many as would not worship the image of the beast should be killed.

16 And he causeth all, both small and great, rich and poor, free and bond, to receive a mark in their right hand, or in their foreheads:

I

Job 21. 20 His eyes shall see his destruction, and he shall drink of the wrath of the Almighty.

Ps. 11. 6 Upon the wicked he shall rain snares, fire and brimstone, and a horrible tempest: *this shall be* the portion of their cup.

Ps. 75. 8 For in the hand of the LORD *there is* a cup, and the wine is red; it is full of mixture; and he poureth out of the same: but the dregs thereof, all the wicked of the earth shall wring *them* out, *and* drink *them*.

Isa. 51. 17 Awake, awake, stand up, O Jerusalem, which hast drunk at the hand of the LORD the cup of his fury; thou hast drunken the dregs of the cup of trembling, *and* wrung *them* out.

Jer. 25. 15 For thus saith the LORD God of Israel unto me; Take the winecup of this fury at my hand, and cause all the nations, to whom I send thee, to drink it.

16 And they shall drink, and be moved, and be mad, because of the sword that I will send among them.

K

Rev. 18. 6 Reward her even as she rewarded

CLOUDS COMING TO JUDGE THE EARTH (Continued).

K—Concluded.

you, and double unto her double according to her works: in the cup which she hath filled, fill to her double.

L

Rev. 16. 19. *See under F.*

M

Gen. 19. 24 Then the LORD rained upon Sodom and upon Gomorrah brimstone and fire from the LORD out of heaven;

Deut. 29. 23 *And that* the whole land thereof *is* brimstone, and salt, *and* burning, *that* it is not sown, nor beareth, nor any grass groweth therein, like the overthrow of Sodom and Gomorrah, Admah and Zeboim, which the LORD overthrew in his anger, and in his wrath:

Job 18. 15 It shall dwell in his tabernacle, because *it is* none of his: brimstone shall be scattered upon his habitation.

Ps. 11. 6. *See under I.*

Isa. 30. 33 For Tophet *is* ordained of old; yea, for the king it is prepared; he hath made *it* deep *and* large: the pile thereof *is* fire and much wood; the breath of the LORD, like a stream of brimstone, doth kindle it.

Isa. 34. 9 And the streams thereof shall be turned into pitch, and the dust thereof into brimstone, and the land thereof shall become burning pitch.

10 It shall not be quenched night nor day; the smoke thereof shall go up for ever: from generation to generation it shall lie waste; none shall pass through it for ever and ever.

Matt. 25. 41 Then shall he say also unto them on the left hand, Depart from me, ye cursed, into everlasting fire, prepared for the devil and his angels;

Rev. 19. 20 And the beast was taken, and with him the false prophet that wrought miracles before him, with which he deceived them that had received the mark of the beast, and them that worshipped his image. These both were cast alive into a lake of fire burning with brimstone.

Rev. 20. 10 And the devil that deceived them was cast into the lake of fire and brimstone, where the beast and the false prophet *are*, and shall be tormented day and night for ever and ever.

Rev. 21. 8 But the fearful, and unbelieving, and the abominable, and murderers, and whoremongers, and sorcerers, and idolaters, and all liars, shall have their part in the lake which burneth with fire and brimstone: which is the second death.

N

Isa. 34. 10. *See under M.*

Rev. 19. 3 And again they said, Alleluia. And her smoke rose up for ever and ever.

O

Rev. 13. 10. *See y, Y, § 589, page 1362.*

P

Rev. 12. 17. *See x, X, § 588, page 1360.*

Q

Eccl. 4. 1 So I returned, and considered all the oppressions that are done under the sun: and behold the tears of *such as were* oppressed, and they had no comforter; and on the side of their oppressors *there was* power; but they had no comforter.

2 Wherefore I praised the dead which are already dead, more than the living which are yet alive.

I Thes. 4. 14 For if we believe that Jesus died and rose again, even so them also which sleep in Jesus will God bring with him.

Rev. 20. 6 Blessed and holy *is* he that hath part in the first resurrection: on such the second death hath no power, but they shall be priests of God and of Christ, and shall reign with him a thousand years.

1

Or, *from henceforth saith the Spirit, Yea.*

R

II Thes. 1. 7 And to you who are troubled rest with us, when the Lord Jesus shall be revealed from heaven with his mighty angels,

Heb. 4. 9 There remaineth therefore a rest to the people of God.

S

Rev. 1. 13. *See l, L, § 570, page 1318.*

T

Rev. 6. 2. *See e, E, § 580, page 1334.*

U

Rev. 16. 17 And the seventh angel poured out his vial into the air; and there came a great voice out of the temple of heaven, from the throne, saying, It is done.

X

Matt. 13. 39. *See d, D, § 66, page 208.*

Y

Jer. 51. 33 For thus saith the LORD of hosts, the God of Israel; The daughter of Babylon *is* like a threshingfloor, *it is* time to thresh her: yet a little while, and the time of her harvest shall come.

Rev. 13. *Read entire chapter.*

2

Or, *dried.*

Z

Rev. 16. 8 And the fourth angel poured out his vial upon the sun; and power was given unto him to scorch men with fire.

§ 592. THE SIGN OF THE SON OF MAN ON THE

CHAP. 14.

thrust in his sickle on the earth; and
the earth was reaped.
17 And another angel came out of
the temple which is in heaven, he
also having a sharp sickle.
18 And another angel came out
from the altar, [z]which had power
over fire; and cried with a loud cry
to him that had the sharp sickle,
saying, [a]Thrust in thy sharp sickle,
and gather the clusters of the vine
of the earth; for her grapes are
fully ripe.
19 And the angel thrust in his sickle
into the earth, and gathered the vine
of the earth, and cast *it* into [b]the
great winepress of the wrath of God.
20 And [c]the winepress was trodden
[d]without the city, [e]and blood came
out of the winepress, even unto the
horse bridles, by the space of a
thousand *and* six hundred furlongs.

§ 593. A SONG OF TRIUMPH. THE SEVEN

15 : 1–8.

1 And [a]I saw another sign in heaven,
great and marvellous, [b]seven angels
having the seven last plagues; [c]for in
them is filled up the wrath of God.
2 And I saw as it were [d]a sea of
glass mingled with fire: and them
that had gotten the victory over the
beast, [e]and over his image, and over
his mark, *and* over the number of
his name, stand on the sea of glass,
[f]having the harps of God.
3 And they sing [g]the song of Moses
the servant of God, and the song
of the Lamb, saying, [h]Great and
marvellous *are* thy works, Lord God
Almighty; [i]just and true *are* thy
ways, thou King of [1]saints.
4 [k]Who shall not fear thee, O Lord,
and glorify thy name? for, *thou* only
art holy: for [l]all nations shall come
and worship before thee; for thy
judgments are made manifest.
5 And after that I looked, and, behold,
the temple of [m]the tabernacle
of the testimony in heaven was
opened:

A

Da. 4. 2 I thought it good to shew the signs and wonders that the high God hath wrought toward me.

3 How great *are* his signs! and how mighty *are* his wonders! his kingdom *is* an everlasting kingdom, and his dominion *is* from generation to generation.

Da. 6. 27 He delivereth and rescueth, and he worketh signs and wonders in heaven and in earth, who hath delivered Daniel from the power of the lions.

Rev. 12. 1 And there appeared a great wonder in heaven; a woman clothed with the sun, and the moon under her feet, and upon her head a crown of twelve stars:

Rev. 12. 3 And there appeared another wonder in heaven; and behold a great red dragon, having seven heads and ten horns, and seven crowns upon his heads.

B

Rev. 8. 2. *See b, B, § 582, page 1342.*

Rev. 16. 1 And I heard a great voice out of the temple saying to the seven angels, Go your ways, and pour out the vials of the wrath of God upon the earth.

Rev. 21. 9 And there came unto me one of the seven angels which had the seven vials full of the seven last plagues, and talked with me, saying, Come hither, I will shew thee the bride, the Lamb's wife.

C

Da. 12. *Read entire chapter.*

Rev. 14. 10. *See i, I, § 592, page 1368.*

CLOUDS COMING TO JUDGE THE EARTH (CONCLUDED).

For Z see preceding page (1369).

A

Joel 3. 13 Put ye in the sickle, for the harvest is ripe: come, get you down; for the press is full, the fats overflow; for their wickedness *is* great.

B

Rev. 19. 15 And out of his mouth goeth a sharp sword, that with it he should smite the nations: and he shall rule them with a rod of iron: and he treadeth the winepress of the fierceness and wrath of Almighty God.

C

Isa. 63. 3 I have trodden the winepress alone; and of the people *there was* none with me: for I will tread them in mine anger, and trample them in my fury;

C—CONCLUDED.

and their blood shall be sprinkled upon my garments, and I will stain all my raiment.

Lam. 1. 15 The Lord hath trodden under foot all my mighty *men* in the midst of me: he hath called an assembly against me to crush my young men: the Lord hath trodden the virgin, the daughter of Judah, *as* in a winepress.

D

Rev. 11. 8. *See u, U, § 585, page 1354.*

E

Rev. 19 13 And he *was* clothed with a vesture dipped in blood: and his name is called The Word of God.

ANGELS HAVING THE SEVEN LAST PLAGUES.

D

Isa. 4. 4 When the Lord shall have washed away the filth of the daughters of Zion, and shall have purged the blood of Jerusalem from the midst thereof by the spirit of judgment, and by the spirit of burning.

Rev. 4. 6 And before the throne *there was* a sea of glass like unto crystal: and in the midst of the throne, and round about the throne, *were* four beasts full of eyes before and behind.

Rev. 21. 18 And the building of the wall of of it was *of* jasper: and the city *was* pure gold, like unto clear glass.

E

Rev. 13. 11-18. *Study § 590, page 1364.*

F

Rev. 5. 8. *See l, L, § 579, page 1332.*

G

Ex. 15. *Read entire chapter.*

Deut. 31. 30 And Moses spake in the ears of all the congregation of Israel the words of this song, until they were ended.

Deut. 32. *Read entire chapter.*

Rev. 14. 3 And they sung as it were a new song before the throne, and before the four beasts, and the elders: and no man could learn that song but the hundred *and* forty *and* four thousand, which were redeemed from the earth.

H

Deut. 32. 4 *He is* the Rock, his work *is* perfect; for all his ways *are* judgment: a God of truth and without iniquity, just and right *is* he.

Ps. 111. 2 The works of the LORD *are* great, sought out of all them that have pleasure therein.

H—CONCLUDED.

Ps. 139. 14 I will praise thee; for I am fearfully *and* wonderfully made: marvellous *are* thy works; and *that* my soul knoweth right well.

I

Hos. 14. 9 Who *is* wise, and he shall understand these *things?* prudent, and he shall know them? for the ways of the LORD *are* right, and the just shall walk in them: but the transgressors shall fall therein.

Rev. 16. 7 And I heard another out of the altar say, Even so, Lord God Almighty, true and righteous *are* thy judgments.

1

Or, *nations*, or, *ages.*

K

Ex. 15. 16 Fear and dread shall fall upon them; by the greatness of thine arm they shall be *as* still as a stone; till thy people pass over, O LORD, till the people pass over, *which* thou hast purchased.

Jer. 10. 7 Who would not fear thee, O King of nations? for to thee doth it appertain: forasmuch as among all the wise *men* of the nations, and in all their kingdoms, *there is* none like unto thee.

L

Isa. 66. 23 And it shall come to pass, *that* from one new moon to another, and from one sabbath to another, shall all flesh come to worship before me, saith the LORD.

For L concl'd and M, see next page (1372).

§ 593. A SONG OF TRIUMPH. THE SEVEN ANGELS

CHAP. 15.

6 And [n]the seven angels came out
of the temple, having the seven
plagues, [o]clothed in pure and white
linen, and having their breasts girded
with golden girdles.

7 And [p]one of the four beasts gave
unto the seven angels seven golden
vials full of the wrath of God, [q]who
liveth for ever and ever.

8 And [r]the temple was filled with
smoke [s]from the glory of God, and
from his power; and no man was
able to enter into the temple, till the
seven plagues of the seven angels
were fulfilled.

L—CONTINUED.

Zech. 2. 11 And many nations shall be joined to the LORD in that day, and shall be my people: and I will dwell in the midst of thee, and thou shalt know that the LORD of hosts hath sent me unto thee.

Zech. 8. 22 Yea, many people and strong nations shall come to seek the LORD of hosts in Jerusalem, and to pray before the LORD.

Zech. 14. 16 And it shall come to pass, *that* every one that is left of all the nations

L—CONCLUDED.

which came against Jerusalem, shall even go up from year to year to worship the King, the LORD of hosts, and to keep the feast of tabernacles.

M

Num. 1. 50 But thou shalt appoint the Levites over the tabernacle of testimony, and over all the vessels thereof, and over all things that *belong* to it: they shall bear the tabernacle, and all the vessels thereof; and they shall minister unto it, and shall encamp round about the tabernacle.

Rev. 11. 9. *See p, P, § 586, page 1356.*

N

Rev. 15. 1. *See text of topic.*

O

Ex. 28. 39 And thou shalt embroider the coat of fine linen, and thou shalt make the mitre *of* fine linen, and thou shalt make the girdle *of* needlework.

40 And for Aaron's sons thou shalt make coats, and thou shalt make for them girdles, and bonnets shalt thou make for them, for glory and for beauty.

41 And thou shall put them upon Aaron thy brother, and his sons with him; and shalt anoint them, and consecrate them, and sanctify them, that they may minister unto me in the priest's office.

§ 594. THE SEVEN PLAGUES POURED FROM

16 : 1–21.

1 And I heard a great voice out of
the temple saying [a]to the seven
angels, Go your ways, and pour out
the vials [b]of the wrath of God upon
the earth.

2 And the first went, and poured
out his vial [c]upon the earth; and
[d]there fell a noisome and grievous
sore upon the men [e]which had the
mark of the beast, and *upon* them
[f]which worshipped his image.

3 And the second angel poured out
his vial [g]upon the sea; and [h]it became as the blood of a dead *man*:
[i]and every living soul died in the sea.

A

Rev. 15. 1. *See b, B, § 593, page 1370.*

B

Rev. 14. 10. *See i, I, § 592, page 1368.*

Rev. 15, 7. *See text of topic § 593.*

C

Rev. 8. 7 The first angel sounded, and there followed hail and fire mingled with blood, and they were cast upon the earth: and the third part of the trees was burnt up, and all green grass was burnt up.

D

Ex. 9. 10 And they took ashes of the furnace, and stood before Pharaoh; and Moses sprinkled it up toward heaven; and it became a boil breaking forth *with* blains upon man, and upon beast.

11 And the magicians could not stand before Moses because of the boils; for the boil was upon the magicians, and upon all the Egyptians.

HAVING THE SEVEN LAST PLAGUES (CONCLUDED).

O—CONCLUDED.

Ex. 28. 42 And thou shalt make them linen
breeches to cover their nakedness;
from the loins even unto the thighs
they shall reach:

Eze. 44. 17 And it shall come to pass, *that*
when they enter in at the gates of the
inner court, they shall be clothed with
linen garments; and no wool shall
come upon them, while they minister in the gates of the inner court,
and within.
18 They shall have linen bonnets
upon their heads, and shall have linen
breeches upon their loins; they shall
not gird *themselves* with any thing that
causeth sweat.

Rev. 19. 8 And to her was granted that she
should be arrayed in fine linen, clean
and white: for the fine linen is the
righteousness of saints.

Rev. 19. 14 And the armies *which were* in
heaven followed him upon white
horses, clothed in fine linen, white and
clean.

P

Rev. 4. 6 And before the throne *there was* a
sea of glass like unto crystal: and in
the midst of the throne, and round
about the throne, *were* four beasts full
of eyes before and behind.

Q

I Thes. 1. 9 For they themselves shew of us
what manner of entering in we had unto

Q—CONCLUDED.

you, and how ye turned to God from
idols to serve the living and true God;

Rev. 4. 9 And when those beasts give glory
and honour and thanks to him that sat
on the throne, who liveth for ever and
ever,

Rev. 10. 6 And sware by him that liveth for
ever and ever, who created heaven,
and the things that therein are, and
the earth, and the things that therein
are, and the sea, and the things which
are therein, that there should be time
no longer:

R

Ex. 40. 34 Then a cloud covered the tent of
the congregation, and the glory of the
LORD filled the tabernacle.

I Ki. 8. 10 And it came to pass, when the
priests were come out of the holy
place, that the cloud filled the house
of the LORD,

II Chr. 5. 14 So that the priests could not stand
to minister by reason of the cloud: for
the glory of the LORD had filled the
house of God.

Isa. 6. 4 And the posts of the door moved
at the voice of him that cried, and the
house was filled with smoke.

S

II Thes. 1 9 Who shall be punished with everlasting destruction from the presence
of the Lord, and from the glory of his
power;

THE VIALS OF THE WRATH OF GOD.

D—CONCLUDED.

Deut. 7. 15 And the LORD will take away
from thee all sickness, and will put
none of the evil diseases of Egypt,
which thou knowest, upon thee; but
will lay them upon all *them* that hate
thee.

Deut. 28. 27 The LORD will smite thee with
the botch of Egypt, and with the emerods, and with the scab, and with the
itch, whereof thou canst not be healed.

I Sa. 5. 6 But the hand of the LORD was
heavy upon them of Ashdod, and he
destroyed them, and smote them with
emerods, *even* Ashdod and the coasts
thereof.

E

Rev. 13. 16, 17. *See i, I, § 590, page 1364.*

F

Rev. 14. 9. *See h, H, § 592, page 1368.*

G

Rev. 8. 8. *See d, D, § 583, page 1344.*

H

Ex. 7. 20 And Moses and Aaron did so, as the
LORD commanded; and he lifted up
the rod, and smote the waters that
were in the river, in the sight of
Pharaoh, and in the sight of his servants; and all the waters that *were*
in the river were turned to blood.
21 And the fish that *was* in the river
died; and the river stank, and the
Egyptians could not drink of the
water of the river; and there was blood
throughout all the land of Egypt.

I

Rev. 8. 9 And the third part of the creatures
which were in the sea, and had life,
died; and the third part of the ships
were destroyed.

K

Rev. 8. 10. *See e, E, § 583, page 1344.*

L

Rom. 3. 21. *See e, E, § 324, page 824.*
Rev. 15. 3. *See i, I, § 593, page 1370.*

§ 594. THE SEVEN PLAGUES POURED FROM THE

CHAP. 16.

4 And [k]the third angel poured out
his vial upon the rivers and fountains
of waters; and they became blood.
5 And I heard the angel of the
waters say, [l]Thou art righteous, O
Lord,[m]which art, and wast, and shalt
be, because thou hast judged thus.
6 For [n]they have shed the blood of
saints and prophets, [o]and thou hast
given them blood to drink; for they
are worthy.
7 And I heard another out of the
altar say, Even so, [p]Lord God Almighty, [q]true and righteous *are* thy
judgments.
8 And the fourth angel poured out
his vial upon the sun; [s]and power
was given unto him to scorch men
with fire.
9 And men were [1]scorched with
great heat, and [t]blasphemed the
name of God, which hath power
over these plagues: and [u]they repented not [x]to give him glory.
10 And the fifth angel poured out
his vial [y]upon the seat of the beast;
[z]and his kingdom was full of darkness; [a]and they gnawed their
tongues for pain,
11 And [b]blasphemed the God of
heaven because of their pains and
[c]their sores, and [d]repented not of
their deeds.
12 And the sixth angel poured out
his vial [e]upon the great river Euphrates; [f]and the water thereof was
dried up, [g]that the way of the kings
of the east might be prepared.
13 And I saw three unclean [h]spirits
like frogs *come* out of the mouth of
[i]the dragon, and out of the mouth
of the beast, and out of the mouth
of [k]the false prophet.
14 For [l]they are the spirits of devils, [m]working miracles, *which* go
forth unto the kings of the earth

For K and L, see preceding page (1373).

M

John 8. 58. *See m, M, § 111, page 333.*

N

Matt. 23. 34. *Study § 167, page 468.*

O

Isa. 49. 26 And I will feed them that oppress thee with their own flesh; and they shall be drunken with their own blood, as with sweet wine: and all flesh shall know that I the LORD *am* thy Saviour and thy Redeemer, the mighty one of Jacob.

P

Rev. 15. 3 And they sing the song of Moses the servant of God, and the song of the Lamb, saying, Great and marvellous *are* thy works, Lord God Almighty; just and true *are* thy ways, thou King of saints.

Q

Rev. 13. 10 He that leadeth into captivity shall go into captivity: he that killeth with the sword must be killed with the sword. Here is the patience and the faith of the saints.

Rev. 14. 10 The same shall drink of the wine of the wrath of God, which is poured out without mixture into the cup of his indignation; and he shall be tormented with fire and brimstone in the presence of the holy angels, and in the presence of the Lamb:

Rev. 19. 2 For true and righteous *are* his judgments: for he hath judged the great whore, which did corrupt the earth with her fornication, and hath avenged the blood of his servants at her hand.

R

Rev. 8. 12. *See i, I, § 583, page 1344.*

S

Rev. 9. 17 And thus I saw the horses in the vision, and them that sat on them, having breastplates of fire, and of jacinth, and brimstone: and the heads of the horses *were* as the heads of lions; and out of their mouths issued fire and smoke and brimstone.

18 By these three was the third part of men killed, by the fire, and by the smoke, and by the brimstone, which issued out of their mouths.

1

Or, *burned.*

T

Rev. 16. 11, 21. *See text of topic.*

VIALS OF THE WRATH OF GOD (CONTINUED).

U

Da. 5. 22 And thou his son, O Belshazzar,
hast not humbled thine heart, though
thou knewest all this;
23 But hast lifted up thyself against
the Lord of heaven; and they have
brought the vessels of his house before thee, and thou, and thy lords, thy
wives, and thy concubines, have drunk
wine in them; and thou hast praised
the gods of silver, and of gold, of
brass, iron, wood, and stone, which
see not, nor hear, nor know: and
the God in whose hand thy breath *is*,
and whose *are* all thy ways, hast thou
not glorified:

Rev. 9. 20. *See n, N, § 583, page 1348.*

X

Rev. 11. 13. *See g, G, § 585, page 1354.*

Y

Rev. 13. 2 And the beast which I saw was
like unto a leopard, and his feet were
as *the feet* of a bear, and his mouth
as the mouth of a lion: and the
dragon gave him his power, and his
seat, and great authority.

Z

Isa. 8. 22 And they shall look unto the
earth; and behold trouble and darkness, dimness of anguish; and *they
shall be* driven to darkness.

Rev. 9. 2 And he opened the bottomless pit;
and there arose a smoke out of the
pit, as the smoke of a great furnace;
and the sun and the air were darkened by reason of the smoke of the pit.

A

Matt. 24. 51. *See h, H, § 174, page 494.*

Rev. 11. 10 And they that dwell upon the
earth shall rejoice over them, and
make merry, and shall send gifts one
to another; because these two prophets tormented them that dwelt on the
earth.

B

Rev. 16. 9, 21. *See text of topic.*

C

Rev. 16. 2. *See text of topic.*

D

Rev. 16. 9. *See text of topic.*

E

Rev. 9. 14. *See g, G, § 583, page 1348.*

F

Jer. 50. 38 A drought *is* upon her waters;
and they shall be dried up: for it *is* the
land of graven images, and they are
mad upon *their* idols.

Jer. 51. 36 Therefore thus saith the LORD;
Behold, I will plead thy cause, and take
vengeance for thee; and I will dry up
her sea, and make her springs dry.

G

Isa. 41. 2 Who raised up the righteous *man*
from the east, called him to his foot,
gave the nations before him, and made
him ruler over kings? he gave *them*
as the dust to his sword, *and* as driven
stubble to his bow.
3 He pursued them, *and* passed
safely; *even* by the way *that* he had
not gone with his feet.

Isa. 41. 25 I have raised up *one* from the
north, and he shall come: from the
rising of the sun shall he call upon
my name: and he shall come upon
princes as *upon* mortar, and as the
potter treadeth clay.

H

I Jno. 4. 1 Beloved, believe not every spirit, but
try the spirits whether they are of
God: because many false prophets are
gone out into the world.
2 Hereby know ye the spirit of God:
Every spirit that confesseth that Jesus
Christ is come in the flesh is of God:
3 And every spirit that confesseth
not that Jesus Christ is come in the
flesh is not of God: and this is that
spirit of antichrist, whereof ye have
heard that it should come; and even
now already is it in the world.

I

Rev. 12. *Study § 587, § 588, page 1358.*

K

II Cor. 11. 13. *See t, T, § 403, page 994.*

Rev. 19. 20 And the beast was taken, and
with him the false prophet that wrought
miracles before him, with which he
deceived them that had received the
mark of the beast, and them that
worshipped his image. These both
were cast alive into a lake of fire
burning with brimstone.

Rev. 20. 10 And the devil that deceived them
was cast into the lake of fire and
brimstone, where the beast and the
false prophet *are*, and shall be tormented day and night for ever and
ever.

L

I Tim. 4. 1. *See d, D, § 478, page 1126.*

Jas. 3. 15 This wisdom descendeth not from
above, but *is* earthly, sensual, devilish.

M

Rev. 13. 13. *See d, D, § 590, page 1364.*

N

Joel 3. 11 Assemble yourselves, and come,
all ye heathen, and gather yourselves
together round about: thither cause thy
mighty ones to come down, O LORD.

§ 594. THE SEVEN PLAGUES POURED FROM THE

CHAP. 16.

and of the whole world, to gather
them to [n]the battle of that great day
of God Almighty.
15 [o]Behold, I come as a thief.
Blessed *is* he that [p]watcheth, and
keepeth his garments, [q]lest he walk
naked, and they see his shame.
16 [r]And he gathered them together
into a place called in the Hebrew
tongue Armageddon.
17 And the seventh angel poured
out his vial into the air; and there
came a great voice out of the temple
of heaven, from the throne, saying,
[s]It is done.
18 And [t]there were voices, and
thunders, and lightnings; [u]and there
was a great earthquake, such as was
not since men were upon the earth,
so mighty an earthquake, *and* so
great.
19 And [x]the great city was divided
into three parts, and the cities of the
nations fell: and great Babylon
[y]came in remembrance before God,
[z]to give unto her the cup of the wine
of the fierceness of his wrath.
20 And [a]every island fled away,
and the mountains were not found.
21 And [b]there fell upon men a
great hail out of heaven, *every stone*
about the weight of a talent: and
[c]men blasphemed God because of
the plague of the hail; for the plague
thereof was exceeding great.

N—CONTINUED. See preceding page (1375).

Joel 3. 12 Let the heathen be wakened, and
come up to the valley of Jehoshaphat:
for there will I sit to judge all the
heathen round about.
13 Put ye in the sickle, for the harvest is ripe: come, get you down; for
the press is full, the fats overflow; for
their wickedness *is* great.
14 Multitudes, multitudes in the valley of decision: for the day of the
LORD *is* near in the valley of decision.

Rev. 17. 14 These shall make war with the
Lamb, and the Lamb shall overcome
them: for he is Lord of lords, and
King of kings: and they that are with
him *are* called, and chosen, and faithful.

§ 595. THE MYSTERY OF BABYLON

17 : 1–18.

1 And there came [a]one of the seven
angels which had the seven vials,
and talked with me, saying unto
me, Come hither; [b]I will shew unto
thee the judgment of [c]the great whore
[d]that sitteth upon many waters:
2 [e]With whom the kings of the
earth have committed fornication,
and [f]the inhabitants of the earth
have been made drunk with the
wine of her fornication.
3 So he carried me away in the
spirit [g]into the wilderness: and I saw
a woman sit [h]upon a scarlet coloured
beast, full of names of blasphemy,

A

Rev. 15. 1. *See b, B, § 593, page 1370.*

B

Rev. 14. 8. *See f, F, § 592, page 1366.*

Rev. 18. 16 And saying, Alas, alas, that great
city, that was clothed in fine linen,
and purple, and scarlet, and decked
with gold, and precious stones, and
pearls!
17 For in one hour so great riches is
come to nought. And every shipmaster, and all the company in ships,
and sailors, and as many as trade by
sea, stood afar off,
18 And cried when they saw the
smoke of her burning, saying, What
city is like unto this great city!
19 And they cast dust on their heads,
and cried, weeping and wailing, saying, Alas, alas, that great city, wherein
were made rich all that had ships in
the sea by reason of her costliness! for
in one hour is she made desolate.

VIALS OF THE WRATH OF GOD (CONCLUDED).

N—CONCLUDED.

Rev. 19. 19 And I saw the beast, and the kings of the earth, and their armies, gathered together to make war against him that sat on the horse, and against his army.

Rev. 20. 8 And shall go out to deceive the nations which are in the four quarters of the earth, Gog and Magog, to gather them together to battle: the number of whom *is* as the sand of the sea.

O

Matt. 24. 43. *See a, A, § 174, page 494.*

P

Matt. 25. 13. *See k, K, § 175, page 496.*

Q

Rev. 3. 18. *See f, F, § 577, page 1328.*

R

Rev. 19. 19. *See under N.*

S

Rev. 21. 6 And he said unto me, It is done. I am Alpha and Omega, the beginning and the end. I will give unto him that is athirst of the fountain of the water of life freely.

T

Rev. 4. 5. *See k, K, § 578, page 1330.*

U

Rev. 11. 13. *See e, E, § 585, page 1354.*

X

Rev. 14. 8. *See f, F, § 592, page 1366.*

Y

Rev. 18. 5 For her sins have reached unto heaven, and God hath remembered her iniquities.

Z

Rev. 14. 10. *See i, I, § 592, page 1368.*

A

Jer. 4. 23 I beheld the earth, and, lo, *it was* without form, and void; and the heavens, and they *had* no light.

24 I beheld the mountains, and, lo, they trembled, and all the hills moved lightly.

Rev. 6. 14. *See e, E, § 580, page 1338.*

B

Ex. 9. 23 And Moses stretched forth his rod toward heaven: and the LORD sent thunder and hail, and the fire ran along upon the ground; and the LORD rained hail upon the land of Egypt.

24 So there was hail, and fire mingled with the hail, very grievous, such as there was none like it in all the land of Egypt since it became a nation.

25 And the hail smote throughout all the land of Egypt all that *was* in the field, both man and beast; and the hail smote every herb of the field, and brake every tree of the field.

Rev. 11. 19 And the temple of God was opened in heaven, and there was seen in his temple the ark of his testament: and there were lightnings, and voices, and thunderings, and an earthquake, and great hail.

C

Rev. 16. 9, 11. *See text of topic, page 1374.*

AND HER JUDGMENT.

C

Nah. 3. 4 Because of the multitude of the whoredoms of the well favoured harlot, the mistress of witchcrafts, that selleth nations through her whoredoms, and families through her witchcrafts.

Rev. 19. 2 For true and righteous *are* his judgments: for he hath judged the great whore, which did corrupt the earth with her fornication, and hath avenged the blood of his servants at her hand.

D

Jer. 51. 13 O thou that dwellest upon many waters, abundant in treasures, thine end is come, *and* the measure of thy covetousness.

E

Rev. 18. 3 For all nations have drunk of the wine of the wrath of her fornication, and the kings of the earth have com-

E—CONCLUDED.

mitted fornication with her, and the merchants of the earth are waxed rich through the abundance of her delicacies.

F

Rev. 14. 8. *See f, F, § 592, page 1366.*

G

Rev. 12. 6. *See n, N, § 587, page 1358.*

H

Rev. 12. 3 And there appeared another wonder in heaven; and behold a great red dragon, having seven heads and ten horns, and seven crowns upon his heads.

Rev. 13. 1 And I stood upon the sand of the sea, and saw a beast rise up out of the sea, having seven heads and ten horns, and upon his horns ten crowns, and upon his heads the name of blasphemy.

I

Rev. 17. 9, 12. *See text of topic.*

§ 595. THE MYSTERY OF BABYLON

CHAP. 17.

[i]having seven heads and ten horns.
4 And the woman [k]was arrayed in
purple and scarlet colour, [l]and [1]decked
with gold and precious stones and
pearls, [m]having a golden cup in her
hand [n]full of abominations and filthiness of her fornication:
5 [o]And upon her forehead *was* a
name written, MYSTERY, BABY-
LON THE GREAT, THE MOTH-
ER OF [2]HARLOTS AND ABOM-
INATIONS OF THE EARTH.
6 And I saw [p]the woman drunken
[q]with the blood of the saints, and
with the blood of [r]the martyrs of
Jesus: and when I saw her, I wondered with great admiration.
7 And the angel said unto me,
Wherefore didst thou marvel? I
will tell thee the mystery of the
woman, and of the beast that car-
rieth her, which hath the seven
heads and ten horns.
8 The beast that thou sawest was,
and is not; and [s]shall ascend out of
the bottomless pit, and [t]go into perdition: and they that dwell on the
earth [u]shall wonder, [x]whose names
were not written in the book of life
from the foundation of the world,
when they behold the beast that
was, and is not, and yet is.
9 And [y]here *is* the mind which hath
wisdom. [z]The seven heads are seven
mountains, on which the woman
sitteth.
10 And there are seven kings: five
are fallen, and one is, *and* the other
is not yet come; and when he cometh, he must continue a short space.
11 And the beast that was, and is
not, even he is the eighth, and is of
the seven, and [a]goeth into perdition.
12 And [b]the ten horns which thou
sawest are ten kings, which have received no kingdom as yet; but re-

CHAP. 17.

ceive power as kings one hour with
the beast.
13 These have one mind, and shall
give their power and strength unto
the beast.
14 [c]These shall make war with the
Lamb, and the Lamb shall overcome them: [d]for he is Lord of
lords, and the King of kings: and
[e]they that are with him *are* called,
and chosen, and faithful.
15 And he saith unto me, [f]The waters

For I, see preceding page (1377).

K

Rev. 18. 7, 16. *Study* § *596.*

L

Da. 11. 38 But in his estate shall he honour the God of forces: and a god whom his fathers knew not shall he honour with gold, and silver, and with precious stones, and pleasant things.

1

Gr. *gilded.*

M

Jer. 51. 7 Babylon *hath been* a golden cup in the LORD'S hand, that made all the earth drunken: the nations have drunken of her wine; therefore the nations are mad.

Rev. 18. 6 Reward her even as she rewarded you, and double unto her double according to her works: in the cup which she hath filled, fill to her double.

N

Rev. 11. 8. *See t, T,* § *585, page 1354.*

O

Isa. 3. 9 The shew of their countenance doth witness against them; and they declare their sin as Sodom, they hide *it* not. Woe unto their soul! for they have rewarded evil unto themselves.

Jer. 51. *Read entire chapter.*

Phil. 3. 19 Whose end *is* destruction, whose God *is their* belly, and *whose* glory *is* in their shame, who mind earthly things.)

IIThes. 2. 7 For the mystery of iniquity doth already work: only he who now letteth *will let*, until he be taken out of the way.

Rev. 14. 8 And there followed another angel, saying, Babylon is fallen, is fallen, that great city, because she made all nations drink of the wine of the wrath of her fornication.

AND HER JUDGMENT (CONTINUED).

O—CONCLUDED.

Rev. 16. 19 And the great city was divided into three parts, and the cities of the nations fell: and great Babylon came in remembrance before God, to give unto her the cup of the wine of the fierceness of his wrath.

Rev. 18. *Read entire chapter.*

Rev. 19. 2 For true and righteous *are* his judgments: for he hath judged the great whore, which did corrupt the earth with her fornication, and hath avenged the blood of his servants at her hand.

2

Or, *fornications.*

P

Rev. 18. 24 And in her was found the blood of prophets, and of saints, and of all that were slain upon the earth.

Q

Rev. 13. 15 And he had power to give life unto the image of the beast, that the image of the beast should both speak, and cause that as many as would not worship the image of the beast should be killed.

Rev. 16. 6 For they have shed the blood of saints and prophets, and thou hast given them blood to drink; for they are worthy.

R

II Cor. 4. 10, 11. *See e, E, § 393, page 972.*

Rev. 6. 9 And when he had opened the fifth seal, I saw under the altar the souls of them that were slain for the word of God, and for the testimony which they held:

10 And they cried with a loud voice, saying, How long, O Lord, holy and true, dost thou not judge and avenge our blood on them that dwell on the earth?

Rev. 12. 11 And they overcame him by the blood of the Lamb, and by the word of their testimony; and they loved not their lives unto the death.

S

Rev. 11. 7 And when they shall have finished their testimony, the beast that ascendeth out of the bottomless pit shall make war against them, and shall overcome them, and kill them.

Rev. 13. 1. *See a, A, § 589, page 1362.*

T

Matt. 26. 52. *See i, I, § 193, page 554.*

Rev. 17. 11. *See text of topic.*

U

Rev. 13. 3 And I saw one of his heads as it were wounded to death; and his deadly wound was healed: and all the world wondered after the beast.

X

Phil. 4. 3. *See f, F, § 446, page 1072.*

Y

Rev. 13. 18. *See m, M, § 590, page 1364.*

Z

Rev. 12. 3. *See d, D, § 587, page 1358.*

Rev. 13. 1. *See a, A, § 589, page 1362.*

A

Rev. 17. 8. *See text of topic.*

B

Da. 7. 20 And of the ten horns that *were* in his head, and of the other which came up, and before whom three fell; even *of* that horn that had eyes, and a mouth that spake very great things, whose look *was* more stout than his fellows.

Zech. 1. 18 Then lifted I up mine eyes, and saw, and behold four horns.

19 And I said unto the angel that talked with me, What *be* these? And he answered me, These *are* the horns which have scattered Judah, Israel, and Jerusalem.

Rev. 13. 1 And I stood upon the sand of the sea, and saw a beast rise up out of the sea, having seven heads and ten horns, and upon his horns ten crowns, and upon his heads the name of blasphemy.

C

Rev. 16. 14. *See n, N, § 594, page 1376.*

D

Deut. 10. 17 For the LORD your God *is* God of gods, and Lord of lords, a great God, a mighty, and a terrible, which regardeth not persons, nor taketh reward:

I Tim. 6. 15. *See l, L, § 482, page 1136.*

E

Jer. 50. 44 Behold, he shall come up like a lion from the swelling of Jordan unto the habitation of the strong: but I will make them suddenly run away from her: and who *is* a chosen *man*, *that* I may appoint over her? for who *is* like me? and who will appoint me the time? and who *is* that shepherd that will stand before me?

Rev. 14. 4 These are they which were not defiled with women; for they are virgins. These are they which follow the Lamb whithersoever he goeth. These were redeemed from among men, *being* the first fruits unto God and to the Lamb.

F

Isa. 8. 7 Now therefore, behold, the Lord bringeth up upon them the waters of the river, strong and many, *even* the king of Assyria, and all his glory:

For F concluded, see next page (1380).

§ 595. THE MYSTERY OF BABYLON

CHAP. 17.

which thou sawest, where the whore
sitteth, [g]are peoples, and multitudes,
and nations, and tongues.
16 And the ten horns which thou
sawest upon the beast, [h]these shall
hate the whore, and shall make her
desolate [i]and naked, and shall eat
her flesh, and [k]burn her with fire.
17 For [l]God hath put in their hearts
to fulfil his will, and to agree, and
give their kingdom unto the beast,

CHAP. 17.

[m]until the words of God shall be fulfilled.
18 And the woman which thou
sawest [n]is that great city, [o]which
reigneth over the kings of the earth.

F—CONCLUDED.

and he shall come up over all his channels, and go over all his banks:

Rev. 17. 1. *See text of topic.*

G

Rev. 13. 7. *See q, Q, § 589, page 1362.*

H

Jer. 50. 41 Behold, a people shall come from the north, and a great nation, and

§ 596. THE FALL OF BABYLON

18 : 1--24.

1 And [a]after these things I saw another angel come down from heaven,
having great power; [b]and the earth
was lightened with his glory.
2 And he cried mightily with a
strong voice, saying, [c]Babylon the
great is fallen, is fallen, and [d]is become the habitation of devils, and
the hold of every foul spirit, and [e]a
cage of every unclean and hateful
bird.
3 For all nations [f]have drunk of
the wine of the wrath of her fornication, and the kings of the earth have
committed fornication with her, [g]and
the merchants of the earth are waxed
rich through the [1]abundance of her
delicacies.
4 And I heard another voice from
heaven, saying, [h]Come out of her,
my people, that ye be not partakers
of her sins, and that ye receive not
of her plagues.
5 [i]For her sins have reached unto
heaven, and [k]God hath remembered
her iniquities.
6 [l]Reward her even as she rewarded

A

Rev. 15. 1. *See b, B, § 593, page 1370.*

B

Eze. 43. 2 And, behold, the glory of the God of Israel came from the way of the east: and his voice *was* like a noise of many waters: and the earth shined with his glory.

C

Isa. 13. *Read entire chapter.*

Isa. 21. 9 And, behold, here cometh a chariot of men, *with* a couple of horsemen. And he answered and said, Babylon is fallen, is fallen; and all the graven images of her gods he hath broken unto the ground.

Jer. 50 and 51. *Read entire chapters.*

Rev. 14. 8. *See f, F, § 592, page 1366.*

D

Isa. 13. 21 But wild beasts of the desert shall lie there; and their houses shall be full of doleful creatures; and owls shall dwell there, and satyrs shall dance there.

Isa. 21. 8 And he cried, A lion: My lord, I stand continually upon the watch-tower in the daytime, and I am set in my ward whole nights:

Isa. 34. 14 The wild beasts of the desert shall also meet with the wild beasts of the island, and the satyr shall cry to his fellow; the screech owl also shall rest there, and find for herself a place of rest.

Jer. 50. 39 Therefore the wild beasts of the desert with the wild beasts of the islands shall dwell *there*, and the

AND HER JUDGMENT (Concluded).

H—Concluded.

many kings shall be raised up from the coasts of the earth.

Jer. 50. 42 They shall hold the bow and the lance: they *are* cruel, and will not shew mercy: their voice shall roar like the sea, and they shall ride upon horses, *every one* put in array, like a man to the battle, against thee, O daughter of Babylon.

Rev. 16. 12 And the sixth angel poured out his vial upon the great river Euphrates; and the water thereof was dried up, that the way of the kings of the east might be prepared.

I

Eze. 16. *Read entire chapter.*

Rev. 18. 16 And saying, Alas, alas, that great

I—Concluded.

city, that was clothed in fine linen, and purple, and scarlet, and decked with gold, and precious stones, and pearls!

K

Rev. 18. 8 Therefore shall her plagues come in one day, death, and mourning, and famine; and she shall be utterly burned with fire: for strong *is* the Lord God who judgeth her.

L

Rom. 1. 24. *See h, H, § 319, page 812.*

M

Rev. 10. 7. *See k, K, § 584, page 1350.*

N

Rev. 14. 8. *See f, F, § 592, page 1366.*

O

Rev. 12. 4. *See f, F, § 587, page 1358.*

AND THE DETAILS THEREOF.

D—Concluded.

owls shall dwell therein: and it shall be no more inhabited for ever; neither shall it be dwelt in from generation to generation.

Jer. 51. 37 And Babylon shall become heaps, a dwellingplace for dragons, an astonishment, and a hissing, without an inhabitant.

E

Isa. 14. 23 I will also make it a possession for the bittern, and pools of water: and I will sweep it with the besom of destruction, saith the Lord of hosts.

Isa. 34. 11 But the cormorant and the bittern shall possess it; the owl also and the raven shall dwell in it: and he shall stretch out upon it the line of confusion, and the stones of emptiness.

Mark 5. 2 And when he was come out of the ship, immediately there met him out of the tombs a man with an unclean spirit.

3 Who had *his* dwelling among the tombs; and no man could bind him, no, not with chains:

F

Rev. 14. 8. *See i, I, § 592, page 1368*

G

Isa. 47. 15 Thus shall they be unto thee with whom thou hast laboured, *even* thy merchants, from thy youth: they shall wander every one to his quarter; none shall save thee.

Rev. 18. 11, 15. *See text of topic.*

1

Or, *power.*

H

Isa. 48. 20 Go ye forth of Babylon, flee ye from the Chaldeans, with a voice of singing declare ye, tell this, utter it *even* to the end of the earth; say ye, The Lord hath redeemed his servant Jacob.

II Cor. 6. 17. *See e, E, § 397, page 980.*

I

Gen. 18. 20 And the Lord said, Because the cry of Sodom and Gomorrah is great, and because their sin is very grievous;

21 I will go down now, and see whether they have done altogether according to the cry of it, which is come unto me; and if not, I will know.

Jer. 51. 9 We would have healed Babylon, but she is not healed: forsake her, and let us go every one into his own country: for her judgment reacheth unto heaven, and is lifted up *even* to the skies.

Jonah 1. 2 Arise, go to Nineveh, that great city, and cry against it; for their wickedness is come up before me.

K

Rev. 16. 19. *See y, Y, § 594, page 1376.*

L

Ps. 137. 8 O daughter of Babylon, who art to be destroyed; happy *shall he be*, that rewardeth thee as thou hast served us.

Jer. 50. 15 Shout against her round about: she hath given her hand: her foundations are fallen, her walls are thrown down: for it *is* the vengeance of the Lord: take vengeance upon her; as she hath done, do unto her.

For L concluded, see next page (1382).

§ 596. THE FALL OF BABYLON AND

CHAP. 18.

you, and double unto her double according to her works: [m]in the cup which she hath filled, [n]fill to her double.

7 [o]How much she hath glorified herself, and lived deliciously, so much torment and sorrow give her: for she saith in her heart, I sit a [p]queen, and am no widow, and shall see no sorrow.

8 Therefore shall her plagues come [q]in one day, death, and mourning, and famine; and [r]she shall be utterly burned with fire: for [s]strong *is* the Lord God who judgeth her.

9 And [t]the kings of the earth, who have committed fornication and lived deliciously with her, [u]shall bewail her, and lament for her, [x]when they shall see the smoke of her burning,

10 Standing afar off for the fear of her torment, saying, [y]Alas, alas, that great city Babylon, that mighty city! [z]for in one hour is thy judgment come.

11 And [a]the merchants of the earth shall weep and mourn over her; for no man buyeth their merchandise any more:

12 [b]The merchandise of gold, and silver, and precious stones, and of pearls, and fine linen, and purple, and silk, and scarlet, and all [2]thyne wood, and all manner vessels of ivory, and all manner vessels of most precious wood, and of brass, and iron, and marble,

13 And cinnamon, and odours, and ointments, and frankincense, and wine, and oil, and fine flour, and wheat, and beasts, and sheep, and horses, and chariots, and [3]slaves, and [c]souls of men.

14 And the fruits that thy soul lusted after are departed from thee, and all things which were dainty and

CHAP. 18.

goodly are departed from thee, and thou shalt find them no more at all.

15 [d]The merchants of these things, which were made rich by her, shall stand afar off for the fear of her torment, weeping and wailing,

16 And saying, Alas, alas, that great city, [e]that was clothed in fine linen, and purple, and scarlet, and decked with gold, and precious stones, and pearls!

17 For [f]in one hour so great riches is come to nought. And [g]every shipmaster, and all the company in ships, and sailors, and as many as trade by sea, stood afar off,

18 [h]And cried when they saw the

L—CONCLUDED.

Jer. 50. 29 Call together the archers against Babylon: all ye that bend the bow, camp against it round about; let none thereof escape: recompense her according to her work; according to all that she hath done, do unto her: for she hath been proud against the LORD, against the Holy One of Israel.

Jer. 51. 24 And I will render unto Babylon and to all the inhabitants of Chaldea all their evil that they have done in Zion in your sight, saith the LORD.

Jer. 51. 49 As Babylon *hath caused* the slain of Israel to fall, so at Babylon shall fall the slain of all the earth.

II Tim. 4. 14. *See g, G, § 492, page 1152.*

M

Rev. 14. 10. *See k, K, 592, page 1368.*

N

Rev. 16. 19 And the great city was divided into three parts, and the cities of the nations fell: and great Babylon came in remembrance before God, to give unto her the cup of the wine of the fierceness of his wrath.

O

Eze. 28. 2 Son of man, say unto the prince of Tyrus, Thus saith the Lord GOD; Because thine heart *is* lifted up, and thou hast said, I *am* a god, I sit *in* the seat of God, in the midst of the seas; yet thou *art* a man, and not God, though thou set thine heart as the heart of God:

THE DETAILS THEREOF (CONTINUED).

P

Isa. 47. 7 And thou saidst, I shall be a lady for ever: *so* that thou didst not lay these *things* to thy heart, neither didst remember the latter end of it.

8 Therefore hear now this, *thou that art* given to pleasures, that dwellest carelessly, that sayest in thine heart, I *am*, and none else besides me; I shall not sit *as* a widow, neither shall I know the loss of children:

Zeph. 2. 15 This *is* the rejoicing city that dwelt carelessly, that said in her heart, I *am* and *there is* none besides me: how is she become a desolation, a place for beasts to lie down in! every one that passeth by her shall hiss, *and* wag his hand.

Q

Isa. 47. 9 But these two *things* shall come to thee in a moment in one day, the loss of children, and widowhood: they shall come upon thee in their perfection for the multitude of thy sorceries, *and* for the great abundance of thine enchantments.

Rev. 18. 10. *See text of topic.*

R

Rev. 17. 16. *See k, K, § 595, page 1380.*

S

Jer. 50. 34 Their Redeemer *is* strong; The LORD of hosts *is* his name: he shall thoroughly plead their cause, that he may give rest to the land, and disquiet the inhabitants of Babylon.

Rev. 11. 17 Saying, We give thee thanks, O Lord God Almighty, which art, and wast, and art to come; because thou hast taken to thee thy great power, and hast reigned.

T

Eze. 26. 16 Then all the princes of the sea shall come down from their thrones, and lay away their robes, and put off their broidered garments: they shall clothe themselves with trembling; they shall sit upon the ground, and shall tremble at *every* moment, and be astonished at thee.

17 And they shall take up a lamentation for thee, and say to thee, How art thou destroyed, *that wast* inhabited of seafaring men, the renowned city, which wast strong in the sea, she and her inhabitants, which cause their terror *to be* on all that haunt it!

Rev. 17. 2 With whom the kings of the earth have committed fornication, and the inhabitants of the earth have been

T—CONCLUDED.

made drunk with the wine of her fornication.

U

Jer. 50. 46 At the noise of the taking of Babylon the earth is moved, and the cry is heard among the nations.

X

Rev. 18. 18. *See text of topic.*

Rev. 19. 3 And again they said, Alleluia. And her smoke rose up for ever and ever.

Y

Rev. 14. 8. *See f, F, § 592, page 1366.*

Z

Rev. 18. 17, 19. *See text of topic.*

A

Eze. 27. 27, etc. *Read to end of chapter.*

B

Rev. 17. 4. *See l, L, § 595, page 1378.*

2

Or, *sweet.*

3

Or, *bodies.*

C

Eze. 27. 13 Javan, Tubal, and Meshech, they *were* thy merchants: they traded the persons of men and vessels of brass in thy market.

D

Rev. 18. 3, 11. *See text of topic.*

E

Luke 16. 19. *See h, H, § 137, page 393.*

Rev. 17. 4 And the woman was arrayed in purple and scarlet colour, and decked with gold and precious stones and pearls, having a golden cup in her hand full of abominations and filthiness of her fornication:

F

Rev. 18. 10. *See text of topic.*

G

Eze. 27. 28 The suburbs shall shake at the sound of the cry of thy pilots.

29 And all that handle the oar, the mariners, *and* all the pilots of the sea, shall come down from their ships, they shall stand upon the land;

H

Eze. 27. 30 And shall cause their voice to be heard against thee, and shall cry bitterly, and shall cast up dust upon their heads, they shall wallow themselves in the ashes:

31 And they shall make themselves utterly bald for thee, and gird them with sackcloth, and they shall weep for thee with bitterness of heart *and* bitter wailing.

For H concluded, see next page (1384).

§ 596. THE FALL OF BABYLON AND

CHAP. 18.

smoke of her burning, saying, What
city is like unto this great city!
19 And [i]they cast dust on their
heads, and cried, weeping and wailing, saying, Alas, alas, that great
city, wherein were made rich all that
had ships in the sea by reason of
her costliness! [k]for in one hour is
she made desolate.
20 [l]Rejoice over her, *thou* heaven,
and *ye* holy apostles and prophets;
[m]for God hath avenged you on her.
21 And a mighty angel took up a
stone like a great millstone, and cast
it into the sea, saying. [n]Thus with
violence shall that great city Babylon be thrown down, and [o]shall be
found no more at all.
22 [p]And the voice of harpers, and
musicians, and of pipers, and trumpeters, shall be heard no more at all
in thee; and no craftsman, of whatsoever craft *he be*, shall be found
any more in thee; and the sound of
a millstone shall be heard no more
at all in thee;
23 And [q]the light of a candle shall
shine no more at all in thee; [r]and
the voice of the bridegroom and of
the bride shall be heard no more at
all in thee: for [s]thy merchants were
the great men of the earth; [t]for by
thy sorceries were all nations deceived.
24 And [u]in her was found the blood
of prophets, and of saints, and of all
that [x]were slain upon the earth.

H—CONCLUDED.

Eze. 27. 32 And in their wailng they shall take up a lamentation for thee, and lament over thee, *saying*, What *city is* like Tyrus, like the destroyed in the midst of the sea?

Rev. 13. 4 And they worshipped the dragon which gave power unto the beast: and they worshipped the beast, saying, Who *is* like unto the beast? who is able to make war with him?

I

Josh. 7. 6 And Joshua rent his clothes, and fell to the earth upon his face before the ark of the LORD until the eventide, he and the elders of Israel, and put dust upon their heads.

I Sa. 4. 12 And there ran a man of Benjamin out of the army, and came to Shiloh the same day with his clothes rent, and with earth upon his head.

Job 2. 12 And when they lifted up their eyes afar off, and knew him not, they lifted up their voice, and wept; and they rent every one his mantle, and sprinkled dust upon their heads toward heaven.

Eze. 27. 30. *See under H.*

K

Rev. 18. 8, 10,17. *See text of topic.*

§ 597. THE TRIUMPHANT SONG AND

19: 1–10.

1 And after these things [a]I heard
a great voice of much people in
heaven, saying, [b]Alleluia; [c]Salvation,
and glory, and honour, and power,
unto the Lord our God:
2 For [d]true and righteous *are* his
judgments: for he hath judged the
great whore, which did corrupt the
earth with her fornication, and [e]hath

CHAP. 19.

avenged the blood of his servants at
her hand.

A

Rev. 11. 15. *See c, C, § 586, page 1354.*

B

Ps. 106. 1 Praise ye the LORD. O give thanks unto the LORD; for *he is* good: for his mercy *endureth* for ever.

Ps. 111. 1 Praise ye the LORD. I will praise the LORD with *my* whole heart, in the assembly of the upright, and *in* the congregation.

THE DETAILS THEREOF (CONCLUDED).

L

Isa. 44. 23 Sing, O ye heavens; for the LORD hath done *it*: shout, ye lower parts of the earth: break forth into singing, ye mountains, O forest, and every tree therein: for the LORD hath redeemed Jacob, and glorified himself in Israel.

Isa. 49. 13 Sing, O heavens; and be joyful, O earth; and break forth into singing, O mountains: for the LORD hath comforted his people, and will have mercy upon his afflicted.

Jer. 51. 48 Then the heaven and the earth, and all that *is* therein, shall sing for Babylon: for the spoilers shall come unto her from the north, saith the LORD.

M

Luke 11. 49, 50. *See o, O, § 56, page 181.*
Rev. 6. 10. *See x, X, § 580, page 1336.*

N

Jer. 51. 64 And thou shalt say, Thus shall Babylon sink, and shall not rise from the evil that I will bring upon her: and they shall be weary. Thus far *are* the words of Jeremiah.

O

Rev. 12. 8 And prevailed not; neither was their place found any more in heaven.

Rev. 16. 20 And every island fled away, and the mountains were not found.

P

Isa. 24. 8 The mirth of tabrets ceaseth, the noise of them that rejoice endeth, the joy of the harp ceaseth.

Jer. 7. 34 Then will I cause to cease from the cites of Judah, and from the streets of Jerusalem, the voice of mirth, and the voice of gladness, the voice of the bridegroom, and the voice of the bride: for the land shall be desolate.

Q

Jer. 25. 10 Moreover I will take from them the voice of mirth, and the voice of gladness, the voice of the bridegroom, and the voice of the bride, the sound of the millstones, and the light of the candle.

R

Jer. 16. 9 For thus saith the LORD of hosts, the God of Israel; Behold, I will cause to cease out of this place in your eyes, and in your days, the voice of mirth, and the voice of gladness, the voice of the bridegroom, and the voice of the bride.

S

Isa. 23. 8 Who hath taken this counsel against Tyre, the crowning *city*, whose merchants *are* princes, whose traffickers *are* the honourable of the earth?

T

II Ki. 9. 22 And it came to pass, when Joram saw Jehu, that he said, *Is it* peace, Jehu? And he answered, What peace, so long as the whoredoms of thy mother Jezebel and her witchcrafts *are so* many?

Nah. 3. 4 Because of the mulitude of the whoredoms of the well favoured harlot, the mistress of witchcrafts, that selleth nations through her whoredoms, and families through her witchcrafts.

Rev. 13. 13, 14. *See d, D, § 590, page 1364.*

U

Rev. 17. 6. *See q, Q, § 595, page 1378.*

X

Jer. 51. 49 As Babylon *hath caused* the slain of Israel to fall, so at Babylon shall fall the slain of all the earth.

THE MARRIAGE OF THE LAMB.

B—CONCLUDED.

Ps. 146. 1 Praise ye the LORD. Praise the LORD, O my soul.

Ps. 148. 1 Praise ye the LORD. Praise ye the LORD from the heavens: praise him in the heights.

Ps. 149. 1 Praise ye the LORD. Sing unto the LORD a new song, *and* his praise in the congregation of saints.

Ps. 150. 1 Praise ye the LORD. Praise God in his sanctuary: praise him in the firmament of his power.

Rev. 19. 3, 4, 6. *See text of topic.*

C

Rev. 7. 10, 12. *See k, K, § 581, page 1340.*

D

Rev. 16. 7. *See q, Q, § 594, page 1374.*

E

Rev. 6. 10. *See x, X, § 580, page 1336.*

F

Isa. 34. 10 It shall not be quenched night nor day; the smoke thereof shall go up for ever: from generation to generation it shall lie waste; none shall pass through it for ever and ever.

Rev. 14. 11 And the smoke of their torment ascendeth up for ever and ever: and

§ 597. THE TRIUMPHANT SONG AND THE

CHAP. 19.

3 And again they said, Alleluia. And [f]her smoke rose up for ever and ever.

4 And the [g]four and twenty elders and the four beasts fell down and worshipped God that sat on the throne, saying, [h]Amen; Alleluia.

5 And a voice came out of the throne, saying, [i]Praise our God, all ye his servants, and ye that fear him, both small and great.

6 [k]And I heard as it were the voice of a great multitude, and as the voice of many waters, and as the voice of mighty thunderings, saying, Alleluia: for [l]the Lord God omnipotent reigneth.

7 Let us be glad and rejoice, and give honour to him: for [m]the marriage of the Lamb is come, and his wife hath made herself ready.

8 And [n]to her was granted that she should be arrayed in fine linen, clean and [1]white: for [o]the fine linen is the righteousness of saints.

9 And he saith unto me, Write, [p]Blessed *are* they which are called unto the marriage supper of the Lamb. And he saith unto me, [q]These are the true sayings of God.

10 [r]And I fell at his feet to worship him. And he said unto me, See *thou do it* not: I am thy fellow servant, and of thy brethren [s]that have the testimony of Jesus: worship God: for the testimony of Jesus is the spirit of prophecy.

F—CONCLUDED. See preceding page (1385).

they have no rest day nor night, who worship the beast and his image, and whosoever receiveth the mark of his name.

Rev. 18. 9 And the kings of the earth, who have committed fornication and lived deliciously with her, shall bewail her, and lament for her, when they shall see the smoke of her burning,

Rev. 18. 18 And cried when they saw the smoke of her burning, saying, What *city is* like unto this great city!

G

Rev. 4. 4 And round about the throne *were* four and twenty seats: and upon the seats I saw four and twenty elders sitting, clothed in white raiment; and they had on their heads crowns of gold.

Rev. 4. 6 And before the throne *there was* a sea of glass like unto crystal: and in the midst of the throne, and round about the throne, *were* four beasts full of eyes before and behind.

Rev. 4. 10 The four and twenty elders fall down before him that sat on the throne, and worship him that liveth for ever and ever, and cast their crowns before the throne, saying,

Rev. 5. 14 And the four beasts said, Amen. And the four *and* twenty elders fell down and worshipped him that liveth for ever and ever.

H

Deut. 27. 26 Cursed *be* he that confirmeth not *all* the words of this law to do them. And all the people shall say, Amen.

1 Chr. 16. 36 Blessed *be* the LORD God of Israel for ever and ever. And all the people said, Amen, and praised the LORD.

Neh. 5. 13 Also I shook my lap, and said, So God shake out every man from his house, and from his labour, that performeth not this promise, even thus be he shaken out, and emptied. And

§ 598. THE KING OF KINGS AND LORD

19 : 11–21.

11 [a]And I saw heaven opened, and behold [b]a white horse; and he that sat upon him *was* called [c]Faithful and True, and [d]in righteousness he doth judge and make war.

A

Rev. 4. 1 After this I looked, and, behold, a door *was* opened in heaven: and the first voice which I heard *was* as it were of a trumpet talking with me; which said, Come up hither, and I will shew thee things which must be hereafter.

MARRIAGE OF THE LAMB (CONCLUDED).

H—CONCLUDED.

all the congregation said, Amen, and praised the LORD. And the people did according to this promise.

Neh. 8. 6 And Ezra blessed the LORD, the great God. And all the people answered, Amen, Amen, with lifting up their hands: and they bowed their heads, and worshipped the LORD with *their* faces to the ground.

Rev. 5. 14. *See under G.*

I

Ps. 134. 1 Behold, bless ye the LORD, all *ye* servants of the LORD, which by night stand in the house of the LORD.

Ps. 135. 1 Praise ye the LORD. Praise ye the name of the LORD; praise *him*, O ye servants of the LORD.

Ps. 150. 6 Let every thing that hath breath praise the LORD. Praise ye the LORD.

K

Rev. 1. 15. *See r, R, § 570, page 1388.*

L

Rev. 11. 15, 17. *See d, D, § 586, page 1354.*

M

Matt. 22. 2 The kingdom of heaven is like unto a certain king, which made a marriage for his son,

Matt. 25. 1, 6. *See a, A, § 175, page 496.*

II Cor. 11. 2 For I am jealous over you with godly jealousy: for I have espoused you to one husband, that I may present *you as* a chaste virgin to Christ.

Eph. 5. 32 This is a great mystery: but I speak concerning Christ and the church.

N

Isa. 61. 10 I will greatly rejoice in the LORD, my soul shall be joyful in my God; for he hath clothed me with the garments of salvation, he hath covered me with the robe of righteousness, as a bridegroom decketh *himself* with ornaments, and as a bride adorneth *herself* with her jewels.

Eze. 16. 10 I clothed thee also with broidered work, and shod thee with badgers'

N—CONCLUDED.

skin, and I girded thee about with fine linen, and I covered thee with silk.

Rev. 15. 6. *See o, O, § 593, page 1372.*

1

Or, *bright.*

O

Ps. 132. 9 Let thy priests be clothed with righteousness; and let thy saints shout for joy.

Rev. 3. 4, 5. *See i, I, § 575, page 1326.*

P

Matt. 22. 2, 3. *See b, B, § 162, page 450.*

Luke 14. 14 And thou shalt be blessed; for they cannot recompense thee: for thou shalt be recompensed at the resurrection of the just.

15 And when one of them that sat at meat with him heard these things, he said unto him, Blessed *is* he that shall eat bread in the kingdom of God.

Q

I Tim. 1. 15. *See i, I, § 474, page 1120.*

Rev. 21. 5 And he that sat upon the throne said, Behold, I make all things new. And he said unto me, Write: for these words are true and faithful.

Rev. 22. 6 And he said unto me, These sayings *are* faithful and true: and the Lord God of the holy prophets sent his angel to show unto his servants the things which must shortly be done.

R

Acts 10. 26. *See r, R, § 254, page 695.*

Rev. 22. 8 And I John saw these things, and heard *them*. And when I had heard and seen, I fell down to worship before the feet of the angel which shewed me these things.

9 Then saith he unto me, See *thou do it* not: for I am thy fellow servant, and of thy brethren the prophets, and of them which keep the sayings of this book: worship God.

S

Rev. 12. 17. *See y, Y, § 588, page 1360.*

OF LORDS RIDES FORTH TO VICTORY.

A—CONCLUDED.

Rev. 11. 19. *See p, P, § 586, page 1356.*

B

Rev. 6. 2. *See c, C, § 580, page 1334.*

C

Rev. 1. 5. *See d, D, § 569, page 1314.*

D

Ps. 45. 3 Gird thy sword upon *thy* thigh, O

D—CONCLUDED.

most Mighty, with thy glory and thy majesty.

Ps. 45. 4 And in thy majesty ride prosperously, because of truth and meekness *and* righteousness; and thy right hand shall teach thee terrible things.

Isa. 11. 4 But with righteousness shall he

For D concluded, see next page (1388).

§ 598. THE KING OF KINGS AND LORD OF

CHAP. 19.

12 [e]His eyes *were* as a flame of fire,
and [f]on his head *were* many crowns;
and [g]he had a name written, that no
man knew, but he himself.
13 And [h]he *was* clothed with a
vesture dipped in blood: and his
name is called [i]The Word of God.
14 And [k]the armies *which were* in
heaven followed him upon white
horses, [l]clothed in fine linen, white
and clean.
15 And [m]out of his mouth goeth a
sharp sword, that with it he should
smite the nations: and he shall rule
them with a rod of iron: and [n]he
treadeth the winepress of the fierceness and wrath of Almighty God.
16 And he hath on *his* vesture and
on his thigh a name written, [o]KING
OF KINGS, AND LORD OF
LORDS.
17 And I saw an angel standing in
the sun; and he cried with a loud
voice, [p]saying to all the fowls that
fly in the midst of heaven, Come
and gather yourselves together unto
the supper of the great God;
18 That ye may eat the flesh of
kings, and the flesh of captains, and
the flesh of mighty men, and the
flesh of horses, and of them that sit
on them, and the flesh of all *men*,
both free and bond, both small and
great.
19 And [q]I saw the beast, and the
kings of the earth, and their armies,
gathered together to make war against
him that sat on the horse, and
against his army.
20 [r]And the beast was taken, and
with him the false prophet that
wrought miracles before him, with
which he deceived them that had received the mark of the beast, and
them that worshipped his image.
[s]These both were cast alive into a

CHAP. 19.

lake of fire burning with brimstone.
21 And the remnant [t]were slain
with the sword of him that sat upon
the horse, which *sword* proceeded
out of his mouth: and [u]all the fowls
were [x]filled with their flesh.

D—CONCLUDED.

judge the poor, and reprove with equity for the meek of the earth: and he shall smite the earth with the rod of his mouth, and with the breath of his lips shall he slay the wicked.

E

Rev. 1. 14. *See p, P, § 570, page 1318.*

F

Ps. 8. 5 For thou hast made him a little lower than the angels, and hast crowned him with glory and honour.

Rev. 6. 2. *See e, E, § 580, page 1344.*

G

Isa. 9. 6 For unto us a child is born, unto us a son is given: and the government shall be upon his shoulder: and his name shall be called Wonderful, Counsellor, The mighty God, The everlasting Father, The Prince of Peace.

Rev. 2. 17. *See k, K, § 573, page 1322.*

Rev. 19. 16. *See text of topic.*

H

Isa. 63. 1 Who *is* this that cometh from Edom, with dyed garments from Bozrah? this *that is* glorious in his apparel, traveling in the greatness of his strength? I that speak in righteousness, mighty to save.

2 Wherefore *art thou* red in thine apparel, and thy garments like him that treadeth in the winefat?

3 I have trodden the winepress alone; and of the people *there was* none with me: for I will tread them in mine anger, and trample them in my fury; and their blood shall be sprinkled upon my garments, and I will stain all my raiment.

I

John 1. 14 And the Word was made flesh, and dwelt among us, (and we beheld his glory, the glory as of the only begotten of the Father,) full of grace and truth.

I Jno. 5. 7. *See l, L, § 557, page 1298.*

LORDS RIDES FORTH TO VICTORY (Concluded).

K

Ps. 68. 17 The chariots of God *are* twenty thousand, *even* thousands of angels: the Lord *is* among them, *as in* Sinai, in the holy *place*.

Rev. 17. 14 These shall make war with the Lamb, and the Lamb shall overcome them: for he is Lord of lords, and King of kings: and they that are with him *are* called, and chosen, and faithful.

L

Rev. 3. 4. *See i, I, § 575, page 1326.*

M

Isa. 11. 4. *See under D.*

Isa. 49. 2 And he hath made my mouth like a sharp sword; in the shadow of his hand hath he hid me, and made me a polished shaft; in his quiver hath he hid me;

Eph. 6. 17. *See n, N, § 437. page 1056.*

IIThes.2. 8 And then shall that Wicked be revealed, whom the Lord shall consume with the spirit of his mouth, and shall destroy with the brightness of his coming:

Rev. 2. 27. *See m, M, § 574, page 1324.*

N

Isa. 63. 3. *See under H.*
Rev. 14. 20. *See under K.*

O

Deut.10. 17 For the LORD your God *is* God of gods, and Lord of lords, a great God, a mighty, and a terrible, which regardeth not persons, nor taketh reward:

Ps. 72. *Read entire Psalm.*

Prov. 8. 15 By me kings reign, and princes decree justice.
16 By me princes rule, and nobles, *even* all the judges of the earth.

Da. 2. 47 The king answered unto Daniel, and said, Of a truth *it is*, that your God *is* a God of gods, and a Lord of kings, and a revealer of secrets, seeing thou couldest reveal this secret.

Phil. 2. 10 That at the name of Jesus every knee should bow, of *things* in heaven, and *things* in earth, and *things* under the earth;

I Tim. 6. 15 Which in his times he shall shew, *who is* the blessed and only Potentate, the King of kings, and Lord of lords;

Rev. 17. 14. *See under K.*

P

Eze. 39. 17 And, thou son of man, thus saith the Lord GOD; Speak unto every feathered fowl, and to every beast of the field, Assemble yourselves, and come; gather yourselves on every side to my sacrifice that I do sacrifice for

P—Concluded.

you, *even* a great sacrifice upon the mountains of Israel, that ye may eat flesh, and drink blood.

Eze. 39. 18 Ye shall eat the flesh of the mighty, and drink the blood of the princes of the earth, of rams, of lambs, and of goats, of bullocks, all of them fatlings of Bashan.
19 And ye shall eat fat till ye be full, and drink blood till ye be drunken, of my sacrifice which I have sacrificed for you.
20 Thus ye shall be filled at my table with horses and chariots, with mighty men, and with all men of war, saith the Lord GOD.

Rev. 19. 21. *See text of topic.*

Q

Rev. 16. 14. *See n, N, § 594, page 1376.*

R

Rev. 14. 8-11. *Study § 592, page 1368.*

S

Da. 7. 11 I beheld then, because of the voice of the great words which the horn spake: I beheld *even* till the beast was slain, and his body destroyed, and given to the burning flame.

Rev. 14. 10. *See m, M, § 592, page 1368.*

Rev. 20. 10 And the devil that deceived them was cast into the lake of fire and brimstone, where the beast and the false prophet *are*, and shall be tormented day and night for ever and ever.

Rev. 20. 14 And death and hell were cast into the lake of fire. This is the second death.
15 And whosoever was not found written in the book of life was cast into the lake of fire.

Rev. 21. 8 But the fearful, and unbelieving, and the abominable, and murderers, and whoremongers, and sorcerers, and idolaters, and all liars, shall have their part in the lake which burneth with fire and brimstone: which is the second death.

T

Rev. 19. 15. *See text of topic.*

U

Rev. 19. 17, 18. *See text of topic.*

X

Rev. 17. 16 And the ten horns which thou sawest upon the beast, these shall hate the whore, and shall make her desolate and naked, and shall eat her flesh, and burn her with fire.

§ 599. THE

20 : 1–6.

1 And I saw an angel come down from heaven, [a]having the key of the bottomless pit and a great chain in his hand.

2 And he laid hold on [b]the dragon, that old serpent, which is the Devil, and Satan, and [c]bound him a thousand years,

3 And cast him into the bottomless pit, and shut him up, and [d]set a seal upon him, [e]that he should deceive the nations no more, till the thousand years should be fulfilled: and after that he must be loosed a little season.

4 And I saw [f]thrones, and they sat upon them, and [g]judgment was given unto them: and *I saw* [h]the souls of them that were beheaded for the witness of Jesus, and for the word of God, and [i]which had not worshipped the beast, neither his image, neither had received *his* mark upon their foreheads, or in their hands; and they lived and [k]reigned with Christ a thousand years.

5 But [l]the rest of the dead lived not again until the thousand years were finished. This *is* the first resurrection.

CHAP. 20.

6 Blessed and holy *is* he that hath part in the first resurrection: on such [m]the second death hath no power, but they shall be [n]priests of God and of Christ, and [o]shall reign with him a thousand years.

A

Rev. 1. 18. *See c, C, § 570, page 1318.*

Rev. 9. 1 And the fifth angel sounded, and I saw a star fall from heaven unto the earth: and to him was given the key of the bottomless pit.

B

Rev. 12. 9. *See d, D, § 558, page 1358.*

C

IIPet. 2. 4 For if God spared not the angels that sinned, but cast *them* down to hell, and delivered *them* into chains of darkness, to be reserved unto judgment;

Jude 6 And the angels which kept not their first estate, but left their own habitation, he hath reserved in everlasting chains under darkness unto the judgment of the great day.

D

Da. 6. 17 And a stone was brought, and laid upon the mouth of the den; and the king sealed it with his own signet, and with the signet of his lords; that the purpose might not be changed concerning Daniel.

E

Rev. 16. 14 For they are the spirits of devils, working miracles, *which* go forth unto the kings of the earth and of the whole world, to gather them to the battle of that great day of God Almighty.

§ 600. SATAN LOOSED TO DECEIVE THE NATIONS, THEN

20 : 7–10.

7 And when the thousand years are expired, [a]Satan shall be loosed out of his prison,

8 And shall go out [b]to deceive the nations which are in the four quarters of the earth, [c]Gog and Magog, [d]to gather them together to battle: the number of whom *is*

CHAP. 20.

as the sand of the sea.

9 And [e]they went up on the breadth of the earth, and compassed the camp of the saints about, and the beloved city: and fire came down from God out of heaven, and devoured them.

10 And [f]the devil that deceived

MILLENNIUM.

E—Concluded.

Rev. 16. 16 And he gathered them together into a place called in the Hebrew tongue Armageddon.

Rev. 20. 8. *See text of topic § 600.*

F

Luke 22. 30. *See p, P, § 181, page 511.*

Da. 7. 9 I beheld till the thrones were cast down, and the Ancient of days did sit, whose garment *was* white as snow, and the hair of his head like the pure wool: his throne *was like* the fiery flame, *and* his wheels *as* burning fire.

Da. 7. 22 Until the Ancient of days came, and judgment was given to the saints of the Most High; and the time came that the saints possessed the kingdom.

Da. 7. 27 And the kingdom and dominion, and the greatness of the kingdom under the whole heaven, shall be given to the people of the saints of the Most High, whose kingdom *is* an everlasting kingdom, and all dominions shall serve and obey him.

G

I Cor. 6. 2 Do ye not know that the saints shall judge the world? and if the world shall be judged by you, are ye unworthy to judge the smallest matters?
3 Know ye not that we shall judge angels? how much more things that pertain to this life?

H

Rev. 6. 9. *See q, Q, § 580, page 1336.*

I

Rev. 13. 12-16. *Study § 590, page 1362.*

K

Da. 2. 44 And in the days of these kings shall the God of heaven set up a kingdom, which shall never be destroyed: and the kingdom shall not be left to

K—Concluded.

other people, *but* it shall break in pieces and consume all these kingdoms, and it shall stand for ever.

Da. 7. 18 But the saints of the Most High shall take the kingdom, and possess the kingdom for ever, even for ever and ever.

Da. 7. 27. *See under F.*

Rom. 8. 17 And if children, then heirs; heirs of God, and joint heirs with Christ; if so be that we suffer with *him*, that we may be also glorified together.

II Tim. 2. 12 If we suffer, we shall also reign with *him*: if we deny *him*, he also will deny us:

Rev. 5. 10 And hast made us unto our God kings and priests: and we shall reign on the earth.

L

Da. 12. 2 And many of them that sleep in the dust of the earth shall awake, some to everlasting life, and some to shame *and* everlasting contempt.

Luke 14. 14 And thou shalt be blessed; for they cannot recompense thee: for thou shalt be recompensed at the resurrection of the just.

John 5. 29 And shall come forth; they that have done good, unto the resurrection of life; and they that have done evil, unto the resurrection of damnation.

Acts 24. 15 And have hope toward God, which they themselves also allow, that there shall be a resurrection of the dead, both of the just and unjust.

M

Rev. 2. 11. *See k, K, § 572, page 1322.*

N

Rev. 1. 6. *See i, I, § 569, page 1316.*

O

Rev. 20. 4. *See text of topic.*

CAST INTO THE LAKE OF FIRE WITH THE FALSE PROPHET.

A

Rev. 20. 2. *See text of topic § 509.*

B

Rev. 20. 3. *See text of topic § 599.*

Rev. 20. 10. *See text of topic.*

C

Eze. 38 and 39. *Read entire chapters.*

D

Rev. 16. 14. *See under E, § 599.*

Rev. 19. 19 And I saw the beast, and the kings of the earth, and their armies, gathered together to make war against him that sat on the horse, and against his army.

E

Isa. 8. 7 Now therefore, behold, the Lord bringeth up upon them the waters of the river, strong and many, *even* the king of Assyria, and all his glory: and he shall come up over all his channels, and go over all his banks:
8 And he shall pass through Judah; he shall overflow and go over, he shall reach *even* to the neck; and the stretching out of his wings shall fill the breadth of thy land, O Immanuel.

For E concluded and F, see next page (1392).

§ 600. SATAN LOOSED TO DECEIVE THE NATIONS, THEN CAST

CHAP. 20.

them was cast into the lake of fire and brimstone, [g]where the beast and the false prophet *are*, and [h]shall be tormented day and night for ever and ever.

E—CONTINUED.

Eze. 38. 9 Thou shalt ascend and come like a storm, thou shalt be like a cloud to cover the land, thou, and all thy bands, and many people with thee.

Eze. 38. 16 And thou shalt come up against my people of Israel, as a cloud to cover the land; it shall be in the latter days, and I will bring thee against my

§ 601. THE JUDGMENT OF

20: 11-15.

11 And I saw a great white throne, and him that sat on it, from whose face [a]the earth and the heaven fled away; [b]and there was found no place for them.

12 And I saw the dead, [c]small and great, stand before God; [d]and the books were opened: and another [e]book was opened, which is *the book* of life: and the dead were judged out of those things which were written in the books, [f]according to their works.

13 And the sea gave up the dead which were in it; [g]and death and [1]hell delivered up the dead which were in them: and [h]they were judged every man according to their works.

14 And [i]death and hell were cast into the lake of fire. [k]This is the second death.

CHAP. 20.

15 And whosoever was not found written in the book of life [l]was cast into the lake of fire.

A

Matt. 24. 35. *See m, M, § 173, page 490.*

II Pet. 3. 7 But the heavens and the earth, which are now, by the same word are kept in store, reserved unto fire against the day of judgment and perdition of ungodly men.

II Pet. 3. 10 But the day of the Lord will come as a thief in the night; in the which the heavens shall pass away with a great noise, and the elements shall melt with fervent heat, the earth also and the works that are therein shall be burned up.

11 *Seeing* then *that* all these things shall be dissolved, what manner *of persons* ought ye to be in *all* holy conversation and godliness,

Rev. 21. 1 And I saw a new heaven and a new earth: for the first heaven and the first earth were passed away; and there was no more sea.

B

Job 9. 6 Which shaketh the earth out of her place, and the pillars thereof tremble.

7 Which commandeth the sun, and it riseth not; and sealeth up the stars;

§ 602. A NEW HEAVEN

21: 1-8.

1 And [a]I saw a new heaven and a new earth: for [b]the first heaven and the first earth were past away; and there was no more sea.

2 And I John saw [c]the holy city, new Jerusalem, coming down from God out of heaven, prepared [d]as a bride adorned for her husband.

A

Isa. 65. 17 For, behold, I create new heavens and a new earth: and the former shall not be remembered, nor come into mind.

Isa. 66. 22 For as the new heavens and the new earth, which I will make, shall remain before me, saith the LORD, so shall your seed and your name remain.

II Pet. 3. 13 Nevertheless we, according to his promise, look for new heavens and a

INTO THE LAKE OF FIRE WITH THE FALSE PROPHET (CONCLUDED).

E—CONCLUDED.

land, that the heathen may know me, when I shall be sanctified in thee, O Gog, before their eyes.

F

Rev. 20. 8. *See text of topic.*

G

Rev. 19. 20. *See s, S, § 598, page 1388.*

H

Rev. 14. 10. *See m, M, § 592, page 1368.*

Rev. 14. 11 And the smoke of their torment ascendeth up for ever and ever: and they have no rest day nor night, who worship the beast and his image, and whosoever receiveth the mark of his name.

THE GREAT WHITE THRONE.

B—CONCLUDED.

Da. 2. 35 Then was the iron, the clay, the brass, the silver, and the gold, broken to pieces together, and became like the chaff of the summer threshing-floors; and the wind carried them away, that no place was found for them: and the stone that smote the image became a great mountain, and filled the whole earth.

C

Rev. 19. 5 And a voice came out of the throne, saying, Praise our God, all ye his servants, and ye that fear him, both small and great.

D

Da. 7. 10 A fiery stream issued and came forth from before him: thousand thousands ministered unto him, and ten thousand times ten thousand stood before him: the judgment was set, and the books were opened.

E

Phil. 4. 3. *See f, F, § 446, page 1072.*

F

Rom. 2. 6. *See h, H, § 320, page 816.*

G

Hos. 13. 14 I will ransom them from the power of the grave; I will redeem them from death: O death, I will be thy plagues; O grave, I will be thy destruction: repentance shall be hid from mine eyes.

G—CONCLUDED.

1Cor. 15. 26 The last enemy *that* shall be destroyed *is* death.

1Cor. 15. 54 So when this corruptible shall have put on incorruption, and this mortal shall have put on immortality, then shall be brought to pass the saying that is written, Death is swallowed up in victory.

55 O death, where *is* thy sting? O grave, where *is* thy victory?

56 The sting of death *is* sin; and the strength of sin *is* the law.

Rev. 6. 8 And I looked, and behold a pale horse: and his name that sat on him was Death, and Hell followed with him. And power was given unto them over the fourth part of the earth, to kill with sword, and with hunger, and with death, and with the beasts of the earth.

1

Or, *the grave.*

H

Rom. 2. 6. *See h, H, § 320, page 816.*

I

Rev. 20. 13. *See text of topic.*

K

Rev. 2. 11. *See k, K, § 572, page 1322.*

L

Rev. 14. 8-11. *Study § 592, page 1368.*

AND A NEW EARTH.

A—CONCLUDED.

new earth, wherein dwelleth righteousness.

B

Matt. 24. 25. *See m, M, § 173, page 490.*
Rev. 20. 11. *See a, A, § 601, page 1392.*

C

Isa. 52. 1 Awake, awake, put on thy strength, O Zion; put on thy beautiful garments, O Jerusalem, the holy city: for henceforth there shall no more come into thee the uncircumcised and the unclean.

C—CONCLUDED.

Gal. 4. 26. *See f, F, § 420, page 1020.*
Heb. 11. 10. *See o, O, § 520, page 1208.*

D

Isa. 54. 5 For thy Maker *is* thine husband; The LORD of hosts *is* his name; and thy Redeemer the Holy One of Israel; The God of the whole earth shall he be called.

Isa. 61. 10 I will greatly rejoice in the LORD, my soul shall be joyful in my God; for

For D concluded see next page (1394).

§ 602. A NEW HEAVEN AND

CHAP. 21.

3 And I heard a great voice out of
heaven saying, Behold, [e]the tabernacle of God *is* with men, and he will
dwell with them, and they shall be
his people, and God himself shall
be with them, *and be* their God.
4 And [f]God shall wipe away all
tears from their eyes; and [g]there
shall be no more death, [h]neither sorrow, nor crying, neither shall there
be any more pain: for the former
things are passed away.
5 And [i]he that sat upon the throne
said, [k]Behold, I make all things
new. And he said unto me, Write:
for [l]these words are true and faithful.
6 And he said unto me, [m]It is
done. [n]I am Alpha and Omega,
the beginning and the end. [o]I will
give unto him that is athirst of the
fountain of the water of life freely.
7 He that overcometh shall inherit [1]all things; and [p]I will be his
God, and he shall be my son.
8 [q]But the fearful, and unbelieving, and the abominable, and murderers, and whoremongers, and sorcerers, and idolaters, and all liars,

CHAP. 21.

shall have their part in [r]the lake
which burneth with fire and brimstone: which is the second death.

D—CONCLUDED.

he hath clothed me with the garments of salvation, he hath covered me with the robe of righteousness, as a bridegroom decketh *himself* with ornaments, and as a bride adorneth *herself* with her jewels.

IICor. 11. 2 For I am jealous over you with godly jealousy: for I have espoused you to one husband, that I may present *you as* a chaste virgin to Christ.

E

II Cor. 6. 16. *See d, D, § 397, page 980.*
Rev. 7. 15. *See r, R, § 581, page 1342.*

F

Rev. 7. 17. *See x, X, § 581, page 1342.*

G

Rev. 20. 13, 14. *See g, G, § 601, page 1392.*

H

Isa. 35. 10 And the ransomed of the LORD shall return, and come to Zion with songs and everlasting joy upon their heads: they shall obtain joy and gladness, and sorrow and sighing shall flee away.

Isa. 61. 3 To appoint unto them that mourn in Zion, to give unto them beauty for ashes, the oil of joy for mourning, the garment of praise for the spirit of heaviness; that they might be called Trees of righteousness, The planting of the LORD, that he might be glorified.

§ 603. THE NEW

21: 9–27; 22: 1–5.

9 And there came unto me one of
[a]the seven angels which had the
seven vials full of the seven last
plagues, and talked with me, saying,
Come hither, I will shew thee [b]the
bride, the Lamb's wife.
10 And he carried me away [c]in the
spirit to a great and high mountain,
[illegible] shewed me [d]that great city, the
holy Jerusalem, descending out of
heaven from God,
11 [e]Having the glory of God: and her

A

Rev. 15. 1. *See b, B, § 593, page 1370.*

Rev. 15. 6 And the seven angels came out of the temple, having the seven plagues, clothed in pure and white linen, and having their breasts girded with golden girdles.

7 And one of the four beasts gave unto the seven angels seven golden vials full of the wrath of God, who liveth for ever and ever.

B

II Cor. 11. 2. *See under D, § 602.*

Eph. 5. 23 For the husband is the head of the wife, even as Christ is the head of the church: and he is the Saviour of the body.

24 Therefore as the church is subject unto Christ, so *let* the wives *be* to their own husbands in every thing.

A NEW EARTH (Concluded).

H—Concluded.

Isa. 65. 19 And I will rejoice in Jerusalem, and joy in my people: and the voice of weeping shall be no more heard in her, nor the voice of crying.

I

Rev. 4. 2. *See e, E, § 578, page 1330.*

Rev. 4. 9 And when those beasts give glory and honour and thanks to him that sat on the throne, who liveth for ever and ever.

Rev. 5. 1 And I saw in the right hand of him that sat on the throne a book written within and on the back side, sealed with seven seals.

Rev. 20. 11 And I saw a great white throne, and him that sat on it, from whose face the earth and the heaven fled away; and there was found no place for them.

K

II Cor. 5. 17. *See l, L, § 395, page 978.*

L

Rev. 19. 9. *See q, Q, § 597, page 1386.*

M

Rev. 16. 17 And the seventh angel poured out his vial into the air; and there came a great voice out of the temple of heaven, from the throne, saying, It is done.

N

Rev. 1. 8. *See n, N, § 569, page 1316.*

O

Isa. 12. 3 Therefore with joy shall ye draw water out of the wells of salvation.

Isa. 55. 1 Ho, every one that thirsteth, come

O—Concluded.

ye to the waters, and he that hath no money; come ye, buy, and eat; yea, come, buy wine and milk without money and without price.

John 4. 10. *See d, D, § 25, page 81.*

John 4. 14 But whosoever drinketh of the water that I shall give him shall never thirst; but the water that I shall give him shall be in him a well of water springing up into everlasting life.

John 7. 37 In the last day, that great *day* of the feast, Jesus stood and cried, saying, If any man thirst, let him come unto me, and drink.

1

Or, *these things.*

P

II Cor. 6. 16. *See d, D, § 397, page 980.*

Q

I Cor. 6. 9. *See f, F, § 360, page 910.*

R

Matt. 25. 41 Then shall he say also unto them on the left hand, Depart from me, ye cursed, into everlasting fire, prepared for the devil and his angels:

Rev. 14. 10. *See m, M, § 592, page 1368.*

Rev. 20. 10 And the devil that deceived them was cast into the lake of fire and brimstone, where the beast and the false prophet *are*, and shall be tormented day and night for ever and ever.

Rev. 20. 14 And death and hell were cast into the lake of fire. This is the second death.

15 And whosoever was not found written in the book of life was cast into the lake of fire.

JERUSALEM.

B—Concluded.

Eph. 5. 25 Husbands, love your wives, even as Christ also loved the church, and gave himself for it;

26 That he might sanctify and cleanse it with the washing of water by the word,

27 That he might present it to himself a glorious church, not having spot, or wrinkle, or any such thing; but that it should be holy and without blemish.

Rev. 19. 7 Let us be glad and rejoice, and give honour to him: for the marriage of the Lamb is come, and his wife hath made herself ready.

8 And to her was granted that she should be arrayed in fine linen, clean and white: for the fine linen is the righteousness of saints.

Rev. 21. 2. *See d, D, § 602, page 1392.*

C

Rev. 1. 10. *See d, D, § 570, page 1316.*

Rev. 17. 3 So he carried me away in the spirit into the wilderness: and I saw a woman sit upon a scarlet coloured beast, full of names of blasphemy, having seven heads and ten horns.

D

Eze. 48. *Read entire chapter.*

Rev. 21. 2. *See c, C, § 602, page 1392.*

E

Isa. 4. 5 And the Lord will create upon every dwelling place of mount Zion, and upon her assemblies a cloud and smoke by day, and the shining of a flaming fire by night: for upon all the glory *shall be* a defence.

Eze. 43. 2 And, behold, the glory of the God

For E concluded, see next page (1396).

CHAP. 21.

light *was* like unto a stone most
precious, even like a jasper stone,
clear as crystal;

12 And had a wall great and high,
and had [f]twelve gates, and at the
gates twelve angels, and names written thereon, which are *the names* of
the twelve tribes of the children of
Israel:

13 On the east three gates; on the
north three gates; on the south
three gates; and on the west three
gates.

14 And the wall of the city had
twelve foundations, and [g]in them
the names of the twelve apostles of
the Lamb.

15 And he that talked with me
[h]had a golden reed to measure the
city, and the gates thereof, and the
wall thereof.

16 And the city lieth foursquare,
and the length is as large as the
breadth: and he measured the city
with the reed, twelve thousand furlongs. The length and the breadth
and the height of it are equal.

17 And he measured the wall
thereof, a hundred *and* forty *and*
four cubits, *according to* the measure
of a man, that is, of the angel.

18 And the building of the wall of
it was *of* jasper: and the city *was*
pure gold, like unto clear glass.

19 And [i]the foundations of the wall
of the city *were* garnished with all
manner of precious stones. The
first foundation *was* jasper; the
second, sapphire; the third, a chal-
cedony; the fourth, an emerald;

20 The fifth, sardonyx; the sixth,
sardius; the seventh, chrysolite; the
eighth, beryl; the ninth, a topaz;
the tenth, a chrysoprasus; the

CHAP. 21.

eleventh, a jacinth; the twelfth, an
amethyst.

21 And the twelve gates *were* twelve
pearls; every several gate was of
one pearl: and [k]the street of the city
was pure gold, as it were transparent
glass.

22 And [l]I saw no temple therein:
for the Lord God Almighty and the
Lamb are the temple of it.

23 And [m]the city had no need of
the sun, neither of the moon, to
shine in it: for the glory of God did
lighten it, and the Lamb *is* the light
thereof.

24 And [n]the nations of them which
are saved shall walk in the light of
it: and the kings of the earth do
bring their glory and honour into it.

25 And the gates of it shall not be
shut at all by day: for [o]there shall
be no night there.

26 And [p]they shall bring the glory
and honour of the nations into it.

27 And [q]there shall in no wise enter
into it any thing that defileth, neither
whatsoever worketh abomination, or
maketh a lie: but they which are
written in the Lamb's [r]book of life.

E—CONCLUDED.

of Israel came from the way of the east: and his voice *was* like a noise of many waters: and the earth shined with his glory.

Rev. 21. 23. *See text of topic.*

Rev. 22. 5 And there shall be no night there; and they need no candle, neither light of the sun; for the Lord God giveth them light: and they shall reign for ever and ever.

F

Eze. 48. 31 And the gates of the city *shall be* after the names of the tribes of Israel: three gates northward; one gate of Reuben, one gate of Judah, one gate of Levi.

32 And at the east side four thousand and five hundred: and three gates; and one gate of Joseph, one gate of Benjamin, one gate of Dan.

JERUSALEM (CONTINUED).

F—CONCLUDED.

Eze. 48. 33 And at the south side four thousand and five hundred measures: and three gates; one gate of Simeon, one gate of Issachar, one gate of Zebulun.

34 At the west side four thousand and five hundred, *with* their three gates; one gate of Gad, one gate of Asher, one gate of Naphtali.

G

Matt. 16. 18 And I say also unto thee, That thou art Peter, and upon this rock I will build my church; and the gates of hell shall not prevail against it.

I Cor. 3. 11 For other foundation can no man lay than that is laid, which is Jesus Christ.

Gal. 2. 9 And when James, Cephas, and John, who seemed to be pillars, perceived the grace that was given unto me, they gave to me and Barnabas the right hands of fellowship; that we *should go* unto the heathen, and they unto the circumcision.

Eph. 2. 20 And are built upon the foundation of the apostles and prophets, Jesus Christ himself being the chief corner *stone;*

H

Rev. 11. 1. *See a, A, § 585, page 1350.*

I

Isa. 54. 11 O thou afflicted, tossed with tempest, *and* not comforted, behold, I will lay thy stones with fair colours, and lay thy foundations with sapphires.

12 And I will make thy windows of agates, and thy gates of carbuncles, and all thy borders of pleasant stones.

K

Rev. 21. 18. *See text of topic.*

Rev. 22. 2 In the midst of the street of it, and on either side of the river, *was there* the tree of life, which bare twelve *manner of* fruits, *and* yielded her fruit every month: and the leaves of the tree *were* for the healing of the nations.

L

John 4. 21 Jesus saith unto her, Woman, believe me, the hour cometh, when ye shall neither in this mountain, nor yet at Jerusalem, worship the Father.

John 4. 23 But the hour cometh, and now is, when the true worshippers shall worship the Father in spirit and in truth: for the Father seeketh such to worship him.

24 God *is* a Spirit: and they that worship him must worship *him* in spirit and in truth.

M

Isa. 24. 23 Then the moon shall be confounded, and the sun ashamed, when the LORD of hosts shall reign in mount Zion, and in Jerusalem, and before his ancients gloriously.

Isa. 60. 19 The sun shall be no more thy light by day; neither for brightness shall the moon give light unto thee: but the LORD shall be unto thee an everlasting light, and thy God thy glory.

20 Thy sun shall no more go down; neither shall thy moon withdraw itself: for the LORD shall be thine everlasting light, and the days of thy mourning shall be ended.

Rev. 22. 5. *See under E.*

N

Isa. 60. 3 And the Gentiles shall come to thy light, and kings to the brightness of thy rising.

Isa. 60. 5 Then thou shalt see, and flow together, and thine heart shall fear, and be enlarged; because the abundance of the sea shall be converted unto thee, the forces of the Gentiles shall come unto thee.

Isa. 60. 11 Therefore thy gates shall be open continually; they shall not be shut day nor night; that *men* may bring unto thee the forces of the Gentiles, and *that* their kings *may be* brought.

Isa. 66. 12 For thus saith the LORD, Behold, I will extend peace to her like a river, and the glory of the Gentiles like a flowing stream: then shall ye suck, ye shall be borne upon *her* sides, and be dandled upon *her* knees.

O

Isa. 60. 20. *See under M.*

Zech. 14. 7 But it shall be one day which shall be known to the LORD, not day, nor night: but it shall come to pass, *that* at evening time it shall be light.

Rev. 22. 5. *See under E.*

P

Rev. 21. 24. *See text of topic.*

Q

Isa. 35. 8 And a highway shall be there, and a way, and it shall be called The way of holiness; the unclean shall not pass over it; but it *shall be* for those: the wayfaring men, though fools, shall not err *therein.*

Isa. 52. 1 Awake, awake; put on thy strength, O Zion; put on thy beautiful gar-

For Q concluded and R, see next page (1398).

§ 603. THE NEW

CHAP. 22.

1 And he shewed me [s]a pure river
of [t]water of life, clear as crystal,
proceeding out of the throne of God
and of the Lamb.

2 [u]In the midst of the street of it,
and on either side of the river, *was
there* [x]the tree of life, which bare
twelve *manner of* fruits, *and* yielded
her fruit every month: and the leaves
of the tree *were* [y]for the healing of
the nations.

3 And [z]there shall be no more
curse: but [a]the throne of God
and of the Lamb shall be in it; and
his servants shall serve him:

4 And [b]they shall see his face; and
[c]his name *shall be* in their foreheads.

5 And [d]there shall be no night
there; and they need no candle,
neither light of the sun; for [e]the
Lord God giveth them light: [f]and
they shall reign for ever and ever.

Q—CONTINUED.

ments, O Jerusalem, the holy city: for henceforth there shall no more come into thee the uncircumcised and the unclean.

Joel 3. 17 So shall ye know that I *am* the LORD your God dwelling in Zion, my holy mountain: then shall Jerusalem be holy, and there shall no strangers pass through her any more.

Matt. 13. 41 The Son of man shall send forth his angels, and they shall gather out of his kingdom all things that offend, and them which do iniquity;

Q—CONCLUDED.

I Cor. 6. 9, 10. *See f, F, § 360, page 910.*

R

Phil. 4. 3. *See f, F, § 446, page 1072.*

S

Ps. 36. 8 They shall be abundantly satisfied with the fatness of thy house; and thou shalt make them drink of the river of thy pleasures.

Ps. 46. 4 *There is* a river, the streams whereof shall make glad the city of God, the holy *place* of the tabernacles of the Most High.

Eze. 47. *Read first twelve verses.*

Zech. 14. 8 And it shall be in that day, *that* living waters shall go out from Jerusalem; half of them toward the former sea, and half of them toward the hinder sea: in summer and in winter shall it be.

T

Ps. 36. 9 For with thee *is* the fountain of life: in thy light shall we see light.

Jer. 2. 13 For my people have committed two evils; they have forsaken me the fountain of living waters, *and* hewed them out cisterns, broken cisterns, that can hold no water.

Rev. 7. 17 For the Lamb which is in the midst of the throne shall feed them, and shall lead them unto living fountains of waters: and God shall wipe away all tears from their eyes.

Rev. 21. 6 And he said unto me, it is done. I am Alpha and Omega, the beginning and the end. I will give unto him that is athirst of the fountain of the water of life freely.

U

Eze. 47. 12 And by the river upon the bank thereof, on this side and on that side, shall grow all trees for meat, whose leaf shall not fade, neither shall the fruit thereof be comsumed: it shall bring forth new fruit according to his

§ 604. A CONFIRMATORY CONCLUSION AND BLESSED

22 : 6–21.

6 And he said unto me, [a]These
sayings *are* faithful and true: and
the Lord God of the holy prophets
[b]sent his angel to shew unto his servants the things which must shortly
be done.

CHAP. 22.

7 [c]Behold, I come quickly: [d]blessed
is he that keepeth the sayings of the
prophecy of this book.

8 And I John saw these things,
and heard *them*. And when I had
heard and seen, [e]I fell down to wor-

JERUSALEM (Concluded).

U—Concluded.

months, because their waters they issued out of the sanctuary: and the fruit thereof shall be for meat, and the leaf thereof for medicine.

Rev. 21. 21 And the twelve gates *were* twelve pearls; every several gate was of one pearl: and the street of the city *was* pure gold, as it were transparent glass.

X

Gen. 2. 9 And out of the ground made the Lord God to grow every tree that is pleasant to the sight, and good for food; the tree of life also in the midst of the garden, and the tree of knowledge of good and evil.

Gen. 3. 22 And the Lord God said, Behold, the man is become as one of us, to know good and evil: and now, lest he put forth his hand, and take also of the tree of life, and eat, and live for ever:

23 Therefore the Lord God sent him forth from the garden of Eden, to till the ground from whence he was taken.

24 So he drove out the man: and he placed at the east of the garden of Eden cherubims, and a flaming sword which turned every way, to keep the way of the tree of life.

Prov. 3. 18 She *is* a tree of life to them that lay hold upon her: and happy *is every one* that retaineth her.

Prov. 11. 30 The fruit of the righteous *is* a tree of life; and he that winneth souls *is* wise.

Prov. 13. 12 Hope deferred maketh the heart sick: but *when* the desire cometh, *it is* a tree of life.

Rev. 2. 7 He that hath an ear, let him hear what the Spirit said unto the churches; To him that overcometh will I give to eat of the tree of life, which is in the midst of the paradise of God.

Rev. 22. 14. *See text of topic, § 604.*

Y

Ps. 147. 3 He healeth the broken in heart, and bindeth up their wounds.

Isa. 57. 19 I create the fruit of the lips; Peace, peace to *him that is* far off, and to *him that is* near, saith the Lord; and I will heal him.

Jer. 17. 14 Heal me, O Lord, and I shall be healed; save me, and I shall be saved: for thou *art* my praise.

Eze. 47. 12. *See under U.*

Z

Zech. 14. 11 And *men* shall dwell in it, and there shall be no more utter destruction; but Jerusalem shall be safely inhabited.

A

Eze. 48. 35 *It was* round about eighteen thousand *measures*: and the name of the city from *that* day *shall be*, The Lord *is* there.

B

I John 3. 2. *See f, F, § 553, page 1290.*

C

Rev. 3. 12. *See p, P, § 576, page 1328.*

D

Rev. 21. 23, 25. *See m, M, § 603, page 1396.*

E

Ps. 36. 9. *See [illegible] T.*

Ps. 84. 11 For the Lord God *is* a sun and shield: the Lord will give grace and glory: no good *thing* will he withhold from them that walk uprightly.

F

Da. 7. 27 And the kingdom and dominion, and the greatness of the kingdom under the whole heaven, shall be given to the people of the saints of the Most High, whose kingdom *is* an everlasting kingdom, and all dominions shall serve and obey him.

Matt. 19. 28. *See d, D, § 145, page 412.*

Matt. 25. 34. *See d, D, § 177, page 502.*

II Tim. 2. 12 If we suffer, we shall also reign with *him*: if we deny *him*, he also will deny us:

INVITATION. A CLOSING WARNING AND BENEDICTION.

A

Rev. 19. 9. *See q, Q, § 597, page 1386.*

B

Rev. 1. 1. *See d, D, § 568, page 1314.*

C

Rev. 3. 11. *See l, L, § 576, page 1326.*

D

Rev. 1. 3. *See f, F, § 568, page 1314.*

E

Rev. 19. 10. *See r, R, § 597, page 1386.*

F

Isa. 8. 16 Bind up the testimony, seal the law among my disciples.

17 And I will wait upon the Lord, that hideth his face from the house of Jacob, and I will look for him.

Da. 8. 26 And the vision of the evening and the morning which was told *is* true: wherefore shut thou up the vision; for it *shall be* for many days.

§ 604. A CONFIRMATORY CONCLUSION AND BLESSED INVITATION.

CHAP. 22.

ship before the feet of the angel which shewed me these things.

9 Then saith he unto me, See *thou do it* not: for I am thy fellow servant, and of thy brethren the prophets, and of them which keep the sayings of this book: worship God.

10 And [f]he saith unto me, Seal not the sayings of the prophecy of this book: for [g]the time is at hand.

11 [h]He that is unjust, let him be unjust still: and he which is filthy, let him be filthy still: and he that is righteous, let him be righteous still: and he that is holy, let him be holy still.

12 And, [i]behold, I come quickly: [k]and my reward *is* with me, [l]to give every man according as his work shall be.

13 [m]I am Alpha and Omega, the beginning and the end, the first and the last.

14 [n]Blessed *are* they that do his commandments, that they may have right [o]to the tree of life, and [p]may enter in through the gates into the city.

15 For [q]without *are* [r]dogs, and sorcerers, and whoremongers, and murderers, and idolaters, and whosoever loveth and maketh a lie.

16 [s]I Jesus have sent mine angel to testify unto you these things in the churches. [t]I am the root and the offspring of David, *and* [u]the bright and morning star.

17 And the Spirit and [x]the bride say, Come. And let him that heareth say, Come. And [y]let him that is athirst come. And whosoever will, let him take the water of life freely.

CHAP. 22.

18 For I testify unto every man that heareth the words of the prophecy of this book, [z]If any man shall add unto these things, God shall add unto him the plagues that are written in this book:

19 And if any man shall take away from the words of the book of this prophecy, [a]God shall take away his part [1]out of the book of life, and out of [b]the holy city, and *from* the things which are written in this book.

20 He which testifieth these things saith, [c]Surely I come quickly. [d]Amen. [e]Even so, come, Lord Jesus.

21 [f]The grace of our Lord Jesus Christ *be* with you all. Amen.

F—CONCLUDED. See preceding page (1399.)

Da. 12. 9 And he said, Go thy way, Daniel: for the words *are* closed up and sealed till the time of the end.

Rev. 10. 4 And when the seven thunders had uttered their voices, I was about to write: and I heard a voice from heaven saying unto me, Seal up those things which the seven thunders uttered, and write them not.

G

Phil. 4. 5. *See h, H, § 446, page 1074.*

Rev. 1. 3 Blessed *is* he that readeth, and they that hear the words of this prophecy, and keep those things which are written therein: for the time *is* at hand.

H

Eze. 3. 27 But when I speak with thee, I will open thy mouth, and thou shalt say unto them, Thus saith the Lord GOD; He that heareth, let him hear; and he that forbeareth, let him forbear: for they *are* a rebellious house.

Da. 12. 10 Many shall be purified, and made white, and tried; but the wicked shall do wickedly: and none of the wicked shall understand; but the wise shall understand.

II Tim. 3. 13. *See b, B, § 490, page 1148.*

A CLOSING WARNING AND BENEDICTION (CONCLUDED).

I

Rev. 3. 11. *See l, L, § 576, page 1326.*

K

Isa. 3. 10 Say ye to the righteous, that *it shall be* well *with him:* for they shall eat the fruit of their doings.

11 Woe unto the wicked! *it shall be* ill *with him:* for the reward of his hands shall be given him.

Isa. 40. 10 Behold, the Lord GOD will come with strong *hand*, and his arm shall rule for him: behold, his reward *is* with him, and his work before him.

Isa. 62. 11 Behold, the LORD hath proclaimed unto the end of the world, Say ye to the daughter of Zion, Behold, thy salvation cometh; behold, his reward *is* with him, and his work before him.

I Cor. 3. 8. *See n, N, § 353, page 898.*

Rev. 11. 18 And the nations were angry, and thy wrath is come, and the time of the dead, that they should be judged, and that thou shouldest give reward unto thy servants the prophets, and to the saints, and them that fear thy name, small and great; and shouldest destroy them which destroy the earth.

L

Rom. 2. 6. *See h, H, § [illegible], page 816.*

M

Rev. 1. 8. *See n, N, § 569, page 1316.*

N

Da. 12. 12 Blessed *is* he that waiteth, and cometh to the thousand three hundred and five and thirty days.

I Jno. 3. 24 And he that keepeth his commandments dwelleth in him, and he in him. And hereby we know that he abideth in us, by the Spirit which he hath given us.

O

Rev. 22. 2. *See x, X, § 603, page 1398.*

P

Rev. 21. 27. *See q, Q, § 603, page 1396.*

Q

I Cor. 6. 9. *See f, F, § 360, [illegible]ge 910.*

R

Phil. 3. 2 Beware of dogs, beware of evil workers, beware of the concision.

S

Rev. 1. 1. *See d, D, § 568, page 1314.*

T

Rom. 15. 12. *See s, S, § 345, page 880.*

U

II Pet. 1. 19. *See n, N, § 546, page 1272.*

X

Rev. 21. 2. *See d, D, § 602, page 1392.*

Y

Rev. 21. 6. *See , O, § 602, page 1394.*

Z

Deut. 4. 2 Ye shall not add unto the word which I command you, neither shall ye diminish *aught* from it, that ye may keep the commandments of the LORD your God which I command you.

Deut. 12. 32 What thing soever I command you, observe to do it: thou shalt not add thereto, nor diminish from it.

Prov. 30. 6 Add thou not unto his words, lest he reprove thee, and thou be found a liar.

A

Ex. 32. 33 And the LORD said unto Moses, Whosoever hath sinned against me, him will I blot out of my book.

Ps. 69. 28 Let them be blotted out of the book of the living, and not be written with the righteous.

Rev. 3. 5 He that overcometh, the same shall be clothed in white raiment; and I will not blot out his name out of the book of life, but I will confess his name before my Father, and before his angels.

Rev. 13. 8 And all that dwell upon the earth shall worship him, whose names are not written in the book of life of the Lamb slain from the foundation of the world.

1

Or, *from the tree of life.*

B

Rev. 21. 2. *See c, C, § 602, page 1392.*

C

Rev. 3. 11. *See l, L, § 576, page 1326.*

D

John 21. 25 And there are also many other things which Jesus did, the which, if they should be written every one, I suppose that even the world itself could not contain the books that should be written. Amen.

E

Acts 1. 11. *See d, D, § 228, page 628.*

II Tim. 4. 8 Henceforth there is laid up for me a crown of righteousness, which the Lord, the righteous judge, shall give me at that day: and not to me only, but unto all them also that love his appearing.

F

Rom. 16. 20, 24. *See r, R, § 347, page 886.*

CHRONOLOGICAL INDEX OF TOPICS.

	TOPICS.	PAGE.	ST. MATT.	ST. MARK.	ST. LUKE.	ST. JOHN.
§ 1.	God the Word	4				1: 1–14
§ 2.	St. Luke's preface to Theophilus	6			1: 1–4	
§ 3.	An angel appears to Zacharias	8			1: 5–25	
§ 4.	An angel appears to Mary	12			1: 26–38	
§ 5.	Mary visits Elizabeth, remaining three months	16			1: 39–56	
§ 6.	Birth of John the Baptist	18			1: 57–80	
§ 7.	The two genealogies	22	1: 1–17		3: 23–38	
§ 8.	The birth of Jesus	28	1: 18–25		2: 1–7	
§ 9.	An angel appears to the shepherds	30			2: 8–20	
§ 10.	The circumcision and presentation in the temple	32			2: 21–38	
§ 11.	The wise men from the east	36	2: 1–12			
§ 12.	Flight into Egypt. Herod's cruelty. The return	38	2: 13–23		2: 39, 40	
§ 13.	Jesus in the temple with the doctors	42			2: 41–52	
§ 14.	Ministry of John the Baptist	44	3: 1–12	1: 1–8	3: 1–18	
§ 15.	Baptism of Jesus Christ	52	3: 13–17	1: 9–11	3: 21, 22	1: 32–34
§ 16.	The Temptation	54	4: 1–11	1: 12, 13	3: 23; 4: 1–13	
§ 17.	Testimony of John the Baptist to Jesus	58				1: 15–31
§ 18.	Andrew and another disciple and Simon Peter	62				1: 35–42
§ 19.	Philip and Nathanael	62				1: 43–51
§ 20.	The marriage of Cana of Galilee	64				2: 1–12
§ 21.	The first passover and cleansing of the temple	68				2: 13–25
§ 22.	Our Lord's discourse with Nicodemus	70				3: 1–21
§ 23.	Christ and John Baptising	74				3: 22–36
§ 24.	Imprisonment of John. Jesus sets out for Galilee	78	4: 12; 14: 3–5	1: 14; 6: 17–20	3: 19, 20; 4: 14	4: 1–3
§ 25.	Discourse with the Samaritan woman	80				4: 4–42
§ 26.	Jesus arrives in Galilee and teaches publicly	86	4: 17	1: 14, 15	4: 14, 15	4: 43–45
§ 27.	Healing of the nobleman's son lying ill at Capernaum	88				4: 46–54
§ 28.	Jesus Rejected at Nazareth	90			4: 16–30	
§ 29.	Jesus leaves Nazareth and dwells at Capernaum	92	4: 13–16		4: 31	
§ 30.	Peter, Andrew, James and John called. Draught of fishes	94	4: 18–22	1: 16–20	5: 1–11	
§ 31.	Healing of a Demoniac in the Synagogue	96		1: 21–28	4: 31–37	
§ 32.	The healing of Peter's wife's mother and many others	98	8: 14–17	1: 29–34	4: 38–41	
§ 33.	Jesus and his disciples go from Capernaum, throughout Galilee	98	4: 23–25	1: 35–39	4: 42–44	
§ 34.	Healing of a leper	100	8: 2–4	1: 40–45	5: 12–16	
§ 35.	The healing of a paralytic	102	9: 2–8	2: 1–12	5: 17–26	
§ 36.	Matthew, the publican	104	9: 9	2: 13, 14	5: 27, 28	
§ 37.	The second passover. Healing of the impotent man at the pool of Bethesda	106				5: 1–16
§ 38.	Discourse subsequent to the miracle at Bethesda	108				5: 17–47
§ 39.	Plucking ears of corn on the Sabbath	114	12: 1–8	2: 23–28	6: 1–5	
§ 40.	The withered hand healed on the Sabbath	118	12: 9–14	3: 1–6	6: 6–11	
§ 41.	Jesus arrives at the Sea of Tiberias followed by multitudes	120	12: 15–21	3: 7–12		
§ 42.	The twelve Apostles chosen	122	10: 2–4	3: 13–19	6: 12–19	
§ 43.	The sermon on the mount	124	5: 1—8: 1		6: 20–49	
	The beatitudes	124				
	Woes pronounced	126				
	The law in its spirit	128				
	The law further explained	132				
	Alms giving, prayer	136				
	Fasting	138				
	Treasure, service	140				
	Trust, judge not	142				
	Ask, enter in, the golden rule	144				
	False prophets	146				
	The wise and foolish builders	148				

	TOPICS.	PAGE.	ST. MATT.	ST. MARK.	ST. LUKE.	ST. JOHN.
§ 44.	Healing of the centurion's servant	150	8: 5–13		7: 1–10	
§ 45.	Raising of the widow's son	152			7: 11–17	
§ 46.	Messengers from John the Baptist and subsequent discourse	154	11: 2–19		7: 18–35	
§ 47.	Favoured cities of Galilee upbraided	160	11: 20–24			
§ 48.	Call to the meek and suffering	160	11: 25–30			
§ 49.	Anointing of the feet of Jesus at the Pharisee's table	162			7: 36–50	
§ 50.	Jesus with the twelve makes a second circuit in Galilee	166			8: 1–3	
§ 51.	The healing of a demoniac, blasphemous scribes and Pharisees reproved	166	12: 22–37	3: 19–30	11: 14, 15, 17–23	
§ 52.	The sign of Jonah: answer to the scribes and Pharisees who seek a sign	172	12: 38–42		11: 16, 29–32	
§ 53.	The unclean spirit's return: a reflection of our Lord	174	12: 43–45		11: 24–28	
§ 54.	The light of the body: a reflection of our Lord	174			11: 33–36	
§ 55.	The true disciples of Christ his nearest relatives	176	12: 46–50	3: 31–35	8: 19–21	
§ 56.	At a Pharisee's table Jesus denounces woes against the Pharisees and others	178			11: 37–54	
§ 57.	Jesus discourses to his disciples and the multitude	182			12: 1–59	
§ 58.	The Galileans that perished. Parable of the barren fig tree	194			13: 1–9	
§ 59.	The parable of the sower	196	13: 1–23	4: 1–20	8: 4–15	
§ 60.	Parable of the candle hid under a bushel	202		4: 21–25	8: 16–18	
§ 61.	Our Lord speaks the parable of the wheat and tares	202	13: 24–30			
§ 62.	Parable of the growth of seed	204		4: 26–29		
§ 63.	Parable of the grain of mustard seed	206	13: 31, 32	4: 30–32		
§ 64.	Parable of the leaven hid in the meal	206	13: 33			
§ 65.	On the teaching by parables	206	13: 34, 35	4: 33, 34		
§ 66.	The wheat and the tares explained	208	13: 36–43			
§ 67.	Parable of the hid treasure, the pearl and the net	210	13: 44–53			
§ 68.	Jesus directs to cross the lake. Unready disciples	212	8: 18–23	4: 35, 36	9: 57–62; 8: 22	
§ 69.	Jesus stills the tempest	212	8: 24–27	4: 37–41	8: 23–25	
§ 70.	The two demoniacs of Gadara	214	8: 28–34; 9: 1	5: 1–21	8: 26–40	
§ 71.	Levi's feast	220	9: 10–13	2: 15–17	5: 29–32	
§ 72.	The disciples of Jesus fast not. Garments and bottles	220	9: 14–17	2: 18–22	5: 33–39	
§ 73.	The raising of Jairus' daughter. The woman healed on the way	222	9: 18–26	5: 22–43	8: 41–56	
§ 74.	Two blind men healed and a dumb spirit cast out	228	9: 27–34			
§ 75.	Jesus again at Nazareth and again rejected	228	13: 54–58	6: 1–6		
§ 76.	Jesus makes a third tour throughout Galilee	230	9: 35–38	6: 6		
§ 77.	The twelve instructed and sent forth	232	10: 1, 5–42; 11: 1	6: 7–13	9: 1–6	
§ 78.	Herod's opinion of Jesus	240	14: 1, 2	6: 14–16	9: 7–9	
§ 79.	The fate of John the Baptist	242	14: 6–12	6: 21–29		
§ 80.	The twelve return. Five thousand are fed	244	14: 13–21	6: 30–44	9: 10–17	6: 1–14
§ 81.	Jesus walks upon the water	248	14: 22–33	6: 45–52		6: 15–21
§ 82.	Many miracles of healing in the land of Gennesaret	250	14: 34–36	6: 53–56		
§ 83.	Discourse to the multitude in the synagogue	250				6: 22–65
§ 84.	Many disciples turn back. Peter's profession of faith	258				6: 66–71; 7: 1
§ 85.	The third passover. Unwashen hands. Pharisaic traditions	260	15: 1–20	7: 1–23		
§ 86.	The daughter of a Syrophœnician woman healed	266	15: 21–28	7: 24–30		
§ 87.	A deaf and dumb man and many others healed	268	15: 29–31	7: 31–37		
§ 88.	Feeding of the four thousand	270	15: 32–39	8: 1–10		
§ 89.	The Pharisees and Sadducees again require a sign	272	16: 1–4	8: 11–13		
§ 90.	Disciples cautioned against the leaven of the Pharisees	272	16: 5–12	8: 14–21		

TOPICS.	PAGE.	ST. MATT.	ST. MARK.	ST. LUKE.	ST. JOHN.
§ 91. A blind man healed	274		8: 22–26		
§ 92. Peter and the rest again profess their faith in Christ.	276	16: 13–20	8: 27–30	9: 18–21	
§ 93. Jesus foretells his death and resurrection	278	16: 21–28	{8: 31–38; 9: 1	9: 22–27	
§ 94. The transfiguration	282	17: 1–9	9: 2–10	9: 28–36	
§ 95. Discourse with the three disciples after the transfiguration	286	17: 10–13	9: 11–13		
§ 96 Jesus heals a lunatic whom the disciples could not heal	286	17: 14–21	9: 14–29	9: 37–42	
§ 97. Jesus again foretells his own death and resurrection.	290	17: 22, 23	9: 30–32	9: 43–45	
§ 98. The fish caught for the tribute money	292	17: 24–27			
§ 99. The little child	294	18: 1–5	9: 33–37	9: 46–48	
§ 100. One casting out devils in Jesus' name	296		9: 38–41	9: 49, 50	
§ 101. Offences. Salted with fire	296	18: 6–9	9: 42–50		
§ 102. The parable of the lost sheep	298	18: 10–14			
§ 103. Forgiveness of injuries	300	18: 15–20			
§ 104. The parable of the unmerciful servant	302	18: 21–35			
§ 105. The seventy instructed and sent out	304			10: 1–16	
§ 106. Jesus goes up to the feast of the tabernacles. Final departure from Galilee	308				7: 2–10
§ 107. James and John ask whether to command fire from heaven	310			9: 51–56	
§ 108. Ten lepers cleansed by Jesus	310			17: 11–19	
§ 109. Jesus teaches at the feast of tabernacles	312				7: 11–53
§ 110. The woman taken in adultery	320				8: 1–11
§ 111. Public teaching. Dispute with the Pharisees. Second attempt to stone Jesus	322				8: 12–59
§ 112. A lawyer instructed. The parable of the good Samaritan	332			10: 25–37	
§ 113. Jesus in the house of Martha and Mary	336			10: 38–42	
§ 114. The disciples again taught how to pray	336			11: 1–4	
§ 115. Prayer effectual	338			11: 5–13	
§ 116. The seventy return	340			10: 17–24	
§ 117. A man born blind healed on the Sabbath	342				9: 1–41
§ 118. The good shepherd. Discourse subsequent to the healing of the blind man	348				10: 1–21
§ 119. Jesus at the feast of the dedication	352				10: 22–39
§ 120. He retires beyond Jordan	356				10: 40–42
§ 121. The raising of Lazarus	356				11: 1–44
§ 122. The counsel of Caiaphas against Jesus. He retires from Jerusalem	364				11: 45–54
§ 123. Jesus beyond Jordan. A woman healed on the Sabbath	366	19: 1, 2	10: 1	13: 10–17	
§ 124. Parable of the grain of mustard seed repeated	368			13: 18, 19	
§ 125. Parable of the leaven hid in the meal repeated	368			13: 20, 21	
§ 126. Journeying toward Jerusalem and teaching on the way	370			13: 22–30	
§ 127. Jesus is warned against Herod	372			13: 31–33	
§ 128. Prophesy against Jerusalem	372			13: 34, 35	
§ 129. Jesus heals a man of dropsy on the Sabbath while dining with a Pharisee	374			14: 1–6	
§ 130. Discourse on choosing chief rooms spoken at the Pharisee's table	374			14: 7–14	
§ 131. The parable of the great supper spoken at the Pharisee's table	376			14: 15–24	
§ 132. What is required of true disciples	378			14: 25–35	
§ 133. Parable of the lost sheep spoken a second time	380			15: 1–7	
§ 134. The parable of the piece of money	382			15: 8–10	
§ 135. The parable of the prodigal son	384			15: 11–32	
§ 136. The parable of the unjust steward	388			16: 1–13	
§ 137. The Pharisee reproved. Parable of the rich man and Lazarus	390			16: 14–31	

TOPICS.	PAGE.	ST. MATT.	ST. MARK.	ST. LUKE.	ST. JOHN.
§ 138. Jesus inculcates forbearance, faith and humility......	394	....	....	17: 1–10	....
§ 139. How the kingdom of God will come..........................	396	....	....	17: 20–37	....
§ 140. The parable of the importunate widow and unjust judge	400	....	....	18: 1–8	....
§ 141. The parable of the Pharisee and the publican...........	402	....	....	18: 9–14	....
§ 142. Precepts of Jesus respecting divorce.........................	402	19: 3–12	10: 2–12	....	....
§ 143. Jesus receives and blesses little children..................	406	19: 13–15	10: 13–16	18: 15–17	....
§ 144. The rich young man........................	408	19: 16–26	10: 17–27	18: 18–27	....
§ 145. Promises to disciples..	412	19: 27–30	10: 28–31	18: 28–30	....
§ 146. The parable of the labourers in the vineyard...........	412	20: 1–16	....	....	....
§ 147. Jesus foretells his death and resurrection a third time	416	20: 17–19	10: 32–34	18: 31–34	....
§ 148. Request of James and John..	418	20: 20–28	10: 35–45	....	....
§ 149. The healing of two blind men.....................................	422	20: 29–34	10: 46–52	{18: 35–43; 19: 1	....
§ 150. Visit to Zaccheus...	424	....	....	19: 2–10	....
§ 151. The parable of the ten pounds..................................	426	....	....	19: 11–28	....
§ 152. Jesus arrives at Bethany six days before the passover..	428	....	....	....	{11: 55–57; 12: 1
§ 153. The supper and anointing by Mary. Hostility of the chief priests..	430	26: 6–13	14: 3–9	....	12: 2–11
§ 154. Our Lord's public entry into Jerusalem.....................	432	{21: 1–11, 17	11: 1–11	19: 29–44	12: 12–19
§ 155. The barren fig tree cursed...	438	21: 18, 19	11: 12–14	....	....
§ 156. The second cleansing of the temple...........................	438	21: 12–16	11: 15–19	{19:45-48; 21: 37,38	....
§ 157. The barren fig tree withers away..............................	440	21: 20–22	11: 20–24	....	....
§ 158. Pray and forgive	440	....	11: 25, 26	....	....
§ 159. Christ's authority questioned.....................................	442	21: 23–27	11: 27–33	20: 1–8	....
§ 160. The parable of the two sons.......................................	444	21: 28–32	....	....	....
§ 161. The parable of the wicked husbandmen.....................	444	21: 33–46	12: 1–12	20: 9–19	....
§ 162. The parable of the wedding garment.........................	450	22: 1–14	....	....	....
§ 163. The tribute money..	454	22: 15–22	12: 13–17	20: 20–26	....
§ 164. The Sadducees and the resurrection...........................	456	22: 23–33	12: 18–27	20: 27–40	....
§ 165. The two great commandments....................................	460	22: 34–40	12: 28–34	....	....
§ 166. David's son and David's Lord.....................................	462	22: 41–46	12: 35–37	20: 41–44	....
§ 167. Warnings against the scribes and Pharisees and the eight woes..	462	23: 1–36	12: 38–40	20: 45–47	....
§ 168. Jesus laments over Jerusalem....................................	470	23: 37–39	....	....	....
§ 169. The poor widow's two mites.......................................	470	....	12: 41–44	21: 1–4	....
§ 170. Certain Greeks desire to see Jesus.............................	472	....	....	....	12: 20–36
§ 171. Reflections of our Lord upon the unbelief of the Jews	476	....	....	....	12: 37–50
§ 172. Destruction of the temple and persecution foretold...	480	24: 1–14	13: 1–13	21: 5–19	....
§ 173. Signs of coming destruction.......................................	486	24: 15–42	13: 14–37	21: 20–36	....
§ 174. Exhortation to watchfulness......................................	494	24: 43–51	....	....	....
§ 175. The parable of the ten virgins...................................	496	25: 1–13	....	....	....
§ 176. The parable of the five talents..................................	498	25: 14–30	....	....	....
§ 177. Scenes of the judgment day.......................................	502	25: 31–46	....	....	....
§ 178. The rulers conspire against Jesus..............................	506	26: 1–5	14: 1, 2	22: 1, 2	....
§ 179. Judas Iscariot covenants to betray Jesus...................	506	26: 14–16	14: 10, 11	22: 3–6	....
§ 180. Preparation for the passover.....................................	508	26: 17–19	14: 12–16	22: 7–13	....
§ 181. The passover meal. Contention among the twelve...	510	26: 20	14: 17	{22: 14–18, 24–30	....
§ 182. Jesus washes the disciples' feet.................................	512	....	....	....	13: 1–20
§ 183. The traitor made known. Judas withdraws...............	516	26: 21–25	14: 18–21	22: 21–23	13: 21–35
§ 184. The Lord's supper instituted.....................................	520	26: 26–29	14: 22–25	22: 19, 20	....
§ 185. Peter's fall foretold..	522	26: 31–35	14: 27–31	22: 31–38	13: 36–38
§ 186. Jesus comforts his disciples.......................................	524	....	....	....	14: 1–31
§ 187. The vine and the branches	530	....	....	....	15: 1–11
§ 188. Mutual love. The disciples hated by the world........	532	....	....	....	15: 12–27

TOPICS.	PAGE.	ST. MATT.	ST. MARK	ST. LUKE.	ST. JOHN.
§ 189. Persecution foretold. Further promise of the Holy Spirit	534	....	....	....	16: 1–16
§ 190. Prayer in the name of Christ	538	....	....	....	16: 17–33
§ 191. Christ's last prayer with his disciples	542	....	....	....	17: 1–26
§ 192. The agony in the garden of Gethsemane	548	{ 26: 30, 36–46	{ 14: 26, 32–42	22: 39–46	18: 1, 2
§ 193. Jesus betrayed and made prisoner	552	26: 47–56	14: 43–52	22: 47–53	18: 3–12
§ 194. Jesus before Annas and Caiaphas. Peter's denial	556	{ 26:57,58, 69–75	{ 14:53,54, 66–72	22: 54–62	{ 18:13-18, 25–27
§ 195. Jesus before Caiaphas and the Sanhedrin	560	26: 59–68	14: 55–65	22: 63–71	18: 19–24
§ 196. The Sanhedrin lead Jesus away to Pilate	564	{ 27: 1, 2, 11–14	15: 1–5	23: 1–5	18: 28–38
§ 197. Jesus before Herod	568	....	....	23: 6–12	....
§ 198. Pilate seeks to release Jesus. Barabbas demanded	568	27: 15–25	15: 6–14	23: 13–23	18: 39, 40
§ 199. Barabbas released. Jesus delivered up to death	572	27: 26–30	15: 15–19	23: 24, 25	19: 1–3
§ 200. Pilate again seeks to release Jesus	574	....	....	....	19: 4–16
§ 201. Judas repents and hangs himself	578	27: 3–10	....	....	....
§ 202. On the way to Golgotha	580	27: 31–34	15: 20–23	23: 26–32	19: 17
§ 203. The crucifixion	582	27: 35–38	15: 24–28	{ 23: 33, 34, 38	19: 18–24
§ 204. Mocked on the cross	584	27: 39–44	15: 29–32	{ 23: 35–37, 39	....
§ 205. The penitent thief	586	....	....	23: 40–43	....
§ 206. The mother of Jesus at the cross	586	....	....	....	19: 25–27
§ 207. Darkness prevails. Christ expires on the cross	588	27: 45–50	15: 33–37	23: 44, 46	19: 28–30
§ 208. The vail of the temple rent, and tombs opened	590	27: 51–56	15: 38–41	{ 23: 45, 47–49	....
§ 209. The side pierced	592	....	....	....	19: 31–37
§ 210. Taken down from the cross, and laid in the tomb	592	27: 57–61	15: 42–47	23: 50–56	19: 38–42
§ 211. The guard at the sepulchre	596	27: 62–66	....	....	....
§ 212. Morning of the resurrection. Women visit the tomb	596	28: 1–4	16: 1–4	24: 1–3	20: 1, 2
§ 213. Vision of angels in the tomb	598	28: 5–7	16: 5–7	24: 4–8	....
§ 214. The women return to the city. Jesus meets them	600	28: 8–10	16: 8	24: 9–11	....
§ 215. Peter and John run to the tomb	600	....	....	24: 12	20: 3–10
§ 216. Our Lord is seen by Mary Magdalene at the tomb	602	....	16: 9–11	....	20: 11–18
§ 217. Report of the guard	604	28: 11–15	....	....	....
§ 218. Jesus appears to two disciples on the way to Emmaus	604	....	16: 12, 13	24: 13–35	....
§ 219. Jesus appears in the midst of the apostles, Thomas being absent	610	....	16: 14–18	24: 36–49	20: 19–23
§ 220. Jesus appears in the midst of the apostles, Thomas being present	614	....	....	....	20: 24–29
§ 221. Jesus appears to seven apostles at the sea of Tiberias	616	28: 16	....	....	21: 1–24
§ 222. Jesus meets the apostles and above five hundred disciples on a mountain in Galilee	622	28: 16–20	....	....	....
§ 223. Our Lord appears to James, and then to all the apostles	622	{ Mentioned only by Luke in ACTS and by Paul in I CORINTHIANS.			
§ 224. The ascension of our Lord	624	....	16: 19, 20	24: 50–53	....
§ 225. Conclusion of John's gospel	624	....	....	....	{ 20:30,31; 21: 25

ROMANS.	PAGE	ROM.
§ 326. Being justified we have peace, hope of glory, reconciliation and salvation through Christ,	830	5: 1-11
§ 327. Through Adam many became sinners. Through Christ many became righteous. The law entered that sin might abound, but grace much more,	834	5: 12-21
§ 328. Continue not in sin for grace. The faithful in Christ are dead unto sin and death, and alive unto God,	834	6: 1-14
§ 329. Freed from sin ye became servants of righteousness. The wages of sin is death. God's gift is eternal life,	838	6: 15-23
§ 330. The dominion of the law and the freedom therefrom illustrated,	838	7: 1-6
§ 331. By the law is the knowledge of sin. It is spiritual. The inward man delights therein. Carnal members war against it. Deliverance is in Christ,	840	7: 7-25
§ 332. No condemnation to them in Christ. Having received the spirit of adoption we become children of God and joint heirs with Christ,	842	8: 1-17
§ 333. All creation awaits redemption, the glory of which will greatly overshadow the present trial and suffering,	846	8: 18-25
§ 334. The Spirit helps, and Christ intercedes for God's elect; therefore nothing shall be able to separate them from the love of God,	848	8: 26-39
§ 335. Not all Israel, God worketh his will in mercy with compassion,	852	9: 1-18
§ 336. The creature shall not reply against the Creator. Gentiles attain to the righteousness of faith at which the Jews stumbled,	854	9: 19-33
§ 337. The Jews though zealous erred in their knowledge of God's righteousness, beholding the letter of the law rather than the spirit thereof,	858	10: 1-15
§ 338. The gospel was proclaimed by Moses and the prophets. The disobedient Jews hearkened not,	860	10: 16-21
§ 339. Israel is not cast off but found not that which was sought; being hardened. The election obtained it, and salvation is come to the Gentiles,	860	11: 1-12
§ 340. The severity of God toward unbelief, and his goodness toward faith are illustrated in the figure of a graft,	864	11: 13-24
§ 341. The Deliverer shall come out of Zion. All Israel shall be saved. The ways of God are past finding out,	864	11: 25-36
§ 342. An exhortation to love God, the faithful performance of duty, and love toward men,	868	12: 1-21
§ 343. An exhortation to be subject to the higher powers, love to man, and a pure and sober life,	872	13: 1-14
§ 344. Admonished to be charitable, not to judge. Put no stumbling blocks, but to follow righteousness, joy, peace and edification,	876	14: 1-23
§ 345. Exhortation to bear with the weak, please our fellowmen unto good as did Christ, and to glorify God as it is written,	878	15: 1-13
§ 346. Paul reminds the Romans of his ministry, declares his purpose to visit them, and solicits their prayers,	880	15: 14-33
§ 347. Paul commends Phebe and sends greetings and salutations to many at Rome,	884	16: 1-27

I. CORINTHIANS.	PAGE	I COR.
§ 348. The Salutation,	888	1: 1-3
§ 349. Thanksgiving for God's grace to them,	888	1: 4-9
§ 350. A rebuke for the contentions and divisions among them,	890	1: 10-17
§ 351. The wisdom of man and the wisdom of God,	892	1: 18-31
§ 352. Paul declares his preaching was of the Spirit with power, which the natural man receiveth not,	894	2: 1-16
§ 353. Rebuke for carnal walk after the manner of men. We are God's fellow-workers,	898	3: 1-9

I. CORINTHIANS.	PAGE	I COR.
§ 354. Christ the foundation. Each builder's work thereon tried by fire,........	898	3: 10-17
§ 355. Let no one glory in men,..	900	3: 18-23
§ 356. Judge nothing before the time. The Lord will bring to light the hidden things of darkness when he comes,..........................	902	4: 1-5
§ 357. Admonished not to be puffed up against each other. The apostles were made spectacles unto the world,..........................	902	4: 6-13
§ 358. Admonished to follow the apostle in the ways of Christ,.............	904	4: 14-21
§ 359. Fornication rebuked, and together with other evil doing to be adjudged unworthy of fellowship,..................................	906	5: 1-13
§ 360. Rebuke for going to law with one another, and that before the unjust, whereas saints shall judge the world and angels,...............	910	6: 1-11
§ 361. All things are lawful, but not expedient. The body is not for fornication, it is a temple of the Holy Spirit,.......................	912	6: 12-20
§ 362. Answer to questions concerning marriage, with special reference to mixed marriages and to bond servants,......................	912	7: 1-24
§ 363. Answer concerning the marriage of virgin daughters,.................	916	7: 25-40
§ 364. Answer concerning things sacrificed to idols, especially meats,........	918	8: 1-13
§ 365. Paul asserts his apostleship and privileges therein, that his abstinence was for the furtherance of the gospel,......................	920	9: 1-27
§ 366. Further warning in the example of Israel against lusting after evil,....	926	10: 1-13
§ 367. All fellowship with idolatry must be renounced. Eat without question, but spare another's conscience,............................	928	10: 14-33
§ 368. Concerning authority and its signs, the covering of heads,...........	932	11: 1-16
§ 369. Paul censures divisions, heresies and profanations, and sets forth the manner and purpose of the Lord's Supper,....................	934	11: 17-34
§ 370. The diversity of gifts, ministrations and workings in the same spirit,....	936	12: 1-11
§ 371. By the figure of the body it is shown how all are baptized into the body of Christ,..	940	12: 12-31
§ 372. Love and its greatness above all,................................	942	13: 1-13
§ 373. Instructions as to the exercise of the gift of prophecy and of tongues,..	944	14: 1-19
§ 374. Tongues are a sign unto the unbelieving, prophecy to the believer,....	946	14: 20-25
§ 375. Instruction as to decency and order in the congregation, and the subjection of women,...	946	14: 26-40
§ 376. Paul sets forth briefly the gospel which he preached,.................	948	15: 1-11
§ 377. The resurrection of Christ the foundation of the faith,...............	950	15: 12-19
§ 378. The importance of the resurrection in the order of dispensation,......	950	15: 20-28
§ 379. No profit in the exercise of the faith if the dead are not raised,........	952	15: 29-34
§ 380. The diverse character of natural and risen bodies and their order set forth in figure and example,...............................	954	15: 35-49
§ 381. The order, manner and victory of the resurrection of the saints,........	954	15: 50-58
§ 382. Concerning the collection for the saints and Paul's visit,.............	956	16: 1-9
§ 383. Instructions concerning Timothy, Apollos, Stephanas, Fortunatus and Achaicus, ...	958	16: 10-18
§ 384. An exhortation of greeting and anathema with concluding salutations,...	960	16: 19-24

II. CORINTHIANS.	PAGE	II COR.
§ 385. The Salutation, ...	962	1: 1-2
§ 386. Paul's thanksgiving for comfort in affliction, and affirmation of a holy and sincere conscience,......................................	962	1: 3-14
§ 387. Paul answers with reasons for delaying his purposed visit,.............	964	1: 15-24 2: 1-4
§ 388. Forgiveness and comfort for the offender,..........................	966	2: 5-11
§ 389. Not finding Titus and having no relief in the Spirit, Paul leaves Troas,	968	2: 12-17
§ 390. The sufficiency of the Spirit's ministration, and the glory of the new covenant, ...	968	3: 1-11
§ 391. The glory of the new covenant reflected,..........................	970	3: 12-18

II. CORINTHIANS.	PAGE	II COR.
§ 392. A veiled gospel to unbelievers, but to believers a light to the knowledge of the glory of God,	972	4: 1-6
§ 393. Our light afflictions work a far more exceeding and eternal weight of glory,	972	4: 7-18
§ 394. A mansion in heaven. In this body we have the earnest of the Spirit that we may strive to please God,	974	5: 1-10
§ 395. All things are of God who gave the ministry of reconciliation. We are ambassadors,	976	5: 11-21
§ 396. With an appeal for faithfulness, Paul sets forth the character of his ministry,	978	6: 1-13
§ 397. Admonished not to have fellowship with unbelievers, to cleanse themselves and be open-hearted,	980	6: 14-18 7: 1-4
§ 398. Paul comforted by the coming of Titus and the good report he brought of the Corinthians,	982	7: 5-16
§ 399. Paul exhorts them to the grace of a liberal offering for the poor saints,	984	8: 1-15
§ 400. Titus and another sent unto the Corinthians,	986	8: 16-24
§ 401. Preparing for the collection for the poor saints. Concerning giving,	988	9: 1-15
§ 402. Paul declares his walk was not according to the flesh. If his word was powerful his deed was the same,	990	10: 1-18
§ 403. Paul exercises a jealous watch over the gospel and warns against false apostles,	992	11: 1-15
§ 404. Paul asserts his fitness and recapitulates his trials, sufferings and perils for the gospel,	996	11: 16-33
§ 405. Paul recounts visions and revelations and declares the power of God perfected in weakness,	998	12: 1-10
§ 406. Paul solicits acknowledgment of his apostleship and offers reasons for the postponement of his visit,	1000	12: 11-21
§ 407. Paul declares his writings to be for the perfecting of the saints,	1002	13: 1-10
§ 408. Concluding admonitions, a salutation and benediction,	1004	13: 11-14

GALATIANS.	PAGE	GAL.
§ 409. The Salutation,	1004	1: 1-5
§ 410. The perverting of the gospel among the Galatians,	1004	1: 6-10
§ 411. Paul declares he received the gospel not of men, but through revelation of Jesus Christ,	1006	1: 11-17
§ 412. Paul recounts his visit to Peter to verify his preaching,	1008	1: 18-24
§ 413. Paul recounts the decision of the council held at Jerusalem,	1008	2: 1-10
§ 414. Paul withstood Peter at Antioch,	1010	2: 11-21
§ 415. The righteous shall live by faith and not by the works of the law,	1012	3: 1-14
§ 416. The law was added because of transgressions and not to disannul the promises,	1014	3: 15-22
§ 417. The law our tutor unto Christ,	1016	3: 23-29
§ 418. Children under bondage of the law are set free and become sons by adoption,	1016	4: 1-7
§ 419. Paul's anxious care for the backsliding Galatians,	1018	4: 8-20
§ 420. The allegory of the two covenants,	1020	4: 21-31 5: 1
§ 421. Neither circumcision availeth anything nor uncircumcision,	1020	5: 2-15
§ 422. The spirit and the flesh discerned and found contrary,	1022	5: 16-26
§ 423. Exhorted to bear with one another and not to weary in well doing,	1024	6: 1-10
§ 424. Glory only in the cross of Christ; conclusion, benediction	1026	6: 11-18

I. THESSALONIANS.	PAGE	I THESS.
§ 457. Salutation. Thanksgiving and commendation for faith and labor of love,	1092	1: 1-10
§ 458. Paul recounts the manner of their entrance and their example,	1094	2: 1-12
§ 459. Thanksgiving for their faithful reception of the word. Satan hinders Paul's coming,	1098	2: 13-20
§ 460. Timothy was sent to establish them, who returned with a comforting report. A prayer,	1100	3: 1-13
§ 461. Exhortation to abstain from fornication and lustful passions,	1102	4: 1-8
§ 462. Exhortation to increase in love and to be diligent and honest in business,	1102	4: 9-12
§ 463. Concerning the saints and the Lord's coming,	1104	4: 13-18
§ 464. The uncertainty of the day of the Lord's coming a motive to sober watchfulness,	1106	5: 1-11
§ 465. Sundry admonitions. Concluding salutation and benediction,	1106	5: 12-28

II. THESSALONIANS.	PAGE	II THESS.
§ 466. Salutation. Thanksgiving. Hope in the Lord's coming for those who suffer persecution, and destruction for the ungodly,	1110	1: 1-2
§ 467. Concerning the coming of our Lord Jesus Christ,	1112	2: 1-12
§ 468. Exhortation to steadfastness and obedience. A benediction,	1114	2: 13-17
§ 469. Paul solicits the prayers of the Thessalonians,	1114	3: 1-5
§ 470. Concerning disorderly walk and diligent work for bread,	1116	3: 6-15
§ 471. Concluding salutation and benediction,	1116	3: 16-18

I. TIMOTHY.	PAGE	I TIM.
§ 472. Salutation,	1118	1: 1-2
§ 473. Timothy is reminded of his commission to the Ephesians,	1118	1: 3-11
§ 474. Paul gives thanks for his calling and charges Timothy to fulfill his commission,	1120	1: 12-20
§ 475. Exhortation to pray and give thanks for all men and rulers. Concerning women,	1122	2: 1-15
§ 476. Concerning bishops, deacons and women,	1124	3: 1-13
§ 477. Paul sets forth his purpose in writing this epistle,	1126	3: 14-16
§ 478. Concerning false teaching in the latter times. Sundry exhortations,	1126	4: 1-16
§ 479. Concerning admonishing and widows,	1130	5: 1-16
§ 480. Concerning elders and other charges,	1132	5: 17-25
§ 481. Concerning bondservants. Rebuke to false and covetous teachers,	1134	6: 1-10
§ 482. Paul charges Timothy to fight a good fight,	1136	6: 11-16
§ 483. A charge to the rich,	1136	6: 17-19
§ 484. Concluding charge and benediction,	1138	6: 20-21

II. TIMOTHY.	PAGE	II TIM.
§ 485. Salutation,	1138	1: 1-2
§ 486. Timothy's faith. He is exhorted to suffer with the gospel in the hope of eternal life,	1138	1: 3-14
§ 487. Paul is abandoned by all in Asia. Onesiphorus is gratefully remembered,	1142	1: 15-18
§ 488. Sundry instructions in duty and exhortations in the gospel,	1142	2: 1-13
§ 489. Sundry instructions as to strife, ungodliness, error and personal conduct,	1144	2: 14-26
§ 490. The perilous character of the last days. Timothy exhorted to steadfastness,	1146	3: 1-17
§ 491. A solemn charge to fulfil a faithful ministry,	1150	4: 1-8

HEBREWS.	PAGE	HEB.
§ 521. Exhortation in the figure of a race. Despise not the chastening of the Lord,	1214	12: 1-13
§ 522. Exhortation to follow peace and sanctification and to shun defiling associations,	1218	12: 14-17
§ 523. The administration of the gospel is superior to that of the law. Its warnings more to be feared,	1218	12: 18-29
§ 524. Exhortation to sundry duties,	1220	13: 1-6
§ 525. Exhortation to remember their instructors and to continue steadfast, bearing reproach,	1222	13: 7-17
§ 526. Solicitation for their prayers, concerning Timothy, closing salutations and benedictions,	1224	13: 18-25

JAMES.	PAGE	JAMES.
§ 527. Introductory greeting,	1226	1: 1
§ 528. Exhortation to bear trial patiently, and to pray for wisdom. Good gifts come from God; evil springs from lust,	1226	1: 2-18
§ 529. Exhortation to bridle the tongue, put away evil. Receive the word; be doers, not only hearers, and follow pure religion,	1228	1: 19-27
§ 530. A rebuke to those who profess faith and show respect to persons,	1230	2: 1-13
§ 531. Faith without works and professions without deeds of mercy, are profitless,	1232	2: 14-26
§ 532. The iniquity of an unbridled tongue illustrated by the bit, helm and fountain,	1234	3: 1-12
§ 533. Worldly and heavenly wisdom defined,	1236	3: 13-18
§ 534. Some sources of evil set forth and some remedies exhorted,	1238	4: 1-17
§ 535. Warnings and sundry exhortations,	1240	5: 1-20

I. PETER.	PAGE	I PETER.
§ 536. Salutation,	1246	1: 1-2
§ 537. Grateful praise for salvation foretold and sought for by the prophets, and comfort for their trials,	1246	1: 3-12
§ 538. Exhortation to holy life, knowing their redemption and royal priestly calling,	1250	1: 11-25 2: 1-10
§ 539. Exhortation concerning worldly walk; subjection to authorities, to servants, and to endure suffering blameless,	1254	2: 11-25
§ 540. Exhortation concerning wives and husbands,	1256	3: 1-7
§ 541. Exhortation concerning social relations, and suffering after the pattern of Christ. The end is at hand,	1258	3: 8-22 4: 1-19
§ 542. Exhortation to elders, to be humble, sober, watchful and steadfast,	1266	5: 1-11
§ 543. Concluding salutations and benedictions,	1268	5: 12-14

II. PETER.	PAGE	II PETER.
§ 544. The Salutation,	1268	1: 1-2
§ 545. Through the promises we become partakers of the divine nature,	1268	1: 3-11
§ 546. Peter, an eye witness of the power and majesty of the Son of God, commends the more sure word of prophecy,	1270	1: 12-21
§ 547. Warnings against false teachers,	1272	2: 1-22
§ 548. Peter defends the Lord's coming against scoffers,	1278	3: 1-18

CHAPTER AND VERSE INDEX.

MATTHEW.

CHAPTER AND VERSE INDEX.

MARK.

LUKE.

LUKE—Concluded.

JOHN.

ALPHABETICAL INDEX.

Where the topics are not obviously included in the headings of pages indicated by index, the reference letters are also given with the pages to locate the topics.

E

F

W.

Y.

Z.

Prophecies and their Fulfillments Relating to Christ.

The fulfillment of prophecies will be found as located below and the prophecies will be found on same pages, under the corresponding reference letters.

TRAVELS OF ST. PAUL
Paul's tour with Barnabus Acts XIII, XIV,
" " " Silas Acts XV, XVIII,
" third miss'y tour Acts XVIII, XIV,
Voyage to Rome
Direction of travel indicted by arrow heads"
Modern Names Thus (Malta)
Scale of Miles
0 50 150 250
Fisk & Co. Engr's N.Y.
BLACK SEA
GREAT OR MEDITERRANEAN SEA
ASIA MINOR
AFRICA
ARABIA
MACEDONIA
THRACE
PAPHLAGONIA
PONTUS
BITHYNIA
GALATIA
CAPPADOCIA
MYSIA
LYDIA
PHRYGIA
PISIDIA
CARIA
LYCIA
Thessaly
Hellas
Achaia
Epirus
CYRENAICA
MARMARICA
ROME
Three Taverns
Appii forum
Neapolis
Luceria
Tarentum
Brundusium
Scodra
Dyrrachium
Philippopolis
Adrianapolis
Byzantium
Constantinopolis
Nicomedia
Gordium
(Broosa)
Ancyra
Sinope
Amasia
Halys
Sebaste (Sivas)
Caesarea
Dorylaeum
Troas
(Adramittium)
Thyatira
Sardis
Philadelphia
Antioch (Pisidia)
Hierapolis
Colosse
Laodicea
Ephesus
Trogyllium
Iconium
Lystria
Derbe
Perga
Pamphylia
Attalia
Taurus
Tarsus
Selucia
Adana
(Marash)
Mts.
Issus
Seleucia
Antioch
Beroea (Aleppo)
Hamath
Emesa
Tripolis
Heliopolis
Berytus
Sidon
Damascus
Tyre
Caesarea
Joppa
Gaza
JERUSALEM
Dead Sea
Kadesh Barnea
Petra
Sin
Pelusium
Zoan
Rameses
Delta
Mouths of the Nile R.
Alexandria
Praetonium
Berenice
Ptolemais
Cyrene
Apollonia
Cyprus
Salamis
Citium
Amathus
Papho
Rhodes
Cnidus
Cos
Patara
Myra
Cyclades
Crete
Salmone Pm.
Phenice
Clauda
Fair Havens
Cythera
Sparta
Peloponnesus
Corinth
Athens
Euboea
Lesbos
Mitylene
Pergamos
Assos
Chios
Samos
Lemnos
Tempe
Amphipolis
Philippi
Neapolis
Apollonia
Thessalonica
Pella
Berea
Axius
Hebrus
Corcyra
Cephallenia
Zacynthus
Narona
Laus
Liparea Is.
Messina
Rhegium
Mt. Etna
Syracuse
Agrigentum
Melita (Malta)
R. Tiber

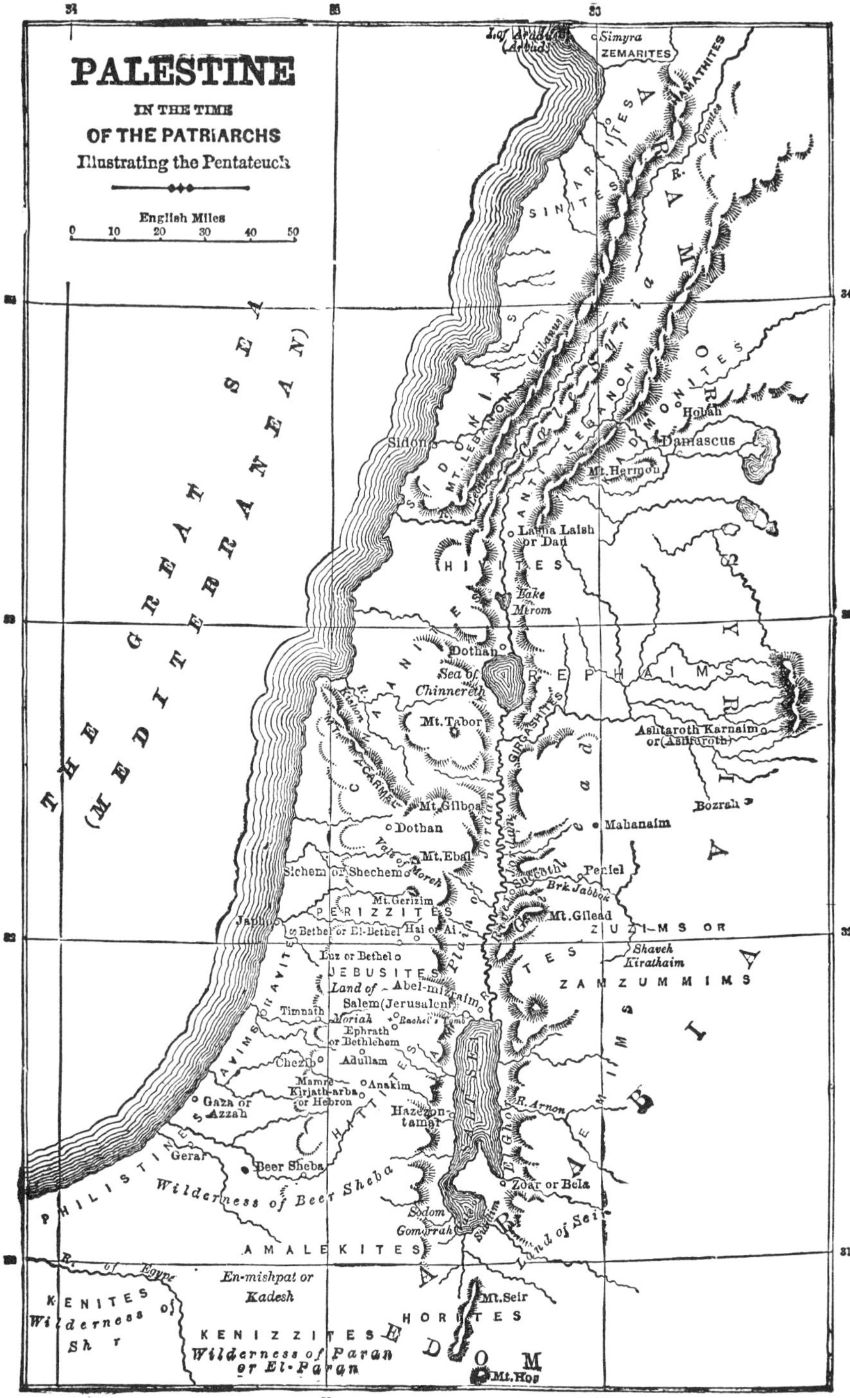

PALESTINE
IN THE TIME
OF THE PATRIARCHS
Illustrating the Pentateuch
English Miles
0 10 20 30 40 50
THE GREAT SEA
(MEDITERRANEAN)
Simyra
ZEMARITES
HAMATHITES
ARAM
SINITES
ARKITES
R. Orontes
Sidon
SIDONIANS
MT. LEBANON
ANTI LEBANON
Mt. Hermon
Damascus
Hobah
AMORITES
ADMONITES
Lasha Laish or Dan
HIVITES
Lake Merom
Dotham
Sea of Chinnereth
REPHAIMS
Mt. Tabor
CANAANITES
R. Kishon
Mt. Carmel
Mt. Gilboa
Dothan
Vale of Moreh
Mt. Ebal
Sichem or Shechem
Mt. Gerizim
PERIZZITES
Japho
Bethel or El-Bethel
Hai or Ai
Luz or Bethel
JEBUSITES
Land of Moriah
Abel-mizraim
Salem (Jerusalem)
Rachel's Tomb
Timnath
Ephrath or Bethlehem
Chezib
Adullam
AVIMS
Mamre
Kirjath-arba or Hebron
Anakim
Gaza or Azzah
Hazezon-tamar
CHATTITES
Gerar
Beer Sheba
PHILISTINES
Wilderness of Beer Sheba
Sodom
Gomorrah
Siddim
AMALEKITES
R. of Egypt
En-mishpat or Kadesh
KENITES
Wilderness of Shur
KENIZZITES
Wilderness of Paran or El-Paran
HORITES
Mt. Seir
EDOM
Mt. Hor
Land of Seir
Zoar or Bela
R. Arnon
EMIMS
ARABIA
ZAMZUMMIMS
ZUZIMS OR
Shaveh Kirathaim
Mt. Gilead
Brk. Jabbok
Peniel
Succoth
Mahanaim
Gilead
GIRGASHITES
Plain of Jordan
Ashtaroth Karnaim or (Ashteroth)
Bozrah
SYRIA
SALT SEA
34 35 36 31 32 33

The

LIFE OF CHRIST

A PRACTICAL STUDY OF OUR LORD'S LIFE
BY THE AID OF

TRACING MAPS

CHRONOLOGICAL ORDER AND THE PARALLEL AND HARMONIC
ARRANGEMENT OF THE GOSPELS AS HEREIN
SET FORTH

FOR

SUNDAY-SCHOOL TEACHERS, FAMILIES AND
GOSPEL READERS EVERYWHERE

BY

I. N. JOHNS.

OUTLINE.

For convenience in study, The Life, Work and Teachings of our Lord as presented in the four Gospels, is divided as follows:

General Instructions.

There are six maps. One to each of the outline divisions except I. and VIII. These require none. The Topic index, pages 1402-1406, will serve as a table of harmony to follow this study in a brief way. For time and place refer to the Topic line of each (§) section throughout the Gospels. The chronological order is that of Dr. Edward Robinson. In reading it follow the sections in their numerical order. The Gospel accounts are printed in ten point (large) type. At a glance it may be seen if there is more than one account. Every verse of each Gospel is found in their respective columns. Consecutive verse and chapter order is sometimes broken, but subjects are never broken. Use the chapter and verse index to locate any portion of any gospel.

In Sunday-schools, if the teacher wishes to be brief, the lecture plan may be used, narrating connectedly Sabbath by Sabbath, noting carefully the intervening events and circumstances, while he points out to his class the various movements from place to place, and time to time. Better, however, to adopt an active working plan for all, and drill the learners in the narrative, and require them to trace the movements upon the maps usually given in the Quarterlies.

Superintendents may draw a plain map of Palestine upon the Blackboard, and if he wishes to be brief, he may narrate, as he traces before the school, in his daily and quarterly reviews. Better, however, if he can draw all the narrative, time, place and salient truths from his school, as time will allow.

In family circles the parent may read the Gospel text of each event in order, day by day, and gather the family about him to look over his shoulder while he traces the movements upon the map, adding the needed note and explanation. Better still, permit all who are able to take part. Let one read Matthew's account; others the parallel accounts, if any, each using a common Bible so that they may become skilled in handling it. Let another observe time and place by these helps; still another may produce a new diagram upon maps. The younger children may be taught by the mother from pictures found in the family Bible or elsewhere; there is an abundance of them. Family worship should be largely for the children's instruction.

The student whose duty it is to teach large classes, congregations, Normal classes, etc., should master one division at a time; by and by he may be able to trace and recite from memory the whole of the Gospel story.

I. Introductions.

§ 1. Is John's prologue or introduction in which he introduces Christ as the Word, the Life, and the Light. § 2. Is Luke's preface, in which he tells to whom and why he wrote his Gospel letter. These two introductory sections could not easily be arranged more appropriately than at the beginning. In this work we cannot begin with Matthew's account, since he does not narrate the earliest events.

II. Childhood, Youth and Ministry to the First Passover.

§ 3. "An angel appears to Zacharias" at Jerusalem, announcing the birth of John, who would "make ready a people prepared for the Lord." § 4. An angel announces the birth of Jesus to Mary at Nazareth. Tracing begins with this section. Follow the upper line across the margin on the map to Nazareth; hold the pencil there. § 5. Mary now visits Elizabeth, the mother of John, her cousin, at Hebron. Trace her journey thither by following the line in the direction of the arrow heads. The Scripture tells us, "She abode with her about three months and returned to her own house." Trace her journey back to Nazareth. § 6. Pertains to John; in this work we have not traced his life. § 7. Is our Lord's genealogy. It requires no tracing. § 8, § 9. Joseph takes Mary with him from Nazareth to Bethlehem to be taxed. Our Lord is Born. § 10. The circumcision takes place. After the purification, they go to Jerusalem to present him to the Lord. Simeon and Anna come in and prophesy. § 11. The wise men come from the East. § 12. Being warned of God they flee to Egypt. Herod slays the children. After Herod's death they return to Nazareth. Egypt adjoins on the southwest of Palestine, but is not shown; therefore the lines are made to cross the margin. § 13. The time of the coming of the wise men, and the sojourn in Egypt is not known. They dwell at Nazareth until the child is twelve years of age. He accompanies them to the feast of the passover at Jerusalem. They return to Nazareth. A period of eighteen years passes by of which there is no record. § 14. The time of John's ministry is at hand. § 15. When Jesus is thirty years of age he leaves his home at Nazareth and goes to Jordan, unto John to be baptized. Probably about Bethabara, beyond Jordan. § 16. He is led of the spirit into the wilderness. Probably the Wilderness of Judea. According to Matthew the Devil takes him to the temple at Jerusalem, then to a mountain. Tradition says near Jericho. § 17. He now goes to John again at Bethabara, beyond Jordan. § 18, § 19. John's disciples come unto him. He finds Philip, the latter finds Nathaniel. § 20. Jesus and these are invited to a marriage at Cana, in Galilee, where he turns the water into wine—his first miracle. He then goes to Capernaum, where he tarries until the time of the passover.

11. Childhood, Youth and Ministry to the First Passover.

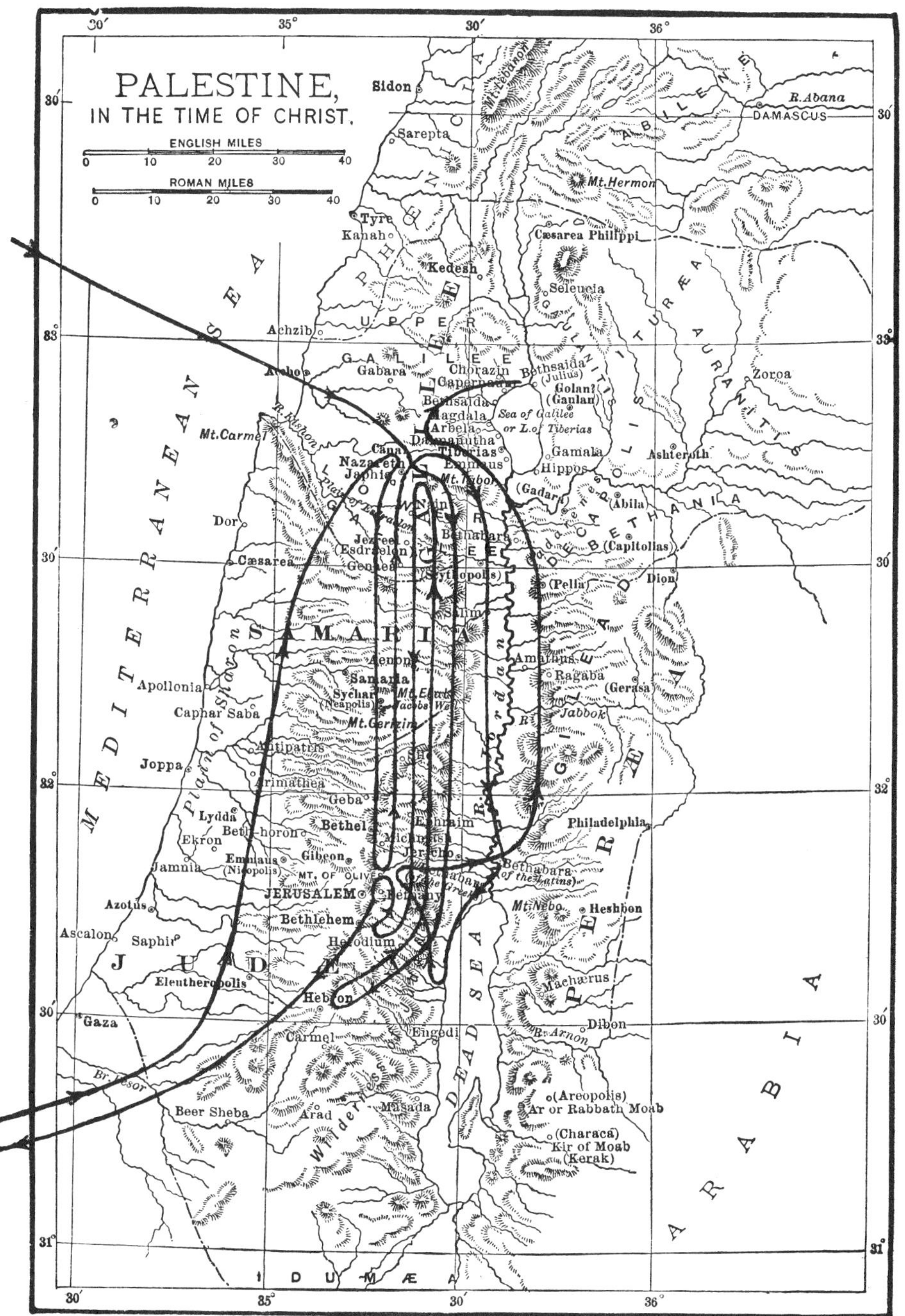

III. First Passover to the Second Passover.

We left Jesus at Capernaum. § 21. John tells us "they continued there not many days." Jesus goes to Jerusalem to the passover. He cleanses the temple. § 22. Nicodemus comes to him by night and is instructed. § 23. Jesus and his disciples tarry in Judea during the summer of A. D. 27, baptizing, while John continues his ministry about Salim and Aenon. § 24. John is now imprisoned by Herod at Machaerus. When Jesus learned of this, he departs from Judea for Galilee, through Samaria. § 25. He meets the woman at the well, at Sychar, and discourses. § 26, § 27. He passes into Galilee teaching publicly. He comes to Cana, where he heals the nobleman's son lying sick at Capernaum. § 28. He comes to Nazareth, his home, and is rejected. § 29. He therefore leaves Nazareth to dwell at Capernaum. § 30. He walks by the seashore, calls four of his disciples, and directs them to a miraculous draft of fish. § 31, § 32. He heals a demoniac in the Synagogue, Peter's wife's mother, and many others. § 33. He now leaves Capernaum and with his disciples makes his first missionary circuit throughout Galilee. § 34. During this circuit, which is indicated by a circle, he heals a leper in an unnamed city; this is signified by an angle in the circle to aid the memory. § 35. They returned to Capernaum and he heals a paralytic. § 36. He calls Matthew, who makes a feast. Dr. Edward Robinson places this feast later; it is found in § 71 and § 72 in the table of Harmony or Topic index, as it is named in this work, on page 1403.

III. First Passover to the Second Passover.

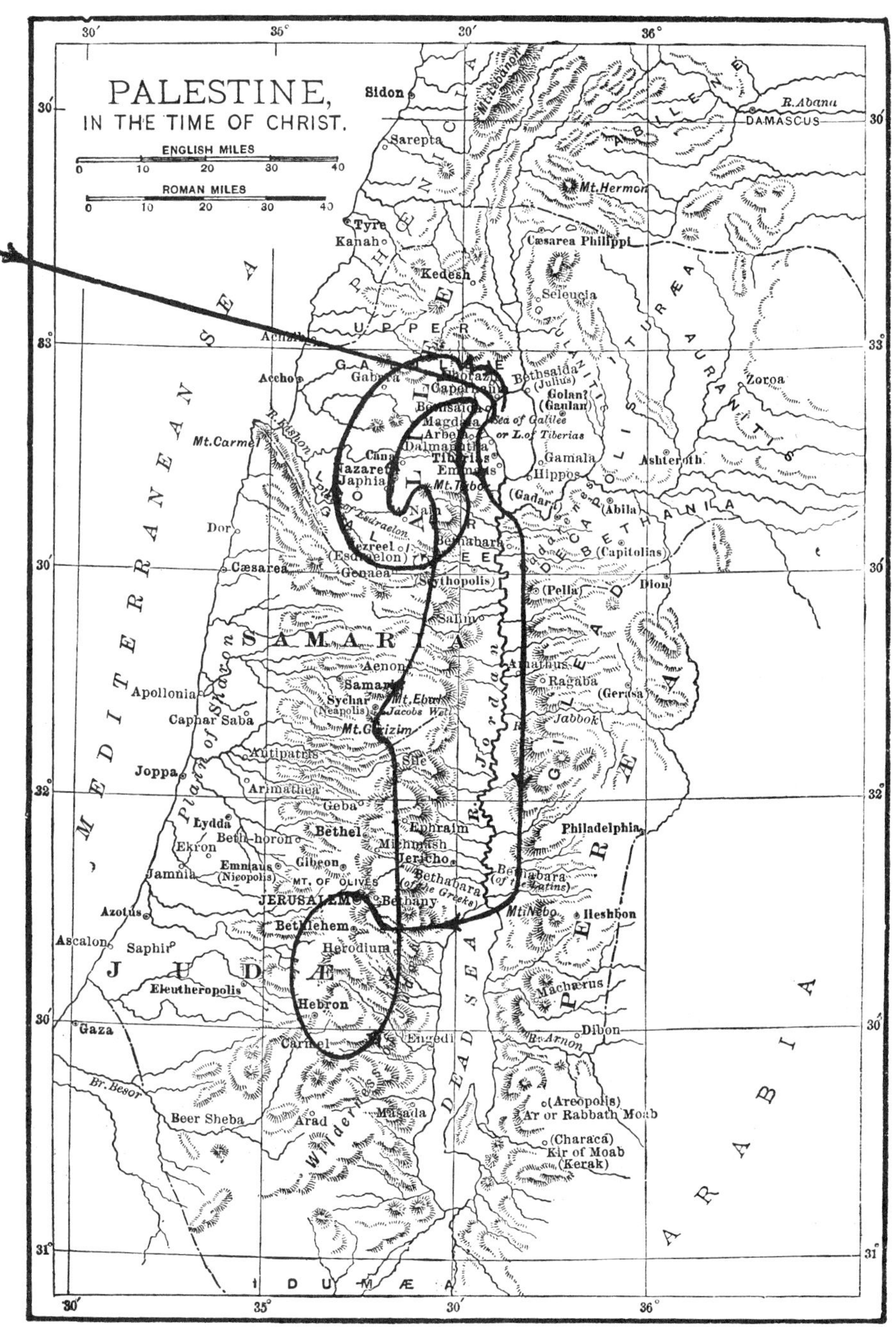

IV. Second Passover to the Third Passover.

We left Jesus at Capernaum. § 37, § 38. He now goes up to Jerusalem to the passover. The impotent man at the pool is healed on the Sabbath and he discourses to the Jews who seek to slay him. § 39. He is on his way to Galilee. While passing through the corn fields on the Sabbath his disciples pluck ears of corn. § 40. Another Sabbath on this journey, he enters the Synagogue of an unnamed city of Galilee and heals the withered hand. The Pharisees take counsel to destroy him. § 41. He withdraws to the sea, followed by multitudes, healing many. Observe that the line does not pass close to the sea on account of other lines, but the general direction of all lines will aid in fixing the order of events. § 42, § 43. Jesus now goes up into a mountain to pray. Probably the Horns of Hatten, near Capernaum. He choses the twelve and delivers the sermon on the mount to them as recorded by Matthew, after which he comes down upon the plain and repeats it as recorded by Luke. § 44. He enters Capernaum and heals the centurian's servant. § 45. The next day he went to Nain, where he raises the widow's son. § 46, § 47, § 48. About this time messengers from John the Baptist come to him. He upbraids the favored cities and calls the meek and suffering. § 49. He goes to Capernaum, where his feet are anointed at a Pharisee's table. § 50. Jesus now makes his second missionary circuit throughout Galilee, with the twelve and the women. § 51–§ 58. Are events that took place and discourses delivered during the second circuit. § 59–§ 67. Jesus seems to have returned again to Capernaum. He goes out by the seaside, where great multitudes come unto him and he teaches by many parables. § 68. He now departs across the lake. § 69. A great storm arises; he stills the tempest. § 70. They come into the country of the Gadarenes, where devils are cast out of two demoniacs. § 71, § 72. Our Lord returns to Capernaum again. Levi gives a feast. By some this feast is given just after his call as noted in § 36.—§ 73. Jarius' daughter is raised from the dead. On the way thither he heals a woman of an issue of blood. § 74. Jesus now leaves Capernaum. He is followed by two blind men whom he heals. §75, §76. He comes to Nazareth a second time and is rejected. He continues his third missionary circuit throughout Galilee. §77. During this circuit he instructs and sends forth the twelve. §78, §79. These events pertain to Herod and John the Baptist who was beheaded about this time. § 80. The twelve return to him. He takes them into a desert place by ship, to rest. Bethsaida (Julius) on the northeast coast of the sea. Multitudes follow him. He feeds the five thousand. § 81. He sends his disciples across the sea. Jesus went up into the mountain to pray. During the night a storm arises. Jesus went unto them, walking on the sea. Peter comes unto him and sinks. §82. They come into the land of Gennesaret (the fertile plain extending several miles south of Capernaum along the sea coast) where he heals many. §83. He comes to Capernaum, whither also came the multitudes whom he had fed. He discourses on the bread of life. §84. Many disciples turn back, but Peter professes faith for the twelve. The time of the third Passover is at hand.

IV. Second Passover to the Third Passover.

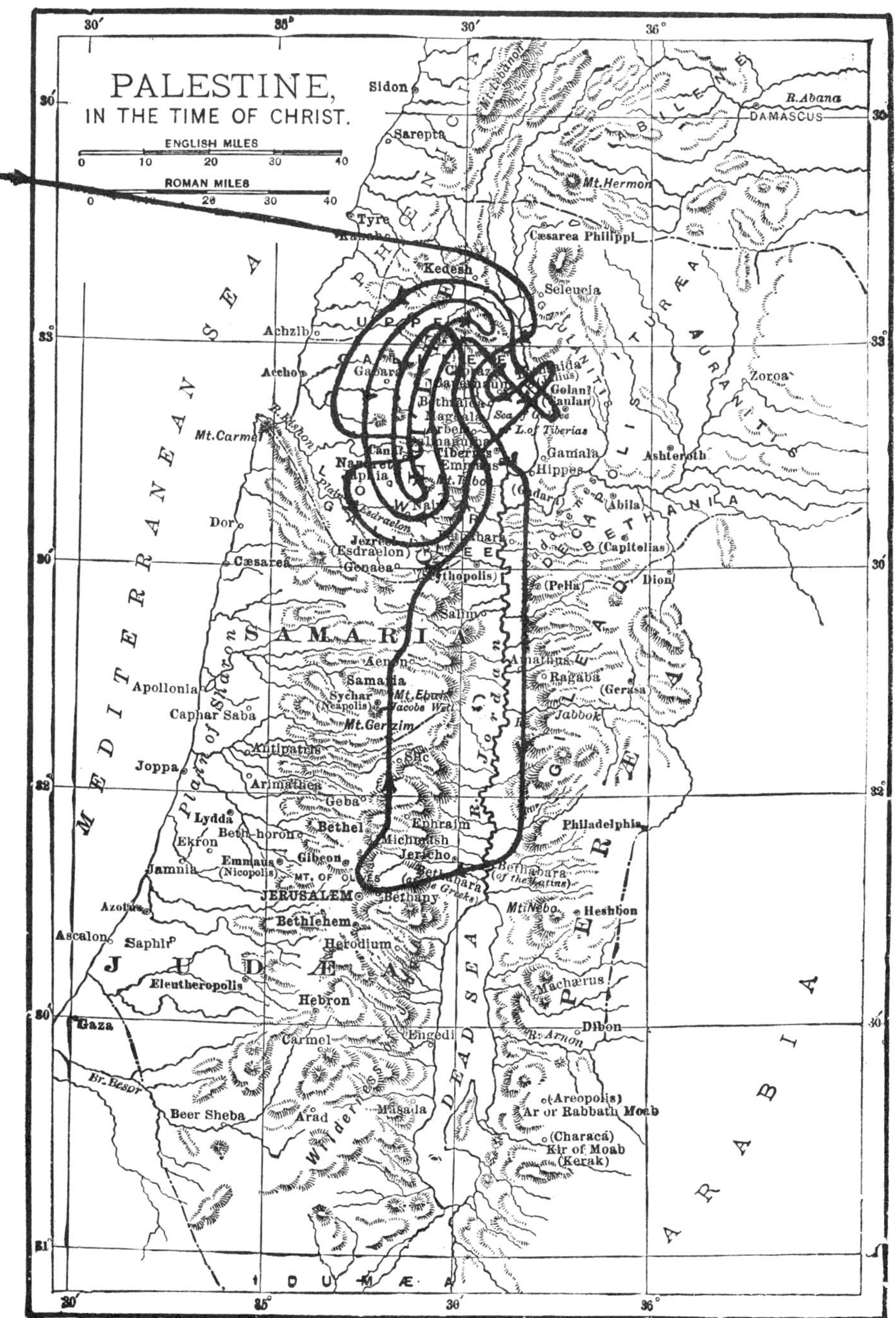

V. Third Passover to the Last Week.

There is no evidence that Jesus attended this passover. §85. Scribes and Pharisees from Jerusalem came to Jesus at Capernaum with fault concerning unwashen hands whom he answers. §86. Jesus now leaves Capernaum and goes into the borders of Tyre and Sidon (Phoenicia). He heals the daughter of a Syrophoenician woman. §87. He departs from thence and came unto the sea of Galilee through the coasts of Decapolis on the eastern shores. His route is not intimated; for convenience we extend it around by the north. A deaf and dumb man is healed, and many others during this journey. §88. He comes to a wilderness by the southeastern coast, where he feeds the four thousand. He takes ship for Magdala. §89. Here Pharisees and Saducees again require a sign. He now departs for the other side. §90. He warns his disciples. §91. They come to Bethsaida (Julius). A blind man is healed. §92. They pass through the region of Caesarea Philippi. Peter for the rest again professes their faith. §93. Jesus fortells his death and resurrection. §94, §95. The transfiguration is witnessed by three—probably on Mt. Hermon. He charges them. §96. When he joins the other disciples and the multitude, he heals a lunatic whom his disciples could not heal. §97. He passes quietly into Galilee and again foretells his death and resurrection. §98–§105. These are events that transpire after they have come to Capernaum. §106. They now go up to Jerusalem to attend the feast of tabernacles. Jesus leaves secretly. §107. The time being at hand he joins them, they come to a village in Samaria, who receive them not. §108. At another village he heals ten lepers. Edward Robinson makes this our Lord's final departure from Galilee. Some others do not; who fix a later journey through these parts and ascribe this event to that time. For simplicity of order we have not traced a later journey, and therefore this event retains this place. §109–§111. Jesus attends the feast of tabernacles and teaches publicly. The woman taken in adultery is brought to him. He disputes with the Pharisees who attempt to stone him again. §112. He answers a lawyer in the parable of the good Samaritan. §113. He visits Martha and Mary. §114–§116. These events transpire while in and about Jerusalem. §117, §118. The man born blind is healed on the Sabbath and discourses on the good shepherd. §119. At the feast of the dedication he is pressed upon by the Jews who seek to take him. §120. He now retires beyond Jordan, where John baptized (Bethabara). §121. Lazarus dies. Jesus is sent for. He goes to Bethany and raises Lazarus. §122. Caiaphas holds a counsel against Jesus. He therefore left Jerusalem and retired to Ephraim. §123. It is at this time that another journey into Galilee is ascribed to our Lord. This may be probable. He now goes beyond Jordan. §125–§148. The parables, public instruction and events recorded in these sections are all ascribed to his ministry beyond Jordan, and are usually referred to as his Peraean ministry. It will be observed that places are not definitely mentioned. §149. Two blind men are healed near Jericho. §150, §151. He visits Zacchaeus at Jericho and gives the parable of the ten pounds. He goes up toward Jerusalem. §152, §153. He arrives at Bethany six days before the passover. He is anointed by Mary.

V. Third Passover to the Last Week.

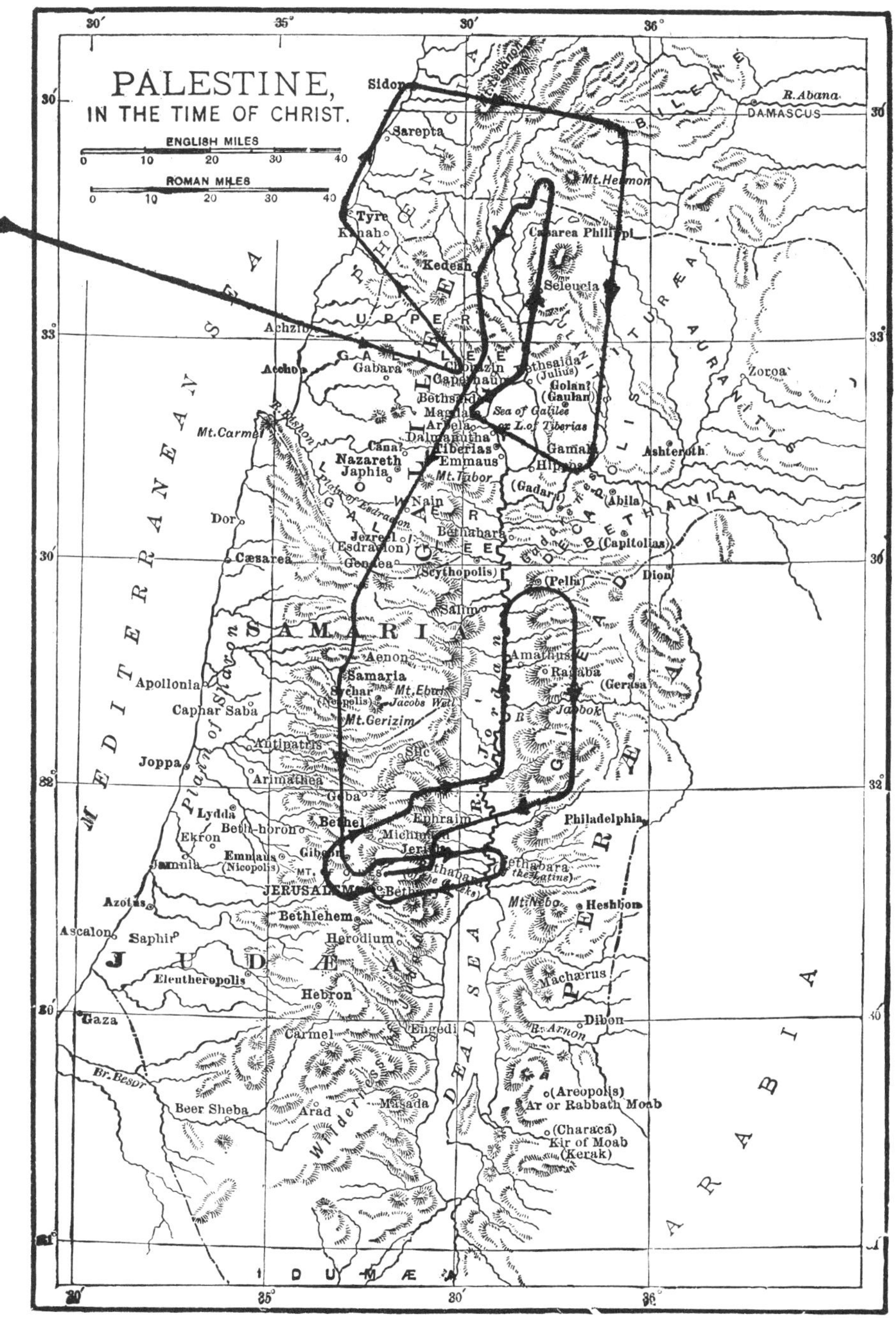

VI. Last Week to the Resurrection Morn.

§ 154. Our Lord makes his public entry journeying from Bethany to the temple at Jerusalem. At eventide he retires to Bethany. This he does three different times during the week which is illustrated by three loops that could not all be made to approach Bethany closely, but which will serve to fix the events in their order. § 155. On his way to the city Monday morning he curses the fig tree. § 156. He cleanses the temple the second time. At even he retires to Bethany. § 157, § 158. Tuesday morning on their way to the city His disciples observe the withered fig tree. §159–§179. These twenty-one sections record the public teachings of our Lord on this day and Judas' covenant to betray him. It is probable that Wednesday was spent in the quiet rest at Bethany with his disciples. §180, §181. Thursday witnesses the preparation for his last, the great passover, which they celebrate in the evening in the upper room at Jerusalem. §182–§191. These sections record the events of the supper and our Lord's final instructions to his disciples, and his prayer. §192. They sing a hymn and go out to the Mount of Olives into the garden of Gethsemane where he passes through agony for the whole world. §193. He is betrayed and made prisoner at midnight. §194–§200. These sections record the various events of His trial. §201. Judas repents and hangs himself. §202-§209. These sections record the events of his crucifixion. §210, §211. He is buried and a guard is set at his tomb.

VI. Last Week to the Resurrection Morn.

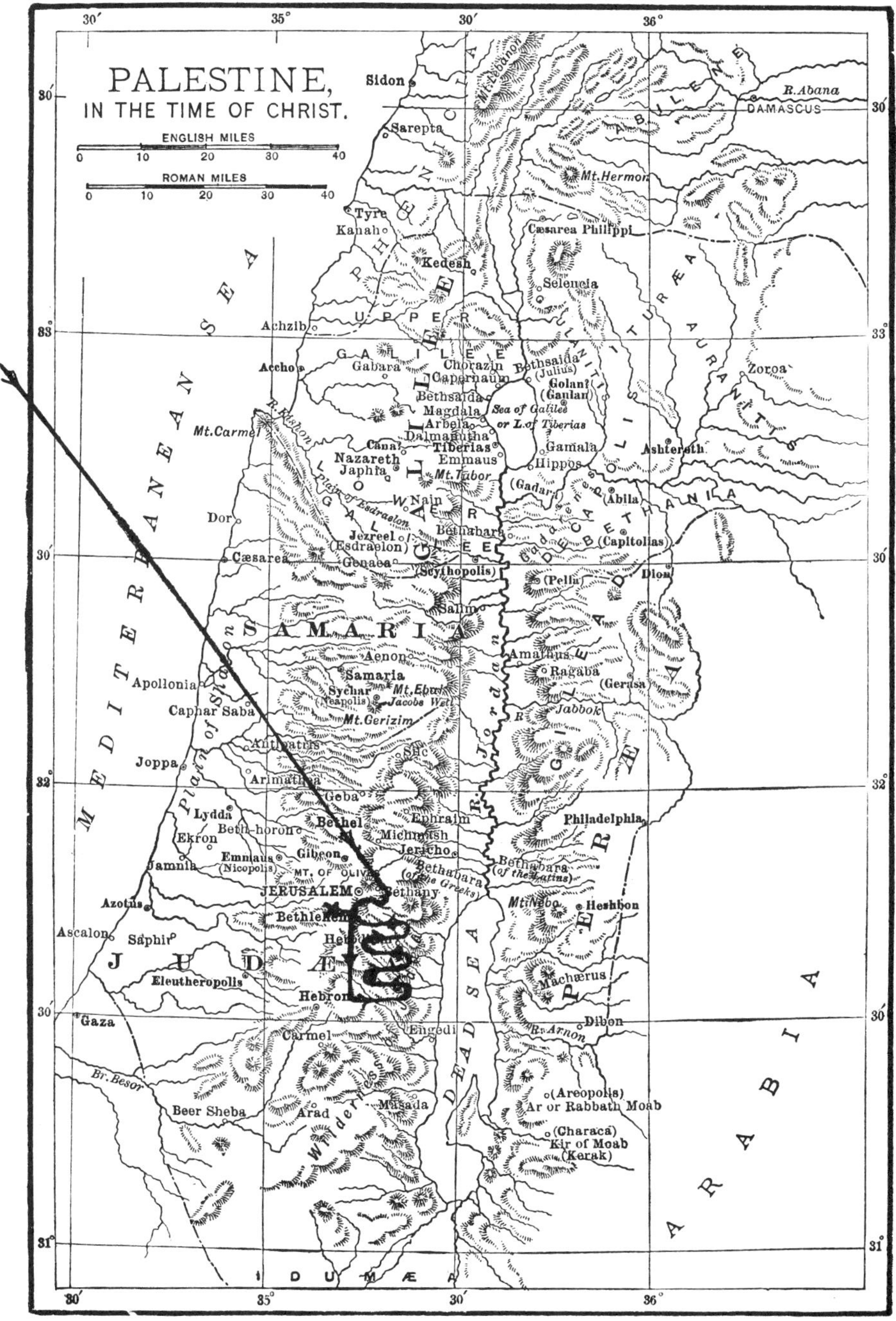

VII. The Forty Days.

In this period the tracings do not refer to our Lord's movements, nor those of his apostles and disciples. They are intended to be some assistance to the mind to observe order.

§212-§217. These sections present the early events of that memorable morn. §218. It is afternoon. Cleopas and his companion walk with Jesus on their way to Emmaus. Probably about the time they had left Jerusalem or after Jesus had left them. He appeared to Peter (Cephas) as recorded by Luke 24:34. §219. It is evening, when the two had returned from Emmaus to Jerusalem, they found the eleven gathered together, except Thomas; Jesus appears in their midst. He bids them tarry in Jerusalem. §220. A week rolls by. They are gathered together again. Thomas is present. He appears in their midst again. §221, §222. These two appearances occurred some time between the last event and May 18 following, the date of the ascension, in Galilee. The one by the sea, the other on an unnamed mountain. §223. He probably sees James at Jerusalem as recorded by Paul—I. Cor. 15:7. Then by the twelve assembled together. §224. He leads them out as far as Bethany and they witness his ascension. Thus closes the most wonderful record the world has ever known. Master this literal study, and there is the promise that its spiritual truth and Life is yours if you desire it.

VIII. Conclusion.

§225. This Gospel begins with an introduction as you have observed at the beginning, both wonderful and profound. Now receive the blessed truth of the whole Gospel as John has epitomized it in this conclusion.

VII. The Forty Days.

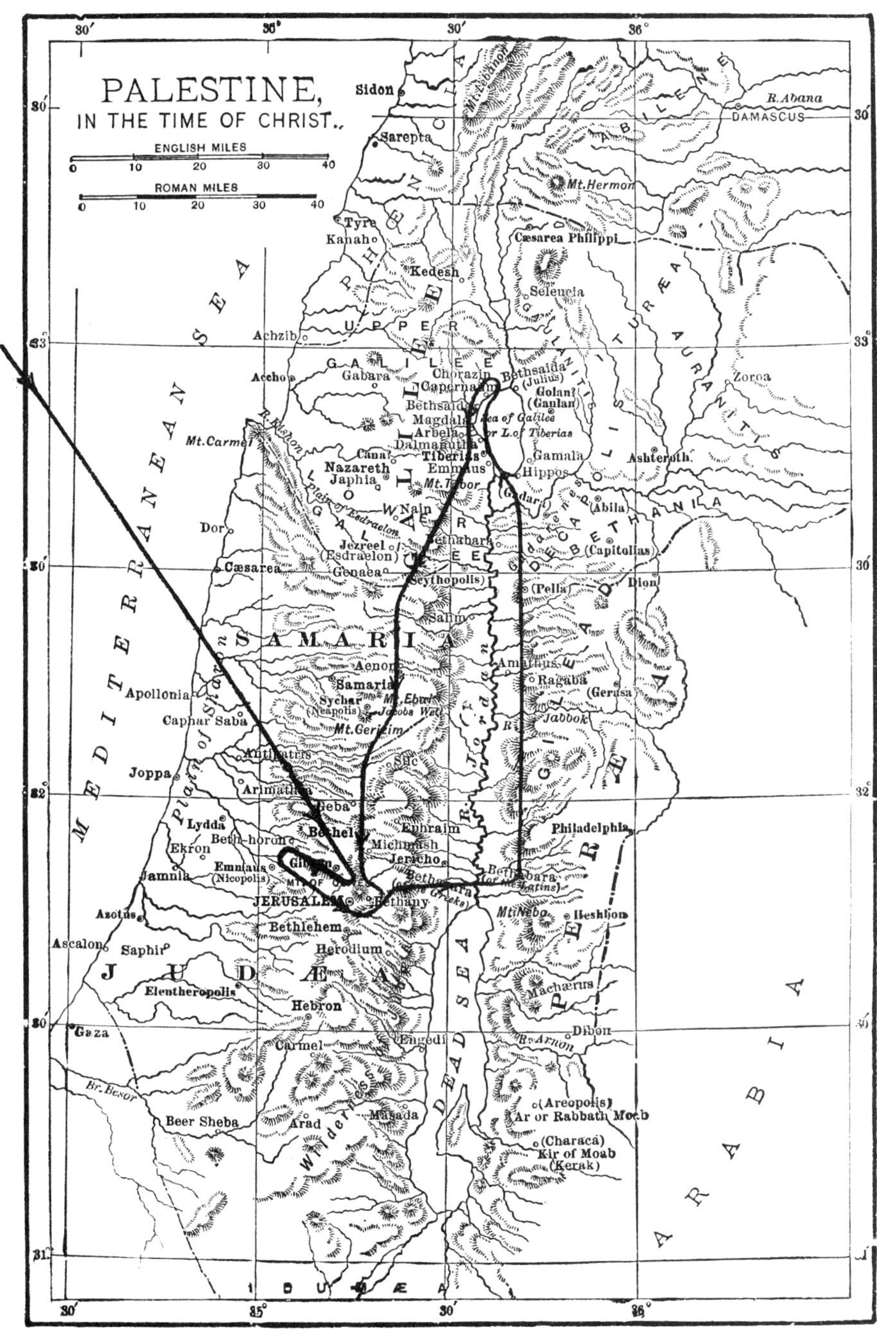